S0-AIJ-723

the Weather Almanac

ISSN 0731-5627

the Weather Almanac

A reference guide to weather, climate, and related issues in the United States and its key cities.

SEVENTH EDITION

Richard A. Wood, Ph.D.
Editor

An ITP Information/Reference Group Company

Changing the Way the World Learns

NEW YORK • LONDON • BONN • BOSTON • DETROIT
MADRID • MELBOURNE • MEXICO CITY • PARIS
SINGAPORE • TOKYO • TORONTO • WASHINGTON
ALBANY NY • BELMONT CA • CINCINNATI OH

Richard A. Wood, Ph.D., *Editor*

Gale Research Staff:

Kimberley A. McGrath, *Project Coordinator*
Jacqueline Longe, *Associate Editor*

Victoria B. Cariappa, *Research Manager*
Maureen Richards, *Research Specialist*

Mary Beth Trimper, *Production Director*
Evi Seoud, *Assistant Production Manager*
Shanna Heilveil, *Production Assistant*

Cynthia D. Baldwin, *Product Design Manager*
Barbara Yarrow, *Graphic Services Manager*
Erin Martin, *Desktop Publisher*
Pamela A. Hayes, *Photography Coordinator*
Randy Bassett, *Image Database Supervisor*
C.J. Jonik, *Keyliner*

Marlene S. Hurst, *Permissions Manager*
Margaret A. Chamberlain, *Permissions Specialist*
Tyra Phillips, *Permissions Assistant*

Benita L. Spight, *Manager Data Entry Services*
Gwendolyn S. Tucker, *Data Entry Supervisor*
Beverly Jendrowski, *Senior Data Entry Associate*

Jeffrey Muhr, Roger Valade, *Editorial Technical Services Associates*

The paper used in this publication meets the minimum requirements of American National Standard for Information Sciences—Permanence Paper for Printed Library Materials, ANSI Z39.48-1984.

This book is printed on recycled paper that meets Environmental Protection Agency Standards.

ISBN: 0-8103-6980-X
ISSN: 0731-5627

Printed in the United States of America

10 9 8 7 6 5 4 3 2 1

Gale Research , an International Thomson Publishing Company.
ITP logo is a trademark under license.

Contents

Foreword

Benjamin Franklin said some 250 years ago: "Some people are weatherwise but most are otherwise." That may have been true a couple of hundred years ago but is no longer the case.

What's happening in the Earth's atmosphere affects numerous aspects of our lives. More and more, individuals are working to increase their awareness, knowledge, and understanding of the weather and its related elements and phenomena.

The changing winds of weather

The United States has more varied severe weather problems than any other country in the world. In fact, each year the U.S. has about 10,000 severe thunderstorms with millions of lightning strikes, 5,000 floods, 1,100 tornadoes, and threatened by about 34 hurricanes and tropical storms with at least several reaching the Atlantic, Pacific, and Gulf of Mexico coastal states.

These changes can be better anticipated and monitored thanks to the numerous changes in weather forecasting since the early 1950s. At that time, there were none of the fine-tuned weather radars, satellites, or the improved forecasting technologies of today.

The first National Weather Service (NWS) office to receive a radar was Miami in 1957 followed shortly by Washington, D.C.; later modifications were made to the radar in 1974. Currently, approximately 160 new Doppler "Next Generation Weather Radars (NEXRAD)" are being posted around the country. To add to the observational data, another 1,000 automated weather systems are also being installed nationwide.

By utilizing new technology to improve forecasting, warnings, and general awareness, countless lives have been saved. About 500 people are killed and at least 2,500 are injured annually in the United States due to atmospheric natural hazards. These totals mark a steady decrease over the years to less than half of the fatalities of fifty years ago, despite the fact that the population has doubled and people, with more free time, spend far more time outdoors than they did in the 1930s.

Expanded atmospheric natural hazard statistics

Statistics play an important part in properly forecasting weather and much can be learned from examining and comparing local, regional, and national statistics—discovering weather patterns. However, key statistics have not always been easy to obtain.

For example, during the early 1980s, the National Weather Service received numerous requests for statistical breakdowns on: who (gender, age, etc.) was being killed or injured during natural hazardous weather events; where the individuals were (home, vehicle, store), and other such information. While tornado, lightning, flash flood/flood, and hurricane fatality statistics had been compiled for more than 50 years, details of this nature had not been compiled or researched. Since 1987, however, tabulation of these types of injury/fatality statistics has become standard practice. By the late 1980s, statistics on dust storms, coastal storms, hail, fog, and high winds (not associated with tornadoes) have also been added to the list of compiled statistics.

Within the pages of *The Weather Almanac* users will find these and hundreds more important and interesting facts and statistics.

Statistics in *The Weather Almanac*

Among the statistics in *The Weather Almanac*, users will find:

- Of the 3,464 killed in atmospheric natural hazards from 1985-93, 69.7% have been males and the remaining 30.3% females.
- The state with the most lightning deaths by far is Florida with 87 fatalities, while Texas has recorded 28.
- Texas exceeds all other states with flash flood/flood fatalities with 121, followed by West Virginia with 52 deaths.
- When Hurricane Andrew struck just south of Miami in August of 1992 causing damages estimates up to $35-40 billion; nearly 200,000 people were left homeless.
- The size and impact of The Great Midwest Flood of 1993 was unprecedented. Approximately 500 forecast points on major rivers and tributary systems exceeded flood stage at some time during the flood.

The Weather Almanac: a ready-reference tool

The Weather Almanac is a convenient and comprehensive

complement to usual sources of day-to-day weather information found in newspapers and broadcast via radio and television. This newly revised edition of *The Weather Almanac* makes available a wide range of maps, charts, and safety rules based upon past records, research, and experience to inform users of what may be expected from our ever-changing atmosphere.

Separate sections in *The Weather Almanac* are devoted to tornadoes, hurricanes, thunderstorms and lightning, flash floods, and winter storms, among others, and have been edited using materials from official National Weather Service and Geological Survey (among other agencies) which serve as a popular basic reference sources for severe weather and extreme conditions. Official records and statistics are included wherever they are useful and available.

Being weather-aware can help save lives—being prepared to act instead of reacting to a natural hazard. For example, the anvil, the flat cloud on top of a thunderstorm, can indicate the direction of movement by which way the anvil is pointed.

Information in this book will help users to better adapt themselves and their activities to the weather and let them prepare for a weather emergency at the best time: before it happens.

Reference to severe weather is only one feature of this book. *The Weather Almanac* offers you a large collection of data from hundreds of sources. *The Weather Almanac* begins with an overview of the various weather conditions (in map and table formats) then extends into underlying weather principals, a glossary of weather terms, and other guides to personal observations.

The Weather Almanac will take users around the world. Besides over 100 cities in the United States, weather statistics for nearly 550 key cities worldwide are provided in this book, including seasonal temperature and precipitation normals. Users will note a slight difference in the appearance of some of the U.S. cities climatic data as the National Climatic Data Center is in the midst of changing somewhat the format of these reports; overall, elements remain the same as prior editions.

Changes in this edition

All sections of the book have been revised as new data on particular subjects and phenomena have become available, but the greatest amount of change occurs in the "Local Climatological Reports." Climatic extremes and other information have been updated through 1993 and normals have been updated a full decade to the period 1961-1990.

Finely detailed weather statistics for each of the 108 cities included typically comprise 40 years, or more, of weather history. Besides temperature and precipitation statistics, heating and cooling degree days are also included.

Also added to this edition is information regarding El Niño. El Niño has become quite noticeable during the past couple of decades in general and the past five years in particular. Floods from California eastward through the southern states to Georgia and even the 1993 Midwest floods can be attributed to El Niño.

The 1994 Northridge Earthquake has been added and compared to the 1989 San Francisco Bay Earthquake. Also included in this edition are passages on Hurricane Andrew, the Great Midwest Flood of 1993, and the winter storm of 1993.

In addition to these major information features, *The Weather Almanac* provides sections examining Weather and Health; Wind Chill; Summer Comfort Index; Livestock Safety; NOAA Weather Radio Warning Network; a Marine Weather Advisories section; how to forecast the weather for yourself, Weather, Climate, and Society; and an assortment of other weather-related subjects.

General note on sources

Much of the information in this book is quoted directly from reports and records prepared by various United States Government departments, agencies, and services which share parts of the nation's great weather and environmental science efforts. For example, safety rules for various atmospheric natural hazards are taken directly from National Oceanic and Atmospheric Administration (NOAA), National Weather Service, publications. Similarly, the United States Geological Survey is the source for comparable safety advice on earthquakes and volcanic activity. It should be noted that these suggested safety rules have helped dramatically to minimize the impact of these hazards.

The city-by-city weather records are worthy of the same confidence, for they come directly from the cumulative records developed by the United States observers around the country and have been coordinated by the staff of the National Climatic Data Center located in Asheville, North Carolina.

The core sections of the information on weather principles: Air Pollution and Weather, Climate, and Society have also been compiled from a wide variety of sources drawn from the Environmental Protection Agency, the President's Council on Environmental Quality, the Department of Agriculture, the Department of Energy, as well as NOAA. The section on Retirement and Health Weather and various introductions are original with *The Weather Almanac*.

The Weather Almanac editorial staff hopes this new edition will be increasingly useful as a source of basic information about our atmosphere and earth.

Comments or suggestions from readers are not only welcome but are encouraged in the quest to constantly improve the book.

Richard A. Wood, Ph.D.
Editor

Introduction

The Weather Almanac Is Your Guide to Weather and Related Phenomena

Now in its seventh edition, *The Weather Almanac* contains information on all types of weather and weather-related phenomena. It furnishes in-depth weather statistics and safety rules, as well as a climatic overview of the country.

Important Features of this Edition

The Weather Almanac has been modified to meet the needs of today's user:

- **Updated Design**. The Almanac's new design provides users with important information in an accessible, clean, and easy-to-use format.
- **Statistics**. Statistics throughout the book have been updated through 1993 (when available).

To further complement its thorough coverage, *The Weather Almanac* uses these important features to help users find information easily:

- **Glossary**—enables users to review, at a glance, fundamental weather terms.
- **General Index**—guides users to important terms and concepts throughout the book.

Availability in Electronic Formats

Diskette/Magnetic Tape. *The Weather Almanac* is available for licensing on magnetic tape or diskette in a fielded format. Either the complete database or a custom selection of entries may be ordered. The database is available for internal data processing and nonpublishing purposes only. For more information, please call 800-877-GALE.

Suggestions Welcome

Comments and suggestions from users on any aspect of *The Weather Almanac* are welcome. Address correspondence to:

The Editor
The Weather Almanac
Gale Research
835 Penobscot Building
Detroit, MI 48226-4094

Acknowledgments

Photographs and illustrations appearing in *The Weather Almanac* were received from the following sources:

-----. Photograph of Mt. St. Helens erupting, May 18, 1980. UPI/Bettmann Newsphotos: **p. 153**; -----. Photograph of tornados. JLM Visuals: **p. 81**; -----. Photograph of Hurricane Diana in 3-D, September 11, 1984, NASA: **pp. 40, 41**; -----. Photograph of earth taken from space. National Oceanic and Atmospheric Administration: **p. 58**; -----. Photograph of Pu'u 'O'o vent erupting on Lilauea's east rift zone, 1983, National Park Service: **p. 158**; -----. Two weather extremes maps. Environmental Sciences Divisions, U.S. Army Topographic Engineering Center: **pp. 241, 275**; Copley, Albert J. Photograph of polluted air over Mexico City. © Albert J. Copley/Visuals Unlimited (reprinted with permission): **p. 173**; © Deeks, John. National Audubon Society Collection/Photo Researchers, Inc. Photograph of cloud types: **p. 201**; Eplett, Robert. Photograph of the separation of an apartment building in Chatsworth, January 17, 1994. Robert A. Eplett/OES: **p. 142**; Eplett, Robert. Photograph of the partial collapse of Golden State (I-5) Freeway, January 17, 1994. Robert A. Eplett/OES: **p. 150**; Eplett, Robert. Photograph of a soft first story at an apartment complex, January 17, 1994. Robert A. Eplett/OES: **p. 147**; Eplett, Robert. Photograph of a missing section of a seating from the rim of the LA Coliseum, January 17, 1994. Robert A. Eplett/OES: **p. 143**; © Garrado, Gordon/ Science Photo Library, National Audubon Society Collection/Photo Researchers, Inc. Photograph of thunderstorm: **p. 106**; Ryan, Anne. Photograph of Midwest Flood in USA TODAY by Anne Ryan. Copyright 1995, USA TODAY (reprinted with permission): **p. 117**.

The editors would also like to acknowledge the National Aeronautics and Space Administration (NASA), the National Climatic Data Center, the National Hurricane Center, the National Oceanic and Atmospheric Administration (NOAA), the National Weather Service, and the U.S. Coast Guard for making relevant data available for use in this publication.

United States Weather in Atlas Format

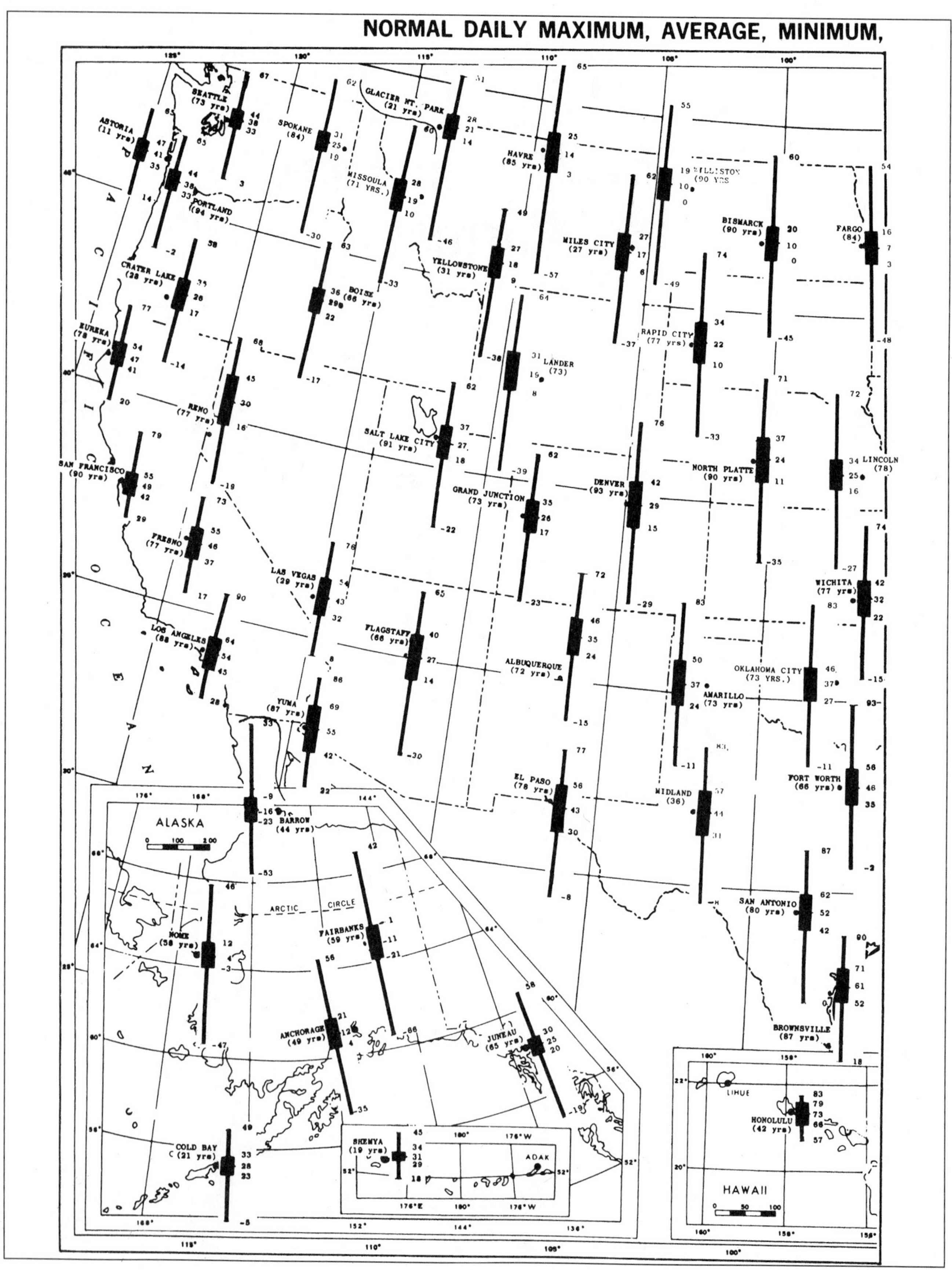
NORMAL DAILY MAXIMUM, AVERAGE, MINIMUM,
SEATTLE (73 yrs)
ASTORIA (11 yrs)
SPOKANE (84)
GLACIER NT. PARK (21 yrs)
MISSOULA (71 YRS.)
HAVRE (85 yrs)
PORTLAND (94 yrs)
WILLISTON (90 YRS)
BISMARCK (90 yrs)
FARGO (84)
MILES CITY (27 yrs)
YELLOWSTONE (31 yrs)
CRATER LAKE (28 yrs)
BOISE (66 yrs)
EUREKA (78 yrs)
RAPID CITY (77 yrs)
LANDER (73)
RENO (77 yrs)
SALT LAKE CITY (91 yrs)
NORTH PLATTE (90 yrs)
LINCOLN (78)
SAN FRANCISCO (90 yrs)
DENVER (93 yrs)
GRAND JUNCTION (73 yrs)
FRESNO (77 yrs)
LAS VEGAS (29 yrs)
WICHITA (77 yrs)
LOS ANGELES (88 yrs)
FLAGSTAFF (66 yrs)
ALBUQUERQUE (72 yrs)
OKLAHOMA CITY (73 YRS.)
AMARILLO (73 yrs)
YUMA (87 yrs)
EL PASO (78 yrs)
MIDLAND (36)
FORT WORTH (66 yrs)
SAN ANTONIO (80 yrs)
BROWNSVILLE (87 yrs)
P A C I F I C O C E A N
ALASKA
BARROW (44 yrs)
ARCTIC CIRCLE
NOME (58 yrs)
FAIRBANKS (59 yrs)
ANCHORAGE (49 yrs)
JUNEAU (65 yrs)
COLD BAY (21 yrs)
SHEMYA (19 yrs)
ADAK
HAWAII
LIHUE
HONOLULU (42 yrs)

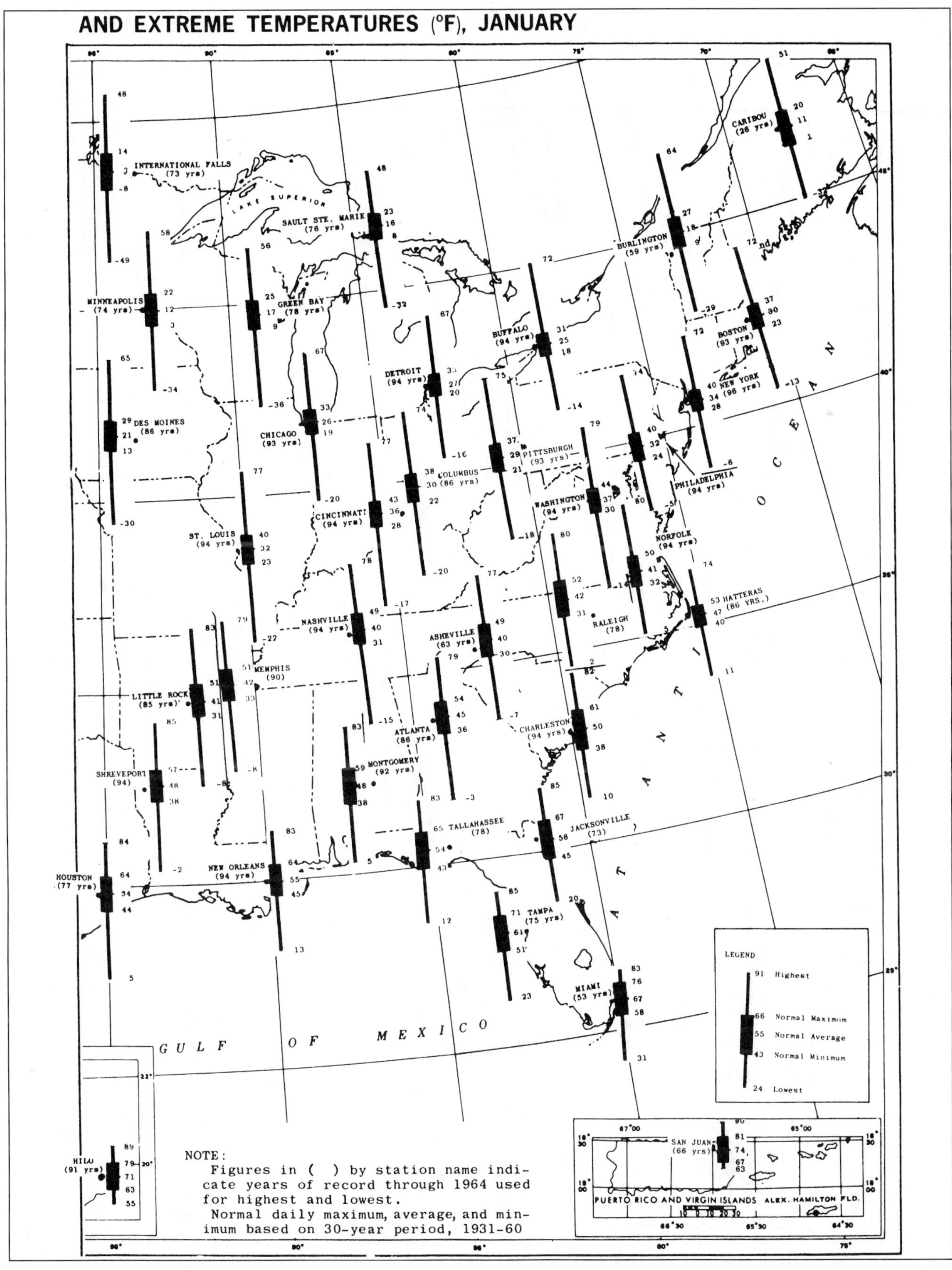
AND EXTREME TEMPERATURES (°F), JANUARY
INTERNATIONAL FALLS (73 yrs)
LAKE SUPERIOR
SAULT STE. MARIE (76 yrs)
CARIBOU (26 yrs)
BURLINGTON (59 yrs)
MINNEAPOLIS (74 yrs)
GREEN BAY (78 yrs)
BUFFALO (94 yrs)
BOSTON (93 yrs)
DETROIT (94 yrs)
NEW YORK (96 yrs)
DES MOINES (86 yrs)
CHICAGO (93 yrs)
PITTSBURGH (93 yrs)
COLUMBUS (86 yrs)
PHILADELPHIA (94 yrs)
CINCINNATI (94 yrs)
WASHINGTON (94 yrs)
ST. LOUIS (94 yrs)
NORFOLK (94 yrs)
HATTERAS (86 YRS.)
RALEIGH (78)
NASHVILLE (94 yrs)
ASHEVILLE (63 yrs)
MEMPHIS (90)
LITTLE ROCK (85 yrs)
ATLANTA (86 yrs)
CHARLESTON (94 yrs)
SHREVEPORT (94)
MONTGOMERY (92 yrs)
TALLAHASSEE (78)
JACKSONVILLE (73)
HOUSTON (77 yrs)
NEW ORLEANS (94 yrs)
TAMPA (75 yrs)
MIAMI (53 yrs)
ATLANTIC OCEAN
GULF OF MEXICO
LEGEND
91 Highest
66 Normal Maximum
55 Normal Average
43 Normal Minimum
24 Lowest
HILO (91 yrs)
SAN JUAN (66 yrs)
PUERTO RICO AND VIRGIN ISLANDS
ALEX. HAMILTON FLD.
NOTE:
Figures in ( ) by station name indicate years of record through 1964 used for highest and lowest.
Normal daily maximum, average, and minimum based on 30-year period, 1931-60

NORMAL DAILY MAXIMUM, AVERAGE, MINIMUM,

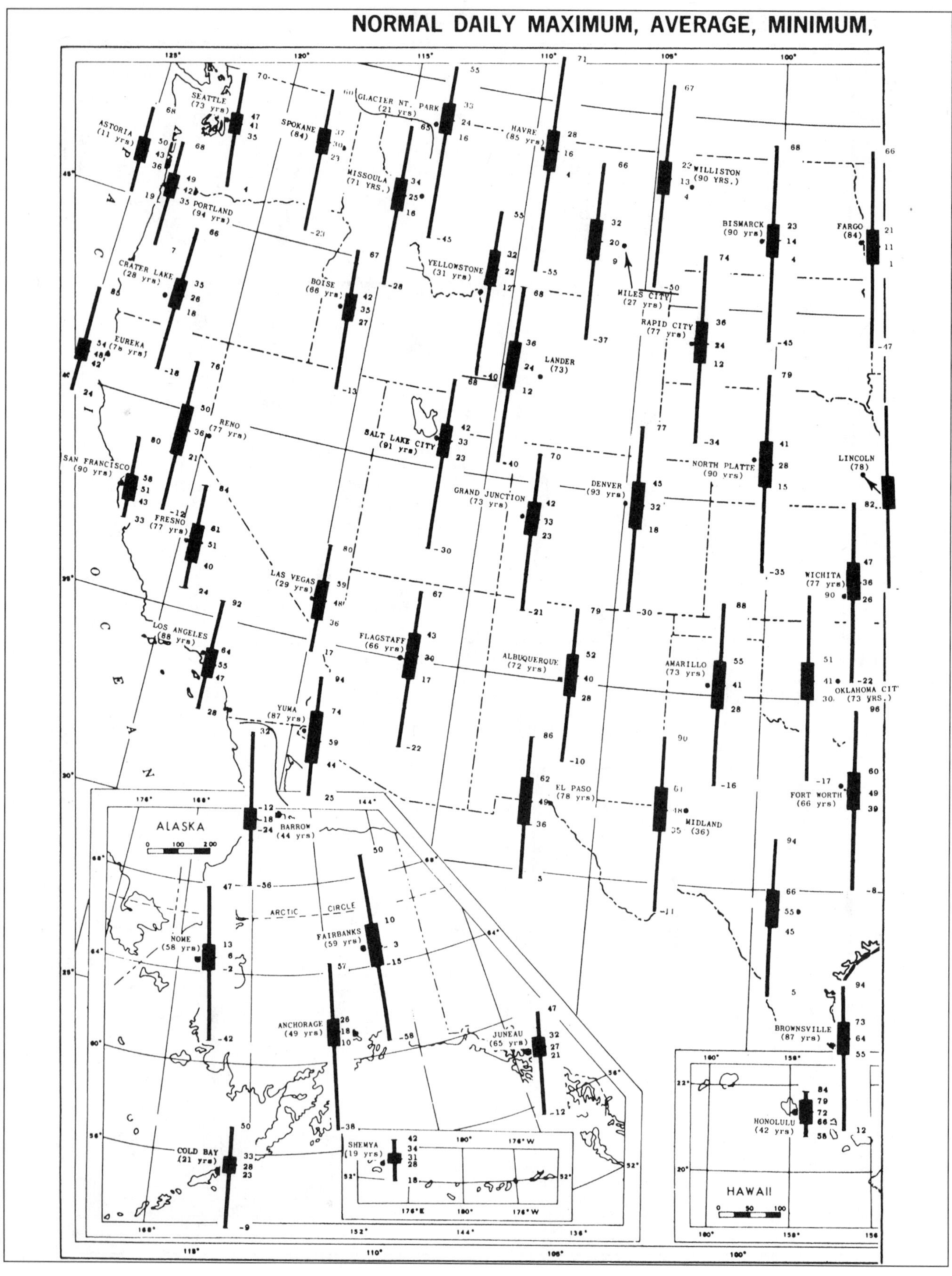

AND EXTREME TEMPERATURES (°F), FEBRUARY

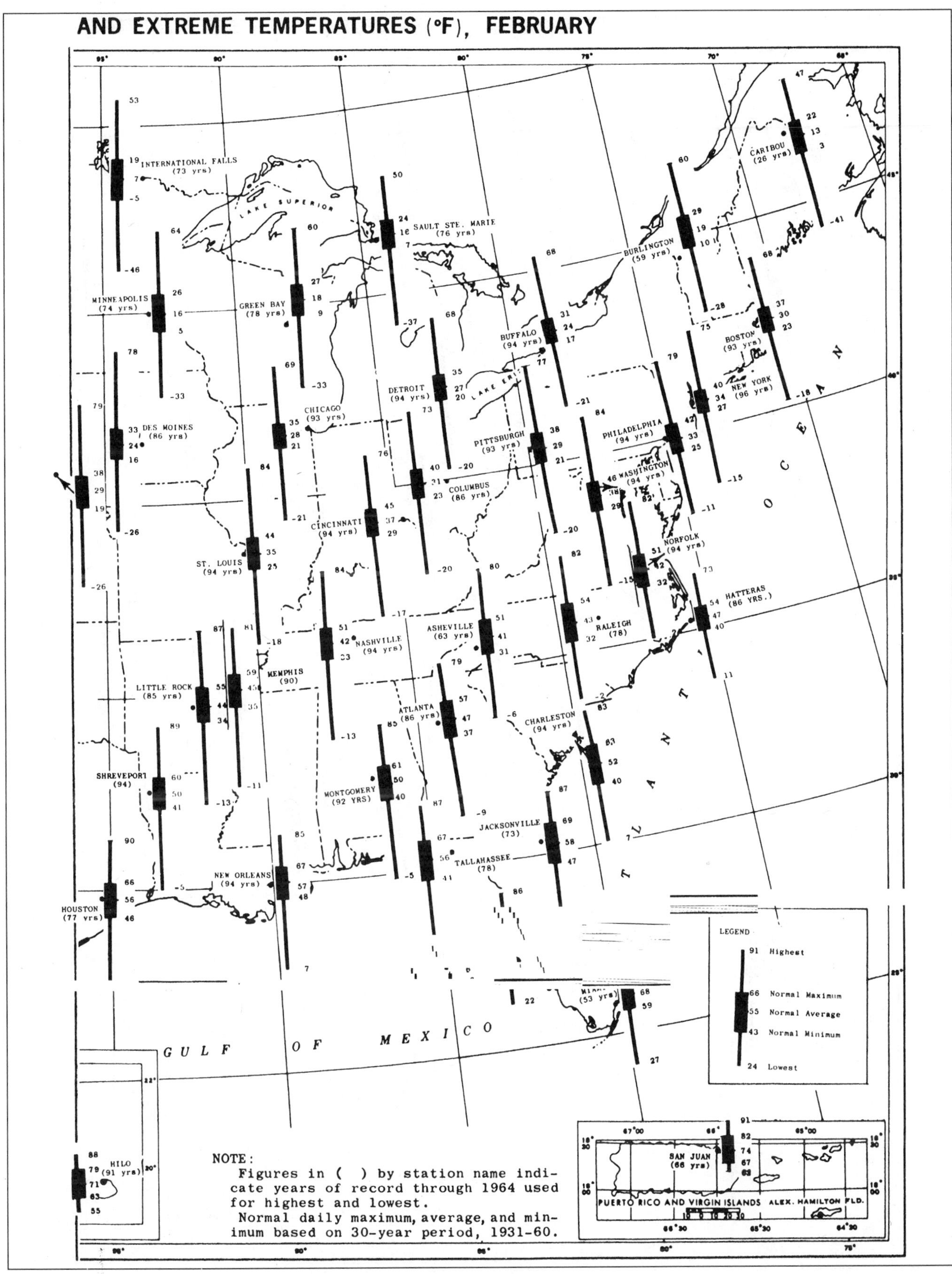

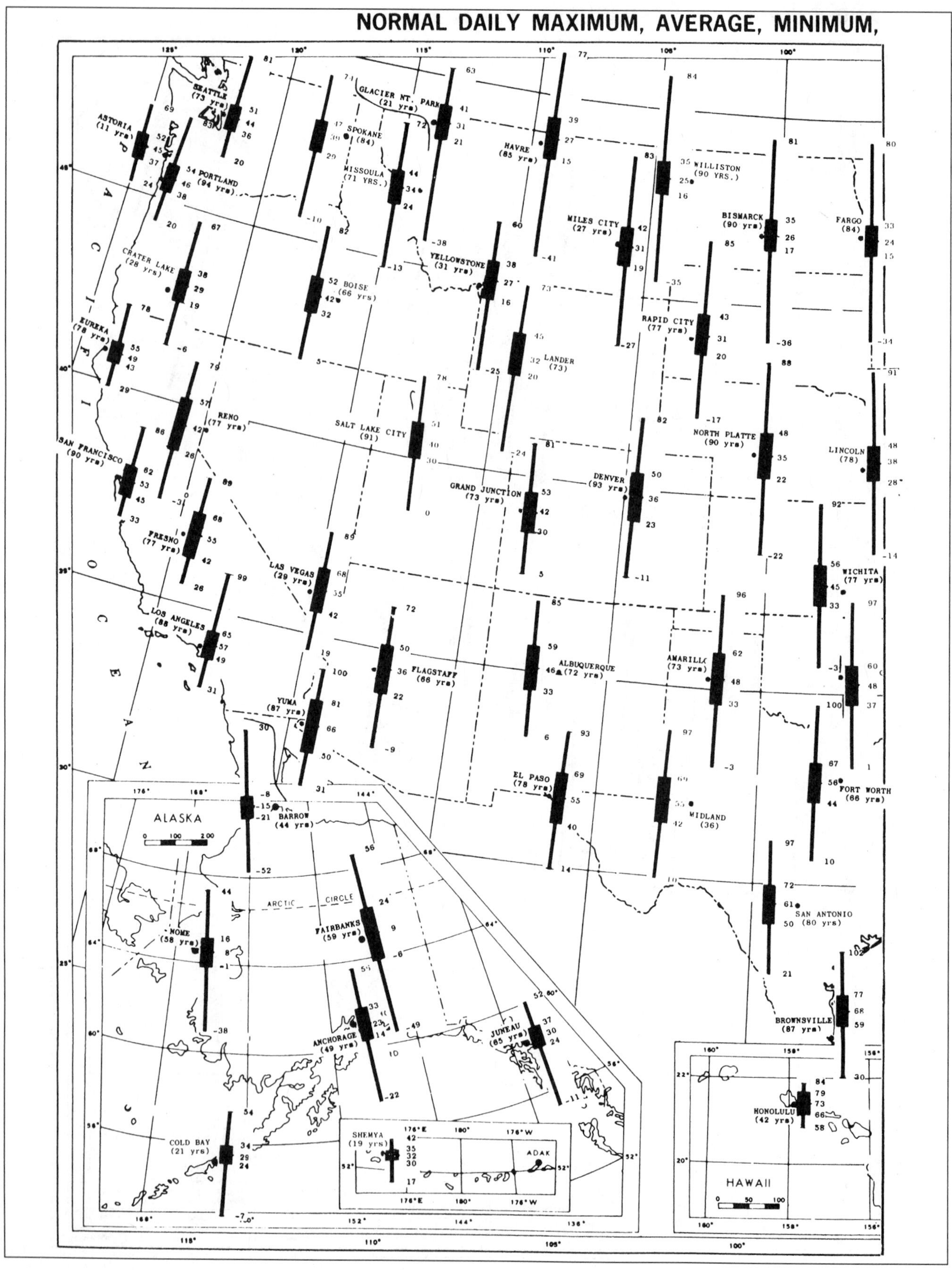
NORMAL DAILY MAXIMUM, AVERAGE, MINIMUM,
SEATTLE (73 yrs)
ASTORIA (11 yrs)
PORTLAND (94 yrs)
GLACIER NT. PARK (21 yrs)
SPOKANE (84)
MISSOULA (71 YRS.)
HAVRE (85 yrs)
WILLISTON (90 YRS.)
MILES CITY (27 yrs)
BISMARCK (90 yrs)
FARGO (84)
CRATER LAKE (28 yrs)
BOISE (66 yrs)
YELLOWSTONE (31 yrs)
EUREKA (78 yrs)
LANDER (73)
RAPID CITY (77 yrs)
RENO (77 yrs)
SALT LAKE CITY (91)
NORTH PLATTE (90 yrs)
LINCOLN (78)
SAN FRANCISCO (90 yrs)
GRAND JUNCTION (73 yrs)
DENVER (93 yrs)
FRESNO (77 yrs)
LAS VEGAS (29 yrs)
WICHITA (77 yrs)
LOS ANGELES (88 yrs)
FLAGSTAFF (66 yrs)
ALBUQUERQUE (72 yrs)
AMARILLO (73 yrs)
YUMA (87 yrs)
EL PASO (78 yrs)
MIDLAND (36)
FORT WORTH (66 yrs)
SAN ANTONIO (80 yrs)
BROWNSVILLE (87 yrs)
ALASKA
BARROW (44 yrs)
ARCTIC CIRCLE
NOME (58 yrs)
FAIRBANKS (59 yrs)
ANCHORAGE (49 yrs)
JUNEAU (85 yrs)
COLD BAY (21 yrs)
SHEMYA (19 yrs)
ADAK
HAWAII
HONOLULU (42 yrs)
P A C I F I C O C E A N

AND EXTREME TEMPERATURES (°F), MARCH

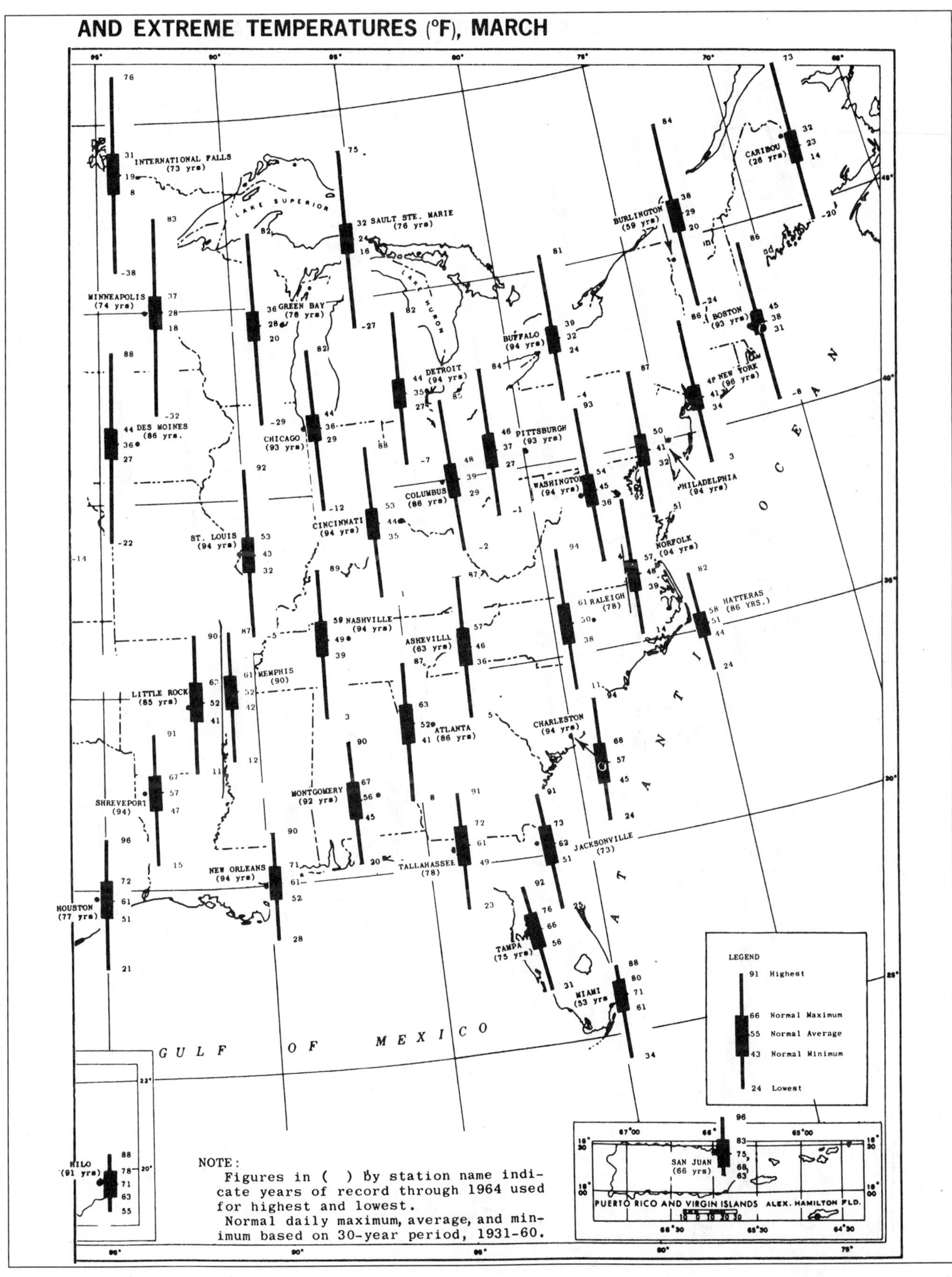

NOTE:
Figures in ( ) by station name indicate years of record through 1964 used for highest and lowest.
Normal daily maximum, average, and minimum based on 30-year period, 1931-60.

NORMAL DAILY MAXIMUM, AVERAGE, MINIMUM,

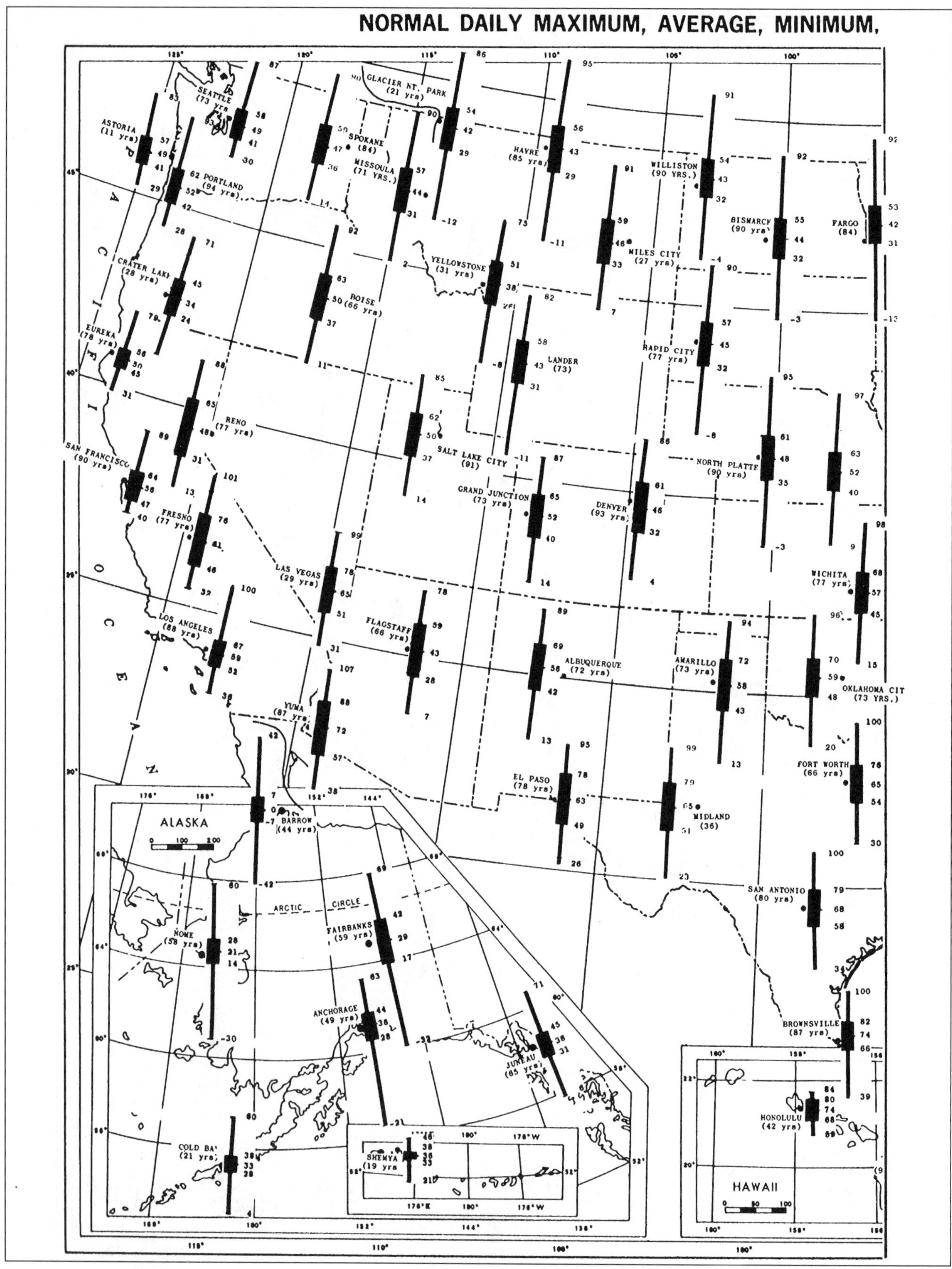

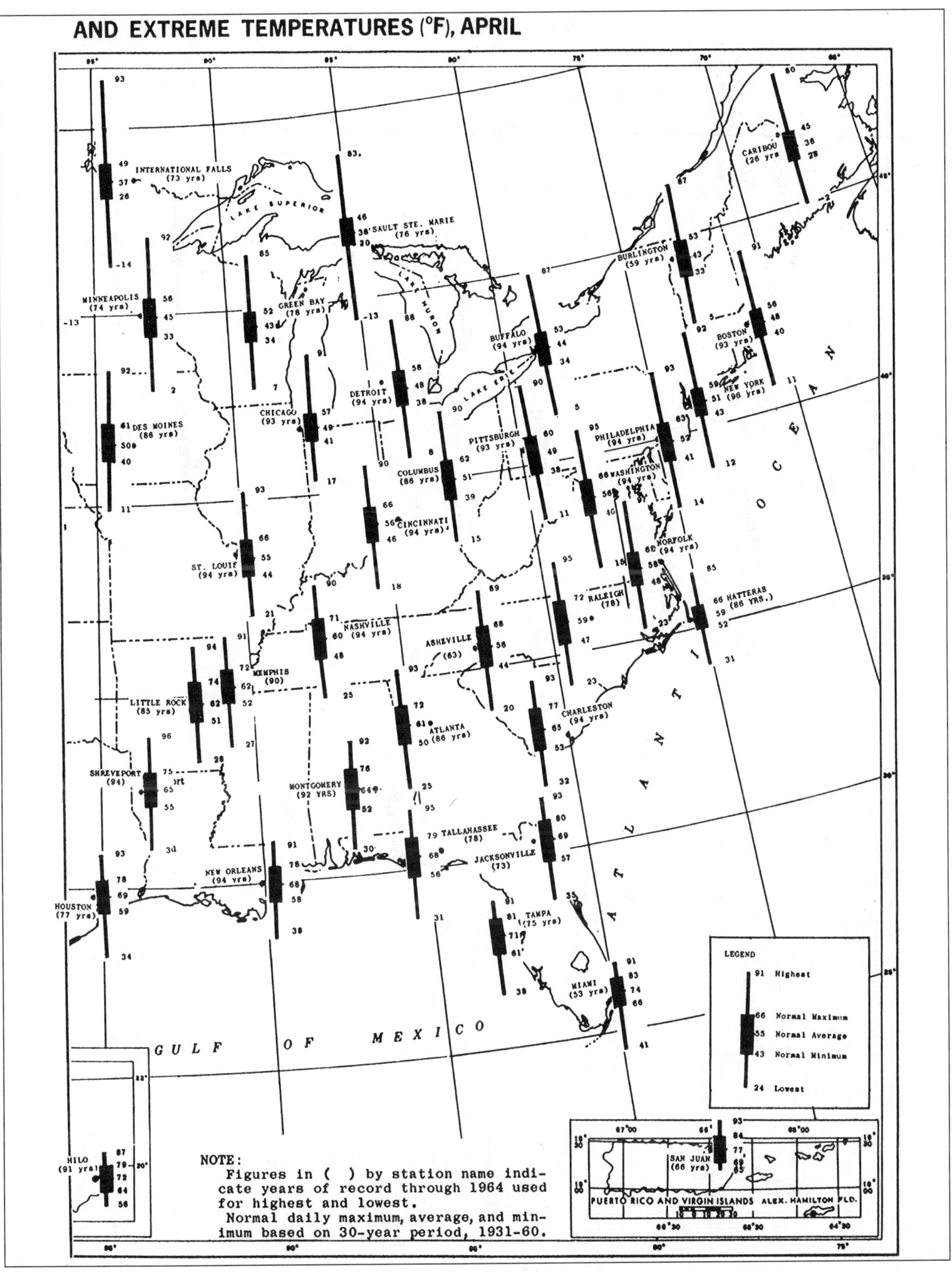
AND EXTREME TEMPERATURES (°F), APRIL
INTERNATIONAL FALLS (73 yrs) 93 49 37 26 -14
LAKE SUPERIOR
SAULT STE. MARIE (76 yrs) 83 46 38 20 -13
MINNEAPOLIS (74 yrs) 92 56 45 33 -13
GREEN BAY (78 yrs) 85 52 43 34 7
LAKE HURON
LAKE ERIE
DES MOINES (86 yrs) 92 61 50 40 11
CHICAGO (93 yrs) 91 57 49 41 17
DETROIT (94 yrs) 88 58 48 38 8
BUFFALO (94 yrs) 87 53 44 34 5
BURLINGTON (59 yrs) 87 53 43 33 5
CARIBOU (26 yrs) 80 45 36 28 -2
BOSTON (93 yrs) 91 56 48 40 11
NEW YORK (96 yrs) 93 59 51 43 12
PHILADELPHIA (94 yrs) 93 63 52 41 14
PITTSBURGH (93 yrs) 90 60 49 38 11
WASHINGTON (94 yrs) 95 66 56 46 15
COLUMBUS (86 yrs) 90 62 51 39 15
CINCINNATI (94 yrs) 90 66 56 46 18
ST. LOUIS (94 yrs) 93 66 55 44 21
NORFOLK (94 yrs) 95 68 58 48 23
HATTERAS (86 YRS.) 85 66 59 52 31
RALEIGH (78) 95 72 59 47 23
ASHEVILLE (63) 89 68 56 44 20
NASHVILLE (94 yrs) 90 71 60 48 25
MEMPHIS (90) 91 72 62 52 27
LITTLE ROCK (85 yrs) 94 74 62 51 28
SHREVEPORT (94) 96 75 65 55 30
ATLANTA (86 yrs) 93 72 61 50 25
MONTGOMERY (92 YRS) 92 76 64 52 30
CHARLESTON (94 yrs) 93 77 65 53 32
TALLAHASSEE (78) 95 79 68 56 31
JACKSONVILLE (73) 93 80 69 57 35
NEW ORLEANS (94 yrs) 91 78 68 58 38
HOUSTON (77 yrs) 93 78 69 59 34
TAMPA (75 yrs) 91 81 71 61 38
MIAMI (53 yrs) 91 83 74 66 41
HILO (91 yrs) 87 79 72 64 56
SAN JUAN (66 yrs) 93 84 77 69 65
PUERTO RICO AND VIRGIN ISLANDS ALEX. HAMILTON FLD.
GULF OF MEXICO
ATLANTIC OCEAN
LEGEND
91 Highest
66 Normal Maximum
55 Normal Average
43 Normal Minimum
24 Lowest
NOTE:
Figures in ( ) by station name indicate years of record through 1964 used for highest and lowest.
Normal daily maximum, average, and minimum based on 30-year period, 1931-60.

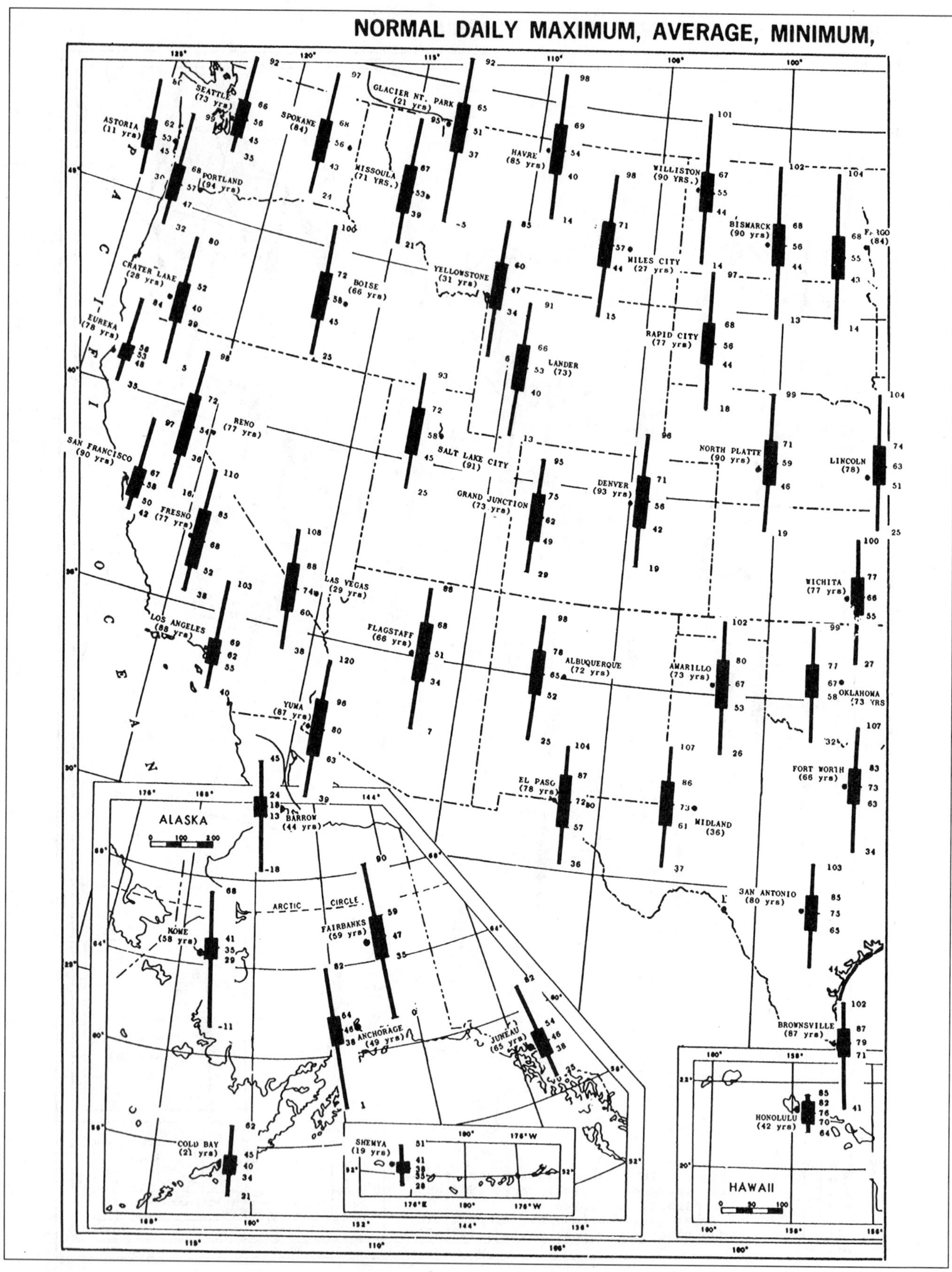
NORMAL DAILY MAXIMUM, AVERAGE, MINIMUM,
ALASKA
HAWAII
ARCTIC CIRCLE

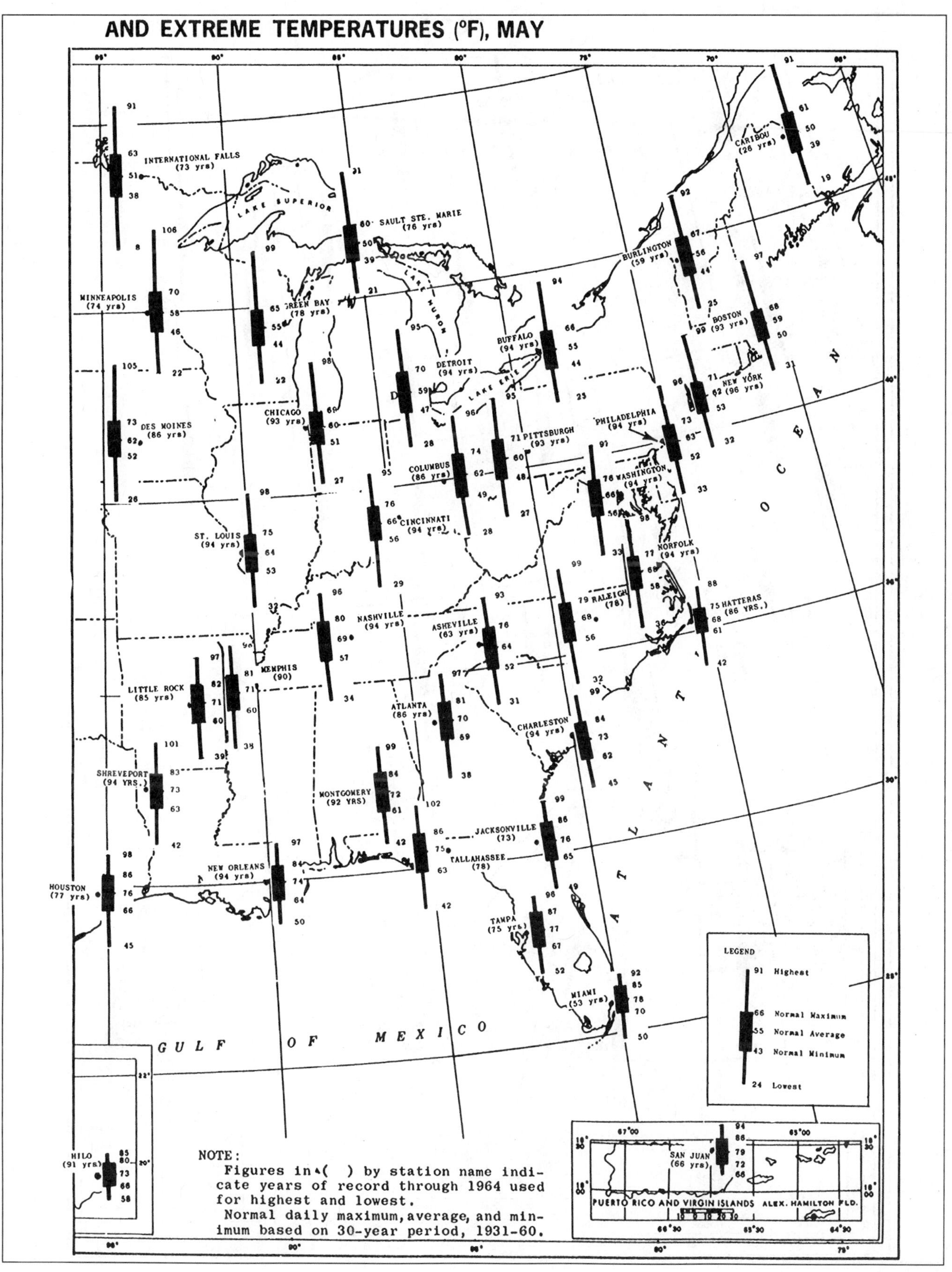
AND EXTREME TEMPERATURES (°F), MAY
INTERNATIONAL FALLS (73 yrs) 91 63 51 38
SAULT STE. MARIE (76 yrs) 91 60 50 39 21
LAKE SUPERIOR
LAKE HURON
LAKE ERIE
MINNEAPOLIS (74 yrs) 106 70 58 46 8
GREEN BAY (78 yrs) 99 65 55 44 22
CARIBOU (26 yrs) 91 61 50 39 19
BURLINGTON (59 yrs) 92 67 56 44 25
BOSTON (93 yrs) 97 68 59 50 31
BUFFALO (94 yrs) 94 66 55 44 25
DETROIT (94 yrs) 95 70 59 47 28
NEW YORK (96 yrs) 96 71 62 53 32
DES MOINES (86 yrs) 105 73 62 52 26
CHICAGO (93 yrs) 98 69 60 51 27
PITTSBURGH (93 yrs) 95 71 60 48 27
PHILADELPHIA (94 yrs) 73 63 52 33
COLUMBUS (86 yrs) 96 74 62 49 28
WASHINGTON (94 yrs) 97 76 66 56 33
CINCINNATI (94 yrs) 95 76 66 56 29
ST. LOUIS (94 yrs) 98 75 64 53 32
NORFOLK (94 yrs) 98 77 68 58 36
RALEIGH (78) 99 79 68 56 32
HATTERAS (86 YRS.) 88 75 68 61 42
NASHVILLE (94 yrs) 96 80 69 57 34
ASHEVILLE (63 yrs) 93 76 64 52 31
MEMPHIS (90) 98 81 71 60 38
LITTLE ROCK (85 yrs) 97 82 71 60 39
ATLANTA (86 yrs) 97 81 70 59 38
CHARLESTON (94 yrs) 99 84 73 62 45
SHREVEPORT (94 YRS.) 101 83 73 63 42
MONTGOMERY (92 YRS) 99 84 72 61 42
JACKSONVILLE (73) 99 86 76 65 49
TALLAHASSEE (78) 102 86 75 63 42
NEW ORLEANS (94 yrs) 97 84 74 64 50
HOUSTON (77 yrs) 98 86 76 66 45
TAMPA (75 yrs) 98 87 77 67 52
MIAMI (53 yrs) 92 85 78 70 50
GULF OF MEXICO
ATLANTIC OCEAN
HILO (91 yrs) 85 80 73 66 58
SAN JUAN (66 yrs) 94 86 79 72 66
PUERTO RICO AND VIRGIN ISLANDS ALEX. HAMILTON FLD.
LEGEND
91 Highest
66 Normal Maximum
55 Normal Average
43 Normal Minimum
24 Lowest
NOTE:
Figures in ( ) by station name indicate years of record through 1964 used for highest and lowest.
Normal daily maximum, average, and minimum based on 30-year period, 1931-60.

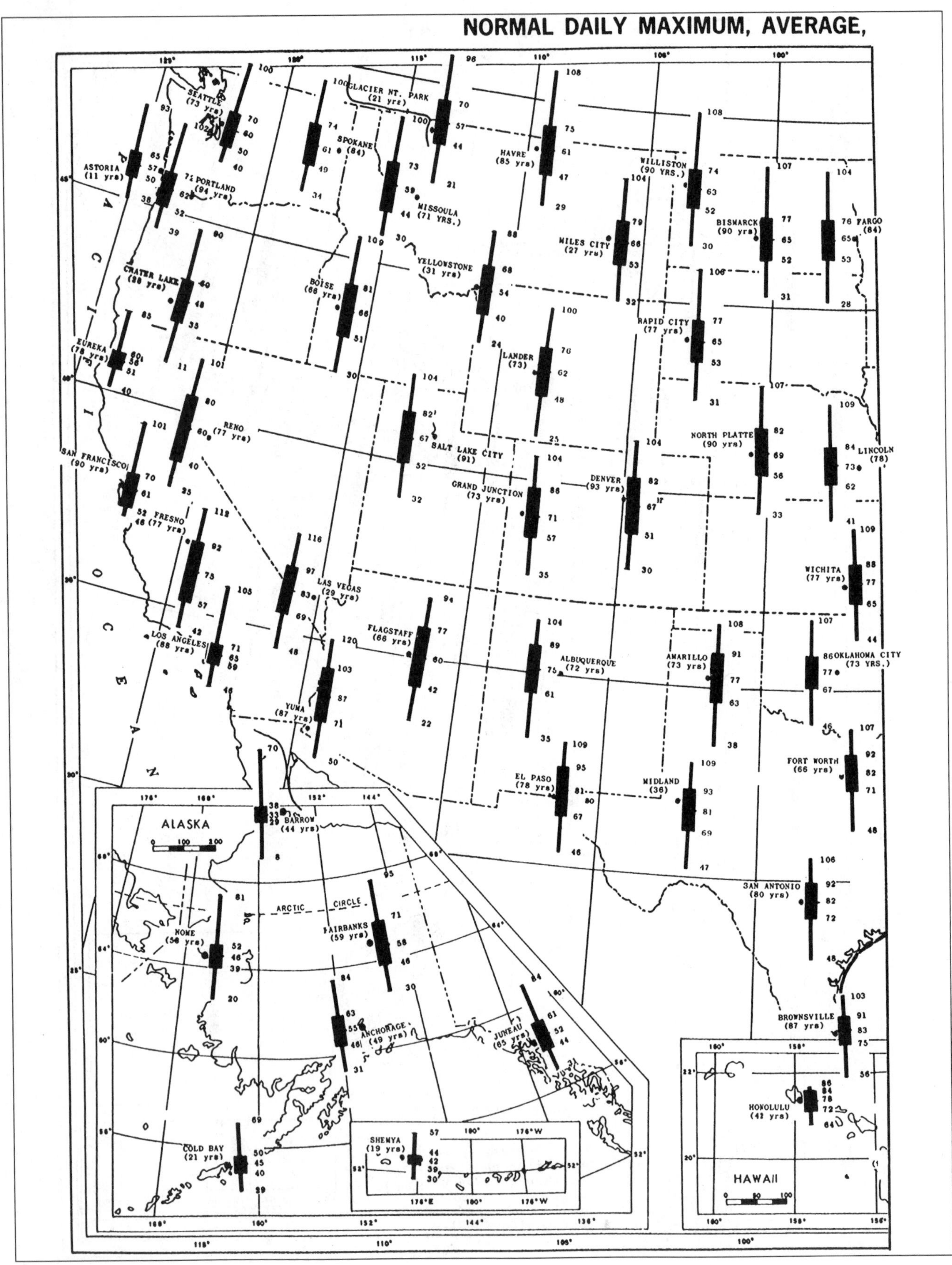
NORMAL DAILY MAXIMUM, AVERAGE,
SEATTLE (73 yrs)
ASTORIA (11 yrs)
PORTLAND (94 yrs)
CRATER LAKE
EUREKA (78 yrs)
SAN FRANCISCO (90 yrs)
RENO (77 yrs)
FRESNO (77 yrs)
LOS ANGELES (88 yrs)
GLACIER NT. PARK (21 yrs)
SPOKANE (84)
MISSOULA (71 YRS.)
BOISE (66 yrs)
YELLOWSTONE (31 yrs)
SALT LAKE CITY (91)
LAS VEGAS (29 yrs)
FLAGSTAFF (66 yrs)
YUMA (87 yrs)
HAVRE (85 yrs)
LANDER (73)
GRAND JUNCTION (73 yrs)
ALBUQUERQUE (72 yrs)
EL PASO (78 yrs)
MILES CITY (27 yrs)
DENVER (93 yrs)
WILLISTON (90 YRS.)
RAPID CITY (77 yrs)
BISMARCK (90 yrs)
FARGO (84)
NORTH PLATTE (90 yrs)
LINCOLN (78)
WICHITA (77 yrs)
OKLAHOMA CITY (73 YRS.)
AMARILLO (73 yrs)
MIDLAND (36)
FORT WORTH (66 yrs)
SAN ANTONIO (80 yrs)
BROWNSVILLE (87 yrs)
ALASKA
BARROW (44 yrs)
ARCTIC CIRCLE
NOME (56 yrs)
FAIRBANKS (59 yrs)
ANCHORAGE (49 yrs)
JUNEAU (65 yrs)
COLD BAY (21 yrs)
SHEMYA (19 yrs)
HAWAII
HONOLULU (42 yrs)

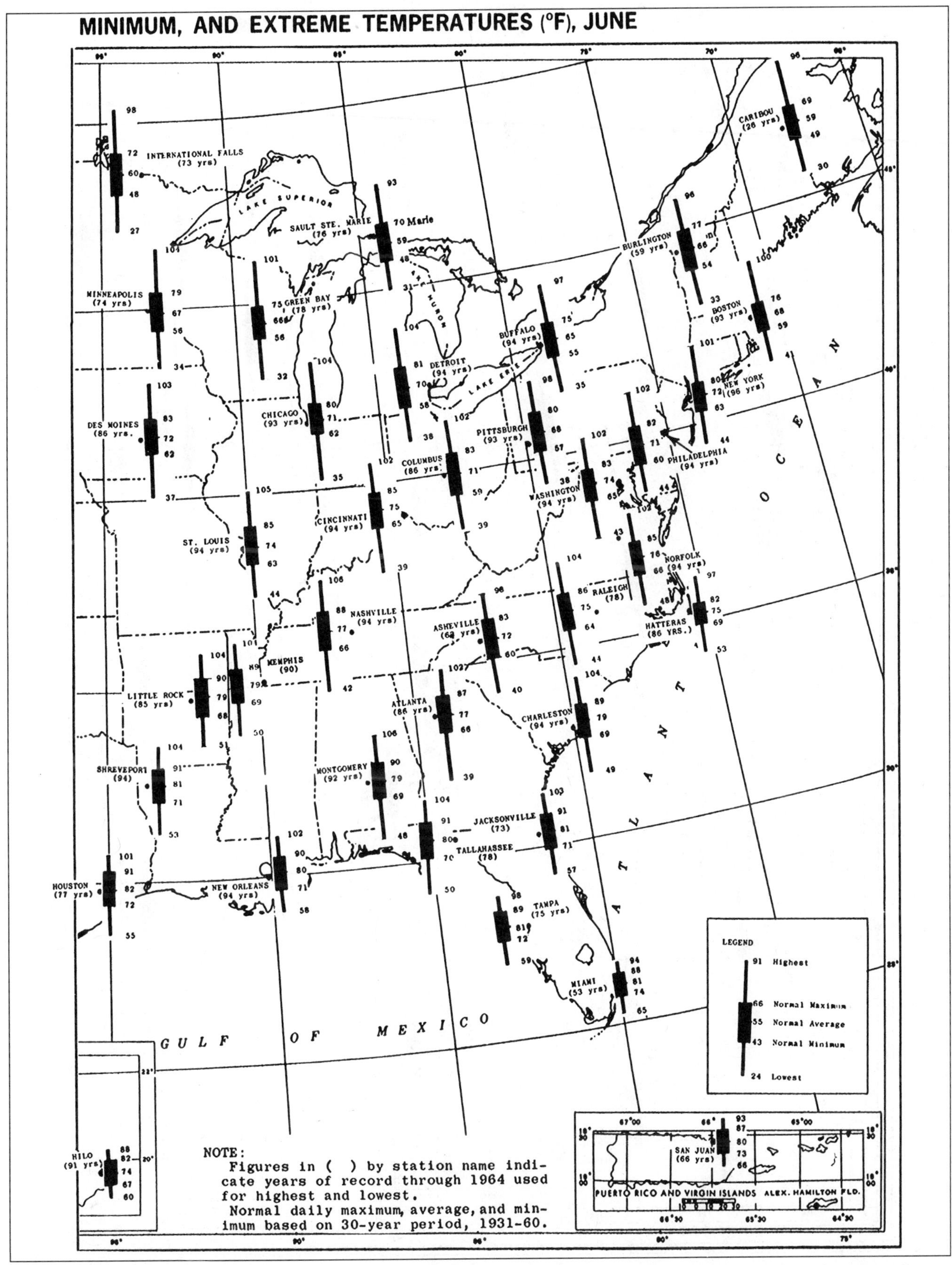
MINIMUM, AND EXTREME TEMPERATURES (°F), JUNE
INTERNATIONAL FALLS (73 yrs) 98 72 60 48 27
SAULT STE. MARIE (76 yrs) 93 70 59 48 31
CARIBOU (26 yrs) 96 69 59 49 30
BURLINGTON (59 yrs) 96 77 66 54 33
MINNEAPOLIS (74 yrs) 104 79 67 56 34
GREEN BAY (78 yrs) 101 75 66 56 32
BUFFALO (94 yrs) 97 75 65 55 35
BOSTON (93 yrs) 100 76 68 59 41
DETROIT (94 yrs) 104 81 70 58 38
NEW YORK (96 yrs) 101 80 72 63 44
DES MOINES (86 yrs.) 103 83 72 62 37
CHICAGO (93 yrs) 104 80 71 62 35
PITTSBURGH (93 yrs) 98 80 68 57 38
PHILADELPHIA (94 yrs) 102 82 71 60 44
COLUMBUS (86 yrs) 102 83 71 59 39
WASHINGTON (94 yrs) 102 83 74 65 43
ST. LOUIS (94 yrs) 105 85 74 63 44
CINCINNATI (94 yrs) 102 85 75 65 39
NORFOLK (94 yrs) 102 85 76 66 48
RALEIGH (78) 104 86 75 64 44
NASHVILLE (94 yrs) 106 88 77 66 42
ASHEVILLE (63 yrs) 96 83 72 60 40
HATTERAS (86 YRS.) 97 82 75 69 53
LITTLE ROCK (85 yrs) 104 90 79 68 50
MEMPHIS (90) 101 89 79 69 51
ATLANTA (86 yrs) 102 87 77 66 39
CHARLESTON (94 yrs) 104 89 79 69 49
SHREVEPORT (94) 104 91 81 71 53
MONTGOMERY (92 yrs) 106 90 79 69 48
JACKSONVILLE (73) 103 91 81 71 57
TALLAHASSEE (78) 104 91 80 70 50
HOUSTON (77 yrs) 101 91 82 72 55
NEW ORLEANS (94 yrs) 102 90 80 71 58
TAMPA (75 yrs) 98 89 81 72 59
MIAMI (53 yrs) 94 88 81 74 65
HILO (91 yrs) 88 82 74 67 60
SAN JUAN (66 yrs) 93 87 80 73 66
LAKE SUPERIOR
LAKE HURON
LAKE ERIE
ATLANTIC OCEAN
GULF OF MEXICO
PUERTO RICO AND VIRGIN ISLANDS
ALEX. HAMILTON FLD.
LEGEND
91 Highest
66 Normal Maximum
55 Normal Average
43 Normal Minimum
24 Lowest
NOTE:
Figures in ( ) by station name indicate years of record through 1964 used for highest and lowest.
Normal daily maximum, average, and minimum based on 30-year period, 1931-60.

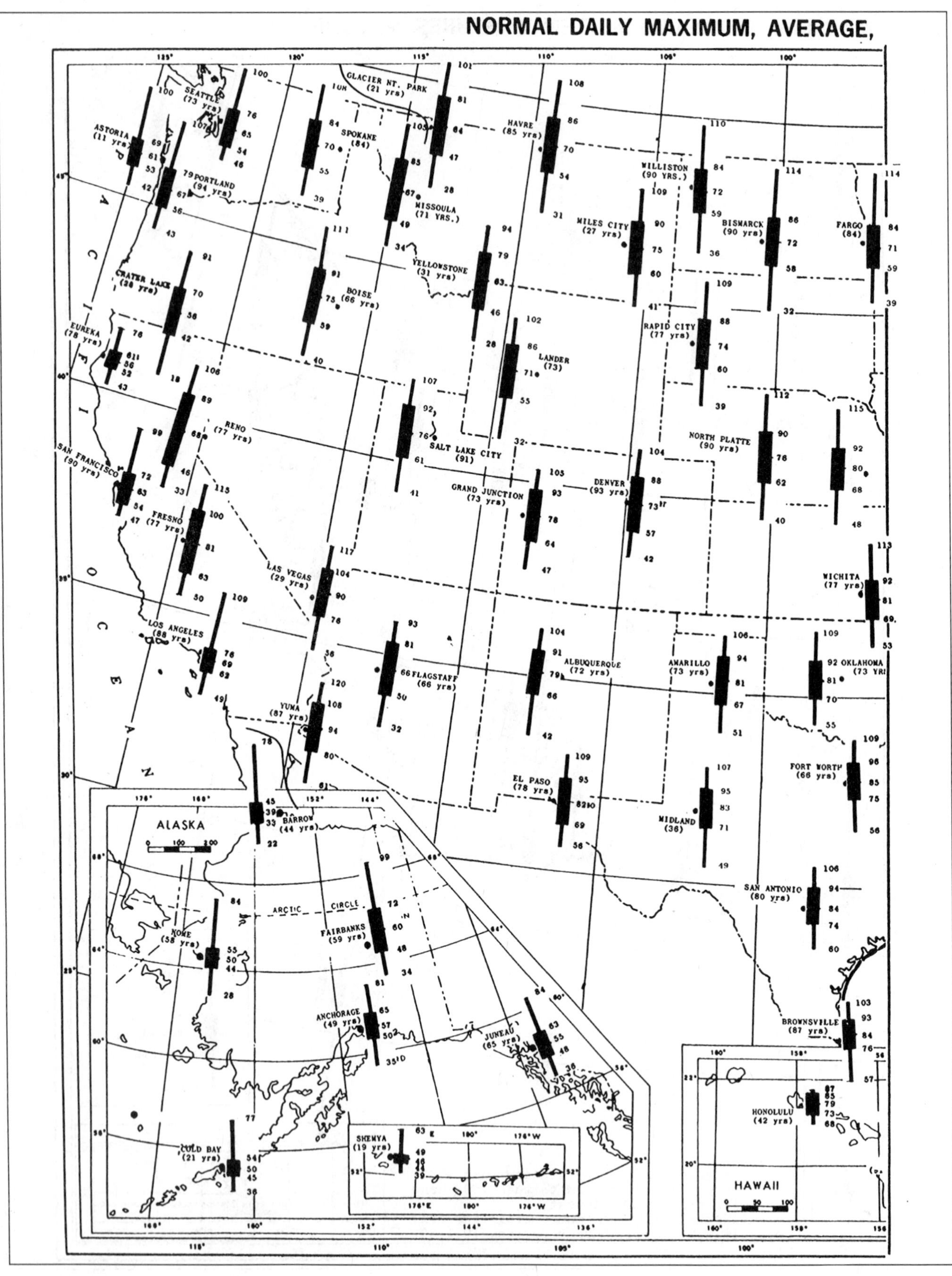

NORMAL DAILY MAXIMUM, AVERAGE,
GLACIER NT. PARK (21 yrs)
SEATTLE (73 yrs)
ASTORIA (11 yrs)
PORTLAND (94 yrs)
SPOKANE (84)
MISSOULA (71 YRS.)
HAVRE (85 yrs)
WILLISTON (90 YRS.)
MILES CITY (27 yrs)
BISMARCK (90 yrs)
FARGO (84)
YELLOWSTONE (31 yrs)
BOISE (66 yrs)
CRATER LAKE (36 yrs)
EUREKA (78 yrs)
LANDER (73)
RAPID CITY (77 yrs)
RENO (77 yrs)
SALT LAKE CITY (91)
NORTH PLATTE (90 yrs)
SAN FRANCISCO (90 yrs)
GRAND JUNCTION (73 yrs)
DENVER (93 yrs)
FRESNO (77 yrs)
LAS VEGAS (29 yrs)
WICHITA (77 yrs)
LOS ANGELES (88 yrs)
FLAGSTAFF (66 yrs)
ALBUQUERQUE (72 yrs)
AMARILLO (73 yrs)
OKLAHOMA
YUMA (87 yrs)
EL PASO (78 yrs)
FORT WORTH (66 yrs)
MIDLAND (36)
SAN ANTONIO (80 yrs)
BROWNSVILLE (87 yrs)
P A C I F I C
O C E A N
ALASKA
BARROW (44 yrs)
ARCTIC CIRCLE
NOME (58 yrs)
FAIRBANKS (59 yrs)
ANCHORAGE (49 yrs)
JUNEAU (65 yrs)
COLD BAY (21 yrs)
SHEMYA (19 yrs)
HAWAII
HONOLULU (42 yrs)

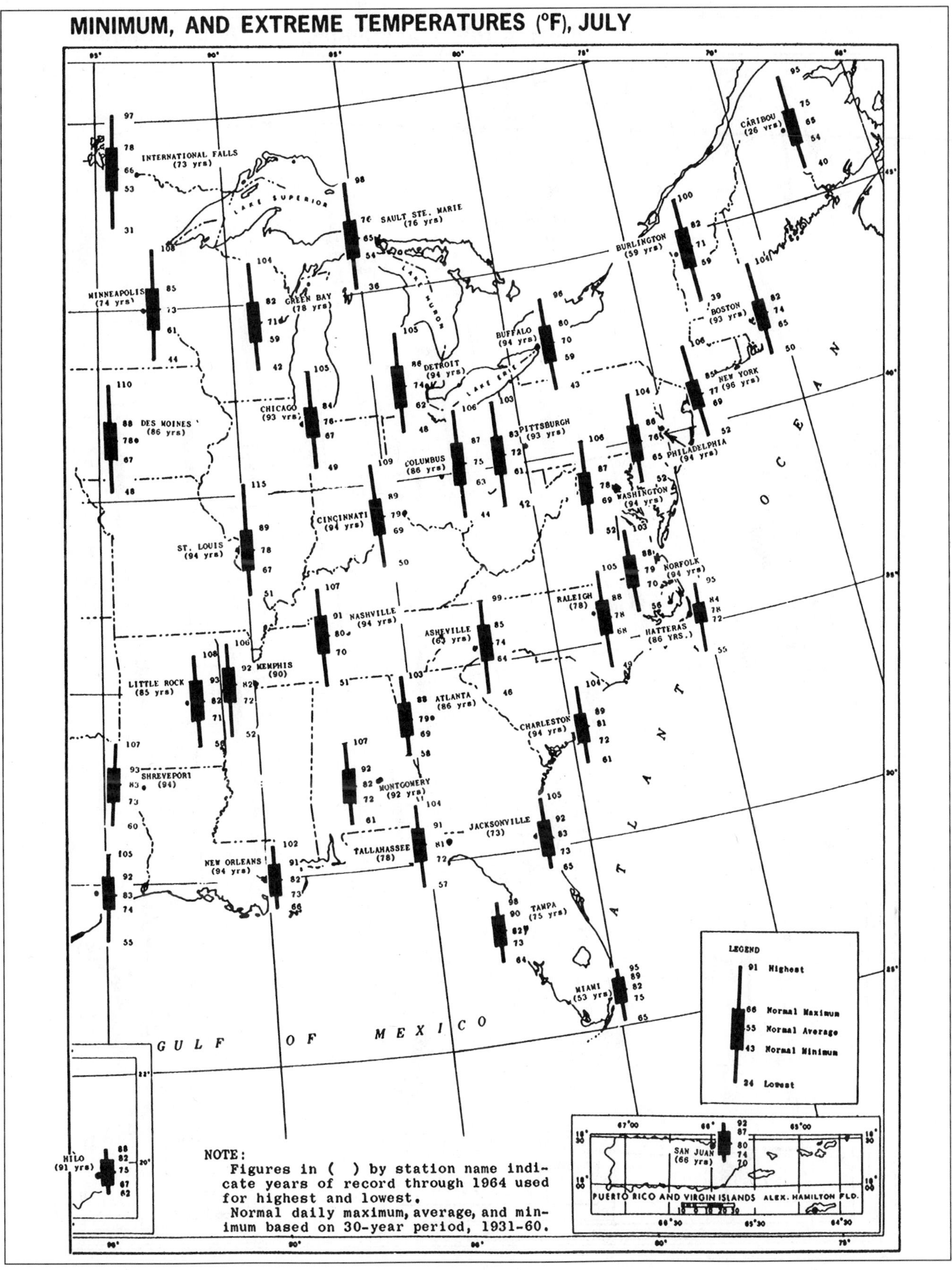
MINIMUM, AND EXTREME TEMPERATURES (°F), JULY
INTERNATIONAL FALLS (73 yrs)
LAKE SUPERIOR
SAULT STE. MARIE (76 yrs)
CARIBOU (26 yrs)
BURLINGTON (59 yrs)
MINNEAPOLIS (74 yrs)
GREEN BAY (78 yrs)
LAKE HURON
BOSTON (93 yrs)
BUFFALO (94 yrs)
DETROIT (94 yrs)
LAKE ERIE
NEW YORK (96 yrs)
DES MOINES (86 yrs)
CHICAGO (93 yrs)
PITTSBURGH (93 yrs)
PHILADELPHIA (94 yrs)
COLUMBUS (86 yrs)
WASHINGTON (94 yrs)
CINCINNATI (94 yrs)
ST. LOUIS (94 yrs)
NORFOLK (94 yrs)
NASHVILLE (94 yrs)
RALEIGH (78)
ASHEVILLE (63 yrs)
HATTERAS (86 YRS.)
MEMPHIS (90)
LITTLE ROCK (85 yrs)
ATLANTA (86 yrs)
CHARLESTON (94 yrs)
SHREVEPORT (94)
MONTGOMERY (92 yrs)
JACKSONVILLE (73)
TALLAHASSEE (78)
NEW ORLEANS (94 yrs)
TAMPA (75 yrs)
MIAMI (53 yrs)
ATLANTIC OCEAN
GULF OF MEXICO
HILO (91 yrs)
SAN JUAN (66 yrs)
PUERTO RICO AND VIRGIN ISLANDS
ALEX. HAMILTON FLD.
LEGEND
91 Highest
66 Normal Maximum
55 Normal Average
43 Normal Minimum
24 Lowest
NOTE:
Figures in ( ) by station name indicate years of record through 1964 used for highest and lowest.
Normal daily maximum, average, and minimum based on 30-year period, 1931-60.

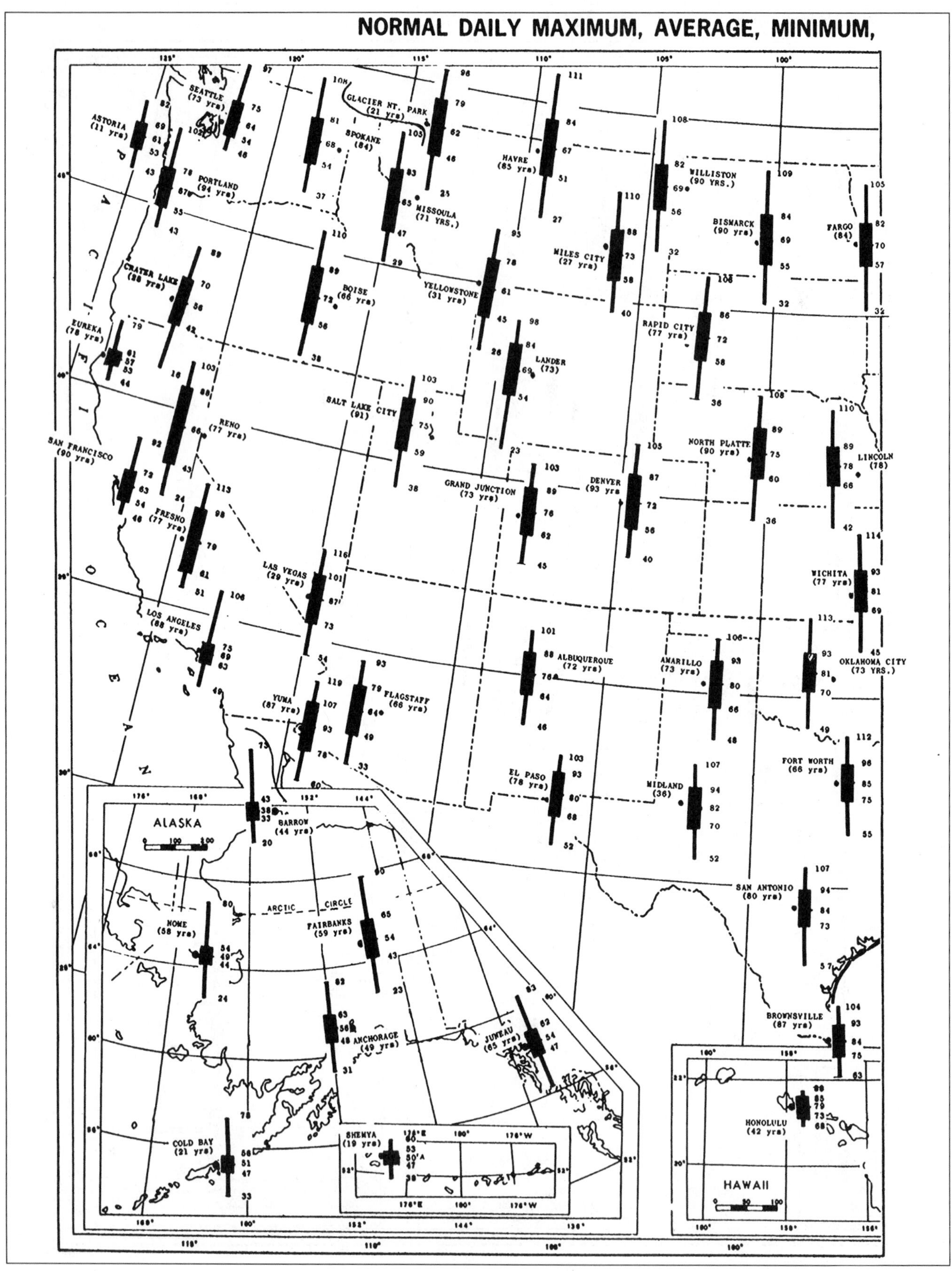
NORMAL DAILY MAXIMUM, AVERAGE, MINIMUM,
SEATTLE (73 yrs)
ASTORIA (11 yrs)
PORTLAND (94 yrs)
GLACIER NT. PARK (21 yrs)
SPOKANE (84)
MISSOULA (71 YRS.)
HAVRE (85 yrs)
WILLISTON (90 YRS.)
BISMARCK (90 yrs)
FARGO (84)
MILES CITY (27 yrs)
CRATER LAKE (28 yrs)
BOISE (66 yrs)
YELLOWSTONE (31 yrs)
EUREKA (78 yrs)
RAPID CITY (77 yrs)
LANDER (73)
RENO (77 yrs)
SALT LAKE CITY (91)
SAN FRANCISCO (90 yrs)
NORTH PLATTE (90 yrs)
LINCOLN (78)
GRAND JUNCTION (73 yrs)
DENVER (93 yrs)
FRESNO (77 yrs)
LAS VEGAS (29 yrs)
WICHITA (77 yrs)
LOS ANGELES (88 yrs)
ALBUQUERQUE (72 yrs)
AMARILLO (73 yrs)
OKLAHOMA CITY (73 YRS.)
YUMA (87 yrs)
FLAGSTAFF (66 yrs)
EL PASO (78 yrs)
MIDLAND (36)
FORT WORTH (66 yrs)
SAN ANTONIO (80 yrs)
BROWNSVILLE (87 yrs)
ALASKA
BARROW (44 yrs)
ARCTIC CIRCLE
NOME (58 yrs)
FAIRBANKS (59 yrs)
ANCHORAGE (49 yrs)
JUNEAU (65 yrs)
COLD BAY (21 yrs)
SHEMYA (19 yrs)
HAWAII
HONOLULU (42 yrs)
P A C I F I C O C E A N

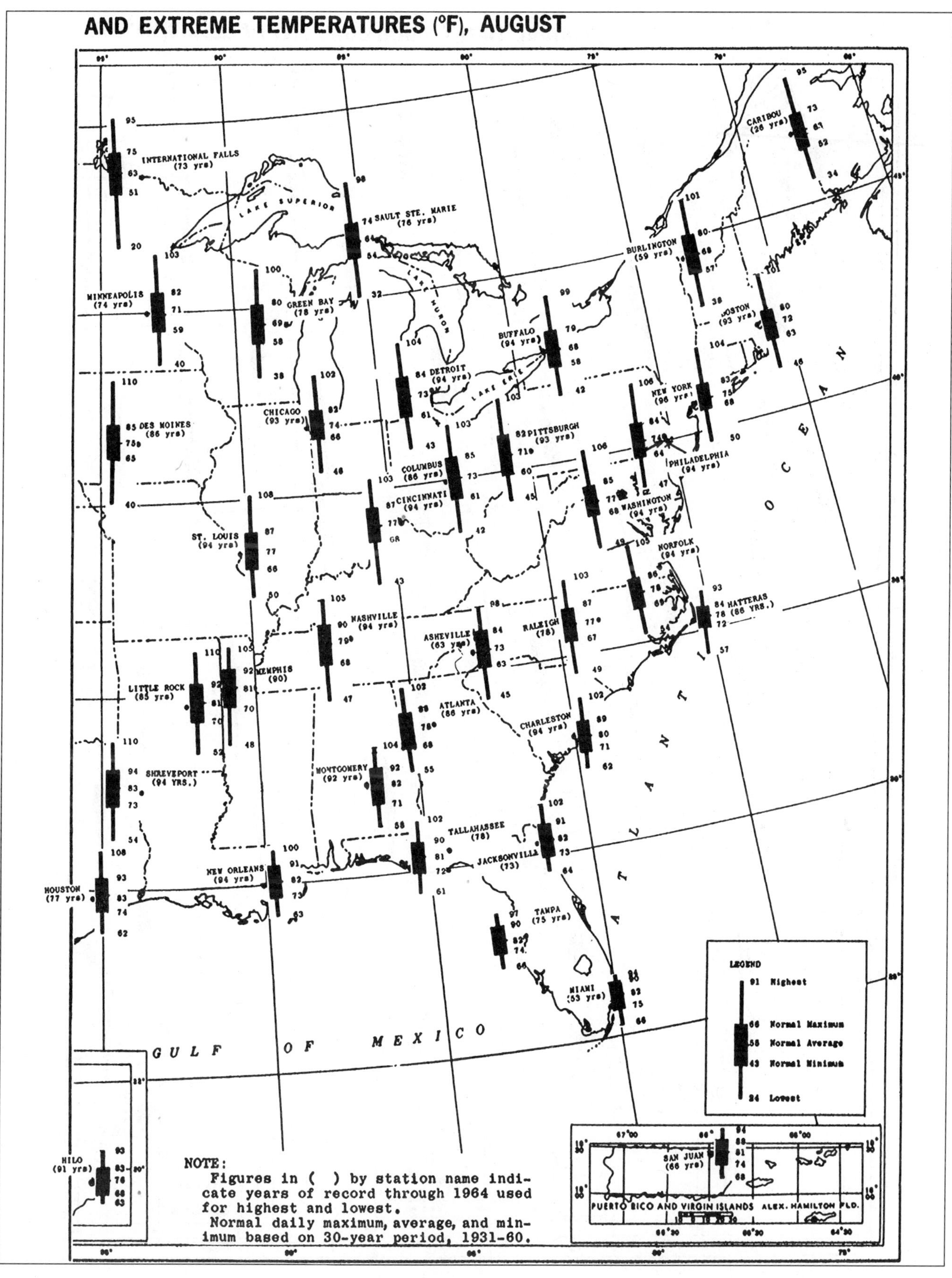
AND EXTREME TEMPERATURES (°F), AUGUST
INTERNATIONAL FALLS (73 yrs)
SAULT STE. MARIE (78 yrs)
CARIBOU (28 yrs)
LAKE SUPERIOR
LAKE HURON
LAKE ERIE
MINNEAPOLIS (74 yrs)
GREEN BAY (78 yrs)
BURLINGTON (59 yrs)
BOSTON (93 yrs)
BUFFALO (94 yrs)
DETROIT (94 yrs)
CHICAGO (93 yrs)
DES MOINES (86 yrs)
PITTSBURGH (93 yrs)
NEW YORK (96 yrs)
PHILADELPHIA (94 yrs)
COLUMBUS (86 yrs)
CINCINNATI (94 yrs)
WASHINGTON (94 yrs)
ST. LOUIS (94 yrs)
NORFOLK (94 yrs)
NASHVILLE (94 yrs)
ASHEVILLE (63 yrs)
RALEIGH (78)
HATTERAS (86 YRS.)
MEMPHIS (90)
LITTLE ROCK (85 yrs)
ATLANTA (86 yrs)
CHARLESTON (94 yrs)
SHREVEPORT (94 YRS.)
MONTGOMERY (92 yrs)
TALLAHASSEE (78)
JACKSONVILLE (73)
NEW ORLEANS (94 yrs)
HOUSTON (77 yrs)
TAMPA (75 yrs)
MIAMI (53 yrs)
ATLANTIC OCEAN
GULF OF MEXICO
HILO (91 yrs)
SAN JUAN (66 yrs)
PUERTO RICO AND VIRGIN ISLANDS
ALEX. HAMILTON FLD.
LEGEND
91 Highest
66 Normal Maximum
55 Normal Average
43 Normal Minimum
24 Lowest
NOTE:
Figures in ( ) by station name indicate years of record through 1964 used for highest and lowest.
Normal daily maximum, average, and minimum based on 30-year period, 1931-60.

NORMAL DAILY MAXIMUM, AVERAGE, MINIMUM,

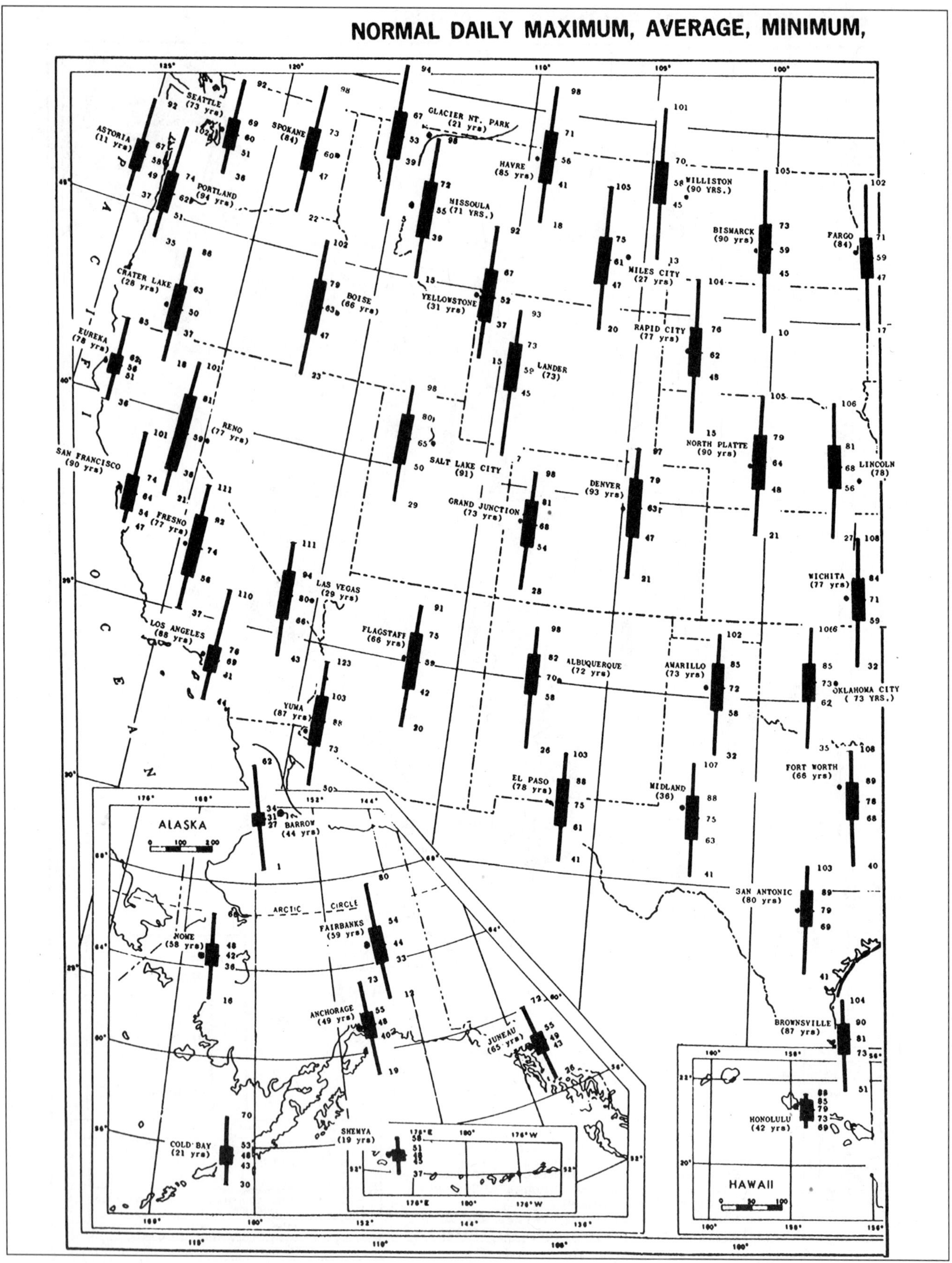

AND EXTREME TEMPERATURES (°F), SEPTEMBER

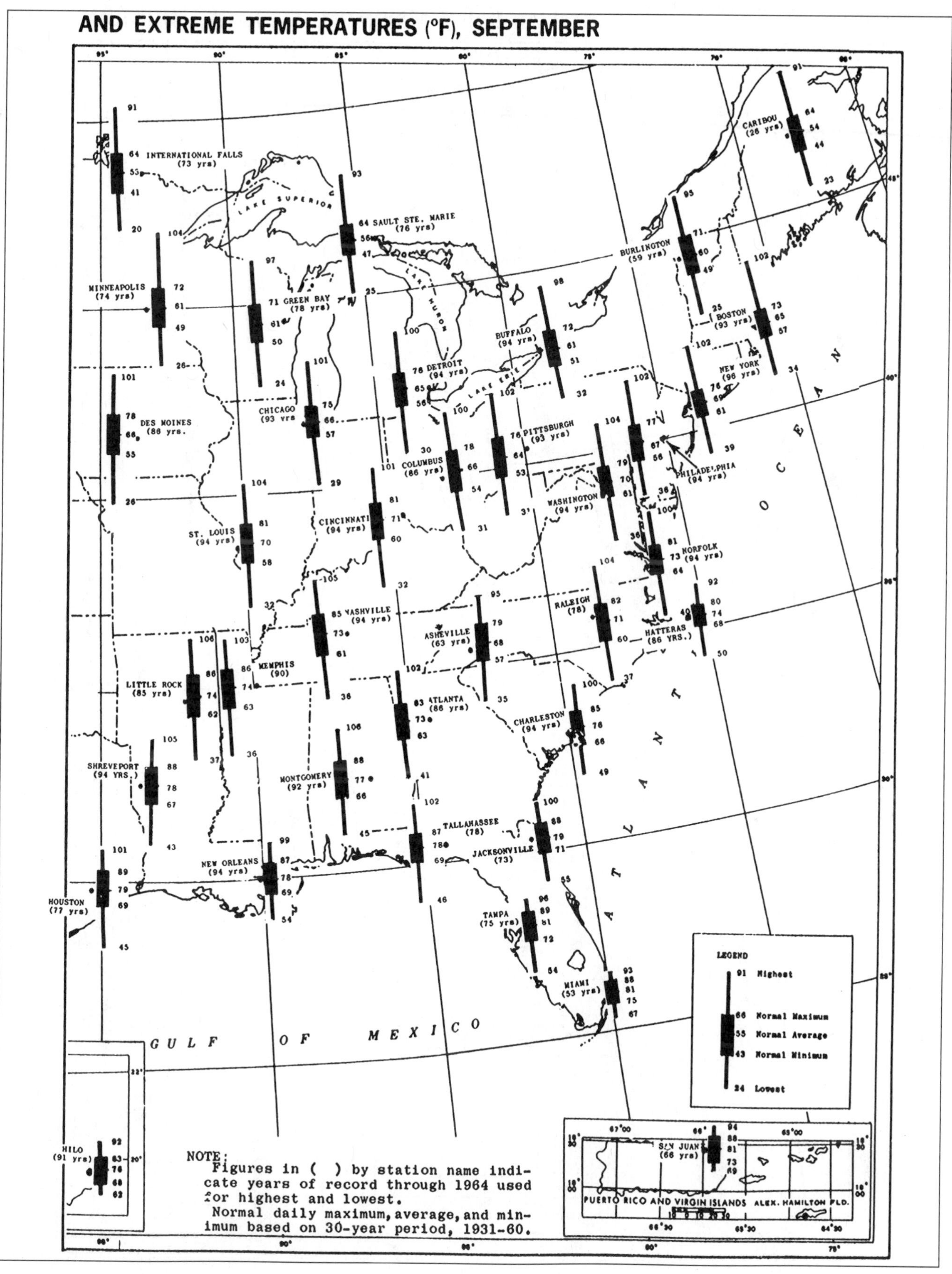

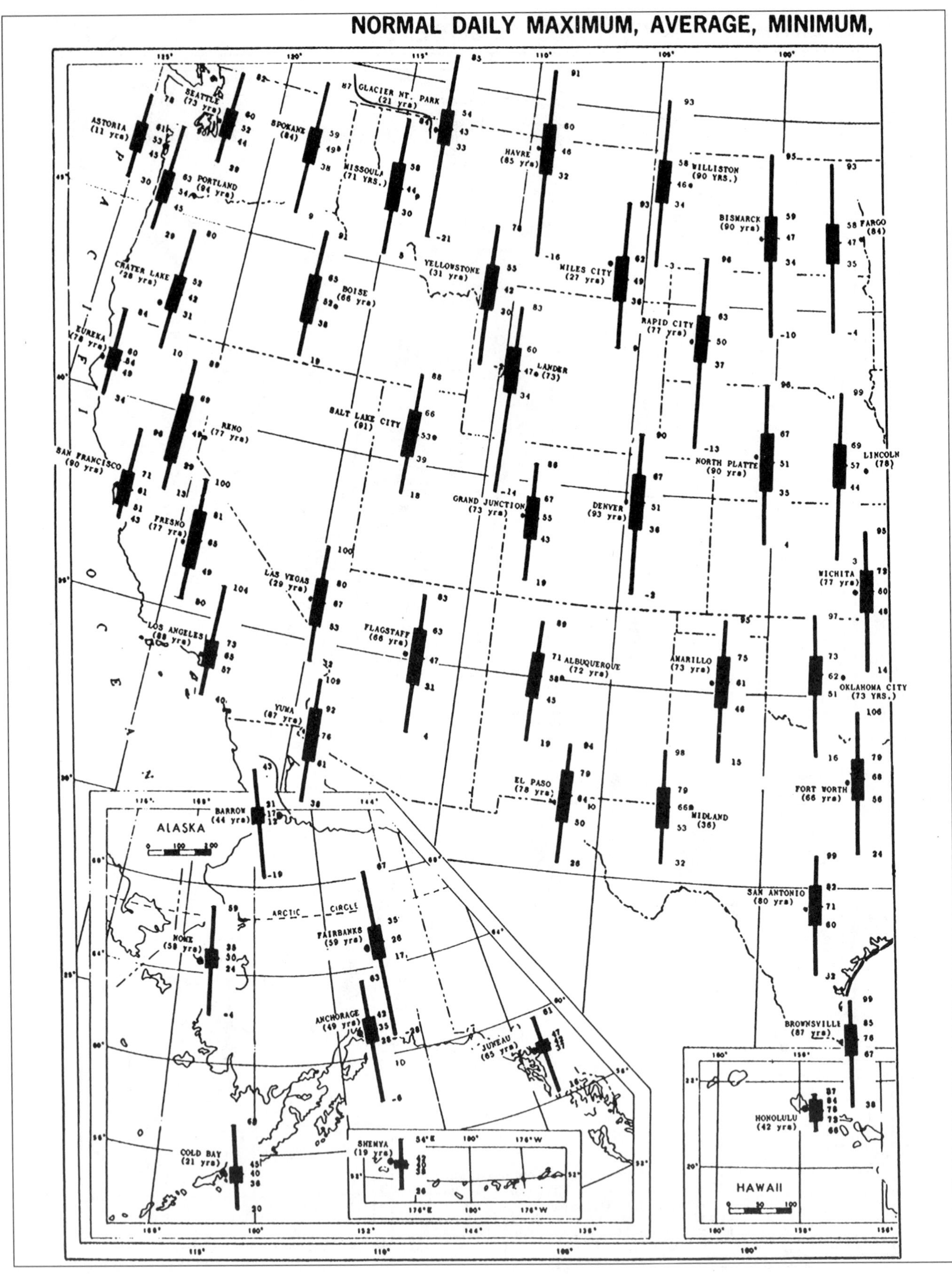
NORMAL DAILY MAXIMUM, AVERAGE, MINIMUM,
SEATTLE (73 yrs)
ASTORIA (11 yrs)
SPOKANE (84)
GLACIER NT. PARK (21 yrs)
MISSOULA (71 YRS.)
HAVRE (65 yrs)
WILLISTON (90 YRS.)
PORTLAND (94 yrs)
BISMARCK (90 yrs)
FARGO (84)
CRATER LAKE (28 yrs)
BOISE (66 yrs)
YELLOWSTONE (31 yrs)
MILES CITY (27 yrs)
RAPID CITY (77 yrs)
EUREKA (78 yrs)
LANDER (73)
RENO (77 yrs)
SALT LAKE CITY (91)
SAN FRANCISCO (90 yrs)
NORTH PLATTE (90 yrs)
LINCOLN (78)
GRAND JUNCTION (73 yrs)
DENVER (93 yrs)
FRESNO (77 yrs)
LAS VEGAS (29 yrs)
WICHITA (77 yrs)
LOS ANGELES (88 yrs)
FLAGSTAFF (66 yrs)
ALBUQUERQUE (72 yrs)
AMARILLO (73 yrs)
OKLAHOMA CITY (73 YRS.)
YUMA (87 yrs)
EL PASO (78 yrs)
MIDLAND (36)
FORT WORTH (66 yrs)
ALASKA
BARROW (44 yrs)
ARCTIC CIRCLE
SAN ANTONIO (80 yrs)
NOME (58 yrs)
FAIRBANKS (59 yrs)
ANCHORAGE (49 yrs)
JUNEAU (65 yrs)
BROWNSVILLE (87 yrs)
COLD BAY (21 yrs)
SHEMYA (19 yrs)
HONOLULU (42 yrs)
HAWAII

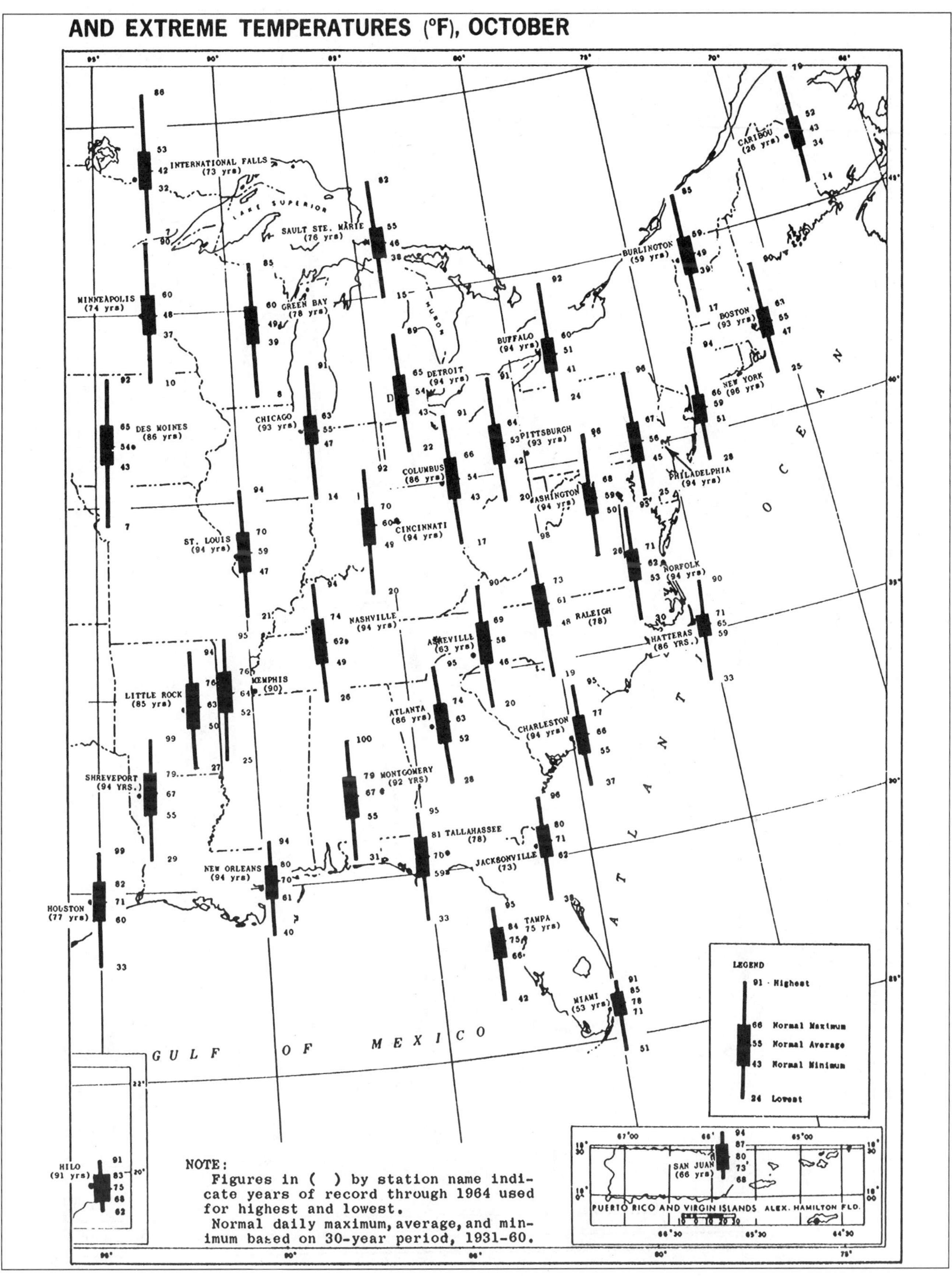
AND EXTREME TEMPERATURES (°F), OCTOBER
INTERNATIONAL FALLS (73 yrs) 86 53 42 32 7
SAULT STE. MARIE (76 yrs) 82 55 46 38 15
LAKE SUPERIOR
HURON
CARIBOU (26 yrs) 79 52 43 34 14
BURLINGTON (59 yrs) 85 59 49 39 17
BOSTON (93 yrs) 90 63 55 47 25
MINNEAPOLIS (74 yrs) 90 60 48 37 10
GREEN BAY (78 yrs) 85 60 49 39 8
BUFFALO (94 yrs) 92 60 51 41 24
DETROIT (94 yrs) 89 65 54 43 22
NEW YORK (96 yrs) 94 66 59 51 28
DES MOINES (86 yrs) 92 65 54 43 7
CHICAGO (93 yrs) 91 63 55 47 14
PITTSBURGH (93 yrs) 91 64 53 42 20
PHILADELPHIA (94 yrs) 96 67 56 45 25
COLUMBUS (86 yrs) 91 66 54 43 17
WASHINGTON (94 yrs) 96 68 59 50 26
CINCINNATI (94 yrs) 92 70 60 49 20
ST. LOUIS (94 yrs) 94 70 59 47 21
NORFOLK (94 yrs) 93 71 62 53 30
NASHVILLE (94 yrs) 94 74 62 49 26
ASHEVILLE (63 yrs) 90 69 58 46 20
RALEIGH (78) 98 73 61 48 19
HATTERAS (86 YRS.) 90 71 65 59 33
MEMPHIS (90) 95 76 64 52 25
LITTLE ROCK (85 yrs) 94 76 63 50 27
ATLANTA (86 yrs) 95 74 63 52 28
CHARLESTON (94 yrs) 95 77 66 55 37
SHREVEPORT (94 YRS.) 99 79 67 55 29
MONTGOMERY (92 YRS) 100 79 67 55 31
TALLAHASSEE (78) 95 81 70 59 33
JACKSONVILLE (73) 96 80 71 62 38
NEW ORLEANS (94 yrs) 94 80 70 61 40
HOUSTON (77 yrs) 99 82 71 60 33
TAMPA (75 yrs) 95 84 75 66 42
MIAMI (53 yrs) 91 85 78 71 51
ATLANTIC OCEAN
GULF OF MEXICO
HILO (91 yrs) 91 83 75 68 62
SAN JUAN (66 yrs) 94 87 80 73 68
PUERTO RICO AND VIRGIN ISLANDS ALEX. HAMILTON FLD.
LEGEND
91 · Highest
66 Normal Maximum
55 Normal Average
43 Normal Minimum
24 Lowest
NOTE:
Figures in ( ) by station name indicate years of record through 1964 used for highest and lowest.
Normal daily maximum, average, and minimum based on 30-year period, 1931-60.

NORMAL DAILY MAXIMUM, AVERAGE, MINIMUM,

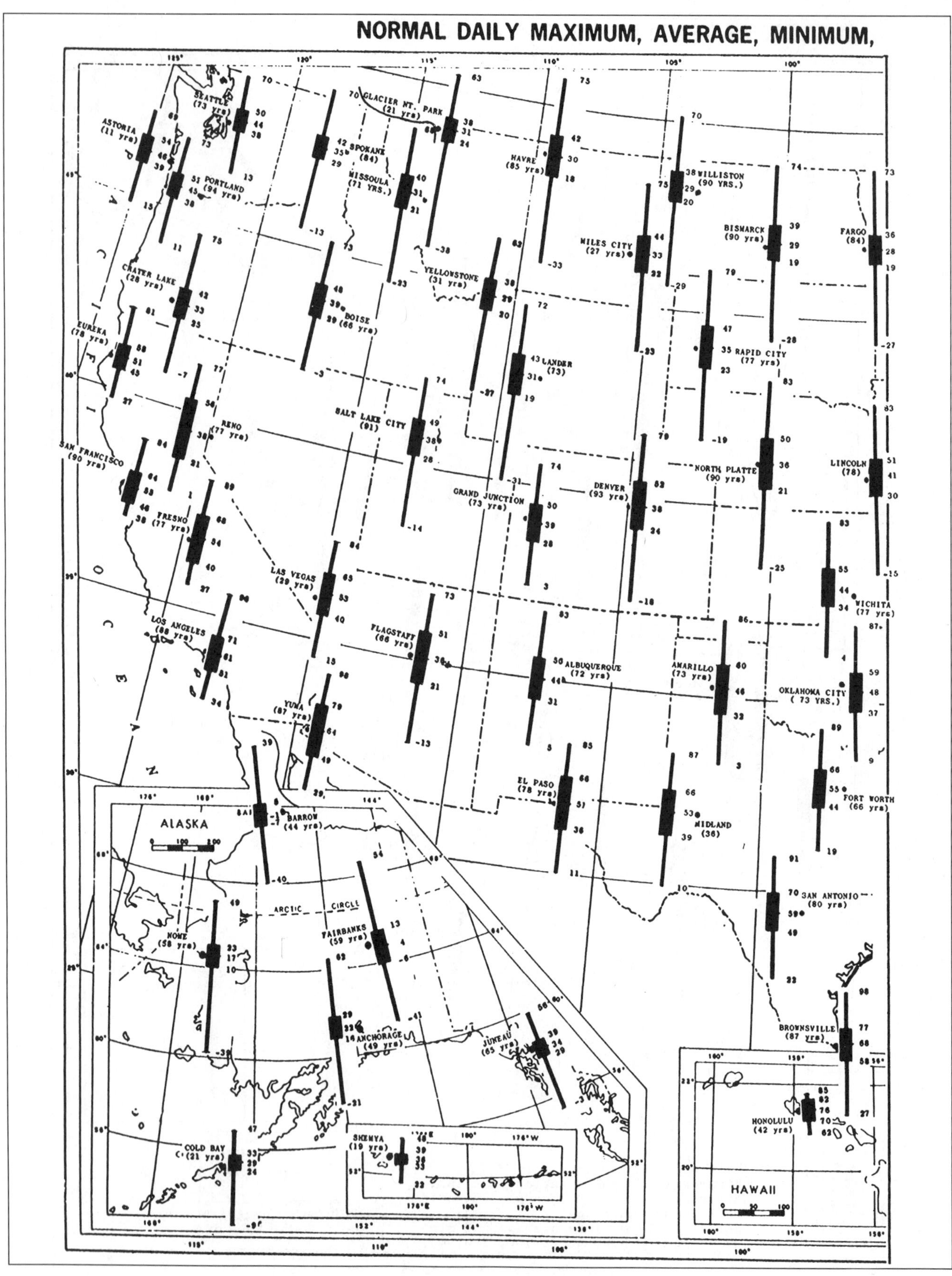

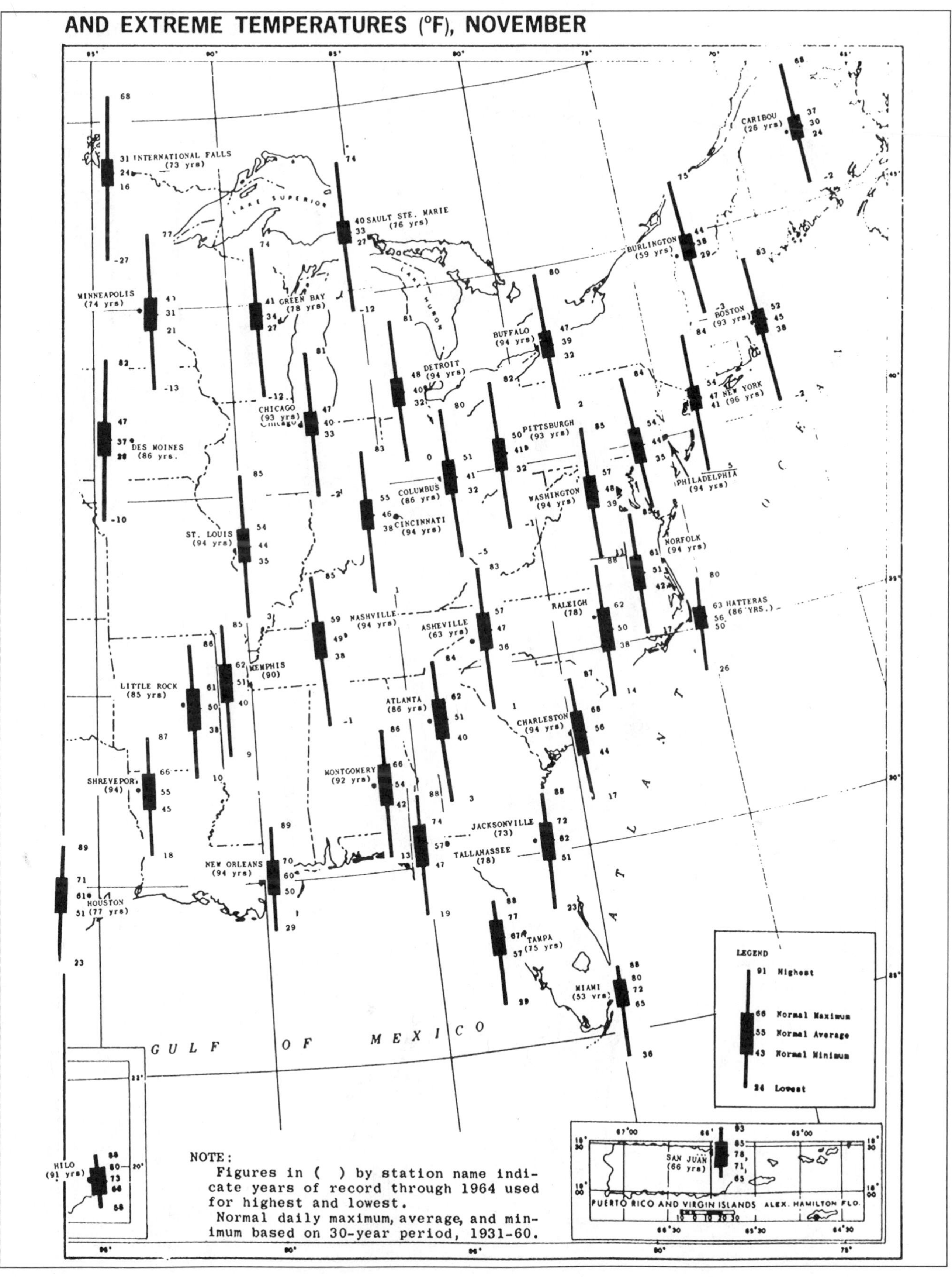
AND EXTREME TEMPERATURES (°F), NOVEMBER
LEGEND
91 Highest
66 Normal Maximum
55 Normal Average
43 Normal Minimum
24 Lowest
GULF OF MEXICO
NOTE:
Figures in ( ) by station name indicate years of record through 1964 used for highest and lowest.
Normal daily maximum, average, and minimum based on 30-year period, 1931-60.
PUERTO RICO AND VIRGIN ISLANDS
SAN JUAN (66 yrs)
HILO (91 yrs)
INTERNATIONAL FALLS (73 yrs)
MINNEAPOLIS (74 yrs)
DES MOINES (86 yrs.
SAULT STE. MARIE (76 yrs)
GREEN BAY (78 yrs)
CHICAGO (93 yrs)
DETROIT (94 yrs)
BUFFALO (94 yrs)
CARIBOU (26 yrs)
BURLINGTON (59 yrs)
BOSTON (93 yrs)
NEW YORK (96 yrs)
PHILADELPHIA (94 yrs)
PITTSBURGH (93 yrs)
WASHINGTON (94 yrs)
COLUMBUS (86 yrs)
CINCINNATI (94 yrs)
ST. LOUIS (94 yrs)
NORFOLK (94 yrs)
RALEIGH (78)
HATTERAS (86 YRS.)
NASHVILLE (94 yrs)
ASHEVILLE (63 yrs)
MEMPHIS (90)
LITTLE ROCK (85 yrs)
ATLANTA (86 yrs)
CHARLESTON (94 yrs)
SHREVEPORT (94)
MONTGOMERY (92 yrs)
JACKSONVILLE (73)
TALLAHASSEE (78)
NEW ORLEANS (94 yrs)
HOUSTON (77 yrs)
TAMPA (75 yrs)
MIAMI (53 yrs)

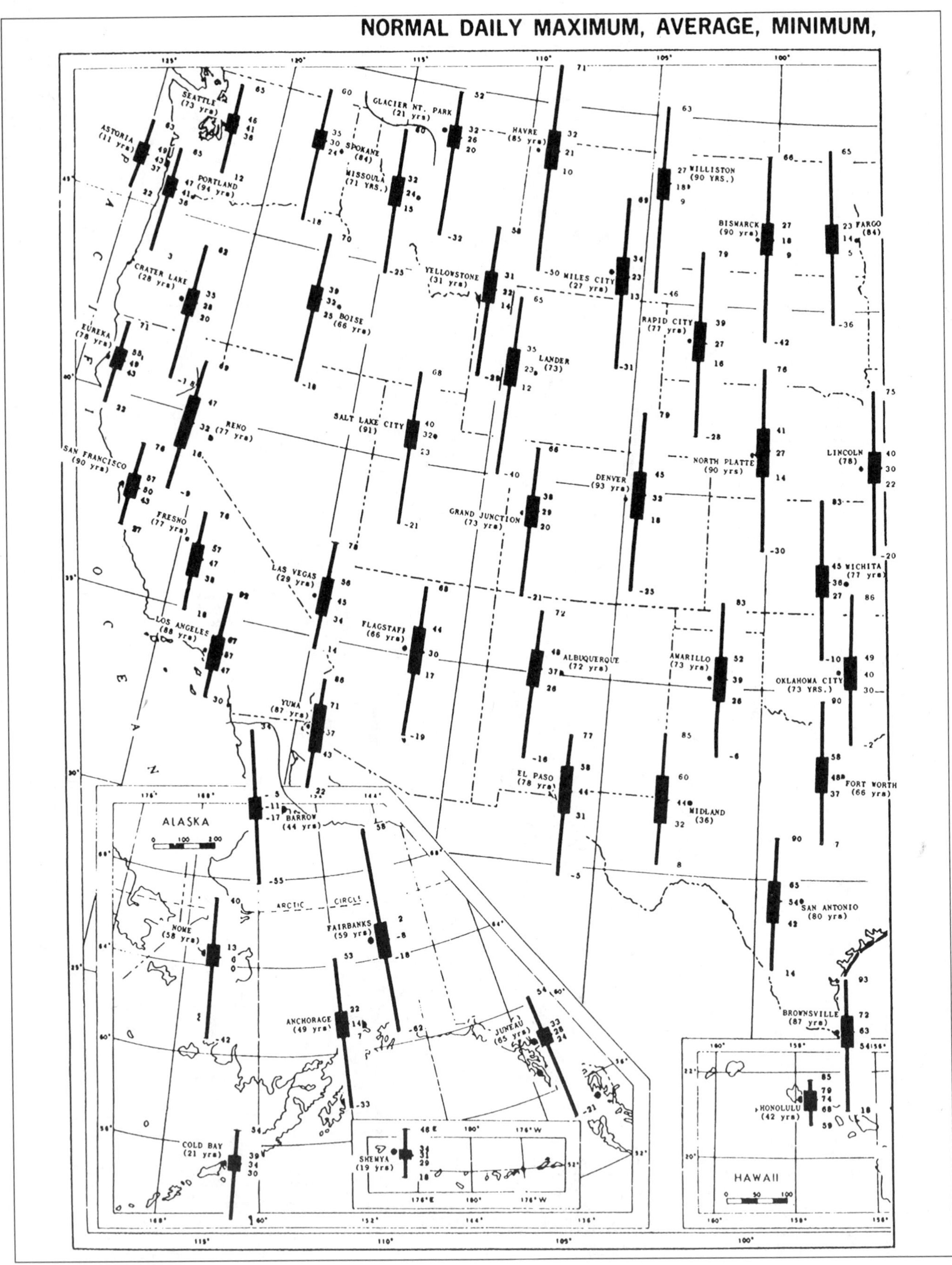
NORMAL DAILY MAXIMUM, AVERAGE, MINIMUM,
SEATTLE (73 yrs)
ASTORIA (11 yrs)
PORTLAND (94 yrs)
SPOKANE (84)
GLACIER NT. PARK (21 yrs)
MISSOULA (71 YRS.)
HAVRE (85 yrs)
WILLISTON (90 YRS.)
BISMARCK (90 yrs)
FARGO (84)
CRATER LAKE (28 yrs)
BOISE (66 yrs)
YELLOWSTONE (31 yrs)
MILES CITY (27 yrs)
EUREKA (78 yrs)
LANDER (73)
RAPID CITY (77 yrs)
SALT LAKE CITY (91)
RENO (77 yrs)
SAN FRANCISCO (90 yrs)
NORTH PLATTE (90 yrs)
LINCOLN (78)
DENVER (93 yrs)
GRAND JUNCTION (73 yrs)
FRESNO (77 yrs)
LAS VEGAS (29 yrs)
WICHITA (77 yrs)
LOS ANGELES (88 yrs)
FLAGSTAFF (66 yrs)
ALBUQUERQUE (72 yrs)
AMARILLO (73 yrs)
OKLAHOMA CITY (73 YRS.)
YUMA (87 yrs)
EL PASO (78 yrs)
MIDLAND (36)
FORT WORTH (66 yrs)
ALASKA
BARROW (44 yrs)
ARCTIC CIRCLE
FAIRBANKS (59 yrs)
NOME (58 yrs)
SAN ANTONIO (80 yrs)
ANCHORAGE (49 yrs)
JUNEAU (65 yrs)
BROWNSVILLE (87 yrs)
COLD BAY (21 yrs)
SHEMYA (19 yrs)
HONOLULU (42 yrs)
HAWAII
PACIFIC OCEAN

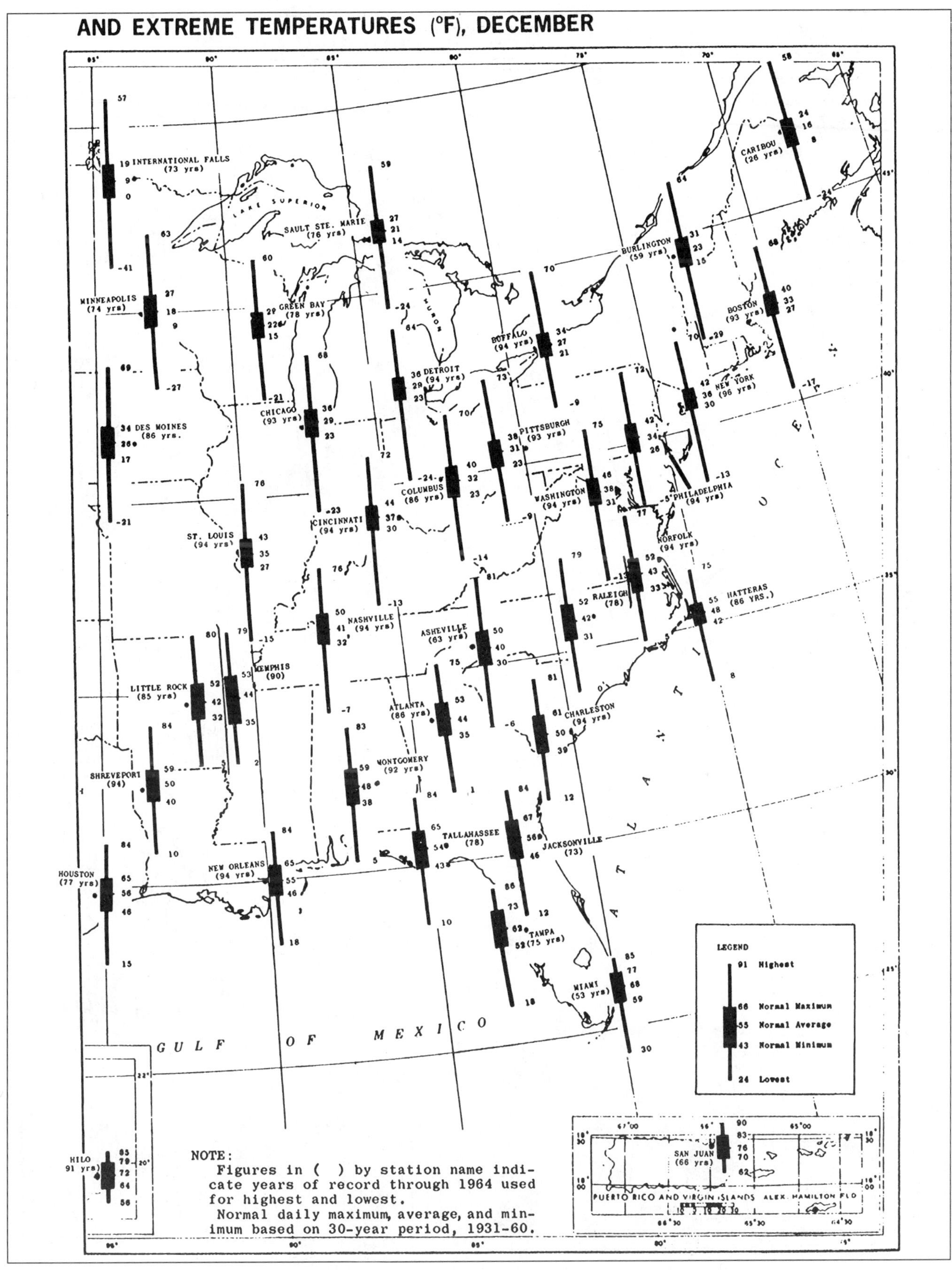
AND EXTREME TEMPERATURES (°F), DECEMBER
INTERNATIONAL FALLS (73 yrs)
LAKE SUPERIOR
SAULT STE. MARIE (76 yrs)
MINNEAPOLIS (74 yrs)
GREEN BAY (78 yrs)
HURON
CARIBOU (26 yrs)
BURLINGTON (59 yrs)
BOSTON (93 yrs)
BUFFALO (94 yrs)
DETROIT (94 yrs)
NEW YORK (96 yrs)
DES MOINES (86 yrs.
CHICAGO (93 yrs)
PITTSBURGH (93 yrs)
PHILADELPHIA (94 yrs)
COLUMBUS (86 yrs)
WASHINGTON (94 yrs)
CINCINNATI (94 yrs)
ST. LOUIS (94 yrs)
NORFOLK (94 yrs)
RALEIGH (78)
HATTERAS (86 YRS.)
NASHVILLE (94 yrs)
ASHEVILLE (63 yrs)
MEMPHIS (90)
LITTLE ROCK (85 yrs)
ATLANTA (86 yrs)
CHARLESTON (94 yrs)
SHREVEPORT (94)
MONTGOMERY (92 yrs)
TALLAHASSEE (78)
JACKSONVILLE (73)
HOUSTON (77 yrs)
NEW ORLEANS (94 yrs)
TAMPA (75 yrs)
MIAMI (53 yrs)
ATLANTIC OCEAN
GULF OF MEXICO
LEGEND
91 Highest
66 Normal Maximum
55 Normal Average
43 Normal Minimum
24 Lowest
HILO 91 yrs
SAN JUAN (66 yrs)
PUERTO RICO AND VIRGIN ISLANDS
NOTE:
Figures in ( ) by station name indicate years of record through 1964 used for highest and lowest.
Normal daily maximum, average, and minimum based on 30-year period, 1931-60.

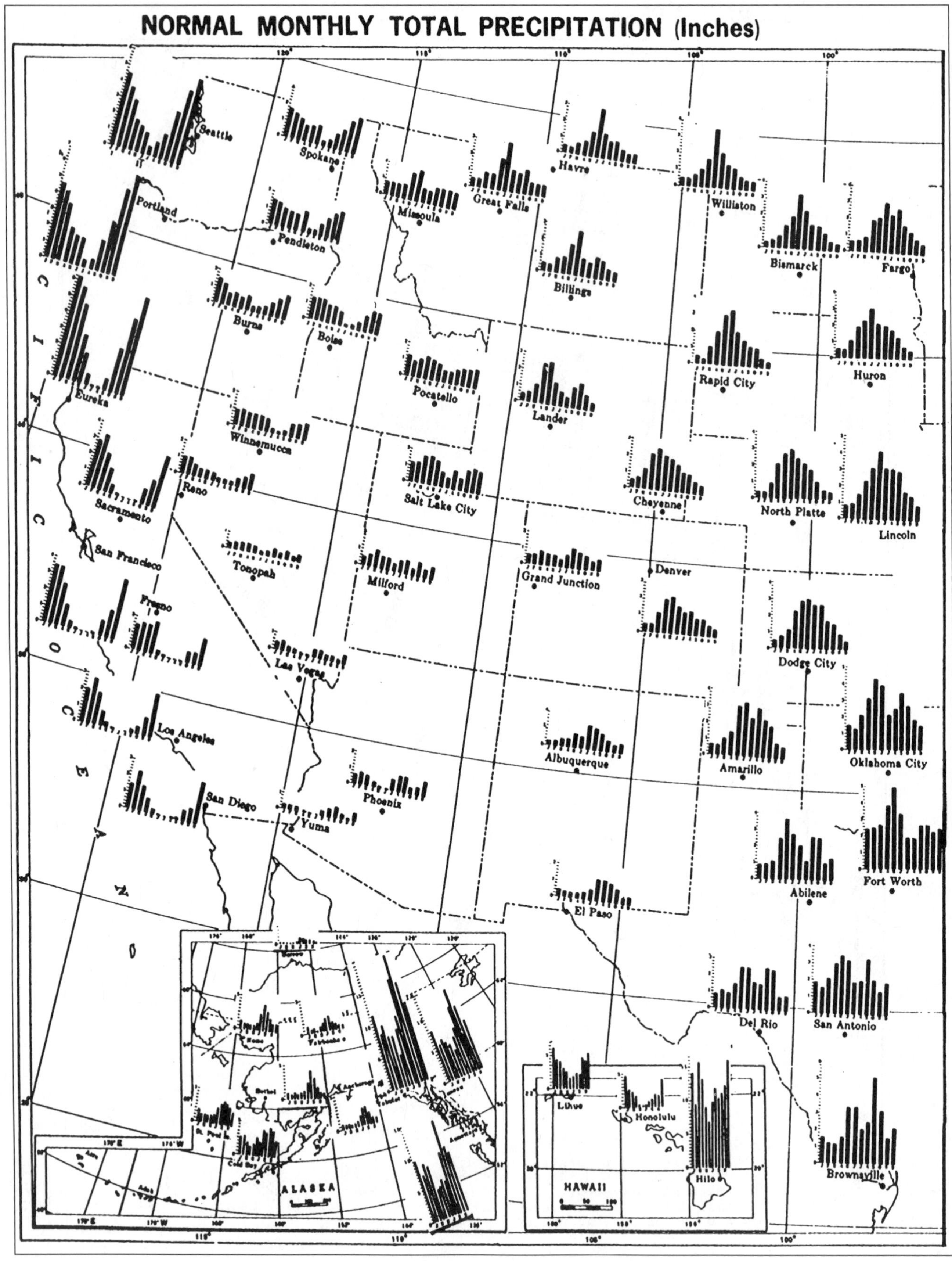
NORMAL MONTHLY TOTAL PRECIPITATION (Inches)
Seattle
Spokane
Havre
Great Falls
Missoula
Williston
Portland
Pendleton
Bismarck
Fargo
Billings
Burns
Boise
Rapid City
Huron
Pocatello
Eureka
Lander
Winnemucca
Cheyenne
North Platte
Reno
Sacramento
Salt Lake City
Lincoln
San Francisco
Tonopah
Grand Junction
Denver
Milford
Fresno
Dodge City
Las Vegas
Los Angeles
Albuquerque
Amarillo
Oklahoma City
Phoenix
San Diego
Yuma
Abilene
Fort Worth
El Paso
Del Rio
San Antonio
Brownsville
P A C I F I C O C E A N
ALASKA
Cold Bay
Lihue
Honolulu
Hilo
HAWAII

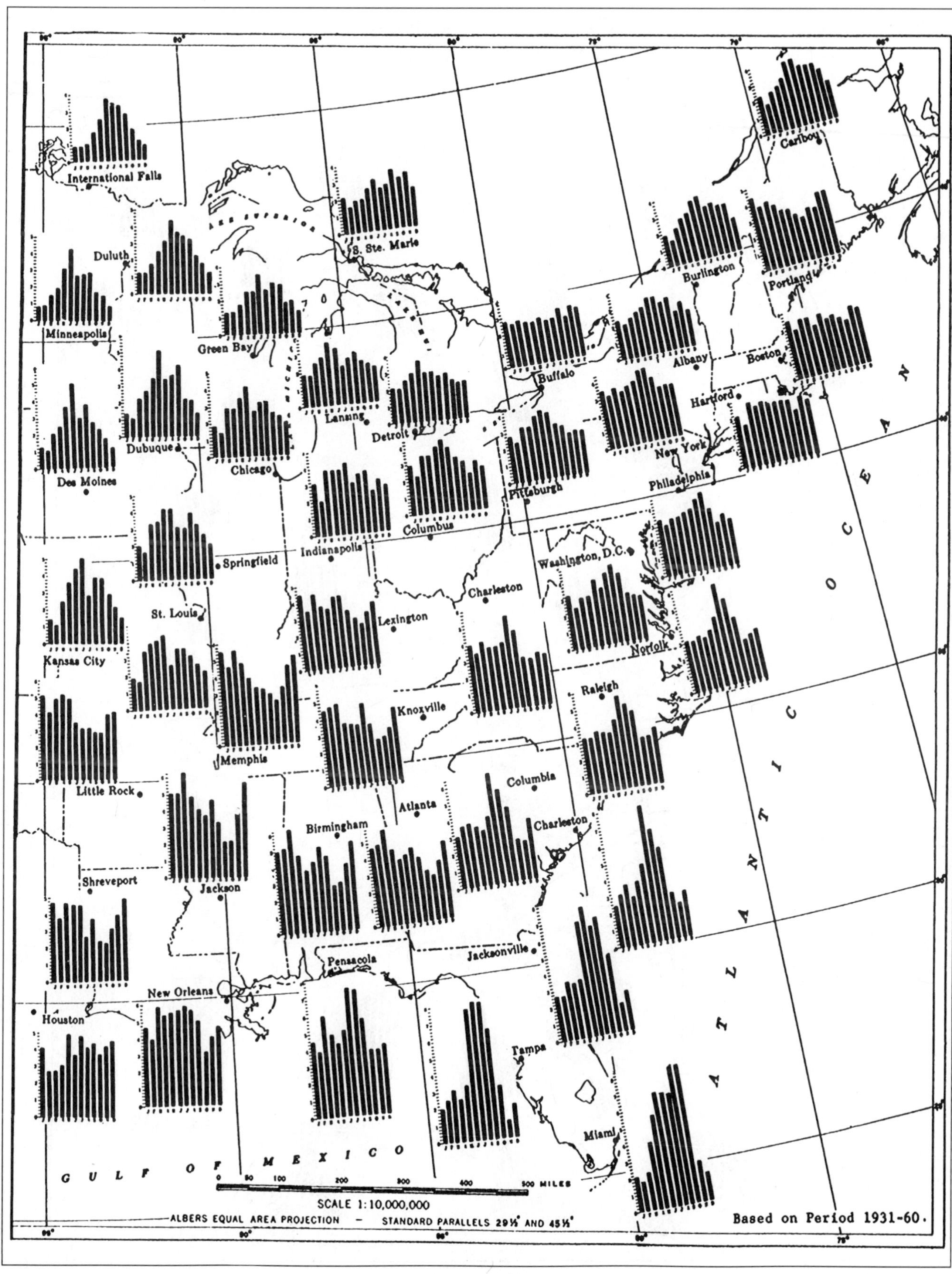

International Falls
Duluth
S. Ste. Marie
Minneapolis
Green Bay
Lansing
Detroit
Dubuque
Chicago
Des Moines
Cariboù
Burlington
Portland
Albany
Boston
Buffalo
Hartford
New York
Philadelphia
Pittsburgh
Columbus
Indianapolis
Springfield
St. Louis
Kansas City
Lexington
Charleston
Washington, D.C.
Norfolk
Raleigh
Knoxville
Memphis
Little Rock
Columbia
Atlanta
Birmingham
Charleston
Shreveport
Jackson
Jacksonville
Pensacola
New Orleans
Houston
Tampa
Miami
GULF OF MEXICO
ATLANTIC OCEAN
0 50 100 200 300 400 500 MILES
SCALE 1:10,000,000
ALBERS EQUAL AREA PROJECTION — STANDARD PARALLELS 29½° AND 45½°
Based on Period 1931-60.

MEAN MONTHLY TOTAL SNOWFALL (Inches)
For Selected Stations*

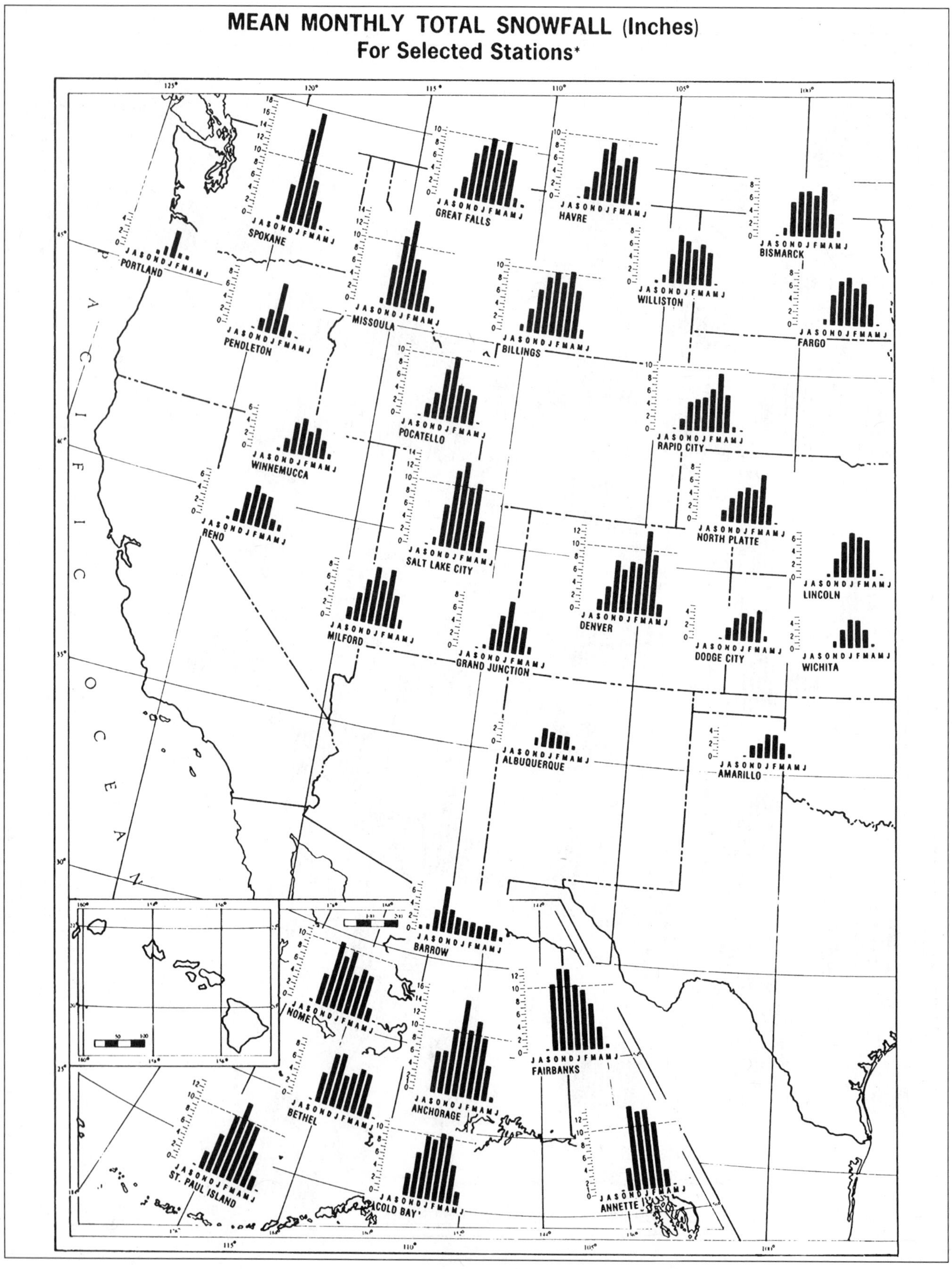

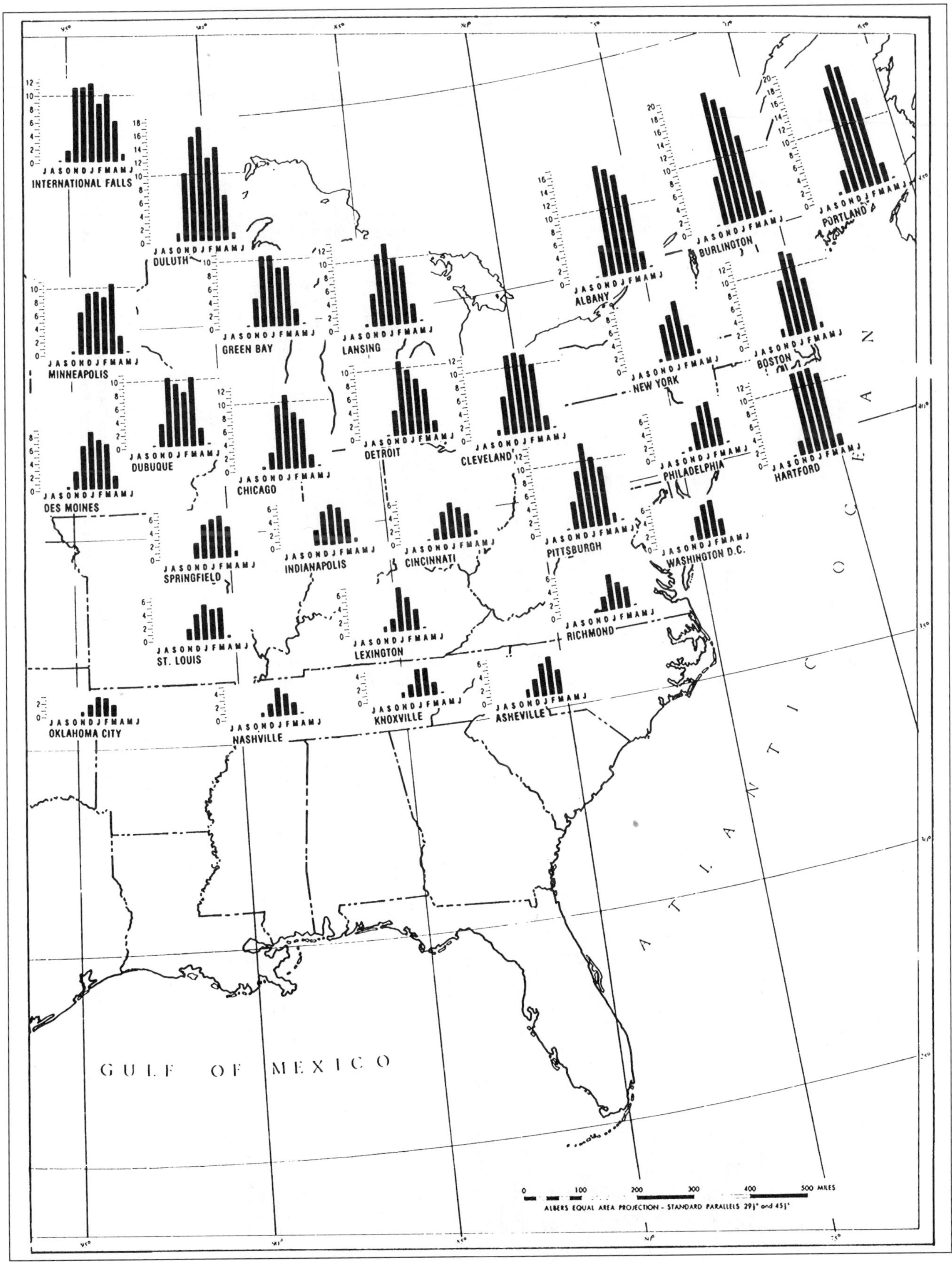
INTERNATIONAL FALLS
DULUTH
MINNEAPOLIS
GREEN BAY
LANSING
ALBANY
BURLINGTON
PORTLAND
DES MOINES
DUBUQUE
CHICAGO
DETROIT
CLEVELAND
NEW YORK
BOSTON
PHILADELPHIA
HARTFORD
SPRINGFIELD
INDIANAPOLIS
CINCINNATI
PITTSBURGH
WASHINGTON D.C.
ST. LOUIS
LEXINGTON
RICHMOND
OKLAHOMA CITY
NASHVILLE
KNOXVILLE
ASHEVILLE
GULF OF MEXICO
ATLANTIC OCEAN
0 100 200 300 400 500 MILES
ALBERS EQUAL AREA PROJECTION - STANDARD PARALLELS 29½° and 45½°

FREEZE DATA AND GROWING SEASON

MEAN DATE OF LAST 32 F. TEMPERATURE IN SPRING, FIRST 32 F. IN AUTUMN, AND MEAN LENGTH OF FREEZE-FREE PERIOD (DAYS)

State and Station	Mean date last 32°F. in spring	Mean date first 32°F. in fall	Mean freeze-free period (no. days)
ALA.Birmingham	Mar. 19	Nov. 14	241
Mobile U	Feb. 17	Dec. 12	298
Montgomery U	Feb. 27	Dec. 3	279
ALASKA.Anchorage	May 18	Sept. 13	118
Barrow	June 27	July 5	8
Cordova	May 10	Oct. 2	145
Fairbanks	May 24	Aug. 29	97
Juneau	Apr. 27	Oct. 19	176
Nome	June 12	Aug. 24	73
ARIZ.Flagstaff	June 8	Oct. 2	116
Phoenix	Jan. 27	Dec. 11	317
Tucson	Mar. 6	Nov. 23	261
Winslow	Apr. 28	Oct. 21	176
Yuma U	Jan. 11	Dec. 27	350
ARK.Fort Smith	Mar. 23	Nov. 9	231
Little Rock	Mar. 16	Nov. 15	244
CALIF.Bakersfield	Feb. 14	Nov. 28	287
Eureka U	Jan. 24	Dec. 25	335
Fresno	Feb. 3	Dec. 3	303
Los Angeles U	*	*	*
Red Bluff	Feb. 25	Nov. 29	277
Sacramento	Jan. 24	Dec. 11	321
San Diego	*	*	*
San Francisco U	*	*	*
COLO.Denver U	May 2	Oct. 14	165
Palisades	Apr. 22	Oct. 17	178
Pueblo	Apr. 28	Oct. 12	167
CONN.Hartford	Apr. 22	Oct. 19	180
New Haven	Apr. 15	Oct. 27	195
D.C.Washington U	Apr. 10	Oct. 28	200
FLA.Apalachicola U	Feb. 2	Dec. 21	322
Fort Myers	*	*	*
Jacksonville U	Feb. 6	Dec. 16	313
Key West	*	*	*
Lakeland	Jan. 10	Dec. 25	349
Miami	*	*	*
Orlando	Jan. 31	Dec. 17	319
Pensacola U	Feb. 18	Dec. 15	300
Tallahassee	Feb. 26	Dec. 3	280
Tampa	Jan. 10	Dec. 26	349
GA.Atlanta U	Mar. 20	Nov. 19	244
Augusta	Mar. 7	Nov. 22	260
Macon	Mar. 12	Nov. 19	252
Savannah	Feb. 21	Dec. 9	291
IDAHO.Boise	Apr. 29	Oct. 16	171
Pocatello	May 8	Sept. 30	145
Salmon	June 4	Sept. 6	94
ILL.Cairo U	Mar. 23	Nov. 11	233
Chicago U	Apr. 19	Oct. 28	192
Freeport	May 8	Oct. 4	149
Peoria	Apr. 22	Oct. 16	177
Springfield U	Apr. 8	Oct. 30	205
IND.Evansville	Apr. 2	Nov. 4	216
Fort Wayne	Apr. 24	Oct. 20	179
Indianapolis U	Apr. 17	Oct. 27	193

NOTE: Narrative descriptions of the climates of most of these cities are contained in the section, *"Weather of U.S. Cities"*. Check the narrative for the city of interest for further notes about the city's growing season and for any updating since this table's compilation.

State and Station	Mean date last 32°F. in spring	Mean date first 32°F. in fall	Mean freeze-free period (no. days)
South Bend	May 3	Oct. 16	165
IOWA.Des Moines U	Apr. 20	Oct. 19	183
Dubuque U	Apr. 19	Oct. 19	184
Keokuk	Apr. 12	Oct. 26	197
Sioux City	Apr. 28	Oct. 12	167
KANS.Concordia U	Apr. 16	Oct. 24	191
Dodge City	Apr. 22	Oct. 24	184
Goodland	May 5	Oct. 9	157
Topeka U	Apr. 9	Oct. 26	200
Wichita	Apr. 5	Nov. 1	210
KY.Lexington	Apr. 13	Oct. 28	198
Louisville U	Apr. 1	Nov. 7	220
LA.Lake Charles	Feb. 18	Dec. 6	291
New Orleans	Feb. 13	Dec. 12	302
Shreveport	Mar. 1	Nov. 27	272
MAINE.Greenville	May 27	Sept. 20	116
Portland	Apr. 29	Oct. 15	169
MD.Annapolis	Mar. 4	Nov. 15	225
Baltimore U	Mar. 28	Nov. 17	234
Frederick	Mar. 24	Oct. 17	176
MASS.Boston	Apr. 16	Oct. 25	192
Nantucket	Apr. 12	Nov. 16	219
MICH.Alpena U	May 6	Oct. 9	156
Detroit	Apr. 25	Oct. 23	181
Escanaba U	May 14	Oct. 6	145
Grand Rapids U	Apr. 25	Oct. 27	185
Marquette U	May 14	Oct. 17	156
S. Ste. Marie	May 18	Oct. 3	138
MINN.Albert Lee	May 3	Oct. 6	156
Big Falls R.S.	June 4	Sept. 7	95
Brainerd	May 16	Sept. 24	131
Duluth	May 22	Sept. 24	125
Minneapolis	Apr. 30	Oct. 13	166
St. Cloud	May 9	Sept. 29	144
MISS.Jackson	Mar. 10	Nov. 13	248
Meridian	Mar. 13	Nov. 14	246
Vicksburg U	Mar. 8	Nov. 15	252
MO.Columbia	Apr. 9	Oct. 24	198
Kansas City	Apr. 5	Oct. 31	210
St. Louis U	Apr. 2	Nov. 8	220
Springfield	Apr. 10	Oct. 31	203
MONT.Billings	May 15	Sept. 24	132
Glasgow U	May 19	Sept. 20	124
Great Falls	May 14	Sept. 26	135
Havre U	May 9	Sept. 23	138
Helena	May 12	Sept. 23	134
Kalispell	May 12	Sept. 23	135
Miles City	May 5	Oct. 3	150
Superior	June 5	Aug. 30	85

* Occurs in less than 1 year in 10. No freeze of record in Key West, Fla.
U Indicates urban.

Charts and tabulation were derived from the Freeze Data tabulation in Climatography of the United States No. 60 - Climates of the States.

MEAN DATE OF LAST 32 F. TEMPERATURE IN SPRING, FIRST 32 F. IN AUTUMN, AND MEAN LENGTH OF FREEZE-FREE PERIOD (continued)

State and Station	Mean date last 32°F. in spring	Mean date first 32°F. in fall	Mean freeze-free period (no. days)
NEBR. Grand Island	Apr. 29	Oct. 6	160
Lincoln	Apr. 20	Oct. 17	180
Norfolk	May 4	Oct. 3	152
North Platte	Apr. 30	Oct. 7	160
Omaha	Apr. 14	Oct. 20	189
Valentine Lakes	May 7	Sept. 30	146
NEV. Elko	June 6	Sept. 3	89
Las Vegas	Mar. 13	Nov. 13	245
Reno	May 14	Oct. 2	141
Winnemucca	May 18	Sept. 21	125
N.H. Concord	May 11	Sept. 30	142
N.J. Cape May	Apr. 4	Nov. 15	225
Trenton U	Apr. 8	Nov. 5	211
N.MEX. Albuquerque	Apr. 16	Oct. 29	196
Roswell	Apr. 9	Nov. 2	208
N.Y. Albany	Apr. 27	Oct. 13	169
Binghamton U	May 4	Oct. 6	154
Buffalo	Apr. 30	Oct. 25	179
New York U	Apr. 7	Nov. 12	219
Rochester	Apr. 28	Oct. 21	176
Syracuse	Apr. 30	Oct. 15	168
N.C. Asheville U	Apr. 12	Oct. 24	195
Charlotte U	Mar. 21	Nov. 15	239
Greenville	Mar. 28	Nov. 5	222
Hatteras	Feb. 25	Dec. 18	296
Raleigh U	Mar. 24	Nov. 16	237
Wilmington U	Mar. 8	Nov. 24	262
N.DAK. Bismarck	May 11	Sept. 24	136
Devils Lake U	May 18	Sept. 22	127
Fargo	May 13	Sept. 27	137
Williston U	May 14	Sept. 23	132
OHIO. Akron-Canton	Apr. 29	Oct. 20	173
Cincinnati (Abbe)	Apr. 15	Oct. 25	192
Cleveland	Apr. 21	Nov. 2	195
Columbus U	Apr. 17	Oct. 30	196
Dayton	Apr. 20	Oct. 21	184
Toledo	Apr. 24	Oct. 25	184
OKLA. Okla. City U	Mar. 28	Nov. 7	223
Tulsa	Mar. 31	Nov. 2	216
OREG. Astoria	Mar. 18	Nov. 24	251
Bend	June 17	Aug. 17	62
Medford	Apr. 25	Oct. 20	178
Pendleton	Apr. 27	Oct. 8	163
Portland U	Feb. 25	Dec. 1	279
Salem	Apr. 14	Oct. 27	197
PA. Allentown	Apr. 20	Oct. 16	180
Harrisburg	Apr. 10	Oct. 28	201
Philadelphia U	Mar. 30	Nov. 17	232
Pittsburgh	Apr. 20	Oct. 23	187
Scranton U	Apr. 24	Oct. 14	174
R.I. Providence U	Apr. 13	Oct. 27	197
S.C. Charleston U	Feb. 19	Dec. 10	294
Columbia U	Mar. 14	Nov. 21	252
Greenville	Mar. 23	Nov. 17	239
S.DAK. Huron U	May 4	Sept. 30	149
Rapid City U	May 7	Oct. 4	150
Sioux Falls U	May 5	Oct. 3	152
TENN. Chattanooga U	Mar. 26	Nov. 10	229
Knoxville U	Mar. 31	Nov. 6	220
Memphis U	Mar. 20	Nov. 12	237
Nashville U	Mar. 28	Nov. 7	224
TEX. Albany	Mar. 30	Nov. 9	224
Balmorhea	Apr. 1	Nov. 12	226
Beeville	Feb. 21	Dec. 6	288
College Station	Mar. 1	Dec. 1	275
Corsicana	Mar. 13	Nov. 27	259
Dalhart Exp. Sta.	Apr. 23	Oct. 18	178
Dallas	Mar. 18	Nov. 22	249
Del Rio	Feb. 12	Dec. 9	300
Encinal	Feb. 15	Dec. 12	301
Houston	Feb. 5	Dec. 11	309
Lampasas	Apr. 1	Nov. 10	223
Matagorda	Feb. 12	Dec. 17	308
Midland	Apr. 3	Nov. 6	218
Mission	Jan. 30	Dec. 21	325
Mount Pleasant	Mar. 23	Nov. 12	233
Nacogdoches	Mar. 15	Nov. 13	243
Plainview	Apr. 10	Nov. 6	211
Presidio	Mar. 20	Nov. 13	238
Quanah	Mar. 31	Nov. 7	221
San Angelo	Mar. 25	Nov. 15	235
Ysleta	Apr. 6	Oct. 30	207
UTAH. Blanding	May 18	Oct. 14	148
Salt Lake City	Apr. 12	Nov. 1	202
VT. Burlington	May 8	Oct. 3	148
VA. Lynchburg	Apr. 6	Oct. 27	205
Norfolk U	Mar. 18	Nov. 27	254
Richmond U	Apr. 2	Nov. 8	220
Roanoke	Apr. 20	Oct. 24	187
WASH. Bumping Lake	June 17	Aug. 16	60
Seattle U	Feb. 23	Dec. 1	281
Spokane	Apr. 20	Oct. 12	175
Tatoosh Island	Jan. 25	Dec. 20	329
Walla Walla U	Mar. 28	Nov. 1	218
Yakima	Apr. 19	Oct. 15	179
W.VA. Charleston	Apr. 18	Oct. 28	193
Parkersburg	Apr. 16	Oct. 21	189
WIS. Green Bay	May 6	Oct. 13	161
La Crosse U	May 1	Oct. 8	161
Madison U	Apr. 26	Oct. 19	177
Milwaukee U	Apr. 20	Oct. 25	188
WYO. Casper	May 18	Sept. 25	130
Cheyenne	May 20	Sept. 27	130
Lander	May 15	Sept. 20	128
Sheridan	May 21	Sept. 21	123

* Occurs in less than 1 year in 10. No freeze of record in Key West, Fla.
U Indicates urban.

Charts and tabulation were derived from the Freeze Data tabulation in Climatography of the United States No. 60 - Climates of the States.

MEAN PERCENTAGE OF POSSIBLE SUNSHINE

STATE AND STATION	YEARS	JAN.	FEB.	MAR.	APR.	MAY	JUNE	JULY	AUG.	SEPT.	OCT.	NOV.	DEC.	ANNUAL
ALA. BIRMINGHAM	56	43	49	56	63	66	67	62	65	66	67	58	44	59
MONTGOMERY	49	51	53	61	69	73	72	66	69	69	71	64	48	64
ALASKA. ANCHORAGE	19	39	46	56	58	50	51	45	39	35	32	33	29	45
FAIRBANKS	20	34	50	61	68	55	53	45	35	31	28	38	29	44
JUNEAU	14	30	32	39	37	34	35	28	30	25	18	21	18	30
NOME	29	44	46	48	53	51	48	32	26	34	35	36	30	41
ARIZ. PHOENIX	64	76	79	83	88	93	94	84	84	89	88	84	77	85
YUMA	52	83	87	91	94	97	98	92	91	93	93	90	83	91
ARK. LITTLE ROCK	66	44	53	57	62	67	72	71	73	71	74	58	47	62
CALIF. EUREKA	49	40	44	50	53	54	56	51	46	52	48	42	39	49
FRESNO	55	46	63	72	83	89	94	97	97	93	87	73	47	78
LOS ANGELES	63	70	69	70	67	68	69	80	81	80	76	79	72	73
RED BLUFF	39	50	60	65	75	79	86	95	94	89	77	64	50	75
SACRAMENTO	48	44	57	67	76	82	90	96	95	92	82	65	44	77
SAN DIEGO	68	68	67	68	66	60	60	67	70	70	70	76	71	68
SAN FRANCISCO	64	53	57	63	69	70	75	68	63	70	70	62	54	66
COLO. DENVER	64	67	67	65	63	61	69	68	68	71	71	67	65	67
GRAND JUNCTION	57	58	62	64	67	71	79	76	72	77	74	67	58	69
CONN. HARTFORD	48	46	55	56	54	57	60	62	60	57	55	46	46	56
D. C. WASHINGTON	66	46	53	56	57	61	64	64	62	62	61	54	47	58
FLA. APALACHICOLA	26	59	62	62	71	77	70	64	63	62	74	66	53	65
JACKSONVILLE	60	58	59	66	71	71	63	62	63	58	58	61	53	62
KEY WEST	45	68	75	78	78	76	70	69	71	65	65	69	66	71
MIAMI BEACH	48	66	72	73	73	68	62	65	67	62	62	65	65	67
TAMPA	63	63	67	71	74	75	66	61	64	64	67	67	61	68
GA. ATLANTA	65	48	53	57	65	68	68	62	63	65	67	60	47	60
HAWAII. HILO	9	48	42	41	34	31	41	44	38	42	41	34	36	39
HONOLULU	53	62	64	60	62	64	66	67	70	70	68	63	60	65
LIHUE	9	48	48	48	46	51	60	58	59	67	58	51	49	54
IDAHO. BOISE	20	40	48	59	67	68	75	89	86	81	66	46	37	66
POCATELLO	21	37	47	58	64	66	72	82	81	78	66	48	36	64
ILL. CAIRO	30	46	53	59	65	71	77	82	79	75	73	56	46	65
CHICAGO	66	44	49	53	56	63	69	73	70	65	61	47	41	59
SPRINGFIELD	59	47	51	54	58	64	69	76	72	73	64	53	45	60
IND. EVANSVILLE	48	42	49	55	61	67	73	78	76	73	67	52	42	64
FT. WAYNE	48	38	44	51	55	62	69	74	69	64	58	41	38	57
INDIANAPOLIS	63	41	47	49	55	62	68	74	70	68	64	48	39	59
IOWA. DES MOINES	66	56	56	56	59	62	66	75	70	64	64	53	48	62
DUBUQUE	54	48	52	52	58	60	63	73	67	61	55	44	40	57
SIOUX CITY	52	55	58	58	59	63	67	75	72	67	65	53	50	63
KANS. CONCORDIA	52	60	60	62	63	65	73	79	76	72	70	64	58	67
DODGE CITY	70	67	66	68	68	68	74	78	78	76	75	70	67	71
WICHITA	46	61	63	64	64	66	73	80	77	73	69	67	59	69
KY. LOUISVILLE	59	41	47	52	57	64	68	72	69	68	64	51	39	59
LA. NEW ORLEANS	69	49	50	57	63	66	64	58	60	64	70	60	46	59
SHREVEPORT	18	48	54	58	60	69	78	79	80	79	77	65	60	69
MAINE. EASTPORT	58	45	51	52	52	51	53	55	57	54	50	37	40	50
MASS. BOSTON	67	47	56	57	56	59	62	64	63	61	58	48	48	57
MICH. ALPENA	45	29	43	52	56	59	64	70	64	52	44	24	22	51
DETROIT	69	34	42	48	52	58	65	69	66	61	54	35	29	53
GRAND RAPIDS	56	26	37	48	54	60	66	72	67	58	50	31	22	49
MARQUETTE	55	31	40	47	52	53	56	63	57	47	38	24	24	47
S. STE. MARIE	60	28	44	50	54	54	59	63	58	45	36	21	22	47
MINN. DULUTH	49	47	55	60	58	58	60	68	63	53	47	36	40	55
MINNEAPOLIS	45	49	54	55	57	60	64	72	69	60	54	40	40	56
MISS. VICKSBURG	66	46	50	57	64	69	73	69	72	74	71	60	45	64
MO. KANSAS CITY	69	55	57	59	60	64	70	76	73	70	67	59	52	65
ST. LOUIS	68	48	49	56	59	64	68	72	68	67	65	54	44	61
SPRINGFIELD	45	48	54	57	60	63	69	77	72	71	65	58	48	63
MONT. HAVRE	55	49	58	61	63	63	65	78	75	64	57	48	46	62
HELENA	65	46	55	58	60	59	63	77	74	63	57	48	43	60
KALISPELL	50	28	40	49	57	58	60	77	73	61	50	28	20	53
NEBR. LINCOLN	55	57	59	60	60	63	69	76	71	67	66	59	55	64
NORTH PLATTE	53	63	63	64	62	64	72	78	74	72	70	62	58	68
NEV. ELY	21	61	64	68	65	67	79	79	81	81	73	67	62	72
LAS VEGAS	19	74	77	78	81	85	91	84	86	92	84	83	75	82
RENO	51	59	64	69	75	77	82	90	89	86	76	68	56	76
WINNEMUCCA	53	52	60	64	70	76	83	90	90	86	75	62	53	74

These charts and tabulation derived from "Normals, Means, and Extremes" table in U. S. Weather Bureau publication Local Climatological Data.

STATE AND STATION	YEARS	JAN.	FEB.	MAR.	APR.	MAY	JUNE	JULY	AUG.	SEPT.	OCT.	NOV.	DEC.	ANNUAL
N. H. CONCORD	44	48	53	55	53	51	56	57	58	55	50	43	43	52
N. J. ATLANTIC CITY	62	51	57	58	59	62	65	67	66	65	54	58	52	60
N. MEX. ALBUQUERQUE	28	70	72	72	76	79	84	76	75	81	80	79	70	76
ROSWELL	47	69	72	75	77	76	80	76	75	74	74	74	69	74
N. Y. ALBANY	63	43	51	53	53	57	62	63	61	58	54	39	38	53
BINGHAMTON	63	31	39	41	44	50	56	54	51	47	43	29	26	44
BUFFALO	49	32	41	49	51	59	67	70	67	60	51	31	28	53
CANTON	43	37	47	50	48	54	61	63	61	54	45	30	31	49
NEW YORK	83	49	56	57	59	62	65	66	64	64	61	53	50	59
SYRACUSE	49	31	38	45	50	58	64	67	63	56	47	29	26	50
N. C. ASHEVILLE	57	48	53	56	61	64	63	59	59	62	64	59	48	58
RALEIGH	61	50	56	59	64	67	65	62	62	63	64	62	52	61
N. DAK. BISMARCK	65	52	58	56	57	58	61	73	69	62	59	49	48	59
DEVILS LAKE	55	53	60	59	60	59	62	71	67	59	56	44	45	58
FARGO	39	47	55	56	58	62	63	73	69	60	57	39	46	59
WILLISTON	43	51	59	60	63	66	66	78	75	65	60	48	48	63
OHIO, CINCINNATI	44	41	46	52	56	62	69	72	68	68	60	46	39	57
CLEVELAND	65	29	36	45	52	61	67	71	68	62	54	32	25	50
COLUMBUS	65	36	44	49	54	63	68	71	68	66	60	44	35	55
OKLA. OKLAHOMA CITY	62	57	60	63	64	65	74	78	78	74	68	64	57	68
OREG. BAKER	46	41	49	56	61	63	67	83	81	74	62	46	37	60
PORTLAND	69	27	34	41	49	52	55	70	65	55	42	28	23	48
ROSEBURG	29	24	32	40	51	57	59	79	77	68	42	28	18	51
PA. HARRISBURG	60	43	52	55	57	61	65	68	63	62	58	47	43	57
PHILADELPHIA	66	45	56	57	58	61	62	64	61	62	61	53	49	57
PITTSBURGH	63	32	39	45	50	57	62	64	61	62	54	39	30	51
R. I. BLOCK ISLAND	48	45	54	47	56	58	60	62	62	60	59	50	44	56
S. C. CHARLESTON	61	58	60	65	72	73	70	66	66	67	68	68	57	66
COLUMBIA	55	53	57	62	68	69	68	63	65	64	68	64	51	63
S. DAK. HURON	62	55	62	60	62	65	68	76	72	66	61	52	49	63
RAPID CITY	53	58	62	63	62	61	66	73	73	69	66	58	54	64
TENN. KNOXVILLE	62	42	49	53	59	64	66	64	59	64	64	53	41	57
MEMPHIS	55	44	51	57	64	68	74	73	74	70	69	58	45	64
NASHVILLE	63	42	47	54	60	65	69	69	68	69	65	55	42	59
TEX. ABILENE	14	64	68	73	66	73	86	83	85	73	71	72	66	73
AMARILLO	54	71	71	75	75	75	82	81	81	79	76	76	70	76
AUSTIN	33	46	50	57	60	62	72	76	79	70	70	57	49	63
BROWNSVILLE	37	44	49	51	57	65	73	78	78	67	70	54	44	61
DEL RIO	36	53	55	61	63	60	66	75	80	69	66	58	52	63
EL PASO	53	74	77	81	85	87	87	78	78	80	82	80	73	80
FT. WORTH	33	56	57	65	66	67	75	78	78	74	70	63	58	68
GALVESTON	66	50	50	55	61	69	76	72	71	70	74	62	49	63
SAN ANTONIO	57	48	51	56	58	60	69	74	75	69	67	55	49	62
UTAH. SALT LAKE CITY	22	48	53	61	68	73	78	82	82	84	73	56	49	69
VT. BURLINGTON	54	34	43	48	47	53	59	62	59	51	43	25	24	46
VA. NORFOLK	60	50	57	60	63	67	66	66	66	63	64	60	51	62
RICHMOND	56	49	55	59	63	67	66	65	62	63	64	58	50	61
WASH. NORTH HEAD	44	28	37	42	48	48	48	50	46	48	41	31	27	41
SEATTLE	26	27	34	42	48	53	48	62	56	53	36	28	24	45
SPOKANE	62	26	41	53	63	64	68	82	79	68	53	28	22	58
TATOOSH ISLAND	49	26	36	39	45	47	46	48	44	47	38	26	23	40
WALLA WALLA	44	24	35	51	63	67	72	86	84	72	59	33	20	60
YAKIMA	18	34	49	62	70	72	74	86	86	74	61	38	29	65
W. VA. ELKINS	55	33	37	42	47	55	55	56	53	55	51	41	33	48
PARKERSBURG	62	30	36	42	49	56	60	63	60	60	53	37	29	48
WIS. GREEN BAY	57	44	51	55	56	58	64	70	65	58	52	40	40	55
MADISON	59	44	49	52	53	58	64	70	66	60	56	41	38	56
MILWAUKEE	59	44	48	53	56	60	65	73	67	62	56	44	39	57
WYO. CHEYENNE	63	65	66	64	61	59	68	70	68	69	69	65	63	66
LANDER	57	66	70	71	66	65	74	76	75	72	67	61	62	69
SHERIDAN	52	56	61	62	61	61	67	76	74	67	60	53	52	64
YELLOWSTONE PARK	35	39	51	55	57	56	63	73	71	65	57	45	38	56
P. R. SAN JUAN	57	64	69	71	66	59	62	65	67	61	63	63	65	65

Based on period of record through December 1959, except in a few instances.

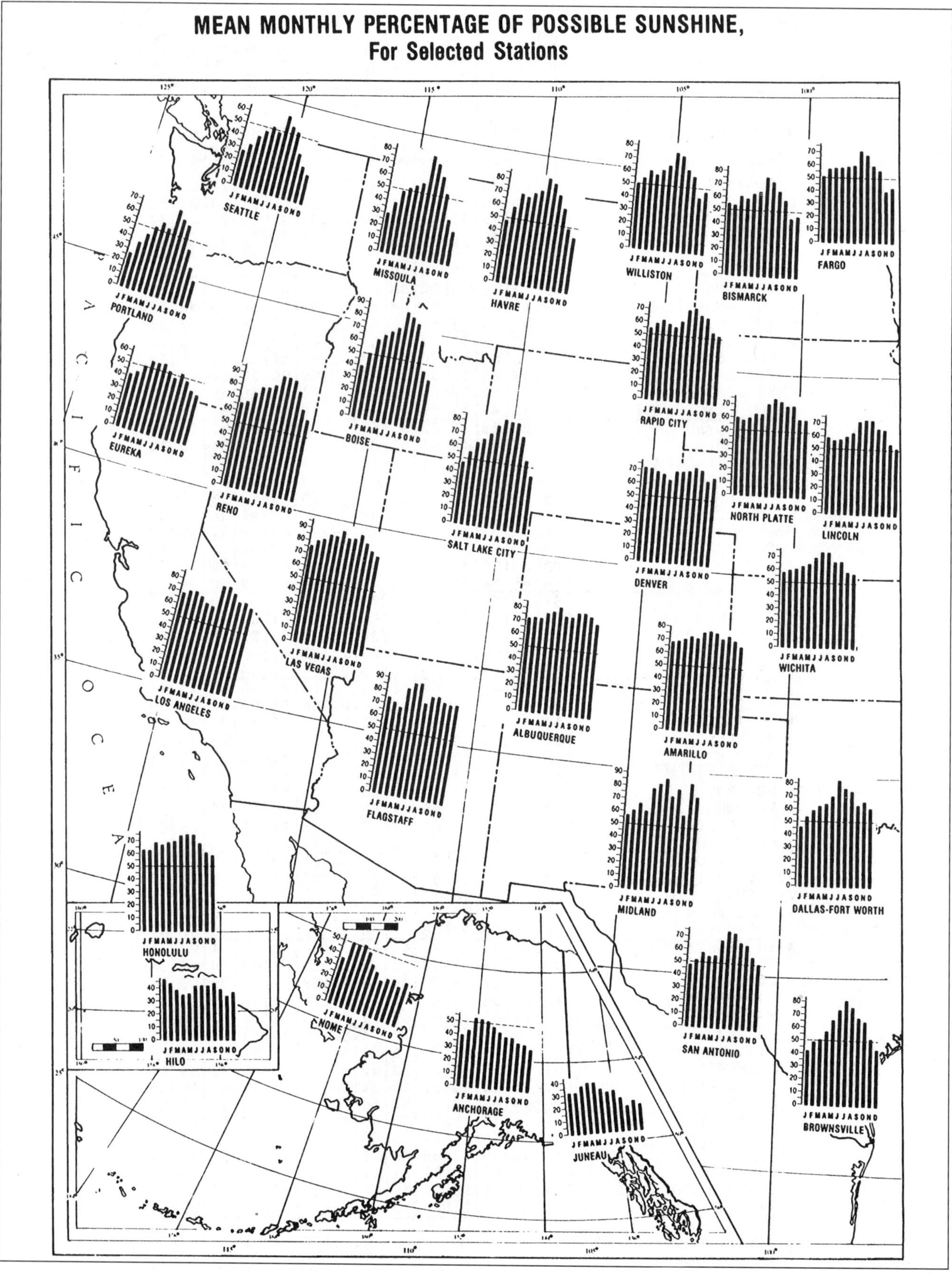
MEAN MONTHLY PERCENTAGE OF POSSIBLE SUNSHINE,
For Selected Stations
SEATTLE
PORTLAND
EUREKA
MISSOULA
HAVRE
WILLISTON
BISMARCK
FARGO
BOISE
RENO
RAPID CITY
SALT LAKE CITY
NORTH PLATTE
LINCOLN
DENVER
LAS VEGAS
LOS ANGELES
WICHITA
ALBUQUERQUE
AMARILLO
FLAGSTAFF
MIDLAND
DALLAS-FORT WORTH
HONOLULU
HILO
NOME
ANCHORAGE
JUNEAU
SAN ANTONIO
BROWNSVILLE
PACIFIC OCEAN

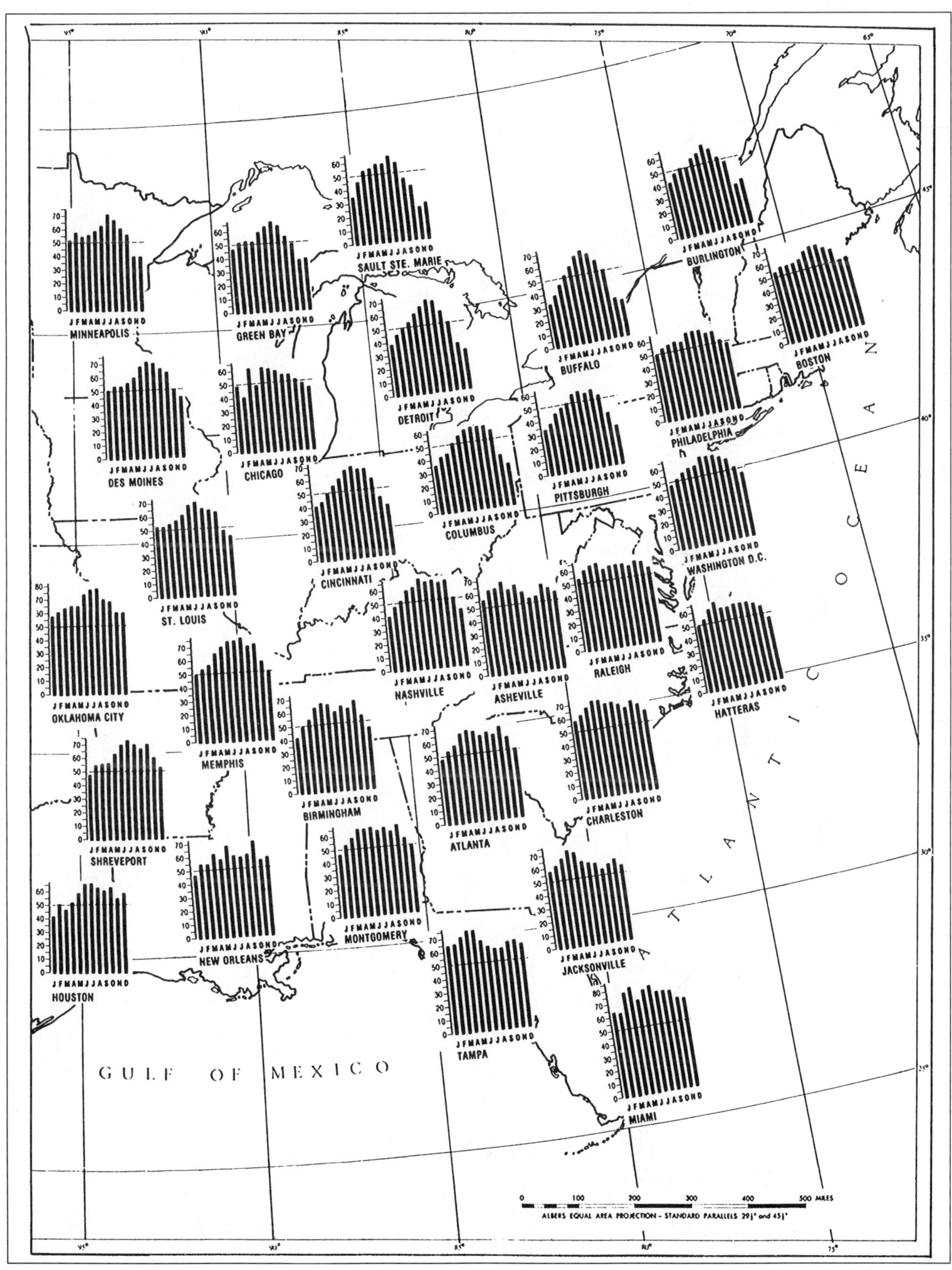
MINNEAPOLIS
GREEN BAY
SAULT STE. MARIE
DETROIT
BUFFALO
BURLINGTON
BOSTON
DES MOINES
CHICAGO
PHILADELPHIA
PITTSBURGH
COLUMBUS
CINCINNATI
ST. LOUIS
WASHINGTON D.C.
OKLAHOMA CITY
NASHVILLE
ASHEVILLE
RALEIGH
HATTERAS
MEMPHIS
BIRMINGHAM
ATLANTA
CHARLESTON
SHREVEPORT
NEW ORLEANS
MONTGOMERY
JACKSONVILLE
HOUSTON
TAMPA
MIAMI
GULF OF MEXICO
ATLANTIC OCEAN
J F M A M J J A S O N D
0 100 200 300 400 500 MILES
ALBERS EQUAL AREA PROJECTION - STANDARD PARALLELS 29½° and 45½°

PREVAILING WIND DIRECTION

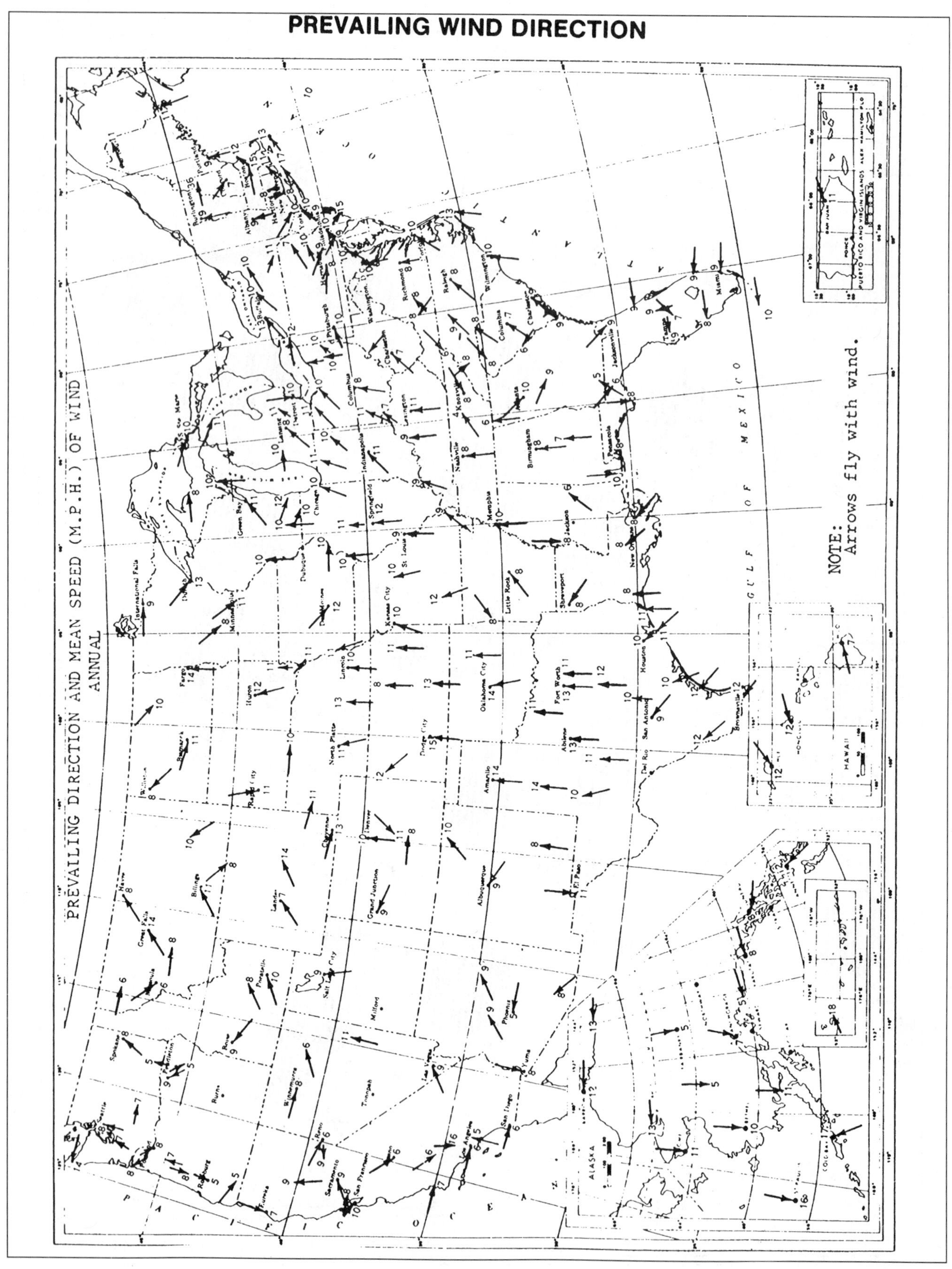

National Climatic Data Center
Research Customer Service Group
Federal Building, Asheville, NC 28801

The U.S. has sustained some very expensive weather-related disasters over the past 15 years. During the 1988-1994 period, the U.S. sustained 11 weather-related disasters with total damages/costs estimated over $ 100 billion. All figures reflect direct and indirect damages, costs, and deaths.

Billion Dollar U.S. Weather Disasters 1980 - 1994

1. **Georgia Flooding** July 1994. Remnants of slow-moving Alberto brought torrential 10-25 inch rains, widespread flooding in parts of Georgia, Alabama, and panhandle of Florida; preliminary estimates up to $1.0 billion damage/costs; 32 deaths.

2. **Southeast Ice Storm** February 1994. Intense ice storm with extensive damage in portions of TX, OK, AR, LA, MS, AL, TN, GA, SC, NC, and VA; estimated over $3.0 billion damage/costs; 9 deaths.

3. **California Wildfires** Fall 1993. Southern California, at least $1.0 billion damage/costs, 4 deaths.

4. **Midwest Flooding** Summer 1993. Central U.S., $15.0-$20.0 billion damage/costs, 48 deaths.

5. **Drought/Heat Wave** Summer 1993. Southeastern U.S., about $1.0 billion damage/costs, death toll undetermined.

6. **Storm/Blizzard** March 1993. Eastern U.S., over $3.0 billion damage/costs, estimated up to 270 deaths.

7. **Hurricane Iniki** September 1992. Hawaiian Island of Kauai, about $1.8 billion damage/costs, 6 deaths.

8. **Hurricane Andrew** August 1992. Florida and Louisiana, about $25.0 billion damage/costs, 58 deaths.

9. **Hurricane Bob** August 1991. Mainly coastal North Carolina, Long Island, and New England, $1.5 billion damage/costs, 18 deaths.

10. **Hurricane Hugo** September 1989. Carolinas, $7.1 billion damage/costs, 57 deaths.

11. **Drought/Heat Wave** Summer 1988. Central and Eastern U.S., estimated $40.0 billion damage/costs, estimated 5,000 to 10,000 deaths (includes heat stress-related).

12. **Hurricane Juan** October-November 1985. Louisiana and Southeast U.S., $1.5 billion damage/costs, 63 deaths.

13. **Hurricane Elena** August-September 1985. Florida to Louisiana, $1.3 billion damage/costs, 4 deaths.

14. **Hurricane Alicia** August 1983. Texas, $2.0 billion damage/costs, 21 deaths.

15. **Drought/Heat Wave** June-September 1980. Central and Eastern U.S., estimated $20.0 billion damage/costs, estimated 1300 deaths (includes heat stress-related).

Storms, Severe Weather & Geophysical Phenomena

• HURRICANES

There is nothing like the hurricane in the atmosphere.

Even seen by sensors on satellites thousands of miles above the earth, the uniqueness of these powerful, tightly coiled storms is clear. Hurricanes are not the largest storm systems in our atmosphere, or the most violent; but they combine those qualities as no other phenomenon does, as if they were designed to be engines of death and destruction.

In our hemisphere, they are called hurricanes, a term which echoes colonial Spanish and Caribbean Indian words for evil spirits and big winds. The storms are products of the tropical ocean and atmosphere, powered by heat from the sea, steered by the easterly trades and temperate westerlies, and their own fierce energy. Around their tranquil core, winds blow with lethal velocity and the ocean develops an inundating surge. What is more, as they move ashore, tornadoes may descend from the advancing bands of thunderclouds.

Tropical storm/hurricane names

The National Hurricane Center near Miami, Florida, keeps a constant watch on oceanic storm-breeding areas for tropical disturbances which may herald the formation of a hurricane. If a disturbance intensifies into a tropical storm with rotary circulation and wind speeds above 39 mph (63 km/hr), the Center will give the storm a name. The tropical disturbance may never reach hurricane intensity, nevertheless it is given a name in anticipation that it may. A separate set of names is used each year beginning with the first name in the set. After the sets have all been used, they will be used again. The 1991 set, for example, will be used again to name storms in 1997. The letters Q, U, X, Y, and Z are not included because of the scarcity of names beginning with those letters.

The name lists have an international flavor because hurricanes affect other nations and are tracked by countries other than the United States. Names for these lists are selected from library sources and agreed upon by nations involved during international meetings of the World Meteorological Organization (WMO).

Hurricane names cut death tolls

Experience shows that the use of short, distinctive given names in written as well as in spoken communications is quicker, and less subject to error than the older more cumbersome latitude-longitude identification methods. These advantages are especially important in exchanging detailed storm information between hundreds of widely scattered stations, airports, coastal bases, and ships at sea. Hurricanes, as poorly understood as they are today, seem to have a single benefit—they are a major source of rain for those continental corners over which their unpredictable tracks carry them. Mostly they are seen as engines of tragedy, which still leave death and destruction in their paths, even though the effectiveness of warnings systems have doubled and redoubled in recent decades.

In Asia, the price in life paid the hurricane has had biblical proportions. As late as 1970, cyclone storm tides along the coast of what now is Bangladesh killed hundreds of thousands of persons. Eleven thousand people perished in a storm that struck that region in 1984, and even more in a storm seven years later.

Our hemisphere has not had such spectacular losses, but the toll has still been high. In August 1893, a storm surge drowned 1,000-2,000 people in Charleston, South Carolina. In October of that same year, nearly 2,000 more perished on the Gulf Coast of Louisiana. The infamous Galveston storm of 1900 took more than 6,000 lives. More than 1,800 perished along the south shore of Florida's Lake Okeechobee in 1928 when hurricane driven waters broached an earthen levee. Cuba lost more than 2,000 to a storm in 1932. Four hundred died in Florida in an intense hurricane in September, 1935—the Labor Day hurricane that, until Hugo hit in 1989, shared with 1969's Camille, the distinction of being

Computer-enhanced photo of Hurricane Diana, September 11, 1984.

the most severe to strike the United States mainland during the years of recordkeeping.

Floods from 1974's Hurricane Fifi caused one of the Western Hemisphere's worst natural disasters in history, with an estimated 5,000 persons dead in Honduras, El Salvador, Guatemala, and Belize.

In the United States, the hurricane death toll has been greatly diminished by timely warnings of approaching storms. But damage to fixed property continues to mount. Camille, in 1969, caused some $1.42 billion (dollars of hurricane damage prior to 1990 have been translated into 1990 dollar equivalents) in property damage. Floods from Agnes in 1972 cost an estimated $2.1 billion and damage from Frederic in 1979 the 1985 season, when eight named in excess of $4 billion. Hugo, in 1989, wrought damage of more than $7 billion while coming ashore as a full-scale hurricane in South Carolina and moving hundreds of miles inland as a furious near-hurricane strength storm.

Hurricane Andrew

Hurricane Andrew slammed into heavily populated south Florida as the most destructive storm in United States history.

Andrew formed as a tropical wave off the African coast on August 14, 1992. By August 22, it was classified as a tropical storm. As it neared the Bahamas and Florida on August 23, Andrew had reached hurricane intensity.

With sustained winds of 145 miles per hour and gusts over 175 miles per hour, Andrew annihilated homes and businesses along a 30-mile (48 km) path through the Dade County towns of Homestead, Leisure City, Goulds, Princeton, Naranja, and Florida City. When it was over, more than 60,000 homes were destroyed and 200,000 people were left homeless.

Andrew had a central pressure of 922 millibars (mb) at landfall making it the third most intense hurricane of the twentieth century. Only the infamous "Labor Day" hurricane that struck the Keys in 1935 and Hurricane Camille in 1969 along the Mississippi/Louisiana coasts were stronger. Damage estimates have been as high $30 billion.

Fifteen people died in Florida as a direct result of Andrew's fury. Another 29 lives were lost as a result of indirect effects of the hurricane within the next three weeks. The relatively low loss of life, compared to the hundreds that died in the 1935 storm and in Camille, stands as a testimony to the success and importance of hurricane awareness campaigns, preparedness planning, and actions by the joint efforts of federal, state, county, and city emergency forces. The news media played a major role in the life-saving actions before, during, and after Andrew hit.

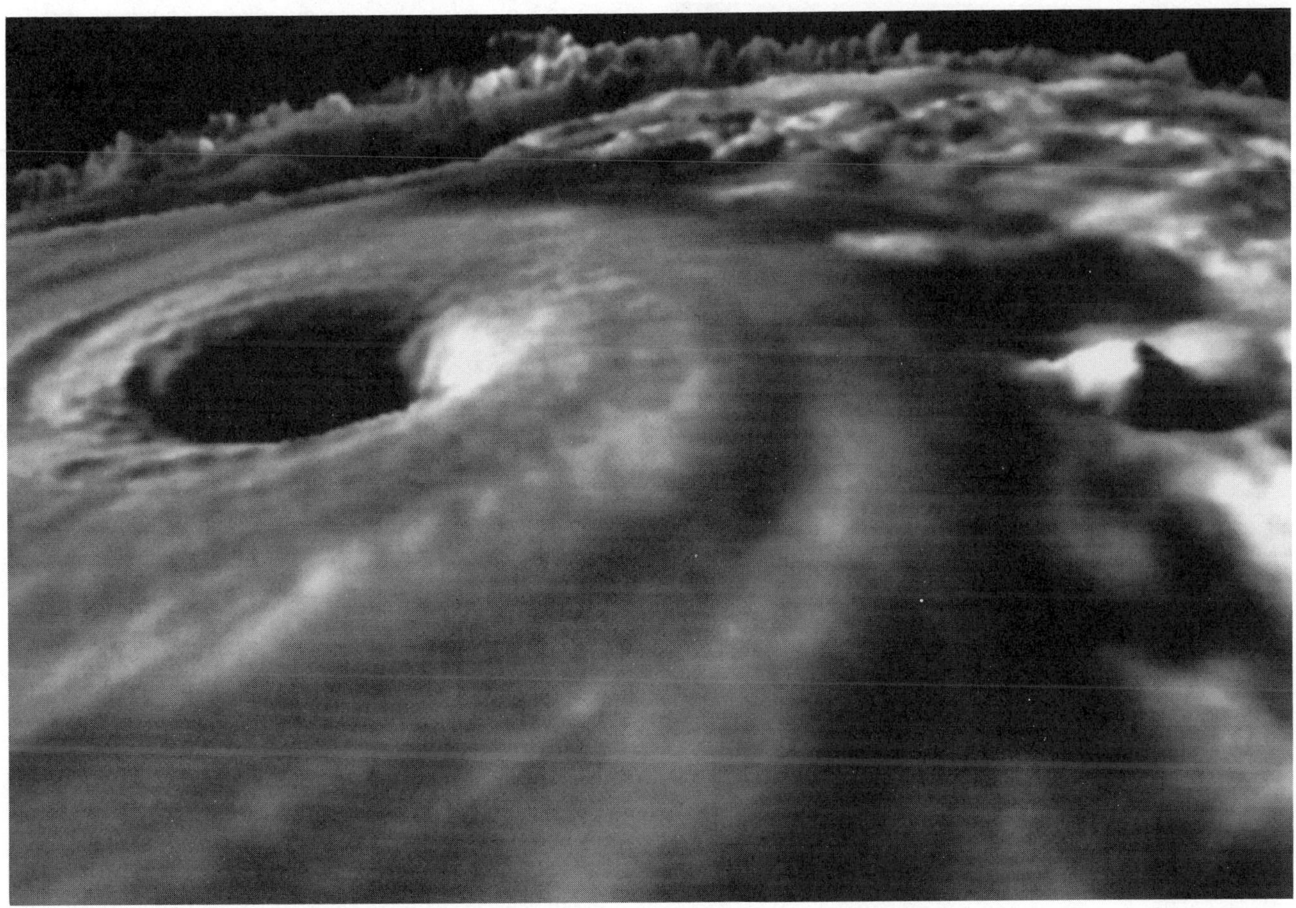

At their strongest, the winds of Diana reached 130 miles per hour.

Storm surge – Historically, such powerful hurricanes have caused great loss of life from the *storm surge*. As Andrew came ashore first in the northwest Bahamas, storm surge reached an astonishing 23 feet (6.9 m). In Florida, a 17-foot (5.18 m) storm tide, which headed inland from Biscayne Bay, is a record for the southeast Florida peninsula. Storm tides of more than 7 feet (2.09 m) in Louisiana also caused severe flooding.

Evacuation from threatened coastal areas is the only defense from the storm surge's potential for death and destruction. After the National Hurricane Center issued hurricane watches and warnings, massive evacuations were ordered in Florida and Louisiana by emergency management officials. It is estimated that more than 2,000,000 people evacuated to safety in Florida and Louisiana as Andrew approached.

Hurricane Hugo

Hurricane Hugo, crossing the coast of South Carolina on September 21, 1989, at that point, was the strongest storm to strike the United States since Camille pounded the Louisiana and Mississippi coasts in 1969.

At one point east of Guadeloupe, a National Oceanic and Atmospheric Administration (NOAA) research aircraft measured winds of 160 mph (257 km/hr) and a central pressure of 27.11 inches (918 mb) which rated Hugo as a category 5—the highest—storm on the Saffir-Simpson Scale. It was somewhat less fierce when it reached the United States mainland.

When Hugo struck the Virgin Islands, Puerto Rico, and the Carolinas, it was classified as a category 4 hurricane. Storm tides of approximately 20 feet (6.7 m) were experienced along part of the South Carolina coast, constituting record storm-tide heights for America's east coast. Although the highest surges struck sparsely populated areas north of Charleston, South Carolina, damage was extensive and lives were lost.

Forty-nine directly-related storm fatalities were recorded, 26 in the United States and its Caribbean Islands. Twenty-three died in other Leeward Islands. It is estimated that Hugo caused more than $9 billion in damage. The mainland of the United States alone accounted for $7 billion.

The season of great storms

It is the coming of summer to the northern hemisphere that ushers in conditions that spawn tropical storms and hurricanes. The movement of our sun—which is not really movement, of course, but a positional shift relative to the

Saffir-Simpson Hurricane Scale

All hurricanes are dangerous, but some are more so than others. The way storm surge, wind, and other factors combine determines the hurricane's destructive power. To make comparisons easier-and to make the predicted hazards of approaching hurricanes clearer to emergency forces, NOAA's hurricane forecasters use a disaster-potential scale, which assigns storms to five categories. Category 1 is a minimum hurricane; category 5 is the worst case. The criteria for each category are shown below.

This can be used to give an estimate of the potential property damage and flooding expected along the coast with a hurricane.

Category Definitions and Effects

ONE Winds 74-95 mph (119-153 km/hr). No real damage to building structures. Damage primarily to unanchored mobile homes, shrubbery and trees. Also, some coastal road flooding and minor pier damage.

TWO Winds 96-110 mph (155-177 km/hr). Some roofing material, door and window damage to buildings. Considerable damage to vegetation, mobile homes and piers. Coastal and low-lying escape routes flood 2-4 hours before arrival of center. Small craft in unprotected anchorages break moorings.

THREE Winds 111-130 mph (179-209 km/hr). Some structural damage to small residences and utility buildings with a minor amount of curtainwall failures. Mobile homes are destroyed. Flooding near the coast destroys smaller structures with larger structures damaged by floating debris. Terrain continuously lower than 5 feet (1.54 m) ASL may be flooded inland as far as 6 miles (9.66 km).

FOUR Winds 131-155 mph (211-250 km/hr). More extensive curtainwall failures with some complete roof structure failure on small residences. Major erosion of beach areas. Major damage to lower floors of structures near the shore. Terrain continuously lower than 10 feet (3 m) ASL may be flooded requiring massive evacuation of residential areas inland as far as 6 miles (9.66 km).

FIVE Winds greater than 155 mph (250 km/hr). Complete roof failure on many residences and industrial buildings. Some complete building failures with small utility buildings blown over or away. Major damage to lower floors of all structure located less than 15 feet (5 m) ASL and within 500 yards (455 m) of the shoreline. Massive evacuation of residential areas on low ground within 10 miles (16.1 km) of the shoreline may be required.

earth caused by our planet's year-long orbit—brings the peak power of the solar radiation northward. The sun's track moves first to the Equator, in March, then toward the Tropic of Cancer, (23°, 27° north latitude), as June, July, and August unfold. Behind this solar track the sea and air grow warmer, and the polar airflows make a steady retreat.

This northward shift of the sun brings the season of tropical cyclones to the Northern Hemisphere. This means it is time to look seaward, along our coasts. This is as true for Asia as for the United States and the Caribbean.

Over the Western Pacific, the tropical cyclone season is never quite over, but varies greatly in intensity. Every year, conditions east of the Philippines send a score of violent storms howling toward Asia; but it is worse from June through October.

Southwest of Mexico, eastern Pacific hurricanes develop during the spring and summer. Most of these will die at sea as they move over colder ocean waters. But there are destructive exceptions when storms occasionally curve back toward Mexico.

Along our Atlantic and Gulf coasts, the nominal hurricane season lasts from June through November. Early in this season, the western Caribbean and Gulf of Mexico are the principal areas of origin. In July and August, this spawning center begins to shift eastward; by early September a few storms are being born as far east as the Cape Verde Islands off Africa's west coast. Again after mid-September, most storms begin in the western Caribbean and Gulf of Mexico.

In an average year, more than 100 disturbances with hurricane potential are observed in the Atlantic, Gulf, and Caribbean; but on an average only ten of these reach the tropical storm stage, and only about six mature into hurricanes. On average, two of these hurricanes strike the United States, where they are apt to kill from about 50-100 people, somewhere between Texas and Maine, and cause hundreds of millions of dollars in property damage. In a worse-than-average year, the same storms cause several hundred deaths, and property damage totaling billions of dollars.

For NOAA, the hurricane season means another hazard from the atmosphere, at a time when tornadoes, and floods, and severe storms are playing seasonal havoc elsewhere on the continent.

Meteorologists with NOAA's National Weather Service (NWS) monitor the massive flow of data that might contain the early indications of a developing storm somewhere over the warm sea. Cloud images from satellites, meteorological data from hundreds of surface stations, balloon probes of the atmosphere, and information from hurricane-hunting aircraft are the tools of the hurricane forecaster.

In NOAA's Environmental Research Laboratories, scientists follow eagerly as nature furnishes additional specimens of the great storms—specimens they can probe and analyze to gather ever-greater understanding of the mechanics of the storms. Such analyses assist the forecaster with his warnings.

Portrait of a hurricane

Given that the hurricane, as an engine, is inefficient and hard to start and sustain, and given, further, that most tropical storms will never reach hurricane proportions, nevertheless some tropical storms will. A certain number every season will manage to accumulate the complex combination of natural forces required. When one does, it is an awesome natural event indeed.

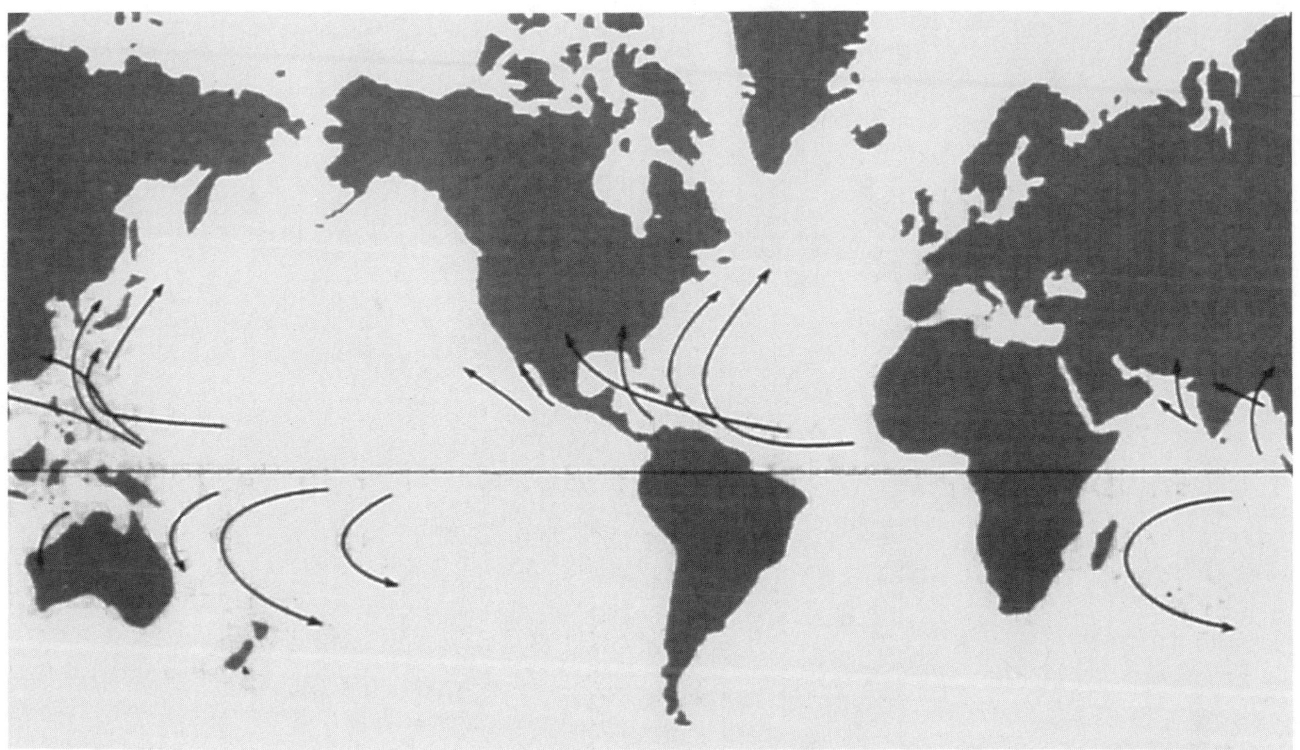

Hurricane breeding places.

The young storm stands upon the sea as a whirlwind of awful violence. Its hurricane-force winds (winds greater than 63 knots) cover thousands of square miles, and tropical storm force winds (winds of 34-63 knots) cover an area ten times larger. Along the twisting contours of its spiral are "rain bands" of dense clouds from which torrential rains fall. These spiral rain bands ascend in "decks" of cumulus and cumulonimbus clouds to the high upper-atmosphere. There condensing water vapor is swept off as ice-crystal wisps of cirrus clouds by high-altitude winds. Lightning glows in almost perpetual pulsations in the rainbands, and this cloudy terrain is whipped by turbulence.

In the lower few thousand feet, air flows in toward the center of the cyclone, and is whirled upward through ascending columns of air near the center. Above 40,000 feet (12,133 m), this cyclone pattern is replaced by an anti-cyclonic circulation—the high-level pump which functions as the "exhaust system" of the hurricane engine. (Anti-cyclonic circulation means, in the Northern Hemisphere, a system of winds rotating in a clockwise direction about a center of relatively low barometric pressure. Contrast this to "cyclonic circulation" which has a counterclockwise pattern. Both of these definitions are reversed in the Southern Hemisphere.)

At the lower levels, where the hurricane is most intense, winds on the rim of the storm follow a wide pattern, like the slower currents on the rim of a whirlpool; like those currents, these winds accelerate as they approach the central vortex. This inner band is the eyewall, where the storm's worst winds are felt, and where moist all entering at the surface is "chimneyed" upward releasing heat to drive the storm. In most hurricanes, these winds exceed 90 knots—in extreme cases they may double that velocity. Maximum winds run still higher in typhoons, the Pacific version of the same type of storm.

Hurricane winds are produced, as all winds are, by difference in atmospheric, pressure, or density. The pressure gradient—the rate of pressure change with distance—produced in hurricanes is the sharpest pressure gradient in the atmosphere, excepting only the pressure change believed to exist across the narrow funnel of a tornado.

Atmospheric pressure is popularly expressed as the height of a column of mercury that can be supported by the weight of the overlying air at a given time. Weather maps show atmospheric pressure in millibars (mb), units equal to a thousandth of a bar. The bar is a unit of measure equal to 29.53 inches of mercury in the English system; and to one million dydnes per square centimeters in the metric system.

Atlantic tropical cyclone names

1995	1996	1997
ALLISON	ARTHUR	ANA
BARRY	BERTHA	BILL
CHANTAL	CESAR	CLAUDETTE
DEAN	DOLLY	DANNY
ERIN	EDOUARD	ERIKA
FELIX	FRAN	FABIAN
GABRIELLE	GUSTAV	GRACE
HUMBERTO	HORTENSE	HENRI
IRIS	ISIDORE	ISABELL
JERRY	JOSEPHINE	JUAN
KAREN	KYLE	KATE
LUIS	LILI	LARRY
MARILYN	MARCO	MINDY
NOEL	NANA	NICHOLAS
OPAL	OMAR	ODETTE
PABLO	PALOMA	PETER
ROXANNE	RENE	ROSE
SEBASTIEN	SALLY	SAM
TANYA	TEDDY	TERESA
VAN	VICKY	VICTOR
WENDY	WILFRED	WANDA
1998	**1999**	**2000**
ALEX	ARLENE	ALBERTO
BONNIE	BRET	BERYL
CHARLEY	CINDY	CHRIS
DANIELLE	DENNIS	DEBBY
EARL	EMILY	ERNESTO
FRANCES	FLOYD	FLORENCE
GEORGES	GERT	GORDON
HERMINE	HARVEY	HELENE
IVAN	IRENE	ISAAC
JEANNE	JOSE	JOYCE
KARL	KATRINA	KEITH
LISA	LENNY	LESLIE
MITCH	MARIA	MICHAEL
NICOLE	NATE	NADINE
OTTO	OPHELIA	OSCAR
PAULA	PHILIPPE	PATTY
RICHARD	RITA	RAFAEL
SHARY	STAN	SANDY
TOMAS	TAMMY	TONY
VIRGINIE	VINCE	VALERIE
WALTER	WILMA	WILLIAM

In North America, barometric measurements at sea level seldom go below 29 inches of mercury (982 mb), and in the tropics the barometer reading is generally close to 30 inches (1,016 mb) under normal conditions. Hurricanes drop the bottom out of those normal categories. The Labor Day hurricane that struck the Florida Keys in 1935 had a central pressure of only 26.35 inches (892 mb). Hurricane Gilbert which wrought havoc in the Caribbean and the Yucatan Peninsula during 1988, was measured at 26.22 inches in its eye. And the pressure change is swift: pressure may drop a full inch (34 mb) per mile. Such pressure contrasts guarantee tremendous wind velocity.

At the center of the storm is a unique atmospheric entity, and a persistent metaphor for order in the midst of chaos—the eye of the hurricane. It is encountered suddenly. From the heated tower of maximum winds and thunderclouds, one bursts into the eye, where winds diminish to something less than 15 knots. Penetrating the opposite wall one is abruptly in the worst of winds again.

A mature hurricane orchestrates more than a million cubic miles of atmosphere. Over the deep ocean, waves generated by hurricane winds call reach heights of 50 feet (15.19 m) or more. Under the storm center tile ocean surface is drawn upward like water in a straw, forming a mound 1-3 feet (30.48-91.44 cm) or so higher than the surrounding ocean surface. This mound may translate into coastal surges of 20 feet (6.1 m) or more. Besides this surge, massive swells pulse out through the upper levels of the sea. (It is not exaggerating to say that Pacific surfers often ride the oceanic memory of distant typhoons, so pronounced are these energy releases of storms).

Hurricane Eloise, which struck the Florida panhandle in September, 1975, taught scientists something new about the influence of passing hurricanes on the marine environment. Expendable bathythermographs dropped from NOAA research aircraft ahead of, into, and in the wake of the storm showed that the ocean was disturbed to depths of hundreds of feet by a passing hurricane. Moreover the ocean "remembered" hurricane passage with internal waves that persisted for weeks after the storm had gone. The same storm also demonstrated that a passing hurricane can be felt deep in the sea-floor sediments.

While a hurricane lives, the transaction of energy within its circulation is immense. The condensation heat energy released by a hurricane in one day can be the equivalent of energy released by fusion of four hundred, 20-megaton hydrogen bombs. One day's released energy, converted to electricity, could supply the United States' electrical needs for about six months.

The fatal thrust toward land

From birth, the hurricane lives in an environment that constantly tries to kill it—and ultimately succeeds.

Eastern Pacific tropical cyclone names

1995	1996	1997
ADOLPH	ALMA	ANDRES
BARBARA	BORIS	BLANCA
COSME	CRISTINA	CARLOS
DALILA	DOUGLAS	DOLORES
ERICK	ELIDA	ENRIQUE
FLOSSIE	FAUSTO	FELICIA
GIL	GENEVIEVE	GUILLERMO
HENRIETTE	HERNAN	HILDA
ISMAEL	ISELLE	IGNACIO
JULIETTE	JULIO	JIMENA
KIKO	KENNA	KEVIN
LORENA	LOWELL	LINDA
MANUEL	MARIE	MARTY
NARDA	NORBERT	NORA
OCTAVE	ODILE	OLAF
PRISILLA	POLO	PAULINE
RAYMOND	RACHEL	RICK
SONIA	SIMON	SANDRA
TICO	TRUDY	TERRY
VELMA	VANCE	VIVIAN
WALLIS	WINNIE	WALDO
XINA	XAVIER	XINA
YORK	YOLANDA	YORK
ZELDA	ZEKE	ZELDA

1998	1999	2000
AGATHA	ADRIAN	ALETTA
BLAS	BEATRIZ	BUD
CELIA	CALVIN	CARLOTTA
DARBY	DORA	DANIEL
ESTELLE	EUGENE	EMILIA
FRANK	FERNANDA	FABIO
GEORGETTE	GREG	GILMA
HOWARD	HILARY	HECTOR
ISIS	IRWIN	ILEANA
JAVIER	JOVA	JOHN
KAY	KENNETH	KRISTY
LESTER	LIDIA	LANE
MADELINE	MAX	MIRIAM
NEWTON	NORMA	NORMAN
ORLENE	OTIS	OLIVIA
PAINE	PILAR	PAUL
ROSLYN	RAMON	ROSA
SEYMOUR	SELMA	SERGIO
TINA	TODD	TARA
VIRGIL	VERONICA	VICENTE
WINIFRED	WILEY	WILLA
XAVIER	XINA	XAVIER
YOLANDA	YORK	YOLANDA
ZEKE	ZELDA	ZEKE

If over 24 tropical cyclones occur in a year, the Greek alphabet will be used following ZEKE or ZELDA.

The hurricane tends to survive while it is over warm water. But its movement is controlled by the forces which drive the storm ashore or over colder water beyond the tropics. In these nonnourishing environments it will fill and die. This thrust away from the tropics is the clockwise curve which propels Atlantic hurricanes into the eastern United States, and which takes eastern Pacific typhoons across the coastlines of Japan and into the Asian mainland.

Even before a hurricane forms, the embryonic storm has forward motion, generally driven by the easterly flow an air movement system of the tropic latitudes, featuring east to west flow of the atmosphere in which it is embedded. As long as this westerly drift is slow—less than about 20 knots—the young hurricane may intensify. More rapid forward motion generally inhibits intensification in the storm's early stages. Entering the temperate latitudes (north of the Tropic of Cancer) some storms may move along at better than 50 knots; but such fast-moving storms soon weaken.

At middle latitudes, the hurricane's end usually comes swiftly. Colder air penetrates the cyclonic vortex; the warm core cools, and acts as a thermal brake on further intensification. Water below 80°F (26.4°C) does not contribute much energy to a hurricane. Even though some large hurricanes may travel for days over cold North Atlantic water, all storms are doomed once they leave the warm tropical waters which sustain them. The farther they venture into higher latitudes, the less fuel they receive from the sea; this lack of fuel finally kills the storms. Over land, hurricanes break up rapidly. Cut off from their oceanic source of energy, and with the added effects of frictional drag, their circulation rapidly weakens and becomes more disorganized. Torrential rains, however, may continue even after the winds are much diminished. In the southeastern United States, about a fourth of the annual rainfall comes from dissipating hurricanes, and the Asian mainland and Japan suffer typhoons to get water from the sky.

Hurricanes are often resurrected into extratropical cyclones at higher latitudes, or their dynamic forces combine with existing temperate-zone disturbances. Many storms moving up our Atlantic coast are in the throes of this transformation when they strike New England, and large continental lows are often invigorated by the remnants of storms born over the tropical sea.

Destruction in a hurricane

Hurricanes are the unstable, unreliable creatures of a moment in our planet's natural history. But their brief life ashore can leave scars that never quite heal. In the mid-1970s, the hand of 1969's Camille could still be seen along the Mississippi Gulf Coast. Most of a hurricane's destructive work is done by the general rise in the height of the seas which accompany the storm. This quick, tidal-like rise in sea level is called storm surge.

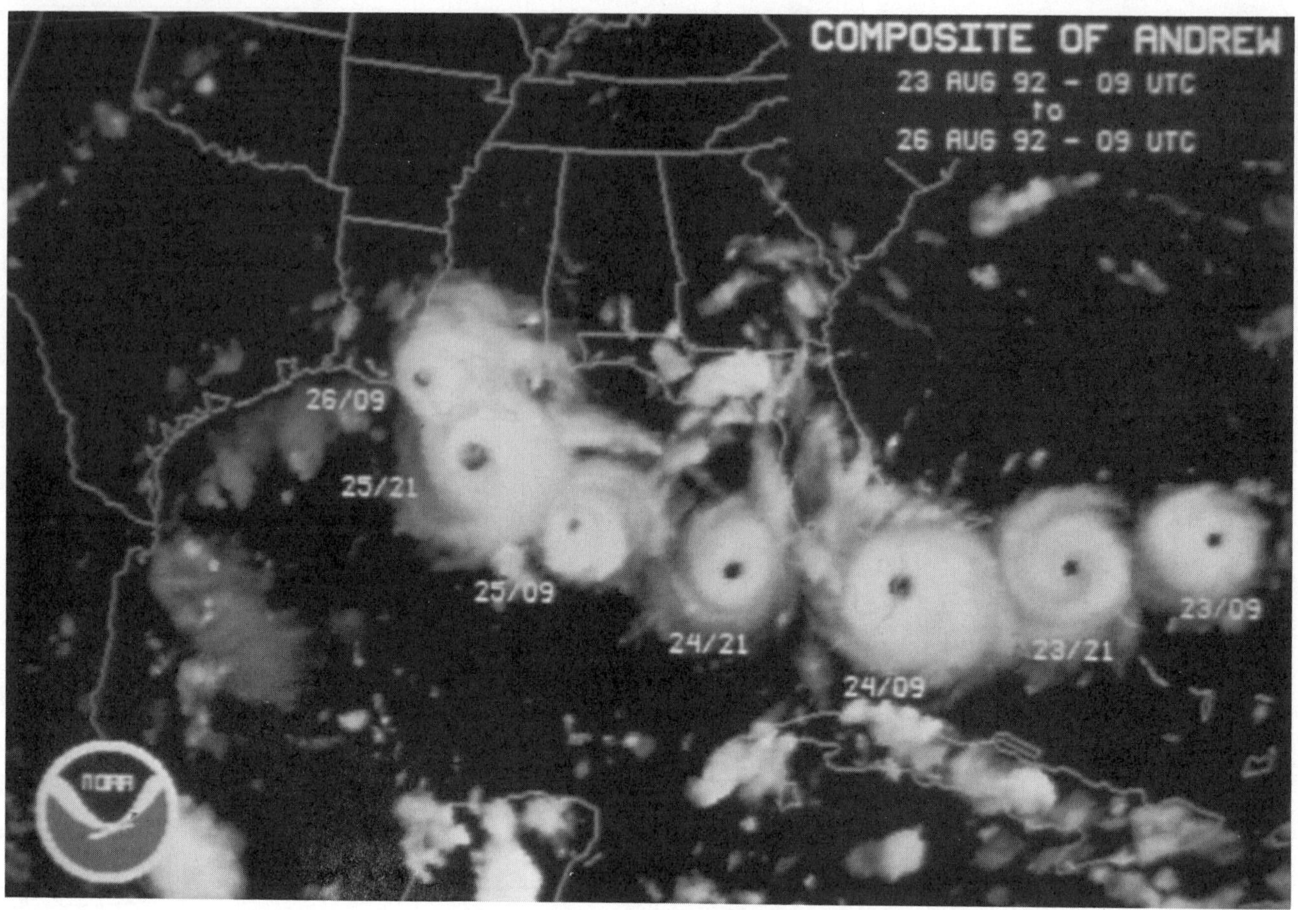

Hurricane Andrew's path of destruction, 1992.

Hurricane winds are a force to be reckoned with by coastal communities deciding how strong their structures should be. As winds increase, pressure against objects is added at a disproportionate rate. Pressure force against a wall mounts with the square of wind speed so that a threefold increase in windspeed gives a ninefold increase in pressure. Thus, a 25 mph (40 km/hr) wind causes about 1.6 lb (.72 kg) of pressure per square foot. A sheet of plywood will be pushed by a force of 50 lb (23 kg). In 75 mph (121 km/hr) winds, that force becomes 450 lb (203 kg) and in 125 mph (201 km/hr), it becomes 1,250 lb (563 kg). For some structures this force is enough to cause failure.

Tall structures like radio towers can be worried to destruction by gusty hurricane-force winds. Winds also carry a barrage of debris that can be extremely dangerous.

All the wind damage does not necessarily come from the hurricane. As the storm moves shoreward, interactions with other weather systems can produce tornadoes, which work around the fringes of the hurricane. Although hurricane-spawned tornadoes are not the most violent form of these whirlwinds, they have added to the toll we pay the hurricane.

Floods from hurricane rainfall are quite destructive. A typical hurricane brings an awesome 6-12 inches (15.24-30.48 cm) of short-duration rainfall to the area it crosses, and some have brought much more. The resulting floods—often sudden flash floods—have caused great damage and loss of life, especially in mountainous area, where heavy rains can mean flash floods. Rains from the dying Hurricane Agnes brought disastrous floods to the entire Atlantic tier of states, causing 118 deaths and some $2.1 billion in property damage.

Storm surge

The hurricane's worst killing blow comes from the sea, in the form of *storm surge*. This subtly approaching smash of tidal wave immensity actually claims nine of each ten victims that fall to a hurricane.

As the storm crosses the continental shelf and moves close to the coast, mean water level may increase 15 feet (4.55 m) or more. The advancing storm surge combines with the normal astronomical tide to create the hurricane storm tide. In addition, wind waves 5-10 feet (1.51-3.03 m) high are superimposed on the storm tide. This buildup of water level can cause severe flooding in coastal areas—particularly when the storm surge coincides with normal high tides. Because much of the United States' densely populated coastline along the Atlantic and Gulf coasts lies less than 10 feet (3.03 m) above mean sea level, the danger from storm surge is multiplied.

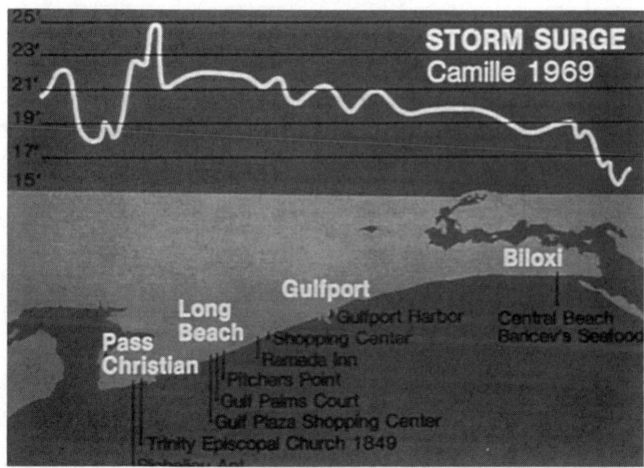

Nearly every coastal location that is exposed to a hurricane is also a candidate for the smashing blow of storm surge.

Wave and current action associated with the surge also causes extensive damage. Water weighs some 1,700 lb/yd^3 (765 kg/m^3); extended pounding by frequent waves can demolish any structures not specifically designed to withstand such forces.

Currents set up along the coast by the gradient in storm surge heights and wind combine with waves to severely erode beaches and coastal highways. Many buildings withstand hurricane winds until, their foundations undermined by erosion, are weakened and fail.

Storm tides, waves, and currents in confined harbors severely damage ships, marinas, and pleasure boats. In estuarine and bayou areas, intrusions of salt water endanger the public health—and can create bizarre effects, like salt-crazed snakes fleeing Louisiana's flooded bayous.

Spotting a hurricane and spreading the word

The day is past when a hurricane could develop to maturity far out to sea and be unreported until it thrust toward land.

Earth-orbiting satellites operated by NOAA keep the earth's atmosphere under virtually continuous surveillance, night and day. Long before a storm has evolved even to the point of ruffling the easterly wave, scientists at NOAA's National Hurricane Center in Miami, Florida, have begun to watch the disturbance.

In the satellite data coming in from both polar-orbiting and geostationary spacecraft, and in reports from ships and aircraft they look for subtle clues that mark the development of hurricanes—cumulus clouds covered by the cirrostratus deck of a highly organized convective system; showers that become steady rains; dropping atmospheric pressure; intensification of the tradewinds, or a westerly wind component there.

Then, if this hint of a disturbance blooms into a tropical storm, a time-honored convention is applied: it receives a name. Naming the storm is a signal which brings the warning systems to readiness.

As an Atlantic hurricane drifts closer to land, it comes under surveillance by weather reconnaissance aircraft to the United States Air Force Reserve, the famous "Hurricane Hunters," who bump through the turbulent interiors of the storms to obtain precise fixes on the position of the eye, and measure winds and pressure fields. Despite the advent of satellites, the aircraft probes are the most detailed information hurricane forecasters receive.

The hurricanes are also probed by the "flying laboratories" from NOAA's Aircraft Operations Center in Miami. Finally, the approaching storm comes within range of a radar network stretching from Texas to Maine, and from Miami to the Lesser Antilles.

Through the lifetime of the hurricane, advisories from the National Hurricane Center warning give the storm's position and what the forecasters in Miami expect the storm to do. As the hurricane drifts to within a day of two of its predicted landfall, these advisories begin to carry watch and warning messages, telling people when and where the hurricane is expected to strike, and what its effects are likely to be. Not until the storm has decayed over land and its cloud elements and great cargo of moisture have blended with other brands of weather does the hurricane emergency end.

This system works well. The death toll in the United States from hurricanes has dropped steadily as NOAA's hurricane tracking and warning apparatus has matured. Although the accuracy of hurricane forecasts has improved over the year any significant improvements must come from quantum leaps in scientific understanding.

The forecasters also know that science will never provide a full solution to the problems of hurricane safety. The rapid development of America's coastal areas has placed millions of people with little or no hurricane experience in the path of these lethal storms. For this vulnerable coastal population, the answer must be community preparedness and public education in the hope that education and planning before the fact will save lives and lessen the impact of the hurricane and its effects are likely to be.

The United States' hurricane problem

The permanent populations of the hurricane-prone coastal counties of the United States continue to grow at a rapid rate. When weekend, seasonal, and holiday populations are considered, the number of people on barrier islands such as at Ocean City, Maryland, Gulf Shores, Alabama, and Padre Island, Texas increase by 10- to 100-fold or more. Also, these areas are subject to inundation from the rapidly rising waters known as the storm surge associated with hurricanes that generally result in catastrophic damage and potentially large losses of life. Over the past several years, the warning system has provided adequate time for the great majority of the people on barrier islands and along the immediate coast to move inland when hurricanes have threatened. However, it is becoming more difficult each year to evacuate people from these areas due to roadway systems that have not kept pace with the rapid population growth. This condition results in

Hurricane Hugo prepares to strike Charleston, SC, 1989.

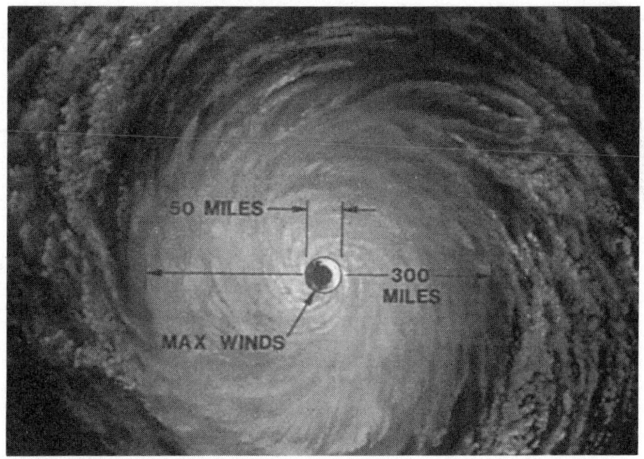

the requirement for longer and longer lead times for safe evacuation. Unfortunately, these extended forecasts suffer from increasing uncertainty. Furthermore, rates of improvements in forecast skills have been far out-paced by rates of population growth in areas vulnerable to hurricanes.

The combination of the growing populations on barrier islands and other vulnerable locations, and the uncertainties in the forecasts poses major dilemmas for forecasters and local and state emergency management officials alike, for example, how do you prevent complacency caused by "false alarms" and yet provide adequate warning times?

Preparations for hurricanes are expensive. When a hurricane is forecast to move inland on a path nearly normal to the coasts, the area placed under warning is about 300 miles (483 km) in length. The average cost of preparation, whether the hurricane strikes or not, is more than $50 million for the Gulf Coast. This estimate covers the cost of boarding up homes, closing down businesses and manufacturing plants, evacuating oil rigs, etc. It does not include economic losses due to disruption of commerce activities such as sales, tourists canceling reservations, etc.

In some locations, the loss for the Labor Day weekend alone can be a substantial portion of the yearly income of coastal businesses. An example of such losses were experienced along the Florida panhandle during Hurricane Elena in 1985.

If the width of the warned area has to be increased by 20% because of greater uncertainties in the forecast, the additional cost for each even would be $10 million. If uncertainties in the hurricane strength require warning for the next higher category of hurricane, then major increases in the number of people evacuated and preparation costs would be required.

Hurricane Gilbert off the Yucatan Peninsula.

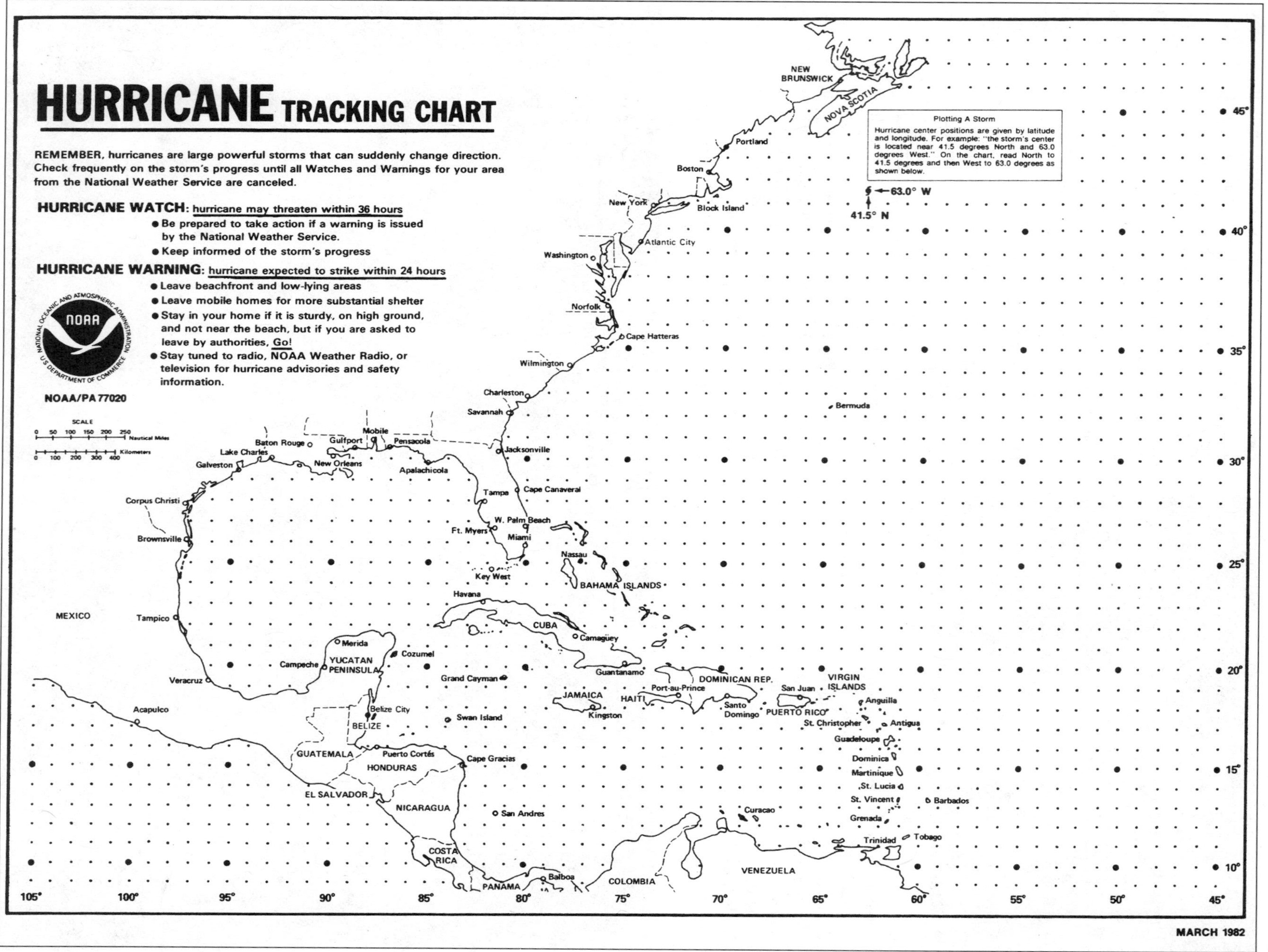
HURRICANE TRACKING CHART
REMEMBER, hurricanes are large powerful storms that can suddenly change direction. Check frequently on the storm's progress until all Watches and Warnings for your area from the National Weather Service are canceled.
HURRICANE WATCH: hurricane may threaten within 36 hours
● Be prepared to take action if a warning is issued by the National Weather Service.
● Keep informed of the storm's progress
HURRICANE WARNING: hurricane expected to strike within 24 hours
● Leave beachfront and low-lying areas
● Leave mobile homes for more substantial shelter
● Stay in your home if it is sturdy, on high ground, and not near the beach, but if you are asked to leave by authorities, Go!
● Stay tuned to radio, NOAA Weather Radio, or television for hurricane advisories and safety information.
NOAA
NATIONAL OCEANIC AND ATMOSPHERIC ADMINISTRATION
U.S. DEPARTMENT OF COMMERCE
NOAA/PA 77020
SCALE
0 50 100 150 200 250 Nautical Miles
0 100 200 300 400 Kilometers
Plotting A Storm
Hurricane center positions are given by latitude and longitude. For example: "the storm's center is located near 41.5 degrees North and 63.0 degrees West." On the chart, read North to 41.5 degrees and then West to 63.0 degrees as shown below.
63.0° W
41.5° N
NEW BRUNSWICK
NOVA SCOTIA
Portland
Boston
Block Island
New York
Atlantic City
Washington
Norfolk
Cape Hatteras
Wilmington
Charleston
Savannah
Bermuda
Jacksonville
Mobile
Baton Rouge
Gulfport
Pensacola
Lake Charles
Galveston
New Orleans
Apalachicola
Tampa
Cape Canaveral
Corpus Christi
W. Palm Beach
Ft. Myers
Miami
Brownsville
Nassau
Key West
BAHAMA ISLANDS
Havana
MEXICO
Tampico
CUBA
Camagüey
Merida
Cozumel
Campeche
YUCATAN PENINSULA
Grand Cayman
Guantanamo
DOMINICAN REP.
VIRGIN ISLANDS
Veracruz
San Juan
Port-au-Prince
JAMAICA
HAITI
Anguilla
Acapulco
Belize City
Santo Domingo
PUERTO RICO
Kingston
Swan Island
St. Christopher
Antigua
BELIZE
Guadeloupe
GUATEMALA
Puerto Cortés
Cape Gracias
Dominica
HONDURAS
Martinique
St. Lucia
EL SALVADOR
St. Vincent
Barbados
NICARAGUA
Curacao
San Andres
Grenada
Trinidad
Tobago
COSTA RICA
VENEZUELA
PANAMA
Balboa
COLOMBIA
45°
40°
35°
30°
25°
20°
15°
10°
105°
100°
95°
90°
85°
80°
75°
70°
65°
60°
55°
50°
45°
MARCH 1982

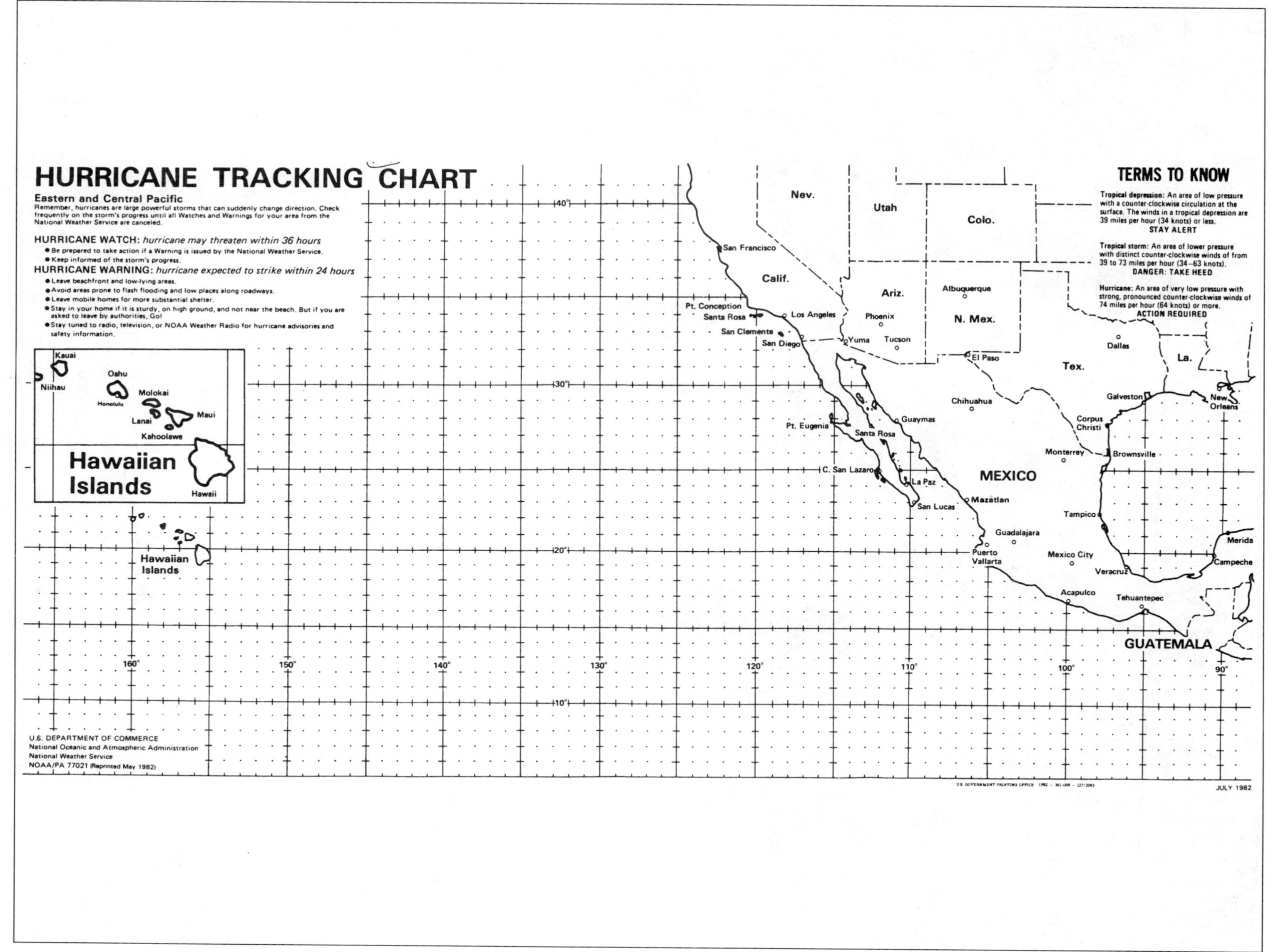
HURRICANE TRACKING CHART
Eastern and Central Pacific
Remember, hurricanes are large powerful storms that can suddenly change direction. Check frequently on the storm's progress until all Watches and Warnings for your area from the National Weather Service are canceled.
HURRICANE WATCH: hurricane may threaten within 36 hours
• Be prepared to take action if a Warning is issued by the National Weather Service.
• Keep informed of the storm's progress.
HURRICANE WARNING: hurricane expected to strike within 24 hours
• Leave beachfront and low-lying areas.
• Avoid areas prone to flash flooding and low places along roadways.
• Leave mobile homes for more substantial shelter.
• Stay in your home if it is sturdy, on high ground, and not near the beach. But if you are asked to leave by authorities, Go!
• Stay tuned to radio, television, or NOAA Weather Radio for hurricane advisories and safety information.
Kauai
Niihau
Oahu
Honolulu
Molokai
Lanai
Maui
Kahoolawe
Hawaii
Hawaiian Islands
Hawaiian Islands
TERMS TO KNOW
Tropical depression: An area of low pressure with a counter-clockwise circulation at the surface. The winds in a tropical depression are 39 miles per hour (34 knots) or less.
STAY ALERT
Tropical storm: An area of lower pressure with distinct counter-clockwise winds of from 39 to 73 miles per hour (34–63 knots).
DANGER: TAKE HEED
Hurricane: An area of very low pressure with strong, pronounced counter-clockwise winds of 74 miles per hour (64 knots) or more.
ACTION REQUIRED
Nev.
Utah
Colo.
Calif.
Ariz.
N. Mex.
Tex.
La.
MEXICO
GUATEMALA
San Francisco
Pt. Conception
Santa Rosa
San Clemente
San Diego
Los Angeles
Yuma
Phoenix
Tucson
Albuquerque
El Paso
Dallas
Chihuahua
Galveston
New Orleans
Corpus Christi
Brownsville
Monterrey
Pt. Eugenia
Santa Rosa
Guaymas
C. San Lazaro
La Paz
San Lucas
Mazatlan
Tampico
Guadalajara
Puerto Vallarta
Mexico City
Veracruz
Acapulco
Tehuantepec
Merida
Campeche
40°
30°
20°
10°
160°
150°
140°
130°
120°
110°
100°
90°
U.S. DEPARTMENT OF COMMERCE
National Oceanic and Atmospheric Administration
National Weather Service
NOAA/PA 77021 (Reprinted May 1982)
JULY 1982

The Mississippi Richelieu Apartments before Camille struck. Defying official pleas to leave, 25 people gathered here for a "hurricane party."

Of course, if these uncertainties meant that major metropolitan areas such as Galveston/Houston, New Orleans Tampa, Miami, or a number of other major coastal cities would or would not be included in the warning area, then the differences in preparation costs would be substantially more than the $10 million. Also, the number of people evacuated would be substantially more than tens of thousands of people. For instance, in the case of the Galveston/Houston area, an increase in storm strength from a category 2 hurricane to a category 3 hurricane on the Saffir-Simpson Scale would require the evacuation of an additional 200,000 people. Likewise, if major industrial areas such as Beaumont/Port Arthur, Texas, or tourist areas such as Atlantic City, New Jersey, were affected by these uncertainties, the financial impact would be quite significant.

Economic factors receive serious consideration from National Hurricane Center, and local and state officials consider not only for direct but also for indirect effects on people response. People will not continually take expensive actions which, afterwards, prove to have been unnecessary. If we consistently over-warn by wide margins, people will not respond and such actions could result in large loss of life. To maintain credibility with the general public, NHC and local and state officials cannot treat all hurricanes as if they were Camilles, Hugos, or Andrews. Such an exaggerated approach may indeed provide maximum protection of life for a given event, but it endangers many more lives the next time when the threat may be even greater.

Finally, the hurricane problem is compounded by the fact that 80-90% of the people who now live in the hurricane-prone areas have never experienced the core of a major hurricane (a category 3 or stronger on the Saffir-Simpson Scale). Many of these people have been through weaker hurricanes or been brushed by the fringe of a major hurricane. The result is a false impression of the damage potential of these storms. This frequently breeds complacency and delayed actions which could result in the loss of many lives. An example of the potential danger are those people living on barrier islands who might be reluctant to evacuate under "blue sky" conditions until they actually see the actual threat (water rising and winds increasing). The result could be people trapped in those areas as waters cut off escape routes. This situation nearly happened for about 200 people on western Galveston Island during Hurricane Alicia of 1983.

This type of response primarily results from three major factors. First, major hurricanes are infrequent events for any

The Richelieu Apartments after Camille swept the coastline. Only two individuals survived the "party."

given location. Second, for the past three decades, major hurricanes striking the United States coast have been less frequent than previous decades. Finally, it has been during this period of low hurricane activity that the great majority of the present coastal residents moved to the coast.

However, with the tremendous increase of populations in high-risk areas along our coastlines, the concern is that we may now not fare as well in the future when hurricane activity inevitably returns to the frequencies experienced during the 1940s-60s.

Hurricane warning service

The hurricane forecast and warning service stands as the finest of its kind in the world, distinguished by its character, credibility and the confidence that our nation has in it. But that wasn't always the case.

The Weather Bureau was created as a civilian agency in 1890 mainly because of a general dissatisfaction with weather forecasting under the military. The hurricane of 1875 that destroyed Indianola, Texas, without much warning was a contributing factor.

It was not until the Spanish American War of 1898 that an effort was made to establish a comprehensive hurricane warning service. President McKinley stated that he was more afraid of a hurricane than he was of the Spanish Navy. He extended the warning service to include warnings for shipping interests as well as the military. Before that, hurricane warnings were only issued for the United States coastal areas. Hurricane warning stations were established throughout the West Indies. A forecast center was established in Kingston, Jamaica and later moved to Havana, Cuba in 1899. The warning service was extended to Mexico and Central America. This recognition of the international responsibility for the United States hurricane warning service continues today under the auspices of the World Meteorological Organization (WMO) of the United Nations.

In 1900, the infamous Galveston hurricane killed 6,000 people—the greatest natural disaster in United States history. There was no formal hurricane warning and this calamity prompted the transfer of the warning service to Washington, D.C., where it remained until 1935.

In the 1920s, there were several hurricanes that hit with little or no warning that led to dissatisfaction with the hurricane service operating out of Washington. The coastal communities felt that Washington was insensitive to the hurricane problem. In 1926, a very strong hurricane (category 4 by today's standard) brought great devastation to southeast Florida, including Miami and Ft. Lauderdale, causing more than 200 deaths. The warnings for that storm were issued at night when most residents were asleep and unaware of the rapidly approaching hurricane. In 1928, another severe hurricane hit south Florida and killed an estimated 1,800 people who drowned when Lake Okeechobee overflowed. In 1933, the largest number of tropical storms—21—developed. Nine of them were hurricanes and two that affected the east coast of the United States including Washington were badly forecast and the public inadequately warned. In 1934, a forecast and warning for an approaching hurricane in the very sensitive Galveston area was badly flubbed by Washington.

Those incidents led Congress and the President to revamp and decentralize the Hurricane Warning Service. Improvements included 24-hour operations with teletypewriter hookup along the Gulf and Atlantic coasts; weather observations at six-hour intervals; hurricane advisories at least four times a day; and a more adequate upper air observing network. New hurricane forecast centers were established at Jacksonville, Florida; New Orleans, Louisiana; San Juan, Puerto Rico; and Boston, Massachusetts (established in 1940).

In 1943, the primary hurricane forecast office at Jacksonville was moved to Miami where the Weather Bureau established a joint hurricane warning service with the Army Air Corps and the Navy under the direction of Grady Norton. It was also in 1943 that Col. Joseph Duckworth made the first intentional plane reconnaissance into the eye of a hurricane. The following year, regular aircraft reconnaissance was begun by the military giving hurricane forecasters the location and intensity of the storms for the first time.

Grady Norton continued as head of the Miami Center until his death in 1954 during Hurricane Hazel that ravaged the east coast of the United States. Norton established a strong and popular reputation as an extraordinary forecaster with the tremendous ability to communicate with residents along the hurricane vulnerable coastlines. Gordon Dunn, who served as his assistant in Jacksonville, was selected as Norton's successor and the Miami office was officially designated as the National Hurricane Center in 1955.

In the 1950s a number of hurricanes in addition to Hazel struck the East Coast causing much damage and flooding. Congress responded with increased appropriations to strengthen the warning service and intensify research into hurricanes. The Weather Bureau organized the National Hurricane Research Project under the direction of Dr. Robert H. Simpson. The Air Force and the Navy provided the first aircraft to be used by the Project to investigate the structure, characteristics, and movement of tropical storms.

In 1960, radars capable of "seeing" out to a distance of 200-250 miles (322-402.5 km) from their coastal sites were established at strategic locations along the Atlantic and Gulf coasts from Maine to Brownsville, Texas. On April 1, 1960, the first weather satellite was placed in orbit giving hurricane forecasters the ability to detect storms before they hit land.

Gordon Dunn retired in 1967 and was succeeded by Dr. Simpson who placed a renewed emphasis on research and development activities at the Center through satellite applications and the development of statistical and dynamic models as forecast aids. Dr. Simpson retired after the 1973 hurricane season and was succeeded by his deputy, Dr. Neil Frank, who served until 1987. Dr. Frank's tenure was marked by great emphasis on the need for hurricane preparedness among the hurricane-prone communities in the United States as well as in the Caribbean. He and his staff created an increased national awareness of the hurricane threat through the cooperation of local and state emergency officials and the enlistment of the news media and other federal agencies in the campaign to substitute education and awareness for the lack of first-band experience among the ever-increasing coastal populations.

Dr. Robert Sheets is the current Director of the National Hurricane Center, at a time where the future holds even greater promise to improve the hurricane warning capability of the National Weather Service. New technology and advances in the science under the weather service's modernization program now underway will lead to more improvement and effectiveness in the forecasting and warning of hurricanes.

Improvements

The next GOES series of satellites is expected to provide more accurate and higher resolution sounding data than presently available from geosynchronous satellites, and similar improvements can be expected from the polar orbit satellite systems.

Major improvements in longer range hurricane forecasts (36-72 hours) will come through improved dynamical models. Global, hemispheric, and regional models show considerable promise.

Present operational reconnaissance aircraft provide invaluable data in the core of the hurricane. Doppler radar are now an integral part of NOAA's research aircraft operations providing entire data fields within several miles-of the aircraft's path.

NEXRAD (Next Generation Radar) will add new dimensions to hurricane warning capabilities. The NEXRAD stations will, provide much needed information on tropical cyclone wind field and the wind fields' changes as they move inland. Local offices will be able to provide accurate short term warnings as rainbands, high winds and possible tornadoes move toward specific inland locations. Heavy rains and flooding frequently occur over widespread inland areas.

Improved observing systems and anticipated improvements in analysis, forecasting, and warning programs require efficient accessing, processing and analysis of large quantities of data from numerous sources. These data also provide the opportunity for improved numerical forecasts. The Class VII computer at the National Meteorological

These diagrams show how hurricane watches and warnings and other advisories change as a hypothetical storm stalks Florida's northern Gulf coast.

First note the *extent* of the hurricane. Its dangerous core of high water and high winds is much larger than any of the communities in its path. When it comes ashore, its worst effects will be felt along some 50 miles of shoreline, with potentially dangerous heavy weather along a reach of coast several hundred miles long.

Then note that NOAA hurricane forecasters "overwarn"—that is, the areas covered by their watches and warnings are larger than the approaching storm. This reflects the state-of-the-art of hurricane forecasting, and the enormous complexity of predicting what a large, destructive, and inherently erratic weather system is going to do.

The hurricane warning area appears in the second panel. It generally covers a much smaller area than the hurricane watch. Beyond the warning area, peripheral gale warnings and small-craft cautionary statements are distributed around the predicted path of the hurricane.

In the third panel, the hurricane has moved ashore, and the watch and warning cycle ends; however, advisories continue to go out, until the ocean and atmosphere behind the hurricane have had a chance to settle down.

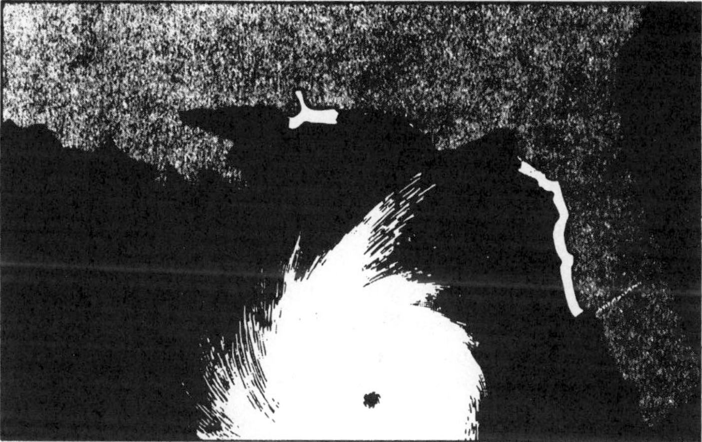

Rain from hurricanes can cause extensive flooding.

Center will permit operational implementation of next generation hurricane prediction models.

Products must be provided to users which optimize the desired response. AWIPS (Advanced Weather Interactive Processing System) will be the primary tool for accomplishing this task. Critical hurricane information needed by local, state, and other federal agencies as well as the private sector will be displayed graphically and transmitted to the user faster and more complete than ever before making more effective warning and evacuation response.

Aerial weather reconnaissance

Aerial weather reconnaissance is vitally important to the forecasters of the National Hurricane Center. Aircraft reports help the meteorologist determine what is going on inside a storm as it actually happens. This, along with the broader view provided by data from satellites, floating buoys, and land and ship reports, makes up the total "package" of information available to the hurricane forecasters who must make forecasts of the speed, intensity, and direction of the storm. Reconnaissance aircraft penetrate to the core of the storm and provide detailed measurements of its strengths as well as accurate location of its center, information that is not available from any other source.

The National Hurricane Center is supported by specially modified aircraft of the United States Air Force Reserve (USAFR) and the National Oceanic and Atmospheric Administration's Aircraft Operations Center (NOAA/AOC) The USAFR crews fly the Lockheed WC-130 *Hercules*, a giant four-engine turboprop aircraft which carries crew of six people and can stay aloft for up to 14 hours. NOAA's Aircraft Operations Center flies Lockheed WP-3 *Orions*, a

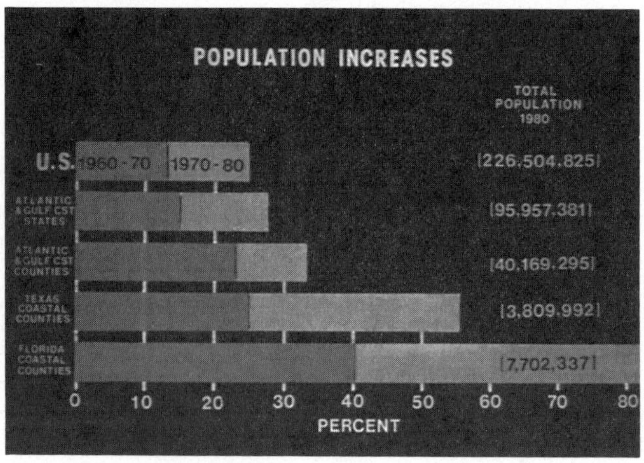

four-engine turboprop aircraft which carries a crew of from 7-17 persons and can stay aloft for up to 12 hours at a time. The NOAA/AOC aircraft and crews are based at Miami International Airport. Both units can be deployed as necessary in the Atlantic, Caribbean, Gulf of Mexico, and Central Pacific Ocean.

Meteorological information obtained from aerial reconnaissance includes measurements of the winds, atmospheric pressure, temperature, and the location of the center of the storm. In addition, these aircraft also drop instruments called "dropsondes" as they fly through the storm's center. This device continuously radios back measurement of pressure, humidity, temperature, and wind direction and speed as it falls toward the sea. This information provides a detailed look at the structure of the storm and an indication of its intensity.

Aerial weather reconnaissance of nature's most powerful destructive force is not without risk. Since aircraft and crews first started flying into hurricanes and typhoons nearly 40 years ago, three have been lost, vanishing without a trace along with their crews. The first of these, a United States Navy P2V *Neptune* fell into the Caribbean Seas while flying into Hurricane Janet on September 26, 1955. Next came a United States Air Force WB-50 *Super Fortress* which crashed into the Pacific Ocean on January 15, 1958 while penetrating Typhoon Ophelia. Also lost was a WC-130 *Hercules* which disappeared in the vicinity of Typhoon Bess in the Philippine Sea south of Taiwan on October 12, 1974.

Flying into a hurricane is like no other experience. Crew members who have flown combat missions say that their feelings before these flights and those involving hurricanes are very similar. There is a blend of excitement and apprehension that is difficult to describe. Adding to the tension is that no two hurricanes are alike. Some are gentle while others seem like raging bulls. Preparations for flying into a hurricane are very thorough. All crew members are fully trained by highly-trained specialists. Special precautions are taken by the crew as they enter the hurricane. All loose objects are tied down or put away and crew members slip into safety harness and belts. When radar picks up the storm, the crew then determines how to get inside. The idea is to make the aircraft mesh with the storm rather than fight it. If it is a well defined storm, getting inside can be a real experience. The winds at flight altitude oftentimes exceed 100 mph (161 km/hr), and the wall cloud surrounding the center, or eye, can be several miles thick. Rain comes down in torrents, and the updrafts and downdrafts are usually strong and frequent. Inside the eye, however, the conditions are much different. The ocean is generally visible, and there is blue sky and sunshine. The flight level winds are nearly calm. After gathering all the information they need, the crew then exits the storm in the same manner they entered.

Making sure the National Hurricane Center gets the aerial weather reconnaissance it needs is the job of a small group of Air Force people assigned to a liaison office in the Center. This office, under a former Chief, Aerial Reconnaissance Coordination, All Hurricanes (CARCAH) is responsible for coordinating requirements and arranging for the supporting flights. This office also records and monitors weather observations radioed back or received through direct satellite communication from the storm by the on-board meteorologists. These data are checked for accuracy and then transmitted to the world-wide meteorological community, through both military and civilian communications circuits.

Aircraft meteorological reconnaissance is a team effort. A host of different organizations, tied together by CARCAH, is dedicated to providing the National Hurricane Center the vital information it needs to make accurate forecasts which help to ensure that communities in the path of a hurricane will be adequately warned. Warnings and forecasts help save countless lives and allow residents to take the necessary precautions to prevent enormous property damage each year.

One of the first images from GOES-8, launched on April 13, 1994.

Terms to Know

By international agreement, **TROPICAL CYCLONE** is the general term for all cyclone circulations originating over tropical waters, classified by form and intensity as follows:

TROPICAL WAVE: A trough of low pressure in the trade-wind easterlies.

TROPICAL DISTURBANCE: A moving area of thunderstorms in the Tropics that maintains its identity for 24 hours or more. A common phenomenon in the tropics.

TROPICAL DEPRESSION: Rotary circulation at surface, highest constant wind speed 38 miles per hour (33 knots) or less.

TROPICAL STORM: Distinct rotary circulation, constant wind speed ranges 39-73 miles per hour (34-63 knots).

HURRICANE: Pronounced rotary circulation, constant wind speed of 74 miles per hour (64 knots) or greater.

SMALL CRAFT CAUTIONARY STATEMENTS: When a tropical cyclone threatens a coastal area, small craft operators are advised to remain in port or not to venture into the open sea.

TROPICAL STORM WATCH: Is issued for a coastal area when there is the threat of tropical storm conditions within 24-36 hours.

TROPICAL STORM WARNINGS: May be issued when winds of 39-73 miles an hour (34-63 knots) are expected. If a hurricane is expected to strike a coastal area, tropical storm warnings will not usually precede hurricane warnings.

HURRICANE WATCH: Is issued for a coastal area when there is a threat of hurricane conditions within 24-36 hours.

HURRICANE WARNING: Is issued when hurricane conditions are expected in a specified coastal area in 24 hours or less.

STORM SURGE: An abnormal rise of the sea along a shore as the result, primarily, of the winds of a storm.

FLASH FLOOD WATCH: Means a flash flood is possible in the area; stay alert.

FLASH FLOOD WARNING: Means a flash flood is imminent; take immediate action.

Hurricane Safety Advice

Be Prepared **BEFORE** the Hurricane Season:

- ✓ Know the storm surge history and elevation of your area.
- ✓ Learn safe routes inland.
- ✓ Learn location of official shelters.
- ✓ Review needs and working condition of emergency equipment, such as flashlights, battery-powered radios, etc.
- ✓ Ensure that enough non-perishable food and water supplies are on hand to last for at least 2 weeks.
- ✓ Obtain and store materials, such as plywood and plastic, necessary to properly secure your home.
- ✓ Check home for loose and clogged rain gutters and downspouts.
- ✓ Keep trees and shrubbery trimmed. Cut weak branches and trees that could fall or bump against the house. When trimming, try to create a channel through the foliage to the center of the tree to allow for air flow.
- ✓ Determine where to move your boat in an emergency.
- ✓ Review your insurance policy to ensure it provides adequate coverage.
- ✓ Individuals with special needs should contact their local office of emergency management.
- ✓ For information and assistance with any of the above, contact your local National Weather Service office, emergency management office, or American Red Cross chapter.

When a "**Hurricane WATCH**" is issued:

- ✓ Frequently monitor radio, TV, NOAA Weather Radio, or hurricane hotline telephone numbers for official bulletins of the storm's progress.
- ✓ Fuel and service family vehicles.
- ✓ Inspect and secure mobile home tie downs.
- ✓ Prepare to cover all window and door openings with shutters or other shielding materials.
- ✓ Check food and water supplies.
  - — Have clean, air-tight containers on hand to store at least 2 weeks of drinking water (14 gallons per person).
  - — Stock up on canned provisions.
  - — Get a camping stove with fuel.
  - — Keep a small cooler with frozen gel packs handy for packing refrigerated items.
- ✓ Check prescription medicines—obtain at least 10 days to 2 weeks supply.
- ✓ Stock up on extra batteries for radios, flashlights, and lanterns.
- ✓ Prepare to store and secure outdoor lawn furniture and other loose, lightweight objects, such as garbage cans, garden tools, potted plants, etc.
- ✓ Check and replenish first-aid supplies.
- ✓ Have on hand an extra supply of cash.

When a **"Hurricane WARNING"** is issued:

- ✓ Closely monitor radio, TV, NOAA Weather Radio, or hurricane hotline telephone numbers for official bulletins.
- ✓ Follow instructions issued by local officials. Leave immediately if ordered to do so.
- ✓ Complete preparation activities, such as putting up storm shutters, storing loose objects, etc.
- ✓ Evacuate areas that might be affected by storm surge flooding.
- ✓ If evacuating, leave early (if possible, in daylight).
- ✓ Leave mobile homes in any case.
- ✓ Notify neighbors and a family member outside of the warned area of your evacuation plans.

If Evacuating:

Plan to evacuate if you...

- — live in a mobile home. Do not stay in a mobile home under any circumstances. They are unsafe in high wind and/or hurricane conditions, no matter how well fastened to the ground.
- — live on the coastline or on an offshore island, or live near a river or in a flood plain.
- — live in a high-rise. Hurricane winds are stronger at higher elevations. Glass doors and windows may be blown out of their casings and weaken the structure.

- ✓ Stay with friends or relatives or at a low-rise inland hotel or motel outside of flood zones. Leave early to avoid heavy traffic, roads blocked by early flood waters, and bridges impassible due to high winds.
- ✓ Put food and water out for pet if you cannot take it with you. Public shelters do not allow pets nor do most motels/hotels.
- ✓ Hurricane shelters will be available for people

The deadliest United States hurricanes of this century.

DEADLIEST HURRICANES, UNITED STATES 1900-1994

(25 or more deaths)

	HURRICANE	YEAR	CATEGORY	DEATHS
1.	TX (Galveston)	1900	4	8000+
2.	FL (SE/Lake Okeechobee)	1928	4	1836
3.	FL (Keys)/S TX	1919	4	600#
4.	New England	1938	3*	600
5.	FL (Keys)	1935	5	408
6.	AUDREY (SW LA/N TX)	1957	4	390
7.	NE U.S.	1944	3*	390@
8.	LA (Grand Isle)	1909	4	350
9.	LA (New Orleans)	1915	4	275
10.	TX (Galveston)	1915	4	275
11.	CAMILLE (MS/SE LA/VA)	1969	5	256
12.	FL(Miami)/MS/AL/Pensacola	1926	4	243
13.	DIANE (NE U.S.)	1955	1	184
14.	SE FL	1906	2	164
15.	MS/AL/Pensacola	1906	3	134
16.	AGNES (FL/NE U.S.)	1972	1	122
17.	HAZEL (SC/NC)	1954	4*	95
18.	BETSY (SE FL/SE LA)	1965	3	75
19.	CAROL (NE U.S.)	1954	3*	60
20.	SE FL/SE LA/MS	1947	4	51
21.	DONNA (FL/Eastern U.S.)	1960	4	50
22.	GA/SC/NC	1940	2	50
23.	CARLA (N & Central TX)	1961	4	46
24.	TX (Velasco)	1909	3	41
25.	TX (Freeport)	1932	4	40
26.	S TX	1933	3	40
27.	HILDA (Central LA)	1964	3	38
28.	SW LA	1918	3	34
29.	SW FL	1910	3	30
30.	ALBERTO (NW FL,GA,AL)	1994	TS&	30
31.	CONNIE (NC)	1955	3	25
32.	LA (Central)	1926	3	25

* Moving more than 30 miles per hour.

\# Over 500 of these lost on ships at sea; 600-900 estimated deaths.

@ Some 344 of these lost on ships at sea.

& Only of Tropical Storm intensity, included because of high death toll.

ADDENDUM

2.	LA	1893	-	2000
3.	SC/GA	1893	-	1000-2000
4.	GA/SC	1881	-	700
24.	SOUTHERN CALIFORNIA	1939	-	45

The costliest United States hurricanes of this century.
(Unadjusted)

COSTLIEST HURRICANES, UNITED STATES 1900-1994
(More than $100,000,000 damage)

	HURRICANE	YEAR	CATEGORY	DAMAGE (U.S.)
1.	ANDREW (SE FL/SE LA)	1992	4	About $25,000,000,000
2.	HUGO (SC)	1989	4	7,000,000,000
3.	FREDERIC (AL/MS)	1979	3	2,300,000,000
4.	AGNES (FL/NE U.S.)	1972	1	2,100,000,000
5.	ALICIA (N TX)	1983	3	2,000,000,000
6.	BOB (NC, NE U.S)	1991	2	1,500,000,000
7.	JUAN (LA)	1985	1	1,500,000,000
8.	CAMILLE (MS/SE LA/VA)	1969	5	1,420,700,000
9.	BETSY (SE FL/SE LA)	1965	3	1,420,500,000
10.	ELENA (MS/AL/NW FL)	1985	3	1,250,000,000
11.	GLORIA (Eastern U.S.)	1985	3*	900,000,000
12.	DIANE (NE U.S.)	1955	1	831,700,000
13.	ALLISON (N TX)	1989	T.S.@	500,000,000
14.	ALBERTO (NW FL,GA,AL)	1994	T.S.@	500,000,000
15	ELOISE (NW FL)	1975	3	490,000,000
16.	CAROL (NE U.S.)	1954	3*	461,000,000
17.	CELIA (S TX)	1970	3	453,000,000
18.	CARLA (N & Central TX)	1961	4	408,000,000
19.	CLAUDETTE (N TX)	1979	T.S.@	400,000,000
20.	GORDON (S&Central FL,NC)	1994	T.S.@	400,000,000
21.	DONNA (FL/Eastern U.S.)	1960	4	387,000,000
22.	DAVID (FL/Eastern U.S.)	1979	2	320,000,000
23.	New England	1938	3*	306,000,000
24.	KATE (FL Keys/NW FL)	1985	2	300,000,000
25.	ALLEN (S TX)	1980	3	300,000,000
26.	HAZEL (SC/NC)	1954	4*	281,000,000
27.	DORA (NE FL)	1964	2	250,000,000
28.	BEULAH (S TX)	1967	3	200,000,000
29.	AUDREY (SW LA/N TX)	1957	4	150,000,000
30.	CARMEN (Central LA)	1974	3	150,000,000
31.	CLEO (SE FL)	1964	2	128,500,000
32.	HILDA (Central LA)	1964	3	125,000,000
33.	FL(Miami)/MS/AL/Pensacola	1926	4	112,000,000
34.	FL SE/SE LA/MS	1947	4	110,000,000
35.	NE U.S.	1944	3*	100,000,000+

* Moving more than 30 miles per hour.
@ Only of Tropical Storm intensity, but included because of high damage amount.

ADDENDUM

6.	INIKI (Kauai, HI)	1992	Unk.	1,800,000,000
22.	OLIVIA (CA)	1982	T.D.	325,000,000
23.	IWA (Kauai, HI)	1982	UNK	312,000,000
24.	NORMAN (CA)	1978	T.D.	300,000,000
29.	KATHLEEN (CA & AZ)	1976	T.D.	160,000,000

The costliest United States hurricanes of this century.
(Adjusted to 1990 dollars) **

COSTLIEST HURRICANES, UNITED STATES 1900-1994
(More than $500,000,000 damage)

	HURRICANE	YEAR	CATEGORY	DAMAGE (U.S.)
1.	ANDREW (SE FL/SE LA)	1992	4	About $25,000,000,000
2.	HUGO (SC)	1989	4	7,155,120,000
3.	BETSY (SE FL/SE LA)	1965	3	6,461,303,000
4.	AGNES (FL/NE U.S.)	1972	1	6,418,143,000
5.	CAMILLE (MS/SE LA/VA)	1969	5	5,242,380,000
6.	DIANE (NE U.S.)	1955	1	4,199,645,000
7.	New England	1938	3*	3,593,853,000
8.	FREDERIC (AL/MS)	1979	3	3,502,942,000
9.	ALICIA (N TX)	1983	3	2,391,854,000
10.	CAROL (NE U.S.)	1954	3*	2,370,215,000
11.	CARLA (N & Central TX)	1961	4	1,926,731,000
12.	DONNA (FL/Eastern U.S.)	1960	4	1,823,605,000
13.	JUAN (LA)	1985	1	1,671,232,000
14.	CELIA (S TX)	1970	3	1,560,440,000
15.	BOB (NC and NE U.S.)	1991	2	1,500,000,000
16.	HAZEL (SC/NC)	1954	4*	1,444,752,000
17.	ELENA(MS/AL/NW FL)	1985	3	1,392,693,000
18.	FL(Miami)/MS/AL/Pensacola	1926	4	1,315,397,000
19.	N TX (Galveston)	1915	4	1,177,937,000[1]
20.	DORA (NE FL)	1964	2	1,157,596,000
21.	ELOISE (NW FL)	1975	3	1,081,854,000
22.	GLORIA (Eastern U.S.)	1985	3*	1,002,739,000
23.	NE U.S.	1944	3*	925,055,000
24.	BEULAH (S TX)	1967	3	844,304,000
25.	N TX (Galveston)	1900	4	706,762,000[2]
26.	SE FL/SE LA/MS	1947	4	703,859,000
27.	AUDREY (SW LA/N TX)	1957	4	696,091,000
28.	CLAUDETTE (N TX)	1979	T.S.@	609,207,000
29.	CLEO (SE FL)	1964	2	595,004,000
30.	SW FL/NE FL	1944	3	582,785,000
31.	HILDA (Central LA)	1964	3	578,798,000
32.	SE FL	1945	3	539,087,000
33.	ALLISON (N TX)	1989	T.S.@	511,080,000
34.	ALBERTO (NW FL,GA,AL)	1994	T.S.@	500,000,000

[1] Unadjusted 1915 damage estimate was considered too high.
[2] Using 1915 cost adjustment base - none available prior to 1915.
* Moving more than 30 miles per hour.
@ Only of Tropical Storm intensity, but included because of high damage amount.
** Adjusted to 1990 dollars on basis of U.S. Department of Commerce composite construction cost indexes.

ADDENDUM

	HURRICANE	YEAR	CATEGORY	DAMAGE (U.S.)
13.	INIKI (Kauai, HI)	1992	Unk.	1,800,000,000
33.	NORMAN (CA)	1978	T.D.	524,000,000

The most intense United States hurricanes of this century.
(at time of landfall)

MOST INTENSE HURRICANES, UNITED STATES 1900-1994
(At time of landfall)

	HURRICANE	YEAR	CATEGORY	MILLIBARS	INCHES
1.	FL (Keys)	1935	5	892	26.35
2.	CAMILLE (MS/SE LA/VA)	1969	5	909	26.84
3.	ANDREW (SE FL/SE LA)	1992	4	922	27.23
4.	FL (Keys)/S TX	1919	4	927	27.37
5.	FL (SE/Lake Okeechobee)	1928	4	929	27.43
6.	DONNA (FL/Eastern U.S.)	1960	4	930	27.46
7.	TX (Galveston)	1900	4	931	27.49
7.	LA (Grand Isle)	1909	4	931	27.49
7.	LA (New Orleans)	1915	4	931	27.49
7.	CARLA (N & Central TX)	1961	4	931	27.49
11.	HUGO (SC)	1989	4	934	27.58
12.	FL(Miami)/MS/AL/Pensacola	1926	4	935	27.61
13.	HAZEL (SC/NC)	1954	4*	938	27.70
14.	SE FL/SE LA/MS	1947	4	940	27.76
15.	N TX	1932	4	941	27.79
16.	GLORIA (Eastern U.S.)	1985	3*&	942	27.82
17.	AUDREY (SW LA/N TX)	1957	4#	945	27.91
17.	TX (Galveston)	1915	4#	945	27.91
17.	CELIA (S TX)	1970	3	945	27.91
17.	ALLEN (S TX)	1980	3@	945	27.91
21.	New England	1938	3*	946	27.94
21.	FREDERIC (AL/MS)	1979	3	946	27.94
23.	NE U.S.	1944	3*	947	27.97
23.	SC/NC	1906	3	947	27.97
25.	BETSY (SE FL/SE LA)	1965	3	948	27.99
25.	SE FL/NW FL	1929	3	948	27.99
25.	SE FL	1933	3	948	27.99
25.	S TX	1916	3	948	27.99
25.	MS/AL	1916	3	948	27.99
30.	DIANA (NC)	1984	3+	949	28.02
30.	S TX	1933	3	949	28.02
32.	BEULAH (S TX)	1967	3	950	28.05
32.	HILDA (Central LA)	1964	3	950	28.05
32.	GRACIE (SC)	1959	3	950	28.05
32.	TX (Central)	1942	3	950	28.05
36.	SE FL	1945	3	951	28.08
37.	FL (Tampa Bay)	1921	3	952	28.11
37.	CARMEN (Central LA)	1974	3	952	28.11

(Continued on next page)

* Moving more than 30 miles per hour.

& Winds and tides did not justify 4.

\# Classified 4 because of estimated winds.

@ Reached Cat. 5 intensity three times along its path through the Caribbean and Gulf of Mexico. The lowest pressure reported was 899 mb (26.55 in.) at 1742 UTC 8/7/80 off the northeastern tip of the Yucatan Peninsula.

\+ Cape Fear, NC area only; was a category 2 at final landfall.

continued

	HURRICANE	YEAR	CATEGORY	MILLIBARS	INCHES
39.	EDNA (New England)	1954	3*	954	28.17
39.	SE FL	1949	3	954	28.17
41.	ELOISE (NW FL)	1975	3	955	28.20
41.	KING (SE FL)	1950	3	955	28.20
41.	Central LA	1926	3	955	28.20
41.	SW LA	1918	3	955	28.20
41.	SW FL	1910	3	955	28.20
46.	NC	1933	3	957	28.26
46.	FL (Keys)	1909	3	957	28.26
48.	EASY (NW FL)	1950	3	958	28.29
48.	N TX	1941	3	958	28.29
48.	NW FL	1917	3	958	28.29
48.	N TX	1909	3	958	28.29
48.	MS/AL	1906	3	958	28.29
53.	ELENA (MS/AL/NW FL)	1985	3	959	28.32
54.	CAROL (NE U.S.)	1954	3*	960	28.35
54.	IONE (NC)	1955	3	960	28.35
54.	EMILY (NC)	1993	3	960	28.35
57.	ALICIA (N TX)	1983	3	962	28.41
57.	CONNIE (NC/VA)	1955	3	962	28.41
57.	SW FL/NE FL	1944	3	962	28.41
57.	Central LA	1934	3	962	28.41
61.	SW FL/SE FL	1948	3	963	28.44
62.	NW FL	1936	3	964	28.47

* Moving more than 30 miles per hour.

ADDENDUM

32.	INIKI (KAUAI, HI)	1992	UNK	950	27.91
41.	DOT (KAUAI, HI)	1959	UNK	955	28.11
62.	IWA (KAUAI, HI)	1982	UNK	964	28.47

DIRECT HITS BY HURRICANES
U.S. GULF & ATLANTIC COASTS
1900-1994

Category 5:	2
4:	15
3:	45
2:	35
1:	57
TOTAL	154

Major hurricanes (categories 3,4,5): 62

This means that during the period 1900-1994, an average of 2 major hurricanes every 3 years made landfall somewhere along the U.S. Gulf or Atlantic coast. (All categories combined average about 5 hurricanes every 3 years for the same period.)

Number of hurricanes of various categories to strike the mainland United States each decade. Updated from Hebert, Jarrell and Mayfield (1993).

	CATEGORY					ALL	MAJOR
DECADE	1	2	3	4	5	1,2,3,4,5	3,4,5
1900-1909	5	5	4	2		16	6
1910-1919	8	3	5	3		19	8
1920-1929	6	4	3	2		15	5
1930-1939	4	5	6	1	1	17	8
1940-1949	7	8	7	1		23	8
1950-1959	8	1	7	2		18	9
1960-1969	4	5	3	2	1	15	6
1970-1979	6	2	4			12	4
1980-1989	9	1	5	1		16	6
1990-1994		1	1	1		3	2
1900-1994	57	35	45	15	2	154	62

Note: Only the highest category to affect the U.S. has been used.

Total and average number of tropical storms and hurricanes in the North Atlantic Ocean, Caribbean Sea, and Gulf of Mexico by month of origin for the period 1886-1994 (updated from Neumann, et al., 1987), and for hurricanes striking the U.S. coast in this century (updated from Hebert, Jarrell and Mayfield, 1993).

	TROPICAL STORMS[1]		HURRICANES		U.S. HURRICANES[2]	
MONTH	TOTAL	AVG.	TOTAL	AVG.	TOTAL	AVG.
JAN-APRIL	4	*	1	*	0	0.0
MAY	14	0.1	3	*	0	0.0
JUNE	58	0.5	23	0.2	11	0.1
JULY	68	0.6	35	0.3	16	0.1
AUGUST	223	2.0	153	1.4	39	0.4
SEPTEMBER	313	2.9	196	1.8	61	0.6
OCTOBER	188	1.7	96	0.9	23	0.2
NOVEMBER	45	0.4	24	0.2	4	*
DECEMBER	6	0.1	3	*	0	0.0
YEAR	919	8.4	534	4.9	154	1.4

[1] Includes subtropical storms after 1967.

[2] 1900-1994.

* Less than 0.05.

Number of hurricanes (direct hits) affecting the U.S. and individual states 1900-1994 according to Saffir/Simpson scale (updated from Hebert, Jarrell and Mayfield, 1993).

AREA	CATEGORY NUMBER 1	2	3	4	5	ALL	MAJOR HURRICANES (≥3)
U.S. (Texas to Maine)	58	34	45	15	2	154	62
Texas	12	9	9	6	0	36	15
(North)	7	3	3	4	0	17	7
(Central)	2	2	1	1	0	6	2
(South)	3	4	5	1	0	13	6
Louisiana	8	5	8	3	1	25	12
Mississippi	1	1	5	0	1	8	6
Alabama	4	1	5	0	0	10	5
Florida	17	15	16	6	1	55	23
(Northwest)	9	7	6	0	0	22	6
(Northeast)	1	7	0	0	0	8	0
(Southwest)	6	3	6	2	1	18	9
(Southeast)	4	10	7	4	0	25	11
Georgia	1	4	0	0	0	5	0
South Carolina	6	4	2	2	0	14	4
North Carolina	10	3	9	1*	0	23	10
Virginia	2	1	1*	0	0	4	1*
Maryland	0	1*	0	0	0	1*	0
Delaware	0	0	0	0	0	0	0
New Jersey	1*	0	0	0	0	1*	0
New York	3	1*	5*	0	0	9	5*
Connecticut	2	3*	3*	0	0	8	3*
Rhode Island	0	2*	3*	0	0	5*	3*
Massachusetts	2	2*	2*	0	0	6	2*
New Hampshire	1*	1*	0	0	0	2*	0
Maine	5*	0	0	0	0	5*	0

* Indicates all hurricanes in this category were moving faster than 30 mph.

Note: State totals will not equal U.S. totals and Texas and Florida sectional totals will not necessarily equal state totals.

Incidence of major hurricanes (direct hits) by months to affect the mainland United States and individual states (1900-1994) according to the Saffir/Simpson Scale (updated from Hebert, Jarrell and Mayfield, 1993).

			MONTH			
AREA	JUNE	JULY	AUG.	SEPT.	OCT.	ALL
U.S. (Texas to Maine)	2	3	15	35	7	62
Texas	1	1	7	6		15
(North)	1	1	3	2		7
(Central)			1	1		2
(South)			3	3		6
Louisiana	2		4	5	1	12
Mississippi		1	1	4		6
Alabama		1		4		5
Florida		1	2	15	5	23
(Northwest)		1		5		6
(Northeast)						0
(Southwest)			1	5	3	9
(Southeast)			2	7	2	11
Georgia						0
South Carolina				3	1	4
North Carolina			2	7	1	10
Virginia				1		1
Maryland						0
Delaware						0
New Jersey						0
New York			1	4		5
Connecticut			1	2		3
Rhode Island			1	2		3
Massachusetts				2		2
New Hampshire						0
Maine						0

Note: State totals will not equal U.S. totals and Texas and Florida sectional totals will not necessarily equal state totals.

Estimated annual deaths and damages (unadjusted and adjusted[1]) in the United States from Gulf and Atlantic hurricanes for each year of this century.

YEAR	DEATHS	DAMAGE ($MILLIONS) UNADJUSTED	DAMAGE ($MILLIONS) ADJUSTED	YEAR	DEATHS	DAMAGE ($MILLIONS) UNADJUSTED	DAMAGE ($MILLIONS) ADJUSTED
1900	8000+	30	(735)[2]	1948	3	18	105
1901	10	1	*	1949	4	59	344
1902	0	Minor	Minor	1950	19	36	206
1903	15	1	*	1951	0	2	10
1904	5	2	*	1952	3	3	15
1905	0	Minor	Minor	1953	2	6	31
1906	298	3+	*	1954	193	756	3887
1907	0	0	0	1955	218	985	4974
1908	0	0	0	1956	19	27	129
1909	406	8	*	1957	400	152	705
1910	30	1	*	1958	2	11	51
1911	17	1+	*	1959	24	23	108
1912	1	Minor	Minor	1960	65	396	1866
1913	5	3	*	1961	46	414	1955
1914	0	0	0	1962	3	2	9
1915	550	63	1544[3]	1963	10	12	55
1916	107	33	672	1964	49	515	2385
1917	5	Minor	Minor	1965	75	1445	6572
1918	34	5	66	1966	54	15	65
1919	287	22	259	1967	18	200	844
1920	2	3	28	1968	9	10	40
1921	6	3	35	1969	256	1421	5244
1922	0	0	0	1970	11	454	1564
1923	0	Minor	Minor	1971	8	213	686
1924	2	Minor	Minor	1972	122	2100	6418
1925	6	Minor	Minor	1973	5	3	8
1926	269	112	1316	1974	1	150	361
1927	0	0	0	1975	21	490	1082
1928	1836	25	293	1976	9	100	213
1929	3	1	11	1977	0	10	19
1930	0	Minor	Minor	1978	36	20	35
1931	0	0	0	1979	22	3045	4638
1932	0	0	0	1980	2	300	411
1933	63	47	652	1981	0	25	32
1934	17	5	63	1982	0	Minor	Minor
1935	414	12	152	1983	22	2000	2392
1936	9	2	26	1984	4	66	77
1937	0	Minor	Minor	1985	30	4000	4457
1938	600	306	3594	1986	9	17	18
1939	3	Minor	Minor	1987	0	8	8
1940	51	5	61	1988	6	9	9
1941	10	8	91	1989	56	7670	7840
1942	8	27	266	1990	13	57	57
1943	16	17	157	1991	16	1500	1500
1944	64	165	1526	1992	24	25000[4]	25000[4]
1945	7	80	719	1993	4	57	57
1946	0	5	38	1994	38	973	973
1947	53	136	870				

[1] Adjusted to 1990 dollars based on the U.S. Commerce Dept. Composite Construction cost index. No downward adjustment is made after 1990.
[2] Using 1915 cost adjustment - none available prior to 1915.
[3] Considered too high in 1915 reference.
[4] Current estimate, subject to change.
* Not available.

Estimated deaths in the United States from Gulf and Atlantic hurricanes for each year of this century ranked according to annual total.

RANK	YEAR	TOTAL	RANK	YEAR	TOTAL
1	1900	8000+	39	1934	17
2	1928	1836	41	1991	16
3	1938	600	41	1943	16
4	1915	550	43	1903	15
5	1935	414	44	1990	13
6	1909	406	45	1970	11
7	1957	400	46	1901	10
8	1906	298	46	1941	10
9	1919	287	46	1963	10
10	1926	269	49	1936	9
11	1969	256	49	1968	9
12	1955	218	49	1976	9
13	1954	193	49	1986	9
14	1972	122	53	1942	8
15	1916	107	53	1971	8
16	1965	75	55	1945	7
17	1960	65	56	1921	6
18	1944	64	56	1925	6
19	1933	63	56	1988	6
20	1989	56	59	1904	5
21	1966	54	59	1913	5
22	1947	53	59	1917	5
23	1940	51	59	1973	5
24	1964	49	63	1949	4
25	1961	46	63	1984	4
26	1994	38	63	1993	4
27	1978	36	66	1929	3
28	1918	34	66	1939	3
29	1910	30	66	1948	3
29	1985	30	66	1952	3
31	1959	24	66	1962	3
31	1992	24	71	1920	2
33	1979	22	71	1924	2
33	1983	22	71	1953	2
35	1975	21	71	1958	2
36	1950	19	71	1980	2
36	1956	19	76	1912	1
38	1967	18	76	1974	1
39	1911	17			

Note 1: There were 18 years in which no deaths occurred...1902, 1905, 1907, 1908, 1914, 1922, 1923, 1927, 1930, 1931, 1932, 1937, 1946, 1951, 1977, 1981, 1982, 1987.

Estimated damages (unadjusted) in the United States from Gulf and Atlantic hurricanes for each year of this century ranked according to annual total.

RANK	YEAR	DAMAGE ($ millions)	RANK	YEAR	DAMAGE ($ millions)
1	1992	Est.$25000	40	1928	25
2	1989	7670	40	1981	25
3	1985	4000	42	1959	23
4	1979	3045	43	1919	22
5	1972	2100	44	1978	20
6	1983	2000	45	1948	18
7	1991	1500	46	1943	17
8	1965	1445	46	1986	17
9	1969	1421	48	1966	15
10	1955	985	49	1935	12
11	1994	973	49	1963	12
12	1954	756	51	1958	11
13	1964	515	52	1968	10
14	1975	490	52	1977	10
15	1970	454	54	1988	9
16	1961	414	55	1909	8
17	1960	396	55	1941	8
18	1938	306	55	1987	8
18	1980	300	58	1953	6
20	1971	213	59	1918	5
21	1967	200	59	1934	5
22	1944	165	59	1940	5
23	1957	152	59	1946	5
24	1974	150	63	1906	3+
25	1947	136	64	1913	3
26	1926	112	64	1920	3
27	1976	100	64	1921	3
28	1945	80	64	1952	3
29	1984	66	64	1973	3
30	1915	63	69	1904	2
31	1949	59	69	1936	2
32	1990	57	69	1951	2
32	1993	57	69	1962	2
34	1933	47	73	1911	1+
35	1950	36	74	1901	1
36	1916	33	74	1903	1
37	1900	30	74	1910	1
38	1942	27	74	1929	1
38	1956	27			

Note 1: Eleven years had minor damage...1902, 1905, 1912, 1917, 1923, 1924, 1925, 1930, 1937, 1939, and 1982.

Note 2: Seven years had no damage...1907, 1908, 1914, 1922, 1927, 1931, and 1932.

Estimated damages (adjusted to 1990 dollars)[1] in the United States from Gulf and Atlantic hurricanes for each year of this century ranked according to annual total.

RANK	YEAR	DAMAGE ($ millions)	RANK	YEAR	DAMAGE ($ millions)
1	1992	Est.$25000	36	1976	213
2	1989	7840	37	1950	206
3	1965	6572	38	1943	157
4	1972	6418	39	1935	152
5	1969	5244	40	1956	129
6	1955	4974	41	1959	108
7	1979	4638	42	1948	105
8	1985	4457	43	1941	91
9	1954	3887	44	1984	77
10	1938	3594	45	1918	66
11	1983	2392	46	1966	65
12	1964	2385	47	1934	63
13	1961	1955	48	1940	61
14	1960	1866	49	1990	57
15	1970	1564	49	1993	57
16	1915	1544[2]	51	1963	55
17	1944	1526	52	1958	51
18	1991	1500	53	1968	40
19	1926	1316	54	1946	38
20	1975	1082	55	1921	35
21	1994	973	56	1978	35
22	1947	870	57	1981	32
23	1967	844	58	1953	31
24	1900	735[3]	59	1920	28
25	1945	719	60	1936	26
26	1957	705	61	1977	19
27	1971	686	62	1986	18
28	1916	672	63	1952	15
29	1933	652	64	1929	11
30	1980	411	65	1951	10
31	1974	361	66	1962	9
32	1949	344	66	1988	9
33	1928	293	68	1973	8
34	1942	266	68	1987	8
35	1919	259			

Notes: Eleven years had minor damage...1902, 1905, 1912, 1917, 1923, 1924, 1925, 1930, 1937, 1939, and 1982. There have been seven years with no damage...1907, 1908, 1914, 1922, 1927, 1931, 1932. Eight years prior to 1915 were not adjusted and do not appear in the table...1901, 1903, 1904, 1906, 1909, 1910, 1911, 1913.

[1] Adjusted to 1990 dollars on basis of U.S. Department of Commerce composite construction cost index. Values after 1990 are not adjusted downward.

[2] Considered too high in 1915 reference.

[3] Using 1915 cost adjustment base - none available prior to 1915.

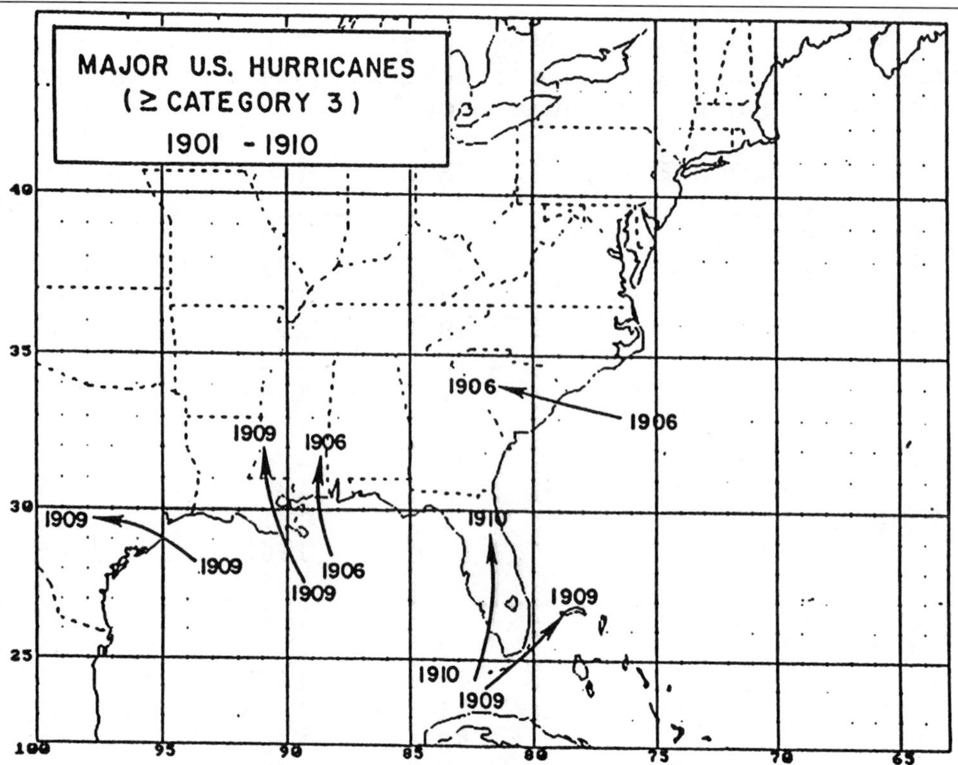

Figure 1. Major landfalling United States hurricanes (greater than or equal to a category 3) during the period 1901-1910.

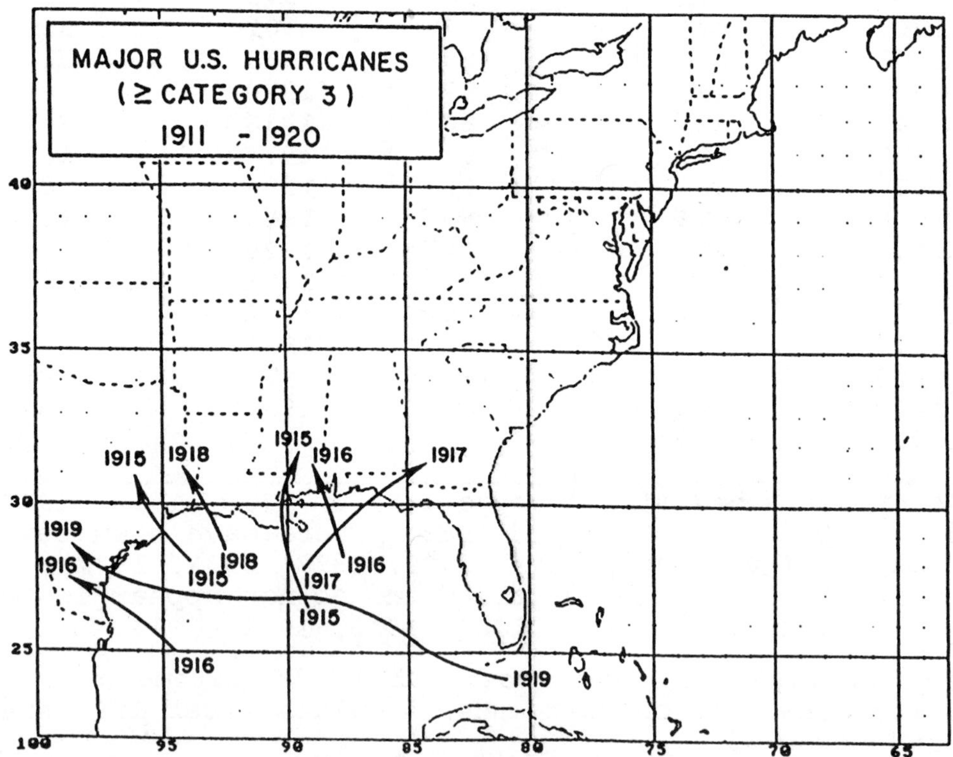

Figure 2. Major landfalling United States hurricanes (greater than or equal to a category 3) during the period 1911-1920.

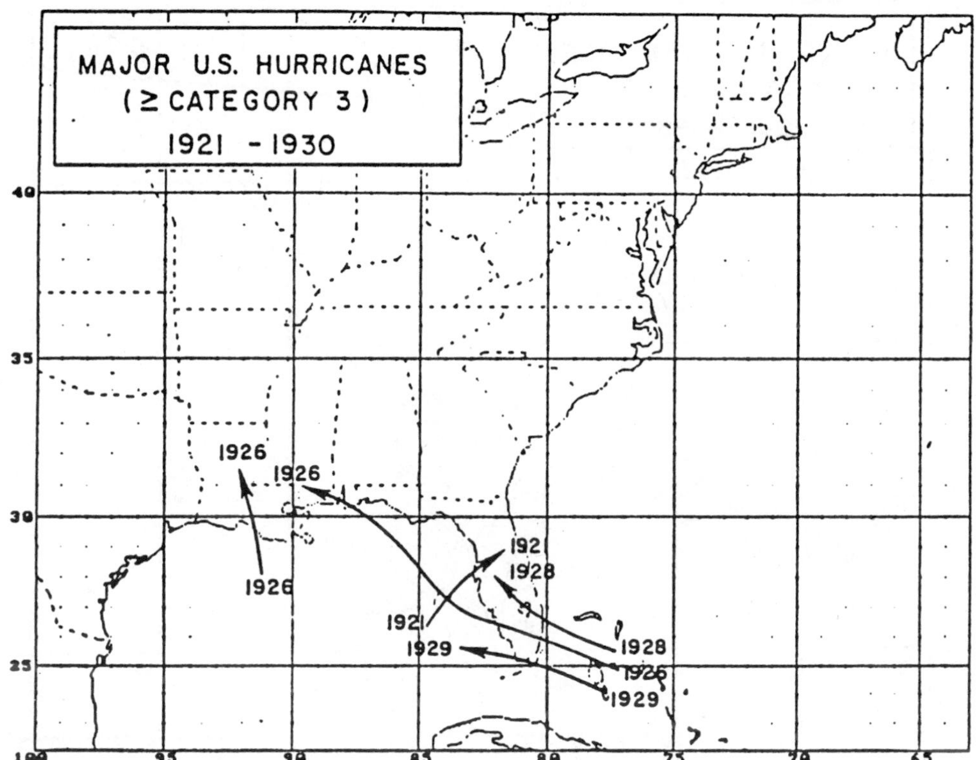

Figure 3. Major landfalling United States hurricanes (greater than or equal to a category 3) during the period 1921-1930.

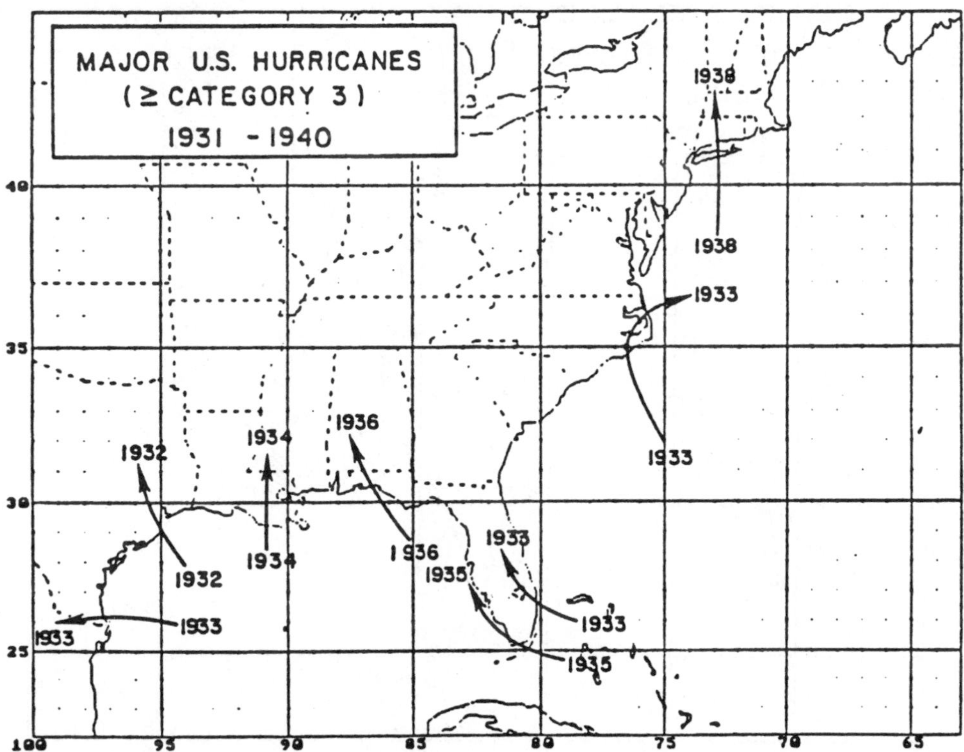

Figure 4. Major landfalling United States hurricanes (greater than or equal to a category 3) during the period 1931-1940.

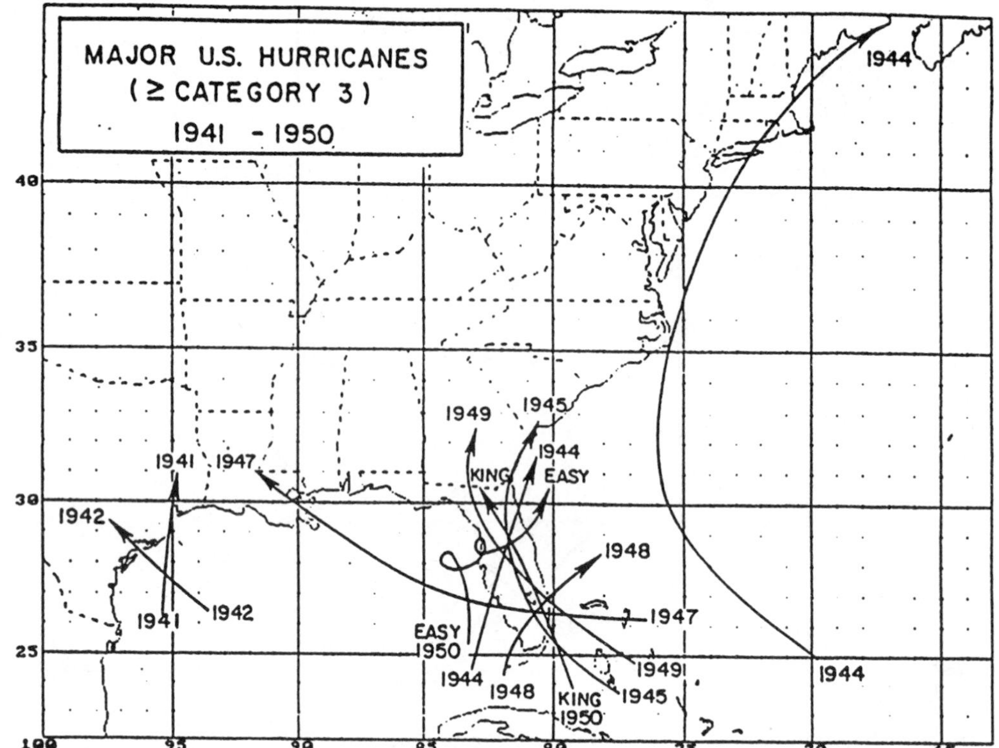

Figure 5. Major landfalling United States hurricanes (greater than or equal to a category 3) during the period 1941-1950.

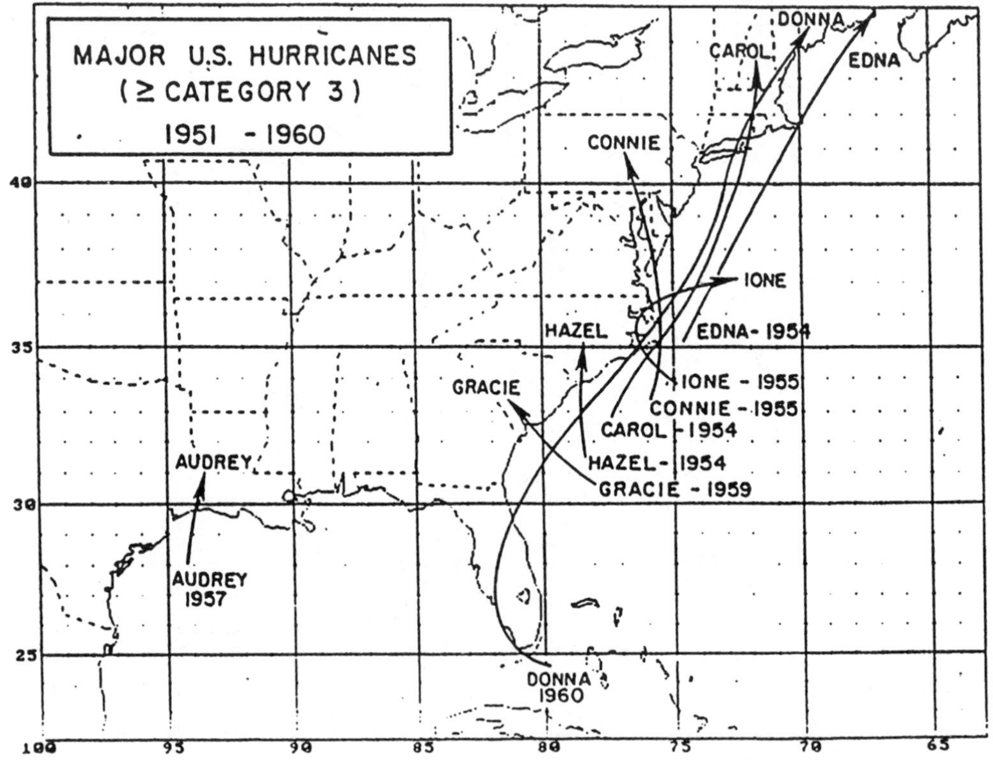

Figure 6. Major landfalling United States hurricanes (greater than or equal to a category 3) during the period 1951-1960.

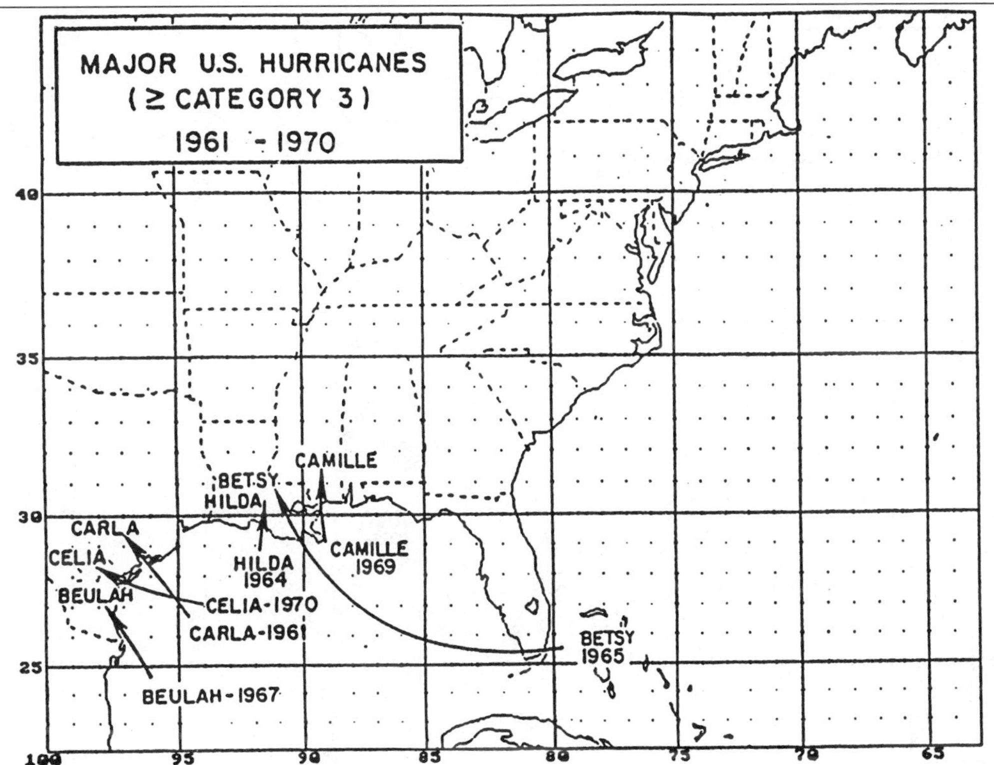

Figure 7. Major landfalling United States hurricanes (greater than or equal to a category 3) during the period 1961-1970.

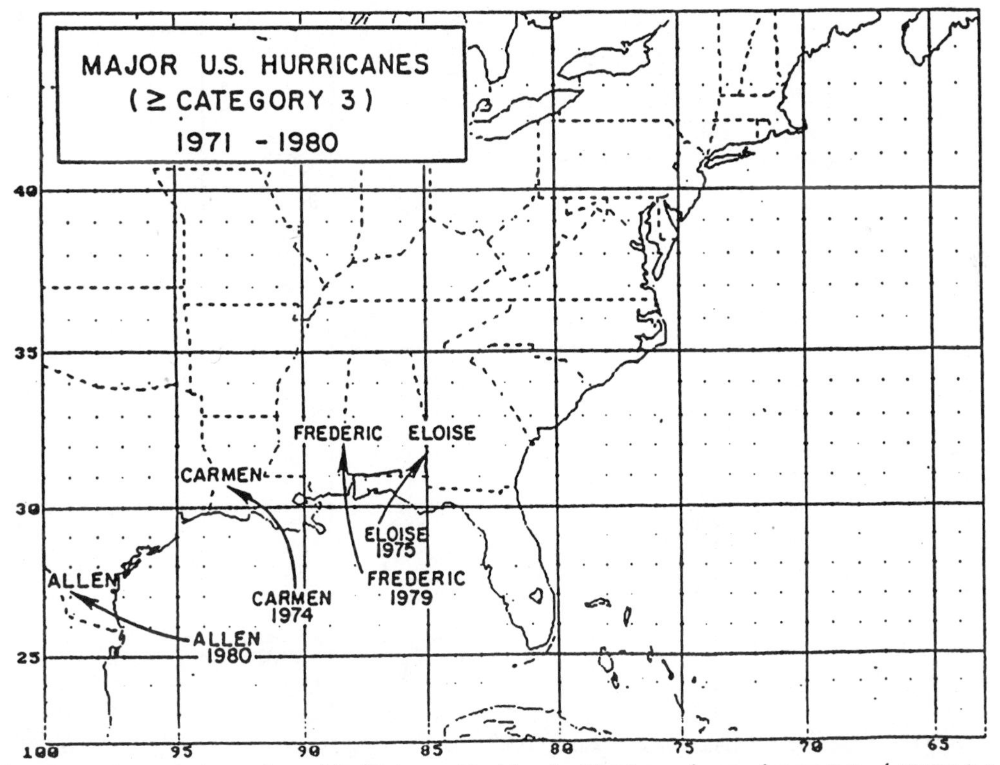

Figure 8. Major landfalling United States hurricanes (greater than or equal to a category 3) during the period 1971-1980.

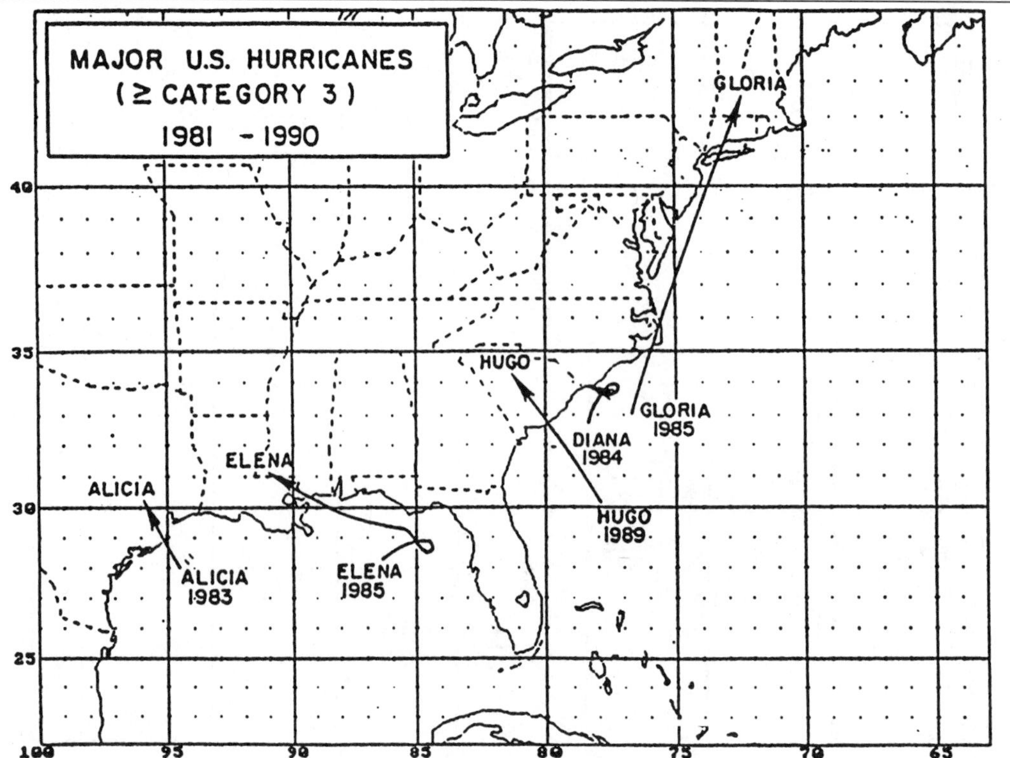

Figure 9. Major landfalling United States hurricanes (greater than or equal to a category 3) during the period 1981-1990.

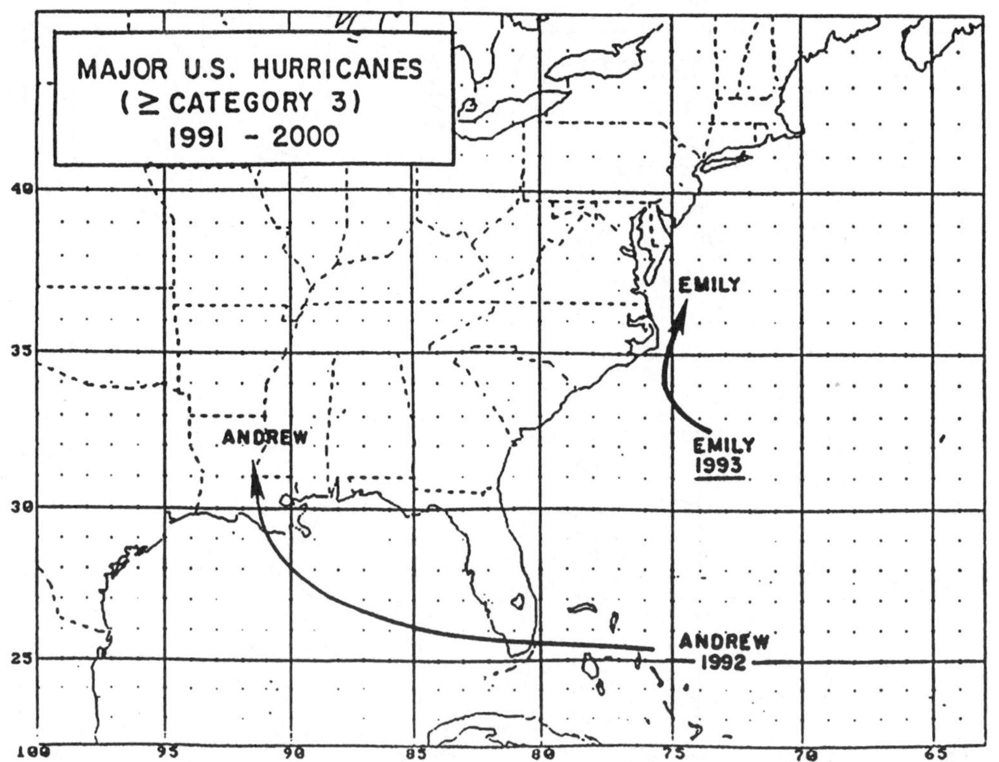

Figure 10. Major landfalling United States hurricanes (greater than or equal to a category 3) during the period 1991-2000.

Number of recorded Atlantic tropical cyclones (excluding depressions and, after 1967, including subtropical cyclones) which reached at least tropical storm intensity in specified month, 1871-1992.

YEAR	JAN	FEB	MAR	APR	MAY	JUN	JUL	AUG	SEP	OCT	NOV	DEC	TOTAL
1871						2		2	2				6
1872							1	1	2	1			5
1873						1		1	3				5
1874							1	1	4	1			7
1875									3	1			4
1876									2	1			3
1877								1	4	2	1		8
1878							1	1	3	4	1		10
1879								3	1	3	1		8
1880						1		4	2	2			9
1881								4	1	1			6
1882									2	1			3
1883								2	1	1			4
1884									2	1			3
1885								3	4	1			8
1886						3	1	2	2	2			10
1887					1		2	2	3	6	1	2	17
1888						1	1	2	2	1	2		9
1889					1	1		1	5	1			9
1890								1					1
1891							1	2	3	4	1		11
1892						1		1	4	3			9
1893						1	1	5	3	1	1		12
1894								2	1	3			6
1895								2	1	3			6
1896							1	1	2	2			6
1897								1	2	2			5
1898								2	5	2			9
1899							1	2	1	2			6
1900								1	3	3			7
1901						1	2	2	3	2			10
1902						2			1	1	1		5
1903							1	1	4	2	1		9
1904						1			1	3			5
1905									3	2			5
1906						2		1	3	4	1		11
1907						1			2	1			4
1908			1				1	1	3	2			8
1909						2	2	2	2	1	1		10
1910								1	2	1			4
1911								2	1	1			4
1912						1	1		1	2	1		6
1913						1		1	1	1			4
1914									1				1
1915							1	3	1				5
1916						1	2	3	4	3	1		14
1917								2	1				3
1918								3	2				5
1919							1		1		1		3
1920									4				4
1921						1			3	2			6
1922						1			1	2			4
1923								1	1	5			7
1924						1		2	2	2	1		8
1925									1		1		2
1926							2	1	5	2	1		11
1927								1	3	3			7
1928								2	3	1			6
1929						1			1	1			3
1930								2					2
1931						1	1	2	3	1	1		9
1932					1			3	3	3	1		11
1933					1	1	3	7	5	3	1		21
1934					1	1	1	2	2	3	1		11
1935								3	1	2			6
1936						3	2	6	4	1			16
1937							1	2	6				9
1938								3	1	3	1		8
1939						1		1	1	2			5
1940					1			3	2	2			8
1941									4	2			6
1942								3	3	3	1		10
1943							1	2	4	3			10
1944							3	2	4	2			11
1945						1	1	4	3	2			11
1946						1	1	1	1	2			6
1947							1	2	3	3			9
1948					1		1	2	3	1	1		9
1949								3	7	2	1		13
1950								4	3	6			13
1951					1			3	3	3			10
1952		1						2	2	2			7
1953					1			3	4	4	1	1	14
1954						1	1	2	4	1	1	1	11
1955							1	4	5	2			12
1956						1	1	1	4		1		8
1957						2		1	4	1			8
1958						1		4	4	1			10
1959					1	2	2	1	3	2			11
1960						1	2	2	2				7
1961							1		6	2	2		11
1962								2	1	2			5
1963								2	5	2			9
1964						1	1	3	5	1	1		12
1965						1		2	2	1			6
1966						1	4	1	4		1		11
1967								1	4	3			8
1968						3		1	3	1			8
1969							1	5	6	5	1		18
1970					1		1	3	3	2			10
1971							1	4	6	1	1		13
1972					1	1		2	2		1		7
1973							2	2	2	2			8
1974						1	1	4	4	1			11
1975						1	1	2	3	1		1	9
1976					1		1	5	2	1			10
1977								1	3	2			6
1978	1						1	4	3	3			12
1979						1	2	3	2	1			9
1980								3	5	1	2		11
1981					1	1		2	5	1	2		12
1982						2		1	2	1			6
1983								2	2				4
1984								4	6	1	1	1	13
1985							2	3	3	2	1		11
1986						2		1	2		1		6
1987								3	3	1			7
1988								3	7	1	1		12
1989						1	2	4	2	1	1		11
1990							2	6	2	4			14
1991							1	1	3	3			8
1992				1				1	4	1			7
1993													
1994													
1995													
1996													
1997													

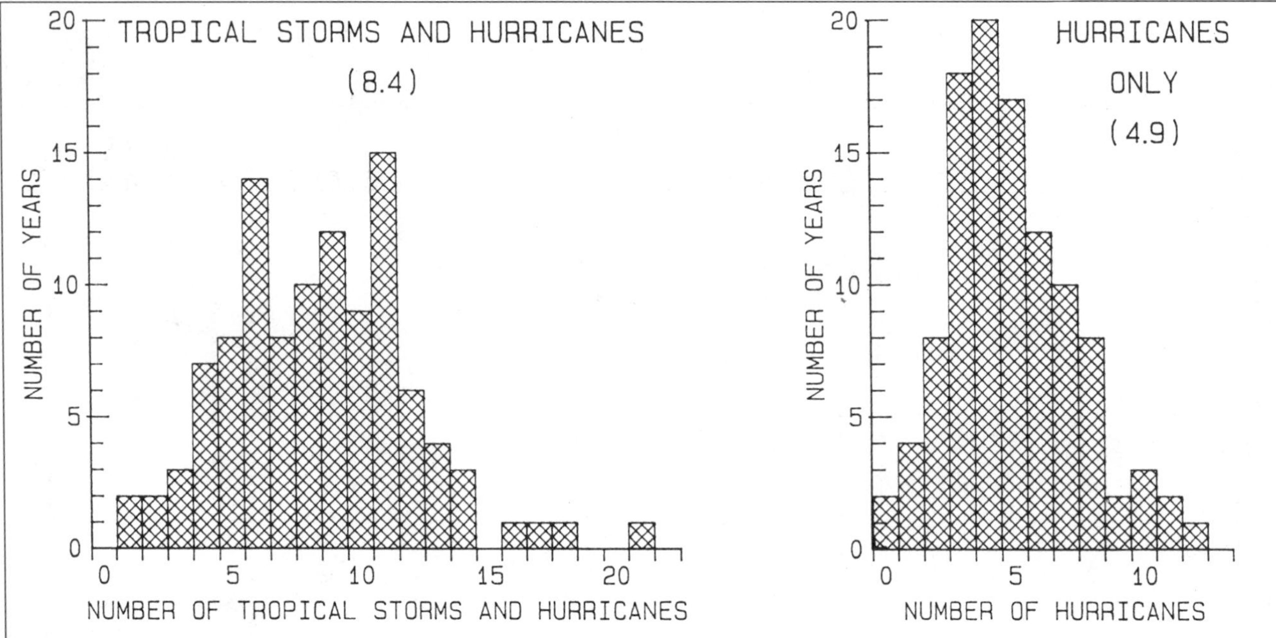

Distribution of annual number of tropical cyclones reaching at least tropical storm strength (left) and hurricane strength (right), 1886 through 1992. The average number of such storms is 8.4 and 4.9, respectively

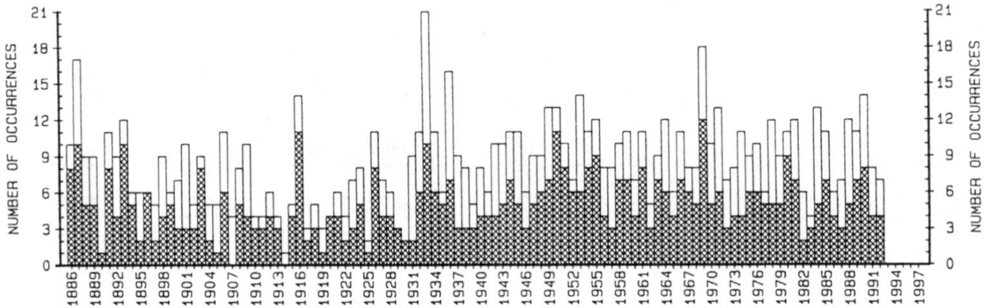

Annual distribution of the 904 Atlantic tropical cyclones reaching at least tropical storm strength (open bar) and the 527 reaching hurricane strength (solid bar), 1886 through 1992. The average number of such storms is 8.4 and 4.9

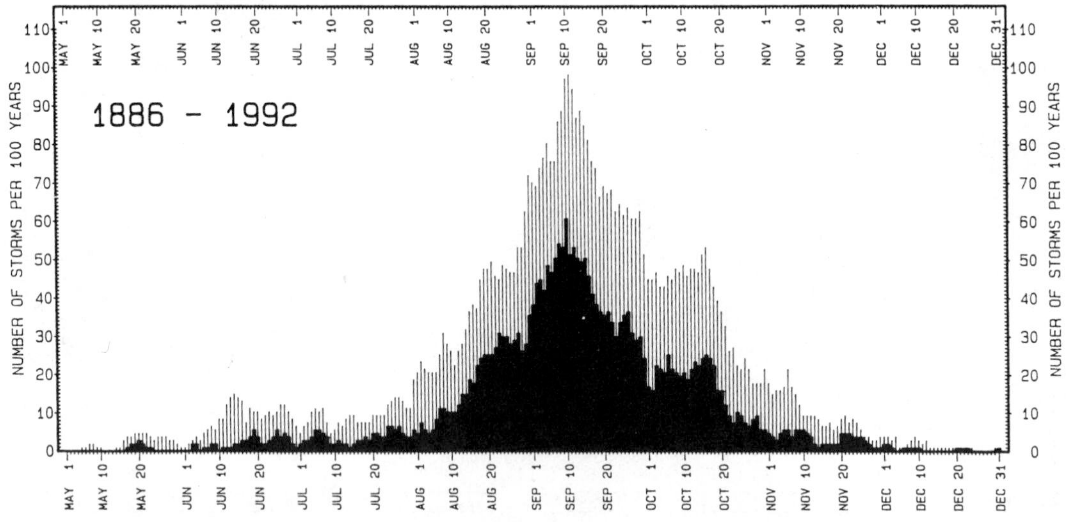

Intra-seasonal variations in the 100-year frequency of tropical cyclone occurrences. Lower bar is for hurricanes and upper bar is for hurricanes and tropical storms combined. Summary is based on period of record, 1886-1992.

Tornadoes

A tornado is a local storm of short duration formed of winds rotating at very high speeds, usually in a counterclockwise direction. This storm is visible as a vortex, a whirlpool structure of winds rotating about a hollow cavity in which centrifugal forces produce a partial vacuum. As condensation occurs around the vortex, a pale cloud appears—the familiar and frightening tornado funnel. Air surrounding the funnel is also part of the tornado vortex; as the storm moves along the ground, this outer ring of rotating winds becomes dark with dust and debris, which may eventually darken the entire funnel.

These small, severe storms form several thousand feet above the earth's surface, usually during warm, humid, unsettled weather, and usually in conjunction with a severe thunderstorm. Sometimes a series of two or more tornadoes is associated with a parent thunderstorm. As the thunderstorm moves, tornadoes may form at intervals along its path, travel for a few miles, and dissipate. The *forward* speed of tornadoes has been observed to range from almost no motion to 70 miles (113 km) per hour.

Funnels usually appear as an extension of the dark, heavy cumulonimbus clouds of thunderstorms, and stretch downward toward the ground. Some never reach the surface; others touch and rise again.

The winds of some tornadoes have been estimated to exceed 350 mph (563.5 km/hr).

• HOW A TORNADO IS FORMED

Tornado formation requires the presence of layers of air with contrasting characteristic of temperature, moisture, density, and wind flow. Complicated energy transformations produce the tornado vortex.

Many theories have been advanced as to the type of energy transformation necessary to generate a tornado, and none has won general acceptance. The two most frequently encountered visualize tornado generation as either the effect of thermally induced rotary circulations, or as the effect of converging rotary winds. Currently, scientists seem to agree that neither process generates tornadoes independently. It is more probable that tornadoes are produced by the combined effects of thermal and mechanical forces, with one or the other force being the stronger generating agent.

Numerous observations of lightning strokes and a variety of luminous features in and around tornado funnels have led scientists to speculate about the relationship between tornado formation and thunderstorm electrification. This hypothesis explores the alternative possibilities that atmospheric electricity accelerates rotary winds to tornado velocities, or that those high-speed rotary winds generate large electrical charges. Here, as in most attempts to understand complex atmospheric relationships, the reach of theory exceeds the grasp of proof.

• SIZE, SPEED & DURATION

Tornadoes vary greatly in size, intensity, and appearance. Most (62%) of the tornadoes that occur each year fall into the "weak" category. Wind speeds are in the range of 100 miles (161 km) an hour or less. Weak tornadoes account for less than 3% of all tornado deaths.

About one out of every three tornadoes is classified as "strong." Wind speeds reach about 200 miles (322 km) an hour with an average path length of 9 miles (14.5 km) and a width of 200 yards (182 m). Almost 30% of all tornado deaths occur each year from this type of storm. Nearly 70% of all tornado fatalities result from "violent" tornadoes. Although very rare (only about 2% are violent), these extreme tornadoes can last for hours. Average path lengths and widths are 26 miles (42 km) and 425 yards (386.75 m), respectively. The largest of these may exceed a mile (1.61 km) or more in width, with wind speeds approaching 300 miles (483 km) an hour.

Tornado Characteristics

Time of day during which tornadoes are most likely to occur is mid-afternoon, generally between 3 and 7 P.M., but they have occurred at all times of day.

Direction of movement is usually from southwest to northeast. (Note: Tornadoes associated with hurricanes may move from an easterly direction).

Length of path averages 4 miles (6 km), but may reach 300 miles (483 km). A tornado traveled 293 miles (472 km) across Illinois and Indiana on May 26, 1917, and lasted 7 hours and 20 minutes.

Width of path averages about 300-400 yards (273-364 m) but tornadoes have cut paths a mile and more in width.

Speed of travel averages from 25-40 miles (40.25-64.4 km) per hour, but speeds ranging from stationary to 68 miles (109.5 km) per hour have been reported.

The cloud directly associated with a tornado is a dark, heavy cumulonimbus (the familiar thunderstorm cloud) from which a whirling funnel-shaped pendant extends to the ground.

Precipitation associated with the tornado usually occurs first as rain just preceding the storm, frequently with hail, and as a heavy downpour immediately to the side of the tornado's path.

Sound occurring during a tornado has been described as a roaring, rushing noise, closely approximating that made by a train speeding through a tunnel or over a trestle, or the roar of many airplanes.

Tornado-Intensity Rating System

The intensity of tornadoes is defined according to the Fujita Scale (or F scale), which ranges from F0 to F6 as outlined below.

F0: 40-72 mph (64-116 km/hr) winds. Damage is light and might include damage to tree branches, chimneys and billboards. Shallow-rooted trees may be pushed over.

F1: 73-112 mph (118-180 km/hr) winds. Damage is moderate; mobile homes may be pushed off foundations and moving autos pushed off the road.

F2: 113-157 mph (182-253 km/hr) winds. Damage is considerable. Roofs can be torn off houses, mobile homes demolished, and large trees uprooted.

F3: 158-206 mph (254-334 km/hr) winds. Damage is severe. Even well-constructed houses may be torn apart, trees uprooted, and cars lifted off the ground.

F4: 207-260 mph (333-419 km/hr) winds. Damage is devastating. Houses can be leveled and cars thrown; objects become deadly missiles.

F5: 261-318 mph (420-512 km/hr) winds. Damage is incredible. Structures are lifted off foundations and carried away; cars become missiles. Less than 2% of all tornadoes reach an intensity of this magnitude.

F6: The maximum tornado wind speeds are not expected to exceed 318 mph (512 km/hr)

• WHERE DO TORNADOES OCCUR?

Tornadoes occur in many parts of the world and in all 50 states. But no area is more favorable to their formation than the continental plains of North America, and no season is free of them. Normally, the number of tornadoes is at its lowest in the United States during December and January and at its peak in May. The months of greatest total frequency are April, May, and June.

In February, when tornado frequency begins to increase, the center of maximum frequency lies over the central Gulf States. Then, during March, this center moves eastward to the southeast Atlantic states, where tornado frequency reaches a peak in April. During May, the center of maximum frequency moves to the southern plains states, and in June, northward to the northern plains and Great Lakes area as far east as western New York state. The reason for this drift is the increasing penetration of warm, moist air while contrasting cool, dry air still surges in from the north and northwest; tornadoes are generated with greatest frequency where these air masses wage their wars. Thus, when the Gulf states are substantially "occupied" by warm air systems after May, there is no cold air intrusion to speak of, and tornado frequency drops. This is the case across the nation after June. Winter cooling permits fewer and fewer encounters between warm and overriding cold systems, and tornado frequency returns to its lowest level by December.

The mathematical chance that a specific location will be struck by a tornado in any one year is quite small. For example, the probability, of a tornado striking a given point in the area most frequently subject to tornadoes is 0.0363, or about once in 250 years. In the far western states, the probability is close to zero.

But tornadoes have provided many unmathematical exceptions. Oklahoma City has been struck by tornadoes 26 times since 1892. Baldwyn, Mississippi, was struck twice by tornadoes during a 25-minute period on March 16, 1942. A third of Irving, Kansas, was left in ruins by two tornadoes which occurred 45 minutes apart on May 30, 1879. Austin, Texas, had two tornadoes in rapid succession on May 4, 1922; and Codell, Kansas, was struck three times in 1916, 1917, and 1918—on May 20.

During the period 1953-69, an average of 642 tornadoes per year occurred in the United States, about half of them during three months—April, May, and June. For the same period, the annual average number of tornadoes days—days on which one or more tornadoes were reported—was 159. Average annual frequency by states for this period ranges from 103 tornadoes in Texas to less than three in most of the northeastern and far western states.

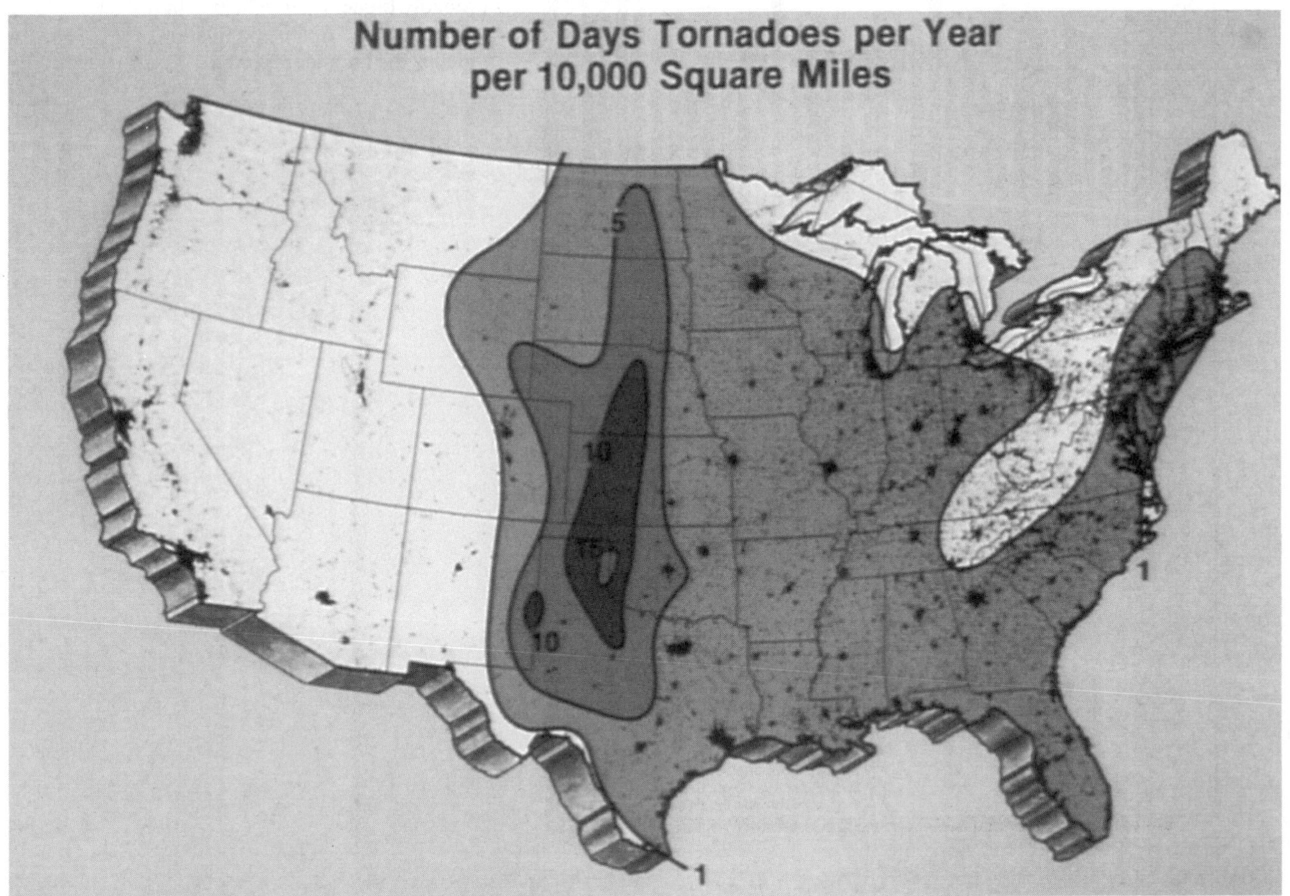

Frequency of Tornadoes

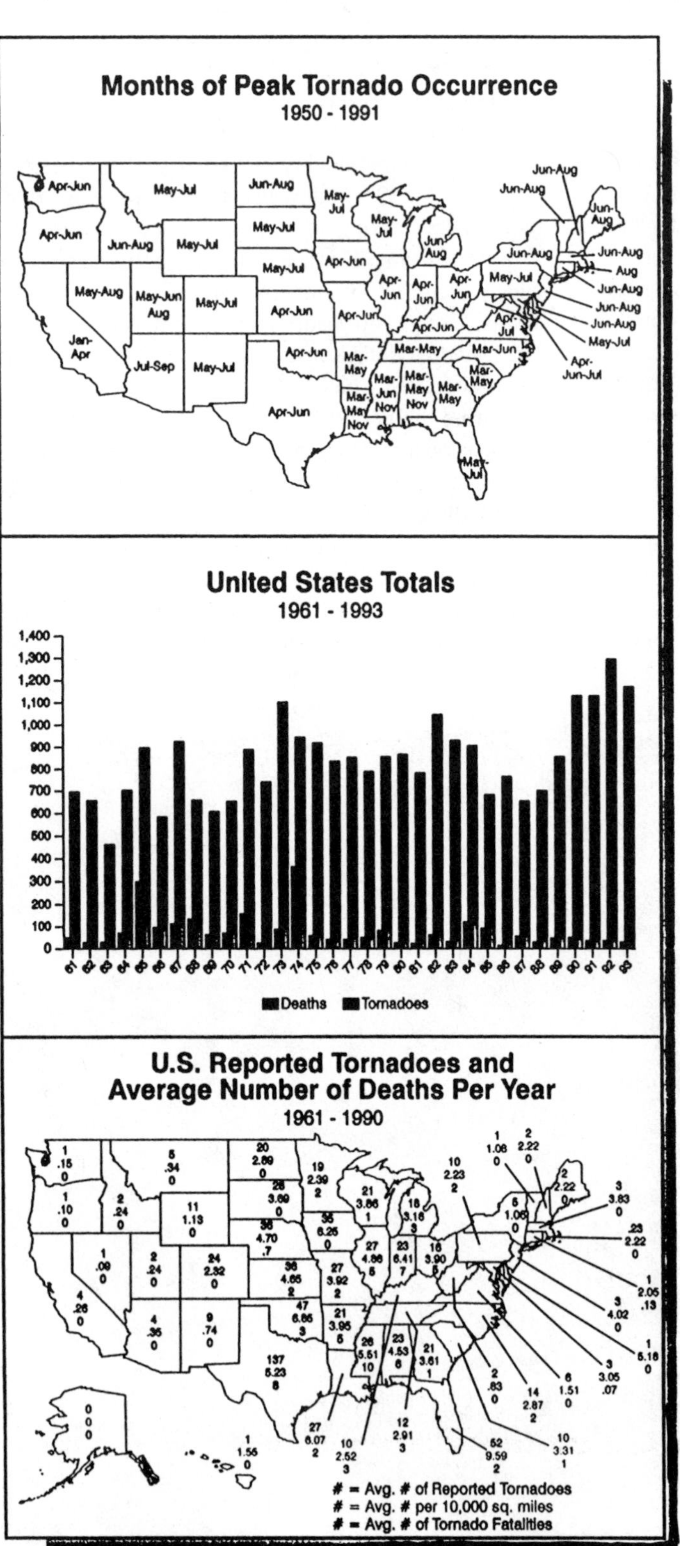

Tornadoes can occur at any time of the year.

- In the southern states, peak tornado occurrence is in March through May, while peak months in the northern states are during the summer.
- Note, in some states, a secondary tornado maximum occurs in the fall.
- Tornadoes are most likely to occur between 3 and 9 p.m. but have been known to occur at all hours of the day or night.
- The average tornado moves from southwest to northeast, but tornadoes have been known to move in any direction. The average forward speed is 30 mph but may vary from nearly stationary to 70 mph.
- The total number of tornadoes is probably higher than indicated in the western states. Sparce population reduces the number reported.

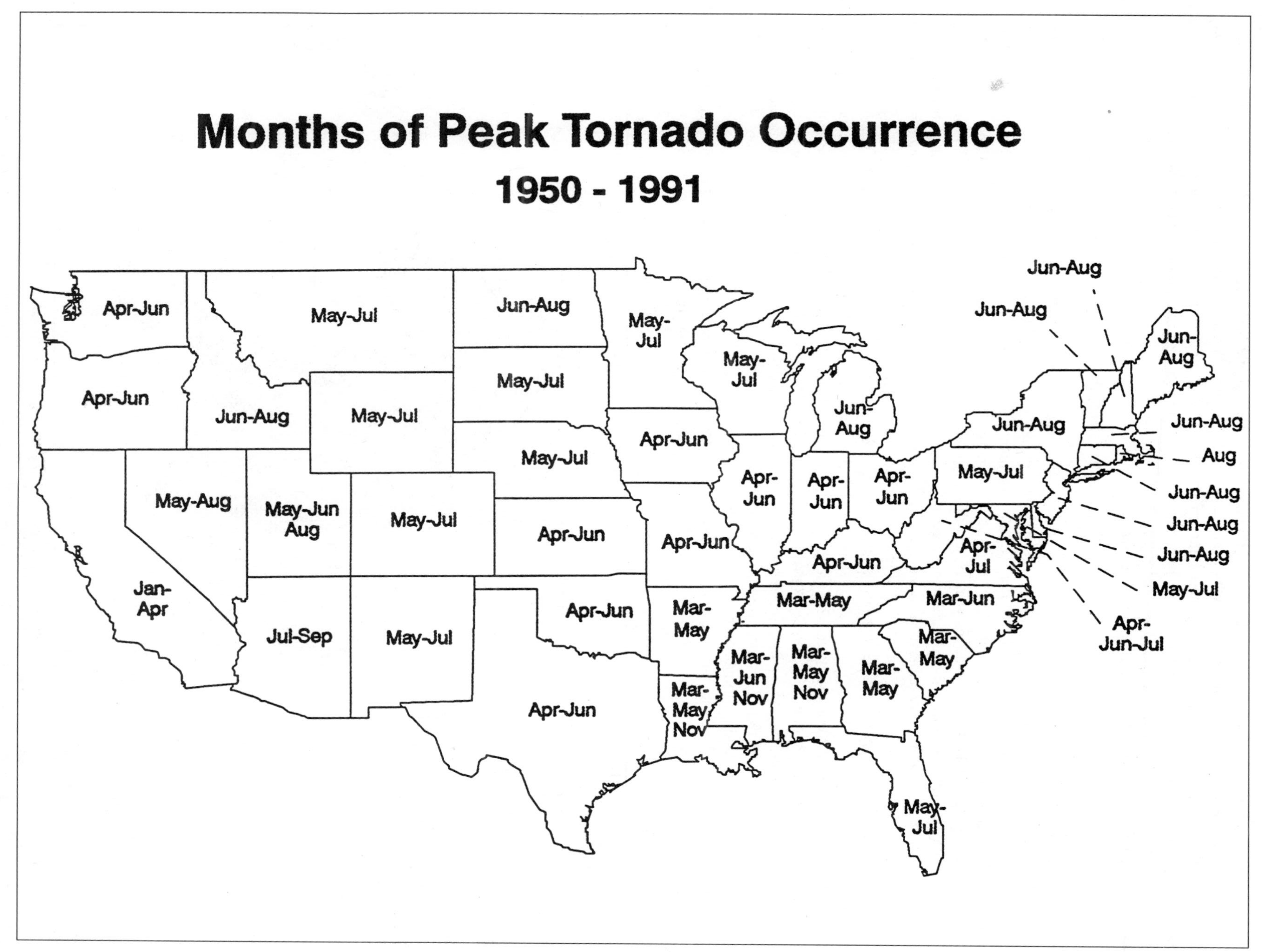

Months of Peak Tornado Occurrence
1950 - 1991
Apr-Jun
May-Jul
Jun-Aug
May-Jul
Jun-Aug
Jun-Aug
Jun-Aug
May-Jul
Apr-Jun
Jun-Aug
May-Jul
Jun-Aug
Jun-Aug
May-Jul
Apr-Jun
Jun-Aug
Aug
Apr-Jun
Apr-Jun
Apr-Jun
May-Jul
Jun-Aug
May-Aug
May-Jun Aug
May-Jul
Apr-Jun
Apr-Jun
Jun-Aug
Apr-Jul
Apr-Jun
Jun-Aug
Jan-Apr
Apr-Jun
Mar-May
Mar-May
Mar-Jun
May-Jul
Jul-Sep
May-Jul
Mar-Jun Nov
Mar-May Nov
Mar-May
Mar-May
Apr-Jun-Jul
Mar-May Nov
Apr-Jun
May-Jul

Tornadoes may occur at any hour of the day or night, but, because of the meteorological combinations which create them, they form most readily during the warmest hours of the day. The greatest number of tornadoes—82% of the total—occurs between noon and midnight, and the greatest single concentration—23% of the total tornado activity—falls between 4 and 6 P.M.

Major tornadoes

The most death-dealing series of tornadoes on record occurred during the late afternoon on March 18, 1925, in portions of Missouri, Indiana, Illinois, Kentucky, and Tennessee. Eight separate and distinct tornadoes were observed. One of these killed 689 persons, injured 1,890 and caused more than $16 million in property damage. The other seven tornadoes of the series increased the total loss of life to 740 and contributed significantly to the total casualty and property damage.

Another major series of tornadoes killed 268 people and injured 1,874 in Alabama on March 21, 1932. Property damage amounted to approximately $5 million. In March, 1990, a series of four separate tornadoes occurred in central Kansas. Two of these tornadoes joined forces at one point and resulted in one of the three most intense to occur during the 1980s. This series cut a path of over 100 miles (161 km) in a two and one-half-hour period. The winds of another tornado in the Wichita, Kansas, area on April 26, 1991, reached 260 miles (419 km) per hour and traveled some 70 miles (113 km) on the ground over a two-hour period.

• TRENDS

From 1916-52, fewer than 300 tornadoes were reported in any one year. In 1953, when the United States Department of Commerce initiated its tornado forecasting effort, more than 437 tornadoes were observed and reported, beginning the first period of reliable statistical history. Since 1953, partly through improved equipment and techniques, partly through increasing public participation, essentially complete tornado records have been available.

In the United States, more tornadoes occurred in 1973 than any year from the beginning of firm records in 1916 through 1989. The year 1973 saw 1,102 tornadoes strike in 46 states, kill 87 persons and cause property damage in the millions of dollars. A harsher year for tornado deaths, however, was 1953 when 515 people died from 421 recorded tornadoes.

Over the ten-year period 1980-89 an average of 820 tornadoes per year occurred in the United States, resulting in

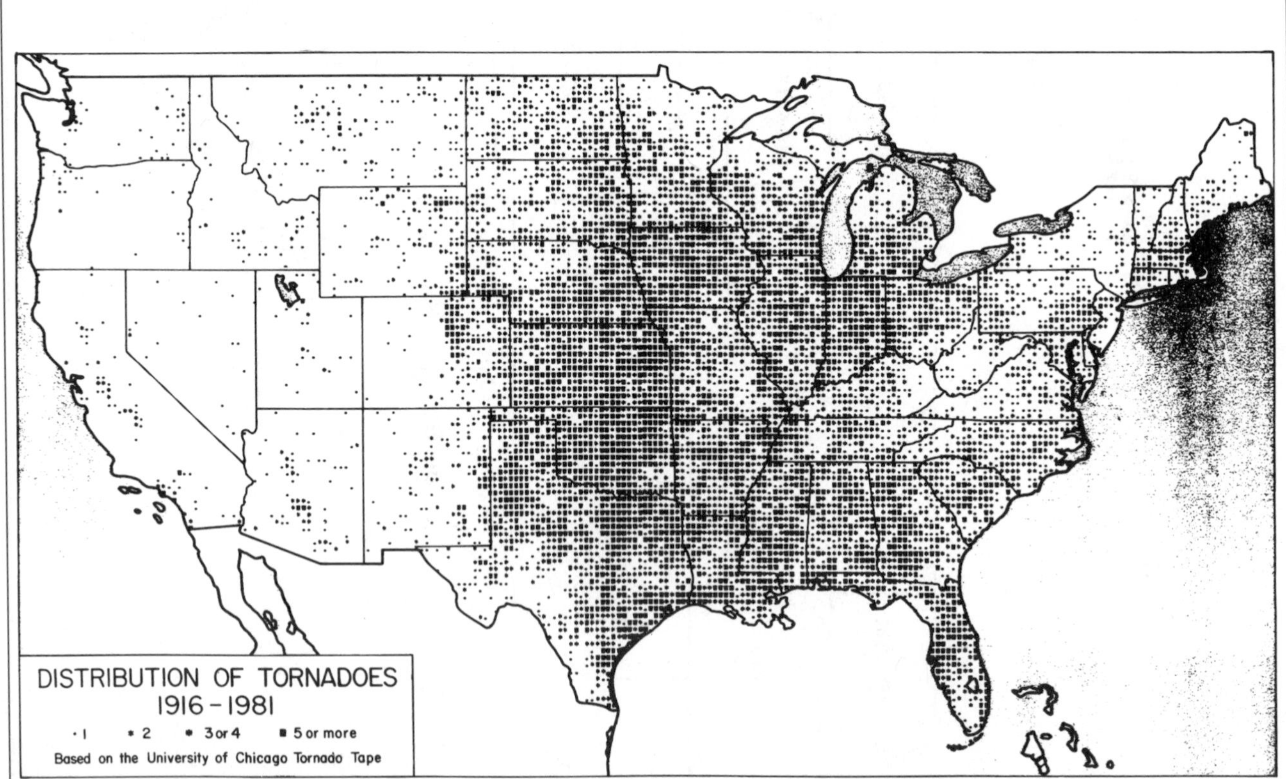

This map includes 26,486 tornadoes between 1916 and 1981 archived in the University of Chicago Tornado Tape. In producing this map, the area of the contiguous United States was divided into 12,734 small subboxes of 15'x15' latitudes and longitudes. Then the number of tornado touchdowns in each subbox was counted by computer and printed on map coordinates. (Produced by T. Theodore Fujita, The University of Chicago.)

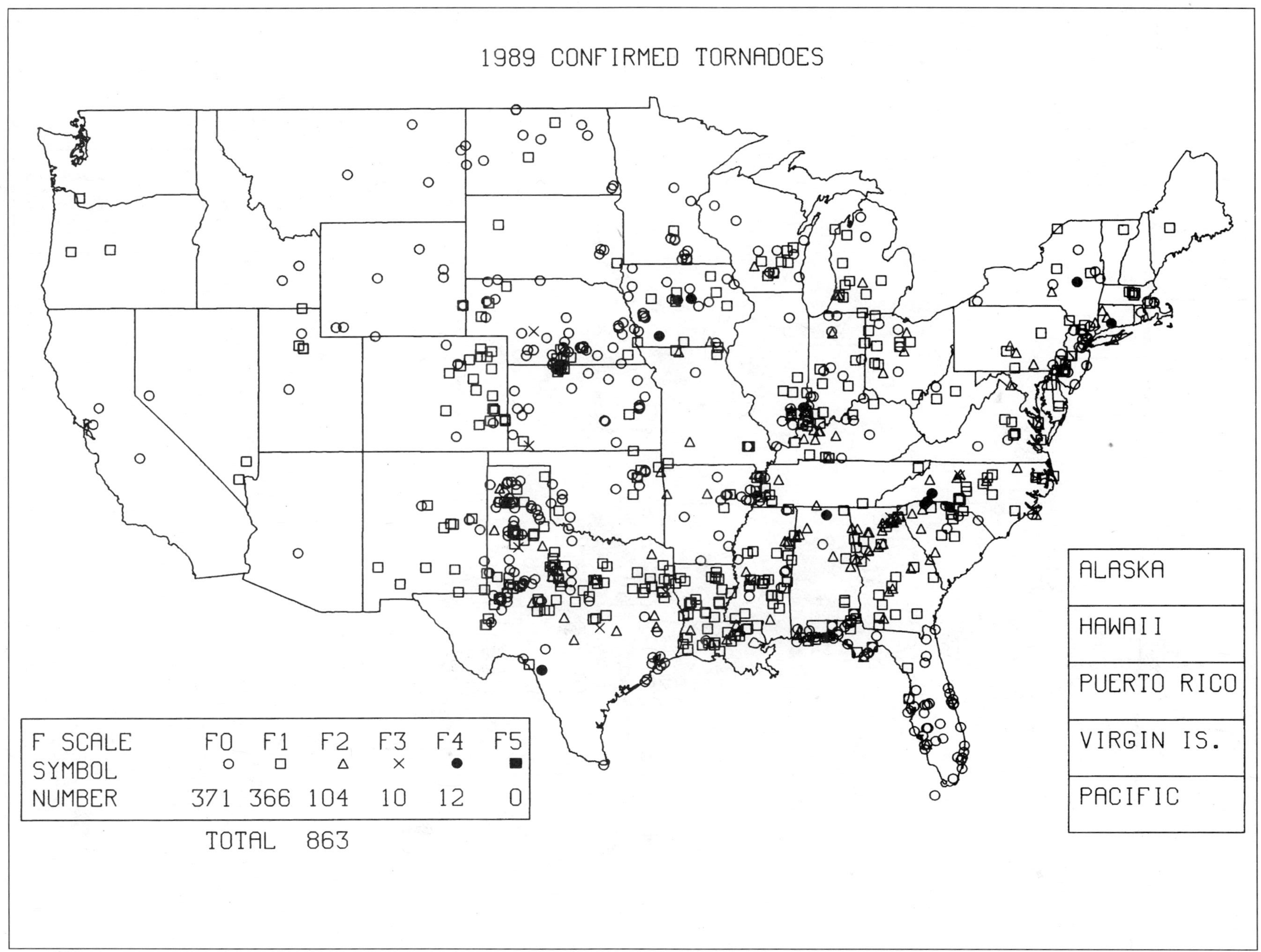
1989 CONFIRMED TORNADOES
ALASKA
HAWAII
PUERTO RICO
VIRGIN IS.
PACIFIC
F SCALE F0 F1 F2 F3 F4 F5
SYMBOL ○ □ △ × ● ■
NUMBER 371 366 104 10 12 0
TOTAL 863

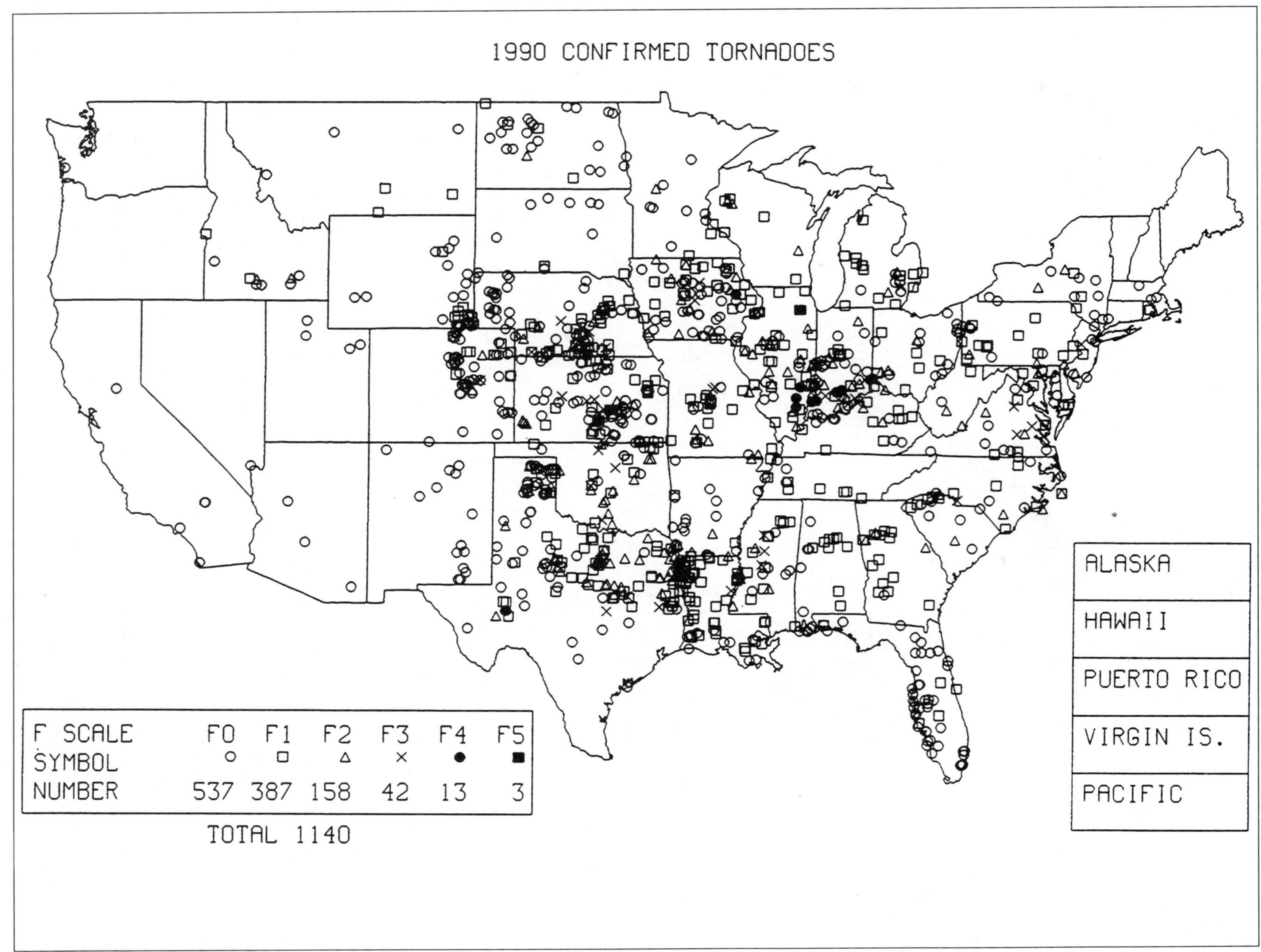
1990 CONFIRMED TORNADOES
F SCALE F0 F1 F2 F3 F4 F5
SYMBOL ○ □ △ × ● ■
NUMBER 537 387 158 42 13 3
TOTAL 1140
ALASKA
HAWAII
PUERTO RICO
VIRGIN IS.
PACIFIC

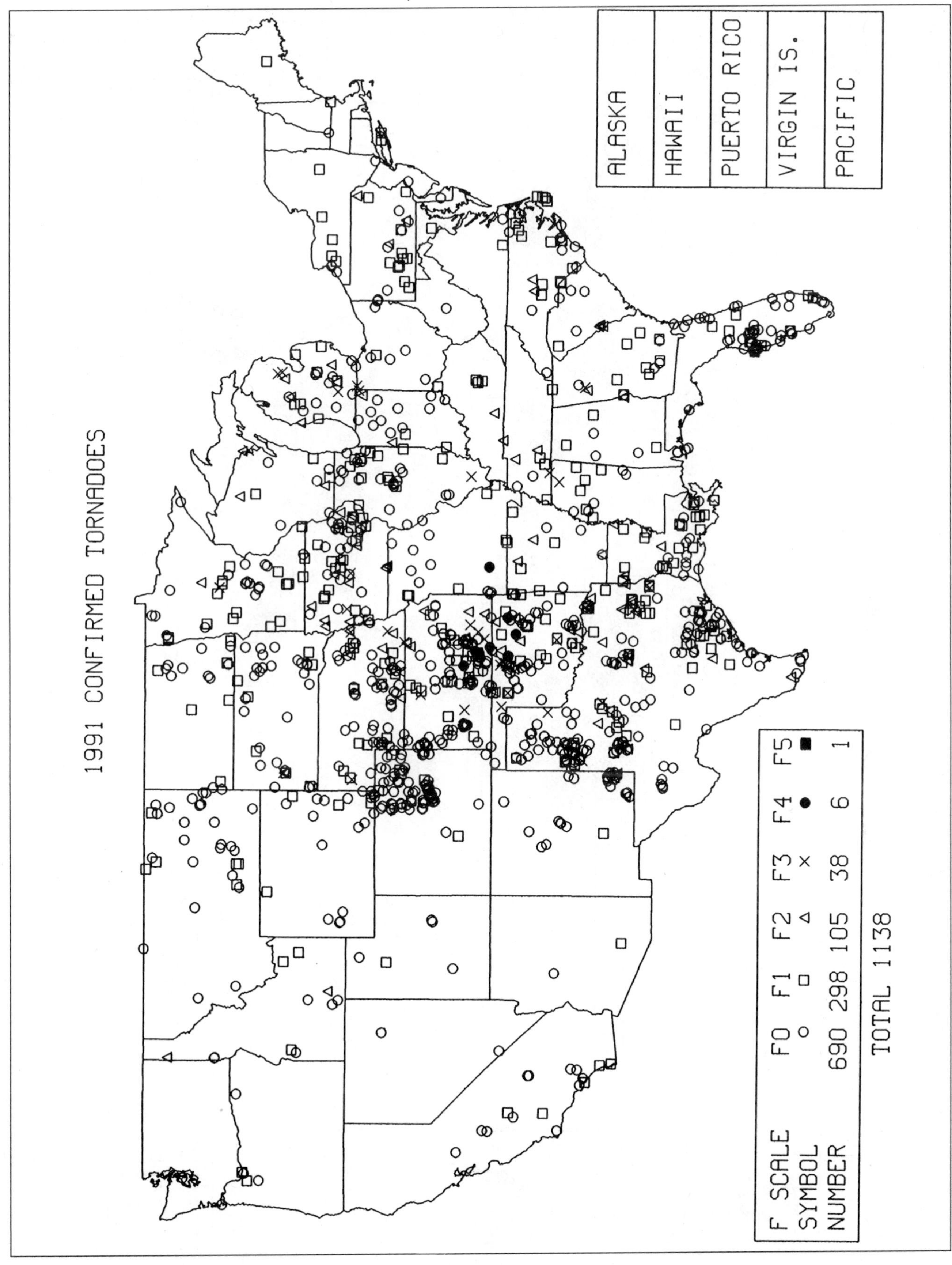
1991 CONFIRMED TORNADOES
ALASKA
HAWAII
PUERTO RICO
VIRGIN IS.
PACIFIC
F SCALE F0 F1 F2 F3 F4 F5
SYMBOL ○ □ △ × ● ■
NUMBER 690 298 105 38 6 1
TOTAL 1138

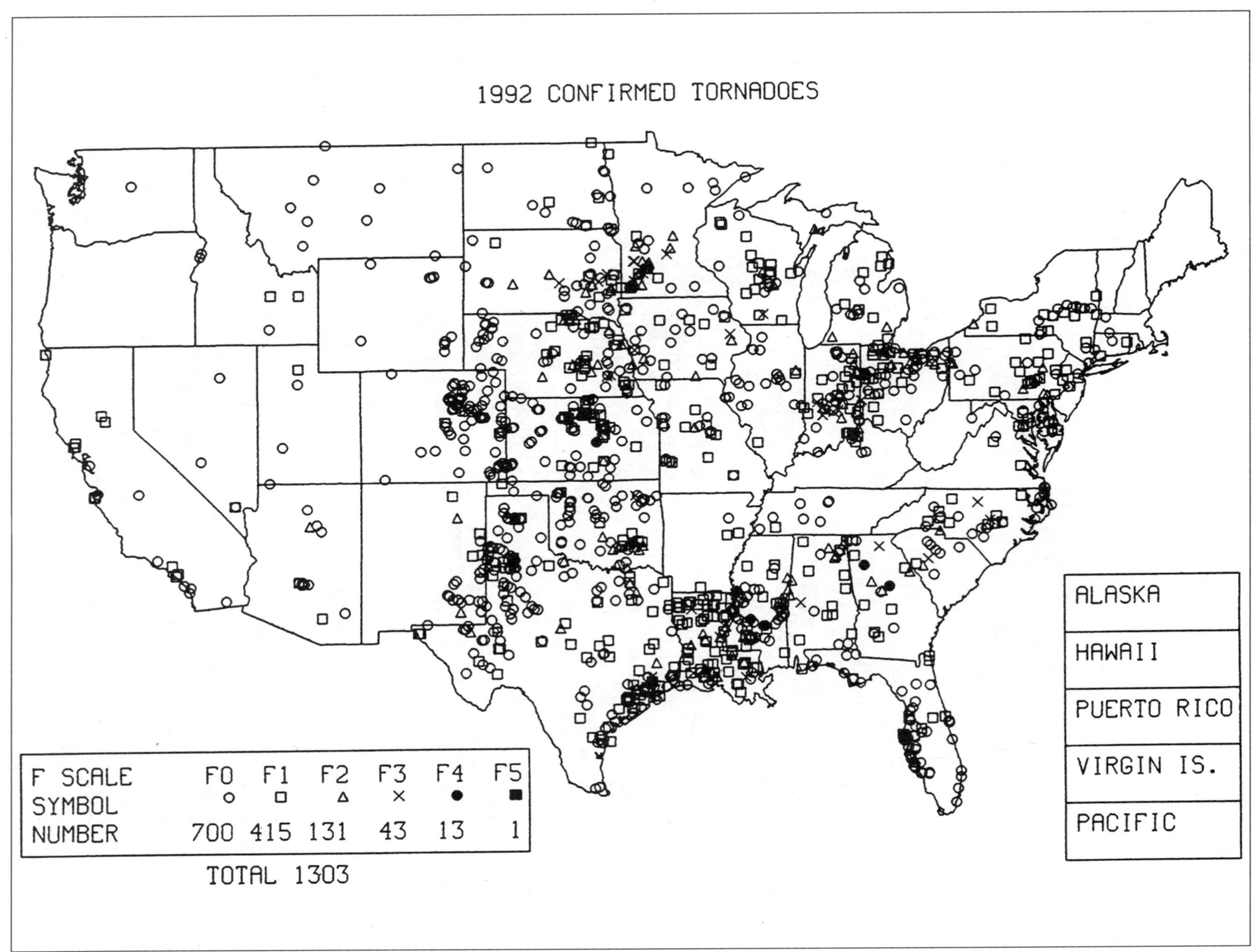
1992 CONFIRMED TORNADOES
ALASKA
HAWAII
PUERTO RICO
VIRGIN IS.
PACIFIC
F SCALE F0 F1 F2 F3 F4 F5
SYMBOL ○ □ △ × ● ■
NUMBER 700 415 131 43 13 1
TOTAL 1303

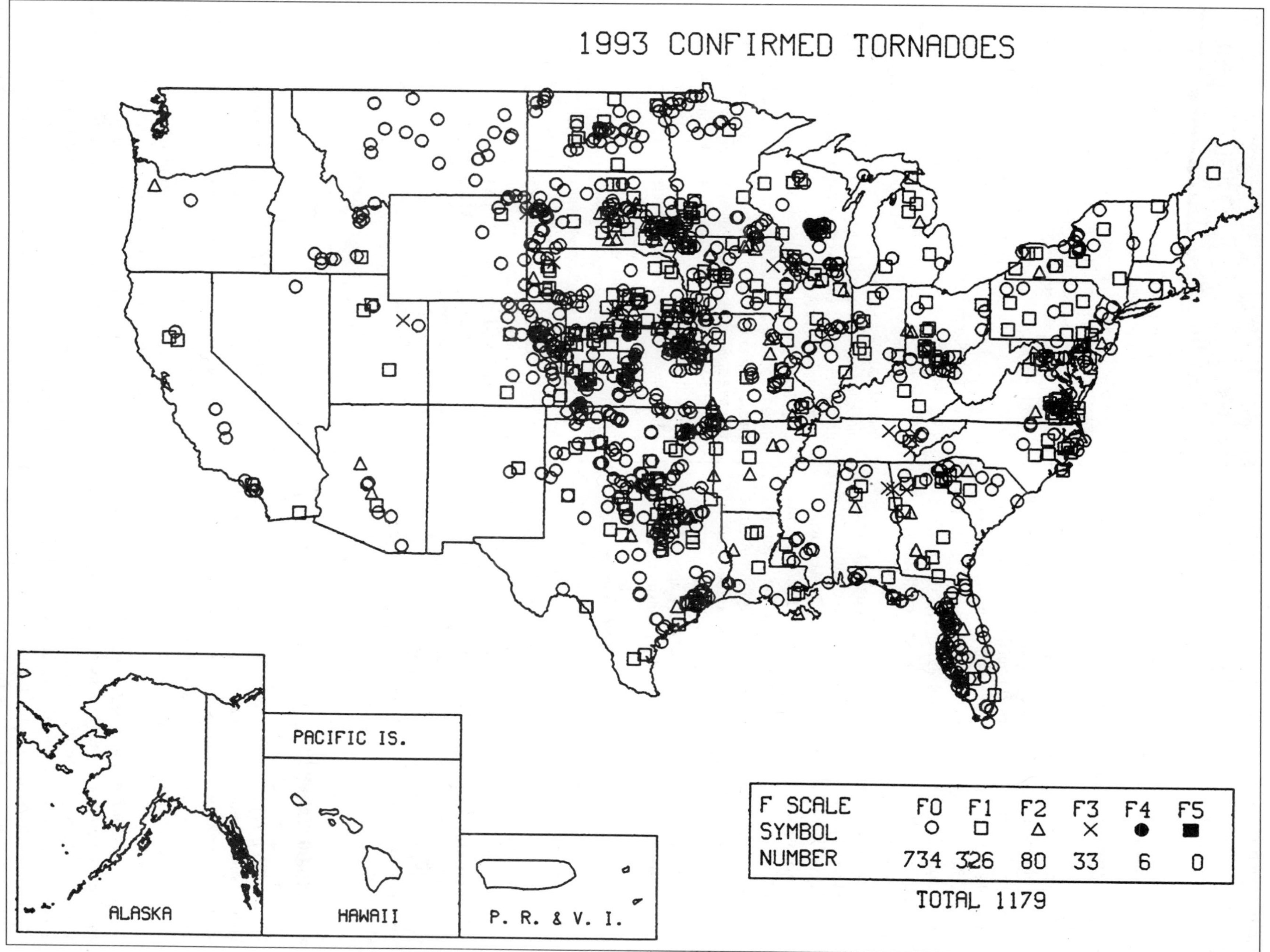
1993 CONFIRMED TORNADOES
ALASKA
PACIFIC IS.
HAWAII
P. R. & V. I.
F SCALE F0 F1 F2 F3 F4 F5
SYMBOL
NUMBER 734 326 80 33 6 0
TOTAL 1179

approximately 62 deaths per year. The average for the forty-year period 1950-89 was about 96 deaths per year. The overall decrease in tornado-related deaths can be attributed in part to improved early-warning systems.

• TORNADO DAMAGE

If there is some question as to the causes of tornadoes, there is none on the destructive effects of these violent storms. The dark funnel of a tornado can destroy solid buildings, make a deadly missile of a piece of straw, uproot large trees, and hurl people and animals for hundreds of yards. In 1931, a tornado in Minnesota carried an 83-ton railroad coach and its 117 passengers 80 feet (24.57 m) through the air, and dropped them in a ditch.

Tornadoes do their destructive work through the combined action of their strong rotary winds and the partial vacuum in the center of the vortex. As a tornado passes over a building, the winds twist and rip at the outside at the same time that the abrupt pressure reduction in the tornado's "eye" causes explosive over-pressures inside the building. Walls collapse or topple outward, windows explode, and the debris of this destruction is driven through the air in a dangerous barrage. Heavy objects like machinery and railroad cars are lifted and carried by the wind for considerable distances.

Tornadoes do their destructive work through the combined action of their strong rotary winds and the impact of windborne debris. In the most simple case, the force of the tornado's winds push the windward wall of a building inward. The roof is lifted up and the other walls fall outward. Until recently, this damage pattern led to the incorrect belief that the structure had exploded as a result of the atmospheric pressure drop associated with the tornado. Mobile homes are particularly vulnerable to strong winds and windborne debris; they should be evacuated for more substantial shelter when tornado warnings are in effect.

Constructing a Shelter

In parts of the country where tornadoes are comparatively frequent, a form of shelter is vital for protection from tornadoes. The shelter may never be needed; but during a tornado emergency, it can be worth many times the effort and cost of preparing it. One of the safest tornado shelters is an underground excavation, known as a **storm cellar**.

1. **Location**. When possible, the storm cellar should be located outside and near the residence, but not so close that failing walls or debris could block the exit. If there is a rise in the ground, the cellar may be dug into it to make use of the rise for protection. The cellar should not be connected in any way with house drains, cesspools, or sewer and gas pipes.

2. **Size**. The size of the shelter depends on the number of persons to be accommodated and the storage needs. A structure 8 feet (2.73 m) long by 6 feet (1.82 m) wide and 7 feet (2 m) high will protect eight people for a short time and provide limited storage space.

3. **Material**. Reinforced concrete is the best material for a tornado shelter. Other suitable building materials include: split logs, 2-inch (5 cm) planks (treated with creosote and covered with tar paper), cinder block, hollow tile, and brick. The roof should be covered with a 3-foot (.91 m) mound of well-pounded dirt, sloped to divert surface water. The entrance door should be of heavy construction, hinged to open inward.

4. **Drainage**. The floor should slope to a drainage outlet if the terrain permits. If not, a dry well can be dug. An outside drain is better, because it will aid ventilation.

5. **Ventilation**. A vertical ventilating shaft about 1 square foot (.09 m^2) can extend from near the floor level through the ceiling. This can be converted into an emergency escape hatch if the opening through the ceiling is made 2 feet (60.96 cm) square and the 1-foot (30.48 cm) shaft below is made easily removable. Slat gratings of heavy wood on the floor also will improve air circulation.

6. **Emergency Equipment**. A lantern and tools—crowbar, pick, shovel, hammer, pliers, screwdriver—should be stored in the cellar to ensure escape if cellar exits are blocked by debris. Stored metal tools should be greased to prevent rusting.

• TORNADO WARNINGS

Although it is not possible to predict exactly where and when severe thunderstorms and tornadoes will occur, it is possible to predict general areas where the probability of severe thunderstorm and tornado development is greatest by detecting the larger-scale events which are usually associated with such storms.

This important function is performed by the National Severe Storms Forecast Center in Kansas City, Missouri. The Kansas City facility is one of several environmental hazards centers of action operated by the National Weather Service, a major element of NOAA, the National Oceanic and Atmospheric Administration of the United States Department of Commerce.

Meteorologists at Kansas City monitor conditions in the North American atmosphere, using surface data from hundreds of points and radar summaries, satellite photographs, meteorological upper-air profile (obtained by sounding balloons), and reports from pilots. From these thousands of pieces of information, meteorologists determine the area that is most likely to experience severe thunderstorms or tornadoes. Information on this area is then issued to National Weather Service offices and the public in the form of a *watch* bulletin.

A severe thunderstorm watch or tornado watch bulletin issued by the Center usually identifies an area about 140 miles (225 km) wide by 240 miles (386 km) long. Although the watch bulletin states approximately where and for how long the severe local storm threat will exist, it does not mean that severe local storms will not occur outside the watch area or time frame—the watch is only an indication of where and when the probabilities are highest.

Watch bulletins are transmitted to all National Weather Service offices. Designated offices prepare and issue a redefining statement which specifies the affected area in terms of counties, towns, and locally well-known geographic landmarks. These messages are disseminated to the public by all possible means, and are used to guide the activities of local government, law enforcement, and emergency agencies in preparing for severe weather.

Watches are not warnings. Until a severe thunderstorm or tornado warning is issued, persons in watch areas should maintain their normal routines, but watch for threatening weather and listen to the radio or television for further severe weather information.

A severe thunderstorm warning or tornado warning bulletin is issued by a local office of the National Weather Service when a severe thunderstorm or tornado has actually been sighted in the area or indicated by radar. Warnings describe the location of the severe thunderstorm or tornado at the time of detection, the area (usually the counties) that could be affected, and the time period (usually one hour) covered by the warning. The length of this area is equal to the distance the storm is expected to travel in one hour.

When a warning is received, persons close to the storm should take cover immediately, especially in the case of a tornado warning. Persons farther away from the storm

Tornado Safety Rules

A tornado **watch** means tornadoes are expected to develop. Keep a battery-operated radio or television set nearby, and listen for weather advisories—even if the sky is blue. A tornado **warning** means a tornado has actually been sighted or indicated by weather radar. Seek inside shelter (in a storm cellar or reinforced building) and stay away from windows. Curl up so that your head and eyes are protected. Keep a battery-operated radio or television nearby, and listen for further advisories.

ON THE STREET OR IN A CAR, leave your car and take shelter in civil defense or other inside shelter areas with basements or storm cellars. Be sure to stay away from large glassed-in areas. If no building is available or if caught out in the open countryside take shelter in a ditch or ravine or lie flat on the ground upwind of your parked car. If an overpass or concrete viaduct is available then take shelter behind the concrete pilings in such a way as to put the concrete between you and approaching tornado.

IN HIGH-RISE OFFICE BUILDINGS AND LARGE APARTMENT BUILDINGS, if possible post a trained spotter or lookout on the roof with a two-way radio. Go to the lower floors or the basement. Take shelter in small interior rooms such as rest rooms, closets and utility rooms as well as interior corridors. Be sure to cover and protect the head from flying and falling debris.

IN HOMES, take shelter in the basement under sturdy items. Concrete laundry tubs, heavy duty work benches, pool tables and staircases offer the greatest safety. If there is no basement take cover under heavily-stuffed furniture in the center of the home or in a bathroom or interior closet. Open some windows on at least two different sides of the home, preferably those on the east and west side, but take shelter away from all windows. Caution: Avoid bathrooms with an outside wall on the south or west side of the home. Also do not lock yourself in a closet that has no inside latch or door handle.

IN SHOPPING CENTERS OR SHOPPING MALLS, if possible post a trained security guard or lookout on the west or south side of the complex with a two way radio. Take shelter in the basement or in shops below ground level. If there is no basement take shelter in interior hallways, small interior rooms or shops on the east or north side of the center. If only one large building or room exists then take shelter in the north end of the room. Be sure to protect your head from flying or falling debris. Caution: Avoid large open malls or walkways with glass or plastic skylights as well as large glass signs and display cases.

IN SCHOOLS, go to a storm cellar or underground shelter if available. If there is no underground shelter area move the pupils into interior hallways or small interior rooms on the lowest floor and on the east or north side of the building. Caution: Avoid auditoriums, gymnasiums, and other large rooms with long freespan roofs as well as southwest to northeast oriented corridors with exposed entrances on the south and west side of the building. Also avoid glass display cases, glassed-in stairwells and all door ways.

IN FACTORIES, post a trained spotter or lookout on the roof with a two-way radio. Workers should move to sections of the plant that are below ground level. If this is not possible then have the workers take shelter in interior corridors or in small interior rooms such as rest rooms, closets and storage rooms on the east or north side of the building. Caution: Avoid the southwest corner of the plant as well as large rooms or work areas with long freespan roofs. Stay away from all windows.

IN MOBILE HOMES, leave your trailer and take shelter in an administration building with a basement or an approved community shelter area. If no shelter is available go to a ditch or ravine on the west or south side of the trailer park and lie down flat against the ground. Make sure you protect your head from flying debris.

IN A BUS,TRUCK, OR LARGE VAN, try to move away from the storm by driving at right angles to its path. If this is not possible or if you experience strong cross winds then park the vehicle pointing into the wind, pull the hand break and unload your passengers. Open as many windows as time will allow on both sides of the vehicles then leave the vehicle and take shelter in a ditch, ravine or other depression in the ground that is upwind from your truck or bus.

should be prepared to take cover if threatening conditions are sighted.

Severe weather statements are prepared by local offices of the National Weather Service to keep the public fully informed of all current information, particularly when watch or warning bulletins are in effect. Statements are issued at least once each hour, and more frequently when the severe weather situation is changing rapidly. In this way, a close watch is kept on weather developments, and information is quickly disseminated to the counties for which the National Weather Service office has responsibility.

All-clear bulletins are issued whenever the threat of severe thunderstorms or tornadoes has ended in the area previously warned in a tornado or a severe thunderstorm warning bulletin. When a warning is canceled, but a watch continues in effect for the same area or a warning is in effect for an adjacent area, a "Severe Weather Bulletin" is issued; this qualified message is also issued when a portion, but not all, of a watch area is canceled. This permits a continuous alert in the path of the storm, with the alert being canceled as the severe weather moves through the watch area.

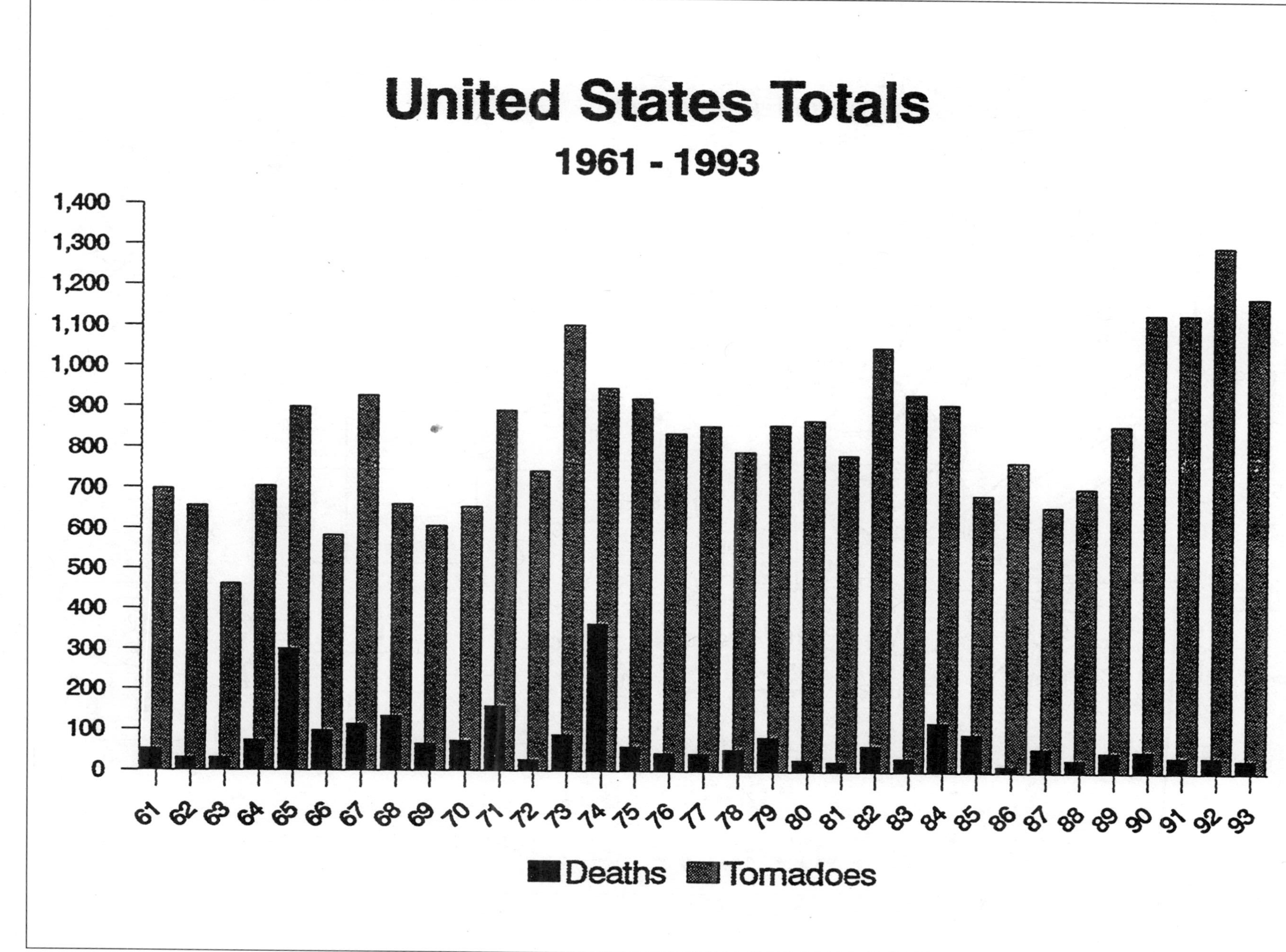
United States Totals
1961 - 1993
1,400
1,300
1,200
1,100
1,000
900
800
700
600
500
400
300
200
100
0
61
62
63
64
65
66
67
68
69
70
71
72
73
74
75
76
77
78
79
80
81
82
83
84
85
86
87
88
89
90
91
92
93
Deaths
Tornadoes

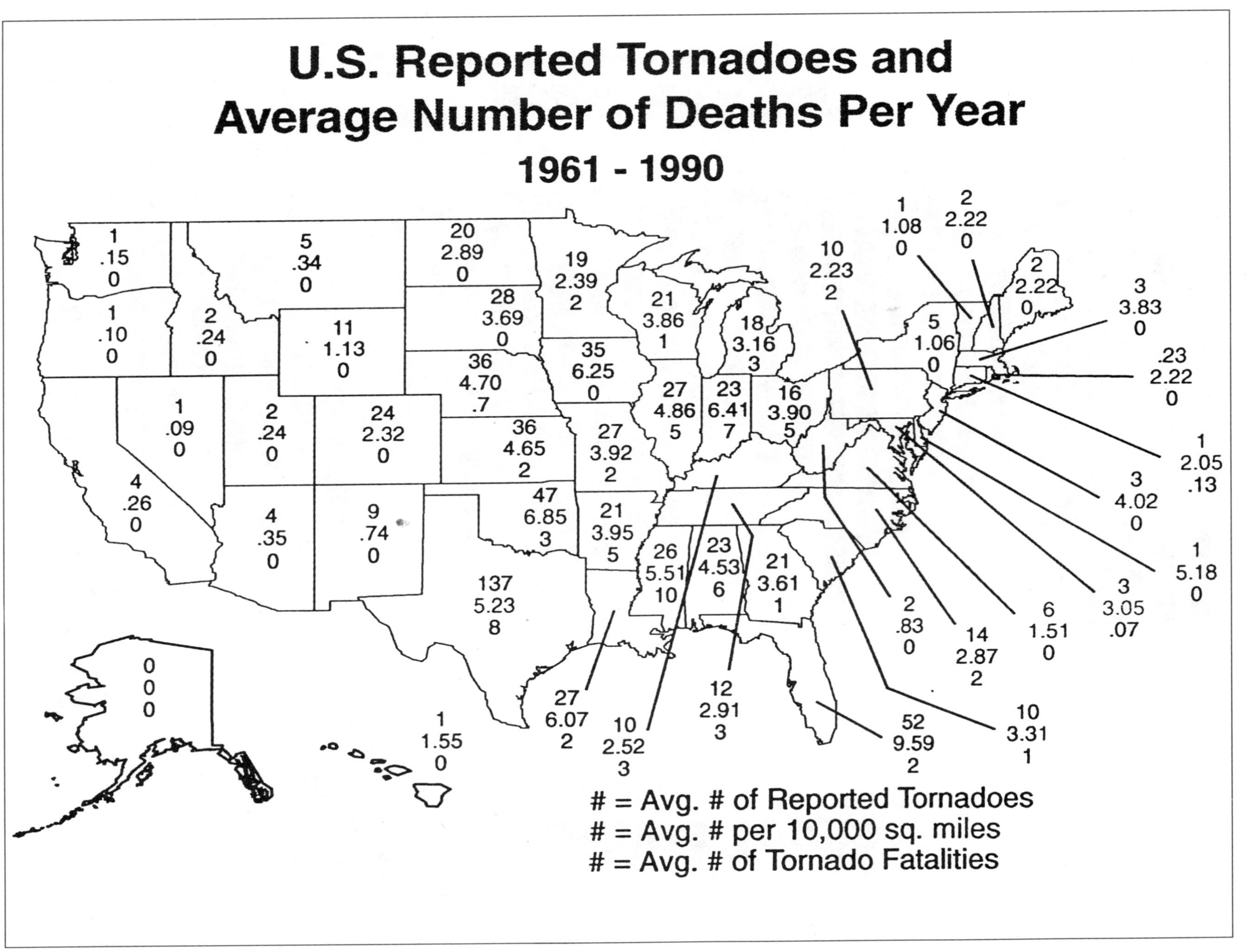
U.S. Reported Tornadoes and
Average Number of Deaths Per Year
1961 - 1990
1 .15 0
1 .10 0
5 .34 0
2 .24 0
11 1.13 0
1 .09 0
4 .26 0
2 .24 0
24 2.32 0
4 .35 0
9 .74 0
20 2.89 0
28 3.69 0
36 4.70 .7
36 4.65 2
47 6.85 3
137 5.23 8
19 2.39 2
35 6.25 0
27 3.92 2
21 3.95 5
21 3.86 1
18 3.16 3
27 4.86 5
23 6.41 7
16 3.90 5
26 5.51 10
23 4.53 6
21 3.61 1
10 2.23 2
5 1.06 0
1 1.08 0
2 2.22 0
2 2.22 0
3 3.83 0
.23 2.22 0
1 2.05 .13
3 4.02 0
1 5.18 0
3 3.05 .07
6 1.51 0
14 2.87 2
2 .83 0
10 3.31 1
52 9.59 2
12 2.91 3
10 2.52 3
27 6.07 2
0 0 0
1 1.55 0
= Avg. # of Reported Tornadoes
= Avg. # per 10,000 sq. miles
= Avg. # of Tornado Fatalities

NATIONAL TORNADOES, TORNADO DAYS, DEATHS AND RESULTING LOSSES BY YEARS, 1916-93

YEAR	NUMBER TORNADOES	TORNADO DAYS	TOTAL DEATHS	MOST DEATHS IN SINGLE TORNADO	TOTAL PROPERTY LOSSES $	PROPERTY LOSS FREQUENCY *		
						CATEGORY 5	CATEGORY 6	CATEGORY 7 AND OVER
1916	90	36	150	30	6	7	1	0
1917	121	38	551	101	7	21	9	0
1918	81	45	136	36	7	20	5	0
1919	64	35	206	59	7	10	2	0
1920	87	50	499	87	7	14	10	0
1921	105	55	202	61	7	22	3	0
1922	108	64	135	16	7	27	5	0
1923	102	59	110	23	6	21	1	0
1924	130	57	376	85	7	26	11	1
1925	119	65	794	689	7	34	2	1
1926	111	57	144	23	6	28	0	0
1927	163	62	540	92	7	42	9	1
1928	203	79	95	14	7	40	7	0
1929	197	74	274	40	7	48	4	0
1930	192	72	179	41	7	38	6	0
1931	94	57	36	6	6	14	1	0
1932	151	67	394	37	7	23	1	1
1933	258	96	362	34	7	46	9	0
1934	147	77	47	6	6	10	3	0
1935	180	77	71	11	6	29	0	0
1936	151	71	552	216	7	17	5	1
1937	147	75	29	5	6	24	0	0
1938	213	76	183	32	7	29	6	0
1939	152	75	91	27	7	21	3	0
1940	124	62	65	18	7	13	2	0
1941	118	57	53	25	6	24	1	0
1942	167	66	384	65	7	42	10	0
1943	152	61	58	5	7	28	8	0
1944	169	68	275	100	7	50	9	0
1945	121	66	210	69	7	21	10	1
1946	106	65	78	15	7	29	7	0
1947	165	78	313	169	7	46	7	1
1948	183	68	139	33	7	62	11	2
1949	249	80	211	58	7	54	13	0
1950	200	88	70	18	7	47	9	0
1951	262	113	34	6	7	35	11	2
1952	240	98	229	57	7	53	19	0
1953	421	136	515	116	8	63	18	7
1954	550	160	36	6	7	63	8	1
1955	593	152	126	80	7	74	13	1
1956	504	155	83	25	7	83	24	1
1957	856	154	192	44	8	129	26	3
1958	564	166	66	19	7	70	8	1
1959	604	156	58	21	7	70	4	1
1960	616	172	46	16	7	65	11	1
1961	697	169	51	16	7	103	21	1
1962	657	152	28	17	7	51	10	0
1963	464	141	31	5	7	77	15	1
1964	704	156	73	22	7	113	17	5
1965	906	181	299	44	8	126	30	11
1966	585	150	98	58	8	79	13	4
1967	926	173	114	33	8	125	33	8
1968	660	171	131	34	8	82	26	6
1969	608	155	66	32	8	98	16	3
1970	653	171	72	26	8	97	24	6
1971	888	192	156	58	8	71	30	5
1972	741	194	27	6	8	100	28	1
1973	1102	206	87	7	9	219	67	9
1974	947	184	361	34	9	166	82	25
1975	920	204	60	9	9	189	31	11
1976	835	169	44	5	8	145	41	5
1977	852	189	43	22	8	173	40	6
1978	788	173	53	16	9	153	53	6
1979	852	186	84	42	9	169	62	11
1980	866	176	28	5	9	201	79	13
1981	783	175	24	5	9	144	43	12
1982	1046	182	64	10	9	254	79	13
1983	931	190	34	3	9	211	85	10
1984	907	166	122	16	9	193	90	35
1985	684	168	94	18	9	114	55	14
1986	764	168	15	3	9	157	66	9
1987	656	151	59	30	8	112	32	6
1988	702	156	32	5	9	148	48	17
1989	856	160	50	21	9	133	60	18
1990	1133	181	53	29	8	215	91	18
1991	1132	179	39	13	8	194	49	15
1992	1297	195	39	12	8	212	83	25
1993	1173	186	33	7	8	186	59	13
MEAN	791	171	90	-	-	132	41	9

NOTE: - THE ABOVE ESTIMATED LOSSES ARE BASED ON VALUES AT TIME OF OCCURRENCE.
MEAN WAS DERIVED FROM DATA FOR PERIOD 1953-1993

$ STORM DAMAGES IN CATEGORIES:

5. $50,000 TO $500,000
6. $500,000 TO $5 MILLION
7. $5 MILLION TO $50 MILLION
8. $50 MILLION TO $500 MILLION
9. $500 MILLION AND OVER

* NUMBER OF TIMES PROPERTY LOSSES REPORTED IN STORM DATA IN CATEGORIES 5,6,7, AND OVER.

TORNADOES, TORNADO DAYS, AND DEATHS BY STATE AND NATION, 1953-93

STATE	TORNADOES							DAYS		DEATHS		
	TOTAL	AVERAGE	GREATEST	YEAR	LEAST	YEAR	PER # 10,000 SQ. MI.	TOTAL	AVERAGE	TOTAL	AVERAGE	PER ' 10,000 SQ. MI.
ALABAMA	849	20	45	1983+	5	1956	3.88	441	10	244	5	47
ALASKA	1	0	1	1959	0	1989+	.00	1	0	0	0	0
ARIZONA	149	3	17	1972	0	1965	.27	118	2	3	0	0
ARKANSAS	798	19	78	1982	2	1987+	3.58	371	9	165	4	31
CALIFORNIA	202	4	20	1992	0	1968+	.25	145	3	0	0	0
COLORADO	1054	25	81	1992	1	1959	2.40	555	13	2	0	0
CONNECTICUT	55	1	8	1973	0	1988+	2.00	48	1	4	0	8
DELAWARE	48	1	6	1992	0	1987+	4.86	39	0	2	0	10
DISTRICT OF COLUMBIA	0	0	0	0+	0	0+	.00	0	0	0	0	0
FLORIDA	1907	46	97	1975	10	1956	7.86	1200	29	79	1	13
GEORGIA	818	19	46	1974+	2	1987	3.23	447	10	87	2	15
HAWAII	27	0	4	1971	0	1987+	.00	23	0	0	0	0
IDAHO	112	2	11	1991+	0	1977+	.24	90	2	0	0	0
ILLINOIS	1099	26	107	1974	4	1953	4.61	509	12	177	4	31
INDIANA	863	21	49	1990	4	1984	5.79	396	9	215	5	59
IOWA	1309	31	71	1990	7	1956	5.51	563	13	60	1	11
KANSAS	1941	47	116	1991	14	1976	5.71	814	19	190	4	23
KENTUCKY	352	8	34	1974	0	1953	1.98	201	4	104	2	26
LOUISIANA	1040	25	79	1992	3	1955	5.15	583	14	101	2	21
MAINE	79	1	11	1971	0	1987+	.30	70	1	1	0	0
MARYLAND	119	2	13	1992	0	1988+	1.89	83	2	2	0	2
MASSACHUSETTS	130	3	12	1958	0	1988+	3.63	92	2	99	2	120
MICHIGAN	693	16	39	1974	2	1959	2.75	385	9	236	5	41
MINNESOTA	787	19	47	1993	5	1988+	2.26	412	10	81	1	10
MISSISSIPPI	971	23	62	1988	1	1979	4.82	469	11	364	8	76
MISSOURI	1110	27	79	1973	6	1987+	3.88	489	11	135	3	19
MONTANA	226	5	30	1991	0	1974+	.34	155	3	1	0	0
NEBRASKA	1594	38	88	1990	10	1966	4.92	716	17	51	1	7
NEVADA	46	1	8	1987	0	1985+	.09	41	1	0	0	0
NEW HAMPSHIRE	70	1	9	1963	0	1987+	1.07	61	1	0	0	0
NEW JERSEY	101	2	17	1989	0	1984+	2.55	73	1	0	0	0
NEW MEXICO	373	9	31	1991	0	1953	.74	270	6	3	0	0
NEW YORK	235	5	25	1992	0	1953	1.01	160	3	21	0	4
NORTH CAROLINA	549	13	38	1973	2	1970	2.47	324	7	81	1	15
NORTH DAKOTA	765	18	52	1976	2	1961	2.55	399	9	21	0	3
OHIO	631	15	61	1992	0	1988	3.64	311	7	171	4	41
OKLAHOMA	2170	52	107	1957	17	1988	7.44	866	21	210	5	30
OREGON	41	1	5	1991	0	1988+	.10	35	0	0	0	0
PENNSYLVANIA	408	9	33	1985+	0	1959	1.99	250	6	74	1	16
PUERTO RICO	9	0	2	1979	0	1989+	.00	8	0	0	0	0
RHODE ISLAND	7	0	3	1986	0	1988+	.00	6	0	0	0	0
SOUTH CAROLINA	379	9	23	1973	1	1986+	2.90	249	6	44	1	14
SOUTH DAKOTA	1096	26	85	1993	1	1958	3.37	495	12	8	0	1
TENNESSEE	447	10	44	1974	1	1987+	2.37	243	5	89	2	21
TEXAS	5255	128	232	1967	32	1953	4.79	1954	47	451	11	17
UTAH	75	1	6	1984+	0	1989+	.12	65	1	0	0	0
VERMONT	32	0	5	1962	0	1985+	.00	29	0	0	0	0
VIRGINIA	263	6	28	1993	1	1982+	1.47	163	3	23	0	6
VIRGIN ISLANDS	2	0	1	1979+	0	1989+	.00	2	0	0	0	0
WASHINGTON	53	1	4	1989+	0	1988+	.15	46	1	6	0	1
WEST VIRGINIA	79	1	6	1980+	0	1988+	.41	62	1	2	0	1
WISCONSIN	796	19	43	1980	3	1953	3.44	404	9	77	1	14
WYOMING	423	10	42	1977	0	1970	1.02	274	6	2	0	0
PACIFIC ISLANDS	2	0	1	1981+	0	1989+	.00	2	0	0	0	0
TOTAL: UNITED STATES	32423*	790	1297	1992	421	1953	2.19	7000&	170	3686	89	10

\+ ALSO IN EARLIER YEAR(S).
* CORRECTED FOR BOUNDARY-CROSSING TORNADOES.
& TORNADO DAYS FOR COUNTRY AS A WHOLE.

\# MEAN ANNUAL TORNADOES PER 10,000 SQUARE MILES.
' NUMBER OF DEATHS PER 10,000 SQUARE MILES.

NATION SUMMARY OF TORNADOES, TORNADO DAYS, AND DEATHS BY MONTH AND ANNUAL, 1953- 93

YEAR	JANUARY			FEBRUARY			MARCH			APRIL		
	NUMBER	DAYS	DEATHS	NUMBER	DAYS	DEATHS	NUMBER	DAYS	DEATHS	NUMBER	DAYS	DEATHS
1953	14	6	0	16	3	3	40	10	24	47	16	34
1954	2	1	0	17	9	2	63	13	10	112	22	3
1955	3	2	0	4	3	0	43	15	5	99	18	7
1956	2	2	0	47	12	8	31	7	1	85	15	67
1957	17	3	13	5	3	0	38	7	1	216	21	29
1958	12	7	0	20	5	13	15	10	0	76	19	4
1959	16	2	3	20	5	21	43	11	9	30	12	1
1960	9	4	0	28	10	0	28	10	0	70	20	7
1961	1	1	0	31	8	0	124	17	7	74	19	3
1962	12	3	1	25	7	0	37	9	17	41	8	1
1963	15	5	1	6	3	0	48	12	8	84	14	16
1964	14	3	10	2	2	0	36	11	6	157	23	15
1965	21	11	0	32	4	0	34	9	2	129	20	267
1966	1	1	0	28	5	0	12	6	58	80	20	12
1967	39	4	7	8	5	0	42	14	3	149	18	73
1968	5	3	0	7	3	0	28	8	0	102	15	40
1969	3	1	32	5	5	0	8	2	1	68	15	2
1970	9	5	0	16	3	0	25	12	2	117	16	29
1971	18	7	1	83	12	131	40	13	2	75	14	11
1972	33	10	5	7	4	0	69	17	0	96	20	16
1973	33	7	1	10	4	0	80	16	17	150	22	10
1974	24	8	2	23	9	0	36	12	1	269	22	313
1975	52	7	12	45	12	7	84	16	12	108	20	13
1976	12	5	0	37	6	5	180	18	21	113	23	1
1977	5	4	0	17	3	2	64	15	0	88	15	26
1978	23	7	2	6	3	0	17	8	0	107	17	4
1979	16	9	0	4	3	0	53	13	1	120	17	58
1980	5	4	0	11	9	0	41	15	2	137	16	4
1981	3	3	0	25	5	2	33	13	1	84	18	13
1982	18	8	1	3	2	0	60	15	6	150	20	30
1983	13	2	2	41	7	1	71	21	0	65	15	6
1984	1	1	0	27	4	0	73	15	64	176	22	33
1985	2	2	0	7	4	0	38	12	2	134	19	5
1986	0	0	0	30	11	2	75	9	6	84	17	2
1987	6	3	0	19	4	6	38	11	1	20	8	1
1988	17	3	5	4	3	0	28	10	1	58	16	4
1989	15	6	0	18	3	0	44	14	1	82	13	0
1990	11	7	0	57	10	1	88	8	3	108	17	0
1991	29	6	1	11	5	0	159	16	13	206	20	21
1992	15	6	0	29	9	0	55	17	5	53	11	0
1993	17	8	0	34	7	3	49	11	5	85	15	10
POR	563	187	99	865	234	207	2170	498	318	4304	708	1191
MEAN	14	5	2	21	6	5	53	12	8	105	17	29

YEAR	MAY			JUNE			JULY			AUGUST		
	NUMBER	DAYS	DEATHS	NUMBER	DAYS	DEATHS	NUMBER	DAYS	DEATHS	NUMBER	DAYS	DEATHS
1953	94	21	161	111	24	244	31	19	0	24	15	0
1954	101	22	9	107	26	5	45	23	0	49	21	1
1955	147	26	103	154	28	2	49	21	5	33	18	0
1956	79	24	4	65	21	0	91	26	1	43	20	2
1957	227	26	87	147	25	14	55	19	0	20	14	0
1958	68	21	0	127	27	42	121	30	1	46	20	1
1959	226	28	8	73	25	2	63	24	0	38	18	0
1960	201	26	34	124	27	3	43	22	0	47	23	1
1961	137	25	23	107	23	2	77	27	0	27	16	0
1962	200	22	3	171	29	0	78	26	0	51	21	6
1963	71	21	1	91	23	0	62	26	0	26	13	2
1964	135	20	16	136	24	0	63	23	0	79	23	2
1965	275	25	17	147	28	6	86	26	0	61	23	1
1966	98	17	0	126	28	19	100	27	3	58	21	0
1967	116	25	3	210	28	6	90	25	1	28	16	2
1968	145	26	72	136	27	11	56	22	2	66	23	2
1969	145	25	4	137	28	7	99	27	0	69	21	19
1970	88	19	26	134	24	6	81	26	3	55	21	0
1971	166	24	7	199	28	1	100	30	1	50	21	0
1972	140	27	0	114	25	2	115	29	0	59	23	2
1973	250	26	35	224	26	2	80	26	0	51	23	4
1974	144	28	10	194	26	31	59	19	0	107	26	0
1975	188	30	5	196	28	6	79	26	2	60	25	2
1976	155	24	8	169	26	3	84	28	2	38	18	1
1977	228	29	4	132	27	0	99	27	1	82	26	6
1978	213	27	7	148	28	17	143	30	11	65	24	1
1979	112	23	2	150	24	8	132	30	1	127	27	5
1980	203	25	8	217	30	7	95	26	5	73	27	0
1981	187	24	0	223	29	8	98	27	0	64	22	0
1982	327	28	14	198	30	4	95	29	0	34	15	0
1983	249	26	14	178	27	2	99	27	4	76	21	0
1984	169	27	6	242	25	14	72	21	0	47	20	0
1985	182	28	78	82	24	3	51	19	0	108	26	3
1986	173	25	1	134	25	0	88	24	3	67	23	1
1987	126	25	31	132	29	2	163	28	0	63	24	1
1988	132	24	3	63	21	0	103	23	0	61	13	3
1989	234	28	9	253	27	5	59	19	0	36	20	0
1990	243	27	5	335	28	11	106	26	0	60	22	29
1991	335	30	0	216	30	1	65	22	1	46	17	0
1992	137	21	0	400	29	1	214	30	0	115	22	3
1993	179	26	2	316	27	1	242	31	0	112	26	6
POR	7025	1021	820	6818	1084	498	3731	1036	47	2421	858	106
MEAN	171	25	20	166	26	12	91	25	1	59	21	3

YEAR	SEPTEMBER			OCTOBER			NOVEMBER			DECEMBER			ANNUAL		
	NUMBER	DAYS	DEATHS	NUMBER	DAYS	DEATHS	NUMBER	DAYS	DEATHS	NUMBER	DAYS	DEATHS	NUMBER	DAYS	DEATHS
1953	5	4	0	6	4	0	12	6	0	21	8	49	421	136	515
1954	21	10	3	14	8	2	2	2	0	17	3	1	550	160	36
1955	15	8	2	23	7	1	20	4	1	3	2	0	593	152	126
1956	16	10	0	29	8	0	7	6	0	9	4	0	504	155	83
1957	17	10	2	18	11	2	58	11	25	38	4	19	856	154	192
1958	24	14	1	9	6	4	45	6	0	1	1	0	564	166	66
1959	58	15	14	24	10	0	11	4	0	2	2	0	604	156	58
1960	22	13	0	18	10	1	25	6	0	1	1	0	616	172	46
1961	53	16	15	14	5	0	36	7	1	16	5	0	697	169	51
1962	24	11	0	11	10	0	5	4	0	2	2	0	657	152	28
1963	33	13	3	13	5	0	15	6	0	0	0	0	464	141	31
1964	25	10	0	22	4	22	17	8	0	18	5	2	704	156	73
1965	64	21	0	16	4	1	34	6	5	7	4	0	906	181	299
1966	22	13	0	29	6	6	20	3	0	11	3	0	585	150	98
1967	139	16	5	36	7	4	8	5	0	61	10	10	926	173	114
1968	25	14	0	14	9	0	44	12	3	32	9	1	660	171	131
1969	20	11	0	26	10	0	5	3	0	23	7	1	608	155	66
1970	54	20	0	50	13	6	10	4	0	14	8	0	653	171	72
1971	47	15	0	38	12	0	16	7	0	56	9	2	888	192	156
1972	49	19	0	34	10	0	17	4	2	8	6	0	741	194	27
1973	69	22	3	25	11	0	81	11	12	49	12	3	1102	206	87
1974	25	11	0	45	10	4	13	8	0	8	5	0	947	184	361
1975	34	17	0	12	7	0	40	8	0	22	8	1	920	204	60
1976	35	15	3	11	5	0	0	0	0	1	1	0	835	169	44
1977	65	21	1	25	5	1	24	10	0	23	7	2	852	189	43
1978	20	10	6	7	5	0	9	5	0	30	9	5	788	173	53
1979	68	19	2	47	12	7	21	8	0	2	1	0	852	186	84
1980	37	14	1	43	7	1	3	2	0	1	1	0	866	176	28
1981	26	16	0	32	12	0	7	5	0	1	1	0	783	175	24
1982	38	12	2	9	4	0	19	6	0	95	13	7	1046	182	64
1983	20	15	0	12	5	0	49	11	0	58	13	5	931	190	34
1984	17	12	0	49	12	4	30	5	1	4	2	0	907	166	122
1985	40	16	0	18	8	0	19	8	3	3	2	0	684	168	94
1986	65	17	0	26	7	0	17	8	0	5	2	0	764	168	15
1987	19	10	0	1	1	0	55	5	11	14	3	6	656	151	59
1988	76	16	1	19	8	0	121	13	14	20	6	1	702	156	32
1989	31	12	0	30	7	4	58	10	31	3	1	0	856	160	50
1990	45	15	0	35	9	2	18	5	0	35	7	2	1133	181	53
1991	26	16	0	22	9	0	20	5	2	3	3	0	1132	179	39
1992	81	17	0	34	10	4	149	14	26	20	9	0	1297	195	39
1993	65	17	2	55	9	4	19	6	0	6	3	0	1173	186	33
POR	1635	583	66	1001	322	80	1179	267	137	743	202	117	32423	7000	3686
MEAN	40	14	2	24	8	2	29	7	3	18	5	3	791	171	90

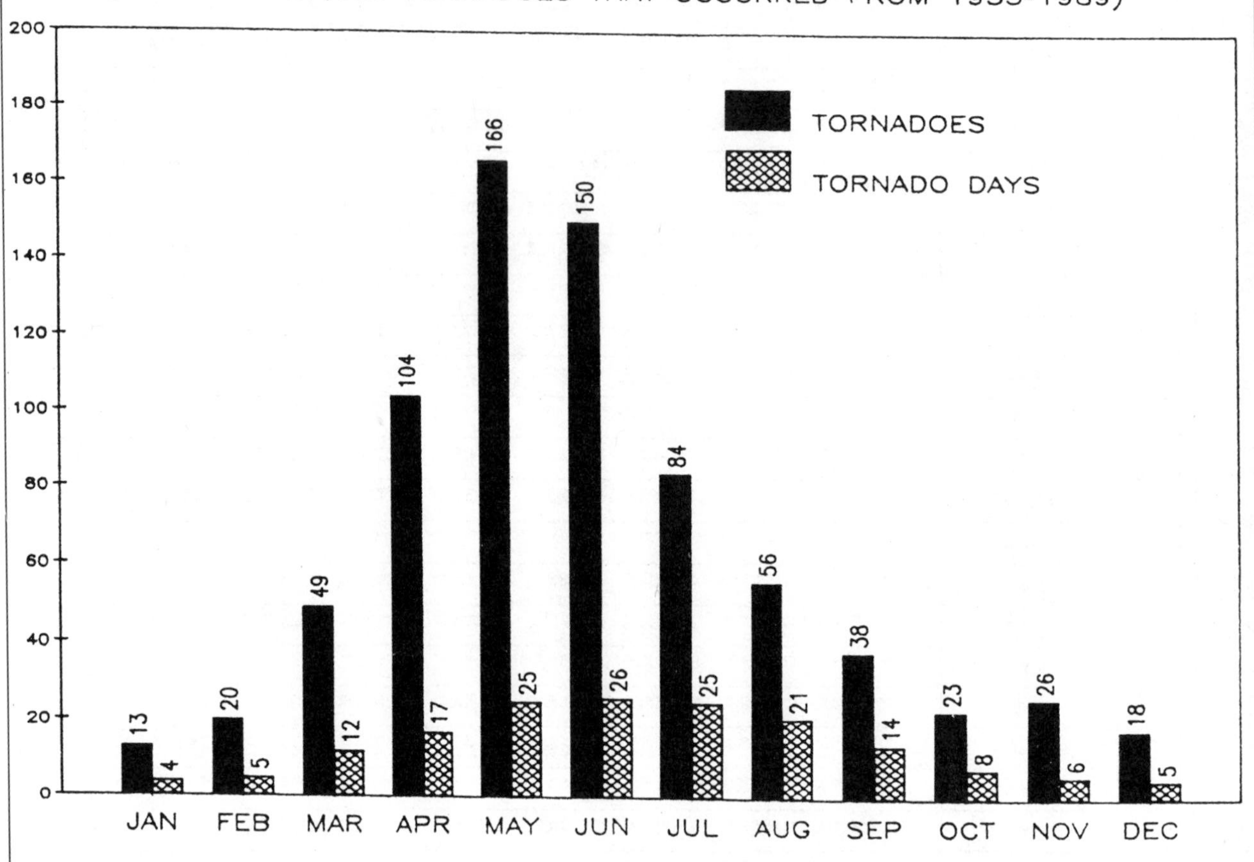
AVERAGE NUMBER OF TORNADOES AND TORNADO DAYS
EACH MONTH IN THE UNITED STATES
(BASED ON 27,688 TORNADOES THAT OCCURRED FROM 1953-1989)
TORNADOES
TORNADO DAYS
200
180
160
140
120
100
80
60
40
20
0
JAN 13 4
FEB 20 5
MAR 49 12
APR 104 17
MAY 166 25
JUN 150 26
JUL 84 25
AUG 56 21
SEP 38 14
OCT 23 8
NOV 26 6
DEC 18 5

Thunderstorms

It is estimated that at any given moment, some 1,800 thunderstorms are in progress over Earth's surface. The frequency with which these giant generators of local weather occur, the quantity of energy they release, and the variety of forms this energy may take, make thunderstorms great destroyers of life and property. For a single household, a single family, they can produce as much tragedy as a war.

• HOW THUNDERSTORMS DEVELOP

Thunderstorms are generated by thermal instability in the atmosphere, and represent a violent example of convection—the vertical circulation produced in a fluid made thermally unstable by the local addition or subtraction of heat and the conversion of potential to kinetic energy. The convective overturning of atmospheric layers that sets up a thunderstorm is dynamically similar to convective circulations observed in the laboratory, where distinct patterns are generated in liquids by unequal heating.

The orderly circulations produced in the laboratory are rarely encountered in the atmosphere, where areas corresponding to the rising core of laboratory convective cells are marked by cumulus and cumulonimbus clouds. Clouds are parcels of air that have been lifted high enough to condense the water vapor they contain into very small, visible particles. These particles are too small and light to fall out as rain. As the lifting process continues, these particles grow in size, by collision and coalescence until they are large

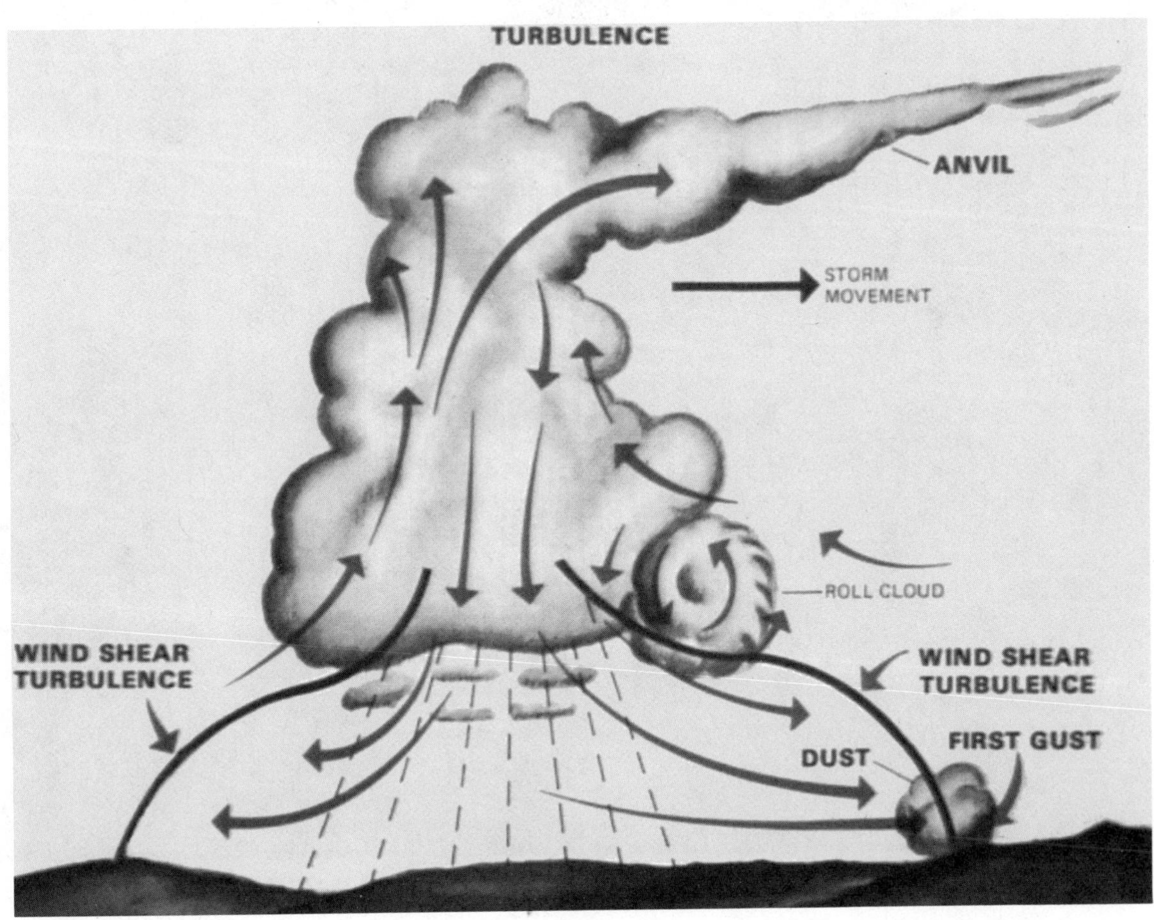

Classic cumulonimbus with anvil.

enough to fall against the updrafts associated with any developing convective clouds. Cumulus (for accumulation) clouds begin their towering movement in response to atmospheric instability and convective overturning. Warmer and lighter than the surrounding air, they rise rapidly around a strong, central updraft. These elements grow vertically, appearing as rising mounds, domes, or towers.

The atmospheric instability in which thunderstorms begin may develop in several ways. Radiational cooling of cloud tops, heating of the cloud base from the ground, and frontal effects may produce an unstable condition. This is compensated in air, as in most fluids, by the convective overturning of layers to put denser layers below less dense layers.

Mechanical processes are also at work. Warm, buoyant air may be forced upward by the wedge-like undercutting of a cold air mass, or lifted by a mountain slope. Convergence of horizontal winds into the center of a low-pressure area forces warm air near that center upward. Where these processes are sustained, and where lifting and cooling of the moist air continues, minor turbulence may generate a cumulus cloud, and then a towering cumulonimbus system.

The history of the vertical movement of air in the center of the cumulus or cumulonimbus cloud system is the history of each convective cell. Most thunderstorms have, at maturity, a series of several cells, each following a life cycle characterized by changes in wind direction, development of precipitation and electrical charge, and other factors.

In the first stage of thunderstorm development, an updraft drives warm air up beyond condensation levels, where clouds form, and where continued upward movement produces cumulus formations. The updraft develops in a region of gently converging surface winds in which the atmospheric pressure is slightly lower than in surrounding areas. As the updraft continues, air flows in through the cloud's sides in a process called entrainment, mixing with and feeding the updraft. The updraft may be further augmented by a chimney effect produced by high winds at altitude.

Heat energy from water

But a developing thunderstorm also feeds on another source of energy. Once the cloud has formed, the phase changes of water result in a release of heat energy, which increases the momentum of the storm's vertical development. The rate at which this energy is released is directly related to the amount of gaseous water vapor converted to liquid water.

As water vapor in the burgeoning cloud is raised to saturation levels, the air is cooled sufficiently to liberate solid and liquid particles of water, and rain and snow begin to fall

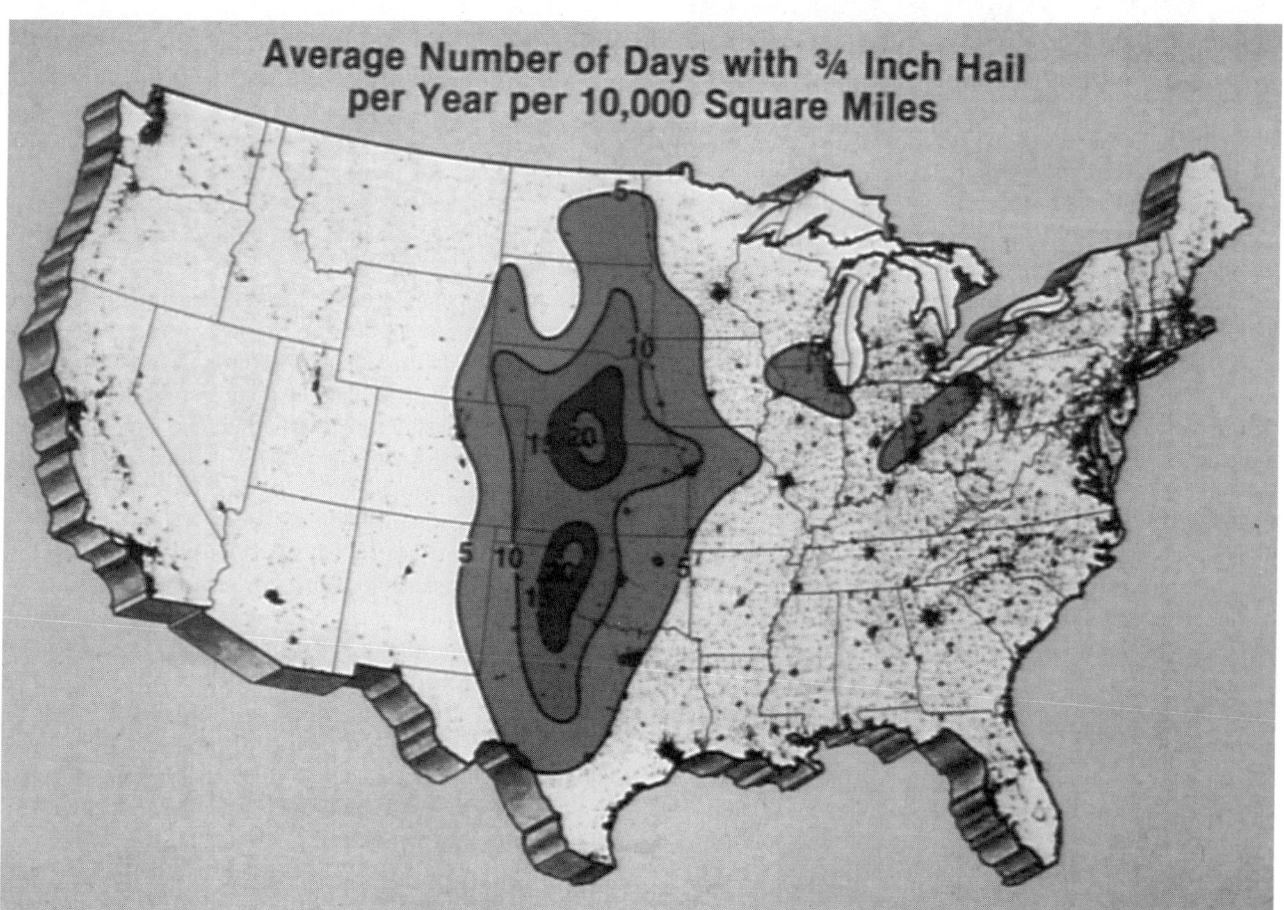

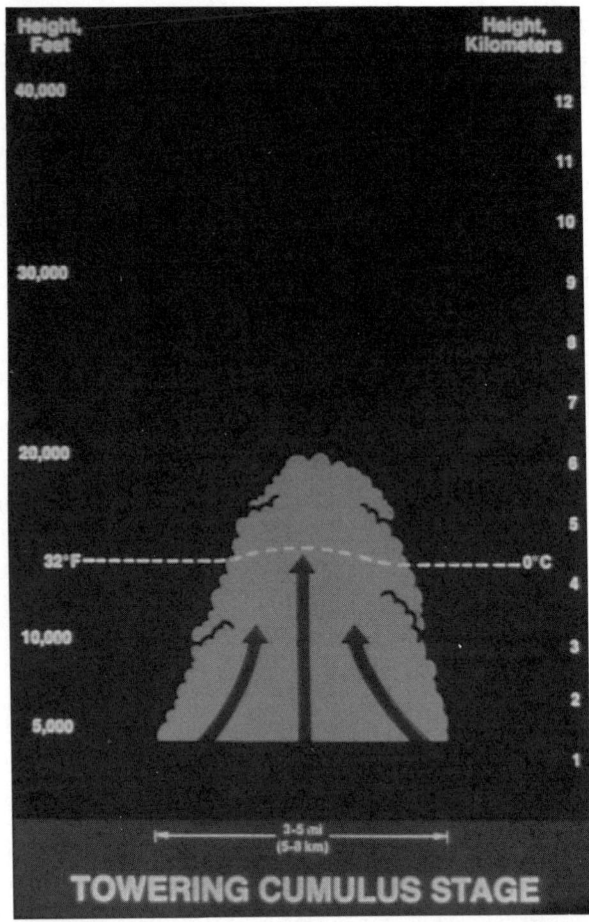

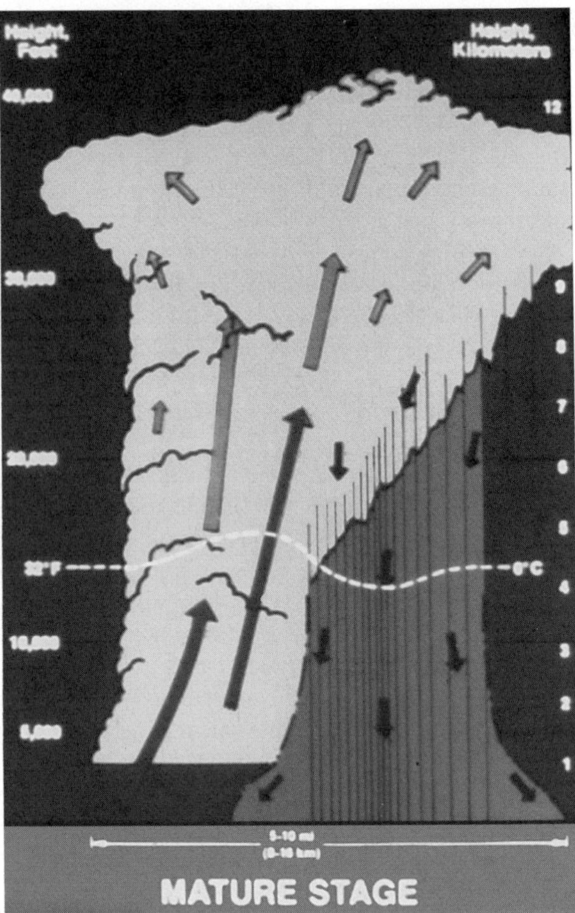

within the cloud. The cloud tower rises beyond the level 1.8-3.1 miles (3-5 km) where fibrous streamers of frozen precipitation elements appear; this apparent ice phase is thought to be a condition of thunderstorm precipitation. The formation and precipitation of particles large enough and in sufficient quantity to fall against the updraft marks the beginning of the second, mature state of the thunderstorm cell.

A thunderstorm's mature stage is marked by a transition in wind direction within the storm cells. The prevailing updraft which initiated the cloud's growth is joined by a downdraft generated by precipitation. The downdraft is fed and strengthened, as the updraft was, by the addition of entrained air, and by evaporational cooling caused by interactions of entrained air and falling precipitation. The mature storm dominates the electrical field and atmospheric circulation for several miles around. Lightning—the discharge of electricity between large charges of opposite sign—occurs soon after precipitation begins, a clue to the relationship of thunderstorm electrification and formation of ice crystals and raindrops.

At maturity, the thunderstorm cloud is several miles across its base and may tower to altitudes of 40,000 feet (12,133 m) or more. The swift winds of the upper troposphere shred the cloud top into the familiar anvil form, visible in dry regions as lonely giants, or as part of a squall line.

On the ground directly beneath the storm system, the mature stage is initially felt as rain, which is soon joined by the strong downdraft. The downdraft spreads out from the cloud in gusting, divergent winds, and brings a marked drop in temperature. Even where the rain has not reached the ground, the thunderstorm's mature stage can be recognized by this cold air stream flowing over the surface. This is nature's warning that the thunderstorm is in its most violent phase. It is in this phase that the thunderstorm unleashes its lightning, hail, heavy rain, high wind, and—most destructive of all—the tornado. But even as it enters maturity, the storm has begun to die. The violent downdraft initially shares the circulation with the sustaining updraft, then strangles it. As the updraft is cut off from its converging low level winds, the storm loses its source of moisture and heat energy. Precipitation weakens, stops, and the cold downdraft ceases. And the thunderstorm, violent creature of an instant, spreads and dies.

Dust storms

Dust storms associated with thunderstorms are common in the southwestern United States in the summer months (June through September) and are found generally in the desert areas of western New Mexico, southern Arizona and in the southeastern deserts of California. Dust storms de-

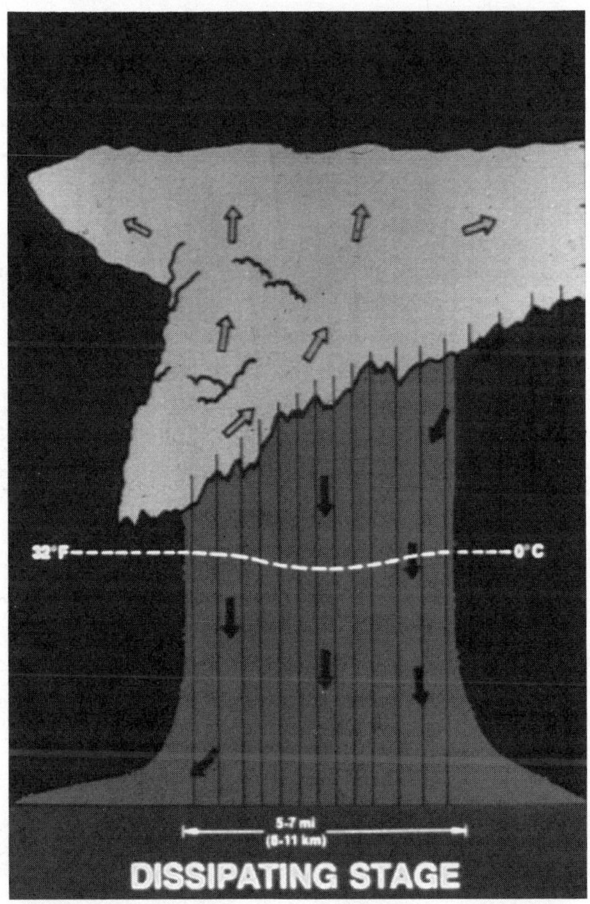

velop due to the cool downdrafts of a thundershower that reach the ground and spread out in all directions picking up dust along the way. Dust storms associated with late winter and early spring storm systems are common during March and April.

Thunderstorm Safety Rules

1. KEEP AN EYE ON THE WEATHER DURING WARM PERIODS AND DURING THE PASSAGE OF COLD FRONTS. When cumulus clouds begin building up and darkening, you are probably in for a thunderstorm. Check the latest weather forecast.

2. KEEP CALM. Thunderstorms are usually of short duration; even squall lines pass in a matter of a few hours. Be cautious, but don't be afraid. Stay indoors and keep informed.

3. KNOW WHAT THE STORM IS DOING. Remember that the mature stage may be marked on the ground by a sudden reversal of wind direction, a noticeable rise in wind speed, and a sharp drop in temperature. Heavy rain, hail, tornadoes, and lightning generally occur only in the mature state of the thunderstorm.

4. CONDITIONS MAY FAVOR TORNADO FORMATION. Tune in your radio or television receiver to determine whether there is a tornado watch or tornado warning out for your area. A tornado watch means tornado formation is likely in the area covered by the watch. A tornado warning means one has been sighted or radar-indicated in your area. If you receive a tornado warning, seek inside shelter in a storm cellar, below ground level, or in reinforced concrete structures; stay away from windows.

5. LIGHTNING IS THE THUNDERSTORM'S WORST KILLER. Stay indoors and away from electrical appliances while the storm is overhead. If lightning catches you outside, remember that it seeks the easiest—not necessarily the shortest—distance between positive and negative centers. Keep yourself lower than the nearest highly conductive object, and maintain a safe distance from it. If the object is a tree, twice its height is considered a safe distance.

6. THUNDERSTORM RAIN MAY PRODUCE FLASH FLOODS. Stay out of dry creek beds during thunderstorms. If you live along a river, listen for flash flood warnings from the National Weather Service.

• LIGHTNING

It is estimated that lightning strikes Earth 100 times each second. The average annual death toll for lightning is greater than for tornadoes or hurricanes.

According to data assembled by the National Center for Health Statistics, lightning kills about 150 Americans per year and injures about 250. Property loss—fire and other damage to structures, aircraft damage, livestock deaths and injuries, forest fires, disruption of electromagnetic transmissions, and other effects—is estimated at more than $100 million annually.

What causes lightning?

Lightning is a secondary effect of electrification within a thunderstorm cloud system. Updrafts of warm, moist air rising into cold air can cause small cumulus clouds to grow into the large cumulonimbus cloud systems we associate with thunderstorms. These turbulent cloud systems tower about their companions, and dominate the atmospheric circulation and electrical field over a wide area. The transition from a small cloud to a turbulent, electrified giant can occur in as little as 30 minutes.

As a thunderstorm cumulonimbus develops, interactions of charged particles, external and internal electrical fields, and complex energy exchanges produce a large electrical field within the cloud. No completely acceptable theory explaining the complex processes of thunderstorm electrification has yet been advanced. But it is believed that electrical charge is important to formation of raindrops and ice crystals, and that thunderstorm electrification closely follows precipitation.

Dust Storm Precautions for Motorists

Dust storms so common to the southwestern United States can wreak havoc for motorists traveling in the area. The sudden dark brown cloud with strong winds and debris is often to blame for tragic, chain-reaction accidents.

If a dust storm *does* develop, motorists should observe the following:

- Pull off to the furthest edge of the shoulder, turn off lights and set emergency brake.
- If conditions prevent pulling off the roadway, a motorist should proceed at an appropriately reduced speed, turn lights on, and use the center line as a guide. A motorist should never stop on the roadway.

The distribution of electricity in a thunderstorm cloud is usually a concentration of positive charge in the frozen upper layers, and a large negative charge around a positive area in the lower portions of the cloud.

Earth is normally negatively charged with respect to the atmosphere. As the thunderstorm passes over the ground, the negative charge in the base of the cloud induces a positive charge on the ground below and several miles around the storm. The ground charge follows the storm like an electrical shadow, growing stronger as the negative cloud charge increases. The attraction between positive and negative charges makes the positive ground current flow up buildings, trees, and other elevated objects in an effort to establish a flow of current. But air, which is a poor conductor of electricity, insulates the cloud and ground charges, preventing a flow of current until large electrical charges are built up.

Lightning occurs when the difference between the positive and negative charges—the electrical potential—becomes great enough to overcome the resistance of the insulating air, and to force a conductive path for current to flow between the two charges. Potential in these cases can be as much as 100 million volts. Lightning strokes represent a flow of current from negative to positive (in most cases), and may proceed from cloud to cloud, cloud to ground, or, where high structures are involved, from ground to cloud.

The typical cloud-to-ground stroke we see most frequently begins as a pilot leader, too faint to be visible, advances downward from the cloud, and sets up the initial portion of the stroke path. A surge of current called a step leader follows the pilot, moving 100 feet (30 m) or more at

It is estimated that lightning strikes Earth 100 times each second.

Electricity in the air can cause hair to stand on end.

Minutes after she left, lightning struck the spot where she was standing.

a time toward the ground, pausing, then repeating the sequence until the conductive path of electrified (ionized) particles is near the ground. There, discharge streamers extending from the ground intercept the leader path and complete the conductive channel between ground and cloud charges. When this path is complete, a return stroke leaps upward at speeds approaching that of light, illuminating the branches of the descending leader track. Because these tracks point downward, the stroke appears to come from the cloud. The bright light of the return stroke is the result of glowing atoms and molecules of air energized by the stroke.

Once the channel has been established and the return stroke has ended, dart leaders from the cloud initiate secondary returns, until the opposing charges are dissipated or the channel is gradually broken up by air movement. Even when luminous lightning is not visible, current may continue to flow along the ionized channel set up by the initial step leader.

Ground-to-cloud discharges are less frequently observed than the familiar cloud-to-ground stroke. In these cases, step leaders generally proceed from a tall conductive or semiconductive structure to the clouds; the initial leader stroke is not followed by a return stroke from the cloud, possibly because charges are less mobile in the cloud than in the highly conducting earth. Once the conductive path is established, however, current flow may set up cloud-to-ground sequences of dart leaders and returns.

Types of lightning

Lightning comes in many forms. *Streak lightning*, a single or multiple line from cloud to ground, is the form seen most frequently. *Forked lightning* shows the conductive channel. *Sheet lightning* is a shapeless flash covering a broad area, often seen in cloud-to-cloud discharges. *Heat lightning* is seen along the horizon during hot weather, and is believed to be the reflection of lightning occurring beyond the horizon. *Ribbon lightning* is streak lightning whose conductive channel is moved by high winds, making successive strokes seem to parallel one another. *Beaded lightning* appears as an interrupted stroke.

Ball lightning is in some ways the most interesting—and most controversial—form. As reported, ball lightning appears as a luminous globe, toroid (doughnut-shape), or ellipsoid which hisses as it hurtles from cloud to earth, maneuvers at high speeds, rolls along structures, or hangs suspended in the air.

The dual character of lightning—it is a carrier of high currents and produces destructive thermal effects—makes it doubly dangerous. The current peaks, which may reach magnitudes of 200,000 amperes or more, produce forces which have a crushing effect upon conductors, and which can build to explosive levels in non-conducting or semiconducting materials like wood or brick. The continuous current produces heat, and is responsible for the numerous fires attributed to lightning.

Work on the lightning problem

At NOAA, the National Oceanic and Atmospheric Administration of the United States Department of Commerce, lightning is the subject of considerable scientific interest. The severe storm warnings of NOAA's National Weather Service carry implicit alerts that lightning can be expected—and avoided. Commerce Department scientists at NOAA's Environmental Research Laboratories are experimenting with lightning suppression techniques, measuring atmospheric electricity over the open ocean, and studying the apparent but elusive connections between lightning and other events in the atmosphere, ionosphere, earth, and geomagnetic field.

• THUNDER

Thunder is the crash and rumble associated with lightning, and is caused by explosive expansion of air heated by the stroke. When lightning is close by, the thunder is a sharp explosive sound. More distant strokes produce the familiar growl and rumble of thunder, a result of sound being refracted and modified by the turbulent environment of a thunderstorm. Because the speed of light is about a million times that of sound, the distance (in miles) to a lightning's stroke can be estimated by counting the number of seconds between lightning and thunder, and dividing by five.

The electromagnetic impulses of a lightning stroke produce whistlers—gliding tones which travel along lines of force in Earth's magnetic field from their lightning source in one hemisphere to a similar point in the opposite hemisphere, often echoing back and forth several times. Their sound is something like the whistle of World War II bombs, occasionally modified in a way that produces musical variations.

Lightning Safety Rules

1. Stay indoors, and don't venture outside, unless absolutely necessary.

2. Stay away from open doors and windows, fireplaces, radiators, stoves, metal pipes, sinks, and plug-in electrical appliances.

3. Don't use plug-in electrical equipment such as hair dryers, electric tooth brushes, or electric razors during the storm.

4. Don't use the telephone during the storm—lightning may strike telephone lines outside.

5. Don't take laundry off the clothesline during the storm.

6. Don't work on fences, telephone or power lines, pipelines, or structural steel fabrication.

7. Don't use metal objects like fishing rods and golf clubs. Golfers wearing cleated shoes are particularly good lightning rods.

8. Don't handle flammable materials in open containers.

9. Stop tractor work, especially when the tractor is pulling metal equipment, and dismount. Tractors and other implements in metallic contact with the ground are often struck by lightning.

10. Get off the water and out of small boats.

11. Stay in your automobile if you are traveling. Automobiles offer excellent lightning protection.

12. Seek shelter in buildings. If no buildings are available, your best protection is a cave, ditch, canyon, or under extremely high clumps of trees in open forest glades.

13. When there is no shelter, avoid the highest object in the area. If only isolated trees are nearby, your best protection is to crouch in the open, keeping twice as far away from isolated trees as the trees can act as lightning rods.

14. Avoid hill tops, open spaces, wire fences, metal clothes lines, exposed sheds, and any electrically conductive elevated objects.

15. When you feel the electrical charge—if your hair stands on end or your skin tingles—lightning may be about to strike you. Drop to the ground immediately.

Persons struck by lightning receive a severe electrical shock and may be burned, but they carry no electrical charge and can be handled safely. A person "killed" by lightning can often be revived by prompt mouth-to-mouth resuscitation, cardiac massage, and prolonged artificial respiration. In a group struck by lightning, the apparently dead should be treated first; those who show vital signs will probably recover spontaneously, although burns and other injuries may require treatment. Recovery from lightning strikes is usually complete except for possible impairment or loss of sight or hearing.

LIGHTNING INJURIES BY STATE, RANK, AND LOCATION OF OCCURRENCE

		1959-1993														1993													
	RANK	OPEN FIELDS, BALL PARKS, AND OPEN SPACES		UNDER TREES		BOATING, FISHING AND WATER RELATED		NEAR TRACTORS HEAVY ROAD EQUIPMENT		GOLF COURSES		AT TELEPHONES		VARIOUS OTHER AND UNKNOWN LOCATIONS		OPEN FIELDS, BALL PARKS, AND OPEN SPACES		UNDER TREES		BOATING, FISHING AND WATER RELATED		NEAR TRACTORS HEAVY ROAD EQUIPMENT		GOLF COURSES		AT TELEPHONES		VARIOUS OTHER AND UNKNOWN LOCATIONS	
STATE		NO.	%	NO.	%	NO.	%	NO.	%	NO.	%	NO.	%	NO.	%	NO.	%	NO.	%	NO.	%	NO.	%	NO.	%	NO.	%	NO.	%
ALABAMA	19	61	31	42	22	3	2	1	1	1	1	11	6	76	39	3	75	0	0	0	0	0	0	0	0	0	0	1	25
ALASKA	52	0	0	0	0	0	0	0	0	0	0	0	0	0	0	0	0	0	0	0	0	0	0	0	0	0	0	0	0
ARIZONA	29	64	64	7	7	2	2	6	6	1	1	0	0	20	20	0	0	0	0	0	0	0	0	0	0	0	0	0	0
ARKANSAS	14	49	22	28	13	14	6	7	3	4	2	11	5	111	50	0	0	0	0	2	50	0	0	0	0	0	0	2	50
CALIFORNIA	40	11	19	10	18	6	11	2	4	0	0	0	0	28	49	0	0	0	0	1	100	0	0	0	0	0	0	0	0
COLORADO	11	116	42	29	10	18	6	7	3	17	6	4	1	88	32	0	0	1	100	0	0	0	0	0	0	0	0	0	0
CONNECTICUT	35	6	8	25	35	4	6	0	0	3	4	3	4	30	42	0	0	3	75	0	0	0	0	0	0	0	0	1	25
DELAWARE	44	9	33	10	37	0	0	0	0	0	0	2	7	6	22	0	0	0	0	0	0	0	0	0	0	0	0	0	0
DISTRICT OF COLUMBIA	48	11	65	3	18	0	0	1	6	1	6	0	0	1	6	0	0	0	0	0	0	0	0	0	0	0	0	0	0
FLORIDA	1	329	32	91	9	150	14	47	5	40	4	27	3	355	34	16	28	3	5	5	9	5	9	1	2	3	5	25	43
GEORGIA	8	118	37	45	14	20	6	3	1	21	7	5	2	103	33	5	28	10	56	0	0	0	0	0	0	0	0	3	17
HAWAII	51	2	67	0	0	0	0	0	0	0	0	1	33	0	0	0	0	0	0	0	0	0	0	0	0	0	0	0	0
IDAHO	36	12	18	7	10	2	3	2	3	2	3	4	6	38	57	0	0	0	0	0	0	0	0	0	0	0	0	0	0
ILLINOIS	12	98	36	70	26	2	1	10	4	17	6	9	3	65	24	5	38	6	46	0	0	1	8	0	0	0	0	1	8
INDIANA	25	25	16	30	19	16	10	10	6	8	5	7	4	63	40	3	23	0	0	4	31	0	0	0	0	3	23	3	23
IOWA	24	28	18	20	13	1	1	1	1	2	1	3	2	105	66	0	0	0	0	0	0	0	0	0	0	1	100	0	0
KANSAS	22	27	15	14	8	2	1	7	4	10	6	7	4	109	62	1	50	0	0	0	0	0	0	0	0	0	0	1	50
KENTUCKY	18	55	20	23	12	9	5	4	2	14	7	7	4	85	43	0	0	0	0	0	0	0	0	1	33	0	0	2	67
LOUISIANA	16	97	45	34	16	20	9	4	2	0	0	3	1	56	26	0	0	1	20	1	20	0	0	0	0	1	20	2	40
MAINE	30	4	4	39	39	4	4	0	0	1	1	2	2	49	49	0	0	0	0	0	0	0	0	0	0	0	0	0	0
MARYLAND *	26	48	36	17	13	17	13	5	4	3	2	1	1	41	31	0	0	0	0	0	0	0	0	0	0	0	0	4	100
MASSACHUSETTS	10	58	20	13	4	9	3	5	2	2	1	6	2	203	69	0	0	1	33	0	0	0	0	0	0	1	33	1	33
MICHIGAN	2	225	38	103	17	26	4	15	3	31	5	17	3	177	30	1	20	0	0	0	0	0	0	0	0	0	0	4	80
MINNESOTA	27	15	14	19	17	7	6	7	6	12	11	11	10	40	36	1	17	0	0	1	17	2	33	0	0	0	0	2	33
MISSISSIPPI	17	71	34	38	18	29	14	2	1	4	2	15	7	48	23	0	0	0	0	0	0	0	0	0	0	0	0	0	0
MISSOURI	31	33	38	16	18	1	1	1	1	3	3	3	3	31	35	1	100	0	0	0	0	0	0	0	0	0	0	0	0
MONTANA	42	14	33	5	12	8	19	1	2	3	7	0	0	11	26	0	0	0	0	0	0	0	0	0	0	0	0	0	0
NEBRASKA	37	22	33	1	2	1	2	5	8	6	9	5	8	26	39	0	0	0	0	0	0	0	0	0	0	0	0	2	100
NEVADA	49	4	40	1	10	0	0	0	0	1	10	0	0	4	40	0	0	0	0	0	0	0	0	1	100	0	0	0	0
NEW HAMPSHIRE	38	14	22	1	2	0	0	1	2	4	6	1	2	44	68	3	100	0	0	0	0	0	0	0	0	0	0	0	0
NEW JERSEY	28	53	48	0	0	8	7	1	1	5	5	2	2	42	38	0	0	0	0	0	0	0	0	0	0	0	0	2	100
NEW MEXICO	23	98	60	23	14	2	1	4	2	5	3	2	1	29	18	2	50	0	0	0	0	0	0	1	25	1	25	0	0
NEW YORK	5	51	12	98	23	27	6	22	5	7	2	9	2	210	50	2	22	2	22	3	33	0	0	0	0	0	0	2	22
NORTH CAROLINA	4	146	32	36	8	28	6	13	3	23	5	9	2	207	45	8	42	1	5	0	0	4	21	1	5	1	5	4	21
NORTH DAKOTA	45	7	30	1	4	1	4	5	22	0	0	1	4	8	35	0	0	0	0	0	0	1	100	0	0	0	0	0	0
OHIO	6	95	23	80	20	12	3	4	1	32	8	11	3	173	43	1	100	0	0	0	0	0	0	0	0	0	0	0	0
OKLAHOMA	13	89	38	15	6	9	4	10	4	5	2	17	7	91	39	2	25	3	38	0	0	0	0	0	0	1	13	2	25
OREGON	46	6	32	0	0	0	0	1	5	0	0	1	5	11	58	0	0	0	0	0	0	0	0	0	0	0	0	0	0
PENNSYLVANIA	3	180	36	29	6	5	1	4	1	10	2	6	1	260	53	21	54	10	26	0	0	2	5	0	0	1	3	5	13
PUERTO RICO	50	1	17	1	17	0	0	0	0	0	0	0	0	4	67	0	0	0	0	0	0	0	0	0	0	0	0	0	0
RHODE ISLAND	41	10	22	15	33	0	0	0	0	2	4	0	0	18	40	0	0	0	0	0	0	0	0	0	0	0	0	0	0
SOUTH CAROLINA	15	56	25	17	8	11	5	7	3	2	1	5	2	124	56	0	0	4	80	0	0	0	0	0	0	0	0	1	20
SOUTH DAKOTA	39	13	22	5	8	2	3	9	15	0	0	2	3	28	47	2	67	0	0	0	0	0	0	0	0	0	0	1	33
TENNESSEE	7	115	35	80	25	4	1	7	2	8	2	15	5	96	30	4	67	0	0	0	0	0	0	0	0	1	17	1	17
TEXAS	9	146	46	37	12	33	11	9	3	4	1	6	2	79	25	0	0	0	0	1	100	0	0	0	0	0	0	0	0
UTAH	34	28	35	18	23	3	4	3	4	5	6	5	6	18	23	2	25	3	38	0	0	1	13	0	0	1	13	1	13
VERMONT	47	5	28	1	6	0	0	0	0	0	0	0	0	12	67	0	0	0	0	0	0	0	0	0	0	0	0	1	100
VIRGINIA	21	17	10	39	22	8	4	2	1	7	4	4	2	101	57	1	10	4	40	0	0	0	0	0	0	1	10	4	40
WASHINGTON	43	15	41	4	11	0	0	1	3	0	0	2	5	15	41	12	92	0	0	0	0	0	0	0	0	0	0	1	8
WEST VIRGINIA	32	16	18	11	13	3	3	1	1	2	2	1	1	54	61	0	0	0	0	0	0	0	0	0	0	0	0	3	100
WISCONSIN	20	67	36	8	4	5	3	6	3	9	5	6	3	85	46	0	0	0	0	1	10	3	30	3	30	0	0	3	30
WYOMING	33	39	48	3	4	13	16	8	10	4	5	0	0	14	17	0	0	0	0	0	0	0	0	0	0	0	0	0	0
UNITED STATES	0	2879	31	1262	14	545	6	271	3	341	4	269	3	3692	40	96	33	52	18	19	6	19	6	8	3	16	5	85	29

USCOM-NOAA-ASHEVILLE, NC 04/95/400

LIGHTNING DEATHS BY STATE, RANK, AND LOCATION OF OCCURRENCE

STATE	RANK	1959-1993														1993													
		OPEN FIELDS, BALL PARKS, AND OPEN SPACES		UNDER TREES		BOATING, FISHING AND WATER RELATED		NEAR TRACTORS HEAVY ROAD EQUIPMENT		GOLF COURSES		AT TELEPHONES		VARIOUS OTHER AND UNKNOWN LOCATIONS		OPEN FIELDS, BALL PARKS, AND OPEN SPACES		UNDER TREES		BOATING, FISHING AND WATER RELATED		NEAR TRACTORS HEAVY ROAD EQUIPMENT		GOLF COURSES		AT TELEPHONES		VARIOUS OTHER AND UNKNOWN LOCATIONS	
		NO.	%	NO.	%	NO.	%	NO.	%	NO.	%	NO.	%	NO.	%	NO.	%	NO.	%	NO.	%	NO.	%	NO.	%	NO.	%	NO.	%
ALABAMA	15	19	23	22	27	8	10	4	5	1	1	2	2	27	33	0	0	0	0	0	0	0	0	0	0	0	0	0	0
ALASKA	52	0	0	0	0	0	0	0	0	0	0	0	0	0	0	0	0	0	0	0	0	0	0	0	0	0	0	0	0
ARIZONA	24	26	46	8	14	5	9	0	0	4	7	3	5	11	19	1	100	0	0	0	0	0	0	0	0	0	0	0	0
ARKANSAS	9	35	32	21	19	11	10	8	7	3	3	0	0	31	28	0	0	0	0	0	0	0	0	0	0	0	0	1	100
CALIFORNIA	35	6	29	3	14	2	10	3	14	0	0	0	0	7	33	1	100	0	0	0	0	0	0	0	0	0	0	0	0
COLORADO	11	46	50	18	20	4	4	3	3	6	7	0	0	15	16	1	100	0	0	0	0	0	0	0	0	0	0	0	0
CONNECTICUT	42	3	23	2	15	0	0	0	0	3	23	0	0	5	38	0	0	0	0	0	0	0	0	0	0	0	0	0	0
DELAWARE	41	5	33	0	0	4	27	1	7	0	0	0	0	5	33	1	100	0	0	0	0	0	0	0	0	0	0	0	0
DISTRICT OF COLUMBIA	48	2	40	2	40	0	0	0	0	1	20	0	0	0	0	0	0	0	0	0	0	0	0	0	0	0	0	0	0
FLORIDA	1	94	28	44	13	84	25	21	6	10	3	0	0	84	25	3	75	0	0	0	0	0	0	0	0	0	0	1	25
GEORGIA	18	22	28	20	25	11	14	1	1	5	6	2	3	18	23	0	0	0	0	0	0	0	0	0	0	0	0	0	0
HAWAII	51	0	0	0	0	0	0	0	0	0	0	0	0	0	0	0	0	0	0	0	0	0	0	0	0	0	0	0	0
IDAHO	39	11	55	3	15	2	10	3	15	1	5	0	0	0	0	0	0	0	0	0	0	0	0	0	0	0	0	0	0
ILLINOIS	17	19	23	15	18	3	4	8	10	7	9	1	1	29	35	2	40	3	60	0	0	0	0	0	0	0	0	0	0
INDIANA	22	12	17	21	29	6	8	7	10	1	1	2	3	23	32	1	100	0	0	0	0	0	0	0	0	0	0	0	0
IOWA	23	8	13	8	13	1	2	7	11	2	3	0	0	37	59	0	0	0	0	0	0	0	0	0	0	0	0	0	0
KANSAS	25	15	27	1	2	4	7	10	18	2	4	0	0	23	42	0	0	0	0	0	0	0	0	0	0	0	0	0	0
KENTUCKY	16	24	29	12	15	4	5	4	5	2	2	1	1	35	43	1	100	0	0	0	0	0	0	0	0	0	0	0	0
LOUISIANA	7	15	13	32	28	37	32	8	7	0	0	0	0	22	19	0	0	1	100	0	0	0	0	0	0	0	0	0	0
MAINE	34	0	0	3	14	7	33	0	0	0	0	0	0	11	52	0	0	0	0	0	0	0	0	0	0	0	0	0	0
MARYLAND *	6	9	8	6	5	16	14	0	0	0	0	0	0	84	73	0	0	1	50	1	50	0	0	0	0	0	0	0	0
MASSACHUSETTS	33	4	17	3	13	1	4	0	0	1	4	1	4	14	58	0	0	0	0	0	0	0	0	0	0	0	0	0	0
MICHIGAN	13	24	27	23	26	10	11	2	2	10	11	2	2	17	19	0	0	0	0	0	0	0	0	0	0	0	0	0	0
MINNESOTA	27	16	31	13	25	5	10	6	12	1	2	2	4	9	17	0	0	0	0	0	0	0	0	0	0	0	0	0	0
MISSISSIPPI	12	29	33	21	24	11	12	6	7	0	0	0	0	22	25	0	0	0	0	0	0	1	100	0	0	0	0	0	0
MISSOURI	21	16	21	17	22	12	16	5	7	3	4	2	3	21	28	0	0	0	0	2	100	0	0	0	0	0	0	0	0
MONTANA	40	7	35	2	10	2	10	5	25	0	0	0	0	4	20	0	0	0	0	0	0	1	100	0	0	0	0	0	0
NEBRASKA	30	17	44	2	5	4	10	10	26	0	0	0	0	6	15	1	100	0	0	0	0	0	0	0	0	0	0	0	0
NEVADA	47	0	0	0	0	1	17	0	0	1	17	0	0	4	67	0	0	0	0	0	0	0	0	1	100	0	0	0	0
NEW HAMPSHIRE	45	2	29	0	0	2	29	0	0	1	14	0	0	2	29	0	0	0	0	1	100	0	0	0	0	0	0	0	0
NEW JERSEY	26	19	35	5	9	13	24	2	4	4	7	2	4	10	18	0	0	0	0	0	0	0	0	0	0	0	0	0	0
NEW MEXICO	19	38	48	14	18	7	9	0	0	1	1	0	0	19	24	0	0	1	50	1	50	0	0	0	0	0	0	0	0
NEW YORK	4	20	16	31	25	17	14	4	3	5	4	1	1	46	37	0	0	0	0	0	0	0	0	0	0	0	0	0	0
NORTH CAROLINA	2	35	21	25	15	22	13	6	4	7	4	1	1	69	42	1	100	0	0	0	0	0	0	0	0	0	0	0	0
NORTH DAKOTA	44	2	18	0	0	0	0	3	27	0	0	0	0	6	55	0	0	0	0	0	0	0	0	0	0	0	0	0	0
OHIO	8	33	30	21	19	15	14	6	5	7	6	1	1	28	25	0	0	1	100	0	0	0	0	0	0	0	0	0	0
OKLAHOMA	14	31	36	11	13	15	17	6	7	1	1	2	2	20	23	1	100	0	0	0	0	0	0	0	0	0	0	0	0
OREGON	46	3	43	1	14	0	0	0	0	0	0	0	0	3	43	0	0	0	0	0	0	0	0	0	0	0	0	0	0
PENNSYLVANIA	10	32	31	13	13	4	4	3	3	11	11	2	2	38	37	1	100	0	0	0	0	0	0	0	0	0	0	0	0
PUERTO RICO	32	11	38	8	28	1	3	0	0	0	0	0	0	9	31	0	0	0	0	0	0	0	0	0	0	0	0	0	0
RHODE ISLAND	49	0	0	0	0	1	25	0	0	0	0	0	0	3	75	0	0	0	0	0	0	0	0	0	0	0	0	0	0
SOUTH CAROLINA	20	16	21	15	19	9	12	10	13	1	1	3	4	23	30	0	0	0	0	1	50	1	50	0	0	0	0	0	0
SOUTH DAKOTA	38	6	30	1	5	2	10	8	40	1	5	0	0	2	10	1	100	0	0	0	0	0	0	0	0	0	0	0	0
TENNESSEE	5	34	28	32	26	9	7	9	7	7	6	2	2	29	24	1	100	0	0	0	0	0	0	0	0	0	0	0	0
TEXAS	3	65	41	25	16	23	15	11	7	4	3	0	0	30	19	1	50	0	0	1	50	0	0	0	0	0	0	0	0
UTAH	31	13	39	10	30	2	6	1	3	1	3	1	3	5	15	0	0	1	50	0	0	1	50	0	0	0	0	0	0
VERMONT	43	1	8	1	8	4	31	0	0	0	0	0	0	7	54	0	0	0	0	0	0	0	0	0	0	0	0	0	0
VIRGINIA	29	9	20	9	20	6	13	3	7	2	4	0	0	16	36	1	100	0	0	0	0	0	0	0	0	0	0	0	0
WASHINGTON	50	2	67	0	0	0	0	1	33	0	0	0	0	0	0	1	100	0	0	0	0	0	0	0	0	0	0	0	0
WEST VIRGINIA	37	6	30	4	20	2	10	0	0	1	5	0	0	7	35	0	0	0	0	0	0	0	0	0	0	0	0	0	0
WISCONSIN	28	8	17	3	7	9	20	5	11	6	13	0	0	15	33	0	0	0	0	0	0	1	100	0	0	0	0	0	0
WYOMING	36	11	52	2	10	3	14	1	5	0	0	0	0	4	19	0	0	0	0	0	0	0	0	0	0	0	0	0	0
UNITED STATES	0	881	28	553	17	421	13	201	6	124	4	33	1	955	30	20	47	8	19	7	16	5	12	1	2	0	0	2	5

* ON DECEMBER 8, 1963 THE CRASH OF A JETLINER KILLING 81 PEOPLE NEAR ELTON, MARYLAND, WAS ATTRIBUTED TO LIGHTNING BY THE CIVIL AERONAUTICS BOARD INVESTIGATORS.

TOTAL INJURIES BY STATE AND NATION FOR PERIOD 1959-93

STATE	JAN	FEB	MAR	APR	MAY	JUN	JUL	AUG	SEP	OCT	NOV	DEC	ANN
ALABAMA	6	1	11	4	11	24	79	52	3	4	0	0	195
ALASKA	0	0	0	0	0	0	0	0	0	0	0	0	0
ARIZONA	2	0	0	0	6	3	30	38	18	3	0	0	100
ARKANSAS	1	2	3	27	32	42	40	61	13	1	0	2	224
CALIFORNIA	1	0	2	13	0	2	15	7	14	1	1	1	57
COLORADO	0	0	0	5	36	88	79	60	11	0	0	0	279
CONNECTICUT	0	0	2	1	7	20	17	15	6	3	0	0	71
DELAWARE	0	0	0	0	8	12	4	1	2	0	0	0	27
DISTRICT OF COLUMBIA	0	0	0	0	10	4	1	1	0	0	1	0	17
FLORIDA	0	2	20	21	46	232	281	240	162	32	0	3	1039
GEORGIA	0	0	5	9	22	78	149	41	5	6	0	0	315
HAWAII	0	0	0	0	0	0	0	3	0	0	0	0	3
IDAHO	0	0	0	1	6	19	15	21	4	1	0	0	67
ILLINOIS	12	0	2	2	22	58	77	53	38	7	0	0	271
INDIANA	0	0	2	7	22	39	46	36	7	0	0	0	159
IOWA	0	0	2	9	22	46	40	21	16	3	1	0	160
KANSAS	0	0	5	11	19	27	46	31	31	5	1	0	176
KENTUCKY	0	0	0	2	22	64	62	36	10	1	0	0	197
LOUISIANA	1	0	6	4	16	18	104	45	15	2	2	1	214
MAINE	0	0	0	0	4	12	28	54	0	0	1	0	99
MARYLAND	0	0	0	0	36	23	39	23	8	3	0	0	132
MASSACHUSETTS	0	0	1	11	21	44	109	77	26	4	2	1	296
MICHIGAN	0	0	2	9	41	142	130	213	51	6	0	0	594
MINNESOTA	0	0	0	0	15	32	30	21	9	4	0	0	111
MISSISSIPPI	1	2	8	3	13	15	109	40	10	2	3	1	207
MISSOURI	0	1	3	8	20	17	8	15	10	2	4	0	88
MONTANA	0	0	0	0	5	14	10	11	2	0	0	0	42
NEBRASKA	0	0	0	4	15	9	14	17	7	0	0	0	66
NEVADA	0	0	0	0	1	2	2	4	1	0	0	0	10
NEW HAMPSHIRE	0	0	0	0	2	21	32	8	2	0	0	0	65
NEW JERSEY	0	0	0	0	5	11	57	22	16	0	0	0	111
NEW MEXICO	0	0	1	1	24	18	60	52	7	0	0	0	163
NEW YORK	0	0	0	1	20	81	149	143	25	4	1	0	424
NORTH CAROLINA	0	2	29	16	42	80	125	132	33	2	1	0	462
NORTH DAKOTA	0	0	0	0	2	4	7	6	4	0	0	0	23
OHIO	0	0	32	3	61	59	74	108	54	4	12	0	407
OKLAHOMA	1	1	3	20	33	40	36	49	26	19	5	3	236
OREGON	0	0	0	1	2	2	0	9	5	0	0	0	19
PENNSYLVANIA	1	6	0	0	22	130	143	142	48	2	0	0	494
PUERTO RICO	0	0	0	0	0	0	3	0	2	1	0	0	6
RHODE ISLAND	0	2	0	0	2	13	12	12	3	0	1	0	45
SOUTH CAROLINA	0	0	0	6	21	24	109	37	23	1	1	0	222
SOUTH DAKOTA	0	0	0	1	5	19	19	12	1	2	0	0	59
TENNESSEE	0	1	4	8	52	63	117	54	21	5	0	0	325
TEXAS	1	2	7	39	46	48	38	50	34	47	2	0	314
UTAH	0	0	0	1	9	19	17	22	9	3	0	0	80
VERMONT	0	0	0	0	0	3	11	4	0	0	0	0	18
VIRGINIA	0	0	1	4	10	21	95	39	8	0	0	0	178
WASHINGTON	0	0	0	0	5	13	9	8	0	1	0	1	37
WEST VIRGINIA	0	0	0	1	3	4	50	28	1	1	0	0	88
WISCONSIN	0	1	2	4	21	29	71	45	9	2	2	0	186
WYOMING	0	0	0	0	4	32	18	21	6	0	0	0	81
TOTAL: UNITED STATES	27	23	153	257	869	1820	2816	2240	816	184	41	13	9259

TOTAL DEATHS BY STATE AND NATION FOR PERIOD 1959–93

STATE	JAN	FEB	MAR	APR	MAY	JUN	JUL	AUG	SEP	OCT	NOV	DEC	ANN
ALABAMA	0	0	2	3	5	23	28	20	1	1	0	0	83
ALASKA	0	0	0	0	0	0	0	0	0	0	0	0	0
ARIZONA	0	0	0	0	4	1	23	16	12	1	0	0	57
ARKANSAS	0	0	8	0	13	33	28	20	6	0	0	1	109
CALIFORNIA	1	0	0	0	0	2	8	5	5	0	0	0	21
COLORADO	0	0	0	3	10	21	38	17	2	1	0	0	92
CONNECTICUT	0	0	0	0	0	4	5	3	1	0	0	0	13
DELAWARE	0	0	0	0	3	2	7	3	0	0	0	0	15
DISTRICT OF COLUMBIA	0	0	0	0	1	2	1	1	0	0	0	0	5
FLORIDA	0	0	5	4	28	81	88	86	39	4	1	1	337
GEORGIA	0	0	2	5	6	18	33	12	2	1	0	0	79
HAWAII	0	0	0	0	0	0	0	0	0	0	0	0	0
IDAHO	0	0	0	1	1	7	5	5	1	0	0	0	20
ILLINOIS	0	0	0	4	10	25	15	15	11	2	0	0	82
INDIANA	0	0	1	2	8	22	18	14	5	2	0	0	72
IOWA	0	0	1	3	11	20	7	13	4	4	0	0	63
KANSAS	0	0	0	4	10	7	14	12	4	2	2	0	55
KENTUCKY	1	0	0	3	10	22	19	15	12	0	0	0	82
LOUISIANA	1	0	1	5	10	22	42	17	11	0	4	1	114
MAINE	0	0	0	0	0	3	6	9	0	3	0	0	21
MARYLAND	0	0	0	0	5	5	10	11	2	1	0	81*	115
MASSACHUSETTS	0	0	0	1	3	4	6	9	1	0	0	0	24
MICHIGAN	0	0	0	1	7	22	28	23	7	0	0	0	88
MINNESOTA	0	0	0	3	3	11	11	13	10	1	0	0	52
MISSISSIPPI	1	0	4	2	12	14	28	22	6	0	0	0	89
MISSOURI	0	0	5	4	20	19	14	10	3	1	0	0	76
MONTANA	0	0	0	0	2	9	6	2	1	0	0	0	20
NEBRASKA	0	0	0	1	4	15	9	6	4	0	0	0	39
NEVADA	0	0	0	0	1	2	0	2	1	0	0	0	6
NEW HAMPSHIRE	0	0	0	0	0	4	3	0	0	0	0	0	7
NEW JERSEY	0	0	0	1	3	8	23	14	6	0	0	0	55
NEW MEXICO	0	0	0	1	8	12	23	30	5	0	0	0	79
NEW YORK	0	0	0	0	9	20	61	26	6	2	0	0	124
NORTH CAROLINA	0	1	5	3	23	37	54	35	7	0	0	0	165
NORTH DAKOTA	0	0	0	0	0	4	4	3	0	0	0	0	11
OHIO	0	0	0	3	10	22	44	18	10	2	2	0	111
OKLAHOMA	1	1	1	10	14	14	7	20	13	3	2	0	86
OREGON	0	0	0	0	2	0	0	1	3	1	0	0	7
PENNSYLVANIA	0	1	0	1	8	26	31	26	9	1	0	0	103
PUERTO RICO	0	0	0	0	0	3	9	9	5	3	0	0	29
RHODE ISLAND	0	0	0	0	0	1	1	0	2	0	0	0	4
SOUTH CAROLINA	0	0	1	0	7	12	32	17	8	0	0	0	77
SOUTH DAKOTA	0	0	0	0	4	2	6	2	3	3	0	0	20
TENNESSEE	0	1	1	7	15	32	26	21	14	2	3	0	122
TEXAS	0	0	1	15	31	19	42	25	17	7	1	0	158
UTAH	0	0	0	3	1	5	8	10	5	1	0	0	33
VERMONT	0	0	0	0	0	4	5	4	0	0	0	0	13
VIRGINIA	0	0	0	0	10	10	11	11	3	0	0	0	45
WASHINGTON	0	0	0	0	0	1	1	1	0	0	0	0	3
WEST VIRGINIA	0	0	0	0	4	2	10	3	1	0	0	0	20
WISCONSIN	0	0	1	1	2	9	12	16	2	1	1	1	46
WYOMING	0	0	0	0	2	4	7	6	2	0	0	0	21
TOTAL: UNITED STATES	5	4	39	94	340	667	917	679	272	50	16	85	3168

* ON DECEMBER 8, 1963 THE CRASH OF A JETLINER KILLING 81 PEOPLE NEAR ELKTON, MARYLAND, WAS ATTRIBUTED TO LIGHTNING BY THE CIVIL AERONAUTICS BOARD INVESTIGATORS.

NATIONAL TOTAL DEATHS BY YEAR FOR PERIOD 1959-93

YEAR	JAN	FEB	MAR	APR	MAY	JUN	JUL	AUG	SEP	OCT	NOV	DEC	ANN
1959	1	0	1	4	18	25	50	39	13	7	0	0	158
1960	0	0	1	5	7	33	25	17	9	0	0	0	97
1961	0	0	1	2	9	23	47	20	10	1	0	0	113
1962	0	0	3	6	27	20	26	28	9	1	0	0	120
1963	0	0	4	3	11	37	42	20	10	2	0	81*	210
1964	0	0	9	6	15	21	29	19	7	1	1	0	108
1965	0	0	2	4	12	34	39	28	4	2	0	0	125
1966	0	0	1	1	8	15	21	16	11	3	0	0	76
1967	1	0	1	2	3	26	21	14	1	2	1	1	73
1968	0	0	0	1	5	24	30	29	9	3	1	1	103
1969	0	0	1	5	13	17	27	13	14	3	0	0	93
1970	0	0	0	1	17	25	27	19	21	1	0	0	111
1971	0	0	2	1	12	27	33	19	19	0	0	0	113
1972	0	0	1	1	5	21	31	28	3	1	0	0	91
1973	0	1	2	3	10	24	31	18	13	2	1	0	105
1974	0	2	0	7	12	21	28	24	6	0	2	0	102
1975	0	1	3	3	11	19	28	18	6	2	0	0	91
1976	0	0	0	1	9	19	19	19	3	2	0	0	72
1977	0	0	0	4	9	19	16	35	14	1	0	0	98
1978	0	0	1	1	9	26	24	22	3	1	0	1	88
1979	0	0	0	3	11	4	20	16	4	3	2	0	63
1980	0	0	0	0	7	16	27	20	5	1	0	0	76
1981	0	0	0	4	5	13	19	19	5	0	2	0	67
1982	1	0	0	3	5	14	29	18	4	3	0	0	77
1983	0	0	1	2	4	8	28	23	8	1	2	0	77
1984	0	0	1	3	10	14	20	10	7	1	1	0	67
1985	0	0	0	5	12	12	26	8	8	1	1	0	73
1986	0	0	0	2	9	13	21	17	5	1	0	0	68
1987	0	0	0	2	14	18	28	15	7	2	0	0	86
1988	0	0	0	3	9	17	21	14	2	1	2	0	69
1989	0	0	1	1	9	14	19	18	4	1	0	0	67
1990	1	0	3	1	3	18	22	15	10	0	0	1	74
1991	0	0	0	2	8	15	23	19	6	0	0	0	73
1992	0	0	0	2	6	6	9	10	8	0	0	0	41
1993	1	0	0	0	6	9	11	12	4	0	0	0	43
TOTAL	5	4	39	94	340	667	917	679	272	50	16	85	3168
MEAN	0	0	1	3	10	19	26	19	8	1	0	2	91

* ON DECEMBER 8, 1963 THE CRASH OF A JETLINER KILLING 81 PEOPLE NEAR ELKTON, MARYLAND, WAS ATTRIBUTED TO LIGHTNING BY THE CIVIL AERONAUTICS BOARD INVESTIGATORS.

NATIONAL TOTAL INJURIES BY YEAR FOR PERIOD 1959-93

YEAR	JAN	FEB	MAR	APR	MAY	JUN	JUL	AUG	SEP	OCT	NOV	DEC	ANN
1959	0	0	0	5	27	52	110	103	23	3	1	1	325
1960	0	0	2	11	12	70	28	50	16	9	4	0	202
1961	0	0	7	14	15	49	83	50	31	5	1	1	256
1962	0	0	3	5	39	38	90	49	12	6	0	0	242
1963	7	0	0	6	14	64	55	44	18	1	0	0	209
1964	0	0	10	15	14	38	99	53	8	1	1	0	239
1965	3	2	2	4	26	42	59	59	19	1	0	0	217
1966	0	2	1	2	37	39	42	44	15	1	0	0	183
1967	0	0	0	4	7	35	59	33	4	2	0	1	145
1968	0	0	4	2	16	52	117	155	14	9	1	0	370
1969	0	0	0	4	19	75	39	23	12	0	0	1	173
1970	0	0	1	5	40	40	82	43	43	4	1	0	259
1971	0	1	0	1	24	71	79	54	22	1	1	0	254
1972	0	0	8	6	12	24	72	54	24	2	1	0	203
1973	0	0	10	2	20	23	74	59	29	9	2	0	228
1974	1	9	1	3	12	27	56	51	12	1	0	0	173
1975	0	3	0	1	30	60	107	154	42	1	0	1	399
1976	0	1	0	7	16	39	73	68	13	1	0	1	219
1977	0	0	0	3	35	58	58	67	62	4	4	0	291
1978	0	0	5	3	19	100	73	54	42	5	0	0	301
1979	0	2	4	26	32	73	55	49	9	2	2	0	254
1980	0	1	2	11	11	49	50	134	16	1	0	0	275
1981	1	0	2	9	34	60	108	52	9	3	13	0	291
1982	1	0	2	6	38	20	54	32	11	4	4	2	174
1983	0	0	24	3	25	24	87	113	30	31	0	0	337
1984	0	0	7	5	13	43	80	53	44	7	1	0	253
1985	0	0	29	4	42	48	61	33	27	4	0	0	248
1986	0	2	4	2	15	68	112	43	22	3	0	0	271
1987	0	0	2	8	66	49	121	70	43	3	1	1	364
1988	0	0	1	14	22	53	133	63	19	5	1	0	311
1989	1	0	8	16	23	70	135	51	12	4	2	0	322
1990	12	0	4	6	10	43	88	62	25	1	0	1	252
1991	0	0	2	30	48	111	94	107	37	3	0	0	432
1992	0	0	4	10	41	38	80	46	31	42	0	0	292
1993	1	0	4	4	15	75	103	65	20	5	0	3	295
TOTAL	27	23	153	257	869	1820	2816	2240	816	184	41	13	9259

Floods

• FLOOD DANGER

The transformation of a tranquil river into a destructive flood occurs hundreds of times each year, in every part of the United States. Every year, some 75,000 Americans are driven from their homes by floods; on the average, 80 persons are killed each year. These destructive overflows have caused property damage in some years estimated at more than $1,000,000,000. Between the years 1960-93, the total number (annual) of floods or flash floods has ranged from 31 (1988), 103 (1993), 188 (1965), 210 (1977), 445 (1969), and 555 (1972). Years with the greatest number of floods can be directly related to the years with major landfalling hurricanes (Camille, 1969; Agnes, 1972).

• WHY FLOODS?

Floods begin when soil and vegetation cannot absorb falling rain or melting snow, and when water runs off the land in such quantities that it cannot be carried in normal stream channels or retained in natural ponds and manmade reservoirs. River Forecast Centers issue flood forecasts and warnings when the rain that has fallen is enough to cause rivers to overflow their banks, and when melting snow combines with rainfall to produce similar effects.

• FLOOD WARNINGS

Early flood warnings allow time for residents to leave low-lying areas, and to move personal property, mobile equipment, and livestock to higher ground. Sometimes valuable crops can be harvested in advance of a destructive flood. Emergency and relief organizations can prepare to handle refugees and to combat the inevitable health hazards caused by floods.

Flood warnings can be issued hours to days in advance of the flood peak on major tributaries. Main river flood forecasts can be issued as far as several days or even weeks in advance. In general, the time lapse between rainfall or snowmelt and the rise in river height increases with the size of the river.

Flood warnings are forecasts of impending floods, and are distributed to the public by radio and television, and through local emergency forces. The warning message tells the expected severity of flooding (minor, moderate, or major), the affected river, and when and where flooding will begin. Careful preparation and prompt response will reduce property loss and ensure personal safety.

• THE GREAT FLOOD OF 1993

In terms of precipitation amounts, record river stages, areal extent of flooding, persons displaced, crop and prop-

Flood Casualties

During the period of 1960-93, a total of 4,297 people lost their lives in the United States, Puerto Rico, and the Virgin Islands combined due to flash floods and floods. Most flash flood fatalities (55%) are vehicle related and more than two-thirds (65%) are males.

The state with the most flash flood/flood deaths during the past 34 years with more than double the next states, is Texas, followed by totals of closely grouped states—South Dakota, California, Virginia, and West Virginia. (Puerto Rico ranks just behind Texas.)

All but 11 of the 248 fatalities in South Dakota occurred during the flash floods in the Rapid City area June 9-10, 1972, and more than half of the Virginia total occurred during August, 1969, floods in the western portion of the state. Most of the Colorado deaths (83%) occurred during the Big Thompson Canyon flash flood, August 1, 1976. *(The flash flood/flood totals include deaths during tropical cyclones.)*

States with Highest Flash Flood/Flood Fatality Statistics, 1960-93

1. Texas (558) 2. South Dakota (248) 3. California (246) 4. Virginia (236) 5. West Virginia (235) 6. Pennsylvania (186) 7. Mississippi (185) 8. Colorado (168) 9. Louisiana (143) 10. Missouri (118)

Sources: Richard A. Wood; National Weather Service, Office of Hydrology, and National Climatic Data Center ("Storm Data" publications).

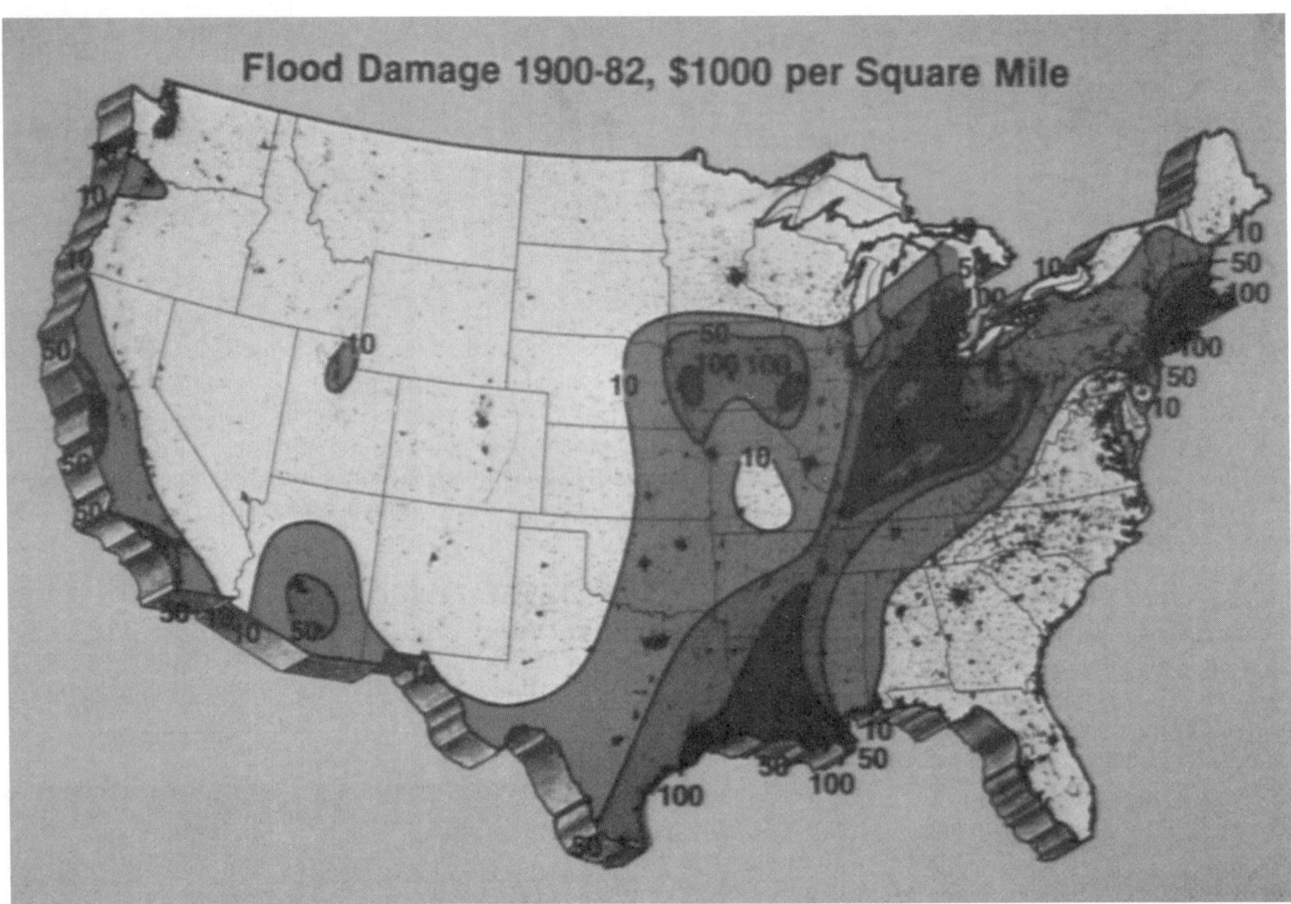

erty damage, and flood duration, the Great Flood of 1993 was perhaps the worst hydrometeorological event to occur since the United States started to provide weather services in the mid-1800s.

Record and near-record precipitation during the spring of 1993, on soil saturated from previous seasonal precipitation, resulted in flooding along many of the major river systems and their tributaries in the upper Midwest during the summer of 1993.

Spring flooding began in March as a result of a previous wet fall, normal to above-normal snow accumulation, and rapid spring snowmelt accompanied by heavy spring rainfall. On May 8, record flooding occurred in South Dakota on Split Rock Creek at Corson and in Minnesota on the Rock River in Luverne. From May 22-24, heavy thunderstorms produced 3-7 inches (7.62-17.78 cm) of rain in three hours over Sioux Falls resulting in major urban and residential flooding across the city. The Big Sioux and Vermillion Rivers in South Dakota went above flood stage in late May and remained in flood through mid-June. Major flooding continued throughout the summer along the Missouri and Mississippi Rivers. For example, on September 1, 1993, the towns of Hannibal, Louisiana and Clarksville, Missouri, had experienced 153 consecutive days of flooding. Flooding at levels above the flood stage continued through the middle of September in many regions along the Mississippi River.

Records broken

Flood records were broken at 44 forecast points on the upper Mississippi River system, at 49 forecast points on the Missouri River system, and at two forecast points on the Red River of the North system. Within the Mississippi River system, 1993 floods of record include those set at 15 forecast points on the main stem, at four forecast points on the Iowa River, at five forecast points on the Des Moines River, and at two forecast points on the Raccoon River.

Within the Missouri river system, 1993 floods of record include those set at 14 forecast points on the main stem and at four forecast points on each of the Saline, Smoky Hill, and Grand Rivers. During the event, near flood of record stage occurred at an additional 23 forecast points on the Missouri River system alone. Record flood stages surpassed old record stages by more than 6 feet (1.82 m) in some cases. For example, in 1993, flood records set more than 42 years ago on the main stem of the Missouri were broken by more than 4 feet (1.18 m) at multiple forecast points. In at least one case, a new flood of record was established early in the event only to be broken by higher water later in the event. The historic flood of record on the Mississippi at St. Louis was established on April 28, 1973, at 43.2 feet (13.1 m); reestablished on July 21, 1993, with a flood stage of 46.9 feet (14.23 m); and reestablished again 11 days later on August 1, 1993, with a record flood stage of 49.58 feet (15 m).

Damages

Damage caused by these record flood stages was massive. Over 17,000 square miles were inundated by the flood (the 1937 flood in the same region affected only 12,700). It's estimated the region suffered over eight billion dollars in damages; President Clinton declared more than 200 counties federal disaster areas, including all 99 counties in Iowa. Amazingly, only 26 individuals died as a direct result of the flood. Compare that figure to 23 killed in the 1973 and 250 in the 1937 floods of the same region and then to the 2,100 killed in the one-day Jamestown, Pennsylvania, flood in 1889. The decreased death tolls can be attributed to: abundant warnings, well-executed evacuation plans, lack of flash floods, and foremost, the protection provided by the system of flood-controlling levees in the area.

St. Louis reestablished a record flood stage of 49.58 feet (15 m) on August 1, 1993.

The duration and magnitude of the Great Flood of 1993, as well as its leading conditions, strongly support the premise that this event was a significant climate variation rather than simply a sequence of meteorological events. It is quite possible that one or more climate-driving forces significantly contributed to this climate variation. (For example, a shift in the jet stream acted as a barrier to a cold front, bringing 150% to 200% more precipitation to the area than usual.) A more thorough analysis of this situation is expected to result in improved understanding of the roles contributing factors may have played.

• FLASH FLOODS

Flash flood waves, moving at incredible speeds, can roll boulders, tear out trees, destroy buildings and bridges, and scour out new channels. Killing walls of water can reach 10-20 feet (3.03-6.06 m). You won't always have a warning that these deadly, sudden floods are coming. But you can save yourself—your family—if you know what to expect and how to react.

Flood Safety Rules

Before the flood:

1. Become familiar with local flood areas and dams; know if flood waters might affect your home and property.
2. Learn flood warning signals and community evacuation routes and shelters.
3. Keep a stock of food that requires no cooking or refrigeration; electric and gas services may be interrupted.
4. Keep a portable radio, emergency cooking equipment, lights and flashlights in working order.
5. Keep first aid supplies and any medicines your family may need on hand.
6. Store materials like sandbags, plywood, plastic sheeting and lumber to protect your house from flood waters and to make quick repairs.
7. Keep your car fueled; in an emergency, filling stations may not be operating.
8. Contact your insurance agent or local government to discuss flood insurance coverage.
9. Install check valves in building sewer traps to prevent flood water from backing up in sewer drains.
10. Arrange for auxiliary electrical supplies for hospitals and other operations which are critically affected by power failure.

When you receive a flood warning:

11. Store drinking water in clean bathtubs and in various closed containers; water service may be disrupted.
12. In coastal areas, board up windows or protect them with storm shutters or tape to prevent flying, broken glass.
13. Put sandbags or other protection in place, but away from outer walls. In the case of deep flooding you may opt to flood a basement with clean water.
14. If forced to leave your home and time permits, move essential items to safe ground or to upper levels of the house; turn off utilities at mainswitches but do not touch electrical equipment if you are wet or standing in water; fill tanks to keep them from moving away; grease immovable machinery; leave a note on your house to advise authorities that you have evacuated.
15. Move to a safe area before access is cut off by flood water. Watch for mud slides, downed electrical lines and areas with high or rising water levels.

During the flood:

16. Avoid areas subject to sudden flooding.
17. Do not drive into flooded areas; if flood waters do rise around your car, abandon it and move to higher ground.
18. Do not swim or dive into the water.

After the flood:

19. Do not visit disaster areas; your presence might hamper rescue and other emergency operations.
20. If you have flood insurance, contact your agent that you have a loss.
21. Tune in to local radio and television for advice on where to obtain medical care and other assistance.
22. Do not enter structures if flood waters covered the first floor; seek expert advice to tell if the building is safe to enter.
23. Use battery-powered lanterns or flashlights (not oil or gas lanterns); if the building may have a gas leak, do not use any kind of light.
24. Flood waters may have swollen doors tightly shut; use windows or other openings.
25. Check with local authorities before using any water; wells should be pumped out and water tested before drinking.
26. Do not use fresh food that has come into contact with flood waters.
27. Do not handle live electrical equipment in wet areas; have an expert check all equipment before returning to service.
28. Pump water out of basements gradually (one-third of the water per day) to lessen damage to walls and foundation.
29. Report broken utility lines to appropriate authorities; have the gas company check for leaks and to turn the gas back on.
30. Watch out for poisonous snakes in previously flooded areas.

Important flood terms:

FLOOD FORECASTS mean rainfall is heavy enough to cause rivers to overflow their banks or melting snow is mixing with rainfall to produce similar effects.

FLOOD WARNINGS or forecasts of impending floods describe the affected river, lake, or tidewater, the severity of flooding (minor, moderate or major), and when and where the flooding will begin.

Flash Flood Safety Rules

BEFORE THE FLOOD know the elevation of your property in relation to nearby streams and other waterways. Investigate the flood history of your area and how human-made changes may affect future flooding. Make advance plans of what you will do and where you will go in a flash flood emergency.

WHEN A FLASH FLOOD WATCH IS ISSUED listen to area radio and television stations for possible Flash Flood Warnings and reports of flooding in progress from the National Weather Service and public safety agencies. Be prepared to move out of danger at a moment's notice. If you are on the road, watch for flooding at highway dips, bridges, and low areas due to heavy rain not observable to you, but which may be indicated by thunder and lightning.

WHEN A FLASH FLOOD WARNING IS ISSUED for your area act quickly to save yourself. You may have only seconds:

1. Get out of areas subject to flooding. Avoid already flooded areas.
2. Do not attempt to cross a flowing stream on foot where water is above your knees.
3. If driving, know the depth of water in a dip before crossing. The road may not be intact under the water. If the vehicle stalls, abandon it immediately and seek higher ground—rapidly rising water may engulf the vehicle and its occupants and sweep them away.
4. Be especially cautious at night when it is harder to recognize flood dangers.
5. When you are out of immediate danger, tune in area radio or television stations for additional information as conditions change and new reports are received.

AFTER THE FLASH FLOOD WATCH OR WARNING IS CANCELLED stay tuned to radio or television for follow-up information. Flash flooding may have ended, but general flooding may come later in headwater streams and major rivers.

Flash flood terms used in forecasts and warnings:

FLASH FLOOD means the occurrence of a dangerous rise in water level of a stream or over a land area in a few hours or less caused by heavy rain, ice jam breakup, earthquake, or dam failure.

FLASH FLOOD WATCH means that heavy rains occurring or expected to occur may soon cause flash flooding in certain areas and citizens should be alert to the possibility of a flood emergency which will require immediate action.

FLASH FLOOD WARNING means that flash flooding is occurring or imminent on certain streams or designated areas and immediate precautions should be taken by those threatened.

On small streams, especially near the headwaters of river basins, water levels may rise quickly in heavy rainstorms, and flash floods can begin before the rain stops falling. There is little time between detection of flood crest. Swift action is essential to the protection of life and property.

Warning systems

NOAA's Weather Service has helped set up flash flood warning systems in about 100 communities. In these, a volunteer network of rainfall and river observing stations is established in the area, and a local flood warning representative is appointed to collect reports from the network. The representative is authorized to issue official flash flood warnings based on a series of graphs prepared by the Weather Service. These graphs show the local flooding that will occur under different conditions of soil moisture and rainfall. On the basis of reported rainfall, the representative can prepare a flood forecast from these graphs, and spread a warning within minutes. Communities within range of a Weather Service radar have the additional protection of advance warning when flood-producing storms approach. Successful operation of a flash flood warning system requires active community participation and planning, but very little financial outlay. Still, the communities with cooperative flash flood warning systems are only a small fraction of the thousands of communities which need them.

Flash flood warnings are the most urgent type of flood warning issued, and are transmitted to the public over radio, television, and by sirens and other signals.

Winter Storms

Winter storms can kill without breaking climatological records. Their danger is persistent, year to year. Since 1936 snowstorms have caused, directly and indirectly, about 100 deaths a year—and a year of 200 deaths is not unusual. Of such deaths, usually just over a third are attributed to automobile and other accidents; just less than a third to overexertion, exhaustion, and consequent fatal heart attack; while only about 11% result from exposure and fatal freezing. The remaining number, about 20%, are deaths due to home fires, carbon-monoxide poisoning in stalled cars, electrocution from downed wires, and building collapse. Large numbers of snow-related deaths—345 and 354—occurred in 1958 and 1960 respectively. About half of these deaths occurred in New England, New York, and Pennsylvania.

• WINTER STORM IMPACT

Nearly everyone east of the Pacific coastal ranges remembers significant winter storms—days of heavy snow, interminable blizzard, inconvenience, economic loss, and sometimes, personal tragedy. Winter brings them all. For Wyoming or Kansas or Texas, the blizzard of 1888 was one of the worst on record. The period January 11-13, in that year brought the most disastrous blizzard ever known in Montana, the Dakotas and Minnesota, combining gale winds, blowing snow, and extreme cold into a lethal, destructive push from the rockies eastward. The eastern seaboard got its big storm of the last century in the same year. March 11-14, 1888, saw the seaboard from Chesapeake Bay to Maine stricken with a blizzard that dumped an average of 40 inches (101.6 cm) of snow over southeastern New York and southern New England. The storm killed 200 in New York City alone; total deaths was over 400.

But every winter is a bad winter for someone. The 1966 season saw the eastern seaboard paralyzed by snow from Virginia to New England, with more than 50 deaths, and thousands marooned. A March storm buried the Dakotas, Minnesota, and Nebraska, with 30-foot (9 m) drifts pushed up by winds gusting to more than 100 miles per hour (161 km/hr). The 1967 winter storm season was not much better, and included a May Day blizzard in the Dakotas and a nor'easter which brought snow and hurricane-force winds to northern New England late in May. Snowfall across middle America was a much as four times normal in early 1968, and 1969 was called "the year of the big snows" in the Midwest.

The winter of 1977-78 was unusually harsh, particularly in the midwest and east. Its most devastating punch was the "Northeast Blizzard of '78" one of the worst of this century. From February 5-7, 1978, it created havoc along the eastern seaboard. In New York City, the 17.7-inch (45 cm) snowfall was the sixth largest since records began in 1869. Boston had over 2 feet (61 cm) of snow, as did Providence, Rhode Island. Winds of more than 55 miles per hour (86 km/hr) caused massive snowdrifts, drove seas through seawalls, undermined homes, destroyed beaches (including Rocky Beaches on Long Island), breached protective dunes, and left many areas from Cape May, New Jersey northward open to further damage from spring coastal storms. The American Red Cross reported 99 deaths and 4,587 injuries or illnesses attributable to the storm. Damage in Massachusetts exceeded one-half billion dollars, while New York and New Jersey losses aggregated to about $94 million.

Superstorm, 1993

In March, 1993, the one of the nation's greatest nontropical weather events occurred, adversely impacting 100 million individuals and severely crippling the commercial activity of the eastern one-third of the United States, as well as the travel activities nationwide.

From March 12-14, 1993, 22 states in the eastern United States were subject to the blizzard conditions (in the north) and high winds, coastal flooding, convective weather (in the south) as the storm swept through the region. Record cold temperatures were noted in all affected areas.

Still recovering from Hurricane Andrew and a rash of tornadoes in Tampa Bay, Florida, reported additional property damage costs of $1.6 billion; about one-third of the storm related deaths occurred there. Thirty storm-related deaths and some $400 million in property damage was reported from the remainder of the United States southeast. The mid-Atlantic and northeast, while sustaining significantly lower storm-related deaths, suffered major economic misfortune due to the extensive slow down of business activity.

• WHERE & WHY WINTER STORMS OCCUR

The storms are generated, as are many of the thunderstorms of summer, from disturbances along the boundary between cold polar and warm tropical air masses, the fronts where air masses of different temperatures and densities wage their perpetual war of instability and equilibrium. The disturbances may become intense low pressure systems, churning over tens of thousands of square miles in a great counter-clockwise sweep.

In the Pacific, these disturbances form along polar fronts off the east coast of Asia and travel northeastward toward Alaska. But some, particularly those forming along the mid-Pacific polar front, take a more southerly track, striking the United States as far south as southern California. Few Pacific disturbances cross the Rockies, but some do, redeveloping to the east. One region of such redevelopment lies east of the Colorado Rockies; the storms which come out of that region are called *Colorado Cyclones*. Another region of storm redevelopment is east of the Canadian Rockies, from which come the so-called *Alberta Cyclones*. Both types take an eastward path, their most frequent ones converging over the Great Lakes. The Lakes themselves are generators of severe local winter storms, and forge others from northward-drifting disturbances originating over the Gulf of Mexico and our southern plains.

On our east coast, winter storms often form along the Atlantic polar front near the coast of Virginia and the Carolinas and in the general area east of the southern Appalachians. These are the notorious Cape Hatteras storms—nor'easters—which develop to great intensity as they move up the coast, then drift seaward toward Iceland, where they finally decay.

Because they form over water, these storms are difficult to forecast, and occasionally surprise the Atlantic megalopolis with paralyzing snows. In 1969, the United States Departments of Commerce, Transportation, and Defense tightened winter storm surveillance with reconnaissance aircraft, an ocean buoy, and a new weather ship. With better hour-to-hour information on the storms, weathermen ashore have begun to ease the burden of unexpected heavy snows in eastern cities.

For some parts of the United States—the Northern Rockies, for example—storms with snow followed by cold are a threat from mid-September to mid-May; during one of the colder months from November to March, it is not unusual for eight separate storms to affect some area across the continent. Intense winter storms are frequently accompanied by cold waves, ice or glaze, heavy snow, blizzards, or a combination of these; often, in a single winter storm, precipitation type changes several times as the storm passes. Their common feature is the ability to completely immobilize large areas and to isolate and kill persons and livestock in their path. In our northland, the severity of these storms makes their threat a seasonal one. Farther south, the occasional penetration of severe winter storms into more moderate climates causes severe hardship and great loss of warm-weather crops.

• FREEZING RAIN & ICE STORMS

Freezing rain or freezing drizzle is rain or drizzle occurring when surface temperatures are below freezing (32°F/0°C). The moisture falls in liquid form but freezes upon impact, resulting in a coating of ice glaze on all exposed objects. The occurrence of freezing rain or drizzle is often called an ice storm when a substantial glaze layer accumulates. Ice forming on exposed objects generally ranges from a thin glaze to coatings about an inch (2.54 cm) thick; but much thicker deposits have been observed. For example, ice deposits to 8 inches (20.32 cm) in diameter were reported on wires in northern Idaho in January 1961, and loadings of 11 pounds (5 kg) per foot of telephone wire were found in Michigan in February 1922. It has been estimated that an evergreen tree 50 feet (15 m) high with an average width of 20 feet (6 m) may be coated with as much as five tons of ice during a severe ice storm. A heavy accumulation of ice, especially when accompanied by high winds, devastates trees and transmission lines. Sidewalks, streets, and highways become extremely hazardous to pedestrians and motorists; over 85% of ice-storm deaths are traffic-related. Freezing rain and drizzle frequently occur for a short time as a transitory condition between the occurrence of rain or drizzle and snow, and therefore usually occur at temperatures slightly below freezing.

Some of the most destructive ice storms have occurred in the southern states, where neither buildings nor crops are designed with severe winter conditions in mind. The most damaging ice storm in the United States was probably that which struck the southland from January 28 to February 4, 1951, causing some $50 million damage in Mississippi, $15 million in Louisiana, and nearly $2 million in Arkansas; this storm also caused 22 deaths. The region of greatest incidence, however, is a broad belt from Nebraska, Kansas, and Oklahoma eastward through the middle Atlantic and New England states.

Not sleet storms

Ice storms are sometimes incorrectly referred to as sleet storms. Sleet can be easily identified as frozen rain drops (ice pellets) which bounce when hitting the ground or other objects. Sleet does not stick to trees and wires; but sleet in sufficient depth does cause hazardous driving conditions.

• WINTER WARNINGS

The terms watch and warning are used for winter storms, as for other natural hazards. The *watch* alerts the public that

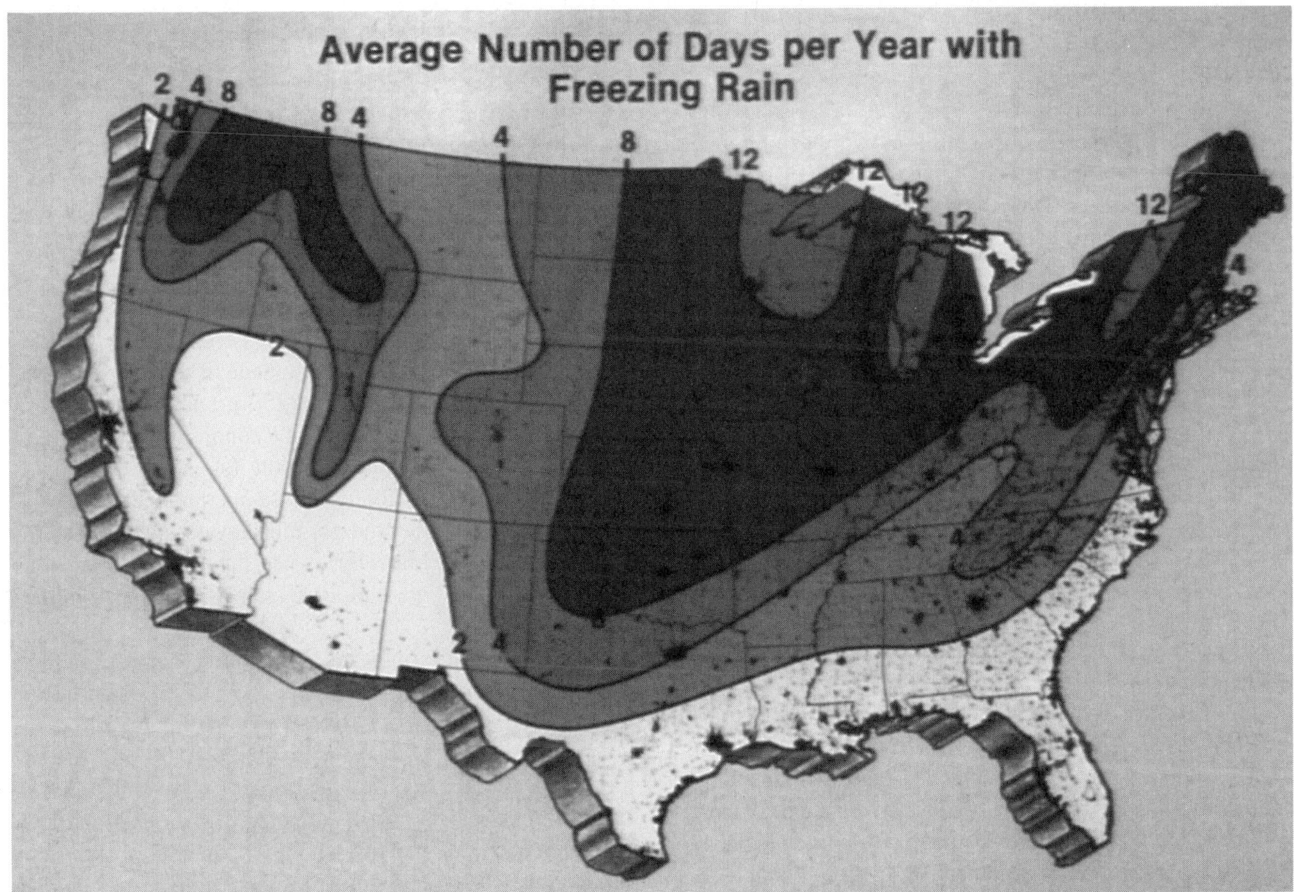

a storm has formed and is approaching the area. People in the alerted area should keep listening for the latest advisories over radio and television, and begin to take precautionary measures. The *warning* means that a storm is imminent and immediate action should be taken to protect life and property.

The word *snow* in a forecast, without a qualifying word such as occasional or intermittent, means that the fall of snow is of a steady nature and will probably continue for several hours without letup.

Heavy snow warnings are issued to the public when a fall of 4 inches (10 cm) or more is expected in a 12-hour period, or a fall of 6 inches (15.24 cm) or more is expected in a 24-hour period. Some variations on these rules may be used in different parts of the country. Where 4-inch snowfalls are common, for example, the emphasis on heavy snow is generally associated with six or more inches of snow. In other parts of the country where heavy snow is infrequent or in metropolitan areas with heavy traffic, a snowfall of 2-3 inches (5-7.6 cm) will justify a heavy snow warning.

Snow flurries are defined as snow falling for short durations at intermittent periods; however, snowfall during the flurries may reduce visibilities to an eighth of a mile or less. Accumulations from snow flurries are generally small.

Snow squalls are brief, intense falls of snow and are comparable to summer rain showers. They are accompanied by gusty surface winds.

Blowing and drifting snow generally occur together and result from strong winds and falling snow or loose snow on the ground. Blowing snow is defined as snow lifted from the surface by the wind and blown about to a degree that horizontal visibility is greatly restricted.

Drifting snow is used in forecasts to indicate that strong winds will blow falling snow or loose snow on the ground into significant drifts. In the northern plains, the combination of blowing and drifting snow, after a substantial snowfall has ended, is often referred to as a ground blizzard.

Blizzards are the most dramatic and perilous of all winter storms, characterized by low temperatures and by strong winds bearing large amounts of snow. Most of the snow accompanying a blizzard is in the form of fine, powdery particles of snow which are whipped in such great quantities that at times visibility is only a few yards.

Blizzard warnings are issued when winds with speeds of at least 35 miles per hour (56 km/hr) are accompanied by considerable falling or blowing snow and temperatures of 20°F (-6.7°C) or lower are expected to prevail for an extended period of time.

Severe blizzard warnings are issued when blizzards of extreme proportions are expected and indicate wind with speeds of at least 45 miles per hour (72 km/hr) plus a great density of falling or blowing snow and a temperature of 10°F (-12.2°C) or lower.

Hazardous driving (travelers') warnings are issued to indicate that falling, blowing or drifting snow, freezing rain or drizzle, sleet or strong winds will make driving difficult.

Livestock (stockmen's) warnings alert ranchers and farmers that livestock will require protection from a large accumulation of snow or ice, a rapid drop in temperature, or strong wind.

A *cold wave warning* indicates an expected rapid fall in temperature within a 24-hour period which will require substantially increased protection to agricultural, industrial, commercial, and social activities. The temperature falls and minimum temperatures required to justify cold wave warnings vary with the changing of the season and with geographic location. Regardless of the month or the section of the country, a cold wave warning is a red flag alert to the public that during a forthcoming forecast period a change to very cold weather will require greater than normal protective measures.

The terms storm, freezing rain, and freezing drizzle warn the public that a coating of ice is expected on the ground and on other exposed surfaces. The qualifying term heavy is used to indicate ice coating which, because of the extra weight of the ice, will cause significant damage to trees, overhead wires, and the like. Damage will be greater if the freezing rain or drizzle is accompanied by high winds.

Blizzard Safety for Livestock

Blizzards take a terrible toll in livestock. For both humane economic reasons, stockmen should take necessary precautions in advance of severe winter storms.

MOVE LIVESTOCK, ESPECIALLY YOUNG LIVESTOCK, INTO SHELTERED AREAS. Shelter belts, properly oriented and laid out, provide better protection for range cattle than shed type shelters, which may cause cattle to overcrowd, with consequental overheating and respiratory disorders.

HAUL EXTRA FEED TO FEEDING AREAS before the storm arrives. Storm duration is the largest determinant of livestock losses; if the storm last more than 48 hours, emergency feed methods are required. Range cattle are hardy and can survive extreme winter weather providing they have some non-confining type of shelter from the wind and are able to feed at frequent intervals.

Autopsies of cattle killed by winter storms have shown the cause of death to be dehydration, not cold or suffocation. Because cattle cannot lick enough snow to satisfy their thirst, stockmen are advised to use heaters in water tanks to provide livestock with water and feed after prolonged exposure to winter storm conditions.

• WIND CHILL INDEX

A reasonably satisfactory solution to that elusive characteristic of weather known as "coldness" was first proposed by Dr. Paul Siple in 1939. The term "wind chill" was used to describe the relative discomfort resulting from combinations of wind and temperature. The method used was not applicable to temperatures above 32°F (0°C). and high wind speeds caused exaggerated wind chill values. During the Antarctic winter of 1941, Siple developed a new formula to determine wind chill from experiments made at Little America. Measurements were made of the time required for the freezing of 8.8 ounces (250 grams) of water in a plastic cylinder under a variety of conditions of wind and temperature. They assumed that the rate of heat loss was proportional to the difference in temperature between the cylinder and the temperature of the surrounding air. The results, expressed in kilocalories per square meter per hour per degree Celsius, were plotted against wind speed in meters per second.

Heat loss occurs by means of radiation, conduction, and convection. Combining all effects, the general equation for heat loss "H" is: $H = (A + B\sqrt{v} + Cv)\,t$. Within the equation, constants **A**, **B**, and **C** are equal to 10.45, 10.00, and -1.0 respectively. **H** is equal to heat loss (wind chill) in kg. cals/m^2/hr.; **v** is wind speed in meters per second; and **t** is the difference in degrees Celsius between neutral skin temperature of 33°F (0.6°C) and air temperature.

The constant **A** includes the cooling caused by radiation and conduction. The value of the constants **A**, **B**, and **C** varies widely in formulae presented by different investigators. This is to be expected since **H** also depends on certain properties of the body being cooled. The above formula measures the cooling power of the wind and temperature in complete shade and does not consider the gain of heat from incoming radiation, either direct or diffuse. Under conditions of bright sunshine, the wind chill index should be reduced by about 200 kg/cals/m^2/hr.

The wind chill index, or equivalent temperature, is based upon a neutral skin temperature of 91°F (33°C). With physical exertion, the body heat production rises, perspiration begins, and heat is removed from the body by vaporization. The body also loses heat through conduction to cold surfaces with which it is in contact, and in breathing cold air which results in the loss of heat from the lungs. The index, therefore, does not take into account all possible losses of the body. It does, however, give a good measure of the convective cooling which is the major source of body heat loss.

The *Wind Chill Index Nomogram* illustrates the amount of cooling produced by various combinations of wind and temperature. The line for 4 miles per hour is accented because this is roughly the wind speed generated by someone walking briskly under calm conditions and is the generally accepted standard wind speed for calculating equivalent temperature. To obtain the temperature equivalent of 4 miles

WIND CHILL (EQUIVALENT TEMPERATURES)

How cold will you feel?

The temperature of the air is not always a reliable indicator of how cold a person will feel outdoors. Other weather elements, such as wind speed, relative humidity and sunshine (solar radiation), also exert an influence. In addition, the type of clothing worn, together with the state of health and the metabolism of an individual also will have an influence upon how cold he will feel. Generally, "coldness" is related to the loss of heat from exposed flesh; it can be assumed to be proportional to the measured rate of heat loss from an object.

Figure 1 (Wind Chill Equivalent Temperature Table) gives equivalent temperatures for various combinations of wind and temperature. In the example shown, a combination of 20° F. and a 10 mph wind has the same cooling power as a temperature of 3° F. and a wind speed of 4 mph.

The next time you want to know how cold it is outdoors, go ahead and check that thermometer! But keep in mind that other things (wind speed, state of nourishment, individual metabolism and protective clothing) all help to determine how "chilly" you feel at a given time and place.

WIND CHILL EQUIVALENT TEMPERATURE TABLE

WIND VELOCITY (MPH) \ DRY BULB TEMPERATURE (°F)	45	40	35	30	25	20	15	10	5	0	−5	−10	−15	−20	−25	−30	−35	−40	−45	
4	45	40	35	30	25	20	15	10	5	0	−5	−10	−15	−20	−25	−30	−35	−40	−45	4
5	43	37	32	27	22	16	11	6	0	−5	−10	−15	−21	−26	−31	−36	−42	−47	−52	5
10	34	28	22	16	10	3	−3	−9	−15	−22	−27	−34	−40	−46	−52	−58	−64	−71	−77	10
15	29	23	16	9	2	−5	−11	−18	−25	−31	−38	−45	−51	−58	−65	−72	−78	−85	−92	15
20	26	19	12	4	−3	−10	−17	−24	−31	−39	−46	−53	−60	−67	−74	−81	−88	−95	−103	20
25	23	16	8	1	−7	−15	−22	−29	−36	−44	−51	−59	−66	−74	−81	−88	−96	−103	−110	25
30	21	13	6	−2	−10	−18	−25	−33	−41	−49	−56	−64	−71	−79	−86	−93	−101	−109	−116	30
35	20	12	4	−4	−12	−20	−27	−35	−43	−52	−58	−67	−74	−82	−89	−97	−105	−113	−120	35
40	19	11	3	−5	−13	−21	−29	−37	−45	−53	−60	−69	−76	−84	−92	−100	−107	−115	−123	40
45	18	10	2	−6	−14	−22	−30	−38	−46	−54	−62	−70	−78	−85	−93	−102	−109	−117	−125	45

VERY COLD — BITTER COLD — EXTREME COLD

EXAMPLE OF TABLE USE-

Suppose the temperature outside is 25°F, and wind velocity is 10 miles-per-hour. To determine wind-chill equivalent temperature, first scan across the top of the chart until 25°F is reached (5th vertical column of the chart). This is the vertical column to be checked. Now scan down the left side of the chart until 10 is reached. This numeral 10, which designates the 3rd horizontal column, is the wind velocity measured in miles-per-hour. Now follow these two vertical and horizontal columns until they intersect. **THE NUMBER IN THE SQUARE IN WHICH THE TWO COLUMNS INTERSECT IS THE WIND-CHILL EQUIVALENT TEMPERATURE YOU SEEK.**

	45	40	35	30	25	20
4	45	40	35	30	25	20
5	43	37	32	27	22	16
10	34	28	22	16	**10**	3
15	29	23	16	9	2 (VERY COLD)	−5

Winter Storm Safety Rules

Keep ahead of the winter storm by listening to the latest weather warnings and bulletins on radio and television.

CHECK BATTERY POWERED EQUIPMENT BEFORE THE STORM ARRIVES. A portable radio or television set may be your only contact with the world outside the winter storm. Also check emergency cooking facilities and flashlights.

CHECK YOUR SUPPLY OF HEATING FUEL. Fuel carriers may not be able to move if a winter storm buries your area in snow.

CHECK YOUR FOOD and stock an extra supply. Your supplies should include food that requires no cooking or refrigeration in case of power failure.

PREVENT FIRE HAZARDS due to overheated coal or oil burning stoves, fireplaces, heaters, or furnaces.

STAY INDOORS DURING STORMS and cold snaps unless in peak physical condition. If you must go out, avoid overexertion.

DON'T KILL YOURSELF SHOVELING SNOW. It is extremely hard work for anyone in less-than-prime physical condition, and can bring on a heart attack, a major cause of death during and after winter storms.

RURAL RESIDENTS: MAKE NECESSARY TRIPS FOR SUPPLIES BEFORE THE STORM DEVELOPS OR NOT AT ALL; arrange for emergency heat supply in case of power failure; be sure camp stoves and lanterns are filled.

DRESS TO FIT THE SEASON. If you spend much time outdoors, wear loose-fitting, lightweight, warm clothing in several layers; layers can be removed to prevent perspiring and subsequent chill. Outer garments should be tightly woven, water repellent, and hooded. The hood should protect much of your face and cover your mouth to ensure warm breathing and protect your lungs from the extremely cold air. Remember that entrapped, insulating air, warmed by body heat, is the best protection against cold. Layers of protective clothing are more effective and efficient than single layers of thick clothing; and mittens, snug at the wrists, are better protection than fingered gloves.

AUTOMOBILE PREPARATIONS. Your automobile can be your best friend—or worst enemy—during winter storms, depending on your preparations. Get your car winterized before the storm season begins. Everything listed should be taken care of before winter storms strike your area: ignition system; heater; battery; brakes perfectly adjusted; lights adjusted; tire tread; wiper blades; cooling system-defroster; fuel system; snow tires installed; lubrication; chains; exhaust system tight-winter-grade oil.

Keep water out of your fuel by maintaining a FULL tank of gasoline.

BE EQUIPPED FOR THE WORST. Carry a winter storm car kit, especially if cross country travel is anticipated or if you live in the northern states.

Suggested Winter Storm Car Kit: blankets or sleeping bags, matches and candles, empty 3-pound coffee can with plastic cover, facial tissue, paper towels, extra clothing, high-calorie, nonperishable food, compass and road maps, knife, first aid kit, shovel, sack of sand, sand, flashlight or signal light, windshield scraper, booster cables, two tow chains, fire extinguisher, catalytic heater, axe.

Winter Auto Travel Safety

Winter travel by automobile is serious business. Take your travel seriously.

1. If the storm exceeds or even tests your limitations, seek available refuge immediately.
2. Plan your travel and select primary and alternate routes.
3. Check latest weather information on your radio.
4. Try not to travel alone; two or three persons are preferable.
5. Travel in convoy with another vehicle, if possible.
6. Always fill gasoline tank before entering open country, even for a short distance.
7. Drive carefully, defensively.

If a Blizzard Catches You in Your Car

AVOID OVEREXERTION AND EXPOSURE. Exertion from attempting to push your car, shovel heavy drifts, and perform other difficult chores during the strong winds, blinding snow, and bitter cold of a blizzard may cause a heart attack—even for persons in apparently good physical condition.

STAY IN YOUR VEHICLE. Do not attempt to walk out of a blizzard. Disorientation comes quickly in blowing and drifting snow. Being lost in open country during a blizzard is almost certain death. You are more likely to be found, and more likely to be sheltered, in your car.

DON'T PANIC.

KEEP FRESH AIR IN YOUR CAR. Freezing wet snow and wind-driven snow can completely seal the passenger compartment.

BEWARE THE GENTLE KILLERS: CARBON MONOXIDE AND OXYGEN STARVATION. Run the motor and heater sparingly, and only with the downwind window open for ventilation.

EXERCISE by clapping hands and moving arms and legs vigorously from time to time, and do not stay in one position for long.

TURN ON DOME LIGHT AT NIGHT, to make the vehicle visible to work crews.

KEEP WATCH. Do not permit all occupants of car to sleep at once.

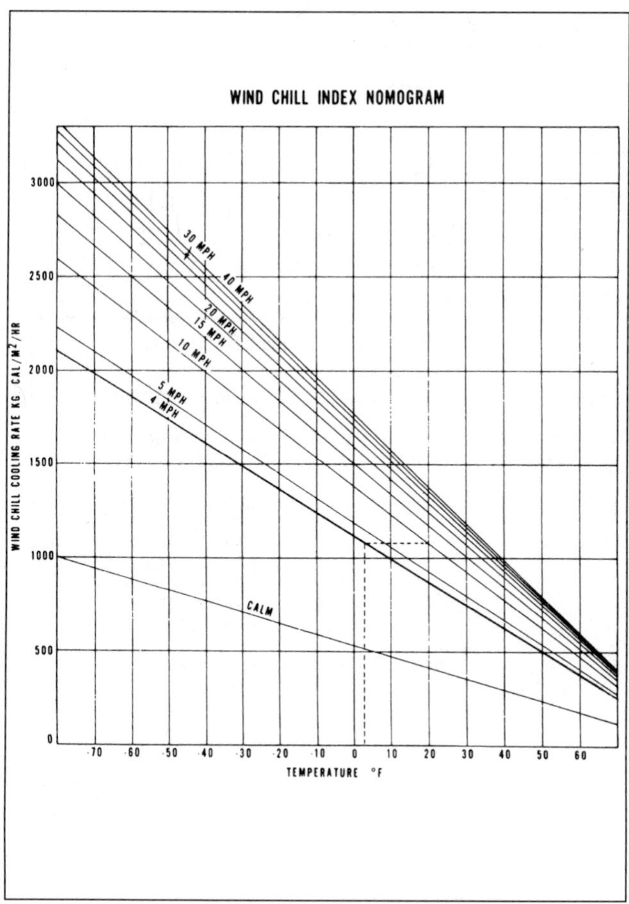

per hour from the graph, move horizontally to the left from the intersection of a given wind and temperature until the 4-mile per hour line is reached. The vertical line intersected is the equivalent temperature. In the example shown, a combination of 20°F (-6.7°C). temperature and a 10-mile per hour wind has an equivalent temperature of 3°F (-16.1°C).

• HUMIDITY & INDOOR WINTER COMFORT

Compared to summer when the moisture content of the air (relative humidity) is an important factor of body discomfort, the amount of moisture in the air in the winter has a lesser effect on the human body during outdoor winter activities. But moisture is a big factor for winter INDOOR comfort because of effects on health and energy consumption.

The colder the outdoor temperature, the more heat must be added indoors to be comfortable. That heat, however, drys the indoor air and lowers the indoor relative humidity. While a room temperature between 71° and 77°F (21.7-25°C) may be comfortable for short periods under very dry conditions, prolonged exposure to dry air has varying effects on the human body and usually causes discomfort.

Dry air has been shown to have four main effects on the human body:

1. Breathing dry air can cause such respiratory ailments as asthma, bronchitis, sinusitis, and nosebleeds or general dehydration since body fluids are depleted during respiration.
2. Skin moisture evaporation can cause skin irritations and eye itching.
3. Irritative effects, such as static electricity, which causes mild shocks when metal is touched, are common when moisture is low.
4. The "apparent temperature" of the air is lower than what the thermometer indicates, and the body "feels" colder.

These problems can be reduced by simply increasing the indoor relative humidity. By increasing the relative humidity to above 50% when the indoor temperature is between 71 and 77°F (21.7-25°C), most average dressed persons will feel comfortable. This can be done by using humidifiers, vaporizers, steam generators, or large pans of water. Even wet towels or water in a bathtub will help. The lower the room temperature the easier the relative humidity can be brought to its desired level. A relative humidity indicator (hygrometer) may be of assistance in determining the humidity in the house.

How cold will you feel?

When the humidity is low, the body feels cooler than what the thermometer indicates. While the indoor temperature may read 75°F (23.9°C), the apparent temperature (what is feels like) may be warmer or cooler depending upon the moisture content (relative humidity) of the air. Apparent temperature can vary as much as 8°F (-13.3°C) when the relative humidity ranges between 10-80%. Why? The human body cools when exposed to dry air because skin moisture evaporates, and the sense of coolness increases as humidity decreases. The dryer the room the cooler the skin feels. With a room temperature of 70°F (21.1°C), for example, a person will feel cooler if the humidity is low than if the humidity is high; this is especially noticeable when entering a dry room after bathing.

APPARENT TEMPERATURE

The apparent temperature is a measure of human discomfort due to combined heat and humidity. It was developed by Dr. R. G. Steadman (1979) and is based on studies of human physiology and textile (clothing) science. The apparent temperature is designed so that apparent temperature exceeds the actual air temperature when humidity is relatively high. The apparent temperature then measures the increased physiological heat stress and discomfort associated with higher than comfortable humidities. Note that the apparent temperature is less than the actual air temperature when humidity is relatively low and that the apparent temperature indicates the reduced stress and increased comfort associated with the higher rate of evaporative cooling of the skin.

Apparent temperatures greater than 80°F (27°C) are likely to produce some discomfort. Values in excess of 105°F (41°C) may be dangerous and even life–threatening, with severe heat exhaustion or heat stroke possible if the exposure is prolonged or physical activity is high. The degree of stress may vary with age, health, and body characteristics.

The apparent temperature as used here does not consider the effects of air movement (wind speed) or exposure to sunshine on the degree of discomfort or stress.

Reference: Steadman, R.G., 1979: The Assessment of Sultriness. Part I: A Temperature–Humidity Index Based on Human Physiology and Clothing Science. (*Journal of Applied Meteorology*, Vol. 18, pp. 861–873.)

GENERAL HEAT STRESS INDEX

DANGER CATEGORY	APPARENT TEMPERATURE	HEAT SYNDROME
IV. EXTREME DANGER	GREATER THAN 130°F	HEATSTROKE OR SUNSTROKE IMMINENT
III. DANGER	105°F – 130°F	SUNSTROKE, HEAT CRAMPS, OR HEAT EXHAUSTION LIKELY. HEAT STROKE POSSIBLE WITH PROLONGED EXPOSURE AND PHYSICAL ACTVITY
II. EXTREME CAUTION	90°F – 105°F	SUNSTROKE, HEAT CRAMPS, AND HEAT EXHAUSTION POSSIBLE WITH PROLONGED EXPOSURE AND PHYSICAL ACTIVITY
I. CAUTION	80°F – 90°F	FATIGUE POSSIBLE WITH PROLONGED EXPOSURE AND PHYSICAL ACTIVITY.

Quasi–empirical formula: AT = 1.03 T + T (exp[(DP – 59) / 17] – 1) / 19–3

AT = Apparent Temperature (°F) T = Observed Temperature (°F) DP = Dew Point (°F) exp = exponential function (raise the mathematical constant "e" to the power of the following bracketed expression).

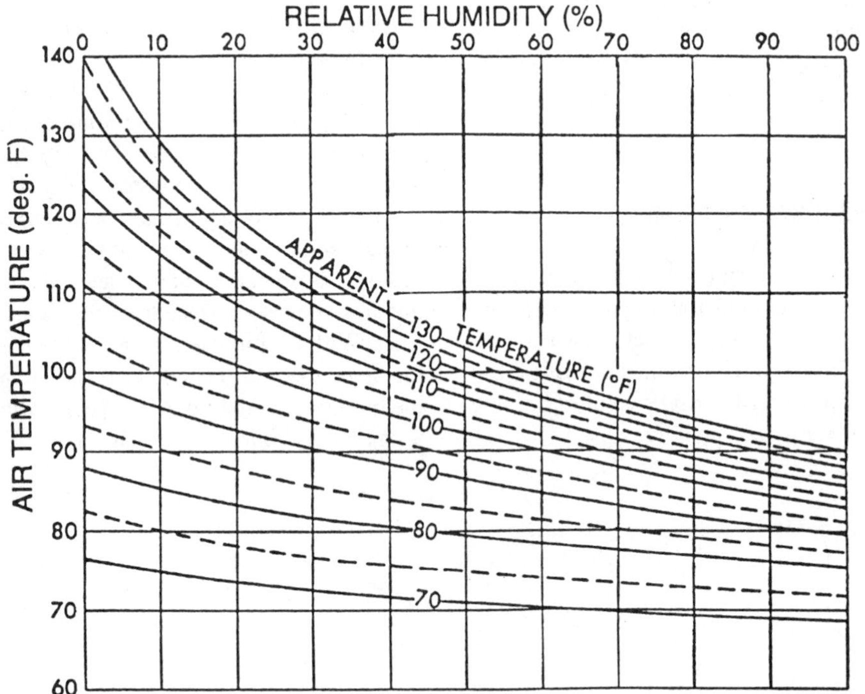

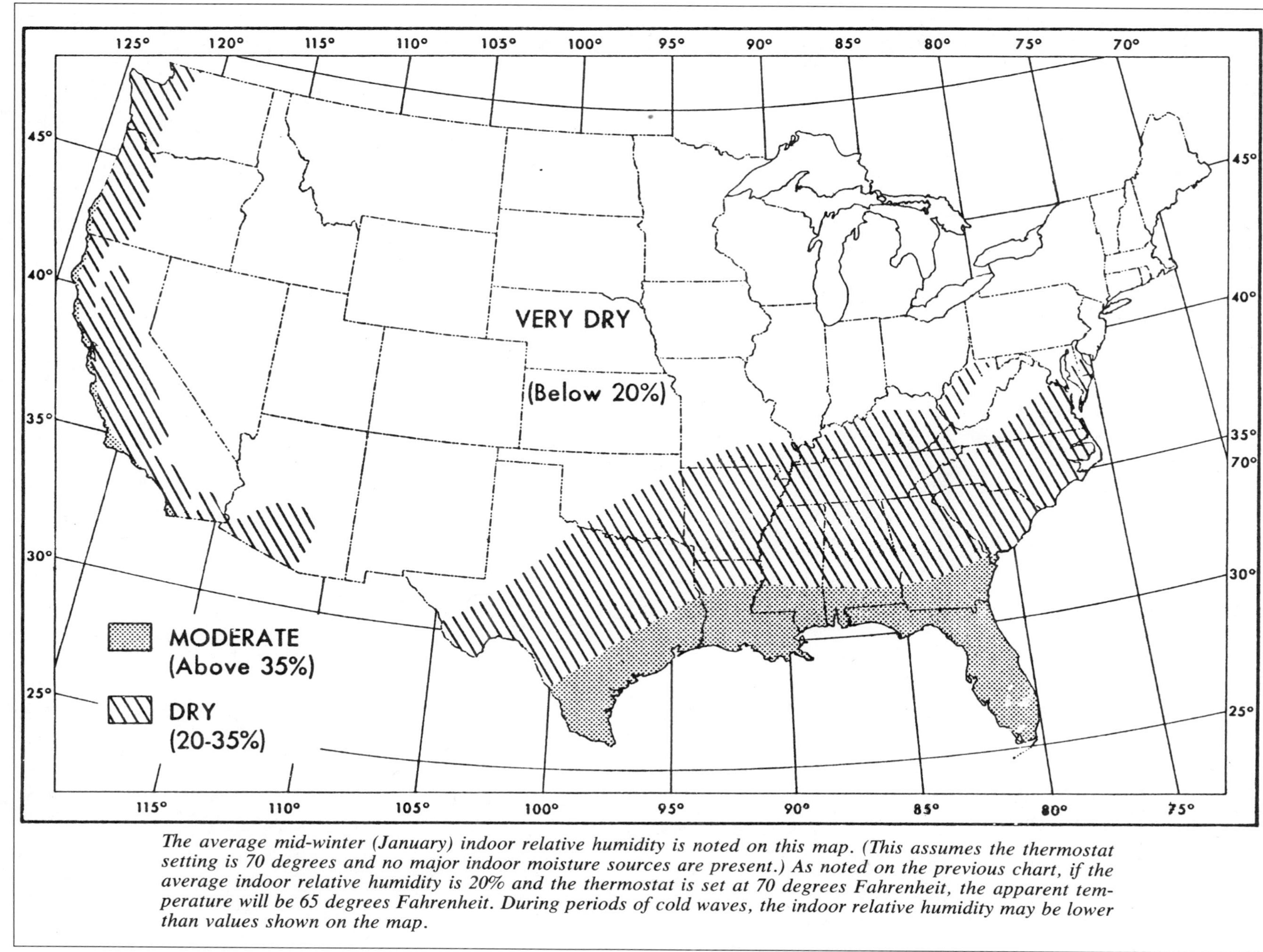

The average mid-winter (January) indoor relative humidity is noted on this map. (This assumes the thermostat setting is 70 degrees and no major indoor moisture sources are present.) As noted on the previous chart, if the average indoor relative humidity is 20% and the thermostat is set at 70 degrees Fahrenheit, the apparent temperature will be 65 degrees Fahrenheit. During periods of cold waves, the indoor relative humidity may be lower than values shown on the map.

Heat & Humidity

• HEATING DEGREE DAYS

Early this century heating engineers developed the concept of heating degree days as a useful index of heating fuel requirements. They found that when the daily mean temperature is lower than 65°F (18.3°C), most buildings require heat to maintain an inside temperature of 70°F (21.1°C). The daily mean temperature is obtained by adding together the maximum and minimum temperatures reported for the day and dividing the total by two. Each degree of mean temperature below 65 is counted as one heating degree day. Thus, if the maximum temperature is 70°F and the minimum 52°F (11.1°C), four heating degree days would be produced. (70 + 52 = 122; 122 divided by 2 = 61; 65—61 = 4). If the daily mean temperature is 65°F or higher, the heating degree day total is zero.

For every additional heating degree day, more fuel is needed to maintain a comfortable 70°F indoors. A day with a mean temperature of 35°F (1.7°C)—30 heating degree days—would require twice as much fuel as a day with a mean temperature of 50—15 heating degree days, assuming, of course, similar meteorological conditions such as wind speed and cloudiness.

Each degree below 70°F (21.1°C) that is called for as indoor temperature will conserve one heating-degree-day where the measure is used in calculating fuel unit requirements.

So valuable has the heating degree concept become that daily, monthly, and seasonal totals are routinely computed for all temperature observing stations in the National Weather Service's network. Daily figures are used by fuel companies for evaluation of fuel use rates and for efficient scheduling of deliveries. For example, if a heating system is known to use one gallon of fuel for every five heating degree days, oil deliveries will be scheduled to meet this burning rate. Gas and electric company dispatchers use the data to anticipate demand and to implement priority procedures when demand exceeds capacity.

The amount of heat required to maintain a certain temperature level is proportional to the heating degree days. A fuel bill usually will be twice as high for a month with 1,000 heating degree days as for a month with 500. For example, it can be estimated that about four times as much fuel will be required to heat a building in Chicago, where the annual average is 6,100 heating degree days as it would to heat a building in New Orleans, where the average is about 1,500. All this is true only if building construction and living habits in these areas are similar. Since such factors are not constant, these ratios must be modified by actual experience. The use of heating degree days has the advantage that consumption rates are fairly constant. i.e., fuel consumed for 100 degree days (37.8°C) is about the same whether the 100 heating degree days were accumulated on only three or four days or were spread over seven or eight days.

Accumulation of temperature data for a particular location has resulted in the establishment of "normal" values based on thirty years of record. Maps and tables of heating degree day normals are published by the National Oceanic and Atmospheric Administration's Environmental Data Service (EDS). The maps are useful only for broad general comparisons, because temperatures, even in a small area, vary considerably depending on differences in altitude, exposure, wind, and other circumstances. Tables of normal monthly and annual heating degree days for United States cities provide a more accurate basis for comparison. The tables show, for instance, that Washington, D.C. (National Airport) has a normal annual total of 4,211 heating degree days, while the normal for Boston, Massachusetts (Logan International Airport) is 5,621.

Heating degree day comparisons within a single area are the most accurate. For example, March heating degree day totals in the Midwest average about 70% of those for January. In Chicago, the coldest six months in order of decreasing coldness are January, December, February, March, November, and April. Annual heating degree day data are published by heating season which runs from July of one year through June of the next year. This enables direct comparison of seasonal heating degree day data and seasonal heating fuel requirements.

• COOLING DEGREE DAYS

The cooling degree day statistic—summer sister of the familiar heating degree day—serves as an index of air-conditioning requirements during the year's warmest months.

According to experts, the need for air-conditioning begins to be felt when the daily maximum temperature climbs to 80°F (26.7°C) and higher. The cooling degree day is therefore a kind of mirror image of the heating degree day.

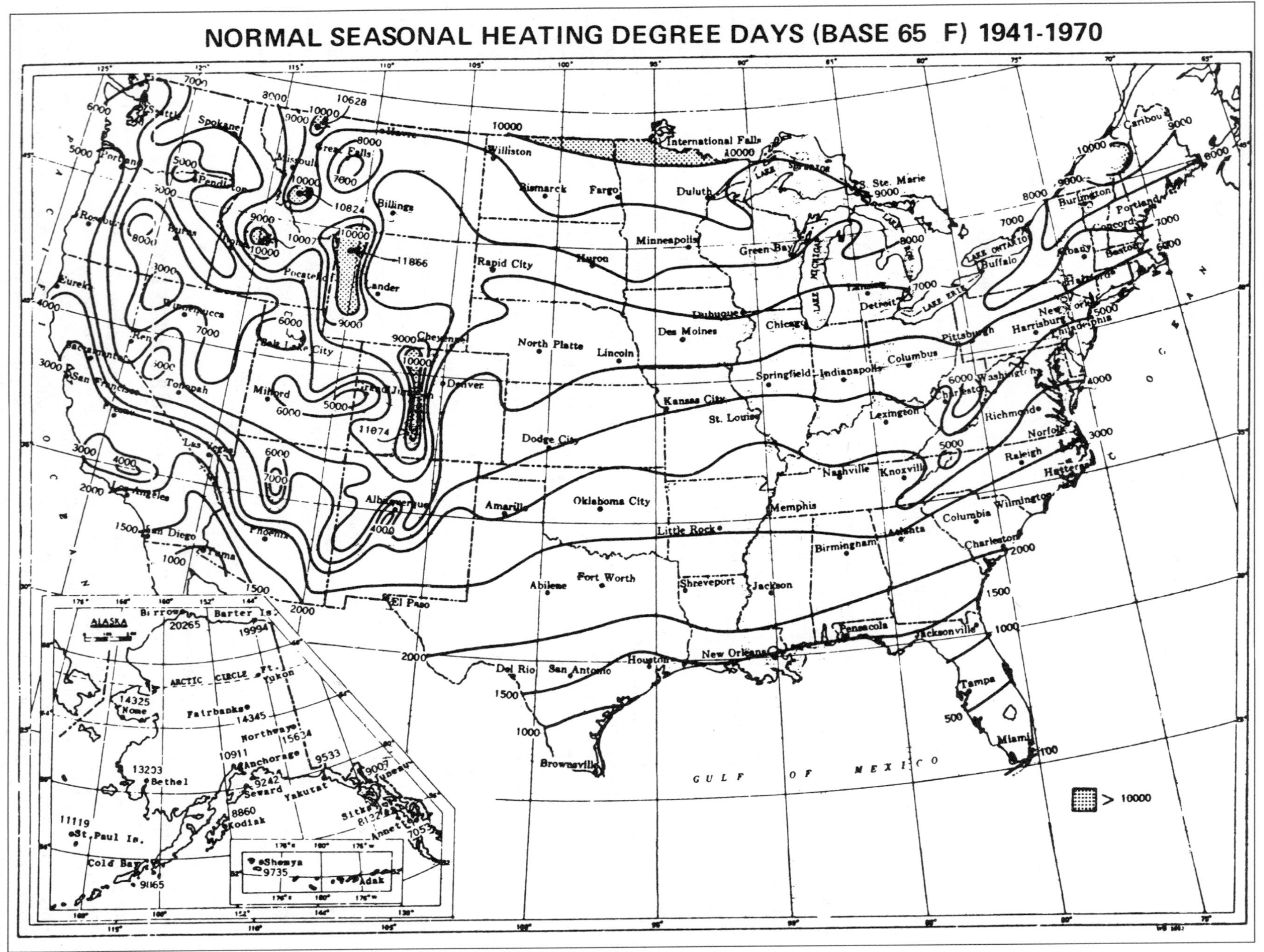
NORMAL SEASONAL HEATING DEGREE DAYS (BASE 65 F) 1941-1970
> 10000
GULF OF MEXICO
ALASKA
ARCTIC CIRCLE

After obtaining the daily mean temperature, by adding together the day's high and low temperatures and dividing the total by two, the base 65 is subtracted from the resulting figure to determine the cooling degree day total. For example, a day with a maximum temperature of 82°F (27.8°C) and a minimum of 60°F (15.6°C) would produce six cooling degree days. (82 + 60 = 142; 142 divided by 2 = 71; 71 - 65 = 6). If the daily mean temperature is 65°F (18.3°C) or lower, the cooling degree day total is zero.

The greater the number of cooling degree days, the more energy is required to maintain indoor temperatures at a comfortable level. However, the relationship between cooling degree days and energy use is less precise than that between heating degree days and fuel consumption. There is considerable controversy among meteorologists, as well as air-conditioning engineers, as to what meteorological variables are most closely related to energy consumption by air-conditioning systems. Many experts argue that because high humidity levels make people feel more uncomfortable as temperatures rise, some measure of moisture should be included in calculating energy needs for air-conditioning. In addition to humidity some experts feel there are other factors, such as cloudiness and wind speed, that should be included in computation of energy needs for air-conditioning. All agree, however, that there is a need for a more effective measure of the influence of weather on air-conditioning loads.

Until a definitive study of the problem is conducted, NOAA's EDS is continuing to use and publish statistics based on simple cooling degree day calculations, employing air temperatures measured at National Weather Service Offices and cooperating stations throughout the country. As with heating degree days, normals of cooling degree days have been established, based on thirty years of record.

It should be noted that heating and cooling degree days do not cancel each other out. Totals for each are accumulated independently.

• HEAT WAVE DANGERS

In a "normal" year, about 175 Americans die from summer heat and too much sun—"excessive heat and insolation" is the vital statistics category. Among our family of natural hazards, only the excessive cold of winter—not lightning, hurricanes, tornadoes, floods, earthquakes, or tsunamis—takes a greater average toll.

Heat waves make a tragic difference

In the period 1950 through 1967, more than 8,000 persons were killed in the United States by the effects of heat and solar radiation. The 1,401 dead in 1952, the 978 in 1954, and the several years with death tolls closer to 600 push the yearly average for this period to about 452 deaths, a high price to pay for warm weather.

These are direct casualties. It is not known how many deaths are encouraged by excessive heat or solar radiation—for example, how many diseased or aging hearts surrender that would not have under better conditions. Heat waves bring great stresses to the human body; among the aged or infirm are many whose systems cannot withstand the extreme summer conditions.

Most summers see heat waves in one section or another of the United States. East of the Rockies, they tend to be periods of high temperatures and humidities—those oppressive, muggy days when human comfort is just an expression—although the worst have been catastrophically dry.

Among the big ones are the hot summer of 1830, which scorched the north central interior, and that of 1860, which dried up the Great Plains. July 1901 may still be talked about by old timers in the middle west, remembering high temperatures, or thinking about someone the heat killed—there were 9,508 heat deaths in that year.

Past heat waves

There is nothing in American climatological annals to touch the heat waves which came with the Dust Bowl droughts of the 1930s. The years 1930, 1934, and 1936 brought progressively more severe summer weather. Record highs of 121°F (48.95°C) in North Dakota and Kansas, and 120°F (48.9°C) in South Dakota, Oklahoma, Arkansas, and Texas were observed in the ugly summer of 1936; July and August of that year saw record highs of 109°F (42.8°C) or better tied or broken in Indiana. Louisiana, Maryland, Michigan, Minnesota, Nebraska, New Jersey, Pennsylvania, West Virginia, and Wisconsin.

These were cruel years in terms of heat deaths. From 1930 through 1936, ranging from a low of 678 deaths in 1932 to 4,768 in 1936, heat killed nearly 15,000 persons. The toll is consistently high, but tends sharply upward with increases in average July temperatures. This relationship between excessive July heat and significant jumps in heat deaths persists to the present day, despite the softening effects of modern consumer technology.

The first half of the 1950s was on the hot side, and its heat death toll is correspondingly high. Many states had their hottest summer of record in 1952; that year's death toll, 1,401, is the highest for the 1950-67 period. The summer of 1954, a year when heat killed 978, was almost as bad.

The heat wave of July 1966 covered much of the eastern and middle continent with high temperatures and very high humidity. Over 400 people died as a result of the heat wave (as compared to nearly 100 in 1965).

Heat waves of 1980 and 1993

One of the most tragic heat waves since the 1930s occurred in 1980, according to the National Center for Health Statistics. That year unusually high temperatures held the central and southwestern United States in their grip for the best part of 15 weeks, and directly or indirectly caused 1,700 deaths. This total, which also includes occupationally-

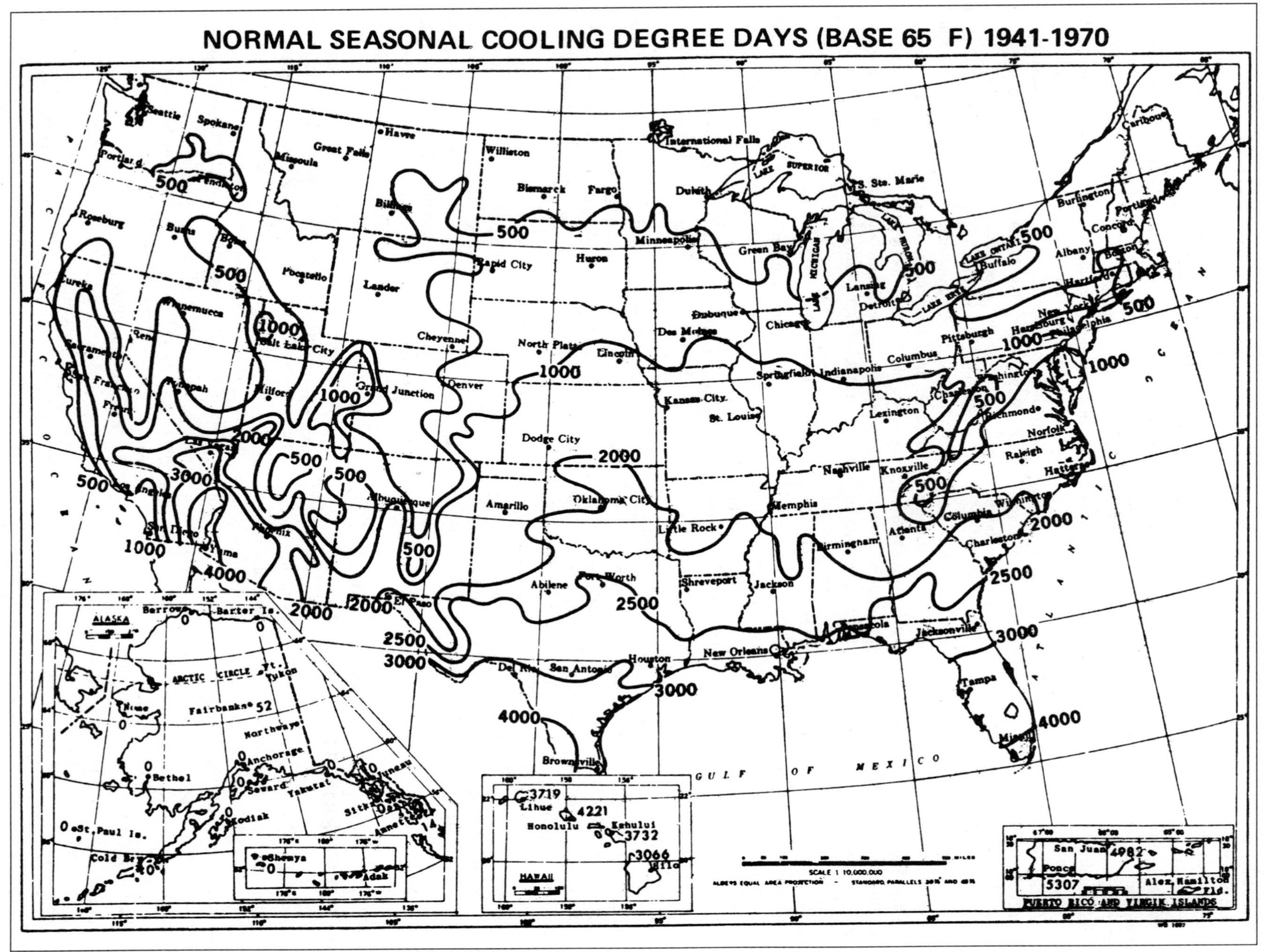
NORMAL SEASONAL COOLING DEGREE DAYS (BASE 65 F) 1941-1970
Seattle
Spokane
Portland
Pendleton
Roseburg
Burns
Boise
Eureka
Winnemucca
Reno
Sacramento
San Francisco
Fresno
Tonopah
Los Angeles
San Diego
Yuma
Phoenix
Las Vegas
Milford
Salt Lake City
Pocatello
Missoula
Great Falls
Havre
Billings
Lander
Cheyenne
Denver
Grand Junction
Albuquerque
El Paso
Williston
Bismarck
Fargo
Rapid City
Huron
North Platte
Lincoln
Dodge City
Amarillo
Oklahoma City
Abilene
Fort Worth
Del Rio
San Antonio
Houston
Brownsville
International Falls
Duluth
Minneapolis
Green Bay
Des Moines
Dubuque
Chicago
Kansas City
St. Louis
Springfield
Indianapolis
Little Rock
Shreveport
Jackson
Memphis
Nashville
Knoxville
Lexington
Columbus
Pittsburgh
Lansing
Detroit
Buffalo
S. Ste. Marie
Birmingham
Atlanta
Columbia
Charleston
Wilmington
Raleigh
Norfolk
Richmond
Washington
Harrisburg
Philadelphia
New York
Hartford
Albany
Boston
Concord
Burlington
Portland
Caribou
New Orleans
Pensacola
Jacksonville
Tampa
Miami
Hatteras
LAKE SUPERIOR
LAKE MICHIGAN
LAKE HURON
LAKE ONTARIO
LAKE ERIE
GULF OF MEXICO
ALASKA
Barrow
Barter Is.
ARCTIC CIRCLE
Ft. Yukon
Fairbanks 52
Nome
Northway
Anchorage
Bethel
Seward
Yakutat
Juneau
Sitka
Annette
Kodiak
St. Paul Is.
Cold Bay
Shemya
Adak
HAWAII
Lihue 3719
Honolulu 4221
Kahului 3732
Hilo 3066
San Juan 4982
Ponce 5307
Alex. Hamilton Fld.
PUERTO RICO AND VIRGIN ISLANDS
SCALE 1:10,000,000
ALBERS EQUAL AREA PROJECTION - STANDARD PARALLELS 29½° AND 45½°

related heat deaths, is more than nine times that of an ordinary year.

The 1980 heat wave, began about June 10, and except for remissions from about July 21 to about August 10, and August 17 to about September 1, lasted continuously through September's third week. As an example of its intensity, the first week of September saw temperatures of 9°F (-12.8°C) above normal over much of the central and eastern states.

On the weekend of July 14, 1993, states throughout the Midwest recorded record-high temperatures. The city of Chicago, experiencing its worst heat emergency ever, attributed over 700 deaths (primarily senior citizens) to the heat or to heat-related activities. Later in the summer, the municipal government developed and implemented heat-crisis plans which included setting up "cooling centers" and contacting senior citizens (to offer fans or transportation to cooling centers, etc.).

• HOW ORDINARY SUMMER HEAT DEVELOPS

Given terrain and geographic situation, North American summers are bound to be hot. As the advancing sun drives back the polar air, the land is opened up to light and solar heat, and occupied by masses of moist warm air spun landward off the tropical ocean. With these rain-filled visitors come the tongues of dry desert air that flick northward out of Mexico, and, occasionally, the hot winds called chinooks which howl down the Rockies' eastern slopes.

Inequalities of atmospheric heating and cooling, of moistness and aridity, are regulated at middle latitudes by horizontal and vertical mixing. The mixing apparatus is the parade of cyclones (low-pressure centers, or Lows) and anticyclones (high-pressure centers, or Highs) which lie at the heart of most weather, good and bad.

The cyclones and anticyclones drift in the mid-latitude westerlies, the prevailing eastward-blowing winds which follow a scalloped path around the Northern Hemisphere. The large-scale undulations of these winds may extend for thousands of miles, and are called planetary waves. Their high-speed core is the jet stream, which snakes across the continent some 6-8 miles (9.66-12.88 km) up, keeping mainly to the cool side of Highs and Lows as they form and spin and die below it.

The kind of weather predominating in an area over a period of time depends largely on the prevailing position and orientation of the jet stream. As the continent warms, the jet stream shifts northward, along with the tracks of surface weather disturbances. Cyclones like the ones which brought April rains to the Gulf states bring June thundershowers to the Plains; the humid spring of Georgia becomes the muggy summer of Illinois.

These semi-regular alternations of instability and equilibrium, hot and cool, moist and dry, combine year-in and year-out to generate the average June-to-September climate for North America.

How heat waves occur

When these alternating processes are somehow interrupted, the climatic "norm" of summer is marred by a heat wave. The anomaly is usually associated with a change in the planetary waves, so that the prevailing winds from the southwestern deserts sweep farther north than usual and blanket a large region with hot, often humid air at ground level. An upper-level High may settle over the mid-continent, destroying cloud cover with its descending, compression-heated currents, until the blessing of fair weather turns to the curse of drought. In addition, heat from the hot, dry ground feeds back into the atmosphere, tending to perpetuate the heat wave circulation.

Whatever the cause, the effect is uncomfortable and dangerous. Continental heat waves live in human memory the fierce winters do.

• THE HUMAN BODY'S REACTION TO HEAT

To keep on the cool side of their upper thermal limits, our bodies dissipate heat by varying the rate and depth of blood circulation, by losing water through the skin and sweat glands, and, as the last extremity is reached, by panting. Under normal conditions, these reflex activities are kept in balance and controlled by the brain's hypothalamus, a comparatively simple sensor of rising and failing environmental temperatures, and a sophisticated manager of temperatures inside.

Like the hot light in a car, the hypothalamus responds to the temperature of coolant, in this case, blood. A surge of blood heated above 98.6°F (37°C) sends the hypothalamus into action. As its orders go out, the heart begins to pump more blood, blood vessels dilate to accommodate the increased flow, and the bundles of tiny capillaries threading through the upper layers of the skin are put into operation. The body's blood is circulated closer to the skin's surface, and excess heat drains off into the cooler atmosphere. At the same time, water diffuses through the skin as insensible perspiration, so-called because it evaporates before it becomes visible, and the skin seems dry to the touch.

Heat loss from increased circulation and insensible perspiration is a comparatively minor correction. If the hypothalamus continues to sense overheating, it calls upon the millions of sweat glands which perforate the outer layer of our skin. These tiny glands can shed great quantities of water (and heat) in what is called sensible perspiration, or sweating. Between sweating and insensible perspiration, the skin handles about 90% of the body's heat-dissipating function.

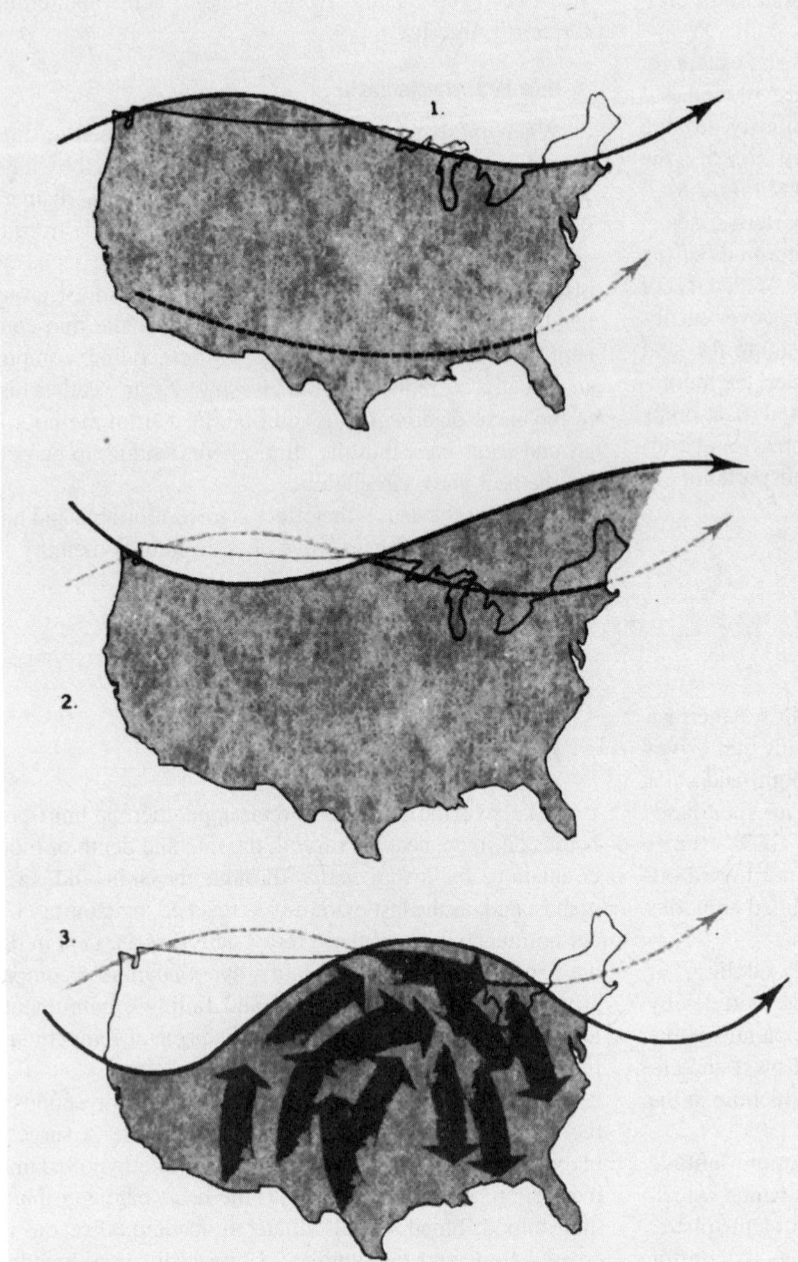

In summer the jet stream can be an ill wind indeed. As the sun drives the polar front back into Canada, the jet stream keeps to the cool side of the boundary, and shifts northward (1). The summer is a"normal" one—hot but not too hot; humid but not too humid. But the polar front and jet stream may be oriented so that their eastern segment is displaced farther to the north (2), setting the stage for a midwestern and eastern heat wave. A persistent High can block the jet stream northward (3), its clockwise, sinking circulation drawing in hot dry air from the southwestern deserts, and dry air from the northwest. This classical Dust Bowl pattern brings hot, dry weather to the mid-continent, but often means cooler-than-normal conditions in New England and the far northwest. (Jet stream position at 500 mb level is shown here.)

As environmental temperature approaches normal body temperature, physical discomfort is replaced by physical danger. The body loses its ability to get rid of heat through the circulatory system, because there is no heat-drawing drop in temperature between the skin and the surrounding aid. At this point, the skin's elimination of heat by sweating becomes virtually the only means of maintaining constant temperature.

Most water enters the atmosphere via the process of evaporation, the jump from liquid to vapor phase; to do this, a water molecule must absorb enough energy to break the tenacious clutch of its fellow molecules. Evaporation, consequently, has the effect of absorbing large quantities of energy in the form of latent heat, which cools the parent body. This is familiar to anyone who has stepped from a bath into a dry room. The breakdown of the evaporation process when one steps from a bath into a hot, moist room is just as familiar.

Sweating, by itself, does nothing to cool the body, unless the water is removed by evaporation—and high relative humidity retards evaporation. Under conditions of high temperature (above 90°F or 32.2°C) and high relative humidity (above 75%), the body is doing everything it can to maintain 98.6°F inside. The heart is pumping a torrent of blood through dilated circulatory vessels, the sweat glands are pouring liquids—and essential dissolved chemicals, like sodium and chloride—onto the surface of the skin. And the body's metabolic heat production goes on, down in the vital organs.

Still, the thermal limits are there. When they are exceeded by very much or for very long, the warm-blooded organism does not doze, reptile fashion. It dies.

A study of three September heat waves in Los Angeles and Orange County, California, shows what excessive temperature alone can do. Without the complicating factors of high humidity or air pollution, the heat waves were accompanied by an increased mortality, especially among the elderly. The California study agreed with other researchers that increased mortality in a heat wave tends to follow maximum temperatures by about one day—the day it takes to overwork a tired circulatory system. The causes of "extra" deaths in September 1963 would seem to bear this out. Most were assigned to coronary and cerebrovascular disease. Heat syndrome was almost absent.

Heat syndrome refers to several clinically recognizable disturbances of the human thermoregulatory system. The disorders generally have to do with a reduction or collapse of the body's ability to shed heat by circulatory changes and sweating, or a chemical (salt) imbalance caused by too much sweating. Ranging in severity from the vague malaise of heat asthenia to the extremely lethal heat stroke, heat syndrome disorders share one common feature: the individual has overexposed or overexercised for his age and physical condition for the thermal environment.

Sunburn, while not categorized as heat syndrome, is pertinent here, for ultraviolet radiation burns can significantly retard the skin's ability to shed excess heat.

Studies of heat syndrome and its victims indicate that it occurs at all ages of man, but, other things being equal, the severity of the disorder tends to increase with age—heat cramps in a 17-year-old may be heat exhaustion in someone 40, and heat stroke in a person over 60.

There is evidence that heat waves are worse in the airless, brick, and asphalt canyons of the "inner cities" than in the better lawned, more open suburbs.

Acclimatization has to do with adjusting sweatsalt concentrations, among other things. In winter and summer, this concentration changes, just as it does when one moves from Boston to Panama. The idea is to lose enough water to regulate body temperature, with the least possible chemical disturbance. Because females appear to be better at this than males—females excrete less sweat and so less salt—heat syndrome usually strikes fewer females.

For people with heart disease, climatic stress is worse than for others. In a hot, humid environment, impaired evaporation and water loss hamper thermal regulation, while physical exertion and heart failure increase the body's rate of heat production. The ensuing cycle is vicious in the extreme.

Heat Wave Safety Rules

1. SLOW DOWN. Your body can't do its best in high temperatures and humidities, and might do its worst.
2. HEED YOUR BODY'S EARLY WARNINGS THAT HEAT SYNDROME IS ON THE WAY. Reduce your level of activities immediately and get to a cooler environment.
3. DRESS FOR SUMMER. Lightweight, light-colored clothing reflects heat and sunlight, and helps your thermoregulatory system maintain normal body temperature.
4. EAT SMALL MEALS AND EAT MORE OFTEN. Avoid foods that are high in protein, which increase metabolic heat.
5. DON'T DRY OUT. Heat wave weather can wring you out before you know it. Drink plenty of water while the hot spell lasts, even if you don't feel thirsty.
6. AVOID THERMAL SHOCK. Acclimatize yourself gradually to warmer weather. Treat yourself extra gently for those first critical two or three hot days.
7. VARY YOUR THERMAL ENVIRONMENT. Physical stress increases with exposure time in heat wave weather. Try to get out of the heat for at least a few hours each day. If you can't do this at home, drop in on a cool store, restaurant, or theater—anything to keep your exposure time down.
8. DON'T GET TOO MUCH SUN. Sunburn makes the job of heat dissipation that much more difficult.
9. KNOW THE HEAT SYNDROME SYMPTOMS AND FIRST AID.

Heat Index

"It isn't the heat; it's the humidity." The job of keeping the body cool falls increasingly upon the evaporation of sweat as the temperature rises. Meanwhile, the other forms of heat dissipation such as radiation and convection, which depend upon temperature differences between the skin and the surroundings, are reduced in effectiveness. In turn, the rate of evaporation of sweat is influenced by the humidity in the surrounding air. (Wind speed and thermal radiation are also factors).

Discomfort is usually a complaint as soon as sweating begins, although to be sure the discomfort and heat stress on the body would be much greater if one could not sweat. "Politeness" aside, it is unfortunate that some people do not sweat as soon or as much as others. Clothing reduces the effectiveness of sweating, but it is needed for protection from the sun. In order to reflect heat and enhance circulation of air, hot weather clothing should be light colored, light weight, porous, and loose fitting. For most individuals, cotton or high cotton blends are still the best hot weather fabrics.

Livestock weather safety index

Livestock, like human beings, are subject to heat stress that is variable not only with temperature but with different combinations of temperature and relative humidity. This is particularly true for animals that are confined or being loaded or transported.

HEAT AND SUN FIRST-AID

Heat Syndrome	Caused by	Symptoms	First Aid
HEAT ASTHENIA (OR CALASTHENIA)	Excessively hot, humid environment.	Easy fatigue, headache, mental and physical inefficiency, poor appetite, insomnia, heavy sweating, high pulse rate, shallow breathing, and sometimes circulatory stress in the ill.	**Respite from heat and humidity, plenty of fluids, and, if sweating is heavy (and no dietary restrictions prevent it) a salt tablet and rest.**
HEAT CRAMPS	Strenuous activity under conditions of high heat and humidity, when evaporative cooling is impaired, stimulating excessive sweating and loss of salts from blood and tissue, causing cramps.	Painful spasms of voluntary muscles, contraction in flexor muscles in fingers, then larger muscles in legs and abdominal wall. Pupils dilate with each spasm, there may be heavy sweating, skin becomes cold and clammy. Unlike severe abdominal disease symptoms, heat cramps are intermittent.	**Usually respond better to firm pressure on cramping muscles than to vigorous kneading. Application of warm wet towels also gives relief.**
HEAT EXHAUSTION	Prolonged hot spell, excessive exposure, physical exertion cause thermoregulatory breakdown involving loss of vasomotor (blood-vessel diameter) control and circulatory shock.	Profuse sweating, weakness, vertigo, and sometimes heat cramps; symptoms similar to calasthenia may herald by several days. Skin is cold and pale, clammy with sweat; pulse is thready and blood pressure is low. Body temperature is normal or sub-normal. Vomiting may occur. Unconsciousness is rare.	**Move to cooler environment immediately. Provide bed rest, salt solution (see above); victims, sometimes nauseated at first, can usually take fluids after a period of rest. Seek medical help for severe heat exhaustion.**

HEAT STROKE (or sunstroke, heat collapse, thermic fever, heat hyperexia)	Failure of thermoregulatory and cardiovascular systems brought about when intensive sweating under conditions of high heat and humidity restrict heat dissipation by sweating, which finally ceases. Advanced age and hot, humid, windless environment are factors.	Weakness, vertigo, nausea, headache, heat cramps, mild heat exhaustion, excessive sweating. Sweating stops just before heat stroke. Then temperature rises sharply, often to 106° or more, pulse is bounding and full, blood pressure elevated. Delirium or coma is common. Armpit and groin areas are dry (they are wet in heat exhaustion). Skin is flushed and pink at first; however, in later stages, it appears ashen or purplish.	**Heat stroke is a very serious emergency. Medical care is urgently needed. Move the victim into cooler, indoor environment, remove his clothing, put him to bed. Primary objective is to reduce body temperature, preferably by iced bath (or by sponging the body with alcohol or lukewarm water) until a tolerable level (about 103° or a pulse rate below 110 per minute) is reached. Caution is necessary here.**
SUNBURN	Overexposure to ultraviolet radiation.	Redness and pain caused by dilation of small blood vessels in skin. In more severe cases, tissue injury brings swelling of skin, blisters, and often fever and headache. Because it impairs thermoregulatory efficiency, sunburn may be accompanied by other heat syndrome disorders.	**Prevent severe sunburn by limiting the time of initial exposure, depending on comfort and conditions. Treat mild sunburn with cold cream or certain oils or greases (e.g., salad oil, shortening). Wash hands before applying. Do not apply butter or oleomargarine. Dressing should be used if blistering appears, injured area should not be exposed to sunlight until healed. Medical care is needed for extensive or severe cases.**

HEAT STROKE IS A SEVERE MEDICAL EMERGENCY. SUMMON A PHYSICIAN OR GET THE PATIENT TO A HOSPITAL IMMEDIATELY. DELAY CAN BE FATAL.

SOURCE: U.S. Dept. of Commerce
National Oceanic and Atmospheric Administration

Heat Index Chart

Air Temperature and Relative Humidity versus Apparent Temperature

RELATIVE HUMIDITY(%)

Heat Index (or Apparent Temperature)

	0	5	10	15	20	25	30	35	40	45	50	55	60	65	70	75	80	85	90	95	100
140	125																				
135	120	128																			
130	117	122	131																		
125	111	116	123	131	141																
120	107	111	116	123	130	139	148														
115	103	107	111	115	120	127	135	143	151												
110	99	102	105	108	112	117	123	130	137	143	150										
105	95	97	100	102	105	109	113	118	123	129	135	142	149								
100	91	93	95	97	99	101	104	107	110	115	120	126	132	138	144						
95	87	88	90	91	93	94	96	98	101	104	107	110	114	119	124	130	136				
90	83	84	85	86	87	88	90	91	93	95	96	98	100	102	106	109	113	117	122		
85	78	79	80	81	82	83	84	85	86	87	88	89	90	91	93	95	97	99	102	105	108
80	73	74	75	76	77	77	78	79	79	80	81	81	82	83	85	86	86	87	88	89	91
75	69	69	70	71	72	72	73	73	74	74	75	75	76	76	77	77	78	78	79	79	80
70	64	64	65	65	66	66	67	67	68	68	69	69	70	70	70	70	71	71	71	71	72

This chart shows how hot it *feels* (apparent temperature) based on the combination of humidity and actual air temperature.

Additional hazard: the effect of calm, cloudless days

Lack of cloud cover and little or no movement of air are additional hazards which can increase stress and should be considered. An emergency situation is most likely to develop when the temperature is 90-95°F (32.2-35°C) early in the day, and higher temperatures are forecast for the period that the livestock will be in the marketing process. Additional stress created by handling livestock should be kept at an absolute minimum.

Reduction of hazard: the effect of wind

The cooling effect of wind can alleviate conditions by lowering temperature a few degrees in open areas. However, when the air temperature approaches the skin temperature of the animal, the cooling effect of wind becomes minimal.

Acclimatization

Hot, humid weather is more detrimental to livestock in the early summer than in mid- or late summer and during any season following an extended cool period. This heat tolerance has not been qualified but should be considered during periods of marginal danger or emergency categories.

Hogs are a special problem

Most livestock do not adjust readily to high temperatures (heat stress). Hogs are especially vulnerable when closely confined in a vehicle, building, or pen. A careful study by Livestock Conservation Inc. (Chicago, IL) of the relationship of hog deaths during the marketing process shows that high temperatures, especially with high relative humidity, cause abnormally high losses.

Heat build up internally in the hog's body if it cannot be thrown off by the lungs or skin. If the internal temperature reaches 105-106°F (40-41°C), heat exhaustion occurs and will be followed by death unless the situation is relieved.

Hogs lose about 80% of their body heat through the lungs when the environmental temperature is above 80° (27°C); only 20% is lost from the skin by radiation and air movement. Hogs must breathe approximately 20 times as much air at 100° (38°C) as at 80°F to maintain a safe internal body temperature (around 102°F (39°C) when their environmental temperature is 100°).

National Weather Service warnings

Many forecast offices of the National Weather Service (U.S. Department of Commerce, National Oceanic and Atmospheric Administration) issue Danger and/or Emergency Warnings. If potential users are unaware of this program they should contact their local weather service office or agricultural extension agent for information on service in their region.

Earthquakes

• BAY AREA'S 1989 EARTHQUAKE TEACHES BASIC LESSONS

There is no substitute for experience in understanding an earthquake. Most of us will never have a significant earthquake experience, but millions had the next thing to it when television was uniquely deployed in San Francisco (for other reasons) and shifted its focus to tell us first-hand how the violent shaking there felt and looked.

At 5:04 P.M., on a quiet, autumnal afternoon—October 17, 1989—the San Andreas fault upset life beyond description in the San Francisco-Oakland Bay area. It heaved its giant breast in the Santa Cruz Mountains and wrought havoc in widening circles that reached throughout the bay area and shook buildings as far as Reno, Nevada, 250 miles (402.5 km) to the east, and quivered skyscrapers 400 miles (644 km) south in Los Angeles. The internationally televised third game of baseball's World Series, about to begin, gave the world the word and picture as it was happening, beginning with views of apprehensive players and fans inside Candlestick Park stadium, and combining them with telephoto visuals of the fires and devastation some 8-10 miles (12.88-16.1 km) to the north. However, virtually no one in the bay area needed the ABC television crew to tell them that the "big one" was happening. Fanning out in every direction from the epicenter, shock waves that reached 6.9 on the Richter scale were sundering the afternoon quiet of uncounted thousands of people—sundering it in a way that visited fright on the entire area, then destruction and, in the next minutes, death (estimates say more than 100 fatalities) as only an earthquake can. The injured persons count topped 3,000, said authorities.

As earthquakes go, the intensity, maintained for a short 15 seconds, was great. But it was nowhere near the 9.2 reading of the 1964 Alaskan quake that destroyed with tidal waves as much as with earth shaking. (Each whole number on the Richter scale equals ten times greater intensity than the previous whole number). The toll in life and property of this 1989 cataclysm (third most lethal of all time) resulted because the epicenter was so close to very large concentrations of population and technology-laced living styles. In the cities of San Francisco, Oakland, and other edge communities, the lives of millions, densely packed into a few square miles, involves structures of all types and descriptions. Very important, it involves the penultimate in steel and concrete structure, a double-deck freeway connecting Oakland and the mainland to San Francisco's peninsula.

Structures that survived, and some that didn't

Safest structures proved to be high-rise office buildings in San Francisco, constructed since a 1971 tremor had spurred new standards; most vulnerable were the restored single homes built 60-90 years ago on landfills in an area known as the Marina district of San Francisco. The former coped with the shocks with well planned engineering provisions, resulting in minimal damage. Meanwhile, more than 50 of the latter (wood and brick structures) collapsed into their foundations, and life loss was high as scores were trapped inside because things happened so fast. The really shocking element of the catastrophe was reserved however for the freeway. Due to reasoning that seems strange in retrospect, the lifeline traffic artery known as the Nimitz Freeway (Interstate Route 80) had been created years before as a double decker with its supports assumed to be, but never tested to be, earthquake resistant. The supports failed this test. Cars and drivers alike were crushed in mid-cruise as the upper deck first undulated with the shock wave then dropped its millions of tons of steel and concrete on the deck below. Drivers were pinned and vehicles crushed as if made of cardboard. The San Francisco-Oakland Bay bridge fared only slightly better, with one end of an upper section falling to meet the lower level, closing it for days.

As terrifying as this quake was, carnage was in one sense light because the early start of the ballgame had drained the streets of much rush hour traffic. That is small consolation to the families of those who died, but a blessing to thousands of others whose route would have placed them directly under the collapsing concrete that repudiated its supports as fast as one could say "deathly inadequate."

• NORTHRIDGE, CALIFORNIA, 1994

Early on the morning of January 17, 1994, Martin Luther King Day, Los Angeles area residents were jolted awake by what was to be the most significant urban earthquake to occur in California since 1906. The initial ten seconds of trembling ground resulted in massive property damage and loss of life.

A Chatsworth apartment is separated (1994).

The powerful quake struck at its epicenter of Northridge at 4:31 A.M. on January 17, reaching a magnitude of 6.8. Residents within an area of approximately 2,192 square miles (5,677 km^2) experienced over 1,000 aftershocks of a magnitude of 1.5 for weeks after the quake.

Nearly 100 deaths and 9,000 injuries resulted from the incident. Over 50,000 people were displaced from their homes; thousands of individuals were forced to move to temporary shelters in schools and churches, or camp in city parks and endure the chilly, less-than-favorable temperatures and rain.

Nearly 114,039 residential and commercial structures were damaged in the area despite the fact that seismic building code provisions and other mitigations had been intensified especially since Loma Prieta earthquake, 1989. Total damage amount has been estimated at $17 billion. This most recent seismic event has brought to light the difficulties in protecting Californians from their rather seismically unsafe environment.

• UNDERSTANDING EARTHQUAKES & WHY THEY ARE ALWAYS A SURPRISE

Most natural hazards can be detected before their threat matures. But *seisms* (from the greek *seismos*, earthquake) have no known precursors, and so they come without warning, like the vengeance of an ancient, lunatic god. For this reason, they continue to kill in some areas at a level usually reserved for wars and epidemics—the 68,000 dead in Peru died on May 31, 1970, not in antiquity. Nor is the horror of lethal earthquake completed with a heavy toll. The homeless living are left to cope with fire, looting, pestilence, fear, and the burden of rebuilding of what the planet so easily shrugs away.

Earthquakes have not been the killers in the United States they have in Eurasia and Africa. A 1972 study revealed that fewer than 1,600 deaths have been caused by earthquakes and tsunamis in the United States, and 700 of these came in the 1906 San Francisco earthquake and fire. Of more than 115,000 deaths from major earthquakes worldwide since 1960, fewer than 300 occurred in the United States.

Property damage is a different story. The San Francisco earthquake of 1906 did an estimated $24 million property damage, and the ensuring fire $500 million more. Between the time of that expensive tremor (imagine what $524 million translates to in 1991 dollars!) and the 1989 Bay area quake, about one billion dollars had been the cost of American earthquakes. Of that total, Alaska's 1964 quake cost about $400 million and $600 million was for 1971's seismic event in California's San Fernando area. Officials' estimates

The Los Angeles Coliseum suffered structural damage due to the 1994 quake.

of the 1989's earthquake are more than $10 billion. And still experts say the worst is still ahead.

Where earthquakes occur

Our planet's most active earthquake-producing feature is the circum-Pacific seismic belt, which trends along the major geologic faults and the deep oceanic trenches of island arcs decorated here and there with the volcanic "Ring of Fire." The mid-Atlantic Ridge, with its fish-skeleton figure of transverse cracks, is also quite active. Other major seismic belts branch from the circum-Pacific system and arc across southeastern and southern Asia into southern Europe, through the Indian Ocean up through the eastern Mediterranean, and up through southern Asia into China.

In an average year, these belts will generate several million tremors, ranging in severity from barely detectable wiggles to great earthquakes of the size which ravaged San Francisco in 1906, and tilted a third of Alaska in 1964. There is always an earthquake in progress somewhere.

Earthquake conditions

The planet Earth is believed to consist of a thin crust 2-3 miles (3.22-4.83 km) thick under the oceans and as much as 25 miles (40.25 km) thick beneath the continents that covers the large, solid sphere of the rock mantle, which descends to about 1,800 miles (2,898 km). Below the mantle is the fluid outer core, and, at about 3,200 miles (5,152 km) depth, the apparently solid inner core. The province of earthquakes recorded thus far is from the crust to a maximum depth of about 450 miles (724.5 km).

Conditions thought to prevail in this hot, dark, high-pressure land cannot be simulated in existing laboratories—at the base of the mantle, pressure is about 11,000 tons per square inch, temperature, 10,000°F (5,482°C). These diamond-mashing pressures produce a rigidity in mantle rock about four times that of ordinary steel, with an average density about that of titanium.

This very solid mantle rock seems to behave, over periods of millions of years, like a very sluggish fluid. Something, perhaps the temperature difference between the white-hot region near the core and the cooler region near the crust, drives slow-moving cycles of rising and descending currents in the mantle rock itself.

Evidently, these currents rise beneath the thin-crusted ocean floor, thrust up the mid-ocean ridges, and generate the stresses which produce their spinelike transverse cracks and shallow earthquakes. This is believed to be the force which causes material to well up through the crust, replacing and spreading the old seafloor, and pushing drifting continents apart.

SURFACE FAULTING DURING HISTORICAL EARTHQUAKES IN CALIFORNIA

No.	Date	Fault	Magnitude (Richter Scale)	Surface Effects
1.	1836	Hayward	7.0*	Ground breakage
2.	1838	San Andreas	7.0*	Ground breakage
3.	1852	Big Pine	No data	Ground breakage questionable
4.	1857	San Andreas	8.0*	Right-lateral slip, possibly as much as 30 feet
5.	1861	Calaveras	No data	Ground breakage
6.	1868	San Andreas	No data	Long fissure in earth at Dos Palmas
7.	1868	Hayward	7.0*	Strike slip
8.	1872	Owens Valley fault zone	8.3*	Right-lateral slip, 16-20 ft.; left-lateral movement may also have occurred; vertical slip, down to east, 23 ft.
9.	1890	San Andreas	No data	Fissures in fault zone; railroad tracks moved; railroad bridge displaced
10.	1899	San Jacinto	6.6*	Surface evidence questionable
11.	1901	San Andreas	6.3*	Ground breakage
12.	1906	San Andreas	8.3	Right-lateral slip, 21 ft.
13.	1922	San Andreas	6.5	Ground breakage
14.	1934	San Andreas	6.0	Ground breakage
15.	1934	San Jacinto fault zone in Colorado River delta	7.1	Distinct fault trace on 1935 aerial photographs
16.	1940	Imperial	7.1	Right-lateral slip, 19 ft.
17.	1947	Manix	6.4	Left-lateral slip, 3 in.
18.	1950	Unnamed fault along west edge Fort Sage Mtns.	5.6	Vertical slip, down to west, 5-8 in.
19.	1951	Superstition Hills	5.6	Right-lateral slip, slight
20.	1952	White Wolf	7.7	South-dipping reverse fault; left-lateral slip, 2 ft.; upthrown, 2 ft.
21.	1956	San Miguel	6.8	Right-lateral slip, 3 ft.; vertical slip, down to southwest, 3 ft.
22.	1966	Imperial	3.6	Right-lateral slip ½ in.
23.	1966	San Andreas	5.5	Right-lateral slip, several inches
24.	1968	Coyote Creek, Superstition Hills, Imperial, and San Andreas	6.4	Right-lateral slip up to 15 inches on Coyote Creek; slight right-lateral slip on Superstition Hills, Imperial, and San Andreas
25.	1971	San Fernando	6.6	Left-lateral slip, up to 5 ft.; thrusting, up to 3 ft. (north side up); shortening 3 ft.
26.	1989	Santa Cruz Mountains	6.9	(Data not avail.)

* Estimated

FAULTS SHOWING CONTINUOUS OR INTERMITTENT CREEP

San Andreas fault from San Juan Bautista to Cholame
Hayward fault
Calaveras fault zone from near Dublin to Hollister
Imperial fault; possible creep after 1940 Imperial Valley earthquake
Manix fault
Garlock fault
Concord fault
Antioch fault

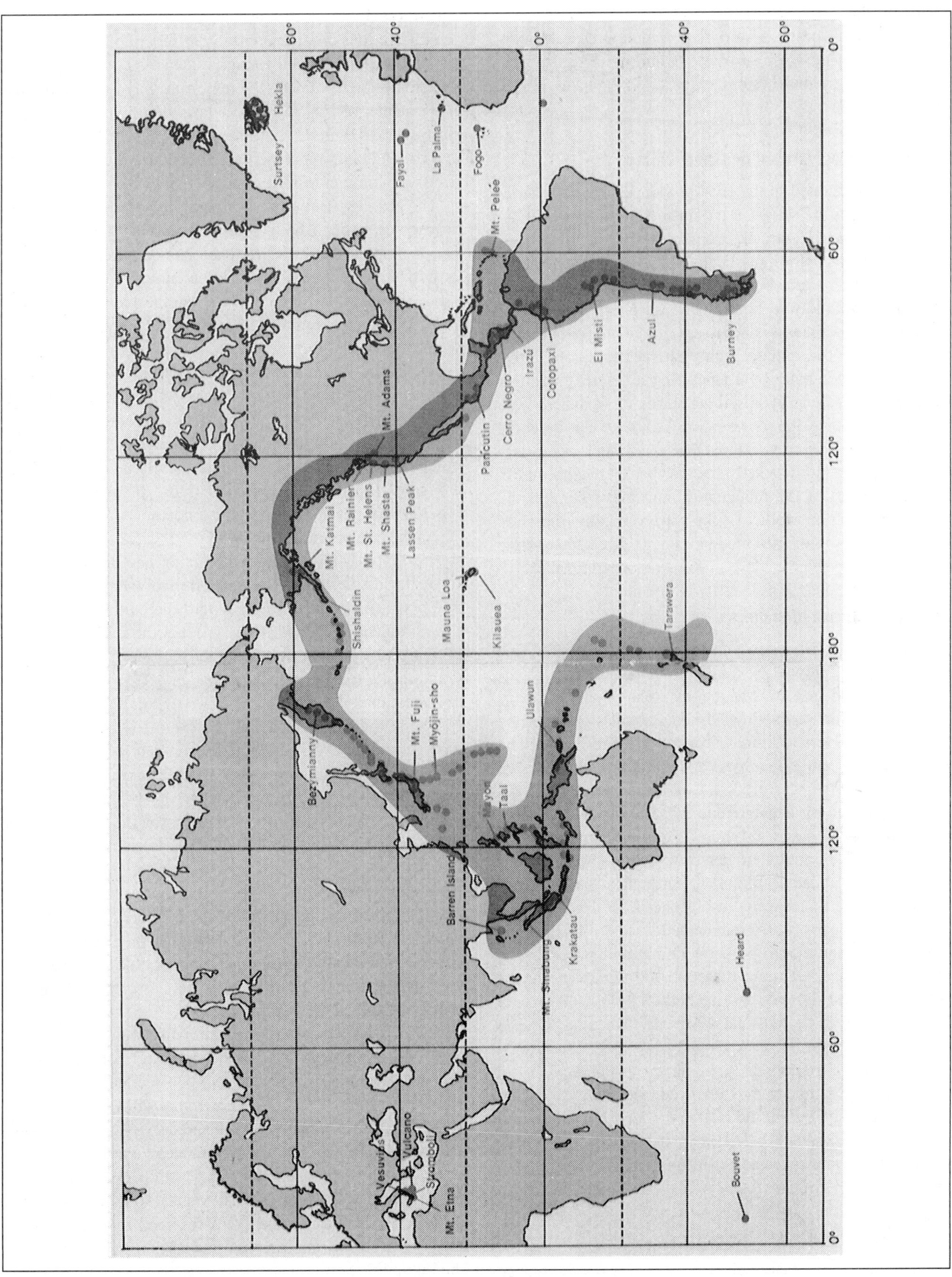
60°
40°
0°
40°
60°
0°
60°
120°
180°
120°
60°
0°
Surtsey
Hekla
Fayal
La Palma
Fogo
Mt. Pelée
Cotopaxi
El Misti
Azul
Burney
Irazú
Cerro Negro
Paricutin
Mt. Adams
Lassen Peak
Mt. Shasta
Mt. St. Helens
Mt. Rainier
Mt. Katmai
Shishaldin
Mauna Loa
Kilauea
Tarawera
Ulawun
Bezymianny
Mt. Fuji
Myōjin-sho
Mayon
Taal
Barren Island
Krakatau
Mt. Sinabung
Heard
Bouvet
Vesuvius
Vulcano
Stromboli
Mt. Etna

“Ring of Fire.”

Where the currents begin their descent at the edges of continents, they produce compressive pressures, and massive folding in the form of trenches and mountain ranges. These regions are the sites of the deeper earthquakes, and of most volcanism.

Earth stresses, strains, and then releases

Stresses generated in the crust and upper mantle by convective currents are stored in the form of strain-physical deformation of the rock structure. Under normal circumstances, the "solid" rocks deform plastically, releasing pent-up energy before it builds to catastrophic levels. But, when stresses accumulate too rapidly to be removed by plastic flow, some structural compensation is necessary. Large blocks of material are slowly forced into highly strained positions along faults, and held in place by a supporting structure of stronger materials. These energy-absorbing zones of weakness continue to shift, like longbows being pulled to the breaking point. Finally, more stress causes the supporting rocks to rupture, triggering the "cocked" fracture back toward equilibrium. The sides of the rebounding fault move horizontally with respect to one another (strike-slip), vertically (dip-slip), or in combinations of such motion, as in the large-scale tilting which accompanied the March 1964 Alaska earthquake.

Foreshocks and aftershocks

Sometimes all the energy to be released goes out in one large wrench, followed by trains of smaller tremors, or aftershocks, produced by continuing collapse and slippage along the fracture. Sometimes the fault shift is preceded by the small structural failures detected as foreshocks. The magnitude 5.9 earthquake which shook Fairbanks, Alaska, on June 21, 1967, was preceded by a magnitude 5.6 foreshock, followed by a magnitude 5.5 aftershock, and then, over the next 24 hours, by more than 2,000 smaller aftershocks. Small tremors were detected for days after the initial event. But all small tremors or earthquake "swarms" do not necessarily indicate that a big one is on the way. The Matsushiro, Japan, swarm maintained an intermittent tremble for more than a year, probably doing more psychic than physical damage. Of more than 600,000 tremors recorded between August 3, 1965, and the end of 1966, 60,000 were strong enough to be felt, and 400 were damaging. During the most active period, in April and May 1966, Matsushiro felt hundreds of tremors daily, all under magnitude 5.

Whatever the time period involved, the energy of strain flows out through the shifted fault in the form of heat, sound, and earthquake waves. These last are the shakers and wreckers, the global messages sent out by earthquakes. They are also man's only window to his planet's deep interior.

How earthquake waves travel

There are four basic seismic waves: two preliminary "body" waves which travel through the Earth, and two which travel only at the surface. Combinations, reflections, and diffractions produce a virtual infinity of other types. The behavior of these is well enough understood that wave speed and amplitude have been the major means of describing the Earth's interior. In addition, a large earthquake generates elastic waves which echo through the planet like vibrations in a ringing bell, and which actually cause the planet to expand and contract infinitesimally.

The primary (P) wave is longitudinal, like a sound wave, propagates through both liquids and solids, and is usually the first signal that an earthquake has occurred. Where the disturbance is near enough or large enough to be felt, the P wave arrives at the surface like a hammerblow from the inside. This is the swiftest seismic wave, its speed varying with the material through which it passes. In the heterogeneous crustal structure, P-wave velocity is usually less than 4 miles (6.4 km) per second—nearly 15,000 miles (24,150 km) per hour. Just below the crust, at a layer called the Mohorovicic discontinuity (the Moho), these speeds jump to 5 miles (8 km) per second and subsequently increase to about 8.5 miles (13.7 km) per second (more than 30,000 miles [48,300 km] per hour) through the core.

As the compressional phase of the P wave passes through the Earth, particles are pushed together and displaced away from the disturbance. The rarefactional phase dilates the particles and displaces them toward the earthquake source. For an object imbedded in the ground, the result is a series of sharp pushes and pulls parallel to the wave path—motions similar to those which the passengers feel when a long train gets under way.

The secondary (S) wave is transverse, like a light or radio wave, and travels barely more than half as fast as the primary wave. Because S waves require a rigid medium to travel in coherent rays, their apparent absence below the mantle gives credence to the theory of a fluid core. About twice the period and amplitude of the associated P waves, these shear waves displace particles at right angles to the direction of wave travel. The vertical component of this movement is somewhat dampened by the opposing force of gravity; but side-to-side shaking in the horizontal can be quite destructive. Where the motion is perceptible, the arrival of the S waves marks the beginning of a new series of shocks, often worse than the P-wave tremor.

Surface waves, named for their discoverers, Love and Rayleigh, are of much greater length and period, e.g., 30 seconds or more, versus less than one second for P waves. Love waves are shear in the horizontal dimension, and the Rayleigh wave induces a retrograde, elliptical motion, something like that in wind-driven ocean waves. The speed of the Love wave is about 2.5 miles (4 km) per second; the Rayleigh wave is about 10% slower. Despite the large proportion of earthquake energy represented by these waves, their long period smooths out the motion they impart, reducing their destructiveness.

Wave motion is not considered in describing the travel of

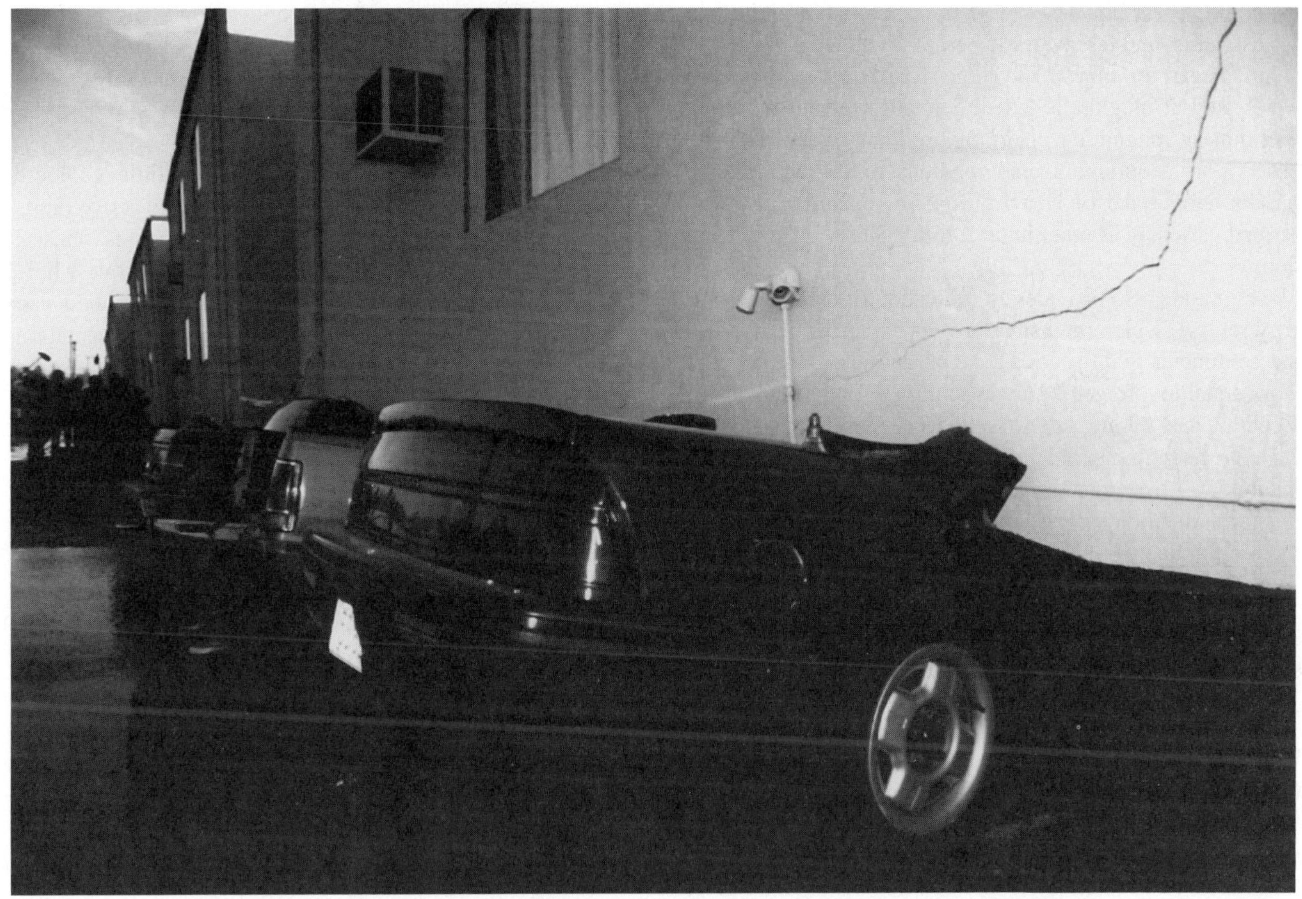

The first floor of many apartment buildings collapsed due to the 1994 Northridge quake.

seismic waves through the earth. Instead, the P and S body waves, and their large family of reflected, combined, or resonated offspring, are treated as rays. If the planet were homogeneous, like a ball of wax, these rays would be straight lines. But in the heterogeneous Earth the rays describe concavely spherical paths away from the earthquake source, and from points of reflection at the surface.

Because they travel at different speeds, seismic waves arrive at a given point on the earth's surface at different times. Near the source, the ground will shake over a slightly longer interval of time than it took the fault to slip. At great distances, the same energy released by a single event may be detected instrumentally for days.

Measuring an earthquake

Intensity is an indication of an earthquake's apparent severity at a specified location, as determined by experienced observers. Through interviews with persons in the stricken area, damage surveys, and studies of earth movement, an earthquake's regional effects can be systematically described. For seismologists and emergency workers, intensity becomes an efficient shorthand for describing what an earthquake has done to a given area.

The Modified Mercalli Intensity Scale generally used in the United States grades observed effects into twelve classes ranging from I, felt only under especially favorable circumstances, to XII, damage total. The older RossiForel Intensity Scale (RF) has ten categories of observed effects, and is still used in Europe. Still other intensity scales are in use in Japan and the former Soviet Union.

Rating earthquakes by intensity has the disadvantage of being always relative. In recent years, intensity ratings have been supplemented by an "objective" scale of earthquake magnitude.

Magnitude expresses the amount of energy released by an earthquake as determined by measuring the amplitudes produced on standardized recording instruments. The persistent misconception that the "Richter Scale" rates the size of earthquakes on a "scale of ten" is extremely misleading, and has tended to mask the clear distinction between magnitude and intensity.

Earthquake magnitudes are similar to stellar magnitudes in that they describe the subject in absolute, not relative, terms, and that they refer to a logarithmic, not an arithmetic, scale. An earthquake of magnitude 8, for example, represents seismograph amplitudes ten times larger than those of a magnitude 7 earthquake, 100 times larger than those of a magnitude 6 earthquake, and so on. There is no highest or lowest value, and it is possible here, as with temperature, to record negative values. The largest earthquakes of record were rated at magnitude 8.9; the smallest, about minus 3. Preliminary magnitude determinations may vary with the observatory, equipment, and methods of estimating—the Alaska earthquake of March 1964, for example, was described variously as magnitude 8.4, 8.5, 8.6 by different stations.

Magnitude also provides an indication of earthquake energy release, which intensity does not. In terms of ergs, (in the centimeter-gram-second system, and erg is the unit of work equal to a force of 1 dyne acting through a distance of 1 centimeter (.39 in); a dyne is the force required to accelerate a freestanding gram mass 1 centimeter per second) a magnitude 1 earthquake releases about one billionth the energy of a magnitude 7 earthquake; a magnitude 5, about one thousandth that of magnitude 7.

• ACTIVE FAULTS OF CALIFORNIA

The most earthquake-prone areas in the contiguous United States are those that are adjacent to the San Andreas fault system of coastal California and the fault system that separates the Sierra Nevada from the Great Basin. Many of the individual faults of these major systems are known to have been active during the last 150-200 years, and others are believed to have been active since the wane of the last great ice advance about 10,000 years ago. Parts of these earthquake-prone areas are among the most densely populated and rapidly urbanizing sections of the western states. A knowledge of the location of these active faults and an understanding of the nature of the earthquake activity that is related to them is necessary for people to accommodate themselves and their work to these hazards.

Earthquakes in California are relatively shallow and clearly related to movement along active faults. During historical times at least 25 California earthquakes have been associated with movements that ruptured the Earth's surface along these faults. On the San Andreas fault, eight moderate-to-severe earthquakes have been accompanied by movements on the fault at the Earth's surface since 1838, and other faults in the California region have also experienced repeated earthquakes. The magnitude of shallow earthquakes can generally be correlated with the amount and length of the associated fault movement. Thus, the largest episode of fault movement (or fault slip) recorded in California accompanied the three great earthquakes of 1857, 1872, and 1906—all of which had estimated magnitudes that were over 8 on the Richter scale.

Many of the California faults have had one or more episodes of sudden slip or of slow movement, called creep, during historical time or a documented history of shallow earthquakes. For other faults, however, recent activity can only be inferred from geologic and topographic relations which indicate that they have been active during the past several thousand years. Such activity suggests that some of these faults will, and that any of them might, slip or creep again.

In parts of California where relatively little geologic work has been done, evidence of other recently active faults will undoubtedly be found as research progresses. This is particularly true of large areas in northern California where topographic features by which recent fault movements can be recognized are commonly obscured by dense vegetation and rapid erosion. Further study may also reveal that some of the faults not definitely known to have been recently active have actually been so, and that some parts of faults thought to be active are actually dead.

Most of the active California faults are vertical or nearly vertical breaks, and movement along these breaks has been predominantly horizontal. If the block on the opposite side of the fault from the observer has moved to the right, the movement is termed right-lateral; movement of the opposite block to the left is termed left-lateral. Note that most of the faults trend northwesterly, and that the movement on these faults has been right-lateral. Notable exceptions to the predominantly northwesterly trend of faults are the west-trending Garlock and Big Pine faults; movement on these faults has been left-lateral.

A few reverse faults have also been active in California. The planes of such faults are inclined to the Earth's surface, and the rocks above the fault have been thrust upward over the rocks below the fault plane. The magnitude 7.7 Arvin-Tehachapi earthquake of 1952 was associated with such movement along the White Horse reverse fault, and the magnitude 6.6 San Fernando earthquake of 1971 was caused by a sudden rupture along a reverse fault at the foot of the San Gabriel Mountains.

Studies of historical fault movement have shown that they occur in two ways. The first and better known is the sudden displacement, or slip, of the ground along a fault. Such displacement is accompanied by earthquakes and occasionally produces spectacular offsets of topographic and even of man-made features. During the 1906 earthquake, the ground was displaced as much as 21 feet (6.37 m) along the San Andreas fault in northern California. During the 1857 earthquake, displacement of the ground along this fault was possibly as much as 30 feet (9.1 m) in southern California. The second type of fault movement, termed creep, is now taking place on portions of several faults in California. This type of movement was well documented for the first time in 1956, and has since been found to be commonplace. It is characterized by continuous or intermittent slight slip without noticeable earthquakes. Recent fault creep on portions of the Hayward, Calaveras, and San Andreas faults has produced cumulative offsets ranging from a fraction of an inch to almost a foot in curbs, streets, and railroad tracks, and has caused some damage to buildings.

Most of the faults are, in reality, zones made up of a number of subsidiary faults or fault strands. These fault zones range in width from several feet to a mile or more. Slip along them during historical time and the recent geologic past has been found to recur repeatedly on only one or a few of the multiple strands that constitute these zones. Most of the strands commonly show no evidence of recent activity, although slip does at times recur on older strands or on entirely new ones. The strong tendency for fault slip and earthquakes to recur along the most recently active strands makes knowledge of the precise location of these strands essential to land-use planning.

The source of the stresses that cause the Earth's crust to break and slip in the California region is unknown, but the stresses appear to be related to crustal distortion on a global scale. Geologists have found abundant evidence that these stresses have been acting for millions of years. Whatever their source, the results is a continuing history of surface displacements and earthquakes along numerous faults in the California region.

The San Andreas Fault

The most important of California's faults is the San Andreas, which is the "master fault" of the intricate network of faults that cuts through rocks of the coastal region of California. It is a fracture in the Earth's crust along which two parts of the crust have slipped with respect to each other.

The presence of the San Andreas fault was dramatically brought to the attention of the world on April 18, 1906, when displacement along the fault resulted in the great San Francisco earthquake and fire. This, however, was but one of many, many earthquakes that have resulted from displacement along the fault throughout its life of possibly 100 million years.

The fault is a huge fracture some 600 miles (966 km) or more long, extending almost vertically into the Earth to a depth of at least 20 miles (32.2 km). In detail it is a complex zone of crushed and broken rock from a few hundred feet to a mile wide. Many smaller faults branch from and join the San Andreas fault zone, and if one examines almost any road cut in the zone, he will find a myriad of small fractures, fault gouge (pulverized rock), and a few solid pieces of rock.

Where is the San Andreas fault?

The San Andreas fault forms a continuous break from northern California southward to Cajon Pass. From Cajon Pass southeastward the identity of the fault becomes confused, because several branching faults such as the San Jacinto, Mission Creek, and Banning faults have similar characteristics. Nevertheless, the San Andreas type of faulting continues unabated southward to and under the Gulf of Lower California.

Over much of its length a linear trough reveals the presence of the fault; and from an airplane the linear arrangement of the lakes, bays, and valleys appears striking. Undoubtedly, however, many people driving near Crystal Springs Reservoir, along Tomales Bay, through Cajon or Tejon Passes, do not realize they are on the San Andreas fault zone. On the ground, the fault zone can be recognized by long straight escarpments, narrow ridges, and small undrained ponds formed by the settling of small blocks within the fault zone. Characteristically, steam channels jog sharply along the fault trace.

Fault movement

Essentially, blocks on opposite sides of the San Andreas fault move horizontally, and if one were to stand on one side of the fault and look across it, the block on the opposite side would appear to be moved to the right. Geologists refer to this as a right-lateral strike-slip fault, or wrench fault.

During the 1906 earthquake, roads, fences, and rows of trees and bushes that crossed the fault were offset several feet, and the road across the head of Tomales Bay was offset 21 feet (6.37 m), the maximum offset recorded. In each case the ground west of the fault moved relatively northward.

Geologists who have studied in detail the fault between Los Angeles and San Francisco have suggested that the total accumulated displacement along the fault may be as much as 350 miles (563.5 km). Similarly, geologic study of a segment of the fault between Tejon Pass and the Salton Sea revealed geologically similar terrains on opposite sides of the fault now separated by 150 miles (241.5 km), indicating that the separation is a result of movement along the San Andreas and branching San Gabriel faults.

It is difficult to imagine this great amount of shifting of the Earth's crust; yet the rate represented by these ancient offsets, seems consistent with the rate measured in historical time. Precise surveying shows a slow drift at the rate of about 2 inches (5.08 cm) per year. At that rate, if the fault has been uniformly active during its possible 100 million years of existence, over 300 miles (483 km) of offset is indeed a possibility.

Since 1934, earthquake activity along the San Andreas fault system has been concentrated in areas of three cities: Eureka, San Francisco, and Los Angeles/San Bernadino. These are areas where historical earthquakes and fault displacements of the Earth's surface have been most common and where fault creep is taking place today. The sections of the state intervening the three areas mentioned above, on the other hand, have had almost no earthquakes or known slip events since the great earthquakes of 1857 in the southernmost segment and 1906 in the segment between Eureka and San Francisco. This implies to some earth scientists that these two segments of the San Andreas fault are temporarily locked, whereas in the other areas stress is being continually relieved by slip, which produces small to moderate earthquakes, and by creep. The lack of such activity in the locked segments could mean that these segments are subject to less frequent but larger fault movements and correspondingly more severe earthquakes.

Many California freeways were subject to partial collapse, such as this section of the Golden Gate Freeway (1994).

The recorded history of earthquakes along the San Andreas fault is an extremely small sample from which, however, a clear pattern of behavior can be determined. Judging from this short history, great earthquakes seem to occur only a few times a century, but smaller earthquakes recorded only on sensitive seismographs occur much more frequently.

It is a popular misconception that once there has been a small earthquake along a segment of the fault, strain is released and further earthquakes are not to be expected for many years. Seismologists have pointed out, however, that the really great earthquakes have been preceded by numerous strong shocks and that large earthquakes seem to cluster in periods of 10-20 years long. Furthermore, the energy released during small earthquakes is insignificant compared to that in earthquakes having the same magnitude as the one in 1906.

Different segments of the fault also behave differently. For example, in the vicinity of Hollister, frequent small shocks are recorded, and slow movement at the rate of 12 millimeters (.47 in) per year has been recorded. In contrast, the segment near San Francisco, except for an earthquake of magnitude 5.3 in 1957, has been relatively quiet since 1906. Perhaps, as some believe, it is gradually bending or accumulating strain that will be adjusted all at once in one large "snap."

What can be done about the fault?

Much is yet to be learned about the nature and behavior of the San Andreas fault and the earthquakes it generates. Some questions geologists would like to answer are: How old is the fault? Has movement been uniform? What movement has there been on branching faults? What is the fundamental cause of the stresses that produced the San Andreas fault? Until these questions and others have been satisfactorily answered the question "what can be done about the fault?" is best responded to, says the United States Geological Survey, in this way: "Though man cannot stop earthquakes from happening, he can learn to live with the problems they cause. Of prime importance are adequate building codes, for experience shows that well-constructed buildings greatly lessen the hazards. In construction projects, greater consideration should be given to foundation conditions. Degree of damage will range widely, between construction on bedrock, water-saturated mud, filled ground, or landslide terrain. For example, in 1906, most buildings on filled or 'made' land near the foot of Market Street in San Francisco suffered particularly intense damage, whereas buildings on solid rock suffered little or no damage. Geologists are horrified to see land developers build rows of houses straddling the trace of the 1906 break..."

Maps showing the most recently active strands or breaks along the San Andreas and related active faults have been prepared by the United States Geological Survey. Contact with this governmental agency can be made at 302 National Center, Reston, Virginia 22092, or 345 Middlefield Road, Menlo Park, California 94025. The Geological Survey also maintains Public Inquiries Offices in San Francisco, and Los Angeles.

• TSUNAMI

What is a tsunami?

The phenomenon we call "tsunami" is a series of traveling ocean waves of great length and long period, generated

Earthquake Safety Rules

An earthquake strikes your area and for a minute or two the "solid" earth moves like the deck of a ship. What you do during and immediately after the tremor may make life-and-death differences for you, your family, and your neighbors. These rules will help you survive.

During an Earthquake

1. Remain calm. Think through the consequences of any action you take. Try to calm and reassure others.
2. If indoors, watch for falling plaster, bricks, light fixtures, and other objects. Watch for high bookcases, china cabinets, shelves, and other furniture which might slide or topple. Stay away from windows, mirrors, and chimneys. If in danger, get under a table, desk, or bed; in a corner away from windows; or in a strong doorway. Encourage others to follow your example. Usually it is best not to run outside.
3. If in a high-rise building, get under a desk. Do not dash for exists, since stairways may be broken and jammed with people. Power for elevators may fail.
4. If in a crowded store, do not rush for a doorway since hundreds may have the same idea. If you must leave the building, choose your exit as carefully as possible.
5. If outside, avoid high buildings, walls, power poles, and other objects which could fall. Do not run through streets. If possible, move to an open area away from all hazards. If in an automobile, stop in the safest place available, preferably an open area.

After an Earthquake

1. Check for injuries in your family and neighborhood. Do not attempt to move seriously injured persons unless they are in immediate danger of further injury.
2. Check for fires or fire hazards.
3. Wear shoes in all areas near debris or broken glass.
4. Check utility lines and appliances for damage. If gas leaks exist, shut off the main gas valve. Shut off electrical power if there is damage to your house wiring. Report damage to the appropriate utility companies and follow their instructions. Do not use matches, lighters, or open-flame appliances until you are sure no gas leaks exist. Do not operate electrical switches or appliances if gas leaks are suspected. This creates sparks which can ignite gas from broken lines.
5. Do not touch downed powerlines or objects touched by the downed wires.
6. Immediately clean up spilled medicines, drugs, and other potentially harmful materials.
7. If water is off, emergency water may be obtained from water heaters, toilet tanks, melted ice cubes, and canned vegetables.
8. Check to see that sewage lines are intact before permitting continued flushing of toilets.
9. Do not eat or drink anything from open containers near shattered glass. Liquids may be strained through a clean handkerchief or cloth if danger of glass contamination exists.
10. If power is off, check your freezer and plan meals to use foods which will spoil quickly.
11. Use outdoor charcoal broilers for emergency cooking.
12. Do not use your telephone except for genuine emergency calls. Turn on your radio for damage reports and information.
13. Check your chimney over its entire length for cracks and damage, particularly in the attic and at the roofline. Unnoticed damage could lead to a fire. The initial check should be made from a distance. Approach chimneys with caution.
14. Check closets and storage shelf areas. Open closets and cupboard doors carefully and watch out for objects failing from shelves.
15. Do not spread rumors. They often do great harm after disasters.
16. Do not go sightseeing immediately, particularly in beach and waterfront areas where seismic sea waves could strike. Keep the streets clear for passage of emergency vehicles.
17. Be prepared for additional earthquake shocks called "aftershocks." Although most of these are smaller than the main shock, some may be large enough to cause additional damage.
18. Respond to requests for help from police, fire fighting, civil defense, and relief organizations, but do not go into damaged areas unless your help has been requested. Cooperate fully with public-safety officials. In some areas, you may be arrested for getting in the way of disaster operations.

There are no rules which can eliminate all earthquake danger. However, damage and injury can be greatly reduced by following these simple rules.

by disturbances associated with earthquakes in oceanic and coastal regions. As the tsunami crosses the deep ocean, its length, from crest to crest may be a hundred miles (161 km) or more, its height from trough to crest only a few feet. It cannot be felt aboard ships in deep water, and cannot be seen from the air. But in deep water, tsunami waves may reach forward speeds exceeding 600 miles (966 km) per hour.

As the tsunami enters the shoaling water of coastlines in its path, the velocity of its waves diminishes and wave height increases. It is in these shallow waters that tsunamis become a threat to life and property for they can crest to heights of more than 100 feet (30.3 m), and strike with devastating force.

The warning system

Development of the NOAA Coast and Geodetic Survey's Pacific Tsunami Warning System was impelled by the disastrous waves of April 1946, which surprised Hawaii and took a heavy toll in life and property. The locally disastrous tsunami caused by the March 1964 Alaska earthquake impelled the development of another type of warning apparatus-the Regional Tsunami Warning System in Alaska.

The Regional Tsunami Warning System is headquartered at the Coast and Geodetic Survey's Seismological Observatory at Palmer, Alaska. This is the nerve center for an elaborate telemetry network linking Palmer with remote seismic and tidal stations along the Alaska coast and in the Aleutian Islands. Seismograph stations in the network are at Palmer Observatory and its two remote stations 25 miles (40.25 km) south and west, and at Biorka, Sitka, Gilmore Creek, Kodiak, and Adak. Tide stations are at Seward, Sitka, Kodiak, Cold Bay, Unalaska, Adak, Yakutat, and Shemya. Data from these stations are recorded continuously at Palmer, where a 24-hour watch is kept.

When an earthquake occurs in the Alaska-Aleutian area, seismologists at Palmer Observatory rapidly determine its epicenter (the point on the earth's surface above the underground source of the earthquake) and magnitude, If the epicenter falls in the Aleutian Island arc or near Alaskan coastal area, and if the earthquake magnitude is great enough to generate a tsunami, Palmer Observatory issues a *tsunami warning* through the Alaska Disaster Office, Alaska Command, and Federal Aviation Administration (FAA) covering the area near the epicenter. A *tsunami watch* is issued for the rest of the Alaskan coastline, alerting the public to the possibility of a tsunami threat. If a tsunami is detected by tide stations, Palmer Observatory extends the tsunami warning to cover the entire coastline of Alaska. If no tsunami is observed, both the watch and warning bulletins are cancelled.

Subsidiary warning centers have been established at Sitka and Adak Observatories. These facilities operate small seismic arrays and have a limited warning responsibility for local areas.

The Pacific Tsunami Warning System has its headquarters at the Coast and Geodetic Survey's Honolulu Observatory. There, seismologists monitor data received from seismic and tidal instruments in Hawaii and around the Pacific Ocean, and provide ocean-wide tsunami watches and warnings. The Pacific system works very closely with its regional counterpart in Alaska. Potentially tsunami-generating earthquakes in the Alaska-Aleutian area are detected and evaluated at Palmer Observatory, and the data relayed directly to Honolulu Observatory. Where there is tidal evidence of a tsunami, the warning is extended by Honolulu to cover the Pacific Ocean basin. For tsunamis generated elsewhere in the Pacific area, tsunami watch and warning bulletins are prepared at Honolulu Observatory and disseminated in Alaska by the Alaska Disaster Office, the military, and FAA.

Tsunami Safety Rules

Tsunamis are generated by some earthquakes. When you hear a tsunami warning, you must assume a dangerous wave is on its way. History shows that when the great waves finally strike, they claim those who have ignored the warning.

REMEMBER:

1. All earthquakes do not cause tsunamis, but many do. When you hear that an earthquake has occurred, stand by for a tsunami emergency.

2. A strong earthquake felt in a low-lying coastal area is a natural warning of possible, immediate danger. Keep calm and move to higher ground, away from the coast.

3. A tsunami is not a single wave, but a series of waves. Stay out of danger areas until an "all-clear" is issued by competent authority.

4. Approaching tsunamis are sometimes heralded by a noticeable rise or fall of coastal water. This is nature's tsunami warning and should be heeded.

5. A small tsunami at one beach can be a giant a few miles away. Don't let the modest size of one make you lose respect for all.

6. All tsunamis—like hurricanes—are potentially dangerous, even though they may not damage every coastline they strike.

7. Never go down to the beach to watch for a tsunami. When you can see the wave you are too close to escape it.

8. During a tsunami emergency, your local Civil Defense, police, and other emergency organizations will try to save your life. Give them your fullest cooperation.

Stay tuned to your radio or television stations during a tsunami emergency—bulletins issued through Civil Defense and NOAA offices can help you save your life!

Volcanic Activity

Since Mount St. Helens volcano, located in the State of Washington, erupted violently on May 18, 1980, volcanism has become a much talked about part of the weather and climate pictures of both the United States and the world. Much of the continuing importance of this spectacular eruption is owed to the fact that it lifted a great volume of ash and debris into the upper atmosphere. Some of the ash from a volcano eruption falls to earth quickly; but a large portion stays aloft, dispersed worldwide, for years. In that case it becomes a factor—as volcanic activity has always been—in meteorological processes that shape weather events globally.

Volcanic activity has played a dominant role in shaping the face of the Earth. Much of the natural beauty of the land, its mineral wealth, and the fertility of the soil is owed to volcanism, especially in the western states. At one time or another during the last 70 million years, volcanic rocks covered nearly all of the Western States of Washington, Oregon, California, Nevada, Arizona, Utah, Idaho, and large parts of Montana, Wyoming, Colorado, New Mexico, and Texas. Still older volcanic rocks, now largely deformed and metamorphosed, are found in nearly every state.

• WHAT ARE VOLCANOES?

Volcanoes are built by the accumulation of their own eruptive products: lava, bombs, ash, and dust. Usually the

Mount St. Helens erupting with Mt. Hood in the background.

volcano is a conical hill or mountain built around a vent that connects with reservoirs of molten rock (known as *magma*) below the Earth's surface. Forced upward by the pressure of contained gas, the molten rock breaks through zones of weakness in the Earth's crust. It spews from the vent as lava flows or shoots into the air as dense clouds of lava fragments.

Larger fragments (bombs and cinders) fall back around the vent. Some of the finer material (ash and dust) may be blown by the wind and eventually fall to the ground many miles away. Very fine particles reach the upper atmosphere (stratosphere) where they can circulate around the Earth for several years.

The gas in lava can be compared with the behavior of the gas in a soda bottle that is shaken and then the top released. The violent separation of gas from lava may produce rock froth known as pumice, which is so light that it floats on water.

Kinds of volcanoes

There are four main kinds of volcanoes—cinder cones, composite cones, shield volcanoes, and lava domes.

1. **Cinder cones**, as the name suggests, are built of lava fragments. They are very numerous in the western United States; for example, Sunset Crater, Arizona, and Craters of the Moon National Monuments, Idaho.

2. **Composite cones** are built of alternating layers of lava flows, volcanic ash, and ash; they are sometimes called strato-volcanoes. Many of the world's large mountains are composite cones; for example, Mount Fuji, Japan, Mount Shasta, California, and Mount St. Helens and Mount Rainier, Washington.

Crater Lake in Oregon is an interesting variation of a composite cone. Originally like Mount Rainier, the volcano lost its summit in a series of tremendous explosions; the remaining parts of the volcano eventually collapsed to form the depression or caldera that is now Crater Lake.

3. **Shield volcanoes** are built almost entirely of lava flows. These flow out in all directions from a central vent of a group of vents. The Hawaiian Islands are clusters of shield volcanoes (Mauna Loa is the world's largest active volcano and rises 13,653 feet [4,141 m] above sea level). In Iceland, lava pours out quietly from long fissures to form broad plateaus.

4. **Lava domes** are built of viscous or pasty lava extruded like toothpaste from a tube. Lassen Peak and Mono Dome in California are examples of lava domes.

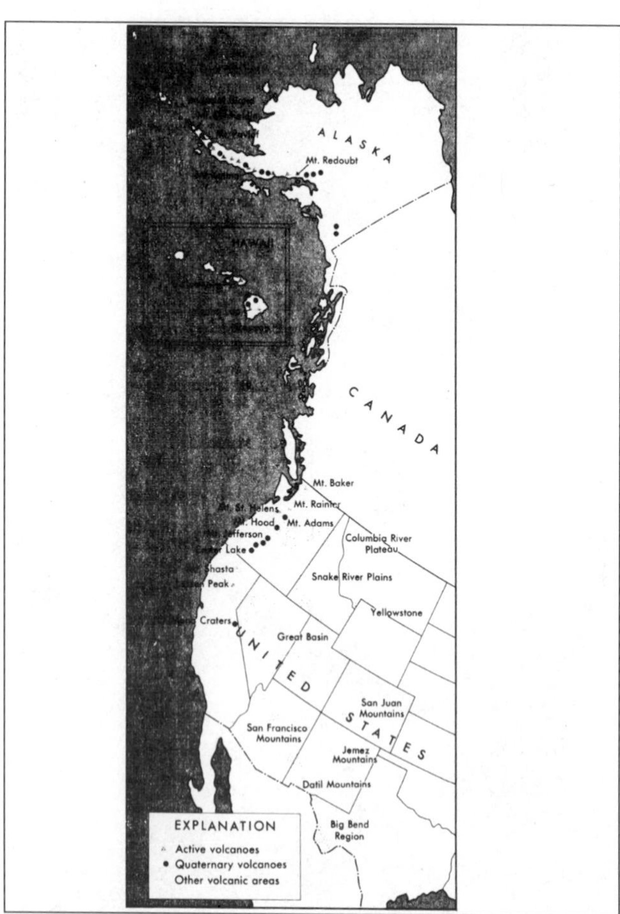

Volcanic areas of the western United States, Alaska, and Hawaii.

Active volcanoes

Active volcanism in the United States is confined to the Hawaiian Islands, the Aleutian Islands, the Alaska Peninsula, and the Cascade Mountains.

The Hawaiian Islands consist entirely of volcanic rocks that form giant shield volcanoes; one rises nearly 30,000 feet (9,100 m) from the ocean floor. By far the dominant rock type is dark gray to black basalt in the form of lava flows, cinders, pumice, ash, and bombs.

On the island of Hawaii are Mauna Loa, the largest volcano in the world, and Kilauea, one of the most active. During an eruption at Kilauea in 1959-60, great fountains of lava, some as high as 1,900 feet (576 m), were observed near the volcano summit. Lava from the fountains ran into an old pit crater and filled it to a depth of 365 feet (110.6 m), forming a lava lake. Late in 1963, nearly four years after the eruption, the crust on top of the lake was nearly 50 feet (15 m) thick and the temperature of the lava below the crust was still about 2,000°F (1,100°C).

The Aleutian Island Arc, including the Alaska Peninsula, is more than 2,000 miles (3,220 km) long and contains about 36 historically active and many extinct volcanoes. Among them are some of the world's most beautiful but little-studied volcanoes. The composite volcanoes Pavlof, Shishaldin, and Pavlof Sister are examples. Bogoslof Island is a disappearing volcano, having emerged and submerged in the sea more than once in historic time. Most of the Aleutian lavas consist of black to gray rocks called basalts and andesites.

Of the several active volcanoes on the Alaskan Peninsula, Mount Katmai (Katmai National Monument) is the most notable. In 1912, one of the most remarkable eruptions

Mount St. Helens.

of historic time occurred near its base. About 2 cubic miles of ash and pumice erupted in the form of incandescent ash flows or avalanches. The "river of sand," as the early explorers called it, flowed for more than 15 miles (24.15 km) down a great glacial valley, filling it to a depth of more than 400 feet (121 m). This valley is known as the "Valley of Ten Thousand Smokes" because of the thousands of fumaroles (gas vents) that formed on the surface of the volcanic deposits and gave off steam and other vapors for many years.

In the Cascade Mountains of Washington, Oregon, and California are the well-known composite cones of Mounts Baker, Rainier, St. Helens, Adams, Hood, Mazama, and Shasta. These High Cascade volcanoes are built primarily of rocks called andesites, which are intermediate in chemical composition between basalts and rhyolites. Andesitic volcanoes are usually great cones of rubble consisting of interlayered lava flows and fragmented deposits called mud flows. These form when eruptions take place through crater lakes, when fragmented lavas and landslides enter streams, or when water from melting snow or rain saturates and mobilizes previously erupted deposits. Volcanic mud flows may be hot or cold and may deposit boulders weighing

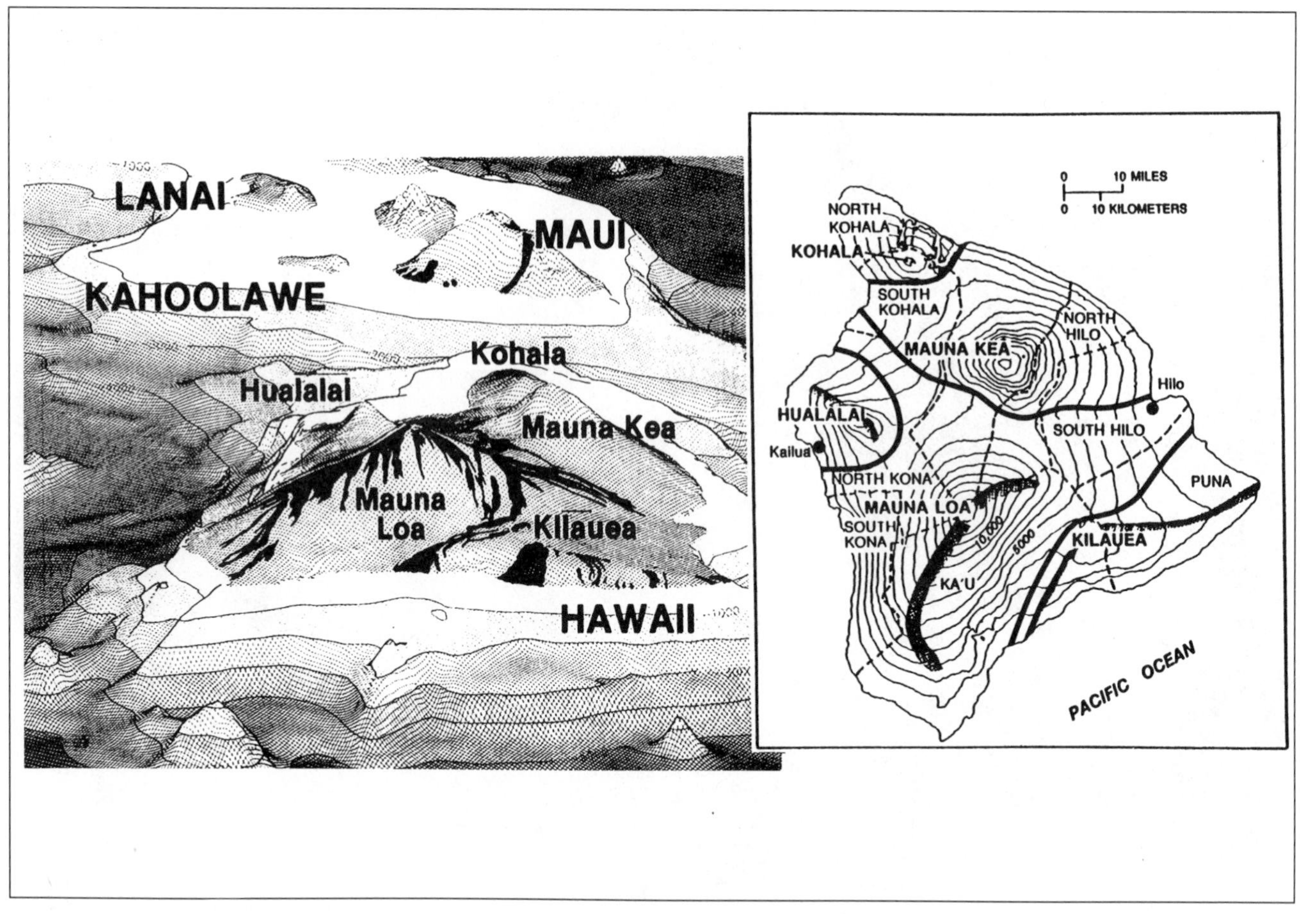

many tons. Very young mud flow deposits are common on the flanks of Mount Rainier and other Cascade cones.

Mud flows—a major cause of destruction

In some areas of the world, mud flows have been the major cause of destruction and loss of life during volcanic catastrophes. Such an eruption in 1919 from Kelud Volcano in Java covered 50 square miles (129.5 km^2) of land with mud and lava blocks. More than 5,000 human lives were lost and 100 villages completely or partly damaged. This great devastation was caused by the ejection of over 1 billion cubic feet of water from Kelud's lake.

Mount Mazama is the volcano that lost most of its top about 7,000 years ago during a tremendous explosive eruption. Nearly 12 cubic miles of ash and pumice erupted, producing under the volcano a void so large that the top caved in to form a great hole 6 miles (9.66 km) across. Depressions formed in the top of volcanoes in this manner are known as calderas. They differ from craters that are produced by explosion rather than by collapse. The caldera of Mount Mazama is now filled with water to a depth of over 1,700 feet (515 m) and is known as Crater Lake.

Lassen Peak is famous among volcanoes because it is one of the largest known plug domes. A plug dome is a part of a volcano formed by the vertical rise of a great sticky mass of lava which remains standing above the crater rim. Commonly great-vertical grooves are formed in the margin of the dome as the material oozes from the orifice. The mechanism may be compare to the squeezing of toothpaste from a tube. Subsequent eruptions from plug domes are among the most dangerous known. Gasses dissolved in the lava may burst forth violently, shatter the dome, and cause the formation of extremely mobile avalanches of hot blocks, rock dust, and gas. Such avalanches may travel at speeds up to 100 miles (161 km) an hour and devastate everything in their paths. It was an eruption of this type in 1902 from Mount Pelee in the West Indies which destroyed the nearby town of St. Pierre and killed nearly 30,000 people.

Mount St. Helens

Mount St. Helens is a symmetrical volcanic cone in southwestern Washington about 45 miles (72.45 km) northeast of Portland, Oregon. Most of the cone that be seen now was formed within the last thousand years—but this overlies an older volcanic center that probably has existed for at least 40,000 years. Mount St. Helens has had a long history of spasmodic explosive activity. It is an especially dangerous volcano because of its past behavior and the high frequency of its eruptions during the past 4,500 years.

Lava flowing from the Kapaianaha vent on Kilauea's rift zone buries a street intersection in a Hawaiian residential area.

Ancient volcanoes

There are several areas in the United States where, for many thousands of years, the only activity has been that of hot springs and solfataras (steam vents). Yellowstone National Park is the most famous of these areas. It is visited each year by thousands of people who come to see the geysers, mud pots, boiling hot springs, steam vents, and beautiful carbonate and silica deposits formed by precipitation from the hot waters. Such phenomena are vestiges of a former period of very active volcanism. It cannot be determined with certainty, however, that some day more violent volcanic activity may not begin again.

The youngest and most dominant volcanic eruptions in Yellowstone Park produced lavas called rhyolite. Chemically, rhyolite is high in silica and is the volcanic equivalent of granite. Among active volcanoes rhyolite is exceedingly rare. In the geologic past, however, rhyolite eruptions were more common and among the most spectacular of natural phenomena. Over 600 cubic miles of rhyolite erupted from the Yellowstone volcanoes alone during their last active periods. Two-thirds of this amount erupted as ash flows like the "river of sand" that caused the "Ten Thousand Smokes" in Alaska in 1912. The remaining 200 cubic miles of material issued as great sticky lava flows.

So great was the volume of flows of ash and pumice that valleys were completely filled and the intervening ridges were covered. The ash flows merged to form flat-topped plateaus thousands of square miles in area. When deposited, these great sheets of ash were so hot that the particles fused together to form rocks known as welded tuffs. Recent geologic studies have revealed that welded tuffs are perhaps the most abundant rhyolitis rocks in the western United States. Tens of thousands of cubic miles are known in Nevada alone, and great volumes are also recognized in the San Juan Mountains of Colorado, southwestern New Mexico, the Big Bend region of Texas, and southwestern Arizona.

In the Jemez Mountains of New Mexico, about one million years ago, eruptions similar to those at Yellowstone produced nearly 50 cubic miles of welded tuffs. Removal of this large volume of material from the abyssal storage chamber caused a great circular block of the Earth's crust (more than 10 miles [16 m] in diameter) to subside several thousand feet, producing a giant caldera at the surface. Formations of this, the Valles Caldera, was similar to that of Crater Lake, but of special interest to geologists is the subsequent, more complex history of the Valles interest to geologists is the Caldera. Renewed pressure from below uplifted and arched the subsided circular block so that its center rose even higher than its original elevation. During and after this uplift, new eruptions of rhyolitic lava broke out along the fracture system around the uplifted circular block and built a ring of 15 new volcanoes.

Detailed studies of the Valles Caldera have allowed geologists to relate this rhyolitic volcanism to more deeply seated processes of granite formation. Volcanism of this type is now known to have occurred in many other area of the United States. The San Juan Mountains of Colorado are an outstanding example, as are the Mono Craters in California. They, like Little Glass and Big Glass Mountains in northeastern California, are famous for black volcanic glass (obsidian) and for the large block of pumice that have recently become so popular as ornamental stones. The Mono Craters include some of the world's finest examples of rhyolitic pumice cones and lava domes. Their forms range from simple, almost perfectly symmetrical cones of pumice and ash, to cones whose craters are partly or completely filled or overflowing with lava. Some cones are completely covered with lava flows that have piled up to form steep-sided lava domes. Those cones containing lava that did not overflow the crater rim are similar to the plug dome of Lassen Peak but are much smaller and formed by more fluid lava.

Recurrently, throughout geologic time, very fluid basaltic lava has erupted from swarms of fissures to form vast lava plateaus. The Columbia River Plateau of Washington and Oregon and the Snake River Plains of Idaho are among the finest examples of this type of volcanism. The Columbia River Plateau has an area of 100,000 square miles (259,000 km^2), and the total volume of basaltic lava approximates 35,000 cubic miles. Individual lava flows can be traced for distances of more than 100 miles (161 km). Such lavas must have been almost as fluid as water to have covered such large areas so uniformly.

On the northern edge of the Snake River Plains is the Craters of the Moon National Monument. Here, basaltic lavas erupted perhaps less than 2,000 years ago. The vents from which the lavas issued are localized on great fissures and show a wide variety of forms, ranging from cinder cones built entirely on very frothy red and black lava cinders, to spatter cones formed by the piling up of liquid lava blobs and droplets around the vent. Both *aa* and *pahoehoe* lavas are found at "Craters of the Moon." Pahoehoe and aa are Hawaiian terms adopted the world over for two principal types of basaltic lavas. Pahoehoe is very fluid lava with smooth to ropy surface and the flows may travel long distances. Aa lava is more viscous lava that forms steep-sided flows seemingly composed only of craggy blocks, but usually containing a continuous fluid interior.

Occasionally the surface and sides of these basaltic lava flows solidify to form a thick outer crust. Yet the hot lava inside continues its forward movement and eventually drains out of its own crust to form lava tunnels or lava tubes. Water entering such tunnels may freeze in the winter and, because of the excellent insulation provided by the basalt crust, may not thaw in the summer even under desert conditions. Excellent examples of these ice caves and lava tunnels may be seen in the Modoc Lava Beds National Monument, California.

Basaltic lava fields in cinder cones are numerous in many parts of the western United States. Some of these are isolated volcanic vents, but basaltic vents are commonly clustered near or around large volcanoes composed of andesitic and similar lavas. Fine examples of the clustered types are the volcanic fields of the San Francisco Mountains, Arizona, and Mount Taylor, New Mexico.

Hundreds of other localities for volcanoes and volcanic rocks are known, and this brief discussion simply serves to emphasize that the United States, particularly the western area, has been one of the most volcanically active areas in the world in recent geologic time. Because we do not yet know the real causes of volcanism, we cannot say whether eruptions will recur in areas like New Mexico, Arizona, or Nevada. We can be sure that in our lifetime volcanoes in Hawaii and Alaska will erupt again.

Volcanic hazards map of the United States

The map shown is abstracted from a preliminary map compiled by D. R. Mullineaux to indicate areas subject to potential volcanic hazard in the contiguous (48) States. The map shows general areas or zones that, over a long period of time, are relatively likely to be affected in one or more places by various kinds of hazardous volcanic events. These hazards include lava flows, mudflows, hot rock avalanches, ashfalls, and floods.

Eruption beginning in 1983 on Kilauea's east rift zone.

The map shows that volcanic hazards are limited to areas in the western United States, principally in the Cascade Mountain Range in California, Oregon, and Washington; in Idaho's Snake River Plain; and in parts of Arizona, New Mexico, and Utah. No hazard areas are shown east of New Mexico.

The immediate risk from volcanic hazards is low because eruptions are so infrequent. Severely destructive effects of eruptions, other than extremely rare ones of catastrophic scale, probably would be limited to areas within a few tens of miles downvalley or downwind from a volcano. Thus, the area seriously endangered by any one eruption would be only a very small part of the western United States.

Except for Mount St. Helens' renewed activity in 1980, the only explosive volcanic eruption in the conterminous states since the area was settled was 10,457-foot (3,172 m) high Mount Lassen in northern California during a series of eruptions in 1914-15. The Mount Lassen eruption was moderate compared to major eruptions at other volcanos in the world during recorded history. No one was killed in the Mount Lassen eruption, and damage was minor.

Eruptions of moderate volume may occur somewhere in the Cascade Range as often as once every 1,000-2,000 years, but very large eruptions may occur no more than once every 10,000 years. A few large cataclysmic eruptions have occurred during the last two million years in and near Yellowstone National Park, at Long Valley, California, and in the Jemez Mountains of New Mexico. These eruptions affected very large regions and deposited ash over much of the Western United States. The sites of these eruptions are shown on the map, but such cataclysmic eruptions were not considered in outlining potential hazard zones. These eruptions are so infrequent that it is not possible to judge whether one might occur during the time for which planning is feasible.

Risk from volcanic hazards decreases as distance from an erupting volcano increases. Lava flows are nearly uniformly destructive to their outer limits. Some other volcanic hazards, especially ashfalls, become less destructive and less frequent with increasing distance. The boundary of such a hazard is indefinite and often dependent upon land use. For example, an ashfall a centimeter or so thick might cause little damage to structures, yet destroy crops.

Copies of the full-size black-and-white map from which this map was taken, identified as MF-786, may be purchased at the United States Geological Survey Public Inquiries Offices or from the Branch of Distribution, United States Geological Survey, P.O. Box 25286, Federal Center, Denver, CO 80225.

Eruption at Mount St. Helens, 1980

On May 18, 1980, a powerful explosion occurred from Mount St. Helens at 8:32 A.M. that was heard 200 miles (322 km) away. The explosion climaxed a series of activi-

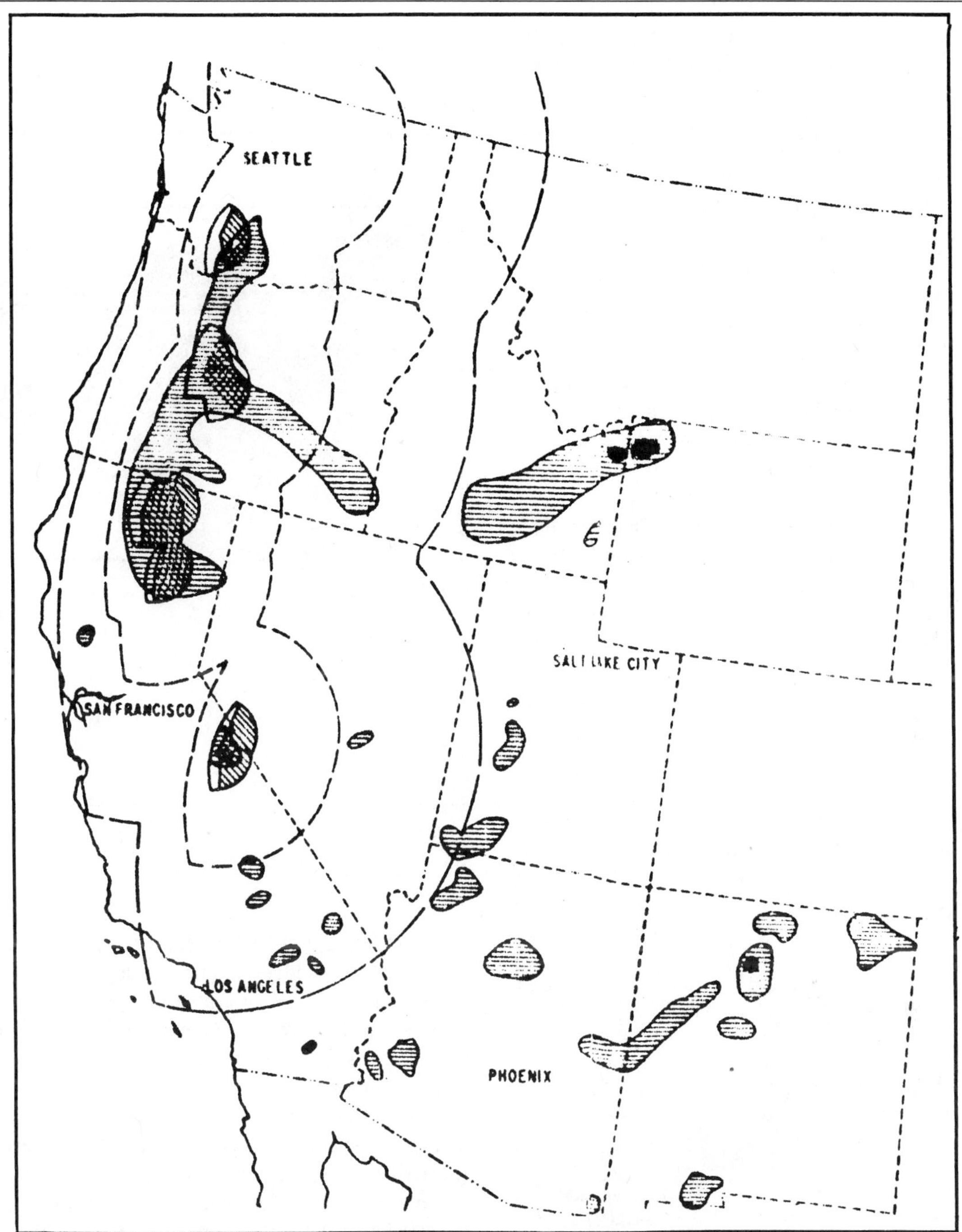

Volcanic hazards map of the United States

U.S. Geological Survey map, prepared by D.R. Mullineaux, shows volcanic hazard zones in the Western United States. Solid black zones are volcanic vent areas that had one or more extremely explosive and voluminous eruptions within the last 2 million years. Zones with horizontal lines are subject to lava flows and small volumes of ash from groups of volcanic vents called "volcanic fields." Zones with diagonal lines would get most of the ashfall from nearby relatively active and explosive volcanoes. The inner dashed line encloses areas subject to 2 inches or more of ash from a large eruption and the outer dashed line encloses areas subject to 2 inches or more of ash from a very large eruption.

ties which began with an earthquake shock of magnitude 4.1 on March 20, 1980. Remarkable photographs, taken as the explosion began, show the north once uplift peeling away from the volcano as a large vertical cloud began to rise from the summit. The once cloud rose very rapidly to more than 10 miles (16 km) above sea level, passing through the tropopause at 7 miles (11.27 km). Winds blew the cloud to the east. Ashfall at Yakima, 90 miles (145 km) away, totaled as much as 4-5 inches (10.16-12.7 cm) and caused respiratory problems for some residents. By mid-afternoon, the ash had reached Spokane, reducing visibility to only 10 feet (3 m), although only half an inch was deposited there. Almost 2 inches (5.08 cm) of ash were reported from areas of Montana west of the Continental Divide, but only a dusting fell on the eastern slopes. Slight ashfall occurred, in Denver on May 19. The ash blew generally eastward for the next several days, causing some problems for aircraft over the Midwest.

The United States Geological Survey identified three components of the initial eruptive event in addition to the vertical cloud:

The first component was a directed blast which leveled the forest on the north and northwest flanks for a distance of up to 15 miles (24.15 km) from the former summit. The blast swept over ridges and flowed down valleys, depositing significant quantities of ash. Although the blast was hot, it did not char fallen or buried trees. Many persons are known to have been killed by the blast, and others in the devastated zone are missing.

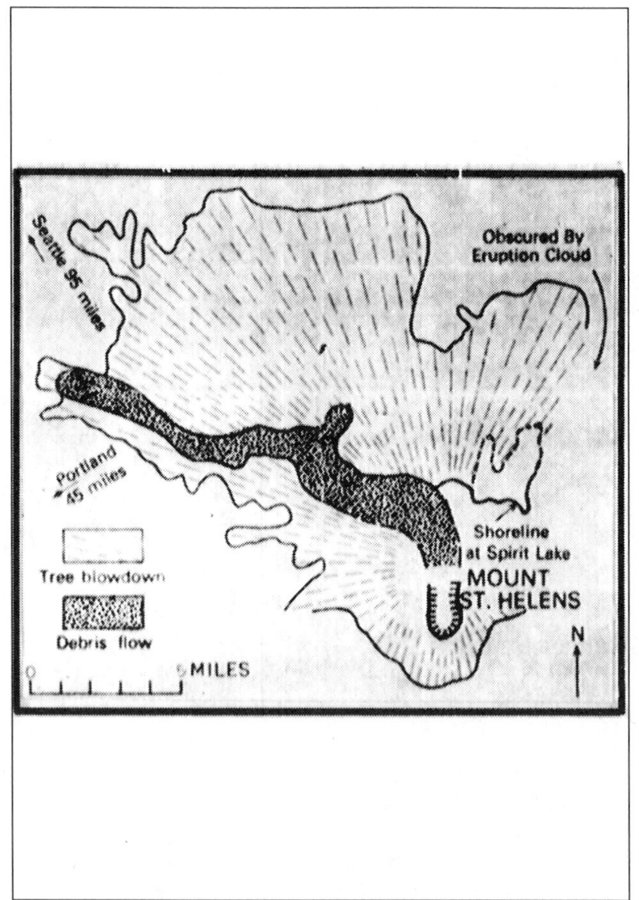

Damage caused on May 18, 1980, in the immediate vicinity of Mount St. Helens.

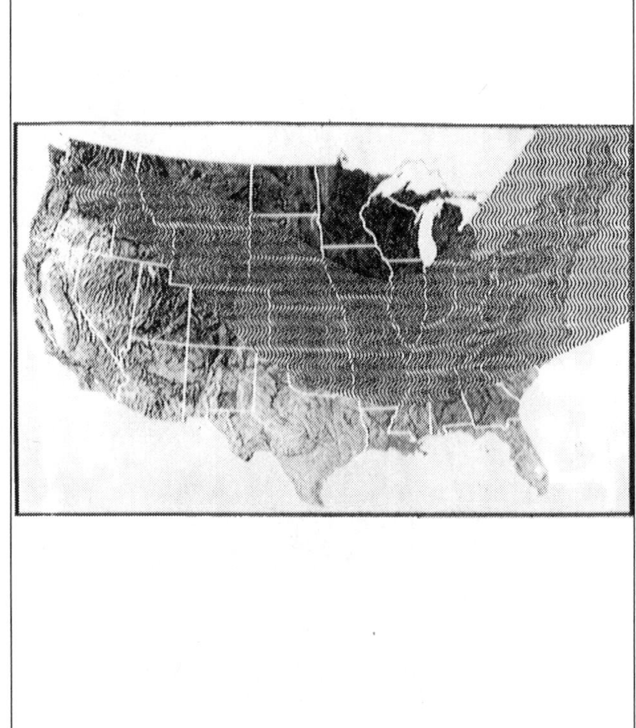

Progress of ashfall of May 18, 1980, eruption of Mount St. Helens.

The second component was a combined pyroclastic flow and landslide that carried the remnants of the north flank uplift across the lower slopes and about 17 miles (27.37 km) down the Toutle River valley, burying it to depths as great as 180 feet (54.6 m). Large quantities of mud, logs, and other debris clogged several valleys around Mount St. Helens and rendered some shipping lanes impassible in the Columbia River.

The third component was a pumiceous pyroclastic flow, funneled northward through the breach formed by the destruction of the north flank bulge. This flow dammed the outlet of Spirit Lake, trapping a large quantity of water.

The volcano maintained an eruption column 10 miles (16 km) high until a relatively sudden diminution of activity occurred in the early morning of May 19. The altitude of the top of the column declined to about 2.5 miles (4 km). Activity continued to weaken through May 22.

Safety Rules—What to do When a Volcano Erupts

Most important, don't panic—keep calm.

If volcanic ash begins to fall:

1. Stay indoors.
2. If you are outside, seek shelter such as a car or a building.
3. If you cannot find shelter, breathe through a cloth, such as a handkerchief, preferably a damp cloth to filter out the ash.
4. When air is full of ash, keep your eyes closed as much as possible.
   - Heavy falls of ash seldom last more than a few hours—only rarely do they last a day or more.
   - Heavy falls of ash may cause darkness during daylight hours and may temporarily interfere with telephone, radio, and television communications.
   - Do not try to drive a car during heavy fall of ash—the chance of accident will be increased by poor visibility.
   - The thick accumulation of ash could increase the load on roofs, and saturation of ash by rain could be an additional load. Ash should be removed from flat or low-pitched roofs to prevent a thick accumulation.
   - Valleys that head on the volcano may be the routes of mudflows which carry boulders and resemble wet flowing concrete. Mudflows can move faster than you can walk or run, but you can drive a car down a valley faster than a mudflow will travel. When driving along a valley that heads on a volcano, watch up the river channel and parts of the valley floor for the occurrence of mudflows.
5. Before crossing a highway bridge, look upstream.
6. Do not cross a bridge while a mudflow is moving beneath it.
7. The danger from a mudflow increases as you approach a river channel and decreases as you move to higher ground.
8. Risk of mudflows also decreases with increasing distance from a volcano.
9. If you become isolated, do not stay near a river channel, move upslope.

DURING AN ERUPTION MOVE AWAY FROM A VOLCANO, NOT TOWARD IT. (In the immediate vicinity of an eruption the hazards to life are much greater than those listed above.)

Source: United States Geological Survey.

A new elliptical crater about a quarter mile (.40 km) deep had been formed by the explosion.

Preliminary analysis of seismic and deformation data indicates that there was no immediate warning of the imminence of a large explosion. A magnitude 5.0 earthquake occurred essentially simultaneously with the explosion at 8:32 A.M. Records of the only surviving tiltmeter, on the south flank, show that rapid inflation began at the same time as the explosion at 8:32 A.M.

Although volume estimates for this eruption are very rough, comparison with previous eruptions in the Smithsonian Institution's Volcano Reference File (a computer data file of the world's volcanoes and their eruptions) indicates that explosions of this size occur only about once a decade.

Climatology and weather experts reported early in 1981 that a considerable amount of Mount St. Helens ash was and will be for years to come distributed throughout the upper atmosphere of the entire world. Efforts to measure this atmosphere-borne ash are expected to go on for years to come; and understanding of its affect on world weather and climate will likewise be a continuing work with few definite answers available early.

Mount St. Helens has erupted 22 times since it came to life on May 18, 1980. On 19 occasions the eruption has been predicted, as scientists use ever-more sensitive equipment to pick up ground vibrations and super-accurate lasers to detect the most minute "bulges" that occur in the slope of the mountain.

Retirement & Health Weather

• A REVIEW OF SOME ATMOSPHERIC FACTORS IN HEALTH & DISEASE

Physicians since before the time of Hippocrates, the "father of medicine," have recognized the inexorable bond between the human organism and its physical environment. Hippocrates'[1] work "On Airs, Waters, and Places," justly regarded as a medical classic and a source of philosophical inspiration in medical analysis, opens with this advice:

Whoever wishes to investigate medicine properly, should proceed thus: in the first place to consider the seasons of the year, and what effects each of them produce (for they are not at all alike, but differ much in themselves and in their changes). Then the winds, the hot and the cold, especially such as are common to all countries, and then such as are peculiar to each locality. We must also consider the qualities of the waters, for as they differ from one another in taste and weight, so also do they differ much in their qualities. In the same manner, when one comes into a city to which he is a stranger, he ought to consider its situation, how it lies as to the winds and the rising of the sun; for its influence is not the same whether it lies to the north or the south, to the rising sun [east] or to the setting sun [west].

Claude Bernard, the great pioneer of scientific medicine in the mid-nineteenth century, recognized that the conditions necessary to life are found neither in the organism nor in the outer environment, but in both at once. The germ theory of disease which is almost exactly one hundred years old did much however to focus medical research on microorganisms and away from the weaker but more pervasive influences of diet and the physical environment. Nevertheless, a hardy and, indeed, at times even foolhardy band of scientists and physicians have continued to probe for an understanding of the vexing relationships between nature and nurture in health and disease.

Scientific disciplines such as biometeorology and medical geography which cut across many research specialties have been developed with increasing success in recent years. The information retrieval problem in cross-disciplinary subjects such as these is difficult because relevant findings may be scattered widely among 50,000 or more scientific and medical publications. Yet, the greatest problems arise because of inherent difficulties in the subject matters of investigation.

The weather is noted for its restless variability. As Frederick Sargent II[2] points out the atmospheric ingredients of weather "are rarely present in exactly the same proportion, and, as a consequence, it has been exceedingly difficult to conceive exact models of the physical environment." Yet, he continues, "the variability of the organism is no less simple. The individual organism, be it plant or animal, has biochemical and physiological individuality. Biochemical, physiological, and behavioral events in plants and animals vary in time [and] are regulated by biological clocks." These clocks have multiple rhythms. Approximate periods vary from one day, to a week, a month, a season, a year, and longer. Given such multiple controls, the variation in factors such as the chemical properties of the blood, functions of important organs or body systems, and overt behavior may be greater in a single individual over a long period of time than between different individuals at the same time.

The theme of the biological and behavioral uniqueness of individuals is an important one. Nothing can be done with it in this review except to note the extraordinary difficulty in making sense of fluctuating series of unique environmental and organismic events. The resulting literature can be exceedingly confusing and contradictory. It is founded too often upon statistical correlations of doubtful significance with the physiological linkages poorly established, for as Nelson Dingle[3] indicates, "in the search for cause and effect relationship in bioclimatological work, one needs to give careful attention to the question whether the data actually contain the required information." As R. E. Munn[4] concludes, "there is a vast literature on medical climatology. In many cases the evidence is inductive and not very convincing." The task of the reviewer is to try to sort the wheat from the chaff.

Meteorotropisms

The Greek term *meteor* refers to atmospheric disturbances and *tropic* to turnings or changes. Hence, a scientific term has been coined to refer to a turn of events related to atmospheric disturbances: meteorotropism. The identification and analysis of such biological events is at the heart of the science of biometeorology. Having stated his ideas on the variability of living individuals, Sargent proceeds as follows:

The main inquiry of biometeorology is to find out how much of this organismic variability is due to the changing atmospheric environment within which the organisms exist... When biological events are ordered in time, deviations from the expected aggregate about certain hours, days, months, etc. When sizable human populations are investigated, it has been found that sudden death, attacks of angina, joint pain, insomnia, and traffic accidents occur with unusual frequency on certain days, or in certain seasons. In some cases, it has been possible to demonstrate by appropriate statistical procedures that characteristic changes in the atmospheric environment are correlated with the biological aggregations. The biological event is then identified as a meteorotropism.

The convincing isolation of a weather-related biological change from those related to some other form of environmental or internally induced stress is not an easy one, as Sargent is the first to acknowledge. Something of the problem can be seen by considering cases of aggravated duodenal ulcers.

Duodenal ulcer aggravation

The monthly summary of the number of patients admitted to the Philadelphia General Hospital with hemorrhaging duodenal ulcers over the period 1949-1953 records cases in every month but shows a tendency to peak in March-April and October-November of any given year. The peak in the fall is somewhat greater than the spring peak. Francis K. Davis, Jr.[5] notes that "since hemorrhage from ulcers is intimately connected with the circulatory system and since this system definitely reacts to temperature changes, an attempt was made to find some relationship between temperature changes and ulcer hemorrhages." The greatest decrease in average temperature from one month to the next during the period under study did in fact occur from October to November, and the greatest increase occurred between March and April. One particular January-February period had a higher incidence of admission than the other comparable periods. This January was characterized by an unusually high monthly average temperature and was followed by an unusually cold February. Moreover, this particular January experienced 16 day-to-day changes of more than 10°F (-12.2°C) in maximum temperature, nine of which were from warm to cold. Thus, the plausible suggestion that "the period of negative temperature change contributes more strongly to circulatory stresses than the period of positive temperature change" receives some support, but "more detailed data than are presently available would be necessary to decide this point." Nevertheless, Davis concludes:

So, there is strong evidence that hemorrhage from duodenal ulcers may be brought on by marked variations in temperatures and the stress that such variations put on the body as it is forced to adjust. This fact, together with the observation that the number of cases is least in midsummer, would suggest that a warm climate with relatively little daily and seasonal variation in temperature would afford the most suitable residence for those prone to suffer from duodenal ulcers. Meanwhile, those northerners who are afflicted with duodenal ulcers might well be on the lookout for cold wave warnings in the fall. Such warnings cause construction workers to stop pouring concrete, prodfarmers into taking special precautions to save crops, and serve to make fuel oil companies prepare for extra deliveries. They might be used to equal advantage by ulcer patients.

Or, can they?

Another study in southern Australia found an increase of reported ulcer cases during May-June, the equivalent of Philadelphia's November-December, thereby seeming to confirm the latter study. Yet, as Munn[4] points out, still another study in Hawaii, where there is a climate like that described by Davis as most suitable for ulcer patients, revealed a variation in frequency of ulcer aggravation through the months similar to that found in Philadelphia. Does this latter finding indicate that the hemorrhages have nothing to do with the weather? Does it indicate that they are related to some weather or environmental circumstance common to both types of settings but as yet not detected? Or does it indicate that the body is somewhat stereotyped in its response to stress and that very different factors can help to bring about the same variation in clinical condition? The prudent person with ulcers may want to follow Davis's advice, at least in so far as it implies elimination of outside activities during periods when the temperature is forecast to change sharply. More properly, that person would also want to consult with a well-read specialist in internal medicine.

Asthma and "hay fever"

The atmosphere is a carrier of countless gases and particles or droplets from natural and human-made sources. Some persons are extremely sensitive by way of allergic reactions to many substances that are quite common in the air. Different types of pollen and fungi spores are found in enormous numbers in various seasons. Asthma symptoms ranging from wheezes to near suffocation result from exposure to many of these substances. Various human-made air pollutants also seem to be implicated.

Fairly good correlations can be found between reported asthma attack rate and levels of air pollution measured variously by indices of sulfur dioxide, nitrates, suspended particulate, and total oxidant. Arlan A. Cohen, M.D. and co-workers[6] conducted an intensive study in New Cumberland, West Virginia where "significant correlations were found between... attack rate and pollution levels after the effects of temperature had been removed from the analysis. These temperature independent air pollution effects occurred at levels of pollution commonly found in large cities, and appeared greater at moderate than at low temperatures." The weather related effects, in themselves, are very interesting and fairly well established by independent investigators.

Sudden changes in the weather can be a very important trigger for the beginning of all types of asthma attacks whether characterized by an allergic reaction to air-borne particles or by bronchial infections. Solco Tromp[7] of the Netherlands has concluded that the frequency of asthma increases rapidly after a sudden increase in the general turbulence of the air combined with rapidly falling temperature. In other words, the increase occurs during the advance and passage of an active fast-moving cold front. The increase is most striking after a long quiet period with moderate temperatures.

On a seasonal basis, the average asthma frequency is low during the winter and spring with significant increases, at least in the Netherlands, at the end of June. The maximum frequency generally occurs sometime between September and November. Studies in the United States seem to indicate that the effects are most pronounced in the early fall during the first or second invasion of cold air when indoor heating has to be reinitiated. Cold frontal passages later in the winter produce less spectacular increases in both the frequency and severity of asthma attacks. These meteorotropisms have been attributed variously to the stirring of allergenic substances in the house with the renewed heating and to the difficulty the body has in adjusting to cold stress after lengthy adaption to warm conditions. Either condition may be expected to decline over the winter months.

A sharp decrease in asthma frequency is observed during the influx of warm tropical air associated with an active warm front and during periods of mild but calm and settled weather. A rapid succession of cold and warm fronts can set up waves of increasing and decreasing asthma frequency. On the other hand, in warm climates, great heat stress is associated with an increase of asthma complaints. To further complicate the picture, Tromp notes that, contrary to patients suffering from noninfectious asthma, the bronchitic patients have the highest degree of complaints in winter, particularly in January and February, and a minimum in the summer. "Hay fever" (seasonal vasomotor rhinitis) is neither caused by hay nor very often associated with fever. It is caused by seasonal allergens produced by plants that often flower around the hay season. The characteristic symptoms such as excessive sneezing, stuffiness, profuse nasal discharge, fatigue, itching eyes, nose, mouth and so forth may also occur on a nonseasonal basis as the result of allergies to substances such as house-dust, animal products, or foods. The weather factors associated with the production, release, and transport of various ragweed pollens of the "late season" from August until first frost have been studied in greater depth than those associated with the aeroallergens of other seasons.

The highest ragweed pollen indices are found in a triangular portion of the United States bounded by the eastern Great Plains, the Gulf of Mexico and the Appalachian Mountains, and the middle Great Lakes. In the southern part of Michigan, a particularly bad area for hay fever, it has been found that high May rainfall and low July rainfall promote the maximum annual yield of pollen. Dingle[3] reports that "on an average midsummer day, with dew at sunrise and sunny weather, the mature flowers begin to swell outward before the dew disappears.... As the relative humidity drops with solar warming, the anthers open in quick succession throughout the local ragweed population." He also notes that the openings take place quickly when the humidity is low, much more slowly when it is high, and perhaps not at all under steady rain.

The vast majority of ragweed pollen falls out within a few hundred feet of the source. Local up-drafts that produce fair weather or "bubble" clouds or the turbulence associated with thunderstorms or approaching cold fronts may, if timed properly with the release of pollen, carry large amounts of pollen to considerable heights. The grains may be swept along for hundreds of miles before falling out or being washed-out by precipitation. Dingle believes that the likelihood of the reflotation of pollen which has fallen out is small in comparison with the amount of fresh daily emissions.

Heart diseases

According to the Department of Health, Education, and Welfare about 1,250,000 heart attacks (acute myocardial infarction) occur annually in the United States of which about 400,000 are deadly. Some 25,000,000 persons suffer from various forms of heart and vascular disease such as stroke and high blood pressure leading to more than 1,000,000 deaths each year. Many studies in western Europe and various parts of the United States have shown significant correlations between these diseases and some form of temperature stress. It is said that persons with coronary artery disease cannot tolerate exposure to cold wind combined with high humidity without experiencing severe chest pain. Such sensitivity of course cannot explain the rather frequent occurrence of heart attacks during rest in a comfortable room or during sleep in a warm bed. Still, certain patterns emerge from the study of weather stresses that help to explain some of the seasonal variations, where they occur. An early study in Los Angeles before World War II could establish no significant seasonal variation in that mild climate. What the situation might be like today with many more social and environmental stresses added to the life of Angelenos would make the basis for an interesting study.

Solco Tromp,[7] who is perhaps the leading European biometeorologist, summarizes the major observed cardiovascular meteorotropic correlations as follows:

1. In the northern countries, the mortality rate of coronary heart diseases, being considerably higher in males than in females, is almost every year highest in January-February and lowest around July-August.
2. The mortality rate for stroke, being higher in females than in males, shows each year the same seasonal pattern as the coronary heart diseases.
3. In very warm countries, such as the southern part of the United States, highest mortality incidence is observed in summer, lowest in winter.

Tromp notes further that winters with abnormally low temperatures are characterized by very high mortality and that during relatively warm winters mortality is relatively low. Similarly, during the summer, even in regions that have relatively low mortality rates in that season, the higher the temperature the more people seem to die from stroke and coronary heart disease. Studies in Philadelphia and Kentucky, where the seasonal extremes are fairly great, reveal a double peak in winter and in summer, at least in males.

One of the most suggestive studies was made in Dallas, Texas. The highest number of heart attacks occurred in the summer and the lowest during the winter season. But a more careful analysis conducted with an eye to strong frontal passages and sudden air mass changes rather than simply to average monthly temperatures revealed an increased frequency of heart attacks in any season during periods of sudden inflow of polar or tropical air masses. The winter cold waves may not last very long, but they can be quite severe, as can the summer heat waves. Thus, while the weather patterns in Dallas and Philadelphia are quite different, as are the patterns of heart disease, the correlations in both places with rapid changes toward hot or cold air masses show considerably unity of result.

Although the basic correlations between heart attacks and weather factors are not clearly established, the findings and opinions of different investigators do not have to be regarded as so widely divergent as they sometimes seem to be. Tromp notes that the findings of significant correlations between meteorological stress (particularly heat and cold) and increased incidence of diseases such as myocardial infraction, angina pectoris, and stroke have been confirmed in artificial climate chambers.

Arthritis

Some persons have an almost legendary sensitivity to weather changes. They have been called variously, cyclonopaths, weather birds, human barometers, and other terms suggesting sensitivity to changing conditions of the atmosphere. Twinges of gout and sciatica are popularly supposed to forecast rain. Most familiar is the conviction expressed in folklore that pains from scars and from arthritis sharpen during weather in the vicinity of a front separating one air mass from another type.

Hippocrates, or one of his followers, tried to relate atmospheric conditions and the personality of individuals in a treatise *On Temperaments and Humors*. The ideas survived in one form or another well past the time of Shakespeare. In the present day, some of the relations between mood or pain and the weather are being put on a fairly sound basis. Some of the more interesting results have been obtained in the Climatron or controlled climate chamber at the Hospital of the University of Pennsylvania.[8]

It should be clear by now that studies of human populations in their usual habitats are frustratingly difficult. Thus, many investigators have taken recourse to artificial chambers where experimental subjects can live for several weeks. Five or more factors can be varied singly or in various combinations. Some of the meteorotropic relations may be clarified in such chambers, although considerable difficulties remain in the attempt to generalize to the "real" world.

The Pennsylvania Climatron can control temperature, humidity, pressure, air flow, and ionization. Experiments with arthritic patients in which the environmental factors were varied one at a time in random order with a return to "standard" conditions in between resulted in no significant effect on the clinical index of well being and joint condition. Large effects however were produced in a group of eight patients with rheumatoid arthritis when they were subjected to simultaneous variations of pressure and humidity. Seven patients were afflicted with greatly increased arthritis in 57-100% of their trial exposures. One patient was insensitive to the same changes through six cycles. Typically, the effects occurred in a cycle when relative humidity was increased from 30% to 80% while the atmospheric pressure was simultaneously decreased by 10% over a six-hour period. It should be noted that these rates of change are considerably higher than those that occur naturally in the atmosphere, except perhaps in rapidly moving hurricanes. The details of the clinical indices varied considerably from patient to patient and for different features of the programmed environmental changes, but the general effects were clear enough to justify the conclusion that

> *From these results, it would appear that at least one condition of changing weather factors—rising humidity with falling barometric pressure—fairly consistently exerts a detrimental effect on arthritic symptoms and signs. It would also appear that the changing conditions, rather than the high humidity or low barometric pressure, are responsible. It now seems reasonable to conclude that weather effect on arthritis is a definite phenomena, and not just another old wives' tale. It is not implied that climatic changes have any direct bearing on the cause of arthritis, nor is it believed that a constant climate would have any fundamentally curative effect.*

• CLIMATE CHANGE

Selecting a climate

An important consideration to be taken into account in choosing a new climate is to learn about it firsthand. Ideally, individuals can spend time (at different times of the year) in the area to which they are thinking of moving—this will ensure exposure to the entire range of weather conditions for the area.

Vacations, however, have traditionally been an attempt for many people to find a more ideal environment, at least for a short period of time. Yet, contemporary folk wisdom tells of the need to take a rest on returning from an otherwise delightful vacation. This bit of folk wisdom has some bearing on the question of moving to a different area. There are many reasons for this advice. One reason is the slowness with which human organisms adapt to major climatic changes. Acclimatization to a new area may take ten years or longer in the opinion of some investigators. It is certainly a process that can take weeks to occur. Clothing habits change quickly enough, and thirst brings about rapid changes in the amount of fluid intake—although to be sure the nature of the fluid imbibed in recreational settings is often inappropriate for a well functioning organism. The quantity and quality of food intake and physical exertion is even more frequently inappropriate to the new setting, and the process of acclimatization can be a long drawn out affair indeed. Motivation plays an important role in speeding the process.

Another consideration for the person thinking of making a "permanent" move to a new location is a possibility of a return to the original environment. Acclimatization is a two way process. After an experience of several years in a new environment, adaptation may be more or less complete. The process of readaptation to the original setting, however, may be even more difficult than the former process. The body is older and, for lack of a better term, may have less "elasticity" in the various vital systems. Also, there may have been adaptive changes that are in principle difficult to reverse. This latter point is highly speculative.

Other key points to consider include: specific weather conditions do not affect every individual to the same degree; not all illness-related factors are equal; weather observations taken at a single location do not necessarily reflect the actual atmospheric conditions at all points in an area.

The search for an "ideal" climate may be a never ending one. Each person is affected in an individual way by his environment and no group could agree on the ideal. The process of acclimation is a complicated interplay of physiological, behavioral, and psychological responses. A person has to feel "at home and wanted." The health and well-being of many persons may be served best by staying in the "native" setting even though it may be regarded as far from ideal. "Air conditioning" in both summer and winter can be a big help in making the old environment do. Of course, in the face of continued ecological decay and energy supplies that will be critical for some time to come and increasingly expensive, people need to consider the possibility of reducing their less essential demands in exchange for the goods and services that make for a healthier way of life.

Effects of changing climate

The effects of many drugs change with changes in the weather. Digitalis, a drug widely used in heart disease, in experimental doses in animals is more toxic during storms than in stable atmospheric conditions. Its toxicity also rises with increased body temperature and increased elevations. It may be the case that these variations in toxicity as well as the variations in the effects of other drugs are related to the permeability of various membranes in the body and thereby to the ease with which the drugs can enter the blood stream. Weather may trigger the body responses that result in these changes, but little is known about the relevant biological mechanisms. At any rate, Helmut Landsberg[9] notes that some sleep-inducing drugs have reduced effects at high temperatures, the response to insulin is apparently slowed by exposure to cold, atropine taken internally to relieve spasms also inhibits sweating and can thereby be dangerous in a hot environment, and some diuretics can cause excess loss of sodium leading to circulatory complications in persons not acclimated to a hot environment. Thus, in this era of high speed business and recreational travel from one climate zone to another, the traveler is well advised to check with a physician about possible changes in medication or dosage.

Jet-lag, or rapid time zone travel fatigue, has made people aware of the difficulties that even healthy individuals may experience in forcing their organism to adapt quickly to a new environment. Some persons can adapt fairly quickly with few ill effects, but many individuals adjust only slowly and with considerable strain.

Many older persons as well as a few younger ones, who are otherwise healthy, may have organic responses to day to day weather changes that are slow enough so that their bodies are never quite "in balance" with the environment. Even though no particular disease may be present, feelings of disease may result. On the other hand, there are schools of medical thought stemming from Hippocrates' time which do not draw sharp distinction between conditions of disease and feelings of disease.

"Inadvertent" changes to climate

A major maladaption of modern societies concerns the disposition of industrial, commercial, transportation, and household wastes. Man has long disposed of these wastes into the air, water, and soil on the assumption that the vastness of these resources could cope adequately with the necessary dispersal, dilution, and assimilation of the waste products. Even before Hippocrates wrote "On Airs, Waters, and Places," air, water, and soil have been known to be vital resources for all living things. It is now clear that these resources cannot continue to be polluted at the accelerating pace of modern society. The possible would wide effects on climate and environmental quality will not be discussed in this review, but the local and regional health effects of air pollutants will be treated briefly.

The large number of deaths in excess of seasonal normals associated with air pollution episodes in places such as Donora, Pennsylvania, and London, England, until as recently as ten or twenty years ago are hopefully things of the past. These earlier episodes involved changes in the expected death rates of 50% or more! They probably were triggered by extraordinarily high levels of pollutants such as sulfur dioxide and particulates: the pollutants produced by uncontrolled heavy industrial processes and the burning of any but the highest grades of coal and fuel oil. In these earlier episodes, the pollutants accumulated to intolerably high levels when the weather pattern over the particular region stagnated for three or more days. Technological remedies of long standing (dating back 40-100 years or more) and newer control techniques coupled with shifts from coal to gas and high grade fuel oil as energy sources finally have been instituted in most highly populated regions of the developed world. Some of the control techniques have not been adequately developed yet and the existing ones have not been universally adopted. With regard to the old fashioned pollutants, most cities are in far better shape today than they were a decade ago. But the difficult improvements lie ahead.

The problem of urban air pollution by the old standby sulfur dioxide and respirable particles has by no means been solved. Out-patient and emergency ward counts in large cities continue to show low correlations with existing air pollution levels of these substances. The effects are truly marginal, and require very nice analytical techniques. Using the best studies available, the correlations involving the various measures of sulfur dioxide, suspended particulate, and total oxidant can be translated even today into thousands of excess hospital and doctor visits for respiratory ailments and associated cardiovascular problems. The dramatic death dealing episodes may be over, at least for a while, but air pollution related deaths continue to occur at lower levels where they tend to be hidden in the noise of normal day-to-day and season-to-season variations in death rates.

Lester Lave and Eugene Seskin[10] believe they have developed techniques of analysis sensitive enough to isolate the proportion of deaths associated with air pollution described by indices of particulates and sulfates. The statistical significance of their findings remains even when climate, home heating, and various social or economic variables are added. They have available only crude measures of the various factors believed to be responsible for most of the observed variation, and one can question whether their air quality and other social and environmental data really contain the necessary information. Still, based on the best available measurements, they conclude that a 50% reduction in the urban levels of particulates and sulfates could cut the urban death rates by 4% and add one full year to life expectancy at birth. According to Lave and Seskin, the social and economic benefits of such a reduction in pollution, which is technologically feasible, would be comparable to the complete eradication of cancer, which is not medically possible at present. The economic cost of such reduction are varied according to different strategies economic management. With no offsetting governmental intervention, for example, the prices of manufactured goods—exclusive of automobiles—might be expected to rise between 0-5% for an average rise of about 2% and net unemployment might be expected to rise by about 0.2% during the first few years of such a phased abatement program.

The sickness and mortality effects of the types of air pollutants associated with automobile exhausts such as hydrocarbons, carbon monoxide, nitrogen oxides, and the oxides of heavy metal additives are more subtle and hence more difficult to isolate than similar effects in the case of heavy industrial effluents and the combustion products of raw coal and low grade oil. Even so, statistical analysis and prudent concern establishes well enough the need for new combustion technology and alternative forms of transportation. The goals set by the Clean Air Act of 1970 for the automobile industry to meet for the 1975 and 1976 model years are very stringent. The economic costs of meeting those standards are roughly twice those mentioned above and they include a significant penalty in consumption of limited fuel resources. Some people argue that the goals for the automobile industry are excessive. More realistically, it might be argued that those goals go somewhat beyond the level required for balanced progress in environmental management. The issue is not one of need, but one of priorities and strategy in achieving responsible environmental stewardship.

The truth is that only a brief respite will have been achieved from human's habit of fouling his nest—someone's waste spaces are someone else's living spaces—unless the search for better technological palliatives is coupled with a less demanding way of life. The sad part of the picture is that the areas with the highest potential for air pollution episodes are precisely the areas with the most stable weather patterns and hence the areas most desirable for many health, recreational, and retirement living purposes. As the pressure mounts to continue the rapid subdivision and economic development of the desirable southeastern, southwestern and west coast areas of the United States, the high potential that they have for weather stagnation and serious air pollution episodes will be fulfilled with increasing frequency. The same conclusion applies to comparable areas in Europe. Existing social and technological mechanisms will have to be maintained even when the economic shoe begins to pinch a little, and new ones developed to make further significant cuts in the witches brew of chemicals that continue to degrade the quality of the air and other life resources. As an aid to the general public in thinking about these issues more deeply, this book draws together for the first time in a single convenient source the best judgments from members of the Environmental Protection Agency about the existing air quality in the various analysis regions of the nation.

Spirit willing and pocketbook able

Americans have always been a mobile people. Freedom of movement for business, recreational, and retirement purposes is a valued privilege of the American way of life. It should not be treated lightly or abused. Knowledge of all the effects of any given movement is, of course, impossible to obtain. Nevertheless, considerable insight about the atmospheric conditions to be found in or near the major urban settings of the nation can be derived from this book. One of its purposes is to provide the basis for that insight in one convenient source. It is like an almanac, the more it is used, the more connections can be seen, and the more valuable the book becomes. On the basis of experience, conversation, and intuition, everyone has some idea of desirable, if not quite ideal, weather patterns. Everyone can extrapolate from known situations to plan for the visit or move that has to be made.

The various tables in this book summarize as far as possible in popular or semi-popular terms the recent weather and air quality history of more than 100 locations in the United States and many additional cities abroad. Each of the standard elements of the observed weather is presented in a way that indicates a great deal about the averages and the amount of deviation that may be expected to occur in any given month. The reader will want to pay attention especially to the information on temperature means and extremes, the persistence of extreme conditions in any month, humidity, sky cover and sunshine.

It is impossible to make forecasts from this book. Not even the *Farmer's Almanac* can do that in any meaningful way. The judicious examination of the various tables of the book, in comparison with the tables for an area known well from first hand experience, can be an aid in planning for both short term and longer term "changes of climate."

Suggestions for further reading:

Landsberg, Helmut E., *Weather and Health*, Doubleday Anchor Science Studies Series S 59, 1969.

Dubos, Rene, *Mirage of Health*, Doubleday Anchor A258, 1959.

Battan, Louis J., *The Unclean Sky*, Doubleday Anchor Science Studies Series S 46, 1966.

[Corman, Rena], *Air Pollution Primer*, National Tuberculosis and Respiratory Disease Association (American Lung Association), 1969.

Dubos, Rene, *Man Adapting*, Yale University Press, 1965.

Licht, Sidney, M.D., (ed.), *Medical Climatology*, Elizabeth Licht, Publisher, 1965.

Sulman, Felix G., M.D., D.V.M., *Short- and Long-Term Changes in Climate*, (2 vol.), C.R.C. Press, 1983.

Tromp, Solco W., *Biometeorology*, Heyden & Son, 1980.

Reference Notes:

[1] Hippocrates. "On Airs, Waters, and Places," *The Theory and Practice of Medicine*, Citadel Press, 1964.

[2] Sargent, Frederick, II, "The Nature and Nurture of Biometeorology," *Bulletin of the American Meteorological Society*, Vol. 44, No. 8 (August 1963), pp. 483-448.

[3] Dingle, A.N., comment, p. 148 in Tromp, S.W. (ed.), *Biometeorology,* Pergamon Press, 1962. Dingle's ideas on pollution by ragweed pollen are found in Licht, Sidney (ed.), *Medical Meteorology*, Licht, 1964, pp. 96-130.

[4] Munn, R.E., *Biometeorological Methods*, Academic Press, 1970, p. 255.

[5] Davis, Francis K., Jr., "Ulcers and Temperature Changes," *Bulletin of American Meteorological Society*, Vol. 39, No. 12 (December 1958), pp. 652-654

[6] Cohen, Arlan A., M.D., et. al., "Asthma and Air Pollution from a Coal-fueled Power Plant," *American Journal of Public Health*, Vol. 62, No. 9 (September 1972), pp. 1181-1188.

[7] Tromp, Solco W., "Biometeorological Aspects of Architectural and Urban Planning and Their Significance for the Thermoregulatory Efficiency, and Physico-Chemical State of the Blood of Human Subjects," Conference on Urban Environment and Second Conference on Biometeorology, 1972. Preprint volume of papers available from the American Meteorological Society, 45 Beacon Street, Boston, Mass., 02108. Tromp's work is also reported extensively in two volumes he edited, *Biometeorology*, Pergamon Press, 1962 and *Medical Meteorology*, Elsevier, 1962.

[8] Hollander, Joseph L. and S.J. Yeostros, "The Effect of Simultaneous Variations of Humidity and Barometric Pressure on Arthritis," *Bulletin of the American Meteorological Society*, Vol. 44, No. 8 (August 1963), pp. 489-494.

[9] Landsberg, Helmut E., *Weather and Health*, Doubleday Anchor, 1969, pp. 126-128.

[10] Lave, Lester B. and Eugene P. Seskin, "Air Pollution, Climate, and Home Heating: Their Effects on U.S. Mortality Rates," *American Journal of Public Health*, Vol. 62, No. 7 (July 1972), pp. 909-916.

• JET-LAG OR TIME-ZONE FATIGUE

The modern jet airplane makes it possible for a person to travel great distances in a few hours under conditions of great comfort and safety. An exception is the physiological and mental stress that most persons encounter if four or more time zones are crossed creating the effects of what is commonly called "jet-lag" or "time-zone fatigue."

More than 100 biological functions and human activities are geared to fluctuate between maximum and minimum values in about 24 hours, the so-called "circadian rhythms" (from the Latin words *circa* and *dies* for approximately one day) or "body clocks." After a jet flight of several hours across a continent or an ocean, a traveler's "body clocks" will be badly out of phase or "desynchronized" with respect to local time. The body rhythms will tend to be in phase with the time of the place of departure rather than the local time of the place of arrival.

The travel induced phase shift between "body time" and "local time" will cause some discomfort and, more dangerously, lapses in alertness, immediate memory, and impairment of normal judgments. Hunger, steep, elimination patterns, and mental functioning may take several days to return to normal. Deep body temperatures, which are commonly highest around 5 P.M. and lowest around 4 or 5 A.M., and the associated biochemical processes, may take a little longer to become resynchronized.

One easy to remember rule of thumb is that most travelers readjust to the new time zone at the rate of about one hour per-day, although each function has its own rate of return and there is marked individual variability in the severity of desynchronization and the rate of recovery.

North-south flights produce few of these effects, although, for reasons to be made clear, such travel within a time zone can cause a high degree of subjective fatigue as well as certain physiological effects keyed to drugs, alcohol, and smoking that need attention by the wise traveler.

In nearly all cases, the effects increase with the age of the traveler.

Social factors

Some studies of adaption to time zone shifts seem to show the importance of social and psychological factors in the readjustment process. Less deterioration seems to take place when persons travel in groups. Related observations reveal that fatigue seems to be less and resynchronization may occur more rapidly in relation to familiar surroundings. The problems may be reduced when the person experiences a high degree of motivation and generally feels "at home."

Anything that interferes with the oxygen up-take of body and brain cells produces an anemia, fatigue, and an impairment of mental functioning. Alcohol from drinking and carbon monoxide from smoking are two common sources of such deterioration. The reduced oxygen pressure at altitudes above 10,000 feet (3,033 m) produces physiological effects similar to those of moderate drinking and smoking in persons acclimatized to near sea level pressures. Fatigue occurs rapidly in such persons at pressure altitudes above about 12,000 feet (3,640 m). With modern airplanes pressurized to between 6,000 and 8,000 feet (1,820-2,427 m), even though flying at altitudes well above 30,000 feet (9,100 m), fatigue and mental impairment are minimized. The various effects are additive, however. A person who drinks or smokes during, or for several hours prior, to a flight can experience a physiological altitude of 10,000 to 12,000 feet (3,033-3,640 m) or more, with the alcohol and smoke having twice the effect of similar amounts at sea level. Thus, for example, two drinks immediately before and during flight might suddenly induce the effects of four drinks under normal circumstances. The effects of these habits on the cardiovascular system and mental functioning are bad enough for north-south flights within a time zone. They aggravate considerably the jet-lag effects of easterly or westerly flights.

Time-zone travel tips

Various common sense rules can be developed from these generalizations. Persons with chronic or acute respiratory and circulatory disorders should abstain from smoking and drinking during and for several hours before any air flight, even if they have not managed to change their behavior for the better in normal circumstances. Consultation with a physician is prudent. All persons should at least moderate their drinking and smoking habits, if not abstain altogether, in order to minimize fatigue and the other effects of long distance high speed travel.

A person should try to adjust sleeping and eating patterns over several days before departure. Eating smaller amounts, more frequently than usual, and, in any case, avoiding a heavy meal just before or just after the flight can be helpful. If possible, sleeping and awakening should be adjusted about an hour a day in each of several days before departure. Thus, before flying toward the east, bedtime and wakeup time can be set one hour earlier in each of several days, or set one hour later in preparation for a westbound flight. Flights of more than 10,000 miles (16,100 km) should include a 24-hour stopover.

A flight can be selected profitably to arrive in the afternoon or evening rather than in the morning in order to move more quickly into the crucial sleep patterns of the new time zone. Evening entertainment or business activities should be avoided on the day of arrival. If adaption is to take place after arrival, important decisions or strenuous sightseeing should be postponed for a day or two. Avoid sleep inducing medications, which reduce the most refreshing REM or rapid eye movement phase of sleep. Light meals, mild exercise such as walking, and warm baths should help to speed adaption to the new sleep cycle.

As a final suggestion, since the effects of many medications can change considerably with pressure altitude, it would be wise to check with your physician before departure about changes in schedule or dosage that might prove to be beneficial.

Suggestions for further reading:

Aschoff, J., "Circadian rhythms in man," *Science*, V. 148 (June 11, 1965), 1427-32.

Brown, F. A. Jr., "The 'clocks' timing biological rhythms," *American Scientist*, V. 60 (December 1972), 756-66.

McFarland, R. A., "Air travel across time zones," *American Scientist*, V. 63 (January-February 1975), 23-30.

Siegel, P. V., et. al., "Time zone effects," *Science*, V. 164 (June 13, 1969), 1249-55.

Strughold, Hubertus, M.D., *Your Body Clock, its significance for the jet traveler*, Charles Scribner's Sons, New York, 1971.

Air Pollution

Air pollution is a general term that covers a broad range of contaminants in the atmosphere. Pollution can occur from natural causes or from human activities. Discussions about the effects of air pollution have focused mainly on human health but attention is being directed to environmental quality and amenity as well. Air pollutants are found as gases or particles; and on a restricted scale, they can be trapped inside buildings as indoor air pollutants. Urban air pollution has long been an important concern for civic administrators; but increasingly, air pollution has become an international problem.

The most characteristic sources of air pollution have always been combustion processes. The most obvious pollutant is smoke; however, the widespread use of fossil fuels have made sulfur and nitrogen oxides pollutants of great concern. With increasing use of petroleum-based fuels, a range of organic compounds have become widespread in the atmosphere.

In urban areas, air pollution has been a matter of concern since historical times. Indeed, there were complaints about smoke in ancient Rome. The use of coal throughout the centuries has caused cities to be very smoky places. Along with smoke, large concentrations of sulfur dioxide were produced. It was this mixture of smoke and sulfur dioxide that typified the foggy streets of victorian London, paced by such figures as Sherlock Holmes and Jack the Ripper, whose images remain linked with smoke and fog. Such situations are far less common in the cities of North America and Europe today. However, until recently, they have been evident in other cities, such as Ankara, Turkey, and Shanghai, China, that rely heavily on coal.

Coal is still burnt in large quantities to produce electricity or to refine metals, but these processes are frequently undertaken outside cities. Within urban areas, fuel use has shifted towards liquid and gaseous hydrocarbons (petrol and natural gas). These fuels typically have a lower concentration of sulfur, so the presence of sulfur dioxide has declined in many urban areas. However the widespread use of liquid fuels in automobiles has meant increased production of carbon monoxide, nitrogen oxides, and volatile organic compounds.

Primary pollutants such as sulfur dioxide or smoke are the direct emission products of the combustion process. Today, many of the key pollutants in the urban atmospheres are secondary pollutants, produced by processes initiated through photochemical reactions. The photochemical-type smog found in Los Angeles, California, is now characteristic of urban atmospheres dominated by secondary pollutants.

Although the automobile is the main source of air pollution in contemporary cities, there are other equally significant sources. Stationary sources are still important and the oil-burning furnaces that have replaced the older coal-burning ones are still responsible for a range of gaseous emissions and fly ash. Incineration is also an important source of complex combustion products, especially where this incineration burns a wide range of refuse. These emissions can include chlorinated hydrocarbons such as dioxin. When plastics, which often contain chlorine, are incinerated, hydrochloric acid results in the waste gas stream. Metals, especially where they are volatile at high temperatures, can migrate to smaller, respirable particles. The accumulation of toxic metals, such as cadmium, on fly ash gives rise to concern over harmful effects from incinerator emissions. In specialized incinerators designed to destroy toxic compounds such as PCBs, many questions have been raised about the completeness of this destruction process. Even under optimum conditions where the furnace operation has been properly maintained, great care needs to be taken to control leaks and losses during transfer operations (fugitive emissions).

The enormous range of compounds used in modern manufacturing processes have also meant that there has been an ever-widening range of emissions from both the industrial processes and the combustion of their wastes. Although the amounts of these toxic compounds are often rather small, they add to the complex range of compounds found in the urban atmosphere. Again, it is not only the deliberate loss of effluents through discharge from pipes and chimneys that needs attention. Fugitive emissions of volatile substances that leak from valves and seals often warrant careful control.

Air pollution control procedures are increasingly an important part of civic administration, although their goals are far from easy to achieve. It is also noticeable that although many urban concentrations of primary pollutants, for example, smoke and sulfur dioxide, are on the decline in developed countries, this is not always true in the developing countries. Here the desire for rapid industrial growth has often lowered urban air quality. Secondary air pollutants are generally proving a more difficult problem to eliminate than primary pollutants like smoke.

Urban air pollutants have a wide range of effects, with health problems being the most enduring concern. In the polluted atmospheres filled with smoke and sulfur dioxide, a range of bronchial diseases were enhanced. While respiratory diseases are still the principal problem, the issues are somewhat more subtle in atmospheres where the air pollutants are not so obvious. In photochemical smog, eye irritation from the secondary pollutant peroxyacetyl nitrate (PAN) is one on the most characteristic direct effects of the smog. High concentrations of carbon monoxide in cities where automobiles operate at high density means that the human heart has to work harder to make up for the oxygen displaced from the blood's hemoglobin by carbon monoxide. This extra stress appears to reveal itself by increased incidence of complaints among people with heart problems. There is a widespread belief that contemporary air pollutants are involved in the increases in asthma, but the links between asthma and air pollution are probably rather complex and related to a whole range of factors. Lead, from automotive exhausts, is thought by many to be a factor in lowering the IQs of urban children.

Air pollution also affects materials in the urban environment. Soiling has long been regarded as a problem, originally the result of the smoke from wood or coal fires, but now increasingly the result of fine black soot from diesel exhausts. The acid gases, particularly sulfur dioxide, increase the rate of destruction of building materials. This is most noticeable with calcareous stones, which are the predominant building material of many important historic structures. Metals also suffer from atmospheric acidity. In modern photochemical smog, natural rubbers crack and deteriorate rapidly.

Table 5.6

Estimates of Adverse Health Effects of Aerosol Acid Sulfates

Effect	Threshold concentration (micrograms per cubic meter)	Duration of exposure
Increased daily mortality (four studies)	25	24 hours or longer
Aggravation of heart and lung disease in elderly (two studies)	25	24 hours or longer
Aggravation of asthma (four studies)	6–10	24 hours or longer
Increased acute respiratory diseases in children (four studies)	13	Several years
Increased risk of chronic bronchitis		
Cigarette smokers	15	Up to 10 years
Nonsmokers	10	Up to 10 years

Source: J. F. Finklen, et al., "Health Effects of Increasing Sulfur Oxides Emissions," Environmental Protection Agency (draft, 1975).

Health problems relating to indoor air pollution are extremely ancient. Anthracosis, or black lung disease, has been found in mummified lung tissue. Recent decades have witnessed a shift from the predominance of concern about outdoor air pollution into a widening interest in indoor air quality.

The production of energy from combustion and the release of solvents is so large in the contemporary world that it causes air pollution problems of a regional and global nature. Acid rain is now widely observed throughout the world. The sheer quantity of carbon dioxide emitted in combustion process is increasing the concentration of carbon dioxide in the atmosphere and enhancing the greenhouse effect. Solvents, such as carbon tetrachloride and aerosol propellants chlorofluorocarbons are now detectable all over the globe and responsible for such problems as ozone layer depletion.

At the other end of the scale, we need to remember that gases leak indoors from the polluted outdoor environment, but more often the serious pollutants arise from processes that take place indoors. There has been particular concern in the generation of nitrogen oxides by sources such as gas stoves. Similarly formaldehyde from insulating foams causes illnesses and adds to concerns about our exposure to a substance that may induce cancer. In the last decade it has become clear that radon leaks from the ground can expose some members of the public to high levels of this radioactive gas within their own homes. Cancers may also result from the emanation of solvents from consumer products, glues, paints, and mineral fibers (asbestos). More generally these compounds and a range of biological materials, animal hair, skin and pollen spores, and dusts can cause allergic reactions in some people. At one end of the spectrum these simply cause annoyance, but in extreme cases, such as found with the bacterium *Legionella,* a large number of deaths can occur.

There are also important issues surrounding the effects of indoor air pollutants on materials. Many industries, especially the electronics industry, must take great care over the purity of indoor air where a speck of dust can destroy a microchip or low concentrations of air pollutants change the composition of surface films in component design. Museums must care for objects over long periods of time, so precautions must be taken to protect delicate dyes from the effects of photochemical smog, paper and books from sulfur dioxide, and metals from sulfide gases.

• AIR QUALITY

Air quality is determined with respect to the total air pollution in a given area as it interacts with meteorological conditions such as humidity, temperature, and wind to produce an overall atmospheric condition. Poor air quality can manifest itself aesthetically (as a displeasing odor, for example), and can also result in harm to plants, animals, people, and even damage to objects.

As early as 1881, cities such as Chicago, Illinois, and Cincinnati, Ohio, had passed laws to control some types of pollution, but it wasn't until several air pollution catastrophes occurred in the twentieth century that governments began to give more attention to air quality problems. In 1930, smog trapped in the Meuse River Valley in Belgium caused 60 deaths. Similarly, in 1948, smog was blamed for 20 deaths in Donora, Pennsylvania. Most dramatically, in 1952 a sulfur-laden fog enshrouded London for five days and caused as many as 4,000 deaths over two weeks.

Disasters such as these prompted governments in a number of industrial countries to initiate programs to protect air quality. The year of the London tragedy, the United States passed the Air Pollution Control Act granting funds to assist the states in controlling airborne pollutants. In 1963, the Clean Air Act, which began to place authority for air quality into the hands of the federal government, was established. Today the Clean Air Act, with its 1970 and 1990 amendments, remains the principal air quality law in the United States.

The Act established a National Ambient Air Quality Standard under which federal, state, and local monitoring stations at thousands of locations, together with temporary stations set up by the Environmental Protection Agency (EPA) and other federal agencies, directly measure pollutant concentrations in the air and compare those concentrations with national standards for six major pollutants: ozone, carbon monoxide, nitrogen oxides, lead, particulates, and sulfur dioxide. When the air we breathe contains amounts of these pollutants in excess of EPA standards, it is deemed unhealthy, and regulatory action is taken to reduce the pollution levels.

In addition, urban and industrial areas maintain an air pollution index. This scale, a composite of several pollutant levels recorded from a particular monitoring site or sites, yields an overall air quality value. If the index exceeds certain values public warnings are given; in severe instances residents might be asked to stay indoors and factories might even be closed down.

Air pollution over Mexico City.

While such air quality emergencies seem increasingly rare in the United States, pollution in developing countries, as well as Eastern European nations, continue to suffer poor air quality, especially in urban areas such as Bangkok, Thailand, and Mexico City, Mexico. In Mexico City, for example, seven out of ten newborns have higher lead levels in their blood than the World Health Organization considers acceptable. At present, many third world countries place national economic development ahead of pollution control—and in many countries with rapid industrialization, high population growth, or increasing per capita income, the best efforts of governments to maintain air quality are outstripped by rapid proliferation of automobiles, escalating factory emissions, and runaway urbanization.

For all the progress the United States has made in reducing ambient air pollution, *indoor* air pollution may pose even greater risks than all of the pollutants we breathe outdoors. The Radon Gas and Indoor Air Quality Act of 1986 directed the EPA to research and implement a public information and technical assistance program on indoor air quality. From this program has come monitoring equipment to measure an individual's "total exposure" to pollutants both in indoor and outdoor air. Studies done using this equipment have shown indoor exposures to toxic air pollutants far exceed outdoor exposures for the simple reason that most people spend 90% of their time in office buildings, homes, and other enclosed spaces. Moreover, nationwide energy conservation efforts following the oil crisis of the 1970s led to building designs that trap pollutants indoors, thereby exacerbating the problem.

• AIR POLLUTION CONTROL

The need to control air pollution was recognized in the earliest cities. In the Mediterranean at the time of Christ, laws were developed to place objectionable sources of odor and smoke downwind or outside city walls. The adoption of fossil fuels in thirteenth century England focused particular concern on the effect of coal smoke on health, with a number of attempts at regulation with regard to fuel type, chimney heights, and time of use. Given the complexity of the air pollution problem it is not surprising that these early attempts at control met with only limited success.

The nineteenth century was typified by a growing interest in urban public health. This developed against a background of continuing industrialization, which saw smoke abatement clauses incorporated into the growing body of sanitary legislation in both Europe and North America. However, a lack of both technology and political will doomed these early efforts to failure, except in the most blatantly destructive situations (for example, industrial settings such as those around Alkali Works in England).

The rise of environmental awareness in the current century has reminded us that air pollution ought not to be seen as a necessary product of industrialization. This has redirected responsibility for air pollution towards those who create it. The notion of "making the polluter pay" is seen as a central feature of air pollution control. The century has also seen the development of a range of broad air pollution control strategies, among them: (1) air quality management strategies that set ambient air quality standards so that emissions from various sources can be monitored and controlled; (2) Emission standards strategy that sets limits for the amount of pollutant that can be emitted from a given source. These may be set to meet air quality standards, but the strategy is optimally seen as one of adopting best available techniques not entailing excessive costs (BATNEEC); (3) Economic strategies that involve charging the party responsible for the pollution. If the level of charge is set correctly, some polluters will find it more economical to install air pollution control equipment than continue to pollute. Other methods utilize a system of tradable pollution rights; (4) Cost-benefit analysis, which attempts to balance economic benefits with environmental costs. This is an appealing strategy but difficult to implement because of its controversial and imprecise nature.

In general air pollution strategies have either been air quality or emission based. In the United Kingdom, emission strategy is frequently used; for example, the Alkali and Works Act of 1863 specifies permissible emissions of hydrochloric acid. By contrast, the United States has aimed to achieve air quality standards, as evidenced by the Clean Air Act. One criticism of using air quality strategy has been that while it improves air in poor areas it leads to degradation in areas with high air quality. Although the emission standards approach is relatively simple, it is criticized for failing to make explicit judgments about air quality and assumes that good practice will lead to an acceptable atmosphere.

Until the mid-twentieth century, legislation was primarily directed towards industrial sources, but the passage of the United Kingdom Clean Air Act (1956), which followed the disastrous smog of December 1952, directed attention towards domestic sources of smoke. While this particular act may have reinforced the improvements already under way, rather than initiating improvements, it has served as a catalyst for much subsequent legislative thinking. Its mode of operation was to initiate a change in fuel, perhaps one of the oldest methods of control. The other well-tried aspects were the creation of smokeless zones and an emphasis on tall chimneys to disperse the pollutants.

As simplistic as such passive control measures seem, they remain at the heart of much contemporary thinking. Changes from coal and oil to the less polluting gas or electricity have contributed to the reduction in smoke and sulfur dioxide concentrations in cities all around the world. Industrial zoning has often kept power and large manufacturing plants away from centers of human population, and "superstacks," chimneys of enormous height are now quite common. Successive changes in automotive fuels—lead-free gasoline, low volatility gas, methanol, or even the interest in the electric automobile—are further indications of continued use of these methods of control.

There are more active forms of air pollution control that seek to clean up the exhaust gases. The earliest of these were smoke and grit arresters that came into increasing use in large electrical stations during the twentieth century. Notable here were the cyclone collectors that removed large particles by driving the exhaust through a tight spiral that threw the grit outward where it could be collected. Finer particles could be removed by electrostatic precipitation. These methods were an important part of the development of the modern pulverized fuel power station. However they failed to address the problem of gaseous emissions. Here it has been necessary to look at burning fuel in ways that reduce the production of nitrogen oxides. Control of sulfur dioxide emissions from large industrial plants can be achieved by desulfurization of the flue gases. This can be quite successful by passing the gas through towers of solid absorbers or spraying solutions through the exhaust gas stream. However, these are not necessarily cheap options.

Catalytic converters are also an important element of active attempts to control air pollutants. Although these can considerably reduce emissions, they have to be offset against the increasing use of the automobile. There is much talk of the development of zero pollution vehicles that do not emit any pollutants.

Legislation and control methods are often associated with monitoring networks that assess the effectiveness of the strategies and inform the general public about air quality where they live. A balanced approach to the control of air pollution in the future may have to look far more broadly than simply at technological controls. It will become necessary to examine the way we structure our lives in order to find more effective solutions to air pollution.

• AIR POLLUTION INDEX

The air pollution index is a value derived from an air quality scale which uses the measured or predicted concentrations of several criteria pollutants and other air quality indicators, such as coefficient of haze (COH) or visibility. The best known index of air pollution is the pollutant standard index (PSI).

The PSI has a scale that spans from 0-500. The index represents the highest value of several subindices; there is a subindex for each pollutant, or in some cases, for a product of pollutant concentrations and a product of pollutant concentrations and COH. If a pollutant is not monitored, its subindex is not used in deriving the PSI.

The subindex of each pollutant or pollutant product is derived from a PSI nomogram which matches concentrations with subindex values. The highest subindex value becomes the PSI. The PSI has five health-related categories: good (0-50); moderate (50-100); unhealthful (100-200); hazardous (300-500).

• CLEAN AIR ACT (1963, 1970, 1990)

The 1970 Clean Air Act and major amendments to the act in 1977 and 1990 serve as the backbone of efforts to control air pollution in the United States. This law established one of the most complex regulatory programs in the country. Efforts to control air pollution in the United States date back to 1881, when Chicago and Cincinnati passed laws to control smoke and soot from factories in the cities. Other municipalities followed suit and the momentum continued to build. In 1952, Oregon became the first state to adopt a significant program to control air pollution, and three years later, the federal government became involved for the first time, when the Air Pollution Control Act was passed. This law granted funds to assist the states in their air pollution control activities.

In 1963, the first Clean Air Act was passed. This act provided permanent federal aid for research, support for the development of state pollution control agencies, and federal involvement in cross-boundary air pollution cases. An amendment to the act in 1965 directed the Department of Health, Education, and Welfare (HEW) to establish federal emission standards for motor vehicles. (At this time, HEW administered air pollution laws. The Environmental Protection Agency (EPA) was not created until 1970.) This represented a significant move by the federal government from a supportive to an active role in setting air pollution policy. The 1967 Air Quality Act provided additional funding to the states, required the states to establish Air Quality Control Regions, and directed HEW to obtain and make available information on the health effects of air pollutants and to identify pollution control techniques. All of these components of the law were designed to assist the states, but they further demonstrated increasing federal involvement in the issue.

The Clean Air Act of 1970 marked a dramatic change in air pollution policy in the United States. Following the passage of this law, the federal government, not the states, would be the focal point for air pollution policy. This act established the framework that continues to be the foundation for air pollution control policy. The impetus for this change was the belief that the current state-based approach was not working and the pressure from rising environmental consciousness across the country. Public sentiment was growing so significantly that environmental issues demanded the attention of high-ranking officials. In fact, the leading policy entrepreneurs on the issue were President Richard Nixon and Senator Edmund Muskie of Maine.

These men and other leaders devised a plan with four key components. First, National Ambient Air Quality Standards

Definition of Pollutant Standard Index (PSI) Values*

Table 5.2

PSI Index Value	Air Quality Level	Pollutant Level: TSP (24-hour), μg/m³	SO_2 (24-hour), μg/m³	CO (8-hour), mg/m³	O_3 (1-hour), μg/m³	NO_2 (1-hour), μg/m³	Health Effect	General Health Effects	Cautionary Statements
500	Significant Harm	1000	2620	57.5	1200	3750			
400	Emergency	875	2100	46.0	1000	3000		Premature death of ill and elderly. Healthy people will experience adverse symptoms that affect their normal activity.	All persons should remain indoors, keeping windows and doors closed. All persons should minimize physical exertion and avoid traffic.
300	Warning	625	1600	34.0	800	2260	Hazardous	Premature onset of certain diseases in addition to significant aggravation of symptoms and decreased exercise tolerance in healthy persons.	Elderly and persons with existing diseases should stay indoors and avoid physical exertion. General population should avoid outdoor activity.
200	Alert	375	800	17.0	400[c]	1130	Very Unhealthful	Significant aggravation of symptoms and decreased exercise tolerance in persons with heart or lung disease, with widespread symptoms in the healthy population.	Elderly and persons with existing heart or lung disease should stay indoors and reduce physical activity.
100	NAAQS	260	365	10.0	240		Unhealthful [a]	Mild aggravation of symptoms in susceptible persons, with irritation symptoms in the healthy population.	Persons with existing heart or respiratory ailments should reduce physical exertion and outdoor activity.
50	50% of NAAQS	75[b]	80[b]	5.0	120		Moderate [a]		
0		0	0	0	0		Good [a]		

[a] No Index values reported at concentration levels below those specified by "Alert Level" criteria.
[b] Annual primary NAAQS.
[c] 400 μg/m³ was used instead of the O_3 Alert Level of 200 μg/m³.

Source: U.S. Environmental Protection Agency, "Guidelines for Public Reporting of Daily Air Quality—Pollutant Standard Index."

*From the 1977 Amendments to the Clean Air Act. See the explanation at the end of this section for the effects the 1990 Amendments may have on these values.

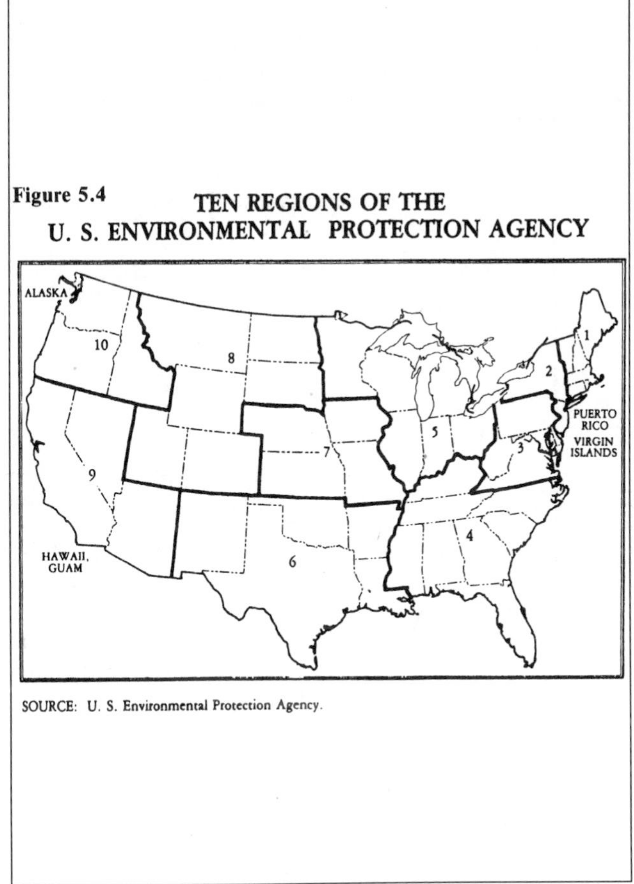

Figure 5.4 TEN REGIONS OF THE U. S. ENVIRONMENTAL PROTECTION AGENCY

SOURCE: U. S. Environmental Protection Agency.

(NAAQSs) were established for six major pollutants: carbon monoxide, lead (in 1977), nitrogen dioxide, ground-level ozone (a key component of smog), particulate matter, and sulfur dioxide. For each of these pollutants, sometimes referred to as criteria pollutants, primary and secondary standards were set. The primary standards were designed to protect human health, the secondary standards were based on protecting crops, forests, and buildings if the primary standards were not capable of doing so. The Act stipulated that these standards must apply to the entire country and be established by the EPA, based on the best available scientific information. The costs of attaining these standards were not among the factors considered. Relatedly, the EPA was to establish standards for less common toxic air pollutants.

Second, New Source Performance Standards (NSPSs) would be established by the EPA. These standards would determine how much air pollution would be allowed by new plants in the various industrial sectors. The standards were based on the best affordable technology available for the control of pollutants at such sources as power plants, steel factories, and chemical plants.

Third, mobile source emission standards were established to control automobile emissions. These standards were specified in the statute (rather than left to the EPA), and schedules for meeting these standards were also written into the law. It was thought that such an approach was crucial in having success with the powerful auto industry. The pollutants regulated were carbon monoxide, hydrocarbons, and nitrogen oxides, with goals of reducing the first two pollutants by 90% by 1975, and nitrogen oxides by 82% by 1975.

The final component of the air quality protection framework involved the implementation of the above procedures. Each state would be encouraged to devise a state implementation plan (SIP), which would indicate how the state would achieve the national standards. This gave each state some flexibility while still maintaining national standards. These plans had to be approved by the EPA; if a state did not have an approved SIP, the EPA would administer the Clean Air Act in that state. However, since the federal government was in charge of establishing pollution standards for new mobile and stationary sources, even the states with an SIP had limited flexibility. The main focal point for the states was the control of existing stationary sources, and if necessary, mobile sources. The states had to set limits in their SIPs that allowed them to achieve the NAAQSs by a statutorily determined deadline (originally 1975, but subsequently delayed). One problem with this approach was the construction of tall smokestacks, which helped move pollution out of a particular airshed but did not reduce overall pollution levels. The states are also charged with monitoring and enforcing the Clean Air Act.

The 1977 amendments to the Clean Air Act dealt with three main issues: nonattainment, auto emissions, and the prevention of air quality deterioration in areas where the air was already relatively clean. The first two issues were resolved primarily by delaying deadlines and increasing penalties. Largely in response to a court decision in favor of environmentalists (*Sierra Club v. Ruckelshaus,* 1972), the 1977 amendments included a program for the prevention of significant deterioration (PSD) of air that was already clean. This program would prevent polluting the air up to the national levels in areas where the air was cleaner than the standards. In Class I areas, areas with near pristine air quality, no new significant air pollution would be allowed. Class I areas are airsheds over larger national parks and wilderness areas. In Class II areas, a moderate degree of air quality deterioration would be allowed. And finally, in Class III areas, air deterioration up to the national secondary standards would be allowed. Most of the country that had air cleaner than the NAAQSs was classified as Class II. Related to the prevention of significant deterioration was a provision to protect and enhance visibility in national parks and wilderness areas even if the air pollution was not a threat to human health. The impetus of this section of the bill was the growing visibility problem in parks, especially in the Southwest.

Throughout the 1980s efforts to further amend the Clean Air Act were stymied. President Ronald Reagan was opposed to any strengthening of the act, which he argued would hurt the economy. In Congress, the controversy over

Table 5-1 National Ambient Air Quality Standards (NAAQS)**

Pollutant	Primary (Health Related)		Secondary (Welfare Related)	
	Averaging Time	Concentration	Averaging Time	Concentration
TSP	Annual Geometric Mean	75 ug/m³	Annual Geometric Mean	60 ug/m³*
	24-hour	260 ug/m³	24-hour	150 ug/m³
SO_2	Annual Arithmetic Mean	(0.03 ppm) 80 ug/m³	3-hour	(0.50 ppm) 1300 ug/m³
	24-hour	(0.14 ppm) 365 ug/m³		
CO	8-hour	(9 ppm) 10 mg/m³	Same as Primary	
	1-hour	(35 ppm) 40 mg/m³	Same as Primary	
NO_2	Annual Arithmetic Mean	(0.053 ppm) 100 ug/m³	Same as Primary	
O_3	Maximum Daily 1-hour Average	0.12 ppm (235 ug/m³)	Same as Primary	
Pb	Maximum Quarterly Average	1.5 ug/m³	Same as Primary	

*This annual geometric mean is a guide used in assessing implementation plans to achieve the 24-hour standards of 150 ug/m³.

Note: The standards are categorized for long- and short-term exposure. Long-term standards specify an annual or quarterly mean that may not be exceeded; short-term standards specify upper limit values for 1-, 3-, 8-, or 24-hour averages. The short-term standards are not to be exceeded more than once per year. For example, the ozone standard requires that the expected number of days per calendar year with daily maximum hourly concentrations exceeding 0.12 parts per million (ppm) be less than or equal to one.

** From 1977 Amendments to the Clean Air Act. See the explanation at the end of this section for comments on the effects the 1990 Amendments will have on the future of these standards.

Figure 5.10

Mandatory Class I Areas *

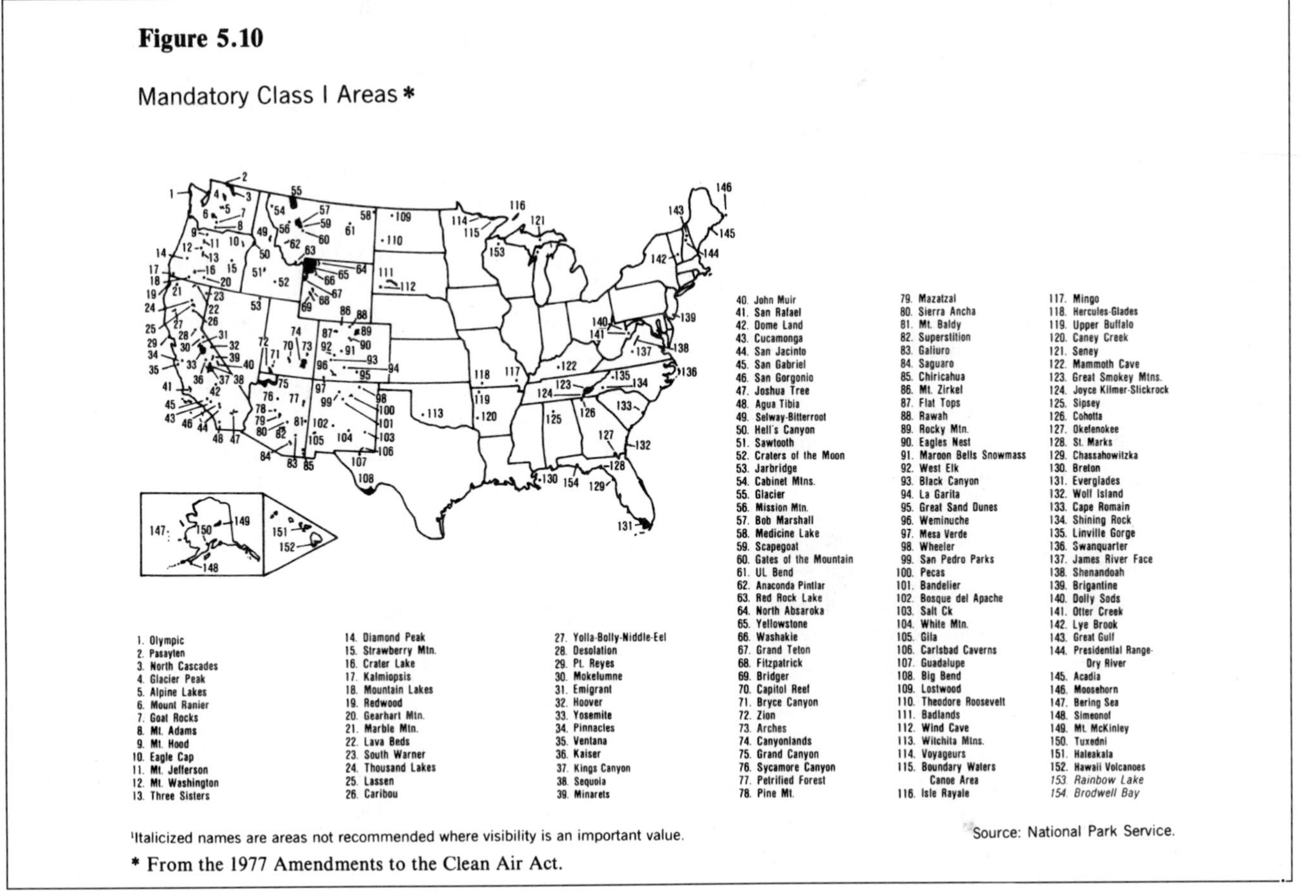

[1]Italicized names are areas not recommended where visibility is an important value.

Source: National Park Service.

* From the 1977 Amendments to the Clean Air Act.

acid rain between members from the Midwest and the Northeast further contributed to the stalemate. Gridlock on the issue broke with the election of George Bush, who supported amendments to the act, and the rise of Senator George Mitchell of Maine to Senate Majority Leader. Over the next two years, the issues were hammered out between environmentalists and industry and between different regions of the country. Major players in Congress were Representatives John Dingell of Michigan and Henry Waxman of California and Senators Robert Byrd of West Virginia and Mitchell.

Major amendments to the Clean Air Act were finally passed in the fall of 1990. These amendments addressed four major topics: (1) acid rain, (2) toxic air pollutants, (3) nonattainment areas, and (4) ozone layer depletion. To address acid rain, a 10 million ton reduction in annual sulfur dioxide emissions (a 40% reduction based on 1980 levels) and a 2 million ton annual reduction in nitrogen oxides by the year 2000 will be required. Most of this reduction will come from old utility power plants. The law also creates marketable pollution allowances, so that a utility that reduces emissions more than required can sell those pollution rights to another source. Economists argue that such an approach should become more widespread for all pollution control, to increase efficiency. Due to the failure of the toxic air pollutant provisions of the 1970 Clean Air Act, new, more stringent provisions were adopted requiring regulations for all major sources of 189 varieties of toxic air pollution within ten years. Areas of the country still in nonattainment for criteria pollutants will be given from three to twenty years to meet these standards. These areas are also required to impose tighter controls to meet these standards. To help these areas and other parts of the country, the Act requires stiffer motor vehicle emissions standards and cleaner gasoline. Finally, three chemical families that contribute to the destruction of the stratospheric ozone layer [chlorofluorocarbons (CFCs), hydrochlorofluorocarbons (HCFCs), and methyl chloroform] are to be phased out of production and use.

The Clean Air Act has met with mixed success. The national average pollutant levels for the criteria pollutants have decreased. Nevertheless, many localities have not achieved these standards and are in perpetual nonattainment. Not surprisingly, major urban areas are those most frequently in nonattainment. The pollutant for which standards are most often exceeded is ozone, or smog. The greatest successes have come with lead, which has been reduced by 96% (largely due to the phase-out of leaded gasoline), and particulates, which were reduced by over 60%. Additionally, despite numerous delays, decreases in carbon monoxide by 96%, hydrocarbon by 96%, and nitrogen oxides by 76%, all from new cars, has occurred over the period from 1967 to 1990. A final point of caution concerning evaluating the Clean Air Act: due to the tremendous complexity of air quality, we cannot conclude that all change in pollutant levels is due to the law. These changes may be due to shifts in the economy at large, changes in weather patterns, or other such variables.

• AIR QUALITY CONTROL REGION (AQCR)

The Clean Air Act defines an Air Quality Control Region as a contiguous area where air quality, and thus air pollution, is relatively uniform. In those cases where topography is a factor in air movement, AQCRs often correspond with airsheds. AQCRs may consist of two or more cities, counties or other governmental entities, and each region is required to adopt consistent pollution control measures across the political jurisdictions involved. AQCRs may even cross state lines and, in these instances, the states must cooperate in developing pollution control strategies. Each AQCR is treated as a unit for the purposes of pollution reduction and achieving National Ambient Air Quality Standards. As of 1993, most AQCRs had achieved national air quality standards; however the remaining AQCRs where standards had not been achieved were a significant group, where a large percentage of the United States population dwelled. AQCRs involving major metro areas like Los Angeles, New York, Houston, Denver, and Philadelphia were not achieving air quality standards because of smog, motor vehicle emissions, and other pollutants.

• OZONE

Ozone is a toxic, colorless gas (but can be blue when in high concentration) with a characteristic acrid odor. A variant of normal oxygen, it had three oxygen atoms per molecule rather than the usual two. Ozone strongly absorbs ultraviolet radiation at wavelengths of 220 through 290 nm with peak absorption at 260.4 nm. Ozone will also absorb infrared radiation at wavelengths in the range 9-10 μm. Ozone occurs naturally in the ozonosphere (ozone layer), which surrounds Earth, protecting living organisms at Earth's surface from ultraviolet radiation. The ozonosphere is located in the stratosphere from 6-31 miles (10-50 km) above Earth's surface, with the highest concentration between 7.5 and 12 miles (12 and 20 km). The concentration of ozone in the ozonosphere is 1 molecule per 100,000 molecules, or if the gas were at standard temperature and pressure, the ozone layer would be 0.12 inch (3 mm) thick. However, the ozone layer absorbs about 90% of incident ultraviolet radiation.

Ozone in the stratosphere results from a chemical equilibrium between oxygen, ozone, and ultraviolet radiation. Ultraviolet radiation is absorbed by oxygen and produces ozone. Simultaneously, ozone absorbs ultraviolet radiation and decomposes to oxygen and other products. Ozone layer depletion occurs as a result of complex reactions in the atmosphere between organic compounds that react with ozone faster than the ozone is replenished. Compounds of most concern include the byproducts of ultraviolet degradation of chlorofluorocarbons (CFCs), chlorine, and fluorine.

Ozone is also a secondary air pollutant at the surface of the earth as a result of complex chemical reactions between sunshine and primary pollutants, such as hydrocarbons and oxides of nitrogen. Ozone can also be generated in the presence of oxygen from equipment that gives off intense light, electrical sparks, or creates intense static electricity, such as photocopiers and laser printers. Human olfactory senses are very sensitive to ozone, being able to detect ozone odor at concentrations between 0.02 and 0.05 parts per million. Toxic symptoms for humans from exposure to ozone include headaches and drying of the throat and respiratory tracts. Ozone is highly toxic to many plant species and destroys or degrades many building materials, such as paint, rubber, and some plastics. The total losses in the United States each year due to ozone damage to crops, livestock, buildings, natural systems, and human health is estimated to be in the tens of billions of dollars. The threshold limit value (TLV) for air quality standards is 0.1 ppm or 0.2 mg O_3 per m^3 of air.

Industrial uses of ozone include chemical manufacturing and air, water, and waste treatment. Industrial quantities of ozone are typically generated from air or pure oxygen by means of silent corona discharge. Ozone is used in water treatment as a disinfectant to kill pathogenic microorganisms or for oxidation of organic and inorganic compounds. Combinations of ozone and hydrogen peroxide or ultraviolet radiation in water can generate powerful oxidants useful in breaking down complex synthetic organic compounds. In wastewater treatment, ozone can be used to disinfect effluents, or decrease their color and odor. In some industrial applications, ozone can be used to enhance biodegradation of complex organic molecules. Industrial cooling tower treatment with ozone prevents transmission of airborne pathogenic organisms and can reduce odor.

• OZONE LAYER DEPLETION

The ozone layer in Earth's upper atmosphere helps make life on the planet possible by shielding it from 95-99% of the sun's potentially deadly ultraviolet radiation. This radiation is harmful and sometimes lethal to wildlife, crops, and vegetation, and can cause fatal skin cancer, cataracts, and immune system damage in humans.

Destroying the ozone shield

Ozone, a form of oxygen consisting of three atoms of oxygen instead of two, is considered an air pollutant when found at ground levels and is a major component of smog. It is formed by the reaction of various air pollutants in the presence of sunlight. Ozone is also used commercially as a bleaching agent and to purify municipal water supplies. Since ozone is toxic, the gas is harmful to health when generated near Earth's surface. Because of its high rate of breakdown, such ozone never reaches the upper atmosphere.

But the ozone that shields Earth from the sun's radiation is found in the stratosphere, a layer of the upper atmosphere found 9-30 miles (15-50 kilometers) above ground. This ozone layer is maintained as follows: the action of ultraviolet light breaks O_2 molecules into atoms of elemental oxygen (O). The elemental oxygen then attaches to other O_2 molecules to form O_3. When it absorbs ultraviolet radiation that would otherwise reach Earth, ozone is, in turn, broken down into $O_2 + O$. The elemental oxygen generated then finds another O_2 molecule to become O_3 once again.

In 1974, chemists F. Sherwood Rowland and Mario J. Molina realized that chlorine from chlorofluorocarbon (CFC) molecules was capable of breaking down ozone in the stratosphere. In time, evidence began accumulating that the ozone layer was indeed being broken apart by these industrial chemicals, and to a lesser extent by nitrogen oxide emissions from jet airplanes as well as hydrogen chloride emissions from large volcanic eruptions.

When released into the environment, CFCs slowly rise into the upper atmosphere, where they are broken apart by solar radiation. This releases chlorine atoms that act as *catalysts*, breaking up molecules of ozone by stripping away one of their oxygen atoms. The chlorine atoms, unaltered by the reaction, are each capable of destroying ozone molecules repeatedly. Without a sufficient quantity of ozone to block its way, ultraviolet radiation from the sun passes through the upper atmosphere and reaches the surface of the earth.

When damage to the ozone layer first became apparent in 1974, propellants in aerosol spray cans were a major source of CFC emissions, and CFC aerosols were banned in the United States in 1978. However, CFCs have since remained in widespread use in thermal insulation, as cooling agents in refrigerators and air conditioners, as cleaning solvents, and as foaming agents in plastics, resulting in continued and accelerating depletion of stratospheric ozone.

The Antarctic ozone hole

The most dramatic evidence of the destruction of the ozone layer has occurred over Antarctica, where a massive "hole" in the ozone layer appears each winter and spring, apparently exacerbated by the area's unique and violent climatological conditions. The destruction of ozone molecules begins during the long, completely dark, and extremely cold Antarctic winter, when swirling winds and ice clouds begin to form in the lower stratosphere. This ice reacts with chlorine compounds in the stratosphere (such as hydrogen chloride and chlorine nitrate) that come from the breakdown of CFCs, creating molecules of chlorine.

When spring returns in August and September, a seasonal vortex—a rotating air mass—causes the ozone to mix with certain chemicals in the presence of sunlight. This helps break down the chlorine molecules into chlorine atoms, which, in turn, react with and break up the molecules of ozone. A single chlorine, bromine, or nitrogen molecule can break up literally thousands of ozone molecules.

During December, the ozone-depleted air can move out of the Antarctic area, as happened in 1987, when levels of ozone over southern Australia and New Zealand sank by 10% over a three week period, causing as much as a 20% increase in ultraviolet radiation reaching Earth. This may have been responsible for a reported increase in skin cancers and damage to some food crops.

The seasonal hole in the ozone layer over Antarctica has been monitored by scientists at the National Aeronautics and Space Administration's (NASA) Goddard Space Flight Center outside Washington, D.C. NASA's NIMBUS-7 satellite first discovered drastically reduced ozone levels over the Southern Hemisphere in 1985, and measurements are also being conducted with instruments on aircraft and balloons. Some of the data that has been gathered is alarming.

In October 1987, ozone levels within the Antarctic ozone hole were found to be 45% below normal, and similar reductions occurred in October 1989. A 1988 study revealed that since 1969, ozone levels had declined by 2% worldwide, and by as much as 3% or more over highly populated areas of North America, Europe, South America, Australia and New Zealand.

In September 1992, the NIMBUS-7 satellite found that the depleted ozone area over the southern polar region had grown 15% from the previous year, to a size three times bigger than the area of the United States, and was 80% thinner than usual. The ozone hole over Antarctica was measured at approximately 8.9 million square miles (23 million square kilometers), as compared to its usual size of 6.5 million square miles (17 square kilometers). The contiguous 48 states are, by comparison, about 3 million square miles (7.8 million square kilometers), and all of North America covers 9.4 million square miles (24.3 million square kilometers). Researchers attributed the increased thinning not only to industrial chemicals but also to the 1991 volcanic eruptions of Mount Pinatubo in the Philippines and Mount Hudson in Chile, which emitted large amounts of sulfur dioxide into the atmosphere.

Dangers of ultraviolet radiation

The major consequence of the thinning of the ozone layer is the penetration of more solar radiation, especially Ultraviolet-B (UV-B) rays, the most dangerous type, which can be extremely damaging to plants, wildlife, and human health. Because UV-B can penetrate the ocean's surface, it is potentially harmful to marine life forms and indeed to the entire chain of life in the seas as well.

UV-B can kill and affect the reproduction of fish, larvae, and other plants and animals, especially those found in shallow waters, including phytoplankton, which forms the basis of the oceanic food chain/web. The National Science Foundation reported in February 1992 that its research ship, on a six week Antarctic cruise, found that the production of phytoplankton decreases at least 6-12% during the period of greatest ozone layer depletion, and that the destructive effects of UV radiation could extend to depths of 90 feet (27 m).

A decrease in phytoplankton would affect all other creatures higher on the food chain and dependent on them, including zooplankton, microscopic ocean creatures that feed on phytoplankton and are also an essential part of the ocean food chain. And marine phytoplankton are the main food source for krill, tiny Antarctic shrimp that are the major food source for fish, squid, penguins, seals, whales, and other creatures in the Southern Hemisphere.

Moreover, phytoplankton are responsible for absorbing, through photosynthesis, great amounts of carbon dioxide (CO_2) and releasing oxygen. It is not known how a depletion of phytoplankton would affect the planet's supply of life-giving oxygen, but more CO_2 in the atmosphere would exacerbate the critical problem of global warming, the so-called greenhouse effect.

There are numerous reports, largely unconfirmed, of animals in the southern polar region being harmed by ultraviolet radiation. Rumors abound in Chile, for example, of pets, livestock, sheep, rabbits, and other wildlife getting cataracts, suffering reproductive irregularities, or even being blinded by solar radiation. Many residents of Chile and Antarctica believe these stories, and wear sunglasses, protective clothing, and sun-blocking lotion in the summer, or even stay indoors much of the day when the sun is out. If the ozone layer's thinning continues to spread, the lifestyles of people across the globe could be similarly disrupted for generations to come.

Particularly frightening have been incidents reported to have taken place in Punta Arenas, Chile's southernmost city, at the tip of Patagonia. After several days of record low levels of ozone were recorded in October 1992, people reported severe burns from short exposure to sunlight. Sheep and cattle became blind, and some starved because they could not find food. Trees wilted and died, and melanoma-type skin cancers seem to have increased dramatically. Similar stories have been reported from other areas of the southern hemisphere. And malignant melanoma, once a rare disorder, is now the fastest rising cancer in the world.

Ozone thinning spreads

Indeed, ozone layer depletion is spreading at an alarming rate. In the 1980s, scientists discovered that an ozone hole was also appearing over the Arctic region in the late winter months, and concern was expressed that similar thinning might begin to occur and threaten heavily populated areas of the globe. These fears were confirmed in April 1991 when the Environmental Protection Agency (EPA) announced that satellite measurements had recorded an ominous decrease in atmospheric ozone, amounting to an average of 5% over the mid-latitudes (including the United States), almost double the loss previously thought to be occurring.

The data showed that ozone levels measured in the late fall, winter, and early spring over large areas of the United States, Europe, and the mid-latitudes of the Northern and Southern Hemisphere had dropped by 4-6% over the last decade—twice the amount estimated in earlier years. The greatest area of ozone thinning in the United States was found north of a line stretching from Philadelphia to Denver to Reno, Nevada. One of the most alarming aspects of the new findings was that the ozone depletion was continuing into April and May, a time when people spend more time outside, and crops are beginning to sprout, making both more vulnerable to ultraviolet radiation.

The new findings led the EPA to project that over the next 50 years, thinning of the ozone layer could cause Americans to suffer some 12 million cases of skin cancer, 200,000 of which would be fatal. Several years earlier, the agency had calculated that over the next century, there could be an additional 155 million cases of skin cancers and 3.2 million deaths if the ozone layer continued to thin at the then current rate. Another EPA projection made in the 1980s was that the increase in radiation could cause Americans to suffer 40 million cases of skin cancer and 800,000 deaths in the following 88 years, plus some 12 million eye cataracts.

No one can say how accurate such varying projections will turn out to be, but evidence of ozone layer thinning is well-documented. In October 1991, additional data of spreading ozone layer destruction were made public. Dr. Robert Watson, a NASA scientist who co-chairs an 80-member panel of scientists from 80 countries, called the situation "extremely serious," saying that "we now see a significant decrease of ozone both in the Northern and Southern Hemispheres, not only in winter but in spring and summer, the time when people sunbathe, putting them at risk for skin cancer, and the time when we grow crops."

In February 1992, a team of NASA scientists announced that they had found record high levels of ozone-depleting chlorine over the Northern Hemisphere. This could, in turn, lead to an ozone "hole" similar to the one that appears over Antarctica developing over populated areas of the United States, Canada, and England. The areas over which increased levels of chlorine monoxide were found extended as far south as New England, France, Britain, and Scandinavia.

Action to protect the ozone layer

As evidence of the critical threats posed by ozone layer depletion has increased, the world community has begun to take steps to address the problem. In 1987, the United States and 22 other nations signed the Montreal Protocol, agreeing, by the year 2000, to cut CFC production in half, and to phase out two ozone-destroying gases, Halon 1301 and Halon 1211. Halons are man-made bromine compounds used mainly in fire extinguishers, and can destroy ozone at a rate 10-40 times more rapidly than CFCs. Fortunately, these restrictions appear to already be having an impact. In 1992, it was found that the rate at which these two Halon gases were accumulating in the atmosphere had fallen significantly since 1987. The rate of increase of levels of Halon 1301 was about 8% a year from 1989 to 1992, about half of the average annual rate of growth over previous years. Similarly, Halon 1211 was increasing at only 3% annually, much less than the previous growth of 15% a year.

Since the Montreal Protocol, other international treaties have been signed limiting the production and use of ozone-destroying chemicals. When alarming new evidence on the destruction of stratospheric ozone became available in 1988, the world's industrialized nations convened at a series of conferences to plan remedial action. In March 1989, the 12-member European Economic Community (EEC) announced plans to end the use of CFCs by the turn of the century, and the United States agreed to join in the ban. A week later, 123 nations met in London to discuss ways to speed the CFC phase-out. The industrial nations agreed to cut their own domestic CFC production in half, while continuing to allow exports of CFCs, in order to accommodate third world nations.

Ironically, the large industrial nations, which have created the CFC problem, are now much more willing to take effective action to ban the compounds than are many developing nations, such as India and China. The latter nations resist restrictions on CFCs on the grounds that the chemicals are necessary for their own economic development.

After the meeting in London, leaders and representatives from 24 countries met in an environmental summit at The Hague, and agreed that the United Nations' authority to protect the world's ozone layer should be strengthened.

In May 1989, members of the EEC and 81 other nations that had signed the 1987 Montreal Protocol decided at a meeting in Helsinki to try to achieve a total phase-out of CFCs by the year 2000, as well as phase-outs as soon as possible of other ozone-damaging chemicals like carbon tetrachloride, halons, and methyl chloroform. In London in June 1990, most of the Montreal Protocol's signatory nations formally adopted a deadline of the year 2000 for industrial nations to phase out the major ozone-destroying chemicals, with 2010 being the goal for developing countries.

Finally, in November 1992, 87 nations meeting in Copenhagen decided to strengthen the action agreed to under the Montreal Protocol and move up the phase-out deadline from 2000 to January 1, 1996 for CFCs, and to January 1, 1994 for halons. A timetable was also agreed to for eliminating hydrochlorofluorocarbons (HCFCs) by the year 2030. HCFCs are being used as substitutes for CFCs even though they also deplete ozone, albeit on a far lesser scale than CFCs. The conference failed to ban the production of the pesticide methyl bromide, which may account for 15% of ozone depletion by the year 2000, but did freeze production at 1991 levels.

Environmentalists were disappointed that stronger action was not taken to protect the ozone layer. But Environmental Protection Agency (EPA) Administrator William K. Reilly, who headed the United States delegation, estimated that the reductions agreed to could, by the year 2075, prevent a million cases of cancer and 20,000 deaths.

Although the restrictions apply to developed nations, which produce most of the ozone-damaging chemicals, it was also agreed to consider moving up a phase-out of such compounds by developing nations from 2010 to 1995. A month after the Copenhagen conference, the nations of the European Community agreed to push bans on the use of CFCs and carbon tetrachloride to 1995 and to cut CFC emissions by 85% by the end of 1993.

The private sector has also taken action to reduce CFC production. The world's largest manufacturer of the chemicals, DuPont Chemical Company announced in 1988 that it was working on a variety of substitutes for CFCs and would phase out production of them by 1996 by partially replacing them with HCFCs. Environmentalists charge that DuPont has been moving too slowly to eliminate production of these chemicals.

There are many ways that individuals can help reduce the release of CFCs into the atmosphere, mainly by avoiding products that contain or are made from CFCs, and by recycling CFCs whenever possible. Although CFCs have not generally been used in spray cans in the United States since 1978, they are still used in many consumer and industrial products, such as styrofoam. Other products manufactured using CFCs include solvents and cleaning liquids used on electrical equipment, polystyrene foam products, and fire extinguishers that use halons.

Refrigerants in cars and home air conditioning units contain CFCs and must be poured into closed containers to be cleaned or recycled, or they will evaporate into the atmosphere. Using foam insulation to seal homes also releases CFCs. Many alternatives to foam insulation exist, such as cellulose fiber, gypsum, fiberboard, and fiberglass.

Unfortunately, whatever steps are taken in the next few years, the problem of ozone layer depletion will continue even after the release of ozone-destroying chemicals is limited or halted. It takes six to eight years for some of these compounds to reach the upper atmosphere, and once there, they will destroy ozone for another 20-25 years. Thus, even if all emissions of destructive chemicals were stopped, compounds already released would continue to damage the ozone layer for another quarter century.

Understanding ozone depletion

As detailed collection of data about interactions in the stratosphere progresses, the observational support for the ozone depletion theory continues to grow more compelling. Yet atmospheric scientists are beginning to realize that their understanding of the upper atmosphere is still quite crude. While certain key reactions which maintain and destroy ozone are theoretically and observationally supported, scientists will have to comprehend the interaction of dozens, if not hundreds, of reactions between natural and artificial species of hydrogen, nitrogen, bromine, chlorine and oxygen before a complete picture of ozone-layer dynamics emerges. The recent eruption of Mt. Pinatubo, for example, made scientists aware that *heterogenous processes*—those reactions which require cloud surfaces to take place—may play a far greater role in causing ozone depletion than originally believed. Such reactions had previously been observed taking place only at the Earth's poles, where stratospheric clouds form during the long winter darkness, but it is now thought that sulfur aerosols ejected by Pinatubo may be serving as a catalyst to speed ozone depletion at nonpolar latitudes.

Ironically, ozone-depleting reactions are best understood around the thinly inhabited polar regions, where stable and isolated conditions over the winter allow scientists to understand stratospheric changes most easily. In contrast, at the temperate latitudes where constantly moving air masses undergo no seasonal isolation, it is difficult to determine whether a fluctuation in a given chemical's density is a result of local reactions or atmospheric turbulence. It is hoped that increasingly detailed measurements using a new generation of equipment (such as NASA's *Perseus* remote-control aircraft) will begin to shed more light on the processes occurring away from the poles. Joe Waters of NASA's Jet Propulsion Laboratory summarizes the urgent task: "We must be able to lay out the catalytic cycles that are destroying ozone at all altitudes all over the globe—from its production region in the tropics to the higher latitudes and the polar regions."

• AIR POLLUTION AND WEATHER

Natural phenomena affecting air quality

The concentration of atmospheric pollutants observed at different locations depends on more than just the quantity of pollutants emitted at the various sources. The atmosphere is the agent that transports and disperses pollutants between sources and receptors. Consequently, the state of the atmosphere helps to determine the concentrations of pollutants observed at receptors. Unlike emissions sources, which can be controlled, the state of the atmosphere is not at present susceptible to man's control.

Some skill has been attained, however, in predicting the future state of the atmosphere. Since meteorological conditions that favor high concentrations of pollutants are known, severe air pollution episodes can therefore be forecast.

In general, three parameters are used to describe atmospheric transport and dispersion processes. These are wind speed, wind direction, and atmospheric stability. For emissions at a given source, a higher wind speed provides the pollutants with a greater air volume within which to disperse. This causes ground level pollutant concentrations, other things being equal, to be inversely proportional to wind speed.

Horizontally, the wind direction is the strongest factor affecting pollutant concentrations. For a given wind direction, nearly all the pollutant transport and dispersion will be downwind. Wind direction determines which sector of the area surrounding a source will receive pollutants from that source.

Atmospheric stability directly affects the vertical dispersion of atmospheric pollutants. Unlike wind direction and wind speed, atmospheric stability cannot be measured directly. Atmospheric stability is a measure of air turbulence and may be defined in terms of the vertical atmospheric temperature profile. When the temperature decreases rapidly with height, vertical motions in the atmosphere are enhanced, and the atmosphere is called unstable. An unstable atmosphere, with its enhanced vertical motions, is more effective for dispersing pollutants, and because of the large volume of air available for the spread of pollutants, ground-level concentrations can be relatively low. When the temperature does not decrease rapidly with height, vertical motions are neither enhanced nor repressed and the stability is described as neutral. Under these conditions, pollutants are also allowed to disperse vertically in the atmosphere, although not as rapidly as for the unstable case.

When the temperature decreases very little, remains the same, or increases with increasing height, the atmosphere is called stable. Under these conditions, the atmosphere inhibits the upward spread of pollutants. Upward-moving smoke, which rapidly assumes the temperature of the surrounding air, reaches a point where it is colder, and hence denser, than the air above it, so it can rise no further. This suppression of upward motion effectively forms a lid beneath which pollutants can freely disperse. The weaker the temperature decrease with height, the higher is the lid. The extreme case is an inversion, when the temperature increases with height. Often, clouds are topped by a stable or inversion layer, which stops their vertical growth.

The well-mixed layer beneath a stable layer is called the mixing layer. When it extends to the ground its vertical extent is known as the mixing height or the mixing depth. Generally, turbulence is enhanced in the early morning hours as the sun heats the ground and temperature decreases with height causing unstable conditions. At night, as the earth cools, temperature increases with height causing less turbulence and stable atmospheric conditions.

Wind speed, wind direction, and atmospheric stability will vary greatly with time. For a certain location, some combinations occur more frequently than others.

Where detailed meteorological records have been kept for a year or more, a stability wind rose can be calculated. This wind rose is a set of tables, one for each stability class (ranging from very stable to very unstable), listing the frequency of occurrence of all possible combinations of wind speed and wind direction. Such roses are available for many locations in the United States from the National Climatic Data Center in Asheville, North Carolina. It should be noted that topographical features such as mountains, hills, valleys, bodies of water, buildings, and other terrain features can change airflow patterns resulting in unexpected pollution effects.

Near a large body of water, local sea breezes influence the spread of pollutants. Early in the morning, when the air is still or the wind is off the land, pollutants can accumulate over their sources or downwind of them. Later in the day, when a local sea breeze develops, a fresh breeze blows in the direction from the water toward land. This breeze brings with it not only the pollutants emitted from the sources at this time of day, but also those accumulated earlier in the day, because they are carried back from water to land. Unexpectedly high pollutant concentrations can occur near the shore when the high pollutant loading blows past. In addition to this effect, which generally occurs close to land, the seabreeze itself can penetrate as far inland as 40 miles (64 km) or more.

Mountains and valleys have characteristic airflow patterns, too. In the evening, as the earth cools, the coldest air will sink into the lowest part of the valley. This creates a stable inversion layer because lighter, warmer air stays above the valley. In this way, pollutants are trapped in the valleys all night. During the daytime when heating occurs, the air in the valley is warmed and rises, permitting the pollutants to escape. Unfortunately, this heating and upward motion does not always occur. During periods when high pressure settles over a region and the air is stagnant, the atmosphere is stable all day long, and pollutants continue to accumulate in the valley. Some of the worst episodes of air pollution have occurred in mountain chains like the Appalachians, where industries are located in the valleys between adjacent hills.

In cities, buildings form the topography. Where rows of tall buildings front on narrow streets, the air flows through the streets as though they were canyons. Since ventilation is determined by building configuration, many distortions in wind, and hence pollution flows, take place in a city. Air flows over a building and into a street downwind of it. The lines show the direction of airflow. The building, because the air cannot flow through it, creates an obstruction in the pattern of the smooth airflow. Downwind of the building, an eddy, or circular movement of air at variance with the main airflow, is formed in its wake, such as the one shown in the figure. The eddy can trap pollutants emitted by cars in the street, and can cause concentrations of pollutants, for example, carbon monoxide, to be as much as three times higher on the side of the street further downwind than at the site of pollutant origin.

High air pollution potential advisories

High Air Pollution Potential Advisories (HAPPA) are prepared at the National Meteorological Center (NMC) in Suitland, Maryland, by meteorologists of the National Oceanographic and Atmospheric Administration (NOAA), Department of Commerce.

Advisories are based both on reports received hourly via teletype from Weather Service stations in the United States and on numerous analyses and forecasts prepared by the NMC. With its electronic computer facilities, the NMC prepares mixing-depth and wind-speed data from all upper-air-observing stations in the contiguous United States (about 70 stations). These data are analyzed, interpreted, and integrated with other meteorological information.

National air pollution potential advisories based on these data are transmitted daily at 12:20 p.m., E.S.T., to Weather Service stations. When meteorological conditions do not warrant issuance of a HAPPA, the teletype message is "none today." When the forecast indicates that an advisory of high air pollution potential should be issued, the message designates the affected areas. The daily message indicates significant changes in the boundaries of advisory areas, including termination of an episode.

Because conditions of atmospheric transport and dispersion typically vary with location and time, the forecasting staff cannot prepare advisories for each city in the United States. For this reason, the NOAA meteorologists limit their forecasts to areas at least as large as 75,000 square miles (roughly the size of Oklahoma), in which stagnation conditions are expected to persist for at least 36 hours. Individual Weather Service stations may modify these generalized forecasts on the basis of local meteorological conditions.

Users of the service should realize that boundaries of the forecast areas of high air pollution potential cannot be delineated exactly. For practical purposes, the lines defining the advisory area should be interpreted as bands roughly 100 miles wide.

To be notified of these advisories, air pollution control or research officials must initiate arrangements with the nearest Weather Service station.

Weather Fundamentals

• THE EARTH'S ATMOSPHERE

Composition

Air is a mixture of several gases. When completely dry, it is about 78% nitrogen and 21% oxygen. The remaining 1% is other gases such as argon, carbon dioxide, neon, helium, and others. However, in nature, air is never completely dry. It always contains some water vapor in amounts varying from almost zero to about 5% by volume. As water vapor content increases, the other gases decrease proportionately.

Vertical structure

The atmosphere is classified into layers, or spheres, by characteristics exhibited in these layers.

The *troposphere* is the layer from the surface to an average altitude of about 7 miles (11.27 km). It is characterized by an overall decrease of temperature with increasing altitude. The height of the troposphere varies with latitude and seasons. It slopes from about 20,000 feet (6,067 m) over the poles to about 65,000 feet (19,717 m) over the Equator; and it is higher in summer than in winter.

At the top of the troposphere is the *tropopause*, a very thin layer marking the boundary between the troposphere and the layer above. The height of the tropopause and certain weather phenomena are related, as will be explained later.

Above the tropopause is the *stratosphere*. This layer is typified by relatively small changes in temperature with height except for a warming trend near the top.

Density

Air is matter and has weight. Since it is gaseous, it is compressible. Pressure the atmosphere exerts on the surface is the result of the weight of the air above. Thus, air near the surface is much more dense than air at high altitudes.

• TEMPERATURE

Temperature scales

Two commonly used temperature scales are Celsius (°C), or Centigrade, and Fahrenheit (°F). The Celsius scale is used exclusively for upper air temperatures and is rapidly becoming the world standard for surface temperatures also.

Traditionally, two common temperature references are the melting point of pure ice and the boiling point of pure water at sea level. The melting point of ice is 0°C or 32°F; the boiling point of water is 100°C, or 212°F. Thus, the difference between melting and boiling is 100°C or 180°F; the ratio between degrees Celsius and Fahrenheit is 100/180 or 5/9. Since O°F is 32°F colder than O°C, you must apply this difference when comparing temperatures on the two scales. You can convert from one scale to the other using one of the following formulae: $C = 5/9\ (F—32)$; $F = 9/5\ C + 32$ where C is degrees Celsius and F is degrees Fahrenheit.

Heat and temperature

Heat is a form of energy. When a substance contains heat, it exhibits degrees of "hotness" or "coldness." A specific amount of heat absorbed by or removed from a substance raises or lowers its temperature a definite amount. However, the amount of temperature change depends on characteristics of the substance. Each substance has its unique temperature change for the specific change in heat. For example, if a land surface and a water surface have the same temperature and an equal amount of heat is added, the land surface becomes hotter than the water surface. Conversely, with equal heat loss, the land becomes colder than the water.

Earth receives energy from the sun in the form of *solar radiation*. Earth and its atmosphere reflect about 55% of the radiation and absorb the remaining 45% by converting it to heat. Earth, in turn, radiates energy, and this outgoing radiation is *terrestrial radiation*. It is evident that the average heat gained from incoming solar radiation must equal heat lost through terrestrial radiation in order to keep the earth from getting progressively hotter or colder. However, this balance is worldwide; regional and local imbalances which create temperature variations should also be considered.

Temperature variations

The amount of solar energy received by any region varies with time of day, with seasons, and with latitude. These differences in solar energy create temperature variations. Temperatures also vary with differences in topographical surface and with altitude. These temperature variations create forces that drive the atmosphere in its endless motions.

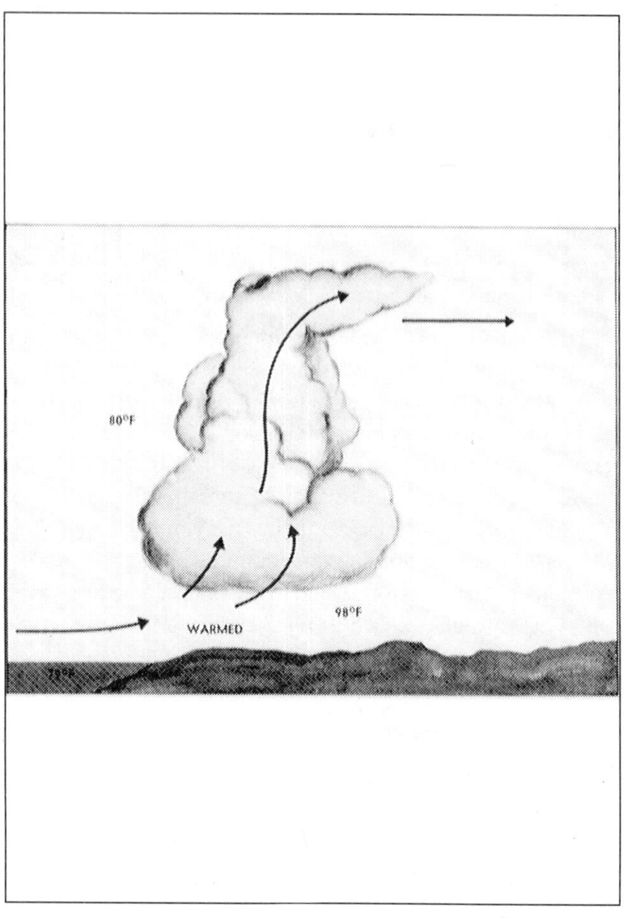

Temperature differences create air movement and, at times, cloudiness.

Day-to-night (diurnal) variation of temperature

Diurnal variation is the change in temperature from day to night brought about by the daily rotation of Earth. Earth receives heat during the day by solar radiation but continually loses heat by terrestrial radiation. Warming and cooling depend on an imbalance of solar and terrestrial radiation. During the day, solar radiation exceeds terrestrial radiation and the surface becomes warmer. At night, solar radiation ceases, but terrestrial radiation continues and cools the surface. Cooling continues after sunrise until solar radiation again exceeds terrestrial radiation. Minimum temperature usually occurs after sunrise, sometimes as much as one hour after. The continued cooling after sunrise is one reason that fog sometimes forms shortly after the sun is above the horizon.

Seasonal variation of temperature

In addition to its daily rotation, Earth revolves in a complete orbit around the sun once each year. Since the axis of Earth tilts to the plane of orbit, the angle of incident solar radiation varies seasonally between hemispheres. The Northern Hemisphere is warmer in June, July, and August because it receives more solar energy than does the Southern Hemisphere. During December, January, and February, the opposite is true; the Southern Hemisphere receives more solar energy and is warmer.

Temperature variation with latitude

The shape of Earth causes a geographical variation in the angle of incident solar radiation. Since the Earth is essentially spherical, the sun is more nearly overhead in equatorial regions than at higher latitudes. Equatorial regions, therefore, receive the most radiant energy and are warmest. Slanting rays of the sun at higher latitudes deliver less energy over a given area with the least being received at the poles. Thus, temperature varies with latitude from the warm Equator to the cold poles.

Temperature variations with topography

Not related to movement or shape of the earth are temperature variations induced by water and terrain. As stated earlier, water absorbs and radiates energy with less temperature change than does land. Large, deep water bodies tend to minimize temperature changes, while continents favor large changes. Wet soil, such as in swamps and marshes, is almost as effective as water in suppressing temperature changes. Thick vegetation tends to control temperature changes since it contains some water and also insulates against heat transfer between the ground and the atmosphere. Arid, barren surfaces permit the greatest temperature changes.

These topographical influences are both diurnal and seasonal. For example, the difference between a daily maximum and minimum may be 10°F (-12.2°C) or less over water, near a shore line, or over a swamp or marsh, while a difference of 50°F (10°C) or more is common over rocky or sandy deserts. In the Northern Hemisphere in July, temperatures are warmer over continents than over oceans; in January they are colder over continents than over oceans. The opposite is true in the Southern Hemisphere, but not as pronounced because of more water surface in the Southern Hemisphere.

To compare land and water effect on seasonal temperature variation, consider northern Asia and southern California near San Diego. In the deep continental interior of northern Asia, July average temperature is about 50°F (10°C); and January average, about-30°F (-34.4°C). Seasonal range is about 80°F (26.7°C). Near San Diego, due to the proximity of the Pacific Ocean, July average is about 70°F (21.1°C) and January average, 50°F (10°C). Seasonal variation is only about 20°F (-6.7°C).

Abrupt temperature differences develop along lake and ocean shores. These variations generate pressure differences and local winds which will be studied further on in this text.

Prevailing wind is also a factor in temperature controls. In an area where prevailing winds are from large water bodies, temperature changes are rather small. Most islands enjoy fairly constant temperatures. On the other hand, temperature changes are more pronounced where prevailing wind is from dry, barren regions.

Air transfers heat slowly from the surface upward. Thus, temperature changes aloft are more gradual than at the surface. The following looks at particulars of temperature changes with altitude.

Temperature variation with altitude

Temperature normally decreases with increasing altitude throughout the troposphere. This decrease of temperature with altitude is defined as lapse rate. The average decrease of temperature-average lapse rate in the troposphere is 35.6°F (2°C) per 1,000 feet (303.3 m). But since this is an average, the exact value seldom exists. In fact, temperature sometimes increases with height through a layer. An increase in temperature with altitude is defined as an inversion, i.e., the lapse rate is inverted.

An inversion often develops near the ground on clear, cool nights when wind is light. The ground radiates and cools much faster than the overlying air. Air in contact with the ground becomes cold while the temperature a few hundred feet above changes very little. Thus, temperature increases with height. Inversions may also occur at any altitude when conditions are favorable. For example, a current of warm air aloft overrunning cold air near the surface produces an inversion aloft. Inversions are common in the stratosphere.

• ATMOSPHERIC PRESSURE & THE BAROMETER

Atmospheric pressure

Atmospheric pressure is the force per unit area exerted by the weight of the atmosphere. Since air is not solid, it can not be weighed with conventional scales. Yet, Toricelli proved three centuries ago that he could weigh the atmosphere by balancing it against a column of mercury. He actually measured pressure converting it directly to weight.

Measuring pressure

The instrument Toricelli designed for measuring pressure is the *barometer*. Weather services and the aviation community use two types of barometers in measuring pressure—the mercurial and aneroid.

The *mercurial barometer*, consists of an open dish of mercury into which we place the open end of an evacuated glass tube. Atmospheric pressure forces mercury to rise in the tube. At stations near sea level, the column of mercury rises on the average to a height of 29.92 inches or 760 millimeters. In other words, a column of mercury of that height weighs the same as column of air having the same cross section as the column of mercury and extending from sea level to the top of the atmosphere.

Why is mercury used in the barometer? Mercury is the heaviest substance available which remains liquid at ordinary temperatures. It permits the instrument to be of manageable size. Water could be used but at sea level the water column would be about 34 feet (10.2 m) high.

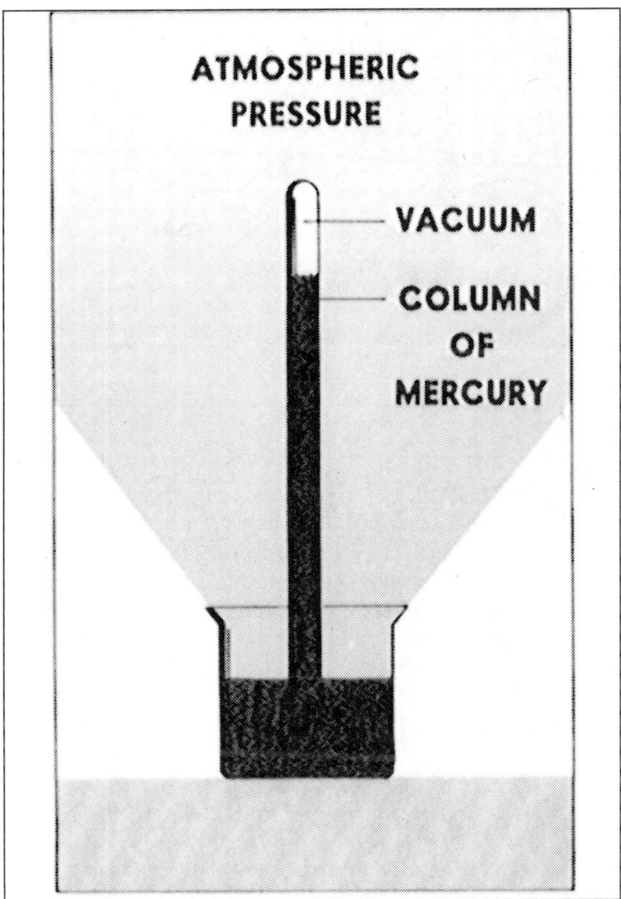

The mercurial barometer. Atmospheric pressure forces mercury from the open dish upward into the evacuated glass tube. The height of the mercury column is a measure of atmospheric pressure.

The *aneroid barometer* comprises the essential features of a flexible metal cell and the registering mechanism. The cell is partially evacuated and contracts or expands as pressure changes. One end of the cell is fixed, while the other end moves the registering mechanism. The coupling mechanism magnifies movement of the cell driving an indicator hand along a scale graduated in pressure units.

Pressure units

Pressure is expressed in many ways throughout the world. The term used depends somewhat on its application and the system of measurement. Two popular units are inches of mercury or millimeters of mercury. Since pressure is force per unit area, a more explicit expression of pressure is pounds per square inch or grams per square centimeter. The term *millibar* (mb) precisely expresses pressure as a force per unit area, one millibar being a force of 1,000 dynes per square centimeter. The millibar is rapidly becoming a universal pressure unit.

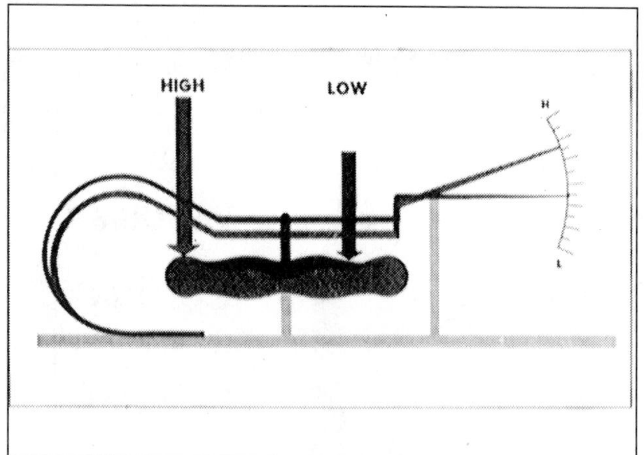

The aneroid barometer. The aneroid consists of a partially evacuated metal cell, a coupling mechanism, and an indicator scale. The cell contracts and expands with changing pressure. The coupling mechanism drives the indicator along a scale graduated in pressure units.

Station pressure

Obviously, pressure can be measured only at the point of measurement. The pressure measured at a station or airport is *station pressure* or the actual pressure at field elevation. For instance, station pressure at Denver is less than at New Orleans. Now look more closely at some factors influencing pressure.

Pressure variation

Pressure varies with altitude and temperature of the air as well as with other minor influences.

Altitude

Moving upward through the atmosphere, weight of the air above becomes less and less. Within the lower few thousand feet of the troposphere, pressure decreases roughly 1 inch (2.54 cm) for each 1,000 feet (303 m) increase in altitude.

Sea level pressure

Since pressure varies with altitude, it is not easy to compare station pressures between stations at different altitudes. To make them comparable, pressure readings must be adjusted to some common level. Mean sea level seems the most feasible common reference. Pressure measured at a 5,000-foot (1,517 m) station is 25 inches (63.5 cm); pressure increases about 1 inch (2.54 cm) for each 1,000 feet or a total of 5 inches (13 cm). Sea level pressure is approximately 25 + 5, or 30 inches (76 cm). The weather observer takes temperature and other effects into account, but this simplified example explains the basic principle of sea level pressure reduction.

Sea level pressure is usually expressed in millibars. Standard sea level pressure is 1013.2 millibars, 29.92 inches (76 cm) of mercury, 760 millimeters of mercury, or about 14.7 pounds per square inch.

Pressure analyses (using isobars)

Sea level pressure are commonly plotted on a map and lines are drawn connecting points of equal pressure. These lines of equal pressure are isobars. Hence, the surface map is an isobaric analysis showing identifiable, organized pressure patterns. Five pressure systems are defined as follow:

1. **LOW**—a center of pressure surrounded on all sides by higher pressure; also called a cyclone. Cyclonic curvature is the curvature of isobars to the left when you stand with lower pressure to your left.
2. **HIGH**—a center of pressure surrounded on all sides by lower pressure, also called an anticyclone. Anticyclonic curvature is the curvature of isobars to the right when you stand with lower pressure to your left.
3. **TROUGH**—an elongated area of low pressure with the lowest pressure along a line marking maximum cyclonic curvature.
4. **RIDGE**—an elongated area of high pressure with the highest pressure along a line marking maximum anticyclonic curvature.
5. **COL**—the neutral area between two highs and two lows. It also is the intersection of a trough and a ridge. The col on a pressure surface is analogous to a mountain pass on a topographic surface. We simply contour the heights of the pressure surface. For example, a 700-millibar constant pressure analysis is a contour map of the heights of the 700-millibar pressure surface. While the contour map is based on variations in height, these variations are small when compared to flight levels, and for all practical purposes, you may regard the 700-millibar chart as a weather map at approximately 10,000 feet or 3,048 meters.

• WIND

What causes wind?

Differences in temperature create differences in pressure. These pressure differences drive a complex system of winds in a never ending attempt to reach equilibrium. Wind also transports water vapor and spreads fog, clouds, and precipitation. To help the reader relate wind to pressure patterns and the movement of weather systems, this text explains convection and the pressure gradient force, describes the effects of the Coriolis and frictional forces, relates convection and these forces to the general circulation, discusses local and small-scale wind systems, introduces the concept of wind shear, and associates wind with weather.

Convection currents

When two surfaces are heated unequally, they heat the overlying air unevenly. The warmer air expands and becomes lighter or less dense than the cool air. The more dense, cool air is drawn to the ground by its greater gravitational force lifting or forcing the warm air upward much as oil is forced to the top of water when the two are mixed. The rising air spreads and cools, eventually descending to complete the convective circulation. As long as the uneven heating persists, convection maintains a continuous *convective current.*

The horizontal air flow in a convective current is wind. Convection of both large and small scales accounts for systems ranging from hemispheric circulations down to local eddies. This horizontal flow, wind, is sometimes called *advection.* However, the term advection more commonly applies to the transport of atmospheric properties by the wind, i.e., warm advection; cold advection; advection of water vapor, etc.

Pressure gradient force of wind

Pressure differences must create a force in order to drive the wind. This force is the pressure gradient force. The force is from higher pressure to lower pressure and is perpendicular to isobars or contours. Whenever a pressure difference develops over an area, the pressure gradient force begins

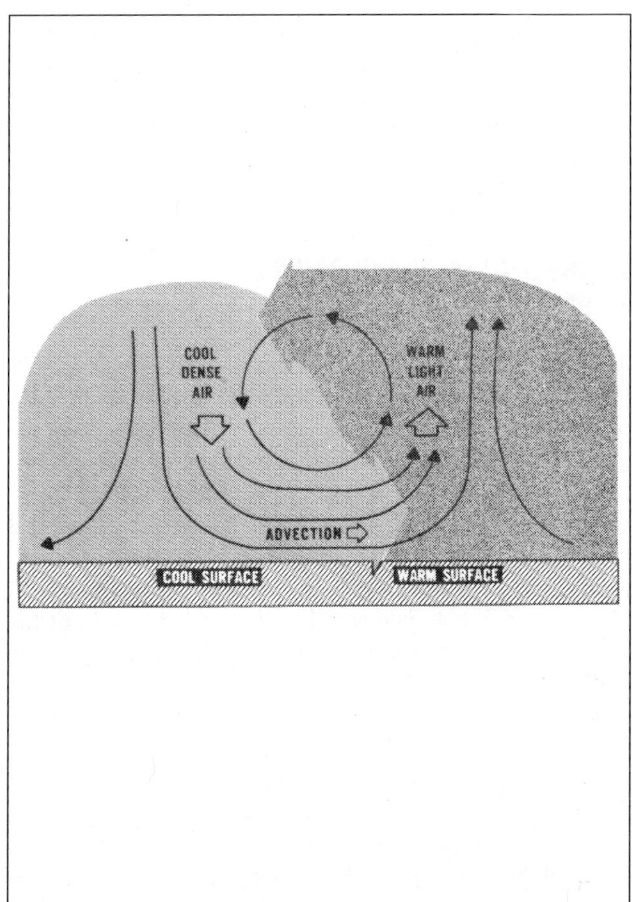

Convective current resulting from uneven heating of air by contrasting surface temperatures. The cool, heavy air forces the warmer air aloft establishing a convective cell. Convection continues as long as the uneven heating persists.

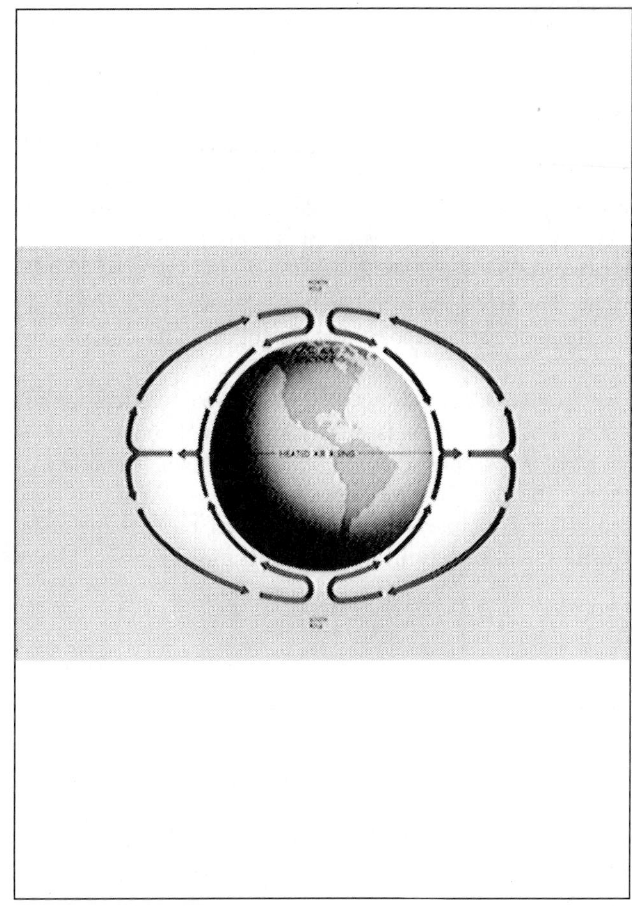

Circulation as it would be on a nonrotating globe. Intense heating at the Equator lowers the density. More dense air flows from the poles toward the Equator forcing the less dense air aloft where it flows toward the poles. The circulation would be two giant hemispherical convective currents.

moving the air directly across the isobars. The closer the spacing of isobars, the stronger is the pressure gradient force. The stronger the pressure gradient force, the stronger is the wind. Thus, closely spaced isobars mean strong winds; widely spaced isobars mean lighter wind. From a pressure analysis, the reader can get a general idea of wind speed from contour or isobar spacing.

Because of uneven heating of the earth, surface pressure is low in warm equatorial regions and high in cold polar regions. A pressure gradient develops from the poles to the Equator. If Earth did not rotate, this pressure gradient force would be the only force acting on the wind. Circulation would be two giant hemispheric convective currents. Cold air would sink at the poles; wind would blow straight from the poles to the Equator; warm air at the Equator would be forced upward; and high level winds would blow directly toward the poles. However, Earth does rotate; and because of its rotation, this simple circulation is greatly distorted.

Coriolis force: it modifies wind direction

A moving mass travels in a straight line until acted on by some outside force. However, if one views the moving mass from a rotating platform, the path of the moving mass relative to his platform appears to be deflected or curved. To illustrate, start rotating the turntable of a record player. Then using a piece of chalk and a ruler, draw a straight line from the center to the outer edge of the turntable. To you, the chalk traveled in a straight line. Now stop the turntable; on it, the line spirals outward from the center. To a viewer on the turntable, some apparent force deflected the chalk to the right.

A similar apparent force deflects moving particles on the earth. Because Earth is spherical, the deflective force is much more complex than the simple turntable example. Although the force is termed apparent, to us on Earth, it is very real. The principle was first explained by a Frenchman, Coriolis, and carries his name—the Coriolis force.

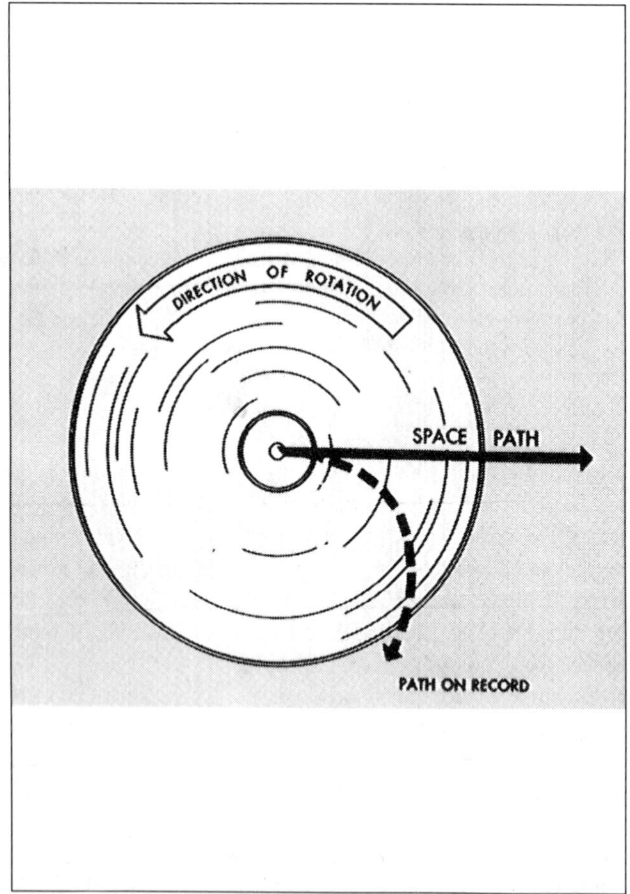

Apparent deflective force due to rotation of a horizontal platform. The "space path" is the path taken by a piece of chalk. The "path of record" is the line traced on the rotating record. Relative to the record, the chalk appeared to curve; in space, it traveled in a straight line.

The Coriolis force affects the paths of aircraft, missiles, flying birds, ocean currents, and, most important to the study of weather, air currents. The force deflects air to the right in the Northern Hemisphere and to the left in the Southern Hemisphere. This text concentrates mostly on deflection to the right in the Northern Hemisphere.

Coriolis force is at a right angle to wind direction and directly proportional to wind speed. That is, as wind speed increases, Coriolis force increases. At a given latitude, double the wind speed and you double the Coriolis force. Why at a given latitude?

Coriolis force varies with latitude from zero at the Equator to a maximum at the poles. It influences wind direction everywhere except immediately at the Equator; but the effects are more pronounced in middle and high latitudes.

Remember that the pressure gradient force drives the wind and is perpendicular to isobars. When a pressure gradient force is first established, wind begins to blow from higher to lower pressure directly across the isobars. However, the instant air begins moving, Coriolis force deflects it to the right. Soon the wind is deflected a full 90° and is parallel to the isobars or contours. At this time, Coriolis force exactly balances pressure gradient force. With the forces in balance, wind will remain parallel to isobars or contours. Surface friction disrupts this balance; but first it should be discussed how Coriolis force distorts the fictitious global circulation.

• THE GENERAL CIRCULATION OF EARTH'S AIR

As air is forced aloft at the Equator and begins its high-level trek northward, the Coriolis force turns it to the right or to the east. Wind becomes westerly at about 30° latitude temporarily blocking further northward movement. Similarly, as air over the poles begins its low-level journey southward toward the Equator, it is deflected to the right and becomes an east wind, halting for a while its southerly progress. As a result, air literally "piles up" at about 30° and 60° latitude in both hemispheres. The added weight of the air increases the pressure into semipermanent high pressure belts.

The building of these high pressure belts creates a temporary impasse disrupting the simple convective transfer between the Equator and the poles. The restless atmosphere cannot live with this impasse in its effort to reach equilibrium. Huge masses of air begin overturning in middle latitudes to complete the exchange.

Large masses of cold air break through the northern barrier plunging southward toward the Tropics. Large midlatitude storms develop between cold outbreaks and carry warm air northward. The result is a midlatitude band of migratory storms with everchanging weather.

Since pressure differences cause wind, seasonal pressure variations determine to a great extent the areas of these cold air outbreaks and midlatitude storms. But, seasonal pressure variations are largely due to seasonal temperature changes. It should be remembered that at the surface, warm temperatures determine low pressure and cold temperatures, as well as high pressure. It should also be recalled that seasonal temperature changes over continents are much greater than over oceans.

During summer, warm continents tend to be areas of low pressure and the relatively cool oceans, high pressure. In winter, the reverse is true—high pressure over the cold continents and low pressure over the relatively warm oceans. The same pressure variations occur in the warm and cold seasons of the Southern Hemisphere, although the effect is not as pronounced because of the much larger water areas of the Southern Hemisphere.

Cold outbreaks are strongest in the cold season and are predominantly from cold continental areas. Summer outbreaks are weaker and more likely to originate from cool water surfaces. Since these outbreaks are masses of cool, dense air, they characteristically are high pressure areas.

As the air tries to blow outward from the high pressure, it is deflected to the right by the Coriolis force. Thus, the wind around a high blows clockwise. The high pressure with its associated wind system is an *anticyclone*.

The storms that develop between high pressure systems are characterized by low pressure. As winds try to blow inward toward the center of low pressure, they also are deflected to the right. Thus, the wind around a low is counterclockwise. The low pressure and its wind system is a *cyclone*.

The high pressure belt at about 30° north latitude forces air outward at the surface to the north and to the south. The northbound air becomes entrained into the midlatitude storms. The southward moving air is again deflected by the Coriolis force becoming the well-known subtropical northeast trade winds. In midlatitudes, high level winds are predominantly from the west and are known as the prevailing westerlies. Polar easterlies dominate low-level circulation north of about 60° latitude.

There are three major wind belts. *Northeasterly* trade winds carry tropical storms from east to west. The *prevailing westerlies* drive midlatitude storms generally from west to east. Few major storm systems develop in the comparatively small Arctic region; the chief influence of the *polar easterlies* is their contribution to the development of midlatitude storms.

Friction effect on wind

Wind flow patterns aloft follow isobars or contours where friction has little effect. However, friction is a significant factor near the surface.

Friction between the wind and the terrain surface slows the wind. The rougher the terrain, the greater is the frictional effect. Also, the stronger the wind speed, the greater is the friction. One may not think of friction as a force, but it is a very real and effective force always acting opposite to wind direction.

As frictional force slows the windspeed, Coriolis force decreases. However, friction does not affect pressure gradient force. Pressure gradient and Coriolis forces are no longer in balance. The stronger pressure gradient force turns the wind at an angle across the isobars toward lower pressure until the three forces balance. Frictional and Coriolis forces combine to just balance pressure gradient force. Surface wind spirals outward from high pressure into low pressure crossing isobars at an angle.

The angle of surface wind to isobars is about 10° over water increasing with roughness of terrain. In mountainous regions, one often has difficulty relating surface wind to pressure gradient because of immense friction and also because of local terrain effects on pressure.

The jet stream

Winds on the average increase with height throughout the troposphere culminating in a maximum near the level of the tropopause. These maximum winds tend to be further concentrated in narrow bands. A *jet stream*, then, is a narrow band of strong winds meandering through the atmosphere at a level near the tropopause.

• LOCAL & SMALL SCALE WINDS

Until now, this text has dealt only with the general circulation and major wind systems. Local terrain features such as mountains and shore lines influence local winds and weather.

Mountain and valley winds

In the daytime, air next to a mountain slope is heated by contact with the ground as it receives radiation from the sun. This air usually becomes warmer than air at the same altitude but farther from the slope.

Colder, denser air in the surroundings settles downward and forces the warmer air near the ground up the mountain slope. This wind is a *valley wind*, so called because the air is flowing up out of the valley.

At night, the air in contact with the mountain slope is cooled by terrestrial radiation and becomes heavier than the surrounding air. It sinks along the slope, producing the *mountain wind* which flows like water down the mountain slope. Mountain winds are usually stronger than valley winds, especially in winter. The mountain wind often continues down the more gentle slopes of canyons and valleys, and in such cases takes the name *drainage wind*. It can become quite strong over some terrain conditions and in extreme cases can become hazardous when flowing through canyon restrictions.

Katabatic wind

A katabatic wind is any wind blowing down an incline when the incline is influential in causing the wind. Thus, the mountain wind is a katabatic wind. Any katabatic wind originates because cold, heavy air spills down sloping terrain displacing warmer, less dense air ahead of it. Air is heated and dried as it flows down the slope. Sometimes the descending air becomes warmer than the air it replaces.

Many katabatic winds recurring in local areas have been given colorful names to highlight their dramatic, local effect. Some of these are the Bora, a cold northerly wind blowing from the Alps to the Mediterranean coast; the Chinook, a warm wind down the east slope of the Rocky Mountains often reaching hundreds of miles into the high plains; the Taku, a cold wind in Alaska blowing off the Taku glacier; and the Santa Ana, a warm wind descending from the Sierras into the Santa Ana Valley of California.

Land and sea breezes

Land surfaces warm and cool more rapidly than do water surfaces; therefore, land is warmer than the sea during the day; wind blows from the cool water to warm land—the *sea breeze*, so called because it blows from the sea. At night, the wind reverses, blowing from cool land to warmer water, and creates a *land breeze*.

Land and sea breezes develop only when the overall pressure gradient is weak. Wind with a stronger pressure gradient mixes the air so rapidly that local temperature and pressure gradients do not develop along the shore line.

Wind shear

Rubbing two objects against each other creates friction. If the objects are solid, no exchange of mass occurs between the two. However, if the objects are fluid currents, friction creates eddies along a common shallow mixing zone, and a mass transfer takes place in the shallow mixing layer. This zone of induced eddies and mixing is a shear zone.

Wind, pressure systems, and weather

It has been noted earlier that wind speed is proportional to the spacing of isobars or contours on a weather map. However, with the same spacing, wind speed at the surface will be less than aloft because of surface friction.

Wind direction can be determined from a weather map. If you face along an isobar or contour with lower pressure on your left, wind will be blowing in the direction you are facing. On a surface map, wind will cross the isobar at an angle toward lower pressure; on an upper air chart, it will be parallel to the contour.

Wind blows counterclockwise (Northern Hemisphere) around a low and clockwise around a high. At the surface where winds cross the isobars at an angle, the transport of air from high to low pressure can be seen. Although winds are virtually parallel to contours on an upper air chart, there still is a slow transport of air from high to low pressure.

At the surface when air converges into a low, it cannot go outward against the pressure gradient, nor can it go downward into the ground; it must go upward. Therefore, a low or trough is an area of rising air.

Rising air is conducive to cloudiness and precipitation; thus we have the general association of low pressure—bad

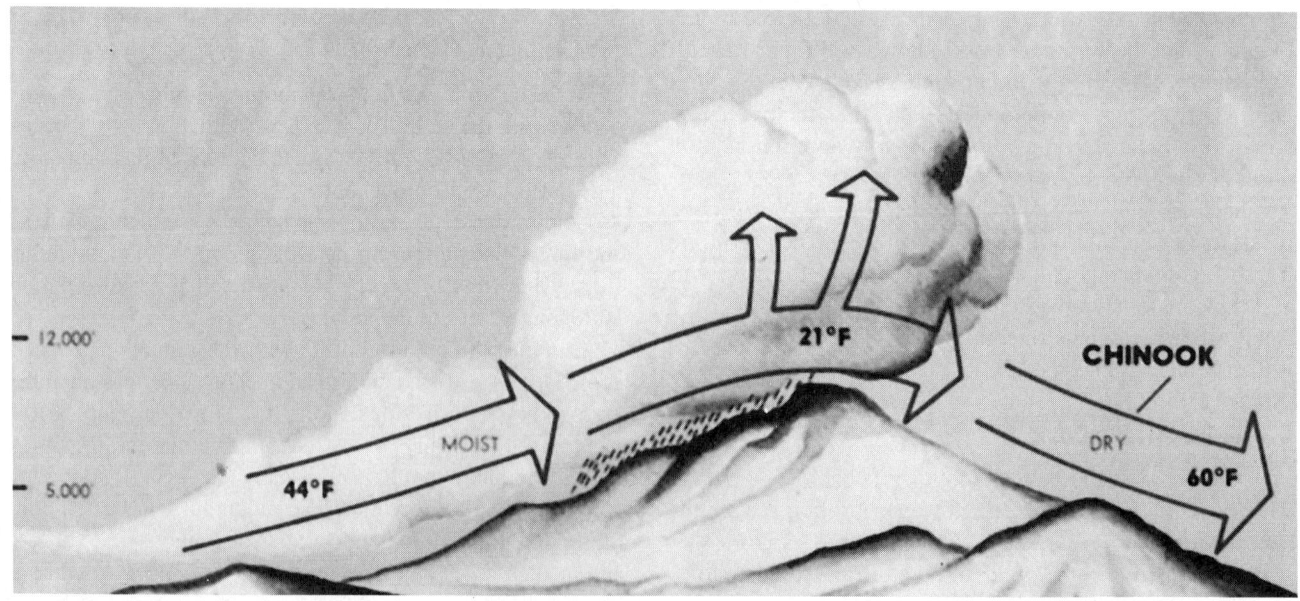

The "Chinook" is a katabatic (downslope) wind. Air cools as it moves upslope and warms as it blows downslope. The Chinook occasionally produces dramatic warming over the plains just east of the Rocky Mountains.

weather. Reasons for the inclement weather are developed further on in this text.

By similar reasoning, air moving out of a high or ridge depletes the quantity of air. Highs and ridges, therefore, are areas of descending air. Descending air favors dissipation of cloudiness; hence the association, high pressure—good weather.

Many times weather is more closely associated with an upper air pattern than with features shown by the surface map. Although features on the two charts are related, they seldom are identical. A weak surface system often loses its identity in the upper air pattern, while another system may be more evident on the upper air chart than on the surface map.

Widespread cloudiness and precipitation often develop in advance of an upper trough or low. A line of showers and thunderstorms is not uncommon with a trough aloft even though the surface pressure pattern shows little or no cause for the development.

On the other hand, downward motion in a high or ridge places a "cap" on convection, preventing any upward motion. Air may become stagnant in a high, trap moisture and contamination in low levels, and restrict ceiling and visibility. Low stratus, fog, haze, and smoke are not uncommon in high pressure areas. However, a high or ridge aloft with moderate surface winds most often produces good flying weather.

• MOISTURE, CLOUD FORMATION & PRECIPITATION

Water vapor

Water evaporates into the air and becomes an ever-present but variable constituent of the atmosphere. Water vapor is invisible just as oxygen and other gases are invisible. However, water vapor can be readily measured and expressed in different ways. Two commonly used terms are (1) relative humidity, and (2) dew point.

Relative humidity

Relative humidity routinely is expressed as a percentage. As the term suggests, relative humidity is "relative." It relates the actual water vapor present to that which could be present.

Temperature largely determines the maximum amount of water vapor air can hold. Warm air can hold more water vapor than cool air. Actually, relative humidity expresses the degree of saturation. Air with 100% relative humidity is saturated; less than 100% is unsaturated.

Dew point

Dew point is the temperature to which air must be cooled to become saturated by the water vapor already present in the air. Aviation weather reports normally include the air temperature and dew point temperature. Dew point when related to air temperature reveals qualitatively how close the air is to saturation.

Temperature—dew point spread

The difference between air temperature and dew point temperature is popularly called the spread. As spread becomes less, relative humidity increases, and it is 100% when temperature and dew point are the same. Surface temperature—dew point spread is important in anticipating fog but has little bearing on precipitation. To support precipitation, air must be saturated through thick layers aloft.

Sometimes the spread at ground level may be quite large, yet at higher altitudes the air is saturated and clouds form. Some rain may reach the ground or it may evaporate as it falls into the drier air. Our neverending weather cycle involves a continual reversible change of water from one state to another.

• CHANGE OF STATE

Evaporation, condensation, sublimation, freezing, and melting are changes of state. Evaporation is the changing of liquid water to invisible water vapor. Condensation is the reverse process. Sublimation is the changing of ice directly to water vapor, or water vapor to ice, bypassing the liquid state in each process. Snow or ice crystals result from the sublimation of water vapor directly to the solid state. The freezing and melting processes are self-explanatory.

Latent heat

Any change of state involves a heat transaction with no change in temperature. Evaporation requires heat energy that comes from the nearest available heat source. This heat energy is known as the *latent heat of vaporization*, and its removal cools the source it comes from. An example is the cooling of your body by evaporation of perspiration.

What becomes of this heat energy used by evaporation? Energy cannot be created or destroyed, so it is hidden or stored in the invisible water vapor. When the water vapor condenses to liquid water or sublimates directly to ice, energy originally used in the evaporation reappears as heat and is released to the atmosphere. This energy is *latent heat* and is quite significant as will be shown later. Melting and freezing involve the exchange of "latent heat of fusion" in a similar manner. The latent heat of fusion is much less than that of condensation and evaporation; however, each in its own way plays an important role in weather.

As air becomes saturated, water vapor begins to condense on the nearest available surface. What surfaces are in the atmosphere on which water vapor may condense?

Condensation nuclei

The atmosphere is never completely clean; an abundance of microscopic solid particles suspended in the air are condensation surfaces. These particles, such as salt, dust, and combustion by products are *condensation nuclei*. Some condensation nuclei have an affinity for water and can induce condensation or sublimation even when air is almost but not completely saturated.

As water vapor condenses or sublimates on condensation nuclei, liquid or ice particles begin to grow. Whether the particles are liquid or ice does not depend entirely on temperature. Liquid water may be present at temperatures well below freezing.

Supercooled water

Freezing is complex and liquid water droplets often condense or persist at temperatures colder than 32°F (0°C). Water droplets colder than O°C are supercooled. When they strike an exposed object, the impact induces freezing. For example, impact freezing of supercooled water can result in aircraft icing.

Supercooled water drops very often are in abundance in clouds at temperatures between 32°F (0°C) and 5°F (-15°C), with decreasing amounts at colder temperatures. Usually, at temperatures colder than 5°F, sublimation is prevalent; and clouds and fog may be mostly ice crystals with a lesser amount of supercooled water. However, strong vertical currents may carry supercooled water to great heights where temperatures are much colder than 5°F. Supercooled water has been observed at temperatures colder than 40°F (4.4°C).

Dew and frost

During clear nights with little or no wind, vegetation often cools by radiation to a temperature at or below the dew point of the adjacent air. Moisture than collects on the leaves just as it does on a pitcher of ice water in a warm room. Heavy dew often collects on grass and plants when none collects on pavements or large solid objects. These more massive objects absorb abundant heat during the day, lose it slowly during the night, and cool below the dew point only in rather extreme cases.

Frost forms in much the same way as dew. The difference is that the dew point of surrounding air must be colder than freezing. Water vapor then sublimates directly as ice crystals or frost rather than condensing as dew. Sometimes dew forms and later freezes; however, frozen dew is easily distinguished from frost. Frozen dew is hard and transparent while frost is white and opaque.

To now, little has been said here about clouds. What brings about the condensation or sublimation that results in cloud formation?

Cloud formation

Normally, air must become saturated for condensation or sublimation to occur. Saturation may result from cooling temperature, increasing dew point, or both. Cooling is far more predominant.

Cooling processes

Three basic processes may cool air to saturation. They are (1) air moving over a colder surface, (2) stagnant air overlying a cooling surface, and (3) expansional cooling in upward moving air. Expansional cooling is the major cause of cloud formation.

Clouds and fog

A cloud is a visible aggregate of minute water or ice particles suspended in air. If the cloud is on the ground, it is fog. When entire layers of air cool to saturation, fog or sheet-like clouds result. Saturation of a localized updraft produces a towering cloud. A cloud may be composed entirely of liquid water, of ice crystals, or a mixture of the two.

Precipitation

Precipitation is an all inclusive term denoting drizzle, rain, snow, ice pellets, hail, and ice crystals. Precipitation occurs when these particles grow in size and weight until the atmosphere no longer can suspend them and they fall. These particles grow primarily in two ways.

Particle growth

Once a water droplet or ice crystal forms, it continues to grow by added condensation or sublimation directly onto the particle. This is the slower of the two methods and usually results in drizzle or very light rain or snow.

Cloud particles collide and merge into a larger drop in the more rapid growth process. This process produces larger precipitation particles and does so more rapidly than the simple condensation growth process. Upward currents enhance the growth rate and also support larger drops. Precipitation formed by merging drops with mild upward currents can produce light to moderate rain and snow. Strong upward currents support the largest drops and build clouds to great heights. They can produce heavy rain, heavy snow, and hail.

Liquid, freezing, and frozen

Precipitation forming and remaining liquid falls as rain or drizzle. Sublimation forms snowflakes, and they reach the ground as snow if temperatures remain below freezing.

Precipitation can change its state as the temperature of its environment changes. Falling snow may melt in warmer layers of air at lower altitudes to form rain. Rain falling through colder air may become supercooled, freezing on impact as freezing rain; or it may freeze during its descent, falling as ice pellets. Ice pellets always indicate freezing rain at higher altitude.

Sometimes strong upward currents sustain large supercooled water drops until some freeze; subsequently, other drops freeze to them forming hailstones.

Precipitation versus cloud thickness

To produce significant precipitation, clouds usually are 4,000 feet (1,213 m) thick or more. The heavier the precipitation, the thicker the clouds are likely to be.

Land and water effects on clouds

Land and water surfaces underlying the atmosphere greatly affect cloud and precipitation development. Large bodies of water such as oceans and large lakes add water vapor to the air.

The greatest frequency of low ceilings, fog, and precipitation can be expected in areas where prevailing winds have an over-water trajectory. The aviator should be especially alert for these hazards when moist winds are blowing upslope.

In winter, cold air frequently moves over relatively warm lakes. The warm water adds heat and water vapor to the air causing showers. In other seasons, the air may be warmer than the lakes. When this occurs, the air may become saturated by evaporation from the water while also becoming cooler in the low levels by contact with the cool water. Fog often becomes extensive and dense to the lee of a lake. Strong cold winds across the Great Lakes often carry precipitation to the Appalachians.

A lake only a few miles across can influence convection and cause a diurnal fluctuation in cloudiness. During the day, cool air over the lake blows toward the land, and convective clouds form over the land. At night, the pattern reverses; clouds tend to form over the lake as cool air from the land flows over the lake creating convective clouds over the water.

Water exists in three states—solid, liquid, and gaseous. Water vapor is an invisible gas. Condensation or sublimation of water vapor creates many common weather extremes. These things may be anticipated:

1. Fog when temperature-dew point spread is 5°F (-15°C) or less and decreasing.
2. Lifting or clearing of low clouds and fog when temperature-dew point spread is increasing.
3. Frost on a clear night when temperature-dew point spread is 5°F or less, is decreasing, and dew point is colder than 32°F (0°C).
4. More cloudiness, fog, and precipitation when wind blows from water than when it blows from land.
5. Cloudiness, fog, and precipitation over higher terrain when moist winds are blowing uphill.
6. Showers to the lee of a lake when air is cold and the lake

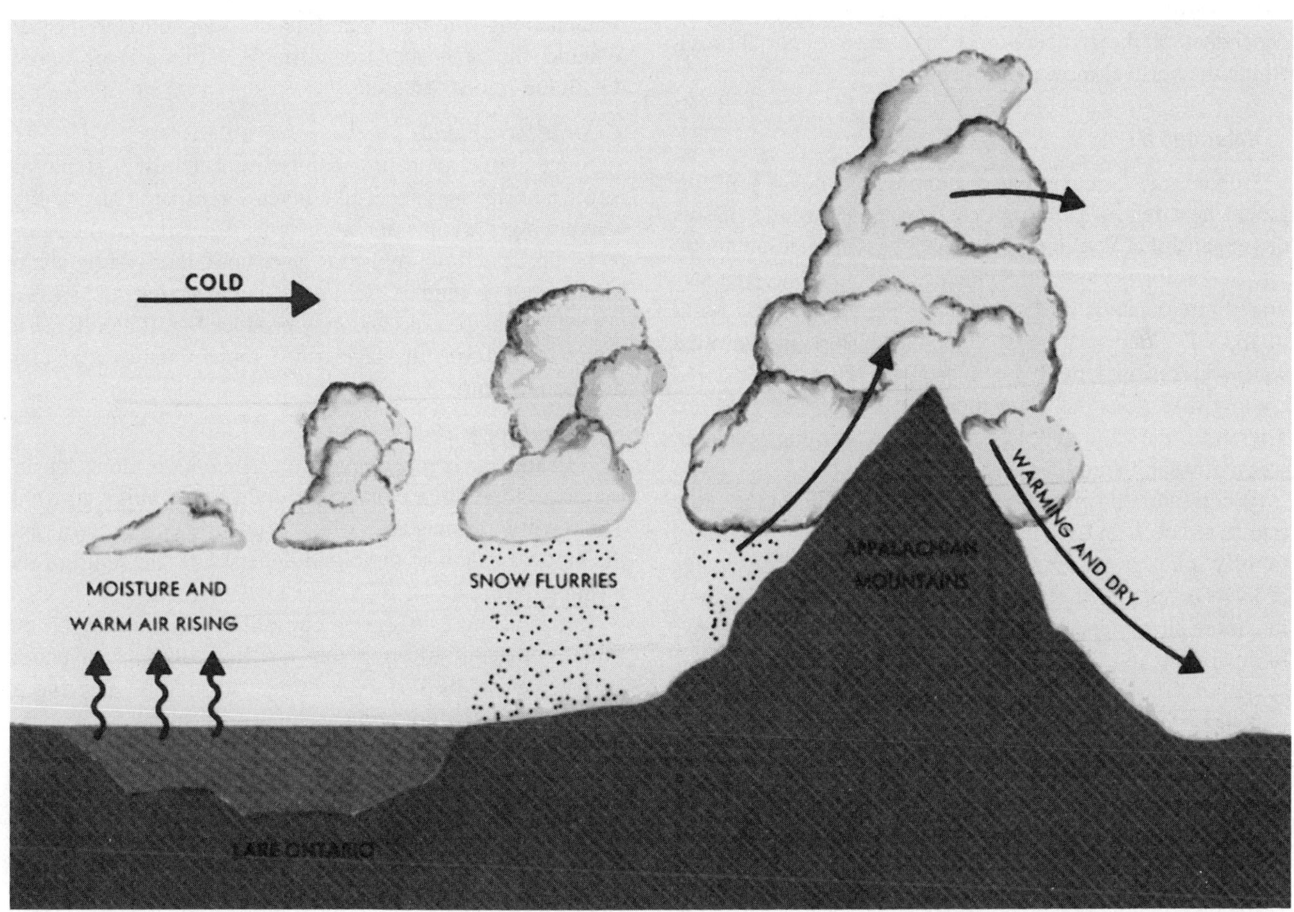

Strong cold winds across the Great Lakes absorb water vapor and may carry showers as far eastward as the Appalachians.

is warm. Expect fog to the lee of the lake when the air is warm and the lake is cold.

7. Clouds to be at least 4,000 feet thick when significant precipitation is reported. The heavier the precipitation, the thicker the clouds are likely to be.

• STABLE & UNSTABLE AIR

Changes within upward and downward moving air

Anytime air moves upward, it expands because of decreasing atmospheric pressure. Conversely, downward moving air is compressed by increasing pressure. But as pressure and volume change, temperature also changes.

When air expands, it cools; and when compressed, it warms. These changes are adiabatic, meaning that no heat is removed from or added to the air. We frequently use the terms expansional or adiabatic cooling and compressional or adiabatic heating. The adiabatic rate of temperature change is virtually fixed in unsaturated air but varies in saturated air.

Unsaturated air

Unsaturated air moving upward and downward cools and warms at about 5.4°F (3.0°C) per 1,000 feet (303.3 m). This rate is the dry adiabatic rate of temperature change and is independent of the temperature of the mass of air through which the vertical movements occur.

Saturated air

Condensation occurs when saturated air moves upward. Latent heat released through condensation partially offsets the expansional cooling. Therefore, the saturated adiabatic rate of cooling is slower than the dry adiabatic rate. The saturated rate depends on saturation temperature or dew point of the air. Condensation of copious moisture in saturated warm air releases more latent heat to offset expansional cooling than does the scant moisture in saturated cold air. Therefore, the saturated adiabatic rate of cooling is less in warm air than in cold air.

When saturated air moves downward, it heats at the same rate as it cools on ascent provided liquid water evaporates rapidly enough to maintain saturation. Minute water droplets evaporate at virtually this rate. Larger drops evaporate more slowly and complicate the moist adiabatic process in downward moving air.

Adiabatic cooling and vertical air movement

If a sample of air is forced upward into the atmosphere, two possibilities must be considered:

1. The air may become colder than the surrounding air.
2. Even though it cools, the air may remain warmer than the surrounding air.

If the upward moving air becomes colder than surrounding air, it sinks; but if it remains warmer, it is accelerated upward as a convective current. Whether it sinks or rises depends on the ambient or existing temperature lapse rate.

Do not confuse existing lapse rate with adiabatic rates of cooling in vertically moving air. Sometimes the dry and moist adiabatic rates of cooling will be called the dry adiabatic lapse rate and the moist adiabatic lapse rate. In this text, lapse rate refers exclusively to the existing, or actual, decrease of temperature with height in a real atmosphere. The dry or moist adiabatic lapse rate signifies a prescribed rate of expansional cooling or compressional heating. An adiabatic lapse rate becomes real only when it becomes a condition brought about by vertically moving air. The difference between the existing lapse rate of a given mass of air and the adiabatic rates of cooling in upward moving air determines if the air is stable or unstable.

• CLOUDS

Clouds—stable or unstable?

Earlier it was stated that when air is cooling and first becomes saturated, condensation, or sublimation, begins to form clouds. Further on in this text cloud types are explained along with their significance as signposts in the sky. Whether the air is stable or unstable within a layer largely determines cloud structure.

Stratiform clouds

Since stable air resists convection, clouds in stable air form in horizontal, sheet-like layers or *strata*. Thus, within a stable layer, clouds are stratiform. Adiabatic cooling may be by upslope flow; by lifting over cold, more dense air; or by converging winds. Cooling by an underlying cold surface is a stabilizing process and may produce fog. If clouds are to remain stratiform, the layer must remain stable after condensation occurs.

Cumuliform clouds

Unstable air favors convection. A *cumulus* cloud, meaning heap, forms in a convective updraft and builds upward. Thus, within an unstable year, clouds are cumuliform; and the vertical extent of the cloud depends on the depth of the unstable layer.

Initial lifting to trigger a cumuliform cloud may be the same as that for lifting stable air. In addition, convection may be set off by surface heating. Air may be unstable or slightly stable before condensation occurs; but for convective cumuliform clouds to develop, it must be unstable after saturation. Cooling in the updraft is now at the slower moist adiabatic rate because of the release of latent heat of condensation. Temperature in the saturated updraft is warmer than ambient temperature, and convection is spontaneous. Updrafts accelerate until temperature within the cloud cools below the ambient temperature. This condition occurs

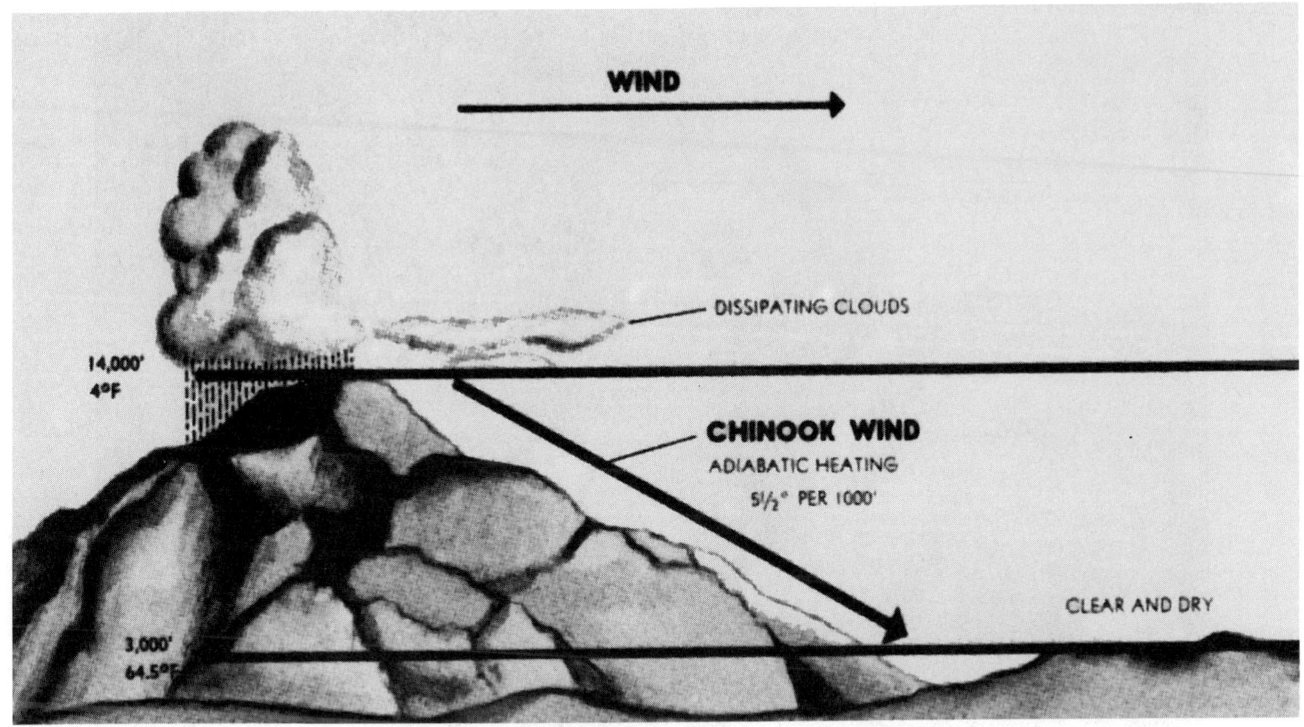

Adiabatic warming of downward moving air produces the warm Chinook wind.

where the unstable layer is capped by a stable layer often marked by a temperature inversion. Vertical heights range from the shallow fair weather cumulus to the giant thunderstorm cumulonimbus—the ultimate in atmospheric instability capped by the tropopause.

When unstable air lies above stable air, convective currents aloft sometimes form middle and high level cumuliform clouds. In relatively shallow layers they occur as altocumulus and ice crystal cirrocumulus clouds. Altocumulus castellans clouds develop in deeper midlevel unstable layers.

Identification

For identification purposes, one needs to be concerned only with the more basic cloud types, which are divided into four families. The families are: high clouds, middle clouds, low clouds, and clouds with extensive vertical development. The first three families are further classified according to the way they are formed. Clouds formed by vertical currents in unstable air are *cumulus*, meaning accumulation or heap; they are characterized by their lumpy, billowy appearance. Clouds formed by the cooling of a stable layer are *stratus*, meaning stratified or layered; they are characterized by their uniform, sheet-like appearance.

In addition to the above, the prefix *nimbo-*, or the suffix *-nimbus*, mean raincloud. Thus, stratified clouds from which rain is falling are nimbostratus. A heavy, swelling cumulus type cloud which produces precipitation is a cumulonimbus. Clouds broken into fragments are often identified by adding the suffix *-fractus*; for example, fragmentary cumulus is cumulus fractus.

High clouds

The high cloud family is cirriform and includes cirrus, cirrocumulus, and cirrostratus. They are composed almost entirely of ice crystals. The height of the bases of these clouds ranges from about 16,500-45,000 feet (5,005-13,650 m) in middle latitudes.

Middle clouds

In the middle cloud family are the altostratus, altocumulus, and nimbostratus clouds. These clouds are primarily water, much of which may be supercooled. The height of the bases of these clouds ranges from about 6,500-23,000 feet (1,971-6,976 m) in middle latitudes.

Low clouds

In the low cloud family are the stratus, stratocumulus, and fair weather cumulus clouds. Low clouds are almost entirely water, but at times the water may be supercooled. Low clouds at sub-freezing temperatures can also contain snow and ice particles. The bases of these clouds range from near the surface to about 6,500 feet (1,971 m) in middle latitudes.

Clouds with extensive vertical development

The vertically developed family of clouds includes towering cumulus and cumulonimbus. These clouds usually contain supercooled water above the freezing level. But when a cumulus grows to great heights, water in the upper part of the cloud freezes into ice crystals forming a cumulonimbus. The

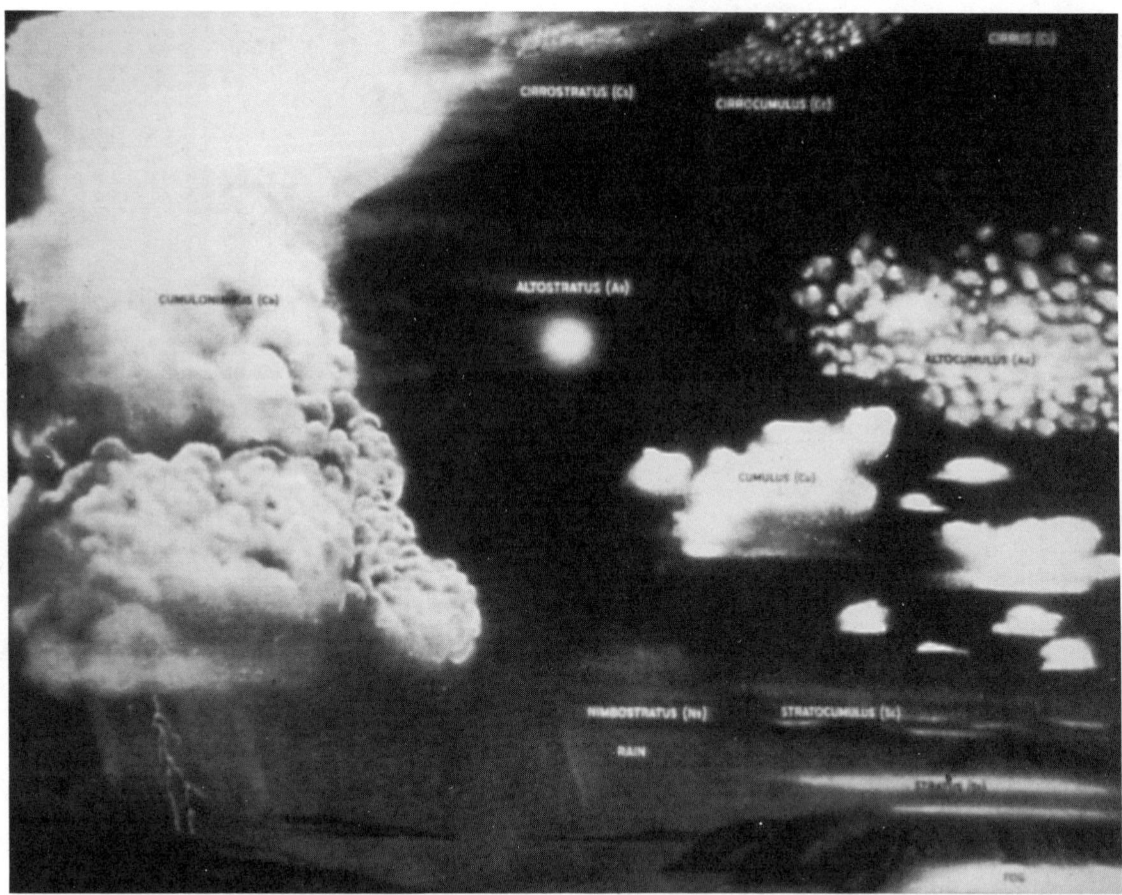

heights of cumuliform cloud bases range from 1,000 feet (303 m) or less to above 10,000 feet (3,033 m).

• FOG

Fog is a surface-based cloud composed of either water droplets or ice crystals.

Small temperature-dew point spread is essential for fog to form. Therefore, fog is prevalent in coastal areas where moisture is abundant. However, fog can occur anywhere. Abundant condensation nuclei enhances the formation of fog. Thus, fog is prevalent in industrial areas where by-products of combustion provide a high concentration of these nuclei. Fog occurs most frequently in the colder months, but the season and frequency of occurrence vary from one area to another.

Fog may form either by cooling air to its dew point, or by adding moisture to air near the ground. Fog is classified by the way it forms. Formation may involve more than one process.

Radiation fog

Radiation fog is relatively shallow fog. It may be dense enough to hide the entire sky or may conceal only part of the sky. "Ground fog" is a form of radiation fog.

Conditions favorable for radiation fog are clear sky, little or no wind, and small temperature-dew point spread (high relative humidity). The fog forms almost exclusively at night or near daybreak. Terrestrial radiation cools the ground; in turn, the cool ground cools the air in contact with it. When the air is cooled to its dew point, fog forms. When rain soaks the ground, followed by clearing skies, radiation fog is not uncommon the following morning.

Radiation fog is restricted to land because water surfaces cool little from nighttime radiation. It is shallow when wind is calm. Winds up to about 5 knots mix the air slightly and tend to deepen the fog by spreading the cooling through a deeper layer. Stronger winds disperse the fog or mix the air through a still deeper layer with stratus clouds forming at the top of the mixing layer.

Ground fog usually "burns off" rather rapidly after sunrise. Other radiation fog generally clears before noon unless clouds move in over the fog.

Advection fog

Advection fog forms when moist air moves over colder ground or water. It is most common along coastal areas but often develops deep in continental areas. At sea it is called *sea fog*. Advection fog deepens as wind speed increases up

Cirrus clouds (top) and cumulus (bottom).

to about 15 knots. Wind much stronger than 15 knots lifts the fog into a layer of low stratus or stratocumulus.

The west coast of the United States is quite vulnerable to advection fog. This fog frequently forms offshore as a result of cold water and then is carried inland by the wind. During the winter, advection fog over the central and eastern United States results when moist air from the Gulf of Mexico spreads northward over cold ground. The fog may extend as far north as the Great Lakes. Water areas in northern latitudes have frequent dense sea fog in summer as a result of warm, moist, tropical air flowing northward over colder Arctic waters.

Advection fog is usually more extensive and much more persistent than radiation fog. Advection fog can move in rapidly regardless of the time of day or night.

Upslope fog

Upslope fog forms as a result of moist, stable air being cooled adiabatically as it moves up sloping terrain. Once the upslope wind ceases, the fog dissipates. Unlike radiation fog, it can form under cloudy skies. Upslope fog is common along the eastern slopes of the Rockies and somewhat less frequent east of the Appalachians. Upslope fog often is quite dense and extends to high altitudes.

Precipitation-induced fog

When relatively warm rain or drizzle falls through cool air, evaporation from the precipitation saturates the cool air and forms fog. Precipitation-induced fog can become quite dense and continue for an extended period of time. This fog may extend over large areas, completely suspending air operations. It is most commonly associated with warm fronts, but can occur with slow moving cold fronts and with stationary fronts.

Ice fog

Ice fog occurs in cold weather when the temperature is much below freezing and water vapor sublimates directly as ice crystals. Conditions favorable for its formation are the same as for radiation fog except for cold temperature, usually -25°F (-31.7°C) or colder. It occurs mostly in the Arctic regions, but is not unknown in middle latitudes during the cold season.

Low stratus clouds

Stratus clouds, like fog, are composed of extremely small water droplets or ice crystals suspended in air. An observer on a mountain in a stratus layer would call it fog. Stratus and fog frequently exist together. In many cases there is no real line of distinction between the fog and stratus; rather, one gradually merges into the other. Stratus tends to be lowest during night and early morning, lifting or dissipating due to solar heating during the late morning or afternoon. Low stratus clouds often occur when moist air mixes with a colder air mass or in any situation where temperature-dew point spread is small.

Haze and smoke

Haze is a concentration of salt particles or other dry particles not readily classified as dust or other phenomenon. It occurs in stable air, is usually only a few thousand feet thick, but sometimes may extend as high as 15,000 feet (4,550 m). Haze layers often have definite tops above which horizontal visibility is good. However, downward visibility from above a haze layer is poor, especially on a slant. Visibility in haze varies greatly depending upon whether the observer is facing the sun.

Smoke concentrations form primarily in industrial areas when air is stable. It is most prevalent at night or early morning under a temperature inversion but it can persist throughout the day.

• AIR MASSES & FRONTS

Air masses

When a body of air comes to rest or moves slowly over an extensive area having fairly uniform properties of temperature and moisture, the air takes on those properties. Thus, the air over the area becomes somewhat of an entity and has fairly uniform horizontal distribution of its properties. The area over which the air mass acquires its identifying distribution of moisture and temperature is its *source region.*

Source regions are many and varied, but the best source regions for air masses are large snow or ice covered polar regions, cold northern oceans, tropical oceans, and large desert areas. Midlatitudes are poor source regions because transitional disturbances dominate these latitudes giving little opportunity for air masses to stagnate and take on the properties of the underlying region.

Air mass modification

Just as an air mass took on the properties of its source region, it tends to take on properties of the underlying surface when it moves away from its source region, thus becoming modified.

The degree of modification depends on the speed with which the air mass moves, the nature of the region over which it moves, and the temperature difference between the new surface and the air mass. Air masses are modified by warming from below, cooling from below, addition of water vapor, and subtraction of water vapor such that

1. Cool air moving over a warm surface is heated from below, generating instability and increasing the possibility of showers.
2. Warm air moving over a cool surface is cooled from below, increasing stability. If air is cooled to its dew point, stratus and/or fog forms.
3. Evaporation from water surfaces and failing precipitation adds water vapor to the air. When the water is warmer than the air, evaporation can raise the dew point sufficiently to saturate the air and form stratus or fog.
4. Water vapor is removed by condensation and precipitation.

Stability

Stability of an air mass determines its typical weather characteristics. When one type of air mass overlies another, conditions change with height. Characteristics typical of an unstable air mass are: cumuliform clouds, showery precipitation, rough air (turbulence), good visibility. Characteristics of stable air include: stratiform clouds and fog, continuous precipitation, smooth air, and fair to poor visibility in haze and smoke.

• FRONTS

As air masses move out of their source regions, they come in contact with other air masses of different properties. The zone between two different air masses is a frontal zone or front. Across this zone, temperature, humidity, and wind often change rapidly over short distances.

Discontinuities

When you pass through a front, the change from the properties of one air mass to those of the other is sometimes quite abrupt. Abrupt changes indicate a narrow frontal zone. At other times, the change of properties is very gradual indicating a broad and diffuse frontal zone.

Temperature—is one of the most easily recognized discontinuities across a front. At the surface, the passage of a front usually causes noticeable temperature change.

Dew Point—Dew point temperature is a measure of the amount of water vapor in the air. Temperature-dew point spread is a measure of the degree of saturation. Dew point and temperature-dew point spread usually differ across a front. The difference helps identify the front and may give a clue to differences of cloudiness and/or fog.

Wind—Wind always changes across a front. Wind discontinuity may be in direction, in speed, or in both.

Pressure—A front lies in a pressure trough, and pressure generally is higher in the cold air. Thus, when a front is crossed directly into colder air, pressure usually rises abruptly. When a front is approached toward warm air, pressure generally falls until the front is crossed, and then remains steady or falls slightly in the warm air. However, pressure patterns vary widely across fronts.

Types of fronts

The three principal types of fronts are the *cold front*, the *warm front*, and the *stationary front*.

Cold front

The leading edge of an advancing cold air mass is a cold front. At the surface, cold air is overtaking and replacing warmer air. Cold fronts move at about the speed of the wind component perpendicular to the front just above the frictional layer. A shallow cold air mass or a slow moving cold front may have a frontal slope more like a warm front.

Warm front

The edge of an advancing warm air mass is a warm front—warmer air is overtaking and replacing colder air. Since the cold air is denser than the warm air, the cold air hugs the ground. The warm air slides up and over the cold air and lacks direct push on the cold air. Thus, the cold air is slow to retreat in advance of the warm air. This slowness of the cold air to retreat produces a frontal slope that is more gradual than the cold frontal slope. Consequently, warm fronts on the surface are seldom as well marked as cold fronts, and they usually move about half as fast when the general wind flows is the same in each case.

Stationary front

When neither air mass is replacing the other, the front is stationary. The opposing forces exerted by adjacent air masses of different densities are such that the frontal surface between them shows little or no movement. In such cases, the surface winds tend to blow parallel to the frontal zone. Slope of a stationary front is normally shallow, although it may be steep depending on wind distribution and density difference.

Frontal waves and occlusion

Frontal waves and cyclones (areas of low pressure) usually form on slow-moving cold fronts or on stationary fronts. The life cycle and movement of a cyclone is dictated to a great extent by the upper wind flow.

In the initial condition of frontal wave development, the winds on both sides of the front are blowing parallel to the front. Small disturbances then may start a wavelike bend in the front.

If this tendency persists and the wave increases in size, a cyclonic (counterclockwise) circulation develops. One section of the front begins to move as a warm front, while the section next to it begins to move as a cold front. This deformation is a *frontal wave*.

The pressure at the peak of the frontal wave falls, and a low-pressure center forms. The cyclonic circulation becomes stronger, and the surface winds are now strong enough to move the fronts; the cold front moves faster than the warm front. When the cold front catches up with the warm front, the two of them occlude (close together). The result is an occluded front or, for brevity, an occlusion. This is the time of maximum intensity for the wave cyclone. Note that the symbol depicting the occlusion is a combination of the symbols for the warm and cold fronts.

As the occlusion continues to grow in length, the cyclonic circulation diminishes in intensity and the frontal movement slows down. Sometimes a new frontal wave begins to form on the long westward-trailing portion of the cold front, or a secondary low pressure system forms at the apex where the cold front and warm front come together to form the occlusion. In the final stage, the two fronts may have become a single stationary front again. The low center with its remnant of the occlusion is disappearing.

Non-frontal lows

Since fronts are boundaries between air masses of different properties, fronts are not associated with lows lying solely in a homogeneous air mass. Nonfrontal lows are infrequent east of the Rocky Mountains in midlatitudes but do not occur occasionally during the warmer months. Small nonfrontal lows over the western mountains are common as is the semistationary thermal low in extreme Southwestern United States. Tropical lows are also nonfrontal.

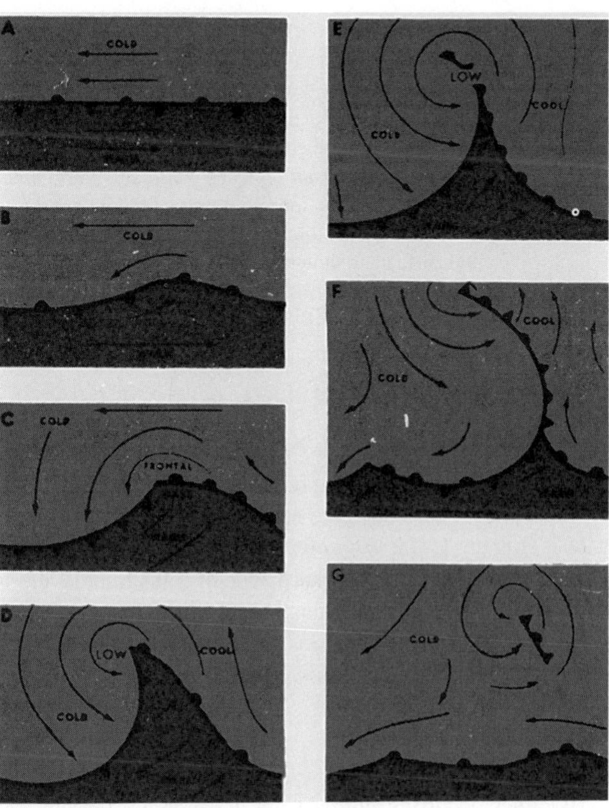

The life cycle of a frontal wave.

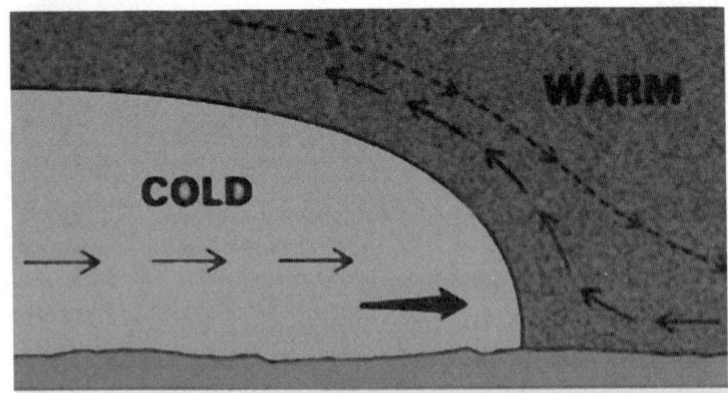

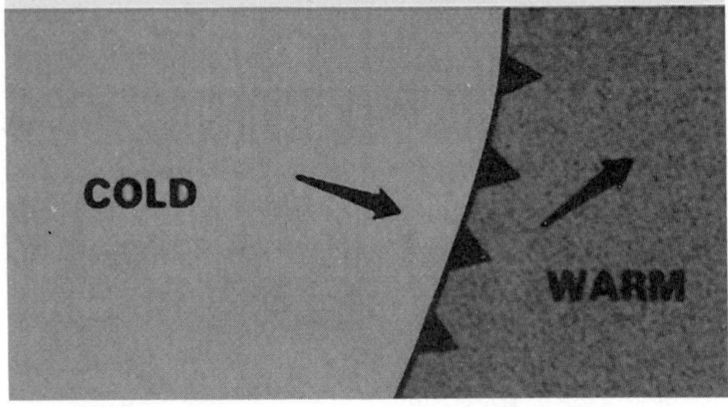

Cross section of a cold front (top) with the weather map symbol (bottom). The symbol is a line with the pointed barbs pointing in the direction of movement. If a map is in color, a blue line represents the cold front. The vertical scale is expanded in the top illustration to show the frontal slope. The frontal slope is steep near the leading edge as cold air replaces warm air. Warm air may descend over the front as indicated by the dashed arrows; but more often, the cold air forces warm air upward over the frontal surface as shown by the solid arrows.

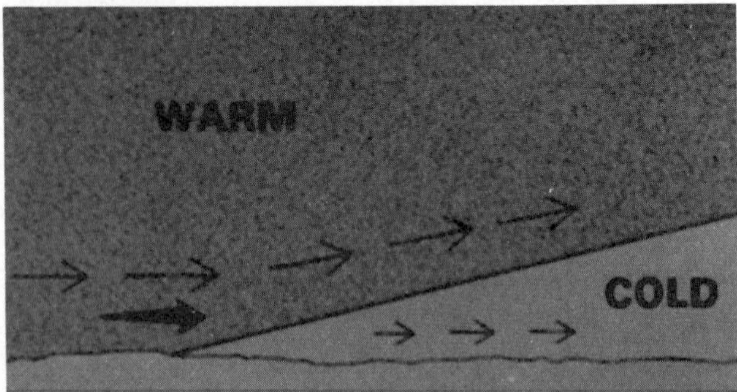

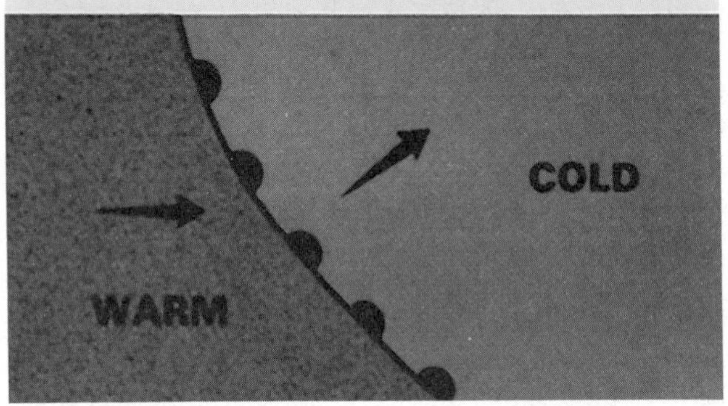

Cross section of a warm front (top) with the weather map symbol (bottom). The symbol is a line with the rounded barbs pointing in the direction of movement. If a map is in color, a red line represents the warm front. Slope of a warm front is generally more shallow than that of a cold front. Movement of a warm front shown by the heavy black arrow is slower than the wind in the warm air represented by the light solid arrows. The warm air gradually erodes the cold air.

Frontolysis

As adjacent air masses modify and as temperature and pressure differences equalize across a front, the front dissipates. This process is *frontolysis*, the generation of a front. It occurs when a relatively sharp zone of transition develops over an area between two air masses which have densities gradually becoming more and more in contrast with each other. The necessary wind flow pattern develops at the same time.

Frontal weather

Weather occurring with a front depends on: the amount of moisture available; the degree of stability of the air that is forced upward; the slope of the front; the speed of frontal movement; and the upper wind flow.

Sufficient moisture must be available for clouds to form,or there will be no clouds. As an inactive front comes into an area of moisture, clouds and precipitation may develop rapidly. A good example of this is a cold front moving eastward from the dry slopes of the Rocky Mountains into a tongue of moist air from the Gulf of Mexico over the Plains states. Thunderstorms may build rapidly.

The degree of stability of the lifted air determines whether cloudiness will be predominately stratiform or cumuliform. If the warm air overriding the front is stable, stratiform clouds develop. If the warm air is unstable, cumuliform clouds develop. Precipitation from stratiform clouds is usually steady and there is little or no turbulence. Precipitation from cumuliform clouds is of a shower type and the clouds are turbulent.

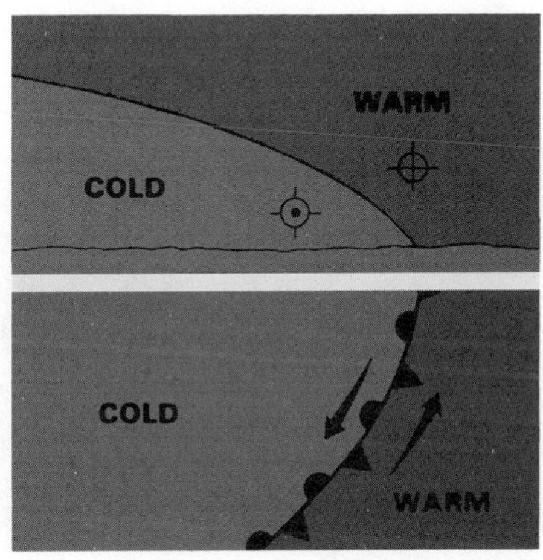

Cross section of a stationary front (top) and its weather symbol (bottom). The symbol is line with alternating pointed and rounded barbs on opposite sides of the line, the pointed barbs pointing away from the cold air and rounded barbs away from the warm air. If a map is in color, the symbol is a line of alternating red and blue segments. The front has little or no movement and winds are nearly parallel to the front. The symbol in the warm air is the tail of a wind arrow into the page. The symbol in the cold air is the point of a wind arrow out of the page. Slope of the front may vary considerably depending on wind and density differences across the front.

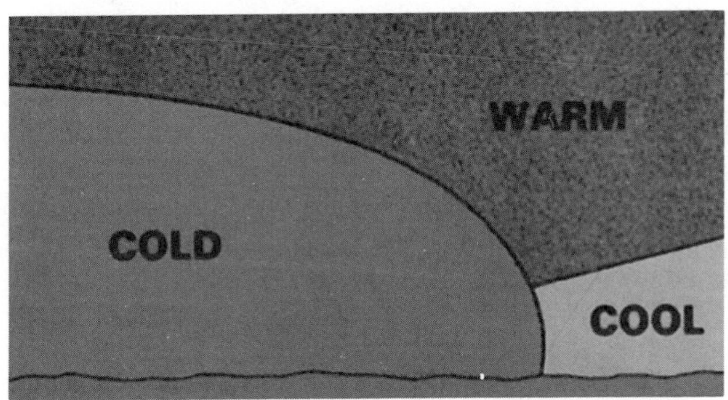

Cross section of a cold front occlusion. Its weather map symbol is the same as that for a warm front occlusion, the coldest air is under the cold front. When it overtakes the warm front, it lifts the warm front aloft; cold air replaces cool air at the surface.

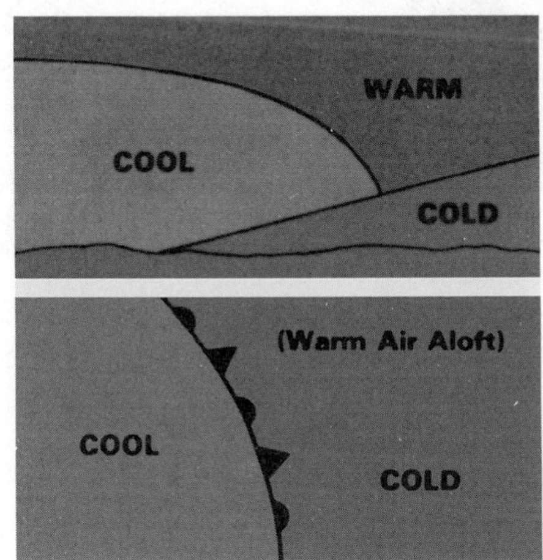

Cross section of a warm front occlusion (top) and its weather symbol (bottom). The symbol is a line with alternating pointed and rounded barbs on the same sid of the line pointing in the direction of movement. Shown in color on a weather map, the line is purple. In the warm front occlusion, air under the cold front is not as cold as air ahead of the warm front; and when the cold front overtakes the warm front, the less cold air rides over the colder air. In a warm front occlusion, cool air replaces cold air at the surface.

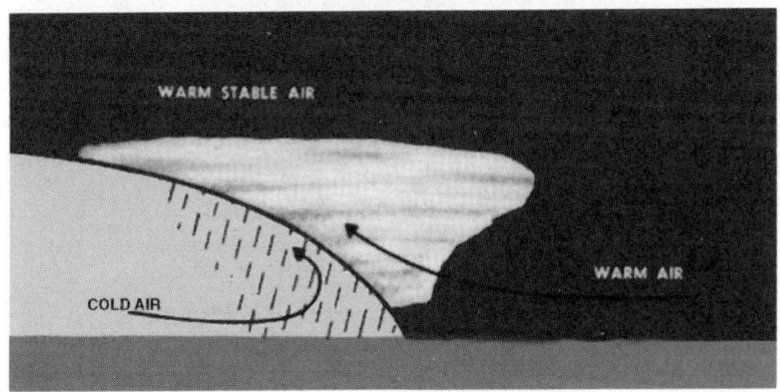

A cold front underrunning warm, moist, stable air. Clouds are stratified and precipitation continuous. Precipitation induces stratus in the cold air.

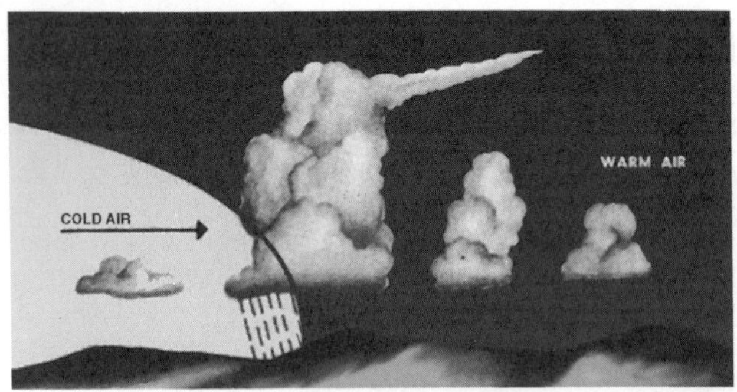

A cold front underrunning warm, moist, unstable air. Clouds cumuliform with possible showers or thunderstorms near the surface position of the front. Convective clouds often develop in the warm air ahead of the front. the warm, wet ground behind the front generates low-level convection and fair weather cumulus in the cold air.

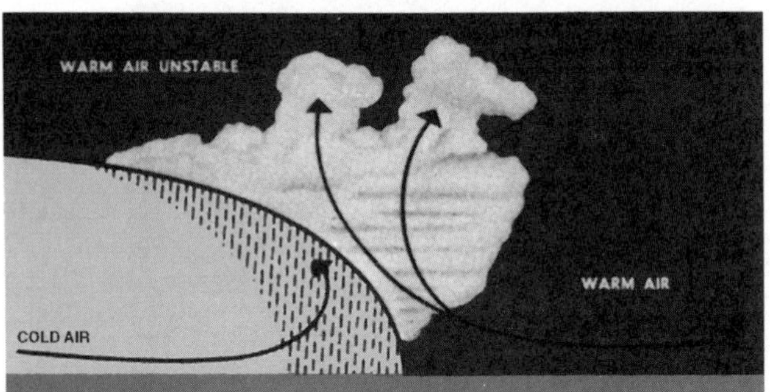

A slow-moving cold front underrunning warm, moist, unstable air. Clouds are stratified with embedded cumulonimbus and thunderstorms. This type of frontal weather is especially hazardous since the individual thunderstorms are hidden and cannot be avoided unless the aircraft is equipped with airborne radar.

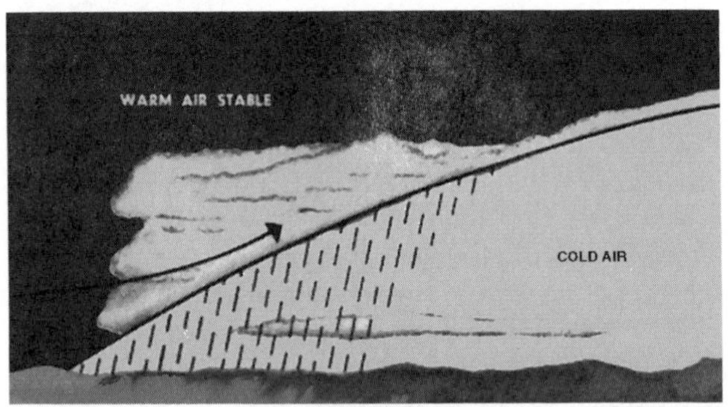

A warm front with overrunning moist, stable air. Clouds are stratiform and widespread over the shallow front. Precipitation is continuous and induces widespread stratus in the cold air.

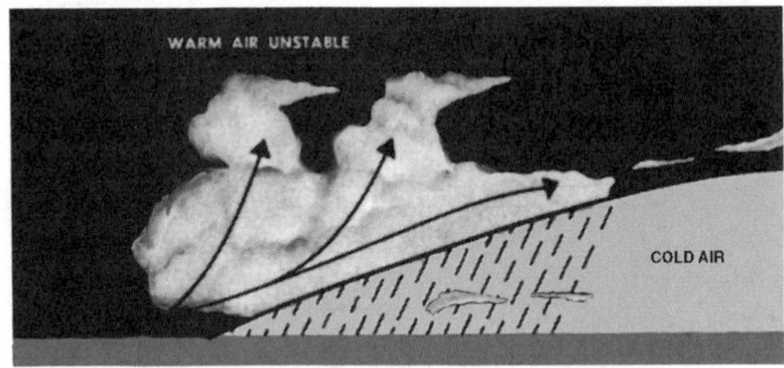

A warm front with overrunning warm, moist, unstable air.

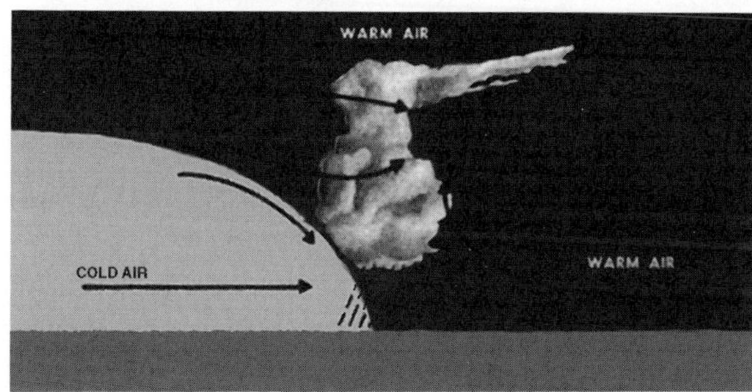

A fast moving cold front underrunning warm, moist, unstable air. Showers and thunderstorms develop along the surface position of the front.

Shallow frontal surfaces tend to give extensive cloudiness with large precipitation areas. Widespread precipitation associated with a gradual sloping front often causes low stratus and fog. In this case, the rain raises the humidity of the cold air to saturation. This and related effects may produce low ceiling and poor visibility over thousands of square miles. If temperature of the cold air near the surface is below freezing but the warmer air aloft is above freezing, precipitation falls as freezing rain or ice pellets; however, if temperature of the warmer air aloft is well below freezing, precipitation forms as snow.

When the warm air overriding a shallow front is moist and unstable, the usual widespread cloud mass forms; but embedded in the cloud mass are altocumulus, cumulus, and even thunderstorms. These embedded storms are more common with warm and stationary fronts but may occur with a slow-moving, shallow cold front.

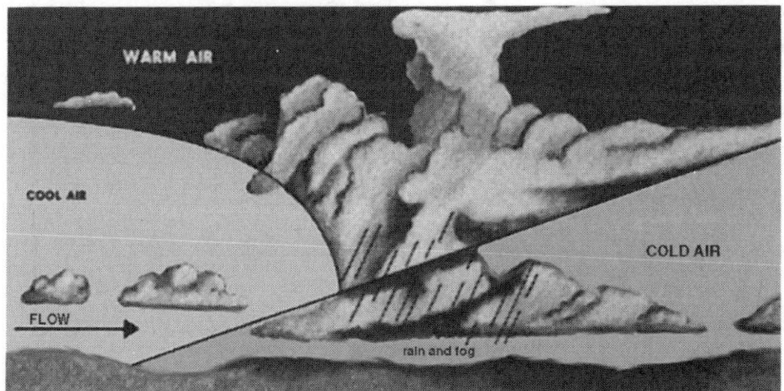

A warm front occlusion lifting warm, moist, unstable air. Note that the associated weather is complex and encompasses all types of weather associated with both the warm and cold fronts when air is moist and unstable.

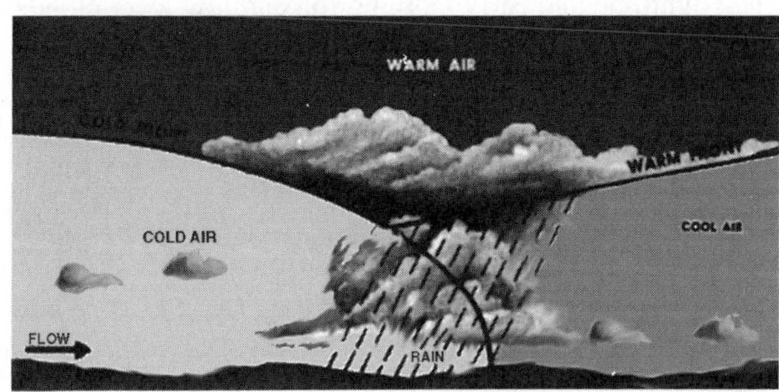

A cold front occlusion lifting warm, moist, stable air. Associated weather encompasses those associated with both warm and cold fronts when air is moist and stable.

A fast-moving, steep cold front forces upward motion of the warm air along its leading edge. If the warm air is moist, precipitation occurs immediately along the surface position of the front.

Since an occluded front develops when a cold front overtakes a warm front, weather with an occluded front is a combination of both warm and cold frontal weather.

A front may have little or no cloudiness associated with it. Dry fronts occur when the warm air aloft is flowing down the frontal slope or the air is so dry that any cloudiness that occurs is at high levels.

The upper wind flow dictates to a great extent the amount of cloudiness and rain accompanying a frontal system as well as movement of the front itself. Remember earlier it was said that systems tend to move with the upper winds. When winds aloft blow across a front,it tends to move with the wind. When winds aloft parallel a front, the front moves slowly if at all. A deep, slow-moving trough aloft forms extensive cloudiness and precipitation, while a rapid moving minor trough more often restricts weather to a rather narrow band. However,the latter often breeds severe, fast-moving, turbulent spring weather.

Instability line

An instability line is a narrow, nonfrontal line or band of convective activity. If the activity is fully developed thunderstorms, the line is a squall line. Instability lines form in moist unstable air. An instability line may develop far from any front. More often, it develops ahead of a cold front, and sometimes a series of these lines move out ahead of the front. A favored location for instability lines which frequently erupt into severe thunderstorms is a dew point front or dry line.

Dew point front or dry line

During a considerable part of the year, dew point fronts are common in western Texas and New Mexico northward over the Plains states. Moist air flowing north from the Gulf of Mexico abuts the dryer and therefore slightly denser air flowing from the southwest. Except for moisture differences, there is seldom any significant air mass contrast across this front; and therefore, it is commonly called a *dry line*. Nighttime and early morning fog and low-level clouds often prevail on the moist side of the line while generally clear skies mark the dry side. In spring and early summer over Texas, Oklahoma, and Kansas, and for some distance eastward, the dry line is a favored spawning area for squall lines and tornadoes.

• TURBULENCE

Convective currents

Convective currents are localized vertical air movements, both ascending and descending. For every rising current, there is a compensating downward current. The downward currents frequently occur over broader areas than do the upward currents, and therefore, they have a slower vertical speed than do the rising currents.

Convective currents are most active on warm summer afternoons when winds are light. Heated air at the surface creates a shallow, unstable layer, and the warm air is forced upward. Convection increases in strength and to greater heights as surface heating increases. Barren surfaces such as sandy or rocky wastelands and plowed fields become hotter than open water or ground covered by vegetation. Thus, air at and near the surface heats unevenly. Because of uneven heating, the strength of convective currents can vary considerably within short distances.

When cold air moves over a warm surface, it becomes unstable in lower levels. Convective currents extend several thousand feet above the surface resulting in rough, choppy turbulence. This condition often occurs in any season after the passage of a cold front.

• HIGH ALTITUDE WEATHER

The tropopause

The tropopause is a thin layer forming the boundary between the troposphere and stratosphere. Height of the tropopause varies from about 65,000 feet (19,716 m) over

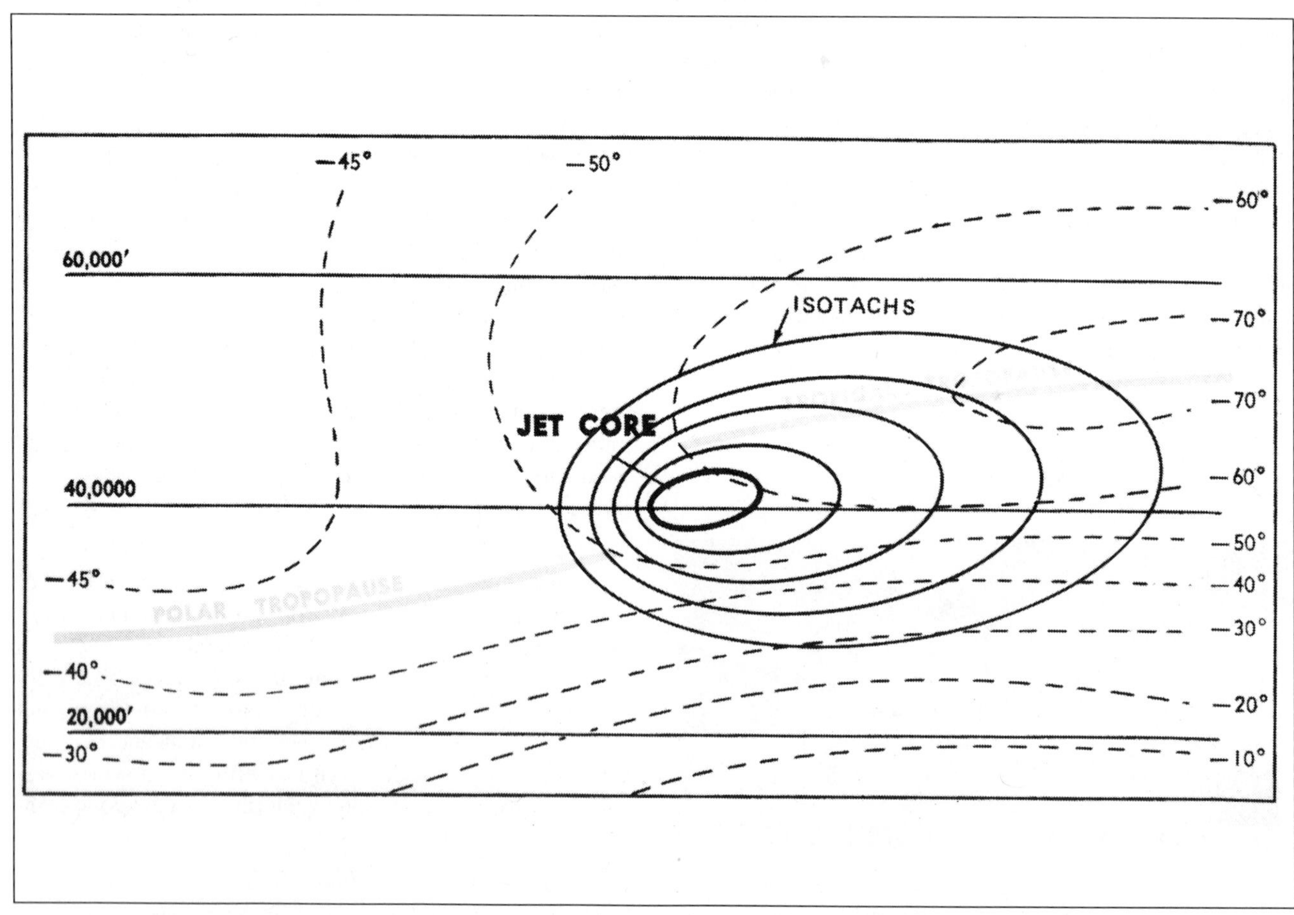

A cross section of the upper troposphere and lower stratosphere showing the tropopause and associated features. Note the "break" between the high tropical and the lower polar tropopause. Maximum winds occur in the vicinity of this break.

the Equator to 20,000 feet (6,066 m) or lower over the poles. The tropopause is not continuous but generally descends step-wise from the Equator to the poles. These steps occur as breaks.

An abrupt change in temperature lapse rate characterizes the tropopause.

Maximum winds generally occur at levels near the tropopause. These strong winds create narrow zones of wind shear which often generate hazardous turbulence for aircraft.

The jet stream

The jet stream is a narrow, shallow, meandering river of maximum winds extending around the globe in a wavelike pattern. A second jet stream is not uncommon, and three at one time are not unknown. A jet may be as far south as the northern Tropics. A jet in midlatitudes generally is stronger than one in or near the Tropics. The jet stream typically occurs in a break in the tropopause. Therefore, a jet stream occurs in an area of intensified temperature gradients characteristic of the break.

The concentrated winds, by arbitrary definition, must be 50 knots or greater to classify as a jet stream. The jet maximum is not constant; rather, it is broken into segments, shaped something like a boomerang.

Jet stream segments move with pressure ridges and troughs in the upper atmosphere. In general they travel faster than pressure systems, and maximum wind speed varies as the segments progress through the systems. In midlatitude, wind speed in the jet stream averages considerably stronger in winter than in summer. Also the jet shifts farther south in winter than in summer.

• CONDENSATION TRAILS

A condensation trail, popularly contracted to *contrail*, is generally defined as a cloud-like streamer which frequently is generated in the wake of aircraft flying in clear, cold, humid air. Two distinct types are observed-exhaust trails and aerodynamic trails.

Exhaust contrails

The exhaust contrail is formed by the addition to the atmosphere of sufficient water vapor from aircraft exhaust gases to cause saturation or super-saturation of the air. Since heat is also added to the atmosphere in the wake of an aircraft, the addition of water vapor must be of such magnitude that it saturates or supersaturates the atmosphere in spite of the added heat. There is evidence to support the idea that the nuclei which are necessary for condensation or sublimation may also be donated to the atmosphere in the exhaust gases of aircraft engines, further aiding contrail formation. These nuclei are relatively large. Recent experiments, however, have revealed that visible exhaust contrails may be prevented by adding very minute nuclei material (dust, for example) to the exhaust. Condensation and sublimation on these smaller nuclei result in contrail particles too small to be visible.

Aerodynamic contrails

In air that is almost saturated, aerodynamic pressure reduction around airfoils, engine nacelles, and propellers cools the air to saturation leaving condensation trails from these components. This type of trail usually is neither as dense nor as persistent as exhaust trails. However, under critical atmospheric conditions, an aerodynamic contrail may trigger the formation and spreading of a deck of cirrus clouds.

Air travels in a corkscrew path around the jet core with upward motion on the equatorial side. Therefore, when high level moisture is available, cirriform clouds form on the equatorial side of the jet. Jet stream cloudiness can form independently of well-defined pressure systems. Such cloudiness ranges primarily from scattered to broken coverage in shallow layers or streaks. Their sometimes fish hook and

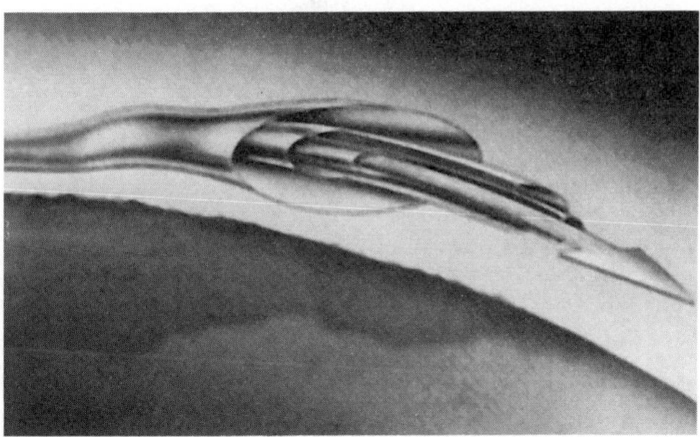

Artist's concept of the jet stream. Broad arrow shows direction of wind.

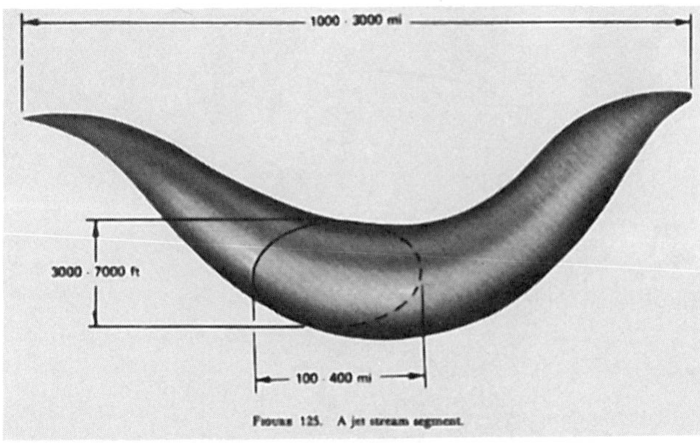

A jet stream segment.

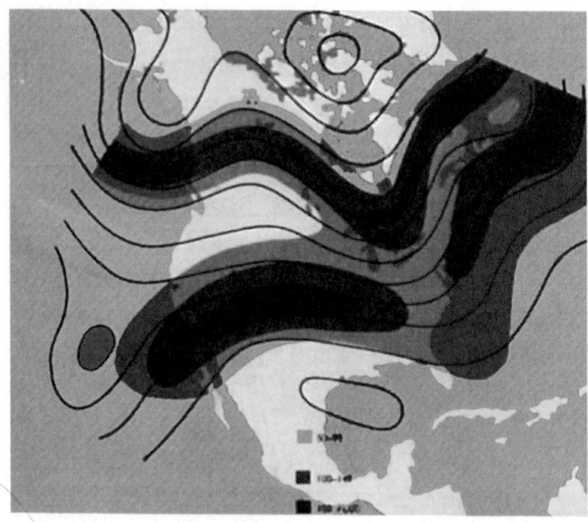

Multiple jet streams. Note the "segments" of maximum winds embedded in the general pattern. Turbulence usually is greatest on the polar sides of these maxima.

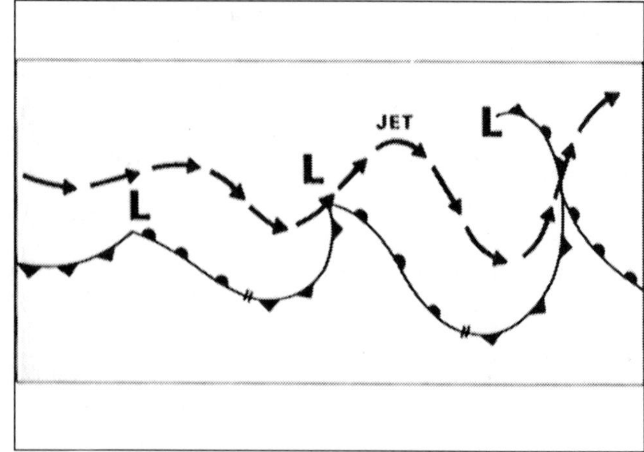

Mean jet positions relative to surface systems. Cyclogenesis (development) of the surface low usually is south of the jet as shown here. The deepening low moves nearer the jet. As it occludes, the low moves north of the jet; the jet then crosses the frontal system near the point of occlusion.

streamlined, wind-swept appearance always indicates very strong upper wind usually quite far from developing or intense weather systems.

The most dense cirriform clouds occur with well-defined systems. They appear in broad bands. Cloudiness is rather dense in an upper trough, thickens downstream, and becomes most dense at the crest of the downwind ridge. The clouds taper off after passing the ridge crest into the area of descending air. The poleward boundary of the cirrus band often is quite abrupt and frequently casts a shadow on lower clouds, especially in an occluded frontal system.

The upper limit of dense, banded cirrus is near the tropopause; a band may be either a single layer of multiple layers 10,000-12,000 feet (3,033-3,640 m) thick. Dense, jet stream cirriform cloudiness is most prevalent along midlatitude and polar jets. However, a cirrus band usually forms along the subtropical jet in winter when a deep upper trough plunges southward into the Tropics.

An important aspect of the jet stream cirrus shield is its association with turbulence. Extensive cirrus cloudiness often occurs with deepening surface and upper lows and these deepening systems produce the greatest turbulence.

Weather Information & Communications

• NATIONAL WEATHER SERVICE

The National Weather Service continues full-scale redevelopment of its systems and its organization.

Applied research conducted over the last ten years in the National Oceanic and Atmospheric Administration's (NOAA) Environmental Research Laboratories and other federal laboratories has demonstrated that state-of-the-art laboratory techniques for analyzing and predicting severe weather and flood phenomena can be practicably applied to Weather Service operations. Because the scientific understanding of the atmosphere and the ability to forecast large- and small-scale weather phenomena has increased dramatically over the last two decades, the Department of Commerce has set an ambitious goal for the National Oceanic and Atmospheric Administration's agency, the National Weather Service (NWS). The Service is to be modernized, to take full advantage of hundreds of new technological tools for upgrading weather forecasting.

In 1988, Public law 100-685 was signed by the President which, in part, specifies conditions on the planning, reporting and accomplishment of the modernization and associated restructuring of the NWS. This strategic plan is the first response to the Congress required by Public law 100-685.

Principles for the modernization and associated restructuring

Throughout the process of change, the NWS will continue to fulfill its mission which is to provide weather and flood warnings, public forecasts and advisories for all of the United States, its territories, adjacent waters and oceans, primarily for the protection of life and property. NWS data and products will continue to be provided to private meteorologists for the provision of all specialized services. Certain principles are essential to meet the operational mission and will be continued during the modernization and associated restructuring transition period.

The need to implement new science and technology

The most deadly of our nation's weather events—tornadoes, severe thunderstorms, and flash floods—are also the most difficult to detect and forecast. The new systems to be installed will enable earlier detection and permit the short range prediction of destructive, violent local storms and floods. The new observational technologies planned for the next decade will provide unprecedented amounts of complex data, thereby requiring that the operational forecasters have higher levels of analytical and interpretive skills. This will require training personnel and the deployment of proven, new observational information processing, and communications technologies.

New equipment, new methods

At present, the vintage technologies that compose part of today's weather service infrastructure are in desperate need of being replaced. As the equipment has aged, it has become costly to maintain. By replacing the equipment with more reliable technologies that support the new scientific capabilities, the nation can move into the future with strengthened confidence in its atmospheric prediction capabilities.

New technological systems are essential in providing the opportunity to improve warning and forecast services and for replacing obsolete and increasingly unreliable existing systems. Each of the new technologies to be installed plays a unique, but complementary role in the modernization process. New observational technologies will yield high resolution, time variant, three-dimensional representations of details on the state of the atmosphere.

At Weather Forecast Offices new data-processing systems will aid the forecaster in the assimilation of changing data and numerical weather prediction outputs. The meteorologist and hydrologist will be able to rapidly manipulate, display, and analyze information, thus enabling them to combine scientific principles and operational experience to produce more accurate and timely warning and forecast services for the nation. The new high-resolution data sets and derived information are an important input to business and economic decision making outside the NWS.

The NWS is joined in its acquisition of much of the major new technologies by the Department of Transportation's Federal Aviation Administration and the Department of Defense, which results in economies of scale and a reduction in purchase costs. Recently purchased geostationary meteorological satellites, newer radars and automated surface observing systems provide data that is shared by each participating agency.

Automated Surface Observing System (ASOS)

Automated Surface Observing System (ASOS) automating surface observations will relieve staff personnel from the time-consuming duty of collecting surface observations manually. These hundreds of ASOS systems nationwide will serve as the primary surface weather-observing network, significantly expanding the information available to forecasters and the aviation community. The system works non-stop, updating observations every minute, everyday.

Getting up-to-the-minute data to forecasters is crucial. This type of information will increase the accuracy and timeliness of forecasts and warnings. This same data will also address and alleviate the safety concerns of the aviation community.

Next Generation Weather Radars (NEXRAD stations)

This is a large step forward in early warnings of tornado and severe thunderstorms. Utilizing Doppler radar technology, the NEXRAD system will observe the presence and calculate the speed and direction of motion of severe weather elements. NEXRAD will also provide quantitative area precipitation measurements so important in hydrologic forecasting of potential flooding. For example, at present, currently limited (obsolescent) radar systems, tornado warnings are usually issued only when visual sightings have been reported. The advent of NEXRAD will not only allow for an earlier detection of the precursors to tornadic activity, but will also provide data on the direction and speed of tornado cells once they form. The national network of NEXRAD systems, when totally deployed, will sharply upgrade uniform coverage way beyond the capability of present day radar network. The NWS will operate the majority of NEXRAD systems; the remainder will be at FAA and Department of Defense locations.

Upgrading satellites

For severe weather and flood warnings and short range forecasts, cloud imagery and atmospheric sounding data from the geostationary meteorological satellites will continue to be a major data source. The new Geostationary Operational Environmental Satellite (GOES) I-M system include separate instrumentation that allows simultaneous image and sounding data to be observed and transmitted to ground stations. The GOES I-M system also provides visible and infrared imagery data updates as frequently as every six minutes during severe weather warning situations over selected areas of the United States.

For longer-range forecasting, soundings from the polar orbiting satellites are a primary data input into the National Meteorological Center numerical forecast models.

National Center advanced computer systems

Warnings and forecasts prepared by NWS offices rely heavily on the basic analyses and advisories provided by the National Meteorological Center (NMC), especially for periods of 36 hours and beyond. These analyses and guidance products result from numerical models of the atmosphere run on high-speed computers. These increased demands require the acquisition of dedicated next generation Class VII computer capabilities with a processing capability that is a full order of magnitude greater than the present Class VI computer.

Advanced Weather Interactive Processing System (AWIPS)

The revised system employed by AWIPS will function as the nerve center of the National Meteorological Centers operations. AWIPS will be the data integrator receiving the high-resolution data from the observation systems, the centrally collected data and the centrally prepared analysis and guidance information developed by the National Meteorological Center. The integration of all of this data from multiple sources represents the information base from which all warning and forecast products will be prepared. The AWIPS system will provide fast-response interactive analysis and display of the data to help support the meteorologists as they make rapid decisions, prepare warnings and forecasts, and disseminate information to users.

AWIPS includes the communications network that interconnects each Weather Forecast Office for exchange of locally generated data. NOAAPORT will provide communications support for the operational distribution of the centrally collected data and centrally produced analysis and guidance products, as well as the satellite imagery and sounding data processed by the National Environmental Satellite, Data and Information Service.

The continued restructuring involves changing the number and location of field offices, a gradual transformation of the workforce to emphasize more professionalism in its makeup, and a reallocation of operational responsibilities between field offices and the National Centers.

The need to restructure is twofold: first, the combination of new operational concepts, new data sets, and an evolving scientific understanding of the dynamic processes associated with the most dangerous weather phenomena requires an increase in the number of meteorologists. The percentage increase of meteorologists in the NWS workforce will improve warnings and forecasts by taking advantage of the capabilities of the new technologies. Second, productivity and efficiency gains will occur as a result of increased integration of the new technological observation, information processing and communication systems with the staff. Key tradeoffs in the restructuring process exist between human capabilities, costs, and programmatic, scientific, and technological opportunities.

The Weather Forecast Office (WFO)

How does the new Weather Forecast Office fit into the scheme? Consider this analogy: think of the surface of a map of the United States...now, consider a uniform arrangement of 115 mutually adjacent cylinders, each with a radius

NEXRAD STATUS
AS OF 4/14/95
LEGEND
(·) NEXRAD TO BE COMMISSIONED 4/13-7/31
★ COMMISSIONED NEXRAD
■ INSTALLED NEXRAD
GUAM

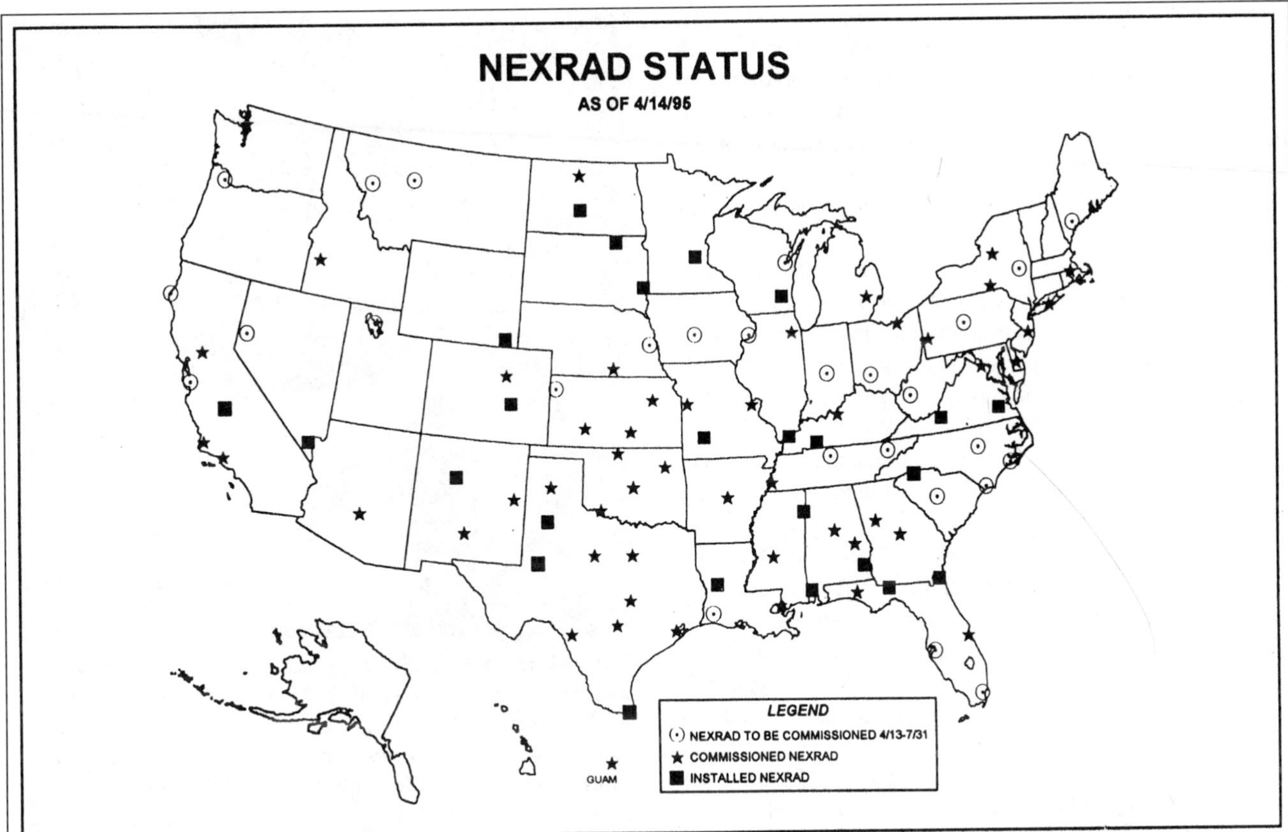

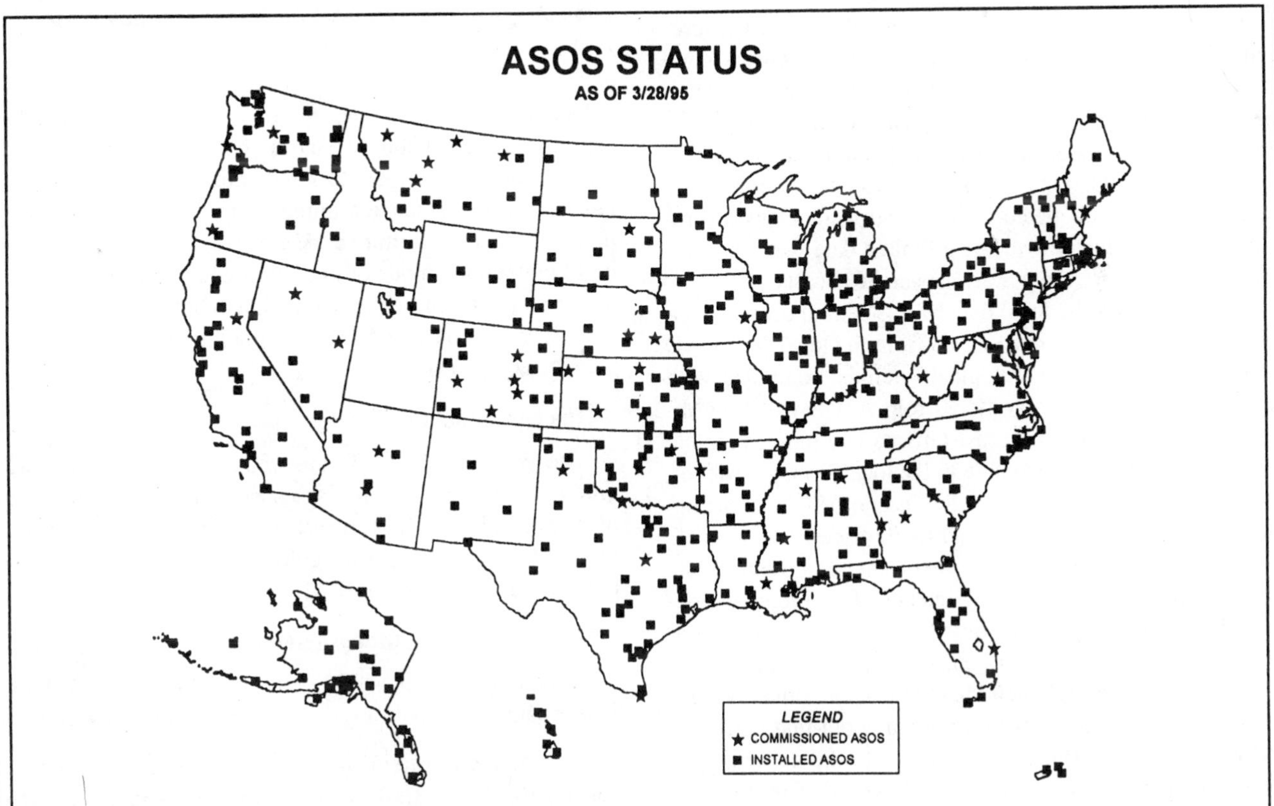

ASOS STATUS
AS OF 3/28/95
LEGEND
★ COMMISSIONED ASOS
■ INSTALLED ASOS

of approximately 125 miles (201.25 km). The cylinders, would each extend upward from Earth's surface up through inside each cylinder represents the "area" of operational responsibility associated with the WFO. A WFO is located in the center of the base of the cylinder. Each section of the country and the coastal ocean area is contained in one of these cylinders, thus the whole of the country is uniformly covered.

The GOES Satellite positioned over the United States is providing to each of these cylinders an Earth image. The regularly updated image represents uniform coverage with visible and infrared imagery of each of the "cylinders." It also provides remote soundings which penetrate each cylinder from above. Associated with each WFO is one or more NEXRAD radars which scan the atmosphere from near Earth's surface to a height sufficient to detect the majority of meteorological events.

Also serving the WFOs are 1,000 ASOS units. They are spread across the surface of the country and each measures surface weather parameters as fast as once every minute, All of these data within the cylinder are sent directly to the AWIPS system in each WFO. The WFO's AWIPS system is also receiving the centrally produced guidance products from the National Centers, generated from globally exchanged data. Subsets of these data are on tap for all other WFOs through the AWIPS communication network.

Integrated operations within the WFO

The future operations will allow forecasters to comprehensively address the air-sea environment in their assigned area. The observation and analysis of current and expected weather conditions can be quickly and reliably completed, critical decisions made, and translated into immediate warnings and forecasts. This is contrasted to current operations where a number of meteorologists and technicians are required to individually evaluate a limited data base and separately derive the various warnings and forecasts.

The concept of the local data base is central to future operations. The high volume of data from the local NEXRAD and geostationary meteorological satellites combined with the high frequency observations from ASOS will flow directly to the Weather Forecast Office. The most complete data sets will only be available to the local WFO. However, summarized data from all NEXRADs and ASOSs in the nation will be made available to all field offices.

The new observing systems are designed to provide data sets which can be immediately integrated into three dimensional depictions of the rapidly changing state of the environment. Each system will contribute a critical part, combining with and complementing data from all other systems to form a complete set of information about that particular cylinder of space from Earth's surface to the upper atmosphere comprising the particular WFO's area of responsibility.

AWIPS work stations will allow the forecaster to quickly update, quality control, and analyze current processes and events detailed within the area of concern. New dedicated supercomputer capabilities and high resolution models running at the National Centers will provide a stream of detailed, frequently updated guidance to forecasters, assisting in the prediction of future conditions. This represents a new, highly integrated mode of operation which greatly increases the productivity of personnel, and also holds the promise of increased accuracy and greater timeliness of forecast services for the nation.

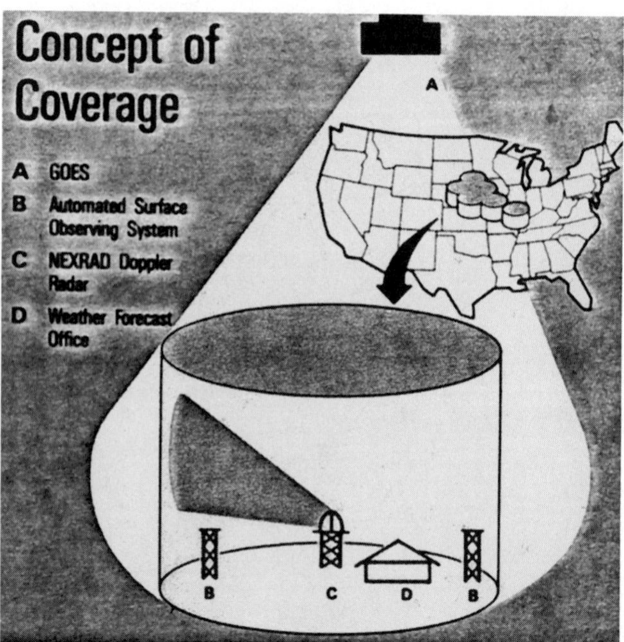

The above schematic suggests how the individual weather forecast offices (WFO) will bear observation and forecast responsibility for an area which has a radius of 125 miles, and reaches to the top of the atmosphere, verically. Each office's "cylinder" of responsibility will abut cylinders around it so that 115 of these cylinders can cover the nation. Many formerly manual operations have been handed to automated gear.

The new structure

The WFO will be the future weather office that will provide all warning and forecast services for its assigned area of responsibility. The forecast and warnings operations at the WFO are supported by guidance products issued from the National Centers and RFC.

Weather Forecast Offices (WFOs)

A total of 115 WFOs will exist in the future that will provide weather and hydrologic services in four major areas:

1. watches and warnings for the general public for severe local storms, floods, flash floods and winter storms, local and zone public forecasts, and fire weather forecasts;
2. local aviation watches and warnings, terminal forecasts, and domestic aviation enroute forecasts;

3. marine warnings and forecasts for coastal areas of the nation and the Great Lakes; and
4. hydrologic services which identify flash flood-prone areas and the development of community supported surveillance systems.

The foundation for the more accurate and timely warnings and forecasts will be the guidance products from the National Centers and RFCs and the data from the new observing systems: ASOS, NEXRAD, and geostationary meteorological satellites.

The basic tool for more accurate and timely warnings and forecasts from the WFO is AWIPS. It will assemble, process and display the observational data and guidance from National Centers. AWIPS will help meteorologists with the warning and forecast decision process through an interactive work station. It will pre-format warning and forecast products and disseminate these products to the users in a timely manner.

River Forecast Center (RFC)

RFCs provide hydrologic forecasts and guidance information in three major categories:

1. mainstem river and flood forecasts regarding about 3,000 locations;
2. flash flood and headwater guidance to WFOs for warning services;
3. long-term, seasonal forecasts providing estimates of snowmelt and water supply outlooks (from excess to drought) at approximately 1,000 locations for periods up to several months in advance.

In the 1990s, the operations of RFCs are expected to change in a several ways. Each of the 13 RFCs will be colocated with a WFO. This will result in a more effective utilization of hydrological and meteorological information facilitated by a Hydrologic Analysis and Support Group in each collocated facility.

National Meteorological Center

The National Meteorological Center has the responsibility for national and international data collection. This data base is first employed for global atmospheric and oceanic analysis. The resultant analyses are distributed to international and domestic users which include the NWS, other government agencies, and private sector meteorologists. The data base is then used as initial input to global atmospheric numerical models. These models produce international aviation forecast products, high seas forecast products, long range national forecast, and forecast guidance for local WFOs and RFCs. New dedicated Class VII computer capabilities will enable increases in the resolution of the models resulting in improved forecast products and guidance. Traditionally the long range national forecasts have begun at three days and beyond. The new computers will reduce this threshold to beyond 36 hours. This will allow local forecasters to devote their attention to short-term weather events that are not aided by the use of centralized computer models.

Climate Analysis Center

This center is a specialized facility which is part of the National Meteorological Center and is colocated with it to take advantage of the facilities available there. The Center's responsibilities are national and international in scope, collecting, organizing, and disseminating climate information for diagnosis of short-term climate change; the Center does research on the physical cause of short-term climate change; and issues forecasts of departures of average weather conditions from climatological means.

National Hurricane Center

This special facility will continue to be responsible for providing the nation its strongest measure of security from tropical storms. It functions by analyzing, predicting, and tracking tropical weather systems, that often become hurricanes. The Center provides leadership and coordination of storm related preparedness. It uses geostationary meteorological satellites to track and monitor tropical storms 24 hours-per-day throughout the cycle of a storm. It will utilize coastal NEXRADs radar systems which are becoming available to provide hurricane understanding well beyond that available at present. NMC's new Class VII computers will run new hurricane models which to greatly assist forecasters at the Hurricane Center. AWIPS at the National Hurricane Center will serve the Center's mission as well as NMC's.

National Severe Storms Forecast Center

In the 1990s, the National Severe Storms Forecast Center will provide national severe weather guidance to WFOs and RFCs. It will issue more timely and specific advisories necessary to support the severe weather and flood warning activities of the WFOs.

National Data Buoy Center

The National Data Buoy Center will continue the operation of deep sea, coastal buoys, and headland systems. Data from the buoys and these coastal systems are essential to marine warnings and forecasts, and numerical weather predictions.

Staffing

The new observing, data processing, and display systems will provide forecasters the opportunity to sample, observe, and analyze the environment to an extent never before possible. This will mean a better product, more efficiently produced. Future field offices will have a core staff of professional scientists at each WFO and RFC to take advantage of these new capabilities. These individuals will provide all warning and forecast services across their area of responsibility. They will have far better data with which to meet these tasks, owing to the systems described.

Taking a quantum leap such as this—improving product while using fewer people—will place great emphasis on a higher level of professional skills and on retraining many technicians. NWS has strategic as well as tactical programs to effect the implied transmutation.

For instance, each WFO will operate 24 hours a day, and a certified meteorologist will be in charge at all times. Other such staffing upgrades will occur. The staffing level will be determined by peak service demands and maximum weather activity, with reduced staff requirements at selected offices during hours of lower threat and service demands.

• NOAA WEATHER RADIO

The National Oceanic and Atmospheric Administration (NOAA) of the United States Department of Commerce provides the service known as *Weather Radio.* This service provides continuous broadcasts of the latest weather information directly from National Weather Service offices. Taped weather messages are repeated every four to six minutes and are routinely revised every one to three hours, or more frequently if needed. Most of the stations operate 24 hours daily.

The broadcasts are tailored to weather information needs of people within the receiving area. For example, stations along the sea coasts and Great Lakes provide specialized weather information for boaters, fishers, and others engaged in marine activities, as well as general weather information.

During severe weather, National Weather Service forecasters can interrupt the routine weather broadcasts and substitute special warning messages. The forecasters can also activate specially designed warning receivers. Such receivers either sound an alarm indicating that an emergency exists, alerting the listener to turn the receiver up to an audible volume; or, when operated in a muted mode, are automatically turned on so that the warning message is heard. "Warning alarm" receivers are especially valuable for schools, hospitals, public-safety agencies, and news media offices.

Under a January, 1975, White House policy statement, NOAA Weather Radio was designated the sole Government-operated radio system to provide direct warnings into private homes for both natural disasters and nuclear attack. This capability is to supplement warnings by sirens and by commercial radio and television.

NOAA Weather Radio broadcasts are made on one of seven high-band FM frequencies as shown on the accompanying chart. The 162.475 MHz frequency is used only in special cases where required to avoid channel interference. These frequencies are not found on the average home radio now in use. However, a number of radios manufacturers offer special weather radios to operate on these frequencies, with or without the emergency warning alarm. Also there are now many radios on the market which offer standard AM/FM frequencies plus the so-called "weather band" as an added feature.

NOAA Weather Radio broadcasts can usually be heard as far as 40 miles (64.4 km) from the antenna site, sometimes more. The effective range depends on many factors, particularly the height of the broadcasting antenna, terrain, quality of the receiver and type of receiving antenna. As a general rule, listeners close to or perhaps beyond the 40-mile (64.4 km) range should have a good quality receiver system if they expect reliable reception.

For more information on NOAA Weather Radio, please contact: National Oceanic and Atmospheric Administration, Silver Spring, Maryland 20910.

Marine weather

Few people are affected more by weather than the mariner. An unexpected change in winds, seas, or visibility can reduce the efficiency of marine operations and threaten the very safety of a vessel and its crew. The National Weather Service (NWS) provides marine warnings and forecasts to serve all who sail for livelihood or recreation.

Aviation weather

The NWS, in cooperation with NOAA, also provides pilots with numerous weather briefings to prepare them for, or assist them with, their flights.

Meteorological and aeronautical information is provided by continuous recorded Transcribed Weather Broadcasts (TWEB), the Pilot's Automatic Telephone Weather Answering Service (PATWAS), and the Telephone Information Briefing Service (TIBS). Complete weather information is available by telephone call or by visit to the nearest Federal Aviation Administration (FAA) Flight Service Station (FSS) or designated NOAA Weather Service Office. Information is also available from private commercial vendors. During periods of marginal weather, briefers are busy and telephone delays may occur. That being the case, pilots may get necessary information from TWEB, PATWAS, or TIBS, but it is recommended pilots wait to hear a briefer's information personally. The latest hourly aviation weather observation from distant stations are normally available by five minutes past each hour.

Marine Advisories and Warnings

These advisories and warnings are "headlined" in marine forecasts. Small Craft Advisories can be issued up to 12 hours and warnings up to 24 hours prior to onset of adverse conditions.

1. **Small Craft Advisory:** Forecast winds of 18-33 knots. Small Craft Advisories may also be issued for hazardous sea conditions or lower wind speeds that may affect small craft operations.
2. **Gale Warning:** Forecast winds of 34-47 knots.
3. **Storm Warning:** Forecast winds of 48 knots or greater.
4. **Tropical Storm Warning:** Forecast winds of 34-63 knots associated with a tropical storm.
5. **Hurricane Warning:** Forecast winds of 64 knots or higher associated with a hurricane.

NOAA WEATHER RADIO NETWORK

Legend—Frequencies are identified as follows:
(1)—162.550 MHz
(2)—162.400 MHz
(3)—162.475 MHz
(4)—162.425 MHz
(5)—162.450 MHz
(6)—162.500 MHz
(7)—162.525 MHz

Revised August 1983

Location	Frequency
Alabama	
Anniston	3
Birmingham	1
*Columbia	4
Demopolis	3
Dozier	1
Florence	3
Huntsville	2
Louisville	3
Mobile	1
Montgomery	2
Tuscaloosa	2
Alaska	
Anchorage	1
Cordova	1
Fairbanks	1
Homer	2
Juneau	1
Ketchikan	1
Kodiak	1
Nome	1
Petersburg	1
Seward	1
Sitka	2
Valdez	1
Wrangell	2
Yakutat	1
Arizona	
Flagstaff	2
Phoenix	1
Tucson	2
Yuma	1
Arkansas	
Fayetteville	3
Fort Smith	2
Gurdon	3
Jonesboro	1
Little Rock	1
Mountain View	2
Star City	2
Texarkana	1
California	
Bakersfield (P)	1
Coachella (P)	2
Eureka	2
Fresno	2
Los Angeles	1
Merced	1
Monterey	2
Point Arena	2
Redding (P)	1
Sacramento	2
San Diego	2
San Francisco	1
San Luis Obispo	1
Santa Barbara	2
Colorado	
Alamosa (P)	3
Colorado Springs	3
Denver	1
Grand Junction	1
Greeley	2
Longmont	1
Pueblo	2
Sterling	2
Connecticut	
Hartford	3
Meriden	2
New London	1
Delaware	
Lewes	1
District of Columbia	
Washington, D.C.	1
Florida	
*Clewiston	2
Daytona Beach	2
Fort Myers	3
Gainesville	3
Jacksonville	1
Key West	2
Melbourne	1
Miami	1
Orlando	3
Panama City	1
Pensacola	2
Tallahassee	2
Tampa	1
West Palm Beach	3
Georgia	
Athens	2
Atlanta	1
Augusta	1
*Baxley	7
Chatsworth	2
Columbus	2
Macon	3
Pelham	1

Location	Frequency
Savannah	2
*Valdosta	6
Waycross	3
Hawaii	
Hilo	1
Honolulu	1
Kokee	2
Mt. Haleakala	2
Waimanalo (R)	2
Idaho	
Boise	1
Lewiston (P)	1
Pocatello	1
Twin Falls	2
Illinois	
Champaign	1
Chicago	1
Marion	4
Moline	1
Peoria	3
Rockford	3
Springfield	2
Indiana	
*Bloomington	5
Evansville	1
Fort Wayne	1
Indianapolis	1
Lafayette	3
South Bend	2
Terre Haute	2
Iowa	
Cedar Rapids	3
Des Moines	1
Dubuque (P)	2
Sioux City	3
Waterloo	1
Kansas	
Chanute	2
Colby	3
Concordia	1
Dodge City	3
Ellsworth	2
Topeka	3
Wichita	1
Kentucky	
Ashland	1
Bowling Green	2
Covington	1
Elizabethtown (R)	2
Hazard	3
Lexington	2
Louisville	3
Mayfield	3
Pikeville (R)	2
Somerset	1
Louisiana	
Alexandria	3
Baton Rouge	2
Buras	3
Lafayette	1
Lake Charles	2
Monroe	1
Morgan City	3
New Orleans	1
Shreveport	2
Maine	
*Caribou	7
*Dresden	3
Ellsworth	2
Portland	1
Maryland	
Baltimore	2
Hagerstown	3
Salisbury	3
Massachusetts	
Boston	3
Hyannis	1
Worcester	1

Location	Frequency
Michigan	
Alpena	1
Detroit	1
Flint	2
Grand Rapids	1
Houghton	2
Marquette	1
Onondaga	2
Sault Sainte Marie	1
Traverse City	2
Minnesota	
Detroit Lakes	3
Duluth	1
International Falls	1
Mankato	2
Minneapolis	1
Rochester	3
Saint Cloud (P)	3
Thief River Falls	1
Willmar (P)	2
Mississippi	
Ackerman	3
Booneville	1
Bude	1
Columbia (R)	2
Gulfport	2
Hattiesburg	3
Inverness	1
Jackson	2
Meridian	1
Oxford	2
Missouri	
Columbia	2
Camdenton	1
Hannibal	3
Hermitage	5
Joplin/Carthage	1
Kansas City	1
St. Joseph	2
St. Louis	1
Sikeston	2
Springfield	2
Montana	
Billings	1
Butte	1
Glasgow	1
Great Falls	1
Havre (P)	2
Helena	2
Kalispell	1
Miles City	2
Missoula	2
Nebraska	
Bassett	3
Grand Island	2
Holdrege	3
Lincoln	3
Merriman	2
Norfolk	1
North Platte	1
Omaha	2
Scottsbluff	1
Nevada	
Elko	1
Ely	2
Las Vegas	1
Reno	1
Winnemucca	2
New Hampshire	
Concord	2
New Jersey	
Atlantic City	2
New Mexico	
Albuquerque	2
Clovis	3
Des Moines	1
Farmington	3
Hobbs	2
Las Cruces	2
Ruidoso	1
Santa Fe	1
New York	
Albany	1
Binghamton	3
Buffalo	1
Elmira	1
Kingston	3
New York City	1
*Riverhead	3

Location	Frequency
Rochester	2
Syracuse	1
North Carolina	
Asheville	2
Cape Hatteras	3
Charlotte	3
Fayetteville	3
New Bern	2
Raleigh/Durham	1
Rocky Mount	3
Wilmington	1
Winston-Salem	2
North Dakota	
Bismarck	2
Dickinson	2
Fargo	2
Jamestown	2
Minot	2
Petersburg	2
Williston	2
Ohio	
Akron	2
Caldwell	3
Cleveland	1
Columbus	1
Dayton	3
Lima	2
*Moscow	4
Sandusky	2
Toledo	1
Oklahoma	
Clinton	3
Enid	3
Lawton	1
McAlester	3
Oklahoma City	2
Tulsa	1
Oregon	
Astoria	2
Brookings	1
Coos Bay	2
Eugene	2
Klamath Falls	1
Medford	2
Newport	1
Pendleton	2
Portland	1
Roseburg	3
Salem	3
Pennsylvania	
Allentown	2
Clearfield	1
Erie	2
Harrisburg	1
Johnstown	2
Philadelphia	3
Pittsburgh	1
State College	3
Wilkes-Barre	1
Williamsport	2
Puerto Rico	
Maricao	1
San Juan	2
Rhode Island	
Providence	2
South Carolina	
Beaufort	3
Charleston	1
Columbia	2
Florence	1
Greenville	1
Myrtle Beach	2
Sumter (R)	3
South Dakota	
Aberdeen	3
Huron	1
Pierre	2
Rapid City	1
Sioux Falls	2

Location	Frequency
Tennessee	
Bristol	1
Chattanooga	1
Cookeville	2
Jackson	1
Knoxville	3
Memphis	3
Nashville	1
Shelbyville	3
Waverly	2
Texas	
Abilene	2
Amarillo	1
Austin	2
Beaumont	3
Big Spring	3
Brownsville	1
Bryan	1
Corpus Christi	1
Dallas	2
Del Rio (P)	2
El Paso	3
Fort Worth	1
Galveston	1
Houston	2
Laredo	3
Lubbock	2
Lufkin	1
Midland	2
Paris	1
Pharr	2
San Angelo	1
San Antonio	1
Sherman	3
Tyler	3
Victoria	2
Waco	3
Wichita Falls	3
Utah	
Logan	2
Cedar City	2
Vernal	2
Salt Lake Cit	1
Vermont	
Burlington	2
*Marlboro	4
Windsor	3
Heathsville	2
Lynchburg	2
Norfolk	1
Richmond	3
Roanoke	3
Washington	
Neah Bay	1
Olympia	3
Seattle	1
Spokane	2
Wenatchee	3
Yakima	1
West Virginia	
Beckley	6
Charleston	2
Clarksburg	1
Gilbert	7
Hinton	4
Romney	7
Spencer	6
Sutton	5
Wisconsin	
La Crosse (P)	1
Green Bay	1
Madison	1
Menomonie	2
Milwaukee	2
Wausau	3
Wyoming	
Casper	1
Cheyenne	3
Lander	3
Sheridan (P)	3

Notes:

1. Stations marked with an asterisk (*) are funded by private interest groups.
2. Stations marked (R) are low powered experimental repeater stations serving a very limited local area.
3. Stations marked (P) operate less than 24 hours/day; however, hours are extended when possible during severe weather.
4. Occasionally the frequency of an existing or planned station must be changed because of unexpected radio frequency interference with adjacent NOAA Weather Radio stations and/or with other government or commercial operators within the area.

Warning display signals –

SMALL CRAFT

DAYTIME: Red Pennant.

NIGHTTIME: Red Light Over White Light.

Indicates: Forecast winds as high as 33 knots and sea conditions considered dangerous to small-craft operations.

GALE

DAYTIME: Two Red Pennants.

NIGHTTIME: White Light over Red Light.

Indicates: Forecast winds in the range 34-47 knots.

STORM

DAYTIME: Square Red Flag With Black Square Centered.

NIGHTTIME: Two Red Lights.

Indicates: Forecast winds 48 knots and above no matter how high the wind speed. If the winds are associated with a tropical cyclone (hurricane), storm warnings indicate forecast winds of 48-63 knots.

HURRICANE

DAYTIME: Two Square Red Flags With Black Square Centered.

NIGHTTIME: White Light Between Two Red Lights.

Indicates: Forecast winds of 64 knots and above, displayed only in connection with a hurricane.

SAFE BOATING WEATHER RULES

BEFORE SETTING OUT

1. Check local weather and sea conditions.

2. Obtain the latest weather forecast for your area from radio broadcasts

When warnings are in effect, don't go out unless you are confident your boat can be navigated safely under forecast conditions of wind and sea. Be cautious when you see warning displays at U. S. Coast Guard stations, yacht clubs, marinas, and at other coastal points.

WHILE AFLOAT:

1. Keep a weather eye out for the approach of dark, threatening clouds, which may foretell a squall or thunderstorm; any steady increase in wind or sea; any increase in wind velocity opposite in direction to a strong tidal current. A dangerous rip tide condition may form steep waves capable of broaching a boat.

2. Heavy static on your AM radio may be an indication of nearby thunderstorm activity.

3. Check radio weather broadcasts for latest forecasts and warnings.

4. If a thunderstorm catches you afloat: –stay below deck if possible. –keep away from metal objects that are not grounded to the boat's protection system. –don't touch more than one grounded object at the same time (or you may become a shortcut for electrical surges through the protection system).

What about navigation? Do you have the NOAA National Ocean Survey charts and other publications covering your part of coastal or Great Lakes waters? Check your local office of the National Weather Service or National Ocean Survey and other essential aids to navigation.

After providing briefers with necessary background information, pilots will receive either a standard, abbreviated, or outlook briefing.

Standard briefings automatically provide pilots with data on adverse conditions, synopsis of prevailing weather systems, current conditions, winds aloft, etc., and any other information the pilot has requested.

Abbreviated briefings are requested when the pilot has used prerecorded or mass media weather information to make a go/no-go decision and only selected additional information is required.

Outlook briefings are requested for long-range flight plans.

Temperature Conversion

Fahrenheit to Celsius

°F	°C	°F	°C	°F	°C
120	48.9	**63**	17.2	**6**	−14.4
119	48.3	**62**	16.7	**5**	−15.0
118	47.8	**61**	16.1	**4**	−15.6
117	47.2	**60**	15.6	**3**	−16.1
116	46.7	**59**	15.0	**2**	−16.7
115	46.1	**58**	14.4	**+1**	−17.2
114	45.6	**57**	13.9	**0**	−17.8
113	45.0	**56**	13.3	**−1**	−18.3
112	44.4	**55**	12.8	**−2**	−18.9
111	43.9	**54**	12.2	**−3**	−19.4
110	43.3	**53**	11.7	**−4**	−20.0
109	42.8	**52**	11.1	**−5**	−20.6
108	42.2	**51**	10.6	**−6**	−21.1
107	41.7	**50**	10.0	**−7**	−21.7
106	41.1	**49**	9.4	**−8**	−22.2
105	40.6	**48**	8.9	**−9**	−22.8
104	40.0	**47**	8.3	**−10**	−23.3
103	39.4	**46**	7.8	**−11**	−23.9
102	38.9	**45**	7.2	**−12**	−24.4
101	38.3	**44**	6.7	**−13**	−25.0
100	37.8	**43**	6.1	**−14**	−25.6
99	37.2	**42**	5.6	**−15**	−26.1
98	36.7	**41**	5.0	**−16**	−26.7
97	36.1	**40**	4.4	**−17**	−27.2
96	35.6	**39**	3.9	**−18**	−27.8
95	35.0	**38**	3.3	**−19**	−28.3
94	34.4	**37**	2.8	**−20**	−28.9
93	33.9	**36**	2.2	**−21**	−29.4
92	33.3	**35**	1.7	**−22**	−30.0
91	32.8	**34**	1.1	**−23**	−30.6
90	32.2	**33**	+0.6	**−24**	−31.1
89	31.7	**32**	0.0	**−25**	−31.7
88	31.1	**31**	−0.6	**−26**	−32.2
87	30.6	**30**	−1.1	**−27**	−32.8
86	30.0	**29**	−1.7	**−28**	−33.3
85	29.4	**28**	−2.2	**−29**	−33.9
84	28.9	**27**	−2.8	**−30**	−34.4
83	28.3	**26**	−3.3	**−31**	−35.0
82	27.8	**25**	−3.9	**−32**	−35.6
81	27.2	**24**	−4.4	**−33**	−36.1
80	26.7	**23**	−5.0	**−34**	−36.7
79	26.1	**22**	−5.6	**−35**	−37.2
78	25.6	**21**	−6.1	**−36**	−37.8
77	25.0	**20**	−6.7	**−37**	−38.3
76	24.4	**19**	−7.2	**−38**	−38.9
75	23.9	**18**	−7.8	**−39**	−39.4
74	23.3	**17**	−8.3	**−40**	−40.0
73	22.8	**16**	−8.9	**−41**	−40.6
72	22.2	**15**	−9.4	**−42**	−41.1
71	21.7	**14**	−10.0	**−43**	−41.7
70	21.1	**13**	−10.6	**−44**	−42.2
69	20.6	**12**	−11.1	**−45**	−42.8
68	20.0	**11**	−11.7	**−46**	−43.3
67	19.4	**10**	−12.2	**−47**	−43.9
66	18.9	**9**	−12.8	**−48**	−44.4
65	18.3	**8**	−13.3	**−49**	−45.0
64	17.8	**7**	−13.9	**−50**	−45.6

Celsius to Fahrenheit

°C	°F	°C	°F
50	122.0	**−7**	19.4
49	120.2	**−8**	17.6
48	118.4	**−9**	15.8
47	116.6	**−10**	14.0
46	114.8	**−11**	12.2
45	113.0	**−12**	10.4
44	111.2	**−13**	8.6
43	109.4	**−14**	6.8
42	107.6	**−15**	5.0
41	105.8	**−16**	3.2
40	104.0	**−17**	+1.4
39	102.2	**−18**	−0.4
38	100.4	**−19**	−2.2
37	98.6	**−20**	−4.0
36	96.8	**−21**	−5.8
35	95.0	**−22**	−7.6
34	93.2	**−23**	−9.4
33	91.4	**−24**	-11.2
32	89.6	**−25**	-13.0
31	87.8	**−26**	-14.8
30	86.0	**−27**	-16.6
29	84.2	**−28**	-18.4
28	82.4	**−29**	-20.2
27	80.6	**−30**	-22.0
26	78.8	**−31**	-23.8
25	77.0	**−32**	-25.6
24	75.2	**−33**	-27.4
23	73.4	**−34**	-29.2
22	71.6	**−35**	-31.0
21	69.8	**−36**	-32.8
20	68.0	**−37**	-34.6
19	66.2	**−38**	-36.4
18	64.4	**−39**	-38.2
17	62.6	**−40**	-40.0
16	60.8	**−41**	-41.8
15	59.0	**−42**	-43.6
14	57.2	**−43**	-45.4
13	55.4	**−44**	-47.2
12	53.6	**−45**	-49.0
11	51.8	**−46**	-50.8
10	50.0		
9	48.2		
8	46.4		
7	44.6		
6	42.8		
5	41.0		
4	39.2		
3	37.4		
2	35.6		
1	33.8		
0	+32.0		
−1	30.2		
−2	28.4		
−3	26.6		
−4	24.8		
−5	23.0		
−6	21.2		

Barometer reduced to sea level.	**Wind direction.**	**Character of weather indicated**
30.10 to 30.20 and steady	**SW. to NW.**	Fair with slight temperature changes for 1 to 2 days.
30.10 to 30.20 and rising rapidly	**SW. to NW.**	Fair followed within 2 days by warmer and rain.
30.10 to 30.20 and falling slowly	**SW. to NW.**	Warmer with rain in 24 to 36 hours.
30.10 to 30.20 and falling rapidly	**SW. to NW.**	Warmer with rain in 18 to 24 hours.
30.20 and above and stationary	**SW. to NW.**	Continued fair with no decided temperature change.
30.20 and above and falling slowly	**SW. to NW.**	Slowly rising temperature and fair for 2 days.
30.10 to 30.20 and falling slowly	**S. to SE.**	Rain within 24 hours.
30.10 to 30.20 and falling rapidly	**S. to SE.**	Wind increasing in force with rain within 12 to 24 hours.
30.10 to 30.20 and falling slowly	**SE. to NE.**	Rain in 12 to 18 hours.
30.10 to 30.20 and falling rapidly	**SE. to. NE.**	Increasing wind with rain within 12 hours.
30.10 and above and falling slowly	**E. to NE.**	In summer with light winds, rain may not fall for several days. In winter rain within 24 hours.
30.10 and above and falling rapidly	**E. to NE.**	In summer rain probable within 12 to 24 hours. In winter rain or snow, with increasing winds, will often set in, when the barometer begins to fall and the wind sets in from the NE.
30 or below and falling slowly	**SE. to NE.**	Rain will continue 1 to 2 days.
30 or below and falling rapidly	**SE. to NE.**	Rain with high wind, followed within 24 hours by clearing and cooler.
30 or below and rising slowly	**S. to SW.**	Clearing within a few hours, and continued fair for several days.
29.80 or below and falling rapidly	**S. to E.**	Severe storm of wind and rain or snow imminent, followed within 24 hours by clearing and colder.
29.80 or below and falling rapidly	**E. to N.**	Severe northeast gales and heavy rain or snow, followed in winter by a cold wave.
29.80 or below and rising rapidly	**Going to W.**	Clearing and colder.

BEAUFORT SCALE OF WIND EFFECTS

Wind speed (miles per hour)	Beaufort Number	Wind Effects on Land	Official Description
Less than 1	0	Calm; smoke rises vertically.	LIGHT
1 – 3	1	Wind direction is seen in direction of smoke; but is not revealed by weather vane.	
4 – 7	2	Wind can be felt on face; leaves rustle; wind vane moves.	
8 – 12	3	Leaves and small twigs in motion; wind extends light flag.	GENTLE
13 – 18	4	Wind raises dust and loose papers. Small branches move.	MODERATE
19 – 24	5	Small trees with leaves begin to sway; crested wavelets appear on inland waters.	FRESH
25 – 31	6	Large branches move; telegraph wires whistle; Umbrellas become difficult to control.	STRONG
32 – 38	7	Whole trees sway and walking into the wind becomes difficult.	
39 – 46	8	Twigs break off trees; cars veer on roads.	GALE
47 – 54	9	Slight structural damage occurs (roof slates may blow away, etc.)	
55 – 63	10	Trees are uprooted; considerable structural damage is caused.	WHOLE GALE
64 – 72	11	Widespread damage is caused.	
73 or more	12	Widespread damage is caused.	HURRICANE

FOR THE ARMCHAIR FORECASTER

Above is the Beaufort Scale which permits the estimating of wind speeds from observations. It also gives the basis for converting wind descriptions used in weather reports to wind speed equivalents, and vice-versa.

Use your barometer and wind indicator to do your own forecasting. It's one of the most popular hobbies in the world. The opposite page gives you a chart combining the weather observations of both professionals and amateurs dating back to such observers as Ben Franklin.

Weather, Climate & Society

• CLIMATE

Climate is a composite of weather conditions over a period of time. It is a standard practice to relate climate in terms of statistical "normals." But normal values do not adequately define the climatic risk. The frequency of occurrences among the various weather elements provides a more complete understanding of climate.

As a natural resource, climate is often overlooked in agricultural planning. Some reasons for this lack of concern are:

1. Climate, as a composite of weather events over a period of time, is very abstract.
2. It is not fixed in time and space like most other natural resource considerations.
3. Climate is often viewed as given and uncontrollable, therefore nothing can be done anyway.

These erroneous views produce a lack of appreciation for climate information and its use in decision making. This lack of use has in turn led to a lack of development in needed climatological data, their acquisition and analysis, in agricultural planning over the past several decades.

As a result, much of the current soil erosion, flood damage, and land management problems in agriculture are traceable, in part, to lack of appreciation and understanding of climate as a manageable resource. The omission of climate information needs to be corrected in future agricultural systems planning.

• AGRICULTURE & CLIMATIC DIVERSITY

An understanding of climate as a natural resource can be gained from examining the general climates in major food crop production regions of the world. The ten largest volume food crops, as well as almost all other crops, are adapted to certain latitude ranges and general climatic conditions.

Botanically, six of these ten major food crops are members of the grass family. They are wheat, rice, maize (corn), barley, sorghum, and sugarcane. Five of the crops produce most of the world's food and feed grains, sugarcane being the only grass family crop not grown for grain production. Of the four remaining major food crops, three are staple root crops—potatoes, cassavas, and sweet potatoes—and one is an oilseed-protein crop, soybeans. When grown under dryland or rain-fed cropping practices, all of these crops have some rather specific climatic resource requirements.

Eight out of ten of these world food and feed crops are successfully grown within the continental limits of the 48 contiguous states. Crops requiring true tropical climates, such as sugarcane and cassava, are not extensively grown within the contiguous states. But true tropical climates do exist in Hawaii and Puerto Rico. As a result, climatic resources of the 50 states and Puerto Rico are diverse enough to contain almost all crop-producing climates in the world.

These extensive and diverse crop-producing climatic resources are a central reason why the United States leads the world in food and feed production.

Ten Major World Food Crops
(Source: U.N.-FAO 1980)

Crop	Climate type (dryland or rain-fed croppings)	Latitudinal Range
Wheat	temperate humid, subhumid to semiarid	25° to 55°
Rice	tropical-subtropical humid	0° to 45°
Maize (Corn)	tropical-warm temperate humid	0° to 45°
Potato	cool temperate	30° to 60°
Barley	cool temperate	35° to 60°
Sweet Potato	subtropical to warm temperate	25° to 40°
Cassava	humid tropical	0° to 30°
Soybeans	subtropical to warm temperate	25° to 45°
Sorghum	semiarid tropics to semiarid warm temperate	0° to 40°
Sugarcane	humid tropics	0° to 30°

Crop belts and climate

A number of regions within the continental limits of the United States are named for their dominant topographic features and associated climatic conditions. Some of these regional labels are used in reporting weather crop-climate conditions.

These general topographic features and associated climates frequently determine the principal crops and cropping systems within a geographical area. This is particularly true for dryland (rain-fed or nonirrigated) cropping systems.

Within the continental United States, several geographical areas are devoted to growing one or two crops. These agricultural patterns or systems are known as crop belts. Some examples are the Cotton Belt, Corn Belt, Spring Wheat Belt, and Winter Wheat Belt.

Climate is usually the dominant natural resource which determines these principal crop production belts. An example of climate as the leading resource is the high latitude spring grain-producing area in the United States, Canada, and around the entire world. These spring grain belts of wheat, barley, and oats are adapted to the high latitude subhumid temperate climates.

On a worldwide basis, the areas are known as cool-temperate grasslands. Spring grain production dominates these geographical areas largely because their annual growth cycle and grain-filling period climatic requirements are met in most years, while requirements of other possible competitive crops are not met in many years.

Grasslands unique

The midlatitude cool-temperate grassland areas are unique the world over in their annual distribution of precipitation, temperature, and solar energy. These climatic elements maximize in phase during late spring or early summer.

Precipitation usually reaches its annual maximum in late May, June, and early July. Temperature reaches maximum levels in July and early August. Sunlight energy peaks in late June and early July during the longest days of the year.

Bismarck, North Dakota, typifies the spring grain belt of the United States and Canada. The spring grain-cropping areas of North America normally receive 12-18 inches (30.48-45.72 cm) of annual precipitation. Bismarck receives an annual average of 16 inches (40.64 cm). But the important feature from a climatic resource viewpoint is the annual distribution of precipitation. Over 60% occurs in the three months of May, June, and July.

During this same period spring grain crops are growing rapidly, and crop water use in the form of evapotranspiration is greatest. As a result, the seasonal distribution of precipitation is in phase with annual spring grain crop needs.

The fact that precipitation, temperature, and sunlight all reach their annual maximum values during the growth and grain-producing season of these annual spring grain crops is the key point of this unique climatic resource.

Winter grain areas

The winter grain crops of wheat, rye, barley, and oats are grown in the lower mid latitude grassland climates in all continents. In the United States, the hard red winter wheat belt lies in the southern half of the Great Plains from Nebraska to Texas.

Climatic resource features of these grassland winter grain areas are roughly similar to the higher latitude spring grain areas of the northern Great Plains. But there are some differences.

In the winter grain belts, the warm season precipitation begins to increase about a month or more earlier. The mean annual maximum period occurs in late May or early June. Therefore, the growing season distribution of precipitation is about a month earlier in the winter grain areas when compared to those in the spring grain areas.

The mean monthly air temperatures are 5°-10°F (-15 to -12.2°C) warmer during the warmest six months of the year in these winter grain areas. But there is a 10° to 20°F (-12.2 to -6.7°C) or more difference between the spring and winter grain areas during the winter months within the Great Plains of North America. In fact the geographical division between spring grain and winter grain cropping belts of both North American and Eurasian continents is determined largely by winter seasonal minimum air temperatures and snow cover.

These specific crop-weather-climate relationships and their frequency of occurrence need more research emphasis in the future.

Normally, winter grains will out yield spring grains in these grassland climates. Therefore, farmers are willing to take some climatic risk of crop failure in favor of growing winter grains rather than spring grains.

In the Great Plains of the United States, the transition from winter grains to spring grains occurs in northern Nebraska and southern South Dakota. This transitional area has a climatic risk of winter grain crop failure due to winter kill of about 20-25%, or one year in four or five. Winter kill in these transitional areas is caused by the normally dry winters with lack of snow cover and low winter minimum air temperatures.

Corn belt uniformity

The Corn Belt of the north central United States is the most valuable and extensive rain-fed cropland area in the world. It completely covers the three states of Iowa, Illinois, and Indiana, plus large portions of the nine surrounding states. Much of the value of this vast mid-continental cropland comes from its climate resource. On an annual basis the climate over the Corn Belt varies from subhumid tallgrass prairie in the western portions to a humid deciduous forest climate in the eastern portions.

From north to south it is a transition climate from a continental cool temperate to a continental warm temperate. The United States Corn Belt climate varies considerably when analyzed on an annual basis. But the uniqueness of that climate occurs during the crop-growing season. The precipitation amounts and temperature levels are amazingly uniform over the entire area from May through September.

Normal growing season rainfall during these five months is about 20 inches (50.8 cm). This occurs with high frequency in both western and eastern portions. Des Moines, in central Iowa, receives an average of about 30 inches (76 cm) annually, but over 65% occurs during the warmest half of the year from April through September. At Indianapolis, Indiana, the warmest seven months from March through September are all above the median. The annual seasonal maximum precipitation occurs in late May and early June at both locations.

The annual temperature change characteristics are slightly more continental in western portions of the Corn Belt. This means the winter temperatures are a little colder and the summer a little warmer in western than in eastern portions.

There are more days above 90°F (32.2°C) in the western areas, primarily because of less carryover soil moisture from dry winters and hot dry winds from the High Plains in the west. Except for higher hail frequency in the western portion, most other forms of climatic risks are exceptionally uniform across the Corn Belt during the growing season.

Dryland cotton

Dryland or rain-fed cotton is grown in most of the southern and southeastern states. The main dryland cotton belt begins in east Texas and continues eastward across the states of Louisiana, Mississippi, Alabama, Georgia, and South Carolina. Lesser acreages of cotton are grown in several other southern states. The climate varies from warm temperate subhumid in eastern Texas to warm temperate humid climate in the states further east.

Annual distribution of mean monthly precipitation and temperature at Jackson, Mississippi, provides a good example of the dryland cotton belt climate of the southern continental United States. Nearly 60% of the annual precipitation normally occurs from November through April. The Cotton Belt usually experiences wet winters which extend well into the early spring planting season. The late summer and early fall months of August, September and October are usually the driest period of the year.

On an annual basis the United States Cotton Belt has a humid warm temperate climate, but the annual distribution of precipitation is somewhat out-of-phase with the summer crop-growing seasonal water demands. This is particularly true for cotton.

Driest months occur in late summer and early fall toward the end of a long annual growing season. This explains why much of the dryland summer crop production in the south and southeastern states experience drought in a high percentage of the years within a humid climate. The annual precipitation distribution, along with soil resources having limited water-retention capacities, produce crop water stress in most years.

West coastal states

The west coastal states of Washington, Oregon, and California are dominated by the winter precipitation climates. Worldwide, these climates are known as the Mediterranean type. They are characterized by wet winters and dry summers. This type of climatic resource is illustrated by Portland, Oregon. Nearly 30 inches (76 cm) of the normal 42 inches (107 cm) of annual precipitation occurs during the coldest half of the year.

Annual winter grain crops and many perennial forage and tree crops are well adapted to these wet winter-dry summer climates. The well-adapted winter annual crops are planted in fall, become dormant in winter due to low temperatures, then complete their growth and reproduction phases before onset of the dry summer. Many perennial forage crops are well adapted to these climates for the same reasons. Forests and perennial tree crops can adapt or survive summer dry climates that are not too hot or too long.

These climates are well suited for irrigated agriculture. The low winter temperatures and relatively high effective precipitation produces water surpluses during the winter season. Therefore, management of stored water is necessary during the annual summer growing season.

Irrigation in these climates makes it possible to bring the surplus winter seasonal precipitation in phase with the summer seasonal temperatures and solar energy. That is why irrigated agriculture is so productive in these warm temperate and subtropical Mediterranean climates the world over.

Intermountain areas

The intermountain regions of the western United States are dominated by a complex of cool semiarid climates in the northern and central portions and arid desert climates in the southern areas. These climatic areas exist largely because of the effect of mountain ranges to the west and east of the region.

The Coastal and Sierra ranges to the west block sources of winter seasonal precipitation from the west, and the Rockies to the east are a barrier to the source of the grassland summer seasonal precipitation from the east. As a result, the dryland agriculture of this intermountain region is largely confined to open range grazing.

The climatic record of Salt Lake City, Utah, provides a good example of these intermountain rangeland climates. The annual precipitation distribution reflects some of the Pacific Coast wet winter climates to the west as well as some lesser influences from the summer maximum precipitation climates to the east.

Irrigated croplands have been developed in many areas where water can be made available through water storage and management. Many different crops are grown with irrigation under highly varied growing season temperature zones in the intermountain regions. These varied growing season temperature conditions are caused by both elevation and latitude throughout the region.

Northeast forest climates

Climatic conditions leading to forest vegetation of the northeastern United States approach the ideal from the standpoint of annual and perennial crop moisture needed.

Mean monthly precipitation and temperature distributions are closely in phase with seasonal crop and forest growth. The highest mean monthly precipitation normally occurs in midsummer when crop and forest water demands are highest. A good example of these cool temperate humid forest climates of the northeast region is Albany, New York.

These climates exist from the upper Ohio Valley eastward across Pennsylvania into New Jersey, then northward through New York and the New England states. The northeast forest climates are characterized by a rather uniform mean monthly distribution of precipitation, with the highest amounts coming in midsummer in phase with the highest mean monthly temperature and evaporation.

Driest months of the year are February and October. The fact that the lowest annual mean monthly precipitation months do not occur consecutively is another unique feature of these climates. This is particularly true for large geographical regions.

Unfortunately, water supply systems in climates with relatively uniform and dependable precipitation are often underdesigned and overcommitted. As a result, when the inevitable drought occurs an acute water shortage develops. This has happened repeatedly in the densely populated northeast United States.

There are other unique climate regions within the continental United States, such as the Great Lakes region and those areas surrounding the Gulf of Mexico.

Great Lakes region

Climate in and around the Great Lakes can best be described as humid and cool with snowy winters and cool pleasant summers. Annual precipitation is rather evenly distributed during the year.

Many small-scale climates exist in land areas surrounding the Great Lakes. There are several snow belts, fruit belts, and other special small-scale climatic areas within the Great Lakes region, which are utilized to produce particular fruit or vegetable crops.

Gulf Coast region

Land areas surrounding the Gulf of Mexico are known as the Gulf Coast region. The climate varies from humid warm temperate to humid subtropical. The frost-free crop growing season is 300 days or more in most of this region. Crops requiring long growing seasons such as sugarcane, cotton, and rice are produced.

The peninsular state of Florida is dominated by humid tropical, subtropical, and warm temperate climates. The main crops are citrus, winter vegetables, and sugarcane in the tropical and subtropical areas. The northern humid warm temperate areas are devoted to several special crops and cattle grazing.

Low desert areas of Arizona and California produce a number of tropical and subtropical crops requiring frost-free climates. Almost all crop production is under irrigation in these southwestern desert climates.

Climatic niches

The large subcontinental land areas of Alaska have a variety of high latitude climates. They range from true Arctic to subarctic and cool marine climates. The agricultural worth of these high latitude climates is limited to certain climatic niches within this huge state.

Much of the true agricultural potential of Alaskan climate resources has not yet been exploited because of a mix of transportation, labor, and energy cost considerations.

A wide diversity of crops are grown within the limits of the 50 states and Puerto Rico. Many of these crops require special climatic niches within the larger or more general climate type briefly discussed here. Some examples are pineapple, cranberries, tobacco, peanuts, and grapes.

These numerous climatic niches within the 50 states add much to the agricultural worth of the United States. Therefore, continued assessment of our collective climatic resources are of great economic value.

• POWER PRODUCTION

Variations in weather and climate affect many areas of society. Areas that are impacted include the productivity of farms, forests and fisheries; land and water resources; commercial, military, and private transportation and communications; and the requirement for power generation and the means by which power is generated. Each area of society has a different tolerance to weather and climatic effects, depending on the institutional structure involved. Now that energy is in short supply, society has become more acutely aware of the interaction between weather and power production. Whether it be intense thunderstorms or intense heat, cold winters or dry winters, mountain runoff or valley winds—all effect how energy is supplied and used.

Weather can loosely be defined as the state of the atmosphere, including such conditions as rain, cloudiness, temperature and winds. Weather is highly variable and includes severe storms, hurricanes, downpours, and intense cold and hot spells. Weather forecasts deal with the near-term and the next few days, over which time relatively accurate descriptions of events can presently be made. Theory indicates that the forecasting time can probably be extended out to a week for weather events with scales of several hundred kilometers. It appears unlikely, however, that extreme local weather conditions can be foreseen much beyond a day, although, as described below, there is hope that anticipated monthly and seasonal average conditions can be forecast.

Beyond the few days over which weather can be forecast, reliance is usually placed on climatology, which is the average of the weather conditions in a region compiled, as a function of season, over a number of years. Climate is defined to include this set of average (or usual) conditions as well as the range of extreme conditions that can occur and the likelihood of their occurrence. In the United States, the period of time used historically to develop averages or normals for a particular period (e.g., a month) has been 30 years with such averages being updated or recalculated every ten years. If climatic conditions were essentially constant, with only year to year fluctuations, the average would remain relatively constant. Climatic conditions are not constant, however and, in fact, it appears that climate has varied over all time scales. Both short (year to year) and long-term variations can be large, and both can be persistent. Thus there can be multiyear periods of drought and multimillenium periods of continental ice sheets. The former are perceived as a fluctuation; the latter (although very large) are often overlooked as being outside the range of consideration and because their presence would be evidenced in the short-term as a very small trend.

At present, there is only very limited improvement over climatology (skill) shown in NOAA forecasts of monthly and seasonal climates. Extensions of work using sea surface temperatures to forecast seasonal climates and incorporation of statistical correlations with solar-terrestrial activity (that may be anticipated several years in advance) offer hope that improvements eventually can be made in the ability to forecast short-and intermediate-term climatic fluctuations.

Atmospheric behavior

In describing the effects of weather and variations on power production, atmospheric behavior is divided into four time-scales.

1. **Short term** is defined to mean that period of time over which detailed forecasting of specific atmospheric properties is reliable (currently up to 3-5 days) and over which responses to energy shortages are based on already in-place supplies. We will, however, restrict this domain to times of at least a day in the future, leaving to those actually producing the energy (as opposed to those planning and allocating it) the responsibility for responding to such shorter-term conditions as tornadoes, etc.
2. **Intermediate term** is defined to mean that period of time over which short-term advance planning can alleviate potential problems of energy shortages, etc. Typically, this period ranges from weeks to a season or year.
3. **Medium term** is defined as a period from one to ten years. This period corresponds to a time over which planning typically occurs to address questions of allocation of capital for energy generation facilities and resource utilization.
4. **Long term** is defined as the period from ten to one-hundred years. This period corresponds to the time over which energy technologies typically can be introduced and become important contributors to national energy supplies or over which new national energy supplies or new technologies mature and their large-scale use may aggravate environmental problems. The still longer time periods are not addressed here.

Short term (days)

Providing the vast amounts of power needed for this country requires reliance on many modes of generation, including domestic and foreign energy supplies. Variations in the weather and climate can influence how energy resources are found, extracted, transported, transformed, distributed and consumed. To some extent the diversity of sources protects us from impacts of unusual weather on any one source or area. But, by being able to better understand what can be expected on a day to day basis and even a few days into the future (i.e., the "short-term"), energy-related activities can be planned so as to reduce overall consumption, and the daily comfort of people in their homes and the efficient functioning of industry can be made more certain.

The focal points in the short-term use of weather data for managing the operation of energy systems include: real-time contingency planning, responses to the impact of extremes of weather on the operation of energy systems or on energy demands, and fuel consumption reports. Problems of interest also include increased energy demands related to extreme cold or heat, icing or freezing rain impacting on the operation of transmission lines, freezing of rivers impeding the availability of barge transportation and normal cooling water, hurricanes interfering with the normal operation of natural gas wells in off-shore environments, precipitation rates in agricultural areas, and coastal forecasts required for liquified natural gas tanker unloading operations. Most of these examples require contingency planning and the identification of alternative supplies for either stand-by or current use.

Intermediate term (weeks)

The past few years have provided examples of the impact monthly and seasonal variations in atmospheric behavior can have on energy supply and distribution.

The intense cold period in the eastern United States during December 1976 and January 1977 led to high demands for natural gas, the effects of which eventually spread to the west coast as gas supplies were diverted to the east. Although the winter as a whole in the east was not much colder than normal and total seasonal supplies were nearly adequate, the intensely cold months created such a large demand that the rate of delivering supplies was not adequate. Accurate forecasting of the weekly, monthly, and seasonal temperature patterns and the resulting energy demands would have permitted better planning of mitigating measures such as fuel switching.

Some impacts can affect the cost of energy. For example, the amount of water stored in mountain snow determines the amount of hydroelectric power that can be produced during the following year. Any shortfall in water supply must be made-up using more costly means of power generation. Accurate forecasts of spring rains and the rate of snow melt would permit more efficient (and therefore less expensive) use of available resources. Intermediate-term weather variations can also affect energy availability. For example, river or lake transport systems may be blocked by ice for extended periods, thus requiring the use of stockpiled fuels or provision of alternate means of delivery.

Medium term (years)

In the design and planning of energy generation and supply facilities, account is already taken of the normal climate and a range of extremes (e.g., flood and hurricane frequency, etc.) that is based on past records.

For the medium term what is needed for energy planning purposes are predictions of trends and cycles of climate that might strain energy supplies in ways that make facilities uneconomical or inadequate to meet energy needs. For example, several years of drought in the western United States have heavily impacted hydroelectric supply capability and limited cooling water supply while at the same time increasing the power demands of some irrigation systems. These are not cases involving direct threats to public safety; rather the existing energy supplies are simply less abundant and plans must be made for augmenting them (e.g., gas turbines, etc.). An increase in the frequency of extreme hot spells during successive summers is an example where the demand for energy might change in a way not normally foreseen by energy planners. Unusually cold or lengthy winters in northern regions where river or sea ice might block access of ships to port facilities would limit the amount and period over which oil might be transported to the United States.

Long term (decades)

The "normal" climate serves as the basis for planning energy needs (demands) and assessing the possibilities for energy supply. Thus, to even a greater extent than for the medium term, understanding trends, cycles, and changes in variability of atmospheric behavior can affect the planning for energy supplies in the future in important ways. Shifts in circulation systems or ocean currents could cause changes in climate which affect energy demand, the availability of such resources as cooling water, and the ability to develop biomass as an energy source. All potential effects could be alleviated to some extent by improved understanding of future climatic events.

• ENERGY TECHNOLOGIES

The by-products of energy production and consumption released to the atmosphere, namely waste heat, gases (including water vapor), and particles, can affect climate on a local or regional scale, usually by affecting the atmospheric radiation balance. In addition, any technology that alters the characteristics of the surface of Earth over extensive areas (such as the projected use of solar collectors) can also have climatic effects by altering the energy and moisture balances at the surface. The effects of energy use in large urban areas, and the resulting impacts on local and regional climate, have received considerable attention in recent years. Effects range from alteration of temperature to modification of precipitation.

Projecting energy use and consumption (and the resulting emission patterns) into the next century, reveals that several effects of energy production and consumption have the potential of extending beyond the regional scale, eventually out to the global scale. A primary source of these effects will be increased concentrations of CO_2, but heat, particles, and possibly other gases may also prove to be important considerations in evaluating future energy policy.

In the discussion of the effects of weather and climate variations on power production it was convenient to subdivide atmospheric behavior into various timescales. Although energy production has diurnal, seasonal and annual cycles, it is more convenient to discuss the effects of energy technologies on weather and climate in terms of the spatial scale of the effect. Some effects of power production may be intermittent, but the most significant effects result from continuous or persistent emissions that either impact the region near the source (e.g., H_2O and particles) or contribute to a build up of the global background concentration (e.g., CO_2, ^{85}Kr).

The spatial scales of importance to power production and climatic effects are:

- local (to distances up to tens of kilometers from the source)
- regional (to distances up to hundreds of kilometers)
- sub-continental (to distances up to thousands of kilometers)
- global (worldwide distribution).

Apart from very limited amounts of permanently stored energy, all energy that is generated is eventually dissipated and ends up as heat, regardless of the means of generation. The released heat may be concentrated at specific sites (e.g., waste heat at power plants) or it may be broadly distributed (e.g., space heating in businesses and residences). The climatic impact depends upon both the total amount of energy released and the amount released in a given area (flux per unit area).

The combined impact of population increases, changing patterns of population densities, and escalating per capita energy consumption has been to concentrate very large energy fluxes per unit area (flux density) in some regions of the world.

In 1971, for example, the world average energy consumption was approximately 1.5×10^9 Btu/km^2 of land area per year (0.05 W/m^2). In the same year, New York City's Manhattan Island had a total energy flux density of approximately 3×10^{12} Btu/km^2 per year (100 W/m^2), which is very nearly equal to the global average net radiation (solar and longwave absorption minus longwave emission) at Earth's surface. Hence, current levels of energy consumption are insignificant in the global heat budget but can be significant on the local or regional scale.

Urban areas are typically warmer than the surrounding rural regions, thus leading to the term "urban heat island." A major portion of the urban heat island effect is caused by changes in the physical parameters of the area, namely radiative properties, moisture properties, evapotranspiration rates, and surface roughness. Another cause is anthropogenic heat rejection, which varies with season and latitude. In the cold northern climates during winter, anthropogenic heat in metropolitan areas may equal or exceed the amount of solar energy received. Energy conservation efforts may reduce the heat island effect.

In addition to waste heat, large-scale particulate and gaseous emissions can also affect the weather and climate. The major sources of atmospheric particles are: wind-raised dust and sea salt, direct products of combustion, volcanic particles, organic products of plant and animal life, and indirect products of combustion (resulting from chemical conversion in the atmosphere of gaseous emissions). The major anthropogenic sources of particles are industrial production and processing of materials such as metals and cement, agriculture, and combustion associated with industrial, commercial and domestic needs. The particles directly emitted tend to be large and are usually radiatively important only on the local and regional scales. Secondary particles, which form from vapors in the atmosphere, are usually sub-micron in size (10^{-6} m in diameter), have optical properties which induce strong scattering of solar radiation, and can be carried by the wind over sub-continental and global distances. Increased energy consumption relying on fuel combustion without adequate controls may increase the atmospheric loading of both primary and secondary (indirect) particles. Atmospheric particles may also affect the nucleation and condensation of water vapor to form cloud droplets and, thus, the rates and pattern of precipitation. Hygroscopic particles may act as cloud condensation nuclei, thus affecting cloudiness and precipitation. Changes in cloudiness or atmospheric particle loading affect the transmission and scattering of solar radiation and the exchange of longwave radiation, thereby further perturbing the radiation balance, which in turn affects temperature patterns.

Gaseous emissions which are radiatively important, such as CO_2, and H_2O, may affect the climate directly by their radiative impact or indirectly by affecting the concentrations of other atmospheric constituents. CO_2, and H_2O are both strong absorbers of infrared radiation, but they are relatively transparent to solar radiation. Consequently, an increase in the atmospheric concentration of these species would act to reduce the flux of infrared radiation emitted to space. To restore the balance with incoming solar radiation, there would be an increase in atmospheric temperature. Estimates of the increase in the global average surface temperature due to a doubling of CO_2, from 300 to 600 ppm range from 34.7-37.4°F (1.5-3.0°C). Predictions of the future CO_2 increase due to combustion of fossil fuels suggest a doubling of the concentration before the middle of the next century.

Heat and moisture from cooling towers have been observed to affect the generation of cumulus clouds. Depending upon the stability of the prevailing air flow, the moisture and heat may lead to decreased stability increasing convective activity, and precipitation. Some have suggested this may lead to an increased frequency of thunderstorms and, possibly, tornadoes if employed on a large scale. Evaporation processes used to dissipate waste heat may also cause fogging and icing.

Other aspects of providing and distributing energy may also affect the weather or climate, but the magnitudes of many of the effects have not yet been assessed. Reservoirs behind hydroelectric dams alter important surface characteristics. Strip mining and similar processes of resource extraction cause vegetation to be removed, thereby exposing soil that has a reflectivity (albedo) different from the natural surface, thus altering the amount of solar radiation absorbed. The moisture retention properties are also altered, so energy that would have been dissipated as latent heat by evaporation is dissipated as sensible heat. In addition, particulate matter may be released to the atmosphere as windblown dust. These effects are likely to be local or regional in scale.

Transportation of crude oil and gasoline has the potential for inadvertent climatic effects. The use of supertankers offers the possibility of large oil spills or slicks at sea in the event of an accident. Very thin oil slicks extending over many square kilometers in higher latitudes or colder water would change the albedo of the ocean and reduce the amount of evaporation. These changes in surface energy balance would affect the ocean atmosphere exchange rates for moisture and sensible heat.

Other examples of how providing and distributing energy may affect weather and climate are given below for various energy technologies.

Fossil fuel combustion (coal, oil, gas)

Combustion of fossil fuels causes atmospheric emissions of primary particles and numerous gaseous species (SO_x, NO_x, CO_x, H_2O and hydrocarbons). The species SO_x, NO_x and hydrocarbons may be converted to secondary particles that can contribute to acid rain on the sub-continental scale and affect radiative processes and precipitation patterns, as already noted above.

Nuclear

Routine emissions of ^{85}Kr, although at very small concentrations, are building up the global background concentration of this species. Ionization caused by ^{85}Kr decay increases the atmospheric conductivity. This increase in turn can affect the atmospheric electric field that is believed to be related to scavenging and precipitation processes in thunderstorms and severe convective activity.

Solar

The technologies being developed to provide electrical power on a large scale using solar energy include photovoltaic, distributed collector, and central receiver systems. The interception and collection of solar radiation by large arrays of reflectors and absorbers will alter the regional radiation budget (solar and longwave) and change the moisture retention properties of Earth's surface. Natural surfaces absorb 70-90% of the incident solar radiation; deserts 70-75%, and vegetated surfaces 80-90%. Portions of the solar energy absorbed are convected away from the surface as heat, used for evaporation, radiated away as longwave radiation, or conducted into the ground. If arrays of mirrors or collectors were placed over soil with a significant moisture content, evaporation would be restricted, thus affecting the moisture and radiation budgets.

Solar thermal collector systems that use large arrays of mirrors or distributed collectors use the absorbed solar radiation to heat a working fluid that in turn powers a steam turbine generator. Cooling towers are used for disposal of the waste heat (approximately 60% of the thermal energy absorbed in the working fluid). The solar thermal collector system reduces the normal amount of energy absorbed at the surface and available for heating the atmosphere in the region. This deficiency would have an effect like a high desert albedo. Cooling towers concentrate the energy and moisture released to the atmosphere, effects that may impact on weather and climate as already noted above.

Biomass

There are two approaches to the use of biomass as a source of energy. One is to cut down existing forests for firewood, such as is done on a large scale in South America and in other tropical locations. The second is to grow special crops for either their oil and rubber content or their combustible mass. Both aspects change the surface conditions (i.e., increase or decrease albedo, affect the moisture flux by changing evaporation or evapotranspiration rates) in ways that may lead to local, regional, or even larger-scale climatic effects. Deforestation also contributes CO_2, to the atmosphere, and biomass crops contribute gaseous and particulate emissions.

Wind

Individual wind turbine generators do not have a significant effect on the planetary boundary layer. However, many such wind turbine generators grouped together may extract energy from a region at a rate that is a significant fraction of the natural rate of kinetic energy replenishment (which averages about 2.5 W/m^2 over the United States). In this case there may be a significant change in the wind flow pattern of the planetary boundary layer, that may affect surface heat and moisture losses, temperature, and the precipitation rate on a regional scale.

Geothermal

Among the various gaseous emissions resulting from the extraction of geothermal energy, H_2S has the greatest potential for affecting weather and climate since it can be converted to sulfate aerosols (particles) through a chain of chemical reactions. As in the case of particles from other energy technologies, these, aerosols may affect the regional climate by perturbing the radiation and condensation nuclei budgets.

Hydroelectric

Reservoirs formed behind dams can alter important surface characteristics. For example, the evaporation rate is enhanced because of the increased water surface area, especially in the West during normally dry summer months. Changing from a vegetated surface to a lake surface also changes the albedo. The net effect is a change in the local and regional temperature and moisture distributions. Dams also help to reduce the effects of extreme weather by controlling flooding and by providing water for irrigation in times of drought.

Ocean thermal energy conversion (OTEC)

These facilities extract energy from the temperature difference between the surface and deeper water. Bringing the cooler, deep water to near the surface will reduce the sea surface temperature and alter salinity gradients. The extent to which ambient surface temperatures are lowered will depend on plant design and site conditions. A 100-240 MW OTEC plant may lower the surface temperature 35.6-37.4°F (2-3°C). Near the equator changes in the sea surface temperature can affect the development of tropical storms. The pumping of large amounts of deep, nutrient rich ocean water to near the ocean surface may cause formation of large plankton blooms, that would change the ocean albedo.

The artificial upwelling of deep ocean water caused by OTEC plants also may have an effect on the concentration Of CO_2 in the atmosphere. The forced upwelling of deep ocean waters (containing about 15% more dissolved carbon than the ocean surface layers) is a potential source of atmospheric CO_2, if the water is discharged from the plant near the ocean surface. The microclimate at OTEC sites could be affected further if open cycle systems are utilized. Degassing procedures needed to ensure operating efficiencies may lead to the venting of concentrations of oxygen, nitrogen, and CO_2. The potential climatic impacts of these changes need to be assessed.

The examples given above for the various energy technologies highlight the climate-related issues associated with primary and alternative sources of power. There is no assurance that all of the critical issues have been identified, nor have assessments of the possible climatic effects been completed. There is a need for constant awareness of potential climatic effects, continued development of improved assessment capabilities, and regular updating of assessments.

• THE CLIMATE SYSTEM & PROCESSES OF CLIMATIC CHANGE

The atmosphere is a dynamic system powered by the sun. The differential heating caused by a surplus of solar radiation at low latitudes and a deficit at high latitudes serves as the forcing function for the varying behavior of the atmosphere. The atmosphere through its motions strives to return to a condition of static stability constrained by the requirements of conserving mass, energy, and momentum. The atmospheric conditions, as they vary from moment to moment and from place to place, are referred to as *weather*. The term *climate* refers loosely to the weather averaged over both time and space as well as the statistical properties of the atmosphere, including weather extremes, joint frequency distributions, and many other measures of weather variability.

The climate at any location on the earth is determined by a combination of influences ranging from the global scale down to details of the local environment. The distribution of solar radiation, for example, affects climate on a global scale (the macroclimate), whereas geographic features may influence climate within smaller regions (the mesoclimate and microclimate).

The global climate system

The global climate system is composed of several components: the atmosphere, oceans, land surfaces, snow and ice masses (the cryosphere), and the biosphere. These major physical components are coupled by the transport of mass, momentum, energy, and water. The coupling is further complicated by many feedback mechanisms, including the radiative effects of trace atmospheric constituents.

The oceans are large heat storage reservoirs that absorb, store, and resupply to the atmosphere vast amounts of energy through the exchange of latent and sensible heat as well as longwave radiation. The energy which is lost to the atmosphere is replenished by absorption of solar radiation. The ocean currents play an important role in affecting the spatial distribution of the energy transferred to the atmosphere. The momentum exchange between the atmosphere and ocean due to wind stress affects both atmospheric and oceanic circulation patterns. Variations in the extent of sea-ice alter the global radiation and energy balances changing the albedo and thermal capacity of the earth's oceans. Factors affecting surface albedo include the amount of snow and ice on land surfaces, soil moisture, and the extent and type vegetation.

The atmospheric composition, including cloudiness, affects the transfer of solar and longwave radiation. The net flux of radiative energy at Earth's surface determines the amount of energy available for evaporation or transfer as sensible heat to the atmosphere. Since cloudiness depends upon temperature, humidity, and wind circulation patterns in addition to convective activity, there is a coupling between atmospheric dynamics and the radiative and hydrological processes. The biosphere affects evapotranspiration of water and release of certain other trace constituents to the atmosphere and is itself regulated by such growth-controlling factors as wind, temperature, moisture, and the solar energy available for photosynthesis.

This complex climate system has undergone many changes in the past, as reflected in the climatic record. In addition to the natural climatic variations to be expected in the future, it is possible that man can also affect the climate by disturbing the delicate balances of heat, radiation, and water on a regional and ultimately on a global scale.

The climatic record

In interpreting and extrapolating the historical records, it is important to realize that the magnitudes of climatic averages themselves vary not only with the location but with the period and length of the record. Thus a particular 30-year period may not be representative. Indeed, the period 1931-60, upon which many statistical analyses are based in defining "normal" climate, was abnormally warm compared to the average for the last thousand years. Further, the climatic record for the past million years shows that the climate has varied over all recorded time scales.

The variation in global mean surface temperature over the past 100 years is about 31°F (0.5°C). From the 1890s to the mid-1940s the global air temperature increased by about 0.5°C. Since 1940 global mean temperatures have fallen by about 0.3°C and appear to have leveled off. Every summer during the 1930s in the corn belt of the United States was warmer than the average for the century. The results of the recent cooling trend can be seen in agricultural records. For example, harvests in England were completed about nine days later on the average during 1960-73 than during the 1940s. Food production may be affected less by cooling or warming trends than by a trend associated with greater variability of the weather and more common occurrence of droughts, floods, hot summers, and severe winters.

The instrumental record of climatic change only spans the last 200-300 years. Climatic variations over much longer time scales have been deduced by analyses of tree rings; fossil flora pollen and fauna in deep ocean sediments and their isotopic composition; fossil pollen in soil and lake sediment layers (varves); isotopic composition in ice cores from Greenland and the polar ice caps; and sealevel changes. Although these data do not give a complete global picture, they do clearly show climatic trends and periods of significant climatic variations.

The variation during the last 1,000 years of the mean temperature for central England inferred from historical data is about 35.6°F (2.0°C). Fluctuations in temperature of this magnitude coincided with significant changes in agricultural practices that caused the migration of civilizations. Around the ninth century Norse settlers in Iceland seem to have flourished in a phase of rapid warming and were able to establish a colony in Greenland. However, within a few hundred years a deterioration in climate occurred that was a major contributing factor in the collapse of the Greenland colony. The Iceland colony barely survived through the Little Ice Age, which extended from the 15th to the 19th centuries.

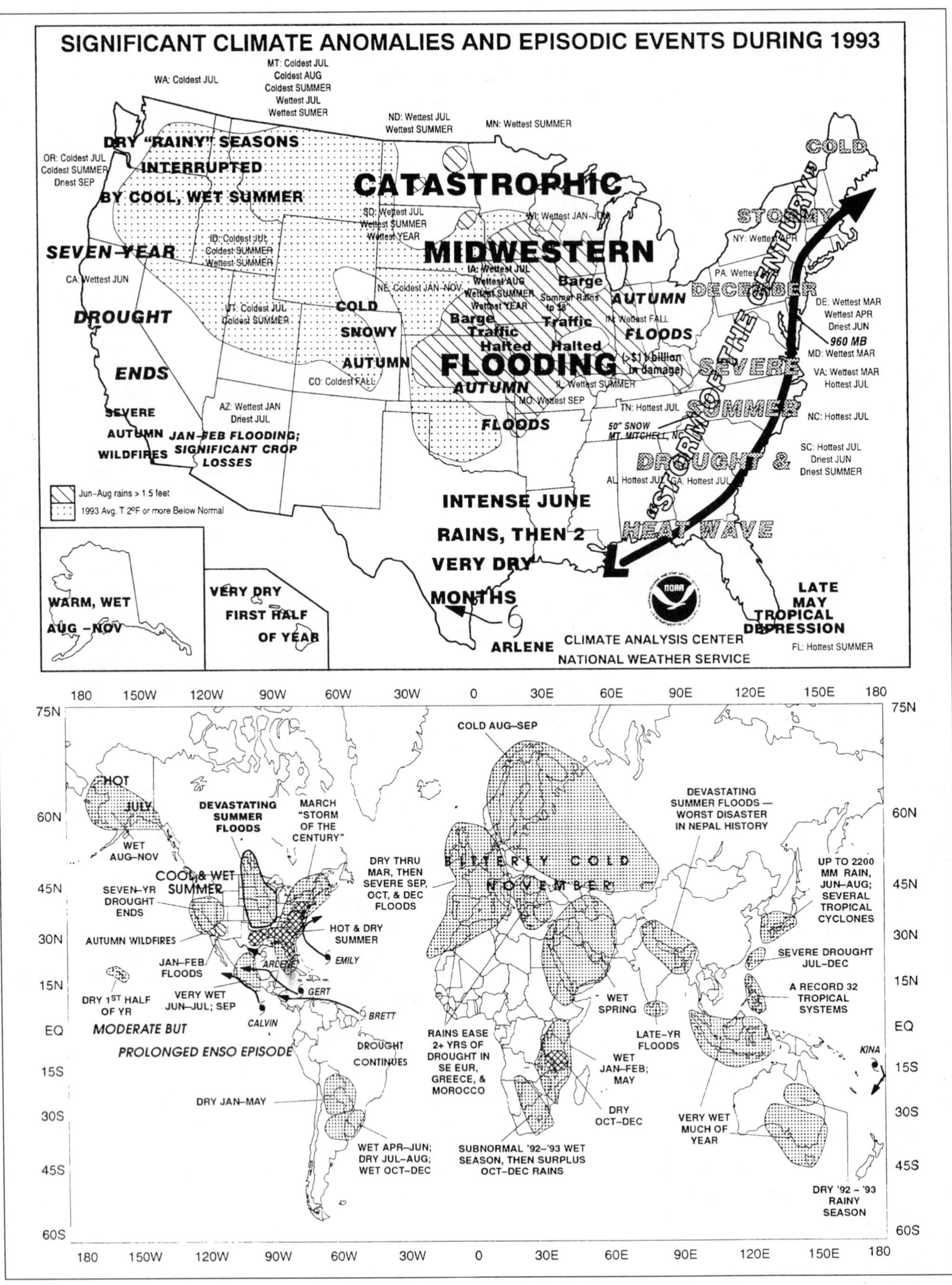
SIGNIFICANT CLIMATE ANOMALIES AND EPISODIC EVENTS DURING 1993
WA: Coldest JUL
MT: Coldest JUL Coldest AUG Coldest SUMMER Wettest JUL Wettest SUMER
ND: Wettest JUL Wettest SUMMER
MN: Wettest SUMMER
OR: Coldest JUL Coldest SUMMER Driest SEP
DRY "RAINY" SEASONS INTERRUPTED BY COOL, WET SUMMER
CATASTROPHIC MIDWESTERN FLOODING
SD: Wettest JUL Wettest SUMMER Wettest YEAR
WI: Wettest JAN–JUN
ID: Coldest JUL Coldest SUMMER Wettest SUMMER
SEVEN-YEAR DROUGHT ENDS
CA: Wettest JUN
IA: Wettest JUL Wettest AUG Wettest SUMMER Wettest YEAR
NE: Coldest JAN–NOV
Barge Traffic Halted
Summer Rains to 58"
UT: Coldest JUL Coldest SUMMER
COLD SNOWY AUTUMN
IN: Wettest FALL
AUTUMN FLOODS
(>$11 billion in damage)
CO: Coldest FALL
AUTUMN FLOODS
IL: Wettest SUMMER
MO: Wettest SEP
AZ: Wettest JAN Driest JUL
SEVERE AUTUMN WILDFIRES
JAN–FEB FLOODING; SIGNIFICANT CROP LOSSES
Jun–Aug rains > 1.5 feet
1993 Avg. T 2°F or more Below Normal
COLD
STORMY
NY: Wettest APR
PA: Wettest
DECEMBER
"STORM OF THE CENTURY"
DE: Wettest MAR Wettest APR Driest JUN
960 MB
MD: Wettest MAR
VA: Wettest MAR Hottest JUL
SEVERE SUMMER
TN: Hottest JUL
NC: Hottest JUL
50" SNOW MT. MITCHELL, NC
DROUGHT &
SC: Hottest JUL Driest JUN Driest SUMMER
AL: Hottest JUL
GA: Hottest JUL
HEAT WAVE
INTENSE JUNE RAINS, THEN 2 VERY DRY MONTHS
WARM, WET AUG–NOV
VERY DRY FIRST HALF OF YEAR
ARLENE
CLIMATE ANALYSIS CENTER NATIONAL WEATHER SERVICE
LATE MAY TROPICAL DEPRESSION
FL: Hottest SUMMER
COLD AUG–SEP
HOT JULY
WET AUG–NOV
DEVASTATING SUMMER FLOODS
MARCH "STORM OF THE CENTURY"
COOL & WET SUMMER
SEVEN-YR DROUGHT ENDS
AUTUMN WILDFIRES
JAN–FEB FLOODS
HOT & DRY SUMMER
EMILY
GERT
DRY 1ST HALF OF YR
VERY WET JUN–JUL; SEP
CALVIN
BRETT
MODERATE BUT PROLONGED ENSO EPISODE
DROUGHT CONTINUES
DRY THRU MAR, THEN SEVERE SEP, OCT, & DEC FLOODS
BITTERLY COLD NOVEMBER
DEVASTATING SUMMER FLOODS — WORST DISASTER IN NEPAL HISTORY
UP TO 2200 MM RAIN, JUN–AUG; SEVERAL TROPICAL CYCLONES
SEVERE DROUGHT JUL–DEC
A RECORD 32 TROPICAL SYSTEMS
WET SPRING
LATE-YR FLOODS
KINA
RAINS EASE 2+ YRS OF DROUGHT IN SE EUR, GREECE, & MOROCCO
WET JAN–FEB; MAY
DRY OCT–DEC
VERY WET MUCH OF YEAR
DRY JAN–MAY
WET APR–JUN; DRY JUL–AUG; WET OCT–DEC
SUBNORMAL '92–'93 WET SEASON, THEN SURPLUS OCT–DEC RAINS
DRY '92 – '93 RAINY SEASON
180 150W 120W 90W 60W 30W 0 30E 60E 90E 120E 150E 180
75N 60N 45N 30N 15N EQ 15S 30S 45S 60S

Mechanisms of climatic change

The causes of past climatic changes have not yet been adequately explained. There are three mechanisms, however, that seem to offer the greatest insight into patterns of climatic change on various time scales over the past 400,000 years. First, there are the long-term cyclic effects produced by subtle, regular variations in Earth's orbital path and inclination around the sun and in the orientation of the spin axis of Earth relative to the sun. These factors induce predictable, systematic changes in the amount of solar energy reaching the top of the atmosphere for different latitudes. In a cycle of approximately 23,000 years, Earth advances in its elliptical orbit so that its closest approach to the sun occurs at different times of the year. Earth and the sun are now closest in January, but in 10,000 years they will be closest in July (a period of approximately 20,000 years). There are also orbital changes affecting climate on time scales greater than 20,000 years. In a cycle of approximately 41,000 years, the orbit tilts so that Earth's axis is sometimes more nearly perpendicular to the planetary plane than at other times (more properly, the tilt changes with respect to the moving ecliptic). In a cycle of approximately 93,000 years, the eccentricity of the earth's orbit changes from nearly circular to more noticeably elliptical.

A second mechanism, which may cause climatic changes on the time scale of a few decades, is variation in the solar output. There is still considerable debate about the link between solar activity (e.g., the 11-year sunspot cycle) and weather. Nevertheless, many features of the observed record of temperature variations since 1600 have been reproduced with a model which incorporated an empirical dependence on solar activity as measured by the Wolf sunspot number. This dependence seems to imply that the solar output is more than 2% less when there is no sunspot activity than when there is moderate activity. More observations by either satellite or balloon-borne instrument systems are needed to confirm such a relationship.

A third mechanism for climatic change is increased atmospheric dust loading due to volcanic activity, which can affect climate on a time scale of years to decades. Intense volcanic eruptions can inject large amounts of dust into the stratosphere where the residence time may range from several months to several years. Dust produced by volcanoes can have a veiling effect that reduces the amount of solar radiation reaching the ground and scatters more incoming solar radiation back to space. The reduction in solar heating of the earth/atmosphere system results in cooler surface temperatures. Climate models including simulation of the effect of volcanic dust have duplicated the major features of the recent climatic record, including the cool temperatures of the Little Ice Age and the decades around 1800 along with the general warming trend between the 1890s and 1940s. None of the above mechanisms, however satisfactorily explains the decline in temperature observed since 1940.

Some have postulated that the cooling since 1940 is due to anthropogenic influences rather than natural climate variability. The suggestion that man has increased the amount of atmospheric dust through agricultural and industrial activities and that this is the cause of the recent cooling is not borne out in global measurements of atmospheric turbidity, although this may partially explain the observed changes in regional climates.

Climatic fluctuations involve processes on a range of spatial scales that can interact in a highly complex way so as to cause climatic anomalies affecting large geographic areas. The intermediate-term anomalies are the result of persistently recurrent weather systems of the same type. The fundamental question involves how and why particular events recur during a given season or sometimes recur for several seasons or years. To cause recurrent events like prolonged droughts or cold waves would seem to require some sort of memory. It is highly unlikely that the atmosphere alone can account for this persistent recurrence because of its highly variable nature and its relatively short thermodynamic relaxation time.

The oceans play a major role in the evolution of intermediate-and medium-term climatic fluctuations. The top 3.27 yards (3 m) of the ocean contain as much heat as the entire atmosphere, and anomalies in ocean temperature have been observed to penetrate down to a few hundred meters. These temperature anomalies create vast heat reservoirs that may affect the course and behavior of storms and jet streams later on. The anomalies are in turn frequently responses to antecedent abnormal atmospheric conditions.

It appears that the abnormal winter of 1976-77 was the result of several factors that operated in a synergistic fashion so that positive feedback processes were amplified in the coupled ocean/air/land system. Extreme cold dominated the eastern half of the United States, record drought affected the far west, and equally abnormal warmth occurred over Alaska and much of the Canadian Arctic. Jerome Namias suggests that interactions between sea surface temperature anomalies in the Pacific, known as El Niño and the atmospheric flow pattern resulted in storms being diverted northward to Alaska rather than coming into the West. The storms moving up to Alaska then created a southward bulge in the jet stream in the eastern United States that moved arctic air masses southward producing snow. Snow-albedo feedback then intensified the cold and the temperature difference between the continent and the Gulf Stream, setting up another set of storms along the eastern seaboard that created more snow and more cold air. The very strong El Niño of 1982-83 produced many new puzzles that require even more complex explanations, possibly involving the volcanic eruption of El Chicon and other poorly understood factors.

El Niño

El Niño is the most powerful weather event on Earth, disrupting weather patterns across half the earth's surface. Its two-to seven-year cycle brings lingering rain to some areas

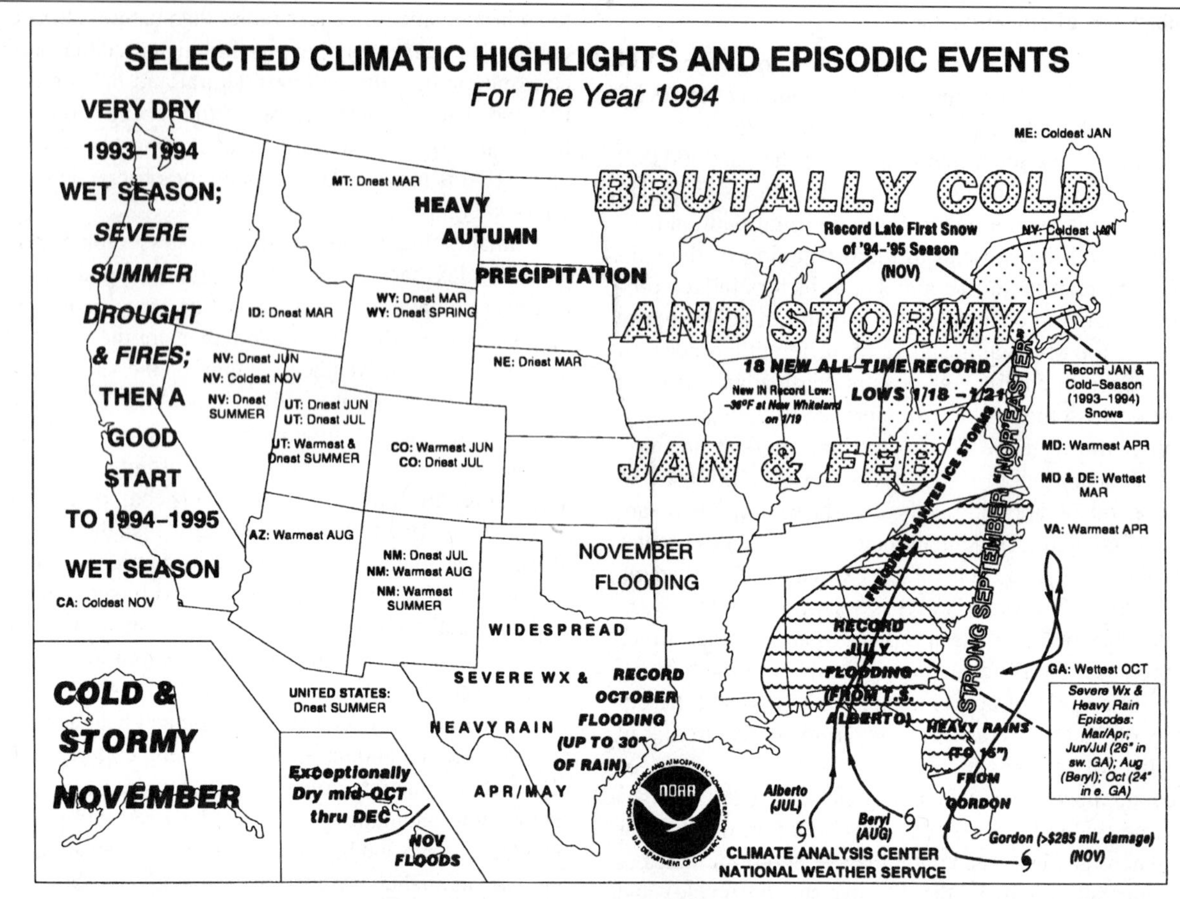
SELECTED CLIMATIC HIGHLIGHTS AND EPISODIC EVENTS
For The Year 1994
VERY DRY 1993–1994 WET SEASON; SEVERE SUMMER DROUGHT & FIRES; THEN A GOOD START TO 1994–1995 WET SEASON
CA: Coldest NOV
MT: Driest MAR
HEAVY AUTUMN PRECIPITATION
ID: Driest MAR
WY: Driest MAR
WY: Driest SPRING
NV: Driest JUN
NV: Coldest NOV
NV: Driest SUMMER
UT: Driest JUN
UT: Driest JUL
UT: Warmest & Driest SUMMER
NE: Driest MAR
CO: Warmest JUN
CO: Driest JUL
AZ: Warmest AUG
NM: Driest JUL
NM: Warmest AUG
NM: Warmest SUMMER
NOVEMBER FLOODING
WIDESPREAD SEVERE WX & HEAVY RAIN APR/MAY
RECORD OCTOBER FLOODING (UP TO 30" OF RAIN)
UNITED STATES: Driest SUMMER
COLD & STORMY NOVEMBER
Exceptionally Dry mid-OCT thru DEC
NOV FLOODS
BRUTALLY COLD AND STORMY JAN & FEB
ME: Coldest JAN
NY: Coldest JAN
Record Late First Snow of '94–'95 Season (NOV)
18 NEW ALL-TIME RECORD LOWS 1/18 – 1/21
New IN Record Low: –36°F at New Whiteland on 1/19
Record JAN & Cold-Season (1993–1994) Snows
MD: Warmest APR
MD & DE: Wettest MAR
VA: Warmest APR
FREQUENT JAN/FEB ICE STORMS
STRONG SEPTEMBER "NOR'EASTER"
RECORD JULY FLOODING (FROM T.S. ALBERTO)
HEAVY RAINS (TO 15") FROM GORDON
GA: Wettest OCT
Severe Wx & Heavy Rain Episodes: Mar/Apr; Jun/Jul (26" in sw. GA); Aug (Beryl); Oct (24" in e. GA)
Alberto (JUL)
Beryl (AUG)
Gordon (>$285 mil. damage) (NOV)
NOAA
CLIMATE ANALYSIS CENTER
NATIONAL WEATHER SERVICE

SIGNIFICANT GLOBAL CLIMATE ANOMALIES AND EPISODIC EVENTS

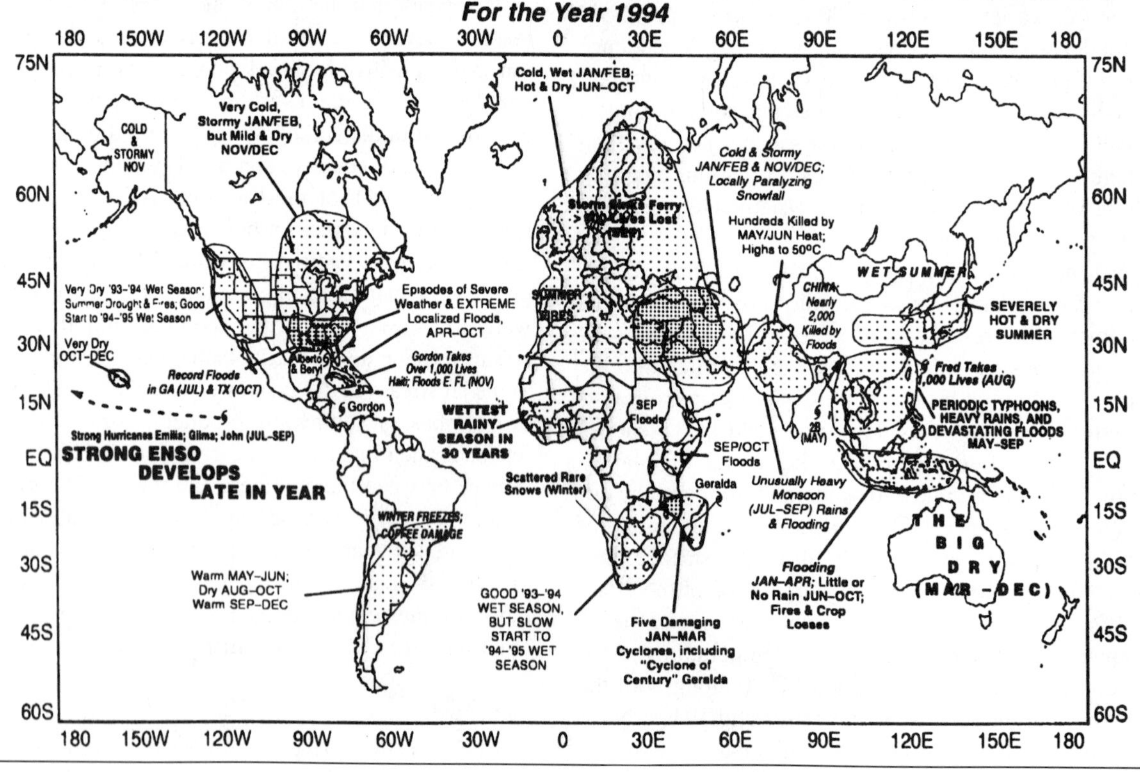
For the Year 1994
180 150W 120W 90W 60W 30W 0 30E 60E 90E 120E 150E 180
75N 60N 45N 30N 15N EQ 15S 30S 45S 60S
COLD & STORMY NOV
Very Cold, Stormy JAN/FEB, but Mild & Dry NOV/DEC
Cold, Wet JAN/FEB; Hot & Dry JUN–OCT
Cold & Stormy JAN/FEB & NOV/DEC; Locally Paralyzing Snowfall
Hundreds Killed by MAY/JUN Heat; Highs to 50°C
Very Dry '93–'94 Wet Season; Summer Drought & Fires; Good Start to '94–'95 Wet Season
Very Dry OCT–DEC
Episodes of Severe Weather & EXTREME Localized Floods, APR–OCT
Gordon Takes Over 1,000 Lives Haiti; Floods E. FL (NOV)
Record Floods in GA (JUL) & TX (OCT)
Alberto & Beryl
Gordon
Strong Hurricanes Emilia; Gilma; John (JUL–SEP)
STRONG ENSO DEVELOPS LATE IN YEAR
WETTEST RAINY SEASON IN 30 YEARS
SEP Floods
SEP/OCT Floods
WET SUMMER
CHINA: Nearly 2,000 Killed by Floods
SEVERELY HOT & DRY SUMMER
Fred Takes 1,000 Lives (AUG)
PERIODIC TYPHOONS, HEAVY RAINS, AND DEVASTATING FLOODS MAY–SEP
2B (MAY)
Scattered Rare Snows (Winter)
Geralda
Unusually Heavy Monsoon (JUL–SEP) Rains & Flooding
THE BIG DRY (MAR – DEC)
WINTER FREEZES; COFFEE DAMAGE
Warm MAY–JUN; Dry AUG–OCT Warm SEP–DEC
GOOD '93–'94 WET SEASON, BUT SLOW START TO '94–'95 WET SEASON
Five Damaging JAN–MAR Cyclones, including "Cyclone of Century" Geralda
Flooding JAN–APR; Little or No Rain JUN–OCT; Fires & Crop Losses

and severe drought to others. El Niño develops when currents in the Pacific Ocean shift, bringing warm water eastward from Australia toward Peru and Ecuador. Heat rising off warmer water shifts patterns of atmospheric pressure, interrupting the high-altitude wind currents of the jet stream and causing climate changes and anomalies.

El Niño, or "Christ child" in Spanish, tends to appear in December. The phenomenon was first noted by Peruvian fishermen in the 1700s, who saw a warming of normally cold Peruvian coastal waters and a simultaneous disappearance of anchovy schools that provided their livelihood.

The most recent El Niño began to develop in 1989, but significant warming of the Pacific did not begin until late in 1991, reaching its peak in early 1992. Typically, El Niño results in unusual weather and short-term climate changes that cause losses in corps and commercial fishing. El Niño contributed to North America's mild 1992 winter, torrential flooding in southern California and the Midwest, and severe droughts in southeastern Africa. Wild animals in central and southern Africa died by the thousands, and 20 million people were plagued by famine. The dried prairie of Alberta, Canada, failed to produce wheat, and Latin America received record flooding. Droughts were felt in the Philippines, Sri Lanka, and Australia, and Turkey experienced heavy snowfall. The South Pacific saw unusual numbers of cyclones during the winter of 1992. El Niño's influence also seems to have suppressed some of the cooling effects of Mount Pinatubo's 1991 explosion.

Recently, scientists mapping the sea floor of the South Pacific near Easter Island have found what may be the greatest concentration of active volcanoes on earth. The discovery has intensified debate over whether undersea volcanic activity could change water temperatures enough to affect weather patterns in the Pacific. Some scientists speculate that periods of extreme volcanic activity underwater could trigger El Niño.

El Niño ends when the warm water is diverted toward the North and South Poles, emptying the moving reservoir of stored energy. Before El Niño can develop again, the western Pacific must "refill" with warm water, which takes at least two years.

This simplified description of climatic change and antecedent events illustrates the complex coupling of physical processes and events. Understanding of these processes has not yet developed to the point, however, where scientific consensus on the causes, trends, and magnitudes of climatic variations has been achieved, let alone understanding to offer prospects for accurate quantitative predictions. Considerable debate still goes on within the scientific community about all these matters. The trends over the next 100-1,000 years may be toward warmer climates or the return of a major Ice Age. Or, perhaps, Earth is in for a prolonged period of highly variable and very disruptive patterns of weather and short term climatic fluctuations. Another Ice Age cannot be ruled out, especially when one considers a time frame beyond a few hundred years. For the moment, however, a moderate degree of consensus has developed among climatological experts that the trends over the next hundred years or more will be toward warmer climates.

• CARBON DIOXIDE

A recent analysis by the National Research Council of the potential climatic effects of the by-products of energy production and consumption (heat, particulate matter, and gases) showed that the combustion product carbon dioxide (CO_2) has the greatest apparent potential for disturbing the global climate over the next few centuries. The perception that there might be a serious CO_2 problem stems from the following:

•There has been a well-documented worldwide increase in atmospheric CO_2 concentrations since 1958; this growth has probably been occurring since the middle of the last century.

•An amount equivalent to about 50% of the CO_2 released from fossil-fuel burning has been accumulating in the atmosphere.

•CO_2 transmits solar radiation but absorbs some of the outgoing longwave radiation from the earth, which is the so-called "greenhouse" effect. Thus, qualitatively, CO_2 should act to warm the lower atmosphere and, by radiating more outgoing energy, cool the stratosphere.

•Different calculations of the "greenhouse" warming indicate that doubling of the CO_2 content of the air could result in a 34.7-37.4°F (1.5-3°C) warming of the lower atmosphere. This global warming is sufficient to cause significant alteration of the present climate.

•While the climatic effects would be worldwide, they will likely not be uniform: some regions of the globe would experience greater changes from the present, others less.

•The doubling of atmospheric CO_2 could take place within the next 75 years. There are sufficient fossil-fuel reserves to raise the atmospheric CO_2 many-fold if they are consumed rapidly enough.

•Natural rates of removal of CO_2 from the air are calculated to be so slow that it might take many centuries before atmospheric CO_2 levels returned to "normal" after emissions ceased.

The crucial questions to be answered include:

1. What will be the potential future atmospheric concentrations of carbon dioxide?
2. What will be the climatic effects of these concentrations?
3. What will be the effect on the biological and physical environment of these changes?
4. What, if any, will be the effects on human societies?
5. What, if any, actions can be taken in order to diminish the climatic changes or mitigate their consequences?

Sources of atmospheric carbon dioxide

The main source of the observed increase in CO_2 is thought to be combustion of fossil fuels. Recently, however, the possibility has been raised that worldwide land-use practices, particularly deforestation and oxidation of humus, could also be contributing to the buildup. It is not thought likely that natural sources, while important over the long history of Earth, are a significant factor in the recent rise.

Volcanoes and other natural venting of CO_2 from Earth's interior, as well as weathering of terrestrial carbonates, is thought to be only a very small fraction of the current annual net input. Recent suggestions that venting of methane along fault lines, and subsequent oxidation, could represent an additional source may need to be checked. No specific study of natural sources is now planned but it should be borne in mind that no comprehensive theory exists to explain the natural cycle of CO_2 over the billions of years of Earth's history—or in fact what atmospheric concentrations of CO_2 actually occurred during this time.

There are three aspects to the problem that should be considered: estimation of the carbon content of fossil fuel reserves in the ground; determination of the annual rate at which these reserves are converted to fuel and used (also other industrial sources such as cement production); and projection of future demand for these fuels.

The available reserves are well enough known today to argue that, if burned rapidly enough, atmospheric CO_2 will continue to increase to several times its present value. Nevertheless, better assessment on a country-by-country basis will be needed to keep track of the potential supply.

A controversy exists whether the carbon in the atmosphere is increasing partly because of deforestation and other land-use practices, or whether the biosphere now acts as a net sink, absorbing a fraction of the fossil fuel CO_2. Current models of oceanic uptake of CO_2 allow, at most, only a small amount of extra non-fossil fuel CO_2 to come from the biosphere. Other investigators have claimed that amounts as great as the fossil-fuel contribution itself could be coming to the air from deforestation. If the latter is the case, then the understanding of the various sinks for atmospheric CO_2 must currently be seriously in error.

Regardless of current and past biospheric trends, it is clear that future levels of atmospheric CO_2 could be substantially increased by large-scale clearing of tropical rain forests followed by oxidation and associated disturbances of the soils. There are reasonably good estimates of past and current fossil fuel usage, but there is very poor knowledge of the current rate of conversion of one type of vegetation to another or to nonvegetated areas like cities and what this means in terms of the total biospheric mass of fixed carbon. These conversions can be deliberate, as with conversion of the forest to agriculture or incidental to other activities, or they may be natural as a result of local climatic shifts. It is desirable to estimate the current changes in the biosphere both to formulate and calibrate models of the carbon cycle as well as to determine the effects of future land-use changes on CO_2 levels.

Sinks for atmospheric CO_2

The ocean is believed to be the major sink for atmospheric CO_2. To provide reliable predictions of future atmospheric CO_2 levels, one must thoroughly understand the dynamics of the CO_2 uptake and the transfer of CO_2 from the surface waters to deeper waters. Several important aspects are involved. The exchange rate of CO_2 between air and sea must be known as a function of temperature, sea state, and possibly wind speed and water chemistry. The thermodynamic distribution coefficient of CO_2 gas between air and sea water (the CO_2 buffer factor) must be known as a function of temperature, alkalinity and total dissolved inorganic carbon concentration. The patterns and rates of vertical transfer within the sea must be determined. The impact of climate changes on these rates must also be anticipated. The vertical flux of particles and organisms transporting carbon downward through the sea should be assessed. The possible influence of environmental changes induced by human's activities on these fluxes must be determined. The role of $CaCO_3$ in determining the uptake of CO_2 from the air should be examined. The dissolution of $CaCO_3$ in marine sediments enhances the capability of the ocean to absorb fossil fuel CO_2 from the air. For the shallow sediments, the critical mineral is high-magnesium calcite; for the deep sea sediments, the critical mineral is calcite.

Most scientists now believe that transfer of CO_2 from the surface waters to deeper waters will constitute the rate-limiting step for oceanic uptake of CO_2 for the next several hundred years. This transfer takes place both by turbulent mixing through the main thermocline and by organized circulations where water previously in contact with the air sinks, mainly at high latitudes. Much of our knowledge of the penetrations of CO_2 into the oceans stems from observations of human-made tracers, notably tritium and ^{14}C, produced in nuclear weapons tests. Continued surveys of these and other transient tracers are likely to be our main tool to provide an understanding of oceanic circulation and mixing.

The rate of future increases in CO_2 concentrations are dependent on how much higher CO_2 levels would enhance the primary production potential of the vegetation and so increase the rate of carbon fixation by the biota. Such fixation would reduce the rate of increase in atmospheric CO_2 from new sources.

To acquire information on the plants' responses to higher CO_2 levels, it will be necessary to consider the effects of increased CO_2 on photosynthesis, nitrogen fixation, water-use efficiency of plants and, of course, actual growth. Photosynthesis is the central process governing the primary productivity of all green plants. The availability of nutrients and water are generally considered to be the major limiting factors to plant productivity, and it is not clear to what extent enhancement of photosynthesis by increased CO_2 will increase carbon fixation. Water used by plants is controlled largely by the stomata, which in turn may be influenced by the ambient CO_2 concentration. It is possible that increased atmospheric CO_2 could result in increased water-use efficiency by allowing the photosynthesis rate to remain unchanged while reducing the demand for water. On the other hand, plants may increase photosynthesis for the same water usage at elevated CO_2 concentrations. Note that increased primary productivity by itself is not sufficient to slow down the atmospheric CO_2 growth. Only if this increased productivity results in a year to year increase in stored biomass or detritus will it increase the strength of the sink for excess CO_2.

Models of the carbon cycle

All the major components of the carbon dioxide research program involve model development as part of their efforts, but an additional component will be devoted to integrating the results of these studies into a global carbon cycle model. Its goal will be to predict the future atmospheric CO_2 concentrations from scenarios of fossil fuel use and land-use changes. To be valid, these models must be able to reproduce not only the currently available data on atmospheric CO_2 growth, but be compatible with the distribution of the isotopes of carbon in the atmosphere, oceans and biosphere.

Progress in this area will depend upon progress in determining the components of the carbon cycle and their reactions to increased atmospheric CO_2 coupled with any attendant climate changes. Attempts to model the carbon cycle will also likely disclose areas needing particular research emphasis in the other components. This effort must proceed, as with all modeling efforts, in close association with data gathering and analysis.

Some modeling of the carbon cycle is now going on both in the United States and abroad. Cooperation among the groups is essential. There is marked similarity in the assumptions and transfer rates among carbon reservoirs, but this may indicate the paucity of information upon which all of the modeled processes are based.

Climate effects of increased CO_2

The consequences to the climate of increased atmospheric CO_2 have been estimated from computer simulations. These simulations, which indicate that a doubling of CO_2 concentrations would increase the global mean temperature of the lower atmosphere by between 34.7 and 37.4°F (1.5 and 3°C), are crude even though they employ the most sophisticated techniques and machines available. Several factors not now included in simulation models are thought to be important and others now unknown could also prove to be significant. In addition, none of the climate models applied to the CO_2 problem have contained a realistic topography or distribution of land and water. Thus, regional climatic changes cannot now be predicted, yet regional modifications of precipitation may be the most crucial consequence of CO_2 increases in the atmosphere.

Knowledge of the climatic history of Earth is important both to anticipate what might happen and to provide data to help validate the computer simulations. Emphasis can be put on periods where the earth was warmer than it is now. Abnormally warm years within the period when instruments were available can also be considered.

Effects of climate change

It is necessary to translate the anticipated climate changes due to increased CO_2 into effects on the biosphere as well as on the cryosphere and ocean circulation. It is likely that some of these effects will feed back to the climate system itself and to the carbon cycle. In addition to the effects already mentioned, the following effects are also possible and in need of further study.

- Marine organisms could be affected by increases in dissolved CO_2. The slow lowering of oceanic pH and lowering of the supersaturation with respect to $CaCO_3$ of surface waters could affect the ability of organisms to form carbonate shells and skeletal structures.
- Changes in atmospheric circulation could produce changes in oceanic circulation. Marine productivity could be reduced if the rate of upwelling were decreased since the latter controls the supply of nutrients to certain surface waters.
- Greatly elevated CO_2 concentrations in the air may have effects on non-photosynthesizing organisms. It is unlikely that mammals would suffer, but possibly invertebrates and microorganisms would be affected.
- Ecosystem stability and the geographic distribution of plants, and the animals associated with them, could be affected. Shifts of temperature and precipitation patterns could rearrange the location of major biomes; some species could suffer, others might prosper.
- Special attention should be given to agricultural effects of climate changes. This, of course, is of current concern because climate changes occur naturally. The reaction of the world's food- and fiber-producing regions to the CO_2-induced climate changes warrants special consideration, however.
- Much concern has been expressed that warming would cause the polar ice sheets to melt and the sea level to rise. It is quite unlikely that this would happen in the next few centuries and the likelihood of its occurrence may have been overstressed. Climatically-induced surges of the ice sheets are possible, but the causes of surges are not well understood. It has been asserted, however, that West Antarctica could deglaciate if the ocean should warm. Because this could produce a 5.45 yards (5 m) sea level rise, this possibility deserves some special attention. The recession of mountain glaciers also should be examined although total melting of them would only raise sea level about 1.09 yards (1 m).

Societal impacts

The ultimate issue is, of course, the impact of increased CO_2 on society. It must be stressed that impacts of climate change will not fall equally on all segments of the world's society despite their global nature. Indeed some regions or countries may find benefits in the altered climate, others may be relatively unaffected, while some could be harmed significantly. Such disparity of effects may make international agreements very difficult to achieve if they are ever needed.

Among the more obvious things to explore are the impacts of shifting agricultural regions and productivity, water availability due to changing precipitation regimes (inter-basin transfer of water to alleviate the problems of local drought), and impacts on energy demand itself. (Is there a positive or negative feedback on CO_2 production?)

The decision to curtail fossil fuel will be made only if and when society's costs are believed to exceed the benefits to continued fossil fuel combustion. Worldwide agreement on reduced consumption of fossil fuel will present very serious international problems. Thus, it seems worthwhile to explore how societies might cope with the climatic consequences of increased CO_2.

Mitigating strategies

Besides reducing fossil-fuel use, one may consider other technological solutions should CO_2 increases be seen as undesirable. Certainly both more efficient use of energy and the development of non-fossil energy sources would help reduce the CO_2 growth and could conceivably delay the onset or even solve the problem.

No technical solution has been proposed so far that seems practicable, but this should not deter the search. One should still explore the possibilities of removing CO_2 from effluent streams or from the air, sequestering it in permanent or quasipermanent reservoirs. Even if such studies fail to uncover a feasible method for doing so, they will serve to demonstrate that technological optimism will not be a substitute for a realistic assessment of the problem.

Record-Setting Weather

• TEMPERATURE EXTREMES, HIGHEST

Temperature extremes depend upon a number of factors, important among which are altitude, latitude, surface conditions, and the density and length of record of observing stations.

The world's highest temperatures, as well as the greatest range of extremes and the greatest and most rapid temperature fluctuations, occur over continental areas in the *Temperate Zones*.

A reading of 136°F (57.2°C), observed at Azizia (elevation about 380 feet [114.6 m]), Tripolitania, Libya, North Africa, on September 13, 1922, is generally accepted as the world's highest temperature recorded under standard conditions.

The highest temperature ever observed in Canada was 115°F (46.1°C) at Gleichen, Alberta, on July 28, 1903. A high of 120°F (48.9°C) or higher has been recorded on all the continents except Antarctica where the high is only 58.3°F (14.4°C).

Greenland Ranch, California, with 134°F (56°C) on July 10, 1913, holds the record for the highest temperature ever officially recorded in the United States. This station is located in barren Death Valley which is about 140 miles (225 km) long and 4-16 miles (6.4-25.75 km) wide and runs north and south in southeastern California and southwestern Nevada. The valley is below sea level and is flanked by towering mountain ranges with Mt. Whitney, the highest landmark in the 48 states, rising to 14,495 feet (4,397 m), less than 100 miles (161 km) to the west. Death Valley has the hottest summers in the Western Hemisphere, and is the only known place in the United States where nighttime temperatures sometime remain above 100°F (37.8°C).

The highest average annual temperature in the world is probably the 88°F (31.1°C) at Lugh, Somalia, East Africa. In the United States the station normally having the highest annual average is Key West, Florida, 77.8°F (25°C); the highest summer average, Death Valley, California, 98.2°F (36.7°C) and the highest winter average, Key West, Florida, 70.2°F (21°C).

Amazing temperature rises of 40-50°F (4.4-10°C) in a few minutes occasionally may be brought about by chinook winds. Some outstanding extreme temperature rises in short periods are:

12 hours: 83°F (28.3°C), Granville, ND, February 21, 1918, from -33°F (-36.1°C) to 50°F (10°C) from early morning to late afternoon.

15 minutes: 42°F (5.6°C), Fort Assiniboine, MT, January 19, 1892, from -5°F (-20.6°C) to 37°F (2.8°C).

7 minutes: 34°F (1.1°C), Kipp, MT, December 1, 1896; observer also reported that a total rise of 80°F (26.7°C) occurred in a few hours and that 30 inches (76.2 cm) of snow disappeared in one-half day.

2 minutes: 49°F (9.4°C), Spearfish, SD, January 22, 1943, from -4°F (-20°C) at 7:30 A.M., to 45°F (7.2°C) at 7:32 A.M.

The range of temperature extremes over large bodies of water is much less than over land. The absolute extremes over the sea, as far as can be ascertained, range from 100°F (37.8°C) recorded by the *SS Titan* on August 8, 1920, in the Red Sea to -40°F (-40°C) observed by the *SS Baychino*, January 27, 1932, when beset by ice at latitude 70° 50' N, longitude 159° 11' W. In the Persian Gulf sea surface temperatures average as high as 88°F (31.1°C) for July and August, and a high of 96°F (35.6°C) measured by the *SS Frankenfels* on August 5, 1924, is at least among the highest if not the highest sea-surface temperature ever observed.

Sunniest U.S. Cities

1. Yuma, AZ
2. Redding, CA
3. Phoenix, AZ
4. Tucson, AZ/Las Vegas, NV
5. El Paso, TX

• TEMPERATURE EXTREMES, LOWEST

Antarctica, a vast elevated, snow-covered continent at the South Pole is one of the most favorable regions in the world for extremely low temperatures. Several stations there now have records dating back through 1957. During the early part of this period, a new world record low temperature was observed on several occasions. The latest, -126.9°F (-88.3°C), was recorded at Vostok (Russian station) on August 24, 1960. At the Amundsen-Scott station (elevation 9,186 ft.) located on a snow plain within a few hundred yards of the geographical South Pole, the average annual temperature for the period 1957-64 was -59°F (-50°C). For July, the average maximum temperature was -69°F (-55°C), the minimum -80°F (61°C) and for January these values were -17°F (-27.2°C) and -22°F (-30°C), respectively. The average temperature at Vostok for the 2-year period 1958-59 was -67°F (-54°C). Even colder locations may exist on the continent.

Other regions favorable for unusually low winter extremes include Greenland, a high snow-covered area located mostly in the north polar regions, and north central Siberia, part of a great land mass at high latitudes. Minima with a temperature of -90°F (-67°C), Verhoyansk at -89.7°F (66.9°C), February 5 and 7, 1892 and Oimekon at -89.9°F, February 6, 1933. The lowest temperature on the Greenland Icecap, -86.8°F (-66.0°C), was observed at Northice on January 9, 1954. Canada's lowest temperature, -81°F (-62°C), was observed at Snag, Yukon territory, near the border of Alaska at an altitude of 2,120 feet (643 m) on February 3, 1947.

In the United States, the lowest temperature on record, -79.8°F (-61.5°C), was recorded at Prospect Creek Camp in the Endicott Mountains of Northern Alaska at latitude 66° 48' N. longitude 150° 40' W. The lowest temperature in the 48 states, -69.7°F (-56°C), occurred at Rogers Pass, in Lewis and Clark County, Montana. This location is in mountainous and heavily forested terrain, about 1/2 mile (.81 km) east of and 140 feet (42.5 m) below the summit of the Continental Divide.

Cloudiest U.S. Cities

1. Quillayute, WA (240)
2. Astoria, OR (239)
3. Olympia, WA (229)
4. Seattle, WA (226)
5. Portland, OR (223)

Shown below are the cloudiest cities within the United States. Average number of cloudy days per year is shown parenthetically.

The lowest average annual temperature recorded in the United States is 9.6°F (-12°C) at Barrow, Alaska, which lies on the Arctic coast. Barrow also has the coolest summers (June, July, August) with an average of 36.7°F (2.6°C). The lowest average winter (December, January, February) temperature is -15.6°F (-26°C) at Barter Island on the Arctic coast of northeast Alaska. In Hawaii, average annual temperatures range from 44°F (6.7°C) at Mauna Loa Slope Observatory (elevation 11,146 feet [3,381 m]) on the island of Hawaii to 75.9°F (24°C) at Honolulu on the island of Oahu.

In the 48 states, Mt. Washington, New Hampshire (elevation 6,262 feet [1,899 m]) has the lowest mean annual temperature, 27°F (-2.8°C), and the lowest mean summer (June, July, August) temperature, 47.2°F (8.3°C). A few stations in the Northeast and upper Rockies have mean annuals in the high 30s; and at the Rockies stations, summers may average in the high 40s. Winter (December, January, February) mean temperature are lowest in northeastern North Dakota where the average is 5.9°F (-14°C) at the Langdon Experiment Farm and northwestern Minnesota where the average is 6.1°F at Hallock.

In continental areas of the Temperate Zone, 40-50°F (4.4-10°C) temperature falls in a few hours caused by advection of cold air masses are not uncommon. Sometimes, following these large drops due to advection, radiation may cause a further temperature fall resulting in remarkable changes. Some outstanding extreme temperature falls are:

24 hours: 100°F (37.8°C), Browning, MT, January 23-24, 1916, from 44-56°F (6.7-13.3°C).

12 hours: 84°F (28.9°C), Fairfield, MT, December 24, 1924, from 63°F (17.2°C) at noon to -21°F (-29.4°C) at midnight.

2 hours: 62°F (16.7°C), Rapid City, SD, January 12, 1911, from 49°F (9.4°C) at 6 A.M. to -13°F (-25°C) at 8 A.M.

27 minutes: 58°F (14.4°C), Spearfish, SD, January 22, 1943, from 54°F (12.2°C) at 9 A.M., to -4°F (-20°C) at 9:27 A.M.

15 minutes: 47°F (8.3°C), Rapid City, SD, January 10, 1911, from 55°F (12.8°C) at 7 A.M., to 8°F (-13.9°C) at 7:15 A.M.

WEATHER EXTREMES IN CANADA AND THE UNITED STATES

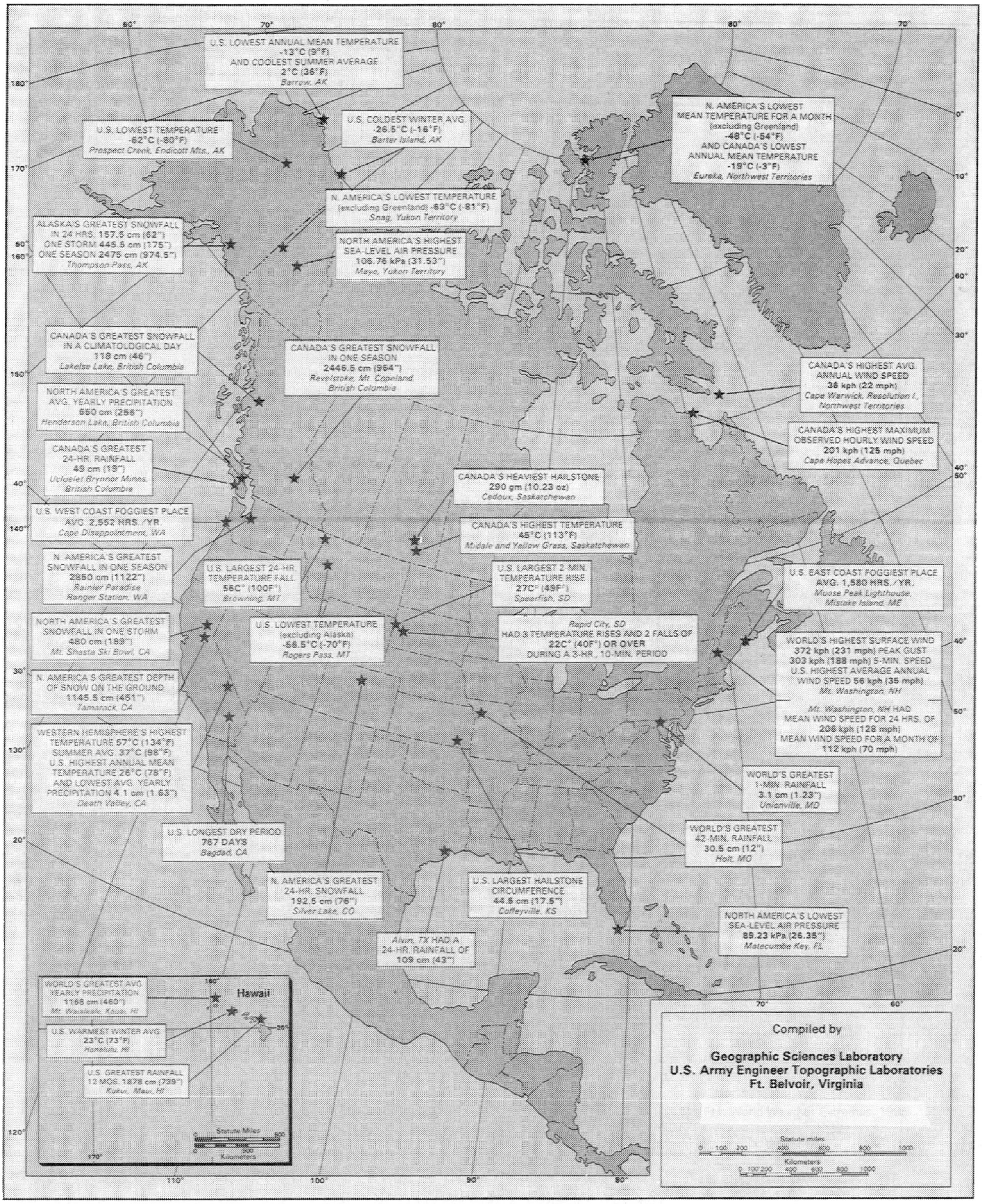

U.S. LOWEST ANNUAL MEAN TEMPERATURE
-13°C (9°F)
AND COOLEST SUMMER AVERAGE
2°C (36°F)
Barrow, AK

U.S. COLDEST WINTER AVG.
-26.5°C (-16°F)
Barter Island, AK

U.S. LOWEST TEMPERATURE
-62°C (-80°F)
Prospect Creek, Endicott Mts., AK

N. AMERICA'S LOWEST
MEAN TEMPERATURE FOR A MONTH
(excluding Greenland)
-48°C (-54°F)
AND CANADA'S LOWEST
ANNUAL MEAN TEMPERATURE
-19°C (-3°F)
Eureka, Northwest Territories

N. AMERICA'S LOWEST TEMPERATURE
(excluding Greenland) -63°C (-81°F)
Snag, Yukon Territory

ALASKA'S GREATEST SNOWFALL
IN 24 HRS. 157.5 cm (62")
ONE STORM 445.5 cm (175")
ONE SEASON 2475 cm (974.5")
Thompson Pass, AK

NORTH AMERICA'S HIGHEST
SEA-LEVEL AIR PRESSURE
106.76 kPa (31.53")
Mayo, Yukon Territory

CANADA'S GREATEST SNOWFALL
IN A CLIMATOLOGICAL DAY
118 cm (46")
Lakelse Lake, British Columbia

CANADA'S GREATEST SNOWFALL
IN ONE SEASON
2446.5 cm (964")
Revelstoke, Mt. Copeland, British Columbia

NORTH AMERICA'S GREATEST
AVG. YEARLY PRECIPITATION
650 cm (256")
Henderson Lake, British Columbia

CANADA'S HIGHEST AVG.
ANNUAL WIND SPEED
36 kph (22 mph)
Cape Warwick, Resolution I., Northwest Territories

CANADA'S HIGHEST MAXIMUM
OBSERVED HOURLY WIND SPEED
201 kph (125 mph)
Cape Hopes Advance, Quebec

CANADA'S GREATEST
24-HR. RAINFALL
49 cm (19")
Ucluelet Brynnor Mines, British Columbia

CANADA'S HEAVIEST HAILSTONE
290 gm (10.23 oz)
Cedoux, Saskatchewan

U.S. WEST COAST FOGGIEST PLACE
AVG. 2,552 HRS./YR.
Cape Disappointment, WA

CANADA'S HIGHEST TEMPERATURE
45°C (113°F)
Midale and Yellow Grass, Saskatchewan

N. AMERICA'S GREATEST
SNOWFALL IN ONE SEASON
2850 cm (1122")
Rainier Paradise Ranger Station, WA

U.S. LARGEST 24-HR.
TEMPERATURE FALL
56C° (100F°)
Browning, MT

U.S. LARGEST 2-MIN.
TEMPERATURE RISE
27C° (49F°)
Spearfish, SD

U.S. EAST COAST FOGGIEST PLACE
AVG. 1,580 HRS./YR.
Moose Peak Lighthouse, Mistake Island, ME

NORTH AMERICA'S GREATEST
SNOWFALL IN ONE STORM
480 cm (189")
Mt. Shasta Ski Bowl, CA

U.S. LOWEST TEMPERATURE
(excluding Alaska)
-56.5°C (-70°F)
Rogers Pass, MT

Rapid City, SD
HAD 3 TEMPERATURE RISES AND 2 FALLS OF
22C° (40F°) OR OVER
DURING A 3-HR., 10-MIN. PERIOD

WORLD'S HIGHEST SURFACE WIND
372 kph (231 mph) PEAK GUST
303 kph (188 mph) 5-MIN. SPEED
U.S. HIGHEST AVERAGE ANNUAL
WIND SPEED 56 kph (35 mph)
Mt. Washington, NH

N. AMERICA'S GREATEST DEPTH
OF SNOW ON THE GROUND
1145.5 cm (451")
Tamarack, CA

Mt. Washington, NH HAD
MEAN WIND SPEED FOR 24 HRS. OF
206 kph (128 mph)
MEAN WIND SPEED FOR A MONTH OF
112 kph (70 mph)

WESTERN HEMISPHERE'S HIGHEST
TEMPERATURE 57°C (134°F)
SUMMER AVG. 37°C (98°F)
U.S. HIGHEST ANNUAL MEAN
TEMPERATURE 26°C (78°F)
AND LOWEST AVG. YEARLY
PRECIPITATION 4.1 cm (1.63")
Death Valley, CA

WORLD'S GREATEST
1-MIN. RAINFALL
3.1 cm (1.23")
Unionville, MD

U.S. LONGEST DRY PERIOD
767 DAYS
Bagdad, CA

WORLD'S GREATEST
42-MIN. RAINFALL
30.5 cm (12")
Holt, MO

N. AMERICA'S GREATEST
24-HR. SNOWFALL
192.5 cm (76")
Silver Lake, CO

U.S. LARGEST HAILSTONE
CIRCUMFERENCE
44.5 cm (17.5")
Coffeyville, KS

NORTH AMERICA'S LOWEST
SEA-LEVEL AIR PRESSURE
89.23 kPa (26.35")
Matecumbe Key, FL

Alvin, TX HAD A
24-HR. RAINFALL OF
109 cm (43")

Hawaii

WORLD'S GREATEST AVG.
YEARLY PRECIPITATION
1168 cm (460")
Mt. Waialeale, Kauai, HI

U.S. WARMEST WINTER AVG.
23°C (73°F)
Honolulu, HI

U.S. GREATEST RAINFALL
12 MOS. 1878 cm (739")
Kukui, Maui, HI

Statute Miles
Kilometers

Compiled by

Geographic Sciences Laboratory
U.S. Army Engineer Topographic Laboratories
Ft. Belvoir, Virginia

Statute miles
Kilometers

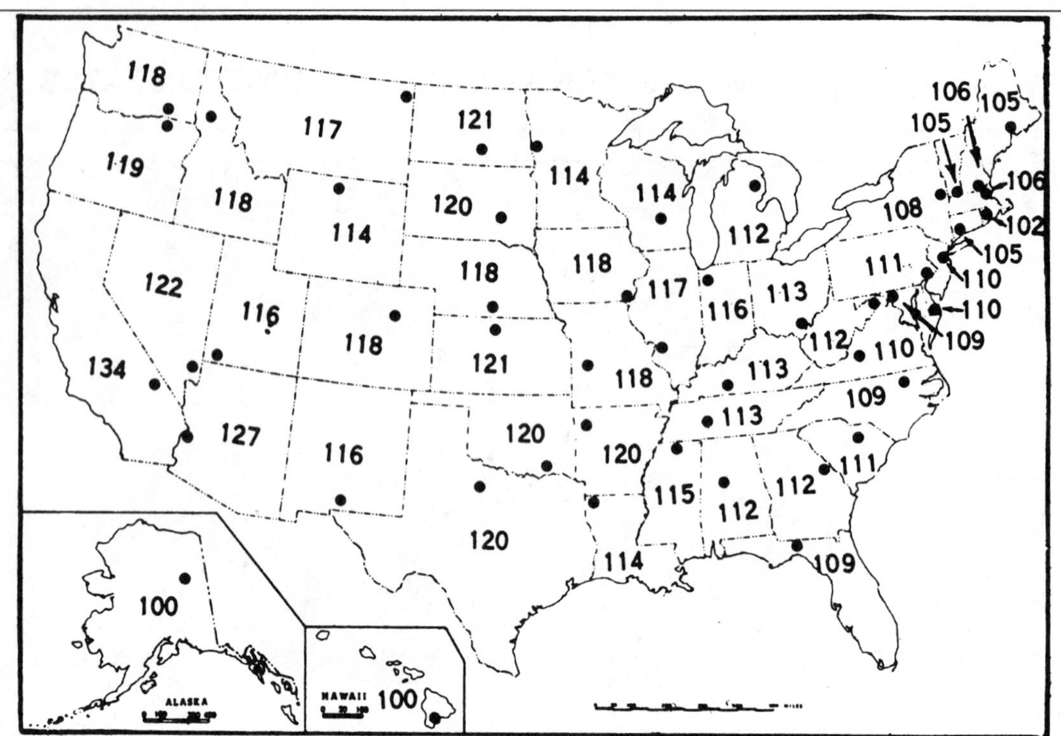

HIGHEST TEMPERATURES OF RECORD AND LOCATIONS, BY STATES

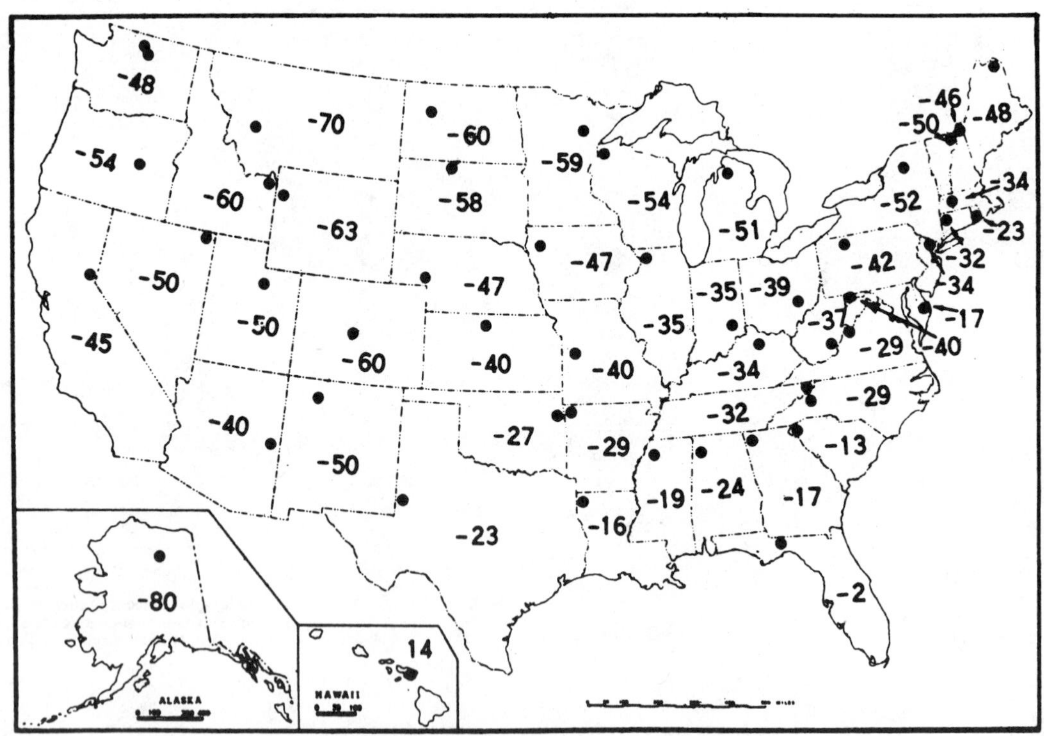

LOWEST TEMPERATURES OF RECORD AND LOCATIONS, BY STATES

RECORD HIGHEST TEMPERATURES BY STATE
(THRU 1992)

State	Temp. °F.	Date	Station	Elevation Feet
Alabama	112	Sep. 5, 1925	Centerville	345
Alaska	100	Jun. 27, 1915	Fort Yukon	est. 420
Arizona	127	Jul. 7, 1905*	Parker	345
Arkansas	120	Aug. 10, 1936	Ozark	396
California	134	Jul. 10, 1913	Greenland Ranch	-178
Colorado	118	Jul. 11, 1888	Bennett	5,484
Connecticut	105	Jul. 21, 1991*	Danbury	450
Delaware	110	Jul. 21, 1930	Millsboro	20
Florida	109	Jun. 29, 1931	Monticello	207
Georgia	112	Jul. 24, 1952	Louisville	132
Hawaii	100	Apr. 27, 1931	Pahala	850
Idaho	118	Jul. 28, 1934	Orofino	1,027
Illinois	117	Jul. 14, 1954	East St. Louis	410
Indiana	116	Jul. 14, 1936	Collegeville	672
Iowa	118	Jul. 20, 1934	Keokuk	614
Kansas	121	Jul. 24, 1936*	Alton (near)	1,651
Kentucky	114	Jul. 28, 1930	Greensburg	581
Louisiana	114	Aug. 10, 1936	Plain Dealing	268
Maine	105	Jul. 10, 1911*	North Bridgton	450
Maryland	109	Jul. 10, 1936*	Cumberland & Frederick	623; 325
Massachusetts	107	Aug. 2, 1975	New Bedford & Chester	120; 640
Michigan	112	Jul. 13, 1936	Mio	963
Minnesota	114	Jul. 6, 1936*	Moorhead	904
Mississippi	115	Jul. 29, 1930	Holly Springs	600
Missouri	118	Jul. 14, 1954*	Warsaw & Union	687; 560
Montana	117	Jul. 5, 1937	Medicine Lake	1,950
Nebraska	118	Jul. 24, 1936*	Minden	2,169
Nevada	122	Jun. 26, 1990*	Laughlin	680
New Hampshire	106	Jul. 4, 1911	Nashua	125
New Jersey	110	Jul. 10, 1936	Runyon	18
New Mexico	116	Jul. 14, 1934*	Orogrande	4,171
New York	108	Jul. 22, 1926	Troy	35
North Carolina	110	Aug. 21, 1983	Fayetteville	213
North Dakota	121	Jul. 6, 1936	Steele	1,857
Ohio	113	Jul. 21, 1934*	Gallipolis (near)	673
Oklahoma	120	Jul. 26, 1943*	Tishomingo	670
Oregon	119	Aug. 10, 1898	Pendleton	1,074
Pennsylvania	111	Jul. 10, 1936*	Phoenixville	100
Rhode Island	104	Aug. 2, 1975	Providence	51
South Carolina	111	Jun. 28, 1954*	Camden	170
South Dakota	120	Jul. 5, 1936	Gannvalley	1,750
Tennessee	113	Aug. 9, 1930*	Perryville	377
Texas	120	Aug. 12, 1936	Seymour	1,291
Utah	117	Jul. 5, 1985	Saint George	2,880
Vermont	105	Jul. 4, 1911	Vernon	310
Virginia	110	Jul. 15, 1954	Balcony Falls	725
Washington	118	Aug. 5, 1961*	Ice Harbor Dam	475
West Virginia	112	Jul. 10, 1936*	Martinsburg	435
Wisconsin	114	Jul. 13, 1936	Wisconsin Dells	900
Wyoming	114	Jul. 12, 1900	Basin	3,500

*Also on earlier dates at the same time or other places.

RECORD LOWEST TEMPERATURES BY STATE
(THRU 1992)

State	Temp. °F.	Date	Station	Elevation Feet
Alabama	-27	Jan. 30, 1966	New Market	760
Alaska	-80	Jan. 23, 1971	Prospect Creek	1,100
Arizona	-40	Jan. 7, 1971	Hawley Lake	8,180
Arkansas	-29	Feb. 13, 1905	Pond	1,250
California	-45	Jan. 20, 1937	Boca	5,532
Colorado	-61	Feb. 1, 1985	Maybell	5,920
Connecticut	-32	Feb. 16, 1943	Falls Village	585
Delaware	-17	Jan. 17, 1893	Millsboro	20
Florida	- 2	Feb. 13, 1899	Tallahassee	193
Georgia	-17	Jan. 27, 1940	CCC Camp F-16	est. 1,000
Hawaii	12	May 17, 1979	Mauna Kea Obs 111.2	13,770
Idaho	-60	Jan. 18, 1943	Island Park Dam	6,285
Illinois	-35	Jan. 22, 1930	Mount Carroll	817
Indiana	-35	Feb. 2, 1951	Greensburg	954
Iowa	-47	Jan. 12, 1912	Washta	1,157
Kansas	-40	Feb. 13, 1905	Lebanon	1,812
Kentucky	-34	Jan. 28, 1963	Cynthiana	684
Louisiana	-16	Feb. 13, 1899	Minden	194
Maine	-48	Jan. 19, 1925	Van Buren	510
Maryland	-40	Jan. 13, 1912	Oakland	2,461
Massachusetts	-35	Jan. 12, 1981	Chester	640
Michigan	-51	Feb. 9, 1934	Vanderbilt	785
Minnesota	-59	Feb. 16, 1903*	Pokegama Dam	1,280
Mississippi	-19	Jan. 30, 1966	Corinth	420
Missouri	-40	Feb. 13, 1905	Warsaw	700
Montana	-70	Jan. 20, 1954	Rogers Pass	5,470
Nebraska	-47	Feb. 12, 1899	Camp Clarke	3,700
Nevada	-50	Jan. 8, 1937	San Jacinto	5,200
New Hampshire	-46	Jan. 28, 1925	Pittsburg	1,575
New Jersey	-34	Jan. 5, 1904	River Vale	70
New Mexico	-50	Feb. 1, 1951	Gavilan	7,350
New York	-52	Feb. 18, 1979*	Old Forge	1,720
North Carolina	-34	Jan. 21, 1985	Mt. Mitchell	6,525
North Dakota	-60	Feb. 15, 1936	Parshall	1,929
Ohio	-39	Feb. 10, 1899	Milligan	800
Oklahoma	-27	Jan. 18, 1930	Watts	958
Oregon	-54	Feb. 10, 1933*	Seneca	4,700
Pennsylvania	-42	Jan. 5, 1904	Smethport	est. 1,500
Rhode Island	-23	Jan. 11, 1942	Kingston	100
South Carolina	-19	Jan. 21, 1985	Caesars Head	3,100
South Dakota	-58	Feb. 17, 1936	McIntosh	2,277
Tennessee	-32	Dec. 30, 1917	Mountain City	2,471
Texas	-23	Feb. 8, 1933*	Seminole	3,275
Utah	-69	Feb. 1, 1985	Peter's Sink	8,092
Vermont	-50	Dec. 30, 1933	Bloomfield	915
Virginia	-30	Jan. 22, 1985	Mtn. Lake Bio. Stn.	3,870
Washington	-48	Dec. 30, 1968	Mazama & Winthrop	2,120;1,765
West Virginia	-37	Dec. 30, 1917	Lewisburg	2,200
Wisconsin	-54	Jan. 24, 1922	Danbury	908
Wyoming	-63	Feb. 9, 1933	Moran	6,770

*Also on earlier dates at the same or other places.

RECORD MAXIMUM ANNUAL PRECIPITATION BY STATE
(THRU 1992)

State	Precip. Inches	Date	Station	Elevation Feet
Alabama	106.57	1853	Mt. Vernon Barracks	49
Alaska	332.29	1976	MacLeod Harbor	40
Arizona	58.92	1978	Hawley Lake	8,180
Arkansas	98.55	1957	Newhope	850
California	153.54	1909	Monumental	2,420
Colorado	92.84	1897	Ruby	est.10,000
Connecticut	78.53*	1955	Burlington Dam	460
Delaware	72.75	1948	Lewes	10
Florida	112.43*	1966	Wewahitchka	50
Georgia	112.16	1959	Flat Top	est. 3,600
Hawaii	704.83	1982	Kukui	5,788
Idaho	81.05	1933	Roland	4,150
Illinois	74.58	1950	New Burnside	560
Indiana	97.38	1890	Marengo	570
Iowa	74.50	1851	Muscatine	680
Kansas	67.02*	1985	Columbus	900
Kentucky	79.68	1950	Russelville	590
Louisiana	113.74*	1991	New Orleans (Audubon)	6
Maine	75.64	1845	Brunswick	70
Maryland	72.59	1948	Salisbury	50
Massachusetts	72.19	1983	Pembroke	74
Michigan	64.01	1881	Adrian	770
Minnesota	51.53	1911	Grand Meadow	1,340
Mississippi	104.36*	1991	Waveland	8
Missouri	92.77	1957	Portageville	280
Montana	55.51	1953	Summit	5,210
Nebraska	64.52	1869	Omaha	980
Nevada	59.03	1969	Mt. Rose Resort	est 7,300
New Hampshire	130.14	1969	Mount Washington	6,260
New Jersey	85.99	1882	Paterson	100
New Mexico	62.45	1941	White Tail	7,450
New York	82.06	1903	Wappingers Falls	200
North Carolina	129.60	1964	Rosman	2,220
North Dakota	37.98	1944	Milnor	2,600
Ohio	70.82	1870	Little Mountain	1,187
Oklahoma	84.47	1957	Kiamichi Tower	2,350
Oregon	168.88	1937	Valsetz	1,150
Pennsylvania	81.64	1952	Mt. Pocono	1,910
Rhode Island	70.21	1983	Kingston	100
South Carolina	101.65	1961	Caesar's Head	3,120
South Dakota	48.42	1946	Deadwood	4,550
Tennessee	114.88	1957	Haw Knob	4,900
Texas	109.38	1873	Clarksville	440
Utah	108.54	1983	Alta	8,700
Vermont	92.88	1983	Mt. Mansfield	3,960
Virginia	81.78	1972	Montebello	2,450
Washington	184.56	1931	Wynoochee Oxbow	670
West Virginia	94.01	1948	Romney	820
Wisconsin	62.07	1884	Embarrass	808
Wyoming	55.46	1945	Grassy Lake Dam	7,240

*At least one month estimated.

RECORD MINIMUM ANNUAL PRECIPITATION BY STATE
(THRU 1992)

State	Precip. Inches	Date	Station	Elevation Feet
Alabama	22.00	1954	Primrose Farm	180
Alaska	1.61	1935	Barrow	31
Arizona	0.07	1956	Davis Dam	660
Arkansas	19.11	1936	Index	300
California	0.00	1929	Death Valley	-282
Colorado	1.69	1939	Buena Vista	7,980
Connecticut	23.60*	1965	Baltic	140
Delaware	21.38	1965	Dover	30
Florida	21.16	1989	Conch Key	6
Georgia	17.14	1954	Swainsboro	320
Hawaii	0.19	1953	Kawaihae	est. 75
Idaho	2.09	1947	Grand View	2,360
Illinois	16.59*	1956	Keithsburg	540
Indiana	18.67	1934	Brooksville	630
Iowa	12.11	1958	Cherokee	1,360
Kansas	4.77	1956	Johnson	3,270
Kentucky	14.51	1968	Jeremiah	1,160
Louisiana	26.44	1936	Shreveport	170
Maine	23.06	1930	Machias	30
Maryland	17.76	1930	Picardy	1,030
Massachusetts	21.76*	1965	Chatham L.S.	20
Michigan	15.64	1936	Croswell	730
Minnesota	7.81	1936	Angus	870
Mississippi	25.97	1936	Yazoo City	120
Missouri	16.14*	1956	La Belle	770
Montana	2.97	1960	Belfry	4,040
Nebraska	6.30	1931	Hull	4,400
Nevada	T	1898	Hot Springs	4,072
New Hampshire	22.31	1930	Bethlehem	1,440
New Jersey	19.85	1965	Canton	20
New Mexico	1.00	1910	Hermanas	4,540
New York	17.64	1941	Lewiston	320
North Carolina	22.69	1930	Mount Airy	1,070
North Dakota	4.02	1934	Parshall	1,930
Ohio	16.96	1963	Elyria	730
Oklahoma	6.53	1956	Regnier	4,280
Oregon	3.33	1939	Warm Springs Reservoir	3,330
Pennsylvania	15.71	1965	Breezewood	1,350
Rhode Island	24.08	1965	Block Island	40
South Carolina	20.73	1954	Rock Hill	667
South Dakota	2.89	1936	Ludlow	2,850
Tennessee	25.23	1941	Halls	310
Texas	1.64*	1956	Presidio	2,580
Utah	1.34	1974	Myton	5,080
Vermont	22.98	1941	Burlington	330
Virginia	12.52	1941	Moores Creek Dam	1,950
Washington	2.61	1930	Wahluke	416
West Virginia	9.50	1930	Upper Tract	1,540
Wisconsin	12.00	1937	Plum Is.	590
Wyoming	1.28	1960	Lysite	5,260

*At least one month estimated.

RECORD MAXIMUM 24-HOUR PRECIPITATION BY STATE
(THRU 1992)

State	Precip Inches	Date	Station	Elevation Feet
Alabama	20.33	Apr. 13, 1955	Axis	36
Alaska	15.20	Oct. 12, 1982	Angoon	15
Arizona	11.40	Sep. 4-5, 1970	Workman Creek	6,970
Arkansas	14.06	Dec. 3, 1982	Big Fork	1,100
California	26.12	Jan. 22-23, 1943	Hoegees Camp	2,760
Colorado	11.08	Jun. 17, 1965	Holly	3,390
Connecticut	12.77	Aug. 19, 1955	Burlington	460
Delaware	8.50	Jul. 13, 1975	Dover	30
Florida	38.70	Sep. 5, 1950	Yankeetown	5
Georgia	18.00	Aug. 28, 1911	St. George	77
Hawaii	38.00	Jan. 24-25, 1956	Kilauea Plantation	180
Idaho	7.17	Nov. 23, 1909	Rattlesnake Creek	4,000
Illinois	16.54	Jun. 14-15, 1957	East St. Louis	410
Indiana	10.50	Aug. 6, 1905	Princeton	480
Iowa	16.70	Aug. 5-6, 1959	Decatur Co.	1,110
Kansas	12.59	May 31-Jun. 1, 1941	Burlington	1,010
Kentucky	10.40	Jun. 28, 1960	Dunmor	610
Louisiana	22.00	Aug. 28-29, 1962	Hackberry	10
Maine	8.05	Sep. 11, 1954	Brunswick	70
Maryland	14.75	Jul. 26-27, 1897	Jewell	152
Massachusetts	18.15	Aug. 18-19, 1955	Westfield	220
Michigan	9.78	Aug. 31-Sep. 1, 1914	Bloomingdale	750
Minnesota	10.84	Jul. 21-22, 1972	Fort Ripley	1,140
Mississippi	15.68	Jul. 9, 1968	Columbus	190
Missouri	18.18	Jul. 20, 1965	Edgarton	850
Montana	11.50	Jun. 20, 1921	Circle	2,440
Nebraska	13.15	Jul. 8-9, 1950	York	1,610
Nevada	7.40	Mar. 19, 1907	Lewers' Ranch	5,200
New Hampshire	10.38	Feb. 10-11, 1970	Mount Washington	6,260
New Jersey	14.81	Aug. 19, 1939	Tuckerton	20
New Mexico	11.28	May 18-19, 1955	Lake Maloya	7,400
New York	11.17	Oct. 9, 1903	NYC Central Park	130
North Carolina	22.22	Jul. 15-16, 1916	Altapass	2,600
North Dakota	8.10	Jun. 29, 1975	Litchville	1,470
Ohio	10.51	Jul. 12, 1966	Sandusky	610
Oklahoma	15.50	Sep. 3-4, 1940	Sapulpa	740
Oregon	10.17	Dec. 21, 1915	Glenora	575
Pennsylvania	34.50*	Jul. 17, 1942	Smethport	1,510
Rhode Island	12.13	Sep. 16-17, 1932	Westerly	40
South Carolina	13.25	Jul. 14-15, 1916	Effingham	110
South Dakota	8.00	Sep. 10, 1900	Elk Point	1,127
Tennessee	11.00	Mar. 28, 1902	McMinnville	900
Texas	43.00*	Jul. 25-26, 1979	Alvin	50
Utah	6.00*	Sep. 5, 1970	Bug Point	6,600
Vermont	8.77	Nov. 3-4, 1927	Somerset	2,080
Virginia	27.00*	Aug. 20, 1969	Nelson Co.	est 500
Washington	14.26	Nov. 23-24, 1986	Mt. Mitchell #2	3,600
West Virginia	19.00*	Jul. 18, 1889	Rockport	700
Wisconsin	11.72	Jun. 24, 1946	Mellen	1,150
Wyoming	6.06	Aug. 1, 1985	Cheyenne	6,126

*Estimated

STATE MONTHLY TEMPERATURE (°F) EXTREMES

(THRU 1992)

STATE	JANUARY Max	JANUARY Min	FEBRUARY Max	FEBRUARY Min	MARCH Max	MARCH Min	APRIL Max	APRIL Min	MAY Max	MAY Min	JUNE Max	JUNE Min	JULY Max	JULY Min	AUGUST Max	AUGUST Min	SEPTEMBER Max	SEPTEMBER Min	OCTOBER Max	OCTOBER Min	NOVEMBER Max	NOVEMBER Min	DECEMBER Max	DECEMBER Min	BEGIN YEAR
Alabama	88	-27	89	-18	94	2	98	19	105	29	110	35	111	41	109	39	112	29	103	19	92	2	88	-10	1884
Alaska	62	-80	66	-75	69	-68	82	-50	92	-25	100	-1	98	20	99	8	86	-13	74	-48	67	-60	62	-70	1907
Arizona	90	-40	105	-37	103	-26	113	-16	121	4	127	13	127	25	124	20	123	11	116	-9	100	-21	91	-32	1895
Arkansas	90	-28	95	-29	98	-14	99	12	107	24	113	35	116	40	120	38	113	28	105	12	96	0	88	-21	1891
California	97	-45	105	-43	105	-29	118	-30	121	-15	129	2	134	12	127	13	126	-5	117	-20	105	-28	100	-40	1897
Colorado	84	-60	90	-61	96	-46	100	-35	106	-10	113	3	118	10	112	5	107	-9	100	-20	93	-41	87	-53	1888
Connecticut	73	-32	77	-32	87	-24	96	-7	98	20	103	24	105	32	104	28	103	17	94	11	84	-8	75	-22	1889
Delaware	78	-17	82	-15	91	1	99	11	100	26	104	34	110	41	107	41	102	31	97	19	88	8	76	-12	1895
Florida	92	2	94	-2	99	13	100	20	106	34	109	43	108	49	105	52	107	35	100	25	96	12	95	5	1891
Georgia	95	-17	90	-12	97	-3	99	12	108	25	110	31	112	40	112	40	111	26	105	14	94	0	89	-9	1892
Hawaii	93	14	93	16	95	18	100	18	98	12	96	23	98	22	98	17	96	23	96	20	96	23	93	17	1905
Idaho	75	-60	76	-57	90	-38	100	-21	107	1	113	2	118	15	116	10	110	-1	98	-16	85	-38	82	-54	1894
Illinois	78	-35	83	-32	94	-21	96	-2	107	12	108	29	117	35	113	31	109	14	98	1	89	-20	79	-29	1890
Indiana	80	-34	83	-35	94	-19	100	1	103	18	111	30	116	37	111	33	108	21	100	8	91	-10	78	-30	1887
Iowa	73	-47	82	-41	95	-35	100	-9	111	10	111	27	118	35	116	20	107	10	97	-15	86	-25	74	-40	1873
Kansas	88	-35	92	-40	100	-25	107	-2	108	14	116	30	121	32	119	33	117	15	104	-3	96	-20	90	-26	1887
Kentucky	83	-34	86	-33	94	-14	98	12	106	20	110	29	114	34	113	33	110	24	98	12	93	-9	87	-24	1889
Louisiana	92	-8	92	-16	95	10	98	24	105	30	110	41	111	50	114	45	110	30	103	21	95	10	90	-1	1891
Maine	65	-48	67	-44	86	-36	94	-14	101	10	105	20	105	29	104	26	100	12	92	1	78	-20	69	-42	1889
Maryland	83	-40	88	-29	93	-20	102	-3	102	16	105	25	109	32	109	30	106	19	100	4	89	-16	80	-32	1895
Massachusetts	72	-35	76	-31	88	-22	100	2	100	6	103	24	106	32	107	15	103	18	92	6	85	-10	74	-33	1889
Michigan	72	-48	70	-51	89	-45	96	-34	100	9	107	12	112	20	108	21	104	9	94	-3	84	-23	69	-41	1887
Minnesota	69	-57	73	-59	88	-49	101	-22	112	4	110	15	114	27	110	21	111	10	95	-16	84	-45	74	-57	1891
Mississippi	89	-19	91	-16	96	7	97	21	104	30	111	39	115	47	110	42	111	31	100	16	92	2	87	-12	1888
Missouri	85	-36	90	-40	98	-26	100	2	110	17	112	28	118	38	116	35	110	17	100	-3	90	-13	83	-34	1888
Montana	74	-70	79	-66	88	-45	97	-30	105	-5	112	11	117	15	112	5	107	-9	99	-30	85	-53	78	-59	1895
Nebraska	82	-45	85	-47	101	-38	106	-17	110	3	114	20	118	29	117	23	113	1	104	-15	92	-32	87	-47	1876
Nevada	84	-50	92	-41	96	-32	106	-12	114	-7	122	12	121	18	122	15	117	0	111	-10	98	-23	81	-45	1889
New Hampshire	68	-46	70	-45	87	-36	95	-17	100	-2	106	13	106	25	105	20	102	13	91	-2	84	-18	70	-44	1889
New Jersey	78	-34	80	-31	92	-15	98	3	102	18	106	29	110	33	108	32	109	18	97	9	88	-7	78	-21	1885
New Mexico	89	-47	100	-50	99	-34	104	-36	110	-2	116	10	116	19	111	23	112	8	101	-15	97	-38	90	-47	1892
New York	75	-46	78	-52	91	-41	97	-24	102	10	105	21	108	25	106	20	107	15	99	2	87	-24	75	-47	1890
North Carolina	86	-34	88	-20	100	-14	99	1	105	11	107	27	109	32	110	31	109	23	101	8	90	-21	86	-21	1887
North Dakota	70	-56	72	-60	90	-48	101	-24	111	-3	111	18	121	23	118	19	109	4	98	-18	88	-38	72	-50	1892
Ohio	79	-37	81	-39	96	-21	97	-4	102	17	108	27	113	34	111	27	107	23	99	7	89	-17	80	-32	1883
Oklahoma	92	-27	99	-27	104	-18	106	6	110	19	117	34	120	41	120	38	115	25	106	9	95	-15	92	-19	1900
Oregon	82	-52	89	-54	99	-30	102	-23	108	0	113	11	119	14	119	13	111	2	104	-9	89	-32	81	-53	1890
Pennsylvania	85	-42	83	-39	92	-31	98	-5	102	10	107	20	111	28	108	23	106	17	100	7	88	-15	82	-29	1888
Rhode Island	69	-23	72	-22	90	-10	98	1	95	25	101	30	102	38	104	33	100	25	99	13	82	1	71	-17	1889
South Carolina	86	-19	89	-11	99	-3	99	18	106	28	111	34	110	45	109	45	111	28	103	16	93	-1	89	-6	1887
South Dakota	79	-57	79	-58	96	-35	102	-17	113	-1	115	14	120	24	116	20	112	5	103	-19	88	-34	79	-45	1890
Tennessee	83	-30	85	-30	94	-11	98	14	102	22	110	28	113	36	113	30	112	19	99	10	89	-8	82	-32	1883
Texas	98	-22	104	-23	108	-12	113	5	116	15	119	32	119	40	120	39	116	25	109	8	102	-10	98	-16	1888
Utah	74	-50	84	-69	89	-37	98	-19	108	0	116	10	117	19	113	17	110	2	99	-16	86	-30	76	-49	1891
Vermont	70	-44	68	-46	84	-37	97	-13	99	5	101	19	105	24	104	24	100	15	92	-5	81	-20	72	-50	1889
Virginia	82	-30	87	-29	96	-15	100	0	105	15	107	26	110	31	108	31	108	20	101	9	91	-17	83	-27	1891
Washington	74	-42	83	-40	88	-25	103	-7	107	11	112	20	118	23	118	20	108	11	99	-5	83	-29	74	-48	1890
West Virginia	88	-36	86	-35	94	-18	101	-4	105	14	109	22	112	20	112	25	107	15	102	3	89	-14	84	-37	1891
Wisconsin	66	-54	68	-52	89	-48	99	-20	109	7	106	20	114	27	108	22	104	10	95	-7	84	-34	66	-52	1891
Wyoming	72	-58	79	-63	86	-50	93	-29	101	-8	114	5	114	10	110	7	108	-15	98	-33	86	-39	78	-58	1892

Round-the-World Weather

• CLIMATES OF THE WORLD

Temperature distribution

The distribution of temperature over the world and its variations throughout the year depend primarily on the amount of distribution of the radiant energy received from the sun in different regions. This, in turn, depends mainly on latitude but is greatly modified by the distribution of continents and oceans, prevailing winds, oceanic circulation, topography, and other factors.

In the winter of the Northern Hemisphere (*Average Temperature maps for January/July*), it will be noted, the poleward temperature gradient (that is, the rate of fall in temperature) north of latitude 15° is very steep over the interior of North America. This is shown by the fact that the lines indicating changes in temperature come very close together. The temperature gradient is also steep toward the cold pole over Asia, the area marked -50°F (-45°C). In western Europe, to the east of the Atlantic Ocean and the North Atlantic Drift, and in the region of prevailing westerly winds, the temperature gradient is much more gradual, as indicated by the fact that the isotherms, or lines of equal temperature, are far apart. In the winter of the Southern Hemisphere, as shown on the map for July (a winter month south of the Equator), the temperature gradient toward the South Pole is very gradual, and the isothermal deflections from the east-west direction (that is, the dipping of the isothermal lines) are of minor importance because continental effects are largely absent.

In the summers of the two hemispheres—July in the north and January in the south—the temperature gradients poleward are very much diminished as compared with those during the winter. This is especially marked over the middle and higher northern latitudes because of the greater warming of the extensive interiors of North America and Eurasia than of the smaller land areas in middle and higher southern latitudes.

Distribution of precipitation

Whether precipitation occurs as rain or snow or in the rarer forms of hail or sleet depends largely on the temperature climate, which may be influenced more by elevation than by latitude, as in the case of the perpetually snow-capped mountain peaks and glaciers on the Equator in both South America and Africa.

The quantity of precipitation is governed by the amount of water vapor in the air and the nature of the process that leads to its condensation into liquid or solid form through cooling. Air may ascend to great elevations through local convection, as in thunderstorms and in tropical regions generally; it may be forced up over topographical elevations across the prevailing wind direction, as on the southern or windward slopes of the Himalayas in the path of the southwest monsoon in India; or it may ascend more or less gradually in migratory low-pressure formations such as those that govern the main features of weather in the United States.

The areas of heaviest precipitation on the map (*World Precipitation*) are generally located, as would be expected, in tropical regions, where the greatest amount of water vapor may be present in the atmosphere and the greatest evaporation takes place—although only where conditions favor condensation can rainfall occur. Outstanding exceptions are certain regions in high latitudes, such as southern Alaska, western Norway, and southern Chile, where relatively warm, moist winds from the sea undergo forced ascent over considerable elevations.

In marked contrast to the rainy regions just named, are the dry polar regions, where the water vapor content of the air is always very low because of the low temperature and very limited evaporation. The dry areas in the subtropical belts of high atmospheric pressure in the vicinity of latitude 30° on all continents, and especially from the extreme western Sahara over a broad, somewhat broken belt to the Gobi Desert and the arid strips on the lee sides of mountains on whose windward slopes precipitation is heavy to excessive, are caused by conditions which, even though the temperature may be high, are unfavorable to the condensation of whatever water vapor may be present in the atmosphere.

The following tables provide data on mean maximum and minimum temperatures for January, April, July, and October, with extremes recorded in the period of record, and monthly and annual precipitation for about 800 selected stations well distributed worldwide.

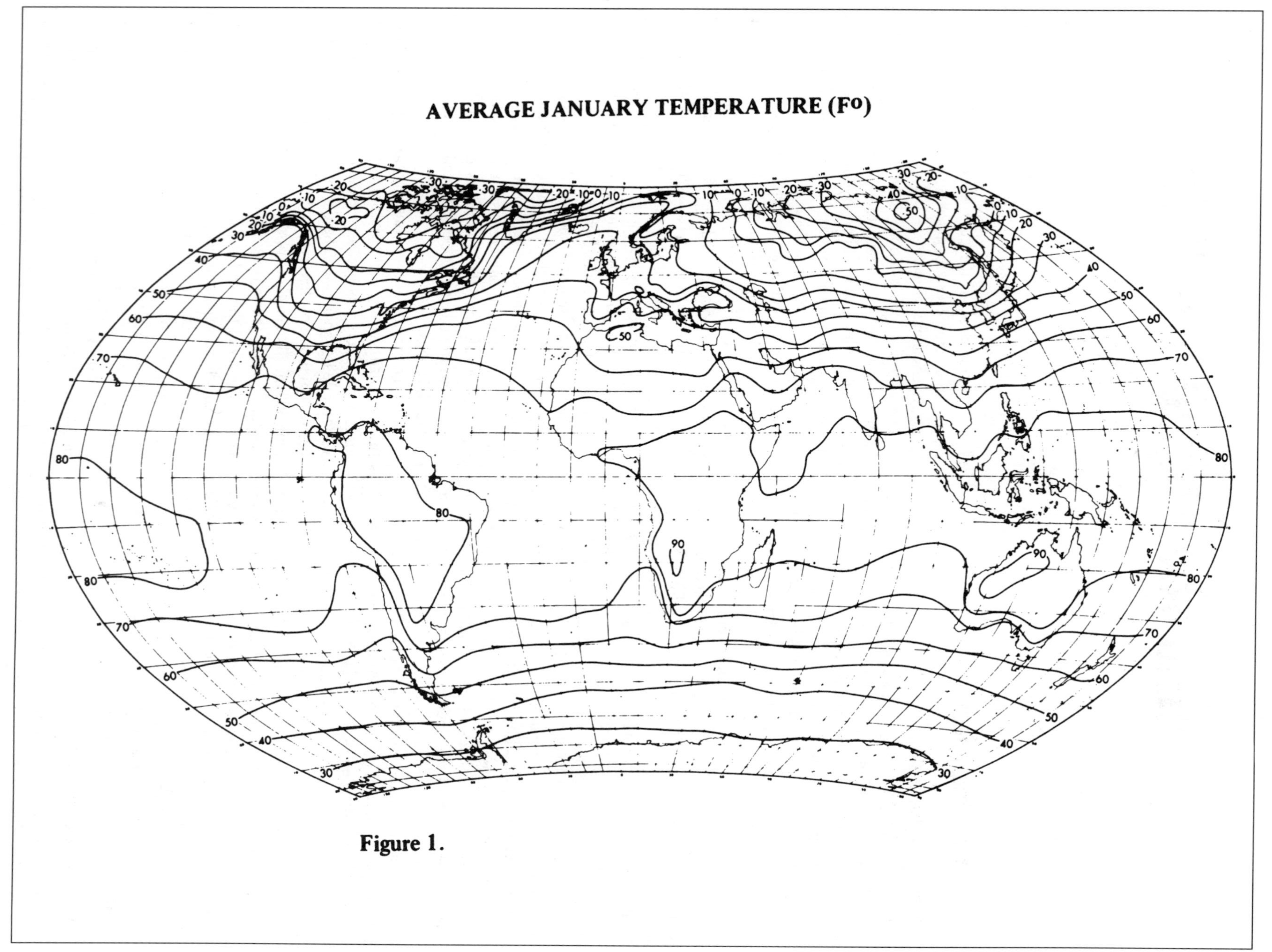

Figure 1.

AVERAGE JULY TEMPERATURE (F°)

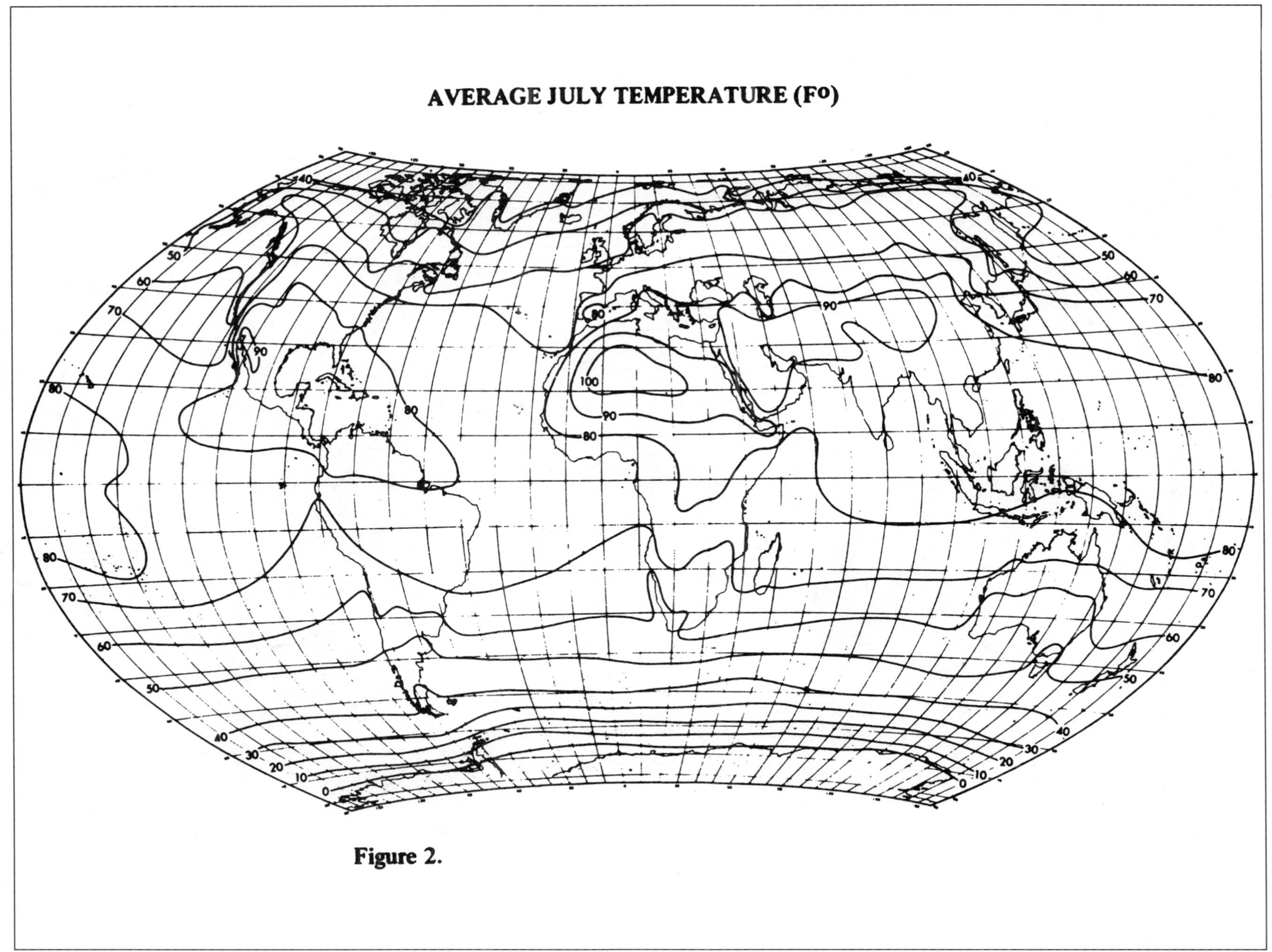

Figure 2.

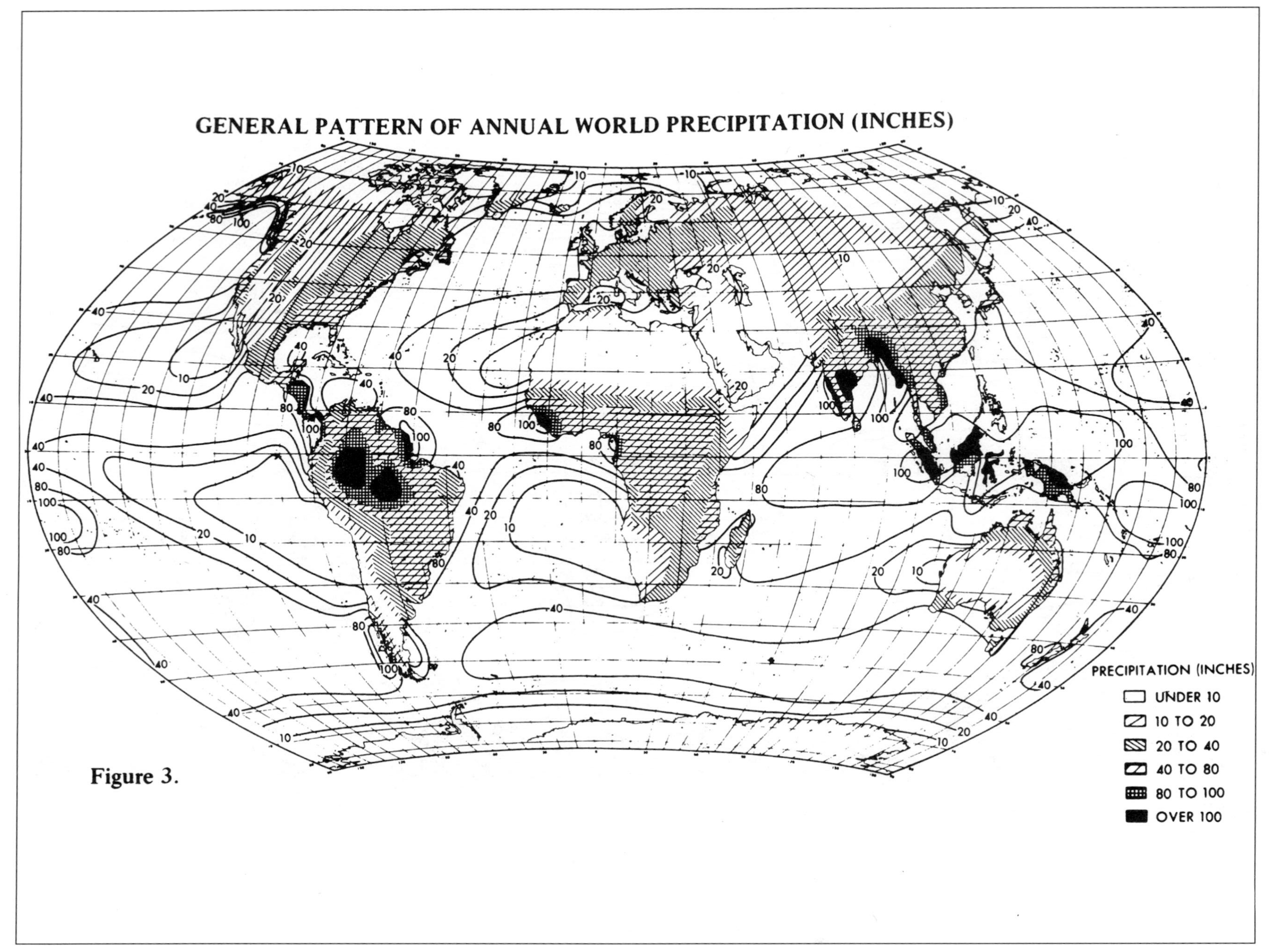
GENERAL PATTERN OF ANNUAL WORLD PRECIPITATION (INCHES)
PRECIPITATION (INCHES)
UNDER 10
10 TO 20
20 TO 40
40 TO 80
80 TO 100
OVER 100

Figure 3.

COUNTRY AND STATION	LATITUDE	LONGITUDE	ELEVATION	TEMPERATURE: LENGTH OF RECORD	AVERAGE DAILY JANUARY MAXIMUM	JANUARY MINIMUM	APRIL MAXIMUM	APRIL MINIMUM	JULY MAXIMUM	JULY MINIMUM	OCTOBER MAXIMUM	OCTOBER MINIMUM	EXTREME MAXIMUM	EXTREME MINIMUM	AVERAGE PRECIPITATION: LENGTH OF RECORD	JANUARY	FEBRUARY	MARCH	APRIL	MAY	JUNE	JULY	AUGUST	SEPTEMBER	OCTOBER	NOVEMBER	DECEMBER	YEAR
	° ′	° ′	FEET	YEAR	°F	°F	°F	°F	°F	°F	°F	°F	°F	°F	YEAR	IN.	IN.	IN.	IN.	IN.	IN.	IN.	IN.	IN.	IN.	IN.	IN.	IN.
NORTH AMERICA																												
United States (Conterminous):																												
Albuquerque, N. Mex.	35 03N	106 37W	5,311	30	46	24	69	42	91	66	71	45	104	-16	30	0.4	0.4	0.5	0.5	0.8	0.6	1.2	1.3	1.0	0.8	0.4	0.5	8.4
Asheville, N.C.	35 26N	82 32W	2,140	30	48	28	67	42	84	61	68	45	99	- 7	30	4.2	4.0	4.8	4.0	3.7	3.5	5.9	4.9	3.6	3.1	2.8	3.6	48.1
Atlanta, Ga.	33 39N	84 26W	1,010	30	52	37	70	50	87	71	72	52	103	- 9	30	4.4	4.5	5.4	4.5	3.2	3.8	4.7	3.6	3.3	2.4	3.0	4.4	47.2
Austin, Tex.	30 18N	97 42W	597	30	60	41	78	57	95	74	82	60	109	- 2	30	2.4	2.6	2.1	3.6	3.7	3.2	2.2	1.9	3.4	2.8	2.1	2.5	32.5
Birmingham, Ala.	33 34N	86 45W	620	30	57	36	76	50	93	71	79	52	107	-10	30	5.0	5.3	6.0	4.5	3.4	4.0	5.2	4.9	3.3	3.0	3.5	5.0	53.1
Bismark, N. Dak.	46 46N	100 45W	1,647	30	20	0	55	32	86	58	59	34	114	-45	30	0.4	0.4	0.8	1.2	2.0	3.4	2.2	1.7	1.2	0.9	0.6	0.4	15.2
Boise, Idaho	43 34N	116 13W	2,838	30	36	22	63	37	91	59	65	38	112	-28	30	1.3	1.3	1.3	1.2	1.3	0.9	0.2	0.2	0.4	0.8	1.2	1.3	11.4
Brownsville, Tex.	25 54N	97 26W	16	30	71	52	82	66	93	76	85	67	104	12	30	1.4	1.5	1.0	1.6	2.4	3.0	1.7	2.8	5.0	3.5	1.3	1.7	26.9
Buffalo, N.Y.	42 56N	78 44W	705	30	31	18	53	34	80	59	60	41	99	-21	30	2.8	2.7	3.2	3.0	3.0	2.5	2.6	3.1	3.1	3.0	3.6	3.0	35.6
Cheyenne, Wyo.	41 09N	104 49W	6,126	30	37	14	56	30	85	55	63	32	100	-38	30	0.5	0.6	1.2	1.9	2.5	2.1	1.8	1.4	1.1	0.8	0.6	0.5	15.0
Chicago, Ill.	41 47N	87 45W	607	30	33	19	57	41	84	67	63	47	105	-23	30	1.9	1.6	2.7	3.0	3.7	4.1	3.4	3.2	2.7	2.8	2.2	1.9	33.2
Des Moines, Iowa	41 32N	93 39W	938	30	29	11	59	38	87	65	66	43	110	-30	30	1.3	1.1	2.1	2.5	4.1	4.7	3.1	3.7	2.9	2.1	1.8	1.1	30.5
Dodge City, Kans.	37 46N	99 58W	2,582	30	42	20	66	41	93	68	71	46	109	-26	30	0.6	0.7	1.2	1.8	3.2	3.0	2.3	2.4	1.5	1.4	0.6	0.5	19.2
El Paso, Tex.	31 48N	106 24W	3,918	30	56	30	78	49	95	69	79	50	109	- 8	30	0.5	0.4	0.4	0.3	0.4	0.7	1.3	1.2	1.1	0.9	0.3	0.5	8.0
Indianapolis, Ind.	39 44N	86 17W	792	30	37	21	61	40	86	64	67	44	107	-25	30	3.1	2.3	3.4	3.7	4.0	4.6	3.5	3.0	3.2	2.6	3.1	2.7	39.2
Jacksonville, Fla.	30 25N	81 39W	20	30	67	45	80	58	92	73	80	62	105	10	30	2.5	2.9	3.5	3.6	3.5	6.3	7.7	6.9	7.6	5.2	1.7	2.2	53.6
Kansas City, Mo.	39 07N	94 36W	742	30	40	23	66	46	92	71	72	49	113	-22	30	1.4	1.2	2.5	3.6	4.4	4.6	3.2	3.8	3.3	2.9	1.8	1.5	34.2
Las Vegas, Nev.	36 05N	115 10W	2,162	30	54	32	78	51	104	76	80	53	117	8	30	0.5	0.4	0.4	0.2	0.1	*	0.5	0.5	0.3	0.2	0.3	0.4	3.8
Los Angeles, Calif.	33 56N	118 23W	97	30	64	45	67	52	76	62	73	57	110	23	30	2.7	2.9	1.8	1.1	0.1	0.1	*	*	0.2	0.4	1.1	2.4	12.8
Louisville, Ky.	38 11N	85 44W	477	30	44	27	66	43	89	67	70	46	107	-20	30	4.1	3.3	4.6	3.8	3.9	4.0	3.4	3 0	2.6	2.3	3.2	3.2	41.4
Miami, Fla.	25 48N	80 16W	7	30	76	58	83	66	89	75	85	71	100	28	30	2.0	1.9	2.3	3.9	6.4	7.4	6.8	7.0	9.5	8.2	2.8	1.7	59.9
Minneapolis, Minn.	44 53N	93 13W	834	30	22	2	56	33	84	61	61	37	108	-34	30	0.7	0.8	1.5	1.9	3.2	4.0	3.3	3.2	2.4	1.6	1.4	0.9	24.9
Missoula, Mont.	46 55N	114 05W	3,190	30	28	10	57	31	85	49	58	30	105	-33	30	0.9	0.9	0.7	1.0	1.9	1.9	0.9	0.7	1.0	1.0	0.9	1.1	12.9
Nashville, Tenn.	36 07N	86 41W	590	30	49	31	71	48	91	70	74	49	107	-15	30	5.5	4.5	5.2	3.7	3.7	3.3	3.7	2.9	2.9	2.3	3.3	4.2	45.2
New Orleans, La.	29 59N	90 15W	3	30	64	45	78	58	91	73	80	61	102	7	30	3.8	4.0	5.3	4.6	4.4	4.4	6.7	5.3	5.0	2.8	3.3	4.1	53.7
New York, N.Y.	40 47N	73 58W	132	30	40	27	60	43	85	68	66	50	106	-15	30	3.3	2.8	4.0	3.4	3.7	3.3	3.7	4.4	3.9	3.1	3.4	3.3	42.3
Oklahoma City, Okla.	35 24N	97 36W	1,285	30	46	28	71	49	93	72	74	52	113	-17	30	1.3	1.4	2.0	3.1	5.2	4.5	2.4	2.5	3.0	2.5	1.6	1.4	30.9
Phoenix, Ariz.	33 26N	112 01W	1,117	30	64	35	84	50	105	75	87	55	118	16	30	0.7	0.9	0.7	0.3	0.1	0.1	0.8	1.1	0.7	0.5	0.5	0.9	7.3
Pittsburgh, Pa.	40 27N	80 00W	747	30	40	25	63	42	85	65	65	45	103	-20	30	2.8	2.3	3.5	3.4	3.8	4.0	3.6	3.5	2.7	2.5	2.3	2.5	36.9
Portland, Maine	43 39N	70 19W	47	30	32	12	53	32	80	57	60	37	103	-39	30	4.4	3.8	4.3	3.7	3.4	3.2	2.9	2.4	3.5	3.2	4.2	3.9	42.9
Portland, Oreg.	45 36N	122 36W	21	30	44	33	62	42	79	56	63	45	107	- 3	30	5.4	4.2	3.8	2.1	2.0	1.7	0.4	0.7	1.6	3.6	5.3	6.4	37.2
Reno, Nev.	39 30N	119 47W	4,404	30	45	16	65	31	89	46	69	29	106	-19	30	1.2	1.0	0.7	0.5	0.5	0.4	0.3	0.2	0.2	0.5	0.6	1.1	7.2
Salt Lake City, Utah	40 46N	111 58W	4,220	30	37	18	63	36	94	60	65	38	107	-30	30	1.4	1.2	1.6	1.8	1.4	1.0	0.6	0.9	0.5	1.2	1.3	1.2	14.1
San Francisco, Calif.	37 37N	122 23W	8	30	55	42	64	47	72	54	71	51	106	20	30	4.0	3.5	2.7	1.3	0.5	0.1	*	*	0.2	0.7	1.6	4.1	18.7
Sault Ste. Marie, Mich.	46 28N	84 22W	721	30	23	8	46	30	76	54	55	38	98	-37	30	2.1	1.5	1.8	2.2	2.8	3.3	2.5	2.9	3.8	2.8	3.3	2.3	31.3
Seattle, Wash.	47 27N	122 18W	400	30	44	33	58	40	76	54	60	44	100	0	30	5.7	4.2	3.8	2.4	1.7	1.6	0.8	1.0	2.1	4.0	5.4	6.3	39.0
Sheridan, Wyo.	44 46N	106 58W	3,964	30	34	9	56	31	87	56	62	33	106	-41	30	0.6	0.7	1.4	2.2	2.6	2.6	1.2	0.9	1.2	1.1	0.8	0.6	15.9
Spokane, Wash.	47 38N	117 32W	2,356	30	31	19	59	36	86	55	60	38	108	-30	30	2.4	1.9	1.5	0.9	1.2	1.5	0.4	0.4	0.8	1.6	2.2	2.4	17.2
Washington, D.C.	38 51N	77 03W	14	30	44	30	66	46	87	69	68	50	106	-15	30	3.0	2.5	3.2	3.2	4.1	3.2	4.2	4.9	3.8	3.1	2.8	2.8	40.8
Wilmington, N.C.	34 16N	77 55W	28	30	58	37	74	51	89	71	76	55	104	5	30	2.9	3.4	4.0	2.9	3.5	4.3	7.7	6.9	6.3	3.0	3.1	3.4	51.4

(See footnotes at end of tables)

COUNTRY AND STATION	LATITUDE	LONGITUDE	ELEVATION	TEMPERATURE											AVERAGE PRECIPITATION													
				LENGTH OF RECORD	AVERAGE DAILY								EXTREME		LENGTH OF RECORD	JANUARY	FEBRUARY	MARCH	APRIL	MAY	JUNE	JULY	AUGUST	SEPTEMBER	OCTOBER	NOVEMBER	DECEMBER	YEAR
					JANUARY		APRIL		JULY		OCTOBER																	
					MAXIMUM	MINIMUM	MAXIMUM	MINIMUM	MAXIMUM	MINIMUM	MAXIMUM	MINIMUM	MAXIMUM	MINIMUM														
	° '	° '	FEET	YEAR	°F	°F	°F	°F	°F	°F	°F	°F	°F	°F	YEAR	IN.	IN.	IN.	IN.	IN.	IN.	IN.	IN.	IN.	IN.	IN.	IN.	IN.
United States, Alaska:																												
Anchorage	61 13N	149 52W	85	30	21	4	44	28	65	50	42	28	86	-38	30	0.8	0.7	0.5	0.4	0.5	1.0	1.9	2.6	2.5	1.9	1.0	0.9	14.7
Annette	55 02N	131 34W	110	30	38	30	50	37	63	51	51	42	90	- 4	30	11.4	8.5	9.6	9.1	7.1	5.7	6.0	7.5	9.9	16.9	14.7	12.1	118.5
Barrow	71 18N	156 47W	31	30	- 9	-23	7	- 7	45	33	21	12	78	-56	30	0.2	0.2	0.1	0.1	0.1	0.4	0.8	0.9	0.6	0.5	0.2	0.2	4.3
Bethel	60 47N	161 48W	125	30	11	- 4	34	18	62	48	38	25	90	-52	30	1.1	1.1	1.0	0.6	1.0	1.2	2.0	4.2	2.6	1.5	1.1	1.0	18.4
Cold Bay	55 12N	162 43W	96	30	33	23	38	28	54	45	45	36	78	- 9	30	2.3	3.2	1.8	1.5	2.3	2.0	1.8	4.3	4.3	4.6	3.8	2.6	34.5
Fairbanks	64 49N	147 52W	436	30	- 1	-21	42	17	72	48	35	17	99	-66	30	0.9	0.5	0.4	0.3	0.7	1.4	1.8	2.2	1.1	0.9	0.6	0.5	11.3
Juneau	58 22N	134 35W	12	30	30	20	45	31	63	48	47	37	89	-21	30	4.0	3.1	3.3	2.9	3.2	3.4	4.5	5.0	6.7	8.3	6.1	4.2	54.7
King Salmon	58 41N	156 39W	49	30	21	6	41	25	63	47	43	29	88	-40	30	1.1	1.0	1.0	0.6	1.0	1.4	2.1	3.4	3.1	2.2	1.5	1.0	19.4
Nome	64 30N	165 26W	13	30	12	- 3	28	14	55	44	35	24	84	-47	30	1.0	0.9	0.9	0.8	0.7	0.9	2.3	3.8	2.7	1.7	1.2	1.0	17.9
St. Paul Island	57 09N	170 13W	22	30	30	21	33	24	49	42	41	33	64	-26	30	1.8	1.2	1.1	1.0	1.3	1.2	2.3	3.3	3.1	3.2	2.5	1.8	23.8
Shemya	52 43N	174 06E	122	30	34	29	38	33	49	44	42	38	63	16	30	2.5	2.3	2.6	2.1	2.4	1.3	2.2	2.1	2.3	2.8	2.7	2.1	27.4
Yakutat	59 31N	139 40W	28	30	34	20	45	29	61	48	49	35	86	-24	30	10.9	8.2	8.7	7.2	8.0	5.1	8.4	10.9	16.6	19.6	16.1	12.3	132.0
Canada:																												
Aklavik, N.W.T.	68 14N	135 00W	30	22	-10	-26	19	- 2	66	47	25	15	93	-62	22	0.5	0.5	0.4	0.5	0.5	0.8	1.4	1.4	0.9	0.9	0.8	0.4	9.0
Alert, N.W.T.	82 31N	62 20W	95	9	-19	-29	- 8	-18	44	36	2	- 7	67	-53	10	0.2	0.3	0.3	0.3	0.5	0.6	0.5	1.1	1.0	0.9	0.2	0.4	6.3
Calgary, Alta.	51 06N	114 01W	3,540	55	24	2	53	27	76	47	54	29	97	-49	55	0.5	0.5	0.8	1.0	2.3	3.1	2.5	2.3	1.5	0.7	0.7	0.6	16.7
Charlottetown, P.E.I.	46 17N	63 08W	181	65	26	10	43	30	73	58	54	41	98	-27	65	3.8	3.0	3.2	2.8	2.7	2.6	3.0	3.4	3.4	4.1	3.8	4.0	39.8
Chatham, N.B.	47 00N	65 27W	109	50	23	2	47	28	77	56	55	37	102	-43	50	3.4	2.7	3.3	3.0	3.2	3.6	3.9	4.0	3.1	4.0	3.4	3.2	40.8
Churchhill, Man.	58 45N	94 04W	94	30	-11	-27	24	4	64	43	34	20	96	-57	30	0.5	0.6	0.9	0.9	0.9	1.9	2.2	2.7	2.3	1.4	1.0	0.7	16.0
Edmonton, Alta.	53 34N	113 31W	2,219	71	16	- 3	52	28	74	50	51	30	99	-57	71	0.9	0.7	0.7	1.0	1.9	3.2	3.3	2.4	1.3	0.8	0.9	0.9	18.0
Fort Nelson, B.C.	58 50N	122 35W	1,253	12	1	-15	47	25	74	51	43	25	98	-61	13	0.9	1.2	0.7	0.8	1.4	2.5	2.4	1.5	1.3	1.0	1.4	1.2	16.3
Fort Simpson, N.W.T.	61 45N	121 14W	554	42	-10	-27	38	14	74	50	36	21	97	-70	42	0.7	0.7	0.5	0.7	1.4	1.5	2.0	1.5	1.3	1.1	0.9	0.8	13.1
Frobisher Bay, N.W.T.	63 45N	68 33W	110	18	- 9	-23	16	- 1	53	39	29	18	76	-49	10	0.7	0.9	0.8	0.8	0.7	0.9	1.5	2.0	1.8	1.1	1.1	1.0	13.3
Gander, Nfld.	48 57N	54 34W	496	14	27	13	40	27	71	52	51	37	96	-17	14	2.6	3.3	2.8	2.6	2.6	2.8	3.6	3.6	3.7	4.1	4.2	3.7	39.6
Halifax, N.S.	44 39N	63 34W	83	75	32	15	47	31	74	55	57	41	99	-21	71	5.4	4.4	4.9	4.5	4.1	4.0	3.8	4.4	4.1	5.4	5.3	5.4	55.7
Kapuskasing, Ont.	49 25N	82 28W	743	19	10	-14	43	19	75	50	47	31	101	-53	19	2.0	1.1	1.6	1.8	2.1	2.3	3.4	2.9	3.5	2.5	2.4	1.9	27.5
Knob Lake, Que.	54 48N	66 49W	1,712	30	- 3	-21	30	12	64	46	37	25	88	-59	10	1.9	1.9	1.4	1.6	1.7	3.3	3.3	4.4	3.4	2.9	2.4	1.5	29.7
Montreal, Que.	45 30N	73 34W	187	67	21	6	50	33	78	61	54	40	97	-35	77	3.8	3.0	3.5	2.6	3.1	3.4	3.7	3.5	3.7	3.4	3.5	3.6	40.8
North Bay, Ont.	46 21N	79 25W	1,216	17	22	2	48	28	78	56	49	36	99	-46	23	2.0	1.5	1.8	2.2	2.5	3.2	3.2	2.7	3.7	3.2	2.7	2.1	30.8
Ottowa, Ont.	45 19N	75 40W	374	65	21	3	51	31	81	58	54	37	102	-38	65	2.9	2.2	2.8	2.7	2.5	3.5	3.4	2.6	3.2	2.9	3.0	2.6	34.3
Penticton, B.C.	49 28N	119 36W	1,129	32	32	21	61	35	84	53	59	38	105	-16	32	1.0	0.7	0.7	0.7	1.1	1.2	0.8	0.8	1.0	0.8	0.9	1.1	10.8
Port Arthur, Ont.	48 22N	89 19W	644	62	17	- 4	44	26	74	52	50	34	104	-42	59	0.9	0.8	1.0	1.5	2.1	2.8	3.6	2.8	3.4	2.5	1.5	0.9	23.8
Prince George, B.C.	53 53N	122 41W	2,218	27	23	3	54	27	75	44	52	30	102	-58	27	1.8	1.2	1.4	0.8	1.3	2.1	1.6	1.9	2.0	2.0	1.9	1.9	19.9
Prince Rupert, B.C.	54 17N	130 23W	170	26	39	30	50	37	62	49	53	42	90	- 3	26	9.8	7.6	8.4	6.7	5.3	4.1	4.8	5.1	7.7	12.2	12.3	11.3	95.3
Quebec, Que.	46 48N	71 23W	239	72	18	2	44	29	76	57	51	37	97	-34	72	3.5	2.7	3.0	2.4	3.1	3.7	4.0	4.0	3.6	3.4	3.2	3.2	39.8
Regina, Sask.	50 26N	104 40W	1,884	55	10	-11	50	26	79	51	52	27	110	-56	49	0.5	0.3	0.7	0.7	1.8	3.3	2.4	1.8	1.3	0.9	0.6	0.4	14.7
Resolute, N.W.T.	74 43N	94 59W	220	13	-20	-33	- 1	-16	45	35	11	0	61	-61	7	0.1	0.1	0.2	0.2	0.5	0.8	0.9	1.1	0.8	0.5	0.2	0.1	5.5
St. John, N.B.	45 17N	66 04W	119	61	28	11	43	32	69	54	54	41	93	-24	61	4.1	3.1	3.7	3.2	3.1	3.2	3.1	3.6	3.7	4.1	3.9	3.8	42.6
St. Johns, Nfld.	47 32N	52 44W	211	68	30	18	41	29	69	51	53	40	93	-21	58	5.3	5.1	4.6	3.8	3.9	3.1	3.1	4.0	3.7	4.8	5.7	6.0	53.1
Saskatoon, Sask.	52 08N	106 38W	1,690	38	9	-11	49	26	77	52	51	27	104	-55	38	0.9	0.5	0.7	0.7	1.4	2.6	2.4	1.9	1.5	0.9	0.5	0.6	14.6

COUNTRY AND STATION	LATITUDE	LONGITUDE	ELEVATION	TEMPERATURE: LENGTH OF RECORD	AVERAGE DAILY: JANUARY MAXIMUM	JANUARY MINIMUM	APRIL MAXIMUM	APRIL MINIMUM	JULY MAXIMUM	JULY MINIMUM	OCTOBER MAXIMUM	OCTOBER MINIMUM	EXTREME: MAXIMUM	EXTREME: MINIMUM	AVERAGE PRECIPITATION: LENGTH OF RECORD	JANUARY	FEBRUARY	MARCH	APRIL	MAY	JUNE	JULY	AUGUST	SEPTEMBER	OCTOBER	NOVEMBER	DECEMBER	YEAR
	° ′	° ′	FEET	YEAR	°F	°F	°F	°F	°F	°F	°F	°F	°F	°F	YEAR	IN.	IN.	IN.	IN.	IN.	IN.	IN.	IN.	IN.	IN.	IN.	IN.	IN.
The Pas, Man.	53 49N	101 15W	890	27	1	-18	45	21	75	54	45	26	100	-54	27	0.6	0.5	0.7	0.8	1.4	2.2	2.2	2.1	2.0	1.2	1.0	0.8	15.5
Toronto, Ont.	43 40N	79 24W	379	105	30	16	50	34	79	59	56	40	105	-26	105	2.7	2.4	2.6	2.5	2.9	2.7	3.0	2.7	2.9	2.4	2.8	2.6	32.2
Vancouver, B.C.	49 17N	123 05W	127	43	41	32	58	40	74	54	57	44	92	2	41	8.6	5.8	5.0	3.3	2.8	2.5	1.2	1.7	3.6	5.8	8.3	8 8	57.4
Whitehorse, Y.T.	60 43N	135 04W	2,303	10	13	- 3	41	22	67	45	41	28	91	-62	10	0.6	0.5	0.6	0.4	0.6	1.0	1.6	1.5	1.3	0.7	1.0	0.8	10.6
Winnipeg, Man.	49 54N	97 14W	783	66	7	-13	48	27	79	55	51	31	108	-54	66	0.9	0.9	1.2	1.4	2.3	3.1	3.1	2.5	2.3	1.5	1.1	0.9	21.2
Yellow Knife, N.W.T.	62 28N	114 27W	674	13	- 8	-23	29	9	69	52	36	26	90	-60	13	0.8	0.6	0.7	0.4	0.7	0.6	1.5	1.4	1.0	1.3	1.0	0.8	10.8
Greenland:																												
Angmagssalik	65 36N	37 33W	95	30	23	10	35	16	54	37	35	25	77	-26	38	2.9	2.4	2.6	2.1	2.0	1.8	1.5	2.1	3.3	4.7	3.0	2.7	31.1
Danmarkshaven	76 46N	19 00W	7	2	- 1	-15	6	-13	47	34	13	2	63	-42	2	1.2	0.7	0.7	0.1	0.2	0.2	0.5	0.6	0.3	0.3	1.0	0.7	6.0
Eismitte	70 53N	40 42W	9,843	1	-33	-53	-14	-37	19	1	-23	-42	27	-85	1	0.6	0.2	0.3	0.2	0.1	0.1	0.1	0.4	0.3	0.5	0.5	1.0	4.3
Godthaab	64 10N	51 43W	66	40	19	10	31	20	52	38	35	26	76	-20	45	1.4	1.7	1.6	1.2	1.7	1.4	2.2	3.1	3.3	2.5	1.9	1.5	23.5
Ivigtut	61 12N	48 10W	98	48	24	12	38	24	57	42	40	29	86	-20	50	3.3	2.6	3.4	2.5	3.5	3.2	3.1	3.7	5.9	5.7	4.6	3.1	44.6
Jacobshavn	69 13N	51 02W	104	32	8	- 7	24	6	51	40	31	20	71	-46	52	0.4	0.4	0.5	0.5	0.6	0.8	1.2	1.4	1.3	0.9	0.7	0.5	9.2
Nord	81 36N	16 40W	118	8	-15	-28	- 5	-18	44	35	3	- 6	61	-60	8	0.8	0.8	0.5	0.3	0.1	0.3	1.0	1.4	1.2	0.6	1.4	0.5	8.9
Scoresbysund	70 29N	21 58W	56	12	12	- 3	22	6	49	36	25	15	63	-42	12	1.8	1.4	0.9	1.4	0.4	0.8	1.5	0.7	1.7	1.4	1.1	1.9	15.0
Thule	76 31N	68 44W	251	12	- 4	-17	10	- 7	46	38	19	8	63	-44	12	0.4	0.3	0.2	0.2	0.3	0.2	0.7	0.6	0.6	0.7	0.5	0.2	4.9
Upernivik	72 47N	56 07W	59	40	- 1	-13	15	- 1	48	35	29	21	69	-44	50	0.4	0.5	0.7	0.6	0.6	0.5	0.9	1.1	1.1	1.1	1.1	0.6	9.2
Mexico:																												
Acapulco	16 50N	99 56W	10	8	85	70	87	71	89	75	88	74	97	60	40	0.3	*	0.0	*	1.4	12.8	9.1	9.3	13.9	6.7	1.2	0.4	55.1
Chihuahua	28 42N	105 57W	4,429	9	65	36	81	51	89	66	79	51	102	12	22	0.2	0.4	0.3	0.2	0.2	1.7	3.6	3.7	3.3	0.9	0.5	0.4	15.4
Guadalajara	20 41N	103 20W	5,194	26	73	45	85	53	79	60	78	56	101	26	33	0.4	0.2	0.2	0.2	1.1	8.8	9.4	8.5	7.2	2.2	0.8	0.7	39.7
Guaymas	27 57N	110 55W	58	9	74	57	84	65	96	82	91	75	117	41	41	0.5	0.2	0.2	0.1	*	0.1	1.7	2.7	2.1	0.7	0.3	0.8	9.4
La Paz	24 07N	110 17W	85	9	74	54	86	58	96	73	90	68	108	31	12	0.2	0.1	0.0	0.0	0.0	0.2	0.4	1.2	1.4	0.6	0.5	1.1	5.7
Lerdo	25 30N	103 32W	3,740	10	72	45	86	57	90	68	82	58	105	23	14	0.4	0.1	0.2	0.3	0.8	1.5	1.5	1.3	2.0	0.8	0.8	0.5	10.2
Manzanillo	19 04N	104 20W	26	17	86	68	87	67	93	76	91	76	103	54	17	0.1	0.2	*	0.0	0.1	4.7	5.7	6.4	14.5	5.1	0.9	1.8	39.5
Mazatlan	23 11N	106 25W	256	10	71	61	76	65	86	77	85	76	93	52	46	0.8	0.5	0.2	0.1	0.1	1.5	5.9	8.3	8.0	2.6	0.9	1.3	30.2
Merida	20 58N	89 38W	72	22	83	62	92	69	92	73	87	71	106	51	40	1.2	0.9	0.7	0.8	3.2	5.6	5.2	5.6	6.8	3.8	1.3	1.3	36.5
Mexico City	19 26N	99 04W	7,340	42	66	42	78	52	74	54	70	50	92	24	48	0.2	0.3	0.5	0.7	1.9	4.1	4.5	4.3	4.1	1.6	0.5	0.3	23.0
Monterrey	25 40N	100 18W	1,732	11	68	48	84	62	90	71	80	64	107	25	33	0.6	0.7	0.8	1.3	1.3	3.0	2.3	2.4	5.2	3.0	1.5	0.8	22.9
Salina Cruz	16 12N	95 12W	184	10	85	72	88	76	89	76	87	75	98	62	22	*	0.4	0.6	0.5	3.3	11.6	4.5	5.5	7.1	4.0	0.9	0.1	38.5
Tampico	22 16N	97 51W	78	12	75	59	83	69	89	75	85	71	104	34	12	1.5	1.2	1.0	1.5	1.9	8.7	4.9	4.8	10.8	5.0	2.0	1.6	44.9
Vera Cruz	19 12N	96 08W	52	10	77	66	83	72	87	74	85	73	98	53	40	0.9	0.6	0.6	0.8	2.6	10.4	4.1	11.1	13.9	6.9	3.0	1.0	65.7
CENTRAL AMERICA																												
British Honduras:																												
Belize	17 31N	88 11W	17	27	81	67	86	74	87	75	86	72	97	49	33	5.4	2.4	1.5	2.2	4.3	7.7	6.4	6.7	9.6	12.0	8.9	7.3	74.4
Canal Zone:																												
Balboa Heights	08 57N	79 33W	118	34	88	71	90	74	87	74	85	73	97	63	46	1.0	0.4	0.7	2.9	8.0	8.4	7.1	7.9	8.2	10.1	10.2	4.8	69.7
Cristobal	09 21N	79 54W	35	36	84	76	86	77	85	76	86	75	97	66	73	3.4	1.5	1.5	4.1	12.5	13.9	15.6	15.3	12.7	15.8	22.3	11.7	130.3
Costa Rica:																												
San Jose	09 56N	84 08W	3,760	8	75	58	79	62	77	62	77	60	92	49	34	0.6	0.2	0.8	1.8	9.0	9.5	8.3	9.5	12.0	11.8	5.7	1.6	70.8

(See footnotes at end of tables)

COUNTRY AND STATION	LATITUDE	LONGITUDE	ELEVATION	TEMPERATURE: LENGTH OF RECORD	AVERAGE DAILY: JANUARY MAXIMUM	JANUARY MINIMUM	APRIL MAXIMUM	APRIL MINIMUM	JULY MAXIMUM	JULY MINIMUM	OCTOBER MAXIMUM	OCTOBER MINIMUM	EXTREME: MAXIMUM	EXTREME: MINIMUM	AVERAGE PRECIPITATION: LENGTH OF RECORD	JANUARY	FEBRUARY	MARCH	APRIL	MAY	JUNE	JULY	AUGUST	SEPTEMBER	OCTOBER	NOVEMBER	DECEMBER	YEAR
	° '	° '	FEET	YEAR	°F	°F	°F	°F	°F	°F	°F	°F	°F	°F	YEAR	IN.	IN.	IN.	IN.	IN.	IN.	IN.	IN.	IN.	IN.	IN.	IN.	IN.
El Salvador:																												
San Salvador	13 42N	89 13W	2,238	39	90	60	93	65	89	65	87	65	105	45	39	0.3	0.2	0.4	1.7	7.7	12.9	11.5	11.7	12.1	9.5	1.6	0.4	70.0
Guatemala:																												
Guatemala City	14 37N	90 31W	4,855	6	73	53	82	58	78	60	76	60	90	41	29	0.3	0.1	0.5	1.2	6.0	10.8	8.0	7.8	9.1	6.8	0.9	0.3	51.8
Honduras:																												
Tela	15 46N	87 27W	41	4	82	67	87	72	88	73	86	71	96	58	20	8.9	5.1	2.6	3.3	4.3	5.0	6.4	9.4	7.7	13.5	15.9	14.0	96.1
WEST INDIES																												
Bridgetown, Barbados	13 08N	59 36W	181	35	83	70	86	72	86	74	86	73	95	61	22	2.6	1.1	1.3	1.4	2.3	4.4	5.8	5.8	6.7	7.0	8.1	3.8	50.3
Camp Jacob, Guadaloupe	16 01N	61 42W	1,750	19	77	64	79	65	81	68	81	68	92	54	21	9.2	6.1	8.1	7.3	11.5	14.1	17.6	15.3	16.4	12.4	12.3	10.1	140.4
Ciudad Trujillo, Dominican Rep	18 29N	69 54W	57	26	84	66	85	69	88	72	87	72	98	59	25	2.4	1.4	1.9	3.9	6.8	6.2	6.4	6.3	7.3	6.0	4.8	2.4	55.8
Fort-de-France, Martinique	14 37N	61 05W	13	22	83	69	86	71	86	74	87	73	96	56	31	4.7	4.3	2.9	3.9	4.7	7.4	9.4	10.3	9.3	9.7	7.9	5.9	80.4
Hamilton, Bermuda	32 17N	64 46W	151	59	68	58	71	59	85	73	79	69	99	40	62	4.4	4.7	4.8	4.1	4.6	4.4	4.5	5.4	5.2	5.8	5.0	4.7	57.6
Havana, Cuba	23 08N	82 21W	80	25	79	65	84	69	89	75	85	73	104	43	72	2.8	1.8	1.8	2.3	4.7	6.5	4.9	5.3	5.9	6.8	3.1	2.3	48.2
Kingston, Jamaica	17 58N	76 48W	110	33	86	67	87	70	90	73	88	73	97	56	59	0.9	0.6	0.9	1.2	4.0	3.5	1.5	3.6	3.9	7.1	2.9	1.4	31.5
La Guerite, St. Christopher (St. Kitts)	17 20N	62 45W	157	19	80	71	83	73	86	76	85	75	91	61	21	4.1	2.0	2.3	2.3	3.8	3.6	4.4	5.2	6.0	5.4	7.3	4.5	50.9
Nassau, Bahamas	25 05N	77 21W	12	35	77	65	81	69	88	75	85	73	94	41	57	1.4	1.5	1.4	2.5	4.6	6.4	5.8	5.3	6.9	6.5	2.8	1.3	46.4
Port-au-Prince, Haiti	18 33N	72 20W	121	42	87	68	89	71	94	74	90	72	101	58	70	1.3	2.3	3.4	6.3	9.1	4.0	2.9	5.7	6.9	6.7	3.4	1.3	53.3
Saint Clair, Trinidad	10 40N	61 31W	67	49	87	69	90	69	88	71	89	71	101	52	97	2.7	1.6	1.8	2.1	3.7	7.6	8.6	9.7	7.6	6.7	7.2	4.9	64.2
Saint Thomas, Virgin Is.	18 20N	64 58W	11	9	82	71	85	74	88	77	87	76	92	63	9	2.5	1.9	1.7	2.2	4.6	3.2	3.2	4.1	6.9	5.6	3.9	3.9	43.7
San Juan, Puerto Rico	18 26N	66 00W	13	30	81	67	84	69	87	74	87	73	94	60	30	4.7	2.9	2.2	3.7	7.1	5.7	6.3	7.1	6.8	5.8	6.5	5.4	64.2
SOUTH AMERICA																												
Argentina:																												
Bahia Blanca	38 43S	62 16W	95	33	88	62	71	51	57	39	71	48	109	18	46	1.7	2.2	2.5	2.3	1.2	0.9	1.0	1.0	1.6	2.2	2.1	1.9	20.6
Buenos Aires	34 35S	58 29W	89	23	85	63	72	53	57	42	69	50	104	22	70	3.1	2.8	4.3	3.5	3.0	2.4	2.2	2.4	3.1	3.4	3.3	3.9	37.4
Cipolletti	38 57S	67 59W	889	9	89	56	72	40	55	29	72	43	107	9	24	0.4	0.4	0.7	0.4	0.6	0.6	0.5	0.3	0.6	0.9	0.5	0.5	6.4
Corrientes	27 28S	58 50W	177	39	93	71	81	63	71	53	82	60	112	30	40	4.7	4.5	5.3	5.6	3.3	1.9	1.7	1.5	2.8	4.7	5.2	5.2	46.4
La Quiaca	22 06S	65 36W	11,345	23	70	41	69	32	60	16	71	32	95	0	25	3.5	2.6	1.8	0.3	*	0.0	*	*	0.1	0.3	1.0	2.7	12.3
Mendoza	32 53S	68 49W	2,625	23	90	60	73	47	59	35	76	50	109	15	46	0.9	1.2	1.1	0.5	0.4	0.3	0.2	0.3	0.5	0.7	0.7	0.7	7.5
Parana	31 44S	60 31W	210	12	91	67	77	58	62	45	75	54	113	21	23	3.1	3.1	3.9	4.9	2.6	1.2	1.2	1.6	2.4	2.8	3.7	4.5	35.0
Puerto Madryn	42 47S	65 01W	26	50	81	57	70	46	55	36	68	45	104	10	50	0.4	0.6	0.7	0.5	0.9	0.6	0.6	0.4	0.6	0.7	0.4	0.6	7.0
Santa Cruz	50 01S	68 32W	39	12	70	48	57	39	41	28	58	39	94	1	20	0.6	0.3	0.3	0.6	0.4	0.5	0.4	0.5	0.3	0.3	0.4	0.7	5.3
Santiago del Estero	27 46S	64 18W	653	28	97	69	82	59	70	44	87	59	116	19	20	3.4	3.0	3.0	1.3	0.6	0.3	0.2	0.2	0.5	1.4	2.5	4.1	20.4
Ushuaia	54 50S	68 20W	26	16	57	41	48	33	39	25	52	35	85	-6	21	2.0	2.6	1.9	2.1	1.5	1.2	1.2	1.1	1.3	1.6	1.5	1.9	19.9
Bolivia:																												
Concepcion	16 15S	62 03W	1,607	5	85	66	86	62	81	54	88	62	101	32	16	7.2	4.7	4.4	1.8	2.0	1.5	1.1	0.9	1.2	2.9	5.0	5.9	38.6
La Paz	16 30S	68 08W	12,001	31	63	43	65	40	62	33	66	40	80	26	50	4.5	4.2	2.6	1.3	0.5	0.3	0.4	0.5	1.1	1.6	1.9	3.7	22.6
Sucre	19 03S	65 17W	9,344	5	63	48	63	45	61	37	65	46	88	25	52	7.3	4.9	3.7	1.6	0.2	0.1	0.2	0.3	1.0	1.6	2.6	4.3	27.8
Brazil:																												
Barra do Corda	05 35S	45 28W	266	9	89	71	89	71	92	64	94	72	103	45	9	6.7	8.7	8.0	6.1	2.3	1.0	0.7	0.7	1.0	2.5	3.9	5.7	47.2

COUNTRY AND STATION	LATITUDE	LONGITUDE	ELEVATION	TEMPERATURE: LENGTH OF RECORD	AVERAGE DAILY JANUARY MAXIMUM	JANUARY MINIMUM	APRIL MAXIMUM	APRIL MINIMUM	JULY MAXIMUM	JULY MINIMUM	OCTOBER MAXIMUM	OCTOBER MINIMUM	EXTREME MAXIMUM	EXTREME MINIMUM	AVERAGE PRECIPITATION: LENGTH OF RECORD	JANUARY	FEBRUARY	MARCH	APRIL	MAY	JUNE	JULY	AUGUST	SEPTEMBER	OCTOBER	NOVEMBER	DECEMBER	YEAR
	° '	° '	FEET	YEAR	°F	°F	°F	°F	°F	°F	°F	°F	°F	°F	YEAR	IN.	IN.	IN.	IN.	IN.	IN.	IN.	IN.	IN.	IN.	IN.	IN.	IN.
Bela Vista	22 06S	56 22W	525	13	91	67	85	61	77	49	87	61	108	20	20	6.6	4.9	4.4	4.3	5.0	2.8	1.3	1.8	2.9	5.4	5.8	7.0	52.2
Belem	01 27S	48 29W	42	16	87	72	87	73	88	71	89	71	98	61	20	12.5	14.1	14.1	12.6	10.2	6.7	5.9	4.4	3.5	3.3	2.6	6.1	96.0
Brasilia	15 51S	47 56W	3,481	3	80	65	82	62	78	51	82	64	93	46	3	9.0	7.8	4.8	3.4	1.4	*	0.0	*	1.3	4.9	9.7	11.7	54.0
Conceicao do Araguaia	08 15S	49 12W	53	5	88	70	91	68	95	63	93	68	102	55	5	14.9	12.1	10.8	4.1	1.9	0.4	*	0.5	1.5	6.6	4.9	8.6	66.2
Corumba	19 00S	57 39W	381	8	94	73	92	73	84	64	93	70	106	33	11	7.3	5.9	5.1	4.6	2.9	1.9	0.3	1.2	2.6	4.0	5.6	7.1	48.5
Florianopolis	27 35S	48 33W	96	17	83	72	74	64	68	57	73	63	102	32	25	7.6	5.6	6.3	4.1	3.6	3.5	2.2	3.7	4.3	5.1	3.5	4.3	53.1
Goias	15 58S	50 04W	1,706	11	86	63	91	63	89	56	94	63	104	41	11	12.5	9.9	10.2	4.6	0.4	0.3	0.0	0.3	2.3	5.3	9.4	9.5	64.8
Guarapuava	25 16S	51 30W	3,592	10	79	61	73	55	66	47	74	53	94	23	5	8.7	5.8	5.4	4.5	4.6	6.5	2.7	3.6	4.6	6.9	6.6	6.1	65.8
Manaus	03 08S	60 01W	144	11	88	75	87	75	89	75	92	76	101	63	25	9.8	9.1	10.3	8.7	6.7	3.3	2.3	1.5	1.8	4.2	5.6	8.0	71.3
Natal	05 46S	35 12W	52	18	87	76	86	73	82	69	85	75	100	61	18	1.9	4.8	7.0	9.2	7.1	8.7	7.7	3.8	1.4	0.8	0.7	1.1	54.2
Parana	12 26S	48 06W	853	19	90	58	90	58	91	48	94	58	105	37	19	11.3	9.3	9.4	4.0	0.5	*	0.1	0.2	1.1	5.0	9.1	12.2	62.3
Porto Alegre	30 02S	51 13W	33	22	87	67	78	60	66	49	74	57	105	25	22	3.5	3.2	3.9	4.1	4.5	5.1	4.5	5.0	5.2	3.4	3.1	3.5	49.1
Quixeramobim	05 12S	39 18W	653	9	92	79	86	76	88	74	93	77	100	63	13	0.7	5.0	6.6	5.0	7.0	1.7	0.7	0.6	0.4	0.6	0.7	0.6	29.6
Recife	08 04S	34 53W	97	27	86	77	85	75	80	71	84	75	94	50	56	2.1	3.3	6.3	8.7	10.5	10.9	10.0	6.0	2.5	1.0	1.0	1.1	63.4
Rio de Janeiro	22 55S	43 12W	201	38	84	73	80	69	75	63	77	66	102	46	84	4.9	4.8	5.1	4.2	3.1	2.1	1.6	1.7	2.6	3.1	4.1	5.4	42.6
Salvador (Bahia)	13 00S	38 30W	154	25	86	74	84	74	79	69	83	71	100	50	20	2.6	5.3	6.1	11.2	10.8	9.4	7.2	4.8	3.3	4.0	4.5	5.6	74.8
Santarem	02 30S	54 42W	66	22	86	73	85	73	87	71	91	73	99	65	22	6.8	10.9	13.2	12.9	11.3	6.9	4.1	1.7	1.5	1.9	2.3	4.1	77.9
Sao Paulo	23 37S	46 39W	2,628	44	77	63	73	59	66	53	68	57	100	32	24	8.8	7.8	6.0	2.2	3.0	2.4	1.5	2.1	3.5	4.6	6.0	9.4	57.3
Sena Madureira	09 04S	68 39W	443	12	92	69	91	68	91	63	93	69	100	41	17	11.2	11.3	10.2	9.4	4.1	2.2	1.1	1.5	4.0	7.0	7.5	11.7	81.2
Uaupes	00 08S	67 05W	272	15	88	72	88	72	85	70	89	71	100	52	10	10.3	7.7	10.0	10.6	12.0	9.2	8.8	7.2	5.1	6.9	7.2	10.4	105.4
Uruguaiana	29 46S	57 07W	246	15	91	69	78	59	66	48	77	55	108	27	12	3.6	3.6	5.6	5.1	3.7	4.2	3.2	2.8	3.6	4.1	2.9	4.1	46.6
Chile:																												
Ancud	41 47S	73 52W	184	30	62	51	57	47	50	42	55	45	82	30	46	3.1	3.7	5.3	7.4	9.9	11.0	10.3	9.4	6.5	4.2	4.7	4.6	80.1
Antofagasta	23 42S	70 24W	308	22	76	63	70	58	63	51	66	55	86	37	32	0.0	0.0	0.0	*	*	0.1	0.2	0.1	*	0.1	*	0.0	0.5
Arica	18 28S	70 20W	95	15	78	64	74	60	66	54	69	58	93	39	25	*	0.0	0.0	0.0	0.0	0.0	0.0	*	0.0	0.0	0.0	*	*
Cabo Raper	46 50S	75 38W	131	8	58	46	54	44	47	38	51	40	72	28	10	7.8	5.8	7.1	7.7	7.5	7.9	9.5	7.5	5.6	7.0	6.7	7.0	87.1
Los Evangelistas	52 23S	75 07W	190	16	50	44	48	41	43	36	45	39	66	19	27	11.7	10.0	11.3	11.4	9.6	9.4	9.4	8.6	9.2	8.8	9.9	10.1	119.4
Potrerillos	26 30S	69 27W	9,350	7	65	49	63	47	57	40	61	44	75	20	7	*	*	0.3	*	0.7	*	0.5	0.3	0.2	0.2	0.0	*	2.2
Puerto Aisen	42 24S	72 42W	33	8	63	50	55	43	45	37	55	42	93	18	11	7.8	7.8	8.3	7.5	14.7	10.4	11.1	11.1	6.5	7.8	7.0	7.9	107.9
Punta Arenas	53 10S	70 54W	26	15	58	45	50	39	40	31	51	38	86	11	15	1.5	0.9	1.3	1.4	1.3	1.6	1.1	1.2	0.9	1.1	0.7	1.4	14.4
Santiago	33 27S	70 42W	1,706	14	85	53	74	45	59	37	72	45	99	24	58	0.1	0.1	0.2	0.5	2.5	3.3	3.0	2.2	1.2	0.6	0.3	0.2	14.2
Valdivia	39 48S	73 14W	16	29	73	52	62	46	52	41	63	44	97	19	60	2.6	2.9	5.2	9.2	14.2	17.7	15.5	12.9	8.2	5.0	4.9	4.1	102.4
Valparaiso	33 01S	71 38W	135	30	72	56	67	52	60	47	65	50	94	32	41	0.1	*	0.3	0.6	4.1	5.9	3.9	2.9	1.3	0.4	0.2	0.2	19.9
Colombia:																												
Andagoya	05 06N	76 40W	197	8	90	75	90	75	89	74	90	74	97	62	15	25.0	21.4	19.5	26.1	25.5	25.8	23.3	25.3	24.6	22.7	22.4	19.5	281.1
Bogota	04 42N	74 08W	8,355	10	67	48	67	51	64	50	66	50	75	30	49	2.3	2.6	4.0	5.8	4.5	2.4	2.0	2.2	2.4	6.3	4.7	2.6	41.8
Cartagena	10 28N	75 30W	39	6	84	73	87	76	88	78	87	77	98	61	10	0.4	0.0	0.4	0.9	3.4	3.4	3.0	0.6	0.5	10.8	8.9	4.5	36.8
Ipiales	00 50N	77 42W	9,680	9	61	50	60	49	57	42	62	49	77	32	13	3.1	2.3	3.5	3.5	2.8	1.9	1.3	1.1	1.4	3.1	3.3	2.6	29.9
Tumaco	01 49N	78 45W	7	10	82	75	84	76	82	75	82	75	90	64	10	16.9	11.7	9.6	14.6	17.4	12.0	7.7	7.3	7.3	5.9	4.9	7.0	122.3
Ecuador:																												
Cuenca	02 53S	78 39W	8,301	7	69	50	69	50	65	47	70	49	81	29	10	2.0	1.8	3.2	4.3	4.3	1.7	0.9	1.1	1.6	3.1	1.8	2.5	28.3

(See footnotes at end of tables)

COUNTRY AND STATION	LATITUDE	LONGITUDE	ELE-VATION	TEMPERATURE: LENGTH OF RECORD	AVERAGE DAILY: JANUARY MAXIMUM	JANUARY MINIMUM	APRIL MAXIMUM	APRIL MINIMUM	JULY MAXIMUM	JULY MINIMUM	OCTOBER MAXIMUM	OCTOBER MINIMUM	EXTREME: MAXIMUM	EXTREME: MINIMUM	AVERAGE PRECIPITATION: LENGTH OF RECORD	JANUARY	FEBRUARY	MARCH	APRIL	MAY	JUNE	JULY	AUGUST	SEPTEMBER	OCTOBER	NOVEMBER	DECEMBER	YEAR
	° '	° '	FEET	YEAR	°F	°F	°F	°F	°F	°F	°F	°F	°F	°F	YEAR	IN.	IN.	IN.	IN.	IN.	IN.	IN.	IN.	IN.	IN.	IN.	IN.	IN.
Guayaquil	02 10S	79 53W	20	5	87	72	88	72	84	67	86	68	98	52	10	8.3	11.4	11.5	8.1	2.1	0.4	0.2	*	*	*	0.1	1.1	43.2
Quito	00 08S	78 29W	9,222	54	67	46	69	47	71	44	71	46	86	25	33	3.9	4.4	5.6	6.9	5.4	1.7	0.8	1.2	2.7	4.4	3.8	3.1	43.9
French Guiana:																												
Cayenne	04 56N	52 27W	20	38	84	74	86	75	88	73	91	74	97	65	51	14.4	12.3	15.8	18.9	21.7	15.5	6.9	2.8	1.2	1.3	4.6	10.7	126.1
Guyana:																												
Georgetown	06 50N	58 12W	6	54	84	74	85	76	85	75	87	76	93	68	35	8.0	4.5	6.9	5.5	11.4	11.9	10.0	6.9	3.2	3.0	6.1	11.3	88.7
Lethem	03 24N	59 38W	270	3	91	73	91	74	87	73	92	76	97	63	9	1.2	1.4	1.3	5.7	11.5	11.9	14.8	9.4	3.4	2.3	4.3	1.3	68.5
Paraguay:																												
Asuncion	25 17S	57 30W	456	15	95	71	84	65	74	53	86	62	110	29	30	5.5	5.1	4.3	5.2	4.6	2.7	2.2	1.5	3.1	5.5	5.9	6.2	51.8
Bahia Negra	20 14S	58 10W	318	20	92	74	87	68	79	61	90	69	106	35	20	5.4	5.3	4.9	2.9	2.3	1.6	1.5	0.6	2.3	4.2	5.3	4.3	40.6
Peru:																												
Arequipa	16 21S	71 34W	8,460	13	67	49	67	48	67	47	68	47	82	25	37	1.3	1.8	0.7	0.2	*	*	*	*	0.0	*	*	0.4	4.4
Cajamarca	07 09S	78 30W	8,662	9	71	48	70	47	70	41	71	47	79	25	9	3.6	4.2	4.6	3.4	1.7	9.5	9.2	9.3	2.3	2.3	1.9	3.2	28.2
Cusco	13 33S	71 59W	10,866	13	68	45	71	40	70	31	72	43	86	16	12	6.4	5.9	4.3	2.0	0.6	0.2	0.2	0.4	1.0	2.6	3.0	5.4	32.0
Iquitos	03 45S	73 13W	384	5	90	71	87	71	88	68	90	70	100	54	5	9.1	10.4	9.4	13.6	10.7	5.7	6.4	5.2	10.5	7.3	9.1	10.3	107.7
Lima	12 05S	77 03W	394	15	82	66	80	63	67	57	71	58	93	49	15	0.1	*	*	*	0.2	0.2	0.3	0.3	0.3	0.1	0.1	*	1.6
Mollendo	17 00S	72 07W	80	10	79	66	76	63	67	57	70	59	90	50	10	*	0.1	*	*	0.1	0.1	*	0.2	0.2	0.1	0.1	*	0.9
Surinam:																												
Paramaribo	05 49N	55 09W	12	35	85	72	86	73	87	73	91	73	99	62	75	8.4	6.5	7.9	9.0	12.2	11.9	9.1	6.2	3.1	3.0	4.9	8.8	91.0
Uruguay:																												
Artigas	30 24S	56 23W	384	13	91	65	77	55	65	45	75	54	107	24	50	4.3	3.9	4.7	5.1	4.1	4.1	2.8	3.0	4.0	4.7	3.8	4.1	48.6
Montevideo	34 52S	56 12W	72	56	83	62	71	53	58	43	68	49	109	25	56	2.9	2.6	3.9	3.9	3.3	3.2	2.9	3.1	3.0	2.6	2.9	3.1	37.4
Venezuela:																												
Caracas	10 30N	66 56W	3,418	30	75	56	81	60	78	61	79	61	91	45	46	0.9	0.4	0.6	1.3	3.1	4.0	4.3	4.3	4.2	4.3	3.7	1.8	32.9
Ciudad Bolivar	08 07N	63 32W	197	10	90	72	93	75	90	75	93	75	100	64	10	1.4	0.8	0.7	1.0	3.8	5.5	6.3	7.1	3.6	4.0	2.8	1.3	38.3
Maracaibo	10 39N	71 36W	20	12	90	73	92	76	94	76	92	76	102	66	36	0.1	*	0.3	0.8	2.7	2.2	1.8	2.2	2.8	5.9	3.3	0.6	22.7
Merida	08 36N	71 10W	5,293	14	73	56	75	60	76	59	75	60	90	48	14	2.5	1.5	3.6	6.7	9.8	7.3	4.7	5.7	6.7	9.5	8.2	3.4	69.7
Santa Elena	04 36N	61 07W	2,976	10	82	61	82	63	81	61	84	61	95	48	10	3.2	3.2	3.2	5.7	9.6	9.5	9.1	7.6	5.3	4.9	4.9	4.5	70.7
PACIFIC ISLANDS																												
Easter Is. (Isla de Pascua)	27 10S	109 26W	98	4	77	64	78	63	70	58	73	58	88	46	10	4.8	3.7	4.6	4.2	4.6	4.3	3.5	3.0	2.7	3.7	4.6	4.9	48.6
Mas a Tierra (Juan Fernandez)	33 37S	78 52W	20	25	72	60	68	57	60	50	61	51	86	39	29	0.8	1.2	1.6	3.4	5.9	6.4	5.8	4.4	2.9	1.9	1.6	1.0	36.9
Seymour Is. (Galapagos Is.)	00 28S	90 18W	36	3	86	72	87	75	81	69	81	67	93	58	3	0.8	1.4	1.1	0.7	*	*	*	*	*	*	*	*	4.0
ATLANTIC ISLANDS																												
Fernando de Noronha	03 50S	32 25W	148	32	84	75	82	75	81	73	82	75	93	63	32	1.7	4.7	7.4	10.5	10.5	7.3	5.4	1.9	0.7	0.3	0.4	0.5	51.3
Cumberland Bay, South Georgia	54 16S	36 30W	8	23	48	35	42	29	34	23	41	28	84	-3	24	3.3	4.3	5.3	5.4	5.2	4.9	5.5	5.3	3.5	2.6	3.4	3.0	51.7
Laurie Is., South Orkneys	60 44S	44 44W	13	48	35	29	31	21	20	4	30	19	54	-40	46	1.4	1.5	1.9	1.6	1.2	1.0	1.3	1.3	1.1	1.1	1.3	1.0	15.7
Stanley, Falkland Isles	51 42S	57 51W	6	25	56	42	49	37	40	31	48	35	76	12	41	2.8	2.3	2.5	2.6	2.6	2.1	2.0	2.0	1.5	1.6	2.0	2.8	26.8

See footnotes at end of table.

COUNTRY AND STATION	LATITUDE	LONGITUDE	ELE-VATION	TEMPERATURE: LENGTH OF RECORD	AVERAGE DAILY JANUARY MAXIMUM	AVERAGE DAILY JANUARY MINIMUM	AVERAGE DAILY APRIL MAXIMUM	AVERAGE DAILY APRIL MINIMUM	AVERAGE DAILY JULY MAXIMUM	AVERAGE DAILY JULY MINIMUM	AVERAGE DAILY OCTOBER MAXIMUM	AVERAGE DAILY OCTOBER MINIMUM	EXTREME MAXIMUM	EXTREME MINIMUM	AVERAGE PRECIPITATION: LENGTH OF RECORD	JANUARY	FEBRUARY	MARCH	APRIL	MAY	JUNE	JULY	AUGUST	SEPTEMBER	OCTOBER	NOVEMBER	DECEMBER	YEAR
			FEET	YEAR	°F	°F	°F	°F	°F	°F	°F	°F	°F	°F	YEAR	IN.	IN.	IN.	IN.	IN.	IN.	IN.	IN.	IN.	IN.	IN.	IN.	IN.
EUROPE																												
Albania:																												
Durres	41 19N	19 28E	23	10	51	42	63	55	83	74	68	58	95	21	10	3.0	3.3	3.9	2.2	1.6	1.9	0.5	1.9	1.7	7.1	8.5	7.3	42.9
Andorra:																												
Les Escaldes	42 30N	01 31E	3,543	5	43	29	59	39	78	55	61	42	91	0	9	1.5	1.7	2.9	2.4	4.7	3.1	2.2	3.4	3.1	3.5	3.3	2.5	34.3
Austria:																												
Innsbruck	47 16N	11 24E	1,909	34	34	20	60	39	78	55	58	40	97	-16	35	2.1	1.8	1.5	2.2	2.9	4.1	5.1	4.5	3.1	2.4	2.2	1.9	33.8
Vienna (Wien)	48 15N	16 22E	664	50	34	26	57	41	75	59	55	44	98	-14	100	1.5	1.4	1.8	2.0	2.8	2.7	3.0	2.7	2.0	2.0	1.9	1.8	25.6
Bulgaria:																												
Sofiya (Sofia)	42 42N	23 20E	1,805	30	34	22	62	41	82	57	63	42	99	-17	27	1.3	1.1	1.7	2.3	3.3	3.2	2.4	2.0	2.3	2.1	1.9	1.4	25.0
Varna	43 12N	27 55E	115	30	40	30	59	43	84	63	67	50	107	-12	20	1.5	0.9	1.2	1.2	1.8	2.6	1.9	1.2	1.5	1.9	1.9	2.0	19.6
Cyprus:																												
Nicosia	35 09N	33 17E	716	40	58	42	74	50	97	69	81	58	116	23	64	2.9	2.0	1.3	0.8	1.1	0.4	*	*	0.2	0.9	1.7	3.0	14.6
Czechoslovakia:																												
Praha (Prague)	50 05N	14 25E	662	40	34	25	55	40	74	58	54	44	98	-16	70	0.9	0.8	1.1	1.5	2.4	2.8	2.6	2.2	1.7	1.2	1.2	0.9	19.3
Prerov	49 27N	17 27E	702	20	34	25	57	38	77	55	56	40	100	-23	21	1.3	1.1	1.1	2.0	2.4	2.9	3.5	3.2	2.0	2.4	1.5	1.4	24.8
Denmark:																												
Copenhagen (Kobenhavn)	55 41N	12 33E	43	30	36	29	50	37	72	55	53	42	91	- 3	30	1.6	1.3	1.2	1.7	1.7	2.1	2.2	3.2	1.9	2.1	2.2	2.1	23.3
Aarhus	56 08N	10 12E	161	21	35	27	51	37	70	54	53	42	87	-12	21	2.3	1.5	1.4	1.8	1.2	2.2	2.5	3.3	3.2	2.6	2.5	2.1	26.6
Finland:																												
Helsinki	60 10N	24 57E	30	20	27	17	43	31	71	57	45	37	89	-23	50	2.2	1.7	1.7	1.7	1.9	2.0	2.3	3.3	2.8	2.9	2.7	2.4	27.6
Kuusamo	65 57N	29 12E	843	20	17	2	35	18	68	50	36	27	90	-40	20	1.1	1.1	1.1	1.1	1.4	2.3	2.8	3.0	2.1	2.1	1.6	1.1	20.8
Vaasa	63 05N	21 36E	13	18	26	16	41	28	69	55	44	36	89	-29	19	1.1	0.8	0.8	1.0	1.4	1.8	2.4	2.5	2.7	2.3	1.7	1.1	19.6
France:																												
Ajaccio (Corsica)	41 52N	08 35E	243	46	56	40	66	48	85	64	72	55	103	23	86	3.0	2.3	2.6	2.2	1.6	0.9	2.8	0.7	1.7	3.8	4.4	3.1	29.1
Bordeaux	44 50N	00 43W	157	51	48	35	63	44	80	58	66	47	102	9	47	2.7	2.8	2.9	2.6	2.5	2.3	2.0	1.9	2.2	3.0	3.9	3.9	32.7
Brest	48 19N	04 47W	56	56	49	40	57	44	70	56	61	49	95	7	56	3.5	3.0	2.5	2.5	1.9	2.0	2.0	2.2	2.3	3.6	4.2	4.4	34.1
Cherbourg	49 39N	01 38W	30	47	47	40	54	43	67	57	59	50	91	14	47	3.3	2.9	2.7	2.0	1.9	1.8	1.9	3.0	2.9	4.6	5.1	5.2	37.3
Lille	50 35N	03 05W	141	40	42	33	58	40	75	55	59	45	96	0	40	2.5	1.9	2.5	2.0	2.4	2.2	2.8	2.3	2.6	3.0	3.0	3.2	30.3
Lyon	45 42N	04 47E	938	70	41	30	61	42	80	58	61	45	105	-13	70	1.4	1.4	1.8	2.1	2.8	2.9	2.8	2.9	3.1	3.1	2.6	1.9	28.8
Marseille	43 18N	05 23E	246	72	53	38	59	41	78	58	76	57	101	9	102	1.9	1.5	1.8	2.0	1.9	1.0	0.6	0.9	2.6	3.7	3.1	2.2	23.2
Paris	48 49N	02 29E	164	66	42	32	60	41	76	55	59	44	105	1	118	1.5	1.3	1.5	1.7	2.0	2.1	2.1	2.0	2.0	2.2	2.0	1.9	22.3
Strasbourg	48 35N	07 46E	465	20	40	31	59	41	78	57	58	43	101	- 8	20	1.6	1.4	1.7	2.6	2.6	3.1	3.4	3.4	3.1	2.7	2.0	1.9	29.5
Toulouse	43 33N	01 23E	538	47	47	35	62	43	82	59	66	48	111	1	47	1.9	1.7	2.3	2.7	2.9	2.4	1.5	2.1	2.3	2.2	2.4	2.3	26.7
Germany:																												
Berlin	52 27N	13 18E	187	50	35	26	55	38	74	55	55	41	96	-15	40	1.9	1.3	1.5	1.7	1.9	2.3	3.1	2.2	1.9	1.7	1.7	1.9	23.1
Bremen	53 05N	08 47E	52	50	37	30	53	38	71	55	54	43	94	- 7	80	1.9	1.6	1.8	1.5	2.1	2.6	3.2	2.8	2.1	2.2	2.0	2.2	26.0
Frankfurt A/M	50 07N	08 40E	338	50	37	29	58	41	75	56	56	43	100	- 7	80	1.7	1.3	1.6	1.5	2.0	2.5	2.8	2.6	1.9	2.2	2.0	2.0	24.1
Hamburg	53 33N	09 58E	66	50	35	28	51	39	69	56	53	44	92	- 4	80	2.1	1.9	2.0	1.8	2.1	2.7	3.4	3.2	2.5	2.6	2.1	2.5	28.9
Munchen (Munich)	48 09N	11 34E	1,739	50	33	23	54	37	72	54	53	40	92	-14	80	1.7	1.4	1.9	2.7	3.7	4.6	4.7	4.2	3.2	2.2	1.9	1.9	34.1
Munster	51 58N	07 38E	207	50	39	29	56	38	73	54	56	42	96	-17	40	2.6	1.9	2.2	2.0	2.2	2.7	3.3	3.1	2.5	2.7	2.4	2.9	30.5
Nurnberg	49 27N	11 03E	1,050	50	35	26	56	38	74	55	55	41	99	-18	80	1.5	1.2	1.3	1.7	2.2	2.5	3.1	3.1	2.1	2.1	1.9	1.7	24.4

(See footnotes at end of tables)

COUNTRY AND STATION	LATITUDE	LONGITUDE	ELE-VATION	TEMPERATURE: LENGTH OF RECORD	AVERAGE DAILY: JANUARY MAXIMUM	JANUARY MINIMUM	APRIL MAXIMUM	APRIL MINIMUM	JULY MAXIMUM	JULY MINIMUM	OCTOBER MAXIMUM	OCTOBER MINIMUM	EXTREME: MAXIMUM	EXTREME: MINIMUM	AVERAGE PRECIPITATION: LENGTH OF RECORD	JANUARY	FEBRUARY	MARCH	APRIL	MAY	JUNE	JULY	AUGUST	SEPTEMBER	OCTOBER	NOVEMBER	DECEMBER	YEAR
	° ′	° ′	FEET	YEAR	°F	°F	°F	°F	°F	°F	°F	°F	°F	°F	YEAR	IN.	IN.	IN.	IN.	IN.	IN.	IN.	IN.	IN.	IN.	IN.	IN.	IN.
Gibraltar:																												
Windmill Hill	36 06N	05 21W	400	12	58	50	64	55	77	66	70	61	97	35	12	4.6	3.4	3.7	2.5	1.4	0.2	*	0.1	0.8	3.5	4.1	5.4	29.7
Greece:																												
Athinai (Athens)	37 58N	23 43E	351	72	54	42	67	52	90	72	74	60	109	20	80	2.2	1.6	1.4	0.8	0.8	0.6	0.2	0.4	0.6	1.7	2.8	2.8	15.8
Iraklion (Crete)	35 20N	25 08E	98	21	60	48	70	54	85	72	77	62	114	32	22	3.7	3.0	1.6	0.9	0.7	0.1	*	0.1	0.7	1.7	2.7	4.0	19.2
Rodhos (Rhodes)	36 26N	28 15E	289	10	59	51	67	59	83	74	76	68	104	30	6	5.7	3.9	2.6	1.7	0.5	0.3	0.0	*	0.4	1.7	5.2	6.7	28.5
Thessaloniki (Salonika)	40 37N	22 57E	78	9	49	37	66	49	90	70	73	56	107	15	26	1.5	1.5	1.6	1.9	2.0	1.2	1.0	0.7	1.2	2.4	2.1	1.9	19.0
Hungary:																												
Budapest	47 31N	19 02E	394	50	35	26	62	44	82	61	61	45	103	-10	50	1.5	1.5	1.7	2.0	2.7	2.6	2.0	1.9	1.8	2.1	2.4	2.0	24.2
Debrecen	47 36N	21 39E	430	50	33	21	61	39	81	57	60	41	102	-22	80	1.2	1.1	1.4	1.8	2.4	2.8	2.5	2.3	1.8	2.2	2.0	1.6	23.1
Iceland:																												
Akureyri	65 41N	18 05W	16	23	34	26	40	30	57	47	43	34	83	- 8	26	1.7	1.5	1.7	1.3	0.6	0.9	1.3	1.6	1.9	2.3	1.9	1.9	18.6
Reykjavik	64 09N	21 56W	92	25	36	28	43	33	58	48	44	36	74	4	30	4.0	3.1	3.0	2.1	1.6	1.7	2.0	2.6	3.1	3.4	3.6	3.7	33.9
Ireland:																												
Cork	51 54N	08 29W	56	27	48	38	55	41	68	53	58	44	85	15	35	4.9	3.6	3.3	2.6	2.9	2.0	2.9	3.1	2.9	3.9	4.5	4.7	41.3
Dublin	53 22N	06 21W	155	30	47	35	54	38	67	51	57	43	86	8	35	2.7	2.2	2.0	1.9	2.3	2.0	2.8	3.0	2.8	2.7	2.7	2.6	29.7
Shannon Airport	52 41N	08 55W	8	9	46	36	55	41	66	53	58	45	87	12	12	3.8	3.0	2.0	2.2	2.4	2.1	3.1	3.0	3.0	3.4	4.2	4.3	36.5
Italy:																												
Ancona	43 37N	13 32E	52	30	46	36	62	50	83	68	67	55	102	18	30	2.6	1.7	1.6	2.3	2.1	1.9	1.5	1.5	3.5	3.7	2.5	3.0	28.0
Cagliari (Sardinia)	39 15N	09 03E	3	30	56	43	66	50	86	67	72	58	102	25	25	2.2	1.5	1.5	1.2	1.5	0.5	0.1	0.4	1.0	3.0	1.8	2.3	17.0
Genova (Genoa)	44 24N	08 55E	318	10	50	41	65	53	82	70	73	58	100	18	10	3.9	4.0	3.3	3.4	4.6	1.4	1.6	2.3	4.7	6.1	7.2	4.1	46.6
Napoli (Naples)	40 51N	14 15E	82	30	54	40	65	52	84	70	71	60	101	24	30	3.7	3.2	3.0	2.6	1.8	1.8	0.6	0.7	2.8	5.1	4.5	5.4	35.2
Palermo (Sicily)	38 07N	13 19E	354	10	58	47	67	53	86	71	75	62	113	31	30	3.8	3.4	2.4	1.9	1.1	0.6	0.2	0.6	2.0	3.7	4.1	4.5	28.3
Rome	41 48N	12 36E	377	10	54	39	68	46	88	64	73	53	104	20	30	3.3	2.9	2.0	2.0	1.9	0.7	0.4	0.7	2.8	4.3	4.4	4.1	29.5
Taranto	40 28N	17 17E	56	10	55	43	59	50	89	70	73	58	108	26	10	1.6	0.9	1.3	0.8	1.0	0.6	0.4	0.7	1.0	2.2	1.8	1.9	14.2
Venezia (Venice)	45 26N	12 23E	82	10	43	33	63	49	82	67	65	52	97	14	30	2.0	2.1	2.4	2.8	3.2	3.3	2.6	2.6	2.6	3.7	3.5	2.6	33.4
Luxembourg:																												
Luxembourg	49 37N	06 03E	1,096	7	36	29	58	40	74	55	56	43	99	-10	100	2.3	2.0	1.9	2.1	2.4	2.5	2.8	2.6	2.4	2.7	2.7	2.8	29.2
Malta:																												
Valletta	35 54N	14 31E	233	90	59	51	66	56	84	72	76	66	105	34	90	3.3	2.3	1.5	0.8	0.4	0.1	*	0.2	1.3	2.7	3.6	3.9	20.3
Monaco:																												
Monaco	43 44N	07 25E	180	60	54	46	61	53	77	70	67	60	93	27	60	2.4	2.3	3.1	2.2	2.1	1.4	0.7	1.1	2.3	4.7	4.3	3.5	30.1
Netherlands:																												
Amsterdam	52 23N	04 55E	5	29	40	34	52	43	69	59	56	48	95	3	29	2.0	1.4	1.3	1.6	1.8	1.8	2.6	2.7	2.8	2.8	2.6	2.2	25.6
Norway:																												
Bergen	60 24N	05 19E	141	49	43	27	55	34	72	51	57	38	89	3	75	7.9	6.0	5.4	4.4	3.9	4.2	5.2	7.3	9.2	9.2	8.0	8.1	78.8
Kristiansand	58 10N	07 59E	175	11	32	25	50	35	71	53	53	39	90	-14	56	5.0	3.6	3.6	2.7	2.5	2.8	3.5	5.3	4.7	6.2	5.7	6.4	52.0
Oslo	59 56N	10 44E	308	44	30	20	50	34	73	56	49	37	93	-21	56	1.7	1.3	1.4	1.6	1.8	2.4	2.9	3.8	2.5	2.9	2.3	2.3	26.9
Tromso	69 39N	18 57E	335	47	30	22	37	27	59	48	40	33	83	- 1	75	4.1	3.8	3.3	2.4	2.1	2.1	2.3	2.9	4.7	4.5	4.0	3.9	40.1
Trondheim	63 25N	10 27E	417	44	31	22	45	32	66	51	46	36	95	-22	65	3.1	2.7	2.6	2.0	1.7	1.9	2.4	3.0	3.4	3.7	2.8	2.8	32.1
Vardo	70 22N	31 06E	43	40	27	19	34	26	53	44	38	32	80	-11	56	2.5	2.5	2.3	1.5	1.3	1.3	1.5	1.7	1.9	2.5	2.1	2.4	23.5

COUNTRY AND STATION	LATITUDE	LONGITUDE	ELEVATION	TEMPERATURE: LENGTH OF RECORD	AVERAGE DAILY: JANUARY MAXIMUM	JANUARY MINIMUM	APRIL MAXIMUM	APRIL MINIMUM	JULY MAXIMUM	JULY MINIMUM	OCTOBER MAXIMUM	OCTOBER MINIMUM	EXTREME: MAXIMUM	EXTREME: MINIMUM	AVERAGE PRECIPITATION: LENGTH OF RECORD	JANUARY	FEBRUARY	MARCH	APRIL	MAY	JUNE	JULY	AUGUST	SEPTEMBER	OCTOBER	NOVEMBER	DECEMBER	YEAR
	° '	° '	FEET	YEAR	°F	°F	°F	°F	°F	°F	°F	°F	°F	°F	YEAR	IN.	IN.	IN.	IN.	IN.	IN.	IN.	IN.	IN.	IN.	IN.	IN.	IN.
Poland:																												
Gdansk (Danzig)	54 24N	18 40E	36	36	33	25	49	37	70	56	53	42	94	-16	35	1.2	1.0	1.3	1.5	1.8	2.3	2.8	2.6	2.1	1.8	1.8	1.5	21.7
Krakow	50 04N	19 57E	723	35	32	22	55	38	76	57	56	41	97	-28	35	1.1	1.3	1.4	1.8	2.8	4.0	4.5	3.8	2.7	2.2	1.7	1.3	28.6
Warsaw	52 13N	21 02E	294	25	30	21	54	38	75	56	54	41	98	-22	113	1.2	1.1	1.3	1.5	1.9	2.6	3.0	3.0	1.9	1.7	1.4	1.4	22.0
Wroclaw (Breslau)	51 07N	17 05E	482	50	35	25	55	39	74	57	55	42	98	-26	40	1.5	1.1	1.5	1.7	2.4	2.4	3.4	2.7	1.8	1.7	1.5	1.5	23.2
Portugal:																												
Braganca	41 49N	06 47W	2,395	11	46	31	59	39	80	54	62	42	103	10	11	11.9	6.9	7.7	3.7	3.0	1.6	0.5	0.6	1.5	3.0	6.3	7.1	53.8
Lagos	37 06N	08 38W	46	21	61	47	67	52	83	64	73	58	107	28	17	3.2	2.6	2.8	1.4	0.8	0.2	*	*	0.4	1.5	2.6	2.8	18.3
Lisbon	38 43N	09 08W	313	75	56	46	64	52	79	63	69	57	103	29	75	3.3	3.2	3.1	2.4	1.7	0.7	0.2	0.2	1.4	3.1	4.2	3.6	27.0
Romania:																												
Bucuresti (Bucharest)	44 25N	26 06E	269	41	33	20	63	41	86	61	65	44	105	-18	41	1.5	1.1	1.7	1.6	2.5	3.8	2.3	1.8	1.5	1.6	1.9	1.5	22.8
Cluj	46 47N	23 40E	1,286	15	31	18	58	38	79	56	60	41	100	-26	16	1.3	1.2	1.0	2.1	3.3	3.3	2.6	3.3	2.0	1.7	1.0	1.2	24.0
Constanta	44 11N	28 39E	13	20	37	25	55	42	79	63	62	49	101	-13	39	1.2	1.2	1.1	1.1	1.3	1.7	1.3	1.1	1.1	1.4	1.2	1.4	15.1
Spain:																												
Almeria	36 51N	02 28W	213	20	61	47	69	54	85	69	76	62	108	34	20	0.9	1.0	0.7	0.9	0.7	0.2	*	0.1	0.6	0.9	1.5	1.1	8.6
Barcelona	41 24N	02 09E	312	20	56	42	64	51	81	69	71	58	98	24	30	1.2	2.1	1.9	1.8	1.8	1.3	1.2	1.7	2.6	3.4	2.7	1.8	23.5
Burgos	42 20N	03 42W	2,825	29	42	30	57	38	77	53	61	43	99	0	29	1.5	1.5	2.1	1.9	2.4	1.7	0.8	0.7	1.4	2.0	2.2	2.0	20.2
Madrid	40 25N	03 41W	2,188	30	47	33	64	44	87	62	66	48	102	14	30	1.1	1.7	1.7	1.7	1.5	1.2	0.4	0.3	1.2	1.9	2.2	1.6	16.5
Sevilla	37 29N	05 59W	98	26	59	41	73	51	96	67	78	57	117	27	26	2.2	2.9	3.3	2.3	1.3	0.9	0.1	0.1	1.1	2.6	3.7	2.8	23.3
Valencia	39 28N	00 23W	79	26	58	41	67	51	83	68	73	57	107	20	29	0.9	1.5	0.9	1.2	1.1	1.3	0.4	0.5	2.2	1.6	2.5	1.3	15.4
Sweden:																												
Abisko	68 21N	18 49E	1,273	11	20	6	33	19	61	45	35	24	82	-30	11	0.7	0.6	0.5	0.5	0.7	1.8	1.6	1.8	1.2	1.0	0.6	0.6	11.7
Goteberg	57 42N	11 58E	55	39	35	27	48	36	69	56	51	42	88	-13	61	2.5	2.0	2.0	1.7	1.9	2.2	2.8	3.7	3.1	3.1	2.7	2.8	30.5
Haparanda	65 50N	24 09E	30	20	22	10	38	23	71	53	39	30	89	-34	20	2.2	1.6	1.2	1.5	1.4	1.7	2.1	2.8	2.6	2.8	2.5	2.0	24.4
Karlstad	59 23N	13 30E	164	30	30	20	49	32	73	56	49	38	93	-21	30	1.9	1.2	1.2	1.4	1.9	1.9	2.6	3.1	2.9	2.4	2.4	1.9	24.8
Sarna	61 41N	13 07E	1,504	20	19	4	42	23	69	46	42	28	91	-51	20	1.6	0.8	0.9	1.2	1.6	2.8	3.6	3.3	2.6	2.3	1.8	1.8	24.3
Stockholm	59 21N	18 04E	146	30	31	23	45	32	70	55	48	39	97	-26	30	1.5	1.1	1.1	1.5	1.6	1.9	2.8	3.1	2.1	2.1	1.9	1.9	22.4
Visby (Gotland)	57 39N	18 18E	36	30	35	28	44	33	67	55	50	41	88	1	30	1.7	1.1	1.2	1.4	1.1	1.4	2.0	2.7	1.7	1.9	2.1	2.0	20.3
Switzerland:																												
Berne	46 57N	07 26E	1,877	30	35	26	56	39	74	56	55	42	96	- 9	77	1.9	2.0	2.6	3.0	3.7	4.4	4.4	4.3	3.5	3.5	2.7	2.5	38.5
Geneve (Geneva)	46 12N	06 09E	1,329	30	39	29	58	41	77	58	58	44	101	- 1	125	1.9	1.8	2.2	2.5	3.0	3.1	2.9	3.6	3.6	3.8	3.1	2.4	33.9
Zurich	47 23N	08 33E	1,617	23	38	28	57	39	76	55	57	42	98	-12	23	2.3	1.9	2.9	3.4	4.0	4.9	5.0	4.6	3.3	3.2	2.5	2.9	40.9
Turkey:																												
Edirne (Adrianople)	41 39N	26 34E	154	18	41	28	66	44	88	63	70	49	107	- 8	18	2.2	1.9	1.7	1.9	1.7	2.1	1.5	1.1	1.1	2.1	2.9	3.0	23.2
Istanbul (Constantinople)	40 58N	28 50E	59	18	45	36	61	45	81	65	67	54	100	17	18	3.7	2.3	2.6	1.9	1.4	1.3	1.7	1.5	2.3	3.8	4.1	4.9	31.5
United Kingdom:																												
Belfast	54 35N	05 56W	57	7	42	34	53	38	65	52	55	44	82	14	30	4.2	2.8	2.3	2.4	2.3	2.5	3.5	3.5	3.4	3.8	3.6	3.9	38.2
Birmingham	52 29N	01 56W	535	30	42	35	53	40	69	54	55	45	92	11	30	2.9	2.1	1.7	2.2	2.5	1.8	2.8	2.7	2.3	2.9	3.2	2.6	29.7
Cardiff	51 28N	03 10W	203	30	45	36	55	41	69	54	57	45	91	2	30	4.6	3.0	2.3	2.5	3.0	2.2	3.4	3.9	3.6	4.5	4.6	4.3	41.9
Dublin	53 22N	06 21W	155	30	47	35	54	38	67	51	57	43	86	8	35	2.7	2.2	2.0	1.9	2.3	2.0	2.8	3.0	2.8	2.7	2.7	2.6	29.7
Edinburgh	55 55N	03 11W	441	30	43	35	50	39	65	52	53	44	83	15	30	2.5	1.6	1.6	1.6	2.2	1.9	3.1	3.1	2.6	2.9	2.4	2.1	27.6
London	51 29N	00 00	149	30	44	35	56	40	73	55	58	44	99	9	30	2.0	1.5	1.4	1.8	1.8	1.6	2.0	2.2	1.8	2.3	2.5	2.0	22.9

(See footnotes at end of tables)

COUNTRY AND STATION	LATITUDE	LONGITUDE	ELE-VATION	TEMPERATURE: LENGTH OF RECORD	AVERAGE DAILY: JANUARY MAXIMUM	JANUARY MINIMUM	APRIL MAXIMUM	APRIL MINIMUM	JULY MAXIMUM	JULY MINIMUM	OCTOBER MAXIMUM	OCTOBER MINIMUM	EXTREME: MAXIMUM	EXTREME: MINIMUM	AVERAGE PRECIPITATION: LENGTH OF RECORD	JANUARY	FEBRUARY	MARCH	APRIL	MAY	JUNE	JULY	AUGUST	SEPTEMBER	OCTOBER	NOVEMBER	DECEMBER	YEAR
	° '	° '	FEET	YEAR	°F	°F	°F	°F	°F	°F	°F	°F	°F	°F	YEAR	IN.	IN.	IN.	IN.	IN.	IN.	IN.	IN.	IN.	IN.	IN.	IN.	IN.
Liverpool	53 24N	03 04W	198	30	44	36	52	41	66	55	55	46	87	15	30	2.7	1.9	1.5	1.6	2.2	2.0	2.8	3.1	2.6	3.0	3.0	2.5	28.9
Perth	56 24N	03 27W	77	30	43	32	53	38	68	51	55	41	89	0	30	3.1	2.2	1.9	1.7	2.3	2.0	3.1	2.9	2.8	3.3	2.7	2.7	30.7
Plymouth	50 21N	04 07W	87	30	47	40	54	43	66	55	58	49	88	16	30	4.3	3.0	2.6	2.3	2.5	2.0	2.6	2.9	2.8	3.8	4.6	4.4	37.8
Wick	58 26N	03 05W	119	30	42	35	48	38	59	50	52	43	80	8	30	2.9	2.1	1.8	2.1	1.8	2.0	2.6	2.6	2.9	3.2	3.1	2.9	30.0
U.S.S.R.:																												
Arkhangelsk	64 33N	40 32E	22	23	9	2	36	23	64	51	36	30	91	-49	25	1.2	1.1	1.1	0.7	1.3	1.9	2.6	2.7	2.2	1.9	1.6	1.3	19.8
Astrakhan	46 21N	48 02E	45	10	23	14	57	40	85	69	56	40	99	-22	25	0.5	0.5	0.4	0.6	0.6	0.7	0.5	0.4	0.6	0.4	0.6	0.6	6.4
Dnepropetrovsk	48 27N	35 04E	259	18	25	16	53	39	80	62	56	40	101	-25	17	1.4	1.1	1.2	1.4	1.8	3.0	1.9	1.6	1.0	1.8	1.6	1.6	19.4
Kaunas	54 54N	23 53E	118	19	26	18	49	34	72	53	50	38	96	-23	19	1.6	1.3	1.3	1.8	2.0	3.2	3.3	3.5	1.9	1.9	1.6	1.6	25.0
Kirov	58 36N	49 41E	594	20	6	- 2	41	27	72	55	37	29	92	-43	29	1.2	1.0	0.9	0.9	1.9	2.5	2.1	2.9	2.3	2.0	1.6	1.3	20.6
Kursk	51 45N	36 12E	773	15	19	11	47	35	74	58	48	36	91	-23	20	1.5	1.3	1.2	1.5	2.2	2.5	3.2	2.3	1.6	1.8	1.5	1.7	22.3
Leningrad	59 56N	30 16E	16	26	23	12	45	31	71	57	45	37	91	-36	95	1.0	0.9	0.9	1.0	1.6	2.0	2.5	2.8	2.1	1.8	1.4	1.2	19.2
Lvov	49 50N	24 01E	978	9	31	22	53	38	77	59	55	43	97	-29	35	1.3	1.5	1.8	2.0	2.8	3.7	4.1	3.1	2.4	2.1	0.8	1.6	28.2
Minsk	53 54N	27 33E	738	12	22	13	47	33	70	54	47	36	92	-27	20	1.4	1.5	1.3	1.5	2.0	2.8	3.0	3.1	1.6	1.5	1.5	1.7	22.9
Moskva (Moscow)	55 46N	37 40E	505	15	21	9	47	31	76	55	46	34	96	-27	11	1.5	1.4	1.1	1.9	2.2	2.9	3.0	2.9	1.9	2.7	1.7	1.6	24.8
Odessa	46 29N	30 44E	214	20	28	22	52	41	79	65	57	47	99	-13	15	1.0	0.7	0.7	1.1	1.1	1.9	1.6	1.4	1.1	1.4	1.1	1.1	14.3
Riga	56 57N	24 06E	67	30	29	20	48	35	72	56	49	39	93	-20	57	1.3	1.0	1.1	1.2	1.7	2.4	3.0	3.0	2.1	2.0	1.9	1.5	22.2
Saratov	51 32N	46 03E	197	14	15	7	50	35	82	64	48	36	102	-27	15	1.0	1.0	0.8	1.0	1.3	1.8	1.2	1.3	1.1	1.4	1.4	1.2	14.5
Sevastopol	44 37N	33 31E	75	20	39	30	55	42	79	65	63	50	97	- 4	30	1.1	1.1	1.1	0.9	0.6	1.1	0.8	0.6	1.1	1.5	1.2	1.1	12.2
Stalingrad	48 42N	44 31E	136	8	15	4	52	36	84	65	53	37	106	-30	12	0.9	1.0	0.6	0.6	1.0	1.9	0.9	0.8	0.7	1.0	1.5	1.3	12.2
Stavropol	45 02N	41 58E	1,886	18	26	17	50	37	76	60	55	42	95	-22	41	1.4	1.1	1.5	2.4	3.0	4.1	3.0	2.0	2.5	2.3	1.8	1.8	26.9
Tallin	59 26N	24 48E	146	15	27	18	42	31	70	55	47	38	89	-19	63	1.1	1.0	0.9	1.1	1.7	1.9	2.1	2.7	2.3	2.1	1.9	1.5	20.2
Tbilisi	41 43N	44 48E	1,325	10	39	26	61	44	83	65	64	48	95	6	10	0.7	0.8	1.3	1.6	3.6	3.1	2.2	1.7	1.9	1.3	2.0	1.2	21.4
Ust'Shchugor	64 16N	57 34E	279	15	4	-14	35	17	65	49	33	23	90	-67	15	1.1	0.8	0.8	0.7	1.4	2.2	3.0	3.2	2.4	2.2	1.5	1.3	20.6
Ufy	54 43N	55 56E	571	20	6	- 3	44	30	75	58	41	31	99	-42	23	1.6	1.3	1.2	0.9	1.6	2.4	2.6	2.2	1.8	2.3	2.2	2.3	22.5
Yugoslavia:																												
Beograd (Belgrade)	44 48N	20 28E	453	16	37	27	64	45	84	61	65	47	107	-14	16	1.6	1.3	1.6	2.2	2.6	2.8	1.9	2.5	1.7	2.7	1.8	1.9	24.6
Skopje	41 59N	21 28E	787	10	40	26	67	42	88	60	65	43	105	-11	10	1.5	1.2	1.3	1.5	1.9	1.9	1.3	1.1	1.1	2.6	2.3	1.8	19.5
Split	43 31N	16 26E	420	14	51	29	65	50	87	68	69	55	100	17	51	3.1	2.5	3.2	3.0	2.5	2.1	1.2	1.6	2.9	4.4	4.2	4.4	35.1
OCEAN ISLANDS																												
Bjornoya, Bear Island	74 31N	19 01E	49	10	26	17	27	16	44	36	36	29	71	-25	25	1.6	1.3	1.3	0.9	0.8	0.7	0.8	1.2	1.8	1.7	1.4	1.6	15.1
Gronfjorden, Spitzbergen	78 02N	14 15E	23	19	10	- 4	15	- 3	46	38	25	17	60	-57	15	1.4	1.3	1.1	0.9	0.5	0.4	0.6	0.9	1.0	1.2	0.9	1.5	11.7
Horta, Azores	38 32N	28 38W	200	30	62	54	64	55	76	65	71	62	88	38	30	4.5	4.1	4.2	3.0	2.9	2.0	1.5	1.9	3.2	4.4	4.1	4.5	40.3
Jan Mayen	71 01N	08 28W	131	5	31	21	31	22	46	38	39	29	60	-18	29	2.1	1.7	1.6	1.4	0.9	0.9	1.4	1.8	2.5	2.5	2.2	2.2	21.2
Lerwick, Shetland Island	60 08N	01 11W	269	30	42	35	46	37	58	49	50	42	71	17	30	4.5	3.4	2.9	2.7	2.2	2.2	2.7	2.9	3.7	4.3	4.5	4.5	40.5
Matochkin Shar, Novaya Zemlya	73 16N	56 24E	61	9	8	- 6	13	- 1	47	36	30	21	68	-41	9	0.6	0.6	0.6	0.4	0.3	0.4	1.4	1.5	1.5	0.6	0.6	0.4	8.9
Ponta Delgada, Azores	37 45N	25 40W	118	30	62	54	64	55	76	64	71	61	85	37	30	4.0	3.5	3.5	2.5	2.3	1.4	1.0	1.2	2.9	3.6	3.7	3.0	32.6
Stornoway, Hebrides	58 11N	06 21W	34	30	44	37	49	39	61	51	53	44	78	11	15	6.4	3.2	3.2	3.1	2.5	2.4	3.0	4.3	4.7	6.2	4.6	5.5	49.1
Thorshavn, Faeroes	62 02N	06 45W	82	50	42	33	45	36	56	47	58	40	70	8	50	6.6	5.2	4.8	3.6	3.4	2.5	3.1	3.5	4.7	5.9	6.3	6.6	56.2

COUNTRY AND STATION	LATITUDE	LONGITUDE	ELEVATION	TEMPERATURE: LENGTH OF RECORD	AVERAGE DAILY: JANUARY MAXIMUM	JANUARY MINIMUM	APRIL MAXIMUM	APRIL MINIMUM	JULY MAXIMUM	JULY MINIMUM	OCTOBER MAXIMUM	OCTOBER MINIMUM	EXTREME: MAXIMUM	EXTREME: MINIMUM	AVERAGE PRECIPITATION: LENGTH OF RECORD	JANUARY	FEBRUARY	MARCH	APRIL	MAY	JUNE	JULY	AUGUST	SEPTEMBER	OCTOBER	NOVEMBER	DECEMBER	YEAR
	° '	° '	FEET	YEAR	°F	°F	°F	°F	°F	°F	°F	°F	°F	°F	YEAR	IN.	IN.	IN.	IN.	IN.	IN.	IN.	IN.	IN.	IN.	IN.	IN.	IN.
AFRICA																												
Algeria:																												
Adrar	27 52N	00 17W	938	15	69	39	92	60	115	82	92	63	124	25	15	*	*	0.1	*	*	*	*	*	*	0.2	0.2	*	0.6
Alger (Algiers)	36 46N	03 03E	194	25	59	49	68	55	83	70	74	63	107	32	25	4.4	3.3	2.9	1.6	1.8	0.6	*	0.2	1.6	3.1	5.1	5.4	30.0
Bone	36 54N	07 46E	66	26	59	46	67	52	85	69	75	61	115	32	26	5.6	4.1	2.9	2.2	1.5	0.6	0.1	0.3	1.2	3.0	4.3	5.2	31.0
El Golea	30 35N	02 53E	1,247	15	63	37	84	56	107	79	87	60	120	23	15	0.1	0.3	0.5	*	*	*	*	*	*	0.3	0.4	0.3	1.9
Fort Flatters	28 06N	06 42E	1,224	15	67	38	90	59	110	78	92	63	124	19	15	0.3	0.1	0.1	0.2	*	*	0.0	*	*	*	0.2	0.2	1.1
Tamanrasset	22 42N	05 31E	4,593	15	67	39	86	56	95	71	85	59	102	20	15	0.2	*	*	0.2	0.4	0.1	0.1	0.4	0.1	*	*	*	1.5
Touggourt	33 07N	06 04E	226	26.	62	38	83	55	107	77	84	59	122	26	26	0.2	0.4	0.5	0.2	0.2	0.2	*	*	0.1	0.3	0.5	0.3	2.9
Angola:																												
Cangamba	13 41S	19 52E	4,331	6	84	62	89	58	82	46	87	59	109	20	7	8.9	7.4	6.8	1.8	0.1	0.0	0.0	0.2	0.2	1.6	5.1	8.5	40.6
Luanda	08 49S	13 13E	194	27	83	74	85	75	74	65	79	71	98	58	59	1.0	1.4	3.0	4.6	0.5	*	*	*	0.1	0.2	1.1	0.8	12.7
Mocamedes	15 12S	12 09E	10	15	79	65	82	66	68	56	74	61	102	44	21	0.3	0.4	0.7	0.5	*	*	*	*	*	*	0.1	0.1	2.1
Nova Lisboa	12 48S	15 45E	5,577	14	78	58	78	57	77	47	81	58	90	36	14	8.7	7.8	9.8	5.7	0.4	0.0	*	*	0.6	5.5	9.6	8.9	57.0
Botswana:																												
Francistown	21 13S	27 30E	3,294	20	88	65	83	56	75	41	90	61	107	24	28	4.2	3.1	2.8	0.7	0.2	0.1	*	*	*	0.9	2.3	3.4	17.7
Maun	19 59S	23 25E	3,091	20	90	66	87	58	77	42	95	64	110	24	20	4.3	3.8	3.5	1.1	0.2	*	0.0	0.0	*	0.5	1.9	2.8	18.2
Tsabong	26 03S	22 27E	3,156	10	94	65	83	51	71	34	88	54	107	15	14	2.0	1.9	1.9	1.3	0.4	0.4	0.1	*	0.2	0.7	1.1	1.5	11.5
Cameroon:																												
Ngaoundere	07 17N	13 19E	3,601	9	87	55	87	64	82	63	82	61	102	46	10	*	*	1.1	5.5	7.0	8.4	10.6	9.6	9.2	5.3	0.5	*	57.2
Yaounde	03 53N	11 32E	2,526	11	85	67	85	66	80	66	81	65	96	57	11	0.9	2.6	5.8	6.7	7.7	6.0	2.9	3.1	8.4	11.6	4.6	0.9	61.2
Central African Republic:																												
Bangui	04 22N	18 34E	1,270	5	90	68	91	71	85	69	87	69	101	57	5	1.0	1.7	5.0	5.3	7.4	4.5	8.9	8.1	5.9	7.9	4.9	0.2	60.8
Ndele	08 24N	20 39E	1,939	3	99	67	98	73	86	69	90	68	109	58	3	0.2	1.3	0.6	1.7	8.4	6.1	8.3	10.1	10.7	7.8	0.6	0.0	55.8
Chad:																												
Am Timan	11 02N	20 17E	1,430	3	98	56	105	68	89	70	96	67	113	43	3	0.0	0.0	0.1	1.2	4.3	5.0	7.3	12.3	5.8	1.2	0.0	0.0	37.2
Fort Lamy	12 07N	15 02E	968	5	93	57	107	74	92	72	97	70	114	47	5	0.0	0.0	0.0	0.1	1.2	2.6	6.7	12.6	4.7	1.4	0.0	0.0	29.3
Largeau (Faya)	18 00N	19 10E	837	5	84	54	104	69	109	76	103	72	121	37	5	0.0	0.0	0.0	0.0	*	0.0	*	0.7	*	0.0	0.0	0.0	0.7
Congo, Democratic Republic of the:																												
Albertville	05 54S	29 12E	2,493	5	85	66	83	67	82	58	87	67	92	50	20	4.2	4.7	6.3	8.4	3.3	0.3	0.1	0.3	0.8	2.8	7.9	6.3	45.4
Kinspasa (Leopoldville)	04 20S	15 18E	1,066	8	87	70	89	71	81	64	88	70	97	58	12	5.3	5.7	7.7	7.7	6.2	0.3	0.1	0.1	1.2	4.7	8.7	5.6	53.3
Luluabourg	05 54S	22 25E	2,198	3	85	68	86	68	85	63	85	68	94	57	14	5.4	5.6	7.7	7.6	3.3	0.8	0.5	2.3	4.6	6.5	9.1	8.9	62.3
Stanleyville	00 26N	25 14E	1,370	8	88	69	88	70	84	67	86	68	97	61	14	2.1	3.3	7.0	6.2	5.4	4.5	5.2	6.5	7.2	8.6	7.8	3.3	67.1
Congo, Republic of:																												
Brazzaville	04 15S	15 15E	1,043	15	88	69	91	71	82	63	89	70	98	54	18	6.3	4.9	7.4	7.0	4.3	0.6	*	*	2.2	5.4	11.5	8.4	58.0
Ouesso	01 37N	16 04E	1,132	4	88	69	91	71	85	69	87	69	106	60	4	2.4	3.6	6.4	3.2	5.8	4.6	2.9	3.7	7.9	10.0	5.7	2.4	58.6
Pointe Noire (Loango)	04 39S	11 48E	164	7	85	73	87	74	78	66	83	72	93	59	7	5.4	6.7	6.4	8.0	3.9	0.0	0.0	0.0	0.4	4.1	6.6	6.6	48.1
Dahomey:																												
Cotonou	06 21N	02 26E	23	5	80	74	83	78	78	74	80	75	95	65	10	1.3	1.3	4.6	4.9	10.0	14.4	3.5	1.5	2.6	5.3	2.3	0.5	52.4

(See footnotes at end of tables)

COUNTRY AND STATION	LATITUDE	LONGITUDE	ELEVATION	TEMPERATURE: LENGTH OF RECORD	AVERAGE DAILY: JANUARY MAXIMUM	JANUARY MINIMUM	APRIL MAXIMUM	APRIL MINIMUM	JULY MAXIMUM	JULY MINIMUM	OCTOBER MAXIMUM	OCTOBER MINIMUM	EXTREME: MAXIMUM	EXTREME: MINIMUM	AVERAGE PRECIPITATION: LENGTH OF RECORD	JANUARY	FEBRUARY	MARCH	APRIL	MAY	JUNE	JULY	AUGUST	SEPTEMBER	OCTOBER	NOVEMBER	DECEMBER	YEAR
	° '	° '	FEET	YEAR	°F	°F	°F	°F	°F	°F	°F	°F	°F	°F	YEAR	IN.	IN.	IN.	IN.	IN.	IN.	IN.	IN.	IN.	IN.	IN.	IN.	IN.
Ethiopia:																												
Addis Ababa	09 20N	38 45E	8,038	15	75	43	77	50	69	50	75	45	94	32	37	0.5	1.5	2.6	3.4	3.4	5.4	11.0	11.8	7.5	0.8	0.6	0.2	48.7
Asmara	15 17N	38 55E	7,628	9	74	44	78	51	71	53	72	53	88	31	17	*	*	0.4	1.5	1.5	1.3	6.7	5.0	1.3	0.3	0.4	*	18.4
Diredawa	09 02N	41 45E	3,937	8	81	58	91	69	90	68	89	67	100	49	8	0.8	0.8	3.3	3.0	2.8	1.5	4.3	3.8	2.2	0.5	0.3	0.8	24.1
Gambela	08 15N	34 35E	1,345	26	98	64	98	71	87	69	92	67	111	48	30	0.2	0.4	1.4	3.2	5.9	6.7	8.5	9.5	7.3	3.5	1.8	0.4	48.8
French Territory of Afars and Issas (F.T.A.I.):																												
Djibouti	11 36N	43 09E	23	16	84	73	90	79	106	87	92	80	117	63	46	0.4	0.5	1.0	0.5	0.2	*	0.1	0.3	0.3	0.4	0.9	0.5	46.0
Gabon:																												
Libreville	00 23N	09 26E	115	11	87	73	89	73	83	68	86	71	99	62	21	9.8	9.3	13.2	13.4	9.6	0.5	0.1	0.7	4.1	13.6	14.7	9.8	98.8
Mayoumba	03 25S	10 38E	200	8	84	73	86	73	78	68	82	72	91	60	8	6.5	9.3	6.2	10.2	2.3	0.1	0.0	0.2	2.6	9.3	10.7	4.6	62.0
Gambia:																												
Bathurst	13 21N	16 40W	90	9	88	59	91	65	86	74	89	72	106	45	9	0.1	0.1	*	*	0.4	2.3	11.1	19.7	12.2	4.3	0.7	0.1	51.0
Ghana:																												
Accra	05 33N	00 12W	88	17	87	73	88	76	81	73	85	74	100	59	65	0.6	1.3	2.2	3.2	5.6	7.0	1.8	0.6	1.4	2.5	1.4	0.9	28.5
Kumasi	06 40N	01 37W	942	10	88	66	89	71	82	70	86	70	100	51	10	0.8	2.3	5.7	5.1	7.5	7.9	4.3	3.1	6.8	7.1	3.7	0.8	55.2
Guinea:																												
Conakry	09 31N	13 43W	23	7	88	72	90	73	83	72	87	73	96	63	10	0.1	0.1	0.4	0.9	6.2	22.0	51.1	41.5	26.9	14.6	4.8	0.4	169.0
Kouroussa	10 39N	09 53W	1,217	9	93	60	99	73	87	69	90	69	109	39	10	0.4	0.3	0.9	2.8	5.3	9.7	11.7	13.6	13.4	6.6	1.3	0.4	66.4
Ifni (now in Morocco):																												
Sidi Ifni	29 27N	10 11W	148	14	66	52	71	59	75	64	75	62	124	40	14	1.0	0.6	0.5	0.6	0.1	0.1	*	*	0.4	0.1	0.9	1.8	6.1
Ivory Coast:																												
Abidjan	05 19N	04 01W	65	13	88	73	90	75	83	73	85	74	96	59	10	1.6	2.1	3.9	4.9	14.2	19.5	8.4	2.1	2.8	6.6	7.9	3.1	77.1
Bouake	07 42N	05 00W	1,194	12	91	68	92	70	85	68	89	68	104	57	10	0.4	1.5	4.1	5.8	5.3	6.0	3.1	4.6	8.2	5.2	1.5	1.0	46.7
Kenya:																												
Mombasa	04 03S	39 39E	52	45	87	75	86	76	81	71	84	74	96	61	54	1.0	0.7	2.5	7.7	12.6	4.7	3.5	2.5	2.5	3.4	3.8	2.4	47.3
Nairobi	01 16S	36 48E	5,971	15	77	54	75	58	69	51	76	55	87	41	17	1.5	2.5	4.9	8.3	6.2	1.8	0.6	0.9	1.2	2.1	4.3	3.4	37.7
Liberia:																												
Monrovia	06 18N	10 48W	75	6	89	71	90	72	80	72	86	72	97	62	4	0.2	0.1	4.4	11.7	13.4	36.1	24.2	18.6	29.9	25.2	8.2	2.9	174.9
Libya:																												
Banghazi (Benghazi)	32 06N	20 04E	82	46	63	50	74	58	84	71	80	66	109	37	46	2.6	1.6	0.8	0.2	0.1	*	*	*	0.1	0.7	1.8	2.6	10.5
Cufra	24 12N	23 21E	1,276	7	69	43	90	62	101	75	90	64	122	26	7	*	0.0	0.0	0.0	*	0.0	0.0	0.0	0.0	0.0	0.0	*	*
Sabhah	27 01N	14 26E	1,457	3	64	41	89	60	102	74	91	64	120	24	10	*	*	*	*	0.1	0.1	0.0	0.0	0.0	*	*	*	0.3
Tarabulus (Triopoli)	32 54N	13 11E	72	47	61	47	72	57	85	71	80	65	114	33	56	3.2	1.8	1.1	0.4	0.2	0.1	*	*	0.4	1.6	2.6	3.7	15.1
Malagasy Republic:																												
Diego Suarez	12 17S	49 17E	100	11	88	75	88	75	84	69	86	72	98	63	31	10.6	9.5	7.6	2.2	0.3	0.2	0.2	0.3	0.3	0.7	1.1	5.8	38.7
Tananarive	18 55S	47 33E	4,500	44	79	61	76	58	68	48	80	54	95	34	62	11.8	11.0	7.0	2.1	0.7	0.3	0.3	0.4	0.7	2.4	5.3	11.3	53.4
Tulear	23 20S	43 41E	20	27	92	72	89	64	81	58	86	65	108	43	15	3.1	3.2	1.4	0.3	0.7	0.4	0.1	0.2	0.3	0.7	1.4	1.7	13.5
Malawi:																												
Karonga	09 57S	33 56E	1,596	8	86	71	85	70	81	59	91	66	99	51	8	7.1	7.0	10.8	6.2	1.7	0.1	*	*	0.0	0.3	0.3	4.7	38.3
Zomba	15 23S	35 19E	3,141	27	80	65	78	62	72	53	85	64	95	41	29	12.1	9.9	10.1	2.7	0.7	0.4	0.3	0.3	0.2	1.0	4.3	10.9	52.9

COUNTRY AND STATION	LATITUDE	LONGITUDE	ELEVATION	TEMPERATURE: LENGTH OF RECORD	AVERAGE DAILY: JANUARY MAXIMUM	JANUARY MINIMUM	APRIL MAXIMUM	APRIL MINIMUM	JULY MAXIMUM	JULY MINIMUM	OCTOBER MAXIMUM	OCTOBER MINIMUM	EXTREME: MAXIMUM	EXTREME: MINIMUM	AVERAGE PRECIPITATION: LENGTH OF RECORD	JANUARY	FEBRUARY	MARCH	APRIL	MAY	JUNE	JULY	AUGUST	SEPTEMBER	OCTOBER	NOVEMBER	DECEMBER	YEAR
	° '	° '	FEET	YEAR	°F	°F	°F	°F	°F	°F	°F	°F	°F	°F	YEAR	IN.	IN.	IN.	IN.	IN.	IN.	IN.	IN.	IN.	IN.	IN.	IN.	IN.
Mali:																												
Araouane	18 54N	03 33W	935	8	81	48	110	67	111	79	103	70	130	37	10	*	*	0.0	0.0	0.0	0.2	0.2	0.5	0.6	0.1	0.1	*	1.7
Bamako	12 39N	07 58W	1,116	11	91	61	103	76	89	71	93	71	117	47	10	*	*	0.1	0.6	2.9	5.4	11.0	13.7	8.1	1.7	0.6	*	44.1
Gao	16 16N	00 03W	902	15	83	58	105	77	97	80	100	78	116	44	19	*	0.0	*	0.1	0.4	1.0	2.9	5.4	1.5	0.2	*	0.0	11.5
Mauritania:																												
Atar	20 31N	13 04W	761	7	84	54	97	67	106	81	98	72	117	39	10	*	0.0	*	*	*	0.1	0.3	1.2	1.1	0.1	*	*	2.8
Nema	16 36N	07 16W	883	9	86	62	105	79	99	78	101	79	120	47	10	0.1	*	*	*	0.7	1.1	2.3	4.7	2.1	0.7	*	0.1	11.6
Nouakchott	18 07N	15 36W	69	5	85	57	90	64	89	74	91	71	115	44	10	*	0.1	*	*	*	0.1	0.5	4.1	0.9	0.4	0.1	*	6.2
Morocco:																												
Casablanca	33 35N	07 39W	164	48	63	45	69	52	79	65	76	58	110	31	40	2.1	1.9	2.2	1.4	0.9	0.2	0.0	*	0.3	1.5	2.6	2.8	15.9
Marrakech	31 36N	08 01W	1,509	35	65	40	79	52	101	67	83	57	120	27	31	1.0	1.1	1.3	1.2	0.6	0.3	0.1	0.1	0.4	0.9	1.2	1.2	9.4
Rabat	34 00N	06 50W	213	35	63	46	71	52	82	63	77	58	118	32	29	2.6	2.5	2.6	1.7	1.1	0.3	*	*	0.4	1.9	3.3	3.4	19.8
Tangier	35 48N	05 49W	239	35	60	47	65	51	80	64	72	59	106	28	35	4.5	4.2	4.8	3.5	1.7	0.6	*	*	0.9	3.9	5.8	5.4	35.3
Mozambique:																												
Beira	19 50S	34 51E	28	37	89	75	86	71	77	61	87	71	109	48	39	10.9	8.4	10.1	4.2	2.2	1.3	1.2	1.1	0.8	5.2	5.3	9.2	59.9
Chicoa	15 36S	32 21E	899	8	96	65	93	63	86	55	101	68	117	32	8	7.8	5.7	4.4	0.6	*	*	*	*	*	1.1	2.6	5.2	27.4
Lourenco Marques	25 58S	32 36E	194	42	86	71	83	66	76	55	82	64	114	45	42	5.1	4.9	4.9	2.1	1.1	0.8	0.5	0.5	1.1	1.9	3.2	3.8	29.9
Niger:																												
Agades	16 59N	07 59E	1,706	8	86	50	105	70	104	75	101	68	115	40	10	0.0	0.0	*	*	0.2	0.3	1.9	3.7	0.7	0.0	0.0	0.0	6.8
Bilma	18 41N	12 55E	1,171	9	81	45	101	63	108	75	101	62	116	29	10	0.0	0.0	0.0	*	*	0.0	0.1	0.5	0.3	0.0	0.0	0.0	0.9
Niamey	13 31N	02 06E	709	10	93	58	108	77	94	74	101	74	114	47	10	*	*	0.2	0.3	1.3	3.2	5.2	7.4	3.7	0.5	*	0.0	21.6
Nigeria:																												
Enugu	06 27N	07 29E	763	11	90	72	91	74	83	71	87	71	99	55	33	0.7	1.1	2.6	5.9	10.4	11.4	7.6	6.7	12.8	9.8	2.1	0.5	71.5
Kaduna	10 35N	06 26E	2,113	18	89	59	95	72	83	68	89	66	105	46	34	*	0.1	0.5	2.5	5.9	7.1	8.5	11.9	10.6	2.9	0.1	*	50.1
Lagos	06 27N	03 24E	10	32	88	74	89	77	83	74	85	74	104	60	47	1.1	1.8	4.0	5.9	10.6	18.1	11.0	2.5	5.5	8.1	2.7	1.0	72.3
Maiduguri	11 51N	13 05E	1,162	15	90	54	104	72	90	73	96	68	112	43	40	*	*	*	0.3	1.6	2.7	7.1	8.7	4.2	0.7	*	0.0	25.3
Portuguese Guinea:																												
Bolama	11 34N	15 26W	62	31	88	67	91	73	84	74	87	74	106	59	37	*	*	*	*	0.8	7.8	23.1	27.6	16.9	8.0	1.6	0.1	85.9
Rhodesia:																												
Bulawayo	20 09S	28 37E	4,405	15	81	61	79	56	70	45	85	59	99	28	50	5.6	4.3	3.3	0.7	0.4	0.1	*	*	0.2	0.8	3.2	4.8	23.4
Salisbury	17 50S	31 08E	4,831	15	78	60	78	55	70	44	83	58	95	32	50	7.7	7.0	4.6	1.1	0.5	0.1	*	0.1	0.2	1.1	3.8	6.4	32.6
Senegal:																												
Dakar	14 42N	17 29W	131	25	79	64	81	65	88	76	89	76	109	53	26	*	*	*	*	*	0.7	3.5	10.0	5.2	1.5	0.1	0.3	21.3
Kaolack	14 08N	16 04W	20	9	93	60	103	68	91	75	93	74	114	48	10	*	0.0	*	*	0.3	2.6	6.9	10.7	7.0	2.7	0.1	*	30.3
Sierra Leone:																												
Freetown/Lungi	08 37N	13 12W	92	8	87	73	88	76	82	73	85	72	98	62	8	0.4	0.2	1.2	3.1	9.5	14.3	29.2	36.5	22.3	14.2	5.5	1.2	137.6
Somalia:																												
Berbera	10 26N	45 02E	45	30	84	68	89	77	107	88	92	76	117	58	30	0.3	0.1	0.2	0.5	0.3	*	*	0.1	*	0.1	0.2	0.2	2.0
Mogadishu (Mogadiscio)	02 02N	45 21E	39	13	86	73	90	78	83	73	86	76	97	59	21	*	*	*	2.3	2.3	3.8	2.5	1.9	1.0	0.9	1.6	0.5	16.9

(See footnotes at end of tables)

COUNTRY AND STATION	LATITUDE	LONGITUDE	ELEVATION	TEMPERATURE: LENGTH OF RECORD	JANUARY MAXIMUM	JANUARY MINIMUM	APRIL MAXIMUM	APRIL MINIMUM	JULY MAXIMUM	JULY MINIMUM	OCTOBER MAXIMUM	OCTOBER MINIMUM	EXTREME MAXIMUM	EXTREME MINIMUM	PRECIPITATION: LENGTH OF RECORD	JANUARY	FEBRUARY	MARCH	APRIL	MAY	JUNE	JULY	AUGUST	SEPTEMBER	OCTOBER	NOVEMBER	DECEMBER	YEAR
	° ′	° ′	FEET	YEAR	°F	°F	°F	°F	°F	°F	°F	°F	°F	°F	YEAR	IN.	IN.	IN.	IN.	IN.	IN.	IN.	IN.	IN.	IN.	IN.	IN.	IN.
South Africa, Republic of:																												
Capetown	33 54S	18 32E	56	19	78	60	72	53	63	45	70	52	103	28	18	0.6	0.3	0.7	1.9	3.1	3.3	3.5	2.6	1.7	1.2	0.7	0.4	20.0
Durban	29 50S	31 02E	16	15	81	69	78	64	72	52	75	62	107	39	78	4.3	4.8	5.1	3.0	2.0	1.3	1.1	1.5	2.8	4.3	4.8	4.7	39.7
Kimberley	28 48S	24 46E	3,927	19	91	64	77	52	65	36	83	54	103	20	57	2.4	2.5	3.1	1.5	0.7	0.2	0.2	0.3	0.6	1.0	1.6	2.0	16.1
Port Elizabeth	33 59S	25 36E	190	14	78	61	73	55	67	45	70	54	104	31	84	1.2	1.3	1.9	1.8	2.4	1.8	1.9	2.0	2.3	2.2	2.2	1.7	22.7
Port Nolloth	29 14S	16 52E	23	20	67	53	66	50	62	45	64	49	107	31	64	0.1	0.1	0.2	0.2	0.3	0.3	0.3	0.3	0.2	0.1	0.1	0.1	2.3
Pretoria	25 45S	28 14E	4,491	13	81	60	75	50	66	37	80	55	96	24	12	5.0	4.3	4.5	1.7	0.9	0.6	0.3	0.2	0.8	2.2	5.2	5.2	30.9
Walvis Bay	22 56S	14 30E	24	20	73	59	75	55	70	47	67	51	104	25	20	*	0.2	0.3	0.1	0.1	*	*	0.1	*	*	*	*	0.9
Southwest Africa:																												
Keetmanshoop	26 35S	18 08E	3,295	17	95	65	85	57	70	42	87	55	108	26	45	0.8	1.1	1.4	0.6	0.2	*	*	*	0.1	0.2	0.3	0.4	5.2
Windhoek	22 34S	17 06E	5,669	30	85	63	77	55	68	43	84	59	97	25	60	3.0	2.9	3.1	1.6	0.3	*	*	*	0.1	0.4	0.9	1.9	14.3
Spanish Sahara:																												
Semara	26 46N	11 31W	1,509	6	73	47	88	58	99	66	88	61	121	37	6	0.1	*	0.0	*	*	0.0	0.0	*	1.0	*	0.4	0.0	1.5
Villa Cisneros	23 42N	15 52W	35	12	71	56	74	60	78	65	80	65	107	48	14	*	*	*	*	0.1	0.0	*	0.2	1.4	0.1	0.2	1.0	3.0
Sudan:																												
El Fasher	13 38N	25 21E	2,395	17	88	50	102	64	96	70	99	64	113	33	17	*	0.0	*	*	0.3	0.7	4.5	5.3	1.2	0.2	0.0	0.0	12.2
Khartoum	15 37N	32 33E	1,279	46	90	59	105	72	101	77	104	75	118	41	46	*	*	*	*	0.1	0.3	2.1	2.8	0.7	0.2	*	0.0	6.2
Port Sudan	19 37N	37 13E	18	30	81	68	89	71	106	83	93	76	117	50	40	0.2	0.1	*	*	*	*	0.3	0.1	*	0.4	1.7	0.9	3.7
Wadi Halfa	21 55N	31 20E	410	39	75	46	98	62	106	74	98	67	127	28	39	*	*	*	*	*	0.0	*	*	*	*	*	0.0	*
Wau	07 42N	28 03E	1,443	38	96	64	99	72	89	69	93	69	115	50	38	*	0.2	0.9	2.6	5.3	6.5	7.5	8.2	6.6	4.9	0.6	*	43.3
Tanzania:																												
Dares Salaam	06 50S	39 18E	47	44	83	77	86	73	83	66	85	69	96	59	49	2.6	2.6	5.1	11.4	7.4	1.3	1.2	1.0	1.2	1.6	2.9	3.6	41.9
Iringa	07 47S	35 42E	5,330	14	76	59	75	59	72	52	80	57	90	42	24	6.8	5.1	7.1	3.5	0.5	*	*	*	0.1	0.2	1.5	4.5	29.3
Kigoma	04 53S	29 38E	2,903	26	80	67	81	67	83	63	84	69	100	53	18	4.8	5.0	5.9	5.1	1.7	0.2	0.1	0.2	0.7	1.9	5.6	5.3	36.5
Togo:																												
Lome	06 10N	01 15E	72	5	85	72	86	74	80	71	83	72	94	58	15	0.6	0.9	1.9	4.6	5.7	8.8	2.8	0.4	1.4	2.4	1.1	0.4	31.0
Tunisia:																												
Gabes	33 53N	10 07E	7	50	61	43	74	54	89	71	81	62	122	27	50	0.9	0.7	0.8	0.4	0.3	*	*	0.1	0.5	1.2	1.2	0.6	6.7
Tunis	36 47N	10 12E	217	50	58	43	70	51	90	68	77	59	118	30	50	2.5	2.0	1.6	1.4	0.7	0.3	0.1	0.3	1.3	2.0	1.9	2.4	16.5
Uganda:																												
Kampala	00 20N	32 36E	4,304	15	83	65	79	64	77	62	81	63	97	53	15	1.8	2.4	5.1	6.9	5.8	2.9	1.8	3.4	3.6	3.8	4.8	3.9	46.2
Lira	02 15N	32 54E	3,560	14	91	61	86	64	81	61	86	61	100	50	14	0.7	1.0	3.5	6.9	7.9	4.9	6.4	10.0	8.3	6.1	3.2	1.8	60.7
United Arab Republic:																												
Alexandria	31 12N	29 53E	105	45	65	51	74	59	85	73	83	68	111	37	61	1.9	0.9	0.4	0.1	*	*	*	*	*	0.2	1.3	2.2	7.0
Aswan	24 02N	32 53E	366	46	74	50	96	66	106	79	98	71	124	35	11	*	*	*	*	*	*	0.0	0.0	0.0	*	*	*	*
Cairo	29 52N	31 20E	381	42	65	47	83	57	96	70	86	65	117	34	42	0.2	0.2	0.2	0.1	0.1	*	0.0	0.0	*	*	0.1	0.2	1.1
Upper Volta:																												
Bobo Dioulasso	11 10N	04 15W	1,411	11	92	58	99	71	87	69	90	70	115	46	10	0.1	0.2	1.1	2.1	4.6	4.8	9.8	12.0	8.5	2.5	0.7	0.0	46.4
Ouagadougou	12 22N	01 31W	991	10	92	60	103	79	91	74	95	74	118	48	15	*	0.1	0.5	0.6	3.3	4.8	8.0	10.9	5.7	1.3	*	0.0	35.2
Zambia:																												
Balovale	13 34S	23 06E	3,577	8	82	65	84	61	81	47	91	64	108	38	9	8.5	6.9	5.8	1.2	*	0.0	0.0	*	0.3	2.3	4.4	8.9	38.3

COUNTRY AND STATION	LATITUDE	LONGITUDE	ELEVATION	TEMPERATURE: LENGTH OF RECORD	AVERAGE DAILY: JANUARY MAXIMUM	JANUARY MINIMUM	APRIL MAXIMUM	APRIL MINIMUM	JULY MAXIMUM	JULY MINIMUM	OCTOBER MAXIMUM	OCTOBER MINIMUM	EXTREME MAXIMUM	EXTREME MINIMUM	AVERAGE PRECIPITATION: LENGTH OF RECORD	JANUARY	FEBRUARY	MARCH	APRIL	MAY	JUNE	JULY	AUGUST	SEPTEMBER	OCTOBER	NOVEMBER	DECEMBER	YEAR
	° ′	° ′	FEET	YEAR	°F	°F	°F	°F	°F	°F	°F	°F	°F	°F	YEAR	IN.	IN.	IN.	IN.	IN.	IN.	IN.	IN.	IN.	IN.	IN.	IN.	IN.
Kasama	10 12S	31 11E	4,544	10	79	61	79	60	76	50	87	62	95	39	10	10.7	9.9	10.9	2.8	0.5	*	*	*	*	0.8	6.4	9.5	51.5
Lusaka	15 25S	28 19E	4,191	10	78	63	79	59	73	49	88	64	100	39	10	9.1	7.5	5.6	0.7	0.1	*	*	0.0	*	0.4	3.6	5.9	32.9
ATLANTIC ISLANDS:																												
Funchal, Madeira Island	32 38N	16 55W	82	30	66	56	67	58	75	66	74	65	103	40	30	2.5	2.9	3.1	1.3	0.7	0.2	*	*	1.0	3.0	3.5	3.3	21.5
Georgetown, Ascension Island	07 56S	14 25W	55	29	85	73	88	75	84	72	83	71	95	65	45	0.2	0.4	0.7	1.1	0.5	0.5	0.5	0.4	0.3	0.3	0.2	0.1	5.2
Hutts Gate, St. Helena	15 57S	05 40W	2,062	30	68	60	69	61	62	55	61	54	82	50	30	2.1	3.1	4.2	3.1	2.8	3.2	4.3	2.6	2.2	1.7	1.2	1.6	32.1
Las Palmas, Canary Islands	28 11N	15 28W	20	45	70	58	71	61	77	67	79	67	99	46	48	1.4	0.9	0.9	0.5	0.2	*	*	*	0.2	1.1	2.1	1.6	8.6
Porto da Praia, Cape Verde Is.	14 54N	23 31W	112	25	77	68	79	69	83	75	85	76	94	56	25	0.1	*	*	*	0.0	*	0.2	3.8	4.5	1.2	0.3	0.1	10.2
Santa Isabel, Fernando Po	03 46N	08 46E	-----	2	87	67	89	70	84	69	86	70	102	61	16	1.3	2.5	4.2	7.2	9.4	11.1	7.4	6.6	9.6	10.4	3.5	1.7	74.9
Sao Tome, Sao Tome	00 20N	06 43E	16	10	86	73	86	73	82	69	84	71	91	56	10	3.2	4.2	5.9	5.0	5.3	1.1	*	*	0.9	4.3	4.6	3.5	38.0
Tristan da Cunha	37 03S	12 19W	75	5	66	59	64	57	57	50	59	51	75	38	5	3.5	3.5	6.4	4.7	7.1	5.9	6.1	6.9	7.9	5.8	4.3	4.0	66.1
INDIAN OCEAN ISLANDS:																												
Agalega Island	10 26S	56 40E	10	3	86	77	87	77	83	75	84	75	91	69	2	5.9	10.1	4.9	6.9	13.2	8.9	8.7	3.2	1.8	4.2	7.0	10.0	84.7
Cocos (Keeling) Island	12 05S	96 53E	15	36	86	77	85	78	82	76	84	76	94	68	38	5.4	7.7	8.5	10.4	7.9	9.0	8.7	4.8	3.7	3.3	4.2	4.6	78.2
Heard Island	53 01S	73 23E	16	5	41	35	39	33	34	27	35	28	58	13	5	5.8	5.8	5.7	6.1	5.8	3.9	3.6	2.2	2.5	3.7	4.0	5.1	54.3
Hellburg, Reunion Island	21 04S	55 22E	3,070	5	74	59	73	56	65	48	69	51	84	40	11	22.4	8.0	16.4	7.2	5.3	4.4	3.1	3.0	2.0	2.3	3.5	12.9	90.5
Port Victoria, Seychelles	04 37S	55 27E	15	60	83	76	86	77	81	75	83	75	92	67	64	15.2	10.5	9.2	7.2	6.7	4.0	3.3	2.7	5.1	6.1	9.1	13.4	92.5
Royal Alfred Observatory, Mauritius	20 06S	57 32E	181	40	86	73	82	70	75	62	80	64	95	50	43	8.5	7.8	8.7	5.0	3.8	2.6	2.3	2.5	1.4	1.6	1.8	4.6	50.6
ASIA – FAR EAST																												
China																												
Canton	23 10N	113 20E	59	26	65	49	77	65	91	77	85	67	101	31	36	0.9	1.9	4.2	6.8	10.6	10.6	8.1	8.5	6.5	3.4	1.2	0.9	63.6
Chanasha	28 15	112 58E	161	14	45	35	70	56	94	78	75	59	109	16	26	1.9	3.7	5.3	5.7	8.2	8.7	4.4	4.3	2.7	3.0	2.7	1.5	52.1
Chungking	29 30N	106 33E	855	27	51	42	73	59	93	76	71	61	111	28	60	0.7	0.8	1.5	3.8	5.7	7.1	5.6	4.7	5.8	4.3	1.9	0.8	42.9
Hankow	30 35N	114 17E	75	29	46	34	69	55	93	78	74	60	108	9	55	1.8	1.9	3.6	5.8	7.0	9.0	7.0	4.1	3.0	3.1	1.9	1.2	49.4
Harbin (Ha-erh-pin)	45 45N	126 38E	476	35	7	-14	54	31	84	65	54	31	102	-43	38	0.2	0.2	0.4	0.9	1.7	3.7	6.6	4.7	2.3	1.2	0.5	0.2	22.6
Kashgar	39 24N	76 07E	4,296	27	33	12	71	48	92	68	71	43	106	-15	18	0.6	0.1	0.5	0.2	0.3	0.2	0.4	0.3	0.1	0.1	0.2	0.3	3.2
Kunming	25 02N	102 43E	6,211	32	61	37	76	51	77	62	70	53	91	22	31	0.4	0.5	0.7	0.8	4.3	6.3	8.8	8.6	5.0	3.0	1.7	0.4	40.5
Lanchow	36 06N	103 55E	5,105	8	33	7	65	40	84	61	62	39	100	- 3	4	0.2	0.2	0.2	0.5	0.8	0.7	3.3	5.1	2.2	0.6	0.0	0.3	14.1
Mukden (Shen-yang)	41 47N	123 24E	138	40	20	- 2	60	36	87	69	62	39	103	-28	42	0.2	0.2	0.7	1.2	2.6	3.8	7.0	6.3	2.9	1.7	0.9	0.4	28.2
Shanghai	31 12N	121 26E	16	56	47	32	67	49	91	75	75	56	104	10	81	1.9	2.4	3.3	3.6	3.8	7.0	5.8	5.5	5.2	2.9	2.1	1.5	45.0
Tientsin	39 10N	117 10E	13	24	33	16	68	45	90	73	68	48	109	- 3	25	0.2	0.1	0.4	0.5	1.1	2.4	7.6	6.0	1.7	0.6	0.4	0.2	21.0
Urumchi	43 45N	87 40E	2,972	6	13	-7	60	36	82	58	50	31	112	-30	6	0.6	0.3	0.5	1.5	1.1	1.5	0.7	1.0	0.6	1.7	1.6	0.4	11.5
Hong Kong:	22 18N	114 10E	109	50	64	56	75	67	87	78	81	73	97	32	50	1.3	1.8	2.9	5.4	11.5	15.5	15.0	14.2	10.1	4.5	1.7	1.2	85.1
Japan:																												
Kushiro	43 02N	144 12E	315	41	30	8	44	31	66	55	58	40	87	-19	41	1.8	1.4	2.8	3.6	3.8	4.1	4.4	4.9	6.6	4.0	3.1	2.0	42.9

(See footnotes at end of tables)

COUNTRY AND STATION	LATITUDE	LONGITUDE	ELEVATION	TEMPERATURE: LENGTH OF RECORD	AVERAGE DAILY JANUARY MAXIMUM	AVERAGE DAILY JANUARY MINIMUM	AVERAGE DAILY APRIL MAXIMUM	AVERAGE DAILY APRIL MINIMUM	AVERAGE DAILY JULY MAXIMUM	AVERAGE DAILY JULY MINIMUM	AVERAGE DAILY OCTOBER MAXIMUM	AVERAGE DAILY OCTOBER MINIMUM	EXTREME MAXIMUM	EXTREME MINIMUM	AVERAGE PRECIPITATION: LENGTH OF RECORD	JANUARY	FEBRUARY	MARCH	APRIL	MAY	JUNE	JULY	AUGUST	SEPTEMBER	OCTOBER	NOVEMBER	DECEMBER	YEAR
	° '	° '	FEET	YEAR	°F	°F	°F	°F	°F	°F	°F	°F	°F	°F	YEAR	IN.	IN.	IN.	IN.	IN.	IN.	IN.	IN.	IN.	IN.	IN.	IN.	IN.
Miyako	39 38N	141 59E	98	30	43	23	58	37	77	62	66	46	99	1	30	2.9	3.0	3.2	3.5	4.5	5.0	5.0	7.2	9.5	6.8	3.0	2.6	56.2
Nagasaki	32 44N	129 53E	436	59	49	36	66	50	85	73	72	58	98	22	59	2.8	3.3	4.9	7.3	6.7	12.3	10.1	6.9	9.8	4.5	3.7	3.2	75.5
Osaka	34 47N	135 26E	49	60	47	32	65	47	87	73	72	55	102	19	60	1.7	2.3	3.8	5.2	4.9	7.4	5.9	4.4	7.0	5.1	3.0	1.9	52.6
Tokyo	35 41N	139 46E	19	60	47	29	63	46	83	70	69	55	101	17	60	1.9	2.9	4.2	5.3	5.8	6.5	5.6	6.0	9.2	8.2	3.8	2.2	61.6
Korea:																												
Pusan	35 10N	129 07E	6	36	43	29	62	47	81	71	70	54	97	7	36	1.7	1.4	2.7	5.5	5.2	7.9	11.6	5.1	6.8	2.9	1.6	1.2	53.6
P'yongyang	39 01N	125 49E	94	43	27	8	61	38	84	69	65	43	100	-19	43	0.6	0.4	1.0	1.8	2.6	3.0	9.3	9.0	4.4	1.8	1.6	0.8	36.4
Seoul	37 31N	126 55E	34	22	32	15	62	41	84	70	67	45	99	-12	22	1.2	0.8	1.5	3.0	3.2	5.1	14.8	10.5	4.7	1.6	1.8	1.0	49.2
Mongolia:																												
Ulan Bator	47 54N	106 56E	4,287	13	- 2	-27	45	18	71	50	44	17	97	-48	15	*	*	0.1	0.2	0.3	1.0	2.9	1.9	0.8	0.2	0.2	0.1	7.7
Taiwan:																												
Tainan	22 57N	120 12E	53	13	72	55	82	67	89	77	86	70	95	39	13	0.7	0.7	1.1	3.2	6.3	15.6	16.0	15.8	8.4	1.2	0.9	0.6	70.5
Taipei	25 04N	121 32E	21	12	66	53	77	64	92	76	80	68	101	32	12	3.8	5.3	4.3	5.3	6.9	8.8	8.8	8.7	8.2	5.5	4.2	2.9	72.7
Union of Soviet Socialist Republics:																												
Alma-Ata	43 16N	76 53E	2,543	19	23	7	56	38	81	60	55	35	100	-30	27	1.3	0.9	2.2	4.0	3.7	2.6	1.4	1.2	1.0	2.0	1.9	1.3	23.5
Chita (Tchita)	52 02N	113 30E	2,218	10	-10	-27	42	19	75	51	38	18	99	-52	24	0.1	0.1	0.1	0.4	1.1	1.8	3.3	3.3	1.2	0.5	0.2	0.2	12.3
Dubinka	69 07N	87 00E	141	5	-23	-31	6	-10	59	47	19	11	84	-62	5	0.3	0.4	0.2	0.3	0.6	1.9	1.5	2.1	1.8	0.9	0.4	0.3	10.7
Irkutsk	52 16N	104 19E	1,532	10	3	-15	42	20	70	50	41	21	98	-58	38	0.5	0.4	0.3	0.6	1.3	2.2	3.1	2.8	1.7	0.7	0.6	0.6	14.9
Kazalinsk	45 46N	62 06E	207	10	16	5	58	27	90	65	57	35	108	-27	19	0.4	0.4	0.5	0.5	0.6	0.2	0.2	0.3	0.3	0.4	0.5	0.6	4.9
Khabarovsk	48 28N	135 03E	165	7	- 2	-13	41	28	75	63	48	34	91	-46	8	0.3	0.2	0.3	0.7	2.0	3.5	4.1	3.3	3.0	0.7	0.6	0.5	19.2
Kirensk	57 47N	108 07E	938	18	-14	-28	38	15	74	51	10	- 4	95	-71	19	0.8	0.5	0.5	0.5	1.0	1.8	2.1	2.1	1.7	1.0	1.0	1.0	14.0
Krasnoyarsk	56 01N	92 52E	498	10	3	-10	34	23	67	55	34	26	103	-47	8	0.1	0.2	0.1	0.2	1.0	1.4	1.2	2.1	1.7	0.9	0.5	0.4	9.8
Markovo	64 45N	170 50E	85	15	-19	-29	5	- 8	59	47	16	9	84	-72	16	0.2	0.2	0.3	0.1	0.3	0.8	1.0	1.9	1.1	0.4	0.4	0.3	7.0
Narym	58 50N	81 39E	197	13	- 7	-18	35	19	71	56	35	25	94	-61	14	0.8	0.5	0.8	0.5	1.3	2.6	2.4	2.7	1.7	1.4	1.1	0.9	16.8
Okhotsk	59 21N	143 17E	18	19	- 6	-17	29	10	57	48	33	21	78	-50	25	0.1	0.1	0.2	0.4	0.9	1.6	2.2	2.6	2.4	1.0	0.2	0.1	11.8
Omsk	54 58N	73 20E	279	19	- 1	-14	39	21	74	56	40	27	102	-56	22	0.6	0.3	0.3	0.5	1.2	2.0	2.0	2.0	1.1	1.0	0.7	0.8	12.5
Petropavlovsk	52 53N	158 42E	286	7	23	11	35	25	56	47	46	34	84	-29	35	3.0	2.2	3.4	2.5	2.2	2.0	3.1	3.2	3.8	3.9	3.6	3.0	35.9
Salehkard	66 31N	66 35E	60	18	-13	-21	18	4	61	49	26	20	85	-65	27	0.3	0.3	0.3	0.3	0.7	1.3	1.9	2.0	1.5	0.7	0.5	0.4	10.2
Semipalatinsk	50 24N	80 13E	709	10	8	- 7	45	26	81	57	46	30	101	-47	10	0.9	0.5	0.5	0.6	1.2	1.5	1.1	1.3	0.7	1.2	1.1	1.0	11.6
Sverdlovsk	56 49N	60 38E	894	21	6	- 5	42	26	70	54	37	28	94	-45	29	0.5	0.4	0.5	0.7	1.9	2.7	2.6	2.7	1.6	1.2	1.1	0.8	16.7
Tashkent	41 20N	69 18E	1,569	19	37	21	65	47	92	64	65	41	106	-19	19	2.1	1.1	2.6	2.3	1.4	0.5	0.2	0.1	0.1	1.2	1.5	1.6	14.7
Verkhoyansk	67 34N	133 51E	328	24	-54	-63	19	-10	66	47	12	- 3	98	-90	44	0.2	0.2	0.1	0.2	0.3	0.9	1.1	1.0	0.5	0.3	0.3	0.2	5.3
Vladivostok	43 07N	131 55E	94	14	13	0	46	34	71	60	55	41	92	-22	53	0.3	0.4	0.7	1.2	2.1	2.9	3.3	4.7	4.3	1.9	1.2	0.6	23.6
Yakutsk	62 01N	129 43E	535	19	-45	-53	27	6	73	54	23	11	97	-84	22	0.3	0.2	0.1	0.3	0.4	1.1	1.6	1.3	1.1	0.5	0.4	0.3	7.4
ASIA – SOUTHEAST																												
Brunei:																												
Brunei	04 55N	114 55E	10	5	85	76	87	77	87	76	86	77	99	70	12	14.6	7.6	7.8	9.8	10.9	9.5	9.0	7.3	11.8	14.5	15.2	13.0	131.0

COUNTRY AND STATION	LATITUDE	LONGITUDE	ELEVATION	TEMPERATURE: LENGTH OF RECORD	AVERAGE DAILY: JANUARY MAXIMUM	JANUARY MINIMUM	APRIL MAXIMUM	APRIL MINIMUM	JULY MAXIMUM	JULY MINIMUM	OCTOBER MAXIMUM	OCTOBER MINIMUM	EXTREME MAXIMUM	EXTREME MINIMUM	AVERAGE PRECIPITATION: LENGTH OF RECORD	JANUARY	FEBRUARY	MARCH	APRIL	MAY	JUNE	JULY	AUGUST	SEPTEMBER	OCTOBER	NOVEMBER	DECEMBER	YEAR
	° ′	° ′	FEET	YEAR	°F	°F	°F	°F	°F	°F	°F	°F	°F	°F	YEAR	IN.	IN.	IN.	IN.	IN.	IN.	IN.	IN.	IN.	IN.	IN.	IN.	IN.
Burma:																												
Mandalay	21 59N	96 06E	252	20	82	55	101	77	93	78	89	73	111	44	20	0.1	0.1	0.2	1.2	5.8	6.3	2.7	4.1	5.4	4.3	2.0	0.4	32.6
Moulmein	16 26N	97 39E	150	43	89	65	95	77	83	74	88	75	103	52	60	0.2	0.2	0.5	3.0	19.9	37.1	47.5	44.2	27.1	8.5	1.7	0.3	190.2
Cambodia:																												
Phnom Penh	11 33N	104 51E	39	37	88	71	95	76	90	76	87	76	105	55	49	0.3	0.4	1.4	3.1	5.7	5.8	6.0	6.1	8.9	9.9	5.5	1.7	54.8
Indonesia:																												
Batavia (Jakarta)	06 11S	106 50E	26	80	84	74	87	75	87	73	87	74	98	66	78	11.8	11.8	8.3	5.8	4.5	3.8	2.5	1.7	2.6	4.4	5.6	8.0	70.8
Manokwari	00 53S	134 03E	10	5	86	73	86	74	86	74	87	74	93	68	40	12.0	9.4	13.2	11.1	7.8	7.2	5.4	5.6	4.9	4.7	6.5	10.3	98.1
Mapanget	01 32N	124 55E	264	21	85	73	86	73	87	73	89	72	97	65	63	18.6	13.8	12.2	8.0	6.4	6.5	4.8	4.0	3.3	4.9	8.9	14.7	106.1
Penfui	10 10S	123 39E	335	21	87	75	89	72	88	70	92	72	101	58	63	15.2	13.7	9.2	2.6	1.2	0.4	0.2	0.0	0.0	0.7	3.3	9.1	55.7
Pontianak	00 00N	109 20E	13	20	87	74	89	75	89	74	89	75	96	68	63	10.8	8.2	9.5	10.9	11.1	8.7	6.5	8.0	9.0	14.4	15.3	12.7	125.1
Tabing	00 52S	100 21E	19	21	87	74	87	75	87	74	86	74	94	68	63	13.9	10.1	12.2	14.5	12.8	11.7	10.5	13.7	16.2	20.1	20.5	19.2	175.4
Tarakan	03 19N	117 33E	20	19	85	73	86	75	87	74	87	74	94	67	31	10.9	10.2	14.0	13.9	13.5	12.6	10.3	12.4	11.6	14.3	15.2	13.4	152.3
Laos:																												
Vientiane	17 58N	102 34E	559	13	83	58	95	73	89	75	88	71	108	32	27	0.2	0.6	1.5	3.9	10.5	11.9	10.5	11.5	11.9	4.3	0.6	0.1	67.5
Malaya, Fed.:																												
Kuala Lumpur	03 06N	101 42E	111	19	90	72	91	74	90	72	89	73	99	64	19	6.2	7.9	10.2	11.5	8.8	5.1	3.9	6.4	8.6	9.8	10.2	7.5	96.1
Singapore	01 18N	103 50E	33	39	86	73	88	75	88	75	87	74	97	66	64	9.9	6.8	7.6	7.4	6.8	6.8	6.7	7.7	7.0	8.2	10.0	10.1	95.0
North Borneo:																												
Sanda Kan	05 54N	118 03E	38	45	85	74	89	76	89	75	88	75	99	70	46	19.0	10.9	8.6	4.5	6.2	7.4	6.7	7.9	9.3	10.2	14.5	18.5	123.7
Philippine Islands:																												
Davao	07 07N	125 38E	88	15	87	72	91	73	88	73	89	73	97	65	34	4.8	4.5	5.2	5.8	9.2	9.1	6.5	6.5	6.7	7.9	5.3	6.1	77.6
Manila	14 31N	121 00E	49	61	86	69	93	73	88	75	88	74	101	58	75	0.9	0.5	0.7	1.3	5.1	10.0	17.0	16.6	14.0	7.6	5.7	2.6	82.0
Sarawak:																												
Kuching	01 29N	110 20E	85	5	85	72	90	73	90	72	89	73	98	64	19	24.0	20.1	12.9	11.0	10.3	7.1	7.7	9.2	8.6	10.5	14.1	18.2	153.7
Thailand:																												
Bangkok	13 44N	100 30E	53	10	89	67	95	78	90	76	88	76	104	50	10	0.2	1.1	1.1	2.3	5.2	6.0	6.9	9.2	14.0	9.9	1.8	0.1	57.8
Viet Nam																												
Hanoi	21 03N	105 52E	20	12	68	58	80	70	92	79	84	72	108	41	12	0.8	1.2	2.5	3.6	4.1	11.2	11.9	15.2	10.0	3.5	2.6	2.8	69.4
Saigon	10 49N	106 39E	33	31	89	70	95	76	88	75	88	74	104	57	33	0.6	0.1	0.5	1.7	8.7	13.0	12.4	10.6	13.2	10.6	4.5	2.2	78.1
ASIA – MIDDLE EAST																												
Aden:																												
Riyan	14 39N	49 19E	83	13	82	67	88	74	92	77	88	72	111	57	13	0.3	0.1	0.6	0.2	*	0.1	0.1	0.1	*	*	0.7	0.3	2.5
Afghanistan:																												
Kabul	34 30N	69 13E	5,955	9	36	18	66	43	92	61	73	42	104	- 6	45	1.3	1.5	3.6	3.3	0.9	0.2	0.1	0.1	*	0.4	0.6	0.6	12.6
Kandhar	31 36N	65 40E	3,462	7	56	31	83	50	102	66	85	44	111	14	7	3.1	1.7	0.8	0.3	0.2	*	0.1	*	0.0	*	*	0.8	7.0
Ceylon:																												
Colombo	06 54N	79 52E	22	25	86	72	88	76	85	77	85	75	99	59	40	3.5	2.7	5.8	9.1	14.6	8.8	5.3	4.3	6.3	13.7	12.4	5.8	92.3
East Pakistan:																												
Dacca	23 46N	90 23E	24	60	77	56	92	74	88	79	88	75	108	43	61	0.3	1.2	2.4	5.4	9.6	12.4	13.0	13.3	9.8	5.3	1.0	0.2	73.9

(See footnotes at end of tables)

COUNTRY AND STATION	LATITUDE	LONGITUDE	ELEVATION	TEMPERATURE: LENGTH OF RECORD	AVERAGE DAILY: JANUARY MAXIMUM	JANUARY MINIMUM	APRIL MAXIMUM	APRIL MINIMUM	JULY MAXIMUM	JULY MINIMUM	OCTOBER MAXIMUM	OCTOBER MINIMUM	EXTREME MAXIMUM	EXTREME MINIMUM	AVERAGE PRECIPITATION: LENGTH OF RECORD	JANUARY	FEBRUARY	MARCH	APRIL	MAY	JUNE	JULY	AUGUST	SEPTEMBER	OCTOBER	NOVEMBER	DECEMBER	YEAR
	° ′	° ′	FEET	YEAR	°F	°F	°F	°F	°F	°F	°F	°F	°F	°F	YEAR	IN.	IN.	IN.	IN.	IN.	IN.	IN.	IN.	IN.	IN.	IN.	IN.	IN.
India:																												
Ahmadabad	23 03N	72 37E	180	45	85	58	104	75	93	79	97	73	118	36	45	*	0.1	0.1	*	0.4	3.7	12.2	8.1	4.2	0.4	0.1	*	29.3
Bangalore	12 57N	77 40E	2,937	60	80	57	93	69	81	66	82	65	102	46	60	0.2	0.3	0.4	1.6	4.2	2.9	3.9	5.0	6.7	5.9	2.7	0.4	34.2
Bombay	19 06N	72 51E	27	60	88	62	93	74	88	75	93	73	110	46	60	0.1	0.1	0.1	*	0.7	19.1	24.3	13.4	10.4	2.5	0.5	0.1	71.2
Calcutta	22 32N	88 20E	21	60	80	55	97	76	90	79	89	74	111	44	60	0.4	1.2	1.4	1.7	5.5	11.7	12.8	12.9	9.9	4.5	0.8	0.2	63.0
Cherrapunji	25 15N	91 44E	4,309	35	60	46	71	59	72	65	72	61	87	33	35	0.7	2.1	7.3	26.2	50.4	106.1	96.3	70.1	43.3	19.4	2.7	0.5	425.1
Hyderabad	17 27N	78 28E	1,741	50	85	59	101	75	87	73	88	68	112	43	45	0.3	0.4	0.5	1.2	1.1	4.4	6.0	5.3	6.5	2.5	1.1	0.3	29.6
Jalpaiguri	26 32N	88 43E	272	50	74	50	90	68	89	77	87	70	104	36	55	0.3	0.7	1.3	3.7	11.8	25.9	32.2	25.3	21.2	5.6	0.5	0.2	128.7
Lucknow	26 45N	80 52E	400	60	74	47	101	71	92	80	91	67	119	34	60	0.8	0.7	0.3	0.3	0.8	4.5	12.0	11.5	7.4	1.3	0.2	0.3	40.1
Madras	13 04N	80 15E	51	60	85	67	95	78	96	79	90	75	113	57	60	1.4	0.4	0.3	0.6	1.0	1.9	3.6	4.6	4.7	12.0	14.0	5.5	50.0
Mormugao	15 22N	73 49E	157	10	86	70	88	79	83	75	86	75	98	59	30	*	*	*	0.7	2.6	29.6	31.2	15.9	9.5	3.8	1.3	0.2	94.8
New Delhi	28 35N	77 12E	695	10	71	43	97	68	95	80	93	64	115	31	75	0.9	0.7	0.5	0.3	0.5	2.9	7.1	6.8	4.6	0.4	0.1	0.4	25.2
Silchar	24 49N	92 48E	95	60	78	52	88	69	90	77	88	72	103	41	53	0.8	2.1	7.9	14.3	15.6	21.7	19.7	19.7	14.4	6.5	1.4	0.4	124.5
Indian Ocean Islands:																												
Port Blair, Andaman Is.	11 40N	92 43E	261	60	84	72	89	75	84	75	84	74	97	62	60	1.8	1.1	1.1	2.4	15.1	21.7	15.4	16.3	17.4	12.5	10.5	7.9	123.2
Amini Divi, Laccadive Is.	11 07N	72 44E	13	29	86	74	92	80	86	77	86	77	99	65	30	0.7	*	*	1.5	3.7	14.3	12.0	7.7	6.3	5.8	2.6	1.3	56.0
Minicoy, Maldive Is.	08 18N	73 00E	9	20	85	73	87	80	85	76	85	76	98	63	50	1.8	0.7	0.9	2.3	7.0	11.6	8.9	7.8	6.3	7.3	5.5	3.4	63.5
Car Nicobar, Nicobar Is.	09 09N	92 49E	47	13	86	77	90	77	86	77	85	75	95	66	30	3.9	1.2	2.1	3.5	12.5	12.4	9.3	10.2	12.9	11.6	11.4	7.8	98.8
Iran:																												
Abadan	30 21N	48 13E	10	12	64	44	90	62	112	81	98	63	127	24	10	1.5	1.7	0.6	0.8	0.1	0.0	0.0	0.0	0.0	0.1	1.0	1.8	7.6
Esfahan (Isfahan)	32 37N	51 41E	5,238	45	47	25	72	46	98	67	78	47	108	- 4	45	0.7	0.6	0.8	0.6	0.3	*	0.1	*	*	0.1	0.4	0.7	4.4
Kermanshah	34 19N	47 07E	4,331	15	45	23	68	38	99	56	79	38	108	-13	15	2.6	2.3	2.8	2.2	1.6	*	*	*	*	0.4	2.0	2.4	16.4
Rezaiyeh	37 32N	45 05E	4,364	3	32	17	67	45	91	64	67	47	99	-11	3	1.9	2.3	2.0	1.7	1.2	0.5	*	0.1	0.2	1.5	0.8	1.6	13.8
Tehran	35 41N	51 19E	3,937	24	45	27	71	49	99	72	76	53	109	- 5	33	1.8	1.5	1.8	1.4	0.5	0.1	0.1	0.1	0.1	0.3	0.8	1.2	9.7
Iraq:																												
Baghdad	33 20N	44 24E	111	15	60	39	85	57	110	76	92	61	121	18	15	0.9	1.0	1.1	0.5	0.1	*	*	*	*	0.1	0.8	1.0	5.5
Basra	30 34N	47 47E	8	10	64	45	85	63	104	81	94	64	123	24	10	1.4	1.1	1.2	1.2	0.2	0.0	*	*	*	*	1.4	0.8	7.3
Mosul	36 19N	43 09E	730	26	54	35	77	49	109	72	88	51	124	12	29	2.8	3.1	2.1	1.9	0.7	*	*	*	*	0.2	1.9	2.4	15.2
Israel:																												
Haifa	32 48N	35 02E	23	16	65	49	77	58	88	75	85	68	112	27	30	6.9	4.3	1.6	1.0	0.2	*	*	*	0.1	1.0	3.7	7.3	26.2
Jerusalem	31 47N	35 13E	2,654	19	55	41	73	50	87	63	81	59	107	26	50	5.1	4.7	2.9	0.9	0.1	*	0.0	0.0	*	0.3	2.2	3.5	19.7
Tel Aviv	32 06N	34 46E	33	10	64	50	70	57	82	72	79	65	102	34	10	4.9	2.7	2.0	0.7	0.1	0.0	0.0	0.0	0.1	0.4	4.1	6.1	21.1
Jammu/Kashmir:																												
Srinagar	33 58N	74 46E	5,458	50	41	24	67	45	88	64	74	41	106	- 4	50	2.9	2.8	3.6	3.7	2.4	1.4	2.3	2.4	1.5	1.2	0.4	1.3	25.9
Jordan:																												
Amman	31 58N	35 59E	2,547	25	54	39	73	49	89	65	81	57	109	21	25	2.7	2.9	1.2	0.6	0.2	0.0	0.0	0.0	*	0.2	1.3	1.8	10.9
Kuwait:																												
Kuwait	29 21N	48 00E	16	14	61	49	83	68	103	86	91	73	119	33	10	0.9	0.9	1.1	0.2	*	0.0	0.0	0.0	0.0	0.1	0.6	1.1	5.1
Lebanon:																												
Beirut	33 54N	35 28E	111	62	62	51	72	58	87	73	81	69	107	30	71	7.5	6.2	3.7	2.2	0.7	0.1	*	*	0.2	2.0	5.2	7.3	35.1

COUNTRY AND STATION	LATITUDE	LONGITUDE	ELEVATION	TEMPERATURE: LENGTH OF RECORD	AVERAGE DAILY: JANUARY MAXIMUM	JANUARY MINIMUM	APRIL MAXIMUM	APRIL MINIMUM	JULY MAXIMUM	JULY MINIMUM	OCTOBER MAXIMUM	OCTOBER MINIMUM	EXTREME: MAXIMUM	EXTREME: MINIMUM	AVERAGE PRECIPITATION: LENGTH OF RECORD	JANUARY	FEBRUARY	MARCH	APRIL	MAY	JUNE	JULY	AUGUST	SEPTEMBER	OCTOBER	NOVEMBER	DECEMBER	YEAR
	° ′	° ′	FEET	YEAR	°F	°F	°F	°F	°F	°F	°F	°F	°F	°F	YEAR	IN.	IN.	IN.	IN.	IN.	IN.	IN.	IN.	IN.	IN.	IN.	IN.	IN.
Nepal:																												
Katmandu	27 42N	85 22E	4,423	27	65	36	84	53	84	69	80	56	99	27	9	0.6	1.6	0.9	2.3	4.8	9.7	14.7	13.6	6.1	1.5	0.3	0.1	56.2
Oman and Muscat:																												
Muscat	23 37N	58 35E	15	23	77	66	90	78	97	87	93	80	116	51	38	1.1	0.7	0.4	0.4	*	0.1	*	*	0.0	0.1	0.4	0.7	3.9
Pakistan (West):																												
Karachi	24 48N	66 59E	13	43	77	55	90	73	91	81	91	72	118	39	59	0.5	0.4	0.3	0.1	0.1	0.7	3.2	1.6	0.5	0.1	0.1	0.2	7.8
Multan	30 11N	71 25E	400	60	68	42	95	68	102	86	94	64	122	29	60	0.4	0.4	0.4	0.3	0.3	0.6	2.0	1.8	0.5	0.1	0.1	0.2	7.1
Rawalpindi	33 35N	73 03E	1,676	60	62	38	86	59	98	77	89	57	118	25	60	2.5	2.5	2.7	1.9	1.3	2.3	8.1	9.2	3.9	0.6	0.3	1.2	36.5
Saudi Arabia:																												
Dhahran	26 16N	50 10E	78	10	69	54	90	69	107	86	95	73	120	40	10	1.1	0.6	0.4	0.2	0.1	0.0	0.0	0.0	0.0	0.0	0.2	0.9	3.5
Jidda	21 28N	39 10E	20	5	84	66	91	70	99	79	95	73	117	49	5	0.2	*	*	*	*	0.0	*	*	*	*	1.0	1.2	2.5
Riyadh	24 39N	46 42E	1,938	3	70	46	89	64	107	78	94	61	113	19	3	0.1	0.8	0.9	1.0	0.4	*	0.0	*	0.0	0.0	*	*	3.2
Syria:																												
Deir Ez Zor	35 21N	40 09E	699	5	53	35	80	52	105	78	86	56	114	16	8	1.6	0.8	0.3	0.8	0.1	*	0.0	0.0	0.0	0.2	1.5	0.9	6.2
Dimashq (Damascus)	33 30N	36 20E	2,362	13	53	36	75	49	96	64	81	54	113	21	7	1.7	1.7	0.3	0.5	0.1	*	*	0.0	0.7	0.4	1.6	1.6	8.6
Halab (Aleppo)	36 14N	37 08E	1,280	8	50	34	75	48	97	69	81	54	117	9	10	3.5	2.5	1.5	1.1	0.3	0.1	0.0	*	*	1.0	2.2	3.3	15.5
Trucial Kingdoms:																												
Sharjah	25 20N	55 24E	18	11	74	54	86	65	100	82	92	71	118	37	12	0.9	0.9	0.4	0.2	0.0	0.0	0.0	0.0	0.0	0.0	0.4	1.4	4.2
Turkey:																												
Adana	36 59N	35 18E	82	21	57	39	74	51	93	71	84	58	109	19	31	4.3	4.0	2.5	1.6	2.0	0.7	0.2	0.2	0.7	1.9	2.4	3.8	24.3
Ankara	39 57N	32 53E	2,825	26	39	24	63	40	86	59	69	44	104	-13	24	1.3	1.2	1.3	1.3	1.9	1.0	0.5	0.4	0.7	0.9	1.2	1.9	13.6
Erzurum	39 54N	41 16E	6,402	16	24	8	50	32	78	53	59	37	93	-22	16	1.4	1.6	2.0	2.5	3.1	2.1	1.3	0.9	1.1	2.3	1.8	1.1	21.2
Izmir (Smyrna)	38 27N	27 15E	92	39	55	39	70	49	92	69	76	55	108	12	58	4.4	3.3	3.0	1.7	1.3	0.6	0.2	0.2	0.8	2.1	3.3	4.8	25.5
Samsun	41 17N	36 19E	131	24	50	38	59	45	79	65	69	56	103	20	27	2.9	2.6	2.7	2.3	1.8	1.5	1.5	1.3	2.4	3.2	3.5	2.4	29.1
Yemen:																												
Kamaran I.	15 20N	42 37E	20	26	82	74	89	79	98	85	93	82	105	66	21	0.2	0.2	0.1	0.1	0.1	*	0.5	0.7	0.1	0.1	0.4	0.9	3.4
AUSTRALIA & PACIFIC ISLANDS																												
Australia:																												
Adelaide	34 57S	138 32E	20	86	86	61	73	55	59	45	73	51	118	32	104	0.8	0.7	1.0	1.8	2.7	3.0	2.6	2.6	2.1	1.7	1.1	1.0	21.1
Alice Springs	23 48S	133 53E	1,791	62	97	70	81	54	67	39	88	58	111	19	30	1.7	1.3	1.1	0.4	0.6	0.5	0.3	0.3	0.3	0.7	1.2	1.5	9.9
Bourke	30 05S	145 58E	361	63	99	70	82	55	65	40	85	56	125	25	72	1.4	1.5	1.1	1.1	1.0	1.1	0.9	0.8	0.8	0.9	1.2	1.4	13.2
Brisbane	27 25S	153 05E	17	53	85	69	79	61	68	49	80	60	110	35	91	6.4	6.3	5.7	3.7	2.8	2.6	2.2	1.9	1.9	2.5	3.7	5.0	44.7
Broome	17 57S	122 13E	56	41	92	79	93	72	82	58	91	72	113	40	50	6.3	5.8	3.9	1.2	0.6	0.9	0.2	0.1	*	*	0.6	3.3	22.9
Burketown	17 45S	139 33E	30	31	93	77	91	69	82	55	93	70	110	40	53	8.2	6.3	5.2	1.0	0.2	0.3	*	*	*	0.4	1.5	4.4	27.5
Canberra	35 18S	149 11E	1,886	23	82	55	67	44	52	33	68	43	109	14	25	1.9	1.7	2.2	1.6	1.8	2.1	1.8	2.2	1.6	2.2	1.9	2.0	23.0
Carnarvon	24 53S	113 40E	13	43	88	72	84	66	71	51	78	61	118	37	57	0.4	0.7	0.7	0.6	1.5	2.4	1.6	0.7	0.2	0.1	*	0.2	9.1
Cloncurry	20 40S	140 30E	622	32	99	77	90	67	77	51	95	68	127	35	59	4.4	4.2	2.4	0.7	0.5	0.6	0.3	0.1	0.3	0.5	1.3	2.7	18.0
Esperance	33 50S	121 55E	14	44	77	60	72	54	62	45	68	50	117	31	60	0.7	0.7	1.2	1.8	3.3	4.1	4.0	3.8	2.7	2.2	1.0	0.9	26.4
Laverton	28 40S	122 23E	1,510	30	96	69	81	57	64	41	82	55	115	25	30	0.8	0.8	1.6	0.8	0.9	0.7	0.6	0.5	0.2	0.3	0.8	0.8	8.8
Melbourne	37 49S	144 58E	115	88	78	57	68	51	56	42	67	48	114	27	88	1.9	1.8	2.2	2.3	2.1	2.1	1.9	1.9	2.3	2.6	2.3	2.3	25.7
Mundiwindi	23 52S	120 10E	1,840	15	101	64	87	61	70	41	89	58	112	22	15	1.0	1.9	2.0	0.8	0.6	0.9	0.1	0.3	0.3	0.5	0.5	1.2	10.1

(See footnotes at end of tables)

COUNTRY AND STATION	LATITUDE	LONGITUDE	ELEVATION	TEMPERATURE: LENGTH OF RECORD	AVERAGE DAILY: JANUARY MAXIMUM	JANUARY MINIMUM	APRIL MAXIMUM	APRIL MINIMUM	JULY MAXIMUM	JULY MINIMUM	OCTOBER MAXIMUM	OCTOBER MINIMUM	EXTREME: MAXIMUM	EXTREME: MINIMUM	AVERAGE PRECIPITATION: LENGTH OF RECORD	JANUARY	FEBRUARY	MARCH	APRIL	MAY	JUNE	JULY	AUGUST	SEPTEMBER	OCTOBER	NOVEMBER	DECEMBER	YEAR
	° '	° '	FEET	YEAR	°F	°F	°F	°F	°F	°F	°F	°F	°F	°F	YEAR	IN.	IN.	IN.	IN.	IN.	IN.	IN.	IN.	IN.	IN.	IN.	IN.	IN
Perth	31 56S	115 58E	64	44	85	63	76	57	63	48	70	53	112	31	63	0.3	0.4	0.8	1.7	5.1	7.1	6.7	5.7	3.4	2.2	0.8	0.5	34.7
Port Darwin	12 25S	130 52E	104	58	90	77	92	76	87	67	93	77	105	55	70	15.2	12.3	10.0	3.8	0.6	0.1	*	0.1	0.5	2.0	4.7	9.4	58.7
Sydney	33 52S	151 02E	62	87	78	65	71	58	60	46	71	56	114	35	87	3.5	4.0	5.0	5.3	5.0	4.6	4.6	3.0	2.9	2.8	2.9	2.9	46.5
Thursday Island	10 35S	142 13E	200	31	87	77	86	77	82	73	86	76	98	64	49	18.2	15.8	13.9	8.0	1.6	0.5	0.4	0.2	0.1	0.3	1.5	7.0	67.5
Townsville	19 15S	146 46E	18	31	87	76	84	70	75	59	83	71	110	39	67	10.9	11.2	7.2	3.3	1.3	1.4	0.6	0.5	0.7	1.3	1.9	5.4	45.7
William Creek	28 55S	136 21E	247	39	96	69	80	55	65	41	84	56	119	25	30	0.5	0.6	0.3	0.3	0.3	0.5	0.2	0.3	0.3	0.5	0.5	0.7	5.0
Windorah	25 26S	142 36E	390	29	101	74	86	59	70	43	91	61	116	26	50	1.4	1.6	1.6	0.9	0.8	0.8	0.5	0.4	0.5	0.6	0.9	1.4	11.4
Tasmania:																												
Hobart	42 53S	147 20E	177	70	71	53	63	48	52	40	63	46	105	28	100	1.9	1.5	1.8	1.9	1.8	2.2	2.1	1.9	2.1	2.3	2.4	2.1	24.0
New Zealand:																												
Auckland	37 00S	174 47E	23	36	73	60	67	56	56	46	63	52	90	33	92	3.1	3.7	3.2	3.8	5.0	5.4	5.7	4.6	4.0	4.0	3.5	3.1	49.1
Christchurch	43 29S	172 32E	118	52	70	53	62	45	50	35	62	44	96	21	64	2.2	1.7	1.9	1.9	2.6	2.6	2.7	1.9	1.8	1.7	1.9	2.2	25.1
Dunedin	45 55S	170 12E	4	77	66	50	59	45	48	37	59	42	94	23	77	3.4	2.8	3.0	2.8	3.2	3.2	3.1	3.0	2.7	3.0	3.2	3.5	36.9
Wellington	41 17S	174 46E	415	66	69	56	63	51	53	42	60	48	88	29	79	3.2	3.2	3.2	3.8	4.6	4.6	5.4	4.6	3.8	4.0	3.5	3.5	47.4
PACIFIC ISLANDS:																												
Canton, Phoenix Is.	02 46S	171 43W	9	12	88	78	89	78	89	78	90	78	98	70	30	2.6	2.2	2.5	3.6	4.3	2.6	2.6	2.5	1.2	1.1	1.6	2.6	29.4
Guam, Marianas Is.	13 33N	144 50E	361	30	84	72	86	73	87	72	86	73	95	54	30	4.6	3.5	2.6	3.0	4.2	5.9	9.0	12.8	13.4	13.1	10.3	6.1	88.5
Honolulu, Hawaii	21 20N	157 55W	7	30	79	66	80	68	85	73	84	72	93	56	30	3.8	3.3	2.9	1.3	1.0	0.3	0.4	0.9	1.0	1.8	2.2	3.0	21.9
Iwo Jima, Bonin Is.	24 47N	141 19E	353	15	71	64	77	69	86	78	84	76	95	46	17	3.2	2.5	2.1	3.7	4.9	4.0	6.4	6.5	4.6	5.9	4.8	4.3	52.8
Madang, New Guinea	05 12S	145 47E	19	12	87	75	88	74	88	74	88	75	98	62	20	12.1	11.9	14.9	16.9	15.1	10.8	7.6	4.8	5.3	10.0	13.3	14.5	137.2
Midway Is.	28 13N	177 23W	29	21	69	62	71	64	81	74	79	72	92	46	20	4.6	3.7	3.1	2.5	1.9	1.3	2.9	3.9	3.7	3.7	3.6	4.2	40.7
Naha, Okinawa	26 12N	127 39E	96	30	67	56	76	64	89	77	81	69	96	41	30	5.3	5.4	6.1	6.1	8.9	10.0	7.1	10.0	7.1	6.6	5.9	4.3	82.8
Noumea, New Caledonia	22 16S	166 27E	246	24	86	72	83	70	76	62	80	65	99	52	52	3.7	5.1	5.7	5.2	4.4	3.7	3.6	2.6	2.5	2.0	2.4	2.6	43.5
Pago Pago, Samoa	14 19S	170 43W	29	2	87	75	87	76	83	74	85	75	98	67	41	24.5	20.5	19.2	16.5	15.4	12.3	10.0	8.2	13.1	14.9	19.2	19.8	193.6
Ponape, Caroline Is.	06 58N	158 13E	123	30	86	75	86	75	87	73	87	72	96	67	30	11.1	9.7	14.6	20.0	20.3	16.7	16.2	16.3	15.8	16.0	16.9	18.3	191.9
Port Moresby, New Guinea	09 29S	147 09E	126	20	89	76	87	75	83	73	86	75	98	64	38	7.0	7.6	6.7	4.2	2.5	1.3	1.1	0.7	1.0	1.4	1.9	4.4	39.8
Rabaul, New Guinea	04 13S	152 11E	28	19	90	73	90	73	89	73	92	73	100	65	24	14.8	10.4	10.2	10.0	5.2	3.3	5.4	3.7	3.5	5.1	7.1	10.1	88.8
Suva, Fiji Is.	18 08S	178 26E	20	43	86	74	84	73	79	68	81	70	98	55	43	11.4	10.7	14.5	12.2	10.1	6.7	4.9	8.3	7.7	8.3	9.8	12.5	117.1
Tahiti, Society Is.	17 33S	149 36W	7	23	89	72	89	72	86	68	87	70	93	61	27	13.2	11.5	6.5	6.8	4.9	3.2	2.6	1.9	2.3	3.4	6.5	11.9	74.7
Tulagi, Solomon Is.	09 05S	160 10E	8	20	88	76	88	76	86	76	87	76	96	68	37	14.3	15.8	15.0	10.0	8.1	6.8	7.6	8.7	8.0	8.7	10.0	10.4	123.4
Wake Is.	19 17N	166 39E	11	30	82	73	83	74	87	77	86	77	92	64	30	1.1	1.4	1.5	1.9	2.0	1.9	4.6	7.1	5.2	5.3	3.1	1.8	36.9
Yap, Caroline Is.	9 31N	138 08E	62	30	85	76	87	77	88	75	88	75	97	69	30	7.9	4.6	5.4	6.4	9.5	10.7	13.8	14.7	14.0	13.2	11.2	10.2	121.6

COUNTRY AND STATION	LATITUDE	LONGITUDE	ELE-VATION	TEMPERATURE: LENGTH OF RECORD	AVERAGE DAILY: JANUARY MAXIMUM	JANUARY MINIMUM	APRIL MAXIMUM	APRIL MINIMUM	JULY MAXIMUM	JULY MINIMUM	OCTOBER MAXIMUM	OCTOBER MINIMUM	EXTREME: MAXIMUM	EXTREME: MINIMUM	AVERAGE PRECIPITATION: LENGTH OF RECORD	JANUARY	FEBRUARY	MARCH	APRIL	MAY	JUNE	JULY	AUGUST	SEPTEMBER	OCTOBER	NOVEMBER	DECEMBER	YEAR
	° ′	° ′	FEET	YEAR	°F	°F	°F	°F	°F	°F	°F	°F	°F	°F	YEAR	IN.	IN.	IN.	IN.	IN.	IN.	IN.	IN.	IN.	IN.	IN.	IN.	IN.
ANTARCTICA																												
Byrd Station	80 01S	119 32W	5,095	6	10	- 2	-11	-30	-25	-45	-15	-33	31	-82	6	0.4	0.4	0.2	0.3	0.4	0.5	0.7	0.7	0.3	0.7	0.0	0.3	4.9
Ellsworth	77 44S	41 07W	139	6	22	12	-10	-25	-21	-35	- 2	-15	36	-70	6	0.3	0.2	0.3	0.6	0.2	0.2	0.2	0.2	0.3	0.4	0.5	0.2	3.6
McMurdo Station	77 53S	166 48W	8	10	30	21	- 1	-13	- 9	-24	2	-12	42	-59	10	0.5	0.7	0.4	0.4	0.4	0.3	0.2	0.3	0.4	0.2	0.2	0.3	4.3
South Pole Station	89 59S	000 00W	9,186	5	-16	-23	-66	-79	-67	-81	-55	-64	6	-107	5	*	0.1	0.0	0.0	0.0	0.0	0.0	0.0	0.0	*	0.0	*	0.1
Wilkes	66 16S	110 31E	31	7	34	28	17	9	8	- 3	16	6	46	-35	7	0.5	0.4	1.7	1.1	1.4	1.2	1.3	0.8	1.5	1.2	0.8	0.3	12.2

NOTES

1. "Length of Record" refers to average daily maximum and minimum temperatures and precipitation. A standard period of the 30 years from 1931-1960 had been used for locations in the United States and some other countries. The length of record of extreme maximum and minimum temperatures includes all available years of data for a given location and is usually for a longer period.

2. * - Less than 0.05"

3. Except for Antarctica, amounts of solid precipitation such as snow or hail have been converted to their water equivalent. Because of the frequent occurrence of blowing snow, it has not been possible to determine the precise amount of precipitation actually falling in Antarctica. The values shown are the average amounts of solid snow accumulating in a given period as determined by snow markers. The liquid content of the accumulation is undetermined.

North America

North America is nearly all within middle and northern latitudes. Consequently it has a large central area in which the continental type of climate with marked seasonal temperature is to be found.

Along the coasts of northern Alaska, western Canada, and the northwestern part of the United States, moderate midsummer temperatures are in marked contrast to those prevailing in the interior east of the mountains. Again, the mild midwinter temperatures in the coastal areas stand out against the severe conditions to be found from the Great Lakes region northward and northwestward.

In the West Indian region, temperature conditions are subtropical; and in Mexico and Central America, climatic zones depend on elevation, ranging from subtropical to temperate in the higher levels.

The prevailing westerly wind movement carries the continental type of climate eastward over the United States, so that the region of maritime climate along the Atlantic Ocean is very narrow.

From the Aleutian Peninsula to northern California west of the crests of the mountains, there is a narrow strip where annual precipitation is over 40 inches (101.6 cm); it exceeds 100 inches (254 cm) locally on the coast of British Columbia. East of this belt there is an abrupt fall-off in precipitation to less than 20 inches (50.8 cm) annually over the western half of the continent from lower California northward, and to even less than 5 inches (12.7 cm) in parts of what used to be called the "Great American Desert," the southwestern part of the United States.

In the eastern part of the continent—that is, from the southeastern part of the United States northeastward to Newfoundland—the average annual precipitation is more than 40 inches (101.6 cm). Rainfall in the West Indies, southern Mexico, and Central America is generally abundant. It is very spotty, however, varying widely even within short distances, especially from the windward to the leeward sides of the mountains.

The northern areas are, of course, very cold; but the midwinter low temperatures fall far short of the records set in the cold-pole area of northeastern Siberia, where the vast extent of land becomes much colder than the partly ice-covered area of northern Canada.

South America

A large part of South America lies within the Tropics and has a characteristically tropical climate. The remaining rather narrow southern portion is not subject to the extremes of heat and cold that are found where wide land areas give full sway to the continental type of climate with its hot summers and cold winters, as in North America and Asia. Temperature anomalies unusual for a given latitude are to be found mainly at the elevated levels of the Andean region stretching from the Isthmus of Panama to Cape Horn.

The Antarctic Current and its cool Humboldt branch skirting the western shores northward to the Equator, together with the prevailing on-shore winds, exert a strong cooling influence over the coastal regions of all the western countries of South America except Colombia. On the east, the southerly moving Brazilian current from tropical waters has the opposite, or warming, effect except along southern Argentina.

In the northern countries of South America the sharply contrasted dry and wet seasons are related to the regime of the trade winds. In the dry season (corresponding to winter in the Northern Hemisphere) these winds sweep the entire region, while the wet season (corresponding to summer in the Northern Hemisphere) calm and variable winds prevail. In the basin of the Amazon River, the rainfall is related to the equatorial belt of low pressure and to the trade winds, which give the maximum amounts of rainfall in the extreme west, where they ascend the Andean slopes.

The desert areas on the west coast of South America, extending from the Equator to the latitude of Santiago, Chile, are due primarily to the cold Humboldt or Peruvian Current and upwelling coastal water. The moist, cool ocean air is warmed in passing over the land, with a consequent decrease in relative humidity, so that the dew point is not reached and condensation of vapor does not occur until the incoming air has reached high elevations in the Andes, where temperatures are very much lower than along the coast.

In southern Chile, the summer has moderate rainfall and winters are excessively wet. The conditions that prevail farther north are not present here, and condensation of moisture from the ocean progresses from the shores up to the crests of the Andes. By the time the air passes these elevations, however, the moisture has been so depleted that the winds in the leeward slopes are dry, becoming more and more so as they are warmed as they reach lower levels. The mountains can be looked upon as casting a great "rain shadow"—an area of little rain—over southern Argentina.

Europe

In Europe there is no extensive north-south mountain system such as is found in both the Americas, and the general east-west direction of the ranges in the south allows the conditions in the maritime west to change rather gradually toward Asia. Generally, rainfall is heaviest on the western coast, where locally it exceeds 60 inches (152.4 cm) annually, and lighter toward the east—except in the elevated Alpine and Caucasus regions—to less than 20 inches (50.8 cm) in eastern Russia. There is a well-defined rain shadow in Scandinavia, with over 60 inches (152 cm) of rain in western Norway and less than 20 inches (51 cm) in eastern Sweden.

Over much of Europe rainfall is both abundant and rather evenly distributed throughout the year. The chief feature of seasonal distribution of precipitation is the marked winter maximum and the extremely dry, even droughty, summers in most of the Mediterranean lands.

Isothermal lines have the general direction of the parallels of latitude except in winter, when the waters of the western ocean, warmed by the Gulf Stream, give them a north-

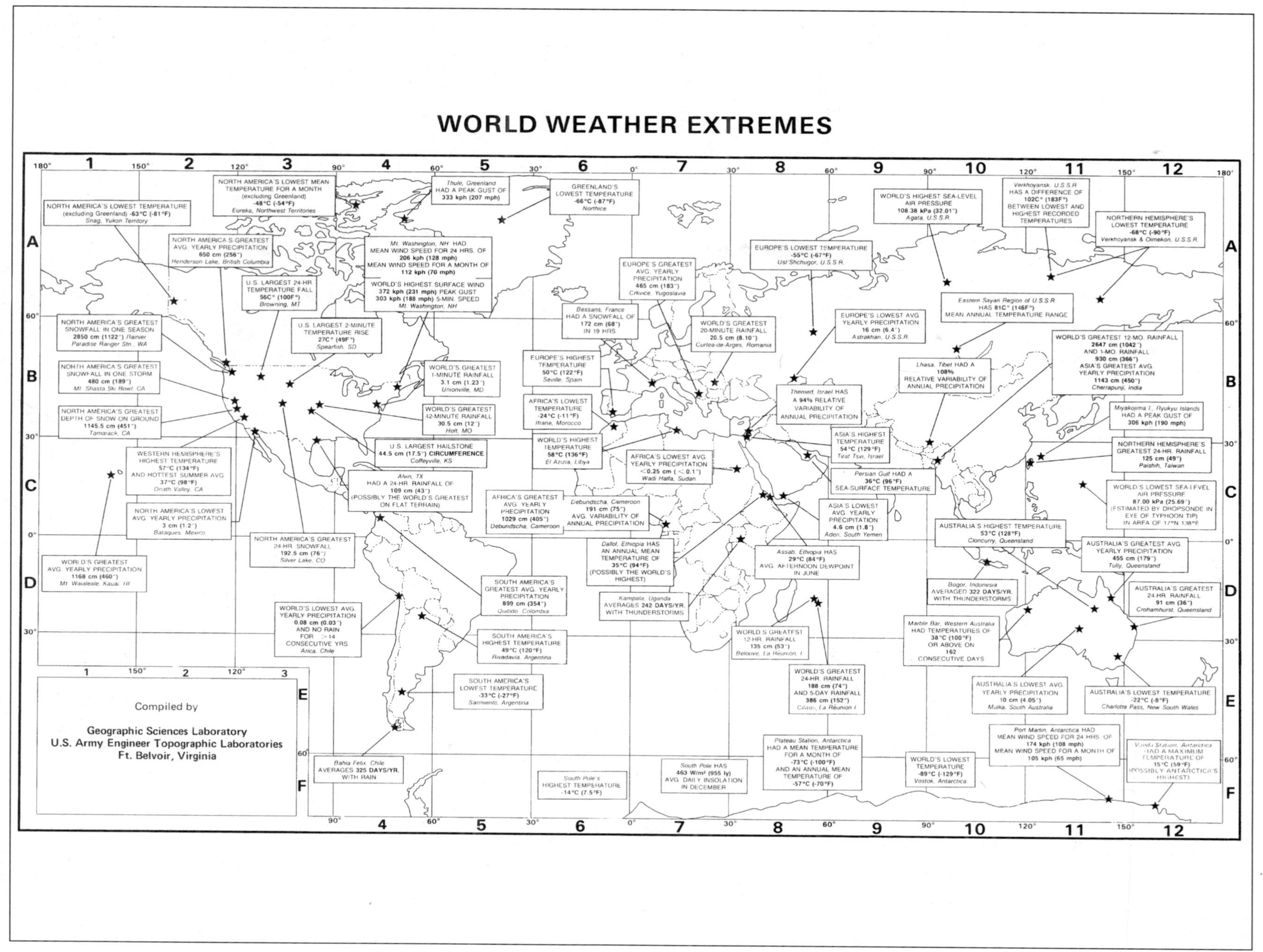
WORLD WEATHER EXTREMES
NORTH AMERICA'S LOWEST TEMPERATURE (excluding Greenland) -63°C (-81°F) Snag, Yukon Territory
NORTH AMERICA'S LOWEST MEAN TEMPERATURE FOR A MONTH (excluding Greenland) -48°C (-54°F) Eureka, Northwest Territories
Thule, Greenland HAD A PEAK GUST OF 333 kph (207 mph)
GREENLAND'S LOWEST TEMPERATURE -66°C (-87°F) Northice
NORTH AMERICA'S GREATEST AVG. YEARLY PRECIPITATION 650 cm (256") Henderson Lake, British Columbia
Mt. Washington, NH HAD MEAN WIND SPEED FOR 24 HRS. OF 206 kph (128 mph) MEAN WIND SPEED FOR A MONTH OF 112 kph (70 mph)
WORLD'S HIGHEST SURFACE WIND 372 kph (231 mph) PEAK GUST 303 kph (188 mph) 5-MIN. SPEED Mt. Washington, NH
U.S. LARGEST 24-HR TEMPERATURE FALL 56C° (100F°) Browning, MT
NORTH AMERICA'S GREATEST SNOWFALL IN ONE SEASON 2850 cm (1122") Rainier Paradise Ranger Stn., WA
U.S. LARGEST 2-MINUTE TEMPERATURE RISE 27C° (49F°) Spearfish, SD
NORTH AMERICA'S GREATEST SNOWFALL IN ONE STORM 480 cm (189") Mt. Shasta Ski Bowl, CA
WORLD'S GREATEST 1-MINUTE RAINFALL 3.1 cm (1.23") Unionville, MD
NORTH AMERICA'S GREATEST DEPTH OF SNOW ON GROUND 1145.5 cm (451") Tamarack, CA
WORLD'S GREATEST 42-MINUTE RAINFALL 30.5 cm (12") Holt, MO
WESTERN HEMISPHERE'S HIGHEST TEMPERATURE 57°C (134°F) AND HOTTEST SUMMER AVG 37°C (98°F) Death Valley, CA
U.S. LARGEST HAILSTONE 44.5 cm (17.5") CIRCUMFERENCE Coffeyville, KS
Alvin, TX HAD A 24-HR. RAINFALL OF 109 cm (43") (POSSIBLY THE WORLD'S GREATEST ON FLAT TERRAIN)
NORTH AMERICA'S LOWEST AVG. YEARLY PRECIPITATION 3 cm (1.2") Bataques, Mexico
NORTH AMERICA'S GREATEST 24-HR. SNOWFALL 192.5 cm (76") Silver Lake, CO
WORLD'S GREATEST AVG. YEARLY PRECIPITATION 1168 cm (460") Mt. Waialeale, Kauai, HI
WORLD'S LOWEST AVG. YEARLY PRECIPITATION 0.08 cm (0.03") AND NO RAIN FOR >14 CONSECUTIVE YRS Arica, Chile
SOUTH AMERICA'S GREATEST AVG. YEARLY PRECIPITATION 899 cm (354") Quibdo, Colombia
SOUTH AMERICA'S HIGHEST TEMPERATURE 49°C (120°F) Rivadavia, Argentina
SOUTH AMERICA'S LOWEST TEMPERATURE -33°C (-27°F) Sarmiento, Argentina
Bahia Felix, Chile AVERAGES 325 DAYS/YR. WITH RAIN
South Pole's HIGHEST TEMPERATURE -14°C (7.5°F)
South Pole HAS 463 W/m² (955 ly) AVG. DAILY INSOLATION IN DECEMBER
Bessans, France HAD A SNOWFALL OF 172 cm (68") IN 19 HRS
EUROPE'S GREATEST AVG. YEARLY PRECIPITATION 465 cm (183") Crkvice, Yugoslavia
EUROPE'S HIGHEST TEMPERATURE 50°C (122°F) Seville, Spain
AFRICA'S LOWEST TEMPERATURE -24°C (-11°F) Ifrane, Morocco
WORLD'S HIGHEST TEMPERATURE 58°C (136°F) El Azizia, Libya
AFRICA'S LOWEST AVG. YEARLY PRECIPITATION <0.25 cm (<0.1") Wadi Halfa, Sudan
AFRICA'S GREATEST AVG. YEARLY PRECIPITATION 1029 cm (405") Debundscha, Cameroon
Debundscha, Cameroon 191 cm (75") AVG. VARIABILITY OF ANNUAL PRECIPITATION
Dallol, Ethiopia HAS AN ANNUAL MEAN TEMPERATURE OF 35°C (94°F) (POSSIBLY THE WORLD'S HIGHEST)
Kampala, Uganda AVERAGES 242 DAYS/YR. WITH THUNDERSTORMS
WORLD'S GREATEST 20-MINUTE RAINFALL 20.5 cm (8.10") Curtea-de-Arges, Romania
EUROPE'S LOWEST TEMPERATURE -55°C (-67°F) Ust'Shchugor, U.S.S.R.
EUROPE'S LOWEST AVG. YEARLY PRECIPITATION 16 cm (6.4") Astrakhan, U.S.S.R.
Themed, Israel HAS A 94% RELATIVE VARIABILITY OF ANNUAL PRECIPITATION
ASIA'S HIGHEST TEMPERATURE 54°C (129°F) Tirat Tsvi, Israel
Persian Gulf HAD A 36°C (96°F) SEA-SURFACE TEMPERATURE
ASIA'S LOWEST AVG. YEARLY PRECIPITATION 4.6 cm (1.8") Aden, South Yemen
Assab, Ethiopia HAS 29°C (84°F) AVG. AFTERNOON DEWPOINT IN JUNE
WORLD'S GREATEST 12-HR. RAINFALL 135 cm (53") Belouve, La Réunion, I.
WORLD'S GREATEST 24-HR. RAINFALL 188 cm (74") AND 5-DAY RAINFALL 386 cm (152") Cilaos, La Réunion I.
Plateau Station, Antarctica HAD A MEAN TEMPERATURE FOR A MONTH OF -73°C (-100°F) AND AN ANNUAL MEAN TEMPERATURE OF -57°C (-70°F)
WORLD'S HIGHEST SEA-LEVEL AIR PRESSURE 108.38 kPa (32.01") Agata, U.S.S.R.
Verkhoyansk, U.S.S.R. HAS A DIFFERENCE OF 102C° (183F°) BETWEEN LOWEST AND HIGHEST RECORDED TEMPERATURES
NORTHERN HEMISPHERE'S LOWEST TEMPERATURE -68°C (-90°F) Verkhoyansk & Oimekon, U.S.S.R.
Eastern Sayan Region of U.S.S.R. HAS 81C° (146F°) MEAN ANNUAL TEMPERATURE RANGE
WORLD'S GREATEST 12-MO. RAINFALL 2647 cm (1042") AND 1-MO. RAINFALL 930 cm (366") ASIA'S GREATEST AVG. YEARLY PRECIPITATION 1143 cm (450") Cherrapunji, India
Lhasa, Tibet HAD A 108% RELATIVE VARIABILITY OF ANNUAL PRECIPITATION
Miyakojima I., Ryukyu Islands HAD A PEAK GUST OF 306 kph (190 mph)
NORTHERN HEMISPHERE'S GREATEST 24-HR. RAINFALL 125 cm (49") Paishih, Taiwan
WORLD'S LOWEST SEA-LEVEL AIR PRESSURE 87.00 kPa (25.69") (ESTIMATED BY DROPSONDE IN EYE OF TYPHOON TIP) IN AREA OF 17°N 138°E
AUSTRALIA'S HIGHEST TEMPERATURE 53°C (128°F) Cloncurry, Queensland
AUSTRALIA'S GREATEST AVG. YEARLY PRECIPITATION 455 cm (179") Tully, Queensland
Bogor, Indonesia AVERAGED 322 DAYS/YR. WITH THUNDERSTORMS
AUSTRALIA'S GREATEST 24-HR. RAINFALL 91 cm (36") Crohamhurst, Queensland
Marble Bar, Western Australia HAD TEMPERATURES OF 38°C (100°F) OR ABOVE ON 162 CONSECUTIVE DAYS
AUSTRALIA'S LOWEST AVG. YEARLY PRECIPITATION 10 cm (4.05") Mulka, South Australia
AUSTRALIA'S LOWEST TEMPERATURE -22°C (-8°F) Charlotte Pass, New South Wales
Port Martin, Antarctica HAD MEAN WIND SPEED FOR 24 HRS. OF 174 kph (108 mph) MEAN WIND SPEED FOR A MONTH OF 105 kph (65 mph)
WORLD'S LOWEST TEMPERATURE -89°C (-129°F) Vostok, Antarctica
Vanda Station, Antarctica HAD A MAXIMUM TEMPERATURE OF 15°C (59°F) (POSSIBLY ANTARCTICA'S HIGHEST)
Compiled by
Geographic Sciences Laboratory
U.S. Army Engineer Topographic Laboratories
Ft. Belvoir, Virginia

south trend. Generally, there are no marked dips in isotherms due to elevation and continental type of climate such as are found in North America. In Scandinavia, however, the winter map shows an abrupt fall in temperature from the western coast of Norway to the eastern coast of Sweden and thence a continued fall eastward, under a type of exposure more and more continental in contrast to the oceanic exposure on the west.

Asia

The vast extent of Asia gives full opportunity for continental conditions to develop a cold area of high barometric pressure in winter and a low-pressure, hot area in summer, the former northeast of the Himalayas and the latter stretching widely from west to east in the latitude of northern India. These distributions of pressure give to India the well-known monsoon seasons, during which the wind comes from one direction for several months, and also affect the yearly distribution of rainfall over eastern Asia.

In winter, the air circulation is outward over the land from the cold pole, and precipitation is very light over the entire continent. In summer, on the contrary, there is an inflow of air from the oceans; even the southeast trade winds flow across the Equator and merge into the southwest monsoon which crosses India. This usually produces abundant rain over most of India, with excessively heavy amounts when the air is forced to rise, even to moderate elevations, in its passage over the land. At Cherrapunji 4,455 feet (1,351 m), on the southern side of the Khasi Hills in Assam, India, the average rainfall in a winter month is about 1 inch (2.54 cm), while in both June and July it is approximately 100 inches (254 cm). However, this heavy summer rainfall meets an impassable barrier in the Himalaya Mountains, while the much lighter summer monsoon rainfall over Japan and eastern Asia does not extend far into China because of lesser elevations. Consequently, while the southeast quadrant of Asia, including the East Indies, also with monsoon winds, has heavy to excessive annual rainfall, the remainder of the continent is dry, with vast areas receiving less than 10 inches (25.4 cm) annually.

North of the Himalayas the low plains are excessively cold in winter and temperatures rise rather high in summer. At Verkhoyansk in the cold-pole area, and north of the Arctic Circle, the mean temperature in January is about -59°F (-50°C), and in July approximately 64°F (17.8°C); the extreme records are a maximum of 98°F (36.7°C), from readings at 1 P.M., and a minimum of -90°F (-67°C).

In southwestern Asia the winter temperature control is still the interior high-pressure area, and temperatures are generally low, especially at high elevations; in summer at low elevations excessively high maxima are recorded, as, for example, in the Tigris-Euphrates Valley.

Africa

Africa, like South America, lies largely within the Tropics. There too, temperature distribution is determined mainly by altitude. Moreover, along the southern portion of the western coast, the cool Benguela Current moves northward, and on the eastern coast are the warm tropical currents of the Indian Ocean, which create conditions closely paralleling those found around the South American continent. In the strictly tropical areas of Africa, conditions are characterized by prevailing low barometric pressure, with conventional rainfall and alternate northward and southward movement of the heat equator; in both the north and the south, the ruling influences are the belts of high barometric pressure.

Except in the Atlas Mountains in the northwest where the considerable elevations set up a barrier in the path of trade winds and produce moderate rainfall, the desert conditions typified by the Sahara extend from the Atlantic to the Red Sea and from the Mediterranean southward well beyond the northern Tropic to about the latitudes of southern Arabia.

South of the Sahara, rainfall increases rapidly, becoming abundant to heavy from the west coast to the central lakes, with annual maxima of over 80 inches (203 cm) in the regions bordering the eastern and western extremes of the Guinea coast. This marked increase in precipitation does not extend to the eastern portion of the middle region of the continent, where the annual amounts received are below 40 inches (101.6 cm) and decrease to less than 10 inches (25.4 cm) on the coasts of Somalia. Also to the south of the central rainy area there is a rapid fall in precipitation toward the and regions of Southwest Africa, where conditions are similar to those in Somalia.

The heavy rainfall over sections of Ethiopia from June to October, when more than 40 inches fall and bring the overflowing of the Nile Valley, is one of Earth's outstanding features of seasonal distribution of rainfall.

Moist equatorial climate is typified by conditions in the Democratic Republic of the Congo; arid torrid climate by those of the United Arab Republic and the Sahara; and moderate plateau climate by those found in parts of Ethiopia, Kenya, and Tanzania.

Australia

In the southern winter the high-pressure belt crosses the interior of Australia, and all except the southernmost parts of the continent are dry. In summer, on the other hand, this pressure belt has moved south of the continent, still giving dry conditions over the southern and western areas. Thus the total annual precipitation is less than 20 inches (50.8 cm) except in the extreme southwest and in a strip circling from southeast to northwest. The average annual precipitation is even less than 10 inches in a large south-central area.

In the south the winter precipitation is the cyclonic type; the heavy summer rains of the north are of monsoon origin; and those of the eastern borders are in large part orographic, owing to the presence of the highlands in the immediate vicinity of the coasts. In the outer border of the rainfall strip along the coastal region, the mean annual rainfall is over 40 inches (101.6 cm) and in many localities over 60 inches (152.4 cm). This is true for the monsoon rains in the north.

Because of the location of Australia, on both sides of the southern Tropic, temperatures far below freezing are to be found only in a small part of the continent, in the south at high elevations. In the arid interior extreme maximum temperatures are very high, ranking with those of the hottest regions on Earth.

Glossary of Weather Terms

A

absolute instability
A state of and layer within the atmosphere in which the vertical distribution of temperature is such that: air parcel, if given an upward or downward push, will move away from its initial level without further outside force being applied.

absolute temperature scale
See Kelvin Temperature Scale

absolute vorticity
See vorticity

adiabatic process
The process by which fixed relationships are maintained during changes in temperature, volume, ad pressure in and body of air without heat being added or removed from the body.

advection
The horizontal transport of air or atmospheric probes. In meteorology, sometimes referred to as the horizontal component of convection.

advection fog
Fog resulting from the transport of warm, humid air over a cold surface.

air density
The mass density of the air in terms of weight per unit volume.

air mass
In meteorology, an extensive body of air within which the conditions of temperature ad moisture in a horizontal plane are essentially uniform.

air mass classification
A system used to identify and characterize the different air masses according to a basic scheme. The system most commonly used classifies air masses primarily according to the thermal properties of their source regions: "tropical" (T); "polar" (P); and "Arctic" or "Antarctic" (A). They are further classified according to moisture characteristics a "continental" (c) or "maritime" (m).

air parcel
See parcel

albedo
The ratio of the amount of electromagnetic radiation reflected by a body to the amount incident upon it, commonly expressed in percentage; in meteorology, usually used in reference to insolation (solar radiation); i.e., the albedo of wet sand is 9, meaning that about 9% of the incident insolation is reflected; albedos of other surfaces range upward to 80-85 for fresh snow cover; average albedo for Earth and its atmosphere has been calculated to rage from 35 to 43.

altimeter
An instrument which determines the altitude of an object with respect to a fixed level.

altimeter setting
The value to which the scale of a pressure altimeter is set so as to read true altitude at field elevation.

altimeter setting indicator
A precision aneroid barometer calibrated to indicate directly the altimeter setting.

altitude
Height expressed in units of distance above a reference plane, usually above mean sea level or above ground.

altocumulus
White or gray layers or patches of cloud, often with a waved appearance; cloud elements appear a rounded masses or rolls; composed mostly of liquid water droplets which may be supercooled; may contain ice crystals at subfreezing temperatures.

altocumulus castellanus
A species of middle cloud of which at least a fraction of its upper part presents some vertically developed, cumuliform protuberances (some of which are taller than they are wide) and which give the cloud a crenelated or turreted appearance; especially evident when seen from the side; elements usually have a common base arranged in lines. This cloud indicates instability and turbulence at the altitudes of occurrence.

anemometer
An instrument for measuring wind speed.

aneroid barometer
A barometer which operates on the principle of having changing atmospheric pressure bend a metallic

surface which, in turn, moves a pointer across a scale graduated in units of pressure.

anticyclone
An area of high atmospheric pressure which has a closed circulation that is anticyclonic, i.e., as viewed from above, the circulation is clockwise in the Northern Hemisphere, counterclockwise in the Southern Hemisphere, undefined at the Equator.

anvil cloud
Popular name given to the top portion of a cumulonimbus having an anvil-like form.

Arctic air
An air mass with characteristics developed mostly in winter over Arctic surfaces of ice and snow. Arctic air extends to great heights, and the surface temperatures are basically, but not always, lower than those of polar air.

Arctic front
The surface of discontinuity between very cold (Arctic) air flowing directly from the Arctic region and another less cold and, consequently, less dense air mass.

astronomical twilight
See twilight

atmosphere
The mass of air surrounding Earth.

atmospheric pressure (barometric pressure)
The pressure exerted by the atmosphere as a consequence of gravitational attraction exerted upon the "column" of air lying directly above the point in question.

atmospherics
Disturbing effects produced in radio-receiving apparatus by atmospheric electrical phenomena such as an electrical storm. Static.

aurora
A luminous, radiant emission over middle and high latitudes confined to the thin air of high altitudes and centered over Earth's magnetic poles. Called "aurora borealis" (northern lights) or "aurora australis" according to its occurrence in the Northern or Southern Hemisphere, respectively.

B

backing
Shifting of the wind in a counterclockwise direction with respect to either space or time; opposite of veering. Commonly used by meteorologists to refer to a cyclonic shift (counterclockwise in the Northern Hemisphere and clockwise in the Southern Hemisphere).

backscatter
Pertaining to radar, the energy reflected or scattered by a target; an echo.

banner cloud (cloud banner)
A banner-like cloud streaming off from a mountain peak.

barograph
A continuous-recording barometer.

barometer
An instrument for measuring the pressure of the atmosphere; the two principle types are mercurial and aneroid.

barometric altimeter
See pressure altimeter

barometric pressure
See atmospheric pressure

barometric tendency
The change of barometric pressure within a specified period of time. In aviation weather observations, routinely determined periodically, usually for a 3-hour period.

Beaufort scale
A scale of wind speeds.

black blizzard
See duststorm

blizzard
A severe weather condition characterized by low temperatures and strong winds hearing a great amount of snow, either falling or picked up from the ground.

blowing dust
A type of lithometeor composed of dust particles picked up locally from the surface and blown about in clouds or sheets.

blowing sand
A type of lithometeor composed of sand picked up locally from the surface and blown about in clouds or sheets.

blowing snow
A type of hydrometeor composed of snow picked up from the surface by the wind and carried to a height of 6 feet (1.82 m) or more.

blowing spray
A type of hydrometeor composed of water particles picked up by the wind from the surface of a large body of water.

Buys Ballot's law
If an observer in the Northern Hemisphere stands with his back to the wind, lower pressure is to his left.

C

calm
The absence of wind or of apparent motion of the air.

cap cloud
A standing or stationary cap-like cloud crowning a mountain summit.

ceiling
In meteorology in the United States, the height above the surface of the base of the lowest layer of clouds or obscuring phenomenon aloft that hides more than half of the sky, or the vertical visibility into an obscuration. *See* summation principle.

Celsius temperature scale (°C)
A temperature scale with zero degrees as the melting point of pure ice and 1OO degrees as the boiling point of pure water at standard sea level atmospheric pressure.

Centigrade temperature scale
See Celsius temperature scale

change of state
In meteorology, the transformation of water from one form, i.e., solid (ice), liquid, or gaseous (water vapor), to any other form. There are six possible transformations designated by the five terms following: (1) condensation: the change of water vapor to liquid water (2) evaporation: the change of liquid water to water vapor (3) freezing: the change of liquid water to ice (4) melting: the change of ice to liquid water (5) sublimation: the change of ice to water vapor or (6) water vapor to ice. *See* latent heat.

Chinook
A warm, dry/foehn wind blowing down the eastern slopes of the Rocky Mountains over the adjacent plains in the United States and Canada.

cirriform
All species and varieties of cirrus, cirrocumulus, and cirrostratus clouds; descriptive of clouds composed mostly or entirely of small ice crystals, usually transparent and white; often producing halo phenomena not observed with other cloud forms. Average height ranges upward from 20,000 feet (6,067 m) in middle latitudes.

cirrocumulus
A cirriform cloud appearing as a thin sheet of small white puffs resembling flakes or patches of cotton without shadows; sometimes confused with altocumulus.

cirrostratus
A cirriform cloud appearing as a whitish veil, usually fibrous, sometimes smooth; often produces halo phenomena; may totally cover the sky.

cirrus
A cirriform cloud in the form of thin, white featherlike clouds in patches or narrow bands; has fibrous and/or silky sheen; large ice crystals often trail downward a considerable vertical distance in fibrous, slanted, or irregularly curved wisps called mare's tails.

civil twilight
See twilight

climate
The statistical collective of the weather conditions of a point or area during a specified interval of time (usually several decades); may be expressed in a variety of ways.

climatology
The study of climate.

clinometer
An instrument used in weather observing for measuring angles of inclination: it is used in conjunction with a ceiling light to determine cloud height at night.

cloudburst
Any sudden and heavy fall of rain, hail almost always of the shower type.

cloud cap
See cap cloud

cold front
Any non-occluded front which moves in such a way that colder air replaces warmer air.

condensation
See change of state

condensation level
The height at which a rising parcel or layer of air would become saturated if lifted adiabatically.

condensation nuclei
Small particles in the air on which water vapor condenses or sublimates.

condensation trail (contrail or vapor trail)
A cloud-like streamer frequently observed to form behind aircraft flying in clear, cold, humid air.

conditionally unstable air
Unsaturated air that will become unstable on the condition it becomes saturated. *See* instability.

conduction
The transfer of heat by molecular action through a substance or from one substance in contact with another; transfer is always from warmer to colder temperature.

constant pressure chart
A chart of a constant pressure surface; may contain analyses of height, wind, temperature, humidity, and/or other elements.

continental polar air
See polar air

continental tropical air
See tropical air

contour
In meteorology, a line of equal height on a constant pressure chart; analogous to contours on a relief map; in radar meteorology, a line on a radar scope of equal echo intensity.

contouring circuit
On weather radar, a circuit which displays multiple contours of echo intensity simultaneously on the plan position indicator or range-height indicator scope. *See* contour

convection
In general, mass motions within a fluid resulting in transport and mixing of the properties of that fluid. In meteorology, atmospheric motions that are predominantly vertical, resulting in vertical transport and mixing of atmospheric properties; distinguished from advection.

convective cloud
See cumuliform

convective condensation level (CCL)
The lowest level at which condensation will occur as a result of convection due to surface heating. When condensation occurs at this level, the layer between the surface and the CCL will be thoroughly mixed, temperature lapse rate will be dry adiabatic, and mixing ratio will he constant.

convective instability
The state of an unsaturated layer of air whose lapse rates of temperature and moisture are such that when lifted adiabatically until the layer becomes saturated, convection is spontaneous.

convergence
The condition that exists when the distribution of winds within a given area is such that there is a net horizontal inflow of air into the area. In convergence at lower levels, the removal of the resulting excess is accomplished by an upward movement of air; consequently, areas of low-level convergent winds are regions favorable to the occurrence of clouds and precipitation. *Compare* with divergence.

Coriolis force
A deflective force resulting from Earth's rotation; it acts to the right of wind direction in the Northern Hemisphere and to the left in the Southern Hemisphere.

corona
A prismatically colored circle or arcs of a circle with the sun or moon at its center; coloration is from blue inside to red outside (opposite that of a halo); varies in size (much smaller) a opposed to the fixed diameter of the halo; characteristic of clouds composed of water droplets and valuable in differentiating between middle and cirriform clouds.

corposant
See St. Elmo's Fire

corrected altitude
See altitude

cumuliform
A term descriptive of all convective clouds exhibiting vertical development in contrast to the horizontally extended stratiform types.

cumulonimbus
A cumuliform cloud type; it is heavy and dense, with considerable vertical extent in the form of massive towers; often with tops in the shape of an anvil or massive plume; under the base of cumulonimbus, which often is very dark, there frequently exists virga, precipitation and low ragged clouds (scud), either merged with it or not; frequently accompanied by lightning, thunder, and sometimes hail; occasionally produces a tornado or a waterspout; the ultimate manifestation of the growth of a cumulus cloud, occasionally extending well into the stratosphere.

cumulonimbus mamma
A cumulonimbus cloud having hanging protuberances, like pouches, festoons, or udders, on the under side of the cloud; usually indicative of seyere turbulence.

cumulus
A cloud in the form of individual detached domes or towers which are usually dense and well defined; develops vertically in the form of rising mounds of which the bulging upper part often resembles a cauliflower; the sunlit parts of these clouds are mostly brilliant white; their bases are relatively dark and nearly horizontal.

cumulus fractus
See fractus

cyclogenesis
Any development or strengthening of cyclonic circulation in the atmosphere.

cyclone
An area of low atmospheric pressure which has a closed circulation that is cyclonic, i.e., as viewed from above, the circulation is counterclockwise in the Northern Hemisphere, clockwise in the Southern Hemisphere, undefined at the Equator. Because cyclonic circulation and relatively low atmospheric pressure usually co-exist, in common practice the terms cyclone and low are used interchangeably. Also, because cyclones often are accompanied by inclement (sometimes destructive) weather, they are frequently referred to simply as storms. The term is frequently misused to denote a tornado. In the Indian Ocean, a tropical cyclone of hurricane or typhoon force.

D

deepening
A decrease in the central pressure of a pressure system; usually applied to a low rather than to a high, although technically, it is acceptable in either sense.

density
The ratio of the mass of any substance to the volume it occupies—weight per unit volume. Also, the ratio of any quantity to the volume or area it occupies, i.e., population per unit area, power density.

density altitude
See altitude

depression
In meteorology, an area of low pressure; a low or trough. This is usually applied to a certain stage in the development of a tropical cyclone, to migratory lows and troughs, and to upper-level lows and troughs that are only weakly developed.

dew
Water condensed onto grass and other objects near the ground, the temperatures of which have fallen below the initial dew point temperature of the surface air, but is still above freezing. *Compare* with frost.

dew point (dew-point temperature)
The temperature to which a sample of air must be cooled, while the mixing ratio and barometric pressure remain constant, in order to attain saturation with respect to water.

discontinuity
A zone with comparatively rapid transition of one or more meteorological elements.

disturbance
In meteorology, applied rather loosely: first, any low pressure or cyclone, but usually one that is relatively small in size; second, an area where weather, wind, pressure, etc., show signs of cyclonic development; third, any deviation in flow or pressure that is associated with a disturbed state of the weather, i.e., cloudiness and precipitation; and finally, any individual circulatory system within the primary circulation of the atmosphere.

diurnal
Daily, especially pertaining to a cycle completed within a 24-hour period, and which recurs every 24 hours.

divergence
The condition that exists when the distribution of winds within a given area is such that there is a net horizontal flow of air outward from the region. In divergence at lower levels, the resulting deficit is compensated for by subsidence of air from aloft; consequently the air is heated and the relative humidity lowered making divergence a warming and drying process. Low-level divergent regions are areas unfavorable to the occurrence of clouds and precipitation. The opposite of convergence.

doldrums
The equatorial belt of calm or light and variable winds between the two tradewind belts. Compare intertropical convergence zone.

downburst
A strong and potentially destructive thunderstorm downdraft; depending on size, either a microburst or a macroburst. *See also* microburst

downdraft
A relative small scale downward current of air; often observed on the lee side of large objects restricting the smooth flow of the air or in precipitation areas in or near cumuliform clouds.

drifting snow
A type of hydrometeor composed of snow particles picked up from the surface, but carried to a height of less than 6 feet (1.82 m).

drizzle
A form of precipitation. Very small water drops that appear to float with the air currents while falling in an irregular path (unlike rain, which falls in a comparatively straight path, and unlike fog droplets which remain suspended in the air).

dropsonde
A radiosonde dropped by parachute from an aircraft to obtain soundings (measurements) of the atmosphere below.

dry adiabatic lapse rate
The rate of decrease of temperature with height when unsaturated air is lifted adiabatically (due to expansion as it is lifted to lower pressure). *See also* adiabatic process

dry bulb
A name given to an ordinary thermometer used to determine temperature of the air.

dry-bulb temperature
The temperature of the air.

dust
A type of lithometeor composed of small earthen particles suspended in the atmosphere.

dust devil
A small, vigorous whirlwind, usually of short duration, rendered visible by dust, sand, and debris picked up from the ground.

duster
See duststorm

duststorm (duster, black blizzard)
An unusual, frequently severe weather condition

characterized by strong winds and dust-filled air over an extensive area.

D-value
Departure of true altitude from pressure altitude; obtained by algebraically subtracting true altitude from pressure altitude; thus it may be plus or minus. On a constant pressure chart, the difference between actual height and standard atmospheric height of a constant pressure surface.

E

eddy
A local irregularity of wind in a larger scale wind flow. Small scale eddies produce turbulent conditions.

El Niño
Name given to the periodic warming of the ocean that occurs in the central and eastern tropical Pacific and can produce extreme weather in many locations of the world.

El Niño/Southern Oscillation (ENSO)
An episode of anomalously high sea-surface temperatures in the equatorial tropical eastern Pacific Ocean.

estimated ceiling
A ceiling classification applied when the ceiling height has been estimated by the observer or has been determined by some other method; but, because of the specified limits of time, distance, or precipitation conditions, a more descriptive classification cannot be applied.

evaporation
See change of state

extratropical low
Any cyclone that is not a tropical cyclone, usually referring to the migratory frontal cyclones of middle and high latitudes.

eye
The roughly circular area of calm or relatively light winds and comparatively fair weather at the center of a well-developed tropical cyclone. A wall cloud marks the outer boundary of the eye.

F

Fahrenheit temperature scale (°F)
A temperature scale with 32°F as the melting point of pure ice and 212°F as the boiling point of pure water at standard sea level atmospheric pressure (29.92 inches or 1013.2 millibars).

Fall wind
A cold wind blowing downslope. Fall wind differs from foehn in that the air is initially cold enough to remain relatively cold despite compressional heating during descent.

filling
An increase in the central pressure of a pressure system; opposite of deepening; more commonly applied to a low rather than a high.

first gust
The leading edge of the spreading downdraft, plow wind, from an approaching thunderstorm.

flow line
A streamline.

foehn
A warm, dry downslope wind; the warmness and dryness being due to adiabatic compression upon descent; characteristic of mountainous regions. *See also* adiabatic process, Chinook, Santa Ana.

fog
A hydrometeor consisting of numerous minute water droplets and based at the surface; droplets are small enough to be suspended in Earth's atmosphere indefinitely. Unlike drizzle, it does not fall to the surface; differs from cloud only in that a cloud is not based at the surface; distinguished from haze by its wetness and gray color.

fractus
Clouds in the form of irregular shreds, appearing as if torn; have a clearly ragged appearance; applies only to stratus and cumulus, i.e., cumulus fractus and stratus fractus.

freezing
See change of state

freezing level
A level in the atmosphere at which the temperature is 0°C (32°F).

front
A surface, interface, or transition zone of discontinuity between two adjacent air masses of different densities; more simply the boundary between two different air masses. *See also* frontal zone.

frontal zone
A front or zone with a marked increase of density gradient; used to denote that fronts are not truly a "surface" of discontinuity but rather a "zone" of rapid transition of meteorological elements.

frontogenesis
The initial formation of a front or frontal zone.

frontolysis
The dissipation of a front.

frost (hoarfrost)
Ice crystal deposits formed by sublimation when temperature and dew point are below freezing.

funnel cloud
A tornado cloud or vortex cloud extending downward from the parent cloud but not reaching the ground.

G

glaze
A coating of ice, generally clear and smooth, formed by freezing of supercooled water on a surface.

gradient
In meteorology, a horizontal decrease in value per unit distance of a parameter in the direction of maximum decrease; most commonly used with pressure, temperature, and moisture.

ground fog
In the United States, a fog that conceals less than 0.6 of the sky and is not contiguous with the base of clouds.

gust
A sudden brief increase in wind; according to United States weather–observing practice, gusts are reported when the variation in wind speed between peaks and lulls is at least 10 knots.

H

hail
A form of precipitation composed of balls or irregular lumps of ice, always produced by convective clouds which are nearly always cumulonimbus.

halo
A prismatically colored or whitish circle or arcs of a circle with the sun or moon at its center; coloration, if not white, is from red inside to blue outside (opposite that of a corona); fixed in size with an angular diameter of 22° (common) or 46° (rare); characteristic of clouds composed of ice crystals; valuable in differentiating between cirriform and forms of lower clouds.

haze
A type of lithometeor composed of fine dust or salt particles dispersed through a portion of the atmosphere, particles are so small they cannot be felt or individually seen with the naked eye (a compared with the larger particles of dust), but diminish the visibility; distinguished from fog by its bluish or yellowish tinge.

high
An area of barometric pressure, with its attendant system of winds; an anticyclone. Also, high pressure system.

hoar frost
See frost

humidity
Water vapor content of the air; may be expressed as specific humidity, relative humidity, or mixing ratio.

hurricane
A tropical cyclone in the Western Hemisphere with winds in excess of 65 knots or 120 km/h.

hydrometer
A general term for particles of liquid water or ice such a rain, fog, frost, etc., formed by modification of water vapor in the atmosphere; also water or ice particles lifted from Earth by the wind such a sea spray or blowing snow.

hydrograph
The record produced by a continuous-recording hygrometer.

hygrometer
An instrument for measuring the water vapor content of the air.

I

ice crystals
A type of precipitation composed of unbranched crystals in the form of needles, columns, or plates; usually having a very slight downward motion, may fall from a cloudless sky.

ice fog
A type of fog composed of minute suspended particles of ice; occurs at very low temperatures and may cause halo phenomena.

ice needles
A form of ice crystals.

ice pellets
Small, transparent or translucent, round or irregularly shaped pellets of ice. They may be hard grains that rebound on striking a hard surface or pellets of snow encased in ice.

indefinite ceiling
A ceiling classification denoting vertical visibility into a surface based obscuration.

indicated altitude
See altitude

insolation
Incoming solar radiation falling upon Earth and its atmosphere.

instability
A general term to indicate various states of the atmosphere in which spontaneous convection will occur when prescribed criteria are met; indicative of turbulence. *See also* absolute instability, conditionally unstable air, convective instability.

intertropical convergence zone
The boundary zone between the trade wind system of the Northern and Southern Hemispheres; it is characterized in maritime climates by showery precipitation with cumulonimbus clouds sometimes extending to great heights.

inversion
An increase in temperature with height—a reversal of the normal decrease with height in the troposphere; may also be applied to other meteorological properties.

isobar
A line of equal or constant barometric pressure.

isoheight
On a weather chart, a line of equal height.

isoline
A line of equal value of a variable quantity, i.e., an isoline of temperature is an isotherm, etc.

isoshear
A line of equal wind shear.

isotach
A line of equal or constant wind speed.

isotherm
A line of equal or constant temperature.

isothermal
Of equal or constant temperature, with respect to either space or time; more commonly, temperature with height; a zero lapse rate.

J

jet stream
A quasi-horizontal streams of winds 50 knots or more concentrated within a narrow band embedded in the westerlies in the high troposphere.

K

katabatic wind
Any wind blowing downslope. *See also* fall wind, foehn.

Kelvin temperature scale (K)
A temperature scale with zero equal to the temperature at which all molecular motion ceases, i.e., absolute zero (0 K =-273°C); the Kelvin degree is identical to the Celsius degree; hence at standard sea level pressure, the melting point is 273 K and the boiling point 373 K.

knot
A unit of speed equal to one nautical mile per hour.

L

La Niña
The condition where the central and eastern tropical Pacific Ocean sea-surface temperatures become cooler than normal.

land breeze
A coastal breeze blowing from land to sea, caused by temperature difference when the sea surface is warmer than the adjacent land. Therefore, it usually blows at night and alternates with a sea breeze, which blows in the opposite direction by day.

lapse rate
The rate of decrease of an atmospheric variable with height; commonly refers to decrease of temperature with height.

latent heat
The amount of heat absorbed (converted to kinetic energy) during the processes of change of liquid water to water vapor, ice to water vapor, or ice to liquid water; or the amount released during the reverse processes. Four basic classifications are: (1) latent heat of condensation: heat released during change of water vapor to water (2) latent heat of fusion: heat released during change of water to ice or the amount absorbed in change of ice to water (3) latent heat of sublimation: heat released during change of water vapor to ice or the amount absorbed in the change of ice to water vapor (4) latent heat of vaporization: heat absorbed in the change of water to water vapor; the negative of latent heat of condensation.

layer
In reference to sky cover, clouds or other obscuring phenomena whose basis are approximately at the same level. The layer may be continuous or composed of detached elements. The term "layer" does not imply that a clear space exists between the layers or that the clouds or obscuring phenomena composing them are of the same type.

lee wave
Any stationary wave disturbance caused by a barrier in a fluid flow. In the atmosphere when sufficient moisture is present, this wave will be evidenced by lenticular clouds to the lee of mountain barriers; also called mountain wave or standing wave.

lenticular cloud (lenticularis)
A species of cloud whose elements have the form of more or less isolated, generally smooth lenses or almonds. These clouds appear most often in formations of orographic origin, the result of lee waves, in which case they remain nearly stationary with respect to the terrain (standing cloud), but they also occur in regions without marked orography.

level of free convection (LFC)
The level at which a parcel of air lifted dry-adiabatically until saturated and moist-adiabatically thereafter would become warmer than its surroundings in a conditionally unstable atmosphere. *See also* conditional instability, adiabatic process.

lifting condensation level (LCL)
The level at which a parcel of unsaturated air lifted dry-adiabatically would become saturated. Compare level of free convection and convective condensation level.

lightning
Generally, any and all forms of visible electrical discharge produced by a thunderstorm.

lithometeor
The general term for dry particles suspended in the atmosphere such as dust, haze, smoke, and sand.

low
An area of low barometric pressure, with its attendant system of winds. Also called a barometric depression or cyclone.

M

macroburst
A downburst that affects a path longer than 2.5 miles (4.0 km).

mammato cumulus
See cumulonimbus mamma

mare's tail
See cirrus

maritime polar air (mP)
See polar air

maritime tropical air (mT)
See tropical air

maximum wind axis
On a constant pressure chart, a line denoting the axis of maximum wind speeds at that constant pressure surface.

mean sea level
The average height of the surface of the sea for all stages of tide; used as reference for elevations throughout the United States.

melting
See change of state

mercurial barometer
A barometer in which pressure is determined by balancing air pressure against the weight of a column of mercury in an evacuated glass tube.

meteorology
The science of the atmosphere.

microbarograph
An aneroid barograph designed to record atmospheric pressure changes of very small magnitudes.

microburst
A downburst that affects a path that is 2.5 miles (4.0 km) or less.

millibar (mb)
An internationally used unit of pressure equal to 1,000 dynes per square centimeter. It is convenient for reporting atmospheric pressure.

mist
A popular expression for drizzle or heavy fog.

mixing ratio
The ratio by weight of the amount of water vapor in a volume of air to the amount of dry air; usually expressed as grams per kilogram (g/kg).

moist-adiabatic lapse rate
See saturated-adiabatic lapse rate

moisture
An all-inclusive term denoting water in any or all of its three states.

monsoon
A wind that in summer blows from sea to a continental interior, bringing copious rain, and in winter blows from the interior to the sea, resulting in sustained dry weather.

mountain wave
A standing wave or lee wave to the lee of a mountain barrier.

N

nautical twilight
See twilight

negative vorticity
See vorticity

nimbostratus
A principal cloud type, gray colored, often dark, the appearance of which is rendered diffuse by more or less continuously falling rain or snow, which in most cases reaches the ground. It is thick enough throughout to blot out the sun.

noctilucent clouds
Clouds of unknown composition which occur at great heights, probably around 75-90 kilometers. They resemble thin cirrus, but usually with a bluish or silverish color, although sometimes orange to red, standing out against a dark night sky. Rarely observed.

normal
In meteorology, the value of an element averaged for a given location over a period of years and recognized as a standard.

numerical forecasting
See numerical weather prediction

numerical weather prediction
Forecasting by digital computers solving mathematical equations; used extensively in weather services worldwide.

O

obscuration
Denotes sky hidden by surface-based obscuring phenomena and vertical visibility restricted overhead.

obscuring phenomena
Any hydrometeor or lithometeor other than clouds; may be surface based or aloft.

occluded front (occlusion, frontal occlusion)
A composite of two fronts as a cold front overtakes a warm front or quasi-stationary front.

orographic
Of, pertaining to, or caused by mountains as in orographic clouds, orographic lift, or orographic precipitation.

ozone
An unstable form of oxygen; heaviest concentrations are in the stratosphere; corrosive to some metals; absorbs most ultraviolet solar radiation.

P

parcel
A small volume of air, small enough to contain uniform distribution of its meteorological properties, and large enough to remain relatively self-contained and respond to all meteorological processes. No specific dimensions have been defined, however, the order of magnitude of 1 cubic foot has been suggested.

partial obscuration
A designation of sky cover when part of the sky is hidden by surface based obscuring phenomena.

pilot balloon
A small free-lift balloon used to determine the speed and direction of winds in the upper air.

pilot balloon observation (PIBAL)
A method of winds-aloft observation by visually tracking a pilot balloon.

plan position indicator (PPI) scope
A radar indicator scope displaying range and azimuth of targets in polar coordinates.

plow wind
The spreading downdraft of a thunderstorm; a strong, straight-line wind in advance of the storm. *See also* first gust.

polar air
An air mass with characteristics developed over high latitudes, especially within the subpolar highs. Continental polar air (cP) has cold surface temperatures, low moisture content, and especially in its source regions, has great stability in the lower layers. It is shallow in comparison with Arctic air. Maritime polar (mP) initially possesses similar properties to those of continental polar air, but in passing over warmer water it becomes unstable with a higher moisture content. Compare tropical air.

polar front
The semipermanent, semicontinuous front-separating air masses of tropical and polar origins.

positive vorticity
See vorticity

precipitation
Any or all forms of water particles, whether liquid or solid, that fall from the atmosphere and reach the surface. It is a major class of hydrometeor, distinguished from cloud and virga in that it must reach the surface.

precipitation attenuation
See attenuation

pressure
See atmospheric pressure

pressure altimeter
An aneroid barometer with a scale graduated in altitude instead of pressure using standard atmospheric pressure-height relationships; shows indicated altitude (not necessarily true altitude); may be set to measure altitude (indicated) from any arbitrarily chosen level.

pressure gradient
The rate of decrease of pressure per unit distance at a fixed time.

pressure jump
A sudden, significant increase in station pressure.

pressure tendency
See barometric tendency

prevailing easterlies
The broad current or pattern of persistent easterly winds in the Tropics and in polar regions.

prevailing visibility
In the United States, the greatest horizontal visibility which is equaled or exceeded throughout half of the horizon circle; it need not be a continuous half.

prevailing westerlies
The dominant west-to-east motion of the atmosphere, centered over middle latitudes of both hemispheres.

prevailing wind
Direction from which the wind blows most frequently.

prognostic chart (PROG)
A chart of expected or forecast conditions.

pseudo-adiabatic lapse rate
See saturated-adiabatic lapse rate

psychrometer
An instrument consisting of a wet-bulb and a dry-bulb thermometer for measuring wet-bulb and dry-bulb temperature; used to determine water vapor content of the air.

pulse
Pertaining to radar, a brief burst of electromagnetic radiation emitted by the radar; of very short time duration. *See also* pulse length.

pulse length
The dimension of a radar pulse; may be expressed as the time duration or the length in linear units. Linear dimension is equal to time duration multiplied by the speed of propagation (approximately the speed of light).

Q

quasi-stationary front (stationary front)
A front which is stationary or nearly so; conventionally, a front which is moving at a speed of less than 5 knots is generally considered to be quasi-stationary.

R

RADAR (radio detection and ranging)
An electronic instrument used for the detection and ranging of distant objects of such composition that they scatter or reflect radio energy. Since hydrometeors can scatter radio energy, weather radars, operating on certain frequency bands, can detect the presence of precipitation, clouds, or both.

radarsonde observation
A rawinsonde observation in which winds are determined by radar tracking a balloon-borne target.

radiation
The emission of energy by a medium and transferred, either through free space or another medium, in the form of electromagnetic waves.

radiation fog
Fog characteristically resulting when radiational cooling of Earth's surface lowers the air temperature near the ground to or below its initial dew point on calm, clear nights.

radiosonde
A balloon-borne instrument for measuring pressure, temperature, and humidity aloft. Radiosonde observation is a sounding made by the instrument.

rain
A form of precipitation; drops are larger than drizzle and fall in relatively straight, although not necessarily vertical, paths as compared to drizzle which falls in irregular paths.

rain shower
See shower

range attenuation
See attenuation

RAOB
A radiosonde observation.

rawin
A rawinsonde observation.

rawinsonde observation
A combined winds aloft and radiosonde observation. Winds are determined by tracking the radiosonde by radio direction finder or radar.

relative humidity
The ratio of the existing amount of water vapor in the air at a given temperature to the maximum amount that could exist at that temperature; usually expressed in percent.

relative vorticity
See vorticity

ridge (ridge line)
In meteorology, an elongated area of relatively high atmospheric pressure; usually associated with and most clearly identified as an area of maximum anticyclonic curvature of the wind flow (isobars, contours, or streamlines).

rocketsonde
A type of radiosonde launched by a rocket and making its measurements during a parachute descent; capable of obtaining soundings to a much greater height than possible by balloon or aircraft.

roll cloud
A dense and horizontal roll-shaped accessory cloud located on the lower leading edge of a cumulonimbus or less often, a rapidly developing cumulus; indicative of turbulence.

rotor cloud
A turbulent cloud formation found in the lee of some large mountain barriers, the air in the cloud rotates around an axis parallel to the range; indicative of possible violent turbulence.

S

St. Elmo's Fire (corposant)
A luminous brush discharge of electricity from protruding objects, such as mats and yardarms of ships, aircraft, lightning rods, steeples, etc., occurring in stormy weather.

Santa Ana
A hot, dry, foehn wind, generally from the northeast or east, occurring west of the Sierra Nevada mountains especially in the pass and river valley near Santa Ana, California.

saturated adiabatic lapse rate
The rate of decrease of temperature with height as saturated air is lifted with no gain or loss of heat from outside sources; varies with temperature, being greatest at low temperatures. *See also* adiabatic process, dry-adiabatic lapse rate.

saturation
The condition of the atmosphere when actual water vapor present is the maximum possible at existing temperature.

scud
Small detached masses of stratus fractus clouds below a layer of higher clouds, usually nimbostratus.

sea breeze
A coastal breeze blowing from sea to land, caused by the temperature difference when the land surface is warmer than the sea surface. Compare land breeze.

sea fog
A type of advection fog formed when air that has been lying over a warm surface is transported over a colder water surface.

sea level pressure
The atmospheric pressure at mean sea level, either directly measured by stations at sea level or empirically determined from the station pressure and temperature by stations not at sea level: used as a common reference for analyses of surface pressure patterns.

sea smoke
See steam fog

sector visibility
Meteorological visibility within a specified sector of the horizon circle.

shear
See wind sheer

shower
Precipitation from a cumuliform cloud; characterized by the suddenness of beginning and ending, by the rapid change of intensity, and usually by rapid change in the appearance of the sky; showery precipitation may be in the form of rain, ice pellets, or snow.

slant visibility
For an airborne observer, the distance at which the pilot can see and distinguish objects on the ground.

sleet
See ice pellets

smog
A mixture of smoke and fog.

smoke
A restriction to visibility resulting from combustion.

snow
Precipitation composed of white or translucent ice crystals, chiefly in complex branched hexagonal form.

snow flurry
Popular term for snow shower, particularly of a very light and brief nature.

snow grains
Precipitation of very small, white opaque grains of ice, similar in structure to snow crystals. The grains are fairly flat or elongated, with diameters generally less than 0.04 inch (1 mm).

snow pellets
Precipitation consisting of white, opaque approximately round (sometimes conical) ice particles having a snow-like structure, and about 0.08 to 0.2 inch in diameter; crisp and easily crushed, differing in this respect from snow grains; rebound from a hard surface and often break up.

snow shower
See shower

solar radiation
The total electromagnetic radiation emitted by the sun. *See also* insolation

sounding
In meteorology, an upper-air observation; a radiosonde observation.

source region
An extensive area of Earth's surface characterized by relatively uniform surface conditions where large masses of air remain long enough to take on characteristic temperature and moisture properties imparted by that surface.

specific humidity
The ratio by weight of water vapor in a sample of air to the combined weight of water vapor and dry air. *Compare* mixing ratio.

squall
A sudden increase in wind speed by at least 15 knots to a peak of 20 knots or more and lasting for at least one minute. Essential difference between a gust and a squall is the duration of the peak speed.

squall line
Any nonfrontal line or narrow band of active thunderstorms (with or without squalls).

stability
A state of the atmosphere in which the vertical distribution of temperature is such that a parcel will resist displacement from its initial level. *See also* instability.

standard atmosphere
A hypothetical atmosphere based on climatological averages comprised of numerous physical constants of which the most important are: (1) A surface temperature of 59°F (15°C) and a surface pressure of 29.92 inches of mercury (1013.2 millibars) at sea level; (2) A lapse rate in the troposphere of 6.5°C per kilometer (approximately 2°C per 1,000 feet [303 m]); (3) A tropopause of 11 kilometers (approximately 36,000 feet [10,920 m]) with a temperature of -56.5° C; and (4) An isothermal lapse rate in the stratosphere to an altitude of 24 kilometers (approximately 80,000 feet [24,266 m]).

standing cloud (standing lenticular altocumulus)
See lenticular cloud

standing wave
A wave that remains stationary in a moving fluid. In aviation operations it is used most commonly to refer to a lee wave or mountain wave.

stationary front
See quasi-stationary front

station pressure
The actual atmospheric pressure at the observing station.

steam fog
Fog formed when cold air moves over relatively warm water or wet ground.

storm detection radar
A weather radar designed to detect hydrometeors of precipitation size; used primarily to detect storms with large drops or hailstones as opposed to clouds and light precipitation of small drop size.

stratiform
Clouds of extensive horizontal development, in contrast to vertically developed cumuliform clouds; characteristic of stable air and, therefore, composed of small water droplets.

stratocumulus
A low cloud, predominantly stratiform, in gray and/or whitish patches or layers, may or may not merge; elements are tessellated, rounded, or roll-shaped with relatively flat tops.

stratosphere
The atmospheric layer above the tropopause, average altitude of base and top, 7 and 22 miles (11.27 and 35.42 km) respectively; characterized by a slight average increase of temperature from base to top and is very stable; also characterized by low moisture content and absence of clouds.

stratus
A low, gray cloud layer or sheet with a fairly uniform base; sometimes appears in ragged patches; seldom produces precipitation but may produce drizzle or snow grains. A stratiform cloud.

stratus fractus
See fractus

streamline
In meteorology, a line whose tangent is the wind direction at any point along the line. A flowline.

sublimation
See change of state

subsidence
A descending motion of air in the atmosphere over a rather broad area; usually associated with divergence.

summation principle
The principle states that the cover assigned to a layer is equal to the summation of the sky cover of the lowest layer plus the additional coverage at all successively higher layers up to and including the layer in question. Thus, no layer can be assigned a sky cover less than a lower layer, and no sky cover can be greater than 1.0 (10/10).

supera diabatic lapse rate
A lapse rate greater than the dry-adiabatic lapse rate. *See also* absolute instability.

supercooled water
Liquid water at temperatures colder than freezing.

surface inversion
An inversion with its base at the surface, often caused by cooling of the air near the surface as a result of terrestrial radiation, especially at night.

surface visibility
Visibility observed from eye-level above the ground.

synoptic chart
A chart, such a the familiar weather map, which depicts the distribution of meteorological conditions over an area at a given time.

T

target
In radar, any of the many types of objects detected by radar.

temperature
In general, the degree of hotness or coldness as measured on some definite temperature scale by means of any of various types of thermometers.

temperature inversion
See inversion

terrestrial radiation
The total infrared radiation emitted by Earth and its atmosphere.

thermograph
A continuous-recording thermometer.

thermometer
An instrument for measuring temperature.

thunderstorm
In general, a local storm invariably produced by a cumulonimbus cloud, and always accompanied by lightning and thunder.

tornado (cyclone or twister)
A violently rotating column of air, pendant from a cumulonimbus cloud, and nearly always observable as "funnel-shaped." It is the most destructive of all small-scale atmospheric phenomena.

towering cumulus
A rapidly growing cumulus in which height exceeds width.

tower visibility
Prevailing visibility determined from the control tower.

trade winds
Prevailing, almost continuous winds blowing with an easterly component from the subtropical high pressure belts toward the intertropical convergence zone northeast in the Northern Hemisphere, southeast in the Southern Hemisphere.

tropical air
An air mass with characteristics developed over low latitudes. Maritime tropical air (mT), the principal type, is produced over the tropical and subtropical sea; very warm and humid. Continental tropical air (cT) is produced over subtropical arid region and is hot and very dry. *Compare* polar air.

tropical cyclone
A general term for a cyclone that originates over tropical oceans. By international agreement, tropical cyclones have been classified according to their intensity, as follows: (1) tropical depression: winds up to 34 knots (64 km/h); (2) tropical storm: winds of 35 to 64 knots (65 to 119 km/h); (3) hurricane or typhoon: winds of 65 knots or higher (120 km/h).

tropical depression
See tropical cyclone

tropical storm
See tropical cyclone

tropopause
The transition zone between the troposphere and stratosphere, usually characterized by an abrupt change of lapse rate.

troposphere
That position of the atmosphere from Earth's surface to the tropopause; that is, the lowest 10 to 20 kilometers of the atmosphere. The troposphere is characterized by decreasing temperature with height, and by appreciable water vapor.

trough (trough line)
In meteorology, an elongated area of relatively low atmospheric pressure, usually associated with and most clearly identified as an area of maximum cyclonic curvature of the wind flow (isobars, contours, or streamlines). *Compare* with ridge.

true altitude
See altitude

true wind direction
The direction, with respect to true north, from which the wind is blowing.

turbulence
In meteorology, any irregular or disturbed flow in the atmosphere.

twilight
The intervals of incomplete darkness following sunset and preceding sunrise. The time at which evening twilight ends or morning twilight begins is determined by arbitrary convention, and several kinds of twilight have been defined and used; most commonly civil, nautical, and astronomical twilight: (1) civil twilight: the period of time before sunrise and after sunset when the sun is not more than 6 degrees below the horizon; (2) nautical twilight: the period of time before sunrise and after sunset when the sun is not more than 12 degrees below the horizon; (3) astronomical twilight: the period of time before sunrise and after sunset when the sun is not more than 18 degrees below the horizon.

twister
In the United States, a colloquial term for tornado.

typhoon
A tropical cyclone (hurricane) in the western tropical Pacific Ocean with winds in excess of 65 knots (120 km/h).

U

undercast
A cloud layer of ten-tenths (1.0) coverage (to the nearest tenth) a viewed from an observation point above the layer.

unlimited ceiling
A clear sky or a sky cover that does not meet the criteria for a ceiling.

unstable
See instability

updraft
A localized upward current of air.

upper front
A front aloft not extending to Earth's surface.

upslope fog
Fog formed when air flows upward over rising terrain and is, consequently, adiabatically cooled to or below its initial dew point.

V

vapor pressure
In meteorology, the pressure of water vapor in the atmosphere. Vapor pressure is that part of the total atmospheric pressure due to water vapor and is independent of the other atmospheric gases or vapors.

vapor trail
See condensation trail

veering
Shifting of the wind in a clockwise direction with respect to either space or time; opposite of backing. Commonly used by meteorologists to refer to an anticyclonic shift (clockwise in the Northern Hemisphere and counterclockwise in the Southern Hemisphere).

vertical visibility
The distance one can see upward into a surface based obscuration; or the maximum height from which a pilot in flight can recognize the ground through a surface based obscuration.

virga
Water or ice particles falling from a cloud, usually in wisps or streaks, and evaporating before reaching the ground.

visibility
The greatest distance one can see and identify prominent objects.

visual range
See runway visual range

vortex
In meteorology, any rotary flow in the atmosphere.

vorticity
Turning of the atmosphere. Vorticity may be imbedded in the total flow and not readily identified by a flow pattern. (1) absolute vorticity: the rotation of Earth imparts vorticity to the atmosphere; absolute vorticity is the combined vorticity due to this rotation and vorticity due to circulation relative to Earth (relative vorticity); (2) negative vorticity: vorticity caused by anticyclonic turning; it is associated with downward motion of the air; (3) positive vorticity: vorticity caused by cyclonic turning; it is associated with upward motion of the air; (4) relative vorticity: vorticity of the air relative to Earth, disregarding the component of vorticity resulting from Earth's rotation.

W

wake turbulence
Turbulence found to the rear of a solid body in motion relative to a fluid. In aviation terminology, the turbulence caused by a moving aircraft.

wall cloud
The well-defined bank of vertically developed clouds having a wall-like appearance which form the outer boundary of the go of a well-developed tropical cyclone.

warm front
Any non-occluded front which moves in such a way that warmer air replaces colder air.

warm sector
The area covered by warm air at the surface and bounded by the warm front and cold front of a wave cyclone.

water equivalent
The depth of water that would result from the melting of snow or ice.

waterspout
See tornado

water vapor
Water in the invisible gaseous form.

wave cyclone
A cyclone which forms and moves along a front. The circulation about the cyclone center tends to produce a wavelike deformation of the front.

weather
The state of the atmosphere, mainly with respect to its effects on life and human activities; refers to instantaneous conditions or short term changes as opposed to climate.

weather radar
Radar specifically designed for observing weather. *See also* cloud detection radar, storm detection radar.

weather vane
See wind vane

wedge
See ridge

wet-bulb temperature
The lowest temperature that can be obtained on a wet-bulb thermometer in any given sample of air, by evaporation of water (or ice) from the muslin wick; used in computing dew point and relative humidity.

wet-bulb thermometer
A thermometer with a muslin-covered bulb used to measure wet-bulb temperature.

whirlwind
A small, rotating column of air; may be visible as a dust devil.

willy-willy
A tropical cyclone of hurricane strength near Australia.

wind
Air in motion relative to the surface of Earth; generally used to denote horizontal movement.

wind direction
The direction from which wind is blowing.

wind speed
Rate of wind movement in distance per unit time.

wind vane
An instrument to indicate wind direction.

wind velocity
A vector term to include both wind direction and wind speed.

wind shear
The rate of change of wind velocity (direction and/or speed) per unit distance; conventionally expressed as vertical or horizontal wind shear.

X, Y, Z

zonal wind
A west wind; the westerly component of a wind. Conventionally used to describe large-scale flow that is neither cyclonic nor anticyclonic.

Local Climatological Data Reports

• INTRODUCTION

Local Climatological Data (LCD) are data observed at principal meteorological stations by trained observers or automated equipment that has been tested and accepted by the controlling agency. The stations are located worldwide and are operated by agencies of the United States government. The controlling agencies are the National Weather Service (NWS), the U.S. Air Force/Air Weather Service (AWS), the U.S. Navy/National Oceanographic Command (NAVOCFANCOM), and the Federal Aviation Administration (FAA). The data are collected on a wide range of time scales from one minute for some current automated equipment to three observations per day for intermittent periods at some remote, part-time locations. The majority of stations collect hourly observations and special (between hour) observations when weather conditions require. The data are used initially for aviation guidance and safety, weather forecasting, and severe weather warnings. The hourly data, special observations, and summaries are generally transmitted over global telecommunication circuits.

In 1992, NWS began automating surface weather observations through the Automated Surface Observing System (ASOS). The measurement of all weather elements included in conventional observations have not been automated. Some of those elements that have not been automated include clouds above 12,000 feet (303 m), snowfall and snow depth, sunshine, and the identification of certain types of weather such as tornado, thunderstorms, hail, drizzle, smoke, and blowing phenomena. Until new automated sensors are designed to measure these elements, the data will be obtained from other sources. ASOS is considered to be only one source of the total surface observation. The total surface observation concept includes the ASOS system, augmentation of ASOS data by station personnel, supplementary data from networks distinct from ASOS (e.g. severe weather spotter networks, hydrological networks, and cooperative networks), and complementary data from other observing technologies such as satellite, radar, and lightning detection systems.

• HOW TO READ THESE REPORTS

Weather statistics on 108 U.S. cities

The information about the history of key cities is easy to find. The reports were planned to be informative, yet easy to read. The terminology used and the standard formats are explained below.

Narrative report

Typically, each report begins with a narrative description of the local area climate prepared by a local climatologist.

The narrative describes the area in terms of terrain, water bodies, and other topographical features as these features exercise key influences on the local weather. They are usually the cause if an area's weather differs sharply from weather in areas only a few miles away. For example, if a lake is near a city, it will always influence the city's weather, and, in fact, may even create climatic differences from one part of the city to another. Mountains, swamps, even plowed fields exercise their influences on air masses as these masses move toward a city.

The report generally discusses temperatures in the city, rainfall tendencies, snowfall history, and other points. It closes with notes about the area's agricultural adaptability. The history of first fall frost and last spring freeze is usually described, along with suggestions about the types of crops for which the area is climatologically suited.

Statistics

The statistics are of two different kinds. The first type distills many years of history to give a profile of the city's weather (e.g., *Normals, Means, and Extremes*). The second group offers data for individual years, allowing the user to see what variances and/or patterns have occurred.

There are several meteorological terms used in the table. The following notes are designed to clarify the information included in the tables.

Location

Precise geographical location is provided at the top of each *Normals, Means, and Extremes* table.

Normal

Term applied as to temperature, degree days, and precipitation refers to the value of that particular element averaged over the period of 1961-90. When the station does not have continuous records from an instrument site with the same "exposure," a difference factor between the old site and the new site is used to adjust the observed values to a common series. The difference factor is determined from a period of simultaneous measurements. The base period is revised every ten years by adding the averages for the most recent decade and dropping them for the first decade of the former normals for 1961-90. *Normal* does not refer to "normalcy" or "expectation," but only to the actual averages for a particular thirty-year period.

Means and extremes (note "a")

Means and extremes are based on the period of years in which observations have been made under comparable conditions of instrument exposure. Data are included for dates through 1985 unless otherwise noted. The Date of an Extreme is the most recent one in cases of repeated occurrences.

Length of observational record

Length of observational record for *Means and Extremes* is based on the length of January data for the present instrument site exposure (15 equals 15 years). The table does not give the all time high or low value if it was recorded at a different site within the area. The *Mean* (or average) values for relative humidity, wind sunshine, sky condition, and the mean number of days with the various other weather conditions listed are also based on length of record noted in each instance. Check the first column for each of these rows to read this length of record for each item.

Average of the highest temperature (°F)

Average of the highest temperature on each day of the month and year for the period 1961-90. This value is obtained by taking the sum of the highest temperature for each day of the period adjusted for site exposure if necessary and dividing by the number of days included.

Average of the lowest temperature (°F)

Average of the lowest temperature on each day of the month and year for the period 1961-90.

Average of all daily temperatures (°F)

Average of all daily temperatures for the month and year for the period 1961-90; computed as being the sum of the minimum and maximum values divided by two. The monthly mean maximum or minimum temperatures are the sum of the daily maximums or minimums divided by the number of days in the month. The monthly average temperature is the sum of the monthly mean maximum and minimum temperatures divided by two.

Extremes—highest temperature (°F)

Highest temperature ever recorded during any month at present site exposure.

Extremes-lowest temperature (°F)

Lowest temperature ever recorded during any month at present site exposure.

Average number of heating degree days

The number of heating degree days (average) for each month and year for the period 1961-90. The statistic is based on the amount that the daily mean temperature falls below 65°F (18.3°C). Each degree of mean temperature below 65 is counted as one heating degree day. If the daily mean temperature is 65°F (18.3°C) or higher, the heating degree day value for that day is zero. Monthly and annual sums are calculated for each period and averaged over the appropriate thirty years of record to establish these "normal" values. Compare this with cooling degree days.

Average number of cooling degree days

The number of cooling degree days (average) for each month and year for the period 1961-90. The concept of this statistic is the mirror image of the concept of heating degree days and is based on the amount that the daily mean temperature exceeds 65°F. Each degree of mean temperature above 65°F is counted as one cooling degree day. If the daily mean temperature is 65°F or below, the cooling degree day is zero. It should be noted that heating and cooling degree days are calculated independently and do not cancel each other out.

Sunshine

The average percent of daytime hours subject to direct radiation from the sun at the present site. The percentage is given without regard for the intensity of sunshine. That is, thin clouds, light haze, or other minor obstructions to direct solar rays may be present but would not mitigate the full counting of an hour.

Mean sky cover

Average amount of daytime sky obscured by any type of cover expressed in tenths (e.g. , 4.8 or, 48%).

Activity limiting weather

Average number of days in month with specified weather conditions (precipitation, storms, etc.) based on present exposure. An (*) indicates less than half a day.

Cloudiness

Average number of days in month at the present site with various amounts of cloud cover. Clear indicates average daytime cloudiness of 0.3 or less; partly cloudy indicates average daytime cloudiness between 0.4 and 0.7; cloudy indicates average daytime cloudiness of 0.8 or more.

Maximum (+) temperature days

Average number of days in month and year when the temperatures at the present site 90°F (32.2°C) or above. (70°F [21.1°C] or above at Alaskan stations.)

Minimum temperature days

Average number of days at the present site when the temperatures remained below 32°F (0°C) at all times.

Freezing days

Average number of days at the present site when the temperature dropped to a minimum of 32°F or below.

Minimum (-) days

Average number of days at present site when the minimum temperature was 0°F or below.

Average station pressure

Given in millibars (mb).

Average relative humidity

Relative humidity levels at various hours of the day. The time is expressed in terms of the 24-hour clock (00 is midnight, 06 is 6 A.M., 12 is noon, and 18 is 6 P.M.). Values are for present site only.

Average precipitation

Precipitation in inches of water equivalent for each month and year during the period 1961-90. As in the other precipitation data, the values are expressed in inches of depth of the liquid water content of all forms of precipitation even if initially frozen. As in all "normal" values, when the station does not have continuous records from the same instrument site, a "ratio factor" between the new and old exposure is used to adjust the observed values to a common series.

Maximum precipitation (month)

Greatest amount (in inches) of water equivalent ever recorded during *any month* at present site.

Minimum precipitation (month)

Least amount (in inches) of water equivalent ever recorded during any month at present site.

Maximum precipitation (day)

Greatest amount (in inches) of water equivalent ever recorded during *any day* at present site.

Summaries for snow, ice pellets, hail

Figures include sleet and are similar to those for total precipitation. The values are expressed in inches of actual snow or ice fall. The water equivalent can be estimated roughly by using the rule-of-thumb that 10 inches of snow equal 1 inch (2.54 cm) of water.

Wind

Average speed of wind is expressed in miles-per-hour without regard of direction.

Prevailing wind direction

The most common single wind direction without regard for wind speed or any minimum amount of persistence. The aggregate total of wind from the other directions may be very much greater than that from the "prevailing" direction. Direction is coded in two different ways, some reports use letters, some use numbers. When letters are used, they have the usual meaning, such as WSW, indicating west-southwest. When numbers are used, they are given in tens of degrees clockwise from true north, so that 09 is 90° clockwise from north (east), 18 is 180° (south), 27 is 270° (west), and 36 is 360° (north).

High wind

The greatest speed in miles per hour of any "mile" of wind passing the station. The accompanying direction and year of occurrence are also given. A mile of wind passing the station one minute has an average speed of 60 mph (97 kph); two minutes—30 mph (48 kph); five minutes—12 mph (19 kph), etc. The wind cups of the particular instrument involved operate much like the wheel of a car in actuating the car's odometer. The instrument does not record the strength of individual wind gusts which usually last less than 20 seconds and which may be very much greater than the value given. The fastest mile however does give some idea of the extremes of wind that can be encountered.

Special symbols

Symbols that appear on many of the individual summaries: (*) less than one half; (**T**) trace, an amount too small to measure; (-) below zero temperatures are preceded by a minus sign.

Weather averages year-by-year

PRECIPITATION refers to the inches of water equivalent in the total of all forms of liquid or frozen precipitation that fell during each month. Snowfall refers to the actual amount of snow in inches that fell during the month. T (trace) is a precipitation amount of less than 0.005 inches. [Note: In estimating the water equivalent of snow, a ratio of 10 inches (25.4 cm) of snow equals 1 inch (2.54 cm) of water is customarily employed.]

AVERAGE TEMPERATURE equals the average of the maximum and minimum temperatures for each day of the month for the given year; afternoon temperatures were typically higher than these values and late night/early morning temperatures were typically below them.

HEATING AND COOLING DEGREE DAYS Heating Degree Days (HDD) provide a well-established index of relative fuel consumption for space heating in a given place—a month of 2,000 HDD requires about twice the amount of space heating energy as one of 1,000 HDD, while 100 HDD will require about the same fuel whether accumulated in two or four days. Regional differences in the Heating Degree Day Index are only partially useful in estimating comparative fuel requirements because the building construction and cultural expectations tend to be different in different parts of the country (e.g., subjective ideas of comfort in relation to temperature will vary). For example, the average standards of efficiency in heating equipment and insulation are generally lower in warmer climates so that fuel requirements tend not to decrease as rapidly as the heating degree days decrease.

The complementary index of Cooling Degree Days provides only a rough guide to relative energy consumption in air conditioning. A proper air–conditioning index will almost certainly require a factor for humidity variation and possibly factors for cloudiness or other weather variables. However, the Cooling Degree Days Index will have some usefulness in indicating relative outdoor comfort and relative indoor air conditioning requirements.

BIRMINGHAM (MUNICIPAL AIRPORT), ALABAMA

Birmingham is located in a hilly area of north-central Alabama in the foothills of the Appalachians about 300 miles inland from the Gulf of Mexico. There is a series of southwest to northeast valleys and ridges in the area.

The city is far enough inland to be protected from destructive tropical hurricanes, yet close enough that the Gulf has a pronounced modifying effect on the climate.

Although summers are long and hot, they are not generally excessively hot. On a typical mid-summer day, the temperature will be nearly 70 degrees at daybreak, approach 90 degrees at mid-day, and level off in the low 90s during the afternoon. It is not unusual for the temperature to remain below 100 degrees for several years in a row. However, every few years an extended heat wave will bring temperatures over 100 degrees. July is normally the hottest month but there is little difference from mid-June to mid-August. Rather persistent high humidity adds to the summer discomfort.

January is normally the coldest month but there is not much difference from mid-December to mid-February. Overall, winters are relatively mild. Even in cold spells, it is unusual for the temperature to remain below freezing all day. Sub-zero cold is extremely rare, occurring only a very few times this century. Extremely low temperatures almost always occur under clear skies after a snowfall.

Snowfall is erratic. Sometimes there is a two- or three-year span with no measurable snow. On rare occasions, there may be a 2 to 4 inch snowstorm. The snow usually melts quickly. Even 1 or 2 inches of snow can effectively shut down this sunbelt city because of the hilly terrain, the wetness of the snow and the unfamiliarity of motorists driving on snow and ice.

Birmingham is blessed with abundant rainfall. It is fairly well distributed throughout the year. However, some of the wetter winter months, plus March and July, have twice the rainfall of October, the driest month. Summer rainfall is almost entirely from scattered afternoon and early evening thunderstorms. Serious droughts are rare and most dry spells are not severe.

The stormiest time of the year with the greatest risk of severe thunderstorms and tornadoes is in spring, especially in March and April.

In a normal year, the last 32 degree minimum temperature in the spring is in mid to late March and the first in autumn is in early November.

NORMALS, MEANS, AND EXTREMES

BIRMINGHAM (MUNICIPAL AIRPORT), ALABAMA

LATITUDE: 33°34'N LONGITUDE: 86°45' W ELEVATION: FT. GRND 620 BARO 622 TIME ZONE: CENTRAL WBAN: 13876

	(a)	JAN	FEB	MAR	APR	MAY	JUNE	JULY	AUG	SEP	OCT	NOV	DEC	YEAR
TEMPERATURE °F:														
Normals														
-Daily Maximum		51.7	56.9	66.1	74.6	81.0	87.4	89.9	89.1	83.9	74.7	64.6	55.7	73.0
-Daily Minimum		31.3	34.5	42.3	49.2	57.7	65.2	69.5	68.8	62.9	50.2	41.6	34.8	50.7
-Monthly		41.5	45.7	54.2	62.0	69.4	76.3	79.8	79.0	73.4	62.5	53.1	45.2	61.8
Extremes														
-Record Highest	50	81	83	89	92	99	102	106	103	100	94	84	80	106
-Year		1949	1962	1982	1987	1962	1954	1980	1990	1990	1954	1961	1951	JUL 1980
-Record Lowest	50	-6	3	2	26	35	42	51	51	37	27	5	1	-6
-Year		1985	1958	1993	1973	1944	1966	1967	1946	1967	1956	1950	1989	JAN 1985
NORMAL DEGREE DAYS:														
Heating (base 65°F)		729	540	350	135	31	0	0	0	7	148	364	614	2918
Cooling (base 65°F)		0	0	15	45	168	339	459	434	259	71	7	0	1797
% OF POSSIBLE SUNSHINE	34	42	50	55	63	66	65	59	63	61	66	55	46	58
MEAN SKY COVER (tenths)														
Sunrise - Sunset	37	6.9	6.5	6.5	5.8	6.0	5.9	6.4	5.8	5.6	4.6	5.7	6.4	6.0
MEAN NUMBER OF DAYS:														
Sunrise to Sunset														
-Clear	37	6.9	7.2	7.4	8.8	8.0	7.1	4.7	6.8	9.5	14.0	10.2	8.4	98.8
-Partly Cloudy	37	6.2	6.4	7.9	8.0	10.9	12.6	14.4	14.5	9.3	7.6	6.8	6.6	111.2
-Cloudy	37	17.9	14.8	15.8	13.2	12.2	10.4	12.0	9.7	11.2	9.4	13.0	15.9	155.3
Precipitation														
.01 inches or more	50	11.2	10.2	11.0	9.2	9.8	9.6	12.4	9.6	8.0	6.2	9.0	10.7	116.9
Snow,Ice pellets,hail														
1.0 inches or more	50	0.3	0.1	0.1	0.*	0.0	0.0	0.0	0.0	0.0	0.0	0.*	0.1	0.6
Thunderstorms	50	1.6	2.3	4.5	5.1	6.9	8.4	11.6	8.8	4.3	1.2	1.8	1.2	57.7
Heavy Fog Visibility 1/4 mile or less	50	1.3	0.6	0.6	0.3	0.3	0.7	0.4	0.5	0.5	0.7	1.0	1.2	8.2
Temperature °F														
-Maximum														
90° and above	30	0.0	0.0	0.0	0.1	1.7	10.8	17.3	15.3	6.3	0.1	0.0	0.0	51.7
32° and below	30	1.4	0.4	0.1	0.0	0.0	0.0	0.0	0.0	0.0	0.0	0.*	0.5	2.5
-Minimum														
32° and below	30	17.0	13.2	6.1	1.2	0.0	0.0	0.0	0.0	0.0	0.5	6.8	14.2	59.0
0° and below	30	0.2	0.0	0.0	0.0	0.0	0.0	0.0	0.0	0.0	0.0	0.0	0.0	0.2
AVG. STATION PRESS.(mb)	21	998.3	997.0	994.6	994.2	993.4	994.0	995.1	995.2	995.4	997.1	997.6	998.5	995.9
RELATIVE HUMIDITY (%)														
Hour 00	30	76	73	72	77	84	84	86	86	85	84	80	77	80
Hour 06 (Local Time)	30	81	79	79	83	86	86	89	90	88	87	84	81	84
Hour 12	30	61	55	52	51	55	56	60	59	59	54	57	60	57
Hour 18	30	65	57	52	52	59	60	65	65	69	70	69	68	63
PRECIPITATION (inches):														
Water Equivalent														
-Normal		5.10	4.72	6.19	4.96	4.85	3.73	5.25	3.59	3.93	2.81	4.33	5.12	54.58
-Maximum Monthly	50	11.00	17.67	15.80	13.75	11.10	8.44	13.70	10.85	10.43	7.52	15.25	13.98	17.67
-Year		1949	1961	1980	1979	1969	1963	1950	1967	1977	1977	1948	1961	FEB 1961
-Minimum Monthly	50	1.09	1.20	1.71	0.42	1.15	0.67	0.30	0.38	T	0.07	0.42	0.81	T
-Year		1981	1968	1985	1986	1951	1968	1983	1989	1955	1991	1949	1980	SEP 1955
-Maximum in 24 hrs	44	5.81	6.57	7.05	5.08	4.63	3.85	5.47	5.13	5.03	3.75	4.87	5.29	7.05
-Year		1949	1961	1970	1966	1969	1957	1985	1952	1977	1977	1948	1961	MAR 1970
Snow,Ice pellets,hail														
-Maximum Monthly	50	6.6	2.3	13.0	5.0	T	T	T	0.0	T	T	1.4	8.0	13.0
-Year		1982	1960	1993	1987	1993	1992	1990		1992	1993	1950	1963	MAR 1993
-Maximum in 24 hrs	44	4.5	2.3	13.0	5.0	T	T	T	0.0	T	T	1.4	8.4	13.0
-Year		1948	1960	1993	1987	1993	1992	1990		1992	1993	1950	1963	MAR 1993
WIND:														
Mean Speed (mph)	50	8.1	8.7	9.1	8.3	6.8	6.1	5.7	5.4	6.3	6.2	7.3	7.8	7.1
Prevailing Direction through 1963		S	N	S	S	S	SSW	SSW	NE	ENE	ENE	N	NNW	S
Fastest Mile														
-Direction (!!)	34	W	SE	SW	SW	NW	SW	SW	NW	SE	W	N	SE	SW
-Speed (MPH)	34	49	59	65	56	65	56	57	50	50	43	52	41	65
-Year		1975	1960	1955	1956	1951	1957	1960	1956	1951	1955	1944	1954	MAR 1955
Peak Gust														
-Direction (!!)														
-Speed (mph)														
-Date														

PRECIPITATION (inches)

BIRMINGHAM (MUNICIPAL AIRPORT), ALABAMA

YEAR	JAN	FEB	MAR	APR	MAY	JUNE	JULY	AUG	SEP	OCT	NOV	DEC	ANNUAL
1964	5.37	4.11	9.44	9.90	3.20	4.08	4.34	2.78	3.26	2.95	3.24	5.09	57.76
1965	3.21	6.22	6.10	2.54	1.37	8.17	4.87	3.55	2.60	0.67	2.80	2.06	44.16
1966	4.74	8.67	3.77	8.37	3.30	2.87	4.99	6.48	5.12	3.13	2.28	2.34	56.06
1967	2.84	4.74	1.79	1.35	9.32	4.37	6.60	10.85	2.84	4.23	6.42	11.49	66.84
1968	5.56	1.20	6.17	6.23	3.51	0.67	9.39	1.81	3.42	1.20	4.66	7.38	51.20
1969	7.78	3.17	5.19	5.32	11.10	3.75	2.91	1.76	6.85	2.51	2.66	6.07	59.07
1970	2.47	2.35	11.36	5.56	2.27	3.55	3.37	7.01	1.05	7.04	2.31	3.32	51.66
1971	3.58	9.28	6.65	4.25	2.64	6.57	8.90	3.68	3.35	1.21	1.76	5.92	57.79
1972	9.30	2.15	4.79	2.56	3.82	2.70	3.55	2.01	8.09	3.35	4.47	5.76	52.55
1973	6.85	2.33	9.71	5.33	8.29	3.74	8.36	5.41	2.64	0.96	4.91	7.58	66.11
1974	6.85	4.94	2.43	5.43	5.43	1.42	4.69	8.28	4.94	1.49	4.13	5.97	56.00
1975	7.23	4.96	7.57	3.19	4.15	2.44	7.33	3.33	3.69	3.74	4.15	3.49	55.27
1976	4.12	1.80	14.15	1.99	9.00	2.75	4.92	3.34	4.91	1.59	2.23	4.35	55.15
1977	5.08	3.89	8.70	6.73	3.51	0.96	6.24	0.87	10.43	7.52	4.10	2.01	60.04
1978	4.54	1.31	3.07	2.64	8.51	5.04	5.09	2.09	1.14	0.22	2.71	5.43	41.79
1979	5.94	4.70	5.69	13.75	6.64	1.19	9.98	2.30	10.40	2.05	5.51	1.55	69.70
1980	6.63	2.36	15.80	9.10	7.30	3.01	2.11	2.84	5.26	3.21	3.04	0.81	61.47
1981	1.09	4.87	7.23	2.45	2.81	2.49	3.88	5.30	0.93	3.34	1.67	5.82	41.88
1982	5.19	6.29	2.71	7.86	3.19	5.39	3.53	2.68	0.66	3.73	7.11	9.51	57.85
1983	3.26	6.42	5.06	8.28	9.57	3.81	0.30	0.99	2.83	3.67	9.14	12.63	65.96
1984	3.96	2.79	4.07	8.61	6.07	1.41	5.06	3.86	0.16	3.91	5.42	2.30	47.62
1985	5.22	5.79	1.71	2.86	4.36	5.34	10.07	4.07	1.97	4.12	2.62	2.54	50.67
1986	1.21	1.79	2.45	0.42	3.66	3.87	1.61	5.56	2.52	5.24	9.66	3.08	41.07
1987	5.89	5.82	4.77	1.03	6.03	4.59	2.30	3.96	3.52	1.16	3.17	3.08	45.32
1988	5.55	2.52	3.18	3.18	1.22	0.79	2.95	3.43	8.57	3.41	6.33	2.84	43.97
1989	4.76	4.31	5.70	3.40	3.82	8.00	6.42	0.38	7.38	1.52	4.63	3.39	53.71
1990	7.38	7.43	5.81	2.38	4.12	2.08	3.16	0.59	2.04	2.98	4.02	5.47	47.46
1991	3.19	4.27	5.42	4.87	8.90	7.52	4.00	4.59	3.02	0.07	4.00	3.64	53.49
1992	3.22	3.96	3.36	2.61	1.18	5.34	7.41	7.43	5.70	2.18	7.94	5.27	55.60
1993	6.11	2.35	4.40	2.99	3.93	1.47	1.16	2.72	4.62	3.22	2.22	4.01	39.20
Record Mean	4.94	4.81	5.97	4.70	4.25	3.95	5.27	4.18	3.53	2.74	3.79	5.02	53.15

AVERAGE TEMPERATURE (deg. F)

BIRMINGHAM (MUNICIPAL AIRPORT), ALABAMA

YEAR	JAN	FEB	MAR	APR	MAY	JUNE	JULY	AUG	SEP	OCT	NOV	DEC	ANNUAL
1964	42.8	42.7	53.9	65.3	71.7	78.2	77.7	78.1	76.0	59.6	55.3	48.0	62.5
1965	45.8	44.6	49.8	64.8	71.8	75.0	77.7	78.0	73.7	60.0	54.8	46.0	61.9
1966	37.7	46.2	52.3	62.2	66.9	73.6	81.3	77.0	71.8	58.8	54.1	44.3	60.5
1967	44.0	41.8	58.3	67.2	67.7	76.2	75.7	74.2	68.4	60.7	48.4	48.5	60.9
1968	42.5	38.7	52.8	62.9	68.3	77.9	78.8	79.4	72.1	63.2	50.3	41.5	60.7
1969	42.6	44.5	46.6	62.7	69.0	76.2	81.7	77.8	70.9	63.9	50.1	43.3	60.8
1970	37.9	44.5	52.6	65.6	71.3	75.7	80.6	78.7	77.0	63.3	48.4	47.9	62.0
1971	43.6	44.2	48.5	60.2	65.3	77.9	77.5	77.8	75.0	67.2	50.7	54.8	61.9
1972	47.2	46.9	53.7	63.1	67.2	74.2	76.9	78.8	75.1	61.7	48.9	47.7	61.8
1973	40.7	42.3	58.6	58.1	67.5	75.9	79.4	77.2	77.2	66.6	56.2	45.0	62.1
1974	52.8	47.3	61.2	61.5	71.0	72.7	79.2	78.4	70.1	60.6	52.7	47.3	62.9
1975	49.1	50.1	53.9	60.5	72.4	76.4	78.1	79.1	70.2	63.5	54.1	44.6	62.7
1976	39.1	54.3	58.7	61.5	64.2	74.4	78.3	77.0	71.9	57.4	45.5	41.2	60.3
1977	31.6	44.8	57.3	65.2	72.4	79.8	83.4	82.1	75.7	59.9	55.0	44.1	62.6
1978	33.5	37.4	50.2	62.9	68.2	77.1	81.5	79.8	76.9	60.6	57.9	46.1	61.0
1979	37.7	44.0	55.2	63.4	69.8	75.1	79.9	78.4	71.4	63.9	52.8	45.9	61.5
1980	45.2	42.3	51.4	60.9	70.0	77.6	84.4	83.0	78.4	60.3	52.4	44.0	62.5
1981	39.2	48.2	51.3	67.1	67.8	80.6	82.2	79.2	71.9	61.8	54.6	42.7	62.2
1982	41.9	47.3	58.9	59.1	72.6	75.7	80.7	79.6	73.1	64.2	54.1	51.2	63.2
1983	40.6	44.8	50.8	56.6	67.3	74.1	80.3	81.7	71.7	63.0	51.9	39.8	60.2
1984	38.5	46.8	52.4	59.0	67.5	77.1	78.2	77.5	72.1	71.1	51.4	54.3	62.2
1985	35.5	43.2	56.7	63.7	69.5	76.2	78.1	78.2	72.0	67.3	61.0	40.2	61.8
1986	41.9	49.9	55.5	61.8	71.2	78.6	82.5	77.8	76.9	63.9	57.4	44.0	63.5
1987	42.1	46.9	54.6	59.5	73.8	76.7	80.5	82.0	73.1	56.8	54.5	49.1	62.5
1988	39.7	43.5	54.1	61.2	67.6	77.5	79.8	81.5	74.4	57.7	55.2	45.8	61.5
1989	48.9	45.7	56.4	60.3	67.7	75.5	79.2	79.5	72.5	61.9	52.9	38.0	61.5
1990	49.0	54.5	57.0	60.7	68.9	77.8	79.8	82.3	77.5	63.9	55.7	49.7	64.7
1991	44.8	49.7	55.8	65.7	73.1	76.9	81.4	80.8	75.4	65.1	50.0	49.3	64.0
1992	43.4	50.6	53.8	61.0	67.4	74.7	80.4	75.6	73.4	61.5	51.7	45.8	61.6
1993	47.0	44.9	50.4	58.8	68.7	78.5	83.8	81.2	73.2	61.9	51.7	44.4	62.0
Record Mean	44.8	47.0	54.8	62.7	70.5	77.6	80.1	79.6	75.0	64.2	53.4	46.2	63.0
Max	54.1	56.9	65.7	74.1	81.4	88.2	90.1	89.7	85.4	75.6	64.2	55.6	73.4
Min	35.5	37.0	44.0	51.3	59.5	67.0	70.1	69.5	64.5	52.7	42.6	36.7	52.5

REFERENCE NOTES

BIRMINGHAM (MUNICIPAL AIRPORT), ALABAMA

GENERAL
T - TRACE AMOUNT.
BLANK ENTRIES DENOTE MISSING/UNREPORTED DATA.
# INDICATES A STATION OR INSTRUMENT RELOCATION.

SPECIFIC

PM - INCLUDES LAST DAY OF PREVIOUS MONTH
ASOS - AUTOMATED SURFACE OBSERVING SYSTEM IN OPERATION DURING THESE MONTHS.

(a) - LENGTH OF RECORD IN YEARS, ALTHOUGH INDIVIDUAL MONTHS MAY BE MISSING.
0.* OR * - THE VALUE IS BETWEEN 0.0 AND 0.05
NORMALS - BASED ON THE 1961-1990 RECORD PERIOD.
EXTREMES - DATES ARE THE MOST RECENT OCCURRENCE.
WIND DIR. - NUMERALS SHOW TENS OF DEGRESS CLOCKWISE FROM TRUE NORTH. "00" INDICATES CALM.
RESULTANT DIRECTIONS ARE GIVEN TO WHOLE DEGREES.
BOLD VALUES INDICATE EXTREME VALUES WHICH OCCURRED AFTER THE ASOS SYSTEM WAS COMMISSIONED.

RECORD = PERIOD OF RECORD
RECORD MEAN PRECIPITATION IS THE MEAN OF ALL DAILY PRECIPITATION AMOUNTS DURING THE PERIOD OF RECORD.
RECORD MAX(MIN) TEMPERATURE IS THE MEAN OF ALL DAILY MAX(MIN) TEMPERATURES DURING THE PERIOD OF RECORD.
RECORD MEAN TEMPERATURE IS THE SUM OF THE RECORD MAX AND RECORD MIN DIVIDED BY 2.
AVERAGE TEMPERATURE IS THE SUM OF THE MEAN DAILY MAX AND MIN TEMPERATURE DIVIDED BY 2.

EXCEPTIONS

1. PERCENT OF POSSIBLE SUNSHINE, MEAN SKY COVER, AND DAYS CLEAR-PARTLY CLOUDY-CLOUDY ARE THROUGH 1977.
2. MAXIMUM 24-HOUR PRECIPITATION AND SNOW, AND FASTEST MILE WINDS ARE THROUGH SEPTEMBER 1978.

RECORD MEANS ARE THROUGH THE CURRENT YEAR, BEGINNING IN 1896 FOR TEMPERATURE
1896 FOR PRECIPITATION
1944 FOR SNOWFALL

HEATING DEGREE DAYS Base 65 deg. F — BIRMINGHAM (MUNICIPAL AIRPORT), ALABAMA

SEASON	JULY	AUG	SEP	OCT	NOV	DEC	JAN	FEB	MAR	APR	MAY	JUNE	TOTAL
1964-65	0	0	0	196	305	520	591	571	478	85	2	0	2748
1965-66	0	0	13	171	305	583	840	520	393	149	34	9	3017
1966-67	0	0	3	203	331	635	643	645	248	51	65	2	2826
1967-68	0	0	41	162	492	510	690	755	387	108	30	0	3175
1968-69	0	0	1	148	434	723	687	566	563	95	26	4	3247
1969-70	0	0	4	110	443	663	830	568	377	91	23	0	3109
1970-71	0	0	10	104	493	523	657	578	500	171	74	0	3110
1971-72	0	0	0	28	437	320	548	526	348	138	21	7	2373
1972-73	0	0	9	135	486	534	749	629	217	228	48	0	3035
1973-74	0	0	3	73	285	615	374	491	161	147	9	0	2158
1974-75	0	0	19	159	378	542	493	412	361	190	2	0	2556
1975-76	0	0	49	105	349	626	795	314	213	129	65	0	2645
1976-77	0	0	7	241	580	732	1026	566	252	73	5	0	3482
1977-78	0	0	0	176	292	640	967	768	452	120	42	0	3457
1978-79	0	0	0	160	220	578	839	584	303	83	33	0	2800
1979-80	0	0	0	101	365	588	604	655	417	144	14	0	2888
1980-81	0	0	7	181	372	642	795	464	428	46	51	0	2986
1981-82	0	0	19	138	314	682	711	490	250	199	4	0	2807
1982-83	0	0	16	134	331	449	751	558	437	262	39	0	2977
1983-84	0	0	26	108	388	774	817	519	392	202	68	2	3296
1984-85	0	0	10	27	410	330	907	604	278	123	16	3	2708
1985-86	0	0	14	62	165	761	711	415	305	132	21	0	2586
1986-87	0	1	0	112	239	644	705	500	320	201	0	0	2722
1987-88	0	0	5	248	315	488	777	616	347	134	18	0	2948
1988-89	0	0	0	234	289	589	492	545	289	200	65	0	2703
1989-90	0	0	27	140	363	834	491	299	265	172	32	0	2623
1990-91	0	0	16	138	282	474	620	421	304	46	7	0	2308
1991-92	0	0	12	97	455	492	663	409	344	173	46	0	2691
1992-93	0	0	6	116	398	587	550	559	452	196	20	0	2884
1993-94	0	0	16	153	411	633							

COOLING DEGREE DAYS Base 65 deg. F — BIRMINGHAM (MUNICIPAL AIRPORT), ALABAMA

YEAR	JAN	FEB	MAR	APR	MAY	JUNE	JULY	AUG	SEP	OCT	NOV	DEC	TOTAL
1969	0	0	0	33	156	346	523	402	188	84	2	0	1734
1970	0	0	2	115	227	330	492	432	377	58	0	0	2033
1971	1	0	0	35	90	394	393	403	309	105	10	13	1753
1972	4	6	7	88	93	291	379	434	318	40	8	2	1670
1973	0	0	24	28	132	333	452	385	376	129	28	0	1887
1974	4	3	52	48	204	238	450	418	180	28	15	0	1640
1975	8	0	26	61	241	351	416	447	211	66	29	2	1858
1976	0	8	25	27	48	290	418	376	219	15	1	0	1427
1977	0	5	21	85	241	450	578	537	329	25	0	1	2272
1978	0	0	0	64	151	370	515	463	365	34	12	1	1975
1979	0	1	8	43	188	308	466	424	198	74	7	2	1719
1980	0	4	6	25	176	386	607	563	413	43	2	0	2225
1981	0	1	9	113	145	475	539	448	231	46	9	0	2016
1982	1	0	65	28	247	327	495	459	265	118	12	27	2044
1983	0	0	7	17	115	281	481	528	233	53	2	0	1717
1984	0	0	11	30	151	373	421	395	230	221	6	6	1844
1985	0	1	27	90	163	349	413	417	233	139	51	1	1884
1986	0	0	16	43	222	413	547	406	364	84	18	0	2113
1987	0	0	5	46	280	357	487	532	254	1	7	3	1972
1988	0	0	13	26	105	382	467	516	292	14	1	0	1816
1989	0	14	27	65	155	323	447	459	257	51	3	0	1801
1990	1	14	21	49	160	393	466	543	398	110	9	4	2168
1991	0	0	28	74	266	364	515	496	333	106	9	1C	2201
1992	0	0	2	59	129	298	484	333	265	14	5	0	1589
1993	0	0	5	19	140	410	591	511	271	63	18	0	2028

SNOWFALL (inches) — BIRMINGHAM (MUNICIPAL AIRPORT), ALABAMA

SEASON	JULY	AUG	SEP	OCT	NOV	DEC	JAN	FEB	MAR	APR	MAY	JUNE	TOTAL
1964-65	0.0	0.0	0.0	0.0	0.0	T	T	T	T	0.0	0.0	0.0	T
1965-66	0.0	0.0	0.0	0.0	0.0	0.0	1.2	T	T	0.0	0.0	0.0	1.2
1966-67	0.0	0.0	0.0	0.0	T	T	T	0.8	T	0.0	0.0	0.0	0.8
1967-68	0.0	0.0	0.0	0.0	T	T	1.0	0.7	T	0.0	0.0	0.0	1.7
1968-69	0.0	0.0	0.0	0.0	T	T	T	T	T	0.0	0.0	0.0	T
1969-70	0.0	0.0	0.0	0.0	T	T	1.7	0.1	T	0.0	0.0	0.0	1.8
1970-71	0.0	0.0	0.0	0.0	T	0.0	T	0.8	T	T	0.0	0.0	0.8
1971-72	0.0	0.0	0.0	0.0	T	0.0	T	T	T	0.0	0.0	0.0	T
1972-73	0.0	0.0	0.0	0.0	0.0	0.0	T	0.0	0.0	0.0	0.0	0.0	T
1973-74	0.0	0.0	0.0	0.0	0.0	T	0.0	T	0.0	0.0	0.0	0.0	T
1974-75	0.0	0.0	0.0	0.0	T	0.4	T	T	T	0.0	0.0	0.0	0.4
1975-76	0.0	0.0	0.0	0.0	T	T	T	0.0	0.0	0.0	0.0	0.0	T
1976-77	0.0	0.0	0.0	0.0	T	T	1.4	T	0.0	0.0	0.0	0.0	1.4
1977-78	0.0	0.0	0.0	0.0	0.0	T	1.9	T	T	0.0	0.0	0.0	1.9
1978-79	0.0	0.0	0.0	0.0	0.0	0.0	T	T	0.0	0.0	0.0	0.0	T
1979-80	0.0	0.0	0.0	0.0	0.0	0.0	T	T	0.3	0.0	0.0	0.0	0.3
1980-81	0.0	0.0	0.0	0.0	T	T	0.0	T	0.0	0.0	0.0	0.0	T
1981-82	0.0	0.0	0.0	0.0	0.0	T	6.6	0.0	T	0.0	0.0	0.0	6.6
1982-83	0.0	0.0	0.0	0.0	0.0	T	1.0	T	1.5	0.0	0.0	0.0	2.5
1983-84	0.0	0.0	0.0	0.0	0.0	T	T	T	2.0	0.0	0.0	0.0	2.0
1984-85	0.0	0.0	0.0	0.0	0.0	T	T	0.3	0.0	0.0	0.0	0.0	0.3
1985-86	0.0	0.0	0.0	0.0	0.0	T	T	T	0.0	0.0	0.0	0.0	T
1986-87	0.0	0.0	0.0	0.0	0.0	T	2.6	0.0	T	5.0	0.0	0.0	7.6
1987-88	0.0	0.0	0.0	0.0	0.0	0.0	1.0	T	0.0	0.0	0.0	0.0	1.0
1988-89	0.0	0.0	0.0	0.0	0.0	T	0.0	T	T	T	0.0	0.0	T
1989-90	0.0	0.0	0.0	0.0	T	0.4	0.0	T	0.0	0.0	T	T	0.4
1990-91	T	0.0	0.0	0.0	0.0	T	T	T	T	T	0.0	T	T
1991-92	0.0	0.0	0.0	0.0	T	0.0	4.4	0.0	T	0.0	T	T	4.4
1992-93	0.0	0.0	T	T	0.0	0.0	0.0	T	13.0	0.0	T	0.0	13.0
1993-94	0.0	0.0	0.0	T	0.0	T							
Record Mean	T	0.0	T	T	T	0.3	0.7	0.2	0.4	0.1	T	T	1.6

MOBILE, ALABAMA

Mobile is located at the head of Mobile Bay and approximately 30 miles from the Gulf of Mexico. Its weather is influenced to a considerable extent by the Gulf.

The summers are consistently warm, but temperatures are seldom as high as they are at inland stations. Normally, in summer, the day begins in the low 70s and the temperature rises rapidly before noon to the high 80s or low 90s, when it is checked by the onset of the sea breeze. On the rare occasions when northerly winds prevail throughout the day, temperatures may reach the high 90s or rise slightly above 100 degrees.

Winter weather is usually mild except for occasional invasions of cold air that last about three days. January is the coldest month in the year. Unusual winters may produce readings that require extensive protective measures as some citrus fruit is grown in the area and outdoor nurseries are numerous.

Based on the 1951–1980 period, the average first occurrence of 32 degrees Fahrenheit in the fall is November 26 and the average last occurrence in the spring is February 27.

The yearly rainfall is among the highest in the United States. It is fairly evenly distributed throughout the year with a slight maximum at the height of the summer thunderstorm season and a slight minimum during the late fall. Rainfall is usually of the shower type and long periods of continuous rain are rare.

Frontal thunderstorms may occur in any month of the year. There may be a thunderstorm every other day in July and August. The summer storms are usually not too violent and seldom produce hail.

The area is subject to hurricanes from the West Indies, the western Caribbean, and the Gulf of Mexico.

NORMALS, MEANS, AND EXTREMES

MOBILE, ALABAMA

LATITUDE: 30°41'N LONGITUDE: 88°15' W ELEVATION: FT. GRND 211 BARO 226 TIME ZONE: CENTRAL WBAN: 13894

	(a)	JAN	FEB	MAR	APR	MAY	JUNE	JULY	AUG	SEP	OCT	NOV	DEC	YEAR
TEMPERATURE °F:														
Normals														
-Daily Maximum		59.7	63.6	70.9	78.5	84.6	90.0	91.3	90.5	86.9	79.5	70.3	62.9	77.4
-Daily Minimum		40.0	42.7	50.1	57.1	64.4	70.7	73.2	72.9	68.7	57.3	49.1	43.1	57.4
-Monthly		49.9	53.2	60.5	67.8	74.5	80.4	82.3	81.8	77.9	68.4	59.8	53.0	67.5
Extremes														
-Record Highest	52	84	82	90	94	100	102	104	102	99	93	87	81	104
-Year		1949	1989	1946	1987	1953	1952	1952	1968	1990	1963	1971	1974	JUL 1952
-Record Lowest	52	3	11	21	32	43	49	60	59	42	30	22	8	3
-Year		1985	1951	1993	1987	1960	1984	1947	1956	1967	1993	1950	1983	JAN 1985
NORMAL DEGREE DAYS:														
Heating (base 65°F)		492	344	177	48	0	0	0	0	0	52	196	393	1702
Cooling (base 65°F)		24	14	38	132	295	462	536	521	387	157	40	21	2627
% OF POSSIBLE SUNSHINE														
MEAN SKY COVER (tenths)														
Sunrise - Sunset	45	6.6	6.2	6.1	5.7	5.7	5.8	6.5	6.0	5.7	4.4	5.3	6.3	5.9
MEAN NUMBER OF DAYS:														
Sunrise to Sunset														
-Clear	45	7.7	7.7	8.8	9.3	8.7	7.1	4.1	6.1	8.8	14.6	11.0	8.9	102.8
-Partly Cloudy	45	6.3	6.7	7.8	8.7	11.2	13.8	15.1	14.8	10.1	7.6	7.1	6.3	115.5
-Cloudy	45	17.0	13.9	14.4	12.0	11.1	9.1	11.8	10.1	11.1	8.9	11.8	15.8	146.9
Precipitation														
.01 inches or more	52	10.8	9.7	10.4	7.4	8.5	11.3	16.2	14.0	10.2	5.7	7.9	10.2	122.3
Snow, Ice pellets, hail														
1.0 inches or more	52	0.*	0.1	0.*	0.0	0.0	0.0	0.0	0.0	0.0	0.0	0.0	0.*	0.2
Thunderstorms	52	2.0	2.3	4.9	4.9	7.2	11.8	18.0	14.4	7.5	2.1	2.3	2.2	79.7
Heavy Fog Visibility														
1/4 mile or less	52	6.1	4.5	5.3	4.6	2.7	0.9	1.0	1.3	1.9	2.7	4.3	4.9	40.4
Temperature °F														
-Maximum														
90° and above	31	0.0	0.0	0.0	0.3	3.7	17.0	22.4	20.6	10.4	1.0	0.0	0.0	75.5
32° and below	31	0.2	0.0	0.0	0.0	0.0	0.0	0.0	0.0	0.0	0.0	0.0	0.1	0.4
-Minimum														
32° and below	31	8.1	5.4	1.2	0.*	0.0	0.0	0.0	0.0	0.0	0.*	1.4	5.6	21.7
0° and below	31	0.0	0.0	0.0	0.0	0.0	0.0	0.0	0.0	0.0	0.0	0.0	0.0	0.0
AVG. STATION PRESS. (mb)	21	1012.8	1011.6	1009.3	1008.7	1007.5	1008.0	1009.3	1008.9	1008.5	1010.5	1011.6	1013.0	1010.0
RELATIVE HUMIDITY (%)														
Hour 00	31	79	78	81	83	85	85	87	88	86	83	82	80	83
Hour 06 (Local Time)	31	82	82	85	87	88	88	90	91	89	86	86	84	87
Hour 12	31	61	56	55	52	54	55	60	61	59	53	57	61	57
Hour 18	31	69	63	63	62	63	67	71	74	72	67	71	72	68
PRECIPITATION (inches):														
Water Equivalent														
-Normal		4.76	5.46	6.41	4.48	5.74	5.04	6.85	6.96	5.91	2.94	4.10	5.31	63.96
-Maximum Monthly	52	16.07	11.89	15.58	17.69	15.08	13.07	19.29	15.19	14.04	13.20	13.65	11.38	19.29
-Year		1991	1983	1946	1955	1980	1961	1949	1984	1988	1985	1948	1953	JUL 1949
-Minimum Monthly	52	0.98	1.31	0.59	0.48	0.45	1.19	1.72	1.46	0.58	T	0.25	1.29	T
-Year		1968	1948	1967	1954	1962	1966	1983	1990	1963	1978	1960	1980	OCT 1978
-Maximum in 24 hrs	52	8.34	5.37	10.57	13.36	8.00	7.38	5.34	6.62	8.55	5.65	7.02	5.50	13.36
-Year		1965	1981	1990	1955	1981	1961	1975	1969	1979	1985	1975	1968	APR 1955
Snow, Ice pellets, hail														
-Maximum Monthly	52	3.5	3.6	2.7	T	T	0.0	T	0.0	0.0	0.0	T	3.0	3.6
-Year		1955	1973	1993	1988	1991		1992				1966	1963	FEB 1973
-Maximum in 24 hrs	52	3.5	3.6	2.7	T	T	0.0	T	0.0	0.0	0.0	T	3.0	3.6
-Year		1955	1973	1993	1988	1991		1992				1966	1963	FEB 1973
WIND:														
Mean Speed (mph)	45	10.3	10.6	10.8	10.2	8.9	7.7	7.0	6.8	7.9	8.2	9.3	10.0	9.0
Prevailing Direction through 1963		N	N	N	S	S	S	S	NE	NE	N	N	N	N
Fastest Obs. 1 Min.														
-Direction (!!)	35	18	23	10	01	32	22	21	14	09	36	36	32	09
-Speed (MPH)	35	44	46	40	44	51	44	60	63	63	46	37	38	63
-Year		1959	1960	1985	1964	1963	1989	1992	1969	1979	1964	1959	1959	SEP 1979
Peak Gust														
-Direction (!!)	10	W	S	SW	SE	SW	SW	SW	E	SE	S	NW	NW	SW
-Speed (mph)	10	45	61	55	46	62	60	64	53	60	52	48	43	64
-Date		1993	1987	1991	1993	1985	1989	1992	1991	1985	1985	1988	1990	JUL 1992

PRECIPITATION (inches)

MOBILE, ALABAMA

YEAR	JAN	FEB	MAR	APR	MAY	JUNE	JULY	AUG	SEP	OCT	NOV	DEC	ANNUAL
1964	7.36	2.73	4.23	13.45	4.32	4.27	8.83	6.20	2.19	2.42	3.73	4.12	63.85
1965	9.35	4.94	4.97	0.60	4.33	3.70	8.13	4.72	10.45	1.59	0.73	3.97	57.48
1966	5.52	9.01	3.21	2.37	4.66	1.19	5.20	6.48	4.32	4.44	1.35	4.60	52.35
1967	5.46	6.13	0.59	2.26	5.05	2.88	7.80	8.86	7.76	6.69	0.36	7.50	61.34
1968	0.98	2.88	1.30	2.24	3.17	3.71	3.08	4.59	6.13	1.13	4.05	10.70	43.96
1969	2.79	3.40	8.15	4.53	7.95	1.33	14.14	12.05	1.95	0.67	0.44	5.58	62.98
1970	3.85	5.32	8.60	1.67	8.84	7.68	9.19	9.20	2.56	5.71	1.54	5.77	69.93
1971	2.15	7.15	6.49	0.99	3.16	2.88	7.75	10.46	7.30	0.03	1.23	5.58	55.17
1972	5.94	4.46	5.87	1.81	7.72	3.65	2.16	2.35	3.28	1.26	5.67	5.59	49.76
1973	1.96	3.40	11.63	9.91	2.97	5.33	6.24	5.46	12.68	2.15	4.52	4.57	70.82
1974	3.89	6.47	6.16	5.91	2.31	3.48	6.60	7.03	10.60	0.88	3.91	4.31	61.55
1975	3.43	3.75	7.45	9.05	7.12	3.76	11.82	8.50	7.37	6.72	12.63	4,98	86.58
1976	1.80	2.36	9.60	1.69	11.11	4.71	4.43	4.77	3.51	5.67	4.64	4.21	58.50
1977	5.54	1.86	6.06	2.73	5.30	1.26	7.77	5.42	9.61	4.57	9.51	4.94	64.57
1978	10.40	3.88	4.08	7.03	9.74	6.13	7.74	7.34	3.04	T	5.05	4.36	68.79
1979	5.14	9.14	8.37	4.05	7.02	3.70	10.80	6.10	11.73	2.80	6.46	3.94	79.25
1980	4.95	1.58	13.46	15.43	15.08	2.57	6.54	6.42	5.94	2.90	1.96	1.29	78.12
1981	1.23	8.75	3.00	0.96	12.51	6.50	6.53	5.06	3.97	0.94	0.85	6.82	57.12
1982	3.56	7.42	6.81	4.48	2.84	11.00	13.14	7.00	4.68	1.61	3.66	8.24	74.44
1983	5.82	11.89	6.89	12.53	1.53	8.09	1.72	11.57	5.97	3.81	5.30	8.34	83.46
1984	6.13	4.79	4.75	3.53	4.28	2.07	2.36	15.19	0.74	6.19	1.67	2.12	53.82
1985	5.06	6.39	5.49	1.22	5.77	3.94	8.31	4.32	10.32	13.20	1.61	4.34	69.97
1986	2.67	4.17	4.53	2.16	4.18	7.53	7.13	5.60	4.41	4.83	8.45	3.68	59.34
1987	5.81	8.64	6.18	0.83	10.69	7.68	4.18	10.33	3.62	0.02	5.54	3.60	67.12
1988	4.64	6.26	7.80	4.19	0.58	2.34	6.04	10.43	14.04	1.83	2.30	1.80	62.25
1989	2.13	1.47	5.57	3.55	6.47	9.82	7.16	3.82	4.55	0.90	11.33	7.23	64.00
1990	7.35	8.13	12.24	4.51	6.47	2.68	2.28	1.46	2.65	1.23	1.77	5.20	55.97
1991	16.07	3.35	4.83	10.43	15.03	7.04	8.15	5.17	1.87	0.86	5.78	3.09	81.67
1992	9.89	9.94	3.61	1.90	1.58	5.24	7.77	8.27	3.26	1.03	12.70	5.27	70.46
1993	8.03	4.48	10.45	4.80	5.24	3.01	5.64	3.52	3.35	5.32	2.87	3.69	60.40
Record Mean	4.87	5.15	6.59	5.04	4.84	5.53	7.42	6.66	5.54	3.20	3.85	5.12	63.82

AVERAGE TEMPERATURE (deg. F)

MOBILE, ALABAMA

YEAR	JAN	FEB	MAR	APR	MAY	JUNE	JULY	AUG	SEP	OCT	NOV	DEC	ANNUAL
1964	49.2	48.1	59.4	69.6	74.9	80.4	80.5	81.5	78.2	64.3	61.1	54.2	66.8
1965	52.5	53.4	58.2	71.4	75.7	79.4	82.4	81.2	79.1	68.7	63.9	53.7	68.3
1966	47.2	52.8	58.8	68.4	75.1	79.1	83.8	81.2	77.9	68.0	60.7	53.2	67.2
1967	53.0	52.2	64.5	74.6	74.6	82.5	81.5	79.8	74.2	66.7	59.5	57.9	68.4
1968	50.3	46.7	58.1	70.3	76.0	83.2	82.7	83.1	78.1	70.1	56.3	49.5	67.0
1969	51.5	53.7	53.8	68.9	74.5	82.4	83.5	80.6	77.5	71.2	58.0	53.7	67.4
1970	45.0	51.4	59.2	71.9	75.3	80.2	83.0	83.0	81.7	70.5	55.9	57.4	67.9
1971	53.7	54.3	59.9	67.9	73.0	82.4	82.3	82.1	79.5	72.9	59.2	63.5	69.2
1972	58.4	55.0	61.8	69.4	74.7	80.7	81.4	83.4	81.6	71.0	56.8	55.5	69.2
1973	50.5	51.7	64.6	65.6	74.6	81.6	84.1	81.4	80.2	73.6	65.3	52.9	68.9
1974	64.0	55.2	64.3	66.1	75.5	77.8	82.2	81.4	75.5	65.5	59.2	55.1	68.5
1975	56.6	59.8	60.7	66.2	76.5	80.7	81.8	81.7	75.3	70.3	60.5	52.1	68.5
1976	49.5	59.4	64.0	69.9	72.7	79.8	83.4	81.0	75.5	61.4	50.6	48.0	66.3
1977	40.9	52.2	62.6	68.2	75.6	82.9	83.5	83.4	80.9	65.2	60.9	50.8	67.3
1978	41.2	45.1	56.7	68.5	75.4	81.2	82.8	83.2	81.6	69.8	65.1	54.4	67.1
1979	45.1	50.7	60.8	69.3	73.3	79.7	81.3	81.1	76.8	68.1	57.2	51.3	66.2
1980	56.2	49.7	61.6	65.9	74.6	81.2	84.6	83.2	81.8	66.3	57.8	51.6	67.9
1981	46.0	53.4	59.5	71.0	71.6	82.6	84.0	82.7	76.8	69.4	63.0	49.9	67.5
1982	49.7	53.3	63.5	67.1	74.4	80.7	81.0	81.0	76.0	68.5	60.4	56.9	67.7
1983	47.1	51.1	55.0	61.8	72.1	76.4	81.8	81.4	73.6	67.4	57.7	47.7	64.4
1984	46.1	52.4	58.6	65.7	72.5	78.1	79.9	78.8	75.6	72.7	56.3	60.4	66.4
1985	43.5	50.7	64.5	67.7	73.7	79.9	79.7	81.0	76.0	71.4	66.1	48.8	66.9
1986	49.7	56.4	59.7	66.1	74.4	81.0	83.3	80.5	79.5	68.5	64.3	51.1	67.9
1987	48.8	53.6	59.2	64.6	75.7	78.9	81.8	82.2	77.2	62.5	59.2	56.5	66.7
1988	46.8	50.6	58.6	67.3	72.8	79.5	81.8	81.3	78.3	65.3	62.7	53.8	66.6
1989	57.1	54.0	61.7	65.9	74.1	79.0	81.0	81.6	76.7	66.1	59.1	44.4	66.7
1990	54.6	59.0	61.7	65.0	73.4	81.1	81.7	83.1	78.6	68.0	60.9	56.7	68.7
1991	52.4	55.9	61.8	69.3	76.0	79.7	81.9	81.3	77.1	69.4	54.1	54.5	67.8
1992	49.4	57.0	60.3	65.4	72.2	79.3	82.4	79.4	77.2	67.4	56.4	55.6	66.8
1993	55.1	52.7	57.0	62.1	71.9	79.9	82.6	82.8	78.3	68.1	56.8	49.8	66.4
Record Mean	51.5	54.2	60.1	67.1	74.2	80.3	81.8	81.5	78.0	68.8	59.0	53.0	67.5
Max	60.4	63.3	69.2	76.2	83.2	88.9	90.1	89.8	86.4	78.5	68.7	61.9	76.4
Min	42.5	45.1	51.0	57.9	65.1	71.6	73.5	73.2	69.5	59.0	49.2	44.0	58.5

REFERENCE NOTES

MOBILE, ALABAMA

GENERAL
T - TRACE AMOUNT.
BLANK ENTRIES DENOTE MISSING/UNREPORTED DATA.
# INDICATES A STATION OR INSTRUMENT RELOCATION.

SPECIFIC

PM - INCLUDES LAST DAY OF PREVIOUS MONTH
ASOS - AUTOMATED SURFACE OBSERVING SYSTEM IN OPERATION DURING THESE MONTHS.

(a) - LENGTH OF RECORD IN YEARS, ALTHOUGH INDIVIDUAL MONTHS MAY BE MISSING.
0.* OR * - THE VALUE IS BETWEEN 0.0 AND 0.05
NORMALS - BASED ON THE 1961-1990 RECORD PERIOD.
EXTREMES - DATES ARE THE MOST RECENT OCCURRENCE.
WIND DIR. - NUMERALS SHOW TENS OF DEGRESS CLOCKWISE FROM TRUE NORTH. "00" INDICATES CALM.
RESULTANT DIRECTIONS ARE GIVEN TO WHOLE DEGREES.
BOLD VALUES INDICATE EXTREME VALUES WHICH OCCURRED AFTER THE ASOS SYSTEM WAS COMMISSIONED.

RECORD = PERIOD OF RECORD
RECORD MEAN PRECIPITATION IS THE MEAN OF ALL DAILY PRECIPITATION AMOUNTS DURING THE PERIOD OF RECORD.
RECORD MAX(MIN) TEMPERATURE IS THE MEAN OF ALL DAILY MAX(MIN) TEMPERATURES DURING THE PERIOD OF RECORD.
RECORD MEAN TEMPERATURE IS THE SUM OF THE RECORD MAX AND RECORD MIN DIVIDED BY 2.
AVERAGE TEMPERATURE IS THE SUM OF THE MEAN DAILY MAX AND MIN TEMPERATURE DIVIDED BY 2.

EXCEPTIONS

RECORD MEANS ARE THROUGH THE CURRENT YEAR, BEGINNING IN 1871 FOR TEMPERATURE
1871 FOR PRECIPITATION
1942 FOR SNOWFALL

HEATING DEGREE DAYS Base 65 deg. F — MOBILE, ALABAMA

SEASON	JULY	AUG	SEP	OCT	NOV	DEC	JAN	FEB	MAR	APR	MAY	JUNE	TOTAL
1964-65	0	0	0	78	167	347	387	342	240	4	0	0	1565
1965-66	0	0	0	43	100	345	554	333	208	27	1	0	1611
1966-67	0	0	0	32	173	374	370	363	100	0	3	0	1415
1967-68	0	0	23	46	202	273	448	525	251	12	0	0	1780
1968-69	0	0	0	50	284	474	420	320	342	8	0	0	1898
1969-70	0	0	0	20	220	345	618	375	190	14	10	0	1792
1970-71	0	0	0	7	273	265	361	308	190	57	6	0	1467
1971-72	0	0	0	8	204	136	244	295	131	35	0	0	1053
1972-73	0	0	0	33	284	308	442	368	86	75	0	0	1596
1973-74	0	0	0	18	91	377	108	288	106	49	0	0	1037
1974-75	0	0	0	58	215	336	276	185	183	70	0	0	1323
1975-76	0	0	9	11	211	402	475	174	100	8	0	0	1390
1976-77	0	0	0	149	430	520	738	355	141	28	0	0	2361
1977-78	0	0	0	73	149	439	731	551	268	16	0	0	2227
1978-79	0	0	0	20	53	355	613	401	152	8	4	0	1606
1979-80	0	0	0	43	246	424	267	454	159	52	0	0	1645
1980-81	0	0	0	63	235	420	581	323	180	9	4	0	1815
1981-82	0	0	5	42	113	463	485	323	161	48	0	0	1640
1982-83	0	0	5	63	185	296	545	383	306	119	4	0	1906
1983-84	0	0	7	60	243	529	582	363	218	69	10	0	2081
1984-85	0	0	2	17	270	172	665	397	84	50	1	0	1658
1985-86	0	0	1	22	69	503	469	251	188	40	0	0	1543
1986-87	0	0	0	43	105	433	500	311	193	106	0	0	1691
1987-88	0	0	0	108	194	283	565	421	214	33	0	0	1818
1988-89	0	0	0	53	122	363	254	335	170	81	2	0	1380
1989-90	0	0	6	71	204	630	326	186	128	71	0	0	1622
1990-91	0	0	2	58	145	287	382	258	156	13	0	0	1301
1991-92	0	0	3	32	344	342	477	236	165	77	16	0	1692
1992-93	0	0	0	18	276	297	307	340	260	110	3	0	1611
1993-94	0	0	0	64	278	464							

COOLING DEGREE DAYS Base 65 deg. F — MOBILE, ALABAMA

YEAR	JAN	FEB	MAR	APR	MAY	JUNE	JULY	AUG	SEP	OCT	NOV	DEC	TOTAL
1969	5	10	4	134	303	527	582	490	380	220	17	4	2676
1970	6	2	16	229	335	467	564	567	505	184	6	36	2917
1971	18	13	37	151	260	531	541	534	441	261	37	94	2918
1972	47	15	40	173	309	478	513	575	505	224	46	20	2945
1973	0	1	80	98	303	508	598	518	462	293	110	10	2981
1974	85	19	91	88	332	392	539	517	323	81	45	36	2548
1975	21	44	57	115	363	475	529	524	325	183	85	11	2732
1976	0	17	74	160	245	454	578	504	321	48	4	0	2405
1977	0	4	74	132	333	543	579	576	482	85	31	7	2846
1978	0	0	17	127	329	496	560	573	507	177	64	34	2884
1979	0	6	28	144	267	448	512	509	361	146	16	5	2442
1980	2	17	61	89	305	495	618	571	512	110	25	9	2814
1981	0	4	15	195	217	538	595	557	366	185	60	4	2736
1982	17	2	119	118	296	475	502	503	342	177	54	53	2658
1983	0	0	4	27	229	351	532	514	271	140	29	2	2099
1984	0	3	24	96	249	401	469	435	327	261	16	34	2315
1985	4	2	77	133	275	452	461	504	339	227	108	7	2589
1986	0	15	31	79	295	486	573	489	444	158	89	8	2667
1987	4	0	21	99	341	422	527	544	373	41	27	28	2427
1988	7	10	21	108	251	442	529	513	404	67	61	20	2433
1989	16	33	74	116	289	431	498	523	366	114	31	0	2491
1990	7	23	34	80	267	493	525	569	417	155	29	36	2635
1991	1	6	66	149	348	448	528	513	371	176	23	22	2651
1992	0	9	31	97	249	437	548	454	373	102	20	13	2333
1993	5	2	21	33	224	455	554	559	408	165	37	0	2463

SNOWFALL (inches) — MOBILE, ALABAMA

SEASON	JULY	AUG	SEP	OCT	NOV	DEC	JAN	FEB	MAR	APR	MAY	JUNE	TOTAL
1970-71	0.0	0.0	0.0	0.0	0.0	0.0	0.0	0.0	T	0.0	0.0	0.0	T
1971-72	0.0	0.0	0.0	0.0	0.0	0.0	0.0	0.0	0.0	0.0	0.0	0.0	0.0
1972-73	0.0	0.0	0.0	0.0	0.0	0.0	T	3.6	0.0	0.0	0.0	0.0	3.6
1973-74	0.0	0.0	0.0	0.0	0.0	T	0.0	0.0	0.0	0.0	0.0	0.0	T
1974-75	0.0	0.0	0.0	0.0	0.0	0.0	0.0	0.0	0.0	0.0	0.0	0.0	0.0
1975-76	0.0	0.0	0.0	0.0	0.0	0.0	0.0	0.0	0.0	0.0	0.0	0.0	0.0
1976-77	0.0	0.0	0.0	0.0	0.0	T	1.9	0.0	0.0	0.0	0.0	0.0	1.9
1977-78	0.0	0.0	0.0	0.0	0.0	0.0	0.4	T	0.0	0.0	0.0	0.0	0.4
1978-79	0.0	0.0	0.0	0.0	0.0	0.0	T	0.0	0.0	0.0	0.0	0.0	T
1979-80	0.0	0.0	0.0	0.0	0.0	0.0	0.0	T	T	0.0	0.0	0.0	T
1980-81	0.0	0.0	0.0	0.0	0.0	0.0	T	T	0.0	0.0	0.0	0.0	T
1981-82	0.0	0.0	0.0	0.0	0.0	0.0	T	0.0	0.0	0.0	0.0	0.0	T
1982-83	0.0	0.0	0.0	0.0	0.0	0.0	0.0	0.0	0.0	0.0	0.0	0.0	0.0
1983-84	0.0	0.0	0.0	0.0	0.0	T	0.0	T	0.0	0.0	0.0	0.0	T
1984-85	0.0	0.0	0.0	0.0	0.0	0.0	T	T	0.0	0.0	0.0	0.0	T
1985-86	0.0	0.0	0.0	0.0	0.0	0.0	0.0	0.0	0.0	0.0	0.0	0.0	0.0
1986-87	0.0	0.0	0.0	0.0	0.0	0.0	T	0.0	0.0	T	0.0	0.0	T
1987-88	0.0	0.0	0.0	0.0	0.0	0.0	0.0	1.7	0.0	T	0.0	0.0	1.7
1988-89	0.0	0.0	0.0	0.0	0.0	0.0	0.0	0.0	T	0.0	0.0	0.0	T
1989-90	T	0.0	0.0	0.0	0.0	T	0.0	0.0	0.0	0.0	0.0	0.0	T
1990-91	0.0	0.0	0.0	0.0	0.0	0.0	0.0	0.0	0.0	0.0	T	0.0	T
1991-92	0.0	0.0	0.0	0.0	0.0	0.0	0.0	0.0	0.0	0.0	0.0	0.0	0.0
1992-93	T	0.0	0.0	0.0	0.0	0.0	0.0	0.0	2.7	0.0	0.0	0.0	2.7
1993-94	0.0	0.0	0.0	0.0	0.0	T							
Record Mean	T	0.0	0.0	0.0	T	0.1	0.1	0.2	0.1	T	T	0.0	0.4

ANCHORAGE, ALASKA

Anchorage is in a broad valley with adjacent narrow bodies of water. Cook Inlet, including Knik Arm and Turnagain Arm, lies approximately 2 miles to the west, north, and south. The terrain rises gradually to the east for about 10 miles, with marshes interspersed with glacial moraines, shallow depressions, small streams, and knolls. Beyond this area, the Chugach Mountains rise abruptly into a range oriented north–northeast to south–southwest, with average elevation 4,000 to 5,000 feet and some peaks to 8,000 or 10,000 feet. The Chugach Range acts as a barrier to the influx of warm, moist air from the Gulf of Alaska, so the average annual precipitation is only 10 to 15 percent of that at stations located on the Gulf of Alaska side of the Chugach Range. The Alaska Mountain Range lies in a long arc from southwest, through northwest, to northeast, approximately 100 miles distant from Anchorage. During the winter, this range is an effective barrier to the influx of very cold air from the north side of the range.

The four seasons are well marked in Anchorage. In the summer, high temperatures average about 60 degrees and low temperatures nearly 50 degrees. Temperatures in the 70s are considered very warm. On summer days, temperatures on the east side of Anchorage may be about 10 degrees warmer than the official airport readings. Rain increases after mid–June. About two–thirds of the days in July and August are cloudy and one–third have rain.

Autumn is brief, beginning in early September and ending in mid–October. Temperatures begin to fall in September with snow becoming more frequent in October.

Winter can be considered as mid–October to early April when streams and lakes are frozen. Temperatures steadily decrease into January when the highs are near 20 degrees and lows near 5 degrees. The coldest weather is normally in January, when very cold days have high temperatures below zero. Cold days generally have clear skies and calm wind. Mild days do occur with temperatures in the 30s. On cold winter nights, temperatures on the east side of Anchorage may be 10–20 degrees lower than airport readings on the west side. Most winter precipitation is snow, but rain may occur on a few days.

Annual snowfall varies from about 70 inches on the west side to about 90 inches on the east side of Anchorage at low elevations. Along the Chugach Mountains, snow totals increase steadily with increasing elevations and winter arrives a month earlier and stays a month longer at the 1,000 to 2,000 foot level. Most snow is light or dry, i.e., low in water content. Freezing rain is extremely rare. Fog, made of water droplets, occurs on about fifteen days. In general, ice–fog does not occur in Anchorage.

Spring begins in late April and May when days are warm and sunny, nights are cool, and precipitation is exceedingly small. Foliage turns green by late May.

The wind in Anchorage is generally light. However, on several days each winter, strong northerly winds, up to 90 mph, affect the entire Anchorage area. Also during the winter there are about eight occurrences of very strong southeast winds which affect only the east side of Anchorage and the slopes of the Chugach Mountains. These winds occur more often above the 800 feet elevation in the Chugach where winds are funneled thru creek canyons. On the east side of Anchorage, damaging winds of over 100 mph have been recorded.

The average occurrence of the first snow is mid–October, but has occurred as early as mid–September. The average date of the last snow is mid–April, but has occurred as late as early May. The growing season is about 125 days. Average occurrence of the last temperature of 32 degrees in spring is mid–May and the first in fall is mid–September. Daylight varies from about 19 hours in late June to 6 hours in late December with 12 hours of daylight occurring in late September and late March.

NORMALS, MEANS, AND EXTREMES

ANCHORAGE, ALASKA

LATITUDE: 61°13'N LONGITUDE: 149°53' W ELEVATION: FT. GRND 114 BARO 157 TIME ZONE: YUKON WBAN: 26451

	(a)	JAN	FEB	MAR	APR	MAY	JUNE	JULY	AUG	SEP	OCT	NOV	DEC	YEAR
TEMPERATURE °F:														
Normals														
-Daily Maximum		21.4	25.8	33.1	42.8	54.4	61.6	65.2	63.0	55.2	40.5	27.2	22.5	42.7
-Daily Minimum		8.4	11.5	18.1	28.6	38.8	47.2	51.7	49.5	41.6	28.7	15.1	10.0	29.1
-Monthly		14.9	18.7	25.7	35.8	46.6	54.4	58.4	56.3	48.4	34.6	21.2	16.3	35.9
Extremes														
-Record Highest	40	50	48	51	65	77	85	82	82	73	61	53	48	85
-Year		1961	1991	1984	1976	1969	1969	1989	1978	1957	1993	1979	1992	JUN 1969
-Record Lowest	40	-34	-26	-24	-4	17	33	38	31	19	-5	-21	-30	-34
-Year		1975	1956	1971	1985	1964	1961	1964	1984	1992	1956	1956	1964	JAN 1975
NORMAL DEGREE DAYS:														
Heating (base 65°F)		1553	1296	1218	876	570	318	205	270	498	942	1314	1510	10570
Cooling (base 65°F)		0	0	0	0	0	0	0	0	0	0	0	0	0
% OF POSSIBLE SUNSHINE	38	36	43	51	51	52	47	44	39	40	37	33	28	42
MEAN SKY COVER (tenths)														
Sunrise - Sunset	40	7.0	7.1	6.8	7.1	7.6	7.9	7.9	7.9	7.8	7.6	7.4	7.5	7.5
MEAN NUMBER OF DAYS:														
Sunrise to Sunset														
-Clear	40	7.1	6.5	7.6	5.7	4.0	2.7	3.5	3.3	3.8	5.2	5.4	5.9	60.7
-Partly Cloudy	40	4.7	3.6	5.4	6.2	6.7	6.9	5.7	6.0	5.4	4.7	4.8	4.0	64.1
-Cloudy	40	19.3	18.1	18.0	18.1	20.3	20.4	21.8	21.7	20.9	21.1	19.8	21.1	240.5
Precipitation														
.01 inches or more	29	7.9	7.9	7.4	6.1	7.2	8.1	11.6	13.6	14.3	12.2	9.6	11.3	117.4
Snow,Ice pellets,hail														
1.0 inches or more	29	2.8	3.1	2.6	1.5	0.0	0.0	0.0	0.0	0.2	2.3	3.4	4.7	20.6
Thunderstorms	40	0.0	0.0	0.0	0.0	0.1	0.1	0.4	0.3	0.1	0.0	0.0	0.0	1.0
Heavy Fog Visibility														
1/4 mile or less	40	6.0	4.3	1.4	0.6	0.3	0.1	0.2	0.9	1.4	2.0	3.8	5.2	26.1
Temperature °F														
-Maximum														
70° and above	29	0.0	0.0	0.0	0.0	0.6	3.1	6.5	3.2	0.1	0.0	0.0	0.0	13.6
32° and below	29	24.6	19.7	11.3	2.1	0.0	0.0	0.0	0.0	0.0	4.7	20.6	24.3	107.2
-Minimum														
32° and below	29	30.5	27.2	28.2	20.9	2.9	0.0	0.0	0.1	3.3	20.0	28.0	30.1	191.2
0° and below	29	9.7	7.2	2.2	0.*	0.0	0.0	0.0	0.0	0.0	0.1	3.2	7.3	29.8
AVG. STATION PRESS.(mb)	21	1000.0	1001.5	1001.5	1004.0	1005.9	1007.9	1010.0	1008.3	1004.1	999.0	998.8	999.4	1003.4
RELATIVE HUMIDITY (%)														
Hour 03	40	73	73	71	72	72	75	80	82	81	77	78	76	76
Hour 09 (Local Time)	40	74	73	70	66	63	67	73	78	79	78	77	77	73
Hour 15	40	72	67	57	53	49	56	62	64	63	66	73	76	63
Hour 21	40	73	71	68	64	59	62	69	75	77	75	77	77	71
PRECIPITATION (inches):														
Water Equivalent														
-Normal		0.79	0.78	0.69	0.67	0.73	1.14	1.71	2.44	2.70	2.03	1.11	1.12	15.91
-Maximum Monthly	40	2.71	3.07	2.76	1.91	1.93	3.40	4.44	9.77	6.64	4.11	2.84	2.67	9.77
-Year		1987	1955	1979	1977	1989	1962	1958	1989	1990	1986	1976	1955	AUG 1989
-Minimum Monthly	40	0.02	0.07	T	T	0.02	0.17	0.42	0.33	0.76	0.35	0.08	0.11	T
-Year		1982	1958	1983	1969	1957	1993	1972	1969	1973	1960	1985	1982	MAR 1983
-Maximum in 24 hrs	40	1.19	1.16	1.25	0.78	1.18	1.84	2.06	4.12	1.92	1.60	1.66	1.62	4.12
-Year		1961	1956	1986	1989	1980	1962	1956	1989	1961	1986	1964	1955	AUG 1989
Snow,Ice pellets,hail														
-Maximum Monthly	40	27.5	48.5	31.0	27.6	3.9	0.0	0.0	0.0	4.6	27.1	32.4	41.6	48.5
-Year		1990	1955	1979	1963	1963				1965	1982	1956	1955	FEB 1955
-Maximum in 24 hrs	40	10.5	12.4	14.5	9.1	3.9	0.0	0.0	0.0	3.5	11.2	16.4	17.7	17.7
-Year		1955	1956	1959	1955	1963				1965	1991	1964	1955	DEC 1955
WIND:														
Mean Speed (mph)	40	6.4	6.8	6.9	7.2	8.4	8.3	7.3	6.9	6.7	6.7	6.5	6.2	7.0
Prevailing Direction through 1963		NNE	N	N	N	S	S	S	S	NNE	N	NNE	NNE	N
Fastest Obs. 1 Min.														
-Direction (!!)	36	03	04	03	15	35	17	16	02	22	03	04	05	03
-Speed (MPH)	36	61	52	51	35	33	30	29	31	35	40	41	41	61
-Year		1971	1979	1989	1964	1964	1971	1957	1987	1993	1966	1978	1964	JAN 1971
Peak Gust														
-Direction (!!)	14	E	NE	NE	SE	S	SE	SE	N	S	S	NE	SE	NE
-Speed (mph)	14	64	61	75	43	43	46	40	44	48	55	55	55	75
-Date		1986	1993	1989	1987	1988	1985	1980	1987	1985	1987	1990	1992	MAR 1989

PRECIPITATION (inches)

ANCHORAGE, ALASKA

YEAR	JAN	FEB	MAR	APR	MAY	JUNE	JULY	AUG	SEP	OCT	NOV	DEC	ANNUAL
#1964	0.35	1.15	1.07	0.89	0.97	1.73	1.08	2.16	0.83	2.31	2.71	0.64	15.89
1965	0.57	0.67	0.83	0.30	0.51	0.96	1.74	1.58	4.60	1.44	1.86	1.44	16.50
1966	0.63	0.80	0.44	0.70	0.75	0.27	0.71	2.47	2.45	0.86	1.11	1.06	12.25
1967	1.25	1.01	0.98	0.49	1.07	1.44	2.47	2.96	2.86	0.51	1.72	2.40	19.16
1968	0.83	1.67	0.29	0.85	1.60	0.62	1.34	0.69	1.05	1.61	1.08	0.45	12.08
1969	0.28	0.73	0.10	T	0.86	0.18	2.14	0.33	0.78	0.90	0.84	0.94	8.08
1970	0.86	0.57	0.29	0.27	0.43	0.85	2.03	2.23	1.11	1.62	1.21	1.62	13.09
1971	0.24	1.49	0.70	0.63	0.52	0.37	2.86	2.58	1.79	2.16	0.67	0.87	14.88
1972	0.56	0.63	0.68	0.73	0.81	0.61	0.42	1.40	4.42	2.89	0.76	0.72	14.63
1973	0.72	0.11	0.65	0.33	0.14	1.07	0.60	3.40	0.76	1.74	0.78	0.38	10.68
1974	0.02	1.15	0.60	0.61	0.34	0.69	1.22	1.62	1.53	2.63	1.01	2.00	13.42
1975	0.43	0.77	0.54	1.71	0.40	0.47	1.33	1.19	4.52	0.69	0.10	0.89	13.04
1976	0.98	0.33	1.77	0.74	0.16	0.33	0.60	0.97	3.50	1.29	2.84	1.03	14.54
1977	1.35	0.52	0.84	1.91	0.46	0.49	1.37	1.35	4.08	1.92	0.53	0.69	15.51
1978	0.39	1.19	0.45	0.02	0.03	3.09	1.78	0.54	2.16	1.65	0.85	2.60	14.75
1979	0.23	0.69	2.76	0.94	0.15	1.79	3.84	1.56	2.73	2.54	2.77	1.15	21.15
1980	1.28	1.18	0.30	0.19	1.68	2.73	2.27	3.06	2.53	3.05	0.49	0.41	19.17
1981	0.93	0.97	0.41	0.19	0.81	0.83	4.39	4.96	2.15	3.49	1.85	0.36	21.34
1982	0.02	0.69	0.42	0.27	0.54	1.56	2.41	2.33	4.66	2.95	1.72	0.11	17.68
1983	0.21	0.23	T	1.36	0.59	0.66	0.55	2.89	2.29	2.67	0.23	0.48	12.16
1984	1.30	1.08	0.08	0.93	0.96	1.10	1.11	3.21	2.59	1.38	0.15	1.08	14.97
1985	0.70	0.67	0.86	0.50	1.45	1.01	0.99	3.54	3.17	1.07	0.08	1.47	15.51
1986	0.20	0.55	1.70	0.42	0.50	0.33	2.02	3.62	2.85	4.11	1.23	1.42	18.95
1987	1.72	0.20	0.17	0.24	0.67	1.09	1.89	0.43	1.91	2.60	1.90	1.12	14.93
1988	0.38	0.32	0.65	0.37	0.56	0.79	0.64	3.77	1.26	2.96	1.11	1.51	14.32
1989	0.26	0.17	0.22	0.98	1.93	1.14	2.89	9.77	3.92	3.63	1.01	1.63	27.55
1990	1.42	1.46	0.46	0.27	0.71	1.52	0.81	1.90	6.64	0.73	1.31	1.78	19.01
1991	0.62	0.42	0.65	0.23	0.12	0.18	2.82	3.54	3.41	1.93	1.57	1.82	17.31
1992	1.17	1.04	0.31	0.08	0.58	1.21	0.79	2.49	2.83	2.08	1.17	0.69	14.44
1993	0.94	1.17	0.29	0.09	1.17	0.17	0.57	4.02	4.27	1.90	2.00	0.30	16.89
Record Mean	0.83	0.79	0.61	0.54	0.64	1.08	1.87	2.55	2.69	1.80	1.06	1.07	15.52

AVERAGE TEMPERATURE (deg. F)

ANCHORAGE, ALASKA

YEAR	JAN	FEB	MAR	APR	MAY	JUNE	JULY	AUG	SEP	OCT	NOV	DEC	ANNUAL
#1964	14.1	20.1	17.3	33.7	41.2	55.9	57.1	54.6	48.7	35.0	21.3	1.0	33.3
1965	10.0	10.3	36.5	39.7	45.4	52.9	59.0	56.3	53.7	30.7	20.5	13.1	35.7
1966	9.7	14.7	16.7	35.3	44.2	55.4	57.9	54.4	46.3	32.3	17.5	10.8	32.9
1967	7.1	14.4	23.2	35.1	47.1	56.1	59.3	58.3	48.1	35.7	30.0	16.0	35.9
1968	12.5	23.1	28.4	35.0	48.2	54.8	59.9	58.2	47.1	33.1	22.1	6.3	35.7
1969	4.6	17.9	28.6	39.4	47.7	57.7	59.3	54.2	48.9	41.2	23.7	28.4	37.7
1970	9.2	29.6	35.4	36.4	48.1	54.8	57.1	54.6	46.4	32.5	24.9	14.9	37.0
1971	2.7	20.6	14.2	33.4	41.6	51.2	55.4	55.0	46.1	32.3	18.3	16.2	32.3
1972	6.4	13.5	15.7	26.8	43.3	51.9	59.0	56.6	44.5	31.7	21.3	12.4	31.9
1973	2.9	13.1	24.2	35.8	43.6	51.4	57.8	53.8	45.7	32.2	13.6	18.3	32.7
1974	6.8	14.1	23.3	37.9	47.9	55.5	57.3	56.3	49.8	34.5	22.6	18.8	35.4
1975	11.9	12.9	22.5	32.9	46.3	53.0	58.6	56.6	49.3	34.6	14.2	11.6	33.7
1976	17.1	12.8	24.1	34.8	44.9	53.7	58.9	56.3	47.4	33.4	30.6	23.1	36.4
1977	32.0	32.7	24.7	35.7	46.9	57.8	62.6	60.3	50.7	38.3	15.3	11.3	39.0
1978	21.2	26.3	29.3	39.1	49.0	54.5	58.8	59.8	51.5	39.3	26.3	21.4	39.7
1979	22.3	10.6	31.6	38.8	50.2	55.9	60.4	58.8	52.0	41.1	33.5	10.0	38.8
1980	14.3	27.4	27.2	39.3	45.8	53.2	57.0	54.4	46.7	37.2	27.6	0.8	35.9
1981	31.5	24.8	34.4	36.0	50.7	53.8	57.4	54.8	47.9	36.0	21.8	15.9	38.8
1982	6.4	15.5	26.3	33.1	44.5	52.9	56.2	54.7	47.5	26.6	21.0	21.5	33.8
1983	16.2	21.4	28.7	37.4	48.7	55.9	58.5	56.1	45.3	34.4	24.9	16.7	37.0
1984	18.8	19.4	36.4	38.8	49.6	58.8	60.8	56.6	49.3	35.5	19.8	18.9	38.6
1985	30.3	13.5	26.7	28.4	45.1	51.9	58.5	55.2	47.6	30.3	14.0	27.5	35.8
1986	25.6	21.8	24.1	31.0	46.6	54.6	58.0	54.3	48.6	39.0	25.0	28.3	38.1
1987	22.8	25.3	26.8	37.9	47.2	51.9	57.1	57.3	48.0	38.9	26.9	18.2	38.2
1988	18.0	22.7	31.3	37.1	48.5	55.2	58.8	56.0	48.0	33.3	20.5	22.0	37.6
1989	3.5	17.6	23.6	39.3	46.3	55.3	59.4	59.0	50.6	34.0	17.2	24.2	35.8
1990	15.5	3.8	28.6	39.9	49.9	57.1	58.6	57.8	49.6	32.3	9.9	14.8	34.8
1991	15.9	19.6	23.7	37.7	46.6	55.7	57.5	55.5	51.0	33.0	25.0	20.5	36.8
1992	20.3	15.0	24.9	35.2	46.1	55.9	59.5	55.8	40.3	31.2	27.1	15.0	35.5
1993	14.5	21.0	28.8	40.6	50.7	56.3	61.1	58.8	48.8	38.7	25.2	24.0	39.0
Record Mean	13.9	17.8	24.6	35.4	46.4	54.4	58.1	56.0	47.9	34.7	21.5	15.4	35.5
Max	21.0	25.6	32.9	43.2	54.7	62.2	65.4	63.2	55.0	41.0	27.8	21.9	42.8
Min	6.8	9.9	16.2	27.5	38.1	46.5	50.8	48.7	40.7	28.4	15.3	8.9	28.2

REFERENCE NOTES

ANCHORAGE, ALASKA

GENERAL
T - TRACE AMOUNT.
BLANK ENTRIES DENOTE MISSING/UNREPORTED DATA.
# INDICATES A STATION OR INSTRUMENT RELOCATION.

SPECIFIC

PM - INCLUDES LAST DAY OF PREVIOUS MONTH
ASOS - AUTOMATED SURFACE OBSERVING SYSTEM IN OPERATION DURING THESE MONTHS.

(a) - LENGTH OF RECORD IN YEARS, ALTHOUGH INDIVIDUAL MONTHS MAY BE MISSING.
0.* OR * - THE VALUE IS BETWEEN 0.0 AND 0.05
NORMALS - BASED ON THE 1961-1990 RECORD PERIOD.
EXTREMES - DATES ARE THE MOST RECENT OCCURRENCE
WIND DIR.- NUMERALS SHOW TENS OF DEGRESS CLOCKWISE FROM TRUE NORTH. "00" INDICATES CALM.
RESULTANT DIRECTIONS ARE GIVEN TO WHOLE DEGREES.
BOLD VALUES INDICATE EXTREME VALUES WHICH OCCURRED AFTER THE ASOS SYSTEM WAS COMMISSIONED.

RECORD = PERIOD OF RECORD
RECORD MEAN PRECIPITATION IS THE MEAN OF ALL DAILY PRECIPITATION AMOUNTS DURING THE PERIOD OF RECORD.
RECORD MAX(MIN) TEMPERATURE IS THE MEAN OF ALL DAILY MAX(MIN) TEMPERATURES DURING THE PERIOD OF RECORD.
RECORD MEAN TEMPERATURE IS THE SUM OF THE RECORD MAX AND RECORD MIN DIVIDED BY 2.
AVERAGE TEMPERATURE IS THE SUM OF THE MEAN DAILY MAX AND MIN TEMPERATURE DIVIDED BY 2.

EXCEPTIONS

RECORD MEANS ARE THROUGH THE CURRENT YEAR, BEGINNING IN 1943 FOR TEMPERATURE
1943 FOR PRECIPITATION
1943 FOR SNOWFALL

HEATING DEGREE DAYS Base 65 deg. F ANCHORAGE, ALASKA

SEASON	JULY	AUG	SEP	OCT	NOV	DEC	JAN	FEB	MAR	APR	MAY	JUNE	TOTAL
1964-65	240	315	485	922	1303	1980	1701	1530	879	754	598	357	11064
1965-66	178	261	333	1055	1328	1603	1713	1402	1493	882	641	285	11174
1966-67	214	324	553	1008	1419	1674	1791	1411	1292	890	547	261	11384
1967-68	172	200	501	901	1042	1513	1625	1209	1129	894	510	301	9997
1968-69	153	208	530	982	1280	1816	1869	1312	1124	761	527	217	10779
1969-70	168	330	478	732	1235	1128	1722	983	910	852	515	298	9351
1970-71	239	312	552	1003	1201	1550	1934	1238	1574	940	717	410	11670
1971-72	291	302	561	1008	1396	1508	1814	1488	1521	1138	666	384	12077
1972-73	185	252	608	1025	1308	1627	1925	1448	1258	866	654	399	11555
1973-74	216	342	573	1012	1532	1440	1797	1416	1285	805	526	279	11223
1974-75	235	263	452	937	1263	1425	1643	1454	1313	954	575	354	10868
1975-76	192	252	463	937	1517	1654	1485	1511	1260	897	615	332	11115
1976-77	184	262	521	972	1028	1294	1017	897	1241	872	554	208	9050
1977-78	75	144	421	820	1486	1659	1349	1077	1100	771	491	308	9701
1978-79	186	160	400	792	1153	1344	1321	1515	1029	781	454	268	9403
1979-80	138	184	384	735	937	1704	1568	1083	1164	764	592	347	9600
1980-81	243	320	542	855	1115	1990	1032	1122	943	863	438	329	9792
1981-82	230	307	507	893	1290	1516	1813	1382	1191	949	625	356	11059
1982-83	261	313	520	1184	1315	1342	1507	1216	1117	821	500	267	10363
1983-84	194	269	585	945	1194	1491	1425	1319	880	778	471	179	9730
1984-85	129	254	464	906	1350	1423	1070	1437	1182	1091	610	388	10304
1985-86	193	298	516	1065	1523	1155	1215	1206	1260	1013	564	307	10315
1986-87	215	325	486	800	1194	1133	1303	1104	1176	805	543	386	9470
1987-88	243	232	506	801	1136	1444	1450	1221	1037	830	504	285	9689
1988-89	184	270	503	975	1331	1326	1908	1322	1277	765	573	286	10720
1989-90	173	181	423	956	1428	1255	1533	1715	1121	746	465	237	10233
1990-91	191	222	457	1006	1648	1552	1518	1265	1273	813	563	273	10781
1991-92	226	287	414	988	1193	1373	1380	1444	1240	891	579	268	10283
1992-93	161	280	735	1039	1131	1543	1563	1226	1117	725	436	252	10208
1993-94	125	187	477	808	1191	1267							

COOLING DEGREE DAYS Base 65 deg. F ANCHORAGE, ALASKA

YEAR	JAN	FEB	MAR	APR	MAY	JUNE	JULY	AUG	SEP	OCT	NOV	DEC	TOTAL
1969	0	0	0	0	0	5	1	2	0	0	0	0	8
1970	0	0	0	0	0	0	0	0	0	0	0	0	0
1971	0	0	0	0	0	0	1	0	0	0	0	0	1
1972	0	0	0	0	0	0	5	0	0	0	0	0	5
1973	0	0	0	0	0	0	0	0	0	0	0	0	0
1974	0	0	0	0	0	0	1	0	0	0	0	0	1
1975	0	0	0	0	0	0	2	0	0	0	0	0	2
1976	0	0	0	0	0	0	3	0	0	0	0	0	3
1977	0	0	0	0	0	0	8	3	0	0	0	0	11
1978	0	0	0	0	0	0	1	7	0	0	0	0	8
1979	0	0	0	0	0	0	4	0	0	0	0	0	4
1980	0	0	0	0	0	0	0	0	0	0	0	0	0
1981	0	0	0	0	0	0	0	0	0	0	0	0	0
1982	0	0	0	0	0	0	0	0	0	0	0	0	0
1983	0	0	0	0	0	0	0	0	0	0	0	0	0
1984	0	0	0	0	0	0	5	1	0	0	0	0	6
1985	0	0	0	0	0	0	0	0	0	0	0	0	0
1986	0	0	0	0	0	0	4	0	0	0	0	0	4
1987	0	0	0	0	0	0	2	0	0	0	0	0	2
1988	0	0	0	0	0	0	0	0	0	0	0	0	0
1989	0	0	0	0	0	0	5	2	0	0	0	0	7
1990	0	0	0	0	0	3	1	2	0	0	0	0	6
1991	0	0	0	0	0	0	0	0	0	0	0	0	0
1992	0	0	0	0	0	0	0	0	0	0	0	0	0
1993	0	0	0	0	0	0	11	0	0	0	0	0	11

SNOWFALL (inches) ANCHORAGE, ALASKA

SEASON	JULY	AUG	SEP	OCT	NOV	DEC	JAN	FEB	MAR	APR	MAY	JUNE	TOTAL
1964-65	0.0	0.0	0.0	10.6	25.8	16.2	8.5	11.5	3.0	2.8	0.2	0.0	78.6
1965-66	0.0	0.0	4.6	16.7	17.9	23.9	9.7	10.7	5.2	6.1	T	0.0	94.8
1966-67	0.0	0.0	0.0	1.9	13.5	13.4	16.7	16.3	8.8	4.0	0.0	0.0	74.6
1967-68	0.0	0.0	0.0	4.8	2.5	26.5	7.3	26.1	3.2	7.8	T	0.0	78.2
1968-69	0.0	0.0	1.3	15.1	14.7	7.9	6.5	10.6	1.1	T	0.0	0.0	57.2
1969-70	0.0	0.0	0.0	0.2	2.6	8.7	16.1	8.7	1.4	4.1	0.0	0.0	41.8
1970-71	0.0	0.0	T	4.2	4.2	11.2	1.2	18.5	11.1	8.3	T	0.0	58.7
1971-72	0.0	0.0	0.0	11.9	8.2	11.4	9.6	8.9	12.0	12.6	T	0.0	74.6
1972-73	0.0	0.0	1.5	3.3	10.7	6.5	8.1	1.0	16.1	1.3	0.0	0.0	48.5
1973-74	0.0	0.0	0.0	6.6	10.6	6.7	0.5	23.3	8.2	1.9	0.0	0.0	57.8
1974-75	0.0	0.0	0.0	4.4	8.4	29.2	5.7	15.4	8.3	16.1	0.4	0.0	87.9
1975-76	0.0	0.0	0.0	T	2.0	11.5	9.7	1.8	30.7	5.6	T	0.0	61.3
1976-77	0.0	0.0	0.0	11.4	11.1	13.8	6.1	2.1	9.5	14.0	0.0	0.0	68.0
1977-78	0.0	0.0	1.0	13.2	12.6	10.6	7.3	20.8	9.5	T	0.0	0.0	75.0
1978-79	0.0	0.0	0.0	3.9	8.5	35.2	3.6	6.2	31.0	2.8	0.0	0.0	91.2
1979-80	0.0	0.0	0.0	4.3	13.7	16.0	12.0	18.7	3.4	0.8	0.0	0.0	68.9
1980-81	0.0	0.0	0.0	10.2	4.2	1.4	5.0	6.6	4.4	1.1	T	0.0	32.9
1981-82	0.0	0.0	1.5	6.3	20.0	7.6	0.5	0.6	5.6	3.5	0.7	0.0	46.3
1982-83	0.0	0.0	0.0	27.1	23.4	1.9	3.7	4.3	T	11.0	0.0	0.0	71.4
1983-84	0.0	0.0	T	23.7	2.1	10.5	15.0	18.9	0.2	9.8	0.0	0.0	80.2
1984-85	0.0	0.0	0.0	3.3	1.8	18.0	9.7	7.9	12.8	7.3	1.3	0.0	62.1
1985-86	0.0	0.0	0.0	0.8	1.5	6.1	5.1	6.1	21.0	5.4	0.1	0.0	46.1
1986-87	0.0	0.0	0.0	T	3.8	10.1	18.5	2.2	2.5	1.6	0.0	0.0	38.7
1987-88	0.0	0.0	0.0	T	29.2	26.3	4.7	9.2	8.5	2.0	0.0	0.0	79.9
1988-89	0.0	0.0	0.0	12.0	15.3	18.6	10.1	2.3	5.1	T	0.2	0.0	63.6
1989-90	0.0	0.0	0.0	16.3	10.1	20.0	27.5	23.0	4.7	0.8	T	0.0	102.4
1990-91	0.0	0.0	0.0	1.6	16.9	21.4	7.7	5.4	12.7	T	0.0	0.0	65.7
1991-92	0.0	0.0	0.0	11.6	19.3	26.2	21.4	18.3	2.7	T	0.2	0.0	99.7
1992-93	0.0	0.0	3.0	13.0	9.1	12.1	13.7	18.3	5.7	0.0	0.0	0.0	74.9
1993-94	0.0	0.0	T	4.4	11.9	5.1							
Record Mean	0.0	0.0	0.3	7.3	10.7	14.8	10.7	11.5	9.0	4.8	0.4	0.0	69.3

FAIRBANKS, ALASKA

Fairbanks is located in the Tanana Valley, in the interior of Alaska. It has a distinctly continental climate, with large variation of temperature from winter to summer.

The climate in Fairbanks is conditioned mainly by the response of the land mass to large changes in solar heat received by the area during the year. The sun is above the horizon from 18 to 21 hours during June and July. During this period, daily average maximum temperatures reach the lower 70s. Temperatures of 80 degrees or higher occur on about 10 days each summer. In contrast, from November to early March, when the period of daylight ranges from 10 to less than 4 hours per day, the lowest temperature readings normally fall below zero quite regularly. Low temperatures of -40 degrees or colder occur each winter. The range of temperatures in summer is comparatively low, from the lower 30s to the mid 90s. In winter, this range is larger, from about 65 below to 45 degrees above. This large winter range of temperature reflects the great difference between frigid weather associated with dry northerly airflow from the Arctic to mild temperatures associated with southerly airflow from the Gulf of Alaska, accompanied by chinook winds off the Alaska Range, 80 miles to the south of Fairbanks.

Snow cover is persistent in Fairbanks, without interruption, from October through April. Snowfalls of 4 inches or more in a day occur only three times during winter. Blizzard conditions are almost never seen, as winds in Fairbanks are above 20 miles an hour less than 1 percent of the time. Precipitation normally reaches a minimum in spring, and a maximum in August, when rainfall is common. During summer, thunderstorms occur in Fairbanks on an average of about eight days. Thunderstorms are about three times more frequent over the hills to the north and east of Fairbanks. Damaging hail or wind rarely accompany thunderstorms around Fairbanks.

There are rolling hills reaching elevations up to 2,000 feet above Fairbanks to the north and east of the city. During winter, the uplands are often warmer than Fairbanks, as cold air settles into the valley. In some months, temperatures in the uplands will average more than 10 degrees warmer than Fairbanks. During summer, the uplands are a few degrees cooler than the city. Precipitation in the uplands around Fairbanks is heavier than it is in the city by roughly 20 to 50 percent. Fairbanks exhibits an urban heat island, especially during winter. Low lying areas nearby, such as the community of North Pole, are often colder than the city, sometimes by as much as 15 degrees.

During winter, with temperatures of -20 degrees or colder, ice fog frequently forms in the city. Cold snaps accompanied by ice fog generally last about a week, but can last three weeks in unusual situations. The fog is almost always less than 300 feet deep, so that the surrounding uplands are usually in the clear, with warmer temperatures. Visibility in the ice fog is sometimes quite low, and this can hinder aircraft operations for as much as a day in severe cases. Aside from the low visibility in winter ice fog, flying weather in Fairbanks is quite favorable, especially from February through May, when crystal clear weather is common and the length of daylight is rapidly increasing.

Hardy vegetables and grains grow luxuriantly. Freezing of local rivers normally begins in the first week of October. The date when ice will normally support a persons weight is October 27. Rivers remain frozen and safe for travel until early April. Breakup of the river ice usually occurs in the first week of May.

NORMALS, MEANS, AND EXTREMES

FAIRBANKS, ALASKA

LATITUDE: 64°49'N LONGITUDE: 147°52' W ELEVATION: FT. GRND 436 BARO 452 TIME ZONE: YUKON WBAN: 26411

	(a)	JAN	FEB	MAR	APR	MAY	JUNE	JULY	AUG	SEP	OCT	NOV	DEC	YEAR
TEMPERATURE °F:														
Normals														
-Daily Maximum		-1.6	7.2	23.8	41.0	59.3	70.1	72.3	66.3	54.8	32.0	10.9	1.8	36.5
-Daily Minimum		-18.5	-14.4	-1.7	20.4	38.0	49.5	52.6	47.2	36.2	18.1	-5.6	-14.8	17.3
-Monthly		-10.1	-3.6	11.0	30.7	48.6	59.8	62.5	56.8	45.5	25.1	2.7	-6.5	26.9
Extremes														
-Record Highest	42	50	47	53	74	89	96	94	90	84	65	46	44	96
-Year		1981	1987	1993	1960	1960	1969	1975	1976	1957	1969	1970	1985	JUN 1969
-Record Lowest	42	-61	-58	-49	-24	-1	31	35	27	3	-27	-46	-62	-62
-Year		1969	1993	1956	1986	1964	1963	1959	1987	1992	1992	1990	1961	DEC 1961
NORMAL DEGREE DAYS:														
Heating (base 65°F)		2328	1921	1674	1029	508	182	123	267	585	1237	1869	2217	13940
Cooling (base 65°F)		0	0	0	0	0	26	45	13	0	0	0	0	84
% OF POSSIBLE SUNSHINE														
MEAN SKY COVER (tenths)														
Sunrise - Sunset	42	6.3	6.2	5.9	6.6	6.9	7.3	7.4	7.8	7.6	7.9	6.9	7.0	7.0
MEAN NUMBER OF DAYS:														
Sunrise to Sunset														
-Clear	42	9.0	8.2	9.9	6.6	4.5	2.9	3.4	3.0	4.2	4.0	6.8	6.8	69.5
-Partly Cloudy	42	6.0	5.9	6.8	7.6	11.0	10.2	8.9	6.7	6.1	5.0	5.2	5.7	85.0
-Cloudy	42	16.1	14.2	14.3	15.8	15.5	16.8	18.7	21.2	19.7	22.0	18.0	18.5	210.7
Precipitation														
.01 inches or more	42	7.7	6.7	5.9	4.7	7.0	10.6	12.3	12.4	9.6	10.7	10.3	9.0	106.9
Snow, Ice pellets, hail														
1.0 inches or more	42	3.4	2.5	2.3	1.1	0.2	0.0	0.0	0.0	0.5	4.2	4.4	4.4	22.9
Thunderstorms	42	0.0	0.0	0.0	0.*	0.4	3.0	2.3	0.9	0.1	0.0	0.0	0.0	6.7
Heavy Fog Visibility														
1/4 mile or less	42	4.6	2.4	0.5	0.3	0.2	0.4	0.8	1.7	1.3	1.7	1.1	3.2	18.1
Temperature °F														
-Maximum														
70° and above	30	0.0	0.0	0.0	0.*	3.9	17.1	21.2	10.8	1.3	0.0	0.0	0.0	54.3
32° and below	30	29.8	26.0	20.8	5.6	0.2	0.0	0.0	0.0	0.4	16.1	27.9	29.6	156.5
-Minimum														
32° and below	30	31.0	28.3	30.9	26.5	6.2	0.0	0.0	0.6	9.1	28.4	30.0	31.0	221.8
0° and below	30	25.9	22.3	16.0	2.2	0.*	0.0	0.0	0.0	0.0	3.7	18.5	24.3	113.0
AVG. STATION PRESS. (mb)	21	993.5	995.7	992.9	993.3	992.9	993.5	995.8	995.3	992.8	990.4	991.5	992.2	993.3
RELATIVE HUMIDITY (%)														
Hour 03	42	69	66	67	68	68	75	81	86	82	79	73	71	74
Hour 09 (Local Time)	42	69	66	66	60	53	60	69	77	78	79	74	71	69
Hour 15	43	69	63	53	46	38	43	50	54	55	67	73	71	57
Hour 21	42	69	66	63	55	47	50	60	70	72	77	74	71	65
PRECIPITATION (inches):														
Water Equivalent														
-Normal		0.47	0.40	0.37	0.32	0.61	1.37	1.87	1.96	0.95	0.90	0.80	0.85	10.87
-Maximum Monthly	42	2.40	1.75	2.24	0.93	1.67	3.52	4.87	6.20	3.05	2.19	3.32	3.23	6.20
-Year		1993	1966	1991	1982	1955	1955	1990	1967	1960	1983	1970	1984	AUG 1967
-Minimum Monthly	42	0.01	0.01	T	T	0.07	0.19	0.35	0.40	0.15	0.08	T	T	T
-Year		1966	1976	1987	1991	1957	1966	1993	1957	1968	1954	1953	1969	APR 1991
-Maximum in 24 hrs	42	0.75	0.97	1.17	0.47	0.88	1.52	1.73	3.42	1.21	2.22	0.84	1.25	3.42
-Year		1993	1966	1991	1979	1955	1955	1990	1967	1954	1976	1970	1968	AUG 1967
Snow, Ice pellets, hail														
-Maximum Monthly	42	40.2	43.1	30.4	11.5	14.1	T	T	T	24.4	25.9	54.0	50.7	54.0
-Year		1993	1966	1991	1992	1992	1993	1990	1969	1992	1982	1970	1984	NOV 1970
-Maximum in 24 hrs	42	10.1	20.1	12.6	6.3	9.4	T	T	T	9.0	10.4	14.6	14.7	20.1
-Year		1993	1966	1963	1992	1992	1993	1990	1969	1992	1974	1970	1968	FEB 1966
WIND:														
Mean Speed (mph)	42	3.1	4.0	5.2	6.6	7.7	7.1	6.6	6.2	6.2	5.4	3.9	3.2	5.4
Prevailing Direction through 1963		N	N	N	N	N	SW	SW	N	N	N	N	N	N
Fastest Obs. 1 Min.														
-Direction (!!)	42	25	27	22	24	23	25	27	27	22	25	25	24	25
-Speed (MPH)	42	31	33	40	32	32	40	32	34	30	40	35	37	40
-Year		1991	1955	1970	1983	1984	1974	1989	1954	1975	1958	1970	1970	JUN 1974
Peak Gust														
-Direction (!!)	9	SW	SW	SW	SW	W	E	NE	S	W	W	W	SW	NE
-Speed (mph)	9	47	40	46	40	44	48	63	38	51	40	35	38	63
-Date		1993	1989	1985	1992	1992	1992	1990	1985	1985	1993	1992	1985	JUL 1990

PRECIPITATION (inches)

FAIRBANKS, ALASKA

YEAR	JAN	FEB	MAR	APR	MAY	JUNE	JULY	AUG	SEP	OCT	NOV	DEC	ANNUAL
1964	0.21	0.46	0.18	0.68	0.97	1.33	1.28	2.37	0.85	0.53	0.86	0.34	10.06
1965	0.07	0.32	0.27	0.47	0.14	1.16	1.39	1.48	2.11	0.74	1.21	1.92	11.28
1966	0.01	1.75	0.34	0.32	0.38	0.19	0.83	0.59	0.15	0.29	2.06	0.16	7.07
1967	0.40	0.25	1.90	0.84	0.43	1.13	3.34	6.20	0.25	0.32	0.93	1.34	17.33
1968	1.19	0.15	T	0.29	0.67	1.52	0.84	0.96	0.15	0.31	0.27	1.38	7.73
1969	0.55	0.10	0.60	T	0.95	0.39	1.33	2.04	0.28	0.10	0.54	T	6.88
1970	0.10	0.32	0.25	0.45	0.42	2.57	1.81	1.98	0.65	1.84	3.32	2.29	16.00
1971	0.33	0.63	0.20	0.11	0.16	0.31	2.08	2.32	2.45	1.35	0.54	1.83	12.31
1972	0.73	0.16	0.27	0.20	0.35	0.55	0.63	1.09	2.08	0.86	0.46	1.13	8.51
1973	0.44	0.11	0.40	0.05	0.99	0.97	1.92	2.19	0.19	0.91	0.80	0.15	9.12
1974	0.14	0.33	0.27	0.21	0.11	1.22	1.17	1.14	0.47	1.08	1.03	0.55	7.72
1975	0.60	0.04	0.22	0.47	0.49	0.99	1.81	2.10	0.20	0.79	0.44	0.31	8.46
1976	0.22	0.01	0.55	0.08	0.94	1.08	1.60	0.69	1.05	0.89	0.13	0.08	7.32
1977	0.31	0.81	0.26	0.36	1.63	3.01	1.58	0.41	2.51	1.11	0.19	0.80	12.98
1978	0.39	0.19	0.09	0.16	0.44	1.71	1.19	1.24	0.98	0.59	1.02	1.40	9.40
1979	0.58	0.02	0.47	0.83	0.88	1.54	2.54	1.22	0.19	0.94	0.63	0.49	10.33
1980	0.52	0.22	0.13	0.10	0.31	1.38	1.37	1.68	0.76	0.39	0.70	0.32	7.88
1981	0.31	0.78	0.07	0.32	0.73	1.91	2.41	1.35	0.80	0.91	0.91	0.58	11.08
1982	0.34	0.38	0.39	0.93	0.96	1.96	2.33	1.67	0.77	1.48	1.49	0.23	12.93
1983	0.24	0.18	0.09	0.27	0.14	0.57	1.71	3.33	0.92	2.19	0.08	0.65	10.37
1984	0.89	0.64	0.03	0.47	1.17	0.48	2.95	1.15	0.22	0.70	0.42	3.23	12.35
1985	0.52	0.48	0.57	0.36	0.41	1.80	1.13	1.88	2.59	1.00	0.90	0.08	11.72
1986	0.13	0.19	0.32	0.07	0.54	0.87	2.12	2.36	0.65	1.79	0.48	0.34	9.86
1987	0.68	0.10	T	0.05	0.21	1.02	1.70	0.56	0.57	0.39	0.64	0.51	6.43
1988	0.32	0.13	0.13	0.21	1.51	2.26	1.02	1.95	0.73	1.07	0.68	0.46	10.47
1989	0.52	0.98	0.13	0.05	0.99	2.53	0.91	0.78	0.72	1.28	0.97	0.57	10.43
1990	0.52	0.72	0.11	0.07	0.40	1.73	4.87	3.60	1.74	0.31	1.51	2.94	18.52
1991	1.17	0.17	2.24	T	0.10	0.36	0.81	1.18	1.16	0.71	0.48	1.02	9.40
1992	0.85	0.66	0.07	0.47	1.23	2.15	2.32	0.59	1.34	0.91	0.93	1.21	12.73
1993	2.40	0.31	0.26	0.03	0.63	1.24	0.35	1.58	2.63	0.61	0.86	0.43	11.33
Record Mean	0.71	0.46	0.41	0.28	0.66	1.38	1.84	2.11	1.06	0.87	0.70	0.70	11.18

AVERAGE TEMPERATURE (deg. F)

FAIRBANKS, ALASKA

YEAR	JAN	FEB	MAR	APR	MAY	JUNE	JULY	AUG	SEP	OCT	NOV	DEC	ANNUAL
1964	-15.7	0.7	-2.2	25.8	38.6	60.1	59.7	56.5	44.9	28.4	2.4	-26.5	22.8
1965	-18.0	-18.1	24.5	30.9	42.9	55.2	60.2	52.7	48.2	13.9	3.9	-14.1	23.5
1966	-27.4	-7.6	-2.5	27.1	45.4	63.3	62.5	57.1	50.1	24.3	0.6	-20.1	22.7
1967	-15.3	-6.9	9.8	31.7	45.7	61.8	59.8	58.3	46.6	24.8	9.5	-1.6	27.1
1968	-11.0	-5.0	12.8	29.2	47.6	59.5	65.8	58.5	42.8	22.1	2.3	-17.7	25.6
1969	-26.7	-7.3	10.1	36.3	49.4	64.9	59.4	49.8	49.1	34.0	1.2	4.0	27.0
1970	-16.2	8.0	20.9	32.0	51.8	58.0	62.4	56.9	40.8	18.9	10.7	-9.8	27.9
1971	-31.7	-4.6	-0.4	26.7	47.3	63.4	61.0	56.1	44.7	27.9	0.5	-5.8	23.8
1972	-16.3	-10.1	-2.8	20.8	47.4	59.4	64.5	58.9	40.1	26.8	7.0	-2.5	24.5
1973	-18.2	-1.5	11.9	35.3	50.6	60.3	62.0	55.0	47.3	25.1	-0.7	-3.4	27.0
1974	-16.7	-17.8	7.6	34.9	51.4	58.7	63.5	59.1	51.4	21.4	0.6	-11.3	25.2
1975	-15.5	-3.4	12.6	30.5	53.5	63.4	68.4	56.1	45.8	23.9	-8.0	-16.1	25.9
1976	-11.5	-13.7	12.1	36.0	47.8	59.6	61.8	59.2	45.4	23.9	15.9	-3.9	27.7
1977	9.8	8.6	4.6	27.8	48.7	59.6	62.8	62.6	45.6	25.6	-7.6	-14.9	27.8
1978	0.1	3.9	14.0	34.8	50.2	54.6	63.5	59.5	46.8	23.3	8.6	3.3	30.2
1979	-7.7	-25.3	12.0	30.9	49.9	57.4	61.3	60.4	46.5	32.4	20.2	-10.2	27.3
1980	-9.5	16.0	17.3	35.9	50.7	56.5	60.9	53.6	43.0	33.0	11.5	-24.0	28.7
1981	18.1	5.1	27.1	31.4	51.3	58.9	56.5	53.6	44.1	29.5	12.3	-4.2	32.0
1982	-18.0	-3.9	13.1	27.7	46.8	58.5	63.1	56.6	49.3	18.5	4.4	2.2	26.6
1983	-11.0	3.4	13.8	37.4	50.4	62.3	64.2	53.5	41.2	23.6	8.6	-3.7	28.6
1984	-5.9	-13.3	21.6	30.3	47.2	61.6	60.9	53.8	46.8	25.9	0.1	-3.1	27.2
1985	11.1	-9.4	14.6	20.8	46.7	57.8	63.1	56.3	42.9	18.8	-4.7	7.7	27.1
1986	-2.1	4.7	6.0	24.0	47.8	62.6	63.6	54.7	46.3	27.1	0.2	7.3	28.5
1987	0.7	1.5	13.5	35.0	50.9	61.9	64.2	57.7	44.1	33.0	6.0	-3.2	30.4
1988	-5.3	3.9	17.8	33.6	52.8	62.9	65.8	58.4	44.4	17.4	-3.1	4.2	29.4
1989	-21.3	3.4	6.7	36.2	47.8	60.1	64.6	60.8	48.6	26.2	-7.1	4.5	27.5
1990	-12.9	-21.7	18.5	38.1	55.1	61.6	65.3	60.0	44.8	24.1	-4.9	-6.3	26.8
1991	-4.7	-1.2	11.9	35.4	51.2	63.8	60.6	54.4	48.0	24.9	0.6	-2.9	28.5
1992	-4.7	-8.7	14.0	26.1	41.8	60.0	64.1	56.5	31.7	17.5	10.4	-7.6	25.1
1993	-3.9	2.4	17.2	41.1	53.7	62.0	65.6	56.1	44.1	29.3	8.4	0.6	31.4
Record Mean	-10.1	-3.4	10.1	30.4	48.0	59.3	61.3	55.6	44.5	25.6	3.1	-7.7	26.4
Max	-1.2	7.7	23.5	41.6	59.1	70.5	71.9	65.7	54.0	33.1	11.3	0.6	36.5
Min	-19.0	-14.5	-3.4	19.2	36.8	48.0	50.7	45.6	35.0	18.1	-5.1	-16.0	16.3

REFERENCE NOTES

FAIRBANKS, ALASKA

GENERAL
T - TRACE AMOUNT.
BLANK ENTRIES DENOTE MISSING/UNREPORTED DATA.
# INDICATES A STATION OR INSTRUMENT RELOCATION.

SPECIFIC

PM - INCLUDES LAST DAY OF PREVIOUS MONTH
ASOS - AUTOMATED SURFACE OBSERVING SYSTEM IN OPERATION DURING THESE MONTHS.

(a) - LENGTH OF RECORD IN YEARS, ALTHOUGH INDIVIDUAL MONTHS MAY BE MISSING.
0.* OR * - THE VALUE IS BETWEEN 0.0 AND 0.05
NORMALS - BASED ON THE 1961-1990 RECORD PERIOD.
EXTREMES - DATES ARE THE MOST RECENT OCCURRENCE
WIND DIR.- NUMERALS SHOW TENS OF DEGRESS CLOCKWISE FROM TRUE NORTH. "00" INDICATES CALM.
RESULTANT DIRECTIONS ARE GIVEN TO WHOLE DEGREES.
BOLD VALUES INDICATE EXTREME VALUES WHICH OCCURRED AFTER THE ASOS SYSTEM WAS COMMISSIONED.

RECORD = PERIOD OF RECORD
RECORD MEAN PRECIPITATION IS THE MEAN OF ALL DAILY PRECIPITATION AMOUNTS DURING THE PERIOD OF RECORD.
RECORD MAX(MIN) TEMPERATURE IS THE MEAN OF ALL DAILY MAX(MIN) TEMPERATURES DURING THE PERIOD OF RECORD.
RECORD MEAN TEMPERATURE IS THE SUM OF THE RECORD MAX AND RECORD MIN DIVIDED BY 2.
AVERAGE TEMPERATURE IS THE SUM OF THE MEAN DAILY MAX AND MIN TEMPERATURE DIVIDED BY 2.

EXCEPTIONS

RECORD MEANS ARE THROUGH THE CURRENT YEAR,
BEGINNING IN 1930 FOR TEMPERATURE
1930 FOR PRECIPITATION
1952 FOR SNOWFALL

HEATING DEGREE DAYS Base 65 deg. F FAIRBANKS, ALASKA

SEASON	JULY	AUG	SEP	OCT	NOV	DEC	JAN	FEB	MAR	APR	MAY	JUNE	TOTAL
1964-65	165	256	595	1133	1876	2841	2574	2334	1249	1019	680	287	15009
1965-66	152	374	496	1580	1833	2455	2872	2039	2092	1132	600	63	15688
1966-67	92	247	441	1255	1929	2643	2496	2014	1704	991	594	138	14544
1967-68	178	213	545	1239	1661	2064	2358	2029	1613	1069	533	169	13671
1968-69	50	208	657	1320	1881	2567	2849	2024	1698	855	475	80	14664
1969-70	170	467	472	955	1914	1892	2524	1595	1365	981	401	203	12939
1970-71	96	244	722	1425	1630	2318	3002	1948	2030	1141	542	117	15215
1971-72	134	271	600	1143	1932	2195	2524	2178	2102	1318	539	205	15141
1972-73	63	184	738	1177	1739	2091	2582	1864	1637	883	439	150	13547
1973-74	111	302	523	1231	1968	2124	2535	2322	1778	895	414	188	14391
1974-75	85	195	402	1342	1935	2370	2497	1918	1620	1028	347	69	13808
1975-76	33	270	570	1270	2195	2513	2372	2285	1631	861	527	156	14683
1976-77	116	188	583	1269	1466	2136	1709	1574	1871	1107	500	155	12674
1977-78	101	124	573	1216	2184	2480	2013	1712	1576	898	454	304	13635
1978-79	65	176	542	1286	1689	1912	2260	2533	1638	1018	463	220	13802
1979-80	124	143	548	1004	1336	2335	2312	1415	1475	868	436	248	12244
1980-81	127	351	654	985	1599	2766	1447	1676	1168	999	418	188	12378
1981-82	255	347	622	1094	1573	2150	2581	1929	1602	1113	555	216	14037
1982-83	86	252	465	1434	1816	1946	2356	1725	1581	823	451	133	13068
1983-84	62	351	705	1280	1688	2126	2201	2277	1338	1035	549	120	13732
1984-85	140	344	538	1205	1950	2111	1666	2086	1558	1321	558	215	13692
1985-86	72	267	654	1430	2095	1776	2079	1686	1825	1224	527	113	13748
1986-87	110	312	559	1169	1943	1787	1994	1776	1594	893	428	128	12693
1987-88	61	218	620	987	1768	2111	2185	1768	1455	934	371	96	12574
1988-89	39	202	611	1469	2045	1883	2676	1722	1804	859	529	149	13988
1989-90	73	134	484	1195	2164	1875	2420	2433	1431	798	310	127	13444
1990-91	74	178	600	1261	2097	2212	2161	1849	1640	877	421	130	13500
1991-92	143	321	504	1234	1935	2105	2163	2140	1577	1160	711	157	14150
1992-93	45	259	995	1463	1636	2253	2134	1751	1478	711	343	103	13171
1993-94	43	273	620	1099	1694	1995							

COOLING DEGREE DAYS Base 65 deg. F FAIRBANKS, ALASKA

YEAR	JAN	FEB	MAR	APR	MAY	JUNE	JULY	AUG	SEP	OCT	NOV	DEC	TOTAL
1969	0	0	0	0	0	83	2	0	0	0	0	0	85
1970	0	0	0	0	0	0	22	0	0	0	0	0	22
1971	0	0	0	0	0	73	16	0	0	0	0	0	89
1972	0	0	0	0	0	40	55	0	0	0	0	0	95
1973	0	0	0	0	0	13	24	2	0	0	0	0	39
1974	0	0	0	0	1	9	44	20	0	0	0	0	74
1975	0	0	0	0	0	28	146	1	0	0	0	0	175
1976	0	0	0	0	0	2	23	14	0	0	0	0	39
1977	0	0	0	0	0	0	44	54	0	0	0	0	98
1978	0	0	0	0	0	0	27	10	0	0	0	0	37
1979	0	0	0	0	0	0	16	7	0	0	0	0	23
1980	0	0	0	0	0	0	8	6	0	0	0	0	14
1981	0	0	0	0	1	11	0	2	0	0	0	0	14
1982	0	0	0	0	0	27	36	0	0	0	0	0	63
1983	0	0	0	0	5	61	40	0	0	0	0	0	106
1984	0	0	0	0	0	22	21	2	0	0	0	0	45
1985	0	0	0	0	0	8	20	4	0	0	0	0	32
1986	0	0	0	0	0	46	74	0	0	0	0	0	120
1987	0	0	0	0	0	42	42	0	0	0	0	0	84
1988	0	0	0	0	0	41	72	2	0	0	0	0	115
1989	0	0	0	0	0	10	67	11	0	0	0	0	88
1990	0	0	0	0	11	32	91	35	0	0	0	0	169
1991	0	0	0	0	0	100	13	0	0	0	0	0	113
1992	0	0	0	0	0	17	21	4	0	0	0	0	42
1993	0	0	0	0	0	18	70	3	0	0	0	0	91

SNOWFALL (inches) FAIRBANKS, ALASKA

SEASON	JULY	AUG	SEP	OCT	NOV	DEC	JAN	FEB	MAR	APR	MAY	JUNE	TOTAL
1964-65	0.0	0.0	0.0	4.7	18.1	14.0	3.0	7.6	1.4	5.8	0.7	0.0	55.3
1965-66	0.0	0.0	T	15.7	18.8	33.5	0.7	43.1	8.9	1.5	1.7	0.0	123.9
1966-67	0.0	0.0	0.0	5.5	36.6	2.9	13.0	5.2	28.4	11.1	T	0.0	102.7
1967-68	0.0	0.0	T	5.8	14.4	16.8	22.6	4.8	0.1	5.0	2.7	0.0	72.2
1968-69	0.0	0.0	0.9	6.7	8.0	20.2	10.8	1.4	11.3	0.4	T	0.0	59.7
1969-70	0.0	T	0.0	3.7	11.4	T	3.6	6.4	4.2	7.1	T	0.0	36.4
1970-71	0.0	0.0	4.1	21.9	54.0	32.5	8.5	16.3	6.4	0.9	1.1	0.0	145.7
1971-72	0.0	0.0	3.5	20.4	9.8	29.6	12.6	4.5	5.7	4.3	0.0	0.0	90.4
1972-73	0.0	0.0	7.8	6.9	12.2	26.9	14.2	1.8	8.7	1.0	T	0.0	79.5
1973-74	0.0	0.0	1.2	8.2	17.5	2.5	3.0	8.7	7.0	1.3	0.0	T	49.4
1974-75	0.0	0.0	0.3	24.4	22.5	17.9	14.1	1.6	5.0	4.4	T	0.0	90.2
1975-76	0.0	0.0	T	14.4	11.4	6.7	6.4	0.5	10.4	1.2	T	0.0	51.0
1976-77	0.0	0.0	T	14.7	4.3	2.6	6.7	19.0	5.5	6.8	T	0.0	59.6
1977-78	0.0	0.0	1.0	17.3	5.1	14.4	4.9	3.0	1.6	0.7	0.1	0.0	48.1
1978-79	0.0	0.0	0.3	7.6	15.1	21.7	9.7	0.5	7.7	3.1	0.0	0.0	65.7
1979-80	0.0	0.0	T	6.5	4.4	11.0	10.8	4.4	3.2	0.8	0.0	0.0	41.1
1980-81	0.0	0.0	3.4	5.1	10.6	4.8	6.2	10.2	0.9	1.9	0.0	0.0	43.1
1981-82	0.0	0.0	0.3	7.8	16.2	10.6	7.6	7.0	7.2	11.4	0.3	0.0	68.4
1982-83	0.0	0.0	0.6	25.9	27.8	3.8	4.8	3.6	2.1	1.9	0.4	0.0	70.9
1983-84	0.0	0.0	0.4	17.3	2.4	14.4	13.8	11.1	0.8	6.7	T	0.0	66.9
1984-85	0.0	0.0	0.0	11.3	8.5	50.7	8.1	8.0	7.4	5.9	1.0	0.0	100.9
1985-86	0.0	0.0	2.1	5.4	14.7	1.8	2.3	2.6	3.7	1.0	0.0	0.0	33.6
1986-87	0.0	0.0	T	11.8	7.4	6.0	12.0	1.5	T	1.0	T	0.0	39.7
1987-88	0.0	0.0	T	3.5	14.1	10.4	6.3	2.5	2.6	0.2	0.3	0.0	39.9
1988-89	0.0	0.0	0.2	12.9	15.2	10.5	10.8	13.4	3.9	0.4	0.8	0.0	68.1
1989-90	0.0	0.0	0.5	19.7	18.1	11.1	10.4	16.0	2.6	T	0.0	T	78.4
1990-91	T	0.0	1.6	6.9	37.3	47.5	20.6	3.0	30.4	T	0.0	0.0	147.3
1991-92	0.0	0.0	0.0	12.2	9.7	18.9	15.5	15.0	1.8	11.5	14.1	0.0	98.7
1992-93	0.0	0.0	24.4	16.7	18.7	28.5	40.2	5.4	5.2	T	0.0	T	139.1
1993-94	0.0	0.0	7.5	7.3	16.3	8.5							
Record Mean	T	T	1.6	10.9	13.6	13.8	10.8	8.6	6.6	3.4	0.8	T	70.1

JUNEAU, ALASKA

Juneau lies well within the area of maritime influences which prevail over the coastal areas of southeastern Alaska, and is in the path of most storms that cross the Gulf of Alaska. Consequently, the area has little sunshine, generally moderate temperatures, and abundant precipitation. In contrast with the characteristic lack of sunshine there are greatly appreciated intervals, sometimes lasting for several days at a stretch, during which clear skies prevail. The rugged terrain exerts a fundamental influence upon local temperatures and the distribution of precipitation, creating considerable variations in both weather elements within relatively short distances.

Temperature variations, both daily and seasonal, are usually confined to relatively narrow limits by the dominant maritime influences. There are, however, periods of comparatively severe cold, which usually start with strong northerly winds, and are most often caused by the flow of cold air from northwestern Canada through nearby mountain passes and over the Juneau ice field. These are generally of brief duration. During such periods strong, gusty winds, known locally as Taku Winds, often occur especially in downtown Juneau, Douglas, and other local areas, but generally they are not felt in the Mendenhall Valley. At times these are strong enough to cause considerable damage. During periods of calm or light winds, temperature differences within short distances are frequently very pronounced. Variations in local sunlight and air drainage patterns produce wide differences in temperatures particularly between upland or sloping areas and areas of low, flat terrain. Juneau International Airport, located on low, flat terrain formed by the Mendenhall River delta, and in the path of drainage air from the Mendenhall Glacier, averages about 10 days a year with minimum readings below zero. Downtown Juneau, located on a sloping portion of a rugged mountain area, experiences on the average only about one day each year with minimum readings below zero. At the airport the growing season averages 146 days, from May 4 to September 28, while the downtown average is 181 days, from April 22 to October 21.

The months of February to June mark the period of lightest precipitation, with monthly averages of about 3 inches. After June the monthly amounts increase gradually, reaching an average of 7.71 inches in October. Due to the rugged topography, precipitation throughout the year tends to vary greatly within short distances. At the Juneau Airport, yearly precipitation is 53 inches while downtown, only 8 miles away, it is 93 inches. The maximum yearly amount received in the city is almost double the maximum received at the airport.

Although a trace of snow has fallen as early as September 9, first falls usually occur in the latter part of October, and sometimes not until the first part of December. On the average there is very little accumulation on the ground at low levels until the last of November, although at higher elevations, and particularly on mountain tops, a cover is usually established in early October. Snow accumulation usually reaches its greatest depth during the middle of February. Individual storms may produce heavy falls as late as the first half of May. However, snow cover is usually gone before the middle of April. Ice accumulations due to alternating thawing and freezing of snow or due to freezing precipitation are frequent problems in the Juneau area during the winter months.

NORMALS, MEANS, AND EXTREMES

JUNEAU, ALASKA

LATITUDE: 58°22'N LONGITUDE: 134°35' W ELEVATION: FT. GRND 12 BARO 20 TIME ZONE: YUKON WBAN: 25309

	(a)	JAN	FEB	MAR	APR	MAY	JUNE	JULY	AUG	SEP	OCT	NOV	DEC	YEAR
TEMPERATURE °F:														
Normals														
-Daily Maximum		29.4	34.1	38.7	47.2	55.1	60.9	63.9	62.7	55.9	47.1	36.7	31.6	46.9
-Daily Minimum		19.0	22.7	26.7	32.1	38.9	45.0	48.1	47.3	42.9	37.2	27.2	22.6	34.1
-Monthly		24.2	28.4	32.7	39.7	47.0	53.0	56.0	55.0	49.4	42.2	32.0	27.1	40.6
Extremes														
-Record Highest	49	57	57	59	71	82	86	90	83	72	61	56	54	90
-Year		1958	1992	1981	1989	1947	1969	1975	1977	1989	1987	1949	1944	JUL 1975
-Record Lowest	49	-22	-22	-15	6	25	31	36	27	23	11	-5	-21	-22
-Year		1972	1968	1972	1963	1972	1971	1950	1948	1972	1984	1966	1949	JAN 1972
NORMAL DEGREE DAYS:														
Heating (base 65°F)		1265	1025	1001	759	558	360	279	310	468	707	990	1175	8897
Cooling (base 65°F)		0	0	0	0	0	0	0	0	0	0	0	0	0
% OF POSSIBLE SUNSHINE	33	32	32	37	39	39	34	31	32	26	19	23	20	30
MEAN SKY COVER (tenths)														
Sunrise - Sunset	43	7.8	8.0	8.1	8.1	8.0	8.1	8.3	8.0	8.5	8.8	8.5	8.5	8.2
MEAN NUMBER OF DAYS:														
Sunrise to Sunset														
-Clear	43	5.6	4.2	4.3	3.5	3.7	3.5	3.0	3.9	2.7	2.3	3.3	3.4	43.3
-Partly Cloudy	43	2.7	2.9	3.2	4.1	4.2	4.1	4.6	4.7	3.2	2.1	2.2	2.0	39.8
-Cloudy	43	22.7	21.2	23.5	22.4	23.1	22.4	23.4	22.4	24.1	26.6	24.5	25.6	282.1
Precipitation														
.01 inches or more	49	18.4	16.7	17.8	16.9	17.0	15.4	16.6	17.6	20.4	23.5	20.1	21.0	221.5
Snow,Ice pellets,hail														
1.0 inches or more	49	7.0	5.3	4.1	0.9	0.0	0.0	0.0	0.0	0.0	0.3	3.5	6.0	27.0
Thunderstorms	49	0.*	0.0	0.0	0.0	0.0	0.1	0.1	0.*	0.1	0.0	0.*	0.0	0.3
Heavy Fog Visibility														
1/4 mile or less	49	2.0	2.4	1.8	1.0	0.8	0.3	0.2	1.1	2.8	3.1	3.2	2.4	20.9
Temperature °F														
-Maximum														
70° and above	49	0.0	0.0	0.0	0.*	1.3	5.1	7.2	5.6	0.2	0.0	0.0	0.0	19.4
32° and below	49	15.9	9.3	3.8	0.2	0.0	0.0	0.0	0.0	0.0	0.2	6.4	12.2	48.0
-Minimum														
32° and below	49	25.4	22.3	23.0	14.7	3.7	0.1	0.0	0.1	1.5	7.8	18.1	23.4	140.1
0° and below	49	4.2	1.7	0.5	0.0	0.0	0.0	0.0	0.0	0.0	0.0	0.2	2.0	8.6
AVG. STATION PRESS.(mb)	12	1011.0	1011.4	1009.2	1012.2	1013.5	1014.5	1015.8	1014.7	1012.7	1008.0	1008.2	1008.9	1011.7
RELATIVE HUMIDITY (%)														
Hour 03	27	81	83	84	87	87	86	87	90	93	89	86	85	87
Hour 09 (Local Time)	27	81	83	82	80	79	79	83	87	91	89	86	85	84
Hour 15	27	78	75	68	63	63	65	70	74	78	79	81	83	73
Hour 21	27	81	82	79	76	72	72	75	81	87	88	86	84	80
PRECIPITATION (inches):														
Water Equivalent														
-Normal		4.54	3.75	3.28	2.77	3.42	3.15	4.16	5.32	6.73	7.84	4.91	4.44	54.31
-Maximum Monthly	49	9.11	8.48	6.37	5.32	9.20	6.02	7.88	12.31	15.14	15.25	11.22	9.89	15.25
-Year		1993	1964	1992	1980	1992	1987	1969	1961	1991	1974	1956	1956	OCT 1974
-Minimum Monthly	49	0.94	0.07	0.59	0.27	1.25	1.08	1.15	0.56	2.34	2.71	1.15	0.49	0.07
-Year		1969	1989	1983	1948	1946	1950	1972	1979	1965	1950	1983	1983	FEB 1989
-Maximum in 24 hrs	49	2.74	2.71	1.81	2.03	2.30	1.92	1.92	2.62	3.17	4.66	3.40	3.56	4.66
-Year		1948	1993	1992	1991	1992	1953	1984	1974	1952	1946	1988	1956	OCT 1946
Snow,Ice pellets,hail														
-Maximum Monthly	49	69.2	86.3	52.6	46.3	1.2	T	0.0	0.0	T	15.6	48.8	54.7	86.3
-Year		1982	1965	1948	1963	1964	1970			1974	1956	1990	1964	FEB 1965
-Maximum in 24 hrs	49	20.1	23.7	31.0	24.2	0.7	T	0.0	0.0	T	8.8	16.5	25.6	31.0
-Year		1975	1949	1948	1963	1945	1970			1974	1956	1963	1962	MAR 1948
WIND:														
Mean Speed (mph)	48	8.3	8.5	8.5	8.6	8.3	7.7	7.5	7.5	8.0	9.5	8.5	9.0	8.3
Prevailing Direction through 1963		ESE	ESE	ESE	ESE	ESE	N	N	N	N	ESE	ESE	ESE	ESE
Fastest Obs. 1 Min.														
-Direction (!!)	23	12	13	11	11	12	13	12	12		12	11	11	
-Speed (MPH)	23	40	44	40	40	40	32	32	38	120	49	58	55	120
-Year		1992	1970	1963	1962	1965	1965	1970	1992	1993	1965	1968	1963	SEP 1993
Peak Gust														
-Direction (!!)														
-Speed (mph)														
-Date														

PRECIPITATION (inches)

JUNEAU, ALASKA

YEAR	JAN	FEB	MAR	APR	MAY	JUNE	JULY	AUG	SEP	OCT	NOV	DEC	ANNUAL
1964	3.19	8.48	4.38	4.04	4.35	3.37	6.94	3.48	2.59	7.35	4.89	5.22	58.28
1965	7.75	5.10	1.66	3.33	4.45	3.11	2.26	4.17	2.34	7.99	1.46	4.26	47.88
1966	4.34	3.13	6.36	2.08	6.33	1.74	3.91	6.37	8.20	6.97	4.39	4.48	58.30
1967	4.04	4.74	1.34	1.12	2.94	2.87	4.26	5.46	8.53	5.71	5.81	3.25	50.07
1968	3.25	5.30	3.85	3.25	1.45	1.95	4.60	2.39	10.14	4.60	5.34	1.90	48.02
1969	0.94	0.68	4.17	1.74	3.38	2.41	7.88	7.54	5.44	3.77	8.69	4.36	51.00
1970	2.37	3.35	4.08	3.69	3.92	2.97	5.01	7.47	9.86	5.87	2.01	2.58	53.18
1971	5.56	3.93	3.33	2.44	4.30	1.74	1.67	6.89	5.36	5.80	4.38	3.23	48.63
1972	3.73	2.71	4.19	3.62	4.03	3.98	1.15	8.62	6.24	8.49	3.35	3.56	53.67
1973	4.37	3.94	3.01	2.41	4.09	2.80	3.65	6.64	4.95	6.07	1.63	2.30	45.86
1974	2.37	6.23	1.15	2.59	1.66	4.92	3.12	5.78	5.96	15.25	7.79	7.03	63.85
1975	4.10	3.76	2.17	3.04	3.59	2.48	4.96	2.78	7.25	3.55	2.83	5.81	46.32
1976	8.19	4.82	3.61	2.14	3.42	3.37	2.48	3.16	8.32	6.19	5.15	5.56	56.41
1977	4.59	4.56	3.31	4.02	1.56	3.47	3.19	3.03	5.57	7.14	4.58	2.16	47.18
1978	1.71	1.50	1.84	2.19	2.86	3.18	3.98	4.39	3.07	13.00	3.90	4.46	46.08
1979	2.19	0.91	3.98	0.98	2.45	2.74	5.44	0.56	4.89	9.06	8.36	7.73	49.29
1980	3.44	2.83	2.75	5.32	2.53	4.37	6.49	5.61	7.91	11.26	7.10	2.27	61.88
1981	4.66	2.57	1.88	2.11	3.27	2.44	4.25	6.19	11.61	6.18	6.93	2.24	54.33
1982	3.74	1.42	2.52	2.44	5.10	1.86	1.73	5.97	5.10	7.97	2.10	1.17	41.12
1983	4.00	1.69	0.59	2.53	5.37	2.69	3.16	9.52	6.13	4.24	1.15	0.49	41.56
1984	6.06	5.40	3.75	2.11	1.84	4.17	6.92	6.26	3.39	6.69			46.59
1985												8.33	8.33
1986	7.00	3.25	6.08	2.98	2.54	2.76	2.38	6.89	2.40	12.33	5.96	6.42	60.99
1987	3.99	3.13	2.12	2.08	2.60	6.02	2.54	4.54	8.92	10.36	7.17	5.32	58.79
1988	2.58	6.55	4.15	2.25	3.91	2.05	5.21	5.53	5.46	9.71	8.62	4.75	60.77
1989	6.77	0.07	1.33	0.87	3.44	1.10	3.81	2.82	7.29	6.37	6.23	6.78	46.88
1990	3.72	4.54	4.86	1.06	1.72	3.32	4.65	5.35	10.63	6.59	4.89	6.03	57.36
1991	4.16	6.55	4.41	4.73	4.72	3.41	4.85	9.60	15.14	8.63	9.63	9.32	85.15
1992	8.69	7.24	6.37	3.63	9.20	2.98	5.18	5.02	11.45	5.90	7.91	5.73	79.30
1993	9.11	8.09	3.50	1.94	2.19	4.92	2.25	3.20	8.44	9.00	11.06	7.89	71.59
Record Mean	4.23	3.66	3.44	2.79	3.46	3.06	4.24	5.23	6.97	7.89	5.62	4.63	55.21

AVERAGE TEMPERATURE (deg. F)

JUNEAU, ALASKA

YEAR	JAN	FEB	MAR	APR	MAY	JUNE	JULY	AUG	SEP	OCT	NOV	DEC	ANNUAL
1964	29.3	35.9	28.8	38.6	45.1	53.6	54.3	53.6	49.7	45.0	32.1	16.6	40.2
1965	23.1	23.6	35.0	37.7	42.4	48.5	55.4	55.1	50.3	43.7	29.9	26.6	39.3
1966	8.6	25.9	30.2	38.1	43.3	52.9	56.2	52.4	49.2	38.6	25.1	26.5	37.2
1967	23.1	30.4	24.1	37.3	45.6	54.8	53.8	55.1	50.0	43.1	32.3	27.3	39.7
1968	18.7	28.8	33.1	37.9	48.4	52.2	56.8	55.7	47.6	39.0	34.1	19.4	39.3
1969	6.8	21.2	30.7	40.6	49.9	57.8	53.7	50.3	47.4	41.4	32.3	35.1	38.9
1970	22.0	35.1	36.5	39.1	45.3	50.7	52.3	51.7	46.3	39.6	27.8	21.6	39.0
1971	13.0	28.1	28.9	38.6	43.5	53.2	57.5	55.4	48.1	38.5	31.4	20.9	38.1
1972	15.8	19.5	26.5	34.6	44.8	50.4	58.0	55.4	47.0	38.7	34.5	23.6	37.4
1973	18.9	24.6	32.9	39.6	45.9	51.3	53.7	51.8	48.0	41.2	23.0	28.0	38.2
1974	14.8	28.8	24.7	39.3	46.8	50.2	53.5	54.7	50.1	42.5	36.4	33.8	39.6
1975	23.1	24.5	30.6	38.3	47.4	51.4	55.9	53.9	51.4	41.8	28.5	24.7	39.3
1976	28.3	25.8	32.4	41.1	45.5	52.0	55.7	55.9	50.6	42.8	40.9	34.4	42.1
1977	35.0	40.1	36.0	42.3	47.7	54.1	57.0	58.5	50.5	42.4	29.4	18.9	42.7
1978	25.1	31.8	33.9	42.0	47.8	54.2	55.2	56.3	50.6	45.1	30.3	28.3	41.7
1979	20.6	11.0	35.6	41.1	47.7	52.2	56.7	58.2	51.0	45.2	37.2	26.5	40.2
1980	19.5	33.8	34.1	42.2	49.4	55.6	55.6	54.7	49.0	44.6	38.7	21.7	41.6
1981	37.6	32.7	39.4	39.1	52.1	54.3	56.1	55.9	49.2	42.8	36.8	26.9	43.6
1982	13.8	21.3	31.8	37.1	45.4	56.3	57.7	54.8	50.3	42.2	30.6	31.6	39.4
1983	30.2	31.8	34.8	42.6	49.7	55.6	57.1	54.6	48.0	42.1	31.8	18.9	41.4
1984	32.0		39.6	43.1	49.1	53.5	55.5	55.3	50.0	40.5			45.5
1985												32.5	32.5
1986	34.3	28.7	35.3	37.3	46.6	54.3	56.8	54.4	50.7	45.8	30.5	36.0	42.6
1987	33.1	34.7	31.8	41.6	47.8	51.6	58.6	57.5	50.1	44.4	40.0	34.3	43.8
1988	27.0	32.6	37.6	41.7	48.5	54.0	53.8	53.9	48.2	44.1	36.2	31.3	42.4
1989	25.5	23.9	29.4	42.7	49.0	55.4	60.1	58.2	52.4	41.7	32.9	36.0	42.3
1990	26.4	25.1	36.4	42.7	49.7	55.0	59.3	58.1	51.2	40.7	26.4	23.7	41.2
1991	24.9	35.3	33.1	41.7	48.2	55.0	55.2	55.0	50.3	40.1	36.3	33.6	42.4
1992	35.7	32.7	36.9	41.1	46.4	55.2	57.0	56.0	46.8	40.5	38.4	25.6	42.7
1993	24.5	30.2	35.8	44.4	52.1	55.8	59.6	57.1	51.2	45.8	36.8	35.9	44.1
Record Mean	24.1	28.0	32.5	39.5	47.1	53.3	56.0	54.8	49.4	42.0	32.8	27.7	40.5
Max	29.5	33.7	38.6	46.9	55.2	61.6	63.9	62.6	55.9	47.0	37.4	32.2	47.0
Min	18.8	22.3	26.4	32.0	39.0	45.0	48.0	47.0	42.8	37.0	28.2	23.1	34.1

REFERENCE NOTES

JUNEAU, ALASKA

GENERAL
T - TRACE AMOUNT.
BLANK ENTRIES DENOTE MISSING/UNREPORTED DATA.
# INDICATES A STATION OR INSTRUMENT RELOCATION.

SPECIFIC

PM - INCLUDES LAST DAY OF PREVIOUS MONTH
ASOS - AUTOMATED SURFACE OBSERVING SYSTEM IN OPERATION DURING THESE MONTHS.

(a) - LENGTH OF RECORD IN YEARS, ALTHOUGH INDIVIDUAL MONTHS MAY BE MISSING.
0.* OR * - THE VALUE IS BETWEEN 0.0 AND 0.05
NORMALS - BASED ON THE 1961-1990 RECORD PERIOD.
EXTREMES - DATES ARE THE MOST RECENT OCCURRENCE
WIND DIR.- NUMERALS SHOW TENS OF DEGRESS CLOCKWISE FROM TRUE NORTH. "00" INDICATES CALM.
RESULTANT DIRECTIONS ARE GIVEN TO WHOLE DEGREES.
BOLD VALUES INDICATE EXTREME VALUES WHICH OCCURRED AFTER THE ASOS SYSTEM WAS COMMISSIONED.

RECORD = PERIOD OF RECORD
RECORD MEAN PRECIPITATION IS THE MEAN OF ALL DAILY PRECIPITATION AMOUNTS DURING THE PERIOD OF RECORD.
RECORD MAX(MIN) TEMPERATURE IS THE MEAN OF ALL DAILY MAX(MIN) TEMPERATURES DURING THE PERIOD OF RECORD.
RECORD MEAN TEMPERATURE IS THE SUM OF THE RECORD MAX AND RECORD MIN DIVIDED BY 2.
AVERAGE TEMPERATURE IS THE SUM OF THE MEAN DAILY MAX AND MIN TEMPERATURE DIVIDED BY 2.

EXCEPTIONS

1. PERCENT OF POSSIBLE SUNSHINE, MEAN SKY COVER, AND DAYS CLEAR-PARTLY CLOUDY-CLOUDY ARE THROUGH 1978.
2. FASTEST OBSERVED WIND IS THROUGH MAY 1979.

ALL PAGES
STATION REDUCED ELEMENTS RECORDED.

RECORD MEANS ARE THROUGH THE CURRENT YEAR,
BEGINNING IN 1944 FOR TEMPERATURE
1944 FOR PRECIPITATION
1944 FOR SNOWFALL

HEATING DEGREE DAYS Base 65 deg. F JUNEAU, ALASKA

SEASON	JULY	AUG	SEP	OCT	NOV	DEC	JAN	FEB	MAR	APR	MAY	JUNE	TOTAL
1964-65	324	347	453	614	980	1496	1291	1154	923	813	693	487	9575
1965-66	292	297	435	654	1045	1182	1746	1090	1071	805	667	355	9639
1966-67	265	382	466	812	1191	1188	1291	963	1261	824	592	300	9535
1967-68	340	303	444	671	973	1162	1432	1043	984	808	508	374	9042
1968-69	248	281	516	802	920	1405	1801	1219	1054	727	464	218	9655
1969-70	343	448	521	724	975	921	1329	830	876	770	601	422	8760
1970-71	387	405	553	783	1110	1343	1607	1029	1112	784	658	346	10117
1971-72	227	290	504	811	1001	1360	1519	1315	1186	906	618	432	10169
1972-73	207	293	535	810	907	1275	1423	1126	986	752	584	404	9302
1973-74	343	404	505	732	1253	1143	1550	1006	1242	765	556	437	9936
1974-75	349	315	437	690	851	957	1296	1129	1063	791	541	402	8821
1975-76	281	337	402	712	1088	1244	1132	1131	1006	706	597	384	9020
1976-77	280	275	427	679	717	938	918	690	893	673	531	320	7341
1977-78	243	196	428	695	1062	1423	1233	922	954	683	525	317	8681
1978-79	298	262	427	612	1037	1134	1370	1505	904	712	528	378	9167
1979-80	251	205	415	609	830	1187	1404	895	949	678	477	278	8178
1980-81	283	308	472	628	783	1333	843	899	786	772	392	316	7815
1981-82	269	275	469	682	841	1175	1579	1214	1021	830	601	257	9213
1982-83	220	310	435	699	1027	1029	1073	924	931	663	470	275	8056
1983-84	237	317	502	701	991	1423	1014		780	649	486	338	
1984-85	286	291	444	754									
1985-86						1001	943	1011	913	822	564	316	
1986-87	249	319	423	587	1028	891	982	841	1020	697	526	394	7957
1987-88	199	222	440	635	744	944	1169	935	844	691	508	324	7655
1988-89	338	338	497	641	855	1040	1217	1144	1097	663	491	283	8604
1989-90	159	210	370	713	959	890	1191	1109	879	661	467	295	7903
1990-91	180	210	407	748	1152	1274	1238	823	981	694	516	298	8521
1991-92	294	303	435	764	855	966	902	930	865	712	571	292	7889
1992-93	240	274	540	750	791	1217	1250	966	899	612	394	271	8204
1993-94	166	240	406	588	838	891							

COOLING DEGREE DAYS Base 65 deg. F JUNEAU, ALASKA

YEAR	JAN	FEB	MAR	APR	MAY	JUNE	JULY	AUG	SEP	OCT	NOV	DEC	TOTAL
1969	0	0	0	0	0	7	0	0	0	0	0	0	7
1970	0	0	0	0	0	0	0	0	0	0	0	0	0
1971	0	0	0	0	0	0	0	0	0	0	0	0	0
1972	0	0	0	0	0	0	0	0	0	0	0	0	0
1973	0	0	0	0	0	0	0	0	0	0	0	0	0
1974	0	0	0	0	0	0	0	0	0	0	0	0	0
1975	0	0	0	0	0	0	7	0	0	0	0	0	7
1976	0	0	0	0	0	0	3	3	0	0	0	0	6
1977	0	0	0	0	0	0	0	1	0	0	0	0	1
1978	0	0	0	0	0	0	0	0	0	0	0	0	0
1979	0	0	0	0	0	0	0	1	0	0	0	0	1
1980	0	0	0	0	0	1	0	0	0	0	0	0	1
1981	0	0	0	0	0	0	0	0	0	0	0	0	0
1982	0	0	0	0	0	2	0	0	0	0	0	0	2
1983	0	0	0	0	0	0	0	0	0	0	0	0	0
1984	0		0	0	0	0	0	0	0	0			0
1985												0	0
1986	0	0	0	0	0	2	0	0	0	0	0	0	2
1987	0	0	0	0	0	0	5	0	0	0	0	0	5
1988	0	0	0	0	0	0	0	0	0	0	0	0	0
1989	0	0	0	0	0	0	14	0	0	0	0	0	14
1990	0	0	0	0	0	1	8	3	0	0	0	0	12
1991	0	0	0	0	0	6	0	0	0	0	0	0	6
1992	0	0	0	0	0	6	0	0	0	0	0	0	6
1993	0	0	0	0	0	0	5	0	0	0	0	0	5

SNOWFALL (inches) JUNEAU, ALASKA

SEASON	JULY	AUG	SEP	OCT	NOV	DEC	JAN	FEB	MAR	APR	MAY	JUNE	TOTAL
1964-65	0.0	0.0	0.0	T	3.1	54.7	45.2	86.3	4.0	0.8	0.2	0.0	194.3
1965-66	0.0	0.0	0.0	0.3	9.6	16.9	54.8	17.6	49.0	1.5	T	0.0	149.7
1966-67	0.0	0.0	0.0	4.3	20.0	19.6	38.2	32.0	6.6	3.0	0.0	0.0	123.7
1967-68	0.0	0.0	0.0	0.0	9.5	21.1	31.1	17.0	8.2	6.1	T	0.0	93.0
1968-69	0.0	0.0	0.0	T	8.7	35.6	28.2	17.1	27.9	T	0.0	0.0	117.5
1969-70	0.0	0.0	0.0	0.0	18.2	0.7	15.8	2.0	1.1	3.5	0.0	T	41.3
1970-71	0.0	0.0	T	0.4	24.3	26.2	51.0	21.5	50.6	1.1	T	0.0	175.1
1971-72	0.0	0.0	0.0	6.9	20.5	37.1	45.1	31.1	27.1	10.3	0.0	0.0	178.1
1972-73	0.0	0.0	0.0	2.2	2.8	31.6	63.8	20.9	9.6	0.5	0.0	0.0	131.4
1973-74	0.0	0.0	0.0	T	18.6	15.7	36.0	32.8	15.3	0.5	0.0	0.0	118.9
1974-75	0.0	0.0	T	0.9	3.5	17.3	41.5	16.5	18.9	4.5	0.0	0.0	103.1
1975-76	0.0	0.0	0.0	5.3	32.5	51.0	32.9	34.1	25.5	2.3	0.0	0.0	183.6
1976-77	0.0	0.0	0.0	1.2	1.1	26.3	5.0	T	12.7	T	0.0	0.0	46.3
1977-78	0.0	0.0	0.0	T	27.4	16.6	5.2	1.1	1.7	0.4	0.0	0.0	52.4
1978-79	0.0	0.0	0.0	0.0	14.9	21.6	24.2	21.4	5.4	T	0.0	0.0	87.5
1979-80	0.0	0.0	0.0	0.0	1.6	48.4	41.6	4.1	2.4	T	0.0	0.0	98.1
1980-81	0.0	0.0	0.0	0.0	0.5	40.5	2.4	16.4	0.5	2.2	0.0	0.0	62.5
1981-82	0.0	0.0	0.0	0.0	4.0	6.0	69.2	29.6	8.4	1.1	T	0.0	118.3
1982-83	0.0	0.0	0.0	2.0	0.4	10.8	40.1	15.7	0.2	T	0.0	0.0	69.2
1983-84	0.0	0.0	0.0	0.0	8.1	13.3	43.1	0.7	1.0	T	T	0.0	66.2
1984-85	0.0	0.0	0.0	0.0									
1985-86						2.0	10.3	7.4	30.4	4.4	T	0.0	
1986-87	0.0	0.0	0.0	T	22.1	1.4	3.3	1.4	7.3	T	0.0	0.0	35.5
1987-88	0.0	0.0	0.0	T	4.6	6.8	3.5	8.0	1.0	0.5	0.0	0.0	24.4
1988-89	0.0	0.0	0.0	0.0	4.8	11.3	44.7	0.2	10.0	T	0.0	0.0	71.0
1989-90	0.0	0.0	0.0	0.6	32.5	6.4	36.5	39.4	0.6	0.0	0.0	0.0	116.0
1990-91	0.0	0.0	0.0	0.0	48.8	33.2	31.8	15.5	9.4	0.8	T	0.0	139.5
1991-92	0.0	0.0	0.0	5.4	7.7	49.3	14.3	12.4	4.1	T	T	0.0	93.2
1992-93	0.0	0.0	0.0	1.1	4.4	25.0	32.5	36.8	2.6	T	0.0	0.0	102.4
1993-94	0.0	0.0	0.0	0.0	4.3	10.4							
Record Mean	0.0	0.0	T	1.1	11.9	22.6	26.0	19.0	14.9	3.5	T	T	98.9

FLAGSTAFF, ARIZONA

Flagstaff, elevation 7,000 feet, is situated on a volcanic plateau at the base of the highest mountains in Arizona. The climate may be classified as vigorous with cold winters, mild, pleasantly cool summers, moderate humidity, and considerable diurnal temperature change. Only limited farming exists due to the short growing season. The stormy months are January, February, March, July, and August.

Based on the 1951-1980 period, the average first occurrence of 32 degrees Fahrenheit in the fall is September 21 and the average last occurrence in the spring is June 13.

Temperatures in Flagstaff are characteristic of high altitude climates. The average daily range of temperature is relatively high, especially in the winter months, October to March, as a result of extensive snow cover and clear skies. Winter minimum temperatures frequently reach zero or below and temperatures of -25 degrees or less have occurred. Summer maximum temperatures are often above 80 degrees and occasionally, temperatures have exceeded 95 degrees.

The Flagstaff area is semi-arid. Several months have recorded little or no precipitation. Over 90 consecutive days without measurable precipitation have occurred. Annual precipitation ranges from less than 10 inches to more than 35 inches. Winter snowfalls can be heavy, exceeding 100 inches during one month and over 200 inches during the winter season. However, accumulations are quite variable from year to year. Some winter months may experience little or no snow and the winter season has produced total snow accumulations of less than 12 inches.

NORMALS, MEANS, AND EXTREMES

FLAGSTAFF, ARIZONA

LATITUDE: 35 °08'N LONGITUDE: 111 °40' W ELEVATION: FT. GRND 7006 BARO 6997 TIME ZONE: MOUNTAIN WBAN: 03103

	(a)	JAN	FEB	MAR	APR	MAY	JUNE	JULY	AUG	SEP	OCT	NOV	DEC	YEAR
TEMPERATURE °F:														
Normals														
-Daily Maximum		42.2	45.3	49.2	57.8	67.4	78.2	81.9	79.3	73.2	63.4	51.1	43.3	61.0
-Daily Minimum		15.2	17.7	21.3	26.7	33.3	41.4	50.5	48.9	41.2	31.0	22.4	15.8	30.5
-Monthly		28.7	31.5	35.3	42.3	50.4	59.8	66.3	64.1	57.3	47.2	36.8	29.6	45.8
Extremes														
-Record Highest	44	66	71	73	80	87	96	97	92	90	85	74	68	97
-Year		1971	1986	1988	1992	1974	1970	1973	1978	1950	1980	1977	1950	JUL 1973
-Record Lowest	44	-22	-23	-16	-2	14	22	32	24	23	-2	-13	-23	-23
-Year		1971	1985	1966	1975	1975	1955	1955	1968	1971	1971	1958	1990	DEC 1990
NORMAL DEGREE DAYS:														
Heating (base 65°F)		1125	938	921	681	453	187	29	65	237	552	846	1097	7131
Cooling (base 65°F)		0	0	0	0	0	31	70	38	6	0	0	0	145
% OF POSSIBLE SUNSHINE	14	76	74	76	83	88	86	75	76	81	79	75	73	79
MEAN SKY COVER (tenths)														
Sunrise - Sunset	42	5.3	5.3	5.3	4.7	4.0	3.0	5.3	5.1	3.7	3.6	4.2	4.8	4.5
MEAN NUMBER OF DAYS:														
Sunrise to Sunset														
-Clear	42	12.3	10.9	11.6	12.5	15.3	18.5	9.1	9.8	15.7	17.1	15.4	13.9	162.0
-Partly Cloudy	42	6.3	6.1	7.9	8.8	9.2	7.7	13.1	13.1	9.6	7.0	6.6	6.5	101.9
-Cloudy	42	12.4	11.3	11.5	8.6	6.5	3.9	8.8	8.1	4.7	6.9	8.0	10.7	101.3
Precipitation														
.01 inches or more	44	7.7	6.9	8.5	5.5	4.5	2.8	11.5	11.5	6.3	4.9	5.3	6.4	81.9
Snow,Ice pellets,hail														
1.0 inches or more	43	4.5	4.0	5.1	2.3	0.6	0.0	0.0	0.0	0.*	0.5	2.1	3.6	22.7
Thunderstorms	30	0.*	0.3	0.6	1.3	2.6	3.7	16.6	15.7	6.7	2.2	0.7	0.2	50.5
Heavy Fog Visibility														
1/4 mile or less	30	1.8	1.8	1.6	1.2	0.2	0.*	0.1	0.3	0.5	0.9	1.1	1.8	11.4
Temperature °F														
-Maximum														
90° and above	44	0.0	0.0	0.0	0.0	0.0	1.3	1.5	0.3	0.*	0.0	0.0	0.0	3.2
32° and below	44	4.4	2.5	1.6	0.2	0.0	0.0	0.0	0.0	0.0	0.1	1.1	4.5	14.4
-Minimum														
32° and below	44	30.4	27.7	30.0	24.8	13.7	2.9	0.1	0.1	2.8	18.0	27.9	30.3	208.5
0° and below	44	3.2	1.4	0.6	0.*	0.0	0.0	0.0	0.0	0.0	0.*	0.4	2.2	8.0
AVG. STATION PRESS.(mb)	5	786.7	786.9	783.0	784.8	786.4	789.2	791.7	791.6	790.6	789.7	788.2	787.6	788.0
RELATIVE HUMIDITY (%)														
Hour 05	36	74	74	72	66	64	55	68	76	73	71	70	72	70
Hour 11 (Local Time)	38	54	51	45	34	29	23	34	40	37	38	44	51	40
Hour 17	30	51	45	41	31	27	21	38	43	36	36	43	52	39
Hour 23	24	68	65	63	54	49	40	59	69	64	63	64	72	61
PRECIPITATION (inches):														
Water Equivalent														
-Normal		2.04	2.09	2.55	1.48	0.72	0.40	2.78	2.75	2.03	1.61	1.95	2.40	22.80
-Maximum Monthly	44	9.55	10.05	6.75	5.62	4.14	2.92	6.62	8.06	6.75	9.86	6.64	7.30	10.05
-Year		1993	1993	1970	1965	1992	1955	1986	1986	1983	1972	1985	1967	FEB 1993
-Minimum Monthly	44	0.00	T	T	T	T	0.00	T	0.26	T	T	T	T	0.00
-Year		1972	1967	1972	1991	1974	1971	1993	1962	1992	1952	1989	1958	JAN 1972
-Maximum in 24 hrs	44	2.71	4.48	2.96	1.79	1.11	2.79	2.55	3.04	3.43	2.73	3.69	3.11	4.48
-Year		1993	1993	1970	1985	1965	1956	1964	1986	1965	1972	1978	1951	FEB 1993
Snow,Ice pellets,hail														
-Maximum Monthly	43	63.4	45.5	79.4	58.3	8.2	T	T	0.3	2.0	24.7	40.7	86.0	86.0
-Year		1980	1990	1991	1965	1975	1993	1992	1992	1965	1971	1985	1967	DEC 1967
-Maximum in 24 hrs	43	23.1	23.1	26.3	17.2	6.6	T	T	0.3	2.0	13.5	19.6	27.3	27.3
-Year		1980	1987	1970	1977	1965	1993	1992	1992	1965	1974	1991	1967	DEC 1967
WIND:														
Mean Speed (mph)	26	6.8	6.7	7.2	7.6	7.3	6.9	5.5	5.1	5.7	5.8	6.8	6.7	6.5
Prevailing Direction through 1963		NE	S	SSW	SSW	SSW	SSW	SSW	S	S	N	NNE	NE	SSW
Fastest Mile														
-Direction (!!!)	11	SW	SW	SW	SW	SW	SW	NW	SW	W	NW	SW	NE	SW
-Speed (MPH)	11	38	34	37	40	46	35	39	30	33	34	39	38	46
-Year		1975	1980	1974	1974	1975	1984	1976	1978	1974	1978	1978	1982	MAY 1975
Peak Gust														
-Direction (!!!)														
-Speed (mph)														
-Date														

PRECIPITATION (inches)

FLAGSTAFF, ARIZONA

YEAR	JAN	FEB	MAR	APR	MAY	JUNE	JULY	AUG	SEP	OCT	NOV	DEC	ANNUAL
1964	1.07	0.14	3.08	2.17	0.84	0.17	5.23	1.32	0.99	0.02	1.27	2.74	19.04
1965	3.05	2.34	3.33	5.62	1.88	0.30	2.34	1.01	4.85	0.27	4.97	6.63	36.59
1966	1.10	1.06	0.95	0.27	T	0.21	1.62	3.55	2.03	0.99	2.33	6.17	20.28
1967	0.93	T	1.11	1.90	0.41	1.05	3.80	2.68	2.25	0.30	0.54	7.30	22.27
1968	1.55	1.29	1.15	2.09	0.55	0.16	3.61	1.13	0.04	1.38	0.87	2.71	16.53
1969	4.63	3.91	3.00	0.11	1.06	0.01	3.81	1.90	1.34	1.14	2.04	0.46	23.41
1970	0.51	0.41	6.75	1.16	T	0.07	2.58	5.15	3.79	0.11	1.37	2.12	24.02
1971	0.08	1.48	0.25	0.55	1.23	0.00	1.97	4.48	2.02	4.37	0.40	4.18	21.01
1972	0.00	0.02	T	0.72	0.14	1.93	1.90	2.82	0.81	9.86	2.34	4.13	24.67
1973	1.89	3.69	6.18	1.21	1.17	0.40	1.87	1.25	T	0.03	1.90	0.12	19.71
1974	3.63	0.26	1.01	0.57	T	T	3.00	2.16	0.93	3.64	1.03	1.18	17.41
1975	1.76	1.90	2.92	2.20	1.16	0.05	2.24	0.74	1.89	0.33	2.96	1.95	20.10
1976	0.17	5.96	2.06	3.09	1.65	T	3.82	0.58	1.16	0.73	0.10	0.80	20.12
1977	1.85	0.84	0.92	1.47	0.96	0.91	3.60	3.72	1.52	1.04	0.76	1.18	18.77
1978	4.09	4.67	5.58	1.60	0.27	0.09	1.17	0.68	0.46	0.56	6.16	5.39	30.72
1979	5.54	1.73	2.52	0.31	2.16	0.18	0.79	2.38	0.13	1.30	1.14	1.50	19.68
1980	6.52	7.81	4.16	1.21	1.79	0.25	2.49	2.19	0.65	1.08	T	1.15	29.30
1981	1.31	1.16	4.04	1.50	0.72	1.09	2.87	3.73	2.54	1.81	2.43	0.17	23.37
1982	4.62	2.55	5.69	0.25	0.86	T	1.89	2.32	3.17	0.71	5.36	3.67	31.09
1983	1.61	3.04	4.36	2.18	0.06	0.28	2.86	3.53	6.75	0.75	1.53	2.52	29.47
1984	0.36	0.13	0.89	0.73	0.21	0.13	4.20	3.86	1.75	1.43	1.40	5.00	20.09
1985	2.38	1.67	2.54	3.39	0.26	0.09	2.36	1.07	3.68	2.44	6.64	0.15	26.67
1986	0.31	1.76	2.60	1.23	0.72	1.16	6.62	8.06	4.80	2.02	1.68	1.43	32.39
1987	2.51	2.54	1.69	0.21	0.70	0.25	1.93	3.74	1.49	4.64	2.91	1.37	23.98
1988	1.64	2.30	0.14	3.83	0.14	1.86	3.48	4.77	0.15	1.23	1.14	1.00	21.68
1989	1.84	1.35	2.08	0.01	0.62	0.23	2.28	3.40	0.30	1.28	T	1.05	14.44
1990	1.54	3.20	2.17	2.32	0.73	0.24	4.32	1.71	6.18	0.49	1.09	1.68	25.67
1991	1.76	2.08	6.00	T	0.14	0.59	1.04	1.64	0.26	1.12	4.47	2.73	21.83
1992	2.03	3.69	4.40	0.78	4.14	0.32	2.67	5.80	T	3.64	0.46	6.78	34.71
1993	9.55	10.05	1.54	0.26	0.44	0.55	T	4.19	1.95	3.29	3.02	0.76	35.60
Record Mean	2.06	2.07	2.11	1.31	0.71	0.51	2.73	2.89	1.78	1.56	1.53	1.95	21.20

AVERAGE TEMPERATURE (deg. F)

FLAGSTAFF, ARIZONA

YEAR	JAN	FEB	MAR	APR	MAY	JUNE	JULY	AUG	SEP	OCT	NOV	DEC	ANNUAL
1964	25.3	26.6	30.5	39.7	49.4	57.4	66.9	63.3	56.7	51.3	31.3	30.3	44.1
1965	31.4	29.7	33.0	39.2	46.7	53.0	65.0	63.7	53.8	49.7	39.7	30.2	44.6
1966	23.5	25.1	37.2	44.7	53.7	59.1	66.4	65.2	58.6	46.9	39.5	29.7	45.8
1967	29.1	35.3	39.0	37.6	48.7	56.2	66.6	64.4	57.9	50.0	40.4	23.1	45.7
1968	25.5	35.8	37.0	40.3	50.2	59.9	64.9	59.5	55.9	46.9	35.7	25.0	44.7
1969	31.8	25.4	27.3	41.7	52.4	57.9	66.2	65.1	58.2	40.5	33.9	33.3	44.5
1970	30.9	37.1	33.7	37.5	52.6	60.4	67.7	66.3	54.4	43.9	39.5	28.5	46.1
1971	29.3	31.1	37.0	41.9	46.8	58.7	67.5	64.0	53.0	38.6	33.5	22.5	43.6
1972	28.4	31.8	40.0	39.8	46.4	57.6	66.5	62.9	56.7	45.9	29.6	21.9	43.9
1973	22.9	28.7	26.8	38.0	52.8	60.5	65.7	64.6	57.7	50.0	37.1	33.0	44.8
1974	27.8	30.5	40.4	43.2	54.8	66.5	66.3	64.7	58.7	47.9	36.8	26.8	47.0
1975	27.7	27.6	33.2	36.2	47.5	57.1	65.9	63.5	57.9	46.5	37.3	29.2	44.2
1976	30.6	35.1	35.4	41.4	52.8	58.9	66.5	62.8	57.1	47.0	39.5	31.6	46.5
1977	26.8	34.2	33.5	44.7	47.4	62.2	67.2	66.2	60.2	50.8	41.0	37.6	47.6
1978	31.5	30.7	40.3	42.2	49.4	61.4	66.6	63.7	57.3	49.8	34.6	24.3	46.0
1979	22.6	25.9	32.3	40.7	47.9	57.8	64.1	60.5	58.8	47.8	31.2	31.2	43.4
1980	30.7	32.8	32.3	41.9	45.6	60.9	69.0	66.3	59.7	49.0	41.4	39.9	47.5
1981	36.2	36.3	36.6	48.5	52.1	66.1	68.2	65.4	58.7	46.7	41.8	36.4	49.4
1982	28.3	30.5	35.3	43.5	49.9	57.1	63.8	65.6	57.6	44.0	35.2	28.1	44.9
1983	31.0	32.3	36.2	37.0	49.9	57.3	65.5	63.8	60.7	48.6	36.9	34.0	46.1
1984	31.7	32.8	38.3	40.7	56.8	58.5	65.7	63.8	59.3	42.4	35.3	29.0	46.2
1985	27.5	28.9	35.5	46.2	51.5	62.6	67.2	65.3	53.1	47.7	33.8	32.4	46.0
1986	37.0	34.2	39.7	44.1	52.0	61.2	64.0	65.7	53.0	43.5	37.6	30.2	46.9
1987	27.6	31.1	32.8	45.9	50.7	61.3	62.8	62.8	56.5	50.4	36.2	27.1	45.4
1988	29.1	34.2	37.4	44.0	50.8	61.5	67.4	64.3	55.9	52.5	36.9	27.9	46.8
1989	26.2	32.3	41.8	50.4	54.2	60.8	68.1	63.6	58.7	47.5	38.4	31.6	47.8
1990	28.6	29.3	38.3	46.1	50.3	64.4	66.9	62.6	59.8	48.9	37.6	25.1	46.5
1991	30.5	37.2	32.2	43.1	49.4	57.3	67.1	66.5	59.6	50.8	36.9	30.2	46.7
1992	27.3	35.2	38.1	49.1	53.3	59.0	65.1	64.2	59.3	50.4	33.8	26.3	46.8
1993	32.2	32.5	40.2	46.4	53.9	60.4	65.5	64.8	57.9	47.4	35.0	30.1	47.2
Record Mean	28.1	31.1	35.8	42.9	50.4	59.4	65.8	63.9	57.4	47.1	36.8	29.7	45.7
Max	41.5	44.2	49.3	57.9	66.8	77.4	81.1	78.6	73.3	63.0	51.4	43.2	60.7
Min	14.7	17.9	22.3	27.8	33.9	41.3	50.4	49.2	41.5	31.2	22.1	16.1	30.7

REFERENCE NOTES

FLAGSTAFF, ARIZONA

GENERAL
T - TRACE AMOUNT.
BLANK ENTRIES DENOTE MISSING/UNREPORTED DATA.
# INDICATES A STATION OR INSTRUMENT RELOCATION.

SPECIFIC

PM - INCLUDES LAST DAY OF PREVIOUS MONTH
ASOS - AUTOMATED SURFACE OBSERVING SYSTEM IN OPERATION DURING THESE MONTHS.

(a) - LENGTH OF RECORD IN YEARS, ALTHOUGH INDIVIDUAL MONTHS MAY BE MISSING.
0.* OR * - THE VALUE IS BETWEEN 0.0 AND 0.05
NORMALS - BASED ON THE 1961-1990 RECORD PERIOD.
EXTREMES - DATES ARE THE MOST RECENT OCCURRENCE
WIND DIR. - NUMERALS SHOW TENS OF DEGRESS CLOCKWISE FROM TRUE NORTH. "00" INDICATES CALM.
RESULTANT DIRECTIONS ARE GIVEN TO WHOLE DEGREES.
BOLD VALUES INDICATE EXTREME VALUES WHICH OCCURRED AFTER THE ASOS SYSTEM WAS COMMISSIONED.

RECORD = PERIOD OF RECORD
RECORD MEAN PRECIPITATION IS THE MEAN OF ALL DAILY PRECIPITATION AMOUNTS DURING THE PERIOD OF RECORD.
RECORD MAX(MIN) TEMPERATURE IS THE MEAN OF ALL DAILY MAX(MIN) TEMPERATURES DURING THE PERIOD OF RECORD.
RECORD MEAN TEMPERATURE IS THE SUM OF THE RECORD MAX AND RECORD MIN DIVIDED BY 2.
AVERAGE TEMPERATURE IS THE SUM OF THE MEAN DAILY MAX AND MIN TEMPERATURE DIVIDED BY 2.

EXCEPTIONS

1. PERCENT OF POSSIBLE SUNSHINE IS 1973-1976 AND 1983 TO DATE.
2. MEAN WIND SPEED, THUNDERSTORMS, AND HEAVY FOG ARE THROUGH 1978.

RECORD MEANS ARE THROUGH THE CURRENT YEAR, BEGINNING IN 1900 FOR TEMPERATURE
1900 FOR PRECIPITATION
1950 FOR SNOWFALL

HEATING DEGREE DAYS Base 65 deg. F — FLAGSTAFF, ARIZONA

SEASON	JULY	AUG	SEP	OCT	NOV	DEC	JAN	FEB	MAR	APR	MAY	JUNE	TOTAL
1964-65	9	72	245	417	1001	1070	1034	983	985	768	560	353	7497
1965-66	22	69	326	467	753	1071	1281	1109	854	603	343	171	7069
1966-67	14	32	185	556	757	1089	1111	824	799	816	498	265	6946
1967-68	11	33	207	461	733	1292	1218	839	861	733	453	172	7013
1968-69	38	164	267	554	872	1234	1021	1105	1164	693	383	207	7702
1969-70	21	37	200	753	926	978	1051	775	962	821	378	174	7076
1970-71	6	16	310	643	758	1125	1098	943	862	683	557	210	7211
1971-72	24	40	352	809	938	1310	1126	956	768	749	573	220	7865
1972-73	22	78	241	584	1055	1330	1297	1006	1176	801	370	164	8124
1973-74	39	45	212	458	829	987	1147	960	754	650	310	67	6458
1974-75	19	34	195	522	841	1178	1150	1041	978	856	536	231	7581
1975-76	23	66	207	566	821	1101	1059	862	912	702	370	190	6879
1976-77	17	71	230	553	757	1027	1177	858	970	603	540	102	6905
1977-78	9	19	157	432	715	843	1032	954	756	677	478	128	6200
1978-79	33	73	227	465	907	1254	1307	1089	1005	722	524	219	7825
1979-80	68	157	186	526	1008	1042	1056	930	1009	684	596	158	7420
1980-81	6	43	153	491	703	774	886	794	873	486	398	50	5657
1981-82	1	39	182	558	689	880	1130	963	911	640	458	230	6681
1982-83	65	22	218	643	888	1136	1046	911	888	835	461	222	7335
1983-84	26	64	134	502	837	952	1025	929	820	722	247	204	6462
1984-85	21	51	165	695	884	1109	1155	1005	911	557	411	102	7066
1985-86	26	31	351	532	931	1005	862	855	777	619	392	119	6500
1986-87	58	28	353	661	816	1069	1150	942	990	566	435	114	7182
1987-88	82	86	246	447	859	1167	1103	885	848	621	434	124	6902
1988-89	9	41	266	381	836	1141	1196	910	710	432	330	139	6391
1989-90	7	67	184	540	792	1030	1124	996	822	558	449	84	6653
1990-91	10	93	167	494	816	1231	1060	772	1008	652	476	225	7004
1991-92	7	12	159	438	835	1071	1159	854	830	470	356	180	6371
1992-93	38	80	163	444	932	1191	1014	903	761	551	339	158	6574
1993-94	29	45	207	538	893	1073							

COOLING DEGREE DAYS Base 65 deg. F — FLAGSTAFF, ARIZONA

YEAR	JAN	FEB	MAR	APR	MAY	JUNE	JULY	AUG	SEP	OCT	NOV	DEC	TOTAL
1969	0	0	0	0	0	1	64	48	0	0	0	0	113
1970	0	0	0	0	0	44	99	64	1	0	0	0	208
1971	0	0	0	0	0	28	108	17	0	0	0	0	153
1972	0	0	0	0	0	4	76	20	0	0	0	0	100
1973	0	0	0	0	0	34	69	40	0	0	0	0	143
1974	0	0	0	0	0	120	66	33	13	0	0	0	232
1975	0	0	0	0	0	0	60	28	0	0	0	0	88
1976	0	0	0	0	0	15	70	13	0	0	0	0	98
1977	0	0	0	0	0	28	82	61	20	0	0	0	191
1978	0	0	0	0	0	25	87	38	2	0	0	0	152
1979	0	0	0	0	0	10	47	24	4	0	0	0	85
1980	0	0	0	0	0	43	133	91	2	0	0	0	269
1981	0	0	0	0	0	91	108	58	0	0	0	0	257
1982	0	0	0	0	0	1	36	46	6	0	0	0	89
1983	0	0	0	0	0	0	45	31	12	0	0	0	88
1984	0	0	0	0	2	14	49	23	2	0	0	0	90
1985	0	0	0	0	0	36	102	47	0	0	0	0	185
1986	0	0	0	0	0	11	33	55	0	0	0	0	99
1987	0	0	0	0	0	13	21	26	0	0	0	0	60
1988	0	0	0	0	0	28	94	28	1	0	0	0	151
1989	0	0	0	0	0	22	111	29	0	0	0	0	162
1990	0	0	0	0	0	76	76	28	18	0	0	0	198
1991	0	0	0	0	0	0	79	65	4	0	0	0	148
1992	0	0	0	0	0	6	48	62	0	0	0	0	116
1993	0	0	0	0	0	26	50	46	1	0	0	0	123

SNOWFALL (inches) — FLAGSTAFF, ARIZONA

SEASON	JULY	AUG	SEP	OCT	NOV	DEC	JAN	FEB	MAR	APR	MAY	JUNE	TOTAL
1964-65	0.0	0.0	0.0	0.0	14.3	13.7	15.1	23.9	34.4	58.3	7.0	0.0	166.7
1965-66	0.0	0.0	2.0	2.2	2.9	38.5	14.5	10.8	7.4	5.1	0.0	0.0	83.4
1966-67	0.0	0.0	0.0	T	11.3	13.4	9.8	T	10.9	17.7	0.0	0.0	63.1
1967-68	0.0	0.0	0.0	0.0	5.1	86.0	15.2	9.3	10.1	22.7	2.0	0.0	150.4
1968-69	0.0	0.0	0.0	T	4.3	27.5	12.0	42.1	43.6	0.6	4.6	0.0	134.7
1969-70	0.0	0.0	0.0	1.5	3.0	4.6	5.2	2.8	67.3	11.3	0.0	0.0	95.7
1970-71	0.0	0.0	0.0	0.0	2.0	24.5	0.8	15.1	3.1	5.0	6.1	0.0	56.6
1971-72	0.0	0.0	T	24.7	4.9	18.8	0.0	0.4	T	1.5	0.0	0.0	50.3
1972-73	0.0	0.0	0.0	11.8	23.2	28.9	21.0	33.8	77.4	10.9	3.0	0.0	210.0
1973-74	0.0	0.0	0.0	T	20.7	1.2	35.3	2.4	8.8	1.6	0.0	0.0	70.0
1974-75	0.0	0.0	0.0	16.6	8.2	15.6	20.1	18.2	29.1	25.1	8.2	0.0	141.1
1975-76	0.0	0.0	0.0	T	25.2	18.9	1.5	31.2	20.4	31.2	3.2	0.0	131.6
1976-77	0.0	0.0	0.0	T	0.7	9.0	21.1	11.2	8.8	17.8	1.6	0.0	70.2
1977-78	0.0	0.0	0.0	0.0	7.0	1.6	40.4	32.1	24.5	9.3	1.3	0.0	116.2
1978-79	0.0	0.0	0.0	0.0	16.5	19.8	59.4	18.1	22.8	4.1	4.8	0.0	145.5
1979-80	0.0	0.0	0.0	0.5	5.5	20.7	63.4	32.9	42.5	11.6	T	0.0	177.1
1980-81	0.0	0.0	0.0	6.9	T	6.8	11.7	11.9	45.6	9.5	0.0	0.0	92.4
1981-82	0.0	0.0			0.0	0.0	47.5	20.4	26.7	1.9	0.4	0.0	
1982-83	0.0	0.0	T	T	22.6	27.1	15.3	25.0	38.5	13.6	0.5	0.0	142.6
1983-84	0.0	0.0	0.0	0.0	14.3	5.8	4.3	1.8	0.3	5.5	0.0	0.0	32.0
1984-85	0.0	0.0	0.0	0.6	9.4	28.7	26.2	31.3	21.3	18.5	0.0	0.0	136.0
1985-86	0.0	0.0	0.0	0.0	40.7	2.6	0.4	26.9	32.8	1.6	0.4	0.0	105.4
1986-87	0.0	0.0	0.9	0.6	4.8	9.5	38.6	40.7	25.0	1.5	0.0	0.0	121.6
1987-88	0.0	0.0	0.0	0.0	2.9	16.7	28.9	21.0	1.5	33.1	0.4	0.0	104.5
1988-89	0.0	0.0	0.0	0.0	11.9	15.0	21.7	12.0	16.6	T	0.5	0.0	77.7
1989-90	0.0	T	T	T	T	13.1	24.2	45.5	25.0	4.2	1.4	0.0	113.4
1990-91	T	T	T	T	9.6	22.3	3.1	13.5	79.4	T	T	0.0	127.9
1991-92	0.0	0.0	T	5.9	39.5	24.0	24.7	24.9	35.9	4.0	T	T	158.9
1992-93	T	0.3	0.0	0.5	2.1	41.7	55.7	35.2	11.9	2.3	0.3	T	150.0
1993-94	0.0	T	T	0.0	23.0	13.4							
Record Mean	T	T	0.1	2.0	10.2	15.9	20.7	18.3	22.3	9.5	1.8	T	100.7

PHOENIX, ARIZONA

Phoenix is located in the Salt River Valley at an elevation of about 1,100 feet. The valley is oval shaped and flat except for scattered precipitous mountains rising a few hundred to as much as 1,500 feet above the valley floor. Sky Harbor Airport, where the weather observations are taken, is in the southern part of the city. Six miles to the south of the airport are the South Mountains rising to 2,500 feet. Eighteen miles southwest, the Estrella Mountains rise to 4,500 feet, and 30 miles to the west are the White Tank Mountains rising to 4,100 feet. The Superstition Mountains, over 30 miles to the east, rise to as much as 5,000 feet. The valley, though located in the Sonora Desert, supports large acreages of cotton, citrus, and other agriculture along with one of the largest urban populations in the United States. The water supply for this complex desert community is partly from reservoirs on the impounded Salt and Verde Rivers, and partly from a large underground water table.

Temperatures range from very hot in summer to mild in winter. Many winter days reach over 70 degrees and typical high temperatures in the middle of the winter are in the 60s. The climate becomes less attractive in the summer. The normal high temperature is over 90 degrees from early May through early October, and over 100 degrees from early June through early September. Many days each summer will exceed 110 degrees in the afternoon and remain above 85 degrees all night. When temperatures are extremely high, the low humidity does not provide much comfort.

Indeed, the climate is very dry. Annual precipitation is only about 7 inches, and afternoon humidities range from about 30 percent in winter to only about 10 percent in June. Rain comes mostly in two seasons. From about Thanksgiving to early April there are periodic rains from Pacific storms. Moisture from the south and southeast results in a summer thunderstorm peak in July and August. Usually the break from extreme dryness in June to the onset of thunderstorms in early July is very abrupt. Afternoon humidities suddenly double to about 20 percent, which with the great heat, gives a feeling of mugginess. Fog is rare, occurring about once per winter, and is unknown in the other seasons.

The valley is characterized by light winds. High winds associated with thunderstorms occur periodically in the summer. These occasionally create duststorms which move large distances across the deserts. Strong thunderstorm winds occur any month of the year, but are rare outside the summer months. Persistent strong winds of 30 mph or more are rare except for two or three events in an average spring due to Pacific storms. Winter storms rarely bring high winds due to the relatively stable air in the valley during that season.

Based on the 1951–1980 period, the average first occurrence of 32 degrees Fahrenheit in the fall is December 13 and the average last occurrence in the spring is February 7.

NORMALS, MEANS, AND EXTREMES

PHOENIX, ARIZONA

LATITUDE: 33°26'N LONGITUDE: 112°01' W ELEVATION: FT. GRND 1110 BARO 1109 TIME ZONE: MOUNTAIN WBAN: 23183

	(a)	JAN	FEB	MAR	APR	MAY	JUNE	JULY	AUG	SEP	OCT	NOV	DEC	YEAR
TEMPERATURE °F:														
Normals														
-Daily Maximum		65.9	70.7	75.5	84.5	93.6	103.5	105.9	103.7	98.3	88.1	74.9	66.2	85.9
-Daily Minimum		41.2	44.7	48.8	55.3	63.9	72.9	81.0	79.2	72.8	60.8	48.9	41.8	59.3
-Monthly		53.6	57.7	62.2	69.9	78.8	88.2	93.5	91.5	85.6	74.5	61.9	54.1	72.6
Extremes														
-Record Highest	56	88	92	100	105	113	122	118	116	118	107	93	88	122
-Year		1971	1986	1988	1992	1984	1990	1989	1975	1950	1980	1988	1950	JUN 1990
-Record Lowest	56	17	22	25	32	40	50	61	60	47	34	25	22	17
-Year		1950	1948	1966	1945	1967	1944	1944	1942	1965	1971	1938	1948	JAN 1950
NORMAL DEGREE DAYS:														
Heating (base 65°F)		362	227	182	75	8	0	0	0	0	17	134	345	1350
Cooling (base 65°F)		8	22	95	222	436	696	884	822	618	311	41	7	4162
% OF POSSIBLE SUNSHINE	98	78	80	84	89	93	94	85	85	89	88	84	78	86
MEAN SKY COVER (tenths)														
Sunrise - Sunset	48	4.7	4.6	4.3	3.4	2.7	1.9	3.7	3.3	2.3	2.8	3.4	4.1	3.4
MEAN NUMBER OF DAYS:														
Sunrise to Sunset														
-Clear	56	13.9	12.6	14.4	17.2	20.8	23.1	16.6	17.6	21.6	20.3	17.7	15.3	211.0
-Partly Cloudy	56	7.0	6.7	8.1	7.3	6.8	4.7	10.3	9.6	5.4	6.2	6.2	6.3	84.6
-Cloudy	56	10.1	8.9	8.5	5.6	3.5	2.2	4.2	3.8	3.0	4.4	6.1	9.4	69.7
Precipitation														
.01 inches or more	54	4.1	3.9	3.7	1.7	1.0	0.7	4.2	4.9	2.9	2.7	2.6	3.9	36.5
Snow, Ice pellets, hail														
1.0 inches or more	56	0.0	0.0	0.0	0.0	0.0	0.0	0.0	0.0	0.0	0.0	0.0	0.0	0.0
Thunderstorms	54	0.4	0.6	0.9	0.7	1.0	1.0	6.1	7.1	3.5	1.4	0.5	0.6	23.7
Heavy Fog Visibility														
1/4 mile or less	56	0.6	0.1	0.1	0.0	0.0	0.0	0.0	0.0	0.0	0.*	0.2	0.5	1.6
Temperature °F														
-Maximum														
90° and above	33	0.0	0.1	2.0	9.8	23.1	29.2	30.9	30.6	27.6	15.2	0.5	0.0	169.0
32° and below	33	0.0	0.0	0.0	0.0	0.0	0.0	0.0	0.0	0.0	0.0	0.0	0.0	0.0
-Minimum														
32° and below	33	3.3	1.3	0.4	0.0	0.0	0.0	0.0	0.0	0.0	0.0	0.2	1.8	7.0
0° and below	33	0.0	0.0	0.0	0.0	0.0	0.0	0.0	0.0	0.0	0.0	0.0	0.0	0.0
AVG. STATION PRESS.(mb)	21	978.3	977.5	974.4	972.6	970.6	969.7	971.2	971.6	971.7	974.0	976.5	978.3	973.9
RELATIVE HUMIDITY (%)														
Hour 05	33	67	60	57	43	35	31	44	51	49	50	57	67	51
Hour 11 (Local Time)	33	46	39	34	23	19	16	28	33	31	30	36	46	32
Hour 17	33	33	27	24	16	13	12	20	23	23	22	27	34	23
Hour 23	33	56	48	43	28	23	20	33	38	38	40	48	57	39
PRECIPITATION (inches):														
Water Equivalent														
-Normal		0.67	0.68	0.88	0.22	0.12	0.13	0.83	0.96	0.86	0.65	0.66	1.00	7.66
-Maximum Monthly	56	5.22	2.23	4.16	2.10	1.06	1.70	5.15	5.56	4.23	4.40	3.04	3.98	5.56
-Year		1993	1944	1941	1941	1976	1972	1984	1951	1939	1972	1952	1967	AUG 1951
-Minimum Monthly	56	0.00	0.00	0.00	0.00	0.00	0.00	T	T	0.00	0.00	0.00	0.00	0.00
-Year		1972	1967	1959	1962	1983	1983	1993	1975	1973	1973	1980	1981	MAY 1983
-Maximum in 24 hrs	56	1.84	1.49	2.04	1.38	0.96	1.64	2.75	3.07	2.43	2.32	2.16	1.89	3.07
-Year		1993	1987	1983	1941	1976	1972	1984	1943	1970	1988	1993	1967	AUG 1943
Snow, Ice pellets, hail														
-Maximum Monthly	56	T	0.6	T	T	T	0.0	0.0	0.0	0.0	T	0.0	0.4	0.6
-Year		1993	1939	1991	1949	1992					1992		1990	FEB 1939
-Maximum in 24 hrs	56	T	0.6	T	T	T	0.0	0.0	0.0	0.0	T	0.0	0.4	0.6
-Year		1993	1939	1991	1949	1992					1992		1990	FEB 1939
WIND:														
Mean Speed (mph)	48	5.3	5.9	6.7	6.9	7.0	6.8	7.1	6.6	6.3	5.8	5.3	5.1	6.2
Prevailing Direction through 1963		E	E	E	E	E	E	W	E	E	E	E	E	E
Fastest Obs. 1 Min.														
-Direction (!!!)	8	27	14	26	27	11	03	08	10	05	21	29	09	26
-Speed (MPH)	8	32	26	35	28	35	31	35	35	35	28	29	26	35
-Year		1988	1992	1992	1986	1992	1986	1991	1989	1990	1986	1990	1988	MAR 1992
Peak Gust														
-Direction (!!!)	56	W	W	W	W	SSE	NE	SE	E	SW	W	W	W	SE
-Speed (mph)	56	60	54	51	49	59	73	86	78	75	61	60	68	86
-Date		1983	1980	1989	1981	1954	1978	1976	1978	1950	1981	1982	1953	JUL 1976

PRECIPITATION (inches)

PHOENIX, ARIZONA

YEAR	JAN	FEB	MAR	APR	MAY	JUNE	JULY	AUG	SEP	OCT	NOV	DEC	ANNUAL
1964	0.22	0.01	0.37	0.10	T	0.00	0.60	1.29	1.80	0.17	0.35	1.09	6.00
1965	1.22	0.91	1.39	1.35	0.16	0.91	0.16	0.18	0.60	0.20	0.92	3.19	11.19
1966	0.35	0.95	0.34	T	T	0.22	0.09	2.17	2.00	0.25	0.38	0.52	7.27
1967	0.25	0.00	0.43	0.08	0.05	0.47	0.99	0.02	0.13	0.67	1.27	3.98	8.34
1968	0.19	1.20	1.04	T	T	0.00	1.70	0.59	0.00	0.35	0.91	0.69	6.67
1969	1.37	0.78	0.56	0.03	0.26	0.00	0.28	0.14	2.11	0.08	0.65	0.68	6.94
1970	T	0.30	2.26	T	T	0.00	0.48	1.02	2.85	0.44	0.02	0.26	7.63
1971	0.22	0.35	T	0.13	T	0.00	0.24	0.99	0.92	0.27	T	0.47	3.59
1972	0.00	T	T	T	T	1.70	0.72	1.20	0.28	4.40	1.01	1.56	10.87
1973	0.13	1.36	1.69	0.07	0.10	T	1.30	T	0.00	0.00	1.36	0.00	6.01
1974	0.57	0.02	1.37	0.01	0.00	0.00	0.84	1.15	1.07	2.12	0.44	0.59	8.18
1975	0.02	0.33	0.63	0.43	T	T	0.38	T	0.82	0.23	0.55	1.12	4.51
1976	T	0.47	0.40	0.67	1.06	0.09	1.48	0.12	1.69	0.70	0.43	0.85	7.96
1977	0.35	0.06	0.27	0.06	0.16	0.10	0.30	0.18	0.53	0.61	T	0.54	3.16
1978	2.33	2.21	2.14	0.20	T	0.01	1.44	1.79	T	0.35	2.30	2.46	15.23
1979	2.16	0.09	1.78	0.02	0.76	0.04	0.34	1.18	0.09	0.09	0.12	0.13	6.80
1980	1.58	2.09	0.86	0.44	0.21	0.03	0.56	0.06	0.13	0.02	0.00	0.08	6.06
1981	0.71	1.08	0.98	0.20	0.03	T	1.14	0.11	0.18	1.34	0.95	0.00	6.72
1982	0.81	0.67	1.30	T	0.50	T	0.43	1.97	0.12	T	2.50	1.64	9.94
1983	0.70	1.17	3.17	0.18	0.00	0.00	0.38	2.48	2.43	0.71	0.43	1.16	12.81
1984	0.31	0.00	0.00	0.91	0.18	0.18	5.15	0.87	3.36	0.31	0.71	2.93	14.91
1985	0.95	0.18	0.46	0.17	T	0.00	0.98	0.21	1.60	0.92	1.59	0.86	7.92
1986	0.07	1.19	1.58	0.01	T	0.01	1.19	1.27	0.47	0.41	0.03	1.38	7.61
1987	0.67	2.06	0.2[illegible]	0.09	0.06	0.01	1.08	0.45	0.57	0.47	1.04	1.62	8.40
1988	0.90	0.23	0.17	1.09	0.00	0.02	0.87	0.63	0.00	2.38	0.78	0.14	7.21
1989	1.19	T	1.25	0.00	T	0.00	0.13	1.11	0.47	0.46	0.14	0.19	4.94
1990	0.80	0.70	0.35	0.17	0.16	0.04	1.05	2.70	1.11	0.04	0.15	0.46	7.73
1991	0.63	0.56	2.05	0.00	0.00	T	0.14	0.12	0.81	1.16	1.25	1.63	8.35
1992	1.62	0.90	2.49	0.49	1.05	0.04	2.95	1.30	0.03	0.26	0.03	3.08	14.24
1993	5.22	1.72	1.62	0.00	0.08	0.01	T	0.55	0.06	1.27	2.79	0.02	13.34
Record Mean	0.82	0.74	0.77	0.33	0.14	0.09	0.93	1.01	0.78	0.53	0.65	0.91	7.71

AVERAGE TEMPERATURE (deg. F)

PHOENIX, ARIZONA

YEAR	JAN	FEB	MAR	APR	MAY	JUNE	JULY	AUG	SEP	OCT	NOV	DEC	ANNUAL
1964	46.7	49.3	56.5	65.2	73.7	82.6	90.6	86.2	80.9	74.9	55.5	52.0	67.8
1965	52.7	52.4	56.1	63.4	71.8	79.0	91.0	89.0	79.2	73.8	62.1	52.9	68.6
1966	48.2	49.7	61.2	69.8	80.1	86.8	93.0	90.9	82.9	70.9	60.5	52.0	70.5
1967	50.7	55.7	62.8	62.4	75.1	81.1	91.6	91.0	84.8	73.5	63.9	48.2	70.1
1968	52.4	59.7	59.9	66.7	76.6	86.2	90.2	86.5	83.6	72.7	59.2	49.5	70.3
1969	54.9	53.0	56.9	68.5	78.3	84.2	93.1	94.4	86.0	69.5	62.1	54.8	71.3
1970	52.1	60.2	59.5	64.7	79.6	88.1	95.0	92.5	82.2	69.1	61.4	52.6	71.4
1971	52.2	56.3	63.3	66.5	73.3	85.3	94.9	89.6	85.6	69.3	59.7	50.2	70.5
1972	51.4	59.1	70.6	71.4	78.3	87.8	94.4	89.9	84.8	71.9	58.1	52.1	72.5
1973	51.2	57.5	56.6	67.2	80.9	88.1	93.5	93.4	84.7	74.4	60.8	55.4	72.0
1974	54.0	56.7	64.5	70.6	80.2	92.2	92.4	91.2	87.2	75.9	61.5	50.6	73.1
1975	52.3	54.0	59.0	62.6	76.7	86.6	94.3	91.9	86.2	72.9	60.9	54.8	71.0
1976	55.4	60.7	61.5	68.7	80.7	87.9	91.6	90.7	83.0	74.0	64.1	55.6	72.8
1977	53.8	61.7	60.8	73.5	75.7	91.4	95.0	94.1	87.6	78.7	65.8	59.9	74.9
1978	56.6	58.7	65.6	69.2	78.5	90.9	94.6	91.4	86.3	78.6	61.5	51.7	73.6
1979	50.1	55.7	60.4	70.1	78.1	89.5	93.8	89.4	90.2	77.2	58.2	55.9	72.4
1980	56.6	60.6	60.7	69.8	76.0	88.9	95.6	92.2	87.3	75.6	64.1	61.3	74.0
1981	59.2	61.4	63.8	76.0	80.5	93.4	95.2	95.8	89.2	73.6	66.1	58.6	76.0
1982	53.9	60.1	62.4	72.5	80.4	88.1	93.7	93.7	86.7	73.5	61.9	54.1	73.4
1983	56.0	58.4	62.2	66.6	80.6	88.6	95.5	92.6	91.0	77.2	62.4	57.2	74.0
1984	57.4	60.1	67.6	70.7	87.0	88.9	91.7	91.2	87.5	71.4	61.9	53.7	74.1
1985	54.3	57.4	62.8	75.1	84.2	92.4	94.9	94.5	82.3	75.1	61.3	55.9	74.2
1986	61.4	61.0	69.3	74.2	82.3	92.8	92.3	94.5	84.1	74.7	65.0	56.4	75.7
1987	54.7	59.7	63.4	77.9	82.6	93.0	93.1	92.2	86.9	80.9	63.1	52.7	75.0
1988	55.1	62.5	66.3	73.0	81.4	93.1	96.2	93.9	87.4	82.4	64.4	55.7	76.0
1989	54.4	61.9	70.1	80.1	83.1	92.1	97.4	93.7	89.9	77.3	66.4	57.0	77.0
1990	55.6	56.6	67.2	76.2	81.1	93.8	93.6	90.8	87.6	78.7	65.9	53.6	75.1
1991	55.9	66.0	60.3	72.2	79.7	87.8	95.1	94.5	88.5	80.2	63.5	57.3	75.1
1992	56.4	62.1	64.7	77.0	83.1	90.1	92.8	92.3	90.5	79.8	61.5	53.8	75.3
1993	58.2	58.2	65.7	73.8	83.7	89.6	92.9	91.6	87.9	76.7	61.4	56.2	74.7
Record Mean	52.4	56.3	61.1	68.7	76.9	86.2	91.5	89.7	84.2	72.7	60.5	53.0	71.1
Max	65.3	69.6	74.9	83.6	92.3	102.1	104.5	102.3	98.0	87.3	74.7	66.1	85.1
Min	39.4	43.0	47.3	53.8	61.4	70.3	78.4	77.0	70.4	58.0	46.2	40.0	57.1

REFERENCE NOTES

PHOENIX, ARIZONA

GENERAL
T - TRACE AMOUNT.
BLANK ENTRIES DENOTE MISSING/UNREPORTED DATA.
# INDICATES A STATION OR INSTRUMENT RELOCATION.

SPECIFIC

PM - INCLUDES LAST DAY OF PREVIOUS MONTH
ASOS - AUTOMATED SURFACE OBSERVING SYSTEM IN OPERATION DURING THESE MONTHS.

(a) - LENGTH OF RECORD IN YEARS, ALTHOUGH INDIVIDUAL MONTHS MAY BE MISSING.
0.* OR * - THE VALUE IS BETWEEN 0.0 AND 0.05
NORMALS - BASED ON THE 1961-1990 RECORD PERIOD.
EXTREMES - DATES ARE THE MOST RECENT OCCURRENCE
WIND DIR.- NUMERALS SHOW TENS OF DEGRESS CLOCKWISE FROM TRUE NORTH. "00" INDICATES CALM.
RESULTANT DIRECTIONS ARE GIVEN TO WHOLE DEGREES.
BOLD VALUES INDICATE EXTREME VALUES WHICH OCCURRED AFTER THE ASOS SYSTEM WAS COMMISSIONED.

RECORD = PERIOD OF RECORD
RECORD MEAN PRECIPITATION IS THE MEAN OF ALL DAILY PRECIPITATION AMOUNTS DURING THE PERIOD OF RECORD.
RECORD MAX(MIN) TEMPERATURE IS THE MEAN OF ALL DAILY MAX(MIN) TEMPERATURES DURING THE PERIOD OF RECORD.
RECORD MEAN TEMPERATURE IS THE SUM OF THE RECORD MAX AND RECORD MIN DIVIDED BY 2.
AVERAGE TEMPERATURE IS THE SUM OF THE MEAN DAILY MAX AND MIN TEMPERATURE DIVIDED BY 2.

EXCEPTIONS

1. PEAK GUST WINDS ARE AS OBSERVED JANUARY 1938 THROUGH OCTOBER 1953 AND FROM RECORDER THEREAFTER.
2. PERCENT OF POSSIBLE SUNSHINE IS FROM CITY OFFICE AUGUST 1895 THROUGH OCTOBER 1953 AND FROM SKY HARBOR AIRPORT THEREAFTER.
3. MEAN SKY COVER IS 1940, 1941, AND 1948 TO DATE.

RECORD MEANS ARE THROUGH THE CURRENT YEAR, BEGINNING IN 1896 FOR TEMPERATURE
1896 FOR PRECIPITATION
1938 FOR SNOWFALL

HEATING DEGREE DAYS Base 65 deg. F PHOENIX, ARIZONA

SEASON	JULY	AUG	SEP	OCT	NOV	DEC	JAN	FEB	MAR	APR	MAY	JUNE	TOTAL
1964-65	0	0	0	0	281	396	375	346	269	133	14	0	1814
1965-66	0	0	4	7	116	370	516	423	145	12	0	0	1593
1966-67	0	0	0	8	139	397	437	256	102	93	10	0	1442
1967-68	0	0	0	6	72	512	384	151	167	39	0	0	1331
1968-69	0	0	0	0	173	473	306	327	265	12	13	0	1569
1969-70	0	0	0	12	95	307	393	134	166	60	0	0	1167
1970-71	0	0	0	19	119	376	396	241	123	53	0	0	1327
1971-72	0	0	0	79	185	455	414	174	22	12	0	0	1341
1972-73	0	0	0	38	205	395	422	200	254	39	0	0	1553
1973-74	0	0	0	2	156	291	333	229	77	5	0	0	1093
1974-75	0	0	0	21	112	439	388	301	191	107	4	0	1563
1975-76	0	0	0	15	159	310	296	123	134	52	0	0	1089
1976-77	0	0	0	2	112	285	339	122	149	33	0	0	1042
1977-78	0	0	0	0	42	155	254	172	67	25	0	0	715
1978-79	0	0	0	1	148	405	455	254	143	30	0	0	1436
1979-80	0	0	0	11	204	277	254	130	129	35	0	0	1040
1980-81	0	0	0	12	108	122	181	131	74	8	0	0	636
1981-82	0	0	0	1	56	196	335	151	99	4	0	0	842
1982-83	0	0	0	1	103	331	272	181	120	53	0	0	1061
1983-84	0	0	0	0	154	236	228	139	16	23	0	0	796
1984-85	0	0	0	7	126	345	328	222	102	5	0	0	1135
1985-86	0	0	0	0	149	274	110	158	66	2	1	0	760
1986-87	0	0	0	0	43	260	318	172	95	4	0	0	892
1987-88	0	0	0	0	98	375	311	100	60	20	2	0	966
1988-89	0	0	0	0	135	284	321	133	46	0	0	0	919
1989-90	0	0	0	1	36	243	291	253	76	0	0	0	900
1990-91	0	0	0	0	65	348	275	27	161	5	0	0	881
1991-92	0	0	0	34	107	233	260	89	56	7	0	0	786
1992-93	0	0	0	0	127	340	205	184	61	0	0	0	917
1993-94	0	0	0	0	125	264							

COOLING DEGREE DAYS Base 65 deg. F PHOENIX, ARIZONA

YEAR	JAN	FEB	MAR	APR	MAY	JUNE	JULY	AUG	SEP	OCT	NOV	DEC	TOTAL
1969	0	0	22	123	433	582	878	918	638	158	16	0	3768
1970	0	4	4	58	459	700	938	862	527	151	18	0	3721
1971	7	2	76	107	265	614	934	773	623	220	30	0	3651
1972	0	11	200	212	419	691	919	780	599	259	4	0	4094
1973	0	0	0	109	499	701	894	885	598	302	36	0	4024
1974	0	2	69	182	477	825	858	821	673	365	13	0	4285
1975	0	0	12	42	374	654	913	839	640	265	45	1	3785
1976	6	4	34	169	495	692	833	804	548	289	91	0	3965
1977	0	36	25	295	334	797	936	907	683	434	73	1	4521
1978	3	1	92	158	422	787	928	828	644	431	49	0	4343
1979	1	0	11	191	411	741	901	763	764	397	7	0	4186
1980	0	5	2	187	344	724	956	852	675	346	88	13	4192
1981	5	36	40	345	489	857	943	961	731	277	95	5	4784
1982	0	21	24	234	481	697	899	897	658	272	12	0	4195
1983	2	1	38	112	489	715	951	861	787	388	85	0	4429
1984	0	2	107	203	688	724	836	821	681	208	41	0	4311
1985	0	17	40	316	603	826	934	920	525	319	47	0	4547
1986	3	52	209	282	543	844	853	921	582	307	51	1	4648
1987	3	30	51	396	553	846	879	850	665	499	48	0	4820
1988	10	31	108	265	520	851	972	904	678	543	124	3	5009
1989	1	49	210	459	566	820	1013	897	751	392	87	0	5245
1990	5	25	150	339	506	873	895	806	683	431	101	0	4814
1991	0	61	22	227	465	691	937	920	712	514	70	0	4619
1992	0	13	54	373	567	762	868	851	771	464	30	0	4753
1993	1	1	89	271	585	746	871	832	695	369	24	0	4484

SNOWFALL (inches) PHOENIX, ARIZONA

SEASON	JULY	AUG	SEP	OCT	NOV	DEC	JAN	FEB	MAR	APR	MAY	JUNE	TOTAL
1964-65	0.0	0.0	0.0	0.0	0.0	0.0	0.0	0.0	0.0	0.0	0.0	0.0	0.0
1965-66	0.0	0.0	0.0	0.0	0.0	0.0	0.0	0.0	0.0	0.0	0.0	0.0	0.0
1966-67	0.0	0.0	0.0	0.0	0.0	0.0	0.0	0.0	0.0	0.0	0.0	0.0	0.0
1967-68	0.0	0.0	0.0	0.0	0.0	T	0.0	0.0	0.0	0.0	0.0	0.0	T
1968-69	0.0	0.0	0.0	0.0	0.0	T	0.0	0.0	0.0	0.0	0.0	0.0	T
1969-70	0.0	0.0	0.0	0.0	0.0	0.0	0.0	0.0	0.0	0.0	0.0	0.0	0.0
1970-71	0.0	0.0	0.0	0.0	0.0	0.0	0.0	0.0	0.0	0.0	0.0	0.0	0.0
1971-72	0.0	0.0	0.0	0.0	0.0	0.0	0.0	0.0	0.0	0.0	0.0	0.0	0.0
1972-73	0.0	0.0	0.0	0.0	0.0	0.0	0.0	0.0	0.0	0.0	0.0	0.0	0.0
1973-74	0.0	0.0	0.0	0.0	0.0	0.0	0.0	0.0	0.0	0.0	0.0	0.0	0.0
1974-75	0.0	0.0	0.0	0.0	0.0	T	0.0	0.0	0.0	0.0	0.0	0.0	T
1975-76	0.0	0.0	0.0	0.0	0.0	0.0	0.0	0.0	T	0.0	0.0	0.0	T
1976-77	0.0	0.0	0.0	0.0	0.0	0.0	0.0	0.0	0.0	0.0	0.0	0.0	0.0
1977-78	0.0	0.0	0.0	0.0	0.0	0.0	0.0	0.0	0.0	0.0	0.0	0.0	0.0
1978-79	0.0	0.0	0.0	0.0	0.0	0.0	0.0	0.0	0.0	0.0	0.0	0.0	0.0
1979-80	0.0	0.0	0.0	0.0	0.0	0.0	0.0	0.0	0.0	0.0	0.0	0.0	0.0
1980-81	0.0	0.0	0.0	0.0	0.0	0.0	0.0	0.0	0.0	0.0	0.0	0.0	0.0
1981-82	0.0	0.0	0.0	0.0	0.0	0.0	0.0	0.0	0.0	0.0	0.0	0.0	0.0
1982-83	0.0	0.0	0.0	0.0	0.0	0.0	0.0	0.0	0.0	0.0	0.0	0.0	0.0
1983-84	0.0	0.0	0.0	0.0	0.0	0.0	0.0	0.0	0.0	0.0	0.0	0.0	0.0
1984-85	0.0	0.0	0.0	0.0	0.0	0.0	0.0	T	0.0	0.0	0.0	0.0	T
1985-86	0.0	0.0	0.0	0.0	0.0	0.1	0.0	0.0	0.0	0.0	0.0	0.0	0.1
1986-87	0.0	0.0	0.0	0.0	0.0	0.0	T	0.0	0.0	0.0	0.0	0.0	T
1987-88	0.0	0.0	0.0	0.0	0.0	0.0	0.0	0.0	0.0	0.0	0.0	0.0	0.0
1988-89	0.0	0.0	0.0	0.0	0.0	0.0	0.0	0.0	0.0	0.0	0.0	0.0	0.0
1989-90	0.0	0.0	0.0	0.0	0.0	0.0	0.0	0.0	0.0	0.0	0.0	0.0	0.0
1990-91	0.0	0.0	0.0	0.0	0.0	0.4	0.0	0.0	T	0.0	0.0	0.0	0.4
1991-92	0.0	0.0	0.0	0.0	0.0	0.0	0.0	0.0	0.0	0.0	T	0.0	T
1992-93	0.0	0.0	0.0	T	0.0	0.0	T	0.0	0.0	0.0	0.0	0.0	T
1993-94	0.0	0.0	0.0	0.0	0.0	0.0							
Record Mean	0.0	0.0	0.0	T	0.0	T	T	T	T	T	T	0.0	T

TUCSON, ARIZONA

Tucson lies at the foot of the Catalina Mountains, north of the airport. The area within about 15 miles of the airport station is flat or gently rolling, with many dry washes. The soil is sandy, and vegetation is mostly brush, cacti, and small trees. Rugged mountains encircle the valley. The mountains to the north, east, and south rise to over 5,000 feet above the airport. The western hills and mountains range from 500 to 4,000 feet.

The climate of Tucson is characterized by a long hot season, from April to October. Temperatures above 90 degrees prevail from May through September. Temperatures of 100 degrees or higher average 41 days annually, including 14 days each for June and July, but these extreme temperatures are moderated by low relative humidities. The temperature range is large, averaging 30 degrees or more a day.

More than 50 percent of the annual precipitation falls between July 1 and September 15, and over 20 percent falls from December through March. During the summer, scattered convective or orographic showers and thunderstorms often fill dry washes to overflowing. On occasion, brief, torrential downpours cause destructive flash floods in the Tucson area. Hail rarely occurs in thunderstorms. The December through March precipitation occurs as prolonged rainstorms that replenish the ground water. During these storms, snow often falls on the higher mountains, but snow in Tucson is infrequent, particularly in accumulations exceeding an inch in depth.

From the first of the year, the humidity decreases steadily until the summer thunderstorm season, when it shows a marked increase. From mid-September, the end of the thunderstorm season, the humidity decreases again until late November. Occasionally during the summer, humidities are high enough to produce discomfort, but only for short periods. During the hot season, humidity values sometimes fall below 5 percent.

Tucson lies in the zone receiving more sunshine than any other section of the United States. Cloudless days are commonplace, and average cloudiness is low.

Surface winds are generally light, with no major seasonal changes in velocity or direction. Occasional duststorms occur in areas where the ground has been disturbed. During the spring, winds may briefly be strong enough to cause some damage to trees and buildings. Wind velocities and directions are influenced by the surrounding mountains, and the general slope of the terrain. Usually local winds tend to be in the southeast quadrant during the night and early morning hours, veering to northwest during the day. Highest velocities usually occur with winds from the southwest and east to south.

While dust and haze are frequently visible, their effect on the general clarity of the atmosphere is not great. Visibility is normally high.

Based on the 1951–1980 period, the average first occurrence of 32 degrees Fahrenheit in the fall is November 29 and the average last occurrence in the spring is February 28.

NORMALS, MEANS, AND EXTREMES

TUCSON, ARIZONA

LATITUDE: 32°07'N LONGITUDE: 110°56' W ELEVATION: FT. GRND 2584 BARO 2589 TIME ZONE: MOUNTAIN WBAN: 23160

	(a)	JAN	FEB	MAR	APR	MAY	JUNE	JULY	AUG	SEP	OCT	NOV	DEC	YEAR
TEMPERATURE °F:														
Normals														
-Daily Maximum		63.9	67.8	72.8	81.2	89.9	99.6	99.4	96.8	93.3	84.3	72.7	64.3	82.2
-Daily Minimum		38.6	41.0	44.6	50.4	58.0	67.9	73.6	72.1	67.5	56.6	45.6	39.8	54.6
-Monthly		51.3	54.4	58.7	65.8	74.0	83.8	86.6	84.5	80.4	70.4	59.2	52.0	68.4
Extremes														
-Record Highest	53	87	92	99	104	107	117	114	112	107	102	90	84	117
-Year		1953	1957	1988	1989	1958	1990	1989	1993	1990	1993	1988	1954	JUN 1990
-Record Lowest	53	16	20	20	27	38	47	59	61	44	26	24	16	16
-Year		1949	1955	1965	1945	1950	1955	1992	1956	1965	1971	1979	1974	DEC 1974
NORMAL DEGREE DAYS:														
Heating (base 65°F)		425	302	229	97	7	0	0	0	0	27	188	403	1678
Cooling (base 65°F)		0	5	33	121	286	564	670	605	462	194	14	0	2954
% OF POSSIBLE SUNSHINE	46	80	82	86	92	93	93	78	80	87	88	85	79	85
MEAN SKY COVER (tenths)														
Sunrise - Sunset	52	4.7	4.6	4.5	3.4	2.8	2.3	5.2	4.6	3.0	2.9	3.5	4.5	3.8
MEAN NUMBER OF DAYS:														
Sunrise to Sunset														
-Clear	53	13.7	12.8	14.7	17.2	20.1	21.5	10.2	12.3	19.3	19.9	17.6	14.8	194.0
-Partly Cloudy	53	7.1	6.4	6.8	7.3	6.8	6.0	12.2	12.1	6.9	6.4	6.1	6.1	90.3
-Cloudy	53	10.3	9.0	9.4	5.5	4.1	2.5	8.6	6.6	3.8	4.8	6.3	10.1	81.0
Precipitation														
.01 inches or more	53	4.7	3.8	4.3	2.0	1.5	1.7	10.3	9.5	4.7	3.4	2.9	4.6	53.3
Snow, Ice pellets, hail														
1.0 inches or more	53	0.2	0.2	0.1	0.*	0.0	0.0	0.0	0.0	0.0	0.0	0.*	0.1	0.5
Thunderstorms	53	0.4	0.3	0.5	0.7	1.6	2.5	13.7	13.6	5.4	2.0	0.5	0.3	41.4
Heavy Fog Visibility														
1/4 mile or less	53	0.3	0.2	0.*	0.0	0.0	0.0	0.0	0.0	0.*	0.0	0.2	0.4	1.0
Temperature °F														
-Maximum														
90° and above	53	0.0	0.*	0.5	4.7	17.7	28.2	29.3	28.6	23.9	9.1	0.*	0.0	142.0
32° and below	53	0.0	0.0	0.0	0.0	0.0	0.0	0.0	0.0	0.0	0.0	0.0	0.0	0.0
-Minimum														
32° and below	53	6.2	4.0	1.1	0.*	0.0	0.0	0.0	0.0	0.0	0.*	1.5	5.0	17.8
0° and below	53	0.0	0.0	0.0	0.0	0.0	0.0	0.0	0.0	0.0	0.0	0.0	0.0	0.0
AVG. STATION PRESS. (mb)	21	927.8	927.1	925.0	924.0	922.8	922.7	924.7	925.0	924.4	925.7	926.9	927.9	925.3
RELATIVE HUMIDITY (%)														
Hour 05	53	63	59	54	42	35	32	57	65	55	52	54	62	53
Hour 11 (Local Time)	53	41	35	29	21	17	16	32	38	32	30	32	40	30
Hour 17	53	33	27	23	16	13	13	28	33	26	25	28	35	25
Hour 23	53	58	50	43	31	24	23	47	53	44	43	48	57	43
PRECIPITATION (inches):														
Water Equivalent														
-Normal		0.87	0.70	0.72	0.30	0.18	0.20	2.37	2.19	1.67	1.06	0.67	1.07	12.00
-Maximum Monthly	53	4.81	2.90	2.26	1.66	1.11	1.46	6.17	7.93	5.11	4.98	1.90	5.02	7.93
-Year		1993	1980	1952	1951	1992	1954	1981	1955	1964	1983	1952	1965	AUG 1955
-Minimum Monthly	53	T	0.00	0.00	0.00	0.00	0.00	0.26	0.23	0.00	0.00	0.00	0.00	0.00
-Year		1970	1972	1956	1972	1974	1983	1993	1976	1953	1982	1980	1981	JUN 1983
-Maximum in 24 hrs	53	1.46	1.49	1.19	0.91	0.89	1.27	3.93	2.48	3.05	3.58	1.86	1.54	3.93
-Year		1993	1942	1952	1988	1943	1954	1958	1961	1964	1983	1968	1967	JUL 1958
Snow, Ice pellets, hail														
-Maximum Monthly	53	4.7	3.9	5.7	2.0	T	0.0	0.0	T	T	T	6.4	6.8	6.8
-Year		1987	1965	1964	1976	1992			1993	1990	1991	1958	1971	DEC 1971
-Maximum in 24 hrs	52	4.3	3.9	5.7	2.0	T	0.0	0.0	T	T	T	6.4	6.8	6.8
-Year		1987	1965	1964	1976	1992			1993	1990	1991	1958	1971	DEC 1971
WIND:														
Mean Speed (mph)	48	7.9	8.1	8.5	8.9	8.8	8.7	8.4	7.9	8.3	8.2	8.1	7.8	8.3
Prevailing Direction through 1963		SE	SE	SE	SE	SE	SSE	SE	SE	SE	SE	SE	SE	SE
Fastest Mile														
-Direction (!!)	45	E	E	SE	SW	SE	SE	SE	NE	SE	SE	E	W	SE
-Speed (MPH)	45	40	59	41	46	43	50	71	54	54	47	55	44	71
-Year		1962	1952	1955	1986	1984	1961	1971	1969	1960	1948	1951	1949	JUL 1971
Peak Gust														
-Direction (!!)	10	SW	E	SE	SW	SE	SW	SE	SE	SE	NW	E	SE	SE
-Speed (mph)	10	45	46	53	55	55	47	66	71	71	47	46	47	71
-Date		1988	1987	1986	1984	1984	1991	1985	1988	1990	1988	1990	1988	SEP 1990

PRECIPITATION (inches)

TUCSON, ARIZONA

YEAR	JAN	FEB	MAR	APR	MAY	JUNE	JULY	AUG	SEP	OCT	NOV	DEC	ANNUAL
1964	0.14	0.13	0.81	0.67	0.00	0.01	4.82	3.90	5.11	0.91	0.68	0.81	17.99
1965	0.45	0.64	0.27	0.23	T	0.01	2.13	1.12	0.82	0.07	0.77	5.02	11.53
1966	1.74	2.25	0.19	0.12	0.11	0.02	2.57	3.31	3.53	0.32	0.06	0.19	14.41
1967	0.04	0.13	0.41	0.29	0.62	0.42	2.72	2.00	1.35	1.03	0.48	3.44	12.93
1968	0.18	0.99	1.79	0.62	T	0.00	1.97	1.12	T	0.09	1.86	0.32	8.94
1969	0.74	0.50	0.34	0.60	0.46	0.00	1.51	2.57	1.31	0.03	1.06	0.82	9.94
1970	T	0.34	1.13	0.45	0.03	0.33	2.53	1.43	3.58	1.73	0.00	0.43	11.98
1971	0.04	0.50	T	0.56	0.01	T	2.18	3.29	1.75	1.18	0.69	1.97	12.17
1972	0.00	0.00	0.01	0.00	0.24	0.68	3.49	2.93	1.09	4.51	1.30	0.61	14.86
1973	0.06	1.60	2.20	0.02	0.09	0.50	1.74	0.54	T	0.00	0.47	0.00	7.22
1974	0.93	T	0.55	T	0.00	0.01	4.44	1.04	1.69	2.12	0.81	0.33	11.92
1975	0.36	0.13	0.95	0.27	0.11	0.00	2.38	0.32	1.26	T	0.34	0.52	6.64
1976	0.06	0.53	0.38	0.57	0.23	0.10	1.18	0.23	1.68	0.37	0.48	0.47	6.28
1977	1.83	0.04	0.74	0.43	0.08	0.06	0.76	0.80	1.41	2.36	0.33	1.33	10.17
1978	2.05	1.75	0.89	0.01	0.61	0.22	0.78	1.59	1.66	1.86	1.58	2.73	15.73
1979	2.94	0.42	0.64	0.04	0.67	0.53	2.04	2.60	0.02	0.33	0.01	0.15	10.39
1980	0.73	2.90	1.22	0.08	T	0.23	1.78	1.95	2.93	0.22	0.00	0.19	12.23
1981	1.29	0.71	1.98	0.56	0.26	0.16	6.17	0.80	1.10	0.06	0.61	0.00	13.70
1982	1.56	0.06	1.26	0.05	0.51	0.13	2.13	2.51	2.69	0.00	1.30	1.59	13.79
1983	1.70	0.94	1.28	0.14	T	0.00	1.98	4.24	4.28	4.98	1.71	0.61	21.86
1984	0.62	0.00	0.00	0.36	0.06	1.05	2.92	4.19	1.81	0.77	0.45	3.30	15.53
1985	1.71	1.08	0.20	0.45	T	0.07	3.14	1.97	1.13	2.03	0.95	0.15	12.88
1986	0.98	1.13	1.30	T	0.44	0.06	1.82	3.56	0.31	0.50	0.42	1.28	11.80
1987	0.59	1.64	0.83	0.80	0.74	0.16	0.37	2.79	2.30	0.34	0.44	1.50	12.50
1988	0.41	0.53	0.35	1.15	0.02	0.15	1.69	3.64	0.80	2.09	0.75	0.05	11.63
1989	0.96	0.23	0.62	0.00	0.13	0.06	1.42	0.90	0.02	1.84	0.12	0.18	6.48
1990	0.96	0.71	0.38	0.10	0.03	0.64	5.45	2.70	1.63	0.58	0.23	1.54	14.95
1991	1.15	0.91	1.40	0.00	0.00	0.20	0.44	2.17	1.54	0.73	0.80	1.44	10.78
1992	1.21	1.80	2.12	0.19	1.11	0.07	0.93	4.55	0.94	0.03	T	3.47	16.42
1993	4.81	1.50	0.49	0.00	0.59	0.02	0.26	4.93	0.46	0.81	0.98	0.14	14.99
Record Mean	0.90	0.83	0.74	0.34	0.21	0.25	2.20	2.22	1.31	0.72	0.74	1.03	11.49

AVERAGE TEMPERATURE (deg. F)

TUCSON, ARIZONA

YEAR	JAN	FEB	MAR	APR	MAY	JUNE	JULY	AUG	SEP	OCT	NOV	DEC	ANNUAL
1964	47.5	47.7	54.8	63.2	73.2	82.0	86.2	81.6	76.3	72.1	55.2	52.4	66.0
1965	53.6	51.1	55.1	64.5	70.1	77.6	85.0	84.0	76.8	71.9	62.6	52.1	67.1
1966	47.7	47.8	60.1	66.8	76.1	82.8	85.3	82.9	78.3	68.1	61.1	52.4	67.4
1967	51.4	55.6	62.1	62.1	71.9	80.7	85.4	84.6	80.7	71.6	62.9	48.6	68.1
1968	52.4	59.1	58.7	63.2	73.3	83.5	84.9	81.3	80.7	71.7	58.3	50.6	68.1
1969	55.5	53.1	54.3	66.6	74.9	80.7	86.1	86.3	81.2	66.8	58.6	52.4	68.0
1970	50.0	57.0	55.9	61.1	75.2	83.4	87.2	84.8	76.4	65.1	60.1	51.8	67.3
1971	50.5	52.3	59.8	62.8	69.3	81.2	87.5	81.3	79.1	64.2	56.8	47.1	66.0
1972	50.4	55.8	65.0	65.8	72.3	81.6	86.6	82.9	78.6	66.5	53.0	49.0	67.3
1973	47.6	53.4	51.6	59.7	73.0	81.4	84.3	84.7	79.6	70.7	58.4	52.3	66.4
1974	50.2	51.9	60.1	66.1	74.3	86.9	83.5	83.0	77.8	69.1	57.5	47.0	67.3
1975	49.8	50.7	55.3	57.9	69.8	80.5	84.2	85.8	80.0	69.5	59.3	53.0	66.3
1976	52.6	58.4	58.2	64.8	74.5	83.4	83.9	85.3	77.7	67.8	60.0	52.2	68.3
1977	50.7	56.9	55.7	67.0	70.8	84.7	87.0	86.4	82.0	73.3	61.7	56.9	69.4
1978	53.1	53.6	61.8	65.2	73.1	85.8	88.1	84.7	80.9	73.8	58.5	49.7	69.0
1979	48.4	53.8	56.4	65.6	72.2	83.1	87.5	83.4	84.2	73.0	56.6	55.0	68.3
1980	54.3	57.9	57.5	65.6	71.5	84.9	88.6	84.6	80.5	69.6	59.5	58.1	69.4
1981	54.8	57.1	57.1	69.1	73.4	86.1	85.2	86.4	80.7	68.1	62.2	55.0	69.6
1982	50.7	54.7	57.7	66.1	72.3	80.5	84.8	83.9	79.2	67.0	57.7	50.1	67.0
1983	52.9	53.8	57.3	60.4	73.8	81.6	86.9	84.0	82.2	69.5	57.4	53.5	67.8
1984	51.8	53.7	60.5	64.0	79.9	83.1	84.2	82.9	81.5	66.3	57.8	51.5	68.1
1985	50.3	53.1	58.7	68.7	75.9	85.8	87.5	86.1	77.4	70.0	58.0	52.9	68.7
1986	58.7	56.9	63.8	69.0	76.8	86.6	85.5	86.0	79.0	69.6	59.8	52.3	70.3
1987	50.9	54.2	57.9	70.1	74.3	86.3	87.4	85.1	79.9	75.1	58.9	50.3	69.2
1988	53.0	59.4	61.4	68.0	76.4	86.8	87.9	85.9	80.4	75.3	59.2	51.9	70.5
1989	49.9	58.2	65.0	73.8	77.4	85.4	90.0	86.6	84.5	71.1	61.7	53.0	71.4
1990	51.8	52.8	61.8	69.7	75.2	88.7	85.0	82.6	82.2	73.1	61.6	51.1	69.6
1991	52.3	59.8	55.4	65.2	73.5	81.5	87.5	86.6	80.7	74.0	58.9	54.3	69.1
1992	51.6	57.3	59.4	70.8	76.7	84.5	86.8	85.1	83.6	74.2	56.1	51.4	69.8
1993	55.2	54.0	61.3	68.6	78.1	85.0	88.0	85.5	81.4	72.6	58.8	53.4	70.2
Record Mean	50.6	53.6	58.0	64.9	73.0	82.4	86.1	84.1	80.1	69.7	58.3	51.5	67.7
Max	64.4	67.8	73.0	81.1	89.7	99.1	99.3	96.8	94.1	84.9	73.1	65.3	82.4
Min	36.8	39.3	43.0	48.8	56.3	65.7	72.9	71.4	66.1	54.5	43.5	37.7	53.0

REFERENCE NOTES

TUCSON, ARIZONA

GENERAL
T - TRACE AMOUNT.
BLANK ENTRIES DENOTE MISSING/UNREPORTED DATA.
# INDICATES A STATION OR INSTRUMENT RELOCATION.

SPECIFIC

PM - INCLUDES LAST DAY OF PREVIOUS MONTH
ASOS - AUTOMATED SURFACE OBSERVING SYSTEM IN OPERATION DURING THESE MONTHS.

(a) - LENGTH OF RECORD IN YEARS, ALTHOUGH INDIVIDUAL MONTHS MAY BE MISSING.
0.* OR * - THE VALUE IS BETWEEN 0.0 AND 0.05
NORMALS - BASED ON THE 1961-1990 RECORD PERIOD.
EXTREMES - DATES ARE THE MOST RECENT OCCURRENCE
WIND DIR.- NUMERALS SHOW TENS OF DEGRESS CLOCKWISE FROM TRUE NORTH. "00" INDICATES CALM.
RESULTANT DIRECTIONS ARE GIVEN TO WHOLE DEGREES.
BOLD VALUES INDICATE EXTREME VALUES WHICH OCCURRED AFTER THE ASOS SYSTEM WAS COMMISSIONED.

RECORD = PERIOD OF RECORD
RECORD MEAN PRECIPITATION IS THE MEAN OF ALL DAILY PRECIPITATION AMOUNTS DURING THE PERIOD OF RECORD.
RECORD MAX(MIN) TEMPERATURE IS THE MEAN OF ALL DAILY MAX(MIN) TEMPERATURES DURING THE PERIOD OF RECORD.
RECORD MEAN TEMPERATURE IS THE SUM OF THE RECORD MAX AND RECORD MIN DIVIDED BY 2.
AVERAGE TEMPERATURE IS THE SUM OF THE MEAN DAILY MAX AND MIN TEMPERATURE DIVIDED BY 2.

EXCEPTIONS

RECORD MEANS ARE THROUGH THE CURRENT YEAR, BEGINNING IN 1900 FOR TEMPERATURE
1900 FOR PRECIPITATION
1941 FOR SNOWFALL

HEATING DEGREE DAYS Base 65 deg. F — TUCSON, ARIZONA

SEASON	JULY	AUG	SEP	OCT	NOV	DEC	JAN	FEB	MAR	APR	MAY	JUNE	TOTAL
1964-65	0	0	0	5	293	383	348	383	305	114	21	0	1852
1965-66	0	0	8	33	110	396	532	473	166	26	0	0	1744
1966-67	0	0	0	20	126	386	416	256	115	113	20	0	1452
1967-68	0	0	0	14	89	502	384	170	200	91	0	0	1450
1968-69	0	0	0	4	204	440	288	328	339	34	35	0	1672
1969-70	0	0	0	55	188	384	455	224	274	132	8	0	1720
1970-71	0	0	0	58	143	403	445	350	200	111	12	0	1722
1971-72	0	0	0	120	249	548	444	259	73	50	0	0	1743
1972-73	0	0	0	96	358	489	533	320	410	174	19	0	2399
1973-74	0	0	0	23	216	390	451	362	161	49	5	0	1657
1974-75	0	0	0	53	218	552	465	393	299	217	29	0	2226
1975-76	0	0	0	38	191	365	378	180	221	88	5	0	1466
1976-77	0	0	0	45	178	390	435	221	287	65	9	0	1630
1977-78	0	0	0	1	117	242	365	313	144	64	24	0	1270
1978-79	0	0	0	15	213	470	511	311	260	76	20	0	1876
1979-80	0	0	0	26	252	302	323	202	227	84	3	0	1419
1980-81	0	0	0	66	197	210	310	220	244	31	0	0	1278
1981-82	0	0	0	34	106	304	437	291	223	46	10	0	1451
1982-83	0	0	0	41	211	456	371	309	239	168	6	0	1801
1983-84	0	0	0	0	232	348	402	323	140	110	0	0	1555
1984-85	0	0	0	49	221	413	448	328	200	41	0	0	1700
1985-86	0	0	0	9	217	369	193	244	117	22	6	0	1177
1986-87	0	0	0	11	154	387	429	299	225	24	0	0	1529
1987-88	0	0	0	0	188	452	366	171	161	46	12	0	1396
1988-89	0	0	0	0	220	402	461	199	82	9	4	0	1377
1989-90	0	0	0	25	107	361	402	340	156	16	3	0	1410
1990-91	0	0	0	5	152	427	384	140	296	47	3	0	1454
1991-92	0	0	0	56	195	325	408	215	169	24	0	0	1392
1992-93	0	0	0	0	261	418	298	299	129	28	0	0	1433
1993-94	0	0	0	5	186	355							

COOLING DEGREE DAYS Base 65 deg. F — TUCSON, ARIZONA

YEAR	JAN	FEB	MAR	APR	MAY	JUNE	JULY	AUG	SEP	OCT	NOV	DEC	TOTAL
1969	0	0	15	87	348	477	658	669	493	118	1	0	2866
1970	0	5	0	25	333	561	693	620	347	68	4	0	2656
1971	6	0	45	51	152	493	706	514	430	101	12	0	2510
1972	0	1	82	82	236	506	678	563	414	150	1	0	2713
1973	0	0	0	21	272	495	603	615	445	206	26	2	2685
1974	0	0	18	87	301	664	581	564	387	185	1	0	2788
1975	0	0	4	11	184	471	604	651	458	182	27	0	2592
1976	2	0	14	89	306	557	597	636	386	139	34	0	2760
1977	0	0	5	133	198	597	691	669	517	266	23	0	3099
1978	0	0	54	76	283	630	721	616	483	293	28	0	3184
1979	0	0	1	101	249	551	706	576	580	282	6	0	3052
1980	0	4	1	109	211	606	742	615	474	216	37	3	3018
1981	0	8	4	159	267	639	633	670	476	137	27	2	3022
1982	0	4	4	82	244	471	622	594	437	112	0	0	2570
1983	0	0	8	36	288	503	688	600	523	145	10	0	2801
1984	0	0	6	87	469	549	601	562	503	96	12	0	2885
1985	0	1	7	159	345	633	704	660	379	173	14	0	3075
1986	2	23	88	150	378	653	643	657	431	158	3	0	3186
1987	0	2	12	184	297	644	702	630	452	325	12	0	3260
1988	2	13	58	142	374	658	716	657	471	327	51	1	3470
1989	0	16	89	281	397	619	780	676	592	221	16	0	3687
1990	0	6	63	164	327	719	625	553	522	262	56	0	3297
1991	0	1	6	58	274	501	703	675	479	345	21	0	3063
1992	0	0	4	204	372	590	683	627	563	291	1	0	3335
1993	1	0	22	142	413	604	721	641	500	250	11	3	3308

SNOWFALL (inches) — TUCSON, ARIZONA

SEASON	JULY	AUG	SEP	OCT	NOV	DEC	JAN	FEB	MAR	APR	MAY	JUNE	TOTAL
1964-65	0.0	0.0	0.0	0.0	0.1	0.0	0.0	3.9	0.0	0.0	0.0	0.0	4.0
1965-66	0.0	0.0	0.0	0.0	0.0	0.3	T	1.2	0.0	0.0	0.0	0.0	1.5
1966-67	0.0	0.0	0.0	0.0	0.0	T	0.0	0.0	0.0	T	0.0	0.0	T
1967-68	0.0	0.0	0.0	0.0	0.0	1.6	0.0	0.0	0.0	0.0	0.0	0.0	1.6
1968-69	0.0	0.0	0.0	0.0	0.0	0.4	0.0	0.0	T	0.0	0.0	0.0	0.4
1969-70	0.0	0.0	0.0	0.0	0.0	T	0.0	0.0	T	T	0.0	0.0	T
1970-71	0.0	0.0	0.0	0.0	0.0	0.0	T	T	0.0	0.0	0.0	0.0	T
1971-72	0.0	0.0	0.0	0.0	0.0	6.8	0.0	0.0	0.0	0.0	0.0	0.0	6.8
1972-73	0.0	0.0	0.0	0.0	0.0	0.0	T	0.0	0.0	0.0	0.0	0.0	T
1973-74	0.0	0.0	0.0	0.0	0.0	0.0	0.4	0.0	T	0.0	0.0	0.0	0.4
1974-75	0.0	0.0	0.0	0.0	0.0	T	0.0	T	0.5	0.0	0.0	0.0	0.5
1975-76	0.0	0.0	0.0	0.0	T	T	0.0	0.0	3.8	2.0	0.0	0.0	5.8
1976-77	0.0	0.0	0.0	0.0	0.0	0.0	0.0	0.0	0.0	0.0	0.0	0.0	0.0
1977-78	0.0	0.0	0.0	0.0	0.0	0.0	0.0	0.0	0.0	0.0	0.0	0.0	0.0
1978-79	0.0	0.0	0.0	0.0	0.0	T	1.2	0.0	0.0	0.0	0.0	0.0	1.2
1979-80	0.0	0.0	0.0	0.0	0.0	0.0	0.0	0.0	T	0.0	0.0	0.0	T
1980-81	0.0	0.0	0.0	0.0	0.0	0.0	0.0	0.0	T	0.0	0.0	0.0	T
1981-82	0.0	0.0	0.0	0.0	0.0	0.0	T	0.0	T	0.0	0.0	0.0	T
1982-83	0.0	0.0	0.0	0.0	0.0	T	0.0	0.0	0.0	0.0	0.0	0.0	T
1983-84	0.0	0.0	0.0	0.0	0.0	0.0	0.0	0.0	0.0	0.0	0.0	0.0	0.0
1984-85	0.0	0.0	0.0	0.0	0.0	T	0.0	2.2	0.0	0.0	0.0	0.0	2.2
1985-86	0.0	0.0	0.0	0.0	0.0	T	0.0	T	0.0	0.0	0.0	0.0	T
1986-87	0.0	0.0	0.0	0.0	0.0	0.0	4.7	0.0	T	0.0	0.0	0.0	4.7
1987-88	0.0	0.0	0.0	0.0	0.0	3.6	0.0	0.0	0.0	0.0	0.0	0.0	3.6
1988-89	0.0	0.0	0.0	0.0	0.0	T	0.0	T	0.0	0.0	0.0	0.0	T
1989-90	0.0	0.0	0.0	0.0	0.0	0.0	2.7	2.3	0.0	T	0.0	0.0	5.0
1990-91	0.0	T	T	0.0	0.0	0.6	0.0	T	0.3	0.0	0.0	0.0	0.9
1991-92	0.0	0.0	0.0	T	0.0	T	0.0	0.0	T	0.0	T	0.0	T
1992-93	0.0	T	0.0	0.0	0.0	0.0	0.0	0.0	0.0	0.0	0.0	0.0	T
1993-94	0.0	T	0.0	0.0	0.0	0.0							
Record Mean	0.0	T	T	-	0.1	0.3	0.3	0.2	0.3	0.1	T	0.0	1.3

LITTLE ROCK, ARKANSAS

Little Rock is located on the Arkansas River near the geographical center of the state. It is situated on the dividing line between the Ouachita Mountains to the west and the flat lowlands comprising the Mississippi River Valley to the east. Elevations range from 222 feet at the river level to 257 feet over much of the flat land, including the airport in the southeast, to near 600 feet in the hilly residential area of the western portions of the city. Two minor temperature variations are observed due to the terrain; somewhat lower minimum temperatures are observed in the airport vicinity and a slight downslope adiabatic heating effect accompanies airflow from the ridges and hills in the west and northwest.

The modified continental climate of Little Rock includes exposure to all of the North American air mass types. However, with its proximity to the Gulf of Mexico, the summer season is marked by prolonged periods of warm and humid weather. The growing season averages 233 days in which 62 percent of the normal precipitation occurs. Winters are mild, but polar and Arctic outbreaks are not uncommon.

Precipitation is fairly well distributed throughout the year. Summer rainfall is almost completely of the convective type. The driest period usually occurs in the late summer and early fall. Snow is almost negligible. Glaze and ice storms, although infrequent, are at times severe. Warm front weather in the winter and early spring, characterized by shallow surface cold air flow from the north under warm moist Gulf air, results in excellent conditions for the production of freezing precipitation.

NORMALS, MEANS, AND EXTREMES

LITTLE ROCK, ARKANSAS

LATITUDE: 34°44'N LONGITUDE: 92°14' W ELEVATION: FT. GRND 257 BARO 260 TIME ZONE: CENTRAL WBAN: 13963

	(a)	JAN	FEB	MAR	APR	MAY	JUNE	JULY	AUG	SEP	OCT	NOV	DEC	YEAR
TEMPERATURE °F:														
Normals														
-Daily Maximum		49.0	53.9	64.0	73.4	81.3	89.3	92.4	91.4	84.6	75.1	62.7	52.5	72.5
-Daily Minimum		29.1	33.2	42.2	50.7	59.0	67.4	71.5	69.8	63.5	50.9	41.5	33.1	51.0
-Monthly		39.1	43.6	53.1	62.1	70.2	78.4	81.9	80.6	74.1	63.0	52.1	42.8	61.8
Extremes														
-Record Highest	52	83	85	91	95	98	105	112	108	106	97	86	80	112
-Year		1950	1986	1974	1987	1964	1988	1986	1980	1947	1963	1955	1956	JUL 1986
-Record Lowest	52	-4	-5	11	28	40	46	54	52	37	29	17	-1	-5
-Year		1962	1951	1951	1971	1971	1969	1972	1986	1942	1989	1976	1989	FEB 1951
NORMAL DEGREE DAYS:														
Heating (base 65°F)		803	599	384	133	25	0	0	0	8	128	387	688	3155
Cooling (base 65°F)		0	0	15	46	187	402	524	484	281	66	0	0	2005
% OF POSSIBLE SUNSHINE	32	46	54	57	62	68	73	71	73	68	69	56	48	62
MEAN SKY COVER (tenths)														
Sunrise - Sunset	35	6.5	6.0	6.2	6.1	6.0	5.4	5.5	5.0	5.2	4.5	5.5	6.2	5.7
MEAN NUMBER OF DAYS:														
Sunrise to Sunset														
-Clear	35	8.6	9.1	8.6	8.7	8.0	9.5	8.8	11.6	11.2	14.4	11.0	9.2	118.7
-Partly Cloudy	35	6.1	5.7	7.0	7.5	10.8	11.6	12.9	10.9	8.6	7.1	5.9	5.9	99.9
-Cloudy	35	16.3	13.5	15.4	13.8	12.3	8.9	9.3	8.5	10.1	9.5	13.1	16.0	146.6
Precipitation														
.01 inches or more	51	9.5	9.0	10.2	10.2	10.2	8.4	8.2	7.0	7.4	6.8	8.2	9.3	104.5
Snow,Ice pellets,hail														
1.0 inches or more	51	0.9	0.5	0.2	0.0	0.0	0.0	0.0	0.0	0.0	0.0	0.1	0.2	1.9
Thunderstorms	51	1.8	2.4	4.8	6.4	7.3	7.6	8.7	6.5	3.7	2.6	3.0	1.8	56.7
Heavy Fog Visibility														
1/4 mile or less	51	2.7	1.7	1.2	0.8	0.8	0.3	0.5	0.7	1.0	1.7	1.8	2.6	15.9
Temperature °F														
-Maximum														
90° and above	33	0.0	0.0	0.*	0.3	3.6	16.1	22.5	19.5	9.0	1.2	0.0	0.0	72.1
32° and below	33	3.4	1.0	0.1	0.0	0.0	0.0	0.0	0.0	0.0	0.0	0.*	1.5	5.9
-Minimum														
32° and below	33	20.0	13.2	4.4	0.5	0.0	0.0	0.0	0.0	0.0	0.2	5.6	15.2	59.1
0° and below	33	0.1	0.0	0.0	0.0	0.0	0.0	0.0	0.0	0.0	0.0	0.0	0.1	0.2
AVG. STATION PRESS.(mb)	21	1012.2	1010.5	1006.8	1006.0	1005.0	1005.6	1006.8	1007.2	1008.0	1009.6	1010.0	1011.5	1008.3
RELATIVE HUMIDITY (%)														
Hour 00	33	76	74	71	75	83	83	83	84	85	82	78	77	79
Hour 06 (Local Time)	33	80	80	79	83	87	87	88	89	89	86	83	80	84
Hour 12	33	61	59	56	56	58	55	56	56	58	53	58	62	57
Hour 18	33	64	59	55	56	60	58	59	60	64	63	65	66	61
PRECIPITATION (inches):														
Water Equivalent														
-Normal		3.91	4.36	5.31	6.21	7.02	7.84	8.19	8.06	7.41	6.30	5.21	4.28	74.10
-Maximum Monthly	52	12.53	11.02	10.40	14.20	12.74	7.82	7.95	14.46	10.17	15.35	13.14	16.48	16.48
-Year		1950	1956	1990	1973	1968	1974	1988	1966	1978	1984	1988	1987	DEC 1987
-Minimum Monthly	52	0.50	0.51	0.73	0.50	0.69	T	0.14	0.19	0.28	0.01	0.28	1.26	T
-Year		1986	1947	1966	1987	1970	1952	1986	1980	1956	1944	1949	1958	JUN 1952
-Maximum in 24 hrs	46	5.18	5.15	4.56	7.96	7.71	4.61	3.58	7.32	4.05	5.67	7.81	7.01	7.96
-Year		1969	1950	1990	1974	1955	1960	1988	1966	1967	1990	1988	1987	APR 1974
Snow,Ice pellets,hail														
-Maximum Monthly	52	13.6	9.8	7.0	T	0.0	0.0	0.0	0.0	0.0	T	4.8	9.8	13.6
-Year		1988	1979	1971	1991						1993	1971	1963	JAN 1988
-Maximum in 24 hrs	46	12.1	9.6	6.7	T	T	0.0	0.0	0.0	0.0	T	4.8	9.8	12.1
-Year		1988	1966	1971	1991	1988					1993	1971	1963	JAN 1988
WIND:														
Mean Speed (mph)	51	8.5	8.9	9.6	9.0	7.7	7.2	6.7	6.3	6.7	6.8	8.0	8.2	7.8
Prevailing Direction through 1963		S	SW	WNW	S	S	SSW	SW	SW	NE	SW	SW	SW	SW
Fastest Mile														
-Direction (!!!)	36	S	SW	SE	NW	NW	NE	NW	NW	NW	SSW	SW	SW	NW
-Speed (MPH)	36	44	57	56	65	61	60	56	54	50	58	49	48	65
-Year		1950	1971	1959	1961	1952	1953	1960	1956	1952	1956	1952	1971	APR 1961
Peak Gust														
-Direction (!!!)														
-Speed (mph)														
-Date														

PRECIPITATION (inches) LITTLE ROCK, ARKANSAS

YEAR	JAN	FEB	MAR	APR	MAY	JUNE	JULY	AUG	SEP	OCT	NOV	DEC	ANNUAL
1964	0.98	2.87	8.22	11.06	1.40	0.31	3.79	3.71	5.46	0.37	3.70	4.37	46.24
1965	4.45	5.73	3.63	1.19	5.42	2.49	2.51	2.03	7.67	0.21	1.54	2.05	38.92
1966	3.03	5.02	0.73	7.29	2.23	0.69	3.54	14.46	1.42	1.95	3.08	4.21	47.65
1967	2.13	2.31	3.11	7.58	8.69	3.02	4.29	1.73	6.25	4.96	1.73	4.95	50.75
1968	4.76	1.08	5.55	4.85	12.74	6.77	5.98	0.26	5.99	2.81	5.30	4.56	60.65
1969	8.06	2.41	3.65	4.30	3.60	2.98	3.40	2.73	2.33	3.60	3.94	8.10	49.10
1970	1.05	4.57	4.87	7.99	0.69	2.30	3.02	2.15	2.82	7.68	2.09	3.85	43.08
1971	2.07	2.21	3.24	1.70	5.37	7.66	4.01	8.62	0.78	2.55	3.38	6.97	48.56
1972	1.71	1.55	3.32	1.81	2.07	2.62	1.77	3.58	6.43	7.63	7.38	5.14	45.01
1973	5.64	2.95	7.89	14.20	3.96	2.66	6.59	1.26	9.09	5.93	9.03	5.19	74.39
1974	5.77	2.60	2.07	9.76	6.26	7.82	4.09	3.20	4.31	3.36	5.73	2.99	57.96
1975	4.64	4.38	7.67	4.14	5.87	1.56	3.98	2.73	1.86	1.62	3.68	2.92	45.05
1976	3.00	5.12	5.43	1.06	4.88	5.69	1.97	0.70	1.82	6.04	1.79	2.30	39.80
1977	2.70	1.96	6.75	4.47	2.89	4.70	5.07	1.37	6.38	0.63	9.34	1.40	47.66
1978	5.44	1.52	3.56	4.22	6.27	5.39	2.70	6.38	10.17	1.01	6.64	11.56	64.86
1979	4.05	5.67	3.10	9.64	11.54	4.45	4.27	6.51	4.35	3.36	4.02	3.53	64.49
1980	2.73	0.89	6.60	5.85	4.57	0.53	0.99	0.19	5.09	2.64	6.28	1.86	38.22
1981	1.11	3.89	4.00	2.75	9.73	7.80	3.15	2.91	1.37	6.11	1.64	1.34	45.80
1982	8.74	3.37	2.87	9.32	5.63	4.10	1.01	4.52	1.47	2.26	9.72	8.28	61.29
1983	2.25	1.49	4.19	6.72	7.58	3.34	1.07	0.79	0.41	3.73	4.47	9.07	45.11
1984	1.31	3.52	5.58	3.77	8.22	1.06	4.15	5.69	3.28	15.35	8.49	3.54	63.96
1985	3.11	2.78	5.27	8.63	2.99	2.40	3.30	3.52	4.36	3.91	5.78	2.97	49.02
1986	0.50	3.45	3.68	7.33	4.07	6.42	0.14	4.56	1.94	6.05	5.67	3.86	47.67
1987	2.07	7.07	3.52	0.50	4.56	4.63	1.60	2.12	7.56	1.37	10.96	16.48	62.44
1988	3.71	3.41	3.50	3.82	2.05	1.04	7.95	2.19	2.54	1.95	13.14	2.91	48.21
1989	3.01	9.55	7.64	2.57	4.04	3.95	7.87	1.21	3.57	1.70	1.95	2.19	49.25
1990	6.50	4.82	10.40	7.73	7.71	0.80	4.63	1.57	4.08	8.75	3.29	6.79	67.07
1991	6.88	3.03	3.56	12.44	2.87	2.28	2.03	6.78	3.01	7.00	5.18	4.59	59.65
1992	1.75	2.05	6.48	1.86	3.67	5.07	6.76	2.14	2.90	0.67	4.71	3.85	41.91
1993	5.06	2.44	3.05	5.40	5.49	2.04	1.24	2.77	1.44	4.10	6.33	4.41	43.77
Record Mean	4.51	3.89	4.70	5.18	5.01	3.64	3.42	3.30	3.36	3.10	4.42	4.30	48.82

AVERAGE TEMPERATURE (deg. F) LITTLE ROCK, ARKANSAS

YEAR	JAN	FEB	MAR	APR	MAY	JUNE	JULY	AUG	SEP	OCT	NOV	DEC	ANNUAL
1964	40.8	41.6	52.7	64.7	72.3	80.6	83.2	79.3	73.7	60.1	54.0	43.9	62.3
1965	44.2	43.2	44.5	65.8	72.7	78.2	82.9	81.7	74.3	61.6	56.5	46.7	62.7
1966	35.4	42.9	54.6	62.4	68.4	78.0	84.2	77.9	72.0	59.2	54.8	43.2	61.1
1967	41.7	40.4	58.9	66.7	68.6	79.5	77.9	75.5	69.0	60.9	49.1	42.7	60.9
1968	37.7	38.0	50.8	60.9	67.6	77.8	77.8	81.4	70.7	62.9	51.2	42.2	59.9
1969	43.5	43.0	45.5	61.8	69.9	77.6	84.8	79.0	72.9	62.4	49.4	40.7	60.9
1970	35.7	42.1	48.2	63.1	71.9	78.7	79.9	81.2	78.1	61.5	50.3	47.2	61.5
1971	41.0	44.4	50.0	59.4	65.6	79.3	80.0	78.0	76.4	69.3	50.5	49.9	62.0
1972	43.6	46.7	53.3	62.5	69.8	79.4	80.4	81.1	75.8	62.6	47.3	41.0	62.0
1973	39.7	42.1	58.2	59.9	68.2	78.6	81.1	80.4	75.7	67.6	56.6	42.8	62.6
1974	42.4	45.7	58.1	60.7	71.3	74.3	83.2	79.0	69.0	62.3	51.9	44.4	61.9
1975	44.6	44.6	48.7	60.7	72.5	78.6	80.2	79.5	69.2	63.0	51.4	42.9	61.3
1976	39.7	52.5	56.5	61.1	64.6	74.4	80.2	78.7	72.1	57.8	45.9	41.9	60.4
1977	31.3	46.9	56.4	64.7	73.7	80.0	82.1	80.4	77.3	62.6	52.9	42.0	62.5
1978	31.7	34.0	51.0	65.9	71.4	78.9	84.1	83.0	76.7	62.0	54.6	43.3	61.4
1979	29.9	38.7	55.5	62.7	70.2	77.9	81.0	79.0	72.7	65.3	50.3	45.8	60.7
1980	44.0	40.9	50.3	61.5	70.6	79.4	88.1	87.0	78.6	60.4	50.4	43.1	62.9
1981	39.7	44.6	52.5	67.5	67.4	80.1	83.5	79.9	75.3	61.4	55.5	43.2	62.5
1982	37.5	41.3	57.1	58.0	72.7	76.6	83.1	82.1	74.2	64.7	53.2	48.3	62.4
1983	39.2	43.8	51.1	54.4	67.7	77.4	82.5	86.1	76.0	64.0	50.8	30.9	60.3
1984	36.7	46.6	50.1	59.7	68.0	79.8	79.7	78.1	71.0	65.0	49.0	52.1	61.3
1985	33.7	39.3	57.6	63.0	70.0	78.2	81.2	80.8	72.5	66.2	56.1	38.1	61.4
1986	42.5	48.2	55.4	63.6	71.4	79.7	86.3	78.1	77.6	63.1	49.7	42.4	63.2
1987	40.2	47.1	53.4	62.4	76.3	79.9	82.2	84.4	74.9	59.1	53.0	45.2	63.2
1988	35.6	42.9	52.2	61.5	70.4	78.8	81.7	82.4	75.8	60.4	53.3	44.4	61.6
1989	46.3	38.4	52.5	62.6	69.6	76.2	79.3	80.2	71.2	63.3	55.3	35.7	60.9
1990	48.1	51.3	55.4	62.0	68.1	80.6	83.2	82.2	77.5	61.5	56.3	43.1	64.1
1991	39.0	49.2	56.2	64.4	74.1	79.5	82.8	80.0	73.7	64.3	49.2	46.8	63.3
1992	42.7	50.6	54.4	62.6	69.0	76.5	81.0	76.5	72.7	64.4	50.1	43.9	62.0
1993	40.4	43.2	51.3	58.3	68.8	78.7	86.0	83.7	73.5	61.4	48.3	44.9	61.5
Record Mean	41.3	44.7	53.1	62.4	70.2	78.3	81.6	80.6	74.2	63.6	51.8	43.7	62.1
Max	50.0	53.9	62.9	72.5	80.0	88.0	91.2	90.4	84.4	74.4	61.6	52.3	71.8
Min	32.5	35.4	43.2	52.3	60.3	68.5	71.9	70.8	63.9	52.8	42.1	35.0	52.4

REFERENCE NOTES LITTLE ROCK, ARKANSAS

GENERAL
T - TRACE AMOUNT.
BLANK ENTRIES DENOTE MISSING/UNREPORTED DATA.
# INDICATES A STATION OR INSTRUMENT RELOCATION

SPECIFIC

PM - INCLUDES LAST DAY OF PREVIOUS MONTH
ASOS - AUTOMATED SURFACE OBSERVING SYSTEM IN OPERATION DURING THESE MONTHS.

(*) - LENGTH OF RECORD IN YEARS, ALTHOUGH INDIVIDUAL MONTHS MAY BE MISSING.
0.* OR * - THE VALUE IS BETWEEN 0.0 AND 0.05
NORMALS - BASED ON THE 1961-1990 RECORD PERIOD.
EXTREMES - DATES ARE THE MOST RECENT OCCURRENCE.
WIND DIR. - NUMERALS SHOW TENS OF DEGRESS CLOCKWISE FROM TRUE NORTH. "00" INDICATES CALM.
RESULTANT DIRECTIONS ARE GIVEN TO WHOLE DEGREES.
BOLD VALUES INDICATE EXTREME VALUES WHICH OCCURRED AFTER THE ASOS SYSTEM WAS COMMISSIONED.

RECORD = PERIOD OF RECORD
RECORD MEAN PRECIPITATION IS THE MEAN OF ALL DAILY PRECIPITATION AMOUNTS DURING THE PERIOD OF RECORD.
RECORD MAX(MIN) TEMPERATURE IS THE MEAN OF ALL DAILY MAX(MIN) TEMPERATURES DURING THE PERIOD OF RECORD.
RECORD MEAN TEMPERATURE IS THE SUM OF THE RECORD MAX AND RECORD MIN DIVIDED BY 2.
AVERAGE TEMPERATURE IS THE SUM OF THE MEAN DAILY MAX AND MIN TEMPERATURE DIVIDED BY 2.

EXCEPTIONS

1. PRECIPITATION DATA DECEMBER 15, 1975 THROUGH OCTOBER 1976 IS FROM NORTH LITTLE ROCK.
2. WIND DATA FROM DECEMBER 15, 1975 THROUGH DECEMBER 1976 IS FROM NORTH LITTLE ROCK.
3. MAXIMUM 24-HOUR PRECIPITATION AND SNOW, FASTEST MILE WINDS, MEAN SKY COVER, AND DAYS CLEAR-PARTLY CLOUDY-CLOUDY ARE THROUGH 1977.
4. PERCENT OF POSSIBLE SUNSHINE IS THROUGH 1975

RECORD MEANS ARE THROUGH THE CURRENT YEAR, BEGINNING IN 1880 FOR TEMPERATURE
1880 FOR PRECIPITATION
1943 FOR SNOWFALL

HEATING DEGREE DAYS Base 65 deg. F — LITTLE ROCK, ARKANSAS

SEASON	JULY	AUG	SEP	OCT	NOV	DEC	JAN	FEB	MAR	APR	MAY	JUNE	TOTAL
1964-65	0	0	14	175	336	646	639	604	629	70	0	0	3113
1965-66	0	0	19	137	257	561	916	611	327	115	42	0	2985
1966-67	0	0	3	198	309	679	717	682	240	52	33	0	2913
1967-68	0	0	39	162	472	685	840	778	440	147	30	0	3593
1968-69	0	0	3	124	412	700	665	611	595	108	16	1	3235
1969-70	0	0	0	175	458	745	905	636	516	124	23	0	3582
1970-71	0	0	4	153	442	554	737	571	470	182	55	0	3168
1971-72	0	0	9	6	437	466	659	525	360	149	20	0	2631
1972-73	0	0	8	142	530	736	777	637	216	186	28	0	3260
1973-74	0	0	2	61	261	680	690	533	255	163	4	0	2649
1974-75	0	0	23	111	401	634	630	566	499	196	5	0	3065
1975-76	0	0	48	130	414	681	777	359	284	146	70	0	2909
1976-77	0	0	1	257	567	710	1041	502	265	70	10	0	3423
1977-78	0	0	0	105	370	709	1025	862	436	68	48	0	3623
1978-79	0	0	0	118	321	667	1083	732	314	110	13	0	3358
1979-80	0	0	0	80	436	588	645	693	450	142	15	0	3049
1980-81	0	0	16	184	437	673	774	565	388	37	45	0	3119
1981-82	0	0	4	186	278	668	847	656	298	223	6	0	3166
1982-83	0	0	12	119	369	536	795	587	425	332	33	0	3208
1983-84	0	0	19	89	422	1050	872	530	460	190	24	0	3656
1984-85	0	0	44	81	476	408	962	713	251	101	8	0	3044
1985-86	0	0	31	82	283	825	691	467	298	91	7	0	2775
1986-87	0	1	0	112	454	694	762	496	353	145	0	0	3017
1987-88	0	0	0	182	358	609	904	637	388	123	4	0	3205
1988-89	0	0	1	163	358	633	573	738	395	156	39	0	3056
1989-90	0	0	23	112	313	898	516	380	316	152	31	0	2741
1990-91	0	0	8	173	260	675	798	438	294	69	10	0	2725
1991-92	0	0	23	97	483	560	682	413	324	134	40	0	2756
1992-93	0	0	14	69	441	647	755	606	423	215	15	1	3186
1993-94	0	0	13	174	506	613							

COOLING DEGREE DAYS Base 65 deg. F — LITTLE ROCK, ARKANSAS

YEAR	JAN	FEB	MAR	APR	MAY	JUNE	JULY	AUG	SEP	OCT	NOV	DEC	TOTAL
1969	4	0	0	21	176	386	622	439	243	100	0	0	1991
1970	3	0	0	77	243	416	471	511	404	51	9	9	2194
1971	0	0	11	19	79	435	470	411	355	146	10	3	1939
1972	2	0	3	81	174	440	484	507	341	76	3	0	2111
1973	0	0	14	41	135	415	506	485	330	147	17	0	2090
1974	0	0	45	37	206	288	572	441	148	36	14	0	1787
1975	6	0	4	73	245	416	475	455	178	73	14	2	1941
1976	0	5	27	37	65	292	480	434	220	42	0	0	1602
1977	0	0	7	67	287	455	537	482	377	40	14	0	2266
1978	0	0	9	104	253	424	599	565	357	31	16	0	2358
1979	0	0	24	48	178	396	502	442	240	95	1	0	1926
1980	0	1	1	42	196	439	725	688	432	50	5	0	2579
1981	0	0	9	117	131	458	580	470	318	78	2	0	2163
1982	0	0	57	21	253	355	570	540	294	114	20	24	2248
1983	0	0	0	21	121	381	550	660	355	63	6	0	2157
1984	0	1	4	38	126	451	462	416	234	88	3	17	1840
1985	0	0	31	48	167	404	508	501	265	125	21	0	2070
1986	0	5	7	56	211	446	668	415	385	63	0	0	2256
1987	0	0	3	74	359	456	540	610	304	8	3	0	2357
1988	0	0	2	24	177	423	523	546	332	25	15	0	2067
1989	0	0	13	91	189	345	450	479	213	70	29	0	1879
1990	0	4	26	67	135	475	571	540	392	73	8	0	2291
1991	0	1	30	56	299	445	558	472	290	82	14	2	2249
1992	0	0	4	70	170	352	505	364	249	60	0	0	1774
1993	0	0	4	22	138	419	656	591	276	69	14	0	2189

SNOWFALL (inches) — LITTLE ROCK, ARKANSAS

SEASON	JULY	AUG	SEP	OCT	NOV	DEC	JAN	FEB	MAR	APR	MAY	JUNE	TOTAL
1964-65	0.0	0.0	0.0	0.0	0.0	0.2	T	2.9	4.3	0.0	0.0	0.0	7.4
1965-66	0.0	0.0	0.0	0.0	0.0	0.0	12.0	9.6	0.0	0.0	0.0	0.0	21.6
1966-67	0.0	0.0	0.0	0.0	T	0.2	1.6	T	T	0.0	0.0	0.0	1.8
1967-68	0.0	0.0	0.0	0.0	T	1.1	1.0	4.3	T	0.0	0.0	0.0	6.4
1968-69	0.0	0.0	0.0	0.0	0.0	0.0	T	2.3	T	0.0	0.0	0.0	2.3
1969-70	0.0	0.0	0.0	0.0	T	T	4.0	T	T	0.0	0.0	0.0	4.0
1970-71	0.0	0.0	0.0	0.0	0.0	T	T	0.7	7.0	T	0.0	0.0	7.7
1971-72	0.0	0.0	0.0	0.0	4.8	0.6	0.1	0.3	0.0	0.0	0.0	0.0	5.8
1972-73	0.0	0.0	0.0	0.0	T	0.7	2.6	T	0.0	T	0.0	0.0	3.3
1973-74	0.0	0.0	0.0	0.0	0.0	T	0.3	T	0.0	0.0	0.0	0.0	0.3
1974-75	0.0	0.0	0.0	0.0	T	T	1.4	0.4	2.4	0.0	0.0	0.0	4.2
1975-76	0.0	0.0	0.0	0.0	0.2	1.0	T	0.0	0.0	0.0	0.0	0.0	1.2
1976-77	0.0	0.0	0.0	0.0	1.0	0.0	3.8	0.0	0.0	0.0	0.0	0.0	4.8
1977-78	0.0	0.0	0.0	0.0	0.0	0.0	10.0	3.4	T	0.0	0.0	0.0	13.4
1978-79	0.0	0.0	0.0	0.0	0.0	T	1.4	9.8	0.0	0.0	0.0	0.0	11.2
1979-80	0.0	0.0	0.0	0.0	0.0	0.0	0.9	0.5	T	T	0.0	0.0	1.4
1980-81	0.0	0.0	0.0	0.0	1.8	T	T	0.0	0.0	0.0	0.0	0.0	1.8
1981-82	0.0	0.0	0.0	0.0	0.0	0.0	5.0	6.3	T	0.0	0.0	0.0	11.3
1982-83	0.0	0.0	0.0	0.0	0.0	T	T	T	T	T	0.0	0.0	T
1983-84	0.0	0.0	0.0	0.0	0.0	0.8	1.5	0.2	4.5	0.0	0.0	0.0	7.0
1984-85	0.0	0.0	0.0	0.0	0.0	T	6.3	5.0	0.0	0.0	0.0	0.0	11.3
1985-86	0.0	0.0	0.0	0.0	0.0	T	0.0	1.5	0.0	0.0	0.0	0.0	1.5
1986-87	0.0	0.0	0.0	0.0	T	0.0	1.0	T	0.8	0.0	0.0	0.0	1.8
1987-88	0.0	0.0	0.0	0.0	0.0	T	13.6	2.5	T	0.0	0.0	0.0	16.1
1988-89	0.0	0.0	0.0	0.0	0.0	T	2.0	T	1.0	0.0	0.0	0.0	3.0
1989-90	0.0	0.0	0.0	0.0	0.0	T	T	0.0	0.0	0.0	0.0	0.0	T
1990-91	0.0	0.0	0.0	0.0	0.0	T	T	T	T	T	0.0	0.0	T
1991-92	0.0	0.0	0.0	0.0	T	T	T	0.0	0.0	0.0	0.0	0.0	T
1992-93	0.0	0.0	0.0	0.0	T	T	0.0	T	T	0.0	0.0	0.0	T
1993-94	0.0	0.0	0.0	T	0.0	0.0							
Record Mean	0.0	0.0	0.0	T	0.2	0.7	2.3	1.4	0.5	T	0.0	0.0	5.1

EUREKA, CALIFORNIA

Humboldt Bay is one-quarter mile north and one mile west of the station. There are no hills in Eureka of any consequence. The land slopes upward gently from the Bay toward the Coast Range, which begins about 3 miles east of the station and reaches the top of its first ridge approximately 10 miles to the east. The elevation of the ridge is 2,000 feet and extends in a semicircle from a point 20 miles north of Eureka to a point 25 miles south.

The climate of Eureka is completely maritime with high humidity prevailing the entire year. There are definite rainy and dry seasons. The rainy season begins in October and continues through April, accounting for about 90 percent of the annual precipitation. The dry season from May through September is marked by considerable fog or low cloudiness that usually clears in the late morning and sunny weather is generally the case during the early afternoon hours.

Temperatures are moderate the entire year. Although record highs have reached the mid 80s and record lows near 20 degrees, the usual yearly range is from lows in the mid 30s to highs in the mid 70s.

The principal industries are lumbering, fishing, tourism, and dairy farming. There is very little truck farming due to the low temperatures and lack of sunshine, however, the climate is nearly ideal for berries and flowers.

Based on the 1951-1980 period, the average first occurrence of 32 degrees Fahrenheit in the fall is December 10 and the average last occurrence in the spring is February 6.

NORMALS, MEANS, AND EXTREMES

EUREKA, CALIFORNIA

LATITUDE: 40°48'N LONGITUDE: 124°10' W ELEVATION: FT. GRND 58 BARO 00079 TIME ZONE: PACIFIC WBAN: 24213

	(a)	JAN	FEB	MAR	APR	MAY	JUNE	JULY	AUG	SEP	OCT	NOV	DEC	YEAR
TEMPERATURE °F:														
Normals														
-Daily Maximum		54.4	55.6	55.4	55.9	57.9	60.3	61.8	62.6	63.0	60.8	58.1	54.8	58.4
-Daily Minimum		41.5	42.9	43.4	44.3	47.5	50.6	52.3	53.1	51.6	48.6	45.2	42.0	46.9
-Monthly		48.0	49.3	49.4	50.2	52.8	55.5	57.0	57.9	57.3	54.7	51.7	48.4	52.7
Extremes														
-Record Highest	83	78	85	78	80	84	85	76	82	86	87	78	77	87
-Year		1986	1930	1914	1989	1939	1945	1992	1991	1983	1993	1987	1963	OCT 1993
-Record Lowest	83	25	27	29	32	36	41	45	44	41	32	29	21	21
-Year		1937	1990	1917	1929	1954	1966	1924	1935	1946	1971	1935	1972	DEC 1972
NORMAL DEGREE DAYS:														
Heating (base 65°F)		527	440	484	444	378	285	248	223	234	319	399	515	4496
Cooling (base 65°F)		0	0	0	0	0	0	0	0	0	0	0	0	0
% OF POSSIBLE SUNSHINE	83	43	46	52	57	58	59	55	50	54	50	44	41	51
MEAN SKY COVER (tenths)														
Sunrise - Sunset	51	7.2	7.4	7.3	7.0	6.7	6.5	6.5	6.9	6.0	6.5	7.1	7.1	6.9
MEAN NUMBER OF DAYS:														
Sunrise to Sunset														
-Clear	83	6.0	5.3	5.6	6.2	6.5	7.2	6.6	5.4	8.7	8.1	6.3	6.5	78.4
-Partly Cloudy	83	6.2	5.8	7.6	8.3	9.8	9.6	10.9	10.7	8.5	8.3	6.6	6.4	98.8
-Cloudy	83	18.8	17.2	17.7	15.5	14.6	13.2	13.6	14.9	12.8	14.5	17.1	18.1	188.1
Precipitation														
.01 inches or more	83	16.0	14.1	15.6	11.8	8.4	5.3	2.2	2.6	4.4	8.6	13.1	15.4	117.4
Snow,Ice pellets,hail														
1.0 inches or more	83	0.1	0.*	0.0	0.0	0.0	0.0	0.0	0.0	0.0	0.0	0.0	0.*	0.1
Thunderstorms	71	0.7	0.6	0.4	0.2	0.2	0.2	0.2	0.1	0.3	0.4	0.6	0.6	4.4
Heavy Fog Visibility														
1/4 mile or less	71	4.1	2.8	1.9	1.7	1.2	2.1	3.5	5.4	7.7	9.6	6.2	4.4	50.6
Temperature °F														
-Maximum														
90° and above	83	0.0	0.0	0.0	0.0	0.0	0.0	0.0	0.0	0.0	0.0	0.0	0.0	0.0
32° and below	83	0.0	0.0	0.0	0.0	0.0	0.0	0.0	0.0	0.0	0.0	0.0	0.0	0.0
-Minimum														
32° and below	83	1.9	0.8	0.2	0.*	0.0	0.0	0.0	0.0	0.0	0.*	0.2	1.4	4.6
0° and below	83	0.0	0.0	0.0	0.0	0.0	0.0	0.0	0.0	0.0	0.0	0.0	0.0	0.0
AVG. STATION PRESS.(mb)														
RELATIVE HUMIDITY (%)														
Hour 04														
Hour 10 (Local Time)														
Hour 16														
Hour 22														
PRECIPITATION (inches):														
Water Equivalent														
-Normal		6.00	4.73	5.32	2.88	1.44	0.51	0.13	0.48	0.89	2.67	6.44	6.04	37.53
-Maximum Monthly	83	13.92	13.94	13.97	10.68	6.05	2.57	1.34	3.42	3.56	13.04	16.58	14.13	16.58
-Year		1969	1938	1938	1963	1960	1954	1916	1983	1925	1950	1973	1983	NOV 1973
-Minimum Monthly	83	0.66	0.50	0.07	0.31	0.03	0.00	0.00	0.00	0.00	0.00	T	0.52	0.00
-Year		1985	1923	1926	1956	1955	1917	1967	1940	1929	1917	1929	1976	JUL 1967
-Maximum in 24 hrs	83	4.42	4.88	4.02	2.56	2.23	1.73	1.18	2.21	1.54	5.83	4.55	4.17	5.83
-Year		1912	1959	1975	1983	1943	1943	1916	1983	1977	1950	1926	1939	OCT 1950
Snow,Ice pellets,hail														
-Maximum Monthly	83	3.0	3.5	1.0	T	0.0	0.0	0.0	0.0	0.0	0.0	0.1	1.9	3.5
-Year		1935	1989	1966	1993							1977	1972	FEB 1989
-Maximum in 24 hrs	83	3.0	2.0	1.0	T	0.0	0.0	0.0	0.0	0.0	0.0	0.1	1.9	3.0
-Year		1935	1989	1966	1993							1977	1972	JAN 1935
WIND:														
Mean Speed (mph)	54	6.9	7.2	7.6	8.0	7.9	7.4	6.8	5.8	5.5	5.6	6.0	6.4	6.8
Prevailing Direction through 1964		SE	SE	N	N	N	N	N	NW	N	N	SE	SE	N
Fastest Mile														
-Direction (!!)	83	S	SW	SW	N	NW	NW	N	N	N	SW	S	S	SW
-Speed (MPH)	83	54	48	48	49	40	39	35	34	44	56	55	56	56
-Year		1955	1960	1953	1915	1955	1949	1986	1920	1941	1962	1981	1931	OCT 1962
Peak Gust														
-Direction (!!)	9	S	N	S	NE	N	N	N	S	N	SE	S	N	S
-Speed (mph)	9	70	60	72	53	60	51	45	45	49	52	62	62	72
-Date		1993	1987	1991	1991	1990	1991	1986	1990	1988	1988	1991	1990	MAR 1991

PRECIPITATION (inches)

EUREKA, CALIFORNIA

YEAR	JAN	FEB	MAR	APR	MAY	JUNE	JULY	AUG	SEP	OCT	NOV	DEC	ANNUAL
1964	11.13	1.20	5.91	0.67	1.59	0.72	0.83	0.03	0.07	1.82	12.11	10.96	47.04
1965	5.82	1.36	1.23	5.60	0.44	0.35	T	0.36	T	0.70	5.20	5.22	26.28
1966	9.44	3.12	6.57	1.34	0.06	0.30	0.25	0.50	1.33	1.02	9.86	6.52	40.31
1967	8.87	1.47	7.44	5.29	1.52	0.32	0.00	T	1.32	2.15	4.40	4.34	37.12
1968	7.59	2.93	3.85	0.40	1.04	0.20	0.04	1.98	0.60	2.81	5.88	8.32	35.64
1969	13.92	7.82	1.56	3.22	1.01	0.34	0.05	T	0.36	3.20	3.49	9.60	44.57
1970	12.46	3.15	2.70	1.54	1.38	0.29	T	T	0.32	2.11	13.20	10.24	47.39
1971	5.41	3.28	7.91	2.92	1.28	1.51	0.16	0.55	2.08	0.92	6.36	6.38	38.76
1972	7.96	5.93	5.08	2.27	1.11	0.88	0.01	0.07	1.06	1.97	5.41	7.42	39.17
1973	6.47	3.85	7.10	0.35	0.85	0.23	T	0.08	2.35	4.14	16.58	7.02	49.02
1974	6.02	5.98	6.98	3.15	0.42	0.33	0.11	0.32	T	1.76	2.75	6.40	34.22
1975	5.20	7.68	10.73	3.29	1.05	0.58	0.10	0.58	0.01	6.77	4.72	5.38	46.09
1976	1.88	7.51	3.12	2.80	0.54	0.14	0.20	1.70	0.04	0.28	2.98	0.52	21.71
1977	1.90	2.24	4.33	1.20	2.10	0.07	T	0.20	3.35	2.79	4.51	6.60	29.29
1978	4.52	6.06	2.88	4.10	0.82	0.34	0.03	0.59	2.72	0.04	2.39	1.16	25.65
1979	3.82	6.26	1.70	3.94	2.25	0.05	0.31	0.13	1.15	6.14	6.19	3.75	35.69
1980	3.19	4.67	6.14	4.18	1.70	0.42	T	0.07	0.14	1.38	2.49	6.10	30.48
1981	7.67	3.72	4.64	0.71	2.02	0.57	T	0.01	0.97	3.71	9.39	9.88	43.29
1982	4.75	5.76	7.06	5.97	0.07	0.78	0.08	0.03	0.62	4.89	7.83	10.30	48.14
1983	8.48	9.18	10.73	5.47	1.12	0.65	0.89	3.42	0.87	1.87	10.40	14.13	67.21
1984	0.76	5.18	4.70	2.76	2.51	1.07	0.03	0.05	0.55	3.67	15.15	4.27	40.70
1985	0.66	3.69	4.68	0.45	1.14	0.89	0.15	0.52	1.06	4.07	2.98	2.78	23.07
1986	7.19	10.08	6.12	1.46	2.34	0.21	0.02	T	2.70	1.75	1.85	3.83	37.55
1987	6.48	3.38	6.10	1.15	0.41	0.26	0.20	0.06	0.02	1.05	4.23	10.92	34.26
1988	7.13	0.54	1.18	2.06	2.70	2.22	0.05	T	0.12	0.41	8.93	6.26	31.60
1989	4.71	2.88	7.63	2.01	1.67	0.21	0.08	0.13	0.85	2.90	1.60	0.80	25.47
1990	7.20	4.50	3.30	1.41	3.74	0.32	0.22	0.71	0.19	1.73	3.07	2.95	29.34
1991	1.65	2.75	6.94	2.52	2.16	0.26	1.13	0.37	T	1.06	1.95	2.36	23.15
1992	3.99	3.80	3.51	2.42	0.06	1.27	0.25	0.01	0.33	2.08	2.21	9.33	29.26
1993	7.15	5.93	4.72	5.94	4.44	1.23	0.37	0.54	0.03	0.56	1.35	7.12	39.38
Record Mean	6.59	5.68	5.29	3.01	1.86	0.72	0.14	0.25	0.86	2.63	5.36	6.29	38.69

AVERAGE TEMPERATURE (deg. F)

EUREKA, CALIFORNIA

YEAR	JAN	FEB	MAR	APR	MAY	JUNE	JULY	AUG	SEP	OCT	NOV	DEC	ANNUAL
1964	46.6	47.0	45.7	47.1	50.4	54.8	56.6	57.0	55.2	54.9	50.0	48.5	51.1
1965	47.3	45.7	48.5	50.1	49.9	51.9	54.8	58.9	53.9	55.7	54.6	47.0	51.6
1966	47.7	46.5	48.0	50.4	50.4	55.5	56.6	55.9	58.0	53.2	52.6	49.5	52.0
1967	47.4	47.6	46.7	46.2	51.9	54.6	56.5	56.8	59.1	56.9	53.3	45.1	51.8
1968	46.6	53.2	50.6	48.1	52.4	55.5	56.3	59.3	57.5	53.3	51.8	46.5	52.6
1969	44.0	46.2	48.3	49.8	53.4	56.6	55.6	55.8	56.5	55.2	51.3	51.3	52.0
1970	52.1	51.4	49.9	47.4	52.3	54.3	54.8	55.3	55.7	52.6	53.5	47.4	52.2
1971	45.7	46.3	47.1	48.1	50.6	54.3	55.2	60.0	56.7	50.6	49.4	45.0	50.8
1972	44.6	49.0	51.2	49.1	51.2	54.6	57.8	58.2	55.8	54.2	51.8	45.7	52.0
1973	47.3	50.7	47.4	50.1	52.0	55.1	55.6	54.8	57.1	52.1	51.4	51.2	52.1
1974	46.7	46.1	50.1	49.7	51.1	54.1	57.7	57.7	55.6	53.2	51.2	48.7	51.8
1975	45.8	48.0	47.6	46.5	51.4	53.2	56.9	55.3	55.2	54.2	48.5	47.4	50.8
1976	46.4	46.9	45.7	48.4	51.1	52.8	57.5	57.9	56.2	54.4	52.2	47.4	51.4
1977	47.4	50.5	46.2	49.2	51.5	54.2	55.1	58.3	57.1	53.8	51.2	51.0	52.1
1978	51.8	50.3	53.5	51.0	53.3	56.0	55.9	57.0	57.6	54.9	48.0	43.3	52.7
1979	46.6	48.0	50.0	51.0	52.7	54.0	58.1	59.4	62.3	57.3	52.4	51.8	53.6
1980	48.3	53.5	48.6	51.9	52.3	55.5	57.3	55.0	56.6	54.3	51.3	51.2	53.0
1981	52.5	51.3	50.2	50.6	53.3	56.5	55.2	58.1	57.9	54.3	53.6	52.1	53.8
1982	44.9	49.5	48.3	50.8	52.8	56.3	58.3	59.6	58.7	57.3	52.1	49.6	53.2
1983	51.3	53.4	53.4	51.8	54.4	58.0	60.5	61.9	60.7	57.9	53.6	50.6	55.6
1984	49.4	50.0	52.8	51.3	55.0	55.2	57.6	60.2	58.3	55.3	52.1	46.8	53.7
1985	48.4	47.9	47.4	51.6	53.9	56.6	58.6	58.5	56.7	54.5	46.6	47.7	52.4
1986	54.3	52.7	53.1	50.7	53.9	59.0	57.4	57.2	57.2	55.6	53.5	51.3	54.7
1987	49.1	51.4	52.7	54.2	56.6	57.7	59.5	58.5	57.3	57.8	54.8	49.7	54.9
1988	50.4	50.2	50.3	52.8	56.3	57.7	58.8	57.7	55.8	55.2	53.3	47.7	53.9
1989	46.0	45.6	51.8	54.6	55.9	57.6	59.4	59.3	56.6	54.9	52.6	49.2	53.6
1990	48.3	45.5	50.2	52.8	54.0	58.2	59.8	60.4	61.6	54.3	49.7	42.8	53.1
1991	47.8	52.8	48.1	50.9	52.2	53.8	57.3	59.9	57.2	56.1	51.4	48.3	53.0
1992	50.3	53.9	54.1	56.4	56.7	58.3	60.6	59.1	57.5	58.0	51.7	46.9	55.3
1993	46.4	49.4	53.4	53.6	57.9	57.9	57.4	59.8	55.8	56.9	49.9	49.5	54.0
Record Mean	47.4	48.3	48.8	50.3	52.7	55.1	56.4	56.9	56.4	54.2	51.3	48.3	52.2
Max	53.6	54.4	54.7	55.8	57.6	59.8	60.7	61.3	61.8	60.2	57.7	54.6	57.7
Min	41.2	42.2	42.9	44.7	47.7	50.4	52.0	52.5	50.9	48.2	44.9	42.0	46.6

REFERENCE NOTES

EUREKA, CALIFORNIA

GENERAL
T - TRACE AMOUNT.
BLANK ENTRIES DENOTE MISSING/UNREPORTED DATA.
# INDICATES A STATION OR INSTRUMENT RELOCATION.

SPECIFIC

PM - INCLUDES LAST DAY OF PREVIOUS MONTH
ASOS - AUTOMATED SURFACE OBSERVING SYSTEM IN OPERATION DURING THESE MONTHS.

(a) - LENGTH OF RECORD IN YEARS, ALTHOUGH INDIVIDUAL MONTHS MAY BE MISSING.
0.* OR * - THE VALUE IS BETWEEN 0.0 AND 0.05
NORMALS - BASED ON THE 1961-1990 RECORD PERIOD.
EXTREMES - DATES ARE THE MOST RECENT OCCURRENCE
WIND DIR.- NUMERALS SHOW TENS OF DEGRESS CLOCKWISE FROM TRUE NORTH. "00" INDICATES CALM.
RESULTANT DIRECTIONS ARE GIVEN TO WHOLE DEGREES.
BOLD VALUES INDICATE EXTREME VALUES WHICH OCCURRED AFTER THE ASOS SYSTEM WAS COMMISSIONED.

RECORD = PERIOD OF RECORD
RECORD MEAN PRECIPITATION IS THE MEAN OF ALL DAILY PRECIPITATION AMOUNTS DURING THE PERIOD OF RECORD.
RECORD MAX(MIN) TEMPERATURE IS THE MEAN OF ALL DAILY MAX(MIN) TEMPERATURES DURING THE PERIOD OF RECORD.
RECORD MEAN TEMPERATURE IS THE SUM OF THE RECORD MAX AND RECORD MIN DIVIDED BY 2.
AVERAGE TEMPERATURE IS THE SUM OF THE MEAN DAILY MAX AND MIN TEMPERATURE DIVIDED BY 2.

EXCEPTIONS

1. PRIOR TO 1965, THUNDERSTORMS AND HEAVY FOG MAY BE INCOMPLETE, DUE TO PART-TIME OPERATIONS.
2. THUNDERSTORM AND HEAVY FOG DATA ARE MISSING FROM 1965 THROUGH 1976.
3. MEAN WIND SPEED IS THROUGH 1964.

RECORD MEANS ARE THROUGH THE CURRENT YEAR, BEGINNING IN 1887 FOR TEMPERATURE
1887 FOR PRECIPITATION
1911 FOR SNOWFALL

HEATING DEGREE DAYS Base 65 deg. F EUREKA, CALIFORNIA

SEASON	JULY	AUG	SEP	OCT	NOV	DEC	JAN	FEB	MAR	APR	MAY	JUNE	TOTAL
1964-65	256	243	288	306	444	505	544	533	505	441	459	385	4909
1965-66	309	183	324	285	305	551	531	510	519	433	443	280	4673
1966-67	254	275	209	358	368	472	541	482	561	560	399	307	4786
1967-68	257	249	170	243	345	611	565	337	441	498	384	279	4379
1968-69	260	179	220	354	388	566	644	519	508	449	352	246	4685
1969-70	284	282	247	295	404	419	392	374	462	521	385	313	4378
1970-71	308	292	274	379	338	539	590	518	548	502	438	318	5044
1971-72	299	154	242	440	463	612	624	456	422	472	423	306	4913
1972-73	217	204	269	328	389	590	542	395	537	439	393	293	4596
1973-74	287	308	230	393	399	419	559	523	455	454	423	321	4771
1974-75	222	220	274	360	407	501	587	469	532	547	417	347	4883
1975-76	244	290	286	328	486	542	569	516	590	490	424	360	5125
1976-77	226	213	258	324	375	535	537	400	577	468	415	317	4645
1977-78	302	200	231	342	408	427	403	404	347	415	357	264	4100
1978-79	274	241	215	307	503	667	562	467	459	412	374	323	4804
1979-80	208	165	92	231	369	404	511	330	500	386	388	280	3864
1980-81	230	303	246	328	402	422	384	377	451	423	357	249	4172
1981-82	299	205	203	324	339	396	616	430	512	419	373	258	4374
1982-83	204	158	181	232	381	468	415	317	355	391	320	203	3625
1983-84	133	90	129	215	336	443	475	429	369	403	301	285	3608
1984-85	222	142	195	295	378	556	507	472	532	396	338	243	4276
1985-86	195	194	244	316	546	533	329	337	365	422	338	169	3988
1986-87	227	236	227	290	341	417	487	372	377	316	260	213	3763
1987-88	163	196	226	221	302	470	446	423	453	358	265	215	3738
1988-89	187	218	274	297	345	529	582	535	403	309	278	214	4171
1989-90	164	171	243	306	365	482	513	541	453	356	332	198	4124
1990-91	154	141	95	325	451	680	528	336	516	418	387	330	4361
1991-92	229	164	225	274	401	511	450	316	329	250	248	193	3590
1992-93	135	176	220	211	393	556	570	433	354	337	214	203	3802
1993-94	229	152	268	253	446	472							

COOLING DEGREE DAYS Base 65 deg. F EUREKA, CALIFORNIA

YEAR	JAN	FEB	MAR	APR	MAY	JUNE	JULY	AUG	SEP	OCT	NOV	DEC	TOTAL
1969	0	0	0	0	0	0	0	0	0	0	0	0	0
1970	0	0	0	0	1	0	0	0	1	0	0	0	2
1971	0	0	0	0	0	0	0	2	0	0	0	0	2
1972	0	0	0	0	0	0	0	1	0	0	0	0	1
1973	0	0	0	0	0	1	0	0	0	0	0	0	1
1974	0	0	0	0	0	0	0	0	0	0	0	0	0
1975	0	0	0	0	0	0	0	0	0	0	0	0	0
1976	0	0	0	0	0	0	0	0	0	0	0	0	0
1977	0	0	0	0	0	0	0	0	0	0	0	0	0
1978	0	0	0	0	0	0	0	0	0	1	0	0	1
1979	0	0	0	0	0	0	0	0	15	0	0	2	17
1980	0	2	0	0	0	0	0	0	0	3	0	0	5
1981	4	0	0	0	0	0	0	0	0	0	0	0	4
1982	0	0	0	0	0	3	0	0	0	2	0	0	5
1983	0	0	0	0	0	0	0	2	7	0	0	0	9
1984	0	0	0	0	0	0	0	0	4	1	0	0	5
1985	0	0	0	0	0	0	1	0	0	2	0	0	3
1986	0	0	0	0	0	0	0	0	0	5	0	0	5
1987	0	0	0	0	3	0	0	0	0	5	0	0	8
1988	0	0	0	0	0	0	0	0	4	0	0	0	4
1989	0	0	0	1	0	0	0	0	0	0	0	0	1
1990	0	0	0	0	0	0	0	4	0	0	0	0	4
1991	0	0	0	0	0	0	0	10	0	4	0	0	14
1992	0	0	0	0	0	0	2	0	3	2	0	0	7
1993	0	3	0	0	3	0	0	0	0	8	0	0	14

SNOWFALL (inches) EUREKA, CALIFORNIA

SEASON	JULY	AUG	SEP	OCT	NOV	DEC	JAN	FEB	MAR	APR	MAY	JUNE	TOTAL
1970-71	0.0	0.0	0.0	0.0	0.0	0.0	T	T	0.0	0.0	0.0	0.0	T
1971-72	0.0	0.0	0.0	0.0	0.0	0.0	1.6	0.0	0.0	0.0	0.0	0.0	1.6
1972-73	0.0	0.0	0.0	0.0	0.0	1.9	0.0	0.0	T	0.0	0.0	0.0	1.9
1973-74	0.0	0.0	0.0	0.0	0.0	0.0	T	0.0	0.0	0.0	0.0	0.0	T
1974-75	0.0	0.0	0.0	0.0	0.0	T	0.0	0.0	0.0	T	0.0	0.0	T
1975-76	0.0	0.0	0.0	0.0	0.0	0.0	0.0	0.0	0.1	0.0	0.0	0.0	0.1
1976-77	0.0	0.0	0.0	0.0	0.0	0.0	0.0	0.0	T	0.0	0.0	0.0	T
1977-78	0.0	0.0	0.0	0.0	0.1	0.0	0.0	0.0	0.0	0.0	0.0	0.0	0.1
1978-79	0.0	0.0	0.0	0.0	0.0	0.0	0.0	0.0	0.0	0.0	0.0	0.0	0.0
1979-80	0.0	0.0	0.0	0.0	0.0	0.0	0.0	0.0	0.0	0.0	0.0	0.0	0.0
1980-81	0.0	0.0	0.0	0.0	0.0	0.0	0.0	0.0	0.0	0.0	0.0	0.0	0.0
1981-82	0.0	0.0	0.0	0.0	0.0	0.0	T	0.0	T	T	0.0	0.0	T
1982-83	0.0	0.0	0.0	0.0	0.0	T	0.0	0.0	T	0.0	0.0	0.0	T
1983-84	0.0	0.0	0.0	0.0	T	1.0	0.0	0.0	0.0	0.0	0.0	0.0	1.0
1984-85	0.0	0.0	0.0	0.0	0.0	0.0	0.0	0.0	0.0	0.0	0.0	0.0	0.0
1985-86	0.0	0.0	0.0	0.0	0.0	0.0	0.0	0.0	0.0	0.0	0.0	0.0	0.0
1986-87	0.0	0.0	0.0	0.0	0.0	0.0	0.0	0.0	0.0	0.0	0.0	0.0	0.0
1987-88	0.0	0.0	0.0	0.0	0.0	T	0.0	0.0	0.0	0.0	0.0	0.0	T
1988-89	0.0	0.0	0.0	0.0	0.0	T	0.0	3.5	0.0	0.0	0.0	0.0	3.5
1989-90	0.0	0.0	0.0	0.0	0.0	0.0	0.0	1.0	0.0	0.0	0.0	0.0	1.0
1990-91	0.0	0.0	0.0	0.0	0.0	T	0.0	0.0	T	0.0	0.0	0.0	T
1991-92	0.0	0.0	0.0	0.0	0.0	T	0.0	0.0	0.0	0.0	0.0	0.0	T
1992-93	0.0	0.0	0.0	0.0	0.0	T	0.0	T	0.0	T	0.0	0.0	T
1993-94	0.0	0.0	0.0	0.0	0.0	0.0							
Record Mean	0.0	0.0	0.0	0.0	T	T	0.1	0.1	T	T	0.0	0.0	0.3

FRESNO, CALIFORNIA

Fresno is located about midway and toward the eastern edge of the San Joaquin Valley, which is oriented northwest to southeast and has a length of about 225 miles and an average width of 50 miles. The San Joaquin Valley is generally flat. About 15 miles east of Fresno the terrain slopes upward with the foothills of the Sierra Nevada. The Sierra Nevada attain an elevation of more than 14,000 feet 50 miles east of Fresno. West of the city 45 miles lie the foothills of the Coastal Range.

The climate of Fresno is dry and mild in winter and hot in summer. Nearly nine-tenths of the annual precipitation falls in the six months from November to April.

Due to clear skies during the summer and the protection of the San Joaquin Valley from marine effects, the normal daily maximum temperature reaches the high 90s during the latter part of July. The daily maximum temperature during the warmest month has ranged from 76 to 115 degrees. Low relative humidities and some wind movement substantially lower the sensible temperature during periods of high readings. Humidity readings of 15 percent are common on summer afternoons, and readings as low as 8 percent have been recorded. In contrast to this, humidity readings average 90 percent during the morning hours of December and January.

Winds flow with the major axis of the San Joaquin Valley, generally from the northwest. This feature is especially beneficial since, during the warmest months, the northwest winds increase during the evenings. These refreshing breezes and the normally large temperature variation of about 35 degrees between the highest and lowest readings of the day, generally result in comfortable evening and night temperatures.

Winter temperatures are usually mild with infrequent cold spells dropping the readings below freezing. Heavy frost occurs almost every year, and the first frost usually occurs during the last week of November. The last frost in spring is usually in early March, however, one year in five will have the last frost after the first of April. The growing season is 291 days.

Although the heaviest rains recorded at Fresno for short periods have occurred in June, usually any rainfall during the summer is very light. Snow is a rare occurrence in Fresno.

Fresno enjoys a very high percentage of sunshine, receiving more than 80 percent of the possible amounts during all but the four months of November, December, January, and February. Reduction of sunshine during these months is caused by fog and short periods of stormy weather.

During foggy periods, at times lasting nearly two weeks, sunshine is reduced to a minimum. This fog frequently lifts to a few hundred feet above the surface of the valley and presents the appearance of a heavy, solid cloud layer.

Spring and autumn are very enjoyable seasons in Fresno, with clear skies, light rainfall and winds and mild temperatures.

NORMALS, MEANS, AND EXTREMES

FRESNO, CALIFORNIA

LATITUDE: 36°46'N LONGITUDE: 119°43' W ELEVATION: FT. GRND 328 BARO 330 TIME ZONE: PACIFIC WBAN: 93193

	(a)	JAN	FEB	MAR	APR	MAY	JUNE	JULY	AUG	SEP	OCT	NOV	DEC	YEAR
TEMPERATURE °F:														
Normals														
-Daily Maximum		54.1	61.7	66.6	75.1	84.2	92.7	98.6	96.7	90.1	79.7	64.7	53.7	76.5
-Daily Minimum		37.4	40.5	43.4	47.3	53.7	60.4	65.1	63.8	58.8	50.7	42.5	37.1	50.1
-Monthly		45.7	51.2	55.1	61.2	69.0	76.6	81.9	80.3	74.5	65.2	53.6	45.4	63.3
Extremes														
-Record Highest	44	78	80	90	100	107	110	112	111	111	102	89	76	112
-Year		1986	1991	1972	1981	1984	1964	1991	1990	1955	1980	1949	1958	JUL 1991
-Record Lowest	44	19	24	26	32	36	44	50	49	37	27	26	18	18
-Year		1963	1990	1966	1982	1975	1955	1955	1966	1950	1972	1975	1990	DEC 1990
NORMAL DEGREE DAYS:														
Heating (base 65°F)		598	386	314	182	34	0	0	0	8	84	342	608	2556
Cooling (base 65°F)		0	0	7	68	158	352	524	474	293	91	0	0	1967
% OF POSSIBLE SUNSHINE	44	47	65	78	85	90	95	97	96	94	88	66	46	79
MEAN SKY COVER (tenths)														
Sunrise - Sunset	44	7.3	6.1	5.4	4.4	3.2	1.9	1.2	1.4	1.7	2.8	5.2	6.9	3.9
MEAN NUMBER OF DAYS:														
Sunrise to Sunset														
-Clear	44	5.4	7.8	11.0	14.0	18.8	23.1	26.7	26.2	23.8	20.2	11.7	6.9	195.6
-Partly Cloudy	44	6.9	7.8	8.0	8.2	7.5	4.5	3.0	3.5	3.9	6.1	7.2	6.2	72.8
-Cloudy	44	18.7	12.7	11.9	7.8	4.7	2.4	1.3	1.4	2.3	4.7	11.1	17.9	96.9
Precipitation														
.01 inches or more	44	7.5	7.1	7.1	4.1	1.9	0.7	0.2	0.3	1.0	2.2	5.2	6.7	44.1
Snow,Ice pellets,hail														
1.0 inches or more	44	0.*	0.0	0.0	0.0	0.0	0.0	0.0	0.0	0.0	0.0	0.0	0.*	*
Thunderstorms	44	0.3	0.4	0.9	0.5	0.5	0.5	0.3	0.3	0.7	0.5	0.2	0.3	5.3
Heavy Fog Visibility														
1/4 mile or less	44	11.8	6.0	1.7	0.3	0.1	0.0	0.0	0.*	0.1	0.9	5.8	12.1	38.8
Temperature °F														
-Maximum														
90° and above	30	0.0	0.0	0.*	2.1	10.1	19.6	28.6	26.3	17.4	4.7	0.0	0.0	108.8
32° and below	30	0.0	0.0	0.0	0.0	0.0	0.0	0.0	0.0	0.0	0.0	0.0	0.1	0.1
-Minimum														
32° and below	30	7.5	3.0	0.7	0.1	0.0	0.0	0.0	0.0	0.0	0.1	1.9	8.7	21.9
0° and below	30	0.0	0.0	0.0	0.0	0.0	0.0	0.0	0.0	0.0	0.0	0.0	0.0	0.0
AVG. STATION PRESS.(mb)	21	1008.9	1007.4	1005.2	1004.3	1001.6	1000.4	1000.3	1000.5	1000.8	1004.1	1007.5	1009.1	1004.2
RELATIVE HUMIDITY (%)														
Hour 04	30	91	89	86	80	71	65	61	67	71	78	87	92	78
Hour 10 (Local Time)	30	85	76	65	51	42	39	38	41	45	52	71	84	57
Hour 16	30	67	55	47	34	26	23	22	25	28	35	53	68	40
Hour 22	30	88	82	75	61	49	44	41	46	51	64	81	89	64
PRECIPITATION (inches):														
Water Equivalent														
-Normal		1.96	1.80	1.89	0.97	0.30	0.08	0.01	0.03	0.24	0.53	1.37	1.42	10.60
-Maximum Monthly	44	8.56	5.97	7.24	4.41	1.65	1.61	0.22	0.25	1.19	2.19	3.50	6.73	8.56
-Year		1969	1962	1991	1967	1990	1993	1992	1964	1976	1992	1972	1955	JAN 1969
-Minimum Monthly	44	0.04	T	0.00	0.02	0.00	0.00	0.00	0.00	0.00	0.00	0.00	0.00	0.00
-Year		1976	1964	1972	1991	1982	1983	1983	1981	1981	1978	1959	1989	DEC 1989
-Maximum in 24 hrs	44	2.59	1.99	1.63	1.39	1.42	1.61	0.22	0.25	0.97	1.76	1.35	1.76	2.59
-Year		1969	1969	1958	1983	1990	1993	1992	1964	1978	1992	1953	1955	JAN 1969
Snow,Ice pellets,hail														
-Maximum Monthly	44	2.2	T	T	0.0	0.0	0.0	0.0	0.0	0.0	T	0.0	1.2	2.2
-Year		1962	1992	1991							1974		1968	JAN 1962
-Maximum in 24 hrs	44	1.5	T	T	0.0	0.0	0.0	0.0	0.0	0.0	T	0.0	1.2	1.5
-Year		1962	1992	1991							1974		1968	JAN 1962
WIND:														
Mean Speed (mph)	44	5.2	5.7	6.7	7.4	8.2	8.3	7.4	6.8	6.1	5.2	4.7	4.9	6.4
Prevailing Direction through 1963		SE	NW	NW	NW	NW	NW	NW	NW	NW	NW	NW	SE	NW
Fastest Obs. 1 Min.														
-Direction (!!)	15	14	31	32	30	32	31	31	31	31	12	30	22	14
-Speed (MPH)	15	39	29	29	32	30	28	23	28	29	23	28	28	39
-Year		1993	1977	1982	1984	1991	1992	1983	1984	1978	1992	1993	1991	JAN 1993
Peak Gust														
-Direction (!!)	10	SE	S	SE	NW	NW	NW	NW	NW	NW	N	N	S	SE
-Speed (mph)	10	55	46	43	41	41	35	28	36	33	46	44	48	55
-Date		1987	1986	1987	1984	1991	1992	1991	1984	1991	1991	1991	1991	JAN 1987

PRECIPITATION (inches)

FRESNO, CALIFORNIA

YEAR	JAN	FEB	MAR	APR	MAY	JUNE	JULY	AUG	SEP	OCT	NOV	DEC	ANNUAL
1964	0.66	T	1.27	0.50	0.35	0.06	T	0.25	0.00	1.23	1.49	2.63	8.44
1965	1.05	0.43	2.38	1.74	T	T	T	0.02	0.00	0.30	2.69	1.73	10.34
1966	0.53	0.54	0.01	0.15	0.10	0.07	0.03	0.00	0.03	0.00	1.57	3.04	6.07
1967	2.21	0.22	3.15	4.41	0.19	0.14	T	T	T	0.07	1.55	1.04	12.98
1968	1.05	1.10	1.49	0.70	0.24	0.00	T	T	0.00	1.54	1.94	2.44	10.50
1969	8.56	5.60	1.16	1.64	0.06	0.04	0.04	0.00	0.04	0.06	0.80	1.14	19.14
1970	3.83	1.27	1.65	0.21	0.00	0.08	T	0.00	0.00	0.01	2.30	2.51	11.86
1971	0.40	0.29	0.58	1.04	1.40	0.00	T	T	0.04	0.03	0.65	2.56	6.99
1972	0.37	0.67	0.00	0.27	0.15	0.60	T	0.00	0.29	0.22	3.50	1.40	7.47
1973	1.91	3.69	2.84	0.09	T	T	0.00	T	0.00	1.02	1.39	1.74	12.68
1974	2.82	0.25	2.56	0.64	0.00	0.00	T	T	0.00	1.44	0.34	1.26	9.31
1975	0.69	0.97	2.44	0.55	T	0.00	T	0.05	0.22	1.07	0.20	0.14	6.33
1976	0.04	4.72	0.44	0.93	T	0.37	0.01	0.21	1.19	1.55	0.87	0.71	11.04
1977	0.68	0.09	1.04	0.04	1.16	0.06	T	T	T	0.01	0.46	3.02	6.56
1978	3.16	4.41	4.25	2.85	0.00	0.00	T	T	1.05	0.00	1.34	0.62	17.68
1979	2.71	2.53	2.27	0.07	0.06	0.00	0.08	0.00	T	0.48	1.01	0.74	9.95
1980	3.83	3.30	2.05	0.25	0.18	T	0.01	0.00	0.00	0.03	0.14	0.49	10.28
1981	2.67	1.29	2.59	1.01	T	0.00	0.00	0.00	0.00	0.58	1.22	0.65	10.01
1982	2.11	0.58	4.76	0.89	0.00	0.31	0.00	T	1.10	1.58	3.16	1.59	16.08
1983	5.14	3.70	4.53	2.76	0.01	0.00	0.00	0.09	1.03	0.09	2.51	1.75	21.61
1984	0.15	1.05	0.48	0.25	0.02	0.20	T	T	0.00	0.70	1.94	1.98	6.77
1985	0.43	0.71	1.73	0.12	0.00	0.33	0.04	0.02	0.43	0.85	3.02	0.72	8.40
1986	2.12	3.66	3.42	0.36	0.16	0.00	T	0.00	0.38	0.00	0.01	2.30	12.41
1987	1.93	1.36	2.39	0.07	0.87	0.01	0.00	0.00	T	0.85	0.52	1.19	9.19
1988	1.52	0.83	0.27	2.41	0.45	0.03	0.00	0.00	0.00	0.00	1.42	2.46	9.39
1989	0.48	1.18	2.25	0.05	0.89	0.00	0.00	0.03	1.11	0.42	0.50	0.00	6.91
1990	2.82	1.33	0.67	0.92	1.65	0.00	T	0.00	0.15	0.05	0.46	0.68	8.73
1991	0.13	1.01	7.24	0.02	0.03	T	0.00	T	T	0.80	0.04	1.22	10.49
1992	1.94	4.73	2.14	0.18	T	T	0.22	T	T	2.19	T	2.68	14.08
1993	5.18	2.44	1.76	0.20	0.25	1.61	0.00	0.00	0.00	0.12	1.16	1.03	13.75
Record Mean	1.82	1.66	1.73	0.94	0.36	0.11	0.01	0.01	0.18	0.55	1.00	1.54	9.90

AVERAGE TEMPERATURE (deg. F)

FRESNO, CALIFORNIA

YEAR	JAN	FEB	MAR	APR	MAY	JUNE	JULY	AUG	SEP	OCT	NOV	DEC	ANNUAL
1964	43.8	47.4	51.3	58.8	64.9	73.3	81.0	78.9	71.0	68.3	51.2	49.0	61.6
1965	46.3	49.6	55.5	60.8	67.5	71.4	78.9	78.8	68.6	65.8	54.7	42.0	61.6
1966	43.4	47.2	56.3	65.5	70.9	76.3	78.2	81.0	72.8	64.8	56.9	45.2	63.2
1967	46.1	48.9	54.4	52.6	68.8	74.3	83.8	83.6	77.4	66.0	56.8	42.6	62.9
1968	44.8	55.8	55.8	61.5	68.1	78.0	82.4	77.2	73.7	63.3	51.9	43.3	63.0
1969	44.8	47.5	53.1	59.7	70.4	72.9	80.9	79.7	75.7	59.7	53.1	46.2	62.0
1970	49.1	52.7	55.3	57.0	70.8	76.5	83.3	79.9	73.0	63.4	55.4	46.3	63.5
1971	45.7	47.6	54.4	59.1	64.2	74.4	81.9	81.1	73.4	60.9	50.7	42.9	61.4
1972	40.6	52.5	60.7	61.1	69.9	77.5	81.5	79.7	71.8	62.6	50.2	40.9	62.4
1973	45.1	51.9	50.4	61.2	72.9	78.6	80.4	78.5	72.0	63.3	52.9	47.2	62.9
1974	47.9	49.1	56.3	60.0	69.5	77.7	81.3	79.3	77.5	66.0	53.1	44.5	63.5
1975	43.4	49.9	51.5	53.9	68.4	74.7	78.1	75.9	75.8	61.4	49.5	43.9	60.6
1976	44.3	49.6	52.4	57.2	69.7	72.9	79.4	72.7	72.2	65.1	53.4	46.5	61.3
1977	44.3	53.5	52.4	65.5	63.6	79.8	81.5	80.6	74.0	66.8	54.6	51.3	64.0
1978	51.4	52.6	60.3	58.9	69.9	76.3	82.4	81.4	73.0	70.0	52.1	42.8	64.2
1979	47.0	51.4	57.4	62.7	71.1	77.9	82.2	79.9	79.5	67.8	54.0	46.9	64.8
1980	49.4	53.8	53.7	61.8	67.2	73.7	84.0	80.7	75.6	68.4	54.2	46.8	64.1
1981	47.9	52.0	54.5	63.2	70.9	82.8	84.9	82.9	76.5	61.4	55.5	47.7	65.0
1982	41.7	50.5	51.4	58.0	69.3	72.9	81.0	80.4	72.3	65.0	51.1	45.4	61.6
1983	45.2	53.1	55.9	57.9	69.7	76.3	79.0	82.1	78.8	68.5	54.6	51.1	64.4
1984	47.8	50.7	58.4	60.8	74.8	77.5	87.0	83.5	81.0	62.4	53.6	46.5	65.3
1985	43.3	51.3	53.1	67.2	69.4	81.8	86.0	80.5	72.3	65.0	52.5	43.8	63.9
1986	53.6	55.7	60.3	62.7	71.2	79.4	81.9	84.2	71.3	66.9	56.7	47.5	66.0
1987	45.3	52.8	55.6	66.7	71.8	78.4	77.0	80.2	75.5	70.1	52.3	44.2	64.2
1988	46.0	52.2	56.8	61.6	67.0	75.6	85.5	81.2	76.4	68.7	54.3	44.5	64.2
1989	42.9	48.8	57.9	67.3	69.6	77.0	82.5	79.3	74.3	65.3	54.3	43.8	63.6
1990	45.5	48.0	57.3	65.7	68.1	76.8	84.0	80.6	75.8	67.7	52.9	41.5	63.7
1991	47.0	55.8	51.5	59.5	66.1	74.7	83.8	78.6	79.9	70.5	55.8	47.0	64.2
1992	42.7	55.5	58.8	66.8	76.0	77.0	81.3	83.2	77.0	68.6	54.3	45.3	65.5
1993	47.1	51.9	60.3	61.7	69.9	75.7	80.2	79.7	75.7	67.8	53.9	45.6	64.1
Record Mean	45.9	51.2	55.2	61.1	68.0	75.5	81.8	80.0	74.1	65.0	54.2	46.3	63.2
Max	54.3	61.4	66.5	74.4	82.6	91.3	98.6	96.7	89.9	79.2	66.0	54.8	76.3
Min	37.4	40.9	43.8	47.8	53.4	59.7	64.9	63.3	58.3	50.8	42.4	37.7	50.0

REFERENCE NOTES

FRESNO, CALIFORNIA

GENERAL
T - TRACE AMOUNT.
BLANK ENTRIES DENOTE MISSING/UNREPORTED DATA.
# INDICATES A STATION OR INSTRUMENT RELOCATION.

SPECIFIC

PM - INCLUDES LAST DAY OF PREVIOUS MONTH
ASOS - AUTOMATED SURFACE OBSERVING SYSTEM IN OPERATION DURING THESE MONTHS.

(a) - LENGTH OF RECORD IN YEARS, ALTHOUGH INDIVIDUAL MONTHS MAY BE MISSING.
0.* OR * - THE VALUE IS BETWEEN 0.0 AND 0.05
NORMALS - BASED ON THE 1961-1990 RECORD PERIOD.
EXTREMES - DATES ARE THE MOST RECENT OCCURRENCE.
WIND DIR. - NUMERALS SHOW TENS OF DEGRESS CLOCKWISE FROM TRUE NORTH. "00" INDICATES CALM.
RESULTANT DIRECTIONS ARE GIVEN TO WHOLE DEGREES.
BOLD VALUES INDICATE EXTREME VALUES WHICH OCCURRED AFTER THE ASOS SYSTEM WAS COMMISSIONED.

RECORD = PERIOD OF RECORD
RECORD MEAN PRECIPITATION IS THE MEAN OF ALL DAILY PRECIPITATION AMOUNTS DURING THE PERIOD OF RECORD.
RECORD MAX(MIN) TEMPERATURE IS THE MEAN OF ALL DAILY MAX(MIN) TEMPERATURES DURING THE PERIOD OF RECORD.
RECORD MEAN TEMPERATURE IS THE SUM OF THE RECORD MAX AND RECORD MIN DIVIDED BY 2.
AVERAGE TEMPERATURE IS THE SUM OF THE MEAN DAILY MAX AND MIN TEMPERATURE DIVIDED BY 2.

EXCEPTIONS

RECORD MEANS ARE THROUGH THE CURRENT YEAR, BEGINNING IN 1888 FOR TEMPERATURE
1878 FOR PRECIPITATION
1939 FOR SNOWFALL

HEATING DEGREE DAYS Base 65 deg. F FRESNO, CALIFORNIA

SEASON	JULY	AUG	SEP	OCT	NOV	DEC	JAN	FEB	MAR	APR	MAY	JUNE	TOTAL
1964-65	0	3	3	41	410	492	572	423	287	191	58	8	2488
1965-66	0	0	12	41	302	707	664	492	271	60	7	1	2557
1966-67	0	0	1	65	238	606	579	444	322	366	59	11	2691
1967-68	0	0	0	29	239	686	619	258	278	139	37	2	2287
1968-69	0	0	12	73	387	665	619	480	366	168	30	0	2800
1969-70	0	0	0	166	349	574	485	340	291	232	25	0	2462
1970-71	0	0	0	108	282	573	593	480	322	181	81	8	2628
1971-72	0	0	20	209	423	678	750	357	142	128	37	0	2744
1972-73	0	0	2	108	437	740	610	358	444	140	12	2	2853
1973-74	0	0	0	94	360	544	522	438	260	160	33	0	2411
1974-75	0	0	0	59	350	628	661	419	409	325	53	3	2907
1975-76	0	0	0	154	455	648	636	440	385	242	10	9	2979
1976-77	0	1	5	63	342	566	636	313	386	42	98	0	2452
1977-78	0	0	0	46	302	417	415	343	143	182	19	0	1867
1978-79	0	0	6	30	382	682	549	372	234	96	34	0	2385
1979-80	0	0	0	56	323	555	473	318	343	129	46	0	2243
1980-81	0	0	0	69	318	553	521	359	316	114	9	0	2259
1981-82	0	0	0	118	278	530	711	398	412	217	21	4	2689
1982-83	0	0	13	62	411	602	607	327	276	206	55	0	2559
1983-84	0	0	1	3	304	421	530	408	198	149	6	0	2020
1984-85	0	0	0	128	335	566	664	378	361	39	8	3	2482
1985-86	0	0	0	63	369	651	345	258	156	98	30	0	1970
1986-87	0	0	13	22	242	537	602	337	282	56	26	0	2117
1987-88	0	0	0	7	374	636	583	366	251	124	69	12	2422
1988-89	0	0	0	20	316	629	679	450	213	52	14	0	2373
1989-90	0	0	7	73	310	649	598	470	236	35	19	1	2398
1990-91	0	0	0	17	356	722	549	253	412	163	65	0	2537
1991-92	0	0	0	81	276	551	683	267	183	25	0	1	2067
1992-93	0	0	0	18	316	602	549	359	145	113	9	12	2123
1993-94	0	0	0	12	326	595							

COOLING DEGREE DAYS Base 65 deg. F FRESNO, CALIFORNIA

YEAR	JAN	FEB	MAR	APR	MAY	JUNE	JULY	AUG	SEP	OCT	NOV	DEC	TOTAL
1969	0	0	4	15	206	241	500	462	331	10	0	0	1769
1970	0	0	0	0	212	353	573	466	245	67	3	0	1919
1971	0	0	0	8	64	296	529	505	279	89	0	0	1770
1972	0	0	17	18	195	383	518	464	213	42	0	0	1850
1973	0	0	0	32	264	419	484	423	218	47	4	0	1891
1974	0	0	0	20	179	384	512	448	381	96	0	0	2020
1975	0	0	0	0	164	303	413	344	329	49	0	0	1602
1976	0	0	2	16	162	254	456	246	228	73	0	0	1437
1977	0	0	0	62	60	451	518	494	275	108	0	0	1968
1978	0	0	3	6	179	342	546	516	250	187	0	0	2029
1979	0	0	2	37	229	396	541	471	442	149	0	0	2267
1980	0	0	0	39	120	265	594	493	326	181	0	0	2018
1981	0	0	0	67	200	545	622	562	352	14	0	0	2362
1982	0	0	0	12	162	251	501	483	240	70	0	0	1719
1983	0	0	0	0	207	343	440	537	422	119	0	0	2068
1984	0	0	1	30	318	382	688	581	487	55	0	0	2542
1985	0	0	0	111	153	516	657	487	227	69	2	0	2222
1986	0	1	18	34	231	440	530	603	206	87	0	0	2150
1987	0	0	0	114	243	409	379	480	323	172	0	0	2120
1988	0	0	3	28	139	338	642	511	349	143	3	0	2156
1989	0	0	4	129	166	366	546	449	291	90	0	0	2041
1990	0	0	2	61	122	360	595	490	333	108	0	0	2071
1991	0	0	0	6	107	298	588	428	454	259	5	0	2145
1992	0	0	0	88	350	366	511	572	365	135	0	0	2387
1993	0	0	3	20	168	342	476	462	331	105	0	0	1907

SNOWFALL (inches) FRESNO, CALIFORNIA

SEASON	JULY	AUG	SEP	OCT	NOV	DEC	JAN	FEB	MAR	APR	MAY	JUNE	TOTAL
1970-71	0.0	0.0	0.0	0.0	0.0	0.0	T	0.0	0.0	0.0	0.0	0.0	T
1971-72	0.0	0.0	0.0	0.0	0.0	0.0	T	0.0	0.0	0.0	0.0	0.0	T
1972-73	0.0	0.0	0.0	0.0	0.0	T	0.0	0.0	T	0.0	0.0	0.0	T
1973-74	0.0	0.0	0.0	0.0	0.0	0.0	0.0	0.0	0.0	0.0	0.0	0.0	0.0
1974-75	0.0	0.0	0.0	T	0.0	0.0	0.0	0.0	0.0	0.0	0.0	0.0	T
1975-76	0.0	0.0	0.0	0.0	0.0	0.0	0.0	T	0.0	0.0	0.0	0.0	T
1976-77	0.0	0.0	0.0	0.0	0.0	0.0	0.0	0.0	0.0	0.0	0.0	0.0	0.0
1977-78	0.0	0.0	0.0	0.0	0.0	0.0	0.0	0.0	0.0	0.0	0.0	0.0	0.0
1978-79	0.0	0.0	0.0	0.0	0.0	0.0	0.0	T	T	0.0	0.0	0.0	T
1979-80	0.0	0.0	0.0	0.0	0.0	0.0	0.0	0.0	0.0	0.0	0.0	0.0	0.0
1980-81	0.0	0.0	0.0	0.0	0.0	0.0	0.0	0.0	0.0	0.0	0.0	0.0	0.0
1981-82	0.0	0.0	0.0	0.0	0.0	0.0	0.0	0.0	0.0	0.0	0.0	0.0	0.0
1982-83	0.0	0.0	0.0	0.0	0.0	0.0	0.0	0.0	0.0	0.0	0.0	0.0	0.0
1983-84	0.0	0.0	0.0	0.0	0.0	0.0	0.0	0.0	0.0	0.0	0.0	0.0	0.0
1984-85	0.0	0.0	0.0	0.0	0.0	0.0	0.0	0.0	0.0	0.0	0.0	0.0	0.0
1985-86	0.0	0.0	0.0	0.0	0.0	0.0	0.0	0.0	0.0	0.0	0.0	0.0	0.0
1986-87	0.0	0.0	0.0	0.0	0.0	0.0	0.0	0.0	0.0	0.0	0.0	0.0	0.0
1987-88	0.0	0.0	0.0	0.0	0.0	0.0	0.0	0.0	0.0	0.0	0.0	0.0	0.0
1988-89	0.0	0.0	0.0	0.0	0.0	0.0	0.0	T	0.0	0.0	0.0	0.0	T
1989-90	0.0	0.0	0.0	0.0	0.0	0.0	0.0	T	0.0	0.0	0.0	0.0	T
1990-91	0.0	0.0	0.0	0.0	0.0	T	0.0	0.0	T	0.0	0.0	0.0	T
1991-92	0.0	0.0	0.0	0.0	0.0	0.0	0.0	T	0.0	0.0	0.0	0.0	T
1992-93	0.0	0.0	0.0	0.0	0.0	0.0	0.0	0.0	0.0	0.0	0.0	0.0	0.0
1993-94	0.0	0.0	0.0	0.0	0.0	0.0							
Record Mean	0.0	0.0	0.0	T	0.0	T	0.1	T	T	0.0	0.0	0.0	0.1

LOS ANGELES, CALIFORNIA
CIVIC CENTER

The climate of Los Angeles is normally pleasant and mild through the year. The Pacific Ocean is the primary moderating influence. The coastal mountain ranges lying along the north and east sides of the Los Angeles coastal basin act as a buffer against extremes of summer heat and winter cold occurring in desert and plateau regions in the interior. A variable balance between mild sea breezes, and either hot or cold winds from the interior, results in some variety in weather conditions, but temperature and humidity are usually well within the limits of human comfort. An important, and somewhat unusual, aspect of the climate of the Los Angeles metropolitan area is the pronounced difference in temperature, humidity, cloudiness, fog, rain, and sunshine over fairly short distances.

These differences are closely related to the distance from, and elevation above, the Pacific Ocean. Both high and low temperatures become more extreme and the average relative humidity becomes lower as one goes inland and up foothill slopes. Relative humidity is frequently high near the coast, but may be quite low along the foothills. During periods of high temperatures, the relative humidity is usually below normal so that discomfort is rare, except for infrequent periods when high temperatures and high humidities occur together.

Like other Pacific Coast areas, most rainfall comes during the winter with nearly 85 percent of the annual total occurring from November through March, while summers are practically rainless. As in many semi-arid regions, there is a marked variability in monthly and seasonal totals. Precipitation generally increases with distance from the ocean, from a yearly total of around inches in coastal sections to the south of th city to over 20 inches in foothill areas. Destructive flash floods occasionally develop in and below some mountain canyons. Snow is (visible on nearby mountains in the winter, but extremely rare in the coastal basin. Thunderstorms are infrequent.

Prevailing winds are from the west during the spring, summer, and early autumn, with northeasterly wind predominating the remainder of the year. At times, the lack of air movement, combined with a frequent and persistent temperature inversion, is associated with concentrations of air pollution in the Los Angeles coastal basin and some adjacent areas. In fall, winter, and early spring months, occasional foehn-like descending Santa Ana winds come from the northeast over ridges and through passes in the coastal mountains. These Santa Ana winds may pick up considerable amounts of dust and reach speeds of 35 to 50 mph in north and east sections of the city, with higher speeds in outlying areas to the north and east, but rarely reach coastal portions of the city.

Sunshine, fog, and clouds depend a great deal on topography and distance from the ocean. Low clouds are common at night and in the morning along the coast during spring and summer, but form later and clear earlier near the foothills so that annual cloudiness and fog frequencies are greatest near the ocean, and sunshine totals are highest on the inland side of the city. The sun shines about 75 percent of daytime hours at the Civic Center. Light fog may accompany the usual night and morning low clouds, but dense fog is more likely to occur during the night and early morning hours of the winter months.

NORMALS, MEANS, AND EXTREMES

LOS ANGELES, CALIFORNIA CIVIC CENTER

LATITUDE: 34 °03'N LONGITUDE: 118 °14' W ELEVATION: FT. GRND 270 BARO TIME ZONE: PACIFIC WBAN: 93134

	(a)	JAN	FEB	MAR	APR	MAY	JUNE	JULY	AUG	SEP	OCT	NOV	DEC	YEAR
TEMPERATURE °F:														
Normals														
-Daily Maximum		67.7	69.4	69.5	72.3	73.9	78.3	84.0	84.5	82.7	79.0	72.4	67.8	75.1
-Daily Minimum		48.9	50.6	51.8	54.2	57.7	61.1	64.5	65.7	64.6	60.3	53.5	48.8	56.8
-Monthly		58.3	60.1	60.7	63.3	65.8	69.7	74.3	75.1	73.7	69.7	63.0	58.3	66.0
Extremes														
-Record Highest	53	95	94	98	106	102	112	107	105	110	108	100	91	112
-Year		1971	1986	1988	1989	1967	1990	1985	1983	1988	1987	1966	1979	JUN 1990
-Record Lowest	53	28	34	35	39	46	50	54	53	51	41	38	30	28
-Year		1949	1989	1976	1975	1964	1953	1952	1943	1948	1971	1978	1978	JAN 1949
NORMAL DEGREE DAYS:														
Heating (base 65°F)		222	170	169	128	72	35	0	0	10	17	105	226	1154
Cooling (base 65°F)		14	32	36	77	97	176	293	316	271	162	45	18	1537
% OF POSSIBLE SUNSHINE	32	69	72	73	70	66	65	82	83	79	73	74	71	73
MEAN SKY COVER (tenths)														
Sunrise - Sunset	34	4.4	4.7	4.7	4.7	4.8	4.3	2.7	2.6	3.0	3.8	3.7	4.2	4.0
MEAN NUMBER OF DAYS:														
Sunrise to Sunset														
-Clear	34	14.3	12.4	12.9	12.0	11.4	13.6	20.9	22.4	18.4	16.1	16.5	15.0	186.0
-Partly Cloudy	34	8.1	6.9	9.3	9.8	11.8	10.5	8.9	7.4	8.4	9.3	7.4	8.0	105.8
-Cloudy	34	8.5	9.0	8.7	8.2	7.8	5.9	1.1	1.2	3.3	5.6	6.1	8.0	73.5
Precipitation														
.01 inches or more	53	5.9	5.4	6.3	3.5	1.2	0.6	0.2	0.6	1.2	1.9	3.4	4.9	35.2
Snow,Ice pellets,hail														
1.0 inches or more	45	0.0	0.0	0.0	0.0	0.0	0.0	0.0	0.0	0.0	0.0	0.0	0.0	0.0
Thunderstorms	24	0.5	1.1	0.9	0.8	0.2	0.1	0.2	0.4	0.4	0.3	0.6	0.7	6.1
Heavy Fog Visibility														
1/4 mile or less	24	1.5	1.8	1.1	1.3	0.5	0.6	0.5	0.8	1.5	2.6	2.5	2.1	16.8
Temperature °F														
-Maximum														
90° and above	53	0.1	0.1	0.2	0.9	1.1	1.5	3.8	4.3	6.0	3.2	0.7	0.*	21.8
32° and below	53	0.0	0.0	0.0	0.0	0.0	0.0	0.0	0.0	0.0	0.0	0.0	0.0	0.0
-Minimum														
32° and below	53	0.1	0.0	0.0	0.0	0.0	0.0	0.0	0.0	0.0	0.0	0.0	0.1	0.2
0° and below	53	0.0	0.0	0.0	0.0	0.0	0.0	0.0	0.0	0.0	0.0	0.0	0.0	0.0
AVG. STATION PRESS.(mb)														
RELATIVE HUMIDITY (%)														
Hour 04	17	63	71	74	78	81	85	84	84	78	76	61	62	75
Hour 10 (Local Time)	10	51	54	52	53	56	59	54	56	52	55	45	45	53
Hour 16	23	50	52	52	54	55	56	53	55	54	56	49	50	53
Hour 22	11	67	70	72	74	75	78	79	79	76	74	62	62	72
PRECIPITATION (inches):														
Water Equivalent														
-Normal		2.92	3.07	2.61	1.03	0.19	0.03	0.01	0.14	0.45	0.31	1.98	2.03	14.77
-Maximum Monthly	53	14.94	12.75	8.37	6.02	3.03	0.76	0.18	2.26	2.82	2.37	9.68	6.57	14.94
-Year		1969	1980	1983	1965	1977	1993	1986	1977	1976	1987	1965	1971	JAN 1969
-Minimum Monthly	53	0.00	T	0.00	0.00	0.00	0.00	0.00	0.00	0.00	0.00	0.00	0.00	0.00
-Year		1976	1951	1959	1979	1981	1982	1983	1982	1980	1980	1980	1990	DEC 1990
-Maximum in 24 hrs	53	6.11	4.02	3.79	2.05	2.41	0.76	0.18	2.22	1.95	1.77	4.07	3.92	6.11
-Year		1956	1944	1978	1956	1977	1993	1986	1977	1986	1983	1970	1965	JAN 1956
Snow,Ice pellets,hail														
-Maximum Monthly	47	0.3	T	0.0	0.0	0.0	0.0	0.0	0.0	0.0	0.0	0.0	T	0.3
-Year		1949	1951										1947	JAN 1949
-Maximum in 24 hrs	44	0.3	T	0.0	0.0	0.0	0.0	0.0	0.0	0.0	0.0	0.0	T	0.3
-Year		1949	1951										1947	JAN 1949
WIND:														
Mean Speed (mph)	24	6.8	6.9	7.0	6.6	6.3	5.7	5.4	5.3	5.3	5.7	6.4	6.6	6.2
Prevailing Direction through 1963		NE	W	W	W	W	W	W	W	W	W	W	NE	W
Fastest Mile														
-Direction (!!)	36	N	NW	NW	NW	NW	N	W	E	NW	N	N	SE	N
-Speed (MPH)	36	49	40	47	40	39	32	21	24	27	48	42	44	49
-Year		1946	1961	1964	1955	1945	1949	1947	1945	1941	1959	1946	1943	JAN 1946
Peak Gust														
-Direction (!!)														
-Speed (mph)														
-Date														

PRECIPITATION (inches)

LOS ANGELES, CALIFORNIA CIVIC CENTER

YEAR	JAN	FEB	MAR	APR	MAY	JUNE	JULY	AUG	SEP	OCT	NOV	DEC	ANNUAL
1964	1.43	T	1.79	0.33	0.01	0.32	T	0.00	0.00	0.33	1.72	2.05	7.98
1965	0.84	0.23	2.49	6.02	0.00	0.01	T	0.01	1.80	0.00	9.68	5.73	26.81
1966	0.96	1.51	0.53	0.00	0.22	0.00	T	T	0.30	0.06	4.07	5.26	12.91
1967	5.93	0.11	2.50	3.76	0.01	0.00	0.00	T	1.02	0.00	8.67	1.66	23.66
1968	0.90	0.49	3.34	0.49	0.00	0.01	0.01	0.11	0.03	0.55	0.37	1.28	7.58
1969	14.94	8.03	1.49	0.63	0.03	T	0.03	0.00	T	0.00	1.11	0.06	26.32
1970	1.59	2.58	2.36	0.00	0.00	0.04	0.00	0.00	0.00	0.00	5.05	4.92	16.54
1971	0.43	0.67	0.53	0.50	0.22	0.00	T	0.00	T	0.04	0.30	6.57	9.26
1972	0.00	0.13	T	0.03	0.03	0.07	0.00	0.35	0.02	0.29	3.26	2.36	6.54
1973	4.39	7.89	2.70	0.00	T	0.00	0.00	0.00	0.00	0.12	1.68	0.67	17.45
1974	8.35	0.14	3.78	0.10	0.08	0.00	0.00	0.00	0.00	0.58	0.07	3.59	16.69
1975	0.12	3.54	4.83	1.53	0.09	0.00	0.00	0.00	0.00	0.27	0.00	0.32	10.70
1976	0.00	3.71	1.81	0.84	0.05	0.22	0.00	0.08	2.82	0.24	0.49	0.75	11.01
1977	2.84	0.17	1.89	0.00	3.03	0.00	0.00	2.26	0.00	0.00	0.08	4.70	14.97
1978	7.70	8.91	8.02	1.77	0.00	0.00	0.00	0.00	0.39	0.05	2.28	1.45	30.57
1979	6.59	3.06	5.85	0.00	0.00	0.00	0.00	0.01	T	0.77	0.21	0.51	17.00
1980	7.50	12.75	4.79	0.31	0.13	0.00	0.00	0.00	0.00	0.00	0.00	0.85	26.33
1981	2.02	1.48	4.10	0.53	0.00	0.00	0.00	0.00	0.02	0.49	1.80	0.48	10.92
1982	2.17	0.70	3.54	1.39	0.12	0.00	0.00	0.00	0.84	0.19	4.41	1.05	14.41
1983	6.49	4.37	8.37	5.16	0.36	0.01	0.00	0.79	1.99	0.75	2.52	3.23	34.04
1984	0.17	0.00	0.28	0.69	0.00	0.01	0.00	0.40	0.23	0.15	1.44	5.53	8.90
1985	0.71	2.84	1.29	0.00	0.23	0.00	0.00	0.00	0.19	0.42	2.91	0.33	8.92
1986	2.19	6.10	5.27	0.45	0.00	0.00	0.18	0.00	1.97	0.53	0.94	0.37	18.00
1987	1.39	1.22	0.95	0.06	0.00	0.05	0.01	0.00	0.09	2.37	1.13	1.84	9.11
1988	1.65	1.72	0.26	3.41	0.00	0.00	0.00	0.05	0.04	0.00	0.70	3.80	9.98
1989	0.73	1.90	0.81	0.00	0.05	0.00	0.00	0.00	0.35	0.43	0.29	0.00	4.56
1990	1.24	3.12	0.17	0.58	1.17	0.00	0.00	0.02	0.00	0.00	0.19	0.00	6.49
1991	1.69	4.13	5.92	0.03	0.00	0.01	0.13	0.00	0.09	0.37	0.00	3.22	15.59
1992	1.74	7.96	7.12	0.33	0.04	0.00	0.08	0.00	0.00	0.70	0.00	4.68	22.65
1993	11.77	6.61	2.74	0.00	0.02	0.76	0.00	0.00	0.00	0.16	0.66	0.78	23.50
Record Mean	3.08	3.17	2.66	1.04	0.30	0.06	0.01	0.06	0.25	0.50	1.34	2.51	14.97

AVERAGE TEMPERATURE (deg. F)

LOS ANGELES, CALIFORNIA CIVIC CENTER

YEAR	JAN	FEB	MAR	APR	MAY	JUNE	JULY	AUG	SEP	OCT	NOV	DEC	ANNUAL
1964	56.7	59.0	58.6	60.5	61.7	64.8	71.8	73.4	70.2	70.5	59.8	56.5	63.6
1965	58.3	58.0	59.0	61.7	63.4	64.1	70.1	75.6	69.6	73.1	62.0	56.9	64.3
1966	55.7	56.2	61.3	64.4	64.5	70.2	74.4	76.6	73.4	71.2	63.6	60.7	66.0
1967	59.2	62.9	61.0	56.1	67.3	66.3	75.7	79.2	75.2	72.5	66.6	55.6	66.5
1968	58.5	63.8	62.9	64.0	65.5	69.2	74.7	74.1	73.4	69.2	63.3	56.2	66.2
1969	58.3	54.9	59.7	63.8	66.6	67.2	73.8	77.0	71.7	67.3	65.2	59.2	65.4
1970	57.6	61.4	61.2	60.9	67.4	70.0	75.3	76.2	74.4	68.3	63.3	57.2	66.1
1971	58.8	59.2	60.3	62.0	64.0	68.8	74.2	78.9	74.6	67.4	60.2	52.8	65.1
1972	55.5	60.3	63.7	63.9	67.6	72.2	78.0	77.4	72.3	67.2	62.2	58.1	66.5
1973	56.4	60.0	57.9	63.1	65.8	72.0	72.4	73.6	70.0	68.8	60.0	59.9	65.0
1974	55.2	59.2	59.6	64.7	65.7	72.2	74.1	72.3	73.2	67.6	64.0	56.2	65.3
1975	57.6	55.8	55.7	56.0	62.7	65.7	72.5	71.9	74.0	66.4	61.2	57.0	63.0
1976	59.4	56.4	58.4	57.8	64.3	71.1	72.6	71.6	72.6	70.7	66.9	60.4	65.2
1977	58.1	63.1	56.9	63.7	61.9	69.2	74.2	75.6	71.8	69.0	66.3	60.8	65.9
1978	58.1	58.9	63.2	60.8	68.6	71.8	73.4	73.7	76.0	70.3	58.4	53.2	65.5
1979	53.3	55.0	57.9	62.7	65.4	71.5	72.1	72.9	77.4	68.7	64.6	63.2	65.4
1980	60.9	64.6	60.9	64.8	63.2	71.8	77.1	76.3	72.6	71.5	65.3	63.7	67.7
1981	61.8	64.3	62.0	66.0	68.9	77.4	77.2	78.3	75.0	68.5	65.0	62.1	68.9
1982	57.1	64.0	59.3	62.2	64.4	65.3	74.0	75.1	73.9	70.9	61.7	58.1	65.5
1983	61.9	63.0	63.9	63.2	70.7	70.7	75.9	80.8	79.1	74.2	63.5	59.8	68.9
1984	61.2	61.9	65.6	65.3	72.4	72.2	78.7	76.4	81.3	68.5	61.0	57.2	68.5
1985	57.5	60.4	59.3	66.8	66.3	73.5	79.2	75.7	71.8	71.3	60.4	61.7	67.0
1986	65.9	62.4	64.5	66.4	68.1	71.2	73.2	76.0	68.8	69.4	66.4	60.1	67.7
1987	57.2	60.3	61.2	67.8	68.1	69.7	70.8	73.0	75.2	71.9	62.9	54.4	66.0
1988	58.3	62.9	64.9	64.1	67.2	67.9	74.3	72.9	72.2	69.7	61.9	57.1	66.8
1989	56.3	56.4	62.4	67.9	66.2	69.8	75.1	72.8	74.5	69.2	66.7	62.7	66.7
1990	59.4	58.0	61.7	65.7	66.9	74.3	77.3	74.0	76.0	73.2	65.6	57.5	67.5
1991	59.2	63.5	56.8	64.2	63.9	67.1	71.0	73.1	73.6	72.1	66.2	59.6	65.9
1992	60.3	62.3	60.8	69.6	69.0	70.4	75.9	78.9	76.6	70.4	65.1	56.5	68.0
1993	57.3	58.3	64.5	67.0	68.9	72.4	73.0	74.4	74.3	71.2	64.6	60.8	67.2
Record Mean	56.3	57.5	58.9	61.3	63.8	67.7	71.9	72.7	71.3	67.2	62.4	57.9	64.1
Max	65.6	66.7	68.0	70.6	72.6	77.0	82.2	82.8	81.5	77.2	72.8	67.3	73.7
Min	47.0	48.3	49.8	52.1	55.1	58.3	61.7	62.5	61.0	57.1	52.0	48.4	54.4

REFERENCE NOTES

LOS ANGELES, CALIFORNIA CIVIC CENTER

GENERAL

T - TRACE AMOUNT.
BLANK ENTRIES DENOTE MISSING/UNREPORTED DATA.
# INDICATES A STATION OR INSTRUMENT RELOCATION.

SPECIFIC

PM - INCLUDES LAST DAY OF PREVIOUS MONTH
ASOS - AUTOMATED SURFACE OBSERVING SYSTEM IN OPERATION DURING THESE MONTHS.

(a) - LENGTH OF RECORD IN YEARS, ALTHOUGH INDIVIDUAL MONTHS MAY BE MISSING.
0.* OR * - THE VALUE IS BETWEEN 0.0 AND 0.05
NORMALS - BASED ON THE 1961-1990 RECORD PERIOD.
EXTREMES - DATES ARE THE MOST RECENT OCCURRENCE.
WIND DIR. - NUMERALS SHOW TENS OF DEGRESS CLOCKWISE FROM TRUE NORTH. "00" INDICATES CALM.
RESULTANT DIRECTIONS ARE GIVEN TO WHOLE DEGREES.
BOLD VALUES INDICATE EXTREME VALUES WHICH OCCURRED AFTER THE ASOS SYSTEM WAS COMMISSIONED.

RECORD = PERIOD OF RECORD
RECORD MEAN PRECIPITATION IS THE MEAN OF ALL DAILY PRECIPITATION AMOUNTS DURING THE PERIOD OF RECORD.
RECORD MAX(MIN) TEMPERATURE IS THE MEAN OF ALL DAILY MAX(MIN) TEMPERATURES DURING THE PERIOD OF RECORD.
RECORD MEAN TEMPERATURE IS THE SUM OF THE RECORD MAX AND RECORD MIN DIVIDED BY 2.
AVERAGE TEMPERATURE IS THE SUM OF THE MEAN DAILY MAX AND MIN TEMPERATURE DIVIDED BY 2.

EXCEPTIONS

1. RELATIVE HUMIDITY IS THROUGH 1963.
2. THUNDERSTORMS AND HEAVY FOG ARE THROUGH 1964 AND MAY BE INCOMPLETE, DUE TO PART-TIME OPERATIONS.
3. MEAN WIND SPEED IS THROUGH 1964.
4. PERCENT OF POSSIBLE SUNSHINE, MEAN SKY COVER AND DAYS CLEAR-PARTLY CLOUDY-CLOUDY ARE THROUGH 1976.
5. FASTEST MILE WIND IS THROUGH NOVEMBER 1977.

RECORD MEANS ARE THROUGH THE CURRENT YEAR, BEGINNING IN 1878 FOR TEMPERATURE
1878 FOR PRECIPITATION
1941 FOR SNOWFALL

HEATING DEGREE DAYS Base 65 deg. F — LOS ANGELES, CALIFORNIA CIVIC CENTER

SEASON	JULY	AUG	SEP	OCT	NOV	DEC	JAN	FEB	MAR	APR	MAY	JUNE	TOTAL
1964-65	0	0	0	5	186	256	224	196	183	168	70	38	1326
1965-66	0	0	0	1	98	264	281	244	126	58	34	0	1106
1966-67	0	0	0	0	88	145	179	81	133	260	43	25	954
1967-68	0	0	0	0	32	287	207	70	99	70	50	7	822
1968-69	0	0	0	4	76	267	219	277	186	68	25	1	1123
1969-70	0	0	0	22	52	182	222	106	128	134	27	1	874
1970-71	0	0	0	8	72	243	255	184	154	127	77	11	1131
1971-72	0	0	0	94	153	369	288	132	61	61	35	0	1193
1972-73	0	0	0	14	97	230	266	136	214	77	32	2	1068
1973-74	0	0	1	8	156	174	300	160	171	54	32	1	1057
1974-75	0	0	0	25	73	268	243	254	283	262	75	21	1504
1975-76	0	0	0	31	132	247	190	246	215	215	50	12	1338
1976-77	0	0	0	0	62	138	215	86	247	57	108	1	914
1977-78	0	0	0	14	51	132	209	174	102	122	24	0	828
1978-79	0	0	0	7	209	361	354	274	226	80	46	6	1563
1979-80	0	0	0	1	59	114	128	60	123	79	75	4	643
1980-81	0	0	0	2	41	85	103	91	97	43	1	0	463
1981-82	0	0	0	11	58	102	238	58	184	113	41	16	821
1982-83	0	0	0	3	117	205	134	73	68	68	2	0	670
1983-84	0	0	0	0	99	158	140	99	29	59	5	0	589
1984-85	0	0	0	4	129	239	225	162	179	40	21	0	999
1985-86	0	0	0	0	163	131	42	125	92	32	7	0	592
1986-87	0	0	8	2	14	151	241	140	131	31	19	0	737
1987-88	0	0	0	3	91	323	216	82	81	88	30	11	925
1988-89	0	0	1	2	98	258	270	271	104	36	27	5	1072
1989-90	0	0	0	2	27	102	173	206	130	26	16	2	684
1990-91	0	0	0	0	42	244	183	63	248	74	72	2	928
1991-92	0	0	0	23	46	168	159	114	125	1	0	0	636
1992-93	0	0	0	1	49	256	235	181	68	9	0	6	805
1993-94	0	0	0	0	45	136							

COOLING DEGREE DAYS Base 65 deg. F — LOS ANGELES, CALIFORNIA CIVIC CENTER

YEAR	JAN	FEB	MAR	APR	MAY	JUNE	JULY	AUG	SEP	OCT	NOV	DEC	TOTAL
1969	19	0	30	39	81	73	276	377	209	100	65	10	1279
1970	0	11	17	17	106	155	326	352	287	118	28	10	1427
1971	71	28	16	46	50	131	291	435	296	176	17	0	1557
1972	0	4	27	34	122	223	409	391	225	89	21	25	1570
1973	9	2	0	25	64	220	236	272	157	133	9	21	1148
1974	3	5	8	51	58	223	288	235	254	115	53	2	1295
1975	21	0	0	0	11	48	241	221	277	82	26	4	931
1976	22	3	20	10	32	203	245	212	233	185	123	2	1290
1977	7	39	3	23	18	135	293	334	210	148	96	8	1314
1978	0	8	52	2	145	212	269	277	338	177	17	0	1497
1979	0	0	14	17	67	209	229	252	379	124	53	62	1406
1980	10	54	3	82	26	215	380	357	233	210	56	53	1679
1981	12	75	13	81	132	380	387	422	306	124	67	17	2016
1982	0	36	15	36	33	32	286	322	275	194	25	0	1254
1983	44	23	41	21	185	174	342	495	432	292	60	4	2113
1984	29	14	56	73	240	222	433	360	496	123	13	6	2065
1985	0	41	10	100	68	264	447	339	210	203	31	35	1748
1986	77	56	83	80	110	194	261	349	132	145	65	6	1558
1987	6	18	21	120	121	147	186	257	312	221	36	1	1446
1988	13	30	84	68	107	107	297	252	223	154	14	20	1356
1989	8	37	31	131	73	154	318	251	290	139	85	41	1558
1990	10	16	36	54	81	291	388	287	336	262	68	20	1849
1991	8	28	0	54	43	72	191	260	265	250	88	6	1265
1992	17	44	1	146	132	168	347	435	353	175	59	0	1877
1993	6	0	59	77	129	232	254	299	287	199	38	12	1592

SNOWFALL (inches) — LOS ANGELES, CALIFORNIA CIVIC CENTER

SEASON	JULY	AUG	SEP	OCT	NOV	DEC	JAN	FEB	MAR	APR	MAY	JUNE	TOTAL
1970-71	0.0	0.0	0.0	0.0	0.0	0.0	0.0	0.0	0.0	0.0	0.0	0.0	0.0
1971-72	0.0	0.0	0.0	0.0	0.0	0.0	0.0	0.0	0.0	0.0	0.0	0.0	0.0
1972-73	0.0	0.0	0.0	0.0	0.0	0.0	0.0	0.0	0.0	0.0	0.0	0.0	0.0
1973-74	0.0	0.0	0.0	0.0	0.0	0.0	0.0	0.0	0.0	0.0	0.0	0.0	0.0
1974-75	0.0	0.0	0.0	0.0	0.0	0.0	0.0	0.0	0.0	0.0	0.0	0.0	0.0
1975-76	0.0	0.0	0.0	0.0	0.0	0.0	0.0	0.0	0.0	0.0	0.0	0.0	0.0
1976-77	0.0	0.0	0.0	0.0	0.0	0.0	0.0	0.0	0.0	0.0	0.0	0.0	0.0
1977-78	0.0	0.0	0.0	0.0	0.0	0.0	0.0	0.0	0.0	0.0	0.0	0.0	0.0
1978-79	0.0	0.0	0.0	0.0	0.0	0.0	0.0	0.0	0.0	0.0	0.0	0.0	0.0
1979-80	0.0	0.0	0.0	0.0	0.0	0.0	0.0	0.0	0.0	0.0	0.0	0.0	0.0
1980-81	0.0	0.0	0.0	0.0	0.0	0.0	0.0	0.0	0.0	0.0	0.0	0.0	0.0
1981-82	0.0	0.0	0.0	0.0	0.0	0.0	0.0	0.0	0.0	0.0	0.0	0.0	0.0
1982-83	0.0	0.0	0.0	0.0	0.0	0.0	0.0	0.0	0.0	0.0	0.0	0.0	0.0
1983-84	0.0	0.0	0.0	0.0	0.0	0.0	0.0	0.0	0.0	0.0			
1984-85													
Record Mean	0.0	0.0	0.0	0.0	0.0	T	T	T	0.0	0.0	0.0	0.0	T

SACRAMENTO, CALIFORNIA

Sacramento, and the lower Sacramento Valley, has a mild climate with abundant sunshine most of the year. A nearly cloud-free sky prevails throughout the summer months, and in much of the spring and fall. The summers are usually dry with warm to hot afternoons and mostly mild nights. The rainy season generally is November through March. About 75 percent of the annual precipitation occurs then, but measurable rain falls only on an average of nine days per month during that period. The shielding effect of mountains to the north, east, and west usually modifies winter storms. The Sierra Nevada snow fields, only 70 miles east of Sacramento, usually provide an adequate water supply during the dry season, and an important recreational area in winter. Heavy snowfall and torrential rains frequently fall on the western Sierra slopes, and may produce flood conditions along the Sacramento River and its tributaries. In the valley, however, excessive rainfall as well as damaging winds are rare.

The prevailing wind at Sacramento is southerly every month but November, when it is northerly. Topographic effects, the north-south alignment of the valley, the coast range, and the Sierra Nevada strongly influence the wind flow in the valley. A sea level gap in the coast range permits cool, oceanic air to flow, occasionally, into the valley during the summer season with a marked lowering of temperature through the Sacramento-San Joaquin River Delta to the capital. In the spring and fall, a large north-to-south pressure gradient develops over the northern part of the state. Air flowing over the Siskiyou mountains to the north warms and dries as it descends to the valley floor. This gusty, blustery north wind is a local variation of the chinook. It apparently carries a form of pollen which may cause allergic responses by susceptible individuals.

As is well known, relative humidity has a marked influence on the reactions of plants and animals to temperature. The extremely low relative humidity that ordinarily accompanies high temperatures in this valley should be considered when comparing temperatures here with those of cities in more humid regions. The extreme hot spells, with temperatures exceeding 100 degrees, are usually caused by air flow from a sub-tropical high pressure area that brings light to nearly calm winds and humidities below 20 percent.

Thunderstorms are few in number, usually mild in character, and occur mainly in the spring. An occasional thunderstorm may drift over the valley from the Sierra Nevada in the summer. Snow falls so rarely, and in such small amounts, that its occurrence may be disregarded as a climatic feature. Heavy fog occurs mostly in midwinter, never in summer, and seldom in spring or autumn. An occasional winter fog, under stagnant atmospheric conditions, may continue for several days. Light and moderate fogs are more frequent, and may come anytime during the wet, cold season. The fog is the radiational cooling type, and is usually confined to the early morning hours.

Sacramento is the geographical center of the great interior valley of California that reaches from Red Bluff in the north to Bakersville in the south. This predominantly agricultural region produces an extremely wide and abundant variety of fruits, grains, and vegetables ranging from the semi-tropical to the hardier varieties.

Based on the 1951-1980 period, the average first occurrence of 32 degrees Fahrenheit in the fall is December 1 and the average last occurrence in the spring is February 14.

NORMALS, MEANS, AND EXTREMES

SACRAMENTO, CALIFORNIA

LATITUDE: 38°31'N LONGITUDE: 121°30' W ELEVATION: FT. GRND 17 BARO 20 TIME ZONE: PACIFIC WBAN: 23232

	(a)	JAN	FEB	MAR	APR	MAY	JUNE	JULY	AUG	SEP	OCT	NOV	DEC	YEAR
TEMPERATURE °F:														
Normals														
-Daily Maximum		52.7	60.0	64.0	71.1	80.3	87.8	93.2	92.1	87.3	77.9	63.1	52.7	73.5
-Daily Minimum		37.7	41.4	43.2	45.5	50.3	55.3	58.1	58.0	55.7	50.4	43.4	37.8	48.1
-Monthly		45.2	50.7	53.6	58.3	65.3	71.6	75.7	75.1	71.5	64.2	53.3	45.3	60.8
Extremes														
-Record Highest	43	70	76	88	93	105	115	114	109	108	101	87	72	115
-Year		1991	1992	1988	1990	1984	1961	1972	1990	1988	1970	1960	1989	JUN 1961
-Record Lowest	43	23	23	26	32	36	41	48	49	43	36	26	18	18
-Year		1979	1989	1971	1953	1974	1990	1983	1978	1978	1989	1993	1990	DEC 1990
NORMAL DEGREE DAYS:														
Heating (base 65°F)		614	400	357	230	80	12	0	0	16	78	351	611	2749
Cooling (base 65°F)		0	0	0	29	89	210	332	313	211	53	0	0	1237
% OF POSSIBLE SUNSHINE	45	48	65	74	82	89	94	97	96	93	86	66	49	78
MEAN SKY COVER (tenths)														
Sunrise - Sunset	45	7.0	6.2	5.6	4.8	3.5	2.2	1.1	1.5	1.8	3.2	5.6	6.7	4.1
MEAN NUMBER OF DAYS:														
Sunrise to Sunset														
-Clear	45	6.6	8.0	10.1	12.0	17.3	21.7	27.0	25.4	23.6	19.2	10.2	7.8	188.8
-Partly Cloudy	45	6.0	6.8	8.3	9.6	8.4	5.9	3.1	4.3	4.2	6.1	7.2	5.9	75.8
-Cloudy	45	18.4	13.4	12.6	8.4	5.3	2.4	0.9	1.3	2.2	5.7	12.6	17.3	100.6
Precipitation														
.01 inches or more	54	9.9	8.7	8.8	5.2	2.7	1.1	0.2	0.4	1.3	3.4	6.8	8.9	57.5
Snow,Ice pellets,hail														
1.0 inches or more	45	0.0	0.*	0.0	0.0	0.0	0.0	0.0	0.0	0.0	0.0	0.0	0.0	*
Thunderstorms	45	0.4	0.6	0.8	0.7	0.4	0.3	0.2	0.2	0.5	0.3	0.2	0.2	4.8
Heavy Fog Visibility														
1/4 mile or less	45	10.2	5.2	1.7	0.3	0.2	0.0	0.0	0.*	0.2	1.4	5.2	9.6	34.0
Temperature °F														
-Maximum														
90° and above	43	0.0	0.0	0.0	0.4	5.3	12.0	22.3	19.4	12.5	2.9	0.0	0.0	74.8
32° and below	43	0.*	0.0	0.0	0.0	0.0	0.0	0.0	0.0	0.0	0.0	0.0	0.*	*
-Minimum														
32° and below	43	6.6	1.7	0.5	0.*	0.0	0.0	0.0	0.0	0.0	0.0	1.3	6.6	16.8
0° and below	43	0.0	0.0	0.0	0.0	0.0	0.0	0.0	0.0	0.0	0.0	0.0	0.0	0.0
AVG. STATION PRESS. (mb)	21	1019.3	1017.6	1015.6	1015.1	1012.5	1011.2	1011.0	1011.2	1011.3	1014.5	1018.0	1019.6	1014.7
RELATIVE HUMIDITY (%)														
Hour 04	33	90	88	85	82	81	78	77	78	78	80	86	90	83
Hour 10 (Local Time)	33	85	78	70	58	50	47	47	50	50	57	73	84	62
Hour 16	33	70	60	54	43	35	31	28	29	31	38	57	70	46
Hour 22	33	86	81	78	73	69	65	61	64	64	70	81	87	73
PRECIPITATION (inches):														
Water Equivalent														
-Normal		3.73	2.87	2.57	1.16	0.27	0.12	0.05	0.07	0.37	1.08	2.72	2.51	17.52
-Maximum Monthly	54	9.14	8.77	7.12	4.76	3.13	1.26	0.79	0.65	2.78	7.51	7.41	12.64	12.64
-Year		1978	1962	1982	1941	1948	1993	1974	1976	1989	1962	1970	1955	DEC 1955
-Minimum Monthly	54	0.16	0.15	0.14	0.00	T	0.00	0.00	0.00	0.00	0.00	0.02	0.00	0.00
-Year		1984	1964	1966	1949	1992	1981	1983	1982	1980	1966	1959	1989	DEC 1989
-Maximum in 24 hrs	45	3.41	3.01	2.30	2.22	0.78	1.21	0.78	0.65	1.79	5.59	2.95	3.64	5.59
-Year		1967	1986	1982	1958	1957	1993	1974	1965	1989	1962	1970	1955	OCT 1962
Snow,Ice pellets,hail														
-Maximum Monthly	45	T	2.0	T	0.0	0.0	0.0	0.0	0.0	0.0	0.0	0.0	T	2.0
-Year		1974	1976	1982									1993	FEB 1976
-Maximum in 24 hrs	45	T	2.0	T	0.0	0.0	0.0	0.0	0.0	0.0	0.0	0.0	T	2.0
-Year		1974	1976	1982									1993	FEB 1976
WIND:														
Mean Speed (mph)	44	7.2	7.5	8.6	8.7	9.2	9.7	9.0	8.6	7.5	6.4	6.0	6.7	7.9
Prevailing Direction through 1963		SE	SSE	SW	SW	SW	SW	SSW	SW	SW	SW	NNW	SSE	SW
Fastest Mile														
-Direction (!!)	45	SE	SE	S	SW	SW	SW	SW	SW	NW	SE	SE	SE	SW
-Speed (MPH)	45	60	51	66	45	74	47	36	38	42	68	70	70	74
-Year		1954	1959	1952	1955	1993	1950	1956	1954	1965	1950	1953	1952	MAY 1993
Peak Gust														
-Direction (!!)														
-Speed (mph)														
-Date														

PRECIPITATION (inches)

SACRAMENTO, CALIFORNIA

YEAR	JAN	FEB	MAR	APR	MAY	JUNE	JULY	AUG	SEP	OCT	NOV	DEC	ANNUAL
1964	3.83	0.15	1.36	0.17	0.23	0.39	0.01	0.11	0.00	1.72	2.70	6.03	16.70
1965	3.01	0.41	1.47	2.70	0.09	T	T	0.65	T	0.11	2.93	2.44	13.81
1966	1.91	1.56	0.14	0.47	0.25	0.02	0.10	T	0.07	0.00	5.73	3.53	13.78
1967	8.42	0.41	3.91	3.40	0.13	0.60	T	0.00	0.04	0.24	1.18	1.29	19.62
1968	3.77	2.13	2.39	0.42	0.16	0.15	T	0.02	0.00	0.60	2.49	2.77	14.90
1969	8.50	6.98	0.94	1.63	0.04	0.08	T	0.00	0.02	0.72	0.60	4.41	23.92
1970	7.88	1.58	1.62	0.18	T	0.16	0.00	0.00	0.00	0.84	7.41	3.40	23.07
1971	0.90	0.56	2.05	0.44	0.77	0.01	0.00	0.00	T	0.13	0.87	4.05	9.78
1972	0.81	1.28	0.29	1.39	0.28	0.19	0.00	0.00	0.90	1.75	5.14	1.88	13.91
1973	6.87	5.64	2.76	0.05	0.13	0.00	0.00	0.00	0.33	1.64	6.27	2.79	26.48
1974	3.58	1.37	3.27	0.96	0.01	0.50	0.79	T	0.00	1.16	0.66	2.86	15.16
1975	0.73	4.59	4.28	0.81	T	T	0.04	0.23	T	2.03	0.29	0.18	13.18
1976	0.36	1.49	0.44	1.53	0.00	0.04	0.00	0.65	0.52	0.02	0.55	0.65	6.25
1977	1.17	1.17	1.27	0.30	0.73	0.00	T	0.00	0.76	0.12	1.92	4.27	11.71
1978	9.14	4.46	3.38	2.31	T	T	0.00	T	0.30	T	3.20	0.95	23.74
1979	5.66	4.55	2.47	0.76	0.14	0.00	0.25	0.00	T	1.62	1.48	3.41	20.34
1980	5.64	7.12	2.62	1.06	0.49	0.04	0.40	0.00	0.00	0.06	0.12	1.79	19.34
1981	4.56	0.87	3.55	0.66	0.50	0.00	0.00	0.00	0.25	2.57	6.09	3.28	22.33
1982	5.50	2.35	7.12	3.07	T	0.15	0.00	0.00	1.81	2.61	5.74	3.25	31.60
1983	4.92	5.56	6.75	4.21	0.25	0.40	0.00	0.11	0.66	0.40	4.91	5.26	33.43
1984	0.16	1.22	1.35	0.34	0.01	0.10	T	0.01	0.07	1.39	3.61	1.23	9.49
1985	0.66	1.52	2.01	T	0.01	0.15	T	0.06	0.56	0.53	3.72	2.34	11.56
1986	3.67	8.60	3.20	0.91	0.07	0.00	0.00	0.00	0.60	0.19	0.14	0.76	18.14
1987	2.29	3.23	3.05	0.20	T	T	0.00	0.00	0.00	1.28	2.53	3.25	15.83
1988	2.96	0.99	0.17	1.58	0.89	0.19	0.00	0.00	0.00	0.19	1.68	2.73	11.38
1989	0.71	1.25	6.29	0.31	0.06	0.43	0.00	0.20	2.78	1.76	1.32	0.00	15.11
1990	4.97	2.91	0.93	0.73	2.10	0.00	T	0.00	0.00	0.09	0.43	1.60	13.76
1991	0.36	3.10	6.14	0.29	0.25	0.53	T	0.14	0.04	1.25	0.19	1.60	13.89
1992	1.39	5.47	2.05	0.92	T	0.15	0.00	T	0.00	1.31	0.28	4.94	16.51
1993	8.63	4.94	2.39	0.63	1.14	1.26	0.00	0.00	0.00	0.47	2.28	1.75	23.49
Record Mean	3.59	3.00	2.53	1.30	0.44	0.13	0.03	0.05	0.28	0.99	2.20	2.89	17.43

AVERAGE TEMPERATURE (deg. F)

SACRAMENTO, CALIFORNIA

YEAR	JAN	FEB	MAR	APR	MAY	JUNE	JULY	AUG	SEP	OCT	NOV	DEC	ANNUAL
1964	45.1	49.4	52.3	58.9	63.0	70.0	75.9	75.8	70.3	66.7	50.3	49.7	60.6
1965	45.4	49.2	53.0	57.3	64.4	67.0	74.4	75.7	67.6	65.9	54.7	41.0	59.6
1966	45.7	47.5	54.3	62.9	66.4	72.6	72.9	76.9	72.0	64.1	54.7	46.1	61.4
1967	45.9	48.4	50.8	49.6	65.2	69.4	78.0	79.0	74.9	65.5	56.2	44.0	60.6
1968	43.4	54.5	55.1	59.8	64.7	73.9	76.2	73.0	72.2	62.0	52.3	43.5	60.9
1969	44.0	47.4	52.4	57.1	66.9	69.0	76.3	77.9	74.0	61.0	53.9	48.0	60.7
1970	49.3	51.9	54.9	56.1	67.6	71.5	76.8	74.7	72.8	62.1	55.3	46.1	61.6
1971	45.3	48.2	52.6	56.4	61.8	70.5	76.2	76.8	72.2	61.2	52.7	43.0	59.8
1972	41.0	51.4	58.6	58.6	66.9	72.5	76.0	75.9	69.5	62.0	49.7	40.6	60.2
1973	44.3	53.1	51.1	60.8	69.4	74.6	76.8	74.2	70.8	63.4	51.9	46.9	61.5
1974	46.3	48.4	54.1	56.6	63.8	70.5	74.1	74.0	72.2	66.3	53.2	46.4	60.5
1975	43.4	49.2	50.3	51.8	68.2	73.2	77.3	76.9	77.4	65.1	54.6	47.4	61.2
1976	47.2	51.9	54.6	57.9	70.1	73.9	76.5	73.4	71.8	66.1	56.7	46.5	62.2
1977	43.8	52.4	51.0	62.2	59.4	72.2	74.2	73.9	68.8	63.9	54.5	49.6	60.5
1978	50.3	51.9	57.2	55.8	66.4	70.0	75.1	75.0	69.6	65.9	49.8	41.7	60.7
1979	45.3	48.8	54.6	56.9	66.7	71.9	75.6	73.1	74.6	64.0	51.7	46.7	60.9
1980	46.9	51.9	51.6	59.6	62.7	66.8	75.0	71.4	69.4	63.7	53.5	45.4	59.9
1981	46.8	50.4	51.2	57.9	64.7	74.8	75.1	74.5	69.7	63.5	60.3	48.6	61.5
1982	42.0	50.5	50.8	55.5	64.6	66.2	72.1	71.7	68.2	61.0	46.9	43.0	57.7
1983	43.1	52.2	53.4	54.7	64.2	70.8	72.2	76.6	74.9	67.5	53.7	51.0	61.2
1984	48.2	50.2	58.1	58.7	70.0	71.7	78.3	75.3	75.5	62.8	53.6	45.1	62.3
1985	42.4	51.4	50.8	61.5	63.2	75.1	77.0	72.9	68.5	63.3	49.8	42.6	59.9
1986	51.4	54.7	58.8	58.4	65.5	71.6	75.0	75.2	66.2	64.8	55.5	45.7	61.9
1987	44.9	51.3	53.8	62.7	69.1	72.4	71.8	74.9	71.8	67.6	53.4	47.2	61.7
1988	48.0	54.2	58.0	60.9	64.7	72.9	80.4	75.9	72.5	66.5	53.8	46.2	62.8
1989	44.1	47.1	55.6	63.2	65.8	71.7	76.2	73.8	69.6	62.4	54.3	44.3	60.7
1990	47.5	48.6	55.4	63.4	65.5	72.4	77.7	76.6	74.0	66.6	53.0	41.0	61.8
1991	47.3	55.0	51.0	58.0	63.3	70.2	77.1	73.2	74.8	68.8	55.9	46.3	61.7
1992	43.6	54.1	56.2	62.1	70.6	70.9	75.3	77.0	72.4	66.6	53.4	44.1	62.2
1993	45.2	49.5	57.9	58.4	64.6	71.7	74.3	74.1	71.5	65.0	51.5	44.3	60.7
Record Mean	45.3	50.4	53.5	58.6	64.9	71.0	75.4	74.4	71.5	63.9	53.0	45.6	60.6
Max	53.0	59.7	64.2	71.4	79.6	87.0	92.8	91.3	87.5	77.7	63.5	53.3	73.4
Min	37.5	41.0	42.9	45.7	50.2	55.0	57.9	57.4	55.5	50.1	42.6	37.9	47.8

REFERENCE NOTES

SACRAMENTO, CALIFORNIA

GENERAL
T - TRACE AMOUNT.
BLANK ENTRIES DENOTE MISSING/UNREPORTED DATA.
# INDICATES A STATION OR INSTRUMENT RELOCATION

SPECIFIC

PM - INCLUDES LAST DAY OF PREVIOUS MONTH
ASOS - AUTOMATED SURFACE OBSERVING SYSTEM IN OPERATION DURING THESE MONTHS.

(a) - LENGTH OF RECORD IN YEARS, ALTHOUGH INDIVIDUAL MONTHS MAY BE MISSING.
0.* OR * - THE VALUE IS BETWEEN 0.0 AND 0.05
NORMALS - BASED ON THE 1961-1990 RECORD PERIOD.
EXTREMES - DATES ARE THE MOST RECENT OCCURRENCE
WIND DIR.- NUMERALS SHOW TENS OF DEGRESS CLOCKWISE FROM TRUE NORTH. "00" INDICATES CALM.
RESULTANT DIRECTIONS ARE GIVEN TO WHOLE DEGREES.
BOLD VALUES INDICATE EXTREME VALUES WHICH OCCURRED AFTER THE ASOS SYSTEM WAS COMMISSIONED.

RECORD = PERIOD OF RECORD
RECORD MEAN PRECIPITATION IS THE MEAN OF ALL DAILY PRECIPITATION AMOUNTS DURING THE PERIOD OF RECORD.
RECORD MAX(MIN) TEMPERATURE IS THE MEAN OF ALL DAILY MAX(MIN) TEMPERATURES DURING THE PERIOD OF RECORD.
RECORD MEAN TEMPERATURE IS THE SUM OF THE RECORD MAX AND RECORD MIN DIVIDED BY 2.
AVERAGE TEMPERATURE IS THE SUM OF THE MEAN DAILY MAX AND MIN TEMPERATURE DIVIDED BY 2.

EXCEPTIONS

RECORD MEANS ARE THROUGH THE CURRENT YEAR,
BEGINNING IN 1941 FOR TEMPERATURE
1940 FOR PRECIPITATION
1949 FOR SNOWFALL

HEATING DEGREE DAYS Base 65 deg. F — SACRAMENTO, CALIFORNIA

SEASON	JULY	AUG	SEP	OCT	NOV	DEC	JAN	FEB	MAR	APR	MAY	JUNE	TOTAL
1964-65	0	4	10	49	436	469	602	434	363	246	86	21	2720
1965-66	0	0	19	32	303	738	591	485	326	96	36	14	2640
1966-67	1	0	4	60	303	580	584	461	435	456	98	34	3016
1967-68	0	0	0	33	259	643	663	296	299	171	80	2	2446
1968-69	0	3	2	97	374	662	644	486	384	230	41	6	2929
1969-70	0	0	1	129	323	519	478	359	304	258	56	9	2436
1970-71	0	0	4	129	286	578	603	466	379	249	114	14	2822
1971-72	0	0	33	191	363	673	731	390	197	190	63	11	2842
1972-73	0	0	6	115	451	749	636	325	424	141	15	1	2863
1973-74	0	0	0	77	384	553	571	456	332	251	93	9	2726
1974-75	7	0	0	44	347	569	661	435	449	389	69	1	2971
1975-76	0	0	0	72	306	539	547	374	315	211	1	3	2368
1976-77	0	0	1	44	252	567	650	345	424	92	187	9	2571
1977-78	0	0	17	68	309	472	451	362	235	269	46	0	2229
1978-79	0	0	11	51	449	715	606	446	313	236	57	2	2886
1979-80	0	0	0	100	391	558	551	373	408	164	107	29	2681
1980-81	2	0	4	134	339	596	557	405	420	229	81	2	2769
1981-82	0	0	9	66	145	498	708	398	434	282	70	40	2650
1982-83	3	0	31	125	532	675	670	353	354	303	99	4	3149
1983-84	3	0	0	7	333	425	514	421	206	191	22	11	2133
1984-85	0	0	0	115	335	611	693	377	433	122	89	11	2786
1985-86	0	2	15	95	450	689	411	284	192	200	73	0	2411
1986-87	0	0	53	47	277	593	614	377	340	95	37	0	2433
1987-88	1	0	0	11	339	544	522	307	212	138	94	27	2195
1988-89	0	0	3	38	329	576	640	496	285	106	50	3	2526
1989-90	0	0	11	107	316	634	536	453	289	71	53	6	2476
1990-91	0	0	0	24	356	739	543	274	427	205	104	6	2678
1991-92	0	0	0	82	267	572	657	310	265	104	0	9	2266
1992-93	0	0	0	24	340	643	605	426	214	202	55	21	2530
1993-94	0	0	5	33	399	634							

COOLING DEGREE DAYS Base 65 deg. F — SACRAMENTO, CALIFORNIA

YEAR	JAN	FEB	MAR	APR	MAY	JUNE	JULY	AUG	SEP	OCT	NOV	DEC	TOTAL
1969	0	0	0	1	108	136	361	409	278	13	0	0	1306
1970	0	0	0	0	143	208	374	305	245	46	0	0	1321
1971	0	0	0	0	22	186	355	375	254	82	0	0	1274
1972	0	0	6	5	129	245	351	349	147	30	0	0	1262
1973	0	0	0	19	156	295	373	293	181	34	0	0	1351
1974	0	0	0	5	61	180	296	285	222	89	0	0	1138
1975	0	0	0	0	177	258	388	375	375	81	0	0	1654
1976	0	0	1	8	167	278	363	270	213	83	8	0	1391
1977	0	0	0	12	19	230	290	284	139	40	0	0	1014
1978	0	0	0	0	98	157	318	315	157	87	0	0	1132
1979	0	0	0	0	117	214	336	260	295	72	0	0	1294
1980	0	0	0	8	42	91	317	207	145	99	0	0	909
1981	0	0	0	26	78	303	318	301	155	28	7	0	1216
1982	0	0	0	2	67	83	230	213	133	9	0	0	737
1983	0	0	0	0	81	183	235	368	304	92	0	0	1263
1984	0	0	0	6	183	216	419	327	320	57	0	0	1528
1985	0	0	0	22	41	319	380	254	128	48	0	0	1192
1986	0	0	10	9	95	207	315	321	95	47	0	0	1099
1987	0	0	0	34	171	234	220	314	212	100	0	0	1285
1988	0	0	5	22	88	269	484	346	233	92	0	0	1539
1989	0	0	1	60	83	211	354	280	158	32	0	0	1179
1990	0	0	0	33	75	236	399	367	276	82	0	0	1468
1991	0	0	0	3	54	171	379	261	300	208	0	0	1376
1992	0	0	0	23	180	193	330	381	231	81	0	0	1419
1993	0	0	1	9	49	227	294	291	207	38	0	0	1116

SNOWFALL (inches) — SACRAMENTO, CALIFORNIA

SEASON	JULY	AUG	SEP	OCT	NOV	DEC	JAN	FEB	MAR	APR	MAY	JUNE	TOTAL
1970-71	0.0	0.0	0.0	0.0	0.0	0.0	0.0	0.0	0.0	0.0	0.0	0.0	0.0
1971-72	0.0	0.0	0.0	0.0	0.0	0.0	0.0	0.0	0.0	0.0	0.0	0.0	0.0
1972-73	0.0	0.0	0.0	0.0	0.0	T	0.0	0.0	0.0	0.0	0.0	0.0	T
1973-74	0.0	0.0	0.0	0.0	0.0	0.0	T	0.0	0.0	0.0	0.0	0.0	T
1974-75	0.0	0.0	0.0	0.0	0.0	0.0	0.0	0.0	0.0	0.0	0.0	0.0	0.0
1975-76	0.0	0.0	0.0	0.0	0.0	0.0	0.0	2.0	0.0	0.0	0.0	0.0	2.0
1976-77	0.0	0.0	0.0	0.0	0.0	0.0	0.0	0.0	0.0	0.0	0.0	0.0	0.0
1977-78	0.0	0.0	0.0	0.0	0.0	0.0	0.0	0.0	0.0	0.0	0.0	0.0	0.0
1978-79	0.0	0.0	0.0	0.0	0.0	0.0	0.0	0.0	0.0	0.0	0.0	0.0	0.0
1979-80	0.0	0.0	0.0	0.0	0.0	0.0	0.0	0.0	0.0	0.0	0.0	0.0	0.0
1980-81	0.0	0.0	0.0	0.0	0.0	0.0	0.0	0.0	0.0	0.0	0.0	0.0	0.0
1981-82	0.0	0.0	0.0	0.0	0.0	0.0	0.0	0.0	T	0.0	0.0	0.0	T
1982-83	0.0	0.0	0.0	0.0	0.0	0.0	0.0	0.0	0.0	0.0	0.0	0.0	0.0
1983-84	0.0	0.0	0.0	0.0	0.0	0.0	0.0	0.0	0.0	0.0	0.0	0.0	0.0
1984-85	0.0	0.0	0.0	0.0	0.0	0.0	0.0	0.0	0.0	0.0	0.0	0.0	0.0
1985-86	0.0	0.0	0.0	0.0	0.0	0.0	0.0	0.0	0.0	0.0	0.0	0.0	0.0
1986-87	0.0	0.0	0.0	0.0	0.0	0.0	0.0	0.0	0.0	0.0	0.0	0.0	0.0
1987-88	0.0	0.0	0.0	0.0	0.0	0.0	0.0	0.0	0.0	0.0	0.0	0.0	0.0
1988-89	0.0	0.0	0.0	0.0	0.0	T	0.0	0.0	0.0	0.0	0.0	0.0	T
1989-90	0.0	0.0	0.0	0.0	0.0	0.0	0.0	0.0	0.0	0.0	0.0	0.0	0.0
1990-91	0.0	0.0	0.0	0.0	0.0	0.0	0.0	0.0	0.0	0.0	0.0	0.0	0.0
1991-92	0.0	0.0	0.0	0.0	0.0	0.0	0.0	0.0	0.0	0.0	0.0	0.0	0.0
1992-93	0.0	0.0	0.0	0.0	0.0	T	0.0	0.0	0.0	0.0	0.0	0.0	T
1993-94	0.0	0.0	0.0	0.0	0.0	T							
Record Mean	0.0	0.0	0.0	0.0	0.0	T	T	T	T	0.0	0.0	0.0	T

SAN DIEGO, CALIFORNIA

The city of San Diego is located on San Diego Bay in the southwest corner of southern California. The prevailing winds and weather are tempered by the Pacific Ocean, with the result that summers are cool and winters warm in comparison with other places along the same general latitude. Temperatures of freezing or below have rarely occurred at the station since the record began in 1871, but hot weather, 90 degrees or above, is more frequent.

Dry easterly winds sometimes blow in the vicinity for several days at a time, bringing temperatures in the 90s and at times even in the 100s in the eastern sections of the city and outlying suburbs. At the National Weather Service station itself, however, there have been relatively few days on which 100 degrees or higher was reached.

As these hot winds are predominant in the fall, highest temperatures occur in the months of September and October. Records show that over 60 percent of the days with 90 degrees or higher have occurred in these two months. High temperatures are almost invariably accompanied by very low relative humidities, which often drop below 20 percent and occasionally below 10 percent.

A marked feature of the climate is the wide variation in temperature within short distances. In nearby valleys daytimes are much warmer in summer and nights noticeably cooler in winter, and freezing occurs much more frequently than in the city. Although records show unusually small daily temperature ranges, only about 15 degrees between the highest and lowest readings, a few miles inland these ranges increase to 30 degrees or more.

Strong winds and gales associated with Pacific, or tropical storms, are infrequent due to the latitude.

The seasonal rainfall is about 10 inches in the city, but increases with elevation and distance from the coast. In the mountains to the north and east the average is between 20 and 40 inches, depending on slope and elevation. Most of the precipitation falls in winter, except in the mountains where there is an occasional thunderstorm. Eighty-five percent of the rainfall occurs from November through March, but wide variations take place in monthly and seasonal totals. Infrequent measurable amounts of hail occur in San Diego, but snow is practically unknown at the Weather Service Office location. In each occurrence of snowfall only a trace was recorded officially, but in some locations amounts up to or slightly exceeding a half-inch fell, and remained on the ground for an hour or more.

As on the rest of the Pacific Coast, a dominant characteristic of spring and summer is the nighttime and early morning cloudiness. Low clouds form regularly and frequently extend inland over the coastal valleys and foothills, but they usually dissipate during the morning and the afternoons are generally clear.

Considerable fog occurs along the coast, but the amount decreases with distance inland. The fall and winter months are usually the foggiest. Thunderstorms are rare, averaging about three a year in the city. Visibilities are good as a rule. The sunshine is plentiful for a marine location, with a marked increase toward the interior.

NORMALS, MEANS, AND EXTREMES

SAN DIEGO, CALIFORNIA

LATITUDE: 32°44'N LONGITUDE: 117°10' W ELEVATION: FT. GRND 13 BARO 33 TIME ZONE: PACIFIC WBAN: 23188

	(a)	JAN	FEB	MAR	APR	MAY	JUNE	JULY	AUG	SEP	OCT	NOV	DEC	YEAR
TEMPERATURE °F:														
Normals														
-Daily Maximum		65.9	66.5	66.3	68.4	69.1	71.6	76.2	77.8	77.1	74.6	69.9	66.1	70.8
-Daily Minimum		48.9	50.7	52.8	55.6	59.1	61.9	65.7	67.3	65.6	60.9	53.9	48.8	57.6
-Monthly		57.4	58.6	59.6	62.0	64.1	66.8	71.0	72.6	71.4	67.7	62.0	57.4	64.2
Extremes														
-Record Highest	53	88	88	93	98	96	101	95	98	111	107	97	88	111
-Year		1953	1954	1988	1989	1953	1979	1985	1955	1963	1961	1976	1963	SEP 1963
-Record Lowest	53	29	36	39	41	48	51	55	57	51	43	38	34	29
-Year		1949	1949	1971	1945	1967	1967	1948	1944	1948	1971	1964	1987	JAN 1949
NORMAL DEGREE DAYS:														
Heating (base 65°F)		245	189	177	113	73	51	13	0	19	24	109	243	1256
Cooling (base 65°F)		9	10	9	23	45	105	199	240	211	107	19	7	984
% OF POSSIBLE SUNSHINE	53	72	72	70	67	59	58	68	70	69	68	75	73	68
MEAN SKY COVER (tenths)														
Sunrise - Sunset	53	5.1	5.2	5.3	5.2	5.7	5.5	4.5	4.2	4.1	4.4	4.2	4.7	4.8
MEAN NUMBER OF DAYS:														
Sunrise to Sunset														
-Clear	53	12.5	10.4	10.9	10.3	8.6	9.2	13.0	14.9	14.9	13.7	14.8	13.6	146.8
-Partly Cloudy	53	7.4	7.5	9.5	10.0	11.4	11.7	13.0	11.6	9.5	9.7	7.8	7.8	116.7
-Cloudy	53	11.2	10.4	10.7	9.8	11.1	9.0	5.0	4.5	5.5	7.6	7.4	9.5	101.7
Precipitation .01 inches or more	53	6.8	6.0	7.0	4.4	2.1	1.0	0.4	0.5	1.1	2.5	4.5	5.8	42.1
Snow,Ice pellets,hail 1.0 inches or more	53	0.0	0.0	0.0	0.0	0.0	0.0	0.0	0.0	0.0	0.0	0.0	0.0	0.0
Thunderstorms	53	0.2	0.3	0.4	0.1	0.1	0.1	0.2	0.2	0.3	0.3	0.3	0.4	3.0
Heavy Fog Visibility 1/4 mile or less	53	3.0	2.5	1.5	1.2	0.6	0.7	0.6	0.6	2.3	3.3	3.5	3.9	23.6
Temperature °F														
-Maximum														
90° and above	33	0.0	0.0	0.1	0.2	0.1	0.5	0.2	0.2	1.3	0.9	0.2	0.0	3.7
32° and below	33	0.0	0.0	0.0	0.0	0.0	0.0	0.0	0.0	0.0	0.0	0.0	0.0	0.0
-Minimum														
32° and below	33	0.*	0.0	0.0	0.0	0.0	0.0	0.0	0.0	0.0	0.0	0.0	0.0	*
0° and below	33	0.0	0.0	0.0	0.0	0.0	0.0	0.0	0.0	0.0	0.0	0.0	0.0	0.0
AVG. STATION PRESS.(mb)	21	1017.2	1016.8	1015.4	1014.5	1013.2	1012.2	1012.5	1012.3	1011.6	1013.7	1015.8	1017.1	1014.4
RELATIVE HUMIDITY (%)														
Hour 04	33	71	74	75	76	77	81	82	82	80	77	72	71	77
Hour 10 (Local Time)	33	55	58	61	60	65	69	69	68	66	61	55	54	62
Hour 16	33	56	59	60	59	64	67	66	67	65	64	61	58	62
Hour 22	33	70	72	73	73	75	78	80	79	78	76	73	71	75
PRECIPITATION (inches):														
Water Equivalent														
-Normal		1.80	1.53	1.77	0.79	0.19	0.07	0.02	0.10	0.24	0.37	1.45	1.57	9.90
-Maximum Monthly	53	9.09	5.40	6.96	3.71	1.79	0.87	0.24	2.13	1.90	2.90	5.82	7.60	9.09
-Year		1993	1976	1991	1988	1977	1990	1991	1977	1963	1941	1965	1943	JAN 1993
-Minimum Monthly	53	T	0.00	T	0.00	0.00	0.00	0.00	0.00	0.00	0.00	0.00	0.02	0.00
-Year		1976	1967	1972	1993	1952	1981	1982	1981	1979	1967	1980	1979	APR 1993
-Maximum in 24 hrs	53	2.65	2.61	2.40	1.98	1.50	0.82	0.23	2.13	1.00	1.39	2.44	3.07	3.07
-Year		1978	1979	1952	1988	1977	1990	1991	1977	1986	1986	1944	1945	DEC 1945
Snow,Ice pellets,hail														
-Maximum Monthly	53	T	0.0	T	0.0	0.0	0.0	0.0	0.0	0.0	0.0	T	T	T
-Year		1949		1985								1985	1967	MAR 1985
-Maximum in 24 hrs	53	T	0.0	T	0.0	0.0	0.0	0.0	0.0	0.0	0.0	T	T	T
-Year		1949		1985								1985	1967	MAR 1985
WIND:														
Mean Speed (mph)	53	5.9	6.6	7.5	7.8	7.9	7.8	7.4	7.3	7.1	6.6	5.9	5.6	7.0
Prevailing Direction through 1963		NE	WNW	WNW	WNW	WNW	SSW	WNW	WNW	NW	WNW	NE	NE	WNW
Fastest Mile														
-Direction (!!!)	49	SE	S	SW	S	S	S	NW	NW	S	N	SE	NW	SE
-Speed (MPH)	49	56	45	46	37	30	26	23	23	31	31	51	39	56
-Year		1980	1980	1945	1958	1977	1948	1968	1982	1978	1961	1944	1982	JAN 1980
Peak Gust														
-Direction (!!!)	10	W	SW	NW	SW	NW	NW	SW	SW	NW	NW	SW	NW	W
-Speed (mph)	10	64	46	41	40	40	28	30	29	31	32	37	44	64
-Date		1988	1993	1985	1988	1988	1988	1985	1991	1989	1991	1985	1991	JAN 1988

PRECIPITATION (inches)

SAN DIEGO, CALIFORNIA

YEAR	JAN	FEB	MAR	APR	MAY	JUNE	JULY	AUG	SEP	OCT	NOV	DEC	ANNUAL
1964	1.30	0.37	0.97	0.20	0.15	0.08	0.00	T	0.00	0.02	1.01	1.17	5.27
1965	0.40	0.52	1.79	3.58	T	0.01	0.02	T	0.29	T	5.82	6.60	19.03
1966	1.29	0.86	0.17	T	0.02	T	T	0.00	T	0.80	0.82	3.22	7.18
1967	2.20	0.00	1.14	2.24	0.05	0.16	0.01	0.14	0.08	0.00	3.53	1.66	11.21
1968	0.35	0.22	1.55	0.34	0.08	T	0.13	T	T	0.04	0.36	0.61	3.68
1969	4.78	4.34	0.94	0.21	0.17	0.02	T	0.01	T	0.04	0.79	0.46	11.76
1970	0.86	2.58	1.50	0.09	0.01	T	T	0.00	T	0.07	2.05	2.22	9.38
1971	0.30	1.27	0.20	0.93	0.95	0.01	T	0.03	T	1.66	0.06	3.27	8.68
1972	0.07	0.10	T	0.02	0.10	0.38	T	0.02	0.44	0.58	3.16	1.61	6.48
1973	1.68	1.63	2.26	0.05	T	T	T	T	0.02	0.01	1.63	0.19	7.47
1974	2.96	0.04	1.70	0.02	0.01	0.02	0.01	T	T	1.03	0.14	2.20	8.13
1975	0.49	0.96	3.79	2.00	0.01	0.02	T	T	T	0.09	0.64	0.37	8.37
1976	T	5.40	0.99	1.33	0.27	0.02	0.02	0.01	1.00	0.38	0.75	1.06	11.23
1977	2.36	0.06	0.61	0.01	1.79	0.03	T	2.13	T	0.50	0.05	1.67	9.21
1978	5.95	2.64	5.00	0.73	0.04	T	0.00	T	0.72	0.05	2.09	2.19	19.41
1979	5.82	0.85	3.71	0.02	0.09	0.01	0.09	0.01	0.00	0.73	0.27	0.02	11.62
1980	5.58	4.47	2.71	1.18	0.65	0.01	T	0.00	T	0.05	0.00	0.31	14.96
1981	1.48	2.26	3.74	0.22	0.04	0.00	T	0.00	0.03	0.14	1.79	0.54	10.24
1982	2.71	0.88	4.74	0.62	0.01	0.04	0.00	T	0.38	0.05	2.10	1.43	12.96
1983	2.10	3.88	6.57	1.74	0.01	T	0.01	0.39	0.21	0.40	1.94	1.53	18.78
1984	0.46	0.09	0.04	0.62	0.00	0.04	0.19	0.06	T	0.29	2.37	4.55	8.71
1985	0.52	0.77	0.58	0.32	T	T	0.00	T	0.20	0.29	4.92	1.06	8.66
1986	0.75	2.59	3.12	1.17	0.00	T	0.01	0.00	1.04	1.39	1.16	0.95	12.18
1987	1.68	1.53	1.04	0.78	0.03	T	0.03	0.01	0.70	1.74	1.33	2.73	11.60
1988	0.89	1.37	0.59	3.71	0.08	0.00	T	T	T	T	1.39	2.23	10.26
1989	0.42	0.70	0.69	0.12	0.04	0.06	0.00	T	0.23	0.47	0.09	1.01	3.83
1990	2.52	1.13	0.25	0.76	0.51	0.87	T	0.01	T	T	0.65	0.59	7.29
1991	1.06	2.46	6.96	0.05	0.01	T	0.24	0.01	0.28	0.69	0.05	1.70	13.51
1992	1.81	3.34	4.42	0.28	0.07	0.04	0.03	0.05	0.00	0.18	0.03	2.56	12.81
1993	9.09	4.73	1.22	0.00	0.01	0.41	0.03	T	T	0.22	0.77	0.78	17.26
Record Mean	1.91	1.91	1.63	0.71	0.26	0.06	0.04	0.09	0.13	0.42	0.99	1.83	9.97

AVERAGE TEMPERATURE (deg. F)

SAN DIEGO, CALIFORNIA

YEAR	JAN	FEB	MAR	APR	MAY	JUNE	JULY	AUG	SEP	OCT	NOV	DEC	ANNUAL
1964	55.3	56.7	57.8	60.2	60.9	64.0	69.2	70.7	67.7	68.6	59.1	55.6	62.1
1965	56.0	55.9	58.6	60.7	62.5	63.7	67.7	72.0	68.5	69.4	60.9	55.1	62.6
1966	53.9	54.6	58.1	61.3	63.5	66.5	69.2	72.6	69.9	67.6	61.9	57.2	63.0
1967	55.0	57.8	59.0	56.5	63.5	63.6	70.4	73.1	72.0	68.1	64.1	55.5	63.2
1968	57.2	60.7	60.7	62.4	63.9	65.8	71.7	72.2	71.3	66.6	61.7	54.9	64.1
1969	58.1	54.9	56.8	61.7	62.9	65.5	69.4	72.8	69.9	66.0	64.1	59.1	63.4
1970	57.0	59.7	60.5	60.1	63.6	65.6	70.4	72.8	69.7	66.3	61.4	55.4	63.5
1971	54.3	55.4	57.8	60.7	61.5	64.9	69.4	75.4	72.2	65.7	59.5	54.2	62.6
1972	54.9	57.8	60.2	62.3	64.7	67.0	72.7	72.2	68.7	65.6	59.8	57.5	63.6
1973	55.6	59.9	58.1	61.5	63.4	68.0	69.1	70.5	68.8	66.8	60.6	58.2	63.4
1974	56.9	58.2	59.1	62.0	63.3	66.9	71.4	70.2	70.3	66.8	62.2	56.3	63.6
1975	56.1	56.4	57.5	58.7	62.2	65.0	69.4	68.9	71.5	65.9	60.4	56.9	62.4
1976	58.9	59.6	60.3	61.0	65.2	69.7	71.1	72.4	73.8	71.2	66.8	60.7	65.9
1977	60.3	61.7	57.5	61.4	61.9	65.8	71.6	73.1	72.2	68.9	64.9	63.3	65.2
1978	61.0	60.9	64.3	63.4	68.2	71.3	71.6	72.9	74.0	70.1	61.7	55.2	66.2
1979	56.9	56.9	60.1	63.4	65.6	70.2	71.8	73.9	76.3	68.7	62.4	60.6	65.6
1980	61.1	63.5	61.5	63.9	63.8	68.5	72.9	74.2	70.4	67.3	62.7	60.8	65.9
1981	61.3	62.2	61.1	64.4	67.3	72.9	75.6	75.8	73.7	67.1	63.5	60.3	67.1
1982	56.6	60.7	60.5	63.8	65.8	66.7	71.9	73.5	73.1	70.1	62.1	57.4	65.2
1983	60.7	60.9	62.0	62.4	66.2	68.1	72.6	77.4	76.8	72.2	64.4	60.6	67.0
1984	61.2	60.2	63.7	64.3	68.1	69.9	77.2	76.6	78.9	68.5	61.4	56.7	67.2
1985	57.0	57.2	58.9	63.6	64.8	69.0	75.3	72.4	69.8	67.9	60.1	58.0	64.5
1986	61.0	58.9	60.5	62.8	64.6	67.4	69.6	71.8	66.9	65.5	62.8	57.6	64.1
1987	55.4	58.0	59.1	63.4	64.7	65.8	67.1	69.9	69.9	69.5	61.8	53.9	63.2
1988	56.7	59.9	61.6	62.4	63.9	64.9	70.4	71.0	70.0	66.7	60.1	56.0	63.6
1989	54.7	56.7	59.8	65.6	63.7	66.0	70.1	71.0	70.4	66.3	63.1	58.7	63.8
1990	56.6	55.2	58.7	63.2	64.3	69.0	72.3	71.6	71.7	68.6	62.7	55.6	64.1
1991	57.4	59.4	56.5	61.7	62.1	64.1	67.4	68.9	69.4	68.0	62.3	57.3	62.9
1992	57.4	61.1	60.4	67.0	68.0	68.1	71.8	74.9	72.4	68.2	62.6	55.3	65.6
1993	56.9	58.0	61.3	63.8	66.0	68.6	69.8	70.2	69.0	67.3	61.6	57.0	64.1
Record Mean	55.5	56.6	58.0	60.3	62.4	65.2	68.8	70.3	68.8	65.2	60.9	57.0	62.4
Max	63.8	64.4	65.1	66.7	67.8	70.4	74.1	75.6	74.9	72.2	69.4	65.5	69.2
Min	47.3	48.8	50.8	53.8	57.0	59.9	63.5	64.9	62.8	58.2	52.3	48.5	55.6

REFERENCE NOTES

SAN DIEGO, CALIFORNIA

GENERAL
T - TRACE AMOUNT.
BLANK ENTRIES DENOTE MISSING/UNREPORTED DATA.
# INDICATES A STATION OR INSTRUMENT RELOCATION.

SPECIFIC

PM - INCLUDES LAST DAY OF PREVIOUS MONTH
ASOS - AUTOMATED SURFACE OBSERVING SYSTEM IN OPERATION DURING THESE MONTHS.

(a) - LENGTH OF RECORD IN YEARS, ALTHOUGH INDIVIDUAL MONTHS MAY BE MISSING.
0.* OR * - THE VALUE IS BETWEEN 0.0 AND 0.05
NORMALS - BASED ON THE 1961-1990 RECORD PERIOD.
EXTREMES - DATES ARE THE MOST RECENT OCCURRENCE.
WIND DIR. - NUMERALS SHOW TENS OF DEGRESS CLOCKWISE FROM TRUE NORTH. "00" INDICATES CALM.
RESULTANT DIRECTIONS ARE GIVEN TO WHOLE DEGREES.
BOLD VALUES INDICATE EXTREME VALUES WHICH OCCURRED AFTER THE ASOS SYSTEM WAS COMMISSIONED.

RECORD = PERIOD OF RECORD
RECORD MEAN PRECIPITATION IS THE MEAN OF ALL DAILY PRECIPITATION AMOUNTS DURING THE PERIOD OF RECORD.
RECORD MAX(MIN) TEMPERATURE IS THE MEAN OF ALL DAILY MAX(MIN) TEMPERATURES DURING THE PERIOD OF RECORD.
RECORD MEAN TEMPERATURE IS THE SUM OF THE RECORD MAX AND RECORD MIN DIVIDED BY 2.
AVERAGE TEMPERATURE IS THE SUM OF THE MEAN DAILY MAX AND MIN TEMPERATURE DIVIDED BY 2.

EXCEPTIONS

RECORD MEANS ARE THROUGH THE CURRENT YEAR, BEGINNING IN 1875 FOR TEMPERATURE
1850 FOR PRECIPITATION
1941 FOR SNOWFALL

HEATING DEGREE DAYS Base 65 deg. F — SAN DIEGO, CALIFORNIA

SEASON	JULY	AUG	SEP	OCT	NOV	DEC	JAN	FEB	MAR	APR	MAY	JUNE	TOTAL
1964-65	0	0	0	8	187	280	277	249	195	138	73	35	1442
1965-66	3	0	0	9	118	303	335	284	209	107	40	4	1412
1966-67	0	0	0	4	113	236	302	197	183	245	72	48	1400
1967-68	0	0	0	3	42	288	239	119	135	85	47	8	966
1968-69	0	0	0	9	104	306	214	274	248	101	63	9	1328
1969-70	0	0	0	14	44	178	240	142	133	143	58	12	964
1970-71	0	0	0	12	107	290	331	266	215	143	109	29	1502
1971-72	0	0	0	78	160	326	310	203	139	78	34	0	1328
1972-73	0	0	0	29	149	224	286	131	208	107	61	1	1196
1973-74	0	0	0	6	132	205	243	184	176	85	55	4	1090
1974-75	0	0	0	14	97	265	273	237	225	182	83	10	1386
1975-76	0	0	0	19	141	246	196	150	148	115	16	0	1031
1976-77	0	0	0	0	39	129	143	94	224	103	88	3	823
1977-78	0	0	0	0	37	55	117	117	52	43	8	0	429
1978-79	0	0	0	0	102	297	244	219	153	45	20	6	1086
1979-80	0	0	0	4	75	136	117	50	104	61	43	1	591
1980-81	0	0	0	6	75	133	113	101	116	40	1	0	585
1981-82	0	0	0	9	57	136	258	119	139	64	9	2	793
1982-83	0	0	0	1	93	228	137	110	88	83	9	0	749
1983-84	0	0	0	0	66	130	123	134	51	43	4	0	551
1984-85	0	0	0	4	104	250	238	219	183	60	18	2	1078
1985-86	0	0	0	3	145	211	118	173	132	85	29	0	896
1986-87	0	0	7	10	66	223	291	197	178	72	21	6	1071
1987-88	0	0	0	0	98	338	250	147	125	85	53	22	1118
1988-89	0	0	0	4	141	275	313	237	158	37	40	14	1219
1989-90	0	0	1	13	67	188	252	268	185	52	39	1	1066
1990-91	0	0	0	3	88	284	227	152	254	104	96	28	1236
1991-92	0	0	0	24	96	231	228	115	136	8	1	0	839
1992-93	0	0	0	0	84	294	240	191	111	44	7	6	977
1993-94	0	0	0	4	103	242							

COOLING DEGREE DAYS Base 65 deg. F — SAN DIEGO, CALIFORNIA

YEAR	JAN	FEB	MAR	APR	MAY	JUNE	JULY	AUG	SEP	OCT	NOV	DEC	TOTAL
1969	5	0	1	9	3	31	144	247	154	53	26	5	678
1970	0	1	1	1	21	40	172	247	145	58	7	0	693
1971	5	3	0	19	7	31	142	327	224	107	1	0	866
1972	0	0	0	4	33	68	247	230	117	53	0	1	753
1973	0	0	0	10	17	97	133	176	121	70	8	1	633
1974	0	0	0	2	9	69	204	169	164	75	19	0	711
1975	0	0	0	0	1	18	142	124	201	54	8	0	548
1976	14	0	10	3	31	147	196	240	269	200	102	0	1212
1977	5	9	0	2	1	34	212	258	224	128	40	8	921
1978	1	7	38	4	115	194	213	251	276	166	11	0	1276
1979	0	0	10	6	46	169	216	283	348	124	5	8	1215
1980	2	13	3	35	15	110	253	289	170	86	15	7	998
1981	7	29	0	26	81	244	335	343	265	80	21	0	1431
1982	0	7	6	32	42	58	219	271	250	164	12	0	1061
1983	11	0	1	9	51	99	242	392	364	231	55	0	1455
1984	13	0	15	31	107	156	387	366	422	119	4	0	1620
1985	0	7	0	22	19	128	325	235	153	104	6	0	999
1986	2	11	4	29	23	78	152	218	73	31	9	0	630
1987	0	6	5	29	17	35	71	158	154	147	10	0	632
1988	0	5	28	16	25	26	176	193	161	64	0	5	699
1989	0	13	2	63	5	48	165	193	168	58	17	0	732
1990	0	0	2	6	21	127	233	211	209	123	25	0	957
1991	0	0	0	9	11	10	80	130	138	122	21	0	521
1992	0	12	1	72	99	100	216	313	228	106	20	0	1167
1993	0	0	4	12	47	119	155	170	126	81	8	0	722

SNOWFALL (inches) — SAN DIEGO, CALIFORNIA

SEASON	JULY	AUG	SEP	OCT	NOV	DEC	JAN	FEB	MAR	APR	MAY	JUNE	TOTAL
1970-71	0.0	0.0	0.0	0.0	0.0	0.0	0.0	0.0	0.0	0.0	0.0	0.0	0.0
1971-72	0.0	0.0	0.0	0.0	0.0	0.0	0.0	0.0	0.0	0.0	0.0	0.0	0.0
1972-73	0.0	0.0	0.0	0.0	0.0	0.0	0.0	0.0	0.0	0.0	0.0	0.0	0.0
1973-74	0.0	0.0	0.0	0.0	0.0	0.0	0.0	0.0	0.0	0.0	0.0	0.0	0.0
1974-75	0.0	0.0	0.0	0.0	0.0	0.0	0.0	0.0	0.0	0.0	0.0	0.0	0.0
1975-76	0.0	0.0	0.0	0.0	0.0	0.0	0.0	0.0	0.0	0.0	0.0	0.0	0.0
1976-77	0.0	0.0	0.0	0.0	0.0	0.0	0.0	0.0	0.0	0.0	0.0	0.0	0.0
1977-78	0.0	0.0	0.0	0.0	0.0	0.0	0.0	0.0	0.0	0.0	0.0	0.0	0.0
1978-79	0.0	0.0	0.0	0.0	0.0	0.0	0.0	0.0	0.0	0.0	0.0	0.0	0.0
1979-80	0.0	0.0	0.0	0.0	0.0	0.0	0.0	0.0	0.0	0.0	0.0	0.0	0.0
1980-81	0.0	0.0	0.0	0.0	0.0	0.0	0.0	0.0	0.0	0.0	0.0	0.0	0.0
1981-82	0.0	0.0	0.0	0.0	0.0	0.0	0.0	0.0	0.0	0.0	0.0	0.0	0.0
1982-83	0.0	0.0	0.0	0.0	0.0	0.0	0.0	0.0	0.0	0.0	0.0	0.0	0.0
1983-84	0.0	0.0	0.0	0.0	0.0	0.0	0.0	0.0	0.0	0.0	0.0	0.0	0.0
1984-85	0.0	0.0	0.0	0.0	0.0	0.0	0.0	0.0	T	0.0	0.0	0.0	T
1985-86	0.0	0.0	0.0	0.0	T	0.0	0.0	0.0	0.0	0.0	0.0	0.0	T
1986-87	0.0	0.0	0.0	0.0	0.0	0.0	0.0	0.0	0.0	0.0	0.0	0.0	0.0
1987-88	0.0	0.0	0.0	0.0	0.0	0.0	0.0	0.0	0.0	0.0	0.0	0.0	0.0
1988-89	0.0	0.0	0.0	0.0	0.0	0.0	0.0	0.0	0.0	0.0	0.0	0.0	0.0
1989-90	0.0	0.0	0.0	0.0	0.0	0.0	0.0	0.0	0.0	0.0	0.0	0.0	0.0
1990-91	0.0	0.0	0.0	0.0	0.0	0.0	0.0	0.0	0.0	0.0	0.0	0.0	0.0
1991-92	0.0	0.0	0.0	0.0	0.0	0.0	0.0	0.0	0.0	0.0	0.0	0.0	0.0
1992-93	0.0	0.0	0.0	0.0	0.0	0.0	0.0	0.0	0.0	0.0	0.0	0.0	0.0
1993-94	0.0	0.0	0.0	0.0	0.0	0.0							
Record Mean	0.0	0.0	0.0	0.0	T	T	T	0.0	T	0.0	0.0	0.0	T

SAN FRANCISCO, CALIFORNIA
MISSION DOLORES

San Francisco is located at the northern end of a narrow peninsula which separates San Francisco Bay from the Pacific Ocean. It is known as the air conditioned city with cool pleasant summers and mild winters. Flowers bloom throughout the year and warm clothing may be needed at times during any month.

Precipitation averages about 20 inches a year with pronounced wet and dry seasons, characteristic of its Mediterranean climate. Little or no rain falls from June through September while about 80 percent of the annual total falls from November through March. Snow is extremely rare. Measurable amounts fall about once every 15 years. Freezing temperatures are also extremely rare. On average, thunderstorms occur on only two days each year. The average annual wind speed is about 9 mph with lighter winds, 6 to 7 mph, occurring in the winter and stronger winds, 10 to 11 mph, in the summer.

San Francisco probably has greater climatic variability by far with respect to temperature, cloudiness, and sunshine within its 49 square mile area than any other similarly sized urban area in the country. Likewise, the San Francisco Bay area has considerably more variability than San Francisco itself.

Sea fogs, and the low stratus clouds associated with them are most common in the summertime, but may occur at any time of the year. In the summer the temperature of the Pacific Ocean is much lower than the temperature inland, particularly in the Central Valley of California. This condition tends to enhance the sea breeze effect common to coastal areas. Brisk westerly winds blow throughout the afternoon and evening hours. The fog is carried inland by these westerly winds in the late afternoon and evening and then evaporates during the subsequent forenoon.

The complex topography of San Francisco causes complex patterns of fog and sun as well as temperature. A range of hills with elevations of nearly 1000 feet above sea level, bisects the city from north to south. This range partially blocks the inland movement of the fog, but gaps in the hills permit small masses of fog to pass through, further complicating the pattern. Occasionally, the fog will reach 50 miles south to San Jose, while the area just to the lee of the highest hills is still mostly clear.

Sunshine varies greatly from one part of the city to another, especially in the summer. Spring and fall are the sunniest seasons. In the summer the sunniest area is a triangular shaped area to the lee of the highest hills and extending to the bay. The least sunny area is along the ocean due to the high frequency of fog there. The percent of possible summer sunshine varies from an estimated 25 to 35 percent at the ocean to 70 to 80 percent in the sunniest area.

The extent and behavior of the summertime fog on a particular day depends on several factors. A typical day would find the fog covering the entire city at sunrise and little wind. During the forenoon the skies become sunny in the eastern part of the city with some partial clearing reaching the ocean for a couple of hours in the early afternoon. By early afternoon the winds pick up and by late afternoon the fog is rolling inland again. The wind usually reaches a maximum velocity in the early evening.

In the winter relatively little difference in the climate is observed from one part of the city to another. This is due to the lack of temperature contrast between the ocean and the land and to the relative frequency of passage of Pacific frontal systems. However, those areas near the ocean have more sunshine than areas further inland. The source region for fog is inland during winter, mainly in the Central Valley, rather than the ocean.

Temperature patterns in the city are the same as those of sunshine. In the winter there is little variation, with average maximums from 55 to 60 degrees and average minimums in the mid to upper 40s. Average temperatures rise until June and remain nearly constant through August with average maximums in the lower 60s near the ocean and upper 60s in the sunny eastern half of the city. Summer minimums range from 50 to 55. The warmest time of the year is September and October when the fog diminishes greatly and some of the warmth from the Central Valley flows westward. At this time of year the average maximums are in the mid 60s near the ocean and in the mid 70s in the warmest areas of the city. The average minimums are about the same as they are during the summer.

NORMALS, MEANS, AND EXTREMES

SAN FRANCISCO, CALIFORNIA MISSION DOLORES

LATITUDE: 37°46'N LONGITUDE: 122°26' W ELEVATION: FT. GRND 75 BARO TIME ZONE: PACIFIC WBAN: 23272

	(a)	JAN	FEB	MAR	APR	MAY	JUNE	JULY	AUG	SEP	OCT	NOV	DEC	YEAR
TEMPERATURE °F:														
Normals														
-Daily Maximum		56.3	60.0	60.8	62.1	62.7	64.1	64.6	65.6	68.7	68.7	62.7	56.4	62.7
-Daily Minimum		45.8	48.7	49.0	49.8	50.5	52.6	53.5	54.6	55.9	55.2	51.6	47.0	51.2
-Monthly		51.1	54.4	54.9	56.0	56.6	58.4	59.1	60.1	62.3	62.0	57.2	51.7	57.0
Extremes														
-Record Highest	57	79	81	83	94	96	101	103	98	101	102	86	76	103
-Year		1962	1986	1952	1989	1976	1961	1988	1993	1971	1987	1966	1958	JUL 1988
-Record Lowest	57	30	31	38	40	44	47	47	48	48	45	41	28	28
-Year		1937	1989	1942	1967	1964	1955	1953	1969	1955	1949	1985	1990	DEC 1990
NORMAL DEGREE DAYS:														
Heating (base 65°F)		431	297	313	275	260	198	187	156	116	123	237	412	3005
Cooling (base 65°F)		0	0	0	0	0	0	0	0	35	30	0	0	65
% OF POSSIBLE SUNSHINE	38	56	62	69	73	72	73	66	65	72	70	62	53	66
MEAN SKY COVER (tenths)														
Sunrise - Sunset														
MEAN NUMBER OF DAYS:														
Sunrise to Sunset														
-Clear														
-Partly Cloudy														
-Cloudy														
Precipitation														
.01 inches or more	57	10.7	10.1	10.7	6.1	3.1	1.3	0.5	0.9	1.5	4.3	7.9	10.1	67.2
Snow, Ice pellets, hail														
1.0 inches or more	37	0.0	0.0	0.0	0.0	0.0	0.0	0.0	0.0	0.0	0.0	0.0	0.0	0.0
Thunderstorms	29	0.3	0.2	0.1	0.3	0.2	0.1	0.2	0.*	0.3	0.2	0.1	0.3	2.2
Heavy Fog Visibility 1/4 mile or less														
Temperature °F														
-Maximum														
90° and above	57	0.0	0.0	0.0	0.1	0.2	0.4	0.2	0.1	1.0	0.4	0.0	0.0	2.3
32° and below	57	0.0	0.0	0.0	0.0	0.0	0.0	0.0	0.0	0.0	0.0	0.0	0.0	0.0
-Minimum														
32° and below	57	0.1	0.*	0.0	0.0	0.0	0.0	0.0	0.0	0.0	0.0	0.0	0.1	0.2
0° and below	57	0.0	0.0	0.0	0.0	0.0	0.0	0.0	0.0	0.0	0.0	0.0	0.0	0.0
AVG. STATION PRESS. (mb)														
RELATIVE HUMIDITY (%)														
Hour 04	7	81	83	81	82	89	89	92	93	87	81	82	80	85
Hour 10 (Local Time)	7	72	70	61	59	65	70	73	73	64	62	69	71	67
Hour 16	7	63	63	61	61	68	72	74	73	66	60	63	63	66
Hour 22	7	76	78	76	80	86	88	90	90	82	74	76	74	81
PRECIPITATION (inches):														
Water Equivalent														
-Normal		4.06	2.95	3.07	1.29	0.25	0.15	0.04	0.07	0.26	1.26	3.21	3.10	19.71
-Maximum Monthly	57	10.69	8.49	9.04	5.47	3.19	1.42	0.62	0.78	2.06	5.51	8.20	11.47	11.47
-Year		1952	1938	1983	1958	1957	1967	1974	1976	1959	1962	1983	1955	DEC 1955
-Minimum Monthly	57	0.31	0.04	0.07	T	0.00	0.00	0.00	0.00	0.00	0.00	T	0.00	0.00
-Year		1976	1953	1988	1949	1982	1983	1982	1982	1980	1980	1959	1989	DEC 1989
-Maximum in 24 hrs	57	4.22	2.34	3.65	2.36	1.47	1.36	0.61	0.49	2.06	3.11	2.72	3.14	4.22
-Year		1982	1940	1940	1953	1990	1967	1974	1965	1959	1962	1973	1945	JAN 1982
Snow, Ice pellets, hail														
-Maximum Monthly	40	T	T	T	0.0	0.0	0.0	0.0	0.0	0.0	0.0	0.0	T	T
-Year		1962	1951	1951									1972	DEC 1972
-Maximum in 24 hrs	36	T	T	T	0.0	0.0	0.0	0.0	0.0	0.0	0.0	0.0	T	T
-Year		1962	1951	1951									1941	JAN 1962
WIND:														
Mean Speed (mph)	28	6.7	7.5	8.5	9.5	10.4	10.9	11.2	10.5	9.1	7.6	6.3	6.5	8.7
Prevailing Direction through 1963		N	W	W	W	W	W	W	W	W	W	W	N	W
Fastest Mile														
-Direction (!!)	36	SE	SW	S	W	W	W	W	W	W	SE	S	SE	SE
-Speed (MPH)	36	47	47	44	38	38	40	38	34	32	43	41	45	47
-Year		1965	1938	1948	1965	1965	1965	1939	1966	1956	1950	1953	1965	JAN 1965
Peak Gust														
-Direction (!!)														
-Speed (mph)														
-Date														

PRECIPITATION (inches)

SAN FRANCISCO, CALIFORNIA MISSION DOLORES

YEAR	JAN	FEB	MAR	APR	MAY	JUNE	JULY	AUG	SEP	OCT	NOV	DEC	ANNUAL
1964	3.37	0.19	2.12	0.01	0.22	0.57	T	0.01	T	1.90	3.99	5.35	17.73
1965	3.97	0.94	2.92	3.21	T	T	0.02	0.49	T	0.01	4.79	3.51	19.86
1966	3.27	2.72	0.80	0.36	0.19	0.17	0.06	0.10	0.10	0.01	4.80	3.87	16.45
1967	9.49	0.22	4.35	4.90	0.09	1.42	0.00	T	0.04	0.53	1.10	2.12	24.26
1968	4.54	2.28	3.15	0.48	0.22	T	T	0.03	0.06	0.62	2.67	3.91	17.96
1969	7.74	7.26	1.01	1.74	T	0.05	T	T	0.01	2.61	0.45	6.15	27.02
1970	7.81	1.56	1.55	0.06	0.03	0.57	T	T	0.00	0.84	6.44	5.39	24.25
1971	2.04	0.26	2.91	0.72	0.19	T	0.01	0.01	0.22	0.11	1.92	3.93	12.32
1972	1.32	2.13	0.23	1.07	T	0.11	0.01	0.04	0.54	5.41	6.40	3.53	20.79
1973	9.38	6.32	2.63	0.02	0.08	0.00	0.00	0.00	0.30	1.62	7.80	3.65	31.80
1974	3.40	1.53	4.49	2.34	0.00	0.10	0.62	0.00	0.00	0.85	0.40	1.53	15.26
1975	2.57	3.72	5.15	1.25	0.02	0.04	0.20	0.02	0.00	2.44	0.43	0.18	16.02
1976	0.31	1.83	1.01	0.70	0.01	0.03	0.00	0.78	0.51	0.38	1.04	2.13	8.73
1977	1.65	0.90	2.01	0.05	0.57	0.00	0.00	0.03	0.86	0.17	1.96	3.30	11.50
1978	6.20	3.54	5.20	3.82	0.00	0.00	0.00	0.00	0.20	0.00	1.67	0.89	21.52
1979	6.74	4.96	1.58	0.87	0.15	0.00	0.07	0.00	0.01	1.66	2.98	3.10	22.12
1980	3.77	4.84	1.25	0.97	0.23	0.02	0.04	0.00	0.00	0.00	0.14	2.95	14.21
1981	4.00	1.78	3.71	0.17	0.12	0.00	0.00	0.00	0.22	1.74	3.73	4.15	19.62
1982	6.84	3.26	7.65	3.03	0.00	0.06	0.00	0.00	0.72	2.79	5.62	2.22	32.19
1983	5.77	8.06	9.04	3.48	0.47	0.00	0.01	0.06	0.68	0.26	8.20	7.72	43.75
1984	0.50	2.34	1.32	0.92	0.16	0.30	0.00	0.24	0.10	2.94	7.45	2.10	18.37
1985	0.59	1.98	3.94	0.27	0.09	0.31	0.00	0.00	0.38	0.80	4.83	2.47	15.66
1986	4.77	8.29	6.25	0.76	0.13	0.00	0.03	0.01	1.32	0.11	0.20	1.64	23.51
1987	4.26	3.77	2.31	0.14	0.06	0.01	0.00	0.00	0.00	1.07	3.09	5.09	19.80
1988	4.93	0.40	0.07	1.73	0.66	0.70	0.00	0.00	0.00	0.64	3.70	4.23	17.06
1989	1.26	1.49	5.28	0.70	0.06	0.07	0.00	0.05	0.98	1.18	1.33	0.00	12.40
1990	4.02	2.45	1.34	0.58	2.38	0.01	0.00	0.04	0.12	0.20	0.52	1.94	13.60
1991	0.60	3.29	5.89	1.07	0.36	0.05	0.00	0.42	0.00	2.35	0.50	2.32	16.85
1992	2.09	6.34	4.41	0.38	0.00	0.39	0.00	0.02	0.00	1.16	0.40	6.03	21.22
1993	9.82	4.48	2.90	0.71	0.87	0.27	0.00	0.00	0.00	0.33	2.16	2.25	23.79
Record Mean	4.54	3.55	3.08	1.47	0.58	0.15	0.02	0.03	0.28	1.01	2.48	4.09	21.27

AVERAGE TEMPERATURE (deg. F)

SAN FRANCISCO, CALIFORNIA MISSION DOLORES

YEAR	JAN	FEB	MAR	APR	MAY	JUNE	JULY	AUG	SEP	OCT	NOV	DEC	ANNUAL
1964	51.0	55.0	53.2	53.8	53.4	57.8	58.9	60.0	62.4	63.1	55.3	53.7	56.5
1965	51.4	54.0	54.4	55.7	54.9	56.2	57.4	61.2	61.2	65.0	58.1	48.3	56.5
1966	52.1	51.8	53.8	57.9	55.1	59.4	58.2	58.8	63.6	62.6	57.2	51.3	56.8
1967	52.6	53.2	52.7	50.8	57.9	57.1	58.9	59.2	63.5	65.5	60.0	51.9	57.0
1968	49.8	56.7	56.7	56.2	55.7	59.0	58.0	62.3	63.1	60.5	56.2	49.8	57.0
1969	48.6	50.1	54.3	54.2	57.0	58.7	57.6	59.4	60.9	61.9	59.3	55.8	56.5
1970	54.0	57.4	57.8	53.3	57.7	56.8	57.8	57.2	64.4	58.6	57.9	50.6	57.0
1971	50.8	51.9	53.3	53.1	54.6	57.3	57.5	61.1	64.7	57.8	55.6	49.0	55.6
1972	48.5	54.0	55.8	55.5	55.5	57.5	60.9	60.2	61.5	61.7	54.9	47.2	56.1
1973	50.1	54.9	52.5	57.2	56.3	60.7	58.6	57.1	61.3	61.0	55.3	52.0	56.4
1974	51.1	52.2	53.3	55.4	54.9	58.2	59.6	59.9	60.3	62.2	56.6	51.1	56.3
1975	51.0	53.3	53.1	51.9	57.2	56.9	58.9	59.5	59.5	59.7	55.6	53.4	55.8
1976	53.4	52.8	52.5	54.1	56.8	61.5	59.2	62.5	62.2	62.8	60.4	54.6	57.8
1977	49.9	56.1	53.2	56.1	55.3	57.1	59.0	61.6	62.0	60.6	58.6	54.9	57.0
1978	55.0	55.2	59.0	56.3	60.7	58.9	58.4	60.6	65.5	61.9	55.9	49.6	58.1
1979	51.0	52.9	55.7	56.5	59.2	58.6	60.2	60.8	66.3	63.2	57.7	55.4	58.1
1980	53.0	57.2	56.0	56.9	55.4	57.9	59.5	58.0	61.3	62.0	58.3	53.4	57.4
1981	52.4	56.1	54.9	55.8	56.8	62.2	57.8	59.2	60.4	59.3	58.3	54.0	57.3
1982	48.5	55.0	52.8	55.6	55.8	56.3	57.9	60.1	62.6	62.8	54.4	52.2	56.2
1983	49.4	54.6	55.3	56.8	59.7	61.8	63.4	65.9	67.1	64.0	56.1	52.8	58.9
1984	51.6	52.6	56.7	54.2	59.9	59.7	63.9	62.8	69.4	61.5	56.0	50.9	58.3
1985	50.0	56.0	53.2	59.8	58.1	63.9	64.1	64.1	64.1	63.2	55.0	51.3	58.6
1986	56.6	58.9	60.4	58.6	60.0	63.2	62.8	61.9	62.8	63.6	60.2	52.5	60.1
1987	51.8	56.4	57.1	60.5	61.1	60.5	61.5	63.5	63.8	65.1	58.8	52.3	59.4
1988	52.8	57.7	59.1	58.8	59.1	61.1	64.2	64.0	63.1	61.5	57.3	53.3	59.3
1989	51.3	50.0	55.4	60.9	59.3	61.6	62.4	63.0	61.8	62.0	58.8	52.6	58.3
1990	52.8	52.0	54.9	59.2	59.0	62.4	62.9	65.3	66.0	64.2	58.0	49.1	58.8
1991	53.4	57.9	53.2	57.1	56.8	58.6	61.3	63.0	63.1	64.4	60.1	53.4	58.5
1992	51.5	58.4	59.2	62.6	62.7	62.5	65.1	63.8	65.8	66.7	59.8	51.7	60.8
1993	51.1	53.8	59.0	59.4	62.5	65.9	63.4	66.6	63.4	64.3	58.2	51.5	59.9
Record Mean	50.5	53.3	54.6	55.9	57.1	59.1	59.2	59.8	62.1	61.3	57.0	51.7	56.8
Max	55.7	59.0	60.7	62.3	63.4	65.6	65.2	65.7	69.0	68.4	63.1	56.7	62.9
Min	45.3	47.5	48.5	49.4	50.8	52.6	53.2	54.0	55.2	54.1	50.9	46.7	50.7

REFERENCE NOTES

SAN FRANCISCO, CALIFORNIA MISSION DOLORES

GENERAL
T - TRACE AMOUNT.
BLANK ENTRIES DENOTE MISSING/UNREPORTED DATA.
# INDICATES A STATION OR INSTRUMENT RELOCATION.

SPECIFIC

PM - INCLUDES LAST DAY OF PREVIOUS MONTH
ASOS - AUTOMATED SURFACE OBSERVING SYSTEM IN OPERATION DURING THESE MONTHS.

(●) - LENGTH OF RECORD IN YEARS, ALTHOUGH INDIVIDUAL MONTHS MAY BE MISSING.
0.* OR * - THE VALUE IS BETWEEN 0.0 AND 0.05
NORMALS - BASED ON THE 1961-1990 RECORD PERIOD.
EXTREMES - DATES ARE THE MOST RECENT OCCURRENCE
WIND DIR.- NUMERALS SHOW TENS OF DEGRESS CLOCKWISE FROM TRUE NORTH. "00" INDICATES CALM.
RESULTANT DIRECTIONS ARE GIVEN TO WHOLE DEGREES.
BOLD VALUES INDICATE EXTREME VALUES WHICH OCCURRED AFTER THE ASOS SYSTEM WAS COMMISSIONED.

RECORD = PERIOD OF RECORD
RECORD MEAN PRECIPITATION IS THE MEAN OF ALL DAILY PRECIPITATION AMOUNTS DURING THE PERIOD OF RECORD.
RECORD MAX(MIN) TEMPERATURE IS THE MEAN OF ALL DAILY MAX(MIN) TEMPERATURES DURING THE PERIOD OF RECORD.
RECORD MEAN TEMPERATURE IS THE SUM OF THE RECORD MAX AND RECORD MIN DIVIDED BY 2.
AVERAGE TEMPERATURE IS THE SUM OF THE MEAN DAILY MAX AND MIN TEMPERATURE DIVIDED BY 2.

EXCEPTIONS

1. THUNDERSTORM DATA ARE THROUGH 1964 AND MAY BE INCOMPLETE, DUE TO PART-TIME OPERATIONS.
2. MEAN WIND SPEED ARE THROUGH 1964.
3. RELATIVE HUMIDITY, SNOW, AND DAYS SNOW 1.0 INCH OR MORE ARE THROUGH 1972.
3. FASTEST MILE WINDS ARE THROUGH MARCH 1973.
4. PERCENT OF POSSIBLE SUNSHINE IS THROUGH 1973.

RECORD MEANS ARE THROUGH THE CURRENT YEAR, BEGINNING IN 1875 FOR TEMPERATURE
1850 FOR PRECIPITATION
1939 FOR SNOWFALL

HEATING DEGREE DAYS Base 65 deg. F — SAN FRANCISCO, CALIFORNIA MISSION DOLORES

SEASON	JULY	AUG	SEP	OCT	NOV	DEC	JAN	FEB	MAR	APR	MAY	JUNE	TOTAL
1964-65	186	152	139	100	284	343	414	302	319	280	306	259	3084
1965-66	230	123	120	73	199	509	393	362	336	217	300	182	3044
1966-67	205	188	78	102	241	417	375	325	372	420	230	229	3182
1967-68	184	173	67	47	158	398	465	235	254	263	280	174	2698
1968-69	213	98	92	148	258	462	505	412	333	315	242	185	3263
1969-70	221	171	132	107	166	277	334	210	222	341	237	242	2660
1970-71	231	246	95	201	208	439	433	359	354	351	317	230	3464
1971-72	225	120	85	229	275	490	506	312	279	278	287	226	3312
1972-73	144	139	110	115	298	546	455	277	380	225	267	167	3123
1973-74	199	239	137	134	285	396	423	353	354	284	309	202	3315
1974-75	167	153	153	119	243	422	428	320	360	386	257	238	3246
1975-76	185	170	177	164	276	352	353	344	378	321	262	179	3161
1976-77	173	86	114	102	152	315	463	242	359	261	294	233	2794
1977-78	197	116	93	139	187	304	304	269	188	254	154	177	2382
1978-79	196	137	43	138	268	471	431	332	281	250	185	197	2929
1979-80	151	125	23	64	213	293	366	221	275	240	291	218	2480
1980-81	165	212	132	128	201	350	384	243	304	284	248	121	2772
1981-82	220	175	136	174	196	334	506	273	369	278	281	253	3195
1982-83	210	151	82	90	311	391	478	283	296	238	174	112	2816
1983-84	83	14	30	52	257	369	408	354	251	321	172	159	2470
1984-85	70	84	19	117	263	430	459	254	359	173	209	57	2494
1985-86	71	49	35	99	302	419	254	172	146	196	154	67	1964
1986-87	78	93	63	84	152	383	399	233	243	140	154	147	2169
1987-88	106	52	50	60	179	387	370	207	183	197	196	125	2112
1988-89	60	53	79	137	229	358	419	416	289	171	181	129	2521
1989-90	86	68	94	113	183	377	371	357	305	170	188	97	2409
1990-91	74	23	8	56	204	487	351	192	358	234	248	188	2423
1991-92	129	74	74	74	150	350	414	186	171	87	75	76	1860
1992-93	30	51	28	31	163	406	423	310	178	163	90	49	1922
1993-94	73	33	74	63	204	411							

COOLING DEGREE DAYS Base 65 deg. F — SAN FRANCISCO, CALIFORNIA MISSION DOLORES

YEAR	JAN	FEB	MAR	APR	MAY	JUNE	JULY	AUG	SEP	OCT	NOV	DEC	TOTAL
1969	0	0	5	0	1	1	0	0	14	20	3	0	44
1970	0	0	5	0	19	1	17	8	82	10	0	0	142
1971	0	0	0	0	0	7	0	6	83	12	0	0	108
1972	0	0	3	0	1	4	22	0	13	20	0	0	63
1973	0	0	0	2	5	43	8	0	34	15	0	0	107
1974	0	0	0	3	4	3	4	3	19	41	0	0	77
1975	0	0	0	0	23	0	4	8	15	5	0	0	55
1976	0	0	0	0	16	82	0	15	37	41	15	0	206
1977	0	0	0	0	0	1	18	17	8	8	0	0	52
1978	0	0	8	2	30	0	0	6	65	46	3	0	160
1979	0	0	0	0	11	13	10	3	72	16	0	0	125
1980	0	0	0	5	0	12	2	3	29	43	3	0	97
1981	0	0	0	13	1	44	6	3	3	5	2	0	77
1982	0	0	0	7	1	0	0	8	16	27	0	0	59
1983	0	0	0	0	16	21	41	50	101	27	0	0	256
1984	0	0	0	5	20	5	42	20	158	14	0	0	264
1985	0	7	0	24	2	28	50	27	16	49	8	0	211
1986	0	7	10	8	6	22	17	1	4	49	12	0	136
1987	0	0	5	12	38	19	5	14	22	68	0	0	183
1988	0	3	6	18	20	12	42	27	30	34	3	0	195
1989	0	0	0	56	9	35	15	12	5	28	2	0	162
1990	0	0	0	5	8	25	18	39	45	40	1	0	181
1991	0	0	0	3	1	5	20	20	26	62	9	0	146
1992	0	2	0	21	13	9	41	23	61	93	10	0	273
1993	0	0	0	1	21	82	32	88	31	48	7	0	310

SNOWFALL (inches) — SAN FRANCISCO, CALIFORNIA MISSION DOLORES

SEASON	JULY	AUG	SEP	OCT	NOV	DEC	JAN	FEB	MAR	APR	MAY	JUNE	TOTAL
1964-65	0.0	0.0	0.0	0.0	0.0	0.0	0.0	0.0	0.0	0.0	0.0	0.0	0.0
1965-66	0.0	0.0	0.0	0.0	0.0	0.0	0.0	0.0	0.0	0.0	0.0	0.0	0.0
1966-67	0.0	0.0	0.0	0.0	0.0	0.0	0.0	0.0	0.0	0.0	0.0	0.0	0.0
1967-68	0.0	0.0	0.0	0.0	0.0	0.0	0.0	0.0	0.0	0.0	0.0	0.0	0.0
1968-69	0.0	0.0	0.0	0.0	0.0	0.0	0.0	0.0	0.0	0.0	0.0	0.0	0.0
1969-70	0.0	0.0	0.0	0.0	0.0	0.0	0.0	0.0	0.0	0.0	0.0	0.0	0.0
1970-71	0.0	0.0	0.0	0.0	0.0	0.0	0.0	0.0	0.0	0.0	0.0	0.0	0.0
1971-72	0.0	0.0	0.0	0.0	0.0	0.0	0.0	0.0	0.0	0.0	0.0	0.0	0.0
1972-73	0.0	0.0	0.0	0.0	0.0	T	0.0	0.0	0.0	0.0			
1973-74													
1975-76													
1976-77													
1977-78													
1978-79													
1979-80													
1980-81													
1981-82													
1982-83													
1983-84													
1984-85													
Record Mean	0.0	0.0	0.0	0.0	0.0	T	T	T	T	0.0	0.0	0.0	T

1993 COLORADO SPRINGS, COLORADO (COS)

At an elevation near 6,200 feet above sea level, Colorado Springs is located in relatively flat semi-arid country on the eastern slope of the Rocky Mountains. Immediately to the west the mountains rise abruptly to heights ranging from 10,000 to 14,000 feet but generally averaging near 11,000 feet. To the east lie gently undulating prairie lands. The land slopes upward to the north, reaching an average height of about 8,000 feet in 20 miles at the top of Palmer Lake Divide.

Colorado Springs is in the Arkansas River drainage basin. The principal tributary feeding the Arkansas from this area is Fountain Creek which rises in the high mountains west of the city and is fed by Monument Creek originating to the north in the Palmer Lake Divide area.

Other topographical features of the area, and particularly its wide range of elevations, help to give Colorado Springs the various and altogether delightful plains and mountain mixture of climate that has established the locality as a highly desirable place to live. The higher elevations immediately to the west and north of the city produce significant differences in temperature and precipitation. Precipitation amounts at these higher elevations are approximately twice those at nearby lower elevations and the number of rainy days is almost triple.

In Colorado Springs itself, precipitation is relatively sparse. Over 80 percent of it falls between April 1 and September 30, mostly as heavy downpours accompanying summer thunderstorms. Temperatures, in view of the station latitude and elevation, are mild. Uncomfortable extremes, in either summer or winter, are comparatively rare and of short duration. Relative humidity is normally low and wind movement moderately high. This is notably true of the west-to-east movement of the chinook winds, that cause rapid rises in winter temperatures and remind us that the Indian meaning of CHINOOK is SNOW EATER.

Colorado Springs is best known as a resort city, but is also important to the high-tech industry and military community. Several military installations, including the United States Air Force Academy and the Space Command are located within or near the city. The surrounding prairie is also important for cattle raising and a considerable amount of grazing land is used for sheep in the summer months. The growing season varies considerably in length but averages from the first week in May to the first week of October.

NORMALS, MEANS, AND EXTREMES FOR 1993

COLORADO SPRINGS, CO (COS)

LATITUDE: 38° 48' 43" N LONGTITUDE: 104° 42' 40" W ELEVATION (FT): GRND: 6145 BARO: 6093 TIME ZONE: MOUNTAIN (UTC+07) WBAN: 93037

	ELEMENT	POR	JAN	FEB	MAR	APR	MAY	JUN	JUL	AUG	SEP	OCT	NOV	DEC	YEAR
TEMPERATURE °F	NORMAL DAILY MAXIMUM	30	41.4	44.6	50.0	59.8	68.7	79.0	84.4	81.3	73.6	63.5	50.7	42.2	61.6
	MEAN DAILY MAXIMUM	45	42.0	45.1	49.8	59.7	68.6	79.3	86.5	83.9	76.3	65.5	51.6	44.4	62.7
	HIGHEST DAILY MAXIMUM	45	72	76	81	87	93	100	100	99	94	86	78	77	100
	YEAR OF OCCURRENCE		1974	1963	1971	1992	1984	1954	1954	1954	1990	1979	1981	1955	JUL 1954
	MEAN OF EXTREME MAXS.	16	62.4	65.6	69.4	79.6	83.9	92.9	95.6	92.1	88.1	79.8	70.7	63.8	78.7
	NORMAL DAILY MINIMUM	30	16.1	19.3	24.6	33.0	42.1	51.1	57.1	55.2	47.1	36.3	24.9	17.4	35.4
	MEAN DAILY MINIMUM	45	16.1	19.3	24.2	32.8	42.3	51.3	58.1	56.5	48.3	37.3	25.1	18.3	35.8
	LOWEST DAILY MINIMUM	45	-26	-27	-11	-3	21	32	42	39	22	5	-8	-24	-27
	YEAR OF OCCURRENCE		1951	1951	1956	1959	1954	1951	1952	1992	1985	1969	1976	1990	FEB 1951
	MEAN OF EXTREME MINS.	16	-1.4	-1.5	8.0	18.7	30.1	40.4	50.2	48.1	33.4	20.1	7.8	-2.4	21.0
	NORMAL DRY BULB	30	28.8	32.0	37.3	46.4	55.4	65.0	70.8	68.3	60.4	49.9	37.8	29.8	48.5
	MEAN DRY BULB	45	29.1	32.2	37.0	46.2	55.5	65.3	72.3	70.2	62.3	51.5	38.4	31.4	49.3
	MEAN WET BULB	44	22.4	25.1	29.0	36.0	44.1	51.7	56.7	55.8	48.6	39.1	29.4	23.8	38.5
	MEAN DEW POINT	44	10.1	12.6	16.4	22.9	33.0	40.8	47.7	47.4	38.0	26.4	17.3	11.5	27.0
	NORMAL NO. DAYS WITH:														
	MAXIMUM ≥ 90°	12	0.0	0.0	0.0	0.0	0.2	4.3	10.8	3.3	0.8	0.0	0.0	0.0	19.4
	MAXIMUM ≤ 32°	12	8.3	6.6	2.7	0.7	0.0	0.0	0.0	0.0	0.1	0.3	3.3	7.8	29.8
	MINIMUM ≤ 32°	12	30.3	26.2	25.1	12.8	2.1	0.0	0.0	0.0	1.1	9.1	24.4	29.3	160.4
	MINIMUM ≤ 0°	12	2.6	2.3	0.3	0.0	0.0	0.0	0.0	0.0	0.0	0.0	0.0	2.3	7.5
H/C	NORMAL HEATING DEG. DAYS	30	1122	924	859	558	302	87	6	18	164	468	816	1091	6415
	NORMAL COOLING DEG. DAYS	30	0	0	0	0	0	87	186	120	26	0	0	0	419
RH	NORMAL (PERCENT)	30	51	50	50	46	49	48	50	54	51	46	50	51	50
	HOUR 05 LST	30	56	59	61	61	66	66	68	70	66	58	59	56	62
	HOUR 11 LST	30	41	40	40	35	37	36	36	40	39	35	39	42	38
	HOUR 17 LST	30	46	41	38	34	36	34	39	41	37	36	44	48	40
	HOUR 23 LST	30	57	58	58	55	59	57	60	64	60	56	58	57	58
S	PERCENT POSSIBLE SUNSHINE														
W/O	MEAN NO. DAYS WITH:														
	HEAVY FOG(VISBY ≤ 1/4 MI)	45	2.3	2.5	2.5	2.0	1.8	0.8	0.5	1.0	1.9	1.8	2.3	2.2	21.6
	THUNDERSTORMS	45	0.0	0.0	0.5	2.3	8.2	11.0	15.6	13.1	4.6	0.8	0.0	0.0	56.1
CLOUDINESS	MEAN:														
	SUNRISE-SUNSET (TENTHS)	1		6.0	7.0	7.0		5.0	4.0	8.0	4.0	5.0	4.0	3.0	
	MIDNIGHT-MIDNIGHT (TENTHS)	1		6.0	8.0	7.0			4.0	8.0	4.0	6.0	4.0	3.0	
	MEAN NO. DAYS WITH:														
	CLEAR	1	13.0	10.0	11.0	8.0	1.0	8.0	11.0	7.0	15.0	13.0	12.0	20.0	129.0
	PARTLY CLOUDY	1	3.0	8.0	5.0	6.0		8.0	6.0	8.0	5.0	2.0	4.0	8.0	
	CLOUDY	1	4.0	9.0	9.0	8.0	1.0	5.0	3.0	13.0	6.0	9.0	3.0	1.0	71.0
PR	MEAN STATION PRESSURE(IN.)	21	23.89	23.89	23.82	23.88	23.90	23.98	24.06	24.07	24.04	24.00	23.91	23.90	23.94
	MEAN SEA-LEVEL PRES. (IN.)	44	30.09	30.06	29.96	29.92	29.90	29.88	29.95	29.97	29.99	30.05	30.08	30.09	30.00
WINDS	MEAN SPEED (MPH)	29	8.9	9.7	11.2	11.6	11.0	10.1	9.2	9.1	9.5	9.7	9.1	9.0	9.8
	PREVAIL.DIR(TENS OF DEGS.)	29	36	36	36	36	36	36	36	36	36	36	36	2	36
	MAXIMUM 2-MINUTE:														
	SPEED (MPH)	1	43	45	40	39	39	38	44	36	36	34	41	53	53
	DIR. (TENS OF DEGS.)	1	31	26	22	30	35	36	33	33	36	33	34	29	29
	YEAR OF OCCURRENCE		1993	1993	1993	1993	1993	1993	1993	1993	1993	1993	1993	1993	DEC 1993
	MAXIMUM 5-SECOND:														
	SPEED (MPH)	1	54	53	46	45	45	46	49	43	41	40	46	59	59
	DIR. (TENS OF DEGS.)	1	33	34	22	30	03	29	33	32	21	34	34	29	29
	YEAR OF OCCURRENCE		1993	1993	1993	1993	1993	1993	1993	1993	1993	1993	1993	1993	DEC 1993
PRECIPITATION	NORMAL TOTAL (IN.)	30	0.29	0.40	0.94	1.19	2.15	2.25	2.90	3.02	1.33	0.84	0.47	0.46	16.24
	MAXIMUM TOTAL (IN.)	45	1.17	2.45	2.38	5.90	5.67	8.00	5.27	6.06	4.28	5.01	2.21	1.05	8.00
	YEAR OF OCCURRENCE		1987	1987	1979	1957	1957	1965	1968	1986	1976	1984	1957	1988	JUN 1965
	MINIMUM TOTAL (IN.)	45	T	T	0.01	0.01	0.33	0.13	0.67	0.15	T	0.01	T	T	T
	YEAR OF OCCURRENCE		1964	1991	1966	1964	1974	1990	1987	1962	1953	1980	1965	1970	DEC 1970
	MAXIMUM IN 24 HOURS (IN.)	45	0.79	1.49	1.51	2.45	2.57	3.09	3.00	3.73	1.73	1.60	1.45	0.69	3.73
	YEAR OF OCCURRENCE		1987	1987	1987	1957	1955	1954	1951	1976	1959	1960	1979	1981	AUG 1976
	NORMAL NO. DAYS WITH:														
	PRECIPITATION ≥ 0.01	12	6.2	5.8	8.3	7.7	12.5	9.7	11.0	14.0	6.8	5.2	4.3	6.4	97.9
	PRECIPITATION ≥ 1.00	12	0.0	0.1	0.1	0.2	0.4	0.2	0.4	0.5	0.2	0.1	0.0	0.0	2.2
SNOWFALL	NORMAL TOTAL (IN.)	12	6.7	7.1	12.1	4.5	2.5	0.0	0.0	0.0	0.2	2.8	5.3	10.2	51.4
	MAXIMUM TOTAL (IN.)	45	28.7	23.2	23.2	42.7	19.4	1.1	T	T	27.9	25.9	26.3	18.2	42.7
	YEAR OF OCCURRENCE		1987	1987	1984	1957	1978	1975	1992	1992	1959	1984	1991	1983	APR 1957
	MAXIMUM IN 24 HOURS (IN.)	45	22.0	14.8	13.3	18.0	17.4	1.1	T	T	17.1	14.6	14.5	9.6	22.0
	YEAR OF OCCURRENCE		1987	1987	1964	1957	1978	1975	1992	1992	1959	1984	1972	1979	JAN 1987
	MAXIMUM SNOW DEPTH (IN.)	13	16	12	14	8	11	0	0	0	2	12	11	10	16
	YEAR OF OCCURRENCE		1987	1987	1985	1979	1978				1985	1984	1979	1979	JAN 1987
	NORMAL NO. DAYS WITH:														
	SNOWFALL ≥ 1.0	12	1.9	1.9	3.1	1.3	0.4	0.0	0.0	0.0	0.1	0.6	1.5	3.0	13.8

PRECIPITATION (inches) 1993 COLORADO SPRINGS, COLORADO (COS)

YEAR	JAN	FEB	MAR	APR	MAY	JUN	JUL	AUG	SEP	OCT	NOV	DEC	ANNUAL
1964	T	0.22	1.08	0.01	2.54	0.96	1.14	0.60	1.33	0.03	0.46	0.22	8.59
1965	0.14	0.72	1.12	1.61	1.81	8.00	5.02	3.83	2.24	0.49	T	0.45	25.43
1966	0.39	0.49	0.01	0.79	0.95	2.56	2.91	2.00	2.12	0.36	0.16	0.17	12.91
1967	0.31	0.15	0.18	2.04	2.18	2.74	5.26	3.09	0.73	1.68	0.25	0.67	19.28
1968	0.10	0.22	0.37	0.54	0.62	0.15	5.27	2.12	1.03	0.43	1.32	0.24	12.41
1969	0.11	0.12	0.77	1.83	4.46	2.72	3.90	2.38	1.13	2.86	0.39	0.32	20.99
1970	0.05	0.17	1.06	0.91	0.33	3.63	3.79	4.24	1.09	0.95	0.27	T	16.49
1971	0.34	0.53	0.34	1.36	2.24	0.39	2.82	1.99	1.36	0.23	0.03	0.23	11.86
1972	0.27	0.25	0.55	0.42	1.46	2.07	4.08	3.55	4.13	1.34	1.08	0.83	20.03
1973	0.06	0.06	1.16	1.72	4.27	0.47	3.31	0.89	1.03	0.35	0.15	0.64	14.11
1974	0.26	0.18	0.52	1.92	0.33	1.29	1.42	1.14	0.43	1.36	0.23	0.42	9.50
1975	0.13	0.29	0.24	0.68	1.00	2.97	2.65	2.06	0.16	0.52	1.00	0.07	11.77
1976	0.32	0.23	0.63	1.63	2.09	2.46	1.75	5.94	4.28	0.49	0.40	0.12	20.34
1977	0.29	0.20	1.18	2.57	1.12	3.87	3.02	5.11	0.45	0.19	0.60	0.18	18.78
1978	0.25	0.38	0.40	1.15	3.58	0.54	2.14	2.51	0.05	0.90	0.37	1.01	13.28
1979	0.53	0.04	2.38	1.83	3.13	1.58	2.73	2.50	0.92	0.55	1.82	1.02	19.03
1980	0.25	0.54	1.30	3.64	4.99	1.60	1.69	4.59	0.65	0.01	0.35	0.05	19.66
1981	0.07	0.12	0.93	0.13	3.14	1.98	3.64	5.24	0.52	0.37	0.03	0.82	16.99
1982	0.25	0.27	0.73	0.76	3.07	3.81	3.64	5.37	3.02	0.22	0.10	0.70	21.94
1983	0.43	0.09	1.79	0.97	3.08	2.41	0.99	2.59	0.37	0.28	1.09	0.70	14.79
1984	0.32	0.09	1.93	1.66	0.74	1.54	3.97	4.03	0.93	5.01	0.14	0.64	21.00
1985	0.42	0.24	1.68	2.07	3.36	0.78	4.92	1.56	1.49	0.52	0.42	0.55	18.01
1986	0.01	0.30	0.31	0.65	1.89	2.47	1.63	6.06	0.61	1.41	0.64	0.28	16.26
1987	1.17	2.45	1.79	0.50	3.82	2.89	0.67	2.77	0.55	0.54	0.44	0.64	18.23
1988	0.43	0.68	0.90	0.27	1.01	1.69	2.07	2.88	1.19	0.08	0.36	1.05	12.61
1989	0.23	1.23	0.49	1.06	1.11	3.42	2.26	2.63	2.30	0.28	0.02	0.41	15.44
1990	0.53	0.59	1.77	2.04	3.90	0.13	5.13	1.45	1.50	1.46	0.30	0.27	19.07
1991	0.09	T	0.42	1.76	0.80	3.07	2.87	4.57	0.56	0.88	2.05	0.45	17.52
1992	0.06	0.02	2.36	0.92	2.07	3.91	0.76	3.37	0.13	0.30	0.75	0.11	14.76
1993	0.52	0.21	0.79	1.02	1.60	1.27	2.38	2.17	1.44	0.91	0.97	0.11	13.39
POR= 45 YRS	0.30	0.35	0.89	1.23	2.22	2.13	2.82	2.80	1.24	0.80	0.51	0.36	15.67

WBAN : 93037

AVERAGE TEMPERATURE (˚F) 1993 COLORADO SPRINGS, COLORADO (COS)

YEAR	JAN	FEB	MAR	APR	MAY	JUN	JUL	AUG	SEP	OCT	NOV	DEC	ANNUAL
1964	30.3	26.1	30.9	46.2	57.6	65.0	75.3	69.3	61.9	52.3	38.4	32.8	48.8
1965	35.4	27.8	25.6	48.3	54.9	62.1	69.4	65.8	55.0	52.9	43.8	34.7	48.0
1966	25.1	26.8	40.8	44.4	57.1	65.7	73.9	66.8	62.1	48.9	40.6	29.4	48.5
1967	33.1	33.0	42.9	48.2	52.4	62.0	69.3	66.1	60.6	52.3	39.6	25.3	48.7
1968	30.7	32.6	38.6	42.5	51.5	66.9	68.4	65.8	60.3	51.5	34.5	29.4	47.7
1969	33.4	33.8	29.6	48.9	56.8	59.7	71.7	70.2	61.9	41.5	37.0	30.8	47.9
1970	28.2	37.2	32.6	42.6	58.2	64.6	71.2	71.4	57.7	44.2	38.2	32.9	48.2
1971	29.8	29.8	37.7	45.3	53.3	67.8	68.8	69.1	56.7	49.3	37.9	30.4	48.0
1972	30.0	36.1	43.3	49.1	55.9	67.8	68.9	67.7	60.8	49.4	29.8	23.5	48.5
1973	25.4	32.3	36.5	40.9	53.3	65.6	68.4	70.6	58.8	52.6	39.6	31.2	47.9
1974	27.0	33.9	42.1	46.0	59.7	66.2	72.6	67.9	58.0	52.6	38.5	28.0	49.4
1975	29.1	29.8	35.6	44.4	53.4	63.8	71.0	70.2	59.4	52.3	36.4	35.3	48.4
1976	30.1	37.8	36.1	47.7	54.7	64.3	72.1	68.1	59.3	45.7	36.2	32.9	48.8
1977	26.8	35.0	37.1	48.3	58.6	68.0	71.4	68.6	64.0	51.5	38.6	34.6	50.2
1978	25.1	27.7	40.9	48.8	52.5	66.2	72.8	67.5	62.8	51.9	36.5	21.9	47.9
1979	16.9	32.5	38.1	48.3	54.0	64.3	70.6	67.5	64.4	51.7	31.2	33.5	47.8
1980	26.7	34.3	35.7	44.3	53.4	69.2	75.3	70.4	62.3	49.9	39.5	39.8	50.1
1981	34.9	34.4	39.3	53.8	54.5	69.4	71.9	67.3	63.4	50.8	43.3	32.7	51.3
1982	29.4	29.0	38.1	45.7	52.7	60.1	70.2	68.5	59.0	47.6	35.4	29.8	47.1
1983	32.5	34.4	35.7	40.1	50.5	61.1	72.3	71.9	63.8	51.3	37.7	18.4	47.5
1984	26.1	33.3	35.3	41.4	58.2	65.1	71.5	68.4	59.5	42.8	38.4	33.1	47.8
1985	25.1	26.3	37.9	48.7	57.2	65.0	70.3	69.8	58.0	49.0	32.1	27.9	47.3
1986	38.2	34.7	44.3	48.5	54.6	65.8	70.4	67.6	59.1	48.0	37.7	29.8	49.9
1987	29.4	33.0	35.3	48.5	56.0	65.1	70.7	66.1	60.0	50.4	39.2	29.0	48.6
1988	24.3	31.8	36.2	48.2	56.4	68.7	70.6	70.4	60.8	53.0	39.2	29.2	49.1
1989	32.8	21.8	43.7	49.0	57.6	62.1	71.8	68.4	61.0	49.7	41.5	27.3	48.9
1990	33.6	31.7	38.9	47.1	53.8	69.5	68.0	68.0	64.5	49.5	42.7	24.3	49.3
1991	28.0	38.0	39.9	45.8	58.0	67.0	69.4	68.1	60.5	50.3	33.0	31.0	49.1
1992	32.6	37.6	41.6	52.1	57.8	62.5	68.4	66.6	62.9	52.4	31.9	29.3	49.6
1993	26.7	29.4	39.8	46.1	55.6	65.0	70.7	67.3	58.1	48.0	32.3	32.3	47.6
POR= 45 YRS	29.0	32.2	37.1	46.3	55.5	65.3	70.8	68.7	60.9	50.3	37.6	30.7	48.7

WBAN : 93037

REFERENCE NOTES:

THE TEMPERATURE GRAPH SHOWS NORMAL MAXIMUM AND NORMAL MINIMUM DAILY TEMPERATURES (SOLID CURVES) AND THE ACTUAL DAILY HIGH AND LOW TEMPERATURES (VERTICAL BARS).

H/C INDICATES HEATING AND COOLING DEGREE DAYS.
RH INDICATES RELATIVE HUMIDITY
W/O INDICATES WEATHER AND OBSTRUCTIONS
S INDICATES SUNSHINE.
PR INDICATES PRESSURE.
CLOUDINESS IS THE SUM OF THE CEILOMETER AND SATELLITE DATA NOT TO EXCEED TEN TENTHS.
MAXIMUM SNOW DEPTH IS THE DEPTH MEASURED AT 12 UTC.

GENERAL:
T INDICATES TRACE PRECIPITATION, AN AMOUNT GREATER THAN ZERO BUT LESS THAN THE LOWEST REPORTABLE VALUE.
+ INDICATES THE VALUE ALSO OCCURS ON EARLIER DATES.
BLANK ENTRIES DENOTE MISSING OR UNREPORTED DATA.
NORMALS ARE 30-YEAR AVERAGES (1961 - 1990).
ASOS INDICATES AUTOMATED SURFACE OBSERVING SYSTEM.
PM INDICATES THE LAST DAY OF THE PREVIOUS MONTH.
POR (PERIOD OF RECORD) INDICATES THE NUMBER OF YEARS USED TO COMPUTE THE MEAN. INDIVIDUAL MONTHS WITHIN THE POR MAY BE MISSING.
WHEN THE POR FOR A NORMAL IS LESS THAN 30 YEARS, THE NORMAL IS PROVISIONAL AND IS BASED ON THE NUMBER OF YEARS INDICATED.
0.* OR * INDICATES THE VALUE OR MEAN DAYS WITH IS BETWEEN 0.00 AND 0.05.
CLOUDINESS FOR ASOS STATIONS DIFFERS FROM THE NON-ASOS OBSERVATION TAKEN BY A HUMAN OBSERVER. ASOS STATION CLOUDINESS IS BASED ON TIME-AVERAGED CEILOMETER DATA FOR CLOUDS AT OR BELOW 12,000 FEET AND ON SATELLITE DATA FOR CLOUDS ABOVE 12,000 FEET.
THE NUMBER OF DAYS WITH CLEAR, PARTLY CLOUDY, AND CLOUDY CONDITIONS FOR ASOS STATIONS IS THE SUM OF THE CEILOMETER AND SATELLITE DATA FOR THE SUNRISE TO SUNSET PERIOD.

GENERAL CONTINUED:
CLEAR INDICATES 0 - 3 TENTHS, PARTLY CLOUDY INDICATES 4 - 7 TENTHS, AND CLOUDY INDICATES 8 OR MORE TENTHS. WHEN AT LEAST ONE OF THE ELEMENTS (CEILOMETER OR SATELLITE) IS MISSING, THE DAILY CLOUDINESS IS NOT COMPUTED.
WIND DIRECTION IS RECORDED IN TENS OF DEGREES (2 DIGITS) CLOCKWISE FROM TRUE NORTH. "00" INDICATES CALM. "36" INDICATES TRUE NORTH.
RESULTANT WIND IS THE VECTOR AVERAGE OF THE SPEED AND DIRECTION.
AVERAGE TEMPERATURE IS THE SUM OF THE MEAN DAILY MAXIMUM AND MINIMUM TEMPERATURE DIVIDED BY 2.
SNOWFALL DATA COMPRISE ALL FORMS OF FROZEN PRECIPITATION, INCLUDING HAIL.
A HEATING (COOLING) DEGREE DAY IS THE DIFFERENCE BETWEEN THE AVERAGE DAILY TEMPERATURE AND 65˚ F.
DRY BULB IS THE TEMPERATURE OF THE AMBIENT AIR.
DEW POINT IS THE TEMPERATURE TO WHICH THE AIR MUST BE COOLED TO ACHIEVE 100 PERCENT RELATIVE HUMIDITY.
WET BULB IS THE TEMPERATURE THE AIR WOULD HAVE IF THE MOISTURE CONTENT WAS INCREASED TO 100 PERCENT RELATIVE HUMIDITY.

HEATING DEGREE DAYS (base 65˚F) 1993 COLORADO SPRINGS, COLORADO (COS)

YEAR	JUL	AUG	SEP	OCT	NOV	DEC	JAN	FEB	MAR	APR	MAY	JUN	TOTAL
1964-65	0	22	151	385	790	992	910	1034	1214	497	306	107	6408
1965-66	10	31	304	366	632	931	1232	1061	744	613	249	63	6236
1966-67	0	33	111	489	728	1099	981	889	679	496	401	95	6001
1967-68	6	52	138	397	758	1223	1057	932	812	669	411	49	6504
1968-69	22	52	149	409	906	1096	969	868	1090	477	260	180	6478
1969-70	1	8	104	720	833	1053	1135	772	998	664	218	95	6601
1970-71	2	3	235	637	797	987	1086	980	837	584	357	32	6537
1971-72	33	5	285	481	806	1067	1080	832	665	469	273	6	6002
1972-73	41	34	136	476	1049	1281	1221	912	877	715	359	76	7177
1973-74	32	1	194	378	754	1041	1172	866	700	566	176	88	5968
1974-75	1	17	229	376	789	1143	1102	980	904	608	350	88	6587
1975-76	0	10	200	391	852	916	1075	782	891	512	314	80	6023
1976-77	0	11	191	593	859	988	1181	837	858	494	192	5	6209
1977-78	2	22	73	413	784	938	1231	1036	741	479	386	98	6203
1978-79	3	44	119	400	848	1329	1484	906	825	494	336	97	6885
1979-80	6	41	88	407	1005	969	1180	883	901	615	351	32	6478
1980-81	0	7	113	463	759	776	928	850	789	335	321	38	5379
1981-82	5	30	70	433	643	993	1095	1001	827	571	374	163	6205
1982-83	8	11	198	532	880	1084	1001	851	904	742	444	159	6814
1983-84	2	0	101	417	811	1438	1198	911	912	700	220	58	6768
1984-85	0	6	200	684	790	982	1233	1077	830	481	242	77	6602
1985-86	5	8	253	487	978	1142	822	840	635	487	315	49	6021
1986-87	4	14	174	519	813	1081	1096	888	912	491	272	50	6314
1987-88	17	74	150	445	767	1108	1256	958	886	499	273	25	6458
1988-89	7	8	154	366	767	1099	989	1207	655	475	247	134	6108
1989-90	0	4	172	473	699	1164	966	928	805	526	345	24	6106
1990-91	28	21	83	473	663	1258	1142	750	773	568	219	33	6011
1991-92	16	16	145	453	954	1048	998	788	717	383	219	96	5833
1992-93	21	53	91	383	990	1101	1179	991	776	558	286	84	6513
1993-	0	40	212	519	972	1008							
POR= 46 YRS	8	18	151	447	816	1054	1106	918	860	556	295	74	6303

WBAN : 93037

COOLING DEGREE DAYS (base 65˚F) 1993 COLORADO SPRINGS, COLORADO (COS)

YEAR	JAN	FEB	MAR	APR	MAY	JUN	JUL	AUG	SEP	OCT	NOV	DEC	ANNUAL
1969	0	0	0	0	11	27	216	177	18	0	0	0	449
1970	0	0	0	0	15	89	200	209	22	0	0	0	535
1971	0	0	0	0	1	126	158	138	41	0	0	0	464
1972	0	0	0	2	0	96	168	124	17	0	0	0	407
1973	0	0	0	0	0	104	145	180	13	0	0	0	442
1974	0	0	0	0	18	130	241	109	26	0	0	0	524
1975	0	0	0	0	0	59	195	180	41	5	0	0	480
1976	0	0	0	0	0	66	227	114	28	0	0	0	435
1977	0	0	0	0	0	103	204	142	49	0	0	0	498
1978	0	0	0	0	4	143	255	127	59	1	0	0	589
1979	0	0	0	0	1	84	185	124	77	2	0	0	473
1980	0	0	0	0	0	169	327	180	41	0	0	0	717
1981	0	0	0	4	2	176	226	105	27	0	0	0	540
1982	0	0	0	0	0	23	176	127	26	0	0	0	352
1983	0	0	0	0	1	48	236	219	71	0	0	0	575
1984	0	0	0	0	17	68	207	119	42	0	0	0	453
1985	0	0	0	0	5	83	179	163	51	0	0	0	481
1986	0	0	0	0	1	82	180	102	3	0	0	0	368
1987	0	0	0	0	0	62	199	113	6	0	0	0	380
1988	0	0	0	0	12	143	190	181	33	0	0	0	559
1989	0	0	0	3	25	54	220	117	57	3	0	0	479
1990	0	0	0	0	6	168	128	121	73	0	0	0	496
1991	0	0	0	0	8	101	161	120	15	4	0	0	409
1992	0	0	0	4	3	28	131	106	32	0	0	0	304
1993	0	0	0	0	2	89	183	117	11	1	0	0	403
POR= 25 YRS	0	0	0	0	4	92	197	140	35	0	0	0	468

WBAN : 93037

SNOWFALL (inches) 1993 COLORADO SPRINGS, COLORADO (COS)

YEAR	JUL	AUG	SEP	OCT	NOV	DEC	JAN	FEB	MAR	APR	MAY	JUN	TOTAL
1964-65	0.0	0.0	0.0	0.0	4.9	4.9	3.2	9.0	14.4	2.2	0.0	0.0	38.6
1965-66	0.0	0.0	0.1	T	T	6.1	6.0	9.7	0.1	4.1	4.2	0.0	30.3
1966-67	0.0	0.0	0.0	3.4	1.7	2.9	4.1	3.6	2.1	13.9	T	0.0	31.7
1967-68	0.0	0.0	0.0	T	3.1	11.7	3.0	4.8	5.7	2.8	0.2	0.0	31.3
1968-69	0.0	0.0	0.0	0.2	12.3	4.9	5.7	2.0	11.3	6.6	0.0	T	43.0
1969-70	0.0	0.0	0.0	21.7	5.6	7.3	0.8	2.4	19.9	7.0	T	T	64.7
1970-71	0.0	0.0	0.8	4.6	1.5	T	8.7	11.5	3.0	2.8	T	0.0	32.9
1971-72	0.0	0.0	9.7	2.9	0.3	3.8	5.2	3.6	7.0	3.3	T	0.0	35.8
1972-73	0.0	0.0	0.0	14.4	16.4	11.4	3.9	2.3	15.6	11.2	0.8	0.0	76.0
1973-74	0.0	0.0	0.0	3.9	1.8	9.1	2.4	2.4	6.8	10.0	0.0	T	36.4
1974-75	0.0	0.0	T	T	1.5	6.3	2.8	4.8	3.5	6.9	0.2	1.1	27.1
1975-76	0.0	0.0	0.0	4.3	9.8	0.9	6.9	5.2	8.6	10.1	0.0	0.0	45.8
1976-77	0.0	0.0	T	2.5	4.9	2.6	4.8	2.5	13.8	4.3	0.0	0.0	35.4
1977-78	0.0	0.0	0.0	0.9	1.9	3.0	4.2	8.6	3.3	1.1	19.4	0.0	42.4
1978-79	0.0	0.0	T	0.5	4.0	15.2	9.9	1.2	20.0	14.6	4.1	0.0	69.5
1979-80	0.0	0.0	0.0	1.3	19.1	17.6	4.7	5.9	12.7	11.3	0.0	0.0	72.6
1980-81	0.0	0.0	0.0	0.2	4.4	1.4	1.0	1.7	9.0	0.3	0.2	0.0	18.2
1981-82	0.0	0.0	0.0	0.4	0.5	9.1	3.6	6.2	8.4	2.3	3.9	0.0	34.4
1982-83	0.0	0.0	0.0	0.2	0.9	8.2	4.0	1.1	16.3	4.8	0.8	0.0	36.3
1983-84	0.0	0.0	0.0	0.0	10.3	18.2	7.8	1.4	23.2	9.0	0.8	0.0	70.7
1984-85	0.0	0.0	0.9	25.9	2.0	10.9	8.0	4.7	22.3	0.8	T	0.0	75.5
1985-86	0.0	0.0	1.9	1.7	8.3	6.3	0.2	4.6	2.9	4.0	T	0.0	29.9
1986-87	0.0	0.0	0.0	1.4	7.3	4.4	28.7	23.2	14.9	3.3	T	0.0	83.2
1987-88	0.0	0.0	0.0	0.0	4.8	9.5	4.9	11.5	12.6	1.0	0.3	0.0	44.6
1988-89	0.0	0.0	0.0	0.0	1.6	13.6	3.0	18.9	T	1.0	0.0	T	38.1
1989-90	T	T	T	2.1	0.2	7.5	8.7	9.3	9.7	11.3	4.2	0.0	53.0
1990-91	0.0	0.0	0.0	8.2	2.7	4.1	0.9	T	5.2	5.9	1.5	0.0	28.5
1991-92	0.0	0.0	0.0	7.5	26.3	4.5	1.2	0.2	3.0	T	0.0	T	42.7
1992-93	T	T	0.0	T	11.4	2.6	7.5	3.3	2.3	1.2	T	T	28.3
1993-	T	0.0	0.1	0.5	12.3	0.5							
POR= 46 YRS	T	T	1.0	3.1	5.6	5.5	5.0	5.1	9.3	6.2	1.5	T	42.3

WBAN : 93037

DENVER, COLORADO

Denver enjoys the invigorating climate that prevails over much of the central Rocky Mountain region, without the extremely cold mornings of the high elevations during winter, or the hot afternoons of summer at lower altitudes. Extremely warm or cold weather in Denver is usually of short duration.

Situated a long distance from any moisture source, and separated from the Pacific Ocean by several high mountain barriers, Denver enjoys low relative humidity, light precipitation, and abundant sunshine.

Air masses from four different sources influence Denver weather. These include arctic air from Canada and Alaska, warm, moist air from the Gulf of Mexico, warm, dry air from Mexico and the southwestern deserts, and Pacific air modified by its passage over mountains to the west.

In winter, the high altitude and mountains to the west combine to moderate temperatures in Denver. Invasions of cold air from the north, intensified by the high altitude, can be abrupt and severe. However, many of the cold air masses that spread southward out of Canada never reach the altitude of Denver, but move off over the lower plains to the east. Surges of air from the west are moderated in their descent down the east face of the Rockies, and reach Denver in the form of chinook winds that often raise temperatures into the 60s, even in midwinter.

In spring, polar air often collides with warm, moist air from the Gulf of Mexico and these collisions result in frequent, rapid and drastic weather changes. Spring is the cloudiest, windiest, and wettest season in the city. Much of the precipitation falls as snow, especially in March and early April. Stormy periods are interspersed with stretches of mild, sunny weather that quickly melt previous snow cover.

Summer precipitation falls mainly from scattered thunderstorms during the afternoon and evening. Mornings are usually clear and sunny, with clouds forming during early afternoon to cut off the sunshine at what would otherwise be the hottest part of the day. Severe thunderstorms, with large hail and heavy rain occasionally occur in the city, but these conditions are more common on the plains to the east.

Autumn is the most pleasant season. Few thunderstorms occur and invasions of cold air are infrequent. As a result, there is more sunshine and less severe weather than at any other time of the year.

Based on the 1951–1980 period, the average first occurrence of 32 degrees Fahrenheit in the fall is October 8 and the average last occurrence in the spring is May 3.

NORMALS, MEANS, AND EXTREMES

DENVER, COLORADO

LATITUDE: 39°45'N LONGITUDE: 104°52' W ELEVATION: FT. GRND 5282 BARO 5287 TIME ZONE: MOUNTAIN WBAN: 23062

	(a)	JAN	FEB	MAR	APR	MAY	JUNE	JULY	AUG	SEP	OCT	NOV	DEC	YEAR
TEMPERATURE °F:														
Normals														
-Daily Maximum		43.2	46.6	52.2	61.8	70.8	81.4	88.2	85.8	76.9	66.3	52.5	44.5	64.2
-Daily Minimum		16.1	20.2	25.8	34.5	43.6	52.4	58.6	56.9	47.6	36.4	25.4	17.4	36.2
-Monthly		29.7	33.4	39.0	48.2	57.2	66.9	73.5	71.4	62.3	51.4	39.0	31.0	50.3
Extremes														
-Record Highest	59	73	76	84	90	96	104	104	101	97	89	79	75	104
-Year		1982	1963	1971	1992	1942	1936	1939	1938	1960	1991	1990	1980	JUL 1939
-Record Lowest	59	-25	-30	-11	-2	22	30	43	41	17	3	-8	-25	-30
-Year		1963	1936	1943	1975	1954	1951	1972	1964	1985	1969	1993	1990	FEB 1936
NORMAL DEGREE DAYS:														
Heating (base 65°F)		1094	885	806	504	253	71	0	0	144	429	780	1054	6020
Cooling (base 65°F)		0	0	0	0	11	128	267	203	63	7	0	0	679
% OF POSSIBLE SUNSHINE	44	71	70	69	67	64	70	71	71	74	72	64	67	69
MEAN SKY COVER (tenths)														
Sunrise - Sunset	45	5.5	5.9	6.2	6.1	6.2	5.1	5.0	5.0	4.4	4.5	5.5	5.3	5.4
MEAN NUMBER OF DAYS:														
Sunrise to Sunset														
-Clear	59	10.3	8.0	7.8	6.7	6.1	9.6	9.2	9.7	13.4	13.3	10.1	10.9	115.2
-Partly Cloudy	59	9.3	8.7	10.1	10.7	12.2	12.2	15.6	13.7	9.0	9.1	9.6	9.6	129.7
-Cloudy	59	11.5	11.5	13.2	12.6	12.7	8.2	6.2	7.6	7.6	8.6	10.3	10.5	120.3
Precipitation														
.01 inches or more	59	5.8	5.9	8.6	8.5	10.8	8.7	9.3	8.8	6.3	5.3	5.6	5.3	89.1
Snow,Ice pellets,hail														
1.0 inches or more	59	2.4	2.4	3.6	2.5	0.4	0.0	0.0	0.0	0.3	1.2	2.6	2.5	17.9
Thunderstorms	59	0.*	0.1	0.3	1.5	6.4	9.9	11.1	8.3	3.5	0.8	0.1	0.0	41.9
Heavy Fog Visibility														
1/4 mile or less	53	1.1	1.6	1.1	0.8	0.5	0.4	0.4	0.6	0.6	0.6	1.2	1.1	9.9
Temperature °F														
-Maximum														
90° and above	33	0.0	0.0	0.0	0.*	0.3	6.3	15.0	9.3	2.2	0.0	0.0	0.0	33.1
32° and below	33	6.5	4.3	2.8	0.4	0.0	0.0	0.0	0.0	0.*	0.4	2.5	5.3	22.2
-Minimum														
32° and below	33	29.8	26.0	24.3	11.4	1.5	0.0	0.0	0.0	0.8	8.6	24.4	29.2	156.1
0° and below	33	3.8	1.7	0.5	0.*	0.0	0.0	0.0	0.0	0.0	0.0	0.2	2.8	9.0
AVG. STATION PRESS.(mb)	21	834.7	834.7	832.3	833.5	834.4	836.4	838.8	839.1	838.5	837.8	835.3	834.9	835.9
RELATIVE HUMIDITY (%)														
Hour 05	33	64	67	68	67	71	69	69	70	69	65	68	65	68
Hour 11 (Local Time)	33	45	44	42	38	39	37	35	37	38	36	44	45	40
Hour 17	33	49	44	40	35	38	35	34	35	34	35	49	52	40
Hour 23	33	63	65	62	58	61	59	57	59	59	59	65	64	61
PRECIPITATION (inches):														
Water Equivalent														
-Normal		0.50	0.57	1.28	1.71	2.40	1.79	1.91	1.51	1.24	0.98	0.87	0.64	15.40
-Maximum Monthly	59	1.44	1.66	4.56	4.17	7.31	4.69	6.41	5.85	4.67	4.17	2.97	2.84	7.31
-Year		1948	1960	1983	1942	1957	1967	1965	1979	1961	1969	1946	1973	MAY 1957
-Minimum Monthly	59	0.01	0.01	0.13	0.03	0.06	0.09	0.17	0.06	T	0.05	0.01	0.03	T
-Year		1952	1970	1945	1963	1974	1980	1939	1960	1944	1962	1949	1977	SEP 1944
-Maximum in 24 hrs	59	1.02	1.01	2.79	3.25	3.55	3.16	2.42	3.43	2.44	1.71	1.29	2.00	3.55
-Year		1962	1953	1983	1967	1973	1970	1965	1951	1936	1947	1975	1982	MAY 1973
Snow,Ice pellets,hail														
-Maximum Monthly	59	24.3	18.3	30.5	28.3	13.6	0.3	T	T	21.3	31.2	39.1	30.8	39.1
-Year		1992	1960	1983	1935	1950	1951	1992	1991	1936	1969	1946	1973	NOV 1946
-Maximum in 24 hrs	59	14.5	9.5	18.0	17.3	10.7	0.3	T	T	19.4	12.4	15.9	23.6	23.6
-Year		1992	1953	1983	1957	1950	1951	1992	1991	1936	1969	1983	1982	DEC 1982
WIND:														
Mean Speed (mph)	45	8.6	8.8	9.7	10.0	9.3	8.9	8.3	8.0	7.9	7.8	8.2	8.4	8.6
Prevailing Direction through 1963		S	S	S	S	S	S	S	S	S	S	S	S	S
Fastest Obs. 1 Min.														
-Direction (!!)	12	32	30	30	33	36	21	29	33	29	01	36	32	33
-Speed (MPH)	12	44	36	41	46	43	38	46	33	36	36	36	38	46
-Year		1982	1989	1991	1993	1983	1987	1993	1989	1988	1992	1987	1981	APR 1993
Peak Gust														
-Direction (!!)	10	W	NW	W	NW	SE	NW	W	NW	W	NW	W	W	NW
-Speed (mph)	10	55	52	59	62	60	60	55	52	56	48	49	51	62
-Date		1993	1990	1989	1986	1991	1988	1993	1989	1984	1990	1990	1990	APR 1986

PRECIPITATION (inches)

DENVER, COLORADO

YEAR	JAN	FEB	MAR	APR	MAY	JUNE	JULY	AUG	SEP	OCT	NOV	DEC	ANNUAL
1964	0.26	1.04	1.38	1.25	2.53	0.82	0.72	0.27	0.41	0.18	0.88	0.40	10.14
1965	1.00	1.27	1.20	1.05	1.82	4.14	6.41	1.06	2.58	0.45	0.36	0.53	21.87
1966	0.30	1.28	0.32	1.46	0.34	1.41	1.04	2.06	1.15	0.96	0.32	0.17	10.81
1967	0.84	0.39	0.79	3.95	4.77	4.69	3.25	0.83	0.60	1.13	1.01	1.06	23.31
1968	0.51	0.74	0.85	2.39	0.71	0.50	1.34	2.53	0.59	0.75	0.71	0.51	12.13
1969	0.17	0.43	1.10	1.33	6.12	2.99	1.81	0.79	1.67	4.17	0.62	0.32	21.52
1970	0.10	0.01	1.34	0.97	0.64	3.83	1.67	0.54	2.47	0.88	1.19	0.09	13.73
1971	0.35	0.78	0.53	1.98	1.34	0.23	1.20	0.85	2.85	0.44	0.16	0.25	10.96
1972	0.36	0.44	0.50	3.52	0.49	2.94	0.63	2.71	2.07	0.82	1.69	0.70	16.87
1973	1.31	0.16	1.76	3.73	5.06	0.20	2.47	1.28	2.85	0.47	0.83	2.84	22.96
1974	1.03	0.82	1.32	2.28	0.06	2.01	2.34	0.16	0.98	1.68	1.06	0.29	14.03
1975	0.23	0.37	1.19	1.14	2.80	2.11	2.78	2.00	0.24	0.30	1.88	0.47	15.51
1976	0.19	0.54	1.34	1.27	1.34	0.63	2.31	2.50	1.88	0.93	0.32	0.16	13.41
1977	0.16	0.27	1.24	2.13	0.34	1.02	2.98	1.00	0.10	0.48	0.59	0.03	10.34
1978	0.27	0.27	1.07	1.82	3.46	1.17	0.54	0.26	0.07	1.45	0.50	0.82	11.70
1979	0.34	0.42	1.25	1.41	3.53	2.39	0.81	5.85	0.36	1.28	1.66	1.06	20.36
1980	0.64	0.45	1.15	2.54	2.73	0.09	2.93	1.65	0.63	0.10	0.66	0.10	13.67
1981	0.29	0.35	2.27	1.01	3.76	0.63	0.90	1.16	0.35	0.79	0.42	0.66	12.59
1982	0.32	0.09	0.18	0.34	3.48	2.26	0.92	1.16	1.38	1.51	0.47	2.34	14.45
1983	0.15	0.07	4.56	2.10	3.62	2.65	1.75	1.51	0.13	0.39	2.63	0.63	20.19
1984	0.18	0.81	1.19	2.42	0.65	1.26	2.11	3.20	0.47	3.47	0.27	0.46	16.49
1985	0.68	0.59	0.69	2.61	1.33	1.46	3.71	0.28	2.33	0.77	1.20	0.66	16.31
1986	0.22	0.65	0.43	2.59	1.30	1.07	1.69	0.53	0.43	1.80	1.07	0.31	12.09
1987	0.69	1.21	1.34	1.03	4.64	3.50	0.76	2.00	0.70	1.24	1.62	1.30	20.03
1988	0.40	0.60	1.28	0.65	4.26	1.28	2.19	1.83	0.90	0.06	0.47	1.04	14.96
1989	1.14	0.66	0.56	1.00	3.83	2.04	1.64	1.28	1.55	0.81	0.15	0.81	15.47
1990	0.74	0.55	3.10	1.01	1.51	0.21	3.57	1.96	1.46	1.03	1.28	0.27	16.69
1991	0.76	0.08	0.76	1.94	2.43	2.20	4.11	3.69	0.79	0.70	2.67	0.19	20.32
1992	1.19	0.09	3.50	0.53	1.13	2.02	2.23	2.33	0.01	0.51	1.46	0.68	15.68
1993	0.25	1.05	0.89	2.08	0.93	1.67	0.91	0.64	2.29	2.27	1.38	0.42	14.78
Record Mean	0.48	0.57	1.16	1.95	2.41	1.51	1.74	1.45	1.09	1.02	0.72	0.63	14.72

AVERAGE TEMPERATURE (deg. F)

DENVER, COLORADO

YEAR	JAN	FEB	MAR	APR	MAY	JUNE	JULY	AUG	SEP	OCT	NOV	DEC	ANNUAL
1964	30.6	27.4	33.0	46.6	58.8	65.0	75.8	70.4	62.5	52.7	40.0	33.2	49.7
1965	35.0	27.4	29.0	51.2	57.1	63.9	72.7	70.2	55.7	55.1	43.3	35.0	49.6
1966	28.6	28.4	42.5	44.6	58.7	64.6	76.9	70.8	65.0	52.2	41.5	31.9	50.5
1967	34.0	35.1	42.9	48.2	52.6	60.6	69.1	68.2	62.1	52.5	40.5	26.5	49.4
1968	29.7	34.2	40.6	43.0	53.9	67.8	71.7	68.1	60.9	51.9	35.7	28.9	48.9
1969	35.0	35.4	32.2	52.2	59.3	61.5	74.7	73.9	64.5	39.0	39.1	32.5	49.9
1970	30.6	38.6	33.5	43.7	58.8	65.2	72.0	73.9	59.5	45.9	39.1	33.3	49.5
1971	32.1	30.6	38.5	47.8	54.2	69.0	70.6	72.8	57.5	49.4	39.1	31.9	49.5
1972	30.5	36.2	44.8	48.5	57.0	68.3	70.2	71.0	62.1	52.1	32.9	24.9	49.9
1973	27.3	35.5	39.9	43.2	55.6	67.5	71.0	73.5	59.9	54.5	39.5	31.6	49.9
1974	23.7	35.2	43.2	47.9	61.6	68.4	74.7	69.5	59.4	52.4	38.0	31.2	50.5
1975	31.7	30.6	37.3	44.1	54.3	64.3	72.7	70.8	59.5	53.2	36.8	37.5	49.4
1976	32.3	39.3	37.1	49.2	56.7	66.3	75.3	70.2	61.8	48.4	39.5	35.5	51.0
1977	29.2	38.0	39.9	51.1	60.7	71.9	74.3	70.2	66.6	53.3	40.3	35.1	52.5
1978	25.8	31.4	43.3	50.3	54.4	66.9	74.7	69.6	65.0	53.1	37.8	24.6	49.7
1979	18.0	34.2	40.5	49.1	54.8	65.8	73.7	69.5	66.3	53.8	33.3	34.5	49.5
1980	26.0	34.5	38.0	47.7	57.1	71.9	76.4	73.2	65.8	52.4	41.9	41.2	52.2
1981	37.3	36.2	41.2	56.4	57.1	70.4	75.9	72.0	68.2	52.6	45.9	35.8	54.1
1982	30.3	32.0	41.1	47.4	55.1	63.1	72.7	73.1	61.7	49.0	35.7	30.9	49.3
1983	31.9	36.6	36.2	41.0	51.4	62.8	73.3	74.4	64.9	52.7	37.0	17.5	48.3
1984	27.3	34.1	37.2	42.3	60.0	66.5	74.9	71.8	60.7	44.8	39.7	32.8	49.3
1985	25.6	27.7	40.8	51.0	60.0	68.0	73.0	72.4	58.8	50.7	29.8	29.4	48.9
1986	40.3	36.1	47.1	49.6	56.7	70.3	73.5	72.2	60.7	49.3	39.0	31.0	52.2
1987	32.2	36.1	38.8	51.9	59.7	69.2	74.4	70.7	62.4	51.7	40.0	28.4	51.3
1988	25.2	34.1	38.5	50.3	59.0	71.9	74.2	73.6	62.3	54.0	40.6	31.1	51.2
1989	33.5	22.4	43.3	51.1	59.0	65.4	75.9	71.7	62.5	51.3	42.8	27.3	50.5
1990	36.4	33.3	39.5	49.1	56.6	72.6	70.8	71.3	66.9	52.3	44.0	25.7	51.5
1991	27.9	40.3	42.8	47.8	60.3	69.4	73.1	71.5	62.5	50.3	34.7	33.1	51.1
1992	31.8	40.1	43.0	54.8	60.6	66.1	70.5	68.4	65.2	53.7	33.9	25.4	51.1
1993	27.3	29.4	42.6	48.5	58.8	66.4	73.0	70.0	60.6	49.2	34.7	34.2	49.6
Record Mean	30.1	33.0	38.9	47.7	56.8	66.8	72.8	71.3	62.8	51.5	39.4	32.1	50.3
Max	42.8	45.4	51.5	60.5	69.6	80.7	86.7	85.0	77.0	65.5	52.4	44.8	63.5
Min	17.4	20.5	26.3	34.9	44.1	52.9	58.9	57.6	48.5	37.5	26.4	19.4	37.0

REFERENCE NOTES

DENVER, COLORADO

GENERAL
T - TRACE AMOUNT.
BLANK ENTRIES DENOTE MISSING/UNREPORTED DATA.
# INDICATES A STATION OR INSTRUMENT RELOCATION.

SPECIFIC

PM - INCLUDES LAST DAY OF PREVIOUS MONTH
ASOS - AUTOMATED SURFACE OBSERVING SYSTEM IN OPERATION DURING THESE MONTHS.

(a) - LENGTH OF RECORD IN YEARS, ALTHOUGH INDIVIDUAL MONTHS MAY BE MISSING.
0.* OR * - THE VALUE IS BETWEEN 0.0 AND 0.05
NORMALS - BASED ON THE 1961-1990 RECORD PERIOD.
EXTREMES - DATES ARE THE MOST RECENT OCCURRENCE
WIND DIR. - NUMERALS SHOW TENS OF DEGRESS CLOCKWISE FROM TRUE NORTH. "00" INDICATES CALM.
RESULTANT DIRECTIONS ARE GIVEN TO WHOLE DEGREES.
BOLD VALUES INDICATE EXTREME VALUES WHICH OCCURRED AFTER THE ASOS SYSTEM WAS COMMISSIONED.

RECORD = PERIOD OF RECORD
RECORD MEAN PRECIPITATION IS THE MEAN OF ALL DAILY PRECIPITATION AMOUNTS DURING THE PERIOD OF RECORD.
RECORD MAX(MIN) TEMPERATURE IS THE MEAN OF ALL DAILY MAX(MIN) TEMPERATURES DURING THE PERIOD OF RECORD.
RECORD MEAN TEMPERATURE IS THE SUM OF THE RECORD MAX AND RECORD MIN DIVIDED BY 2.
AVERAGE TEMPERATURE IS THE SUM OF THE MEAN DAILY MAX AND MIN TEMPERATURE DIVIDED BY 2.

EXCEPTIONS

1. FASTEST MILE WINDS ARE THROUGH AUGUST 1981.

RECORD MEANS ARE THROUGH THE CURRENT YEAR, BEGINNING IN 1872 FOR TEMPERATURE
1872 FOR PRECIPITATION
1935 FOR SNOWFALL

HEATING DEGREE DAYS Base 65 deg. F DENVER, COLORADO

SEASON	JULY	AUG	SEP	OCT	NOV	DEC	JAN	FEB	MAR	APR	MAY	JUNE	TOTAL
1964-65	0	16	123	375	743	981	921	1044	1108	411	245	63	6030
1965-66	6	7	296	302	645	924	1122	1017	691	604	204	82	5900
1966-67	0	9	61	391	699	1018	954	832	679	498	388	135	5664
1967-68	4	16	108	389	729	1186	1086	885	751	655	343	38	6190
1968-69	10	35	145	399	871	1114	925	821	1011	378	204	144	6057
1969-70	2	0	56	801	769	998	1061	734	969	632	200	78	6300
1970-71	0	0	198	584	770	977	1018	958	817	508	329	25	6184
1971-72	24	0	273	479	771	1019	1063	832	621	486	246	4	5818
1972-73	42	15	107	397	960	1239	1162	820	771	646	290	56	6505
1973-74	8	0	166	321	758	1029	1277	831	671	507	137	67	5772
1974-75	0	9	199	381	803	1043	1024	957	852	621	332	85	6306
1975-76	0	4	195	363	840	843	1006	740	859	469	254	64	5637
1976-77	0	7	142	509	759	907	1105	749	771	414	137	0	5500
1977-78	2	14	38	358	737	920	1206	936	665	435	335	87	5733
1978-79	0	20	96	366	811	1245	1450	854	751	473	313	81	6460
1979-80	0	20	58	347	941	939	1204	876	828	514	247	9	5983
1980-81	0	4	56	386	683	731	853	801	727	260	243	26	4770
1981-82	0	12	19	375	570	898	1071	918	733	522	306	92	5516
1982-83	3	0	151	487	875	1050	1017	789	885	712	419	129	6517
1983-84	3	0	87	372	833	1469	1163	889	854	673	183	51	6577
1984-85	0	1	183	622	753	990	1215	1041	742	412	167	42	6168
1985-86	0	1	241	435	1051	1094	758	802	548	456	260	22	5668
1986-87	0	0	145	477	775	1045	1012	803	805	392	170	22	5646
1987-88	11	21	110	410	743	1125	1227	889	811	437	215	14	6013
1988-89	7	0	129	333	723	1043	969	1193	665	432	213	76	5783
1989-90	0	0	153	424	658	1162	879	882	781	469	265	7	5680
1990-91	12	3	64	388	623	1211	1143	684	682	510	174	16	5510
1991-92	6	4	118	449	902	982	1022	714	673	309	158	35	5372
1992-93	10	35	58	346	926	1219	1162	992	686	489	195	71	6189
1993-94	1	20	152	488	900	948							

COOLING DEGREE DAYS Base 65 deg. F DENVER, COLORADO

YEAR	JAN	FEB	MAR	APR	MAY	JUNE	JULY	AUG	SEP	OCT	NOV	DEC	TOTAL
1969	0	0	0	0	35	44	312	284	46	0	0	0	721
1970	0	0	0	0	16	93	222	282	40	0	0	0	653
1971	0	0	0	0	0	149	203	248	53	0	0	0	653
1972	0	0	0	0	6	110	210	207	28	1	0	0	562
1973	0	0	0	0	2	138	199	270	21	1	0	0	631
1974	0	0	0	0	36	176	307	157	39	0	0	0	715
1975	0	0	0	0	3	69	246	192	39	5	0	0	554
1976	0	0	0	0	3	112	324	176	52	0	0	0	667
1977	0	0	0	2	11	214	297	182	93	0	0	0	799
1978	0	0	0	0	12	152	308	171	103	2	0	0	748
1979	0	0	0	0	2	112	275	163	102	7	0	0	661
1980	0	0	0	2	10	224	358	263	88	1	0	0	946
1981	0	0	0	7	6	195	346	236	121	1	0	0	912
1982	0	0	0	0	6	42	247	257	59	0	0	0	611
1983	0	0	0	0	7	69	264	301	91	0	0	0	732
1984	0	0	0	0	33	104	315	218	60	0	0	0	730
1985	0	0	0	1	19	137	256	238	63	0	0	0	714
1986	0	0	0	0	11	188	271	227	20	0	0	0	717
1987	0	0	0	3	12	153	309	205	36	2	0	0	720
1988	0	0	0	1	35	225	300	277	55	0	0	0	893
1989	0	0	0	19	34	96	345	214	83	5	0	0	796
1990	0	0	0	0	9	244	196	203	129	1	0	0	782
1991	0	0	0	1	34	156	267	211	50	1	0	0	720
1992	0	0	0	9	29	76	187	148	74	1	0	0	524
1993	0	0	0	0	10	121	256	185	30	5	0	0	607

SNOWFALL (inches) DENVER, COLORADO

SEASON	JULY	AUG	SEP	OCT	NOV	DEC	JAN	FEB	MAR	APR	MAY	JUNE	TOTAL
1964-65	0.0	0.0	0.0	T	6.0	4.4	13.2	17.1	14.9	0.3	T	0.0	55.9
1965-66	0.0	0.0	5.5	0.0	5.5	5.6	3.6	14.6	2.8	6.4	2.9	0.0	46.9
1966-67	0.0	0.0	T	8.3	3.0	1.9	9.9	4.4	6.6	3.6	3.0	0.0	40.7
1967-68	0.0	0.0	0.0	1.7	9.4	13.1	3.0	7.3	9.2	15.1	T	0.0	58.8
1968-69	0.0	0.0	0.0	0.4	5.8	6.9	2.8	4.2	13.2	T	0.0	0.0	33.3
1969-70	0.0	0.0	0.0	31.2	5.1	3.1	0.9	0.3	20.5	4.7	T	0.0	65.8
1970-71	0.0	0.0	4.6	5.9	9.2	0.9	8.6	11.9	9.6	6.0	T	0.0	56.7
1971-72	0.0	0.0	17.2	3.1	1.4	8.4	10.9	9.1	7.1	17.2	0.0	0.0	74.4
1972-73	0.0	0.0	0.0	9.7	19.4	9.8	12.1	3.0	15.1	24.8	1.0	0.0	94.9
1973-74	0.0	0.0	0.0	2.3	9.3	30.8	8.2	10.3	12.8	17.8	0.0	T	91.5
1974-75	0.0	0.0	1.8	1.0	11.9	2.1	3.6	4.0	14.3	10.9	6.1	0.0	55.7
1975-76	0.0	0.0	0.0	2.7	15.2	7.3	3.2	6.4	18.7	1.2	0.0	0.0	54.7
1976-77	0.0	0.0	0.0	7.2	4.5	3.1	2.4	3.1	9.6	4.7	0.0	0.0	34.6
1977-78	0.0	0.0	0.0	3.3	4.1	0.7	5.5	6.2	8.6	4.6	13.5	0.0	46.5
1978-79	0.0	0.0	T	2.7	6.9	14.2	9.1	5.8	18.2	8.1	8.2	0.0	73.2
1979-80	0.0	0.0	0.0	2.7	22.3	16.5	12.3	9.6	12.1	10.0	T	0.0	85.5
1980-81	0.0	0.0	0.0	1.5	7.1	1.2	4.1	4.3	24.0	2.9	T	0.0	45.1
1981-82	0.0	0.0	0.0	2.8	3.3	9.9	4.8	1.8	2.1	2.0	T	0.0	26.7
1982-83	0.0	0.0	0.0	1.2	1.8	27.1	1.3	0.8	30.5	11.3	7.6	0.0	81.6
1983-84	0.0	0.0	T	T	29.3	11.5	3.4	7.9	12.0	16.8	T	0.0	80.9
1984-85	0.0	0.0	5.2	13.1	2.3	5.0	12.5	8.7	7.6	0.8	T	0.0	55.2
1985-86	0.0	0.0	8.7	1.9	17.0	10.3	2.4	6.2	2.6	14.0	0.0	0.0	63.1
1986-87	0.0	0.0	0.0	4.3	11.5	4.9	17.0	12.2	11.5	9.9	0.0	0.0	71.3
1987-88	0.0	0.0	0.0	T	11.2	21.5	5.8	7.0	13.5	2.0	1.3	0.0	62.3
1988-89	0.0	0.0	0.0	0.0	2.8	12.3	13.0	8.2	4.8	9.0	T	T	50.1
1989-90	0.0	0.0	2.3	7.8	1.6	11.8	8.4	7.0	21.9	3.6	0.1	0.0	64.5
1990-91	T	T	0.0	7.6	12.0	4.7	14.1	0.8	4.2	14.3	T	T	57.7
1991-92	T	T	0.0	7.3	29.6	1.9	24.3	0.3	15.6	0.0	0.0	T	79.0
1992-93	T	0.0	0.0	0.1	20.1	11.0	3.7	16.9	4.9	3.7	0.0	T	60.4
1993-94	0.0	0.0	5.4	5.4	17.4	5.6							
Record Mean	T	T	1.6	3.8	8.9	7.4	8.2	7.4	12.6	8.9	1.6	T	60.4

GRAND JUNCTION, COLORADO

Grand Junction is located at the junction of the Colorado and Gunnison Rivers. It is on the west slope of the Rockies, in a large mountain valley. The area has a climate marked by the wide seasonal range usual to interior localities at this latitude. Thanks, however, to the protective topography of the vicinity, sudden and severe weather changes are very infrequent. The valley floor slopes from 4,800 feet near Palisade to 4,400 feet at the west end near Fruita. Mountains are on all sides at distances of from 10 to 60 miles and reach heights of 9,000 to over 12,000 feet.

This mountain valley location, with attendant valley breezes, provides protection from spring and fall frosts. This results in a growing season averaging 191 days in the city. This varies considerably in the outlying districts. It is about the same in the upper valley around Palisade, and 3 to 4 weeks shorter near the river west of Grand Junction. The growing season is sufficiently long to permit commercial growth of almost all fruits except citrus varieties. Summer grazing of cattle and sheep on nearby mountain ranges is extensive.

The interior, continental location, ringed by mountains on all sides, results in quite low precipitation in all seasons. Consequently, agriculture is dependent on irrigation. Adequate supplies of water are available from mountain snows and rains. Summer rains occur chiefly as scattered light showers and thunderstorms which develop over nearby mountains. Winter snows are fairly frequent, but are mostly light and quick to melt. Even the infrequent snows of from 4 to 8 inches seldom remain on the ground for prolonged periods. Blizzard conditions in the valley are extremely rare.

Temperatures above 100 degrees are infrequent, and about one-third of the winters have no readings below zero. Summer days with maximum temperatures in the middle 90s and minimums in the low 60s are common. Relative humidity is very low during the summer, with values similar to other dry locations such as the southern parts of New Mexico and Arizona. Spells of cold winter weather are sometimes prolonged due to cold air becoming trapped in the valley. Winds are usually very light during the coldest weather. Changes in winter are normally gradual, and abrupt changes are much less frequent than in eastern Colorado. Cold waves are rare. Sunny days predominate in all seasons.

The prevailing wind is from the east-southeast due to the valley breeze effect. The strongest winds are associated with thunderstorms or with pre-frontal weather. They usually are from the south or southwest.

NORMALS, MEANS, AND EXTREMES

GRAND JUNCTION, COLORADO

LATITUDE: 39°07'N LONGITUDE: 108°32' W ELEVATION: FT. GRND 4843 BARO 4836 TIME ZONE: MOUNTAIN WBAN: 23066

	(a)	JAN	FEB	MAR	APR	MAY	JUNE	JULY	AUG	SEP	OCT	NOV	DEC	YEAR
TEMPERATURE °F:														
Normals														
-Daily Maximum		35.5	45.4	55.6	65.8	76.0	87.7	93.6	90.5	81.1	67.7	51.4	38.7	65.8
-Daily Minimum		14.5	23.5	31.3	38.5	47.9	57.1	63.9	62.2	52.8	41.6	29.4	18.7	40.1
-Monthly		25.0	34.5	43.4	52.2	62.0	72.4	78.8	76.4	67.0	54.7	40.4	28.7	53.0
Extremes														
-Record Highest	47	60	68	81	89	95	105	105	103	98	88	75	64	105
-Year		1971	1986	1971	1992	1956	1990	1976	1969	1977	1963	1977	1980	JUN 1990
-Record Lowest	47	-23	-18	5	11	26	34	44	43	29	18	-2	-17	-23
-Year		1963	1989	1948	1975	1970	1976	1993	1968	1978	1993	1976	1990	JAN 1963
NORMAL DEGREE DAYS:														
Heating (base 65°F)		1240	854	670	389	132	13	0	0	55	332	738	1125	5548
Cooling (base 65°F)		0	0	0	0	39	235	428	353	115	13	0	0	1183
% OF POSSIBLE SUNSHINE	47	61	65	64	70	73	81	79	77	79	74	63	61	71
MEAN SKY COVER (tenths)														
Sunrise - Sunset	47	6.1	6.2	6.2	5.9	5.5	4.0	4.2	4.4	3.6	4.2	5.4	5.8	5.1
MEAN NUMBER OF DAYS:														
Sunrise to Sunset														
-Clear	47	9.3	7.6	7.9	8.1	9.7	15.0	13.8	13.4	16.4	15.0	10.7	9.7	136.6
-Partly Cloudy	47	7.0	7.4	8.5	9.4	10.9	9.4	11.6	11.4	8.2	7.9	7.4	7.9	106.9
-Cloudy	47	14.6	13.3	14.6	12.6	10.4	5.7	5.6	6.2	5.4	8.2	11.8	13.4	121.8
Precipitation														
.01 inches or more	47	7.0	6.0	7.8	6.5	6.5	4.1	5.2	6.6	5.7	5.6	5.7	6.2	72.8
Snow,Ice pellets,hail														
1.0 inches or more	47	2.6	1.2	1.3	0.3	0.*	0.0	0.0	0.0	0.*	0.2	0.9	2.1	8.7
Thunderstorms	47	0.1	0.3	0.8	2.1	4.6	4.9	7.6	7.9	5.1	1.5	0.4	0.1	35.3
Heavy Fog Visibility														
1/4 mile or less	47	2.9	1.9	0.6	0.1	0.*	0.0	0.0	0.0	0.0	0.1	0.8	2.0	8.3
Temperature °F														
-Maximum														
90° and above	30	0.0	0.0	0.0	0.0	1.2	14.0	24.4	19.4	4.2	0.0	0.0	0.0	63.2
32° and below	30	11.9	2.3	0.2	0.0	0.0	0.0	0.0	0.0	0.0	0.0	0.7	7.0	22.1
-Minimum														
32° and below	30	30.2	25.0	16.4	6.5	0.5	0.0	0.0	0.0	0.1	3.1	20.8	29.6	132.2
0° and below	30	3.8	0.7	0.0	0.0	0.0	0.0	0.0	0.0	0.0	0.0	0.*	1.1	5.7
AVG. STATION PRESS.(mb)	21	855.1	853.6	849.6	849.8	849.6	850.9	853.1	853.6	853.5	854.3	853.9	855.1	852.7
RELATIVE HUMIDITY (%)														
Hour 05	30	78	73	64	57	54	45	48	51	52	58	70	77	61
Hour 11 (Local Time)	30	65	54	43	34	31	25	29	32	33	39	51	62	42
Hour 17	30	64	48	36	28	25	19	22	24	26	33	47	60	36
Hour 23	30	77	68	57	47	42	33	37	40	41	51	65	75	53
PRECIPITATION (inches):														
Water Equivalent														
-Normal		0.56	0.48	0.90	0.75	0.87	0.50	0.65	0.81	0.82	0.98	0.71	0.61	8.64
-Maximum Monthly	47	2.46	1.56	2.02	1.95	1.99	2.07	1.92	3.48	2.81	3.45	2.00	1.89	3.48
-Year		1957	1948	1979	1965	1993	1969	1983	1957	1982	1972	1983	1951	AUG 1957
-Minimum Monthly	47	T	T	0.02	0.06	T	T	0.03	0.04	T	0.00	T	0.01	0.00
-Year		1961	1972	1972	1958	1970	1980	1972	1956	1953	1952	1989	1976	OCT 1952
-Maximum in 24 hrs	47	0.71	0.69	1.15	1.33	1.13	1.57	1.42	1.21	1.35	1.24	0.83	1.16	1.57
-Year		1989	1989	1993	1965	1983	1969	1974	1953	1965	1957	1983	1951	JUN 1969
Snow,Ice pellets,hail														
-Maximum Monthly	47	33.7	18.4	14.9	14.3	5.0	0.0	0.0	T	3.1	6.1	12.1	19.0	33.7
-Year		1957	1948	1948	1975	1979			1993	1965	1975	1964	1983	JAN 1957
-Maximum in 24 hrs	47	9.1	9.0	6.1	8.9	5.0	0.0	0.0	T	3.1	6.1	8.4	6.0	9.1
-Year		1957	1989	1948	1975	1979			1993	1965	1975	1954	1967	JAN 1957
WIND:														
Mean Speed (mph)	47	5.7	6.7	8.3	9.4	9.6	9.7	9.3	9.1	9.0	7.9	6.8	5.9	8.1
Prevailing Direction through 1963		ESE	ESE	ESE	ESE	ESE	ESE	ESE	ESE	ESE	ESE	ESE	ESE	ESE
Fastest Obs. 1 Min.														
-Direction (!!)	14	18	24	28	29	20	27	08	25	28	32	31	27	27
-Speed (MPH)	14	35	32	35	46	46	53	40	37	38	35	39	32	53
-Year		1982	1993	1985	1985	1989	1981	1988	1988	1992	1990	1982	1982	JUN 1981
Peak Gust														
-Direction (!!)	10	SW	SW	W	S	W	S	SW	S	W	W	W	NW	S
-Speed (mph)	10	41	43	52	78	62	66	64	74	64	54	49	41	78
-Date		1993	1993	1988	1985	1989	1991	1993	1984	1992	1985	1984	1990	APR 1985

PRECIPITATION (inches)

GRAND JUNCTION, COLORADO

YEAR	JAN	FEB	MAR	APR	MAY	JUNE	JULY	AUG	SEP	OCT	NOV	DEC	ANNUAL
1964	0.47	0.02	0.70	1.37	0.41	0.16	0.65	1.16	0.36	T	1.05	0.53	6.88
1965	0.66	0.94	0.87	1.95	1.35	1.33	0.89	0.67	2.52	1.40	0.82	0.76	14.16
1966	0.65	0.44	0.04	0.83	0.71	0.13	0.31	0.52	0.26	1.23	0.62	1.78	7.52
1967	0.25	0.22	0.18	0.08	1.52	1.34	1.03	0.59	0.37	0.63	0.33	1.14	7.68
1968	0.26	1.13	0.44	0.67	1.14	0.05	0.49	1.37	0.07	0.94	0.42	0.47	7.45
1969	1.03	0.40	0.67	0.33	0.45	2.07	0.21	0.88	1.45	2.01	0.45	0.36	10.31
1970	0.52	0.05	1.75	0.76	T	0.91	0.60	0.44	0.78	1.56	0.54	0.39	8.30
1971	0.19	0.13	0.02	0.42	1.10	0.03	0.15	1.02	0.58	1.13	0.56	0.67	6.00
1972	0.20	T	0.02	0.11	0.44	0.64	0.03	0.29	0.72	3.45	0.69	0.74	7.33
1973	0.79	0.12	0.65	0.86	1.45	0.87	0.52	0.62	0.33	0.20	0.91	0.62	7.94
1974	1.20	0.40	0.81	1.03	0.01	0.14	1.53	0.48	0.38	0.72	1.18	0.32	8.20
1975	0.53	0.49	1.74	1.38	1.23	0.43	1.39	0.09	0.16	0.85	0.39	0.50	9.18
1976	0.13	0.81	0.75	0.40	1.49	0.14	0.20	0.31	0.67	0.32	0.04	0.01	5.27
1977	0.37	0.06	0.50	0.54	0.59	0.04	0.89	0.59	0.52	0.50	0.70	0.38	5.68
1978	1.08	0.64	1.19	1.19	0.55	0.01	0.25	0.54	0.49	0.03	0.62	1.30	7.89
1979	1.36	0.63	2.02	0.42	1.45	0.78	0.08	0.61	0.01	0.25	1.02	0.27	8.90
1980	0.57	1.10	1.77	0.53	1.17	T	0.96	1.39	0.58	1.31	0.52	0.24	10.14
1981	0.44	0.16	1.35	0.56	1.49	0.17	0.41	0.82	0.25	2.06	0.47	0.60	8.78
1982	0.29	0.41	0.79	0.09	0.75	0.21	0.35	0.94	2.81	0.83	0.48	0.27	8.22
1983	0.50	0.64	1.59	0.90	1.68	1.54	1.92	0.73	1.11	0.36	2.00	1.85	14.82
1984	0.28	0.11	1.57	1.21	0.55	1.68	0.62	1.77	0.34	2.65	0.38	0.43	11.59
1985	0.51	0.26	0.92	1.78	1.09	0.39	1.21	0.24	1.67	2.32	1.10	0.73	12.22
1986	0.13	0.33	0.25	0.71	1.15	0.15	0.94	0.97	1.52	1.22	1.02	0.47	8.86
1987	0.30	1.21	1.95	0.46	1.51	0.23	1.51	0.83	0.13	0.65	1.92	0.83	11.53
1988	1.07	0.21	0.72	0.99	1.10	0.21	0.18	1.37	0.76	0.02	1.02	0.20	7.85
1989	0.98	1.33	0.51	0.23	0.39	0.24	0.27	1.01	0.33	0.14	T	0.08	5.51
1990	0.59	0.55	1.07	0.71	0.05	0.26	0.96	0.49	1.23	0.95	0.57	0.98	8.41
1991	0.92	0.13	0.70	0.87	0.20	0.30	0.40	0.57	2.30	1.20	1.10	0.54	9.23
1992	0.24	0.35	1.71	0.15	1.81	0.17	1.03	0.84	0.33	1.45	0.76	0.35	9.19
1993	1.36	1.09	1.72	1.30	1.99	0.03	0.04	1.42	0.41	1.34	0.41	0.57	11.68
Record Mean	0.60	0.58	0.83	0.75	0.78	0.43	0.62	1.01	0.89	0.92	0.63	0.58	8.63

AVERAGE TEMPERATURE (deg. F)

GRAND JUNCTION, COLORADO

YEAR	JAN	FEB	MAR	APR	MAY	JUNE	JULY	AUG	SEP	OCT	NOV	DEC	ANNUAL
1964	25.5	29.5	37.0	50.3	62.3	70.2	81.3	74.1	66.6	58.0	38.1	30.4	51.9
1965	32.3	32.9	40.4	53.9	62.4	70.3	78.9	76.6	63.4	58.1	48.3	33.8	54.3
1966	24.5	30.6	46.1	53.6	65.4	72.0	80.9	77.0	69.1	56.5	43.9	29.5	54.1
1967	23.9	36.4	48.5	51.6	59.5	68.6	77.7	76.2	67.5	55.3	41.0	18.3	52.0
1968	15.4	37.0	43.8	46.3	59.1	72.8	78.0	70.3	64.2	53.8	38.0	22.7	50.1
1969	28.5	33.6	38.1	53.8	66.4	67.7	80.3	79.5	69.3	47.4	39.2	32.7	53.1
1970	29.3	40.9	39.8	45.9	63.3	71.4	79.1	78.7	64.1	48.8	41.0	31.9	52.9
1971	27.7	34.1	41.1	52.2	60.1	74.1	80.2	78.5	63.2	52.3	38.4	25.9	52.3
1972	30.0	36.6	46.6	53.3	63.1	74.3	80.2	77.1	68.1	54.0	37.1	22.7	53.6
1973	11.5	29.1	42.1	48.1	61.5	70.5	78.1	77.4	65.7	56.4	41.2	30.1	51.0
1974	16.9	19.9	48.2	51.0	65.0	74.9	78.3	75.6	66.4	56.2	39.6	27.1	51.6
1975	20.0	33.0	41.0	46.4	57.1	67.5	78.3	75.4	67.1	53.5	36.2	27.4	50.2
1976	21.7	38.2	38.7	51.9	61.8	70.4	79.6	75.3	66.9	51.2	39.1	27.6	51.9
1977	23.9	37.1	40.8	56.9	63.7	79.1	80.2	78.3	70.2	58.2	40.3	33.3	55.2
1978	29.4	34.4	46.7	52.3	58.8	73.0	78.4	74.5	65.7	54.7	40.2	16.0	52.0
1979	16.6	23.5	41.1	52.5	60.3	71.0	78.7	74.6	72.0	58.9	33.2	26.9	50.8
1980	32.6	39.2	40.9	51.4	59.1	74.0	78.6	75.3	67.9	53.8	42.3	40.1	54.6
1981	36.8	37.9	44.0	56.8	60.9	76.4	79.4	76.8	69.2	50.7	41.6	31.3	55.1
1982	26.0	34.7	46.0	51.3	61.4	72.2	79.0	78.2	67.5	51.9	41.2	33.0	53.5
1983	34.3	40.9	45.9	48.7	58.7	69.8	78.3	80.4	71.4	58.2	42.1	30.5	54.9
1984	20.7	31.7	44.4	49.0	66.2	70.1	78.0	76.6	68.3	50.2	40.8	32.6	52.4
1985	31.1	32.0	43.9	54.5	63.6	73.0	77.6	77.1	62.4	52.8	38.8	31.9	53.2
1986	34.2	40.4	49.0	52.5	60.6	74.3	76.0	75.6	63.2	51.5	40.8	32.4	54.2
1987	27.4	36.8	40.1	54.5	61.2	73.5	75.2	72.9	66.2	56.8	39.6	27.9	52.7
1988	17.4	29.2	41.0	53.1	60.9	76.5	80.6	76.2	64.5	58.9	40.7	30.0	52.4
1989	20.2	27.7	47.5	57.0	63.8	71.0	80.5	74.4	68.3	54.9	40.6	29.2	52.9
1990	28.5	35.4	46.8	55.7	61.3	75.2	78.0	76.6	69.7	53.2	39.5	20.6	53.4
1991	17.6	32.0	42.0	48.8	62.0	72.5	77.6	76.2	66.5	55.0	37.7	26.2	51.2
1992	19.9	37.6	47.2	59.0	64.5	71.2	75.1	75.1	67.7	57.8	35.9	24.5	53.0
1993	31.9	36.2	45.6	50.0	61.9	70.1	76.7	73.2	65.9	51.7	35.6	29.2	52.3
Record Mean	25.8	33.5	43.0	52.3	61.8	71.9	78.3	75.7	66.9	54.2	39.8	28.6	52.7
Max	36.2	44.2	54.6	65.2	75.3	86.7	92.4	89.2	80.6	67.2	51.2	38.7	65.1
Min	15.3	22.9	31.3	39.4	48.3	57.2	64.1	62.1	53.2	41.2	28.4	18.4	40.2

REFERENCE NOTES

GRAND JUNCTION, COLORADO

GENERAL
T - TRACE AMOUNT.
BLANK ENTRIES DENOTE MISSING/UNREPORTED DATA.
# INDICATES A STATION OR INSTRUMENT RELOCATION.

SPECIFIC

PM - INCLUDES LAST DAY OF PREVIOUS MONTH
ASOS - AUTOMATED SURFACE OBSERVING SYSTEM IN OPERATION DURING THESE MONTHS.

(a) - LENGTH OF RECORD IN YEARS, ALTHOUGH INDIVIDUAL MONTHS MAY BE MISSING.
0.* OR * - THE VALUE IS BETWEEN 0.0 AND 0.05
NORMALS - BASED ON THE 1961-1990 RECORD PERIOD.
EXTREMES - DATES ARE THE MOST RECENT OCCURRENCE
WIND DIR.- NUMERALS SHOW TENS OF DEGRESS CLOCKWISE FROM TRUE NORTH. "00" INDICATES CALM.
RESULTANT DIRECTIONS ARE GIVEN TO WHOLE DEGREES.
BOLD VALUES INDICATE EXTREME VALUES WHICH OCCURRED AFTER THE ASOS SYSTEM WAS COMMISSIONED.

RECORD = PERIOD OF RECORD
RECORD MEAN PRECIPITATION IS THE MEAN OF ALL DAILY PRECIPITATION AMOUNTS DURING THE PERIOD OF RECORD.
RECORD MAX(MIN) TEMPERATURE IS THE MEAN OF ALL DAILY MAX(MIN) TEMPERATURES DURING THE PERIOD OF RECORD.
RECORD MEAN TEMPERATURE IS THE SUM OF THE RECORD MAX AND RECORD MIN DIVIDED BY 2.
AVERAGE TEMPERATURE IS THE SUM OF THE MEAN DAILY MAX AND MIN TEMPERATURE DIVIDED BY 2.

EXCEPTIONS

RECORD MEANS ARE THROUGH THE CURRENT YEAR,
BEGINNING IN 1892 FOR TEMPERATURE
1892 FOR PRECIPITATION
1947 FOR SNOWFALL

HEATING DEGREE DAYS Base 65 deg. F — GRAND JUNCTION, COLORADO

SEASON	JULY	AUG	SEP	OCT	NOV	DEC	JAN	FEB	MAR	APR	MAY	JUNE	TOTAL
1964-65	0	2	39	219	800	1067	1004	893	758	334	158	8	5282
1965-66	0	0	138	209	496	960	1246	959	582	337	59	4	4990
1966-67	0	2	16	256	628	1092	1268	795	508	396	213	21	5195
1967-68	0	0	28	320	714	1442	1532	805	648	552	218	24	6283
1968-69	0	12	86	346	804	1302	1125	874	826	332	52	34	5793
1969-70	0	0	20	545	764	995	1100	671	772	564	115	39	5585
1970-71	0	0	93	495	714	1019	1152	858	734	378	182	4	5629
1971-72	0	0	134	389	792	1204	1076	813	563	346	139	0	5456
1972-73	0	0	31	335	832	1303	1651	999	705	499	139	49	6543
1973-74	0	0	72	266	708	1075	1487	1260	513	415	66	32	5894
1974-75	0	0	60	266	756	1167	1387	888	736	551	249	51	6111
1975-76	0	0	35	358	858	1161	1335	775	807	386	122	25	5862
1976-77	0	0	41	421	769	1153	1267	775	743	250	94	0	5513
1977-78	0	1	17	214	736	975	1098	852	561	373	210	9	5046
1978-79	0	6	95	313	737	1510	1493	1154	732	377	192	37	6646
1979-80	0	3	0	209	945	1175	999	741	740	405	195	4	5416
1980-81	0	2	21	359	674	765	864	754	645	247	153	15	4499
1981-82	0	0	12	439	696	1039	1203	841	581	405	136	6	5358
1982-83	2	0	61	397	704	983	946	668	586	482	238	22	5089
1983-84	0	0	27	208	678	1064	1366	959	631	474	89	44	5540
1984-85	0	0	54	452	719	996	1044	919	646	310	81	12	5233
1985-86	0	0	139	371	779	1018	949	685	489	366	168	3	4967
1986-87	0	0	130	414	718	1001	1159	785	765	314	143	0	5429
1987-88	0	6	34	248	754	1147	1469	1031	741	350	172	8	5960
1988-89	0	0	106	183	724	1078	1379	1038	534	258	113	8	5421
1989-90	0	0	40	316	729	1103	1124	820	557	271	139	20	5119
1990-91	0	0	28	360	759	1371	1464	919	706	478	136	18	6239
1991-92	0	2	37	304	815	1193	1390	788	540	195	53	8	5325
1992-93	0	6	25	222	868	1245	1018	799	597	446	144	33	5403
1993-94	4	0	59	410	875	1102							

COOLING DEGREE DAYS Base 65 deg. F — GRAND JUNCTION, COLORADO

YEAR	JAN	FEB	MAR	APR	MAY	JUNE	JULY	AUG	SEP	OCT	NOV	DEC	TOTAL
1969	0	0	0	3	104	124	481	458	158	1	0	0	1329
1970	0	0	0	0	67	238	442	430	72	0	0	0	1249
1971	0	0	0	0	36	284	479	425	86	3	0	0	1313
1972	0	0	0	0	86	288	479	381	130	3	0	0	1367
1973	0	0	0	0	35	222	410	393	101	6	0	0	1167
1974	0	0	0	1	73	335	420	335	109	0	0	0	1273
1975	0	0	0	0	9	133	419	328	106	9	0	0	1004
1976	0	0	0	0	32	195	460	324	103	0	0	0	1114
1977	0	0	0	16	60	429	477	420	180	10	0	0	1592
1978	0	0	0	0	25	258	420	308	123	1	0	0	1135
1979	0	0	0	6	52	225	428	310	215	27	0	0	1263
1980	0	0	0	1	16	280	427	325	115	19	0	0	1183
1981	0	0	0	9	31	367	456	375	143	0	0	0	1381
1982	0	0	0	0	33	229	443	415	144	0	0	0	1264
1983	0	0	0	0	49	171	421	483	226	3	0	0	1353
1984	0	0	0	0	134	200	408	368	159	0	0	0	1269
1985	0	0	0	4	45	261	396	382	67	0	0	0	1155
1986	0	0	0	0	39	289	348	334	82	0	0	0	1092
1987	0	0	0	5	30	262	324	256	76	2	0	0	955
1988	0	0	0	0	51	360	489	357	98	4	0	0	1359
1989	0	0	0	26	85	195	489	300	145	11	0	0	1251
1990	0	0	0	1	34	331	412	368	174	3	0	0	1323
1991	0	0	0	0	50	247	398	356	88	0	0	0	1139
1992	0	0	0	21	43	203	319	328	114	7	0	0	1035
1993	0	0	0	0	56	193	371	260	92	6	0	0	978

SNOWFALL (inches) — GRAND JUNCTION, COLORADO

SEASON	JULY	AUG	SEP	OCT	NOV	DEC	JAN	FEB	MAR	APR	MAY	JUNE	TOTAL
1964-65	0.0	0.0	0.0	0.0	12.1	3.0	5.9	7.5	3.8	0.2	T	0.0	32.5
1965-66	0.0	0.0	3.1	0.0	2.8	3.5	11.0	5.9	0.3	0.8	T	0.0	27.4
1966-67	0.0	0.0	0.0	1.9	4.2	6.3	2.8	T	0.2	0.4	T	0.0	15.8
1967-68	0.0	0.0	0.0	T	0.5	16.7	3.7	0.9	0.3	0.6	T	0.0	22.7
1968-69	0.0	0.0	0.0	0.0	0.2	7.8	3.4	3.8	9.5	T	T	0.0	24.7
1969-70	0.0	0.0	0.0	0.6	0.5	4.8	5.2	T	12.4	1.2	0.0	0.0	24.7
1970-71	0.0	0.0	0.0	3.1	T	4.1	3.2	1.5	0.2	1.1	T	0.0	13.2
1971-72	0.0	0.0	0.0	0.5	3.9	10.4	4.0	T	0.0	T	0.0	0.0	18.8
1972-73	0.0	0.0	0.0	5.7	1.3	9.7	12.8	1.2	1.3	2.0	T	0.0	34.0
1973-74	0.0	0.0	0.0	0.0	7.7	5.7	17.0	5.5	T	1.2	0.0	0.0	37.1
1974-75	0.0	0.0	0.0	T	0.1	4.6	7.9	4.4	8.8	14.3	1.3	0.0	41.4
1975-76	0.0	0.0	0.0	6.1	3.9	7.2	1.7	4.0	6.8	0.2	0.0	0.0	29.9
1976-77	0.0	0.0	0.0	0.0	T	0.1	4.2	T	2.3	1.7	0.0	0.0	8.3
1977-78	0.0	0.0	0.0	T	3.3	2.5	12.0	2.5	0.6	T	T	0.0	20.9
1978-79	0.0	0.0	0.0	0.0	2.9	11.8	18.7	9.6	3.4	1.1	5.0	0.0	52.5
1979-80	0.0	0.0	0.0	0.0	8.2	3.5	2.2	0.5	7.3	0.2	0.0	0.0	21.9
1980-81	0.0	0.0	0.0	0.0	T	0.0	3.9	0.8	1.2	T	0.0	0.0	5.9
1981-82	0.0	0.0	0.0	0.5	3.3	3.4	3.4	4.0	0.8	T	0.0	0.0	15.4
1982-83	0.0	0.0	0.0	T	T	1.9	6.1	3.1	1.5	2.2	T	0.0	14.8
1983-84	0.0	0.0	0.0	0.0	4.2	19.0	3.7	0.6	6.1	2.9	0.0	0.0	36.5
1984-85	0.0	0.0	0.0	0.7	2.0	2.7	5.0	2.7	5.6	0.1	0.0	0.0	18.8
1985-86	0.0	0.0	0.0	0.0	4.6	4.4	1.8	0.7	T	0.2	T	0.0	11.7
1986-87	0.0	0.0	0.0	2.2	1.2	1.0	3.0	5.5	9.4	0.6	T	0.0	22.9
1987-88	0.0	0.0	0.0	0.0	1.1	7.1	12.2	2.2	4.3	0.0	0.0	0.0	26.9
1988-89	0.0	0.0	0.0	0.0	0.9	3.1	10.2	16.0	1.1	T	T	0.0	31.3
1989-90	0.0	0.0	0.0	0.0	0.0	1.1	6.2	8.6	1.8	0.8	0.0	0.0	18.5
1990-91	0.0	0.0	0.0	0.0	1.5	5.1	12.7	0.3	3.7	4.7	0.0	0.0	28.0
1991-92	0.0	0.0	T	2.5	1.9	7.6	2.7	1.9	T	0.0	T	0.0	16.6
1992-93	0.0	0.0	0.0	0.0	2.0	4.4	6.0	8.4	0.0	0.4	T	0.0	21.2
1993-94	0.0	T	0.0	0.0	0.6	5.9							
Record Mean	0.0	T	0.1	0.5	2.7	5.3	7.3	4.2	3.8	1.1	0.1	0.0	25.2

HARTFORD, CONNECTICUT

Bradley International Airport is located about 3 miles west of the Connecticut River on a slight rise of ground in a broad portion of the Connecticut River Valley between north-south mountain ranges whose heights do not exceed 1,200 feet.

The station is in the northern temperate climate zone. The prevailing west to east movement of air brings the majority of weather systems into Connecticut from the west. The average wintertime position of the Polar Front boundary between cold, dry polar air and warm, moist tropical air is just south of New England, which helps to explain the extensive winter storm activity and day to day variability of local weather. In summer, the Polar Front has an average position along the New England-Canada border with this station in a warm and pleasant atmosphere.

The location of Hartford, relative to continent and ocean, is also significant. Rapid weather changes result when storms move northward along the mid-Atlantic coast, frequently producing strong and persistent northeast winds associated with storms known locally as coastals or northeasters. Seasonally, weather characteristics vary from the cold and dry continental-polar air of winter to the warm and humid maritime air of summer.

Summer thunderstorms develop in the Berkshire Mountains to the west and northwest, move over the Connecticut Valley, and when accompanied by wind and hail, sometimes cause considerable damage to crops, particularly tobacco. During the winter, rain often falls through cold air trapped in the valley, creating extremely hazardous ice conditions. On clear nights in the late summer or early autumn, cool air drainage into the valley, and moisture from the Connecticut River, produce steam and/or ground fog which becomes quite dense throughout the valley, hampering ground and air transportation.

The mean date of the last springtime temperature of 32 degrees or lower is April 22, and the mean date of the first autumn temperature of 32 degrees is October 15.

NORMALS, MEANS, AND EXTREMES

HARTFORD, CONNECTICUT

LATITUDE: 41°56'N LONGITUDE: 72°41' W ELEVATION: FT. GRND 169 BARO 201 TIME ZONE: EASTERN WBAN: 14740

	(a)	JAN	FEB	MAR	APR	MAY	JUNE	JULY	AUG	SEP	OCT	NOV	DEC	YEAR
TEMPERATURE °F:														
Normals														
-Daily Maximum		33.2	36.4	46.8	59.9	71.6	80.0	85.0	82.7	74.8	63.7	51.0	37.5	60.2
-Daily Minimum		15.8	18.6	28.1	37.5	47.6	56.9	62.2	60.4	51.8	40.7	32.8	21.3	39.5
-Monthly		24.6	27.5	37.5	48.7	59.6	68.5	73.7	71.6	63.3	52.2	41.9	29.5	49.9
Extremes														
-Record Highest	39	65	73	87	96	97	100	102	101	99	91	81	74	102
-Year		1967	1985	1977	1976	1979	1964	1966	1975	1983	1963	1974	1984	JUL 1966
-Record Lowest	39	-26	-21	-6	9	28	37	44	36	30	17	1	-14	-26
-Year		1961	1961	1967	1970	1985	1986	1962	1965	1979	1978	1989	1980	JAN 1961
NORMAL DEGREE DAYS:														
Heating (base 65°F)		1252	1050	853	489	194	20	0	6	96	397	693	1101	6151
Cooling (base 65°F)		0	0	0	0	27	125	270	210	45	0	0	0	677
% OF POSSIBLE SUNSHINE	39	55	57	56	55	57	60	62	62	59	57	46	48	56
MEAN SKY COVER (tenths)														
Sunrise - Sunset	39	6.4	6.5	6.7	6.7	6.8	6.6	6.4	6.3	6.1	5.9	6.9	6.7	6.5
MEAN NUMBER OF DAYS:														
Sunrise to Sunset														
-Clear	39	7.7	6.8	6.7	6.4	5.6	5.7	5.8	6.7	8.5	9.3	5.7	6.9	81.6
-Partly Cloudy	39	7.9	7.5	8.5	8.4	9.7	10.4	12.1	10.9	8.8	8.7	8.3	7.6	108.8
-Cloudy	39	15.4	13.9	15.8	15.2	15.7	13.9	13.2	13.4	12.7	13.0	16.1	16.5	174.8
Precipitation														
.01 inches or more	39	10.5	10.3	11.4	11.2	11.7	11.3	9.7	9.8	9.5	8.5	11.2	11.9	127.0
Snow,Ice pellets,hail														
1.0 inches or more	39	2.9	2.6	2.5	0.5	0.*	0.0	0.0	0.0	0.0	0.*	0.5	3.2	12.3
Thunderstorms	39	0.1	0.2	0.7	1.2	2.2	3.9	4.5	3.7	2.1	1.0	0.4	0.1	20.2
Heavy Fog Visibility 1/4 mile or less	39	2.2	2.4	2.2	1.3	1.7	2.3	1.9	2.3	3.2	3.6	2.2	2.9	28.4
Temperature °F														
-Maximum														
90° and above	34	0.0	0.0	0.0	0.3	1.2	3.4	7.6	4.8	1.3	0.*	0.0	0.0	18.8
32° and below	34	13.6	9.1	1.9	0.1	0.0	0.0	0.0	0.0	0.0	0.0	0.5	9.4	34.5
-Minimum														
32° and below	34	28.7	25.6	21.5	8.4	0.7	0.0	0.0	0.0	0.4	6.4	16.5	26.9	135.1
0° and below	34	2.8	1.6	0.*	0.0	0.0	0.0	0.0	0.0	0.0	0.0	0.0	1.1	5.5
AVG. STATION PRESS.(mb)	21	1010.0	1010.4	1009.3	1007.7	1008.4	1007.9	1008.5	1010.3	1011.7	1012.0	1011.1	1011.1	1009.9
RELATIVE HUMIDITY (%)														
Hour 01	34	69	68	68	69	76	81	82	84	86	81	75	73	76
Hour 07 (Local Time)	34	71	72	72	70	73	77	78	83	86	83	79	76	77
Hour 13	34	56	54	50	45	47	51	51	53	55	51	56	59	52
Hour 19	34	62	60	56	53	56	60	62	66	71	67	67	67	62
PRECIPITATION (inches):														
Water Equivalent														
-Normal		3.41	3.23	3.63	3.85	4.12	3.75	3.19	3.65	3.79	3.57	4.04	3.91	44.14
-Maximum Monthly	39	9.61	7.27	6.86	9.90	12.00	13.60	8.43	21.87	9.02	11.61	8.53	8.36	21.87
-Year		1978	1981	1983	1983	1989	1982	1988	1955	1975	1955	1972	1969	AUG 1955
-Minimum Monthly	39	0.38	0.45	0.27	1.38	0.73	0.67	1.07	0.54	0.84	0.35	0.51	0.78	0.27
-Year		1981	1987	1981	1966	1959	1988	1983	1981	1986	1963	1976	1955	MAR 1981
-Maximum in 24 hrs	39	2.56	2.16	2.62	3.01	4.90	6.14	3.48	12.12	5.28	4.45	2.90	3.12	12.12
-Year		1979	1965	1987	1979	1989	1982	1960	1955	1960	1959	1988	1973	AUG 1955
Snow,Ice pellets,hail														
-Maximum Monthly	39	37.0	32.2	43.3	14.3	1.3	T	0.0	0.0	0.0	1.7	8.7	35.4	43.3
-Year		1978	1969	1956	1982	1977	1993				1979	1986	1969	MAR 1956
-Maximum in 24 hrs	39	14.7	21.0	14.8	14.1	1.3	T	0.0	0.0	0.0	1.7	8.6	13.9	21.0
-Year		1978	1983	1993	1982	1977	1993				1979	1980	1969	FEB 1983
WIND:														
Mean Speed (mph)	39	9.0	9.5	10.0	10.0	8.8	8.1	7.4	7.2	7.3	7.8	8.5	8.7	8.5
Prevailing Direction through 1963		NW	NW	NW	S	S	S	S	S	S	N	S	N	S
Fastest Obs. 1 Min.														
-Direction (!!!)	8	30	29	18	29	05	30	35	18	17	26	19	31	17
-Speed (MPH)	8	30	37	37	33	28	26	35	40	43	33	40	39	43
-Year		1993	1989	1987	1988	1987	1986	1991	1988	1985	1986	1989	1992	SEP 1985
Peak Gust														
-Direction (!!!)	10	NW	NW	S	NW	NW	W	SW	NW	S	S	S	NW	SW
-Speed (mph)	10	49	49	62	48	48	53	89	55	66	72	60	55	89
-Date		1993	1990	1987	1988	1990	1993	1988	1991	1985	1990	1989	1992	JUL 1988

PRECIPITATION (inches)

HARTFORD, CONNECTICUT

YEAR	JAN	FEB	MAR	APR	MAY	JUNE	JULY	AUG	SEP	OCT	NOV	DEC	ANNUAL
1964	5.54	3.43	3.63	3.76	0.87	1.68	3.07	2.46	1.42	1.98	2.20	4.51	34.55
1965	2.73	4.43	1.50	2.14	1.20	1.98	1.68	1.09	3.50	4.97	2.21	2.02	29.45
1966	3.05	4.40	3.15	1.38	3.01	2.72	3.96	1.90	6.05	4.23	3.82	3.60	41.27
1967	2.01	2.00	4.43	4.18	6.34	3.82	2.59	4.34	2.85	2.59	3.13	6.77	45.05
1968	1.92	1.14	4.55	2.74	3.93	6.65	1.58	2.53	2.88	2.03	5.46	5.22	40.63
1969	1.19	3.32	3.11	5.63	3.13	2.63	5.79	3.32	3.53	1.45	6.17	8.36	47.63
1970	0.39	5.15	4.28	4.12	3.59	2.49	1.49	3.18	3.20	2.08	4.31	4.15	38.43
1971	2.80	4.60	3.24	2.85	4.08	0.71	3.23	5.31	4.24	4.46	5.68	3.55	44.75
1972	2.02	5.12	6.71	4.61	7.49	9.66	3.84	3.45	1.84	4.20	8.53	7.08	64.55
1973	3.28	3.05	3.22	6.59	5.95	5.07	1.77	4.50	3.73	3.47	2.14	8.31	51.08
1974	4.10	1.95	4.49	3.64	3.03	2.38	2.39	3.36	8.57	2.34	2.62	4.52	43.39
1975	4.30	3.22	3.82	2.99	3.29	3.83	6.11	4.60	9.02	5.28	4.57	4.31	55.34
1976	5.57	3.11	2.86	3.93	4.45	2.86	3.51	5.76	2.55	4.10	0.51	2.97	42.18
1977	2.41	2.81	6.57	4.89	3.70	3.99	3.37	2.44	8.17	5.45	4.38	5.68	53.86
1978	9.61	1.42	3.63	1.51	4.61	2.94	2.51	3.61	2.67	1.75	2.12	4.23	40.61
1979	9.12	2.83	4.25	5.88	3.48	0.91	1.97	4.44	2.95	4.76	3.46	2.57	46.62
1980	0.72	0.98	5.87	5.39	1.65	3.81	2.65	1.60	1.40	2.58	4.22	0.82	31.69
1981	0.38	7.27	0.27	2.92	2.17	1.37	4.21	0.54	4.49	5.19	2.34	4.00	35.15
1982	4.76	2.83	2.23	4.12	3.30	13.60	2.60	4.41	2.41	3.31	3.12	1.32	48.01
1983	4.68	3.83	6.86	9.90	4.82	2.61	1.07	2.55	2.10	5.52	6.09	5.97	56.00
1984	1.80	4.72	3.93	4.24	11.55	2.16	4.22	1.32	1.20	2.76	2.49	2.46	42.85
1985	0.73	1.72	2.16	1.54	2.77	3.55	4.55	6.44	3.83	2.27	6.04	1.28	36.88
1986	5.34	3.02	2.72	1.55	2.28	6.79	4.44	3.44	0.84	2.18	5.57	6.15	44.32
1987	6.20	0.45	4.44	5.23	2.18	3.66	2.27	4.25	7.19	3.67	3.66	1.57	44.77
1988	3.36	3.99	2.06	2.35	3.46	0.67	8.43	2.12	1.88	2.29	7.84	1.35	39.80
1989	0.88	1.85	3.02	3.33	12.00	6.65	3.40	6.81	4.67	7.62	2.89	1.49	54.61
1990	4.03	3.37	2.46	4.55	6.38	3.59	2.09	8.32	2.13	7.63	3.76	4.86	53.17
1991	2.45	1.78	4.52	3.54	5.18	2.37	2.90	8.69	5.67	3.17	4.03	2.96	47.26
1992	2.73	2.23	3.79	3.13	3.21	5.77	4.62	3.60	2.43	1.95	4.19	4.33	41.98
1993	2.63	2.90	6.67	4.71	1.92	2.63	4.90	1.80	5.35	4.15	3.27	4.16	45.09
Record Mean	3.50	3.17	3.74	3.76	3.71	3.59	3.57	3.91	3.62	3.24	3.83	3.71	43.35

AVERAGE TEMPERATURE (deg. F)

HARTFORD, CONNECTICUT

YEAR	JAN	FEB	MAR	APR	MAY	JUNE	JULY	AUG	SEP	OCT	NOV	DEC	ANNUAL
1964	27.1	25.9	37.7	48.8	62.6	68.3	75.0	68.1	63.0	51.3	43.3	29.7	50.1
1965	22.5	26.6	36.1	47.5	64.4	68.9	72.4	71.7	64.1	51.1	39.6	33.8	49.9
1966	26.4	28.8	39.1	46.9	56.4	70.7	75.8	73.4	63.4	51.9	46.2	31.8	50.9
1967	32.8	24.5	33.3	47.1	53.7	70.6	74.0	70.2	62.8	52.8	38.0	32.1	49.4
1968	21.1	25.8	39.9	52.4	58.2	67.4	75.1	70.8	65.0	54.7	38.9	25.4	49.6
1969	24.0	26.8	34.5	51.1	58.8	68.2	70.6	73.3	63.8	51.7	41.2	26.9	49.2
1970	16.8	28.2	35.1	49.0	61.5	67.8	75.2	73.8	65.4	54.9	44.1	26.8	49.9
1971	19.4	29.0	35.4	46.3	58.1	71.0	73.7	72.2	67.7	58.3	39.6	32.8	50.3
1972	27.9	26.0	34.6	44.3	60.1	65.9	73.8	71.1	64.3	48.9	38.7	30.8	48.9
1973	29.4	27.2	43.3	50.4	58.0	71.8	75.0	76.4	64.7	54.7	43.6	32.9	52.3
1974	28.2	27.0	36.8	50.7	56.6	67.3	73.7	72.7	63.3	47.3	40.7	30.7	49.6
1975	31.2	29.7	35.9	45.8	64.6	68.3	76.1	71.8	61.7	55.7	48.2	28.5	51.4
1976	19.5	34.8	40.3	53.3	58.4	72.7	72.4	71.0	62.4	49.9	38.3	24.8	49.8
1977	18.7	27.6	42.9	51.2	63.6	68.0	74.5	72.8	64.0	52.0	44.4	28.0	50.6
1978	23.6	22.1	35.1	48.1	59.9	69.2	71.9	70.0	58.6	49.0	38.6	29.3	47.9
1979	26.6	18.0	41.2	49.0	64.1	69.0	74.6	70.8	61.6	50.7	45.5	33.6	50.4
1980	27.6	24.3	35.2	49.2	61.0	66.4	74.2	73.2	64.9	50.3	37.9	24.6	49.1
1981	17.8	35.3	38.1	52.0	61.6	69.6	74.8	70.6	62.5	49.3	43.7	31.0	50.6
1982	18.8	29.2	36.7	45.8	61.4	65.0	74.4	69.5	63.0	51.5	45.8	36.0	49.8
1983	27.1	29.1	39.2	48.9	56.8	69.9	74.9	72.7	66.5	52.5	42.7	28.1	50.7
1984	21.8	34.3	31.4	48.0	56.0	69.8	71.8	73.2	59.8	55.2	41.5	35.7	49.9
1985	21.5	29.9	39.7	50.7	60.6	63.7	72.4	70.2	63.4	51.9	43.2	27.5	49.6
1986	27.4	26.2	38.7	51.0	61.7	66.0	72.3	69.5	61.8	51.4	38.3	33.1	49.8
1987	25.0	26.7	39.8	49.7	60.8	68.8	74.2	69.0	62.9	49.2	41.4	33.2	50.1
1988	23.1	28.3	38.5	47.4	59.7	66.7	75.2	74.5	62.2	47.6	42.3	29.3	49.6
1989	30.8	28.6	37.4	46.5	60.4	68.3	72.6	71.4	63.9	53.4	40.9	18.1	49.4
1990	34.7	33.0	40.2	49.2	56.7	69.0	74.4	73.3	64.0	57.4	44.5	36.7	52.8
1991	27.0	33.9	40.5	53.3	65.8	70.5	73.7	73.1	62.1	55.1	42.7	32.8	52.5
1992	28.6	30.3	34.6	46.4	58.5	66.4	69.9	69.1	62.6	49.2	40.6	31.2	49.0
1993	28.8	23.8	34.5	49.6	61.2	68.6	74.3	73.4	63.0	49.8	40.8	30.9	49.9
Record Mean	26.6	27.9	37.2	48.2	59.3	67.9	73.2	71.0	63.5	53.0	42.1	30.4	50.0
Max	34.8	36.4	46.1	58.5	70.4	78.7	83.7	81.4	74.1	63.7	50.7	38.2	59.7
Min	18.5	19.3	28.2	37.9	48.1	57.1	62.6	60.6	52.8	42.2	33.4	22.6	40.3

REFERENCE NOTES

HARTFORD, CONNECTICUT

GENERAL
T - TRACE AMOUNT.
BLANK ENTRIES DENOTE MISSING/UNREPORTED DATA.
# INDICATES A STATION OR INSTRUMENT RELOCATION.

SPECIFIC

PM - INCLUDES LAST DAY OF PREVIOUS MONTH
ASOS - AUTOMATED SURFACE OBSERVING SYSTEM IN OPERATION DURING THESE MONTHS.

(a) - LENGTH OF RECORD IN YEARS, ALTHOUGH INDIVIDUAL MONTHS MAY BE MISSING.
0.* OR * - THE VALUE IS BETWEEN 0.0 AND 0.05
NORMALS - BASED ON THE 1961-1990 RECORD PERIOD.
EXTREMES - DATES ARE THE MOST RECENT OCCURRENCE
WIND DIR.- NUMERALS SHOW TENS OF DEGRESS CLOCKWISE FROM TRUE NORTH. "00" INDICATES CALM.
RESULTANT DIRECTIONS ARE GIVEN TO WHOLE DEGREES.
BOLD VALUES INDICATE EXTREME VALUES WHICH OCCURRED AFTER THE ASOS SYSTEM WAS COMMISSIONED.

RECORD = PERIOD OF RECORD
RECORD MEAN PRECIPITATION IS THE MEAN OF ALL DAILY PRECIPITATION AMOUNTS DURING THE PERIOD OF RECORD.
RECORD MAX(MIN) TEMPERATURE IS THE MEAN OF ALL DAILY MAX(MIN) TEMPERATURES DURING THE PERIOD OF RECORD.
RECORD MEAN TEMPERATURE IS THE SUM OF THE RECORD MAX AND RECORD MIN DIVIDED BY 2.
AVERAGE TEMPERATURE IS THE SUM OF THE MEAN DAILY MAX AND MIN TEMPERATURE DIVIDED BY 2.

EXCEPTIONS

RECORD MEANS ARE THROUGH THE CURRENT YEAR, BEGINNING IN
1905 FOR TEMPERATURE
1905 FOR PRECIPITATION
1955 FOR SNOWFALL

HEATING DEGREE DAYS Base 65 deg. F — HARTFORD, CONNECTICUT

SEASON	JULY	AUG	SEP	OCT	NOV	DEC	JAN	FEB	MAR	APR	MAY	JUNE	TOTAL
1964-65	2	16	128	419	644	1084	1311	1068	888	518	99	45	6222
1965-66	2	34	110	426	753	961	1186	1008	792	534	275	31	6112
1966-67	0	0	98	398	554	1019	993	1126	976	530	349	18	6061
1967-68	0	10	112	380	803	1013	1353	1134	771	374	205	46	6201
1968-69	0	16	56	326	775	1219	1262	1063	938	415	221	27	6318
1969-70	8	7	116	409	707	1175	1485	1026	922	483	161	37	6536
1970-71	0	0	89	322	619	1177	1410	1001	911	556	215	17	6317
1971-72	2	11	55	214	756	992	1140	1125	935	619	172	50	6071
1972-73	6	9	82	494	782	1054	1097	1051	665	444	229	13	5926
1973-74	0	0	102	322	635	988	1134	1056	868	435	287	37	5864
1974-75	2	1	121	542	725	1057	1040	986	894	567	111	43	6089
1975-76	0	11	121	292	503	1125	1403	869	759	391	213	20	5707
1976-77	0	16	118	467	794	1242	1429	1038	684	419	130	45	6382
1977-78	1	8	112	399	610	1141	1276	1192	920	500	220	25	6404
1978-79	9	15	209	489	790	1102	1184	1310	730	473	81	26	6418
1979-80	16	30	152	442	578	965	1151	1174	916	466	146	68	6104
1980-81	0	0	99	449	808	1246	1456	824	828	380	149	10	6249
1981-82	0	9	115	481	635	1048	1427	996	871	569	128	64	6343
1982-83	1	30	96	416	575	894	1170	1002	793	483	261	24	5745
1983-84	0	7	106	404	662	1135	1332	884	1035	503	286	32	6386
1984-85	3	3	186	298	698	896	1341	975	776	428	167	76	5847
1985-86	0	14	119	401	648	1157	1159	1081	809	413	174	63	6038
1986-87	14	32	135	422	793	981	1230	1065	773	452	191	29	6117
1987-88	1	31	100	481	700	981	1292	1057	817	523	186	75	6244
1988-89	9	23	112	539	672	1101	1054	1012	847	553	175	31	6128
1989-90	0	22	103	354	715	1444	935	890	763	478	251	21	5976
1990-91	5	0	112	276	608	873	1170	863	755	373	107	16	5158
1991-92	1	0	156	311	663	990	1122	1002	936	553	218	37	5989
1992-93	9	16	138	486	722	1042	1114	1148	935	454	139	43	6246
1993-94	3	4	142	464	722	1049							

COOLING DEGREE DAYS Base 65 deg. F — HARTFORD, CONNECTICUT

YEAR	JAN	FEB	MAR	APR	MAY	JUNE	JULY	AUG	SEP	OCT	NOV	DEC	TOTAL
1969	0	0	0	4	35	131	189	273	88	5	0	0	725
1970	0	0	0	8	58	129	322	280	108	16	0	0	921
1971	0	0	0	0	7	201	274	243	142	11	4	0	882
1972	0	0	0	3	30	83	286	203	70	1	0	0	676
1973	0	0	0	11	19	221	318	362	99	8	0	0	1038
1974	0	0	0	11	34	110	282	247	77	0	3	0	764
1975	0	0	0	0	106	147	348	229	27	7	6	0	870
1976	0	0	0	47	18	257	236	208	47	6	0	0	819
1977	0	0	4	13	93	144	303	259	88	1	0	0	905
1978	0	0	0	0	71	159	228	173	26	0	0	0	657
1979	0	0	0	0	60	151	320	218	56	6	0	0	811
1980	0	0	0	0	31	117	296	263	107	1	0	0	815
1981	0	0	0	0	53	152	311	190	48	0	0	0	754
1982	0	0	0	0	22	70	298	176	45	2	3	0	616
1983	0	0	0	5	16	177	313	253	158	23	0	0	945
1984	0	0	0	0	11	182	218	265	38	4	0	0	718
1985	0	0	0	3	37	44	234	182	78	3	0	0	581
1986	0	0	0	0	79	103	249	179	48	7	0	0	665
1987	0	0	0	3	70	150	292	161	42	0	0	0	718
1988	0	0	0	0	27	134	331	326	37	6	0	0	861
1989	0	0	0	0	37	136	240	224	77	0	0	0	714
1990	0	0	0	13	1	146	305	263	89	48	1	0	866
1991	0	0	0	29	139	191	278	257	76	12	0	0	982
1992	0	0	0	0	21	85	170	151	74	2	0	0	503
1993	0	0	0	0	28	155	297	271	89	0	0	0	840

SNOWFALL (inches) — HARTFORD, CONNECTICUT

SEASON	JULY	AUG	SEP	OCT	NOV	DEC	JAN	FEB	MAR	APR	MAY	JUNE	TOTAL
1964-65	0.0	0.0	0.0	T	T	12.3	28.7	6.0	7.8	1.7	0.0	0.0	56.5
1965-66	0.0	0.0	0.0	0.0	T	4.5	18.4	19.1	10.6	T	0.0	0.0	52.6
1966-67	0.0	0.0	0.0	0.0	T	20.0	3.0	25.2	33.2	1.4	T	0.0	82.8
1967-68	0.0	0.0	0.0	0.0	3.7	21.7	7.5	1.6	6.8	0.0	0.0	0.0	41.3
1968-69	0.0	0.0	0.0	0.0	7.9	13.9	3.4	32.2	4.4	0.0	0.0	0.0	61.8
1969-70	0.0	0.0	0.0	T	T	35.4	3.2	6.7	14.7	2.0	0.0	0.0	62.0
1970-71	0.0	0.0	0.0	T	T	27.0	17.7	8.4	12.8	4.0	0.0	0.0	69.9
1971-72	0.0	0.0	0.0	0.0	8.2	6.6	2.9	24.9	13.2	2.7	0.0	0.0	58.5
1972-73	0.0	0.0	0.0	0.4	2.1	12.0	14.1	5.9	0.4	0.3	0.0	0.0	35.2
1973-74	0.0	0.0	0.0	0.0	T	3.1	14.3	5.8	4.8	2.1	0.0	0.0	30.1
1974-75	0.0	0.0	0.0	T	0.8	8.5	10.2	16.0	2.5	0.3	0.0	0.0	38.3
1975-76	0.0	0.0	0.0	0.0	0.3	13.4	15.6	5.0	12.3	0.0	0.0	0.0	46.6
1976-77	0.0	0.0	0.0	0.0	0.4	7.3	20.0	9.1	11.0	0.3	1.3	0.0	49.4
1977-78	0.0	0.0	0.0	0.0	1.3	12.6	37.0	18.1	13.3	T	0.0	0.0	82.3
1978-79	0.0	0.0	0.0	0.0	4.3	10.3	8.6	9.2	T	3.6	0.0	0.0	36.0
1979-80	0.0	0.0	0.0	1.7	0.0	0.9	0.2	7.7	5.9	T	0.0	0.0	16.4
1980-81	0.0	0.0	0.0	0.0	8.6	3.9	4.1	0.9	0.2	0.0	0.0	0.0	17.7
1981-82	0.0	0.0	0.0	T	T	13.1	16.7	5.8	6.5	14.3	0.0	0.0	56.4
1982-83	0.0	0.0	0.0	0.0	T	5.7	10.2	29.4	0.2	0.9	0.0	0.0	46.4
1983-84	0.0	0.0	0.0	0.0	T	7.9	14.7	1.3	19.3	T	0.0	0.0	43.2
1984-85	0.0	0.0	0.0	0.0	0.1	3.8	6.9	9.4	2.1	1.4	0.0	0.0	23.7
1985-86	0.0	0.0	0.0	0.0	2.0	5.4	5.1	11.8	0.2	0.8	0.0	0.0	25.3
1986-87	0.0	0.0	0.0	0.0	8.7	4.9	34.0	1.6	1.7	0.4	0.0	0.0	51.3
1987-88	0.0	0.0	0.0	T	8.6	5.8	22.6	17.6	4.9	T	T	0.0	59.5
1988-89	0.0	0.0	0.0	0.0	0.0	6.3	0.6	4.6	3.4	T	T	0.0	14.9
1989-90	0.0	0.0	0.0	0.0	5.3	12.4	10.5	9.0	4.3	1.5	0.0	0.0	43.0
1990-91	0.0	0.0	0.0	0.0	T	8.1	10.2	5.8	5.7	0.0	0.0	0.0	29.8
1991-92	0.0	0.0	0.0	0.0	0.7	6.0	1.7	5.3	7.3	2.6	0.0	0.0	23.6
1992-93	0.0	0.0	0.0	T	T	6.7	10.5	13.8	31.1	T	0.0	T	62.1
1993-94	0.0	0.0	0.0	0.0	T	6.7							
Record Mean	0.0	0.0	0.0	0.1	2.0	10.3	12.0	11.4	9.9	1.6	T	T	47.1

WILMINGTON, DELAWARE

Delaware is part of the Atlantic Coastal Plain consisting mainly of flat low land with many marshes. Small streams and tidal estuaries comprise the drainage of the State. Wilmington, at the northern end of the State, marks the beginning of low rolling hills extending northward and northwestward into Pennsylvania. The Delaware River, the Delaware Bay, and the Atlantic Ocean are along the eastern boundary of the State. The broad Chesapeake Bay lies 35 miles, or less, to the west of the western boundary of nearly the entire State. These large water areas considerably influence the climate of the Wilmington, Delaware region.

Summers are warm and humid, winters are usually mild. During the summer maximum temperatures are usually in the 80s. The temperature reaches 100 degrees on the average once in six years. During January, the coldest month of the year, the daily average temperature is 32 degrees. Temperatures of zero may be expected once in four years. Most of the winter precipitation falls as rain. Seasonal snowfall has been as little as 1 inch, and as much as 50 inches. Snow is frequently mixed with rain and sleet, and seldom remains on the ground more than a few days.

The proximity of large water areas and the inflow of southerly winds cause the relative humidity to be quite high all year. During the summer months the relative humidity is approximately 75 percent. Fog is relatively frequent and may occur in any month. Light southeast winds blowing up the Delaware Bay favor the formation of fog. Light north–northeast winds bring in smoke from Philadelphia and from the heavy industry area located along the Delaware River north of Wilmington.

Rainfall distribution throughout the year is fairly uniform, however, the greatest amounts normally come during the summer months. Mostly, the summer rainfall comes in the form of thunderstorms. Moisture deficiencies for crops occur occasionally, but severe droughts are rare. During the fall, winter, and spring seasons, much of the rainfall comes from storms forming over the southern states or the South Atlantic and moving northward along the coast. During the late summer and early fall, hurricanes occasionally cause heavy rainfall, but winds seldom reach hurricane force in Wilmington. Heavy rains occasionally cause minor flooding, but the streams and rivers of northern Delaware are not subject to major flooding. Strong easterly and southeasterly winds sometimes cause high tides in the Delaware Bay and the Delaware River, resulting in the flooding of lowlands and damage to bay front and river front properties.

Based on the 1951–1980 period, the average first occurrence of 32 degrees Fahrenheit in the fall is October 29 and the average last occurrence in the spring is April 13.

NORMALS, MEANS, AND EXTREMES

WILMINGTON, DELAWARE

LATITUDE: 39°40'N LONGITUDE: 75°36' W ELEVATION: FT. GRND 74 BARO 96 TIME ZONE: EASTERN WBAN: 13781

	(a)	JAN	FEB	MAR	APR	MAY	JUNE	JULY	AUG	SEP	OCT	NOV	DEC	YEAR
TEMPERATURE °F:														
Normals														
-Daily Maximum		38.7	41.9	52.1	62.6	72.9	81.4	85.6	84.1	77.7	66.6	55.5	43.9	63.6
-Daily Minimum		22.4	24.8	33.1	41.8	52.2	61.6	67.1	65.9	58.2	45.7	37.0	27.6	44.8
-Monthly		30.6	33.4	42.7	52.2	62.5	71.5	76.4	75.0	68.0	56.2	46.3	35.8	54.2
Extremes														
-Record Highest	46	75	78	86	94	95	99	102	101	100	91	85	74	102
-Year		1950	1985	1948	1985	1962	1952	1966	1955	1983	1951	1950	1984	JUL 1966
-Record Lowest	46	-14	-6	2	18	30	41	48	43	36	24	14	-7	-14
-Year		1985	1979	1984	1982	1978	1972	1988	1982	1974	1976	1955	1983	JAN 1985
NORMAL DEGREE DAYS:														
Heating (base 65°F)		1066	885	691	384	122	0	0	0	35	288	561	905	4937
Cooling (base 65°F)		0	0	0	0	44	199	353	310	125	15	0	0	1046
% OF POSSIBLE SUNSHINE														
MEAN SKY COVER (tenths)														
Sunrise - Sunset	46	6.6	6.4	6.4	6.4	6.5	6.0	5.9	5.8	5.7	5.5	6.4	6.6	6.2
MEAN NUMBER OF DAYS:														
Sunrise to Sunset														
-Clear	46	7.2	7.3	7.8	7.2	6.6	7.7	8.0	9.1	10.0	10.8	7.6	7.6	96.9
-Partly Cloudy	46	7.2	6.7	8.1	8.3	10.0	10.8	11.3	10.2	8.0	8.3	8.1	7.4	104.3
-Cloudy	46	16.6	14.2	15.2	14.5	14.4	11.5	11.7	11.7	12.0	11.9	14.3	16.0	164.1
Precipitation														
.01 inches or more	46	10.7	9.4	11.0	10.9	11.3	9.6	9.2	8.9	8.2	7.7	9.4	9.9	116.1
Snow,Ice pellets,hail														
1.0 inches or more	46	2.1	1.5	0.9	0.1	0.0	0.0	0.0	0.0	0.0	0.*	0.2	0.9	5.7
Thunderstorms	46	0.2	0.3	1.2	2.1	4.3	5.8	6.2	5.7	2.4	0.9	0.6	0.2	29.8
Heavy Fog Visibility														
1/4 mile or less	46	4.0	3.4	2.9	2.0	2.2	1.7	1.6	2.3	2.5	3.9	3.5	3.6	33.7
Temperature °F														
-Maximum														
90° and above	46	0.0	0.0	0.0	0.2	0.9	3.9	8.2	5.2	1.7	0.*	0.0	0.0	20.1
32° and below	46	7.3	4.4	0.8	0.0	0.0	0.0	0.0	0.0	0.0	0.0	0.1	4.0	16.5
-Minimum														
32° and below	46	25.4	22.0	15.2	3.0	0.*	0.0	0.0	0.0	0.0	1.6	10.3	22.2	99.8
0° and below	46	0.5	0.2	0.0	0.0	0.0	0.0	0.0	0.0	0.0	0.0	0.0	0.1	0.7
AVG. STATION PRESS.(mb)	21	1015.8	1015.7	1014.0	1012.4	1012.7	1012.4	1013.0	1014.5	1015.8	1016.6	1016.4	1016.5	1014.7
RELATIVE HUMIDITY (%)														
Hour 01	46	73	72	71	73	79	82	83	85	85	83	77	75	78
Hour 07 (Local Time)	46	75	74	74	73	76	78	79	83	85	84	80	76	78
Hour 13	46	60	57	52	50	53	53	54	57	56	54	56	60	55
Hour 19	46	68	64	61	60	64	64	66	70	71	70	69	69	66
PRECIPITATION (inches):														
Water Equivalent														
-Normal		3.03	2.91	3.43	3.39	3.84	3.55	4.23	3.40	3.43	2.88	3.27	3.48	40.84
-Maximum Monthly	46	8.41	7.02	7.50	6.80	7.38	7.49	12.63	12.09	9.53	6.41	7.84	7.90	12.63
-Year		1978	1979	1993	1983	1983	1972	1989	1955	1960	1971	1972	1969	JUL 1989
-Minimum Monthly	46	0.52	0.83	0.81	0.35	0.22	0.21	0.16	0.25	0.82	0.21	0.49	0.19	0.16
-Year		1981	1980	1966	1985	1964	1988	1955	1972	1970	1963	1976	1955	JUL 1955
-Maximum in 24 hrs	46	2.12	2.29	3.11	2.56	2.72	4.35	6.83	4.11	5.62	3.88	3.83	2.33	6.83
-Year		1978	1966	1978	1961	1990	1972	1989	1971	1960	1966	1956	1992	JUL 1989
Snow,Ice pellets,hail														
-Maximum Monthly	46	21.4	27.5	20.3	2.6	T	T	T	0.0	0.0	2.5	11.9	21.5	27.5
-Year		1987	1979	1958	1982	1991	1992	1990			1979	1953	1966	FEB 1979
-Maximum in 24 hrs	46	12.1	16.5	15.6	2.4	T	T	T	0.0	0.0	2.5	11.9	12.4	16.5
-Year		1987	1979	1958	1987	1991	1992	1990			1979	1953	1966	FEB 1979
WIND:														
Mean Speed (mph)	45	9.8	10.4	11.1	10.5	9.0	8.4	7.8	7.4	7.8	8.2	9.1	9.3	9.1
Prevailing Direction through 1963		WNW	NW	WNW	WNW	S	S	NW	S	S	NW	NW	WNW	S
Fastest Obs. 1 Min.														
-Direction (!!)	45	29	29	06	29	30	34	27	35	07	20	16	32	20
-Speed (MPH)	45	46	46	43	45	46	43	48	46	40	58	46	46	58
-Year		1957	1956	1984	1963	1984	1991	1963	1971	1956	1954	1950	1988	OCT 1954
Peak Gust														
-Direction (!!)	10	NW	NW	NE	NW	NW	NW	S	NW	NW	W	NW	NW	NW
-Speed (mph)	10	51	51	59	47	71	52	66	60	64	58	59	69	71
-Date		1986	1987	1993	1993	1984	1989	1993	1990	1985	1987	1989	1988	MAY 1984

PRECIPITATION (inches)

WILMINGTON, DELAWARE

YEAR	JAN	FEB	MAR	APR	MAY	JUNE	JULY	AUG	SEP	OCT	NOV	DEC	ANNUAL
1964	4.13	3.37	2.20	5.97	0.22	1.02	3.70	1.83	2.77	1.29	1.62	4.70	32.82
1965	2.38	2.17	3.20	1.76	1.41	1.62	3.84	2.04	2.41	1.59	0.94	1.54	24.90
1966	2.82	4.90	0.81	3.16	3.35	0.70	3.09	1.42	8.53	5.17	1.75	3.81	39.51
1967	1.67	1.90	5.45	2.69	3.79	3.01	4.45	11.16	1.16	2.05	2.08	5.24	44.65
1968	2.29	1.52	4.75	1.57	4.78	2.81	1.83	1.17	1.50	3.28	3.92	2.33	31.75
1969	1.68	1.76	1.71	1.58	3.21	3.62	6.48	2.34	6.84	1.47	1.79	7.90	40.38
1970	1.00	2.13	3.61	5.56	0.94	6.16	6.03	2.31	0.82	2.64	4.09	3.02	38.31
1971	2.22	6.29	2.29	2.15	4.51	2.50	3.65	8.38	6.99	6.41	5.52	1.33	52.24
1972	2.50	5.43	2.40	4.47	3.85	7.49	2.07	0.25	1.64	4.20	7.84	5.99	48.13
1973	3.81	3.42	4.02	6.57	5.56	5.19	2.82	2.44	3.02	2.22	0.67	7.31	47.05
1974	2.92	1.73	4.56	3.08	3.96	3.97	1.49	5.11	5.65	1.77	1.19	4.18	39.61
1975	4.23	2.95	4.63	3.03	5.65	6.16	5.53	2.55	6.19	3.06	2.63	3.00	49.61
1976	4.21	1.70	2.25	1.40	5.05	2.14	4.33	2.00	2.11	6.12	0.49	1.79	33.59
1977	2.18	1.09	4.55	3.91	0.96	4.41	1.38	4.82	1.29	3.59	6.14	5.81	40.13
1978	8.41	1.77	5.59	2.16	6.94	3.00	5.53	5.97	2.18	1.48	2.69	5.56	51.28
1979	7.61	7.02	2.61	4.03	3.10	4.01	4.76	6.11	5.94	3.45	3.23	1.44	53.31
1980	2.44	0.83	6.22	4.55	2.40	4.23	3.49	1.09	1.44	3.99	2.41	0.83	33.92
1981	0.52	3.23	1.26	3.54	5.05	4.50	2.52	3.38	3.82	2.84	0.67	3.95	35.28
1982	3.75	2.71	2.87	5.41	3.72	4.70	2.70	4.68	2.30	1.97	3.87	2.39	41.07
1983	2.98	3.55	6.84	6.80	7.38	3.94	2.33	1.29	3.44	3.87	5.48	6.80	54.70
1984	1.25	4.27	5.40	4.24	5.03	4.54	6.53	1.56	2.02	3.31	1.63	1.94	41.72
1985	1.56	2.05	2.03	0.35	5.52	1.37	6.91	2.28	4.56	1.84	4.46	0.80	33.73
1986	4.21	2.77	1.19	2.77	1.69	4.05	3.99	2.88	2.75	4.04	6.42	6.11	42.87
1987	4.35	1.52	1.16	2.63	3.15	2.31	4.09	4.21	4.85	2.31	3.50	1.90	35.98
1988	2.46	4.14	1.82	2.59	4.95	0.21	8.29	3.03	2.18	1.94	5.29	0.90	37.80
1989	2.48	2.75	3.69	2.76	6.57	5.43	12.63	1.97	4.31	3.92	1.99	1.27	49.77
1990	3.56	1.35	2.15	3.42	7.03	3.94	4.27	6.15	2.64	2.85	1.61	5.16	44.13
1991	4.30	0.97	4.64	3.28	1.98	3.41	3.71	5.38	5.36	1.27	1.26	4.26	39.82
1992	1.05	1.81	4.36	1.76	4.48	3.14	4.34	2.21	4.30	1.11	4.27	4.21	37.04
1993	2.64	3.11	7.50	5.87	3.95	1.60	4.04	2.65	6.26	2.77	2.85	3.51	46.75
Record Mean	3.29	3.04	3.70	3.51	3.69	3.73	4.54	4.50	3.65	2.99	3.24	3.44	43.30

AVERAGE TEMPERATURE (deg. F)

WILMINGTON, DELAWARE

YEAR	JAN	FEB	MAR	APR	MAY	JUNE	JULY	AUG	SEP	OCT	NOV	DEC	ANNUAL
1964	33.2	31.6	43.1	49.4	64.3	72.1	75.8	71.5	67.2	52.8	47.6	37.3	53.8
1965	29.0	33.6	38.4	49.3	66.0	70.2	74.5	73.3	69.4	53.6	45.0	37.7	53.3
1966	29.3	31.9	42.9	47.9	60.3	72.5	77.2	74.8	65.3	53.6	46.6	34.8	53.1
1967	36.2	29.4	39.4	51.5	55.4	71.2	74.4	72.8	65.1	54.7	40.7	36.8	52.3
1968	28.0	30.5	44.6	54.1	59.6	71.4	76.7	77.1	69.7	59.0	47.0	34.2	54.3
1969	30.8	33.6	39.6	55.1	64.2	73.4	75.7	75.4	68.2	56.0	44.6	32.7	54.1
1970	24.5	33.5	38.9	51.9	64.8	71.7	76.6	76.7	72.1	60.4	48.5	35.9	54.6
1971	27.4	35.5	40.7	51.1	60.4	73.4	75.9	74.0	71.1	62.9	45.7	42.1	55.0
1972	36.1	32.6	41.3	50.0	62.5	68.6	76.9	75.5	69.6	53.5	45.2	41.6	54.4
1973	35.6	35.5	49.4	54.7	61.4	75.8	78.1	78.1	70.4	59.9	49.1	37.7	57.2
1974	36.2	33.1	44.3	55.5	62.4	70.4	76.7	76.1	66.5	53.2	46.6	38.9	55.0
1975	37.5	35.9	40.6	47.5	65.2	71.5	75.7	76.3	65.4	60.0	51.0	36.2	55.2
1976	27.7	41.2	46.5	54.7	59.9	72.4	74.2	73.7	66.9	52.5	40.4	31.0	53.4
1977	20.8	33.3	47.2	54.4	63.9	68.9	76.4	75.4	69.3	53.4	46.6	33.4	53.6
1978	27.2	22.8	37.6	50.3	60.3	70.6	73.4	77.1	66.7	54.1	46.8	37.2	52.0
1979	31.4	22.1	45.4	50.6	63.8	67.9	75.3	75.0	68.2	55.0	49.6	38.1	53.5
1980	32.4	29.9	40.0	54.6	64.9	68.9	77.7	78.2	71.3	54.8	43.3	33.1	54.1
1981	25.4	37.9	40.2	55.0	62.5	72.3	77.1	73.5	66.9	53.0	45.3	34.2	53.6
1982	24.2	34.2	41.8	50.6	65.0	69.9	77.3	72.0	67.4	56.0	47.5	41.3	53.9
1983	35.2	35.3	45.9	53.1	61.0	71.8	77.6	77.0	69.3	56.9	46.7	32.1	55.2
1984	24.8	38.6	35.6	50.7	61.2	73.8	75.2	75.2	63.7	61.2	43.3	42.1	53.8
1985	27.5	37.4	47.1	58.0	65.9	70.6	76.6	74.4	69.1	58.3	51.0	32.9	55.7
1986	32.2	31.6	43.6	52.4	65.7	72.1	77.1	72.5	67.5	57.2	44.1	37.3	54.4
1987	31.4	31.9	44.6	52.3	63.1	73.5	79.1	74.3	68.3	51.7	47.4	38.6	54.7
1988	27.4	34.8	44.2	50.8	62.9	71.6	79.4	77.3	65.8	51.0	46.7	35.1	53.9
1989	36.0	34.3	42.1	51.6	62.1	74.3	75.9	74.4	68.4	57.6	44.6	25.0	53.9
1990	40.5	41.1	46.0	53.7	61.5	72.1	77.4	74.6	66.7	60.0	48.4	41.0	56.9
1991	34.3	39.7	44.9	54.7	69.1	73.6	77.3	76.7	67.2	57.6	46.8	39.5	56.8
1992	35.2	37.2	41.5	52.0	60.7	69.6	76.3	72.2	67.3	53.2	47.2	38.3	54.2
1993	37.6	31.0	39.0	52.8	65.3	72.8	79.4	77.8	68.7	55.7	47.4	36.4	55.3
Record Mean	32.3	33.3	42.1	52.3	62.8	71.3	76.1	74.3	67.8	56.5	45.8	35.3	54.2
Max	40.1	41.6	51.5	62.8	73.4	81.6	85.7	83.7	77.6	66.5	54.6	43.1	63.5
Min	24.4	24.9	32.7	41.8	52.1	61.1	66.5	64.8	58.1	46.6	37.0	27.5	44.8

REFERENCE NOTES

WILMINGTON, DELAWARE

GENERAL
T - TRACE AMOUNT.
BLANK ENTRIES DENOTE MISSING/UNREPORTED DATA.
# INDICATES A STATION OR INSTRUMENT RELOCATION.

SPECIFIC

PM - INCLUDES LAST DAY OF PREVIOUS MONTH
ASOS - AUTOMATED SURFACE OBSERVING SYSTEM IN OPERATION DURING THESE MONTHS.

(a) - LENGTH OF RECORD IN YEARS, ALTHOUGH INDIVIDUAL MONTHS MAY BE MISSING.
0.* OR * - THE VALUE IS BETWEEN 0.0 AND 0.05
NORMALS - BASED ON THE 1961-1990 RECORD PERIOD.
EXTREMES - DATES ARE THE MOST RECENT OCCURRENCE
WIND DIR.- NUMERALS SHOW TENS OF DEGRESS CLOCKWISE FROM TRUE NORTH. "00" INDICATES CALM.
RESULTANT DIRECTIONS ARE GIVEN TO WHOLE DEGREES.
BOLD VALUES INDICATE EXTREME VALUES WHICH OCCURRED AFTER THE ASOS SYSTEM WAS COMMISSIONED.

RECORD = PERIOD OF RECORD
RECORD MEAN PRECIPITATION IS THE MEAN OF ALL DAILY PRECIPITATION AMOUNTS DURING THE PERIOD OF RECORD.
RECORD MAX(MIN) TEMPERATURE IS THE MEAN OF ALL DAILY MAX(MIN) TEMPERATURES DURING THE PERIOD OF RECORD.
RECORD MEAN TEMPERATURE IS THE SUM OF THE RECORD MAX AND RECORD MIN DIVIDED BY 2.
AVERAGE TEMPERATURE IS THE SUM OF THE MEAN DAILY MAX AND MIN TEMPERATURE DIVIDED BY 2.

EXCEPTIONS

RECORD MEANS ARE THROUGH THE CURRENT YEAR, BEGINNING IN 1895 FOR TEMPERATURE
1894 FOR PRECIPITATION
1948 FOR SNOWFALL

HEATING DEGREE DAYS Base 65 deg. F — WILMINGTON, DELAWARE

SEASON	JULY	AUG	SEP	OCT	NOV	DEC	JAN	FEB	MAR	APR	MAY	JUNE	TOTAL
1964-65	0	9	49	372	514	854	1108	873	816	467	63	27	5152
1965-66	0	12	40	349	593	839	1103	921	676	507	186	24	5250
1966-67	0	0	84	346	545	931	888	991	788	402	295	5	5275
1967-68	0	0	80	327	722	866	1139	994	626	319	171	6	5250
1968-69	0	0	7	205	532	949	1052	874	780	298	92	1	4790
1969-70	0	0	41	288	606	993	1250	876	803	389	95	1	5342
1970-71	0	0	25	175	487	895	1159	821	746	411	153	3	4875
1971-72	0	2	23	93	585	702	889	935	732	443	105	27	4536
1972-73	0	0	20	356	586	716	902	820	477	322	143	0	4342
1973-74	0	0	15	179	469	839	886	887	635	300	137	7	4354
1974-75	0	0	65	362	553	805	847	808	753	520	84	5	4802
1975-76	0	0	56	177	418	888	1149	681	567	341	178	31	4486
1976-77	0	4	44	387	734	1047	1361	884	546	333	107	32	5479
1977-78	0	1	31	353	550	975	1165	1179	842	433	191	17	5737
1978-79	6	0	60	337	542	854	1037	1197	605	424	89	28	5179
1979-80	4	7	31	318	458	827	1004	1009	768	307	83	35	4851
1980-81	0	0	20	322	645	985	1222	752	763	299	135	4	5147
1981-82	0	0	57	370	585	947	1259	855	715	426	69	12	5295
1982-83	0	14	29	305	519	724	919	822	587	368	163	7	4457
1983-84	0	0	74	275	542	1013	1240	758	904	422	162	5	5395
1984-85	0	2	113	149	641	701	1154	766	550	248	73	7	4404
1985-86	0	0	45	213	411	986	1011	930	653	373	99	11	4732
1986-87	0	27	36	276	619	848	1032	923	628	374	143	2	4908
1987-88	0	2	22	406	521	811	1159	869	637	419	121	38	5005
1988-89	3	0	52	434	541	923	893	854	710	395	142	0	4947
1989-90	0	2	54	236	605	1231	749	661	593	368	127	6	4632
1990-91	2	1	69	214	494	734	943	700	617	320	61	5	4160
1991-92	0	0	64	244	541	785	914	799	723	386	169	12	4637
1992-93	0	1	57	363	527	817	843	945	799	360	64	12	4788
1993-94	0	0	55	286	526	879							

COOLING DEGREE DAYS Base 65 deg. F — WILMINGTON, DELAWARE

YEAR	JAN	FEB	MAR	APR	MAY	JUNE	JULY	AUG	SEP	OCT	NOV	DEC	TOTAL
1969	0	0	0	8	73	258	336	330	143	14	0	0	1162
1970	0	0	0	2	97	211	365	371	244	38	0	0	1328
1971	0	0	0	0	16	261	345	287	214	34	16	0	1173
1972	0	0	2	0	35	143	376	334	165	8	0	0	1063
1973	0	0	0	19	42	332	416	413	183	29	0	0	1434
1974	0	0	0	24	64	175	370	355	113	2	6	0	1109
1975	0	0	0	0	97	207	337	355	73	27	5	0	1101
1976	0	0	0	37	25	260	291	278	106	6	0	0	1003
1977	0	0	5	20	80	156	360	328	166	0	5	0	1120
1978	0	0	0	0	48	188	273	383	117	7	0	0	1016
1979	0	0	4	1	57	123	327	324	138	16	0	0	990
1980	0	0	0	0	83	159	400	417	214	10	0	0	1283
1981	0	0	0	9	62	228	381	270	120	3	0	0	1073
1982	0	0	0	2	75	163	391	238	107	32	1	0	1009
1983	0	0	0	17	47	218	398	378	209	29	0	0	1296
1984	0	0	0	0	50	276	321	327	80	34	0	0	1088
1985	0	0	4	47	106	181	366	300	174	13	0	0	1191
1986	0	0	0	0	129	227	379	267	116	40	0	0	1158
1987	0	0	0	3	91	264	446	295	129	0	0	0	1228
1988	0	0	0	0	62	242	455	389	80	5	0	0	1233
1989	0	0	6	0	61	287	345	299	162	17	0	0	1177
1990	0	0	10	36	23	227	395	304	127	66	0	0	1188
1991	0	0	1	18	197	271	390	371	135	23	2	0	1408
1992	0	0	0	3	39	156	358	230	134	3	0	0	923
1993	0	0	0	1	79	252	452	405	176	3	4	0	1372

SNOWFALL (inches) — WILMINGTON, DELAWARE

SEASON	JULY	AUG	SEP	OCT	NOV	DEC	JAN	FEB	MAR	APR	MAY	JUNE	TOTAL
1964-65	0.0	0.0	0.0	0.0	T	1.6	8.4	1.7	5.8	0.6	0.0	0.0	18.1
1965-66	0.0	0.0	0.0	0.0	0.0	0.0	17.2	10.0	T	T	0.0	0.0	27.2
1966-67	0.0	0.0	0.0	0.0	T	21.5	0.6	18.7	2.7	T	0.0	0.0	43.5
1967-68	0.0	0.0	0.0	0.0	6.8	4.0	1.6	0.9	1.3	0.0	0.0	0.0	14.6
1968-69	0.0	0.0	0.0	0.0	T	0.6	2.9	5.5	7.8	0.0	0.0	0.0	16.8
1969-70	0.0	0.0	0.0	T	0.1	6.8	9.7	1.5	0.4	0.0	0.0	0.0	18.5
1970-71	0.0	0.0	0.0	0.0	0.0	3.2	5.8	0.2	2.4	0.6	0.0	0.0	12.2
1971-72	0.0	0.0	0.0	0.0	T	T	2.1	7.0	0.3	0.1	0.0	0.0	9.5
1972-73	0.0	0.0	0.0	T	T	T	T	1.2	T	T	0.0	0.0	1.2
1973-74	0.0	0.0	0.0	0.0	0.0	6.1	2.4	11.5	T	T	0.0	0.0	20.0
1974-75	0.0	0.0	0.0	0.0	T	T	5.1	4.8	1.1	T	0.0	0.0	11.0
1975-76	0.0	0.0	0.0	0.0	0.0	0.3	4.5	1.7	6.7	T	0.0	0.0	13.2
1976-77	0.0	0.0	0.0	0.0	0.1	3.2	14.5	T	0.0	T	0.0	0.0	17.8
1977-78	0.0	0.0	0.0	0.0	0.4	0.9	16.0	18.4	9.9	T	0.0	0.0	45.6
1978-79	0.0	0.0	0.0	0.0	4.5	T	12.0	27.5	0.2	T	0.0	0.0	44.2
1979-80	0.0	0.0	0.0	2.5	0.0	1.4	6.1	0.8	5.1	0.0	0.0	0.0	15.9
1980-81	0.0	0.0	0.0	0.0	0.5	1.4	6.5	T	3.7	0.0	0.0	0.0	12.1
1981-82	0.0	0.0	0.0	0.0	T	2.8	14.6	4.5	0.4	2.6	0.0	0.0	24.9
1982-83	0.0	0.0	0.0	0.0	T	5.8	T	18.5	0.3	0.5	0.0	0.0	25.1
1983-84	0.0	0.0	0.0	0.0	T	T	9.7	T	5.2	T	0.0	0.0	14.9
1984-85	0.0	0.0	0.0	0.0	T	0.3	14.2	0.7	T	0.4	0.0	0.0	15.6
1985-86	0.0	0.0	0.0	0.0	0.0	1.4	3.1	9.7	T	T	0.0	0.0	14.2
1986-87	0.0	0.0	0.0	0.0	T	0.3	21.4	15.7	0.2	2.4	0.0	0.0	40.0
1987-88	0.0	0.0	0.0	0.0	0.7	2.1	10.8	1.1	T	T	0.0	0.0	14.7
1988-89	0.0	0.0	0.0	0.0	T	0.2	6.7	2.9	1.2	0.0	0.0	0.0	11.0
1989-90	0.0	0.0	0.0	0.0	5.6	8.9	1.5	1.0	1.3	1.6	0.0	0.0	19.9
1990-91	T	0.0	0.0	0.0	0.0	6.4	5.2	0.6	0.9	T	T	0.0	13.1
1991-92	0.0	0.0	0.0	0.0	T	0.2	1.5	1.3	0.5	T	0.0	T	3.5
1992-93	0.0	0.0	0.0	0.0	T	0.1	1.4	10.0	13.9	0.0	0.0	0.0	25.4
1993-94	0.0	0.0	0.0	0.0	T	2.4							
Record Mean	T	0.0	0.0	0.1	0.9	3.3	6.6	6.0	3.3	0.2	T	T	20.4

WASHINGTON, D.C.
NATIONAL AIRPORT

Washington lies at the western edge of the mid Atlantic Coastal Plain, about 50 miles east of the Blue Ridge Mountains and 35 miles west of Chesapeake Bay, adjacent to the Potomac and Anacostia Rivers. Elevations range from a few feet above sea level to about 400 feet in parts of the northwest section of the city.

Observations have been kept continuously since November 1870. Since June 1941 the official observations have been taken at Washington National Airport.

National Airport is located at the center of the urban heat island. As a result, low temperatures are the highest for the area. Differences between the airport and suburban locations are often 10 to 15 degrees. There is less variation in the high temperatures.

Summers are warm and humid and winters are cold, but not severe. Periods of pleasant weather often occur in the spring and fall. The summertime temperature is in the upper 80s and the winter is in the upper 20s. Precipitation is rather uniformly distributed throughout the year.

Thunderstorms can occur at any time but are most frequent during the late spring and summer. The storms are most often accompanied by downpours and gusty winds, but are not usually severe.

Tornadoes, which infrequently occur, have resulted in significant damage. Severe hailstorms have occurred in the spring.

Tropical storms can bring heavy rain, high winds and flooding, but extensive damage from wind and tidal flooding is rare. Wind gusts of nearly 100 mph and rainfall over 7 inches have occurred during the passage of tropical storms and hurricanes.

Major flooding of the Potomac River can result from heavy rains over the basin, occasionally augmented by snowmelt, and above normal tides associated with hurricanes or severe storms along the coast. Flooding may also occur after a cold winter when the Potomac may be blocked with ice.

Although a snowfall of 10 inches or more in 24 hours is unusual, several notable falls of more than 25 inches have occurred. Normal snowfall during the winter season is 18 inches.

The average date of the last freezing temperature in the spring is April 1 and the average date for the first freezing temperature in the fall is November 10.

NORMALS, MEANS, AND EXTREMES

WASHINGTON, D.C. NATIONAL AIRPORT

LATITUDE: 38°51'N LONGITUDE: 77°02' W ELEVATION: FT. GRND 10 BARO 75 TIME ZONE: EASTERN WBAN: 13743

	(a)	JAN	FEB	MAR	APR	MAY	JUNE	JULY	AUG	SEP	OCT	NOV	DEC	YEAR
TEMPERATURE °F:														
Normals														
-Daily Maximum		42.3	45.9	56.5	66.7	76.2	84.7	88.5	86.9	80.1	69.1	58.3	47.0	66.9
-Daily Minimum		26.8	29.1	37.7	46.4	56.6	66.5	71.4	70.0	62.5	50.3	41.1	31.7	49.2
-Monthly		34.6	37.5	47.2	56.5	66.4	75.6	80.0	78.5	71.3	59.7	49.8	39.4	58.0
Extremes														
-Record Highest	52	79	82	89	95	99	101	104	103	101	94	86	75	104
-Year		1950	1948	1990	1976	1991	1988	1988	1988	1980	1954	1974	1984	JUL 1988
-Record Lowest	52	-5	4	11	24	34	47	54	49	39	29	16	1	-5
-Year		1982	1961	1943	1982	1947	1972	1988	1986	1963	1969	1955	1942	JAN 1982
NORMAL DEGREE DAYS:														
Heating (base 65°F)		942	770	552	264	60	0	0	0	14	195	456	794	4047
Cooling (base 65°F)		0	0	0	9	104	318	465	419	203	31	0	0	1549
% OF POSSIBLE SUNSHINE	45	47	51	55	56	58	64	62	62	61	59	51	46	56
MEAN SKY COVER (tenths)														
Sunrise - Sunset	45	6.6	6.5	6.5	6.4	6.4	6.0	6.0	5.8	5.7	5.5	6.2	6.5	6.2
MEAN NUMBER OF DAYS:														
Sunrise to Sunset														
-Clear	45	7.4	7.2	7.4	7.0	7.0	7.5	7.6	8.8	9.7	10.9	8.0	8.1	96.7
-Partly Cloudy	45	7.2	6.6	8.4	9.1	10.0	11.2	11.7	10.3	8.4	7.8	8.0	6.6	105.5
-Cloudy	45	16.3	14.5	15.1	14.0	14.0	11.2	11.7	11.9	11.9	12.3	14.0	16.3	163.1
Precipitation														
.01 inches or more	52	10.2	8.9	11.0	9.8	11.0	9.4	9.9	9.1	7.9	7.4	8.5	9.3	112.3
Snow,Ice pellets,hail														
1.0 inches or more	50	1.6	1.3	0.7	0.0	0.0	0.0	0.0	0.0	0.0	0.0	0.2	0.8	4.6
Thunderstorms	45	0.2	0.2	1.2	2.7	4.6	5.7	6.8	5.1	2.3	1.1	0.6	0.*	30.4
Heavy Fog Visibility														
1/4 mile or less	45	1.7	1.4	0.9	0.8	0.4	0.2	0.2	0.1	0.4	1.4	1.2	1.8	10.3
Temperature °F														
-Maximum														
90° and above	33	0.0	0.0	0.0	0.4	1.7	7.5	14.2	10.2	3.7	0.1	0.0	0.0	37.7
32° and below	33	4.8	2.2	0.2	0.0	0.0	0.0	0.0	0.0	0.0	0.0	0.*	2.1	9.4
-Minimum														
32° and below	33	22.0	18.4	8.5	0.8	0.0	0.0	0.0	0.0	0.0	0.4	4.3	15.7	70.2
0° and below	33	0.1	0.0	0.0	0.0	0.0	0.0	0.0	0.0	0.0	0.0	0.0	0.0	0.1
AVG. STATION PRESS.(mb)	21	1017.1	1016.8	1015.0	1013.3	1013.4	1013.2	1013.8	1015.2	1016.5	1017.4	1017.4	1017.7	1015.6
RELATIVE HUMIDITY (%)														
Hour 01	33	67	66	65	67	74	77	77	80	80	77	72	69	73
Hour 07 (Local Time)	33	70	70	70	70	74	75	76	80	81	80	75	72	74
Hour 13	33	55	52	50	49	52	52	53	55	56	53	54	57	53
Hour 19	33	60	56	54	52	59	60	61	64	66	64	62	62	60
PRECIPITATION (inches):														
Water Equivalent														
-Normal		2.72	2.71	3.17	2.71	3.66	3.38	3.80	3.91	3.31	3.02	3.12	3.12	38.63
-Maximum Monthly	52	7.11	5.71	7.43	6.88	10.69	11.53	11.06	14.31	12.36	8.18	6.70	6.54	14.31
-Year		1978	1961	1953	1983	1953	1972	1945	1955	1975	1942	1963	1969	AUG 1955
-Minimum Monthly	52	0.31	0.42	0.64	0.03	0.75	0.95	0.93	0.55	0.20	T	0.29	0.22	T
-Year		1955	1978	1945	1985	1986	1988	1966	1962	1967	1963	1981	1955	OCT 1963
-Maximum in 24 hrs	50	2.13	1.94	3.43	3.08	4.32	7.19	4.69	6.39	5.31	4.98	4.03	2.86	7.19
-Year		1976	1983	1958	1970	1953	1972	1970	1955	1975	1955	1993	1977	JUN 1972
Snow,Ice pellets,hail														
-Maximum Monthly	50	21.3	30.6	17.1	0.6	T	0.0	T	T	0.0	0.3	11.5	16.2	30.6
-Year		1966	1979	1960	1972	1993		1990	1992		1979	1987	1962	FEB 1979
-Maximum in 24 hrs	50	13.8	18.7	7.9	0.6	T	0.0	T	T	0.0	0.3	11.5	11.4	18.7
-Year		1966	1979	1960	1972	1993		1990	1992		1979	1987	1957	FEB 1979
WIND:														
Mean Speed (mph)	45	10.0	10.4	10.9	10.5	9.3	8.9	8.3	8.1	8.4	8.7	9.3	9.6	9.4
Prevailing Direction through 1963		NW	S	NW	S	S	S	S	S	S	SSW	S	NW	S
Fastest Obs. 1 Min.														
-Direction (!!)	8	29	33	06	33	32	36	31	34	32	23	33	34	32
-Speed (MPH)	8	35	37	38	35	46	38	38	37	33	39	36	38	46
-Year		1992	1991	1993	1992	1993	1986	1990	1988	1985	1990	1989	1993	MAY 1993
Peak Gust														
-Direction (!!)	10	NW	NW	NE	S	NW	N	W	NW	NW	SW	NW	NW	W
-Speed (mph)	10	51	49	55	48	60	53	63	53	54	58	59	56	63
-Date		1985	1987	1993	1988	1984	1986	1991	1988	1985	1990	1992	1985	JUL 1991

PRECIPITATION (inches)

WASHINGTON, D.C. NATIONAL AIRPORT

YEAR	JAN	FEB	MAR	APR	MAY	JUNE	JULY	AUG	SEP	OCT	NOV	DEC	ANNUAL
1964	3.98	3.38	2.53	4.37	1.46	1.30	1.87	1.89	3.07	1.34	1.42	2.87	29.48
1965	2.73	1.89	4.37	1.65	1.72	1.88	2.98	4.44	2.12	2.32	0.37	0.47	26.94
1966	3.95	3.57	1.44	3.33	2.74	2.02	0.93	1.67	6.87	4.72	1.50	3.28	36.02
1967	1.35	2.32	3.49	0.80	4.27	1.51	5.24	9.17	0.20	1.77	2.10	5.93	38.15
1968	1.97	0.80	3.66	1.53	4.23	7.40	1.31	3.95	2.97	3.17	3.62	2.22	36.83
1969	1.69	2.08	1.60	1.71	1.20	3.46	9.44	6.98	5.07	1.14	2.39	6.54	43.30
1970	1.24	2.69	2.82	5.35	2.79	2.80	8.12	1.09	1.57	2.05	5.77	3.33	39.62
1971	1.86	5.44	1.93	2.10	6.80	1.72	4.97	7.18	2.48	6.12	3.76	1.66	46.02
1972	2.45	5.27	2.27	3.99	4.78	11.53	3.43	2.82	1.27	3.56	6.05	4.55	51.97
1973	2.26	2.68	2.97	4.19	3.39	2.11	2.68	4.41	1.58	1.71	0.97	6.03	34.98
1974	2.66	0.95	4.21	2.26	4.37	3.40	1.15	5.77	4.39	1.13	1.24	4.43	35.96
1975	3.09	1.56	5.33	2.13	4.71	2.15	7.16	3.54	12.36	2.38	2.05	4.04	50.50
1976	3.56	1.55	2.51	1.17	3.57	1.21	4.54	2.13	7.23	7.76	0.85	1.99	38.07
1977	1.50	0.66	2.17	2.66	1.73	3.28	4.06	4.74	0.32	5.35	4.81	4.86	36.14
1978	7.11	0.42	4.48	1.38	5.13	2.43	4.28	5.85	1.01	1.16	2.31	4.00	39.56
1979	6.64	5.62	2.45	1.88	3.55	2.99	3.43	5.41	6.64	5.54	2.33	0.85	47.33
1980	2.85	1.16	5.04	3.28	2.64	1.68	3.86	1.11	1.90	2.59	2.56	0.65	29.32
1981	0.38	2.82	1.49	2.63	3.42	2.55	5.69	3.02	1.94	3.64	0.29	2.80	30.67
1982	2.27	3.33	2.64	3.19	5.11	5.41	2.98	2.68	1.71	1.75	2.96	1.74	35.77
1983	1.69	3.09	4.84	6.88	4.62	7.09	1.78	3.11	2.90	4.87	5.09	5.91	51.87
1984	1.71	3.43	6.14	3.71	3.80	2.01	4.09	2.30	2.51	3.18	3.66	1.19	37.73
1985	2.11	3.07	1.88	0.03	5.79	2.05	2.91	2.35	6.67	3.85	4.47	0.68	35.86
1986	2.38	3.49	0.74	1.98	0.75	1.29	3.79	5.33	0.60	2.01	5.23	4.98	32.57
1987	4.90	2.11	1.54	2.28	2.54	3.90	2.59	2.07	5.11	2.53	4.49	2.57	36.63
1988	3.14	2.52	2.27	2.00	4.50	0.95	3.74	2.39	1.85	1.75	5.33	1.30	31.74
1989	2.49	2.80	4.30	3.50	7.77	6.02	5.66	1.15	6.68	5.48	2.37	2.10	50.32
1990	2.95	1.30	2.57	4.09	5.20	3.14	3.78	6.74	0.87	3.30	2.17	4.73	40.84
1991	2.90	0.83	4.42	1.39	1.57	1.27	3.76	2.03	3.50	2.03	0.85	5.07	29.62
1992	2.78	2.23	3.48	2.55	3.41	2.35	5.34	2.48	3.49	2.03	3.38	2.86	36.38
1993	2.90	2.27	6.82	3.62	3.40	1.73	1.36	3.87	3.68	2.62	4.76	4.38	41.41
Record Mean	2.74	2.52	3.35	2.81	3.88	3.30	3.98	4.24	3.31	2.98	3.05	3.10	39.26

AVERAGE TEMPERATURE (deg. F)

WASHINGTON, D.C. NATIONAL AIRPORT

YEAR	JAN	FEB	MAR	APR	MAY	JUNE	JULY	AUG	SEP	OCT	NOV	DEC	ANNUAL
1964	36.3	36.9	47.5	54.1	68.1	76.0	79.1	75.5	69.9	55.1	51.0	39.9	57.5
1965	33.4	36.8	41.4	51.8	69.1	72.6	78.2	77.2	72.6	57.5	49.5	41.5	56.8
1966	32.4	36.2	47.5	52.7	65.0	76.0	80.9	78.7	68.6	57.0	49.5	37.6	56.8
1967	41.0	34.0	45.0	57.6	60.0	74.7	77.2	76.2	68.0	57.9	45.0	39.9	56.4
1968	31.4	34.3	49.7	58.0	63.7	74.1	79.9	79.2	72.0	61.3	50.0	36.6	57.5
1969	34.2	36.9	43.0	58.7	68.4	77.1	79.5	76.3	70.1	58.8	47.2	36.3	57.2
1970	30.0	37.1	41.9	55.3	68.3	75.2	79.2	79.0	75.0	62.5	49.3	39.7	57.7
1971	31.3	39.1	43.2	55.0	63.7	75.9	78.3	76.7	73.0	64.7	48.2	45.5	57.9
1972	38.5	36.5	45.6	54.1	64.6	70.2	77.5	75.9	71.0	56.0	46.8	43.6	56.7
1973	37.6	37.0	51.1	56.0	62.8	77.1	79.2	79.9	74.3	63.3	51.6	41.9	59.3
1974	42.9	39.2	49.2	58.3	65.1	71.5	79.0	78.4	70.2	57.3	50.9	43.1	58.8
1975	40.9	40.6	45.2	53.6	69.7	76.4	79.3	80.1	68.5	63.2	54.4	40.5	59.4
1976	33.9	46.9	51.3	59.9	65.0	77.6	78.4	76.7	70.4	55.4	43.0	35.5	57.9
1977	25.4	38.8	52.7	60.1	69.4	74.3	80.9	78.8	73.9	59.0	51.8	38.1	58.6
1978	32.5	31.4	44.4	57.7	65.8	76.7	78.8	81.3	73.6	59.4	52.2	43.1	58.1
1979	35.1	28.4	51.5	56.0	67.7	72.4	78.6	78.5	71.6	58.6	54.4	43.7	58.1
1980	37.2	36.1	46.2	60.1	69.5	74.8	82.3	82.8	77.1	59.9	48.6	39.8	59.5
1981	33.0	43.7	47.6	62.1	66.2	78.7	80.2	77.0	71.0	58.3	51.4	38.5	59.0
1982	28.1	38.3	45.7	54.0	69.0	72.8	80.3	75.4	70.6	60.2	51.8	45.5	57.7
1983	38.1	38.7	48.8	53.3	64.9	75.0	81.2	81.0	72.6	60.5	50.3	36.0	58.4
1984	32.2	43.8	41.8	54.9	64.9	76.9	76.5	77.8	68.3	65.2	46.0	45.6	57.8
1985	30.8	37.8	47.7	61.6	68.1	72.3	79.0	76.7	71.9	61.2	54.3	36.4	58.2
1986	35.4	35.3	47.4	56.2	68.1	76.6	81.1	74.6	70.9	61.1	46.5	39.8	57.8
1987	34.7	37.0	47.7	54.8	67.2	76.4	82.6	78.7	72.1	54.4	49.9	41.5	58.1
1988	31.0	37.3	47.2	54.4	65.8	74.4	81.9	80.7	68.9	54.4	49.9	38.7	57.1
1989	39.9	37.8	46.1	55.4	64.1	76.8	78.3	77.1	71.4	60.5	48.0	27.9	56.9
1990	43.6	45.2	50.2	56.8	64.3	75.0	79.4	76.5	69.6	62.8	52.0	44.5	60.0
1991	38.6	43.0	48.8	58.2	73.0	76.8	81.4	80.0	71.0	60.4	48.8	42.3	60.2
1992	38.2	41.2	45.0	55.4	62.3	71.7	79.5	74.0	69.2	56.0	48.8	39.6	56.7
1993	39.7	34.3	42.2	54.8	67.4	75.3	83.1	79.6	71.0	58.1	48.8	38.1	57.7
Record Mean	35.7	38.0	46.3	56.3	66.1	74.7	79.0	77.3	70.7	59.5	48.9	38.8	57.6
Max	43.3	46.4	55.4	66.6	75.9	84.0	87.9	86.0	79.5	68.8	57.6	46.3	66.5
Min	28.1	29.6	37.1	46.1	56.3	65.3	70.1	68.7	61.8	50.1	40.2	31.2	48.7

REFERENCE NOTES

WASHINGTON, D.C. NATIONAL AIRPORT

GENERAL
T - TRACE AMOUNT.
BLANK ENTRIES DENOTE MISSING/UNREPORTED DATA.
# INDICATES A STATION OR INSTRUMENT RELOCATION.

SPECIFIC

PM - INCLUDES LAST DAY OF PREVIOUS MONTH
ASOS - AUTOMATED SURFACE OBSERVING SYSTEM IN OPERATION DURING THESE MONTHS.

(a) - LENGTH OF RECORD IN YEARS, ALTHOUGH INDIVIDUAL MONTHS MAY BE MISSING.
0.* OR * - THE VALUE IS BETWEEN 0.0 AND 0.05
NORMALS - BASED ON THE 1961-1990 RECORD PERIOD.
EXTREMES - DATES ARE THE MOST RECENT OCCURRENCE
WIND DIR.- NUMERALS SHOW TENS OF DEGRESS CLOCKWISE FROM TRUE NORTH. "00" INDICATES CALM.
RESULTANT DIRECTIONS ARE GIVEN TO WHOLE DEGREES.
BOLD VALUES INDICATE EXTREME VALUES WHICH OCCURRED AFTER THE ASOS SYSTEM WAS COMMISSIONED.

RECORD = PERIOD OF RECORD
RECORD MEAN PRECIPITATION IS THE MEAN OF ALL DAILY PRECIPITATION AMOUNTS DURING THE PERIOD OF RECORD.
RECORD MAX(MIN) TEMPERATURE IS THE MEAN OF ALL DAILY MAX(MIN) TEMPERATURES DURING THE PERIOD OF RECORD.
RECORD MEAN TEMPERATURE IS THE SUM OF THE RECORD MAX AND RECORD MIN DIVIDED BY 2.
AVERAGE TEMPERATURE IS THE SUM OF THE MEAN DAILY MAX AND MIN TEMPERATURE DIVIDED BY 2.

EXCEPTIONS

RECORD MEANS ARE THROUGH THE CURRENT YEAR,
BEGINNING IN 1872 FOR TEMPERATURE
1871 FOR PRECIPITATION
1944 FOR SNOWFALL

HEATING DEGREE DAYS Base 65 deg. F — WASHINGTON, D.C. NATIONAL AIRPORT

SEASON	JULY	AUG	SEP	OCT	NOV	DEC	JAN	FEB	MAR	APR	MAY	JUNE	TOTAL
1964-65	0	0	29	300	415	771	974	785	724	395	27	24	4444
1965-66	0	1	18	236	458	723	1001	800	535	374	99	11	4256
1966-67	0	0	41	246	462	843	735	859	611	249	178	3	4227
1967-68	0	0	34	240	592	773	1033	886	471	216	87	0	4332
1968-69	0	0	0	162	445	875	949	780	671	208	40	0	4130
1969-70	0	0	18	226	525	883	1077	773	713	294	56	0	4565
1970-71	0	0	17	131	464	777	1034	722	670	294	85	2	4196
1971-72	0	0	12	61	518	597	815	817	599	326	56	21	3822
1972-73	0	0	8	278	543	654	843	777	423	286	109	0	3921
1973-74	0	0	4	103	399	708	677	716	490	228	85	4	3414
1974-75	0	0	26	250	446	674	740	677	608	345	24	0	3790
1975-76	0	0	20	102	328	752	956	524	415	236	80	0	3413
1976-77	0	0	11	306	652	907	1221	729	389	188	32	3	4438
1977-78	0	0	1	196	406	829	1001	933	633	219	86	0	4304
1978-79	0	0	9	192	378	671	918	1019	425	273	30	0	3915
1979-80	0	0	5	231	313	654	857	830	573	149	28	0	3640
1980-81	0	0	4	189	487	774	984	592	536	133	75	0	3774
1981-82	0	0	19	219	399	818	1135	743	592	328	19	3	4275
1982-83	0	2	9	193	402	597	827	730	497	365	77	0	3699
1983-84	0	0	32	177	433	890	1009	610	710	302	95	4	4262
1984-85	0	0	54	59	561	594	1053	757	533	166	30	6	3813
1985-86	0	0	14	147	320	879	913	824	542	267	61	3	3970
1986-87	0	13	18	180	548	775	931	777	527	304	68	0	4141
1987-88	0	0	4	325	448	719	1047	796	544	317	69	25	4294
1988-89	0	0	18	330	442	807	771	755	596	297	112	0	4128
1989-90	0	0	35	167	507	1144	656	550	481	285	64	4	3893
1990-91	0	0	38	153	381	630	810	608	502	237	22	0	3381
1991-92	0	0	27	175	486	696	824	686	614	295	127	5	3935
1992-93	0	0	43	282	477	781	779	855	700	307	32	3	4259
1993-94	0	0	33	217	487	825							

COOLING DEGREE DAYS Base 65 deg. F — WASHINGTON, D.C. NATIONAL AIRPORT

YEAR	JAN	FEB	MAR	APR	MAY	JUNE	JULY	AUG	SEP	OCT	NOV	DEC	TOTAL
1969	0	0	0	24	151	367	458	360	180	39	1	0	1580
1970	0	0	0	10	166	311	449	442	324	60	0	0	1762
1971	0	0	0	0	52	337	422	372	258	60	22	0	1523
1972	0	0	3	5	50	184	393	346	195	8	2	0	1186
1973	0	0	2	21	47	371	448	469	288	57	3	0	1706
1974	0	0	4	33	96	205	441	422	192	17	27	0	1437
1975	1	0	0	12	177	344	448	475	132	50	15	0	1654
1976	0	4	1	92	86	383	424	370	179	15	0	0	1554
1977	0	0	10	49	177	289	496	434	274	18	15	0	1762
1978	0	0	0	10	117	358	434	514	274	25	0	0	1732
1979	0	0	14	9	120	231	431	425	208	39	2	0	1479
1980	0	0	0	9	174	301	546	563	374	38	1	0	2006
1981	0	0	6	49	118	417	478	380	204	18	0	0	1670
1982	0	0	0	6	155	244	479	330	185	51	13	1	1464
1983	0	0	0	21	81	310	510	504	269	42	0	0	1737
1984	0	0	0	4	99	368	365	404	157	73	0	0	1470
1985	0	0	6	70	135	232	444	373	228	37	6	0	1531
1986	0	0	5	10	162	358	503	318	202	70	1	0	1629
1987	0	0	0	8	146	347	554	431	222	0	0	0	1708
1988	0	0	1	4	101	313	534	490	144	11	0	0	1598
1989	0	0	16	14	91	362	417	381	233	33	1	0	1548
1990	0	0	30	46	50	309	451	364	183	88	0	0	1521
1991	0	0	5	38	278	362	517	472	214	41	5	0	1932
1992	0	0	0	16	53	214	457	285	175	8	0	0	1208
1993	0	0	0	5	114	319	569	460	218	9	8	0	1702

SNOWFALL (inches) — WASHINGTON, D.C. NATIONAL AIRPORT

SEASON	JULY	AUG	SEP	OCT	NOV	DEC	JAN	FEB	MAR	APR	MAY	JUNE	TOTAL
1964-65	0.0	0.0	0.0	0.0	0.2	0.5	9.1	1.9	5.4	0.0	0.0	0.0	17.1
1965-66	0.0	0.0	0.0	0.0	0.0	0.2	21.3	6.9	T	0.0	0.0	0.0	28.4
1966-67	0.0	0.0	0.0	0.0	T	16.1	1.3	19.0	0.7	0.0	0.0	0.0	37.1
1967-68	0.0	0.0	0.0	0.0	6.9	6.3	2.8	2.4	3.0	0.0	0.0	0.0	21.4
1968-69	0.0	0.0	0.0	0.0	T	T	0.2	2.2	6.7	0.0	0.0	0.0	9.1
1969-70	0.0	0.0	0.0	0.0	T	6.8	3.6	3.6	T	0.0	0.0	0.0	14.0
1970-71	0.0	0.0	0.0	0.0	T	5.2	4.8	0.3	1.4	T	0.0	0.0	11.7
1971-72	0.0	0.0	0.0	0.0	1.4	0.1	0.3	14.4	T	0.6	0.0	0.0	16.8
1972-73	0.0	0.0	0.0	T	T	0.0	T	0.1	T	T	0.0	0.0	0.1
1973-74	0.0	0.0	0.0	0.0	0.0	11.0	1.5	4.2	T	T	0.0	0.0	16.7
1974-75	0.0	0.0	0.0	T	T	0.1	6.6	5.8	0.3	T	0.0	0.0	12.8
1975-76	0.0	0.0	0.0	0.0	0.0	0.4	0.1	0.9	0.8	0.0	0.0	0.0	2.2
1976-77	0.0	0.0	0.0	0.0	0.8	0.6	9.7	0.0	0.0	T	0.0	0.0	11.1
1977-78	0.0	0.0	0.0	0.0	0.1	0.2	10.3	3.8	8.3	0.0	0.0	0.0	22.7
1978-79	0.0	0.0	0.0	0.0	3.1	T	4.0	30.6	T	0.0	0.0	0.0	37.7
1979-80	0.0	0.0	0.0	0.3	0.0	T	8.6	5.1	6.1	0.0	0.0	0.0	20.1
1980-81	0.0	0.0	0.0	0.0	T	0.3	4.2	T	T	0.0	0.0	0.0	4.5
1981-82	0.0	0.0	0.0	0.0	T	1.7	15.3	5.3	0.2	T	0.0	0.0	22.5
1982-83	0.0	0.0	0.0	0.0	0.0	6.6	T	21.0	0.0	T	0.0	0.0	27.6
1983-84	0.0	0.0	0.0	0.0	0.3	T	6.5	T	1.8	T	0.0	0.0	8.6
1984-85	0.0	0.0	0.0	0.0	T	0.3	10.0	T	T	T	0.0	0.0	10.3
1985-86	0.0	0.0	0.0	0.0	0.0	0.7	1.8	12.9	T	T	0.0	0.0	15.4
1986-87	0.0	0.0	0.0	0.0	0.0	T	20.8	10.3	T	T	0.0	0.0	31.1
1987-88	0.0	0.0	0.0	0.0	11.5	T	13.1	T	0.4	T	0.0	0.0	25.0
1988-89	0.0	0.0	0.0	0.0	0.0	1.2	2.9	1.2	0.4	0.0	0.0	0.0	5.7
1989-90	0.0	0.0	0.0	0.0	3.5	9.0	0.2	T	2.4	0.2	0.0	0.0	15.3
1990-91	T	0.0	0.0	0.0	0.0	3.0	4.8	0.3	T	0.0	T	0.0	8.1
1991-92	0.0	0.0	0.0	0.0	T	0.0	4.0	2.6	T	0.0	0.0	0.0	6.6
1992-93	0.0	T	0.0	0.0	T	1.0	T	4.1	6.6	0.0	T	0.0	11.7
1993-94	0.0	0.0	0.0	0.0	T	2.6							
Record Mean	T	T	0.0	T	0.8	3.1	5.3	5.3	2.1	T	T	0.0	16.6

DAYTONA BEACH, FLORIDA

Daytona Beach is located on the Atlantic Ocean. The Halifax River, part of the Florida Inland Waterway, runs through the city. The terrain in the area is flat and the soil is mostly sandy. Elevations in the area range from 3 to 15 feet above mean sea level near the ocean to about 31 feet at the airport and on a ridge running along the western city limits.

Nearness to the ocean results in a climate tempered by the effect of land and sea breezes. In the summer, while maximum temperatures reach 90 degrees or above during the late morning or early afternoon, the number of hours of 90 degrees or above is relatively small due to the beginning of the sea breeze near midday and the occurrence of local afternoon convective thunderstorms which lower the temperature to the comfortable 80s. Winters, although subject to invasions of cold air, are relatively mild due to the nearness of the ocean and latitudinal location.

The rainy season from June through mid-October produces 60 percent of the annual rainfall. The major portion of the summer rainfall occurs in the form of local convective thunderstorms which are occasionally heavy and produce as much as 2 or 3 inches of rain. The more severe thunderstorms may be attended by strong gusty winds. Almost all rainfall during the winter months is associated with frontal passages.

Long periods of cloudiness and rain are infrequent, usually not lasting over 2 or 3 days. These periods are usually associated with a stationary front, a so-called northeaster, or a tropical disturbance.

Tropical disturbances or hurricanes are not considered a great threat to this area of the state. Generally hurricanes in this latitude tend to pass well offshore or lose much of their intensity while crossing the state before reaching this area. Only in gusts have hurricane-force winds been recorded at this station.

Heavy fog occurs mostly during the winter and early spring. These fogs usually form by radiational cooling at night and dissipate soon after sunrise. On rare occasions sea fog moves in from the ocean and persists for two or three days. There is no significant source in the area for air pollution.

NORMALS, MEANS, AND EXTREMES

DAYTONA BEACH, FLORIDA

LATITUDE: 29°11'N LONGITUDE: 81°03' W ELEVATION: FT. GRND 29 BARO 34 TIME ZONE: EASTERN WBAN: 12834

	(a)	JAN	FEB	MAR	APR	MAY	JUNE	JULY	AUG	SEP	OCT	NOV	DEC	YEAR
TEMPERATURE °F:														
Normals														
-Daily Maximum		68.0	69.5	74.8	80.0	84.5	88.0	89.8	89.1	86.8	81.5	75.5	70.4	79.8
-Daily Minimum		46.9	48.4	53.9	58.6	64.9	70.8	72.5	72.9	71.9	65.2	56.3	49.7	61.0
-Monthly		57.5	59.0	64.3	69.3	74.7	79.4	81.2	81.0	79.4	73.4	65.9	60.1	70.4
Extremes														
-Record Highest	50	87	89	91	96	100	102	102	100	99	95	89	88	102
-Year		1991	1985	1977	1968	1953	1944	1981	1989	1944	1959	1948	1990	JUL 1981
-Record Lowest	50	15	24	26	35	44	52	60	65	52	41	27	19	15
-Year		1985	1958	1980	1950	1971	1984	1981	1984	1956	1993	1950	1983	JAN 1985
NORMAL DEGREE DAYS:														
Heating (base 65°F)		282	205	112	21	0	0	0	0	0	0	82	207	909
Cooling (base 65°F)		50	37	90	150	301	432	502	496	432	265	109	55	2919
% OF POSSIBLE SUNSHINE														
MEAN SKY COVER (tenths)														
Sunrise - Sunset	45	5.8	5.7	5.6	5.0	5.3	6.2	6.2	6.2	6.3	5.7	5.4	5.9	5.8
MEAN NUMBER OF DAYS:														
Sunrise to Sunset														
-Clear	50	9.3	8.7	9.6	10.9	10.1	5.6	4.7	4.9	5.4	9.5	9.9	9.2	97.9
-Partly Cloudy	50	9.1	8.0	9.5	10.6	11.3	12.7	14.5	15.2	12.7	10.3	9.8	9.0	132.6
-Cloudy	50	12.6	11.5	11.8	8.5	9.6	11.7	11.8	10.9	11.9	11.2	10.3	12.8	134.7
Precipitation														
.01 inches or more	50	7.1	7.8	8.0	5.8	8.2	12.3	13.2	13.8	13.1	10.5	7.4	7.3	114.4
Snow,Ice pellets,hail														
1.0 inches or more	50	0.0	0.0	0.0	0.0	0.0	0.0	0.0	0.0	0.0	0.0	0.0	0.0	0.0
Thunderstorms	49	1.1	1.8	3.4	3.7	7.7	13.4	17.5	15.6	8.7	3.1	1.2	1.1	78.2
Heavy Fog Visibility														
1/4 mile or less	49	5.3	3.2	3.2	1.8	1.5	1.0	1.0	1.2	0.6	1.4	2.8	4.5	27.6
Temperature °F														
-Maximum														
90° and above	50	0.0	0.0	0.2	1.6	5.0	11.0	17.0	14.6	6.3	0.8	0.0	0.0	56.5
32° and below	50	0.0	0.0	0.0	0.0	0.0	0.0	0.0	0.0	0.0	0.0	0.0	0.0	0.0
-Minimum														
32° and below	50	2.3	1.1	0.3	0.0	0.0	0.0	0.0	0.0	0.0	0.0	0.2	1.5	5.5
0° and below	50	0.0	0.0	0.0	0.0	0.0	0.0	0.0	0.0	0.0	0.0	0.0	0.0	0.0
AVG. STATION PRESS.(mb)	21	1018.8	1018.0	1016.5	1015.9	1014.8	1015.1	1016.6	1016.0	1014.9	1015.8	1017.6	1019.1	1016.6
RELATIVE HUMIDITY (%)														
Hour 01	49	85	84	84	83	85	88	89	90	88	85	86	86	86
Hour 07 (Local Time)	49	87	86	86	85	85	87	89	91	90	87	88	87	87
Hour 13	49	59	57	55	53	57	63	65	67	67	63	61	60	61
Hour 19	49	77	73	70	69	71	76	78	80	80	77	79	79	76
PRECIPITATION (inches):														
Water Equivalent														
-Normal		2.75	3.11	2.90	2.23	3.45	5.99	5.40	6.16	6.34	4.13	2.84	2.59	47.89
-Maximum Monthly	50	7.16	9.13	8.11	7.12	12.33	15.19	14.58	19.89	15.20	13.00	10.96	11.98	19.89
-Year		1986	1960	1991	1949	1976	1966	1944	1953	1979	1950	1972	1983	AUG 1953
-Minimum Monthly	50	0.15	0.29	0.25	T	0.08	1.03	0.16	2.01	0.42	0.19	T	0.06	T
-Year		1950	1944	1956	1967	1965	1981	1992	1963	1972	1967	1967	1956	APR 1967
-Maximum in 24 hrs	50	5.73	4.39	5.74	4.03	4.22	6.28	4.21	4.76	6.34	9.29	5.83	5.22	9.29
-Year		1989	1971	1953	1982	1947	1966	1986	1974	1964	1953	1979	1983	OCT 1953
Snow,Ice pellets,hail														
-Maximum Monthly	50	T	T	T	0.0	0.0	T	0.0	0.0	0.0	0.0	0.0	T	T
-Year		1977	1951	1993			1989						1989	MAR 1993
-Maximum in 24 hrs	50	T	T	T	0.0	0.0	T	0.0	0.0	0.0	0.0	0.0	T	T
-Year		1977	1951	1993			1989						1989	MAR 1993
WIND:														
Mean Speed (mph)	48	8.9	9.6	9.9	9.6	8.9	8.1	7.4	7.1	8.3	9.2	8.6	8.5	8.7
Prevailing Direction through 1963		NW	NNW	SSW	E	E	SW	SSW	E	E	NE	NW	NW	E
Fastest Obs. 1 Min.														
-Direction (!!)	45	26	20	24	18	24	33	25	11	11	05	27	34	24
-Speed (MPH)	45	43	44	58	46	41	40	40	50	58	53	37	40	58
-Year		1978	1960	1993	1953	1989	1989	1963	1949	1960	1950	1963	1954	MAR 1993
Peak Gust														
-Direction (!!)	10	W	W	SW	SW	SW	NW	SW	W	S	W	SW	NW	SW
-Speed (mph)	10	52	58	77	49	69	67	59	68	48	56	47	43	77
-Date		1986	1992	1993	1988	1989	1989	1989	1989	1984	1985	1988	1989	MAR 1993

PRECIPITATION (inches)

DAYTONA BEACH, FLORIDA

YEAR	JAN	FEB	MAR	APR	MAY	JUNE	JULY	AUG	SEP	OCT	NOV	DEC	ANNUAL
1964	5.29	2.65	4.84	3.61	2.58	4.73	7.67	10.81	11.39	3.54	3.13	2.52	62.76
1965	2.22	3.00	3.05	1.00	0.08	9.00	3.72	2.97	4.33	3.65	0.97	2.14	36.13
1966	2.89	5.58	0.36	2.56	6.77	15.19	7.09	7.93	4.49	4.60	1.19	1.60	60.25
1967	1.26	3.98	0.31	T	0.73	7.51	9.04	3.02	5.56	0.19	T	2.98	34.58
1968	0.42	1.73	1.79	0.40	4.79	14.38	6.25	11.09	6.07	7.44	2.43	1.38	58.17
1969	1.53	2.03	2.74	0.12	6.47	2.47	2.61	9.40	8.89	6.97	1.96	5.03	50.22
1970	3.94	3.79	3.59	2.08	1.68	2.62	3.65	3.61	3.54	3.87	0.31	0.72	33.40
1971	0.61	5.48	2.00	2.57	3.12	4.73	3.20	3.97	7.20	9.53	1.33	2.49	46.23
1972	2.37	3.97	6.66	1.41	4.02	7.06	3.22	8.29	0.42	3.08	10.96	2.48	53.94
1973	4.66	2.02	2.63	3.09	2.41	4.32	4.69	7.58	5.14	4.40	0.75	2.54	44.23
1974	0.30	1.10	3.19	0.44	2.66	8.65	6.31	9.96	10.50	1.42	0.48	2.20	47.21
1975	1.66	2.27	1.52	2.96	2.99	9.00	6.89	3.16	6.61	5.84	1.46	0.83	45.19
1976	0.60	0.70	2.03	4.27	12.33	11.14	1.07	3.80	5.10	1.90	3.38	6.00	52.32
1977	4.69	2.45	1.43	0.41	4.61	1.15	2.23	7.91	6.55	1.46	3.04	4.74	40.67
1978	2.89	5.98	2.31	3.30	0.56	7.48	5.53	7.99	4.63	8.31	0.07	4.89	53.94
#1979	7.10	1.94	4.08	3.96	6.13	3.03	11.69	5.24	15.20	2.13	7.96	0.56	69.02
1980	3.75	0.76	2.41	2.54	3.62	5.57	5.82	4.13	1.83	2.42	3.12	1.39	37.36
1981	0.32	5.54	3.00	0.29	1.74	1.03	4.69	7.19	7.59	1.08	2.57	4.64	39.68
1982	2.46	2.08	5.81	6.04	4.68	8.29	5.31	3.21	4.96	3.23	1.58	2.53	50.18
1983	2.51	5.96	7.71	6.17	3.86	6.37	1.92	6.82	8.57	10.11	2.01	11.98	73.99
1984	1.46	3.44	1.31	5.29	6.04	2.84	6.77	4.02	10.73	1.09	3.52	0.20	46.71
1985	0.79	0.58	1.49	3.14	3.42	6.81	2.16	9.83	10.62	4.08	0.41	2.05	45.38
1986	7.16	1.28	1.85	0.44	0.99	3.50	14.43	3.47	3.58	3.47	5.08	2.76	48.01
1987	2.21	6.64	7.94	0.28	2.65	3.81	2.78	4.89	5.63	2.77	5.87	0.25	45.72
1988	5.36	1.72	4.57	1.68	1.78	2.39	2.94	4.79	6.81	1.24	6.70	0.93	40.91
1989	6.82	0.64	2.01	2.92	2.02	1.84	2.44	4.47	5.04	11.64	0.88	3.93	44.65
1990	1.42	5.61	1.94	1.48	1.45	2.71	5.85	7.00	1.61	5.88	0.83	0.34	36.12
1991	2.25	1.65	8.11	5.57	6.79	12.67	11.97	7.60	5.52	2.94	0.61	1.51	67.19
1992	2.42	1.71	2.28	2.81	3.13	10.64	0.16	8.86	6.57	5.21	2.15	0.47	46.41
1993	4.29	3.02	5.56	0.33	0.65	2.19	5.05	2.66	2.74	5.53	1.83	1.86	35.71
Record Mean	2.38	2.97	3.30	2.53	3.06	6.01	6.14	6.30	6.75	4.91	2.48	2.27	49.11

AVERAGE TEMPERATURE (deg. F)

DAYTONA BEACH, FLORIDA

YEAR	JAN	FEB	MAR	APR	MAY	JUNE	JULY	AUG	SEP	OCT	NOV	DEC	ANNUAL
1964	56.7	56.4	64.2	71.1	74.8	80.6	81.0	80.8	78.3	70.4	67.9	62.9	70.4
1965	57.5	61.3	63.6	70.8	72.3	77.3	78.7	79.9	79.1	71.6	65.5	59.7	69.8
1966	57.0	59.2	61.9	68.2	75.6	77.6	81.6	81.2	79.1	74.2	64.1	58.4	69.8
1967	60.6	58.5	67.0	72.4	75.5	78.0	79.4	78.7	76.0	71.3	64.5	63.2	70.5
1968	58.2	52.9	60.0	72.2	75.1	78.6	80.7	80.8	79.1	73.2	61.6	56.2	69.0
1969	58.0	55.2	57.9	70.5	74.4	80.5	82.8	80.4	79.7	77.1	63.5	56.5	69.7
1970	54.5	56.1	65.5	73.1	76.1	80.8	82.7	83.5	82.4	76.9	60.6	61.5	71.1
1971	58.6	59.9	60.0	68.0	73.3	78.7	80.5	80.7	79.6	76.1	65.9	67.8	70.7
1972	65.5	59.0	64.7	70.8	74.4	79.6	80.7	80.2	78.7	75.0	67.3	63.5	71.6
1973	58.9	56.3	68.2	68.7	75.2	79.8	81.9	80.3	80.8	75.0	69.6	58.4	71.1
1974	69.5	59.5	68.5	69.3	76.0	78.6	79.2	80.3	80.5	72.0	65.5	59.5	71.5
1975	63.6	65.7	65.6	70.1	77.2	79.5	80.5	80.5	79.6	75.2	66.8	58.6	71.9
1976	54.4	61.1	68.1	67.7	73.3	77.4	80.9	80.0	78.3	70.4	60.5	59.4	69.3
1977	50.6	55.5	68.9	70.0	74.8	82.3	82.6	82.6	80.8	70.8	67.1	58.3	70.3
1978	53.9	52.1	62.3	71.3	77.3	81.5	82.7	82.3	80.7	74.2	71.1	65.6	71.3
#1979	56.7	57.1	64.4	72.3	75.5	78.7	82.1	80.0	80.2	72.9	66.1	59.6	70.4
1980	57.7	55.3	66.3	68.8	74.9	79.2	82.8	82.1	80.3	72.7	65.3	57.0	70.2
1981	48.8	59.2	60.4	70.5	73.5	82.0	82.8	81.5	77.7	73.8	62.7	57.1	69.2
1982	56.6	64.4	66.8	69.4	72.6	79.5	80.0	79.9	77.9	71.5	68.8	64.0	70.9
1983	53.9	57.2	60.2	64.3	72.4	77.0	81.7	81.1	77.8	73.5	62.6	58.1	68.3
1984	55.1	58.0	61.8	66.8	72.4	76.3	79.0	81.4	79.5	75.7	66.5	65.2	69.8
1985	53.7	61.0	66.6	69.4	76.1	81.7	80.6	81.4	78.3	76.8	71.2	56.1	71.1
1986	56.7	62.4	63.1	66.3	73.8	79.9	81.4	81.4	79.6	75.3	72.5	64.7	71.4
1987	55.8	59.7	63.3	65.1	74.3	79.7	81.9	82.3	79.6	70.0	66.5	61.9	70.0
1988	55.1	56.8	62.8	69.1	72.6	79.0	81.2	81.5	80.6	70.7	67.5	59.8	69.7
1989	64.8	61.9	67.8	69.5	75.4	80.3	82.7	81.8	80.5	73.4	65.9	53.3	71.4
1990	62.7	67.5	66.4	69.6	77.3	80.7	81.9	81.9	80.5	76.0	67.4	65.1	73.1
1991	63.4	61.9	65.6	73.7	78.5	80.3	82.5	82.4	80.8	73.8	64.4	63.5	72.6
1992	56.5	61.7	63.3	67.2	72.5	80.5	83.4	80.7	79.8	72.3	69.1	61.4	70.7
1993	64.5	57.5	62.9	65.5	72.7	80.0	82.5	81.9	79.6	73.7	66.9	56.4	70.3
Record Mean	58.3	59.6	64.3	69.2	74.7	79.3	81.0	80.9	79.3	73.3	65.7	59.9	70.4
Max	69.1	70.3	75.0	79.8	84.7	88.3	89.9	89.4	87.0	81.5	75.4	70.3	80.1
Min	47.6	48.9	53.5	58.6	64.6	70.2	72.1	72.4	71.7	65.0	56.0	49.4	60.8

REFERENCE NOTES

DAYTONA BEACH, FLORIDA

GENERAL
T - TRACE AMOUNT.
BLANK ENTRIES DENOTE MISSING/UNREPORTED DATA.
# INDICATES A STATION OR INSTRUMENT RELOCATION.

SPECIFIC

PM - INCLUDES LAST DAY OF PREVIOUS MONTH
ASOS - AUTOMATED SURFACE OBSERVING SYSTEM IN OPERATION DURING THESE MONTHS.

(a) - LENGTH OF RECORD IN YEARS, ALTHOUGH INDIVIDUAL MONTHS MAY BE MISSING.
0.* OR * - THE VALUE IS BETWEEN 0.0 AND 0.05
NORMALS - BASED ON THE 1961-1990 RECORD PERIOD.
EXTREMES - DATES ARE THE MOST RECENT OCCURRENCE.
WIND DIR.- NUMERALS SHOW TENS OF DEGRESS CLOCKWISE FROM TRUE NORTH. "00" INDICATES CALM.
RESULTANT DIRECTIONS ARE GIVEN TO WHOLE DEGREES.
BOLD VALUES INDICATE EXTREME VALUES WHICH OCCURRED AFTER THE ASOS SYSTEM WAS COMMISSIONED.

RECORD = PERIOD OF RECORD
RECORD MEAN PRECIPITATION IS THE MEAN OF ALL DAILY PRECIPITATION AMOUNTS DURING THE PERIOD OF RECORD.
RECORD MAX(MIN) TEMPERATURE IS THE MEAN OF ALL DAILY MAX(MIN) TEMPERATURES DURING THE PERIOD OF RECORD.
RECORD MEAN TEMPERATURE IS THE SUM OF THE RECORD MAX AND RECORD MIN DIVIDED BY 2.
AVERAGE TEMPERATURE IS THE SUM OF THE MEAN DAILY MAX AND MIN TEMPERATURE DIVIDED BY 2.

EXCEPTIONS

RECORD MEANS ARE THROUGH THE CURRENT YEAR, BEGINNING IN 1935 FOR TEMPERATURE
1935 FOR PRECIPITATION
1944 FOR SNOWFALL

HEATING DEGREE DAYS Base 65 deg. F — DAYTONA BEACH, FLORIDA

SEASON	JULY	AUG	SEP	OCT	NOV	DEC	JAN	FEB	MAR	APR	MAY	JUNE	TOTAL
1964-65	0	0	0	18	22	126	246	138	136	9	1	0	696
1965-66	0	0	0	10	57	173	263	192	120	26	0	0	841
1966-67	0	0	0	3	88	217	168	192	37	5	0	0	710
1967-68	0	0	0	6	72	108	227	344	185	0	0	0	942
1968-69	0	0	0	27	152	301	216	275	228	2	0	0	1201
1969-70	0	0	0	0	105	272	330	252	80	2	0	0	1041
1970-71	0	0	0	0	164	143	230	199	194	55	7	0	992
1971-72	0	0	0	0	71	19	85	182	69	15	0	0	441
1972-73	0	0	0	0	62	139	226	251	38	29	0	0	745
1973-74	0	0	0	10	15	239	0	197	30	24	0	0	515
1974-75	0	0	0	0	69	201	108	69	91	30	0	0	568
1975-76	0	0	0	0	102	222	334	143	34	16	0	0	851
1976-77	0	0	0	11	168	209	444	273	53	20	0	0	1178
1977-78	0	0	0	23	63	241	352	356	132	5	0	0	1172
#1978-79	0	0	0	0	4	71	279	244	79	5	0	0	682
1979-80	0	0	0	0	75	183	234	297	84	16	0	0	889
1980-81	0	0	0	11	93	247	497	184	171	0	1	0	1204
1981-82	0	0	0	0	127	284	273	72	63	26	0	0	845
1982-83	0	0	0	24	21	125	345	220	167	74	2	0	978
1983-84	0	0	0	2	126	255	323	215	148	37	3	0	1109
1984-85	0	0	0	0	63	77	372	173	44	21	0	0	750
1985-86	0	0	0	0	24	303	261	119	141	30	0	0	878
1986-87	0	0	0	0	11	84	301	160	99	81	0	0	736
1987-88	0	0	0	10	74	146	316	259	120	23	0	0	948
1988-89	0	0	0	1	39	187	70	154	68	20	1	0	540
1989-90	0	0	0	31	59	369	120	47	37	14	0	0	677
1990-91	0	0	0	9	35	96	114	126	83	9	0	0	472
1991-92	0	0	0	0	110	114	264	139	106	43	15	0	791
1992-93	0	0	0	0	70	136	104	210	107	49	0	0	676
1993-94	0	0	0	12	62	281							

COOLING DEGREE DAYS Base 65 deg. F — DAYTONA BEACH, FLORIDA

YEAR	JAN	FEB	MAR	APR	MAY	JUNE	JULY	AUG	SEP	OCT	NOV	DEC	TOTAL
1969	7	4	17	173	300	473	559	483	447	383	66	13	2925
1970	13	9	101	253	351	478	557	580	532	373	37	40	3324
1971	39	65	45	150	270	420	484	495	445	348	106	113	2980
1972	107	16	67	193	299	447	494	477	415	317	138	98	3068
1973	45	14	148	148	324	450	527	482	483	326	156	40	3143
1974	147	50	145	159	349	414	447	480	469	223	90	40	3013
1975	71	95	118	191	386	441	488	487	445	325	163	29	3239
1976	12	36	136	104	264	378	497	471	406	186	39	40	2569
1977	4	12	181	177	310	527	553	554	478	212	131	41	3180
1978	14	0	56	198	388	499	553	543	477	295	192	94	3309
#1979	26	28	68	231	332	419	538	471	462	252	111	23	2961
1980	12	21	131	135	315	435	559	538	467	258	109	5	2985
1981	0	25	37	172	269	516	559	521	385	282	65	47	2878
1982	19	61	127	166	240	440	472	470	392	234	141	97	2859
1983	6	6	28	57	238	369	521	504	391	270	62	46	2498
1984	22	20	55	96	238	345	442	515	441	338	114	91	2717
1985	29	67	101	160	348	506	490	511	405	373	217	35	3242
1986	13	50	89	79	280	452	516	515	444	324	246	82	3090
1987	20	17	52	92	297	449	530	543	442	171	125	58	2796
1988	17	27	62	155	242	425	509	518	474	185	121	32	2767
1989	71	74	162	162	331	468	553	530	474	299	94	11	3229
1990	55	124	85	161	385	478	531	528	470	355	114	107	3393
1991	71	45	113	278	426	465	548	548	480	278	98	74	3424
1992	8	51	60	118	256	472	577	492	448	231	196	35	2944
1993	95	7	48	71	245	456	551	534	446	289	126	23	2891

SNOWFALL (inches) — DAYTONA BEACH, FLORIDA

SEASON	JULY	AUG	SEP	OCT	NOV	DEC	JAN	FEB	MAR	APR	MAY	JUNE	TOTAL
1970-71	0.0	0.0	0.0	0.0	0.0	0.0	0.0	0.0	0.0	0.0	0.0	0.0	0.0
1971-72	0.0	0.0	0.0	0.0	0.0	0.0	0.0	0.0	0.0	0.0	0.0	0.0	0.0
1972-73	0.0	0.0	0.0	0.0	0.0	0.0	0.0	0.0	0.0	0.0	0.0	0.0	0.0
1973-74	0.0	0.0	0.0	0.0	0.0	0.0	0.0	0.0	0.0	0.0	0.0	0.0	0.0
1974-75	0.0	0.0	0.0	0.0	0.0	0.0	0.0	0.0	0.0	0.0	0.0	0.0	0.0
1975-76	0.0	0.0	0.0	0.0	0.0	0.0	0.0	0.0	0.0	0.0	0.0	0.0	0.0
1976-77	0.0	0.0	0.0	0.0	0.0	0.0	T	0.0	0.0	0.0	0.0	0.0	T
1977-78	0.0	0.0	0.0	0.0	0.0	0.0	0.0	0.0	0.0	0.0	0.0	0.0	0.0
#1978-79	0.0	0.0	0.0	0.0	0.0	0.0	0.0	0.0	0.0	0.0	0.0	0.0	0.0
1979-80	0.0	0.0	0.0	0.0	0.0	0.0	0.0	0.0	0.0	0.0	0.0	0.0	0.0
1980-81	0.0	0.0	0.0	0.0	0.0	0.0	0.0	0.0	0.0	0.0	0.0	0.0	0.0
1981-82	0.0	0.0	0.0	0.0	0.0	0.0	0.0	0.0	0.0	0.0	0.0	0.0	0.0
1982-83	0.0	0.0	0.0	0.0	0.0	0.0	0.0	0.0	0.0	0.0	0.0	0.0	0.0
1983-84	0.0	0.0	0.0	0.0	0.0	0.0	0.0	0.0	0.0	0.0	0.0	0.0	0.0
1984-85	0.0	0.0	0.0	0.0	0.0	0.0	0.0	0.0	0.0	0.0	0.0	0.0	0.0
1985-86	0.0	0.0	0.0	0.0	0.0	0.0	0.0	0.0	0.0	0.0	0.0	0.0	0.0
1986-87	0.0	0.0	0.0	0.0	0.0	0.0	0.0	0.0	0.0	0.0	0.0	0.0	0.0
1987-88	0.0	0.0	0.0	0.0	0.0	0.0	0.0	0.0	0.0	0.0	0.0	0.0	0.0
1988-89	0.0	0.0	0.0	0.0	0.0	0.0	0.0	0.0	0.0	0.0	0.0	T	T
1989-90	0.0	0.0	0.0	0.0	0.0	T	0.0	0.0	0.0	0.0	0.0	0.0	T
1990-91	0.0	0.0	0.0	0.0	0.0	0.0	0.0	0.0	0.0	0.0	0.0	0.0	0.0
1991-92	0.0	0.0	0.0	0.0	0.0	0.0	0.0	0.0	0.0	0.0	0.0	0.0	0.0
1992-93	0.0	0.0	0.0	0.0	0.0	0.0	0.0	0.0	T	0.0	0.0	0.0	T
1993-94	0.0	0.0	0.0	0.0	0.0	0.0							
Record Mean	0.0	0.0	0.0	0.0	0.0	T	T	T	T	0.0	0.0	T	T

MIAMI, FLORIDA

Miami is located on the lower east coast of Florida. To the east of the city lies Biscayne Bay, an arm of the ocean, about 15 miles long and 3 miles wide. East of the bay is the island of Miami Beach, a mile or less wide and about 10 miles long, and beyond Miami Beach is the Atlantic Ocean. The surrounding countryside is level and sparsely wooded.

The climate of Miami is essentially subtropical marine, featured by a long and warm summer, with abundant rainfall, followed by a mild, dry winter. The marine influence is evidenced by the low daily range of temperature and the rapid warming of cold air masses which pass to the east of the state. The Miami area is subject to winds from the east or southeast about half the time, and in several specific respects has a climate whose features differ from those farther inland.

One of these features is the annual precipitation for the area. During the early morning hours more rainfall occurs at Miami Beach than at the airport, while during the afternoon the reverse is true. The airport office is about 9 miles inland.

An even more striking difference appears in the annual number of days with temperatures reaching 90 degrees or higher, with inland stations having about four times more than the beach. Minimum temperature contrasts also are particularly marked under proper conditions, with the difference between inland locations and the Miami Beach station frequently reaching to 15 degrees or more, especially in winter.

Freezing temperatures occur occasionally in the suburbs and farming districts southwest, west, and northwest of the city, but rarely near the ocean.

Hurricanes occasionally affect the area. The months of greatest frequency are September and October. Destructive tornadoes are very rare. Funnel clouds are occasionally sighted and a few touch the ground briefly but significant damage is seldom reported. Waterspouts are often visible from the beaches during the summer months, however, significant damage is seldom reported. June, July, and August have the highest frequency of dangerous lightning events.

NORMALS, MEANS, AND EXTREMES

MIAMI, FLORIDA

LATITUDE: 25°49'N LONGITUDE: 80°17' W ELEVATION: FT. GRND 7 BARO 12 TIME ZONE: EASTERN WBAN: 12839

	(a)	JAN	FEB	MAR	APR	MAY	JUNE	JULY	AUG	SEP	OCT	NOV	DEC	YEAR
TEMPERATURE °F:														
Normals														
-Daily Maximum		75.2	76.5	79.1	82.4	85.3	87.6	89.0	89.0	87.8	84.5	80.4	76.7	82.8
-Daily Minimum		59.2	60.4	64.2	67.8	72.1	75.1	76.2	76.7	75.9	72.1	66.7	61.5	69.0
-Monthly		67.2	68.5	71.7	75.2	78.7	81.4	82.6	82.8	81.9	78.3	73.6	69.1	75.9
Extremes														
-Record Highest	51	88	89	92	96	95	98	98	98	97	95	89	87	98
-Year		1987	1991	1977	1971	1990	1985	1983	1990	1987	1980	1989	1989	AUG 1990
-Record Lowest	51	30	32	32	46	53	60	69	68	68	51	39	30	30
-Year		1985	1947	1980	1971	1945	1984	1985	1950	1983	1943	1950	1989	DEC 1989
NORMAL DEGREE DAYS:														
Heating (base 65°F)		88	51	14	0	0	0	0	0	0	0	6	41	200
Cooling (base 65°F)		156	149	221	306	425	492	546	552	507	412	264	168	4198
% OF POSSIBLE SUNSHINE	17	67	67	74	76	72	69	73	73	72	71	66	63	70
MEAN SKY COVER (tenths)														
Sunrise - Sunset	45	5.3	5.3	5.4	5.2	5.8	6.7	6.5	6.5	6.7	5.9	5.5	5.4	5.9
MEAN NUMBER OF DAYS:														
Sunrise to Sunset														
-Clear	44	9.4	8.5	8.6	8.6	6.4	3.1	2.6	2.5	2.2	6.7	7.5	9.1	75.1
-Partly Cloudy	44	13.2	12.2	14.0	14.7	15.2	14.4	17.3	17.8	15.6	14.2	13.9	12.8	175.3
-Cloudy	44	8.5	7.7	8.4	6.7	9.4	12.5	11.0	10.7	12.2	10.1	8.6	9.1	114.9
Precipitation														
.01 inches or more	51	6.7	6.0	6.1	6.0	10.2	14.9	16.0	17.2	17.4	14.1	8.6	6.4	129.5
Snow, Ice pellets, hail														
1.0 inches or more	44	0.0	0.0	0.0	0.0	0.0	0.0	0.0	0.0	0.0	0.0	0.0	0.0	0.0
Thunderstorms	44	0.9	1.2	1.8	2.6	6.5	12.3	15.1	15.9	11.8	4.6	1.2	0.7	74.5
Heavy Fog Visibility														
1/4 mile or less	45	1.3	0.8	0.6	0.6	0.3	0.0	0.1	0.1	0.1	0.2	0.9	0.9	5.9
Temperature °F														
-Maximum														
90° and above	29	0.0	0.0	0.2	1.4	3.3	9.4	15.0	14.8	9.9	2.4	0.0	0.0	56.3
32° and below	29	0.0	0.0	0.0	0.0	0.0	0.0	0.0	0.0	0.0	0.0	0.0	0.0	0.0
-Minimum														
32° and below	29	0.1	0.0	0.*	0.0	0.0	0.0	0.0	0.0	0.0	0.0	0.0	0.1	0.2
0° and below	29	0.0	0.0	0.0	0.0	0.0	0.0	0.0	0.0	0.0	0.0	0.0	0.0	0.0
AVG. STATION PRESS. (mb)	21	1019.4	1018.7	1017.6	1016.7	1015.6	1016.3	1017.9	1016.8	1015.2	1015.4	1017.4	1019.4	1017.2
RELATIVE HUMIDITY (%)														
Hour 01	29	81	79	77	76	78	83	82	83	84	82	81	80	81
Hour 07 (Local Time)	29	84	83	82	80	80	84	84	85	87	86	85	83	84
Hour 13	29	59	57	56	54	59	65	63	64	66	63	62	59	61
Hour 19	29	69	67	65	64	69	74	72	74	76	73	72	70	70
PRECIPITATION (inches):														
Water Equivalent														
-Normal		2.01	2.08	2.39	2.85	6.21	9.33	5.70	7.58	7.63	5.64	2.66	1.83	55.91
-Maximum Monthly	51	6.66	8.07	10.57	17.29	18.54	22.36	13.51	16.88	24.40	21.64	13.84	6.39	24.40
-Year		1969	1983	1986	1979	1968	1968	1947	1943	1960	1991	1992	1958	SEP 1960
-Minimum Monthly	51	0.04	0.01	0.02	0.05	0.44	1.81	1.77	1.65	2.63	1.25	0.09	0.12	0.01
-Year		1951	1944	1956	1981	1965	1945	1963	1954	1951	1977	1970	1988	FEB 1944
-Maximum in 24 hrs	51	2.68	5.73	7.07	16.21	11.59	8.20	4.55	6.92	7.58	9.95	8.01	4.38	16.21
-Year		1973	1966	1949	1979	1977	1977	1952	1964	1960	1948	1992	1964	APR 1979
Snow, Ice pellets, hail														
-Maximum Monthly		0.0	0.0	0.0	0.0	0.0	0.0	0.0	0.0	0.0	0.0	0.0	0.0	
-Year														
-Maximum in 24 hrs	51	0.0	0.0	0.0	0.0	0.0	0.0	0.0	0.0	0.0	0.0	0.0	0.0	
-Year														
WIND:														
Mean Speed (mph)	44	9.5	10.2	10.6	10.5	9.7	8.4	8.0	7.9	8.2	9.3	9.7	9.2	9.3
Prevailing Direction through 1963		NNW	ESE	SE	ESE	ESE	SE	SE	SE	ESE	ENE	N	N	ESE
Fastest Obs. 1 Min.														
-Direction (!!!)	36	24	25	04	24	32	13	25	12	06	05	07	32	12
-Speed (MPH)	36	46	41	46	35	52	37	43	86	69	41	38	38	86
-Year		1978	1983	1966	1993	1980	1967	1990	1992	1965	1966	1985	1967	AUG 1992
Peak Gust														
-Direction (!!!)	10	SW	W	SW	NW	SE	S	NE	E	SW	S	E	NE	E
-Speed (mph)	10	45	47	59	55	46	58	56	115	44	47	48	40	115
-Date		1987	1992	1993	1984	1991	1989	1992	1992	1988	1990	1985	1991	AUG 1992

PRECIPITATION (inches)

MIAMI, FLORIDA

YEAR	JAN	FEB	MAR	APR	MAY	JUNE	JULY	AUG	SEP	OCT	NOV	DEC	ANNUAL
1964	0.45	2.21	0.50	3.31	4.67	10.48	5.51	9.84	4.22	9.77	3.00	6.24	60.20
1965	1.98	2.98	3.97	1.20	0.44	6.55	6.56	4.97	11.38	16.79	0.96	0.62	58.40
1966	3.97	6.56	3.25	1.80	5.53	21.37	8.50	7.62	8.00	10.88	3.84	0.74	82.06
1967	2.75	1.14	3.60	0.15	1.68	15.98	5.55	8.13	9.18	12.88	3.81	1.37	66.22
1968	1.92	2.77	0.88	1.27	18.54	22.36	6.15	8.34	11.11	8.71	1.21	0.13	83.39
1969	6.66	2.02	1.98	4.63	8.02	11.42	8.48	4.31	8.24	13.57	1.01	1.15	71.49
1970	2.64	1.77	2.61	0.95	10.98	5.53	4.48	3.60	8.89	3.01	0.09	0.17	44.72
1971	0.51	0.80	0.40	0.07	4.13	11.65	4.72	6.02	9.63	7.48	0.98	4.33	50.72
1972	1.60	2.71	3.01	2.67	13.71	10.90	7.13	6.49	5.08	2.86	2.77	4.18	63.11
1973	3.41	2.21	1.76	2.24	1.08	8.93	6.14	14.60	6.59	3.36	0.46	2.46	53.24
1974	2.54	0.10	2.27	2.11	2.63	8.12	6.09	9.29	6.38	3.68	4.62	1.17	49.00
1975	1.39	0.90	0.61	0.53	4.94	6.37	4.99	5.19	4.69	6.25	2.80	0.44	39.10
1976	0.95	3.54	0.23	4.17	10.45	6.81	3.83	9.45	7.75	4.42	2.69	1.61	55.90
1977	1.44	2.10	0.91	1.97	15.82	12.42	5.23	8.28	7.04	1.25	5.94	2.55	64.95
1978	2.07	3.44	2.92	3.50	5.66	5.29	2.69	3.93	3.42	7.68	3.17	2.06	45.83
1979	1.28	0.57	0.30	17.29	5.29	4.06	5.06	4.81	13.36	3.63	1.62	2.84	60.11
1980	1.89	0.88	3.17	10.20	2.14	3.02	9.40	11.32	5.60	6.05	3.47	0.20	57.34
1981	0.61	4.66	1.32	0.05	4.94	5.49	2.78	12.25	14.79	1.62	2.14	0.14	50.79
1982	0.44	1.22	4.22	9.27	8.80	10.82	3.84	5.79	7.62	7.12	7.09	1.18	67.41
1983	5.36	8.07	2.82	1.79	1.44	8.66	6.20	5.88	7.48	3.52	2.01	4.19	57.42
1984	0.18	0.70	6.12	4.51	10.91	7.24	7.38	5.44	10.45	2.35	4.04	0.70	60.02
1985	0.35	0.06	1.35	3.27	3.19	6.33	11.23	11.88	8.59	5.17	1.37	3.47	56.26
1986	5.04	1.72	10.57	0.71	8.24	9.06	7.81	7.67	4.38	3.96	4.75	2.21	66.12
1987	0.87	2.62	3.82	0.38	4.99	5.48	5.17	3.24	10.17	4.33	4.92	4.28	50.27
1988	1.88	0.61	0.39	1.82	5.28	10.36	10.90	7.89	3.09	1.49	0.76	0.12	44.59
1989	0.67	0.71	0.89	2.14	0.99	10.83	3.53	12.78	5.83	2.65	0.99	0.62	42.63
1990	0.24	1.19	2.28	6.96	7.79	6.84	4.31	11.06	3.52	4.82	1.67	1.03	51.71
1991	1.59	2.04	2.32	5.16	2.50	7.51	7.29	8.84	11.17	21.64	1.18	0.18	71.42
1992	1.80	1.49	2.67	2.43	0.55	13.17	4.21	7.22	6.48	2.02	13.84	1.94	57.82
1993	5.04	2.14	5.98	3.08	4.13	3.64	7.28	5.13	12.59	7.23	6.06	0.49	62.79
Record Mean	2.02	1.92	2.35	3.57	5.96	8.58	6.63	7.38	8.40	6.88	2.99	1.75	58.43

AVERAGE TEMPERATURE (deg. F)

MIAMI, FLORIDA

YEAR	JAN	FEB	MAR	APR	MAY	JUNE	JULY	AUG	SEP	OCT	NOV	DEC	ANNUAL
#1964	67.4	65.7	74.6	77.1	77.6	81.2	82.8	83.6	82.3	76.9	74.9	72.2	76.4
1965	67.0	70.9	73.1	76.7	78.5	80.7	81.3	81.7	79.9	78.1	74.2	69.3	76.0
1966	66.0	68.9	69.2	72.8	77.6	78.2	81.1	81.7	81.2	77.9	70.2	66.6	74.3
1967	71.4	68.9	72.8	74.7	79.3	79.9	82.4	81.8	81.3	76.2	71.2	70.3	75.8
1968	66.1	62.7	67.0	75.9	77.6	79.6	81.6	83.9	82.2	77.8	71.0	66.6	74.3
1969	67.6	65.2	67.8	77.3	79.6	82.3	84.1	83.5	82.5	80.3	70.4	65.9	75.5
1970	63.8	64.7	71.8	79.0	79.1	82.0	82.7	84.0	82.2	79.5	69.6	70.9	75.8
1971	68.2	70.9	70.3	75.0	79.1	81.0	82.7	81.9	80.7	78.9	73.9	74.2	76.4
1972	73.0	68.4	72.1	75.0	77.6	79.9	80.9	81.7	80.4	77.9	73.3	70.8	75.9
1973	70.3	65.3	74.5	75.6	79.6	81.3	81.8	81.3	81.8	77.6	76.2	67.0	76.1
1974	74.3	68.9	75.6	76.2	80.0	82.1	82.6	84.0	84.1	78.1	72.9	69.0	77.3
1975	72.7	73.1	73.4	77.5	79.4	81.5	81.1	82.6	82.0	79.2	72.3	69.0	77.0
1976	64.7	68.8	75.8	75.1	78.5	79.1	83.1	81.9	80.4	76.3	71.5	68.2	75.3
1977	61.1	66.1	74.9	74.8	77.0	81.7	83.7	83.2	83.0	76.5	74.0	69.1	75.4
1978	64.0	63.2	68.9	74.0	79.2	81.9	82.5	82.6	82.0	78.8	75.7	73.0	75.5
1979	65.0	64.9	69.2	77.8	80.6	81.9	83.2	82.1	80.7	77.9	75.4	70.2	75.7
1980	67.5	64.0	73.2	75.4	79.0	81.4	82.6	82.8	82.1	80.1	74.3	67.3	75.8
1981	59.7	69.5	70.1	77.8	79.6	83.7	85.0	83.2	81.2	79.7	71.4	67.8	75.7
1982	67.8	74.4	74.7	77.9	77.2	82.0	84.3	84.0	82.7	77.9	75.0	72.6	77.6
1983	67.2	67.5	67.6	71.9	78.2	81.8	85.0	83.3	81.6	78.3	72.5	69.8	75.4
1984	67.0	68.6	70.4	73.2	77.1	79.8	81.9	82.6	80.1	78.2	71.5	71.1	75.1
1985	62.1	68.4	72.5	74.2	79.1	82.4	81.0	82.4	80.6	80.5	75.6	66.0	75.4
1986	65.2	69.4	68.6	71.7	77.5	81.3	83.1	83.5	83.3	80.3	79.3	73.6	76.4
1987	66.1	70.8	71.9	70.6	78.7	84.2	84.2	85.4	83.6	77.6	75.3	69.8	76.5
1988	67.9	67.7	70.7	76.1	77.9	82.0	83.1	83.6	84.0	79.1	76.9	70.5	76.6
1989	72.7	70.8	73.6	77.1	81.0	82.7	83.3	84.3	84.0	79.0	76.2	65.0	77.5
1990	73.6	74.0	73.7	75.2	80.3	83.0	83.5	83.7	83.1	80.4	74.4	72.9	78.2
1991	72.9	69.7	73.9	78.4	81.5	82.9	83.5	84.6	82.4	78.9	73.1	72.2	77.8
1992	67.4	70.5	71.9	74.0	77.8	81.5	84.9	84.4	83.2	79.5	76.8	71.6	77.0
1993	73.2	68.9	71.5	74.0	79.2	83.3	84.6	84.8	83.0	80.8	75.9	68.9	77.3
Record Mean	67.3	68.2	71.5	74.9	78.3	81.3	82.6	82.9	81.8	78.2	73.1	68.9	75.7
Max	75.6	76.7	79.5	82.6	85.5	88.1	89.4	89.8	88.3	84.8	80.3	76.9	83.1
Min	59.0	59.7	63.4	67.2	71.0	74.4	75.7	76.0	75.3	71.5	65.9	60.9	68.3

REFERENCE NOTES

MIAMI, FLORIDA

GENERAL
T - TRACE AMOUNT.
BLANK ENTRIES DENOTE MISSING/UNREPORTED DATA.
# INDICATES A STATION OR INSTRUMENT RELOCATION.

SPECIFIC

PM - INCLUDES LAST DAY OF PREVIOUS MONTH
ASOS - AUTOMATED SURFACE OBSERVING SYSTEM IN OPERATION DURING THESE MONTHS.

(a) - LENGTH OF RECORD IN YEARS, ALTHOUGH INDIVIDUAL MONTHS MAY BE MISSING.
0.* OR * - THE VALUE IS BETWEEN 0.0 AND 0.05
NORMALS - BASED ON THE 1961-1990 RECORD PERIOD.
EXTREMES - DATES ARE THE MOST RECENT OCCURRENCE.
WIND DIR.- NUMERALS SHOW TENS OF DEGRESS CLOCKWISE FROM TRUE NORTH. "00" INDICATES CALM.
RESULTANT DIRECTIONS ARE GIVEN TO WHOLE DEGREES.
BOLD VALUES INDICATE EXTREME VALUES WHICH OCCURRED AFTER THE ASOS SYSTEM WAS COMMISSIONED.

RECORD = PERIOD OF RECORD
RECORD MEAN PRECIPITATION IS THE MEAN OF ALL DAILY PRECIPITATION AMOUNTS DURING THE PERIOD OF RECORD.
RECORD MAX(MIN) TEMPERATURE IS THE MEAN OF ALL DAILY MAX(MIN) TEMPERATURES DURING THE PERIOD OF RECORD.
RECORD MEAN TEMPERATURE IS THE SUM OF THE RECORD MAX AND RECORD MIN DIVIDED BY 2.
AVERAGE TEMPERATURE IS THE SUM OF THE MEAN DAILY MAX AND MIN TEMPERATURE DIVIDED BY 2.

EXCEPTIONS

RECORD MEANS ARE THROUGH THE CURRENT YEAR, BEGINNING IN 1940 FOR TEMPERATURE
1940 FOR PRECIPITATION
1940 FOR SNOWFALL

HEATING DEGREE DAYS Base 65 deg. F MIAMI, FLORIDA

SEASON	JULY	AUG	SEP	OCT	NOV	DEC	JAN	FEB	MAR	APR	MAY	JUNE	TOTAL
#1964-65	0	0	0	0	0	4	63	25	18	0	0	0	110
1965-66	0	0	0	0	0	16	70	41	16	0	0	0	143
1966-67	0	0	0	0	27	41	28	41	0	0	0	0	137
1967-68	0	0	0	0	0	25	56	101	57	0	0	0	239
1968-69	0	0	0	0	32	80	18	54	49	0	0	0	233
1969-70	0	0	0	0	21	53	117	58	19	0	0	0	268
1970-71	0	0	0	0	42	23	67	45	31	5	0	0	213
1971-72	0	0	0	0	0	0	2	39	0	0	0	0	41
1972-73	0	0	0	0	3	30	41	64	0	0	0	0	138
1973-74	0	0	0	0	1	93	0	37	0	0	0	0	131
1974-75	0	0	0	0	2	32	14	1	10	0	0	0	59
1975-76	0	0	0	0	33	49	93	27	0	0	0	0	202
1976-77	0	0	0	0	9	32	165	62	3	0	0	0	271
1977-78	0	0	0	0	6	58	123	99	34	0	0	0	320
1978-79	0	0	0	0	0	1	84	82	13	0	0	0	180
1979-80	0	0	0	0	6	10	50	95	39	0	0	0	200
1980-81	0	0	0	0	7	59	168	25	12	0	0	0	271
1981-82	0	0	0	0	1	80	65	1	3	0	0	0	150
1982-83	0	0	0	0	0	22	50	25	38	2	0	0	137
1983-84	0	0	0	0	4	69	54	37	17	0	0	0	181
1984-85	0	0	0	0	9	18	135	61	4	1	0	0	228
1985-86	0	0	0	0	2	78	76	22	54	0	0	0	232
1986-87	0	0	0	0	0	0	83	15	6	27	0	0	131
1987-88	0	0	0	0	3	29	49	38	26	0	0	0	145
1988-89	0	0	0	0	0	36	1	49	18	0	0	0	104
1989-90	0	0	0	1	0	110	7	4	0	0	0	0	122
1990-91	0	0	0	0	0	4	2	31	5	0	0	0	42
1991-92	0	0	0	0	7	0	38	7	6	0	0	0	58
1992-93	0	0	0	0	2	10	5	7	21	0	0	0	45
1993-94	0	0	0	0	4	31							

COOLING DEGREE DAYS Base 65 deg. F MIAMI, FLORIDA

YEAR	JAN	FEB	MAR	APR	MAY	JUNE	JULY	AUG	SEP	OCT	NOV	DEC	TOTAL
1969	104	66	145	375	459	526	597	581	532	478	191	88	4142
1970	85	59	239	425	446	518	558	596	522	457	185	213	4303
1971	176	219	202	315	444	488	558	531	476	443	274	292	4418
1972	262	144	227	307	398	454	498	523	471	408	261	217	4170
1973	212	81	301	324	459	499	531	516	511	394	343	163	4334
1974	294	150	335	342	471	518	551	596	578	414	245	163	4657
1975	261	233	276	382	456	501	508	553	517	448	257	178	4570
1976	92	144	336	309	424	429	569	530	470	361	209	141	4014
1977	50	97	318	299	381	508	587	574	549	364	284	191	4202
1978	97	54	163	273	449	515	547	552	513	437	329	254	4183
1979	90	81	149	391	492	516	572	537	481	407	324	178	4218
1980	138	75	296	321	441	501	555	563	519	476	292	135	4312
1981	10	154	177	389	460	568	625	570	492	460	198	173	4276
1982	161	270	311	394	385	518	606	596	537	406	304	264	4752
1983	125	101	124	213	417	514	628	576	503	419	236	221	4077
1984	124	144	194	252	380	452	532	554	460	416	213	214	3935
1985	55	164	244	285	445	529	505	546	476	488	329	114	4180
1986	86	150	175	207	395	495	569	582	556	483	432	272	4402
1987	122	186	227	202	430	580	603	639	565	401	314	182	4451
1988	145	123	209	339	408	516	571	584	578	445	364	216	4498
1989	247	219	292	367	502	540	576	603	578	442	346	114	4826
1990	279	262	276	314	479	547	578	587	552	486	287	254	4901
1991	254	167	288	408	515	547	583	614	531	437	255	231	4830
1992	121	173	226	277	404	503	624	609	553	454	366	222	4532
1993	269	123	227	277	449	557	613	622	550	497	338	159	4681

SNOWFALL (inches) MIAMI, FLORIDA

SEASON	JULY	AUG	SEP	OCT	NOV	DEC	JAN	FEB	MAR	APR	MAY	JUNE	TOTAL
1970-71	0.0	0.0	0.0	0.0	0.0	0.0	0.0	0.0	0.0	0.0	0.0	0.0	0.0
1971-72	0.0	0.0	0.0	0.0	0.0	0.0	0.0	0.0	0.0	0.0	0.0	0.0	0.0
1972-73	0.0	0.0	0.0	0.0	0.0	0.0	0.0	0.0	0.0	0.0	0.0	0.0	0.0
1973-74	0.0	0.0	0.0	0.0	0.0	0.0	0.0	0.0	0.0	0.0	0.0	0.0	0.0
1974-75	0.0	0.0	0.0	0.0	0.0	0.0	0.0	0.0	0.0	0.0	0.0	0.0	0.0
1975-76	0.0	0.0	0.0	0.0	0.0	0.0	0.0	0.0	0.0	0.0	0.0	0.0	0.0
1976-77	0.0	0.0	0.0	0.0	0.0	0.0	0.0	0.0	0.0	0.0	0.0	0.0	0.0
1977-78	0.0	0.0	0.0	0.0	0.0	0.0	0.0	0.0	0.0	0.0	0.0	0.0	0.0
1978-79	0.0	0.0	0.0	0.0	0.0	0.0	0.0	0.0	0.0	0.0	0.0	0.0	0.0
1979-80	0.0	0.0	0.0	0.0	0.0	0.0	0.0	0.0	0.0	0.0	0.0	0.0	0.0
1980-81	0.0	0.0	0.0	0.0	0.0	0.0	0.0	0.0	0.0	0.0	0.0	0.0	0.0
1981-82	0.0	0.0	0.0	0.0	0.0	0.0	0.0	0.0	0.0	0.0	0.0	0.0	0.0
1982-83	0.0	0.0	0.0	0.0	0.0	0.0	0.0	0.0	0.0	0.0	0.0	0.0	0.0
1983-84	0.0	0.0	0.0	0.0	0.0	0.0	0.0	0.0	0.0	0.0	0.0	0.0	0.0
1984-85	0.0	0.0	0.0	0.0	0.0	0.0	0.0	0.0	0.0	0.0	0.0	0.0	0.0
1985-86	0.0	0.0	0.0	0.0	0.0	0.0	0.0	0.0	0.0	0.0	0.0	0.0	0.0
1986-87	0.0	0.0	0.0	0.0	0.0	0.0	0.0	0.0	0.0	0.0	0.0	0.0	0.0
1987-88	0.0	0.0	0.0	0.0	0.0	0.0	0.0	0.0	0.0	0.0	0.0	0.0	0.0
1988-89	0.0	0.0	0.0	0.0	0.0	0.0	0.0	0.0	0.0	0.0	0.0	0.0	0.0
1989-90	0.0	0.0	0.0	0.0	0.0	0.0	0.0	0.0	0.0	0.0	0.0	0.0	0.0
1990-91	0.0	0.0	0.0	0.0	0.0	0.0	0.0	0.0	0.0	0.0	0.0	0.0	0.0
1991-92	0.0	0.0	0.0	0.0	0.0	0.0	0.0	0.0	0.0	0.0	0.0	0.0	0.0
1992-93	0.0	0.0	0.0	0.0	0.0	0.0	0.0	0.0	0.0	0.0	0.0	0.0	0.0
1993-94	0.0	0.0	0.0	0.0	0.0	0.0							
Record Mean	0.0	0.0	0.0	0.0	0.0	0.0	0.0	0.0	0.0	0.0	0.0	0.0	0.0

ORLANDO, FLORIDA

Orlando is located in the central section of the Florida peninsula, surrounded by many lakes. Relative humidities remain high the year-round, with values near 90 percent at night and 40 to 50 percent in the afternoon. On some winter days, the humidity may drop to 20 percent.

The rainy season extends from June through September, sometimes through October when tropical storms are near. During this period, scattered afternoon thunderstorms are an almost daily occurrence, and these bring a drop in temperature to make the climate bearable. Summer temperatures above 95 degrees are rather rare. There is usually a breeze which contributes to the general comfort.

During the winter months rainfall is light. While temperatures, on infrequent occasion, may drop at night to near freezing, they rise rapidly during the day and, in brilliant sunshine, afternoons are pleasant.

Frozen precipitation in the form of snowflakes, snow pellets, or sleet is rare. However, hail is occasionally reported during thunderstorms.

Hurricanes are usually not considered a great threat to Orlando, since, to reach this area, they must pass over a substantial stretch of land and, in so doing, lose much of their punch. Sustained hurricane winds of 75 mph or higher rarely occur. Orlando, being inland, is relatively safe from high water, although heavy rains sometimes briefly flood sections of the city.

NORMALS, MEANS, AND EXTREMES

ORLANDO, FLORIDA

LATITUDE: 28°26'N LONGITUDE: 81°19' W ELEVATION: FT. GRND 96 BARO 94 TIME ZONE: EASTERN WBAN: 12815

	(a)	JAN	FEB	MAR	APR	MAY	JUNE	JULY	AUG	SEP	OCT	NOV	DEC	YEAR
TEMPERATURE °F:														
Normals														
-Daily Maximum		70.8	72.7	78.0	83.0	87.8	90.5	91.5	91.5	89.7	84.6	78.5	72.9	82.6
-Daily Minimum		48.6	49.7	55.2	59.4	65.9	71.8	73.1	73.4	72.4	65.8	57.5	51.3	62.0
-Monthly		59.7	61.2	66.7	71.2	76.9	81.1	82.3	82.5	81.0	75.2	68.0	62.1	72.3
Extremes														
-Record Highest	51	87	90	92	96	102	100	100	100	98	95	89	90	102
-Year		1991	1962	1970	1968	1945	1985	1961	1980	1988	1986	1992	1978	MAY 1945
-Record Lowest	51	19	28	25	38	48	53	64	64	56	43	29	20	19
-Year		1985	1970	1980	1987	1992	1984	1981	1957	1956	1957	1950	1983	JAN 1985
NORMAL DEGREE DAYS:														
Heating (base 65°F)		234	164	65	5	0	0	0	0	0	0	54	164	686
Cooling (base 65°F)		70	58	117	191	369	483	536	543	480	316	144	74	3381
% OF POSSIBLE SUNSHINE														
MEAN SKY COVER (tenths)														
Sunrise - Sunset	45	5.7	5.7	5.6	5.1	5.4	6.4	6.4	6.4	6.5	5.5	5.2	5.7	5.8
MEAN NUMBER OF DAYS:														
Sunrise to Sunset														
-Clear	45	9.0	8.6	9.2	10.2	8.8	4.2	3.4	3.1	3.8	9.6	10.2	9.8	89.9
-Partly Cloudy	45	10.2	8.7	10.4	11.4	13.5	14.3	16.7	17.0	14.6	11.2	10.2	9.2	147.3
-Cloudy	45	11.8	11.0	11.4	8.4	8.7	11.5	10.9	10.9	11.6	10.2	9.6	12.1	128.1
Precipitation														
.01 inches or more	51	6.3	6.9	7.7	5.5	8.5	14.0	17.1	16.0	13.6	8.5	5.7	5.9	115.8
Snow, Ice pellets, hail														
1.0 inches or more	51	0.0	0.0	0.0	0.0	0.0	0.0	0.0	0.0	0.0	0.0	0.0	0.0	0.0
Thunderstorms	49	1.0	1.5	2.9	3.4	7.6	14.6	19.3	17.5	9.7	2.6	1.1	1.1	82.3
Heavy Fog Visibility														
1/4 mile or less	45	5.5	3.2	2.5	1.4	1.4	0.8	0.5	0.9	1.2	1.7	2.7	4.3	26.1
Temperature °F														
-Maximum														
90° and above	30	0.0	0.0	0.4	3.9	10.7	19.6	25.2	25.5	18.7	3.4	0.0	0.*	107.5
32° and below	30	0.0	0.0	0.0	0.0	0.0	0.0	0.0	0.0	0.0	0.0	0.0	0.0	0.0
-Minimum														
32° and below	30	1.5	0.5	0.1	0.0	0.0	0.0	0.0	0.0	0.0	0.0	0.1	0.6	2.8
0° and below	30	0.0	0.0	0.0	0.0	0.0	0.0	0.0	0.0	0.0	0.0	0.0	0.0	0.0
AVG. STATION PRESS. (mb)	21	1016.6	1015.8	1014.3	1013.6	1012.4	1012.9	1014.4	1013.8	1012.6	1013.4	1015.3	1016.8	1014.3
RELATIVE HUMIDITY (%)														
Hour 01	29	85	83	84	84	86	89	90	91	90	87	87	87	87
Hour 07 (Local Time)	30	88	87	88	87	88	89	90	92	92	89	89	88	89
Hour 13	30	56	52	50	46	49	57	58	60	60	56	56	57	55
Hour 19	30	69	63	61	58	62	72	75	77	77	74	73	73	70
PRECIPITATION (inches):														
Water Equivalent														
-Normal		2.30	3.02	3.21	1.80	3.55	7.32	7.25	6.78	6.01	2.42	2.30	2.15	48.11
-Maximum Monthly	51	7.23	8.32	11.38	9.10	10.36	18.28	19.57	16.11	15.87	14.51	10.29	5.33	19.57
-Year		1986	1983	1987	1992	1976	1968	1960	1972	1945	1950	1987	1983	JUL 1960
-Minimum Monthly	51	0.15	0.10	0.16	0.14	0.43	1.97	2.60	2.92	0.43	0.35	0.03	T	T
-Year		1950	1944	1956	1977	1961	1948	1992	1980	1972	1967	1967	1944	DEC 1944
-Maximum in 24 hrs	51	4.19	4.38	5.03	5.65	3.18	8.40	8.19	5.29	9.67	7.74	5.87	3.61	9.67
-Year		1986	1970	1960	1992	1980	1945	1960	1949	1945	1950	1988	1969	SEP 1945
Snow, Ice pellets, hail														
-Maximum Monthly	21	T	0.0	T	T	0.0	0.0	T	T	0.0	0.0	0.0	0.0	T
-Year		1977		1992	1992			1993	1989					JUL 1993
-Maximum in 24 hrs	21	T	0.0	T	T	0.0	0.0	T	T	0.0	0.0	0.0	0.0	T
-Year		1977		1992	1992			1993	1989					JUL 1993
WIND:														
Mean Speed (mph)	45	9.0	9.6	9.9	9.4	8.8	8.0	7.4	7.2	7.6	8.6	8.7	8.6	8.5
Prevailing Direction through 1963		NNE	S	S	SE	SE	SW	S	S	ENE	N	N	NNE	S
Fastest Obs. 1 Min.														
-Direction (!!)	44	25	25	24	02	17	32	14	32	24	05	26	07	32
-Speed (MPH)	44	42	46	46	50	46	64	46	50	46	48	46	32	64
-Year		1953	1969	1993	1956	1981	1970	1961	1957	1969	1950	1968	1968	JUN 1970
Peak Gust														
-Direction (!!)	10	NW	W	W	E	S	W	W	SW	NW	W	NE	W	W
-Speed (mph)	10	48	51	62	53	68	62	68	58	54	40	41	43	68
-Date		1991	1991	1993	1992	1991	1985	1991	1991	1988	1990	1984	1984	JUL 1991

PRECIPITATION (inches)

ORLANDO, FLORIDA

YEAR	JAN	FEB	MAR	APR	MAY	JUNE	JULY	AUG	SEP	OCT	NOV	DEC	ANNUAL
1964	6.18	3.42	4.65	2.14	2.74	6.11	6.68	9.00	9.47	1.64	0.45	1.91	54.39
1965	1.79	3.67	3.02	0.66	0.52	7.36	11.55	5.49	5.99	4.06	1.06	2.23	47.40
1966	4.45	6.31	2.57	1.92	6.57	9.77	6.73	7.76	6.25	1.98	0.09	0.99	55.39
1967	0.84	5.49	1.31	0.28	1.69	11.16	4.63	6.83	5.88	0.35	0.03	2.42	40.91
1968	0.65	2.76	2.27	0.30	3.72	18.28	5.60	3.44	5.91	5.47	2.82	0.88	52.10
1969	2.22	3.30	5.52	2.38	1.40	5.04	6.73	7.17	6.44	9.45	0.87	4.66	55.18
1970	4.05	6.77	3.66	0.45	4.08	4.92	5.97	5.91	3.25	2.60	0.24	2.06	43.96
1971	0.45	2.98	1.46	1.52	4.31	4.39	8.29	7.51	2.98	3.06	1.21	1.93	40.09
1972	0.99	4.96	5.06	1.39	3.76	6.33	3.98	16.11	0.43	2.34	4.11	1.89	51.35
1973	4.82	2.73	4.13	2.82	4.74	6.63	6.24	7.33	11.53	1.10	0.74	2.56	55.37
#1974	0.18	0.63	3.67	1.17	2.69	15.28	6.01	6.56	5.78	0.48	0.31	1.62	44.38
1975	0.98	1.49	1.10	1.36	7.52	9.70	9.26	4.75	4.97	4.74	0.66	0.51	47.04
1976	0.37	0.83	1.72	2.16	10.36	9.93	7.05	3.25	5.87	0.74	2.03	2.77	47.08
1977	1.81	1.76	1.82	0.14	1.47	4.47	6.61	6.28	7.03	0.43	2.60	3.70	38.12
1978	2.49	5.45	2.14	0.61	3.16	10.00	11.92	5.13	4.31	1.51	0.18	3.69	50.59
1979	6.48	1.45	3.24	1.08	7.66	4.00	7.95	5.88	9.19	0.43	1.93	0.94	50.23
1980	2.45	1.64	1.51	4.07	6.96	5.25	5.14	2.92	3.70	0.55	6.55	0.47	41.21
1981	0.21	4.36	1.85	0.18	2.02	12.49	3.53	5.60	8.26	3.13	2.50	2.97	47.10
1982	1.72	1.34	4.85	6.27	5.29	6.06	11.81	5.03	6.96	0.74	0.53	1.01	51.61
1983	2.08	8.32	5.37	3.21	1.77	7.82	6.49	4.83	5.16	3.78	1.36	5.33	55.52
1984	2.01	2.73	1.85	6.21	3.20	5.32	6.19	7.89	6.19	0.56	2.10	0.19	44.44
1985	0.91	1.27	4.59	1.69	3.00	4.54	7.28	11.63	5.45	2.55	0.82	3.46	47.19
1986	7.23	1.84	2.63	0.49	0.88	9.50	5.85	5.99	4.50	5.63	1.69	3.60	49.83
1987	1.27	1.74	11.38	0.59	1.40	3.54	7.95	6.07	8.64	3.41	10.29	0.51	56.79
1988	3.12	1.38	6.07	2.02	2.82	4.17	9.44	7.94	5.67	1.42	7.44	1.00	52.49
1989	3.80	0.15	1.35	2.28	2.38	6.79	4.74	6.20	10.29	1.75	1.44	4.49	45.66
1990	0.23	4.13	1.92	1.73	0.55	6.22	6.68	3.78	2.46	2.10	1.05	0.83	31.68
1991	2.37	0.98	6.66	7.72	9.48	5.98	10.78	7.13	4.53	4.76	0.27	0.24	60.90
1992	1.35	2.42	3.67	9.10	1.19	8.68	2.60	8.03	7.13	5.17	2.74	0.88	52.96
1993	4.89	1.48	6.26	1.78	2.32	4.47	6.49	5.95	5.35	4.61	0.17	0.76	44.53
Record Mean	2.23	2.70	3.53	2.62	3.40	6.98	7.83	6.68	6.74	3.36	1.88	1.91	49.84

AVERAGE TEMPERATURE (deg. F)

ORLANDO, FLORIDA

YEAR	JAN	FEB	MAR	APR	MAY	JUNE	JULY	AUG	SEP	OCT	NOV	DEC	ANNUAL
1964	58.5	58.3	68.1	74.1	77.1	82.4	81.6	82.8	79.8	72.5	70.5	64.4	72.5
1965	60.0	64.1	67.0	74.8	77.1	79.0	80.5	82.2	80.8	74.2	69.5	62.6	72.7
1966	58.7	62.3	64.4	70.5	77.4	78.0	82.3	82.3	80.1	75.8	65.8	60.1	71.5
1967	63.2	60.0	68.3	74.3	78.3	80.2	82.4	82.0	79.7	74.0	67.5	65.9	73.0
1968	59.6	54.8	61.4	73.5	76.7	78.8	81.3	82.3	80.3	74.3	63.4	58.7	70.4
1969	59.8	57.8	60.4	72.5	76.9	82.9	84.4	82.2	81.2	77.9	64.0	58.7	71.6
1970	55.1	58.7	67.0	75.8	77.7	81.8	83.8	82.3	83.6	77.0	63.4	64.6	72.6
1971	62.0	64.1	64.8	72.1	78.2	81.7	83.1	83.3	81.8	79.0	69.5	71.4	74.2
1972	68.9	62.0	68.7	72.7	77.4	82.2	83.2	82.8	81.8	76.8	68.9	66.1	74.3
1973	62.4	59.7	71.1	71.1	78.3	83.1	84.2	81.8	81.4	75.6	70.9	60.4	73.3
#1974	71.6	60.5	70.2	71.4	78.0	80.3	80.7	82.0	81.8	72.6	67.6	60.9	73.1
1975	65.8	67.6	67.4	72.4	79.1	80.8	80.5	82.3	80.7	76.6	67.4	60.2	73.4
1976	56.5	63.7	70.4	71.3	76.8	79.7	82.4	81.9	80.5	72.6	63.0	60.1	71.6
1977	50.6	57.4	69.7	70.6	75.2	82.6	82.0	81.5	82.6	72.9	69.6	61.0	71.3
1978	56.8	55.8	66.3	73.4	79.3	82.9	82.6	82.6	81.7	75.0	72.3	66.8	73.0
1979	58.2	58.4	64.6	73.4	75.4	80.7	83.3	82.4	81.3	74.4	68.3	62.6	71.9
1980	60.5	57.2	68.2	70.4	76.4	80.1	83.6	83.6	81.7	75.4	67.1	59.0	71.9
1981	51.3	61.7	64.0	73.1	76.7	83.2	84.1	82.9	80.0	76.4	65.3	60.5	71.6
1982	60.0	68.4	70.4	72.6	75.3	82.0	82.6	82.2	80.2	74.1	70.8	66.7	73.8
1983	58.0	59.9	63.5	68.6	76.4	80.5	83.2	83.5	80.6	76.5	65.8	61.2	71.5
1984	57.8	61.2	64.7	69.2	75.6	78.4	80.7	81.5	78.9	75.4	65.8	66.0	71.3
1985	54.7	62.2	68.4	70.7	77.2	82.4	82.1	82.3	79.8	79.4	73.0	58.8	72.6
1986	59.8	64.3	65.4	69.3	76.7	81.7	82.3	83.3	81.7	77.5	75.8	67.3	73.8
1987	58.8	62.7	65.9	66.8	76.8	83.1	83.5	85.0	82.7	72.2	69.0	64.2	72.6
1988	58.5	60.4	65.5	72.0	75.5	80.3	80.7	82.8	83.9	73.7	70.5	62.4	72.2
1989	66.9	64.5	69.7	71.9	77.9	81.9	83.2	83.3	82.2	75.3	69.0	55.5	73.4
1990	65.8	69.1	69.3	71.5	79.4	81.9	82.8	83.5	82.0	77.1	69.3	66.3	74.8
1991	66.3	64.2	67.7	75.3	79.5	81.1	82.6	83.0	81.7	75.3	65.8	65.5	74.0
1992	59.7	64.8	66.4	69.9	74.9	81.2	84.5	82.3	81.6	73.4	70.4	63.5	72.7
1993	66.3	60.6	64.8	68.3	75.5	81.9	83.9	83.2	81.2	75.1	68.3	58.9	72.3
Record Mean	60.5	62.2	66.8	71.8	77.2	81.2	82.4	82.6	81.0	74.8	67.6	62.1	72.5
Max	71.6	73.4	78.0	83.1	88.1	90.9	91.8	91.6	89.6	84.0	77.8	72.8	82.7
Min	49.5	50.9	55.5	60.4	66.3	71.5	73.0	73.5	72.4	65.6	57.4	51.3	62.3

REFERENCE NOTES

ORLANDO, FLORIDA

GENERAL
T - TRACE AMOUNT.
BLANK ENTRIES DENOTE MISSING/UNREPORTED DATA.
# INDICATES A STATION OR INSTRUMENT RELOCATION.

SPECIFIC

PM - INCLUDES LAST DAY OF PREVIOUS MONTH
ASOS - AUTOMATED SURFACE OBSERVING SYSTEM IN OPERATION DURING THESE MONTHS.

(a) - LENGTH OF RECORD IN YEARS, ALTHOUGH INDIVIDUAL MONTHS MAY BE MISSING.
0.* OR * - THE VALUE IS BETWEEN 0.0 AND 0.05
NORMALS - BASED ON THE 1961-1990 RECORD PERIOD.
EXTREMES - DATES ARE THE MOST RECENT OCCURRENCE
WIND DIR.- NUMERALS SHOW TENS OF DEGRESS CLOCKWISE FROM TRUE NORTH. "00" INDICATES CALM.
RESULTANT DIRECTIONS ARE GIVEN TO WHOLE DEGREES.
BOLD VALUES INDICATE EXTREME VALUES WHICH OCCURRED AFTER THE ASOS SYSTEM WAS COMMISSIONED.

RECORD = PERIOD OF RECORD
RECORD MEAN PRECIPITATION IS THE MEAN OF ALL DAILY PRECIPITATION AMOUNTS DURING THE PERIOD OF RECORD.
RECORD MAX(MIN) TEMPERATURE IS THE MEAN OF ALL DAILY MAX(MIN) TEMPERATURES DURING THE PERIOD OF RECORD.
RECORD MEAN TEMPERATURE IS THE SUM OF THE RECORD MAX AND RECORD MIN DIVIDED BY 2.
AVERAGE TEMPERATURE IS THE SUM OF THE MEAN DAILY MAX AND MIN TEMPERATURE DIVIDED BY 2.

EXCEPTIONS

RECORD MEANS ARE THROUGH THE CURRENT YEAR, BEGINNING IN 1943 FOR TEMPERATURE
1943 FOR PRECIPITATION
1943 FOR SNOWFALL

HEATING DEGREE DAYS Base 65 deg. F ORLANDO, FLORIDA

SEASON	JULY	AUG	SEP	OCT	NOV	DEC	JAN	FEB	MAR	APR	MAY	JUNE	TOTAL
1964-65	0	0	0	7	14	84	178	89	82	0	0	0	454
1965-66	0	0	0	1	19	112	215	122	72	5	0	0	546
1966-67	0	0	0	2	70	169	119	157	25	0	0	0	542
1967-68	0	0	0	0	29	80	191	293	149	0	0	0	742
1968-69	0	0	0	19	120	237	168	206	169	0	0	0	919
1969-70	0	0	0	0	93	204	316	187	58	0	0	0	858
1970-71	0	0	0	0	120	79	165	115	92	20	0	0	591
1971-72	0	0	0	0	26	9	51	124	24	6	0	0	240
1972-73	0	0	0	0	54	105	160	169	12	9	0	0	509
#1973-74	0	0	0	6	13	193	0	173	15	8	0	0	408
1974-75	0	0	0	0	40	163	73	44	57	10	0	0	387
1975-76	0	0	0	0	85	174	278	104	18	1	0	0	660
1976-77	0	0	0	4	118	197	440	218	41	8	0	0	1026
1977-78	0	0	0	6	38	179	275	255	71	0	0	0	824
1978-79	0	0	0	0	0	56	230	214	71	0	0	0	571
1979-80	0	0	0	0	47	119	161	245	61	4	0	0	637
1980-81	0	0	0	1	67	190	416	119	76	1	0	0	870
1981-82	0	0	0	0	75	205	204	21	33	7	0	0	545
1982-83	0	0	0	14	16	94	233	148	105	13	0	0	623
1983-84	0	0	0	0	63	188	252	137	86	18	0	0	744
1984-85	0	0	0	0	68	71	340	146	22	12	0	0	659
1985-86	0	0	0	0	14	228	180	82	105	4	0	0	613
1986-87	0	0	0	0	0	42	216	97	48	66	0	0	469
1987-88	0	0	0	0	39	97	221	169	71	7	0	0	604
1988-89	0	0	0	0	11	135	32	119	59	4	0	0	360
1989-90	0	0	0	21	27	308	71	34	11	5	0	0	477
1990-91	0	0	0	6	14	69	75	88	52	0	0	0	304
1991-92	0	0	0	0	85	76	187	79	51	19	8	0	505
1992-93	0	0	0	0	47	102	73	131	80	12	0	0	445
1993-94	0	0	0	10	45	201							

COOLING DEGREE DAYS Base 65 deg. F ORLANDO, FLORIDA

YEAR	JAN	FEB	MAR	APR	MAY	JUNE	JULY	AUG	SEP	OCT	NOV	DEC	TOTAL
1969	12	10	32	232	376	544	608	540	495	406	68	16	3339
1970	19	14	128	330	399	511	586	544	565	380	77	72	3625
1971	77	97	90	238	411	505	569	573	510	440	167	214	3891
1972	181	44	146	243	391	524	570	561	509	374	179	148	3870
1973	88	28	207	198	421	548	602	529	501	341	199	58	3720
#1974	213	51	183	207	410	463	492	536	510	241	125	43	3474
1975	105	121	141	237	442	481	489	541	479	366	167	32	3601
1976	18	75	194	196	374	449	549	529	474	247	65	49	3219
1977	1	13	192	182	324	534	537	521	536	257	185	62	3344
1978	26	3	116	259	449	541	550	553	508	321	225	115	3666
1979	26	31	65	260	330	479	575	546	498	299	153	53	3315
1980	27	25	169	172	362	459	586	582	508	331	138	12	3371
1981	0	34	52	253	372	552	602	559	458	359	89	73	3403
1982	56	123	211	241	325	518	550	542	465	303	196	152	3682
1983	22	11	68	129	361	473	573	582	476	362	95	77	3229
1984	37	35	84	151	332	411	490	520	426	331	99	107	3023
1985	27	74	137	191	386	531	539	548	451	454	262	45	3645
1986	25	69	124	139	372	506	543	573	507	392	333	121	3704
1987	32	38	82	127	376	549	582	627	540	230	163	78	3424
1988	26	43	95	223	336	466	496	559	573	275	182	61	3335
1989	101	111	213	216	408	509	573	579	523	346	153	19	3751
1990	102	156	156	206	453	514	559	581	518	388	149	116	3898
1991	121	71	143	315	455	490	553	565	508	326	118	98	3763
1992	28	79	101	175	325	496	612	540	507	265	217	62	3407
1993	120	14	80	118	334	514	591	573	492	331	146	18	3331

SNOWFALL (inches) ORLANDO, FLORIDA

SEASON	JULY	AUG	SEP	OCT	NOV	DEC	JAN	FEB	MAR	APR	MAY	JUNE	TOTAL
1970-71	0.0	0.0	0.0	0.0	0.0	0.0	0.0	0.0	0.0	0.0	0.0	0.0	0.0
1971-72	0.0	0.0	0.0	0.0	0.0	0.0	0.0	0.0	0.0	0.0	0.0	0.0	0.0
1972-73	0.0	0.0	0.0	0.0	0.0	0.0	0.0	0.0	0.0	0.0	0.0	0.0	0.0
#1973-74	0.0	0.0	0.0	0.0	0.0	0.0	0.0	0.0	0.0	0.0	0.0	0.0	0.0
1974-75	0.0	0.0	0.0	0.0	0.0	0.0	0.0	0.0	0.0	0.0	0.0	0.0	0.0
1975-76	0.0	0.0	0.0	0.0	0.0	0.0	0.0	0.0	0.0	0.0	0.0	0.0	0.0
1976-77	0.0	0.0	0.0	0.0	0.0	0.0	T	0.0	0.0	0.0	0.0	0.0	T
1977-78	0.0	0.0	0.0	0.0	0.0	0.0	0.0	0.0	0.0	0.0	0.0	0.0	0.0
1978-79	0.0	0.0	0.0	0.0	0.0	0.0	0.0	0.0	0.0	0.0	0.0	0.0	0.0
1979-80	0.0	0.0	0.0	0.0	0.0	0.0	0.0	0.0	0.0	0.0	0.0	0.0	0.0
1980-81	0.0	0.0	0.0	0.0	0.0	0.0	0.0	0.0	0.0	0.0	0.0	0.0	0.0
1981-82	0.0	0.0	0.0	0.0	0.0	0.0	0.0	0.0	0.0	0.0	0.0	0.0	0.0
1982-83	0.0	0.0	0.0	0.0	0.0	0.0	0.0	0.0	0.0	0.0	0.0	0.0	0.0
1983-84	0.0	0.0	0.0	0.0	0.0	0.0	0.0	0.0	0.0	0.0	0.0	0.0	0.0
1984-85	0.0	0.0	0.0	0.0	0.0	0.0	0.0	0.0	0.0	0.0	0.0	0.0	0.0
1985-86	0.0	0.0	0.0	0.0	0.0	0.0	0.0	0.0	0.0	0.0	0.0	0.0	0.0
1986-87	0.0	0.0	0.0	0.0	0.0	0.0	0.0	0.0	0.0	0.0	0.0	0.0	0.0
1987-88	0.0	0.0	0.0	0.0	0.0	0.0	0.0	0.0	0.0	0.0	0.0	0.0	0.0
1988-89	0.0	0.0	0.0	0.0	0.0	0.0	0.0	0.0	0.0	0.0	0.0	0.0	0.0
1989-90	0.0	T	0.0	0.0	0.0	0.0	0.0	0.0	0.0	0.0	0.0	0.0	T
1990-91	0.0	0.0	0.0	0.0	0.0	0.0	0.0	0.0	0.0	0.0	0.0	0.0	0.0
1991-92	T	0.0	0.0	0.0	0.0	0.0	0.0	0.0	T	T	0.0	0.0	T
1992-93	0.0	0.0	0.0	0.0	0.0	0.0	0.0	0.0	0.0	0.0	0.0	0.0	0.0
1993-94	T	0.0	0.0	0.0	0.0	0.0							
Record Mean	T	T	0.0	0.0	0.0	0.0	T	0.0	T	T	0.0	0.0	T

TAMPA, FLORIDA

Tampa is on west central coast of the Florida Peninsula. Very near the Gulf of Mexico at the upper end of Tampa Bay, land and sea breezes modify the subtropical climate. Major rivers flowing into the area are the Hillsborough, the Alafia, and the Little Manatee.

Winters are mild. Summers are long, rather warm, and humid. Low temperatures are about 50 degrees in the winter and 70 degrees during the summer. Afternoon highs range from the low 70s in the winter to around 90 degrees from June through September. Invasions of cold northern air produce an occasional cool winter morning. Freezing temperatures occur on one or two mornings per year during December, January, and February. In some years no freezing temperatures occur. Temperatures rarely fail to recover to the 60s on the cooler winter days. Temperatures above the low 90s are uncommon because of the afternoon sea breezes and thunderstorms. An outstanding feature of the Tampa climate is the summer thunderstorm season. Most of the thunderstorms occur in the late afternoon hours from June through September. The resulting sudden drop in temperature from about 90 degrees to around 70 degrees makes for a pleasant change. Between a dry spring and a dry fall, some 30 inches of rain, about 60 percent of the annual total, falls during the summer months. Snowfall is very rare. Measurable snows under 1/2 inch have occurred only a few times in the last one hundred years.

A large part of the generally flat sandy land near the coast has an elevation of under 15 feet above sea level. This does make the area vulnerable to tidal surges. Tropical storms threaten the area on a few occasions most years. The greatest risk of hurricanes has been during the months of June and October. Many hurricanes, by replenishing the soil moisture and raising the water table, do far more good than harm. The heaviest rains in a 24-hour period, around 12 inches, have been associated with hurricanes.

Fittingly named the Suncoast, the sun shines more than 65 percent of the possible, with the sunniest months being April and May. Afternoon humidities are usually 60 percent or higher in the summer months, but range from 50 to 60 percent the remainder of the year.

Night ground fogs occur frequently during the cooler winter months. Prevailing winds are easterly, but westerly afternoon and early evening sea breezes occur most months of the year. Winds in excess of 25 mph are not common and usually occur only with thunderstorms or tropical disturbances.

Based on the 1951-1980 period, the average first occurrence of 32 degrees Fahrenheit in the fall is December 26 and the average last occurrence in the spring is February 3.

NORMALS, MEANS, AND EXTREMES

TAMPA, FLORIDA

LATITUDE: 27°58'N LONGITUDE: 82°32' W ELEVATION: FT. GRND 19 BARO 41 TIME ZONE: EASTERN WBAN: 12842

	(a)	JAN	FEB	MAR	APR	MAY	JUNE	JULY	AUG	SEP	OCT	NOV	DEC	YEAR
TEMPERATURE °F:														
Normals														
-Daily Maximum		69.8	71.4	76.6	81.7	87.2	89.5	90.2	90.2	89.0	84.3	77.7	72.1	81.6
-Daily Minimum		50.0	51.6	56.5	60.8	67.5	72.9	74.5	74.5	72.8	65.2	57.2	52.3	63.0
-Monthly		59.9	61.5	66.6	71.3	77.4	81.3	82.4	82.4	80.9	74.8	67.5	62.2	72.4
Extremes														
-Record Highest	47	86	88	91	93	98	99	97	98	96	94	90	86	99
-Year		1991	1971	1949	1975	1975	1985	1993	1975	1991	1990	1971	1991	JUN 1985
-Record Lowest	47	21	24	29	40	49	53	63	67	57	40	23	18	18
-Year		1985	1958	1980	1987	1992	1984	1970	1973	1981	1964	1970	1962	DEC 1962
NORMAL DEGREE DAYS:														
Heating (base 65°F)		234	160	81	7	0	0	0	0	0	0	72	171	725
Cooling (base 65°F)		76	62	130	196	384	489	539	539	477	304	147	84	3427
% OF POSSIBLE SUNSHINE	46	63	66	71	75	75	67	62	61	61	65	64	62	66
MEAN SKY COVER (tenths)														
Sunrise - Sunset	47	5.6	5.5	5.4	4.8	5.1	6.1	6.6	6.5	6.2	5.1	5.0	5.5	5.6
MEAN NUMBER OF DAYS:														
Sunrise to Sunset														
-Clear	47	9.6	9.1	10.6	11.4	10.6	5.5	2.8	3.2	5.2	11.6	11.6	10.2	101.5
-Partly Cloudy	47	9.7	9.0	10.0	11.0	12.6	14.4	16.3	16.7	13.9	10.4	9.5	9.8	143.3
-Cloudy	47	11.7	10.1	10.5	7.6	7.8	10.1	11.8	11.1	11.0	8.9	8.9	11.1	120.5
Precipitation														
.01 inches or more	47	6.5	6.8	6.9	4.7	6.4	11.7	15.5	16.5	12.9	6.9	5.5	6.1	106.3
Snow,Ice pellets,hail														
1.0 inches or more	47	0.0	0.0	0.0	0.0	0.0	0.0	0.0	0.0	0.0	0.0	0.0	0.0	0.0
Thunderstorms	47	0.9	1.5	2.7	2.6	5.5	13.7	20.7	20.4	11.7	2.9	1.2	1.2	85.1
Heavy Fog Visibility														
1/4 mile or less	47	5.5	3.0	2.7	1.1	0.4	0.3	0.1	0.2	0.3	1.1	2.6	4.0	21.2
Temperature °F														
-Maximum														
90° and above	30	0.0	0.0	0.0	0.8	8.2	16.6	20.9	21.5	16.3	2.7	0.*	0.0	87.1
32° and below	30	0.0	0.0	0.0	0.0	0.0	0.0	0.0	0.0	0.0	0.0	0.0	0.0	0.0
-Minimum														
32° and below	30	1.7	0.6	0.1	0.0	0.0	0.0	0.0	0.0	0.0	0.0	0.1	0.8	3.3
0° and below	30	0.0	0.0	0.0	0.0	0.0	0.0	0.0	0.0	0.0	0.0	0.0	0.0	0.0
AVG. STATION PRESS.(mb)	20	1020.0	1019.1	1017.7	1016.8	1015.7	1016.1	1017.7	1016.9	1015.6	1016.6	1018.4	1020.2	1017.6
RELATIVE HUMIDITY (%)														
Hour 01	30	85	83	83	82	82	84	86	87	87	86	86	85	85
Hour 07 (Local Time)	30	87	86	87	87	86	87	87	90	91	89	88	87	88
Hour 13	30	59	56	55	51	52	60	63	64	61	57	57	59	58
Hour 19	30	73	69	67	62	63	69	73	76	75	72	74	74	71
PRECIPITATION (inches):														
Water Equivalent														
-Normal		1.99	3.08	3.01	1.15	3.10	5.48	6.58	7.61	5.98	2.02	1.77	2.15	43.92
-Maximum Monthly	47	8.02	7.95	12.64	6.59	17.64	13.75	20.59	18.59	13.98	7.36	6.12	6.66	20.59
-Year		1948	1963	1959	1957	1979	1974	1960	1949	1979	1952	1963	1950	JUL 1960
-Minimum Monthly	47	T	0.21	0.06	T	0.10	1.86	1.65	2.35	1.28	0.09	T	0.07	T
-Year		1950	1950	1956	1981	1992	1951	1981	1952	1972	1988	1960	1984	APR 1981
-Maximum in 24 hrs	47	3.29	3.68	5.20	3.70	11.84	5.53	12.11	5.37	4.99	2.93	4.48	3.28	12.11
-Year		1953	1981	1960	1951	1979	1974	1960	1949	1985	1985	1988	1969	JUL 1960
Snow,Ice pellets,hail														
-Maximum Monthly	47	0.2	T	T	0.0	0.0	0.0	0.0	0.0	0.0	0.0	0.0	T	0.2
-Year		1977	1951	1980									1989	JAN 1977
-Maximum in 24 hrs	47	0.2	T	T	0.0	0.0	0.0	0.0	0.0	0.0	0.0	0.0	T	0.2
-Year		1977	1951	1980									1989	JAN 1977
WIND:														
Mean Speed (mph)	47	8.6	9.2	9.4	9.2	8.7	7.9	7.1	6.9	7.7	8.4	8.4	8.4	8.3
Prevailing Direction through 1963		N	E	S	ENE	E	E	E	ENE	ENE	NNE	NNE	N	E
Fastest Obs. 1 Min.														
-Direction (!!)	41	29	32	29	29	36	31	32	11	34	02	29	36	31
-Speed (MPH)	41	35	50	43	37	46	67	58	38	56	38	40	45	67
-Year		1959	1954	1956	1961	1958	1964	1963	1961	1960	1953	1963	1953	JUN 1964
Peak Gust														
-Direction (!!)	10	W	NW	W	W	N	E	E	S	W	SW	NE	N	E
-Speed (mph)	10	44	46	58	49	51	61	60	48	45	41	47	36	61
-Date		1991	1984	1993	1991	1986	1988	1988	1990	1984	1985	1988	1989	JUN 1988

PRECIPITATION (inches)

TAMPA, FLORIDA

YEAR	JAN	FEB	MAR	APR	MAY	JUNE	JULY	AUG	SEP	OCT	NOV	DEC	ANNUAL
1964	5.08	5.37	3.92	0.53	3.58	6.64	9.75	10.73	5.89	2.86	0.38	3.19	57.92
1965	1.56	2.57	2.28	1.10	0.67	7.30	9.70	5.59	7.36	1.43	0.88	2.34	42.78
1966	4.05	3.08	1.16	1.57	0.71	6.44	7.62	4.75	4.12	1.22	0.39	0.94	36.05
1967	1.32	4.30	0.66	T	0.63	4.70	10.30	10.34	2.20	2.42	0.45	2.04	39.36
1968	0.41	1.52	1.23	0.74	2.08	6.72	8.39	6.79	3.58	4.16	3.14	0.59	39.35
1969	1.78	2.11	5.33	0.05	6.23	4.39	7.39	11.88	4.09	3.12	2.68	5.17	54.22
1970	3.10	4.02	6.12	0.49	4.12	2.05	2.77	8.43	3.95	0.89	1.08	1.25	38.27
1971	0.86	4.25	0.54	1.80	4.09	2.54	7.74	7.46	10.16	4.70	1.40	0.79	46.33
1972	0.54	4.44	3.01	0.38	1.88	5.24	6.65	9.78	1.28	3.29	3.53	2.16	42.18
1973	3.75	2.54	4.21	2.42	0.17	4.19	4.77	9.43	8.91	0.98	2.82	5.52	49.71
1974	0.17	0.89	2.35	0.38	1.11	13.75	3.43	4.67	4.00	0.23	0.12	2.80	33.90
1975	0.91	1.56	1.09	0.91	2.07	8.73	6.65	4.24	11.25	4.94	0.22	0.87	43.44
1976	0.40	0.49	1.64	1.83	8.13	7.22	4.58	7.02	6.04	1.30	1.59	2.05	42.29
1977	2.75	2.41	0.73	0.86	0.73	2.66	5.36	5.98	4.28	0.42	1.89	3.40	31.47
1978	2.82	5.17	2.44	0.94	5.00	2.03	5.85	5.97	3.08	3.42	0.01	3.12	39.85
1979	5.72	2.87	2.43	0.55	17.64	2.07	5.93	12.76	13.98	0.16	0.83	1.52	66.46
1980	1.72	2.01	3.09	4.38	3.94	3.81	5.66	7.62	4.05	1.27	2.68	0.37	40.60
1981	0.44	5.34	1.70	T	1.68	9.37	1.65	7.71	5.87	0.87	0.43	3.58	38.64
1982	1.86	2.09	2.99	1.87	5.90	8.34	10.49	7.20	10.76	2.17	0.85	1.29	55.81
1983	1.25	7.35	7.59	2.76	4.10	7.17	6.37	8.89	6.61	1.74	2.33	4.71	60.87
1984	1.62	3.32	1.31	1.51	3.19	3.24	7.15	5.68	4.21	0.29	0.72	0.07	32.31
1985	2.06	2.07	1.80	0.96	0.22	6.43	6.48	8.65	9.04	4.77	0.99	1.13	44.60
1986	2.37	1.49	4.27	0.95	2.46	5.00	6.24	5.46	3.87	6.21	1.33	1.95	41.60
1987	3.29	1.50	12.01	0.39	2.86	3.39	6.06	8.50	4.76	1.46	4.36	0.50	49.08
1988	2.76	1.44	4.09	1.83	1.27	5.19	3.40	11.09	13.56	0.09	5.97	1.64	52.33
1989	1.54	0.41	1.79	0.71	0.24	7.41	8.86	7.90	6.11	1.89	2.05	4.72	43.63
1990	0.53	4.58	1.71	1.47	1.76	5.16	10.01	3.27	2.42	2.63	0.66	0.19	34.39
1991	2.41	0.41	4.73	1.54	6.88	3.78	9.92	7.35	3.43	0.78	1.26	0.67	43.16
1992	1.47	3.67	0.95	2.17	0.10	7.03	2.80	8.22	2.95	2.20	2.43	0.99	34.98
1993	3.60	2.32	3.93	2.45	1.74	3.18	2.92	5.06	6.60	4.23	0.22	1.28	37.53
Record Mean	2.22	2.77	3.03	2.00	3.04	6.76	7.62	7.92	6.48	2.61	1.64	2.01	48.10

AVERAGE TEMPERATURE (deg. F)

TAMPA, FLORIDA

YEAR	JAN	FEB	MAR	APR	MAY	JUNE	JULY	AUG	SEP	OCT	NOV	DEC	ANNUAL
1964	58.6	57.1	68.0	74.0	76.7	81.8	82.0	81.5	79.3	70.9	67.7	63.2	71.7
1965	58.6	63.8	66.4	72.7	76.3	79.5	80.3	81.5	80.5	72.5	67.0	60.6	71.7
1966	57.0	59.9	63.1	69.2	78.5	79.2	81.7	82.5	80.6	75.3	65.1	59.2	70.9
1967	62.3	59.5	67.8	73.2	77.3	79.9	80.8	80.3	79.2	73.5	65.3	64.8	72.0
1968	59.4	54.3	60.9	72.5	75.7	79.6	80.2	82.0	79.6	73.2	62.3	57.6	69.8
1969	58.5	55.8	58.2	72.3	76.2	82.1	83.1	80.9	80.5	76.9	62.9	58.1	70.5
1970	54.0	57.6	64.9	73.2	76.2	80.1	82.8	82.9	81.9	76.1	61.9	62.4	71.2
1971	60.0	63.1	62.2	69.4	75.8	81.2	82.3	81.8	80.3	77.5	67.7	69.4	72.6
1972	67.0	60.7	66.8	71.4	76.6	81.0	81.9	82.1	81.3	76.1	68.2	65.1	73.2
1973	61.9	57.4	70.2	69.3	76.8	81.8	83.2	81.8	81.7	75.8	70.8	60.1	72.6
1974	71.1	61.1	70.9	70.9	78.2	80.1	81.1	82.8	82.8	72.9	67.9	61.9	73.5
1975	65.1	66.6	67.6	74.0	81.5	82.6	83.2	83.7	81.9	77.9	68.3	60.2	74.4
1976	56.6	63.1	70.5	70.6	76.1	79.0	81.7	81.6	79.3	71.0	62.8	59.6	71.0
1977	51.2	57.5	70.9	71.5	76.5	83.7	82.9	83.0	82.3	72.5	67.7	58.7	71.6
1978	55.0	53.2	64.2	72.3	78.7	82.4	83.0	82.8	81.4	75.1	71.7	66.2	72.2
1979	57.8	59.3	65.4	74.2	75.9	80.8	83.9	82.2	81.9	75.2	68.7	63.0	72.3
1980	62.0	56.6	68.1	70.1	77.2	81.6	84.0	83.0	81.3	74.0	66.4	57.5	71.8
1981	50.4	61.4	62.8	72.4	75.4	81.5	82.5	81.7	78.6	74.5	64.4	59.2	70.4
1982	59.8	67.9	68.1	71.4	74.4	81.5	82.1	82.1	80.2	74.3	70.8	67.6	73.4
1983	58.9	60.3	63.3	68.6	76.8	80.9	82.2	82.2	79.4	75.8	65.9	59.9	71.2
1984	58.0	62.6	66.0	71.0	78.0	80.4	81.5	82.4	79.9	75.7	64.9	67.3	72.3
1985	55.9	63.6	69.4	72.5	79.8	83.7	82.4	83.1	80.5	79.2	73.6	59.0	73.6
1986	59.3	65.0	65.4	69.1	77.4	81.8	83.0	82.6	82.3	76.8	76.3	66.5	73.8
1987	59.2	63.2	66.4	66.4	77.8	82.7	83.1	83.7	81.4	71.3	68.9	64.3	72.4
1988	58.6	59.1	65.6	70.6	75.3	81.0	82.7	82.9	82.0	73.5	70.8	63.0	72.1
1989	67.1	64.9	69.8	72.0	78.4	82.4	83.3	83.0	82.4	75.4	68.9	56.2	73.7
1990	66.1	69.2	69.7	72.1	80.5	82.7	82.5	83.9	82.8	77.6	70.2	66.9	75.4
1991	66.7	64.2	68.4	76.8	81.2	81.3	82.3	83.2	81.9	75.3	65.8	64.6	74.3
1992	59.8	63.6	64.8	69.4	74.3	82.1	83.8	82.4	82.0	72.7	70.0	64.3	72.4
1993	67.0	60.2	64.3	67.2	76.1	81.8	83.8	83.7	81.9	75.8	69.1	59.5	72.5
Record Mean	60.9	62.2	66.7	71.4	77.0	80.8	82.0	82.1	80.7	74.7	67.3	62.0	72.3
Max	70.3	71.7	76.2	81.1	86.4	89.2	89.8	90.0	88.7	83.3	76.7	71.5	81.2
Min	51.4	52.7	57.2	61.7	67.5	72.4	74.1	74.2	72.6	66.0	57.9	52.6	63.3

REFERENCE NOTES

TAMPA, FLORIDA

GENERAL
T - TRACE AMOUNT.
BLANK ENTRIES DENOTE MISSING/UNREPORTED DATA.
# INDICATES A STATION OR INSTRUMENT RELOCATION.

SPECIFIC

PM - INCLUDES LAST DAY OF PREVIOUS MONTH
ASOS - AUTOMATED SURFACE OBSERVING SYSTEM IN OPERATION DURING THESE MONTHS.

(a) - LENGTH OF RECORD IN YEARS, ALTHOUGH INDIVIDUAL MONTHS MAY BE MISSING.
0.* OR * - THE VALUE IS BETWEEN 0.0 AND 0.05
NORMALS - BASED ON THE 1961-1990 RECORD PERIOD.
EXTREMES - DATES ARE THE MOST RECENT OCCURRENCE
WIND DIR.- NUMERALS SHOW TENS OF DEGRESS CLOCKWISE FROM TRUE NORTH. "00" INDICATES CALM.
RESULTANT DIRECTIONS ARE GIVEN TO WHOLE DEGREES.
BOLD VALUES INDICATE EXTREME VALUES WHICH OCCURRED AFTER THE ASOS SYSTEM WAS COMMISSIONED.

RECORD = PERIOD OF RECORD
RECORD MEAN PRECIPITATION IS THE MEAN OF ALL DAILY PRECIPITATION AMOUNTS DURING THE PERIOD OF RECORD.
RECORD MAX(MIN) TEMPERATURE IS THE MEAN OF ALL DAILY MAX(MIN) TEMPERATURES DURING THE PERIOD OF RECORD.
RECORD MEAN TEMPERATURE IS THE SUM OF THE RECORD MAX AND RECORD MIN DIVIDED BY 2.
AVERAGE TEMPERATURE IS THE SUM OF THE MEAN DAILY MAX AND MIN TEMPERATURE DIVIDED BY 2.

EXCEPTIONS

RECORD MEANS ARE THROUGH THE CURRENT YEAR,
BEGINNING IN 1890 FOR TEMPERATURE
1890 FOR PRECIPITATION
1947 FOR SNOWFALL

HEATING DEGREE DAYS Base 65 deg. F — TAMPA, FLORIDA

SEASON	JULY	AUG	SEP	OCT	NOV	DEC	JAN	FEB	MAR	APR	MAY	JUNE	TOTAL
1964-65	0	0	0	22	24	114	204	96	84	2	0	0	546
1965-66	0	0	0	5	37	160	267	172	93	18	0	0	752
1966-67	0	0	0	7	85	198	129	175	23	0	0	0	617
1967-68	0	0	0	0	69	95	193	306	157	0	0	0	820
1968-69	0	0	0	27	138	264	201	252	220	0	0	0	1102
1969-70	0	0	0	0	111	218	343	209	81	0	0	0	962
1970-71	0	0	0	0	145	115	201	134	139	36	0	0	770
1971-72	0	0	0	0	41	13	62	139	26	5	0	0	286
1972-73	0	0	0	0	65	130	166	223	18	21	0	0	623
1973-74	0	0	0	6	24	200	0	159	17	12	0	0	418
1974-75	0	0	0	0	39	138	84	64	61	5	0	0	391
1975-76	0	0	0	0	88	183	268	109	18	2	0	0	668
1976-77	0	0	0	11	122	208	422	214	28	6	0	0	1011
1977-78	0	0	0	18	53	222	320	323	99	4	0	0	1039
1978-79	0	0	0	0	2	75	245	190	53	0	0	0	565
1979-80	0	0	0	0	47	112	136	262	64	8	0	0	629
1980-81	0	0	0	1	65	233	447	127	103	2	0	0	978
1981-82	0	0	0	0	83	223	209	24	53	8	0	0	600
1982-83	0	0	0	12	18	95	218	148	103	20	0	0	614
1983-84	0	0	0	0	57	214	252	115	68	5	0	0	711
1984-85	0	0	0	0	87	61	306	119	17	5	0	0	595
1985-86	0	0	0	0	9	238	185	78	105	7	0	0	622
1986-87	0	0	0	0	0	53	202	88	42	64	0	0	449
1987-88	0	0	0	4	46	107	221	195	85	14	0	0	672
1988-89	0	0	0	0	9	127	41	116	45	7	0	0	345
1989-90	0	0	0	17	27	285	70	32	13	5	0	0	449
1990-91	0	0	0	7	11	70	72	84	46	0	0	0	290
1991-92	0	0	0	0	93	94	179	90	69	32	5	0	562
1992-93	0	0	0	0	57	83	58	137	84	24	0	0	443
1993-94	0	0	0	6	44	185							

COOLING DEGREE DAYS Base 65 deg. F — TAMPA, FLORIDA

YEAR	JAN	FEB	MAR	APR	MAY	JUNE	JULY	AUG	SEP	OCT	NOV	DEC	TOTAL
1969	8	2	14	224	353	521	568	498	471	377	55	10	3101
1970	12	10	85	255	352	464	557	563	514	353	58	40	3263
1971	54	86	58	174	342	490	541	526	463	396	128	155	3413
1972	131	20	90	204	365	487	528	536	497	352	168	141	3519
1973	75	15	188	158	374	510	574	529	510	348	205	55	3541
1974	196	55	204	197	413	460	506	562	540	250	130	48	3561
1975	93	115	151	282	521	536	572	585	512	407	191	39	4004
1976	17	63	199	175	348	424	525	517	440	202	63	45	3018
1977	2	9	218	210	364	567	559	565	526	258	139	36	3453
1978	18	0	79	232	431	529	565	557	500	319	208	121	3559
1979	28	36	73	283	344	482	592	543	515	322	164	55	3437
1980	45	22	164	165	386	506	598	564	493	284	115	7	3349
1981	0	32	43	230	331	501	552	525	414	303	71	49	3051
1982	56	114	156	208	299	499	537	537	467	311	197	182	3563
1983	36	24	57	137	369	487	540	541	439	342	91	64	3127
1984	42	52	104	190	410	468	517	546	454	337	92	135	3347
1985	30	88	163	237	464	569	547	566	475	445	275	58	3917
1986	15	85	123	139	391	510	565	551	526	374	348	107	3734
1987	27	43	91	114	405	538	567	583	497	207	169	91	3332
1988	30	32	110	188	326	489	554	562	517	271	191	74	3344
1989	112	120	202	224	425	528	575	564	529	344	151	18	3792
1990	107	154	164	225	487	537	549	592	541	406	176	139	4077
1991	131	68	158	361	509	498	543	572	515	326	126	88	3895
1992	25	55	70	170	301	519	589	544	518	248	212	72	3323
1993	126	12	72	95	352	511	593	587	513	347	174	21	3403

SNOWFALL (inches) — TAMPA, FLORIDA

SEASON	JULY	AUG	SEP	OCT	NOV	DEC	JAN	FEB	MAR	APR	MAY	JUNE	TOTAL
1970-71	0.0	0.0	0.0	0.0	0.0	0.0	0.0	0.0	0.0	0.0	0.0	0.0	0.0
1971-72	0.0	0.0	0.0	0.0	0.0	0.0	0.0	0.0	0.0	0.0	0.0	0.0	0.0
1972-73	0.0	0.0	0.0	0.0	0.0	0.0	0.0	0.0	0.0	0.0	0.0	0.0	0.0
1973-74	0.0	0.0	0.0	0.0	0.0	0.0	0.0	0.0	0.0	0.0	0.0	0.0	0.0
1974-75	0.0	0.0	0.0	0.0	0.0	0.0	0.0	0.0	0.0	0.0	0.0	0.0	0.0
1975-76	0.0	0.0	0.0	0.0	0.0	0.0	0.0	0.0	0.0	0.0	0.0	0.0	0.0
1976-77	0.0	0.0	0.0	0.0	0.0	0.0	0.2	0.0	0.0	0.0	0.0	0.0	0.2
1977-78	0.0	0.0	0.0	0.0	0.0	0.0	0.0	0.0	0.0	0.0	0.0	0.0	0.0
1978-79	0.0	0.0	0.0	0.0	0.0	0.0	0.0	0.0	0.0	0.0	0.0	0.0	0.0
1979-80	0.0	0.0	0.0	0.0	0.0	0.0	0.0	0.0	T	0.0	0.0	0.0	T
1980-81	0.0	0.0	0.0	0.0	0.0	0.0	0.0	0.0	0.0	0.0	0.0	0.0	0.0
1981-82	0.0	0.0	0.0	0.0	0.0	0.0	0.0	0.0	0.0	0.0	0.0	0.0	0.0
1982-83	0.0	0.0	0.0	0.0	0.0	0.0	0.0	0.0	0.0	0.0	0.0	0.0	0.0
1983-84	0.0	0.0	0.0	0.0	0.0	0.0	0.0	0.0	0.0	0.0	0.0	0.0	0.0
1984-85	0.0	0.0	0.0	0.0	0.0	0.0	0.0	0.0	0.0	0.0	0.0	0.0	0.0
1985-86	0.0	0.0	0.0	0.0	0.0	0.0	0.0	0.0	0.0	0.0	0.0	0.0	0.0
1986-87	0.0	0.0	0.0	0.0	0.0	0.0	0.0	0.0	0.0	0.0	0.0	0.0	0.0
1987-88	0.0	0.0	0.0	0.0	0.0	0.0	0.0	0.0	0.0	0.0	0.0	0.0	0.0
1988-89	0.0	0.0	0.0	0.0	0.0	0.0	0.0	0.0	0.0	0.0	0.0	0.0	0.0
1989-90	0.0	0.0	0.0	0.0	0.0	T	0.0	0.0	0.0	0.0	0.0	0.0	T
1990-91	0.0	0.0	0.0	0.0	0.0	0.0	0.0	0.0	0.0	0.0	0.0	0.0	0.0
1991-92	0.0	0.0	0.0	0.0	0.0	0.0	0.0	0.0	0.0	0.0	0.0	0.0	0.0
1992-93	0.0	0.0	0.0	0.0	0.0	0.0	0.0	0.0	0.0	0.0	0.0	0.0	0.0
1993-94	0.0	0.0	0.0	0.0	0.0	0.0							
Record Mean	0.0	0.0	0.0	0.0	0.0	T	T	T	T	0.0	0.0	0.0	T

ATLANTA, GEORGIA

Atlanta is located in the foothills of the southern Appalachians in north-central Georgia. The terrain is rolling to hilly and slopes downward toward the east, west, and south so that drainage of the major river systems is generally into the Gulf of Mexico from the western and southern sections of the city and to the Atlantic from the eastern portions of the city.

The Gulf of Mexico and the Atlantic Ocean are approximately 250 miles south and southeast of the city, respectively. Both the Appalachian chain of mountains and the two nearby maritime bodies exert an important influence on the Atlanta climate. Temperatures are moderated throughout the year while abundant precipitation fosters natural vegetation and growth of crops. Summer temperatures in Atlanta are moderated somewhat by elevation but are still rather warm. However, prolonged periods of hot weather are unusual and 100 degree heat is rarely experienced.

With the mountains to the north tending to retard the southward movement of Polar air masses, Atlanta winters are rather mild. Cold spells are not unusual but they are rather short-lived and seldom disrupt outdoor activities for an extended period of time. Late March is the average date of the last temperature of 32 degrees in the spring and mid-November is the average date of the first temperature of 32 degrees in the fall, which gives an average growing season of about 234 days.

Minimum dry precipitation periods occur mainly during the late summer and early autumn. Maximum thunderstorm activity occurs during July, but severe local thunderstorms occur most frequently in March, April, and May, some spawning highly damaging tornadoes.

The average annual snowfall varies widely from year to year. A fall of 4 inches or more occurs about once every five years. Most snows melt in a short period of time due to the rapid warming which often follows the storm. Ice storms, freezing rain or glaze, occur about two out of every three years, causing hazardous travel and disruption of utilities. Severe ice storms occur about once in ten years, causing major disruption of utilities and significant property damage.

The Bermuda High pressure area has a dominant effect on Atlanta weather, particularly in the summer months. East or northeast winds produce the most unpleasant weather although southerly winds are quite humid during the summer. The generally light wind conditions contribute to the formation of an occasional early morning fog.

NORMALS, MEANS, AND EXTREMES

ATLANTA, GEORGIA

LATITUDE: 33°39'N LONGITUDE: 84°25' W ELEVATION: FT. GRND 1010 BARO 1110 TIME ZONE: EASTERN WBAN: 13874

	(a)	JAN	FEB	MAR	APR	MAY	JUNE	JULY	AUG	SEP	OCT	NOV	DEC	YEAR
TEMPERATURE °F:														
Normals														
-Daily Maximum		50.4	55.0	64.3	72.7	79.6	85.8	88.0	87.1	81.8	72.7	63.4	54.0	71.2
-Daily Minimum		31.5	34.5	42.5	50.2	58.7	66.2	69.5	69.0	63.5	51.9	42.8	35.0	51.3
-Monthly		41.0	44.8	53.5	61.5	69.2	76.0	78.8	78.1	72.7	62.3	53.1	44.5	61.3
Extremes														
-Record Highest	45	79	80	85	93	95	101	105	102	98	95	84	79	105
-Year		1949	1989	1991	1986	1953	1952	1980	1980	1954	1954	1961	1991	JUL 1980
-Record Lowest	45	-8	5	10	26	37	46	53	55	36	28	3	0	-8
-Year		1985	1958	1960	1973	1971	1956	1967	1992	1967	1976	1950	1983	JAN 1985
NORMAL DEGREE DAYS:														
Heating (base 65°F)		744	566	365	138	27	0	0	0	10	138	367	636	2991
Cooling (base 65°F)		0	0	8	33	157	330	428	406	241	54	10	0	1667
% OF POSSIBLE SUNSHINE	58	49	54	58	66	68	67	63	64	63	67	58	50	61
MEAN SKY COVER (tenths)														
Sunrise - Sunset	59	6.4	6.2	6.1	5.5	5.7	5.8	6.1	5.8	5.5	4.6	5.4	6.2	5.8
MEAN NUMBER OF DAYS:														
Sunrise to Sunset														
-Clear	59	8.3	8.0	8.8	10.1	9.1	7.8	6.3	7.4	9.7	14.0	11.6	9.2	110.4
-Partly Cloudy	59	6.4	6.2	7.5	8.2	10.5	11.8	13.2	13.1	9.9	7.2	6.0	6.4	106.4
-Cloudy	59	16.3	14.0	14.6	11.8	11.4	10.3	11.6	10.4	10.4	9.8	12.4	15.4	148.5
Precipitation														
.01 inches or more	59	11.5	10.1	11.4	8.9	9.2	9.9	11.9	9.5	7.6	6.4	8.5	10.3	115.1
Snow,Ice pellets,hail														
1.0 inches or more	59	0.3	0.2	0.1	0.0	0.0	0.0	0.0	0.0	0.0	0.0	0.*	0.1	0.6
Thunderstorms	59	1.1	1.9	3.6	4.2	6.0	8.6	10.3	8.0	3.1	1.0	1.0	0.7	49.6
Heavy Fog Visibility 1/4 mile or less	59	5.0	3.3	2.7	1.4	1.4	1.0	1.5	1.7	1.9	2.2	3.0	4.5	29.6
Temperature °F														
-Maximum														
90° and above	33	0.0	0.0	0.0	0.1	1.0	8.0	12.5	9.5	3.4	0.0	0.0	0.0	34.4
32° and below	33	1.5	0.3	0.*	0.0	0.0	0.0	0.0	0.0	0.0	0.0	0.*	0.4	2.3
-Minimum														
32° and below	33	15.8	12.3	4.9	0.5	0.0	0.0	0.0	0.0	0.0	0.2	4.8	12.8	51.4
0° and below	33	0.2	0.0	0.0	0.0	0.0	0.0	0.0	0.0	0.0	0.0	0.0	0.*	0.2
AVG. STATION PRESS.(mb)	21	982.6	981.6	979.8	979.6	979.2	979.9	981.0	981.3	981.4	982.5	982.7	983.2	981.2
RELATIVE HUMIDITY (%)														
Hour 01	33	74	69	69	69	77	80	85	85	83	78	76	74	77
Hour 07 (Local Time)	33	78	75	78	78	82	84	88	90	88	84	81	79	82
Hour 13	33	59	54	51	49	53	56	60	60	59	53	55	58	56
Hour 19	33	63	56	53	50	58	61	66	67	67	63	63	64	61
PRECIPITATION (inches):														
Water Equivalent														
-Normal		4.75	4.81	5.77	4.26	4.29	3.56	5.01	3.66	3.42	3.05	3.86	4.33	50.77
-Maximum Monthly	59	10.82	12.77	11.66	11.86	8.37	9.99	11.26	8.69	11.64	7.53	15.72	9.92	15.72
-Year		1936	1961	1980	1979	1980	1991	1948	1967	1989	1966	1948	1961	NOV 1948
-Minimum Monthly	59	0.84	0.77	1.86	0.49	0.32	0.16	0.76	0.50	0.04	T	0.41	0.69	T
-Year		1981	1978	1985	1986	1936	1988	1980	1976	1984	1963	1939	1979	OCT 1963
-Maximum in 24 hrs	59	3.91	5.67	5.74	5.58	5.13	4.22	5.44	5.05	5.87	5.41	4.11	3.85	5.87
-Year		1973	1961	1990	1979	1948	1991	1948	1940	1992	1989	1935	1961	SEP 1992
Snow,Ice pellets,hail														
-Maximum Monthly	59	8.3	4.4	7.9	T	0.0	0.0	0.0	0.0	0.0	T	1.0	2.8	8.3
-Year		1940	1979	1983	1990						1993	1968	1993	JAN 1940
-Maximum in 24 hrs	59	8.3	4.2	7.9	T	0.0	0.0	0.0	0.0	0.0	T	1.0	2.8	8.3
-Year		1940	1979	1983	1990						1993	1968	1993	JAN 1940
WIND:														
Mean Speed (mph)	55	10.4	10.8	10.8	10.1	8.7	8.1	7.6	7.2	8.0	8.5	9.1	9.8	9.1
Prevailing Direction through 1963		NW	NW	NW	NW	NW	NW	SW	NW	ENE	NW	NW	NW	NW
Fastest Obs. 1 Min.														
-Direction (!!)	17	23	29	31	31	27	24	30	32	27	09	24	30	30
-Speed (MPH)	17	46	52	49	41	54	51	60	41	37	30	37	33	60
-Year		1978	1990	1993	1989	1984	1989	1984	1986	1980	1985	1984	1984	JUL 1984
Peak Gust														
-Direction (!!)	10	W	W	NW	W	W	SW	NW	N	E	E	NW	NW	NW
-Speed (mph)	10	48	68	61	61	72	60	77	55	45	45	56	47	77
-Date		1992	1990	1993	1985	1984	1989	1984	1990	1985	1985	1986	1993	JUL 1984

PRECIPITATION (inches)

ATLANTA, GEORGIA

YEAR	JAN	FEB	MAR	APR	MAY	JUNE	JULY	AUG	SEP	OCT	NOV	DEC	ANNUAL
1964	6.01	4.17	9.51	8.68	2.59	2.88	7.14	4.10	1.38	5.63	3.11	4.93	60.13
1965	3.74	4.31	5.94	3.10	2.51	7.15	4.59	1.53	3.02	2.35	2.32	1.70	42.26
1966	5.94	7.04	4.02	4.19	5.84	2.95	3.32	3.94	2.15	7.53	4.82	4.60	56.34
1967	4.85	3.75	3.63	2.81	4.95	3.06	6.46	8.69	1.90	2.51	5.52	6.71	54.84
1968	4.07	1.40	4.54	6.33	6.42	2.65	5.34	4.13	1.29	2.99	4.81	4.89	48.86
1969	2.85	3.20	4.00	5.70	7.68	1.00	2.64	6.12	3.74	1.53	2.67	3.27	44.40
1970	2.95	2.99	6.94	3.24	3.01	2.62	3.59	3.26	1.82	6.29	1.86	3.68	42.25
1971	4.40	5.77	8.65	4.09	2.12	3.33	8.22	2.76	3.32	0.31	3.42	2.79	49.18
1972	9.26	3.16	4.49	2.31	4.28	4.04	3.81	2.78	1.86	3.04	3.96	7.62	50.61
1973	8.89	3.44	9.53	4.03	7.14	3.35	2.10	1.35	4.16	0.75	2.31	8.11	55.16
1974	5.36	6.37	2.44	3.72	3.83	3.20	4.64	6.26	1.06	1.22	3.89	5.31	47.30
1975	6.19	8.98	8.31	4.28	4.62	5.52	8.52	3.30	2.99	5.31	4.62	3.36	66.00
1976	5.15	1.84	10.95	1.49	6.99	2.36	4.29	0.50	0.72	3.55	4.11	4.01	45.96
1977	3.49	2.14	6.28	1.77	2.04	3.03	4.26	4.23	4.90	5.00	7.18	2.36	46.68
1978	7.03	0.77	2.63	3.49	7.28	2.86	2.56	5.66	0.94	1.42	2.96	3.75	41.35
1979	5.03	5.71	3.19	11.86	2.43	1.46	3.62	7.28	6.08	2.17	5.19	0.69	54.71
1980	5.69	2.69	11.66	1.88	8.37	4.49	0.76	1.59	4.77	1.61	2.14	1.29	46.94
1981	0.84	6.62	3.93	2.06	3.89	2.69	2.74	2.76	5.27	3.01	1.85	6.25	41.91
1982	4.75	6.99	3.79	6.02	2.60	6.09	6.31	1.45	3.00	5.83	4.15	5.23	56.21
1983	3.09	4.99	6.68	4.79	1.42	1.52	1.85	1.06	7.52	1.97	7.46	9.27	51.62
1984	4.66	5.97	5.83	6.62	6.57	0.74	11.21	6.46	0.04	1.54	2.10	3.65	55.39
1985	4.11	4.98	1.86	2.75	4.69	2.04	9.92	4.57	2.63	5.74	4.23	2.28	49.80
1986	0.88	2.46	4.13	0.49	2.95	2.18	3.27	6.08	3.68	5.15	6.20	3.03	40.50
1987	5.63	6.13	5.44	1.16	2.74	6.36	7.35	1.22	3.02	0.70	2.36	4.13	46.24
1988	4.64	3.32	2.57	6.06	1.71	0.16	5.04	4.92	6.35	5.00	4.87	1.21	45.85
1989	2.57	4.30	3.85	5.24	6.42	9.34	7.65	2.13	11.64	1.71	3.97	4.49	63.31
1990	8.47	9.75	8.36	2.76	5.26	1.39	3.49	4.64	3.01	6.12	1.27	3.04	57.56
1991	4.66	3.10	6.98	5.28	7.35	9.99	5.82	4.37	2.03	0.39	3.19	2.69	55.85
1992	3.58	3.94	3.81	1.03	1.73	4.14	9.03	5.04	8.55	2.84	10.04	6.38	60.11
1993	3.94	4.43	5.73	2.77	4.87	6.01	3.05	2.96	3.91	3.83	4.01	2.54	48.05
Record Mean	4.72	4.69	5.55	4.01	3.71	3.79	4.82	3.95	3.31	2.66	3.32	4.41	48.94

AVERAGE TEMPERATURE (deg. F)

ATLANTA, GEORGIA

YEAR	JAN	FEB	MAR	APR	MAY	JUNE	JULY	AUG	SEP	OCT	NOV	DEC	ANNUAL
1964	40.8	40.3	51.2	60.6	68.9	77.8	76.5	76.0	72.6	58.8	55.6	46.5	60.4
1965	43.2	43.9	48.8	63.3	71.8	71.7	76.6	77.3	72.9	60.3	53.8	44.8	60.7
1966	36.6	43.2	50.2	60.6	67.6	73.4	78.2	75.4	70.6	59.4	52.1	43.4	59.2
1967	43.9	41.8	56.7	65.0	66.2	72.5	74.1	74.0	66.5	59.4	48.5	47.7	59.7
1968	39.2	38.3	52.3	60.9	67.4	75.7	77.7	79.0	71.5	61.7	50.1	40.2	59.5
1969	40.2	42.7	46.9	62.8	69.2	77.4	80.8	76.1	70.9	62.5	50.1	41.7	60.1
1970	35.9	43.9	52.9	64.4	70.1	74.6	78.7	79.1	77.0	65.2	49.5	47.4	61.6
1971	42.9	44.3	47.5	60.8	66.7	77.2	76.3	76.7	73.7	66.8	50.7	52.3	61.3
1972	46.8	42.6	52.4	61.3	66.5	72.2	76.8	77.7	74.6	61.1	49.6	48.3	60.8
1973	41.4	42.8	57.4	57.6	65.0	75.6	78.9	77.4	75.6	64.7	55.6	44.2	61.3
1974	53.2	45.8	57.8	61.1	71.0	72.5	77.9	76.7	70.2	61.3	52.4	44.3	62.0
1975	47.2	47.1	50.5	59.8	71.0	75.3	76.4	77.9	70.3	63.3	54.0	43.4	61.4
1976	38.5	51.5	56.4	61.7	65.4	73.8	76.4	76.0	69.8	56.2	44.2	39.8	59.1
1977	29.3	42.0	55.3	63.0	69.9	77.1	79.5	77.7	73.5	59.6	54.3	42.1	60.3
1978	33.7	39.3	51.6	61.5	67.6	76.3	78.6	78.3	76.3	62.5	58.5	46.1	60.8
1979	37.3	41.7	56.2	62.7	70.1	75.7	78.8	80.1	72.7	62.4	54.3	46.7	61.6
1980	44.9	41.9	52.1	62.6	72.0	79.1	85.1	83.8	78.9	61.5	51.9	44.9	63.2
1981	39.5	46.8	51.8	67.7	67.6	81.3	82.2	77.7	72.4	60.2	54.5	39.1	61.8
1982	38.5	47.4	56.5	58.4	72.5	76.3	79.1	77.5	70.5	62.7	53.7	49.9	61.9
1983	40.4	44.4	51.3	56.4	67.8	74.0	81.4	81.4	70.8	62.1	51.5	39.9	60.1
1984	39.6	47.5	51.7	58.1	67.5	78.3	76.8	77.5	71.3	69.8	50.6	53.7	61.9
1985	36.3	44.2	56.8	64.0	69.9	77.5	78.4	77.6	72.5	66.4	62.0	41.4	62.3
1986	43.4	49.8	54.4	62.9	71.0	80.0	84.1	77.4	74.6	64.0	57.9	45.1	63.7
1987	41.9	45.7	53.2	60.3	73.2	77.8	81.0	82.0	74.1	59.7	55.7	48.8	62.8
1988	39.2	45.5	54.9	63.0	70.0	78.6	80.5	81.0	73.4	59.3	55.0	46.6	62.3
1989	49.7	47.5	56.8	62.9	68.8	76.9	79.8	79.4	72.9	64.2	54.3	39.1	62.7
1990	49.8	54.4	57.7	61.9	70.4	78.6	80.6	80.6	75.7	64.4	56.5	49.1	65.0
1991	44.3	49.2	56.2	65.9	72.8	76.7	81.0	79.2	74.8	64.6	51.0	49.1	63.7
1992	45.1	51.8	54.0	61.9	68.1	74.5	80.2	76.1	73.2	61.9	51.5	44.5	61.9
1993	47.0	45.2	51.7	59.4	71.1	79.3	85.4	82.1	76.7	63.3	53.9	45.3	63.4
Record Mean	43.0	45.7	52.8	61.3	69.6	76.5	78.8	78.0	73.2	62.8	52.3	44.8	61.6
Max	51.5	54.9	62.7	71.6	79.5	86.0	87.8	86.8	82.1	72.3	61.6	53.2	70.8
Min	34.6	36.5	42.9	51.1	59.6	67.0	69.7	69.1	64.2	53.2	43.0	36.3	52.3

REFERENCE NOTES

ATLANTA, GEORGIA

GENERAL
T - TRACE AMOUNT.
BLANK ENTRIES DENOTE MISSING/UNREPORTED DATA.
# INDICATES A STATION OR INSTRUMENT RELOCATION.

SPECIFIC

PM - INCLUDES LAST DAY OF PREVIOUS MONTH
ASOS - AUTOMATED SURFACE OBSERVING SYSTEM IN OPERATION DURING THESE MONTHS.

(●) - LENGTH OF RECORD IN YEARS, ALTHOUGH INDIVIDUAL MONTHS MAY BE MISSING.
0.* OR * - THE VALUE IS BETWEEN 0.0 AND 0.05
NORMALS - BASED ON THE 1961-1990 RECORD PERIOD.
EXTREMES - DATES ARE THE MOST RECENT OCCURRENCE
WIND DIR.- NUMERALS SHOW TENS OF DEGRESS CLOCKWISE FROM TRUE NORTH. "00" INDICATES CALM.
RESULTANT DIRECTIONS ARE GIVEN TO WHOLE DEGREES.
BOLD VALUES INDICATE EXTREME VALUES WHICH OCCURRED AFTER THE ASOS SYSTEM WAS COMMISSIONED.

RECORD = PERIOD OF RECORD
RECORD MEAN PRECIPITATION IS THE MEAN OF ALL DAILY PRECIPITATION AMOUNTS DURING THE PERIOD OF RECORD.
RECORD MAX(MIN) TEMPERATURE IS THE MEAN OF ALL DAILY MAX(MIN) TEMPERATURES DURING THE PERIOD OF RECORD.
RECORD MEAN TEMPERATURE IS THE SUM OF THE RECORD MAX AND RECORD MIN DIVIDED BY 2.
AVERAGE TEMPERATURE IS THE SUM OF THE MEAN DAILY MAX AND MIN TEMPERATURE DIVIDED BY 2.

EXCEPTIONS

RECORD MEANS ARE THROUGH THE CURRENT YEAR, BEGINNING IN
1879 FOR TEMPERATURE
1879 FOR PRECIPITATION
1934 FOR SNOWFALL

HEATING DEGREE DAYS Base 65 deg. F ATLANTA, GEORGIA

SEASON	JULY	AUG	SEP	OCT	NOV	DEC	JAN	FEB	MAR	APR	MAY	JUNE	TOTAL
1964-65	0	0	2	201	288	567	669	586	500	110	0	3	2926
1965-66	0	0	3	176	332	619	874	605	451	171	26	5	3262
1966-67	0	0	5	177	379	663	645	642	270	67	78	20	2946
1967-68	0	0	52	193	490	530	792	769	389	154	31	0	3400
1968-69	0	2	0	157	441	760	761	620	555	93	28	0	3417
1969-70	0	0	13	125	445	719	895	586	371	95	15	0	3264
1970-71	0	0	3	64	457	537	681	572	533	156	56	0	3059
1971-72	0	0	0	36	436	390	559	643	387	161	21	5	2638
1972-73	0	0	3	136	465	511	725	617	240	230	72	0	2999
1973-74	0	0	1	86	295	639	357	531	241	155	5	0	2310
1974-75	0	0	26	148	381	633	547	493	451	192	2	0	2873
1975-76	0	0	28	113	342	665	814	384	265	124	48	4	2787
1976-77	0	0	10	277	618	775	1099	640	300	102	11	0	3832
1977-78	0	0	4	178	313	701	966	714	412	137	57	0	3482
1978-79	0	0	0	112	194	580	853	646	279	97	16	0	2777
1979-80	0	0	5	122	320	559	616	668	399	113	3	0	2805
1980-81	0	0	18	154	391	618	786	502	410	36	43	0	2958
1981-82	0	0	17	179	314	795	819	486	282	204	2	0	3098
1982-83	0	0	16	139	341	466	755	571	423	261	24	0	2996
1983-84	0	0	32	123	400	770	780	503	409	221	50	0	3288
1984-85	0	0	13	22	426	346	882	576	265	111	14	1	2656
1985-86	0	0	15	71	131	725	663	422	331	133	14	0	2505
1986-87	0	11	2	107	243	609	709	534	359	191	6	0	2771
1987-88	0	0	0	172	279	494	791	559	310	104	6	0	2715
1988-89	0	0	0	188	291	566	468	490	284	160	44	0	2491
1989-90	0	0	29	103	318	797	462	297	250	150	20	0	2426
1990-91	0	0	12	109	252	488	636	437	281	54	8	0	2277
1991-92	0	0	8	76	419	499	611	377	345	161	50	2	2548
1992-93	0	0	12	110	398	627	548	549	417	184	13	0	2858
1993-94	0	0	6	129	346	604							

COOLING DEGREE DAYS Base 65 deg. F ATLANTA, GEORGIA

YEAR	JAN	FEB	MAR	APR	MAY	JUNE	JULY	AUG	SEP	OCT	NOV	DEC	TOTAL
1969	0	0	1	31	162	379	494	348	197	51	0	0	1663
1970	0	0	0	80	178	292	430	442	371	77	0	0	1870
1971	0	0	0	38	115	374	358	371	265	95	13	5	1634
1972	0	0	3	56	72	227	370	396	297	25	7	0	1453
1973	0	0	11	15	78	322	438	388	323	79	20	0	1674
1974	0	1	24	42	198	229	405	368	187	41	11	0	1506
1975	0	0	6	44	195	313	359	406	193	63	21	0	1600
1976	0	1	8	30	67	273	359	346	159	11	0	0	1254
1977	0	0	3	51	171	367	456	403	266	17	1	0	1735
1978	0	0	2	40	144	346	428	420	345	40	7	1	1773
1979	0	0	13	33	181	327	436	475	243	49	5	0	1762
1980	0	4	4	49	227	428	632	589	440	51	0	0	2424
1981	0	0	9	124	131	494	540	398	246	36	4	0	1982
1982	2	0	25	13	243	346	446	394	192	73	8	6	1748
1983	0	0	3	10	118	278	515	512	212	40	0	0	1688
1984	0	0	2	21	132	405	372	397	210	178	1	2	1720
1985	0	0	18	88	172	381	423	401	248	119	49	0	1899
1986	0	0	11	74	208	455	599	401	300	83	34	0	2165
1987	0	0	2	60	266	391	502	531	281	12	6	2	2053
1988	0	0	5	49	169	416	490	502	258	18	0	0	1907
1989	0	7	36	101	170	364	467	452	273	85	6	0	1961
1990	0	5	26	66	194	415	490	488	341	98	2	0	2125
1991	0	0	20	89	258	358	502	446	305	70	4	13	2065
1992	0	1	13	73	155	292	478	349	265	20	0	0	1646
1993	0	0	11	22	208	435	639	536	364	80	19	0	2314

SNOWFALL (inches) ATLANTA, GEORGIA

SEASON	JULY	AUG	SEP	OCT	NOV	DEC	JAN	FEB	MAR	APR	MAY	JUNE	TOTAL
1964-65	0.0	0.0	0.0	0.0	0.0	T	2.4	0.1	0.5	0.0	0.0	0.0	3.0
1965-66	0.0	0.0	0.0	0.0	0.0	0.0	0.7	T	T	0.0	0.0	0.0	0.7
1966-67	0.0	0.0	0.0	0.0	T	0.0	0.0	2.0	0.0	0.0	0.0	0.0	2.0
1967-68	0.0	0.0	0.0	0.0	0.0	0.0	0.7	3.5	T	0.0	0.0	0.0	4.2
1968-69	0.0	0.0	0.0	0.0	1.0	T	T	1.2	0.0	0.0	0.0	0.0	2.2
1969-70	0.0	0.0	0.0	0.0	T	T	0.6	T	0.0	0.0	0.0	0.0	0.6
1970-71	0.0	0.0	0.0	0.0	0.0	T	T	1.0	T	T	0.0	0.0	1.0
1971-72	0.0	0.0	0.0	0.0	T	1.0	T	T	T	0.0	0.0	0.0	1.0
1972-73	0.0	0.0	0.0	0.0	0.0	0.0	1.0	T	0.0	0.0	0.0	0.0	1.0
1973-74	0.0	0.0	0.0	0.0	0.0	T	0.0	T	T	0.0	0.0	0.0	T
1974-75	0.0	0.0	0.0	0.0	0.0	T	T	T	T	0.0	0.0	0.0	T
1975-76	0.0	0.0	0.0	0.0	0.6	0.0	T	T	T	0.0	0.0	0.0	0.6
1976-77	0.0	0.0	0.0	0.0	0.0	0.0	1.0	0.0	0.0	0.0	0.0	0.0	1.0
1977-78	0.0	0.0	0.0	0.0	0.0	T	T	0.3	T	0.0	0.0	0.0	0.3
1978-79	0.0	0.0	0.0	0.0	0.0	0.0	0.2	4.4	0.0	0.0	0.0	0.0	4.6
1979-80	0.0	0.0	0.0	0.0	0.0	0.0	T	1.7	2.7	0.0	0.0	0.0	4.4
1980-81	0.0	0.0	0.0	0.0	0.0	0.0	T	T	0.0	0.0	0.0	0.0	T
1981-82	0.0	0.0	0.0	0.0	0.0	T	7.0	0.7	0.0	0.0	0.0	0.0	7.7
1982-83	0.0	0.0	0.0	0.0	0.0	0.0	1.9	0.5	7.9	0.0	0.0	0.0	10.3
1983-84	0.0	0.0	0.0	0.0	0.0	T	T	1.3	T	0.0	0.0	0.0	1.3
1984-85	0.0	0.0	0.0	0.0	0.0	T	0.4	1.5	0.0	0.0	0.0	0.0	1.9
1985-86	0.0	0.0	0.0	0.0	0.0	T	0.4	T	0.0	0.0	0.0	0.0	0.4
1986-87	0.0	0.0	0.0	0.0	0.0	0.0	3.6	T	1.2	T	0.0	0.0	4.8
1987-88	0.0	0.0	0.0	0.0	0.0	0.0	4.2	T	0.0	0.0	0.0	0.0	4.2
1988-89	0.0	0.0	0.0	0.0	0.0	T	0.0	0.7	0.0	T	0.0	0.0	0.7
1989-90	0.0	0.0	0.0	0.0	0.0	1.3	0.0	0.0	0.0	T	0.0	0.0	1.3
1990-91	0.0	0.0	0.0	0.0	0.0	0.0	2.1	T	T	0.0	0.0	0.0	2.1
1991-92	0.0	0.0	0.0	0.0	0.0	0.0	5.0	0.0	T	0.0	0.0	0.0	5.0
1992-93	0.0	0.0	0.0	0.0	0.0	T	0.0	T	4.2	0.0	0.0	0.0	4.2
1993-94	0.0	0.0	0.0	T	0.0	2.8							
Record Mean	0.0	0.0	0.0	T	T	0.2	0.9	0.5	0.4	T	0.0	0.0	2.1

SAVANNAH, GEORGIA

Savannah is surrounded by flat terrain, low and marshy to the north and east, and rising to several feet above sea level to the west and south. About half the land to the west and south is cleared and the other half is wooded and swampy.

The area has a temperate climate, with a seasonal low temperature of 51 degrees in winter, 66 degrees in spring, 80 degrees in summer, and 66 degrees in autumn. The lowest temperatures are below 10 degrees and the highest temperatures are about 100 degrees.

The normal annual rainfall is about 49 inches. About half falls in the thunderstorm season of June 15 through September 15. The remainder, produced principally by squall-line and frontal showers, is spread over the other nine months with a minor peak in March. Considerable periods of fair, mild weather are experienced in October, November, April, and to a less extent, in May. Snow is a rarity and even a trace does not occur on an average of once a year. The heaviest snowfalls are under 5 inches. Severe tropical storms affect this area about once in ten years. Rainfall from these storms constitute the heaviest sustained precipitation. Accumulations exceeding 22 inches have occurred.

The present exposure of the thermometers gives readings more nearly commensurate with those of suburban street levels of Savannah than was the case of previous locations atop various buildings. During that time, especially on still, clear nights, temperatures near the ground and in lower inland areas were as much as 15 degrees lower than the official low temperature. Present differences on comparable nights range from 3 - 8 degrees.

Sunshine is adequate at all seasons and seldom are there two or more days in succession without it. Sea- and land-breeze effect is usually not felt in Savannah, though it is a daily feature on the nearby islands. Dry, continental air masses reach this area in summer mostly by sliding down the Atlantic coast and giving cooler northeast winds. Such masses reaching this area from the northwest or west in summer bring mostly clear skies and high temperatures.

Based on the 1951-1980 period, the average first occurrence of 32 degrees Fahrenheit in the fall is November 15 and the average last occurrence in the spring is March 10.

NORMALS, MEANS, AND EXTREMES

SAVANNAH, GEORGIA

LATITUDE: 32°08'N LONGITUDE: 81°12' W ELEVATION: FT. GRND 46 BARO 52 TIME ZONE: EASTERN WBAN: 03822

	(a)	JAN	FEB	MAR	APR	MAY	JUNE	JULY	AUG	SEP	OCT	NOV	DEC	YEAR
TEMPERATURE °F:														
Normals														
-Daily Maximum		59.7	62.4	70.1	77.5	84.0	88.8	91.1	89.7	85.2	77.5	70.0	62.3	76.5
-Daily Minimum		38.1	41.1	48.3	54.5	62.9	69.2	72.4	72.2	67.8	56.9	48.1	41.0	56.0
-Monthly		48.9	51.8	59.2	66.0	73.5	79.1	81.8	81.0	76.6	67.3	59.1	51.7	66.3
Extremes														
-Record Highest	43	84	86	91	95	100	104	105	104	98	97	89	83	105
-Year		1957	1989	1974	1986	1953	1985	1986	1954	1986	1986	1961	1971	JUL 1986
-Record Lowest	43	3	14	20	32	39	51	61	57	43	28	15	9	3
-Year		1985	1958	1980	1987	1963	1984	1972	1986	1967	1952	1970	1983	JAN 1985
NORMAL DEGREE DAYS:														
Heating (base 65°F)		516	378	204	47	0	0	0	0	0	63	213	426	1847
Cooling (base 65°F)		16	9	24	77	266	423	521	496	348	135	36	14	2365
% OF POSSIBLE SUNSHINE	43	54	57	62	70	68	65	64	62	58	64	62	55	62
MEAN SKY COVER (tenths)														
Sunrise - Sunset	43	6.2	6.1	6.0	5.4	5.7	6.1	6.3	6.2	6.2	5.1	5.4	6.0	5.9
MEAN NUMBER OF DAYS:														
Sunrise to Sunset														
-Clear	43	9.2	8.4	9.0	10.7	9.3	6.9	5.4	5.7	7.0	12.1	11.1	9.3	104.1
-Partly Cloudy	43	6.0	6.3	8.5	8.5	10.0	11.2	13.6	13.7	10.5	7.8	6.9	7.0	110.0
-Cloudy	43	15.8	13.6	13.5	10.8	11.8	11.9	12.0	11.6	12.5	11.1	12.0	14.7	151.1
Precipitation														
.01 inches or more	43	9.4	8.7	9.1	6.9	8.7	11.1	13.5	12.8	10.0	5.9	6.4	8.0	110.6
Snow,Ice pellets,hail														
1.0 inches or more	43	0.*	0.1	0.*	0.0	0.0	0.0	0.0	0.0	0.0	0.0	0.0	0.*	0.2
Thunderstorms	43	1.0	1.2	3.0	3.8	7.2	10.1	14.9	12.6	5.7	1.5	0.5	0.6	62.0
Heavy Fog Visibility 1/4 mile or less	43	4.7	3.1	3.3	2.6	3.1	2.3	1.2	2.0	3.7	3.4	4.9	4.6	38.8
Temperature °F														
-Maximum														
90° and above	29	0.0	0.0	0.1	1.4	5.0	14.4	22.0	18.2	8.1	0.7	0.0	0.0	69.8
32° and below	29	0.2	0.0	0.*	0.0	0.0	0.0	0.0	0.0	0.0	0.0	0.0	0.1	0.3
-Minimum														
32° and below	29	10.0	6.9	1.9	0.*	0.0	0.0	0.0	0.0	0.0	0.*	2.2	7.4	28.6
0° and below	29	0.0	0.0	0.0	0.0	0.0	0.0	0.0	0.0	0.0	0.0	0.0	0.0	0.0
AVG. STATION PRESS.(mb)	21	1018.9	1018.0	1016.0	1015.3	1014.5	1014.7	1015.8	1015.8	1015.7	1017.2	1018.4	1019.5	1016.7
RELATIVE HUMIDITY (%)														
Hour 01	29	78	76	77	79	84	86	87	89	88	85	83	79	83
Hour 07 (Local Time)	29	81	80	83	83	85	87	88	91	91	88	86	82	85
Hour 13	29	55	50	48	46	51	55	57	60	60	53	52	54	53
Hour 19	29	66	60	60	58	63	68	72	75	75	72	72	69	68
PRECIPITATION (inches):														
Water Equivalent														
-Normal		3.59	3.22	3.78	3.03	4.09	5.66	6.38	7.46	4.47	2.39	2.19	2.96	49.22
-Maximum Monthly	43	8.98	7.92	9.57	10.57	10.08	14.39	20.10	14.94	13.47	12.50	5.26	5.80	20.10
-Year		1991	1964	1959	1991	1957	1963	1964	1971	1953	1990	1993	1977	JUL 1964
-Minimum Monthly	43	0.45	0.26	0.18	0.38	0.51	0.84	1.35	1.02	0.35	0.02	0.15	0.12	0.02
-Year		1989	1991	1955	1986	1953	1954	1972	1980	1991	1963	1966	1984	OCT 1963
-Maximum in 24 hrs	43	3.58	3.46	4.65	5.62	5.67	4.06	6.36	7.04	6.80	5.79	5.02	3.47	7.04
-Year		1984	1964	1959	1976	1976	1963	1957	1971	1979	1990	1969	1964	AUG 1971
Snow,Ice pellets,hail														
-Maximum Monthly	43	2.0	3.6	1.1	0.0	0.0	T	0.0	0.0	0.0	0.0	0.0	3.6	3.6
-Year		1977	1968	1986			1989						1989	DEC 1989
-Maximum in 24 hrs	43	1.3	3.6	1.1	0.0	0.0	T	0.0	0.0	0.0	0.0	0.0	3.4	3.6
-Year		1977	1968	1986			1989						1989	FEB 1968
WIND:														
Mean Speed (mph)	43	8.5	9.2	9.2	8.7	7.7	7.5	7.2	6.6	7.2	7.5	7.5	7.9	7.9
Prevailing Direction through 1963		WNW	NE	WNW	SSE	SW	SW	SW	SW	NE	NNE	NNE	NE	SW
Fastest Obs. 1 Min.														
-Direction (!!)	13	31	29	32	23	22	27	35	25	29	31	23	30	32
-Speed (MPH)	13	30	30	46	35	44	31	37	29	35	35	40	29	46
-Year		1989	1981	1981	1991	1984	1989	1986	1986	1989	1990	1985	1982	MAR 1981
Peak Gust														
-Direction (!!)	10	NW	NW	W	NE	SW	NW	SW	W	W	NW	S	NW	W
-Speed (mph)	10	51	49	68	53	68	66	63	58	54	61	62	48	68
-Date		1989	1991	1993	1991	1984	1991	1993	1990	1989	1990	1985	1993	MAR 1993

PRECIPITATION (inches)

SAVANNAH, GEORGIA

YEAR	JAN	FEB	MAR	APR	MAY	JUNE	JULY	AUG	SEP	OCT	NOV	DEC	ANNUAL
1964	6.29	7.92	2.71	2.64	4.66	2.55	20.10	8.37	3.93	6.94	2.90	4.16	73.17
1965	0.83	4.34	7.75	1.39	2.62	5.63	7.46	4.56	4.82	1.33	2.09	2.99	45.81
1966	6.05	3.66	3.79	1.88	6.73	6.61	7.89	3.73	1.78	1.19	0.15	1.93	45.39
1967	7.18	2.80	0.50	1.38	2.94	4.38	6.23	8.57	2.12	1.36	0.84	2.97	41.27
1968	1.79	1.16	0.89	2.09	4.80	5.86	6.35	3.83	0.48	3.53	2.59	3.97	37.34
1969	1.77	1.59	5.11	0.71	8.74	9.99	7.57	10.33	3.74	4.04	3.82	3.43	60.84
1970	3.11	2.32	8.51	0.95	5.41	5.21	5.76	10.61	5.88	2.29	0.42	3.37	53.84
1971	3.40	2.60	2.63	3.53	3.56	6.98	9.07	14.94	1.67	8.01	1.26	3.69	61.34
1972	3.99	4.61	3.84	1.20	5.84	6.54	1.35	12.62	0.36	0.54	4.91	2.77	48.57
1973	3.61	4.46	5.36	4.43	1.23	9.19	2.89	6.45	3.65	0.19	0.68	3.26	45.40
1974	1.37	2.79	1.87	2.75	7.25	6.00	6.48	7.90	2.61	0.10	0.96	1.85	41.93
1975	3.17	3.01	3.99	4.71	6.00	2.08	11.55	3.13	8.01	1.25	1.09	3.19	51.18
1976	2.19	1.24	2.51	5.62	6.33	7.49	7.56	7.28	10.07	4.75	4.83	3.87	63.74
1977	3.14	1.83	2.72	1.94	1.03	2.00	5.62	8.01	6.52	1.16	2.07	5.80	41.84
1978	4.02	3.14	1.93	3.68	4.50	2.19	3.61	4.43	2.61	0.60	1.85	2.85	35.41
1979	3.96	4.14	2.42	3.83	8.49	7.37	10.78	2.65	12.20	0.70	2.70	2.68	61.92
1980	2.95	1.29	7.75	3.68	4.50	3.47	2.38	1.02	5.81	1.62	2.04	1.33	37.84
1981	1.03	2.94	3.91	1.75	2.10	3.01	5.42	10.91	2.88	1.29	1.65	3.17	40.06
1982	3.47	2.94	1.64	6.25	4.18	9.15	6.70	9.18	2.98	1.74	0.40	3.63	52.26
1983	5.90	5.23	9.01	5.15	1.07	5.81	5.30	3.67	3.39	1.03	4.18	4.77	54.51
1984	8.87	3.21	5.13	3.41	5.29	1.48	7.88	3.46	7.43	1.23	3.15	0.12	50.66
1985	0.51	1.37	1.65	1.37	2.18	6.72	5.00	9.42	0.76	3.37	4.28	2.01	38.64
1986	2.03	5.28	2.85	0.38	2.06	2.98	5.49	12.31	0.49	1.99	4.40	5.07	45.33
1987	8.62	4.39	5.33	0.50	3.82	8.03	4.37	9.46	8.16	0.33	2.06	1.41	56.48
1988	3.44	4.09	2.11	5.05	3.52	2.63	1.80	10.68	9.62	2.81	1.43	0.99	48.17
1989	0.45	0.67	1.41	3.59	3.10	7.30	4.91	6.29	7.98	4.71	1.26	5.20	46.87
1990	3.91	3.08	3.79	1.75	2.07	0.97	1.92	7.25	1.26	12.50	2.48	2.10	43.08
1991	8.98	0.26	5.48	10.57	7.13	5.12	15.41	10.51	0.35	1.60	1.26	1.75	68.42
1992	6.60	2.24	3.97	2.08	2.04	13.01	2.03	7.69	8.42	3.60	5.15	1.53	58.36
1993	5.52	3.35	7.96	3.22	1.31	2.48	4.34	3.04	6.84	2.58	5.26	2.15	48.05
Record Mean	2.98	3.13	3.60	2.95	3.40	5.53	6.65	7.09	5.58	2.77	2.06	2.80	48.55

AVERAGE TEMPERATURE (deg. F)

SAVANNAH, GEORGIA

YEAR	JAN	FEB	MAR	APR	MAY	JUNE	JULY	AUG	SEP	OCT	NOV	DEC	ANNUAL
#1964	48.2	47.8	58.4	66.8	73.2	81.4	79.1	79.6	74.7	63.1	60.1	53.7	65.5
1965	49.9	52.4	56.8	66.4	74.8	76.4	79.8	80.6	76.7	66.2	58.0	50.1	65.7
1966	44.9	51.2	55.6	64.7	71.6	74.6	80.9	79.6	76.4	67.3	57.1	49.5	64.4
1967	51.4	49.6	61.7	69.0	73.2	77.2	79.9	79.4	71.6	64.4	56.4	55.3	65.7
1968	45.7	44.6	57.0	68.0	72.5	79.1	81.6	82.1	76.5	68.7	54.8	47.6	64.8
1969	47.4	47.1	52.4	66.1	71.0	79.7	82.2	78.9	75.4	69.9	53.9	47.7	64.3
1970	42.4	49.2	59.2	68.3	73.0	78.2	81.6	81.8	78.9	70.2	54.8	54.1	66.0
1971	50.1	52.4	54.5	64.6	71.1	80.5	80.9	80.8	78.6	72.4	58.0	60.6	67.0
1972	57.5	51.3	59.3	66.7	71.6	75.7	81.0	81.0	77.3	68.1	58.1	57.1	67.1
1973	49.8	49.6	63.6	64.0	73.5	79.3	82.2	80.0	79.0	68.9	61.6	51.2	66.9
1974	62.9	53.0	63.8	65.6	74.5	76.8	79.2	79.6	76.3	64.6	57.7	53.1	67.3
1975	55.3	57.7	59.5	65.4	76.7	79.5	78.4	81.7	76.5	70.0	59.3	50.5	67.5
1976	45.9	56.4	62.6	64.3	69.7	75.8	81.7	78.2	74.9	62.5	51.5	49.0	64.4
1977	39.9	49.2	62.1	67.6	74.0	82.0	83.3	81.1	78.9	64.1	61.2	50.0	66.1
1978	43.9	43.6	56.3	68.0	73.7	80.0	82.2	82.3	78.2	67.0	64.7	53.4	66.1
1979	45.4	49.0	59.8	67.7	73.9	76.8	82.1	81.4	77.4	67.5	60.4	50.7	66.0
1980	50.7	48.5	57.1	66.2	73.3	79.7	84.4	83.4	80.4	65.4	56.7	48.1	66.1
1981	43.5	52.6	56.8	69.0	71.6	84.5	84.4	79.2	75.2	65.4	57.7	48.3	65.7
1982	48.7	55.9	62.1	64.8	74.3	80.2	81.3	81.0	75.5	67.6	61.8	57.4	67.5
1983	46.1	50.8	58.0	62.8	73.0	78.2	84.1	82.9	75.7	69.7	57.7	48.5	65.6
1984	47.7	53.7	59.3	65.7	72.9	79.2	80.6	81.5	75.0	73.2	55.7	59.5	67.0
1985	45.3	53.0	61.5	66.9	74.6	81.3	82.7	80.7	76.6	72.2	67.5	48.9	67.6
1986	47.6	56.9	59.1	66.8	75.0	82.5	85.7	81.6	79.7	70.0	65.0	53.9	68.7
1987	49.0	50.4	58.2	63.9	74.1	80.6	83.6	84.5	77.8	61.5	60.4	54.7	66.6
1988	45.0	50.2	58.2	66.1	72.4	77.7	82.7	82.5	77.4	64.2	61.3	51.1	65.7
1989	56.6	56.1	60.6	65.6	72.3	81.0	82.9	80.7	76.8	68.6	59.5	43.7	67.0
1990	55.7	60.0	62.6	65.0	74.3	81.5	84.4	82.4	78.9	70.7	60.8	56.5	69.4
1991	52.2	56.2	62.4	70.0	77.5	79.4	83.2	82.2	77.9	68.4	56.6	55.6	68.5
1992	49.9	55.7	59.2	64.5	71.7	78.6	84.3	81.0	77.1	66.6	60.6	52.0	66.8
1993	54.8	50.3	57.0	62.4	73.6	81.3	86.7	83.1	79.6	68.1	59.9	49.7	67.2
Record													
Mean	51.3	53.3	59.4	66.1	73.6	79.4	81.7	81.0	77.0	67.8	58.8	52.3	66.8
Max	60.8	63.1	69.3	76.1	83.1	88.4	90.4	89.4	85.1	77.1	68.8	62.0	76.2
Min	41.7	43.6	49.5	56.1	64.0	70.3	72.9	72.6	68.9	58.6	48.8	42.6	57.5

REFERENCE NOTES

SAVANNAH, GEORGIA

GENERAL
T - TRACE AMOUNT.
BLANK ENTRIES DENOTE MISSING/UNREPORTED DATA.
# INDICATES A STATION OR INSTRUMENT RELOCATION.

SPECIFIC

PM - INCLUDES LAST DAY OF PREVIOUS MONTH
ASOS - AUTOMATED SURFACE OBSERVING SYSTEM IN OPERATION DURING THESE MONTHS.

(a) - LENGTH OF RECORD IN YEARS, ALTHOUGH INDIVIDUAL MONTHS MAY BE MISSING.
0.* OR * - THE VALUE IS BETWEEN 0.0 AND 0.05
NORMALS - BASED ON THE 1961-1990 RECORD PERIOD.
EXTREMES - DATES ARE THE MOST RECENT OCCURRENCE
WIND DIR.- NUMERALS SHOW TENS OF DEGRESS CLOCKWISE FROM TRUE NORTH. "00" INDICATES CALM.
RESULTANT DIRECTIONS ARE GIVEN TO WHOLE DEGREES.
BOLD VALUES INDICATE EXTREME VALUES WHICH OCCURRED AFTER THE ASOS SYSTEM WAS COMMISSIONED.

RECORD = PERIOD OF RECORD
RECORD MEAN PRECIPITATION IS THE MEAN OF ALL DAILY PRECIPITATION AMOUNTS DURING THE PERIOD OF RECORD.
RECORD MAX(MIN) TEMPERATURE IS THE MEAN OF ALL DAILY MAX(MIN) TEMPERATURES DURING THE PERIOD OF RECORD.
RECORD MEAN TEMPERATURE IS THE SUM OF THE RECORD MAX AND RECORD MIN DIVIDED BY 2.
AVERAGE TEMPERATURE IS THE SUM OF THE MEAN DAILY MAX AND MIN TEMPERATURE DIVIDED BY 2.

EXCEPTIONS

1. FASTEST MILE WIND IS THROUGH OCTOBER 1980.

RECORD MEANS ARE THROUGH THE CURRENT YEAR, BEGINNING IN 1874 FOR TEMPERATURE
1871 FOR PRECIPITATION
1951 FOR SNOWFALL

HEATING DEGREE DAYS Base 65 deg. F SAVANNAH, GEORGIA

SEASON	JULY	AUG	SEP	OCT	NOV	DEC	JAN	FEB	MAR	APR	MAY	JUNE	TOTAL
#1964-65	0	0	0	116	157	355	463	359	282	66	0	0	1798
1965-66	0	0	0	92	204	454	612	387	294	88	11	0	2142
1966-67	0	0	0	50	259	480	413	428	159	26	12	1	1828
1967-68	0	0	12	82	269	306	592	582	270	34	3	0	2150
1968-69	0	0	0	73	309	533	539	498	395	48	3	0	2398
1969-70	0	0	0	38	332	530	698	437	199	57	8	0	2299
1970-71	0	0	1	20	303	340	458	359	338	100	15	0	1934
1971-72	0	0	0	10	236	187	256	400	183	74	1	0	1347
1972-73	0	0	0	25	239	261	462	423	98	85	4	0	1597
1973-74	0	0	0	47	148	435	107	340	124	73	1	0	1275
1974-75	0	0	2	79	243	368	315	232	212	86	0	0	1537
1975-76	0	0	0	25	228	446	586	256	134	69	11	0	1755
1976-77	0	0	0	142	405	490	771	437	152	42	2	0	2441
1977-78	0	0	0	96	165	457	645	594	283	35	2	0	2277
1978-79	0	0	0	45	53	378	602	448	181	17	1	0	1725
1979-80	0	0	0	41	183	438	436	489	257	43	7	0	1894
1980-81	0	0	0	72	252	518	659	342	263	25	8	0	2139
1981-82	0	0	3	59	231	513	501	258	149	76	0	0	1790
1982-83	0	0	0	73	139	266	579	392	228	115	0	0	1792
1983-84	0	0	2	19	232	513	531	320	200	68	7	0	1892
1984-85	0	0	1	8	299	185	615	360	157	60	2	0	1687
1985-86	0	0	1	16	51	504	531	240	215	59	4	0	1621
1986-87	0	5	0	48	101	349	491	401	231	110	5	0	1741
1987-88	0	0	0	122	185	332	612	426	218	52	1	0	1948
1988-89	0	0	0	84	141	423	268	289	193	110	13	0	1521
1989-90	0	0	1	59	191	653	286	175	135	81	0	0	1581
1990-91	0	0	0	55	143	279	395	260	139	14	0	0	1285
1991-92	0	0	0	34	270	315	461	274	204	101	22	0	1681
1992-93	0	0	1	45	194	401	320	406	254	113	0	0	1734
1993-94	0	0	1	45	193	470							

COOLING DEGREE DAYS Base 65 deg. F SAVANNAH, GEORGIA

YEAR	JAN	FEB	MAR	APR	MAY	JUNE	JULY	AUG	SEP	OCT	NOV	DEC	TOTAL
1969	0	4	8	86	194	450	539	438	320	199	8	1	2247
1970	4	0	26	163	262	403	521	528	423	188	4	9	2531
1971	1	13	18	92	210	474	502	495	414	248	34	56	2557
1972	28	8	14	130	214	328	505	503	379	125	38	23	2295
1973	0	0	63	63	275	434	540	473	429	177	52	13	2519
1974	52	9	96	99	302	360	448	462	347	74	32	8	2289
1975	20	33	48	104	374	439	423	528	351	187	65	2	2574
1976	0	12	68	53	164	331	526	416	306	70	7	1	1954
1977	0	1	71	130	289	517	574	508	421	74	58	0	2643
1978	0	0	22	132	281	456	538	543	403	115	51	29	2570
1979	0	5	28	105	282	360	537	516	378	126	51	2	2390
1980	0	16	19	87	270	449	607	579	468	90	8	2	2595
1981	0	1	14	150	219	589	609	444	319	80	17	4	2446
1982	6	10	67	79	292	463	514	503	323	158	48	42	2505
1983	0	0	16	55	253	400	598	562	332	171	18	6	2411
1984	0	0	31	94	261	431	486	517	309	270	24	19	2442
1985	11	31	58	123	307	496	557	496	355	248	133	7	2822
1986	0	18	40	121	321	532	651	525	449	212	107	13	2989
1987	0	0	26	85	292	474	583	611	392	22	50	21	2556
1988	0	3	11	92	238	386	555	547	378	66	35	1	2312
1989	13	45	64	135	248	488	563	493	362	177	33	0	2621
1990	4	41	69	90	296	503	608	549	422	237	25	24	2868
1991	7	18	64	169	397	441	572	540	393	143	25	29	2798
1992	0	11	29	94	234	414	603	504	370	101	69	7	2436
1993	12	0	10	43	271	497	678	567	447	149	46	1	2721

SNOWFALL (inches) SAVANNAH, GEORGIA

SEASON	JULY	AUG	SEP	OCT	NOV	DEC	JAN	FEB	MAR	APR	MAY	JUNE	TOTAL
1970-71	0.0	0.0	0.0	0.0	0.0	0.0	T	0.0	0.0	0.0	0.0	0.0	T
1971-72	0.0	0.0	0.0	0.0	0.0	0.0	0.0	0.0	0.0	0.0	0.0	0.0	0.0
1972-73	0.0	0.0	0.0	0.0	0.0	0.0	T	3.2	0.0	0.0	0.0	0.0	3.2
1973-74	0.0	0.0	0.0	0.0	0.0	0.0	0.0	0.0	0.0	0.0	0.0	0.0	0.0
1974-75	0.0	0.0	0.0	0.0	0.0	0.0	0.0	0.0	0.0	0.0	0.0	0.0	0.0
1975-76	0.0	0.0	0.0	0.0	0.0	0.0	T	0.0	0.0	0.0	0.0	0.0	T
1976-77	0.0	0.0	0.0	0.0	0.0	0.0	2.0	T	0.0	0.0	0.0	0.0	2.0
1977-78	0.0	0.0	0.0	0.0	0.0	0.0	0.0	0.0	0.0	0.0	0.0	0.0	0.0
1978-79	0.0	0.0	0.0	0.0	0.0	0.0	0.0	T	0.0	0.0	0.0	0.0	T
1979-80	0.0	0.0	0.0	0.0	0.0	0.0	0.0	0.0	T	0.0	0.0	0.0	T
1980-81	0.0	0.0	0.0	0.0	0.0	T	0.0	0.0	0.0	0.0	0.0	0.0	T
1981-82	0.0	0.0	0.0	0.0	0.0	0.0	0.0	0.0	0.0	0.0	0.0	0.0	0.0
1982-83	0.0	0.0	0.0	0.0	0.0	0.0	T	0.0	T	0.0	0.0	0.0	T
1983-84	0.0	0.0	0.0	0.0	0.0	0.0	T	0.0	0.0	0.0	0.0	0.0	T
1984-85	0.0	0.0	0.0	0.0	0.0	0.0	0.0	0.0	0.0	0.0	0.0	0.0	0.0
1985-86	0.0	0.0	0.0	0.0	0.0	0.0	0.3	0.0	1.1	0.0	0.0	0.0	1.4
1986-87	0.0	0.0	0.0	0.0	0.0	0.0	T	0.0	0.0	0.0	0.0	0.0	T
1987-88	0.0	0.0	0.0	0.0	0.0	0.0	T	T	0.0	0.0	0.0	0.0	T
1988-89	0.0	0.0	0.0	0.0	0.0	T	0.0	1.0	0.0	0.0	0.0	T	1.0
1989-90	0.0	0.0	0.0	0.0	0.0	3.6	0.0	0.0	0.0	0.0	0.0	0.0	3.6
1990-91	0.0	0.0	0.0	0.0	0.0	0.0	0.0	T	0.0	0.0	0.0	0.0	T
1991-92	0.0	0.0	0.0	0.0	0.0	0.0	0.0	0.0	0.0	0.0	0.0	0.0	0.0
1992-93	0.0	0.0	0.0	0.0	0.0	0.0	0.0	0.0	0.2	0.0	0.0	0.0	0.2
1993-94	0.0	0.0	0.0	0.0	0.0	T							
Record Mean	0.0	0.0	0.0	0.0	0.0	0.1	0.1	0.2	T	0.0	0.0	T	0.4

HILO, HAWAII

The city of Hilo is located near the midpoint of the eastern shore of the Island of Hawaii. This island is by far the largest of the Hawaiian group, with an area of 4,038 square miles, more than twice that of all the other islands combined. Its topography is dominated by the great volcanic masses of Mauna Loa (13,653 feet), Mauna Kea (13,796 feet), and of Haulalai, the Kohala Mountains, and Kilauea. In fact, the island consists entirely of the slopes of these mountains and of the broad saddles between them. Mauna Loa and Kilauea, which occupy the southern half of the island, are still active volcanoes.

Hawaii lies well within the belt of northeasterly trade winds generated by the semi-permanent Pacific high pressure cell to the north and east. The climate provides equable temperatures from day to day and season to season. In Hilo, July and August are the warmest months, with average daily highs and lows of 83 and 68 degrees. January and February, the coolest months, have highs of 80 degrees and lows of 63 degrees. Greater variations occur in localities with less rain and cloud, but temperatures in the mid-90s and low 50s are uncommon anywhere on the island near sea level.

Over the windward slopes of Hawaii , rainfall occurs principally as orographic showers within the ascending moist trade winds. Mean annual rainfall, except for the semi-sheltered Hamakua district, increases from 100 inches or more along the coasts to a maximum of over 300 inches at elevations of 2,000 to 3,000 feet, and then declines to about 15 inches at the summits of Mauna Kea and Mauna Loa. Leeward areas are topographically sheltered from the trades and are therefore drier, although sea breezes created by daytime heating of the land move onshore and upslope, causing afternoon and evening cloudiness and showers. The driest locality on the island, and in the State, with an annual rainfall of less than 10 inches, is the coastal strip just leeward of the southern portion of the Kohala Mountains and of the saddle between the Kohalas and Mauna Kea.

Within the city of Hilo, average rainfall varies from about 130 inches a year near the shore to as much as 200 upslope. The wettest part of the island, with a mean annual rainfall exceeding 300 inches, lies about 6 miles upslope from the city limits. Relative humidity at Hilo is in the moderate range, however, due to the natural ventilation provided by the prevailing winds, the weather is seldom oppressive.

The trade winds prevail throughout the year and profoundly influence the climate. The islands entire western coast is sheltered from the trades by high mountains, except that unusually strong trade winds may sweep through the saddle between the Kohala Mountains and Mauna Kea and reach the areas to the lee. But even places exposed to the trades may be affected by local mountain circulations. Except for heavy rain, really severe weather seldom occurs. During the winter, cold fronts or the cyclonic storms of subtropical origin may bring blizzards to the upper slopes of Mauna Loa and Mauna Kea, with snow extending at times to 9,000 feet or below and icing nearer the summit.

Storms crossing the Pacific a thousand miles to the north, low pressure or tropical storms, may generate seas that cause heavy swell and surf.

NORMALS, MEANS, AND EXTREMES

HILO, HAWAII

LATITUDE: 19°43'N LONGITUDE: 155°04'W ELEVATION: FT. GRND 27 BARO 34 TIME ZONE: BERING WBAN: 21504

	(a)	JAN	FEB	MAR	APR	MAY	JUNE	JULY	AUG	SEP	OCT	NOV	DEC	YEAR
TEMPERATURE °F:														
Normals														
-Daily Maximum		79.8	79.8	79.5	79.8	81.2	82.7	83.0	83.6	83.8	83.2	81.4	80.0	81.5
-Daily Minimum		63.6	63.6	64.4	65.5	66.5	67.6	68.6	68.9	68.6	68.1	66.8	64.8	66.4
-Monthly		71.7	71.7	72.0	72.7	73.9	75.2	75.8	76.3	76.2	75.7	74.2	72.4	74.0
Extremes														
-Record Highest	47	91	92	93	89	94	90	89	93	92	91	90	93	94
-Year		1979	1968	1972	1978	1966	1969	1986	1950	1951	1979	1985	1980	MAY 1966
-Record Lowest	47	54	53	54	56	58	60	62	63	61	62	58	55	53
-Year		1980	1962	1983	1949	1947	1946	1970	1955	1970	1985	1985	1977	FEB 1962
NORMAL DEGREE DAYS:														
Heating (base 65°F)		0	0	0	0	0	0	0	0	0	0	0	0	0
Cooling (base 65°F)		208	188	217	231	276	306	335	350	336	332	276	229	3284
% OF POSSIBLE SUNSHINE	43	47	46	41	36	37	44	42	42	43	39	34	37	41
MEAN SKY COVER (tenths)														
Sunrise - Sunset	47	6.4	6.6	7.5	8.0	7.8	7.5	7.6	7.3	7.0	7.2	7.3	6.8	7.3
MEAN NUMBER OF DAYS:														
Sunrise to Sunset														
-Clear	47	6.3	5.2	2.8	1.0	1.2	1.6	1.3	1.8	3.1	2.7	3.3	5.1	35.6
-Partly Cloudy	47	11.4	10.2	10.1	8.9	10.7	11.1	11.5	12.2	12.1	11.7	10.4	10.7	131.0
-Cloudy	47	13.3	12.8	18.1	20.1	19.0	17.3	18.2	17.0	14.8	16.6	16.3	15.2	198.7
Precipitation .01 inches or more	51	17.3	17.0	23.4	25.2	25.2	24.5	27.5	26.5	23.4	23.7	23.2	21.4	278.3
Snow, Ice pellets, hail 1.0 inches or more	51	0.0	0.0	0.0	0.0	0.0	0.0	0.0	0.0	0.0	0.0	0.0	0.0	0.0
Thunderstorms	48	0.9	1.2	1.5	1.1	0.6	0.1	0.3	0.3	0.5	1.2	1.1	0.9	9.8
Heavy Fog Visibility 1/4 mile or less	48	0.0	0.0	0.0	0.0	0.0	0.0	0.0	0.0	0.0	0.0	0.0	0.0	0.0
Temperature °F														
-Maximum														
90° and above	48	0.1	0.1	0.*	0.0	0.*	0.*	0.0	0.1	0.2	0.3	0.*	0.1	0.9
32° and below	48	0.0	0.0	0.0	0.0	0.0	0.0	0.0	0.0	0.0	0.0	0.0	0.0	0.0
-Minimum														
32° and below	48	0.0	0.0	0.0	0.0	0.0	0.0	0.0	0.0	0.0	0.0	0.0	0.0	0.0
0° and below	48	0.0	0.0	0.0	0.0	0.0	0.0	0.0	0.0	0.0	0.0	0.0	0.0	0.0
AVG. STATION PRESS. (mb)	21	1014.4	1014.9	1016.9	1016.7	1016.4	1016.3	1015.6	1015.0	1014.1	1014.3	1014.5	1014.8	1015.3
RELATIVE HUMIDITY (%)														
Hour 02	44	83	83	86	88	88	87	88	88	87	87	87	85	86
Hour 18 (Local Time)	44	79	78	80	81	80	78	81	81	79	80	81	81	80
Hour 14	44	66	66	67	69	68	65	68	69	68	69	71	69	68
Hour 20	44	82	81	82	83	82	81	82	83	84	85	86	84	83
PRECIPITATION (inches):														
Water Equivalent														
-Normal		9.88	10.29	13.92	15.26	9.91	6.20	9.71	9.34	8.53	9.60	14.51	12.04	129.19
-Maximum Monthly	51	32.24	45.55	49.93	43.24	25.01	15.50	28.59	26.92	18.47	26.10	45.75	50.82	50.82
-Year		1979	1979	1980	1986	1964	1943	1982	1991	1990	1951	1990	1954	DEC 1954
-Minimum Monthly	51	0.36	0.58	0.88	2.93	1.18	1.80	3.83	2.66	1.59	2.40	1.01	0.28	0.28
-Year		1953	1986	1972	1962	1945	1985	1975	1971	1974	1962	1989	1980	DEC 1980
-Maximum in 24 hrs	51	10.90	22.30	17.05	11.07	10.26	4.21	7.11	11.57	7.23	8.88	15.59	11.45	22.30
-Year		1990	1979	1980	1971	1965	1978	1982	1991	1986	1951	1959	1987	FEB 1979
Snow, Ice pellets, hail														
-Maximum Monthly		0.0	0.0	0.0	0.0	0.0	0.0	0.0	0.0	0.0	0.0	0.0	0.0	
-Year														
-Maximum in 24 hrs	51	0.0	0.0	0.0	0.0	0.0	0.0	0.0	0.0	0.0	0.0	0.0	0.0	
-Year														
WIND:														
Mean Speed (mph)	44	7.5	7.7	7.7	7.5	7.4	7.1	6.9	6.9	6.8	6.7	6.8	7.2	7.2
Prevailing Direction through 1963		SW	SW	SW	WSW	WSW	WSW	WSW	WSW	WSW	SW	WSW	SW	WSW
Fastest Obs. 1 Min.														
-Direction (!!)	14	36	35	35	34	35	11	05	36	04	34	02	36	36
-Speed (MPH)	14	35	35	28	26	29	25	25	25	25	29	28	29	35
-Year		1987	1987	1987	1987	1987	1982	1984	1993	1987	1983	1987	1989	JAN 1987
Peak Gust														
-Direction (!!)	10	NW	W	N	N	N	NE	SE	N	SE	SE	S	NW	W
-Speed (mph)	10	47	55	40	40	41	32	36	36	37	33	36	45	55
-Date		1992	1986	1993	1989	1987	1987	1986	1991	1992	1988	1988	1989	FEB 1986

PRECIPITATION (inches)

HILO, HAWAII

YEAR	JAN	FEB	MAR	APR	MAY	JUNE	JULY	AUG	SEP	OCT	NOV	DEC	ANNUAL
1964	14.65	18.22	19.58	11.03	25.01	7.01	6.39	7.33	12.62	11.56	23.39	9.65	166.44
1965	9.28	3.71	8.33	18.49	21.05	8.85	7.15	4.79	5.72	5.80	19.18	14.94	127.29
1966	12.56	7.63	5.59	5.24	5.04	7.49	13.26	7.22	8.37	15.69	20.83	15.09	124.01
1967	8.04	10.35	9.46	21.26	9.84	6.26	14.03	19.55	6.78	10.08	21.25	17.10	154.00
1968	4.77	11.46	10.21	29.68	2.71	8.72	7.43	9.62	8.53	5.97	10.22	24.82	134.14
1969	19.66	43.66	30.64	14.57	7.83	2.76	11.75	17.50	7.24	3.19	6.33	8.10	173.23
1970	2.76	2.56	4.89	28.60	20.26	5.60	12.27	20.53	5.61	8.44	7.21	35.25	153.98
1971	13.47	5.31	12.04	27.82	6.49	2.79	4.13	2.66	8.63	7.28	17.88	32.19	140.69
1972	10.96	10.13	0.88	17.79	4.71	4.58	9.07	8.77	5.20	9.52	13.23	4.01	98.85
1973	3.45	5.51	18.84	7.34	8.34	3.69	4.40	3.54	8.07	9.72	26.88	8.19	107.97
1974	5.88	7.57	13.47	19.11	8.07	4.76	7.81	4.25	1.59	6.65	14.56	19.20	112.92
1975	19.62	9.28	10.40	10.23	3.01	4.20	3.83	8.13	2.73	8.88	11.15	8.47	99.93
1976	15.62	11.63	25.00	11.58	6.01	2.97	5.46	5.13	5.31	11.35	7.24	7.37	114.67
1977	1.22	9.56	15.49	10.90	10.86	2.46	6.36	7.60	4.19	10.30	8.78	2.66	90.38
1978	5.41	4.26	12.95	6.53	9.64	10.99	11.19	13.53	5.44	10.12	20.21	8.82	119.09
1979	32.24	45.55	5.32	9.90	4.10	10.45	6.54	7.04	3.64	5.03	21.56	7.40	158.77
1980	0.91	4.14	49.93	11.01	5.88	9.66	9.17	8.24	13.70	7.69	7.13	0.28	127.74
1981	1.51	4.95	5.66	4.63	4.16	2.43	4.32	8.97	12.79	10.23	11.73	18.53	89.91
1982	13.58	1.35	48.50	12.00	6.89	6.03	28.59	25.45	9.92	6.53	4.74	6.78	170.36
1983	0.90	0.83	1.98	10.31	9.60	3.94	7.21	7.48	12.08	8.06	2.33	3.37	68.09
1984	10.76	10.06	3.37	12.08	6.59	4.28	6.63	9.36	4.05	2.52	18.38	12.00	100.08
1985	2.25	16.14	21.28	10.61	17.04	1.80	9.86	6.71	11.78	8.19	4.71	2.59	112.96
1986	4.95	0.58	15.37	43.24	8.61	9.11	11.17	10.64	14.36	11.53	35.72	5.75	171.03
1987	9.02	5.06	4.79	9.24	15.65	12.91	18.26	3.69	11.56	14.21	15.83	22.19	142.41
1988	10.31	9.95	13.09	12.90	7.77	5.11	5.50	16.56	11.30	8.50	25.74	13.46	140.19
1989	27.46	6.54	7.33	37.19	19.80	7.03	22.93	8.82	9.73	13.16	1.01	5.71	166.71
1990	29.13	15.24	10.80	4.02	8.13	10.04	10.78	7.80	18.47	20.96	45.75	30.10	211.22
1991	3.81	9.32	37.88	11.02	8.08	9.85	9.82	26.92	9.41	5.15	6.74	15.04	153.04
1992	1.33	1.29	3.90	6.62	2.99	9.36	17.63	13.62	17.59	3.38	25.16	17.02	119.89
1993	2.17	2.67	11.96	9.04	7.54	6.63	18.43	11.38	4.99	12.83	10.74	16.11	114.49
Record Mean	9.61	11.33	13.82	13.29	9.14	6.40	10.03	10.33	7.91	9.86	14.79	14.00	130.50

AVERAGE TEMPERATURE (deg. F)

HILO, HAWAII

YEAR	JAN	FEB	MAR	APR	MAY	JUNE	JULY	AUG	SEP	OCT	NOV	DEC	ANNUAL
1964	72.1	70.2	70.8	71.7	72.0	75.0	75.2	75.4	75.0	73.7	72.7	73.2	73.1
1965	71.7	68.4	69.7	72.4	74.5	74.1	75.2	75.8	76.8	75.4	73.7	69.9	73.1
1966	69.7	69.9	71.6	71.8	75.0	75.1	76.6	77.1	77.4	77.0	75.6	74.3	74.3
1967	71.9	73.9	74.1	74.3	77.1	77.5	77.8	77.1	77.0	77.2	75.4	73.3	75.6
1968	72.9	74.9	74.5	73.8	75.7	76.6	76.8	76.5	76.8	77.1	76.2	73.7	75.5
1969	71.4	72.2	72.5	72.8	74.5	76.2	75.8	76.2	75.0	74.5	73.3	71.5	73.8
1970	72.0	71.1	71.1	72.4	73.7	73.7	74.2	74.9	74.8	75.3	73.9	72.7	73.3
1971	71.3	71.9	69.4	70.9	72.2	75.0	76.6	76.6	76.6	75.4	73.8	70.9	73.4
1972	70.1	70.7	73.8	72.7	73.0	75.3	75.4	76.5	76.4	76.0	73.3	71.4	73.7
1973	72.2	71.1	72.5	72.2	72.9	74.6	75.7	76.3	76.3	75.8	75.4	73.8	74.1
1974	74.5	72.6	73.1	73.5	73.8	75.3	76.1	76.9	77.3	76.9	73.6	72.3	74.6
1975	71.0	71.9	71.2	72.4	73.1	74.4	74.8	75.7	75.5	74.7	73.5	72.2	73.4
1976	71.3	71.2	71.6	72.1	73.0	73.6	74.5	76.2	76.9	76.2	74.5	73.2	73.7
1977	73.9	74.0	73.3	74.2	74.7	76.2	77.1	78.1	77.5	76.9	75.2	73.7	75.4
1978	71.7	72.5	73.2	74.2	76.2	76.5	77.1	76.8	76.2	75.5	74.1	71.1	74.6
1979	69.8	70.4	71.5	73.8	73.8	74.2	74.6	75.6	76.5	76.1	73.0	72.8	73.5
1980	71.6	72.6	72.3	74.5	77.3	77.6	77.8	75.0	75.7	74.8	73.8	74.2	74.8
1981	73.5	72.7	71.6	72.8	74.2	76.0	76.1	76.1	76.2	74.6	73.9	72.0	74.1
1982	71.9	71.8	70.3	71.2	72.9	76.3	76.7	76.9	76.1	74.9	74.6	71.8	73.8
1983	71.4	71.9	72.5	71.9	72.6	74.3	74.8	75.2	74.9	74.1	73.8	72.9	73.3
1984	72.4	71.5	73.8	73.0	74.0	74.7	75.2	75.3	75.4	76.5	73.6	71.1	73.9
1985	69.8	70.5	69.4	69.8	71.4	74.4	75.4	75.7	75.7	74.3	73.0	71.6	72.6
1986	71.1	73.6	74.7	73.6	75.4	76.6	77.8	78.5	77.9	76.4	75.1	72.8	75.3
1987	71.8	70.7	71.6	72.2	72.5	75.4	76.7	77.9	77.8	76.6	74.7	73.1	74.3
1988	71.9	72.3	72.2	72.6	74.2	74.7	75.7	76.0	76.6	77.9	76.3	74.9	74.6
1989	72.2	71.4	72.4	71.1	72.7	74.7	75.2	75.0	74.6	75.6	73.6	71.3	73.3
1990	72.1	70.4	71.2	73.5	74.1	75.0	76.0	77.0	77.2	76.2	75.4	72.5	74.2
1991	72.0	72.8	70.8	72.6	74.2	74.8	76.0	76.9	76.9	76.2	75.8	72.9	74.3
1992	71.2	71.4	72.3	72.4	74.8	76.2	76.2	77.2	77.8	77.7	75.2	73.6	74.7
1993	71.1	70.1	71.6	73.5	73.3	75.4	75.8	77.0	77.1	76.0	73.4	71.7	73.8
Record Mean	71.3	71.3	71.5	72.3	73.4	74.8	75.5	76.0	75.9	75.4	73.7	72.0	73.6
Max	79.3	79.3	79.0	79.4	80.7	82.3	82.6	83.2	83.5	82.9	80.9	79.4	81.1
Min	63.3	63.2	63.9	65.1	66.2	67.3	68.3	68.8	68.3	67.8	66.5	64.5	66.1

REFERENCE NOTES

HILO, HAWAII

GENERAL
T - TRACE AMOUNT.
BLANK ENTRIES DENOTE MISSING/UNREPORTED DATA.
# INDICATES A STATION OR INSTRUMENT RELOCATION.

SPECIFIC

PM - INCLUDES LAST DAY OF PREVIOUS MONTH
ASOS - AUTOMATED SURFACE OBSERVING SYSTEM IN OPERATION DURING THESE MONTHS.

(a) - LENGTH OF RECORD IN YEARS, ALTHOUGH INDIVIDUAL MONTHS MAY BE MISSING.
0.* OR * - THE VALUE IS BETWEEN 0.0 AND 0.05
NORMALS - BASED ON THE 1961-1990 RECORD PERIOD.
EXTREMES - DATES ARE THE MOST RECENT OCCURRENCE
WIND DIR. - NUMERALS SHOW TENS OF DEGRESS CLOCKWISE FROM TRUE NORTH. "00" INDICATES CALM.
RESULTANT DIRECTIONS ARE GIVEN TO WHOLE DEGREES.
BOLD VALUES INDICATE EXTREME VALUES WHICH OCCURRED AFTER THE ASOS SYSTEM WAS COMMISSIONED.

RECORD = PERIOD OF RECORD
RECORD MEAN PRECIPITATION IS THE MEAN OF ALL DAILY PRECIPITATION AMOUNTS DURING THE PERIOD OF RECORD.
RECORD MAX(MIN) TEMPERATURE IS THE MEAN OF ALL DAILY MAX(MIN) TEMPERATURES DURING THE PERIOD OF RECORD.
RECORD MEAN TEMPERATURE IS THE SUM OF THE RECORD MAX AND RECORD MIN DIVIDED BY 2.
AVERAGE TEMPERATURE IS THE SUM OF THE MEAN DAILY MAX AND MIN TEMPERATURE DIVIDED BY 2.

EXCEPTIONS

RECORD MEANS ARE THROUGH THE CURRENT YEAR, BEGINNING IN 1947 FOR TEMPERATURE
1943 FOR PRECIPITATION

HEATING DEGREE DAYS Base 65 deg. F HILO, HAWAII

SEASON	JULY	AUG	SEP	OCT	NOV	DEC	JAN	FEB	MAR	APR	MAY	JUNE	TOTAL
1983-84	0	0	0	0	0	0	0	0	0	0	0	0	0
1984-85	0	0	0	0	0	0	0	0	0	0	0	0	0
1985-86	0	0	0	0	0	0	0	0	0	0	0	0	0
1986-87	0	0	0	0	0	0	0	0	0	0	0	0	0
1987-88	0	0	0	0	0	0	0	0	0	0	0	0	0
1988-89	0	0	0	0	0	0	0	0	0	0	0	0	0
1989-90	0	0	0	0	0	0	0	0	0	0	0	0	0
1990-91	0	0	0	0	0	0	0	0	0	0	0	0	0
1991-92	0	0	0	0	0	0	0	0	0	0	0	0	0
1992-93	0	0	0	0	0	0	0	0	0	0	0	0	0
1993-94	0	0	0	0	0	0							

COOLING DEGREE DAYS Base 65 deg. F HILO, HAWAII

YEAR	JAN	FEB	MAR	APR	MAY	JUNE	JULY	AUG	SEP	OCT	NOV	DEC	TOTAL
1969	207	209	240	239	298	341	344	351	308	300	253	208	3298
1970	223	173	195	229	273	270	290	313	303	325	276	246	3116
1971	203	201	142	185	232	306	366	367	354	328	271	188	3143
1972	163	171	281	236	256	316	330	365	349	348	256	207	3278
1973	233	180	239	222	253	294	341	358	345	340	321	278	3404
1974	299	219	261	263	276	315	351	375	375	376	262	235	3607
1975	192	201	197	232	257	288	311	339	323	309	262	233	3144
1976	201	186	214	222	255	268	302	355	364	357	291	261	3276
1977	280	260	264	281	307	343	379	415	382	374	312	274	3871
1978	216	215	263	283	353	351	383	375	341	332	279	195	3586
1979	155	160	210	271	278	280	302	338	351	350	246	248	3189
1980	213	227	234	293	390	385	405	316	328	313	269	295	3668
1981	271	220	210	242	293	338	350	348	345	302	274	225	3418
1982	220	196	170	194	252	348	369	379	340	317	293	219	3297
1983	207	200	239	214	240	287	313	324	303	288	272	250	3137
1984	236	194	282	247	284	298	324	326	320	363	261	195	3330
1985	154	161	142	152	204	290	329	339	329	294	248	211	2853
1986	196	246	308	264	329	356	404	423	396	363	309	250	3844
1987	218	163	212	226	241	319	369	407	389	365	299	259	3467
1988	221	216	233	238	293	298	338	349	353	405	345	315	3604
1989	227	188	238	189	248	297	327	315	294	335	264	202	3124
1990	227	157	200	260	290	308	349	379	376	353	317	237	3453
1991	223	222	188	234	296	301	348	378	365	351	333	251	3490
1992	197	192	235	229	312	343	355	384	387	402	315	275	3626
1993	193	148	213	263	263	318	343	380	370	350	260	217	3318

SNOWFALL (inches) HILO, HAWAII

SEASON	JULY	AUG	SEP	OCT	NOV	DEC	JAN	FEB	MAR	APR	MAY	JUNE	TOTAL
1971-72	0.0	0.0	0.0	0.0	0.0	0.0	0.0	0.0	0.0	0.0	0.0	0.0	0.0
1972-73	0.0	0.0	0.0	0.0	0.0	0.0	0.0	0.0	0.0	0.0	0.0	0.0	0.0
1973-74	0.0	0.0	0.0	0.0	0.0	0.0	0.0	0.0	0.0	0.0	0.0	0.0	0.0
1974-75	0.0	0.0	0.0	0.0	0.0	0.0	0.0	0.0	0.0	0.0	0.0	0.0	0.0
1975-76	0.0	0.0	0.0	0.0	0.0	0.0	0.0	0.0	0.0	0.0	0.0	0.0	0.0
1976-77	0.0	0.0	0.0	0.0	0.0	0.0	0.0	0.0	0.0	0.0	0.0	0.0	0.0
1977-78	0.0	0.0	0.0	0.0	0.0	0.0	0.0	0.0	0.0	0.0	0.0	0.0	0.0
1978-79	0.0	0.0	0.0	0.0	0.0	0.0	0.0	0.0	0.0	0.0	0.0	0.0	0.0
1979-80	0.0	0.0	0.0	0.0	0.0	0.0	0.0	0.0	0.0	0.0	0.0	0.0	0.0
1980-81	0.0	0.0	0.0	0.0	0.0	0.0	0.0	0.0	0.0	0.0	0.0	0.0	0.0
1981-82	0.0	0.0	0.0	0.0	0.0	0.0	0.0	0.0	0.0	0.0	0.0	0.0	0.0
1982-83	0.0	0.0	0.0	0.0	0.0	0.0	0.0	0.0	0.0	0.0	0.0	0.0	0.0
1983-84	0.0	0.0	0.0	0.0	0.0	0.0	0.0	0.0	0.0	0.0	0.0	0.0	0.0
1984-85	0.0	0.0	0.0	0.0	0.0	0.0	0.0	0.0	0.0	0.0	0.0	0.0	0.0
1985-86	0.0	0.0	0.0	0.0	0.0	0.0	0.0	0.0	0.0	0.0	0.0	0.0	0.0
1986-87	0.0	0.0	0.0	0.0	0.0	0.0	0.0	0.0	0.0	0.0	0.0	0.0	0.0
1987-88	0.0	0.0	0.0	0.0	0.0	0.0	0.0	0.0	0.0	0.0	0.0	0.0	0.0
1988-89	0.0	0.0	0.0	0.0	0.0	0.0	0.0	0.0	0.0	0.0	0.0	0.0	0.0
1989-90	0.0	0.0	0.0	0.0	0.0	0.0	0.0	0.0	0.0	0.0	0.0	0.0	0.0
1990-91	0.0	0.0	0.0	0.0	0.0	0.0	0.0	0.0	0.0	0.0	0.0	0.0	0.0
1991-92	0.0	0.0	0.0	0.0	0.0	0.0	0.0	0.0	0.0	0.0	0.0	0.0	0.0
1992-93	0.0	0.0	0.0	0.0	0.0	0.0	0.0	0.0	0.0	0.0	0.0	0.0	0.0
1993-94	0.0	0.0	0.0	0.0	0.0	0.0							
Record Mean	0.0	0.0	0.0	0.0	0.0	0.0	0.0	0.0	0.0	0.0	0.0	0.0	0.0

HONOLULU, HAWAII

Oahu, on which Honolulu is located, is the third largest of the Hawaiian Islands. The Koolau Range, at an average elevation of 2,000 feet parallels the northeastern coast. The Waianae Mountains, somewhat higher in elevation, parallel the west coast. Honolulu Airport, the business and Waikiki districts, and a number of the residential areas of Honolulu lie along the southern coastal plain.

The climate of Hawaii is unusually pleasant for the tropics. Its outstanding features are the persistence of the trade winds, the remarkable variability in rainfall over short distances, the sunniness of the leeward lowlands in contrast to the persistent cloudiness over nearby mountain crests, the equable temperature, and the general infrequency of severe storms.

The prevailing wind throughout the year is the northeasterly trade wind, although its average frequency varies from more than 90 percent during the summer to only 50 percent in January.

Heavy mountain rainfall sustains extensive irrigation of cane fields and the water supply for Honolulu. Oahu is driest along the coast west of the Waianaes where rainfall drops to about 20 inches a year. Daytime showers, usually light, often occur while the sun continues to shine, a phenomenon referred to locally as liquid sunshine.

The moderate temperature range is associated with the small seasonal variation in the energy received from the sun and the tempering effect of the surrounding ocean. Honolulu Airport has recorded as high as the lower 90s and as low as the lower 50s.

Because of the trade winds, even the warmest months are usually comfortable. But when the trades diminish or give way to southerly winds, a situation known locally as kona weather, or kona storms when stormy, the humidity may become oppressively high.

Intense rains of the October to April winter season sometimes cause serious, flash flooding. Thunderstorms are infrequent and usually mild and hail seldom occurs. Infrequently, a small tornado or a waterspout may do some damage. Only a few tropical cyclones have struck Hawaii, although others have come near enough for their outlying winds, waves, clouds, and rain to affect the Islands.

NORMALS, MEANS, AND EXTREMES

HONOLULU, HAWAII

LATITUDE: 21°20'N LONGITUDE: 157°56' W ELEVATION: FT. GRND 7 BARO 18 TIME ZONE: BERING WBAN: 22521

	(a)	JAN	FEB	MAR	APR	MAY	JUNE	JULY	AUG	SEP	OCT	NOV	DEC	YEAR
TEMPERATURE °F:														
Normals														
-Daily Maximum		80.1	80.5	81.6	82.8	84.7	86.5	87.5	88.7	88.5	86.9	84.1	81.2	84.4
-Daily Minimum		65.6	65.4	67.2	68.7	70.3	72.2	73.5	74.2	73.5	72.3	70.3	67.0	70.0
-Monthly		72.9	73.0	74.4	75.8	77.5	79.4	80.5	81.4	81.0	79.6	77.2	74.1	77.2
Extremes														
-Record Highest	24	87	88	88	89	93	92	92	93	94	94	93	89	94
-Year		1987	1984	1987	1990	1988	1992	1992	1987	1988	1984	1986	1983	SEP 1988
-Record Lowest	24	53	53	55	57	60	65	66	67	66	61	57	54	53
-Year		1972	1983	1976	1985	1989	1982	1990	1984	1985	1993	1990	1962	FEB 1983
NORMAL DEGREE DAYS:														
Heating (base 65°F)		0	0	0	0	0	0	0	0	0	0	0	0	0
Cooling (base 65°F)		245	224	291	324	388	432	481	508	480	453	366	282	4474
% OF POSSIBLE SUNSHINE	41	64	66	70	69	70	72	75	76	76	69	62	61	69
MEAN SKY COVER (tenths) Sunrise - Sunset	47	5.4	5.5	5.8	6.1	5.9	5.5	5.3	5.2	5.2	5.7	5.7	5.6	5.6
MEAN NUMBER OF DAYS:														
Sunrise to Sunset														
-Clear	44	9.4	8.2	7.5	5.7	6.5	6.4	7.6	8.2	8.2	7.4	7.2	8.2	90.4
-Partly Cloudy	44	13.1	12.4	14.0	14.4	15.4	17.2	18.2	16.8	16.1	15.1	13.8	13.6	180.1
-Cloudy	44	8.5	7.7	9.4	9.9	9.1	6.4	5.2	6.0	5.7	8.5	9.1	9.2	94.7
Precipitation .01 inches or more	44	9.5	9.2	8.8	8.8	7.3	5.8	7.3	6.3	7.0	8.8	9.2	10.3	98.4
Snow,Ice pellets,hail 1.0 inches or more	44	0.0	0.0	0.0	0.0	0.0	0.0	0.0	0.0	0.0	0.0	0.0	0.0	0.0
Thunderstorms	44	0.8	1.1	0.9	0.5	0.3	0.1	0.2	0.1	0.5	0.8	0.8	0.7	6.7
Heavy Fog Visibility 1/4 mile or less	44	0.0	0.0	0.0	0.0	0.0	0.0	0.0	0.0	0.0	0.0	0.0	0.0	0.0
Temperature °F														
-Maximum														
90° and above	24	0.0	0.0	0.0	0.0	0.3	1.6	4.7	10.4	10.1	4.0	0.3	0.0	31.3
32° and below	24	0.0	0.0	0.0	0.0	0.0	0.0	0.0	0.0	0.0	0.0	0.0	0.0	0.0
-Minimum														
32° and below	24	0.0	0.0	0.0	0.0	0.0	0.0	0.0	0.0	0.0	0.0	0.0	0.0	0.0
0° and below	24	0.0	0.0	0.0	0.0	0.0	0.0	0.0	0.0	0.0	0.0	0.0	0.0	0.0
AVG. STATION PRESS.(mb)	21	1014.9	1015.5	1017.3	1017.1	1016.9	1016.7	1016.0	1015.4	1014.5	1014.7	1014.9	1015.3	1015.8
RELATIVE HUMIDITY (%)														
Hour 02	24	81	79	76	75	74	73	73	74	75	76	78	80	76
Hour 18 (Local Time)	24	81	78	73	69	67	66	67	68	68	70	75	79	72
Hour 14	24	61	59	57	55	53	52	51	52	52	55	58	60	55
Hour 20	24	73	71	70	69	68	68	68	69	69	70	72	74	70
PRECIPITATION (inches):														
Water Equivalent														
-Normal		3.55	2.21	2.20	1.54	1.13	0.50	0.59	0.44	0.78	2.28	3.00	3.80	22.02
-Maximum Monthly	47	14.74	13.68	20.79	8.92	7.23	2.46	2.33	3.08	2.74	11.15	14.72	17.29	20.79
-Year		1949	1955	1951	1963	1965	1971	1989	1959	1947	1978	1965	1987	MAR 1951
-Minimum Monthly	47	0.18	0.06	0.01	0.01	0.05	T	0.03	T	0.05	0.11	0.03	0.06	T
-Year		1986	1983	1957	1960	1949	1959	1950	1974	1977	1957	1962	1976	AUG 1974
-Maximum in 24 hrs	44	6.72	6.88	17.07	4.21	3.44	2.28	2.20	2.35	1.40	7.57	9.15	8.25	17.07
-Year		1963	1955	1958	1972	1965	1967	1989	1959	1963	1978	1954	1987	MAR 1958
Snow,Ice pellets,hail														
-Maximum Monthly		0.0	0.0	0.0	0.0	0.0	0.0	0.0	0.0	0.0	0.0	0.0	0.0	
-Year														
-Maximum in 24 hrs	47	0.0	0.0	0.0	0.0	0.0	0.0	0.0	0.0	0.0	0.0	0.0	0.0	
-Year														
WIND:														
Mean Speed (mph)	44	9.5	10.2	11.4	11.8	11.8	12.7	13.2	12.8	11.2	10.5	10.7	10.4	11.3
Prevailing Direction through 1963		ENE	ENE	ENE	ENE	ENE	ENE	ENE	ENE	ENE	ENE	ENE	ENE	ENE
Fastest Obs. 1 Min.														
-Direction (!!)	13	07	07	06	06	13	05	07	04	13	07	20	06	20
-Speed (MPH)	13	32	35	30	31	30	26	28	28	38	25	46	33	46
-Year		1982	1990	1990	1980	1985	1981	1980	1982	1992	1981	1982	1993	NOV 1982
Peak Gust														
-Direction (!!)	10	NE	NE	NE	NE	E	NE	NE	NE	SE	SE	NE	NE	SE
-Speed (mph)	10	41	46	46	41	39	35	40	35	49	35	40	46	49
-Date		1987	1990	1985	1986	1985	1993	1984	1990	1992	1991	1986	1993	SEP 1992

PRECIPITATION (inches)

HONOLULU, HAWAII

YEAR	JAN	FEB	MAR	APR	MAY	JUNE	JULY	AUG	SEP	OCT	NOV	DEC	ANNUAL
1964	2.18	0.52	5.21	0.88	0.21	0.08	1.34	0.46	0.97	0.34	2.36	5.57	20.12
1965	3.02	0.80	0.99	1.48	7.23	0.25	1.37	0.87	0.52	3.56	14.72	7.97	42.78
1966	1.39	3.71	0.39	0.46	0.41	0.04	0.43	0.82	0.16	2.95	9.44	2.98	23.18
1967	0.79	2.53	6.78	1.29	2.12	2.43	1.21	2.53	0.42	1.53	2.78	9.93	34.34
1968	8.17	2.91	2.49	3.14	1.22	0.24	0.29	0.10	1.30	2.13	5.64	9.63	37.26
1969	8.20	0.48	3.00	0.10	0.81	0.23	0.63	0.11	0.87	0.96	5.77	1.34	22.50
1970	1.81	0.77	0.07	0.74	0.21	0.23	2.01	0.21	0.39	1.88	5.94	1.23	15.49
1971	6.19	2.37	5.57	2.19	0.43	2.46	0.04	0.26	1.03	2.27	0.95	2.88	26.64
1972	5.28	5.00	2.45	5.15	0.12	0.79	0.20	0.46	0.92	2.39	0.59	3.59	26.94
1973	0.67	0.60	0.40	0.72	0.89	0.09	0.46	0.32	0.64	1.78	3.73	3.94	14.24
1974	4.21	1.28	3.49	4.13	0.82	1.52	0.44	T	2.08	2.77	2.69	0.59	24.02
1975	6.42	2.36	2.02	0.51	0.19	0.03	0.40	0.03	0.11	0.18	11.54	0.60	24.39
1976	1.29	6.08	2.67	0.71	0.26	0.18	0.24	0.17	0.33	0.45	0.46	0.06	12.90
1977	0.52	0.32	2.36	1.81	4.76	0.11	0.14	0.08	0.05	0.15	0.61	1.45	12.36
1978	0.34	0.75	1.37	2.07	3.39	1.06	0.20	0.83	0.28	11.15	1.55	2.06	25.05
1979	4.57	7.21	0.77	0.55	0.21	0.32	0.13	0.15	0.47	0.53	0.52	1.50	16.93
1980	8.91	2.26	3.04	1.13	0.78	1.76	0.37	0.36	0.41	0.30	0.21	7.37	26.90
1981	0.81	0.97	0.71	1.01	0.94	0.14	0.42	0.70	0.39	1.84	1.01	4.47	13.41
1982	12.82	2.16	3.73	1.28	0.13	0.35	0.20	1.98	0.52	7.24	1.32	3.19	34.92
1983	0.32	0.06	0.53	0.42	0.35	0.26	0.22	0.29	1.16	0.23	0.13	1.06	5.03
1984	0.21	0.60	1.08	2.41	0.16	0.08	0.23	0.04	1.36	1.89	3.58	5.44	17.08
1985	1.46	3.87	1.26	0.20	1.11	0.13	0.53	0.16	1.28	5.08	2.11	0.19	17.38
1986	0.18	1.38	0.17	0.35	0.81	0.36	1.54	0.90	2.00	1.23	4.23	0.78	13.93
1987	0.42	0.86	0.31	0.65	0.73	0.46	0.33	0.22	1.13	0.20	0.93	17.29	23.53
1988	3.05	1.31	0.67	0.50	1.25	0.04	0.12	0.34	0.86	0.23	1.39	6.71	16.47
1989	2.07	6.48	2.58	1.23	0.29	0.11	2.33	0.08	0.15	10.37	0.51	1.32	27.52
1990	4.32	4.15	0.86	0.30	0.30	0.08	0.49	0.01	0.98	0.47	2.96	4.92	19.84
1991	0.80	2.09	6.24	1.00	0.48	0.26	0.16	0.16	0.56	3.43	1.52	1.24	17.94
1992	0.43	1.35	0.72	0.11	1.13	0.10	2.01	0.97	2.08	2.57	1.04	6.49	19.00
1993	0.70	0.41	0.02	0.23	0.19	0.11	0.69	1.03	0.10	1.63	0.46	0.27	5.84
Record Mean	3.76	2.50	2.68	1.32	0.96	0.38	0.56	0.59	0.76	2.02	2.66	3.57	21.77

AVERAGE TEMPERATURE (deg. F)

HONOLULU, HAWAII

YEAR	JAN	FEB	MAR	APR	MAY	JUNE	JULY	AUG	SEP	OCT	NOV	DEC	ANNUAL
1964	75.1	74.7	74.7	75.7	76.4	77.9	79.3	80.4	80.2	78.3	76.4	74.9	77.0
1965	71.9	69.8	72.1	75.0	77.0	79.1	79.9	79.7	80.0	78.2	77.1	73.3	76.1
1966	72.6	72.0	75.2	75.1	77.1	80.6	80.8	82.0	82.4	80.9	77.2	74.6	77.6
1967	72.5	73.9	73.8	74.7	78.2	79.7	81.5	82.1	82.4	80.6	77.6	74.0	77.6
1968	73.0	73.4	74.8	76.7	78.4	80.4	81.5	82.9	82.0	80.6	78.8	72.7	77.9
1969	69.1	73.9	73.6	74.7	76.7	79.1	80.9	83.2	82.0	80.5	78.7	76.5	77.4
#1970	74.2	73.3	76.9	78.3	80.4	81.1	82.2	83.8	79.0	78.5	75.8	74.7	78.2
#1971	71.7	74.4	73.9	75.6	76.2	77.3	78.9	79.5	79.1	78.0	75.7	73.3	76.1
1972	70.4	70.6	72.8	75.0	77.3	78.9	80.4	81.1	80.5	79.3	76.7	71.6	76.2
1973	72.9	72.6	76.1	75.5	77.1	79.2	80.5	81.2	81.0	79.4	77.0	73.8	77.2
1974	74.5	74.4	74.0	77.4	78.2	79.3	79.9	81.2	80.0	79.5	75.7	75.8	77.5
1975	72.4	72.8	73.0	74.5	75.7	78.1	79.0	80.1	79.4	79.1	77.1	73.0	76.2
1976	73.7	72.0	73.6	75.1	77.5	78.2	79.8	80.8	80.7	79.1	75.3	75.3	76.8
1977	73.7	75.6	76.2	76.3	77.6	79.5	80.9	82.2	81.6	81.1	78.6	75.1	78.2
1978	74.2	73.2	75.7	76.8	78.2	78.7	79.0	80.5	80.5	77.8	74.7	72.4	76.8
1979	69.9	72.1	72.8	74.8	78.0	80.0	80.9	80.4	81.1	81.0	77.4	75.3	77.0
1980	71.9	72.4	75.0	76.1	78.3	79.5	80.9	81.0	81.6	80.1	78.0	74.4	77.5
1981	73.2	73.6	74.7	75.9	77.3	80.6	79.7	80.1	80.7	78.3	76.7	74.0	77.1
1982	73.2	71.7	74.0	75.4	78.3	79.6	80.6	81.4	81.4	79.4	75.7	72.0	76.9
1983	71.9	71.3	73.5	74.6	75.7	78.9	79.7	82.4	82.3	81.1	80.1	75.1	77.2
1984	74.6	74.6	75.8	77.0	78.7	79.3	81.0	81.7	81.3	80.2	79.0	74.1	78.1
1985	71.4	73.9	74.5	74.5	76.5	79.2	81.6	81.9	81.1	79.8	75.1	73.3	76.9
1986	72.8	72.6	76.5	77.5	78.3	80.0	81.6	82.9	82.1	80.6	79.2	75.1	78.3
1987	73.4	71.2	74.0	76.0	75.7	80.4	82.1	82.7	82.9	81.4	78.8	75.8	77.9
1988	73.1	74.7	76.0	77.3	78.9	80.8	81.8	82.1	82.1	80.1	79.9	75.6	78.5
1989	74.5	73.6	75.3	74.5	78.4	80.9	81.6	81.4	81.9	78.6	76.7	72.9	77.5
1990	74.7	71.5	73.1	76.6	78.1	80.0	80.8	82.3	82.3	80.9	77.3	74.1	77.6
1991	72.4	73.4	72.9	75.9	77.8	79.4	81.2	82.4	81.5	80.0	79.5	76.2	77.7
1992	72.9	73.2	74.9	75.6	77.8	81.3	81.5	82.2	81.3	79.4	77.0	76.7	77.8
1993	70.9	71.1	74.0	77.4	77.2	80.2	80.6	81.3	81.1	79.7	76.3	75.0	77.1
Record Mean	72.6	72.7	73.8	75.3	76.8	78.8	79.8	80.6	80.4	79.0	76.7	74.1	76.8
Max	79.7	79.9	80.7	82.0	83.7	85.6	86.5	87.3	87.4	85.9	83.3	80.7	83.6
Min	65.5	65.4	66.9	68.5	70.0	72.0	73.1	73.9	73.4	72.1	70.0	67.4	69.9

REFERENCE NOTES

HONOLULU, HAWAII

GENERAL
T - TRACE AMOUNT.
BLANK ENTRIES DENOTE MISSING/UNREPORTED DATA.
# INDICATES A STATION OR INSTRUMENT RELOCATION.

SPECIFIC

PM - INCLUDES LAST DAY OF PREVIOUS MONTH
ASOS - AUTOMATED SURFACE OBSERVING SYSTEM IN OPERATION DURING THESE MONTHS.

(a) - LENGTH OF RECORD IN YEARS, ALTHOUGH INDIVIDUAL MONTHS MAY BE MISSING.
0.* OR * - THE VALUE IS BETWEEN 0.0 AND 0.05
NORMALS - BASED ON THE 1961-1990 RECORD PERIOD.
EXTREMES - DATES ARE THE MOST RECENT OCCURRENCE
WIND DIR.- NUMERALS SHOW TENS OF DEGRESS CLOCKWISE FROM TRUE NORTH. "00" INDICATES CALM.
RESULTANT DIRECTIONS ARE GIVEN TO WHOLE DEGREES.
BOLD VALUES INDICATE EXTREME VALUES WHICH OCCURRED AFTER THE ASOS SYSTEM WAS COMMISSIONED.

RECORD = PERIOD OF RECORD
RECORD MEAN PRECIPITATION IS THE MEAN OF ALL DAILY PRECIPITATION AMOUNTS DURING THE PERIOD OF RECORD.
RECORD MAX(MIN) TEMPERATURE IS THE MEAN OF ALL DAILY MAX(MIN) TEMPERATURES DURING THE PERIOD OF RECORD.
RECORD MEAN TEMPERATURE IS THE SUM OF THE RECORD MAX AND RECORD MIN DIVIDED BY 2.
AVERAGE TEMPERATURE IS THE SUM OF THE MEAN DAILY MAX AND MIN TEMPERATURE DIVIDED BY 2.

EXCEPTIONS

RECORD MEANS ARE THROUGH THE CURRENT YEAR, BEGINNING IN 1947 THRU 1964 AND
1970 TO DATE FOR TEMPERATURE
1947 FOR PRECIPITATION

HEATING DEGREE DAYS Base 65 deg. F — HONOLULU, HAWAII

SEASON	JULY	AUG	SEP	OCT	NOV	DEC	JAN	FEB	MAR	APR	MAY	JUNE	TOTAL
1983-84	0	0	0	0	0	0	0	0	0	0	0	0	0
1984-85	0	0	0	0	0	0	0	0	0	0	0	0	0
1985-86	0	0	0	0	0	0	0	0	0	0	0	0	0
1986-87	0	0	0	0	0	0	0	0	0	0	0	0	0
1987-88	0	0	0	0	0	0	0	0	0	0	0	0	0
1988-89	0	0	0	0	0	0	0	0	0	0	0	0	0
1989-90	0	0	0	0	0	0	0	0	0	0	0	0	0
1990-91	0	0	0	0	0	0	0	0	0	0	0	0	0
1991-92	0	0	0	0	0	0	0	0	0	0	0	0	0
1992-93	0	0	0	0	0	0	0	0	0	0	0	0	0
1993-94	0	0	0	0	0	0							

COOLING DEGREE DAYS Base 65 deg. F — HONOLULU, HAWAII

YEAR	JAN	FEB	MAR	APR	MAY	JUNE	JULY	AUG	SEP	OCT	NOV	DEC	TOTAL
1969	133	255	269	295	369	428	500	572	517	488	419	365	4610
1970	293	239	378	409	485	490	540	586	429	426	332	306	4913
1971	216	269	284	326	355	376	435	456	431	408	328	265	4149
1972	178	170	249	307	386	425	484	506	470	450	357	209	4191
1973	252	219	353	322	382	432	485	512	484	455	367	279	4542
1974	300	270	285	378	415	434	468	509	458	457	328	341	4643
1975	235	224	256	292	337	400	438	475	438	442	372	257	4166
1976	278	209	275	311	393	402	464	498	479	446	315	325	4395
1977	276	305	355	344	396	441	498	541	505	507	417	320	4905
1978	292	238	336	361	417	418	439	489	473	401	298	239	4401
1979	159	209	250	299	412	458	500	485	489	504	378	326	4469
1980	222	220	317	340	418	442	501	504	503	476	395	295	4633
1981	263	249	311	335	385	474	463	477	477	419	355	284	4492
1982	261	195	288	318	421	442	493	514	499	452	326	225	4434
1983	223	182	270	295	335	425	461	544	525	508	461	318	4547
1984	304	285	340	366	432	438	501	527	494	475	425	291	4878
1985	205	256	300	293	364	437	521	532	491	464	310	264	4437
1986	251	217	366	384	421	457	519	561	521	491	433	318	4939
1987	267	178	285	337	337	465	537	556	544	516	418	342	4782
1988	260	289	346	373	437	482	527	537	520	478	455	336	5040
1989	301	244	325	291	425	482	521	517	512	431	358	252	4659
1990	306	189	258	354	412	456	498	543	525	501	377	289	4708
1991	236	243	250	333	404	442	508	547	501	474	443	353	4734
1992	251	244	316	327	404	495	518	540	495	452	369	368	4779
1993	190	180	285	381	387	463	491	515	491	465	345	314	4507

SNOWFALL (inches) — HONOLULU, HAWAII

SEASON	JULY	AUG	SEP	OCT	NOV	DEC	JAN	FEB	MAR	APR	MAY	JUNE	TOTAL
1971-72	0.0	0.0	0.0	0.0	0.0	0.0	0.0	0.0	0.0	0.0	0.0	0.0	0.0
1972-73	0.0	0.0	0.0	0.0	0.0	0.0	0.0	0.0	0.0	0.0	0.0	0.0	0.0
1973-74	0.0	0.0	0.0	0.0	0.0	0.0	0.0	0.0	0.0	0.0	0.0	0.0	0.0
1974-75	0.0	0.0	0.0	0.0	0.0	0.0	0.0	0.0	0.0	0.0	0.0	0.0	0.0
1975-76	0.0	0.0	0.0	0.0	0.0	0.0	0.0	0.0	0.0	0.0	0.0	0.0	0.0
1976-77	0.0	0.0	0.0	0.0	0.0	0.0	0.0	0.0	0.0	0.0	0.0	0.0	0.0
1977-78	0.0	0.0	0.0	0.0	0.0	0.0	0.0	0.0	0.0	0.0	0.0	0.0	0.0
1978-79	0.0	0.0	0.0	0.0	0.0	0.0	0.0	0.0	0.0	0.0	0.0	0.0	0.0
1979-80	0.0	0.0	0.0	0.0	0.0	0.0	0.0	0.0	0.0	0.0	0.0	0.0	0.0
1980-81	0.0	0.0	0.0	0.0	0.0	0.0	0.0	0.0	0.0	0.0	0.0	0.0	0.0
1981-82	0.0	0.0	0.0	0.0	0.0	0.0	0.0	0.0	0.0	0.0	0.0	0.0	0.0
1982-83	0.0	0.0	0.0	0.0	0.0	0.0	0.0	0.0	0.0	0.0	0.0	0.0	0.0
1983-84	0.0	0.0	0.0	0.0	0.0	0.0	0.0	0.0	0.0	0.0	0.0	0.0	0.0
1984-85	0.0	0.0	0.0	0.0	0.0	0.0	0.0	0.0	0.0	0.0	0.0	0.0	0.0
1985-86	0.0	0.0	0.0	0.0	0.0	0.0	0.0	0.0	0.0	0.0	0.0	0.0	0.0
1986-87	0.0	0.0	0.0	0.0	0.0	0.0	0.0	0.0	0.0	0.0	0.0	0.0	0.0
1987-88	0.0	0.0	0.0	0.0	0.0	0.0	0.0	0.0	0.0	0.0	0.0	0.0	0.0
1988-89	0.0	0.0	0.0	0.0	0.0	0.0	0.0	0.0	0.0	0.0	0.0	0.0	0.0
1989-90	0.0	0.0	0.0	0.0	0.0	0.0	0.0	0.0	0.0	0.0	0.0	0.0	0.0
1990-91	0.0	0.0	0.0	0.0	0.0	0.0	0.0	0.0	0.0	0.0	0.0	0.0	0.0
1991-92	0.0	0.0	0.0	0.0	0.0	0.0	0.0	0.0	0.0	0.0	0.0	0.0	0.0
1992-93	0.0	0.0	0.0	0.0	0.0	0.0	0.0	0.0	0.0	0.0	0.0	0.0	0.0
1993-94	0.0	0.0	0.0	0.0	0.0	0.0							
Record Mean	0.0	0.0	0.0	0.0	0.0	0.0	0.0	0.0	0.0	0.0	0.0	0.0	0.0

BOISE, IDAHO

Boise is situated in the Boise River Valley about 8 miles below the mouth of a mountain canyon where the valley proper begins. Sheltered by large shade trees and averaging 2,710 feet in elevation, the denser part of the city covers a gentle alluvial slope about 2 miles wide, stretching southwest from the foothills of the Boise Mountains to the river. The Boise Mountains immediately north of the city rise 5,000 to 6,000 feet above sea level in about 8 miles, the slopes partly mantled with sagebrush and then chaparral giving way near the summit to ridges of fir, spruce, and pine. Across the river, the land rises in two irregular steps, or benches, for several miles, finally reaching the low divide between the Boise and Snake Rivers. Downstream the valley widens, merging with the valley of the Snake about 40 miles to the northwest. Once semi-arid, the entire area is now irrigated from the upstream reservoirs.

Although air masses from the Pacific are considerably modified by the time they reach Boise, their influence, particularly in winter, alternates with that of atmospheric developments from other directions. The result is almost a typical upland continental type of climate in summer, while winters are usually tempered by periods of cloudy or stormy and mild weather. Autumns have prolonged periods of near ideal weather, while springtime is noted by changeable weather and varied temperatures. The Boise climate in general may be described as dry and temperate, with sufficient variation to be stimulating.

Summer hot periods rarely last longer than a few days. Temperatures of 100 degrees or higher occur nearly every year.

Winter cold spells with temperatures of 10 degrees or lower generally last longer than the summer hot spells. During cold weather, however, there is ordinarily little wind to add to the discomfort.

The normal precipitation pattern in the Boise area shows a winter high and a very pronounced summer low. Total amounts and intensity are generally greatest near the foothills, dwindling to westward and southward.

Tornadoes are very rare as are destructive force winds. Northwesterly winds, drying and rather raw in character, although of moderate velocity, are common from March through May. Diurnal southeasterly winds, descending from nearby foothills at night, frequently have a moderating effect on winter temperatures. There is an occasional, but moderate, duststorm during the warmer months, usually occurring at times of cold frontal passage.

Relative humidity is low but widespread irrigation maintains humidity several percent above the general dryness of western arid conditions in summer. Thunderstorms occur primarily during spring and summer, with less frequency during fall and occasionally during winter. December and January are the months of heavy fog or low stratus cloud conditions. Only a moderate amount of sunshine is received in the average winter, but protracted periods of clear, sunny weather are the rule in summer. Ice storms are practically unknown.

Based on the 1951-1980 period, the average first occurrence of 32 degrees Fahrenheit in the fall is October 9 and the average last occurrence in the spring is May 8.

NORMALS, MEANS, AND EXTREMES

BOISE, IDAHO

LATITUDE: 43°34'N LONGITUDE: 116°13'W ELEVATION: FT. GRND 2838 BARO 2875 TIME ZONE: MOUNTAIN WBAN: 24131

	(a)	JAN	FEB	MAR	APR	MAY	JUNE	JULY	AUG	SEP	OCT	NOV	DEC	YEAR
TEMPERATURE °F:														
Normals														
-Daily Maximum		36.4	44.2	52.9	61.4	71.0	80.9	90.2	88.1	77.0	64.6	48.7	37.7	62.8
-Daily Minimum		21.6	27.5	31.9	36.7	43.9	52.1	57.7	56.8	48.2	39.0	31.1	22.5	39.1
-Monthly		29.0	35.9	42.4	49.1	57.5	66.5	74.0	72.5	62.6	51.8	39.9	30.1	50.9
Extremes														
-Record Highest	54	63	71	81	92	98	109	111	110	102	94	74	65	111
-Year		1953	1992	1978	1987	1986	1940	1960	1961	1945	1992	1988	1964	JUL 1960
-Record Lowest	54	-17	-15	6	19	22	31	35	34	23	11	-3	-25	-25
-Year		1950	1989	1971	1968	1982	1984	1986	1992	1970	1971	1985	1990	DEC 1990
NORMAL DEGREE DAYS:														
Heating (base 65°F)		1116	815	701	477	242	75	6	20	160	414	753	1082	5861
Cooling (base 65°F)		0	0	0	0	9	120	285	252	88	0	0	0	754
% OF POSSIBLE SUNSHINE	51	40	51	62	68	72	76	87	85	81	69	43	39	64
MEAN SKY COVER (tenths)														
Sunrise - Sunset	54	7.7	7.3	6.9	6.5	5.8	4.8	2.8	3.3	3.6	5.1	7.0	7.5	5.7
MEAN NUMBER OF DAYS:														
Sunrise to Sunset														
-Clear	54	4.5	4.5	6.1	6.5	8.5	11.5	20.4	18.4	17.0	12.1	6.1	4.9	120.4
-Partly Cloudy	54	5.0	6.4	7.3	8.8	9.9	10.2	7.2	8.0	7.0	8.2	6.3	5.7	90.1
-Cloudy	54	21.6	17.4	17.6	14.7	12.4	8.3	3.3	4.6	6.0	10.7	17.6	20.4	154.6
Precipitation														
.01 inches or more	54	11.8	10.2	9.7	8.3	7.8	6.1	2.4	2.6	3.7	5.9	10.1	11.1	89.7
Snow,Ice pellets,hail														
1.0 inches or more	54	2.4	1.3	0.5	0.2	0.*	0.0	0.0	0.0	0.0	0.1	0.9	2.2	7.7
Thunderstorms	54	0.*	0.3	0.6	0.9	2.8	2.8	2.5	2.5	1.5	0.6	0.3	0.1	14.8
Heavy Fog Visibility														
1/4 mile or less	54	5.8	3.3	0.8	0.3	0.2	0.1	0.0	0.*	0.1	0.5	3.0	5.8	19.9
Temperature °F														
-Maximum														
90° and above	54	0.0	0.0	0.0	0.1	1.3	5.4	18.3	15.2	3.3	0.1	0.0	0.0	43.6
32° and below	54	10.4	2.9	0.2	0.0	0.0	0.0	0.0	0.0	0.0	0.0	1.0	6.7	21.3
-Minimum														
32° and below	54	26.3	20.8	17.6	8.1	1.8	0.*	0.0	0.0	0.5	5.6	18.0	25.6	124.3
0° and below	54	1.8	0.4	0.0	0.0	0.0	0.0	0.0	0.0	0.0	0.0	0.1	1.1	3.4
AVG. STATION PRESS.(mb)	21	920.0	918.0	914.3	914.5	913.5	913.8	914.4	914.4	915.8	917.8	918.4	920.1	916.2
RELATIVE HUMIDITY (%)														
Hour 05	54	81	80	74	70	69	67	54	52	59	67	78	81	69
Hour 11 (Local Time)	54	74	68	55	47	44	41	33	33	39	47	65	74	52
Hour 17	54	70	60	45	36	34	30	22	23	29	39	60	71	43
Hour 23	54	80	77	68	61	58	53	39	40	49	60	75	80	62
PRECIPITATION (inches):														
Water Equivalent														
-Normal		1.45	1.07	1.29	1.24	1.08	0.81	0.35	0.43	0.80	0.75	1.48	1.36	12.11
-Maximum Monthly	54	3.87	3.70	3.46	3.04	4.07	3.41	1.62	2.37	2.93	2.25	3.36	4.23	4.23
-Year		1970	1986	1989	1955	1990	1941	1982	1968	1986	1956	1988	1983	DEC 1983
-Minimum Monthly	54	0.12	0.19	0.17	0.09	T	0.01	0.00	T	0.00	0.00	0.14	0.09	0.00
-Year		1949	1964	1992	1949	1992	1966	1947	1992	1987	1988	1976	1976	OCT 1988
-Maximum in 24 hrs	54	1.48	1.00	1.65	1.27	2.05	2.24	0.94	1.61	1.74	0.76	0.88	1.16	2.24
-Year		1953	1951	1981	1969	1990	1958	1960	1979	1976	1947	1971	1955	JUN 1958
Snow,Ice pellets,hail														
-Maximum Monthly	54	21.4	25.2	11.9	8.0	4.0	T	T	T	0.0	2.7	18.6	26.2	26.2
-Year		1964	1949	1951	1967	1964	1954	1970	1989		1971	1985	1983	DEC 1983
-Maximum in 24 hrs	54	8.5	13.0	6.4	7.2	4.0	T	T	T	0.0	1.7	6.5	6.7	13.0
-Year		1950	1949	1952	1969	1964	1954	1970	1989		1971	1964	1983	FEB 1949
WIND:														
Mean Speed (mph)	54	8.0	8.9	9.9	9.9	9.5	9.0	8.4	8.2	8.2	8.3	8.4	8.1	8.7
Prevailing Direction through 1963		SE	SE	SE	SE	NW	NW	NW	NW	SE	SE	SE	SE	SE
Fastest Mile														
-Direction (!!)	54	SE	W	W	W	W	SW	W	SE	SE	SE	NW	NW	W
-Speed (MPH)	54	50	56	52	50	50	50	61	56	50	56	57	56	61
-Year		1941	1954	1957	1942	1954	1948	1944	1963	1960	1950	1953	1950	JUL 1944
Peak Gust														
-Direction (!!)	10	N	W	NW	W	NW	NW	S	W	W	S	SW	SE	S
-Speed (mph)	10	59	45	48	58	49	54	71	54	43	43	54	44	71
-Date		1986	1989	1984	1986	1992	1987	1987	1984	1992	1992	1984	1992	JUL 1987

PRECIPITATION (inches)

BOISE, IDAHO

YEAR	JAN	FEB	MAR	APR	MAY	JUNE	JULY	AUG	SEP	OCT	NOV	DEC	ANNUAL
1964	2.46	0.19	0.64	1.35	1.76	2.00	0.41	0.53	0.70	0.21	2.33	3.19	15.77
1965	2.89	0.31	0.43	2.81	0.80	1.20	0.25	0.88	0.55	0.28	1.51	0.61	12.52
1966	0.81	0.73	0.60	0.61	0.32	0.01	0.06	0.01	0.19	0.29	1.60	1.41	6.64
1967	1.49	0.35	0.37	1.47	0.49	1.07	0.05	T	0.58	0.42	0.89	0.50	7.68
1968	0.43	1.86	0.71	0.35	0.40	0.60	T	2.37	0.10	0.70	1.50	1.95	10.97
1969	3.50	1.00	0.26	1.35	0.50	2.00	0.02	T	0.68	0.64	0.59	1.77	12.31
1970	3.87	0.30	1.04	0.93	0.73	1.72	0.28	0.10	1.00	0.81	2.03	1.37	14.18
1971	2.04	0.65	1.50	0.40	0.25	1.58	0.12	0.18	0.64	0.53	2.32	1.63	11.84
1972	2.15	0.91	1.50	0.62	0.32	0.90	0.21	0.05	1.11	0.64	1.11	1.79	11.31
1973	1.14	0.42	0.65	1.49	0.74	0.19	0.07	0.03	0.82	1.15	2.44	2.23	11.37
1974	1.35	0.66	1.50	0.67	0.10	0.60	0.53	0.22	T	1.45	0.67	1.71	9.46
1975	0.59	2.62	1.92	1.53	0.88	0.78	0.82	0.48	0.01	1.99	0.78	1.29	13.69
1976	1.49	1.31	0.72	1.60	0.46	1.66	1.15	0.95	2.11	0.52	0.14	0.09	12.20
1977	0.65	0.57	0.86	0.19	1.80	1.26	0.41	0.73	1.20	0.21	1.86	2.46	12.20
1978	2.37	1.50	1.43	2.34	0.36	0.56	0.48	0.24	0.89	T	1.06	0.60	11.83
1979	1.93	1.20	0.48	1.60	1.28	0.18	0.01	1.81	0.04	1.50	1.30	0.74	12.07
1980	1.56	1.29	2.14	1.20	3.77	0.58	0.03	T	1.59	0.30	1.26	1.49	15.21
1981	1.20	1.02	2.76	1.93	0.95	0.77	0.23	0.13	0.36	0.97	2.24	2.72	15.28
1982	1.42	1.54	1.39	0.79	0.39	0.35	1.62	0.19	1.38	1.74	1.10	1.92	13.83
1983	1.67	1.26	2.70	2.29	1.93	0.17	1.16	0.28	0.65	0.56	1.87	4.23	18.77
1984	0.80	0.86	1.43	1.62	1.06	1.47	0.23	1.24	0.69	0.85	2.36	0.63	13.24
1985	0.20	0.55	0.97	0.90	1.52	0.37	0.85	0.04	1.81	0.84	1.85	1.24	11.14
1986	0.98	3.70	2.01	1.55	1.10	0.35	0.17	0.07	2.93	0.33	1.00	0.12	14.31
1987	0.73	1.24	2.01	0.38	0.69	0.58	0.70	0.11	0.00	T	1.00	1.05	8.49
1988	1.30	0.43	1.45	1.80	1.33	0.47	0.02	0.09	0.24	0.00	3.36	0.81	11.30
1989	1.14	1.15	3.46	0.46	0.21	0.08	0.03	0.78	1.20	1.24	0.59	0.10	10.44
1990	0.84	0.79	0.77	2.14	4.07	0.11	0.42	0.39	0.50	0.45	0.61	0.98	12.07
1991	0.96	0.46	0.55	1.65	1.57	0.64	0.37	0.04	0.21	0.91	1.76	0.35	9.47
1992	0.36	0.92	0.17	0.66	T	2.07	0.03	T	0.30	0.90	1.37	0.89	7.67
1993	1.65	0.96	2.45	2.09	0.92	2.10	0.52	0.24	T	0.47	0.38	0.98	12.76
Record Mean	1.44	1.25	1.32	1.21	1.20	0.89	0.29	0.26	0.58	0.92	1.35	1.32	12.03

AVERAGE TEMPERATURE (deg. F)

BOISE, IDAHO

YEAR	JAN	FEB	MAR	APR	MAY	JUNE	JULY	AUG	SEP	OCT	NOV	DEC	ANNUAL
1964	26.0	26.3	37.6	45.3	55.1	62.5	74.9	69.2	59.6	52.9	36.9	35.2	48.5
1965	34.1	36.9	39.2	50.2	54.9	64.7	73.3	71.1	57.1	56.4	44.3	30.1	51.0
1966	32.4	33.3	43.2	49.2	61.5	65.0	73.2	72.1	66.2	49.4	43.0	31.3	51.6
1967	36.2	38.3	42.0	43.9	56.5	66.1	78.5	78.0	68.6	50.7	40.7	27.8	52.3
1968	29.5	41.1	45.9	46.3	57.8	67.9	77.3	68.7	63.0	52.4	42.0	35.1	52.2
1969	34.3	36.2	42.5	50.5	61.1	66.3	72.9	72.4	64.2	45.9	39.7	34.6	51.7
1970	36.2	41.2	41.4	43.8	57.5	68.9	76.3	75.8	57.8	47.5	43.2	33.5	51.9
1971	33.9	37.5	40.2	49.2	60.0	64.9	74.7	78.6	59.2	49.0	39.7	30.2	51.4
1972	30.9	36.5	45.5	46.7	60.6	67.6	73.5	74.5	58.8	51.7	40.5	23.8	50.9
1973	30.7	39.4	43.0	49.1	60.5	67.6	75.6	73.0	63.1	52.4	41.7	38.4	52.9
1974	29.4	38.7	42.6	49.7	55.4	71.7	73.8	71.7	65.3	52.2	41.7	33.2	52.1
1975	28.2	36.9	41.5	44.5	56.2	64.4	78.3	70.0	65.5	52.3	39.5	31.4	50.7
1976	32.2	34.2	37.1	47.3	59.3	62.6	73.1	67.7	64.1	50.8	40.9	29.3	49.9
1977	19.0	33.8	39.8	54.1	53.7	70.2	72.7	73.6	62.0	53.2	39.6	37.3	50.8
1978	37.0	38.2	48.7	48.5	54.3	64.5	72.8	69.9	61.4	52.8	36.7	27.0	51.0
1979	16.2	34.3	43.2	48.7	57.8	66.7	74.1	71.2	67.3	54.4	34.7	35.8	50.3
1980	30.3	39.8	41.1	52.6	57.2	62.6	72.9	67.2	62.6	51.6	39.8	33.1	50.9
1981	33.9	36.8	44.5	50.3	54.7	63.2	71.0	74.2	63.7	48.7	44.0	35.3	51.7
1982	24.8	30.0	41.3	45.2	54.9	65.8	70.1	72.7	60.4	50.9	36.0	31.5	48.6
1983	35.9	41.5	44.6	47.1	56.5	63.8	69.4	74.9	60.8	53.8	42.0	23.2	51.2
1984	21.2	30.2	41.9	45.9	54.8	61.7	74.2	75.5	60.1	46.9	39.1	22.9	47.9
1985	19.1	25.8	36.0	51.6	58.5	67.2	77.7	69.2	56.2	48.4	27.7	12.6	45.8
1986	29.4	41.0	48.0	48.3	59.1	72.0	69.6	75.9	57.4	52.6	40.4	28.0	51.8
1987	27.8	37.6	44.2	56.0	62.2	70.2	71.2	70.0	65.6	54.9	40.7	32.9	52.8
1988	26.1	37.8	42.6	52.7	57.9	70.7	74.6	71.6	61.7	59.9	40.7	27.0	51.9
1989	24.7	23.2	43.7	53.1	56.3	68.5	77.0	70.0	63.3	51.2	39.4	30.4	50.1
1990	34.2	34.1	44.3	54.7	55.7	66.9	76.2	74.0	69.9	51.0	41.2	18.1	51.7
1991	24.4	41.6	43.0	48.3	54.9	62.6	75.7	76.6	65.8	51.8	37.4	31.7	51.2
1992	33.1	42.1	48.9	54.9	64.3	69.8	71.4	73.9	63.4	54.4	34.5	28.5	53.3
1993	24.8	28.9	41.7	48.1	63.1	61.9	65.0	68.6	63.0	53.2	32.8	33.3	48.7
Record Mean	29.4	35.4	42.4	49.8	57.7	65.6	74.2	72.4	62.7	52.3	40.2	31.5	51.1
Max	36.7	43.5	52.5	61.8	70.8	79.4	89.9	87.8	76.9	64.8	49.2	38.7	62.7
Min	22.1	27.3	32.3	37.8	44.6	51.7	58.4	56.9	48.4	39.8	31.1	24.2	39.5

REFERENCE NOTES

BOISE, IDAHO

GENERAL
T - TRACE AMOUNT.
BLANK ENTRIES DENOTE MISSING/UNREPORTED DATA.
# INDICATES A STATION OR INSTRUMENT RELOCATION.

SPECIFIC

PM - INCLUDES LAST DAY OF PREVIOUS MONTH
ASOS - AUTOMATED SURFACE OBSERVING SYSTEM IN OPERATION DURING THESE MONTHS.

(a) - LENGTH OF RECORD IN YEARS, ALTHOUGH INDIVIDUAL MONTHS MAY BE MISSING.
0.* OR * - THE VALUE IS BETWEEN 0.0 AND 0.05
NORMALS - BASED ON THE 1961-1990 RECORD PERIOD.
EXTREMES - DATES ARE THE MOST RECENT OCCURRENCE
WIND DIR.- NUMERALS SHOW TENS OF DEGRESS CLOCKWISE FROM TRUE NORTH. "00" INDICATES CALM.
RESULTANT DIRECTIONS ARE GIVEN TO WHOLE DEGREES.
BOLD VALUES INDICATE EXTREME VALUES WHICH OCCURRED AFTER THE ASOS SYSTEM WAS COMMISSIONED.

RECORD = PERIOD OF RECORD
RECORD MEAN PRECIPITATION IS THE MEAN OF ALL DAILY PRECIPITATION AMOUNTS DURING THE PERIOD OF RECORD.
RECORD MAX(MIN) TEMPERATURE IS THE MEAN OF ALL DAILY MAX(MIN) TEMPERATURES DURING THE PERIOD OF RECORD.
RECORD MEAN TEMPERATURE IS THE SUM OF THE RECORD MAX AND RECORD MIN DIVIDED BY 2.
AVERAGE TEMPERATURE IS THE SUM OF THE MEAN DAILY MAX AND MIN TEMPERATURE DIVIDED BY 2.

EXCEPTIONS

RECORD MEANS ARE THROUGH THE CURRENT YEAR, BEGINNING IN 1900 FOR TEMPERATURE
1900 FOR PRECIPITATION
1940 FOR SNOWFALL

HEATING DEGREE DAYS Base 65 deg. F BOISE, IDAHO

SEASON	JULY	AUG	SEP	OCT	NOV	DEC	JAN	FEB	MAR	APR	MAY	JUNE	TOTAL
1964-65	0	62	166	370	835	916	951	781	793	435	317	82	5708
1965-66	7	30	234	266	613	1075	1004	884	668	467	172	97	5517
1966-67	7	18	68	476	654	1039	885	742	707	627	279	79	5581
1967-68	0	0	49	434	723	1146	1092	688	586	555	235	58	5566
1968-69	0	59	119	382	684	918	945	797	689	432	147	75	5247
1969-70	3	13	91	585	751	935	886	659	724	631	249	79	5606
1970-71	0	0	240	537	650	969	958	765	763	465	176	78	5601
1971-72	10	6	210	492	753	1069	1047	818	598	543	194	45	5785
1972-73	11	0	222	406	727	1270	1056	708	673	470	182	91	5816
1973-74	4	13	103	382	692	817	1099	728	687	452	304	42	5323
1974-75	10	11	53	391	689	983	1132	782	721	607	275	76	5730
1975-76	6	21	74	399	759	1035	1013	886	858	524	189	132	5896
1976-77	3	36	76	434	720	1097	1418	868	772	342	358	7	6131
1977-78	8	32	145	362	758	853	859	744	500	488	329	74	5152
1978-79	5	38	173	370	841	1171	1503	855	668	481	241	72	6418
1979-80	5	2	26	326	903	899	1070	725	736	367	257	133	5449
1980-81	0	41	104	409	750	983	957	783	631	432	315	97	5502
1981-82	15	5	137	497	624	915	1240	974	729	586	312	86	6120
1982-83	27	2	182	432	863	1030	897	653	622	530	309	82	5629
1983-84	38	0	145	338	682	1290	1353	1004	710	566	328	162	6616
1984-85	0	8	204	557	771	1299	1412	1093	895	398	226	53	6916
1985-86	0	26	259	509	1113	1619	1097	668	522	499	280	15	6607
1986-87	35	2	259	376	733	1141	1149	761	639	287	140	41	5563
1987-88	23	18	86	306	722	990	1198	780	686	359	261	59	5488
1988-89	4	5	157	178	724	1169	1242	1166	656	356	276	30	5963
1989-90	0	29	97	421	759	1064	951	858	633	303	286	82	5483
1990-91	6	10	26	430	710	1449	1252	651	676	493	306	100	6109
1991-92	0	0	55	409	822	1026	982	657	492	308	92	54	4897
1992-93	6	40	118	340	907	1124	1239	1004	715	501	140	155	6289
1993-94	53	45	124	367	960	975							

COOLING DEGREE DAYS Base 65 deg. F BOISE, IDAHO

YEAR	JAN	FEB	MAR	APR	MAY	JUNE	JULY	AUG	SEP	OCT	NOV	DEC	TOTAL
1969	0	0	0	0	32	121	256	251	75	0	0	0	735
1970	0	0	0	0	24	201	357	341	30	0	0	0	953
1971	0	0	0	0	31	81	320	435	42	2	0	0	911
1972	0	0	0	0	62	129	283	303	40	0	0	0	817
1973	0	0	0	0	51	177	341	269	51	1	0	0	890
1974	0	0	0	0	13	252	289	226	71	0	0	0	851
1975	0	0	0	0	10	64	426	182	96	11	0	0	789
1976	0	0	0	0	19	66	263	130	55	2	0	0	535
1977	0	0	0	20	10	170	255	306	61	0	0	0	822
1978	0	0	1	0	6	64	254	200	72	0	0	0	597
1979	0	0	0	0	27	129	293	199	101	3	0	0	752
1980	0	0	0	3	25	68	251	117	38	2	0	0	504
1981	0	0	0	1	3	52	205	296	101	0	0	0	658
1982	0	0	0	0	2	117	194	248	50	0	0	0	611
1983	0	0	0	0	55	50	180	313	26	0	0	0	624
1984	0	0	0	0	19	70	291	340	64	2	0	0	786
1985	0	0	0	2	28	125	402	165	4	0	0	0	726
1986	0	0	0	1	103	235	184	348	37	0	0	0	908
1987	0	0	0	23	61	202	223	180	111	0	0	0	800
1988	0	0	0	0	46	237	308	215	66	24	0	0	896
1989	0	0	0	6	14	140	376	191	56	0	0	0	783
1990	0	0	0	3	5	145	357	293	180	6	0	0	989
1991	0	0	0	0	0	36	337	368	85	6	0	0	832
1992	0	0	0	11	76	202	208	321	77	20	0	0	915
1993	0	0	0	0	86	68	61	162	71	8	0	0	456

SNOWFALL (inches) BOISE, IDAHO

SEASON	JULY	AUG	SEP	OCT	NOV	DEC	JAN	FEB	MAR	APR	MAY	JUNE	TOTAL
1964-65	0.0	0.0	0.0	0.0	7.3	8.7	18.4	0.4	0.4	1.3	T	0.0	36.5
1965-66	0.0	0.0	0.0	T	0.7	4.5	3.6	7.1	0.2	0.1	0.0	0.0	16.2
1966-67	0.0	0.0	0.0	0.1	T	9.0	2.0	1.9	0.3	8.0	T	0.0	21.3
1967-68	0.0	0.0	0.0	0.0	1.3	4.3	3.3	0.1	0.8	0.3	T	0.0	10.1
1968-69	0.0	0.0	0.0	0.0	1.3	11.4	14.4	5.5	1.3	7.2	0.0	0.0	41.1
1969-70	0.0	0.0	0.0	1.2	0.3	4.8	2.9	0.1	2.3	1.1	0.5	0.0	13.2
1970-71	T	0.0	0.0	0.3	0.1	4.4	4.0	2.1	1.6	T	0.0	0.0	12.5
1971-72	0.0	0.0	0.0	2.7	0.4	14.8	5.0	3.5	0.6	1.6	0.0	0.0	28.6
1972-73	0.0	0.0	0.0	T	T	12.6	7.3	0.3	0.6	T	0.0	0.0	20.8
1973-74	0.0	0.0	0.0	0.0	8.8	4.5	6.0	2.4	5.7	T	0.0	0.0	27.4
1974-75	0.0	0.0	0.0	0.0	0.9	4.6	5.4	6.3	2.2	2.6	0.9	0.0	22.9
1975-76	0.0	0.0	0.0	T	3.9	4.2	6.3	6.7	3.9	0.2	0.0	0.0	25.2
1976-77	0.0	0.0	0.0	0.0	T	1.1	7.2	3.5	2.9	T	T	0.0	14.7
1977-78	0.0	0.0	0.0	T	4.7	4.4	1.6	7.3	T	T	T	0.0	18.0
1978-79	0.0	0.0	0.0	0.0	0.2	3.1	11.9	4.3	0.8	0.2	T	0.0	20.5
1979-80	0.0	0.0	0.0	0.0	6.6	1.4	3.8	0.8	2.7	T	0.0	0.0	15.3
1980-81	0.0	0.0	0.0	0.0	3.2	1.7	3.6	0.7	T	0.5	0.0	0.0	9.7
1981-82	0.0	0.0	0.0	0.0	2.8	11.1	12.2	1.4	3.6	1.4	0.0	0.0	32.5
1982-83	0.0	0.0	0.0	0.0	2.1	6.4	1.6	0.9	T	T	0.8	0.0	11.8
1983-84	0.0	0.0	0.0	0.0	2.2	26.2	4.3	4.4	T	0.3	T	0.0	37.4
1984-85	0.0	0.0	0.0	T	0.2	7.7	2.6	5.3	1.5	1.0	0.0	0.0	18.3
1985-86	0.0	0.0	0.0	T	18.6	12.6	3.9	4.4	0.0	T	0.0	0.0	39.5
1986-87	0.0	0.0	0.0	0.0	5.9	0.9	0.5	0.6	T	0.0	0.0	0.0	7.9
1987-88	0.0	0.0	0.0	0.0	0.5	3.0	3.9	0.3	2.9	1.2	0.0	0.0	11.8
1988-89	0.0	0.0	0.0	0.0	2.5	10.8	8.0	0.7	T	T	0.0	0.0	22.0
1989-90	0.0	T	0.0	T	0.4	T	5.2	6.5	0.4	T	T	0.0	12.5
1990-91	0.0	0.0	0.0	0.0	0.1	15.7	1.5	T	1.2	T	0.0	0.0	18.5
1991-92	0.0	0.0	0.0	1.1	2.8	T	0.3	T	0.0	T	0.0	0.0	4.2
1992-93	0.0	0.0	0.0	T	3.6	5.7	14.6	10.4	0.2	T	T	0.0	34.5
1993-94	0.0	0.0	0.0	0.0	1.9	0.2							
Record Mean	T	T	0.0	0.1	2.2	5.8	6.8	3.6	1.7	0.6	0.1	T	20.9

CHICAGO, OHARE INTERNATIONAL AIRPORT, ILLINOIS

Chicago is located along the southwest shore of Lake Michigan and occupies a plain which, for the most part, is only some tens of feet above the lake. Lake Michigan averages 579 feet above sea level. Natural water drainage over most of the city would be into Lake Michigan, and from areas west of the city is into the Mississippi River System. But actual drainage over most of the city is artificially channeled also into the Mississippi system. Topography does not significantly affect air flow in or near the city except that lesser frictional drag over Lake Michigan causes winds to be frequently stronger along the lakeshore, and often permits air masses moving from the north to reach shore areas an hour or more before affecting western parts of the city.

Chicago is in a region of frequently changeable weather. The climate is predominately continental, ranging from relatively warm in summer to relatively cold in winter. However, the continentality is partially modified by Lake Michigan, and to a lesser extent by other Great Lakes. In late autumn and winter, air masses that are initially very cold often reach the city only after being tempered by passage over one or more of the lakes. Similarly, in late spring and summer, air masses reaching the city from the north, northeast, or east are cooler because of movement over the Great Lakes. Very low winter temperatures most often occur in air that flows southward to the west of Lake Superior before reaching the Chicago area. In summer the higher temperatures are with south or southwest flow and are therefore not influenced by the lakes, the only modifying effect being a local lake breeze. Strong south or southwest flow may overcome the lake breeze and cause high temperatures to extend over the entire city.

During the warm season, when the lake is cold relative to land, there is frequently a lake breeze that reduces daytime temperature near the shore, sometimes by 10 degrees or more below temperatures farther inland. When the breeze off the lake is light this effect usually reaches inland only a mile or two, but with stronger on-shore winds the whole city is cooled. On the other hand, temperatures at night are warmer near the lake so that 24-hour averages on the whole are only slightly different in various parts of the city and suburbs.

At the OHare International Airport temperatures of 96 degrees or higher occur in about half the summers, while about half the winters have a minimum as low as -15 degrees. The average occurrence of the first temperature as low as 32 degrees in the fall is mid-October and the average occurrence of the last temperature as low as 32 degrees in the spring is late April.

Precipitation falls mostly from air that has passed over the Gulf of Mexico. But in winter there is sometimes snowfall, light inland but locally heavy near the lakeshore, with Lake Michigan as the principal moisture source. The heavy lakeshore snow occurs when initially colder air moves from the north with a long trajectory over Lake Michigan and impinges on the Chicago lakeshore. In this situation the air mass is warmed and its moisture content increased up to a height of several thousand feet. Snowfall is produced by upward currents that become stronger, because of frictional effects, when the air moves from the lake onto land. This type of snowfall therefore tends to be heavier and to extend farther inland in south-shore areas of the city and in Indiana suburbs, where the angle between wind-flow and shoreline is greatest. The effect of Lake Michigan, both on winter temperatures and lake-produced snowfall, is enhanced by non-freezing of much of the lake during the winter, even though areas and harbors are often ice-choked.

Summer thunderstorms are often locally heavy and variable, parts of the city may receive substantial rainfall and other parts none. Longer periods of continuous precipitation are mostly in autumn, winter, and spring. About one-half the precipitation in winter, and about 10 percent of the yearly total precipitation, falls as snow. Snowfall from month to month and year to year is greatly variable. There is a 50 percent likelihood that the first and last 1-inch snowfall of a season will occur by December 5 and March 20, respectively.

Channeling of winds between tall buildings often causes locally stronger gusts in the central business area. However, the nickname, windy city, is a misnomer as the average wind speed is not greater than in many other parts of the U.S.

NORMALS, MEANS, AND EXTREMES

CHICAGO, OHARE INTERNATIONAL AIRPORT, ILLINOIS

LATITUDE: 42°00'N LONGITUDE: 87°53' W ELEVATION: FT. GRND 658 BARO 697 TIME ZONE: CENTRAL WBAN: 94846

	(a)	JAN	FEB	MAR	APR	MAY	JUNE	JULY	AUG	SEP	OCT	NOV	DEC	YEAR
TEMPERATURE °F:														
Normals														
-Daily Maximum		29.0	33.5	45.8	58.6	70.1	79.6	83.7	81.8	74.8	63.3	48.4	34.0	58.6
-Daily Minimum		12.9	17.2	28.5	38.6	47.7	57.5	62.6	61.6	53.9	42.2	31.6	19.1	39.5
-Monthly		21.0	25.4	37.2	48.6	58.9	68.6	73.2	71.7	64.4	52.8	40.0	26.6	49.0
Extremes														
-Record Highest	35	65	71	88	91	93	104	102	101	99	91	78	71	104
-Year		1989	1976	1986	1980	1977	1988	1988	1991	1985	1963	1978	1982	JUN 1988
-Record Lowest	35	-27	-17	-8	7	24	36	40	41	28	17	1	-25	-27
-Year		1985	1967	1962	1982	1966	1972	1965	1965	1974	1981	1976	1983	JAN 1985
NORMAL DEGREE DAYS:														
Heating (base 65°F)		1364	1109	862	492	235	35	5	19	84	391	750	1190	6536
Cooling (base 65°F)		0	0	0	0	46	143	259	226	66	12	0	0	752
% OF POSSIBLE SUNSHINE	13	46	47	50	50	57	67	65	63	58	56	39	44	54
MEAN SKY COVER (tenths)														
Sunrise - Sunset	35	6.9	6.9	7.2	6.9	6.2	5.9	5.7	5.7	5.8	6.0	7.3	7.2	6.5
MEAN NUMBER OF DAYS:														
Sunrise to Sunset														
-Clear	35	7.0	5.8	4.9	6.1	7.2	7.2	8.2	8.9	8.6	8.7	5.3	5.9	83.8
-Partly Cloudy	35	6.2	6.5	8.3	7.6	9.9	11.5	12.3	11.5	9.7	8.8	6.4	6.2	105.0
-Cloudy	35	17.8	15.9	17.7	16.3	13.9	11.2	10.5	10.7	11.6	13.5	18.3	18.9	176.4
Precipitation														
.01 inches or more	35	11.0	9.4	12.5	12.6	10.8	9.8	9.9	9.3	9.6	9.4	10.8	11.3	126.3
Snow,Ice pellets,hail														
1.0 inches or more	35	3.3	2.6	2.1	0.4	0.0	0.0	0.0	0.0	0.0	0.1	0.6	2.4	11.6
Thunderstorms	35	0.3	0.4	2.1	4.0	4.9	6.4	6.0	5.8	4.6	1.8	1.1	0.6	37.9
Heavy Fog Visibility														
1/4 mile or less	35	1.5	1.8	2.2	0.9	1.2	0.6	0.5	0.7	0.5	0.9	1.3	1.9	13.9
Temperature °F														
-Maximum														
90° and above	35	0.0	0.0	0.0	0.*	0.7	3.7	6.5	4.4	1.7	0.1	0.0	0.0	17.2
32° and below	35	17.7	12.7	4.2	0.1	0.0	0.0	0.0	0.0	0.0	0.0	2.0	11.6	48.3
-Minimum														
32° and below	35	28.7	25.3	21.3	7.7	0.9	0.0	0.0	0.0	0.2	5.2	16.7	26.5	132.4
0° and below	35	6.5	3.0	0.3	0.0	0.0	0.0	0.0	0.0	0.0	0.0	0.0	2.6	12.4
AVG. STATION PRESS.(mb)	21	993.5	993.9	991.2	990.4	990.4	990.3	991.6	992.8	993.3	993.4	992.5	993.5	992.2
RELATIVE HUMIDITY (%)														
Hour 00	35	76	76	76	72	74	75	79	81	81	77	77	78	77
Hour 06 (Local Time)	35	77	78	79	77	77	78	82	86	85	82	81	80	80
Hour 12	35	67	65	61	55	54	55	57	57	57	56	64	70	60
Hour 18	35	72	70	65	58	54	55	58	62	63	64	71	72	64
PRECIPITATION (inches):														
Water Equivalent														
-Normal		1.53	1.36	2.69	3.64	3.32	3.78	3.66	4.22	3.82	2.41	2.92	2.47	35.82
-Maximum Monthly	35	4.11	3.46	5.91	7.69	7.14	9.96	8.33	17.10	11.44	7.36	8.22	8.56	17.10
-Year		1965	1985	1976	1983	1970	1993	1982	1987	1961	1991	1985	1982	AUG 1987
-Minimum Monthly	35	0.10	0.12	0.63	0.97	0.30	0.95	1.18	0.51	0.02	0.16	0.65	0.23	0.02
-Year		1981	1969	1981	1971	1992	1991	1977	1969	1979	1964	1976	1962	SEP 1979
-Maximum in 24 hrs	35	2.00	1.90	2.39	2.78	3.45	3.09	2.90	9.35	3.00	4.62	2.99	4.53	9.35
-Year		1960	1985	1985	1983	1981	1967	1993	1987	1978	1969	1990	1982	AUG 1987
Snow,Ice pellets,hail														
-Maximum Monthly	35	34.3	21.5	24.7	11.1	1.6	T	T	T	T	6.6	10.4	35.3	35.3
-Year		1979	1967	1965	1975	1966	1992	1992	1989	1967	1967	1959	1978	DEC 1978
-Maximum in 24 hrs	35	18.1	9.7	10.6	10.9	1.6	T	T	T	T	6.6	5.8	11.0	18.1
-Year		1967	1990	1970	1975	1966	1992	1992	1989	1967	1967	1975	1969	JAN 1967
WIND:														
Mean Speed (mph)	35	11.7	11.5	12.0	12.0	10.5	9.3	8.3	8.2	8.9	10.0	11.1	11.0	10.4
Prevailing Direction														
Fastest Obs. 1 Min.														
-Direction (!!)	35	28	25	01	24	34	24	36	32	23	20	23	26	23
-Speed (MPH)	35	47	45	54	54	52	41	55	46	58	48	51	46	58
-Year		1971	1967	1964	1965	1962	1970	1980	1960	1959	1971	1958	1970	SEP 1959
Peak Gust														
-Direction (!!)	9	W	N	SW	S	S	S	W	W	N	SW	SW	SW	SW
-Speed (mph)	9	58	54	84	69	55	63	54	64	58	49	51	53	84
-Date		1989	1990	1991	1984	1988	1990	1992	1987	1989	1990	1991	1992	MAR 1991

PRECIPITATION (inches)

CHICAGO, OHARE INTERNATIONAL AIRPORT, ILLINOIS

YEAR	JAN	FEB	MAR	APR	MAY	JUNE	JULY	AUG	SEP	OCT	NOV	DEC	ANNUAL
1964	0.72	0.52	3.45	5.22	2.26	2.86	4.23	1.95	3.96	0.16	2.90	1.51	29.74
1965	4.11	1.18	3.06	3.48	2.36	3.44	3.66	6.40	5.03	1.57	1.47	3.32	39.08
1966	1.09	1.75	2.64	6.28	4.77	2.95	2.19	1.00	0.55	2.16	4.74	1.88	32.00
1967	2.22	1.82	2.30	3.97	1.61	7.94	1.87	2.60	2.45	3.89	2.19	2.41	35.27
1968	1.77	0.87	0.90	2.31	2.99	4.15	2.03	5.32	3.88	1.04	3.70	2.77	31.73
1969	1.62	0.12	1.93	4.02	3.17	7.76	3.43	0.51	3.01	6.55	1.11	1.18	34.41
1970	0.82	0.59	2.12	4.29	7.14	7.14	4.08	1.50	8.69	2.48	2.78	1.77	43.40
1971	0.93	1.94	1.54	0.97	2.23	2.62	3.57	3.97	2.39	0.72	1.32	5.37	27.57
1972	1.01	0.73	3.45	4.77	3.02	3.55	4.97	6.97	8.14	2.92	3.05	2.89	45.47
1973	1.24	1.38	3.91	4.99	3.69	2.87	5.27	0.67	6.01	2.86	1.50	3.71	38.10
1974	3.29	2.11	2.40	4.27	5.09	4.69	2.96	2.60	1.47	1.88	2.47	2.12	35.35
1975	3.69	2.48	2.02	5.50	3.02	5.07	2.19	7.37	0.80	1.90	2.53	3.05	39.62
1976	0.85	1.87	5.91	4.05	4.03	2.93	1.44	1.29	1.49	1.41	0.65	0.64	26.56
1977	0.55	0.71	3.67	2.62	1.88	5.12	1.18	5.39	6.07	1.36	2.05	1.96	32.56
1978	1.48	0.43	1.16	3.94	2.80	6.36	4.61	1.96	6.88	1.08	2.24	4.41	37.35
1979	2.81	1.02	4.49	4.92	2.58	4.63	2.19	7.57	0.02	1.49	2.80	2.58	37.10
1980	1.04	1.24	1.96	3.41	3.22	3.42	3.56	8.54	5.65	2.09	1.10	3.43	38.66
1981	0.10	2.35	0.63	6.14	5.85	4.46	4.50	6.60	3.25	1.80	2.46	1.05	39.19
1982	2.90	0.41	4.15	2.78	2.08	1.56	8.33	3.93	1.15	1.88	6.95	8.56	44.68
1983	0.66	2.06	3.56	7.69	6.26	4.11	4.25	2.08	5.41	4.41	5.87	2.99	49.35
1984	1.15	1.39	3.00	4.11	4.49	2.02	3.19	2.10	3.84	3.15	2.64	2.92	34.00
1985	1.48	3.46	4.73	1.48	2.79	1.97	3.75	3.90	1.82	4.98	8.22	1.49	40.07
1986	0.39	2.58	1.49	1.85	3.11	3.49	4.30	1.15	7.12	3.75	1.41	1.09	31.73
1987	1.67	0.99	1.59	2.34	2.21	2.19	4.19	17.10	0.94	1.59	2.77	3.77	41.35
1988	1.88	1.29	2.15	2.08	1.19	1.05	2.74	3.29	3.79	5.05	6.45	2.40	33.36
1989	0.82	0.77	1.67	1.37	1.59	2.01	5.89	7.31	3.91	1.49	2.16	0.46	29.45
1990	1.97	2.25	3.09	1.79	6.85	4.50	2.25	7.75	1.03	4.10	5.60	1.94	43.12
1991	1.41	0.62	3.54	4.00	5.20	0.95	1.32	2.81	2.51	7.36	3.59	1.71	35.02
1992	0.87	1.39	2.67	2.21	0.30	1.35	3.77	3.56	4.31	1.79	5.41	2.49	30.12
1993	3.83	0.82	4.52	4.57	1.83	9.96	4.45	5.74	4.47	2.19	1.52	1.00	44.90
Record Mean	1.62	1.37	2.74	3.58	3.22	3.76	3.68	4.12	3.69	2.54	2.87	2.29	35.49

AVERAGE TEMPERATURE (deg. F)

CHICAGO, OHARE INTERNATIONAL AIRPORT, ILLINOIS

YEAR	JAN	FEB	MAR	APR	MAY	JUNE	JULY	AUG	SEP	OCT	NOV	DEC	ANNUAL
1964	27.7	26.6	33.7	49.1	62.7	69.0	72.1	67.7	63.3	48.0	41.4	24.7	48.9
1965	21.4	24.3	26.6	46.6	61.7	64.9	69.4	68.0	63.8	53.2	40.3	35.3	47.9
1966	16.3	26.1	39.6	45.2	53.4	68.5	74.5	69.6	62.5	51.4	42.5	27.1	48.1
1967	27.7	19.8	36.5	48.4	53.8	69.8	68.4	66.2	61.7	52.9	37.3	30.3	47.7
1968	23.8	23.6	42.7	52.3	57.0	70.2	72.0	73.7	65.5	54.7	40.0	27.8	50.3
1969	21.1	29.9	34.4	50.8	60.4	64.3	73.0	73.9	65.3	51.8	38.3	28.0	49.3
1970	16.3	26.1	34.8	51.7	61.9	69.4	74.7	72.9	65.2	55.4	40.7	30.8	50.0
1971	18.9	28.2	35.0	48.6	57.2	73.5	71.5	72.0	69.7	61.7	41.7	34.2	51.0
1972	19.6	23.6	34.0	44.8	61.0	65.7	73.6	73.8	63.5	49.3	37.7	23.9	47.6
1973	28.2	28.7	44.0	48.1	54.8	71.1	74.7	74.6	66.0	57.9	41.9	28.1	51.5
1974	24.8	27.4	38.6	52.3	56.8	65.5	73.6	70.0	60.5	52.8	40.6	30.2	49.4
1975	27.3	26.2	34.1	43.3	62.3	70.5	75.5	76.3	61.4	55.8	47.2	31.5	50.9
1976	19.9	35.2	42.8	52.3	55.9	70.1	74.0	70.8	62.7	48.3	32.4	19.4	48.6
1977	10.7	26.9	44.9	55.0	67.2	69.3	77.5	71.9	66.0	51.5	40.0	24.2	50.4
1978	15.7	16.8	31.9	47.5	58.3	67.6	72.0	72.4	68.8	51.4	40.8	25.8	47.4
1979	12.5	16.2	36.4	45.5	59.3	69.2	72.0	71.0	66.1	53.3	40.6	33.7	48.0
1980	23.4	21.5	32.6	46.5	59.7	65.3	75.7	75.7	66.0	48.4	39.9	28.0	48.6
1981	22.6	28.0	37.6	51.8	55.3	69.8	72.5	71.2	61.7	49.1	40.8	24.9	48.8
1982	12.2	21.5	35.1	44.5	64.3	62.1	74.1	68.8	62.1	53.2	39.1	36.0	47.8
1983	26.3	30.5	37.4	43.4	53.2	69.7	76.7	77.3	64.6	52.8	41.1	14.3	49.0
1984	17.1	33.9	29.5	45.8	55.5	70.3	70.3	72.8	61.1	54.7	37.9	31.0	48.3
1985	14.4	20.4	39.4	52.6	60.2	63.6	71.4	69.2	65.4	52.5	37.8	17.0	47.0
1986	22.8	24.0	40.4	51.5	59.5	66.3	74.9	68.5	66.8	53.7	36.0	30.6	49.6
1987	25.9	33.9	40.8	50.6	63.4	72.4	76.7	71.9	65.1	47.3	43.9	32.2	52.0
1988	19.8	22.7	38.1	48.2	61.0	71.7	76.8	76.8	65.9	46.1	41.7	27.7	49.7
1989	32.4	19.6	36.6	46.8	57.8	67.5	73.9	71.4	62.0	54.0	37.7	17.4	48.1
1990	33.9	31.3	41.3	49.9	56.2	69.6	71.7	71.9	65.9	51.6	44.7	28.6	51.4
1991	20.8	31.0	40.4	52.0	65.6	71.9	75.5	73.6	63.7	53.2	35.2	30.3	51.1
1992	28.1	33.3	37.5	46.1	56.9	64.9	69.3	67.0	62.7	50.4	38.3	28.6	48.6
1993	26.2	24.4	34.2	45.0	59.7	66.4	74.3	73.3	59.2	49.5	38.7	29.8	48.4
Record Mean	21.4	25.8	36.6	48.5	59.2	68.3	73.2	71.8	64.3	52.5	39.8	27.0	49.0
Max	29.3	33.7	45.2	58.5	70.3	79.5	83.6	82.0	74.7	63.0	48.0	34.4	58.5
Min	13.5	17.9	28.0	38.5	48.0	57.2	62.7	61.7	53.9	42.1	31.5	19.5	39.5

REFERENCE NOTES

CHICAGO, OHARE INTERNATIONAL AIRPORT, ILLINOIS

GENERAL
T - TRACE AMOUNT.
BLANK ENTRIES DENOTE MISSING/UNREPORTED DATA.
# INDICATES A STATION OR INSTRUMENT RELOCATION.

SPECIFIC

PM - INCLUDES LAST DAY OF PREVIOUS MONTH
ASOS - AUTOMATED SURFACE OBSERVING SYSTEM IN OPERATION DURING THESE MONTHS.

(a) - LENGTH OF RECORD IN YEARS, ALTHOUGH INDIVIDUAL MONTHS MAY BE MISSING.
0.* OR * - THE VALUE IS BETWEEN 0.0 AND 0.05
NORMALS - BASED ON THE 1961-1990 RECORD PERIOD.
EXTREMES - DATES ARE THE MOST RECENT OCCURRENCE.
WIND DIR. - NUMERALS SHOW TENS OF DEGRESS CLOCKWISE FROM TRUE NORTH. "00" INDICATES CALM.
RESULTANT DIRECTIONS ARE GIVEN TO WHOLE DEGREES.
BOLD VALUES INDICATE EXTREME VALUES WHICH OCCURRED AFTER THE ASOS SYSTEM WAS COMMISSIONED.

RECORD = PERIOD OF RECORD
RECORD MEAN PRECIPITATION IS THE MEAN OF ALL DAILY PRECIPITATION AMOUNTS DURING THE PERIOD OF RECORD.
RECORD MAX(MIN) TEMPERATURE IS THE MEAN OF ALL DAILY MAX(MIN) TEMPERATURES DURING THE PERIOD OF RECORD.
RECORD MEAN TEMPERATURE IS THE SUM OF THE RECORD MAX AND RECORD MIN DIVIDED BY 2.
AVERAGE TEMPERATURE IS THE SUM OF THE MEAN DAILY MAX AND MIN TEMPERATURE DIVIDED BY 2.

EXCEPTIONS

RECORD MEANS ARE THROUGH THE CURRENT YEAR, BEGINNING IN 1958 FOR TEMPERATURE
1958 FOR PRECIPITATION
1958 FOR SNOWFALL

HEATING DEGREE DAYS Base 65 deg. F — CHICAGO, OHARE INTERNATIONAL AIRPORT, ILLINOIS

SEASON	JULY	AUG	SEP	OCT	NOV	DEC	JAN	FEB	MAR	APR	MAY	JUNE	TOTAL
1964-65	10	52	148	521	699	1240	1345	1134	1185	545	157	77	7113
1965-66	12	53	110	370	733	915	1502	1079	782	587	371	53	6567
1966-67	1	12	127	420	669	1170	1148	1257	878	491	362	19	6554
1967-68	39	53	160	395	827	1068	1274	1192	682	376	257	28	6351
1968-69	14	12	59	355	740	1146	1355	976	941	419	204	124	6345
1969-70	4	0	75	423	794	1138	1506	1086	929	418	168	44	6585
1970-71	2	0	85	302	725	1055	1422	1026	923	484	262	14	6300
1971-72	7	3	64	154	693	948	1405	1197	954	602	178	80	6285
1972-73	15	10	109	481	811	1269	1135	1012	645	503	311	0	6301
1973-74	0	0	72	244	687	1139	1240	1046	812	383	266	63	5952
1974-75	0	1	176	384	724	1072	1160	1078	951	643	152	30	6371
1975-76	1	0	147	303	531	1033	1392	859	681	411	285	17	5660
1976-77	0	9	119	522	973	1408	1679	1060	616	332	115	41	6874
1977-78	0	8	42	413	741	1254	1521	1346	1020	518	264	46	7173
1978-79	1	4	59	418	718	1206	1622	1360	879	580	233	30	7110
1979-80	16	19	62	382	722	967	1281	1254	995	558	198	83	6537
1980-81	0	3	71	511	746	1140	1308	1031	846	397	313	6	6372
1981-82	8	6	135	489	719	1236	1632	1213	922	608	93	118	7179
1982-83	7	37	152	372	772	891	1194	961	847	643	364	38	6278
1983-84	16	0	125	383	714	1568	1479	894	1095	575	300	18	7167
1984-85	19	1	189	320	807	1046	1563	1245	787	418	183	103	6681
1985-86	0	6	141	380	813	1480	1302	1142	765	417	202	74	6722
1986-87	3	29	64	343	863	1060	1205	866	742	432	162	14	5783
1987-88	4	19	74	541	629	1011	1396	1221	828	503	176	40	6442
1988-89	0	9	63	583	693	1149	1003	1265	882	540	261	43	6491
1989-90	0	5	131	344	813	1471	956	938	733	491	271	33	6186
1990-91	10	5	103	425	605	1120	1365	945	756	393	142	13	5882
1991-92	0	0	163	367	887	1066	1137	913	847	560	284	77	6301
1992-93	9	37	136	449	795	1122	1196	1133	948	595	184	69	6673
1993-94	0	3	185	479	784	1084							

COOLING DEGREE DAYS Base 65 deg. F — CHICAGO, OHARE INTERNATIONAL AIRPORT, ILLINOIS

YEAR	JAN	FEB	MAR	APR	MAY	JUNE	JULY	AUG	SEP	OCT	NOV	DEC	TOTAL
1971	0	0	0	0	27	275	213	228	213	59	0	0	1015
1972	0	0	0	0	64	106	289	289	72	0	0	0	820
1973	0	0	0	5	3	189	308	301	108	32	0	0	946
1974	0	0	0	10	21	83	274	162	48	12	0	0	610
1975	0	0	0	0	76	203	332	358	46	24	1	0	1040
1976	0	0	0	36	6	178	286	196	56	8	0	0	766
1977	0	0	0	39	191	178	395	229	76	0	0	0	1108
1978	0	0	0	0	60	132	227	243	181	2	0	0	845
1979	0	0	0	2	61	164	241	213	99	26	0	0	806
1980	0	0	0	10	43	101	338	342	107	2	0	0	943
1981	0	0	0	9	20	157	248	204	44	0	0	0	682
1982	0	0	0	0	79	38	295	161	69	14	0	0	656
1983	0	0	1	0	4	189	385	388	122	10	0	0	1099
1984	0	0	0	5	11	184	190	254	77	8	0	0	729
1985	0	0	0	53	42	71	204	142	158	0	0	0	670
1986	0	0	7	17	37	118	318	145	123	3	0	0	768
1987	0	0	0	6	116	241	377	238	83	0	1	0	1062
1988	0	0	0	5	59	247	373	383	96	1	0	0	1164
1989	0	0	2	0	44	121	282	207	48	11	0	0	715
1990	0	0	7	43	8	179	226	224	137	11	1	0	836
1991	0	0	0	11	167	226	334	273	132	10	0	0	1153
1992	0	0	0	1	40	79	152	106	75	4	0	0	457
1993	0	0	0	0	28	118	294	266	19	5	0	0	730

SNOWFALL (inches) — CHICAGO, OHARE INTERNATIONAL AIRPORT, ILLINOIS

SEASON	JULY	AUG	SEP	OCT	NOV	DEC	JAN	FEB	MAR	APR	MAY	JUNE	TOTAL
1964-65	0.0	0.0	0.0	0.0	2.3	11.1	11.7	11.5	24.7	T	0.0	0.0	61.3
1965-66	0.0	0.0	0.0	T	0.2	6.6	15.5	4.3	0.7	T	1.6	0.0	28.9
1966-67	0.0	0.0	0.0	T	0.5	8.4	25.1	21.5	8.8	3.4	T	0.0	67.7
1967-68	0.0	0.0	T	6.6	2.4	2.9	10.4	3.8	1.5	0.1	0.0	0.0	27.7
1968-69	0.0	0.0	0.0	0.0	0.7	10.9	3.7	2.3	4.7	0.0	T	0.0	22.3
1969-70	0.0	0.0	0.0	0.0	2.0	19.3	9.5	6.3	11.8	7.2	0.0	0.0	56.1
1970-71	0.0	0.0	0.0	0.0	0.2	2.7	10.0	1.4	8.0	0.8	T	0.0	23.1
1971-72	0.0	0.0	0.0	0.0	1.3	0.2	7.6	7.7	16.8	3.3	0.0	0.0	36.9
1972-73	0.0	0.0	0.0	0.1	0.9	11.2	0.5	9.3	3.4	0.2	T	0.0	25.6
1973-74	0.0	0.0	0.0	0.0	T	18.8	7.4	9.6	1.4	T	0.0	0.0	37.2
1974-75	0.0	0.0	0.0	0.0	1.0	9.4	3.5	8.2	4.5	11.1	0.0	0.0	37.7
1975-76	0.0	0.0	0.0	0.0	6.4	6.8	10.0	1.6	1.9	0.8	T	0.0	27.5
1976-77	0.0	0.0	0.0	1.6	0.5	6.5	7.2	4.0	4.9	T	0.0	0.0	24.7
1977-78	0.0	0.0	0.0	0.0	5.2	12.7	21.9	7.9	4.5	0.2	0.0	0.0	52.4
1978-79	0.0	0.0	0.0	0.0	5.2	35.3	34.3	6.8	2.0	0.1	0.0	0.0	83.7
1979-80	0.0	0.0	0.0	0.0	4.0	0.9	6.2	14.7	11.6	4.2	0.0	0.0	41.6
1980-81	0.0	0.0	0.0	T	5.1	9.7	2.0	15.9	2.3	0.0	0.0	0.0	35.0
1981-82	0.0	0.0	0.0	T	3.6	4.9	21.1	4.8	14.3	10.6	0.0	0.0	59.3
1982-83	0.0	0.0	0.0	0.0	0.4	2.1	5.0	8.9	9.0	1.2	0.0	0.0	26.6
1983-84	0.0	0.0	0.0	0.0	1.0	16.5	17.2	1.9	9.7	2.7	0.0	0.0	49.0
1984-85	0.0	0.0	0.0	0.0	T	6.6	18.9	13.3	0.3	T	0.0	0.0	39.1
1985-86	0.0	0.0	0.0	0.0	1.1	5.2	6.9	10.9	4.1	0.8	0.0	0.0	29.0
1986-87	0.0	0.0	0.0	T	3.8	0.4	17.3	T	4.7	T	0.0	0.0	26.2
1987-88	0.0	0.0	0.0	0.1	1.0	18.7	5.4	15.5	1.9	T	0.0	0.0	42.6
1988-89	0.0	0.0	0.0	T	0.9	5.0	0.4	15.1	2.0	0.6	0.5	0.0	24.5
1989-90	0.0	T	0.0	6.3	3.9	5.4	3.2	13.6	1.3	0.1	T	0.0	33.8
1990-91	0.0	0.0	0.0	T	T	3.2	11.1	3.3	5.9	T	0.0	0.0	23.5
1991-92	0.0	0.0	0.0	T	1.2	7.6	5.6	1.3	11.6	1.1	0.0	T	28.4
1992-93	T	0.0	0.0	0.3	0.2	5.7	15.2	8.0	13.8	3.7	0.0	0.0	46.9
1993-94	0.0	0.0	0.0	T	0.2	1.2							
Record Mean	T	T	T	0.4	1.9	8.3	10.7	8.1	7.0	1.7	0.1	T	38.2

PEORIA, ILLINOIS

The airport station is situated on a rather level tableland surrounded by well-drained and gently rolling terrain. It is set back a mile from the rim of the Illinois River Valley and is almost 200 feet above the river bed. Exposures of all instruments are good. The climate of this area is typically continental as shown by its changeable weather and the wide range of temperature extremes.

June and September are usually the most pleasant months of the year. Then during October or the first of November, Indian Summer is often experienced with an extended period of warm, dry weather.

Precipitation is normally heaviest during the growing season and lowest during midwinter.

The earliest snowfalls have occurred in September and the latest in the spring have occurred as late as May. Heavy snowfalls have rarely exceeded 20 inches.

Based on the 1951–1980 period, the average first occurrence of 32 degrees Fahrenheit in the fall is October 20 and the average last occurrence in the spring is April 24.

NORMALS, MEANS, AND EXTREMES

PEORIA, ILLINOIS

LATITUDE: 40°40'N LONGITUDE: 89°41' W ELEVATION: FT. GRND 652 BARO 683 TIME ZONE: CENTRAL WBAN: 14842

	(a)	JAN	FEB	MAR	APR	MAY	JUNE	JULY	AUG	SEP	OCT	NOV	DEC	YEAR
TEMPERATURE °F:														
Normals														
-Daily Maximum		29.9	34.9	48.1	62.0	72.8	82.2	85.7	83.1	76.9	64.8	49.8	34.6	60.4
-Daily Minimum		13.2	17.7	29.8	40.8	50.9	60.7	65.4	63.1	55.2	43.1	32.5	19.3	41.0
-Monthly		21.6	26.3	39.0	51.4	61.9	71.5	75.5	73.1	66.1	54.0	41.2	27.0	50.7
Extremes														
-Record Highest	54	70	72	86	92	93	105	103	103	100	90	81	71	105
-Year		1989	1976	1986	1986	1987	1988	1940	1988	1953	1963	1950	1982	JUN 1988
-Record Lowest	54	-25	-18	-10	14	25	39	47	41	26	19	-2	-23	-25
-Year		1977	1979	1960	1982	1966	1993	1972	1986	1942	1972	1977	1989	JAN 1977
NORMAL DEGREE DAYS:														
Heating (base 65°F)		1345	1084	806	408	183	11	0	9	54	356	714	1178	6148
Cooling (base 65°F)		0	0	0	0	87	206	326	261	87	15	0	0	982
% OF POSSIBLE SUNSHINE	50	47	50	51	55	60	67	68	67	64	61	43	42	56
MEAN SKY COVER (tenths)														
Sunrise - Sunset	50	6.8	6.8	7.0	6.8	6.4	6.0	5.6	5.5	5.3	5.4	6.8	7.0	6.3
MEAN NUMBER OF DAYS:														
Sunrise to Sunset														
-Clear	50	7.4	6.7	6.0	6.2	7.2	7.1	8.9	10.0	10.9	11.1	6.8	6.7	95.0
-Partly Cloudy	50	5.9	5.7	7.3	8.0	9.5	10.6	11.8	10.5	8.6	7.7	5.9	5.8	97.6
-Cloudy	50	17.7	15.8	17.7	15.8	14.3	12.2	10.2	10.5	10.5	12.1	17.3	18.5	172.6
Precipitation .01 inches or more	54	9.3	8.3	11.0	11.8	11.3	9.5	9.0	8.3	8.7	7.9	9.4	9.8	114.4
Snow,Ice pellets,hail 1.0 inches or more	50	2.2	1.7	1.4	0.3	0.0	0.0	0.0	0.0	0.0	0.*	0.6	1.9	8.1
Thunderstorms	50	0.6	0.6	2.7	5.1	6.7	8.3	7.9	6.6	5.0	2.5	1.3	0.6	47.9
Heavy Fog Visibility 1/4 mile or less	50	3.0	2.8	2.3	0.9	0.9	0.6	1.0	1.4	1.4	1.5	2.1	3.4	21.3
Temperature °F														
-Maximum														
90° and above	34	0.0	0.0	0.0	0.1	0.5	4.4	8.0	5.3	1.7	0.*	0.0	0.0	19.9
32° and below	34	16.9	11.5	3.7	0.1	0.0	0.0	0.0	0.0	0.0	0.0	1.9	12.4	46.6
-Minimum														
32° and below	34	29.3	25.4	19.5	5.8	0.4	0.0	0.0	0.0	0.1	4.6	16.8	26.6	128.6
0° and below	34	6.1	3.1	0.2	0.0	0.0	0.0	0.0	0.0	0.0	0.0	0.1	2.7	12.2
AVG. STATION PRESS.(mb)	21	995.4	995.1	991.8	990.8	990.7	991.0	992.3	993.4	993.9	994.4	993.7	995.1	993.1
RELATIVE HUMIDITY (%)														
Hour 00	34	78	79	77	72	75	77	82	84	82	78	80	81	79
Hour 06 (Local Time)	34	79	81	81	79	81	82	87	89	88	85	84	83	83
Hour 12	34	69	67	63	56	56	56	59	60	59	57	67	72	62
Hour 18	34	72	71	64	56	56	56	61	64	64	63	71	76	65
PRECIPITATION (inches):														
Water Equivalent														
-Normal		1.51	1.42	2.91	3.77	3.70	3.99	4.20	3.10	3.87	2.65	2.69	2.44	36.25
-Maximum Monthly	54	8.11	5.18	6.95	8.66	7.96	11.69	10.15	8.61	13.09	10.80	7.62	6.34	13.09
-Year		1965	1942	1973	1947	1957	1974	1993	1965	1961	1941	1985	1949	SEP 1961
-Minimum Monthly	54	0.22	0.33	0.39	0.71	0.82	0.60	0.33	0.25	0.03	0.03	0.43	0.33	0.03
-Year		1986	1947	1958	1971	1992	1988	1988	1992	1979	1964	1953	1962	SEP 1979
-Maximum in 24 hrs	50	4.45	1.92	3.39	5.06	3.62	4.44	4.22	4.32	4.15	3.70	4.32	3.38	5.06
-Year		1965	1954	1944	1950	1956	1974	1993	1955	1961	1969	1990	1949	APR 1950
Snow,Ice pellets,hail														
-Maximum Monthly	50	24.7	15.2	16.9	13.4	0.1	0.0	T	0.0	T	1.8	9.1	21.7	24.7
-Year		1979	1989	1960	1982	1966		1990		1992	1967	1974	1977	JAN 1979
-Maximum in 24 hrs	50	12.2	7.6	9.0	6.1	0.1	0.0	T	0.0	T	1.8	7.2	10.2	12.2
-Year		1979	1944	1946	1982	1966		1990		1992	1967	1951	1973	JAN 1979
WIND:														
Mean Speed (mph)	50	11.1	11.1	12.1	11.8	10.0	8.9	7.8	7.6	8.4	9.4	11.0	10.8	10.0
Prevailing Direction through 1963		S	WNW	WNW	S	S	S	S	S	S	S	S	S	S
Fastest Obs. 1 Min.														
-Direction (!!!)	8	30	31	25	36	31	30	26	01	29	27	20	06	20
-Speed (MPH)	8	37	37	46	37	35	44	40	33	35	31	48	46	48
-Year		1985	1990	1991	1989	1991	1987	1990	1987	1992	1985	1988	1987	NOV 1988
Peak Gust														
-Direction (!!!)	10	NW	NW	W	N	NW	NW	W	NW	W	W	S	NE	W
-Speed (mph)	10	53	53	68	69	61	63	67	54	75	48	62	59	75
-Date		1985	1990	1991	1989	1992	1987	1992	1990	1991	1985	1988	1987	SEP 1991

PRECIPITATION (inches)

PEORIA, ILLINOIS

YEAR	JAN	FEB	MAR	APR	MAY	JUNE	JULY	AUG	SEP	OCT	NOV	DEC	ANNUAL
1964	1.02	0.54	3.77	6.92	1.04	4.22	1.59	2.06	3.63	0.03	3.01	1.12	28.95
1965	8.11	0.93	3.40	5.58	3.85	1.04	3.31	8.61	8.17	0.69	1.22	3.35	48.26
1966	1.49	2.60	1.78	3.98	4.50	2.29	3.66	2.56	3.06	1.80	2.42	3.00	33.14
1967	1.08	1.07	2.33	5.47	2.80	2.03	5.74	2.34	2.72	5.56	2.18	2.63	35.95
1968	1.12	1.55	0.93	2.20	4.70	6.16	4.32	1.71	4.83	0.58	2.99	2.80	33.89
1969	2.43	0.56	1.20	2.94	2.37	4.93	5.55	2.82	3.31	5.67	0.79	1.13	33.70
1970	0.56	0.64	1.60	7.18	3.89	3.92	5.46	3.21	11.49	4.36	1.11	1.30	44.72
1971	0.59	1.64	1.09	0.71	2.80	0.98	5.21	2.19	3.07	1.71	1.43	4.96	26.38
1972	0.81	0.74	2.48	4.38	1.30	5.97	3.54	4.26	5.21	2.50	2.56	2.48	36.23
1973	1.76	0.99	6.95	4.26	4.51	6.46	6.04	0.90	7.58	5.18	1.48	4.11	50.22
1974	3.09	1.65	2.69	4.11	6.26	11.69	2.63	0.81	1.45	2.07	4.13	1.93	42.51
1975	2.59	2.85	1.73	3.92	5.19	3.90	4.26	5.62	2.74	3.63	2.75	2.04	41.22
1976	0.78	2.56	4.25	4.86	5.11	2.92	2.98	2.30	1.78	2.48	0.83	0.38	31.23
1977	1.22	0.95	4.41	1.24	3.54	2.06	3.43	7.28	6.26	4.00	1.77	2.25	38.41
1978	0.69	0.59	1.56	4.69	7.72	1.96	3.47	1.28	2.32	1.73	2.54	3.54	32.09
1979	2.48	1.37	4.42	4.48	1.96	1.77	4.81	0.87	0.03	1.70	2.76	2.33	28.98
1980	0.59	1.06	2.79	2.78	2.05	8.94	1.43	6.16	4.09	2.44	0.67	2.25	35.25
1981	0.48	2.41	0.92	5.71	5.77	6.22	7.08	5.61	1.31	1.37	1.64	1.24	39.76
1982	2.88	1.13	4.80	5.40	3.15	3.15	7.53	3.97	1.24	1.47	4.95	5.45	45.12
1983	0.53	1.01	2.84	7.06	6.66	4.48	1.99	1.09	5.08	3.01	5.58	2.65	41.98
1984	0.59	2.28	3.95	5.18	4.84	2.90	5.02	0.78	2.38	5.07	3.95	3.82	40.76
1985	0.99	2.62	5.77	1.14	3.14	5.11	3.43	3.70	3.43	4.61	7.62	2.24	43.80
1986	0.22	1.79	0.87	1.39	2.95	6.53	7.00	1.74	6.39	4.64	1.32	2.60	37.44
1987	1.49	0.84	1.98	1.84	1.69	3.27	2.90	4.02	1.62	0.73	2.88	4.15	27.41
1988	1.99	0.71	2.83	1.59	1.68	0.60	0.33	2.11	2.82	1.08	4.19	2.23	22.16
1989	1.00	1.17	1.14	4.39	2.23	1.28	2.22	2.86	2.87	1.57	0.93	0.87	22.53
1990	1.73	3.59	3.95	2.32	6.19	7.99	9.18	5.31	1.03	3.17	7.19	3.70	55.35
1991	1.19	0.57	3.67	2.97	5.94	1.50	0.35	3.41	3.59	7.31	3.57	2.06	36.13
1992	1.06	1.55	2.58	1.61	0.82	0.80	8.19	0.25	5.81	1.33	5.58	2.99	32.57
1993	3.55	1.68	4.08	4.89	3.25	5.70	10.15	7.38	7.56	2.42	2.22	1.19	54.07
Record Mean	1.75	1.77	2.82	3.52	3.91	3.87	3.88	3.10	3.69	2.50	2.41	2.08	35.29

AVERAGE TEMPERATURE (deg. F)

PEORIA, ILLINOIS

YEAR	JAN	FEB	MAR	APR	MAY	JUNE	JULY	AUG	SEP	OCT	NOV	DEC	ANNUAL
1964	28.7	28.1	36.0	52.2	66.3	72.7	76.2	72.4	65.4	50.8	43.5	25.7	51.5
1965	24.3	27.0	28.0	50.9	66.7	71.3	73.7	71.2	64.7	52.5	41.2	35.4	50.6
1966	19.5	27.8	40.7	48.1	57.1	70.4	78.4	70.3	63.8	51.3	42.6	29.2	49.9
1967	27.6	21.8	40.2	52.7	56.4	72.3	72.0	68.1	63.3	52.6	36.8	29.8	49.5
1968	22.1	23.7	43.0	52.4	57.7	72.4	73.2	73.8	64.3	53.9	40.4	27.6	50.4
1969	20.3	30.4	33.0	52.6	61.4	66.4	75.6	73.1	64.8	51.5	37.5	25.8	49.4
1970	15.1	25.9	35.3	52.2	64.2	69.8	74.9	72.3	65.8	53.6	39.1	29.9	49.8
1971	19.2	27.7	35.5	51.9	57.7	76.8	71.2	71.6	68.9	60.0	40.5	34.3	51.3
1972	19.7	24.5	36.9	48.9	63.2	68.0	73.2	72.4	66.2	50.0	36.2	23.8	48.6
1973	27.4	28.9	46.5	50.9	57.9	71.8	75.0	74.7	67.0	57.7	42.4	24.8	52.1
1974	23.1	29.4	41.1	53.6	59.3	66.7	76.9	72.2	61.1	53.6	39.6	29.9	50.5
1975	27.5	26.1	33.8	47.0	64.6	72.1	73.8	74.7	60.9	55.3	44.9	30.2	50.9
1976	19.5	34.9	43.9	54.1	58.2	70.5	75.3	70.3	63.3	47.3	32.0	21.0	49.2
1977	8.6	27.0	44.6	57.1	68.6	70.2	78.2	71.4	66.4	51.3	40.3	22.8	50.5
1978	13.3	15.4	32.4	51.2	60.3	71.3	75.0	73.2	70.5	52.1	41.3	26.8	48.6
1979	9.4	14.7	37.9	47.7	60.5	71.2	73.0	72.5	65.6	52.6	38.0	31.8	47.9
1980	23.6	19.9	35.6	49.2	63.0	69.3	78.5	76.9	67.9	49.6	40.7	28.9	50.2
1981	23.7	27.8	40.7	55.4	58.7	73.2	75.4	72.8	65.9	53.4	45.0	27.3	51.6
1982	15.8	24.8	37.7	46.5	68.4	67.2	75.7	71.3	64.9	55.0	41.5	37.4	50.5
1983	28.2	33.5	40.3	46.8	58.6	72.6	80.2	80.8	67.9	55.3	44.9	15.2	52.0
1984	20.6	35.5	31.3	49.6	58.8	74.3	73.0	74.9	64.0	57.6	40.3	33.9	51.2
1985	16.8	23.2	43.8	57.0	64.3	68.7	73.7	70.2	66.6	55.5	39.0	18.6	49.8
1986	26.6	23.5	43.2	55.4	64.0	72.3	77.4	68.9	68.9	55.2	36.2	30.9	51.9
1987	25.2	35.7	44.1	54.1	68.4	74.0	79.0	73.7	65.7	48.0	44.6	32.4	53.7
1988	22.7	23.5	39.9	51.1	65.4	73.1	78.6	78.5	68.2	48.2	41.5	29.7	51.7
1989	33.9	18.7	39.2	50.7	59.1	69.8	75.3	72.4	62.2	54.9	39.8	16.2	49.4
1990	34.8	33.7	43.4	50.0	57.8	71.0	72.6	72.1	66.1	51.9	45.2	27.7	52.2
1991	21.5	32.4	42.8	55.8	68.0	74.7	75.4	74.3	65.4	53.9	36.0	32.0	52.7
1992	30.1	35.6	42.3	50.0	61.0	69.7	72.4	68.6	64.2	53.1	39.8	29.5	51.4
1993	27.4	25.1	36.4	49.8	63.6	70.4	76.1	75.0	61.4	51.7	39.4	31.4	50.6
Record Mean	24.0	27.7	38.8	51.0	61.8	71.3	75.6	73.6	66.2	54.3	40.3	28.3	51.1
Max	32.1	36.0	48.1	61.5	72.7	82.2	86.4	84.3	77.2	65.2	49.1	35.9	60.9
Min	15.9	19.4	29.4	40.6	50.8	60.5	64.8	62.9	55.1	43.4	31.6	20.7	41.3

REFERENCE NOTES

PEORIA, ILLINOIS

GENERAL
T - TRACE AMOUNT.
BLANK ENTRIES DENOTE MISSING/UNREPORTED DATA.
# INDICATES A STATION OR INSTRUMENT RELOCATION.

SPECIFIC

PM - INCLUDES LAST DAY OF PREVIOUS MONTH
ASOS - AUTOMATED SURFACE OBSERVING SYSTEM IN OPERATION DURING THESE MONTHS.

(a) - LENGTH OF RECORD IN YEARS, ALTHOUGH INDIVIDUAL MONTHS MAY BE MISSING.
0.* OR * - THE VALUE IS BETWEEN 0.0 AND 0.05
NORMALS - BASED ON THE 1961-1990 RECORD PERIOD.
EXTREMES - DATES ARE THE MOST RECENT OCCURRENCE
WIND DIR.- NUMERALS SHOW TENS OF DEGRESS CLOCKWISE FROM TRUE NORTH. "00" INDICATES CALM.
RESULTANT DIRECTIONS ARE GIVEN TO WHOLE DEGREES.
BOLD VALUES INDICATE EXTREME VALUES WHICH OCCURRED AFTER THE ASOS SYSTEM WAS COMMISSIONED.

RECORD = PERIOD OF RECORD
RECORD MEAN PRECIPITATION IS THE MEAN OF ALL DAILY PRECIPITATION AMOUNTS DURING THE PERIOD OF RECORD.
RECORD MAX(MIN) TEMPERATURE IS THE MEAN OF ALL DAILY MAX(MIN) TEMPERATURES DURING THE PERIOD OF RECORD.
RECORD MEAN TEMPERATURE IS THE SUM OF THE RECORD MAX AND RECORD MIN DIVIDED BY 2.
AVERAGE TEMPERATURE IS THE SUM OF THE MEAN DAILY MAX AND MIN TEMPERATURE DIVIDED BY 2.

EXCEPTIONS

RECORD MEANS ARE THROUGH THE CURRENT YEAR,
BEGINNING IN 1905 FOR TEMPERATURE
1856 FOR PRECIPITATION
1944 FOR SNOWFALL

HEATING DEGREE DAYS Base 65 deg. F

PEORIA, ILLINOIS

SEASON	JULY	AUG	SEP	OCT	NOV	DEC	JAN	FEB	MAR	APR	MAY	JUNE	TOTAL
1964-65	2	8	108	435	637	1212	1254	1058	1139	416	72	1	6342
1965-66	0	18	100	391	707	914	1406	1037	746	502	260	22	6103
1966-67	0	10	106	419	666	1103	1151	1205	766	371	291	7	6095
1967-68	10	30	113	394	841	1083	1323	1192	673	371	229	13	6272
1968-69	5	7	68	377	732	1150	1377	962	984	367	172	73	6274
1969-70	0	0	77	443	818	1211	1545	1088	914	402	115	28	6641
1970-71	2	3	84	353	774	1080	1418	1035	906	402	241	0	6298
1971-72	17	5	85	186	728	945	1402	1167	866	475	150	42	6068
1972-73	9	19	87	461	855	1271	1161	1005	566	423	216	0	6073
1973-74	0	0	54	253	671	1237	1292	991	736	348	214	42	5838
1974-75	0	1	157	354	756	1081	1156	1085	959	534	92	17	6192
1975-76	13	1	171	306	596	1069	1404	868	648	351	221	5	5653
1976-77	0	9	106	556	981	1357	1747	1061	623	273	60	17	6790
1977-78	0	6	39	418	734	1301	1595	1383	1006	405	222	14	7123
1978-79	0	4	49	390	704	1174	1722	1403	833	510	194	10	6993
1979-80	3	19	70	401	804	1022	1279	1300	907	474	123	26	6428
1980-81	0	0	65	470	722	1112	1273	1037	748	295	221	1	5944
1981-82	1	0	60	360	594	1163	1520	1119	839	548	29	28	6261
1982-83	0	13	94	325	697	849	1133	875	758	537	206	17	5504
1983-84	2	0	92	311	595	1541	1371	849	1038	467	206	1	6473
1984-85	1	1	153	246	734	956	1489	1164	656	284	71	38	5793
1985-86	0	6	111	287	774	1432	1184	1156	683	314	92	7	6046
1986-87	0	26	37	305	858	1048	1228	814	640	340	53	2	5351
1987-88	0	16	68	520	609	1001	1306	1198	772	409	64	12	5975
1988-89	0	4	38	517	698	1090	958	1290	796	442	231	25	6089
1989-90	0	3	134	317	749	1509	929	871	672	475	226	16	5901
1990-91	8	3	99	409	589	1148	1341	909	683	285	86	0	5560
1991-92	0	0	143	347	863	1017	1078	847	698	444	180	19	5636
1992-93	0	23	109	367	748	1094	1159	1110	878	450	96	48	6082
1993-94	0	0	135	408	761	1035							

COOLING DEGREE DAYS Base 65 deg. F

PEORIA, ILLINOIS

YEAR	JAN	FEB	MAR	APR	MAY	JUNE	JULY	AUG	SEP	OCT	NOV	DEC	TOTAL
1969	0	0	0	0	67	122	334	260	80	30	0	0	893
1970	0	0	0	24	99	178	317	239	109	6	0	0	972
1971	0	0	0	14	22	359	217	214	210	37	0	0	1073
1972	0	0	0	0	103	140	273	253	130	3	0	0	902
1973	0	0	0	7	3	211	315	306	121	35	0	0	998
1974	0	0	0	12	43	99	377	233	47	6	0	0	817
1975	0	0	0	0	83	237	292	307	55	14	0	0	988
1976	0	0	0	28	14	176	326	180	62	14	0	0	800
1977	0	0	0	42	176	179	416	209	88	0	0	0	1110
1978	0	0	0	0	81	208	316	267	221	0	0	0	1093
1979	0	0	0	0	62	206	259	258	95	23	0	0	903
1980	0	0	0	6	70	160	425	378	156	1	0	0	1196
1981	0	0	0	13	33	250	331	250	93	6	1	0	977
1982	0	0	0	0	141	101	338	215	96	26	0	0	917
1983	0	0	0	0	14	250	479	494	188	17	0	0	1442
1984	0	0	0	12	24	285	256	315	129	22	0	0	1043
1985	0	0	3	48	54	155	279	173	164	0	0	0	876
1986	0	0	15	30	68	234	392	157	161	6	0	0	1063
1987	0	0	0	19	166	278	440	293	92	0	3	0	1291
1988	0	0	0	2	84	266	431	428	140	5	0	0	1356
1989	0	0	2	20	56	177	324	240	57	11	0	0	887
1990	0	0	9	34	8	204	251	230	138	9	0	0	883
1991	0	0	4	16	189	296	331	293	159	11	0	0	1299
1992	0	0	0	1	62	171	237	140	90	6	0	0	707
1993	0	0	0	2	60	218	350	321	33	6	0	0	990

SNOWFALL (inches)

PEORIA, ILLINOIS

SEASON	JULY	AUG	SEP	OCT	NOV	DEC	JAN	FEB	MAR	APR	MAY	JUNE	TOTAL
1964-65	0.0	0.0	0.0	0.0	1.0	7.2	5.5	5.8	13.5	0.0	0.0	0.0	33.0
1965-66	0.0	0.0	0.0	0.0	0.1	4.2	0.6	2.0	0.8	T	0.1	0.0	7.8
1966-67	0.0	0.0	0.0	0.0	T	3.8	10.0	3.6	2.7	1.4	0.0	0.0	21.5
1967-68	0.0	0.0	0.0	1.8	2.5	2.2	8.4	1.6	1.1	T	0.0	0.0	17.6
1968-69	0.0	0.0	0.0	0.0	1.5	4.6	4.6	2.2	4.1	0.0	0.0	0.0	17.0
1969-70	0.0	0.0	0.0	0.0	0.6	11.0	7.3	5.9	8.3	4.6	0.0	0.0	37.7
1970-71	0.0	0.0	0.0	0.0	T	3.4	5.4	0.6	5.8	0.0	0.0	0.0	15.2
1971-72	0.0	0.0	0.0	0.0	4.0	T	10.2	6.2	8.0	0.9	0.0	0.0	29.3
1972-73	0.0	0.0	0.0	0.3	7.3	4.7	0.8	2.7	1.2	0.7	0.0	0.0	17.7
1973-74	0.0	0.0	0.0	0.0	0.1	18.9	6.7	1.9	0.9	1.2	0.0	0.0	29.7
1974-75	0.0	0.0	0.0	0.0	9.1	6.2	8.8	12.8	3.8	1.6	0.0	0.0	42.3
1975-76	0.0	0.0	0.0	0.0	8.1	1.4	8.6	2.5	2.0	0.0	0.0	0.0	22.6
1976-77	0.0	0.0	0.0	T	0.4	4.1	16.3	4.1	2.4	1.4	0.0	0.0	28.7
1977-78	0.0	0.0	0.0	0.0	6.4	21.7	7.0	7.0	5.0	0.0	0.0	0.0	47.1
1978-79	0.0	0.0	0.0	0.0	2.6	14.2	24.7	3.6	6.5	T	0.0	0.0	51.6
1979-80	0.0	0.0	0.0	0.0	0.8	0.1	3.7	11.3	5.3	6.3	0.0	0.0	27.5
1980-81	0.0	0.0	0.0	T	4.1	3.3	5.9	10.5	T	0.0	0.0	0.0	23.8
1981-82	0.0	0.0	0.0	0.0	0.1	9.8	11.0	6.1	6.5	13.4	0.0	0.0	46.9
1982-83	0.0	0.0	0.0	0.0	0.9	2.0	5.6	4.8	5.7	0.1	0.0	0.0	19.1
1983-84	0.0	0.0	0.0	0.0	3.3	15.9	6.9	4.1	6.0	0.0	0.0	0.0	36.2
1984-85	0.0	0.0	0.0	0.0	T	0.9	9.8	6.2	T	T	0.0	0.0	16.9
1985-86	0.0	0.0	0.0	0.0	1.0	6.2	1.3	13.9	0.4	0.1	0.0	0.0	22.9
1986-87	0.0	0.0	0.0	0.0	1.0	T	18.0	0.1	T	0.0	0.0	0.0	19.1
1987-88	0.0	0.0	0.0	T	0.3	9.8	1.9	9.7	1.9	0.0	0.0	0.0	23.6
1988-89	0.0	0.0	0.0	0.0	0.7	4.7	0.3	15.2	T	0.9	T	0.0	21.8
1989-90	0.0	0.0	0.0	0.6	T	10.5	4.8	6.2	T	T	0.0	0.0	22.1
1990-91	T	0.0	0.0	T	T	3.8	9.8	1.0	6.9	0.0	0.0	0.0	21.5
1991-92	0.0	0.0	0.0	T	3.6	5.1	6.4	0.4	4.1	T	0.0	0.0	19.6
1992-93	0.0	0.0	T	T	0.7	6.1	6.8	12.4	3.5	0.7	0.0	0.0	30.2
1993-94	0.0	0.0	0.0	T	3.6	2.4							
Record Mean	T	0.0	T	0.1	2.1	5.9	6.6	5.4	4.1	0.9	T	0.0	25.0

SPRINGFIELD, ILLINOIS

The location of Springfield near the center of North America gives it a typical continental climate with warm summers and fairly cold winters. The surrounding country is nearly level. There are no large hills in the vicinity, but rolling terrain is found near the Sangamon River and Spring Creek.

Monthly temperatures range from the upper 20s for January to the upper 70s for July. Considerable variation may take place within the seasons. Temperatures of 70 degrees or higher may occur in winter and temperatures near 50 degrees are sometimes recorded during the summer months.

There are no wet and dry seasons. Monthly precipitation ranges from a little over 4 inches in May and June to about 2 inches in January. There is some variation in rainfall totals from year to year. Thunderstorms are common during hot weather, and these are sometimes locally severe with brief but heavy showers. The average year has about fifty thunderstorms of which two-thirds occur during the months of May through August. Damaging hail accompanies only a few of the thunderstorms and the areas affected are usually small.

Sunshine is particularly abundant during the summer months when days are long and not very cloudy. January is the cloudiest month, with only about a third as much sunshine as July or August. March is the windiest month, and August the month with the least wind. Velocities of more than 40 mph are not unusual for brief periods in most months of the year. The prevailing wind direction is southerly during most of the year with northwesterly winds during the late fall and early spring months.

An overall description of the climate of Springfield would be one indicating pleasant conditions with sharp seasonal changes, but no extended periods of severely cold weather. Summer weather is often uncomfortably warm and humid.

Based on the 1951–1980 period, the average first occurrence of 32 degrees Fahrenheit in the fall is October 19 and the average last occurrence in the spring is April 17.

NORMALS, MEANS, AND EXTREMES

SPRINGFIELD, ILLINOIS

LATITUDE: 39°50'N LONGITUDE: 89°40' W ELEVATION: FT. GRND 588 BARO 597 TIME ZONE: CENTRAL WBAN: 93822

	(a)	JAN	FEB	MAR	APR	MAY	JUNE	JULY	AUG	SEP	OCT	NOV	DEC	YEAR
TEMPERATURE °F:														
Normals														
-Daily Maximum		32.5	37.2	50.0	63.9	74.7	83.9	86.9	84.2	78.7	66.8	51.7	37.3	62.3
-Daily Minimum		15.9	20.2	31.6	42.5	52.3	61.9	66.1	63.3	55.9	44.4	34.0	21.9	42.5
-Monthly		24.2	28.7	40.8	53.2	63.5	72.9	76.5	73.7	67.3	55.6	42.9	29.7	52.4
Extremes														
-Record Highest	46	71	74	87	90	95	103	112	103	101	93	83	74	112
-Year		1950	1972	1981	1986	1967	1954	1954	1964	1984	1954	1950	1984	JUL 1954
-Record Lowest	46	-21	-22	-12	19	28	40	48	43	32	17	-3	-21	-22
-Year		1985	1963	1960	1982	1966	1966	1975	1986	1984	1952	1964	1989	FEB 1963
NORMAL DEGREE DAYS:														
Heating (base 65°F)		1265	1016	750	361	166	7	0	8	44	314	663	1094	5688
Cooling (base 65°F)		0	0	0	7	120	244	357	278	113	22	0	0	1141
% OF POSSIBLE SUNSHINE	45	49	51	51	56	64	68	71	70	68	63	48	44	59
MEAN SKY COVER (tenths)														
Sunrise - Sunset	46	6.7	6.6	7.0	6.6	6.1	5.8	5.4	5.3	5.1	5.2	6.6	6.9	6.1
MEAN NUMBER OF DAYS:														
Sunrise to Sunset														
-Clear	46	7.3	7.2	6.4	7.0	8.0	8.5	9.9	10.9	11.8	12.0	7.8	7.0	103.9
-Partly Cloudy	46	6.5	5.7	6.9	7.8	9.4	9.3	10.7	10.0	7.9	7.2	6.2	6.3	93.9
-Cloudy	46	17.2	15.3	17.7	15.2	13.6	12.2	10.4	10.1	10.4	11.7	16.0	17.7	167.5
Precipitation														
.01 inches or more	46	9.1	8.7	11.9	11.6	10.4	9.7	9.0	8.3	8.3	7.7	9.5	9.9	114.1
Snow,Ice pellets,hail														
1.0 inches or more	46	1.8	1.8	1.3	0.3	0.0	0.0	0.0	0.0	0.0	0.0	0.5	1.6	7.3
Thunderstorms	46	0.5	0.8	2.6	5.4	6.8	7.9	8.7	6.8	4.5	2.4	1.5	0.6	48.5
Heavy Fog Visibility														
1/4 mile or less	46	2.6	2.7	1.9	0.9	0.8	0.3	0.7	1.1	1.1	1.0	1.6	2.5	17.1
Temperature °F														
-Maximum														
90° and above	34	0.0	0.0	0.0	0.*	1.6	7.1	10.5	6.7	3.1	0.1	0.0	0.0	29.2
32° and below	34	14.5	9.4	2.5	0.*	0.0	0.0	0.0	0.0	0.0	0.0	1.2	9.5	37.1
-Minimum														
32° and below	34	28.0	23.5	16.9	4.2	0.1	0.0	0.0	0.0	0.*	3.7	14.6	25.1	116.1
0° and below	34	4.5	2.4	0.1	0.0	0.0	0.0	0.0	0.0	0.0	0.0	0.*	1.9	9.0
AVG. STATION PRESS.(mb)	20	997.6	996.9	993.4	992.4	992.2	992.3	993.7	994.8	995.5	996.2	995.6	997.0	994.8
RELATIVE HUMIDITY (%)														
Hour 00	34	78	78	77	73	76	77	81	84	82	77	79	81	79
Hour 06 (Local Time)	34	79	81	82	80	80	82	85	89	89	83	83	83	83
Hour 12	34	68	68	64	56	54	54	58	60	56	54	65	72	61
Hour 18	34	72	71	65	56	55	55	60	64	63	62	70	76	64
PRECIPITATION (inches):														
Water Equivalent														
-Normal		1.51	1.77	3.24	3.68	3.62	3.43	3.52	3.29	3.33	2.60	2.53	2.73	35.25
-Maximum Monthly	46	5.67	4.89	7.89	9.91	8.84	9.22	10.76	8.37	8.57	6.41	6.94	8.94	10.76
-Year		1949	1990	1973	1964	1990	1990	1981	1981	1986	1991	1985	1982	JUL 1981
-Minimum Monthly	46	0.04	0.51	0.63	0.73	0.52	0.23	0.91	0.46	T	0.16	0.43	0.15	T
-Year		1986	1958	1956	1971	1992	1959	1974	1992	1979	1964	1949	1955	SEP 1979
-Maximum in 24 hrs	46	2.78	2.54	2.84	4.45	3.95	4.73	4.43	4.79	5.12	3.51	2.46	6.12	6.12
-Year		1975	1990	1972	1979	1990	1958	1981	1956	1959	1973	1964	1982	DEC 1982
Snow,Ice pellets,hail														
-Maximum Monthly	46	21.1	16.0	20.3	7.3	T	0.0	0.0	0.0	0.0	0.3	9.2	22.7	22.7
-Year		1977	1993	1960	1980	1989					1989	1951	1973	DEC 1973
-Maximum in 24 hrs	46	8.8	10.3	8.2	6.1	T	0.0	0.0	0.0	0.0	0.3	8.0	10.9	10.9
-Year		1964	1965	1978	1980	1989					1989	1951	1973	DEC 1973
WIND:														
Mean Speed (mph)	46	12.5	12.3	13.5	13.1	11.2	9.7	8.4	7.9	9.0	10.4	12.4	12.4	11.1
Prevailing Direction through 1963		NW	NW	NW	S	SSW	SSW	SSW	SSW	SSW	S	S	S	SSW
Fastest Obs. 1 Min.														
-Direction (!!)	14	28	17	24	24	23	28	15	29	18	24	24	25	24
-Speed (MPH)	14	35	33	56	46	39	41	35	41	39	38	46	36	56
-Year		1990	1988	1991	1988	1987	1993	1992	1987	1988	1983	1988	1990	MAR 1991
Peak Gust														
-Direction (!!)	10	W	NW	SW	SW	NE	N	SE	W	NE	SW	SW	S	SW
-Speed (mph)	10	51	49	71	63	67	59	60	69	54	53	58	60	71
-Date		1990	1990	1991	1984	1990	1993	1992	1987	1989	1988	1988	1984	MAR 1991

PRECIPITATION (inches)

SPRINGFIELD, ILLINOIS

YEAR	JAN	FEB	MAR	APR	MAY	JUNE	JULY	AUG	SEP	OCT	NOV	DEC	ANNUAL
1964	1.64	1.27	4.00	9.91	1.82	2.26	1.32	2.20	1.24	0.16	4.19	1.01	31.02
1965	3.17	1.88	2.62	4.59	1.67	6.54	2.05	5.90	6.43	0.85	0.89	2.49	39.08
1966	0.36	2.20	1.04	5.75	3.54	1.35	0.96	2.71	4.72	2.37	3.08	2.62	30.70
1967	2.41	0.91	2.61	2.11	4.42	2.54	3.39	2.51	4.03	4.20	1.18	6.00	36.31
1968	1.79	1.15	1.25	2.44	5.69	3.25	4.67	0.99	3.29	1.43	3.08	2.64	31.67
1969	2.50	1.96	2.00	5.35	0.96	2.68	4.60	2.34	3.97	5.80	1.13	1.39	34.68
1970	0.54	0.67	1.99	9.10	2.26	4.68	2.55	4.20	7.73	2.50	0.70	1.33	38.25
1971	1.24	2.36	1.18	0.73	3.59	0.96	5.96	1.06	3.76	0.99	1.41	4.38	27.62
1972	1.03	0.82	4.03	3.35	1.88	2.72	1.70	4.52	3.95	1.40	3.27	3.36	32.03
1973	1.31	0.84	7.89	5.29	2.62	7.29	3.36	1.66	3.28	5.46	1.43	3.86	44.29
1974	2.61	3.15	3.39	3.11	6.37	5.00	0.91	7.70	2.17	1.39	3.58	1.44	40.82
1975	4.28	3.63	1.91	2.89	5.90	4.38	2.71	3.34	2.84	1.37	2.50	1.91	37.66
1976	0.98	3.67	5.60	1.07	1.96	1.41	2.29	2.33	2.20	3.00	0.53	0.66	25.70
1977	1.51	1.21	5.09	2.78	5.78	4.26	1.16	5.95	5.94	5.16	1.63	2.24	42.71
1978	0.72	0.83	4.20	2.84	5.81	1.73	2.99	4.04	1.58	1.57	2.13	3.39	31.83
1979	1.90	1.09	3.75	7.17	1.32	0.94	4.63	2.85	T	1.34	1.98	2.36	29.33
1980	0.72	1.42	4.29	2.22	2.22	3.23	2.08	3.91	4.95	1.47	0.57	1.99	29.07
1981	0.43	2.12	2.27	4.57	6.17	5.80	10.76	8.37	1.13	1.94	2.21	2.35	48.12
1982	4.48	1.81	3.04	3.40	4.12	2.54	2.53	3.68	2.75	2.69	4.50	8.94	44.48
1983	0.46	0.96	3.44	5.02	4.53	2.62	1.60	0.84	1.36	3.63	4.71	3.50	32.67
1984	0.70	1.97	4.00	5.45	6.32	2.26	3.46	0.63	4.80	4.74	4.36	3.91	42.60
1985	0.65	2.96	4.19	1.46	1.75	5.82	2.95	6.03	0.64	3.08	6.94	2.43	38.90
1986	0.04	1.80	1.45	1.57	2.56	6.23	5.39	1.13	8.57	3.63	1.95	1.40	35.72
1987	1.46	0.73	2.08	2.59	0.56	4.08	4.12	3.23	0.99	1.26	3.25	5.00	29.35
1988	2.17	1.39	2.69	1.27	1.76	0.62	1.74	1.56	2.84	1.68	4.37	3.22	25.31
1989	0.88	1.27	1.68	5.50	4.18	0.89	3.13	2.57	5.49	1.02	0.84	0.58	28.03
1990	1.49	4.89	3.41	1.28	8.84	9.22	5.48	2.68	1.91	5.03	3.47	4.97	52.67
1991	1.29	0.71	2.64	3.57	5.74	1.26	3.22	4.03	4.35	6.41	3.31	1.38	37.91
1992	1.03	1.59	2.39	2.82	0.52	2.31	6.86	0.46	1.54	1.47	6.14	2.36	29.49
1993	3.97	1.48	2.48	4.59	2.05	7.26	9.46	3.21	6.05	2.92	3.04	1.07	47.58
Record Mean	1.92	2.01	3.08	3.54	4.02	3.96	3.29	3.01	3.38	2.68	2.51	2.20	35.58

AVERAGE TEMPERATURE (deg. F)

SPRINGFIELD, ILLINOIS

YEAR	JAN	FEB	MAR	APR	MAY	JUNE	JULY	AUG	SEP	OCT	NOV	DEC	ANNUAL
1964	30.7	29.1	38.3	55.1	68.7	75.1	77.9	74.5	69.0	53.3	46.5	29.4	53.9
1965	27.3	30.0	31.1	54.6	70.3	73.2	74.2	72.4	68.6	55.1	45.6	38.2	52.4
1966	21.9	29.5	43.1	49.5	57.7	71.5	80.8	72.0	64.0	52.3	44.1	30.5	51.4
1967	29.5	26.4	43.8	56.5	59.3	73.8	72.9	68.6	63.7	54.9	38.5	31.4	51.6
1968	23.8	25.6	42.8	52.9	59.0	74.5	75.8	75.2	66.7	54.8	41.3	29.1	51.8
1969	23.4	31.5	32.6	54.6	64.2	70.7	77.9	74.0	66.4	54.0	39.7	28.2	51.5
1970	17.9	28.7	37.9	54.7	66.5	71.5	76.4	74.0	69.2	56.2	41.7	34.0	52.4
1971	23.7	30.7	39.1	54.4	60.4	79.0	72.4	72.5	71.2	62.9	43.8	38.5	54.1
1972	24.4	29.0	40.8	52.5	64.7	70.5	75.9	73.8	68.7	52.9	38.3	26.7	51.5
1973	29.7	30.7	48.3	51.9	59.6	73.2	76.0	76.0	69.8	60.7	45.5	28.0	54.1
1974	26.1	32.6	44.2	54.8	61.6	68.3	78.8	72.9	61.9	55.8	42.2	32.7	52.7
1975	31.1	29.4	37.4	50.4	66.5	73.6	74.7	76.6	63.8	57.7	47.1	33.4	53.5
1976	23.5	39.6	45.4	55.0	59.7	72.4	77.4	71.6	65.2	49.4	34.6	24.1	51.5
1977	10.3	29.5	47.6	59.9	71.0	71.6	79.4	72.8	68.6	53.8	42.8	27.0	52.9
1978	15.6	16.7	33.6	53.9	62.3	74.2	76.3	73.1	70.9	53.7	45.2	31.4	50.6
1979	12.4	17.1	40.3	50.4	64.0	74.9	75.4	74.0	67.7	55.7	42.0	35.8	50.8
1980	27.8	21.8	37.1	51.1	64.6	72.0	81.4	79.3	68.7	52.8	42.3	31.7	52.6
1981	26.4	32.4	44.1	60.4	60.3	74.9	77.1	73.8	67.2	54.6	45.3	26.8	53.6
1982	17.0	24.2	40.3	48.1	70.0	68.3	77.1	72.5	66.1	55.4	43.0	38.8	51.7
1983	28.7	34.9	40.6	47.8	59.9	73.8	80.4	80.0	69.1	57.2	45.7	16.1	52.9
1984	22.3	35.9	31.8	50.4	60.3	75.2	74.5	76.9	65.7	59.9	41.7	35.9	52.5
1985	18.5	24.9	45.7	57.8	65.2	69.7	74.3	70.8	67.9	58.1	42.8	21.5	51.4
1986	29.1	26.9	45.3	57.4	65.9	74.7	78.8	70.0	70.4	56.1	37.9	32.6	53.8
1987	26.1	36.6	45.4	54.7	70.5	75.4	78.8	75.3	67.6	50.6	46.2	34.6	55.2
1988	25.6	25.6	41.5	52.8	65.8	73.8	78.6	78.7	68.7	49.7	43.0	31.6	53.0
1989	36.0	20.3	40.6	52.3	59.3	70.5	75.4	73.3	63.8	56.9	42.0	18.7	50.8
1990	37.1	36.1	45.5	50.8	59.9	73.1	75.2	74.0	68.4	53.5	47.8	30.0	54.3
1991	24.0	35.3	45.1	57.3	69.2	75.6	75.3	74.5	66.8	55.8	38.5	34.7	54.3
1992	32.1	38.1	43.7	52.2	62.3	69.6	74.3	70.9	67.0	56.1	42.4	32.8	53.5
1993	29.8	27.6	38.6	50.9	64.3	72.0	77.2	76.0	62.4	52.9	40.5	33.1	52.1
Record Mean	26.9	30.2	40.8	53.3	63.7	73.2	77.2	74.9	67.8	56.3	42.5	31.3	53.2
Max	34.7	38.3	49.8	63.3	74.1	83.4	87.5	85.1	78.5	66.7	50.9	38.6	62.6
Min	19.1	22.1	31.9	43.2	53.3	62.9	66.9	64.7	57.2	46.0	34.0	24.0	43.8

REFERENCE NOTES

SPRINGFIELD, ILLINOIS

GENERAL
T - TRACE AMOUNT.
BLANK ENTRIES DENOTE MISSING/UNREPORTED DATA.
# INDICATES A STATION OR INSTRUMENT RELOCATION.

SPECIFIC

PM - INCLUDES LAST DAY OF PREVIOUS MONTH
ASOS - AUTOMATED SURFACE OBSERVING SYSTEM IN OPERATION DURING THESE MONTHS.

(a) - LENGTH OF RECORD IN YEARS, ALTHOUGH INDIVIDUAL MONTHS MAY BE MISSING.
0.* OR * - THE VALUE IS BETWEEN 0.0 AND 0.05
NORMALS - BASED ON THE 1961-1990 RECORD PERIOD.
EXTREMES - DATES ARE THE MOST RECENT OCCURRENCE
WIND DIR.- NUMERALS SHOW TENS OF DEGRESS CLOCKWISE FROM TRUE NORTH. "00" INDICATES CALM.
RESULTANT DIRECTIONS ARE GIVEN TO WHOLE DEGREES.
BOLD VALUES INDICATE EXTREME VALUES WHICH OCCURRED AFTER THE ASOS SYSTEM WAS COMMISSIONED.

RECORD = PERIOD OF RECORD
RECORD MEAN PRECIPITATION IS THE MEAN OF ALL DAILY PRECIPITATION AMOUNTS DURING THE PERIOD OF RECORD.
RECORD MAX(MIN) TEMPERATURE IS THE MEAN OF ALL DAILY MAX(MIN) TEMPERATURES DURING THE PERIOD OF RECORD.
RECORD MEAN TEMPERATURE IS THE SUM OF THE RECORD MAX AND RECORD MIN DIVIDED BY 2.
AVERAGE TEMPERATURE IS THE SUM OF THE MEAN DAILY MAX AND MIN TEMPERATURE DIVIDED BY 2.

EXCEPTIONS

RECORD MEANS ARE THROUGH THE CURRENT YEAR,
BEGINNING IN 1897 FOR TEMPERATURE
1897 FOR PRECIPITATION
1948 FOR SNOWFALL

HEATING DEGREE DAYS Base 65 deg. F SPRINGFIELD, ILLINOIS

SEASON	JULY	AUG	SEP	OCT	NOV	DEC	JAN	FEB	MAR	APR	MAY	JUNE	TOTAL
1964-65	0	10	66	356	554	1100	1158	973	1041	320	36	0	5614
1965-66	0	13	54	321	575	822	1329	987	670	459	242	15	5487
1966-67	0	5	100	388	618	1065	1091	1074	662	289	230	10	5532
1967-68	9	34	104	337	789	1032	1271	1134	684	358	203	8	5963
1968-69	1	2	31	353	703	1107	1282	934	995	314	130	31	5883
1969-70	0	0	59	370	748	1135	1457	1013	830	332	83	26	6053
1970-71	0	1	41	281	690	952	1275	952	793	342	168	0	5495
1971-72	9	1	65	130	633	820	1253	1040	745	375	114	27	5212
1972-73	3	11	58	375	795	1181	1089	957	512	398	174	0	5553
1973-74	0	0	30	191	578	1140	1200	901	642	316	167	29	5194
1974-75	0	2	135	299	680	996	1044	992	848	435	63	7	5501
1975-76	10	0	125	253	528	973	1280	732	601	321	188	2	5013
1976-77	0	3	84	497	905	1260	1693	989	532	222	44	12	6241
1977-78	0	2	21	340	661	1172	1521	1348	968	334	186	4	6557
1978-79	0	0	36	349	591	1035	1627	1336	758	435	119	0	6286
1979-80	0	9	50	323	684	898	1146	1249	857	421	95	8	5740
1980-81	0	0	49	395	675	1028	1193	906	648	181	184	0	5259
1981-82	0	0	51	332	581	1175	1483	1139	760	502	9	20	6052
1982-83	0	5	86	325	656	806	1117	836	749	510	169	14	5273
1983-84	0	0	75	269	574	1512	1320	835	1023	446	170	1	6225
1984-85	0	0	127	194	691	899	1437	1116	601	262	67	32	5426
1985-86	0	11	99	223	658	1340	1105	1060	618	261	74	1	5450
1986-87	0	19	25	284	807	999	1199	788	599	325	34	0	5079
1987-88	0	3	44	440	565	934	1216	1139	720	360	59	11	5491
1988-89	0	5	33	475	654	1027	890	1242	749	405	224	19	5723
1989-90	0	4	106	269	683	1431	856	803	613	459	168	10	5402
1990-91	7	2	72	360	512	1080	1262	827	612	243	69	0	5046
1991-92	0	0	120	295	787	932	1007	771	651	382	154	20	5119
1992-93	0	8	82	296	671	991	1083	1041	813	419	85	35	5524
1993-94	0	0	117	382	730	979							

COOLING DEGREE DAYS Base 65 deg. F SPRINGFIELD, ILLINOIS

YEAR	JAN	FEB	MAR	APR	MAY	JUNE	JULY	AUG	SEP	OCT	NOV	DEC	TOTAL
1969	0	0	0	6	110	206	407	288	108	37	0	0	1162
1970	0	0	0	31	136	229	361	284	174	17	0	0	1232
1971	0	0	0	32	33	425	248	241	254	69	2	0	1304
1972	0	0	0	6	114	199	347	291	178	10	0	0	1145
1973	0	0	0	12	12	251	350	348	184	64	0	0	1221
1974	0	0	7	14	70	136	437	252	49	17	2	0	984
1975	0	0	0	2	115	271	315	367	94	36	0	0	1200
1976	0	0	3	28	34	228	393	214	98	23	0	0	1021
1977	0	0	0	76	238	217	452	251	134	0	1	0	1369
1978	0	0	1	8	107	289	358	258	222	5	5	0	1253
1979	0	0	0	2	93	305	327	295	138	41	0	0	1201
1980	0	0	0	10	88	228	515	452	169	20	0	0	1482
1981	0	0	8	50	43	303	380	280	121	13	0	0	1198
1982	0	0	0	1	173	131	379	244	126	32	1	1	1088
1983	0	0	1	1	17	289	483	471	205	34	0	0	1501
1984	0	0	0	16	30	312	303	375	155	44	0	1	1236
1985	0	0	7	52	80	178	293	202	191	17	0	0	1020
1986	0	0	14	38	109	299	434	182	193	14	0	0	1283
1987	0	0	0	21	212	318	436	329	130	0	8	0	1454
1988	0	0	0	3	93	281	430	437	150	6	0	0	1400
1989	0	0	2	30	57	190	332	268	77	24	0	0	980
1990	0	0	14	39	18	261	328	289	182	12	1	0	1144
1991	0	0	5	20	207	327	326	302	184	18	0	0	1389
1992	0	0	0	4	75	166	294	199	150	28	0	0	916
1993	0	0	0	1	71	253	386	352	46	13	0	0	1122

SNOWFALL (inches) SPRINGFIELD, ILLINOIS

SEASON	JULY	AUG	SEP	OCT	NOV	DEC	JAN	FEB	MAR	APR	MAY	JUNE	TOTAL
1964-65	0.0	0.0	0.0	0.0	4.4	1.6	9.1	14.2	11.1	T	0.0	0.0	40.4
1965-66	0.0	0.0	0.0	0.0	T	1.7	0.4	8.6	3.5	T	T	0.0	14.2
1966-67	0.0	0.0	0.0	0.0	0.3	2.0	6.4	3.7	2.4	0.1	0.0	0.0	14.9
1967-68	0.0	0.0	0.0	0.1	2.8	6.4	13.0	1.7	4.5	T	0.0	0.0	28.5
1968-69	0.0	0.0	0.0	0.0	0.7	4.7	5.0	6.8	7.0	0.0	0.0	0.0	24.2
1969-70	0.0	0.0	0.0	0.0	0.5	10.2	7.0	3.9	4.3	1.1	0.0	0.0	27.0
1970-71	0.0	0.0	0.0	0.0	T	0.9	4.2	3.4	0.7	3.8	0.0	0.0	13.0
1971-72	0.0	0.0	0.0	0.0	4.4	T	8.1	6.0	3.6	T	0.0	0.0	22.1
1972-73	0.0	0.0	0.0	0.0	5.4	3.1	0.6	3.1	0.3	0.9	0.0	0.0	13.4
1973-74	0.0	0.0	0.0	0.0	1.3	22.7	7.3	5.3	4.4	0.4	0.0	0.0	41.4
1974-75	0.0	0.0	0.0	0.0	6.8	2.5	4.5	14.2	4.5	0.4	0.0	0.0	32.9
1975-76	0.0	0.0	0.0	0.0	8.5	4.3	8.5	2.1	2.2	0.0	0.0	0.0	25.6
1976-77	0.0	0.0	0.0	T	T	6.9	21.1	8.9	0.6	1.1	0.0	0.0	38.6
1977-78	0.0	0.0	0.0	0.0	6.4	8.9	8.9	9.4	18.5	T	0.0	0.0	52.1
1978-79	0.0	0.0	0.0	0.0	T	3.2	15.9	4.6	8.1	T	0.0	0.0	31.8
1979-80	0.0	0.0	0.0	0.0	0.8	0.1	5.1	11.7	5.5	7.3	0.0	0.0	30.5
1980-81	0.0	0.0	0.0	T	3.5	2.1	2.7	8.6	0.6	0.0	0.0	0.0	17.5
1981-82	0.0	0.0	0.0	0.0	0.1	21.6	12.0	11.4	0.7	4.6	0.0	0.0	50.4
1982-83	0.0	0.0	0.0	0.0	0.2	0.9	2.4	1.3	5.4	0.2	0.0	0.0	10.4
1983-84	0.0	0.0	0.0	T	T	16.2	3.9	9.8	5.7	0.0	0.0	0.0	35.6
1984-85	0.0	0.0	0.0	0.0	1.8	0.7	9.3	2.5	T	T	0.0	0.0	14.3
1985-86	0.0	0.0	0.0	0.0	T	4.3	0.2	15.1	0.6	0.1	0.0	0.0	20.3
1986-87	0.0	0.0	0.0	0.0	0.5	T	20.3	T	0.0	0.0	0.0	0.0	20.8
1987-88	0.0	0.0	0.0	0.0	0.1	5.7	0.4	10.2	5.0	0.0	0.0	0.0	21.4
1988-89	0.0	0.0	0.0	0.0	T	5.5	0.3	13.7	5.2	T	T	0.0	24.7
1989-90	0.0	0.0	0.0	0.3	T	6.7	0.6	0.5	1.2	T	0.0	0.0	9.3
1990-91	0.0	0.0	0.0	0.0	T	9.4	6.8	0.8	3.1	0.0	0.0	0.0	20.1
1991-92	0.0	0.0	0.0	T	3.2	0.5	4.6	0.9	2.2	T	0.0	0.0	11.4
1992-93	0.0	0.0	0.0	0.0	1.2	2.5	7.0	16.0	2.9	0.4	0.0	0.0	30.0
1993-94	0.0	0.0	0.0	0.2	0.8	1.7							
Record Mean	0.0	0.0	0.0	T	1.7	4.9	5.8	6.4	4.1	0.7	T	0.0	23.5

INDIANAPOLIS, INDIANA

Indianapolis is located in the central part of the state and is situated on level or slightly rolling terrain. The greater part of the city lies east of the White River which flows in a general north to south direction.

The National Weather Service Forecast Office is located approximately 7 miles southwest of the central part of the city at the Indianapolis International Airport. From a field elevation of 797 feet above sea level at the Indianapolis International Airport the terrain slopes gradually downward to a little below 645 feet at the White River, then upward to just over 910 feet in the northwest corner and eastern sections of the county. The street elevation at the former city office located in the Old Federal Building is 718 feet.

Indianapolis has a temperate climate, with very warm summers and without a dry season. Very cold temperatures may be produced by the invasion of continental polar air in the winter from northern latitudes. The polar air can be quite frigid with very low humidity. The arrival of maritime tropical air from the Gulf in the summer brings warm temperatures and moderate humidity. One of the longest and most severe heat waves brought temperatures of 100 degrees or more for nine consecutive days.

Precipitation is distributed fairly evenly throughout the year, and therefore there is no pronounced wet or dry season. Rainfall in the spring and summer is produced mostly by showers and thunderstorms. A rainfall of about 2 1/2 inches in a 24-hour period can be expected about once a year. Snowfalls of 3 inches or more occur on an average of two or three times in the winter.

Local levees and/or channel improvements now protect some formerly flood-prone areas.

Based on the 1951-1980 period, the average first occurrence of 32 degrees Fahrenheit in the fall is October 20 and the average last occurrence in the spring is April 22.

NORMALS, MEANS, AND EXTREMES

INDIANAPOLIS, INDIANA

LATITUDE: 39°42'N LONGITUDE: 86°16' W ELEVATION: FT. GRND 790 BARO 837 TIME ZONE: EASTERN WBAN: 93819

	(a)	JAN	FEB	MAR	APR	MAY	JUNE	JULY	AUG	SEP	OCT	NOV	DEC	YEAR
TEMPERATURE °F:														
Normals														
-Daily Maximum		33.7	38.3	50.9	63.3	73.8	82.7	85.5	83.6	77.6	65.8	51.9	38.5	62.1
-Daily Minimum		17.2	20.9	31.9	41.5	51.7	61.0	65.2	62.8	55.6	43.5	34.1	23.2	42.4
-Monthly		25.5	29.6	41.4	52.4	62.8	71.9	75.4	73.2	66.6	54.7	43.0	30.9	52.3
Extremes														
-Record Highest	54	71	74	85	89	93	102	104	102	100	90	81	74	104
-Year		1950	1972	1981	1970	1988	1988	1954	1988	1954	1954	1950	1982	JUL 1954
-Record Lowest	54	-22	-21	-7	16	28	37	44	41	28	17	-2	-23	-23
-Year		1985	1982	1980	1940	1966	1992	1942	1965	1942	1942	1958	1989	DEC 1989
NORMAL DEGREE DAYS:														
Heating (base 65°F)		1225	991	732	378	165	5	0	6	58	338	660	1057	5615
Cooling (base 65°F)		0	0	0	0	96	212	322	260	106	18	0	0	1014
% OF POSSIBLE SUNSHINE	49	41	49	50	54	60	66	66	68	65	61	41	38	55
MEAN SKY COVER (tenths)														
Sunrise - Sunset	51	7.3	7.0	7.2	6.9	6.5	6.1	5.8	5.6	5.5	5.5	7.1	7.4	6.5
MEAN NUMBER OF DAYS:														
Sunrise to Sunset														
-Clear	62	5.9	5.6	5.6	6.0	7.1	7.1	8.5	9.1	10.5	11.0	6.4	5.1	87.9
-Partly Cloudy	62	5.9	6.3	7.0	7.3	8.9	10.5	12.4	11.7	8.7	7.5	6.5	6.2	98.9
-Cloudy	62	19.2	16.4	18.4	16.7	15.0	12.4	10.1	10.2	10.8	12.5	17.2	19.8	178.6
Precipitation														
.01 inches or more	54	11.8	10.2	13.1	12.2	12.1	9.8	9.7	8.7	7.9	8.2	10.5	11.9	126.0
Snow,Ice pellets,hail														
1.0 inches or more	52	2.0	2.0	1.2	0.2	0.0	0.0	0.0	0.0	0.0	0.1	0.6	1.8	7.7
Thunderstorms	51	0.7	0.7	2.7	4.5	6.3	7.3	7.8	6.2	3.7	1.8	1.1	0.5	43.3
Heavy Fog Visibility														
1/4 mile or less	51	3.3	2.5	1.6	0.6	0.8	0.7	1.1	1.7	1.5	1.3	1.6	2.9	19.5
Temperature °F														
-Maximum														
90° and above	34	0.0	0.0	0.0	0.0	0.5	3.6	7.0	4.3	1.9	0.0	0.0	0.0	17.3
32° and below	34	13.3	8.9	2.3	0.*	0.0	0.0	0.0	0.0	0.0	0.0	1.0	8.6	34.1
-Minimum														
32° and below	34	27.4	23.5	17.1	5.4	0.3	0.0	0.0	0.0	0.*	4.3	14.2	24.9	117.1
0° and below	34	4.0	2.0	0.2	0.0	0.0	0.0	0.0	0.0	0.0	0.0	0.0	1.8	8.0
AVG. STATION PRESS.(mb)	21	989.9	989.5	986.9	986.2	986.2	986.5	987.7	988.8	989.3	989.9	989.2	990.0	988.4
RELATIVE HUMIDITY (%)														
Hour 01	34	78	77	75	73	77	79	84	86	85	80	80	81	80
Hour 07 (Local Time)	34	81	81	80	79	82	82	87	90	90	87	84	83	84
Hour 13	34	70	67	62	56	56	56	60	61	58	57	67	72	62
Hour 19	34	73	70	65	58	57	58	62	66	66	64	72	76	66
PRECIPITATION (inches):														
Water Equivalent														
-Normal		2.32	2.46	3.79	3.70	4.00	3.49	4.47	3.64	2.87	2.63	3.23	3.34	39.94
-Maximum Monthly	54	12.69	5.35	10.74	8.09	10.10	9.74	11.79	8.34	8.06	8.36	8.50	7.72	12.69
-Year		1950	1971	1963	1964	1943	1942	1992	1980	1989	1941	1985	1990	JAN 1950
-Minimum Monthly	54	0.21	0.36	1.03	0.98	1.06	0.36	0.99	0.68	0.24	0.17	0.82	0.45	0.17
-Year		1944	1978	1941	1976	1988	1988	1941	1964	1963	1963	1976	1976	OCT 1963
-Maximum in 24 hrs	51	3.47	2.50	3.05	2.56	3.53	3.80	5.32	4.72	3.07	3.90	4.15	2.83	5.32
-Year		1950	1977	1963	1961	1961	1963	1987	1976	1961	1959	1993	1990	JUL 1987
Snow,Ice pellets,hail														
-Maximum Monthly	62	30.6	18.0	10.5	4.0	0.2	T	0.0	T	0.0	9.3	8.3	27.5	30.6
-Year		1978	1979	1975	1940	1989	1992		1989		1989	1966	1973	JAN 1978
-Maximum in 24 hrs	51	12.2	12.5	5.6	3.1	0.2	T	0.0	T	0.0	7.5	8.2	11.5	12.5
-Year		1978	1965	1948	1953	1989	1992		1989		1989	1966	1973	FEB 1965
WIND:														
Mean Speed (mph)	45	10.9	10.8	11.7	11.2	9.5	8.5	7.5	7.2	8.0	8.8	10.4	10.5	9.6
Prevailing Direction through 1963		NW	WNW	WNW	SW	SW	SW	SW	SW	SW	SW	SW	SW	SW
Fastest Obs. 1 Min.														
-Direction (!!)	14	29	33	27	33	32	29	36	32	27	23	31	22	33
-Speed (MPH)	14	39	38	38	46	37	46	40	40	31	35	33	40	46
-Year		1980	1980	1991	1988	1986	1980	1987	1980	1990	1988	1992	1987	APR 1988
Peak Gust														
-Direction (!!)	10	SW	SW	W	NW	NW	SW	SW	NW	NW	SW	SW	SW	NW
-Speed (mph)	10	48	53	54	74	62	62	55	70	46	48	67	64	74
-Date		1990	1988	1991	1988	1986	1992	1992	1985	1993	1991	1991	1987	APR 1988

PRECIPITATION (inches)

INDIANAPOLIS, INDIANA

YEAR	JAN	FEB	MAR	APR	MAY	JUNE	JULY	AUG	SEP	OCT	NOV	DEC	ANNUAL
1964	2.04	2.01	7.20	8.09	1.42	2.73	4.09	0.68	1.27	0.64	3.13	3.05	36.35
1965	3.86	4.33	2.17	5.80	1.44	3.49	3.18	3.25	5.16	1.05	1.41	2.97	38.11
1966	1.13	2.91	1.31	3.32	1.47	1.28	2.71	1.31	5.73	1.60	4.72	5.23	32.72
1967	1.81	1.84	3.33	3.00	5.00	1.07	2.34	2.38	0.80	5.72	2.54	4.92	34.75
1968	2.96	1.51	3.73	2.86	9.25	2.51	2.19	4.45	1.54	1.13	4.74	4.18	41.05
1969	6.19	1.23	1.33	4.42	1.82	4.16	8.02	2.98	2.89	4.83	2.86	2.04	42.77
1970	1.17	1.86	2.51	6.53	2.43	1.97	4.43	1.82	2.41	3.66	2.12	2.07	32.98
1971	1.98	5.35	1.49	1.16	4.25	3.39	5.68	1.93	3.10	1.84	1.29	6.02	37.48
1972	1.57	1.15	2.48	5.81	1.89	6.04	2.01	2.94	5.65	2.25	5.65	2.83	40.27
1973	2.27	1.11	5.63	2.76	1.79	5.91	6.67	2.74	2.43	3.11	3.62	4.27	42.31
1974	3.39	2.58	3.60	3.45	6.27	5.15	1.20	5.63	3.25	0.99	2.99	2.81	41.31
1975	4.37	4.13	4.16	4.14	2.42	5.73	4.63	4.68	2.32	2.80	3.63	3.71	46.72
1976	2.29	2.90	3.46	0.98	3.10	3.97	3.09	7.95	2.02	2.79	0.82	0.45	33.82
1977	1.50	3.62	3.83	1.91	2.78	3.86	2.57	4.47	3.40	2.79	3.01	4.31	38.05
1978	3.80	0.36	3.54	3.59	4.21	4.43	5.04	6.89	0.85	3.82	2.38	4.03	42.94
1979	3.24	2.86	2.43	3.14	2.23	3.93	11.06	6.09	0.36	2.32	4.37	2.57	44.60
1980	1.67	1.84	4.26	2.10	2.26	4.15	2.87	8.34	3.31	1.87	1.41	0.78	34.86
1981	0.36	2.88	1.22	5.81	9.23	1.64	5.75	1.69	2.04	2.35	1.12	3.40	37.49
1982	5.64	1.62	4.73	2.40	5.94	5.16	3.44	1.00	1.20	0.91	4.16	5.78	41.98
1983	1.05	1.03	2.94	4.47	4.68	4.53	1.58	2.79	1.28	3.87	4.55	3.43	36.20
1984	0.97	3.16	3.14	3.90	4.35	1.51	4.83	3.27	4.69	2.60	5.38	4.33	42.13
1985	1.37	3.73	5.94	2.60	4.60	3.06	4.06	5.29	2.71	1.82	8.50	3.30	46.98
1986	0.73	2.84	3.93	4.34	7.37	3.58	4.88	1.18	5.68	7.84	2.32	1.71	46.40
1987	1.55	1.28	1.84	2.68	1.77	4.11	9.22	0.86	1.41	1.36	2.60	4.77	33.45
1988	2.35	3.04	3.22	4.02	1.06	0.36	4.71	1.46	1.14	3.07	4.39	2.50	31.32
1989	1.75	1.32	3.72	4.32	5.79	3.80	6.15	8.05	8.06	2.92	2.79	1.90	50.57
1990	1.79	5.17	3.93	2.44	7.59	3.11	3.68	4.46	2.68	4.64	3.23	7.72	50.44
1991	1.59	1.94	6.41	4.34	4.64	0.91	2.17	3.54	1.12	5.47	3.95	1.45	37.53
1992	1.40	1.15	2.61	4.17	1.56	4.07	11.79	1.42	3.40	2.84	7.88	1.89	44.18
1993	3.29	2.31	3.72	3.75	2.76	5.15	4.94	6.42	5.69	2.25	8.30	2.18	50.76
Record Mean	2.85	2.52	3.78	3.67	3.93	4.00	3.97	3.33	3.14	2.72	3.30	2.95	40.18

AVERAGE TEMPERATURE (deg. F)

INDIANAPOLIS, INDIANA

YEAR	JAN	FEB	MAR	APR	MAY	JUNE	JULY	AUG	SEP	OCT	NOV	DEC	ANNUAL
1964	30.7	29.0	40.6	54.7	65.6	73.4	74.6	72.5	67.2	51.7	45.3	32.2	53.1
1965	27.5	29.5	33.7	54.4	68.3	71.7	72.9	71.1	67.5	53.7	44.7	38.6	52.8
1966	22.4	30.4	43.3	51.3	58.4	72.4	79.2	73.2	65.2	51.9	43.8	32.7	52.0
1967	32.6	27.7	44.0	53.6	59.3	73.9	73.8	71.1	65.9	55.2	39.4	33.7	52.5
1968	25.1	26.4	42.8	53.7	58.6	72.3	75.3	74.5	65.8	54.4	42.9	30.6	51.9
1969	25.7	31.7	35.7	54.0	63.4	69.8	75.8	72.7	65.2	53.8	37.5	28.2	51.1
1970	17.9	28.6	38.1	55.1	65.6	71.5	75.2	74.2	69.1	55.2	40.9	34.7	52.2
1971	23.4	28.9	37.3	51.0	58.9	75.6	72.3	71.3	69.4	62.0	43.1	38.4	52.7
1972	26.5	28.4	39.8	52.1	65.0	68.8	74.6	73.1	68.3	51.5	39.9	31.9	51.7
1973	30.7	31.5	49.4	51.3	59.5	73.3	76.0	74.4	69.9	59.4	46.4	30.9	54.4
1974	31.6	32.4	45.3	55.0	62.1	68.6	76.0	71.8	60.6	52.5	42.5	32.9	52.6
1975	32.0	32.0	36.9	48.9	65.5	71.5	73.5	76.1	62.6	55.9	46.4	32.8	52.8
1976	23.9	38.8	46.6	53.4	58.8	71.3	73.9	71.3	63.6	48.7	34.7	24.6	50.8
1977	10.3	28.2	46.5	57.1	70.6	71.2	78.0	74.0	69.6	54.2	45.9	29.2	52.9
1978	18.2	17.8	36.7	55.2	63.5	74.0	77.2	75.0	70.4	52.7	45.7	34.4	51.7
1979	18.0	18.8	43.4	49.8	61.1	71.1	73.0	72.4	64.9	53.1	41.3	34.9	50.2
1980	28.5	22.5	36.0	49.1	64.0	69.1	78.5	76.6	67.9	50.9	40.3	31.8	51.3
1981	23.5	33.0	39.9	57.4	59.9	73.3	75.4	72.8	64.6	53.1	44.2	27.8	52.1
1982	20.1	26.4	42.5	48.6	68.6	67.8	76.2	71.7	64.4	55.7	44.2	40.2	52.2
1983	30.6	35.5	42.9	48.2	58.2	71.8	79.7	80.1	69.4	57.5	44.1	20.2	53.2
1984	22.8	37.3	33.0	50.0	58.8	75.3	72.4	74.3	64.2	61.3	43.0	38.9	52.6
1985	20.4	26.1	44.6	57.1	64.9	70.6	74.3	71.2	66.2	57.6	46.6	22.5	51.8
1986	28.5	31.4	43.9	53.8	63.5	72.8	77.5	70.1	69.8	55.6	39.8	32.3	53.3
1987	27.6	35.5	44.5	52.5	68.1	73.7	75.8	73.6	68.1	48.6	46.3	35.8	54.2
1988	25.9	27.2	41.4	51.9	64.4	73.4	78.3	77.5	67.3	48.2	44.2	31.7	52.6
1989	36.3	27.2	42.5	51.4	59.4	71.4	75.7	71.8	64.4	55.4	40.9	18.8	51.3
1990	37.3	37.6	46.2	51.4	60.1	71.3	73.9	72.5	66.9	53.9	47.5	34.6	54.4
1991	26.9	35.3	43.7	55.3	68.3	74.6	76.7	75.2	67.9	57.5	40.2	35.7	54.8
1992	31.5	38.4	43.2	52.1	60.5	68.1	73.5	69.5	65.1	53.4	43.2	33.3	52.7
1993	31.6	27.4	39.1	50.7	63.5	71.0	77.2	75.3	62.2	51.6	42.2	32.4	52.0
Record Mean	28.0	30.7	40.4	52.0	62.5	71.8	75.8	73.6	66.8	55.3	42.2	31.8	52.5
Max	35.8	38.8	49.3	61.8	72.6	81.7	85.7	83.6	77.2	65.4	50.4	39.0	61.8
Min	20.3	22.6	31.5	42.2	52.4	61.8	65.8	63.6	56.5	45.1	33.9	24.5	43.3

REFERENCE NOTES

INDIANAPOLIS, INDIANA

GENERAL
T - TRACE AMOUNT.
BLANK ENTRIES DENOTE MISSING/UNREPORTED DATA.
# INDICATES A STATION OR INSTRUMENT RELOCATION.

SPECIFIC

PM - INCLUDES LAST DAY OF PREVIOUS MONTH
ASOS - AUTOMATED SURFACE OBSERVING SYSTEM IN OPERATION DURING THESE MONTHS.

(a) - LENGTH OF RECORD IN YEARS, ALTHOUGH INDIVIDUAL MONTHS MAY BE MISSING.
0.* OR * - THE VALUE IS BETWEEN 0.0 AND 0.05
NORMALS - BASED ON THE 1961-1990 RECORD PERIOD.
EXTREMES - DATES ARE THE MOST RECENT OCCURRENCE
WIND DIR.- NUMERALS SHOW TENS OF DEGRESS CLOCKWISE FROM TRUE NORTH. "00" INDICATES CALM.
RESULTANT DIRECTIONS ARE GIVEN TO WHOLE DEGREES.
BOLD VALUES INDICATE EXTREME VALUES WHICH OCCURRED AFTER THE ASOS SYSTEM WAS COMMISSIONED.

RECORD = PERIOD OF RECORD
RECORD MEAN PRECIPITATION IS THE MEAN OF ALL DAILY PRECIPITATION AMOUNTS DURING THE PERIOD OF RECORD.
RECORD MAX(MIN) TEMPERATURE IS THE MEAN OF ALL DAILY MAX(MIN) TEMPERATURES DURING THE PERIOD OF RECORD.
RECORD MEAN TEMPERATURE IS THE SUM OF THE RECORD MAX AND RECORD MIN DIVIDED BY 2.
AVERAGE TEMPERATURE IS THE SUM OF THE MEAN DAILY MAX AND MIN TEMPERATURE DIVIDED BY 2.

EXCEPTIONS

RECORD MEANS ARE THROUGH THE CURRENT YEAR, BEGINNING IN 1871 FOR TEMPERATURE
1871 FOR PRECIPITATION
1932 FOR SNOWFALL

HEATING DEGREE DAYS Base 65 deg. F — INDIANAPOLIS, INDIANA

SEASON	JULY	AUG	SEP	OCT	NOV	DEC	JAN	FEB	MAR	APR	MAY	JUNE	TOTAL
1964-65	2	16	73	405	581	1009	1155	989	964	323	39	0	5556
1965-66	0	18	66	355	603	811	1312	962	668	412	223	11	5441
1966-67	0	0	77	402	631	995	997	1040	652	353	219	2	5368
1967-68	3	9	83	327	761	964	1232	1112	680	333	205	11	5720
1968-69	4	13	49	354	656	1057	1211	925	904	329	121	38	5661
1969-70	0	0	85	358	816	1137	1458	1012	829	316	95	11	6117
1970-71	4	0	51	301	715	930	1281	1006	852	417	198	0	5755
1971-72	3	1	49	129	648	813	1186	1054	774	389	89	35	5170
1972-73	8	4	36	413	746	1018	1059	937	477	416	184	0	5298
1973-74	0	0	20	211	552	1052	1028	905	617	314	158	18	4875
1974-75	0	5	163	380	671	988	1016	918	866	481	78	22	5588
1975-76	8	0	137	288	551	992	1265	754	564	363	203	1	5126
1976-77	0	2	79	503	904	1249	1693	1025	567	276	45	19	6362
1977-78	0	0	30	326	575	1104	1443	1313	873	292	150	4	6110
1978-79	0	0	36	377	571	944	1453	1288	665	455	170	5	5964
1979-80	3	13	87	384	705	929	1123	1224	893	474	93	36	5964
1980-81	0	0	45	438	734	1022	1279	889	769	244	180	1	5601
1981-82	1	0	94	368	621	1146	1388	1075	690	486	26	18	5913
1982-83	0	2	110	325	621	764	1062	819	681	498	211	21	5114
1983-84	1	0	64	246	619	1386	1304	796	987	447	211	1	6062
1984-85	1	0	119	138	653	803	1375	1082	631	269	85	16	5172
1985-86	0	1	97	245	544	1311	1126	935	652	344	114	7	5376
1986-87	0	24	30	312	750	1009	1150	820	627	378	51	0	5151
1987-88	2	5	37	504	553	900	1205	1090	726	390	84	15	5511
1988-89	0	2	37	517	618	1024	882	1052	693	419	226	11	5481
1989-90	0	8	106	313	718	1426	851	760	588	432	153	19	5374
1990-91	4	1	86	348	518	932	1175	824	651	292	71	0	4902
1991-92	0	0	103	254	739	902	1035	766	670	390	185	34	5078
1992-93	2	7	88	353	645	973	1028	1046	796	424	103	35	5500
1993-94	0	1	129	409	680	1005							

COOLING DEGREE DAYS Base 65 deg. F — INDIANAPOLIS, INDIANA

YEAR	JAN	FEB	MAR	APR	MAY	JUNE	JULY	AUG	SEP	OCT	NOV	DEC	TOTAL
1969	0	0	0	5	78	190	344	245	95	18	0	0	975
1970	0	0	0	26	122	213	327	292	182	5	0	0	1167
1971	0	0	0	2	17	324	237	202	189	40	0	0	1011
1972	0	0	0	8	95	156	313	266	141	0	0	0	979
1973	0	0	0	11	20	256	349	302	172	44	1	0	1155
1974	0	0	11	19	73	131	346	225	40	3	2	0	850
1975	0	0	0	3	100	222	281	355	71	14	0	0	1046
1976	0	0	0	21	15	198	284	205	43	4	0	0	770
1977	0	0	3	45	226	212	410	286	175	0	6	0	1363
1978	0	0	0	4	110	282	382	318	203	1	0	0	1300
1979	0	0	0	7	57	197	255	250	92	24	0	0	882
1980	0	0	0	3	68	168	425	368	139	6	0	0	1177
1981	0	0	1	23	29	256	332	249	88	5	0	0	983
1982	0	0	0	0	146	109	356	214	98	40	3	1	967
1983	0	0	1	3	9	231	464	474	202	18	0	0	1402
1984	0	0	0	6	25	318	237	291	103	28	0	0	1008
1985	0	0	5	36	90	190	296	199	143	21	0	0	980
1986	0	0	6	12	74	249	395	189	181	24	0	0	1130
1987	0	0	0	6	156	265	343	279	137	0	0	0	1186
1988	0	0	1	3	72	274	422	395	114	2	0	0	1283
1989	0	0	1	20	57	215	338	227	94	21	0	0	973
1990	0	0	13	30	10	215	289	241	147	10	1	0	956
1991	0	0	0	7	178	294	367	323	196	30	0	0	1395
1992	0	0	0	10	53	137	274	152	99	1	0	0	726
1993	0	0	0	0	64	223	389	328	51	0	0	0	1055

SNOWFALL (inches) — INDIANAPOLIS, INDIANA

SEASON	JULY	AUG	SEP	OCT	NOV	DEC	JAN	FEB	MAR	APR	MAY	JUNE	TOTAL
1964-65	0.0	0.0	0.0	0.0	2.6	1.1	12.2	15.3	5.3	T	0.0	0.0	36.5
1965-66	0.0	0.0	0.0	0.0	T	2.9	2.5	6.3	0.8	T	T	0.0	12.5
1966-67	0.0	0.0	0.0	0.0	8.3	3.3	2.4	8.1	3.0	0.0	0.0	0.0	25.1
1967-68	0.0	0.0	0.0	T	6.3	3.5	17.0	1.1	8.8	T	0.0	0.0	36.7
1968-69	0.0	0.0	0.0	0.0	0.6	1.6	9.3	0.8	6.4	T	0.0	0.0	18.7
1969-70	0.0	0.0	0.0	0.0	2.5	12.9	7.8	9.2	5.6	0.2	0.0	0.0	38.2
1970-71	0.0	0.0	0.0	0.0	0.2	0.4	1.5	8.2	2.8	T	0.0	0.0	13.1
1971-72	0.0	0.0	0.0	0.0	4.4	0.4	7.9	6.3	0.3	0.6	0.0	0.0	19.9
1972-73	0.0	0.0	0.0	T	1.9	1.1	0.4	1.4	2.0	1.1	0.0	0.0	7.9
1973-74	0.0	0.0	0.0	0.0	0.4	27.5	3.8	8.0	3.0	2.1	0.0	0.0	44.8
1974-75	0.0	0.0	0.0	0.0	3.8	5.8	6.8	4.8	10.5	0.1	0.0	0.0	31.8
1975-76	0.0	0.0	0.0	0.0	4.5	8.1	5.6	0.6	2.3	0.0	0.0	0.0	21.1
1976-77	0.0	0.0	0.0	0.0	0.4	3.1	20.9	3.6	1.6	0.4	0.0	0.0	30.0
1977-78	0.0	0.0	0.0	0.0	2.8	15.2	30.6	3.9	5.4	0.0	0.0	0.0	57.9
1978-79	0.0	0.0	0.0	0.0	T	0.7	19.1	18.0	0.2	0.4	0.0	0.0	38.4
1979-80	0.0	0.0	0.0	0.0	0.8	0.2	5.0	14.5	3.6	0.7	0.0	0.0	24.8
1980-81	0.0	0.0	0.0	T	3.4	2.1	3.9	7.2	0.7	0.0	0.0	0.0	17.3
1981-82	0.0	0.0	0.0	T	0.4	15.6	21.8	13.6	3.5	3.3	0.0	0.0	58.2
1982-83	0.0	0.0	0.0	0.0	0.1	0.4	2.8	2.5	1.3	T	0.0	0.0	7.1
1983-84	0.0	0.0	0.0	0.0	0.1	8.3	7.2	17.1	9.2	T	0.0	0.0	41.9
1984-85	0.0	0.0	0.0	0.0	2.5	3.6	10.6	11.0	T	0.1	0.0	0.0	27.8
1985-86	0.0	0.0	0.0	0.0	T	8.1	1.7	9.5	1.1	T	0.0	0.0	20.4
1986-87	0.0	0.0	0.0	0.0	T	1.6	11.6	5.3	1.4	T	0.0	0.0	19.9
1987-88	0.0	0.0	0.0	0.0	T	1.1	2.9	4.8	2.5	T	0.0	0.0	11.3
1988-89	0.0	0.0	0.0	T	0.4	6.8	0.1	2.4	1.9	1.7	0.2	0.0	13.5
1989-90	0.0	T	0.0	9.3	0.6	8.2	4.1	2.5	1.3	T	0.0	0.0	26.0
1990-91	0.0	0.0	0.0	0.0	0.0	9.6	5.4	2.4	0.1	0.0	T	0.0	17.5
1991-92	0.0	0.0	0.0	0.0	3.0	0.2	7.1	0.2	2.9	1.3	0.0	T	14.7
1992-93	0.0	0.0	0.0	0.1	1.4	3.7	3.1	17.2	3.0	T	0.0	0.0	28.5
1993-94	0.0	0.0	0.0	2.4	1.1	5.6							
Record Mean	0.0	T	0.0	0.2	1.8	4.9	6.1	5.8	3.4	0.5	T	T	22.7

SOUTH BEND, INDIANA

South Bend is located on the Saint Joseph River in the northern portion of Saint Joseph County, situated on mostly level to gently rolling terrain and some former marshland. Drainage for the area is through the Saint Joseph River and Kankakee River.

South Bend is under the climatic influence of Lake Michigan with its nearest shore 20 miles to the northwest. The lake has a moderating effect on the temperature. Temperatures of 100 degrees or higher are rare and cold waves are less severe than at many locations at the same latitude. This results in favorable conditions for orchard and vegetable growth.

Based on the 1951-1980 period, the average first occurrence of 32 degrees Fahrenheit in the fall is October 18 and the average last occurrence in the spring is May 1.

Precipitation is fairly evenly distributed throughout the year with the greatest amounts during the growing season. The predominant snow season is from November through March, although there are also generally lighter amounts in October and April.

Winter is marked by considerable cloudiness and rather high humidity along with frequent periods of snow. Heavy snowfalls, resulting from a cold northwest wind passing over Lake Michigan are not uncommon.

NORMALS, MEANS, AND EXTREMES

SOUTH BEND, INDIANA

LATITUDE: 41 °42'N LONGITUDE: 86 °19' W ELEVATION: FT. GRND 773 BARO 782 TIME ZONE: EASTERN WBAN: 14848

	(a)	JAN	FEB	MAR	APR	MAY	JUNE	JULY	AUG	SEP	OCT	NOV	DEC	YEAR
TEMPERATURE °F:														
Normals														
-Daily Maximum		30.4	34.1	45.6	58.7	70.0	79.5	82.9	80.7	74.1	62.3	48.5	35.4	58.5
-Daily Minimum		16.1	18.7	29.1	38.7	48.8	58.6	63.0	61.1	53.7	42.8	33.4	22.3	40.5
-Monthly		23.3	26.4	37.4	48.7	59.4	69.1	72.9	70.9	63.9	52.6	40.9	28.9	49.5
Extremes														
-Record Highest	54	68	69	85	91	95	104	101	103	99	92	82	70	104
-Year		1950	1976	1981	1942	1942	1988	1991	1988	1953	1963	1950	1982	JUN 1988
-Record Lowest	54	-22	-17	-13	11	24	35	44	40	29	20	-7	-16	-22
-Year		1943	1951	1943	1972	1968	1972	1972	1965	1942	1988	1950	1960	JAN 1943
NORMAL DEGREE DAYS:														
Heating (base 65°F)		1293	1081	856	489	233	28	7	22	85	395	723	1119	6331
Cooling (base 65°F)		0	0	0	0	59	151	251	205	52	10	0	0	728
% OF POSSIBLE SUNSHINE														
MEAN SKY COVER (tenths)														
Sunrise - Sunset	48	8.0	7.7	7.5	6.9	6.3	6.1	5.7	5.7	5.9	6.1	7.8	8.2	6.8
MEAN NUMBER OF DAYS:														
Sunrise to Sunset														
-Clear	54	3.4	3.6	4.7	5.9	6.9	7.2	8.3	8.6	8.8	8.6	3.6	2.9	72.5
-Partly Cloudy	54	6.0	5.5	7.2	7.7	9.6	10.4	12.6	12.2	8.9	8.1	6.0	5.5	99.6
-Cloudy	54	21.6	19.1	19.2	16.5	14.5	12.4	10.1	10.1	12.3	14.3	20.4	22.6	193.1
Precipitation .01 inches or more	54	15.5	12.4	14.1	13.3	11.3	10.5	9.5	9.4	9.3	10.1	13.0	15.4	143.9
Snow,Ice pellets,hail 1.0 inches or more	54	5.8	5.0	2.9	0.7	0.0	0.0	0.0	0.0	0.*	0.3	2.5	5.5	22.8
Thunderstorms	54	0.4	0.4	2.4	4.4	5.1	8.0	7.3	6.4	4.4	2.0	1.0	0.4	42.2
Heavy Fog Visibility 1/4 mile or less	54	2.5	2.3	2.0	1.3	1.4	1.1	1.2	2.2	1.9	2.1	1.9	3.2	23.1
Temperature °F														
-Maximum														
90° and above	30	0.0	0.0	0.0	0.0	0.6	3.0	5.3	3.2	0.7	0.0	0.0	0.0	12.8
32° and below	30	16.4	12.4	3.9	0.1	0.0	0.0	0.0	0.0	0.0	0.0	1.8	10.0	44.7
-Minimum														
32° and below	30	28.0	24.4	20.0	7.7	0.7	0.0	0.0	0.0	0.*	3.3	14.0	25.0	123.1
0° and below	30	3.7	2.4	0.1	0.0	0.0	0.0	0.0	0.0	0.0	0.0	0.0	1.3	7.5
AVG. STATION PRESS.(mb)	21	989.4	989.8	987.4	986.7	986.8	986.9	988.2	989.4	989.8	989.9	988.9	989.5	988.6
RELATIVE HUMIDITY (%)														
Hour 01	30	80	78	77	74	75	77	82	85	84	79	80	81	79
Hour 07 (Local Time)	30	81	81	80	78	79	80	84	88	88	84	83	83	82
Hour 13	30	72	69	62	57	54	55	57	59	60	60	69	76	63
Hour 19	30	75	72	66	60	56	57	60	64	67	68	74	79	67
PRECIPITATION (inches):														
Water Equivalent														
-Normal		2.23	1.90	3.10	3.82	3.22	4.11	3.82	3.67	3.62	3.08	3.27	3.30	39.14
-Maximum Monthly	54	5.28	5.23	7.96	9.20	6.86	10.86	7.47	8.30	9.01	9.75	6.72	5.50	10.86
-Year		1959	1976	1976	1947	1990	1993	1982	1979	1977	1954	1985	1965	JUN 1993
-Minimum Monthly	54	0.44	0.54	0.54	0.50	1.17	0.48	0.02	0.32	0.01	0.42	1.37	0.60	0.01
-Year		1945	1969	1958	1971	1992	1988	1946	1950	1979	1950	1962	1943	SEP 1979
-Maximum in 24 hrs	54	2.81	2.64	2.33	3.14	2.99	4.70	3.64	3.70	3.00	3.49	3.95	3.33	4.70
-Year		1960	1954	1972	1947	1976	1968	1989	1966	1977	1988	1990	1965	JUN 1968
Snow,Ice pellets,hail														
-Maximum Monthly	54	86.1	35.1	33.9	14.0	0.6	T	T	T	1.2	8.8	30.3	41.9	86.1
-Year		1978	1958	1960	1982	1966	1992	1989	1989	1942	1989	1977	1962	JAN 1978
-Maximum in 24 hrs	54	16.7	14.4	14.8	8.7	0.6	T	T	T	1.0	8.8	17.5	13.7	17.5
-Year		1978	1993	1960	1982	1966	1992	1989	1989	1942	1989	1977	1981	NOV 1977
WIND:														
Mean Speed (mph)	45	11.9	11.3	12.0	11.6	10.2	9.1	8.2	7.7	8.6	9.6	11.1	11.3	10.2
Prevailing Direction through 1963		SW	SW	NNW	NNW	SSW	SSW	SSW	SSW	SSW	SSW	SSW	SW	SSW
Fastest Obs. 1 Min.														
-Direction (!!!)	44	22	20	20	27	27	27	34	32	31	25	22	23	27
-Speed (MPH)	44	52	47	51	55	68	50	45	63	35	38	58	43	68
-Year		1975	1953	1961	1962	1989	1950	1951	1953	1992	1955	1988	1953	MAY 1989
Peak Gust														
-Direction (!!!)	10	NW	NW	SW	SW	W	SW	W	SW	W	SW	SW	W	W
-Speed (mph)	10	59	58	54	66	86	71	66	45	63	59	74	54	86
-Date		1985	1987	1991	1984	1989	1987	1992	1988	1988	1991	1988	1987	MAY 1989

PRECIPITATION (inches)

SOUTH BEND, INDIANA

YEAR	JAN	FEB	MAR	APR	MAY	JUNE	JULY	AUG	SEP	OCT	NOV	DEC	ANNUAL
1964	1.57	1.03	5.01	5.37	1.32	4.45	4.80	3.42	3.39	0.89	2.33	2.54	36.12
1965	4.74	2.70	3.35	4.87	1.67	2.24	2.22	5.43	5.55	2.53	1.65	5.50	42.45
1966	1.54	1.73	2.58	5.72	3.89	1.90	4.40	5.48	1.10	1.32	4.89	4.73	39.28
1967	3.56	2.26	1.73	4.96	1.57	5.49	2.11	2.77	2.59	5.01	3.34	4.08	39.47
1968	2.06	3.21	1.24	2.40	2.44	9.09	2.06	3.17	4.38	1.43	4.42	3.42	39.32
1969	3.61	0.54	1.92	5.51	4.26	5.17	4.88	0.44	1.42	4.70	2.29	1.25	35.99
1970	1.34	0.76	2.81	5.43	3.35	3.92	4.14	3.37	5.37	3.68	3.57	1.78	39.52
1971	1.55	2.12	2.10	0.50	1.64	1.13	4.16	2.80	5.16	2.23	1.83	4.58	29.80
1972	1.82	1.39	3.63	3.23	3.01	2.72	4.52	3.85	7.67	3.76	2.90	4.78	43.28
1973	1.64	1.02	3.85	3.88	3.61	4.85	3.33	1.29	2.11	3.49	1.45	4.30	34.82
1974	3.24	2.20	2.81	4.17	4.82	4.08	1.17	1.70	4.65	2.46	3.21	3.00	37.51
1975	4.58	3.26	2.96	6.02	2.08	5.46	2.58	7.55	1.15	1.31	4.73	3.72	45.40
1976	2.21	5.23	7.96	5.20	6.67	6.60	5.96	2.44	3.34	3.23	3.23	2.21	54.28
1977	1.63	1.27	7.05	2.75	1.92	5.71	2.68	6.03	9.01	3.08	4.27	3.65	49.05
1978	4.03	0.86	2.37	4.35	3.35	3.79	5.21	3.80	3.07	3.99	2.79	4.43	42.04
1979	3.22	1.51	4.03	5.80	3.03	4.66	1.75	8.30	0.01	4.79	4.88	3.66	45.64
1980	1.52	1.51	3.74	3.44	1.65	5.97	3.29	7.84	5.64	3.35	1.47	3.91	43.33
1981	0.68	1.92	0.88	5.28	6.79	6.97	3.71	2.30	3.81	1.23	2.23	1.81	37.61
1982	2.95	1.17	4.54	1.46	5.51	3.12	7.47	2.84	2.51	0.91	4.52	3.40	40.40
1983	0.77	0.79	2.46	5.36	4.83	2.04	2.45	1.28	2.81	1.66	2.60	3.23	30.28
1984	0.86	1.45	2.10	4.22	4.02	3.43	1.76	1.47	4.02	4.38	2.73	4.42	34.86
1985	2.58	4.32	3.86	1.93	1.50	2.88	3.80	3.82	1.88	3.36	6.72	2.51	39.16
1986	1.24	2.46	2.09	1.87	3.42	5.06	6.15	1.90	4.27	3.81	2.90	1.67	36.84
1987	2.31	1.32	1.18	2.67	3.50	3.57	3.61	3.34	3.64	3.20	2.11	4.12	34.57
1988	2.21	1.98	3.03	2.91	1.40	0.48	1.28	5.63	4.42	6.68	5.72	2.91	38.65
1989	1.58	1.05	2.27	2.83	2.72	3.49	5.90	5.65	3.78	1.45	3.55	1.83	36.10
1990	2.36	3.66	2.79	2.91	6.86	4.40	5.45	4.60	3.76	7.09	6.69	5.04	55.61
1991	1.64	1.79	2.79	4.58	4.01	0.62	1.32	3.68	2.71	8.75	2.75	1.67	36.31
1992	1.64	1.73	2.93	2.19	1.17	1.74	5.24	2.07	8.84	1.60	5.54	3.99	38.68
1993	3.35	1.20	2.62	3.64	2.34	10.86	1.51	4.38	7.76	4.09	2.39	1.50	45.64
Record Mean	2.27	1.82	2.87	3.42	3.54	3.67	3.36	3.46	3.43	3.07	2.89	2.65	36.45

AVERAGE TEMPERATURE (deg. F)

SOUTH BEND, INDIANA

YEAR	JAN	FEB	MAR	APR	MAY	JUNE	JULY	AUG	SEP	OCT	NOV	DEC	ANNUAL
1964	29.3	27.3	35.8	50.4	63.5	71.1	74.0	69.0	63.0	48.9	43.2	27.5	50.2
1965	24.7	27.0	28.7	46.9	64.2	67.5	69.9	68.1	63.7	51.6	40.6	36.4	49.1
1966	20.3	28.1	39.1	45.3	52.2	68.8	72.9	67.2	62.3	51.7	42.8	29.9	48.4
1967	29.0	21.1	36.5	48.9	54.3	70.6	69.8	67.9	62.5	51.7	36.0	30.5	48.2
1968	22.3	22.3	39.7	50.0	55.2	68.9	71.0	71.6	64.6	53.7	40.7	27.0	48.9
1969	22.3	27.8	32.9	50.3	59.5	64.9	73.1	73.0	63.6	51.4	37.2	27.5	48.6
1970	16.8	25.7	32.3	48.8	61.0	67.8	72.0	70.4	64.4	54.4	39.4	30.4	48.6
1971	20.0	28.6	33.9	46.2	56.3	73.9	69.5	68.1	67.1	60.4	40.9	36.0	50.1
1972	23.9	26.5	33.4	45.4	60.0	63.6	71.4	69.4	62.9	49.7	38.1	28.8	47.8
1973	29.9	30.0	46.7	50.1	56.1	72.3	74.4	74.1	67.0	58.3	44.4	29.2	52.7
1974	27.9	28.1	39.6	51.7	57.3	66.8	75.0	71.9	62.0	53.0	42.4	32.9	50.7
1975	30.0	27.8	34.4	43.6	63.2	70.3	71.8	73.6	60.1	55.9	48.1	32.7	51.0
1976	21.6	35.3	43.6	52.5	57.0	70.9	72.8	69.0	61.3	47.9	33.2	22.8	49.0
1977	12.3	26.8	44.1	55.4	68.7	67.1	76.2	69.8	65.3	50.5	42.6	25.9	50.4
1978	18.5	14.8	31.2	48.7	59.5	69.2	71.7	71.9	68.9	51.9	42.9	29.5	48.2
1979	17.9	16.3	39.2	46.2	58.5	70.1	72.3	71.3	65.4	54.2	42.3	34.8	49.0
1980	27.1	23.6	35.5	49.0	62.1	67.8	76.6	75.0	66.3	50.4	41.6	31.1	50.5
1981	23.4	32.1	40.7	52.5	56.6	69.2	71.4	70.6	62.8	50.0	41.5	27.6	49.9
1982	15.6	22.7	35.1	44.7	66.0	64.5	73.3	68.9	63.3	54.0	42.5	39.0	49.1
1983	29.3	33.2	40.2	45.5	55.3	72.0	78.7	78.3	66.5	53.8	43.8	18.4	51.3
1984	18.5	35.9	30.0	48.2	56.1	72.3	71.7	74.4	63.8	57.1	41.0	34.4	50.3
1985	19.6	23.7	41.3	55.2	63.1	66.8	73.1	69.8	65.6	54.6	41.6	20.1	49.5
1986	25.8	24.8	40.4	51.3	59.9	67.7	74.8	67.6	65.9	53.0	36.1	31.2	49.9
1987	25.3	30.8	40.0	50.4	64.7	72.8	75.8	71.7	64.6	46.8	43.7	32.8	51.6
1988	21.3	22.7	37.3	48.4	62.2	72.0	76.4	75.9	64.5	45.9	42.5	28.8	49.8
1989	33.4	22.2	37.0	47.3	57.2	68.0	73.9	70.6	61.8	52.9	38.8	17.7	48.4
1990	34.0	31.3	40.9	48.7	56.7	68.8	71.2	69.9	65.0	52.3	45.9	31.8	51.4
1991	24.2	32.3	41.5	52.6	67.5	74.0	75.7	73.2	63.2	54.9	36.6	32.1	52.3
1992	29.1	33.2	37.4	46.1	58.4	65.1	70.0	67.4	62.3	51.4	40.0	30.9	49.3
1993	28.3	24.4	35.0	46.9	60.7	67.7	74.5	73.6	58.9	50.5	39.4	29.7	49.1
Record Mean	24.5	26.1	36.4	48.2	59.3	68.9	73.3	71.5	64.6	53.2	40.1	28.6	49.5
Max	31.9	34.0	45.2	58.5	70.4	79.8	84.1	82.3	75.2	63.2	47.9	35.4	59.0
Min	17.0	18.2	27.6	37.9	48.2	57.9	62.4	60.6	53.9	43.2	32.3	21.7	40.1

REFERENCE NOTES

SOUTH BEND, INDIANA

GENERAL
T - TRACE AMOUNT.
BLANK ENTRIES DENOTE MISSING/UNREPORTED DATA.
# INDICATES A STATION OR INSTRUMENT RELOCATION.

SPECIFIC

PM - INCLUDES LAST DAY OF PREVIOUS MONTH
ASOS - AUTOMATED SURFACE OBSERVING SYSTEM IN OPERATION DURING THESE MONTHS.

(a) - LENGTH OF RECORD IN YEARS, ALTHOUGH INDIVIDUAL MONTHS MAY BE MISSING.
0.* OR * - THE VALUE IS BETWEEN 0.0 AND 0.05
NORMALS - BASED ON THE 1961-1990 RECORD PERIOD.
EXTREMES - DATES ARE THE MOST RECENT OCCURRENCE
WIND DIR. - NUMERALS SHOW TENS OF DEGRESS CLOCKWISE FROM TRUE NORTH. "00" INDICATES CALM.
RESULTANT DIRECTIONS ARE GIVEN TO WHOLE DEGREES.
BOLD VALUES INDICATE EXTREME VALUES WHICH OCCURRED AFTER THE ASOS SYSTEM WAS COMMISSIONED.

RECORD = PERIOD OF RECORD
RECORD MEAN PRECIPITATION IS THE MEAN OF ALL DAILY PRECIPITATION AMOUNTS DURING THE PERIOD OF RECORD.
RECORD MAX(MIN) TEMPERATURE IS THE MEAN OF ALL DAILY MAX(MIN) TEMPERATURES DURING THE PERIOD OF RECORD.
RECORD MEAN TEMPERATURE IS THE SUM OF THE RECORD MAX AND RECORD MIN DIVIDED BY 2.
AVERAGE TEMPERATURE IS THE SUM OF THE MEAN DAILY MAX AND MIN TEMPERATURE DIVIDED BY 2.

EXCEPTIONS

RECORD MEANS ARE THROUGH THE CURRENT YEAR, BEGINNING IN 1894 FOR TEMPERATURE
1894 FOR PRECIPITATION
1940 FOR SNOWFALL

HEATING DEGREE DAYS Base 65 deg. F — SOUTH BEND, INDIANA

SEASON	JULY	AUG	SEP	OCT	NOV	DEC	JAN	FEB	MAR	APR	MAY	JUNE	TOTAL
1964-65	5	40	155	493	648	1157	1244	1058	1120	535	99	36	6590
1965-66	3	56	121	411	727	879	1377	1028	796	584	402	47	6431
1966-67	4	31	128	412	658	1079	1109	1220	880	474	337	8	6340
1967-68	31	30	137	429	861	1064	1317	1233	779	444	311	35	6671
1968-69	11	27	69	372	724	1171	1316	1034	988	433	226	105	6476
1969-70	0	0	110	421	826	1158	1485	1094	1007	497	181	68	6847
1970-71	18	11	93	327	766	1066	1387	1012	959	562	280	7	6488
1971-72	16	13	86	171	716	892	1269	1110	972	582	197	109	6133
1972-73	24	35	112	468	801	1115	1080	977	561	446	268	0	5887
1973-74	0	4	60	229	611	1102	1142	1028	780	403	250	51	5660
1974-75	0	3	144	378	672	985	1077	1035	944	634	136	37	6045
1975-76	13	1	175	300	503	992	1338	856	658	407	253	9	5505
1976-77	0	19	139	525	949	1302	1628	1063	640	327	85	68	6745
1977-78	2	18	58	443	669	1206	1436	1401	1041	480	233	41	7028
1978-79	5	4	57	399	656	1095	1453	1356	795	560	241	22	6643
1979-80	3	17	73	353	672	928	1172	1195	908	482	147	58	6008
1980-81	0	1	62	449	694	1047	1282	915	749	374	271	6	5850
1981-82	4	8	132	460	700	1154	1523	1178	922	604	64	72	6821
1982-83	2	30	114	353	668	798	1100	886	760	581	298	30	5620
1983-84	6	0	94	352	628	1440	1431	838	1080	503	290	4	6666
1984-85	7	0	128	244	714	940	1401	1153	727	339	116	47	5816
1985-86	0	4	121	319	694	1381	1208	1117	760	425	192	46	6267
1986-87	3	48	81	369	858	1038	1224	950	766	436	139	16	5928
1987-88	5	25	78	558	638	993	1347	1220	851	498	158	37	6408
1988-89	1	11	72	581	670	1116	972	1190	865	528	271	40	6317
1989-90	0	12	147	381	779	1462	954	936	751	521	257	46	6246
1990-91	6	14	110	408	565	1021	1260	910	722	378	106	2	5502
1991-92	0	1	167	318	844	1012	1104	915	850	561	247	75	6094
1992-93	6	25	139	417	742	1049	1130	1130	925	536	157	55	6311
1993-94	0	7	198	450	765	1087							

COOLING DEGREE DAYS Base 65 deg. F — SOUTH BEND, INDIANA

YEAR	JAN	FEB	MAR	APR	MAY	JUNE	JULY	AUG	SEP	OCT	NOV	DEC	TOTAL
1969	0	0	0	0	59	109	257	256	73	3	0	0	757
1970	0	0	0	19	63	158	240	185	82	5	0	0	752
1971	0	0	0	3	17	283	163	114	155	34	0	0	769
1972	0	0	0	0	47	74	226	180	55	0	0	0	582
1973	0	0	0	7	1	226	297	292	126	29	0	0	978
1974	0	0	0	10	17	114	321	222	60	11	0	0	755
1975	0	0	0	0	86	203	232	274	32	25	1	0	853
1976	0	0	1	37	13	192	249	150	36	4	0	0	682
1977	0	0	0	47	206	137	355	173	74	0	2	0	994
1978	0	0	0	0	70	173	218	227	179	0	1	0	868
1979	0	0	0	2	48	181	236	220	93	21	0	0	801
1980	0	0	0	9	65	145	367	319	107	6	0	0	1018
1981	0	0	2	6	15	137	211	191	72	0	0	0	634
1982	0	0	0	3	105	65	266	159	71	17	0	0	686
1983	0	0	0	1	3	247	440	417	146	13	0	0	1267
1984	0	0	0	5	19	228	226	298	98	7	0	0	881
1985	0	0	0	52	64	109	260	159	147	3	0	0	794
1986	0	0	4	22	41	135	312	136	113	2	0	0	765
1987	0	0	0	3	136	256	345	240	71	0	3	0	1054
1988	0	0	0	3	77	254	362	357	65	0	0	0	1118
1989	0	0	1	6	37	137	283	194	55	11	0	0	724
1990	0	0	9	37	8	167	203	171	117	21	0	0	733
1991	0	0	0	13	189	281	338	264	121	11	0	0	1217
1992	0	0	0	2	50	90	168	103	66	2	0	0	481
1993	0	0	0	0	29	144	302	284	18	9	0	0	786

SNOWFALL (inches) — SOUTH BEND, INDIANA

SEASON	JULY	AUG	SEP	OCT	NOV	DEC	JAN	FEB	MAR	APR	MAY	JUNE	TOTAL
1964-65	0.0	0.0	0.0	T	13.5	18.5	14.7	20.1	20.5	0.4	0.0	0.0	87.7
1965-66	0.0	0.0	0.0	2.4	7.3	8.6	26.9	10.7	11.4	5.4	0.6	0.0	73.3
1966-67	0.0	0.0	T	T	16.2	18.2	30.4	31.6	11.3	2.9	0.0	0.0	110.6
1967-68	0.0	0.0	0.0	5.0	7.0	12.5	12.6	20.1	8.7	1.5	T	0.0	67.4
1968-69	0.0	0.0	0.0	T	8.8	27.9	24.1	10.0	6.8	T	0.0	0.0	77.6
1969-70	0.0	0.0	0.0	T	10.5	17.1	24.8	11.2	16.7	7.9	0.0	0.0	88.2
1970-71	0.0	0.0	0.0	0.0	11.0	20.0	22.5	7.5	19.1	2.6	0.0	0.0	82.7
1971-72	0.0	0.0	0.0	0.0	16.3	4.4	19.2	21.2	16.1	7.1	0.0	0.0	84.3
1972-73	0.0	0.0	0.0	1.5	12.6	19.7	5.5	10.6	4.7	1.7	0.0	0.0	56.3
1973-74	0.0	0.0	0.0	0.0	1.0	22.6	14.4	11.9	9.4	1.2	0.0	0.0	60.5
1974-75	0.0	0.0	0.0	0.6	7.9	19.9	9.2	13.9	17.8	5.4	0.0	0.0	74.7
1975-76	0.0	0.0	0.0	0.0	10.7	14.0	31.2	13.9	3.8	0.6	0.1	0.0	74.3
1976-77	0.0	0.0	0.0	0.8	21.6	37.6	37.2	13.9	15.8	2.3	0.0	0.0	129.2
1977-78	0.0	0.0	0.0	0.3	30.3	33.6	86.1	16.6	5.1	T	0.0	0.0	172.0
1978-79	0.0	0.0	0.0	0.0	7.5	26.4	45.1	15.9	6.3	0.1	0.0	0.0	101.3
1979-80	0.0	0.0	0.0	T	7.5	13.6	11.5	22.3	9.8	1.7	0.0	0.0	66.4
1980-81	0.0	0.0	0.0	1.1	8.8	24.3	23.8	20.7	6.3	T	0.0	0.0	85.0
1981-82	0.0	0.0	0.0	0.1	9.1	41.3	41.3	19.2	10.2	14.0	0.0	0.0	135.2
1982-83	0.0	0.0	0.0	0.0	2.1	2.5	8.0	9.6	12.0	1.1	0.0	0.0	35.3
1983-84	0.0	0.0	0.0	0.0	1.4	35.6	16.7	15.9	11.1	0.4	0.0	0.0	81.1
1984-85	0.0	0.0	0.0	0.0	0.6	14.1	40.0	28.9	1.6	3.1	0.0	0.0	88.3
1985-86	0.0	0.0	0.0	0.0	2.2	40.4	26.3	11.3	3.6	0.2	0.0	0.0	84.0
1986-87	0.0	0.0	0.0	0.0	9.7	4.8	31.4	5.9	2.0	1.5	0.0	0.0	55.3
1987-88	0.0	0.0	T	T	1.6	13.1	11.4	22.9	12.1	T	0.0	0.0	61.1
1988-89	0.0	0.0	0.0	0.3	7.8	14.8	3.1	16.3	2.5	1.7	T	T	46.5
1989-90	T	T	0.0	8.8	15.2	29.4	1.2	13.9	3.4	1.1	0.0	0.0	73.0
1990-91	0.0	0.0	0.0	T	T	17.5	15.7	23.4	2.4	T	T	0.0	59.0
1991-92	0.0	0.0	0.0	T	7.6	11.7	19.9	10.9	16.7	0.9	0.0	T	67.7
1992-93	0.0	0.0	0.0	1.2	7.7	12.6	8.1	32.2	19.0	1.4	0.0	0.0	82.2
1993-94	0.0	0.0	0.1	T	2.2	11.3							
Record Mean	T	T	T	0.7	8.0	17.7	18.9	14.9	9.1	2.0	T	T	71.3

DES MOINES, IOWA

Located in the heart of North America, Des Moines has a climate which is continental in character. This results in a marked seasonal contrast in both temperature and precipitation. There is a gently rolling terrain in and around the Des Moines metropolitan area. Drainage of the area is generally to the southeast to the Des Moines River and its tributaries.

Since agriculture and services for it are the mainstay of the area, it is convenient to separate the year into arbitrary seasons corresponding to the growing seasons of the principal crops of the section. The winter season, when most plant life is dormant, is from mid-November to late March. The summer season, when corn and soybeans can be grown, lasts from early May to early October. The spring growing season, including part of the growing season of oats and forage crops, and the fall harvest season, each runs about 6 weeks. There is a large variation in annual precipitation from a minimum of about 17 inches to a maximum of about 56 inches. The average annual snowfall is 32 inches. Annual variation of snowfall is also large, ranging from a minimum of about 8 inches to as much as 72 inches.

The winter is a season of cold dry air, interrupted by occasional storms of short duration. At the beginning and the end of the season, the precipitation may occur as rain, but during the major portion of the season it falls as snow. Drifting snow may be extensive and impede transportation. The average precipitation for this season is approximately 20 percent of the annual amount. Although occasional cold waves follow the storms, bitterly cold days on which the temperatures fail to rise above zero occur on an average of only 3 days in 4 years.

The average growing season with temperatures above 32 degrees normally spans 160 to 165 days between late April and mid-October. The growing season is characterized by prevailing southerly winds and precipitation falling primarily as showers and thunderstorms, occasionally with damaging wind, erosive downpours or hail. Some 60 percent of the annual precipitation falls during the crop season with the maximum rate normally in late May and June. The autumn is characteristically sunny with diminishing precipitation, a condition favorable for drying and harvesting crops.

NORMALS, MEANS, AND EXTREMES

DES MOINES, IOWA

LATITUDE: 41°32'N LONGITUDE: 93°39' W ELEVATION: FT. GRND 938 BARO 966 TIME ZONE: CENTRAL WBAN: 14933

	(a)	JAN	FEB	MAR	APR	MAY	JUNE	JULY	AUG	SEP	OCT	NOV	DEC	YEAR
TEMPERATURE °F:														
Normals														
-Daily Maximum		28.1	33.7	46.9	61.8	73.0	82.2	86.7	84.2	75.6	64.3	48.0	32.6	59.8
-Daily Minimum		10.7	15.6	27.6	40.0	51.5	61.2	66.5	63.6	54.5	42.7	29.9	16.1	40.0
-Monthly		19.4	24.7	37.3	50.9	62.3	71.8	76.6	73.9	65.1	53.5	39.0	24.4	49.9
Extremes														
-Record Highest	54	65	73	91	93	98	103	105	108	101	95	76	69	108
-Year		1989	1972	1986	1980	1967	1988	1955	1983	1939	1963	1990	1984	AUG 1983
-Record Lowest	54	-24	-20	-22	9	30	38	47	40	26	14	-4	-22	-24
-Year		1970	1958	1962	1975	1967	1945	1971	1950	1942	1972	1991	1989	JAN 1970
NORMAL DEGREE DAYS:														
Heating (base 65°F)		1414	1128	859	428	165	10	0	11	71	372	780	1259	6497
Cooling (base 65°F)		0	0	0	5	81	214	360	287	74	15	0	0	1036
% OF POSSIBLE SUNSHINE	43	52	54	55	56	61	68	72	70	66	62	49	46	59
MEAN SKY COVER (tenths)														
Sunrise - Sunset	44	6.5	6.5	6.8	6.5	6.4	5.8	5.2	5.2	5.1	5.3	6.5	6.8	6.0
MEAN NUMBER OF DAYS:														
Sunrise to Sunset														
-Clear	44	7.9	7.6	6.8	7.3	7.6	8.2	10.4	10.8	11.8	11.7	7.5	7.1	104.7
-Partly Cloudy	44	7.3	5.8	7.3	7.5	8.5	10.5	11.0	10.4	7.4	7.2	6.8	6.7	96.5
-Cloudy	44	15.8	14.9	16.9	15.1	14.8	11.3	9.6	9.8	10.8	12.1	15.7	17.2	164.0
Precipitation														
.01 inches or more	54	7.6	7.3	10.2	10.6	11.4	10.7	9.5	9.2	8.7	7.6	7.3	8.0	108.1
Snow,Ice pellets,hail														
1.0 inches or more	54	2.4	2.3	1.9	0.5	0.0	0.0	0.0	0.0	0.0	0.1	0.9	2.2	10.2
Thunderstorms	54	0.3	0.4	2.1	4.3	7.2	9.2	8.4	7.4	5.1	2.7	1.1	0.3	48.5
Heavy Fog Visibility														
1/4 mile or less	44	2.1	2.4	2.1	0.9	0.8	0.6	0.6	1.2	1.2	1.2	1.8	2.8	17.6
Temperature °F														
-Maximum														
90° and above	32	0.0	0.0	0.*	0.2	0.5	4.3	9.7	6.8	1.7	0.1	0.0	0.0	23.4
32° and below	32	17.4	12.8	4.5	0.2	0.0	0.0	0.0	0.0	0.0	0.0	3.4	13.7	52.0
-Minimum														
32° and below	32	30.0	25.7	20.4	6.3	0.2	0.0	0.0	0.0	0.2	4.9	18.7	28.7	135.0
0° and below	32	7.9	3.9	0.2	0.0	0.0	0.0	0.0	0.0	0.0	0.0	0.3	3.7	16.0
AVG. STATION PRESS.(mb)	21	984.7	984.0	980.2	979.4	979.1	979.3	980.9	981.8	982.4	982.7	982.0	983.7	981.7
RELATIVE HUMIDITY (%)														
Hour 00	32	74	76	73	69	70	73	76	79	79	73	76	78	75
Hour 06 (Local Time)	32	76	78	78	78	78	80	82	85	85	79	79	80	80
Hour 12	32	67	65	61	55	55	56	58	58	59	55	64	69	60
Hour 18	32	69	66	59	53	53	53	57	58	60	58	67	72	60
PRECIPITATION (inches):														
Water Equivalent														
-Normal		0.96	1.11	2.33	3.36	3.66	4.46	3.78	4.20	3.53	2.62	1.79	1.32	33.12
-Maximum Monthly	54	4.38	2.99	5.82	7.76	7.88	14.19	10.51	13.68	10.19	7.29	6.52	3.43	14.19
-Year		1960	1951	1990	1976	1991	1947	1958	1977	1961	1941	1983	1982	JUN 1947
-Minimum Monthly	54	0.07	0.13	0.37	0.23	1.23	1.02	0.04	0.25	0.41	0.03	0.03	0.12	0.03
-Year		1954	1968	1989	1985	1949	1992	1975	1984	1950	1952	1969	1976	NOV 1969
-Maximum in 24 hrs	54	2.97	1.77	2.42	3.80	2.79	5.50	5.14	6.18	4.47	2.81	3.35	1.69	6.18
-Year		1960	1961	1945	1974	1954	1947	1958	1975	1961	1947	1952	1982	AUG 1975
Snow,Ice pellets,hail														
-Maximum Monthly	54	19.8	21.3	18.8	15.6	0.2	T	T	0.0	T	7.4	14.7	23.9	23.9
-Year		1942	1962	1948	1982	1944	1993	1992		1992	1980	1991	1961	DEC 1961
-Maximum in 24 hrs	54	19.8	12.1	8.5	10.4	0.2	T	T	0.0	T	7.4	11.8	11.0	19.8
-Year		1942	1950	1957	1973	1944	1993	1992		1992	1980	1968	1961	JAN 1942
WIND:														
Mean Speed (mph)	44	11.5	11.4	12.7	12.7	11.1	10.2	8.9	8.6	9.4	10.3	11.3	11.2	10.8
Prevailing Direction through 1963		NW	NW	NW	NW	SE	S	S	S	S	S	NW	NW	NW
Fastest Mile														
-Direction (!!)	40	NW	W	S	W	W	NW	W	SSE	NW	W	W	SW	W
-Speed (MPH)	40	66	56	66	76	70	76	73	60	55	56	72	61	76
-Year		1953	1952	1953	1965	1955	1953	1968	1960	1953	1952	1952	1951	APR 1965
Peak Gust														
-Direction (!!)	10	NW	NW	W	SW	E	SW	S	NW	W	NW	SW	NW	S
-Speed (mph)	10	55	62	58	66	54	58	83	63	54	60	62	55	83
-Date		1990	1984	1985	1989	1988	1990	1993	1989	1985	1985	1986	1985	JUL 1993

PRECIPITATION (inches)

DES MOINES, IOWA

YEAR	JAN	FEB	MAR	APR	MAY	JUNE	JULY	AUG	SEP	OCT	NOV	DEC	ANNUAL
1964	0.51	0.28	1.25	3.29	2.90	6.49	3.37	3.94	4.28	0.29	0.95	0.87	28.42
1965	1.62	1.14	3.02	4.18	3.89	4.80	1.93	1.93	7.23	0.79	1.79	1.64	33.96
1966	0.96	0.25	1.56	1.74	5.37	5.22	2.43	2.09	0.75	0.29	0.70	0.49	21.85
1967	0.77	0.28	1.64	2.25	2.22	7.39	0.81	0.79	2.54	1.93	0.47	0.73	21.82
1968	0.78	0.13	0.93	4.19	2.62	3.42	4.48	4.05	2.63	1.47	1.90	1.71	28.31
1969	1.01	0.97	1.41	4.46	4.75	7.32	4.34	1.83	2.43	2.87	0.03	1.01	32.43
1970	0.26	0.24	3.28	2.28	4.21	2.45	1.96	4.95	6.51	5.20	1.46	0.83	33.63
1971	1.75	2.34	0.41	1.54	3.87	4.31	2.16	1.83	2.19	3.51	3.29	1.12	28.32
1972	0.44	0.63	1.05	3.56	3.05	2.58	5.86	6.65	5.45	2.36	2.43	1.96	36.02
1973	2.09	2.21	4.15	4.67	5.01	2.04	9.17	1.37	7.07	3.26	1.49	2.65	45.18
1974	1.51	0.84	1.99	6.31	7.19	4.62	1.33	2.81	2.08	3.96	1.20	1.83	35.67
1975	1.41	1.48	1.90	2.65	3.41	5.98	0.04	9.73	1.70	0.63	2.20	0.48	31.61
1976	0.23	2.43	3.04	7.76	2.84	7.25	1.87	2.26	1.00	1.11	0.10	0.12	30.01
1977	0.50	0.36	3.57	2.45	2.29	1.25	2.63	13.68	2.82	5.10	0.69	1.81	37.15
1978	0.28	1.27	0.90	4.57	3.49	2.74	2.95	3.10	6.39	1.14	3.16	1.37	31.36
1979	1.72	0.52	4.23	3.23	2.50	5.78	2.96	5.07	0.97	3.23	1.43	0.20	31.84
1980	1.80	0.64	1.15	0.86	1.94	5.56	1.52	7.24	1.03	1.90	0.45	1.00	25.09
1981	0.25	0.97	0.39	2.00	2.46	5.02	5.76	6.32	2.30	2.06	2.63	1.14	31.30
1982	2.63	0.78	3.30	5.03	5.79	2.59	7.00	5.25	2.94	3.44	2.62	3.43	44.80
1983	1.17	1.95	3.72	3.80	3.93	3.65	2.44	3.01	3.87	5.54	6.52	1.57	41.17
1984	0.99	0.82	1.65	5.85	5.58	7.81	6.22	0.25	2.76	6.28	1.16	2.41	41.78
1985	0.64	1.98	3.37	0.23	1.56	3.72	2.04	2.83	5.42	3.75	1.65	1.31	28.50
1986	0.12	1.76	2.92	5.66	4.35	7.08	3.90	4.52	6.41	3.89	0.99	0.98	42.58
1987	0.42	1.38	2.99	2.92	3.75	2.10	5.08	10.04	1.40	1.03	3.27	2.59	36.97
1988	0.37	0.59	0.66	0.75	1.46	2.75	4.78	3.05	2.89	0.59	3.38	0.84	22.11
1989	1.30	1.05	0.37	1.95	3.62	2.22	3.65	6.53	5.41	2.28	0.19	0.57	29.14
1990	1.43	0.89	5.82	3.43	4.36	9.52	8.75	1.83	1.40	1.80	2.52	2.18	43.93
1991	0.95	0.17	3.90	7.54	7.88	2.87	1.14	3.65	0.90	4.96	3.61	2.20	39.77
1992	0.97	2.12	2.13	3.99	1.45	1.02	7.76	1.39	4.99	0.51	5.20	1.98	33.51
1993	1.59	1.52	3.22	2.96	7.51	7.68	9.75	12.24	5.79	1.70	1.06	0.86	55.88
Record Mean	1.11	1.14	2.03	2.97	4.19	4.64	3.53	3.82	3.39	2.44	1.68	1.23	32.17

AVERAGE TEMPERATURE (deg. F)

DES MOINES, IOWA

YEAR	JAN	FEB	MAR	APR	MAY	JUNE	JULY	AUG	SEP	OCT	NOV	DEC	ANNUAL
1964	27.8	26.3	30.4	48.0	64.3	69.9	77.2	70.4	63.6	50.8	41.2	23.3	49.4
1965	17.6	20.2	22.7	48.1	66.2	70.3	74.8	72.9	61.0	55.3	41.0	35.3	48.8
1966	14.2	24.7	41.0	46.0	57.7	70.4	78.6	70.8	62.4	52.9	38.4	24.8	48.5
1967	23.7	22.2	40.3	51.1	57.1	69.0	72.1	70.3	62.3	51.5	36.5	28.9	48.8
1968	22.3	23.9	42.6	51.1	57.0	72.4	74.2	73.0	63.3	53.8	34.8	21.3	49.2
1969	16.2	25.9	28.2	52.5	62.9	67.3	76.0	74.7	66.1	50.0	39.0	23.8	48.5
1970	12.7	27.1	32.9	51.7	65.8	72.4	76.6	73.9	65.5	54.1	39.8	28.8	50.1
1971	15.7	23.1	35.2	52.1	58.7	76.8	72.1	73.2	68.1	60.5	39.6	28.2	50.3
1972	16.6	19.9	37.1	48.9	62.5	70.2	73.9	72.4	64.6	48.0	33.9	18.4	47.2
1973	22.0	27.7	45.6	49.2	59.8	73.6	76.4	76.9	65.7	59.0	40.7	22.1	51.6
1974	19.5	28.0	39.8	53.0	60.3	69.1	80.9	71.1	60.9	55.0	39.6	28.2	50.4
1975	22.7	22.4	29.7	46.9	65.9	72.3	77.9	77.1	61.8	57.2	43.5	29.9	50.6
1976	22.9	34.1	39.7	55.4	60.7	71.4	77.2	73.8	65.7	48.5	32.6	21.8	50.3
1977	10.1	29.8	44.7	58.5	69.5	74.7	81.0	72.1	66.5	52.3	39.1	23.2	51.8
1978	11.0	13.3	33.2	50.5	61.6	72.8	75.8	75.1	70.5	52.4	39.0	23.0	48.2
1979	7.5	13.8	35.2	47.0	61.1	70.9	74.5	74.3	66.8	54.3	38.0	31.6	47.9
1980	23.4	21.3	34.7	52.0	63.5	71.2	79.9	76.2	66.8	49.6	41.6	26.6	50.6
1981	25.7	29.8	42.7	57.6	60.4	72.9	76.1	72.4	66.0	51.7	42.8	25.5	51.9
1982	9.6	22.9	35.4	46.9	64.7	67.1	76.9	73.2	64.9	54.6	38.4	31.6	48.8
1983	27.3	32.3	39.4	45.4	58.4	73.2	80.9	83.3	67.7	52.6	40.7	9.8	50.9
1984	19.7	35.5	31.1	48.8	58.7	73.2	75.9	77.5	62.4	52.8	39.5	27.6	50.2
1985	15.8	22.2	42.0	55.2	65.1	68.4	76.5	71.9	64.8	52.6	30.0	13.4	48.2
1986	26.9	21.7	42.5	53.9	62.6	73.3	77.2	69.3	67.4	52.6	33.3	28.8	50.8
1987	26.6	35.7	42.7	54.6	66.8	74.7	78.5	72.1	65.2	48.2	43.1	30.0	53.2
1988	19.6	21.6	40.2	51.4	67.4	75.6	78.5	78.8	66.9	47.9	39.8	28.8	51.4
1989	32.5	15.4	37.1	52.3	61.0	68.9	77.1	73.3	62.2	54.1	36.0	16.9	48.9
1990	31.7	31.1	42.0	50.0	57.9	71.6	73.8	74.4	68.1	52.4	43.7	22.9	51.6
1991	16.8	33.5	42.5	53.6	66.7	74.8	76.1	73.7	65.0	52.5	30.9	30.6	51.4
1992	30.7	34.9	42.4	48.9	62.0	70.3	71.2	68.3	63.1	53.4	34.9	27.1	50.6
1993	21.3	21.5	34.1	47.1	61.0	69.0	73.8	73.8	59.2	50.4	36.4	28.4	48.0
Record Mean	20.8	24.9	36.7	50.6	61.7	71.2	76.2	73.8	65.3	53.8	38.4	25.9	49.9
Max	29.5	33.8	45.9	60.9	71.9	81.2	86.5	84.1	75.9	64.4	47.5	34.1	59.6
Min	12.0	16.0	27.4	40.3	51.4	61.2	65.8	63.5	54.8	43.2	29.2	17.8	40.2

REFERENCE NOTES

DES MOINES, IOWA

GENERAL
T - TRACE AMOUNT.
BLANK ENTRIES DENOTE MISSING/UNREPORTED DATA.
# INDICATES A STATION OR INSTRUMENT RELOCATION.

SPECIFIC

PM - INCLUDES LAST DAY OF PREVIOUS MONTH
ASOS - AUTOMATED SURFACE OBSERVING SYSTEM IN OPERATION DURING THESE MONTHS.

(a) - LENGTH OF RECORD IN YEARS, ALTHOUGH INDIVIDUAL MONTHS MAY BE MISSING.
0.* OR * - THE VALUE IS BETWEEN 0.0 AND 0.05
NORMALS - BASED ON THE 1961-1990 RECORD PERIOD.
EXTREMES - DATES ARE THE MOST RECENT OCCURRENCE
WIND DIR.- NUMERALS SHOW TENS OF DEGRESS CLOCKWISE FROM TRUE NORTH. "00" INDICATES CALM.
RESULTANT DIRECTIONS ARE GIVEN TO WHOLE DEGREES.
BOLD VALUES INDICATE EXTREME VALUES WHICH OCCURRED AFTER THE ASOS SYSTEM WAS COMMISSIONED.

RECORD = PERIOD OF RECORD
RECORD MEAN PRECIPITATION IS THE MEAN OF ALL DAILY PRECIPITATION AMOUNTS DURING THE PERIOD OF RECORD.
RECORD MAX(MIN) TEMPERATURE IS THE MEAN OF ALL DAILY MAX(MIN) TEMPERATURES DURING THE PERIOD OF RECORD.
RECORD MEAN TEMPERATURE IS THE SUM OF THE RECORD MAX AND RECORD MIN DIVIDED BY 2.
AVERAGE TEMPERATURE IS THE SUM OF THE MEAN DAILY MAX AND MIN TEMPERATURE DIVIDED BY 2.

EXCEPTIONS

RECORD MEANS ARE THROUGH THE CURRENT YEAR,
BEGINNING IN 1878 FOR TEMPERATURE
1877 FOR PRECIPITATION
1940 FOR SNOWFALL

HEATING DEGREE DAYS Base 65 deg. F — DES MOINES, IOWA

SEASON	JULY	AUG	SEP	OCT	NOV	DEC	JAN	FEB	MAR	APR	MAY	JUNE	TOTAL
1964-65	0	28	124	433	707	1286	1465	1247	1305	509	86	1	7191
1965-66	0	14	154	310	715	915	1568	1122	737	565	256	16	6372
1966-67	0	13	136	375	789	1239	1276	1192	767	421	308	22	6538
1967-68	14	18	109	440	850	1112	1317	1184	685	411	260	24	6424
1968-69	2	11	92	378	898	1351	1508	1086	1135	368	159	50	7038
1969-70	0	0	45	478	773	1270	1617	1055	987	422	99	9	6755
1970-71	0	0	100	352	748	1114	1521	1167	915	393	211	0	6521
1971-72	8	4	96	184	756	1132	1495	1303	857	478	149	23	6485
1972-73	7	10	112	523	925	1442	1326	1039	594	470	173	0	6621
1973-74	0	0	68	209	719	1325	1406	1033	775	363	189	20	6107
1974-75	0	12	168	307	755	1131	1308	1185	1090	539	81	11	6587
1975-76	0	0	148	267	637	1085	1297	890	780	302	160	4	5570
1976-77	0	1	76	527	964	1333	1700	981	624	234	25	2	6467
1977-78	0	3	35	388	769	1289	1667	1442	988	427	181	9	7198
1978-79	0	0	48	385	776	1293	1779	1433	912	532	163	13	7334
1979-80	1	10	57	339	801	1031	1281	1263	932	408	124	9	6256
1980-81	0	0	77	473	695	1182	1214	979	684	241	177	0	5722
1981-82	6	2	57	406	660	1218	1713	1175	911	536	73	30	6787
1982-83	0	6	113	326	791	1026	1162	908	787	587	219	17	5942
1983-84	0	0	96	394	720	1709	1401	851	1043	488	217	1	6920
1984-85	0	0	172	376	759	1154	1520	1192	707	335	59	27	6301
1985-86	0	0	172	378	1046	1596	1181	1208	702	344	116	2	6745
1986-87	0	25	51	378	941	1114	1184	813	687	336	58	6	5593
1987-88	0	24	54	513	648	1083	1399	1254	764	400	33	3	6175
1988-89	0	6	35	524	749	1114	1002	1384	866	417	170	31	6298
1989-90	0	6	140	345	865	1489	1025	943	703	469	221	21	6227
1990-91	3	0	85	394	633	1301	1491	875	699	355	112	0	5948
1991-92	0	1	144	395	1019	1058	1054	868	691	486	152	9	5877
1992-93	0	26	135	363	897	1169	1344	1210	953	528	151	42	6818
1993-94	0	2	185	460	851	1129							

COOLING DEGREE DAYS Base 65 deg. F — DES MOINES, IOWA

YEAR	JAN	FEB	MAR	APR	MAY	JUNE	JULY	AUG	SEP	OCT	NOV	DEC	TOTAL
1969	0	0	0	0	99	129	349	308	84	20	0	0	989
1970	0	0	0	31	131	238	368	280	123	20	0	0	1191
1971	0	0	0	13	26	362	234	263	194	52	0	0	1144
1972	0	0	0	3	77	184	289	247	109	0	0	0	909
1973	0	0	0	2	19	267	358	378	98	30	0	0	1152
1974	0	0	0	9	52	149	499	209	52	4	0	0	974
1975	0	0	0	3	116	237	408	383	58	32	0	0	1237
1976	0	0	0	19	36	203	385	283	104	20	0	0	1050
1977	0	0	0	48	172	298	505	232	86	1	0	0	1342
1978	0	0	6	0	83	251	341	321	221	3	0	0	1226
1979	0	0	0	0	48	194	304	305	118	15	0	0	984
1980	0	0	0	22	83	200	469	353	138	2	0	0	1267
1981	0	0	1	27	42	243	358	239	95	2	0	0	1007
1982	0	0	0	0	71	101	374	269	120	11	0	0	946
1983	0	0	0	4	20	272	502	574	183	19	0	0	1574
1984	0	0	0	8	27	254	345	397	101	2	0	0	1134
1985	0	0	0	46	69	134	361	221	174	0	0	0	1005
1986	0	0	11	17	46	258	386	162	130	0	0	0	1010
1987	0	0	0	31	121	304	426	250	65	0	0	0	1197
1988	0	0	0	1	112	329	425	444	101	3	0	0	1415
1989	0	0	6	44	53	156	379	269	61	15	0	0	983
1990	0	0	1	26	5	226	283	297	184	11	2	0	1035
1991	0	0	9	19	172	302	349	279	150	14	0	0	1294
1992	0	0	0	10	64	174	197	134	86	10	0	0	675
1993	0	0	0	0	31	167	281	280	19	15	0	0	793

SNOWFALL (inches) — DES MOINES, IOWA

SEASON	JULY	AUG	SEP	OCT	NOV	DEC	JAN	FEB	MAR	APR	MAY	JUNE	TOTAL
1964-65	0.0	0.0	0.0	T	0.5	2.6	7.4	7.6	17.3	0.0	0.0	0.0	35.4
1965-66	0.0	0.0	0.0	0.0	T	2.4	3.6	0.5	1.8	T	T	0.0	8.3
1966-67	0.0	0.0	0.0	T	T	7.1	4.0	2.3	0.5	0.9	T	0.0	14.8
1967-68	0.0	0.0	0.0	2.4	0.7	2.6	8.5	2.1	T	0.1	T	0.0	16.4
1968-69	0.0	0.0	0.0	T	13.5	5.2	6.8	12.3	2.8	0.0	0.0	0.0	40.6
1969-70	0.0	0.0	0.0	T	T	12.0	3.2	1.2	9.8	3.9	0.0	0.0	30.1
1970-71	0.0	0.0	0.0	0.0	0.2	1.4	15.9	13.7	5.3	0.4	0.0	0.0	36.9
1971-72	0.0	0.0	0.0	0.0	10.3	2.9	5.8	9.0	1.6	0.6	0.0	0.0	30.2
1972-73	0.0	0.0	0.0	T	10.2	9.5	15.3	4.6	T	15.1	0.0	0.0	54.7
1973-74	0.0	0.0	0.0	0.0	T	9.6	10.6	6.1	1.9	1.2	0.0	0.0	29.4
1974-75	0.0	0.0	0.0	0.0	9.3	9.1	13.3	17.9	5.6	4.5	0.0	0.0	59.7
1975-76	0.0	0.0	0.0	0.0	7.0	0.5	2.4	11.8	0.9	0.0	T	0.0	22.6
1976-77	0.0	0.0	0.0	T	1.1	2.8	7.6	0.9	4.8	1.9	0.0	0.0	19.1
1977-78	0.0	0.0	0.0	0.0	2.2	22.0	2.7	18.6	9.9	0.3	0.0	0.0	55.7
1978-79	0.0	0.0	0.0	0.0	5.8	11.0	16.6	8.2	4.1	8.0	0.0	0.0	53.7
1979-80	0.0	0.0	0.0	T	0.7	0.4	7.9	5.7	5.8	2.8	0.0	0.0	23.3
1980-81	0.0	0.0	0.0	7.4	T	2.7	3.7	6.6	T	0.0	0.0	0.0	20.4
1981-82	0.0	0.0	0.0	0.4	3.2	10.7	18.5	2.6	11.9	15.6	0.0	0.0	62.9
1982-83	0.0	0.0	0.0	0.8	0.3	3.6	4.2	16.8	13.2	12.6	0.0	0.0	51.5
1983-84	0.0	0.0	0.0	T	9.8	19.6	12.5	1.3	13.7	0.1	0.0	0.0	57.0
1984-85	0.0	0.0	0.0	T	2.7	7.6	7.7	6.9	6.7	T	0.0	0.0	31.6
1985-86	0.0	0.0	T	0.0	8.1	15.9	1.3	6.7	0.2	0.1	0.0	0.0	32.3
1986-87	0.0	0.0	0.0	T	3.1	2.9	5.1	2.8	5.5	0.0	0.0	0.0	19.4
1987-88	0.0	0.0	0.0	T	0.1	13.0	1.2	7.6	0.8	0.0	0.0	0.0	22.7
1988-89	0.0	0.0	0.0	0.0	1.1	1.0	0.1	16.3	1.2	0.6	T	0.0	20.3
1989-90	0.0	0.0	0.0	T	1.7	6.6	11.3	7.4	0.1	T	0.0	0.0	27.1
1990-91	0.0	0.0	0.0	T	1.3	12.1	9.9	0.4	0.2	T	T	0.0	23.9
1991-92	0.0	0.0	0.0	T	14.7	1.2	1.9	4.5	0.2	0.1	0.0	0.0	22.6
1992-93	T	0.0	T	T	10.0	3.7	11.1	10.1	5.1	1.5	T	T	41.5
1993-94	0.0	0.0	0.0	0.2	0.9	2.0							
Record Mean	T	0.0	T	0.2	3.0	6.6	8.1	7.2	6.2	1.9	T	T	33.3

1993 TOPEKA, KANSAS (TOP)

Topeka, is located near the geographical center of the United States, and the middle of the temperate zone. The city straddles the Kansas River about 60 miles above its junction with the Missouri River. The Kansas River flows in an easterly direction through northeastern Kansas. Near Topeka, the river valley ranges from 2 to 4 miles wide, and is bordered on both sides by rolling prairie uplands of some 200 to 300 feet. The city is built on both banks of the Kansas River and along two tributaries, Soldier Creek in north Topeka and Shunganunga Creek in the south and east part of town. Flooding is always a threat following periods of heavy rains but protective construction has reduced the problem.

Seventy percent of the annual precipitation normally falls during the six crop-growing months, April through September. The rains of this period are usually of short duration, predominantly of the thunderstorm type. They occur more frequently during the nighttime and early morning hours than at other times of the day. Excessive precipitation rates may occur with warm-season thunderstorms. Rainfall accumulations over 8 inches in 24 hours have occurred in Topeka. Tornadoes have occurred in the area on several occasions and caused severe damage and numerous injuries.

Individual summers show wide departures from average conditions. Hottest summers may produce temperatures of 100 degrees or higher on more than 50 days. On the other hand, 25 percent of the summers pass with two or fewer 100 degree days. Similarly, precipitation has shown a wide range for June, July, and August, varying from under 3 inches to more than 27 inches during the 3 months. Summers are hot with low relative humidity and persistent southerly winds. Oppressively warm periods with high relative humidity are usually of short duration.

Winter temperatures average about 45 degrees cooler than summer. Cold spells are seldom prolonged. Only on rare occasions do daytime temperatures fail to rise above freezing. Winter precipitation is often in the form of snow, sleet, or glaze, but storms of such severity to prevent normal movement of traffic or to interfere with scheduled activity are not common.

In the transitional spring and fall seasons, the numerous days of fair weather are interspersed with short intervals of stormy weather. Strong, blustery winds are quite common in late winter and spring. Autumn is characteristically a season of warm days, cool nights, and infrequent precipitation, with cold air invasions gradually increasing in intensity as the season progresses.

Nearly all crops of the temperate zone can be produced in the vicinity of Topeka. Wheat and other small grains, clover, soybeans, fruit, and berries do well, and the area supports an extensive dairy industry.

Based on the 1951-1980 period, the average first occurrence of 32 degrees Fahrenheit in the fall is October 14 and the average last occurrence in the spring is April 21.

NORMALS, MEANS, AND EXTREMES FOR 1993

TOPEKA, KS (TOP)

LATITUDE:	LONGTITUDE:	ELEVATION (FT):		TIME ZONE:	WBAN: 13996
39° 04' 08" N	95° 37' 20" W	GRND: 877	BARO: 884	CENTRAL (UTC+06)	

	ELEMENT	POR	JAN	FEB	MAR	APR	MAY	JUN	JUL	AUG	SEP	OCT	NOV	DEC	YEAR
TEMPERATURE °F	NORMAL DAILY MAXIMUM	30	37.0	42.6	55.0	66.9	75.8	84.2	89.3	87.5	79.7	69.0	54.0	40.5	65.1
	MEAN DAILY MAXIMUM	47	37.4	42.1	53.8	66.5	75.9	84.6	89.3	88.2	82.3	71.3	54.8	42.7	65.7
	HIGHEST DAILY MAXIMUM	47	73	84	89	95	97	107	110	110	109	96	85	73	110
	YEAR OF OCCURRENCE		1967	1972	1986	1987	1975	1953	1980	1984	1947	1963	1980	1984	AUG 1984
	MEAN OF EXTREME MAXS.	46	61.1	65.0	78.3	86.2	89.7	95.7	99.2	99.3	94.6	87.1	74.4	63.5	82.9
	NORMAL DAILY MINIMUM	30	16.3	21.7	32.1	42.8	53.3	62.9	67.6	64.9	55.7	43.6	32.0	21.0	42.8
	MEAN DAILY MINIMUM	47	16.9	21.5	31.2	42.7	53.3	63.1	67.4	65.3	57.2	45.2	32.4	22.3	43.2
	LOWEST DAILY MINIMUM	47	-20	-23	-7	10	26	43	43	41	29	19	2	-26	-26
	YEAR OF OCCURRENCE		1974	1979	1978	1975	1963	1993	1972	1988	1984	1993	1976	1989	DEC 1989
	MEAN OF EXTREME MINS.	46	-3.8	0.7	12.4	26.1	36.9	49.1	55.1	51.8	38.0	27.0	14.6	1.3	25.8
	NORMAL DRY BULB	30	26.7	32.2	43.6	54.9	64.6	73.6	78.5	76.2	67.8	56.3	43.0	30.8	54.0
	MEAN DRY BULB	47	27.2	31.8	42.5	54.6	64.6	73.8	78.3	76.8	69.8	58.3	43.6	32.5	54.5
	MEAN WET BULB	44	24.2	28.9	37.2	48.0	57.9	66.8	70.4	68.7	60.9	50.2	38.2	28.5	48.3
	MEAN DEW POINT	44	17.9	22.6	30.3	41.3	53.0	62.9	66.8	64.8	56.4	44.4	32.2	22.6	42.9
	NORMAL NO. DAYS WITH:														
	MAXIMUM ≥ 90°	30	0.0	0.0	0.0	0.4	1.1	6.7	15.5	12.8	4.7	0.6	0.0	0.0	41.8
	MAXIMUM ≤ 32°	30	10.9	6.8	1.4	*	0.0	0.0	0.0	0.0	0.0	0.0	1.1	7.7	27.9
	MINIMUM ≤ 32°	30	29.0	23.1	16.7	4.3	0.3	0.0	0.0	0.0	0.2	4.0	16.1	27.1	120.8
	MINIMUM ≤ 0°	30	4.1	2.0	0.1	0.0	0.0	0.0	0.0	0.0	0.0	0.0	0.0	1.9	8.1
H/C	NORMAL HEATING DEG. DAYS	30	1187	918	663	312	121	5	0	0	56	283	660	1060	5265
	NORMAL COOLING DEG. DAYS	30	0	0	0	9	109	263	419	351	140	13	0	0	1304
RH	NORMAL (PERCENT)	30	70	69	66	64	68	71	70	71	72	68	71	72	69
	HOUR 00 LST	30	75	75	73	72	78	81	78	80	82	77	78	77	77
	HOUR 06 LST	30	77	78	79	80	84	87	86	87	88	83	81	80	82
	HOUR 12 LST	30	63	62	57	54	57	60	59	58	58	54	60	65	59
	HOUR 18 LST	30	64	60	53	51	55	58	56	57	60	57	64	68	58
S	PERCENT POSSIBLE SUNSHINE	44	57	56	57	58	61	66	71	71	67	64	55	52	61
W/O	MEAN NO. DAYS WITH:														
	HEAVY FOG(VISBY ≤ 1/4 MI)	47	2.1	1.8	1.0	0.9	0.9	0.6	0.5	1.1	1.0	1.5	1.1	2.0	14.5
	THUNDERSTORMS	47	0.4	0.7	2.6	5.5	9.1	10.1	8.9	8.0	6.1	3.3	1.2	0.4	56.3
CLOUDINESS	MEAN:														
	SUNRISE-SUNSET (TENTHS)	1		8.0	8.0	9.0	8.0		8.0	4.0	5.0	6.0	6.0	6.0	
	MIDNIGHT-MIDNIGHT (TENTHS)	1		8.0	8.0	9.0	8.0		8.0	4.0	5.0	7.0	5.0	6.0	
	MEAN NO. DAYS WITH:														
	CLEAR	1	5.0	11.0	6.0	6.0	9.0	8.0	5.0	15.0	14.0	10.0	9.0	14.0	112.0
	PARTLY CLOUDY	1	6.0	2.0	9.0	4.0	6.0	5.0	5.0	6.0	1.0	1.0	2.0	6.0	53.0
	CLOUDY	1	9.0	11.0	10.0	11.0	8.0	5.0	9.0	6.0	9.0	10.0	10.0	10.0	108.0
PR	MEAN STATION PRESSURE(IN.)	21	29.19	29.15	29.02	29.00	28.99	29.00	29.04	29.06	29.09	29.11	29.10	29.17	29.08
	MEAN SEA-LEVEL PRES. (IN.)	44	30.16	30.12	30.01	29.95	29.92	29.91	29.96	29.98	30.01	30.06	30.08	30.12	30.02
WINDS	MEAN SPEED (MPH)	30	9.7	9.9	10.5	10.4	9.5	8.9	8.6	8.3	8.9	8.5	9.4	9.9	9.4
	PREVAIL.DIR(TENS OF DEGS.)	30	32	36	36	18	18	18	18	18	18	18	18	30	18
	MAXIMUM 2-MINUTE:														
	SPEED (MPH)	1	25	24	31	37	32	37	44	31	34	26	31	33	44
	DIR. (TENS OF DEGS.)	1	01	31	14	26	16	36	34	34	16	25	31	32	34
	YEAR OF OCCURRENCE		1993	1993	1993	1993	1993	1993	1993	1993	1993	1993	1993	1993	JUL 1993
	MAXIMUM 5-SECOND:														
	SPEED (MPH)	1	32	30	36	46	39	45	52	36	40	31	36	41	52
	DIR. (TENS OF DEGS.)	1	02	09	14	25	16	36	35	34	16	34	31	30	35
	YEAR OF OCCURRENCE		1993	1993	1993	1993	1993	1993	1993	1993	1993	1993	1993	1993	JUL 1993
PRECIPITATION	NORMAL TOTAL (IN.)	30	0.95	1.04	2.46	3.08	4.45	5.54	3.59	3.89	3.81	3.06	1.93	1.43	35.23
	MAXIMUM TOTAL (IN.)	47	5.24	3.49	8.44	8.12	9.39	15.20	12.02	11.18	12.71	7.24	6.27	4.30	15.20
	YEAR OF OCCURRENCE		1949	1971	1973	1967	1982	1967	1950	1977	1973	1980	1964	1973	JUN 1967
	MINIMUM TOTAL (IN.)	47	T	0.02	0.10	0.62	0.41	0.56	0.59	0.26	0.66	0.04	T	0.05	T
	YEAR OF OCCURRENCE		1986	1991	1966	1989	1966	1980	1983	1971	1952	1 952	1989	1979	NOV 1989
	MAXIMUM IN 24 HOURS (IN.)	47	1.55	2.33	3.76	3.59	3.62	5.52	4.19	4.48	4.80	4.10	4.66	2.65	5.52
	YEAR OF OCCURRENCE		1988	1971	1987	1967	1978	1967	1951	1962	1989	1985	1964	1980	JUN 1967
	NORMAL NO. DAYS WITH:														
	PRECIPITATION ≥ 0.01	30	5.9	5.9	8.7	9.8	11.0	10.3	7.9	8.3	8.3	6.8	6.5	6.6	96.0
	PRECIPITATION ≥ 1.00	30	0.1	0.1	0.5	0.7	1.3	1.8	1.2	1.3	1.2	1.1	0.3	0.2	9.8
SNOWFALL	NORMAL TOTAL (IN.)	30	5.8	4.7	2.8	0.6	0.0	0.0	0.0	0.0	0.0	0.*	1.2	5.6	20.7
	MAXIMUM TOTAL (IN.)	47	23.0	22.4	22.1	6.8	T	T	T	0.0	0.0	0.8	9.4	18.8	23.0
	YEAR OF OCCURRENCE		1993	1971	1960	1970	1991	1992	1992			1970	1972	1983	JAN 1993
	MAXIMUM IN 24 HOURS (IN.)	47	15.2	15.2	8.4	7.6	T	T	T	0.0	0.0	0.8	7.4	9.0	15.2
	YEAR OF OCCURRENCE		1993	1971	1960	1970	1991	1992	1992	1993	1993	1970	1975	1973	FEB 1971
	MAXIMUM SNOW DEPTH (IN.)	44	12	12	18	4	0	T	0	T	0	T	8	9	18
	YEAR OF OCCURRENCE		1979	1971	1960	1970		1993		1949		1957	1975	1983	MAR 1960
	NORMAL NO. DAYS WITH:														
	SNOWFALL ≥ 1.0	30	1.9	1.5	1.0	0.2	0.0	0.0	0.0	0.0	0.0	0.0	0.4	1.8	6.8

PRECIPITATION (inches) 1993 TOPEKA, KANSAS (TOP)

YEAR	JAN	FEB	MAR	APR	MAY	JUN	JUL	AUG	SEP	OCT	NOV	DEC	ANNUAL
1964	0.54	0.29	1.73	4.70	2.09	8.10	1.81	8.24	1.13	0.14	6.27	0.94	35.98
1965	1.60	1.27	1.58	2.31	3.41	10.14	3.33	3.53	7.22	0.92	0.20	2.46	37.97
1966	0.16	0.54	0.10	1.98	0.41	8.83	0.75	3.62	1.46	0.42	0.24	0.79	19.30
1967	1.06	0.21	1.91	8.12	5.07	15.20	3.06	1.84	4.64	6.01	0.41	3.11	50.64
1968	0.89	0.56	0.46	4.20	3.37	3.18	10.17	7.40	2.50	4.19	1.56	2.10	40.58
1969	0.84	0.42	1.37	7.14	3.77	8.46	3.26	0.87	2.03	3.98	0.10	1.24	33.48
1970	0.19	0.34	1.03	3.49	5.46	5.82	1.39	0.83	7.70	2.49	1.23	1.65	31.62
1971	1.20	3.49	0.64	1.08	4.83	3.10	4.07	0.26	1.35	3.87	3.03	1.83	28.75
1972	0.47	0.56	1.37	3.93	2.90	1.14	4.81	3.26	4.89	2.11	3.99	1.78	31.21
1973	2.67	1.71	8.44	4.03	4.37	2.96	10.16	2.83	12.71	4.57	2.14	4.30	60.89
1974	0.99	1.20	1.22	2.78	3.59	3.72	2.90	4.89	1.40	5.16	2.19	1.18	31.22
1975	1.50	1.67	1.66	3.26	3.88	4.85	0.68	1.69	4.35	0.05	4.44	1.12	29.15
1976	0.41	0.51	1.38	4.85	4.63	1.69	2.04	0.86	1.12	3.01	0.04	0.21	20.75
1977	0.90	0.22	2.06	2.46	7.83	10.91	1.37	11.18	3.22	4.92	3.38	0.26	48.71
1978	0.19	0.84	1.63	2.35	5.75	4.57	2.26	2.89	6.65	0.36	3.22	0.55	31.26
1979	1.81	0.63	3.95	2.37	2.25	5.63	5.84	4.05	2.17	4.15	1.80	0.05	34.70
1980	1.34	0.91	4.15	1.03	4.85	0.56	0.87	5.86	1.19	7.24	0.25	3.86	32.11
1981	0.32	0.21	1.61	1.98	5.93	9.40	7.63	3.92	2.03	3.72	3.63	0.22	40.60
1982	1.67	0.59	1.14	1.58	9.39	5.99	5.08	4.53	1.17	1.25	2.26	3.61	38.26
1983	0.69	0.63	4.39	6.29	4.93	6.08	0.59	0.62	2.25	5.19	3.61	1.34	36.61
1984	0.11	1.35	4.57	4.26	3.45	10.17	1.66	1.04	4.24	4.10	0.72	2.36	38.03
1985	0.70	2.02	2.38	3.60	3.79	5.15	2.90	7.97	8.16	5.20	2.02	0.71	44.60
1986	T	1.55	1.35	3.15	7.53	2.51	4.21	5.50	6.21	3.30	0.87	1.20	37.38
1987	1.09	2.71	5.92	2.33	3.89	4.86	2.78	5.90	1.81	1.86	1.94	1.87	36.96
1988	2.04	0.48	0.73	2.93	3.08	3.13	1.74	1.34	1.94	0.26	0.86	0.86	19.39
1989	1.24	0.86	3.11	0.62	4.05	4.76	5.21	6.22	8.65	3.44	T	0.61	38.77
1990	1.22	2.31	3.75	1.01	4.45	5.57	3.01	5.69	0.83	2.71	2.91	0.97	34.43
1991	0.76	0.00	2.98	3.63	7.09	1.49	1.47	1.76	2.15	3.20	2.20	2.44	29.17
1992	0.89	1.18	5.29	3.25	1.75	3.35	6.37	1.24	3.92	1.41	5.27	2.01	35.93
1993	1.11	1.61	2.56	5.43	6.95	2.18	10.98	5.32	7.03	1.37	1.12	0.90	46.56
POR= 47 YRS	0.97	1.11	2.47	3.14	4.35	5.13	4.26	3.88	3.41	2.78	1.77	1.40	34.66

WBAN : 13996

AVERAGE TEMPERATURE (˚F) 1993 TOPEKA, KANSAS (TOP)

YEAR	JAN	FEB	MAR	APR	MAY	JUN	JUL	AUG	SEP	OCT	NOV	DEC	ANNUAL
1964	34.2	34.3	40.0	56.4	68.9	72.1	81.2	74.5	68.1	54.6	46.2	29.8	55.0
1965	31.0	30.8	33.0	57.2	68.6	73.1	77.0	74.9	66.9	57.3	45.7	39.9	54.6
1966	26.0	31.9	47.0	50.8	63.8	72.7	83.1	74.8	65.8	55.4	44.1	30.7	53.8
1967	31.5	33.4	47.0	57.4	60.8	72.1	75.0	72.1	63.6	54.7	41.7	33.0	53.5
1968	26.6	31.6	46.4	53.5	59.1	74.1	76.4	75.5	66.6	57.3	40.0	29.0	53.0
1969	25.8	33.9	37.1	55.5	65.3	68.7	79.4	75.5	69.0	52.7	42.5	29.9	52.9
1970	23.3	35.9	39.5	53.5	68.1	71.8	77.8	80.6	69.1	54.2	41.2	34.3	54.1
1971	24.1	26.8	41.1	56.3	61.4	77.5	74.5	75.9	71.6	61.6	45.4	34.8	54.2
1972	25.6	31.8	46.7	54.7	63.6	74.3	74.4	74.7	68.5	54.6	39.4	27.7	53.0
1973	27.5	33.9	47.5	52.6	61.3	74.9	77.4	77.1	66.6	60.4	44.8	29.9	54.5
1974	22.3	35.9	46.9	56.8	67.2	70.0	80.6	74.1	61.9	58.4	43.1	32.7	54.2
1975	30.7	28.8	37.8	54.4	67.3	74.2	77.3	79.3	64.0	59.3	45.5	34.5	54.4
1976	27.8	42.7	45.4	57.0	60.4	72.7	78.0	76.9	69.0	50.3	35.4	28.5	53.7
1977	15.2	37.4	49.6	60.2	70.1	75.2	79.4	76.4	71.6	56.7	42.7	30.1	55.4
1978	17.3	20.4	38.4	55.9	63.0	74.6	77.3	75.7	72.9	54.6	43.0	30.0	51.9
1979	11.8	19.2	42.6	51.6	63.1	72.4	77.8	76.9	68.0	57.0	40.0	35.5	51.3
1980	28.6	26.0	40.8	53.7	62.8	76.5	86.4	80.7	70.0	53.9	45.0	32.6	54.8
1981	31.4	35.5	46.1	60.6	60.9	75.5	79.5	73.1	68.0	56.1	47.2	30.1	55.3
1982	21.9	28.5	43.2	50.2	63.7	69.0	78.7	75.5	66.5	55.9	42.0	35.8	52.6
1983	32.5	36.1	44.9	49.4	62.5	73.5	81.1	83.0	72.2	58.7	45.8	14.4	54.5
1984	26.0	40.2	38.1	51.7	62.4	73.9	77.0	78.0	66.5	56.6	45.5	36.8	54.4
1985	19.9	25.6	48.6	58.7	66.5	72.0	79.7	72.8	66.8	56.6	36.7	25.1	52.4
1986	35.8	32.5	49.8	57.7	65.9	77.0	80.4	72.3	71.6	56.6	38.3	34.6	56.0
1987	29.7	40.3	46.7	57.1	70.4	76.2	78.1	75.5	68.2	52.6	47.4	35.9	56.5
1988	28.1	30.8	43.4	53.9	68.8	75.1	76.7	79.5	70.3	52.8	45.2	35.3	55.0
1989	38.0	22.9	44.4	57.9	64.2	71.4	77.6	74.8	62.3	57.1	42.3	21.0	52.8
1990	37.3	36.2	45.5	51.9	60.3	77.2	77.7	76.5	71.6	57.0	49.1	29.6	55.8
1991	25.2		48.2	57.7	69.4	77.1	80.2	77.3	69.3	58.6	37.9	37.4	
1992	37.2	41.5	47.8	54.7	62.5	69.1	75.9	71.7	67.9	56.5	39.1	32.6	54.7
1993	26.4	29.9	40.8	50.2	63.1	72.9	78.2	77.8	63.4	54.0	39.3	34.8	52.6
POR= 47 YRS	27.2	32.5	42.5	54.6	64.7	73.9	78.3	76.8	68.3	57.1	42.7	31.9	54.2

WBAN : 13996

REFERENCE NOTES:

THE TEMPERATURE GRAPH SHOWS NORMAL MAXIMUM AND NORMAL MINIMUM DAILY TEMPERATURES (SOLID CURVES) AND THE ACTUAL DAILY HIGH AND LOW TEMPERATURES (VERTICAL BARS).

H/C INDICATES HEATING AND COOLING DEGREE DAYS.
RH INDICATES RELATIVE HUMIDITY
W/O INDICATES WEATHER AND OBSTRUCTIONS
S INDICATES SUNSHINE.
PR INDICATES PRESSURE.
CLOUDINESS IS THE SUM OF THE CEILOMETER AND SATELLITE DATA NOT TO EXCEED TEN TENTHS.
MAXIMUM SNOW DEPTH IS THE DEPTH MEASURED AT 12 UTC.

GENERAL:
T INDICATES TRACE PRECIPITATION, AN AMOUNT GREATER THAN ZERO BUT LESS THAN THE LOWEST REPORTABLE VALUE.
+ INDICATES THE VALUE ALSO OCCURS ON EARLIER DATES.
BLANK ENTRIES DENOTE MISSING OR UNREPORTED DATA.
NORMALS ARE 30-YEAR AVERAGES (1961 - 1990).
ASOS INDICATES AUTOMATED SURFACE OBSERVING SYSTEM.
PM INDICATES THE LAST DAY OF THE PREVIOUS MONTH.
POR (PERIOD OF RECORD) INDICATES THE NUMBER OF YEARS USED TO COMPUTE THE MEAN. INDIVIDUAL MONTHS WITHIN THE POR MAY BE MISSING.
WHEN THE POR FOR A NORMAL IS LESS THAN 30 YEARS, THE NORMAL IS PROVISIONAL AND IS BASED ON THE NUMBER OF YEARS INDICATED.
0.* OR * INDICATES THE VALUE OR MEAN DAYS WITH IS BETWEEN 0.00 AND 0.05.
CLOUDINESS FOR ASOS STATIONS DIFFERS FROM THE NON-ASOS OBSERVATION TAKEN BY A HUMAN OBSERVER. ASOS STATION CLOUDINESS IS BASED ON TIME-AVERAGED CEILOMETER DATA FOR CLOUDS AT OR BELOW 12,000 FEET AND ON SATELLITE DATA FOR CLOUDS ABOVE 12,000 FEET.
THE NUMBER OF DAYS WITH CLEAR, PARTLY CLOUDY, AND CLOUDY CONDITIONS FOR ASOS STATIONS IS THE SUM OF THE CEILOMETER AND SATELLITE DATA FOR THE SUNRISE TO SUNSET PERIOD.

GENERAL CONTINUED:
CLEAR INDICATES 0 - 3 TENTHS, PARTLY CLOUDY INDICATES 4 - 7 TENTHS, AND CLOUDY INDICATES 8 OR MORE TENTHS. WHEN AT LEAST ONE OF THE ELEMENTS (CEILOMETER OR SATELLITE) IS MISSING, THE DAILY CLOUDINESS IS NOT COMPUTED.
WIND DIRECTION IS RECORDED IN TENS OF DEGREES (2 DIGITS) CLOCKWISE FROM TRUE NORTH. "00" INDICATES CALM. "36" INDICATES TRUE NORTH.
RESULTANT WIND IS THE VECTOR AVERAGE OF THE SPEED AND DIRECTION.
AVERAGE TEMPERATURE IS THE SUM OF THE MEAN DAILY MAXIMUM AND MINIMUM TEMPERATURE DIVIDED BY 2.
SNOWFALL DATA COMPRISE ALL FORMS OF FROZEN PRECIPITATION, INCLUDING HAIL.
A HEATING (COOLING) DEGREE DAY IS THE DIFFERENCE BETWEEN THE AVERAGE DAILY TEMPERATURE AND 65˚F.
DRY BULB IS THE TEMPERATURE OF THE AMBIENT AIR.
DEW POINT IS THE TEMPERATURE TO WHICH THE AIR MUST BE COOLED TO ACHIEVE 100 PERCENT RELATIVE HUMIDITY.
WET BULB IS THE TEMPERATURE THE AIR WOULD HAVE IF THE MOISTURE CONTENT WAS INCREASED TO 100 PERCENT RELATIVE HUMIDITY.

HEATING DEGREE DAYS (base 65°F) 1993 TOPEKA, KANSAS (TOP)

YEAR	JUL	AUG	SEP	OCT	NOV	DEC	JAN	FEB	MAR	APR	MAY	JUN	TOTAL
1964-65	0	9	67	316	572	1087	1044	955	984	263	30	0	5327
1965-66	0	0	74	253	572	770	1202	922	552	423	107	6	4881
1966-67	0	2	64	316	620	1053	1032	875	570	247	205	15	4999
1967-68	1	7	87	356	690	985	1184	965	572	338	202	5	5392
1968-69	0	1	35	282	745	1108	1210	866	857	282	94	42	5522
1969-70	0	0	17	408	666	1083	1284	811	785	376	45	29	5504
1970-71	0	0	57	344	706	945	1262	1065	735	274	144	0	5532
1971-72	4	0	69	143	580	927	1216	958	567	324	109	10	4907
1972-73	10	0	59	337	764	1152	1158	864	537	378	129	0	5388
1973-74	0	0	58	191	603	1082	1317	807	558	258	64	7	4945
1974-75	0	3	134	213	649	991	1056	1008	839	352	46	7	5298
1975-76	2	0	137	230	581	941	1148	639	599	269	178	5	4729
1976-77	0	0	45	471	881	1126	1537	767	469	180	11	0	5487
1977-78	0	0	6	263	662	1075	1473	1240	824	280	156	6	5985
1978-79	0	0	34	319	655	1078	1643	1277	693	401	129	9	6238
1979-80	0	4	45	267	741	908	1123	1123	744	344	129	3	5431
1980-81	0	0	65	344	591	1001	1035	822	579	175	176	0	4788
1981-82	0	2	46	283	529	1076	1329	1014	664	449	76	32	5500
1982-83	0	0	93	303	683	896	1002	804	615	466	120	13	4995
1983-84	0	0	56	223	570	1565	1204	713	830	405	137	0	5703
1984-85	0	0	145	276	578	871	1389	1098	501	228	35	8	5129
1985-86	0	0	127	259	844	1228	899	906	491	252	49	0	5055
1986-87	0	9	27	263	792	934	1084	688	560	292	16	0	4665
1987-88	0	3	24	376	531	893	1136	988	662	331	16	5	4965
1988-89	2	4	24	383	587	912	832	1174	641	296	125	5	4985
1989-90	0	2	155	276	672	1360	851	801	600	413	176	4	5310
1990-91	1	1	39	276	477	1093	1227		523	233	48	0	
1991-92	0	0	95	262	808	849	855	673	528	326	132	7	4535
1992-93	0	2	68	278	770	995	1189	979	744	440	101	22	5588
1993-	0	1	108	356	763	930							
POR= 47 YRS	0	1	61	272	662	1022	1164	911	693	328	100	8	5222

WBAN : 13996

COOLING DEGREE DAYS (base 65°F) 1993 TOPEKA, KANSAS (TOP)

YEAR	JAN	FEB	MAR	APR	MAY	JUN	JUL	AUG	SEP	OCT	NOV	DEC	ANNUAL
1969	0	0	0	4	107	158	456	330	146	32	0	0	1233
1970	0	0	0	35	149	239	407	490	188	16	0	0	1524
1971	0	0	3	21	42	381	309	345	273	42	0	0	1416
1972	0	0	5	22	74	297	308	309	169	20	0	0	1204
1973	0	0	0	13	21	304	394	384	115	52	0	0	1283
1974	0	0	6	21	140	165	490	292	47	12	0	0	1173
1975	0	0	0	38	129	289	390	448	116	61	3	0	1474
1976	0	0	1	34	40	242	410	376	171	20	0	0	1294
1977	0	0	0	40	176	311	453	360	209	14	0	0	1563
1978	0	0	6	15	101	298	390	339	277	5	3	0	1434
1979	0	0	4	7	76	237	401	379	144	27	0	0	1275
1980	0	0	0	9	69	356	670	496	220	9	0	0	1829
1981	0	0	0	53	58	321	457	260	143	17	0	0	1309
1982	0	0	0	11	43	157	432	334	147	28	0	0	1152
1983	0	0	0	7	50	274	509	564	278	33	2	0	1717
1984	0	0	0	14	67	274	379	407	196	20	0	3	1360
1985	0	0	0	46	88	225	461	249	188	6	0	0	1263
1986	0	0	26	42	85	363	488	243	233	9	0	0	1489
1987	0	0	0	61	192	344	410	335	126	0	9	0	1477
1988	0	0	0	4	140	314	375	458	191	11	0	0	1493
1989	0	0	11	90	107	206	399	311	81	41	0	0	1246
1990	0	0	1	26	39	377	403	366	241	37	7	0	1497
1991	0	0	11	22	192	371	478	387	229	69	0	0	1759
1992	0	0	0	25	61	134	344	217	162	20	0	0	963
1993	0	0	0	0	48	269	417	405	64	22	0	0	1225
POR= 25 YRS	0	0	2	25	91	275	424	362	173	24	0	0	1376

WBAN : 13996

SNOWFALL (inches) 1993 TOPEKA, KANSAS (TOP)

YEAR	JUL	AUG	SEP	OCT	NOV	DEC	JAN	FEB	MAR	APR	MAY	JUN	TOTAL
1964-65	0.0	0.0	0.0	0.0	1.3	4.3	2.9	7.3	5.0	0.0	0.0	0.0	20.8
1965-66	0.0	0.0	0.0	0.0	T	3.6	0.5	0.6	T	T	0.0	0.0	4.7
1966-67	0.0	0.0	0.0	0.0	T	8.3	3.4	1.9	0.8	0.0	0.0	0.0	14.4
1967-68	0.0	0.0	0.0	0.0	T	11.1	4.7	5.7	T	T	0.0	0.0	21.5
1968-69	0.0	0.0	0.0	0.0	T	0.8	6.2	3.4	2.0	0.0	0.0	0.0	12.4
1969-70	0.0	0.0	0.0	0.0	0.8	9.4	2.1	T	4.9	6.8	0.0	0.0	24.0
1970-71	0.0	0.0	0.0	0.8	T	7.9	2.1	22.4	7.5	T	0.0	0.0	40.7
1971-72	0.0	0.0	0.0	0.0	2.4	1.2	3.0	6.7	3.0	T	0.0	0.0	16.3
1972-73	0.0	0.0	0.0	0.0	9.4	4.0	13.5	1.7	0.0	0.1	0.0	0.0	28.7
1973-74	0.0	0.0	0.0	0.0	T	15.2	7.8	2.1	1.5	1.3	0.0	0.0	27.9
1974-75	0.0	0.0	0.0	0.0	1.3	1.4	5.0	6.7	7.8	3.6	0.0	0.0	25.8
1975-76	0.0	0.0	0.0	0.0	8.3	2.7	6.4	0.7	2.9	0.0	0.0	0.0	21.0
1976-77	0.0	0.0	0.0	T	0.3	T	13.6	0.1	T	0.2	0.0	0.0	14.2
1977-78	0.0	0.0	0.0	0.0	0.1	0.2	3.9	12.4	6.2	0.0	0.0	0.0	22.8
1978-79	0.0	0.0	0.0	0.0	T	11.1	20.1	3.1	7.5	1.1	0.0	0.0	42.9
1979-80	0.0	0.0	0.0	0.0	T	T	3.5	11.4	3.4	0.0	0.0	0.0	18.3
1980-81	0.0	0.0	0.0	T	0.0	3.8	2.6	2.5	0.0	0.0	0.0	0.0	8.9
1981-82	0.0	0.0	0.0	0.0	T	1.4	3.2	8.0	0.3	0.5	0.0	0.0	13.4
1982-83	0.0	0.0	0.0	0.0	1.1	5.0	6.1	10.1	0.6	4.5	0.0	0.0	27.4
1983-84	0.0	0.0	0.0	0.0	4.1	18.8	2.6	T	4.2	0.0	0.0	0.0	29.7
1984-85	0.0	0.0	0.0	0.0	T	9.8	18.2	7.9	0.5	0.0	0.0	0.0	36.4
1985-86	0.0	0.0	0.0	0.0	3.3	5.8	T	1.5	T	0.0	0.0	0.0	10.6
1986-87	0.0	0.0	0.0	T	0.7	1.7	15.1	2.3	0.5	0.0	0.0	0.0	20.3
1987-88	0.0	0.0	0.0	0.0	0.9	9.6	0.6	6.0	4.7	0.0	0.0	0.0	21.8
1988-89	0.0	0.0	0.0	0.0	0.7	0.8	T	9.0	1.6	0.0	T	T	12.1
1989-90	0.0	0.0	0.0	0.0	T	9.5	1.0	0.1	7.6	0.0	0.0	0.0	18.2
1990-91	0.0	0.0	0.0	0.0	0.0	2.9	9.6		T	T	T	0.0	
1991-92	0.0	0.0	0.0	T	6.2	0.1	T	T	0.9	T	0.0	T	7.2
1992-93	T	0.0	0.0	T	4.5	0.9	23.0	14.2	0.6	T		T	
1993-	0.0	0.0	0.0	T	T	3.3							
POR= 47 YRS	T	0.0	0.0	T	1.3	4.8	6.1	4.8	3.7	0.5	T	T	21.2

WBAN : 13996

1993 WICHITA, KANSAS (ICT)

Wichita is in the Central Great Plains where masses of warm, moist air from the Gulf of Mexico collide with cold, dry air from the Arctic region to create a wide range of weather the year around. Summers are usually warm and humid, and can be very hot and dry. The winters are usually mild, with brief periods of very cold weather.

The elevation is just over 1,300 feet above sea level. The terrain is basically flat with natural tree areas mainly along the Arkansas River and its tributaries.

The temperature extremes for the period of weather records at Wichita range from more than 110 degrees to less than -20 degrees. Temperatures above 90 degrees occur an average of 63 days per year, while very cold temperatures below zero occur about 2 days per year.

Precipitation averages about 30 inches per year, with 70 percent of that falling from April through September during the growing season. The wettest years have recorded over 50 inches. The driest years less than 15 inches.

Thunderstorms occur mainly during the spring and early summer. They can be severe and cause damage from heavy rain, large hail, strong winds and tornadoes.

The city of Wichita is protected against floods from the Arkansas River and its local tributaries by the Wichita-Vally Center Flood Control Project, which is designed to protect against floods up to the 75 to 100 year frequency class.

Snowfall normally is 15 inches per year, falling from December through March. Monthly snowfalls in excess of 20 inches and 24-hour snowfalls of more than 13 inches have occurred.

The prevailing wind direction is south with the windiest months March and April. July has the least wind. Strong north winds often occur with the passage of cold fronts from late fall through early spring. Extremely low wind chill factors are experienced with very cold outbreaks during the mid winter. On rare occasions during the summer, strong, hot, dry southwest winds can do considerable damage to crops.

NORMALS, MEANS, AND EXTREMES FOR 1993

WICHITA, KS (ICT)

LATITUDE: 37° 39′ 00″ N　LONGTITUDE: 97° 25′ 58″ W　ELEVATION (FT): GRND: 1321 BARO: 1342　TIME ZONE: CENTRAL (UTC+06)　WBAN: 03928

	ELEMENT	POR	JAN	FEB	MAR	APR	MAY	JUN	JUL	AUG	SEP	OCT	NOV	DEC	YEAR
TEMPERATURE °F	NORMAL DAILY MAXIMUM	30	39.8	45.9	57.2	68.3	76.9	86.8	92.8	90.7	81.4	70.6	55.3	43.0	67.4
	MEAN DAILY MAXIMUM	40	40.0	46.2	56.6	68.2	76.8	87.0	93.1	91.3	81.9	70.6	55.0	45.0	67.7
	HIGHEST DAILY MAXIMUM	41	75	84	89	96	100	110	113	110	107	95	85	83	113
	YEAR OF OCCURRENCE		1967	1976	1989	1972	1967	1980	1954	1984	1990	1979	1980	1955	JUL 1954
	MEAN OF EXTREME MAXS.	41	62.2	69.0	79.5	85.9	90.8	99.7	104.0	103.4	97.2	88.1	73.7	64.4	84.8
	NORMAL DAILY MINIMUM	30	19.2	23.7	33.6	44.5	54.3	64.6	69.9	67.9	59.2	46.6	33.9	23.0	45.0
	MEAN DAILY MINIMUM	40	19.8	24.4	33.3	44.7	54.7	64.5	69.8	67.9	59.3	46.8	33.6	24.6	45.3
	LOWEST DAILY MINIMUM	41	-12	-21	-2	15	31	43	51	48	31	18	1	-16	-21
	YEAR OF OCCURRENCE		1962	1982	1960	1975	1976	1969	1975	1967	1984	1993	1975	1989	FEB 1982
	MEAN OF EXTREME MINS.	41	0.9	5.0	14.8	27.8	39.3	51.5	59.2	56.6	42.6	30.4	17.3	6.3	29.3
	NORMAL DRY BULB	30	29.5	34.8	45.4	56.4	65.6	75.7	81.4	79.3	70.3	58.6	44.7	33.0	56.2
	MEAN DRY BULB	40	29.9	35.3	45.0	56.5	65.8	75.7	81.5	79.7	70.6	58.7	44.3	34.8	56.5
	MEAN WET BULB	38	26.3	30.7	38.9	49.2	58.4	66.3	69.8	68.5	61.8	51.4	39.4	30.0	49.2
	MEAN DEW POINT	38	20.1	24.1	31.4	42.2	53.2	61.4	64.0	62.8	56.5	45.1	33.2	23.9	43.2
	NORMAL NO. DAYS WITH:														
	MAXIMUM ≥ 90°	30	0.0	0.0	0.0	0.3	2.0	12.1	21.9	18.9	7.0	0.8	0.0	0.0	63.0
	MAXIMUM ≤ 32°	30	9.4	5.5	1.0	*	0.0	0.0	0.0	0.0	0.0	0.0	0.7	6.0	22.6
	MINIMUM ≤ 32°	30	28.4	22.5	14.6	2.8	0.1	0.0	0.0	0.0	*	1.3	14.3	26.8	110.8
	MINIMUM ≤ 0°	30	2.2	1.0	0.1	0.0	0.0	0.0	0.0	0.0	0.0	0.0	0.0	0.9	4.2
H/C	NORMAL HEATING DEG. DAYS	30	1101	846	608	278	102	5	0	0	29	221	609	992	4791
	NORMAL COOLING DEG. DAYS	30	0	0	0	20	121	326	508	443	188	22	0	0	1628
RH	NORMAL (PERCENT)	30	70	68	64	63	67	64	59	61	67	65	70	72	66
	HOUR 00 LST	30	75	74	71	71	76	74	67	69	75	73	76	76	73
	HOUR 06 LST	30	78	78	77	78	82	82	78	79	83	80	80	80	80
	HOUR 12 LST	30	62	60	55	52	56	53	48	50	56	53	59	63	56
	HOUR 18 LST	30	64	59	52	50	54	49	44	46	53	54	64	67	55
S	PERCENT POSSIBLE SUNSHINE	40	61	61	62	64	65	70	76	76	69	66	59	58	65
W/O	MEAN NO. DAYS WITH:														
	HEAVY FOG(VISBY ≤ 1/4 MI)	40	2.9	2.8	1.5	0.9	0.7	0.3	0.2	0.2	1.0	1.3	2.0	3.2	17.0
	THUNDERSTORMS	40	0.3	0.8	2.9	5.3	8.9	9.8	7.7	7.3	5.8	3.2	1.2	0.3	53.5
CLOUDINESS	MEAN:														
	SUNRISE-SUNSET (TENTHS)	1		8.0	7.0	8.0	7.0	5.0	3.0	3.0	4.0	6.0	5.0	5.0	
	MIDNIGHT-MIDNIGHT (TENTHS)	1		8.0	8.0	7.0	7.0	5.0	3.0	3.0	4.0	6.0	5.0	5.0	
	MEAN NO. DAYS WITH:														
	CLEAR	1	6.0	7.0	8.0	7.0	8.0	7.0	12.0	18.0	12.0	10.0	11.0	16.0	122.0
	PARTLY CLOUDY	1	2.0	6.0	5.0	2.0	7.0	7.0	5.0	6.0	6.0	6.0	3.0	5.0	60.0
	CLOUDY	1	11.0	12.0	13.0	10.0	7.0	4.0	2.0	3.0	5.0	7.0	7.0	9.0	90.0
PR	MEAN STATION PRESSURE(IN.)	21	28.69	28.66	28.53	28.53	28.51	28.52	28.57	28.59	28.61	28.63	28.62	28.68	28.60
	MEAN SEA-LEVEL PRES. (IN.)	38	30.15	30.10	29.99	29.93	29.91	29.90	29.94	29.95	29.99	30.04	30.07	30.12	30.01
WINDS	MEAN SPEED (MPH)	30	9.4	9.8	10.8	10.4	9.2	8.8	9.0	8.1	8.7	8.6	9.7	9.5	9.3
	PREVAIL.DIR(TENS OF DEGS.)	30	36	36	18	18	18	18	18	18	18	18	18	36	18
	MAXIMUM 2-MINUTE:														
	SPEED (MPH)	1	31	31	38	37	38	38	59	33	39	49	38	39	59
	DIR. (TENS OF DEGS.)	1	32	31	31	28	30	01	03	36	18	31	34	17	03
	YEAR OF OCCURRENCE		1993	1993	1993	1993	1993	1993	1993	1993	1993	1993	1993	1993	JUL 1993
	MAXIMUM 5-SECOND:														
	SPEED (MPH)	1	39		47	41	46	49	101	37	46	53	46	44	
	DIR. (TENS OF DEGS.)	1	33		30	28	30	21	04	36	20	31	31	36	
	YEAR OF OCCURRENCE		1993		1993	1993	1993	1993	1993	1993	1993	1993	1993	1993	
PRECIPITATION	NORMAL TOTAL (IN.)	30	0.79	0.96	2.43	2.38	3.81	4.31	3.13	3.02	3.49	2.22	1.59	1.20	29.33
	MAXIMUM TOTAL (IN.)	40	2.73	3.33	9.17	5.57	9.62	10.46	9.22	7.91	9.46	6.13	5.88	4.71	10.46
	YEAR OF OCCURRENCE		1973	1987	1973	1976	1993	1957	1962	1960	1973	1959	1964	1984	JUN 1957
	MINIMUM TOTAL (IN.)	40	T	T	0.01	0.22	0.52	0.94	0.05	0.31	0.03	T	T	0.03	T
	YEAR OF OCCURRENCE		1986	1991	1971	1963	1973	1954	1975	1976	1956	1958	1989	1955	NOV 1989
	MAXIMUM IN 24 HOURS (IN.)	40	1.72	1.53	2.65	2.51	4.70	4.98	3.86	4.50	3.29	5.03	4.33	2.60	5.03
	YEAR OF OCCURRENCE		1980	1973	1961	1988	1963	1965	1983	1991	1989	1985	1964	1984	OCT 1985
	NORMAL NO. DAYS WITH:														
	PRECIPITATION ≥ 0.01	30	5.1	5.3	7.9	8.0	10.6	9.3	7.1	7.7	7.9	6.2	5.2	5.8	86.1
	PRECIPITATION ≥ 1.00	30	0.1	0.1	0.7	0.5	1.1	1.3	0.9	0.8	1.1	0.6	0.5	0.2	7.9
SNOWFALL	NORMAL TOTAL (IN.)	30	4.7	4.5	2.1	0.3	0.0	0.0	0.0	0.0	0.0	-1.1	1.4	3.8	16.8
	MAXIMUM TOTAL (IN.)	40	19.7	16.7	16.5	4.6	T	T	T	0.0	T	1.5	7.1	13.8	19.7
	YEAR OF OCCURRENCE		1987	1971	1970	1979	1991	1992	1993		1992	1991	1972	1983	JAN 1987
	MAXIMUM IN 24 HOURS (IN.)	40	13.0	11.9	13.5	4.6	T	T	T	0.0	T	1.5	6.8	9.0	13.5
	YEAR OF OCCURRENCE		1962	1971	1970	1979	1991	1992	1993	1993	1992	1991	1984	1983	MAR 1970
	MAXIMUM SNOW DEPTH (IN.)	39	17	13	13	3	0	0	0	0	0	T	5	8	17
	YEAR OF OCCURRENCE		1962	1971	1970	1979						1993	1987	1987	JAN 1962
	NORMAL NO. DAYS WITH:														
	SNOWFALL ≥ 1.0	30	1.4	1.3	0.4	0.1	0.0	0.0	0.0	0.0	0.0	0.0	0.4	1.2	4.8

PRECIPITATION (inches) 1993 WICHITA, KANSAS (ICT)

YEAR	JAN	FEB	MAR	APR	MAY	JUN	JUL	AUG	SEP	OCT	NOV	DEC	ANNUAL
1964	0.71	0.53	0.89	2.97	5.84	3.73	2.23	6.10	2.66	1.64	5.88	1.03	34.21
1965	0.56	1.39	0.48	2.63	6.26	8.00	3.62	4.91	8.44	0.32	0.11	2.25	38.97
1966	0.23	1.44	0.26	2.21	0.76	2.67	1.78	1.09	0.72	0.47	0.09	0.43	12.15
1967	0.28	0.09	0.57	1.30	1.42	5.62	4.28	1.91	3.19	2.98	0.39	1.41	23.44
1968	0.14	0.20	1.36	2.16	4.37	2.38	3.65	6.41	5.91	3.06	2.47	1.31	33.42
1969	0.45	1.35	1.73	4.30	3.28	6.82	6.23	1.07	4.77	2.80	0.01	1.36	34.17
1970	0.28	0.21	2.70	4.49	1.58	6.72	0.47	2.37	4.04	1.88	0.05	0.49	25.28
1971	0.98	1.70	0.01	2.35	3.02	2.70	6.65	1.49	1.73	5.54	2.49	0.95	29.61
1972	0.15	0.28	0.56	3.32	2.47	2.02	3.86	3.31	1.31	2.00	3.06	0.97	23.31
1973	2.73	1.20	9.17	3.78	0.52	1.21	6.07	0.68	9.46	3.43	0.91	2.80	41.96
1974	0.56	0.25	2.36	4.29	4.65	2.79	0.09	4.11	1.08	3.44	2.69	2.22	28.53
1975	1.28	2.12	1.72	1.57	8.60	6.88	0.05	2.77	1.19	0.08	2.89	0.48	29.63
1976	0.04	0.25	1.50	5.57	2.69	3.12	6.13	0.31	2.02	1.82	0.06	0.07	23.58
1977	0.54	0.08	1.42	3.32	8.85	3.15	3.98	6.31	4.35	1.19	2.38	0.19	35.76
1978	0.49	1.71	2.10	2.71	2.24	3.19	1.49	1.90	3.58	0.05	2.21	0.59	22.26
1979	1.57	0.23	4.47	1.46	3.05	6.54	2.18	0.67	1.54	2.96	2.05	1.99	28.71
1980	1.82	0.81	3.99	1.07	2.66	1.34	0.47	3.76	0.67	1.25	0.54	2.11	20.49
1981	0.25	0.22	2.15	0.38	6.33	4.25	1.27	2.65	2.25	4.69	2.93	0.29	27.66
1982	1.68	0.77	2.05	0.73	7.82	8.28	0.56	1.51	1.08	0.41	0.73	1.51	27.13
1983	1.66	1.23	4.26	3.80	4.08	7.38	3.86	1.39	2.53	2.97	2.39	1.13	36.68
1984	0.20	1.23	7.57	3.71	1.15	2.30	0.30	0.75	2.18	2.78	1.44	4.71	28.32
1985	0.26	2.07	1.64	2.28	2.01	4.79	3.97	2.86	5.97	5.58	1.60	0.61	33.64
1986	T	1.26	1.22	1.80	2.98	5.39	3.42	6.00	3.81	3.61	0.58	1.22	31.29
1987	1.40	3.33	4.13	0.61	8.01	4.50	2.14	7.69	2.10	0.90	1.50	2.25	38.56
1988	0.51	0.18	2.91	4.46	2.40	1.86	0.91	1.10	0.53	0.94	0.77	0.50	17.07
1989	0.79	0.39	2.38	0.23	4.96	7.96	4.07	5.72	7.38	0.37	T	0.44	34.69
1990	1.73	2.19	2.68	0.80	1.29	1.91	1.72	2.01	1.95	0.64	2.01	0.78	19.71
1991	0.58	T	0.71	2.27	4.09	1.34	2.65	7.57	2.08	1.00	2.38	2.07	26.74
1992	0.67	0.47	3.60	1.42	3.44	7.26	4.77	1.94	2.94	2.80	4.91	1.16	35.38
1993	1.12	2.25	1.75	2.11	9.62	4.44	6.21	1.31	1.77	1.68	0.55	0.30	33.11
POR= 40 YRS	0.75	0.94	2.27	2.23	4.04	4.23	3.34	2.99	3.30	2.43	1.51	1.11	29.13

WBAN : 03928

AVERAGE TEMPERATURE (°F) 1993 WICHITA, KANSAS (ICT)

YEAR	JAN	FEB	MAR	APR	MAY	JUN	JUL	AUG	SEP	OCT	NOV	DEC	ANNUAL
1964	36.8	36.1	42.1	59.2	70.2	76.9	85.0	76.8	70.8	58.7	47.2	31.2	57.6
1965	35.2	34.4	36.8	60.4	68.8	76.3	81.9	78.2	68.5	60.4	50.5	41.2	57.7
1966	28.3	33.6	49.1	53.5	65.7	76.2	84.9	76.1	68.6	58.0	48.3	32.7	56.2
1967	34.3	36.3	50.5	61.5	64.0	74.5	76.2	74.7	65.9	57.7	43.2	34.6	56.1
1968	32.5	33.8	48.0	55.5	61.0	76.1	80.3	77.9	67.9	59.3	41.7	30.7	55.4
1969	30.1	36.1	36.1	56.4	65.2	71.0	82.9	78.9	71.9	54.6	44.5	34.6	55.2
1970	27.3	38.5	39.7	55.1	69.3	74.5	81.3	83.2	69.7	53.9	41.5	36.9	55.9
1971	28.8	28.8	44.0	57.0	63.9	78.9	78.0	76.8	70.8	60.6	43.9	35.8	55.6
1972	27.0	34.8	47.9	55.3	64.1	76.7	77.1	78.4	71.0	55.6	39.8	28.5	54.7
1973	27.4	35.6	48.4	52.2	61.9	76.8	80.3	79.8	67.8	61.1	46.7	31.9	55.8
1974	24.9	38.7	47.9	56.4	68.3	72.5	84.4	76.7	64.1	60.5	44.9	35.1	56.2
1975	33.4	28.5	40.4	54.7	64.0	73.6	79.2	81.4	65.8	60.3	44.8	36.0	55.2
1976	32.0	45.5	46.3	57.5	60.2	73.7	78.4	79.7	69.8	52.4	38.3	33.7	55.6
1977	24.5	41.7	50.2	59.8	69.2	78.3	83.6	77.9	73.2	59.8	46.1	35.0	58.3
1978	20.5	23.8	43.6	59.0	65.0	76.8	85.1	81.2	76.3	58.6	45.0	32.0	55.6
1979	16.7	24.0	46.9	54.1	64.1	74.5	80.4	79.8	72.7	61.9	41.8	37.7	54.6
1980	31.4	28.2	41.5	54.3	63.5	79.9	90.5	85.3	75.2	58.8	46.9	36.9	57.7
1981	34.1	40.1	47.6	63.7	62.6	77.9	83.6	78.1	72.0	55.9	47.0	32.9	58.0
1982	25.5	28.0	46.0	53.5	65.3	70.4	81.5	82.0	71.9	58.0	43.0	36.1	55.1
1983	31.7	35.5	43.3	48.0	60.5	71.5	81.6	85.0	72.7	58.5	45.5	16.4	54.2
1984	26.7	41.4	40.7	51.8	63.6	77.7	81.6	82.8	70.3	58.3	45.5	37.2	56.5
1985	25.2	31.2	49.1	59.9	67.7	74.0	81.7	77.5	69.8	57.4	39.4	28.8	55.1
1986	38.1	37.8	51.9	58.7	66.7	78.7	83.0	75.9	73.6	57.6	39.9	35.8	58.1
1987	29.3	42.3	47.0	57.4	69.7	76.4	80.1	78.7	70.4	55.7	47.7	34.9	57.5
1988	27.0	34.1	44.2	53.9	68.3	78.6	80.9	83.0	72.0	56.7	47.5	38.5	57.1
1989	38.5	27.5	47.0	59.6	66.0	72.0	79.0	77.0	65.7	60.7	45.5	25.2	55.3
1990	39.5	38.8	46.9	54.3	63.7	81.7	81.7	80.8	74.3	58.4	50.4	30.2	58.4
1991	28.9	44.6	49.7	58.9	70.4	79.3	83.8	80.5	69.6	59.4	39.5	39.1	58.6
1992	39.0	44.9	50.0	56.7	63.3	71.2	78.9	73.8	71.0	59.1	41.3	33.3	56.9
1993	28.6	32.2	43.1	52.5	63.5	74.5	81.7	81.0	67.4	55.3	40.8	37.8	54.9
POR= 40 YRS	29.9	35.3	45.0	56.5	65.7	75.8	81.5	79.6	70.6	58.7	44.3	34.0	56.4

WBAN : 03928

REFERENCE NOTES:

THE TEMPERATURE GRAPH SHOWS NORMAL MAXIMUM AND NORMAL MINIMUM DAILY TEMPERATURES (SOLID CURVES) AND THE ACTUAL DAILY HIGH AND LOW TEMPERATURES (VERTICAL BARS).

H/C INDICATES HEATING AND COOLING DEGREE DAYS.
RH INDICATES RELATIVE HUMIDITY
W/O INDICATES WEATHER AND OBSTRUCTIONS
S INDICATES SUNSHINE.
PR INDICATES PRESSURE.
CLOUDINESS ON IS THE SUM OF THE CEILOMETER AND SATELLITE DATA NOT TO EXCEED TEN TENTHS.
MAXIMUM SNOW DEPTH IS THE DEPTH MEASURED AT 12 UTC.

GENERAL:
T INDICATES TRACE PRECIPITATION, AN AMOUNT GREATER THAN ZERO BUT LESS THAN THE LOWEST REPORTABLE VALUE.
+ INDICATES THE VALUE ALSO OCCURS ON EARLIER DATES.
BLANK ENTRIES DENOTE MISSING OR UNREPORTED DATA.
NORMALS ARE 30-YEAR AVERAGES (1961 - 1990).
ASOS INDICATES AUTOMATED SURFACE OBSERVING SYSTEM.
PM INDICATES THE LAST DAY OF THE PREVIOUS MONTH.
POR (PERIOD OF RECORD) INDICATES THE NUMBER OF YEARS USED TO COMPUTE THE MEAN. INDIVIDUAL MONTHS WITHIN THE POR MAY BE MISSING.
WHEN THE POR FOR A NORMAL IS LESS THAN 30 YEARS, THE NORMAL IS PROVISIONAL AND IS BASED ON THE NUMBER OF YEARS INDICATED.
0.* OR * INDICATES THE VALUE OR MEAN DAYS WITH IS BETWEEN 0.00 AND 0.05.
CLOUDINESS FOR ASOS STATIONS DIFFERS FROM THE NON-ASOS OBSERVATION TAKEN BY A HUMAN OBSERVER. ASOS STATION CLOUDINESS IS BASED ON TIME-AVERAGED CEILOMETER DATA FOR CLOUDS AT OR BELOW 12,000 FEET AND ON SATELLITE DATA FOR CLOUDS ABOVE 12,000 FEET.
THE NUMBER OF DAYS WITH CLEAR, PARTLY CLOUDY, AND CLOUDY CONDITIONS FOR ASOS STATIONS IS THE SUM OF THE CEILOMETER AND SATELLITE DATA FOR THE SUNRISE TO SUNSET PERIOD.

GENERAL CONTINUED:
CLEAR INDICATES 0 - 3 TENTHS, PARTLY CLOUDY INDICATES 4 - 7 TENTHS, AND CLOUDY INDICATES 8 OR MORE TENTHS. WHEN AT LEAST ONE OF THE ELEMENTS (CEILOMETER OR SATELLITE) IS MISSING, THE DAILY CLOUDINESS IS NOT COMPUTED.
WIND DIRECTION IS RECORDED IN TENS OF DEGREES (2 DIGITS) CLOCKWISE FROM TRUE NORTH. "00" INDICATES CALM. "36" INDICATES TRUE NORTH.
RESULTANT WIND IS THE VECTOR AVERAGE OF THE SPEED AND DIRECTION.
AVERAGE TEMPERATURE IS THE SUM OF THE MEAN DAILY MAXIMUM AND MINIMUM TEMPERATURE DIVIDED BY 2.
SNOWFALL DATA COMPRISE ALL FORMS OF FROZEN PRECIPITATION, INCLUDING HAIL.
A HEATING (COOLING) DEGREE DAY IS THE DIFFERENCE BETWEEN THE AVERAGE DAILY TEMPERATURE AND 65°F.
DRY BULB IS THE TEMPERATURE OF THE AMBIENT AIR.
DEW POINT IS THE TEMPERATURE TO WHICH THE AIR MUST BE COOLED TO ACHIEVE 100 PERCENT RELATIVE HUMIDITY.
WET BULB IS THE TEMPERATURE THE AIR WOULD HAVE IF THE MOISTURE CONTENT WAS INCREASED TO 100 PERCENT RELATIVE HUMIDITY.

HEATING DEGREE DAYS (base 65°F) 1993 WICHITA, KANSAS (ICT)

YEAR	JUL	AUG	SEP	OCT	NOV	DEC	JAN	FEB	MAR	APR	MAY	JUN	TOTAL
1964-65	0	1	34	200	531	1038	918	851	868	176	23	0	4640
1965-66	0	1	73	179	428	733	1131	871	490	342	100	2	4350
1966-67	0	0	33	247	499	996	945	798	463	160	143	5	4289
1967-68	2	1	63	280	645	936	998	899	525	285	153	1	4788
1968-69	0	5	22	224	691	1054	1076	804	887	254	77	20	5114
1969-70	0	0	2	361	610	939	1163	738	778	312	43	26	4972
1970-71	1	0	64	358	696	866	1118	1005	643	253	95	0	5099
1971-72	4	0	77	165	628	897	1171	871	524	310	109	0	4756
1972-73	2	0	46	319	750	1123	1159	816	506	386	125	0	5232
1973-74	0	0	58	159	541	1021	1237	732	529	263	42	1	4583
1974-75	0	0	92	156	596	920	974	1016	757	333	72	9	4925
1975-76	0	0	98	201	596	892	1015	562	575	238	173	2	4352
1976-77	0	0	38	409	794	966	1253	646	456	170	12	0	4744
1977-78	0	0	1	176	558	926	1375	1149	663	194	112	6	5160
1978-79	0	0	18	210	598	1016	1491	1143	560	333	104	3	5476
1979-80	0	0	10	156	690	838	1038	1063	723	318	116	0	4952
1980-81	0	0	28	239	535	864	954	692	533	104	126	0	4075
1981-82	0	0	24	292	537	990	1214	1033	583	356	54	17	5100
1982-83	0	0	37	239	653	889	1022	818	664	507	168	20	5017
1983-84	0	0	47	221	582	1504	1180	680	747	394	95	0	5450
1984-85	0	0	103	237	576	856	1224	938	487	184	33	8	4646
1985-86	0	0	111	230	762	1116	826	755	416	220	41	0	4477
1986-87	0	3	11	233	747	899	1099	631	551	263	14	0	4451
1987-88	0	2	7	282	523	924	1170	891	637	330	33	0	4799
1988-89	0	0	16	265	519	813	817	1044	556	238	90	8	4366
1989-90	0	0	105	193	578	1228	783	728	555	332	112	0	4614
1990-91	0	0	18	238	445	1074	1114	567	475	201	53	0	4185
1991-92	0	0	71	242	759	793	802	574	461	259	113	10	4084
1992-93	0	2	25	209	703	975	1122	913	670	368	100	10	5097
1993-	0	0	59	321	718	837							
POR= 40 YRS	0	0	41	228	613	955	1081	831	616	274	82	5	4726

WBAN : 03928

COOLING DEGREE DAYS (base 65°F) 1993 WICHITA, KANSAS (ICT)

YEAR	JAN	FEB	MAR	APR	MAY	JUN	JUL	AUG	SEP	OCT	NOV	DEC	ANNUAL
1969	0	0	0	1	90	208	563	437	214	45	0	0	1558
1970	0	0	2	24	187	315	513	573	212	22	0	0	1848
1971	0	0	0	19	65	425	414	372	259	34	0	0	1588
1972	0	0	2	26	88	358	385	421	234	34	0	0	1548
1973	0	0	0	7	39	360	482	468	149	47	0	0	1552
1974	0	0	4	12	149	233	608	368	69	23	0	0	1466
1975	0	0	0	32	49	275	450	515	128	63	0	0	1512
1976	0	0	2	19	32	270	420	464	187	23	0	0	1417
1977	0	0	3	19	152	404	581	404	254	24	0	0	1841
1978	0	0	6	20	122	366	631	510	364	23	5	0	2047
1979	0	0	5	14	81	294	488	465	249	67	0	0	1663
1980	0	0	0	3	75	456	796	635	340	52	1	0	2358
1981	0	0	0	72	56	393	582	412	240	17	0	0	1772
1982	0	0	1	16	70	186	516	534	253	29	0	0	1605
1983	0	0	0	2	34	220	521	628	286	28	5	0	1724
1984	0	0	0	6	61	388	520	558	272	35	0	0	1840
1985	0	0	0	36	122	285	523	394	262	1	0	0	1623
1986	0	0	17	40	102	419	563	349	275	10	0	0	1775
1987	0	0	0	42	166	350	473	434	177	3	10	0	1655
1988	0	0	0	3	140	415	497	566	235	15	0	0	1871
1989	0	0	5	81	129	225	442	379	132	70	0	0	1463
1990	0	0	0	17	79	508	525	497	306	41	11	0	1984
1991	0	0	9	25	225	433	592	484	214	77	0	0	2059
1992	0	0	0	17	66	203	441	281	213	37	0	0	1258
1993	0	0	0	0	59	304	526	502	134	27	0	0	1552
POR= 25 YRS	0	0	1	22	97	330	521	465	226	33	0	0	1695

WBAN : 03928

SNOWFALL (inches) 1993 WICHITA, KANSAS (ICT)

YEAR	JUL	AUG	SEP	OCT	NOV	DEC	JAN	FEB	MAR	APR	MAY	JUN	TOTAL
1964-65	0.0	0.0	0.0	0.0	0.1	5.4	3.3	2.7	T	0.0	0.0	0.0	11.5
1965-66	0.0	0.0	0.0	0.0	0.0	0.9	4.7	0.8	T	0.0	0.0	0.0	6.4
1966-67	0.0	0.0	0.0	0.0	T	5.0	2.1	T	0.7	0.0	0.0	0.0	7.8
1967-68	0.0	0.0	0.0	0.0	2.2	9.7	0.6	1.0	T	0.0	0.0	0.0	13.5
1968-69	0.0	0.0	0.0	0.0	0.3	2.8	T	8.3	5.1	0.0	0.0	0.0	16.5
1969-70	0.0	0.0	0.0	0.0	T	3.5	2.8	T	16.5	0.1	0.0	0.0	22.9
1970-71	0.0	0.0	0.0	T	T	T	T	16.7	T	0.0	0.0	0.0	16.7
1971-72	0.0	0.0	0.0	0.0	2.3	2.4	1.7	4.4	0.8	0.0	0.0	0.0	11.6
1972-73	0.0	0.0	0.0	0.0	7.1	2.7	17.7	0.2	T	2.3	0.0	0.0	30.0
1973-74	0.0	0.0	0.0	0.0	T	8.7	4.1	0.7	2.0	0.3	0.0	0.0	15.8
1974-75	0.0	0.0	0.0	0.0	1.8	2.2	7.6	15.2	7.6	T	0.0	0.0	34.4
1975-76	0.0	0.0	0.0	0.0	5.5	T	0.6	0.9	T	0.0	0.0	0.0	7.0
1976-77	0.0	0.0	0.0	T	0.3	T	3.6	T	T	T	0.0	0.0	3.9
1977-78	0.0	0.0	0.0	0.0	T	T	7.4	7.8	0.3	0.0	0.0	0.0	15.5
1978-79	0.0	0.0	0.0	0.0	T	6.7	13.9	1.9	1.6	4.6	0.0	0.0	28.7
1979-80	0.0	0.0	0.0	0.0	T	T	T	12.3	0.4	0.0	0.0	0.0	12.7
1980-81	0.0	0.0	0.0	T	T	0.4	T	2.5	0.2	0.0	0.0	0.0	3.1
1981-82	0.0	0.0	0.0	0.0	T	1.2	0.0	12.7	T	0.0	0.0	0.0	13.9
1982-83	0.0	0.0	0.0	0.0	T	1.4	13.0	8.9	1.5	0.7	0.0	0.0	25.5
1983-84	0.0	0.0	0.0	0.0	4.1	13.8	4.3	T	6.9	0.0	0.0	0.0	29.1
1984-85	0.0	0.0	0.0	0.0	6.8	7.6	3.5	3.6	0.2	0.0	0.0	0.0	21.7
1985-86	0.0	0.0	0.0	0.0	1.0	3.0	0.0	7.5	0.0	0.0	0.0	0.0	11.5
1986-87	0.0	0.0	0.0	0.0	T	0.4	19.7	6.0	T	0.0	0.0	0.0	26.1
1987-88	0.0	0.0	0.0	0.0	6.2	12.6	8.5	1.1	11.0	0.0	0.0	0.0	39.4
1988-89	0.0	0.0	0.0	0.0	3.0	0.7	0.3	0.8	T	T	T	T	4.8
1989-90	0.0	0.0	0.0	0.0	T	4.4	0.3	7.0	0.7	0.1	0.0	0.0	12.5
1990-91	0.0	0.0	0.0	0.0	0.0	4.8	2.1	0.0	T	T	T	T	6.9
1991-92	0.0	0.0	0.0	1.5	0.3	0.0	T	T	T	T	0.0	T	1.8
1992-93	0.0	0.0	T	T	3.8	3.3	7.7	5.1	2.2	T	0.0	0.0	22.1
1993-	T	0.0	0.0	T	T	0.1							
POR= 40 YRS	T	0.0	T	T	1.3	3.2	4.6	4.2	2.4	0.3	T	T	16.0

WBAN : 03928

LEXINGTON, KENTUCKY

Lexington, County Seat of Fayette County, is located in the heart of the famed Kentucky Blue Grass Region. Fayette County is a gently rolling plateau with the elevation varying between 900 and 1,050 feet above sea level. It is noted for its beauty, the fertility of its soil, excellent grass, stock farms, and burley tobacco. The soil has a high phosphorus content and this is very valuable in growing pasture grasses for the grazing of cattle and horses. Lexington has a decided continental climate with a rather large diurnal temperature range. The climate is temperate and well suited to a varied plant and animal life. There are no bodies of water close enough to have any effect on the climate. The closest river is the Kentucky which makes an arc about 15 to 20 miles to the southeast, south, and southwest on its course to the Ohio River. There are numerous small creeks that rise in the county and flow into the river. The reservoirs of the Lexington Water Company are about 5 miles southeast of the city and are the largest bodies of water in the area.

Lexington is subject to rather sudden and large changes in temperature with the spells generally of rather short duration. Temperatures above 100 degrees and below zero degrees are relatively rare. The average temperature for the winter is 35 degrees, spring 62 degrees, fall 50 degrees, and summer 74 degrees.

Precipitation is evenly distributed throughout the winter, spring, and summer, with about 12 inches recorded on the average for each of these seasons. The fall season averages nearly 8 1/2 inches. Snowfall amounts are variable and the ground does not retain snow cover more than a few days at a time.

The months of September and October are the most pleasant of the year. They have the least amount of precipitation, the greatest number of clear days, and generally comfortable temperatures are the rule during these months.

Based on the 1951–1980 period, the average first occurrence of 32 degrees Fahrenheit in the fall is October 25 and the average last occurrence in the spring is April 17.

NORMALS, MEANS, AND EXTREMES

LEXINGTON, KENTUCKY

LATITUDE: 38°02'N LONGITUDE: 84°36' W ELEVATION: FT. GRND 966 BARO 990 TIME ZONE: EASTERN WBAN: 93820

	(a)	JAN	FEB	MAR	APR	MAY	JUNE	JULY	AUG	SEP	OCT	NOV	DEC	YEAR
TEMPERATURE °F:														
Normals														
-Daily Maximum		39.1	43.6	55.3	65.5	74.3	82.7	85.8	84.9	78.3	67.2	54.9	44.2	64.7
-Daily Minimum		22.4	25.3	35.3	44.2	53.5	61.5	65.7	64.4	58.0	46.0	37.0	27.6	45.1
-Monthly		30.8	34.5	45.3	54.8	64.0	72.2	75.8	74.7	68.2	56.7	46.0	35.9	54.9
Extremes														
-Record Highest	49	76	76	83	88	92	101	103	103	103	91	83	75	103
-Year		1950	1945	1945	1962	1987	1988	1988	1983	1954	1959	1987	1982	JUL 1988
-Record Lowest	49	-21	-15	-2	18	26	39	47	42	34	20	-3	-19	-21
-Year		1963	1951	1960	1982	1966	1966	1972	1965	1993	1976	1950	1989	JAN 1963
NORMAL DEGREE DAYS:														
Heating (base 65°F)		1060	854	611	312	135	5	0	0	47	287	570	902	4783
Cooling (base 65°F)		0	0	0	6	104	221	335	301	143	30	0	0	1140
% OF POSSIBLE SUNSHINE														
MEAN SKY COVER (tenths)														
Sunrise - Sunset	49	7.3	7.1	7.1	6.6	6.3	6.0	5.8	5.5	5.4	5.3	6.7	7.3	6.4
MEAN NUMBER OF DAYS:														
Sunrise to Sunset														
-Clear	49	5.7	5.9	5.7	6.3	7.0	7.0	8.0	9.3	10.5	11.7	6.8	5.8	89.7
-Partly Cloudy	49	5.8	5.6	7.4	8.5	10.0	11.6	12.3	12.0	8.4	7.2	6.6	5.9	101.1
-Cloudy	49	19.5	16.8	18.0	15.2	14.0	11.4	10.7	9.7	11.1	12.1	16.6	19.4	174.4
Precipitation .01 inches or more	49	12.3	11.2	12.9	12.2	11.9	10.5	11.2	9.1	8.1	8.0	10.8	11.6	130.0
Snow,Ice pellets,hail 1.0 inches or more	49	1.7	1.5	0.7	0.1	0.0	0.0	0.0	0.0	0.0	0.0	0.4	0.8	5.1
Thunderstorms	49	0.8	0.9	2.9	3.9	6.3	7.9	9.2	6.7	3.2	1.4	1.0	0.4	44.6
Heavy Fog Visibility 1/4 mile or less	49	2.4	2.0	1.4	0.7	1.0	1.1	1.5	1.9	2.1	1.8	1.3	2.0	19.2
Temperature °F														
-Maximum														
90° and above	30	0.0	0.0	0.0	0.0	0.2	3.3	7.5	6.2	1.7	0.0	0.0	0.0	18.9
32° and below	30	9.1	5.7	0.9	0.0	0.0	0.0	0.0	0.0	0.0	0.0	0.5	4.7	21.0
-Minimum														
32° and below	30	23.9	20.2	13.6	3.3	0.1	0.0	0.0	0.0	0.0	2.3	10.9	20.0	94.3
0° and below	30	1.6	0.7	0.1	0.0	0.0	0.0	0.0	0.0	0.0	0.0	0.0	0.4	2.8
AVG. STATION PRESS.(mb)	21	983.7	982.9	980.7	980.1	980.1	980.7	981.8	982.5	983.2	983.8	983.4	983.8	982.2
RELATIVE HUMIDITY (%)														
Hour 01	29	76	75	71	69	77	81	83	83	83	77	76	77	77
Hour 07 (Local Time)	30	80	79	77	75	81	83	86	88	88	84	81	81	82
Hour 13	30	68	64	58	54	57	57	58	59	59	56	63	68	60
Hour 19	30	70	66	59	55	60	61	63	64	66	64	68	72	64
PRECIPITATION (inches):														
Water Equivalent														
-Normal		2.86	3.21	4.40	3.88	4.47	3.66	5.00	3.93	3.20	2.57	3.39	3.98	44.55
-Maximum Monthly	49	16.65	10.12	10.38	9.30	10.84	11.69	10.64	11.18	9.69	6.13	6.87	10.17	16.65
-Year		1950	1989	1975	1970	1983	1960	1958	1974	1979	1983	1951	1990	JAN 1950
-Minimum Monthly	49	0.37	0.67	0.99	0.79	1.20	0.61	1.83	0.56	0.24	0.33	0.45	0.61	0.24
-Year		1981	1978	1966	1946	1965	1988	1951	1984	1959	1963	1976	1965	SEP 1959
-Maximum in 24 hrs	49	2.98	3.79	3.85	4.39	3.24	5.88	4.73	3.56	4.35	3.21	2.71	3.77	5.88
-Year		1951	1989	1952	1948	1983	1960	1978	1968	1979	1962	1988	1978	JUN 1960
Snow,Ice pellets,hail														
-Maximum Monthly	49	21.9	16.4	17.7	5.9	T	T	T	T	0.0	0.2	9.7	10.7	21.9
-Year		1978	1960	1960	1987	1989	1993	1989	1989		1972	1950	1967	JAN 1978
-Maximum in 24 hrs	49	9.4	7.3	9.5	4.9	T	T	T	T	0.0	0.2	7.5	7.8	9.5
-Year		1966	1971	1947	1987	1989	1993	1989	1989		1972	1966	1967	MAR 1947
WIND:														
Mean Speed (mph)	46	10.9	10.8	11.2	10.6	8.7	7.9	7.3	6.9	7.6	8.2	10.0	10.6	9.2
Prevailing Direction through 1963		S	SSW	SSW	SSW	S	S	SSW	S	S	S	S	S	S
Fastest Obs. 1 Min.														
-Direction (!!)	32	27	32	27	32	22	34	29	22	32	26	15	19	32
-Speed (MPH)	32	41	46	36	46	35	38	37	39	32	32	39	37	46
-Year		1978	1962	1962	1963	1965	1992	1966	1964	1980	1965	1983	1971	APR 1963
Peak Gust														
-Direction (!!)	10	SW	W	E	S	NW	N	W	NW	NW	SW	W	SW	N
-Speed (mph)	10	53	56	47	61	51	64	56	51	40	40	49	54	64
-Date		1985	1993	1986	1993	1993	1992	1987	1988	1989	1984	1992	1985	JUN 1992

PRECIPITATION (inches)

LEXINGTON, KENTUCKY

YEAR	JAN	FEB	MAR	APR	MAY	JUNE	JULY	AUG	SEP	OCT	NOV	DEC	ANNUAL
1964	2.83	2.52	10.06	2.86	1.68	3.55	3.99	1.96	4.91	0.57	2.37	6.18	43.48
1965	2.83	2.92	5.45	3.24	1.20	3.28	3.64	1.92	3.55	2.44	1.02	0.61	32.10
1966	3.99	3.64	0.99	7.16	4.85	1.36	5.74	4.55	4.03	1.44	4.01	4.60	46.36
1967	1.35	2.29	6.03	3.61	6.94	2.65	5.87	3.63	2.97	2.11	4.15	3.99	45.59
1968	1.44	0.71	6.76	3.23	6.87	2.83	4.54	5.27	2.98	2.57	3.23	2.89	43.32
1969	4.26	1.60	1.50	3.83	3.78	4.61	4.37	5.96	0.49	1.53	3.42	4.15	39.50
1970	0.95	3.60	4.72	9.30	3.18	3.81	3.39	2.61	5.71	2.37	2.35	5.51	47.50
1971	3.29	4.72	2.02	2.10	6.14	7.84	7.64	0.88	3.51	0.52	1.71	4.30	44.67
1972	4.10	5.60	4.04	8.75	3.84	3.61	5.58	3.95	4.30	2.71	4.21	6.92	57.61
1973	1.53	1.58	5.08	5.67	8.22	6.06	5.15	3.58	1.40	2.65	6.58	3.42	50.92
1974	6.39	2.24	5.89	3.33	5.52	7.21	4.82	11.18	4.18	1.53	4.08	3.72	60.09
1975	3.66	5.70	10.38	6.17	2.69	2.23	5.60	3.96	6.46	5.09	2.93	4.24	59.11
1976	3.59	4.67	3.72	1.24	3.16	3.34	6.74	1.26	4.23	3.86	0.45	1.22	37.48
1977	2.30	1.03	4.21	3.42	1.51	4.80	4.59	4.83	2.71	3.77	3.95	3.04	40.16
1978	6.38	0.67	2.87	3.15	5.74	1.94	7.60	10.00	3.10	3.20	3.11	9.97	57.73
1979	4.07	2.92	3.22	4.92	4.17	2.80	4.72	6.20	9.69	2.96	4.52	3.81	54.00
1980	1.63	1.17	6.04	2.82	2.27	1.88	5.55	5.10	2.47	2.07	2.02	1.67	34.69
1981	0.37	4.76	1.76	4.88	5.10	2.29	5.27	2.72	1.97	2.44	1.99	3.10	36.65
1982	5.48	2.16	3.89	2.19	2.51	3.95	3.82	4.01	1.21	1.56	3.45	4.53	38.76
1983	1.29	1.61	1.48	5.18	10.84	2.18	2.41	1.26	1.33	6.13	3.59	3.46	40.76
1984	1.64	3.31	4.09	5.02	5.34	2.20	4.80	0.56	1.36	3.87	5.19	4.89	42.27
1985	1.91	1.11	3.69	2.34	4.34	4.98	3.37	3.76	1.93	4.23	4.96	1.13	37.75
1986	0.53	2.48	2.43	1.65	3.24	1.29	5.64	2.67	3.08	2.06	6.49	3.30	34.86
1987	1.30	3.62	3.13	2.23	1.80	6.59	3.48	4.18	0.91	0.55	2.72	6.17	36.68
1988	2.94	3.06	2.34	2.93	3.02	0.61	3.51	4.18	5.96	1.34	5.39	3.62	38.90
1989	3.99	10.12	6.08	2.60	5.39	4.26	4.20	3.98	4.98	3.38	2.38	1.80	53.16
1990	4.17	3.43	1.89	2.37	5.41	4.59	6.45	4.36	2.12	4.49	2.69	10.17	52.14
1991	2.57	3.91	5.80	2.70	3.95	2.91	3.60	3.08	2.09	2.70	1.27	7.22	41.80
1992	3.63	1.84	4.70	2.11	4.68	7.74	10.27	4.73	3.44	0.65	3.50	1.80	49.09
1993	2.42	4.15	3.77	3.53	2.43	5.46	3.38	4.52	3.00	4.19	5.42	3.31	45.58
Record Mean	3.94	3.24	4.44	3.63	3.90	4.09	4.53	3.54	2.89	2.45	3.27	3.72	43.62

AVERAGE TEMPERATURE (deg. F)

LEXINGTON, KENTUCKY

YEAR	JAN	FEB	MAR	APR	MAY	JUNE	JULY	AUG	SEP	OCT	NOV	DEC	ANNUAL
1964	35.0	32.0	45.3	58.3	66.9	74.3	75.2	75.0	68.2	52.7	48.0	37.4	55.7
1965	32.2	34.3	37.9	55.9	68.9	71.3	73.7	74.5	68.8	53.9	46.2	39.6	54.8
1966	25.3	33.3	44.6	52.6	60.5	71.6	77.4	72.6	65.3	54.2	45.7	35.5	53.2
1967	37.3	30.2	50.0	58.8	62.0	72.1	72.5	70.6	64.9	56.1	40.7	39.0	54.5
1968	29.6	28.0	46.0	55.1	62.1	72.0	75.9	75.5	67.8	56.6	46.4	34.6	54.1
1969	32.1	36.2	38.9	56.3	65.5	72.8	77.8	74.7	67.8	57.9	42.8	32.7	54.6
1970	25.8	32.4	40.5	57.2	66.5	71.3	74.1	74.6	72.7	57.7	43.6	38.3	54.5
1971	29.7	34.8	40.3	52.0	59.2	73.7	73.9	73.9	72.5	64.7	47.2	45.7	55.6
1972	35.4	33.2	42.2	53.7	63.2	67.6	73.8	72.9	69.8	53.0	44.5	40.9	54.2
1973	35.1	35.2	53.8	52.9	60.1	73.6	75.8	74.9	72.2	60.9	48.5	36.4	56.6
1974	40.7	37.4	48.5	55.8	63.6	67.2	74.4	73.3	62.6	54.3	45.7	37.8	55.1
1975	37.3	39.5	41.4	52.2	67.4	73.5	76.4	77.5	63.4	57.4	48.5	35.8	55.9
1976	28.4	43.9	50.0	54.5	60.6	71.1	73.0	71.2	64.1	49.7	37.1	30.9	52.9
1977	17.8	34.9	50.8	59.6	69.8	72.3	78.4	75.7	72.2	56.1	49.0	33.4	55.8
1978	21.6	21.3	40.4	57.0	61.1	73.1	76.0	74.1	70.9	53.7	48.4	37.9	53.0
1979	23.6	26.9	48.0	53.8	63.1	70.9	74.0	74.0	66.9	55.6	45.7	37.9	53.4
1980	32.4	28.3	41.5	52.5	64.8	71.2	78.8	78.2	70.6	53.7	43.6	36.0	54.3
1981	27.5	37.0	42.6	59.6	60.4	73.8	75.8	73.4	65.8	55.6	45.9	33.0	54.2
1982	28.2	34.9	47.1	50.6	69.8	68.5	77.1	72.9	65.6	58.3	48.4	44.2	55.5
1983	33.8	37.2	46.3	50.8	60.7	72.8	79.8	80.5	70.2	59.0	46.5	28.4	55.5
1984	27.6	41.2	39.7	53.1	60.6	76.0	72.9	74.9	66.5	63.5	41.8	45.4	55.3
1985	23.8	30.5	48.5	58.5	64.7	70.3	75.1	72.8	67.6	60.5	53.0	29.6	54.6
1986	33.2	38.6	46.8	57.3	65.5	74.2	78.6	72.9	71.0	58.0	44.9	35.7	56.4
1987	31.9	38.0	46.8	53.7	70.3	75.0	77.1	77.5	70.0	52.0	50.0	38.9	56.8
1988	29.8	33.7	44.8	54.2	64.5	74.3	79.1	77.9	67.8	49.6	46.1	36.5	54.9
1989	40.5	33.1	47.3	54.2	60.6	71.6	76.5	74.1	67.6	57.0	45.0	23.0	54.2
1990	41.6	43.1	48.9	53.2	61.6	72.2	75.3	73.8	68.5	56.4	49.9	40.4	57.1
1991	33.9	39.1	47.4	58.1	70.5	74.3	77.6	75.8	68.8	58.7	43.4	40.1	57.3
1992	35.2	41.3	45.4	56.1	62.0	69.4	75.6	70.9	67.0	55.8	45.9	37.0	55.1
1993	37.4	33.1	42.0	52.7	65.0	72.1	80.1	76.5	66.0	55.1	44.6	35.0	55.0
Record Mean	33.1	35.2	44.2	54.3	64.1	72.7	76.3	74.8	68.8	57.2	45.0	36.0	55.2
Max	41.1	43.8	53.7	64.5	74.2	82.6	86.0	84.7	79.1	67.5	53.7	43.8	64.6
Min	25.1	26.5	34.6	44.1	54.0	62.7	66.5	65.0	58.6	46.9	36.2	28.1	45.7

REFERENCE NOTES

LEXINGTON, KENTUCKY

GENERAL
T - TRACE AMOUNT.
BLANK ENTRIES DENOTE MISSING/UNREPORTED DATA.
# INDICATES A STATION OR INSTRUMENT RELOCATION.

SPECIFIC

PM - INCLUDES LAST DAY OF PREVIOUS MONTH
ASOS - AUTOMATED SURFACE OBSERVING SYSTEM IN OPERATION DURING THESE MONTHS.

(a) - LENGTH OF RECORD IN YEARS, ALTHOUGH INDIVIDUAL MONTHS MAY BE MISSING.
0.* OR * - THE VALUE IS BETWEEN 0.0 AND 0.05
NORMALS - BASED ON THE 1961-1990 RECORD PERIOD.
EXTREMES - DATES ARE THE MOST RECENT OCCURRENCE
WIND DIR. - NUMERALS SHOW TENS OF DEGRESS CLOCKWISE FROM TRUE NORTH. "00" INDICATES CALM.
RESULTANT DIRECTIONS ARE GIVEN TO WHOLE DEGREES.
BOLD VALUES INDICATE EXTREME VALUES WHICH OCCURRED AFTER THE ASOS SYSTEM WAS COMMISSIONED.

RECORD = PERIOD OF RECORD
RECORD MEAN PRECIPITATION IS THE MEAN OF ALL DAILY PRECIPITATION AMOUNTS DURING THE PERIOD OF RECORD.
RECORD MAX(MIN) TEMPERATURE IS THE MEAN OF ALL DAILY MAX(MIN) TEMPERATURES DURING THE PERIOD OF RECORD.
RECORD MEAN TEMPERATURE IS THE SUM OF THE RECORD MAX AND RECORD MIN DIVIDED BY 2.
AVERAGE TEMPERATURE IS THE SUM OF THE MEAN DAILY MAX AND MIN TEMPERATURE DIVIDED BY 2.

EXCEPTIONS

RECORD MEANS ARE THROUGH THE CURRENT YEAR, BEGINNING IN 1871 FOR TEMPERATURE
1871 FOR PRECIPITATION
1945 FOR SNOWFALL

HEATING DEGREE DAYS Base 65 deg. F LEXINGTON, KENTUCKY

SEASON	JULY	AUG	SEP	OCT	NOV	DEC	JAN	FEB	MAR	APR	MAY	JUNE	TOTAL
1964-65	0	11	61	375	502	850	1010	851	834	277	26	8	4805
1965-66	0	9	52	346	558	777	1225	883	631	373	167	21	5042
1966-67	0	3	62	340	570	908	851	967	468	223	138	23	4553
1967-68	1	4	83	289	722	800	1090	1065	581	298	124	8	5065
1968-69	0	5	20	296	552	938	1011	799	800	261	77	17	4776
1969-70	0	0	44	274	657	996	1209	908	750	251	84	1	5174
1970-71	6	0	31	229	637	821	1087	838	759	382	198	0	4988
1971-72	0	0	8	69	536	591	909	917	700	343	96	47	4216
1972-73	10	1	20	366	612	739	920	827	353	371	167	0	4386
1973-74	0	1	21	172	490	880	744	767	514	289	128	37	4043
1974-75	0	0	125	338	578	836	852	705	726	387	51	4	4602
1975-76	0	0	128	249	488	895	1130	606	468	339	158	2	4463
1976-77	1	4	64	474	829	1050	1457	836	444	208	52	19	5438
1977-78	0	0	6	277	498	972	1338	1219	755	254	179	6	5504
1978-79	0	0	20	348	492	834	1277	1061	522	337	110	15	5016
1979-80	0	5	40	307	574	833	1005	1057	721	371	88	17	5018
1980-81	0	0	23	358	633	892	1156	777	687	182	180	0	4888
1981-82	0	0	77	286	568	985	1134	840	549	429	14	9	4891
1982-83	0	1	75	259	500	646	961	772	580	422	151	7	4374
1983-84	0	0	59	201	550	1128	1152	685	778	370	178	3	5104
1984-85	2	0	89	84	689	601	1275	959	510	228	66	23	4526
1985-86	0	0	72	179	360	1092	978	735	561	259	94	2	4332
1986-87	0	15	14	250	595	903	1016	749	559	342	39	0	4482
1987-88	0	0	17	399	447	804	1085	901	620	328	90	18	4709
1988-89	0	3	30	474	560	877	750	887	548	351	196	8	4684
1989-90	0	6	61	267	592	1297	720	608	505	378	128	17	4579
1990-91	0	3	57	288	453	757	955	719	544	215	34	0	4025
1991-92	0	0	77	230	642	765	915	682	600	293	159	17	4380
1992-93	0	5	64	288	566	863	847	884	705	363	64	27	4676
1993-94	0	0	67	313	608	922							

COOLING DEGREE DAYS Base 65 deg. F LEXINGTON, KENTUCKY

YEAR	JAN	FEB	MAR	APR	MAY	JUNE	JULY	AUG	SEP	OCT	NOV	DEC	TOTAL
1969	0	0	0	7	97	260	404	309	134	57	0	0	1268
1970	0	0	0	26	137	199	295	306	266	11	0	0	1240
1971	0	0	0	0	25	266	281	285	239	65	10	0	1171
1972	0	0	0	11	47	130	287	250	171	0	4	0	900
1973	0	0	12	18	21	266	342	314	245	51	0	0	1269
1974	0	0	10	21	94	108	296	264	60	11	4	0	868
1975	0	0	0	11	130	267	357	394	86	18	0	0	1263
1976	0	0	9	30	26	193	257	205	46	4	0	0	770
1977	0	0	11	52	206	241	422	337	232	8	23	0	1532
1978	0	0	0	19	69	257	349	290	202	4	0	0	1190
1979	0	0	2	8	57	199	287	292	102	21	0	0	968
1980	0	0	0	4	87	210	438	415	199	17	0	0	1370
1981	0	0	1	29	43	270	341	267	109	2	0	0	1062
1982	0	0	0	4	171	121	383	252	101	62	9	7	1110
1983	0	0	4	3	27	248	465	487	219	21	0	0	1474
1984	0	0	0	17	50	340	254	312	141	44	1	0	1159
1985	0	0	5	40	67	189	317	245	155	49	4	0	1071
1986	0	0	4	34	115	285	427	269	197	42	0	0	1373
1987	0	0	0	10	212	304	383	395	173	2	5	0	1484
1988	0	0	1	8	81	306	442	407	120	5	0	0	1370
1989	0	0	8	34	66	214	362	296	146	27	0	0	1153
1990	0	0	13	29	32	239	326	285	168	26	5	0	1123
1991	0	0	3	15	210	285	398	341	198	41	0	0	1491
1992	0	0	0	35	76	155	340	192	132	8	0	0	938
1993	0	0	0	2	74	247	474	365	103	13	3	0	1281

SNOWFALL (inches) LEXINGTON, KENTUCKY

SEASON	JULY	AUG	SEP	OCT	NOV	DEC	JAN	FEB	MAR	APR	MAY	JUNE	TOTAL
1964-65	0.0	0.0	0.0	0.0	0.7	0.7	9.9	1.8	2.8	0.0	0.0	0.0	15.9
1965-66	0.0	0.0	0.0	0.0	T	1.3	12.4	6.5	1.2	T	0.0	0.0	21.4
1966-67	0.0	0.0	0.0	0.0	8.4	0.3	1.5	11.1	4.3	0.0	0.0	0.0	25.6
1967-68	0.0	0.0	0.0	0.0	T	10.7	12.1	3.1	8.6	0.0	0.0	0.0	34.5
1968-69	0.0	0.0	0.0	0.0	1.0	1.5	1.9	6.1	1.7	0.0	0.0	0.0	12.2
1969-70	0.0	0.0	0.0	0.0	1.4	5.2	8.4	9.9	6.2	T	0.0	0.0	31.1
1970-71	0.0	0.0	0.0	0.0	T	1.2	4.0	9.1	5.3	0.0	0.0	0.0	19.6
1971-72	0.0	0.0	0.0	0.0	0.7	T	1.4	6.3	2.4	T	0.0	0.0	10.8
1972-73	0.0	0.0	0.0	0.2	1.7	0.4	1.0	1.4	0.4	0.2	0.0	0.0	5.3
1973-74	0.0	0.0	0.0	0.0	0.0	4.3	T	3.6	0.7	T	0.0	0.0	8.6
1974-75	0.0	0.0	0.0	T	1.4	2.8	4.6	1.5	5.6	T	0.0	0.0	15.9
1975-76	0.0	0.0	0.0	0.0	T	0.9	6.5	0.4	2.2	0.0	0.0	0.0	10.0
1976-77	0.0	0.0	0.0	0.0	2.9	1.6	18.5	3.5	0.1	0.8	0.0	0.0	27.4
1977-78	0.0	0.0	0.0	0.0	1.7	3.0	21.9	7.1	8.4	0.0	0.0	0.0	42.1
1978-79	0.0	0.0	0.0	0.0	0.0	0.7	11.4	11.6	0.1	T	0.0	0.0	23.8
1979-80	0.0	0.0	0.0	0.0	0.1	T	11.9	4.0	4.2	0.3	0.0	0.0	20.5
1980-81	0.0	0.0	0.0	0.0	0.1	0.5	2.2	0.4	0.5	0.0	0.0	0.0	3.7
1981-82	0.0	0.0	0.0	0.0	0.4	1.7	5.6	3.9	0.3	0.7	0.0	0.0	12.6
1982-83	0.0	0.0	0.0	0.0	0.0	T	0.2	7.5	0.3	T	0.0	0.0	8.0
1983-84	0.0	0.0	0.0	0.0	T	1.7	8.4	4.6	0.3	0.0	0.0	0.0	15.0
1984-85	0.0	0.0	0.0	0.0	T	4.9	10.2	10.7	T	0.5	0.0	0.0	26.3
1985-86	0.0	0.0	0.0	0.0	0.0	3.5	1.2	8.9	0.7	T	0.0	0.0	14.3
1986-87	0.0	0.0	0.0	0.0	0.2	T	3.6	3.5	2.1	5.9	0.0	0.0	15.3
1987-88	0.0	0.0	0.0	0.0	1.0	1.8	3.3	3.4	0.7	0.0	0.0	0.0	10.2
1988-89	0.0	0.0	0.0	0.0	T	0.7	T	1.5	T	T	T	0.0	2.2
1989-90	T	T	0.0	T	1.1	9.3	0.2	T	3.7	T	0.0	0.0	14.3
1990-91	0.0	0.0	0.0	0.0	0.0	0.8	0.1	3.2	1.7	0.0	0.0	0.0	5.8
1991-92	0.0	0.0	0.0	0.0	T	0.2	0.7	0.6	1.3	0.4	0.0	0.0	3.2
1992-93	0.0	0.0	0.0	T	1.8	2.5	0.4	11.5	7.1	T	0.0	T	23.3
1993-94	0.0	0.0	0.0	T	0.1	7.4							
Record Mean	T	T	0.0	T	0.6	1.9	5.4	4.8	2.7	0.3	T	T	15.7

LOUISVILLE, KENTUCKY

Louisville is located on the south bank of the Ohio River, 604 miles below Pittsburgh, Pennsylvania, and 377 miles above the mouth of the river at Cairo, Illinois. The city is divided by Beargrass Creek and its south fork into two portions with entirely different types of topography. The eastern portion is rolling, containing several creeks, and consists of plateaus and rolling hillsides. The highest elevation in this area is 565 feet. The western portion is mostly flat with an average elevation about 100 feet lower than the eastern area. Much of the western section lies in the flood plain of the Ohio River. Nearly all of the industries in the city are located in the western portion, while the eastern portion is almost entirely residential. A range of low hills about five miles northwest of Louisville, on the Indiana side of the Ohio River, present a partial barrier to arctic blasts in the winter months. During colder months, snow is frequently observed on the summits of these hills when there is no snow in the city of Louisville or in riverside communities on the Indiana side of the Ohio River.

The climate of Louisville, while continental in type, is of a variable nature because of its position with respect to the paths of high and low pressure systems and the occasional influx of warm moist air from the Gulf of Mexico. In winter and summer there are occasional cold and hot spells of short duration. As a whole, winters are moderately cold and summers are quite warm. Temperatures of 100 degrees or more in summer and zero degrees or less in winter are rare.

Thunderstorms with high rainfall intensities are common during the spring and summer months. The precipitation in Louisville is nonseasonal and varies from year to year. The fall months are usually the driest. Generally, March has the most rainfall and October the least. Snowfall usually occurs from November through March. As with rainfall, amounts vary from year to year and month to month. Some snow has also been recorded in the months of October and April. Mean total amounts for the months of January, February, and March are about the same with January showing a slight edge in total amount. Relative humidity remains rather high throughout the summer months. Cloud cover is about equally distributed throughout the year with the winter months showing somewhat of an increase in amount. The percentage of possible sunshine at Louisville varies from month to month with the greatest amount during the summer months as a result of the decreasing sky cover during that season. Heavy fog is unusual and there is only an average of 10 days during the year with heavy fog and these occur generally in the months of September through March.

The average date for the last occurrence in the spring of temperatures as low as 32 degrees is mid-April, and the first occurrence in the fall is generally in late October.

The prevailing direction of the wind has a southerly component and the velocity averages under 10 mph. The strongest winds are usually associated with thunderstorms.

NORMALS, MEANS, AND EXTREMES

LOUISVILLE, KENTUCKY

LATITUDE: 38°11'N LONGITUDE: 85°44' W ELEVATION: FT. GRND 477 BARO 485 TIME ZONE: EASTERN WBAN: 93821

	(a)	JAN	FEB	MAR	APR	MAY	JUNE	JULY	AUG	SEP	OCT	NOV	DEC	YEAR
TEMPERATURE °F:														
Normals														
-Daily Maximum		40.3	44.8	56.3	67.3	76.0	83.5	87.0	85.7	80.3	69.2	56.8	45.1	66.0
-Daily Minimum		23.2	26.5	36.2	45.4	54.7	62.9	67.3	65.8	58.7	45.8	37.3	28.6	46.0
-Monthly		31.7	35.7	46.3	56.3	65.3	73.2	77.2	75.8	69.5	57.6	47.1	36.9	56.1
Extremes														
-Record Highest	46	77	77	86	91	95	102	105	101	104	92	84	76	105
-Year		1950	1972	1981	1960	1959	1952	1954	1988	1954	1959	1958	1982	JUL 1954
-Record Lowest	46	-20	-19	-1	22	31	42	50	46	33	23	-1	-15	-20
-Year		1963	1951	1960	1982	1966	1966	1972	1986	1949	1952	1950	1989	JAN 1963
NORMAL DEGREE DAYS:														
Heating (base 65°F)		1032	820	580	273	105	6	0	0	36	254	537	871	4514
Cooling (base 65°F)		0	0	0	12	115	252	378	335	171	25	0	0	1288
% OF POSSIBLE SUNSHINE	46	42	48	50	55	60	66	67	66	64	61	46	40	55
MEAN SKY COVER (tenths) Sunrise - Sunset	46	7.3	7.0	7.0	6.6	6.3	5.9	5.7	5.3	5.4	5.3	6.7	7.2	6.3
MEAN NUMBER OF DAYS:														
Sunrise to Sunset														
-Clear	46	5.7	5.9	5.8	6.3	7.5	7.6	8.0	10.2	10.5	11.5	7.4	6.1	92.7
-Partly Cloudy	46	5.7	6.3	7.5	8.8	9.4	11.2	12.7	11.5	8.8	7.6	6.0	6.1	101.5
-Cloudy	46	19.6	16.1	17.6	14.9	14.0	11.1	10.3	9.3	10.7	11.9	16.4	18.8	170.8
Precipitation .01 inches or more	46	11.2	10.6	13.0	11.7	11.7	9.8	10.5	8.4	8.1	7.6	10.4	11.5	124.7
Snow, Ice pellets, hail 1.0 inches or more	46	1.6	1.2	0.7	0.1	0.0	0.0	0.0	0.0	0.0	0.*	0.3	0.7	4.5
Thunderstorms	46	0.8	1.1	3.2	4.3	6.6	7.3	8.4	6.9	3.3	1.7	1.4	0.5	45.6
Heavy Fog Visibility 1/4 mile or less	46	0.9	0.9	0.5	0.2	0.3	0.3	0.5	0.9	1.0	1.5	0.7	0.7	8.4
Temperature °F														
-Maximum														
90° and above	33	0.0	0.0	0.0	0.*	0.5	6.1	11.6	9.4	3.0	0.0	0.0	0.0	30.7
32° and below	33	8.6	4.9	0.6	0.0	0.0	0.0	0.0	0.0	0.0	0.0	0.3	4.2	18.7
-Minimum														
32° and below	33	24.0	19.8	11.8	2.2	0.1	0.0	0.0	0.0	0.0	1.5	9.1	19.9	88.5
0° and below	33	1.2	0.2	0.0	0.0	0.0	0.0	0.0	0.0	0.0	0.0	0.0	0.3	1.8
AVG. STATION PRESS. (mb)	21	1002.5	1001.6	998.8	997.9	997.4	997.8	998.7	999.6	1000.4	1001.4	1001.4	1002.3	1000.0
RELATIVE HUMIDITY (%)														
Hour 01	33	72	72	69	68	77	80	81	82	83	78	75	74	76
Hour 07 (Local Time)	33	76	77	76	76	82	83	85	88	88	85	79	78	81
Hour 13	33	64	61	57	52	55	56	58	58	59	55	61	65	58
Hour 19	33	65	62	57	52	57	58	60	61	63	61	65	68	61
PRECIPITATION (inches):														
Water Equivalent														
-Normal		2.86	3.30	4.66	4.23	4.62	3.46	4.51	3.54	3.16	2.71	3.70	3.64	44.39
-Maximum Monthly	46	11.38	9.02	14.91	11.10	11.57	10.11	10.05	8.79	10.49	6.47	9.12	8.86	14.91
-Year		1950	1989	1964	1970	1990	1960	1979	1974	1979	1983	1957	1990	MAR 1964
-Minimum Monthly	46	0.45	0.76	1.02	0.76	1.37	0.49	0.99	0.23	0.27	0.39	0.72	0.65	0.23
-Year		1981	1978	1966	1976	1977	1984	1983	1953	1953	1987	1976	1976	AUG 1953
-Maximum in 24 hrs	46	3.00	3.66	6.97	4.85	4.60	5.14	5.46	3.13	4.97	3.25	3.58	2.79	6.97
-Year		1988	1990	1964	1970	1961	1960	1979	1992	1979	1977	1948	1978	MAR 1964
Snow, Ice pellets, hail														
-Maximum Monthly	46	28.4	15.9	22.9	1.6	T	T	0.0	0.0	0.0	2.4	13.2	9.3	28.4
-Year		1978	1993	1960	1973	1989	1993				1993	1966	1961	JAN 1978
-Maximum in 24 hrs	46	14.1	11.0	12.1	1.6	T	T	0.0	0.0	0.0	2.4	13.0	5.0	14.1
-Year		1978	1966	1968	1973	1989	1993				1993	1966	1961	JAN 1978
WIND:														
Mean Speed (mph)	46	9.6	9.6	10.2	9.7	8.0	7.4	6.8	6.4	6.8	7.2	8.9	9.2	8.3
Prevailing Direction through 1963		S	NW	NW	SW	SE	S	S	N	SE	SE	S	S	S
Fastest Obs. 1 Min.														
-Direction (!!!)	8	W	30	22	33	27	27	32	32	29	27	27	29	32
-Speed (MPH)	8	34	32	36	37	35	41	46	26	39	29	40	31	46
-Year		1984	1990	1986	1988	1985	1985	1987	1986	1986	1992	1993	1984	JUL 1987
Peak Gust														
-Direction (!!!)	10	W	NW	NW	S	S	W	NW	S	NW	SE	W	S	NW
-Speed (mph)	10	48	52	60	49	60	72	78	53	48	44	51	52	78
-Date		1990	1990	1986	1985	1985	1990	1987	1984	1984	1984	1993	1987	JUL 1987

AVERAGE TEMPERATURE (deg. F)

LOUISVILLE, KENTUCKY

YEAR	JAN	FEB	MAR	APR	MAY	JUNE	JULY	AUG	SEP	OCT	NOV	DEC	ANNUAL
1964	35.9	33.4	45.3	58.4	66.8	75.1	76.4	76.2	69.1	53.4	48.0	38.0	56.3
1965	34.3	35.9	38.9	58.3	70.0	73.4	76.3	75.2	70.5	55.7	47.3	42.3	56.5
1966	27.1	34.1	46.1	53.4	62.3	73.1	81.1	75.6	67.4	54.6	47.2	35.6	54.8
1967	36.3	30.9	50.6	59.7	62.4	73.4	74.5	72.2	65.7	57.2	42.7	39.4	55.4
1968	30.3	30.1	45.7	56.8	63.4	74.0	77.7	77.9	69.0	57.4	48.0	35.7	55.5
1969	33.1	36.9	39.9	58.0	66.2	73.5	78.7	74.7	67.5	57.3	43.3	33.5	55.2
1970	27.9	33.6	42.3	59.3	67.2	72.9	75.8	76.0	73.4	58.1	45.3	39.6	56.0
1971	30.9	35.0	42.0	54.7	61.5	76.5	74.8	74.1	72.2	64.4	47.0	45.1	56.5
1972	35.2	34.9	44.8	56.2	65.5	70.6	77.1	76.1	72.3	55.3	44.0	39.1	55.9
1973	35.0	36.4	53.7	54.4	61.5	75.6	78.4	77.0	73.6	62.3	49.8	37.1	57.9
1974	39.8	39.3	49.8	57.2	65.1	68.7	75.9	75.0	63.2	54.9	47.0	39.1	56.3
1975	38.1	40.2	43.3	54.4	69.0	75.4	77.7	79.3	66.2	59.4	50.6	38.9	57.7
1976	31.3	45.4	52.4	57.5	62.9	72.9	76.8	74.2	66.8	52.5	39.5	33.1	55.4
1977	18.6	36.9	51.7	60.3	71.2	73.9	80.2	77.5	72.5	55.5	49.6	34.6	56.9
1978	22.9	23.8	41.7	58.0	63.8	75.7	78.5	77.1	73.7	55.5	50.0	40.0	55.1
1979	24.6	28.0	48.3	55.0	64.2	73.9	75.3	76.1	69.4	58.2	46.9	39.2	54.9
1980	33.5	29.6	41.8	53.6	66.8	73.4	81.5	81.0	73.5	55.8	46.3	38.3	56.3
1981	30.4	38.8	45.7	62.4	62.9	76.2	78.8	76.1	67.7	56.5	47.4	33.8	56.4
1982	28.6	34.9	47.1	51.3	70.3	69.3	78.0	73.5	66.8	59.0	48.7	44.9	56.0
1983	34.7	37.5	46.7	51.7	62.1	73.4	81.1	81.7	71.0	59.1	47.8	28.4	56.3
1984	28.9	41.5	40.4	55.0	62.6	77.7	75.5	76.0	67.2	63.9	44.0	45.9	56.6
1985	25.4	32.8	50.2	60.3	66.5	72.1	77.2	74.8	69.2	61.4	53.7	30.4	56.2
1986	34.5	39.9	48.3	58.5	67.0	75.7	80.3	74.3	73.1	59.5	45.9	36.7	57.8
1987	33.7	39.5	47.9	55.4	71.5	76.2	78.9	78.2	71.2	52.6	50.8	40.2	58.0
1988	31.0	34.7	46.1	57.0	67.1	75.6	80.3	80.0	70.1	52.3	47.8	38.0	56.7
1989	41.6	34.0	48.4	56.7	62.6	73.5	78.1	76.6	69.4	58.4	46.7	25.3	55.9
1990	43.1	44.3	51.2	55.5	64.2	75.1	78.5	77.5	71.8	58.7	52.0	40.8	59.4
1991	34.1	40.5	49.4	60.3	73.1	78.3	81.3	79.2	71.7	61.5	45.0	41.4	59.7
1992	37.1	43.7	47.9	58.2	63.9	72.1	78.5	73.2	69.1	58.1	47.9	38.6	57.4
1993	38.5	34.0	44.0	54.9	66.8	74.5	82.0	79.0	68.0	55.9	45.8	36.5	56.7
Record													
Mean	34.2	36.8	45.8	56.4	66.0	74.6	78.4	76.8	70.3	58.7	46.6	37.2	56.8
Max	42.2	45.3	55.2	66.4	76.1	84.4	88.2	86.6	80.5	69.1	55.2	45.0	66.2
Min	26.2	28.2	36.4	46.3	55.9	64.7	68.6	66.9	60.1	48.2	37.9	29.3	47.4

PRECIPITATION (inches)

LOUISVILLE, KENTUCKY

YEAR	JAN	FEB	MAR	APR	MAY	JUNE	JULY	AUG	SEP	OCT	NOV	DEC	ANNUAL
1964	2.45	2.45	14.91	3.06	1.85	2.24	3.03	2.63	4.16	0.62	3.32	5.86	46.58
1965	2.76	4.67	4.82	3.28	1.60	2.27	4.86	2.12	8.41	2.54	1.33	1.14	39.80
1966	5.73	5.01	1.02	9.56	3.91	0.75	2.13	5.18	2.59	1.04	3.67	4.33	44.92
1967	1.11	2.01	4.37	4.39	4.62	4.41	7.33	4.30	1.73	3.06	3.08	3.51	43.92
1968	2.13	0.80	6.23	3.94	5.16	1.70	3.07	3.68	2.61	1.00	3.34	3.62	37.28
1969	5.31	1.65	1.94	3.77	3.91	2.97	4.05	3.65	1.08	1.69	3.08	3.69	36.79
1970	1.40	2.87	4.52	11.10	1.85	5.20	3.33	7.65	3.57	4.79	1.75	4.18	52.21
1971	2.64	6.28	2.12	2.16	6.15	2.64	6.74	1.83	4.72	1.96	2.06	2.98	42.28
1972	2.87	3.94	4.07	8.48	4.46	1.08	3.64	2.45	4.24	2.55	6.31	5.29	49.38
1973	1.96	1.60	6.26	5.77	7.04	6.20	9.38	0.91	2.34	2.28	7.59	2.64	53.97
1974	4.38	1.64	5.41	2.74	3.86	2.58	2.04	8.79	3.52	2.09	3.03	2.85	42.93
1975	4.87	4.53	9.65	6.47	4.50	3.15	1.91	3.89	2.64	6.12	3.69	4.89	56.31
1976	3.85	3.13	2.87	0.76	5.09	4.71	2.10	3.18	3.10	3.99	0.72	0.65	34.15
1977	2.33	1.45	4.69	3.40	1.37	7.59	3.29	6.12	3.67	4.76	6.11	4.32	49.10
1978	5.90	0.76	3.76	3.33	4.76	2.67	3.77	5.50	0.96	2.26	5.14	7.64	46.45
1979	3.81	4.49	2.71	7.32	3.59	3.03	10.05	2.37	10.49	2.27	5.85	3.82	59.80
1980	1.71	1.09	4.80	2.63	4.58	3.70	5.41	3.76	3.17	3.37	2.42	1.25	37.89
1981	0.45	3.23	1.54	4.44	4.63	3.23	3.98	3.21	3.22	1.60	2.40	2.02	33.95
1982	5.28	1.55	5.89	3.05	2.96	3.86	3.72	3.74	3.46	1.26	5.50	5.11	45.38
1983	1.63	1.52	2.16	7.10	10.58	4.42	0.99	2.39	1.13	6.47	5.03	3.96	47.38
1984	0.92	1.68	4.41	5.53	6.78	0.49	6.94	5.08	3.70	2.12	5.87	5.86	49.38
1985	2.20	2.08	4.43	1.69	3.93	4.37	3.45	4.49	1.48	4.24	4.43	0.96	37.75
1986	0.91	3.90	2.69	1.04	4.28	2.32	7.04	2.19	2.75	3.08	4.62	2.69	37.51
1987	0.81	4.42	3.05	2.35	1.61	3.58	5.31	2.66	1.15	0.39	2.62	4.70	32.65
1988	4.00	3.58	2.97	3.52	2.68	0.87	4.68	3.00	1.48	1.54	5.76	3.45	37.53
1989	3.68	9.02	5.50	4.93	4.39	5.26	6.90	2.20	2.42	2.65	2.57	1.45	50.97
1990	3.90	6.72	2.78	3.46	11.57	6.13	1.96	3.21	2.57	3.97	2.34	8.86	57.47
1991	3.29	3.72	4.79	2.61	4.02	1.23	2.99	3.35	2.74	2.31	1.87	5.23	38.15
1992	1.97	1.74	5.88	2.66	3.51	3.04	6.51	4.71	3.50	0.96	4.71	1.60	40.79
1993	3.50	4.20	5.20	3.57	2.80	4.05	4.58	5.74	3.90	4.03	3.26	2.56	47.39
Record													
Mean	3.74	3.38	4.50	3.91	3.99	3.81	3.85	3.32	2.80	2.60	3.52	3.58	43.01

REFERENCE NOTES

LOUISVILLE, KENTUCKY

GENERAL
T - TRACE AMOUNT.
BLANK ENTRIES DENOTE MISSING/UNREPORTED DATA.
# INDICATES A STATION OR INSTRUMENT RELOCATION.

SPECIFIC

PM - INCLUDES LAST DAY OF PREVIOUS MONTH
ASOS - AUTOMATED SURFACE OBSERVING SYSTEM IN OPERATION DURING THESE MONTHS.

(*) - LENGTH OF RECORD IN YEARS, ALTHOUGH INDIVIDUAL MONTHS MAY BE MISSING.
0.* OR * - THE VALUE IS BETWEEN 0.0 AND 0.05
NORMALS - BASED ON THE 1961-1990 RECORD PERIOD.
EXTREMES - DATES ARE THE MOST RECENT OCCURRENCE
WIND DIR.- NUMERALS SHOW TENS OF DEGRESS CLOCKWISE FROM TRUE NORTH. "00" INDICATES CALM.
RESULTANT DIRECTIONS ARE GIVEN TO WHOLE DEGREES.
BOLD VALUES INDICATE EXTREME VALUES WHICH OCCURRED AFTER THE ASOS SYSTEM WAS COMMISSIONED.

RECORD = PERIOD OF RECORD
RECORD MEAN PRECIPITATION IS THE MEAN OF ALL DAILY PRECIPITATION AMOUNTS DURING THE PERIOD OF RECORD.
RECORD MAX(MIN) TEMPERATURE IS THE MEAN OF ALL DAILY MAX(MIN) TEMPERATURES DURING THE PERIOD OF RECORD.
RECORD MEAN TEMPERATURE IS THE SUM OF THE RECORD MAX AND RECORD MIN DIVIDED BY 2.
AVERAGE TEMPERATURE IS THE SUM OF THE MEAN DAILY MAX AND MIN TEMPERATURE DIVIDED BY 2.

EXCEPTIONS

RECORD MEANS ARE THROUGH THE CURRENT YEAR,
BEGINNING IN 1873 FOR TEMPERATURE
1873 FOR PRECIPITATION
1948 FOR SNOWFALL

HEATING DEGREE DAYS Base 65 deg. F — LOUISVILLE, KENTUCKY

SEASON	JULY	AUG	SEP	OCT	NOV	DEC	JAN	FEB	MAR	APR	MAY	JUNE	TOTAL
1964-65	0	5	44	349	502	829	943	808	802	223	20	0	4525
1965-66	0	2	45	304	526	697	1170	857	580	353	127	8	4669
1966-67	0	0	35	324	531	907	882	949	453	209	139	13	4442
1967-68	0	0	68	259	660	788	1069	1007	590	247	98	4	4790
1968-69	0	1	10	276	511	903	987	778	771	213	61	14	4525
1969-70	0	0	42	282	645	971	1141	875	697	200	70	0	4923
1970-71	0	0	23	220	582	781	1052	833	707	303	137	0	4638
1971-72	0	0	13	65	537	610	914	866	623	282	61	19	3990
1972-73	0	0	16	298	628	793	927	796	349	343	129	0	4279
1973-74	0	0	13	144	450	860	772	714	487	257	99	19	3815
1974-75	0	0	122	314	543	794	830	688	665	333	22	0	4311
1975-76	0	0	73	205	431	801	1040	562	405	266	111	1	3895
1976-77	0	0	29	393	757	982	1435	780	421	183	36	7	5023
1977-78	0	0	6	295	472	935	1294	1145	720	221	142	1	5231
1978-79	0	0	4	293	442	765	1246	1030	514	301	94	5	4694
1979-80	0	0	19	244	534	792	969	1021	713	342	68	8	4710
1980-81	0	0	12	309	555	821	1065	728	595	142	122	0	4349
1981-82	0	0	61	268	523	960	1124	837	549	408	13	3	4746
1982-83	0	1	56	246	495	624	933	763	571	399	121	5	4214
1983-84	0	0	54	196	509	1128	1115	673	757	315	141	0	4888
1984-85	0	0	73	84	623	584	1222	896	458	180	52	16	4188
1985-86	0	0	53	160	347	1067	941	696	516	224	69	0	4073
1986-87	0	12	5	210	570	869	962	706	526	294	21	0	4175
1987-88	0	0	9	377	423	762	1048	872	580	244	38	7	4360
1988-89	0	0	13	398	510	833	720	860	513	291	156	4	4298
1989-90	0	0	49	230	539	1222	672	574	445	320	82	13	4146
1990-91	0	0	34	229	387	745	949	677	482	167	27	0	3697
1991-92	0	0	52	168	590	725	855	610	523	244	124	8	3899
1992-93	0	0	40	219	505	813	819	859	644	299	44	18	4260
1993-94	0	0	48	289	572	875							

COOLING DEGREE DAYS Base 65 deg. F — LOUISVILLE, KENTUCKY

YEAR	JAN	FEB	MAR	APR	MAY	JUNE	JULY	AUG	SEP	OCT	NOV	DEC	TOTAL
1969	0	0	0	9	106	277	431	308	127	49	0	0	1307
1970	0	0	0	36	147	244	343	346	283	15	0	0	1414
1971	0	0	0	2	35	351	310	291	237	58	3	0	1287
1972	0	0	3	25	81	193	386	351	242	2	4	0	1287
1973	0	0	7	29	28	325	422	380	280	71	2	0	1544
1974	0	0	22	31	109	136	345	319	75	8	10	0	1055
1975	0	0	0	24	152	320	402	451	116	36	5	0	1506
1976	0	0	21	47	51	243	372	294	92	10	0	0	1130
1977	0	0	14	50	234	281	479	396	238	5	20	0	1717
1978	0	0	0	20	110	323	425	383	270	6	2	0	1539
1979	0	0	5	10	73	279	326	350	154	39	0	0	1236
1980	0	0	0	8	134	266	519	504	276	31	1	0	1739
1981	0	0	5	68	63	343	435	348	150	10	0	0	1422
1982	0	0	1	2	183	139	408	274	118	68	13	8	1214
1983	0	0	7	8	39	264	504	524	240	19	0	0	1605
1984	0	0	0	20	69	386	333	349	145	56	0	1	1359
1985	0	2	8	48	106	233	387	311	185	55	14	0	1349
1986	0	0	5	37	138	330	481	306	255	46	0	0	1598
1987	0	0	0	14	232	342	439	416	203	1	4	0	1651
1988	0	0	4	10	111	333	481	472	173	10	0	0	1594
1989	0	0	6	48	88	264	412	364	188	30	0	0	1400
1990	0	0	22	44	65	323	427	392	244	42	7	0	1566
1991	0	0	8	31	286	406	514	445	262	68	0	0	2020
1992	0	0	2	48	100	229	424	262	169	14	0	0	1248
1993	0	0	0	4	106	310	534	442	146	12	3	0	1557

SNOWFALL (inches) — LOUISVILLE, KENTUCKY

SEASON	JULY	AUG	SEP	OCT	NOV	DEC	JAN	FEB	MAR	APR	MAY	JUNE	TOTAL
1964-65	0.0	0.0	0.0	0.0	0.9	0.2	11.8	3.9	4.6	0.0	0.0	0.0	21.4
1965-66	0.0	0.0	0.0	0.0	0.0	T	7.0	11.4	1.3	0.4	0.0	0.0	20.1
1966-67	0.0	0.0	0.0	0.0	13.2	0.5	0.4	7.8	9.3	0.0	0.0	0.0	31.2
1967-68	0.0	0.0	0.0	0.0	T	2.7	13.8	1.8	12.7	0.0	0.0	0.0	31.0
1968-69	0.0	0.0	0.0	0.0	0.3	1.1	3.2	6.3	2.2	0.0	0.0	0.0	13.1
1969-70	0.0	0.0	0.0	0.0	0.7	7.7	7.9	7.4	10.7	T	0.0	0.0	34.4
1970-71	0.0	0.0	0.0	0.0	0.3	0.8	3.2	11.9	5.2	0.1	0.0	0.0	21.5
1971-72	0.0	0.0	0.0	0.0	5.4	T	1.6	3.4	1.2	T	0.0	0.0	11.6
1972-73	0.0	0.0	0.0	0.0	2.0	2.2	1.1	1.1	0.5	1.6	0.0	0.0	8.5
1973-74	0.0	0.0	0.0	0.0	0.0	4.5	1.0	0.9	2.8	T	0.0	0.0	9.2
1974-75	0.0	0.0	0.0	0.0	1.0	1.2	3.0	1.3	10.0	T	0.0	0.0	16.5
1975-76	0.0	0.0	0.0	0.0	0.1	0.7	2.5	0.1	0.7	0.0	0.0	0.0	4.1
1976-77	0.0	0.0	0.0	0.0	1.6	1.1	19.6	0.8	0.1	0.8	0.0	0.0	24.0
1977-78	0.0	0.0	0.0	0.0	4.8	2.2	28.4	5.3	9.4	T	0.0	0.0	50.1
1978-79	0.0	0.0	0.0	0.0	0.0	T	8.5	10.9	0.9	T	0.0	0.0	20.3
1979-80	0.0	0.0	0.0	0.0	0.1	T	10.7	3.6	3.9	T	0.0	0.0	18.3
1980-81	0.0	0.0	0.0	T	T	T	2.5	0.3	0.1	0.0	0.0	0.0	2.9
1981-82	0.0	0.0	0.0	0.0	0.1	3.6	2.7	2.9	0.3	1.4	0.0	0.0	11.0
1982-83	0.0	0.0	0.0	0.0	T	0.0	0.6	4.5	0.1	T	0.0	0.0	5.2
1983-84	0.0	0.0	0.0	0.0	0.0	0.6	3.1	8.8	1.0	0.0	0.0	0.0	13.5
1984-85	0.0	0.0	0.0	0.0	T	4.8	7.4	6.7	T	T	0.0	0.0	18.9
1985-86	0.0	0.0	0.0	0.0	0.0	1.6	1.1	8.8	0.1	0.0	0.0	0.0	11.6
1986-87	0.0	0.0	0.0	0.0	T	T	2.2	6.7	9.3	T	0.0	0.0	18.2
1987-88	0.0	0.0	0.0	0.0	T	T	3.0	5.0	0.5	0.0	0.0	0.0	8.5
1988-89	0.0	0.0	0.0	0.0	T	0.3	T	0.6	T	0.0	T	0.0	0.9
1989-90	0.0	0.0	0.0	1.4	T	6.5	1.9	0.8	4.1	T	0.0	0.0	14.7
1990-91	0.0	0.0	0.0	0.0	0.0	4.1	0.3	1.5	0.2	0.0	0.0	0.0	6.1
1991-92	0.0	0.0	0.0	0.0	0.5	0.1	0.9	0.1	0.9	0.7	0.0	0.0	3.2
1992-93	0.0	0.0	0.0	0.0	0.9	1.0	T	15.9	1.1	T	0.0	T	18.9
1993-94	0.0	0.0	0.0	2.4	T	3.6							
Record Mean	0.0	0.0	0.0	0.1	1.0	2.2	5.1	4.5	3.2	0.1	T	T	16.2

NEW ORLEANS, LOUISIANA

The New Orleans metropolitan area is virtually surrounded by water. Lake Pontchartrain, some 610 square miles in area, borders the city on the north and is connected to the Gulf of Mexico through Lake Borgne on the east. In other directions there are bayous, lakes, and marshy delta land. The proximity of the Gulf of Mexico also has a great influence on the climate. Elevations in the city vary from a few feet below to a few feet above mean sea level. A massive levee system surrounding the city and along the Mississippi River offers protection against flooding from the river and tidal surges. The New Orleans International Airport is located 12 miles west of downtown New Orleans, between the Mississippi River and Lake Pontchartrain.

The climate of the city can best be described as humid with the surrounding water modifying the temperature and decreasing the range between the extremes. Almost daily sporadic afternoon thunderstorms from mid-June through September keep the temperature from rising much above 90 degrees. From about mid-November to mid-March, the area is subjected alternately to the southerly flow of warm tropical air and to the northerly flow of cold continental air in periods of varying lengths. The usual track of winter storms is to the north of New Orleans, but occasionally one moves this far south, bringing large and rather sudden drops in temperature. However, the cold spells seldom last over three or four days. The lowest temperatures observed are below 10 degrees. In about two-thirds of the years, the lowest temperature is about 24 degrees or warmer. The lowest temperatures in some years are entirely above freezing.

During the winter and spring, the cold Mississippi River water enhances the formation of river fogs, particularly when light southerly winds bring warm, moist air into the area from the Gulf of Mexico. The nearby lakes and marshes also contribute to fog formation. Even so, the fog usually does not seriously affect automobile traffic except for brief periods. However, air travel will be suspended for several hours and river traffic, at times, will be unable to move between New Orleans and the Gulf for several days.

Rather frequent and sometimes very heavy rains are typical for this area. There are an average of 120 days of measurable rain per year and an annual average accumulation of over 60 inches. A fairly definite rainy period occurs from mid-December to mid-March. Precipitation during this period is most likely to be steady rain for two to three day periods. April, May, October, and November are generally dry, but there have been some extremely heavy showers in those months. The greatest 24-hour amounts have exceeded 14 inches. Snowfall is rather infrequent and light. However, on rare occasions, snowstorms have produced accumulations over 8 inches.

While thunder occurs with most of the showers in the area, thunderstorms with damaging winds are infrequent. Hail of a damaging nature seldom occurs, and tornadoes are extremely rare. However, waterspouts are observed quite often on nearby lakes. Hurricanes have effected the area.

The lower Mississippi River floods result from runoff upstream. If the water level in the river becomes dangerously high, the spillways upriver can be opened to divert the floodwaters. Rainfall in the New Orleans area is pumped into the surrounding lakes and bayous. Local street and minor urban flooding of short duration result from occasional downpours.

Air pollution is not a serious problem. The area is not highly industrialized, and long periods of air stagnation are rare.

Based on the 1951-1980 period, the average first occurrence of 32 degrees Fahrenheit in the fall is December 5 and the average last occurrence in the spring is February 20.

NORMALS, MEANS, AND EXTREMES

NEW ORLEANS, LOUISIANA

LATITUDE: 29°59'N LONGITUDE: 90°15' W ELEVATION: FT. GRND 4 BARO 20 TIME ZONE: CENTRAL WBAN: 12916

	(a)	JAN	FEB	MAR	APR	MAY	JUNE	JULY	AUG	SEP	OCT	NOV	DEC	YEAR
TEMPERATURE °F:														
Normals														
-Daily Maximum		60.8	64.1	71.6	78.5	84.4	89.2	90.6	90.2	86.6	79.4	71.1	64.3	77.6
-Daily Minimum		41.8	44.4	51.6	58.4	65.2	70.8	73.1	72.8	69.5	58.7	51.0	44.8	58.5
-Monthly		51.3	54.3	61.6	68.5	74.8	80.0	81.9	81.5	78.1	69.1	61.1	54.5	68.1
Extremes														
-Record Highest	47	83	85	89	92	96	100	101	102	101	92	87	84	102
-Year		1982	1972	1982	1987	1953	1954	1981	1980	1980	1990	1986	1978	AUG 1980
-Record Lowest	47	14	19	25	32	41	50	60	60	42	35	24	11	11
-Year		1985	1970	1980	1971	1960	1984	1967	1968	1967	1993	1970	1989	DEC 1989
NORMAL DEGREE DAYS:														
Heating (base 65°F)		450	316	162	28	0	0	0	0	0	30	178	349	1513
Cooling (base 65°F)		25	17	56	133	304	450	524	512	393	157	61	23	2655
% OF POSSIBLE SUNSHINE	20	46	51	58	63	64	64	60	61	61	66	55	48	58
MEAN SKY COVER (tenths)														
Sunrise - Sunset	45	6.8	6.3	6.3	5.8	5.6	5.6	6.4	5.8	5.5	4.4	5.4	6.4	5.9
MEAN NUMBER OF DAYS:														
Sunrise to Sunset														
-Clear	45	6.7	7.6	7.9	8.0	9.0	8.2	4.6	7.2	9.5	14.6	10.3	7.8	101.4
-Partly Cloudy	45	7.3	6.5	8.0	10.4	11.2	12.6	14.7	13.8	10.5	7.8	8.2	7.4	118.3
-Cloudy	45	17.0	14.1	15.1	11.6	10.8	9.2	11.7	10.1	10.0	8.6	11.5	15.8	145.6
Precipitation														
.01 inches or more	45	10.2	9.1	8.8	7.2	8.0	10.7	14.5	13.2	9.8	5.7	7.4	9.9	114.5
Snow,Ice pellets,hail														
1.0 inches or more	45	0.0	0.*	0.0	0.0	0.0	0.0	0.0	0.0	0.0	0.0	0.0	0.*	*
Thunderstorms	45	1.9	2.9	3.9	4.4	6.0	9.4	15.0	12.8	6.9	1.9	2.0	2.1	69.2
Heavy Fog Visibility														
1/4 mile or less	45	6.0	4.1	3.9	1.7	0.8	0.2	0.1	0.1	0.2	1.6	3.6	4.9	27.3
Temperature °F														
-Maximum														
90° and above	47	0.0	0.0	0.0	0.2	3.3	16.2	20.8	20.0	9.3	1.0	0.0	0.0	70.8
32° and below	47	0.1	0.0	0.0	0.0	0.0	0.0	0.0	0.0	0.0	0.0	0.0	0.1	0.2
-Minimum														
32° and below	47	4.9	2.8	0.5	0.*	0.0	0.0	0.0	0.0	0.0	0.0	0.9	3.7	12.8
0° and below	47	0.0	0.0	0.0	0.0	0.0	0.0	0.0	0.0	0.0	0.0	0.0	0.0	0.0
AVG. STATION PRESS.(mb)	21	1020.0	1018.7	1016.0	1015.3	1013.9	1014.5	1016.0	1015.4	1015.1	1017.3	1018.5	1020.0	1016.7
RELATIVE HUMIDITY (%)														
Hour 00	45	82	81	82	84	86	87	89	89	86	84	84	83	85
Hour 06 (Local Time)	45	85	84	85	88	89	90	91	92	89	88	86	86	88
Hour 12	45	66	63	60	59	60	63	66	66	65	59	61	66	63
Hour 18	45	72	67	64	65	65	68	72	73	74	72	75	75	70
PRECIPITATION (inches):														
Water Equivalent														
-Normal		5.05	6.01	4.90	4.50	4.56	5.84	6.12	6.17	5.51	3.05	4.42	5.75	61.88
-Maximum Monthly	47	19.25	12.59	19.09	16.12	14.33	15.01	13.15	16.12	16.74	13.20	19.81	10.77	19.81
-Year		1991	1983	1948	1980	1959	1987	1991	1977	1971	1985	1989	1967	NOV 1989
-Minimum Monthly	47	0.54	0.15	0.24	0.28	0.95	0.23	1.92	1.68	0.24	0.00	0.21	1.46	0.00
-Year		1968	1989	1955	1976	1992	1979	1981	1980	1953	1978	1949	1958	OCT 1978
-Maximum in 24 hrs	47	6.08	5.60	7.87	8.08	9.86	7.40	4.30	4.96	6.50	4.51	12.66	6.81	12.66
-Year		1978	1961	1948	1988	1959	1988	1966	1992	1971	1985	1989	1990	NOV 1989
Snow,Ice pellets,hail														
-Maximum Monthly	47	0.4	2.0	T	T	T	0.0	0.0	0.0	0.0	0.0	T	2.7	2.7
-Year		1985	1958	1993	1991	1989						1950	1963	DEC 1963
-Maximum in 24 hrs	47	0.4	2.0	T	T	T	0.0	0.0	0.0	0.0	0.0	T	2.7	2.7
-Year		1985	1958	1993	1991	1989						1950	1963	DEC 1963
WIND:														
Mean Speed (mph)	45	9.3	9.8	9.9	9.4	8.2	6.9	6.1	6.0	7.3	7.6	8.7	9.1	8.2
Prevailing Direction														
Fastest Obs. 1 Min.														
-Direction (!!)	34	21	26	16	27	36	05	13	33	09	17	27	28	09
-Speed (MPH)	34	46	43	38	35	55	48	44	42	69	40	33	46	69
-Year		1975	1970	1987	1993	1973	1971	1979	1969	1965	1964	1992	1973	SEP 1965
Peak Gust														
-Direction (!!)	10	W	S	N	W	W	W	NE	SE	NE	NE	NW	SW	SE
-Speed (mph)	10	48	49	53	62	60	54	51	66	58	49	41	48	66
-Date		1991	1984	1993	1993	1989	1992	1992	1992	1990	1985	1989	1990	AUG 1992

PRECIPITATION (inches)

NEW ORLEANS, LOUISIANA

YEAR	JAN	FEB	MAR	APR	MAY	JUNE	JULY	AUG	SEP	OCT	NOV	DEC	ANNUAL
1964	9.60	5.35	5.45	5.66	1.69	5.52	5.90	3.88	4.93	3.50	3.51	3.10	58.09
1965	4.48	5.25	1.95	0.33	3.62	2.21	5.26	6.34	10.03	1.03	1.49	7.35	49.34
1966	12.62	10.11	1.90	4.92	9.31	2.10	9.42	2.84	5.55	3.15	0.72	5.44	68.08
1967	4.22	6.80	1.60	2.18	3.56	2.40	6.42	7.51	3.73	3.79	0.45	10.77	53.43
1968	0.54	3.02	3.49	3.59	4.13	3.69	4.96	4.78	2.44	1.40	4.97	6.14	43.15
1969	3.12	4.80	7.08	6.04	5.51	2.47	6.64	7.80	1.08	0.51	1.73	5.26	52.04
1970	2.53	2.28	7.22	0.43	4.68	4.97	3.70	10.21	4.25	4.94	0.85	4.28	50.34
1971	1.13	4.87	3.61	1.53	1.38	8.02	4.55	5.75	16.74	0.58	2.63	6.64	57.43
1972	6.98	6.03	6.07	1.64	6.31	3.10	3.90	4.92	3.29	4.64	8.45	8.65	63.98
1973	2.68	5.40	12.17	10.47	4.68	6.08	5.94	3.37	11.07	5.07	4.04	8.31	79.28
1974	8.46	5.53	6.64	5.52	9.84	3.83	5.66	6.70	7.58	2.26	5.88	4.89	72.79
1975	2.95	3.64	5.32	6.69	8.03	12.28	8.35	10.11	3.97	4.00	11.35	3.81	80.50
1976	2.61	3.85	3.08	0.28	5.58	3.36	5.67	1.69	1.57	5.08	5.80	8.81	47.38
1977	5.62	2.75	3.96	6.38	2.59	1.74	2.91	16.12	13.48	4.33	8.77	4.15	72.80
1978	13.63	2.53	2.67	3.44	9.72	7.82	10.34	14.68	2.98	0.00	4.67	4.42	76.90
1979	5.55	12.49	3.31	4.90	4.38	0.23	11.43	4.57	4.55	1.49	4.27	3.07	60.24
1980	6.37	3.09	10.08	16.12	9.65	3.69	4.84	1.68	6.31	5.87	3.85	1.54	73.09
1981	0.94	8.34	2.70	2.28	5.35	8.47	1.92	11.10	4.78	2.03	1.10	5.50	54.51
1982	2.76	7.88	2.56	5.86	1.19	5.43	13.07	1.92	5.40	3.84	5.45	10.26	65.62
1983	3.31	12.59	4.88	14.86	3.71	10.64	2.95	6.29	5.72	4.88	6.32	9.15	85.30
1984	4.10	5.27	4.90	1.72	3.54	7.21	3.86	9.51	3.79	2.84	2.80	2.53	52.07
1985	4.83	9.28	7.07	2.11	1.16	4.56	6.92	6.37	5.74	13.20	0.96	4.78	66.98
1986	3.49	2.93	1.88	1.50	1.61	8.87	3.60	6.74	1.42	2.87	7.90	5.05	47.86
1987	8.88	7.38	4.39	2.27	3.46	15.01	6.38	5.05	1.29	0.72	2.92	2.88	60.63
1988	3.74	11.31	8.90	9.25	1.68	11.28	6.78	7.53	5.86	2.87	1.26	3.94	74.40
1989	2.47	0.15	7.14	3.20	3.50	8.22	8.34	3.31	4.53	0.51	19.81	6.28	67.46
1990	7.59	11.45	5.98	4.59	5.87	1.01	2.30	2.45	4.55	2.38	3.21	9.67	61.05
1991	19.25	5.42	6.27	15.29	14.28	10.71	13.15	7.86	3.44	1.88	2.19	2.63	102.37
1992	9.94	8.73	6.69	2.52	0.95	9.52	5.75	9.64	6.63	0.55	15.27	5.68	81.87
1993	6.21	2.34	5.65	6.82	7.23	4.96	5.77	2.26	2.47	3.67	2.43	2.90	52.71
Record Mean	5.03	5.17	5.30	4.88	4.79	5.33	6.71	6.02	5.33	3.07	4.45	5.09	61.16

AVERAGE TEMPERATURE (deg. F)

NEW ORLEANS, LOUISIANA

YEAR	JAN	FEB	MAR	APR	MAY	JUNE	JULY	AUG	SEP	OCT	NOV	DEC	ANNUAL
1964	50.0	49.8	60.5	70.6	74.6	78.9	80.6	81.7	77.0	64.8	61.8	56.4	67.2
1965	54.9	54.4	58.9	70.9	75.5	78.5	81.0	77.7	76.2	66.7	64.5	54.0	67.8
1966	46.9	52.0	59.0	68.7	75.0	77.1	82.2	80.4	77.0	68.9	61.6	53.3	66.9
1967	52.5	52.5	63.2	72.2	73.8	81.6	80.5	80.0	75.1	65.6	60.3	58.2	68.0
1968	51.6	47.2	55.9	68.1	74.1	80.4	82.4	81.0	75.4	68.5	55.5	50.8	65.9
1969	54.2	54.6	53.8	68.8	73.3	80.3	82.1	80.1	76.7	71.1	58.5	54.5	67.3
1970	47.3	51.7	60.1	70.7	74.2	79.6	81.6	81.5	80.1	68.7	55.4	57.9	67.4
1971	55.1	53.9	59.2	66.9	72.9	80.0	81.4	81.1	78.9	71.7	59.2	63.4	68.6
1972	58.6	56.1	61.9	69.8	73.9	80.8	79.4	81.1	79.6	70.4	56.6	55.3	68.6
1973	50.3	52.6	65.5	64.2	72.5	81.7	84.4	81.7	79.7	73.4	66.6	54.1	68.9
1974	63.3	55.9	67.3	69.0	75.8	78.1	80.3	80.4	77.0	66.9	59.8	55.3	69.1
1975	57.2	58.9	61.4	66.8	75.1	79.4	80.2	80.5	75.1	69.9	61.2	51.9	68.2
1976	50.6	58.2	64.8	68.5	72.3	78.3	81.2	81.5	77.8	64.0	52.7	50.6	66.7
1977	43.4	53.8	65.0	69.0	75.9	82.4	83.9	81.9	80.2	68.2	62.9	54.3	68.4
1978	44.1	45.0	59.9	71.4	76.9	81.2	82.6	83.2	81.1	69.7	67.1	55.9	68.2
1979	45.9	52.9	62.6	71.1	74.6	81.1	83.6	82.9	79.3	71.0	58.0	52.5	68.0
1980	56.1	52.0	62.0	66.2	77.9	83.3	85.8	85.5	83.5	68.8	60.0	53.6	69.6
1981	48.5	55.3	61.9	71.4	74.8	83.8	85.0	83.1	77.9	71.1	64.9	54.5	69.4
1982	54.5	55.0	65.9	69.8	76.5	81.5	81.4	82.2	76.8	70.4	62.5	59.4	69.6
1983	50.2	53.8	58.3	64.3	74.0	77.6	81.5	82.4	75.3	69.1	60.0	49.5	66.3
1984	46.6	53.9	59.3	67.5	73.7	77.4	78.8	79.2	76.3	73.5	58.8	62.4	67.3
1985	45.2	52.3	65.3	69.0	74.7	79.3	80.2	81.6	77.0	72.6	67.3	51.0	68.0
1986	51.2	59.2	60.6	67.2	76.7	81.0	83.2	81.6	81.0	70.4	66.3	53.2	69.3
1987	50.0	56.3	60.3	66.2	76.8	79.9	82.9	83.5	78.2	64.4	61.6	59.0	68.3
1988	49.4	53.2	60.9	68.4	73.3	78.5	81.6	81.4	79.8	68.0	65.6	56.0	68.0
1989	60.2	55.9	62.8	67.0	76.4	79.4	81.4	81.7	76.9	67.5	62.4	46.9	68.2
1990	57.2	61.3	63.3	67.6	76.2	82.6	82.3	83.0	79.6	68.1	62.3	59.0	70.2
1991	52.8	58.2	64.2	71.2	77.5	81.3	83.5	81.7	78.2	71.6	55.9	57.6	69.5
1992	51.1	58.3	62.0	66.4	72.8	80.6	83.1	79.6	78.5	69.5	57.4	58.2	68.1
1993	57.2	54.7	58.8	64.0	71.9	80.4	83.3	83.6	79.7	69.9	58.0	52.2	67.8
Record Mean	53.3	56.0	61.8	68.7	75.3	80.7	82.3	82.1	78.7	70.3	60.9	55.4	68.8
Max	62.1	65.2	71.1	78.0	84.3	89.5	90.6	90.3	86.7	79.7	70.3	64.4	77.7
Min	44.5	46.8	52.5	59.3	66.2	71.9	74.0	73.8	70.7	60.9	51.4	46.3	59.9

REFERENCE NOTES

NEW ORLEANS, LOUISIANA

GENERAL
T - TRACE AMOUNT.
BLANK ENTRIES DENOTE MISSING/UNREPORTED DATA.
# INDICATES A STATION OR INSTRUMENT RELOCATION.

SPECIFIC

PM - INCLUDES LAST DAY OF PREVIOUS MONTH
ASOS - AUTOMATED SURFACE OBSERVING SYSTEM IN OPERATION DURING THESE MONTHS.

(a) - LENGTH OF RECORD IN YEARS, ALTHOUGH INDIVIDUAL MONTHS MAY BE MISSING.
0.* OR * - THE VALUE IS BETWEEN 0.0 AND 0.05
NORMALS - BASED ON THE 1961-1990 RECORD PERIOD.
EXTREMES - DATES ARE THE MOST RECENT OCCURRENCE
WIND DIR.- NUMERALS SHOW TENS OF DEGRESS CLOCKWISE FROM TRUE NORTH. "00" INDICATES CALM.
RESULTANT DIRECTIONS ARE GIVEN TO WHOLE DEGREES.
BOLD VALUES INDICATE EXTREME VALUES WHICH OCCURRED AFTER THE ASOS SYSTEM WAS COMMISSIONED.

RECORD = PERIOD OF RECORD
RECORD MEAN PRECIPITATION IS THE MEAN OF ALL DAILY PRECIPITATION AMOUNTS DURING THE PERIOD OF RECORD.
RECORD MAX(MIN) TEMPERATURE IS THE MEAN OF ALL DAILY MAX(MIN) TEMPERATURES DURING THE PERIOD OF RECORD.
RECORD MEAN TEMPERATURE IS THE SUM OF THE RECORD MAX AND RECORD MIN DIVIDED BY 2.
AVERAGE TEMPERATURE IS THE SUM OF THE MEAN DAILY MAX AND MIN TEMPERATURE DIVIDED BY 2.

EXCEPTIONS

RECORD MEANS ARE THROUGH THE CURRENT YEAR,
BEGINNING IN 1947 FOR TEMPERATURE
1947 FOR PRECIPITATION
1947 FOR SNOWFALL

HEATING DEGREE DAYS Base 65 deg. F — NEW ORLEANS, LOUISIANA

SEASON	JULY	AUG	SEP	OCT	NOV	DEC	JAN	FEB	MAR	APR	MAY	JUNE	TOTAL
1964-65	0	0	0	73	163	297	315	316	231	11	1	0	1407
1965-66	0	0	0	54	84	339	560	361	201	31	0	0	1630
1966-67	0	0	0	33	150	376	390	353	129	2	3	0	1436
1967-68	0	0	20	56	187	265	407	511	303	29	2	0	1780
1968-69	0	0	0	55	303	435	353	304	339	12	0	0	1801
1969-70	0	0	0	19	224	330	561	367	171	24	5	0	1701
1970-71	0	0	0	24	284	248	329	328	216	88	2	0	1519
1971-72	0	0	0	10	208	137	245	278	126	25	0	0	1029
1972-73	0	0	0	28	293	314	447	351	72	114	9	0	1628
1973-74	0	0	0	18	80	355	117	274	71	16	0	0	931
1974-75	0	0	0	24	194	341	270	210	183	73	0	0	1295
1975-76	0	0	6	16	222	417	445	205	98	21	0	0	1430
1976-77	0	0	0	93	375	438	664	318	117	18	0	0	2023
1977-78	0	0	0	43	113	342	646	556	191	2	0	0	1893
1978-79	0	0	0	16	39	324	586	347	128	8	2	0	1450
1979-80	0	0	0	13	230	396	278	385	154	38	0	0	1494
1980-81	0	0	0	35	195	363	504	275	123	12	0	0	1507
1981-82	0	0	0	36	100	333	365	278	127	29	0	0	1268
1982-83	0	0	0	31	146	234	453	309	217	81	1	0	1472
1983-84	0	0	1	37	183	483	564	321	197	48	2	0	1836
1984-85	0	0	2	14	214	146	605	359	62	28	0	0	1430
1985-86	0	0	0	12	49	443	421	195	160	28	0	0	1308
1986-87	0	0	0	28	85	370	464	242	168	75	0	0	1432
1987-88	0	0	0	58	149	222	490	351	166	23	0	0	1459
1988-89	0	0	0	12	92	301	186	292	155	60	0	0	1098
1989-90	0	0	0	53	142	559	253	136	101	41	0	0	1285
1990-91	0	0	0	62	122	244	371	196	105	8	0	0	1108
1991-92	0	0	0	22	312	262	426	203	128	54	5	0	1412
1992-93	0	0	0	2	240	218	248	285	209	82	0	0	1284
1993-94	0	0	0	42	259	399							

COOLING DEGREE DAYS Base 65 deg. F — NEW ORLEANS, LOUISIANA

YEAR	JAN	FEB	MAR	APR	MAY	JUNE	JULY	AUG	SEP	OCT	NOV	DEC	TOTAL
1969	28	17	1	133	266	462	537	474	360	213	34	9	2534
1970	20	0	25	200	297	442	520	520	460	148	2	32	2666
1971	29	25	44	151	252	456	514	508	424	221	40	92	2756
1972	50	26	38	175	281	479	453	507	446	200	48	19	2722
1973	0	9	96	99	247	507	607	524	448	289	136	24	2986
1974	71	27	147	144	345	402	484	484	368	93	45	45	2655
1975	34	45	80	132	321	440	479	491	314	171	114	16	2637
1976	4	18	100	132	234	404	509	518	390	68	13	0	2390
1977	0	10	123	145	345	528	593	532	463	151	56	16	2962
1978	5	0	39	203	380	493	553	569	489	169	110	49	3059
1979	0	14	63	198	307	491	581	559	435	206	25	16	2895
1980	10	13	70	85	409	554	653	640	561	160	51	17	3223
1981	0	12	35	210	311	570	627	565	396	231	102	12	3071
1982	49	6	160	182	366	504	517	541	363	208	78	66	3040
1983	0	0	16	67	286	385	518	545	317	171	42	10	2357
1984	0	6	31	130	281	379	436	448	351	286	33	71	2452
1985	0	10	78	154	308	437	480	521	366	251	124	13	2742
1986	0	40	32	99	370	487	573	524	488	203	127	9	2952
1987	3	4	30	120	373	456	562	580	402	48	53	42	2673
1988	14	15	49	131	263	411	523	513	448	113	118	30	2628
1989	46	43	95	124	363	439	515	525	365	137	70	6	2728
1990	17	40	56	127	353	538	545	567	448	166	50	62	2969
1991	2	12	88	202	396	496	580	524	402	233	47	40	3022
1992	0	18	41	103	258	472	568	459	408	149	20	14	2510
1993	13	4	26	61	222	468	572	585	447	200	57	8	2663

SNOWFALL (inches) — NEW ORLEANS, LOUISIANA

SEASON	JULY	AUG	SEP	OCT	NOV	DEC	JAN	FEB	MAR	APR	MAY	JUNE	TOTAL
1970-71	0.0	0.0	0.0	0.0	0.0	0.0	0.0	0.0	0.0	0.0	0.0	0.0	0.0
1971-72	0.0	0.0	0.0	0.0	0.0	0.0	0.0	0.0	0.0	0.0	0.0	0.0	0.0
1972-73	0.0	0.0	0.0	0.0	0.0	0.0	0.1	0.6	0.0	0.0	0.0	0.0	0.7
1973-74	0.0	0.0	0.0	0.0	0.0	T	0.0	0.0	0.0	0.0	0.0	0.0	T
1974-75	0.0	0.0	0.0	0.0	0.0	0.0	0.0	0.0	0.0	0.0	0.0	0.0	0.0
1975-76	0.0	0.0	0.0	0.0	0.0	0.0	0.0	0.0	0.0	0.0	0.0	0.0	0.0
1976-77	0.0	0.0	0.0	0.0	0.0	0.0	T	0.0	0.0	0.0	0.0	0.0	T
1977-78	0.0	0.0	0.0	0.0	0.0	0.0	T	T	0.0	0.0	0.0	0.0	T
1978-79	0.0	0.0	0.0	0.0	0.0	0.0	T	0.0	0.0	0.0	0.0	0.0	T
1979-80	0.0	0.0	0.0	0.0	0.0	0.0	0.0	0.0	T	0.0	0.0	0.0	T
1980-81	0.0	0.0	0.0	0.0	0.0	0.0	0.0	0.0	0.0	0.0	0.0	0.0	0.0
1981-82	0.0	0.0	0.0	0.0	0.0	0.0	T	0.0	0.0	0.0	0.0	0.0	T
1982-83	0.0	0.0	0.0	0.0	0.0	0.0	0.0	0.0	0.0	0.0	0.0	0.0	0.0
1983-84	0.0	0.0	0.0	0.0	0.0	0.0	0.0	0.0	0.0	0.0	0.0	0.0	0.0
1984-85	0.0	0.0	0.0	0.0	0.0	0.0	0.4	0.0	0.0	0.0	0.0	0.0	0.4
1985-86	0.0	0.0	0.0	0.0	0.0	0.0	0.0	0.0	0.0	0.0	0.0	0.0	0.0
1986-87	0.0	0.0	0.0	0.0	0.0	0.0	0.0	0.0	0.0	0.0	0.0	0.0	0.0
1987-88	0.0	0.0	0.0	0.0	0.0	0.0	0.0	T	0.0	0.0	0.0	0.0	T
1988-89	0.0	0.0	0.0	0.0	0.0	0.0	0.0	0.0	T	0.0	T	0.0	T
1989-90	0.0	0.0	0.0	0.0	0.0	0.5	0.0	0.0	0.0	T	0.0	0.0	0.5
1990-91	0.0	0.0	0.0	0.0	0.0	0.0	0.0	0.0	T	T	0.0	0.0	T
1991-92	0.0	0.0	0.0	0.0	0.0	0.0	0.0	0.0	T	0.0	0.0	0.0	T
1992-93	0.0	0.0	0.0	0.0	0.0	0.0	0.0	0.0	T	0.0	0.0	0.0	T
1993-94	0.0	0.0	0.0	0.0	0.0	0.0							
Record Mean	0.0	0.0	0.0	0.0	T	0.1	T	0.1	T	T	T	0.0	0.1

SHREVEPORT, LOUISIANA

Shreveport is located in the northwestern section of Louisiana, some 30 miles south of Arkansas and 15 miles east of Texas. A portion of the city is situated in the Red River bottom lands and the remainder in gently rolling hills that begin about 1 mile west of the river. The NOAA National Weather Service Office is at the Shreveport Regional Airport, about 7 miles southwest of the downtown area. Elevations in the Shreveport area range from about 170 to 280 feet above sea level. The climate of Shreveport is transitional between the subtropical humid type prevalent to the south and the continental climates of the Great Plains and Middle West to the north. During winter, masses of moderate to severely cold air move periodically through the area. Rainfall is abundant with the normal annual total near 45 inches. Amounts are substantial from late autumn to spring and there is a summer-early autumn low amount with monthly averages less than 3 inches in August, September, and October.

The winter months are normally mild with cold spells generally of short duration. Freezing temperatures are recorded on an average of 34 days during the year. The average first occurrence of 32 degrees in the autumn is mid-November, and the last occurrence in the spring is early March Although temperatures have fallen below zero degrees, they normally drop below about 15 degrees in about one-half the years. Temperatures recorded at the NWS Office at the airport on clear, calm nights are normally 2 to 5 degrees warmer than those experienced in the river bottom lands. The summer months are consistently quite warm and humid with temperatures exceeding 100 degrees on about 10 days a year and exceeding 95 degrees about 45 days per year. Late afternoon humidity rarely drops below 55 percent.

Measurable snow occurs only once every other year on average. Many consecutive years may pass with no measurable snow. The heaviest snowstorms in the Shreveport area have produced more than 10 inches. More troublesome than the infrequent heavy snowfall are ice and sleet storms which may cause considerable damage to trees and utility lines, as well as make travel very difficult.

Thunderstorms occur each month, but are most frequent in spring and summer months. Severe local storms, including hailstorms, tornadoes, and local windstorms have occurred over small areas in all seasons, but are most frequent during the spring months, with a secondary peak from late November through early January. Large hail of a damaging nature is infrequent, although hail as large as grapefruit has fallen on a few occasions.

Tropical cyclones are in the dissipating stages by the time they reach this portion of the state and winds from them are usually not a destructive factor. Associated heavy rainfall can contribute to local flooding.

NORMALS, MEANS, AND EXTREMES

SHREVEPORT, LOUISIANA

LATITUDE: 32°28'N LONGITUDE: 93°49' W ELEVATION: FT. GRND 254 BARO 268 TIME ZONE: CENTRAL WBAN: 13957

	(a)	JAN	FEB	MAR	APR	MAY	JUNE	JULY	AUG	SEP	OCT	NOV	DEC	YEAR
TEMPERATURE °F:														
Normals														
-Daily Maximum		55.4	60.6	69.2	77.1	83.2	89.7	93.0	93.1	87.3	78.7	68.0	58.5	76.2
-Daily Minimum		34.8	38.0	45.8	54.1	62.0	69.0	72.3	71.3	66.0	54.3	45.3	37.3	54.2
-Monthly		45.1	49.3	57.5	65.6	72.6	79.4	82.7	82.2	76.7	66.5	56.7	48.0	65.2
Extremes														
-Record Highest	41	84	89	92	94	95	101	106	107	103	97	88	84	107
-Year		1972	1986	1974	1987	1977	1988	1980	1962	1980	1954	1984	1955	AUG 1962
-Record Lowest	41	3	12	20	31	42	52	58	53	42	28	16	5	3
-Year		1962	1978	1980	1989	1960	1977	1972	1992	1984	1993	1976	1989	JAN 1962
NORMAL DEGREE DAYS:														
Heating (base 65°F)		623	448	262	69	0	0	0	0	0	63	264	535	2264
Cooling (base 65°F)		6	8	30	87	239	432	549	533	351	110	15	8	2368
% OF POSSIBLE SUNSHINE	41	49	55	58	59	64	71	74	73	69	70	59	52	63
MEAN SKY COVER (tenths)														
Sunrise - Sunset	41	6.7	6.3	6.3	6.2	6.1	5.4	5.3	5.1	5.1	4.7	5.5	6.2	5.8
MEAN NUMBER OF DAYS:														
Sunrise to Sunset														
-Clear	41	7.8	8.0	8.6	7.9	7.6	8.6	10.2	10.8	11.3	13.3	10.9	9.2	114.3
-Partly Cloudy	41	5.2	5.4	6.2	7.7	10.2	12.6	11.9	12.3	9.1	7.6	5.9	6.3	100.3
-Cloudy	41	17.9	14.8	16.2	14.4	13.2	8.8	8.8	7.9	9.6	10.2	13.2	15.6	150.7
Precipitation														
.01 inches or more	41	9.8	8.2	9.3	8.7	9.2	7.9	7.8	6.7	6.8	6.6	8.2	9.3	98.5
Snow,Ice pellets,hail														
1.0 inches or more	41	0.2	0.2	0.1	0.0	0.0	0.0	0.0	0.0	0.0	0.0	0.*	0.*	0.6
Thunderstorms	41	1.8	2.8	4.9	5.7	7.2	7.3	8.0	6.6	4.2	2.9	3.1	2.1	56.6
Heavy Fog Visibility														
1/4 mile or less	41	3.4	2.1	1.4	1.2	1.0	0.5	0.3	0.4	1.0	2.3	2.6	2.9	19.1
Temperature °F														
-Maximum														
90° and above	41	0.0	0.0	0.*	0.3	4.1	18.0	25.6	25.0	14.1	2.4	0.0	0.0	89.5
32° and below	41	1.0	0.3	0.*	0.0	0.0	0.0	0.0	0.0	0.0	0.0	0.0	0.4	1.7
-Minimum														
32° and below	41	12.7	7.7	2.5	0.1	0.0	0.0	0.0	0.0	0.0	0.2	3.4	10.0	36.5
0° and below	41	0.0	0.0	0.0	0.0	0.0	0.0	0.0	0.0	0.0	0.0	0.0	0.0	0.0
AVG. STATION PRESS.(mb)	21	1011.7	1010.1	1006.5	1005.8	1004.6	1005.4	1007.0	1006.8	1007.2	1009.1	1009.7	1011.3	1007.9
RELATIVE HUMIDITY (%)														
Hour 00	41	78	76	75	79	84	84	83	82	82	81	80	80	80
Hour 06 (Local Time)	41	84	83	83	87	90	91	91	91	91	89	87	85	88
Hour 12	41	63	59	56	57	59	58	57	55	57	54	58	62	58
Hour 18	41	65	58	54	56	60	60	58	57	61	62	67	68	61
PRECIPITATION (inches):														
Water Equivalent														
-Normal		3.88	3.92	3.59	3.75	5.18	4.29	3.67	2.43	3.12	3.73	4.45	4.10	46.11
-Maximum Monthly	41	10.09	8.57	7.23	21.84	11.78	17.11	9.46	9.23	9.59	12.05	10.81	10.00	21.84
-Year		1974	1983	1969	1991	1967	1989	1972	1991	1968	1984	1987	1982	APR 1991
-Minimum Monthly	41	0.27	0.90	0.56	0.43	0.42	0.13	0.15	0.35	0.17	0.00	0.71	0.59	0.00
-Year		1971	1954	1966	1987	1988	1988	1964	1985	1956	1963	1967	1981	OCT 1963
-Maximum in 24 hrs	41	4.35	3.53	3.63	10.44	5.27	7.28	4.30	4.64	5.39	3.88	6.51	3.35	10.44
-Year		1990	1965	1979	1991	1978	1993	1972	1955	1961	1957	1987	1965	APR 1991
Snow,Ice pellets,hail														
-Maximum Monthly	41	5.9	4.4	4.0	0.3	T	0.0	0.0	0.0	0.0	T	1.3	5.4	5.9
-Year		1978	1985	1965	1987	1991					1992	1980	1983	JAN 1978
-Maximum in 24 hrs	41	5.6	4.4	4.0	0.3	T	0.0	0.0	0.0	0.0	T	1.3	5.4	5.6
-Year		1982	1985	1965	1987	1991					1992	1980	1983	JAN 1982
WIND:														
Mean Speed (mph)	41	9.2	9.6	10.1	9.7	8.3	7.5	7.1	6.7	7.2	7.4	8.5	8.9	8.3
Prevailing Direction through 1963		S	S	S	S	S	S	S	S	ENE	SSE	S	S	S
Fastest Obs. 1 Min.														
-Direction (!!)	31	25	27	29	28	35	36	29	25	19	31	29	14	35
-Speed (MPH)	31	37	40	41	52	58	46	46	37	44	35	38	37	58
-Year		1992	1965	1964	1975	1991	1992	1982	1963	1965	1966	1975	1965	MAY 1991
Peak Gust														
-Direction (!!)	10	NW	N	NW	W	N	N	NW	W	NW	NW	NW	W	N
-Speed (mph)	10	49	54	58	81	83	66	66	56	54	41	63	64	83
-Date		1993	1990	1986	1991	1991	1992	1989	1991	1992	1985	1992	1987	MAY 1991

PRECIPITATION (inches)

SHREVEPORT, LOUISIANA

YEAR	JAN	FEB	MAR	APR	MAY	JUNE	JULY	AUG	SEP	OCT	NOV	DEC	ANNUAL
1964	2.57	2.74	4.24	7.27	1.41	1.87	0.15	4.71	2.51	0.64	1.65	2.55	32.31
1965	3.77	6.51	3.39	1.16	5.40	3.18	1.49	1.82	6.55	0.36	1.20	6.29	41.12
1966	4.22	3.45	0.56	8.02	3.78	2.05	0.58	1.71	3.27	1.62	0.97	3.63	33.86
1967	1.36	2.91	1.02	2.11	11.78	0.89	6.15	4.67	1.27	1.34	0.71	3.92	38.13
1968	8.33	2.22	1.89	9.38	6.05	2.78	4.68	1.89	9.59	1.90	5.85	3.27	57.83
1969	1.14	4.32	7.23	6.63	5.18	1.16	1.06	0.50	0.97	3.16	7.50	3.95	42.80
1970	1.23	4.70	4.30	5.12	4.36	1.14	3.94	2.04	1.64	7.44	2.09	3.80	41.80
1971	0.27	4.13	2.11	1.06	5.26	0.97	6.15	2.99	1.30	3.86	3.75	3.65	35.50
1972	5.97	0.94	2.45	2.06	4.13	2.76	9.46	1.27	2.10	6.32	5.32	4.18	46.96
1973	5.65	1.52	5.01	6.44	2.00	5.84	7.63	0.77	6.39	5.38	5.16	6.37	58.16
1974	10.09	3.67	3.60	3.09	4.58	6.29	7.73	3.84	6.64	3.79	5.80	2.34	61.46
1975	4.55	4.51	5.84	3.91	5.31	3.48	3.45	1.65	0.98	3.87	4.44	1.88	43.87
1976	2.07	2.45	6.67	1.75	5.95	4.42	3.47	2.96	6.28	2.08	1.63	3.77	43.50
1977	3.00	3.68	4.94	2.05	2.40	2.41	3.89	4.28	0.53	0.31	2.11	2.58	32.18
1978	4.89	1.90	2.66	2.79	7.92	1.21	1.74	3.90	2.40	2.74	4.18	5.13	41.46
1979	9.22	4.98	5.74	7.42	7.99	3.04	7.50	1.86	4.33	3.96	4.76	3.12	63.92
1980	4.67	3.10	3.75	5.34	4.42	2.60	1.83	0.42	1.63	2.48	3.59	0.74	34.57
1981	1.43	3.83	3.33	1.97	9.96	6.45	2.36	0.94	3.32	5.63	1.49	0.59	41.30
1982	3.59	3.19	2.59	2.72	2.32	1.84	4.25	2.20	1.11	5.19	5.72	10.00	44.72
1983	2.45	8.57	3.68	1.47	8.22	6.60	1.18	1.67	3.12	0.79	4.90	7.18	49.83
1984	2.10	5.66	3.58	2.52	5.86	3.56	2.20	0.87	2.61	12.05	4.46	2.88	48.35
1985	2.38	4.42	4.28	3.05	1.96	4.57	8.40	0.35	4.40	9.87	4.25	3.37	51.30
1986	0.49	3.48	0.75	3.50	6.60	14.67	2.92	1.68	3.51	6.63	9.19	4.69	58.11
1987	2.26	7.80	1.48	0.43	6.67	5.43	1.21	3.50	0.94	5.49	10.81	8.12	54.14
1988	2.06	3.59	3.89	3.45	0.42	0.13	3.12	3.52	1.61	4.44	5.44	4.71	36.38
1989	7.20	4.06	3.41	2.41	10.07	17.11	4.46	3.94	1.08	1.50	2.32	3.34	60.90
1990	10.02	6.92	4.90	4.29	10.48	2.56	3.53	2.88	2.93	4.33	8.81	3.99	65.64
1991	7.70	5.13	2.89	21.84	10.71	2.53	3.47	9.23	3.45	3.59	3.94	7.51	81.99
1992	4.63	6.41	5.94	3.26	2.81	3.95	3.36	1.24	5.15	4.13	4.69	5.84	51.41
1993	4.63	4.80	5.94	4.19	3.30	15.73	0.27	4.09	3.51	4.43	4.85	1.44	57.18
Record Mean	4.16	3.73	4.15	4.63	4.64	3.62	3.51	2.61	2.91	3.16	3.99	4.47	45.58

AVERAGE TEMPERATURE (deg. F)

SHREVEPORT, LOUISIANA

YEAR	JAN	FEB	MAR	APR	MAY	JUNE	JULY	AUG	SEP	OCT	NOV	DEC	ANNUAL
1964	46.5	45.6	56.8	68.7	75.1	81.0	84.2	84.0	78.5	64.2	59.3	50.1	66.2
1965	50.8	49.4	49.6	70.1	73.7	78.4	83.0	82.1	77.2	66.1	63.2	52.0	66.3
1966	42.3	47.5	58.1	66.2	72.7	79.0	85.0	81.0	75.3	64.0	60.4	46.9	64.9
1967	47.6	46.5	63.5	71.0	71.1	80.9	79.8	80.0	73.2	66.5	57.1	48.9	65.5
1968	45.4	43.6	55.9	66.5	72.7	80.1	81.0	82.0	73.6	66.6	53.7	46.6	64.0
1969	49.3	49.2	50.1	65.1	72.4	80.5	86.6	84.3	78.2	67.8	54.7	48.3	65.5
1970	42.0	49.4	53.8	67.4	72.7	78.8	81.7	84.3	81.1	65.1	54.7	54.3	65.5
1971	50.6	50.6	55.4	64.3	70.8	81.7	83.3	80.6	78.1	70.7	56.4	55.4	66.5
1972	49.4	51.9	59.8	66.9	72.3	80.8	81.0	82.6	80.2	67.2	50.9	45.5	65.7
1973	44.7	49.5	60.9	62.0	71.7	78.5	81.1	78.2	74.9	68.2	61.5	46.8	64.8
1974	47.8	51.2	63.6	64.3	74.0	76.6	82.1	80.1	71.0	66.2	55.6	47.3	65.0
1975	50.2	48.4	55.6	63.7	72.4	78.2	80.9	80.7	73.7	68.0	56.3	49.3	64.8
1976	47.1	59.2	60.2	67.3	67.9	75.7	78.6	78.7	74.3	59.9	49.3	46.3	63.7
1977	37.3	50.8	59.6	65.5	74.1	79.5	83.5	80.3	78.7	66.3	56.5	47.3	64.9
1978	34.9	38.1	52.8	65.5	73.6	80.5	85.4	83.3	77.8	66.0	60.0	48.0	63.8
1979	37.4	46.6	59.1	66.0	70.2	78.0	81.2	80.3	74.2	67.0	52.8	48.9	63.5
1980	48.3	47.9	54.9	63.0	74.3	83.4	86.9	85.5	82.1	63.5	54.2	49.1	66.1
1981	44.7	49.8	56.0	70.0	69.2	80.2	82.8	81.3	73.9	65.0	56.8	46.9	64.7
1982	46.1	45.6	61.5	63.3	74.4	78.6	83.3	83.2	75.6	64.6	55.4	51.2	65.2
1983	44.6	48.8	55.0	59.7	70.0	77.4	82.3	84.0	75.7	66.7	55.9	37.5	63.1
1984	40.6	50.4	58.0	64.9	72.1	79.3	81.1	82.1	75.0	70.6	56.4	60.0	65.9
1985	40.0	46.2	61.4	67.0	72.8	79.3	83.1	84.8	76.3	68.5	61.5	44.2	65.4
1986	49.0	54.4	59.7	66.5	72.3	79.9	83.7	80.8	79.4	65.2	55.6	46.1	66.1
1987	44.8	51.7	55.7	64.2	75.3	79.1	82.3	85.3	76.7	64.1	56.1	50.2	65.5
1988	42.2	49.3	56.3	65.2	71.8	79.8	83.3	83.7	77.8	64.1	58.6	49.2	65.1
1989	51.5	45.8	56.7	65.6	73.8	76.7	81.2	81.0	73.7	66.5	58.6	40.8	64.3
1990	52.5	56.4	59.4	65.6	72.6	82.7	82.2	83.3	79.7	65.0	58.9	48.5	67.2
1991	44.2	52.0	60.0	68.6	75.3	80.6	82.6	81.2	75.7	68.7	52.1	51.2	66.0
1992	47.2	54.7	59.5	65.1	71.4	78.5	82.9	78.6	76.0	67.0	52.0	49.5	65.2
1993	46.4	49.3	55.2	61.3	70.7	80.2	84.6	84.8	77.3	64.4	52.0	49.1	64.6
Record Mean	47.0	50.5	58.0	66.0	73.2	80.3	83.1	82.7	77.1	66.9	56.1	49.1	65.8
Max	56.1	60.3	68.3	76.4	83.1	90.2	93.0	92.9	87.4	78.1	66.5	58.4	75.9
Min	37.9	40.7	47.6	55.6	63.2	70.3	73.1	72.4	66.8	55.8	45.7	39.7	55.7

REFERENCE NOTES

SHREVEPORT, LOUISIANA

GENERAL
T - TRACE AMOUNT.
BLANK ENTRIES DENOTE MISSING/UNREPORTED DATA.
# INDICATES A STATION OR INSTRUMENT RELOCATION.

SPECIFIC

PM - INCLUDES LAST DAY OF PREVIOUS MONTH
ASOS - AUTOMATED SURFACE OBSERVING SYSTEM IN OPERATION DURING THESE MONTHS.

(a) - LENGTH OF RECORD IN YEARS, ALTHOUGH INDIVIDUAL MONTHS MAY BE MISSING.
0.* OR * - THE VALUE IS BETWEEN 0.0 AND 0.05
NORMALS - BASED ON THE 1961-1990 RECORD PERIOD.
EXTREMES - DATES ARE THE MOST RECENT OCCURRENCE
WIND DIR. - NUMERALS SHOW TENS OF DEGRESS CLOCKWISE FROM TRUE NORTH. "00" INDICATES CALM.
RESULTANT DIRECTIONS ARE GIVEN TO WHOLE DEGREES.
BOLD VALUES INDICATE EXTREME VALUES WHICH OCCURRED AFTER THE ASOS SYSTEM WAS COMMISSIONED.

RECORD = PERIOD OF RECORD
RECORD MEAN PRECIPITATION IS THE MEAN OF ALL DAILY PRECIPITATION AMOUNTS DURING THE PERIOD OF RECORD.
RECORD MAX(MIN) TEMPERATURE IS THE MEAN OF ALL DAILY MAX(MIN) TEMPERATURES DURING THE PERIOD OF RECORD.
RECORD MEAN TEMPERATURE IS THE SUM OF THE RECORD MAX AND RECORD MIN DIVIDED BY 2.
AVERAGE TEMPERATURE IS THE SUM OF THE MEAN DAILY MAX AND MIN TEMPERATURE DIVIDED BY 2.

EXCEPTIONS

RECORD MEANS ARE THROUGH THE CURRENT YEAR, BEGINNING IN 1875 FOR TEMPERATURE
1872 FOR PRECIPITATION
1953 FOR SNOWFALL

HEATING DEGREE DAYS Base 65 deg. F — SHREVEPORT, LOUISIANA

SEASON	JULY	AUG	SEP	OCT	NOV	DEC	JAN	FEB	MAR	APR	MAY	JUNE	TOTAL
1964-65	0	0	6	93	216	479	446	432	473	28	0	0	2173
1965-66	0	0	3	78	103	400	703	485	238	62	8	0	2080
1966-67	0	0	0	99	181	570	553	511	140	13	13	0	2080
1967-68	0	0	15	72	244	500	604	614	308	49	0	0	2406
1968-69	0	0	0	57	346	560	495	438	455	44	2	0	2397
1969-70	0	0	0	86	314	510	713	429	344	58	14	0	2468
1970-71	0	0	0	97	324	351	459	398	316	94	15	0	2054
1971-72	0	0	4	7	282	304	499	382	185	62	0	0	1725
1972-73	0	0	6	92	419	597	621	429	135	145	9	0	2453
1973-74	0	0	0	40	164	557	533	386	152	78	2	0	1912
1974-75	0	0	14	32	312	541	473	457	305	124	0	0	2258
1975-76	0	0	4	39	286	492	551	186	202	38	17	0	1815
1976-77	0	0	0	199	471	574	851	399	188	46	0	0	2728
1977-78	0	0	0	72	260	549	933	746	374	61	30	0	3025
1978-79	0	0	0	57	181	528	849	517	216	50	11	0	2409
1979-80	0	0	0	52	366	498	508	494	312	96	4	0	2330
1980-81	0	0	3	128	340	488	620	425	279	14	20	0	2317
1981-82	0	0	8	129	246	554	588	537	202	125	4	0	2393
1982-83	0	0	9	120	309	457	624	449	308	186	12	0	2474
1983-84	0	0	15	69	305	848	747	421	247	81	11	0	2744
1984-85	0	0	19	36	286	208	770	528	151	42	1	0	2041
1985-86	0	0	11	49	174	638	490	331	176	44	1	0	1914
1986-87	0	0	0	86	299	579	618	366	286	117	0	0	2351
1987-88	0	0	0	79	279	456	701	453	278	54	1	0	2301
1988-89	0	0	0	76	218	482	418	535	295	93	2	0	2119
1989-90	0	0	17	85	244	743	382	243	216	92	3	0	2025
1990-91	0	0	6	126	208	509	634	357	197	26	6	0	2069
1991-92	0	0	9	36	401	422	544	297	185	84	23	0	2001
1992-93	0	0	2	33	381	480	569	435	307	154	3	0	2364
1993-94	0	0	5	132	404	490							

COOLING DEGREE DAYS Base 65 deg. F — SHREVEPORT, LOUISIANA

YEAR	JAN	FEB	MAR	APR	MAY	JUNE	JULY	AUG	SEP	OCT	NOV	DEC	TOTAL
1969	15	0	0	57	241	470	675	604	402	177	11	0	2652
1970	9	0	5	138	259	420	528	606	492	106	23	28	2614
1971	22	1	24	82	203	510	576	488	403	191	28	9	2537
1972	22	10	31	128	235	480	501	553	467	167	1	0	2595
1973	0	2	16	64	223	412	504	417	305	145	66	0	2154
1974	7	6	115	63	288	355	541	477	200	77	35	0	2164
1975	23	0	21	91	238	403	501	493	271	141	34	12	2228
1976	2	26	58	116	112	326	428	432	288	48	7	0	1843
1977	0	7	28	69	289	443	580	479	419	119	12	9	2454
1978	5	0	3	84	303	472	637	570	391	96	39	8	2608
1979	0	8	39	86	178	395	509	483	284	124	8	2	2116
1980	1	6	6	43	298	560	686	643	522	86	22	1	2874
1981	0	5	10	171	157	463	558	511	284	135	6	0	2300
1982	14	0	99	81	300	413	573	573	333	115	24	32	2557
1983	0	0	7	34	176	381	540	595	343	126	39	0	2241
1984	0	5	38	83	235	436	511	540	329	219	35	61	2492
1985	0	8	49	109	252	436	568	620	356	163	78	0	2639
1986	2	41	17	95	236	454	586	494	438	101	24	0	2488
1987	1	0	7	99	327	431	544	634	357	57	19	5	2481
1988	3	3	14	67	220	449	575	587	390	53	37	1	2399
1989	8	7	43	121	283	358	508	503	286	140	57	0	2314
1990	2	9	50	115	244	538	536	572	453	132	30	3	2684
1991	0	1	47	141	334	475	550	509	336	158	20	5	2576
1992	0	4	21	93	227	412	561	428	339	99	1	4	2189
1993	0	0	10	50	189	461	614	620	381	121	20	4	2470

SNOWFALL (inches) — SHREVEPORT, LOUISIANA

SEASON	JULY	AUG	SEP	OCT	NOV	DEC	JAN	FEB	MAR	APR	MAY	JUNE	TOTAL
1970-71	0.0	0.0	0.0	0.0	0.0	0.0	0.8	0.6	0.3	0.0	0.0	0.0	1.7
1971-72	0.0	0.0	0.0	0.0	T	0.0	T	0.0	0.0	0.0	0.0	0.0	T
1972-73	0.0	0.0	0.0	0.0	0.0	0.0	0.6	T	0.0	0.0	0.0	0.0	0.6
1973-74	0.0	0.0	0.0	0.0	0.0	T	0.0	0.0	0.0	0.0	0.0	0.0	T
1974-75	0.0	0.0	0.0	0.0	0.0	0.0	3.4	T	T	0.0	0.0	0.0	3.4
1975-76	0.0	0.0	0.0	0.0	T	0.0	0.0	0.0	0.0	0.0	0.0	0.0	T
1976-77	0.0	0.0	0.0	0.0	T	0.0	5.4	0.0	0.0	0.0	0.0	0.0	5.4
1977-78	0.0	0.0	0.0	0.0	0.0	0.0	5.9	2.0	0.3	0.0	0.0	0.0	8.2
1978-79	0.0	0.0	0.0	0.0	0.0	0.0	T	1.5	0.0	0.0	0.0	0.0	1.5
1979-80	0.0	0.0	0.0	0.0	T	0.0	0.0	1.4	T	0.0	0.0	0.0	1.4
1980-81	0.0	0.0	0.0	0.0	1.3	0.0	0.7	0.1	0.0	0.0	0.0	0.0	2.1
1981-82	0.0	0.0	0.0	0.0	0.0	T	5.6	T	T	0.0	0.0	0.0	5.6
1982-83	0.0	0.0	0.0	0.0	0.0	T	T	T	0.0	0.0	0.0	0.0	T
1983-84	0.0	0.0	0.0	0.0	0.0	5.4	T	T	0.0	0.0	0.0	0.0	5.4
1984-85	0.0	0.0	0.0	0.0	0.0	0.0	0.4	4.4	0.0	0.0	0.0	0.0	4.8
1985-86	0.0	0.0	0.0	0.0	0.0	0.0	T	T	0.0	0.0	0.0	0.0	T
1986-87	0.0	0.0	0.0	0.0	0.0	T	0.0	T	T	0.3	0.0	0.0	0.3
1987-88	0.0	0.0	0.0	0.0	0.0	0.0	1.2	0.8	0.0	0.0	0.0	0.0	2.0
1988-89	0.0	0.0	0.0	0.0	0.0	0.0	T	T	T	0.0	T	0.0	T
1989-90	0.0	0.0	0.0	0.0	0.0	T	0.0	T	0.0	0.0	0.0	0.0	T
1990-91	0.0	0.0	0.0	0.0	0.0	T	0.0	T	0.0	T	T	0.0	T
1991-92	0.0	0.0	0.0	0.0	0.0	0.0	T	T	T	0.0	0.0	0.0	T
1992-93	0.0	0.0	0.0	T	T	0.0	T	T	1.0	T	0.0	0.0	1.0
1993-94	0.0	0.0	0.0	0.0	0.0	T							
Record Mean	0.0	0.0	0.0	T	T	0.2	0.8	0.5	0.2	T	T	0.0	1.7

CARIBOU, MAINE

The Caribou Municipal Airport is located in Aroostook County, the largest and northernmost county in the state. The airport lies on top of high land which is about on the same level as most of the surrounding gently rolling hills. The Aroostook River, which runs about 1 mile to the east and southeast of the station, has little effect on the local weather. Even though Caribou is located only 150 miles from the Atlantic coast, its climate can be justly classed as a severe typical continental type. Winters are particularly long and windy, and seasonal snowfalls averaging over 100 inches are not unusual. While the extreme low temperatures may be less severe than one might expect, temperatures of zero or lower normally occur over 40 times per year. A study of heating degree day data will show the outstanding part that cold weather plays here.

Summers are cool and generally favored with abundant rainfall, which is one of the most important factors in the high yield of the potato and grain crops throughout the county. Our location high up in the St. Lawrence Valley allows Aroostook County to come under the influence of the Summer Polar Front, resulting in practically no dry periods of more than 3 or 4 days in the growing season. The growing season at Caribou averages more than 120 days, with the average last freeze in the spring in mid-May and the average first freeze in autumn in late September.

Autumn climate is nearly ideal, with mostly sunny warm days and crisp cool nights predominating. Aroostook County, even with its relatively short growing season, provides profitable farming. The principal crops are potatoes, peas, a variety of grains, and some hardy vegetables.

Probably unknown to many victims of hay fever and similar afflictions, the immediate Caribou area offers sparkling visibility and relatively pollen-free air in the late summer months. This latter condition is principally due to the extremely high degree of cultivation of all available land.

NORMALS, MEANS, AND EXTREMES

CARIBOU, MAINE

LATITUDE: 46°52'N LONGITUDE: 68°01' W ELEVATION: FT. GRND 624 BARO 630 TIME ZONE: EASTERN WBAN: 14607

	(a)	JAN	FEB	MAR	APR	MAY	JUNE	JULY	AUG	SEP	OCT	NOV	DEC	YEAR
TEMPERATURE °F:														
Normals														
-Daily Maximum		19.4	23.0	34.3	46.7	61.7	71.9	76.5	73.6	64.0	52.0	37.6	24.0	48.7
-Daily Minimum		-1.6	0.7	14.9	29.0	40.1	49.1	54.5	52.1	43.2	34.4	23.7	5.5	28.8
-Monthly		8.9	11.9	24.6	37.9	50.9	60.5	65.5	62.8	53.7	43.2	30.7	14.8	38.8
Extremes														
-Record Highest	54	52	52	73	86	96	96	95	95	91	79	68	58	96
-Year		1986	1990	1962	1990	1977	1944	1991	1975	1945	1968	1956	1950	MAY 1977
-Record Lowest	54	-32	-41	-21	-2	18	30	36	34	23	14	-5	-31	-41
-Year		1976	1955	1992	1964	1974	1958	1969	1982	1980	1972	1989	1989	FEB 1955
NORMAL DEGREE DAYS:														
Heating (base 65°F)		1739	1487	1252	813	437	143	61	115	343	676	1029	1556	9651
Cooling (base 65°F)		0	0	0	0	0	8	76	47	0	0	0	0	131
% OF POSSIBLE SUNSHINE														
MEAN SKY COVER (tenths)														
Sunrise - Sunset	48	6.8	6.8	6.8	7.2	7.3	7.3	7.0	6.8	6.8	7.2	8.0	7.3	7.1
MEAN NUMBER OF DAYS:														
Sunrise to Sunset														
-Clear	52	6.9	6.2	7.0	5.2	4.1	3.3	3.1	4.6	5.5	4.8	2.9	5.6	59.1
-Partly Cloudy	52	7.0	6.2	6.8	6.8	9.0	9.8	12.9	11.4	9.2	7.8	6.2	6.6	99.7
-Cloudy	52	17.1	15.8	17.2	18.0	17.9	16.9	15.0	14.9	15.4	18.4	20.9	18.9	206.4
Precipitation														
.01 inches or more	54	14.6	12.4	12.8	12.9	13.4	13.6	13.8	13.2	12.3	12.7	14.5	14.6	160.6
Snow,Ice pellets,hail														
1.0 inches or more	52	6.0	5.7	4.9	2.6	0.3	0.0	0.0	0.0	0.*	0.5	3.1	6.3	29.3
Thunderstorms	25	0.*	0.0	0.1	0.5	1.9	4.3	6.7	4.1	1.3	1.0	0.*	0.0	20.1
Heavy Fog Visibility														
1/4 mile or less	25	2.0	1.6	1.7	2.2	1.0	1.6	2.6	2.3	3.2	2.3	3.7	2.7	26.9
Temperature °F														
-Maximum														
90° and above	54	0.0	0.0	0.0	0.0	0.1	0.4	1.0	0.5	0.*	0.0	0.0	0.0	2.1
32° and below	54	26.2	22.9	13.1	1.8	0.*	0.0	0.0	0.0	0.0	0.3	9.1	23.5	96.9
-Minimum														
32° and below	54	30.7	28.0	29.0	21.7	5.4	0.1	0.0	0.0	2.9	14.3	25.0	30.3	187.4
0° and below	54	16.1	12.9	4.4	0.*	0.0	0.0	0.0	0.0	0.0	0.0	0.3	10.1	43.8
AVG. STATION PRESS.(mb)	10	987.8	989.3	988.7	988.0	990.0	989.6	989.2	991.8	992.1	991.7	990.2	989.9	989.9
RELATIVE HUMIDITY (%)														
Hour 01	19	74	75	76	79	79	84	84	89	89	86	85	79	82
Hour 07 (Local Time)	49	74	74	76	76	73	78	83	86	87	86	85	80	80
Hour 13	49	66	63	60	57	52	56	58	59	60	62	71	70	61
Hour 19	48	72	69	67	65	60	65	70	73	75	75	79	79	71
PRECIPITATION (inches):														
Water Equivalent														
-Normal		2.42	1.92	2.43	2.45	3.07	2.91	4.01	4.07	3.45	3.10	3.55	3.22	36.60
-Maximum Monthly	54	5.10	4.13	5.13	5.26	6.27	7.11	6.83	12.09	8.14	8.73	8.15	7.97	12.09
-Year		1978	1955	1953	1973	1947	1940	1957	1981	1954	1990	1983	1973	AUG 1981
-Minimum Monthly	54	0.12	0.26	0.66	0.54	0.47	0.88	0.96	0.93	0.86	0.63	0.45	0.74	0.12
-Year		1944	1978	1965	1967	1982	1983	1991	1957	1968	1955	1939	1963	JAN 1944
-Maximum in 24 hrs	54	1.52	1.38	1.70	2.11	2.25	2.37	2.92	6.89	6.23	4.07	2.27	2.80	6.89
-Year		1992	1988	1984	1958	1948	1957	1957	1981	1954	1970	1983	1973	AUG 1981
Snow,Ice pellets,hail														
-Maximum Monthly	54	41.4	41.0	47.1	36.4	10.9	T	T	0.0	2.5	12.1	34.9	59.9	59.9
-Year		1978	1960	1955	1982	1967	1991	1992		1991	1963	1974	1972	DEC 1972
-Maximum in 24 hrs	54	15.9	18.2	28.6	21.1	5.8	T	T	0.0	2.5	9.4	21.0	19.7	28.6
-Year		1986	1952	1984	1982	1967	1991	1992		1991	1963	1986	1989	MAR 1984
WIND:														
Mean Speed (mph)	15	12.4	12.0	12.9	11.7	11.4	10.4	9.8	9.3	10.4	10.9	11.1	11.5	11.2
Prevailing Direction through 1962		NW	NW	NW	NW	NW	WSW	WSW	WSW	WSW	NNW	WSW	WSW	WSW
Fastest Obs. 1 Min.														
-Direction (!!)		25	33	32	34	34	34	32	33	23	26	28	32	34
-Speed (MPH)	4	30	28	29	28	31	35	32	24	25	25	31	32	35
-Year		1993	1992	1993	1993	1991	1991	1992	1993	1993	1990	1990	1992	JUN 1991
Peak Gust														
-Direction (!!)														
-Speed (mph)														
-Date														

PRECIPITATION (inches) CARIBOU, MAINE

YEAR	JAN	FEB	MAR	APR	MAY	JUNE	JULY	AUG	SEP	OCT	NOV	DEC	ANNUAL
1964	2.64	0.56	3.12	2.07	2.81	1.80	3.58	3.38	1.33	4.19	2.28	2.98	30.74
1965	1.21	2.33	0.66	1.10	2.35	1.25	3.71	3.60	3.07	4.14	4.75	1.56	29.73
1966	2.06	1.49	2.61	0.73	1.73	2.06	3.27	1.54	3.19	3.47	3.60	2.17	27.92
1967	2.23	1.75	1.07	0.54	3.95	1.69	4.18	4.81	6.61	2.81	2.79	4.58	37.01
1968	2.31	1.46	4.01	2.15	1.33	1.65	4.24	2.01	0.86	3.51	3.98	4.16	31.67
1969	3.00	2.25	1.49	2.60	2.88	3.47	3.73	4.02	6.80	1.55	4.36	3.59	39.74
1970	0.31	2.09	2.25	3.56	4.26	3.25	2.54	3.18	5.46	6.35	1.85	2.58	37.68
1971	1.71	2.16	3.20	2.09	2.06	2.62	2.79	3.39	2.62	3.43	3.31	2.46	31.84
1972	1.32	2.38	4.72	1.09	3.69	4.97	4.21	5.07	3.88	4.03	2.76	5.28	43.40
1973	2.60	2.89	2.48	5.26	5.03	2.13	4.62	2.95	2.62	1.47	2.63	7.97	42.65
1974	1.89	1.37	3.56	3.81	3.61	2.82	3.39	3.98	3.40	1.15	4.16	2.05	35.19
1975	2.71	1.66	1.94	1.95	3.04	2.40	4.28	1.39	2.98	1.51	3.40	4.05	31.31
1976	3.51	3.43	2.57	3.31	5.11	2.85	6.74	6.17	2.52	5.46	2.33	4.63	48.63
1977	3.42	2.99	2.36	1.83	0.74	6.44	1.75	7.86	3.54	5.30	1.63	3.59	41.45
1978	5.10	0.26	2.69	2.33	1.98	3.70	5.56	1.95	2.74	1.94	1.84	3.04	33.13
1979	4.49	2.22	3.70	3.08	4.27	3.39	3.36	4.98	4.68	1.68	2.90	3.05	41.80
1980	1.55	0.82	3.15	2.57	2.05	2.19	5.42	2.28	4.06	2.51	3.21	2.74	32.55
1981	1.68	2.39	3.43	2.17	3.18	4.15	2.62	12.09	2.38	6.28	2.51	3.81	46.69
1982	2.46	2.17	2.72	4.01	0.47	3.08	4.25	4.78	3.70	1.61	5.50	2.51	37.26
1983	2.95	1.77	3.84	4.20	5.28	0.88	5.92	3.86	2.70	1.81	8.15	5.01	46.37
1984	2.10	3.06	2.55	1.74	5.72	5.90	4.52	1.65	1.54	1.81	2.01	3.00	35.60
1985	0.99	2.77	1.87	1.80	2.64	2.89	5.05	1.74	2.30	1.42	3.50	2.24	29.21
1986	4.86	1.13	2.32	2.29	2.13	1.96	4.21	4.97	3.58	1.47	3.96	1.66	34.54
1987	2.29	0.33	1.24	1.75	2.46	3.59	3.16	1.82	4.37	2.18	2.33	2.56	28.08
1988	2.79	2.65	1.23	1.99	1.84	2.37	2.28	5.65	1.82	3.09	4.10	1.00	30.81
1989	1.88	1.43	1.40	2.24	4.13	2.29	2.63	5.41	3.52	1.62	3.88	2.35	32.78
1990	3.36	1.84	1.16	2.28	3.53	4.56	4.15	3.23	3.78	8.73	4.22	5.60	46.44
1991	2.06	1.13	4.71	2.62	3.51	1.98	0.96	6.72	3.45	4.46	1.61	2.10	35.31
1992	3.76	2.68	1.87	2.57	1.83	4.58	4.49	6.28	1.51	3.52	1.60	1.58	36.27
1993	2.18	2.10	1.72	3.48	3.58	4.54	2.48	3.57	5.11	4.31	2.94	3.99	40.00
Record Mean	2.32	2.05	2.41	2.55	3.01	3.42	3.93	4.03	3.36	3.21	3.36	2.93	36.57

AVERAGE TEMPERATURE (deg. F) CARIBOU, MAINE

YEAR	JAN	FEB	MAR	APR	MAY	JUNE	JULY	AUG	SEP	OCT	NOV	DEC	ANNUAL
1964	13.4	15.9	24.1	37.1	51.8	58.8	65.8	58.6	50.8	41.0	29.3	16.9	38.6
1965	8.7	11.5	25.6	37.0	49.1	61.1	61.5	60.9	53.9	41.0	25.1	15.9	37.6
1966	16.7	15.3	28.2	37.6	49.0	60.4	64.1	62.0	51.7	42.7	34.8	21.1	40.3
1967	14.3	6.7	17.4	34.4	42.7	62.1	68.4	64.2	55.8	44.2	31.4	17.3	38.2
1968	6.1	9.9	25.7	41.0	49.7	59.1	66.3	59.1	58.5	48.4	28.2	18.0	39.2
1969	15.3	17.8	25.4	35.6	48.2	60.7	62.9	64.0	52.8	41.1	34.9	21.9	40.0
1970	4.9	13.1	25.3	38.2	50.6	61.7	69.7	66.0	53.9	47.4	34.6	10.1	39.6
1971	5.8	14.3	25.4	36.1	51.6	59.3	64.0	61.3	56.2	46.4	27.9	11.7	38.3
1972	8.2	6.4	18.3	34.7	52.4	61.5	64.7	60.5	54.2	38.3	27.1	7.6	36.2
1973	9.7	12.6	29.6	37.9	48.9	63.0	68.6	66.4	52.9	43.9	27.5	23.9	40.4
1974	6.7	10.8	21.0	36.8	45.2	62.7	64.7	64.3	52.7	39.3	31.4	18.5	37.9
1975	9.6	11.5	23.1	35.1	53.7	61.4	68.6	64.4	54.5	42.3	32.8	10.9	39.0
1976	5.3	13.5	22.7	38.4	51.2	64.0	63.7	62.6	51.5	39.2	25.6	7.9	37.1
1977	6.0	12.9	32.3	36.4	53.3	58.8	65.2	64.2	51.2	43.5	33.3	16.9	39.5
1978	9.9	12.5	20.8	34.9	55.3	60.8	66.2	64.9	50.4	41.6	27.7	16.3	38.4
1979	15.4	10.4	31.8	41.2	54.6	63.0	68.6	61.9	54.4	45.2	35.8	19.2	41.8
1980	13.3	11.9	24.0	42.6	51.2	59.4	64.8	66.0	50.8	40.9	30.1	9.0	38.7
1981	5.6	27.6	28.0	39.5	54.2	61.2	66.3	64.5	53.1	40.4	31.9	23.1	41.3
1982	4.0	11.3	24.5	35.1	53.6	60.3	66.4	58.7	54.9	44.4	32.7	22.1	39.0
1983	14.9	15.3	27.0	41.1	48.9	61.9	64.5	64.3	57.2	43.6	32.2	14.5	40.4
1984	6.7	22.4	19.3	39.8	49.2	59.2	65.8	65.5	51.7	44.5	33.4	18.4	39.7
1985	6.0	16.2	23.5	35.3	49.5	58.2	66.0	62.2	56.1	43.8	28.3	12.1	38.1
1986	11.8	12.2	24.4	42.8	52.2	56.9	62.6	60.7	50.5	41.2	25.9	16.2	38.1
1987	9.9	12.5	28.0	43.9	50.6	60.3	65.8	61.1	54.5	44.2	29.0	18.7	39.9
1988	12.1	13.6	23.1	39.4	54.6	58.5	67.4	64.4	52.4	40.5	33.5	13.8	39.4
1989	12.3	10.4	19.5	36.7	56.7	60.1	64.7	63.5	55.4	45.0	27.6	3.5	38.0
1990	17.3	11.7	24.7	39.6	49.0	62.9	66.2	66.6	53.5	44.7	31.0	20.5	40.6
1991	7.1	15.1	27.0	39.6	52.5	61.4	65.8	65.3	52.1	44.8	32.8	13.5	39.8
1992	10.4	10.9	20.2	36.4	53.2	60.2	60.3	63.7	56.2	41.1	29.3	19.6	38.5
1993	8.6	4.2	23.3	39.9	51.2	59.9	64.8	65.8	54.1	39.2	29.7	19.4	38.3
Record Mean	10.1	12.9	23.8	37.3	50.6	60.0	65.2	62.8	53.8	43.1	30.8	15.8	38.8
Max	19.5	23.0	33.2	46.1	61.4	70.7	75.9	73.6	64.2	51.9	37.6	24.0	48.4
Min	0.7	2.8	14.3	28.5	39.8	49.2	54.4	52.1	43.3	34.3	24.0	7.6	29.2

REFERENCE NOTES CARIBOU, MAINE

GENERAL
T - TRACE AMOUNT.
BLANK ENTRIES DENOTE MISSING/UNREPORTED DATA.
# INDICATES A STATION OR INSTRUMENT RELOCATION.

SPECIFIC

PM - INCLUDES LAST DAY OF PREVIOUS MONTH
ASOS - AUTOMATED SURFACE OBSERVING SYSTEM IN OPERATION DURING THESE MONTHS.

(a) - LENGTH OF RECORD IN YEARS, ALTHOUGH INDIVIDUAL MONTHS MAY BE MISSING.
0.* OR * - THE VALUE IS BETWEEN 0.0 AND 0.05
NORMALS - BASED ON THE 1961-1990 RECORD PERIOD.
EXTREMES - DATES ARE THE MOST RECENT OCCURRENCE.
WIND DIR.- NUMERALS SHOW TENS OF DEGRESS CLOCKWISE FROM TRUE NORTH. "00" INDICATES CALM.
RESULTANT DIRECTIONS ARE GIVEN TO WHOLE DEGREES.
BOLD VALUES INDICATE EXTREME VALUES WHICH OCCURRED AFTER THE ASOS SYSTEM WAS COMMISSIONED.

RECORD = PERIOD OF RECORD
RECORD MEAN PRECIPITATION IS THE MEAN OF ALL DAILY PRECIPITATION AMOUNTS DURING THE PERIOD OF RECORD.
RECORD MAX(MIN) TEMPERATURE IS THE MEAN OF ALL DAILY MAX(MIN) TEMPERATURES DURING THE PERIOD OF RECORD.
RECORD MEAN TEMPERATURE IS THE SUM OF THE RECORD MAX AND RECORD MIN DIVIDED BY 2.
AVERAGE TEMPERATURE IS THE SUM OF THE MEAN DAILY MAX AND MIN TEMPERATURE DIVIDED BY 2.

EXCEPTIONS

1. RELATIVE HUMIDITY HOUR 01, AND MEAN WIND SPEED ARE THROUGH 1962.
2. THUNDERSTORMS AND HEAVY FOG ARE THROUGH 1964 AND MAY BE INCOMPLETE, DUE TO PART-TIME OPERATIONS.

RECORD MEANS ARE THROUGH THE CURRENT YEAR, BEGINNING IN 1939 FOR TEMPERATURE
1939 FOR PRECIPITATION
1939 FOR SNOWFALL

HEATING DEGREE DAYS Base 65 deg. F — CARIBOU, MAINE

SEASON	JULY	AUG	SEP	OCT	NOV	DEC	JAN	FEB	MAR	APR	MAY	JUNE	TOTAL
1964-65	46	199	419	737	1063	1484	1743	1493	1213	831	485	164	9877
1965-66	115	161	351	737	1191	1514	1489	1388	1135	813	499	160	9553
1966-67	64	106	393	683	899	1354	1567	1629	1468	912	682	121	9878
1967-68	14	55	276	636	1000	1471	1823	1594	1211	715	468	171	9434
1968-69	48	191	199	515	1097	1452	1534	1316	1219	876	512	167	9126
1969-70	109	86	364	732	895	1331	1861	1449	1221	800	440	142	9430
1970-71	17	80	328	540	905	1697	1833	1415	1224	860	411	199	9509
1971-72	59	141	274	569	1106	1648	1759	1698	1440	903	405	134	10136
1972-73	55	145	326	818	1130	1775	1711	1464	1092	807	491	122	9936
1973-74	9	44	373	649	1117	1270	1810	1512	1359	837	609	81	9670
1974-75	40	66	369	789	998	1433	1717	1498	1295	890	343	158	9596
1975-76	19	93	310	700	960	1674	1849	1489	1302	793	426	123	9738
1976-77	84	132	405	793	1175	1765	1828	1453	1002	850	406	203	10096
1977-78	56	93	408	657	944	1489	1702	1467	1364	894	333	156	9563
1978-79	53	86	434	717	1114	1503	1534	1527	1018	708	326	104	9124
1979-80	34	146	327	612	870	1413	1593	1534	1265	664	420	200	9078
1980-81	71	41	425	740	1042	1733	1839	1040	1141	757	333	125	9287
1981-82	37	77	355	757	984	1292	1891	1499	1251	890	355	145	9533
1982-83	60	199	310	632	961	1325	1544	1387	1171	712	493	148	8942
1983-84	75	78	257	656	978	1562	1804	1229	1412	748	493	199	9491
1984-85	38	57	396	630	940	1441	1822	1363	1281	884	472	198	9522
1985-86	43	118	272	650	1094	1636	1646	1473	1255	660	394	246	9487
1986-87	105	147	427	733	1167	1505	1704	1465	1140	629	442	142	9606
1987-88	79	152	314	641	1071	1430	1636	1485	1289	760	321	232	9410
1988-89	47	114	373	752	939	1583	1627	1524	1402	841	257	181	9640
1989-90	66	101	303	613	1116	1905	1471	1490	1241	759	490	107	9662
1990-91	57	47	337	623	1014	1370	1791	1392	1172	755	383	158	9099
1991-92	55	66	383	619	959	1595	1691	1564	1382	852	381	163	9710
1992-93	145	73	273	732	1064	1402	1747	1699	1284	748	423	175	9765
1993-94	73	53	327	791	1051	1407							

COOLING DEGREE DAYS Base 65 deg. F — CARIBOU, MAINE

YEAR	JAN	FEB	MAR	APR	MAY	JUNE	JULY	AUG	SEP	OCT	NOV	DEC	TOTAL
1969	0	0	0	0	0	45	48	62	4	0	0	0	159
1970	0	0	0	0	2	47	164	117	1	0	0	0	331
1971	0	0	0	0	2	36	38	33	16	0	0	0	125
1972	0	0	0	0	21	35	51	11	9	0	0	0	127
1973	0	0	0	0	0	67	126	97	17	0	0	0	307
1974	0	0	0	0	2	21	38	50	5	0	0	0	116
1975	0	0	0	0	0	54	137	80	0	0	0	0	271
1976	0	0	0	0	6	104	52	65	4	0	0	0	231
1977	0	0	0	0	52	24	69	77	1	0	0	0	223
1978	0	0	0	0	38	35	97	93	1	0	0	0	264
1979	0	0	0	0	8	50	153	57	16	6	0	0	290
1980	0	0	0	0	0	37	71	78	8	0	0	0	194
1981	0	0	0	0	3	17	83	68	4	0	0	0	175
1982	0	0	0	0	11	10	110	9	12	0	0	0	152
1983	0	0	0	0	0	62	65	66	32	1	0	0	226
1984	0	0	0	0	9	33	72	79	0	0	0	0	193
1985	0	0	0	0	0	0	82	40	10	0	0	0	132
1986	0	0	0	0	5	10	39	20	1	0	0	0	75
1987	0	0	0	0	2	10	111	38	8	0	0	0	169
1988	0	0	0	0	6	45	131	103	1	0	0	0	286
1989	0	0	0	0	9	37	64	63	19	0	0	0	192
1990	0	0	0	2	0	51	102	106	0	0	0	0	261
1991	0	0	0	0	2	55	89	85	4	0	0	0	235
1992	0	0	0	0	23	26	5	40	12	0	0	0	106
1993	0	0	0	0	0	31	72	83	6	0	0	0	192

SNOWFALL (inches) — CARIBOU, MAINE

SEASON	JULY	AUG	SEP	OCT	NOV	DEC	JAN	FEB	MAR	APR	MAY	JUNE	TOTAL
1964-65	0.0	0.0	0.0	0.9	12.9	37.2	18.7	14.8	6.1	4.0	0.0	0.0	94.6
1965-66	0.0	0.0	0.0	1.2	27.0	17.8	30.3	20.9	10.7	2.8	8.2	0.0	118.9
1966-67	0.0	0.0	0.0	0.4	7.1	24.2	27.8	26.0	10.5	2.2	10.9	0.0	109.1
1967-68	0.0	0.0	0.0	T	9.3	31.3	33.5	5.3	26.3	T	0.0	0.0	105.7
1968-69	0.0	0.0	0.0	T	28.0	31.2	29.5	29.7	19.5	14.1	0.0	0.0	152.0
1969-70	0.0	0.0	0.0	2.3	4.6	28.6	6.0	15.0	19.8	11.7	T	0.0	88.0
1970-71	0.0	0.0	0.0	7.6	11.0	32.4	16.6	16.3	38.6	12.2	0.0	T	134.7
1971-72	0.0	0.0	0.0	T	18.9	26.3	15.7	25.1	41.4	9.4	T	0.0	136.8
1972-73	0.0	0.0	0.0	1.7	13.3	59.9	20.3	27.8	7.8	22.2	0.0	0.0	153.0
1973-74	0.0	0.0	T	T	14.5	23.4	20.7	11.9	21.6	13.1	4.2	0.0	109.4
1974-75	0.0	0.0	T	0.4	34.9	12.6	31.2	9.8	18.2	15.1	0.0	0.0	122.2
1975-76	0.0	0.0	0.0	T	10.4	36.4	30.1	30.2	23.3	1.5	0.5	0.0	132.4
1976-77	0.0	0.0	0.0	3.7	10.2	31.9	39.1	34.4	16.0	10.6	T	0.0	145.9
1977-78	0.0	0.0	0.0	0.0	5.5	37.7	41.4	4.4	13.7	15.3	0.8	0.0	118.8
1978-79	0.0	0.0	0.0	T	9.2	40.3	32.1	18.1	8.6	14.9	T	0.0	123.2
1979-80	0.0	0.0	0.0	0.7	3.0	18.0	7.9	12.6	27.6	0.8	0.0	T	70.6
1980-81	0.0	0.0	T	0.2	12.0	28.9	35.2	8.6	36.4	1.4	0.2	0.0	122.9
1981-82	0.0	0.0	T	2.6	4.8	34.3	30.9	25.1	23.7	36.4	1.0	0.0	158.8
1982-83	0.0	0.0	0.0	T	14.6	4.0	22.8	22.8	13.9	4.8	T	0.0	82.9
1983-84	0.0	0.0	0.0	T	21.0	26.6	27.3	20.1	35.4	3.9	0.2	0.0	134.5
1984-85	0.0	0.0	0.0	0.8	3.8	30.7	10.5	26.8	11.9	5.0	1.3	0.0	90.8
1985-86	0.0	0.0	0.0	T	14.8	18.3	30.0	11.9	18.6	11.3	T	0.0	104.9
1986-87	0.0	0.0	T	0.4	28.1	8.5	26.4	4.1	12.3	5.2	T	0.0	85.0
1987-88	0.0	0.0	T	T	5.2	22.6	32.1	28.2	3.9	6.4	T	0.0	98.4
1988-89	0.0	0.0	0.0	1.2	13.8	11.5	18.4	16.6	11.9	9.4	0.0	0.0	82.8
1989-90	0.0	0.0	T	0.1	14.3	38.0	28.5	18.3	7.6	10.7	0.6	T	118.1
1990-91	0.0	0.0	0.0	T	12.0	22.6	21.5	12.2	24.0	2.5	0.0	T	94.8
1991-92	0.0	0.0	2.5	T	7.1	19.4	14.8	38.6	4.2	7.4	T	0.0	94.0
1992-93	T	0.0	T	0.4	5.3	15.9	5.6	22.8	23.4	7.1	T	0.0	80.5
1993-94	0.0	0.0	0.0	0.2	10.5	13.9							
Record Mean	T	0.0	T	1.7	12.1	23.0	23.3	21.6	19.2	8.4	0.7	T	109.9

PORTLAND, MAINE

The Portland City Airport is located 2 3/4 miles west of the site of the former city office. The surrounding country is mostly open, rolling and sloping generally toward the Fore River, a body of brackish water about 1,000 feet wide at a distance of about 1/2 mile from the station and forming one boundary (north through east) of the field. The airport is about 5 1/2 miles west-northwest of the open ocean. A slight rise reaching an elevation of 100 feet, lying northwest of the field, cuts down the wind slightly from that direction. The older portion of the city is situated on a hill rising abruptly from sea level to 170 feet, 1 1/2 miles east of the airport and on the opposite side of the Fore River. A line of low hills southeast of the airport, near the ocean, which reach a maximum height of 160 feet, shuts off sight of the ocean from the airport. Sebago Lake with an area of 44 square miles is situated about 15 miles to the northwest and 45 miles farther are the White Mountains, averaging 3,000 to 5,000 feet in height.

As a rule, Portland has very pleasant summers and falls, cold winters with frequent thaws, and disagreeable springs. Very few summer nights are too warm and humid for comfortable sleeping. Autumn has the greatest number of sunny days and the least cloudiness. Winters are quite severe, but begin late and then extend deeply into the normal springtime.

Heavy seasonal snowfalls, over 100 inches, normally occur about each 10 years. True blizzards are very rare. The White Mountains, to the northwest, keep considerable snow from reaching the Portland area and also moderate the temperature. Normal monthly precipitation is remarkably uniform throughout the year.

Winds are generally quite light with the highest velocities being confined mostly to March and November. Even in these months the occasional northeasterly gales have usually lost much of their severity before reaching the coast of Maine.

Temperatures well below zero are recorded frequently each winter. Cold waves sometimes come in on strong winds, but extremely low temperatures are generally accompanied by light winds.

The average freeze-free season at the airport station is 139 days. Mid-May is the average occurrence of the last freeze in spring, and the average occurrence of the first freeze in fall is late September. The freeze-free period is longer in the city proper, but may be even shorter at susceptible places further inland.

Daily maximum temperatures at the present airport site agree closely with those near the former intown office, but minimum temperatures on clear, quiet mornings range as much as 15 degrees lower at the airport.

NORMALS, MEANS, AND EXTREMES

PORTLAND, MAINE

LATITUDE: 43°39'N LONGITUDE: 70°18'W ELEVATION: FT. GRND 43 BARO 78 TIME ZONE: EASTERN WBAN: 14764

	(a)	JAN	FEB	MAR	APR	MAY	JUNE	JULY	AUG	SEP	OCT	NOV	DEC	YEAR
TEMPERATURE °F:														
Normals														
-Daily Maximum		30.3	33.1	41.4	52.3	63.2	72.7	78.8	77.4	69.3	58.7	47.0	35.1	54.9
-Daily Minimum		11.4	13.5	24.5	34.1	43.4	52.1	58.3	57.1	48.9	38.3	30.4	17.8	35.8
-Monthly		20.8	23.3	33.0	43.3	53.3	62.4	68.6	67.3	59.1	48.5	38.7	26.5	45.4
Extremes														
-Record Highest	53	64	64	86	85	94	98	99	103	95	88	74	69	103
-Year		1950	1957	1946	1957	1987	1991	1977	1975	1983	1963	1987	1982	AUG 1975
-Record Lowest	53	-26	-39	-21	8	23	33	40	33	23	15	3	-21	-39
-Year		1971	1943	1950	1954	1956	1944	1965	1965	1941	1976	1989	1963	FEB 1943
NORMAL DEGREE DAYS:														
Heating (base 65°F)		1370	1168	992	651	363	100	11	39	189	512	789	1194	7378
Cooling (base 65°F)		0	0	0	0	0	22	123	111	12	0	0	0	268
% OF POSSIBLE SUNSHINE	53	56	59	56	54	55	59	63	63	62	58	48	53	57
MEAN SKY COVER (tenths)														
Sunrise - Sunset	50	6.1	6.1	6.4	6.7	6.7	6.5	6.3	5.9	5.7	5.8	6.6	6.2	6.2
MEAN NUMBER OF DAYS:														
Sunrise to Sunset														
-Clear	53	10.0	8.6	8.7	7.4	6.3	6.8	7.2	9.1	10.3	10.4	7.5	9.2	101.3
-Partly Cloudy	53	6.5	7.1	7.0	7.1	9.5	10.0	11.2	10.7	7.8	7.6	7.1	7.2	99.0
-Cloudy	53	14.5	12.5	15.3	15.5	15.2	13.2	12.6	11.2	11.9	12.9	15.4	14.6	164.9
Precipitation														
.01 inches or more	53	11.0	10.0	11.4	11.8	12.5	11.5	9.7	9.5	8.5	9.5	11.6	11.5	128.5
Snow,Ice pellets,hail														
1.0 inches or more	53	4.5	3.8	3.4	0.8	0.1	0.0	0.0	0.0	0.0	0.1	1.0	3.7	17.3
Thunderstorms	53	0.*	0.1	0.4	0.5	2.0	4.1	4.5	3.5	1.5	0.6	0.3	0.1	17.7
Heavy Fog Visibility														
1/4 mile or less	53	1.9	2.1	3.3	3.1	5.3	5.2	6.4	5.6	5.3	4.8	3.5	1.9	48.3
Temperature °F														
-Maximum														
90° and above	53	0.0	0.0	0.0	0.0	0.2	1.1	2.0	1.6	0.3	0.0	0.0	0.0	5.2
32° and below	53	16.7	12.2	4.4	0.1	0.0	0.0	0.0	0.0	0.0	0.0	0.8	11.7	46.0
-Minimum														
32° and below	53	29.8	26.8	25.8	13.8	2.3	0.0	0.0	0.0	1.0	9.0	19.5	28.7	156.8
0° and below	53	5.9	4.1	0.6	0.0	0.0	0.0	0.0	0.0	0.0	0.0	0.0	2.8	13.5
AVG. STATION PRESS.(mb)	21	1013.0	1013.6	1012.8	1011.6	1012.6	1011.4	1011.9	1014.0	1015.3	1015.7	1014.4	1014.1	1013.4
RELATIVE HUMIDITY (%)														
Hour 01	53	74	73	75	79	84	87	89	89	89	85	81	77	82
Hour 07 (Local Time)	53	76	76	74	73	75	78	80	83	85	84	82	79	79
Hour 13	53	60	58	57	55	58	60	59	59	60	59	62	61	59
Hour 19	53	68	67	68	69	71	73	74	77	79	77	75	71	72
PRECIPITATION (inches):														
Water Equivalent														
-Normal		3.53	3.33	3.67	4.08	3.62	3.44	3.09	2.87	3.09	3.90	5.17	4.55	44.34
-Maximum Monthly	53	11.92	7.10	9.97	9.90	9.64	6.75	7.48	15.22	9.81	12.27	13.50	9.69	15.22
-Year		1979	1981	1953	1973	1984	1982	1976	1991	1954	1962	1983	1969	AUG 1991
-Minimum Monthly	53	0.76	0.04	0.81	0.71	0.49	0.70	0.61	0.27	0.30	0.26	0.90	0.98	0.04
-Year		1970	1987	1965	1941	1965	1941	1965	1947	1948	1947	1976	1955	FEB 1987
-Maximum in 24 hrs	53	3.56	3.41	3.47	5.26	4.66	5.58	2.68	7.83	7.49	7.71	4.70	3.82	7.83
-Year		1977	1981	1951	1973	1989	1967	1979	1991	1954	1962	1990	1969	AUG 1991
Snow,Ice pellets,hail														
-Maximum Monthly	53	62.4	61.2	49.0	15.9	7.0	0.0	0.0	0.0	T	3.8	15.6	54.8	62.4
-Year		1979	1969	1993	1982	1945				1992	1969	1972	1970	JAN 1979
-Maximum in 24 hrs	53	27.1	21.5	18.6	15.9	7.0	0.0	0.0	0.0	T	3.6	11.1	22.8	27.1
-Year		1979	1969	1993	1982	1945				1992	1969	1972	1970	JAN 1979
WIND:														
Mean Speed (mph)	53	9.2	9.4	10.0	10.0	9.2	8.3	7.6	7.5	7.9	8.4	8.8	9.0	8.8
Prevailing Direction through 1963		N	N	W	S	S	S	S	S	S	N	W	N	S
Fastest Obs. 1 Min.														
-Direction (!!)	8	17	32	07	18	16	28	26	01	25	07	15	26	01
-Speed (MPH)	8	36	29	37	30	30	35	29	40	29	31	35	35	40
-Year		1992	1992	1993	1993	1990	1991	1988	1991	1993	1988	1993	1993	AUG 1991
Peak Gust														
-Direction (!!)	10	S	NW	E	NE	SE	W	NW	N	SE	N	SE	SE	SE
-Speed (mph)	10	53	47	53	49	45	49	55	61	70	53	52	56	70
-Date		1992	1992	1993	1991	1989	1991	1990	1991	1985	1991	1993	1986	SEP 1985

PRECIPITATION (inches) PORTLAND, MAINE

YEAR	JAN	FEB	MAR	APR	MAY	JUNE	JULY	AUG	SEP	OCT	NOV	DEC	ANNUAL
1964	4.74	2.66	3.64	3.27	1.56	2.01	3.47	1.77	1.02	3.45	3.25	3.75	34.59
1965	1.68	6.36	0.81	2.93	0.49	2.27	0.61	1.84	2.31	2.49	3.96	2.40	28.15
1966	4.97	3.43	3.77	1.00	1.96	3.04	0.96	4.99	3.84	3.61	5.01	3.46	40.04
1967	2.52	4.63	2.16	4.74	5.34	6.23	3.46	2.57	2.68	1.31	2.52	6.00	44.16
1968	3.00	1.26	4.16	3.37	3.81	4.04	0.65	2.00	1.40	2.00	7.74	7.70	41.13
1969	3.63	6.28	3.36	2.86	1.67	3.53	5.45	2.20	5.28	2.51	8.54	9.69	55.00
1970	0.76	4.31	4.22	4.14	3.15	2.91	0.95	5.12	4.49	3.87	2.38	5.14	41.44
1971	2.25	6.76	4.74	1.86	4.09	1.09	3.14	3.24	3.55	3.95	4.13	2.85	41.65
1972	2.09	5.14	6.01	2.53	3.17	4.24	2.05	0.80	4.31	3.92	7.87	6.49	48.62
1973	2.58	2.57	3.33	9.90	6.28	4.87	1.70	3.48	2.23	3.38	2.40	9.57	52.29
1974	3.41	2.07	3.82	3.82	4.20	4.69	3.66	1.45	5.43	1.74	4.85	4.41	43.55
1975	4.40	2.51	3.20	3.71	1.09	4.87	2.06	3.89	4.34	4.50	6.01	8.14	48.72
1976	4.44	2.84	2.47	2.42	3.99	1.53	7.48	4.87	1.86	5.37	0.90	3.22	41.39
1977	6.46	3.75	6.92	3.46	2.04	3.38	2.83	2.79	4.63	8.30	6.46	6.61	57.63
1978	6.91	0.87	4.19	4.46	4.36	2.42	1.67	2.36	0.59	3.23	2.26	3.15	36.47
1979	11.92	3.50	4.17	6.48	5.15	1.97	5.90	5.53	3.28	6.71	3.95	2.59	61.15
1980	0.98	1.36	4.54	5.78	1.83	3.34	1.99	2.14	3.00	2.99	4.75	1.18	33.88
1981	0.93	7.10	1.44	3.46	2.27	4.59	5.44	2.31	6.14	4.71	2.80	4.51	45.70
1982	5.17	2.53	3.20	4.54	2.91	6.75	2.61	3.35	1.90	1.93	3.61	1.18	39.68
1983	4.59	3.94	9.75	6.82	5.98	1.35	4.31	2.58	1.35	3.38	13.50	8.78	66.33
1984	2.56	4.99	5.12	4.81	9.64	3.87	3.86	2.09	0.84	3.26	3.69	3.44	48.17
1985	1.03	1.54	3.15	1.25	2.03	2.74	3.30	3.18	2.97	4.07	6.36	2.39	34.01
1986	6.58	2.61	4.21	3.49	2.51	3.91	3.44	1.87	2.64	2.09	5.18	5.91	44.44
1987	5.21	0.04	4.29	6.33	2.62	5.01	1.79	2.48	4.64	2.54	3.82	2.01	40.78
1988	1.97	3.34	1.85	3.68	4.27	2.36	5.89	5.24	1.50	3.47	8.84	1.21	43.62
1989	1.15	2.37	2.14	2.94	8.74	4.49	2.50	1.73	4.48	4.81	3.97	2.23	41.55
1990	3.19	2.49	1.42	5.16	5.23	4.12	3.21	1.89	3.12	7.46	7.50	7.90	52.69
1991	2.91	1.85	6.19	6.71	3.77	1.47	2.35	15.22	5.44	2.83	4.34	4.06	57.14
1992	4.80	3.42	3.93	2.47	1.15	3.99	4.06	2.59	3.11	2.48	4.39	2.12	38.51
1993	2.80	3.84	6.26	5.69	1.14	2.89	2.73	1.21	4.10	3.74	4.05	5.40	43.85
Record Mean	3.86	3.66	3.95	3.65	3.43	3.27	3.12	3.07	3.21	3.39	4.12	3.96	42.70

AVERAGE TEMPERATURE (deg. F) PORTLAND, MAINE

YEAR	JAN	FEB	MAR	APR	MAY	JUNE	JULY	AUG	SEP	OCT	NOV	DEC	ANNUAL
1964	24.4	23.0	31.9	40.9	54.8	62.6	67.6	61.1	55.6	47.1	36.2	25.3	44.2
1965	19.8	21.6	33.3	41.1	54.8	63.1	66.3	66.5	58.0	47.6	36.6	27.9	44.7
1966	22.3	22.6	32.7	39.9	50.4	63.1	67.7	66.2	56.2	47.1	41.1	26.7	44.7
1967	24.4	17.2	26.5	41.5	47.3	63.3	67.5	66.8	59.9	49.7	34.8	27.8	43.9
1968	16.6	19.2	33.2	45.1	51.0	60.0	70.0	66.4	61.7	52.8	36.7	25.2	44.8
1969	24.2	25.0	31.1	43.0	52.8	62.6	67.6	71.3	60.9	48.9	41.1	28.7	46.5
1970	16.7	25.4	32.4	43.6	55.7	63.5	70.1	68.8	61.0	51.7	41.3	19.6	45.8
1971	12.2	21.9	31.6	41.6	52.7	64.3	69.0	68.9	61.3	52.5	35.4	27.3	44.9
1972	22.2	21.1	28.9	40.6	52.6	59.6	67.5	65.3	58.7	45.2	35.0	24.0	43.4
1973	23.1	23.4	37.7	45.5	51.3	63.8	70.8	70.9	58.4	49.2	37.7	33.5	47.1
1974	23.2	24.5	33.9	45.1	50.6	61.3	68.2	67.9	58.8	44.7	39.3	30.2	45.6
1975	26.7	25.0	29.8	40.0	55.6	61.5	70.1	66.8	57.2	49.3	43.0	24.3	45.8
1976	15.7	28.2	31.5	45.0	52.3	65.9	65.9	65.4	57.3	43.6	36.1	19.4	43.9
1977	14.6	21.9	36.2	42.4	54.4	59.0	68.2	66.6	57.6	48.1	39.4	25.4	44.5
1978	21.1	19.2	30.2	40.6	52.7	61.0	68.0	68.6	57.8	48.2	36.4	26.1	44.2
1979	23.7	15.6	35.6	42.2	55.3	62.7	69.3	64.8	57.4	47.5	42.4	29.8	45.5
1980	22.7	20.5	32.0	44.3	53.7	61.0	69.6	71.2	61.5	45.9	36.2	21.3	45.0
1981	13.8	32.3	35.7	45.2	55.3	63.9	68.8	66.0	58.6	46.6	38.9	29.2	46.2
1982	15.0	23.3	32.1	42.0	54.6	58.3	69.2	64.4	59.2	48.1	41.3	32.0	45.0
1983	25.2	26.2	35.8	44.4	52.0	63.8	69.7	67.6	63.0	47.9	40.2	26.1	46.8
1984	19.8	32.0	28.2	43.3	53.0	63.9	69.6	69.1	57.8	49.6	39.2	31.2	46.4
1985	16.2	26.4	34.8	44.1	53.7	61.7	69.8	66.6	60.7	50.8	39.9	24.6	45.8
1986	25.0	23.4	34.6	46.5	53.6	60.9	66.3	66.2	57.4	47.9	36.3	29.6	45.6
1987	21.6	23.0	34.0	44.9	54.6	63.8	68.0	66.2	59.6	47.1	38.1	30.2	45.9
1988	21.6	25.7	34.2	43.5	54.7	63.8	71.1	71.1	59.4	46.5	41.0	26.0	46.6
1989	26.8	24.0	31.6	41.1	55.6	63.9	69.4	68.0	60.5	49.8	37.3	14.1	45.2
1990	30.2	25.7	34.7	44.6	51.8	62.4	70.3	69.8	59.8	52.4	41.8	33.7	48.1
1991	23.4	29.8	37.0	45.9	58.1	65.5	70.1	69.9	58.2	50.8	40.4	26.4	48.0
1992	23.9	25.9	30.9	41.4	51.9	63.4	65.8	66.8	58.9	47.3	37.6	28.9	45.2
1993	23.4	16.8	29.8	43.3	54.8	64.5	69.8	69.5	59.6	46.2	39.0	29.9	45.6
Record													
Mean	22.3	23.5	32.4	42.9	53.3	62.4	68.3	66.8	59.5	49.3	38.7	26.9	45.5
Max	30.8	32.3	40.3	51.3	62.3	71.7	77.5	75.7	68.5	58.1	46.3	34.7	54.1
Min	13.7	14.8	24.5	34.5	44.3	53.1	59.1	57.8	50.4	40.5	31.0	19.0	36.9

REFERENCE NOTES PORTLAND, MAINE

GENERAL
T - TRACE AMOUNT.
BLANK ENTRIES DENOTE MISSING/UNREPORTED DATA.
# INDICATES A STATION OR INSTRUMENT RELOCATION.

SPECIFIC

PM - INCLUDES LAST DAY OF PREVIOUS MONTH
ASOS - AUTOMATED SURFACE OBSERVING SYSTEM IN OPERATION DURING THESE MONTHS.

(*) - LENGTH OF RECORD IN YEARS, ALTHOUGH INDIVIDUAL MONTHS MAY BE MISSING.
0.* OR * - THE VALUE IS BETWEEN 0.0 AND 0.05
NORMALS - BASED ON THE 1961-1990 RECORD PERIOD.
EXTREMES - DATES ARE THE MOST RECENT OCCURRENCE
WIND DIR.- NUMERALS SHOW TENS OF DEGRESS CLOCKWISE FROM TRUE NORTH. "00" INDICATES CALM.
RESULTANT DIRECTIONS ARE GIVEN TO WHOLE DEGREES.
BOLD VALUES INDICATE EXTREME VALUES WHICH OCCURRED AFTER THE ASOS SYSTEM WAS COMMISSIONED.

RECORD = PERIOD OF RECORD
RECORD MEAN PRECIPITATION IS THE MEAN OF ALL DAILY PRECIPITATION AMOUNTS DURING THE PERIOD OF RECORD.
RECORD MAX(MIN) TEMPERATURE IS THE MEAN OF ALL DAILY MAX(MIN) TEMPERATURES DURING THE PERIOD OF RECORD.
RECORD MEAN TEMPERATURE IS THE SUM OF THE RECORD MAX AND RECORD MIN DIVIDED BY 2.
AVERAGE TEMPERATURE IS THE SUM OF THE MEAN DAILY MAX AND MIN TEMPERATURE DIVIDED BY 2.

EXCEPTIONS

RECORD MEANS ARE THROUGH THE CURRENT YEAR, BEGINNING IN 1874 FOR TEMPERATURE
1871 FOR PRECIPITATION
1941 FOR SNOWFALL

HEATING DEGREE DAYS Base 65 deg. F — PORTLAND, MAINE

SEASON	JULY	AUG	SEP	OCT	NOV	DEC	JAN	FEB	MAR	APR	MAY	JUNE	TOTAL
1964-65	28	134	293	549	857	1222	1396	1212	975	710	320	125	7821
1965-66	41	61	242	532	845	1145	1315	1183	994	745	449	108	7660
1966-67	19	29	264	549	710	1181	1254	1330	1187	699	544	92	7858
1967-68	15	27	155	467	900	1147	1496	1320	981	590	424	164	7686
1968-69	8	46	110	375	841	1228	1259	1112	1043	652	377	118	7169
1969-70	30	7	179	494	710	1120	1491	1104	1005	637	283	93	7153
1970-71	7	14	159	408	704	1400	1634	1202	1028	695	373	81	7705
1971-72	3	20	147	381	878	1164	1322	1265	1112	725	379	155	7551
1972-73	27	53	190	607	893	1264	1292	1157	842	575	419	99	7418
1973-74	0	9	231	480	813	970	1290	1126	958	595	444	131	7047
1974-75	15	17	206	624	762	1071	1177	1112	1086	746	286	146	7248
1975-76	13	59	230	480	653	1258	1522	1061	1030	594	389	94	7383
1976-77	45	73	229	660	858	1404	1559	1199	888	674	354	184	8127
1977-78	29	54	233	518	761	1219	1353	1276	1071	724	377	134	7749
1978-79	39	32	230	513	852	1201	1272	1380	905	677	311	97	7509
1979-80	21	82	240	539	672	1083	1305	1284	1018	613	346	163	7366
1980-81	16	6	163	584	855	1349	1578	910	901	588	312	54	7316
1981-82	16	45	189	566	778	1102	1543	1161	1014	684	320	198	7616
1982-83	20	78	185	519	704	1015	1225	1080	895	612	393	101	6827
1983-84	8	38	139	527	738	1198	1397	949	1132	642	368	110	7246
1984-85	11	13	223	469	767	1043	1506	1076	930	620	347	115	7120
1985-86	4	32	157	433	747	1245	1236	1161	935	548	354	138	6990
1986-87	47	52	242	523	855	1092	1336	1172	955	597	343	77	7291
1987-88	20	58	171	548	798	1070	1339	1130	950	641	323	112	7160
1988-89	13	32	180	569	713	1201	1174	1141	1028	708	286	91	7136
1989-90	6	25	167	464	824	1573	1071	1093	935	607	402	107	7274
1990-91	12	24	170	388	690	964	1283	979	861	568	236	76	6251
1991-92	11	16	228	433	730	1191	1267	1127	1051	700	414	84	7252
1992-93	47	30	208	543	814	1112	1280	1344	1084	645	311	81	7499
1993-94	15	5	192	575	774	1080							

COOLING DEGREE DAYS Base 65 deg. F — PORTLAND, MAINE

YEAR	JAN	FEB	MAR	APR	MAY	JUNE	JULY	AUG	SEP	OCT	NOV	DEC	TOTAL
1969	0	0	0	0	3	56	118	211	59	0	0	0	447
1970	0	0	0	0	4	55	172	136	41	0	0	0	408
1971	0	0	0	0	0	66	135	149	43	1	0	0	394
1972	0	0	0	0	0	3	114	71	8	0	0	0	196
1973	0	0	0	0	1	71	189	201	40	0	0	0	502
1974	0	0	0	2	4	26	121	115	28	0	0	0	296
1975	0	0	0	0	1	49	179	120	2	0	0	0	351
1976	0	0	0	0	2	128	80	93	5	0	0	0	308
1977	0	0	0	1	32	12	135	109	19	0	0	0	308
1978	0	0	0	0	6	22	138	150	20	0	0	0	336
1979	0	0	0	0	15	34	162	83	19	3	0	0	316
1980	0	0	0	0	1	50	163	205	67	0	0	0	486
1981	0	0	0	0	20	30	138	84	5	0	0	0	277
1982	0	0	0	0	6	4	158	66	17	0	0	0	251
1983	0	0	0	0	0	73	161	125	84	3	0	0	446
1984	0	0	0	0	0	84	162	147	12	0	0	0	405
1985	0	0	0	0	5	25	161	92	35	1	0	0	319
1986	0	0	0	0	8	23	93	96	19	0	0	0	239
1987	0	0	0	0	28	47	121	103	17	0	0	0	316
1988	0	0	0	0	11	85	209	227	17	2	0	0	551
1989	0	0	0	0	2	67	151	126	38	0	0	0	384
1990	0	0	0	0	0	34	181	179	19	7	0	0	420
1991	0	0	0	0	29	96	178	176	31	0	0	0	510
1992	0	0	0	0	13	43	76	93	30	0	0	0	255
1993	0	0	0	0	1	72	170	150	37	0	0	0	430

SNOWFALL (inches) — PORTLAND, MAINE

SEASON	JULY	AUG	SEP	OCT	NOV	DEC	JAN	FEB	MAR	APR	MAY	JUNE	TOTAL
1964-65	0.0	0.0	0.0	0.0	T	20.5	15.8	13.2	3.4	2.6	0.0	0.0	55.5
1965-66	0.0	0.0	0.0	T	0.6	9.1	38.2	21.3	2.8	0.7	2.0	0.0	74.7
1966-67	0.0	0.0	0.0	0.0	0.0	14.7	12.4	45.8	17.5	15.7	0.1	0.0	106.2
1967-68	0.0	0.0	0.0	0.0	3.6	18.9	20.0	4.5	11.9	0.0	0.0	0.0	58.9
1968-69	0.0	0.0	0.0	T	15.3	18.8	5.4	61.2	9.3	T	0.0	0.0	110.0
1969-70	0.0	0.0	0.0	3.8	T	24.7	6.2	9.8	20.7	2.9	0.0	0.0	68.1
1970-71	0.0	0.0	0.0	T	0.0	54.8	17.2	35.6	24.7	9.2	0.0	0.0	141.5
1971-72	0.0	0.0	0.0	0.0	6.2	12.5	7.0	38.0	21.7	6.3	0.0	0.0	91.7
1972-73	0.0	0.0	0.0	T	15.6	35.1	9.6	6.6	0.5	2.3	0.0	0.0	69.7
1973-74	0.0	0.0	0.0	0.0	0.0	7.2	15.0	4.3	6.2	8.3	0.0	0.0	41.0
1974-75	0.0	0.0	0.0	T	3.2	8.2	15.4	11.6	6.3	1.7	0.0	0.0	46.4
1975-76	0.0	0.0	0.0	T	3.6	25.3	18.1	4.9	22.2	T	0.0	0.0	74.1
1976-77	0.0	0.0	0.0	0.0	1.5	23.3	35.2	7.9	19.3	1.4	T	0.0	88.6
1977-78	0.0	0.0	0.0	0.0	1.9	23.1	30.7	8.2	12.5	0.8	0.0	0.0	77.2
1978-79	0.0	0.0	0.0	0.0	3.6	18.9	62.4	4.5	T	2.9	0.0	0.0	92.3
1979-80	0.0	0.0	0.0	1.7	T	1.8	6.0	11.2	6.8	0.0	0.0	0.0	27.5
1980-81	0.0	0.0	0.0	0.0	8.9	13.0	9.2	4.6	3.1	T	0.0	0.0	38.8
1981-82	0.0	0.0	0.0	0.0	T	24.0	25.9	11.0	8.5	15.9	0.0	0.0	85.3
1982-83	0.0	0.0	0.0	0.0	0.6	5.7	12.4	24.5	2.1	T	0.0	0.0	45.3
1983-84	0.0	0.0	0.0	0.0	T	12.6	28.3	3.3	26.4	T	0.0	0.0	70.6
1984-85	0.0	0.0	0.0	0.0	T	17.0	12.1	7.2	13.1	2.4	0.0	0.0	51.8
1985-86	0.0	0.0	0.0	0.0	3.1	11.2	18.6	12.0	6.4	T	0.0	0.0	51.3
1986-87	0.0	0.0	0.0	0.0	5.2	4.0	50.7	0.8	14.3	3.4	0.0	0.0	78.4
1987-88	0.0	0.0	T	0.0	5.4	9.1	19.8	20.8	3.0	4.2	0.0	0.0	62.3
1988-89	0.0	0.0	0.0	T	T	3.5	4.0	13.8	8.9	0.7	0.0	0.0	30.9
1989-90	0.0	0.0	0.0	0.0	5.0	15.6	20.4	25.6	3.2	T	0.0	0.0	69.8
1990-91	0.0	0.0	T	0.0	0.2	6.8	13.4	6.3	5.7	T	0.0	0.0	32.4
1991-92	0.0	0.0	0.0	0.0	T	22.5	2.4	10.3	13.4	10.0	0.0	0.0	58.6
1992-93	0.0	0.0	T	T	2.8	2.1	17.1	33.5	49.0	11.1	0.0	0.0	115.6
1993-94	0.0	0.0	0.0	0.2	T	12.3							
Record Mean	0.0	0.0	T	0.2	3.0	14.6	19.0	17.4	13.0	3.1	0.2	0.0	70.5

BALTIMORE, MARYLAND

Baltimore–Washington International Airport lies in a region about midway between the rigorous climates of the North and the mild climates of the South, and adjacent to the modifying influences of the Chesapeake Bay and Atlantic Ocean to the east and the Appalachian Mountains to the west. Since this region is near the average path of the low pressure systems which move across the country, changes in wind direction are frequent and contribute to the changeable character of the weather. The net effect of the mountains to the west and the bay and ocean to the east is to produce a more equable climate compared with other continental locations farther inland at the same latitude.

Rainfall distribution throughout the year is rather uniform, however, the greatest intensities are confined to the summer and early fall months, the season for hurricanes and severe thunderstorms. Moisture deficiencies for crops occur occasionally during the growing season, but severe droughts are rare. Rainfall during the growing season occurs principally in the form of thunderstorms, and rainfall totals during these months vary appreciably.

The average date for the last occurrence in spring of temperatures as low as 32 degrees is mid–April. The average date for the first occurrence in fall of temperatures as low as 32 degrees is late October. The freeze–free period is approximately 194 days.

In summer, the area is under the influence of the large semi–permanent high pressure system commonly known as the Bermuda High and centered over the Atlantic Ocean near 30 degrees N Latitude. This pressure system brings warm humid air to the area. The proximity of large water areas and the inflow of southerly winds contribute to high relative humidities during much of the year.

January is the coldest month, and July, the warmest. Snowfall occurs on about eleven days per year on the average, however, an average of only about six days annually produces snowfalls of 1 inch or greater. Snow is frequently mixed with rain and sleet, and snow seldom remains on the ground more than a few days.

Glaze or freezing rain which is hazardous to highway traffic occurs on an average of two to three times per year, generally in January or February. Some years pass without the occurrence of freezing rain, while in others it occurs on as many as eight to ten days. Sleet is observed on about five days annually with the greatest frequency of occurrence in January.

The annual prevailing wind direction is from the west. Winter and spring months have the highest average wind speed. Destructive velocities are rare and occur mostly during summer thunderstorms. Only rarely have hurricanes in the vicinity caused widespread damage, then primarily through flooding.

NORMALS, MEANS, AND EXTREMES

BALTIMORE, MARYLAND

LATITUDE: 39°11'N LONGITUDE: 76°40' W ELEVATION: FT. GRND 148 BARO 197 TIME ZONE: EASTERN WBAN: 93721

	(a)	JAN	FEB	MAR	APR	MAY	JUNE	JULY	AUG	SEP	OCT	NOV	DEC	YEAR
TEMPERATURE °F:														
Normals														
-Daily Maximum		40.2	43.7	54.0	64.3	74.2	83.2	87.2	85.4	78.5	67.3	56.5	45.2	65.0
-Daily Minimum		23.4	25.9	34.1	42.5	52.6	61.8	66.8	65.7	58.4	45.9	37.1	28.2	45.2
-Monthly		31.8	34.8	44.1	53.4	63.4	72.5	77.0	75.6	68.5	56.6	46.8	36.7	55.1
Extremes														
-Record Highest	43	75	79	87	94	98	100	104	105	100	92	83	77	105
-Year		1975	1985	1979	1960	1991	1988	1988	1983	1983	1954	1974	1984	AUG 1983
-Record Lowest	43	-7	-3	6	20	32	40	50	45	35	25	13	0	-7
-Year		1984	1979	1960	1965	1966	1972	1988	1986	1963	1969	1955	1983	JAN 1984
NORMAL DEGREE DAYS:														
Heating (base 65°F)		1029	846	648	348	108	0	0	0	29	276	546	877	4707
Cooling (base 65°F)		0	0	0	0	59	227	372	329	134	16	0	0	1137
% OF POSSIBLE SUNSHINE	40	51	55	56	56	56	62	64	62	60	58	51	49	57
MEAN SKY COVER (tenths)														
Sunrise - Sunset	43	6.3	6.3	6.3	6.2	6.2	5.7	5.6	5.6	5.4	5.2	6.1	6.4	5.9
MEAN NUMBER OF DAYS:														
Sunrise to Sunset														
-Clear	43	8.1	7.7	7.9	7.7	7.7	8.4	9.2	9.4	10.6	11.9	8.3	8.3	105.3
-Partly Cloudy	43	7.7	6.8	8.8	9.0	10.3	11.6	11.8	10.8	8.5	8.0	8.3	7.2	108.7
-Cloudy	43	15.2	13.7	14.3	13.3	13.0	10.0	10.0	10.8	10.9	11.1	13.3	15.6	151.2
Precipitation .01 inches or more	43	10.4	9.0	10.8	10.7	10.9	9.2	9.0	9.5	7.7	7.5	9.0	9.3	113.1
Snow,Ice pellets,hail 1.0 inches or more	43	2.0	1.8	1.2	0.*	0.0	0.0	0.0	0.0	0.0	0.0	0.3	1.0	6.3
Thunderstorms	43	0.3	0.2	0.9	2.4	4.0	5.3	6.0	5.1	2.0	1.0	0.4	0.1	27.6
Heavy Fog Visibility 1/4 mile or less	43	3.0	3.2	2.6	1.8	1.7	0.9	0.8	1.0	1.3	2.7	2.4	3.4	25.0
Temperature °F														
-Maximum														
90° and above	43	0.0	0.0	0.0	0.4	1.5	6.2	11.4	8.0	3.1	0.1	0.0	0.0	30.7
32° and below	43	6.2	3.8	0.6	0.0	0.0	0.0	0.0	0.0	0.0	0.0	0.1	3.6	14.3
-Minimum														
32° and below	43	24.9	21.2	14.4	3.0	0.*	0.0	0.0	0.0	0.0	1.7	10.9	21.2	97.4
0° and below	43	0.4	0.1	0.0	0.0	0.0	0.0	0.0	0.0	0.0	0.0	0.0	0.*	0.5
AVG. STATION PRESS.(mb)	21	1013.3	1013.1	1011.4	1009.7	1009.9	1009.9	1010.5	1011.9	1013.1	1013.9	1013.8	1013.9	1012.0
RELATIVE HUMIDITY (%)														
Hour 01	40	69	67	67	68	77	81	81	83	83	80	74	71	75
Hour 07 (Local Time)	40	72	71	72	72	77	79	80	84	85	83	78	74	77
Hour 13	40	57	54	51	49	52	52	53	55	55	54	55	58	54
Hour 19	40	62	59	55	54	60	62	64	67	69	68	65	65	63
PRECIPITATION (inches):														
Water Equivalent														
-Normal		3.05	3.12	3.38	3.09	3.72	3.67	3.69	3.92	3.41	2.98	3.32	3.41	40.76
-Maximum Monthly	43	7.84	7.16	8.12	8.15	8.71	9.95	8.18	18.35	8.62	8.09	7.68	7.44	18.35
-Year		1979	1979	1993	1952	1989	1972	1960	1955	1975	1976	1952	1969	AUG 1955
-Minimum Monthly	43	0.29	0.56	0.93	0.39	0.37	0.15	0.30	0.77	0.21	T	0.31	0.20	T
-Year		1955	1978	1966	1985	1986	1954	1955	1951	1967	1963	1981	1955	OCT 1963
-Maximum in 24 hrs	43	3.11	3.26	3.18	2.80	3.64	5.23	5.86	8.35	6.04	3.49	3.43	3.39	8.35
-Year		1976	1983	1958	1952	1960	1972	1952	1955	1985	1955	1952	1977	AUG 1955
Snow,Ice pellets,hail														
-Maximum Monthly	43	25.1	33.1	21.6	0.7	T	0.0	T	0.0	0.0	0.3	8.4	20.4	33.1
-Year		1987	1979	1960	1985	1963		1992			1979	1967	1966	FEB 1979
-Maximum in 24 hrs	43	12.3	22.8	13.0	0.7	T	0.0	T	0.0	0.0	0.3	8.4	14.1	22.8
-Year		1987	1983	1962	1985	1963		1992			1979	1967	1960	FEB 1983
WIND:														
Mean Speed (mph)	43	9.7	10.3	10.8	10.5	9.1	8.5	8.0	7.8	8.0	8.6	9.2	9.3	9.2
Prevailing Direction through 1963		WNW	NW	WNW	WNW	W	WNW	W	W	S	NW	WNW	WNW	WNW
Fastest Mile														
-Direction (!!)	43	NE	W	SE	W	SW	SW	NW	NE	W	SE	E	W	SE
-Speed (MPH)	43	63	68	80	70	65	80	57	54	56	73	58	57	80
-Year		1958	1956	1952	1954	1961	1952	1962	1955	1952	1954	1952	1953	MAR 1952
Peak Gust														
-Direction (!!)	10	SW	NW	W	NW	NW	NW	NW	SW	NW	S	NW	NW	NW
-Speed (mph)	10	53	51	58	49	55	45	68	55	45	47	64	77	77
-Date		1992	1987	1985	1993	1993	1985	1987	1987	1985	1990	1989	1988	DEC 1988

PRECIPITATION (inches)

BALTIMORE, MARYLAND

YEAR	JAN	FEB	MAR	APR	MAY	JUNE	JULY	AUG	SEP	OCT	NOV	DEC	ANNUAL
1964	5.27	4.36	2.98	4.37	0.43	2.40	2.66	1.96	2.61	1.19	2.51	3.94	34.68
1965	3.09	2.89	4.31	1.72	1.79	1.94	2.61	4.72	1.94	1.90	0.68	0.63	28.22
1966	4.15	4.24	0.93	4.39	4.53	1.18	1.48	1.87	8.50	4.80	2.78	3.53	42.38
1967	0.99	2.25	4.39	1.73	3.79	1.89	3.56	8.87	0.21	1.34	2.60	5.31	36.93
1968	3.42	0.72	4.41	1.61	5.41	3.35	2.75	4.16	4.39	3.13	3.85	2.60	39.80
1969	1.38	1.75	1.63	1.80	1.46	3.65	5.22	3.81	2.60	1.10	1.74	7.44	33.58
1970	0.94	3.34	3.07	4.53	1.69	4.10	4.32	1.33	0.46	3.04	5.11	3.50	35.43
1971	2.02	6.21	1.90	1.75	6.12	2.92	4.03	10.91	5.55	6.88	3.75	1.29	53.33
1972	2.82	6.01	2.38	5.30	4.11	9.95	2.81	2.22	1.15	3.51	7.05	5.02	52.33
1973	2.81	2.82	3.96	6.41	3.73	3.16	4.22	3.35	4.87	2.86	1.28	6.36	45.83
1974	2.92	0.94	4.12	2.59	3.58	2.84	0.85	5.85	5.45	1.53	1.39	5.70	37.76
1975	3.47	2.47	5.17	2.73	4.63	3.82	7.15	4.23	8.62	2.89	2.03	4.61	51.82
1976	4.10	2.16	2.23	1.27	5.03	2.49	5.56	2.98	6.93	8.09	0.56	2.04	43.44
1977	1.36	0.63	3.93	3.05	1.49	3.44	2.62	3.31	0.62	5.17	5.01	5.76	36.39
1978	7.34	0.56	4.74	1.26	5.49	2.81	6.83	3.39	1.03	0.71	2.70	4.63	41.49
1979	7.84	7.16	2.05	3.37	4.15	5.74	3.71	9.38	6.73	5.53	2.45	0.87	58.98
1980	2.58	1.06	5.46	4.24	3.58	3.04	3.25	4.00	1.00	3.08	2.72	0.70	34.71
1981	0.49	2.93	1.14	2.04	3.63	5.40	4.59	1.93	2.89	2.57	0.31	3.30	31.22
1982	3.37	4.04	3.03	3.61	1.85	5.70	2.16	0.95	3.63	2.31	3.13	2.39	36.17
1983	2.21	4.81	6.80	6.55	5.47	5.23	1.31	1.57	1.76	3.58	5.02	6.72	51.03
1984	1.96	3.90	5.79	2.95	4.29	1.65	3.27	4.11	2.38	1.94	3.01	1.71	36.96
1985	2.03	3.03	2.37	0.39	6.01	2.44	2.53	3.72	6.22	2.48	4.71	0.84	36.77
1986	2.16	3.78	0.96	2.64	0.37	1.46	4.12	4.26	0.58	1.86	5.96	5.52	33.67
1987	5.85	2.22	0.99	1.86	4.16	2.63	5.05	1.61	7.34	2.25	5.05	2.07	41.08
1988	3.24	3.25	2.35	2.44	4.37	0.84	3.78	2.64	2.05	1.59	4.78	0.97	32.30
1989	3.07	3.36	4.24	3.16	8.71	5.98	7.35	3.38	3.64	4.90	1.97	2.12	51.88
1990	3.71	1.48	2.54	4.23	4.92	2.55	5.68	6.17	1.07	2.57	2.10	4.86	41.88
1991	3.54	0.73	5.65	1.68	1.16	1.08	1.76	2.54	3.05	3.20	1.69	4.08	30.16
1992	1.27	2.49	4.58	1.76	2.92	1.89	5.07	2.19	5.96	2.73	3.44	4.63	38.93
1993	2.73	2.84	8.12	3.68	3.66	2.56	1.71	2.55	4.09	3.02	3.09	4.45	42.50
Record Mean	2.92	2.99	3.73	3.20	3.60	3.54	3.84	4.10	3.45	2.98	3.20	3.39	40.93

AVERAGE TEMPERATURE (deg. F)

BALTIMORE, MARYLAND

YEAR	JAN	FEB	MAR	APR	MAY	JUNE	JULY	AUG	SEP	OCT	NOV	DEC	ANNUAL
1964	33.8	33.2	44.4	50.9	65.3	72.7	77.0	73.5	68.1	53.3	49.8	39.1	55.1
1965	30.8	34.9	39.2	50.3	66.9	70.1	76.8	75.5	70.8	53.9	45.6	38.3	54.4
1966	29.8	30.5	43.3	49.5	61.7	72.9	78.9	76.5	66.7	53.4	46.4	35.6	53.8
1967	37.4	30.7	41.8	54.0	57.0	72.7	75.2	73.4	65.3	55.3	42.0	37.3	53.5
1968	29.2	32.2	46.6	54.0	59.7	72.6	78.2	78.7	70.3	59.7	48.2	34.6	55.3
1969	31.7	34.9	40.7	56.2	65.5	74.9	77.4	76.5	69.5	57.7	46.1	35.2	55.5
1970	27.8	35.4	40.4	53.3	66.6	73.0	77.2	77.4	73.7	61.5	48.6	38.2	56.1
1971	30.0	37.4	41.8	52.7	61.2	74.0	76.5	74.2	70.9	62.9	46.4	43.7	56.0
1972	37.6	34.3	43.6	51.6	62.7	68.1	76.9	75.4	69.8	53.5	43.2	40.4	54.8
1973	34.6	34.3	48.3	53.1	59.6	73.5	75.9	76.9	69.8	58.2	47.3	37.3	55.7
1974	37.9	33.8	45.2	55.3	61.9	68.5	76.5	75.0	67.5	55.3	48.2	40.3	55.4
1975	38.5	39.1	42.1	50.4	66.3	73.0	76.1	77.9	66.0	60.7	51.9	37.2	56.6
1976	30.8	44.1	48.1	56.9	62.1	74.8	75.0	73.9	67.5	52.9	40.9	32.6	55.0
1977	22.9	36.5	50.0	57.9	66.7	71.4	79.0	77.7	72.1	56.0	49.2	35.6	56.3
1978	29.2	27.3	41.7	54.2	62.4	73.1	75.9	78.1	69.7	56.1	48.7	40.2	54.7
1979	33.1	25.6	48.5	53.1	64.7	70.7	75.9	75.7	68.8	55.7	50.6	40.3	55.2
1980	33.8	31.5	41.5	55.7	65.5	71.3	78.2	78.7	72.2	55.3	44.2	35.5	55.3
1981	27.9	38.8	41.9	57.0	62.2	74.3	77.3	74.4	67.7	53.2	46.2	34.5	54.6
1982	25.5	35.8	42.9	50.7	66.1	69.4	77.1	73.0	67.3	56.3	48.4	42.0	54.6
1983	34.6	34.7	45.4	51.8	61.5	72.1	78.7	78.0	69.5	57.3	47.1	33.2	55.3
1984	28.5	41.7	38.2	51.5	61.3	73.4	73.9	75.0	64.8	62.2	43.9	44.1	54.9
1985	29.3	38.7	46.0	57.9	65.1	70.4	76.4	74.5	69.4	58.8	52.4	33.8	56.1
1986	33.2	32.9	45.0	53.5	66.7	74.4	79.4	73.1	68.9	58.9	44.8	38.2	55.8
1987	32.5	34.3	46.2	53.1	65.0	74.5	80.0	76.1	69.3	51.5	47.8	39.8	55.8
1988	28.7	35.9	45.1	52.0	64.0	73.0	80.3	78.5	66.8	51.3	48.1	36.3	55.0
1989	37.9	36.5	43.8	52.5	62.0	73.9	76.0	74.4	69.0	58.3	44.8	25.4	54.5
1990	42.0	42.3	47.6	54.8	62.3	73.3	78.4	74.6	67.3	60.7	49.6	42.2	57.9
1991	35.5	40.7	46.7	55.9	70.6	74.6	79.5	77.8	69.0	57.8	45.8	38.7	57.7
1992	34.6	37.1	41.3	52.0	60.8	70.1	77.4	72.3	67.7	54.3	47.2	38.9	54.5
1993	37.9	31.4	39.4	52.5	65.0	72.2	80.2	76.7	68.8	55.5	46.5	36.2	55.2
Record Mean	32.8	35.3	43.4	53.8	63.5	72.3	77.1	75.5	68.6	56.8	46.4	36.7	55.2
Max	41.2	44.3	53.2	64.7	74.3	83.0	87.3	85.3	78.7	67.5	56.1	45.2	65.1
Min	24.3	26.4	33.5	42.9	52.7	61.6	66.9	65.6	58.4	46.1	36.7	28.2	45.3

REFERENCE NOTES

BALTIMORE, MARYLAND

GENERAL
T - TRACE AMOUNT.
BLANK ENTRIES DENOTE MISSING/UNREPORTED DATA.
# INDICATES A STATION OR INSTRUMENT RELOCATION.

SPECIFIC

PM - INCLUDES LAST DAY OF PREVIOUS MONTH
ASOS - AUTOMATED SURFACE OBSERVING SYSTEM IN OPERATION DURING THESE MONTHS.

(a) - LENGTH OF RECORD IN YEARS, ALTHOUGH INDIVIDUAL MONTHS MAY BE MISSING.
0.* OR * - THE VALUE IS BETWEEN 0.0 AND 0.05
NORMALS - BASED ON THE 1961-1990 RECORD PERIOD.
EXTREMES - DATES ARE THE MOST RECENT OCCURRENCE
WIND DIR.- NUMERALS SHOW TENS OF DEGRESS CLOCKWISE FROM TRUE NORTH. "00" INDICATES CALM.
RESULTANT DIRECTIONS ARE GIVEN TO WHOLE DEGREES.
BOLD VALUES INDICATE EXTREME VALUES WHICH OCCURRED AFTER THE ASOS SYSTEM WAS COMMISSIONED.

RECORD = PERIOD OF RECORD
RECORD MEAN PRECIPITATION IS THE MEAN OF ALL DAILY PRECIPITATION AMOUNTS DURING THE PERIOD OF RECORD.
RECORD MAX(MIN) TEMPERATURE IS THE MEAN OF ALL DAILY MAX(MIN) TEMPERATURES DURING THE PERIOD OF RECORD.
RECORD MEAN TEMPERATURE IS THE SUM OF THE RECORD MAX AND RECORD MIN DIVIDED BY 2.
AVERAGE TEMPERATURE IS THE SUM OF THE MEAN DAILY MAX AND MIN TEMPERATURE DIVIDED BY 2.

EXCEPTIONS

RECORD MEANS ARE THROUGH THE CURRENT YEAR, BEGINNING IN 1951 FOR TEMPERATURE
1951 FOR PRECIPITATION
1951 FOR SNOWFALL

HEATING DEGREE DAYS Base 65 deg. F — BALTIMORE, MARYLAND

SEASON	JULY	AUG	SEP	OCT	NOV	DEC	JAN	FEB	MAR	APR	MAY	JUNE	TOTAL
1964-65	0	0	41	358	448	797	1052	838	792	433	55	44	4858
1965-66	0	5	34	336	576	819	1085	961	665	460	157	23	5121
1966-67	0	0	68	353	555	905	846	955	715	338	254	6	4995
1967-68	0	0	75	318	684	851	1100	943	566	324	173	1	5035
1968-69	0	1	4	197	500	934	1028	835	748	273	69	0	4589
1969-70	0	0	26	251	561	916	1148	822	752	346	77	0	4899
1970-71	0	0	20	149	484	824	1080	766	712	364	134	2	4535
1971-72	0	0	24	96	571	652	841	884	663	396	94	42	4263
1972-73	2	0	16	357	649	759	935	854	511	365	191	1	4640
1973-74	0	0	24	221	524	852	830	868	613	309	148	14	4403
1974-75	0	0	49	303	509	759	818	720	702	436	66	2	4364
1975-76	0	0	50	156	397	853	1050	603	518	293	133	11	4064
1976-77	0	0	34	377	716	1001	1296	790	469	245	62	18	5008
1977-78	0	0	9	278	476	904	1101	1048	715	318	141	9	4999
1978-79	0	0	33	280	483	763	984	1100	520	354	75	6	4598
1979-80	2	3	22	311	425	757	962	967	723	273	74	6	4525
1980-81	0	0	20	311	620	908	1145	727	706	252	148	1	4838
1981-82	0	0	51	363	557	940	1218	808	677	422	58	20	5114
1982-83	0	5	42	289	495	707	936	842	602	410	152	6	4486
1983-84	0	0	70	257	530	979	1123	671	825	397	169	9	5030
1984-85	0	1	96	123	625	643	1101	731	589	252	79	10	4250
1985-86	0	0	41	201	378	962	980	892	613	342	86	6	4501
1986-87	0	23	34	236	598	822	1002	853	576	357	106	1	4608
1987-88	0	1	15	412	511	774	1120	838	613	389	96	27	4796
1988-89	2	0	39	424	504	882	834	792	663	374	145	0	4659
1989-90	0	0	51	229	600	1221	707	631	552	341	102	5	4439
1990-91	1	0	63	195	454	701	907	674	562	289	55	4	3905
1991-92	0	0	49	246	570	809	936	802	730	387	161	8	4698
1992-93	0	1	51	328	529	801	834	934	787	369	61	11	4706
1993-94	0	0	52	292	553	886							

COOLING DEGREE DAYS Base 65 deg. F — BALTIMORE, MARYLAND

YEAR	JAN	FEB	MAR	APR	MAY	JUNE	JULY	AUG	SEP	OCT	NOV	DEC	TOTAL
1969	0	0	0	16	93	304	392	364	169	33	0	0	1371
1970	0	0	0	4	134	246	389	390	291	45	0	0	1499
1971	0	0	0	0	24	278	363	293	208	36	20	0	1222
1972	0	0	5	1	29	140	379	331	166	7	0	0	1058
1973	0	0	0	15	29	263	344	376	173	19	0	0	1219
1974	0	0	4	24	57	126	361	317	130	8	11	0	1038
1975	0	0	0	4	112	252	351	404	85	27	10	0	1245
1976	0	1	0	58	51	315	317	284	114	9	0	0	1149
1977	0	0	10	37	124	217	439	401	229	7	10	0	1474
1978	0	0	0	0	63	260	344	413	182	12	0	0	1274
1979	0	0	15	4	72	183	348	341	145	28	1	0	1137
1980	0	0	0	0	97	203	415	431	245	17	0	0	1408
1981	0	0	0	19	69	287	389	296	141	5	0	0	1206
1982	0	0	0	4	99	160	381	259	119	26	4	1	1053
1983	0	0	0	18	51	228	430	410	214	24	0	0	1375
1984	0	0	0	0	59	268	281	316	98	41	0	2	1065
1985	0	2	7	43	89	179	363	298	178	17	5	0	1181
1986	0	0	0	1	143	295	452	281	158	54	0	0	1384
1987	0	0	0	7	115	292	473	352	152	0	0	0	1391
1988	0	0	2	4	71	274	485	427	100	8	0	0	1371
1989	0	0	14	5	58	276	351	298	178	25	1	0	1206
1990	0	0	19	38	26	261	422	303	137	68	0	0	1274
1991	0	0	2	24	233	303	462	402	177	29	2	0	1634
1992	0	0	0	6	39	168	392	232	139	4	0	0	980
1993	0	0	0	0	70	235	476	371	175	3	5	0	1335

SNOWFALL (inches) — BALTIMORE, MARYLAND

SEASON	JULY	AUG	SEP	OCT	NOV	DEC	JAN	FEB	MAR	APR	MAY	JUNE	TOTAL
1964-65	0.0	0.0	0.0	0.0	T	0.8	8.3	1.1	8.4	0.0	0.0	0.0	18.6
1965-66	0.0	0.0	0.0	0.0	0.0	T	21.4	11.4	0.0	T	0.0	0.0	32.8
1966-67	0.0	0.0	0.0	0.0	T	20.4	0.4	20.1	2.5	0.0	0.0	0.0	43.4
1967-68	0.0	0.0	0.0	0.0	8.4	4.6	2.5	2.6	5.3	0.0	0.0	0.0	23.4
1968-69	0.0	0.0	0.0	0.0	4.3	T	0.1	6.4	7.8	0.0	0.0	0.0	18.6
1969-70	0.0	0.0	0.0	0.0	T	9.0	6.1	4.0	1.9	T	0.0	0.0	21.0
1970-71	0.0	0.0	0.0	0.0	0.0	6.3	4.1	0.6	2.0	T	0.0	0.0	13.0
1971-72	0.0	0.0	0.0	0.0	1.0	T	1.1	11.4	0.2	0.3	0.0	0.0	14.0
1972-73	0.0	0.0	0.0	T	T	T	T	1.2	T	T	0.0	0.0	1.2
1973-74	0.0	0.0	0.0	0.0	0.0	8.3	1.2	7.6	T	T	0.0	0.0	17.1
1974-75	0.0	0.0	0.0	0.0	T	0.4	5.1	5.5	1.2	T	0.0	0.0	12.2
1975-76	0.0	0.0	0.0	0.0	0.0	0.7	1.7	1.3	7.8	0.0	0.0	0.0	11.5
1976-77	0.0	0.0	0.0	0.0	1.1	1.5	8.5	T	T	T	0.0	0.0	11.1
1977-78	0.0	0.0	0.0	T	0.6	0.5	12.4	12.3	8.5	T	0.0	0.0	34.3
1978-79	0.0	0.0	0.0	0.0	3.7	0.0	5.7	33.1	T	T	0.0	0.0	42.5
1979-80	0.0	0.0	0.0	0.3	T	0.1	4.7	3.8	5.7	0.0	0.0	0.0	14.6
1980-81	0.0	0.0	0.0	0.0	T	0.2	4.1	T	0.3	0.0	0.0	0.0	4.6
1981-82	0.0	0.0	0.0	0.0	T	2.4	14.8	7.6	0.7	T	0.0	0.0	25.5
1982-83	0.0	0.0	0.0	0.0	0.0	7.2	1.2	27.2	T	T	0.0	0.0	35.6
1983-84	0.0	0.0	0.0	0.0	T	T	8.4	T	6.1	T	0.0	0.0	14.5
1984-85	0.0	0.0	0.0	0.0	T	0.1	9.1	0.4	T	0.7	0.0	0.0	10.3
1985-86	0.0	0.0	0.0	0.0	0.0	0.7	1.9	13.0	T	T	0.0	0.0	15.6
1986-87	0.0	0.0	0.0	0.0	0.0	T	25.1	10.1	T	T	0.0	0.0	35.2
1987-88	0.0	0.0	0.0	0.0	6.0	0.5	13.7	0.2	T	T	0.0	0.0	20.4
1988-89	0.0	0.0	0.0	0.0	0.0	0.9	6.0	1.1	0.3	0.0	0.0	0.0	8.3
1989-90	0.0	0.0	0.0	0.0	3.8	10.2	0.5	T	2.7	0.1	0.0	0.0	17.3
1990-91	0.0	0.0	0.0	0.0	0.0	4.8	4.2	0.1	0.3	0.0	0.0	0.0	9.4
1991-92	T	0.0	0.0	0.0	T	T	2.2	1.9	T	T	0.0	0.0	4.1
1992-93	T	0.0	0.0	0.0	T	1.5	1.4	8.8	12.7	T	0.0	0.0	24.4
1993-94	0.0	0.0	0.0	0.0	T	2.9							
Record Mean	T	0.0	0.0	T	1.0	3.5	5.9	6.5	3.8	0.1	T	0.0	20.6

BOSTON, MASSACHUSETTS

Climate is the composite of numerous weather elements. Three important influences are responsible for the main features of the Boston climate. First, the latitude places the city in the zone of prevailing west to east atmospheric flow. Both polar and tropical air masses influence the region. Secondly, Boston is situated on or near several tracks frequently followed by low pressure storm systems. The weather fluctuates regularly from fair to cloudy to stormy conditions and assures an adequate amount of precipitation. The third factor is the east-coast location of Boston. The ocean has a moderating influence on temperature extremes of winter and summer.

Hot summer afternoons are frequently relieved by the locally celebrated sea breeze, as air flows inland from the cool water surface to displace the warm air over the land. This refreshing east wind is more commonly experienced along the shore than in the interior of the city or the western suburbs. In winter, under appropriate conditions, the severity of cold waves is reduced by the nearness of the relatively warm ocean. The average last occurrence of freezing temperature in spring is early April and the first occurrence of freezing temperature in autumn is early November. In suburban areas, especially away from the coast, these dates are later in spring and earlier in autumn by up to one month in the more susceptible localities.

Boston has no dry season. Most growing seasons have several shorter dry spells during which irrigation for high-value crops may be useful. Much of the rainfall from June to September comes from showers and thunderstorms. During the rest of the year, low pressure systems pass more or less regularly and produce precipitation on an average of roughly one day in three. Coastal storms, or northeasters, are prolific producers of rain and snow. The main snow season extends from December through March. Periods when the ground is bare or nearly bare of snow may occur at any time in the winter.

Relative humidity has been known to fall as low as 5 percent but such desert dryness is very rare. Heavy fog occurs on an average of about two days per month with its prevalence increasing eastward from the interior of Boston Bay to the open waters beyond.

Although winds of 30 mph or higher may be expected on at least one day in every month of the year, gales are both more common and more severe in winter.

NORMALS, MEANS, AND EXTREMES

BOSTON, MASSACHUSETTS

LATITUDE: 42°22'N LONGITUDE: 71°02' W ELEVATION: FT. GRND 15 BARO 30 TIME ZONE: EASTERN WBAN: 14739

	(a)	JAN	FEB	MAR	APR	MAY	JUNE	JULY	AUG	SEP	OCT	NOV	DEC	YEAR
TEMPERATURE °F:														
Normals														
-Daily Maximum		35.7	37.5	45.8	55.9	66.6	76.3	81.8	79.8	72.8	62.7	52.2	40.4	59.0
-Daily Minimum		21.6	23.0	31.3	40.2	49.8	59.1	65.1	64.0	56.8	46.9	38.3	26.7	43.6
-Monthly		28.6	30.3	38.6	48.1	58.2	67.7	73.5	71.9	64.8	54.8	45.3	33.6	51.3
Extremes														
-Record Highest	42	63	70	81	94	95	100	102	102	100	90	78	73	102
-Year		1990	1985	1989	1976	1979	1952	1977	1975	1953	1963	1993	1984	JUL 1977
-Record Lowest	42	-12	-4	6	16	34	45	50	47	38	28	15	-7	-12
-Year		1957	1961	1984	1982	1956	1986	1988	1986	1965	1976	1989	1980	JAN 1957
NORMAL DEGREE DAYS:														
Heating (base 65°F)		1128	972	818	507	221	32	0	6	72	321	591	973	5641
Cooling (base 65°F)		0	0	0	0	10	113	264	220	66	5	0	0	678
% OF POSSIBLE SUNSHINE	58	53	56	57	56	59	63	66	65	63	60	50	52	58
MEAN SKY COVER (tenths)														
Sunrise - Sunset	58	6.2	6.2	6.4	6.6	6.6	6.3	6.2	5.7	5.6	5.6	6.4	6.3	6.2
MEAN NUMBER OF DAYS:														
Sunrise to Sunset														
-Clear	58	9.0	8.2	7.8	7.0	6.3	6.6	6.7	9.1	10.3	10.8	7.9	8.6	98.4
-Partly Cloudy	58	6.8	6.7	8.1	8.1	9.9	10.5	12.2	10.8	8.1	7.8	7.3	7.5	103.7
-Cloudy	58	15.1	13.3	15.1	14.9	14.8	12.9	12.1	11.1	11.7	12.4	14.8	14.9	163.2
Precipitation .01 inches or more	42	11.4	10.5	11.9	11.3	11.5	10.6	9.2	9.9	8.7	9.1	10.9	11.6	126.5
Snow, Ice pellets, hail 1.0 inches or more	58	3.1	2.6	2.1	0.3	0.0	0.0	0.0	0.0	0.0	0.0	0.4	2.1	10.7
Thunderstorms	58	0.2	0.2	0.6	1.0	2.2	3.7	4.3	3.6	1.6	0.7	0.4	0.2	18.6
Heavy Fog Visibility 1/4 mile or less	58	1.8	1.6	2.0	1.7	2.8	1.9	2.2	1.8	1.9	2.2	1.8	1.3	23.2
Temperature °F														
-Maximum														
90° and above	29	0.0	0.0	0.0	0.1	0.5	2.6	5.4	3.4	0.8	0.0	0.0	0.0	12.9
32° and below	29	11.1	7.7	2.1	0.*	0.0	0.0	0.0	0.0	0.0	0.0	0.3	5.7	27.0
-Minimum														
32° and below	29	26.0	23.3	16.6	2.4	0.0	0.0	0.0	0.0	0.0	0.6	7.0	21.6	97.4
0° and below	29	0.5	0.3	0.0	0.0	0.0	0.0	0.0	0.0	0.0	0.0	0.0	0.2	1.0
AVG. STATION PRESS. (mb)	21	1015.0	1015.4	1014.6	1013.2	1014.1	1013.3	1013.8	1015.7	1017.1	1017.3	1016.3	1016.1	1015.2
RELATIVE HUMIDITY (%)														
Hour 01	29	65	65	67	69	74	77	77	79	80	76	71	68	72
Hour 07 (Local Time)	29	67	67	69	69	72	73	73	77	79	77	74	70	72
Hour 13	29	57	56	57	55	59	58	57	59	60	58	59	59	58
Hour 19	29	61	59	62	62	65	66	66	69	71	68	66	63	65
PRECIPITATION (inches):														
Water Equivalent														
-Normal		3.59	3.62	3.69	3.60	3.25	3.09	2.84	3.24	3.06	3.30	4.22	4.01	41.51
-Maximum Monthly	42	10.55	7.81	11.00	9.46	13.38	13.20	8.12	17.09	8.31	8.68	8.89	9.74	17.09
-Year		1979	1984	1953	1987	1954	1982	1959	1955	1954	1962	1983	1969	AUG 1955
-Minimum Monthly	42	0.61	0.72	0.62	1.24	0.53	0.48	0.52	0.83	0.35	0.96	0.64	0.81	0.35
-Year		1989	1987	1981	1966	1964	1953	1952	1972	1957	1967	1976	1989	SEP 1957
-Maximum in 24 hrs	42	2.72	2.68	4.13	3.32	5.74	4.17	2.43	8.40	5.64	4.26	3.76	5.14	8.40
-Year		1979	1969	1968	1991	1954	1984	1988	1955	1954	1962	1992	1992	AUG 1955
Snow, Ice pellets, hail														
-Maximum Monthly	58	35.9	41.3	38.9	13.3	0.5	0.0	0.0	0.0	0.0	0.2	10.0	27.9	41.3
-Year		1978	1969	1993	1982	1977					1979	1938	1970	FEB 1969
-Maximum in 24 hrs	58	21.0	23.6	17.7	13.2	0.5	0.0	0.0	0.0	0.0	0.2	8.0	13.0	23.6
-Year		1978	1978	1960	1982	1977					1979	1987	1960	FEB 1978
WIND:														
Mean Speed (mph)	36	13.8	13.8	13.7	13.2	12.2	11.5	11.0	10.8	11.3	12.0	12.9	13.6	12.5
Prevailing Direction through 1963		NW	WNW	NW	WNW	SW	SW	SW	SW	SW	SW	SW	WNW	SW
Fastest Obs. 1 Min.														
-Direction (!!)	8	18	30	06	05	09	28	35	08	21	09	31	05	06
-Speed (MPH)	8	40	37	54	38	33	45	37	47	35	41	38	51	54
-Year		1992	1991	1993	1991	1992	1988	1989	1991	1989	1988	1989	1992	MAR 1993
Peak Gust														
-Direction (!!)	10	S	NW	NE	NE	S	W	NW	NW	S	NE	NW	NE	NE
-Speed (mph)	10	59	58	81	55	52	68	54	64	76	55	55	78	81
-Date		1992	1991	1993	1991	1989	1988	1989	1991	1985	1991	1989	1992	MAR 1993

PRECIPITATION (inches)

BOSTON, MASSACHUSETTS

YEAR	JAN	FEB	MAR	APR	MAY	JUNE	JULY	AUG	SEP	OCT	NOV	DEC	ANNUAL
1964	4.56	4.67	3.48	3.69	0.53	1.91	3.12	1.78	2.65	2.82	2.18	5.08	36.47
1965	2.64	3.17	2.22	2.32	0.93	2.99	0.55	1.48	2.01	1.59	2.08	1.73	23.71
1966	5.29	3.48	1.98	1.24	2.66	3.40	3.21	1.25	3.42	2.62	4.43	3.03	36.01
1967	2.28	4.05	4.67	4.83	7.32	3.48	2.47	5.74	2.00	0.96	3.38	6.42	47.60
1968	3.85	1.15	7.86	1.72	3.26	5.65	0.55	1.63	1.79	1.85	6.74	6.23	42.28
1969	2.26	7.08	2.63	4.37	1.96	0.63	2.98	1.89	4.42	1.64	8.18	9.74	47.78
1970	0.89	4.65	4.32	2.79	3.01	4.62	1.27	4.12	2.60	2.63	4.09	6.92	41.91
1971	1.88	5.05	3.08	2.92	3.72	1.74	2.84	1.59	1.55	2.16	6.74	2.40	35.67
1972	2.05	5.29	5.37	3.34	5.26	6.76	2.19	0.83	5.94	2.98	7.02	6.08	53.11
1973	3.12	2.13	2.20	5.65	3.76	4.68	4.83	2.78	1.95	2.71	1.74	7.20	42.75
1974	3.22	3.24	4.01	3.86	2.87	2.29	1.54	3.41	7.03	3.12	1.73	3.92	40.24
1975	5.70	3.37	2.74	2.40	1.78	2.10	2.35	5.52	5.49	4.41	5.13	4.80	45.79
1976	5.29	2.45	2.42	2.00	1.98	0.58	4.30	7.99	1.56	4.16	0.64	3.35	36.72
1977	4.41	2.40	4.76	4.07	3.52	2.49	2.21	2.91	4.03	4.63	2.54	6.20	44.17
1978	8.12	2.87	2.46	1.79	4.50	1.53	1.48	4.62	1.30	3.13	2.21	3.63	37.64
1979	10.55	3.46	3.03	3.19	4.24	0.86	2.36	5.02	3.61	3.14	3.29	1.42	44.17
1980	0.74	0.88	5.37	4.36	2.30	3.05	2.20	1.55	0.82	4.14	3.01	0.97	29.39
1981	0.95	6.65	0.62	3.14	1.17	1.65	3.47	1.04	2.54	3.43	4.78	6.27	35.71
1982	4.69	2.66	2.17	3.42	2.58	13.20	4.22	2.22	1.57	3.19	3.42	1.27	44.61
1983	5.03	5.00	9.72	6.86	2.94	1.07	1.07	3.28	1.06	3.74	8.89	4.94	53.60
1984	2.31	7.81	6.82	4.43	8.77	3.06	4.43	1.60	1.22	5.18	1.68	2.93	50.24
1985	1.12	1.83	2.29	1.62	3.36	3.94	3.51	6.67	3.00	1.65	6.39	1.21	36.59
1986	3.42	2.83	3.42	1.59	1.31	7.74	3.96	3.32	1.08	3.27	6.01	6.38	44.33
1987	7.28	0.72	4.27	9.46	1.75	2.62	0.82	2.93	7.29	2.73	3.49	2.12	45.48
1988	2.50	3.93	3.52	1.47	2.86	1.29	7.62	1.11	1.29	1.60	6.57	1.02	34.78
1989	0.61	2.51	3.07	3.58	3.54	2.84	5.09	5.92	4.61	5.71	4.13	0.81	42.42
1990	3.78	3.60	1.71	5.94	6.53	0.69	4.08	6.57	1.67	7.36	1.39	3.18	46.50
1991	3.24	1.58	4.33	4.84	0.92	2.89	1.95	5.27	6.32	4.27	4.06	2.58	42.25
1992	3.11	2.28	3.59	2.34	1.40	4.61	2.66	4.25	3.46	1.62	6.14	8.26	43.72
1993	2.17	4.94	7.67	4.86	1.04	1.75	1.75	1.32	4.64	3.61	2.86	6.60	43.21
Record Mean	3.62	3.38	3.86	3.61	3.22	3.15	3.15	3.60	3.19	3.29	3.91	3.65	41.62

AVERAGE TEMPERATURE (deg. F)

BOSTON, MASSACHUSETTS

YEAR	JAN	FEB	MAR	APR	MAY	JUNE	JULY	AUG	SEP	OCT	NOV	DEC	ANNUAL
#1964	31.7	29.1	38.7	46.1	60.3	67.1	71.5	66.4	62.0	52.5	44.1	32.4	50.2
1965	25.4	28.0	35.8	44.2	59.5	67.4	71.0	70.5	62.5	52.8	42.1	36.1	49.6
1966	28.8	31.3	39.8	45.9	57.3	69.4	74.9	71.3	63.5	54.5	46.9	34.2	51.5
1967	35.1	26.4	33.2	44.9	51.7	67.2	73.0	70.9	62.7	53.8	40.1	35.0	49.5
1968	25.6	26.1	39.1	49.6	56.1	64.9	75.2	70.7	65.0	57.9	43.8	30.9	50.4
1969	29.3	29.5	35.4	50.6	58.5	69.3	71.0	74.3	63.7	54.3	44.9	33.4	51.2
1970	23.0	32.3	37.4	49.0	59.6	67.0	74.3	73.6	65.6	54.9	44.8	28.9	50.9
1971	23.8	30.5	36.7	45.1	55.7	69.1	73.4	73.4	68.0	59.8	43.1	36.3	51.2
1972	33.0	29.6	36.3	44.9	57.6	65.4	73.8	71.5	65.7	51.8	42.3	33.0	50.4
1973	31.4	30.1	43.3	49.9	57.0	70.0	74.3	74.8	64.4	55.6	45.8	39.6	53.0
1974	31.7	29.1	38.7	50.9	54.7	64.8	72.4	72.0	63.7	50.1	45.3	37.8	50.9
1975	34.9	32.1	36.9	45.1	61.5	67.5	75.9	72.9	63.9	57.3	51.8	34.4	52.8
1976	26.1	37.3	41.2	55.1	60.2	73.4	72.9	72.0	64.9	52.3	41.9	29.0	52.2
1977	23.3	30.7	44.7	51.3	62.6	67.4	74.9	73.4	64.4	55.3	48.1	34.2	52.5
1978	28.5	27.1	36.2	48.8	59.3	68.3	72.1	71.6	61.4	52.5	43.6	35.3	50.4
1979	32.5	23.1	42.5	48.7	61.1	68.2	74.5	71.7	64.9	52.7	48.6	36.7	52.1
1980	29.4	27.9	36.9	48.7	59.4	66.3	75.8	74.2	67.0	52.4	41.2	28.6	50.6
1981	21.4	36.4	39.1	51.7	60.4	70.7	74.6	72.1	63.7	51.2	43.9	33.2	51.5
1982	22.9	30.8	38.7	48.2	57.8	63.3	74.9	70.3	64.1	54.2	47.6	39.6	51.0
1983	31.2	32.8	40.6	49.1	58.2	70.7	78.0	73.6	70.6	55.2	46.1	32.1	53.2
1984	26.7	37.6	31.9	46.1	58.0	70.5	74.7	74.6	62.1	53.3	44.6	39.5	51.6
1985	24.4	32.8	40.4	49.3	59.3	64.8	73.5	70.4	65.4	55.4	45.4	31.3	51.0
1986	31.4	28.9	40.7	48.4	58.4	66.1	71.0	70.5	63.2	54.0	42.3	35.5	50.9
1987	28.9	29.1	38.5	45.1	57.2	65.1	71.7	70.3	65.4	54.3	43.9	36.1	50.5
1988	27.8	32.2	39.2	46.8	57.6	68.5	73.7	75.5	64.6	50.8	46.7	32.8	51.4
1989	34.5	30.5	37.3	45.9	59.4	67.8	72.8	71.6	64.7	55.3	42.8	21.7	50.4
1990	36.4	34.1	40.1	47.6	54.9	66.6	73.1	73.3	64.6	58.3	48.5	40.7	53.2
1991	29.4	36.1	41.6	51.3	63.3	70.0	74.6	73.8	63.7	56.4	45.2	36.0	53.5
1992	31.0	32.4	35.4	46.4	55.6	67.8	69.5	70.4	63.9	52.5	42.9	34.8	50.2
1993	32.4	27.1	36.4	48.3	60.3	69.5	74.7	73.6	64.8	52.3	45.6	34.2	51.6
Record Mean	28.8	29.4	37.1	47.2	57.9	67.2	72.7	71.0	64.1	54.0	43.7	32.8	50.5
Max	36.3	37.1	44.6	55.2	66.5	75.9	81.1	78.9	72.1	62.0	50.8	39.8	58.4
Min	21.3	21.8	29.6	39.1	49.3	58.4	64.3	63.0	56.1	46.1	36.5	25.7	42.6

REFERENCE NOTES

BOSTON, MASSACHUSETTS

GENERAL
T - TRACE AMOUNT.
BLANK ENTRIES DENOTE MISSING/UNREPORTED DATA.
# INDICATES A STATION OR INSTRUMENT RELOCATION.

SPECIFIC

PM - INCLUDES LAST DAY OF PREVIOUS MONTH
ASOS - AUTOMATED SURFACE OBSERVING SYSTEM IN OPERATION DURING THESE MONTHS.

(a) - LENGTH OF RECORD IN YEARS, ALTHOUGH INDIVIDUAL MONTHS MAY BE MISSING.
0.* OR * - THE VALUE IS BETWEEN 0.0 AND 0.05
NORMALS - BASED ON THE 1961-1990 RECORD PERIOD.
EXTREMES - DATES ARE THE MOST RECENT OCCURRENCE
WIND DIR.- NUMERALS SHOW TENS OF DEGRESS CLOCKWISE FROM TRUE NORTH. "00" INDICATES CALM.
RESULTANT DIRECTIONS ARE GIVEN TO WHOLE DEGREES.
BOLD VALUES INDICATE EXTREME VALUES WHICH OCCURRED AFTER THE ASOS SYSTEM WAS COMMISSIONED.

RECORD = PERIOD OF RECORD
RECORD MEAN PRECIPITATION IS THE MEAN OF ALL DAILY PRECIPITATION AMOUNTS DURING THE PERIOD OF RECORD.
RECORD MAX(MIN) TEMPERATURE IS THE MEAN OF ALL DAILY MAX(MIN) TEMPERATURES DURING THE PERIOD OF RECORD.
RECORD MEAN TEMPERATURE IS THE SUM OF THE RECORD MAX AND RECORD MIN DIVIDED BY 2.
AVERAGE TEMPERATURE IS THE SUM OF THE MEAN DAILY MAX AND MIN TEMPERATURE DIVIDED BY 2.

EXCEPTIONS

RECORD MEANS ARE THROUGH THE CURRENT YEAR, BEGINNING IN 1872 FOR TEMPERATURE
1871 FOR PRECIPITATION
1936 FOR SNOWFALL

HEATING DEGREE DAYS Base 65 deg. F BOSTON, MASSACHUSETTS

SEASON	JULY	AUG	SEP	OCT	NOV	DEC	JAN	FEB	MAR	APR	MAY	JUNE	TOTAL
1964-65	14	26	140	380	620	1004	1220	1032	900	617	195	80	6228
1965-66	2	37	136	371	680	888	1115	936	776	566	258	46	5811
1966-67	0	1	88	322	535	950	921	1075	977	596	403	58	5926
1967-68	0	4	110	347	739	923	1214	1122	797	454	270	76	6056
1968-69	1	9	46	247	630	1050	1099	987	911	430	208	21	5639
1969-70	2	3	107	326	595	973	1295	909	846	473	184	52	5765
1970-71	0	0	68	314	598	1113	1269	962	868	586	287	25	6090
1971-72	0	2	37	169	651	882	985	1021	883	598	250	54	5532
1972-73	3	4	51	405	673	985	1033	971	666	450	258	24	5523
1973-74	0	2	94	289	570	782	1023	1000	809	429	335	77	5410
1974-75	0	2	102	458	587	836	925	918	866	590	162	59	5505
1975-76	0	8	70	239	395	941	1198	800	733	331	166	16	4897
1976-77	1	10	55	393	688	1108	1290	956	623	414	158	43	5739
1977-78	0	4	85	304	498	948	1127	1057	885	480	209	18	5615
1978-79	11	11	150	381	635	916	1002	1169	691	481	149	19	5615
1979-80	2	15	80	390	484	873	1096	1071	866	481	185	66	5609
1980-81	2	5	72	387	706	1120	1344	794	796	393	200	7	5826
1981-82	2	6	91	419	628	979	1300	948	811	496	231	113	6024
1982-83	2	19	71	338	515	783	1040	896	749	478	223	22	5136
1983-84	0	8	42	327	561	1012	1182	790	1020	563	239	36	5780
1984-85	3	0	142	359	605	781	1255	897	758	471	204	71	5546
1985-86	3	11	65	298	580	1035	1035	1008	746	490	258	66	5595
1986-87	21	16	98	344	674	904	1112	997	814	588	285	76	5929
1987-88	8	18	57	326	626	888	1145	945	792	541	253	61	5660
1988-89	9	10	64	443	541	992	938	959	853	565	196	51	5621
1989-90	2	4	88	294	660	1336	880	857	762	524	307	60	5774
1990-91	4	5	84	236	496	744	1096	803	721	407	126	35	4757
1991-92	1	8	111	273	586	894	1049	937	913	552	317	37	5678
1992-93	21	14	109	386	656	930	1002	1056	880	493	167	31	5745
1993-94	3	1	89	387	579	946							

COOLING DEGREE DAYS Base 65 deg. F BOSTON, MASSACHUSETTS

YEAR	JAN	FEB	MAR	APR	MAY	JUNE	JULY	AUG	SEP	OCT	NOV	DEC	TOTAL
1969	0	0	0	9	13	156	196	297	74	1	0	0	746
1970	0	0	0	0	25	118	294	273	91	9	0	0	810
1971	0	0	0	0	6	155	269	271	132	15	1	0	849
1972	0	0	0	0	26	74	279	213	79	0	0	0	671
1973	0	0	0	7	18	180	296	316	84	3	0	0	904
1974	0	0	0	10	22	81	235	226	68	1	3	0	646
1975	0	0	0	0	60	139	345	261	44	9	4	0	862
1976	0	0	0	43	25	276	251	231	61	8	0	0	895
1977	0	0	1	13	92	124	314	272	75	6	0	0	897
1978	0	0	0	0	40	122	237	221	48	0	0	0	668
1979	0	0	0	0	35	122	304	226	85	17	0	0	789
1980	0	0	0	0	18	114	347	299	137	1	0	0	916
1981	0	0	0	0	67	185	306	232	60	0	0	0	850
1982	0	0	0	0	15	67	314	192	49	10	2	0	649
1983	0	0	0	7	18	200	410	283	217	27	0	0	1162
1984	0	0	0	3	31	207	312	306	62	3	0	0	924
1985	0	0	0	5	30	72	271	183	83	8	0	0	652
1986	0	0	0	0	60	105	211	190	55	10	0	0	631
1987	0	0	0	0	48	87	221	189	76	0	2	0	623
1988	0	0	0	0	31	173	287	342	59	11	0	0	903
1989	0	0	1	0	29	142	248	214	89	0	0	0	723
1990	0	0	0	10	2	116	261	268	77	34	8	0	776
1991	0	0	0	3	79	189	304	287	79	15	0	0	956
1992	0	0	0	0	30	126	165	189	83	5	0	0	598
1993	0	0	0	0	28	173	310	273	89	0	2	0	875

SNOWFALL (inches) BOSTON, MASSACHUSETTS

SEASON	JULY	AUG	SEP	OCT	NOV	DEC	JAN	FEB	MAR	APR	MAY	JUNE	TOTAL
1964-65	0.0	0.0	0.0	T	T	12.2	22.2	4.7	9.7	1.6	0.0	0.0	50.4
1965-66	0.0	0.0	0.0	0.0	T	2.3	26.4	12.1	3.3	T	T	0.0	44.1
1966-67	0.0	0.0	0.0	0.0	0.0	9.9	0.5	23.5	22.9	3.3	T	0.0	60.1
1967-68	0.0	0.0	0.0	0.0	2.2	14.7	17.7	3.4	6.8	0.0	0.0	0.0	44.8
1968-69	0.0	0.0	0.0	0.0	0.4	5.1	0.9	41.3	6.1	T	0.0	0.0	53.8
1969-70	0.0	0.0	0.0	T	T	12.6	7.4	10.5	18.2	0.1	0.0	0.0	48.8
1970-71	0.0	0.0	0.0	T	T	27.9	12.0	8.1	7.4	1.9	0.0	0.0	57.3
1971-72	0.0	0.0	0.0	0.0	2.8	7.9	7.8	16.5	12.1	0.4	0.0	0.0	47.5
1972-73	0.0	0.0	0.0	T	0.6	3.3	3.6	2.5	0.3	T	0.0	0.0	10.3
1973-74	0.0	0.0	0.0	0.0	0.0	T	16.0	17.8	0.1	3.0	0.0	0.0	36.9
1974-75	0.0	0.0	0.0	0.0	2.0	3.6	2.2	17.0	1.8	1.0	0.0	0.0	27.6
1975-76	0.0	0.0	0.0	T	0.1	19.3	15.0	1.4	10.8	T	0.0	0.0	46.6
1976-77	0.0	0.0	0.0	0.0	1.0	17.2	23.2	5.9	10.7	T	0.5	0.0	58.5
1977-78	0.0	0.0	0.0	0.0	0.7	5.2	35.9	27.2	16.1	T	0.0	0.0	85.1
1978-79	0.0	0.0	0.0	0.0	4.2	5.8	10.5	6.6	T	0.4	0.0	0.0	27.5
1979-80	0.0	0.0	0.0	0.2	T	2.0	0.4	6.5	3.6	T	0.0	0.0	12.7
1980-81	0.0	0.0	0.0	0.0	2.4	5.6	11.9	1.9	0.5	0.0	0.0	0.0	22.3
1981-82	0.0	0.0	0.0	0.0	T	17.6	18.0	7.6	5.3	13.3	0.0	0.0	61.8
1982-83	0.0	0.0	0.0	0.0	T	5.5	4.7	22.3	0.2	T	0.0	0.0	32.7
1983-84	0.0	0.0	0.0	0.0	T	2.6	21.1	0.3	19.0	T	0.0	0.0	43.0
1984-85	0.0	0.0	0.0	0.0	T	3.7	7.0	10.2	3.7	2.0	0.0	0.0	26.6
1985-86	0.0	0.0	0.0	0.0	3.0	1.3	0.8	10.4	2.6	T	0.0	0.0	18.1
1986-87	0.0	0.0	0.0	0.0	3.5	3.4	24.3	3.7	3.5	4.1	0.0	0.0	42.5
1987-88	0.0	0.0	0.0	0.0	9.0	7.5	17.0	14.1	5.0	T	0.0	0.0	52.6
1988-89	0.0	0.0	0.0	T	0.0	3.7	1.5	6.7	3.2	0.4	0.0	0.0	15.5
1989-90	0.0	0.0	0.0	0.0	4.5	6.2	7.0	16.9	4.1	0.5	0.0	0.0	39.2
1990-91	0.0	0.0	0.0	0.0	T	1.2	11.7	2.8	3.4	0.0	0.0	0.0	19.1
1991-92	0.0	0.0	0.0	0.0	T	5.8	0.4	4.0	10.8	1.0	0.0	0.0	22.0
1992-93	0.0	0.0	0.0	0.0	0.6	9.7	12.9	19.6	38.9	2.2	0.0	0.0	83.9
1993-94	0.0	0.0	0.0	0.0	T	11.6							
Record Mean	0.0	0.0	0.0	T	1.3	7.5	12.0	11.3	7.9	0.9	T	0.0	41.0

WORCESTER, MASSACHUSETTS

Worcester Municipal Airport is located on the crest of a hill, 1,000 feet above sea level. It is about 500 feet above and 3 1/2 miles northwest of the city proper. The airport is surrounded by ridges and valleys with many of the valleys containing reservoirs. Only two of the ridges extend above the airport elevation. One is 400 feet higher and 2 1/2 miles to the northwest, and the other is 1,000 feet higher and 15 miles to the north.

The proximity to the Atlantic Ocean, Long Island Sound, and the Berkshire Hills plays an important part in determining the weather and, hence, the climate of Worcester. Rapid weather changes occur when storms move up the east coast after developing off the Carolina Coast. In the majority of these cases, they pass to the south and east, resulting in northeast and easterly winds with rain or snow and fog. Storms developing in the Texas–Oklahoma area normally travel up the St. Lawrence River Valley and, depending on the movement and intensity, usually deposit little precipitation over the area. However, they do bring an influx of warm air into the region. Wintertime cold snaps are quite frequent, but temperatures are usually modified by the passage of the air over land and mountains before reaching the county. Summertime thunderstorms develop over the hills to the west, with a majority moving toward the northeast. From the use of radar, we find many break up just before reaching Worcester, or pass either north or south of the city proper.

Airport site temperatures are moderate. The normal mean for the warmest month, July, is around 70 degrees. Though winters are reasonably cold, prolonged periods of severe cold weather are extremely rare. The three coldest months, December through February, have an average temperature of over 25 degrees. A review of Worcester Cooperative records since 1901 shows maximum temperatures above 100 degrees and minimum temperatures below –24 degrees.

Precipitation is usually plentiful and well distributed throughout the year. The annual snowfall for all Worcester sites since 1901, averages slightly less than 60 inches. The airport location averages slightly higher.

Based on the 1951–1980 period, the average first occurrence of 32 degrees Fahrenheit in the fall is October 17 and the average last occurrence in the spring is April 27.

NORMALS, MEANS, AND EXTREMES

WORCESTER, MASSACHUSETTS

LATITUDE: 42°16'N LONGITUDE: 71°52' W ELEVATION: FT. GRND 986 BARO 1001 TIME ZONE: EASTERN WBAN: 94746

	(a)	JAN	FEB	MAR	APR	MAY	JUNE	JULY	AUG	SEP	OCT	NOV	DEC	YEAR
TEMPERATURE °F:														
Normals														
-Daily Maximum		30.7	33.0	42.4	54.0	65.9	74.5	79.3	77.3	69.7	59.5	47.4	34.7	55.7
-Daily Minimum		15.0	16.5	24.9	34.7	45.1	53.9	60.1	58.6	50.5	40.5	31.3	20.1	37.6
-Monthly		22.8	24.8	33.7	44.4	55.5	64.2	69.7	68.0	60.2	50.0	39.4	27.4	46.7
Extremes														
-Record Highest	38	60	67	81	91	92	94	96	96	91	85	78	70	96
-Year		1974	1985	1990	1976	1962	1988	1988	1975	1983	1963	1982	1984	JUL 1988
-Record Lowest	38	-19	-12	-4	11	28	36	43	38	30	20	6	-13	-19
-Year		1957	1967	1986	1982	1970	1986	1988	1965	1992	1969	1989	1962	JAN 1957
NORMAL DEGREE DAYS:														
Heating (base 65°F)		1308	1126	970	618	301	69	6	25	157	465	768	1166	6979
Cooling (base 65°F)		0	0	0	0	6	45	151	118	13	0	0	0	333
% OF POSSIBLE SUNSHINE														
MEAN SKY COVER (tenths)														
Sunrise - Sunset	37	6.2	6.2	6.5	6.6	6.7	6.4	6.3	6.0	5.9	5.7	6.7	6.4	6.3
MEAN NUMBER OF DAYS:														
Sunrise to Sunset														
-Clear	38	8.8	7.7	7.7	6.6	6.1	6.0	6.0	8.0	9.0	10.1	7.0	7.6	90.4
-Partly Cloudy	38	7.8	6.9	7.8	8.6	9.8	10.7	12.1	11.1	8.5	8.2	7.6	7.8	106.9
-Cloudy	38	14.4	13.7	15.5	14.8	15.2	13.3	12.9	11.9	12.4	12.7	15.4	15.7	167.9
Precipitation														
.01 inches or more	38	11.6	10.9	12.3	11.4	12.2	11.3	10.1	10.1	9.4	9.0	11.8	12.7	132.6
Snow, Ice pellets, hail														
1.0 inches or more	38	4.2	3.7	3.2	1.0	0.1	0.0	0.0	0.0	0.0	0.1	0.8	3.6	16.8
Thunderstorms	23	0.*	0.1	0.7	1.2	3.0	4.2	5.3	4.1	1.5	1.0	0.5	0.1	21.6
Heavy Fog Visibility														
1/4 mile or less	23	5.7	5.6	7.6	7.0	7.1	8.0	6.3	6.2	8.2	7.2	7.9	7.0	83.8
Temperature °F														
-Maximum														
90° and above	38	0.0	0.0	0.0	0.1	0.1	0.7	1.5	0.7	0.*	0.0	0.0	0.0	3.2
32° and below	38	17.6	13.7	5.5	0.2	0.0	0.0	0.0	0.0	0.0	0.0	1.7	13.2	51.8
-Minimum														
32° and below	38	29.6	26.8	25.3	11.1	0.6	0.0	0.0	0.0	0.1	4.9	16.8	27.8	143.1
0° and below	38	3.0	1.8	0.1	0.0	0.0	0.0	0.0	0.0	0.0	0.0	0.0	0.9	5.9
AVG. STATION PRESS. (mb)	21	977.1	977.8	977.4	976.8	978.1	978.1	978.9	980.5	981.4	980.9	979.4	978.7	978.8
RELATIVE HUMIDITY (%)														
Hour 01	32	69	69	68	68	73	78	79	81	83	78	76	73	75
Hour 07 (Local Time)	38	72	72	70	68	69	74	76	79	81	78	77	75	74
Hour 13	38	58	57	55	50	51	56	57	59	61	57	61	62	57
Hour 19	38	65	63	60	57	59	66	68	72	75	69	69	69	66
PRECIPITATION (inches):														
Water Equivalent														
-Normal		3.68	3.46	3.95	3.91	4.33	3.88	3.85	3.82	4.01	4.32	4.49	4.05	47.75
-Maximum Monthly	38	11.16	8.37	7.96	8.79	9.94	12.17	8.11	8.01	13.13	10.19	10.40	9.83	13.13
-Year		1979	1981	1972	1987	1984	1982	1959	1991	1974	1990	1972	1973	SEP 1974
-Minimum Monthly	38	0.89	0.25	0.74	1.26	0.86	0.79	0.74	1.03	0.69	1.46	0.67	0.74	0.25
-Year		1970	1987	1981	1985	1959	1979	1987	1981	1986	1963	1976	1989	FEB 1987
-Maximum in 24 hrs	38	2.97	2.46	4.56	3.15	3.03	3.98	3.87	5.00	4.79	3.91	2.98	3.00	5.00
-Year		1978	1973	1987	1987	1967	1986	1985	1991	1960	1990	1972	1986	AUG 1991
Snow, Ice pellets, hail														
-Maximum Monthly	38	46.8	45.2	44.1	21.0	12.7	0.1	0.0	0.0	T	7.5	20.7	37.0	46.8
-Year		1987	1962	1993	1987	1977	1992			1992	1979	1971	1992	JAN 1987
-Maximum in 24 hrs	38	18.7	24.0	19.7	17.0	12.7	0.1	0.0	0.0	T	7.5	14.8	28.1	28.1
-Year		1961	1962	1993	1987	1977	1992			1992	1979	1971	1992	DEC 1992
WIND:														
Mean Speed (mph)	29	11.9	11.6	11.4	11.0	10.0	8.9	8.4	8.3	8.6	9.4	10.2	10.9	10.0
Prevailing Direction through 1963		WSW	WNW	W	W	SW	SW	SW	SW	SW	WSW	WSW	WSW	SW
Fastest Obs. 1 Min.														
-Direction (!!)	37	25	32	29	05	27	25	32	36	14	25	20	23	32
-Speed (MPH)	37	60	76	76	54	48	39	43	44	36	43	54	51	76
-Year		1959	1956	1956	1956	1956	1958	1957	1991	1985	1958	1956	1957	FEB 1956
Peak Gust														
-Direction (!!)	10	W	NW	NW	SW	S	W	NW	N	SE	NW	S	W	SE
-Speed (mph)	10	62	63	66	54	61	58	48	69	71	59	62	62	71
-Date		1992	1990	1993	1990	1989	1993	1984	1991	1985	1992	1989	1993	SEP 1985

PRECIPITATION (inches)

WORCESTER, MASSACHUSETTS

YEAR	JAN	FEB	MAR	APR	MAY	JUNE	JULY	AUG	SEP	OCT	NOV	DEC	ANNUAL
1964	5.42	3.54	3.65	4.01	1.18	1.77	3.02	2.93	1.78	2.26	3.17	4.92	37.65
1965	1.71	4.30	2.37	3.56	1.51	3.14	1.03	3.40	2.83	3.02	2.90	2.21	31.98
1966	4.22	4.05	2.52	1.62	3.21	1.91	3.76	1.95	5.59	4.13	4.93	3.05	40.94
1967	2.38	3.15	3.73	5.10	7.01	3.72	5.91	3.47	5.06	1.83	3.65	5.72	50.73
1968	3.00	1.26	7.67	2.24	6.83	7.78	1.06	1.25	1.94	1.88	5.75	6.16	46.82
1969	1.29	3.04	2.53	5.30	3.09	1.26	3.81	3.34	6.16	1.78	6.81	7.69	46.10
1970	0.89	5.47	3.51	3.44	4.18	3.88	1.08	5.86	2.17	3.47	3.75	3.09	40.79
1971	1.97	5.60	1.93	1.71	5.22	1.88	5.27	4.67	4.23	3.66	5.01	2.68	43.83
1972	2.34	4.91	7.96	4.29	7.83	9.25	6.39	2.89	4.98	4.93	10.40	5.49	71.66
1973	4.04	3.30	3.50	6.33	4.73	6.98	3.82	4.29	3.80	4.63	2.00	9.83	57.25
1974	3.54	2.75	5.05	3.24	5.15	4.35	3.22	3.50	13.13	3.45	3.06	6.04	56.48
1975	5.35	3.52	3.37	2.66	2.07	3.32	3.92	4.59	7.21	6.06	5.28	4.61	51.96
1976	6.03	2.57	2.74	2.45	3.46	2.95	3.28	5.72	2.38	4.99	0.67	3.20	40.44
1977	2.76	2.46	5.75	3.69	2.20	4.00	3.84	2.73	6.54	6.33	3.69	4.99	48.98
1978	9.90	2.08	3.22	2.24	3.69	1.57	3.57	5.00	1.02	3.85	2.07	3.56	41.77
1979	11.16	2.64	3.71	4.49	4.14	0.79	5.74	7.39	3.80	4.36	3.58	1.89	53.69
1980	0.95	0.73	6.86	4.77	2.23	4.55	3.59	1.95	1.82	6.16	4.58	1.06	39.25
1981	0.93	8.37	0.74	3.85	4.48	2.45	7.90	1.03	4.66	5.49	3.13	5.94	48.97
1982	5.00	3.22	3.67	4.30	2.96	12.17	3.61	3.36	2.69	2.67	4.32	1.70	49.67
1983	4.85	4.67	7.84	8.59	5.97	2.56	1.32	6.26	1.38	5.77	8.75	6.37	64.33
1984	2.44	5.78	5.47	4.23	9.94	2.85	5.69	1.17	1.68	3.99	2.71	2.84	48.79
1985	1.16	2.72	2.89	1.26	5.46	5.24	6.35	3.74	3.77	3.12	6.41	1.93	44.05
1986	5.56	3.14	2.93	1.59	3.14	7.21	4.83	3.20	0.69	2.72	5.63	7.25	47.89
1987	5.52	0.25	6.57	8.79	1.55	4.55	0.74	4.61	6.37	4.18	2.77	1.85	47.75
1988	2.71	2.78	3.46	3.45	4.47	1.25	6.27	2.19	2.70	3.66	7.91	1.42	42.27
1989	1.18	2.47	2.66	4.25	6.17	5.27	5.67	5.65	4.71	8.21	4.00	0.74	50.98
1990	3.75	3.88	1.52	4.78	7.65	1.74	2.44	6.84	1.73	10.19	2.41	5.46	52.39
1991	2.98	2.08	4.92	5.04	4.16	3.06	2.78	8.01	6.40	3.44	5.47	2.89	51.23
1992	3.01	2.51	4.15	2.59	2.54	4.68	5.25	4.83	3.58	2.36	4.94	4.61	45.05
1993	2.56	2.38	5.46	4.00	1.79	2.36	3.34	1.90	8.85	3.88	4.85	5.11	46.48
Record Mean	3.65	3.31	4.05	4.03	4.00	3.63	3.74	4.29	3.99	4.23	4.57	4.02	47.52

AVERAGE TEMPERATURE (deg. F)

WORCESTER, MASSACHUSETTS

YEAR	JAN	FEB	MAR	APR	MAY	JUNE	JULY	AUG	SEP	OCT	NOV	DEC	ANNUAL
1964	27.2	23.9	35.2	43.7	58.9	64.3	68.6	63.4	59.3	49.6	41.2	28.4	47.0
1965	20.9	24.3	31.3	42.9	58.9	63.7	68.2	67.4	61.1	49.1	36.7	30.1	46.2
1966	22.2	25.8	34.2	42.0	52.9	65.4	70.7	68.1	58.2	49.0	43.1	28.0	46.7
1967	29.4	20.5	28.8	41.7	48.8	66.1	70.7	67.8	60.6	51.5	34.4	29.8	45.9
1968	19.2	20.0	35.6	48.5	53.8	62.2	71.2	68.0	63.5	53.0	37.1	24.0	46.3
1969	23.2	25.1	30.8	48.8	56.3	66.3	68.4	70.4	60.8	49.7	39.1	25.3	47.0
1970	14.9	24.2	30.4	44.6	56.9	63.7	71.1	70.1	60.6	51.7	40.2	22.2	45.9
1971	17.7	25.9	29.9	42.5	54.2	65.6	70.6	68.2	63.4	56.5	36.6	30.5	46.8
1972	26.4	23.3	30.4	40.4	55.7	62.2	71.1	66.9	59.7	44.7	34.9	27.6	45.3
1973	26.1	24.7	40.9	46.3	54.2	67.4	71.1	71.7	60.1	51.3	39.8	31.9	48.8
1974	26.4	23.9	33.5	47.5	52.4	64.0	69.7	69.7	59.7	45.8	39.4	30.4	46.9
1975	27.5	25.2	31.3	40.8	60.1	63.6	71.8	67.5	57.3	51.5	45.2	27.3	47.4
1976	19.2	31.2	35.1	49.1	55.0	68.0	67.8	67.2	58.9	46.4	34.6	21.9	46.2
1977	16.2	24.9	39.1	45.9	58.1	62.4	69.3	68.6	59.6	49.3	41.1	26.0	46.7
1978	20.9	20.0	30.8	42.4	56.6	64.3	68.2	68.1	57.6	48.4	39.2	28.8	45.4
1979	25.3	16.5	38.2	44.7	57.7	63.6	71.2	67.7	60.0	49.0	44.3	31.9	47.5
1980	25.0	22.2	33.1	46.0	57.0	61.5	71.3	69.9	61.1	47.3	36.4	24.2	46.3
1981	15.9	32.8	34.7	47.4	57.9	66.0	70.7	67.4	58.2	46.7	39.1	27.8	47.1
1982	17.1	25.7	33.8	43.6	58.3	61.5	71.5	65.9	61.3	50.8	43.8	34.8	47.3
1983	26.1	29.1	36.6	46.6	54.7	67.9	72.3	70.2	64.9	50.3	42.0	27.3	49.0
1984	22.7	34.0	29.2	45.6	55.4	68.1	70.0	71.4	59.6	53.9	41.1	34.9	48.8
1985	20.1	28.6	37.2	47.4	57.8	61.4	70.4	67.9	62.0	51.7	40.9	25.3	47.6
1986	25.9	23.1	36.4	48.1	57.9	62.6	68.2	66.8	59.4	49.6	37.1	30.3	47.1
1987	24.0	24.5	36.8	45.7	57.6	65.8	70.7	66.6	60.6	48.8	39.4	30.8	47.6
1988	23.0	26.6	35.0	43.8	57.3	64.6	72.6	72.3	60.2	45.5	41.7	27.2	47.5
1989	28.5	24.4	33.0	42.4	57.0	64.0	68.7	67.3	60.6	50.7	36.5	15.1	45.7
1990	31.3	28.8	36.2	43.9	51.5	64.6	69.2	68.8	59.3	53.0	42.1	34.0	48.6
1991	23.8	30.3	36.5	48.2	61.2	64.7	70.0	69.1	58.7	51.9	40.2	29.7	48.7
1992	25.3	27.1	30.7	42.3	55.5	63.5	65.9	65.5	59.2	46.8	37.8	28.7	45.7
1993	26.0	19.6	31.3	45.7	57.8	64.5	70.4	70.0	59.5	47.2	39.7	28.9	46.7
Record Mean	23.8	25.6	33.4	45.1	56.0	64.7	70.0	68.2	60.2	50.3	39.7	28.0	47.0
Max	31.5	33.7	41.7	54.6	66.3	74.6	79.3	77.2	69.2	59.3	47.3	35.3	55.8
Min	16.0	17.4	25.1	35.6	45.7	54.8	60.7	59.2	51.2	41.3	32.0	20.6	38.3

REFERENCE NOTES

WORCESTER, MASSACHUSETTS

GENERAL
T - TRACE AMOUNT.
BLANK ENTRIES DENOTE MISSING/UNREPORTED DATA.
# INDICATES A STATION OR INSTRUMENT RELOCATION.

SPECIFIC

PM - INCLUDES LAST DAY OF PREVIOUS MONTH
ASOS - AUTOMATED SURFACE OBSERVING SYSTEM IN OPERATION DURING THESE MONTHS.

(a) - LENGTH OF RECORD IN YEARS, ALTHOUGH INDIVIDUAL MONTHS MAY BE MISSING.
0.* OR * - THE VALUE IS BETWEEN 0.0 AND 0.05
NORMALS - BASED ON THE 1961-1990 RECORD PERIOD.
EXTREMES - DATES ARE THE MOST RECENT OCCURRENCE.
WIND DIR. - NUMERALS SHOW TENS OF DEGRESS CLOCKWISE FROM TRUE NORTH. "00" INDICATES CALM.
RESULTANT DIRECTIONS ARE GIVEN TO WHOLE DEGREES.
BOLD VALUES INDICATE EXTREME VALUES WHICH OCCURRED AFTER THE ASOS SYSTEM WAS COMMISSIONED.

RECORD = PERIOD OF RECORD
RECORD MEAN PRECIPITATION IS THE MEAN OF ALL DAILY PRECIPITATION AMOUNTS DURING THE PERIOD OF RECORD.
RECORD MAX(MIN) TEMPERATURE IS THE MEAN OF ALL DAILY MAX(MIN) TEMPERATURES DURING THE PERIOD OF RECORD.
RECORD MEAN TEMPERATURE IS THE SUM OF THE RECORD MAX AND RECORD MIN DIVIDED BY 2.
AVERAGE TEMPERATURE IS THE SUM OF THE MEAN DAILY MAX AND MIN TEMPERATURE DIVIDED BY 2.

EXCEPTIONS

1. THUNDERSTORMS, AND HEAVY FOG ARE THROUGH 1977.

RECORD MEANS ARE THROUGH THE CURRENT YEAR, BEGINNING IN 1948 FOR TEMPERATURE
1948 FOR PRECIPITATION
1956 FOR SNOWFALL

HEATING DEGREE DAYS Base 65 deg. F — WORCESTER, MASSACHUSETTS

SEASON	JULY	AUG	SEP	OCT	NOV	DEC	JAN	FEB	MAR	APR	MAY	JUNE	TOTAL
1964-65	36	80	189	472	704	1122	1362	1136	1040	658	206	118	7123
1965-66	14	61	163	486	843	1076	1320	1093	948	685	376	80	7145
1966-67	4	19	218	489	649	1141	1097	1242	1115	691	493	73	7231
1967-68	4	28	151	422	912	1087	1414	1300	904	490	343	126	7181
1968-69	8	31	79	375	830	1264	1286	1111	1056	487	282	49	6858
1969-70	19	15	163	468	773	1224	1547	1137	1068	604	261	99	7378
1970-71	2	12	174	410	738	1319	1461	1087	1083	667	327	61	7341
1971-72	3	35	98	258	844	1061	1189	1203	1065	733	290	116	6895
1972-73	16	41	171	622	897	1152	1200	1120	738	555	338	37	6887
1973-74	6	8	202	420	750	1017	1191	1145	969	520	391	82	6701
1974-75	6	9	190	592	760	1063	1158	1110	1037	721	180	104	6930
1975-76	2	47	223	413	586	1161	1412	972	920	511	310	60	6617
1976-77	17	46	192	571	905	1331	1508	1115	798	571	244	115	7413
1977-78	16	32	189	481	711	1202	1359	1255	1054	674	288	69	7330
1978-79	33	38	229	511	767	1116	1225	1354	824	601	243	80	7021
1979-80	25	53	180	500	614	1019	1235	1233	983	562	246	148	6798
1980-81	2	19	165	540	853	1259	1516	894	934	521	241	42	6986
1981-82	1	29	204	562	772	1145	1478	1094	961	639	212	127	7224
1982-83	7	55	140	436	632	929	1199	996	871	548	318	44	6175
1983-84	5	20	115	459	682	1163	1303	892	1099	577	300	54	6669
1984-85	9	1	184	338	713	928	1382	1011	855	518	230	121	6290
1985-86	2	25	128	406	713	1223	1206	1166	879	501	262	119	6630
1986-87	48	49	182	471	830	1069	1266	1130	867	571	273	58	6814
1987-88	9	56	152	495	761	1052	1298	1107	922	629	253	115	6849
1988-89	19	32	155	597	693	1166	1123	1129	984	674	257	90	6919
1989-90	7	38	172	436	846	1540	1035	1006	884	632	413	58	7067
1990-91	22	30	192	379	683	957	1270	965	877	501	167	80	6123
1991-92	13	16	222	402	739	1090	1222	1092	1056	676	321	82	6931
1992-93	40	55	203	558	810	1117	1204	1259	1039	574	229	74	7162
1993-94	10	5	201	545	754	1115							

COOLING DEGREE DAYS Base 65 deg. F — WORCESTER, MASSACHUSETTS

YEAR	JAN	FEB	MAR	APR	MAY	JUNE	JULY	AUG	SEP	OCT	NOV	DEC	TOTAL
1969	0	0	0	5	17	98	131	192	44	1	0	0	488
1970	0	0	0	0	16	70	197	177	50	6	0	0	516
1971	0	0	0	0	0	87	184	141	57	2	0	0	471
1972	0	0	0	0	9	41	215	109	20	0	0	0	394
1973	0	0	0	1	11	118	201	224	62	0	0	0	617
1974	0	0	0	4	8	59	159	164	36	0	0	0	430
1975	0	0	0	0	33	69	218	132	0	1	0	0	453
1976	0	0	0	37	7	154	110	119	16	0	0	0	443
1977	0	0	2	4	37	44	156	150	32	0	0	0	425
1978	0	0	0	0	32	57	138	137	14	0	0	0	378
1979	0	0	0	0	24	44	225	142	38	10	0	0	483
1980	0	0	0	0	8	48	206	178	57	0	0	0	497
1981	0	0	0	0	29	78	184	110	10	0	0	0	411
1982	0	0	0	0	8	29	216	92	34	0	0	0	379
1983	0	0	0	4	4	138	238	188	118	11	0	0	701
1984	0	0	0	2	10	156	171	209	30	0	0	0	578
1985	0	0	0	0	15	22	177	120	47	0	0	0	381
1986	0	0	0	0	50	54	151	111	21	2	0	0	389
1987	0	0	0	0	49	90	193	110	25	0	0	0	467
1988	0	0	0	0	24	112	260	266	17	1	0	0	680
1989	0	0	0	0	16	70	131	116	47	0	0	0	380
1990	0	0	0	6	0	52	159	153	25	10	0	0	405
1991	0	0	0	4	57	79	173	149	40	2	0	0	504
1992	0	0	0	0	30	44	75	78	37	0	0	0	264
1993	0	0	0	0	12	67	181	163	44	0	0	0	467

SNOWFALL (inches) — WORCESTER, MASSACHUSETTS

SEASON	JULY	AUG	SEP	OCT	NOV	DEC	JAN	FEB	MAR	APR	MAY	JUNE	TOTAL
1964-65	0.0	0.0	0.0	2.1	T	11.7	18.7	5.9	17.7	6.7	0.0	0.0	62.8
1965-66	0.0	0.0	0.0	T	0.6	2.3	44.0	19.7	5.8	0.8	T	0.0	73.2
1966-67	0.0	0.0	0.0	0.0	0.7	13.6	2.5	35.5	34.6	7.3	T	0.0	94.2
1967-68	0.0	0.0	0.0	0.0	9.8	22.2	18.6	6.4	9.2	T	0.0	0.0	66.2
1968-69	0.0	0.0	0.0	0.0	15.3	12.2	1.8	39.5	6.9	T	0.0	0.0	75.7
1969-70	0.0	0.0	0.0	T	0.3	29.5	7.7	11.4	19.9	3.3	T	0.0	72.1
1970-71	0.0	0.0	0.0	T	T	32.1	16.6	11.4	12.1	7.8	0.0	0.0	80.0
1971-72	0.0	0.0	0.0	0.0	20.7	9.6	6.7	35.0	20.1	7.2	0.0	0.0	99.3
1972-73	0.0	0.0	0.0	T	6.1	13.8	17.9	5.8	0.4	0.4	0.0	0.0	44.4
1973-74	0.0	0.0	0.0	0.0	T	0.9	12.5	15.0	1.7	3.7	0.0	0.0	33.8
1974-75	0.0	0.0	0.0	T	1.2	13.1	22.6	21.9	4.9	1.4	0.0	0.0	65.1
1975-76	0.0	0.0	0.0	T	1.5	18.1	21.6	4.7	16.4	T	T	0.0	62.3
1976-77	0.0	0.0	0.0	T	3.0	13.5	21.7	13.8	21.5	1.0	12.7	0.0	87.2
1977-78	0.0	0.0	0.0	0.0	2.2	13.7	34.2	20.8	15.0	T	T	0.0	85.9
1978-79	0.0	0.0	0.0	0.0	5.4	13.1	16.0	6.5	1.3	5.4	0.0	0.0	47.7
1979-80	0.0	0.0	0.0	7.5	0.0	2.1	0.8	6.5	9.7	T	0.0	0.0	26.6
1980-81	0.0	0.0	0.0	0.0	9.0	6.8	12.5	11.4	3.3	T	T	0.0	43.0
1981-82	0.0	0.0	0.0	T	T	24.6	16.7	6.5	11.0	15.1	0.0	0.0	73.9
1982-83	0.0	0.0	0.0	0.0	0.5	6.4	18.6	32.1	3.5	2.3	T	0.0	63.4
1983-84	0.0	0.0	0.0	T	1.1	17.2	24.1	3.3	30.9	T	T	0.0	76.6
1984-85	0.0	0.0	0.0	0.0	T	7.0	9.7	11.0	7.2	4.9	0.0	0.0	39.8
1985-86	0.0	0.0	0.0	0.0	6.9	9.1	5.8	14.5	2.3	0.1	0.3	0.0	39.0
1986-87	0.0	0.0	0.0	0.0	11.5	4.9	46.8	3.0	6.4	21.0	0.0	0.0	93.6
1987-88	0.0	0.0	0.0	0.0	10.2	12.9	25.2	15.8	6.4	0.6	0.0	0.0	71.1
1988-89	0.0	0.0	0.0	0.4	T	5.0	2.8	7.7	8.5	3.7	0.0	0.0	28.1
1989-90	0.0	0.0	0.0	0.0	7.9	10.2	11.3	15.2	6.4	2.1	0.0	T	53.1
1990-91	0.0	0.0	0.0	0.0	0.7	5.0	11.3	9.1	9.3	0.2	0.0	0.0	35.6
1991-92	0.0	0.0	0.0	0.0	5.8	14.5	2.7	8.4	11.8	2.7	0.0	0.1	46.0
1992-93	0.0	0.0	T	0.0	1.9	37.0	14.6	19.7	44.1	2.8	0.0	T	120.1
1993-94	0.0	0.0	0.0	T	0.2	12.9							
Record Mean	0.0	0.0	T	0.5	3.6	13.4	16.1	15.9	14.1	3.8	0.3	T	67.8

DETROIT, METROPOLITAN AIRPORT
MICHIGAN

Detroit and the immediate suburbs, including nearby urban areas in Canada, occupy an area approximately 25 miles in radius. The waterway, consisting of the Detroit and St. Clair Rivers, Lake St. Clair, and the west end of Lake Erie, lies at an elevation of 568 to 580 feet above sea level. Nearly flat land slopes up gently from the waters edge northwestward for about 10 miles and then gives way to increasingly rolling terrain. The Irish Hills, parallel to and about 40 miles northwest of the waterway, have tops 1,000 to 1,250 feet above sea level. On the Canadian side of the waterway the land is relatively level.

Northwest winds in winter bring snow flurry accumulations to all of Michigan except in the Detroit Metropolitan area while summer showers moving from the northwest weaken and sometimes dissipate as they approach Detroit. On the other hand, much of the heaviest precipitation in winter comes from southeast winds, especially to the northwest suburbs of the city.

The climate of Detroit is influenced by its location with respect to major storm tracks and the influence of the Great Lakes. The normal wintertime storm track is south of the city, which brings on the average, about 3 inch snowfalls. Winter storms can bring combinations of rain, snow, freezing rain, and sleet with heavy snowfall accumulations possible at times. In summer, most storms pass to the north allowing for intervals of warm, humid, sunny skies with occasional thunderstorms followed by days of mild, dry, and fair weather. Temperatures of 90 degrees or higher are reached during each summer.

The most pronounced lake effect occurs in the winter when arctic air moving across the lakes is warmed and moistened. This produces an excess of cloudiness but a moderation of cold wave temperatures.

Local climatic variations are due largely to the immediate effect of Lake St. Clair and the urban heat island. On warm days in late spring or early summer, lake breezes often lower temperatures by 10 to 15 degrees in the eastern part of the city and the northeastern suburbs. The urban heat island effect shows up mainly at night where minimum temperatures at the Metropolitan Airport average 4 degrees lower than downtown Detroit. On humid summer nights or on very cold winter nights, this difference can exceed 10 degrees.

The growing season averages 180 days and has ranged from 145 days to 205 days. On average, the last freezing temperature occurs in late April while the average first freezing temperature occurs in late October. A freeze has occurred as late as mid-May and as early as late September.

Air pollution comes primarily from heavy industry spread along both shores of the waterway from Port Huron to Toledo. However, wind dispersion is usually sufficient to keep it from becoming a major hazard.

NORMALS, MEANS, AND EXTREMES

DETROIT, METROPOLITAN AIRPORT MICHIGAN

LATITUDE: 42°14'N LONGITUDE: 83°20' W ELEVATION: FT. GRND 633 BARO 647 TIME ZONE: EASTERN WBAN: 94847

	(a)	JAN	FEB	MAR	APR	MAY	JUNE	JULY	AUG	SEP	OCT	NOV	DEC	YEAR
TEMPERATURE °F:														
Normals														
-Daily Maximum		30.3	33.3	44.4	57.7	69.6	78.9	83.3	81.3	73.9	61.5	48.1	35.2	58.1
-Daily Minimum		15.6	17.6	27.0	36.8	47.1	56.3	61.3	59.6	52.5	40.9	32.2	21.4	39.0
-Monthly		22.9	25.4	35.7	47.3	58.4	67.6	72.3	70.5	63.2	51.2	40.2	28.3	48.6
Extremes														
-Record Highest	35	62	65	81	89	93	104	102	100	98	91	77	68	104
-Year		1965	1976	1986	1977	1988	1988	1988	1988	1976	1963	1968	1982	JUN 1988
-Record Lowest	35	-21	-15	-4	10	25	36	41	38	29	17	9	-10	-21
-Year		1984	1985	1978	1982	1966	1972	1965	1982	1974	1974	1969	1983	JAN 1984
NORMAL DEGREE DAYS:														
Heating (base 65°F)		1305	1109	908	531	243	38	0	16	102	435	744	1138	6569
Cooling (base 65°F)		0	0	0	0	38	116	231	186	48	7	0	0	626
% OF POSSIBLE SUNSHINE	28	40	46	51	54	61	65	68	68	61	51	35	30	53
MEAN SKY COVER (tenths)														
Sunrise - Sunset	35	7.6	7.2	7.1	6.8	6.3	5.9	5.6	5.7	6.1	6.4	7.7	8.0	6.7
MEAN NUMBER OF DAYS:														
Sunrise to Sunset														
-Clear	35	4.2	4.7	5.7	6.0	6.8	7.8	8.8	9.0	8.0	7.5	3.9	3.4	75.8
-Partly Cloudy	35	6.7	6.9	7.3	7.6	10.4	11.1	12.4	11.2	9.7	8.8	6.6	6.1	104.9
-Cloudy	35	20.1	16.7	18.0	16.4	13.8	11.1	9.7	10.8	12.3	14.7	19.5	21.5	184.6
Precipitation														
.01 inches or more	35	13.2	11.1	13.2	12.7	11.1	10.2	9.5	9.5	9.9	9.8	11.9	13.7	136.0
Snow,Ice pellets,hail														
1.0 inches or more	35	3.2	2.9	2.2	0.5	0.0	0.0	0.0	0.0	0.0	0.1	1.1	3.2	13.2
Thunderstorms	35	0.2	0.5	1.6	3.2	3.9	5.9	5.8	5.5	4.1	1.3	0.6	0.4	33.1
Heavy Fog Visibility														
1/4 mile or less	35	2.1	2.3	2.4	1.0	0.7	0.7	0.6	1.3	1.7	2.2	1.8	3.2	19.9
Temperature °F														
-Maximum														
90° and above	35	0.0	0.0	0.0	0.0	0.4	2.7	5.0	3.0	0.9	0.1	0.0	0.0	12.1
32° and below	35	16.8	13.1	4.4	0.2	0.0	0.0	0.0	0.0	0.0	0.0	1.4	11.4	47.1
-Minimum														
32° and below	35	29.0	25.6	22.6	9.5	0.8	0.0	0.0	0.0	0.1	4.8	16.5	26.1	135.0
0° and below	35	3.5	1.9	0.1	0.0	0.0	0.0	0.0	0.0	0.0	0.0	0.0	1.3	6.8
AVG. STATION PRESS.(mb)	21	992.8	993.7	991.7	990.6	990.7	990.6	991.7	993.0	993.7	993.9	992.9	993.2	992.4
RELATIVE HUMIDITY (%)														
Hour 01	35	78	77	76	74	76	79	81	83	84	80	79	79	79
Hour 07 (Local Time)	35	80	79	79	78	78	79	82	86	87	84	82	81	81
Hour 13	35	69	65	61	55	53	54	54	56	57	57	65	71	60
Hour 19	35	73	70	66	59	56	57	58	63	67	68	73	76	66
PRECIPITATION (inches):														
Water Equivalent														
-Normal		1.76	1.74	2.55	2.95	2.92	3.61	3.18	3.43	2.89	2.10	2.67	2.82	32.62
-Maximum Monthly	35	3.92	5.02	4.48	5.40	6.20	7.04	6.02	7.83	7.52	4.87	5.68	6.00	7.83
-Year		1993	1990	1973	1961	1991	1987	1969	1975	1986	1967	1982	1965	AUG 1975
-Minimum Monthly	35	0.27	0.15	0.82	0.92	0.87	0.97	0.59	0.72	0.43	0.35	0.79	0.46	0.15
-Year		1961	1969	1981	1971	1988	1988	1974	1982	1960	1964	1976	1960	FEB 1969
-Maximum in 24 hrs	35	1.72	2.36	1.69	1.97	2.87	2.84	3.19	3.21	3.52	2.57	2.20	3.71	3.71
-Year		1967	1990	1985	1965	1968	1983	1966	1964	1990	1985	1982	1965	DEC 1965
Snow,Ice pellets,hail														
-Maximum Monthly	35	29.6	20.8	16.1	9.0	T	0.0	0.0	0.0	T	2.9	11.8	34.9	34.9
-Year		1978	1986	1965	1982	1991				1990	1980	1966	1974	DEC 1974
-Maximum in 24 hrs	35	11.1	10.3	9.2	7.4	T	0.0	0.0	0.0	T	2.9	5.6	19.2	19.2
-Year		1992	1965	1973	1982	1991				1990	1980	1977	1974	DEC 1974
WIND:														
Mean Speed (mph)	35	11.9	11.5	11.8	11.6	10.2	9.3	8.5	8.3	8.8	9.9	11.3	11.5	10.4
Prevailing Direction through 1963		WSW	WSW	WSW	WSW	WSW	SW	SW	SW	SW	WSW	SW	SW	SW
Fastest Obs. 1 Min.														
-Direction (!!!)	14	22	31	25	28	31	23	33	25	28	26	17	22	22
-Speed (MPH)	14	48	38	44	44	39	37	40	32	35	36	37	48	48
-Year		1990	1990	1989	1982	1988	1990	1980	1984	1992	1993	1988	1987	JAN 1990
Peak Gust														
-Direction (!!!)	10	SW	NW	W	SW	S	NW	W	W	NW	W	SW	SW	SW
-Speed (mph)	10	66	51	60	64	58	56	54	47	54	52	53	59	66
-Date		1990	1987	1989	1991	1984	1991	1991	1990	1987	1985	1991	1987	JAN 1990

PRECIPITATION (inches)

DETROIT, METROPOLITAN AIRPORT MICHIGAN

YEAR	JAN	FEB	MAR	APR	MAY	JUNE	JULY	AUG	SEP	OCT	NOV	DEC	ANNUAL
1964	2.20	0.68	2.98	4.13	1.72	3.84	1.11	7.70	1.31	0.35	0.80	1.92	28.74
1965	3.63	2.54	3.59	3.30	1.15	2.28	2.38	6.94	1.91	3.89	1.49	6.00	39.10
1966	0.61	1.64	2.62	2.65	2.18	4.16	5.24	5.03	1.51	1.15	3.13	4.53	34.45
1967	2.34	1.28	1.03	3.67	1.63	4.23	2.85	2.01	1.96	4.87	2.77	5.19	33.83
1968	2.30	1.48	2.04	1.71	5.88	4.99	5.14	1.83	1.87	1.09	3.31	3.59	35.23
1969	2.83	0.15	1.62	3.77	3.74	4.26	6.02	1.06	0.68	1.41	2.46	1.33	29.33
1970	1.11	0.86	2.62	3.32	3.01	3.90	3.30	2.75	1.63	1.91	2.73	1.61	28.75
1971	1.03	2.68	1.59	0.92	1.97	2.17	1.95	1.62	2.72	1.01	1.34	3.79	22.79
1972	1.28	1.00	2.55	3.63	2.68	3.30	2.21	3.07	3.40	2.24	3.19	3.11	31.66
1973	1.65	1.08	4.48	1.42	3.72	4.86	4.66	1.67	1.82	2.01	3.21	3.51	34.09
1974	3.26	2.37	4.20	2.75	3.49	2.38	0.59	2.95	2.22	0.81	2.86	4.00	31.88
1975	2.90	2.65	1.66	2.50	2.82	2.39	1.98	7.83	3.18	1.29	2.39	3.00	34.59
1976	1.91	2.87	4.24	3.15	3.26	3.26	1.47	1.68	3.66	2.01	0.79	0.79	29.09
1977	0.98	1.64	3.57	4.17	2.40	3.16	3.28	2.23	4.23	1.37	2.88	2.97	32.88
1978	3.16	0.45	2.05	2.49	3.58	2.69	1.97	1.73	1.82	2.49	2.41	2.81	27.65
1979	1.52	0.57	2.44	4.97	2.82	4.04	4.96	2.99	0.94	1.24	4.19	2.36	33.04
1980	0.69	1.00	3.88	4.23	3.22	6.42	4.33	6.09	2.94	1.26	0.88	2.30	37.24
1981	0.57	3.13	0.82	3.44	2.60	3.33	4.29	2.32	5.47	3.92	1.26	2.38	33.53
1982	3.43	1.10	3.14	1.60	2.83	4.11	4.78	0.72	2.55	1.01	5.68	3.29	34.24
1983	0.84	0.89	1.87	4.20	5.47	4.88	4.53	1.57	2.49	2.85	4.28	3.78	37.65
1984	0.78	1.31	3.12	2.48	3.62	1.04	0.95	3.00	2.30	2.28	2.49	2.90	26.27
1985	2.63	3.83	4.42	2.11	3.11	1.62	3.96	4.88	2.59	3.91	5.51	1.51	40.08
1986	1.30	3.46	2.29	2.73	1.36	5.75	2.47	3.52	7.52	3.05	1.88	2.28	37.61
1987	2.35	0.53	2.19	2.14	2.50	7.04	2.20	6.87	2.69	2.00	3.17	4.60	38.28
1988	1.30	2.02	1.16	1.50	0.87	0.97	2.43	3.13	3.65	3.57	4.29	1.97	26.86
1989	1.28	0.77	2.16	2.22	4.16	3.79	4.21	2.14	3.03	1.73	2.53	1.24	29.26
1990	1.80	5.02	1.91	2.72	3.74	4.92	1.47	3.85	6.06	4.14	2.64	4.37	42.64
1991	1.44	0.94	1.41	2.66	6.20	1.89	1.23	4.31	0.90	4.14	2.61	1.91	29.64
1992	1.78	1.54	3.34	4.34	1.33	2.35	5.91	2.50	5.55	2.01	4.33	2.35	37.33
1993	3.92	1.27	2.12	3.32	1.24	6.05	2.17	1.60	4.26	2.21	1.69	0.78	30.63
Record Mean	1.87	1.72	2.48	3.00	2.92	3.63	3.11	3.38	2.90	2.22	2.65	2.65	32.52

AVERAGE TEMPERATURE (deg. F)

DETROIT, METROPOLITAN AIRPORT MICHIGAN

YEAR	JAN	FEB	MAR	APR	MAY	JUNE	JULY	AUG	SEP	OCT	NOV	DEC	ANNUAL
1964	28.1	25.9	34.3	47.6	60.9	66.2	72.9	65.3	60.7	46.5	41.2	28.1	48.1
1965	24.7	25.9	30.1	45.1	62.4	66.8	69.2	68.0	63.3	48.2	40.5	35.0	48.3
1966	20.4	27.4	37.1	44.4	51.9	68.4	73.5	69.1	62.2	51.0	41.8	28.7	48.0
1967	29.3	23.8	35.9	48.0	51.9	70.4	69.0	67.3	60.4	50.7	35.2	30.9	47.7
1968	20.9	24.3	38.2	50.9	56.1	68.4	71.7	72.5	65.5	53.5	41.0	28.1	49.3
1969	23.1	28.2	33.5	49.4	57.4	64.7	73.2	73.1	64.8	51.4	37.9	26.4	48.6
1970	16.6	24.4	32.9	49.3	60.9	68.4	72.6	72.1	64.5	54.2	40.0	29.0	48.8
1971	20.7	27.4	32.0	45.2	56.4	70.8	69.6	70.3	66.6	58.5	38.5	33.3	49.1
1972	23.8	24.6	32.6	44.6	60.3	64.2	71.2	69.1	63.0	47.3	37.4	29.4	47.3
1973	28.8	25.3	43.3	48.8	55.5	69.9	72.6	72.9	64.9	56.2	41.4	28.7	50.7
1974	26.5	23.6	35.7	49.2	55.2	65.9	72.5	72.3	59.7	48.8	40.6	28.6	48.2
1975	28.3	27.5	32.5	40.9	62.8	69.0	72.2	72.3	59.1	52.9	46.8	29.1	49.5
1976	19.2	33.3	40.4	50.0	56.4	70.6	72.7	70.2	62.1	47.4	33.5	21.5	48.1
1977	12.8	25.2	41.5	52.4	64.4	65.5	75.8	70.6	65.1	47.9	40.5	25.5	48.9
1978	19.6	16.3	30.0	45.5	59.3	66.8	70.6	71.9	67.5	50.2	40.5	28.9	47.3
1979	18.6	16.5	37.7	44.6	56.5	66.6	70.4	67.9	62.6	50.1	39.5	31.9	46.9
1980	24.5	22.2	31.3	45.9	59.8	63.7	72.7	72.7	63.8	46.3	37.4	26.0	47.2
1981	19.0	28.8	36.5	49.8	55.9	68.0	72.4	70.0	60.9	47.6	41.1	27.8	48.2
1982	17.1	20.7	33.0	43.2	64.3	64.2	72.4	67.7	61.8	52.6	41.6	37.3	48.0
1983	28.7	31.6	38.4	44.2	54.4	68.2	74.5	73.6	64.0	51.6	41.2	20.8	49.3
1984	18.0	33.3	28.9	47.8	54.5	70.8	70.8	72.7	61.2	54.9	38.6	34.0	48.8
1985	20.4	23.5	38.4	51.0	60.1	62.8	71.3	69.2	64.3	53.0	42.4	22.2	48.2
1986	23.9	24.6	37.6	50.6	61.3	67.3	75.0	68.9	65.9	52.6	37.3	31.7	49.7
1987	26.1	29.6	39.8	50.8	63.3	71.3	76.1	71.6	64.6	46.6	43.5	33.6	51.4
1988	23.8	23.4	36.9	48.5	62.0	70.4	77.1	75.1	63.3	46.0	42.2	28.7	49.8
1989	32.8	24.1	35.2	45.1	57.5	67.5	73.0	69.9	61.9	52.1	38.2	18.0	47.9
1990	33.6	30.7	39.5	49.0	56.6	68.5	72.2	71.2	64.5	52.8	44.2	32.8	51.3
1991	25.0	31.2	40.3	52.0	66.5	72.4	74.9	73.4	63.1	54.8	38.5	32.1	52.0
1992	28.3	30.8	35.5	46.3	58.3	65.5	68.8	66.7	61.4	49.7	40.5	33.2	48.8
1993	29.4	24.2	34.7	47.8	60.2	67.5	75.5	74.5	61.0	51.9	41.2	30.8	49.9
Record													
Mean	23.4	25.8	35.5	47.5	58.7	67.7	72.3	70.7	63.3	51.3	40.1	28.6	48.8
Max	30.6	33.5	44.2	57.8	69.9	78.8	83.2	81.4	73.8	61.5	47.9	35.4	58.2
Min	16.1	18.0	26.8	37.1	47.5	56.5	61.4	60.0	52.7	41.1	32.2	21.8	39.3

REFERENCE NOTES

DETROIT, METROPOLITAN AIRPORT MICHIGAN

GENERAL
T - TRACE AMOUNT.
BLANK ENTRIES DENOTE MISSING/UNREPORTED DATA.
# INDICATES A STATION OR INSTRUMENT RELOCATION.

SPECIFIC

PM - INCLUDES LAST DAY OF PREVIOUS MONTH
ASOS - AUTOMATED SURFACE OBSERVING SYSTEM IN OPERATION DURING THESE MONTHS.

(*) - LENGTH OF RECORD IN YEARS, ALTHOUGH INDIVIDUAL MONTHS MAY BE MISSING.
0.* OR * - THE VALUE IS BETWEEN 0.0 AND 0.05
NORMALS - BASED ON THE 1961-1990 RECORD PERIOD.
EXTREMES - DATES ARE THE MOST RECENT OCCURRENCE
WIND DIR.- NUMERALS SHOW TENS OF DEGRESS CLOCKWISE FROM TRUE NORTH. "00" INDICATES CALM.
RESULTANT DIRECTIONS ARE GIVEN TO WHOLE DEGREES.
BOLD VALUES INDICATE EXTREME VALUES WHICH OCCURRED AFTER THE ASOS SYSTEM WAS COMMISSIONED.

RECORD = PERIOD OF RECORD
RECORD MEAN PRECIPITATION IS THE MEAN OF ALL DAILY PRECIPITATION AMOUNTS DURING THE PERIOD OF RECORD.
RECORD MAX(MIN) TEMPERATURE IS THE MEAN OF ALL DAILY MAX(MIN) TEMPERATURES DURING THE PERIOD OF RECORD.
RECORD MEAN TEMPERATURE IS THE SUM OF THE RECORD MAX AND RECORD MIN DIVIDED BY 2.
AVERAGE TEMPERATURE IS THE SUM OF THE MEAN DAILY MAX AND MIN TEMPERATURE DIVIDED BY 2.

EXCEPTIONS

RECORD MEANS ARE THROUGH THE CURRENT YEAR,
BEGINNING IN 1959 FOR TEMPERATURE
1959 FOR PRECIPITATION
1959 FOR SNOWFALL

HEATING DEGREE DAYS Base 65 deg. F — DETROIT, METROPOLITAN AIRPORT MICHIGAN

SEASON	JULY	AUG	SEP	OCT	NOV	DEC	JAN	FEB	MAR	APR	MAY	JUNE	TOTAL
1964-65	4	82	175	566	710	1137	1239	1088	1074	591	131	45	6842
1965-66	18	48	128	510	729	927	1377	1046	860	612	406	53	6714
1966-67	0	13	136	427	688	1119	1097	1148	894	505	406	9	6442
1967-68	32	29	158	452	886	1050	1360	1173	823	416	275	29	6683
1968-69	3	17	71	384	714	1137	1289	1024	972	464	259	102	6436
1969-70	0	0	93	418	804	1189	1491	1130	993	479	168	49	6814
1970-71	8	8	108	339	742	1105	1368	1047	1015	588	278	22	6628
1971-72	13	6	72	213	788	977	1272	1165	997	608	174	91	6376
1972-73	24	28	113	539	822	1096	1115	1103	667	480	289	3	6279
1973-74	0	10	98	276	702	1119	1189	1152	901	476	308	54	6285
1974-75	0	2	189	495	726	1123	1129	1043	996	714	142	41	6600
1975-76	4	0	178	375	537	1107	1413	914	757	473	269	6	6033
1976-77	1	15	133	540	938	1341	1609	1106	721	395	122	85	7006
1977-78	1	17	85	524	729	1218	1400	1357	1077	580	235	65	7288
1978-79	17	0	73	452	728	1112	1432	1355	843	604	291	55	6962
1979-80	12	29	126	471	758	1019	1249	1233	1036	568	191	104	6796
1980-81	0	0	110	578	822	1201	1418	1008	878	452	293	19	6779
1981-82	3	9	167	534	710	1144	1477	1237	985	647	75	70	7058
1982-83	2	39	145	383	696	852	1119	928	816	618	323	59	5980
1983-84	6	0	125	418	708	1367	1450	912	1112	507	334	9	6948
1984-85	11	4	164	310	785	955	1377	1154	818	435	177	93	6283
1985-86	2	8	129	366	672	1317	1271	1125	842	435	166	48	6381
1986-87	1	33	76	380	824	1028	1198	984	776	423	158	11	5892
1987-88	4	30	69	566	639	969	1273	1201	864	486	138	46	6285
1988-89	2	3	90	590	679	1118	991	1138	916	591	254	33	6405
1989-90	0	11	151	400	797	1451	966	955	785	506	258	27	6307
1990-91	1	1	112	380	618	994	1234	939	761	394	125	5	5564
1991-92	0	0	151	319	788	1013	1129	985	906	555	224	59	6129
1992-93	15	30	153	469	725	976	1097	1138	931	506	161	51	6252
1993-94	0	2	155	404	710	1050							

COOLING DEGREE DAYS Base 65 deg. F — DETROIT, METROPOLITAN AIRPORT MICHIGAN

YEAR	JAN	FEB	MAR	APR	MAY	JUNE	JULY	AUG	SEP	OCT	NOV	DEC	TOTAL
1969	0	0	0	1	28	98	260	259	91	4	0	0	741
1970	0	0	0	17	50	161	249	236	100	12	0	0	825
1971	0	0	0	0	14	205	161	177	128	17	0	0	702
1972	0	0	0	0	36	73	222	160	59	0	0	0	550
1973	0	0	0	3	2	156	241	261	104	11	0	0	778
1974	0	0	0	8	10	91	237	237	36	1	0	0	620
1975	0	0	0	0	82	171	233	232	7	6	0	0	731
1976	0	0	0	30	10	182	246	182	53	3	0	0	706
1977	0	0	0	25	108	107	341	198	94	0	0	0	873
1978	0	0	0	0	63	122	200	221	154	0	0	0	760
1979	0	0	0	0	32	109	184	124	57	16	0	0	522
1980	0	0	0	3	38	69	246	248	79	3	0	0	686
1981	0	0	0	1	17	118	241	168	51	0	0	0	596
1982	0	0	0	0	58	55	237	129	57	5	0	0	541
1983	0	0	0	2	0	160	306	272	104	6	0	0	850
1984	0	0	0	0	15	189	197	252	55	2	0	0	710
1985	0	0	0	25	32	32	201	146	116	0	0	0	552
1986	0	0	0	10	55	120	319	160	110	3	0	0	777
1987	0	0	0	4	111	207	355	245	64	0	1	0	987
1988	0	0	0	0	52	214	385	322	46	8	0	0	1027
1989	0	0	0	0	29	114	256	171	64	5	0	0	639
1990	0	0	1	32	8	139	234	200	101	11	0	0	726
1991	0	0	0	10	179	233	315	268	104	9	0	0	1118
1992	0	0	0	0	27	80	143	91	51	0	0	0	392
1993	0	0	0	0	21	135	334	302	41	5	0	0	838

SNOWFALL (inches) — DETROIT, METROPOLITAN AIRPORT MICHIGAN

SEASON	JULY	AUG	SEP	OCT	NOV	DEC	JAN	FEB	MAR	APR	MAY	JUNE	TOTAL
1964-65	0.0	0.0	0.0	T	4.3	7.2	11.7	17.3	16.1	2.5	0.0	0.0	59.1
1965-66	0.0	0.0	0.0	T	0.4	1.6	8.4	3.9	2.5	1.8	0.0	0.0	18.6
1966-67	0.0	0.0	0.0	0.0	11.8	14.9	5.4	11.0	5.8	1.7	0.0	0.0	50.6
1967-68	0.0	0.0	0.0	T	1.4	4.5	11.8	2.8	10.0	0.1	0.0	0.0	30.6
1968-69	0.0	0.0	0.0	T	T	5.9	6.3	2.3	2.3	0.3	0.0	0.0	17.1
1969-70	0.0	0.0	0.0	T	3.9	10.0	10.9	9.4	6.7	4.2	T	0.0	45.1
1970-71	0.0	0.0	0.0	0.0	1.7	9.8	8.7	5.9	8.7	0.6	0.0	0.0	35.4
1971-72	0.0	0.0	0.0	0.0	4.2	2.6	7.9	9.3	2.5	2.5	0.0	0.0	29.0
1972-73	0.0	0.0	0.0	T	7.1	12.5	2.4	12.8	10.1	0.1	T	0.0	45.0
1973-74	0.0	0.0	0.0	0.0	0.1	16.4	14.1	11.2	5.7	1.7	T	0.0	49.2
1974-75	0.0	0.0	0.0	T	7.7	34.9	4.9	7.5	4.5	3.6	0.0	0.0	63.1
1975-76	0.0	0.0	0.0	0.0	6.5	19.8	15.1	4.9	7.5	2.1	T	0.0	55.9
1976-77	0.0	0.0	0.0	T	1.4	9.8	14.7	5.0	12.3	0.7	0.0	0.0	43.9
1977-78	0.0	0.0	0.0	0.0	7.4	16.6	29.6	5.3	2.5	0.3	0.0	0.0	61.7
1978-79	0.0	0.0	0.0	0.0	6.1	6.6	13.3	3.9	2.7	3.0	0.0	0.0	35.6
1979-80	0.0	0.0	0.0	T	3.2	2.3	2.8	5.5	11.7	1.4	0.0	0.0	26.9
1980-81	0.0	0.0	0.0	2.9	3.4	10.5	7.6	13.4	0.6	0.0	0.0	0.0	38.4
1981-82	0.0	0.0	0.0	0.1	0.7	17.3	20.0	13.3	13.6	9.0	0.0	0.0	74.0
1982-83	0.0	0.0	0.0	T	1.8	1.4	1.5	4.3	7.6	3.4	0.0	0.0	20.0
1983-84	0.0	0.0	0.0	0.0	3.5	19.9	9.9	8.7	9.7	0.1	0.0	0.0	51.8
1984-85	0.0	0.0	0.0	0.0	4.1	6.2	20.9	16.9	6.1	0.9	0.0	0.0	55.1
1985-86	0.0	0.0	0.0	0.0	2.0	14.1	8.6	20.8	7.4	1.3	0.0	0.0	54.2
1986-87	0.0	0.0	0.0	T	3.3	6.0	24.0	2.0	13.3	1.1	0.0	0.0	49.7
1987-88	0.0	0.0	0.0	T	0.7	15.3	7.0	19.2	2.7	0.2	0.0	0.0	45.1
1988-89	0.0	0.0	0.0	T	1.0	6.3	5.3	9.6	2.4	0.5	T	0.0	25.1
1989-90	0.0	0.0	0.0	2.7	2.4	11.8	4.0	11.1	7.8	2.0	0.0	0.0	41.8
1990-91	0.0	0.0	T	0.0	T	13.2	8.8	9.2	0.2	T	T	0.0	31.4
1991-92	0.0	0.0	0.0	T	2.2	8.6	18.4	2.4	11.7	0.2	0.0	0.0	43.5
1992-93	0.0	0.0	0.0	0.4	0.9	5.0	11.0	15.2	15.7	4.0	0.0	0.0	52.2
1993-94	0.0	0.0	0.0	0.4	0.6	1.9							
Record Mean	0.0	0.0	T	0.2	3.0	10.2	10.2	9.1	7.0	1.7	T	0.0	41.2

GRAND RAPIDS, MICHIGAN

Grand Rapids, Michigan, is located in the west-central part of Kent County, in the picturesque Grand River valley about 30 air miles east of Lake Michigan. The Grand River, the longest stream in Michigan, flows through the city and bisects it into east and west sections. High hills rise on either side of the valley. Elevations range from 602 feet on the valley floor to 1,020 feet in the extreme southern part of Kent County, southwest of the airport.

Grand Rapids is under the natural climatic influence of Lake Michigan. In spring the cooling effect of Lake Michigan helps retard the growth of vegetation until the danger of frost has passed. The warming effect in the fall retards frost until most of the crops have matured. Fall is a colorful time of year in western Michigan, compensating for the late spring. During the winter, excessive cloudiness and numerous snow flurries occur with strong westerly winds. The tempering effect of Lake Michigan on cold waves coming in from the west and northwest is quite evident.

The tempering effect of the lake promotes the growth of a great variety of fruit trees and berries, especially apples, peaches, cherries, and blueberries. The intense cold of winter is modified, thus reducing winter kill of fruit trees. Summer days are pleasantly warm and most summer nights are quite comfortable, although there are about three weeks of hot, humid weather during most summers. Prolonged severe cold waves with below-zero temperatures are infrequent. The temperature usually rises to above zero during the daytime hours regardless of early morning readings.

July is the sunniest month and December is the month with the least sunshine. November through January is usually a period of excessive cloudiness and minimal sunshine.

Precipitation is usually ample for the growth and development of all vegetation. About one-half of the annual precipitation falls during the growing season, May through September. Droughts occur occasionally, but are seldom of protracted length. The snowfall season extends from mid-November to mid-March. Some winters have had continuous snow cover throughout this period, although there is usually a mid-winter thaw. The Grand River flows through the city and reaches critical heights a couple of times each year, generally once in January-February and again in March-April. Overflow is generally limited to the lowlands of the flood plain.

November is one of the windiest months and although violent windstorms are infrequent, gusts have on occasion exceeded 65 mph. Summer thunderstorms occasionally produce gusty winds over 60 mph.

NORMALS, MEANS, AND EXTREMES

GRAND RAPIDS, MICHIGAN

LATITUDE: 42°53'N LONGITUDE: 85°31' W ELEVATION: FT. GRND 784 BARO 819 TIME ZONE: EASTERN WBAN: 94860

	(a)	JAN	FEB	MAR	APR	MAY	JUNE	JULY	AUG	SEP	OCT	NOV	DEC	YEAR
TEMPERATURE °F:														
Normals														
-Daily Maximum		29.0	31.6	42.8	56.6	69.3	78.7	82.8	80.5	72.0	59.8	45.8	33.5	56.9
-Daily Minimum		14.7	15.8	25.4	35.4	45.6	55.3	60.4	58.4	49.9	39.1	30.2	20.7	37.6
-Monthly		21.8	23.7	34.1	46.0	57.5	67.0	71.6	69.5	61.0	49.5	38.0	27.1	47.2
Extremes														
-Record Highest	30	62	67	78	88	92	98	100	100	93	87	77	67	100
-Year		1967	1976	1986	1970	1978	1988	1988	1964	1973	1975	1975	1982	JUL 1988
-Record Lowest	30	-21	-19	-8	3	22	33	41	39	27	18	5	-18	-21
-Year		1979	1973	1978	1982	1966	1972	1983	1976	1991	1988	1977	1983	JAN 1979
NORMAL DEGREE DAYS:														
Heating (base 65°F)		1339	1156	958	570	273	50	0	18	139	485	810	1175	6973
Cooling (base 65°F)		0	0	0	0	40	110	208	157	19	0	0	0	534
% OF POSSIBLE SUNSHINE	30	30	40	45	51	56	61	63	61	54	44	27	21	46
MEAN SKY COVER (tenths)														
Sunrise - Sunset	30	8.3	7.7	7.4	6.9	6.4	6.1	5.9	5.9	6.4	6.9	8.2	8.6	7.1
MEAN NUMBER OF DAYS:														
Sunrise to Sunset														
-Clear	30	2.6	3.5	4.8	6.0	7.1	6.7	7.8	8.3	7.0	5.7	2.7	2.2	64.4
-Partly Cloudy	30	5.1	5.9	6.9	7.0	9.1	11.1	12.3	11.3	9.2	8.3	5.3	4.0	95.4
-Cloudy	30	23.3	18.9	19.3	17.0	14.8	12.2	10.9	11.5	13.8	16.9	22.0	24.8	205.5
Precipitation														
.01 inches or more	30	16.2	11.8	12.7	13.3	10.4	10.0	9.4	9.4	10.8	11.4	13.6	16.1	145.1
Snow,Ice pellets,hail														
1.0 inches or more	30	6.7	4.1	2.9	0.8	0.0	0.0	0.0	0.0	0.0	0.2	2.6	6.1	23.4
Thunderstorms	30	0.3	0.3	1.7	3.4	3.7	5.7	6.2	5.4	4.3	1.7	1.3	0.4	34.3
Heavy Fog Visibility 1/4 mile or less	30	2.0	2.3	2.5	1.8	1.5	1.5	1.4	2.0	2.1	2.1	2.1	3.3	24.6
Temperature °F														
-Maximum														
90° and above	30	0.0	0.0	0.0	0.0	0.5	2.2	4.9	2.6	0.4	0.0	0.0	0.0	10.7
32° and below	30	18.9	14.8	5.7	0.4	0.0	0.0	0.0	0.0	0.0	0.0	2.4	13.6	55.8
-Minimum														
32° and below	30	29.2	26.3	23.8	11.7	2.1	0.0	0.0	0.0	0.4	6.4	17.5	27.7	145.1
0° and below	30	3.7	2.7	0.4	0.0	0.0	0.0	0.0	0.0	0.0	0.0	0.0	1.4	8.3
AVG. STATION PRESS.(mb)	21	987.2	988.3	986.3	985.4	985.7	985.6	986.9	988.2	988.6	988.4	987.3	987.6	987.1
RELATIVE HUMIDITY (%)														
Hour 01	30	80	79	77	75	76	80	83	86	86	82	81	82	81
Hour 07 (Local Time)	30	82	81	80	79	79	81	84	89	89	85	83	83	83
Hour 13	30	72	68	64	57	53	55	56	58	61	62	70	75	63
Hour 19	30	76	72	67	59	55	57	58	63	71	72	76	79	67
PRECIPITATION (inches):														
Water Equivalent														
-Normal		1.83	1.42	2.63	3.37	3.13	3.68	3.19	3.57	4.24	2.81	3.32	2.85	36.04
-Maximum Monthly	30	4.36	3.34	5.12	6.11	8.29	8.21	8.83	8.46	11.85	6.30	7.81	6.63	11.85
-Year		1975	1986	1974	1981	1981	1967	1992	1987	1986	1969	1966	1971	SEP 1986
-Minimum Monthly	30	0.47	0.33	1.08	1.79	0.94	0.25	0.81	0.14	T	0.60	0.95	0.66	T
-Year		1981	1969	1968	1989	1987	1988	1976	1969	1979	1964	1986	1969	SEP 1979
-Maximum in 24 hrs	30	2.16	1.52	1.78	2.63	5.48	3.28	3.38	3.68	4.55	3.19	3.00	2.79	5.48
-Year		1993	1985	1985	1991	1981	1972	1992	1987	1986	1993	1990	1982	MAY 1981
Snow,Ice pellets,hail														
-Maximum Monthly	30	45.5	25.1	36.0	12.4	0.2	0.0	T	T	T	8.4	25.3	34.8	45.5
-Year		1979	1989	1965	1982	1990		1990	1993	1967	1967	1991	1983	JAN 1979
-Maximum in 24 hrs	30	16.1	9.1	13.2	9.8	0.2	0.0	T	T	T	8.4	10.4	15.1	16.1
-Year		1978	1985	1970	1975	1990		1990	1993	1967	1967	1991	1970	JAN 1978
WIND:														
Mean Speed (mph)	30	11.5	10.7	11.1	11.0	9.7	8.9	8.2	7.9	8.3	9.4	10.5	10.7	9.8
Prevailing Direction														
Fastest Obs. 1 Min.														
-Direction (!!)	14	26	33	25	24	27	24	29	20	36	25	25	24	25
-Speed (MPH)	14	39	37	41	41	39	39	35	31	31	36	44	39	44
-Year		1980	1987	1982	1984	1990	1992	1980	1989	1989	1993	1991	1982	NOV 1991
Peak Gust														
-Direction (!!)	10	W	NW	W	SW	SW	SW	NW	N	N	W	SW	SW	SW
-Speed (mph)	10	51	55	56	63	68	63	51	61	52	45	55	51	68
-Date		1990	1987	1991	1984	1987	1992	1991	1984	1989	1993	1991	1992	MAY 1987

PRECIPITATION (inches)

GRAND RAPIDS, MICHIGAN

YEAR	JAN	FEB	MAR	APR	MAY	JUNE	JULY	AUG	SEP	OCT	NOV	DEC	ANNUAL
1964	1.42	0.73	3.54	5.28	3.96	4.12	2.14	3.19	3.16	0.60	2.13	2.01	32.28
1965	3.99	1.58	3.11	2.49	1.53	2.89	1.96	5.36	6.62	2.10	2.35	4.23	38.21
1966	1.22	2.28	2.65	4.62	2.16	2.36	1.95	3.82	1.92	2.33	7.81	4.01	37.13
1967	1.94	1.13	2.49	4.27	1.86	8.21	2.77	3.34	2.37	4.42	4.35	3.60	40.75
1968	1.55	2.12	1.08	2.40	2.67	5.02	2.74	2.86	4.21	4.05	4.28	3.16	36.14
1969	2.39	0.33	1.29	5.16	3.40	4.74	6.42	0.14	0.93	6.30	3.00	0.66	34.76
1970	1.18	0.51	2.43	3.27	4.24	6.53	6.32	2.89	7.18	3.65	3.42	1.89	43.51
1971	1.04	2.48	1.77	2.27	1.05	2.01	2.46	0.92	6.30	1.39	2.84	6.63	31.16
1972	1.26	0.90	2.11	3.85	1.99	4.64	3.72	5.01	3.96	2.92	2.06	4.96	37.38
1973	1.66	1.15	3.34	3.47	4.31	3.58	2.06	1.45	2.47	4.12	3.54	3.28	34.43
1974	3.23	2.09	5.12	2.93	4.01	4.43	0.97	4.61	2.05	2.44	3.11	1.83	36.82
1975	4.36	1.92	2.28	4.07	2.08	5.97	2.31	7.38	2.00	1.04	3.82	4.02	41.25
1976	1.67	2.13	4.99	4.75	6.63	2.79	0.81	1.03	1.21	2.00	1.51	1.05	30.57
1977	1.59	1.35	3.81	4.04	1.33	3.50	5.16	4.77	4.26	2.28	2.34	3.35	37.78
1978	2.22	0.54	2.01	2.55	2.91	4.65	2.83	5.00	5.62	3.05	1.83	3.32	36.53
1979	2.09	0.61	3.72	3.56	1.37	4.16	2.27	4.33	T	2.10	5.46	2.97	32.64
1980	1.76	1.76	1.74	3.64	3.19	4.00	5.90	3.18	4.57	1.99	1.57	3.60	36.90
1981	0.47	2.03	1.29	6.11	8.29	4.22	3.74	2.95	9.52	2.54	2.58	1.10	44.84
1982	2.98	0.36	3.36	2.11	3.63	2.45	3.81	3.07	1.92	1.42	5.36	6.49	36.96
1983	1.33	1.12	3.30	5.06	4.64	2.09	4.76	1.49	4.87	2.66	3.00	2.79	37.11
1984	0.94	1.15	2.77	2.10	4.77	0.62	2.12	1.49	2.16	3.34	2.85	4.37	28.68
1985	1.94	3.26	4.20	2.54	1.36	1.68	3.09	6.48	4.26	4.64	5.45	2.00	40.90
1986	1.07	3.34	2.35	2.58	3.88	7.14	5.27	5.30	11.85	2.76	0.95	1.04	47.53
1987	0.67	0.37	1.15	2.40	0.94	3.56	2.93	8.46	4.47	2.33	2.49	3.29	33.06
1988	2.39	1.14	2.12	3.11	1.07	0.25	3.69	3.04	7.49	5.37	4.82	1.88	36.37
1989	0.95	1.01	2.47	1.79	4.33	5.02	1.29	4.78	4.90	1.53	4.86	0.97	33.90
1990	2.39	2.08	1.96	2.23	4.39	3.00	3.73	3.40	4.22	5.05	7.14	2.97	42.56
1991	1.32	0.64	3.58	5.58	4.44	1.76	6.24	3.79	2.93	5.61	6.41	2.63	44.93
1992	1.52	1.06	3.51	3.98	1.45	1.61	8.83	3.55	5.60	2.34	5.64	3.27	42.36
1993	4.21	1.13	2.31	4.93	2.17	6.05	1.83	7.73	8.20	4.32	2.12	1.47	46.47
Record Mean	2.18	1.82	2.51	3.01	3.29	3.54	2.98	2.88	3.60	2.80	2.84	2.48	33.93

AVERAGE TEMPERATURE (deg. F)

GRAND RAPIDS, MICHIGAN

YEAR	JAN	FEB	MAR	APR	MAY	JUNE	JULY	AUG	SEP	OCT	NOV	DEC	ANNUAL
1964	27.5	25.0	34.5	48.2	62.0	68.9	73.1	67.3	61.4	47.2	41.8	26.0	48.6
1965	22.5	23.8	26.2	42.8	62.3	65.9	70.0	67.9	62.3	50.0	40.0	33.5	47.3
1966	19.1	25.5	37.1	43.8	52.0	69.2	73.6	68.5	61.4	51.2	42.1	29.2	47.7
1967	28.6	20.4	34.1	46.4	51.9	69.3	68.6	66.0	60.3	49.9	34.5	29.9	46.7
1968	21.0	21.4	38.0	48.8	54.0	66.7	69.8	70.6	63.7	51.8	37.9	24.3	47.3
1969	20.8	24.4	29.3	46.4	55.7	61.8	71.3	72.1	62.4	47.9	33.5	25.0	45.9
1970	17.0	22.4	28.8	46.8	59.4	66.8	72.1	70.1	61.7	52.2	38.3	25.7	46.8
1971	18.3	24.1	29.0	43.9	54.0	70.9	69.2	68.6	65.6	58.3	38.0	32.0	47.6
1972	20.8	21.9	29.7	42.3	59.3	63.5	70.3	68.7	62.0	46.1	35.9	26.6	45.6
1973	27.4	22.8	41.9	46.8	53.7	69.9	72.4	72.7	63.4	55.0	39.9	26.2	49.3
1974	25.7	21.1	33.6	47.2	53.2	63.0	71.1	67.3	56.4	46.9	37.6	28.4	46.0
1975	25.2	24.3	28.8	39.8	60.7	67.6	70.6	70.5	57.0	53.0	44.7	27.3	47.5
1976	18.9	31.0	37.9	48.2	53.9	69.5	72.5	68.9	60.2	45.7	31.5	19.1	46.4
1977	12.7	22.8	40.0	52.1	65.8	64.5	74.0	67.9	62.9	48.6	39.5	25.9	48.1
1978	19.3	14.4	27.9	45.3	59.9	66.8	70.4	68.1	63.7	47.2	37.6	26.6	45.6
1979	17.1	15.0	36.9	44.5	57.7	67.6	71.1	68.5	63.4	51.5	40.5	33.0	47.2
1980	25.1	22.7	32.5	47.0	59.9	64.4	72.7	72.6	62.7	45.8	37.5	25.1	47.3
1981	20.8	30.2	35.1	47.3	55.5	68.6	72.1	70.7	60.9	48.2	39.8	28.7	48.2
1982	17.2	22.1	32.5	41.8	65.0	62.8	73.1	68.6	61.9	53.6	40.8	36.2	48.0
1983	27.6	30.9	36.9	42.6	52.8	67.7	74.7	72.2	62.4	50.7	40.7	19.2	48.2
1984	17.1	34.0	28.9	47.3	53.5	70.1	70.1	73.0	60.5	54.2	40.3	32.2	48.4
1985	18.6	21.3	36.2	51.7	60.4	63.8	70.7	67.4	63.6	50.6	38.4	22.3	47.1
1986	22.7	22.5	36.7	49.7	58.8	64.4	72.5	66.0	62.8	50.2	35.0	29.8	47.6
1987	25.4	29.9	37.3	50.1	62.6	71.2	74.1	69.3	62.2	45.0	41.1	31.5	50.0
1988	20.8	20.7	34.1	47.1	60.9	68.5	74.7	73.4	61.3	44.2	40.7	27.3	47.8
1989	30.5	19.7	31.8	43.9	55.8	65.9	71.9	68.4	59.4	51.1	35.7	17.2	45.9
1990	32.1	28.1	37.1	47.7	55.0	67.1	70.3	69.0	62.8	49.9	43.3	30.0	49.4
1991	22.2	29.2	37.9	50.8	64.6	71.2	72.4	70.5	60.1	52.0	35.7	29.4	49.7
1992	27.5	30.3	33.7	44.0	57.4	64.3	67.2	65.0	59.7	48.2	38.2	30.5	47.2
1993	25.9	21.9	32.4	44.0	58.2	65.2	72.7	71.4	56.5	48.0	37.9	27.8	46.8
Record Mean	24.0	24.4	34.0	46.6	58.0	67.8	72.6	70.4	62.9	51.5	39.1	28.2	48.3
Max	30.5	31.6	42.2	56.5	68.9	78.7	83.3	81.0	73.0	60.8	46.0	34.1	57.2
Min	17.5	17.2	25.8	36.7	47.1	56.8	61.8	59.8	52.7	42.2	32.2	22.3	39.3

REFERENCE NOTES

GRAND RAPIDS, MICHIGAN

GENERAL
T - TRACE AMOUNT.
BLANK ENTRIES DENOTE MISSING/UNREPORTED DATA.
# INDICATES A STATION OR INSTRUMENT RELOCATION.

SPECIFIC

PM - INCLUDES LAST DAY OF PREVIOUS MONTH
ASOS - AUTOMATED SURFACE OBSERVING SYSTEM IN OPERATION DURING THESE MONTHS.

(a) - LENGTH OF RECORD IN YEARS, ALTHOUGH INDIVIDUAL MONTHS MAY BE MISSING.
0.* OR * - THE VALUE IS BETWEEN 0.0 AND 0.05
NORMALS - BASED ON THE 1961-1990 RECORD PERIOD.
EXTREMES - DATES ARE THE MOST RECENT OCCURRENCE
WIND DIR.- NUMERALS SHOW TENS OF DEGRESS CLOCKWISE FROM TRUE NORTH. "00" INDICATES CALM.
RESULTANT DIRECTIONS ARE GIVEN TO WHOLE DEGREES.
BOLD VALUES INDICATE EXTREME VALUES WHICH OCCURRED AFTER THE ASOS SYSTEM WAS COMMISSIONED.

RECORD = PERIOD OF RECORD
RECORD MEAN PRECIPITATION IS THE MEAN OF ALL DAILY PRECIPITATION AMOUNTS DURING THE PERIOD OF RECORD.
RECORD MAX(MIN) TEMPERATURE IS THE MEAN OF ALL DAILY MAX(MIN) TEMPERATURES DURING THE PERIOD OF RECORD.
RECORD MEAN TEMPERATURE IS THE SUM OF THE RECORD MAX AND RECORD MIN DIVIDED BY 2.
AVERAGE TEMPERATURE IS THE SUM OF THE MEAN DAILY MAX AND MIN TEMPERATURE DIVIDED BY 2.

EXCEPTIONS

RECORD MEANS ARE THROUGH THE CURRENT YEAR, BEGINNING IN 1894 FOR TEMPERATURE
1870 FOR PRECIPITATION
1964 FOR SNOWFALL

HEATING DEGREE DAYS Base 65 deg. F GRAND RAPIDS, MICHIGAN

SEASON	JULY	AUG	SEP	OCT	NOV	DEC	JAN	FEB	MAR	APR	MAY	JUNE	TOTAL
1964-65	12	54	179	545	690	1202	1310	1145	1197	657	142	57	7190
1965-66	5	50	145	462	743	968	1414	1102	860	632	400	47	6828
1966-67	0	12	146	426	680	1102	1120	1242	950	554	410	9	6651
1967-68	38	47	179	477	909	1080	1356	1255	827	482	342	70	7062
1968-69	30	36	90	434	805	1254	1360	1132	1102	550	300	151	7244
1969-70	3	2	145	524	938	1232	1481	1186	1117	559	216	61	7464
1970-71	13	17	150	397	798	1210	1441	1140	1110	626	342	35	7279
1971-72	15	11	107	233	800	1016	1365	1240	1089	675	204	102	6857
1972-73	28	41	126	577	867	1185	1162	1178	708	552	341	4	6769
1973-74	1	7	136	314	748	1196	1212	1225	967	532	364	113	6815
1974-75	5	22	275	555	816	1127	1227	1133	1113	750	191	61	7275
1975-76	16	5	242	382	602	1161	1420	980	835	526	342	18	6529
1976-77	0	32	185	591	999	1415	1616	1177	765	401	106	91	7378
1977-78	3	48	99	501	759	1204	1407	1413	1140	584	213	62	7433
1978-79	15	22	124	545	816	1182	1477	1393	863	607	264	42	7350
1979-80	7	31	109	431	731	984	1230	1221	1000	541	189	106	6580
1980-81	0	4	115	588	821	1227	1363	969	919	525	298	8	6837
1981-82	7	5	173	513	749	1116	1475	1196	998	689	91	98	7110
1982-83	6	34	140	361	717	884	1151	949	866	663	373	61	6205
1983-84	16	2	149	440	721	1413	1480	892	1107	532	353	13	7118
1984-85	16	4	189	333	735	1014	1431	1216	886	428	173	81	6506
1985-86	9	17	157	436	790	1316	1302	1186	871	466	214	75	6839
1986-87	11	56	118	452	894	1084	1220	978	849	440	178	20	6300
1987-88	18	36	118	610	712	1032	1364	1277	950	531	169	60	6877
1988-89	3	21	135	639	722	1162	1062	1263	1023	625	297	51	7003
1989-90	2	23	203	424	874	1477	1014	1026	865	549	306	45	6808
1990-91	11	15	139	475	645	1077	1323	997	830	430	157	18	6117
1991-92	5	4	211	404	871	1098	1155	1001	964	626	262	75	6676
1992-93	25	66	197	512	794	1060	1204	1203	1004	624	227	84	7000
1993-94	1	16	259	524	810	1150							

COOLING DEGREE DAYS Base 65 deg. F GRAND RAPIDS, MICHIGAN

YEAR	JAN	FEB	MAR	APR	MAY	JUNE	JULY	AUG	SEP	OCT	NOV	DEC	TOTAL
1969	0	0	0	0	21	61	202	229	76	1	0	0	590
1970	0	0	0	19	49	122	242	180	55	6	0	0	673
1971	0	0	0	0	8	218	154	129	132	31	0	0	672
1972	0	0	0	0	37	61	200	163	42	0	0	0	503
1973	0	0	0	10	0	157	238	255	96	12	0	0	768
1974	0	0	0	4	6	60	201	103	23	3	0	0	400
1975	0	0	0	0	65	148	199	184	8	15	0	0	619
1976	0	0	0	27	4	158	239	161	49	0	0	0	638
1977	0	0	0	19	137	85	286	143	44	0	0	0	714
1978	0	0	0	0	62	123	188	125	90	0	0	0	588
1979	0	0	0	0	46	129	204	147	69	19	0	0	614
1980	0	0	0	6	34	96	247	245	53	0	0	0	681
1981	0	0	0	0	13	124	236	190	55	0	0	0	618
1982	0	0	0	0	99	40	263	153	55	12	0	0	622
1983	0	0	0	0	2	146	325	234	76	5	0	0	788
1984	0	0	0	7	5	174	179	259	60	6	0	0	690
1985	0	0	0	36	39	52	193	99	119	0	0	0	538
1986	0	0	0	14	26	64	252	94	61	0	0	0	511
1987	0	0	0	2	110	213	306	174	38	0	0	0	843
1988	0	0	0	0	50	170	310	289	29	2	0	0	850
1989	0	0	0	0	19	84	223	135	40	0	0	0	501
1990	0	0	6	37	6	115	185	144	83	13	0	0	589
1991	0	0	0	12	155	211	240	182	71	7	0	0	878
1992	0	0	0	2	36	60	99	74	44	1	0	0	316
1993	0	0	0	0	21	94	244	222	10	5	0	0	596

SNOWFALL (inches) GRAND RAPIDS, MICHIGAN

SEASON	JULY	AUG	SEP	OCT	NOV	DEC	JAN	FEB	MAR	APR	MAY	JUNE	TOTAL
1964-65	0.0	0.0	0.0	T	5.8	13.4	24.1	16.7	36.0	5.4	0.0	0.0	101.4
1965-66	0.0	0.0	T	0.0	9.1	9.6	25.9	15.0	4.6	2.8	T	0.0	67.0
1966-67	0.0	0.0	0.0	0.0	16.6	17.6	29.8	17.5	10.3	T	T	0.0	91.8
1967-68	0.0	0.0	T	8.4	11.0	9.6	11.8	8.5	4.2	1.6	0.0	0.0	55.1
1968-69	0.0	0.0	0.0	0.0	4.2	26.2	27.7	6.3	7.9	0.0	0.0	0.0	72.3
1969-70	0.0	0.0	0.0	T	14.3	11.8	23.2	8.2	19.3	7.8	0.0	0.0	84.6
1970-71	0.0	0.0	0.0	0.0	6.1	33.3	27.2	4.4	25.9	4.1	0.0	0.0	101.0
1971-72	0.0	0.0	0.0	0.0	14.9	3.7	22.6	16.9	14.2	7.5	0.0	0.0	79.8
1972-73	0.0	0.0	0.0	0.9	11.0	19.8	7.0	13.2	8.5	5.0	0.1	0.0	65.5
1973-74	0.0	0.0	0.0	0.0	0.4	20.0	13.3	18.4	11.3	1.0	T	0.0	64.4
1974-75	0.0	0.0	0.0	0.4	8.9	16.5	10.7	10.6	11.8	10.0	0.0	0.0	68.9
1975-76	0.0	0.0	0.0	0.0	6.6	23.3	25.0	6.5	3.5	4.2	0.1	0.0	69.2
1976-77	0.0	0.0	0.0	2.0	8.5	17.7	26.1	5.0	9.5	2.0	0.0	0.0	70.8
1977-78	0.0	0.0	0.0	0.0	10.6	23.2	35.8	8.8	6.2	T	0.0	0.0	84.6
1978-79	0.0	0.0	0.0	T	6.2	30.0	45.5	5.3	7.2	1.8	0.0	0.0	96.0
1979-80	0.0	0.0	0.0	T	9.4	2.6	13.3	12.6	6.6	4.0	T	0.0	48.5
1980-81	0.0	0.0	0.0	0.4	5.5	17.3	8.1	18.8	1.4	T	0.0	0.0	51.5
1981-82	0.0	0.0	0.0	T	4.4	8.9	30.3	6.7	11.8	12.4	0.0	0.0	74.5
1982-83	0.0	0.0	0.0	0.0	5.2	8.2	5.7	2.9	13.2	0.7	0.0	0.0	35.9
1983-84	0.0	0.0	0.0	T	4.7	34.8	19.6	1.6	10.6	0.1	T	0.0	71.4
1984-85	0.0	0.0	0.0	0.0	T	15.7	22.6	21.3	6.7	3.3	0.0	0.0	69.6
1985-86	0.0	0.0	0.0	0.0	3.5	30.7	18.4	20.2	6.1	0.2	0.0	0.0	79.1
1986-87	0.0	0.0	0.0	0.0	5.3	12.7	19.2	0.9	5.7	3.8	0.0	0.0	47.6
1987-88	0.0	0.0	0.0	1.6	0.7	18.2	21.9	18.1	3.4	0.3	0.0	0.0	64.2
1988-89	0.0	0.0	0.0	0.2	5.5	14.4	8.7	25.1	6.3	2.2	T	0.0	62.4
1989-90	0.0	0.0	0.0	5.8	19.4	25.2	10.6	23.8	2.7	2.1	0.2	0.0	89.8
1990-91	T	0.0	0.0	T	2.0	18.6	27.7	9.5	2.8	T	0.0	0.0	60.6
1991-92	0.0	0.0	0.0	0.3	25.3	27.9	13.4	3.5	15.1	2.3	0.0	0.0	87.8
1992-93	0.0	0.0	0.0	2.3	4.2	14.2	11.1	18.6	11.6	3.3	0.0	0.0	65.3
1993-94	0.0	T	0.0	T	1.9	17.7							
Record Mean	T	T	T	0.7	7.7	18.1	20.2	11.9	10.0	3.0	T	0.0	71.6

HOUGHTON LAKE, MICHIGAN

Houghton Lake is located in north-central lower Michigan. The present station is on the northeast shore of Houghton Lake, the largest inland lake in Michigan, with a circumference of about 32 miles. The Muskegon River source is Higgins Lake, 8 miles to the north. It flows through Houghton Lake, then southwestward to Lake Michigan. The station lies within an elongated bowl shaped 1,000-foot plateau, which extends roughly 50 miles north, 75 miles southwest, and about 20 miles southeast of Houghton Lake. In the immediate area, the land is level to rolling, but there are hills and ridges from 100 to 300 feet higher in elevation surrounding the station. Soils are generally sand, or sandy loam supporting little agricultural production, but the area is rich in natural resources of forests, lakes, and streams.

The interior location diminishes the influence of the larger Great Lakes, which lie 70 to 80 miles east and west of Houghton Lake. Hence, the daily temperature range is larger, especially in summer, and temperature extremes are greater than are found nearer the shores of either Lake Michigan or Lake Huron. Temperatures reach the 100 degree mark about one summer out of ten, and at the other extreme, fall below zero an average of twenty-two times during the winter season.

Precipitation is normally a little heavier during the summer season. About 60 percent of the annual total falls in the six-month period from April through September. The heaviest precipitation occurs with summertime thunderstorms.

Snowfall averages above 80 inches per year at Houghton Lake, with considerable variation from year to year. Much heavier snows, averaging over 100 inches a season, fall within a 30- to 60-mile radius to the north and west of Houghton Lake. Seasonal totals have ranged from 24 inches to over 124 inches. Measurable amounts of snow have occurred in nine of the twelve months, and the average number of months with measurable snowfall is six.

Cloudiness is greatest in the late fall and early winter, while sunshine percentage is highest in the spring and summer. Cloudiness is increased in the late fall due to the moisture and warmth picked up by the westerly and northwesterly winds while crossing Lake Michigan.

The growing season is normally quite short, averaging about 90 days between spring and fall freezes.

NORMALS, MEANS, AND EXTREMES

HOUGHTON LAKE, MICHIGAN

LATITUDE: 44°22'N LONGITUDE: 84°41'W ELEVATION: FT. GRND 1149 BARO 1157 TIME ZONE: EASTERN WBAN: 94814

	(a)	JAN	FEB	MAR	APR	MAY	JUNE	JULY	AUG	SEP	OCT	NOV	DEC	YEAR
TEMPERATURE °F:														
Normals														
-Daily Maximum		25.3	28.1	38.2	52.7	66.1	74.8	79.6	76.4	67.8	55.8	42.0	29.5	53.0
-Daily Minimum		8.4	8.2	18.2	31.6	42.0	50.6	55.4	53.8	46.9	37.5	28.4	15.7	33.1
-Monthly		16.9	18.2	28.2	42.2	54.1	62.7	67.5	65.1	57.3	46.7	35.2	22.6	43.1
Extremes														
-Record Highest	29	53	59	76	86	90	95	98	94	92	85	70	63	98
-Year		1973	1984	1990	1980	1988	1987	1987	1988	1985	1971	1990	1982	JUL 1987
-Record Lowest	29	-26	-34	-23	3	21	29	33	29	21	16	-2	-21	-34
-Year		1981	1979	1967	1982	1966	1972	1965	1982	1989	1969	1989	1976	FEB 1979
NORMAL DEGREE DAYS:														
Heating (base 65°F)		1491	1310	1141	684	358	120	35	70	234	567	894	1314	8218
Cooling (base 65°F)		0	0	0	0	20	51	112	73	0	0	0	0	256
% OF POSSIBLE SUNSHINE														
MEAN SKY COVER (tenths)														
Sunrise - Sunset	28	8.0	7.4	7.0	6.8	6.4	6.1	5.8	5.9	6.6	7.2	8.4	8.4	7.0
MEAN NUMBER OF DAYS:														
Sunrise to Sunset														
-Clear	28	2.9	4.2	5.9	6.2	6.9	6.6	7.5	8.0	6.3	5.1	2.4	2.3	64.3
-Partly Cloudy	28	6.4	6.6	7.1	7.1	9.6	11.5	13.2	11.2	9.1	7.8	4.9	5.8	100.3
-Cloudy	28	21.7	17.4	18.0	16.6	14.2	11.9	10.0	11.8	14.6	18.0	22.6	22.9	199.8
Precipitation														
.01 inches or more	29	14.8	11.3	12.0	11.9	10.1	10.5	9.1	9.9	11.7	11.9	13.5	15.3	142.0
Snow,Ice pellets,hail														
1.0 inches or more	29	6.0	4.6	3.4	1.4	0.1	0.0	0.0	0.0	0.0	0.3	2.9	5.4	24.1
Thunderstorms	29	0.1	0.1	0.8	2.0	4.0	5.2	5.7	5.9	4.0	1.4	0.5	0.2	30.1
Heavy Fog Visibility														
1/4 mile or less	29	1.9	1.5	2.7	1.5	1.4	1.2	2.0	3.6	3.6	2.8	2.8	2.8	27.8
Temperature °F														
-Maximum														
90° and above	29	0.0	0.0	0.0	0.0	0.*	0.8	1.9	0.6	0.*	0.0	0.0	0.0	3.3
32° and below	29	23.5	18.4	9.0	1.0	0.0	0.0	0.0	0.0	0.0	0.0	5.2	18.9	76.0
-Minimum														
32° and below	29	30.8	27.8	27.6	17.0	4.9	0.3	0.0	0.*	1.6	9.6	22.2	29.6	171.3
0° and below	29	8.4	7.9	3.0	0.0	0.0	0.0	0.0	0.0	0.0	0.0	0.1	3.1	22.5
AVG. STATION PRESS.(mb)	7	972.5	972.5	972.2	973.1	971.9	972.4	973.9	975.7	975.5	975.6	973.1	971.9	973.4
RELATIVE HUMIDITY (%)														
Hour 01	14	83	81	80	77	78	84	84	88	88	85	86	86	83
Hour 07 (Local Time)	29	83	82	84	81	78	81	85	91	91	88	87	85	85
Hour 13	29	73	68	63	55	50	55	55	60	63	65	73	77	63
Hour 19	29	77	73	67	58	53	57	58	66	73	74	80	81	68
PRECIPITATION (inches):														
Water Equivalent														
-Normal		1.50	1.16	2.02	2.22	2.57	3.02	2.58	3.37	3.41	2.18	2.27	1.95	28.25
-Maximum Monthly	29	3.13	3.36	5.67	4.73	5.99	6.67	4.96	7.18	9.49	8.08	5.10	4.48	9.49
-Year		1974	1971	1976	1991	1983	1969	1975	1975	1986	1991	1988	1971	SEP 1986
-Minimum Monthly	29	0.60	0.29	0.62	0.97	0.40	0.85	0.55	0.85	0.01	0.47	0.45	0.65	0.01
-Year		1977	1982	1993	1987	1966	1988	1989	1969	1979	1971	1986	1976	SEP 1979
-Maximum in 24 hrs	29	1.39	1.43	2.18	1.81	1.94	2.59	3.83	3.12	2.55	2.31	1.82	1.70	3.83
-Year		1974	1971	1976	1991	1973	1969	1984	1981	1985	1991	1988	1971	JUL 1984
Snow,Ice pellets,hail														
-Maximum Monthly	29	38.0	23.6	28.7	11.6	2.3	0.0	T	T	0.1	4.4	18.9	30.4	38.0
-Year		1982	1971	1971	1979	1979		1970	1993	1967	1980	1968	1968	JAN 1982
-Maximum in 24 hrs	29	15.4	8.5	11.7	7.6	2.3	0.0	T	T	0.1	3.5	14.4	13.2	15.4
-Year		1978	1974	1970	1979	1979		1970	1993	1967	1980	1981	1980	JAN 1978
WIND:														
Mean Speed (mph)	14	10.1	9.2	9.3	9.8	9.0	8.0	7.6	7.2	8.0	9.1	9.9	9.6	8.9
Prevailing Direction														
Fastest Obs. 1 Min.														
-Direction (!!)	16	26	27	22	30	34	27	32	26	23	23	27	27	26
-Speed (MPH)	16	40	35	31	36	36	40	32	26	32	32	40	32	40
-Year		1972	1979	1977	1979	1992	1969	1966	1977	1970	1968	1970	1970	JAN 1972
Peak Gust														
-Direction (!!)	10	W	NW	W	SW	S	NW	NW	SW	NW		NW	NE	S
-Speed (mph)	10	46	48	55	53	60	58	58	59	46	54	59	55	60
-Date		1990	1987	1991	1984	1988	1992	1987	1988	1985	1991	1989	1990	MAY 1988

PRECIPITATION (inches) — HOUGHTON LAKE, MICHIGAN

YEAR	JAN	FEB	MAR	APR	MAY	JUNE	JULY	AUG	SEP	OCT	NOV	DEC	ANNUAL
#1964	1.10	0.39	1.55	2.64	2.56	1.25	3.03	2.77	3.61	1.29	2.78	1.11	24.08
1965	2.47	1.40	1.83	2.85	2.81	2.43	1.26	5.05	5.76	1.97	2.41	2.73	32.97
1966	1.02	1.02	2.30	2.08	0.40	0.95	1.74	1.92	2.25	1.79	4.81	3.46	23.74
1967	2.02	0.88	1.32	4.56	2.41	5.65	1.28	1.66	1.73	2.73	2.82	2.41	29.47
1968	1.03	1.57	0.85	1.28	2.62	5.54	1.84	1.32	4.17	3.09	2.47	2.50	28.28
1969	1.87	0.32	0.86	2.59	3.57	6.67	3.57	0.85	1.63	5.45	2.19	0.94	30.51
1970	1.16	0.70	1.86	1.50	2.67	4.15	3.93	1.26	5.85	2.75	3.79	2.00	31.62
1971	1.30	3.36	1.79	2.19	1.52	2.84	3.14	1.76	1.20	0.47	1.96	4.48	26.01
1972	0.82	0.99	2.36	1.40	1.79	2.00	2.52	4.63	2.67	2.50	0.99	3.48	26.15
1973	1.22	1.33	1.95	1.66	4.88	2.84	2.34	2.29	1.95	3.11	1.34	1.81	26.72
1974	3.13	1.14	1.44	3.47	2.92	4.60	4.70	2.78	2.53	1.40	1.41	1.43	30.95
1975	1.97	1.14	1.50	2.63	2.79	3.79	4.96	7.18	1.52	0.85	2.20	1.33	31.86
1976	1.77	2.49	5.67	1.86	2.86	2.77	1.22	1.07	0.99	1.31	0.75	0.65	23.41
1977	0.60	1.46	2.40	2.29	1.39	0.94	1.72	5.70	4.19	1.89	2.14	2.20	26.92
1978	1.93	0.55	1.20	1.35	2.42	2.38	0.91	4.10	6.70	1.43	1.28	2.08	26.33
1979	1.51	0.63	3.05	3.18	1.85	4.46	0.87	3.90	0.01	2.43	2.47	1.71	26.07
1980	1.61	0.69	1.10	3.30	1.55	3.44	2.29	2.01	3.75	1.91	1.55	1.95	25.15
1981	0.79	2.10	0.88	3.88	1.73	4.02	1.89	7.06	1.89	2.61	2.07	1.08	30.00
1982	2.43	0.29	2.41	2.46	2.98	3.21	3.31	3.25	3.58	1.86	2.52	3.47	31.77
1983	1.20	0.79	3.11	1.86	5.99	0.95	1.40	3.89	4.63	3.66	1.60	1.69	30.77
1984	1.06	0.88	2.28	1.96	2.60	3.01	4.30	2.95	2.74	2.17	1.99	2.93	28.87
1985	1.64	1.99	3.55	2.42	1.87	1.71	2.28	4.76	6.14	1.63	3.56	2.14	33.69
1986	1.06	1.73	2.20	1.73	3.20	5.43	4.38	1.76	9.49	1.75	0.45	0.85	34.03
1987	1.06	0.61	0.78	0.97	1.56	1.04	1.62	6.69	4.35	2.21	2.63	2.45	25.97
1988	2.09	0.75	2.39	2.37	0.56	0.85	2.49	4.50	3.63	3.38	5.10	1.86	29.97
1989	0.97	0.70	2.99	0.98	3.19	2.90	0.55	2.62	1.03	1.30	2.08	0.92	20.23
1990	2.43	1.09	1.47	1.77	4.15	2.57	3.82	3.28	3.00	2.94	2.90	1.55	30.97
1991	1.22	0.62	3.02	4.73	5.03	1.48	4.43	2.36	3.05	8.08	1.88	1.76	37.66
1992	1.29	1.35	1.84	3.13	0.49	1.91	2.86	3.45	3.63	2.75	4.65	1.98	29.33
1993	1.73	0.89	0.62	2.96	2.50	4.84	1.28	5.67	2.10	1.78	1.58	0.74	26.69
Record Mean	1.45	1.23	1.92	2.42	2.78	3.03	2.69	2.96	3.17	2.59	2.36	1.77	28.39

AVERAGE TEMPERATURE (deg. F) — HOUGHTON LAKE, MICHIGAN

YEAR	JAN	FEB	MAR	APR	MAY	JUNE	JULY	AUG	SEP	OCT	NOV	DEC	ANNUAL
#1964	23.7	23.9	30.0	45.3	59.6	65.0	68.2	62.3	56.3	43.5	38.5	21.8	44.8
1965	15.5	18.3	22.5	37.9	57.9	61.4	63.0	63.0	56.7	45.7	35.4	28.9	42.1
1966	12.9	21.7	31.9	39.3	47.6	64.7	69.1	64.7	55.8	45.6	34.4	23.0	42.6
1967	21.7	11.9	27.0	42.1	48.4	66.4	65.2	62.1	55.4	46.2	30.7	24.2	41.8
1968	17.6	14.8	32.3	45.3	50.7	62.6	65.7	65.6	60.2	48.9	34.7	21.0	43.3
1969	18.3	19.4	23.2	43.1	52.9	56.9	67.5	68.4	57.2	45.4	33.4	21.6	42.3
1970	12.5	15.8	22.9	42.2	53.9	63.2	69.2	66.1	58.1	49.5	35.5	21.9	42.6
1971	14.7	18.7	23.4	38.8	51.6	67.0	64.7	63.4	60.8	54.7	34.4	26.2	43.2
1972	16.3	16.4	22.3	36.6	56.9	59.1	66.5	64.4	56.8	41.7	33.6	22.0	41.1
1973	22.1	18.1	38.1	43.1	50.6	64.9	67.7	68.9	57.4	51.3	35.8	22.9	45.1
1974	20.3	14.4	27.0	43.2	50.0	61.6	67.8	65.0	53.9	44.3	36.3	26.1	42.5
1975	22.0	20.7	24.3	37.0	59.7	64.1	68.1	65.0	53.7	49.6	40.8	23.8	44.1
1976	14.0	24.1	30.8	45.5	50.8	66.1	67.0	64.6	55.6	42.3	28.3	13.8	41.9
1977	8.7	17.8	34.8	46.6	60.3	61.0	70.1	62.1	58.3	45.1	35.8	21.4	43.5
1978	14.5	10.8	23.6	39.1	56.9	61.6	65.1	66.4	58.6	44.3	35.9	21.8	41.6
1979	11.5	10.4	30.9	40.0	52.6	62.3	66.9	62.7	59.2	45.7	35.0	27.6	42.0
1980	19.1	15.7	25.0	41.9	56.0	59.2	67.4	68.0	56.7	41.6	33.9	18.9	41.9
1981	14.8	24.0	32.5	44.3	53.0	63.6	66.8	65.6	55.9	42.9	35.6	25.3	43.7
1982	11.4	17.9	25.8	37.3	60.9	57.4	68.6	61.9	57.2	48.9	36.2	31.2	42.9
1983	21.8	25.9	32.4	40.3	48.5	63.3	71.5	68.6	59.7	46.4	36.6	16.8	44.3
1984	12.4	28.2	24.1	44.8	50.1	65.2	66.4	68.8	56.1	49.2	35.4	27.0	44.0
1985	14.9	17.9	30.3	46.5	57.0	59.5	66.1	63.9	59.8	47.5	34.5	18.0	43.0
1986	17.3	18.4	30.9	47.3	56.9	60.5	69.7	62.8	58.1	46.8	32.3	26.8	44.0
1987	21.6	23.4	33.6	47.3	58.1	67.1	71.4	65.6	59.5	43.9	37.7	28.7	46.5
1988	17.3	16.3	28.0	43.7	58.6	64.8	71.4	68.8	57.9	42.4	36.6	23.7	44.1
1989	24.9	15.5	25.0	41.1	54.5	62.2	69.5	64.8	56.2	47.9	30.7	12.9	42.1
1990	26.2	21.3	32.1	44.9	51.9	63.4	66.8	65.0	57.9	45.3	38.9	25.8	45.0
1991	16.1	24.5	33.1	46.9	61.1	67.7	68.6	68.0	55.8	47.9	33.4	25.4	45.7
1992	22.8	24.1	28.6	39.4	54.3	60.4	63.0	62.0	56.8	44.8	33.6	26.1	43.0
1993	21.0	16.2	28.7	40.2	54.6	61.9	70.2	68.8	52.9	44.6	34.7	25.9	43.3
Record Mean	18.7	19.5	28.5	42.3	54.5	63.5	67.6	65.6	58.0	47.6	35.2	23.8	43.7
Max	27.2	29.5	39.0	53.9	67.8	76.9	81.2	78.5	69.8	58.2	42.6	30.8	54.6
Min	10.2	9.5	18.0	30.6	41.1	50.1	54.0	52.6	46.2	36.9	27.8	16.7	32.8

REFERENCE NOTES — HOUGHTON LAKE, MICHIGAN

GENERAL
T - TRACE AMOUNT.
BLANK ENTRIES DENOTE MISSING/UNREPORTED DATA.
# INDICATES A STATION OR INSTRUMENT RELOCATION.

SPECIFIC

PM - INCLUDES LAST DAY OF PREVIOUS MONTH
ASOS - AUTOMATED SURFACE OBSERVING SYSTEM IN OPERATION DURING THESE MONTHS.

(a) - LENGTH OF RECORD IN YEARS, ALTHOUGH INDIVIDUAL MONTHS MAY BE MISSING.
0.* OR * - THE VALUE IS BETWEEN 0.0 AND 0.05
NORMALS - BASED ON THE 1961-1990 RECORD PERIOD.
EXTREMES - DATES ARE THE MOST RECENT OCCURRENCE
WIND DIR.- NUMERALS SHOW TENS OF DEGRESS CLOCKWISE FROM TRUE NORTH. "00" INDICATES CALM.
RESULTANT DIRECTIONS ARE GIVEN TO WHOLE DEGREES.
BOLD VALUES INDICATE EXTREME VALUES WHICH OCCURRED AFTER THE ASOS SYSTEM WAS COMMISSIONED.

RECORD = PERIOD OF RECORD
RECORD MEAN PRECIPITATION IS THE MEAN OF ALL DAILY PRECIPITATION AMOUNTS DURING THE PERIOD OF RECORD.
RECORD MAX(MIN) TEMPERATURE IS THE MEAN OF ALL DAILY MAX(MIN) TEMPERATURES DURING THE PERIOD OF RECORD.
RECORD MEAN TEMPERATURE IS THE SUM OF THE RECORD MAX AND RECORD MIN DIVIDED BY 2.
AVERAGE TEMPERATURE IS THE SUM OF THE MEAN DAILY MAX AND MIN TEMPERATURE DIVIDED BY 2.

EXCEPTIONS

1. MEAN WIND SPEED IS THROUGH 1978.
2. FASTEST OBSERVED WIND IS THROUGH JUNE 1979.
3. THUNDERSTORMS AND HEAVY FOG MAY BE INCOMPLETE, DUE TO PART-TIME OPERATIONS.

RECORD MEANS ARE THROUGH THE CURRENT YEAR, BEGINNING IN 1918 FOR TEMPERATURE
1918 FOR PRECIPITATION
1965 FOR SNOWFALL

HEATING DEGREE DAYS Base 65 deg. F — HOUGHTON LAKE, MICHIGAN

SEASON	JULY	AUG	SEP	OCT	NOV	DEC	JAN	FEB	MAR	APR	MAY	JUNE	TOTAL
1964-65	38	136	283	659	789	1331	1533	1303	1314	807	237	144	8574
1965-66	109	123	266	593	883	1114	1607	1205	1020	763	535	91	8309
1966-67	19	65	280	592	911	1295	1335	1484	1168	678	510	33	8370
1967-68	69	116	288	579	1022	1260	1468	1453	1005	582	438	137	8417
1968-69	71	100	159	510	903	1353	1444	1272	1290	651	378	254	8385
1969-70	38	28	250	601	939	1342	1621	1373	1296	682	348	122	8640
1970-71	30	54	225	478	878	1330	1556	1289	1282	781	415	65	8383
1971-72	70	95	183	327	912	1197	1502	1401	1320	847	254	191	8299
1972-73	77	92	242	716	933	1326	1324	1307	829	653	442	54	7995
1973-74	26	25	280	420	871	1298	1380	1411	1171	649	463	135	8129
1974-75	27	56	337	633	856	1197	1327	1234	1254	836	215	101	8073
1975-76	44	68	333	472	720	1272	1575	1180	1054	590	434	53	7795
1976-77	24	92	296	698	1094	1582	1743	1315	932	544	199	159	8678
1977-78	29	134	200	610	869	1347	1556	1513	1276	769	289	144	8736
1978-79	79	46	220	636	869	1333	1655	1530	1053	742	396	135	8694
1979-80	48	109	196	597	893	1153	1416	1424	1233	690	286	209	8254
1980-81	18	27	258	716	928	1423	1553	1143	1001	613	368	80	8128
1981-82	50	44	280	676	872	1222	1658	1315	1209	824	148	224	8522
1982-83	12	139	255	494	855	1040	1331	1087	1003	733	505	116	7570
1983-84	25	29	209	569	846	1487	1628	1062	1262	599	458	53	8227
1984-85	42	28	270	481	881	1168	1547	1313	1071	571	248	172	7792
1985-86	46	88	209	535	908	1451	1474	1297	1048	532	274	148	8010
1986-87	23	109	212	557	975	1179	1335	1159	963	523	271	57	7363
1987-88	41	60	169	649	813	1117	1473	1406	1140	636	225	106	7835
1988-89	7	75	218	692	847	1276	1236	1381	1234	711	333	126	8136
1989-90	19	79	277	520	1025	1607	1196	1217	1009	627	398	97	8071
1990-91	32	51	248	604	773	1208	1509	1127	985	540	219	33	7329
1991-92	37	30	295	525	939	1219	1298	1178	1123	763	341	161	7909
1992-93	83	132	257	619	934	1196	1359	1358	1119	737	331	123	8248
1993-94	4	37	358	627	904	1205							

COOLING DEGREE DAYS Base 65 deg. F — HOUGHTON LAKE, MICHIGAN

YEAR	JAN	FEB	MAR	APR	MAY	JUNE	JULY	AUG	SEP	OCT	NOV	DEC	TOTAL
1969	0	0	0	0	10	18	120	138	24	0	0	0	310
1970	0	0	0	6	15	74	167	95	24	1	0	0	382
1971	0	0	0	0	5	131	68	50	62	17	0	0	333
1972	0	0	0	0	11	19	131	78	4	0	0	0	243
1973	0	0	0	1	0	58	119	155	60	2	0	0	395
1974	0	0	0	1	6	41	120	62	11	0	0	0	241
1975	0	0	0	0	58	83	146	78	2	2	0	0	369
1976	0	0	0	13	0	92	93	86	24	0	0	0	308
1977	0	0	0	0	61	46	192	50	5	0	0	0	354
1978	0	0	0	0	44	49	85	96	34	0	0	0	308
1979	0	0	0	0	18	58	112	45	31	7	0	0	271
1980	0	0	0	2	17	43	98	124	16	0	0	0	300
1981	0	0	0	0	3	47	114	70	13	0	0	0	247
1982	0	0	0	0	27	3	132	52	29	3	0	0	246
1983	0	0	0	0	0	73	235	148	56	0	0	0	512
1984	0	0	0	1	2	65	90	151	11	0	0	0	320
1985	0	0	0	22	8	11	86	61	60	0	0	0	248
1986	0	0	0	8	29	22	175	46	15	0	0	0	295
1987	0	0	0	1	64	125	250	86	12	0	0	0	538
1988	0	0	0	0	35	108	213	199	11	0	0	0	566
1989	0	0	0	0	10	49	164	83	19	0	0	0	325
1990	0	0	0	29	0	55	94	56	41	0	0	0	275
1991	0	0	0	2	104	120	157	130	26	0	0	0	539
1992	0	0	0	0	15	31	28	46	19	0	0	0	139
1993	0	0	0	0	16	34	175	161	4	0	0	0	390

SNOWFALL (inches) — HOUGHTON LAKE, MICHIGAN

SEASON	JULY	AUG	SEP	OCT	NOV	DEC	JAN	FEB	MAR	APR	MAY	JUNE	TOTAL
1964-65	0.0	0.0	0.0	4.1	3.8	12.5	26.5	12.9	17.9	10.8	0.0	0.0	88.5
1965-66	0.0	0.0	T	0.3	6.5	11.8	19.5	7.3	9.2	7.1	0.1	0.0	61.8
1966-67	0.0	0.0	0.0	T	15.1	15.4	22.6	14.3	9.4	4.5	T	0.0	81.3
1967-68	0.0	0.0	0.1	3.0	12.6	10.6	9.0	15.6	4.9	0.7	0.0	0.0	56.5
1968-69	0.0	0.0	0.0	1.0	18.9	30.4	25.8	8.7	9.5	0.4	0.3	0.0	95.0
1969-70	0.0	0.0	0.0	2.0	17.6	20.0	22.7	12.8	24.5	3.8	T	0.0	103.4
1970-71	T	0.0	0.0	T	17.7	23.1	27.5	23.6	28.7	3.5	T	0.0	124.1
1971-72	0.0	0.0	0.0	T	16.7	16.7	15.0	18.7	26.8	2.9	0.0	0.0	96.8
1972-73	0.0	0.0	0.0	0.6	4.1	29.2	8.3	15.2	5.3	7.9	0.8	0.0	71.4
1973-74	0.0	0.0	0.0	T	4.8	13.0	11.2	17.5	12.3	3.1	1.0	0.0	62.9
1974-75	0.0	0.0	T	T	6.0	18.0	11.8	12.4	14.0	4.5	0.0	0.0	66.7
1975-76	0.0	0.0	T	T	5.9	14.6	29.6	20.8	17.6	6.0	0.6	0.0	95.1
1976-77	0.0	0.0	0.0	0.7	13.6	18.6	16.3	11.4	3.9	2.7	0.0	0.0	67.2
1977-78	0.0	0.0	0.0	T	16.0	14.0	33.3	13.1	12.5	0.3	0.0	0.0	89.2
1978-79	0.0	0.0	0.0	T	10.5	29.0	21.8	8.3	5.7	11.6	2.3	0.0	89.2
1979-80	0.0	0.0	0.0	0.7	5.0	7.1	14.4	12.3	12.1	7.7	0.0	0.0	59.3
1980-81	0.0	0.0	0.0	4.4	3.2	25.6	19.3	16.3	5.4	0.2	0.0	0.0	74.4
1981-82	0.0	0.0	0.0	3.0	16.1	15.7	38.0	6.1	14.3	5.5	0.0	0.0	98.7
1982-83	0.0	0.0	0.0	0.2	7.7	4.8	15.4	6.4	13.3	2.7	1.0	0.0	51.5
1983-84	0.0	0.0	0.0	0.0	5.0	19.8	17.0	6.3	6.5	5.1	0.4	0.0	60.1
1984-85	0.0	0.0	0.0	0.0	0.6	11.7	25.3	18.7	14.1	10.0	0.0	0.0	80.4
1985-86	0.0	0.0	0.0	0.0	12.6	23.1	12.7	14.0	8.9	0.3	0.0	0.0	71.6
1986-87	0.0	0.0	0.0	T	3.4	10.3	14.1	6.4	2.3	2.0	0.0	0.0	38.5
1987-88	0.0	0.0	0.0	2.4	8.7	18.6	13.4	12.9	10.3	1.4	0.0	0.0	67.7
1988-89	0.0	0.0	0.0		7.8	12.3	9.3	13.5	18.7	3.1	T	0.0	
1989-90	0.0	0.0	T	0.6	12.2	15.0	21.7	11.0	2.4	2.1	0.9	0.0	65.9
1990-91	0.0	0.0	0.0	T	9.1	15.3	22.6	8.5	4.5	1.8	0.0	0.0	61.8
1991-92	0.0	0.0	T	T	4.9	17.5	15.0	15.8	9.5	3.6	0.0	0.0	66.3
1992-93	0.0	0.0	0.0	3.2	11.8	14.3	14.7	13.1	8.1	2.9	0.0	0.0	68.1
1993-94	0.0	T	0.0	0.1	2.3	9.0							
Record Mean	T	T	T	0.8	9.5	16.7	19.1	12.9	11.5	4.1	0.3	0.0	74.8

MARQUETTE COUNTY AIRPORT, MICHIGAN

The Marquette County Airport lies about 7.5 miles southwest of the nearest shoreline of Lake Superior and about 8 miles west of the city of Marquette. Lake Superior is the largest body of fresh water in the world and the deepest and coldest of the Great Lakes. An irregular northwest-southeast ridge line lies just to the east of the airport. There are several water storage basins in the vicinity of the station. One basin, about 20 miles long, is 3 miles northwest and another, about 8 miles in diameter, is 3 miles west.

The climate is influenced considerably by the proximity of Lake Superior. As a consequence of the cool expanse of water in the summer, there is rarely a long period of sweltering hot weather. Periods of drought are extremely rare. In the winter, cold outbreaks are tempered considerably by the waters of Lake Superior if the lake is unfrozen. However, winds blowing across these relatively warmer waters pick up moisture and cause cloudy weather throughout the winter, as well as frequent periods of light snow. Lake-formed snow showers and snow squalls are intensified near the station by upslope winds, especially from the northwest through northeast. With a northeast through east wind, especially in autumn, the upslope condition will cause light snow at the airport, while along the lakeshore, only drizzle or no precipitation may occur.

The growing season averages 117 days. Precipitation is rather evenly distributed throughout the year, with an average precipitation of 4 inches or more in June and September and less than 2 inch averages only in January and February. One hundred inches or more of snow occur in nine of ten winter seasons.

NORMALS, MEANS, AND EXTREMES

MARQUETTE COUNTY AIRPORT, MICHIGAN

LATITUDE: 46°32'N LONGITUDE: 87°34' W ELEVATION: FT. GRND 1415 BARO 1417 TIME ZONE: EASTERN WBAN: 94850

	(a)	JAN	FEB	MAR	APR	MAY	JUNE	JULY	AUG	SEP	OCT	NOV	DEC	YEAR
TEMPERATURE °F:														
Normals														
-Daily Maximum		20.5	23.9	33.5	47.5	61.9	70.9	76.6	73.3	63.8	52.3	36.9	24.6	48.8
-Daily Minimum		3.3	4.0	13.6	27.0	38.4	47.4	53.5	51.7	44.1	34.8	23.3	9.9	29.3
-Monthly		11.9	14.0	23.6	37.3	50.2	59.2	65.1	62.5	54.0	43.6	30.1	17.3	39.1
Extremes														
-Record Highest	15	46	61	68	92	93	95	99	95	92	87	69	59	99
-Year		1981	1981	1989	1980	1986	1988	1988	1988	1983	1992	1990	1982	JUL 1988
-Record Lowest	15	-25	-34	-23	-5	17	28	36	34	24	14	-5	-28	-34
-Year		1982	1979	1982	1979	1983	1986	1989	1992	1993	1984	1989	1983	FEB 1979
NORMAL DEGREE DAYS:														
Heating (base 65°F)		1646	1428	1283	831	471	193	74	122	330	663	1047	1479	9567
Cooling (base 65°F)		0	0	0	0	13	19	78	45	0	0	0	0	155
% OF POSSIBLE SUNSHINE	12	33	39	45	49	56	56	61	57	48	40	28	27	45
MEAN SKY COVER (tenths)														
Sunrise - Sunset														
MEAN NUMBER OF DAYS:														
Sunrise to Sunset														
-Clear														
-Partly Cloudy														
-Cloudy														
Precipitation														
.01 inches or more	15	17.7	12.9	14.4	12.5	10.7	11.5	10.7	12.5	14.4	15.5	15.8	17.9	166.4
Snow,Ice pellets,hail														
1.0 inches or more	15	11.2	7.1	7.1	3.5	0.2	0.0	0.0	0.0	0.1	2.5	6.4	9.2	47.3
Thunderstorms	15	0.0	0.1	0.5	1.2	3.1	5.6	6.1	5.5	4.2	1.5	0.1	0.0	27.9
Heavy Fog Visibility														
1/4 mile or less	15	0.9	1.4	2.3	2.7	2.9	1.4	2.3	3.9	3.5	3.1	1.6	1.9	27.7
Temperature °F														
-Maximum														
90° and above	15	0.0	0.0	0.0	0.1	0.1	0.5	1.7	0.7	0.1	0.0	0.0	0.0	3.2
32° and below	15	26.3	20.4	13.1	2.5	0.1	0.0	0.0	0.0	0.0	0.6	9.9	23.5	96.4
-Minimum														
32° and below	15	31.0	28.0	29.2	21.5	8.5	0.6	0.0	0.0	2.8	17.8	27.3	30.5	197.2
0° and below	15	11.4	11.0	4.7	0.1	0.0	0.0	0.0	0.0	0.0	0.0	0.7	7.6	35.5
AVG. STATION PRESS.(mb)														
RELATIVE HUMIDITY (%)														
Hour 01														
Hour 07														
Hour 13 (Local Time)														
Hour 19														
PRECIPITATION (inches):														
Water Equivalent														
-Normal		2.17	1.73	2.77	2.64	3.03	3.48	2.88	3.41	4.08	3.61	2.89	2.61	35.30
-Maximum Monthly	15	4.02	3.68	6.08	6.56	6.49	6.61	5.40	8.59	6.94	7.59	8.25	4.33	8.59
-Year		1988	1984	1979	1985	1983	1981	1991	1988	1980	1979	1988	1981	AUG 1988
-Minimum Monthly	15	0.92	0.59	0.56	1.48	0.06	0.61	0.57	0.81	1.21	1.98	1.00	0.52	0.06
-Year		1991	1982	1980	1989	1986	1992	1981	1991	1989	1992	1990	1986	MAY 1986
-Maximum in 24 hrs	14	2.23	2.05	2.40	3.09	3.44	2.80	2.64	2.34	2.34	3.66	2.97	2.48	3.66
-Year		1988	1983	1986	1985	1983	1989	1985	1988	1993	1985	1988	1985	OCT 1985
Snow,Ice pellets,hail														
-Maximum Monthly	15	68.8	51.4	59.1	29.2	22.6	T	0.0	T	1.7	18.6	48.9	82.6	82.6
-Year		1982	1985	1985	1982	1990	1990		1989	1993	1979	1991	1981	DEC 1981
-Maximum in 24 hrs	14	23.3	20.6	25.4	20.0	17.2	T	0.0	T	1.7	12.7	19.1	25.8	25.8
-Year		1988	1983	1986	1985	1990	1990		1989	1993	1989	1991	1985	DEC 1985
WIND:														
Mean Speed (mph)														
Prevailing Direction														
Fastest Mile														
-Direction (!!)	6	NW	NW	NW	NW	N	NW	NW	NW	W	SE	NW	SW	NW
-Speed (MPH)	6	44	31	40	44	34	38	35	37	35	38	31	35	44
-Year		1980	1985	1982	1982	1981	1984	1982	1984	1983	1984	1979	1982	APR 1982
Peak Gust														
-Direction (!!)														
-Speed (mph)														
-Date														

PRECIPITATION (inches)

MARQUETTE COUNTY AIRPORT, MICHIGAN

YEAR	JAN	FEB	MAR	APR	MAY	JUNE	JULY	AUG	SEP	OCT	NOV	DEC	ANNUAL
1964	1.31	1.42	1.74	2.91	3.13	2.50	2.95	5.04	3.91	1.79	2.65	2.13	31.48
1965	1.16	1.61	1.72	1.43	3.61	1.51	2.10	3.02	4.25	2.23	3.51	2.02	28.17
1966	1.33	0.72	4.46	1.58	1.10	2.46	1.80	3.90	3.10	3.18	3.62	2.79	30.04
1967	2.71	1.35	1.33	3.06	1.63	3.67	1.44	2.80	1.20	5.50	1.71	0.73	27.13
1968	1.24	3.08	0.76	3.11	2.86	7.07	1.81	2.44	7.22	2.47	1.68	3.96	37.70
1969	2.39	0.79	1.82	2.49	2.22	2.76	1.48	0.53	3.23	5.20	1.86	2.11	26.88
1970	1.90	1.20	1.17	1.55	4.86	1.46	5.36	0.94	5.47	2.29	2.68	1.75	30.63
1971	3.57	2.54	2.06	1.41	2.53	4.12	2.22	1.45	3.80	4.71	2.33	2.89	33.63
1972	1.53	1.43	3.25	2.62	2.50	1.70	2.85	4.12	5.32	1.96	3.39	3.03	33.70
1973	1.47	0.99	2.37	3.01	7.16	3.42	2.16	2.93	2.03	2.53	1.16	2.43	31.66
1974	1.31	1.42	0.61	3.28	2.49	3.57	1.80	3.87	4.01	3.05	2.87	0.81	29.09
1975	2.85	2.10	2.11	2.41	3.53	4.59	1.06	2.97	2.80	1.34	3.16	1.87	30.79
1976	2.65	2.22	3.95	1.83	2.95	1.63	1.52	0.50	1.32	2.24	1.68	1.79	24.28
1977	1.01	1.57	4.09	3.19	2.04	3.10	3.89	3.55	5.17	2.65	2.52	3.24	36.02
1978	3.03	0.89	0.56	1.49	3.34	2.68	4.10	4.47	4.54	1.72	2.72	2.18	31.72
#1979	2.43	1.99	6.08	1.84	2.70	6.13	4.63	1.41	2.09	7.59	2.47	1.56	40.92
1980	2.95	1.47	0.56	4.11	1.87	2.51	3.18	3.49	6.94	2.71	1.92	2.21	33.92
1981	1.96	2.18	2.30	3.10	2.43	6.61	0.57	2.28	2.11	4.63	2.00	4.33	34.50
1982	3.80	0.59	1.89	4.45	2.76	1.24	4.65	3.45	5.00	3.87	2.53	2.83	37.06
1983	2.67	3.14	4.85	3.17	6.49	1.62	1.45	3.21	4.98	5.75	5.68	3.35	46.36
1984	1.27	3.68	3.99	2.46	0.79	2.81	1.92	4.29	4.29	2.03	2.35	2.60	32.48
1985	2.96	2.91	4.63	6.56	3.59	1.49	3.76	4.78	6.32	4.88	5.74	3.97	51.59
1986	2.94	1.21	4.77	2.36	0.06	2.45	3.07	4.62	2.85	4.50	1.04	0.52	30.39
1987	1.42	1.53	2.07	2.30	3.93	2.01	4.88	3.58	2.66	4.31	4.05	3.56	36.30
1988	4.02	0.95	3.66	1.48	1.34	0.71	1.46	8.59	3.97	5.01	8.25	2.36	41.80
1989	1.82	1.60	2.89	1.48	2.15	5.36	0.91	2.61	1.21	3.49	3.43	2.58	29.53
1990	1.74	1.96	1.88	2.32	4.25	3.13	2.01	2.70	4.76	5.27	1.00	1.71	32.73
1991	0.92	1.78	3.75	3.50	2.64	3.06	5.40	0.81	3.10	4.73	5.87	1.51	37.07
1992	1.28	2.66	2.57	2.12	1.76	0.61	4.93	3.28	3.35	1.98	4.27	2.46	31.27
1993	2.39	0.68	0.99	4.11	4.61	2.42	1.95	3.98	4.41	3.32	2.84	1.31	33.01
Record Mean	2.06	1.71	2.17	2.49	2.92	3.33	3.02	2.87	3.53	2.90	2.95	2.29	32.24

AVERAGE TEMPERATURE (deg. F)

MARQUETTE COUNTY AIRPORT, MICHIGAN

YEAR	JAN	FEB	MAR	APR	MAY	JUNE	JULY	AUG	SEP	OCT	NOV	DEC	ANNUAL
1964	25.3	23.5	25.4	40.9	56.5	58.8	67.6	62.2	56.0	47.4	36.5	21.0	43.4
1965	15.8	15.8	23.3	38.2	54.2	60.1	63.1	62.6	53.1	47.4	33.9	28.9	41.4
1966	15.4	21.1	31.6	37.8	47.1	63.0	69.9	64.0	58.5	46.6	32.9	23.9	42.7
1967	20.4	13.1	28.3	39.2	45.8	60.5	64.6	63.6	59.0	45.5	31.0	24.7	41.3
1968	17.8	16.2	33.6	42.3	48.6	56.4	66.1	64.3	60.3	50.5	35.0	24.1	42.9
1969	21.3	22.6	25.6	41.7	51.9	55.4	65.3	70.8	59.3	44.5	34.6	25.6	43.2
1970	14.9	17.5	25.1	40.2	47.0	60.8	68.8	67.8	58.8	50.7	35.2	24.2	42.6
1971	14.4	19.2	26.3	39.7	48.4	61.3	64.2	63.4	61.1	53.6	34.9	25.4	42.7
1972	13.6	14.9	22.8	34.9	52.3	57.0	63.9	63.3	54.6	43.6	33.3	18.9	39.4
1973	22.1	20.5	35.2	39.8	45.4	60.3	67.0	69.1	58.6	53.4	35.1	23.0	44.1
1974	17.1	16.4	26.7	39.9	47.7	59.7	69.1	64.5	52.9	46.7	36.6	29.4	42.2
1975	20.4	23.2	26.5	35.4	54.7	61.1	70.3	67.1	54.2	50.1	39.4	23.1	43.8
1976	15.6	26.1	28.4	43.1	48.5	64.1	66.5	67.6	56.8	43.4	29.1	14.6	42.0
1977	10.1	19.9	34.3	43.8	58.4	59.2	67.3	61.8	56.6	48.4	35.0	22.0	43.1
1978	17.9	18.6	27.4	37.3	53.3	60.5	65.1	66.4	58.7	47.0	34.2	20.1	42.2
#1979	5.6	6.9	24.4	34.4	46.2	58.1	64.7	60.8	55.6	39.5	28.8	23.5	37.4
1980	13.1	12.8	21.3	39.1	54.5	56.9	65.7	64.5	52.9	38.6	29.8	15.4	38.7
1981	13.9	18.4	27.3	39.0	48.1	59.6	65.7	63.8	52.0	40.1	34.5	18.7	40.1
1982	4.8	12.1	23.1	32.8	54.9	54.0	66.0	59.8	53.8	45.4	29.1	23.3	38.2
1983	18.0	21.9	26.0	33.8	44.1	60.5	70.1	67.9	57.5	43.2	31.9	8.7	40.3
1984	9.0	25.3	17.5	40.3	48.2	62.0	64.4	65.4	52.4	46.7	30.5	18.7	40.0
1985	11.3	11.8	26.7	40.9	52.1	56.8	62.6	61.4	54.7	44.0	26.2	9.7	38.2
1986	14.4	14.8	26.4	42.0	54.8	57.1	66.3	60.0	53.2	42.7	25.2	21.3	39.9
1987	18.0	22.9	30.1	44.6	53.7	63.8	67.8	62.7	56.9	39.0	32.6	23.5	43.0
1988	11.6	10.8	23.1	38.5	54.7	62.3	68.6	65.0	54.9	38.0	31.8	16.3	39.6
1989	19.1	8.4	19.4	34.7	50.8	57.5	66.7	63.2	55.7	45.3	24.8	9.2	37.9
1990	22.0	18.1	28.5	42.3	46.9	59.9	63.7	63.2	53.7	41.3	34.0	18.0	41.0
1991	10.0	20.1	26.7	42.2	55.7	62.9	64.9	65.2	52.4	41.0	27.0	19.8	40.7
1992	17.0	19.8	22.6	34.6	52.6	56.3	58.4	59.2	53.5	41.4	28.4	20.2	38.7
1993	16.9	13.9	25.6	34.4	49.8	57.8	66.1	65.4	49.9	40.3	27.0	20.8	39.0
Record Mean	16.8	17.6	25.9	38.7	49.5	59.3	65.8	64.3	57.0	46.7	33.1	22.4	41.5
Max	23.8	25.3	33.5	46.5	58.5	69.0	75.1	72.9	65.2	54.0	39.0	28.3	49.3
Min	9.8	10.0	18.2	30.8	40.5	49.5	56.5	55.8	48.8	39.3	27.2	16.5	33.6

REFERENCE NOTES

MARQUETTE COUNTY AIRPORT, MICHIGAN

GENERAL
T - TRACE AMOUNT.
BLANK ENTRIES DENOTE MISSING/UNREPORTED DATA.
# INDICATES A STATION OR INSTRUMENT RELOCATION.

SPECIFIC

PM - INCLUDES LAST DAY OF PREVIOUS MONTH
ASOS - AUTOMATED SURFACE OBSERVING SYSTEM IN OPERATION DURING THESE MONTHS.

(*) - LENGTH OF RECORD IN YEARS, ALTHOUGH INDIVIDUAL MONTHS MAY BE MISSING.
0.* OR * - THE VALUE IS BETWEEN 0.0 AND 0.05
NORMALS - BASED ON THE 1961-1990 RECORD PERIOD.
EXTREMES - DATES ARE THE MOST RECENT OCCURRENCE
WIND DIR. - NUMERALS SHOW TENS OF DEGRESS CLOCKWISE FROM TRUE NORTH. "00" INDICATES CALM.
RESULTANT DIRECTIONS ARE GIVEN TO WHOLE DEGREES.
BOLD VALUES INDICATE EXTREME VALUES WHICH OCCURRED AFTER THE ASOS SYSTEM WAS COMMISSIONED.

RECORD = PERIOD OF RECORD
RECORD MEAN PRECIPITATION IS THE MEAN OF ALL DAILY PRECIPITATION AMOUNTS DURING THE PERIOD OF RECORD.
RECORD MAX(MIN) TEMPERATURE IS THE MEAN OF ALL DAILY MAX(MIN) TEMPERATURES DURING THE PERIOD OF RECORD.
RECORD MEAN TEMPERATURE IS THE SUM OF THE RECORD MAX AND RECORD MIN DIVIDED BY 2.
AVERAGE TEMPERATURE IS THE SUM OF THE MEAN DAILY MAX AND MIN TEMPERATURE DIVIDED BY 2.

EXCEPTIONS

RECORD MEANS ARE THROUGH THE CURRENT YEAR, BEGINNING IN 1875 FOR TEMPERATURE
1872 FOR PRECIPITATION
1938 FOR SNOWFALL

HEATING DEGREE DAYS Base 65 deg. F — MARQUETTE COUNTY AIRPORT, MICHIGAN

SEASON	JULY	AUG	SEP	OCT	NOV	DEC	JAN	FEB	MAR	APR	MAY	JUNE	TOTAL
1964-65	43	137	268	540	850	1355	1520	1370	1287	795	344	187	8696
1965-66	105	131	355	547	929	1113	1533	1223	1026	809	559	149	8479
1966-67	24	84	225	565	956	1267	1375	1448	1131	767	587	172	8601
1967-68	85	118	203	598	1010	1243	1459	1411	963	676	501	263	8530
1968-69	81	106	166	465	890	1262	1349	1182	1214	692	436	297	8140
1969-70	93	21	209	628	905	1215	1548	1323	1234	739	557	186	8658
1970-71	49	44	224	443	887	1257	1563	1279	1189	754	513	162	8364
1971-72	90	123	182	350	897	1218	1586	1447	1304	897	403	257	8754
1972-73	103	121	305	653	950	1423	1323	1239	916	752	598	159	8542
1973-74	59	37	244	360	889	1296	1482	1354	1180	747	535	192	8375
1974-75	27	77	360	563	843	1097	1376	1165	1188	880	320	176	8072
1975-76	49	45	317	455	762	1290	1525	1120	1128	653	506	94	7944
1976-77	36	79	293	668	1069	1556	1695	1253	946	630	239	193	8657
1977-78	50	126	244	504	894	1329	1455	1295	1156	826	381	183	8443
#1978-79	64	57	220	554	918	1385	1840	1626	1254	914	577	214	9623
1979-80	93	153	295	785	1080	1282	1604	1508	1350	772	340	271	9533
1980-81	53	68	361	813	1050	1532	1581	1303	1160	776	519	168	9384
1981-82	73	78	384	766	907	1425	1864	1480	1292	960	313	326	9868
1982-83	37	190	350	598	1069	1289	1446	1201	1205	929	638	207	9159
1983-84	35	38	264	672	989	1740	1737	1145	1469	733	517	124	9463
1984-85	71	72	369	560	1028	1431	1658	1486	1178	724	400	249	9226
1985-86	111	146	323	645	1156	1709	1564	1400	1191	684	334	250	9513
1986-87	71	169	349	684	1185	1348	1450	1171	1075	606	387	106	8601
1987-88	58	130	247	800	964	1278	1650	1569	1295	787	347	166	9291
1988-89	37	101	305	833	988	1504	1416	1584	1412	902	432	245	9759
1989-90	65	117	283	610	1199	1727	1324	1308	1123	702	556	176	9190
1990-91	104	111	347	726	921	1454	1703	1250	1182	678	334	115	8925
1991-92	74	112	385	739	1133	1394	1483	1308	1306	905	398	276	9513
1992-93	208	202	340	732	1092	1383	1485	1424	1215	910	474	233	9698
1993-94	38	78	446	760	1130	1366							

COOLING DEGREE DAYS Base 65 deg. F — MARQUETTE COUNTY AIRPORT, MICHIGAN

YEAR	JAN	FEB	MAR	APR	MAY	JUNE	JULY	AUG	SEP	OCT	NOV	DEC	TOTAL
1969	0	0	0	0	35	14	109	210	44	0	0	0	412
1970	0	0	0	0	6	66	176	139	46	7	0	0	440
1971	0	0	0	0	6	57	73	81	73	4	0	0	294
1972	0	0	0	0	14	26	76	73	0	0	0	0	189
1973	0	0	0	0	0	25	127	172	59	6	0	0	389
1974	0	0	0	0	5	40	162	70	3	0	0	0	280
1975	0	0	0	0	9	67	218	118	1	0	0	0	413
1976	0	0	0	3	0	75	92	166	53	4	0	0	393
1977	0	0	0	0	44	24	126	35	0	0	0	0	229
1978	0	0	0	0	25	53	76	108	38	2	0	0	302
#1979	0	0	0	0	0	15	92	29	19	0	0	0	155
1980	0	0	0	2	21	36	83	61	5	0	0	0	208
1981	0	0	0	0	1	13	103	50	2	0	0	0	169
1982	0	0	0	0	7	2	75	35	23	0	0	0	142
1983	0	0	0	0	0	78	200	135	47	1	0	0	461
1984	0	0	0	0	3	42	59	89	0	0	0	0	193
1985	0	0	0	7	7	10	44	41	21	0	0	0	130
1986	0	0	0	1	21	17	119	21	0	0	0	0	179
1987	0	0	0	3	41	77	150	65	13	0	0	0	349
1988	0	0	0	0	32	89	157	106	8	0	0	0	392
1989	0	0	0	0	1	27	123	70	13	1	0	0	235
1990	0	0	0	24	0	29	70	63	14	0	0	0	200
1991	0	0	0	0	51	60	77	126	13	0	0	0	327
1992	0	0	0	0	21	22	8	30	3	5	0	0	89
1993	0	0	0	0	10	22	79	97	0	0	0	0	208

SNOWFALL (inches) — MARQUETTE COUNTY AIRPORT, MICHIGAN

SEASON	JULY	AUG	SEP	OCT	NOV	DEC	JAN	FEB	MAR	APR	MAY	JUNE	TOTAL
1964-65	0.0	0.0	0.0	1.7	14.9	27.9	17.0	20.1	22.4	2.9	T	0.0	106.9
1965-66	0.0	0.0	T	0.1	12.6	7.6	20.6	13.0	31.5	12.4	0.3	0.0	98.1
1966-67	0.0	0.0	0.0	1.1	28.0	32.6	29.8	23.5	10.4	2.4	4.5	0.0	132.3
1967-68	0.0	0.0	0.0	5.4	17.4	6.2	11.6	44.4	4.1	5.5	T	0.0	94.6
1968-69	0.0	0.0	0.0	2.0	15.6	41.1	29.5	12.2	17.7	1.0	0.1	0.0	119.2
1969-70	0.0	0.0	0.0	4.3	7.5	30.9	30.8	18.3	11.1	0.9	1.6	0.0	105.4
1970-71	0.0	0.0	T	0.1	11.0	26.6	52.6	22.7	15.9	2.7	3.9	0.0	135.5
1971-72	0.0	0.0	0.0	0.0	11.2	25.3	22.6	23.2	34.3	14.4	0.0	0.0	131.0
1972-73	0.0	0.0	0.0	2.2	6.5	37.7	14.8	12.8	0.4	2.5	3.1	0.0	80.0
1973-74	0.0	0.0	0.0	T	7.4	27.9	15.5	18.2	5.2	13.2	2.3	0.0	89.7
1974-75	0.0	0.0	5.1	5.8	10.3	10.6	34.7	28.7	29.0	0.2	0.0	0.0	124.4
1975-76	0.0	0.0	T	0.1	16.9	15.3	45.6	25.9	44.3	1.4	4.3	0.0	153.8
1976-77	0.0	0.0	T	17.5	17.6	33.3	16.7	17.5	16.7	13.5	T	0.0	132.8
1977-78	0.0	0.0	0.0	T	12.2	38.3	43.3	16.3	6.1	1.0	0.0	0.0	117.2
#1978-79	0.0	0.0	0.0	0.4	13.0	24.2	39.6	23.1	43.9	11.8	T	0.0	156.0
1979-80	0.0	0.0	0.0	18.6	24.8	18.9	33.9	30.2	7.0	11.3	1.4	0.0	146.1
1980-81	0.0	0.0	0.1	11.9	13.1	41.5	41.9	29.5	34.0	4.1	T	0.0	176.1
1981-82	0.0	0.0	0.0	14.2	15.3	82.6	68.8	9.6	24.1	29.2	0.0	0.0	243.8
1982-83	0.0	0.0	0.0	7.2	15.1	17.4	42.4	42.9	54.1	20.2	T	0.0	199.3
1983-84	0.0	0.0	T	2.5	31.6	54.3	30.2	38.1	46.3	1.1	T	0.0	204.1
1984-85	0.0	0.0	T	T	13.6	30.6	56.2	51.4	59.1	18.1	0.0	0.0	229.0
1985-86	0.0	0.0	0.0	T	28.1	56.4	49.8	17.4	49.1	6.8	0.1	0.0	207.7
1986-87	0.0	T	0.0	2.3	15.7	10.5	21.9	27.7	19.3	11.3	0.1	0.0	108.8
1987-88	0.0	0.0	T	8.3	21.4	36.1	62.8	28.0	49.0	5.8	0.0	0.0	211.4
1988-89	0.0	0.0	0.0	10.9	4.2	41.7	43.1	33.7	44.3	7.8	0.2	0.0	185.9
1989-90	0.0	T	0.5	16.6	41.7	58.4	26.4	35.8	16.3	17.1	22.6	T	235.4
1990-91	0.0	0.0	T	9.6	2.5	27.8	25.7	35.2	21.1	9.0	0.6	0.0	131.5
1991-92	0.0	0.0	T	2.9	48.9	30.7	33.3	49.6	23.3	16.7	T	0.0	205.4
1992-93	0.0	0.0	T	11.5	30.0	25.7	40.9	19.9	18.1	29.1	T	0.0	175.2
1993-94	0.0	0.0	1.7	8.7	29.0	22.9							
Record Mean	0.0	T	0.2	4.0	16.8	26.7	27.1	22.9	21.1	9.0	1.4	T	129.3

DULUTH, MINNESOTA

Duluth, Minnesota is located at the western tip of Lake Superior. The city, about 20 miles long, lies at the base of a range of hills that rise abruptly to 600 - 800 feet above the level of Lake Superior. The range runs in a northeast and southwest direction. Two or 3 miles from the lake the land becomes a slightly rolling plateau.

Duluth in the summer is known as the Air Conditioned City. Being situated below high terrain and along the lake, any easterly component winds automatically cool the city. However, with westerly flow in the summer, the wind generally abates at night, thus, allowing cool lake air to move back into the city area near the lake.

An important influence on the climate is the passage of a succession of high and low pressure systems west and east. The proximity of Lake Superior, which is the largest and coldest of the Great Lakes, modifies the local weather. Summer temperatures are cooler and winter temperatures are warmer. The lake effect at Duluth is most prevalent when low pressure systems pass to the south creating easterly winds. In the summer, warm, moist air flowing over the cold lake surface has a stabilizing effect that results in cool, cloudy weather over Duluth. However, during the winter cold air flowing over the warm open lake surface absorbs moisture that is later precipitated over Duluth as snow. The lake effect is further reflected from the low frequency of severe storms such as wind, hail, tornadoes, freezing rain (glaze), and blizzards when compared to other areas that are a further distance from the lake.

Easterly component winds at Duluth occur 40 to 50 percent of the time from March through August and 20 to 25 percent of the time from November through February. During the winter 60 to 70 percent of the winds are from a westerly component.

The climate of Duluth is predominantly continental with significant local Lake Superior effects. Duluth averages 143 days between the last occurrence of 32 degrees in mid-May and the first in early October. At the Duluth Airport about six miles away from the lake, the average first and last occurrences of 32 degrees are late May and late September, giving a freeze-free period of 123 days.

Fall colors throughout this area are outstanding. Reds, yellows, browns, and combinations of these are an experience to see. Recreation is superb from December through March for cross-country and down-hill skiing and snowmobiling. The snow is dry.

Ice in the harbor forms about mid-November and generally is gone by mid-April. The shipping season can vary from year to year depending on temperatures and the winds that move the ice around. In most years there is little or no shipping during February and March on Lake Superior.

NORMALS, MEANS, AND EXTREMES

DULUTH, MINNESOTA

LATITUDE: 46°50'N LONGITUDE: 92°11' W ELEVATION: FT. GRND 1428 BARO 1430 TIME ZONE: CENTRAL WBAN: 14913

	(a)	JAN	FEB	MAR	APR	MAY	JUNE	JULY	AUG	SEP	OCT	NOV	DEC	YEAR
TEMPERATURE °F:														
Normals														
-Daily Maximum		16.2	21.7	32.9	48.2	61.9	71.0	77.1	73.9	63.8	52.3	35.2	20.7	47.9
-Daily Minimum		-2.2	2.8	15.7	28.9	39.6	48.5	55.1	53.3	44.5	35.1	21.5	4.9	29.0
-Monthly		7.0	12.3	24.4	38.6	50.8	59.8	66.1	63.7	54.2	43.7	28.4	12.8	38.5
Extremes														
-Record Highest	52	52	55	78	88	90	93	97	97	95	86	70	55	97
-Year		1942	1976	1946	1952	1986	1980	1988	1947	1976	1953	1978	1962	JUL 1988
-Record Lowest	52	-39	-33	-29	-5	17	27	35	32	22	8	-23	-34	-39
-Year		1972	1988	1989	1975	1967	1972	1988	1986	1942	1976	1964	1983	JAN 1972
NORMAL DEGREE DAYS:														
Heating (base 65°F)		1798	1476	1259	792	445	170	60	113	329	660	1098	1618	9818
Cooling (base 65°F)		0	0	0	0	0	14	94	72	0	0	0	0	180
% OF POSSIBLE SUNSHINE	43	48	53	54	55	57	58	65	60	51	46	35	39	52
MEAN SKY COVER (tenths)														
Sunrise - Sunset	45	6.8	6.5	6.8	6.8	6.6	6.6	6.0	6.0	6.6	6.8	7.6	7.2	6.7
MEAN NUMBER OF DAYS:														
Sunrise to Sunset														
-Clear	45	7.2	7.3	7.1	6.2	6.3	5.1	6.9	7.4	6.4	6.6	4.5	6.0	77.1
-Partly Cloudy	45	6.9	6.1	7.0	7.8	9.5	11.1	13.1	12.2	8.6	7.9	5.7	5.9	101.8
-Cloudy	45	16.8	14.8	17.0	15.9	15.2	13.8	11.0	11.4	15.0	16.5	19.8	19.1	186.4
Precipitation														
.01 inches or more	52	11.7	9.5	10.7	10.5	12.3	12.6	11.4	11.4	12.0	9.5	11.1	11.7	134.3
Snow,Ice pellets,hail														
1.0 inches or more	50	4.5	3.5	3.8	1.8	0.3	0.0	0.0	0.0	0.*	0.4	3.2	4.3	21.8
Thunderstorms	51	0.1	0.*	0.6	1.6	3.5	6.9	8.0	7.2	4.0	1.3	0.4	0.1	33.8
Heavy Fog Visibility														
1/4 mile or less	45	2.3	2.3	3.7	3.6	5.5	6.5	5.3	6.5	5.7	4.5	3.4	3.3	52.5
Temperature °F														
-Maximum														
90° and above	32	0.0	0.0	0.0	0.0	0.1	0.1	1.1	0.7	0.1	0.0	0.0	0.0	2.1
32° and below	32	28.0	22.4	15.1	1.9	0.0	0.0	0.0	0.0	0.0	0.7	12.5	26.3	107.0
-Minimum														
32° and below	32	31.0	28.1	29.0	20.1	5.3	0.5	0.0	0.*	2.5	12.6	25.8	30.8	185.7
0° and below	32	17.2	12.8	4.6	0.1	0.0	0.0	0.0	0.0	0.0	0.0	1.6	12.2	48.4
AVG. STATION PRESS.(mb)	21	963.6	965.1	963.5	963.5	963.2	962.5	964.2	965.1	964.7	964.3	963.4	963.8	963.9
RELATIVE HUMIDITY (%)														
Hour 00	32	75	73	73	70	72	80	82	85	84	77	78	79	77
Hour 06 (Local Time)	32	77	76	78	76	76	81	85	88	87	82	81	80	81
Hour 12	32	70	65	63	56	53	60	59	63	64	62	70	74	63
Hour 18	32	70	64	62	54	52	58	59	64	68	66	72	75	64
PRECIPITATION (inches):														
Water Equivalent														
-Normal		1.22	0.80	1.91	2.25	3.03	3.82	3.61	3.99	3.84	2.49	1.80	1.24	30.00
-Maximum Monthly	52	4.70	2.37	5.12	5.84	7.67	8.04	8.48	10.31	9.38	7.53	5.01	3.70	10.31
-Year		1969	1971	1965	1948	1962	1986	1949	1972	1991	1949	1983	1968	AUG 1972
-Minimum Monthly	52	0.14	0.13	0.22	0.24	0.15	0.83	0.97	0.71	0.19	0.13	0.19	0.16	0.13
-Year		1961	1988	1959	1987	1976	1987	1947	1970	1952	1944	1976	1979	FEB 1988
-Maximum in 24 hrs	44	1.74	1.38	2.38	2.27	3.25	4.05	3.68	5.79	3.77	2.90	2.64	2.12	5.79
-Year		1975	1965	1977	1954	1979	1958	1987	1978	1972	1973	1968	1950	AUG 1978
Snow,Ice pellets,hail														
-Maximum Monthly	50	46.8	31.5	45.5	31.5	8.1	0.2	T	T	2.4	8.1	50.1	44.3	50.1
-Year		1969	1955	1965	1950	1954	1945	1992	1989	1991	1966	1991	1950	NOV 1991
-Maximum in 24 hrs	50	14.7	17.0	19.4	11.6	4.3	0.2	T	T	2.4	7.9	24.1	25.4	25.4
-Year		1982	1948	1965	1983	1954	1945	1992	1989	1991	1966	1991	1950	DEC 1950
WIND:														
Mean Speed (mph)	44	11.6	11.2	11.8	12.4	11.6	10.5	9.4	9.4	10.5	11.1	11.6	11.2	11.0
Prevailing Direction through 1963		NW	NW	WNW	NW	E	E	WNW	E	WNW	WNW	WNW	NW	WNW
Fastest Obs. 1 Min.														
-Direction (!!)	8	30	08	E	08	09	27	10	11	24	30	24	30	E
-Speed (MPH)	8	45	32	57	37	39	46	29	30	32	32	39	32	57
-Year		1986	1987	1985	1986	1989	1986	1992	1993	1985	1987	1986	1992	MAR 1985
Peak Gust														
-Direction (!!)	10	W	NW	E	E	E	W	N	E	SW	NW	NW	NW	E
-Speed (mph)	10	56	47	71	60	59	69	47	45	60	70	54	49	71
-Date		1990	1987	1985	1986	1989	1986	1991	1993	1991	1987	1993	1989	MAR 1985

PRECIPITATION (inches)

DULUTH, MINNESOTA

YEAR	JAN	FEB	MAR	APR	MAY	JUNE	JULY	AUG	SEP	OCT	NOV	DEC	ANNUAL
1964	1.10	0.57	1.10	4.10	5.74	3.50	1.47	6.57	6.58	0.59	1.84	1.79	34.95
1965	0.89	1.73	5.12	1.64	2.96	4.51	3.57	3.76	5.56	3.30	3.33	1.67	38.04
1966	0.98	1.31	3.84	1.99	1.53	4.14	6.13	6.42	1.52	3.56	1.17	1.56	34.15
1967	3.12	0.24	0.66	1.99	0.80	5.21	2.91	2.31	1.34	1.44	0.50	0.91	21.43
1968	0.77	0.22	1.89	4.83	4.02	5.39	3.60	2.07	3.42	5.28	3.10	3.70	38.29
1969	4.70	0.26	0.39	1.46	2.82	2.18	3.03	2.18	4.13	2.42	1.25	2.67	27.49
1970	0.51	0.43	1.15	3.16	2.81	1.68	3.58	0.71	2.01	6.07	3.39	1.97	27.47
1971	1.56	2.37	2.02	1.29	3.45	3.25	3.91	4.50	2.67	6.09	2.07	1.22	34.40
1972	2.28	1.47	1.45	2.17	2.00	3.70	6.71	10.31	5.30	0.83	1.37	2.02	39.61
1973	0.67	0.29	1.54	1.35	3.81	2.43	2.36	8.46	4.28	4.56	1.61	0.69	32.05
1974	0.97	0.82	0.78	2.07	3.09	4.07	4.85	3.79	0.98	1.57	1.36	1.15	25.50
1975	3.69	0.76	2.59	2.21	1.44	5.59	2.26	2.52	2.32	1.20	4.19	0.64	29.41
1976	1.57	1.05	3.67	0.73	0.15	6.16	2.60	1.84	1.84	0.48	0.19	0.39	20.67
1977	0.36	0.47	4.43	1.27	3.50	3.97	3.91	3.26	5.97	3.20	2.37	1.31	34.02
1978	0.52	0.35	0.47	1.96	3.49	2.96	7.67	7.49	1.52	0.77	1.27	1.19	29.66
1979	0.76	1.89	3.58	1.15	6.01	4.33	5.45	2.10	2.01	3.01	0.47	0.16	30.92
1980	1.55	0.56	1.02	0.41	0.82	2.35	3.94	5.34	6.61	1.64	0.70	0.63	25.57
1981	0.32	1.50	1.05	4.48	1.15	5.83	3.26	2.84	2.42	3.59	0.96	0.97	28.37
1982	2.02	0.48	2.06	2.06	4.30	1.97	6.21	1.60	4.19	5.07	3.08	1.19	34.23
1983	1.34	0.49	2.05	2.28	2.12	2.00	3.51	3.37	5.57	2.32	5.01	1.97	32.03
1984	0.78	0.61	0.54	2.34	1.83	5.70	1.33	1.96	3.82	5.19	0.82	1.91	26.83
1985	0.39	0.66	1.85	2.35	4.44	3.18	4.16	3.91	6.02	1.76	2.33	0.78	31.83
1986	0.66	0.74	0.88	4.11	2.59	8.04	4.58	5.29	6.26	0.66	2.01	0.45	36.27
1987	0.69	0.31	0.60	0.24	4.02	0.83	5.46	1.87	2.93	0.96	1.26	0.67	19.84
1988	0.78	0.13	2.55	0.44	3.96	4.56	1.14	6.82	6.18	1.05	3.44	1.12	32.17
1989	1.87	0.34	1.49	2.11	3.50	3.81	1.09	5.02	4.40	1.02	1.01	0.63	26.29
1990	0.51	0.51	3.35	3.76	1.48	4.83	2.42	5.39	6.49	3.51	0.65	0.49	33.39
1991	0.52	0.55	1.17	3.90	6.11	5.64	5.33	2.49	9.38	2.85	4.89	0.61	43.44
1992	0.60	0.58	0.84	2.87	2.87	5.04	3.64	4.13	3.90	1.13	1.84	1.23	28.67
1993	1.79	0.38	0.44	2.42	4.74	6.95	5.75	3.63	1.81	0.56	2.60	1.28	32.35
Record Mean	1.11	0.90	1.64	2.20	3.13	4.03	3.73	3.54	3.45	2.20	1.73	1.12	28.77

AVERAGE TEMPERATURE (deg. F)

DULUTH, MINNESOTA

YEAR	JAN	FEB	MAR	APR	MAY	JUNE	JULY	AUG	SEP	OCT	NOV	DEC	ANNUAL
1964	16.9	16.4	19.8	38.7	54.3	58.4	66.3	59.1	52.4	44.4	30.2	8.4	38.8
1965	5.2	6.0	15.8	38.0	52.0	58.0	61.9	61.1	48.0	44.8	27.8	21.1	36.6
1966	-1.3	12.3	27.1	34.7	47.3	61.1	68.0	61.5	54.8	43.2	25.2	13.5	37.3
1967	11.2	3.7	24.8	37.0	45.6	58.2	64.1	61.7	56.0	42.4	26.6	16.3	37.3
1968	9.1	9.3	32.0	40.5	48.4	57.4	64.2	61.7	56.6	46.2	28.9	11.9	38.8
1969	7.5	14.4	21.4	40.6	50.6	53.8	64.0	68.5	56.7	40.7	28.9	17.5	38.7
1970	2.4	8.4	21.1	38.7	46.6	60.8	68.8	66.0	55.5	44.4	27.8	12.7	37.8
1971	0.6	12.6	21.8	38.3	48.1	61.7	62.0	62.4	57.3	47.7	28.1	14.7	37.9
1972	0.2	6.4	17.9	33.3	53.5	58.4	61.2	61.9	50.0	38.9	25.9	7.2	34.6
1973	11.6	13.7	31.8	38.3	47.8	59.1	64.8	65.5	53.6	48.2	27.9	11.7	39.5
1974	5.6	11.0	20.6	37.9	46.6	58.6	67.1	60.1	47.9	42.8	29.2	19.5	37.2
1975	9.6	12.0	18.2	31.0	53.3	57.9	68.7	62.0	50.9	46.7	31.3	11.8	37.8
1976	4.7	20.7	22.0	42.6	50.6	63.2	66.1	64.9	55.3	37.1	22.1	4.5	37.8
1977	-0.2	17.2	31.4	44.4	57.4	60.0	65.9	58.6	53.2	44.3	28.0	11.3	39.3
1978	5.1	10.5	25.6	38.3	54.8	60.2	64.7	63.6	57.3	44.9	26.2	10.1	38.5
1979	0.6	5.0	23.0	34.5	47.2	59.8	66.1	62.0	56.9	43.0	29.4	22.2	37.5
1980	8.7	10.7	19.7	41.4	54.9	59.5	67.6	63.6	52.9	38.9	30.1	11.6	38.3
1981	11.9	16.3	28.3	39.2	50.2	58.7	65.5	64.3	52.9	40.5	34.7	14.8	39.8
1982	-3.2	10.6	20.8	35.7	52.8	54.8	64.5	60.8	54.3	45.1	24.4	19.6	36.7
1983	13.2	21.1	25.6	35.1	46.7	59.9	69.6	69.7	56.6	44.9	31.6	1.8	39.6
1984	7.1	23.0	18.7	42.4	50.5	61.4	66.6	67.7	51.9	45.7	28.4	13.2	39.7
1985	6.5	11.6	30.3	42.1	54.9	56.5	64.6	59.7	52.1	42.7	19.9	3.0	37.0
1986	11.7	11.5	28.5	42.1	51.8	58.9	64.7	60.8	52.7	43.4	24.0	18.8	39.1
1987	15.3	23.7	31.6	46.1	53.1	63.1	67.6	63.5	57.2	39.4	32.2	20.4	42.8
1988	4.8	6.2	24.4	40.1	56.0	62.8	70.0	64.5	55.4	38.6	28.9	13.5	38.8
1989	14.3	3.4	18.9	36.8	51.7	58.4	68.6	64.8	55.9	44.4	23.2	4.1	37.0
1990	18.7	14.9	27.1	40.2	48.3	61.5	64.6	64.1	56.2	42.1	31.4	12.6	40.1
1991	5.9	19.4	26.1	42.7	54.7	61.7	63.8	66.3	53.0	40.4	22.0	15.9	39.3
1992	16.7	21.2	25.9	36.2	53.8	56.3	59.4	60.5	53.8	41.7	27.3	15.9	39.1
1993	11.9	14.5	27.1	37.2	50.3	57.1	63.6	65.0	49.5	40.0	24.4	17.0	38.1
Record Mean	8.5	12.6	24.2	38.3	49.5	58.6	65.2	63.7	55.0	44.2	28.6	14.5	38.5
Max	17.3	21.7	32.6	47.2	59.7	69.1	75.5	73.4	64.0	52.5	35.4	22.2	47.5
Min	-0.3	3.5	15.8	29.4	39.3	48.1	54.9	54.0	45.9	35.8	21.7	6.8	29.6

REFERENCE NOTES

DULUTH, MINNESOTA

GENERAL
T - TRACE AMOUNT.
BLANK ENTRIES DENOTE MISSING/UNREPORTED DATA.
# INDICATES A STATION OR INSTRUMENT RELOCATION.

SPFCIFIC

PM - INCLUDES LAST DAY OF PREVIOUS MONTH
ASOS - AUTOMATED SURFACE OBSERVING SYSTEM IN OPERATION DURING THESE MONTHS.

(a) - LENGTH OF RECORD IN YEARS, ALTHOUGH INDIVIDUAL MONTHS MAY BE MISSING.
0.* OR * - THE VALUE IS BETWEEN 0.0 AND 0.05
NORMALS - BASED ON THE 1961-1990 RECORD PERIOD.
EXTREMES - DATES ARE THE MOST RECENT OCCURRENCE
WIND DIR.- NUMERALS SHOW TENS OF DEGRESS CLOCKWISE FROM TRUE NORTH. "00" INDICATES CALM.
RESULTANT DIRECTIONS ARE GIVEN TO WHOLE DEGREES.
BOLD VALUES INDICATE EXTREME VALUES WHICH OCCURRED AFTER THE ASOS SYSTEM WAS COMMISSIONED.

RECORD = PERIOD OF RECORD
RECORD MEAN PRECIPITATION IS THE MEAN OF ALL DAILY PRECIPITATION AMOUNTS DURING THE PERIOD OF RECORD.
RECORD MAX(MIN) TEMPERATURE IS THE MEAN OF ALL DAILY MAX(MIN) TEMPERATURES DURING THE PERIOD OF RECORD.
RECORD MEAN TEMPERATURE IS THE SUM OF THE RECORD MAX AND RECORD MIN DIVIDED BY 2.
AVERAGE TEMPERATURE IS THE SUM OF THE MEAN DAILY MAX AND MIN TEMPERATURE DIVIDED BY 2.

EXCEPTIONS

RECORD MEANS ARE THROUGH THE CURRENT YEAR, BEGINNING IN 1904 FOR TEMPERATURE
1904 FOR PRECIPITATION
1944 FOR SNOWFALL

HEATING DEGREE DAYS Base 65 deg. F DULUTH, MINNESOTA

SEASON	JULY	AUG	SEP	OCT	NOV	DEC	JAN	FEB	MAR	APR	MAY	JUNE	TOTAL
1964-65	50	215	377	631	1037	1751	1854	1650	1519	802	397	209	10492
1965-66	127	158	506	617	1109	1355	2053	1473	1166	903	546	165	10178
1966-67	36	145	304	670	1187	1589	1662	1714	1243	832	592	210	10184
1967-68	80	144	269	694	1147	1504	1730	1611	1017	729	507	227	9659
1968-69	90	140	254	576	1073	1644	1780	1411	1346	725	449	332	9820
1969-70	99	20	258	746	1075	1466	1939	1581	1355	781	573	162	10055
1970-71	38	67	311	630	1107	1616	1996	1464	1332	794	518	124	9997
1971-72	111	133	273	531	1099	1553	2012	1698	1458	946	357	211	10382
1972-73	134	146	440	802	1167	1792	1654	1429	1022	793	526	171	10076
1973-74	72	66	354	513	1106	1651	1843	1508	1373	806	565	206	10063
1974-75	45	160	507	684	1069	1404	1713	1479	1447	1013	358	226	10105
1975-76	46	129	418	561	1003	1642	1867	1279	1325	667	440	101	9478
1976-77	35	112	310	860	1280	1871	2017	1334	1033	612	242	170	9876
1977-78	46	196	347	636	1101	1662	1852	1520	1212	794	324	176	9866
1978-79	71	99	262	615	1159	1699	1999	1679	1293	910	549	172	10507
1979-80	52	115	252	674	1059	1317	1745	1573	1398	702	326	201	9414
1980-81	39	76	357	800	1043	1650	1644	1358	1133	769	455	185	9509
1981-82	74	62	363	752	903	1549	2117	1523	1363	875	370	303	10254
1982-83	66	161	332	609	1212	1398	1598	1226	1214	887	562	185	9450
1983-84	30	9	285	615	996	1959	1792	1210	1429	671	446	116	9558
1984-85	40	40	391	588	1093	1601	1809	1494	1067	679	314	252	9368
1985-86	57	178	394	686	1349	1925	1646	1492	1127	680	416	196	10146
1986-87	76	151	361	663	1224	1426	1537	1153	1027	561	376	112	8667
1987-88	34	100	234	782	977	1377	1862	1704	1253	741	300	146	9510
1988-89	22	97	287	812	1081	1590	1567	1721	1424	839	405	206	10051
1989-90	27	78	272	633	1249	1887	1428	1398	1166	745	506	130	9519
1990-91	76	94	273	700	1003	1623	1833	1273	1201	661	332	129	9198
1991-92	97	67	363	754	1284	1515	1492	1266	1207	859	355	271	9530
1992-93	174	167	332	717	1121	1518	1638	1408	1171	825	451	239	9761
1993-94	73	71	459	769	1214	1485							

COOLING DEGREE DAYS Base 65 deg. F DULUTH, MINNESOTA

YEAR	JAN	FEB	MAR	APR	MAY	JUNE	JULY	AUG	SEP	OCT	NOV	DEC	TOTAL
1969	0	0	0	0	11	4	76	135	16	0	0	0	242
1970	0	0	0	0	8	42	162	102	30	0	0	0	344
1971	0	0	0	0	0	32	24	60	47	1	0	0	164
1972	0	0	0	0	8	22	24	59	0	0	0	0	113
1973	0	0	0	0	0	1	72	84	18	0	0	0	175
1974	0	0	0	0	0	19	115	15	0	0	0	0	149
1975	0	0	0	0	2	18	168	41	0	0	0	0	229
1976	0	0	0	0	0	53	75	117	26	0	0	0	271
1977	0	0	0	0	12	24	80	6	0	0	0	0	122
1978	0	0	0	0	17	34	70	64	39	0	0	0	224
1979	0	0	0	0	4	25	95	30	15	0	0	0	169
1980	0	0	0	0	25	46	126	40	3	0	0	0	240
1981	0	0	0	0	2	2	97	48	6	0	0	0	155
1982	0	0	0	0	0	0	58	36	18	0	0	0	112
1983	0	0	0	0	0	42	179	165	42	0	0	0	428
1984	0	0	0	0	4	13	96	133	4	0	0	0	250
1985	0	0	0	0	9	4	54	20	15	0	0	0	102
1986	0	0	0	0	13	18	74	26	0	0	0	0	131
1987	0	0	0	0	13	62	121	60	7	0	0	0	263
1988	0	0	0	0	27	83	183	89	4	0	0	0	386
1989	0	0	0	0	0	17	147	80	7	0	0	0	251
1990	0	0	0	7	0	32	70	73	16	0	0	0	198
1991	0	0	0	0	20	35	69	117	8	0	0	0	249
1992	0	0	0	0	13	18	9	37	3	3	0	0	83
1993	0	0	0	0	0	8	36	76	0	0	0	0	120

SNOWFALL (inches) DULUTH, MINNESOTA

SEASON	JULY	AUG	SEP	OCT	NOV	DEC	JAN	FEB	MAR	APR	MAY	JUNE	TOTAL
1964-65	0.0	0.0	T	T	8.6	24.3	10.6	19.3	45.5	1.6	1.0	0.0	110.9
1965-66	0.0	0.0	T	T	25.9	8.6	11.8	4.3	24.5	10.2	1.7	0.0	87.0
1966-67	0.0	0.0	T	8.1	7.6	15.4	36.7	2.7	6.9	1.6	1.3	0.0	80.3
1967-68	0.0	0.0	0.0	0.8	4.2	4.3	10.8	2.7	4.1	8.7	3.7	0.0	39.3
1968-69	0.0	0.0	0.0	T	21.8	37.7	46.8	3.0	3.0	8.7	T	0.0	121.0
1969-70	0.0	0.0	0.0	4.3	9.1	38.8	7.5	8.9	9.9	14.8	1.6	0.0	94.9
1970-71	0.0	0.0	0.0	0.2	16.8	20.9	31.8	27.4	12.7	6.5	0.6	0.0	116.9
1971-72	0.0	0.0	0.0	0.2	6.4	17.5	30.9	20.7	11.0	20.4	T	0.0	107.1
1972-73	0.0	0.0	T	0.5	6.7	20.0	9.2	3.0	2.1	2.8	1.5	0.0	45.8
1973-74	0.0	0.0	0.0	T	7.6	15.7	13.4	15.3	15.1	5.2	1.0	0.0	73.3
1974-75	0.0	0.0	0.3	0.8	4.5	19.1	32.7	12.3	30.3	0.4	T	0.0	100.4
1975-76	0.0	0.0	0.0	0.1	25.7	7.8	20.6	8.8	26.4	0.0	T	0.0	89.4
1976-77	0.0	0.0	0.0	0.8	2.7	7.8	8.8	5.1	15.3	0.1	0.0	0.0	40.6
1977-78	0.0	0.0	0.0	1.7	16.0	12.0	13.5	11.4	8.3	6.8	0.0	0.0	69.7
1978-79	0.0	0.0	0.0	T	10.1	20.8	11.9	23.3	17.0	4.2	1.4	0.0	88.7
1979-80	0.0	0.0	0.0	0.8	6.0	2.0	21.9	10.3	12.6	1.5	T	0.0	55.1
1980-81	0.0	0.0	0.0	1.3	1.6	7.1	4.7	13.3	4.2	4.3	T	0.0	36.5
1981-82	0.0	0.0	T	1.4	12.5	15.5	34.2	8.0	17.8	6.3	0.0	0.0	95.7
1982-83	0.0	0.0	0.0	0.8	16.0	21.4	15.7	9.0	9.9	23.7	T	0.0	96.5
1983-84	0.0	0.0	T	T	37.7	32.1	20.0	4.0	9.9	3.3	0.3	0.0	107.3
1984-85	0.0	0.0	T	3.5	2.4	8.2	15.3	12.0	26.7	0.1	0.0	0.0	68.2
1985-86	0.0	0.0	0.7	2.3	34.1	18.8	11.5	10.3	11.4	0.2	T	0.0	89.3
1986-87	0.0	0.0	0.0	1.8	8.2	7.3	11.2	5.1	6.7	0.3	T	0.0	40.6
1987-88	0.0	0.0	0.0	3.9	5.8	11.3	16.7	2.3	13.7	0.1	0.0	0.0	53.8
1988-89	0.0	0.0	0.0	0.3	24.3	20.7	31.2	5.3	17.6	19.0	0.7	0.0	119.1
1989-90	0.0	T	0.0	0.6	8.4	14.2	5.5	15.0	11.6	2.4	0.6	T	58.3
1990-91	0.0	0.0	0.0	3.2	5.1	13.5	11.4	9.7	9.5	8.5	2.9	0.0	63.8
1991-92	0.0	0.0	2.4	4.3	50.1	12.9	9.3	10.6	0.7	9.7	0.0	0.0	100.0
1992-93	T	0.0	T	5.1	29.4	15.5	24.9	10.0	5.8	3.5	T	0.0	94.2
1993-94	0.0	0.0	T	0.6	28.5	15.1							
Record Mean	T	T	0.1	1.4	12.5	15.4	16.8	11.2	13.3	6.5	0.8	T	77.9

MINNEAPOLIS – ST. PAUL, MINNESOTA

The Twin Cities of Minneapolis and St. Paul are located at the confluence of the Mississippi and Minnesota Rivers over the heart of an artesian water basin. Its flat or gently rolling terrain varies little in elevation from that of the official observation station at International Airport. Numerous lakes dot the surrounding area. Minneapolis alone boasts of 22 lakes within the city park system. The largest body of water, nearly 15,000 acres, is Lake Minnetonka, located about 15 miles west of the airport. Most bodies of water are relatively small and shallow and are ice covered during winter.

The climate of the Minneapolis–St. Paul area is predominantly continental. Seasonal temperature variations are quite large. Temperatures range from less than −30 degrees to over 100 degrees. The growing season is 166 days. Because of this favorable growing season, all crops generally mature before the autumn freeze occurs.

The Twin Cities lie near the northern edge of the influx of moisture from the Gulf of Mexico. Severe storms such as blizzards, freezing rain (glaze), tornadoes, wind and hail storms do occur. The total annual precipitation is important. Even more significant is its proper distribution during the growing season. During the five month growing season, May through September, the major crops produced are corn, soybeans, small grains, and hay. During this period, the normal rainfall is over 16 inches, approximately 65 percent of the annual precipitation. Winter snowfall is nearly 48 inches. Winter recreational weather is excellent because of the dry snow. These conditions exist from about Christmas into early March. Snow depths average 6 to 8 inches in the city and 8 to 10 inches in the suburbs during this period.

Floods occur along the Mississippi River due to spring snow melt, excessive rainfall, or both. Occasionally an ice jam forms and creates a local flood condition. The flood problem at St. Paul is complicated because the Minnesota River empties into the Mississippi River between the two cities. Consequently, high water or flooding on the Minnesota River creates a greater flood potential at St. Paul. Flood stage at St. Paul can be expected on the average once in every eight years.

NORMALS, MEANS, AND EXTREMES

MINNEAPOLIS - ST. PAUL, MINNESOTA

LATITUDE: 44°53'N LONGITUDE: 93°13' W ELEVATION: FT. GRND 834 BARO 860 TIME ZONE: CENTRAL WBAN: 14922

	(a)	JAN	FEB	MAR	APR	MAY	JUNE	JULY	AUG	SEP	OCT	NOV	DEC	YEAR
TEMPERATURE °F:														
Normals														
-Daily Maximum		20.7	26.6	39.2	56.5	69.4	78.8	84.0	80.7	70.7	58.8	41.0	25.5	54.3
-Daily Minimum		2.8	9.2	22.7	36.2	47.6	57.6	63.1	60.3	50.3	38.8	25.2	10.2	35.3
-Monthly		11.8	17.9	31.0	46.4	58.5	68.2	73.6	70.5	60.5	48.8	33.2	17.9	44.9
Extremes														
-Record Highest	55	58	60	83	95	96	102	105	102	98	89	75	63	105
-Year		1944	1981	1986	1980	1978	1985	1988	1947	1976	1953	1944	1982	JUL 1988
-Record Lowest	55	-34	-28	-32	2	18	34	43	39	26	15	-17	-29	-34
-Year		1970	1965	1962	1962	1967	1945	1972	1967	1974	1972	1964	1983	JAN 1970
NORMAL DEGREE DAYS:														
Heating (base 65°F)		1649	1319	1054	558	244	41	11	22	167	502	954	1460	7981
Cooling (base 65°F)		0	0	0	0	43	137	278	192	32	0	0	0	682
% OF POSSIBLE SUNSHINE	55	53	59	57	58	61	65	72	69	62	55	39	42	58
MEAN SKY COVER (tenths)														
Sunrise - Sunset	55	6.3	6.3	6.7	6.5	6.4	6.1	5.3	5.3	5.6	5.8	7.1	7.0	6.2
MEAN NUMBER OF DAYS:														
Sunrise to Sunset														
-Clear	55	8.3	7.7	7.1	7.0	7.1	7.2	9.9	10.2	9.8	9.9	5.5	6.4	96.1
-Partly Cloudy	55	7.4	6.9	7.3	7.7	9.1	10.4	11.8	11.1	8.6	7.6	6.5	6.4	100.8
-Cloudy	55	15.3	13.7	16.6	15.2	14.8	12.3	9.3	9.7	11.6	13.5	18.0	18.2	168.3
Precipitation .01 inches or more	55	8.7	7.3	10.3	10.3	11.3	11.7	9.8	10.0	9.6	7.9	8.5	9.4	114.7
Snow,Ice pellets,hail 1.0 inches or more	55	3.2	2.7	3.0	0.7	0.1	0.0	0.0	0.0	0.*	0.1	2.2	3.1	15.1
Thunderstorms	55	0.*	0.2	1.0	2.6	5.1	7.5	7.6	6.5	4.3	1.8	0.6	0.1	37.4
Heavy Fog Visibility 1/4 mile or less	55	1.1	1.4	1.3	0.4	0.5	0.5	0.3	0.6	0.9	0.9	1.1	1.3	10.5
Temperature °F														
-Maximum														
90° and above	34	0.0	0.0	0.0	0.1	0.8	2.7	6.1	3.6	0.8	0.0	0.0	0.0	14.2
32° and below	34	23.4	17.9	8.7	0.3	0.0	0.0	0.0	0.0	0.0	0.1	7.0	21.2	78.5
-Minimum														
32° and below	34	30.8	27.3	25.2	11.0	1.1	0.0	0.0	0.0	0.5	7.8	23.0	29.9	156.4
0° and below	34	13.5	8.1	1.9	0.0	0.0	0.0	0.0	0.0	0.0	0.0	0.7	8.0	32.3
AVG. STATION PRESS.(mb)	21	987.5	988.3	985.2	984.2	983.6	983.0	984.7	985.6	986.0	986.3	985.9	987.4	985.6
RELATIVE HUMIDITY (%)														
Hour 00	34	73	74	72	67	68	72	75	77	79	74	77	76	74
Hour 06 (Local Time)	34	74	76	76	75	76	79	81	84	85	81	80	78	79
Hour 12	34	67	65	61	52	52	54	54	57	59	58	66	70	60
Hour 18	34	68	66	61	51	50	52	53	56	61	60	69	73	60
PRECIPITATION (inches):														
Water Equivalent														
-Normal		0.95	0.88	1.94	2.42	3.39	4.05	3.53	3.62	2.72	2.19	1.55	1.08	28.32
-Maximum Monthly	55	3.63	2.14	4.75	5.88	8.03	9.82	17.90	9.31	7.53	5.68	5.29	4.27	17.90
-Year		1967	1981	1965	1986	1962	1990	1987	1977	1942	1971	1991	1982	JUL 1987
-Minimum Monthly	55	0.10	0.06	0.32	0.16	0.61	0.22	0.58	0.43	0.41	0.01	0.02	T	T
-Year		1990	1964	1958	1987	1967	1988	1975	1946	1940	1952	1939	1943	DEC 1943
-Maximum in 24 hrs	55	1.21	1.10	1.66	2.23	3.03	3.00	10.00	7.36	3.55	2.95	2.91	2.47	10.00
-Year		1967	1966	1965	1975	1965	1986	1987	1977	1942	1966	1940	1982	JUL 1987
Snow,Ice pellets,hail														
-Maximum Monthly	55	46.4	26.5	40.0	21.8	3.0	T	T	T	1.7	8.2	46.9	33.2	46.9
-Year		1982	1962	1951	1983	1946	1989	1993	1992	1942	1991	1991	1969	NOV 1991
-Maximum in 24 hrs	55	18.5	9.3	14.7	13.6	3.0	T	T	T	1.7	8.2	21.0	16.5	21.0
-Year		1982	1939	1985	1983	1946	1989	1993	1992	1942	1991	1991	1982	NOV 1991
WIND:														
Mean Speed (mph)	55	10.5	10.4	11.3	12.2	11.1	10.5	9.4	9.3	10.0	10.5	10.9	10.4	10.5
Prevailing Direction through 1963		NW	NW	NW	NW	SE	SE	S	SE	S	SE	NW	NW	NW
Fastest Obs. 1 Min.														
-Direction (!!)	14	32	34	08	19	23	01	35	20	18	33	25	34	32
-Speed (MPH)	14	51	37	33	41	35	46	43	44	36	33	41	35	51
-Year		1986	1987	1985	1984	1986	1980	1980	1983	1988	1981	1986	1989	JAN 1986
Peak Gust														
-Direction (!!)	10	NW	NW	W	SW	N	S	NW	W	N	NW	W	NW	W
-Speed (mph)	10	67	55	60	61	67	51	51	71	52	53	66	48	71
-Date		1986	1987	1988	1984	1985	1992	1984	1988	1989	1987	1986	1989	AUG 1988

PRECIPITATION (inches)

MINNEAPOLIS – ST. PAUL, MINNESOTA

YEAR	JAN	FEB	MAR	APR	MAY	JUNE	JULY	AUG	SEP	OCT	NOV	DEC	ANNUAL
1964	0.47	0.06	1.35	2.98	3.44	2.18	2.02	5.42	5.21	0.57	1.19	1.08	25.97
1965	0.47	1.59	4.75	3.52	7.86	4.01	4.69	4.04	4.90	0.90	1.98	1.23	39.94
1966	0.95	1.55	2.48	0.89	1.46	3.51	2.47	4.40	1.69	3.53	0.39	1.02	24.34
1967	3.63	1.59	0.96	4.07	0.61	7.53	1.36	2.79	0.63	1.73	0.09	0.45	25.44
1968	0.71	0.13	1.89	2.94	3.74	6.78	6.46	0.75	6.16	5.62	0.54	2.21	37.93
1969	2.05	0.31	0.90	1.55	1.98	2.93	2.95	0.99	0.49	2.53	0.65	2.06	19.39
1970	0.47	0.16	2.05	3.55	4.77	1.27	3.66	2.19	3.19	4.97	3.82	0.43	30.53
1971	1.22	1.74	1.21	1.11	3.14	3.52	3.94	1.78	2.73	5.68	2.67	0.70	29.44
1972	0.84	0.49	1.25	1.69	2.18	3.31	5.12	2.48	1.96	1.77	1.11	1.57	23.77
1973	0.92	0.84	1.12	2.32	2.48	1.06	2.90	3.05	2.08	1.29	1.97	1.10	21.13
1974	0.17	1.06	1.00	2.42	2.08	5.21	1.14	2.75	0.58	1.69	0.66	0.35	19.11
1975	2.82	0.79	1.67	5.40	3.81	7.99	0.58	4.92	1.31	0.27	4.80	0.79	35.15
1976	0.87	0.59	2.83	0.80	1.13	3.86	2.45	1.39	1.42	0.49	0.16	0.51	16.50
1977	0.65	0.93	2.66	1.84	2.86	3.57	3.72	9.31	4.43	2.34	1.42	1.15	34.88
1978	0.38	0.24	0.79	3.63	3.79	7.09	3.19	5.77	2.47	0.19	1.84	0.88	30.26
1979	1.09	1.39	2.55	0.66	4.55	4.78	2.34	7.04	2.20	3.16	0.98	0.33	31.07
1980	0.94	0.67	1.12	0.83	2.29	5.52	2.30	3.26	3.68	0.66	0.26	0.24	21.77
1981	0.30	2.14	0.71	2.17	2.18	4.42	4.09	4.73	1.46	2.69	2.16	0.92	27.97
1982	2.45	0.43	2.09	1.62	4.99	1.44	0.92	3.80	1.50	3.45	3.27	4.27	30.23
1983	0.67	1.19	3.22	3.97	6.20	5.22	3.07	3.12	3.34	2.61	4.93	1.53	39.07
1984	0.88	1.64	1.47	3.86	2.29	7.95	3.03	5.15	2.65	5.48	0.31	2.24	36.95
1985	0.87	0.50	4.48	1.81	3.65	2.18	2.20	5.02	4.37	3.66	1.72	1.20	31.66
1986	0.90	0.84	2.03	5.88	3.48	5.34	4.11	4.44	6.90	1.77	0.62	0.31	36.62
1987	0.63	0.13	0.64	0.16	1.88	1.95	17.90	3.67	1.28	0.60	2.07	1.25	32.16
1988	1.37	0.30	1.33	1.58	1.70	0.22	1.17	4.29	2.79	0.80	2.86	0.67	19.08
1989	0.52	1.04	2.19	2.66	3.38	3.50	3.50	2.92	1.28	0.53	1.38	0.42	23.32
1990	0.10	0.77	3.66	3.80	3.36	9.82	5.06	1.71	1.88	1.23	0.65	1.01	33.05
1991	0.49	1.03	2.29	3.58	6.35	2.57	2.95	3.14	5.43	2.52	5.29	1.05	36.69
1992	0.66	0.57	1.56	1.99	1.15	3.68	5.21	4.54	5.20	2.11	1.95	1.05	29.67
1993	1.25	0.39	1.25	1.99	4.02	6.28	5.58	6.50	2.04	0.79	1.57	0.55	32.21
Record Mean	0.83	0.85	1.60	2.17	3.38	4.17	3.55	3.40	2.89	2.01	1.45	0.94	27.26

AVERAGE TEMPERATURE (deg. F)

MINNEAPOLIS – ST. PAUL, MINNESOTA

YEAR	JAN	FEB	MAR	APR	MAY	JUNE	JULY	AUG	SEP	OCT	NOV	DEC	ANNUAL
1964	20.0	23.9	25.8	46.8	61.5	68.7	76.0	68.5	58.9	48.2	35.0	14.8	45.7
1965	10.0	11.8	19.5	41.8	58.7	66.5	70.5	68.6	52.8	50.7	33.1	28.0	42.7
1966	3.3	16.3	35.8	42.2	53.6	68.4	76.8	68.2	60.3	47.5	30.1	18.1	43.4
1967	14.6	8.7	29.8	44.7	52.3	66.9	68.8	66.2	60.3	46.3	30.7	21.8	42.6
1968	14.3	15.2	38.8	48.5	53.4	67.2	71.1	70.7	61.1	50.7	34.0	16.9	45.2
1969	9.4	19.3	24.1	49.3	60.6	61.8	73.6	74.4	63.0	46.5	33.6	20.3	44.7
1970	5.6	15.4	26.0	46.1	58.5	71.2	75.2	71.9	61.2	49.6	32.7	18.2	44.3
1971	6.5	17.0	28.0	47.0	55.4	71.5	68.8	69.6	62.8	51.4	32.7	18.4	44.1
1972	5.5	10.5	26.5	41.9	61.3	66.0	68.5	69.8	57.9	43.7	32.2	11.3	41.3
1973	17.4	21.6	40.2	44.4	55.2	69.5	73.8	73.4	60.1	53.8	34.3	16.7	46.7
1974	11.9	16.9	29.5	47.1	54.4	65.5	76.6	67.3	55.3	49.8	33.7	24.4	44.4
1975	14.5	15.5	22.1	38.9	60.9	68.8	76.3	71.7	57.7	52.8	37.5	21.3	44.8
1976	11.6	27.8	31.4	51.8	58.9	71.7	76.1	73.3	61.8	44.6	28.3	13.6	45.9
1977	0.3	22.7	37.5	53.0	66.9	68.4	74.8	66.1	60.5	47.1	30.8	14.4	45.2
1978	5.5	11.6	30.0	45.2	61.8	67.8	71.1	72.2	67.3	49.8	32.5	15.2	44.2
1979	3.2	10.0	28.9	44.0	55.5	67.3	73.6	69.9	63.4	46.6	31.7	26.0	43.3
1980	15.3	15.3	27.3	49.2	61.5	67.6	75.2	70.7	59.5	45.1	36.6	19.8	45.2
1981	18.0	23.4	37.7	49.1	57.1	67.0	70.9	69.3	60.0	46.7	38.0	17.5	46.2
1982	2.3	15.8	29.0	43.8	62.5	63.7	75.6	71.8	60.9	50.3	31.5	25.7	44.4
1983	19.6	26.9	34.2	42.3	54.6	68.0	77.2	76.8	62.6	48.4	34.0	3.7	45.7
1984	12.0	27.5	24.8	47.1	56.0	69.7	72.2	73.5	57.2	50.7	33.3	17.9	45.2
1985	10.1	16.5	35.6	52.1	62.2	63.9	73.9	67.6	59.9	47.5	24.8	7.7	43.5
1986	17.5	15.7	33.9	49.6	59.4	68.6	73.9	67.1	59.8	49.2	28.2	24.7	45.6
1987	21.2	31.6	38.7	53.5	63.5	72.8	76.0	69.0	62.5	44.6	37.9	25.0	49.7
1988	10.4	13.9	33.8	47.4	65.4	74.4	78.1	73.9	62.4	44.0	32.7	20.5	46.4
1989	21.2	8.6	26.6	45.3	57.5	68.4	76.4	70.8	60.9	49.9	28.0	10.6	43.7
1990	26.3	23.7	35.7	46.8	56.3	69.5	71.3	70.6	64.4	48.1	37.4	16.9	47.3
1991	12.5	24.4	34.3	49.1	61.9	72.9	72.3	71.1	59.0	47.2	24.5	21.2	45.9
1992	21.9	28.0	33.1	43.6	60.5	65.6	65.8	65.9	59.6	47.4	31.4	21.2	45.3
1993	14.6	17.2	29.5	44.2	57.2	64.5	70.3	70.4	55.0	46.5	30.6	22.2	43.5
Record Mean	13.2	17.3	30.1	46.0	58.3	67.9	73.2	70.6	61.4	49.5	32.8	19.2	45.0
Max	21.8	25.9	38.4	55.8	68.5	77.8	83.2	80.5	71.3	59.0	40.4	26.7	54.1
Min	4.6	8.6	21.8	36.3	48.0	58.0	63.1	60.7	51.5	40.1	25.2	11.7	35.8

REFERENCE NOTES

MINNEAPOLIS – ST. PAUL, MINNESOTA

GENERAL
T - TRACE AMOUNT.
BLANK ENTRIES DENOTE MISSING/UNREPORTED DATA.
# INDICATES A STATION OR INSTRUMENT RELOCATION.

SPECIFIC

PM - INCLUDES LAST DAY OF PREVIOUS MONTH
ASOS - AUTOMATED SURFACE OBSERVING SYSTEM IN OPERATION DURING THESE MONTHS.

(a) - LENGTH OF RECORD IN YEARS, ALTHOUGH INDIVIDUAL MONTHS MAY BE MISSING.
0.* OR * - THE VALUE IS BETWEEN 0.0 AND 0.05
NORMALS - BASED ON THE 1961-1990 RECORD PERIOD.
EXTREMES - DATES ARE THE MOST RECENT OCCURRENCE
WIND DIR.- NUMERALS SHOW TENS OF DEGRESS CLOCKWISE FROM TRUE NORTH. "00" INDICATES CALM.
RESULTANT DIRECTIONS ARE GIVEN TO WHOLE DEGREES.
BOLD VALUES INDICATE EXTREME VALUES WHICH OCCURRED AFTER THE ASOS SYSTEM WAS COMMISSIONED.

RECORD = PERIOD OF RECORD
RECORD MEAN PRECIPITATION IS THE MEAN OF ALL DAILY PRECIPITATION AMOUNTS DURING THE PERIOD OF RECORD.
RECORD MAX(MIN) TEMPERATURE IS THE MEAN OF ALL DAILY MAX(MIN) TEMPERATURES DURING THE PERIOD OF RECORD.
RECORD MEAN TEMPERATURE IS THE SUM OF THE RECORD MAX AND RECORD MIN DIVIDED BY 2.
AVERAGE TEMPERATURE IS THE SUM OF THE MEAN DAILY MAX AND MIN TEMPERATURE DIVIDED BY 2.

EXCEPTIONS

RECORD MEANS ARE THROUGH THE CURRENT YEAR,
BEGINNING IN 1891 FOR TEMPERATURE
1891 FOR PRECIPITATION
1939 FOR SNOWFALL

HEATING DEGREE DAYS Base 65 deg. F — MINNEAPOLIS - ST. PAUL, MINNESOTA

SEASON	JULY	AUG	SEP	OCT	NOV	DEC	JAN	FEB	MAR	APR	MAY	JUNE	TOTAL
1964-65	0	63	224	515	894	1551	1702	1486	1405	690	211	19	8760
1965-66	7	40	368	447	950	1140	1909	1358	899	678	357	41	8194
1966-67	0	40	185	536	1042	1446	1556	1572	1086	600	404	30	8497
1967-68	36	65	166	577	1024	1335	1567	1440	808	491	358	62	7929
1968-69	10	28	143	451	922	1486	1723	1274	1261	461	204	136	8099
1969-70	5	0	131	580	933	1379	1842	1382	1204	577	249	20	8302
1970-71	3	5	190	476	959	1443	1811	1341	1139	537	297	18	8219
1971-72	16	22	164	413	962	1438	1844	1576	1188	687	204	73	8587
1972-73	34	52	218	651	974	1664	1474	1208	761	611	299	13	7959
1973-74	1	3	185	350	915	1493	1642	1344	1092	535	338	72	7970
1974-75	0	48	289	467	933	1252	1561	1379	1324	775	188	39	8255
1975-76	15	7	231	387	818	1346	1650	1074	1031	405	195	11	7170
1976-77	0	4	162	632	1092	1590	2005	1180	844	365	75	17	7966
1977-78	0	35	145	548	1016	1565	1842	1488	1080	584	162	46	8511
1978-79	5	7	89	464	968	1538	1914	1537	1112	623	307	38	8602
1979-80	0	24	105	566	992	1203	1536	1436	1165	484	184	34	7729
1980-81	0	12	194	611	845	1396	1453	1160	838	472	249	28	7258
1981-82	11	11	172	564	803	1466	1945	1374	1111	629	117	71	8274
1982-83	0	14	168	448	997	1212	1400	1061	947	673	313	49	7282
1983-84	2	0	161	514	923	1901	1641	1082	1240	531	284	7	8286
1984-85	5	12	251	435	943	1453	1694	1355	904	403	123	104	7682
1985-86	0	28	240	537	1201	1774	1466	1377	957	454	212	30	8276
1986-87	0	43	177	480	1096	1243	1352	929	809	347	134	13	6623
1987-88	2	29	106	623	804	1236	1688	1479	962	523	76	4	7532
1988-89	1	16	116	646	963	1373	1353	1576	1184	583	251	44	8106
1989-90	0	6	159	470	1105	1683	1194	1151	899	569	274	37	7547
1990-91	2	5	136	516	820	1484	1624	1130	945	481	197	3	7343
1991-92	7	8	228	548	1206	1354	1333	1067	981	636	190	72	7630
1992-93	32	52	182	542	1003	1351	1557	1335	1096	617	243	70	8080
1993-94	3	18	302	566	1025	1322							

COOLING DEGREE DAYS Base 65 deg. F — MINNEAPOLIS - ST. PAUL, MINNESOTA

YEAR	JAN	FEB	MAR	APR	MAY	JUNE	JULY	AUG	SEP	OCT	NOV	DEC	TOTAL
1969	0	0	0	0	76	49	276	298	77	12	0	0	788
1970	0	0	0	17	54	213	323	225	83	5	0	0	920
1971	0	0	0	2	5	218	141	168	106	3	0	0	643
1972	0	0	0	0	94	109	148	208	13	0	0	0	572
1973	0	0	0	1	4	158	280	271	47	8	0	0	769
1974	0	0	0	5	18	93	369	127	6	1	0	0	619
1975	0	0	0	0	66	159	371	220	18	16	0	0	850
1976	0	0	0	14	14	223	351	269	72	7	0	0	950
1977	0	0	0	12	145	129	310	76	19	0	0	0	691
1978	0	0	0	0	72	138	201	236	164	0	0	0	811
1979	0	0	0	0	17	113	275	181	65	0	0	0	651
1980	0	0	0	16	82	121	322	194	38	1	0	0	774
1981	0	0	0	0	10	96	200	151	28	0	0	0	485
1982	0	0	0	0	46	40	338	232	53	0	0	0	709
1983	0	0	0	0	0	145	389	368	98	8	0	0	1008
1984	0	0	0	0	13	155	237	280	24	0	0	0	709
1985	0	0	0	22	43	77	284	118	93	0	0	0	637
1986	0	0	0	1	45	148	286	115	32	0	0	0	627
1987	0	0	0	11	95	253	348	159	37	0	0	0	903
1988	0	0	0	1	96	296	412	302	45	0	0	0	1152
1989	0	0	0	0	26	153	359	192	41	8	0	0	779
1990	0	0	0	28	11	178	206	191	125	1	0	0	740
1991	0	0	0	8	109	246	238	205	51	0	0	0	857
1992	0	0	0	3	56	96	64	88	28	2	0	0	337
1993	0	0	0	0	12	60	176	195	8	0	0	0	451

SNOWFALL (inches) — MINNEAPOLIS - ST. PAUL, MINNESOTA

SEASON	JULY	AUG	SEP	OCT	NOV	DEC	JAN	FEB	MAR	APR	MAY	JUNE	TOTAL
1964-65	0.0	0.0	0.0	T	4.3	8.1	10.5	11.7	37.1	2.0	T	0.0	73.7
1965-66	0.0	0.0	0.0	0.0	1.6	1.2	11.9	6.8	14.2	0.4	T	0.0	36.1
1966-67	0.0	0.0	0.0	0.2	3.4	12.7	35.3	23.7	2.6	0.2	0.3	0.0	78.4
1967-68	0.0	0.0	0.0	0.3	0.8	2.4	10.6	2.2	0.8	0.4	0.0	0.0	17.5
1968-69	0.0	0.0	0.0	T	4.9	28.7	21.6	5.3	7.3	0.3	0.0	0.0	68.1
1969-70	0.0	0.0	0.0	2.4	3.8	33.2	9.8	4.3	8.6	1.3	T	0.0	63.4
1970-71	0.0	0.0	0.0	T	6.3	5.5	19.9	13.9	7.0	1.9	0.2	0.0	54.7
1971-72	0.0	0.0	0.0	0.0	13.2	12.8	12.2	7.6	10.4	8.0	0.0	0.0	64.2
1972-73	0.0	0.0	T	T	1.1	15.3	11.6	11.3	0.4	2.0	0.0	0.0	41.7
1973-74	0.0	0.0	0.0	0.0	0.1	17.9	2.5	15.7	7.7	7.3	0.0	0.0	51.2
1974-75	0.0	0.0	0.0	0.0	1.2	6.1	27.4	9.0	18.3	2.2	0.0	0.0	64.2
1975-76	0.0	0.0	0.0	0.0	16.2	5.6	12.8	5.1	13.6	0.0	1.2	0.0	54.5
1976-77	0.0	0.0	0.0	2.3	1.4	8.3	13.4	1.8	14.6	1.8	0.0	0.0	43.6
1977-78	0.0	0.0	0.0	3.0	11.7	14.2	6.8	4.6	8.5	1.9	0.0	0.0	50.7
1978-79	0.0	0.0	0.0	0.0	16.5	15.1	14.2	13.5	8.4	0.7	0.0	0.0	68.4
1979-80	0.0	0.0	0.0	T	7.7	1.7	12.9	8.8	13.7	8.5	0.0	0.0	53.3
1980-81	0.0	0.0	0.0	T	0.9	2.8	4.6	11.0	0.1	1.7	0.0	0.0	21.1
1981-82	0.0	0.0	0.0	0.9	14.0	10.6	46.4	7.4	10.9	4.8	0.0	0.0	95.0
1982-83	0.0	0.0	0.0	1.4	3.6	19.3	3.2	10.8	14.3	21.8	0.0	0.0	74.4
1983-84	0.0	0.0	0.0	T	30.4	21.0	10.6	9.3	17.3	9.8	0.0	0.0	98.4
1984-85	0.0	0.0	0.0	0.3	2.0	16.3	13.1	4.2	36.8	T	0.0	0.0	72.7
1985-86	0.0	0.0	0.4	T	23.9	13.5	10.3	12.3	8.7	0.4	0.0	0.0	69.5
1986-87	0.0	0.0	0.0	T	4.4	4.2	5.5	1.2	2.1	T	0.0	0.0	17.4
1987-88	0.0	0.0	0.0	0.3	4.5	7.5	19.5	4.5	3.7	2.4	0.0	0.0	42.4
1988-89	0.0	0.0	0.0	0.2	15.8	7.2	6.0	17.3	22.7	0.8	0.1	T	70.1
1989-90	0.0	0.0	0.0	0.0	11.3	7.0	1.1	10.7	3.2	2.2	0.0	0.0	35.5
1990-91	0.0	0.0	0.0	T	5.0	11.7	6.5	14.2	4.4	1.5	0.3	0.0	43.6
1991-92	0.0	T	0.0	8.2	46.9	6.7	5.0	5.9	10.8	0.6	0.0	0.0	84.1
1992-93	0.0	T	T	1.3	12.2	9.2	12.0	5.3	6.9	0.5	0.0	0.0	47.4
1993-94	T	0.0	0.0	T	7.7	4.5							
Record Mean	T	T	T	0.5	7.9	9.3	9.8	8.4	10.7	2.8	0.1	T	49.6

JACKSON, MISSISSIPPI

Jackson is located on the west bank of the Pearl River, about 45 miles east of the Mississippi River and 150 miles north of the Gulf of Mexico. The nearby terrain is gently rolling with no topographic features that appreciably influence the weather. The National Weather Service Office is nearly 7 miles east-northeast of the Jackson Post Office and over 5 miles southwest of the Ross Barnett Reservoir. Alluvial plains up to 3 miles wide extend along the river near Jackson, where some levees have been built on both sides of the river.

The climate is significantly humid during most of the year, with relatively short mild winters and long warm summers. The Gulf of Mexico has a moderating effect on the climate. Cold spells are fairly frequent in winter, but are usually of short duration. Sub-zero temperatures rarely occur. Temperatures occasionally exceed 80 degrees in mid-winter. In summer, temperatures reach 90 degrees or higher on about two-thirds of the days. 100 degree readings are infrequent. Extended periods of very hot weather are rare. On unusual occasions, temperatures at night may drop into the 50s, even in July or August.

Snowfall averages less than two inches per season, with nearly two-thirds of the seasons having only a trace of snow or none at all. Ice storms occasionally cause major damage to trees and power lines during the winter or early spring season. Rainfall is abundant and fairly well-distributed throughout the year. The area does not have a true dry season. However, the six-month period, June through November, is relatively dry in comparison with the December through May period when 60 percent of the annual precipitation can be expected.

Excessive rainfall may occur in any season. In spite of the normally abundant rainfall, fairly serious droughts occasionally occur during the summer or fall season. Tropical disturbances, including hurricanes and their remnants, are infrequent. However, those that pass near or visit the Mississippi Coast in the summer or early fall may bring several days of heavy rain to the Jackson area.

Thunderstorms can be expected on an average of 65 days a year, usually occurring in each month. They are most frequent in summer when they occur on about one-third of the days. At other times of the year, thunderstorms are usually associated with passing weather systems and are likely to be attended by higher winds than in summer. Severe thunderstorms normally affect portions of the metropolitan area a few times each year.

NORMALS, MEANS, AND EXTREMES

JACKSON, MISSISSIPPI

LATITUDE: 32°19'N LONGITUDE: 90°05' W ELEVATION: FT. GRND 291 BARO 297 TIME ZONE: CENTRAL WBAN: 03940

	(a)	JAN	FEB	MAR	APR	MAY	JUNE	JULY	AUG	SEP	OCT	NOV	DEC	YEAR
TEMPERATURE °F:														
Normals														
-Daily Maximum		55.6	60.1	69.3	77.4	84.0	90.6	92.4	92.0	88.0	79.1	69.2	59.5	76.4
-Daily Minimum		32.7	35.7	44.1	51.9	60.0	67.1	70.5	69.7	63.7	50.3	42.3	36.1	52.0
-Monthly		44.1	47.9	56.7	64.6	72.0	78.8	81.5	80.9	75.9	64.7	55.8	47.8	64.2
Extremes														
-Record Highest	30	82	85	89	94	99	105	106	102	104	95	88	84	106
-Year		1972	1989	1982	1987	1964	1988	1980	1981	1980	1986	1971	1978	JUL 1980
-Record Lowest	30	2	11	15	27	38	47	51	**55**	35	**26**	17	4	2
-Year		1985	1970	1980	1987	1971	1984	1967	**1992**	1967	**1993**	1976	1989	JAN 1985
NORMAL DEGREE DAYS:														
Heating (base 65°F)		656	485	285	87	7	0	0	0	6	104	295	542	2467
Cooling (base 65°F)		8	6	28	75	224	414	512	493	333	94	19	9	2215
% OF POSSIBLE SUNSHINE	29	48	54	60	65	62	70	65	66	64	68	57	48	61
MEAN SKY COVER (tenths)														
Sunrise - Sunset	30	6.7	6.3	6.2	5.8	5.9	5.5	5.8	5.4	5.3	4.5	5.6	6.4	5.8
MEAN NUMBER OF DAYS:														
Sunrise to Sunset														
-Clear	30	7.8	7.9	8.8	9.4	8.3	8.8	7.5	9.0	10.4	14.8	9.8	8.5	111.2
-Partly Cloudy	30	5.9	6.1	6.9	7.4	10.4	12.0	13.2	12.9	9.2	6.6	7.3	6.3	104.2
-Cloudy	30	17.2	14.3	15.3	13.1	12.3	9.2	10.3	9.1	10.4	9.7	12.9	16.1	149.9
Precipitation														
.01 inches or more	30	10.9	9.3	10.1	8.5	9.5	8.4	10.4	9.6	8.3	6.2	8.3	10.0	109.6
Snow, Ice pellets, hail														
1.0 inches or more	30	0.2	0.1	0.1	0.0	0.0	0.0	0.0	0.0	0.0	0.0	0.0	0.0	0.3
Thunderstorms	30	1.9	2.7	5.5	5.7	7.3	8.7	12.6	10.5	5.3	2.1	2.7	2.5	67.5
Heavy Fog Visibility														
1/4 mile or less	30	3.4	2.1	1.7	1.5	1.0	0.6	1.2	1.5	1.5	2.2	2.3	3.1	22.1
Temperature °F														
-Maximum														
90° and above	30	0.0	0.0	0.0	0.3	4.8	18.7	24.2	22.6	12.2	1.0	0.0	0.0	83.8
32° and below	30	0.8	0.3	0.0	0.0	0.0	0.0	0.0	0.0	0.0	0.0	0.*	0.3	1.4
-Minimum														
32° and below	30	14.7	10.9	4.1	0.4	0.0	0.0	0.0	0.0	0.0	0.5	6.2	12.0	48.8
0° and below	30	0.0	0.0	0.0	0.0	0.0	0.0	0.0	0.0	0.0	0.0	0.0	0.0	0.0
AVG. STATION PRESS. (mb)	21	1009.4	1007.8	1004.9	1004.4	1003.3	1003.9	1005.2	1004.9	1005.1	1007.0	1007.8	1009.2	1006.1
RELATIVE HUMIDITY (%)														
Hour 00	30	84	82	82	85	87	88	91	91	90	89	87	84	87
Hour 06 (Local Time)	30	87	87	87	91	92	92	94	95	94	93	90	88	91
Hour 12	30	65	60	56	54	56	56	59	58	58	53	57	63	58
Hour 18	30	71	63	58	58	61	61	66	67	70	72	73	74	66
PRECIPITATION (inches):														
Water Equivalent														
-Normal		5.24	4.70	5.82	5.57	5.05	3.18	4.51	3.77	3.55	3.26	4.81	5.91	55.37
-Maximum Monthly	30	14.10	10.28	15.13	15.95	10.82	8.17	13.25	**8.33**	9.61	9.13	9.98	17.70	17.70
-Year		1979	1987	1976	1991	1967	1989	1979	**1992**	1965	1970	1977	1982	DEC 1982
-Minimum Monthly	30	0.75	1.43	2.05	1.21	0.29	0.10	1.04	0.61	0.56	0.00	0.51	0.91	0.00
-Year		1986	1976	1966	1987	1988	1988	1987	1990	1969	1963	1985	1980	OCT 1963
-Maximum in 24 hrs	30	5.63	3.46	4.69	8.42	3.43	3.38	5.37	**4.79**	5.86	6.99	4.34	6.71	8.42
-Year		1979	1974	1991	1979	1989	1989	1981	**1992**	1965	1975	1983	1982	APR 1979
Snow, Ice pellets, hail														
-Maximum Monthly	30	6.3	3.6	5.3	1.1	0.0	0.0	**0.0**	**0.0**	**0.0**	**0.0**	0.2	3.1	6.3
-Year		1982	1968	1968	1987							1976	1963	JAN 1982
-Maximum in 24 hrs	30	6.0	3.6	5.3	1.1	0.0	0.0	**0.0**	**0.0**	**0.0**	**0.0**	0.2	1.8	6.0
-Year		1982	1968	1968	1987							1976	1963	JAN 1982
WIND:														
Mean Speed (mph)	30	8.4	8.6	9.2	8.5	7.3	6.4	5.9	5.6	6.4	6.5	7.6	8.3	7.4
Prevailing Direction														
Fastest Obs. 1 Min.														
-Direction (!!)	17	35	19	16	12	22	35	33	17	14	34	14	35	35
-Speed (MPH)	17	46	36	44	35	35	40	44	37	30	26	41	35	46
-Year		1990	1986	1986	1991	1987	1984	1982	1981	1991	1990	1987	1976	JAN 1990
Peak Gust														
-Direction (!!)	10	N	N	SE	SW	W	SW	**NE**	**E**	W	NE	SW	W	SW
-Speed (mph)	10	59	51	51	63	49	55	**51**	**56**	52	40	69	48	69
-Date		1990	1984	1987	1985	1990	1992	**1992**	**1992**	1984	1985	1987	1987	NOV 1987

PRECIPITATION (inches) JACKSON, MISSISSIPPI

YEAR	JAN	FEB	MAR	APR	MAY	JUNE	JULY	AUG	SEP	OCT	NOV	DEC	ANNUAL
1964	5.21	2.32	10.92	11.88	2.18	2.45	5.17	6.43	3.67	7.83	6.44	6.95	71.45
1965	2.86	7.90	6.66	1.25	1.36	2.54	1.92	3.61	9.61	0.84	1.79	3.65	43.99
1966	8.23	7.84	2.05	5.76	7.96	1.45	3.14	6.65	4.87	1.63	3.66	4.83	58.07
1967	1.86	3.56	2.32	1.66	10.82	3.76	4.05	3.49	1.80	2.78	0.93	8.68	45.71
1968	4.56	2.54	2.83	7.20	7.54	1.02	2.24	3.90	1.95	0.28	5.55	5.58	45.19
1969	0.86	3.02	4.90	6.59	1.52	1.29	5.46	3.35	0.56	2.26	1.87	7.22	38.90
1970	2.09	2.63	5.40	2.75	2.43	2.54	2.34	5.64	6.48	9.13	2.70	4.23	48.36
1971	3.02	5.68	7.68	6.86	8.05	3.40	6.28	2.64	6.00	0.09	2.54	9.82	62.06
1972	5.94	3.09	5.57	2.44	4.52	2.01	3.31	2.84	5.04	2.08	3.52	9.67	50.03
1973	4.59	4.23	6.12	9.44	5.96	0.32	1.99	2.38	4.44	2.72	6.15	6.71	55.05
1974	11.00	6.72	3.50	6.74	3.01	3.39	1.54	6.17	5.06	1.74	4.12	7.22	60.21
1975	4.57	6.18	4.86	5.07	6.53	7.44	9.81	6.21	2.68	8.25	4.34	4.29	70.23
1976	3.64	1.43	15.13	2.08	8.01	2.80	4.96	5.26	3.78	3.52	3.34	3.44	57.39
1977	6.18	2.26	6.41	7.98	0.74	2.17	6.22	1.45	3.93	2.79	9.98	3.47	53.58
1978	5.32	2.36	3.37	3.54	10.48	1.03	3.65	1.80	2.90	1.21	3.30	8.37	47.33
1979	14.10	8.35	4.67	14.38	5.52	4.38	13.25	7.44	5.93	1.76	8.79	4.18	92.75
1980	7.53	3.19	13.57	14.33	6.60	1.74	2.91	1.45	3.25	3.47	4.11	0.91	63.06
1981	1.41	2.63	6.19	1.26	6.64	3.66	6.51	2.81	3.51	5.12	1.97	4.90	46.61
1982	4.48	5.22	5.13	6.59	0.77	6.27	9.29	4.97	1.05	6.73	7.43	17.70	75.63
1983	8.17	6.55	6.00	15.53	9.41	2.93	1.70	3.70	2.70	1.52	8.11	6.95	73.27
1984	2.64	4.64	4.84	3.96	5.61	3.18	3.07	4.56	0.93	7.68	6.48	2.17	49.76
1985	4.05	7.55	3.13	3.31	0.86	1.74	4.43	7.06	3.94	7.17	0.51	3.61	47.36
1986	0.75	1.53	3.34	1.75	10.00	3.72	4.78	2.03	2.63	5.10	9.40	4.98	50.01
1987	4.66	10.28	5.47	1.21	4.98	6.17	1.04	4.03	1.50	0.27	4.20	3.50	47.31
1988	2.25	3.89	7.46	5.37	0.29	0.10	2.73	3.02	2.28	6.14	5.66	4.80	43.99
1989	4.38	2.52	4.53	2.13	7.92	8.17	4.47	1.74	5.40	0.23	6.86	4.20	52.55
1990	12.17	8.30	3.55	3.66	6.34	1.46	2.84	0.61	4.83	1.24	3.33	5.71	54.04
1991	4.98	5.30	7.50	15.95	7.11	3.35	3.32	1.49	3.45	2.95	2.39	5.27	63.06
1992	4.27	3.83	2.11	1.48	1.22	4.75	4.48	8.33	3.80	1.55	8.27	4.32	48.41
1993	4.72	3.40	3.84	4.09	4.31	3.79	7.00	2.47	2.04	4.08	5.39	2.89	48.02
Record Mean	4.95	4.77	5.54	5.39	4.64	3.75	4.52	3.60	2.87	2.52	4.06	5.47	52.09

AVERAGE TEMPERATURE (deg. F) JACKSON, MISSISSIPPI

YEAR	JAN	FEB	MAR	APR	MAY	JUNE	JULY	AUG	SEP	OCT	NOV	DEC	ANNUAL
#1964	45.3	44.4	56.3	68.1	74.7	80.7	81.3	81.7	77.1	62.5	59.4	50.5	65.2
1965	48.5	47.2	50.2	67.8	74.0	77.7	81.5	79.5	76.3	62.6	60.1	49.4	64.6
1966	40.8	46.3	54.7	64.8	70.9	76.1	82.4	78.3	74.4	61.1	56.2	46.5	62.7
1967	46.4	44.2	60.5	69.3	69.6	78.3	77.3	77.0	69.8	61.4	52.7	50.1	63.1
1968	43.4	39.9	53.9	65.9	71.2	79.6	80.7	80.9	73.3	66.2	52.7	45.7	62.8
1969	48.0	48.1	49.3	65.1	72.3	80.3	83.5	79.6	75.2	66.2	52.4	47.1	63.9
1970	41.2	46.3	54.0	68.1	72.9	79.1	80.8	81.6	80.1	64.7	52.8	52.7	64.5
1971	48.7	49.1	52.4	62.2	67.9	79.9	81.0	80.5	78.3	70.1	54.7	57.9	65.2
1972	51.5	51.2	58.8	66.4	71.9	79.6	80.4	82.8	81.5	68.0	52.0	50.1	66.2
1973	44.3	46.9	62.1	62.5	70.9	81.3	83.7	80.1	77.6	68.6	61.7	49.3	65.7
1974	55.1	50.1	62.4	63.1	73.8	74.8	80.4	79.3	72.0	64.1	55.6	50.4	65.1
1975	51.8	52.9	56.8	63.5	74.1	78.3	81.2	80.6	72.3	66.2	56.6	47.4	65.1
1976	44.3	56.7	60.0	65.4	67.9	76.7	80.8	80.2	74.8	59.9	47.2	45.0	63.2
1977	35.3	49.3	59.7	66.3	75.5	81.7	82.7	82.0	78.4	62.0	57.1	47.5	64.8
1978	36.5	39.6	52.5	65.4	71.9	80.0	83.4	82.0	78.4	63.6	60.3	48.8	63.6
1979	38.3	46.0	57.4	64.8	70.3	76.7	80.2	79.7	73.8	64.1	50.9	46.2	62.4
1980	47.4	45.5	54.3	61.6	72.8	80.7	85.8	84.7	82.4	61.4	53.2	46.2	64.7
1981	41.8	48.7	55.1	71.0	69.9	81.8	83.6	82.6	73.2	65.4	58.6	46.6	64.9
1982	47.2	48.8	62.1	63.8	74.7	79.5	82.4	81.8	74.1	65.1	56.4	52.9	65.7
1983	43.7	47.4	53.9	60.1	70.7	76.6	82.9	82.7	74.1	65.8	55.1	41.8	62.9
1984	39.9	49.7	56.5	63.9	71.0	78.9	80.6	79.9	74.6	71.2	53.6	58.3	64.8
1985	38.0	44.8	61.3	65.2	72.2	78.8	80.5	80.3	74.0	68.0	62.5	42.7	64.0
1986	45.3	52.6	57.0	64.1	72.9	80.4	83.2	80.5	79.8	66.1	60.1	46.6	65.7
1987	44.4	51.3	55.5	62.2	75.9	79.0	82.0	82.9	75.2	59.9	56.6	52.1	64.8
1988	41.7	47.5	55.8	64.6	70.8	79.8	82.5	82.6	77.9	61.6	59.3	49.3	64.5
1989	52.5	48.2	58.8	63.2	72.0	78.4	80.6	80.8	74.1	63.9	57.1	40.4	64.2
1990	51.0	56.2	60.0	63.7	71.8	81.3	81.5	82.3	78.4	63.7	58.0	51.8	66.6
1991	46.6	51.7	59.3	68.0	75.6	79.9	82.9	81.4	76.0	67.2	52.4	52.0	66.1
1992	45.6	53.7	57.6	64.1	71.1	77.7	82.0	77.8	75.6	65.0	52.7	50.1	64.4
1993	49.9	49.2	54.4	61.0	71.0	80.9	82.5	82.9	75.9	62.3	52.1	45.8	64.0
Record Mean	47.4	50.5	57.3	65.1	72.5	79.6	81.9	81.4	76.8	66.0	55.7	49.1	65.3
Max	57.9	61.6	68.9	76.9	84.0	90.8	92.6	92.4	88.4	79.3	68.1	59.8	76.7
Min	36.8	39.4	45.7	53.2	61.0	68.3	71.2	70.4	65.1	52.7	43.2	38.4	53.8

REFERENCE NOTES JACKSON, MISSISSIPPI

GENERAL
T - TRACE AMOUNT.
BLANK ENTRIES DENOTE MISSING/UNREPORTED DATA.
# INDICATES A STATION OR INSTRUMENT RELOCATION.

SPECIFIC

PM - INCLUDES LAST DAY OF PREVIOUS MONTH
ASOS - AUTOMATED SURFACE OBSERVING SYSTEM IN OPERATION DURING THESE MONTHS.

(a) - LENGTH OF RECORD IN YEARS, ALTHOUGH INDIVIDUAL MONTHS MAY BE MISSING.
0.* OR * - THE VALUE IS BETWEEN 0.0 AND 0.05
NORMALS - BASED ON THE 1961-1990 RECORD PERIOD.
EXTREMES - DATES ARE THE MOST RECENT OCCURRENCE
WIND DIR.- NUMERALS SHOW TENS OF DEGRESS CLOCKWISE FROM TRUE NORTH. "00" INDICATES CALM.
RESULTANT DIRECTIONS ARE GIVEN TO WHOLE DEGREES.
BOLD VALUES INDICATE EXTREME VALUES WHICH OCCURRED AFTER THE ASOS SYSTEM WAS COMMISSIONED.

RECORD = PERIOD OF RECORD
RECORD MEAN PRECIPITATION IS THE MEAN OF ALL DAILY PRECIPITATION AMOUNTS DURING THE PERIOD OF RECORD.
RECORD MAX(MIN) TEMPERATURE IS THE MEAN OF ALL DAILY MAX(MIN) TEMPERATURES DURING THE PERIOD OF RECORD.
RECORD MEAN TEMPERATURE IS THE SUM OF THE RECORD MAX AND RECORD MIN DIVIDED BY 2.
AVERAGE TEMPERATURE IS THE SUM OF THE MEAN DAILY MAX AND MIN TEMPERATURE DIVIDED BY 2.

EXCEPTIONS

RECORD MEANS ARE THROUGH THE CURRENT YEAR,
BEGINNING IN 1909 FOR TEMPERATURE
1909 FOR PRECIPITATION
1964 FOR SNOWFALL

HEATING DEGREE DAYS Base 65 deg. F — JACKSON, MISSISSIPPI

SEASON	JULY	AUG	SEP	OCT	NOV	DEC	JAN	FEB	MAR	APR	MAY	JUNE	TOTAL
1964-65	0	0	0	124	219	465	512	500	459	48	2	0	2329
1965-66	0	0	9	129	173	481	747	520	326	98	13	0	2496
1966-67	0	0	0	155	270	581	570	574	192	20	26	0	2388
1967-68	0	0	35	141	368	461	662	721	362	64	12	0	2826
1968-69	0	0	0	93	369	592	523	470	476	65	3	0	2591
1969-70	0	0	0	95	372	550	741	516	340	72	23	0	2709
1970-71	0	0	0	85	367	388	507	444	394	147	40	0	2372
1971-72	0	0	0	19	328	235	431	410	216	76	1	0	1716
1972-73	0	0	4	71	400	466	634	503	135	146	19	0	2378
1973-74	0	0	0	61	173	486	327	419	165	115	1	0	1747
1974-75	0	0	6	79	308	465	429	348	293	138	0	0	2066
1975-76	0	0	26	59	304	543	635	252	201	59	18	0	2097
1976-77	0	0	0	197	528	614	913	435	196	43	1	0	2927
1977-78	0	0	0	136	246	538	881	706	377	73	14	0	2971
1978-79	0	0	0	98	164	519	821	531	262	69	20	0	2484
1979-80	0	0	0	98	421	580	540	570	337	124	3	0	2673
1980-81	0	0	0	158	363	575	711	454	312	20	18	0	2611
1981-82	0	0	16	104	217	568	569	451	199	123	4	0	2251
1982-83	0	0	19	120	286	421	653	487	347	176	12	0	2521
1983-84	0	0	21	83	315	716	770	440	289	113	29	0	2776
1984-85	0	0	12	27	350	249	832	562	158	92	2	0	2284
1985-86	0	0	14	54	148	685	606	360	261	90	8	0	2226
1986-87	0	0	0	79	183	566	632	378	297	150	0	0	2285
1987-88	0	0	0	161	271	408	716	502	292	74	4	0	2428
1988-89	0	0	0	134	208	484	392	495	239	135	20	0	2107
1989-90	0	0	11	109	265	754	429	261	209	125	9	0	2172
1990-91	0	0	5	145	227	427	566	368	229	35	2	0	2004
1991-92	0	0	4	67	404	403	593	323	233	118	18	0	2163
1992-93	0	0	1	45	364	452	461	437	327	163	5	0	2255
1993-94	0	0	10	161	401	588							

COOLING DEGREE DAYS Base 65 deg. F — JACKSON, MISSISSIPPI

YEAR	JAN	FEB	MAR	APR	MAY	JUNE	JULY	AUG	SEP	OCT	NOV	DEC	TOTAL
1969	3	0	0	75	235	465	577	460	312	137	3	0	2267
1970	7	0	5	173	274	431	496	522	460	81	7	18	2474
1971	9	7	10	69	138	453	503	487	406	181	29	20	2312
1972	20	17	30	126	221	445	487	561	506	169	15	16	2613
1973	1	0	51	77	210	498	583	477	382	181	81	5	2546
1974	25	8	91	64	279	298	487	451	223	57	34	19	2036
1975	26	17	46	96	290	407	509	487	255	101	59	7	2300
1976	0	17	52	76	116	357	497	481	300	47	0	0	1943
1977	0	3	39	89	331	508	555	534	409	47	16	4	2535
1978	2	0	0	92	235	456	576	536	409	60	31	24	2421
1979	0	2	35	69	190	357	482	461	269	76	4	2	1947
1980	0	11	11	28	253	476	652	619	527	52	14	1	2644
1981	0	3	12	207	174	514	582	555	267	127	30	2	2473
1982	25	3	116	93	310	443	544	530	297	130	35	51	2577
1983	0	0	13	35	194	354	564	555	300	115	24	6	2160
1984	0	5	35	87	221	422	489	470	310	227	19	49	2334
1985	0	3	54	105	233	424	486	480	290	153	79	0	2307
1986	0	21	18	70	259	469	572	487	446	122	44	2	2510
1987	0	0	9	72	344	429	533	560	311	14	22	15	2309
1988	0	1	14	67	193	452	552	552	395	34	45	3	2308
1989	8	30	54	87	245	406	489	498	293	84	36	0	2230
1990	3	25	60	92	226	494	515	544	412	113	24	24	2532
1991	0	3	59	129	337	456	562	515	341	142	37	7	2588
1992	0	1	10	97	213	383	532	403	324	51	2	0	2016
1993	0	1	6	48	197	485	547	562	340	82	19	0	2287

SNOWFALL (inches) — JACKSON, MISSISSIPPI

SEASON	JULY	AUG	SEP	OCT	NOV	DEC	JAN	FEB	MAR	APR	MAY	JUNE	TOTAL
1964-65	0.0	0.0	0.0	0.0	T	T	T	T	T	0.0	0.0	0.0	T
1965-66	0.0	0.0	0.0	0.0	0.0	0.0	T	0.0	0.0	0.0	0.0	0.0	T
1966-67	0.0	0.0	0.0	0.0	T	T	0.0	T	0.0	0.0	0.0	0.0	T
1967-68	0.0	0.0	0.0	0.0	0.0	T	T	3.6	5.3	0.0	0.0	0.0	8.9
1968-69	0.0	0.0	0.0	0.0	0.0	0.0	0.0	0.0	0.0	0.0	0.0	0.0	0.0
1969-70	0.0	0.0	0.0	0.0	0.0	T	T	0.0	T	0.0	0.0	0.0	T
1970-71	0.0	0.0	0.0	0.0	0.0	0.0	T	T	T	T	0.0	0.0	T
1971-72	0.0	0.0	0.0	0.0	T	0.0	0.0	T	0.0	0.0	0.0	0.0	T
1972-73	0.0	0.0	0.0	0.0	0.0	0.0	T	T	0.0	0.0	0.0	0.0	T
1973-74	0.0	0.0	0.0	0.0	0.0	0.3	0.0	0.0	0.0	0.0	0.0	0.0	0.3
1974-75	0.0	0.0	0.0	0.0	T	0.0	T	0.0	T	0.0	0.0	0.0	T
1975-76	0.0	0.0	0.0	0.0	T	T	T	0.0	0.0	0.0	0.0	0.0	T
1976-77	0.0	0.0	0.0	0.0	0.2	0.0	5.8	0.0	0.0	0.0	0.0	0.0	6.0
1977-78	0.0	0.0	0.0	0.0	0.0	0.0	1.1	T	0.1	0.0	0.0	0.0	1.2
1978-79	0.0	0.0	0.0	0.0	0.0	T	T	T	0.0	0.0	0.0	0.0	T
1979-80	0.0	0.0	0.0	0.0	0.0	0.0	T	T	T	0.0	0.0	0.0	T
1980-81	0.0	0.0	0.0	0.0	0.0	T	T	T	0.0	0.0	0.0	0.0	T
1981-82	0.0	0.0	0.0	0.0	0.0	T	6.3	T	T	0.0	0.0	0.0	6.3
1982-83	0.0	0.0	0.0	0.0	0.0	0.0	T	T	0.0	T	0.0	0.0	T
1983-84	0.0	0.0	0.0	0.0	0.0	T	T	T	0.0	0.0	0.0	0.0	T
1984-85	0.0	0.0	0.0	0.0	0.0	T	0.3	1.4	0.0	0.0	0.0	0.0	1.7
1985-86	0.0	0.0	0.0	0.0	0.0	T	0.0	T	0.0	0.0	0.0	0.0	T
1986-87	0.0	0.0	0.0	0.0	0.0	0.0	T	0.0	T	1.1	0.0	0.0	1.1
1987-88	0.0	0.0	0.0	0.0	0.0	0.0	T	T	0.0	0.0	0.0	0.0	T
1988-89	0.0	0.0	0.0	0.0	0.0	T	0.0	T	T	T	0.0	0.0	T
1989-90	0.0	0.0	0.0	0.0	T	0.1	0.0	0.0	0.0	0.0	0.0	0.0	0.1
1990-91	0.0	0.0	0.0	0.0	0.0	T	0.0	0.0	0.0	T	0.0	0.0	T
1991-92	0.0	0.0	0.0	0.0	T	0.0	0.2	0.0	0.0	0.0	0.0	0.0	0.2
1992-93	0.0	0.0	0.0	0.0	T	0.0	T	0.0	1.6	0.0	0.0	0.0	1.6
1993-94	0.0	0.0	0.0	0.0	0.0	T							
Record Mean	0.0	0.0	0.0	0.0	T	T	0.5	0.2	0.2	T	0.0	0.0	1.0

INTERNATIONAL AIRPORT, KANSAS CITY, MISSOURI

The National Weather Service Office at Kansas City is very near the geographical center of the United States. The surrounding terrain is gently rolling. It has a modified continental climate. There are no natural topographic obstructions to prevent the free sweep of air from all directions. The influx of moist air from the Gulf of Mexico, or dry air from the semi-arid regions of the southwest, determine whether wet or dry conditions will prevail. There is often conflict between the warm moist gulf air and the cold polar continental air from the north in this area.

Early spring brings a period of frequent and rapid fluctuations in weather, with the fluctuations generally less frequent as spring progresses. The summer season is characterized by warm days and mild nights, with moderate humidities. July is the warmest month. The fall season is normally mild and usually includes a period near the middle of the season characterized by mild, sunny days, and cool nights. Winters are not severely cold. January is the coldest month. Falls of snow to a depth of 10 inches or more are comparatively rare. The distribution of measurable snow normally extends from November to April.

Nearly 60 percent of the annual precipitation occurs during the six months from April through September. More than 75 percent of the annual moisture normally falls during the growing season. The frequency and distribution of precipitation over a normal day is also important. The maximum frequency of precipitation, from April through October, occurs during the six hours following midnight and the minimum frequency occurs during the six hours following noon.

NORMALS, MEANS, AND EXTREMES

INTERNATIONAL AIRPORT, KANSAS CITY, MISSOURI

LATITUDE: 39°19'N LONGITUDE: 94°43' W ELEVATION: FT. GRND 973 BARO 975 TIME ZONE: CENTRAL WBAN: 03947

	(a)	JAN	FEB	MAR	APR	MAY	JUNE	JULY	AUG	SEP	OCT	NOV	DEC	YEAR
TEMPERATURE °F:														
Normals														
-Daily Maximum		34.7	40.6	52.8	65.1	74.3	83.3	88.7	86.4	78.1	67.5	52.6	38.8	63.6
-Daily Minimum		16.7	21.8	32.6	43.8	53.9	63.1	68.2	65.7	56.9	45.7	33.6	21.9	43.7
-Monthly		25.7	31.2	42.7	54.5	64.1	73.2	78.5	76.1	67.5	56.6	43.1	30.4	53.6
Extremes														
-Record Highest	21	69	76	86	93	92	105	107	109	102	92	82	70	109
-Year		1989	1981	1986	1987	1985	1980	1974	1984	1990	1976	1990	1980	AUG 1984
-Record Lowest	21	-17	-19	-10	12	30	42	52	43	33	17	1	-23	-23
-Year		1982	1982	1978	1975	1976	1990	1973	1986	1991	1993	1991	1989	DEC 1989
NORMAL DEGREE DAYS:														
Heating (base 65°F)		1218	946	691	325	135	7	0	6	56	279	657	1073	5393
Cooling (base 65°F)		0	0	0	10	107	253	419	350	131	18	0	0	1288
% OF POSSIBLE SUNSHINE	21	59	55	58	63	62	67	72	67	66	61	49	50	61
MEAN SKY COVER (tenths)														
Sunrise - Sunset	21	5.9	6.2	6.5	6.1	6.2	5.5	4.6	4.8	4.9	5.0	6.1	6.0	5.7
MEAN NUMBER OF DAYS:														
Sunrise to Sunset														
-Clear	21	10.3	7.9	7.4	8.6	7.7	9.6	13.2	12.6	12.2	12.8	8.6	9.8	120.7
-Partly Cloudy	21	6.3	6.1	7.6	7.1	9.4	9.9	10.3	10.5	8.0	7.1	6.9	6.2	95.6
-Cloudy	21	14.4	14.2	16.0	14.2	13.9	10.5	7.5	7.9	9.8	11.1	14.5	15.0	149.0
Precipitation .01 inches or more	21	7.3	6.9	10.4	10.8	11.5	10.1	8.7	8.9	8.5	7.5	8.1	7.8	106.5
Snow, Ice pellets, hail 1.0 inches or more	21	2.0	1.7	0.8	0.3	0.0	0.0	0.0	0.0	0.0	0.0	0.5	1.1	6.5
Thunderstorms	21	0.3	0.6	2.6	5.0	8.3	9.0	8.3	7.3	5.7	3.0	1.2	0.4	51.8
Heavy Fog Visibility 1/4 mile or less	21	2.3	3.0	2.3	1.2	1.0	0.7	0.5	1.3	1.3	1.5	2.0	3.2	20.3
Temperature °F														
-Maximum														
90° and above	21	0.0	0.0	0.0	0.4	0.2	5.7	15.5	11.7	3.7	0.1	0.0	0.0	37.3
32° and below	21	12.1	8.2	1.7	0.1	0.0	0.0	0.0	0.0	0.0	0.0	2.2	7.8	32.2
-Minimum														
32° and below	21	28.1	22.0	14.5	3.7	0.*	0.0	0.0	0.0	0.0	2.4	13.9	26.2	110.8
0° and below	21	3.7	2.3	0.1	0.0	0.0	0.0	0.0	0.0	0.0	0.0	0.0	2.0	8.0
AVG. STATION PRESS. (mb)	21	982.9	982.0	977.9	977.2	976.9	977.4	978.8	979.7	980.4	981.1	980.5	982.2	979.8
RELATIVE HUMIDITY (%)														
Hour 00	21	73	74	72	70	76	78	76	78	79	73	74	75	75
Hour 06 (Local Time)	21	77	78	78	78	83	85	84	86	86	80	79	79	81
Hour 12	21	64	64	59	56	59	59	58	59	59	55	62	65	60
Hour 18	21	65	63	57	53	57	57	55	58	60	59	66	68	60
PRECIPITATION (inches):														
Water Equivalent														
-Normal		1.09	1.10	2.51	3.12	5.04	4.72	4.38	4.01	4.86	3.29	1.92	1.58	37.62
-Maximum Monthly	21	2.66	2.69	9.08	6.82	10.07	7.44	15.47	9.58	11.34	7.67	5.12	5.42	15.47
-Year		1982	1985	1973	1984	1974	1981	1992	1982	1977	1977	1992	1980	JUL 1992
-Minimum Monthly	21	0.02	0.20	1.18	1.02	1.05	1.80	0.25	0.75	1.13	0.21	T	0.05	T
-Year		1986	1991	1974	1980	1992	1988	1975	1984	1974	1988	1989	1979	NOV 1989
-Maximum in 24 hrs	21	1.83	1.39	1.98	4.69	4.26	2.67	5.08	6.19	8.82	4.92	2.08	3.67	8.82
-Year		1982	1987	1992	1975	1974	1976	1986	1982	1977	1973	1990	1980	SEP 1977
Snow, Ice pellets, hail														
-Maximum Monthly	21	14.2	15.7	11.4	7.2	T	T	T	0.0	T	T	7.1	13.2	15.7
-Year		1977	1993	1978	1983	1990	1993	1992		1992	1993	1975	1983	FEB 1993
-Maximum in 24 hrs	21	9.5	10.8	9.2	4.0	T	T	T	0.0	T	T	6.1	10.8	10.8
-Year		1993	1993	1990	1983	1990	1993	1992		1992	1993	1975	1987	FEB 1993
WIND:														
Mean Speed (mph)	21	11.4	11.3	12.6	12.4	10.4	9.9	9.5	9.1	9.6	10.5	11.5	11.2	10.8
Prevailing Direction														
Fastest Obs. 1 Min.														
-Direction (!!)	9	23	32	22	16	33	35	18	31	29	19	18	20	35
-Speed (MPH)	9	35	35	39	32	45	48	46	40	40	38	35	39	48
-Year		1990	1991	1991	1991	1987	1990	1990	1987	1988	1992	1990	1988	JUN 1990
Peak Gust														
-Direction (!!)	10	NW	NW	SW	SW	NW	N	NW	NW	N	NW	NW	NW	NW
-Speed (mph)	10	58	56	63	62	59	67	75	54	63	54	52	55	75
-Date		1984	1984	1991	1984	1991	1990	1992	1987	1987	1990	1991	1993	JUL 1992

PRECIPITATION (inches)

INTERNATIONAL AIRPORT, KANSAS CITY, MISSOURI

YEAR	JAN	FEB	MAR	APR	MAY	JUNE	JULY	AUG	SEP	OCT	NOV	DEC	ANNUAL
1964	1.20	1.50	3.20	5.40	5.50	5.40	2.94	3.79	3.07	0.36	4.73	1.73	38.82
1965	2.35	1.81	3.51	2.21	2.19	7.50	9.83	6.27	7.75	1.83	0.24	2.25	47.74
1966	0.21	0.76	1.88	3.04	2.48	8.63	0.89	4.24	2.67	0.45	1.05	0.91	27.21
1967	2.09	0.35	2.85	6.86	6.04	9.71	1.81	0.31	7.87	8.63	0.45	1.72	48.69
1968	0.27	1.20	0.73	3.91	5.19	2.33	5.13	4.32	1.04	3.52	3.03	1.29	31.96
1969	1.31	0.49	1.36	4.77	3.89	10.57	10.29	8.70	3.67	6.50	0.08	0.72	52.35
1970	0.21	0.46	1.02	3.95	4.75	5.32	0.62	4.02	10.79	2.30	0.94	1.74	36.12
1971	1.48	0.89	0.87	1.29	3.02	3.20	3.13	1.04	2.70	3.47	1.68	3.82	26.59
#1972	0.56	0.41	2.13	3.98	2.18	2.71	3.43	2.90	2.69	2.29	3.00	1.47	27.75
1973	2.05	1.35	9.08	2.91	5.65	2.84	8.71	1.60	10.32	5.80	2.36	2.59	55.26
1974	1.05	1.12	1.18	2.94	10.07	2.16	1.13	4.98	1.13	7.22	1.62	1.52	36.12
1975	2.14	1.59	1.49	6.61	3.45	2.46	0.25	4.85	6.10	0.35	2.75	2.03	34.07
1976	0.53	0.66	2.53	3.30	5.49	5.08	0.77	0.76	1.41	2.84	0.21	0.10	23.68
1977	1.15	0.57	2.59	2.35	5.43	6.18	2.74	7.99	11.34	7.67	1.36	0.37	49.74
1978	0.39	1.32	1.77	5.36	4.98	2.64	5.49	2.66	4.04	0.33	3.93	1.05	33.96
#1979	2.35	0.78	2.96	2.35	3.00	5.37	4.68	3.66	1.16	3.56	1.83	0.05	31.75
1980	1.60	1.44	3.64	1.02	3.06	2.52	1.99	4.89	1.63	4.13	0.45	5.42	31.79
1981	0.49	0.31	1.43	1.94	9.46	7.44	8.43	2.43	2.71	4.14	2.84	0.45	42.07
1982	2.66	1.13	2.94	1.55	9.81	6.04	2.73	9.58	1.58	3.04	2.21	3.94	47.21
1983	0.58	0.57	2.93	5.52	6.03	5.03	0.26	0.86	1.89	3.85	3.94	1.42	32.88
1984	0.14	1.96	4.52	6.82	2.26	4.14	3.91	0.75	3.42	6.04	1.24	3.57	38.77
1985	0.94	2.69	2.05	1.75	7.00	3.56	5.82	6.98	9.23	7.51	3.95	1.24	52.72
1986	0.02	1.25	1.34	2.12	4.76	2.48	8.36	3.16	10.40	3.17	1.18	1.20	39.44
1987	0.77	2.26	2.85	2.24	4.74	4.58	3.00	4.64	3.66	1.32	1.88	2.05	33.99
1988	1.40	0.72	1.43	2.15	2.14	1.80	1.21	1.87	8.48	0.21	1.96	0.85	24.22
1989	0.98	0.59	2.13	1.50	4.56	3.44	4.76	7.38	8.87	2.88	T	0.55	37.64
1990	1.20	2.11	3.90	2.47	7.36	6.27	4.40	5.04	1.28	2.46	3.01	1.11	40.61
1991	1.37	0.20	2.36	4.99	3.69	3.06	1.72	1.35	2.12	3.71	2.05	2.08	28.70
1992	1.21	2.01	3.79	4.92	1.05	3.84	15.47	2.37	5.69	1.38	5.12	3.78	50.63
1993	1.96	1.28	2.21	5.59	7.30	5.67	10.90	3.98	7.63	1.75	2.07	1.12	51.46
Record Mean	1.30	1.42	2.60	3.37	4.78	4.75	4.02	3.94	4.39	2.98	1.92	1.50	36.97

AVERAGE TEMPERATURE (deg. F)

INTERNATIONAL AIRPORT, KANSAS CITY, MISSOURI

YEAR	JAN	FEB	MAR	APR	MAY	JUNE	JULY	AUG	SEP	OCT	NOV	DEC	ANNUAL
1964	37.2	36.2	41.8	57.4	70.1	73.7	82.5	76.0	69.4	57.6	49.9	32.3	57.0
1965	31.4	32.3	34.0	58.5	71.6	74.6	78.5	77.1	69.9	60.5	48.2	44.0	56.7
1966	28.0	33.7	49.1	52.8	65.6	73.3	83.4	74.9	68.8	59.7	49.1	34.8	56.1
1967	33.9	33.6	47.8	58.9	61.7	72.9	76.5	75.1	67.9	58.6	44.4	35.4	55.6
1968	28.4	32.3	48.1	57.0	62.2	77.6	79.4	77.8	69.5	59.6	41.2	29.7	55.3
1969	26.5	34.2	37.6	56.3	66.1	70.2	81.4	78.9	71.8	55.7	46.1	33.1	54.8
1970	26.1	36.7	42.0	57.4	72.1	74.5	80.8	82.4	71.6	58.6	44.4	38.9	57.1
1971	27.7	31.5	43.7	59.7	64.4	79.4	76.4	78.3	72.6	64.0	46.9	37.0	56.8
#1972	27.3	33.2	47.1	57.4	67.1	76.9	77.2	77.3	70.9	53.9	39.6	27.5	54.6
1973	27.3	33.8	47.7	51.8	61.5	74.5	76.6	77.1	66.7	60.7	45.5	30.1	54.5
1974	23.8	35.3	46.9	56.2	65.6	70.5	82.1	73.0	61.6	57.7	42.8	32.2	54.0
1975	29.9	27.8	36.5	52.8	67.1	74.2	80.9	79.8	63.5	58.9	45.9	34.1	54.3
1976	27.5	42.7	45.0	56.3	60.0	71.3	79.0	77.7	69.0	50.8	35.9	29.0	53.7
1977	15.6	35.1	48.0	59.7	69.0	74.5	79.7	74.4	69.0	55.7	42.3	29.5	54.4
1978	16.8	19.5	37.6	55.5	62.1	74.6	79.3	76.5	73.6	56.4	44.4	31.0	52.3
#1979	12.5	20.9	42.2	51.6	63.5	72.2	75.9	75.7	68.6	57.7	40.7	35.2	51.4
1980	28.7	25.2	38.7	54.6	63.9	75.3	85.2	80.3	69.6	54.1	44.5	32.1	54.4
1981	30.3	33.4	45.2	61.1	60.5	74.1	78.3	72.9	68.4	55.3	45.6	29.0	54.5
1982	18.6	27.8	42.5	51.1	65.5	68.8	79.4	75.0	67.5	55.6	41.9	35.5	52.4
1983	30.1	35.9	43.1	46.3	59.6	70.8	81.5	83.5	71.2	57.2	44.3	13.2	53.1
1984	25.0	38.9	36.0	50.3	60.4	74.3	76.1	79.0	66.1	56.8	43.9	35.5	53.5
1985	18.7	25.3	47.4	57.9	66.0	68.8	77.0	72.1	66.7	56.5	36.8	22.9	51.3
1986	34.5	30.5	48.5	57.1	65.2	76.5	79.7	72.0	71.8	56.9	37.9	34.5	55.4
1987	29.7	39.4	47.1	56.8	70.6	76.0	79.9	76.4	67.8	52.0	46.7	35.1	56.5
1988	26.7	27.9	43.2	54.5	69.1	78.1	79.6	81.3	70.5	52.2	44.8	35.2	55.3
1989	37.7	22.8	43.8	56.9	63.2	71.1	77.8	75.5	63.2	57.9	42.3	21.1	52.8
1990	37.9	36.2	45.7	52.7	60.4	75.5	77.3	77.1	72.1	57.1	50.1	29.3	56.0
1991	22.9	39.4	47.2	56.7	67.6	76.1	80.6	77.7	68.8	57.6	36.7	36.1	55.6
1992	35.9	39.8	46.9	53.1	62.6	69.7	74.4	70.7	66.1	56.6	39.0	32.9	54.0
1993	25.9	28.6	39.8	50.4	63.5	72.9	77.6	77.8	62.8	53.6	39.4	34.5	52.2
Record Mean	29.1	32.8	43.3	55.3	65.1	74.4	79.4	77.7	69.7	58.5	44.3	33.1	55.2
Max	37.7	41.8	53.0	65.2	74.6	83.8	88.9	87.4	79.6	68.6	53.2	41.2	64.6
Min	20.5	23.8	33.5	45.4	55.5	65.0	69.8	68.0	59.8	48.3	35.3	25.0	45.8

REFERENCE NOTES

INTERNATIONAL AIRPORT, KANSAS CITY, MISSOURI

GENERAL
T - TRACE AMOUNT.
BLANK ENTRIES DENOTE MISSING/UNREPORTED DATA.
# INDICATES A STATION OR INSTRUMENT RELOCATION.

SPECIFIC

PM - INCLUDES LAST DAY OF PREVIOUS MONTH
ASOS - AUTOMATED SURFACE OBSERVING SYSTEM IN OPERATION DURING THESE MONTHS.

(*) - LENGTH OF RECORD IN YEARS, ALTHOUGH INDIVIDUAL MONTHS MAY BE MISSING.
0.* OR * - THE VALUE IS BETWEEN 0.0 AND 0.05
NORMALS - BASED ON THE 1961-1990 RECORD PERIOD.
EXTREMES - DATES ARE THE MOST RECENT OCCURRENCE
WIND DIR.- NUMERALS SHOW TENS OF DEGRESS CLOCKWISE FROM TRUE NORTH. "00" INDICATES CALM.
RESULTANT DIRECTIONS ARE GIVEN TO WHOLE DEGREES.
BOLD VALUES INDICATE EXTREME VALUES WHICH OCCURRED AFTER THE ASOS SYSTEM WAS COMMISSIONED.

RECORD = PERIOD OF RECORD
RECORD MEAN PRECIPITATION IS THE MEAN OF ALL DAILY PRECIPITATION AMOUNTS DURING THE PERIOD OF RECORD.
RECORD MAX(MIN) TEMPERATURE IS THE MEAN OF ALL DAILY MAX(MIN) TEMPERATURES DURING THE PERIOD OF RECORD.
RECORD MEAN TEMPERATURE IS THE SUM OF THE RECORD MAX AND RECORD MIN DIVIDED BY 2.
AVERAGE TEMPERATURE IS THE SUM OF THE MEAN DAILY MAX AND MIN TEMPERATURE DIVIDED BY 2.

EXCEPTIONS

RECORD MEANS ARE THROUGH THE CURRENT YEAR,
BEGINNING IN 1889 FOR TEMPERATURE
1889 FOR PRECIPITATION
1936 FOR SNOWFALL

HEATING DEGREE DAYS Base 65 deg. F — INTERNATIONAL AIRPORT, KANSAS CITY, MISSOURI

SEASON	JULY	AUG	SEP	OCT	NOV	DEC	JAN	FEB	MAR	APR	MAY	JUNE	TOTAL
1964-65	0	2	49	235	473	1004	1033	911	955	237	15	0	4914
1965-66	0	0	44	175	497	646	1141	869	492	365	95	9	4333
1966-67	0	2	29	203	478	931	956	874	548	213	193	11	4438
1967-68	0	3	48	255	609	909	1125	941	528	245	131	3	4797
1968-69	0	1	13	224	706	1090	1186	857	845	258	86	24	5290
1969-70	0	0	3	330	562	984	1198	785	707	280	26	22	4897
1970-71	0	0	25	231	610	801	1151	931	659	208	92	0	4708
1971-72	4	0	57	87	538	863	1163	920	557	263	71	0	4523
#1972-73	1	0	37	355	751	1155	1160	868	529	394	127	0	5377
1973-74	0	0	53	173	578	1077	1272	823	559	270	84	6	4895
1974-75	0	6	141	227	660	1009	1084	1036	878	381	42	5	5469
1975-76	0	0	142	226	567	954	1155	640	616	277	178	6	4761
1976-77	0	0	45	469	865	1108	1527	832	521	192	22	0	5581
1977-78	0	0	21	293	673	1094	1487	1266	848	291	172	6	6151
#1978-79	0	0	28	272	618	1050	1624	1230	698	400	115	5	6040
1979-80	5	5	35	247	720	918	1118	1148	809	327	98	3	5433
1980-81	0	0	63	347	609	1011	1069	880	607	169	179	2	4936
1981-82	0	2	40	309	573	1112	1432	1037	690	416	51	32	5694
1982-83	0	2	78	307	688	911	1074	810	675	557	180	29	5311
1983-84	0	0	57	271	617	1602	1234	750	891	443	175	1	6041
1984-85	0	0	143	269	624	907	1431	1102	538	256	41	19	5330
1985-86	0	3	131	260	841	1297	940	960	528	267	60	0	5287
1986-87	0	12	23	251	805	938	1088	712	549	298	15	0	4691
1987-88	0	3	30	398	552	922	1180	1069	668	311	19	0	5152
1988-89	2	1	18	394	599	915	836	1176	658	319	135	7	5060
1989-90	0	1	138	267	675	1360	836	800	601	398	167	10	5253
1990-91	1	0	44	278	452	1104	1296	709	553	258	62	0	4757
1991-92	0	0	96	277	841	888	898	724	554	367	137	6	4788
1992-93	0	7	80	271	773	987	1203	1011	775	431	88	26	5652
1993-94	0	2	118	365	760	938							

COOLING DEGREE DAYS Base 65 deg. F — INTERNATIONAL AIRPORT, KANSAS CITY, MISSOURI

YEAR	JAN	FEB	MAR	APR	MAY	JUNE	JULY	AUG	SEP	OCT	NOV	DEC	TOTAL
#1969	0	0	0	4	126	188	513	435	216	52	0	0	1534
1970	0	0	0	58	250	317	493	546	232	39	0	0	1935
1971	0	0	5	54	81	437	366	421	295	64	3	0	1726
1972	0	3	7	41	146	368	386	389	219	16	0	0	1575
1973	0	0	0	4	30	291	368	382	110	46	0	0	1231
1974	0	0	4	13	109	176	538	264	47	8	0	0	1159
1975	0	0	0	22	117	284	498	464	105	43	1	0	1534
1976	0	0	0	22	29	199	444	399	169	34	0	0	1296
1977	0	0	0	39	154	291	463	298	147	11	0	0	1403
1978	0	0	5	14	86	300	452	364	295	11	8	0	1535
#1979	0	0	1	3	77	229	348	340	147	29	0	0	1174
1980	0	0	0	21	69	316	632	483	210	15	0	0	1746
1981	0	0	0	58	44	279	418	253	149	14	0	0	1215
1982	0	0	0	8	75	154	452	320	158	26	0	0	1193
1983	0	0	3	5	19	210	517	582	251	31	1	0	1619
1984	0	0	0	9	41	287	353	445	184	23	0	0	1342
1985	0	0	0	49	77	137	379	230	191	5	0	0	1068
1986	0	0	24	35	73	352	466	237	232	7	0	0	1426
1987	0	0	0	58	196	336	474	364	118	1	9	0	1556
1988	0	0	2	5	151	400	459	514	188	5	0	0	1724
1989	0	0	9	85	88	196	402	334	87	56	0	0	1257
1990	0	0	8	33	33	331	394	384	263	40	11	0	1497
1991	0	0	9	16	154	339	490	399	219	54	0	0	1680
1992	0	0	1	20	71	154	298	191	121	19	0	0	875
1993	0	0	0	0	49	271	398	406	55	19	0	0	1198

SNOWFALL (inches) — INTERNATIONAL AIRPORT, KANSAS CITY, MISSOURI

SEASON	JULY	AUG	SEP	OCT	NOV	DEC	JAN	FEB	MAR	APR	MAY	JUNE	TOTAL
1964-65	0.0	0.0	0.0	0.0	2.1	6.2	4.2	7.7	9.6	0.0	0.0	0.0	29.8
1965-66	0.0	0.0	0.0	0.0	T	2.5	T	3.7	3.5	T	T	0.0	9.7
1966-67	0.0	0.0	0.0	0.0	T	7.2	7.6	0.9	1.1	T	0.0	0.0	16.8
1967-68	0.0	0.0	0.0	T	0.2	7.0	2.8	2.7	T	T	0.0	0.0	12.7
1968-69	0.0	0.0	0.0	0.0	3.2	0.8	6.0	1.6	2.8	0.0	0.0	0.0	14.4
1969-70	0.0	0.0	0.0	0.0	0.6	3.8	2.5	2.2	1.0	4.6	0.0	0.0	14.7
1970-71	0.0	0.0	0.0	T	T	3.6	1.3	8.2	7.4	0.0	0.0	0.0	20.5
1971-72	0.0	0.0	0.0	0.0	0.2	1.0	3.0	2.9	3.3	T	0.0	0.0	10.4
#1972-73	0.0	0.0	0.0	0.0	3.6	3.1	10.9	0.3	0.0	1.3	0.0	0.0	19.2
1973-74	0.0	0.0	0.0	0.0	T	8.0	4.8	0.3	0.5	0.3	0.0	0.0	13.9
1974-75	0.0	0.0	0.0	0.0	1.4	1.2	5.4	4.6	5.9	2.3	0.0	0.0	20.8
1975-76	0.0	0.0	0.0	0.0	7.1	2.8	5.2	5.2	1.5	0.0	0.0	0.0	21.8
1976-77	0.0	0.0	0.0	T	0.8	0.2	14.2	0.3	T	0.6	0.0	0.0	16.1
1977-78	0.0	0.0	0.0	0.0	T	1.2	3.9	12.7	11.4	0.0	0.0	0.0	29.2
#1978-79	0.0	0.0	0.0	0.0	0.2	11.7	13.3	1.5	4.7	2.0	0.0	0.0	33.4
1979-80	0.0	0.0	0.0	0.0	T	T	5.4	12.7	5.4	0.0	0.0	0.0	23.5
1980-81	0.0	0.0	0.0	T	T	3.2	4.0	2.9	0.1	0.0	0.0	0.0	10.2
1981-82	0.0	0.0	0.0	0.0	0.1	5.3	6.0	12.7	4.0	1.3	0.0	0.0	29.4
1982-83	0.0	0.0	0.0	0.0	0.5	0.7	6.3	7.4	1.3	7.2	0.0	0.0	23.4
1983-84	0.0	0.0	0.0	0.0	0.7	13.2	1.3	0.5	8.7	0.0	0.0	0.0	24.4
1984-85	0.0	0.0	0.0	0.0	0.4	7.0	11.8	6.9	0.3	0.0	0.0	0.0	26.4
1985-86	0.0	0.0	0.0	0.0	3.5	5.4	T	4.5	T	T	0.0	0.0	13.4
1986-87	0.0	0.0	0.0	T	0.6	1.2	10.5	5.0	T	0.0	0.0	0.0	17.3
1987-88	0.0	0.0	0.0	T	2.0	11.9	0.9	9.3	2.2	0.0	0.0	0.0	26.3
1988-89	0.0	0.0	0.0	0.0	0.1	0.1	0.2	6.5	T	0.0	T	T	6.9
1989-90	0.0	0.0	0.0	0.0	T	6.8	1.0	2.1	9.6	0.0	T	0.0	19.5
1990-91	0.0	0.0	0.0	0.0	1.7	1.6	12.1	T	1.2	T	0.0	0.0	16.6
1991-92	0.0	0.0	0.0	0.0	4.6	0.2	T	2.0	0.5	2.8	0.0	0.0	10.1
1992-93	T	0.0	T	T	4.1	0.8	12.0	15.7	1.1	0.6	0.0	T	34.3
1993-94	0.0	0.0	0.0	T	0.5	2.7							
Record Mean	T	0.0	T	T	1.1	4.4	5.8	4.5	3.6	0.8	T	T	20.1

ST. LOUIS, MISSOURI

Saint Louis is located at the confluence of the Missouri and Mississippi Rivers and near the geographical center of the United States. Thus, with a somewhat modified continental climate, it is in the enviable position of being able to enjoy the changes of a four-season climate without the undue hardship of prolonged periods of extreme heat or high humidity. To the south is the warm, moist air of the Gulf of Mexico, and to the north, in Canada, is a favored region of cold air masses. The alternate invasion of Saint Louis by air masses from these sources, and the conflict along the frontal zones where they come together, produce a variety of weather conditions, none of which are likely to persist to the point of monotony.

Winters are brisk and stimulating, seldom severe. Records since 1870 show that temperatures drop to zero or below an average of two or three days per year. Temperatures remain as cold as 32 degrees or lower less than 25 days in most years. Snowfall has averaged a little over 18 inches per winter season. Snowfall of an inch or more is received on five to ten days in most years.

The long-term record for Saint Louis (since 1870) indicates that temperatures of 90 degrees or higher occur on about 35-40 days a year. Extremely hot days of 100 degrees or more are expected on no more than five days per year.

Normal annual precipitation for the Saint Louis area, is a little less than 34 inches. The three winter months are the driest, with an average total of about 6 inches of precipitation. The spring months of March through May are normally the wettest with normal total precipitation of just under 10 1/2 inches. It is not unusual to have extended dry periods of one to two weeks during the growing season.

Thunderstorms occur normally on between 40 and 50 days per year. During any year, there are usually a few of these that can be classified as severe storms with hail and damaging winds. Tornadoes have produced extensive damage and loss of life in the Saint Louis area.

NORMALS, MEANS, AND EXTREMES

ST. LOUIS, MISSOURI

LATITUDE: 38°45'N LONGITUDE: 90°22' W ELEVATION: FT. GRND 535 BARO 565 TIME ZONE: CENTRAL WBAN: 13994

	(a)	JAN	FEB	MAR	APR	MAY	JUNE	JULY	AUG	SEP	OCT	NOV	DEC	YEAR
TEMPERATURE °F:														
Normals														
-Daily Maximum		37.7	42.6	54.6	66.9	76.1	85.2	89.3	87.3	79.9	68.5	54.7	41.7	65.4
-Daily Minimum		20.8	25.1	35.5	46.4	56.0	65.7	70.4	67.9	60.5	48.3	37.7	26.0	46.7
-Monthly		29.3	33.9	45.1	56.7	66.1	75.4	79.8	77.6	70.2	58.4	46.2	33.9	56.1
Extremes														
-Record Highest	36	76	85	89	93	93	102	107	107	104	94	85	76	107
-Year		1970	1972	1985	1989	1991	1988	1980	1984	1984	1963	1989	1970	AUG 1984
-Record Lowest	36	-18	-10	-5	22	31	43	51	47	36	23	1	-16	-18
-Year		1985	1979	1960	1975	1976	1969	1972	1986	1974	1976	1964	1989	JAN 1985
NORMAL DEGREE DAYS:														
Heating (base 65°F)		1107	871	617	266	111	0	0	0	21	237	564	964	4758
Cooling (base 65°F)		0	0	0	17	145	312	459	391	177	33	0	0	1534
% OF POSSIBLE SUNSHINE	34	51	52	53	56	59	66	68	64	63	59	46	43	57
MEAN SKY COVER (tenths)														
Sunrise - Sunset	45	6.7	6.6	6.8	6.5	6.3	6.0	5.6	5.4	5.2	5.1	6.3	6.8	6.1
MEAN NUMBER OF DAYS:														
Sunrise to Sunset														
-Clear	45	7.5	6.8	6.5	6.9	7.2	7.2	9.2	10.0	11.4	12.3	8.6	7.2	100.9
-Partly Cloudy	45	6.6	6.4	8.1	8.1	9.5	10.9	11.4	11.1	8.2	7.4	6.5	6.5	100.9
-Cloudy	45	16.9	15.1	16.4	14.9	14.2	11.9	10.4	9.8	10.4	11.3	14.9	17.3	163.5
Precipitation														
.01 inches or more	36	8.4	8.2	11.4	11.3	10.7	9.3	8.9	7.8	8.0	8.4	9.6	9.4	111.1
Snow, Ice pellets, hail														
1.0 inches or more	36	1.8	1.5	1.0	0.2	0.0	0.0	0.0	0.0	0.0	0.0	0.5	1.3	6.2
Thunderstorms	36	0.7	0.9	3.1	5.7	6.5	7.1	7.4	6.4	3.9	2.6	1.7	0.7	46.8
Heavy Fog Visibility														
1/4 mile or less	36	2.1	1.7	1.5	0.6	0.6	0.3	0.2	0.4	0.5	0.8	1.1	1.9	11.5
Temperature °F														
-Maximum														
90° and above	33	0.0	0.0	0.0	0.3	1.3	8.1	15.1	11.7	4.3	0.2	0.0	0.0	41.1
32° and below	33	11.2	6.8	1.2	0.0	0.0	0.0	0.0	0.0	0.0	0.0	0.8	6.6	26.6
-Minimum														
32° and below	33	26.4	21.0	13.2	2.6	0.1	0.0	0.0	0.0	0.0	1.5	11.0	22.9	98.8
0° and below	33	2.1	0.5	0.*	0.0	0.0	0.0	0.0	0.0	0.0	0.0	0.0	1.0	3.6
AVG. STATION PRESS. (mb)	21	1000.0	999.0	995.4	994.5	994.2	994.5	995.7	996.8	997.5	998.3	997.9	999.4	996.9
RELATIVE HUMIDITY (%)														
Hour 00	33	77	77	74	70	75	76	77	79	80	75	77	79	76
Hour 06 (Local Time)	33	81	82	81	78	82	82	84	87	88	84	83	83	83
Hour 12	33	66	63	59	54	55	55	56	56	58	55	63	68	59
Hour 18	33	69	65	59	53	55	55	56	57	60	60	67	72	61
PRECIPITATION (inches):														
Water Equivalent														
-Normal		1.81	2.12	3.58	3.50	3.97	3.72	3.85	2.85	3.12	2.68	3.28	3.03	37.51
-Maximum Monthly	36	5.38	4.68	6.67	9.09	9.59	9.43	10.71	6.44	9.16	7.12	9.95	7.82	10.71
-Year		1975	1986	1978	1970	1990	1985	1981	1970	1993	1984	1985	1982	JUL 1981
-Minimum Monthly	36	0.10	0.25	1.09	0.99	1.02	0.44	0.60	0.08	T	0.21	0.44	0.32	T
-Year		1986	1963	1966	1977	1972	1991	1970	1971	1979	1975	1969	1958	SEP 1979
-Maximum in 24 hrs	36	2.43	2.56	2.95	4.91	3.62	3.29	3.47	3.17	3.50	2.70	3.71	4.03	4.91
-Year		1975	1959	1977	1979	1990	1960	1982	1993	1986	1986	1985	1982	APR 1979
Snow, Ice pellets, hail														
-Maximum Monthly	57	23.9	20.8	22.3	6.5	0.6	T	0.0	0.0	0.0	T	11.3	26.3	26.3
-Year		1977	1993	1960	1971	1993	1993				1993	1951	1973	DEC 1973
-Maximum in 24 hrs	57	13.9	11.7	10.7	6.1	0.6	T	0.0	0.0	0.0	T	10.3	12.0	13.9
-Year		1982	1993	1989	1971	1993	1993				1993	1951	1973	JAN 1982
WIND:														
Mean Speed (mph)	44	10.6	10.7	11.7	11.3	9.5	8.8	8.0	7.6	8.2	8.9	10.1	10.4	9.7
Prevailing Direction through 1963		NW	NW	WNW	WNW	S	S	S	S	S	S	S	WNW	S
Fastest Obs. 1 Min.														
-Direction (!!)	14	29	30	27	27	34	27	36	31	25	28	11	29	28
-Speed (MPH)	14	40	45	48	49	46	48	46	40	41	52	41	39	52
-Year		1984	1980	1984	1982	1990	1982	1987	1987	1986	1981	1987	1985	OCT 1981
Peak Gust														
-Direction (!!)	10	NW	W	W	SW	N	NW	N	S	W	NW	W	SW	W
-Speed (mph)	10	53	54	66	58	59	60	62	53	49	58	64	55	66
-Date		1992	1991	1984	1984	1990	1990	1987	1985	1986	1988	1984	1984	MAR 1984

PRECIPITATION (inches) — ST. LOUIS, MISSOURI

YEAR	JAN	FEB	MAR	APR	MAY	JUNE	JULY	AUG	SEP	OCT	NOV	DEC	ANNUAL
1964	1.70	2.30	3.84	4.99	2.68	2.73	4.25	2.39	1.47	0.73	3.84	1.24	32.16
1965	2.51	1.16	2.34	3.67	1.38	3.03	3.17	3.59	3.00	0.46	0.78	3.17	28.26
1966	0.65	4.12	1.09	6.03	4.59	1.59	1.26	3.72	2.15	2.18	2.47	2.49	32.34
1967	2.89	1.72	2.77	3.40	4.73	4.46	3.84	1.36	4.33	3.45	2.15	6.20	41.30
1968	1.86	1.09	2.06	1.48	6.78	0.90	3.92	1.60	3.74	0.69	5.74	2.63	32.49
1969	3.61	2.04	2.47	4.01	2.11	8.65	7.08	0.52	5.03	5.77	0.44	1.99	43.72
1970	0.22	0.64	2.17	9.09	2.04	5.08	0.60	6.44	5.54	2.21	0.77	1.40	36.20
1971	0.66	3.08	1.81	1.65	5.66	2.43	4.70	0.08	3.98	1.51	1.67	6.50	33.73
1972	0.77	0.74	2.93	4.49	1 02	1.19	3.10	2.69	6.21	1.47	5.59	3.54	33.74
1973	1.40	1.04	5.81	4.25	3.92	4.23	2.85	2.46	3.52	2.33	3.65	4.36	39.82
1974	3.51	4.17	2.58	2.40	5.90	3.45	0.90	5.05	2.50	1.51	3.15	1.71	36.83
1975	5.38	3.59	4.08	4.56	3.23	3.78	2.56	5.44	2.48	0.21	2.62	2.28	40.21
1976	0.83	1.08	4.28	1.37	3.90	2.32	2.28	1.27	0.90	3.37	0.73	1.13	23.46
1977	2.38	2.47	6.28	0.99	2.13	5.47	4.28	5.34	3.64	3.76	4.33	2.34	43.41
1978	1.70	1.60	6.67	3.21	3.69	2.39	6.03	0.76	3.10	2.28	4.47	1.81	37.71
1979	1.95	1.48	3.63	7.47	1.62	1.67	3.67	2.26	T	1.81	2.07	1.85	29.48
1980	0.63	1.54	3.98	1.54	3.40	2.19	3.56	2.72	3.12	2.89	1.25	0.66	27.48
1981	0.64	2.18	2.97	3.40	6.79	5.82	10.71	3.31	1.17	3.81	2.71	2.01	45.52
1982	4.90	1.37	2.88	2.55	4.85	5.96	7.91	5.27	5.27	2.30	3.89	7.82	54.97
1983	0.72	0.95	3.54	7.30	6.32	4.32	1.23	2.24	1.24	5.40	7.79	3.75	44.80
1984	0.84	3.43	5.37	6.29	5.19	2.74	0.76	0.64	8.88	7.12	5.50	4.89	51.65
1985	0.53	3.77	5.18	3.60	3.30	9.43	5.23	3.66	0.43	1.96	9.95	3.69	50.73
1986	0.10	4.68	1.22	1.23	2.42	4.43	2.61	2.22	7.99	5.34	1.58	1.06	34.88
1987	1.98	1.40	2.16	1.74	2.00	3.59	5.04	5.56	1.62	1.74	4.09	7.46	38.38
1988	3.30	2.27	4.73	1.15	1.44	1.97	3.02	2.31	1.99	1.86	6.65	3.24	33.93
1989	2.58	1.43	4.53	2.10	4.11	2.34	4.59	3.00	1.69	0.95	0.59	0.69	28.60
1990	1.42	3.53	2.66	3.07	9.59	3.02	3.34	2.84	0.78	4.96	3.36	6.52	45.09
1991	1.52	0.98	3.20	3.27	3.87	0.44	5.18	0.98	2.98	5.70	3.26	2.10	33.48
1992	1.12	1.89	3.45	2.46	1.45	1.19	4.31	3.45	2.98	1.21	6.32	3.66	33.49
1993	3.54	2.75	3.31	6.16	3.94	7.12	5.06	4.78	9.16	2.61	4.85	1.48	54.76
Record Mean	2.14	2.28	3.35	3.68	4.08	4.04	3.45	2.96	3.19	2.73	2.85	2.36	37.11

AVERAGE TEMPERATURE (deg. F) — ST. LOUIS, MISSOURI

YEAR	JAN	FEB	MAR	APR	MAY	JUNE	JULY	AUG	SEP	OCT	NOV	DEC	ANNUAL
1964	34.7	34.3	42.3	58.7	69.6	74.8	78.5	76.5	69.3	54.0	47.3	31.9	56.0
1965	31.9	33.8	34.5	58.4	70.5	75.1	76.8	75.8	69.1	56.4	48.5	41.7	56.1
1966	25.0	32.1	46.7	51.7	61.7	73.7	82.9	74.2	65.6	54.2	47.1	34.8	54.1
1967	34.7	31.3	48.3	58.5	60.8	74.0	74.9	72.4	66.5	57.5	42.0	34.8	54.7
1968	28.6	29.3	46.1	55.6	61.9	77.0	77.6	77.5	68.0	56.9	43.5	32.3	54.5
1969	29.2	35.3	37.8	56.9	65.7	72.5	80.5	77.0	69.3	56.1	43.4	32.1	54.7
1970	24.8	33.0	40.6	58.0	69.3	72.3	77.9	76.3	71.8	56.1	43.6	37.0	55.1
1971	27.4	33.9	41.7	55.9	62.3	78.9	75.4	75.7	72.5	63.7	46.0	40.6	56.2
1972	29.9	34.3	45.0	56.1	66.4	73.4	77.5	76.3	71.1	54.8	39.8	30.4	54.6
1973	32.6	34.5	50.9	53.7	61.7	74.6	78.7	76.9	70.0	60.7	47.0	30.0	55.9
1974	29.8	36.1	48.1	57.5	65.0	69.5	79.8	74.5	62.3	57.8	44.0	34.0	54.9
1975	33.2	32.0	39.0	53.4	67.6	74.9	77.8	77.9	64.7	59.0	48.3	35.5	55.3
1976	28.1	43.5	48.8	56.5	60.8	72.7	79.5	74.3	68.2	50.9	37.0	28.5	54.1
1977	15.1	34.8	49.6	60.8	71.1	74.7	81.2	76.4	70.7	55.5	44.7	30.6	55.4
1978	19.6	21.1	37.9	56.2	63.6	74.4	78.5	76.4	73.1	55.6	47.5	35.0	53.2
1979	16.6	23.1	44.1	52.9	65.5	76.5	79.2	78.4	70.8	59.2	44.5	38.7	54.1
1980	31.4	27.9	41.0	54.5	66.9	75.5	85.0	83.5	72.5	55.9	46.4	36.6	56.4
1981	31.2	36.8	46.7	63.1	60.7	75.7	78.7	76.1	69.2	55.7	48.7	31.1	56.1
1982	22.5	28.6	45.3	51.5	70.7	70.6	79.3	75.2	68.0	58.3	46.3	41.6	54.9
1983	32.3	38.1	44.5	50.3	62.3	75.3	83.5	84.2	72.0	59.7	48.2	20.5	55.9
1984	28.3	40.4	37.1	54.1	63.2	79.5	78.3	80.7	68.2	61.8	44.3	40.7	56.4
1985	22.6	30.5	49.5	60.4	67.6	71.6	79.3	74.7	70.9	61.4	46.5	27.3	55.2
1986	34.9	34.5	49.2	60.8	68.2	78.3	82.8	74.0	73.3	58.3	41.5	35.4	57.6
1987	30.6	40.1	48.6	56.9	72.6	77.9	81.0	78.9	70.5	53.8	49.1	38.0	58.2
1988	29.2	30.5	45.2	57.1	69.0	77.7	81.6	82.7	72.5	53.9	47.2	37.2	57.0
1989	41.2	28.2	45.0	57.7	64.3	74.8	79.3	77.8	67.4	61.3	47.1	24.1	55.7
1990	42.9	41.3	49.8	55.7	63.6	77.2	80.2	77.9	74.1	58.1	52.7	34.7	59.0
1991	29.3	41.7	50.1	61.5	73.0	79.9	80.9	79.7	72.4	60.5	42.4	39.2	59.2
1992	37.0	42.7	48.5	57.8	65.1	73.8	79.0	73.4	69.2	59.4	44.3	35.7	57.2
1993	32.1	31.7	41.5	54.2	66.4	75.1	81.9	80.4	66.4	56.1	43.9	37.2	55.6
Record Mean	31.3	34.7	44.5	56.1	65.9	75.2	79.5	77.6	70.1	58.8	45.4	35.0	56.2
Max	39.5	43.3	53.8	65.8	75.6	84.5	88.8	87.0	79.8	68.5	53.9	42.8	65.3
Min	23.0	26.1	35.1	46.4	56.3	65.8	70.2	68.1	60.4	49.0	36.8	27.3	47.1

REFERENCE NOTES — ST. LOUIS, MISSOURI

GENERAL
T - TRACE AMOUNT.
BLANK ENTRIES DENOTE MISSING/UNREPORTED DATA.
# INDICATES A STATION OR INSTRUMENT RELOCATION.

SPECIFIC

PM - INCLUDES LAST DAY OF PREVIOUS MONTH
ASOS - AUTOMATED SURFACE OBSERVING SYSTEM IN OPERATION DURING THESE MONTHS.

(a) - LENGTH OF RECORD IN YEARS, ALTHOUGH INDIVIDUAL MONTHS MAY BE MISSING.
0.* OR * - THE VALUE IS BETWEEN 0.0 AND 0.05
NORMALS - BASED ON THE 1961-1990 RECORD PERIOD.
EXTREMES - DATES ARE THE MOST RECENT OCCURRENCE
WIND DIR.- NUMERALS SHOW TENS OF DEGRESS CLOCKWISE FROM TRUE NORTH. "00" INDICATES CALM.
RESULTANT DIRECTIONS ARE GIVEN TO WHOLE DEGREES.
BOLD VALUES INDICATE EXTREME VALUES WHICH OCCURRED AFTER THE ASOS SYSTEM WAS COMMISSIONED.

RECORD = PERIOD OF RECORD
RECORD MEAN PRECIPITATION IS THE MEAN OF ALL DAILY PRECIPITATION AMOUNTS DURING THE PERIOD OF RECORD.
RECORD MAX(MIN) TEMPERATURE IS THE MEAN OF ALL DAILY MAX(MIN) TEMPERATURES DURING THE PERIOD OF RECORD.
RECORD MEAN TEMPERATURE IS THE SUM OF THE RECORD MAX AND RECORD MIN DIVIDED BY 2.
AVERAGE TEMPERATURE IS THE SUM OF THE MEAN DAILY MAX AND MIN TEMPERATURE DIVIDED BY 2.

EXCEPTIONS

RECORD MEANS ARE THROUGH THE CURRENT YEAR, BEGINNING IN 1873 FOR TEMPERATURE
1871 FOR PRECIPITATION
1937 FOR SNOWFALL

HEATING DEGREE DAYS Base 65 deg. F — ST. LOUIS, MISSOURI

SEASON	JULY	AUG	SEP	OCT	NOV	DEC	JAN	FEB	MAR	APR	MAY	JUNE	TOTAL
1964-65	0	2	55	333	526	1019	1016	869	938	250	19	0	5027
1965-66	0	7	49	286	489	717	1233	915	570	397	156	4	4823
1966-67	0	0	78	336	534	931	932	940	530	257	188	12	4738
1967-68	3	7	67	268	682	928	1121	1031	587	290	137	2	5123
1968-69	0	2	14	293	640	1008	1106	826	834	247	85	15	5070
1969-70	0	0	27	313	644	1013	1241	893	751	257	55	20	5214
1970-71	0	0	24	287	635	863	1159	866	718	303	122	0	4977
1971-72	0	0	47	97	574	751	1081	884	619	295	80	10	4438
1972-73	2	0	29	317	751	1069	997	849	430	348	121	0	4913
1973-74	0	0	31	182	538	1077	1083	804	539	253	101	21	4629
1974-75	0	0	127	242	625	954	979	919	803	353	48	1	5051
1975-76	2	0	110	228	498	910	1137	619	505	288	158	0	4455
1976-77	0	0	24	456	832	1125	1541	839	471	190	36	3	5517
1977-78	0	0	11	291	601	1059	1401	1223	840	275	158	5	5864
1978-79	0	0	24	292	528	923	1496	1167	644	364	80	0	5518
1979-80	0	0	16	223	610	810	1035	1071	740	331	54	0	4890
1980-81	0	0	30	305	553	877	1039	784	569	127	168	0	4452
1981-82	0	0	35	298	483	1048	1308	1015	603	407	9	11	5217
1982-83	0	0	49	261	569	721	1008	745	632	437	117	7	4546
1983-84	0	0	58	192	498	1376	1133	705	860	342	115	0	5279
1984-85	0	0	103	151	616	746	1308	960	487	200	42	10	4623
1985-86	0	0	64	145	550	1159	929	850	506	194	44	0	4441
1986-87	0	11	12	221	699	910	1062	691	501	267	10	0	4384
1987-88	0	0	12	346	490	830	1102	995	610	241	17	3	4646
1988-89	0	0	5	354	528	854	730	1029	625	293	128	4	4550
1989-90	0	0	73	183	536	1261	679	657	496	327	85	9	4306
1990-91	3	0	24	250	375	934	1101	648	474	154	21	0	3984
1991-92	0	0	67	191	674	796	859	642	509	264	95	5	4102
1992-93	0	3	46	204	615	902	1014	927	726	327	52	13	4829
1993-94	0	0	58	292	628	852							

COOLING DEGREE DAYS Base 65 deg. F — ST. LOUIS, MISSOURI

YEAR	JAN	FEB	MAR	APR	MAY	JUNE	JULY	AUG	SEP	OCT	NOV	DEC	TOTAL
1969	0	0	0	9	113	246	486	381	162	43	0	0	1440
1970	0	0	0	54	195	247	410	360	236	17	0	0	1519
1971	0	0	2	35	45	427	326	340	279	62	10	0	1526
1972	0	0	5	35	129	268	394	358	219	9	0	0	1417
1973	0	0	1	17	25	294	435	375	187	57	4	0	1395
1974	0	0	24	36	109	164	463	300	52	25	2	0	1175
1975	0	0	2	12	133	308	405	406	110	51	4	0	1431
1976	0	0	8	38	34	239	458	298	129	25	0	0	1229
1977	0	0	2	69	231	302	509	360	190	4	0	0	1667
1978	0	0	7	17	120	295	426	360	276	10	8	0	1519
1979	0	0	2	9	102	354	446	420	195	50	0	0	1578
1980	0	0	0	23	120	320	626	580	262	31	2	0	1964
1981	0	0	7	77	42	327	431	353	166	13	1	0	1417
1982	0	0	0	7	191	186	453	322	146	63	15	4	1387
1983	0	0	3	3	41	322	578	603	274	36	2	0	1862
1984	0	0	0	24	67	442	423	493	202	57	2	1	1711
1985	0	0	14	70	128	214	451	310	245	43	2	0	1477
1986	0	0	25	75	150	407	561	298	267	21	0	0	1804
1987	0	0	0	32	251	393	501	439	183	5	20	0	1824
1988	0	0	4	10	144	389	521	556	238	16	0	0	1878
1989	0	0	11	80	111	305	450	403	151	75	6	0	1592
1990	0	0	30	55	47	382	480	408	304	41	12	0	1759
1991	0	0	19	56	277	452	498	463	295	58	3	0	2121
1992	0	0	7	54	104	277	440	268	182	36	0	0	1368
1993	0	0	1	9	102	320	529	483	107	23	0	0	1574

SNOWFALL (inches) — ST. LOUIS, MISSOURI

SEASON	JULY	AUG	SEP	OCT	NOV	DEC	JAN	FEB	MAR	APR	MAY	JUNE	TOTAL
1964-65	0.0	0.0	0.0	0.0	3.1	0.3	7.3	5.7	8.7	0.0	0.0	0.0	25.1
1965-66	0.0	0.0	0.0	0.0	T	0.1	2.5	7.1	0.9	T	0.0	0.0	10.6
1966-67	0.0	0.0	0.0	0.0	T	0.1	1.4	0.9	1.2	0.0	0.0	0.0	3.6
1967-68	0.0	0.0	0.0	T	1.6	4.2	6.9	0.4	7.7	0.0	0.0	0.0	20.8
1968-69	0.0	0.0	0.0	0.0	T	1.3	2.3	5.8	2.7	0.0	0.0	0.0	12.1
1969-70	0.0	0.0	0.0	0.0	T	10.2	2.1	3.7	5.0	1.0	0.0	0.0	22.0
1970-71	0.0	0.0	0.0	0.0	T	0.9	0.4	1.4	0.2	6.5	0.0	0.0	9.4
1971-72	0.0	0.0	0.0	0.0	1.3	0.0	4.1	1.9	0.3	T	0.0	0.0	7.6
1972-73	0.0	0.0	0.0	0.0	5.2	1.0	2.2	3.0	0.2	0.2	0.0	0.0	11.8
1973-74	0.0	0.0	0.0	0.0	0.0	26.3	4.2	4.5	7.4	0.0	0.0	0.0	42.4
1974-75	0.0	0.0	0.0	0.0	1.2	1.5	4.1	12.1	6.3	T	0.0	0.0	25.2
1975-76	0.0	0.0	0.0	0.0	7.6	3.9	4.5	4.5	4.8	0.0	0.0	0.0	25.3
1976-77	0.0	0.0	0.0	0.0	0.3	5.2	23.9	6.7	0.1	0.1	0.0	0.0	36.3
1977-78	0.0	0.0	0.0	0.0	6.7	11.7	22.9	9.3	15.4	0.0	0.0	0.0	66.0
1978-79	0.0	0.0	0.0	0.0	0.0	1.4	18.4	4.8	2.0	0.0	0.0	0.0	26.6
1979-80	0.0	0.0	0.0	0.0	0.3	T	4.2	7.4	8.7	5.0	0.0	0.0	25.6
1980-81	0.0	0.0	0.0	0.0	8.0	1.1	0.6	8.2	0.2	0.0	0.0	0.0	18.1
1981-82	0.0	0.0	0.0	0.0	T	7.9	16.6	9.0	0.4	2.7	0.0	0.0	36.6
1982-83	0.0	0.0	0.0	0.0	T	T	3.3	0.3	1.4	2.4	0.0	0.0	7.4
1983-84	0.0	0.0	0.0	0.0	T	6.5	2.3	9.9	5.2	0.0	0.0	0.0	23.9
1984-85	0.0	0.0	0.0	0.0	1.7	1.8	5.1	1.3	T	0.0	0.0	0.0	9.9
1985-86	0.0	0.0	0.0	0.0	T	5.7	1.0	6.1	0.2	T	0.0	0.0	13.0
1986-87	0.0	0.0	0.0	0.0	T	T	23.6	0.6	T	0.0	0.0	0.0	24.2
1987-88	0.0	0.0	0.0	0.0	T	7.3	1.4	6.7	2.8	0.0	0.0	0.0	18.2
1988-89	0.0	0.0	0.0	0.0	2.9	5.9	0.1	3.9	11.0	0.0	0.0	0.0	23.8
1989-90	0.0	0.0	0.0	T	T	9.1	0.2	6.9	8.4	T	T	T	24.6
1990-91	0.0	0.0	0.0	0.0	T	13.2	1.9	T	1.7	0.0	0.0	0.0	16.8
1991-92	0.0	0.0	0.0	T	3.9	0.4	3.8	2.3	3.1	0.0	0.0	0.0	13.5
1992-93	0.0	0.0	0.0	0.0	T	0.7	5.5	20.8	3.0	0.3	0.6	T	30.9
1993-94	0.0	0.0	0.0	T	1.6	1.1							
Record Mean	0.0	0.0	0.0	T	1.4	3.8	5.3	4.7	4.2	0.4	T	T	19.8

HELENA, MONTANA

Helena is located on the south side of an intermountain valley bounded on the west and south by the main chain of the Continental Divide. The valley is approximately 25 miles in width from north to south and 35 miles long from east to west. The average height of the mountains above the valley floor is about 3,000 feet.

The climate of Helena may be described as modified continental. Several factors enter into modifying the continental climate characteristics. Some of these are invasion by Pacific Ocean air masses, drainage of cool air into the valley from the surrounding mountains, and the protecting mountain shield in all directions.

The mountains to the north and east sometimes deflect shallow masses of invading cold Arctic air to the east. Following periods of extreme cold, when the return circulation of maritime air has brought warming to most of the eastern part of the state, cold air may remain trapped in the valley for several days before being replaced by warmer air. During these periods of transition from cold-to-warm temperatures, inversions are often quite pronounced.

As may be expected in a northern latitude, cold waves may occur from November through February, with temperatures occasionally dropping to zero or lower.

Summertime temperatures are moderate, with maximum readings generally under 90 degrees and very seldom reaching 100 degrees. Like all mountain stations, there is usually a marked change in temperature from day to night. During the summer this tends to produce an agreeable combination of fairly warm days and cool nights.

Most of the precipitation falls from April through July from frequent showers or thunderstorms, but usually with some steady rains in June, the wettest month of the year. Like summer, fall and winter months are relatively dry. During the April to September growing season, precipitation varies considerably.

Thunderstorms are rather frequent from May through August. Snow can be expected from September through May, but amounts during the spring and fall are usually light, and snow on the ground ordinarily lasts only a day or two. During the winter months snow may remain on the ground for several weeks at a time. There is little drifting of snow in the valley, and blizzard conditions are very infrequent.

Severe ice, sleet, and hailstorms are very seldom observed. Since 1880, only a few hailstorms have caused extensive damage in the city of Helena.

In winter, hours of sunshine are more than would be expected at a mountain location.

Due to the sheltering influence of the mountains, Foehn (Chinook) winds are not as pronounced as might be expected for a location on the eastern slopes of the Rocky Mountains. Strong winds can occur at any time throughout the year, but generally do not last more than a few hours at a time.

Based on the 1951-1980 period, the average first occurrence of 32 degrees Fahrenheit in the fall is September 18 and the average last occurrence in the spring is May 18.

NORMALS, MEANS, AND EXTREMES

HELENA, MONTANA

LATITUDE: 46°36'N LONGITUDE: 112°00'W ELEVATION: FT. GRND 3828 BARO 3898 TIME ZONE: MOUNTAIN WBAN: 24144

	(a)	JAN	FEB	MAR	APR	MAY	JUNE	JULY	AUG	SEP	OCT	NOV	DEC	YEAR
TEMPERATURE °F:														
Normals														
-Daily Maximum		29.6	36.9	44.8	56.1	65.4	75.8	85.0	83.2	69.8	58.5	42.4	31.3	56.6
-Daily Minimum		9.6	15.9	22.3	30.6	39.6	48.3	53.4	51.7	41.0	31.6	20.7	11.2	31.3
-Monthly		19.6	26.4	33.6	43.4	52.5	62.1	69.2	67.4	55.4	45.1	31.6	21.2	44.0
Extremes														
-Record Highest	53	62	68	77	86	92	100	102	105	99	85	72	64	105
-Year		1992	1950	1978	1992	1986	1988	1981	1969	1967	1992	1990	1980	AUG 1969
-Record Lowest	53	-42	-33	-30	1	17	30	36	28	18	-8	-39	-38	-42
-Year		1957	1989	1955	1954	1954	1969	1971	1992	1970	1991	1959	1964	JAN 1957
NORMAL DEGREE DAYS:														
Heating (base 65°F)		1407	1081	973	648	388	137	34	65	321	617	1002	1358	8031
Cooling (base 65°F)		0	0	0	0	0	50	164	139	33	0	0	0	386
% OF POSSIBLE SUNSHINE	53	46	55	60	59	60	63	78	74	67	60	44	42	59
MEAN SKY COVER (tenths)														
Sunrise - Sunset	53	7.5	7.3	7.3	7.2	6.8	6.3	4.1	4.6	5.3	6.1	7.2	7.5	6.4
MEAN NUMBER OF DAYS:														
Sunrise to Sunset														
-Clear	53	4.7	4.3	3.9	3.8	4.9	5.7	14.5	12.8	10.5	8.3	4.6	4.0	82.1
-Partly Cloudy	53	6.2	6.7	8.2	8.7	9.9	11.2	10.6	11.0	8.6	8.6	7.5	7.3	104.4
-Cloudy	53	20.1	17.2	18.9	17.5	16.2	13.0	5.9	7.2	10.9	14.1	17.9	19.7	178.7
Precipitation														
.01 inches or more	53	7.9	6.5	8.5	8.2	11.0	11.3	7.6	7.6	6.6	5.6	7.0	7.8	95.7
Snow, Ice pellets, hail														
1.0 inches or more	53	2.7	1.9	2.4	1.4	0.4	0.*	0.0	0.*	0.4	0.8	1.7	2.4	14.2
Thunderstorms	53	0.1	0.1	0.1	0.9	4.2	7.6	8.8	7.9	1.8	0.3	0.1	0.*	32.2
Heavy Fog Visibility														
1/4 mile or less	53	1.6	1.2	0.8	0.2	0.2	0.1	0.1	0.2	0.3	0.5	1.2	2.0	8.2
Temperature °F														
-Maximum														
90° and above	30	0.0	0.0	0.0	0.0	0.2	2.2	7.6	6.9	1.1	0.0	0.0	0.0	18.0
32° and below	30	14.8	8.3	3.9	0.5	0.0	0.0	0.0	0.0	0.0	0.7	5.4	14.6	48.1
-Minimum														
32° and below	30	29.5	26.5	27.2	17.6	3.6	0.1	0.0	0.*	3.5	17.0	26.9	29.6	181.5
0° and below	30	8.7	4.5	1.5	0.0	0.0	0.0	0.0	0.0	0.0	0.2	1.9	6.2	23.0
AVG. STATION PRESS. (mb)	21	881.5	881.0	878.4	879.4	879.3	880.2	881.9	882.1	882.7	882.7	881.2	881.5	881.0
RELATIVE HUMIDITY (%)														
Hour 05	28	71	72	72	70	71	72	67	67	72	73	74	73	71
Hour 11 (Local Time)	30	67	63	55	47	44	44	39	42	48	52	62	68	53
Hour 17	30	63	54	46	38	38	37	30	31	36	42	58	66	45
Hour 23	30	70	69	66	60	59	59	52	53	59	64	70	72	63
PRECIPITATION (inches):														
Water Equivalent														
-Normal		0.63	0.41	0.73	0.97	1.78	1.87	1.10	1.29	1.15	0.60	0.48	0.59	11.60
-Maximum Monthly	53	2.78	1.20	1.62	3.00	6.09	4.74	4.70	4.23	3.37	2.68	1.50	1.48	6.09
-Year		1969	1986	1982	1975	1981	1944	1993	1974	1965	1975	1950	1977	MAY 1981
-Minimum Monthly	53	T	0.02	0.02	0.10	0.29	0.08	0.08	0.02	0.08	0.02	0.04	0.04	T
-Year		1987	1991	1959	1977	1979	1985	1973	1988	1972	1978	1969	1976	JAN 1987
-Maximum in 24 hrs	53	0.77	0.58	1.01	1.25	2.31	1.78	2.26	1.86	1.61	0.85	0.82	0.51	2.31
-Year		1969	1953	1957	1951	1981	1979	1983	1974	1980	1954	1959	1982	MAY 1981
Snow, Ice pellets, hail														
-Maximum Monthly	53	35.6	19.7	21.6	20.6	12.7	2.7	T	6.2	13.7	11.0	32.9	22.8	35.6
-Year		1969	1959	1955	1967	1967	1969	1993	1992	1965	1969	1959	1967	JAN 1969
-Maximum in 24 hrs	53	11.5	11.7	8.7	12.9	12.5	2.7	T	6.2	13.3	7.4	21.5	10.7	21.5
-Year		1969	1993	1955	1960	1967	1969	1993	1992	1957	1969	1959	1991	NOV 1959
WIND:														
Mean Speed (mph)	53	6.7	7.3	8.3	9.2	8.9	8.5	7.8	7.4	7.4	7.1	7.1	6.8	7.7
Prevailing Direction through 1963		W	W	W	W	W	W	W	W	W	W	W	W	W
Fastest Mile														
-Direction (!!!)	53	SW	W	SW	W	SW	W	SW	S	NW	W	SW	NW	W
-Speed (MPH)	53	73	73	61	52	56	56	65	65	54	62	56	59	73
-Year		1944	1949	1955	1950	1975	1970	1975	1947	1943	1948	1962	1946	FEB 1949
Peak Gust														
-Direction (!!!)	10	W	W	W	W	W	S	W	S	W	W	SW	W	W
-Speed (mph)	10	64	63	52	55	58	58	64	58	51	60	61	58	64
-Date		1990	1988	1987	1989	1989	1988	1990	1992	1984	1991	1990	1992	JUL 1990

PRECIPITATION (inches)

HELENA, MONTANA

YEAR	JAN	FEB	MAR	APR	MAY	JUNE	JULY	AUG	SEP	OCT	NOV	DEC	ANNUAL
1964	0.31	0.27	0.51	1.56	3.52	2.98	0.83	1.91	0.16	0.04	0.53	0.99	13.61
1965	0.36	0.49	0.85	0.98	2.20	3.85	0.60	1.92	3.37	0.13	0.62	0.15	15.52
1966	0.46	0.33	0.28	0.51	0.43	0.96	0.32	0.42	0.34	0.75	1.04	0.62	6.46
1967	0.61	0.62	1.43	2.38	2.08	2.36	0.46	0.58	0.68	1.50	0.31	1.39	14.40
1968	0.59	0.16	0.53	1.21	1.62	2.68	0.26	2.00	2.22	0.23	0.92	0.75	13.17
1969	2.78	0.22	0.57	0.60	1.13	3.50	1.77	0.38	0.33	1.06	0.04	0.31	12.69
1970	0.51	0.67	0.96	0.81	1.20	2.11	0.93	0.63	0.36	0.58	0.44	0.54	9.74
1971	1.38	0.63	0.41	0.58	1.77	0.93	0.56	1.22	0.89	0.39	0.34	1.02	10.12
1972	1.12	0.54	0.63	0.41	0.77	1.12	0.56	1.63	0.08	0.57	0.33	0.46	8.22
1973	0.22	0.13	0.05	0.66	1.08	0.73	0.08	0.56	0.43	0.66	1.03	0.63	6.26
1974	0.66	0.23	0.38	0.76	2.07	0.34	0.49	4.23	0.22	0.51	0.30	0.26	10.45
1975	1.26	0.72	0.88	3.00	1.95	2.83	3.89	2.47	0.47	2.68	0.48	0.31	20.94
1976	0.26	0.38	0.41	1.34	0.87	2.74	0.29	1.58	1.82	0.04	0.30	0.04	10.07
1977	0.65	0.13	1.11	0.10	1.82	1.37	1.37	0.72	1.93	0.17	0.48	1.48	11.33
1978	0.96	0.61	0.31	0.94	1.20	0.44	2.83	0.59	1.11	0.02	1.19	0.76	10.96
1979	0.77	0.72	1.34	2.26	0.29	2.75	0.32	0.79	0.12	0.38	0.06	0.59	10.39
1980	0.62	0.74	0.88	0.63	4.32	3.16	1.92	0.28	2.57	1.21	0.32	0.40	17.05
1981	0.15	0.10	1.10	0.75	6.09	1.15	1.78	0.10	0.90	0.82	0.54	0.33	13.81
1982	0.80	0.58	1.62	0.54	1.77	2.99	0.49	0.74	2.74	0.35	0.31	1.05	13.98
1983	0.24	0.07	0.36	0.29	1.79	2.20	3.48	2.67	1.56	0.35	0.26	0.76	14.03
1984	0.17	0.15	0.49	1.45	1.03	2.14	0.11	1.11	0.73	0.74	0.47	0.41	9.00
1985	0.16	0.38	0.32	0.46	0.75	0.08	0.10	2.64	2.11	0.76	0.84	0.35	8.95
1986	0.32	1.20	0.49	1.08	0.83	1.56	1.37	1.84	2.45	0.03	0.54	0.38	12.09
1987	T	0.03	1.19	0.76	1.90	1.50	2.88	0.38	0.80	0.05	0.12	0.42	10.03
1988	0.27	0.50	0.45	1.32	1.82	1.50	0.36	0.02	2.09	0.69	0.69	0.32	10.03
1989	1.42	0.82	1.35	0.72	1.00	1.43	1.55	1.61	1.31	0.54	0.26	0.48	12.49
1990	0.47	0.14	0.91	0.43	1.54	0.92	0.40	2.57	0.11	0.11	0.36	0.47	8.43
1991	0.27	0.02	0.90	0.75	1.71	3.27	0.72	0.70	1.26	0.65	0.88	0.79	11.92
1992	0.29	0.10	0.60	0.55	0.64	2.36	1.06	1.01	0.09	1.87	0.19	0.57	9.33
1993	0.80	1.03	0.56	1.63	1.71	3.14	4.70	2.79	1.25	0.71	0.36	0.13	18.81
Record Mean	0.70	0.52	0.74	0.97	1.87	2.18	1.13	0.96	1.14	0.75	0.61	0.62	12.20

AVERAGE TEMPERATURE (deg. F)

HELENA, MONTANA

YEAR	JAN	FEB	MAR	APR	MAY	JUNE	JULY	AUG	SEP	OCT	NOV	DEC	ANNUAL
1964	22.0	27.2	29.9	41.8	51.7	59.0	70.2	63.4	53.8	47.4	30.5	19.1	43.0
1965	29.6	26.6	24.6	44.4	50.1	59.5	67.7	65.8	45.6	49.3	34.7	27.5	43.8
1966	20.6	27.0	36.5	42.5	56.5	59.3	71.5	66.7	62.7	46.4	33.8	27.4	45.9
1967	28.7	32.7	29.0	37.8	52.1	59.9	70.5	71.4	61.9	47.4	33.0	19.0	45.3
1968	15.7	28.9	39.6	39.7	49.6	58.3	68.2	63.2	55.0	44.4	33.5	16.7	42.8
1969	7.2	14.5	21.3	46.7	55.2	57.8	67.9	70.1	58.0	38.1	33.5	25.9	41.4
1970	18.8	32.5	28.2	36.5	51.5	62.3	68.2	67.9	51.1	40.2	29.3	20.6	42.2
1971	19.0	28.5	31.9	41.5	51.4	57.0	63.2	69.0	49.7	42.0	33.6	15.6	41.9
1972	12.4	26.8	39.1	39.8	50.9	61.8	61.7	66.0	50.9	39.0	31.1	13.6	41.1
1973	17.7	22.8	36.0	40.3	52.9	61.2	68.9	66.8	54.4	45.8	24.5	28.2	43.3
1974	18.1	32.8	33.9	46.0	48.6	64.9	70.4	61.5	53.5	45.8	34.7	27.7	44.8
1975	21.1	13.7	28.8	32.9	48.6	56.9	69.2	61.2	54.1	43.3	29.9	26.0	40.5
1976	24.9	29.5	30.4	43.2	54.1	56.6	67.6	64.8	57.9	44.9	33.8	28.7	44.7
1977	18.0	34.1	32.4	46.9	50.4	63.6	66.3	63.6	56.3	45.6	31.2	20.7	44.1
1978	16.9	22.8	38.8	47.7	53.2	63.2	67.2	65.5	57.9	46.5	22.7	15.2	43.2
1979	1.1	20.1	34.7	42.7	53.2	62.0	69.2	67.7	61.3	47.8	29.0	28.2	43.1
1980	14.3	25.3	31.3	49.0	55.4	59.8	67.3	62.9	56.8	45.4	34.9	26.9	44.1
1981	28.4	29.7	38.0	46.4	52.8	58.9	67.7	69.5	58.8	43.8	36.4	25.3	46.3
1982	16.5	23.7	33.9	40.5	50.9	61.2	68.6	69.1	55.5	44.9	27.4	22.7	42.9
1983	30.6	35.3	38.3	43.1	51.5	60.2	66.0	70.8	53.5	46.0	34.7	5.5	44.6
1984	27.3	32.4	37.2	43.5	52.8	60.0	70.0	69.8	52.3	41.7	33.1	11.6	44.3
1985	12.3	18.8	33.4	46.9	56.2	63.3	75.0	63.1	49.6	42.3	12.6	15.0	40.7
1986	25.5	21.8	42.9	43.3	53.6	66.4	64.2	68.0	51.2	45.3	29.0	18.6	44.2
1987	23.3	31.9	37.0	50.2	55.9	64.4	66.2	62.8	59.9	46.8	34.7	24.7	46.5
1988	18.8	29.1	36.1	47.1	55.5	68.4	71.3	68.6	56.4	50.3	33.8	23.1	46.5
1989	24.5	6.1	27.6	44.5	51.7	62.2	72.0	64.3	55.6	45.1	36.8	23.8	42.9
1990	28.8	26.9	34.9	45.8	51.0	61.5	69.4	68.4	63.6	45.3	37.4	14.0	45.6
1991	19.0	37.5	35.3	43.8	52.8	59.5	70.8	72.8	58.4	43.3	29.8	22.9	45.5
1992	23.7	34.2	42.7	47.7	57.5	64.9	64.3	64.7	56.7	46.7	32.8	14.7	45.9
1993	12.3	15.0	36.4	44.3	57.3	58.5	59.5	61.5	54.0	43.8	26.8	30.0	41.6
Record Mean	19.8	24.5	32.7	43.6	52.3	60.0	67.8	66.3	55.8	45.4	32.4	23.8	43.7
Max	28.8	34.0	42.8	55.0	64.0	72.2	82.0	80.6	68.7	57.0	41.9	32.5	55.0
Min	10.7	15.0	22.6	32.2	40.5	47.9	53.6	52.0	42.8	33.8	22.8	15.1	32.4

REFERENCE NOTES

HELENA, MONTANA

GENERAL
T - TRACE AMOUNT.
BLANK ENTRIES DENOTE MISSING/UNREPORTED DATA.
# INDICATES A STATION OR INSTRUMENT RELOCATION.

SPECIFIC

PM - INCLUDES LAST DAY OF PREVIOUS MONTH
ASOS - AUTOMATED SURFACE OBSERVING SYSTEM IN OPERATION DURING THESE MONTHS.

(a) - LENGTH OF RECORD IN YEARS, ALTHOUGH INDIVIDUAL MONTHS MAY BE MISSING.
0.* OR * - THE VALUE IS BETWEEN 0.0 AND 0.05
NORMALS - BASED ON THE 1961-1990 RECORD PERIOD.
EXTREMES - DATES ARE THE MOST RECENT OCCURRENCE
WIND DIR.- NUMERALS SHOW TENS OF DEGRESS CLOCKWISE FROM TRUE NORTH. "00" INDICATES CALM.
RESULTANT DIRECTIONS ARE GIVEN TO WHOLE DEGREES.
BOLD VALUES INDICATE EXTREME VALUES WHICH OCCURRED AFTER THE ASOS SYSTEM WAS COMMISSIONED.

RECORD = PERIOD OF RECORD
RECORD MEAN PRECIPITATION IS THE MEAN OF ALL DAILY PRECIPITATION AMOUNTS DURING THE PERIOD OF RECORD.
RECORD MAX(MIN) TEMPERATURE IS THE MEAN OF ALL DAILY MAX(MIN) TEMPERATURES DURING THE PERIOD OF RECORD.
RECORD MEAN TEMPERATURE IS THE SUM OF THE RECORD MAX AND RECORD MIN DIVIDED BY 2.
AVERAGE TEMPERATURE IS THE SUM OF THE MEAN DAILY MAX AND MIN TEMPERATURE DIVIDED BY 2.

EXCEPTIONS

RECORD MEANS ARE THROUGH THE CURRENT YEAR,
BEGINNING IN 1881 FOR TEMPERATURE
1881 FOR PRECIPITATION
1941 FOR SNOWFALL

HEATING DEGREE DAYS Base 65 deg. F HELENA, MONTANA

SEASON	JULY	AUG	SEP	OCT	NOV	DEC	JAN	FEB	MAR	APR	MAY	JUNE	TOTAL
1964-65	1	101	332	542	1028	1420	1090	1070	1250	612	454	169	8069
1965-66	14	69	578	478	903	1153	1370	1058	874	670	267	188	7622
1966-67	8	51	117	570	930	1157	1120	898	1107	807	396	171	7332
1967-68	0	1	130	539	954	1422	1525	1042	780	751	472	206	7822
1968-69	23	102	294	633	937	1493	1788	1407	1348	543	301	226	9095
1969-70	35	14	219	826	938	1207	1427	904	1132	849	409	153	8113
1970-71	22	12	413	763	1063	1372	1422	1013	1020	699	414	251	8464
1971-72	91	22	454	707	936	1524	1628	1102	796	747	430	120	8557
1972-73	136	49	418	798	1010	1588	1465	1174	892	732	374	155	8791
1973-74	23	47	317	588	1208	1136	1452	897	956	564	500	99	7787
1974-75	16	130	338	588	905	1149	1355	1429	1114	954	501	235	8714
1975-76	14	119	322	666	1045	1199	1236	1023	1064	649	331	257	7925
1976-77	15	45	219	615	928	1120	1449	862	1005	535	443	90	7326
1977-78	52	92	270	593	1008	1367	1485	1175	806	512	361	87	7808
1978-79	32	60	244	564	1263	1540	1979	1250	930	665	359	128	9014
1979-80	11	15	127	528	1072	1138	1566	1148	1039	473	304	164	7585
1980-81	25	81	242	602	899	1175	1127	986	832	552	371	191	7083
1981-82	21	16	195	650	853	1227	1497	1153	959	726	428	136	7861
1982-83	30	16	304	618	1120	1306	1059	828	823	649	417	152	7322
1983-84	76	0	351	584	901	1842	1164	941	856	640	380	174	7909
1984-85	2	7	377	716	954	1654	1625	1291	973	538	266	97	8500
1985-86	3	105	455	696	1571	1545	1218	1202	677	645	380	42	8539
1986-87	66	23	409	602	1077	1432	1288	923	862	437	276	77	7472
1987-88	75	104	163	556	901	1241	1426	1034	889	529	297	63	7278
1988-89	10	13	282	449	934	1292	1251	1650	1156	610	407	107	8161
1989-90	0	92	274	611	839	1268	1116	1058	925	573	426	177	7359
1990-91	15	31	78	604	823	1579	1420	767	914	630	373	159	7393
1991-92	2	0	220	666	1053	1297	1273	884	687	513	237	94	6926
1992-93	68	141	246	564	960	1552	1631	1397	879	617	228	214	8497
1993-94	179	122	323	652	1139	1080							

COOLING DEGREE DAYS Base 65 deg. F HELENA, MONTANA

YEAR	JAN	FEB	MAR	APR	MAY	JUNE	JULY	AUG	SEP	OCT	NOV	DEC	TOTAL
1969	0	0	0	0	1	18	128	178	20	0	0	0	345
1970	0	0	0	0	0	76	130	109	5	0	0	0	320
1971	0	0	0	0	0	14	42	154	0	0	0	0	210
1972	0	0	0	0	2	30	42	89	0	0	0	0	163
1973	0	0	0	0	4	45	151	108	3	0	0	0	311
1974	0	0	0	0	0	102	190	31	0	0	0	0	323
1975	0	0	0	0	0	1	154	12	0	0	0	0	167
1976	0	0	0	0	0	14	102	45	10	0	0	0	171
1977	0	0	0	0	0	57	101	54	13	0	0	0	225
1978	0	0	0	0	3	37	109	85	37	0	0	0	271
1979	0	0	0	0	1	45	152	103	21	0	0	0	322
1980	0	0	0	0	14	14	104	25	4	0	0	0	161
1981	0	0	0	0	0	15	109	165	16	0	0	0	305
1982	0	0	0	0	0	30	147	151	25	0	0	0	353
1983	0	0	0	0	4	16	115	186	12	0	0	0	333
1984	0	0	0	0	10	31	165	163	4	0	0	0	373
1985	0	0	0	0	2	55	318	54	0	0	0	0	429
1986	0	0	0	0	35	91	45	123	1	0	0	0	295
1987	0	0	0	0	3	66	122	41	15	0	0	0	247
1988	0	0	0	0	8	170	211	132	30	0	0	0	551
1989	0	0	0	0	0	30	222	82	0	0	0	0	334
1990	0	0	0	0	0	77	159	142	42	0	0	0	420
1991	0	0	0	0	0	2	188	250	29	0	0	0	469
1992	0	0	0	0	10	96	55	140	3	0	0	0	304
1993	0	0	0	0	2	24	15	23	0	0	0	0	64

SNOWFALL (inches) HELENA, MONTANA

SEASON	JULY	AUG	SEP	OCT	NOV	DEC	JAN	FEB	MAR	APR	MAY	JUNE	TOTAL
1964-65	0.0	0.0	0.0	0.0	6.3	13.2	2.3	9.4	12.9	6.3	5.0	0.0	55.4
1965-66	0.0	0.0	13.7	0.0	2.1	1.4	6.3	5.1	2.3	1.9	T	0.0	32.8
1966-67	0.0	0.0	0.0	T	9.5	5.7	7.3	10.5	14.9	20.6	12.7	0.0	81.2
1967-68	0.0	0.0	0.0	T	2.7	22.8	8.7	0.9	0.8	10.0	T	0.0	45.9
1968-69	0.0	0.0	3.0	0.4	7.4	11.0	35.6	3.6	7.0	2.6	0.7	2.7	74.0
1969-70	0.0	0.0	0.0	11.0	0.1	6.1	7.0	9.5	9.0	7.9	1.4	0.0	52.0
1970-71	0.0	0.0	T	1.4	5.4	7.5	16.2	3.5	2.5	0.7	T	0.0	37.2
1971-72	0.0	0.0	T	0.8	4.6	14.5	14.9	3.3	4.5	3.8	T	0.0	46.4
1972-73	T	0.0	0.3	4.7	0.7	7.8	3.2	1.8	0.1	6.5	T	0.0	25.1
1973-74	0.0	0.0	1.3	7.2	12.5	7.2	9.9	5.9	2.2	1.5	0.2	0.0	47.9
1974-75	0.0	0.0	T	1.5	0.8	2.7	15.2	10.7	12.3	15.4	0.2	0.0	58.8
1975-76	0.0	0.0	0.0	6.3	4.9	3.9	3.3	4.4	6.7	10.9	0.0	0.0	40.4
1976-77	0.0	0.0	0.0	T	2.9	0.9	13.8	0.8	14.1	0.5	1.0	0.0	34.0
1977-78	0.0	0.0	0.0	0.4	6.8	19.5	15.7	13.3	2.6	0.9	T	0.0	59.2
1978-79	0.0	0.0	T	T	22.1	13.8	11.7	7.2	12.4	9.3	T	T	76.5
1979-80	0.0	0.0	0.0	0.2	0.6	6.5	9.3	10.5	10.1	3.1	0.0	0.0	40.3
1980-81	0.0	0.0	0.0	3.7	1.2	3.8	2.7	2.1	3.3	0.1	T	0.0	16.9
1981-82	0.0	0.0	0.0	5.2	3.4	6.1	18.4	4.8	13.9	4.1	0.8	0.0	56.7
1982-83	0.0	0.0	6.5	0.5	4.1	11.3	3.2	0.2	2.2	1.1	9.9	0.0	39.0
1983-84	0.0	0.0	6.4	0.0	1.3	13.0	1.3	1.5	5.7	2.3	0.8	0.0	32.3
1984-85	0.0	0.0	6.3	9.0	5.7	7.5	3.9	6.2	4.0	0.8	0.0	0.0	43.4
1985-86	0.0	0.0	2.9	8.8	10.4	8.5	4.2	15.6	1.2	11.6	0.2	0.0	63.4
1986-87	0.0	0.0	0.0	T	7.6	5.0	0.2	0.2	9.1	4.3	3.8	0.0	30.2
1987-88	0.0	0.0	0.0	0.3	0.9	1.2	4.4	8.0	5.2	2.9	0.0	0.0	22.9
1988-89	0.0	0.0	5.9	1.5	6.0	5.0	23.0	13.0	20.7	7.9	3.5	T	86.5
1989-90	0.0	T	T	2.6	1.8	9.4	4.3	1.8	14.0	0.8	0.1	0.0	34.8
1990-91	0.0	0.5	0.0	0.5	8.6	11.6	5.9	0.8	12.2	5.6	0.4	0.5	46.6
1991-92	0.0	T	0.0	7.3	8.8	15.7	4.7	1.3	T	2.2	T	0.0	40.0
1992-93	T	6.2	T	8.6	1.5	11.8	10.2	17.9	2.3	2.5	T	0.2	61.2
1993-94	T	0.0	T	4.6	7.3	1.1							
Record Mean	T	0.1	1.5	2.4	6.4	8.5	8.7	6.2	7.4	4.8	1.4	0.1	47.5

NORTH PLATTE, NEBRASKA

The climate of North Platte is characterized throughout the year by frequent rapid changes in the weather. During the winter, most North Pacific lows cross the country north of North Platte. The passage usually brings little or no snowfall, and only a moderate drop in temperature. Only when there is a major outbreak of cold air from Canada does the temperature fall to zero or below. The duration of below-zero temperature is hardly more than two mornings, and by the third or fourth day the temperature is ordinarily rising to the 40s or higher. Snowfall at the onset of a cold outbreak is usually less than 2 inches.

Only when a low moves from the middle Rockies through Nebraska, allowing easterly winds to draw moist air into the low circulation, does snowfall of appreciable amounts occur. Few of these storms move slowly enough, or are intense enough, to deposit much precipitation in the North Platte area. However, during some winters the cold outbreak and intense low from the mid-Rockies combine to produce severe cold and snow several inches in depth, with blizzard conditions following. During and after these snowfalls and blizzards, rail and highway traffic may be stalled until the snow is cleared. Widespread loss of unsheltered livestock and wild life results from such conditions.

The sudden and frequent weather changes of the winter continue through spring with decreasing intensity of temperature changes but increasing precipitation. The summer and fall months bring frequent changes from hot to cool weather. Most summer and fall precipitation is associated with thunderstorms, so the amounts are extremely variable. The surrounding area is occasionally damaged by locally severe winds and hailstorms.

Temperatures may reach into the upper 90s and lower 100s frequently during the summer months, but the elevation and clear skies bring rapid cooling after sunset to lows in the 60s or below by daybreak. Since the humidity is generally low, the extremely hot days of summer are not uncomfortable.

Based on the 1951-1980 period, the average first occurrence of 32 degrees Fahrenheit in the fall is September 24 and the average last occurrence in the spring is May 11.

NORMALS, MEANS, AND EXTREMES

NORTH PLATTE, NEBRASKA

LATITUDE: 41°08'N LONGITUDE: 100°41' W ELEVATION: FT. GRND 2775 BARO 2782 TIME ZONE: CENTRAL WBAN: 24023

	(a)	JAN	FEB	MAR	APR	MAY	JUNE	JULY	AUG	SEP	OCT	NOV	DEC	YEAR
TEMPERATURE °F:														
Normals														
-Daily Maximum		34.6	40.9	49.9	62.5	71.8	81.7	87.8	86.0	76.6	65.7	49.5	37.2	62.0
-Daily Minimum		8.6	14.3	23.0	33.9	44.6	54.1	60.1	57.6	46.2	33.5	21.3	11.2	34.0
-Monthly		21.6	27.6	36.5	48.2	58.2	67.9	74.0	71.8	61.4	49.7	35.4	24.2	48.0
Extremes														
-Record Highest	42	73	79	86	98	97	107	112	105	102	94	82	75	112
-Year		1990	1962	1986	1992	1953	1952	1954	1954	1990	1990	1980	1980	JUL 1954
-Record Lowest	42	-23	-22	-22	7	19	29	40	35	17	10	-13	-34	-34
-Year		1979	1981	1962	1975	1989	1969	1990	1976	1984	1993	1976	1989	DEC 1989
NORMAL DEGREE DAYS:														
Heating (base 65°F)		1345	1047	884	504	234	49	0	11	158	474	888	1265	6859
Cooling (base 65°F)		0	0	0	0	23	136	282	222	50	0	0	0	713
% OF POSSIBLE SUNSHINE	41	61	60	60	64	65	71	76	75	71	69	60	60	66
MEAN SKY COVER (tenths)														
Sunrise - Sunset	41	6.1	6.3	6.6	6.3	6.4	5.3	4.7	4.9	4.7	5.0	6.0	5.8	5.7
MEAN NUMBER OF DAYS:														
Sunrise to Sunset														
-Clear	41	8.5	7.1	7.3	7.1	6.7	10.2	12.1	11.6	13.0	12.6	8.9	9.6	114.8
-Partly Cloudy	41	8.6	7.5	7.7	9.1	10.2	10.5	12.0	11.4	8.3	8.4	8.0	7.9	109.6
-Cloudy	41	13.9	13.6	16.0	13.8	14.1	9.3	7.0	8.0	8.7	10.0	13.0	13.5	140.8
Precipitation .01 inches or more	41	4.9	5.5	7.0	8.0	11.0	9.5	9.8	7.8	6.5	5.0	4.7	4.3	84.0
Snow,Ice pellets,hail 1.0 inches or more	41	1.7	1.7	2.0	0.8	0.1	0.0	0.0	0.0	0.*	0.5	1.1	1.4	9.2
Thunderstorms	41	0.*	0.1	0.8	2.6	6.6	10.0	10.3	8.2	4.1	1.2	0.2	0.0	44.2
Heavy Fog Visibility 1/4 mile or less	41	1.3	2.3	2.1	0.9	0.9	0.8	1.0	1.7	1.9	2.0	2.3	1.5	18.8
Temperature °F														
-Maximum														
90° and above	29	0.0	0.0	0.0	0.3	0.8	5.7	12.8	10.8	3.8	0.3	0.0	0.0	34.4
32° and below	29	12.3	8.2	3.8	0.2	0.*	0.0	0.0	0.0	0.0	0.2	3.8	10.5	39.1
-Minimum														
32° and below	29	31.0	27.9	26.6	12.6	2.4	0.*	0.0	0.0	2.3	14.4	27.8	30.8	175.8
0° and below	29	7.9	3.7	0.6	0.0	0.0	0.0	0.0	0.0	0.0	0.0	0.8	4.6	17.6
AVG. STATION PRESS.(mb)	21	918.9	918.6	915.3	915.4	915.4	916.2	918.0	918.5	918.8	919.1	918.0	918.6	917.6
RELATIVE HUMIDITY (%)														
Hour 00 (Local Time)	29	77	77	74	71	74	75	74	76	74	73	76	77	75
Hour 06	29	79	79	80	80	83	84	83	85	83	81	81	79	81
Hour 12	29	63	59	53	47	51	52	50	51	48	46	55	61	53
Hour 18	29	64	56	49	43	48	48	47	47	46	47	58	63	51
PRECIPITATION (inches):														
Water Equivalent														
-Normal		0.36	0.43	1.20	1.99	3.43	3.37	3.06	1.74	1.61	0.98	0.66	0.47	19.30
-Maximum Monthly	42	1.12	1.98	2.98	5.01	8.01	6.81	7.05	6.30	6.03	2.91	2.89	1.22	8.01
-Year		1960	1978	1992	1984	1962	1965	1979	1992	1963	1969	1979	1977	MAY 1962
-Minimum Monthly	42	T	0.01	0.09	0.10	0.77	0.33	0.42	0.06	T	0.05	0.02	T	T
-Year		1964	1954	1967	1989	1966	1952	1955	1967	1953	1988	1989	1988	DEC 1988
-Maximum in 24 hrs	42	0.75	1.15	2.26	2.42	2.95	3.80	3.15	2.93	2.53	1.37	1.48	0.79	3.80
-Year		1992	1971	1959	1971	1962	1965	1964	1957	1963	1982	1979	1978	JUN 1965
Snow,Ice pellets,hail														
-Maximum Monthly	42	17.1	20.6	21.9	14.5	3.6	T	T	T	3.1	15.7	17.5	14.1	21.9
-Year		1976	1978	1980	1984	1967	1993	1993	1992	1985	1969	1979	1973	MAR 1980
-Maximum in 24 hrs	42	11.9	9.7	15.1	8.5	2.3	T	T	T	3.1	8.8	8.8	8.6	15.1
-Year		1976	1955	1980	1984	1967	1993	1993	1992	1985	1969	1979	1968	MAR 1980
WIND:														
Mean Speed (mph)	41	9.3	9.8	11.7	12.6	11.7	10.4	9.6	9.4	9.7	9.5	9.6	9.2	10.2
Prevailing Direction through 1963		NW	NW	N	N	SE	SE	SE	SSE	SSE	SSE	NW	NW	NW
Fastest Obs. 1 Min.														
-Direction (!!!)	14	34	35	02	32	07	32	31	18	18	33	03	02	02
-Speed (MPH)	14	43	39	47	45	46	52	46	41	38	37	41	52	52
-Year		1992	1981	1992	1986	1992	1981	1981	1985	1986	1990	1983	1982	DEC 1982
Peak Gust														
-Direction (!!!)	10	NW	NW	NE	S	NE	NW	W	NE	S	W	N	NW	S
-Speed (mph)	10	60	55	64	76	72	62	64	74	58	55	52	56	76
-Date		1987	1988	1992	1985	1985	1986	1993	1990	1986	1985	1989	1988	APR 1985

PRECIPITATION (inches) NORTH PLATTE, NEBRASKA

YEAR	JAN	FEB	MAR	APR	MAY	JUNE	JULY	AUG	SEP	OCT	NOV	DEC	ANNUAL
1964	T	0.62	1.26	3.76	2.06	4.78	4.52	2.63	1.02	0.17	0.04	0.10	20.96
1965	0.61	0.35	0.25	1.42	4.18	6.81	6.68	1.82	5.69	0.73	0.05	1.02	29.61
1966	0.30	0.15	1.12	1.05	0.77	5.14	3.35	2.74	2.09	0.31	0.04	0.51	17.57
1967	0.47	0.03	0.09	1.03	3.94	6.05	3.74	0.06	1.12	0.58	0.19	0.15	17.45
1968	0.12	0.36	0.11	3.04	1.72	2.25	1.82	3.97	0.82	1.50	0.46	0.87	17.04
1969	0.94	0.26	0.17	0.15	1.35	4.20	2.52	1.61	0.80	2.91	0.18	0.10	15.19
1970	0.23	0.28	0.97	2.46	1.31	4.33	1.68	0.28	2.27	1.27	0.91	0.22	16.21
1971	0.47	1.28	0.97	3.94	2.54	5.84	3.48	0.91	2.01	1.75	0.90	0.16	24.25
1972	0.16	0.08	0.65	1.19	3.18	2.96	3.58	0.95	1.46	0.62	1.12	0.42	16.37
1973	0.40	0.10	2.45	1.45	3.85	0.88	2.87	2.82	3.98	1.26	0.54	1.13	21.73
1974	0.27	0.08	0.42	1.17	1.64	3.86	2.27	1.15	0.24	0.61	0.04	0.42	12.17
1975	0.26	0.17	0.92	1.77	2.12	6.12	2.51	0.25	0.56	0.14	1.15	0.22	16.19
1976	0.99	0.14	2.03	2.80	2.88	2.43	0.92	2.87	2.03	1.18	0.08	0.01	18.36
1977	0.18	0.27	2.89	4.85	5.90	1.31	4.41	1.79	1.48	0.18	0.39	1.22	24.87
1978	0.52	1.98	0.40	1.96	4.84	1.75	3.70	1.92	0.33	0.43	1.03	0.99	19.85
1979	0.86	0.09	2.78	1.46	2.96	3.37	7.05	1.49	0.45	1.32	2.89	0.28	25.00
1980	0.52	0.82	2.56	0.77	2.59	1.89	0.64	3.04	0.34	1.00	0.13	0.02	14.32
1981	0.07	0.05	2.72	2.47	5.37	2.32	5.09	2.48	0.25	0.60	1.94	0.43	23.79
1982	0.20	0.15	0.99	1.42	6.32	2.35	1.78	1.18	1.26	2.44	0.73	1.08	19.90
1983	0.33	0.25	1.54	2.12	3.20	3.32	3.74	1.98	0.14	0.56	1.56	0.46	19.20
1984	0.36	0.87	1.20	5.01	2.82	4.37	0.94	1.38	0.39	2.41	0.69	0.72	21.16
1985	0.55	0.14	0.44	1.84	4.01	0.87	3.98	1.16	3.23	1.24	1.09	0.79	19.34
1986	0.02	1.10	0.70	3.77	2.80	1.70	2.57	1.22	1.02	1.58	0.19	0.27	16.94
1987	0.16	1.55	1.65	1.01	3.19	3.95	2.81	1.19	1.16	1.67	1.26	0.81	20.41
1988	0.72	0.03	0.37	2.02	3.59	3.12	3.03	3.93	1.59	0.05	0.40	T	18.85
1989	0.55	0.73	0.38	0.10	3.02	3.51	1.86	2.37	1.11	0.08	0.02	0.28	14.01
1990	0.27	0.18	1.75	1.52	3.65	1.90	1.99	1.79	0.31	1.48	0.87	0.09	15.80
1991	0.35	0.21	1.00	3.00	5.39	2.78	1.81	0.53	1.75	2.14	0.92	0.67	20.55
1992	0.89	1.42	2.98	0.18	3.18	2.61	3.75	6.30	0.25	0.92	0.20	0.33	23.01
1993	0.74	1.37	0.61	1.80	2.47	6.12	5.47	3.78	0.71	1.59	1:32	0.22	26.20
Record Mean	0.41	0.50	0.98	2.05	3.03	3.24	2.75	2.20	1.52	1.05	0.55	0.49	18.77

AVERAGE TEMPERATURE (deg. F) NORTH PLATTE, NEBRASKA

YEAR	JAN	FEB	MAR	APR	MAY	JUNE	JULY	AUG	SEP	OCT	NOV	DEC	ANNUAL
#1964	28.1	24.9	32.3	47.0	60.9	67.2	77.5	69.8	63.1	50.3	35.8	25.2	48.5
1965	26.3	23.4	25.5	51.4	60.1	67.1	73.1	70.5	53.8	54.0	40.9	28.9	47.9
1966	15.6	21.4	38.5	43.8	60.0	68.8	77.6	67.8	62.1	50.5	36.0	24.5	47.2
1967	24.9	30.8	39.9	49.3	51.9	64.6	70.3	68.8	61.2	49.8	33.9	22.8	47.3
1968	22.2	27.1	39.9	46.2	53.3	69.5	72.6	71.6	61.1	51.1	34.4	19.0	47.4
1969	16.2	24.2	29.0	51.4	61.0	62.8	73.0	73.6	65.8	41.7	38.3	28.4	47.1
1970	22.3	31.8	31.3	45.6	61.9	68.1	74.3	75.6	60.8	45.4	34.8	26.8	48.2
1971	22.1	24.5	33.4	48.0	54.7	70.2	69.8	72.2	59.7	49.5	37.1	27.6	47.4
1972	20.7	29.9	40.7	46.6	58.1	68.4	70.4	70.8	61.2	46.4	29.8	17.2	46.7
1973	21.5	30.3	40.4	45.8	56.0	67.7	72.8	73.7	58.4	51.7	35.0	23.2	48.0
1974	16.0	33.0	40.1	50.0	59.5	66.5	77.5	67.1	57.5	52.9	34.8	24.2	48.3
1975	25.7	23.4	31.5	46.6	57.1	65.7	74.6	73.2	58.5	50.9	30.2	26.4	47.0
1976	17.8	32.7	34.0	47.4	53.1	64.6	72.8	70.6	59.8	45.2	30.5	28.2	46.4
1977	16.6	32.0	37.0	51.7	63.1	70.5	74.5	68.5	63.8	50.0	35.8	24.9	49.0
1978	11.2	14.7	35.1	48.4	56.6	68.2	74.5	71.0	65.4	49.2	32.1	14.6	45.1
1979	6.0	17.2	37.0	48.4	57.4	68.1	74.1	72.9	67.1	53.8	32.2	34.0	47.3
1980	25.1	26.8	35.5	50.5	60.2	72.5	78.0	74.0	63.7	48.9	38.5	32.0	50.5
1981	29.7	29.1	40.2	55.8	54.8	68.6	73.8	70.1	63.0	49.0	39.9	26.7	50.1
1982	17.1	28.1	36.3	44.8	57.3	63.4	75.0	73.1	61.7	49.2	33.3	28.1	47.3
1983	27.1	35.1	37.2	42.3	54.0	65.2	75.3	78.0	64.8	51.3	36.7	7.5	47.9
1984	20.4	33.2	34.1	43.3	58.1	68.0	73.7	75.5	58.4	48.0	37.2	22.5	47.7
1985	18.3	23.1	40.5	52.2	60.8	65.4	75.3	70.1	59.8	48.6	24.6	19.2	46.5
1986	31.6	27.0	44.3	48.9	58.0	71.4	75.6	71.3	63.0	50.4	35.5	30.2	50.6
1987	29.5	35.8	36.7	51.3	63.1	70.2	75.7	70.3	61.3	47.0	38.2	27.7	50.6
1988	16.4	26.5	37.8	48.5	60.7	74.6	74.5	73.4	62.0	48.7	38.0	30.3	49.3
1989	30.2	17.8	35.7	51.1	59.0	65.8	74.3	71.7	61.0	50.7	37.6	20.6	48.0
1990	30.6	30.9	40.0	48.5	56.7	71.1	73.7	74.0	67.6	50.2	38.1	21.9	50.3
1991	23.1	37.5	40.5	49.3	61.8	71.0	74.9	73.7	63.6	48.4	32.2	33.4	50.8
1992	32.1	37:3	41.8	50.6	58.7	65.7	68.5	66.5	63.0	49.9	32.4	22.5	49.1
1993	18.5	18.0	37.0	45.5	58.7	65.3	71.5	70.3	58.3	48.5	32.7	30.4	46.2
Record Mean	23.3	27.8	36.5	48.7	58.7	68.6	74.7	72.8	63.3	51.0	36.5	27.0	49.1
Max	35.7	40.3	49.4	61.8	71.2	81.1	87.6	86.1	77.6	66.0	50.1	39.3	62.2
Min	10.9	15.2	23.6	35.5	46.2	56.0	61.7	59.6	49.0	36.0	23.0	14.6	35.9

REFERENCE NOTES NORTH PLATTE, NEBRASKA

GENERAL
T - TRACE AMOUNT.
BLANK ENTRIES DENOTE MISSING/UNREPORTED DATA.
# INDICATES A STATION OR INSTRUMENT RELOCATION.

SPECIFIC

PM - INCLUDES LAST DAY OF PREVIOUS MONTH
ASOS - AUTOMATED SURFACE OBSERVING SYSTEM IN OPERATION DURING THESE MONTHS.

(a) - LENGTH OF RECORD IN YEARS, ALTHOUGH INDIVIDUAL MONTHS MAY BE MISSING.
0.* OR * - THE VALUE IS BETWEEN 0.0 AND 0.05
NORMALS - BASED ON THE 1961-1990 RECORD PERIOD.
EXTREMES - DATES ARE THE MOST RECENT OCCURRENCE.
WIND DIR.- NUMERALS SHOW TENS OF DEGRESS CLOCKWISE FROM TRUE NORTH. "00" INDICATES CALM.
RESULTANT DIRECTIONS ARE GIVEN TO WHOLE DEGREES.
BOLD VALUES INDICATE EXTREME VALUES WHICH OCCURRED AFTER THE ASOS SYSTEM WAS COMMISSIONED.

RECORD = PERIOD OF RECORD
RECORD MEAN PRECIPITATION IS THE MEAN OF ALL DAILY PRECIPITATION AMOUNTS DURING THE PERIOD OF RECORD.
RECORD MAX(MIN) TEMPERATURE IS THE MEAN OF ALL DAILY MAX(MIN) TEMPERATURES DURING THE PERIOD OF RECORD.
RECORD MEAN TEMPERATURE IS THE SUM OF THE RECORD MAX AND RECORD MIN DIVIDED BY 2.
AVERAGE TEMPERATURE IS THE SUM OF THE MEAN DAILY MAX AND MIN TEMPERATURE DIVIDED BY 2.

EXCEPTIONS

RECORD MEANS ARE THROUGH THE CURRENT YEAR, BEGINNING IN 1875 FOR TEMPERATURE
1875 FOR PRECIPITATION
1953 FOR SNOWFALL

HEATING DEGREE DAYS Base 65 deg. F — NORTH PLATTE, NEBRASKA

SEASON	JULY	AUG	SEP	OCT	NOV	DEC	JAN	FEB	MAR	APR	MAY	JUNE	TOTAL
#1964-65	0	43	143	450	870	1229	1189	1158	1217	405	173	26	6903
1965-66	0	11	345	335	718	1113	1530	1213	815	628	199	48	6955
1966-67	0	34	136	442	863	1250	1240	950	771	465	427	70	6648
1967-68	19	29	132	479	926	1305	1321	1096	770	558	363	26	7024
1968-69	17	18	150	428	911	1421	1509	1133	1106	399	178	122	7392
1969-70	1	0	45	716	795	1129	1315	923	1041	582	136	55	6738
1970-71	2	1	214	600	899	1177	1320	1127	974	501	311	13	7139
1971-72	12	0	210	472	829	1157	1368	1013	745	549	250	32	6637
1972-73	24	15	169	567	1047	1479	1343	967	756	567	283	34	7251
1973-74	10	0	219	407	892	1290	1518	889	765	445	190	62	6687
1974-75	0	40	256	373	900	1262	1216	1160	1032	558	247	62	7106
1975-76	6	0	228	437	1035	1191	1460	929	956	521	363	70	7196
1976-77	0	13	178	608	1028	1133	1493	920	858	395	81	2	6709
1977-78	2	34	96	458	869	1236	1662	1400	924	491	275	71	7518
1978-79	5	24	99	488	982	1560	1828	1335	862	491	259	56	7989
1979-80	4	11	52	341	975	957	1233	1102	909	439	166	10	6199
1980-81	0	6	107	491	790	1019	1089	1000	762	283	318	26	5891
1981-82	9	4	101	492	749	1179	1479	1030	885	601	239	111	6879
1982-83	0	18	160	484	946	1138	1167	833	854	672	343	90	6705
1983-84	2	0	128	419	840	1780	1379	915	953	647	236	33	7332
1984-85	0	0	247	519	829	1312	1440	1168	752	393	156	83	6899
1985-86	0	23	252	502	1205	1416	1029	1060	634	479	219	2	6821
1986-87	0	14	98	446	878	1074	1093	810	868	420	102	15	5818
1987-88	13	36	139	551	796	1152	1501	1109	839	490	170	3	6799
1988-89	0	13	128	498	803	1067	1072	1316	902	430	211	67	6507
1989-90	2	7	180	437	815	1374	1061	948	771	502	259	15	6371
1990-91	15	1	84	457	797	1331	1290	762	754	466	149	5	6111
1991-92	3	1	148	508	977	971	1010	797	714	436	219	45	5829
1992-93	18	60	113	466	970	1310	1436	1311	862	578	204	73	7401
1993-94	2	24	218	513	965	1066							

COOLING DEGREE DAYS Base 65 deg. F — NORTH PLATTE, NEBRASKA

YEAR	JAN	FEB	MAR	APR	MAY	JUNE	JULY	AUG	SEP	OCT	NOV	DEC	TOTAL
1969	0	0	0	0	58	63	257	276	76	0	0	0	730
1970	0	0	0	4	48	155	300	341	96	0	0	0	944
1971	0	0	0	0	1	177	167	229	59	1	0	0	634
1972	0	0	0	0	43	137	199	202	64	0	0	0	645
1973	0	0	0	0	11	121	260	278	29	3	0	0	702
1974	0	0	0	5	24	117	394	115	40	3	0	0	698
1975	0	0	0	10	11	89	311	260	39	7	0	0	727
1976	0	0	0	0	5	62	247	192	27	0	0	0	533
1977	0	0	0	2	26	174	305	149	64	0	0	0	720
1978	0	0	0	1	21	174	307	218	117	5	0	0	843
1979	0	0	0	0	27	156	294	262	123	0	0	0	862
1980	0	0	0	10	27	243	411	289	74	0	0	0	1054
1981	0	0	0	10	9	141	288	168	47	1	0	0	664
1982	0	0	0	0	8	70	314	276	68	0	0	0	736
1983	0	0	0	0	8	103	331	412	128	1	0	0	983
1984	0	0	0	0	27	129	281	331	55	2	0	0	825
1985	0	0	0	14	32	100	326	189	100	0	0	0	761
1986	0	0	0	3	11	201	334	217	43	0	0	0	809
1987	0	0	0	16	48	176	352	208	35	0	0	0	835
1988	0	0	0	1	41	293	301	282	46	0	0	0	964
1989	0	0	0	21	35	99	295	220	67	2	0	0	739
1990	0	0	0	15	10	205	291	289	165	5	0	0	980
1991	0	0	0	3	59	194	317	276	112	2	0	0	963
1992	0	0	0	13	31	68	135	116	60	1	0	0	424
1993	0	0	0	0	15	88	212	194	24	6	0	0	539

SNOWFALL (inches) — NORTH PLATTE, NEBRASKA

SEASON	JULY	AUG	SEP	OCT	NOV	DEC	JAN	FEB	MAR	APR	MAY	JUNE	TOTAL
1964-65	0.0	0.0	0.0	0.0	T	1.8	9.2	7.2	5.0	T	0.0	0.0	23.2
1965-66	0.0	0.0	T	0.0	0.5	6.3	10.5	1.7	9.6	5.0	0.2	0.0	33.8
1966-67	0.0	0.0	0.0	1.4	0.5	8.5	9.3	0.8	0.7	4.5	3.6	0.0	29.3
1967-68	0.0	0.0	0.0	T	2.9	3.4	1.6	3.0	0.8	2.2	0.0	0.0	13.9
1968-69	0.0	0.0	0.0	0.0	0.3	10.3	12.4	3.2	1.8	T	T	0.0	28.0
1969-70	0.0	0.0	0.0	15.7	0.8	1.8	3.6	4.0	18.4	0.4	0.0	0.0	44.7
1970-71	0.0	0.0	0.0	9.0	3.6	1.8	5.6	2.7	19.0	0.8	T	0.0	42.5
1971-72	0.0	0.0	0.0	2.0	2.5	2.1	2.6	1.9	0.1	0.1	0.0	0.0	11.3
1972-73	0.0	0.0	0.0	0.8	8.0	8.7	3.8	0.4	1.6	1.7	0.0	0.0	25.0
1973-74	0.0	0.0	0.0	T	4.3	14.1	4.2	1.0	2.3	0.7	0.0	0.0	26.6
1974-75	0.0	0.0	0.0	0.0	T	4.5	2.2	2.6	3.9	3.0	0.0	0.0	16.2
1975-76	0.0	0.0	0.0	0.8	10.9	1.2	17.1	1.6	5.2	T	0.0	0.0	36.8
1976-77	0.0	0.0	0.0	1.0	0.6	T	2.5	2.2	9.9	8.1	0.0	0.0	24.3
1977-78	0.0	0.0	0.0	T	0.3	6.4	6.2	20.6	2.0	T	T	0.0	35.5
1978-79	0.0	0.0	0.0	T	7.6	10.3	6.3	0.3	5.9	2.3	T	0.0	32.7
1979-80	0.0	0.0	0.0	2.9	17.5	2.3	5.2	9.1	21.9	7.4	0.0	0.0	66.3
1980-81	0.0	0.0	0.0	0.6	1.2	T	0.7	0.5	0.5	0.4	0.0	0.0	3.9
1981-82	0.0	0.0	0.0	T	5.3	6.4	4.4	1.7	6.4	0.9	0.0	0.0	25.1
1982-83	0.0	0.0	0.0	1.0	2.0	9.7	1.6	0.1	5.9	5.4	0.0	0.0	25.7
1983-84	0.0	0.0	T	0.0	12.1	7.3	5.3	9.6	8.8	14.5	0.2	0.0	57.8
1984-85	0.0	0.0	T	0.3	0.9	8.7	8.5	0.8	2.1	0.0	0.0	0.0	21.3
1985-86	0.0	0.0	3.1	T	13.0	8.1	0.2	8.7	3.8	T	0.0	0.0	36.9
1986-87	0.0	0.0	0.0	2.0	1.0	2.6	1.6	9.2	7.2	0.1	0.0	0.0	23.7
1987-88	0.0	0.0	0.0	1.3	8.2	7.2	12.6	0.6	3.8	2.1	0.0	0.0	35.8
1988-89	0.0	0.0	0.0	T	2.5	T	6.1	10.6	4.3	0.3	T	0.0	23.8
1989-90	T	0.0	T	T	T	2.2	5.9	1.9	5.3	0.3	T	T	15.6
1990-91	0.0	0.0	0.0	2.0	9.7	0.8	4.1	1.1	5.6	T	T	0.0	23.3
1991-92	0.0	0.0	0.0	7.3	1.6	1.8	5.4	1.2	5.1	0.3	T	0.0	22.7
1992-93	T	T	0.0	T	2.2	3.9	10.1	17.2	2.7	2.0	T	T	38.1
1993-94	T	0.0	T	T	3.9	3.3							
Record Mean	T	T	0.1	1.4	4.0	4.7	5.4	5.2	6.8	2.7	0.1	T	30.3

OMAHA (EPPLEY AIRFIELD), NEBRASKA

Omaha, Nebraska, is situated on the west bank of the Missouri River. The river level at Omaha is normally about 965 feet above sea level and the rolling hills in and around Omaha rise to about 1,300 feet above sea level. The climate is typically continental with relatively warm summers and cold, dry winters. It is situated midway between two distinctive climatic zones, the humid east and the dry west. Fluctuations between these two zones produce weather conditions for periods that are characteristic of either zone, or combinations of both. Omaha is also affected by most low pressure systems that cross the country. This causes periodic and rapid changes in weather, especially during the winter months.

Most of the precipitation in Omaha falls during sharp showers or thunderstorms, and these occur mostly during the growing season from April to September. Of the total precipitation, about 75 percent falls during this six-month period. The rain occurs mostly as evening or nighttime showers and thunderstorms. Although winters are relatively cold, precipitation is light, with only 10 percent of the total annual precipitation falling during the winter months.

Sunshine is fairly abundant, ranging around 50 percent of the possible in the winter to 75 percent of the possible in the summer.

NORMALS, MEANS, AND EXTREMES

OMAHA (EPPLEY AIRFIELD), NEBRASKA

LATITUDE: 41°18'N LONGITUDE: 95°54' W ELEVATION: FT. GRND 997 BARO 985 TIME ZONE: CENTRAL WBAN: 14942

	(a)	JAN	FEB	MAR	APR	MAY	JUNE	JULY	AUG	SEP	OCT	NOV	DEC	YEAR
TEMPERATURE °F:														
Normals														
-Daily Maximum		31.3	37.1	49.4	63.8	74.0	83.7	87.9	85.2	76.5	65.6	49.3	34.6	61.5
-Daily Minimum		10.9	16.7	27.7	39.9	50.9	60.4	65.9	62.9	53.6	41.2	28.7	15.6	39.5
-Monthly		21.1	26.9	38.6	51.9	62.4	72.1	76.9	74.1	65.1	53.4	39.0	25.1	50.6
Extremes														
-Record Highest	57	69	78	89	97	99	105	114	110	104	96	80	72	114
-Year		1944	1972	1986	1989	1939	1953	1936	1936	1939	1938	1980	1939	JUL 1936
-Record Lowest	57	-23	-21	-16	5	27	38	44	43	25	13	-9	-23	-23
-Year		1982	1981	1948	1975	1980	1983	1972	1967	1984	1972	1964	1989	DEC 1989
NORMAL DEGREE DAYS:														
Heating (base 65°F)		1361	1067	818	398	164	14	0	9	80	372	780	1237	6300
Cooling (base 65°F)		0	0	0	5	84	227	369	292	83	12	0	0	1072
% OF POSSIBLE SUNSHINE														
MEAN SKY COVER (tenths)														
Sunrise - Sunset	48	6.1	6.3	6.7	6.4	6.3	5.7	4.9	4.9	4.9	4.9	6.1	6.4	5.8
MEAN NUMBER OF DAYS:														
Sunrise to Sunset														
-Clear	48	8.8	7.4	6.9	7.3	7.3	8.1	11.3	12.3	12.3	12.9	8.6	8.0	111.2
-Partly Cloudy	48	7.9	7.4	8.1	8.5	9.5	11.3	12.0	10.1	7.6	8.1	7.4	7.5	105.4
-Cloudy	48	14.3	13.5	16.0	14.2	14.1	10.6	7.7	8.6	10.2	10.1	13.9	15.4	148.6
Precipitation .01 inches or more	57	6.4	6.6	8.8	9.6	11.6	10.6	9.4	9.1	8.5	6.4	5.8	6.5	99.1
Snow,Ice pellets,hail 1.0 inches or more	58	2.3	1.9	2.0	0.4	0.*	0.0	0.0	0.0	0.0	0.1	0.9	1.8	9.4
Thunderstorms	58	0.1	0.4	1.6	3.8	7.4	9.4	8.5	7.8	5.3	2.3	0.8	0.2	47.7
Heavy Fog Visibility 1/4 mile or less	58	1.8	2.0	1.4	0.6	0.8	0.4	0.6	1.5	1.4	1.5	1.6	2.1	15.7
Temperature °F														
-Maximum														
90° and above	29	0.0	0.0	0.0	0.5	1.4	7.0	12.8	8.8	2.9	0.2	0.0	0.0	33.7
32° and below	29	14.3	10.1	3.5	0.1	0.0	0.0	0.0	0.0	0.0	0.*	2.7	11.4	42.1
-Minimum														
32° and below	29	30.0	26.1	21.2	6.6	0.4	0.0	0.0	0.0	0.4	6.2	20.7	29.3	141.0
0° and below	29	6.9	3.5	0.3	0.0	0.0	0.0	0.0	0.0	0.0	0.0	0.3	3.3	14.4
AVG. STATION PRESS.(mb)	11	982.7	983.6	979.1	978.4	977.9	977.6	979.3	980.5	981.2	982.2	981.4	983.2	980.6
RELATIVE HUMIDITY (%)														
Hour 00	29	76	77	73	69	73	76	79	81	82	76	77	78	76
Hour 06 (Local Time)	29	78	79	79	77	80	82	85	87	87	82	81	80	81
Hour 12	29	65	63	57	52	54	55	58	59	59	55	62	67	59
Hour 18	29	67	64	54	48	51	52	56	58	59	56	65	71	58
PRECIPITATION (inches):														
Water Equivalent														
-Normal		0.74	0.77	2.04	2.66	4.52	3.87	3.51	3.24	3.72	2.28	1.49	1.02	29.86
-Maximum Monthly	57	3.70	2.97	5.96	6.45	10.33	10.81	10.34	10.16	13.75	4.99	4.70	5.42	13.75
-Year		1949	1965	1973	1951	1959	1947	1993	1987	1965	1961	1983	1984	SEP 1965
-Minimum Monthly	57	T	0.09	0.12	0.23	0.56	1.03	0.39	0.61	0.41	T	0.03	T	T
-Year		1986	1981	1956	1936	1948	1972	1983	1984	1953	1952	1976	1943	JAN 1986
-Maximum in 24 hrs	51	1.52	2.24	1.45	2.56	4.16	3.48	3.37	5.27	6.47	3.13	2.53	3.03	6.47
-Year		1967	1954	1990	1938	1987	1942	1958	1987	1965	1968	1948	1984	SEP 1965
Snow,Ice pellets,hail														
-Maximum Monthly	58	25.7	25.4	27.2	10.0	2.0	T	0.0	0.0	T	7.2	12.0	19.9	27.2
-Year		1936	1965	1948	1992	1945	1993			1985	1941	1957	1969	MAR 1948
-Maximum in 24 hrs	51	13.1	18.3	13.0	9.9	2.0	T	0.0	0.0	T	7.2	8.7	10.2	18.3
-Year		1949	1965	1948	1992	1945	1993			1985	1941	1957	1969	FEB 1965
WIND:														
Mean Speed (mph)	57	10.9	11.0	12.3	12.7	10.9	10.1	8.9	8.9	9.4	9.8	10.9	10.7	10.5
Prevailing Direction through 1963		NNW	NNW	NNW	NNW	SSE	SSE	SSE	SSE	SSE	SSE	SSE	SSE	SSE
Fastest Obs. 1 Min.														
-Direction (!!)		33	35	35	28	27	24	28	31	19	30	33	34	28
-Speed (MPH)	7	44	37	38	40	52	40	58	40	36	36	35	37	58
-Year		1990	1988	1987	1989	1991	1991	1986	1988	1989	1990	1991	1992	JUL 1986
Peak Gust														
-Direction (!!)														
-Speed (mph)														
-Date														

PRECIPITATION (inches)

OMAHA (EPPLEY AIRFIELD), NEBRASKA

YEAR	JAN	FEB	MAR	APR	MAY	JUNE	JULY	AUG	SEP	OCT	NOV	DEC	ANNUAL
1964	0.54	0.36	1.58	4.40	7.46	6.39	4.61	4.13	2.60	0.50	2.34	0.84	35.75
1965	0.60	2.97	2.63	3.71	6.19	5.15	4.39	2.06	13.75	0.76	1.24	1.40	44.85
1966	0.81	0.41	0.88	0.83	3.67	5.93	4.70	1.85	2.16	0.64	0.22	0.62	22.72
1967	2.00	0.16	0.82	2.61	2.26	9.86	4.33	1.53	4.15	1.69	0.28	0.79	30.48
1968	0.49	0.10	0.57	3.93	4.35	4.44	2.61	3.30	5.74	4.62	1.50	2.04	33.69
1969	1.10	1.33	1.25	3.95	4.48	3.27	4.27	5.06	1.33	2.24	0.11	1.80	30.19
1970	0.20	0.14	0.85	2.84	2.64	2.48	1.98	4.66	4.93	4.88	1.23	0.42	27.25
1971	0.95	2.43	0.49	0.90	7.21	3.30	1.77	1.60	0.57	4.20	3.12	1.05	27.59
1972	0.38	0.36	1.14	4.63	5.13	1.03	7.28	2.60	4.93	3.21	3.25	1.62	35.56
1973	1.44	0.87	5.96	3.60	4.94	1.56	4.98	1.27	8.04	2.60	1.43	1.65	38.34
1974	0.63	0.16	0.80	1.72	2.65	1.79	0.79	4.17	2.54	2.74	1.41	0.81	20.21
1975	2.01	1.06	1.78	3.37	3.72	4.30	0.46	1.80	2.16	0.01	2.85	0.46	23.98
1976	0.11	1.39	2.13	2.98	3.55	2.84	1.52	0.62	1.64	1.35	0.03	0.21	18.37
1977	0.93	0.38	3.72	3.28	6.05	2.40	4.69	8.63	5.05	4.38	2.90	0.35	42.76
1978	0.15	0.76	1.04	4.61	5.05	2.19	5.89	3.87	6.01	0.96	1.09	0.50	32.12
1979	1.11	0.30	4.59	2.58	2.84			2.07	3.36	3.12	1.23	0.14	
1980	0.93	0.52	1.40	1.72	2.50	8.99	3.63	6.98	0.82	2.70	0.11	0.04	30.34
1981	0.20	0.09	0.88	1.33	4.13	2.14	1.87	4.80	1.51	1.92	2.60	0.86	22.33
1982	1.83	0.26	1.90	1.22	9.92	4.16	2.46	3.21	2.27	1.10	1.81	1.17	31.31
1983	0.86	0.68	3.65	1.00	2.81	6.52	0.39	1.24	2.45	2.16	4.70	0.63	27.09
1984	0.38	0.62	2.32	4.77	4.92	5.56	1.58	0.61	2.55	3.87	0.52	5.42	33.12
1985	0.56	1.88	1.36	3.16	2.46	1.73	3.27	1.50	2.71	1.36	0.85	0.37	21.21
1986	T	1.00	2.51	4.96	4.88	2.37	2.77	3.86	8.11	4.86	0.99	0.89	37.20
1987	0.08	0.55	4.14	2.24	8.64	3.29	6.72	10.16	1.56	1.33	1.60	1.01	41.32
1988	0.42	0.18	0.14	1.57	4.68	1.60	2.68	1.78	2.63	0.14	2.55	0.95	19.32
1989	1.10	0.86	0.40	1.80	0.83	5.05	3.06	1.80	6.46	1.55	0.15	0.74	23.80
1990	0.59	0.34	4.01	0.36	5.08	3.88	6.36	0.81	0.81	1.71	1.15	1.18	26.28
1991	1.08	0.26	2.85	4.46	4.07	7.79	2.96	3.67	1.37	3.76	3.51	1.75	37.53
1992	1.41	1.18	3.08	3.19	2.27	1.44	7.31	1.57	6.86	2.22	3.01	1.15	34.69
1993	1.42	0.93	2.67	2.26	4.90	8.03	10.34	7.53	2.29	1.18	0.66	0.51	42.72
Record Mean	0.74	0.87	1.54	2.64	3.89	4.48	3.71	3.43	3.18	2.10	1.29	0.91	28.78

AVERAGE TEMPERATURE (deg. F)

OMAHA (EPPLEY AIRFIELD), NEBRASKA

YEAR	JAN	FEB	MAR	APR	MAY	JUNE	JULY	AUG	SEP	OCT	NOV	DEC	ANNUAL
1964	28.6	30.5	33.7	52.8	68.0	71.9	80.1	70.5	65.3	53.7	42.2	25.2	51.9
1965	23.0	22.2	27.1	53.2	68.1	71.8	75.7	74.1	61.0	57.2	42.4	36.9	51.1
1966	18.4	28.8	44.1	48.2	61.0	72.6	79.4	71.0	63.7	53.9	40.1	28.3	50.8
1967	25.5	28.4	45.5	55.6	59.1	70.8	74.4	71.7	62.5	52.1	38.4	28.4	51.1
1968	22.6	27.3	44.6	52.5	58.0	74.0	76.4	75.0	65.4	55.8	37.4	24.0	51.1
1969	18.7	26.7	31.5	53.1	63.2	67.9	78.2	75.6	67.7	50.1	41.0	24.8	49.9
1970	16.3	32.0	35.9	53.0	68.1	74.3	77.3	76.3	66.2	51.7	38.2	29.8	51.6
1971	17.8	25.3	37.2	54.4	60.4	77.8	74.2	74.7	67.8	58.8	41.2	28.9	51.5
1972	20.0	25.4	40.8	51.2	62.4	72.6	74.6	73.6	65.4	49.1	37.1	21.1	49.5
1973	22.6	28.6	44.3	50.4	59.4	73.3	75.5	77.6	64.2	57.3	39.8	22.7	51.3
1974	18.8	30.6	42.1	52.6	61.9	69.8	82.2	70.5	59.7	55.3	40.7	28.9	51.1
1975	22.5	22.4	31.7	49.4	66.2	72.5	78.9	79.7	62.6	58.2	41.6	30.9	51.4
1976	25.5	37.5	40.4	56.8	60.2	72.7	79.0	76.3	67.4	48.5	33.3	24.1	51.8
1977	13.3	33.2	41.6	59.0	70.2	75.1	80.6	72.5	67.4	53.1	39.7	26.2	53.0
1978	12.0	15.7	35.7	52.6	61.7	73.7	77.3	75.5	71.1	53.7	39.6	24.4	49.4
1979	10.7	17.3	39.8	50.0	61.8	72.7	76.0	75.7	66.7		35.8	30.3	
1980	22.4	20.3	32.9	50.7	61.6	73.1	79.6	76.6	64.7	49.0	40.3	26.1	49.8
1981	24.1	28.4	40.8	57.4	58.6	72.6	76.6	71.0	64.8	50.2	40.6	22.9	50.6
1982	9.4	22.6	34.8	47.7	62.9	65.5	77.1	72.6	64.7	55.0	37.1	28.3	48.1
1983	24.9	30.1	37.3	43.5	56.5	69.6	79.4	81.5	67.0	52.2	38.5	7.3	48.9
1984	19.6	33.2	30.3	46.6	57.7	71.8	75.1	76.5	61.9	52.2	39.4	27.1	49.3
1985	19.1	23.6	43.4	54.9	63.4	67.2	74.1	69.4	62.1	52.7	28.5	16.4	47.9
1986	29.4	22.8	42.8	51.9	61.3	73.9	77.9	70.1	67.9	53.7	34.4	29.4	51.3
1987	28.6	36.8	42.8	55.3	67.3	74.2	77.8	70.9	64.8	48.3	43.4	30.9	53.4
1988	21.1	23.9	40.7	50.5	67.3	76.3	76.4	77.3	66.2	49.1	40.0	29.5	51.5
1989	32.4	16.0	37.9	54.6	62.4	69.4	77.4	74.4	63.0	53.9	36.2	17.7	49.6
1990	33.5	31.3	42.7	50.8	58.5	73.5	74.8	75.3	69.0	53.3	42.9	21.2	52.2
1991	16.3	34.2	42.5	54.2	67.3	74.6	75.8	74.3	66.0	52.1	30.6	31.8	51.6
1992	32.6	36.7	43.6	50.0	61.8	69.4	71.1	68.4	64.0	53.5	35.4	27.9	51.2
1993	19.5	22.2	35.6	47.7	61.4	70.0	75.1	75.2	59.7	50.9	35.0	29.4	48.5
Record Mean	22.0	26.6	37.8	51.7	62.6	72.2	77.3	75.0	66.2	54.5	39.0	27.1	51.0
Max	31.2	35.9	47.6	62.4	73.0	82.5	87.6	85.2	76.9	65.5	48.5	35.7	61.0
Min	12.7	17.2	27.9	41.0	52.2	61.9	67.0	64.8	55.5	43.6	29.5	18.5	41.0

REFERENCE NOTES

OMAHA (EPPLEY AIRFIELD), NEBRASKA

GENERAL
T - TRACE AMOUNT.
BLANK ENTRIES DENOTE MISSING/UNREPORTED DATA.
# INDICATES A STATION OR INSTRUMENT RELOCATION.

SPECIFIC

PM - INCLUDES LAST DAY OF PREVIOUS MONTH
ASOS - AUTOMATED SURFACE OBSERVING SYSTEM IN OPERATION DURING THESE MONTHS.

(*) - LENGTH OF RECORD IN YEARS, ALTHOUGH INDIVIDUAL MONTHS MAY BE MISSING.
0.* OR * - THE VALUE IS BETWEEN 0.0 AND 0.05
NORMALS - BASED ON THE 1961-1990 RECORD PERIOD.
EXTREMES - DATES ARE THE MOST RECENT OCCURRENCE
WIND DIR.- NUMERALS SHOW TENS OF DEGRESS CLOCKWISE FROM TRUE NORTH. "00" INDICATES CALM.
RESULTANT DIRECTIONS ARE GIVEN TO WHOLE DEGREES.
BOLD VALUES INDICATE EXTREME VALUES WHICH OCCURRED AFTER THE ASOS SYSTEM WAS COMMISSIONED.

RECORD = PERIOD OF RECORD
RECORD MEAN PRECIPITATION IS THE MEAN OF ALL DAILY PRECIPITATION AMOUNTS DURING THE PERIOD OF RECORD.
RECORD MAX(MIN) TEMPERATURE IS THE MEAN OF ALL DAILY MAX(MIN) TEMPERATURES DURING THE PERIOD OF RECORD.
RECORD MEAN TEMPERATURE IS THE SUM OF THE RECORD MAX AND RECORD MIN DIVIDED BY 2.
AVERAGE TEMPERATURE IS THE SUM OF THE MEAN DAILY MAX AND MIN TEMPERATURE DIVIDED BY 2.

EXCEPTIONS

1. MEAN SKY COVER, AND DAYS CLEAR-PARTLY CLOUDY-CLOUDY ARE THROUGH 1976.
2. MAXIMUM 24-HOUR PRECIPITATION AND SNOW, AND FASTEST MILE WINDS ARE THROUGH MAY 1977.

RECORD MEANS ARE THROUGH THE CURRENT YEAR, BEGINNING IN 1873 FOR TEMPERATURE
1871 FOR PRECIPITATION
1936 FOR SNOWFALL

HEATING DEGREE DAYS Base 65 deg. F — OMAHA (EPPLEY AIRFIELD), NEBRASKA

SEASON	JULY	AUG	SEP	OCT	NOV	DEC	JAN	FEB	MAR	APR	MAY	JUNE	TOTAL
1964-65	0	24	93	353	676	1227	1298	1191	1168	361	55	0	6446
1965-66	0	5	169	257	670	864	1440	1008	642	501	185	13	5754
1966-67	0	13	107	354	741	1132	1216	1020	615	295	249	17	5759
1967-68	8	15	109	417	791	1129	1307	1085	631	380	228	11	6111
1968-69	2	1	60	313	824	1268	1430	1066	1028	353	140	56	6541
1969-70	0	0	25	478	714	1242	1507	917	894	388	68	2	6235
1970-71	0	0	105	426	799	1085	1458	1106	853	319	172	1	6324
1971-72	5	1	95	228	707	1113	1392	1143	741	408	147	12	5992
1972-73	6	7	106	488	831	1357	1307	1014	636	437	191	0	6380
1973-74	0	0	90	254	750	1302	1427	955	702	379	140	31	6030
1974-75	0	15	191	300	726	1115	1311	1189	1024	469	72	11	6423
1975-76	0	0	141	251	695	1051	1219	791	757	261	177	4	5347
1976-77	0	0	61	522	947	1265	1598	883	579	219	10	1	6085
1977-78	0	1	28	361	754	1196	1637	1375	910	372	160	17	6811
1978-79	0	0	39	350	754	1255	1676	1333	775	451	156	12	6801
1979-80	1	6	65		867	1070	1318	1290	987	440	158	4	
1980-81	0	3	108	491	735	1198	1259	1018	743	241	221	0	6017
1981-82	7	3	85	452	723	1299	1721	1183	930	518	102	56	7079
1982-83	0	13	115	315	829	1131	1240	971	854	638	278	37	6421
1983-84	0	0	102	405	789	1786	1401	916	1071	552	243	7	7272
1984-85	0	3	184	391	766	1166	1416	1153	666	325	88	45	6203
1985-86	0	13	217	378	1089	1501	1095	1176	689	389	134	1	6682
1986-87	0	15	40	338	913	1096	1122	784	685	322	67	7	5389
1987-88	1	32	67	512	639	1048	1353	1185	748	433	29	6	6053
1988-89	1	7	56	488	744	1095	1002	1368	844	380	143	23	6151
1989-90	0	7	140	356	855	1460	973	935	684	460	206	15	6091
1990-91	4	1	75	371	662	1350	1506	859	695	338	108	0	5969
1991-92	0	0	123	402	1027	1022	999	816	656	449	154	11	5659
1992-93	2	26	114	359	881	1141	1403	1192	904	514	140	34	6710
1993-94	0	1	171	448	895	1097							

COOLING DEGREE DAYS Base 65 deg. F — OMAHA (EPPLEY AIRFIELD), NEBRASKA

YEAR	JAN	FEB	MAR	APR	MAY	JUNE	JULY	AUG	SEP	OCT	NOV	DEC	TOTAL
1969	0	0	0	2	95	149	416	338	113	25	0	0	1138
1970	0	0	0	32	172	286	386	361	148	20	0	0	1405
1971	0	0	0	12	34	393	295	308	188	42	0	0	1272
1972	0	0	0	3	74	249	314	280	124	1	0	0	1045
1973	0	0	0	3	23	257	332	395	74	22	0	0	1106
1974	0	0	0	11	52	182	540	193	39	4	0	0	1021
1975	0	0	0	7	115	242	441	464	76	44	0	0	1389
1976	0	0	0	21	34	240	440	358	139	17	0	0	1249
1977	0	0	0	45	179	310	489	236	105	0	0	0	1364
1978	0	0	7	5	67	287	386	333	231	5	0	0	1321
1979	0	0	0	8	64	249	344	345	122		0	0	
1980	0	0	0	15	61	254	459	368	107	0	0	0	1264
1981	0	0	0	24	29	235	372	196	85	0	0	0	941
1982	0	0	0	5	43	78	383	252	113	12	0	0	886
1983	0	0	0	0	20	183	453	519	167	17	0	0	1359
1984	0	0	0	6	22	220	320	366	96	4	0	0	1034
1985	0	0	0	30	44	116	290	156	137	1	0	0	774
1986	0	0	10	5	26	276	408	181	133	0	0	0	1039
1987	0	0	0	39	145	292	407	221	69	2	1	0	1176
1988	0	0	0	5	109	351	364	394	99	3	0	0	1325
1989	0	0	10	77	68	159	395	306	89	19	0	0	1123
1990	0	0	0	41	9	277	316	327	199	12	4	0	1185
1991	0	0	5	21	184	295	345	295	161	9	0	0	1315
1992	0	0	0	7	63	150	198	136	90	11	0	0	655
1993	0	0	0	0	35	188	322	324	21	19	0	0	909

SNOWFALL (inches) — OMAHA (EPPLEY AIRFIELD), NEBRASKA

SEASON	JULY	AUG	SEP	OCT	NOV	DEC	JAN	FEB	MAR	APR	MAY	JUNE	TOTAL
1964-65	0.0	0.0	0.0	0.0	2.6	5.4	6.8	25.4	16.1	0.0	0.0	0.0	56.3
1965-66	0.0	0.0	0.0	0.0	0.1	1.7	2.8	1.3	8.3	T	T	0.0	14.2
1966-67	0.0	0.0	0.0	T	0.1	6.8	7.2	0.8	0.3	0.7	1.0	0.0	16.9
1967-68	0.0	0.0	0.0	1.5	T	5.7	4.6	1.1	T	T	T	0.0	12.9
1968-69	0.0	0.0	0.0	0.0	4.7	8.6	8.3	14.0	3.2	0.0	0.0	0.0	38.8
1969-70	0.0	0.0	0.0	T	0.5	19.9	3.2	1.1	5.8	T	0.0	0.0	30.5
1970-71	0.0	0.0	0.0	3.5	T	0.5	13.1	17.4	4.3	0.5	0.0	0.0	39.3
1971-72	0.0	0.0	0.0	0.0	9.0	4.4	1.9	5.0	3.1	1.5	0.0	0.0	24.9
1972-73	0.0	0.0	0.0	T	9.7	5.9	15.8	4.6	T	2.3	0.0	0.0	38.3
1973-74	0.0	0.0	0.0	0.0	4.1	10.7	11.5	2.4	4.2	0.8	0.0	0.0	33.7
1974-75	0.0	0.0	0.0	0.0	5.4	8.1	22.7	11.9	5.1	4.6	0.0	0.0	57.8
1975-76	0.0	0.0	0.0	0.0	6.3	0.6	1.8	7.1	4.2	0.0	0.0	0.0	20.0
1976-77	0.0	0.0	0.0	1.4	0.5	2.8	14.4	0.1	3.7	1.6	0.0	0.0	24.5
1977-78	0.0	0.0	0.0	0.0	T	4.0	1.4	17.0	6.5	T	0.0	0.0	28.9
1978-79	0.0	0.0	0.0	0.0	2.0	5.6	10.0	1.4	6.0	1.1	0.0	0.0	26.1
1979-80	0.0	0.0	0.0	2.0	T	1.3	5.0	3.0	9.2	T	0.0	0.0	20.5
1980-81	0.0	0.0	0.0	2.0	T	0.5	3.6	3.0	T	0.0	0.0	0.0	9.1
1981-82	0.0	0.0	0.0	T	1.0	7.0	2.4	3.0	8.0	2.9	0.0	0.0	24.3
1982-83	0.0	0.0	0.0	T	T	4.0	6.5	9.0	9.0	3.0	0.0	0.0	31.5
1983-84	0.0	0.0	0.0	0.0	6.9	13.5	3.3	2.0	14.2	T	0.0	0.0	39.9
1984-85	0.0	0.0	0.0	T	T	5.0	4.0	4.0	6.0	T	0.0	0.0	19.0
1985-86	0.0	0.0	T	0.0	5.0	4.5	T	7.7	T	0.3	0.0	0.0	17.5
1986-87	0.0	0.0	0.0	0.0	1.8	5.5	1.2	1.6	10.5	T	0.0	0.0	20.6
1987-88	0.0	0.0	0.0	T	9.0	2.0	2.0	2.2	0.8	0.0	0.0	0.0	16.0
1988-89	0.0	0.0	0.0	0.0	4.3	2.7	1.4	11.8	3.3	T	T	0.0	23.5
1989-90	0.0	0.0	0.0	T	1.2	5.3	5.2	4.0	6.7	0.1	0.0	T	22.5
1990-91	0.0	0.0	0.0	T	1.1	10.1	14.9	0.3	4.1	1.1	0.0	T	31.6
1991-92	0.0	0.0	0.0	2.5	8.8	T	0.3	1.1	0.4	10.0	0.0	0.0	23.1
1992-93	0.0	0.0	0.0	0.0	5.8	3.9	13.0	8.5	4.1	1.5	0.0	T	36.8
1993-94	0.0	0.0	0.0	T	2.8	3.1							
Record Mean	0.0	0.0	T	0.3	2.6	5.5	7.4	6.6	6.4	1.0	0.1	T	29.9

LAS VEGAS, NEVADA

Las Vegas is situated near the center of a broad desert valley, which is almost surrounded by mountains ranging from 2,000 to 10,000 feet higher than the floor of the valley. This Vegas Valley, comprising about 600 square miles, runs from northwest to southeast, and slopes gradually upward on each side toward the surrounding mountains. Weather observations are taken at McCarran Airport, 7 miles south of downtown Las Vegas, and about 5 miles southwest and 300 feet higher than the lower portions of the valley. Since mountains encircle the valley, drainage winds are usually downslope toward the center, or lowest portion of the valley. This condition also affects minimum temperatures, which in lower portions of the valley can be from 15 to 25 degrees colder than recorded at the airport on clear, calm nights.

The four seasons are well defined. Summers display desert conditions, with maximum temperatures usually in the 100 degree range. The proximity of the mountains contributes to the relatively cool summer nights, with the majority of minimum temperatures in the mid 70s. During about 2 weeks almost every summer warm, moist air predominates in this area, and causes scattered thunderstorms, occasionally quite severe, together with higher than average humidity. Soil erosion, especially near the mountains and foothills surrounding the valley, is evidence of the intensity of some of the thunderstorm activity. Winters, on the whole, are mild and pleasant. Daytime temperatures average near 60 degrees with mostly clear skies. The spring and fall seasons are generally considered most ideal, although rather sharp temperature changes can occur during these months. There are very few days during the spring and fall months when outdoor activities are affected in any degree by the weather.

The Sierra Nevada Mountains of California and the Spring Mountains immediately west of the Vegas Valley, the latter rising to elevations over 10,000 feet above the valley floor, act as effective barriers to moisture moving eastward from the Pacific Ocean. It is mainly these barriers that result in a minimum of dark overcast and rainy days. Rainy days average less than one in June to three per month in the winter months. Snow rarely falls in this valley and it usually melts as it falls, or shortly thereafter. Notable exceptions have occurred.

Strong winds, associated with major storms, usually reach this valley from the southwest or through the pass from the northwest. Winds over 50 mph are infrequent but, when they do occur, are probably the most provoking of the elements experienced in the Vegas Valley, because of the blowing dust and sand associated with them.

Based on the 1951–1980 period, the average first occurrence of 32 degrees Fahrenheit in the fall is November 21 and the average last occurrence in the spring is March 7.

NORMALS, MEANS, AND EXTREMES

LAS VEGAS, NEVADA

LATITUDE: 36 °05'N LONGITUDE: 115 °10' W ELEVATION: FT. GRND 2162 BARO 2179 TIME ZONE: PACIFIC WBAN: 23169

	(a)	JAN	FEB	MAR	APR	MAY	JUNE	JULY	AUG	SEP	OCT	NOV	DEC	YEAR
TEMPERATURE °F:														
Normals														
-Daily Maximum		57.3	63.3	68.8	77.5	87.8	100.3	105.9	103.2	94.7	82.1	67.4	57.5	80.5
-Daily Minimum		33.6	38.8	43.8	50.7	60.2	69.4	76.2	74.2	66.2	54.3	42.6	33.9	53.7
-Monthly		45.5	51.1	56.3	64.1	74.0	84.9	91.1	88.7	80.5	68.3	55.0	45.7	67.1
Extremes														
-Record Highest	45	77	87	91	99	109	115	116	116	113	103	87	77	116
-Year		1975	1986	1966	1981	1951	1970	1985	1979	1950	1978	1988	1980	JUL 1985
-Record Lowest	45	8	16	23	31	40	48	60	56	46	26	21	11	8
-Year		1963	1989	1971	1975	1964	1993	1987	1968	1965	1971	1952	1990	JAN 1963
NORMAL DEGREE DAYS:														
Heating (base 65°F)		605	389	292	143	14	0	0	0	0	62	304	598	2407
Cooling (base 65°F)		0	0	22	116	293	597	809	735	465	164	0	0	3201
% OF POSSIBLE SUNSHINE	44	77	80	83	87	88	93	88	88	91	87	81	79	85
MEAN SKY COVER (tenths)														
Sunrise - Sunset	45	4.8	4.7	4.6	3.8	3.4	2.1	2.8	2.5	2.1	2.8	3.9	4.4	3.5
MEAN NUMBER OF DAYS:														
Sunrise to Sunset														
-Clear	45	13.8	12.4	13.6	15.8	17.9	22.2	20.1	21.6	22.6	20.4	15.9	14.9	211.1
-Partly Cloudy	45	6.4	6.9	8.5	7.6	8.0	5.2	7.5	6.6	5.0	6.3	7.3	6.7	82.0
-Cloudy	45	10.9	9.0	8.9	6.6	5.1	2.6	3.4	2.8	2.4	4.2	6.8	9.4	72.2
Precipitation														
.01 inches or more	45	3.2	2.8	3.2	1.8	1.4	0.7	2.6	2.9	1.6	1.8	2.0	2.6	26.5
Snow,Ice pellets,hail														
1.0 inches or more	45	0.3	0.*	0.0	0.0	0.0	0.0	0.0	0.0	0.0	0.0	0.1	0.*	0.4
Thunderstorms	45	0.*	0.2	0.4	0.5	1.0	1.0	4.0	4.0	1.6	0.5	0.2	0.*	13.4
Heavy Fog Visibility														
1/4 mile or less	45	0.3	0.1	0.1	0.0	0.0	0.0	0.0	0.0	0.*	0.*	0.1	0.2	0.8
Temperature °F														
-Maximum														
90° and above	33	0.0	0.0	0.*	3.3	15.4	25.7	30.5	29.8	22.2	6.0	0.0	0.0	132.9
32° and below	33	0.1	0.0	0.0	0.0	0.0	0.0	0.0	0.0	0.0	0.0	0.0	0.*	0.2
-Minimum														
32° and below	33	12.5	4.3	1.2	0.1	0.0	0.0	0.0	0.0	0.0	0.1	2.2	11.2	31.5
0° and below	33	0.0	0.0	0.0	0.0	0.0	0.0	0.0	0.0	0.0	0.0	0.0	0.0	0.0
AVG. STATION PRESS.(mb)	21	942.3	940.7	937.3	935.9	933.9	933.6	934.9	935.6	936.0	938.7	940.8	942.5	937.7
RELATIVE HUMIDITY (%)														
Hour 04	33	56	51	46	35	32	25	29	35	33	37	46	55	40
Hour 10 (Local Time)	33	42	36	31	22	19	15	19	24	22	25	32	40	27
Hour 16	33	31	27	22	16	14	11	15	17	17	19	26	32	21
Hour 22	33	50	43	37	26	23	17	22	26	26	30	40	49	32
PRECIPITATION (inches):														
Water Equivalent														
-Normal		0.48	0.48	0.42	0.21	0.28	0.12	0.35	0.49	0.28	0.21	0.43	0.38	4.13
-Maximum Monthly	45	2.41	2.52	4.80	2.44	0.96	0.97	2.48	2.59	1.58	1.22	2.22	1.71	4.80
-Year		1949	1993	1992	1965	1969	1990	1984	1957	1963	1992	1965	1992	MAR 1992
-Minimum Monthly	45	T	0.00	0.00	0.00	0.00	0.00	0.00	0.00	0.00	0.00	0.00	0.00	0.00
-Year		1984	1977	1972	1962	1970	1982	1981	1980	1971	1979	1980	1981	JUN 1982
-Maximum in 24 hrs	45	1.09	1.30	1.27	0.97	0.83	0.97	1.36	2.59	1.07	1.09	1.78	0.95	2.59
-Year		1990	1993	1992	1965	1987	1990	1984	1957	1963	1992	1960	1977	AUG 1957
Snow,Ice pellets,hail														
-Maximum Monthly	45	16.7	1.4	0.1	T	0.0	0.0	0.0	T	0.0	T	4.0	2.0	16.7
-Year		1949	1990	1976	1970				1989		1956	1964	1967	JAN 1949
-Maximum in 24 hrs	45	9.0	6.9	0.1	T	0.0	0.0	0.0	T	0.0	T	4.0	2.0	9.0
-Year		1974	1979	1976	1970				1989		1956	1964	1967	JAN 1974
WIND:														
Mean Speed (mph)	45	7.4	8.6	10.2	11.0	11.1	11.1	10.3	9.6	9.0	8.1	7.8	7.3	9.3
Prevailing Direction through 1963		W	SW	SW	SW	SW	SW	SW	SW	SW	WSW	W	W	SW
Fastest Obs. 1 Min.														
-Direction (!!)	8	23	23	23	22	32	34	10	14	22	31	21	30	32
-Speed (MPH)	8	39	50	51	49	53	48	38	40	35	47	43	40	53
-Year		1987	1989	1989	1988	1991	1989	1984	1989	1989	1989	1985	1984	MAY 1991
Peak Gust														
-Direction (!!)	10	SW	NW	NW	W	NW	NE	SW	SE	SW	SW	SW	SW	SE
-Speed (mph)	10	54	67	82	69	72	59	53	90	49	52	68	54	90
-Date		1987	1984	1984	1988	1991	1984	1984	1989	1989	1984	1987	1990	AUG 1989

PRECIPITATION (inches)

LAS VEGAS, NEVADA

YEAR	JAN	FEB	MAR	APR	MAY	JUNE	JULY	AUG	SEP	OCT	NOV	DEC	ANNUAL
1964	0.05	0.02	0.02	0.03	0.05	0.03	0.24	0.05	T	T	0.63	T	1.12
1965	0.05	0.45	0.74	2.44	0.40	T	0.28	0.38	T	T	2.22	1.00	7.96
1966	T	0.07	0.04	0.01	T	0.15	0.30	0.09	0.35	0.09	0.33	0.48	1.91
1967	0.47	0.00	T	0.09	0.21	0.82	0.20	0.38	1.03	0.00	1.52	0.82	5.54
1968	0.01	0.22	0.22	0.10	T	0.31	0.11	0.04	0.01	T	0.02	0.07	1.11
1969	1.57	0.96	0.57	T	0.96	0.23	0.06	0.33	0.08	0.27	0.06	T	5.09
1970	0.01	0.86	0.28	0.04	0.00	0.18	0.58	1.79	0.00	0.02	0.38	0.15	4.29
1971	T	0.03	T	T	0.84	T	0.08	0.90	0.00	0.06	0.12	0.51	2.54
1972	0.00	T	0.00	0.07	0.46	0.32	0.13	0.84	0.63	1.12	1.09	0.19	4.85
1973	0.49	1.64	1.83	0.35	0.09	0.03	T	0.08	T	0.02	0.14	0.01	4.68
1974	2.00	0.11	0.16	T	T	0.00	0.58	0.08	0.16	0.61	0.23	0.59	4.52
1975	0.01	0.05	1.07	0.42	0.35	T	0.26	0.06	1.17	0.03	T	0.05	3.47
1976	0.00	2.49	0.02	0.13	0.34	0.00	1.95	0.00	1.09	0.70	0.02	0.03	6.77
1977	0.21	0.00	0.28	0.01	0.72	0.05	T	1.38	0.19	0.06	0.01	1.06	3.97
1978	1.00	1.51	1.13	0.36	0.54	0.00	0.19	0.53	0.03	0.62	0.59	1.15	7.65
1979	2.18	0.07	0.96	0.06	0.35	0.00	0.78	2.12	T	0.00	0.03	0.24	6.79
1980	1.45	2.25	0.94	0.18	0.15	T	0.43	0.00	0.18	0.04	0.00	0.01	5.63
1981	0.09	0.20	1.44	0.02	0.50	T	0.00	0.20	0.25	0.15	0.29	0.00	3.14
1982	0.09	1.10	0.29	0.01	0.31	0.00	0.05	0.71	0.07	0.04	0.60	0.72	3.99
1983	0.43	0.32	0.90	0.45	0.16	T	0.06	1.25	0.50	0.26	0.10	0.43	4.86
1984	T	0.03	T	0.04	0.00	0.22	2.48	0.99	0.47	T	0.94	1.68	6.85
1985	0.19	0.02	0.06	0.31	T	0.02	0.13	0.00	0.08	0.07	0.37	0.02	1.27
1986	0.23	0.15	0.32	0.10	0.28	T	0.13	0.04	0.05	0.07	0.81	0.47	2.65
1987	1.13	0.45	0.49	0.17	0.90	0.13	0.13	0.01	T	0.49	1.80	0.89	6.59
1988	0.65	0.26	0.00	0.76	T	0.04	0.04	0.46	T	0.00	T	0.08	2.29
1989	0.51	0.06	0.05	T	0.64	T	0.05	0.80	T	T	0.00	T	2.11
1990	1.18	0.37	T	0.18	T	0.97	0.59	T	0.19	0.17	0.10	T	3.75
1991	0.21	0.54	1.01	T	0.05	0.19	0.54	0.78	0.06	0.06	0.38	0.24	4.06
1992	0.45	1.30	4.80	0.02	0.05	0.09	0.03	0.21	0.00	1.22	0.00	1.71	9.88
1993	1.63	2.52	0.14	0.01	0.01	0.08	0.00	0.26	0.00	0.02	0.17	0.21	5.05
Record Mean	0.53	0.48	0.51	0.22	0.18	0.08	0.41	0.48	0.30	0.24	0.37	0.40	4.21

AVERAGE TEMPERATURE (deg. F)

LAS VEGAS, NEVADA

YEAR	JAN	FEB	MAR	APR	MAY	JUNE	JULY	AUG	SEP	OCT	NOV	DEC	ANNUAL
1964	42.0	45.6	52.3	61.8	70.9	80.9	90.7	87.6	78.4	72.0	50.0	45.3	64.8
1965	47.1	49.5	53.2	61.2	69.6	78.0	88.7	87.9	74.8	69.8	55.9	45.0	65.1
1966	42.7	45.8	57.9	66.4	77.5	83.9	89.3	89.6	80.1	66.5	55.4	46.1	66.8
1967	45.3	50.6	59.3	56.2	72.5	79.6	91.7	90.3	80.0	69.1	56.7	41.6	66.1
1968	44.2	55.7	57.5	62.0	73.5	84.0	89.0	83.5	79.7	67.0	54.5	40.8	66.0
1969	47.5	46.3	53.0	64.4	76.8	81.4	89.7	92.2	82.5	62.8	53.5	45.8	66.3
1970	44.0	52.5	54.9	58.6	75.3	83.4	91.1	88.8	77.2	63.8	55.0	44.5	65.8
1971	44.4	49.7	55.8	63.0	68.0	83.3	92.8	89.0	77.6	61.7	50.9	41.4	64.8
1972	42.3	52.0	63.7	65.1	74.5	84.7	93.1	86.5	78.0	63.5	49.7	41.3	66.2
1973	40.9	49.6	50.7	62.2	76.7	85.2	91.7	87.6	78.9	67.7	53.4	46.2	65.9
1974	41.0	48.9	59.5	63.4	77.0	89.1	88.8	87.7	83.4	69.3	54.8	44.4	67.3
1975	45.3	48.8	53.9	56.6	72.5	83.8	90.3	87.5	81.7	66.1	53.0	48.2	65.6
1976	46.9	53.2	53.4	62.6	77.8	81.5	86.9	85.5	78.7	66.5	58.0	46.4	66.5
1977	45.7	54.2	52.6	68.6	67.7	88.0	92.4	90.1	80.6	71.4	57.2	51.9	68.3
1978	47.9	52.1	59.9	63.1	73.1	87.1	91.9	89.0	79.0	73.5	54.2	42.9	67.8
1979	41.1	48.4	56.0	66.1	75.4	85.5	91.1	85.9	85.3	70.7	51.6	47.2	67.1
1980	49.5	53.2	54.2	63.5	69.0	83.9	92.0	90.2	81.4	68.9	56.8	52.7	67.9
1981	51.1	52.5	56.4	70.6	74.3	88.8	92.7	90.0	82.5	64.4	58.0	48.8	69.2
1982	45.6	50.5	55.1	63.8	73.6	81.5	88.1	87.3	77.9	63.0	50.5	44.5	65.1
1983	46.6	51.7	56.4	58.5	72.8	82.8	88.5	83.8	82.5	67.8	55.3	47.9	66.2
1984	47.1	50.1	57.9	63.1	80.7	83.5	88.2	85.4	81.7	63.0	52.7	44.0	66.5
1985	44.4	47.4	54.9	68.2	76.9	87.4	92.0	89.9	75.4	67.3	51.7	48.3	67.0
1986	51.7	55.8	63.0	66.2	76.6	87.8	87.6	91.2	75.4	65.0	55.8	46.0	68.5
1987	44.7	51.4	54.6	68.4	74.5	86.3	86.9	88.2	81.2	71.0	53.4	42.5	66.9
1988	45.1	52.4	58.1	64.2	73.4	85.3	92.6	86.9	79.1	74.9	56.0	46.0	67.8
1989	43.9	50.0	63.4	72.7	75.7	85.3	93.4	86.9	80.0	67.2	57.3	48.0	68.7
1990	45.2	48.8	60.5	68.8	74.5	85.9	90.8	87.8	82.0	69.2	55.1	40.2	67.4
1991	45.5	55.9	52.7	64.2	69.9	82.1	90.2	87.8	81.9	72.2	55.2	47.0	67.1
1992	45.9	54.1	56.8	70.5	77.7	83.2	88.7	90.5	83.7	70.9	52.7	43.6	68.2
1993	45.7	50.1	60.9	67.5	77.0	82.5	89.4	88.5	81.3	69.1	51.5	46.3	67.5
Record Mean	44.6	49.9	55.8	64.6	73.9	83.5	89.8	87.7	80.0	67.3	53.5	45.7	66.3
Max	56.5	62.4	68.9	78.5	88.3	98.6	104.5	102.2	94.8	81.7	66.6	57.7	80.0
Min	32.7	37.4	42.7	50.6	59.4	68.3	75.0	73.2	65.1	53.0	40.4	33.6	52.6

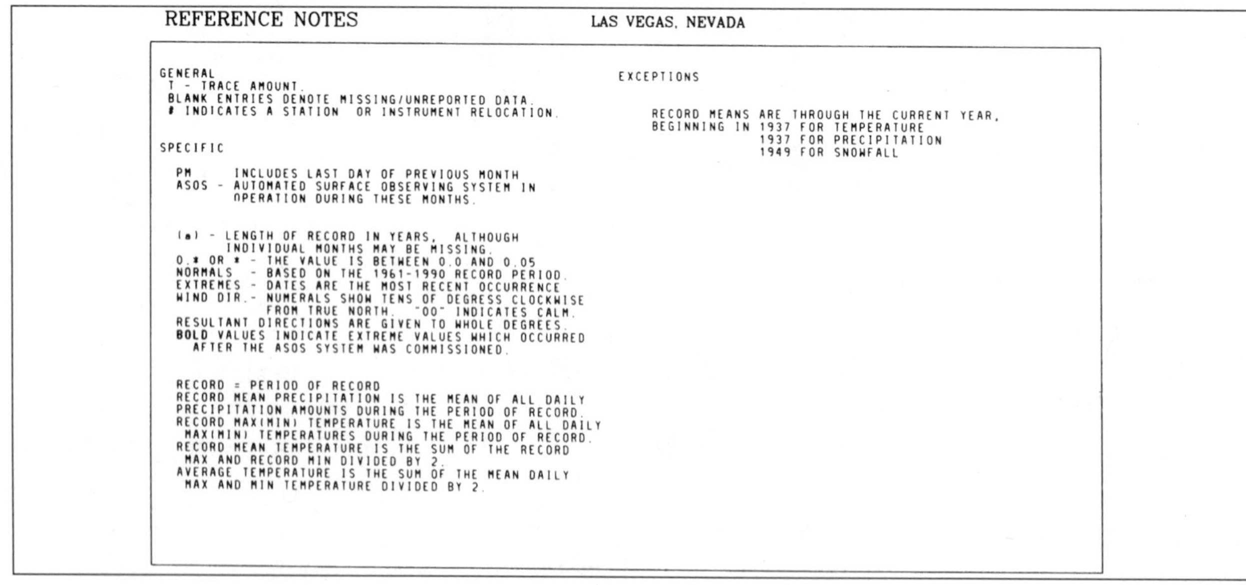

REFERENCE NOTES

LAS VEGAS, NEVADA

GENERAL
T - TRACE AMOUNT.
BLANK ENTRIES DENOTE MISSING/UNREPORTED DATA.
# INDICATES A STATION OR INSTRUMENT RELOCATION.

SPECIFIC

PM INCLUDES LAST DAY OF PREVIOUS MONTH
ASOS - AUTOMATED SURFACE OBSERVING SYSTEM IN OPERATION DURING THESE MONTHS.

(a) - LENGTH OF RECORD IN YEARS, ALTHOUGH INDIVIDUAL MONTHS MAY BE MISSING.
0.* OR * - THE VALUE IS BETWEEN 0.0 AND 0.05
NORMALS - BASED ON THE 1961-1990 RECORD PERIOD.
EXTREMES - DATES ARE THE MOST RECENT OCCURRENCE
WIND DIR.- NUMERALS SHOW TENS OF DEGRESS CLOCKWISE FROM TRUE NORTH. "00" INDICATES CALM.
RESULTANT DIRECTIONS ARE GIVEN TO WHOLE DEGREES.
BOLD VALUES INDICATE EXTREME VALUES WHICH OCCURRED AFTER THE ASOS SYSTEM WAS COMMISSIONED.

RECORD = PERIOD OF RECORD
RECORD MEAN PRECIPITATION IS THE MEAN OF ALL DAILY PRECIPITATION AMOUNTS DURING THE PERIOD OF RECORD.
RECORD MAX(MIN) TEMPERATURE IS THE MEAN OF ALL DAILY MAX(MIN) TEMPERATURES DURING THE PERIOD OF RECORD.
RECORD MEAN TEMPERATURE IS THE SUM OF THE RECORD MAX AND RECORD MIN DIVIDED BY 2.
AVERAGE TEMPERATURE IS THE SUM OF THE MEAN DAILY MAX AND MIN TEMPERATURE DIVIDED BY 2.

EXCEPTIONS

RECORD MEANS ARE THROUGH THE CURRENT YEAR, BEGINNING IN 1937 FOR TEMPERATURE
1937 FOR PRECIPITATION
1949 FOR SNOWFALL

HEATING DEGREE DAYS Base 65 deg. F — LAS VEGAS, NEVADA

SEASON	JULY	AUG	SEP	OCT	NOV	DEC	JAN	FEB	MAR	APR	MAY	JUNE	TOTAL
1964-65	0	0	0	12	444	606	551	427	358	220	49	0	2667
1965-66	0	0	15	17	266	615	685	529	235	54	0	0	2416
1966-67	0	0	0	47	286	578	606	397	189	261	25	0	2389
1967-68	0	0	0	18	244	716	638	265	231	110	8	0	2230
1968-69	0	0	1	28	304	743	536	518	381	74	16	0	2601
1969-70	0	0	0	112	341	589	643	344	304	208	8	0	2549
1970-71	0	0	0	111	295	631	630	421	306	105	47	0	2546
1971-72	0	0	4	207	417	724	697	373	99	69	6	0	2596
1972-73	0	0	0	108	453	727	744	428	437	132	12	0	3041
1973-74	0	0	0	42	349	576	738	443	188	82	13	0	2431
1974-75	0	0	0	55	300	634	607	446	340	249	37	0	2668
1975-76	0	0	0	73	354	516	553	339	357	124	1	0	2317
1976-77	0	0	0	39	212	569	593	297	374	45	56	0	2185
1977-78	0	0	0	3	226	399	522	356	168	91	16	0	1781
1978-79	0	0	1	2	324	676	737	458	270	66	18	0	2552
1979-80	0	0	0	44	395	546	474	335	328	108	32	0	2262
1980-81	0	0	0	82	255	374	426	344	263	29	2	0	1775
1981-82	0	0	0	74	214	497	594	398	301	98	9	0	2185
1982-83	0	0	10	84	429	631	564	364	263	198	21	0	2564
1983-84	0	0	0	3	297	524	548	424	216	111	0	0	2123
1984-85	0	0	0	127	363	641	629	487	308	41	0	0	2596
1985-86	0	0	1	31	393	512	404	270	125	57	11	0	1804
1986-87	0	0	14	53	268	586	622	375	316	40	1	0	2275
1987-88	0	0	0	18	342	689	612	357	225	83	33	0	2359
1988-89	0	0	0	0	291	581	647	425	118	23	16	0	2101
1989-90	0	0	0	70	224	519	606	449	172	12	0	0	2052
1990-91	0	0	0	23	290	761	597	247	376	57	25	2	2378
1991-92	0	0	0	77	297	552	584	308	248	7	0	0	2073
1992-93	0	0	0	16	364	655	591	410	143	32	3	8	2222
1993-94	0	0	0	33	398	573							

COOLING DEGREE DAYS Base 65 deg. F — LAS VEGAS, NEVADA

YEAR	JAN	FEB	MAR	APR	MAY	JUNE	JULY	AUG	SEP	OCT	NOV	DEC	TOTAL
1969	0	0	13	62	390	500	772	852	532	54	0	0	3175
1970	0	0	0	21	334	560	818	748	371	81	1	0	2934
1971	0	0	24	53	148	556	871	752	390	112	0	0	2906
1972	0	2	66	80	308	597	876	675	398	69	0	0	3071
1973	0	0	0	54	382	612	833	708	424	134	8	0	3155
1974	0	0	24	43	394	731	744	713	559	195	0	0	3403
1975	0	0	2	2	276	570	792	704	508	117	2	0	2973
1976	0	0	2	57	404	500	687	641	419	93	6	0	2809
1977	0	0	0	161	149	694	858	781	476	210	3	0	3332
1978	0	0	17	40	277	672	841	752	425	268	8	0	3300
1979	0	0	0	104	346	625	813	656	614	229	0	0	3387
1980	0	0	0	68	160	575	842	788	498	211	15	0	3157
1981	0	0	5	205	296	721	866	781	531	64	12	0	3481
1982	0	0	2	70	281	501	721	699	404	30	0	0	2708
1983	0	0	2	9	269	541	735	589	534	94	10	0	2783
1984	0	0	3	61	496	563	724	641	508	74	1	0	3071
1985	0	0	0	143	377	678	844	778	319	110	2	0	3251
1986	0	20	69	98	379	693	707	821	332	59	0	0	3178
1987	0	0	0	148	302	645	685	729	495	211	0	0	3215
1988	0	0	16	64	300	615	864	685	434	312	31	0	3321
1989	0	11	74	259	351	614	887	687	456	143	0	0	3482
1990	0	0	42	134	302	634	810	713	516	163	0	0	3314
1991	0	0	0	42	187	524	788	714	515	307	12	0	3089
1992	0	0	0	180	402	552	742	798	571	206	3	0	3454
1993	0	0	21	114	381	537	765	737	494	166	0	0	3215

SNOWFALL (inches) — LAS VEGAS, NEVADA

SEASON	JULY	AUG	SEP	OCT	NOV	DEC	JAN	FEB	MAR	APR	MAY	JUNE	TOTAL
1970-71	0.0	0.0	0.0	0.0	0.0	T	T	0.0	0.0	0.0	0.0	0.0	T
1971-72	0.0	0.0	0.0	0.0	0.0	T	0.0	0.0	0.0	0.0	0.0	0.0	T
1972-73	0.0	0.0	0.0	0.0	0.0	0.0	0.3	0.0	T	0.0	0.0	0.0	0.3
1973-74	0.0	0.0	0.0	0.0	0.0	0.0	13.4	0.0	0.0	0.0	0.0	0.0	13.4
1974-75	0.0	0.0	0.0	0.0	0.0	T	0.0	T	T	0.0	0.0	0.0	T
1975-76	0.0	0.0	0.0	0.0	T	0.0	0.0	0.0	0.1	0.0	0.0	0.0	0.1
1976-77	0.0	0.0	0.0	0.0	0.0	0.0	0.0	0.0	0.0	0.0	0.0	0.0	0.0
1977-78	0.0	0.0	0.0	0.0	0.0	0.0	0.0	0.0	0.0	0.0	0.0	0.0	0.0
1978-79	0.0	0.0	0.0	0.0	0.0	T	9.9	0.3	0.0	0.0	0.0	0.0	10.2
1979-80	0.0	0.0	0.0	0.0	0.0	0.0	0.0	0.0	0.0	0.0	0.0	0.0	0.0
1980-81	0.0	0.0	0.0	0.0	0.0	0.0	0.0	0.0	0.0	0.0	0.0	0.0	0.0
1981-82	0.0	0.0	0.0	0.0	0.0	0.0	0.0	0.0	0.0	0.0	0.0	0.0	0.0
1982-83	0.0	0.0	0.0	0.0	0.0	0.0	0.0	0.0	0.0	0.0	0.0	0.0	0.0
1983-84	0.0	0.0	0.0	0.0	0.0	0.0	0.0	0.0	0.0	0.0	0.0	0.0	0.0
1984-85	0.0	0.0	0.0	0.0	0.0	T	0.0	T	0.0	0.0	0.0	0.0	T
1985-86	0.0	0.0	0.0	0.0	0.0	T	0.0	0.0	0.0	0.0	0.0	0.0	T
1986-87	0.0	0.0	0.0	0.0	0.0	0.0	T	0.6	0.0	0.0	0.0	0.0	0.6
1987-88	0.0	0.0	0.0	0.0	0.0	0.0	0.0	T	0.0	0.0	0.0	0.0	T
1988-89	0.0	0.0	0.0	0.0	0.0	T	0.0	0.3	0.0	0.0	0.0	0.0	0.3
1989-90	0.0	T	0.0	0.0	0.0	0.0	T	1.4	0.0	0.0	0.0	0.0	1.4
1990-91	0.0	0.0	0.0	0.0	0.0	0.0	0.0	0.0	0.0	0.0	0.0	0.0	0.0
1991-92	0.0	0.0	0.0	0.0	0.0	0.0	0.0	0.0	T	0.0	0.0	0.0	T
1992-93	0.0	0.0	0.0	0.0	0.0	T	0.0	0.0	0.0	0.0	0.0	0.0	T
1993-94	0.0	0.0	0.0	0.0	0.0	0.0							
Record Mean	0.0	T	0.0	T	0.1	0.1	1.0	0.1	T	T	0.0	0.0	1.2

CONCORD, NEW HAMPSHIRE

Concord, the Capital of New Hampshire, is situated near the geographical center of New England at an altitude of approximately 300 feet above sea level on the Merrimack River. Its surroundings are hilly with many lakes and ponds. The countryside is generously wooded, mostly on land reclaimed from fields which were formerly cleared for farming. From the coast about 50 miles to the southeast, the terrain slopes gently upward to the city. West of the city, the land rises some 2,000 feet higher in only half that distance. Mount Washington, at an elevation of 6,288 feet is in the White Mountains 75 miles north of town.

Northwesterly winds are prevalent. They bring cold, dry air during the winter and pleasantly cool, dry air in the summer. Stronger southerly winds occur during July and August, and easterly winds usually accompany summer and winter storms. Winter breezes are somewhat lighter, and winds are frequently calm during the night and early morning hours. Low temperatures, as a rule, do not interrupt normal out-of-doors activity because winds are calm or light, producing a low wind chill factor.

Very hot summer weather is infrequent. During any month, temperatures considerably above the average maxima and much below the normal minima are observed.

The average amount of precipitation for the warmer half of the year differs little from that for the colder half. Precipitation occurrences average approximately one day of three for the year, with a somewhat higher frequency for the April–May period, offsetting the lower frequency of August–October. The more significant rains and heavier snowfalls are associated with easterly winds, especially northeasterly winds. The first snowfall of an inch or more is likely to come between the middle of November and the middle of December. The snow cover normally lasts from mid-December until the last week of March, but bare ground is not rare in the winter, nor is a snowscape rare earlier or later in the season. Rain, sleet, or freezing rain may also occur.

Agriculture is neither intensive nor large-scale in the vicinity of the station. Potatoes and other frost-resistant vegetables, hardy fruits such as apples, forage for the dairy industry, and maple sugar are the principal crops.

Based on the 1951–1980 period, the average first occurrence of 32 degrees Fahrenheit in the fall is September 22 and the average last occurrence in the spring is May 23. Freezing temperatures have occurred as late as June and as early as August.

NORMALS, MEANS, AND EXTREMES

CONCORD, NEW HAMPSHIRE

LATITUDE: 43°12'N LONGITUDE: 71°30' W ELEVATION: FT. GRND 342 BARO 343 TIME ZONE: EASTERN WBAN: 14745

	(a)	JAN	FEB	MAR	APR	MAY	JUNE	JULY	AUG	SEP	OCT	NOV	DEC	YEAR
TEMPERATURE °F:														
Normals														
-Daily Maximum		29.8	33.0	42.8	56.3	68.9	77.3	82.4	79.8	71.6	60.7	47.1	34.2	57.0
-Daily Minimum		7.4	10.4	22.1	31.5	41.4	51.2	56.5	54.7	46.0	34.9	27.0	14.4	33.1
-Monthly		18.6	21.8	32.4	43.9	55.2	64.2	69.5	67.3	58.8	47.8	37.1	24.3	45.1
Extremes														
-Record Highest	52	68	66	85	95	97	98	102	101	98	90	80	68	102
-Year		1950	1957	1977	1976	1962	1980	1966	1975	1953	1963	1950	1982	JUL 1966
-Record Lowest	52	-33	-37	-16	8	21	30	35	29	21	10	-5	-22	-37
-Year		1984	1943	1967	1969	1966	1972	1965	1965	1947	1972	1989	1951	FEB 1943
NORMAL DEGREE DAYS:														
Heating (base 65°F)		1438	1210	1011	633	312	70	13	39	196	533	837	1262	7554
Cooling (base 65°F)		0	0	0	0	8	46	153	111	10	0	0	0	328
% OF POSSIBLE SUNSHINE	52	52	55	53	53	55	59	63	60	56	53	43	47	54
MEAN SKY COVER (tenths)														
Sunrise - Sunset	52	6.1	6.2	6.4	6.6	6.7	6.3	6.2	5.9	6.0	5.9	6.8	6.4	6.3
MEAN NUMBER OF DAYS:														
Sunrise to Sunset														
-Clear	52	9.2	7.6	7.8	7.0	6.1	6.1	6.7	8.0	8.6	9.2	6.3	7.8	90.5
-Partly Cloudy	52	7.1	7.6	8.0	8.0	9.9	11.8	12.5	11.5	9.1	9.0	7.6	7.9	109.8
-Cloudy	52	14.8	13.1	15.2	14.9	14.9	12.2	11.8	11.4	12.3	12.8	16.1	15.3	164.8
Precipitation														
.01 inches or more	52	10.6	9.6	10.9	11.6	11.9	10.9	10.1	9.8	8.9	9.0	11.4	10.9	125.5
Snow, Ice pellets, hail														
1.0 inches or more	52	4.5	3.8	3.1	0.6	0.*	0.0	0.0	0.0	0.0	0.*	1.3	4.0	17.3
Thunderstorms	52	0.*	0.1	0.3	0.8	2.3	4.3	5.3	3.8	1.8	0.6	0.1	0.*	19.4
Heavy Fog Visibility 1/4 mile or less	52	2.2	1.8	2.8	1.9	3.2	3.6	5.2	6.8	9.0	6.3	3.6	2.7	49.1
Temperature °F														
-Maximum														
90° and above	28	0.0	0.0	0.0	0.2	1.0	2.2	4.8	3.0	0.5	0.0	0.0	0.0	11.5
32° and below	28	17.7	13.2	4.4	0.2	0.0	0.0	0.0	0.0	0.0	0.*	1.7	13.1	50.3
-Minimum														
32° and below	28	30.4	27.3	25.8	16.9	5.2	0.2	0.0	0.1	2.3	14.1	21.5	29.1	172.9
0° and below	28	9.4	6.6	1.1	0.0	0.0	0.0	0.0	0.0	0.0	0.0	0.2	5.1	22.4
AVG. STATION PRESS. (mb)	21	1002.9	1003.4	1002.6	1001.5	1002.3	1001.6	1002.3	1004.2	1005.5	1005.6	1004.3	1003.9	1003.3
RELATIVE HUMIDITY (%)														
Hour 01	27	74	73	73	76	83	88	90	91	91	86	81	78	82
Hour 07 (Local Time)	28	75	76	77	76	77	82	84	88	91	88	84	80	82
Hour 13	28	58	55	52	47	47	52	51	53	55	53	59	61	54
Hour 19	28	66	62	59	55	58	63	65	70	76	73	73	71	66
PRECIPITATION (inches):														
Water Equivalent														
-Normal		2.51	2.53	2.72	2.91	3.14	3.15	3.23	3.32	2.81	3.23	3.66	3.16	36.37
-Maximum Monthly	52	8.09	7.77	7.81	5.88	9.52	10.10	6.53	7.26	7.78	8.78	7.36	7.52	10.10
-Year		1979	1981	1953	1983	1984	1944	1988	1991	1960	1962	1983	1973	JUN 1944
-Minimum Monthly	52	0.40	0.03	0.86	1.02	0.60	0.64	0.96	0.95	0.41	0.59	0.75	0.58	0.03
-Year		1970	1987	1981	1985	1965	1979	1955	1944	1948	1947	1976	1943	FEB 1987
-Maximum in 24 hrs	52	2.12	2.26	2.27	2.27	2.59	4.47	2.54	3.97	4.12	4.24	2.89	3.31	4.47
-Year		1979	1981	1974	1987	1984	1944	1971	1991	1960	1962	1947	1969	JUN 1944
Snow, Ice pellets, hail														
-Maximum Monthly	52	45.4	49.8	38.3	15.3	5.0	T	0.0	0.0	T	2.1	18.4	38.1	49.8
-Year		1987	1969	1956	1982	1945	1993			1992	1969	1971	1956	FEB 1969
-Maximum in 24 hrs	52	19.0	14.2	16.8	13.9	5.0	T	0.0	0.0	T	2.1	9.5	14.6	19.0
-Year		1944	1972	1993	1982	1945	1993			1992	1969	1961	1946	JAN 1944
WIND:														
Mean Speed (mph)	51	7.2	7.8	8.2	7.8	7.0	6.4	5.7	5.4	5.5	6.0	6.7	7.1	6.7
Prevailing Direction through 1963		NW	NW	NW	NW	NW	NW	NW	NW	NW	NW	NW	NW	NW
Fastest Mile														
-Direction (!!)	50	NW	N	NE	NW	NW	SW	SW	E	E	NW	NE	NW	NE
-Speed (MPH)	50	44	42	71	52	48	44	45	56	42	39	72	52	72
-Year		1972	1950	1950	1945	1945	1986	1971	1934	1960	1944	1950	1962	NOV 1950
Peak Gust														
-Direction (!!)	10	W	E	NW	NW	NW	SW	N	NW	SE	SW	NW	W	E
-Speed (mph)	10	52	60	49	48	45	59	53	45	44	44	53	58	60
-Date		1992	1988	1993	1985	1993	1986	1987	1987	1985	1990	1989	1993	FEB 1988

PRECIPITATION (inches)

CONCORD, NEW HAMPSHIRE

YEAR	JAN	FEB	MAR	APR	MAY	JUNE	JULY	AUG	SEP	OCT	NOV	DEC	ANNUAL
1964	3.64	1.93	3.01	2.05	1.15	0.81	3.37	2.74	0.42	2.24	3.47	3.07	27.90
1965	0.97	3.06	0.93	2.49	0.60	2.72	1.73	3.12	1.87	2.71	2.45	1.52	24.17
1966	2.69	2.13	2.19	1.16	2.16	1.78	2.30	4.05	5.40	3.31	3.01	2.42	32.60
1967	1.23	2.36	1.75	3.52	3.92	3.82	5.91	1.97	2.04	0.99	2.86	3.82	34.19
1968	1.79	0.93	3.80	2.85	5.20	5.90	1.62	3.60	2.34	2.23	5.24	5.82	41.32
1969	1.34	3.69	2.36	2.75	1.26	4.70	4.40	2.84	4.43	1.56	5.87	7.10	42.30
1970	0.40	4.27	2.78	3.38	3.04	2.26	2.33	3.06	3.40	3.64	3.03	3.08	34.67
1971	1.63	3.87	2.28	2.19	3.36	1.67	5.14	2.79	1.91	2.69	2.91	2.36	32.80
1972	1.44	2.60	4.16	2.71	4.20	3.54	5.40	2.12	2.55	2.23	6.57	4.55	42.07
1973	2.44	1.91	2.58	4.55	4.20	4.86	1.05	6.88	1.77	2.46	1.82	7.52	42.04
1974	2.80	2.32	3.98	2.58	3.74	1.82	1.41	2.20	4.74	1.64	3.20	4.02	34.45
1975	4.12	2.36	3.12	2.47	1.22	3.87	3.71	3.94	5.15	4.29	4.91	3.12	42.28
1976	3.40	2.36	2.02	2.43	3.90	2.74	3.20	2.66	2.73	4.05	0.75	2.27	32.51
1977	2.16	2.02	4.51	4.04	2.44	3.47	1.26	3.51	5.64	5.52	3.07	4.00	41.64
1978	6.32	0.67	2.16	2.06	2.67	3.18	1.08	2.87	0.46	2.72	1.77	2.91	28.87
1979	8.09	2.29	2.85	3.10	4.86	0.64	3.45	4.20	3.15	3.79	2.92	1.93	41.27
1980	0.43	0.78	3.37	3.72	0.86	2.83	2.35	3.99	2.19	2.63	3.12	0.79	27.06
1981	0.48	7.77	0.86	3.12	3.21	2.81	5.54	3.25	4.61	6.51	3.51	4.17	45.84
1982	3.98	2.88	2.47	3.08	1.91	7.84	2.83	2.54	1.85	1.52	2.93	0.91	34.74
1983	3.92	2.17	7.07	5.88	5.19	2.52	2.07	2.07	1.21	3.28	7.36	5.35	48.09
1984	1.89	5.06	2.92	3.74	9.52	2.83	4.44	0.97	1.08	4.42	2.67	2.70	42.24
1985	0.95	1.99	2.86	1.02	2.05	3.05	2.83	2.51	3.78	3.62	4.58	1.65	30.89
1986	4.78	2.23	3.58	1.85	1.44	4.95	4.77	3.72	2.27	1.71	4.48	4.50	40.28
1987	3.00	0.03	3.47	4.71	1.08	5.77	3.77	2.84	3.94	4.14	2.50	1.55	36.80
1988	1.97	2.24	1.32	2.75	3.35	0.80	6.53	5.44	1.56	1.23	5.06	1.05	33.30
1989	0.74	2.05	2.18	3.40	5.11	4.25	3.62	3.55	4.22	4.86	3.34	0.91	38.23
1990	2.82	2.63	1.64	3.00	5.09	2.51	1.79	7.19	2.31	4.93	3.25	4.12	41.28
1991	1.85	1.42	3.01	2.61	2.51	1.72	1.80	7.26	5.52	3.32	4.84	3.62	39.48
1992	1.97	1.30	2.77	1.78	2.39	3.28	3.50	2.13	2.48	2.41	3.54	2.23	29.78
1993	1.51	1.63	3.04	3.77	0.97	1.95	2.10	1.97	4.01	3.58	3.72	3.36	31.61
Record Mean	2.88	2.58	3.06	3.00	3.14	3.29	3.53	3.43	3.37	3.19	3.47	3.04	37.97

AVERAGE TEMPERATURE (deg. F)

CONCORD, NEW HAMPSHIRE

YEAR	JAN	FEB	MAR	APR	MAY	JUNE	JULY	AUG	SEP	OCT	NOV	DEC	ANNUAL
1964	22.9	22.4	33.6	43.6	58.8	65.6	70.8	62.7	57.4	47.4	37.1	25.1	45.6
#1965	18.9	22.2	31.9	41.3	57.1	62.5	65.9	66.6	58.8	46.8	34.8	27.3	44.5
1966	20.4	22.5	34.6	42.2	53.4	66.8	72.2	69.6	57.0	48.0	41.5	26.2	46.2
1967	24.8	17.5	27.1	42.0	48.8	66.1	70.2	67.2	58.4	49.3	32.7	27.8	44.3
1968	15.8	18.0	34.8	44.8	51.1	62.0	69.3	64.6	61.0	51.2	34.8	22.5	44.2
1969	21.9	23.2	28.3	44.3	52.3	63.0	65.4	68.9	59.7	47.5	38.9	23.7	44.8
1970	11.0	22.6	30.7	45.8	57.3	63.1	70.9	68.7	60.6	51.0	39.3	20.3	45.1
1971	12.5	23.3	30.4	42.1	54.1	65.5	68.3	67.0	61.1	51.9	32.4	26.6	44.6
1972	22.0	21.2	27.9	40.2	56.8	62.8	69.3	64.1	57.5	42.3	31.2	23.4	43.2
1973	21.0	20.2	35.5	45.0	52.9	66.9	70.3	72.3	58.8	48.2	36.1	28.9	46.3
1974	21.4	21.1	31.8	45.8	51.1	62.8	67.5	67.0	58.9	42.5	35.9	26.7	44.4
1975	21.6	21.5	30.1	40.4	61.3	65.0	72.9	66.5	56.1	47.6	39.9	21.9	45.4
1976	10.9	24.7	31.9	46.7	53.6	68.9	66.8	65.3	57.2	45.0	31.7	16.1	43.3
1977	10.6	20.5	36.7	45.1	58.3	62.9	69.0	68.0	58.5	47.0	39.4	21.0	44.8
1978	17.5	13.5	28.0	40.6	57.5	65.2	69.7	69.6	55.9	46.7	35.3	22.7	43.5
1979	23.3	15.1	37.6	44.2	56.3	63.8	71.2	67.5	59.8	47.4	42.2	29.4	46.5
1980	22.4	19.1	31.8	44.4	55.6	62.8	70.6	68.4	58.2	45.1	34.8	19.2	44.4
1981	12.5	30.8	34.2	47.1	57.5	66.1	69.9	66.6	58.7	45.2	37.8	25.4	46.0
1982	10.9	20.8	30.2	41.6	57.3	60.9	69.5	65.4	60.2	47.6	41.7	32.4	44.9
1983	23.1	26.1	35.9	45.2	53.1	65.1	70.1	69.3	62.3	48.2	39.4	23.4	46.8
1984	16.0	30.5	28.2	44.6	52.9	65.9	68.7	69.3	57.8	50.4	38.3	30.3	46.1
1985	15.9	25.8	35.7	45.2	56.1	62.2	70.3	66.7	60.5	49.2	38.5	22.0	45.7
1986	23.0	21.3	35.5	48.2	57.5	61.3	67.3	66.1	57.3	47.4	34.1	29.0	45.7
1987	20.0	22.0	34.5	46.8	56.7	64.4	70.6	65.1	58.7	45.8	36.9	28.1	45.8
1988	18.5	23.5	33.4	43.9	57.3	62.9	72.6	70.5	57.8	44.9	39.1	23.2	45.6
1989	25.7	22.6	31.8	41.4	58.3	65.0	69.5	67.7	60.8	49.1	35.8	11.9	45.0
1990	28.6	24.6	34.7	45.6	52.8	65.3	70.8	69.8	59.7	51.8	40.1	30.9	47.9
1991	20.2	28.3	36.0	47.6	60.2	65.6	69.2	69.9	57.7	50.8	39.7	25.5	47.6
1992	23.3	26.0	30.2	42.5	55.0	64.0	66.0	67.1	59.7	44.9	35.6	26.5	45.1
1993	23.5	15.7	30.5	45.7	56.9	64.9	71.4	70.0	58.8	45.3	36.4	26.8	45.5
Record Mean	21.0	22.8	32.1	44.4	56.2	64.8	69.9	67.3	59.6	48.9	37.5	25.4	45.8
Max	31.3	33.5	41.8	56.0	68.8	77.1	82.1	79.1	71.4	60.5	47.0	34.7	56.9
Min	10.7	12.0	22.4	32.8	43.5	52.5	57.8	55.6	47.8	37.2	28.1	16.1	34.7

REFERENCE NOTES

CONCORD, NEW HAMPSHIRE

GENERAL
T - TRACE AMOUNT.
BLANK ENTRIES DENOTE MISSING/UNREPORTED DATA.
# INDICATES A STATION OR INSTRUMENT RELOCATION.

SPECIFIC

PM - INCLUDES LAST DAY OF PREVIOUS MONTH
ASOS - AUTOMATED SURFACE OBSERVING SYSTEM IN OPERATION DURING THESE MONTHS.

(a) - LENGTH OF RECORD IN YEARS, ALTHOUGH INDIVIDUAL MONTHS MAY BE MISSING.
0.* OR * - THE VALUE IS BETWEEN 0.0 AND 0.05
NORMALS - BASED ON THE 1961-1990 RECORD PERIOD.
EXTREMES - DATES ARE THE MOST RECENT OCCURRENCE
WIND DIR. - NUMERALS SHOW TENS OF DEGRESS CLOCKWISE FROM TRUE NORTH. "00" INDICATES CALM.
RESULTANT DIRECTIONS ARE GIVEN TO WHOLE DEGREES.
BOLD VALUES INDICATE EXTREME VALUES WHICH OCCURRED AFTER THE ASOS SYSTEM WAS COMMISSIONED.

RECORD = PERIOD OF RECORD
RECORD MEAN PRECIPITATION IS THE MEAN OF ALL DAILY PRECIPITATION AMOUNTS DURING THE PERIOD OF RECORD.
RECORD MAX(MIN) TEMPERATURE IS THE MEAN OF ALL DAILY MAX(MIN) TEMPERATURES DURING THE PERIOD OF RECORD.
RECORD MEAN TEMPERATURE IS THE SUM OF THE RECORD MAX AND RECORD MIN DIVIDED BY 2.
AVERAGE TEMPERATURE IS THE SUM OF THE MEAN DAILY MAX AND MIN TEMPERATURE DIVIDED BY 2.

EXCEPTIONS

RECORD MEANS ARE THROUGH THE CURRENT YEAR,
BEGINNING IN 1871 FOR TEMPERATURE
1855 FOR PRECIPITATION
1942 FOR SNOWFALL

HEATING DEGREE DAYS Base 65 deg. F — CONCORD, NEW HAMPSHIRE

SEASON	JULY	AUG	SEP	OCT	NOV	DEC	JAN	FEB	MAR	APR	MAY	JUNE	TOTAL
#1964-65	8	106	246	539	831	1230	1418	1191	1015	704	257	133	7678
1965-66	50	78	227	556	899	1163	1376	1184	935	681	362	73	7584
1966-67	6	5	244	520	697	1196	1241	1323	1164	683	496	57	7632
1967-68	8	34	208	482	965	1144	1520	1358	928	598	424	118	7787
1968-69	18	92	133	424	899	1311	1330	1165	1128	613	389	119	7621
1969-70	64	40	193	534	777	1275	1668	1179	1055	572	256	108	7721
1970-71	4	25	181	431	760	1379	1622	1165	1064	682	332	73	7718
1971-72	26	49	165	396	970	1185	1327	1267	1142	736	262	112	7637
1972-73	27	82	223	695	1007	1284	1357	1250	905	596	370	78	7874
1973-74	15	9	244	518	860	1112	1345	1223	1025	573	432	99	7455
1974-75	34	26	213	694	865	1182	1339	1218	1075	730	152	98	7626
1975-76	10	78	260	532	747	1330	1672	1162	1019	565	356	60	7791
1976-77	37	84	234	615	992	1506	1683	1242	870	594	259	119	8235
1977-78	37	58	222	551	760	1360	1466	1435	1138	725	270	72	8094
1978-79	45	34	275	563	882	1304	1284	1392	841	617	280	99	7616
1979-80	33	64	199	546	675	1098	1317	1324	1022	610	290	123	7301
1980-81	13	33	245	611	899	1417	1626	953	951	530	267	40	7585
1981-82	12	43	192	608	810	1222	1674	1233	1072	695	246	136	7943
1982-83	25	66	169	535	692	1007	1291	1086	895	588	364	82	6800
1983-84	14	33	167	521	760	1283	1516	993	1135	607	382	85	7496
1984-85	19	27	238	446	792	1072	1514	1092	901	588	286	106	7081
1985-86	9	38	166	485	785	1326	1295	1216	907	499	267	140	7133
1986-87	41	67	251	538	919	1109	1390	1199	939	542	296	77	7368
1987-88	18	89	201	589	837	1138	1436	1194	971	626	254	137	7490
1988-89	19	60	219	622	769	1289	1211	1182	1022	703	219	80	7395
1989-90	6	53	169	484	865	1639	1121	1121	933	585	369	67	7412
1990-91	22	15	183	409	737	1049	1381	1024	893	517	186	58	6474
1991-92	19	7	238	438	754	1216	1286	1123	1070	669	319	90	7229
1992-93	52	33	203	617	875	1190	1277	1372	1062	574	248	85	7588
1993-94	6	15	229	600	851	1177							

COOLING DEGREE DAYS Base 65 deg. F — CONCORD, NEW HAMPSHIRE

YEAR	JAN	FEB	MAR	APR	MAY	JUNE	JULY	AUG	SEP	OCT	NOV	DEC	TOTAL
1969	0	0	0	0	4	65	82	168	44	0	0	0	363
1970	0	0	0	1	27	58	196	145	56	6	0	0	489
1971	0	0	0	0	0	95	135	118	55	0	0	0	403
1972	0	0	0	0	17	52	167	60	5	0	0	0	301
1973	0	0	0	3	2	145	184	242	67	2	0	0	645
1974	0	0	0	3	9	40	118	92	40	0	0	0	302
1975	0	0	0	0	48	108	263	134	0	0	0	0	553
1976	0	0	0	18	9	184	100	99	8	1	0	0	419
1977	0	0	0	5	57	64	168	156	38	0	0	0	488
1978	0	0	0	0	46	83	198	186	8	0	0	0	521
1979	0	0	0	1	15	69	232	150	46	6	0	0	519
1980	0	0	0	0	5	64	193	145	51	0	0	0	458
1981	0	0	0	0	38	80	172	101	11	0	0	0	402
1982	0	0	0	0	11	17	171	87	31	0	0	0	317
1983	0	0	0	0	2	93	179	172	93	5	0	0	544
1984	0	0	0	0	15	117	139	165	28	0	0	0	464
1985	0	0	0	0	16	27	184	93	36	1	0	0	357
1986	0	0	0	0	44	37	118	109	23	0	0	0	331
1987	0	0	0	1	45	64	198	96	21	0	0	0	425
1988	0	0	0	0	19	81	262	238	7	4	0	0	611
1989	0	0	0	0	17	87	153	141	50	0	0	0	448
1990	0	0	0	10	0	80	210	170	30	8	0	0	508
1991	0	0	0	2	44	84	157	166	29	4	0	0	486
1992	0	0	0	2	15	66	90	105	52	0	0	0	330
1993	0	0	0	0	7	90	212	176	49	0	0	0	534

SNOWFALL (inches) — CONCORD, NEW HAMPSHIRE

SEASON	JULY	AUG	SEP	OCT	NOV	DEC	JAN	FEB	MAR	APR	MAY	JUNE	TOTAL
1964-65	0.0	0.0	0.0	T	T	12.4	13.2	6.5	5.2	1.3	0.0	0.0	38.6
1965-66	0.0	0.0	0.0	T	1.0	4.6	32.9	17.7	3.7	T	1.1	0.0	61.0
1966-67	0.0	0.0	0.0	0.0	T	14.3	8.3	32.6	19.6	6.0	T	0.0	80.8
1967-68	0.0	0.0	0.0	0.0	15.0	15.0	15.8	6.7	7.4	0.0	0.0	0.0	59.9
1968-69	0.0	0.0	0.0	0.0	11.6	13.4	4.7	49.8	5.7	T	0.0	0.0	85.2
1969-70	0.0	0.0	0.0	2.1	T	20.7	5.0	13.8	14.2	2.8	0.0	0.0	58.6
1970-71	0.0	0.0	0.0	0.0	T	30.1	15.6	19.8	24.0	6.3	0.0	0.0	95.8
1971-72	0.0	0.0	0.0	0.0	18.4	17.4	10.8	29.8	13.6	10.0	0.0	0.0	100.0
1972-73	0.0	0.0	0.0	0.0	12.9	23.2	13.1	5.6	0.1	3.4	0.0	0.0	58.3
1973-74	0.0	0.0	0.0	0.0	T	6.6	15.4	7.0	6.5	3.9	0.0	0.0	39.4
1974-75	0.0	0.0	0.0	0.0	2.9	18.3	19.5	17.1	4.7	5.5	0.0	0.0	68.0
1975-76	0.0	0.0	0.0	0.0	2.2	25.1	14.7	8.4	24.3	T	0.0	0.0	74.7
1976-77	0.0	0.0	0.0	T	3.1	11.6	37.1	11.7	22.3	0.5	T	0.0	86.3
1977-78	0.0	0.0	0.0	0.0	1.5	20.2	37.1	13.5	11.5	0.4	T	0.0	84.2
1978-79	0.0	0.0	0.0	0.0	10.5	16.2	42.3	4.5	0.2	5.1	0.0	0.0	78.8
1979-80	0.0	0.0	0.0	1.3	T	2.1	3.1	11.9	8.6	T	0.0	0.0	27.0
1980-81	0.0	0.0	0.0	T	9.4	9.8	9.2	20.9	5.4	T	0.0	0.0	54.7
1981-82	0.0	0.0	0.0	0.0	T	33.0	26.2	9.0	6.5	15.3	0.0	0.0	90.0
1982-83	0.0	0.0	0.0	0.0	1.3	3.6	9.0	20.8	4.0	T	T	0.0	38.7
1983-84	0.0	0.0	0.0	0.0	T	17.5	20.4	12.7	25.0	T	T	0.0	75.6
1984-85	0.0	0.0	0.0	0.0	T	16.5	11.6	11.0	12.4	1.0	0.0	0.0	52.5
1985-86	0.0	0.0	0.0	0.0	8.3	11.2	15.1	11.5	4.4	T	T	0.0	50.5
1986-87	0.0	0.0	0.0	0.0	14.4	7.7	45.4	0.6	7.0	9.4	0.0	0.0	84.5
1987-88	0.0	0.0	0.0	0.0	5.8	12.0	19.3	23.7	4.6	0.1	0.0	0.0	65.5
1988-89	0.0	0.0	0.0	T	0.5	5.0	5.6	7.0	10.2	0.8	T	0.0	29.1
1989-90	0.0	0.0	0.0	0.0	4.7	12.0	23.1	22.0	1.3	T	0.0	0.0	63.1
1990-91	0.0	0.0	0.0	0.0	0.6	8.8	11.2	6.8	6.0	0.2	0.0	0.0	33.6
1991-92	0.0	0.0	0.0	0.0	1.3	13.5	3.8	5.3	6.8	4.5	0.0	0.0	35.2
1992-93	0.0	0.0	T	T	1.1	10.9	19.7	24.0	35.8	6.6	0.0	T	98.1
1993-94	0.0	0.0	0.0	T	0.2	10.0							
Record Mean	0.0	0.0	T	0.1	3.8	13.6	17.7	14.6	10.9	2.4	0.1	T	63.2

ATLANTIC CITY, NEW JERSEY
STATE MARINA

The Atlantic City State Marina is located on Abescon Island on the southeast coast of New Jersey. Surrounding terrain, composed of tidal marshes and beach sand, is flat and lies slightly above sea level. The climate is principally continental in character. However, the moderating influence of the Atlantic Ocean is apparent throughout the year, being more marked in the city than at the airport. As a result, summers are relatively cooler and winters milder than elsewhere at the same latitude.

Land and sea breezes, local circulations resulting from the differential heating and cooling of the land and sea, often prevail. These winds occur when moderate or intense storms are not present in the area, thus enabling the local circulation to overcome the general wind pattern. During the warm season sea breezes in the late morning and afternoon hours prevent excessive heating. Frequently, the temperature at Atlantic City during the afternoon hours in the summer averages several degrees lower than at the airport and the airport averages several degrees lower than localities farther inland. On occasions, sea breezes have lowered the temperature as much as 15 to 20 degrees within a half hour. However, the major effect of the sea breeze at the airport is preventing the temperature from rising above the 80s. Because the change in ocean temperature lags behind the air temperature from season to season, the weather tends to remain comparatively mild late into the fall, but on the other hand, warming is retarded in the spring. Normal ocean temperatures range from an average near 37 degrees in January to near 72 degrees in August.

Precipitation is moderate and well distributed throughout the year, with June the driest month and August the wettest. Tropical storms or hurricanes occasionally bring excessive rainfall to the area. The bulk of winter precipitation results from storms which move northeastward along or near the east coast of the United States. Snowfall is considerably less than elsewhere at the same latitude and does not remain long on the ground. Precipitation, often beginning as snow, will frequently become mixed with or change to rain while continuing as snow over more interior sections. In addition, ice storms and resultant glaze are relatively infrequent.

NORMALS, MEANS, AND EXTREMES

ATLANTIC CITY, NEW JERSEY STATE MARINA

LATITUDE: 39°23'N LONGITUDE: 74°26' W ELEVATION: FT. GRND 11 BARO TIME ZONE: EASTERN WBAN: 13724

	(a)	JAN	FEB	MAR	APR	MAY	JUNE	JULY	AUG	SEP	OCT	NOV	DEC	YEAR
TEMPERATURE °F:														
Normals														
-Daily Maximum														
-Daily Minimum														
-Monthly														
Extremes														
-Record Highest	33	70	72	76	91	94	97	100	102	92	88	78	72	102
-Year		1967	1976	1991	1960	1969	1991	1983	1983	1985	1986	1993	1984	AUG 1983
-Record Lowest	33	-2	1	2	22	36	45	53	50	42	27	19	4	-2
-Year		1985	1961	1991	1982	1966	1972	1988	1986	1974	1974	1987	1983	JAN 1985
NORMAL DEGREE DAYS:														
Heating (base 65°F)														
Cooling (base 65°F)														
% OF POSSIBLE SUNSHINE														
MEAN SKY COVER (tenths)														
Sunrise - Sunset														
MEAN NUMBER OF DAYS:														
Sunrise to Sunset														
-Clear														
-Partly Cloudy														
-Cloudy														
Precipitation														
.01 inches or more	32	10.2	9.5	10.5	10.0	9.9	8.7	8.6	8.5	7.8	7.5	9.1	10.2	110.5
Snow,Ice pellets,hail														
1.0 inches or more														
Thunderstorms														
Heavy Fog Visibility														
1/4 mile or less														
Temperature °F														
-Maximum														
90° and above	32	0.0	0.0	0.0	0.1	0.3	0.8	2.2	1.3	0.3	0.0	0.0	0.0	4.9
32° and below	32	6.8	3.9	0.6	0.0	0.0	0.0	0.0	0.0	0.0	0.0	0.1	2.3	13.6
-Minimum														
32° and below	32	21.9	18.3	10.2	1.3	0.0	0.0	0.0	0.0	0.0	0.3	4.2	15.6	71.6
0° and below	32	0.*	0.0	0.0	0.0	0.0	0.0	0.0	0.0	0.0	0.0	0.0	0.0	*
AVG. STATION PRESS.(mb)														
RELATIVE HUMIDITY (%)														
Hour 01														
Hour 07 (Local Time)														
Hour 13														
Hour 19														
PRECIPITATION (inches):														
Water Equivalent														
-Normal														
-Maximum Monthly	33	8.40	6.29	8.20	6.68	6.01	7.28	15.69	14.77	5.55	5.47	7.57	6.56	15.69
-Year		1987	1979	1993	1987	1984	1973	1959	1967	1964	1959	1972	1969	JUL 1959
-Minimum Monthly	33	0.35	0.79	0.68	0.82	0.28	0.61	0.57	0.93	0.39	0.02	0.82	0.71	0.02
-Year		1981	1980	1966	1976	1986	1971	1981	1964	1959	1963	1965	1985	OCT 1963
-Maximum in 24 hrs	33	3.40	2.40	3.30	2.73	3.13	4.10	6.62	8.60	2.54	2.67	3.90	3.32	8.60
-Year		1962	1966	1993	1991	1978	1968	1969	1967	1971	1972	1977	1993	AUG 1967
Snow,Ice pellets,hail														
-Maximum Monthly		0.0	0.0	0.0	0.0	0.0	0.0	0.0	0.0	0.0	0.0	0.0	0.0	
-Year														
-Maximum in 24 hrs														
-Year														
WIND:														
Mean Speed (mph)														
Prevailing Direction														
Fastest Mile														
-Direction (!!!)	28	W		W	SSW	SW	NW	W	SE	NNW	SE	E	ENE	SE
-Speed (MPH)	28	60	59	54	53	46	49	48	63	63	48	62	58	63
-Year		1966	1972	1964	1970	1974	1972	1965	1971	1961	1965	1968	1974	AUG 1971
Peak Gust														
-Direction (!!!)	6	SSW	WNW	ENE	NE	NE	SW	SE	ENE	WSW	SE	NW	E	ENE
-Speed (mph)	6	58	60	87	63	52	64	52	67	78	77	55	67	87
-Date		1992	1985	1984	1987	1985	1986	1984	1986	1985	1991	1987	1992	MAR 1984

PRECIPITATION (inches)

ATLANTIC CITY, NEW JERSEY STATE MARINA

YEAR	JAN	FEB	MAR	APR	MAY	JUNE	JULY	AUG	SEP	OCT	NOV	DEC	ANNUAL
1964	5.84	4.04	2.65	6.62	1.30	1.21	1.37	0.93	5.55	2.35	1.21	2.62	35.69
1965	3.48	1.99	3.28	2.30	2.39	1.87	4.92	5.50	1.57	0.61	0.82	1.32	30.05
1966	3.12	4.84	0.68	2.58	4.62	2.22	2.70	4.11	4.35	2.81	1.44	4.58	38.05
1967	0.87	2.98	2.82	2.78	3.33	1.33	2.62	14.77	2.01	2.64	1.09	4.93	42.17
1968	2.09	1.41	4.05	1.13	5.04	6.24	1.26	1.07	2.17	2.36	3.08	3.85	33.75
1969	2.24	2.92	2.63	3.76	1.43	1.64	11.11	4.15	2.46	0.51	4.56	6.55	43.96
1970	1.54	3.39	3.26	4.77	2.46	4.60	3.72	1.24	0.47	3.35	4.37	2.30	35.47
1971	2.89	4.31	1.84	1.35	2.14	0.61	4.20	10.37	5.47	3.60	4.29	2.85	43.92
1972	3.25	3.76	3.87	3.97	5.10	5.21	3.73	1.46	4.35	4.43	7.57	4.98	51.68
1973	2.87	3.51	2.64	4.03	2.83	7.28	3.21	1.06	2.96	1.80	1.33	5.23	38.75
1974	2.78	2.35	4.33	1.75	2.44	2.01	2.57	6.31	2.56	1.59	1.00	3.31	33.00
1975	4.29	3.08	3.39	3.94	2.73	3.72	5.63	2.05	3.82	1.74	2.93	2.57	39.89
1976	3.66	2.98	0.91	0.82	2.19	1.59	1.74	5.01	3.08	4.94	0.95	2.42	30.29
1977	2.48	2.10	2.30	1.89	0.90	1.78	2.17	4.10	1.81	3.05	6.77	5.12	34.47
1978	5.59	1.11	3.82	1.33	6.00	2.07	4.20	4.01	0.87	1.35	2.48	3.95	36.78
1979	6.96	6.29	3.28	4.00	3.55	3.12	2.21	5.93	3.68	2.07	3.80	1.56	46.45
1980	2.97	0.79	6.39	4.38	1.47	2.73	2.25	1.41	2.08	3.63	3.11	1.13	32.34
1981	0.35	4.08	1.98	4.96	2.16	2.49	0.57	3.75	2.09	2.98	1.28	3.83	30.52
1982	2.81	2.03	2.48	3.98	2.24	2.88	4.14	2.08	1.16	1.11	4.05	3.04	32.00
1983	2.22	2.82	5.63	5.17	3.75	2.50	0.71	2.43	1.88	3.41	6.64	3.47	40.63
1984	2.38	4.32	6.50	4.46	6.01	1.44	4.24	1.03	2.08	1.53	2.28	1.53	37.80
1985	2.04	1.73	2.58	0.97	5.01	2.39	3.37	3.43	2.07	1.08	2.16	0.71	27.54
1986	2.46	2.83	1.46	2.79	0.28			6.11	1.88	3.55	4.19	5.01	
1987	8.40	1.55	4.10	6.68	3.84	0.71	3.11	2.91	3.27	2.81	2.41	1.99	41.78
1988	3.07	3.74	2.00	2.37	3.28	1.55	2.95	3.73	2.22				24.91
1990						1.65	4.06	3.70	1.44	1.98	1.95	3.67	
1991	5.81	1.36	4.90	5.41	0.34	0.81	2.59	4.86	2.86	2.70	1.38	4.29	37.31
1992	1.20	2.40	2.97	1.43	2.81	1.75	5.89	5.11	5.01	1.42	3.25	4.25	37.49
1993	2.75	2.39	8.20	1.96	2.24	1.17	1.89	4.53	1.24	3.81	1.29	5.21	36.68
Record Mean	3.23	3.05	3.64	3.24	2.90	2.45	3.94	4.12	2.68	2.64	3.05	3.36	38.30

AVERAGE TEMPERATURE (deg. F)

ATLANTIC CITY, NEW JERSEY STATE MARINA

YEAR	JAN	FEB	MAR	APR	MAY	JUNE	JULY	AUG	SEP	OCT	NOV	DEC	ANNUAL
1964	36.6	34.6	42.6	48.9	61.9	69.7	73.6	72.4	69.2	56.3	50.6	39.4	54.7
1965	31.8	34.4	39.6	48.3	62.8	68.0	73.0	73.3	59.0	55.8	47.2	39.5	53.6
1966	31.8	34.3	42.6	48.2	58.3	68.4	76.6	73.8	67.1	56.4	49.3	37.7	53.7
1967	38.9	32.5	39.1	51.2	55.4	68.6	75.3	73.5	66.0	58.3	45.2	40.6	53.7
1968	32.0	32.5	44.8	52.6	60.2	70.6	76.5	76.2	71.0	60.2	48.4	35.6	55.1
1969	32.4	33.6	38.6	52.8	61.4	70.8	75.2	75.4	69.3	58.6	47.8	37.9	54.5
1970	29.5	36.7	41.0	51.1	61.4	69.3	72.5	74.9	68.3	58.5	48.3	38.2	54.1
1971	31.5	38.1	40.9	48.7	56.9	67.9	71.9	71.0	67.9	60.0	46.2	44.9	53.8
1972	38.6	36.6	40.4	48.3	58.1	64.5	73.1	72.0	67.5	54.3	46.4	43.6	53.6
1973	39.0	38.4	48.4	54.0	57.2	68.8	73.7	75.1	69.8	60.4	48.9	40.8	56.2
1974	39.1	34.1	43.6	52.5	59.8	67.5	75.6	73.4	65.8	53.3	47.4	39.5	54.3
1975	37.4	36.0	39.4	45.9	61.3	68.8	73.5	74.9	64.7	59.3	50.8	38.5	54.2
1976	32.7	42.0	45.0	53.4	58.0	69.1	71.8	71.4	65.9	53.1	41.6	34.5	53.2
1977	24.4	35.6	45.7	52.2	60.9	67.1	75.3	76.1	71.1	56.6	48.9	36.9	54.2
1978	31.2	27.9	39.8	49.6	55.3	65.8	70.6	74.4	65.0	55.2	48.2	39.3	51.9
1979	33.1	27.4	43.3	50.5	59.3	66.6	72.8	73.1	67.5	56.2	51.4	41.9	53.6
1980	35.5	32.7	40.7	52.2	62.3	67.0	72.9	75.1	69.4	55.6		36.7	
1981	29.9	39.1	41.4	53.2	60.7	71.4	77.5	74.7	67.3	54.6	46.9	37.9	54.5
1982	29.1	35.8	42.2	48.7	60.2	66.1	72.8	69.6	66.0	56.3	48.8	40.7	53.0
1983	34.7	39.0	46.0	51.3	59.0	67.5	76.0	74.6	68.7	57.6	48.3	35.4	54.9
1984	30.4	41.3	39.6	51.1	60.7	72.8	73.4	77.4	67.4	62.8	47.6	47.2	56.0
1985	30.6	36.9	46.4	54.1	62.0	68.4	75.0	74.4	70.4	61.7	54.4	36.4	55.9
1986	35.5	34.0	43.6	51.5	62.4	69.4	77.0	73.3	68.3	59.8	48.4	41.1	55.4
1987	35.1	34.8	44.1	49.8		70.4	76.3	74.5	69.0	54.4	49.4	40.6	55.1
1988	30.5	35.2	43.0	49.4	59.4	68.4	73.6	73.8	66.2				55.5
1990						69.9	75.0	75.4	67.9	62.2	50.1	44.0	
1991	37.5	40.9	44.9	53.0	66.0	71.8	76.4	76.7	68.3	59.1	48.6	41.5	57.1
1992	36.9	37.9	41.0	48.7	56.8	66.7	74.9	72.6	67.8	55.7	48.7	40.3	54.0
1993	39.8	32.9	39.2	49.2	61.4	69.6	78.1	75.1	68.8	57.9	49.3	38.4	55.0
Record Mean	33.7	35.3	42.0	50.7	59.7	68.5	74.3	74.1	67.9	57.7	48.4	38.7	54.3
Max	40.0	41.7	48.3	57.2	65.8	74.6	80.2	79.8	73.8	64.3	54.9	45.3	60.5
Min	27.3	28.8	35.6	44.1	53.6	62.4	68.5	68.3	61.9	51.1	41.8	32.1	48.0

REFERENCE NOTES

ATLANTIC CITY, NEW JERSEY STATE MARINA

GENERAL
T - TRACE AMOUNT.
BLANK ENTRIES DENOTE MISSING/UNREPORTED DATA.
# INDICATES A STATION OR INSTRUMENT RELOCATION.

SPECIFIC

PM - INCLUDES LAST DAY OF PREVIOUS MONTH
ASOS - AUTOMATED SURFACE OBSERVING SYSTEM IN OPERATION DURING THESE MONTHS.

(a) - LENGTH OF RECORD IN YEARS, ALTHOUGH INDIVIDUAL MONTHS MAY BE MISSING.
0.* OR * - THE VALUE IS BETWEEN 0.0 AND 0.05
NORMALS - BASED ON THE 1961-1990 RECORD PERIOD.
EXTREMES - DATES ARE THE MOST RECENT OCCURRENCE
WIND DIR.- NUMERALS SHOW TENS OF DEGRESS CLOCKWISE FROM TRUE NORTH. "00" INDICATES CALM.
RESULTANT DIRECTIONS ARE GIVEN TO WHOLE DEGREES.
BOLD VALUES INDICATE EXTREME VALUES WHICH OCCURRED AFTER THE ASOS SYSTEM WAS COMMISSIONED.

RECORD = PERIOD OF RECORD
RECORD MEAN PRECIPITATION IS THE MEAN OF ALL DAILY PRECIPITATION AMOUNTS DURING THE PERIOD OF RECORD.
RECORD MAX(MIN) TEMPERATURE IS THE MEAN OF ALL DAILY MAX(MIN) TEMPERATURES DURING THE PERIOD OF RECORD.
RECORD MEAN TEMPERATURE IS THE SUM OF THE RECORD MAX AND RECORD MIN DIVIDED BY 2.
AVERAGE TEMPERATURE IS THE SUM OF THE MEAN DAILY MAX AND MIN TEMPERATURE DIVIDED BY 2.

EXCEPTIONS

WINDS ARE FASTEST OBSERVED 1-MINUTE WINDS WITH DIRECTIONS IN COMPASS POINTS.

RECORD MEANS ARE THROUGH THE CURRENT YEAR, BEGINNING IN 1959 FOR TEMPERATURE
1959 FOR PRECIPITATION
1959 FOR SNOWFALL

FOR REPRESENTITIVE SNOWFALL DATA FOR THE ATLANTIC CITY AREA, CONSULT THE ANNUAL ISSUE OF THE ATLANTIC CITY AIRPORT OFFICE, ATLANTIC CITY NEW JERSEY, N.A.F.E.C.

HEATING DEGREE DAYS Base 65 deg. F ATLANTIC CITY, NEW JERSEY STATE MARINA

SEASON	JULY	AUG	SEP	OCT	NOV	DEC	JAN	FEB	MAR	APR	MAY	JUNE	TOTAL
1964-65	0	0	17	272	426	785	1022	851	778	492	126	38	4807
1965-66	0	8	23	284	528	783	1023	854	688	498	217	26	4932
1966-67	0	0	47	263	463	835	800	903	796	405	293	8	4813
1967-68	0	0	49	226	591	751	1016	937	618	371	156	1	4716
1968-69	0	0	1	180	490	903	1005	872	810	358	141	2	4762
1969-70	0	0	25	222	509	833	1093	789	736	411	142	3	4763
1970-71	0	0	33	204	493	823	1029	749	738	480	246	30	4825
1971-72	0	2	27	158	560	615	812	818	755	494	209	47	4497
1972-73	2	0	23	328	553	658	796	738	508	330	245	9	4190
1973-74	0	0	16	163	476	742	798	860	655	379	173	24	4286
1974-75	0	0	57	358	524	784	848	805	786	567	151	11	4891
1975-76	0	0	49	188	422	814	994	664	612	356	212	29	4340
1976-77	0	3	38	366	696	936	1253	816	590	384	154	36	5272
1977-78	0	0	11	267	477	862	1043	1031	776	455	302	41	5265
1978-79	6	0	62	297	497	791	979	1045	666	427	173	22	4965
1979-80	5	3	27	275	404	708	906	931	746	376	115	43	4539
1980-81	0	0	19	288		871	1080	720	723	350	160	3	
1981-82	0	0	51	315	538	834	1106	813	698	482	155	39	5031
1982-83	1	10	36	280	486	749	931	722	584	405	179	17	4400
1983-84	1	9	63	236	496	911	1065	681	781	406	139	5	4793
1984-85	0	0	56	96	514	543	1059	783	571	336	119	16	4093
1985-86	0	0	19	132	313	876	910	860	654	399	144	15	4322
1986-87	0	9	20	201	491	735	922	842	641	452		3	
1987-88	0	0	14	324	460	747	1062	859	675	465	200	51	4857
1988-89	1	2	40										
1989-90												13	
1990-91	0	0	42	154	437	646	847	668	616	357	79	8	3854
1991-92	0	0	36	205	484	722	865	780	738	484	267	23	4604
1992-93	0	0	37	292	482	759	776	890	792	467	136	19	4650
1993-94	0	0	33	214	469	819							

COOLING DEGREE DAYS Base 65 deg. F ATLANTIC CITY, NEW JERSEY STATE MARINA

YEAR	JAN	FEB	MAR	APR	MAY	JUNE	JULY	AUG	SEP	OCT	NOV	DEC	TOTAL
1969	0	0	0	0	38	181	322	327	160	32	0	0	1060
1970	0	0	0	0	37	138	240	315	141	11	0	0	882
1971	0	0	0	0	2	122	219	194	336	7	2	0	882
1972	0	0	0	0	0	39	258	224	103	2	0	0	626
1973	0	0	0	3	9	233	278	319	168	29	0	0	1039
1974	0	0	0	10	18	125	334	266	91	0	1	0	845
1975	0	0	0	0	42	131	269	313	50	16	0	0	821
1976	0	0	0	14	2	160	219	210	69	2	0	0	676
1977	0	0	0	6	37	105	324	355	200	10	0	0	1037
1978	0	0	0	0	9	72	186	297	69	0	0	0	633
1979	0	0	0	0	5	74	252	263	111	8	0	0	713
1980	0	0	0	0	39	109	250	319	159	2		0	
1981	0	0	0	3	33	200	392	305	125	1	0	0	1059
1982	0	0	0	0	13	77	247	160	70	20	3	0	590
1983	0	0	0	2	0	96	349	313	181	14	0	0	955
1984	0	0	0	0	12	246	269	393	135	36	0	0	1091
1985	0	0	2	12	34	124	315	298	188	35	0	0	1008
1986	0	0	0	0	70	154	378	274	126	47	0	0	1049
1987	0	0	0	0		173	357	299	142	0	0	0	1042
1988	0	0	0	0	34	160	275	280	83				832
1990						166	318	330	136	74	1	0	
1991	0	0	0	3	116	219	359	370	143	30	0	0	1240
1992	0	0	0	0	21	83	315	243	126	8	0	0	796
1993	0	0	0	0	30	164	415	319	155	2	4	0	1089

SNOWFALL (inches) ATLANTIC CITY, NEW JERSEY STATE MARINA

SEASON	JULY	AUG	SEP	OCT	NOV	DEC	JAN	FEB	MAR	APR	MAY	JUNE	TOTAL
Record Mean													

NEWARK, NEW JERSEY

Terrain in vicinity of the station is flat and rather marshy. To the northwest are ridges oriented roughly in a south-southwest to north-northeast direction. They rise to an elevation of about 200 feet at 4.5 to 5 miles and to 500 to 600 feet at 7 to 8 miles. All winds between west-northwest and north-northwest are downslope and therefore are subject to some adiabatic temperature increase. This effect is evident in the rapid improvement which normally occurs with shift of wind to westerly, following a coastal storm or frontal passage. The drying effect of the downslope winds accounts for the relatively few local thunderstorms occurring at the station, compared to areas to the west. Easterly winds, particularly southeasterly, moderate the temperature because of the influence of the Atlantic Ocean.

Temperature falls of 5 to 15 degrees, depending on the season, are not uncommon when the wind backs from southwesterly to southeasterly. Periods of very hot weather, lasting as long as a week, are associated with a west-southwest air flow which has a long trajectory over land. Extremes of cold are related to rapidly moving outbreaks of cold air traveling southeastward from the Hudson Bay region. Temperatures of zero or below occur in one winter out of four, but are much more common several miles to the west of the station. Average dates of the last occurrence in spring and the first occurrence in autumn of temperatures as low as 32 degrees are in mid-April and the end of October or early November. Areas to the west of the station experience a growing season at least a month shorter than that at the airport.

A considerable amount of precipitation is realized from the Northeasters of the Atlantic coast. These storms, more typical of the fall and winter, generally last for a period of two days and commonly produce between 1 and 2 inches of precipitation. Storms producing 4 inches or more of snow occur from two to five times a winter. Snowstorms producing 8 inches or more have occurred in about one-half the winters. As many as three such storms have been experienced in one winter. The frequency and intensity of snow storms and the duration of snow cover increase dramatically within a few miles to the west of the station.

NORMALS, MEANS, AND EXTREMES

NEWARK, NEW JERSEY

LATITUDE: 40°42'N LONGITUDE: 74°10' W ELEVATION: FT. GRND 7 BARO 29 TIME ZONE: EASTERN WBAN: 14734

	(a)	JAN	FEB	MAR	APR	MAY	JUNE	JULY	AUG	SEP	OCT	NOV	DEC	YEAR
TEMPERATURE °F:														
Normals														
-Daily Maximum		37.7	40.5	50.8	61.9	72.4	82.3	87.0	85.4	77.6	66.7	55.4	42.9	63.4
-Daily Minimum		23.4	25.4	33.4	42.7	53.2	62.8	68.6	67.4	59.9	48.2	39.2	29.1	46.1
-Monthly		30.6	33.0	42.1	52.3	62.8	72.6	77.8	76.4	68.8	57.5	47.3	36.0	54.8
Extremes														
-Record Highest	52	74	76	89	94	98	102	105	103	105	92	85	72	105
-Year		1950	1949	1945	1990	1992	1993	1993	1948	1953	1949	1950	1982	JUL 1993
-Record Lowest	52	-8	-7	6	16	33	43	52	45	35	28	15	-1	-8
-Year		1985	1943	1943	1982	1947	1945	1945	1982	1947	1969	1955	1980	JAN 1985
NORMAL DEGREE DAYS:														
Heating (base 65°F)		1066	896	710	381	127	0	0	0	26	252	531	899	4888
Cooling (base 65°F)		0	0	0	0	59	232	397	353	140	20	0	0	1201
% OF POSSIBLE SUNSHINE														
MEAN SKY COVER (tenths)														
Sunrise - Sunset	47	6.5	6.3	6.3	6.4	6.5	6.1	6.2	6.0	5.7	5.5	6.4	6.5	6.2
MEAN NUMBER OF DAYS:														
Sunrise to Sunset														
-Clear	51	7.8	7.4	8.0	7.2	6.3	6.8	6.6	7.7	9.5	10.8	7.5	7.9	93.5
-Partly Cloudy	51	7.8	7.5	8.5	8.8	10.8	11.0	12.2	11.7	8.9	8.4	8.3	8.0	111.7
-Cloudy	51	15.5	13.4	14.6	14.0	13.9	12.2	12.2	11.7	11.5	11.8	14.2	15.1	160.0
Precipitation .01 inches or more	52	10.8	9.6	11.3	11.1	11.7	10.3	10.1	9.5	8.5	7.9	10.0	10.9	121.6
Snow, Ice pellets, hail 1.0 inches or more	52	2.1	1.9	1.3	0.2	0.0	0.0	0.0	0.0	0.0	0.0	0.2	1.4	7.0
Thunderstorms	52	0.3	0.2	1.0	1.5	3.6	4.8	6.0	4.7	2.3	1.1	0.5	0.2	26.1
Heavy Fog Visibility 1/4 mile or less	52	2.1	1.7	1.5	1.1	1.7	1.2	0.4	0.5	0.8	1.9	1.8	1.8	16.4
Temperature °F														
-Maximum														
90° and above	28	0.0	0.0	0.0	0.2	1.5	4.8	9.3	7.0	1.6	0.0	0.0	0.0	24.3
32° and below	28	9.3	5.4	0.9	0.*	0.0	0.0	0.0	0.0	0.0	0.0	0.1	3.9	19.5
-Minimum														
32° and below	28	23.7	20.9	12.7	1.5	0.0	0.0	0.0	0.0	0.0	0.5	5.7	18.9	84.0
0° and below	28	0.5	0.2	0.0	0.0	0.0	0.0	0.0	0.0	0.0	0.0	0.0	0.1	0.7
AVG. STATION PRESS. (mb)	20	1017.0	1016.9	1015.9	1013.8	1014.4	1014.0	1014.4	1016.0	1017.6	1018.1	1017.9	1018.0	1016.2
RELATIVE HUMIDITY (%)														
Hour 01	28	70	68	66	66	72	73	73	76	78	76	72	72	72
Hour 07 (Local Time)	28	74	72	70	66	70	70	72	75	78	78	77	74	73
Hour 13	28	58	54	51	48	51	51	51	53	55	53	56	59	53
Hour 19	28	63	60	57	54	59	58	59	62	65	64	64	64	61
PRECIPITATION (inches):														
Water Equivalent														
-Normal		3.39	3.04	3.87	3.84	4.13	3.22	4.50	3.91	3.66	3.05	3.91	3.45	43.97
-Maximum Monthly	52	10.10	4.94	11.14	11.14	10.22	6.40	9.98	11.84	10.28	8.20	11.53	9.47	11.84
-Year		1979	1979	1983	1983	1984	1975	1988	1955	1944	1943	1977	1983	AUG 1955
-Minimum Monthly	52	0.45	1.22	1.10	0.90	0.52	0.07	0.89	0.50	0.95	0.21	0.51	0.27	0.07
-Year		1981	1968	1981	1963	1964	1949	1966	1964	1951	1963	1976	1955	JUN 1949
-Maximum in 24 hrs	40	3.59	2.45	2.83	3.73	4.22	2.97	3.63	7.84	5.27	3.04	7.22	2.77	7.84
-Year		1979	1961	1991	1984	1979	1992	1988	1971	1971	1973	1977	1983	AUG 1971
Snow, Ice pellets, hail														
-Maximum Monthly	52	27.4	26.1	26.0	13.8	T	0.0	0.0	0.0	0.0	0.3	5.7	29.1	29.1
-Year		1978	1979	1956	1982	1977					1952	1989	1947	DEC 1947
-Maximum in 24 hrs	52	17.8	20.0	17.6	12.8	T	0.0	0.0	0.0	0.0	0.3	5.7	26.0	26.0
-Year		1978	1961	1956	1982	1977					1952	1989	1947	DEC 1947
WIND:														
Mean Speed (mph)	49	11.2	11.5	11.9	11.2	10.0	9.5	8.9	8.7	9.0	9.4	10.2	10.8	10.2
Prevailing Direction through 1963		NE	NW	NW	WNW	SW	SW	SW	SW	SW	SW	SW	SW	SW
Fastest Obs. 1 Min.														
-Direction (!!!)	45	30	23	27	27	32	26	35	09	05	11	09	32	09
-Speed (MPH)	45	52	46	43	50	50	58	52	46	51	48	82	55	82
-Year		1964	1965	1950	1951	1963	1984	1988	1955	1960	1954	1950	1962	NOV 1950
Peak Gust														
-Direction (!!!)	10	SW	NW	NE	NW	NW	W	NW	N	W	SW	NW	NW	W
-Speed (mph)	10	54	58	62	55	58	83	69	68	67	53	63	60	83
-Date		1992	1984	1993	1993	1988	1984	1988	1985	1985	1990	1989	1988	JUN 1984

PRECIPITATION (inches)

NEWARK, NEW JERSEY

YEAR	JAN	FEB	MAR	APR	MAY	JUNE	JULY	AUG	SEP	OCT	NOV	DEC	ANNUAL
1964	5.12	2.59	2.27	5.56	0.52	3.09	4.74	0.50	1.30	1.55	2.08	4.10	33.42
1965	2.86	2.91	2.81	2.60	1.23	1.23	1.73	2.87	2.20	2.31	1.48	1.86	26.09
1966	2.29	4.41	1.12	3.01	4.86	0.49	0.89	3.08	7.86	3.78	3.06	3.01	37.86
1967	1.15	3.00	5.86	2.84	3.57	3.31	7.53	5.53	1.35	2.87	2.35	4.65	44.01
1968	1.71	1.22	3.59	2.24	6.28	4.37	1.87	2.41	2.48	2.02	4.38	4.32	36.89
1969	1.47	2.68	3.53	3.51	2.73	2.53	7.11	2.24	6.63	1.75	2.80	4.97	41.95
1970	0.87	3.29	3.42	3.52	2.64	2.41	3.68	3.91	1.83	2.36	4.41	2.05	34.39
1971	2.74	4.44	3.29	1.35	3.65	1.48	6.98	10.63	7.88	2.96	3.86	1.51	50.77
1972	2.26	4.01	3.09	3.08	6.02	6.02	4.70	2.30	1.03	4.83	8.42	4.10	49.86
1973	3.65	3.39	3.63	5.77	3.56	4.03	3.63	3.36	3.39	3.35	1.29	7.24	46.29
1974	2.84	1.44	4.11	2.37	3.49	3.60	1.31	7.17	5.76	1.85	0.80	4.02	38.76
1975	3.99	2.56	2.94	2.29	3.27	6.40	8.02	4.36	9.00	3.24	3.67	2.91	52.65
1976	5.04	2.52	2.33	2.50	4.12	1.54	3.91	2.98	2.50	5.07	0.51	2.17	35.19
1977	1.55	2.77	5.67	3.16	1.31	3.89	1.51	4.29	3.99	3.53	11.53	4.77	47.97
1978	7.76	2.26	4.58	2.60	7.97	2.05	4.99	7.30	4.23	1.64	2.66	5.37	53.41
1979	10.10	4.94	3.65	3.66	7.78	2.73	3.39	4.38	5.72	4.58	3.09	2.08	56.10
1980	1.66	1.28	9.13	7.28	2.61	3.27	2.78	0.92	1.87	3.37	3.71	0.63	38.51
1981	0.45	4.81	1.10	3.15	3.88	2.61	4.51	0.57	3.42	3.47	1.75	5.32	35.04
1982	6.77	2.36	2.82	6.20	2.96	5.28	2.86	2.78	2.39	1.68	3.16	1.32	40.58
1983	4.37	3.03	11.14	11.14	4.22	2.81	1.59	3.46	2.93	5.80	5.54	9.47	65.50
1984	2.78	4.57	6.96	6.36	10.22	4.77	8.65	1.74	2.46	3.93	2.88	3.69	59.01
1985	1.22	2.58	1.59	1.17	4.23	4.29	4.52	2.58	4.19	1.29	8.32	1.31	37.29
1986	4.44	3.88	1.95	5.88	1.41	1.71	6.62	4.16	1.96	1.93	6.78	5.23	45.95
1987	6.21	1.30	3.81	5.06	2.55	4.13	4.66	5.26	3.87	3.37	2.94	2.37	45.53
1988	3.74	4.15	2.13	1.97	5.86	1.06	9.98	1.82	1.66	2.45	7.71	0.98	43.51
1989	1.98	2.70	4.42	3.25	8.80	5.41	5.23	7.03	6.45	5.40	2.57	0.75	53.99
1990	4.72	1.71	2.81	3.98	6.87	3.68	4.98	7.71	2.72	5.11	2.82	5.19	52.30
1991	3.72	1.81	5.49	3.91	4.80	2.95	5.21	5.63	3.24	1.29	2.04	3.67	43.76
1992	1.27	1.37	3.48	1.35	3.46	4.67	4.79	3.37	2.60	0.73	5.02	4.63	36.74
1993	2.75	2.87	7.22	4.59	1.77	1.21	2.15	2.84	6.29	3.98	1.95	4.89	42.51
Record Mean	3.34	2.88	4.04	3.66	3.86	3.31	4.08	4.16	3.73	3.03	3.61	3.38	43.08

AVERAGE TEMPERATURE (deg. F)

NEWARK, NEW JERSEY

YEAR	JAN	FEB	MAR	APR	MAY	JUNE	JULY	AUG	SEP	OCT	NOV	DEC	ANNUAL
1964	34.3	31.9	42.6	49.1	65.4	71.2	76.0	73.9	68.9	55.9	49.4	35.9	54.6
#1965	28.3	32.4	39.0	50.0	67.3	71.6	75.7	74.5	68.4	54.0	44.4	38.8	53.7
1966	30.4	33.2	41.7	48.2	59.3	73.8	79.6	76.5	66.6	55.5	48.9	36.5	54.2
1967	36.9	29.4	37.6	50.9	54.3	72.0	74.2	73.5	66.6	56.4	42.2	38.3	52.7
1968	27.8	29.9	43.1	54.0	59.6	69.7	78.2	76.9	70.7	59.7	45.7	32.5	54.0
1969	31.3	31.3	38.8	54.6	64.1	72.8	74.2	77.3	67.5	56.2	45.5	33.1	53.9
1970	24.2	33.0	39.0	51.9	64.6	70.9	77.2	77.3	70.6	59.5	49.1	35.3	54.4
1971	27.3	35.2	41.2	51.4	60.6	74.8	77.8	76.0	71.8	63.2	46.2	41.4	55.6
1972	35.4	31.3	40.5	50.0	63.0	68.8	77.9	75.9	69.8	53.3	44.8	39.7	54.2
1973	35.5	33.3	48.6	54.2	60.4	74.6	78.7	79.6	71.0	60.3	48.8	39.4	57.0
1974	35.4	31.9	43.4	56.5	62.7	70.1	77.1	76.5	66.6	53.9	47.5	38.9	55.0
1975	36.9	35.1	39.7	47.3	65.8	71.6	76.9	75.1	64.3	59.1	51.7	35.4	54.9
1976	26.8	39.3	44.0	55.2	61.1	73.6	74.9	74.4	66.5	52.6	39.9	29.1	53.1
1977	20.9	32.8	46.8	53.7	65.4	70.3	78.2	75.1	68.0	54.5	47.1	33.3	53.9
1978	27.2	25.5	38.5	51.0	60.5	71.6	75.1	76.7	66.1	57.5	48.8	38.1	53.1
1979	32.5	23.5	46.2	52.0	64.5	69.4	77.0	76.6	69.1	56.5	51.8	40.2	54.9
1980	34.0	30.8	38.9	52.6	65.9	70.2	78.9	78.6	70.8	55.0	42.9	30.4	54.1
1981	24.1	37.6	40.2	55.3	64.0	74.6	79.3	75.1	67.2	53.1	46.0	34.6	54.3
1982	24.2	36.2	41.8	50.6	63.2	67.9	78.4	72.5	66.7	56.9	48.8	42.8	54.2
1983	35.0	35.9	44.7	52.2	60.8	73.5	79.6	77.6	70.6	57.8	47.8	34.2	55.8
1984	27.8	40.8	36.5	52.7	62.2	75.0	76.6	77.3	65.4	62.3	45.3	40.8	55.2
1985	24.9	33.5	44.5	57.0	67.1	69.4	76.3	75.6	70.2	58.5	49.5	33.3	55.0
1986	33.0	31.1	44.2	53.4	66.7	72.7	76.9	74.2	68.6	58.0	45.0	38.1	55.2
1987	31.5	33.0	45.0	53.9	63.9	74.5	79.4	75.3	68.7	53.7	47.6	38.4	55.4
1988	28.7	34.4	43.9	51.1	63.4	73.0	80.5	79.8	68.0	52.6	48.9	35.5	55.0
1989	37.0	34.2	42.4	52.5	63.2	74.3	77.2	76.3	69.9	59.1	45.0	25.6	54.7
1990	40.4	39.8	44.9	53.3	61.1	73.4	77.8	76.6	68.6	62.4	50.0	42.3	57.6
1991	33.6	38.6	44.4	54.8	68.9	74.2	77.9	77.7	68.0	58.3	47.6	38.8	56.9
1992	35.2	36.0	39.3	50.2	61.7	72.6	76.9	75.1	69.6	55.7	47.8	38.8	54.9
1993	37.6	31.0	40.2	54.3	67.0	75.8	82.6	79.2	69.2	56.4	47.8	37.2	56.5
Record Mean	31.6	32.9	41.1	51.7	62.5	71.6	76.8	75.1	67.8	56.9	46.3	35.4	54.1
Max	38.7	40.6	49.4	60.9	72.1	81.0	85.8	83.9	76.7	66.1	54.2	42.4	62.6
Min	24.5	25.2	32.8	42.4	52.8	62.1	67.7	66.3	58.8	47.7	38.4	28.3	45.6

REFERENCE NOTES

NEWARK, NEW JERSEY

GENERAL
T - TRACE AMOUNT.
BLANK ENTRIES DENOTE MISSING/UNREPORTED DATA.
# INDICATES A STATION OR INSTRUMENT RELOCATION.

SPECIFIC

PM - INCLUDES LAST DAY OF PREVIOUS MONTH
ASOS - AUTOMATED SURFACE OBSERVING SYSTEM IN OPERATION DURING THESE MONTHS.

(a) - LENGTH OF RECORD IN YEARS, ALTHOUGH INDIVIDUAL MONTHS MAY BE MISSING.
0.* OR * - THE VALUE IS BETWEEN 0.0 AND 0.05
NORMALS - BASED ON THE 1961-1990 RECORD PERIOD.
EXTREMES - DATES ARE THE MOST RECENT OCCURRENCE
WIND DIR.- NUMERALS SHOW TENS OF DEGRESS CLOCKWISE FROM TRUE NORTH. "00" INDICATES CALM.
RESULTANT DIRECTIONS ARE GIVEN TO WHOLE DEGREES.
BOLD VALUES INDICATE EXTREME VALUES WHICH OCCURRED AFTER THE ASOS SYSTEM WAS COMMISSIONED.

RECORD = PERIOD OF RECORD
RECORD MEAN PRECIPITATION IS THE MEAN OF ALL DAILY PRECIPITATION AMOUNTS DURING THE PERIOD OF RECORD.
RECORD MAX(MIN) TEMPERATURE IS THE MEAN OF ALL DAILY MAX(MIN) TEMPERATURES DURING THE PERIOD OF RECORD.
RECORD MEAN TEMPERATURE IS THE SUM OF THE RECORD MAX AND RECORD MIN DIVIDED BY 2.
AVERAGE TEMPERATURE IS THE SUM OF THE MEAN DAILY MAX AND MIN TEMPERATURE DIVIDED BY 2.

EXCEPTIONS

RECORD MEANS ARE THROUGH THE CURRENT YEAR, BEGINNING IN 1931 FOR TEMPERATURE
1931 FOR PRECIPITATION
1942 FOR SNOWFALL

HEATING DEGREE DAYS Base 65 deg. F — NEWARK, NEW JERSEY

SEASON	JULY	AUG	SEP	OCT	NOV	DEC	JAN	FEB	MAR	APR	MAY	JUNE	TOTAL
#1964-65	1	0	40	278	461	895	1133	905	799	442	55	17	5026
1965-66	0	11	50	339	610	807	1066	882	717	500	212	14	5208
1966-67	0	0	63	286	480	876	864	991	842	425	331	5	5163
1967-68	0	1	58	285	677	823	1148	1012	676	325	167	12	5184
1968-69	0	0	6	193	573	1003	1039	938	804	317	101	2	4976
1969-70	0	0	49	284	575	984	1255	892	796	390	97	5	5327
1970-71	0	0	24	199	472	914	1160	827	732	402	155	7	4892
1971-72	0	1	12	95	569	724	909	969	757	444	93	19	4592
1972-73	0	0	22	356	599	776	906	882	504	339	163	1	4548
1973-74	0	0	18	166	479	787	909	921	661	273	127	12	4353
1974-75	0	0	62	341	521	802	864	832	775	524	84	6	4811
1975-76	0	1	59	195	400	913	1177	738	645	338	141	17	4624
1976-77	0	4	56	381	745	1107	1361	895	563	352	89	24	5577
1977-78	0	0	50	319	527	975	1168	1099	814	411	190	13	5566
1978-79	6	0	66	239	481	830	1001	1155	577	386	68	11	4820
1979-80	2	4	28	289	393	763	953	987	802	366	62	24	4673
1980-81	0	0	28	314	654	1066	1261	762	764	290	96	0	5235
1981-82	0	0	52	360	563	934	1258	802	712	433	85	42	5241
1982-83	0	13	36	267	493	679	923	810	622	395	162	5	4405
1983-84	0	0	52	249	510	949	1144	696	874	366	128	9	4977
1984-85	0	0	83	114	584	745	1235	877	641	268	62	15	4624
1985-86	0	0	21	212	462	971	985	942	642	341	89	7	4672
1986-87	0	11	22	240	594	826	1030	893	616	331	140	3	4706
1987-88	0	1	25	342	518	818	1117	880	647	410	120	28	4906
1988-89	1	0	18	386	476	906	859	853	698	366	132	6	4701
1989-90	0	0	37	190	594	1215	756	699	622	369	122	2	4606
1990-91	1	1	50	163	446	697	967	734	630	330	63	4	4086
1991-92	0	0	55	227	513	804	917	834	790	441	148	4	4733
1992-93	0	0	38	295	510	807	842	946	765	318	42	4	4567
1993-94	0	0	48	263	513	853							

COOLING DEGREE DAYS Base 65 deg. F — NEWARK, NEW JERSEY

YEAR	JAN	FEB	MAR	APR	MAY	JUNE	JULY	AUG	SEP	OCT	NOV	DEC	TOTAL
1969	0	0	0	15	80	243	293	390	131	17	0	0	1169
1970	0	0	0	4	94	187	384	387	201	33	0	0	1290
1971	0	0	0	0	25	307	403	350	222	46	12	0	1365
1972	0	0	3	4	41	142	406	347	175	3	0	0	1121
1973	0	0	0	20	26	296	432	459	205	28	0	0	1466
1974	0	0	0	28	64	172	381	361	115	1	3	0	1125
1975	0	0	0	0	117	211	375	321	46	20	10	0	1100
1976	0	0	0	50	30	281	317	305	110	6	0	0	1099
1977	0	0	6	18	111	191	414	321	146	1	0	0	1208
1978	0	0	0	0	59	217	325	367	105	15	0	0	1088
1979	0	0	0	2	59	147	381	372	158	34	3	0	1156
1980	0	0	0	0	97	187	435	427	209	10	0	0	1365
1981	0	0	0	6	75	293	446	319	124	0	0	0	1263
1982	0	0	0	6	39	136	421	249	95	24	12	0	982
1983	0	0	0	19	39	268	458	396	226	36	0	0	1442
1984	0	0	0	2	47	316	365	388	102	36	0	0	1256
1985	0	0	11	36	134	152	357	335	183	19	3	0	1230
1986	0	0	2	2	149	243	380	303	136	30	0	0	1245
1987	0	0	0	6	116	293	453	327	143	0	1	0	1339
1988	0	0	0	0	75	274	488	465	115	10	0	0	1427
1989	0	0	3	1	81	294	385	360	194	16	0	0	1334
1990	0	0	7	23	11	262	403	365	165	89	2	0	1327
1991	0	0	0	28	190	288	406	399	151	28	0	0	1490
1992	0	0	0	4	52	242	373	323	185	15	0	0	1194
1993	0	0	0	5	113	340	553	450	182	9	4	0	1656

SNOWFALL (inches) — NEWARK, NEW JERSEY

SEASON	JULY	AUG	SEP	OCT	NOV	DEC	JAN	FEB	MAR	APR	MAY	JUNE	TOTAL
1964-65	0.0	0.0	0.0	0.0	0.0	3.9	16.1	1.8	4.6	0.7	0.0	0.0	27.1
1965-66	0.0	0.0	0.0	T	0.0	T	10.2	8.6	T	0.0	0.0	0.0	18.8
1966-67	0.0	0.0	0.0	0.0	0.0	12.6	1.3	25.4	18.0	T	0.0	0.0	57.3
1967-68	0.0	0.0	0.0	0.0	3.1	3.9	4.6	0.6	1.7	0.0	0.0	0.0	13.9
1968-69	0.0	0.0	0.0	0.0	0.4	4.7	1.1	16.5	5.9	0.0	0.0	0.0	28.6
1969-70	0.0	0.0	0.0	0.0	T	8.5	9.1	5.5	4.3	T	0.0	0.0	27.4
1970-71	0.0	0.0	0.0	0.0	0.0	2.9	13.2	1.1	4.2	2.2	0.0	0.0	23.6
1971-72	0.0	0.0	0.0	0.0	T	0.4	3.1	12.3	1.0	T	0.0	0.0	16.8
1972-73	0.0	0.0	0.0	T	T	T	0.7	0.6	0.6	T	0.0	0.0	1.9
1973-74	0.0	0.0	0.0	0.0	0.0	2.1	6.8	8.1	3.1	0.3	0.0	0.0	20.4
1974-75	0.0	0.0	0.0	0.0	T	1.2	1.4	12.7	1.1	T	0.0	0.0	16.4
1975-76	0.0	0.0	0.0	0.0	T	2.4	7.2	6.1	4.2	T	0.0	0.0	19.9
1976-77	0.0	0.0	0.0	0.0	T	6.7	10.8	5.8	1.7	T	T	0.0	25.0
1977-78	0.0	0.0	0.0	0.0	1.5	0.2	27.4	25.3	10.5	T	0.0	0.0	64.9
1978-79	0.0	0.0	0.0	0.0	2.6	T	9.4	26.1	T	T	0.0	0.0	38.1
1979-80	0.0	0.0	0.0	T	0.0	3.7	2.5	1.8	6.3	T	0.0	0.0	14.3
1980-81	0.0	0.0	0.0	0.0	0.4	3.1	6.9	T	9.1	0.0	0.0	0.0	19.5
1981-82	0.0	0.0	0.0	0.0	T	3.4	12.3	0.5	0.8	13.8	0.0	0.0	30.8
1982-83	0.0	0.0	0.0	0.0	T	2.9	2.3	21.5	0.2	4.1	0.0	0.0	31.0
1983-84	0.0	0.0	0.0	0.0	1.2	2.4	13.7	0.3	11.3	T	0.0	0.0	28.9
1984-85	0.0	0.0	0.0	0.0	T	6.8	8.9	7.4	0.1	T	0.0	0.0	23.2
1985-86	0.0	0.0	0.0	0.0	0.6	4.6	2.8	13.9	T	0.1	0.0	0.0	22.0
1986-87	0.0	0.0	0.0	0.0	T	2.3	21.4	6.5	2.4	0.0	0.0	0.0	32.6
1987-88	0.0	0.0	0.0	0.0	1.5	2.3	15.4	2.7	0.9	T	0.0		
1988-89	0.0	0.0	0.0	0.0	0.0	0.1	4.1	0.6	2.7	0.0	0.0	0.0	7.5
1989-90	0.0	0.0	0.0	0.0	5.7	0.5	2.4	2.8	2.5	0.6	0.0	0.0	14.5
1990-91	0.0	0.0	0.0	0.0	T	7.6	8.5	5.2	0.2	0.0	0.0	0.0	21.5
1991-92	0.0	0.0	0.0	0.0	T	0.5	1.0	1.0	11.4	T	0.0	0.0	13.9
1992-93	0.0	0.0	0.0	0.0	T	0.5	0.8	10.7	16.8	0.0	0.0	0.0	28.8
1993-94	0.0	0.0	0.0	0.0	T	3.9							
Record Mean	0.0	0.0	0.0	T	0.5	5.5	7.5	7.9	4.9	0.7	T	0.0	26.9

ALBUQUERQUE, NEW MEXICO

The Albuquerque metropolitan area is largely situated in the Rio Grande Valley and on the mesas and piedmont slopes which rise either side of the valley floor. The Rio Grande flows from north to south through the area. The Sandia and Manzano Mountains rise abruptly at the eastern edge of the city with Tijeras Canyon separating the two ranges. West of the city the land gradually rises to the Continental Divide, some 90 miles away.

The climate of Albuquerque is best described as arid continental with abundant sunshine, low humidity, scant precipitation, and a wide yet tolerable seasonal range of temperatures. Sunny days and low humidity are renowned features of the climate. More than three-fourths of the daylight hours have sunshine, even in the winter months. The air is normally dry and muggy days are rare. The combination of dry air and plentiful solar radiation allows widespread use of energy-efficient devices such as evaporative coolers and solar collectors.

Precipitation within the valley area is adequate only for native desert vegetation and deep-rooted imports. However, irrigation supports successful farming and fruit growing in the Rio Grande Valley. On the east slopes of the Sandias and Manzanos, precipitation is sufficient for thick stands of timber and good grass cover.

Meager amounts of precipitation fall in the winter, much of it as snow. Snowfalls of an inch or more occur about four times a year in the Rio Grande Valley, while the mountains receive substantial snowfall on occasion. Snow seldom remains on the ground more than 24 hours in the city proper. However, snow cover on the east slopes of the Sandias is sufficient for skiing during most winters.

Nearly half of the annual precipitation in Albuquerque results from afternoon and evening thunderstorms during the summer. Thunderstorm frequency increases rapidly around July 1st, peaks during August, then tapers off by the end of September. Thunderstorms are usually brief, sometimes produce heavy rainfall, and often lower afternoon temperatures noticeably. Hailstorms are infrequent and tornadoes rare.

Temperatures in Albuquerque are those characteristic of a dry, high altitude, continental climate. The average daily range of temperature is relatively high, but extreme temperatures are rare. High temperatures during the winter are near 50 degrees with only a few days on which the temperature fails to rise above the freezing mark. In the summer, daytime maxima are about 90 degrees, but with the large daily range, the nights usually are comfortably cool.

The average number of days between the last freezing temperature in spring and the first freeze in fall varies widely across the Albuquerque metropolitan area. The growing season in Albuquerque and adjacent suburbs ranges from around 170 days in the Rio Grande Valley to about 200 days in parts of the northeast section of the city.

Sustained winds of 12 mph or less occur approximately 80 percent of the time at the Albuquerque International Airport, while sustained winds greater than 25 mph have a frequency less than 3 percent. Late winter and spring storms along with occasional east winds out of Tijeras Canyon are the main sources of strong wind conditions. Blowing dust, the least attractive feature of the climate, often accompanies the occasional strong winds of winter and spring.

NORMALS, MEANS, AND EXTREMES

ALBUQUERQUE, NEW MEXICO

LATITUDE: 35°03'N　LONGITUDE: 106°37' W　ELEVATION: FT. GRND 5311 BARO 5313　TIME ZONE: MOUNTAIN　WBAN: 23050

	(a)	JAN	FEB	MAR	APR	MAY	JUNE	JULY	AUG	SEP	OCT	NOV	DEC	YEAR
TEMPERATURE °F:														
Normals														
-Daily Maximum		46.8	53.5	61.4	70.8	79.7	90.0	92.5	89.0	81.9	71.0	57.3	47.5	70.1
-Daily Minimum		21.7	26.4	32.2	39.6	48.6	58.3	64.4	62.6	55.2	43.0	31.2	23.1	42.2
-Monthly		34.2	40.0	46.9	55.2	64.2	74.2	78.5	75.9	68.6	57.0	44.3	35.3	56.2
Extremes														
-Record Highest	54	69	76	85	89	98	105	105	101	100	91	77	72	105
-Year		1971	1986	1971	1989	1951	1980	1980	1979	1979	1979	1975	1958	JUN 1980
-Record Lowest	54	-17	-5	8	19	28	40	52	50	37	21	-7	-7	-17
-Year		1971	1951	1948	1980	1975	1980	1985	1992	1971	1991	1976	1990	JAN 1971
NORMAL DEGREE DAYS:														
Heating (base 65°F)		955	700	561	301	89	0	0	0	18	259	621	921	4425
Cooling (base 65°F)		0	0	0	7	64	279	419	338	126	11	0	0	1244
% OF POSSIBLE SUNSHINE	54	72	72	73	77	80	83	76	75	79	79	76	71	76
MEAN SKY COVER (tenths)														
Sunrise - Sunset	54	4.9	5.0	5.1	4.6	4.2	3.4	4.5	4.4	3.6	3.5	4.0	4.6	4.3
MEAN NUMBER OF DAYS:														
Sunrise to Sunset														
-Clear	54	13.0	10.9	11.4	12.6	14.2	17.4	12.0	13.3	16.8	17.2	15.1	13.9	167.9
-Partly Cloudy	54	7.7	7.6	9.6	9.5	10.4	8.6	14.1	12.4	7.6	7.8	7.6	7.3	110.5
-Cloudy	54	10.4	9.7	9.9	7.9	6.4	3.9	4.8	5.2	5.6	6.1	7.2	9.8	86.9
Precipitation														
.01 inches or more	54	4.1	4.1	4.6	3.3	4.5	4.0	8.8	9.6	5.7	4.8	3.5	4.3	61.3
Snow,Ice pellets,hail														
1.0 inches or more	54	1.0	0.9	0.6	0.2	0.*	0.0	0.0	0.0	0.0	0.*	0.5	0.9	4.3
Thunderstorms	54	0.1	0.3	0.9	1.5	4.0	5.1	10.8	10.8	4.6	2.3	0.5	0.2	41.2
Heavy Fog Visibility														
1/4 mile or less	54	1.1	1.0	0.6	0.2	0.*	0.*	0.1	0.*	0.1	0.3	0.6	1.6	5.8
Temperature °F														
-Maximum														
90° and above	33	0.0	0.0	0.0	0.0	2.5	17.0	23.0	15.9	3.8	0.1	0.0	0.0	62.3
32° and below	33	2.2	0.7	0.1	0.0	0.0	0.0	0.0	0.0	0.0	0.0	0.2	1.8	5.0
-Minimum														
32° and below	33	28.8	22.5	15.4	4.3	0.2	0.0	0.0	0.0	0.0	2.1	16.5	28.5	118.2
0° and below	33	0.4	0.0	0.0	0.0	0.0	0.0	0.0	0.0	0.0	0.0	0.1	0.1	0.5
AVG. STATION PRESS.(mb)	21	838.9	837.9	835.2	835.7	836.1	837.9	840.2	840.8	840.2	840.0	838.8	839.2	838.4
RELATIVE HUMIDITY (%)														
Hour 05	33	71	65	56	49	48	46	60	67	62	61	65	70	60
Hour 11 (Local Time)	33	51	44	34	26	25	24	34	40	40	38	42	50	37
Hour 17	33	41	33	25	19	19	18	27	31	30	29	36	44	29
Hour 23	33	61	53	44	35	35	33	47	53	52	49	54	61	48
PRECIPITATION (inches):														
Water Equivalent														
-Normal		0.44	0.46	0.54	0.52	0.50	0.59	1.37	1.64	1.00	0.89	0.43	0.50	8.88
-Maximum Monthly	54	1.32	1.82	2.18	1.97	3.07	2.57	3.33	3.30	2.63	3.08	1.93	1.85	3.33
-Year		1978	1993	1973	1942	1941	1986	1968	1967	1988	1972	1991	1959	JUL 1968
-Minimum Monthly	54	T	T	T	T	T	T	0.08	T	T	0.00	0.00	0.00	0.00
-Year		1970	1984	1966	1993	1945	1975	1980	1962	1957	1952	1949	1981	DEC 1981
-Maximum in 24 hrs	54	0.87	0.80	1.11	1.66	1.14	1.64	1.77	1.75	1.92	1.80	1.67	1.35	1.92
-Year		1962	1993	1973	1969	1969	1952	1961	1980	1955	1969	1991	1958	SEP 1955
Snow,Ice pellets,hail														
-Maximum Monthly	54	9.5	10.3	13.9	8.1	1.0	T	T	T	T	3.2	9.3	14.7	14.7
-Year		1973	1986	1973	1973	1979	1992	1990	1993	1971	1986	1940	1959	DEC 1959
-Maximum in 24 hrs	54	5.1	6.0	10.7	10.9	1.0	T	T	T	T	3.2	5.5	14.2	14.2
-Year		1973	1986	1973	1988	1979	1992	1990	1993	1971	1986	1946	1958	DEC 1958
WIND:														
Mean Speed (mph)	54	8.0	8.8	10.0	10.8	10.5	9.9	9.0	8.2	8.5	8.2	7.9	7.7	9.0
Prevailing Direction through 1963		N	N	SE	S	S	S	SE	SE	SE	SE	N	N	SE
Fastest Obs. 1 Min.														
-Direction (!!)	9	09	09	19	17	28	16	36	27	25	10	27	09	09
-Speed (MPH)	9	52	40	49	46	46	40	52	41	40	38	48	47	52
-Year		1990	1989	1991	1985	1986	1991	1990	1990	1985	1991	1988	1987	JAN 1990
Peak Gust														
-Direction (!!)	10	E	W	SW	E	SW	N	N	E	W	NW	W	E	SW
-Speed (mph)	10	70	63	77	64	70	68	72	63	61	51	63	71	77
-Date		1990	1984	1991	1990	1991	1992	1990	1989	1985	1986	1988	1987	MAR 1991

PRECIPITATION (inches)

ALBUQUERQUE, NEW MEXICO

YEAR	JAN	FEB	MAR	APR	MAY	JUNE	JULY	AUG	SEP	OCT	NOV	DEC	ANNUAL
1964	0.07	1.12	0.13	0.61	0.35	T	1.87	0.98	1.57	0.04	0.21	0.49	7.44
1965	0.47	0.60	0.49	0.49	0.19	0.99	1.65	0.61	1.18	0.89	0.33	1.42	9.31
1966	0.42	0.30	T	0.04	0.02	1.66	1.63	1.06	1.04	0.54	0.09	0.01	6.81
1967	0.01	0.44	0.25	T	0.04	1.71	0.61	3.30	0.79	0.18	0.15	0.56	8.04
1968	0.01	0.98	1.48	0.51	0.99	0.05	3.33	1.49	0.30	0.12	0.59	0.82	10.67
1969	0.08	0.34	0.41	1.76	1.31	0.59	0.94	0.95	1.08	2.37	0.01	0.72	10.56
1970	T	0.27	0.42	0.05	0.33	0.40	1.22	2.24	0.79	0.25	0.08	0.23	6.28
1971	0.27	0.21	0.03	0.78	0.16	0.02	1.05	0.87	1.44	1.15	0.67	1.40	8.05
1972	0.12	0.12	0.08	T	0.18	0.55	1.00	2.93	1.00	3.08	0.69	0.36	10.11
1973	0.85	0.33	2.18	0.91	0.66	1.37	1.80	1.19	1.13	0.35	0.08	0.03	10.88
1974	0.88	0.11	0.85	0.14	0.01	0.22	2.40	0.79	1.58	1.96	0.38	0.51	9.83
1975	0.26	0.99	0.95	0.10	0.66	T	1.43	1.40	1.66	T	0.28	0.28	8.01
1976	0.00	0.40	0.09	0.31	0.82	0.60	1.32	0.73	0.45	0.03	0.24	0.20	5.19
1977	0.88	0.13	0.63	1.07	0.10	0.04	0.69	2.28	0.78	0.76	0.42	0.13	7.91
1978	1.32	1.02	0.54	0.05	0.69	1.05	0.24	2.49	0.59	1.22	1.00	0.76	10.97
1979	1.07	0.62	0.14	0.24	2.48	1.02	0.80	1.53	0.40	0.27	0.91	0.87	10.35
1980	0.87	0.58	0.60	0.60	0.56	0.01	0.08	2.61	1.83	0.09	0.30	0.74	8.87
1981	0.05	0.67	0.80	0.30	0.53	0.35	1.07	1.68	0.41	1.43	0.37	0.00	7.66
1982	0.32	0.20	0.84	0.05	0.52	0.09	1.32	1.09	1.34	0.26	0.60	0.78	7.41
1983	1.10	0.71	0.61	0.02	0.32	1.21	0.55	0.27	0.91	1.20	0.44	0.42	7.76
1984	0.33	T	0.62	0.50	0.16	0.48	1.13	2.70	1.13	3.04	0.63	1.36	12.08
1985	0.49	0.54	0.70	1.69	1.12	0.53	1.16	0.49	1.53	2.15	0.19	0.16	10.75
1986	0.22	1.01	0.17	0.33	1.11	2.57	1.51	2.26	0.53	1.54	1.29	0.44	12.98
1987	0.66	0.61	0.07	1.00	0.58	0.13	0.91	2.98	0.20	0.44	0.42	0.34	8.34
1988	0.15	0.07	0.85	1.42	0.62	1.25	2.26	3.29	2.63	0.32	0.22	0.03	13.11
1989	0.57	0.35	0.48	T	0.02	0.02	1.51	0.48	0.31	0.97	T	0.28	4.99
1990	0.21	0.49	0.41	1.71	0.45	0.27	2.36	1.79	0.96	0.15	0.86	0.59	10.25
1991	0.60	0.06	0.14	T	1.14	0.65	2.63	1.26	1.43	0.26	1.93	1.49	11.59
1992	0.60	0.20	0.63	0.22	1.81	0.67	2.01	2.17	0.79	0.70	1.12	1.16	12.08
1993	0.94	1.82	0.22	T	0.20	0.44	0.23	3.05	0.49	0.64	0.97	0.03	9.03
Record Mean	0.40	0.39	0.45	0.54	0.64	0.60	1.41	1.42	0.93	0.83	0.46	0.47	8.53

AVERAGE TEMPERATURE (deg. F)

ALBUQUERQUE, NEW MEXICO

YEAR	JAN	FEB	MAR	APR	MAY	JUNE	JULY	AUG	SEP	OCT	NOV	DEC	ANNUAL
1964	30.0	29.1	41.5	51.7	65.8	73.6	78.2	76.8	69.3	59.4	43.7	35.5	54.5
1965	38.8	39.4	44.6	54.8	61.7	69.4	77.9	75.4	66.6	58.0	48.4	35.8	55.9
1966	30.1	33.2	45.6	54.6	67.2	72.8	79.8	75.7	68.4	56.8	46.7	34.3	55.4
1967	33.2	40.5	52.0	57.8	63.8	71.5	79.2	74.5	68.4	58.2	46.1	32.4	56.5
1968	36.8	43.3	46.7	53.4	62.7	75.2	76.1	72.4	68.0	58.3	42.8	30.0	55.5
1969	38.0	38.5	41.1	57.4	66.2	73.6	80.2	79.0	70.0	53.8	41.4	39.1	56.6
1970	34.5	42.8	44.1	52.5	66.2	72.7	79.6	77.8	67.5	52.6	44.5	36.4	56.0
1971	33.6	38.9	47.7	53.3	61.7	73.8	78.1	73.9	66.4	53.8	45.2	31.9	54.8
1972	36.1	42.5	53.6	56.9	64.0	73.7	78.6	74.1	68.1	57.6	40.1	35.0	56.7
1973	31.8	35.9	45.1	50.2	62.7	73.5	78.4	78.0	67.5	56.4	44.6	34.0	54.8
1974	33.6	37.9	52.8	56.4	68.5	80.1	77.0	72.7	66.1	58.1	45.0	32.0	56.7
1975	30.8	38.0	45.0	49.9	61.0	73.0	76.8	76.1	66.3	56.5	42.6	35.6	54.3
1976	33.2	43.3	44.3	54.6	62.8	73.4	77.0	75.0	68.0	53.1	40.6	33.0	54.9
1977	29.8	40.7	43.2	56.5	64.2	75.5	78.6	77.4	69.4	58.9	46.4	40.4	56.8
1978	36.8	39.3	50.2	57.7	60.5	75.5	81.6	75.5	69.1	60.3	47.5	34.3	57.4
1979	32.9	41.1	48.4	56.9	63.7	73.3	80.6	77.1	72.3	61.5	41.0	37.7	57.2
1980	40.2	44.2	46.1	52.1	61.1	77.2	82.7	77.4	69.9	54.5	43.5	40.5	57.4
1981	38.0	42.9	46.2	59.0	64.5	77.0	79.8	76.4	69.7	55.7	47.0	40.5	58.0
1982	35.9	39.4	47.4	56.1	63.0	74.8	79.1	77.4	69.5	54.8	42.9	34.4	56.2
1983	35.0	39.7	46.9	50.2	63.0	73.4	80.4	79.4	73.4	58.3	45.1	36.7	56.8
1984	34.1	40.1	46.8	52.8	69.9	73.6	78.9	75.7	68.8	51.6	43.7	35.6	56.0
1985	33.8	38.3	47.5	57.4	64.0	74.1	77.1	76.6	65.9	57.5	45.4	37.6	56.3
1986	41.3	43.0	50.9	56.5	63.7	72.7	74.7	76.0	66.5	54.6	42.0	36.3	56.5
1987	32.3	39.2	43.7	54.8	62.8	73.0	77.8	74.7	68.8	61.3	45.2	35.3	55.7
1988	34.6	43.9	47.0	55.1	64.3	74.4	78.1	75.0	66.3	61.1	45.4	33.9	56.6
1989	35.5	41.9	52.8	61.4	68.8	75.6	78.6	74.3	69.4	56.7	46.4	35.1	58.0
1990	34.6	38.5	48.6	57.3	63.6	79.0	76.8	73.8	70.9	58.3	45.0	32.1	56.5
1991	35.7	44.6	46.1	56.0	65.5	73.4	76.9	75.5	68.1	59.6	43.4	37.3	56.8
1992	32.7	42.3	48.9	60.0	64.6	72.4	76.2	75.0	70.3	60.8	39.7	32.8	56.3
1993	39.7	42.5	48.8	57.1	65.7	75.1	79.9	75.6	69.1	56.2	43.3	37.3	57.5
Record Mean	34.6	39.8	46.5	55.0	63.9	73.6	77.4	75.3	68.4	56.8	43.9	35.3	55.9
Max	47.0	53.1	60.9	70.1	79.1	89.1	91.3	88.7	82.2	71.1	57.4	47.5	69.8
Min	22.2	26.5	32.1	39.9	48.7	58.0	63.5	61.9	54.7	42.6	30.4	23.1	42.0

REFERENCE NOTES

ALBUQUERQUE, NEW MEXICO

GENERAL
T - TRACE AMOUNT.
BLANK ENTRIES DENOTE MISSING/UNREPORTED DATA.
# INDICATES A STATION OR INSTRUMENT RELOCATION.

SPECIFIC

PM - INCLUDES LAST DAY OF PREVIOUS MONTH
ASOS - AUTOMATED SURFACE OBSERVING SYSTEM IN OPERATION DURING THESE MONTHS.

(a) - LENGTH OF RECORD IN YEARS, ALTHOUGH INDIVIDUAL MONTHS MAY BE MISSING.
0.* OR * - THE VALUE IS BETWEEN 0.0 AND 0.05
NORMALS - BASED ON THE 1961-1990 RECORD PERIOD.
EXTREMES - DATES ARE THE MOST RECENT OCCURRENCE
WIND DIR.- NUMERALS SHOW TENS OF DEGRESS CLOCKWISE FROM TRUE NORTH. "00" INDICATES CALM.
RESULTANT DIRECTIONS ARE GIVEN TO WHOLE DEGREES.
BOLD VALUES INDICATE EXTREME VALUES WHICH OCCURRED AFTER THE ASOS SYSTEM WAS COMMISSIONED.

RECORD = PERIOD OF RECORD
RECORD MEAN PRECIPITATION IS THE MEAN OF ALL DAILY PRECIPITATION AMOUNTS DURING THE PERIOD OF RECORD.
RECORD MAX(MIN) TEMPERATURE IS THE MEAN OF ALL DAILY MAX(MIN) TEMPERATURES DURING THE PERIOD OF RECORD.
RECORD MEAN TEMPERATURE IS THE SUM OF THE RECORD MAX AND RECORD MIN DIVIDED BY 2.
AVERAGE TEMPERATURE IS THE SUM OF THE MEAN DAILY MAX AND MIN TEMPERATURE DIVIDED BY 2.

EXCEPTIONS

RECORD MEANS ARE THROUGH THE CURRENT YEAR, BEGINNING IN 1893 FOR TEMPERATURE
1893 FOR PRECIPITATION
1940 FOR SNOWFALL

HEATING DEGREE DAYS Base 65 deg. F — ALBUQUERQUE, NEW MEXICO

SEASON	JULY	AUG	SEP	OCT	NOV	DEC	JAN	FEB	MAR	APR	MAY	JUNE	TOTAL
1964-65	2	0	20	173	632	909	805	709	624	300	128	24	4326
1965-66	0	0	56	217	492	895	1074	882	595	305	53	0	4569
1966-67	0	0	15	247	541	942	980	682	396	211	109	0	4123
1967-68	0	0	13	220	557	1003	870	623	559	343	107	8	4303
1968-69	2	0	12	208	660	1080	831	735	735	228	84	0	4575
1969-70	0	0	1	348	701	795	938	612	644	367	63	11	4480
1970-71	0	0	58	380	605	878	968	725	533	343	122	5	4617
1971-72	0	0	101	341	587	1022	889	648	346	244	76	0	4254
1972-73	0	3	14	244	740	925	1020	811	607	440	113	3	4920
1973-74	0	0	43	257	606	955	963	754	373	255	29	4	4239
1974-75	0	2	68	212	593	1020	1051	748	614	449	143	6	4906
1975-76	0	0	47	256	664	905	979	622	634	304	99	1	4511
1976-77	0	0	35	367	726	985	1084	675	669	250	61	0	4852
1977-78	0	0	1	192	551	757	870	713	454	215	175	2	3930
1978-79	0	0	20	167	521	945	988	665	509	241	100	12	4168
1979-80	0	0	23	148	715	840	763	595	577	379	139	2	4181
1980-81	0	0	6	335	640	752	827	611	575	197	62	2	4007
1981-82	0	0	3	280	534	754	895	709	538	268	94	0	4075
1982-83	0	0	23	314	658	941	922	703	556	439	127	0	4683
1983-84	0	0	11	198	592	875	948	714	559	362	22	3	4284
1984-85	0	0	51	411	631	903	960	744	536	220	74	7	4537
1985-86	0	0	61	228	581	842	727	610	431	249	80	8	3817
1986-87	0	0	51	313	680	882	1004	717	653	300	81	2	4683
1987-88	0	0	2	133	589	914	937	605	551	290	103	2	4126
1988-89	0	5	39	118	579	959	909	640	373	133	31	0	3786
1989-90	0	0	10	260	551	918	934	735	501	233	103	0	4245
1990-91	0	0	14	202	595	1013	903	563	581	263	60	12	4206
1991-92	0	0	21	188	645	851	994	651	493	170	53	5	4071
1992-93	0	0	8	128	752	991	778	624	496	238	69	3	4087
1993-94	0	0	15	284	642	853							

COOLING DEGREE DAYS Base 65 deg. F — ALBUQUERQUE, NEW MEXICO

YEAR	JAN	FEB	MAR	APR	MAY	JUNE	JULY	AUG	SEP	OCT	NOV	DEC	TOTAL
1969	0	0	0	6	127	263	478	442	158	7	0	0	1481
1970	0	0	0	0	105	246	461	405	141	4	0	0	1362
1971	0	0	5	0	26	277	414	282	149	0	0	0	1153
1972	0	0	0	5	52	267	428	294	113	23	0	0	1182
1973	0	0	0	0	48	267	422	409	124	0	0	0	1270
1974	0	0	0	5	144	464	380	247	107	6	0	0	1353
1975	0	0	0	0	25	256	372	351	96	0	0	0	1100
1976	0	0	0	0	38	260	382	319	137	5	0	0	1141
1977	0	0	0	0	44	324	427	392	141	7	0	0	1335
1978	0	0	0	4	41	324	521	330	151	27	0	0	1398
1979	0	0	0	5	67	269	491	382	249	45	0	0	1508
1980	0	0	0	0	27	375	557	392	160	15	0	0	1526
1981	0	0	0	28	51	368	470	360	152	1	0	0	1430
1982	0	0	0	6	38	301	441	394	163	4	0	0	1347
1983	0	0	0	1	72	260	484	450	267	1	0	0	1535
1984	0	0	0	4	179	266	441	340	169	1	0	0	1400
1985	0	0	0	0	51	289	383	368	97	0	0	0	1188
1986	0	0	0	1	50	245	310	349	103	0	0	0	1058
1987	0	0	0	0	17	251	404	308	120	25	0	0	1125
1988	0	0	0	1	85	288	411	322	86	3	0	0	1196
1989	0	0	0	31	154	323	426	295	150	10	0	0	1389
1990	0	0	0	10	66	426	374	281	200	2	0	0	1359
1991	0	0	0	0	87	269	375	331	120	25	0	0	1207
1992	0	0	0	27	49	235	354	318	171	5	0	0	1159
1993	0	0	0	8	101	312	470	337	145	16	0	0	1389

SNOWFALL (inches) — ALBUQUERQUE, NEW MEXICO

SEASON	JULY	AUG	SEP	OCT	NOV	DEC	JAN	FEB	MAR	APR	MAY	JUNE	TOTAL
1964-65	0.0	0.0	0.0	0.0	T	0.3	1.4	3.6	T	T	0.0	0.0	5.3
1965-66	0.0	0.0	0.0	0.0	T	3.0	5.4	1.0	0.0	T	0.0	0.0	9.4
1966-67	0.0	0.0	0.0	0.0	T	T	T	1.0	1.1	T	0.0	0.0	2.1
1967-68	0.0	0.0	0.0	0.2	1.0	2.8	T	2.0	1.4	T	0.0	0.0	7.4
1968-69	0.0	0.0	0.0	0.0	T	7.4	T	1.8	5.5	T	0.0	0.0	14.7
1969-70	0.0	0.0	0.0	0.0	T	1.1	T	2.7	3.3	0.0	0.0	0.0	7.1
1970-71	0.0	0.0	0.0	0.5	T	0.5	3.0	2.3	0.5	T	0.0	0.0	6.8
1971-72	0.0	0.0	T	T	T	6.8	1.2	1.1	0.0	T	0.0	0.0	9.1
1972-73	0.0	0.0	0.0	T	2.9	1.2	9.5	1.8	13.9	8.1	0.0	0.0	37.4
1973-74	0.0	0.0	0.0	0.3	0.6	0.1	9.3	0.6	2.0	0.0	0.0	0.0	12.9
1974-75	0.0	0.0	0.0	0.0	T	4.9	0.9	6.7	3.8	0.2	0.0	0.0	16.5
1975-76	0.0	0.0	0.0	0.0	0.2	2.9	0.0	T	0.5	0.2	0.0	0.0	3.8
1976-77	0.0	0.0	0.0	T	2.4	1.2	8.4	1.4	2.3	2.6	0.0	0.0	18.3
1977-78	0.0	0.0	0.0	0.0	0.0	T	6.0	3.4	2.0	0.0	0.1	0.0	11.5
1978-79	0.0	0.0	0.0	0.0	T	1.0	2.6	6.0	T	0.5	1.0	0.0	11.1
1979-80	0.0	0.0	0.0	0.9	0.8	2.7	T	0.9	3.1	T	T	0.0	8.4
1980-81	0.0	0.0	0.0	T	2.8	7.4	0.5	2.6	0.9	T	0.0	0.0	14.2
1981-82	0.0	0.0	0.0	0.0	0.0	0.0	3.6	1.2	0.7	T	0.0	0.0	5.5
1982-83	0.0	0.0	0.0	0.0	0.9	3.3	7.3	4.2	1.0	T	T	0.0	16.7
1983-84	0.0	0.0	0.0	0.0	0.8	0.8	4.1	T	0.1	3.0	0.0	0.0	8.8
1984-85	0.0	0.0	0.0	T	T	3.4	2.0	2.9	0.6	0.0	0.0	0.0	8.9
1985-86	0.0	0.0	0.0	0.0	0.7	0.9	2.9	10.3	0.3	0.0	T	0.0	15.1
1986-87	0.0	0.0	0.0	3.2	0.6	0.2	4.9	4.9	0.2	2.2	0.0	0.0	16.2
1987-88	0.0	0.0	0.0	0.0	1.1	1.7	1.2	T	7.9	4.2	0.0	0.0	16.1
1988-89	0.0	0.0	0.0	0.0	1.7	0.3	3.4	3.2	3.1	0.0	0.0	0.0	11.7
1989-90	0.0	0.0	0.0	0.0	T	2.5	1.8	4.8	T	0.3	T	T	9.4
1990-91	T	0.0	0.0	0.0	2.2	6.3	0.9	T	0.8	T	0.0	0.0	10.2
1991-92	0.0	0.0	0.0	2.5	1.5	2.1	5.6	T	1.0	0.0	T	T	12.7
1992-93	0.0	T	0.0	0.0	5.9	7.6	0.8	2.0	0.2	0.0	T	0.0	16.5
1993-94	0.0	T	0.0	T	4.1	0.2							
Record Mean	T	T	T	0.1	1.3	2.6	2.5	2.1	1.8	0.6	T	T	11.1

ALBANY,
NEW YORK

Albany is located on the west bank of the Hudson River some 150 miles north of New York City, and 8 miles south of the confluence of the Mohawk and Hudson Rivers. The river-front portion of the city is only a few feet above sea level, and there is a tidal effect upstream to Troy. Eleven miles west of Albany the Helderberg escarpment rises to 1,800 feet. Between it and the Hudson River the valley floor is gently rolling, ranging some 200 to 500 feet above sea level. East of the city there is more rugged terrain 5 or 6 miles wide with elevations of 300 to 600 feet. Farther to the east the terrain rises more sharply. It reaches a north-south range of hills 12 miles east of Albany with elevations ranging to 2,000 feet.

The climate at Albany is primarily continental in character, but is subjected to some modification by the Atlantic Ocean. The moderating effect on temperatures is more pronounced during the warmer months than in winter when outbursts of cold air sweep down from Canada. In the warmer seasons, temperatures rise rapidly in the daytime. However, temperatures also fall rapidly after sunset so that the nights are relatively cool. Occasionally there are extended periods of oppressive heat up to a week or more in duration.

Winters are usually cold and sometimes fairly severe. Maximum temperatures during the colder winters are often below freezing and nighttime lows are frequently below 10 degrees. Sub-zero readings occur about twelve times a year. Snowfall throughout the area is quite variable and snow flurries are quite frequent during the winter. Precipitation is sufficient to serve the economy of the region in most years, and only occasionally do periods of drought exist. Most of the rainfall in the summer is from thunderstorms. Tornadoes are quite rare and hail is not usually of any consequence.

Wind velocities are moderate. The north-south Hudson River Valley has a marked effect on the lighter winds and in the warm months, average wind direction is usually southerly. Destructive winds rarely occur.

The area enjoys one of the highest percentages of sunshine in the entire state. Seldom does the area experience long periods of cloudy days and long periods of smog are rare.

Based on the 1951-1980 period, the average first occurrence of 32 degrees Fahrenheit in the fall is September 29 and the average last occurrence in the spring is May 7.

NORMALS, MEANS, AND EXTREMES

ALBANY, NEW YORK

LATITUDE: 42°45'N LONGITUDE: 73°48' W ELEVATION: FT. GRND 275 BARO 296 TIME ZONE: EASTERN WBAN: 14735

	(a)	JAN	FEB	MAR	APR	MAY	JUNE	JULY	AUG	SEP	OCT	NOV	DEC	YEAR
TEMPERATURE °F:														
Normals														
-Daily Maximum		30.2	33.2	44.0	57.5	69.7	79.0	84.0	81.4	73.2	61.8	48.7	34.9	58.1
-Daily Minimum		11.0	13.8	24.5	35.1	45.4	54.6	59.6	57.8	49.4	38.6	30.7	18.2	36.6
-Monthly		20.6	23.5	34.3	46.4	57.6	66.9	71.8	69.6	61.3	50.2	39.7	26.5	47.4
Extremes														
-Record Highest	47	62	67	86	92	94	99	100	99	100	89	82	71	100
-Year		1974	1976	1986	1990	1981	1952	1953	1955	1953	1963	1950	1984	JUL 1953
-Record Lowest	47	-28	-21	-21	10	26	36	40	34	24	16	5	-22	-28
-Year		1971	1973	1948	1965	1968	1986	1978	1982	1947	1969	1972	1969	JAN 1971
NORMAL DEGREE DAYS:														
Heating (base 65°F)		1376	1162	952	558	247	34	0	12	141	459	759	1194	6894
Cooling (base 65°F)		0	0	0	0	18	91	213	155	30	0	0	0	507
% OF POSSIBLE SUNSHINE	55	46	52	53	54	56	60	63	60	57	52	36	38	52
MEAN SKY COVER (tenths)														
Sunrise - Sunset	55	7.0	6.9	6.9	6.9	6.9	6.6	6.3	6.2	6.1	6.3	7.5	7.4	6.8
MEAN NUMBER OF DAYS:														
Sunrise to Sunset														
-Clear	55	5.4	5.6	6.1	5.6	5.1	5.2	5.7	6.7	7.6	7.5	3.6	4.8	69.0
-Partly Cloudy	55	8.1	7.2	7.8	8.0	9.3	11.4	13.2	11.8	9.9	9.4	8.1	6.9	111.1
-Cloudy	55	17.5	15.5	17.1	16.4	16.5	13.5	12.1	12.6	12.5	14.1	18.4	19.3	185.2
Precipitation														
.01 inches or more	47	12.2	10.6	11.9	12.2	13.0	11.1	10.2	10.4	9.6	9.0	11.9	12.3	134.5
Snow,Ice pellets,hail														
1.0 inches or more	47	3.9	3.3	2.5	0.7	0.*	0.0	0.0	0.0	0.0	0.*	1.0	4.0	15.4
Thunderstorms	55	0.1	0.1	0.5	1.3	3.3	5.3	6.3	4.7	2.3	0.9	0.3	0.1	25.4
Heavy Fog Visibility														
1/4 mile or less	55	1.2	1.0	1.3	0.8	1.3	1.2	1.4	2.5	3.7	4.1	1.6	1.7	21.7
Temperature °F														
-Maximum														
90° and above	28	0.0	0.0	0.0	0.2	0.4	1.6	4.3	2.1	0.4	0.0	0.0	0.0	8.9
32° and below	28	16.9	13.0	4.0	0.2	0.0	0.0	0.0	0.0	0.0	0.0	1.1	11.3	46.4
-Minimum														
32° and below	28	29.4	26.1	24.2	12.2	1.6	0.0	0.0	0.0	0.6	8.7	18.3	27.4	148.5
0° and below	28	6.5	4.2	0.5	0.0	0.0	0.0	0.0	0.0	0.0	0.0	0.0	2.3	13.4
AVG. STATION PRESS.(mb)	21	1006.7	1007.3	1005.9	1004.2	1004.6	1004.2	1004.8	1006.6	1007.9	1008.3	1007.6	1007.7	1006.3
RELATIVE HUMIDITY (%)														
Hour 01	28	76	74	72	71	78	83	84	88	88	83	79	78	80
Hour 07 (Local Time)	28	77	76	75	72	76	79	81	86	89	86	81	79	80
Hour 13	28	63	58	53	49	52	56	55	58	59	57	62	65	57
Hour 19	28	70	66	61	55	59	63	64	70	75	72	72	73	67
PRECIPITATION (inches):														
Water Equivalent														
-Normal		2.36	2.27	2.93	2.99	3.41	3.62	3.18	3.47	2.95	2.83	3.23	2.93	36.17
-Maximum Monthly	47	6.44	5.02	5.90	7.95	8.96	7.36	6.96	7.33	7.89	8.83	8.07	6.73	8.96
-Year		1978	1981	1977	1983	1953	1973	1975	1950	1960	1955	1972	1973	MAY 1953
-Minimum Monthly	47	0.42	0.24	0.26	1.14	1.05	0.65	0.49	0.73	0.40	0.20	0.91	0.64	0.20
-Year		1980	1987	1981	1963	1980	1964	1968	1947	1964	1963	1978	1958	OCT 1963
-Maximum in 24 hrs	47	1.91	1.74	2.38	2.20	2.17	3.48	3.42	4.52	3.66	3.31	2.26	4.02	4.52
-Year		1978	1990	1986	1968	1968	1952	1993	1971	1960	1987	1991	1948	AUG 1971
Snow,Ice pellets,hail														
-Maximum Monthly	47	47.8	34.5	34.7	17.7	1.6	T	T	0.0	T	6.5	24.6	57.5	57.5
-Year		1987	1962	1956	1982	1977	1991	1989		1989	1987	1972	1969	DEC 1969
-Maximum in 24 hrs	47	21.2	17.9	26.6	17.5	1.6	T	T	0.0	T	6.5	21.9	18.3	26.6
-Year		1983	1958	1993	1982	1977	1991	1989		1989	1987	1971	1966	MAR 1993
WIND:														
Mean Speed (mph)	55	9.8	10.2	10.6	10.4	9.0	8.3	7.5	7.0	7.4	8.1	9.1	9.3	8.9
Prevailing Direction through 1963		WNW	WNW	WNW	WNW	S	S	S	S	S	S	S	S	S
Fastest Obs. 1 Min.														
-Direction (!!!)	10	28	27	28	30	30	31	30	30	18	32	36	31	31
-Speed (MPH)	10	36	33	38	33	30	35	32	36	30	29	35	41	41
-Year		1985	1985	1984	1989	1993	1991	1993	1988	1989	1992	1989	1991	DEC 1991
Peak Gust														
-Direction (!!!)	10	W	W	W	W	NW	NW	W	NW	S	W	W	NW	NW
-Speed (mph)	10	58	56	53	47	49	59	52	55	47	56	58	56	59
-Date		1992	1985	1993	1992	1992	1991	1993	1990	1989	1992	1988	1985	JUN 1991

PRECIPITATION (inches)

ALBANY, NEW YORK

YEAR	JAN	FEB	MAR	APR	MAY	JUNE	JULY	AUG	SEP	OCT	NOV	DEC	ANNUAL
1964	3.35	1.63	2.93	2.17	1.31	0.65	1.29	2.55	0.40	0.54	1.45	3.28	21.55
1965	1.95	1.92	1.73	2.38	1.22	1.91	3.52	4.32	3.76	2.37	1.89	0.97	27.94
1966	2.29	2.71	3.63	1.46	2.35	2.95	3.88	1.44	5.61	2.22	1.79	3.04	33.37
1967	1.22	1.76	2.56	3.69	3.36	2.85	3.38	2.17	2.23	3.48	2.68	3.90	33.28
1968	1.48	0.36	2.62	2.64	4.79	4.38	0.49	1.77	1.49	2.18	5.48	4.60	32.28
1969	2.13	1.66	1.32	3.51	2.64	5.30	5.08	2.18	2.06	1.55	5.56	6.51	39.50
1970	0.81	1.98	2.87	3.01	1.78	3.14	1.93	3.35	3.79	2.49	1.48	3.89	30.52
1971	1.78	4.10	3.11	2.00	3.48	2.81	3.89	7.04	2.40	2.09	3.78	3.09	39.57
1972	1.21	3.04	4.05	3.63	5.98	6.84	3.10	1.48	1.99	3.60	8.07	4.19	47.18
1973	2.16	1.34	1.99	4.47	5.45	7.36	1.68	2.89	1.33	2.07	1.27	6.73	38.74
1974	2.04	2.12	3.10	2.80	3.47	3.31	4.84	3.53	5.37	1.49	3.83	2.57	38.47
1975	2.75	3.58	2.72	2.18	2.96	3.80	6.96	5.98	4.57	5.88	2.89	2.78	47.05
1976	3.78	2.60	3.57	3.63	4.89	5.37	2.60	5.04	2.61	5.65	1.41	1.39	42.54
1977	1.51	2.63	5.90	3.41	2.29	2.87	2.31	3.66	6.66	4.00	4.85	4.21	44.30
1978	6.44	0.88	1.99	1.68	1.96	4.60	4.04	3.06	1.87	2.95	0.91	3.08	33.46
1979	6.37	1.71	1.83	3.89	4.13	1.94	2.78	2.67	4.05	3.42	3.41	0.94	37.14
1980	0.42	0.89	4.44	3.02	1.05	4.90	2.69	6.45	2.24	2.27	2.99	1.23	32.59
1981	0.59	5.02	0.26	1.99	2.44	2.78	3.50	1.76	3.45	3.55	1.56	3.54	30.44
1982	3.18	2.14	3.23	2.46	2.60	6.48	2.43	2.01	1.42	0.99	3.80	1.33	32.07
1983	3.73	2.03	5.33	7.95	6.26	1.95	1.34	3.41	2.28	2.18	4.73	5.10	46.29
1984	1.28	2.98	3.04	4.29	7.92	1.74	3.97	3.25	1.53	2.50	2.15	2.48	37.13
1985	0.81	1.18	3.67	1.44	2.71	4.12	1.86	2.23	3.07	1.81	5.00	2.05	29.95
1986	3.17	3.00	3.72	1.49	3.11	5.43	6.68	4.09	2.61	2.12	4.62	3.92	43.96
1987	4.23	0.24	1.99	4.25	1.57	3.54	2.50	3.67	6.98	6.90	1.78	1.64	39.29
1988	1.95	3.00	1.62	2.22	2.95	1.42	3.12	4.77	1.50	1.40	4.58	1.02	29.55
1989	0.46	1.60	2.69	2.68	5.92	6.52	5.91	2.90	2.81	5.53	1.90	0.75	39.67
1990	3.84	3.94	3.66	3.87	6.12	2.66	1.68	6.66	1.81	4.60	3.67	3.50	46.01
1991	2.15	1.67	2.53	4.14	2.74	1.69	1.65	4.32	3.33	3.82	4.76	2.92	35.72
1992	1.86	1.30	1.66	2.77	3.61	1.96	4.26	2.05	2.43	2.80	3.66	3.02	31.38
1993	2.14	2.86	5.12	5.39	1.37	2.87	6.55	1.54	3.22	3.31	3.80	3.08	41.25
Record Mean	2.47	2.35	2.77	2.81	3.34	3.67	3.69	3.52	3.27	3.07	2.96	2.64	36.57

AVERAGE TEMPERATURE (deg. F)

ALBANY, NEW YORK

YEAR	JAN	FEB	MAR	APR	MAY	JUNE	JULY	AUG	SEP	OCT	NOV	DEC	ANNUAL
#1964	23.9	22.3	34.9	45.7	61.7	66.5	74.4	66.2	61.0	49.2	41.4	27.9	47.9
1965	18.1	22.3	31.2	42.2	59.6	66.9	68.9	69.4	63.6	51.2	37.6	30.8	46.8
1966	21.5	23.3	34.3	44.0	53.9	67.4	72.2	69.2	58.0	48.5	42.3	27.3	46.8
1967	27.0	18.0	29.0	43.5	50.4	69.9	71.6	69.3	61.3	51.0	34.8	28.9	46.2
1968	14.7	21.1	37.1	51.1	54.9	66.7	72.7	68.6	63.7	53.3	38.5	23.5	47.2
1969	20.9	24.7	31.1	47.6	56.3	66.0	69.7	70.6	62.4	49.0	39.7	21.6	46.6
1970	9.7	23.1	32.0	48.7	60.5	65.9	72.0	69.6	63.3	52.9	41.9	21.6	46.8
1971	13.9	25.4	30.6	42.3	54.9	66.3	68.4	66.8	64.8	54.7	36.9	30.0	46.3
1972	22.9	21.1	30.5	41.2	59.5	63.6	70.9	67.2	60.7	45.7	35.1	28.9	45.6
1973	27.0	22.0	41.9	48.8	55.3	68.7	72.8	72.9	60.5	51.0	39.9	28.2	49.1
1974	23.3	21.3	32.4	48.1	54.1	65.0	69.3	67.9	58.3	44.4	38.6	28.9	46.0
1975	25.7	24.9	30.8	40.7	61.9	65.1	72.8	70.0	59.4	53.3	45.5	26.1	48.0
1976	16.0	31.5	36.7	49.7	55.0	69.4	68.5	67.4	59.0	46.5	34.9	21.4	46.3
1977	15.5	24.5	40.0	46.8	60.2	64.6	71.7	67.8	61.4	49.7	42.6	26.7	47.6
1978	21.5	18.2	30.8	43.4	58.4	64.4	68.9	69.2	56.8	48.6	38.6	28.7	45.6
1979	22.1	14.4	38.9	45.4	60.0	66.0	72.5	69.0	61.2	50.2	44.1	31.4	47.9
1980	24.1	19.8	33.3	48.0	59.5	63.3	72.2	70.7	62.6	47.4	34.8	19.9	46.3
1981	14.0	33.1	34.7	48.1	58.9	66.7	69.3	68.5	58.8	44.8	37.7	25.7	46.7
1982	14.3	23.4	32.8	44.3	59.5	62.9	70.1	65.5	60.5	50.6	43.0	33.7	46.7
1983	24.3	26.8	37.6	46.7	54.9	67.2	72.2	69.8	62.6	49.6	39.2	24.0	47.9
1984	18.1	32.4	29.0	47.6	53.2	66.4	68.9	71.8	60.2	53.8	40.3	33.8	48.0
1985	19.9	26.8	37.3	49.7	60.0	62.2	70.7	68.7	63.3	50.2	40.1	24.5	47.8
1986	23.0	22.8	37.2	50.5	61.3	64.6	71.3	67.8	60.1	48.9	35.7	30.8	47.8
1987	21.7	21.7	37.7	50.4	60.0	68.3	73.5	67.2	60.6	46.6	40.1	30.7	48.2
1988	20.6	24.1	34.2	46.6	59.5	65.1	75.0	72.3	60.0	46.0	41.0	26.6	47.6
1989	27.8	24.2	33.5	44.6	59.5	68.0	71.6	69.8	62.5	51.5	39.3	13.7	47.2
1990	32.8	28.2	37.8	48.9	55.3	67.3	73.0	70.9	61.7	53.1	41.8	33.6	50.4
1991	23.2	30.0	37.4	51.2	63.2	69.0	71.6	71.2	59.9	53.2	40.1	28.9	49.9
1992	24.5	26.9	31.5	44.7	58.5	65.2	67.6	67.4	61.4	46.5	38.9	29.8	46.9
1993	26.6	18.3	31.4	48.4	59.5	66.3	73.1	71.7	60.5	48.6	38.4	27.4	47.5
Record Mean	22.8	23.9	33.7	46.6	58.5	67.4	72.3	70.1	62.4	51.1	39.6	27.6	48.0
Max	31.1	32.6	42.3	56.5	69.3	78.0	82.8	80.4	72.7	60.9	47.3	35.1	57.4
Min	14.4	15.2	25.1	36.7	47.7	56.8	61.7	59.7	52.1	41.3	31.9	20.1	38.5

REFERENCE NOTES

ALBANY, NEW YORK

GENERAL
T - TRACE AMOUNT.
BLANK ENTRIES DENOTE MISSING/UNREPORTED DATA.
# INDICATES A STATION OR INSTRUMENT RELOCATION.

SPECIFIC

PM - INCLUDES LAST DAY OF PREVIOUS MONTH
ASOS - AUTOMATED SURFACE OBSERVING SYSTEM IN OPERATION DURING THESE MONTHS.

(a) - LENGTH OF RECORD IN YEARS, ALTHOUGH INDIVIDUAL MONTHS MAY BE MISSING.
0.* OR * - THE VALUE IS BETWEEN 0.0 AND 0.05
NORMALS - BASED ON THE 1961-1990 RECORD PERIOD.
EXTREMES - DATES ARE THE MOST RECENT OCCURRENCE
WIND DIR.- NUMERALS SHOW TENS OF DEGRESS CLOCKWISE FROM TRUE NORTH. "00" INDICATES CALM.
RESULTANT DIRECTIONS ARE GIVEN TO WHOLE DEGREES.
BOLD VALUES INDICATE EXTREME VALUES WHICH OCCURRED AFTER THE ASOS SYSTEM WAS COMMISSIONED.

RECORD = PERIOD OF RECORD
RECORD MEAN PRECIPITATION IS THE MEAN OF ALL DAILY PRECIPITATION AMOUNTS DURING THE PERIOD OF RECORD.
RECORD MAX(MIN) TEMPERATURE IS THE MEAN OF ALL DAILY MAX(MIN) TEMPERATURES DURING THE PERIOD OF RECORD.
RECORD MEAN TEMPERATURE IS THE SUM OF THE RECORD MAX AND RECORD MIN DIVIDED BY 2.
AVERAGE TEMPERATURE IS THE SUM OF THE MEAN DAILY MAX AND MIN TEMPERATURE DIVIDED BY 2.

EXCEPTIONS

RECORD MEANS ARE THROUGH THE CURRENT YEAR,
BEGINNING IN 1874 FOR TEMPERATURE
1826 FOR PRECIPITATION
1947 FOR SNOWFALL

HEATING DEGREE DAYS Base 65 deg. F — ALBANY, NEW YORK

SEASON	JULY	AUG	SEP	OCT	NOV	DEC	JAN	FEB	MAR	APR	MAY	JUNE	TOTAL
#1964-65	1	48	169	484	702	1141	1449	1193	1041	679	197	68	7172
1965-66	11	49	120	421	817	1051	1342	1162	948	623	347	57	6948
1966-67	3	5	216	502	673	1163	1169	1312	1111	639	447	11	7251
1967-68	0	19	153	429	899	1112	1557	1269	857	412	304	46	7057
1968-69	7	45	76	359	787	1281	1360	1122	1043	518	284	55	6937
1969-70	13	22	137	491	749	1339	1708	1168	1016	495	165	75	7378
1970-71	3	7	127	377	686	1336	1580	1104	1059	672	315	50	7316
1971-72	20	45	109	311	838	1080	1298	1269	1060	707	175	97	7009
1972-73	16	38	154	590	890	1113	1168	1198	709	486	299	47	6708
1973-74	2	3	200	431	750	1136	1285	1216	1005	511	343	54	6936
1974-75	17	14	227	631	786	1113	1212	1115	1053	722	145	88	7123
1975-76	0	19	173	357	580	1199	1511	964	871	472	315	43	6504
1976-77	7	40	196	564	895	1345	1526	1127	764	545	205	85	7299
1977-78	7	51	156	471	666	1179	1340	1306	1051	642	245	84	7198
1978-79	43	19	256	503	784	1119	1324	1414	803	579	188	63	7095
1979-80	19	37	163	468	619	1036	1259	1303	974	503	190	106	6677
1980-81	0	7	140	539	900	1393	1575	885	930	502	235	30	7136
1981-82	8	22	204	622	816	1209	1564	1160	992	617	182	87	7483
1982-83	20	65	156	436	657	969	1255	1062	843	539	312	58	6372
1983-84	5	24	150	479	766	1265	1448	939	1109	517	363	60	7125
1984-85	12	8	170	344	737	959	1389	1062	852	458	184	106	6281
1985-86	7	16	123	452	740	1246	1295	1177	859	432	154	75	6576
1986-87	17	46	173	495	872	1053	1332	1207	842	433	210	29	6709
1987-88	2	56	154	567	741	1056	1370	1181	946	546	198	99	6916
1988-89	8	30	160	584	714	1185	1146	1133	968	607	194	35	6764
1989-90	0	22	134	413	766	1584	990	1026	839	500	298	44	6616
1990-91	5	6	148	388	689	964	1290	973	850	417	141	22	5893
1991-92	6	0	197	372	740	1111	1248	1098	1034	605	210	56	6677
1992-93	17	27	167	565	773	1082	1183	1300	1034	492	185	67	6892
1993-94	0	11	185	500	791	1161							

COOLING DEGREE DAYS Base 65 deg. F — ALBANY, NEW YORK

YEAR	JAN	FEB	MAR	APR	MAY	JUNE	JULY	AUG	SEP	OCT	NOV	DEC	TOTAL
1969	0	0	0	2	23	95	165	203	68	0	0	0	556
1970	0	0	0	12	36	107	225	160	83	7	0	0	630
1971	0	0	0	0	9	98	132	107	109	1	0	0	456
1972	0	0	0	0	12	58	208	112	31	0	0	0	421
1973	0	0	0	7	6	164	248	255	71	2	0	0	753
1974	0	0	0	11	12	59	157	111	35	0	1	0	386
1975	0	0	0	0	58	97	248	180	12	0	2	0	597
1976	0	0	0	19	11	184	120	120	22	0	0	0	476
1977	0	0	0	8	66	79	222	146	53	0	0	0	574
1978	0	0	0	0	47	70	169	154	16	0	0	0	456
1979	0	0	0	0	39	99	258	168	55	17	0	0	636
1980	0	0	0	0	28	63	230	189	73	0	0	0	583
1981	0	0	0	2	53	87	149	137	25	0	0	0	453
1982	0	0	0	0	19	31	184	88	29	0	4	0	355
1983	0	0	0	0	8	134	236	179	86	6	0	0	649
1984	0	0	0	0	3	107	140	226	35	3	0	0	514
1985	0	0	0	5	37	27	191	140	80	2	0	0	482
1986	0	0	6	4	46	69	220	140	33	1	0	0	519
1987	0	0	0	4	62	136	271	133	29	0	0	0	635
1988	0	0	0	0	36	110	326	263	16	4	0	0	755
1989	0	0	1	0	31	132	213	178	63	0	0	0	618
1990	0	0	2	22	1	119	261	197	55	24	0	0	681
1991	0	0	0	9	92	147	221	198	50	14	0	0	731
1992	0	0	0	2	15	70	106	112	65	0	0	0	370
1993	0	0	0	0	17	116	259	224	55	2	0	0	673

SNOWFALL (inches) — ALBANY, NEW YORK

SEASON	JULY	AUG	SEP	OCT	NOV	DEC	JAN	FEB	MAR	APR	MAY	JUNE	TOTAL
1964-65	0.0	0.0	0.0	T	T	11.2	20.4	3.7	8.4	2.1	0.0	0.0	45.8
1965-66	0.0	0.0	0.0	T	0.5	2.7	28.8	24.5	9.2	T	1.4	0.0	67.1
1966-67	0.0	0.0	0.0	0.0	T	29.4	5.7	16.3	26.2	3.1	0.2	0.0	80.9
1967-68	0.0	0.0	0.0	T	9.0	17.8	8.0	1.8	5.6	0.0	0.0	0.0	42.2
1968-69	0.0	0.0	0.0	0.0	13.5	18.1	6.3	20.7	4.5	0.2	0.0	0.0	63.3
1969-70	0.0	0.0	0.0	T	3.2	57.5	7.2	7.4	11.2	1.2	T	0.0	87.7
1970-71	0.0	0.0	0.0	T	T	43.8	15.2	17.6	32.0	3.9	0.0	0.0	112.5
1971-72	0.0	0.0	0.0	0.0	24.0	10.1	8.5	24.8	15.9	6.0	0.0	0.0	89.3
1972-73	0.0	0.0	0.0	T	24.6	22.5	11.2	12.5	T	0.1	0.0	0.0	70.9
1973-74	0.0	0.0	0.0	0.0	0.1	18.9	10.0	12.4	5.6	11.3	0.0	0.0	58.3
1974-75	0.0	0.0	0.0	T	2.2	12.5	14.0	21.2	2.9	1.8	0.0	0.0	54.6
1975-76	0.0	0.0	0.0	0.0	3.6	16.4	15.0	4.4	14.8	T	T	0.0	54.2
1976-77	0.0	0.0	0.0	T	5.7	7.8	22.1	17.9	15.2	0.3	1.6	0.0	70.6
1977-78	0.0	0.0	0.0	0.0	8.4	19.8	40.8	15.8	7.4	0.2	T	0.0	92.4
1978-79	0.0	0.0	0.0	0.0	3.4	19.9	26.5	4.6	0.9	8.2	0.0	0.0	63.5
1979-80	0.0	0.0	0.0	T	0.0	5.8	0.6	10.2	10.8	0.0	0.0	0.0	27.4
1980-81	0.0	0.0	0.0	0.0	11.8	12.8	11.9	6.9	1.5	T	0.0	0.0	44.9
1981-82	0.0	0.0	0.0	0.0	1.1	31.4	18.2	9.6	19.1	17.7	0.0	0.0	97.1
1982-83	0.0	0.0	0.0	0.0	0.6	5.5	27.5	17.4	9.2	14.7	0.1	0.0	75.0
1983-84	0.0	0.0	0.0	0.0	1.7	11.6	16.5	7.2	28.2	T	0.0	0.0	65.2
1984-85	0.0	0.0	0.0	0.0	2.2	11.7	8.4	10.1	8.7	0.2	0.0	0.0	41.3
1985-86	0.0	0.0	0.0	0.0	11.8	11.5	18.0	16.1	3.4	1.7	T	0.0	62.5
1986-87	0.0	0.0	0.0	0.0	8.3	20.3	47.8	2.8	0.8	0.6	0.0	0.0	80.6
1987-88	0.0	0.0	0.0	6.5	6.2	11.4	21.7	26.0	4.8	0.1	0.0	0.0	76.7
1988-89	0.0	0.0	0.0	T	T	7.8	1.3	5.1	4.7	0.1	0.0	0.0	19.0
1989-90	T	0.0	T	0.0	1.9	8.0	20.3	22.8	4.9	T	0.0	0.0	57.9
1990-91	0.0	0.0	0.0	T	0.4	8.5	11.2	5.3	3.3	0.0	0.0	T	28.7
1991-92	0.0	0.0	0.0	0.0	1.5	12.7	3.4	6.3	4.9	1.9	0.0	0.0	30.7
1992-93	0.0	0.0	0.0	T	2.8	12.6	14.3	28.6	34.3	1.6	0.0	0.0	94.2
1993-94	0.0	0.0	0.0	T	0.7	6.1							-
Record Mean	T	0.0	T	0.2	4.1	14.9	16.0	14.2	11.1	2.7	0.1	T	63.2

BUFFALO, NEW YORK

The country surrounding Buffalo is comparatively low and level to the west. To the east and south the land is gently rolling, rising to pronounced hills within 12 to 18 miles, and to 1,000 feet above the level of Lake Erie about 35 miles south-southeast of the city. An escarpment of 50 to 100 feet lies east-west 1-1/2 miles to the north. The eastern end of Lake Erie is 9 miles to the west-southwest, while Lake Ontario lies 25 miles to the north, the two being connected by the Niagara River, which flows north-northwestward from the end of Lake Erie.

Buffalo is located near the mean position of the polar front. Its weather is varied and changeable, characteristic of the latitude. Wide seasonal swings of temperature from hot to cold are tempered appreciably by the proximity of Lakes Erie and Ontario. Lake Erie lies to the southwest, the direction of the prevailing wind. Wind flow throughout the year is somewhat higher due to this exposure. The vigorous interplay of warm and cold air masses during the winter and early spring months causes one or more windstorms. Precipitation is moderate and fairly evenly divided throughout the twelve months.

The spring season is more cloudy and cooler than points not affected by the cold lake. Spring growth of vegetation is retarded, protecting it from late spring frosts. With heavy winter ice accumulations in the lake, typical spring conditions are delayed until late May or early June.

Summer comes suddenly in mid-June. Lake breezes temper the extreme heat of the summer season. Temperatures of 90 degrees and above are infrequent. There is more summer sunshine here than in any other section of the state. Due to the stabilizing effects of Lake Erie, thunderstorms are relatively infrequent. Most of them are caused by frontal action. To the north and south of the city thunderstorms occur more often.

Autumn has long, dry periods and is frost free usually until mid-October. Cloudiness increases in November, continuing mostly cloudy throughout the winter and early spring. Snow flurries off the lake begin in mid-November or early December. Outbreaks of Arctic air in December and throughout the winter months produce locally heavy snowfalls from the lake. At the same time, temperatures of well below zero over Canada and the midwest are raised 10 to 30 degrees in crossing the lakes. Only on rare occasions do polar air masses drop southward from eastern Hudson Bay across Lake Ontario without appreciable warming.

NORMALS, MEANS, AND EXTREMES

BUFFALO, NEW YORK

LATITUDE: 42°56'N LONGITUDE: 78°44' W ELEVATION: FT. GRND 705 BARO 715 TIME ZONE: EASTERN WBAN: 14733

	(a)	JAN	FEB	MAR	APR	MAY	JUNE	JULY	AUG	SEP	OCT	NOV	DEC	YEAR
TEMPERATURE °F:														
Normals														
-Daily Maximum		30.2	31.6	41.7	54.2	66.1	75.3	80.2	77.9	70.8	59.4	47.1	35.3	55.8
-Daily Minimum		17.0	17.4	25.9	36.2	47.0	56.5	61.9	60.1	53.0	42.7	33.9	22.9	39.5
-Monthly		23.6	24.5	33.8	45.2	56.6	65.9	71.1	69.0	61.9	51.1	40.5	29.1	47.7
Extremes														
-Record Highest	50	72	65	81	94	90	96	97	99	98	87	80	74	99
-Year		1950	1981	1945	1990	1991	1988	1988	1948	1953	1951	1961	1982	AUG 1948
-Record Lowest	50	-16	-20	-7	12	26	35	43	38	32	20	9	-10	-20
-Year		1982	1961	1984	1982	1947	1945	1945	1982	1991	1965	1971	1980	FEB 1961
NORMAL DEGREE DAYS:														
Heating (base 65°F)		1283	1134	967	594	279	59	5	17	130	431	735	1113	6747
Cooling (base 65°F)		0	0	0	0	19	86	194	141	37	0	0	0	477
% OF POSSIBLE SUNSHINE	50	31	38	45	51	58	65	67	64	57	49	29	27	48
MEAN SKY COVER (tenths)														
Sunrise - Sunset	50	8.4	8.2	7.6	7.1	6.8	6.2	6.0	6.1	6.4	6.7	8.4	8.5	7.2
MEAN NUMBER OF DAYS:														
Sunrise to Sunset														
-Clear	50	1.4	2.2	3.8	4.9	5.6	6.3	6.9	7.0	6.4	6.3	2.1	1.3	54.1
-Partly Cloudy	50	6.1	5.6	7.6	8.0	9.7	11.5	13.1	11.8	9.9	8.4	5.4	6.1	103.1
-Cloudy	50	23.5	20.5	19.6	17.1	15.7	12.2	11.0	12.3	13.7	16.3	22.6	23.5	208.1
Precipitation														
.01 inches or more	50	19.8	17.2	16.1	14.2	12.4	10.4	9.9	10.6	11.0	11.8	16.1	19.5	168.9
Snow,Ice pellets,hail														
1.0 inches or more	50	7.1	5.5	3.5	1.0	0.1	0.0	0.0	0.0	0.0	0.1	3.0	6.1	26.4
Thunderstorms	50	0.2	0.2	1.3	2.3	3.1	5.2	5.7	6.0	3.8	1.6	1.1	0.4	30.9
Heavy Fog Visibility														
1/4 mile or less	50	1.4	1.7	2.6	2.2	2.3	1.2	0.8	0.9	1.0	1.3	1.2	1.2	17.9
Temperature °F														
-Maximum														
90° and above	33	0.0	0.0	0.0	0.*	0.1	0.5	1.5	0.6	0.*	0.0	0.0	0.0	2.9
32° and below	33	17.1	15.2	7.2	0.5	0.0	0.0	0.0	0.0	0.0	0.0	1.9	11.9	53.8
-Minimum														
32° and below	33	28.5	25.8	23.8	10.3	0.6	0.0	0.0	0.0	0.1	3.3	14.0	25.6	132.1
0° and below	33	2.0	1.5	0.2	0.0	0.0	0.0	0.0	0.0	0.0	0.0	0.0	0.6	4.4
AVG. STATION PRESS.(mb)	21	990.5	991.6	990.2	989.1	989.5	989.5	990.4	991.8	992.4	992.4	991.3	991.2	990.8
RELATIVE HUMIDITY (%)														
Hour 01	33	77	79	78	75	76	79	79	83	83	79	79	79	79
Hour 07 (Local Time)	33	79	80	80	76	75	77	78	83	84	82	80	81	80
Hour 13	33	72	70	65	58	55	56	55	58	60	60	69	73	63
Hour 19	33	76	75	72	64	62	61	60	66	72	72	76	77	69
PRECIPITATION (inches):														
Water Equivalent														
-Normal		2.70	2.31	2.68	2.87	3.14	3.55	3.08	4.17	3.49	3.09	3.83	3.67	38.58
-Maximum Monthly	50	6.88	5.90	5.97	5.90	7.22	8.36	8.93	10.67	8.99	9.13	9.75	8.71	10.67
-Year		1982	1990	1991	1961	1989	1987	1992	1977	1977	1954	1985	1990	AUG 1977
-Minimum Monthly	50	1.03	0.81	1.20	1.27	1.21	0.11	0.93	1.10	0.77	0.30	1.44	0.69	0.11
-Year		1946	1968	1967	1946	1965	1955	1989	1948	1964	1963	1944	1943	JUN 1955
-Maximum in 24 hrs	50	2.57	2.31	2.14	2.09	3.52	5.01	3.38	3.88	4.94	3.49	2.51	2.33	5.01
-Year		1982	1954	1954	1991	1986	1987	1963	1963	1979	1945	1949	1990	JUN 1987
Snow,Ice pellets,hail														
-Maximum Monthly	50	68.3	54.2	29.3	15.0	7.9	T	T	T	T	3.1	31.3	68.4	68.4
-Year		1977	1958	1993	1975	1989	1980	1993	1991	1993	1972	1976	1985	DEC 1985
-Maximum in 24 hrs	50	25.3	19.4	17.2	6.8	7.9	T	T	T	T	2.8	19.9	24.3	25.3
-Year		1982	1984	1993	1975	1989	1980	1993	1991	1993	1993	1955	1945	JAN 1982
WIND:														
Mean Speed (mph)	54	14.2	13.5	13.2	12.6	11.4	10.9	10.3	9.8	10.3	11.1	12.7	13.3	11.9
Prevailing Direction through 1963		WSW	SW	SW	SW	SW	SW	SW	SW	S	S	S	WSW	SW
Fastest Mile														
-Direction (!!)	47	SW	SW	W	W	SW	NW	NW	SW	SW	SW	SW	S	SW
-Speed (MPH)	47	91	70	68	67	63	56	59	56	59	63	66	60	91
-Year		1950	1946	1959	1957	1950	1954	1953	1944	1954	1954	1948	1945	JAN 1950
Peak Gust														
-Direction (!!)	10	SW	S	W	W	SW	SW	SW	W	S	SW	SW	SW	W
-Speed (mph)	10	71	55	72	74	61	59	53	71	62	61	72	66	74
-Date		1985	1988	1986	1985	1990	1990	1990	1988	1987	1993	1992	1985	APR 1985

PRECIPITATION (inches)

BUFFALO, NEW YORK

YEAR	JAN	FEB	MAR	APR	MAY	JUNE	JULY	AUG	SEP	OCT	NOV	DEC	ANNUAL
1964	2.12	1.09	3.72	3.36	2.91	1.55	2.57	5.02	0.77	1.89	2.09	2.58	29.67
1965	3.27	2.99	1.97	1.99	1.21	1.50	3.69	4.12	2.37	5.07	4.69	2.60	35.47
1966	3.74	2.11	2.78	2.06	1.36	1.97	4.92	3.60	2.65	0.93	4.50	2.25	32.87
1967	1.18	1.39	1.20	2.60	3.69	2.50	1.57	4.04	6.36	4.78	3.13	2.16	34.60
1968	2.18	0.81	2.67	1.78	3.30	4.45	1.19	5.33	5.63	3.03	4.47	3.42	38.26
1969	3.85	0.97	1.62	4.16	3.75	3.51	3.83	2.48	2.04	2.77	4.09	3.09	36.16
1970	2.06	1.74	1.72	2.54	2.87	2.55	4.02	2.01	4.55	4.20	3.20	3.25	34.71
1971	1.46	3.03	2.07	1.48	1.56	4.25	4.50	4.43	1.88	1.57	3.07	3.61	32.91
1972	2.17	3.44	3.99	2.99	3.64	6.06	0.99	4.19	3.06	2.96	4.28	3.86	41.63
1973	2.03	1.98	3.27	3.56	2.99	1.68	3.68	2.98	1.44	4.27	4.07	4.89	36.84
1974	2.44	2.19	3.19	3.15	3.36	3.86	1.80	3.64	2.42	1.75	5.38	3.13	36.31
1975	2.11	2.93	2.92	1.86	3.31	3.65	2.34	8.49	2.44	1.13	2.77	4.58	38.53
1976	3.19	3.43	5.59	4.01	4.70	3.36	5.65	1.65	5.39	3.61	2.11	3.83	46.52
1977	3.38	1.59	2.42	3.60	1.39	2.79	3.64	10.67	8.99	2.61	4.45	8.02	53.55
1978	6.29	1.36	1.72	1.84	3.95	2.42	1.48	3.51	4.40	3.72	1.55	3.50	35.74
1979	5.43	2.03	2.48	3.16	1.63	2.18	3.51	6.26	5.61	3.88	4.14	3.43	43.74
1980	1.97	1.08	4.05	2.43	1.60	5.82	3.55	3.58	4.53	4.69	2.36	2.65	38.31
1981	1.11	3.50	1.70	3.09	2.56	3.68	5.05	3.13	4.24	3.31	2.22	2.87	36.46
1982	6.88	1.28	2.64	2.33	3.66	3.14	1.50	4.62	3.37	2.06	6.31	3.32	41.11
1983	1.44	1.30	3.20	2.55	3.28	2.99	2.01	3.51	2.11	4.62	5.19	7.30	39.50
1984	1.54	3.59	1.77	2.53	4.67	6.86	1.37	4.16	3.73	0.87	2.66	3.67	37.42
1985	4.27	3.34	4.42	1.33	3.46	3.21	1.81	4.63	1.20	3.73	9.75	4.85	46.00
1986	2.31	2.60	1.95	3.33	4.42	4.15	2.82	2.73	3.88	4.34	3.11	4.02	39.66
1987	2.90	0.85	3.66	3.40	1.35	8.36	3.09	3.38	5.32	2.62	4.44	2.78	42.15
1988	1.58	4.07	2.99	2.96	2.74	1.56	6.35	2.69	2.07	6.08	3.37	2.15	38.61
1989	1.77	2.54	3.15	1.88	7.22	7.83	0.93	1.84	3.85	2.98	4.83	2.34	41.16
1990	2.69	5.90	1.50	5.22	6.08	3.55	3.14	3.25	3.65	4.59	2.61	8.71	50.89
1991	2.07	2.06	5.97	5.83	3.10	0.86	3.34	2.84	3.19	3.11	4.02	3.81	40.20
1992	2.01	2.45	2.93	4.68	3.48	2.21	8.93	3.79	5.56	2.80	4.92	3.80	47.56
1993	4.35	1.92	3.02	2.55	1.79	4.99	1.78	3.86	5.53	3.69	3.58	3.60	40.66
Record Mean	3.06	2.69	2.79	2.75	2.95	2.92	2.96	3.23	3.13	3.09	3.34	3.32	36.23

AVERAGE TEMPERATURE (deg. F)

BUFFALO, NEW YORK

YEAR	JAN	FEB	MAR	APR	MAY	JUNE	JULY	AUG	SEP	OCT	NOV	DEC	ANNUAL
1964	29.3	23.5	34.0	46.9	59.2	65.7	73.1	64.9	60.9	48.1	42.1	29.5	48.1
1965	23.6	25.8	30.0	41.2	59.6	64.3	67.6	67.8	63.5	47.8	40.0	34.3	47.1
1966	20.4	24.9	34.7	43.3	52.2	67.4	71.4	68.5	58.7	48.8	41.5	28.6	46.7
1967	29.8	20.6	30.9	46.1	50.1	72.5	71.2	68.1	60.7	51.9	36.3	33.0	47.6#
1968	19.9	20.7	35.7	49.2	53.4	64.8	71.2	69.4	66.1	53.5	40.7	26.8	47.6
1969	25.0	24.6	30.9	46.8	54.4	64.4	70.5	71.2	62.2	51.0	39.1	24.8	47.1
1970	17.6	24.8	30.1	46.9	57.3	66.0	71.0	70.2	64.0	54.5	41.6	27.4	47.6
1971	20.9	27.0	29.8	41.8	54.5	67.6	68.7	67.8	65.4	58.7	39.1	33.5	47.9
1972	25.5	22.0	30.1	41.1	59.1	62.6	71.0	67.7	62.8	46.2	36.0	30.8	46.3
1973	27.6	22.9	42.4	46.9	54.5	68.2	72.3	71.8	61.7	54.3	40.8	29.0	49.4
1974	27.1	22.3	33.0	46.2	53.1	65.6	69.9	69.9	59.6	49.2	40.2	31.7	47.3
1975	30.1	29.1	30.8	39.3	62.1	68.0	72.3	69.7	58.3	53.1	46.9	28.3	49.0
1976	19.7	31.8	37.2	46.5	53.4	68.4	67.8	67.5	60.1	46.3	34.1	22.0	46.3
1977	13.8	24.6	39.8	47.0	60.3	64.4	72.0	68.1	62.6	49.6	43.3	27.9	47.8
1978	20.4	15.5	28.2	42.5	57.4	65.1	70.4	70.3	60.8	49.5	40.4	30.4	45.9
1979	20.5	14.9	38.2	44.3	56.9	66.5	71.3	67.5	61.9	50.7	43.5	33.4	47.5
1980	25.8	21.2	31.8	46.1	58.1	61.9	71.7	72.6	62.4	48.7	39.4	25.3	47.1
1981	19.3	32.9	33.9	47.2	56.4	66.2	71.8	70.0	60.9	48.2	40.4	29.0	48.0
1982	17.2	23.2	32.5	41.6	61.0	62.2	71.8	65.0	61.6	52.6	43.0	37.5	47.5
1983	27.0	29.6	36.7	43.6	53.9	67.6	74.2	71.2	63.7	51.7	40.8	22.7	48.6
1984	20.4	33.8	27.1	47.7	52.9	67.8	70.3	70.3	58.5	53.2	39.0	35.6	48.1
1985	21.1	24.8	35.6	49.5	59.5	62.7	69.7	69.2	64.2	52.5	42.0	25.6	48.0
1986	25.5	24.5	36.2	47.8	59.7	64.1	71.1	67.9	61.8	50.9	37.7	32.4	48.3
1987	26.1	25.0	37.7	50.0	60.5	68.9	74.2	68.9	63.4	47.9	42.5	34.3	50.0
1988	26.6	24.3	35.2	46.1	59.7	64.0	74.8	72.4	62.1	46.9	43.0	30.0	48.8
1989	31.3	22.7	33.0	41.9	55.1	65.9	71.5	68.5	60.8	51.5	37.9	17.4	46.5
1990	33.4	29.3	36.9	48.5	54.9	66.7	71.4	70.4	61.7	52.5	43.4	34.4	50.3
1991	26.0	30.6	37.8	50.5	64.3	69.1	71.9	71.0	62.0	53.1	39.3	31.3	50.6
1992	27.1	27.7	31.6	43.8	57.3	63.4	66.8	66.3	61.6	47.9	40.2	31.9	47.1
1993	29.5	20.7	30.7	47.3	57.0	66.0	73.4	72.0	59.4	49.2	39.6	29.6	47.9
Record Mean	25.0	24.7	32.6	43.8	55.1	64.8	70.5	69.0	62.4	51.5	40.0	29.5	47.4
Max	31.4	31.6	39.9	52.0	63.7	72.7	78.3	77.0	70.5	59.1	46.3	35.4	54.8
Min	18.5	17.7	25.3	35.5	46.4	56.9	62.6	60.9	54.3	44.0	33.8	23.6	40.0

REFERENCE NOTES

BUFFALO, NEW YORK

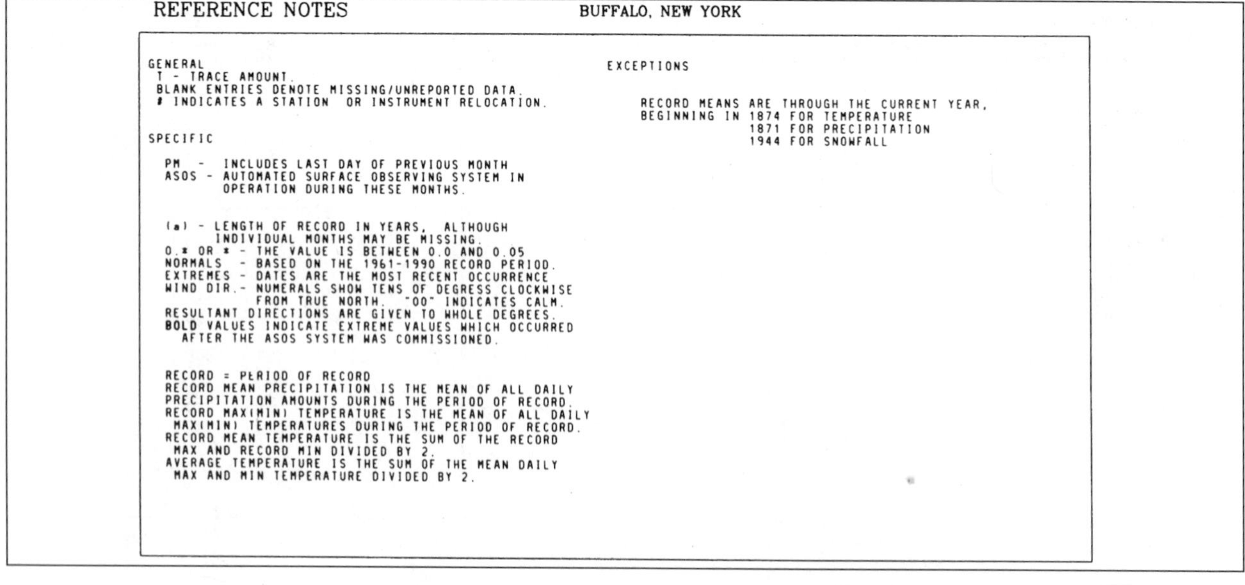

GENERAL
T - TRACE AMOUNT.
BLANK ENTRIES DENOTE MISSING/UNREPORTED DATA.
# INDICATES A STATION OR INSTRUMENT RELOCATION.

SPECIFIC

PM - INCLUDES LAST DAY OF PREVIOUS MONTH
ASOS - AUTOMATED SURFACE OBSERVING SYSTEM IN OPERATION DURING THESE MONTHS.

(a) - LENGTH OF RECORD IN YEARS, ALTHOUGH INDIVIDUAL MONTHS MAY BE MISSING.
0.* OR * - THE VALUE IS BETWEEN 0.0 AND 0.05
NORMALS - BASED ON THE 1961-1990 RECORD PERIOD.
EXTREMES - DATES ARE THE MOST RECENT OCCURRENCE
WIND DIR.- NUMERALS SHOW TENS OF DEGRESS CLOCKWISE FROM TRUE NORTH. "00" INDICATES CALM.
RESULTANT DIRECTIONS ARE GIVEN TO WHOLE DEGREES.
BOLD VALUES INDICATE EXTREME VALUES WHICH OCCURRED AFTER THE ASOS SYSTEM WAS COMMISSIONED.

RECORD = PERIOD OF RECORD
RECORD MEAN PRECIPITATION IS THE MEAN OF ALL DAILY PRECIPITATION AMOUNTS DURING THE PERIOD OF RECORD.
RECORD MAX(MIN) TEMPERATURE IS THE MEAN OF ALL DAILY MAX(MIN) TEMPERATURES DURING THE PERIOD OF RECORD.
RECORD MEAN TEMPERATURE IS THE SUM OF THE RECORD MAX AND RECORD MIN DIVIDED BY 2.
AVERAGE TEMPERATURE IS THE SUM OF THE MEAN DAILY MAX AND MIN TEMPERATURE DIVIDED BY 2.

EXCEPTIONS

RECORD MEANS ARE THROUGH THE CURRENT YEAR, BEGINNING IN
1874 FOR TEMPERATURE
1871 FOR PRECIPITATION
1944 FOR SNOWFALL

HEATING DEGREE DAYS Base 65 deg. F — BUFFALO, NEW YORK

SEASON	JULY	AUG	SEP	OCT	NOV	DEC	JAN	FEB	MAR	APR	MAY	JUNE	TOTAL
1964-65	5	68	176	518	680	1097	1277	1092	1080	706	186	100	6985
1965-66	23	46	122	525	742	942	1374	1114	931	648	401	68	6936
1966-67	7	19	199	495	700	1124	1086	1239	1047	560	457	4	6937
1967-68	12	26	162	403	853	985	1393	1281	901	469	352	84	6921
1968-69	11	29	58	374	722	1180	1233	1125	1052	540	325	102	6751
1969-70	13	16	147	433	769	1240	1459	1121	1076	552	255	66	7147
1970-71	6	6	93	328	695	1161	1361	1057	1085	691	327	36	6846
1971-72	11	29	87	202	771	971	1218	1237	1070	707	187	112	6602
1972-73	16	33	113	574	860	1054	1152	1173	696	542	318	24	6555
1973-74	2	14	171	326	720	1107	1167	1187	989	553	365	51	6652
1974-75	2	0	187	483	738	1024	1077	1001	1053	764	175	32	6536
1975-76	3	15	197	368	535	1134	1400	958	853	557	358	40	6418
1976-77	15	35	180	573	921	1328	1580	1123	775	544	207	90	7371
1977-78	5	40	110	473	646	1146	1376	1378	1130	670	282	81	7337
1978-79	14	3	154	472	732	1067	1371	1400	823	619	285	65	7005
1979-80	16	35	134	455	636	973	1208	1265	1022	559	240	142	6685
1980-81	2	0	128	498	759	1224	1411	895	956	527	269	33	6702
1981-82	6	11	170	514	732	1108	1476	1163	1002	698	147	95	7122
1982-83	4	65	140	382	656	848	1172	987	868	636	342	71	6171
1983-84	5	10	125	418	722	1304	1378	899	1167	519	385	35	6967
1984-85	11	22	210	360	774	905	1354	1120	902	476	196	95	6425
1985-86	8	12	114	378	685	1215	1215	1128	885	519	197	80	6436
1986-87	4	42	137	430	811	1003	1199	1115	837	447	213	28	6266
1987-88	3	25	91	527	665	948	1184	1174	916	560	186	113	6392
1988-89	5	17	122	560	654	1078	1038	1177	985	687	321	60	6704
1989-90	1	28	170	411	806	1466	970	995	866	518	311	46	6588
1990-91	5	2	141	395	640	941	1203	956	836	431	141	22	5713
1991-92	1	1	166	376	762	1037	1169	1076	1027	633	254	93	6595
1992-93	28	41	148	525	738	1021	1095	1235	1053	526	257	60	6727
1993-94	0	8	212	486	752	1089							

COOLING DEGREE DAYS Base 65 deg. F — BUFFALO, NEW YORK

YEAR	JAN	FEB	MAR	APR	MAY	JUNE	JULY	AUG	SEP	OCT	NOV	DEC	TOTAL
1969	0	0	0	0	1	88	192	212	69	6	0	0	568
1970	0	0	0	16	21	108	197	173	72	12	0	0	599
1971	0	0	0	0	9	119	136	122	107	15	0	0	508
1972	0	0	0	0	12	48	210	123	57	0	0	0	450
1973	0	0	0	6	2	126	233	230	78	3	0	0	678
1974	0	0	0	0	7	71	163	158	29	0	0	0	428
1975	0	0	0	0	90	129	238	171	3	3	0	0	634
1976	0	0	0	8	7	149	109	119	40	0	0	0	432
1977	0	0	0	12	68	78	228	142	45	0	1	0	574
1978	0	0	0	0	52	91	189	173	35	0	0	0	540
1979	0	0	0	6	40	118	217	120	49	20	0	0	570
1980	0	0	0	0	32	56	217	242	58	2	0	0	607
1981	0	0	0	2	13	78	225	173	55	0	0	0	546
1982	0	0	0	3	31	18	221	74	45	2	0	2	396
1983	0	0	0	0	5	157	300	214	90	15	0	0	781
1984	0	0	0	5	16	123	183	193	23	1	0	0	544
1985	0	0	0	18	32	32	161	151	96	0	1	0	491
1986	0	0	0	7	38	60	200	137	46	0	0	0	488
1987	0	0	0	4	79	151	298	152	49	0	0	0	733
1988	0	0	0	0	29	88	315	255	41	8	0	0	736
1989	0	0	0	0	21	97	207	143	50	0	0	0	518
1990	0	0	3	29	4	104	208	176	47	14	0	0	585
1991	0	0	0	3	125	153	221	193	83	13	0	0	791
1992	0	0	0	1	24	53	90	90	55	0	0	0	313
1993	0	0	0	0	14	97	267	231	51	3	0	0	663

SNOWFALL (inches) — BUFFALO, NEW YORK

SEASON	JULY	AUG	SEP	OCT	NOV	DEC	JAN	FEB	MAR	APR	MAY	JUNE	TOTAL
1964-65	0.0	0.0	0.0	T	5.4	15.2	19.2	9.4	17.5	4.2	0.0	0.0	70.9
1965-66	0.0	0.0	0.0	1.2	12.2	7.0	48.0	15.2	11.4	3.2	0.1	0.0	98.3
1966-67	0.0	0.0	0.0	0.0	10.0	12.1	11.6	19.8	10.8	0.6	1.2	0.0	66.1
1967-68	0.0	0.0	0.0	T	19.7	10.4	19.1	11.7	10.6	0.1	0.0	0.0	71.6
1968-69	0.0	0.0	0.0	T	11.6	11.7	31.2	12.8	8.0	3.1	0.0	0.0	78.4
1969-70	0.0	0.0	0.0	1.0	22.1	23.4	38.0	21.9	12.6	1.5	T	0.0	120.5
1970-71	0.0	0.0	0.0	0.0	2.6	32.3	17.2	19.4	22.6	2.9	0.0	0.0	97.0
1971-72	0.0	0.0	0.0	0.0	18.7	12.9	27.6	31.4	14.1	5.2	0.0	0.0	109.9
1972-73	0.0	0.0	0.0	3.1	18.9	19.8	9.9	16.1	8.5	2.4	0.1	0.0	78.8
1973-74	0.0	0.0	0.0	0.0	3.0	23.1	19.7	22.8	12.9	7.1	0.1	0.0	88.7
1974-75	0.0	0.0	0.0	T	22.1	23.6	11.0	16.3	7.6	15.0	0.0	0.0	95.6
1975-76	0.0	0.0	0.0	T	5.5	27.3	21.6	8.3	17.3	2.5	T	0.0	82.5
1976-77	0.0	0.0	0.0	0.2	31.3	60.7	68.3	22.7	13.5	2.2	0.5	0.0	199.4
1977-78	0.0	0.0	0.0	T	15.0	53.4	56.5	21.7	5.8	1.8	0.1	0.0	154.3
1978-79	0.0	0.0	0.0	T	3.0	10.1	42.6	28.3	4.6	8.7	0.0	0.0	97.3
1979-80	0.0	0.0	0.0	T	12.6	19.7	10.2	11.7	13.9	0.3	T	T	68.4
1980-81	0.0	0.0	0.0	T	6.7	21.6	14.4	5.0	13.2	T	0.0	0.0	60.9
1981-82	0.0	0.0	0.0	T	1.8	24.8	53.2	12.7	9.0	10.9	0.0	0.0	112.4
1982-83	0.0	0.0	0.0	0.0	15.8	12.9	9.0	5.5	6.9	2.3	T	0.0	52.4
1983-84	0.0	0.0	0.0	T	17.7	52.0	13.4	32.5	16.0	0.9	T	0.0	132.5
1984-85	0.0	0.0	0.0	0.0	1.4	11.2	65.9	20.9	6.3	1.5	0.0	0.0	107.2
1985-86	0.0	0.0	0.0	0.0	5.2	68.4	17.3	17.3	4.8	1.7	T	0.0	114.7
1986-87	0.0	0.0	0.0	0.0	13.7	4.8	28.5	7.7	10.8	2.0	0.0	0.0	67.5
1987-88	0.0	0.0	0.0	T	0.9	9.8	6.9	31.9	6.1	0.8	0.0	0.0	56.4
1988-89	0.0	0.0	0.0	0.5	0.6	10.8	5.4	29.6	10.1	2.5	7.9	0.0	67.4
1989-90	0.0	0.0	0.0	T	7.8	34.8	11.8	28.0	1.4	9.9	T	0.0	93.7
1990-91	0.0	0.0	0.0	T	0.7	15.4	16.6	16.1	8.5	0.2	T	0.0	57.5
1991-92	0.0	T	0.0	0.2	18.0	21.4	18.4	7.0	22.8	5.0	0.0	0.0	92.8
1992-93	0.0	0.0	0.0	0.6	13.7	16.5	13.1	19.5	29.3	0.5	T	0.0	93.2
1993-94	T	0.0	T	2.9	4.8	27.9							
Record Mean	T	T	T	0.3	11.5	22.7	23.3	18.2	11.7	3.1	0.3	T	91.0

NEW YORK, CENTRAL PARK, NEW YORK

New York City, in area exceeding 300 square miles, is located on the Atlantic coastal plain at the mouth of the Hudson River. The terrain is laced with numerous waterways, all but one of the five boroughs in the city are situated on islands. Elevations range from less than 50 feet over most of Manhattan, Brooklyn, and Queens to almost 300 feet in northern Manhattan and the Bronx, and over 400 feet in Staten Island. Extensive suburban areas on Long Island, and in Connecticut, New York State and New Jersey border the city on the east, north, and west. About 30 miles to the west and northwest, hills rise to about 1,500 feet and to the north in upper Westchester County to 800 feet. To the southwest and to the east are the low-lying land areas of the New Jersey coastal plain and of Long Island, bordering on the Atlantic.

The New York Metropolitan area is close to the path of most storm and frontal systems which move across the North American continent. Therefore, weather conditions affecting the city most often approach from a westerly direction. New York City can thus experience higher temperatures in summer and lower ones in winter than would otherwise be expected in a coastal area. However, the frequent passage of weather systems often helps reduce the length of both warm and cold spells, and is also a major factor in keeping periods of prolonged air stagnation to a minimum.

Although continental influence predominates, oceanic influence is by no means absent. During the summer local sea breezes, winds blowing onshore from the cool water surface, often moderate the afternoon heat. The effect of the sea breeze diminishes inland. On winter mornings, ocean temperatures which are warm relative to the land reinforce the effect of the city heat island and low temperatures are often 10-20 degrees lower in the inland suburbs than in the central city. The relatively warm water temperatures also delay the advent of winter snows. Conversely, the lag in warming of water temperatures keeps spring temperatures relatively cool. One year-round measure of the ocean influence is the small average daily variation in temperature.

Precipitation is moderate and distributed fairly evenly throughout the year. Most of the rainfall from May through October comes from thunderstorms, usually of brief duration and sometimes intense. Heavy rains of long duration associated with tropical storms occur infrequently in late summer or fall. For the other months of the year precipitation is more likely to be associated with widespread storm areas, so that day-long rain, snow or a mixture of both is more common. Coastal storms, occurring most often in the fall and winter months, produce on occasion considerable amounts of precipitation and have been responsible for record rains, snows, and high winds.

The average annual precipitation is reasonably uniform within the city but is higher in the northern and western suburbs and less on eastern Long Island. Annual snowfall totals also show a consistent increase to the north and west of the city with lesser amounts along the south shores and the eastern end of Long Island, reflecting the influence of the ocean waters.

Local Climatological Data is published for three locations in New York City, Central Park, La Guardia Airport, and John F. Kennedy International Airport. Other nearby locations for which it is published are Newark, New Jersey, and Bridgeport, Connecticut.

Based on the 1951-1980 period, the average first occurrence of 32 degrees Fahrenheit in the fall is November 11 and the average last occurrence in the spring is April 1.

NORMALS, MEANS, AND EXTREMES

NEW YORK, CENTRAL PARK, NEW YORK

LATITUDE: 40°47'N LONGITUDE: 73°58' W ELEVATION: FT. GRND 132 BARO 87 TIME ZONE: EASTERN WBAN: 94728

	(a)	JAN	FEB	MAR	APR	MAY	JUNE	JULY	AUG	SEP	OCT	NOV	DEC	YEAR
TEMPERATURE °F:														
Normals														
-Daily Maximum		37.6	40.3	50.0	61.2	71.7	80.1	85.2	83.7	76.2	65.3	54.0	42.5	62.3
-Daily Minimum		25.3	26.9	34.8	43.8	53.7	63.0	68.4	67.3	60.1	49.7	41.1	30.7	47.1
-Monthly		31.5	33.6	42.4	52.5	62.7	71.6	76.8	75.5	68.2	57.5	47.6	36.6	54.7
Extremes														
-Record Highest	125	72	75	86	96	99	101	106	104	102	94	84	72	106
-Year		1950	1985	1945	1976	1962	1966	1936	1918	1953	1941	1950	1982	JUL 1936
-Record Lowest	125	-6	-15	3	12	32	44	52	50	39	28	5	-13	-15
-Year		1882	1934	1872	1923	1891	1945	1943	1986	1912	1936	1875	1917	FEB 1934
NORMAL DEGREE DAYS:														
Heating (base 65°F)		1039	879	701	375	125	0	0	0	34	250	522	880	4805
Cooling (base 65°F)		0	0	0	0	54	203	366	326	130	17	0	0	1096
% OF POSSIBLE SUNSHINE	107	51	55	57	58	61	64	65	64	62	61	52	49	58
MEAN SKY COVER (tenths)														
Sunrise - Sunset	42	6.0	5.8	5.7	6.0	5.7	5.6	5.5	5.5	5.2	4.9	5.8	5.9	5.6
MEAN NUMBER OF DAYS:														
Sunrise to Sunset														
-Clear	42	8.1	8.3	8.8	7.6	8.0	8.0	8.5	9.2	10.6	11.8	9.0	8.9	106.7
-Partly Cloudy	42	9.2	8.7	10.1	10.5	12.4	12.4	13.0	12.1	10.0	9.7	9.5	9.1	126.7
-Cloudy	42	13.7	11.2	12.1	11.9	10.7	9.6	9.5	9.7	9.4	9.5	11.5	13.0	131.8
Precipitation														
.01 inches or more	124	11.1	9.8	11.4	10.7	11.0	10.1	10.5	9.8	8.4	8.3	9.2	10.4	120.6
Snow,Ice pellets,hail														
1.0 inches or more	123	2.2	2.2	1.5	0.2	0.0	0.0	0.0	0.0	0.0	0.0	0.3	1.5	7.9
Thunderstorms	30	0.1	0.2	0.9	1.0	2.4	3.8	4.1	3.7	1.2	0.7	0.4	0.1	18.7
Heavy Fog Visibility														
1/4 mile or less	6	0.0	0.0	0.0	0.0	0.0	0.0	0.0	0.0	0.0	0.0	0.0	0.0	0.0
Temperature °F														
-Maximum														
90° and above	80	0.0	0.0	0.0	0.1	1.0	3.2	6.8	4.6	1.4	0.1	0.0	0.0	17.3
32° and below	80	8.4	5.6	1.2	0.*	0.0	0.0	0.0	0.0	0.0	0.0	0.2	4.8	20.3
-Minimum														
32° and below	80	22.5	20.1	12.4	1.4	0.*	0.0	0.0	0.0	0.0	0.3	4.6	17.9	79.2
0° and below	80	0.2	0.2	0.0	0.0	0.0	0.0	0.0	0.0	0.0	0.0	0.0	0.1	0.4
AVG. STATION PRESS. (mb)	10	1013.9	1013.7	1012.3	1011.5	1011.3	1012.3	1012.5	1014.2	1014.7	1015.1	1014.5	1014.5	1013.4
RELATIVE HUMIDITY (%)														
Hour 01	49	65	64	64	64	70	73	74	76	76	72	69	67	70
Hour 07 (Local Time)	61	68	68	67	67	71	74	75	78	79	76	73	69	72
Hour 13	61	60	58	55	51	53	55	55	57	57	55	59	60	56
Hour 19	61	60	59	57	56	60	61	63	66	66	63	63	62	61
PRECIPITATION (inches):														
Water Equivalent														
-Normal		3.42	3.27	4.08	4.20	4.42	3.67	4.35	4.01	3.89	3.56	4.47	3.91	47.25
-Maximum Monthly	124	10.52	6.87	10.41	8.77	10.24	9.78	11.89	12.36	16.85	13.31	12.41	9.98	16.85
-Year		1979	1869	1980	1874	1989	1903	1889	1990	1882	1903	1972	1973	SEP 1882
-Minimum Monthly	124	0.58	0.46	0.90	0.95	0.30	0.02	0.49	0.24	0.21	0.14	0.34	0.25	0.02
-Year		1981	1895	1885	1881	1903	1949	1910	1964	1884	1963	1976	1955	JUN 1949
-Maximum in 24 hrs	81	3.91	3.04	4.25	4.22	4.88	4.74	3.60	5.78	8.30	11.17	8.09	3.21	11.17
-Year		1979	1973	1876	1984	1968	1884	1971	1971	1882	1903	1977	1909	OCT 1903
Snow,Ice pellets,hail														
-Maximum Monthly	125	27.4	27.9	30.5	13.5	T	0.0	T	0.0	0.0	0.8	19.0	29.6	30.5
-Year		1925	1934	1896	1875	1977		1990			1925	1898	1947	MAR 1896
-Maximum in 24 hrs	125	13.6	17.6	18.1	10.2	T	0.0	T	0.0	0.0	0.8	10.0	26.4	26.4
-Year		1978	1983	1941	1915	1977		1990			1925	1898	1947	DEC 1947
WIND:														
Mean Speed (mph)	58	10.7	10.8	11.0	10.5	8.8	8.1	7.6	7.6	8.1	8.9	9.9	10.4	9.4
Prevailing Direction through 1963		NW	NW	NW	NW	SW	SW	SW	SW	SW	SW	NW	NW	SW
Fastest Obs. 1 Min.														
-Direction (!!)	10	06	05	04	05	18	29	35	05	27	20	31	05	05
-Speed (MPH)	10	25	28	35	26	24	25	29	21	23	25	29	39	39
-Year		1992	1988	1984	1986	1989	1985	1986	1992	1985	1991	1989	1992	DEC 1992
Peak Gust														
-Direction (!!)	10	NE	NE	NE	SE	ENE	N	WSW	S	W	NE	NW	NE	NE
-Speed (mph)	10	43	51	63	46	44	41	37	43	52	46	58	64	64
-Date		1992	1984	1984	1984	1989	1990	1988	1986	1985	1988	1989	1992	DEC 1992

PRECIPITATION (inches)

NEW YORK, CENTRAL PARK, NEW YORK

YEAR	JAN	FEB	MAR	APR	MAY	JUNE	JULY	AUG	SEP	OCT	NOV	DEC	ANNUAL
1964	4.62	2.93	2.57	5.09	0.57	2.67	4.17	0.24	1.69	1.73	2.55	4.16	32.99
1965	3.09	3.66	2.49	2.90	1.58	1.27	1.33	2.73	1.70	2.16	1.46	1.72	26.09
1966	2.63	4.96	0.94	2.69	4.26	1.17	1.25	1.89	8.82	4.64	3.47	3.18	39.90
1967	1.39	2.68	5.97	3.45	4.08	4.64	6.99	5.94	1.84	3.47	2.59	6.08	49.12
1968	2.04	1.13	4.79	2.82	7.06	6.15	2.63	2.88	1.97	2.20	5.75	4.15	43.57
1969	1.10	3.05	3.73	3.99	2.67	3.16	7.37	2.53	8.32	1.97	3.58	7.07	48.54
1970	0.66	4.52	4.18	3.48	3.34	2.27	2.19	2.47	1.74	2.48	5.14	2.82	35.29
1971	2.67	5.33	3.80	2.95	4.24	2.31	7.20	9.37	7.36	4.14	5.64	1.76	56.77
1972	2.41	5.90	4.55	3.92	8.39	9.30	4.54	1.92	1.33	6.27	12.41	6.09	67.03
1973	4.53	4.55	3.60	8.05	4.51	4.55	5.89	3.08	2.75	3.92	1.82	9.98	57.23
1974	3.80	1.49	5.76	3.83	4.29	3.29	1.33	5.99	8.05	2.59	0.94	6.33	47.69
1975	4.76	3.33	3.32	3.04	3.38	7.58	11.77	3.05	9.32	3.70	4.33	3.63	61.21
1976	5.78	3.13	2.99	2.80	4.77	2.78	1.42	6.52	3.15	5.31	0.34	2.29	41.28
1977	2.25	2.51	7.41	3.75	1.71	3.83	1.60	4.57	4.75	5.03	12.26	5.06	54.73
1978	8.27	1.59	2.73	2.38	9.15	1.69	4.48	5.50	4.06	1.50	2.85	5.61	49.81
1979	10.52	4.58	4.40	4.04	6.23	1.56	1.76	4.27	4.83	3.87	3.38	2.69	52.13
1980	1.72	1.04	10.41	8.26	2.33	3.84	5.26	1.16	1.98	3.86	4.11	0.58	44.55
1981	0.58	6.04	1.19	3.42	3.56	2.71	6.21	0.59	3.45	3.49	1.69	5.18	38.11
1982	6.46	2.37	2.56	5.67	2.43	5.12	3.14	4.66	1.77	2.31	3.44	1.47	41.40
1983													
1984	1.87	4.86	6.30	6.62	9.74	5.76	7.03	1.38	2.51	3.63	4.07	3.26	57.03
1985	1.00	2.41	1.91	1.41	5.72	4.41	4.41	2.58	4.75	1.30	8.09	0.83	38.82
1986	4.23	2.86	1.46	3.93	1.68	1.86	5.56	4.24	2.20	1.92	6.85	6.16	42.95
1987	5.81	1.01	4.93	5.90	1.45	3.94	4.12	4.89	5.25	3.89	3.08	2.17	46.44
1988	3.64	3.91	2.10	2.20	5.27	1.29	8.14	2.19	2.34	3.56	8.90	1.13	44.67
1989	2.29	3.03	4.93	4.26	10.24	8.79	5.13	8.44	6.90	7.48	2.79	0.83	65.11
1990	5.34	2.33	3.64	5.12	9.10	2.50	3.51	12.36	2.24	6.38	2.82	5.58	60.92
1991	3.38	1.93	5.16	3.68	3.11	4.16	4.57	7.13	3.71	2.13	1.96	4.26	45.18
1992	1.68	1.87	4.08	1.76	4.02	4.77	4.49	3.49	4.89	1.16	5.64	5.50	43.35
1993	3.44	2.81	6.64	4.28	1.56	1.49	1.70	5.41	5.25	4.55	2.20	4.95	44.28
Record Mean	3.43	3.34	3.88	3.54	3.64	3.46	4.27	4.35	3.73	3.50	3.52	3.48	44.14

AVERAGE TEMPERATURE (deg. F)

NEW YORK, CENTRAL PARK, NEW YORK

YEAR	JAN	FEB	MAR	APR	MAY	JUNE	JULY	AUG	SEP	OCT	NOV	DEC	ANNUAL
1964	35.7	32.9	43.1	49.7	65.4	71.6	75.4	72.9	67.2	55.0	49.4	36.4	54.6
1965	29.7	33.9	40.0	50.6	66.4	70.1	74.3	73.2	67.5	57.3	46.8	40.5	54.2
1966	32.2	35.1	42.7	49.7	61.6	75.4	79.7	76.9	66.5	56.2	48.9	35.7	55.1
1967	37.4	29.2	37.6	49.6	55.2	72.8	75.3	73.9	66.7	57.2	42.5	38.2	53.0
1968	26.7	28.9	43.3	55.0	59.6	69.7	77.3	76.0	70.6	60.5	46.9	34.3	54.1
1969	31.8	32.6	40.1	55.9	65.3	73.1	74.8	77.4	69.0	57.7	46.4	33.4	54.8
1970	25.1	33.0	38.7	52.1	64.0	70.9	77.1	77.6	70.8	58.9	48.5	34.4	54.3
1971	27.0	35.1	40.1	50.8	61.4	74.2	77.8	75.9	71.6	62.7	45.1	40.8	55.2
1972	35.1	31.4	39.8	50.1	63.3	67.9	77.2	75.6	69.5	53.5	44.4	38.5	53.8
1973	35.5	32.5	46.4	53.4	59.5	73.4	77.4	77.6	69.5	60.2	48.3	39.0	56.1
1974	35.3	31.7	42.1	55.2	61.0	69.0	77.2	76.4	66.7	54.1	48.2	39.4	54.7
1975	37.3	35.8	40.2	47.9	65.8	70.5	75.8	74.4	64.2	59.2	52.3	35.9	54.9
1976	27.4	39.9	44.4	55.0	60.2	73.2	74.8	74.3	66.6	52.9	41.7	29.9	53.4
1977	22.1	33.5	46.8	53.7	65.0	70.2	79.0	75.7	68.2	54.9	47.3	35.7	54.3
1978	28.0	27.2	39.0	51.6	61.5	71.3	74.4	76.0	65.0	54.9	47.8	38.9	53.0
1979	33.6	25.5	46.9	52.6	65.3	69.2	76.9	76.8	70.5	57.3	52.5	41.1	55.7
1980	33.7	31.4	41.2	54.5	65.6	70.3	79.3	80.3	70.8	55.2	44.6	32.5	55.0
1981	26.3	39.3	42.3	56.2	64.8	73.0	78.5	76.0	67.6	54.4	47.7	36.5	55.2
1982	26.1	35.3	42.0	51.2	64.1	68.6	77.9	73.2	68.3	58.5	50.4	42.8	54.9
1983	34.5	36.4	44.0	52.3	60.2	73.4	79.5	77.7	71.8	57.9	48.9	35.2	56.0
1984	29.9	40.6	36.7	51.9	61.6	74.5	74.7	76.7	65.9	61.8	47.3	43.8	55.5
1985	28.8	36.6	45.8	55.5	65.3	68.6	76.2	75.4	70.5	59.5	50.0	34.2	55.5
1986	34.1	32.0	45.1	54.5	66.0	71.6	76.0	73.1	67.9	58.0	45.7	39.0	55.3
1987	32.3	33.2	45.2	53.4	63.6	72.8	78.0	74.2	67.7	53.8	47.7	39.5	55.1
1988	29.5	35.0	43.6	51.2	62.7	71.8	79.3	78.8	67.4	52.8	49.4	35.9	54.8
1989	37.4	34.5	42.4	52.2	62.1	72.0	75.0	74.0	68.1	58.2	45.7	25.9	54.0
1990	41.4	39.8	45.1	53.5	60.2	72.1	76.8	75.3	67.5	61.9	50.4	42.6	57.2
1991	34.9	40.0	44.6	55.7	68.7	74.1	77.7	77.1	67.5	58.4	48.3	39.6	57.2
1992	35.7	36.4	40.0	50.5	61.0	70.3	74.2	73.0	67.2	54.5	46.5	37.9	53.9
1993	36.3	30.8	39.7	53.3	65.7	73.3	80.2	77.2	67.3	56.0	48.8	37.3	55.5
Record Mean	32.2	33.1	41.2	51.5	62.2	71.1	76.3	74.8	68.1	57.7	47.0	36.0	54.3
Max	38.5	40.0	48.7	60.0	71.2	79.8	84.8	83.1	76.3	65.6	53.5	42.0	62.0
Min	25.8	26.2	33.6	43.1	53.2	62.3	67.8	66.6	59.8	49.8	40.4	29.9	46.6

REFERENCE NOTES

NEW YORK, CENTRAL PARK, NEW YORK

GENERAL
T - TRACE AMOUNT.
BLANK ENTRIES DENOTE MISSING/UNREPORTED DATA.
# INDICATES A STATION OR INSTRUMENT RELOCATION.

SPECIFIC

PM - INCLUDES LAST DAY OF PREVIOUS MONTH
ASOS - AUTOMATED SURFACE OBSERVING SYSTEM IN OPERATION DURING THESE MONTHS.

(a) - LENGTH OF RECORD IN YEARS, ALTHOUGH INDIVIDUAL MONTHS MAY BE MISSING.
0.* OR * - THE VALUE IS BETWEEN 0.0 AND 0.05
NORMALS - BASED ON THE 1961-1990 RECORD PERIOD.
EXTREMES - DATES ARE THE MOST RECENT OCCURRENCE
WIND DIR.- NUMERALS SHOW TENS OF DEGRESS CLOCKWISE FROM TRUE NORTH. "00" INDICATES CALM.
RESULTANT DIRECTIONS ARE GIVEN TO WHOLE DEGREES.
BOLD VALUES INDICATE EXTREME VALUES WHICH OCCURRED AFTER THE ASOS SYSTEM WAS COMMISSIONED.

RECORD = PERIOD OF RECORD
RECORD MEAN PRECIPITATION IS THE MEAN OF ALL DAILY PRECIPITATION AMOUNTS DURING THE PERIOD OF RECORD.
RECORD MAX(MIN) TEMPERATURE IS THE MEAN OF ALL DAILY MAX(MIN) TEMPERATURES DURING THE PERIOD OF RECORD.
RECORD MEAN TEMPERATURE IS THE SUM OF THE RECORD MAX AND RECORD MIN DIVIDED BY 2.
AVERAGE TEMPERATURE IS THE SUM OF THE MEAN DAILY MAX AND MIN TEMPERATURE DIVIDED BY 2.

EXCEPTIONS

1. MEAN SKY COVER, AND DAYS CLEAR-PARTLY CLOUDY-CLOUDY ARE THROUGH 1966.
2. PERCENT OF POSSIBLE SUNSHINE, AND MEAN WIND SPEED ARE THROUGH 1976.
3. FASTEST MILE WINDS ARE THROUGH MARCH 1977 AND FEBRUARY 1980 THROUGH OCTOBER 1981.
4. RELATIVE HUMIDITY IS THROUGH 1980.
5. LIQUID PRECIPITATION FOR 1983 IS NOT CONSIDERED IN DETERMINING EXTREMES.

RECORD MEANS ARE THROUGH THE CURRENT YEAR, BEGINNING IN 1912 FOR TEMPERATURE
1869 FOR PRECIPITATION
1869 FOR SNOWFALL

HEATING DEGREE DAYS Base 65 deg. F — NEW YORK, CENTRAL PARK, NEW YORK

SEASON	JULY	AUG	SEP	OCT	NOV	DEC	JAN	FEB	MAR	APR	MAY	JUNE	TOTAL
1964-65	3	0	63	308	461	879	1088	867	765	426	64	30	4954
1965-66	0	13	54	239	538	755	1007	830	685	451	166	9	4747
1966-67	0	0	63	270	475	901	849	999	843	462	305	5	5172
1967-68	0	4	55	264	671	825	1179	1042	668	292	170	15	5185
1968-69	0	0	3	183	538	944	1023	902	768	285	74	0	4720
1969-70	0	0	28	240	551	974	1227	890	809	387	109	6	5221
1970-71	0	0	27	210	490	940	1173	830	764	419	135	9	4997
1971-72	0	0	14	106	596	743	920	965	775	445	94	26	4684
1972-73	2	0	25	355	611	812	907	903	572	362	188	2	4739
1973-74	0	0	29	162	493	800	913	925	704	309	165	27	4527
1974-75	1	0	59	333	502	789	852	812	764	507	86	11	4716
1975-76	0	3	62	193	387	898	1163	723	630	360	167	18	4604
1976-77	0	4	44	373	692	1082	1322	877	560	354	100	27	5435
1977-78	0	0	56	307	524	903	1140	1051	797	394	179	13	5364
1978-79	5	0	75	311	510	802	969	1100	554	369	55	14	4764
1979-80	4	4	20	271	373	734	963	969	731	310	67	22	4468
1980-81	0	0	31	305	602	1000	1194	715	698	264	78	3	4890
1981-82	0	0	48	320	513	876	1198	825	707	413	74	36	5010
1982-83	0	5	24	229	446	679	936	793	644	393	161	3	4313
1983-84	0	0	34	249	480	914	1082	698	870	389	137	9	4862
1984-85	0	0	69	114	525	654	1113	789	596	305	79	24	4268
1985-86	0	0	17	188	448	947	950	917	615	312	89	11	4494
1986-87	0	10	27	236	572	797	1008	883	608	348	146	8	4643
1987-88	0	2	29	343	512	780	1093	867	656	409	133	31	4855
1988-89	3	0	23	385	459	896	844	849	696	376	143	14	4688
1989-90	0	1	54	217	572	1205	724	702	612	366	150	4	4607
1990-91	3	2	57	166	436	686	927	696	625	311	61	3	3973
1991-92	0	0	60	222	496	782	902	827	767	434	160	12	4662
1992-93	0	3	54	324	547	834	882	953	779	347	57	14	4794
1993-94	0	0	65	275	483	852							

COOLING DEGREE DAYS Base 65 deg. F — NEW YORK, CENTRAL PARK, NEW YORK

YEAR	JAN	FEB	MAR	APR	MAY	JUNE	JULY	AUG	SEP	OCT	NOV	DEC	TOTAL
1969	0	0	0	20	88	250	310	392	154	20	0	0	1234
1970	0	0	0	8	86	190	385	398	207	30	0	0	1304
1971	0	0	0	0	29	290	404	347	218	40	7	0	1335
1972	0	0	0	5	47	118	384	338	169	3	0	0	1064
1973	0	0	0	20	23	260	390	401	171	22	2	0	1289
1974	0	0	0	19	47	155	385	360	115	1	6	0	1088
1975	0	0	0	0	120	185	341	299	43	22	15	0	1025
1976	0	0	0	65	24	270	310	299	103	5	0	0	1076
1977	0	0	3	22	110	189	442	338	159	0	0	0	1263
1978	0	0	0	0	77	209	301	348	81	4	0	0	1020
1979	0	0	0	4	71	149	378	376	192	43	5	0	1218
1980	0	0	0	1	94	188	448	480	213	11	0	0	1435
1981	0	0	0	4	78	252	425	347	129	0	0	0	1235
1982	0	0	0	7	55	152	405	266	129	36	16	0	1066
1983	0	0	0	19	16	259	460	404	244	35	0	0	1437
1984	0	0	0	3	39	301	306	367	106	26	0	0	1148
1985	0	0	8	28	95	139	353	329	189	21	5	0	1167
1986	0	0	5	4	127	214	348	269	120	27	0	0	1114
1987	0	0	0	5	110	251	406	295	118	0	2	0	1187
1988	0	0	0	0	66	243	455	435	104	12	0	0	1315
1989	0	0	4	0	61	231	313	287	151	10	0	0	1057
1990	0	0	4	25	8	225	375	328	140	77	4	0	1186
1991	0	0	0	38	182	280	403	382	142	24	1	0	1452
1992	0	0	0	5	46	174	292	256	127	8	0	0	908
1993	0	0	0	0	82	269	474	386	140	3	4	0	1358

SNOWFALL (inches) — NEW YORK, CENTRAL PARK, NEW YORK

SEASON	JULY	AUG	SEP	OCT	NOV	DEC	JAN	FEB	MAR	APR	MAY	JUNE	TOTAL
1964-65	0.0	0.0	0.0	0.0	0.0	3.1	14.8	2.5	2.8	1.2	0.0	0.0	24.4
1965-66	0.0	0.0	0.0	T	0.0	T	11.6	9.8	T	0.0	0.0	0.0	21.4
1966-67	0.0	0.0	0.0	0.0	0.0	9.1	1.4	23.6	17.4	T	0.0	0.0	51.5
1967-68	0.0	0.0	0.0	0.0	3.2	5.5	3.6	1.1	6.1	0.0	0.0	0.0	19.5
1968-69	0.0	0.0	0.0	0.0	T	7.0	1.0	16.6	5.6	0.0	0.0	0.0	30.2
1969-70	0.0	0.0	0.0	0.0	T	6.8	8.4	6.4	4.0	T	0.0	0.0	25.6
1970-71	0.0	0.0	0.0	0.0	0.0	2.4	11.4	T	1.3	0.4	0.0	0.0	15.5
1971-72	0.0	0.0	0.0	0.0	T	T	2.8	17.8	2.3	T	0.0	0.0	22.9
1972-73	0.0	0.0	0.0	T	T	T	1.8	0.8	0.2	T	0.0	0.0	2.8
1973-74	0.0	0.0	0.0	0.0	0.0	2.8	7.8	9.4	3.2	0.3	0.0	0.0	23.5
1974-75	0.0	0.0	0.0	0.0	0.1	0.1	2.0	10.6	0.3	T	0.0	0.0	13.1
1975-76	0.0	0.0	0.0	0.0	T	2.3	5.6	5.0	4.4	T	0.0	0.0	17.3
1976-77	0.0	0.0	0.0	0.0	T	5.1	13.0	5.8	0.6	T	T	0.0	24.5
1977-78	0.0	0.0	0.0	0.0	0.2	0.4	20.3	23.0	6.8	T	0.0	0.0	50.7
1978-79	0.0	0.0	0.0	0.0	2.2	0.5	6.6	20.1	T	T	0.0	0.0	29.4
1979-80	0.0	0.0	0.0	T	0.0	3.5	2.0	2.7	4.6	T	0.0	0.0	12.8
1980-81	0.0	0.0	0.0	0.0	T	2.8	8.0	T	8.6	0.0	0.0	0.0	19.4
1981-82	0.0	0.0	0.0	0.0	0.0	2.1	11.8	0.4	0.7	9.6	0.0	0.0	24.6
1982-83	0.0	0.0	0.0	0.0	0.0	3.0	1.9	23.5	T	0.8	0.0	0.0	29.2
1983-84	0.0	0.0	0.0	0.0	T	1.6	11.7	0.2	11.9	0.0	0.0	0.0	25.4
1984-85	0.0	0.0	0.0	0.0	T	5.5	8.4	10.0	0.2	T	0.0	0.0	24.1
1985-86	0.0	0.0	0.0	0.0	T	0.9	2.2	9.9	T	T	0.0	0.0	13.0
1986-87	0.0	0.0	0.0	0.0	T	0.6	13.6	7.0	1.9	0.0	0.0	0.0	23.1
1987-88	0.0	0.0	0.0	0.0	1.1	2.6	13.9	1.5	T	0.0	0.0	0.0	19.1
1988-89	0.0	0.0	0.0	0.0	0.0	0.3	5.0	0.3	2.5	0.0	0.0	0.0	8.1
1989-90	0.0	0.0	0.0	0.0	4.7	1.4	1.8	1.8	3.1	0.6	0.0	0.0	13.4
1990-91	T	0.0	0.0	0.0	0.0	7.2	8.4	9.1	0.2	0.0	0.0	0.0	24.9
1991-92	0.0	0.0	0.0	0.0	T	0.7	1.5	1.0	9.4	T	0.0	0.0	12.6
1992-93	0.0	0.0	0.0	0.0	0.0	0.4	1.5	10.7	11.9	0.0	0.0	0.0	24.5
1993-94	0.0	0.0	0.0	0.0	T	6.9							
Record Mean	T	0.0	0.0	T	0.9	5.4	7.5	8.4	5.0	0.9	T	0.0	28.2

ROCHESTER, NEW YORK

Rochester is located at the mouth of the Genesee River at about the mid point of the south shore of Lake Ontario. The river flows northward from northwest Pennsylvania and empties into Lake Ontario. The land slopes from a lakeshore elevation of 246 feet to over 1,000 feet some 20 miles south. The airport is located just south of the city.

Lake Ontario plays a major role in the Rochester weather. In the summer its cooling effect inhibits the temperature from rising much above the low to mid 90s. In the winter the modifying temperature effect prevents temperatures from falling below -15 degrees most of the time, although temperatures at locations more than 15 miles inland do drop below -30 degrees.

The lake plays a major role in winter snowfall distribution. Well inland from the lake and toward the airport, the seasonal snowfall is usually less than in the area north of the airport and toward the lakeshore where wide variations occur. This is due to what is called the lake effect. Snowfalls of one to two feet or more in 24 hours are common near the lake in winter due the lake effect alone. The lake rarely freezes over because of its depth. The area is also prone to other heavy snowstorms and blizzards because of its proximity to the paths of low pressure systems coming up the east coast, out of the Ohio Valley, or, to a lesser extent, from the Alberta area. The climate is favorable for winter sports activities with a continuous snow cover likely from December through March.

Moisture in the air from the lake enhances the climatic conditions for fruit growing. Apples, peaches, pears, cantaloupes, plums, cherries, and grapes are grown abundantly in Greater Rochester and the Western Finger Lakes Region.

Precipitation is rather evenly distributed throughout the year. Excessive rains occur infrequently but may be caused by slowly moving thunderstorms, slowly moving or stalled major low pressure systems, or by hurricanes and tropical storms that move inland. Hail occurs occasionally and heavy fog is rare.

The growing season averages 150 to 180 days. The years first frost usually occurs in late September and the last frost typically occurs in mid-May.

NORMALS, MEANS, AND EXTREMES

ROCHESTER, NEW YORK

LATITUDE: 43°07'N LONGITUDE: 77°40' W ELEVATION: FT. GRND 547 BARO 547 TIME ZONE: EASTERN WBAN: 14768

	(a)	JAN	FEB	MAR	APR	MAY	JUNE	JULY	AUG	SEP	OCT	NOV	DEC	YEAR
TEMPERATURE °F:														
Normals														
-Daily Maximum		30.9	32.5	42.7	55.9	67.8	75.8	80.7	78.1	71.8	60.5	47.8	35.8	56.7
-Daily Minimum		16.3	16.6	25.7	35.9	46.3	54.3	59.6	57.8	51.7	41.6	33.3	22.4	38.5
-Monthly		23.6	24.6	34.3	45.9	57.1	65.1	70.2	68.0	61.7	51.1	40.5	29.1	47.6
Extremes														
-Record Highest	53	74	67	84	93	94	100	98	99	99	91	81	72	100
-Year		1950	1947	1945	1990	1987	1953	1993	1948	1953	1951	1950	1982	JUN 1953
-Record Lowest	53	-16	-19	-6	13	26	35	42	36	28	20	5	-16	-19
-Year		1957	1979	1980	1982	1979	1949	1963	1965	1947	1972	1971	1942	FEB 1979
NORMAL DEGREE DAYS:														
Heating (base 65°F)		1283	1131	952	573	270	62	10	33	137	435	735	1113	6734
Cooling (base 65°F)		0	0	0	0	25	65	171	126	38	0	0	0	425
% OF POSSIBLE SUNSHINE	53	36	40	49	54	59	67	69	66	59	49	31	31	51
MEAN SKY COVER (tenths)														
Sunrise - Sunset	53	8.2	7.9	7.3	6.8	6.6	6.0	5.8	6.0	6.2	6.7	8.2	8.4	7.0
MEAN NUMBER OF DAYS:														
Sunrise to Sunset														
-Clear	53	2.0	2.4	4.5	6.2	6.1	7.2	7.9	7.7	7.0	6.3	2.2	2.0	61.4
-Partly Cloudy	53	6.7	6.6	8.2	7.8	9.6	10.8	12.4	11.7	10.5	8.4	6.2	5.6	104.5
-Cloudy	53	22.2	19.2	18.3	16.1	15.4	11.9	10.6	11.6	12.5	16.2	21.7	23.4	199.3
Precipitation														
.01 inches or more	53	17.6	15.9	14.6	13.4	11.9	10.6	9.6	10.0	10.8	11.7	15.2	17.5	158.8
Snow, Ice pellets, hail														
1.0 inches or more	53	7.3	6.9	4.0	1.0	0.1	0.0	0.0	0.0	0.0	0.1	2.0	6.2	27.6
Thunderstorms	53	0.1	0.1	1.0	2.0	3.5	5.2	6.2	5.7	3.1	1.0	0.4	0.2	28.3
Heavy Fog Visibility														
1/4 mile or less	53	0.9	0.6	1.6	1.1	1.2	1.1	0.6	0.8	1.3	1.7	0.7	1.0	12.7
Temperature °F														
-Maximum														
90° and above	30	0.0	0.0	0.0	0.1	0.3	1.6	4.3	2.0	0.6	0.0	0.0	0.0	8.9
32° and below	30	16.5	14.3	6.5	0.4	0.0	0.0	0.0	0.0	0.0	0.0	1.5	10.5	49.7
-Minimum														
32° and below	30	28.6	25.6	23.1	10.7	0.9	0.0	0.0	0.0	0.1	4.6	15.2	25.5	134.2
0° and below	30	2.7	2.1	0.2	0.0	0.0	0.0	0.0	0.0	0.0	0.0	0.0	0.7	5.8
AVG. STATION PRESS. (mb)	21	996.4	997.5	996.1	994.8	995.0	994.8	995.6	997.1	998.0	998.2	997.2	997.2	996.5
RELATIVE HUMIDITY (%)														
Hour 01	30	77	77	76	76	78	82	83	87	87	82	80	80	80
Hour 07 (Local Time)	30	77	79	79	77	77	80	82	87	88	85	82	81	81
Hour 13	30	69	67	62	56	54	55	54	58	61	61	68	72	61
Hour 19	30	74	73	69	61	60	60	60	67	74	74	77	78	69
PRECIPITATION (inches):														
Water Equivalent														
-Normal		2.08	2.10	2.28	2.61	2.72	3.00	2.71	3.40	2.97	2.44	2.92	2.73	31.96
-Maximum Monthly	53	5.79	5.07	5.42	4.90	6.62	6.77	9.70	6.00	6.30	7.85	6.99	5.05	9.70
-Year		1978	1950	1942	1944	1974	1980	1947	1984	1977	1955	1985	1944	JUL 1947
-Minimum Monthly	53	0.72	0.66	0.47	1.28	0.36	0.22	0.98	0.76	0.28	0.23	0.44	0.62	0.22
-Year		1988	1987	1958	1971	1977	1963	1989	1951	1960	1963	1976	1958	JUN 1963
-Maximum in 24 hrs	53	1.64	2.43	2.21	2.22	3.85	2.86	3.25	2.39	3.54	2.98	3.13	1.60	3.85
-Year		1966	1950	1942	1991	1974	1950	1987	1968	1979	1980	1945	1978	MAY 1974
Snow, Ice pellets, hail														
-Maximum Monthly	53	60.4	64.8	40.3	20.2	10.9	0.0	T	T	T	2.6	17.6	46.1	64.8
-Year		1978	1958	1959	1979	1989		1990	1965	1993	1993	1983	1981	FEB 1958
-Maximum in 24 hrs	53	18.2	22.8	22.2	10.4	10.8	0.0	T	T	T	2.6	11.2	19.1	22.8
-Year		1966	1978	1993	1990	1989		1990	1965	1993	1993	1953	1978	FEB 1978
WIND:														
Mean Speed (mph)	53	11.6	11.3	11.0	10.7	9.3	8.6	8.0	7.7	8.0	8.8	10.2	10.7	9.7
Prevailing Direction through 1963		WSW	WSW	WSW	WSW	WSW	SW	SW	SW	SW	SW	WSW	WSW	WSW
Fastest Obs. 1 Min.														
-Direction (!!)	8	28	25	24	25	30	31	24	28	25	24	25	26	24
-Speed (MPH)	8	35	35	52	38	35	35	31	40	37	38	46	37	52
-Year		1992	1988	1991	1991	1991	1993	1990	1986	1993	1993	1992	1991	MAR 1991
Peak Gust														
-Direction (!!)	10	W	SW	SW	SW	NW	N	NW	W	W	SW	SW	W	SW
-Speed (mph)	10	63	52	68	67	64	52	45	62	48	56	67	53	68
-Date		1988	1988	1991	1984	1991	1988	1988	1986	1993	1993	1992	1991	MAR 1991

PRECIPITATION (inches)

ROCHESTER, NEW YORK

YEAR	JAN	FEB	MAR	APR	MAY	JUNE	JULY	AUG	SEP	OCT	NOV	DEC	ANNUAL
1964	1.99	0.89	2.89	3.54	2.77	1.13	1.52	2.74	0.58	0.76	1.60	2.04	22.45
1965	3.05	2.24	2.07	1.85	0.50	0.64	1.46	2.94	1.98	2.82	3.40	2.21	25.16
1966	4.10	2.51	1.42	2.04	1.26	1.85	2.77	2.14	2.47	0.68	3.12	1.75	26.11
1967	0.94	1.67	1.31	1.69	2.74	1.57	2.68	4.64	3.84	4.35	2.89	1.52	29.84
1968	1.91	0.74	2.38	1.33	2.84	2.84	1.42	5.95	1.86	2.89	4.28	3.31	31.75
1969	2.46	0.91	1.16	3.48	2.25	4.69	1.83	1.82	1.77	1.69	3.42	3.66	29.14
1970	1.80	2.28	1.49	2.58	3.03	3.74	4.91	3.88	2.49	3.96	3.50	4.12	37.78
1971	2.66	4.21	3.43	1.28	1.71	3.52	5.59	3.18	1.79	1.34	1.96	3.49	34.16
1972	1.50	3.96	2.19	2.68	3.32	6.56	1.43	3.14	3.84	2.25	4.83	2.58	38.28
1973	1.28	1.70	2.92	3.21	2.68	2.84	1.14	1.94	1.41	2.67	3.82	3.62	29.23
1974	1.75	2.06	3.61	2.60	6.62	2.59	2.82	3.64	3.48	1.34	3.23	2.86	36.60
1975	1.83	2.82	2.74	1.43	2.85	5.35	1.18	2.31	3.15	1.83	1.35	3.76	30.60
1976	2.33	1.67	3.54	3.81	2.63	3.37	5.15	3.04	2.13	4.73	0.44	1.48	34.32
1977	1.49	0.97	2.18	2.49	0.36	1.33	3.26	5.65	6.30	2.64	3.78	4.65	35.10
1978	5.79	2.40	1.48	2.25	2.03	1.30	2.17	2.66	3.63	2.56	1.14	4.35	31.76
1979	4.18	2.40	1.76	3.78	3.14	1.85	3.16	2.05	5.32	2.60	1.80	2.86	34.90
1980	1.11	1.16	3.83	2.35	1.49	6.77	1.90	3.44	3.57	3.73	2.52	2.45	34.32
1981	1.24	3.13	1.04	1.95	2.27	2.70	4.60	4.44	5.37	3.29	2.18	2.78	34.99
1982	4.16	1.01	1.73	1.63	1.77	3.92	3.13	3.00	3.57	1.79	3.95	2.17	31.83
1983	1.43	1.23	2.45	3.50	3.44	2.40	1.13	5.43	1.56	3.26	4.91	4.47	35.21
1984	1.62	2.97	2.08	3.05	5.47	1.67	1.90	6.00	3.34	0.76	1.47	3.31	33.64
1985	2.49	1.78	3.47	1.30	2.08	2.63	1.86	1.11	2.49	2.34	6.99	1.46	30.00
1986	1.63	2.46	1.90	3.80	1.64	4.27	3.13	3.29	5.11	3.56	1.93	3.56	36.28
1987	1.89	0.66	1.98	3.68	1.19	3.94	5.85	3.92	4.60	1.65	2.74	1.98	34.08
1988	0.72	2.18	1.62	2.32	1.73	1.10	4.30	3.81	1.69	2.34	1.68	1.11	24.60
1989	1.18	1.55	3.69	1.62	5.99	5.65	0.98	2.46	2.82	3.13	2.01	1.58	32.66
1990	1.61	3.93	1.56	3.58	5.76	2.88	3.05	3.59	3.36	4.37	2.27	4.18	40.14
1991	1.69	1.16	4.70	4.07	2.43	1.19	2.37	1.80	2.86	1.65	2.39	2.92	29.23
1992	1.46	1.87	3.53	3.43	2.83	1.98	6.03	4.45	3.02	1.78	2.90	2.98	36.26
1993	2.32	1.52	2.44	3.07	1.24	2.76	1.67	1.67	4.37	3.21	3.27	1.60	29.14
Record Mean	2.44	2.35	2.62	2.60	2.90	2.98	3.08	2.89	2.78	2.75	2.69	2.59	32.67

AVERAGE TEMPERATURE (deg. F)

ROCHESTER, NEW YORK

YEAR	JAN	FEB	MAR	APR	MAY	JUNE	JULY	AUG	SEP	OCT	NOV	DEC	ANNUAL
1964	28.3	24.0	34.4	47.2	60.3	65.8	73.8	66.2	61.2	48.7	42.3	29.6	48.5
1965	21.6	25.7	29.5	41.3	60.1	64.4	67.5	68.4	63.8	48.8	39.8	34.6	47.1
1966	22.6	25.5	36.6	44.4	53.0	67.8	73.0	68.9	59.2	50.1	43.5	30.8	48.0
1967	31.1	21.4	32.5	46.4	49.1	70.4	69.4	67.6	60.4	52.1	36.3	32.3	47.4
1968	19.8	20.8	36.0	49.5	53.2	64.7	70.7	69.4	64.8	53.8	41.2	27.7	47.6
1969	25.2	26.0	32.0	47.6	55.6	65.0	70.7	72.0	63.6	50.9	40.1	25.1	47.8
1970	18.0	23.7	30.8	48.4	59.5	68.1	72.2	70.1	63.0	53.9	41.4	25.5	47.9
1971	19.5	26.9	28.5	41.1	54.0	67.5	68.8	68.8	67.4	59.0	38.4	30.9	47.6
1972	26.0	23.4	30.3	42.2	60.4	65.2	73.0	69.8	64.3	47.6	37.0	33.1	47.7
1973	28.7	22.2	42.5	48.0	56.1	70.7	73.4	73.0	62.5	55.0	43.0	31.2	50.5
1974	27.1	22.5	33.0	49.4	53.9	65.7	71.3	70.6	59.2	47.6	39.5	31.4	47.6
1975	29.5	28.4	31.6	39.3	63.2	67.1	73.0	70.0	58.4	53.1	47.2	27.8	49.0
1976	19.8	33.3	37.2	48.6	55.4	69.8	69.2	68.4	60.9	47.5	35.4	23.6	47.4
1977	15.5	25.4	39.8	47.9	60.7	64.8	72.9	68.7	62.7	49.4	43.6	28.4	48.3
1978	22.9	16.2	29.7	43.6	60.2	67.4	72.6	71.6	62.4	51.0	41.0	30.0	47.4
1979	21.5	13.7	38.6	44.0	56.4	66.2	72.3	67.1	61.3	50.3	43.0	32.3	47.2
1980	24.0	19.7	32.4	47.8	60.0	63.1	72.9	74.3	63.7	48.8	38.8	24.7	47.5
1981	15.7	32.3	34.5	48.0	57.2	67.3	71.9	69.4	59.8	47.3	39.9	28.7	47.7
1982	16.1	23.0	33.5	43.2	60.9	63.6	72.0	66.1	62.8	52.7	43.4	37.4	47.9
1983	27.4	29.1	37.2	43.9	53.8	66.7	73.8	70.7	63.9	52.9	40.7	25.1	48.8
1984	20.4	33.2	26.5	47.5	52.6	66.8	69.2	72.0	60.6	54.9	40.7	35.9	48.4
1985	21.9	25.6	36.7	49.6	58.6	61.7	68.8	68.7	63.8	51.0	41.4	25.0	47.7
1986	25.0	24.5	37.0	47.9	59.8	63.3	69.8	65.7	59.8	49.9	36.9	31.7	47.6
1987	25.3	23.6	37.1	49.7	59.9	67.9	72.7	67.3	61.6	47.1	40.6	32.6	48.8
1988	25.0	23.7	34.7	45.0	58.7	64.2	73.7	71.1	60.1	45.8	42.6	29.4	47.8
1989	30.3	22.5	32.3	42.1	56.3	67.4	72.8	68.5	61.7	52.6	38.1	17.1	46.8
1990	33.6	29.3	37.3	48.8	54.4	67.2	70.7	69.9	60.7	52.1	42.4	33.8	50.0
1991	25.1	30.5	37.0	50.0	62.8	68.3	72.3	70.3	60.5	52.1	39.0	30.7	49.9
1992	26.2	27.2	30.2	44.1	57.1	63.5	66.6	66.3	60.9	46.4	38.9	30.2	46.5
1993	27.5	18.7	30.0	46.9	56.6	65.5	72.4	71.4	59.0	48.0	39.0	28.4	47.0
Record Mean	24.7	24.6	32.9	45.2	56.8	66.4	71.3	69.3	62.5	51.3	39.8	29.0	47.8
Max	31.6	32.0	40.6	54.2	66.8	76.6	81.3	78.9	72.1	60.1	46.6	35.3	56.3
Min	17.7	17.2	25.2	36.2	46.8	56.2	61.3	59.7	52.9	42.4	33.0	22.7	39.3

REFERENCE NOTES

ROCHESTER, NEW YORK

GENERAL
T - TRACE AMOUNT.
BLANK ENTRIES DENOTE MISSING/UNREPORTED DATA.
# INDICATES A STATION OR INSTRUMENT RELOCATION.

SPECIFIC

PM - INCLUDES LAST DAY OF PREVIOUS MONTH
ASOS - AUTOMATED SURFACE OBSERVING SYSTEM IN OPERATION DURING THESE MONTHS.

(a) - LENGTH OF RECORD IN YEARS, ALTHOUGH INDIVIDUAL MONTHS MAY BE MISSING.
0.* OR * - THE VALUE IS BETWEEN 0.0 AND 0.05
NORMALS - BASED ON THE 1961-1990 RECORD PERIOD.
EXTREMES - DATES ARE THE MOST RECENT OCCURRENCE
WIND DIR.- NUMERALS SHOW TENS OF DEGRESS CLOCKWISE FROM TRUE NORTH. "00" INDICATES CALM.
RESULTANT DIRECTIONS ARE GIVEN TO WHOLE DEGREES.
BOLD VALUES INDICATE EXTREME VALUES WHICH OCCURRED AFTER THE ASOS SYSTEM WAS COMMISSIONED.

RECORD = PERIOD OF RECORD
RECORD MEAN PRECIPITATION IS THE MEAN OF ALL DAILY PRECIPITATION AMOUNTS DURING THE PERIOD OF RECORD.
RECORD MAX(MIN) TEMPERATURE IS THE MEAN OF ALL DAILY MAX(MIN) TEMPERATURES DURING THE PERIOD OF RECORD.
RECORD MEAN TEMPERATURE IS THE SUM OF THE RECORD MAX AND RECORD MIN DIVIDED BY 2.
AVERAGE TEMPERATURE IS THE SUM OF THE MEAN DAILY MAX AND MIN TEMPERATURE DIVIDED BY 2.

EXCEPTIONS

RECORD MEANS ARE THROUGH THE CURRENT YEAR, BEGINNING IN 1872 FOR TEMPERATURE
1829 FOR PRECIPITATION
1941 FOR SNOWFALL

HEATING DEGREE DAYS Base 65 deg. F — ROCHESTER, NEW YORK

SEASON	JULY	AUG	SEP	OCT	NOV	DEC	JAN	FEB	MAR	APR	MAY	JUNE	TOTAL
1964-65	3	48	169	500	674	1090	1337	1096	1095	706	192	114	7024
1965-66	24	53	122	496	748	937	1307	1098	871	612	382	57	6707
1966-67	0	16	190	458	639	1053	1046	1216	998	551	486	8	6661
1967-68	25	28	164	401	856	1005	1399	1275	894	463	357	78	6945
1968-69	15	36	67	369	710	1150	1229	1087	1013	517	302	86	6581
1969-70	18	10	126	437	737	1231	1448	1149	1053	506	209	49	6973
1970-71	3	11	126	349	699	1218	1405	1059	1122	707	342	49	7090
1971-72	17	33	74	194	792	1048	1200	1199	1071	677	161	78	6544
1972-73	7	24	92	534	833	982	1118	1189	690	519	279	17	6284
1973-74	2	14	162	305	653	1040	1167	1187	983	475	352	59	6399
1974-75	1	1	209	535	755	1034	1096	1017	1031	764	139	52	6634
1975-76	4	14	194	365	525	1146	1395	914	858	507	300	35	6257
1976-77	11	27	173	538	879	1279	1524	1103	777	523	204	89	7127
1977-78	9	44	113	477	634	1127	1298	1360	1087	634	220	63	7066
1978-79	5	1	136	428	711	1077	1342	1432	813	626	310	79	6960
1979-80	13	37	155	468	655	1006	1264	1306	1003	510	195	125	6737
1980-81	1	0	108	498	782	1243	1522	908	938	507	260	26	6793
1981-82	6	12	201	546	748	1119	1510	1171	972	648	162	67	7162
1982-83	10	54	113	377	643	847	1161	998	854	627	347	78	6109
1983-84	9	8	121	387	723	1228	1376	917	1187	520	395	50	6921
1984-85	14	7	162	307	724	897	1330	1097	869	471	217	119	6214
1985-86	15	23	121	429	700	1231	1235	1129	864	506	206	100	6559
1986-87	16	62	175	462	840	1026	1223	1153	858	454	234	39	6542
1987-88	7	50	139	547	722	997	1232	1192	933	594	220	126	6759
1988-89	6	40	164	596	664	1095	1070	1184	1009	682	288	33	6831
1989-90	0	33	149	383	801	1478	967	993	853	520	327	46	6550
1990-91	7	6	171	406	669	959	1230	957	862	458	170	29	5924
1991-92	2	1	196	408	776	1057	1195	1088	1069	621	259	89	6761
1992-93	26	46	172	571	774	1071	1158	1289	1077	538	263	66	7051
1993-94	0	10	214	525	775	1127							

COOLING DEGREE DAYS Base 65 deg. F — ROCHESTER, NEW YORK

YEAR	JAN	FEB	MAR	APR	MAY	JUNE	JULY	AUG	SEP	OCT	NOV	DEC	TOTAL
1969	0	0	0	0	18	94	202	233	92	7	0	0	646
1970	0	0	0	16	47	148	235	176	69	13	0	0	704
1971	0	0	0	0	10	133	143	159	155	15	0	0	615
1972	0	0	0	0	24	94	261	179	79	0	0	0	637
1973	0	0	0	15	6	194	267	269	96	4	0	0	851
1974	0	0	0	13	14	88	204	181	40	0	0	0	540
1975	0	0	0	0	89	121	257	178	5	6	0	0	656
1976	0	0	0	24	9	189	150	138	55	1	0	0	566
1977	0	0	3	16	80	88	260	164	50	0	1	0	662
1978	0	0	0	0	77	141	245	212	66	3	0	0	744
1979	0	0	0	1	52	121	244	112	49	18	0	0	597
1980	0	0	0	0	46	73	253	294	76	2	0	0	744
1981	0	0	0	5	23	102	228	156	50	0	0	0	564
1982	0	0	0	3	40	30	232	95	52	3	1	0	456
1983	0	0	0	0	7	136	289	192	96	20	0	0	740
1984	0	0	0	1	14	113	152	233	35	1	0	0	549
1985	0	0	0	15	23	27	139	145	90	0	0	0	439
1986	0	0	1	0	50	53	168	94	28	0	0	0	394
1987	0	0	0	1	82	131	254	127	42	0	0	0	637
1988	0	0	0	0	34	107	284	232	29	7	0	0	693
1989	0	0	0	0	26	111	248	153	60	3	0	0	601
1990	0	0	3	41	5	122	192	164	45	14	0	0	586
1991	0	0	0	14	108	135	234	175	68	14	0	0	748
1992	0	0	0	1	19	51	84	96	57	0	0	0	308
1993	0	0	0	0	9	86	239	214	42	5	0	0	595

SNOWFALL (inches) — ROCHESTER, NEW YORK

SEASON	JULY	AUG	SEP	OCT	NOV	DEC	JAN	FEB	MAR	APR	MAY	JUNE	TOTAL
1964-65	0.0	0.0	0.0	T	5.1	11.6	26.6	10.3	15.6	1.9	0.0	0.0	71.1
1965-66	0.0	T	0.0	0.9	8.0	6.0	60.2	21.0	6.2	0.9	T	0.0	103.2
1966-67	0.0	0.0	0.0	0.0	3.0	14.4	12.7	27.6	16.0	T	0.3	0.0	74.0
1967-68	0.0	0.0	0.0	T	10.0	6.9	24.2	20.4	15.2	T	0.0	0.0	76.7
1968-69	0.0	0.0	0.0	T	8.6	22.2	25.6	17.8	4.6	1.0	0.0	0.0	79.8
1969-70	0.0	0.0	0.0	T	5.8	42.0	37.9	27.7	4.9	1.3	T	0.0	119.6
1970-71	0.0	0.0	0.0	0.2	3.6	44.2	34.1	29.7	29.7	1.2	0.0	0.0	142.7
1971-72	0.0	0.0	0.0	0.0	11.2	13.8	18.1	35.7	19.0	7.3	0.0	0.0	105.1
1972-73	0.0	0.0	0.0	0.2	16.9	22.7	8.9	18.4	4.4	1.5	T	0.0	73.0
1973-74	0.0	0.0	0.0	0.0	4.2	23.4	14.4	26.6	22.3	8.2	T	0.0	99.1
1974-75	0.0	0.0	0.0	0.3	4.6	26.5	10.8	23.2	10.9	14.9	0.0	0.0	91.2
1975-76	0.0	0.0	0.0	T	1.8	28.3	29.9	8.8	15.2	1.8	0.4	0.0	86.2
1976-77	0.0	0.0	0.0	0.5	6.5	24.5	30.2	15.0	13.0	1.8	0.6	0.0	92.1
1977-78	0.0	0.0	0.0	T	12.7	35.2	60.4	40.7	7.5	4.2	0.2	0.0	160.9
1978-79	0.0	0.0	0.0	T	3.3	30.9	36.8	39.1	8.2	20.2	0.0	0.0	138.5
1979-80	0.0	0.0	0.0	0.2	1.2	12.2	13.1	24.0	21.2	0.3	0.0	0.0	72.2
1980-81	0.0	0.0	0.0	T	8.4	31.8	31.5	9.3	12.0	1.4	0.0	0.0	94.4
1981-82	0.0	0.0	0.0	0.1	2.4	46.1	43.6	14.9	8.9	12.4	0.0	0.0	128.4
1982-83	0.0	0.0	0.0	T	3.0	11.6	10.2	13.6	9.3	12.2	T	0.0	59.9
1983-84	0.0	0.0	0.0	0.0	17.6	19.6	23.4	27.8	29.1	0.5	T	0.0	118.0
1984-85	0.0	0.0	0.0	0.0	1.6	11.6	36.8	26.1	8.4	2.6	0.0	0.0	87.1
1985-86	0.0	0.0	0.0	0.0	7.6	18.3	15.5	17.9	9.3	2.1	T	0.0	70.7
1986-87	0.0	0.0	0.0	0.0	7.4	9.3	29.6	13.0	5.3	2.5	0.0	0.0	67.1
1987-88	0.0	0.0	0.0	T	4.6	19.3	9.8	29.4	5.6	1.1	0.0	0.0	69.8
1988-89	0.0	0.0	0.0	0.1	0.2	10.3	15.0	30.6	15.6	3.9	10.9	0.0	86.6
1989-90	0.0	0.0	0.0	T	6.5	32.8	14.0	31.3	5.4	15.8	T	0.0	105.8
1990-91	T	0.0	0.0	T	4.4	18.2	26.5	16.1	2.0	1.1	0.0	0.0	68.3
1991-92	0.0	0.0	0.0	0.0	13.7	23.9	18.3	12.8	38.1	3.8	0.0	0.0	110.6
1992-93	0.0	0.0	0.0	T	9.5	29.3	22.4	31.2	37.1	2.0	T	0.0	131.5
1993-94	0.0	0.0	T	2.6	9.8	14.0							
Record Mean	T	T	T	0.2	6.7	19.6	22.7	22.4	14.4	3.6	0.3	0.0	89.8

SYRACUSE, NEW YORK

Syracuse is located approximately at the geographical center of the state. Gently rolling terrain stretches northward for about 30 miles to the eastern end of Lake Ontario. Oneida Lake is about 8 miles northeast of Syracuse. Approximately 5 miles south of the city, hills rise to 1,500 feet. Immediately to the west, the terrain is gently rolling with elevations 500 to 800 feet above sea level.

The climate of Syracuse is primarily continental in character and comparatively humid. Nearly all cyclonic systems moving from the interior of the country through the St. Lawrence Valley will affect the Syracuse area. Seasonal and diurnal changes are marked and produce an invigorating climate.

In the summer and in portions of the transitional seasons, temperatures usually rise rapidly during the daytime to moderate levels and as a rule fall rapidly after sunset. The nights are relatively cool and comfortable. There are only a few days in a year when atmospheric humidity causes great personal discomfort.

Winters are usually cold and are sometimes severe in part. Daytime temperatures average in the low 30s with nighttime lows in the teens. Low winter temperatures below -25 degrees have been recorded. The autumn, winter, and spring seasons display marked variability.

Based on the 1951-1980 period, the average first occurrence of 32 degrees Fahrenheit in the fall is October 16 and the average last occurrence in the spring is April 28.

Precipitation in the Syracuse area is derived principally from cyclonic storms which pass from the interior of the country through the St. Lawrence Valley. Lake Ontario provides the source of significant winter precipitation. The lake is quite deep and never freezes so cold air flowing over the lake is quickly saturated and produces the cloudiness and snow squalls which are a well-known feature of winter weather in the Syracuse area.

The area enjoys sufficient precipitation in most years to meet the needs of agriculture and water supplies. The precipitation is uncommonly well distributed, averaging about 3 inches per month throughout the year. Snowfall is moderately heavy with an average just over 100 inches. There are about 30 days per year with thunderstorms, mostly during the warmer months.

Wind velocities are moderate, but during the winter months there are numerous days with sufficient winds to cause blowing and drifting snow.

During December, January, and February there is much cloudiness. Syracuse receives only about one-third of possible sunshine during winter months. Approximately two-thirds of possible sunshine is received during the warm months.

NORMALS, MEANS, AND EXTREMES

SYRACUSE, NEW YORK

LATITUDE: 43°07'N LONGITUDE: 76°07' W ELEVATION: FT. GRND 410 BARO 420 TIME ZONE: EASTERN WBAN: 14771

	(a)	JAN	FEB	MAR	APR	MAY	JUNE	JULY	AUG	SEP	OCT	NOV	DEC	YEAR
TEMPERATURE °F:														
Normals														
-Daily Maximum		30.6	32.5	42.7	56.0	68.3	76.7	81.7	79.0	71.6	60.3	48.0	35.4	56.9
-Daily Minimum		14.2	15.4	25.1	35.5	46.0	53.8	59.0	57.7	51.4	41.1	33.0	21.1	37.8
-Monthly		22.4	24.0	33.9	45.7	57.1	65.3	70.4	68.4	61.5	50.7	40.5	28.3	47.4
Extremes														
-Record Highest	44	70	69	87	92	96	98	97	97	97	87	81	70	98
-Year		1967	1981	1986	1990	1977	1953	1990	1987	1953	1963	1950	1966	JUN 1953
-Record Lowest	44	-26	-26	-16	9	25	35	45	40	28	19	5	-22	-26
-Year		1966	1979	1950	1972	1966	1966	1976	1965	1991	1976	1976	1980	FEB 1979
NORMAL DEGREE DAYS:														
Heating (base 65°F)		1321	1148	964	579	268	61	10	28	139	443	735	1138	6834
Cooling (base 65°F)		0	0	0	0	23	70	178	133	34	0	0	0	438
% OF POSSIBLE SUNSHINE	44	34	39	46	50	55	59	64	59	53	44	26	26	46
MEAN SKY COVER (tenths)														
Sunrise - Sunset	44	8.1	7.9	7.4	6.9	6.6	6.2	5.9	6.2	6.3	6.8	8.3	8.4	7.1
MEAN NUMBER OF DAYS:														
Sunrise to Sunset														
-Clear	44	2.6	3.2	4.8	6.2	6.1	7.2	7.8	6.9	6.8	6.4	2.2	2.3	62.6
-Partly Cloudy	44	6.5	5.8	6.9	6.7	9.8	10.5	12.2	11.4	10.2	7.7	5.5	4.9	98.1
-Cloudy	44	21.8	19.3	19.3	17.1	15.0	12.3	11.0	12.7	13.0	16.9	22.3	23.8	204.6
Precipitation														
.01 inches or more	44	19.0	16.0	16.7	14.3	12.9	11.3	10.9	11.0	11.3	12.4	16.4	19.1	171.2
Snow,Ice pellets,hail														
1.0 inches or more	44	8.7	7.6	5.0	1.4	0.*	0.0	0.0	0.0	0.0	0.3	2.8	7.8	33.6
Thunderstorms	44	0.2	0.2	0.8	1.8	3.3	5.3	6.1	5.5	2.6	1.0	0.6	0.1	27.4
Heavy Fog Visibility														
1/4 mile or less	44	0.7	0.7	0.8	0.6	0.7	0.5	0.5	0.7	0.9	1.2	0.6	0.8	8.8
Temperature °F														
-Maximum														
90° and above	30	0.0	0.0	0.0	0.*	0.3	1.4	3.7	1.8	0.3	0.0	0.0	0.0	7.5
32° and below	30	16.5	14.1	5.9	0.3	0.0	0.0	0.0	0.0	0.0	0.0	1.4	11.2	49.4
-Minimum														
32° and below	30	28.6	25.5	23.5	11.7	0.9	0.0	0.0	0.0	0.2	5.3	14.8	26.2	136.7
0° and below	30	4.4	3.0	0.7	0.0	0.0	0.0	0.0	0.0	0.0	0.0	0.0	1.6	9.6
AVG. STATION PRESS.(mb)	21	1001.7	1002.7	1001.3	999.7	1000.0	999.7	1000.4	1002.0	1003.0	1003.4	1002.5	1002.6	1001.6
RELATIVE HUMIDITY (%)														
Hour 01	30	76	76	76	75	79	83	84	87	86	82	80	79	80
Hour 07 (Local Time)	30	77	78	78	76	77	79	81	86	88	85	81	80	81
Hour 13	30	68	65	60	53	55	56	56	59	62	61	67	71	61
Hour 19	30	74	72	67	59	60	63	63	70	76	75	76	77	69
PRECIPITATION (inches):														
Water Equivalent														
-Normal		2.34	2.15	2.77	3.33	3.28	3.79	3.81	3.51	3.79	3.24	3.72	3.20	38.93
-Maximum Monthly	44	5.77	5.38	6.84	8.12	7.41	12.30	9.52	8.41	8.81	8.29	6.79	5.50	12.30
-Year		1978	1951	1955	1976	1976	1972	1974	1956	1975	1955	1972	1983	JUN 1972
-Minimum Monthly	44	1.02	0.63	1.01	1.22	0.75	1.10	0.90	1.33	0.75	0.21	1.25	1.73	0.21
-Year		1970	1987	1981	1985	1977	1962	1969	1980	1964	1963	1978	1958	OCT 1963
-Maximum in 24 hrs	44	1.47	1.99	1.77	2.85	3.13	3.88	4.07	4.27	4.14	3.60	2.09	2.18	4.27
-Year		1958	1961	1993	1976	1969	1972	1974	1954	1975	1955	1967	1952	AUG 1954
Snow,Ice pellets,hail														
-Maximum Monthly	44	72.2	72.6	54.4	16.4	1.2	T	T	0.0	T	5.7	25.9	64.6	72.6
-Year		1978	1958	1993	1983	1973	1992	1992		1992	1988	1976	1989	FEB 1958
-Maximum in 24 hrs	44	24.5	21.4	35.6	7.1	1.2	T	T	0.0	T	2.9	12.1	17.3	35.6
-Year		1966	1961	1993	1975	1973	1992	1992		1992	1988	1973	1991	MAR 1993
WIND:														
Mean Speed (mph)	44	10.8	10.7	10.8	10.5	9.0	8.3	8.0	7.7	8.2	8.8	10.2	10.4	9.4
Prevailing Direction through 1963		WSW	WNW	WNW	WNW	WNW	WNW	WNW	WSW	S	WSW	WSW	WSW	WNW
Fastest Mile														
-Direction (!!)	44	W	W	SE	NW	30	NW	NW	NW	W	SE	E	W	SE
-Speed (MPH)	44	60	62	56	52	52	49	47	43	52	63	59	52	63
-Year		1974	1967	1956	1957	1991	1961	1982	1958	1962	1954	1950	1962	OCT 1954
Peak Gust														
-Direction (!!)	10	W	SW	SW	W	NW	SE	NW	W	W	NW	**W**	NW	NW
-Speed (mph)	10	58	56	54	61	76	67	64	46	48	45	**58**	63	76
-Date		1992	1985	1986	1985	1991	1989	1993	1987	1989	1992	**1992**	1991	MAY 1991

PRECIPITATION (inches)

SYRACUSE, NEW YORK

YEAR	JAN	FEB	MAR	APR	MAY	JUNE	JULY	AUG	SEP	OCT	NOV	DEC	ANNUAL
1964	2.18	1.13	3.83	3.66	2.31	1.41	2.15	3.09	0.75	1.52	2.20	2.87	27.10
1965	2.28	2.82	1.63	3.53	1.61	2.04	1.34	1.95	3.60	2.70	2.97	1.92	28.39
1966	3.98	2.96	2.27	3.05	1.79	2.73	2.09	2.64	4.75	0.90	2.05	3.93	33.14
1967	1.47	1.49	1.34	2.11	3.33	1.56	6.33	5.00	2.73	3.52	4.48	2.66	36.02
1968	2.08	1.10	3.13	2.40	3.46	6.14	3.77	4.17	3.43	5.81	4.07	4.67	44.23
1969	3.37	1.49	1.08	3.95	4.34	3.74	0.90	1.77	1.13	2.30	4.56	3.42	32.05
1970	1.02	1.84	2.45	3.68	2.79	2.93	4.42	4.07	4.33	3.84	3.53	3.33	38.23
1971	1.90	4.07	2.90	2.19	3.40	3.26	6.49	4.01	2.56	1.62	3.52	3.26	39.18
1972	1.10	2.87	2.49	4.03	6.19	12.30	3.45	3.76	4.12	4.36	6.79	3.95	55.41
1973	1.85	1.71	3.45	6.91	5.58	7.07	3.62	2.97	4.57	3.81	6.73	4.38	52.65
1974	2.08	1.70	4.34	3.09	5.78	4.67	9.52	4.60	4.45	1.58	4.95	3.47	50.23
1975	2.54	3.05	2.67	2.01	2.74	4.08	9.32	5.35	8.81	3.69	3.54	4.10	51.90
1976	2.79	2.71	4.62	8.12	7.41	7.42	5.24	6.73	3.27	6.53	1.53	1.80	58.17
1977	1.84	1.62	3.47	3.04	0.75	3.30	4.76	4.93	6.54	4.75	5.31	4.33	44.64
1978	5.77	0.80	3.08	1.87	1.90	3.58	2.78	3.31	3.93	2.68	1.25	4.12	35.07
1979	4.70	2.54	2.73	3.89	3.07	2.33	2.33	3.69	5.25	2.91	3.25	1.84	38.53
1980	1.47	1.38	4.34	3.33	1.34	4.45	2.57	1.33	3.40	2.56	2.64	3.27	32.08
1981	1.34	2.72	1.01	2.04	2.61	1.89	2.68	2.63	5.58	6.66	3.09	2.96	35.21
1982	3.59	1.26	2.63	1.71	2.87	4.64	3.83	2.60	4.22	0.72	4.52	2.55	35.14
1983	1.92	1.07	2.30	6.34	3.33	1.50	2.31	2.80	2.98	1.98	4.30	5.50	36.33
1984	1.30	2.88	2.39	3.16	4.97	2.02	3.66	5.17	2.61	1.95	3.48	4.38	37.97
1985	2.49	1.55	2.61	1.22	3.39	2.80	2.75	1.44	3.88	3.39	5.18	1.80	32.50
1986	2.41	2.27	2.82	3.42	2.67	4.89	5.23	3.36	5.47	3.32	3.74	3.33	42.93
1987	3.03	0.63	1.86	3.31	1.41	5.04	2.16	2.12	5.99	3.13	3.02	1.99	33.69
1988	1.50	2.13	1.79	2.70	3.05	2.46	5.72	3.77	1.88	3.57	3.95	1.92	34.44
1989	1.06	1.71	3.13	1.52	4.27	5.41	2.20	2.68	5.96	4.08	2.78	2.13	36.93
1990	2.13	3.95	3.70	4.09	5.62	2.92	3.72	5.33	3.45	6.09	3.23	5.24	49.47
1991	2.44	1.54	4.07	3.90	3.90	1.67	2.86	4.03	4.20	2.62	2.72	3.10	37.05
1992	2.62	2.46	3.80	3.54	5.21	1.78	8.00	2.64	4.55	2.69	3.75	2.57	43.61
1993	3.08	2.45	3.75	6.55	2.25	2.93	4.76	4.71	3.83	2.91	3.19	3.20	43.61
Record Mean	2.66	2.48	3.08	3.14	3.07	3.54	3.53	3.34	3.19	3.08	3.03	2.96	37.09

AVERAGE TEMPERATURE (deg. F)

SYRACUSE, NEW YORK

YEAR	JAN	FEB	MAR	APR	MAY	JUNE	JULY	AUG	SEP	OCT	NOV	DEC	ANNUAL
1964	25.9	23.7	35.1	46.5	61.6	66.0	73.2	67.5	61.6	49.5	43.6	29.6	48.6
1965	20.5	24.6	30.3	42.3	59.4	63.7	67.5	69.1	62.8	47.9	38.7	32.1	46.6
1966	19.0	23.1	34.4	42.6	51.2	65.7	71.1	70.4	59.5	49.5	42.9	29.2	46.6
1967	30.6	19.2	31.6	44.9	50.2	69.5	67.7	66.6	60.7	51.8	37.6	32.7	46.9
1968	18.5	21.1	33.2	48.1	53.6	64.9	69.9	68.8	64.8	52.5	40.0	27.2	46.9
1969	24.3	23.6	30.4	46.9	55.7	64.5	69.9	71.3	63.8	51.1	40.4	23.8	47.1
1970	16.1	24.1	31.7	47.2	57.5	63.5	69.7	68.0	61.4	52.3	41.7	25.4	46.5
1971	18.5	26.5	31.2	42.8	55.8	67.9	69.0	67.1	65.6	56.6	36.9	33.2	47.6
1972	26.4	22.9	29.4	40.5	58.5	64.5	72.9	69.2	63.5	46.5	37.0	30.8	46.9
1973	28.4	21.4	42.6	46.8	54.3	69.6	72.7	73.5	62.0	53.7	40.7	29.5	49.6
1974	26.0	21.6	32.3	48.8	54.1	65.6	69.1	68.9	59.1	46.5	40.6	30.4	46.9
1975	29.4	28.1	31.7	39.9	62.9	67.1	71.7	68.2	57.1	53.2	46.6	27.6	48.6
1976	18.1	32.5	36.6	48.4	54.2	67.9	66.7	66.0	59.8	46.9	35.8	22.6	46.3
1977	15.7	26.0	40.1	48.2	60.3	62.7	70.8	67.3	62.5	50.6	44.0	27.3	48.0
1978	21.3	17.6	29.4	42.2	58.3	64.8	71.9	71.7	59.9	49.6	40.3	30.6	46.4
1979	22.4	12.9	39.1	45.1	58.6	66.0	71.7	67.9	61.4	50.9	44.5	33.4	47.8
1980	25.6	19.8	32.4	47.8	59.8	63.0	72.5	73.8	63.4	48.8	37.6	22.6	47.3
1981	15.0	33.7	36.4	50.0	59.2	68.0	73.3	70.4	61.6	47.9	39.0	29.0	48.6
1982	14.8	25.1	33.2	43.9	59.4	63.1	70.4	65.3	60.6	50.4	43.9	34.1	47.0
1983	23.4	26.4	35.7	44.3	53.7	66.7	72.0	69.0	62.5	50.3	39.0	22.5	47.1
1984	18.7	32.0	24.5	46.0	52.4	65.4	68.0	68.8	57.7	52.2	38.3	33.5	46.5
1985	22.0	27.3	36.3	47.8	59.5	62.0	69.8	68.9	63.5	51.4	41.2	26.0	48.0
1986	23.9	23.4	37.4	49.2	61.0	64.3	71.0	66.8	60.5	49.7	36.8	31.6	48.0
1987	23.8	21.7	38.0	51.9	60.3	68.3	73.6	68.5	61.1	47.7	40.9	32.3	49.0
1988	23.1	24.6	34.4	45.7	59.7	64.1	74.0	71.8	60.8	46.6	43.0	27.8	48.0
1989	28.6	22.7	32.9	43.5	58.2	67.3	71.1	68.2	61.8	51.7	38.8	14.7	46.6
1990	33.2	29.0	37.5	49.3	54.5	67.3	71.8	70.3	61.2	52.8	42.2	33.5	50.2
1991	24.3	29.8	37.7	51.0	62.8	68.4	72.4	71.8	60.5	53.1	40.0	30.7	50.2
1992	24.7	26.5	29.3	44.4	57.5	64.0	67.3	67.5	61.3	46.6	39.7	31.0	46.7
1993	27.5	17.0	30.1	46.9	58.0	65.2	72.5	70.7	60.0	48.2	38.6	26.9	46.8
Record Mean	23.9	24.2	33.5	45.6	57.1	66.1	71.2	69.2	62.0	51.2	40.2	28.2	47.7
Max	31.7	32.2	41.7	55.0	67.4	76.3	81.2	79.0	71.7	60.3	47.3	35.1	56.6
Min	16.1	16.1	25.3	36.2	46.8	55.9	61.1	59.4	52.4	42.1	33.1	21.3	38.8

REFERENCE NOTES

SYRACUSE, NEW YORK

GENERAL
T - TRACE AMOUNT.
BLANK ENTRIES DENOTE MISSING/UNREPORTED DATA.
# INDICATES A STATION OR INSTRUMENT RELOCATION.

SPECIFIC

PM - INCLUDES LAST DAY OF PREVIOUS MONTH
ASOS - AUTOMATED SURFACE OBSERVING SYSTEM IN OPERATION DURING THESE MONTHS.

(a) - LENGTH OF RECORD IN YEARS, ALTHOUGH INDIVIDUAL MONTHS MAY BE MISSING.
0.* OR * - THE VALUE IS BETWEEN 0.0 AND 0.05
NORMALS - BASED ON THE 1961-1990 RECORD PERIOD.
EXTREMES - DATES ARE THE MOST RECENT OCCURRENCE
WIND DIR.- NUMERALS SHOW TENS OF DEGRESS CLOCKWISE FROM TRUE NORTH. "00" INDICATES CALM.
RESULTANT DIRECTIONS ARE GIVEN TO WHOLE DEGREES.
BOLD VALUES INDICATE EXTREME VALUES WHICH OCCURRED AFTER THE ASOS SYSTEM WAS COMMISSIONED.

RECORD = PERIOD OF RECORD
RECORD MEAN PRECIPITATION IS THE MEAN OF ALL DAILY PRECIPITATION AMOUNTS DURING THE PERIOD OF RECORD.
RECORD MAX(MIN) TEMPERATURE IS THE MEAN OF ALL DAILY MAX(MIN) TEMPERATURES DURING THE PERIOD OF RECORD.
RECORD MEAN TEMPERATURE IS THE SUM OF THE RECORD MAX AND RECORD MIN DIVIDED BY 2.
AVERAGE TEMPERATURE IS THE SUM OF THE MEAN DAILY MAX AND MIN TEMPERATURE DIVIDED BY 2.

EXCEPTIONS

RECORD MEANS ARE THROUGH THE CURRENT YEAR, BEGINNING IN 1902 FOR TEMPERATURE
1902 FOR PRECIPITATION
1950 FOR SNOWFALL

HEATING DEGREE DAYS Base 65 deg. F — SYRACUSE, NEW YORK

SEASON	JULY	AUG	SEP	OCT	NOV	DEC	JAN	FEB	MAR	APR	MAY	JUNE	TOTAL
1964-65	2	30	154	475	636	1087	1370	1125	1069	676	215	132	6971
1965-66	27	50	144	521	782	1011	1422	1168	945	665	429	80	7244
1966-67	6	7	186	473	652	1104	1059	1275	1030	595	453	13	6853
1967-68	24	35	154	407	812	995	1438	1266	979	501	345	83	7039
1968-69	27	41	54	391	745	1163	1256	1152	1063	536	306	103	6837
1969-70	22	20	134	425	730	1269	1508	1139	1027	536	244	115	7169
1970-71	7	27	150	388	692	1222	1437	1069	1040	658	295	50	7035
1971-72	13	51	96	256	840	980	1189	1216	1098	731	204	84	6758
1972-73	9	23	98	567	833	1053	1128	1217	687	547	325	31	6518
1973-74	2	12	164	344	723	1094	1200	1206	1004	493	339	52	6633
1974-75	16	3	202	565	726	1069	1100	1026	1026	749	138	46	6666
1975-76	3	32	230	357	545	1154	1449	936	872	509	329	47	6463
1976-77	24	45	179	556	869	1303	1520	1086	767	511	209	111	7180
1977-78	14	60	121	444	624	1162	1348	1322	1097	677	252	92	7213
1978-79	10	1	184	470	735	1062	1315	1457	796	591	242	74	6937
1979-80	19	39	146	454	607	971	1215	1302	1007	511	194	115	6580
1980-81	3	0	120	496	814	1307	1544	869	882	446	221	27	6729
1981-82	2	4	145	523	775	1110	1552	1114	978	626	183	79	7091
1982-83	13	57	152	449	628	951	1280	1073	902	615	351	67	6538
1983-84	11	25	140	457	769	1312	1432	949	1246	563	386	68	7358
1984-85	16	33	227	390	797	971	1329	1048	882	514	193	109	6509
1985-86	10	18	121	415	702	1200	1266	1156	856	471	172	76	6463
1986-87	12	50	155	468	838	1027	1270	1208	831	395	211	35	6500
1987-88	7	27	138	529	717	1007	1290	1167	942	571	187	131	6713
1988-89	9	33	150	574	653	1148	1120	1175	989	639	242	38	6770
1989-90	3	36	151	406	779	1554	976	1001	849	496	319	43	6613
1990-91	4	4	160	386	675	967	1253	980	839	428	153	24	5873
1991-92	1	0	189	378	743	1056	1240	1112	1099	617	245	79	6759
1992-93	15	33	164	562	753	1047	1156	1337	1074	537	230	68	6976
1993-94	2	10	190	515	785	1172							

COOLING DEGREE DAYS Base 65 deg. F — SYRACUSE, NEW YORK

YEAR	JAN	FEB	MAR	APR	MAY	JUNE	JULY	AUG	SEP	OCT	NOV	DEC	TOTAL
1969	0	0	0	0	22	94	183	222	102	1	0	0	624
1970	0	0	0	8	22	74	160	127	51	3	0	0	445
1971	0	0	0	0	17	145	145	124	117	4	0	0	552
1972	0	0	0	0	9	78	262	160	61	0	0	0	570
1973	0	0	0	7	0	177	249	281	79	2	0	0	795
1974	0	0	0	14	6	77	148	128	31	1	0	0	405
1975	0	0	0	0	80	114	221	138	1	1	0	0	555
1976	0	0	0	16	2	141	84	83	31	0	0	0	357
1977	0	0	1	12	71	47	202	138	49	0	0	0	520
1978	0	0	0	0	49	92	231	215	36	0	0	0	623
1979	0	0	0	2	50	109	232	134	46	22	0	0	595
1980	0	0	0	0	41	62	243	279	80	1	0	0	706
1981	0	0	3	4	47	125	264	180	49	0	0	0	672
1982	0	0	0	0	18	25	186	72	25	0	3	0	329
1983	0	0	0	0	2	125	236	155	70	7	0	0	595
1984	0	0	0	0	4	88	119	154	14	1	0	0	380
1985	0	0	0	7	30	26	165	144	87	0	0	0	459
1986	0	0	5	1	52	62	201	112	28	0	0	0	461
1987	0	0	0	7	73	142	280	143	29	0	0	0	674
1988	0	0	0	0	33	112	296	251	32	9	0	0	733
1989	0	0	0	0	37	112	198	144	59	0	0	0	550
1990	0	0	5	33	2	118	222	177	51	16	0	0	624
1991	0	0	0	16	89	136	237	218	61	16	0	0	773
1992	0	0	0	5	21	54	94	118	60	0	0	0	352
1993	0	0	0	0	17	81	241	195	48	0	0	0	582

SNOWFALL (inches) — SYRACUSE, NEW YORK

SEASON	JULY	AUG	SEP	OCT	NOV	DEC	JAN	FEB	MAR	APR	MAY	JUNE	TOTAL
1964-65	0.0	0.0	0.0	0.3	4.0	18.3	31.8	24.9	13.3	4.7	0.0	0.0	97.3
1965-66	0.0	0.0	0.0	1.8	2.7	7.1	71.0	27.0	7.8	0.5	0.9	0.0	118.8
1966-67	0.0	0.0	0.0	0.0	T	33.0	18.3	21.0	10.4	0.3	T	0.0	83.0
1967-68	0.0	0.0	0.0	T	14.4	14.4	18.5	23.2	10.7	T	0.0	0.0	81.2
1968-69	0.0	0.0	0.0	0.8	16.5	25.4	24.5	21.3	9.4	T	0.0	0.0	97.9
1969-70	0.0	0.0	0.0	1.7	9.7	52.5	21.7	25.8	12.7	1.2	0.2	0.0	125.5
1970-71	0.0	0.0	0.0	0.8	7.0	51.9	30.3	25.2	37.2	4.8	0.0	0.0	157.2
1971-72	0.0	0.0	0.0	0.0	16.7	18.3	18.2	50.0	22.7	7.8	0.0	0.0	133.7
1972-73	0.0	0.0	0.0	0.3	15.8	29.8	11.9	13.3	3.6	5.3	1.2	0.0	81.2
1973-74	0.0	0.0	0.0	T	20.6	24.4	15.5	23.7	31.2	7.8	T	0.0	123.2
1974-75	0.0	0.0	0.0	2.8	4.8	26.2	11.8	27.3	20.6	12.0	0.0	0.0	105.5
1975-76	0.0	0.0	0.0	T	2.8	27.0	35.8	12.7	16.6	0.9	T	0.0	95.8
1976-77	0.0	0.0	0.0	0.3	25.9	25.7	52.3	24.4	13.5	1.9	1.0	0.0	145.0
1977-78	0.0	0.0	0.0	0.0	11.3	40.1	72.2	26.1	11.1	0.4	T	0.0	161.2
1978-79	0.0	0.0	0.0	T	3.9	40.9	27.9	20.7	14.9	10.2	0.0	0.0	118.5
1979-80	0.0	0.0	0.0	0.1	1.5	13.8	24.5	32.8	20.5	0.2	0.0	0.0	93.4
1980-81	0.0	0.0	0.0	T	7.3	28.8	23.4	8.5	10.6	0.4	0.0	0.0	79.0
1981-82	0.0	0.0	0.0	0.5	12.1	37.3	48.2	11.6	14.4	13.0	0.0	0.0	137.1
1982-83	0.0	0.0	0.0	T	1.9	10.9	20.3	8.2	8.3	16.4	T	0.0	66.0
1983-84	0.0	0.0	0.0	0.0	7.6	24.2	21.8	19.7	40.3	T	0.0	0.0	113.6
1984-85	0.0	0.0	0.0	0.0	5.0	23.4	57.3	21.6	7.1	2.0	0.0	0.0	116.4
1985-86	0.0	0.0	0.0	0.0	8.0	28.2	29.9	26.1	11.0	1.7	T	0.0	104.9
1986-87	0.0	0.0	0.0	0.0	16.1	8.8	49.2	15.1	3.0	1.3	0.0	0.0	93.5
1987-88	0.0	0.0	0.0	T	10.8	20.7	18.0	46.1	10.2	5.6	0.0	0.0	111.4
1988-89	0.0	0.0	0.0	5.7	0.2	34.4	19.4	21.7	9.9	6.5	0.0	0.0	97.8
1989-90	0.0	0.0	T	T	12.9	64.6	27.4	33.3	15.2	8.6	0.0	0.0	162.0
1990-91	0.0	0.0	0.0	0.2	7.8	24.5	30.9	27.7	2.8	3.0	0.0	0.0	96.9
1991-92	0.0	0.0	0.0	0.0	5.5	37.9	50.5	27.6	41.3	4.1	0.0	T	166.9
1992-93	T	0.0	T	1.4	10.1	19.8	42.9	51.3	54.4	12.2	0.0	0.0	192.1
1993-94	0.0	0.0	0.0	1.0	17.1	34.0							
Record Mean	T	0.0	T	0.6	9.3	26.8	29.6	26.2	17.4	4.0	0.1	T	113.9

ASHEVILLE, NORTH CAROLINA

The city of Asheville is located on both banks of the French Broad River, near the center of the French Broad Basin. Upstream from Asheville, the valley runs south for 18 miles and then curves toward the south-southwest. Downstream from the city, the valley is oriented toward the north-northwest. Two miles upstream from the principal section of Asheville, the Swannanoa River joins the French Broad from the east. The entire valley is known as the Asheville Plateau, having an average elevation near 2,200 feet above sea level, and is flanked by mountain ridges to the east and west, whose peaks range from 2,000 to 4,400 feet above the valley floor. At the Carolina-Tennessee border, about 25 miles north-northwest of Asheville, a relatively high ridge of mountains blocks the northern end of the valley. Thirty miles south, the Blue Ridge Mountains form an escarpment, having a general elevation of about 2,700 feet above sea level. The tallest peaks near Asheville are Mt. Mitchell, 6,684 feet above sea level, 20 miles northeast of the city, and Big Pisgah Mountain, 5,721 feet above sea level, 16 miles to the southwest.

Asheville has a temperate, but invigorating, climate. Considerable variation in temperature often occurs from day to day in summer, as well as during the other seasons.

While the office was located in the city, the combination of roof exposure conditions and a smoke blanket, caused by inversions in temperature in the valley on quiet nights, resulted in higher early morning temperatures at City Office sites than were experienced nearer ground level in nearby rural areas. The growing season in this area is of sufficient length for commercial crops, the average length of freeze-free period being about 195 days. The average last occurrence in spring of a temperature 32 degrees or lower is mid-April and the average first occurrence in fall of 32 degrees is late October.

The orientation of the French Broad Valley appears to have a pronounced influence on the wind direction. Prevailing winds are from the northwest during all months of the year. Also, the shielding effect of the nearby mountain barriers apparently has a direct bearing on the annual amount of precipitation received in this vicinity. In an area northwest of Asheville, the average annual precipitation is the lowest in North Carolina. Precipitation increases sharply in all other directions, especially to the south and southwest.

Destructive events caused directly by meteorological conditions are infrequent. The most frequent, occurring at approximately 12-year intervals, are floods on the French Broad River. These floods are usually associated with heavy rains caused by storms moving out of the Gulf of Mexico. Snowstorms which have seriously disrupted normal life in this community are infrequent. Hailstorms that cause property damage are extremely rare.

NORMALS, MEANS, AND EXTREMES

ASHEVILLE, NORTH CAROLINA

LATITUDE: 35°26'N LONGITUDE: 82°33' W ELEVATION: FT. GRND 2140 BARO 2161 TIME ZONE: EASTERN WBAN: 03812

	(a)	JAN	FEB	MAR	APR	MAY	JUNE	JULY	AUG	SEP	OCT	NOV	DEC	YEAR
TEMPERATURE °F:														
Normals														
-Daily Maximum		46.5	50.0	59.2	67.8	75.0	80.4	83.0	82.1	76.9	68.3	59.3	50.3	66.6
-Daily Minimum		24.8	27.4	35.4	42.6	50.9	58.3	62.7	61.9	55.5	43.5	35.7	28.6	43.9
-Monthly		35.7	38.7	47.4	55.2	63.0	69.4	72.8	72.0	66.2	55.9	47.5	39.5	55.3
Extremes														
-Record Highest	29	78	77	83	89	91	96	96	100	92	86	81	78	100
-Year		1975	1989	1985	1972	1969	1969	1988	1983	1991	1986	1974	1971	AUG 1983
-Record Lowest	29	-16	-2	2	22	28	35	44	42	30	21	8	-7	-16
-Year		1985	1967	1993	1987	1989	1966	1988	1986	1967	1976	1970	1983	JAN 1985
NORMAL DEGREE DAYS:														
Heating (base 65°F)		908	736	546	298	117	18	5	5	64	295	525	791	4308
Cooling (base 65°F)		0	0	0	0	55	150	247	222	100	13	0	0	787
% OF POSSIBLE SUNSHINE	29	55	59	60	65	61	63	60	54	56	61	58	55	59
MEAN SKY COVER (tenths)														
Sunrise - Sunset	29	6.1	5.9	6.0	5.6	6.2	6.1	6.3	6.4	6.2	5.1	5.5	6.0	6.0
MEAN NUMBER OF DAYS:														
Sunrise to Sunset														
-Clear	29	9.3	9.0	9.0	9.8	7.3	6.4	5.4	4.9	6.9	12.1	10.7	9.8	100.7
-Partly Cloudy	29	7.4	6.3	8.2	8.5	10.3	12.1	13.8	13.7	10.6	8.0	7.1	7.2	113.1
-Cloudy	29	14.2	12.9	13.8	11.7	13.4	11.5	11.8	12.4	12.4	10.9	12.2	14.0	151.4
Precipitation														
.01 inches or more	29	10.2	9.3	11.4	9.4	11.9	11.1	11.8	12.7	9.6	8.0	9.4	9.8	124.6
Snow, Ice pellets, hail														
1.0 inches or more	29	1.3	1.2	0.7	0.2	0.0	0.0	0.0	0.0	0.0	0.0	0.2	0.5	4.1
Thunderstorms	29	0.3	0.8	2.2	3.3	6.9	7.7	9.3	8.8	3.3	0.8	0.8	0.3	44.4
Heavy Fog Visibility														
1/4 mile or less	29	4.0	3.0	2.3	2.4	5.7	7.8	9.1	13.9	12.0	8.1	4.3	4.5	77.2
Temperature °F														
-Maximum														
90° and above	29	0.0	0.0	0.0	0.0	0.1	1.8	5.1	2.4	0.3	0.0	0.0	0.0	9.8
32° and below	29	3.1	1.5	0.3	0.0	0.0	0.0	0.0	0.0	0.0	0.0	0.1	1.0	5.9
-Minimum														
32° and below	29	23.2	20.1	13.3	4.2	0.3	0.0	0.0	0.0	0.*	4.2	13.4	20.8	99.5
0° and below	29	0.5	0.*	0.0	0.0	0.0	0.0	0.0	0.0	0.0	0.0	0.0	0.1	0.6
AVG. STATION PRESS. (mb)	21	941.7	941.2	940.3	940.2	941.0	942.2	943.4	944.0	944.0	944.0	943.3	942.7	942.3
RELATIVE HUMIDITY (%)														
Hour 01	29	81	78	79	78	89	93	94	96	96	91	85	82	87
Hour 07 (Local Time)	29	85	83	85	85	92	94	95	97	97	94	88	85	90
Hour 13	29	59	55	53	50	57	59	62	63	63	56	57	59	58
Hour 19	29	68	62	60	55	67	70	74	78	81	73	70	70	69
PRECIPITATION (inches):														
Water Equivalent														
-Normal		3.25	3.91	4.63	3.36	4.43	4.23	4.52	4.69	3.87	3.59	3.59	3.52	47.59
-Maximum Monthly	29	7.47	8.07	9.86	7.26	8.83	10.73	9.92	11.28	9.12	8.82	7.76	8.48	11.28
-Year		1978	1990	1975	1979	1973	1989	1982	1967	1977	1990	1979	1973	AUG 1967
-Minimum Monthly	29	0.45	0.44	0.77	0.25	1.06	0.90	0.46	0.52	0.16	0.19	1.19	0.16	0.16
-Year		1981	1978	1985	1976	1988	1990	1986	1981	1984	1991	1981	1965	SEP 1984
-Maximum in 24 hrs	29	2.95	3.47	5.13	3.06	4.95	3.93	4.02	5.10	3.41	3.06	4.03	2.66	5.13
-Year		1978	1982	1968	1973	1973	1987	1969	1990	1975	1990	1977	1973	MAR 1968
Snow, Ice pellets, hail														
-Maximum Monthly	29	17.6	25.5	18.2	11.5	T	T	0.0	T	0.0	T	9.6	16.3	25.5
-Year		1966	1969	1993	1987	1993	1991		1990		1993	1968	1971	FEB 1969
-Maximum in 24 hrs	29	14.0	11.7	16.5	11.5	T	T	0.0	T	0.0	T	5.7	16.3	16.5
-Year		1988	1969	1993	1987	1993	1991		1990		1993	1968	1971	MAR 1993
WIND:														
Mean Speed (mph)	29	9.5	9.5	9.4	8.8	7.1	6.1	5.9	5.4	5.7	6.7	8.2	8.9	7.6
Prevailing Direction														
Fastest Obs. 1 Min.														
-Direction (!!!)	29	34	34	33	22	34	36	35	34	32	33	32	34	34
-Speed (MPH)	29	40	60	48	44	40	40	43	40	35	35	40	44	60
-Year		1975	1972	1993	1970	1971	1977	1966	1973	1980	1972	1974	1965	FEB 1972
Peak Gust														
-Direction (!!!)	10	NW	NW	NW	N	N	N	S	NW	N	NW	N	NW	NW
-Speed (mph)	10	49	54	64	51	44	52	60	43	37	40	49	49	64
-Date		1984	1987	1993	1988	1992	1987	1990	1993	1992	1990	1989	1992	MAR 1993

PRECIPITATION (inches)

ASHEVILLE, NORTH CAROLINA

YEAR	JAN	FEB	MAR	APR	MAY	JUNE	JULY	AUG	SEP	OCT	NOV	DEC	ANNUAL
#1964	2.83	3.58	5.13	5.21	0.94	0.80	3.29	8.88	5.37	8.46	2.51	2.88	49.88
1965	2.16	4.60	5.10	2.62	3.33	4.12	4.47	4.03	4.69	2.92	1.30	0.16	39.50
1966	3.37	6.56	2.59	5.47	4.73	2.46	3.24	7.73	4.55	5.37	3.32	2.36	51.75
1967	2.02	2.20	2.86	1.11	6.79	4.45	6.90	11.28	2.53	3.30	2.54	6.13	52.11
1968	2.93	0.62	6.65	2.37	2.92	5.06	7.18	3.31	2.64	5.02	2.98	3.10	44.78
1969	2.64	5.08	4.01	3.53	3.32	3.82	7.53	6.47	3.04	2.63	1.91	4.63	48.61
1970	1.75	2.42	2.62	2.96	1.72	2.72	5.02	2.46	1.17	5.55	1.83	2.72	32.94
1971	2.53	4.93	3.48	2.06	3.54	5.00	5.47	3.03	3.80	7.05	2.84	4.32	48.05
1972	3.57	2.02	3.19	1.49	6.63	6.54	4.66	1.88	5.29	4.44	4.42	3.89	48.02
1973	4.26	4.23	8.91	5.71	8.83	3.87	6.95	4.57	3.12	2.41	3.57	8.48	64.91
1974	3.44	4.24	3.18	4.99	5.58	3.73	3.93	7.34	4.13	1.28	4.22	2.38	48.44
1975	3.86	4.56	9.86	0.61	8.17	2.12	3.31	3.63	7.53	3.94	4.89	4.44	56.92
1976	3.51	2.20	4.96	0.25	8.67	5.51	3.18	4.23	3.50	5.59	1.58	4.05	47.23
1977	2.09	1.02	7.29	4.05	3.96	5.11	1.03	3.68	9.12	3.79	6.88	2.43	50.45
1978	7.47	0.44	5.22	2.97	4.65	2.29	0.63	6.91	2.57	0.30	2.49	4.32	40.26
1979	6.81	5.14	5.72	7.26	5.35	2.20	5.52	3.63	5.60	1.40	7.76	1.05	57.44
1980	2.85	0.53	8.26	4.77	4.54	4.68	2.21	2.38	4.36	2.62	3.04	0.59	40.83
1981	0.45	4.80	3.24	2.07	7.50	4.41	2.06	0.52	1.36	2.19	1.19	4.79	34.58
1982	5.41	7.02	1.92	3.62	3.78	3.98	9.92	1.73	1.33	3.48	4.59	4.04	50.82
1983	3.39	5.63	6.27	5.27	3.48	3.71	1.06	0.95	5.66	4.43	4.77	8.30	52.92
1984	2.36	6.43	4.82	4.05	6.62	3.69	5.88	5.02	0.16	2.73	2.61	1.34	45.71
1985	2.95	4.74	0.77	2.74	1.59	1.47	4.37	7.04	1.25	3.41	4.91	0.70	35.94
1986	1.11	1.85	2.75	0.57	3.55	1.28	0.46	6.10	3.15	4.19	5.28	4.28	34.57
1987	3.49	6.17	2.85	3.67	1.87	8.94	1.86	1.79	6.79	0.36	3.09	2.33	43.21
1988	3.71	0.88	1.31	3.46	1.06	0.94	2.65	1.78	2.79	3.12	3.47	1.41	26.58
1989	1.65	4.61	2.91	3.17	5.54	10.73	8.33	4.98	8.17	2.98	4.27	3.29	60.63
1990	3.27	8.07	5.95	1.96	5.09	0.90	6.55	7.78	1.43	8.82	1.55	4.50	55.87
1991	3.25	1.66	6.13	5.38	2.41	5.27	6.07	3.83	1.27	0.19	3.34	4.86	43.66
1992	3.08	3.66	3.52	3.99	6.18	6.62	1.10	7.64	3.15	4.15	7.24	3.71	54.04
1993	3.82	2.03	6.16	3.21	4.59	1.12	2.07	5.29	1.56	1.21	3.32	3.59	37.97
Record Mean	3.21	3.74	4.57	3.29	4.69	4.03	4.26	4.52	3.65	3.41	3.63	3.52	46.51

AVERAGE TEMPERATURE (deg. F)

ASHEVILLE, NORTH CAROLINA

YEAR	JAN	FEB	MAR	APR	MAY	JUNE	JULY	AUG	SEP	OCT	NOV	DEC	ANNUAL
#1964	38.1	34.7	46.3	57.3	65.3	72.8	72.9	71.7	66.0	53.0	51.4	42.9	56.1
1965	37.0	37.9	42.4	57.4	65.8	66.8	72.2	71.1	66.8	53.8	46.4	40.3	54.8
1966	30.1	36.2	43.5	52.0	60.1	66.1	71.1	69.9	62.9	51.7	45.0	37.6	52.2
1967	38.7	35.0	49.8	57.6	59.7	66.8	68.7	68.5	60.2	53.5	42.7	41.8	53.6
1968	34.3	32.4	46.6	54.8	61.0	69.5	73.1	74.1	64.1	56.7	46.0	36.2	54.0
1969	36.7	37.8	41.3	56.7	65.2	73.1	75.9	70.7	65.8	56.2	44.0	36.5	55.0
1970	30.9	39.1	46.8	57.6	63.7	70.1	74.4	73.1	70.7	59.0	46.0	42.8	56.2
1971	36.5	39.5	43.1	55.2	61.1	72.4	72.5	72.2	69.5	61.8	45.8	47.7	56.5
1972	42.1	37.6	46.5	55.8	61.2	66.5	72.3	72.5	69.0	55.0	45.5	45.2	55.7
1973	37.5	38.5	52.7	52.8	60.3	71.0	74.1	74.2	70.0	58.8	49.1	39.8	56.5
1974	48.2	40.5	51.1	54.9	64.2	66.7	72.9	72.3	65.7	54.6	47.4	40.3	56.6
1975	41.7	42.5	44.8	54.1	66.0	68.8	72.4	72.9	65.2	57.3	48.2	38.6	56.1
1976	33.6	45.3	50.6	54.9	59.5	68.1	71.2	70.2	63.1	51.5	41.2	36.2	53.8
1977	24.8	37.4	50.7	58.2	64.6	69.7	75.7	73.8	69.1	54.3	49.3	36.8	55.3
1978	29.3	33.4	45.9	56.8	62.0	71.1	73.4	74.1	70.0	55.7	51.8	41.0	55.4
1979	34.2	35.8	50.0	55.9	64.3	68.8	72.2	73.2	66.5	55.3	49.2	42.0	55.6
1980	40.5	35.1	46.2	56.5	64.8	71.7	77.5	74.8	70.2	54.7	47.1	39.6	56.5
1981	33.3	39.9	44.9	60.1	60.7	74.3	75.0	71.7	66.1	54.5	48.2	35.8	55.4
1982	32.3	41.2	50.0	53.6	67.3	71.5	74.6	71.7	64.5	56.3	47.1	44.9	56.3
1983	36.7	38.8	46.7	51.1	61.6	69.0	75.7	76.5	66.6	57.5	47.3	36.4	55.3
1984	34.0	40.5	44.8	51.7	59.9	70.0	70.6	71.6	62.8	62.7	43.1	46.3	54.8
1985	30.5	38.3	48.1	56.6	62.6	69.8	72.2	70.9	64.2	60.5	56.0	34.7	55.4
1986	35.0	42.2	46.0	56.0	63.3	71.7	76.1	70.9	68.0	57.4	50.7	39.8	56.4
1987	35.3	38.9	46.5	52.6	66.7	71.2	74.7	74.7	66.5	50.1	47.0	42.2	55.5
1988	32.1	37.1	47.1	54.6	61.1	69.3	73.8	74.6	66.3	50.2	46.7	38.7	54.3
1989	42.1	39.8	50.3	54.5	59.4	70.0	73.3	71.9	65.8	56.1	46.2	31.6	55.1
1990	42.8	45.6	50.4	54.2	63.3	70.9	73.8	73.9	67.6	57.8	49.9	45.5	58.0
1991	39.2	42.4	49.6	58.4	67.3	70.3	75.2	72.1	67.3	57.0	45.5	43.4	57.3
1992	40.7	44.2	46.3	55.9	59.9	68.1	74.9	70.4	67.8	54.4	46.2	39.2	55.7
1993	42.0	38.0	43.0	52.6	63.2	71.4	78.0	73.9	67.8	55.0	46.0	36.8	55.6
Record Mean	36.3	39.0	47.0	55.3	62.7	69.8	73.7	72.5	66.5	55.8	47.0	39.9	55.5
Max	46.9	50.4	59.1	68.1	74.7	81.2	84.3	82.8	77.2	68.2	58.7	50.7	66.9
Min	25.6	27.6	35.0	42.4	50.7	58.4	63.1	62.1	55.8	43.4	35.3	29.1	44.1

REFERENCE NOTES

ASHEVILLE, NORTH CAROLINA

GENERAL
T - TRACE AMOUNT.
BLANK ENTRIES DENOTE MISSING/UNREPORTED DATA.
# INDICATES A STATION OR INSTRUMENT RELOCATION.

SPECIFIC

PM - INCLUDES LAST DAY OF PREVIOUS MONTH
ASOS - AUTOMATED SURFACE OBSERVING SYSTEM IN OPERATION DURING THESE MONTHS.

(a) - LENGTH OF RECORD IN YEARS, ALTHOUGH INDIVIDUAL MONTHS MAY BE MISSING.
0.* OR * - THE VALUE IS BETWEEN 0.0 AND 0.05
NORMALS - BASED ON THE 1961-1990 RECORD PERIOD.
EXTREMES - DATES ARE THE MOST RECENT OCCURRENCE
WIND DIR.- NUMERALS SHOW TENS OF DEGRESS CLOCKWISE FROM TRUE NORTH. "00" INDICATES CALM.
RESULTANT DIRECTIONS ARE GIVEN TO WHOLE DEGREES.
BOLD VALUES INDICATE EXTREME VALUES WHICH OCCURRED AFTER THE ASOS SYSTEM WAS COMMISSIONED.

RECORD = PERIOD OF RECORD
RECORD MEAN PRECIPITATION IS THE MEAN OF ALL DAILY PRECIPITATION AMOUNTS DURING THE PERIOD OF RECORD.
RECORD MAX(MIN) TEMPERATURE IS THE MEAN OF ALL DAILY MAX(MIN) TEMPERATURES DURING THE PERIOD OF RECORD.
RECORD MEAN TEMPERATURE IS THE SUM OF THE RECORD MAX AND RECORD MIN DIVIDED BY 2.
AVERAGE TEMPERATURE IS THE SUM OF THE MEAN DAILY MAX AND MIN TEMPERATURE DIVIDED BY 2.

EXCEPTIONS

RECORD MEANS ARE THROUGH THE CURRENT YEAR,
BEGINNING IN 1965 FOR TEMPERATURE
1965 FOR PRECIPITATION
1965 FOR SNOWFALL

HEATING DEGREE DAYS Base 65 deg. F   ASHEVILLE, NORTH CAROLINA

SEASON	JULY	AUG	SEP	OCT	NOV	DEC	JAN	FEB	MAR	APR	MAY	JUNE	TOTAL
#1964-65	0	20	46	372	399	679	863	751	691	232	23	27	4103
1965-66	0	7	39	344	550	759	1075	800	660	383	149	42	4808
1966-67	1	1	87	405	593	838	810	834	465	226	185	51	4496
1967-68	7	2	158	351	660	713	947	939	566	306	150	7	4806
1968-69	0	20	42	258	563	884	873	755	729	246	70	9	4449
1969-70	0	8	59	280	623	875	1050	720	557	236	86	3	4497
1970-71	0	0	29	194	565	682	875	707	672	290	137	0	4151
1971-72	0	0	6	129	576	530	704	790	569	294	116	35	3749
1972-73	3	0	8	304	578	605	846	737	374	362	158	0	3975
1973-74	0	0	7	205	473	772	516	680	423	299	83	24	3482
1974-75	0	0	65	316	519	760	715	624	619	331	46	7	4002
1975-76	0	0	77	232	498	812	966	566	439	296	168	33	4087
1976-77	2	3	83	411	706	884	1239	768	437	198	66	25	4822
1977-78	0	0	14	331	466	868	1101	878	586	241	139	0	4624
1978-79	0	0	12	283	390	741	951	810	457	268	71	18	4001
1979-80	5	0	44	299	468	707	753	861	573	258	65	2	4035
1980-81	0	0	37	315	533	778	978	696	615	152	152	0	4256
1981-82	0	1	57	326	499	897	1006	659	458	333	38	0	4274
1982-83	0	0	74	274	531	616	872	725	562	410	127	13	4204
1983-84	0	0	84	229	527	882	955	706	618	391	176	9	4577
1984-85	1	0	107	91	648	576	1064	737	520	249	109	19	4121
1985-86	0	6	111	156	266	932	923	633	581	273	91	2	3974
1986-87	0	32	16	268	419	774	913	725	567	369	40	1	4124
1987-88	0	0	47	452	532	702	1013	802	545	308	132	31	4564
1988-89	5	0	33	453	544	808	702	698	454	331	200	4	4232
1989-90	1	8	74	279	558	1028	679	535	446	321	91	3	4023
1990-91	0	0	55	229	445	601	793	627	472	204	53	16	3495
1991-92	0	1	64	242	578	663	748	596	573	274	169	25	3933
1992-93	0	0	34	324	558	794	708	751	677	365	82	9	4302
1993-94	0	0	44	310	563	866							

COOLING DEGREE DAYS Base 65 deg. F   ASHEVILLE, NORTH CAROLINA

YEAR	JAN	FEB	MAR	APR	MAY	JUNE	JULY	AUG	SEP	OCT	NOV	DEC	TOTAL
1969	0	0	0	4	85	262	343	196	92	15	0	0	997
1970	0	0	0	22	52	159	296	259	206	17	0	0	1011
1971	0	0	0	3	25	232	238	231	149	37	8	0	923
1972	0	0	0	24	6	84	236	237	134	0	1	0	722
1973	0	0	0	1	16	190	288	292	163	19	0	0	969
1974	0	0	0	3	65	82	254	234	92	1	0	0	731
1975	0	0	0	11	82	124	237	252	89	0	0	0	795
1976	0	0	0	0	5	135	198	170	35	2	0	0	545
1977	0	0	0	2	59	173	340	279	146	7	1	0	1007
1978	0	0	0	2	53	188	266	292	168	4	0	0	973
1979	0	0	0	1	55	141	234	261	96	4	0	0	792
1980	0	0	0	8	64	210	396	311	198	4	0	0	1191
1981	0	0	0	10	25	286	316	213	98	7	0	0	955
1982	0	0	0	0	117	206	305	215	64	16	0	0	923
1983	0	0	0	0	25	139	335	362	141	5	0	0	1007
1984	0	0	0	0	25	165	180	211	49	27	0	0	657
1985	0	0	5	2	43	170	229	194	90	25	4	0	762
1986	0	0	0	8	43	209	353	222	112	38	0	0	985
1987	0	0	0	7	97	192	310	309	97	0	0	0	1012
1988	0	0	0	0	18	168	282	304	79	3	0	0	854
1989	0	0	5	23	34	159	264	229	107	11	0	0	832
1990	0	0	0	3	48	187	279	283	141	11	0	0	952
1991	0	0	3	13	132	181	324	227	139	3	0	0	1022
1992	0	0	0	7	20	125	313	174	125	0	0	0	764
1993	0	0	0	0	37	210	411	285	133	5	0	0	1081

SNOWFALL (inches)   ASHEVILLE, NORTH CAROLINA

SEASON	JULY	AUG	SEP	OCT	NOV	DEC	JAN	FEB	MAR	APR	MAY	JUNE	TOTAL
#1964-65	0.0	0.0	0.0	0.0	T	T	5.5	4.3	5.0	0.0	0.0	0.0	14.8
1965-66	0.0	0.0	0.0	0.0	T	T	17.6	6.2	0.2	T	0.0	0.0	24.0
1966-67	0.0	0.0	0.0	0.0	1.3	0.8	1.5	4.2	T	0.0	0.0	0.0	7.8
1967-68	0.0	0.0	0.0	0.0	0.0	1.9	7.2	6.0	0.1	0.0	0.0	0.0	15.2
1968-69	0.0	0.0	0.0	0.0	9.6	T	0.1	25.5	13.0	0.0	0.0	0.0	48.2
1969-70	0.0	0.0	0.0	0.0	T	10.9	4.8	1.1	0.5	0.0	0.0	0.0	17.3
1970-71	0.0	0.0	0.0	0.0	T	6.1	0.1	0.1	8.9	0.2	0.0	0.0	15.4
1971-72	0.0	0.0	0.0	0.0	0.6	16.3	T	7.4	7.4	0.0	0.0	0.0	31.7
1972-73	0.0	0.0	0.0	0.0	0.6	T	7.1	0.5	1.0	T	0.0	0.0	9.2
1973-74	0.0	0.0	0.0	0.0	0.0	3.0	T	0.3	1.1	T	0.0	0.0	4.4
1974-75	0.0	0.0	0.0	0.0	3.1	3.0	0.4	4.3	3.7	T	0.0	0.0	14.5
1975-76	0.0	0.0	0.0	0.0	5.0	0.4	1.6	3.5	T	0.0	0.0	0.0	10.5
1976-77	0.0	0.0	0.0	0.0	0.1	0.3	11.9	0.7	0.0	0.0	0.0	0.0	13.0
1977-78	0.0	0.0	0.0	T	T	1.5	9.7	5.3	5.3	T	0.0	0.0	21.8
1978-79	0.0	0.0	0.0	0.0	0.0	T	5.2	17.8	T	0.0	T	0.0	23.0
1979-80	0.0	0.0	0.0	0.0	T	T	2.1	6.3	5.4	T	0.0	0.0	13.8
1980-81	0.0	0.0	0.0	0.0	T	T	4.7	T	9.9	0.0	0.0	0.0	14.6
1981-82	0.0	0.0	0.0	0.0	T	2.0	8.6	8.1	0.1	3.0	0.0	0.0	21.8
1982-83	0.0	0.0	0.0	0.0	0.0	0.4	10.5	9.3	4.5	2.0	0.0	0.0	26.7
1983-84	0.0	0.0	0.0	0.0	T	T	0.2	2.9	T	0.0	0.0	0.0	3.1
1984-85	0.0	0.0	0.0	0.0	0.0	T	4.5	3.1	0.1	0.4	0.0	0.0	8.1
1985-86	0.0	0.0	0.0	0.0	0.0	0.4	0.8	3.7	0.1	T	0.0	0.0	5.0
1986-87	0.0	0.0	0.0	0.0	T	T	15.0	2.7	0.3	11.5	0.0	0.0	29.5
1987-88	0.0	0.0	0.0	0.0	0.3	0.5	14.2	T	T	1.2	0.0	0.0	16.2
1988-89	0.0	0.0	0.0	0.0	0.0	T	1.2	6.0	T	1.0	0.0	0.0	8.2
1989-90	0.0	0.0	0.0	T	T	3.0	T	T	T	0.0	0.0	0.0	3.0
1990-91	0.0	T	0.0	0.0	0.0	T	T	0.4	3.1	0.0	0.0	T	3.5
1991-92	0.0	0.0	0.0	0.0	1.0	0.0	T	T	0.5	0.0	T	0.0	1.5
1992-93	0.0	0.0	0.0	0.0	T	T	T	3.0	18.2	T	T	0.0	21.2
1993-94	0.0	0.0	0.0	T	T	8.0							
Record Mean	0.0	T	0.0	T	0.7	2.0	4.6	4.6	3.0	0.7	T	T	15.7

RALEIGH, NORTH CAROLINA

The Raleigh-Durham Airport is located in the zone of transition between the Coastal Plain and the Piedmont Plateau. The surrounding terrain is rolling, with an average elevation of around 400 feet, the range over a 10-mile radius is roughly between 200 and 550 feet. Being centrally located between the mountains on the west and the coast on the south and east, the Raleigh-Durham area enjoys a favorable climate. The mountains form a partial barrier to cold air masses moving eastward from the interior of the nation. As a result, there are few days in the heart of the winter season when the temperature falls below 20 degrees. Tropical air is present over the eastern and central sections of North Carolina during much of the summer season, bringing warm temperatures and rather high humidities to the Raleigh-Durham area. Afternoon temperatures reach 90 degrees or higher on about one-fourth of the days in the middle of summer, but reach 100 degrees less than once per year. Even in the hottest weather, early morning temperatures almost always drop into the lower 70s.

Rainfall is well distributed throughout the year as a whole. July and August have the greatest amount of rainfall, and October and November the least. There are times in spring and summer when soil moisture is scanty. This usually results from too many days between rains rather than from a shortage of total rainfall, but occasionally the accumulated total during the growing season falls short of plant needs. Most summer rain is produced by thunderstorms, which may occasionally be accompanied by strong winds, intense rains, and hail. The Raleigh-Durham area is far enough from the coast so that the bad weather effects of coastal storms are reduced. While snow and sleet usually occur each year, excessive accumulations of snow are rare.

From September 1887 to December 1950, the office was located in the downtown areas of Raleigh. The various buildings occupied were within an area of three blocks. All thermometers were exposed on the roof, and this, plus the smoke over the city, had an effect on the temperature record of that period. Lowest temperatures at the city office were frequently from 2 to 5 degrees higher than those recorded in surrounding rural areas. Maximum temperatures in the city were generally a degree or two lower. These observations are supported by a period of simultaneous record from the Municipal Airport and the city office location between 1937 and 1940.

From September 1946 to May 1954, simultaneous records were kept at a surface location on the North Carolina State College campus in Raleigh, and at the Raleigh-Durham Airport 10 1/2 air miles to the northwest.

Based on the 1951-1980 period, the average first occurrence of 32 degrees Fahrenheit in the fall is October 27 and the average last occurrence in the spring is April 11.

NORMALS, MEANS, AND EXTREMES

RALEIGH, NORTH CAROLINA

LATITUDE: 35°52'N LONGITUDE: 78°47' W ELEVATION: FT. GRND 416 BARO 415 TIME ZONE: EASTERN WBAN: 13722

	(a)	JAN	FEB	MAR	APR	MAY	JUNE	JULY	AUG	SEP	OCT	NOV	DEC	YEAR
TEMPERATURE °F:														
Normals														
-Daily Maximum		48.9	52.6	62.1	71.7	78.6	85.0	88.0	86.8	81.1	71.6	62.6	52.7	70.1
-Daily Minimum		28.8	31.3	38.7	46.2	55.3	63.6	68.1	67.5	61.1	48.4	39.7	32.4	48.4
-Monthly		38.9	42.0	50.4	59.0	67.0	74.3	78.1	77.1	71.1	60.1	51.2	42.6	59.3
Extremes														
-Record Highest	49	79	84	92	95	97	104	105	105	104	98	88	79	105
-Year		1952	1977	1945	1980	1953	1954	1952	1988	1954	1954	1950	1978	AUG 1988
-Record Lowest	49	-9	5	11	23	31	38	48	46	37	19	11	4	-9
-Year		1985	1971	1980	1985	1977	1977	1975	1965	1983	1962	1970	1983	JAN 1985
NORMAL DEGREE DAYS:														
Heating (base 65°F)		809	644	458	193	47	0	0	0	9	189	414	694	3457
Cooling (base 65°F)		0	0	6	13	109	279	406	375	192	37	0	0	1417
% OF POSSIBLE SUNSHINE	39	53	56	60	63	58	61	60	58	58	61	57	53	58
MEAN SKY COVER (tenths)														
Sunrise - Sunset	44	6.2	6.0	6.0	5.6	6.0	5.8	6.0	6.0	5.7	5.0	5.4	5.9	5.8
MEAN NUMBER OF DAYS:														
Sunrise to Sunset														
-Clear	45	9.0	8.7	9.4	9.6	8.2	7.7	7.3	7.2	9.5	12.9	11.4	9.9	110.7
-Partly Cloudy	45	6.9	6.1	7.4	9.0	10.0	11.8	12.0	12.4	9.2	7.0	7.2	7.0	106.0
-Cloudy	45	15.1	13.5	14.2	11.4	12.8	10.5	11.8	11.4	11.3	11.1	11.4	14.1	148.6
Precipitation														
.01 inches or more	49	10.0	9.7	10.3	9.0	10.3	9.3	11.3	10.0	7.6	7.0	8.2	9.1	111.8
Snow, Ice pellets, hail														
1.0 inches or more	49	0.8	0.7	0.3	0.*	0.0	0.0	0.0	0.0	0.0	0.0	0.1	0.3	2.2
Thunderstorms	49	0.4	0.9	2.0	3.4	6.2	7.1	10.6	7.8	3.4	1.3	0.8	0.3	44.0
Heavy Fog Visibility														
1/4 mile or less	44	3.5	2.8	2.2	1.5	2.4	1.9	2.6	3.3	3.4	3.5	3.1	3.5	33.6
Temperature °F														
-Maximum														
90° and above	29	0.0	0.0	0.*	0.6	1.3	7.1	12.9	10.2	3.0	0.2	0.0	0.0	35.3
32° and below	29	2.1	0.5	0.1	0.0	0.0	0.0	0.0	0.0	0.0	0.0	0.*	0.8	3.6
-Minimum														
32° and below	29	20.1	17.2	9.8	2.2	0.*	0.0	0.0	0.0	0.0	1.4	9.1	17.2	77.1
0° and below	29	0.2	0.0	0.0	0.0	0.0	0.0	0.0	0.0	0.0	0.0	0.0	0.0	0.2
AVG. STATION PRESS. (mb)	21	1003.7	1003.1	1001.4	1000.2	1000.3	1000.6	1001.4	1002.3	1003.0	1003.9	1004.3	1004.5	1002.4
RELATIVE HUMIDITY (%)														
Hour 01	29	73	70	71	73	84	86	88	89	88	85	79	75	80
Hour 07 (Local Time)	29	79	77	80	81	86	87	89	92	92	89	84	80	85
Hour 13	29	55	52	49	45	54	56	58	60	58	53	52	55	54
Hour 19	29	63	58	56	53	66	67	70	74	77	76	67	66	66
PRECIPITATION (inches):														
Water Equivalent														
-Normal		3.48	3.69	3.77	2.59	3.92	3.68	4.01	4.02	3.19	2.86	2.98	3.24	41.43
-Maximum Monthly	49	7.52	6.42	7.78	6.10	7.67	9.38	10.27	12.18	12.94	7.53	8.22	6.65	12.94
-Year		1954	1989	1983	1978	1974	1973	1991	1986	1945	1971	1948	1983	SEP 1945
-Minimum Monthly	49	0.87	0.69	1.03	0.23	0.92	0.33	0.80	0.81	0.23	0.44	0.61	0.25	0.23
-Year		1981	1991	1985	1976	1964	1993	1953	1950	1985	1963	1973	1965	SEP 1985
-Maximum in 24 hrs	49	3.11	3.22	3.70	4.04	4.40	3.44	3.89	5.20	5.16	4.10	4.70	3.18	5.20
-Year		1984	1973	1983	1978	1957	1967	1952	1955	1944	1954	1963	1958	AUG 1955
Snow, Ice pellets, hail														
-Maximum Monthly	49	14.4	17.2	14.0	1.8	0.0	0.0	T	0.0	0.0	0.0	2.6	10.6	17.2
-Year		1955	1979	1960	1983			1993				1975	1958	FEB 1979
-Maximum in 24 hrs	49	9.0	10.4	9.3	1.8	0.0	0.0	T	0.0	0.0	0.0	2.6	9.1	10.4
-Year		1966	1979	1969	1983			1993				1975	1958	FEB 1979
WIND:														
Mean Speed (mph)	44	8.5	8.9	9.3	9.0	7.7	7.0	6.7	6.4	6.8	7.1	7.6	8.0	7.7
Prevailing Direction through 1963		SW	SW	SW	SW	SW	SW	SW	NE	NE	NNE	SW	SW	SW
Fastest Obs. 1 Min.														
-Direction (!!)	40	27	12	32	14	20	33	17	33	23	29	32	21	17
-Speed (MPH)	40	41	44	44	40	54	39	153	46	35	73	35	35	153
-Year		1971	1984	1967	1961	1972	1977	1993	1969	1972	1954	1969	1968	JUL 1993
Peak Gust														
-Direction (!!)	10	NW	SE	W	NW	W	N	N	SW	S	SE	S	NW	SE
-Speed (mph)	10	48	62	52	56	55	48	45	61	46	36	41	45	62
-Date		1989	1984	1993	1987	1984	1993	1991	1986	1989	1990	1989	1987	FEB 1984

PRECIPITATION (inches)

RALEIGH, NORTH CAROLINA

YEAR	JAN	FEB	MAR	APR	MAY	JUNE	JULY	AUG	SEP	OCT	NOV	DEC	ANNUAL
1964	3.66	4.11	2.93	3.39	0.92	3.41	4.06	5.68	5.29	3.95	1.38	4.13	42.91
1965	1.47	2.40	4.08	1.51	2.20	8.32	5.54	3.00	2.65	1.77	1.23	0.25	34.42
1966	5.42	4.76	1.81	2.02	4.95	3.68	0.91	5.79	3.58	2.01	2.06	2.61	39.60
1967	1.64	3.80	1.62	3.02	4.15	4.57	3.49	6.22	1.74	2.26	2.14	4.93	39.58
1968	2.88	1.00	2.22	3.03	3.82	1.74	5.15	2.50	1.77	5.15	3.59	2.75	35.60
1969	1.55	3.60	3.95	1.43	2.85	4.81	4.40	6.31	6.21	2.09	1.01	3.31	41.52
1970	2.26	3.47	4.04	2.07	3.36	0.87	5.64	4.47	1.20	4.47	1.59	2.57	36.01
1971	3.28	3.85	3.69	2.59	4.68	2.79	4.56	6.26	2.91	7.53	1.81	1.69	45.64
1972	1.97	4.13	2.50	1.92	5.34	4.16	6.80	4.17	5.80	3.96	5.98	5.01	51.74
1973	2.67	5.50	4.06	4.40	3.99	9.38	3.12	4.60	1.13	0.60	0.61	6.38	46.44
1974	4.39	2.87	3.34	1.32	7.67	4.02	1.56	4.82	3.71	1.23	1.79	4.02	40.74
1975	6.09	2.85	6.26	1.64	3.84	1.66	6.74	2.11	5.77	1.23	4.60	4.04	46.83
1976	3.07	1.54	3.17	0.23	4.74	2.55	1.00	1.52	5.99	3.97	1.89	4.04	33.71
1977	2.82	2.13	5.63	1.89	3.94	0.84	0.89	4.12	3.86	5.06	2.22	3.70	37.10
1978	7.03	1.43	4.40	6.10	4.20	4.06	3.63	1.86	1.37	1.46	4.17	3.26	42.97
#1979	5.71	5.55	2.69	2.63	4.71	3.27	4.84	1.66	6.76	1.88	4.73	0.94	45.37
1980	4.39	1.91	5.87	1.97	2.33	4.89	2.11	1.87	3.76	2.25	2.87	1.42	35.64
1981	0.87	3.02	2.35	1.03	4.28	0.55	5.69	5.34	2.70	4.64	0.95	4.96	36.38
1982	3.43	4.97	3.02	3.33	4.20	8.39	3.34	1.83	1.55	3.93	2.34	4.02	44.35
1983	1.79	6.00	7.78	3.54	5.89	3.09	1.10	1.81	2.13	3.59	3.86	6.65	47.23
1984	4.93	5.65	5.40	4.45	5.43	3.08	9.20	1.13	2.31	0.73	1.64	2.32	46.27
1985	4.83	4.44	1.03	0.64	3.95	2.87	6.28	3.73	0.23	1.75	7.61	0.81	38.17
1986	1.88	1.65	3.06	1.01	2.98	1.92	4.32	12.18	0.95	1.28	2.77	2.95	36.95
1987	6.53	5.52	2.88	4.68	1.19	2.11	1.78	5.80	5.48	1.71	1.39	3.02	42.09
1988	3.15	2.42	1.76	3.56	2.85	2.88	2.69	3.40	4.90	5.67	3.34	1.04	37.66
1989	1.35	6.42	5.40	4.91	3.88	7.30	5.46	5.08	3.96	3.44	3.94	3.01	54.15
1990	3.07	3.82	5.02	2.19	6.97	1.03	2.22	2.65	0.30	5.69	1.51	3.08	37.55
1991	4.12	0.69	4.59	1.04	2.89	2.05	10.27	1.87	3.16	1.40	0.73	2.65	35.46
1992	3.80	2.23	2.95	1.93	2.60	5.12	3.45	7.63	2.22	3.79	5.02	2.44	43.18
1993	4.50	2.22	6.13	4.84	3.32	0.33	2.11	1.77	3.50	2.95	2.66	3.72	38.05
Record Mean	3.43	3.67	3.75	3.21	3.88	4.06	5.15	4.99	3.61	2.91	2.63	3.24	44.52

AVERAGE TEMPERATURE (deg. F)

RALEIGH, NORTH CAROLINA

YEAR	JAN	FEB	MAR	APR	MAY	JUNE	JULY	AUG	SEP	OCT	NOV	DEC	ANNUAL
#1964	41.2	39.4	50.6	59.6	68.1	75.6	76.4	74.9	69.3	55.2	52.7	43.3	58.9
1965	40.5	42.9	44.6	58.3	71.9	71.9	76.2	77.2	72.7	58.8	50.9	43.8	59.1
1966	35.8	42.3	49.7	57.0	66.5	73.4	79.1	77.7	71.0	58.6	50.8	41.9	58.7
1967	44.8	38.9	53.7	62.5	63.9	72.0	76.9	76.3	67.5	59.4	46.8	46.3	59.1
1968	37.1	36.4	52.6	58.1	63.9	73.6	76.9	79.2	70.9	62.0	51.7	38.8	58.4
1969	37.4	40.9	43.4	58.7	66.2	74.7	78.0	73.8	67.5	58.6	46.1	37.7	56.9
1970	32.9	38.9	46.2	59.4	66.0	72.7	76.1	75.3	73.3	61.0	49.4	42.7	57.8
1971	37.0	42.1	45.1	56.4	64.4	75.4	76.6	75.3	72.0	64.8	48.7	50.3	59.0
1972	44.7	40.0	49.5	58.0	64.3	69.9	77.1	75.6	70.4	57.4	48.1	46.2	58.5
1973	39.3	40.0	54.8	57.9	64.5	75.1	76.5	76.6	73.2	62.2	54.6	42.5	59.8
1974	49.3	42.9	54.4	60.2	67.4	71.8	76.5	76.0	69.0	56.5	48.7	43.2	59.7
1975	43.8	43.7	47.1	55.8	68.2	73.7	75.6	78.3	71.1	62.2	53.5	42.0	59.6
1976	37.6	50.1	56.2	60.7	66.8	74.7	78.6	75.4	69.7	55.7	42.5	37.1	58.7
1977	26.6	39.3	53.3	62.6	68.4	73.3	80.6	78.1	72.8	56.4	51.8	39.9	58.6
1978	35.3	33.1	48.2	59.2	66.0	75.8	78.0	79.9	73.7	59.5	55.1	44.9	59.1
1979	39.1	36.5	52.2	59.7	66.8	69.8	75.4	77.2	71.2	59.9	52.0	43.4	58.6
1980	40.6	36.5	46.5	62.0	69.8	75.0	78.9	79.6	74.9	58.7	49.1	40.7	59.3
1981	33.4	43.9	46.2	61.7	64.0	78.9	80.8	74.6	68.3	57.2	50.7	39.7	58.3
1982	35.5	45.5	51.7	57.4	71.0	74.7	79.1	76.5	70.5	60.6	51.9	47.5	60.2
1983	38.1	40.7	50.7	55.1	65.4	72.5	79.1	79.1	70.7	60.4	50.9	39.5	58.5
1984	36.3	45.7	47.2	55.9	65.5	75.5	74.9	76.6	67.5	66.3	47.1	49.7	59.0
1985	34.0	41.9	52.7	62.0	67.3	73.9	76.8	75.2	69.7	63.7	58.4	39.4	59.6
1986	38.5	44.5	51.7	61.2	67.4	78.4	81.7	75.6	72.3	63.0	52.9	42.6	60.8
1987	38.3	40.4	49.2	56.9	69.3	76.3	81.2	79.2	73.0	54.6	52.8	44.5	59.6
1988	34.7	41.9	50.6	57.8	66.0	72.4	79.0	80.3	70.3	54.4	52.0	42.4	58.5
1989	44.8	42.9	50.7	58.0	65.0	77.0	78.1	76.2	71.7	61.3	51.4	34.6	59.3
1990	48.0	51.0	54.9	60.3	67.4	75.2	80.0	78.0	72.2	64.1	54.2	48.1	62.8
1991	41.9	46.8	54.3	62.3	72.3	75.8	80.6	77.8	71.6	61.1	50.0	47.0	61.8
1992	43.4	46.2	50.5	59.2	63.2	72.0	80.4	74.1	71.5	58.1	51.9	42.5	59.4
1993	43.3	40.9	47.9	56.9	69.0	76.1	82.5	78.2	73.7	59.6	51.8	40.3	60.0
Record Mean	41.2	42.9	50.5	59.3	67.9	75.2	78.3	77.2	71.7	60.7	50.8	42.8	59.8
Max	50.6	53.0	61.4	70.9	79.0	85.7	88.2	86.7	81.5	71.5	61.3	52.3	70.2
Min	31.7	32.8	39.5	47.6	56.8	64.7	68.5	67.6	61.8	49.9	40.3	33.2	49.5

REFERENCE NOTES

RALEIGH, NORTH CAROLINA

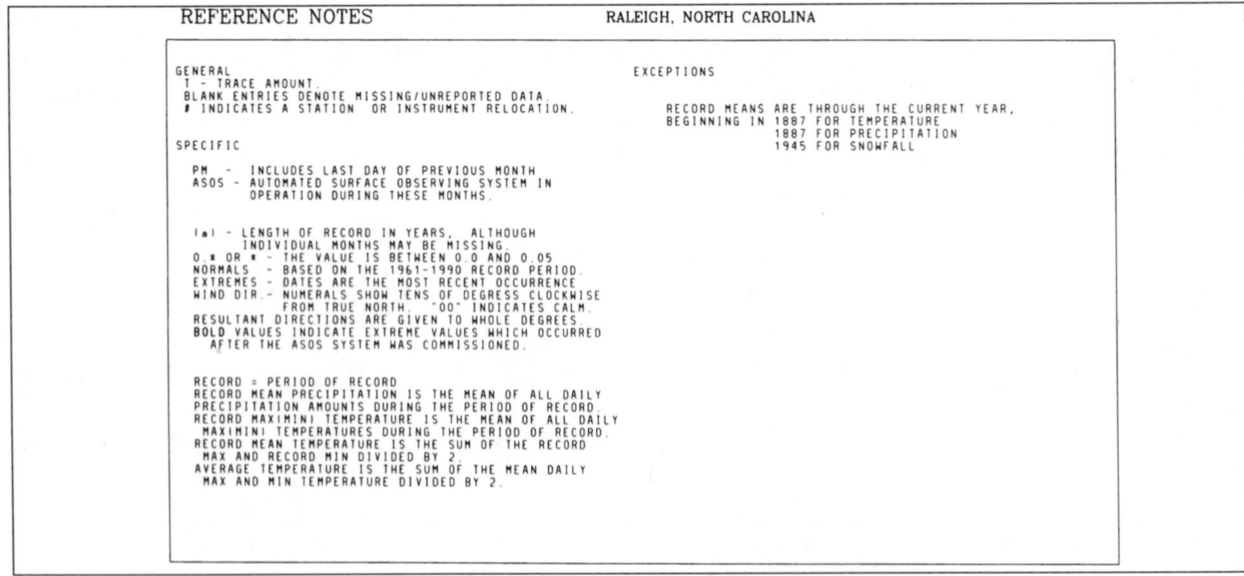

GENERAL
T - TRACE AMOUNT.
BLANK ENTRIES DENOTE MISSING/UNREPORTED DATA.
# INDICATES A STATION OR INSTRUMENT RELOCATION.

SPECIFIC

PM - INCLUDES LAST DAY OF PREVIOUS MONTH
ASOS - AUTOMATED SURFACE OBSERVING SYSTEM IN OPERATION DURING THESE MONTHS.

(a) - LENGTH OF RECORD IN YEARS, ALTHOUGH INDIVIDUAL MONTHS MAY BE MISSING.
0.* OR * - THE VALUE IS BETWEEN 0.0 AND 0.05
NORMALS - BASED ON THE 1961-1990 RECORD PERIOD.
EXTREMES - DATES ARE THE MOST RECENT OCCURRENCE
WIND DIR.- NUMERALS SHOW TENS OF DEGRESS CLOCKWISE FROM TRUE NORTH. "00" INDICATES CALM.
RESULTANT DIRECTIONS ARE GIVEN TO WHOLE DEGREES.
BOLD VALUES INDICATE EXTREME VALUES WHICH OCCURRED AFTER THE ASOS SYSTEM WAS COMMISSIONED.

RECORD = PERIOD OF RECORD
RECORD MEAN PRECIPITATION IS THE MEAN OF ALL DAILY PRECIPITATION AMOUNTS DURING THE PERIOD OF RECORD.
RECORD MAX(MIN) TEMPERATURE IS THE MEAN OF ALL DAILY MAX(MIN) TEMPERATURES DURING THE PERIOD OF RECORD.
RECORD MEAN TEMPERATURE IS THE SUM OF THE RECORD MAX AND RECORD MIN DIVIDED BY 2.
AVERAGE TEMPERATURE IS THE SUM OF THE MEAN DAILY MAX AND MIN TEMPERATURE DIVIDED BY 2.

EXCEPTIONS

RECORD MEANS ARE THROUGH THE CURRENT YEAR, BEGINNING IN 1887 FOR TEMPERATURE
1887 FOR PRECIPITATION
1945 FOR SNOWFALL

HEATING DEGREE DAYS Base 65 deg. F RALEIGH, NORTH CAROLINA

SEASON	JULY	AUG	SEP	OCT	NOV	DEC	JAN	FEB	MAR	APR	MAY	JUNE	TOTAL
#1964-65	0	1	25	305	365	665	754	616	628	232	0	15	3606
1965-66	0	5	7	208	416	650	898	629	473	263	72	12	3633
1966-67	0	0	11	216	425	709	623	723	361	151	105	13	3337
1967-68	0	0	35	199	539	574	855	824	391	213	87	0	3717
1968-69	0	0	0	151	396	805	848	667	667	195	61	0	3790
1969-70	0	0	45	222	561	841	989	725	576	200	74	0	4233
1970-71	0	0	22	154	460	684	863	636	611	258	87	0	3775
1971-72	0	0	3	61	496	456	623	718	478	237	51	16	3139
1972-73	0	0	9	238	504	576	790	692	334	231	88	0	3462
1973-74	0	0	2	126	312	690	481	614	346	187	48	0	2806
1974-75	0	0	44	268	501	668	651	589	553	293	34	0	3601
1975-76	0	0	17	117	351	705	843	426	300	194	52	6	3011
1976-77	0	0	7	302	668	857	1183	715	358	132	49	14	4285
1977-78	0	0	4	283	411	768	914	883	514	196	83	0	4056
1978-79	0	0	7	184	292	627	793	792	398	183	43	8	3327
1979-80	0	0	13	196	394	661	753	820	564	130	33	0	3564
1980-81	0	0	16	225	477	747	973	583	579	149	99	0	3848
1981-82	0	4	31	253	425	776	907	538	411	244	15	0	3604
1982-83	0	0	14	182	392	542	828	675	438	305	79	7	3462
1983-84	0	0	59	180	417	784	882	553	545	283	83	5	3791
1984-85	0	0	63	42	530	468	954	644	395	146	42	4	3288
1985-86	0	0	36	96	207	789	812	569	415	157	59	0	3140
1986-87	0	11	12	149	370	687	820	681	484	248	29	0	3491
1987-88	0	0	1	319	362	631	932	665	444	228	62	22	3666
1988-89	0	0	8	336	386	695	619	623	459	257	102	0	3485
1989-90	0	3	30	167	404	934	518	390	357	186	37	0	3026
1990-91	0	0	18	124	323	520	709	501	354	153	18	0	2720
1991-92	0	0	24	156	451	562	659	537	446	226	114	3	3178
1992-93	0	0	29	224	390	691	666	670	524	244	15	0	3453
1993-94	0	0	19	198	405	758							

COOLING DEGREE DAYS Base 65 deg. F RALEIGH, NORTH CAROLINA

YEAR	JAN	FEB	MAR	APR	MAY	JUNE	JULY	AUG	SEP	OCT	NOV	DEC	TOTAL
1969	0	0	0	12	105	295	413	283	128	28	0	0	1264
1970	0	0	0	41	113	236	350	327	278	38	0	0	1383
1971	0	0	0	6	78	320	364	329	222	61	17	5	1402
1972	0	0	5	37	36	170	382	336	177	6	6	2	1157
1973	0	0	24	26	81	310	363	365	254	48	7	0	1478
1974	0	0	25	51	130	210	363	347	169	9	21	0	1325
1975	0	0	3	22	141	269	337	421	209	38	12	0	1452
1976	0	3	31	71	116	304	428	330	157	19	0	0	1459
1977	0	2	4	68	162	272	490	414	245	25	19	0	1701
1978	0	0	2	30	120	330	412	468	275	21	3	10	1671
1979	0	0	6	28	105	159	332	384	205	46	10	0	1275
1980	0	0	0	45	190	306	441	460	321	38	6	0	1807
1981	0	0	2	56	75	425	497	309	139	19	0	0	1522
1982	0	0	3	24	208	299	443	363	183	53	5	7	1588
1983	0	0	0	16	97	238	441	447	239	42	0	0	1520
1984	0	0	0	16	108	324	311	366	143	90	0	0	1358
1985	0	3	20	65	121	277	373	323	181	64	14	0	1441
1986	0	0	7	51	142	408	526	349	237	96	15	0	1831
1987	0	0	0	11	170	347	508	447	250	0	2	0	1735
1988	0	3	5	17	98	249	438	482	172	14	3	0	1481
1989	0	11	23	54	110	367	412	359	237	59	4	0	1636
1990	0	3	49	51	117	312	472	410	239	102	4	5	1764
1991	0	0	28	78	253	333	493	403	230	40	9	13	1880
1992	0	0	3	58	65	218	487	285	228	15	3	0	1362
1993	0	0	0	12	147	338	550	417	286	34	17	0	1801

SNOWFALL (inches) RALEIGH, NORTH CAROLINA

SEASON	JULY	AUG	SEP	OCT	NOV	DEC	JAN	FEB	MAR	APR	MAY	JUNE	TOTAL
1964-65	0.0	0.0	0.0	0.0	0.4	0.0	9.7	3.4	T	0.0	0.0	0.0	13.5
1965-66	0.0	0.0	0.0	0.0	0.0	0.0	12.3	T	0.0	0.0	0.0	0.0	12.3
1966-67	0.0	0.0	0.0	0.0	T	1.0	0.5	9.1	0.0	0.0	0.0	0.0	10.6
1967-68	0.0	0.0	0.0	0.0	T	1.4	3.0	1.3	T	0.0	0.0	0.0	5.7
1968-69	0.0	0.0	0.0	0.0	1.2	0.7	T	0.8	9.3	0.0	0.0	0.0	12.0
1969-70	0.0	0.0	0.0	0.0	0.0	0.0	2.0	T	T	0.0	0.0	0.0	2.0
1970-71	0.0	0.0	0.0	0.0	0.0	0.6	T	T	5.3	0.0	0.0	0.0	5.9
1971-72	0.0	0.0	0.0	0.0	T	3.7	0.0	1.4	2.6	0.0	0.0	0.0	7.7
1972-73	0.0	0.0	0.0	0.0	T	0.0	6.4	4.5	0.4	0.0	0.0	0.0	11.3
1973-74	0.0	0.0	0.0	0.0	0.0	2.8	0.0	T	2.9	0.0	0.0	0.0	5.7
1974-75	0.0	0.0	0.0	0.0	0.0	T	T	T	0.6	0.0	0.0	0.0	0.6
1975-76	0.0	0.0	0.0	0.0	2.6	T	0.4	T	0.0	0.0	0.0	0.0	3.0
1976-77	0.0	0.0	0.0	0.0	T	T	2.1	1.5	0.0	0.0	0.0	0.0	3.6
1977-78	0.0	0.0	0.0	0.0	T	T	T	9.0	1.6	0.0	0.0	0.0	10.6
1978-79	0.0	0.0	0.0	0.0	0.0	0.0	0.4	17.2	T	0.0	0.0	0.0	17.6
#1979-80	0.0	0.0	0.0	0.0	0.0	0.0	2.2	5.0	11.1	0.0	0.0	0.0	18.3
1980-81	0.0	0.0	0.0	0.0	0.0	3.1	2.6	0.0	T	0.0	0.0	0.0	5.7
1981-82	0.0	0.0	0.0	0.0	0.0	T	6.0	0.6	0.0	0.0	0.0	0.0	6.6
1982-83	0.0	0.0	0.0	0.0	0.0	T	T	2.7	7.3	1.8	0.0	0.0	11.8
1983-84	0.0	0.0	0.0	0.0	0.0	0.0	T	6.9	T	0.0	0.0	0.0	6.9
1984-85	0.0	0.0	0.0	0.0	0.0	0.0	4.1	T	0.0	0.0	0.0	0.0	4.1
1985-86	0.0	0.0	0.0	0.0	0.0	T	T	0.9	T	0.0	0.0	0.0	0.9
1986-87	0.0	0.0	0.0	0.0	T	0.0	0.6	10.2	T	T	0.0	0.0	10.8
1987-88	0.0	0.0	0.0	0.0	0.6	0.0	7.3	T	0.0	0.0	0.0	0.0	7.9
1988-89	0.0	0.0	0.0	0.0	0.0	0.1	0.0	11.1	0.5	0.3	0.0	0.0	12.0
1989-90	0.0	0.0	0.0	0.0	0.0	2.7	0.0	T	T	0.0	0.0	0.0	2.7
1990-91	0.0	0.0	0.0	0.0	0.0	T	T	T	T	0.0	0.0	0.0	T
1991-92	0.0	0.0	0.0	0.0	T	0.0	T	T	0.0	0.0	0.0	0.0	T
1992-93	0.0	0.0	0.0	0.0	0.0	T	T	1.6	0.9	0.0	0.0	0.0	2.5
1993-94	T	0.0	0.0	0.0	0.0	3.1							
Record Mean	T	0.0	0.0	0.0	0.1	0.8	2.2	2.6	1.3	T	0.0	0.0	7.1

FARGO, NORTH DAKOTA

Moorhead, Minnesota, and Fargo are twin cities in the Red River Valley of the north. The Red River of the north flows northward between the two cities and is a part of the Hudson Bay drainage area. The Red River is approximately 2 miles east of the airport at its nearest point and has no significant effect on the weather. In recent years, spring floods due to melting snow have been common. Summer floods caused by heavy rains are infrequent.

The surrounding terrain is flat and open. Northerly winds blowing up the valley occasionally causing low cloudiness and fog. However, this upslope cloudiness is very infrequent. Aside from this, there are no pronounced climatic differences due to geographical features in the immediate area.

The summers are generally comfortable with very few days of hot and humid weather. Nights, with few exceptions, are comfortably cool. The winter months are cold and dry with temperatures rising above freezing only on an average of six days each month, and nighttime lows dropping below zero approximately half of the time.

Precipitation is the most important climatic factor in the area. The Red River Valley lies in an area where lighter amounts fall to the west and heavier amounts to the east. Seventy-five percent of the precipitation occurs during the growing season (April to September) and is often accompanied by electrical storms and heavy falls in a short time. Winter precipitation is light, indicating that heavy snowfall is the exception rather than the rule. The first light snow in the fall occasionally falls in September, but usually very little, if any, occurs until October or November. The latest fall is generally in April.

With the flat terrain, surface friction has little effect on the wind in the area and this fact has led to the legendary Dakota blizzards. Strong winds with even light snowfall cause much drifting and blowing snow, reducing visibility to near zero. Fortunately, these conditions occur only several times during the winter months.

NORMALS, MEANS, AND EXTREMES

FARGO, NORTH DAKOTA

LATITUDE: 46°54'N LONGITUDE: 96°48' W ELEVATION: FT. GRND 896 BARO 911 TIME ZONE: CENTRAL WBAN: 14914

	(a)	JAN	FEB	MAR	APR	MAY	JUNE	JULY	AUG	SEP	OCT	NOV	DEC	YEAR
TEMPERATURE °F:														
Normals														
-Daily Maximum		15.4	21.1	34.6	53.8	68.5	77.4	83.4	81.3	69.4	56.7	36.8	20.1	51.5
-Daily Minimum		-3.6	2.7	17.3	32.1	43.8	53.6	58.8	56.4	45.9	34.6	19.4	3.1	30.3
-Monthly		5.9	12.0	25.9	43.0	56.2	65.5	71.1	68.8	57.7	45.7	28.1	11.6	41.0
Extremes														
-Record Highest	41	52	66	78	100	98	99	106	106	102	93	74	57	106
-Year		1981	1958	1967	1980	1964	1959	1988	1976	1959	1963	1990	1962	JUL 1988
-Record Lowest	41	-35	-34	-23	-7	20	30	36	33	19	7	-24	-32	-35
-Year		1977	1962	1980	1975	1966	1969	1967	1982	1965	1976	1985	1967	JAN 1977
NORMAL DEGREE DAYS:														
Heating (base 65°F)		1832	1484	1212	660	307	93	19	48	239	598	1107	1655	9254
Cooling (base 65°F)		0	0	0	0	35	108	209	165	20	0	0	0	537
% OF POSSIBLE SUNSHINE	51	50	56	57	59	61	61	71	69	59	54	40	42	57
MEAN SKY COVER (tenths)														
Sunrise - Sunset	48	6.7	6.7	7.0	6.6	6.4	6.2	5.2	5.2	5.8	6.2	7.2	7.0	6.3
MEAN NUMBER OF DAYS:														
Sunrise to Sunset														
-Clear	51	6.8	6.2	5.4	6.5	7.0	6.5	10.1	10.4	8.7	8.7	5.5	6.1	88.0
-Partly Cloudy	51	7.5	7.3	8.9	8.8	9.7	10.9	13.4	11.9	9.1	8.3	6.3	7.2	109.4
-Cloudy	51	16.8	14.8	16.6	14.7	14.3	12.6	7.5	8.7	12.1	14.0	18.2	17.7	167.9
Precipitation .01 inches or more	51	8.5	7.0	7.8	8.2	10.0	10.7	9.6	9.0	7.9	6.3	6.3	8.2	99.4
Snow,Ice pellets,hail 1.0 inches or more	51	2.4	1.7	2.1	1.1	0.*	0.0	0.0	0.0	0.0	0.3	1.9	2.3	11.8
Thunderstorms	51	0.0	0.*	0.3	1.3	3.8	7.3	8.4	7.0	2.9	0.9	0.1	0.*	32.0
Heavy Fog Visibility 1/4 mile or less	51	0.8	1.6	1.9	0.5	0.4	0.6	0.8	1.0	0.9	0.9	1.4	1.8	12.5
Temperature °F														
-Maximum														
90° and above	34	0.0	0.0	0.0	0.1	0.7	2.2	5.1	5.3	1.0	0.1	0.0	0.0	14.6
32° and below	34	26.9	21.3	12.3	1.1	0.*	0.0	0.0	0.0	0.0	0.5	10.9	24.9	98.0
-Minimum														
32° and below	34	31.0	28.2	27.6	16.3	4.0	0.*	0.0	0.0	1.8	13.1	27.0	30.9	179.9
0° and below	34	18.4	12.4	4.4	0.1	0.0	0.0	0.0	0.0	0.0	0.0	2.1	13.3	50.7
AVG. STATION PRESS.(mb)	21	985.2	986.1	983.0	982.0	980.5	979.5	981.2	982.0	982.4	983.0	983.5	984.7	982.8
RELATIVE HUMIDITY (%)														
Hour 00	34	75	77	80	73	67	76	78	77	78	74	79	78	76
Hour 06 (Local Time)	34	75	77	82	79	77	82	85	86	85	80	82	78	81
Hour 12	34	72	72	70	57	50	56	55	54	58	58	70	74	62
Hour 18	34	73	74	71	53	46	52	51	50	55	59	73	76	61
PRECIPITATION (inches):														
Water Equivalent														
-Normal		0.67	0.45	1.06	1.82	2.45	2.82	2.70	2.43	1.99	1.68	0.73	0.65	19.45
-Maximum Monthly	52	1.85	1.74	2.27	5.28	7.30	9.40	8.42	8.52	6.13	7.03	4.58	2.19	9.40
-Year		1989	1979	1983	1986	1977	1975	1952	1944	1957	1982	1977	1951	JUN 1975
-Minimum Monthly	52	0.09	0.03	0.03	0.01	0.46	0.58	0.42	0.18	0.13	0.05	0.02	0.04	0.01
-Year		1961	1954	1958	1988	1976	1972	1950	1984	1974	1986	1990	1958	APR 1988
-Maximum in 24 hrs	52	1.00	1.22	1.16	1.91	4.10	4.02	5.10	4.72	3.97	3.22	1.99	0.87	5.10
-Year		1989	1946	1950	1963	1977	1975	1993	1943	1957	1982	1977	1960	JUL 1993
Snow,Ice pellets,hail														
-Maximum Monthly	52	31.5	19.5	18.7	12.8	1.0	T	0.0	T	0.6	8.1	24.3	20.3	31.5
-Year		1989	1979	1975	1970	1950	1991		1989	1942	1951	1985	1951	JAN 1989
-Maximum in 24 hrs	52	19.4	11.2	11.5	8.6	1.0	T	0.0	T	0.6	7.8	12.6	9.3	19.4
-Year		1989	1951	1990	1970	1950	1991		1989	1942	1951	1977	1988	JAN 1989
WIND:														
Mean Speed (mph)	51	12.7	12.4	13.1	13.9	12.9	11.6	10.5	11.0	11.9	12.6	12.8	12.3	12.3
Prevailing Direction through 1963		SSE	N	N	N	N	SSE	S	SSE	SSE	SSE	S	S	SSE
Fastest Obs. 1 Min.														
-Direction (!!)	8	30	33	34	14	32	08	30	29	31	31	31	30	31
-Speed (MPH)	8	40	38	36	37	37	41	37	40	45	46	37	41	46
-Year		1990	1988	1989	1992	1989	1993	1987	1987	1988	1993	1986	1992	OCT 1993
Peak Gust														
-Direction (!!)	10	NW	N	SE	NW	NW	SW	NW	NW	NW	NW	NW	NW	NW
-Speed (mph)	10	60	59	53	51	62	66	69	60	62	54	52	59	69
-Date		1990	1984	1985	1991	1988	1991	1987	1988	1988	1993	1991	1992	JUL 1987

PRECIPITATION (inches)

FARGO, NORTH DAKOTA

YEAR	JAN	FEB	MAR	APR	MAY	JUNE	JULY	AUG	SEP	OCT	NOV	DEC	ANNUAL
1964	0.54	0.27	0.92	3.76	0.87	4.85	0.77	2.85	1.70	0.10	0.72	0.91	18.26
1965	0.10	0.14	1.36	3.04	3.06	3.10	4.81	2.55	3.50	0.55	0.79	1.01	24.01
1966	0.40	0.26	1.92	1.78	1.27	2.91	4.01	3.80	0.54	1.40	0.18	0.50	18.97
1967	1.03	0.21	0.34	4.14	1.00	2.54	0.60	0.41	0.31	1.06	0.04	1.36	13.04
1968	0.37	0.27	1.29	4.09	2.08	3.94	1.49	1.61	2.23	1.75	0.37	1.11	20.60
1969	1.27	0.46	0.54	1.55	2.36	2.03	5.92	0.38	1.55	1.51	0.14	0.81	18.52
1970	0.10	0.20	1.52	2.30	2.83	2.63	0.43	1.24	3.61	1.61	0.96	0.47	17.90
1971	0.81	0.34	0.56	1.10	2.68	3.51	2.80	0.92	4.30	4.42	0.83	0.59	22.86
1972	0.94	0.61	0.74	0.96	3.52	0.58	2.78	3.45	1.22	1.25	0.22	1.51	17.78
1973	0.12	0.13	1.25	0.70	1.65	1.78	3.60	3.85	4.98	1.54	0.90	1.02	21.52
1974	0.35	0.36	0.71	3.40	4.03	0.90	4.75	6.46	0.13	3.10	0.48	0.32	24.99
1975	1.32	0.27	1.48	3.24	1.45	9.40	2.42	2.90	1.24	1.76	0.64	0.18	26.30
1976	1.25	0.35	1.00	1.19	0.46	2.34	0.63	0.41	0.55	0.16	0.26	0.24	8.84
1977	0.65	1.24	1.72	0.84	7.30	1.64	5.36	2.53	3.21	2.46	4.58	0.75	32.28
1978	0.16	0.18	0.43	1.15	1.78	4.40	2.92	3.79	0.92	0.13	1.11	0.47	17.44
1979	0.44	1.74	2.00	3.04	2.02	2.92	3.38	0.90	0.31	2.60	0.48	0.14	19.97
1980	1.23	0.57	0.62	0.02	0.64	2.68	0.76	4.24	2.52	1.06	0.47	0.30	15.11
1981	0.11	0.49	0.67	0.61	3.46	2.56	3.21	1.76	1.11	2.36	0.40	0.85	17.59
1982	1.32	0.54	1.25	0.45	1.82	1.61	2.64	1.12	1.12	7.03	1.13	0.17	20.20
1983	0.46	0.21	2.27	0.42	2.00	2.34	4.16	2.56	1.63	1.62	1.04	0.96	19.67
1984	0.79	0.90	1.12	1.68	0.61	5.38	0.64	0.18	1.23	6.76	0.18	0.90	20.37
1985	0.20	0.18	1.35	0.60	5.03	1.44	3.91	2.30	1.39	1.12	1.06	0.59	19.17
1986	0.85	0.27	0.19	5.28	1.00	3.98	4.78	1.72	3.67	0.05	1.43	0.29	23.51
1987	0.27	0.86	0.49	0.12	3.46	0.66	2.86	3.23	1.70	0.18	0.48	0.69	15.00
1988	1.62	0.22	1.02	0.01	1.82	1.24	0.46	2.14	3.22	0.49	1.18	1.11	14.53
1989	1.85	0.21	1.49	1.03	2.60	1.51	0.62	6.07	2.10	0.31	1.18	0.24	19.21
1990	0.13	0.58	1.54	1.78	1.52	6.05	0.78	0.99	1.75	1.22	0.02	0.77	17.13
1991	0.29	1.27	0.97	3.15	2.38	6.26	1.86	1.87	1.28	0.71	0.46	0.37	20.87
1992	0.89	0.51	1.05	0.89	2.32	6.47	0.83	2.35	2.55	0.26	1.73	0.56	20.41
1993	0.79	0.19	0.83	0.74	2.67	4.28	7.71	1.13	0.49	0.19	1.88	1.00	21.90
Record Mean	0.64	0.59	0.92	1.92	2.45	3.42	3.09	2.74	1.94	1.50	0.87	0.66	20.74

AVERAGE TEMPERATURE (deg. F)

FARGO, NORTH DAKOTA

YEAR	JAN	FEB	MAR	APR	MAY	JUNE	JULY	AUG	SEP	OCT	NOV	DEC	ANNUAL
1964	15.6	18.9	20.8	46.4	61.1	67.2	74.0	64.9	55.4	45.2	29.2	3.8	41.9
1965	-1.2	7.1	13.7	41.6	54.4	63.9	68.5	66.5	48.9	47.3	26.0	19.2	38.0
1966	-6.4	6.2	29.7	37.2	51.4	66.1	73.8	65.5	58.2	44.0	23.1	11.9	38.4
1967	9.3	3.8	26.8	38.3	49.7	62.6	67.9	66.7	60.8	44.0	29.0	15.1	39.5
1968	7.7	9.9	34.1	43.9	52.9	64.1	69.6	68.1	59.3	46.7	31.0	8.9	41.4
1969	-1.6	12.8	15.3	45.4	54.8	57.3	68.4	72.4	59.0	40.3	30.5	15.6	39.2
1970	0.6	10.9	18.6	39.1	51.7	67.9	71.8	69.7	59.7	46.8	27.8	9.3	39.5
1971	-0.7	12.7	27.6	44.5	54.2	67.5	65.1	68.3	58.5	47.4	29.6	12.2	40.6
1972	2.7	4.1	23.9	41.0	59.8	66.9	68.4	70.5	56.9	42.4	28.6	3.8	39.1
1973	10.3	16.3	36.0	41.4	54.2	64.7	68.3	71.7	54.8	50.2	25.1	10.1	41.9
1974	1.7	9.6	22.9	42.2	51.1	64.4	73.7	64.3	53.4	47.5	29.2	20.9	40.1
1975	12.3	10.1	18.4	35.9	56.6	65.2	74.3	68.1	55.4	49.4	31.1	14.8	41.0
1976	7.7	21.4	23.0	47.0	55.8	68.5	71.8	73.6	60.0	39.5	23.2	6.9	41.5
1977	-3.3	17.5	32.0	49.5	66.5	66.6	72.2	62.5	57.9	47.1	25.6	6.5	41.7
1978	-1.4	3.4	23.5	42.5	59.1	64.7	69.5	69.1	63.6	46.4	22.8	7.3	39.2
1979	-4.2	-1.5	20.4	36.0	50.4	65.4	71.9	67.3	62.0	42.6	24.5	20.7	38.0
1980	6.6	8.3	20.7	49.0	61.4	65.7	71.9	67.5	56.9	42.4	33.1	12.7	41.6
1981	11.8	19.6	33.5	45.6	55.5	62.8	71.1	69.6	57.4	44.5	35.4	8.7	43.0
1982	-7.0	8.9	22.9	40.7	58.1	59.1	70.9	68.5	57.5	45.7	24.1	20.9	39.2
1983	16.1	21.8	29.9	40.2	52.1	66.1	73.5	72.9	56.7	44.4	31.3	-0.3	42.1
1984	9.7	24.9	23.4	45.6	54.2	65.8	70.6	73.3	54.4	47.4	29.7	9.6	42.4
1985	5.1	10.9	32.9	46.6	60.2	60.0	69.0	64.5	53.9	44.6	15.4	3.9	38.9
1986	13.8	10.5	31.6	43.9	57.5	67.5	71.5	65.6	56.1	45.3	23.1	20.8	42.3
1987	18.2	27.5	31.4	51.5	61.7	69.1	74.0	66.8	59.6	42.6	33.4	20.6	46.4
1988	5.9	9.3	29.5	44.5	63.9	73.8	75.8	72.2	58.5	42.9	27.5	15.2	43.3
1989	11.4	1.7	20.1	42.2	58.2	64.1	75.9	70.8	58.5	45.8	24.0	4.3	39.8
1990	21.8	17.6	31.4	43.6	55.0	67.0	70.0	71.1	62.3	45.6	32.1	12.2	44.1
1991	6.4	20.5	30.4	48.0	61.5	70.1	70.2	72.7	58.8	42.0	22.0	18.8	43.5
1992	17.3	23.5	32.6	41.4	58.7	62.0	64.3	64.8	56.8	45.1	27.3	10.5	42.0
1993	7.5	9.8	25.6	43.3	56.7	63.1	67.0	69.2	54.7	43.9	26.6	16.0	40.3
Record Mean	5.5	10.2	24.6	42.5	55.2	64.8	70.1	68.1	58.0	45.5	27.4	12.7	40.4
Max	15.0	19.7	33.7	53.2	67.3	76.1	81.9	80.2	69.7	56.4	36.0	21.4	50.9
Min	-4.0	0.7	15.5	31.8	43.1	53.5	58.3	56.0	46.2	34.6	18.7	4.0	29.9

REFERENCE NOTES

FARGO, NORTH DAKOTA

GENERAL
T - TRACE AMOUNT.
BLANK ENTRIES DENOTE MISSING/UNREPORTED DATA.
# INDICATES A STATION OR INSTRUMENT RELOCATION.

SPECIFIC

PM - INCLUDES LAST DAY OF PREVIOUS MONTH
ASOS - AUTOMATED SURFACE OBSERVING SYSTEM IN OPERATION DURING THESE MONTHS.

(a) - LENGTH OF RECORD IN YEARS, ALTHOUGH INDIVIDUAL MONTHS MAY BE MISSING.
0.* OR * - THE VALUE IS BETWEEN 0.0 AND 0.05
NORMALS - BASED ON THE 1961-1990 RECORD PERIOD.
EXTREMES - DATES ARE THE MOST RECENT OCCURRENCE
WIND DIR. - NUMERALS SHOW TENS OF DEGRESS CLOCKWISE FROM TRUE NORTH. "00" INDICATES CALM.
RESULTANT DIRECTIONS ARE GIVEN TO WHOLE DEGREES.
BOLD VALUES INDICATE EXTREME VALUES WHICH OCCURRED AFTER THE ASOS SYSTEM WAS COMMISSIONED.

RECORD = PERIOD OF RECORD
RECORD MEAN PRECIPITATION IS THE MEAN OF ALL DAILY PRECIPITATION AMOUNTS DURING THE PERIOD OF RECORD.
RECORD MAX(MIN) TEMPERATURE IS THE MEAN OF ALL DAILY MAX(MIN) TEMPERATURES DURING THE PERIOD OF RECORD.
RECORD MEAN TEMPERATURE IS THE SUM OF THE RECORD MAX AND RECORD MIN DIVIDED BY 2.
AVERAGE TEMPERATURE IS THE SUM OF THE MEAN DAILY MAX AND MIN TEMPERATURE DIVIDED BY 2.

EXCEPTIONS

RECORD MEANS ARE THROUGH THE CURRENT YEAR, BEGINNING IN 1881 FOR TEMPERATURE
1881 FOR PRECIPITATION
1943 FOR SNOWFALL

HEATING DEGREE DAYS Base 65 deg. F FARGO, NORTH DAKOTA

SEASON	JULY	AUG	SEP	OCT	NOV	DEC	JAN	FEB	MAR	APR	MAY	JUNE	TOTAL
1964-65	5	94	304	604	1065	1902	2051	1618	1582	695	324	66	10310
1965-66	19	59	477	544	1161	1415	2216	1649	1089	829	430	86	9974
1966-67	0	84	230	644	1253	1642	1723	1716	1178	795	480	96	9841
1967-68	65	49	158	645	1073	1544	1773	1592	952	628	375	79	8933
1968-69	31	66	201	565	1015	1736	2066	1460	1536	582	348	230	9836
1969-70	20	10	229	757	1028	1522	1996	1511	1431	773	407	55	9739
1970-71	16	26	251	560	1109	1723	2035	1461	1153	609	333	30	9306
1971-72	57	36	241	535	1052	1630	1931	1763	1269	718	231	60	9523
1972-73	25	41	261	695	1089	1897	1688	1361	893	701	328	79	9058
1973-74	32	3	309	451	1187	1698	1963	1550	1298	676	431	86	9684
1974-75	3	91	345	537	1066	1362	1630	1535	1438	867	265	79	9218
1975-76	14	22	284	492	1012	1550	1774	1257	1296	533	285	55	8574
1976-77	13	9	227	788	1247	1797	2119	1327	1015	466	74	30	9112
1977-78	7	95	211	549	1178	1817	2061	1721	1284	668	209	90	9890
1978-79	15	39	179	571	1262	1788	2147	1863	1377	861	457	64	10623
1979-80	3	45	139	689	1209	1367	1808	1644	1363	493	206	61	9027
1980-81	3	35	267	696	951	1616	1645	1266	971	574	298	84	8406
1981-82	14	10	250	627	881	1742	2236	1570	1298	725	222	187	9762
1982-83	0	66	257	589	1219	1359	1513	1206	1082	738	390	74	8493
1983-84	16	2	301	631	1004	2023	1714	1154	1280	576	344	52	9097
1984-85	15	13	339	541	1053	1715	1853	1514	988	550	172	179	8932
1985-86	13	72	329	625	1487	1895	1585	1527	1027	627	266	45	9498
1986-87	0	69	268	602	1251	1360	1447	1047	1036	415	163	39	7697
1987-88	15	59	177	688	940	1369	1832	1614	1092	609	131	8	8534
1988-89	3	25	207	677	1118	1537	1658	1771	1386	677	224	96	9379
1989-90	0	17	224	599	1224	1881	1332	1324	1034	666	314	58	8673
1990-91	8	18	173	594	982	1637	1813	1242	1066	505	211	6	8255
1991-92	3	3	234	708	1284	1425	1473	1198	998	709	247	137	8419
1992-93	66	84	252	613	1125	1686	1780	1542	1214	643	269	111	9385
1993-94	35	19	310	652	1144	1514							

COOLING DEGREE DAYS Base 65 deg. F FARGO, NORTH DAKOTA

YEAR	JAN	FEB	MAR	APR	MAY	JUNE	JULY	AUG	SEP	OCT	NOV	DEC	TOTAL
1969	0	0	0	0	39	5	131	249	59	0	0	0	483
1970	0	0	0	0	2	146	233	180	95	3	0	0	659
1971	0	0	0	0	3	109	65	142	56	0	0	0	375
1972	0	0	0	0	74	125	135	217	23	0	0	0	574
1973	0	0	0	0	0	76	140	219	13	0	0	0	448
1974	0	0	0	0	9	75	281	75	3	1	0	0	444
1975	0	0	0	0	11	92	308	126	1	15	0	0	553
1976	0	0	0	0	4	164	228	283	83	4	0	0	766
1977	0	0	0	6	129	86	235	23	8	0	0	0	487
1978	0	0	0	0	31	86	165	176	146	0	0	0	604
1979	0	0	0	0	12	85	225	124	58	0	0	0	504
1980	0	0	0	18	102	89	222	119	31	1	0	0	582
1981	0	0	0	0	9	25	212	159	26	0	0	0	431
1982	0	0	0	2	11	20	189	179	39	0	0	0	440
1983	0	0	0	0	2	113	288	252	55	0	0	0	710
1984	0	0	0	0	18	81	196	279	24	4	0	0	602
1985	0	0	0	6	31	35	143	63	4	0	0	0	282
1986	0	0	0	0	41	126	208	92	10	0	0	0	477
1987	0	0	0	17	66	169	303	121	25	0	0	0	701
1988	0	0	0	0	102	280	346	252	22	0	0	0	1002
1989	0	0	0	0	19	76	345	201	34	11	0	0	686
1990	0	0	0	29	10	123	172	214	98	1	0	0	647
1991	0	0	0	2	107	166	171	250	54	0	0	0	750
1992	0	0	0	9	58	52	49	85	11	3	0	0	267
1993	0	0	0	0	19	61	107	155	9	4	0	0	355

SNOWFALL (inches) FARGO, NORTH DAKOTA

SEASON	JULY	AUG	SEP	OCT	NOV	DEC	JAN	FEB	MAR	APR	MAY	JUNE	TOTAL
1964-65	0.0	0.0	0.0	T	2.7	11.9	1.2	1.7	13.1	2.5	T	0.0	33.1
1965-66	0.0	0.0	T	0.0	6.1	6.1	5.0	1.1	15.4	5.0	0.0	0.0	38.7
1966-67	0.0	0.0	0.0	1.2	1.3	3.4	15.1	2.6	4.9	5.0	T	0.0	33.5
1967-68	0.0	0.0	0.0	0.7	0.7	10.3	4.0	2.4	2.0	11.6	0.4	0.0	32.1
1968-69	0.0	0.0	0.0	0.8	3.9	11.4	14.5	7.8	3.0	T	T	0.0	41.4
1969-70	0.0	0.0	0.0	2.0	1.9	9.5	2.3	3.6	9.1	12.8	T	0.0	41.2
1970-71	0.0	0.0	0.0	0.9	6.4	8.3	15.1	4.8	1.8	1.0	T	0.0	38.3
1971-72	0.0	0.0	0.0	3.8	2.3	10.0	16.5	10.9	7.1	3.1	0.0	0.0	53.7
1972-73	0.0	0.0	T	3.8	1.7	18.5	1.7	1.4	1.4	2.4	0.0	0.0	30.9
1973-74	0.0	0.0	0.0	T	3.9	12.3	6.1	7.1	10.5	2.7	0.0	0.0	42.6
1974-75	0.0	0.0	0.0	0.4	1.0	5.1	18.3	5.9	18.7	3.7	T	0.0	53.1
1975-76	0.0	0.0	0.0	0.4	3.8	1.9	14.0	6.2	14.0	T	0.1	0.0	40.4
1976-77	0.0	0.0	0.0	0.1	2.7	5.5	12.6	10.7	4.6	2.1	0.0	0.0	38.3
1977-78	0.0	0.0	0.0	T	24.2	7.2	4.6	3.9	7.1	2.8	0.0	0.0	49.8
1978-79	0.0	0.0	0.0	T	8.5	11.7	7.8	19.5	4.3	2.7	0.8	0.0	55.3
1979-80	0.0	0.0	0.0	1.4	6.0	1.5	17.3	7.2	6.5	T	0.0	0.0	39.9
1980-81	0.0	0.0	0.0	0.5	1.1	4.6	2.1	4.5	0.3	T	0.0	0.0	13.1
1981-82	0.0	0.0	T	2.3	2.2	9.9	30.0	10.9	14.0	0.2	0.0	0.0	69.5
1982-83	0.0	0.0	0.0	0.0	6.8	0.3	3.8	2.0	7.4	2.9	T	0.0	23.2
1983-84	0.0	0.0	T	T	5.3	11.8	11.5	3.1	7.7	0.5	0.0	0.0	39.9
1984-85	0.0	0.0	T	T	1.4	7.4	3.7	3.1	12.6	T	0.0	0.0	28.2
1985-86	0.0	0.0	0.0	T	24.3	10.4	11.2	6.7	0.7	3.7	T	0.0	57.0
1986-87	0.0	0.0	0.0	T	5.3	3.8	2.8	10.4	1.2	T	0.0	0.0	23.5
1987-88	0.0	0.0	0.0	T	3.0	6.6	24.3	4.4	6.2	T	0.0	0.0	44.5
1988-89	0.0	0.0	0.0	T	11.6	14.9	31.5	2.3	12.4	0.9	T	0.0	73.6
1989-90	0.0	T	T	T	16.3	2.6	0.8	7.9	11.5	7.2	T	0.0	46.3
1990-91	0.0	0.0	0.0	1.3	0.2	12.4	4.0	15.3	10.9	4.2	T	T	48.3
1991-92	0.0	0.0	T	0.3	5.2	5.9	10.5	2.1	0.2	3.3	T	0.0	27.5
1992-93	0.0	0.0	T	1.8	16.4	9.2	16.7	3.3	6.4	T	0.0	0.0	53.8
1993-94	0.0	0.0	0.0	T	21.5	13.8							
Record Mean	0.0	T	T	0.7	5.8	7.1	8.6	5.9	6.7	3.1	0.1	T	37.9

CINCINNATI, (GREATER CINCINNATI AIRPORT) OHIO

Greater Cincinnati Airport is located on a gently rolling plateau about 12 miles southwest of downtown Cincinnati and 2 miles south of the Ohio River at its nearest point. The river valley is rather narrow and steep-sided varying from 1 to 3 miles in width and the river bed is 500 feet below the level of the airport.

The climate is continental with a rather wide range of temperatures from winter to summer. A precipitation maximum occurs during winter and spring with a late summer and fall minimum. On the average, the maximum snowfall occurs during January, although the heaviest 24-hour amounts have been recorded during late November and February.

The heaviest precipitation, as well as the precipitation of the longest duration, is normally associated with low pressure disturbances moving in a general southwest to northeast direction through the Ohio valley and south of the Cincinnati area.

Summers are warm and rather humid. The temperature will reach 100 degrees or more in 1 year out of 3. However, the temperature will reach 90 degrees or higher on about 19 days each year. Winters are moderately cold with frequent periods of extensive cloudiness.

The freeze free period lasts on the average 187 days from mid-April to the latter part of October.

NORMALS, MEANS, AND EXTREMES

CINCINNATI, (GREATER CINCINNATI AIRPORT) OHIO

LATITUDE: 39°03'N LONGITUDE: 84°40' W ELEVATION: FT. GRND 869 BARO 888 TIME ZONE: EASTERN WBAN: 93814

	(a)	JAN	FEB	MAR	APR	MAY	JUNE	JULY	AUG	SEP	OCT	NOV	DEC	YEAR
TEMPERATURE °F:														
Normals														
-Daily Maximum		36.6	40.8	53.0	64.2	74.0	82.0	85.5	84.1	77.9	66.0	53.3	41.5	63.2
-Daily Minimum		19.5	22.7	33.1	42.2	51.8	60.0	64.8	62.9	56.6	44.2	35.3	25.3	43.2
-Monthly		28.1	31.8	43.0	53.2	62.9	71.0	75.1	73.5	67.3	55.1	44.3	33.5	53.2
Extremes														
-Record Highest	32	69	73	84	89	93	102	103	102	98	88	81	75	103
-Year		1967	1972	1986	1976	1962	1988	1988	1962	1964	1963	1987	1982	JUL 1988
-Record Lowest	32	-25	-11	-11	17	27	39	47	43	31	16	1	-20	-25
-Year		1977	1982	1980	1964	1963	1972	1963	1986	1993	1962	1976	1989	JAN 1977
NORMAL DEGREE DAYS:														
Heating (base 65°F)		1144	930	682	354	151	11	0	0	51	327	621	977	5248
Cooling (base 65°F)		0	0	0	0	86	191	313	266	120	20	0	0	996
% OF POSSIBLE SUNSHINE	10	37	43	47	56	56	62	62	62	62	53	37	32	51
MEAN SKY COVER (tenths)														
Sunrise - Sunset	42	7.5	7.3	7.3	6.9	6.7	6.2	6.0	5.7	5.6	5.6	7.1	7.6	6.6
MEAN NUMBER OF DAYS:														
Sunrise to Sunset														
-Clear	42	5.2	5.1	5.3	5.8	6.0	7.0	7.7	8.3	9.7	10.5	5.9	5.1	81.6
-Partly Cloudy	42	6.0	5.9	6.7	7.5	9.7	10.5	11.6	11.9	8.8	7.4	5.9	5.8	97.8
-Cloudy	42	19.7	17.2	19.0	16.6	15.3	12.5	11.6	10.8	11.5	13.1	18.2	20.1	185.9
Precipitation														
.01 inches or more	46	12.0	11.3	13.3	12.5	11.7	10.5	10.2	9.1	8.0	8.3	11.2	12.2	130.2
Snow,Ice pellets,hail														
1.0 inches or more	46	2.1	1.8	1.2	0.2	0.0	0.0	0.0	0.0	0.0	0.1	0.5	1.2	7.2
Thunderstorms	46	0.7	0.8	2.4	4.2	5.7	6.9	8.2	7.5	3.2	1.4	1.2	0.5	42.6
Heavy Fog Visibility														
1/4 mile or less	30	2.3	2.0	1.5	0.8	1.2	1.2	1.7	2.7	3.3	2.5	1.6	2.5	23.4
Temperature °F														
-Maximum														
90° and above	31	0.0	0.0	0.0	0.0	0.5	4.1	8.0	5.3	1.8	0.0	0.0	0.0	19.7
32° and below	31	11.4	7.6	1.3	0.0	0.0	0.0	0.0	0.0	0.0	0.0	0.7	6.4	27.4
-Minimum														
32° and below	31	26.2	22.4	15.9	4.5	0.2	0.0	0.0	0.0	0.*	3.5	12.6	21.9	107.3
0° and below	31	2.9	1.5	0.1	0.0	0.0	0.0	0.0	0.0	0.0	0.0	0.0	1.1	5.7
AVG. STATION PRESS.(mb)	21	987.5	987.0	984.7	984.0	983.9	984.5	985.6	986.5	987.1	987.7	987.2	987.7	986.1
RELATIVE HUMIDITY (%)														
Hour 01	31	76	74	73	71	77	81	83	84	83	78	75	77	78
Hour 07 (Local Time)	31	79	78	78	76	80	82	85	88	88	84	80	80	82
Hour 13	31	68	64	59	54	55	56	57	58	58	55	63	69	60
Hour 19	31	70	65	61	55	58	59	61	64	67	65	69	72	64
PRECIPITATION (inches):														
Water Equivalent														
-Normal		2.59	2.69	4.24	3.75	4.28	3.84	4.24	3.35	2.88	2.86	3.46	3.15	41.33
-Maximum Monthly	46	9.43	6.72	12.18	7.19	9.48	7.36	8.36	7.71	8.61	8.60	7.51	7.90	12.18
-Year		1950	1955	1964	1970	1968	1977	1962	1982	1979	1983	1985	1990	MAR 1964
-Minimum Monthly	46	0.57	0.25	1.14	1.04	1.13	0.95	1.18	0.31	0.18	0.25	0.43	0.51	0.18
-Year		1981	1978	1960	1971	1964	1965	1951	1953	1963	1963	1949	1976	SEP 1963
-Maximum in 24 hrs	46	4.33	2.84	5.21	2.72	3.71	3.45	4.28	3.12	4.54	4.47	3.36	2.96	5.21
-Year		1959	1990	1964	1950	1956	1974	1988	1957	1979	1985	1948	1948	MAR 1964
Snow,Ice pellets,hail														
-Maximum Monthly	46	31.5	19.9	13.0	3.7	0.2	T	T	0.0	0.0	6.2	12.1	12.5	31.5
-Year		1978	1993	1968	1977	1989	1993	1991			1993	1966	1989	JAN 1978
-Maximum in 24 hrs	46	8.1	9.3	9.8	3.6	0.2	T	T	0.0	0.0	5.9	9.0	7.5	9.8
-Year		1978	1966	1968	1977	1989	1993	1991			1993	1966	1990	MAR 1968
WIND:														
Mean Speed (mph)	46	10.7	10.4	11.1	10.7	8.7	8.0	7.2	6.8	7.4	8.2	9.7	10.2	9.1
Prevailing Direction														
through 1963		SSW	SSW	SSW	SSW	SSW	SSW	SSW	SSW	SSW	SSW	SSW	SSW	SSW
Fastest Obs. 1 Min.														
-Direction (!!)	30	28	29	25	25	31	24	34	31	30	27	21	21	25
-Speed (MPH)	30	46	40	44	46	37	40	35	37	32	35	35	40	46
-Year		1976	1967	1977	1982	1986	1971	1980	1983	1990	1967	1988	1973	APR 1982
Peak Gust														
-Direction (!!)	10	SW	SW	SW	S	W	SW	W	NE	NW	SW	W	SW	SW
-Speed (mph)	10	51	55	64	61	53	60	49	47	45	43	56	59	64
-Date		1990	1988	1986	1985	1987	1992	1990	1990	1990	1986	1988	1987	MAR 1986

PRECIPITATION (inches)

CINCINNATI, (GREATER CINCINNATI AIRPORT) OHIO

YEAR	JAN	FEB	MAR	APR	MAY	JUNE	JULY	AUG	SEP	OCT	NOV	DEC	ANNUAL
1964	2.88	1.98	12.18	6.73	1.13	4.32	2.56	2.25	1.65	0.59	2.69	4.92	43.88
1965	3.11	5.07	2.86	4.90	1.46	0.95	4.42	3.24	6.06	3.81	1.26	1.19	38.33
1966	3.84	3.73	1.22	5.38	2.42	2.52	4.06	4.31	3.13	0.57	4.18	3.31	38.67
1967	0.75	1.86	3.63	3.66	5.64	1.72	4.99	0.77	1.79	2.65	3.84	3.94	35.24
1968	1.79	0.64	4.24	3.47	9.48	2.43	7.50	2.26	2.16	1.35	3.21	4.01	42.54
1969	4.64	1.27	1.42	3.59	2.05	4.91	3.28	2.15	2.87	1.53	3.67	2.59	33.97
1970	1.27	1.68	4.71	7.19	1.88	5.73	3.47	2.96	3.87	2.44	2.29	3.32	40.81
1971	2.47	5.89	2.55	1.04	3.31	5.18	3.70	3.45	6.56	1.44	1.68	3.39	40.66
1972	1.96	2.20	3.68	5.89	6.02	2.41	1.50	2.64	5.96	2.55	6.26	4.23	45.30
1973	1.79	1.58	6.11	5.81	3.46	6.27	7.16	2.62	2.63	4.39	4.95	2.66	49.43
1974	3.65	1.63	4.39	5.08	5.53	4.38	3.82	5.75	4.44	1.07	4.19	2.83	46.76
1975	4.05	3.38	6.76	4.16	3.11	5.09	1.62	1.97	3.64	4.59	2.50	3.36	44.23
1976	3.00	2.37	2.14	1.21	1.80	5.94	2.33	4.36	1.95	3.85	0.83	0.51	30.29
1977	1.90	1.29	4.52	4.16	1.53	7.36	1.90	5.45	1.80	3.74	3.90	4.00	41.55
1978	4.52	0.25	1.99	2.28	5.30	6.63	6.86	4.41	0.43	5.03	2.67	6.46	46.83
1979	3.68	3.77	2.05	4.90	4.00	5.92	5.49	4.80	8.61	1.77	4.86	2.91	52.76
1980	2.26	1.04	4.50	1.96	4.59	4.13	5.51	4.19	1.83	3.28	2.58	1.26	37.13
1981	0.57	3.86	1.72	5.05	5.07	3.34	3.66	2.15	1.47	2.33	2.94	2.39	34.55
1982	7.17	1.17	4.67	2.18	4.60	3.61	2.44	7.71	1.27	0.99	5.08	4.25	45.14
1983	1.56	1.14	2.02	4.84	8.89	2.22	1.96	3.23	1.22	8.60	4.20	2.84	42.72
1984	0.75	2.40	3.61	4.88	4.82	2.11	2.57	3.30	3.50	3.85	6.00	4.21	42.00
1985	1.68	2.25	6.90	1.34	6.18	4.55	3.59	2.02	0.76	5.83	7.51	1.52	44.13
1986	1.01	2.85	3.07	1.57	3.59	1.46	3.33	3.78	3.53	3.08	3.79	2.58	33.64
1987	0.92	1.62	4.65	2.88	2.73	4.62	5.07	2.27	1.17	1.42	1.82	3.43	32.60
1988	2.75	4.94	3.42	3.92	1.99	1.19	6.85	2.44	3.05	1.86	4.78	2.78	39.97
1989	3.21	4.67	6.40	5.19	4.64	3.04	5.97	5.33	2.97	3.18	3.05	1.96	49.61
1990	2.59	5.82	2.75	3.22	9.41	5.01	3.68	5.67	4.13	5.09	2.31	7.90	57.58
1991	2.84	3.99	6.20	3.62	3.41	1.39	2.66	5.04	2.60	1.37	1.89	5.08	40.09
1992	2.99	0.93	4.19	2.71	2.84	3.65	7.00	3.17	3.23	1.11	4.31	1.36	37.49
1993	3.83	3.43	3.60	3.13	2.33	4.80	1.26	4.20	2.68	2.61	4.31	2.53	38.71
Record Mean	3.19	2.90	3.97	3.52	3.97	3.86	4.16	3.21	2.82	2.69	3.42	3.10	40.82

AVERAGE TEMPERATURE (deg. F)

CINCINNATI, (GREATER CINCINNATI AIRPORT) OHIO

YEAR	JAN	FEB	MAR	APR	MAY	JUNE	JULY	AUG	SEP	OCT	NOV	DEC	ANNUAL
1964	32.1	30.2	43.1	56.1	65.8	71.9	74.2	73.7	67.1	52.7	47.1	35.5	54.1
1965	30.6	32.9	36.6	53.3	67.1	71.9	73.2	72.5	67.1	53.4	44.2	38.8	53.5
1966	23.8	31.5	42.9	50.1	60.4	73.1	78.8	74.5	66.5	51.0	44.7	33.6	52.6
1967	35.4	27.5	44.8	55.4	60.5	73.0	72.9	71.1	65.3	55.5	40.3	36.8	53.2
1968	26.8	28.1	45.2	55.5	60.7	72.9	75.7	75.3	67.4	55.9	45.6	33.7	53.6
1969	30.2	33.7	37.3	55.2	65.0	71.9	77.3	74.0	66.5	55.7	40.3	30.6	53.1
1970	24.0	30.6	39.0	56.8	66.8	72.2	75.5	75.1	73.7	58.6	45.0	38.0	54.6
1971	28.3	33.3	40.2	53.1	60.8	75.8	74.8	72.4	70.3	61.4	43.2	41.2	54.6
1972	30.2	29.5	40.6	52.5	63.1	65.3	75.5	73.4	68.7	51.7	40.3	36.1	52.3
1973	31.7	33.0	50.6	51.1	58.4	72.3	74.8	73.7	69.6	59.0	45.4	33.6	54.4
1974	35.7	33.9	45.9	54.3	61.9	67.7	75.2	74.3	61.6	53.2	44.4	34.4	53.5
1975	34.0	37.1	39.8	50.6	67.6	72.3	74.6	76.9	62.4	57.5	49.1	37.4	54.9
1976	27.1	41.7	47.0	56.1	60.0	71.5	73.6	71.2	63.6	48.8	34.9	27.6	52.0
1977	12.0	29.8	46.5	56.3	68.2	68.7	77.9	73.9	69.8	52.3	45.4	28.7	52.5
1978	18.4	18.2	36.4	53.4	60.1	72.2	75.0	73.0	70.8	52.6	46.4	36.0	51.0
1979	21.3	21.4	46.6	50.9	60.2	69.4	73.4	72.3	66.1	54.3	44.2	36.2	51.4
1980	29.9	24.0	38.5	50.3	64.9	70.1	76.6	76.5	68.6	50.6	41.5	32.9	52.0
1981	24.1	34.2	40.1	58.1	59.8	72.3	75.9	73.6	65.2	53.9	43.7	29.0	52.5
1982	23.9	30.6	44.3	49.6	68.1	67.4	77.0	71.3	66.9	59.3	48.4	42.9	54.1
1983	31.6	35.3	44.7	49.4	59.0	71.6	79.2	78.3	67.2	55.7	44.7	24.6	53.4
1984	23.7	38.2	34.4	51.1	58.9	74.1	72.2	74.3	65.7	61.5	42.0	42.4	53.2
1985	22.7	29.4	47.5	57.9	65.4	69.9	75.1	72.5	67.5	59.3	49.9	26.2	53.6
1986	30.9	35.2	45.2	55.3	64.5	72.9	77.6	72.0	70.1	56.4	42.7	34.0	54.7
1987	30.7	37.3	45.0	53.0	69.3	73.6	76.1	75.2	68.3	49.3	48.0	36.8	55.2
1988	27.5	30.5	42.2	52.4	64.4	72.4	78.5	77.5	67.2	48.5	45.0	34.1	53.4
1989	38.6	30.8	45.4	52.9	60.1	71.3	76.7	73.5	66.4	55.7	43.9	21.6	53.1
1990	40.0	40.8	48.2	52.8	61.6	71.8	74.7	73.7	67.7	55.9	48.9	38.3	56.2
1991	31.0	37.3	45.4	56.9	70.4	75.4	77.9	74.8	68.6	58.6	41.4	37.3	56.3
1992	32.9	39.7	43.6	54.1	61.2	68.0	73.5	69.6	64.5	53.3	44.2	35.6	53.4
1993	34.5	29.3	40.2	52.0	63.3	70.9	79.1	76.2	63.9	53.0	43.5	32.8	53.2
Record Mean	29.7	33.1	42.4	53.5	63.3	71.7	75.7	74.1	67.3	55.6	43.9	33.9	53.7
Max	37.9	42.0	52.0	64.2	74.2	82.4	86.1	84.8	78.1	66.4	52.8	41.8	63.6
Min	21.4	24.2	32.7	42.8	52.3	60.9	65.3	63.4	56.4	44.7	35.0	26.0	43.8

REFERENCE NOTES

CINCINNATI, (GREATER CINCINNATI AIRPORT) OHIO

GENERAL
T - TRACE AMOUNT.
BLANK ENTRIES DENOTE MISSING/UNREPORTED DATA.
# INDICATES A STATION OR INSTRUMENT RELOCATION.

SPECIFIC

PM - INCLUDES LAST DAY OF PREVIOUS MONTH
ASOS - AUTOMATED SURFACE OBSERVING SYSTEM IN OPERATION DURING THESE MONTHS.

(a) - LENGTH OF RECORD IN YEARS, ALTHOUGH INDIVIDUAL MONTHS MAY BE MISSING.
0.* OR * - THE VALUE IS BETWEEN 0.0 AND 0.05
NORMALS - BASED ON THE 1961-1990 RECORD PERIOD.
EXTREMES - DATES ARE THE MOST RECENT OCCURRENCE
WIND DIR.- NUMERALS SHOW TENS OF DEGRESS CLOCKWISE FROM TRUE NORTH. "00" INDICATES CALM.
RESULTANT DIRECTIONS ARE GIVEN TO WHOLE DEGREES.
BOLD VALUES INDICATE EXTREME VALUES WHICH OCCURRED AFTER THE ASOS SYSTEM WAS COMMISSIONED.

RECORD = PERIOD OF RECORD
RECORD MEAN PRECIPITATION IS THE MEAN OF ALL DAILY PRECIPITATION AMOUNTS DURING THE PERIOD OF RECORD.
RECORD MAX(MIN) TEMPERATURE IS THE MEAN OF ALL DAILY MAX(MIN) TEMPERATURES DURING THE PERIOD OF RECORD.
RECORD MEAN TEMPERATURE IS THE SUM OF THE RECORD MAX AND RECORD MIN DIVIDED BY 2.
AVERAGE TEMPERATURE IS THE SUM OF THE MEAN DAILY MAX AND MIN TEMPERATURE DIVIDED BY 2.

EXCEPTIONS

RECORD MEANS ARE THROUGH THE CURRENT YEAR,
BEGINNING IN 1948 FOR TEMPERATURE
1948 FOR PRECIPITATION
1948 FOR SNOWFALL

HEATING DEGREE DAYS Base 65 deg. F CINCINNATI, (GREATER CINCINNATI AIRPORT) OHIO

SEASON	JULY	AUG	SEP	OCT	NOV	DEC	JAN	FEB	MAR	APR	MAY	JUNE	TOTAL
1964-65	0	14	68	376	529	907	1058	894	872	350	43	0	5111
1965-66	2	15	64	362	614	803	1270	931	681	442	181	15	5380
1966-67	0	0	70	428	602	969	910	1043	622	305	175	9	5133
1967-68	0	2	82	313	736	867	1178	1063	609	284	151	6	5291
1968-69	0	4	32	316	576	965	1072	872	852	298	84	29	5100
1969-70	0	0	66	309	737	1058	1265	954	797	264	91	2	5543
1970-71	4	0	28	212	591	829	1133	881	758	351	157	0	4944
1971-72	0	0	31	128	649	731	1073	1024	751	374	116	79	4956
1972-73	2	3	24	404	733	891	1025	888	445	425	206	3	5049
1973-74	0	1	27	217	583	964	901	863	591	332	161	31	4671
1974-75	0	0	147	371	614	942	953	774	778	435	50	10	5074
1975-76	5	0	142	244	474	848	1168	670	558	321	176	5	4611
1976-77	0	4	72	498	893	1157	1640	980	571	276	67	36	6194
1977-78	0	2	32	391	586	1118	1440	1303	880	346	207	10	6315
1978-79	0	0	21	381	552	891	1348	1216	563	425	179	15	5591
1979-80	1	14	60	346	616	887	1080	1182	814	434	92	24	5550
1980-81	0	0	48	446	697	988	1261	858	768	230	191	6	5493
1981-82	0	0	87	344	634	1107	1268	956	635	460	28	19	5538
1982-83	0	1	56	244	505	682	1029	825	627	466	199	21	4655
1983-84	1	0	89	288	600	1247	1274	773	939	425	219	4	5859
1984-85	0	0	101	128	684	692	1306	992	543	256	72	22	4796
1985-86	0	0	78	212	450	1195	1056	828	613	305	105	3	4845
1986-87	0	21	25	292	664	955	1058	766	612	365	52	2	4812
1987-88	0	1	39	477	505	868	1156	991	699	374	84	22	5216
1988-89	1	0	38	509	595	949	811	949	608	380	211	14	5065
1989-90	0	4	77	297	630	1335	770	671	531	390	127	21	4853
1990-91	0	1	66	296	477	821	1046	773	602	250	44	0	4376
1991-92	0	0	81	232	700	853	988	727	658	339	172	27	4777
1992-93	0	8	97	358	617	907	937	997	762	384	103	40	5210
1993-94	0	0	101	370	640	992							

COOLING DEGREE DAYS Base 65 deg. F CINCINNATI, (GREATER CINCINNATI AIRPORT) OHIO

YEAR	JAN	FEB	MAR	APR	MAY	JUNE	JULY	AUG	SEP	OCT	NOV	DEC	TOTAL
1969	0	0	0	9	92	240	389	285	116	31	0	0	1162
1970	0	0	0	28	151	225	336	320	292	21	0	0	1373
1971	0	0	0	0	33	335	313	236	195	25	0	0	1137
1972	0	0	0	7	65	96	334	268	142	0	0	0	912
1973	0	0	4	13	7	228	310	278	170	36	0	0	1046
1974	0	0	8	17	70	121	323	297	50	12	2	0	900
1975	0	0	0	8	138	236	309	376	72	19	3	0	1161
1976	0	0	6	59	28	207	276	202	39	5	0	0	822
1977	0	0	7	22	171	152	407	285	181	4	5	0	1234
1978	0	0	0	4	63	231	315	255	200	2	0	0	1070
1979	0	0	2	8	38	154	271	248	102	22	0	0	845
1980	0	0	0	0	98	187	364	363	166	5	0	0	1183
1981	0	0	1	31	34	234	343	275	99	9	0	0	1026
1982	0	0	0	5	129	99	381	203	120	73	13	8	1031
1983	0	0	4	4	18	225	448	417	161	8	0	0	1285
1984	0	0	0	13	38	289	233	295	130	29	0	0	1027
1985	0	0	6	47	93	174	318	241	162	41	5	0	1087
1986	0	0	4	22	97	247	399	243	183	30	0	0	1225
1987	0	0	0	12	193	266	353	325	147	0	4	0	1300
1988	0	0	2	3	70	251	425	392	111	6	0	0	1260
1989	0	0	7	26	67	210	369	275	125	17	0	0	1096
1990	0	0	17	32	27	230	309	276	155	21	3	0	1070
1991	0	0	0	14	218	317	408	310	195	42	0	0	1504
1992	0	0	0	19	59	126	273	158	88	2	0	0	725
1993	0	0	0	0	56	224	443	353	75	5	0	0	1156

SNOWFALL (inches) CINCINNATI, (GREATER CINCINNATI AIRPORT) OHIO

SEASON	JULY	AUG	SEP	OCT	NOV	DEC	JAN	FEB	MAR	APR	MAY	JUNE	TOTAL
1964-65	0.0	0.0	0.0	0.0	1.7	0.9	9.3	5.9	6.2	T	0.0	0.0	24.0
1965-66	0.0	0.0	0.0	0.0	T	2.5	6.8	9.5	1.2	0.1	T	0.0	20.1
1966-67	0.0	0.0	0.0	0.0	12.1	1.6	2.5	7.3	8.1	0.0	0.0	0.0	31.6
1967-68	0.0	0.0	0.0	T	3.1	3.1	8.7	3.6	13.0	0.0	0.0	0.0	31.5
1968-69	0.0	0.0	0.0	0.0	0.4	2.0	1.0	0.3	2.8	0.0	0.0	0.0	6.5
1969-70	0.0	0.0	0.0	0.0	1.1	6.0	6.7	4.3	12.0	T	0.0	0.0	30.1
1970-71	0.0	0.0	0.0	0.0	0.4	0.4	3.2	13.3	9.7	T	0.0	0.0	27.0
1971-72	0.0	0.0	0.0	0.0	3.0	T	1.6	10.8	0.1	0.5	0.0	0.0	16.0
1972-73	0.0	0.0	0.0	T	6.5	1.9	0.5	3.1	3.9	1.8	0.0	0.0	17.7
1973-74	0.0	0.0	0.0	0.0	0.4	2.0	1.7	3.2	3.4	0.5	0.0	0.0	11.2
1974-75	0.0	0.0	0.0	T	5.0	5.6	2.0	2.2	6.8	0.2	0.0	0.0	21.8
1975-76	0.0	0.0	0.0	0.0	3.7	1.7	8.0	0.1	0.6	0.0	0.0	0.0	14.1
1976-77	0.0	0.0	0.0	0.0	2.7	1.0	30.3	4.2	5.4	3.7	0.0	0.0	47.3
1977-78	0.0	0.0	0.0	0.0	4.0	6.3	31.5	4.6	7.5	0.0	0.0	0.0	53.9
1978-79	0.0	0.0	0.0	0.0	T	0.7	17.5	11.7	0.6	0.1	0.0	0.0	30.6
1979-80	0.0	0.0	0.0	0.0	1.0	1.0	8.3	11.9	7.9	T	0.0	0.0	30.1
1980-81	0.0	0.0	0.0	T	1.2	3.7	4.0	2.6	2.5	0.0	0.0	0.0	14.0
1981-82	0.0	0.0	0.0	T	0.3	10.9	7.1	3.9	0.5	1.5	0.0	0.0	24.2
1982-83	0.0	0.0	0.0	0.0	T	T	0.8	5.5	0.3	T	0.0	0.0	6.6
1983-84	0.0	0.0	0.0	0.0	T	1.7	4.1	6.7	4.1	0.0	0.0	0.0	16.6
1984-85	0.0	0.0	0.0	0.0	1.4	7.3	12.2	9.5	0.4	1.7	0.0	0.0	32.5
1985-86	0.0	0.0	0.0	0.0	0.0	5.0	2.8	11.3	0.8	T	0.0	0.0	19.9
1986-87	0.0	0.0	0.0	0.0	T	0.8	1.6	2.4	8.8	2.3	0.0	0.0	15.9
1987-88	0.0	0.0	0.0	0.0	0.1	0.2	4.3	4.7	2.3	T	0.0	0.0	11.6
1988-89	0.0	0.0	0.0	0.0	0.7	2.9	T	3.0	1.2	0.3	0.2	0.0	8.3
1989-90	0.0	0.0	0.0	5.9	0.2	12.5	1.3	3.6	5.6	T	0.0	0.0	29.1
1990-91	0.0	0.0	0.0	0.0	0.0	8.6	4.3	2.6	T	0.0	0.0	0.0	15.5
1991-92	T	0.0	0.0	0.0	1.9	0.5	3.6	1.2	3.6	2.9	0.1	0.0	13.8
1992-93	0.0	0.0	0.0	T	1.6	3.8	0.3	19.9	3.9	T	0.0	T	29.5
1993-94	0.0	0.0	0.0	6.2	0.8	5.4							
Record Mean	T	0.0	0.0	0.3	2.1	3.9	6.7	5.5	4.2	0.5	T	T	23.2

CLEVELAND, OHIO

Cleveland is on the south shore of Lake Erie in northeast Ohio. The metropolitan area has a lake frontage of 31 miles. The surrounding terrain is generally level except for an abrupt ridge on the eastern edge of the city which rises some 500 feet above the shore terrain. The Cuyahoga River, which flows through a rather deep but narrow north-south valley, bisects the city.

Local climate is continental in character but with strong modifying influences by Lake Erie. West to northerly winds blowing off Lake Erie tend to lower daily high temperatures in summer and raise temperatures in winter. Temperatures at Hopkins Airport which is 5 miles south of the lakeshore average from 2-4 degrees higher than the lakeshore in summer, while overnight low temperatures average from 2-4 degrees lower than the lakefront during all seasons.

In this area, summers are moderately warm and humid with occasional days when temperatures exceed 90 degrees. Winters are relatively cold and cloudy with an average of 5 days with sub-zero temperatures. Weather changes occur every few days from the passing of cold fronts.

The daily range in temperature is usually greatest in late summer and least in winter. Annual extremes in temperature normally occur soon after late June and December. Maximum temperatures below freezing occur most often in December, January, and February. Temperatures of 100 degrees or higher are rare. On the average, freezing temperatures in fall are first recorded in October while the last freezing temperature in spring normally occurs in April.

As is characteristic of continental climates, precipitation varies widely from year to year. However, it is normally abundant and well distributed throughout the year with spring being the wettest season. Showers and thunderstorms account for most of the rainfall during the growing season. Thunderstorms are most frequent from April through August. Snowfall may fluctuate widely. Mean annual snowfall increases from west to east in Cuyahoga County ranging from about 45 inches in the west to more than 90 inches in the extreme east.

Damaging winds of 50 mph or greater are usually associated with thunderstorms. Tornadoes, one of the most destructive of all atmospheric storms, occasionally occur in Cuyahoga County.

NORMALS, MEANS, AND EXTREMES

CLEVELAND, OHIO

LATITUDE: 41°25'N LONGITUDE: 81°52' W ELEVATION: FT. GRND 777 BARO 779 TIME ZONE: EASTERN WBAN: 14820

	(a)	JAN	FEB	MAR	APR	MAY	JUNE	JULY	AUG	SEP	OCT	NOV	DEC	YEAR
TEMPERATURE °F:														
Normals														
-Daily Maximum		31.9	35.0	46.3	57.9	68.6	78.3	82.4	80.5	73.6	62.1	50.0	37.4	58.7
-Daily Minimum		17.6	19.3	28.2	37.3	47.3	56.8	61.4	60.3	54.2	43.5	35.0	24.5	40.5
-Monthly		24.8	27.2	37.3	47.6	58.0	67.6	71.9	70.4	63.9	52.8	42.6	30.9	49.6
Extremes														
-Record Highest	52	73	69	83	88	92	104	103	102	101	90	82	77	104
-Year		1950	1961	1945	1986	1959	1988	1941	1948	1953	1946	1950	1982	JUN 1988
-Record Lowest	52	-19	-15	-5	10	25	31	41	38	32	19	3	-15	-19
-Year		1963	1963	1984	1964	1966	1972	1968	1982	1942	1988	1976	1989	JAN 1963
NORMAL DEGREE DAYS:														
Heating (base 65°F)		1246	1058	859	522	250	40	0	11	99	387	672	1057	6201
Cooling (base 65°F)		0	0	0	0	33	118	218	178	66	8	0	0	621
% OF POSSIBLE SUNSHINE	50	31	37	44	52	58	65	67	63	59	52	31	26	49
MEAN SKY COVER (tenths)														
Sunrise - Sunset	52	8.3	7.9	7.5	7.1	6.6	6.1	5.7	5.7	6.0	6.3	8.0	8.4	7.0
MEAN NUMBER OF DAYS:														
Sunrise to Sunset														
-Clear	52	2.8	2.9	4.4	5.0	6.2	6.8	8.3	8.7	7.9	8.0	2.9	2.5	66.4
-Partly Cloudy	52	4.8	5.5	6.4	7.9	9.8	11.1	11.9	11.2	9.6	8.0	5.9	4.7	96.7
-Cloudy	52	23.5	19.8	20.2	17.1	15.1	12.2	10.8	11.2	12.5	15.0	21.2	23.8	202.1
Precipitation .01 inches or more	52	16.2	14.3	15.4	14.4	12.9	10.8	10.2	9.8	10.0	11.2	14.5	16.3	156.0
Snow,Ice pellets,hail 1.0 inches or more	52	4.2	4.0	3.3	0.8	0.*	0.0	0.0	0.0	0.0	0.2	1.8	4.2	18.4
Thunderstorms	52	0.1	0.5	1.7	3.4	4.9	6.5	6.4	5.2	3.3	1.6	1.0	0.3	34.8
Heavy Fog Visibility 1/4 mile or less	52	1.3	1.7	1.9	1.2	1.3	0.7	0.4	0.9	0.6	0.8	0.6	1.1	12.5
Temperature °F														
-Maximum														
90° and above	33	0.0	0.0	0.0	0.0	0.3	1.8	4.0	2.1	0.6	0.0	0.0	0.0	8.7
32° and below	33	15.0	12.4	4.8	0.2	0.0	0.0	0.0	0.0	0.0	0.0	1.1	10.0	43.5
-Minimum														
32° and below	33	27.8	24.3	20.9	9.1	0.8	0.*	0.0	0.0	0.0	2.9	12.5	24.5	122.8
0° and below	33	3.0	2.0	0.1	0.0	0.0	0.0	0.0	0.0	0.0	0.0	0.0	0.8	5.9
AVG. STATION PRESS. (mb)	21	988.8	989.2	987.4	986.5	986.7	987.0	987.9	989.2	989.7	990.0	989.2	989.4	988.4
RELATIVE HUMIDITY (%)														
Hour 01	33	75	76	75	73	77	80	81	83	82	77	75	76	78
Hour 07 (Local Time)	33	78	78	78	76	78	79	81	85	85	80	77	77	79
Hour 13	33	69	68	63	57	57	57	57	60	60	59	65	70	62
Hour 19	33	72	72	69	61	60	61	61	66	70	69	71	74	67
PRECIPITATION (inches):														
Water Equivalent														
-Normal		2.04	2.19	2.91	3.14	3.49	3.70	3.52	3.40	3.44	2.54	3.17	3.09	36.63
-Maximum Monthly	52	7.01	4.70	6.07	6.61	9.14	9.06	9.12	8.96	7.33	9.50	8.80	8.59	9.50
-Year		1950	1990	1954	1961	1989	1972	1992	1975	1990	1954	1985	1990	OCT 1954
-Minimum Monthly	52	0.36	0.48	0.78	1.18	1.00	0.65	1.21	0.53	0.74	0.61	0.80	0.71	0.36
-Year		1961	1978	1958	1946	1963	1988	1982	1969	1964	1952	1976	1958	JAN 1961
-Maximum in 24 hrs	52	2.33	2.33	2.76	2.24	3.73	4.00	2.87	3.07	3.30	3.44	2.73	2.81	4.00
-Year		1959	1959	1948	1961	1955	1972	1969	1947	1990	1954	1985	1992	JUN 1972
Snow,Ice pellets,hail														
-Maximum Monthly	52	42.8	39.1	26.3	14.5	2.1	T	T	0.0	T	8.0	22.3	30.3	42.8
-Year		1978	1993	1954	1943	1974	1993	1993		1993	1962	1950	1962	JAN 1978
-Maximum in 24 hrs	52	10.5	14.8	16.0	11.6	2.1	T	T	0.0	T	6.7	15.0	12.2	16.0
-Year		1978	1993	1987	1982	1974	1993	1993		1993	1962	1950	1974	MAR 1987
WIND:														
Mean Speed (mph)	52	12.2	11.8	12.1	11.5	10.0	9.3	8.6	8.3	9.0	9.9	11.8	12.1	10.5
Prevailing Direction through 1963		SW	S	W	S	S	S	S	S	S	S	S	S	S
Fastest Obs. 1 Min.														
-Direction (!!)	16	22	23	27	23	20	18	23	31	34	23	21	21	22
-Speed (MPH)	16	53	39	41	44	42	37	36	36	31	37	39	43	53
-Year		1978	1988	1986	1982	1983	1992	1983	1988	1986	1983	1988	1982	JAN 1978
Peak Gust														
-Direction (!!)	10	SW	SW	SW	SW	NW	W	NW	NW	W	W	S	SW	SW
-Speed (mph)	10	55	58	63	69	54	56	67	49	45	52	59	63	69
-Date		1985	1988	1986	1984	1988	1988	1992	1988	1986	1988	1988	1987	APR 1984

PRECIPITATION (inches) CLEVELAND, OHIO

YEAR	JAN	FEB	MAR	APR	MAY	JUNE	JULY	AUG	SEP	OCT	NOV	DEC	ANNUAL
1964	1.45	1.49	5.21	4.87	3.02	2.06	3.37	3.82	0.74	1.78	0.92	2.67	31.40
1965	4.45	3.00	1.66	1.83	2.29	3.05	3.01	3.58	2.53	2.55	1.89	2.07	31.91
1966	1.53	2.31	2.26	3.61	2.21	1.83	3.89	3.48	1.66	1.18	5.16	2.84	31.96
1967	0.97	2.35	2.08	3.12	3.82	1.17	1.90	1.85	2.08	2.11	2.88	2.46	26.79
1968	3.27	0.79	2.07	2.25	4.08	2.32	3.58	1.82	3.36	2.90	4.35	3.94	34.73
1969	2.84	0.75	1.82	4.49	5.73	4.61	6.47	0.53	4.92	1.90	2.86	2.46	39.38
1970	1.28	1.35	2.32	2.64	2.95	4.98	4.14	0.92	3.16	3.98	3.69	2.25	33.66
1971	1.35	3.69	2.01	1.24	3.29	3.79	3.72	0.91	4.27	1.61	2.02	3.90	31.80
1972	1.95	2.01	2.97	3.40	3.74	9.06	4.44	6.38	4.91	1.64	4.58	3.26	48.34
1973	1.62	2.40	3.48	3.40	4.79	6.72	2.94	3.11	2.69	3.95	2.62	3.53	41.25
1974	2.56	2.43	3.88	3.64	4.78	3.57	1.90	3.29	3.06	1.19	4.72	4.86	39.88
1975	3.06	3.20	3.47	1.31	3.23	4.10	2.54	8.96	3.35	1.73	2.09	3.77	40.81
1976	3.38	3.97	3.11	2.17	2.94	3.64	3.48	3.50	3.71	2.54	0.80	1.57	34.81
1977	1.29	1.38	4.49	3.56	1.02	4.91	3.94	3.92	2.52	1.93	3.62	3.51	36.09
1978	3.67	0.48	2.17	3.02	3.01	3.30	2.40	3.58	3.68	3.23	1.19	2.96	32.69
1979	2.61	2.74	2.33	3.09	4.77	3.47	3.76	4.46	3.66	1.79	3.16	4.00	39.84
1980	1.18	1.27	3.66	2.65	3.13	2.69	4.77	4.38	3.11	2.38	1.29	2.10	32.61
1981	0.76	2.72	1.61	4.62	2.19	4.68	5.31	2.61	6.75	2.33	1.99	3.44	39.01
1982	4.00	1.41	3.77	1.62	2.65	5.01	1.21	2.66	4.82	0.93	5.17	3.68	36.93
1983	1.08	0.77	3.54	4.48	4.17	3.45	4.16	3.15	2.87	4.14	5.89	2.92	40.62
1984	1.25	3.82	3.80	2.29	5.95	3.40	3.35	5.51	2.43	2.20	3.95	3.38	41.33
1985	1.78	2.60	4.97	1.38	3.45	2.93	3.23	4.01	2.05	3.45	8.80	2.63	41.28
1986	2.23	3.08	2.44	3.90	4.34	2.97	3.10	3.58	6.41	2.83	3.01	2.82	40.71
1987	1.98	0.49	3.84	2.97	2.40	7.94	3.36	5.51	2.07	3.41	1.02	2.96	37.95
1988	1.03	2.84	2.20	3.47	1.33	0.65	3.42	3.35	1.77	2.51	4.63	2.49	29.69
1989	2.07	1.73	3.46	3.73	9.14	5.22	3.02	1.09	4.61	4.50	3.61	1.72	43.90
1990	2.35	4.70	0.86	4.57	6.10	1.72	5.62	4.79	7.33	4.92	2.28	8.59	53.83
1991	2.18	2.31	3.64	4.22	3.24	1.37	1.69	2.79	3.40	2.65	2.92	2.26	32.67
1992	3.32	2.65	3.05	3.77	3.01	2.66	9.12	4.58	3.25	2.27	6.54	4.31	48.53
1993	4.44	2.61	3.85	3.16	1.56	5.18	2.58	1.52	5.94	3.52	4.06	2.21	40.63
Record Mean	2.49	2.34	2.90	2.86	3.22	3.37	3.44	3.06	3.22	2.63	2.78	2.56	34.87

AVERAGE TEMPERATURE (deg. F) CLEVELAND, OHIO

YEAR	JAN	FEB	MAR	APR	MAY	JUNE	JULY	AUG	SEP	OCT	NOV	DEC	ANNUAL
1964	29.8	25.5	37.1	48.8	60.7	67.5	72.2	67.5	63.5	49.2	44.2	32.2	49.8
1965	27.2	28.0	31.7	45.6	63.2	66.9	69.0	68.7	67.4	51.3	42.5	37.4	49.9
1966	21.9	26.7	37.8	46.2	54.2	68.9	72.7	68.8	60.9	50.3	42.8	30.5	48.5
1967	32.4	25.9	37.2	49.7	52.3	71.7	69.7	68.8	61.7	54.0	38.6	34.7	49.7
1968	23.0	22.6	37.6	49.4	54.4	66.5	70.0	71.7	63.9	52.1	42.4	30.0	48.6
1969	25.4	27.9	34.3	49.4	58.6	65.5	72.4	71.8	63.6	51.9	40.2	27.2	49.0
1970	18.9	27.2	33.8	50.2	62.7	69.8	71.9	69.9	66.0	54.4	41.6	32.2	49.9
1971	21.4	27.9	31.6	43.2	56.5	71.0	69.5	68.9	67.7	59.9	41.4	38.1	49.8
1972	27.3	25.7	34.8	46.0	58.6	62.7	71.4	68.9	63.8	49.1	39.6	34.5	48.5
1973	30.4	27.9	46.5	50.2	56.7	70.4	72.6	73.2	66.3	57.7	44.6	34.3	52.6
1974	32.0	27.8	39.6	51.3	56.4	66.2	72.2	70,4	59.9	51.2	42.9	31.7	50.1
1975	31.9	30.4	34.6	41.8	62.3	69.8	71.3	72.3	58.6	53.8	47.0	32.0	50.5
1976	21.6	36.0	45.0	49.1	55.3	69.5	71.6	68.4	61.1	48.1	33.7	23.3	48.6
1977	11.0	25.0	42.7	51.4	61.8	63.3	73.1	69.6	65.6	52.6	45.4	29.2	49.3
1978	20.1	16.8	32.4	47.0	59.4	69.0	72.2	73.0	69.2	53.2	44.2	33.7	49.2
1979	22.0	19.1	42.9	46.6	56.9	66.9	71.1	71.5	65.0	52.4	42.3	33.7	49.2
1980	25.5	21.9	33.6	46.1	58.5	64.0	72.3	73.2	64.7	47.9	39.4	28.5	48.0
1981	20.1	31.5	36.0	50.6	55.7	68.2	71.3	70.0	62.4	50.0	42.6	30.6	49.1
1982	19.8	25.2	37.1	44.6	64.9	64.1	73.6	67.9	62.7	55.3	45.4	40.5	50.1
1983	30.7	33.9	40.8	47.1	55.7	69.0	75.2	73.7	65.1	53.4	43.9	23.2	51.0
1984	20.7	34.5	28.4	46.8	54.0	69.5	68.7	70.6	61.1	56.3	40.9	36.5	49.0
1985	20.8	25.2	40.3	53.6	60.4	62.7	71.1	68.9	64.9	54.0	46.0	24.3	49.4
1986	26.7	28.8	39.5	49.8	60.8	67.2	73.1	69.0	67.0	54.3	40.3	32.6	50.8
1987	27.4	30.5	39.0	49.1	63.0	70.2	75.2	70.8	63.5	47.5	46.1	34.8	51.4
1988	25.6	25.8	37.5	47.9	59.7	68.9	75.9	74.2	64.0	47.1	43.8	31.3	50.1
1989	35.0	26.1	38.1	45.3	57.6	68.3	73.4	71.0	64.0	54.0	41.0	19.2	49.4
1990	35.8	34.1	42.0	49.4	56.3	67.6	71.2	69.8	63.4	53.7	45.3	35.6	52.0
1991	27.3	32.8	40.7	52.6	66.9	71.1	74.7	72.7	64.5	55.7	40.2	34.8	52.8
1992	30.2	32.7	36.6	47.9	57.9	64.1	70.7	67.6	63.3	49.9	42.0	34.1	49.8
1993	32.3	25.6	33.6	47.6	59.2	67.9	75.0	73.2	62.2	51.3	41.8	30.5	50.0
Record Mean	27.1	27.8	36.2	47.3	58.4	67.8	72.3	70.7	64.6	53.6	41.7	31.3	49.9
Max	34.0	35.1	44.0	56.0	67.4	76.7	80.8	79.1	73.2	61.9	48.6	37.5	57.8
Min	20.2	20.5	28.3	38.5	49.3	59.0	63.7	62.2	55.9	45.2	34.8	25.0	41.9

REFERENCE NOTES CLEVELAND, OHIO

GENERAL
T - TRACE AMOUNT.
BLANK ENTRIES DENOTE MISSING/UNREPORTED DATA.
# INDICATES A STATION OR INSTRUMENT RELOCATION.

SPECIFIC

PM - INCLUDES LAST DAY OF PREVIOUS MONTH
ASOS - AUTOMATED SURFACE OBSERVING SYSTEM IN OPERATION DURING THESE MONTHS.

(a) - LENGTH OF RECORD IN YEARS, ALTHOUGH INDIVIDUAL MONTHS MAY BE MISSING.
0.* OR * - THE VALUE IS BETWEEN 0.0 AND 0.05
NORMALS - BASED ON THE 1961-1990 RECORD PERIOD.
EXTREMES - DATES ARE THE MOST RECENT OCCURRENCE.
WIND DIR.- NUMERALS SHOW TENS OF DEGRESS CLOCKWISE FROM TRUE NORTH. "00" INDICATES CALM.
RESULTANT DIRECTIONS ARE GIVEN TO WHOLE DEGREES.
BOLD VALUES INDICATE EXTREME VALUES WHICH OCCURRED AFTER THE ASOS SYSTEM WAS COMMISSIONED.

RECORD = PERIOD OF RECORD
RECORD MEAN PRECIPITATION IS THE MEAN OF ALL DAILY PRECIPITATION AMOUNTS DURING THE PERIOD OF RECORD.
RECORD MAX(MIN) TEMPERATURE IS THE MEAN OF ALL DAILY MAX(MIN) TEMPERATURES DURING THE PERIOD OF RECORD.
RECORD MEAN TEMPERATURE IS THE SUM OF THE RECORD MAX AND RECORD MIN DIVIDED BY 2.
AVERAGE TEMPERATURE IS THE SUM OF THE MEAN DAILY MAX AND MIN TEMPERATURE DIVIDED BY 2.

EXCEPTIONS

RECORD MEANS ARE THROUGH THE CURRENT YEAR, BEGINNING IN 1871 FOR TEMPERATURE
1871 FOR PRECIPITATION
1942 FOR SNOWFALL

HEATING DEGREE DAYS Base 65 deg. F — CLEVELAND, OHIO

SEASON	JULY	AUG	SEP	OCT	NOV	DEC	JAN	FEB	MAR	APR	MAY	JUNE	TOTAL
1964-65	3	46	117	483	617	1009	1165	1032	1025	576	130	64	6267
1965-66	24	49	67	418	671	852	1328	1067	837	562	346	53	6274
1966-67	6	15	162	452	655	1063	1000	1087	858	461	393	17	6169
1967-68	21	19	137	351	784	934	1295	1224	845	459	328	59	6456
1968-69	26	34	93	414	672	1080	1220	1032	946	471	234	100	6322
1969-70	1	7	121	406	736	1166	1425	1052	960	462	154	39	6529
1970-71	9	12	86	332	696	1009	1344	1032	1031	650	277	16	6494
1971-72	9	13	63	168	704	828	1160	1133	930	564	196	124	5892
1972-73	32	27	95	485	752	937	1067	1033	569	450	254	3	5704
1973-74	3	9	73	234	605	946	1015	1035	777	419	280	49	5445
1974-75	2	5	176	423	660	1026	1021	962	934	691	154	38	6092
1975-76	5	4	187	345	532	1015	1336	836	614	493	309	25	5701
1976-77	0	25	150	519	932	1286	1672	1113	689	423	166	115	7090
1977-78	4	26	60	378	592	1103	1387	1343	1005	534	218	43	6693
1978-79	7	2	43	362	620	965	1328	1281	680	552	290	60	6190
1979-80	20	11	87	403	670	967	1218	1244	967	561	223	103	6474
1980-81	3	2	97	521	763	1125	1385	935	894	430	298	30	6483
1981-82	11	11	145	458	664	1059	1393	1109	860	608	78	75	6471
1982-83	5	42	136	310	586	760	1056	864	742	533	294	56	5384
1983-84	7	0	116	362	628	1291	1366	878	1126	544	347	19	6684
1984-85	16	17	174	270	716	877	1364	1110	757	370	187	99	5957
1985-86	2	7	118	338	565	1255	1180	1009	785	459	172	52	5942
1986-87	3	40	63	332	736	999	1158	958	795	473	170	23	5750
1987-88	3	22	90	535	562	929	1213	1129	848	506	208	60	6105
1988-89	8	5	83	557	629	1040	922	1084	831	585	272	33	6049
1989-90	0	6	108	350	716	1416	898	858	718	492	270	56	5888
1990-91	7	3	121	350	585	906	1163	897	748	379	111	11	5281
1991-92	0	0	123	310	738	930	1074	929	872	513	243	90	5822
1992-93	8	26	118	462	682	952	1009	1097	967	519	192	56	6088
1993-94	0	3	134	420	691	1063							

COOLING DEGREE DAYS Base 65 deg. F — CLEVELAND, OHIO

YEAR	JAN	FEB	MAR	APR	MAY	JUNE	JULY	AUG	SEP	OCT	NOV	DEC	TOTAL
1969	0	0	0	10	41	120	237	223	84	10	0	0	725
1970	0	0	0	22	89	189	230	171	121	10	0	0	832
1971	0	0	0	0	22	198	158	143	152	19	0	0	692
1972	0	0	0	1	5	63	239	157	64	0	0	0	529
1973	0	0	0	13	7	168	244	273	119	17	0	0	841
1974	0	0	0	14	18	91	231	180	30	3	2	0	569
1975	0	0	0	0	75	187	206	241	6	5	0	0	720
1976	0	0	3	23	14	167	214	138	39	2	0	0	600
1977	0	0	4	22	74	73	262	175	84	0	9	0	703
1978	0	0	0	0	53	170	237	256	177	3	0	0	896
1979	0	0	0	6	42	122	213	218	93	21	0	0	715
1980	0	0	0	0	27	83	235	263	97	0	0	0	705
1981	0	0	0	4	16	132	214	175	73	0	0	0	614
1982	0	0	0	3	84	54	278	140	73	17	6	6	661
1983	0	0	0	5	12	185	327	277	127	12	0	0	945
1984	0	0	0	3	13	159	139	197	60	5	0	0	576
1985	0	0	0	38	52	34	201	131	122	4	2	0	584
1986	0	0	1	9	48	128	259	168	131	8	0	0	752
1987	0	0	0	0	114	183	322	209	53	0	3	0	884
1988	0	0	0	0	47	185	348	297	58	9	0	0	944
1989	0	0	4	0	46	138	268	199	83	14	0	0	752
1990	0	0	10	31	8	141	208	158	80	8	1	0	645
1991	0	0	1	14	176	200	307	245	114	26	0	0	1083
1992	0	0	0	8	28	68	191	114	74	0	0	0	483
1993	0	0	0	0	17	147	316	262	62	2	0	0	806

SNOWFALL (inches) — CLEVELAND, OHIO

SEASON	JULY	AUG	SEP	OCT	NOV	DEC	JAN	FEB	MAR	APR	MAY	JUNE	TOTAL
1964-65	0.0	0.0	0.0	T	1.0	8.7	13.6	15.6	12.9	0.4	0.0	0.0	52.2
1965-66	0.0	0.0	0.0	T	1.2	1.2	15.3	10.1	7.0	2.5	T	0.0	37.3
1966-67	0.0	0.0	0.0	0.0	8.8	10.9	2.0	18.5	7.3	0.1	0.0	0.0	47.6
1967-68	0.0	0.0	0.0	0.1	9.1	2.8	14.5	8.9	7.7	0.2	T	0.0	43.3
1968-69	0.0	0.0	0.0	T	6.8	8.3	5.8	5.6	9.0	1.5	T	0.0	37.0
1969-70	0.0	0.0	0.0	0.6	6.6	17.4	10.5	6.6	11.5	0.2	T	0.0	53.4
1970-71	0.0	0.0	T	T	5.2	6.0	8.6	14.3	16.6	0.7	0.0	0.0	51.4
1971-72	0.0	0.0	0.0	0.0	5.3	1.9	15.0	14.8	6.3	2.3	0.0	0.0	45.6
1972-73	0.0	0.0	0.0	5.5	7.8	15.2	9.8	20.4	8.3	0.9	0.6	0.0	68.5
1973-74	0.0	0.0	0.0	T	3.3	13.8	8.9	16.9	7.1	6.4	2.1	0.0	58.5
1974-75	0.0	0.0	0.0	1.6	5.3	24.1	9.7	9.9	15.2	1.2	0.0	0.0	67.0
1975-76	0.0	0.0	0.0	0.0	5.6	13.1	21.5	6.8	5.8	1.6	T	0.0	54.4
1976-77	0.0	0.0	T	1.6	8.9	16.3	21.1	9.6	4.2	1.7	0.0	0.0	63.4
1977-78	0.0	0.0	0.0	T	9.7	23.1	42.8	10.8	3.5	0.2	0.0	0.0	90.1
1978-79	0.0	0.0	0.0	0.0	1.9	2.5	15.1	16.0	2.4	0.4	0.0	0.0	38.3
1979-80	0.0	0.0	0.0	0.2	0.5	4.0	11.3	19.2	3.5	T	T	0.0	38.7
1980-81	0.0	0.0	0.0	T	5.4	13.5	15.0	9.7	16.9	T	0.0	0.0	60.5
1981-82	0.0	0.0	0.0	4.0	2.9	27.1	28.1	7.6	17.6	13.2	0.0	0.0	100.5
1982-83	0.0	0.0	0.0	T	2.2	6.3	6.5	8.3	11.3	3.4	0.0	0.0	38.0
1983-84	0.0	0.0	0.0	0.0	7.1	13.0	12.9	27.1	19.3	T	0.0	0.0	79.4
1984-85	0.0	0.0	0.0	0.0	4.0	8.9	25.5	18.2	1.2	5.9	0.0	0.0	63.7
1985-86	0.0	0.0	0.0	0.0	T	23.4	17.2	10.8	6.7	0.2	0.0	0.0	58.3
1986-87	0.0	0.0	0.0	0.0	3.1	1.1	16.4	5.0	26.2	4.0	0.0	0.0	55.8
1987-88	0.0	0.0	0.0	T	1.0	16.4	8.7	22.9	20.4	1.9	0.0	0.0	71.3
1988-89	0.0	0.0	0.0	T	1.7	17.9	6.6	13.8	9.9	4.9	T	0.0	54.8
1989-90	0.0	0.0	0.0	T	9.1	24.0	10.5	9.9	4.4	4.7	0.0	0.0	62.6
1990-91	0.0	0.0	0.0	T	T	7.4	16.6	18.9	4.2	T	0.0	0.0	47.1
1991-92	0.0	0.0	0.0	0.0	3.5	9.4	23.8	6.2	18.4	4.4	0.0	0.0	65.7
1992-93	0.0	0.0	0.0	T	7.1	7.1	8.7	39.1	25.4	1.1	0.0	T	88.5
1993-94	T	0.0	T	0.2	3.0	19.0							
Record Mean	T	0.0	T	0.6	5.0	11.9	12.6	12.3	10.6	2.3	0.1	T	55.4

COLUMBUS, OHIO

Columbus is located in the center of the state and in the drainage area of the Ohio River. The airport is located at the eastern boundary of the city approximately 7 miles from the center of the business district.

Four nearly parallel streams run through or adjacent to the city. The Scioto River is the principal stream and flows from the northwest into the center of the city and then flows straight south toward the Ohio River. The Olentangy River runs almost due south and empties into the Scioto just west of the business district. Two minor streams run through portions of Columbus or skirt the eastern and southern fringes of the area. They are Alum Creek and Big Walnut Creek. Alum Creek empties into the Big Walnut southeast of the city and the Big Walnut empties into the Scioto a few miles downstream. The Scioto and Olentangy are gorge-like in character with very little flood plain and the two creeks have only a little more flood plain or bottomland.

The narrow valleys associated with the streams flowing through the city supply the only variation in the micro-climate of the area. The city proper shows the typical metropolitan effect with shrubs and flowers blossoming earlier than in the immediate surroundings and in retarding light frost on clear quiet nights. Many small areas to the southeast and to the north and northeast show marked effects of air drainage as evidenced by the frequent formation of shallow ground fog at daybreak during the summer and fall months and the higher frequency of frost in the spring and fall.

The average occurrence of the last freezing temperature in the spring within the city proper is mid-April, and the first freeze in the fall is very late October, but in the immediate surroundings there is much variation. For example, at Valley Crossing located at the southeastern outskirts of the city, the average occurrence of the last 32 degree temperature in the spring is very early May, while the first 32 degree temperature in the fall is mid-October.

The records show a high frequency of calm or very low wind speeds during the late evening and early morning hours, from June through September. The rolling landscape is conducive to air drainage and from the Weather Service location at the airport the air drainage is toward the northwest with the wind direction indicated as southeast. Air drainage takes place at speeds generally 4 mph or less and frequently provides the only perceptible breeze during the night.

Columbus is located in the area of changeable weather. Air masses from central and northwest Canada frequently invade this region. Air from the Gulf of Mexico often reachs central Ohio during the summer and to a much lesser extent in the fall and winter. There are also occasional weather changes brought about by cool outbreaks from the Hudson Bay region of Canada, especially during the spring months. At infrequent intervals the general circulation will bring showers or snow to Columbus from the Atlantic. Although Columbus does not have a wet or dry season as such, the month of October usually has the least amount of precipitation.

NORMALS, MEANS, AND EXTREMES

COLUMBUS, OHIO

LATITUDE: 40 °00'N LONGITUDE: 82 °53' W ELEVATION: FT. GRND 813 BARO 816 TIME ZONE: EASTERN WBAN: 14821

	(a)	JAN	FEB	MAR	APR	MAY	JUNE	JULY	AUG	SEP	OCT	NOV	DEC	YEAR
TEMPERATURE °F:														
Normals														
-Daily Maximum		34.1	38.0	50.5	62.0	72.3	80.4	83.7	82.1	76.2	64.5	51.4	39.2	61.2
-Daily Minimum		18.5	21.2	31.2	40.0	50.1	58.0	62.7	60.8	54.8	42.9	34.3	24.6	41.6
-Monthly		26.4	29.6	40.9	51.0	61.2	69.2	73.2	71.5	65.5	53.7	42.9	31.9	51.4
Extremes														
-Record Highest	54	74	73	85	89	94	102	100	101	100	90	80	76	102
-Year		1950	1957	1945	1948	1941	1944	1988	1983	1951	1951	1987	1982	JUN 1944
-Record Lowest	54	-19	-13	-6	14	25	35	43	39	31	20	5	-17	-19
-Year		1985	1977	1984	1982	1966	1972	1972	1965	1963	1962	1976	1989	JAN 1985
NORMAL DEGREE DAYS:														
Heating (base 65°F)		1197	991	747	420	187	23	0	12	81	361	663	1026	5708
Cooling (base 65°F)		0	0	0	0	69	149	258	214	96	11	0	0	797
% OF POSSIBLE SUNSHINE	42	36	42	43	51	56	60	60	60	60	55	37	31	49
MEAN SKY COVER (tenths)														
Sunrise - Sunset	44	7.7	7.6	7.4	7.0	6.6	6.2	6.1	5.9	5.7	5.8	7.4	7.9	6.8
MEAN NUMBER OF DAYS:														
Sunrise to Sunset														
-Clear	44	4.3	4.0	4.9	5.3	6.1	6.2	6.6	7.1	9.0	10.1	4.8	4.0	72.4
-Partly Cloudy	44	6.4	6.1	6.7	7.8	10.2	11.3	13.2	12.9	9.2	7.4	6.5	5.8	103.4
-Cloudy	44	20.4	18.1	19.4	16.9	14.8	12.6	11.2	11.0	11.8	13.5	18.8	21.2	189.5
Precipitation														
.01 inches or more	54	13.3	11.4	13.9	13.0	12.6	10.9	10.8	9.3	8.5	8.9	11.6	12.8	137.1
Snow,Ice pellets,hail														
1.0 inches or more	45	2.6	2.2	1.4	0.2	0.0	0.0	0.0	0.0	0.0	0.1	0.7	1.8	8.9
Thunderstorms	54	0.4	0.6	2.1	4.0	6.3	7.9	8.2	6.1	3.1	1.3	1.0	0.3	41.3
Heavy Fog Visibility														
1/4 mile or less	44	1.8	1.5	1.1	0.6	0.9	1.0	1.0	1.6	1.8	1.4	1.2	1.6	15.4
Temperature °F														
-Maximum														
90° and above	34	0.0	0.0	0.0	0.0	0.6	3.4	5.9	3.8	1.3	0.0	0.0	0.0	15.1
32° and below	34	12.8	9.2	2.7	0.1	0.0	0.0	0.0	0.0	0.0	0.0	1.1	8.7	34.6
-Minimum														
32° and below	34	26.9	23.5	18.4	6.5	0.6	0.0	0.0	0.0	0.1	4.0	13.6	23.6	117.3
0° and below	34	2.7	1.4	0.1	0.0	0.0	0.0	0.0	0.0	0.0	0.0	0.0	0.9	5.1
AVG. STATION PRESS.(mb)	21	988.9	988.6	986.5	985.7	985.7	986.1	987.2	988.2	988.9	989.4	988.9	989.2	987.8
RELATIVE HUMIDITY (%)														
Hour 01	34	75	74	70	71	77	81	83	84	84	79	77	77	78
Hour 07 (Local Time)	34	77	77	75	75	79	81	84	87	87	82	80	79	80
Hour 13	34	67	64	57	53	55	55	56	58	57	55	63	69	59
Hour 19	34	69	67	60	55	57	58	60	63	65	64	69	73	63
PRECIPITATION (inches):														
Water Equivalent														
-Normal		2.18	2.24	3.27	3.21	3.93	4.04	4.31	3.72	2.96	2.15	3.22	2.86	38.09
-Maximum Monthly	54	8.29	5.15	9.59	6.36	9.11	9.75	12.36	8.63	6.76	5.24	10.67	6.98	12.36
-Year		1950	1990	1964	1964	1968	1958	1992	1979	1979	1954	1985	1990	JUL 1992
-Minimum Monthly	54	0.53	0.29	0.61	0.67	0.95	0.71	0.48	0.58	0.51	0.11	0.60	0.46	0.11
-Year		1944	1978	1941	1971	1977	1984	1940	1951	1963	1963	1976	1955	OCT 1963
-Maximum in 24 hrs	46	4.81	2.15	3.40	2.37	2.72	2.93	5.16	3.79	4.86	2.21	2.47	1.83	5.16
-Year		1959	1975	1964	1957	1968	1958	1992	1972	1979	1986	1985	1990	JUL 1992
Snow,Ice pellets,hail														
-Maximum Monthly	46	34.4	16.4	13.5	12.6	0.8	T	0.0	0.0	T	4.6	15.2	17.3	34.4
-Year		1978	1979	1962	1987	1989	1990			1967	1993	1950	1960	JAN 1978
-Maximum in 24 hrs	46	7.5	8.9	8.6	12.3	0.8	T	0.0	0.0	T	4.6	8.2	8.7	12.3
-Year		1978	1971	1962	1987	1989	1990			1967	1993	1950	1960	APR 1987
WIND:														
Mean Speed (mph)	44	9.9	9.7	10.2	9.7	8.1	7.3	6.6	6.2	6.5	7.4	9.1	9.6	8.4
Prevailing Direction through 1963		SSW	NW	SSW	WNW	S	SSW	SSW	NNW	S	S	S	W	S
Fastest Obs. 1 Min.														
-Direction (!!)	12	23	18	28	22	25	26	23	27	20	25	27	23	25
-Speed (MPH)	12	37	30	35	40	52	31	35	38	27	35	39	35	52
-Year		1985	1988	1985	1982	1982	1983	1981	1984	1983	1981	1992	1987	MAY 1982
Peak Gust														
-Direction (!!)	10	W	SW	W	S	W	SW	W	W	S	W	W	SW	W
-Speed (mph)	10	51	51	53	52	52	40	47	56	38	39	53	55	56
-Date		1985	1988	1985	1985	1985	1989	1991	1984	1985	1993	1988	1987	AUG 1984

PRECIPITATION (inches) COLUMBUS, OHIO

YEAR	JAN	FEB	MAR	APR	MAY	JUNE	JULY	AUG	SEP	OCT	NOV	DEC	ANNUAL
1964	1.82	1.68	9.59	6.36	1.95	5.71	2.97	3.19	1.66	0.38	1.81	4.09	41.21
1965	2.70	3.76	2.90	5.90	4.00	2.42	3.76	4.62	6.18	3.98	1.19	1.24	42.65
1966	2.87	2.59	1.04	4.89	3.13	1.28	5.91	4.90	3.56	0.79	4.05	3.33	38.34
1967	0.78	2.46	4.40	3.29	4.59	2.92	4.22	1.51	2.63	1.39	3.22	2.55	33.96
1968	2.22	0.38	3.01	2.20	9.11	2.96	2.80	3.08	1.77	2.59	4.26	3.40	37.78
1969	3.40	1.17	1.32	3.10	3.04	8.19	7.65	3.25	1.40	1.52	3.87	2.30	40.21
1970	1.60	1.68	3.04	5.52	5.37	5.65	3.73	3.94	3.95	2.07	2.88	2.50	41.93
1971	1.57	3.16	2.70	0.67	3.66	4.16	4.22	2.81	3.08	1.32	1.73	4.61	33.69
1972	1.40	1.74	2.86	3.74	6.56	3.98	2.60	7.96	5.13	1.74	4.40	3.49	45.60
1973	2.46	1.29	3.43	3.72	3.36	8.77	4.07	4.97	2.82	3.29	5.37	2.70	46.25
1974	2.40	2.30	4.38	2.66	3.29	5.04	1.14	4.88	3.32	1.51	3.39	2.68	36.99
1975	3.21	3.47	4.10	2.71	3.17	3.53	2.04	4.51	5.46	2.29	1.54	3.01	39.04
1976	3.15	2.03	2.17	1.44	1.41	4.52	5.12	5.08	2.54	2.86	0.60	0.93	31.85
1977	1.57	1.02	3.88	4.04	0.95	4.02	2.52	4.76	3.48	2.57	3.77	3.54	36.12
1978	5.89	0.29	2.98	3.02	4.15	3.65	1.81	5.23	1.16	2.39	1.56	5.01	37.14
1979	3.32	2.88	1.01	4.01	3.27	4.23	8.06	8.63	6.76	1.26	3.91	1.83	49.17
1980	1.69	1.38	3.77	1.59	4.56	5.17	4.58	6.26	1.86	2.53	2.07	1.96	37.42
1981	0.70	4.60	1.11	5.38	6.50	5.73	4.14	1.41	2.28	1.40	1.65	2.88	37.78
1982	4.77	1.49	3.99	1.90	4.68	3.37	3.90	1.02	4.25	0.92	5.19	3.84	39.32
1983	1.20	0.74	1.69	5.58	5.06	4.59	2.80	2.23	1.91	4.45	5.00	3.16	38.41
1984	1.07	1.97	3.89	3.10	4.93	0.71	3.15	2.96	1.48	2.91	4.41	2.84	33.42
1985	1.31	1.67	3.78	0.73	4.96	1.41	6.88	2.34	1.18	1.93	10.67	1.81	38.67
1986	1.54	2.96	2.61	1.31	2.47	5.53	3.60	1.61	3.44	4.16	3.00	2.81	35.04
1987	1.14	0.59	2.04	2.02	2.85	3.60	3.89	2.96	1.53	1.57	1.63	2.88	26.70
1988	2.14	4.26	2.54	2.24	2.27	1.34	7.80	2.68	3.52	1.70	3.59	2.49	36.57
1989	1.97	3.10	4.16	3.30	4.69	6.36	6.79	4.30	2.16	2.49	2.65	1.79	43.76
1990	2.43	5.15	1.32	2.82	7.01	5.25	8.00	1.86	5.26	5.05	2.03	6.98	53.16
1991	1.97	2.30	3.97	4.15	2.47	2.81	2.14	2.02	4.05	1.76	1.31	3.79	32.74
1992	1.79	0.85	3.40	2.83	3.40	2.33	12.36	3.75	2.14	1.40	4.03	1.32	39.60
1993	4.14	1.82	3.50	4.49	2.47	3.33	5.95	0.74	1.75	3.05	4.45	2.16	37.85
Record Mean	2.84	2.45	3.90	3.14	3.70	3.71	3.91	3.20	2.63	2.25	2.80	2.62	37.16

AVERAGE TEMPERATURE (deg. F) COLUMBUS, OHIO

YEAR	JAN	FEB	MAR	APR	MAY	JUNE	JULY	AUG	SEP	OCT	NOV	DEC	ANNUAL
1964	30.1	27.7	41.1	53.6	63.4	70.3	74.4	71.2	65.0	51.1	45.1	33.9	52.3
1965	28.3	29.1	34.8	51.4	68.1	69.4	72.0	71.0	68.3	54.4	43.3	36.6	52.2
1966	22.2	29.4	41.8	49.4	56.1	71.4	75.6	71.3	63.2	50.7	42.4	32.6	50.5
1967	34.8	25.8	40.4	52.6	55.4	71.8	71.7	68.3	60.4	51.9	36.7	34.3	50.3
1968	23.6	25.7	43.3	53.1	58.5	71.5	74.1	73.0	65.5	54.1	44.0	31.1	51.5
1969	27.0	31.4	35.3	51.5	61.7	68.5	74.1	71.2	63.8	53.9	39.3	26.8	50.4
1970	20.6	28.5	36.9	53.4	64.9	69.8	73.5	72.4	68.9	55.6	42.4	34.3	51.8
1971	24.3	30.8	36.6	49.0	58.0	73.5	70.5	68.9	67.8	59.8	40.4	38.4	51.5
1972	28.2	27.7	37.0	48.8	60.8	63.6	71.9	70.1	64.6	49.6	40.5	36.1	49.9
1973	31.2	31.4	50.4	51.1	59.5	72.6	74.3	74.2	68.9	58.6	45.1	33.7	54.3
1974	33.2	31.2	44.6	54.3	60.8	67.7	74.4	74.0	62.2	52.8	44.5	34.0	52.8
1975	32.5	33.4	37.3	46.7	66.6	72.4	75.1	77.3	62.7	54.7	47.5	33.5	53.3
1976	24.0	37.4	46.5	50.9	58.1	70.5	72.0	68.3	61.7	47.5	33.9	24.8	49.6
1977	11.4	26.5	45.6	54.8	66.8	67.5	76.2	72.0	68.2	52.0	45.1	29.5	51.3
1978	19.0	16.6	34.5	50.6	59.6	70.4	73.5	73.2	69.8	51.5	44.4	34.4	49.8
1979	21.4	19.3	44.3	50.1	60.5	69.6	71.8	71.9	65.1	53.3	43.6	35.1	50.5
1980	29.3	25.2	37.2	49.5	62.4	67.4	75.9	75.9	68.3	50.8	40.8	32.5	51.3
1981	23.3	34.0	40.2	55.8	59.5	70.9	71.9	70.4	62.3	51.1	40.9	30.6	50.9
1982	21.2	29.2	40.4	46.4	66.8	65.8	74.4	69.2	63.5	56.2	45.4	40.4	51.6
1983	29.9	34.0	43.3	48.4	57.6	69.4	76.7	76.2	67.1	54.5	44.0	24.8	52.2
1984	23.3	37.4	32.3	50.0	57.6	73.1	71.2	72.9	63.1	59.4	40.6	39.5	51.7
1985	21.7	26.0	43.7	56.3	62.6	66.9	72.7	71.2	66.6	57.3	48.2	26.0	51.6
1986	30.1	32.7	42.5	54.5	64.3	70.6	75.7	71.0	69.2	56.3	41.3	33.3	53.5
1987	29.9	34.9	44.3	52.1	66.0	72.7	76.6	74.3	66.9	49.1	47.6	35.7	54.2
1988	26.5	29.3	40.2	50.3	62.6	69.6	77.5	75.3	65.2	47.4	43.9	31.6	51.6
1989	36.6	28.7	42.0	48.2	57.2	68.8	73.9	71.2	65.2	54.2	42.1	19.8	50.7
1990	37.7	37.5	45.3	50.7	59.1	70.3	73.6	72.5	66.4	55.1	46.2	37.2	54.3
1991	29.7	35.7	43.9	56.1	70.9	75.0	77.6	75.0	66.2	55.9	41.0	36.4	55.3
1992	32.2	36.8	40.7	51.8	59.9	67.3	73.5	69.4	64.7	51.9	44.8	34.7	52.3
1993	34.3	27.8	38.6	50.3	62.2	69.8	76.2	75.7	64.9	53.0	43.5	32.9	52.4
Record Mean	29.0	30.8	40.2	51.2	61.9	70.7	74.8	72.8	66.4	54.7	42.4	32.4	52.3
Max	36.5	38.8	49.2	61.4	72.5	81.2	85.2	83.2	77.1	65.0	50.6	39.5	61.7
Min	21.4	22.7	31.1	40.9	51.3	60.2	64.3	62.4	55.8	44.4	34.2	25.3	42.8

REFERENCE NOTES COLUMBUS, OHIO

GENERAL
T - TRACE AMOUNT.
BLANK ENTRIES DENOTE MISSING/UNREPORTED DATA.
# INDICATES A STATION OR INSTRUMENT RELOCATION.

SPECIFIC

PM - INCLUDES LAST DAY OF PREVIOUS MONTH
ASOS - AUTOMATED SURFACE OBSERVING SYSTEM IN OPERATION DURING THESE MONTHS.

(a) - LENGTH OF RECORD IN YEARS, ALTHOUGH INDIVIDUAL MONTHS MAY BE MISSING.
0.* OR * - THE VALUE IS BETWEEN 0.0 AND 0.05
NORMALS - BASED ON THE 1961-1990 RECORD PERIOD.
EXTREMES - DATES ARE THE MOST RECENT OCCURRENCE
WIND DIR.- NUMERALS SHOW TENS OF DEGRESS CLOCKWISE FROM TRUE NORTH. "00" INDICATES CALM.
RESULTANT DIRECTIONS ARE GIVEN TO WHOLE DEGREES.
BOLD VALUES INDICATE EXTREME VALUES WHICH OCCURRED AFTER THE ASOS SYSTEM WAS COMMISSIONED.

RECORD = PERIOD OF RECORD
RECORD MEAN PRECIPITATION IS THE MEAN OF ALL DAILY PRECIPITATION AMOUNTS DURING THE PERIOD OF RECORD.
RECORD MAX(MIN) TEMPERATURE IS THE MEAN OF ALL DAILY MAX(MIN) TEMPERATURES DURING THE PERIOD OF RECORD.
RECORD MEAN TEMPERATURE IS THE SUM OF THE RECORD MAX AND RECORD MIN DIVIDED BY 2.
AVERAGE TEMPERATURE IS THE SUM OF THE MEAN DAILY MAX AND MIN TEMPERATURE DIVIDED BY 2.

EXCEPTIONS

1. FASTEST MILE WINDS ARE THROUGH JUNE 1981.

RECORD MEANS ARE THROUGH THE CURRENT YEAR,
BEGINNING IN 1879 FOR TEMPERATURE
1879 FOR PRECIPITATION
1948 FOR SNOWFALL

HEATING DEGREE DAYS Base 65 deg. F — COLUMBUS, OHIO

SEASON	JULY	AUG	SEP	OCT	NOV	DEC	JAN	FEB	MAR	APR	MAY	JUNE	TOTAL
1964-65	0	28	90	424	589	957	1132	999	932	403	39	26	5619
1965-66	4	28	53	330	645	873	1325	989	710	465	286	29	5737
1966-67	1	5	106	440	671	999	929	1093	756	374	300	9	5683
1967-68	7	23	164	406	843	942	1276	1133	667	351	205	6	6023
1968-69	6	20	57	362	624	1043	1173	933	916	402	143	54	5733
1969-70	0	2	107	359	763	1175	1369	1017	861	365	119	13	6150
1970-71	10	0	58	297	674	944	1256	950	871	475	230	4	5769
1971-72	3	5	52	181	733	815	1133	1077	860	482	146	101	5588
1972-73	22	18	77	473	727	889	1041	934	444	427	184	0	5236
1973-74	0	3	35	219	589	963	977	940	628	332	178	31	4895
1974-75	0	0	130	374	609	954	999	878	850	542	73	18	5427
1975-76	0	0	110	321	520	973	1263	791	570	440	229	4	5221
1976-77	1	25	118	537	925	1241	1659	1071	601	324	91	64	6657
1977-78	1	17	36	394	594	1091	1420	1346	938	424	223	23	6507
1978-79	0	0	38	411	610	943	1346	1270	637	449	185	18	5907
1979-80	11	16	83	376	632	920	1099	1148	855	458	133	53	5784
1980-81	0	0	46	435	717	1000	1286	864	761	287	195	14	5605
1981-82	8	5	141	429	713	1061	1351	997	758	556	45	33	6097
1982-83	3	19	107	304	585	759	1081	863	669	493	239	30	5152
1983-84	6	0	83	325	626	1236	1284	796	1007	447	254	3	6067
1984-85	6	3	143	182	727	782	1339	1086	654	286	134	35	5377
1985-86	0	2	96	249	500	1202	1076	901	694	328	113	19	5180
1986-87	0	26	41	287	702	974	1083	838	637	393	103	9	5093
1987-88	0	4	53	489	521	900	1187	1029	762	433	119	49	5546
1988-89	3	7	57	547	624	1032	873	1009	711	499	274	28	5664
1989-90	0	11	90	345	680	1394	840	766	613	444	190	26	5399
1990-91	0	3	83	310	558	857	1089	817	649	282	42	0	4690
1991-92	0	0	105	296	714	878	1011	814	747	402	190	35	5192
1992-93	0	8	101	403	600	932	942	1034	811	434	130	51	5446
1993-94	0	1	84	366	637	989							

COOLING DEGREE DAYS Base 65 deg. F — COLUMBUS, OHIO

YEAR	JAN	FEB	MAR	APR	MAY	JUNE	JULY	AUG	SEP	OCT	NOV	DEC	TOTAL
1969	0	0	0	3	45	165	290	203	76	18	0	0	800
1970	0	0	0	22	125	166	281	237	179	13	0	0	1023
1971	0	0	0	0	21	266	181	135	144	24	0	0	771
1972	0	0	0	1	24	67	245	183	71	0	0	0	591
1973	0	0	3	14	17	236	295	292	160	25	0	0	1042
1974	0	0	4	20	58	117	296	286	52	3	0	0	836
1975	0	0	0	1	130	248	320	389	48	10	1	0	1147
1976	0	0	3	23	23	174	223	135	25	2	0	0	608
1977	0	0	8	24	151	148	354	242	139	0	7	0	1073
1978	0	0	0	0	59	190	270	261	188	0	0	0	968
1979	0	0	0	7	54	163	230	239	93	22	0	0	808
1980	0	0	0	0	61	132	343	344	151	3	0	0	1034
1981	0	0	0	16	32	198	231	181	64	4	0	0	726
1982	0	0	0	4	111	66	301	154	67	39	7	4	753
1983	0	0	1	2	17	167	377	355	152	9	0	0	1080
1984	0	0	0	8	30	253	205	254	94	14	0	0	858
1985	0	0	2	32	64	97	245	201	152	19	2	0	814
1986	0	0	2	19	95	194	339	221	171	25	0	0	1066
1987	0	0	0	11	142	246	366	299	116	0	5	0	1185
1988	0	0	0	0	54	194	396	333	70	5	0	0	1052
1989	0	0	5	2	40	149	282	211	106	12	0	0	807
1990	0	0	11	21	13	191	273	244	133	9	3	0	898
1991	0	0	0	21	232	307	402	317	147	23	0	0	1449
1992	0	0	0	13	37	115	272	152	99	2	0	0	690
1993	0	0	0	0	48	204	352	343	89	2	0	0	1038

SNOWFALL (inches) — COLUMBUS, OHIO

SEASON	JULY	AUG	SEP	OCT	NOV	DEC	JAN	FEB	MAR	APR	MAY	JUNE	TOTAL
1964-65	0.0	0.0	0.0	0.0	1.0	3.2	10.2	7.6	8.6	T	0.0	0.0	30.6
1965-66	0.0	0.0	0.0	0.0	0.2	1.1	7.6	6.7	1.2	0.7	T	0.0	17.5
1966-67	0.0	0.0	0.0	T	10.4	6.4	2.8	15.6	11.4	0.0	0.0	0.0	46.6
1967-68	0.0	0.0	T	T	6.5	5.2	11.6	2.8	6.1	T	0.0	0.0	32.2
1968-69	0.0	0.0	0.0	0.0	1.0	6.8	2.5	2.5	1.9	0.5	0.0	0.0	15.2
1969-70	0.0	0.0	0.0	0.0	1.8	9.7	18.4	3.2	10.3	0.9	0.0	0.0	44.3
1970-71	0.0	0.0	0.0	0.0	0.9	1.4	6.5	12.3	12.3	T	0.0	0.0	33.4
1971-72	0.0	0.0	0.0	0.0	5.0	0.6	5.8	6.6	5.0	0.6	0.0	0.0	23.6
1972-73	0.0	0.0	0.0	T	6.3	2.8	4.4	1.8	2.1	7.1	0.0	0.0	24.5
1973-74	0.0	0.0	0.0	0.0	T	6.4	2.3	5.0	4.5	0.3	0.0	0.0	18.5
1974-75	0.0	0.0	0.0	T	0.3	7.4	8.1	3.7	2.6	T	0.0	0.0	22.1
1975-76	0.0	0.0	0.0	0.0	1.1	2.9	12.4	1.8	1.0	T	0.0	0.0	19.2
1976-77	0.0	0.0	0.0	T	3.1	4.6	18.1	6.7	0.3	0.1	0.0	0.0	32.9
1977-78	0.0	0.0	0.0	0.0	2.2	7.5	34.4	4.5	5.5	T	0.0	0.0	54.1
1978-79	0.0	0.0	0.0	T	1.3	1.8	17.3	16.4	0.8	0.3	0.0	0.0	37.9
1979-80	0.0	0.0	0.0	0.0	0.1	0.2	7.0	8.1	1.2	T	0.0	0.0	16.6
1980-81	0.0	0.0	0.0	T	8.0	7.3	7.8	3.7	3.3	0.0	0.0	0.0	30.1
1981-82	0.0	0.0	0.0	0.0	1.9	9.8	11.8	3.7	3.2	4.7	0.0	0.0	35.1
1982-83	0.0	0.0	0.0	0.0	T	1.5	2.6	4.5	2.8	0.1	0.0	0.0	11.5
1983-84	0.0	0.0	0.0	0.0	0.5	5.7	9.0	10.8	9.8	0.3	0.0	0.0	36.1
1984-85	0.0	0.0	0.0	0.0	0.9	7.3	21.9	12.5	T	0.8	0.0	0.0	43.4
1985-86	0.0	0.0	0.0	0.0	0.0	8.6	4.8	9.8	1.8	T	0.0	0.0	25.0
1986-87	0.0	0.0	0.0	0.0	0.4	0.4	2.7	1.2	5.9	12.6	0.0	0.0	23.2
1987-88	0.0	0.0	0.0	T	0.6	4.6	8.4	6.5	3.8	T	0.0	0.0	23.9
1988-89	0.0	0.0	0.0	T	0.8	5.9	0.6	3.9	6.6	0.1	0.8	0.0	18.7
1989-90	0.0	0.0	0.0	0.4	0.3	9.4	3.3	6.0	1.4	0.4	0.0	T	21.2
1990-91	0.0	0.0	0.0	0.0	0.0	3.7	3.4	4.5	4.0	T	0.0	0.0	15.6
1991-92	0.0	0.0	0.0	T	0.6	1.6	12.2	1.8	1.6	1.1	0.0	0.0	18.9
1992-93	0.0	0.0	0.0	T	3.0	2.4	1.5	14.6	8.9	0.2	0.0	0.0	30.6
1993-94	0.0	0.0	0.0	4.6	0.8	4.2							
Record Mean	0.0	0.0	T	0.1	2.3	5.5	8.1	6.2	4.5	0.9	T	T	27.7

TOLEDO, OHIO

Toledo is located on the western end of Lake Erie at the mouth of the Maumee River. Except for a bank up from the river about 30 feet, the terrain is generally level with only a slight slope toward the river and Lake Erie. The city has quite a diversified industrial section and excellent harbor facilities, making it a large transportation center for rail, water, and motor freight. Generally rich agricultural land is found in the surrounding area, especially up the Maumee Valley toward the Indiana state line.

Rainfall is usually sufficient for general agriculture. The terrain is level and drainage rather poor, therefore, a little less than the normal precipitation during the growing season is better than excessive amounts. Snowfall is generally light in this area, distributed throughout the winter from November to March with frequent thaws.

The nearness of Lake Erie and the other Great Lakes has a moderating effect on the temperature, and extremes are seldom recorded. On average, only fifteen days a year experience temperatures of 90 degrees or higher, and only eight days when it drops to zero or lower. The growing season averages 160 days, but has ranged from over 220 to less than 125 days.

Humidity is rather high throughout the year in this area, and there is an excessive amount of cloudiness. In the winter months the sun shines during only about 30 percent of the daylight hours. December and January, the cloudiest months, sometimes have as little as 16 percent of the possible hours of sunshine.

Severe windstorms, causing more than minor damage, occur infrequently. There are on the average twenty-three days per year having a sustained wind velocity of 32 mph or more.

Flooding in the Toledo area is produced by several factors. Heavy rains of 1 inch or more will cause a sudden rise in creeks and drainage ditches to the point of overflow. The western shores of Lake Erie are subject to flooding when the lake level is high and prolonged periods of east to northeast winds prevail.

NORMALS, MEANS, AND EXTREMES

TOLEDO, OHIO

LATITUDE: 41°36'N LONGITUDE: 83°48'W ELEVATION: FT. GRND 669 BARO 694 TIME ZONE: EASTERN WBAN: 94830

	(a)	JAN	FEB	MAR	APR	MAY	JUNE	JULY	AUG	SEP	OCT	NOV	DEC	YEAR
TEMPERATURE °F:														
Normals														
-Daily Maximum		30.2	33.4	45.5	58.8	70.5	79.8	83.4	81.3	74.4	62.4	48.5	35.2	58.6
-Daily Minimum		14.9	17.0	26.8	36.4	46.7	56.0	60.6	58.4	51.5	40.0	31.5	20.5	38.4
-Monthly		22.5	25.2	36.2	47.6	58.6	67.9	72.1	69.9	63.0	51.2	40.0	27.9	48.5
Extremes														
-Record Highest	38	62	68	80	88	95	104	103	99	98	91	78	68	104
-Year		1989	1957	1986	1990	1962	1988	1988	1993	1978	1963	1987	1982	JUN 1988
-Record Lowest	38	-20	-14	-6	8	25	32	40	34	26	15	2	-19	-20
-Year		1984	1982	1984	1982	1974	1972	1988	1982	1974	1976	1958	1989	JAN 1984
NORMAL DEGREE DAYS:														
Heating (base 65°F)		1318	1114	893	522	238	33	0	16	109	436	750	1150	6579
Cooling (base 65°F)		0	0	0	0	40	120	225	168	49	8	0	0	610
% OF POSSIBLE SUNSHINE	38	42	47	49	52	60	64	65	63	60	54	37	33	52
MEAN SKY COVER (tenths)														
Sunrise - Sunset	38	7.5	7.3	7.3	6.9	6.4	6.0	5.7	5.7	5.9	6.1	7.7	7.9	6.7
MEAN NUMBER OF DAYS:														
Sunrise to Sunset														
-Clear	38	4.6	4.6	5.1	5.8	6.7	7.0	7.6	8.4	8.1	8.1	3.7	3.3	72.7
-Partly Cloudy	38	6.7	6.7	7.1	7.8	10.4	11.5	13.4	12.2	9.8	8.9	7.0	6.2	107.7
-Cloudy	38	19.7	17.0	18.8	16.4	13.9	11.5	10.1	10.5	12.1	14.0	19.4	21.5	184.8
Precipitation														
.01 inches or more	38	13.1	10.8	13.3	12.8	11.9	10.0	9.6	9.1	10.2	9.3	12.0	14.2	136.3
Snow,Ice pellets,hail														
1.0 inches or more	38	2.8	2.5	2.0	0.5	0.0	0.0	0.0	0.0	0.0	0.1	1.1	2.7	11.6
Thunderstorms	38	0.2	0.5	2.0	3.7	4.9	6.9	6.9	6.2	3.8	1.3	0.7	0.2	37.3
Heavy Fog Visibility														
1/4 mile or less	38	1.4	1.9	1.7	0.9	0.7	0.9	0.8	1.8	1.8	1.9	1.5	2.2	17.6
Temperature °F														
-Maximum														
90° and above	38	0.0	0.0	0.0	0.0	0.8	3.5	5.1	3.5	1.1	0.*	0.0	0.0	14.1
32° and below	38	16.9	12.7	4.4	0.2	0.0	0.0	0.0	0.0	0.0	0.0	2.1	11.6	47.9
-Minimum														
32° and below	38	29.1	25.8	22.8	10.5	1.4	0.*	0.0	0.0	0.4	6.8	17.3	26.4	140.6
0° and below	38	4.2	2.7	0.2	0.0	0.0	0.0	0.0	0.0	0.0	0.0	0.0	1.8	8.9
AVG. STATION PRESS. (mb)	21	992.6	993.2	991.1	990.0	990.1	990.2	991.3	992.6	993.1	993.4	992.6	993.0	991.9
RELATIVE HUMIDITY (%)														
Hour 01	38	76	76	75	76	78	82	84	88	88	82	80	82	81
Hour 07 (Local Time)	38	80	80	81	80	80	82	86	91	91	86	83	83	84
Hour 13	38	70	66	61	55	52	54	55	58	58	57	66	73	60
Hour 19	38	74	71	66	59	56	58	61	67	71	70	74	78	67
PRECIPITATION (inches):														
Water Equivalent														
-Normal		1.75	1.73	2.66	2.96	2.91	3.75	3.27	3.25	2.85	2.10	2.81	2.93	32.97
-Maximum Monthly	38	4.61	5.39	5.70	6.10	5.13	8.48	6.75	8.47	8.10	5.53	6.86	6.81	8.48
-Year		1965	1990	1985	1977	1968	1981	1969	1965	1972	1991	1982	1967	JUN 1981
-Minimum Monthly	38	0.27	0.27	0.58	0.88	0.96	0.27	0.52	0.40	0.58	0.28	0.55	0.54	0.27
-Year		1961	1969	1958	1962	1964	1988	1991	1976	1963	1964	1976	1958	JUN 1988
-Maximum in 24 hrs	38	1.78	2.59	2.60	3.43	2.34	3.21	4.39	2.42	3.97	3.21	3.17	3.53	4.39
-Year		1959	1990	1985	1977	1991	1978	1969	1972	1972	1988	1982	1967	JUL 1969
Snow,Ice pellets,hail														
-Maximum Monthly	38	30.8	14.4	17.7	12.0	1.3	0.0	T	T	T	2.0	17.9	24.2	30.8
-Year		1978	1967	1993	1957	1989		1992	1993	1993	1989	1966	1977	JAN 1978
-Maximum in 24 hrs	38	10.4	7.7	9.7	9.8	1.3	0.0	T	T	T	1.8	8.3	13.9	13.9
-Year		1978	1981	1993	1957	1989		1992	1993	1993	1989	1966	1974	DEC 1974
WIND:														
Mean Speed (mph)	38	10.9	10.6	11.1	10.9	9.5	8.4	7.4	7.1	7.6	8.8	10.2	10.5	9.4
Prevailing Direction through 1963		WSW	WSW	WSW	E	WSW	SW	WSW	SW	SSW	WSW	WSW	SW	WSW
Fastest Mile														
-Direction (!!)	38	W	SW	W	SW	W	W	NW	W	NW	SW	SW	SW	SW
-Speed (MPH)	38	47	56	56	72	45	50	54	47	47	40	65	45	72
-Year		1972	1967	1957	1956	1957	1969	1970	1965	1969	1956	1957	1971	APR 1956
Peak Gust														
-Direction (!!)	10	SW	NW	SW	SW	W	SW	SW	SE	NW	SW	NW	SW	SE
-Speed (mph)	10	62	52	64	59	58	55	66	75	54	49	51	56	75
-Date		1990	1990	1991	1991	1989	1992	1992	1988	1986	1990	1989	1987	AUG 1988

PRECIPITATION (inches) TOLEDO, OHIO

YEAR	JAN	FEB	MAR	APR	MAY	JUNE	JULY	AUG	SEP	OCT	NOV	DEC	ANNUAL
1964	1.87	0.95	4.88	3.49	0.96	1.89	1.58	3.80	1.61	0.28	0.77	2.20	24.28
1965	4.61	1.96	1.77	2.07	3.80	2.57	2.03	8.47	4.93	3.28	1.75	3.61	40.85
1966	0.46	1.46	1.82	2.81	1.88	3.42	3.73	4.60	1.17	0.97	4.63	5.12	32.07
1967	1.29	2.12	1.72	2.77	2.28	1.92	3.95	0.81	2.14	3.07	2.85	6.81	31.73
1968	1.91	1.29	2.26	3.01	5.13	3.40	4.50	1.45	1.52	1.11	3.52	3.97	33.07
1969	3.70	0.27	1.54	3.64	3.74	4.82	6.75	1.15	2.70	1.58	3.81	2.10	35.80
1970	1.09	0.89	2.61	4.26	4.05	4.59	5.99	3.00	5.78	2.00	2.09	1.49	37.84
1971	0.82	2.59	1.34	1.08	2.33	2.64	2.77	1.10	1.84	1.77	1.17	3.73	23.18
1972	1.42	0.77	2.33	3.74	2.63	4.09	2.77	4.47	8.10	1.46	3.55	3.08	38.41
1973	1.63	1.05	4.20	1.79	2.85	6.51	3.17	1.18	1.09	2.76	3.27	3.17	32.67
1974	2.27	2.00	2.93	2.55	4.18	3.31	0.68	1.61	1.41	0.70	3.57	3.41	28.62
1975	2.57	2.57	1.90	2.34	3.83	4.21	4.99	5.52	2.70	2.42	2.17	3.35	38.57
1976	2.80	4.43	3.56	2.79	1.72	3.70	2.08	0.40	3.68	2.14	0.55	0.93	28.78
1977	1.29	1.99	4.43	6.10	1.53	3.48	1.83	5.79	4.27	1.77	2.72	3.56	38.76
1978	3.14	0.54	2.34	3.74	2.48	5.34	1.86	1.67	3.19	1.65	2.48	3.31	31.74
1979	1.24	0.70	2.55	4.03	3.15	4.23	3.96	4.71	2.90	2.02	4.25	2.46	36.20
1980	0.74	0.96	3.65	3.13	2.93	3.26	4.49	5.89	1.63	1.79	0.97	2.48	31.92
1981	0.48	3.27	0.63	3.54	2.38	8.48	3.72	2.28	6.05	3.79	0.84	2.93	38.39
1982	3.61	1.15	3.74	1.53	2.61	2.01	1.97	1.38	2.03	1.14	6.86	3.48	31.51
1983	0.88	0.59	1.86	4.28	3.98	4.06	3.39	2.15	1.42	3.59	5.56	3.91	35.67
1984	0.99	1.18	2.95	5.15	3.48	1.49	2.30	3.87	2.02	1.75	2.74	3.22	31.14
1985	2.02	3.23	5.70	1.40	1.85	2.90	3.86	4.30	2.53	3.05	5.89	1.62	38.35
1986	0.99	2.46	2.16	2.81	2.72	5.32	3.37	5.93	4.75	4.78	1.66	1.87	38.82
1987	1.87	0.53	1.78	1.72	2.32	5.62	1.51	4.45	2.31	2.21	2.59	3.80	30.71
1988	1.17	1.33	1.69	1.45	1.37	0.27	3.76	5.11	1.80	4.37	4.27	1.96	28.55
1989	1.80	0.74	2.03	3.50	4.87	6.74	6.31	3.59	3.30	1.36	1.89	1.29	37.42
1990	2.18	5.39	3.46	2.09	4.63	3.14	1.89	3.32	1.72	2.63	2.27	5.69	38.41
1991	1.41	1.42	1.42	4.29	4.82	1.51	0.52	1.94	0.73	5.53	2.15	1.51	27.25
1992	1.70	1.68	3.05	3.41	3.18	1.28	6.51	2.40	4.01	1.77	4.45	3.60	37.04
1993	3.17	1.71	3.46	3.06	1.13	4.60	1.60	1.15	4.50	1.51	2.73	1.25	29.87
Record Mean	2.12	1.91	2.59	2.85	3.15	3.47	3.00	2.93	2.67	2.32	2.45	2.42	31.89

AVERAGE TEMPERATURE (deg. F) TOLEDO, OHIO

YEAR	JAN	FEB	MAR	APR	MAY	JUNE	JULY	AUG	SEP	OCT	NOV	DEC	ANNUAL
1964	28.5	25.9	35.0	48.6	62.6	68.8	73.8	67.8	62.5	47.5	42.3	27.8	49.2
1965	24.7	25.8	29.8	46.8	63.5	66.9	68.5	67.2	63.7	49.1	39.5	34.1	48.3
1966	20.2	27.0	38.1	45.6	53.8	70.8	74.1	69.1	61.7	50.4	40.4	27.7	48.2
1967	29.1	23.0	34.8	49.0	52.4	71.1	69.1	65.4	58.4	51.2	34.8	31.6	47.5
1968	22.1	24.5	38.6	49.5	55.9	69.6	71.9	74.0	65.2	52.0	40.6	26.6	49.2
1969	21.6	27.4	33.2	49.3	58.4	64.6	71.8	71.4	62.9	50.5	37.6	25.7	47.9
1970	16.2	24.3	31.8	48.9	61.1	67.2	71.1	69.6	64.4	54.0	39.8	28.9	48.1
1971	20.3	27.9	32.9	46.1	56.4	71.3	69.0	69.0	66.8	59.0	37.6	33.6	49.1
1972	23.4	24.4	34.1	46.1	60.4	63.9	71.4	68.4	62.2	47.2	37.7	30.3	47.5
1973	28.2	25.2	44.1	48.3	55.7	70.1	72.3	71.3	64.4	55.7	41.9	27.5	50.4
1974	26.1	23.2	36.2	48.8	56.0	65.4	72.5	71.5	59.6	49.5	40.4	28.9	48.2
1975	29.2	28.3	33.3	42.7	62.5	69.0	70.8	72.0	57.4	51.9	45.3	28.9	49.3
1976	19.8	32.8	41.6	49.3	56.0	69.3	72.2	68.2	60.5	45.6	32.3	19.9	47.3
1977	9.6	24.3	41.6	53.3	63.6	65.0	74.6	69.3	65.0	49.3	41.0	24.7	48.4
1978	16.7	11.8	28.7	45.8	58.9	67.6	70.9	70.4	68.0	49.8	40.3	30.1	46.6
1979	17.6	15.1	38.7	45.5	57.9	67.7	70.1	68.8	63.0	51.3	40.6	32.1	47.4
1980	24.3	21.4	32.4	46.8	59.5	65.5	73.6	73.3	63.8	46.8	37.4	26.0	47.6
1981	17.6	28.5	36.5	49.9	55.4	68.4	71.7	69.8	61.3	47.7	39.6	27.4	47.8
1982	15.8	20.2	33.4	42.7	64.4	64.3	72.6	67.5	61.9	52.7	41.8	36.6	47.8
1983	27.6	30.5	37.9	44.2	54.8	67.9	74.7	73.8	64.2	51.9	41.3	20.0	49.1
1984	16.6	33.0	27.6	46.8	54.4	71.2	69.8	71.2	60.8	55.2	38.7	34.0	48.3
1985	19.5	22.6	39.3	53.5	61.6	64.8	73.2	69.1	64.0	53.3	43.9	22.3	48.9
1986	25.6	25.0	39.2	50.0	60.3	66.8	73.8	67.0	65.3	53.2	37.2	31.6	49.6
1987	25.8	30.0	39.7	50.3	62.5	70.8	74.9	71.0	63.8	45.4	44.4	33.0	51.0
1988	23.8	23.3	37.5	48.1	61.0	69.3	75.9	73.9	62.5	45.2	41.8	28.0	49.2
1989	33.1	24.5	36.7	45.5	57.2	68.2	73.2	69.8	61.8	52.2	38.5	16.8	48.1
1990	34.3	32.4	41.1	49.4	56.6	69.1	71.8	70.0	63.7	51.8	44.3	33.1	51.5
1991	25.2	31.6	40.3	52.6	67.0	72.6	74.6	73.0	62.9	55.0	37.9	33.0	52.1
1992	28.8	31.9	36.1	47.4	57.9	65.1	70.1	67.8	61.9	49.6	40.8	32.9	49.2
1993	30.2	24.7	34.3	48.3	60.6	68.1	76.1	74.3	61.1	49.8	39.7	29.5	49.7
Record Mean	25.6	26.9	36.0	47.7	59.0	68.7	73.2	71.1	64.3	52.7	40.4	29.5	49.6
Max	32.7	34.4	44.3	57.2	69.1	78.7	83.2	81.0	74.2	62.2	47.9	36.2	58.4
Min	18.4	19.3	27.6	38.1	48.9	58.7	63.1	61.1	54.3	43.2	32.9	22.8	40.7

REFERENCE NOTES TOLEDO, OHIO

GENERAL
T - TRACE AMOUNT.
BLANK ENTRIES DENOTE MISSING/UNREPORTED DATA.
# INDICATES A STATION OR INSTRUMENT RELOCATION.

SPECIFIC

PM - INCLUDES LAST DAY OF PREVIOUS MONTH
ASOS - AUTOMATED SURFACE OBSERVING SYSTEM IN OPERATION DURING THESE MONTHS.

(a) - LENGTH OF RECORD IN YEARS, ALTHOUGH INDIVIDUAL MONTHS MAY BE MISSING.
0.* OR * - THE VALUE IS BETWEEN 0.0 AND 0.05
NORMALS - BASED ON THE 1961-1990 RECORD PERIOD.
EXTREMES - DATES ARE THE MOST RECENT OCCURRENCE
WIND DIR.- NUMERALS SHOW TENS OF DEGRESS CLOCKWISE FROM TRUE NORTH. "00" INDICATES CALM.
RESULTANT DIRECTIONS ARE GIVEN TO WHOLE DEGREES.
BOLD VALUES INDICATE EXTREME VALUES WHICH OCCURRED AFTER THE ASOS SYSTEM WAS COMMISSIONED.

RECORD = PERIOD OF RECORD
RECORD MEAN PRECIPITATION IS THE MEAN OF ALL DAILY PRECIPITATION AMOUNTS DURING THE PERIOD OF RECORD.
RECORD MAX(MIN) TEMPERATURE IS THE MEAN OF ALL DAILY MAX(MIN) TEMPERATURES DURING THE PERIOD OF RECORD.
RECORD MEAN TEMPERATURE IS THE SUM OF THE RECORD MAX AND RECORD MIN DIVIDED BY 2.
AVERAGE TEMPERATURE IS THE SUM OF THE MEAN DAILY MAX AND MIN TEMPERATURE DIVIDED BY 2.

EXCEPTIONS

RECORD MEANS ARE THROUGH THE CURRENT YEAR,
BEGINNING IN 1874 FOR TEMPERATURE
1871 FOR PRECIPITATION
1956 FOR SNOWFALL

HEATING DEGREE DAYS Base 65 deg. F TOLEDO, OHIO

SEASON	JULY	AUG	SEP	OCT	NOV	DEC	JAN	FEB	MAR	APR	MAY	JUNE	TOTAL
1964-65	1	55	150	536	676	1149	1242	1088	1084	538	123	51	6693
1965-66	27	57	129	486	759	953	1381	1058	828	579	348	30	6635
1966-67	1	15	147	451	729	1150	1105	1170	929	479	390	16	6582
1967-68	27	57	206	437	900	1031	1324	1168	814	458	284	27	6733
1968-69	8	17	71	424	726	1184	1340	1047	976	470	239	107	6609
1969-70	3	7	126	446	818	1213	1507	1130	1022	495	176	70	7013
1970-71	14	11	118	345	749	1111	1379	1035	987	561	272	22	6604
1971-72	18	12	78	197	813	966	1283	1169	952	560	158	95	6301
1972-73	28	36	134	543	810	1073	1135	1106	639	499	285	3	6291
1973-74	3	16	114	289	686	1157	1197	1166	885	483	295	71	6362
1974-75	2	0	190	478	730	1108	1104	1021	974	664	148	45	6464
1975-76	7	6	227	406	585	1110	1393	927	717	497	277	16	6168
1976-77	1	33	162	596	976	1393	1708	1135	718	381	135	91	7329
1977-78	3	29	71	481	713	1241	1490	1484	1121	573	243	43	7492
1978-79	11	11	74	466	732	1076	1461	1390	808	577	259	42	6907
1979-80	16	33	121	440	724	1009	1258	1256	1005	542	199	83	6686
1980-81	0	3	113	560	822	1206	1464	1015	879	450	309	24	6845
1981-82	7	15	169	529	754	1160	1522	1250	972	665	81	76	7200
1982-83	3	47	148	386	690	871	1154	958	833	624	311	55	6080
1983-84	8	0	127	407	705	1389	1494	920	1151	545	341	9	7096
1984-85	11	15	173	297	782	951	1404	1182	791	368	158	58	6190
1985-86	0	16	138	356	626	1316	1216	1113	793	449	185	54	6262
1986-87	2	54	87	365	828	1027	1209	972	778	439	173	20	5954
1987-88	5	34	89	601	611	986	1269	1202	845	498	159	53	6352
1988-89	4	5	104	613	691	1141	979	1127	869	578	270	29	6410
1989-90	0	14	159	396	789	1488	947	907	742	492	262	31	6227
1990-91	4	3	125	415	612	981	1228	928	758	377	115	7	5553
1991-92	0	0	167	315	806	986	1116	953	889	525	245	62	6064
1992-93	7	25	146	473	719	987	1072	1123	943	493	156	48	6192
1993-94	0	3	151	465	756	1095							

COOLING DEGREE DAYS Base 65 deg. F TOLEDO, OHIO

YEAR	JAN	FEB	MAR	APR	MAY	JUNE	JULY	AUG	SEP	OCT	NOV	DEC	TOTAL
1969	0	0	0	7	43	101	220	215	69	1	0	0	656
1970	0	0	0	19	62	142	210	159	107	10	0	0	709
1971	0	0	0	1	13	219	148	143	138	18	0	0	680
1972	0	0	0	0	22	67	236	148	55	0	0	0	528
1973	0	0	0	5	3	163	237	222	103	9	0	0	742
1974	0	0	0	4	25	91	243	206	34	5	0	0	608
1975	0	0	0	0	79	172	197	230	7	7	0	0	692
1976	0	0	0	31	10	155	230	137	34	2	0	0	599
1977	0	0	0	37	95	99	309	167	77	0	0	0	784
1978	0	0	0	0	58	128	200	184	170	1	0	0	741
1979	0	0	0	0	46	127	182	158	67	22	0	0	602
1980	0	0	0	3	35	106	275	265	84	4	0	0	772
1981	0	0	1	2	17	132	220	170	64	0	0	0	606
1982	0	0	0	0	68	61	245	132	62	11	0	0	579
1983	0	0	0	4	2	148	311	279	109	11	0	0	864
1984	0	0	0	5	17	203	168	214	51	1	0	0	659
1985	0	0	0	29	60	58	263	147	116	0	0	0	673
1986	0	0	1	4	48	113	282	125	103	4	0	0	680
1987	0	0	0	5	105	202	318	225	59	0	4	0	918
1988	0	0	0	0	43	190	350	286	39	5	0	0	913
1989	0	0	2	0	34	132	259	168	69	5	0	0	669
1990	0	0	7	32	11	164	222	164	91	14	0	0	705
1991	0	0	0	14	185	244	305	256	111	13	0	0	1128
1992	0	0	0	3	32	66	170	120	59	2	0	0	452
1993	0	0	0	0	26	148	351	297	41	1	0	0	864

SNOWFALL (inches) TOLEDO, OHIO

SEASON	JULY	AUG	SEP	OCT	NOV	DEC	JAN	FEB	MAR	APR	MAY	JUNE	TOTAL
1964-65	0.0	0.0	0.0	0.0	3.6	7.4	9.0	12.6	10.2	1.4	0.0	0.0	44.2
1965-66	0.0	0.0	0.0	0.0	0.1	0.9	5.3	4.5	7.9	1.1	T	0.0	19.8
1966-67	0.0	0.0	0.0	0.0	17.9	13.6	4.1	14.4	9.8	0.8	0.0	0.0	60.6
1967-68	0.0	0.0	T	T	1.9	5.1	10.4	5.6	11.2	0.2	0.0	0.0	34.4
1968-69	0.0	0.0	0.0	0.0	1.8	8.2	9.2	2.5	4.9	1.5	0.0	0.0	28.1
1969-70	0.0	0.0	0.0	T	5.7	19.0	14.2	7.7	8.3	4.5	0.0	0.0	59.4
1970-71	0.0	0.0	0.0	0.0	3.6	8.1	8.5	8.0	5.2	T	0.0	0.0	33.4
1971-72	0.0	0.0	0.0	0.0	5.7	1.4	10.1	7.6	3.3	1.8	0.0	0.0	29.9
1972-73	0.0	0.0	0.0	0.2	5.0	7.7	3.0	11.6	4.0	T	0.0	0.0	31.5
1973-74	0.0	0.0	0.0	0.0	0.2	13.8	7.5	11.6	2.9	1.1	T	0.0	37.1
1974-75	0.0	0.0	0.0	T	2.8	23.9	5.4	5.5	5.3	1.8	0.0	0.0	44.7
1975-76	0.0	0.0	0.0	0.0	5.7	12.2	14.5	8.4	4.0	1.3	0.0	0.0	46.1
1976-77	0.0	0.0	0.0	T	1.3	11.1	17.2	8.7	15.0	0.6	0.0	0.0	53.9
1977-78	0.0	0.0	0.0	0.0	6.6	24.2	30.8	9.0	2.5	T	0.0	0.0	73.1
1978-79	0.0	0.0	0.0	0.0	2.8	2.3	7.6	5.1	1.2	4.0	0.0	0.0	23.0
1979-80	0.0	0.0	0.0	T	1.6	1.5	4.1	6.4	3.4	0.5	T	0.0	17.5
1980-81	0.0	0.0	0.0	0.9	3.5	11.6	6.9	11.2	3.6	0.0	0.0	0.0	37.7
1981-82	0.0	0.0	0.0	T	0.8	14.9	18.4	14.3	10.7	9.1	0.0	0.0	68.2
1982-83	0.0	0.0	0.0	T	2.2	1.2	0.7	4.1	3.6	0.7	0.0	0.0	12.5
1983-84	0.0	0.0	0.0	0.0	3.4	13.4	12.2	6.3	9.8	T	T	0.0	45.1
1984-85	0.0	0.0	0.0	0.0	2.4	5.1	14.0	12.4	2.6	2.0	0.0	0.0	38.5
1985-86	0.0	0.0	0.0	0.0	2.5	8.7	6.6	10.2	2.2	0.2	0.0	0.0	30.4
1986-87	0.0	0.0	0.0	T	4.5	1.3	20.5	0.5	10.0	2.4	0.0	0.0	39.2
1987-88	0.0	0.0	0.0	T	0.1	11.1	8.3	14.3	4.2	T	0.0	0.0	38.0
1988-89	0.0	0.0	0.0	T	2.3	6.6	2.4	4.8	2.6	0.7	1.3	0.0	20.7
1989-90	0.0	0.0	0.0	2.0	2.3	6.5	2.5	10.4	3.5	0.3	0.0	0.0	27.5
1990-91	0.0	0.0	0.0	0.0	T	8.2	5.0	10.1	T	T	0.0	0.0	23.3
1991-92	0.0	0.0	0.0	T	1.7	2.5	10.5	3.0	12.5	0.1	0.0	0.0	30.3
1992-93	T	0.0	0.0	1.0	0.2	5.2	6.3	10.2	17.7	0.8	0.0	0.0	41.4
1993-94	0.0	T	T	0.8	1.1	6.9							
Record Mean	T	T	T	0.1	2.9	8.5	9.3	8.2	6.3	1.5	T	0.0	36.9

1993 OKLAHOMA CITY, OKLAHOMA (OKC)

Oklahoma City is located along the North Canadian River, a frequently nearly-dry stream, at the geographic center of the state. It is not quite 1,000 miles south of the Canadian Border and a little less than 500 miles north of the Gulf of Mexico. The surrounding country is gently rolling with the nearest hills or low mountains, the Arbuckles, 80 miles south. The elevation ranges around 1,250 feet above sea level.

Although some influence is exerted at times by warm, moist air currents from the Gulf of Mexico, the climate of Oklahoma City falls mainly under continental controls characteristic of the Great Plains Region. The continental effect produces pronounced daily and seasonal temperature changes and considerable variation in seasonal and annual precipitation. Summers are long and usually hot. Winters are comparatively mild and short.

During the year, temperatures of 100 degrees or more occur on an average of 10 days, but have occurred on as many as 50 days or more. While summers are usually hot, the discomforting effect of extreme heat is considerably mitigated by low humidity and the prevalence of a moderate southerly breeze. Approximately one winter in three has temperatures of zero or lower.

The length of the growing season varies from 180 to 251 days. Average date of last freeze is early April and average date of first freeze is early November. Freezes have occurred in early October.

During an average year, skies are clear approximately 40 percent of the time, partly cloudy 25 percent, and cloudy 35 percent of the time. The city is almost smoke-free as a result of favorable atmospheric conditions and the almost exclusive use of natural gas for heating. Flying conditions are generally very good with flight by visual flight rules possible about 96 percent of the time.

Summer rainfall comes mainly from showers and thunderstorms. Winter precipitation is generally associated with frontal passages. Measurable precipitation has occurred on as many as 122 days and as few as 55 days during the year. The seasonal distribution of precipitation is normally 12 percent in winter, 34 percent in spring, 30 percent in summer, and 24 percent in fall. The The period with the least number of days with precipitation is November through January, and the month with the most rainy days is May. Thunderstorms occur most often in late spring and early summer. Large hail and/or destructive winds on occasion accompany these thunderstorms.

Snowfall averages less than 10 inches per year and seldom remains on the ground very long. Occasional brief periods of freezing rain and sleet storms occur.

Heavy fogs are infrequent. Prevailing winds are southerly except in January and February when northerly breezes predominate.

NORMALS, MEANS, AND EXTREMES FOR 1993

OKLAHOMA CITY, OK (OKC)

LATITUDE: 35° 23′ 35″ N LONGTITUDE: 97° 36′ 02″ W ELEVATION (FT): GRND: 1285 BARO: 1283 TIME ZONE: CENTRAL (UTC+06) WBAN: 13967

	ELEMENT	POR	JAN	FEB	MAR	APR	MAY	JUN	JUL	AUG	SEP	OCT	NOV	DEC	YEAR
TEMPERATURE °F	NORMAL DAILY MAXIMUM	30	46.7	52.1	62.0	71.9	79.1	87.3	93.4	92.5	83.8	73.6	60.4	49.9	71.1
	MEAN DAILY MAXIMUM	55	46.8	52.2	61.3	72.8	80.3	88.9	94.6	94.3	86.0	75.4	60.9	51.2	72.0
	HIGHEST DAILY MAXIMUM	40	80	84	93	100	104	105	109	110	102	96	87	86	110
	YEAR OF OCCURRENCE		1986	1981	1967	1972	1985	1980	1986	1980	1985	1972	1980	1955	AUG 1980
	MEAN OF EXTREME MAXS.	46	69.0	74.5	82.2	87.7	91.4	96.8	101.0	101.6	96.7	87.3	77.7	70.7	86.4
	NORMAL DAILY MINIMUM	30	25.2	29.6	38.5	48.8	57.7	66.1	70.6	69.6	62.2	50.4	38.6	28.6	48.8
	MEAN DAILY MINIMUM	55	26.1	30.5	38.0	49.8	58.9	67.7	72.0	71.1	63.2	51.9	38.6	30.1	49.8
	LOWEST DAILY MINIMUM	40	-4	-3	3	20	37	47	53	51	36	16	11	-8	-8
	YEAR OF OCCURRENCE		1988	1979	1960	1957	1981	1954	1971	1956	1989	1993	1991	1989	DEC 1989
	MEAN OF EXTREME MINS.	46	7.2	12.4	19.8	32.3	44.5	55.7	62.3	59.9	46.5	33.1	21.5	11.8	33.9
	NORMAL DRY BULB	30	35.9	40.9	50.3	60.4	68.4	76.7	82.0	81.1	73.0	62.0	49.6	39.3	60.0
	MEAN DRY BULB	55	36.5	41.4	49.6	61.3	69.6	78.3	83.4	82.7	74.6	63.7	49.8	40.7	61.0
	MEAN WET BULB	47	31.7	35.8	42.7	52.2	60.9	68.3	70.9	70.0	64.0	54.3	42.9	34.7	52.4
	MEAN DEW POINT	47	25.1	28.9	35.0	45.2	56.2	64.3	66.0	64.8	58.9	48.1	36.0	28.0	46.4
	NORMAL NO. DAYS WITH:														
	MAXIMUM ≥ 90°	30	0.0	0.0	0.1	0.5	2.2	12.0	22.4	22.4	8.8	1.2	0.0	0.0	69.6
	MAXIMUM ≤ 32°	30	5.2	2.4	0.2	0.0	0.0	0.0	0.0	0.0	0.0	0.0	0.1	2.9	10.8
	MINIMUM ≤ 32°	30	23.1	17.0	8.4	0.9	0.0	0.0	0.0	0.0	0.0	0.4	7.9	20.0	77.7
	MINIMUM ≤ 0°	30	0.5	0.1	0.0	0.0	0.0	0.0	0.0	0.0	0.0	0.0	0.0	0.2	0.8
H/C	NORMAL HEATING DEG. DAYS	30	902	675	464	176	31	0	0	0	15	137	462	797	3659
	NORMAL COOLING DEG. DAYS	30	0	0	9	38	136	351	527	499	255	44	0	0	1859
RH	NORMAL (PERCENT)	30	67	66	61	61	68	67	61	62	67	64	67	68	65
	HOUR 00 LST	30	72	72	68	69	76	77	70	70	76	72	74	73	72
	HOUR 06 LST	30	77	77	75	76	83	84	80	80	83	79	79	78	79
	HOUR 12 LST	30	58	58	52	51	57	56	49	50	55	52	56	58	54
	HOUR 18 LST	30	58	54	48	48	54	53	46	46	53	54	60	62	53
S	PERCENT POSSIBLE SUNSHINE	39	60	61	65	67	67	75	80	79	73	70	62	59	68
W/O	MEAN NO. DAYS WITH:														
	HEAVY FOG(VISBY ≤ 1/4 MI)	45	3.8	3.2	1.8	1.0	0.7	0.4	0.3	0.4	0.8	1.5	2.1	3.3	19.3
	THUNDERSTORMS	54	0.5	1.4	3.2	5.5	9.1	8.7	6.2	6.4	5.0	3.1	1.3	0.6	51.0
CLOUDINESS	MEAN:														
	SUNRISE-SUNSET (TENTHS)	1		8.0	7.0	6.0	7.0		2.0	4.0	3.0	4.0	4.0	5.0	
	MIDNIGHT-MIDNIGHT (TENTHS)	1		8.0	6.0	6.0	7.0		2.0	3.0	3.0	4.0	5.0	5.0	
	MEAN NO. DAYS WITH:														
	CLEAR	1	3.0	9.0	11.0	9.0	8.0	7.0	15.0	17.0	14.0	14.0	9.0	14.0	130.0
	PARTLY CLOUDY	1	3.0	4.0	4.0	2.0	6.0	6.0	3.0	4.0	6.0	5.0	5.0	7.0	55.0
	CLOUDY	1	13.0	12.0	10.0	8.0	7.0	5.0	2.0	5.0	4.0	5.0	5.0	9.0	85.0
PR	MEAN STATION PRESSURE(IN.)	21	28.74	28.70	28.59	28.58	28.55	28.58	28.63	28.64	28.66	28.69	28.68	28.73	28.65
	MEAN SEA-LEVEL PRES. (IN.)	47	30.14	30.09	29.98	29.94	29.91	29.90	29.96	29.96	29.99	30.04	30.08	30.12	30.01
WINDS	MEAN SPEED (MPH)	30	11.2	12.1	13.5	13.1	11.3	10.6	10.2	9.7	10.1	10.7	11.5	11.4	11.3
	PREVAIL.DIR(TENS OF DEGS.)	30	36	36	17	16	16	17	18	16	17	17	16	36	17
	MAXIMUM 2-MINUTE:														
	SPEED (MPH)	1	39	32	36	40	44	41	39	34	32	38	34	38	44
	DIR. (TENS OF DEGS.)	1	32	31	33	32	21	25	20	24	21	02	36	32	21
	YEAR OF OCCURRENCE		1993	1993	1993	1993	1993	1993	1993	1993	1993	1993	1993	1993	MAY 1993
	MAXIMUM 5-SECOND:														
	SPEED (MPH)	1	43	37	43	47	57	51	47	40	40	44	41	47	57
	DIR. (TENS OF DEGS.)	1	33	19	33	33	22	26	20	25	22	01	36	32	22
	YEAR OF OCCURRENCE		1993	1993	1993	1993	1993	1993	1993	1993	1993	1993	1993	1993	MAY 1993
PRECIPITATION	NORMAL TOTAL (IN.)	30	1.13	1.56	2.71	2.77	5.22	4.31	2.61	2.60	3.84	3.23	1.98	1.40	33.36
	MAXIMUM TOTAL (IN.)	54	5.68	4.63	7.85	10.78	12.07	14.66	8.44	6.77	11.85	13.18	5.46	8.14	14.66
	YEAR OF OCCURRENCE		1949	1990	1988	1947	1982	1989	1959	1966	1991	1983	1964	1984	JUN 1989
	MINIMUM TOTAL (IN.)	54	0.00	T	T	0.17	0.33	0.63	T	0.25	T	T	T	0.03	0.0
	YEAR OF OCCURRENCE		1985	1947	1940	1989	1942	1952	1983	1978	1948	1958	1949	1955	JAN 1985
	MAXIMUM IN 24 HOURS (IN.)	54	3.10	2.21	3.44	3.80	7.56	4.56	5.75	3.56	7.68	8.95	2.21	2.89	8.95
	YEAR OF OCCURRENCE		1982	1978	1944	1970	1993	1989	1981	1989	1970	1983	1986	1991	OCT 1983
	NORMAL NO. DAYS WITH:														
	PRECIPITATION ≥ 0.01	30	5.1	6.1	7.2	7.4	9.6	8.1	6.1	6.7	7.7	6.5	5.7	5.6	81.8
	PRECIPITATION ≥ 1.00	30	0.3	0.3	0.8	0.8	1.5	1.4	0.7	0.9	1.1	0.9	0.6	0.4	9.7
SNOWFALL	NORMAL TOTAL (IN.)	30	2.8	2.7	1.2	0.*	0.0	0.0	0.0	0.0	0.0	0.0	0.6	1.8	9.1
	MAXIMUM TOTAL (IN.)	54	17.3	12.0	13.9	0.7	T	T	0.0	0.0	T	0.1	7.5	8.3	17.3
	YEAR OF OCCURRENCE		1949	1978	1968	1957	1992	1992			1992	1993	1972	1987	JAN 1949
	MAXIMUM IN 24 HOURS (IN.)	54	8.9	6.5	8.4	0.7	T	T	0.0	0.0	T	0.1	5.5	8.3	8.9
	YEAR OF OCCURRENCE		1988	1986	1948	1957	1992	1992	1993	1993	1992	1993	1972	1987	JAN 1988
	MAXIMUM SNOW DEPTH (IN.)	43	12	8	8	T	0	0	0	0	0	T	3	7	12
	YEAR OF OCCURRENCE		1988	1951	1948	1973						1993	1980	1987	JAN 1988
	NORMAL NO. DAYS WITH:														
	SNOWFALL ≥ 1.0	30	0.9	1.1	0.3	0.0	0.0	0.0	0.0	0.0	0.0	0.0	0.2	0.6	3.1

PRECIPITATION (inches) 1993 OKLAHOMA CITY, OKLAHOMA (OKC)

YEAR	JAN	FEB	MAR	APR	MAY	JUN	JUL	AUG	SEP	OCT	NOV	DEC	ANNUAL
1964	0.83	2.17	1.30	2.06	5.21	0.77	2.01	4.91	2.96	0.84	5.46	0.62	29.14
1965	0.98	0.85	0.86	3.24	2.14	3.65	1.57	3.37	3.94	1.00	0.06	2.51	24.17
1966	1.05	2.39	1.30	3.68	0.88	2.63	2.38	6.77	2.82	0.37	0.84	0.45	25.56
1967	0.77	0.20	2.49	5.71	4.25	2.27	1.21	1.40	3.15	2.92	0.40	1.04	25.81
1968	2.19	1.02	2.84	3.03	8.40	2.39	1.41	3.75	2.64	2.40	4.11	1.33	35.51
1969	0.20	1.93	3.01	1.66	3.99	4.92	1.42	2.38	6.51	1.58	0.06	1.44	29.10
1970	0.32	0.29	2.09	5.33	6.53	2.45	1.30	0.80	9.64	3.29	1.03	0.26	33.33
1971	0.75	1.95	0.07	0.62	2.68	5.15	4.13	2.13	4.25	2.62	0.29	2.79	27.43
1972	0.21	0.43	1.13	3.10	4.03	1.36	3.22	1.82	2.04	7.17	2.28	0.84	27.63
1973	3.39	0.31	6.76	2.32	3.61	6.31	3.38	1.36	8.00	3.05	2.81	0.47	41.77
1974	0.10	2.68	3.12	4.66	5.01	3.36	0.48	4.42	6.24	5.57	2.34	1.47	39.45
1975	1.99	1.90	1.72	1.92	8.76	4.82	7.71	0.60	1.92	0.84	1.77	1.30	35.25
1976	T	0.33	3.09	2.94	4.36	0.88	1.38	1.46	1.53	1.78	0.12	0.19	18.06
1977	0.32	1.40	1.30	2.88	7.97	2.00	4.10	3.08	1.20	2.41	1.59	0.34	28.59
1978	1.26	3.23	1.32	1.65	10.12	4.04	3.75	0.25	0.96	1.02	2.88	0.70	31.18
1979	1.55	0.63	2.73	2.78	7.29	9.94	5.62	3.78	0.72	1.58	1.93	2.57	41.12
1980	1.69	1.29	1.38	2.16	9.00	2.52	0.42	0.60	2.21	0.99	0.51	1.58	24.35
1981	0.19	1.15	2.87	2.97	2.73	7.49	6.45	3.61	1.48	7.70	2.11	0.20	38.95
1982	3.68	0.98	1.63	1.92	12.07	4.06	2.11	1.13	2.86	1.03	2.78	1.94	36.19
1983	2.62	1.71	2.51	2.34	6.88	3.18	T	3.18	0.90	13.18	1.90	0.70	39.10
1984	0.35	1.16	4.70	1.79	1.62	3.48	0.30	2.35	1.01	6.64	2.05	8.14	33.59
1985	0.92	3.71	6.60	5.35	1.49	8.34	1.33	2.63	4.59	5.23	3.73	0.26	44.18
1986	0.00	0.68	1.75	4.42	8.21	3.11	0.38	3.29	9.54	8.00	4.63	1.16	45.17
1987	2.45	4.05	2.33	0.41	11.86	6.50	2.99	1.83	4.58	1.82	1.92	3.75	44.49
1988	1.24	0.41	7.85	3.19	1.07	3.59	1.92	1.60	5.19	2.04	2.45	1.39	31.94
1989	1.17	2.20	2.72	0.17	4.33	14.66	1.91	5.55	4.51	3.26	0.09	0.32	40.89
1990	1.85	4.63	4.43	5.11	5.79	1.25	2.65	3.16	7.35	1.27	1.59	1.46	40.54
1991	0.89	0.03	1.59	2.10	6.39	3.85	1.98	3.24	11.85	3.98	1.94	5.90	43.74
1992	1.15	1.28	1.08	3.64	4.88	6.35	4.01	5.82	2.92	1.13	4.51	3.08	39.85
1993	1.90	3.21	2.82	2.50	10.90	2.65	1.24	1.86	7.05	0.47	1.34	1.27	37.21
POR= 55 YRS	1.21	1.49	2.33	3.05	5.49	4.41	2.67	2.56	3.63	2.92	1.72	1.47	32.95

AVERAGE TEMPERATURE (˚F) 1993 OKLAHOMA CITY, OKLAHOMA (OKC)

YEAR	JAN	FEB	MAR	APR	MAY	JUN	JUL	AUG	SEP	OCT	NOV	DEC	ANNUAL
1964	40.1	38.5	47.1	64.1	70.0	77.4	85.3	80.8	72.3	60.3	49.9	37.9	60.3
1965	38.8	39.5	40.7	65.5	71.3	78.0	84.6	80.6	73.9	62.8	56.3	48.8	61.7
1966	33.8	38.6	52.8	57.8	68.7	77.9	86.4	78.8	70.5	60.9	54.3	37.8	59.9
1967	41.8	41.7	56.4	65.4	66.9	77.4	79.7	79.3	70.9	62.6	49.4	39.8	60.9
1968	36.6	36.4	50.7	58.1	64.7	74.8	79.8	80.0	70.5	62.1	46.2	38.1	58.2
1969	38.8	42.3	42.0	60.4	67.7	75.0	83.9	80.2	73.3	57.6	48.7	40.4	59.2
1970	31.8	42.7	45.0	60.2	69.2	76.3	82.1	83.6	75.1	57.9	46.0	43.9	59.5
1971	36.9	39.1	49.1	60.4	67.3	78.6	80.7	77.2	73.3	63.4	49.0	42.2	59.8
1972	34.9	42.1	53.4	63.2	67.6	79.0	79.8	80.4	75.8	61.1	43.4	34.4	59.6
1973	33.3	39.8	52.5	56.0	66.8	75.2	79.8	79.7	70.6	64.3	53.1	39.3	59.2
1974	35.0	44.4	54.8	60.0	71.5	74.1	82.7	78.5	65.5	63.5	49.3	39.6	59.9
1975	40.3	36.5	46.1	58.7	67.4	75.1	78.0	80.1	68.3	63.4	50.7	41.8	58.9
1976	39.0	52.2	52.4	61.6	63.6	74.8	79.8	81.3	72.6	56.5	43.9	38.8	59.7
1977	29.2	45.9	54.1	62.5	70.0	79.6	83.0	80.7	78.0	62.7	50.9	40.0	61.4
1978	26.3	29.4	49.1	64.5	68.1	77.3	87.0	82.6	79.7	64.7	50.4	36.9	59.7
1979	25.4	31.5	51.2	58.1	65.8	75.2	81.0	80.0	73.1	65.7	46.5	43.3	58.1
1980	38.2	38.2	46.3	56.7	69.0	81.4	88.3	88.0	76.3	61.1	50.3	41.9	61.3
1981	37.7	43.9	51.9	65.6	65.7	78.4	84.2	78.8	74.1	60.1	50.3	39.1	60.8
1982	35.3	37.7	52.7	57.5	68.2	72.2	81.0	84.1	74.5	62.7	48.6	43.2	59.8
1983	38.6	42.6	48.8	54.0	64.6	73.4	81.6	84.0	74.9	62.7	50.4	25.8	58.5
1984	34.0	45.4	46.4	56.5	68.4	78.6	81.6	82.6	71.5	61.6	49.7	43.0	59.9
1985	30.6	37.2	53.0	62.7	70.0	76.0	80.9	81.3	73.1	61.2	46.1	35.1	58.9
1986	43.6	44.8	55.5	62.8	69.0	79.0	85.9	80.0	74.8	61.6	44.8	40.8	61.9
1987	35.1	45.9	50.3	61.8	72.6	77.1	80.1	82.2	72.4	60.0	50.5	40.6	60.7
1988	34.2	40.3	49.5	58.9	70.3	78.4	81.6	82.8	73.5	59.3	51.2	43.9	60.3
1989	42.8	33.1	51.1	63.4	69.4	74.3	79.6	78.3	67.8	63.1	52.2	32.7	59.0
1990	45.9	46.0	52.6	59.2	68.6	82.0	80.7	81.6	77.0	60.9	54.9	37.1	62.2
1991	34.9	49.0	54.3	62.5	72.3	78.0	82.2	81.2	70.9	62.6	45.0	44.1	61.4
1992	42.0	49.9	54.1	61.3	66.5	74.1	81.1	74.8	72.5	62.3	45.9	39.8	60.4
1993	36.5	38.8	48.0	56.2	66.0	76.8	83.6	82.3	69.8	57.1	44.2	42.0	58.4
POR= 55 YRS	36.5	41.4	49.7	60.2	68.4	76.9	81.8	81.2	73.2	62.6	48.9	39.9	60.1

REFERENCE NOTES:

THE TEMPERATURE GRAPH SHOWS NORMAL MAXIMUM AND NORMAL MINIMUM DAILY TEMPERATURES (SOLID CURVES) AND THE ACTUAL DAILY HIGH AND LOW TEMPERATURES (VERTICAL BARS).

H/C INDICATES HEATING AND COOLING DEGREE DAYS.
RH INDICATES RELATIVE HUMIDITY
W/O INDICATES WEATHER AND OBSTRUCTIONS
S INDICATES SUNSHINE.
PR INDICATES PRESSURE.
CLOUDINESS IS THE SUM OF THE CEILOMETER AND SATELLITE DATA NOT TO EXCEED TEN TENTHS.
MAXIMUM SNOW DEPTH IS THE DEPTH MEASURED AT 12 UTC.

GENERAL:
T INDICATES TRACE PRECIPITATION, AN AMOUNT GREATER THAN ZERO BUT LESS THAN THE LOWEST REPORTABLE VALUE.
+ INDICATES THE VALUE ALSO OCCURS ON EARLIER DATES.
BLANK ENTRIES DENOTE MISSING OR UNREPORTED DATA.
NORMALS ARE 30-YEAR AVERAGES (1961 - 1990).
ASOS INDICATES AUTOMATED SURFACE OBSERVING SYSTEM.
PM INDICATES THE LAST DAY OF THE PREVIOUS MONTH.
POR (PERIOD OF RECORD) INDICATES THE NUMBER OF YEARS USED TO COMPUTE THE MEAN. INDIVIDUAL MONTHS WITHIN THE POR MAY BE MISSING.
WHEN THE POR FOR A NORMAL IS LESS THAN 30 YEARS, THE NORMAL IS PROVISIONAL AND IS BASED ON THE NUMBER OF YEARS INDICATED.
0.* OR * INDICATES THE VALUE OR MEAN DAYS WITH IS BETWEEN 0.00 AND 0.05.
CLOUDINESS FOR ASOS STATIONS DIFFERS FROM THE NON-ASOS OBSERVATION TAKEN BY A HUMAN OBSERVER. ASOS STATION CLOUDINESS IS BASED ON TIME-AVERAGED CEILOMETER DATA FOR CLOUDS AT OR BELOW 12,000 FEET AND ON SATELLITE DATA FOR CLOUDS ABOVE 12,000 FEET.
THE NUMBER OF DAYS WITH CLEAR, PARTLY CLOUDY, AND CLOUDY CONDITIONS FOR ASOS STATIONS IS THE SUM OF THE CEILOMETER AND SATELLITE DATA FOR THE SUNRISE TO SUNSET PERIOD.

GENERAL CONTINUED:
CLEAR INDICATES 0 - 3 TENTHS, PARTLY CLOUDY INDICATES 4 - 7 TENTHS, AND CLOUDY INDICATES 8 OR MORE TENTHS. WHEN AT LEAST ONE OF THE ELEMENTS (CEILOMETER OR SATELLITE) IS MISSING, THE DAILY CLOUDINESS IS NOT COMPUTED.
WIND DIRECTION IS RECORDED IN TENS OF DEGREES (2 DIGITS) CLOCKWISE FROM TRUE NORTH. "00" INDICATES CALM. "36" INDICATES TRUE NORTH.
RESULTANT WIND IS THE VECTOR AVERAGE OF THE SPEED AND DIRECTION.
AVERAGE TEMPERATURE IS THE SUM OF THE MEAN DAILY MAXIMUM AND MINIMUM TEMPERATURE DIVIDED BY 2.
SNOWFALL DATA COMPRISE ALL FORMS OF FROZEN PRECIPITATION, INCLUDING HAIL.
A HEATING (COOLING) DEGREE DAY IS THE DIFFERENCE BETWEEN THE AVERAGE DAILY TEMPERATURE AND 65˚ F.
DRY BULB IS THE TEMPERATURE OF THE AMBIENT AIR.
DEW POINT IS THE TEMPERATURE TO WHICH THE AIR MUST BE COOLED TO ACHIEVE 100 PERCENT RELATIVE HUMIDITY.
WET BULB IS THE TEMPERATURE THE AIR WOULD HAVE IF THE MOISTURE CONTENT WAS INCREASED TO 100 PERCENT RELATIVE HUMIDITY.

HEATING DEGREE DAYS (base 65°F) 1993 OKLAHOMA CITY, OKLAHOMA (OKC)

YEAR	JUL	AUG	SEP	OCT	NOV	DEC	JAN	FEB	MAR	APR	MAY	JUN	TOTAL
1964-65	0	0	24	150	454	831	808	706	745	71	2	0	3791
1965-66	0	0	28	129	262	496	961	734	388	223	62	0	3283
1966-67	0	0	6	166	338	837	713	647	307	71	77	0	3162
1967-68	0	0	27	155	464	773	872	826	444	215	71	0	3847
1968-69	0	0	0	152	561	829	808	629	708	158	38	2	3885
1969-70	0	0	0	274	481	752	1022	620	615	187	31	12	3994
1970-71	0	0	18	254	559	651	866	718	492	163	36	0	3757
1971-72	0	0	59	88	475	702	923	660	365	144	46	0	3462
1972-73	0	0	23	225	640	940	975	701	380	283	55	0	4222
1973-74	0	0	37	99	362	787	922	573	330	168	8	0	3286
1974-75	0	0	56	88	463	784	763	792	583	235	29	0	3793
1975-76	0	0	64	126	430	713	801	367	406	128	100	0	3135
1976-77	0	0	19	306	629	805	1103	529	338	107	7	0	3843
1977-78	0	0	0	115	420	766	1192	990	493	90	64	0	4130
1978-79	0	0	2	89	437	866	1221	932	434	217	81	0	4279
1979-80	0	0	2	92	551	669	823	771	572	249	24	0	3753
1980-81	0	0	23	180	444	710	839	587	400	69	69	0	3321
1981-82	0	0	22	189	434	797	913	759	382	248	25	13	3782
1982-83	0	0	14	156	490	671	809	622	496	345	96	9	3708
1983-84	0	0	25	117	439	1207	955	561	572	263	45	0	4184
1984-85	0	0	75	162	462	676	1059	773	377	108	10	0	3702
1985-86	0	0	63	146	562	921	656	562	308	122	17	0	3357
1986-87	0	0	2	137	599	742	918	528	450	177	3	0	3556
1987-88	0	0	1	165	442	748	948	712	473	204	14	0	3707
1988-89	0	0	8	196	408	644	679	887	441	140	38	0	3441
1989-90	0	0	78	135	386	993	583	525	387	202	52	0	3341
1990-91	0	0	9	169	307	860	925	444	339	110	25	0	3188
1991-92	0	0	37	150	594	642	704	430	332	154	59	2	3104
1992-93	0	1	5	115	563	774	878	725	525	265	53	0	3904
1993-	0	1	27	269	619	706							
POR= 50 YRS	0	0	20	146	479	776	879	661	474	185	45	1	3666

COOLING DEGREE DAYS (base 65°F) 1993 OKLAHOMA CITY, OKLAHOMA (OKC)

YEAR	JAN	FEB	MAR	APR	MAY	JUN	JUL	AUG	SEP	OCT	NOV	DEC	ANNUAL
1969	0	0	0	29	128	310	593	477	255	52	0	0	1844
1970	0	0	1	47	169	357	536	582	328	38	0	0	2058
1971	0	0	4	31	117	416	493	388	313	45	3	0	1810
1972	0	2	11	97	133	429	470	483	351	109	0	0	2085
1973	0	0	0	19	119	312	465	462	216	83	11	0	1687
1974	0	0	22	26	217	280	553	426	80	47	0	0	1651
1975	0	0	1	53	108	310	410	476	170	83	4	0	1615
1976	0	1	23	33	62	300	468	512	253	50	0	0	1702
1977	0	1	8	37	170	445	565	491	395	49	2	0	2163
1978	0	0	8	80	165	378	690	553	450	87	7	0	2418
1979	0	0	10	18	112	314	505	471	252	121	2	0	1805
1980	0	0	0	7	155	498	729	721	366	65	11	2	2554
1981	0	4	0	94	98	409	603	435	304	47	0	0	1994
1982	0	0	9	28	130	234	503	598	305	90	3	1	1901
1983	0	0	0	20	91	266	523	599	329	54	8	0	1890
1984	0	0	0	16	159	414	521	551	279	64	5	0	2009
1985	0	0	12	43	172	336	501	512	313	38	0	0	1927
1986	0	2	21	63	147	425	653	473	301	40	0	0	2125
1987	0	0	0	88	242	371	475	543	230	18	12	0	1979
1988	0	0	1	29	186	410	525	558	270	25	1	0	2005
1989	0	0	16	100	179	285	459	419	170	83	8	0	1719
1990	0	0	12	33	169	517	495	522	378	48	13	0	2187
1991	0	0	15	45	257	398	542	507	219	85	1	0	2069
1992	0	0	3	51	114	283	508	312	239	36	0	1	1547
1993	0	0	4	9	89	362	584	545	177	32	0	0	1802
POR= 25 YRS	0	0	6	43	146	362	534	503	276	58	2	0	1930

SNOWFALL (inches) 1993 OKLAHOMA CITY, OKLAHOMA (OKC)

YEAR	JUL	AUG	SEP	OCT	NOV	DEC	JAN	FEB	MAR	APR	MAY	JUN	TOTAL
1964-65	0.0	0.0	0.0	0.0	T	T	2.0	0.9	0.1	0.0	0.0	0.0	3.0
1965-66	0.0	0.0	0.0	0.0	0.0	T	5.8	2.3	0.0	0.0	0.0	0.0	8.1
1966-67	0.0	0.0	0.0	0.0	T	0.6	T	0.1	0.4	0.0	0.0	0.0	1.1
1967-68	0.0	0.0	0.0	T	1.2	1.2	0.4	7.7	13.9	0.0	0.0	0.0	24.4
1968-69	0.0	0.0	0.0	0.0	1.4	1.3	T	1.3	8.2	0.0	0.0	0.0	12.2
1969-70	0.0	0.0	0.0	0.0	0.0	4.2	0.4	T	2.3	T	0.0	0.0	6.9
1970-71	0.0	0.0	0.0	0.0	T	T	T	5.1	0.7	0.0	0.0	0.0	5.8
1971-72	0.0	0.0	0.0	0.0	0.5	5.2	0.8	4.9	0.0	0.0	0.0	0.0	11.4
1972-73	0.0	0.0	0.0	0.0	7.5	1.4	8.3	0.2	T	T	0.0	0.0	17.4
1973-74	0.0	0.0	0.0	0.0	0.0	0.6	0.7	1.0	0.5	0.0	0.0	0.0	2.8
1974-75	0.0	0.0	0.0	0.0	1.0	2.0	0.6	0.9	0.1	0.0	0.0	0.0	4.6
1975-76	0.0	0.0	0.0	0.0	0.7	3.9	T	0.3	0.0	0.0	0.0	0.0	4.9
1976-77	0.0	0.0	0.0	0.0	0.3	T	2.8	0.4	0.0	0.0	0.0	0.0	3.5
1977-78	0.0	0.0	0.0	0.0	T	0.0	8.4	12.0	T	0.0	0.0	0.0	20.4
1978-79	0.0	0.0	0.0	0.0	0.0	3.3	4.0	6.1	0.0	0.0	0.0	0.0	13.4
1979-80	0.0	0.0	0.0	0.0	T	T	T	1.8	T	0.0	0.0	0.0	1.8
1980-81	0.0	0.0	0.0	0.0	4.0	0.0	T	T	0.0	0.0	0.0	0.0	4.0
1981-82	0.0	0.0	0.0	0.0	0.0	T	1.0	3.9	2.5	0.0	0.0	0.0	7.4
1982-83	0.0	0.0	0.0	0.0	T	T	5.1	4.3	T	0.0	0.0	0.0	9.4
1983-84	0.0	0.0	0.0	0.0	T	1.9	5.6	2.0	T	0.0	0.0	0.0	9.5
1984-85	0.0	0.0	0.0	0.0	T	6.1	1.5	2.3	0.0	0.0	0.0	0.0	9.9
1985-86	0.0	0.0	0.0	0.0	T	2.9	0.0	10.9	0.0	0.0	0.0	0.0	13.8
1986-87	0.0	0.0	0.0	0.0	0.0	T	10.0	1.0	T	0.0	0.0	0.0	11.0
1987-88	0.0	0.0	0.0	0.0	2.0	8.3	12.1	0.2	0.9	0.0	0.0	0.0	23.5
1988-89	0.0	0.0	0.0	0.0	0.6	2.0	4.8	T	4.0	0.6	T	0.0	12.0
1989-90	0.0	0.0	0.0	0.0	T	1.7	0.0	1.7	0.1	0.0	0.0	0.0	3.5
1990-91	0.0	0.0	0.0	0.0	0.0	4.2	T	0.0	T	0.0	0.0	0.0	4.2
1991-92	0.0	0.0	0.0	T	2.1	1.0	5.0	0.0	T	0.0	T	T	8.1
1992-93	0.0	0.0	T		T	3.3	0.4	1.8	T	T		0.0	
1993-	0.0	0.0	0.0	0.1	0.0	T							
POR= 52 YRS	0.0	0.0	T	T	0.5	1.8	3.0	2.4	1.2	T	T	T	8.9

1993 TULSA, OKLAHOMA (TUL)

The city of Tulsa lies along the Arkansas River at an elevation of 700 feet above sea level. The surrounding terrain is gently rolling.

At latitude 36 degrees, Tulsa is far enough north to escape the long periods of heat in summer, yet far enough south to miss the extreme cold of winter. The influence of warm moist air from the Gulf of Mexico is often noted, due to the high humidity, but the climate is essentially continental characterized by rapid changes in temperature. Generally the winter months are mild. Temperatures occasionally fall below zero but only last a very short time. Temperatures of 100 degrees or higher are often experienced from late July to early September, but are usually accompanied by low relative humidity and a good southerly breeze. The fall season is long with a great number of pleasant, sunny days and cool, bracing nights.

Rainfall is ample for most agricultural pursuits and is distributed favorably throughout the year. Spring is the wettest season, having an abundance of rain in the form of showers and thunderstorms. The steady rains of fall are a contrast to the spring and summer showers and provide a good supply of moisture and more ideal conditions for the growth of winter grains and pastures. The greatest amounts of snow are received in January and early March. The snow is usually light and only remains on the ground for brief periods.

The average date of the last 32 degree temperature occurrence is late March and the average date of the first 32 degree occurrence is early November. The average growing season is 216 days.

The Tulsa area is occasionally subjected to large hail and violent windstorms which occur mostly during spring and early summer, although occurrences have been noted throughout the year.

Prevailing surface winds are southerly during most of the year. Heavy fogs are infrequent. Sunshine is abundant. The prevalence of good flying weather throughout the year has contributed to the development of Tulsa as an aviation center.

NORMALS, MEANS, AND EXTREMES FOR 1993

TULSA, OK (TUL)

LATITUDE: 36° 11' 54" N LONGTITUDE: 95° 53' 17" W ELEVATION (FT): GRND: 650 BARO: 669 TIME ZONE: CENTRAL (UTC+06) WBAN: 13968

	ELEMENT	POR	JAN	FEB	MAR	APR	MAY	JUN	JUL	AUG	SEP	OCT	NOV	DEC	YEAR
TEMPERATURE °F	NORMAL DAILY MAXIMUM	30	45.4	51.0	62.1	73.0	79.7	87.7	93.7	92.5	83.6	73.8	60.3	48.8	71.0
	MEAN DAILY MAXIMUM	58	46.6	52.0	61.2	73.3	80.6	87.6	93.3	92.7	84.7	74.7	60.1	50.9	71.5
	HIGHEST DAILY MAXIMUM	55	79	86	96	102	96	103	112	110	109	98	87	80	112
	YEAR OF OCCURRENCE		1950	1962	1974	1972	1985	1953	1954	1970	1939	1979	1945	1966	JUL 1954
	MEAN OF EXTREME MAXS.	46	68.7	74.4	83.2	88.3	90.6	96.4	101.9	102.0	96.5	87.6	78.9	71.0	86.6
	NORMAL DAILY MINIMUM	30	24.9	29.5	39.1	49.9	58.8	67.7	72.8	70.6	63.0	50.7	39.5	28.9	49.6
	MEAN DAILY MINIMUM	58	26.3	30.4	38.4	50.6	59.6	67.5	72.1	70.4	62.3	50.7	38.3	30.5	49.8
	LOWEST DAILY MINIMUM	55	-8	-7	-3	22	35	49	51	52	35	18	10	-8	-8
	YEAR OF OCCURRENCE		1947	1979	1948	1957	1961	1954	1971	1988	1984	1993	1976	1989	DEC 1989
	MEAN OF EXTREME MINS.	46	6.4	11.9	20.1	33.4	44.2	55.7	62.3	59.3	46.3	33.3	21.7	11.0	33.8
	NORMAL DRY BULB	30	35.2	40.3	50.6	61.5	69.3	77.7	83.3	81.5	73.3	62.2	49.9	38.9	60.3
	MEAN DRY BULB	58	36.5	41.2	49.8	62.0	70.1	77.6	82.7	81.6	73.5	62.7	49.2	40.7	60.6
	MEAN WET BULB	44	31.6	35.7	43.0	52.7	62.0	69.7	72.6	71.2	65.0	54.6	43.4	35.0	53.0
	MEAN DEW POINT	44	24.8	28.6	35.1	45.6	57.5	65.8	68.2	66.6	60.3	48.6	36.5	28.3	47.2
	NORMAL NO. DAYS WITH:														
	MAXIMUM ≥ 90°	30	0.0	0.0	0.3	0.8	2.1	13.3	24.0	22.0	9.4	1.6	0.0	0.0	73.5
	MAXIMUM ≤ 32°	30	5.8	2.6	0.3	0.0	0.0	0.0	0.0	0.0	0.0	0.0	0.2	3.1	12.0
	MINIMUM ≤ 32°	30	23.9	17.2	8.5	0.5	0.0	0.0	0.0	0.0	0.0	0.3	7.6	20.1	78.1
	MINIMUM ≤ 0°	30	0.6	0.1	0.0	0.0	0.0	0.0	0.0	0.0	0.0	0.0	0.0	0.4	1.1
H/C	NORMAL HEATING DEG. DAYS	30	924	692	457	151	41	0	0	0	20	144	453	809	3691
	NORMAL COOLING DEG. DAYS	30	0	0	11	46	174	381	567	512	269	57	0	0	2017
RH	NORMAL (PERCENT)	30	67	65	62	61	69	69	64	64	70	66	67	68	66
	HOUR 00 LST	30	72	70	68	68	78	78	72	73	79	75	74	73	73
	HOUR 06 LST	30	78	77	76	78	85	86	82	84	86	82	80	79	81
	HOUR 12 LST	30	59	57	53	51	58	58	53	53	58	53	57	60	56
	HOUR 18 LST	30	58	55	49	48	56	56	49	50	57	55	59	61	54
S	PERCENT POSSIBLE SUNSHINE	51	54	55	58	59	59	68	75	74	67	65	56	53	61
W/O	MEAN NO. DAYS WITH:														
	HEAVY FOG(VISBY ≤ 1/4 MI)	55	2.0	1.6	0.9	0.2	0.4	0.3	0.2	0.1	0.6	1.1	1.2	1.6	10.2
	THUNDERSTORMS	55	0.7	1.3	3.3	6.0	8.8	8.2	5.6	6.0	5.2	3.1	1.5	0.8	50.5
CLOUDINESS	MEAN:														
	SUNRISE-SUNSET (TENTHS)	1		8.0	8.0	8.0	8.0		4.0	4.0	5.0	6.0	6.0	5.0	
	MIDNIGHT-MIDNIGHT (TENTHS)	1		8.0	8.0	8.0	8.0		3.0	4.0	5.0	5.0	6.0	6.0	
	MEAN NO. DAYS WITH:														
	CLEAR	1	5.0	9.0	8.0	8.0	6.0	3.0	13.0	16.0	14.0	11.0	9.0	14.0	116.0
	PARTLY CLOUDY	1	1.0	4.0	2.0	1.0	3.0	10.0	5.0	5.0	5.0	3.0	2.0	7.0	48.0
	CLOUDY	1	13.0	11.0	14.0	11.0	10.0	6.0	3.0	7.0	6.0	8.0	9.0	8.0	106.0
PR	MEAN STATION PRESSURE(IN.)	21	29.43	29.38	29.25	29.23	29.20	29.22	29.26	29.28	29.31	29.34	29.34	29.41	29.30
	MEAN SEA-LEVEL PRES. (IN.)	44	30.15	30.10	30.00	29.94	29.92	29.92	29.96	29.97	30.00	30.05	30.08	30.12	30.02
WINDS	MEAN SPEED (MPH)	30	9.6	10.3	11.6	11.5	10.2	9.8	9.4	8.9	8.9	9.2	10.0	9.8	9.9
	PREVAIL.DIR(TENS OF DEGS.)	30	18	18	18	18	18	18	18	18	18	18	18	18	18
	MAXIMUM 2-MINUTE:														
	SPEED (MPH)	1	31	36	32	55	37	48	51	31	34	30	31	31	55
	DIR. (TENS OF DEGS.)	1	35	24	27	34	31	14	19	33	36	01	36	19	34
	YEAR OF OCCURRENCE		1993	1993	1993	1993	1993	1993	1993	1993	1993	1993	1993	1993	APR 1993
	MAXIMUM 5-SECOND:														
	SPEED (MPH)	1	34	46	44	63	44	55	55	36	40	37	39	41	63
	DIR. (TENS OF DEGS.)	1	35	25	27	34	30	25	19	33	35	02	36	32	34
	YEAR OF OCCURRENCE		1993	1993	1993	1993	1993	1993	1993	1993	1993	1993	1993	1993	APR 1993
PRECIPITATION	NORMAL TOTAL (IN.)	30	1.54	1.97	3.46	3.72	5.60	4.44	3.09	3.12	4.70	3.66	3.13	2.16	40.59
	MAXIMUM TOTAL (IN.)	55	6.65	5.73	11.94	9.23	18.00	11.17	10.88	7.47	18.81	16.51	7.57	8.70	18.81
	YEAR OF OCCURRENCE		1949	1985	1973	1947	1943	1948	1961	1942	1971	1941	1946	1984	SEP 1971
	MINIMUM TOTAL (IN.)	55	0.00	0.38	0.08	0.34	1.17	0.53	0.03	0.21	T	T	0.01	0.16	0.0
	YEAR OF OCCURRENCE		1993	1991	1971	1989	1988	1963	1954	1945	1948	1952	1949	1950	JAN 1993
	MAXIMUM IN 24 HOURS (IN.)	55	2.25	4.34	2.67	4.58	9.27	5.01	7.54	5.37	6.39	5.80	5.14	3.27	9.27
	YEAR OF OCCURRENCE		1946	1985	1969	1964	1984	1941	1963	1989	1940	1983	1974	1984	MAY 1984
	NORMAL NO. DAYS WITH:														
	PRECIPITATION ≥ 0.01	30	6.1	6.7	8.4	8.8	10.1	8.5	5.9	6.8	8.0	6.5	6.5	6.7	89.0
	PRECIPITATION ≥ 1.00	30	0.2	0.4	1.1	1.0	1.6	1.3	0.9	1.1	1.5	1.3	1.0	0.6	12.0
SNOWFALL	NORMAL TOTAL (IN.)	30	2.8	2.5	1.5	0.*	0.0	0.0	0.0	0.0	0.0	0.0	0.4	1.9	9.1
	MAXIMUM TOTAL (IN.)	55	12.7	10.1	11.8	1.7	T	0.0	0.0	0.0	T	0.3	5.6	9.9	12.7
	YEAR OF OCCURRENCE		1979	1960	1968	1957	1991				1990	1993	1972	1958	JAN 1979
	MAXIMUM IN 24 HOURS (IN.)	55	9.0	6.5	9.8	1.7	T	0.0	0.0	0.0	T	0.3	4.0	8.8	9.8
	YEAR OF OCCURRENCE		1944	1993	1968	1957	1991	1993	1993	1993	1990	1993	1972	1954	MAR 1968
	MAXIMUM SNOW DEPTH (IN.)	44	11	6	10	T	0	0	0	0	0	0	2	8	11
	YEAR OF OCCURRENCE		1988	1949	1968	1993							1971	1954	JAN 1988
	NORMAL NO. DAYS WITH:														
	SNOWFALL ≥ 1.0	30	1.0	0.9	0.3	0.0	0.0	0.0	0.0	0.0	0.0	0.0	0.2	0.8	3.2

PRECIPITATION (inches) 1993 TULSA, OKLAHOMA (TUL)

YEAR	JAN	FEB	MAR	APR	MAY	JUN	JUL	AUG	SEP	OCT	NOV	DEC	ANNUAL
1964	0.63	2.17	3.96	5.87	4.77	5.79	1.80	6.14	3.33	1.24	6.90	1.67	44.27
1965	1.56	1.45	0.73	3.00	3.91	3.76	3.39	3.72	4.59	0.26	0.03	4.29	30.69
1966	0.69	2.35	0.86	4.84	1.86	2.56	2.00	4.59	2.68	1.39	0.51	2.53	26.86
1967	1.51	0.65	1.42	5.09	5.34	4.60	6.88	0.57	4.89	3.75	1.09	1.12	36.91
1968	3.26	1.08	3.49	4.40	3.56	4.08	1.37	1.90	2.80	2.64	5.19	2.01	35.78
1969	1.63	1.34	3.25	1.56	1.98	6.40	1.08	3.24	1.67	5.86	0.32	1.62	29.95
1970	0.41	0.57	2.05	5.66	4.20	4.60	0.13	1.85	6.73	5.83	0.84	1.15	34.02
1971	1.37	4.18	0.08	1.37	6.59	3.27	3.34	1.86	18.81	7.99	1.21	6.34	56.41
1972	0.17	0.49	0.91	4.45	2.43	2.69	2.68	5.16	2.95	7.58	5.00	1.03	35.54
1973	3.39	0.74	11.94	7.22	5.30	7.69	6.47	4.70	6.56	6.16	6.32	3.39	69.88
1974	0.79	3.17	2.62	3.65	6.94	7.88	0.55	5.30	11.78	6.40	7.30	2.88	59.26
1975	2.61	3.44	5.45	2.20	7.22	6.75	2.14	3.52	3.34	1.47	3.53	3.04	44.71
1976	0.21	0.84	3.95	8.27	6.75	1.87	4.37	1.17	2.60	2.65	0.68	0.55	33.91
1977	1.43	1.57	5.58	2.05	5.72	6.69	2.00	4.86	5.57	2.75	2.31	0.93	41.46
1978	0.81	2.84	2.99	7.14	9.28	6.06	0.36	1.37	0.13	0.95	5.48	0.78	38.19
1979	2.07	0.81	3.97	4.47	6.15	8.90	2.68	4.77	0.28	2.20	5.60	0.45	42.35
1980	2.07	1.32	3.59	3.44	7.23	5.57	0.09	2.34	3.47	2.05	0.79	1.37	33.33
1981	0.69	1.63	1.67	1.90	6.70	3.31	6.22	2.47	3.11	6.73	2.25	0.20	36.88
1982	3.58	0.67	1.04	1.28	9.30	4.13	1.65	1.42	2.95	1.22	4.61	3.39	35.24
1983	2.95	1.98	2.19	3.88	6.85	1.47	0.58	0.65	2.11	9.33	2.14	0.61	34.74
1984	1.00	1.95	6.72	2.44	11.25	1.72	0.48	1.96	2.77	6.98	2.80	8.70	48.77
1985	1.24	5.74	5.39	5.62	4.19	7.63	2.38	1.91	3.29	6.26	6.27	1.39	51.31
1986	0.00	1.22	2.28	5.10	6.97	4.23	1.15	3.96	8.36	5.53	2.99	0.97	42.76
1987	2.21	4.72	2.20	0.70	10.02	2.31	4.20	3.72	3.52	1.27	5.17	5.87	45.91
1988	1.11	1.03	6.52	3.18	1.17	0.58	4.20	2.43	5.37	1.43	4.38	1.82	33.22
1989	2.94	2.26	3.14	0.34	3.95	5.16	4.09	6.69	3.32	2.80	0.15	0.26	35.10
1990	2.93	4.14	6.51	5.31	5.21	1.08	0.24	1.83	4.19	2.15	2.41	2.94	38.94
1991	1.47	0.38	1.02	2.58	5.11	3.64	0.35	1.17	6.15	5.12	1.98	4.57	33.54
1992	0.48	1.32	1.37	4.75	5.65	8.41	2.12	3.09	2.66	3.53	4.83	5.21	43.42
1993	0.00	2.86	2.76	4.59	6.86	3.79	2.42	2.29	6.90	1.13	1.69	1.76	37.05
POR= 57 YRS	1.59	1.85	2.83	3.96	5.53	4.61	3.06	3.04	4.18	3.47	2.55	2.01	38.67

AVERAGE TEMPERATURE (°F) 1993 TULSA, OKLAHOMA (TUL)

YEAR	JAN	FEB	MAR	APR	MAY	JUN	JUL	AUG	SEP	OCT	NOV	DEC	ANNUAL
1964	40.9	39.4	46.9	65.7	71.7	78.2	84.9	80.7	73.0	60.1	52.7	39.1	61.1
1965	39.8	39.4	40.5	66.2	72.6	78.1	83.2	81.7	75.3	63.3	55.7	46.8	61.9
1966	32.8	39.0	52.7	57.9	67.6	77.3	87.3	78.5	70.3	59.5	53.4	37.2	59.5
1967	39.6	38.9	55.1	64.3	65.2	76.5	77.5	76.0	69.2	61.2	48.2	39.7	59.3
1968	36.0	37.0	49.8	59.3	65.5	76.8	80.6	80.9	71.9	62.2	46.7	36.8	58.6
1969	36.9	41.4	42.7	61.6	69.9	75.0	85.9	80.8	74.9	59.5	48.1	39.3	59.7
1970	29.7	41.9	44.6	60.7	70.7	76.9	82.8	84.8	74.5	58.9	45.6	42.5	59.5
1971	36.5	39.0	49.9	60.2	66.7	79.4	80.0	79.0	73.0	65.0	50.1	43.7	60.2
1972	34.8	41.8	53.0	62.8	68.0	79.5	80.4	81.7	75.5	60.9	43.6	33.7	59.6
1973	34.0	39.8	54.3	58.2	67.5	76.7	81.2	79.3	72.3	65.0	53.4	38.1	60.0
1974	34.1	43.7	55.2	61.8	72.1	73.8	85.4	78.3	64.7	63.0	49.1	39.7	60.1
1975	39.9	36.9	45.3	60.4	69.1	76.0	81.2	82.2	69.2	63.2	50.8	40.1	59.5
1976	37.2	51.1	51.9	61.5	63.0	75.0	81.4	79.7	72.8	56.1	43.1	37.1	59.2
1977	26.9	46.6	55.0	64.4	72.6	81.0	84.8	81.7	75.6	62.2	51.1	39.0	61.7
1978	24.9	29.4	47.5	63.5	68.3	77.6	87.8	84.3	80.6	63.5	51.6	38.0	59.7
1979	23.1	30.2	52.4	61.0	68.7	77.8	83.4	81.8	74.7	66.2	47.5	44.4	59.3
1980	38.6	37.1	48.3	61.1	70.6	82.5	91.7	89.7	78.3	61.5	50.5	42.3	62.7
1981	37.6	43.6	53.3	68.0	65.9	80.0	85.9	79.4	73.9	60.9	51.4	38.5	61.5
1982	33.6	38.2	55.3	59.3	72.9	74.7	84.2	85.3	74.6	63.4	50.6	44.4	61.4
1983	39.1	42.9	49.0	55.4	67.0	76.6	84.7	88.1	77.4	64.5	52.9	26.7	60.4
1984	34.4	46.4	48.3	58.0	67.5	80.1	82.0	82.7	71.5	63.8	50.4	44.7	60.8
1985	30.2	35.9	54.7	63.3	70.6	75.8	82.9	81.7	74.6	63.1	47.8	34.5	59.6
1986	42.8	43.2	55.0	62.6	69.4	79.7	86.6	78.2	74.7	61.0	43.6	40.0	61.4
1987	36.0	45.4	51.5	63.2	74.1	78.9	81.9	83.1	72.4	59.3	51.6	41.4	61.6
1988	34.8	39.3	49.3	59.5	71.0	79.9	82.6	83.0	73.2	58.5	51.7	43.4	60.5
1989	43.4	31.9	49.3	63.3	69.2	74.8	80.2	80.4	68.7	64.0	52.7	31.6	59.1
1990	46.1	46.1	53.2	59.6	67.4	82.1	83.2	83.5	78.3	61.2	56.4	38.5	63.0
1991	34.7	48.3	55.1	63.8	73.7	80.0	84.9	82.9	72.7	64.3	45.8	44.6	62.6
1992	42.8	50.1	54.9	61.6	67.6	74.7	81.8	76.6	72.8	60.8	45.9	38.6	60.7
1993	35.7	37.8	46.8	55.8	66.0	76.8	84.4	83.5	68.6	56.2	44.5	42.3	58.2
POR= 58 YRS	36.5	41.2	49.8	60.9	68.9	77.6	82.7	81.5	73.5	62.7	49.2	40.0	60.4

REFERENCE NOTES:

THE TEMPERATURE GRAPH SHOWS NORMAL MAXIMUM AND NORMAL MINIMUM DAILY TEMPERATURES (SOLID CURVES) AND THE ACTUAL DAILY HIGH AND LOW TEMPERATURES (VERTICAL BARS).

H/C INDICATES HEATING AND COOLING DEGREE DAYS.
RH INDICATES RELATIVE HUMIDITY
W/O INDICATES WEATHER AND OBSTRUCTIONS
S INDICATES SUNSHINE.
PR INDICATES PRESSURE.
CLOUDINESS IS THE SUM OF THE CEILOMETER AND SATELLITE DATA NOT TO EXCEED TEN TENTHS.
MAXIMUM SNOW DEPTH IS THE DEPTH MEASURED AT 12 UTC.

GENERAL:
T INDICATES TRACE PRECIPITATION, AN AMOUNT GREATER THAN ZERO BUT LESS THAN THE LOWEST REPORTABLE VALUE.
+ INDICATES THE VALUE ALSO OCCURS ON EARLIER DATES.
BLANK ENTRIES DENOTE MISSING OR UNREPORTED DATA.
NORMALS ARE 30-YEAR AVERAGES (1961 - 1990).
ASOS INDICATES AUTOMATED SURFACE OBSERVING SYSTEM.
PM INDICATES THE LAST DAY OF THE PREVIOUS MONTH.
POR (PERIOD OF RECORD) INDICATES THE NUMBER OF YEARS USED TO COMPUTE THE MEAN. INDIVIDUAL MONTHS WITHIN THE POR MAY BE MISSING.
WHEN THE POR FOR A NORMAL IS LESS THAN 30 YEARS, THE NORMAL IS PROVISIONAL AND IS BASED ON THE NUMBER OF YEARS INDICATED.
0.* OR * INDICATES THE VALUE OR MEAN DAYS WITH IS BETWEEN 0.00 AND 0.05.
CLOUDINESS FOR ASOS STATIONS DIFFERS FROM THE NON-ASOS OBSERVATION TAKEN BY A HUMAN OBSERVER. ASOS STATION CLOUDINESS IS BASED ON TIME-AVERAGED CEILOMETER DATA FOR CLOUDS AT OR BELOW 12,000 FEET AND ON SATELLITE DATA FOR CLOUDS ABOVE 12,000 FEET.
THE NUMBER OF DAYS WITH CLEAR, PARTLY CLOUDY, AND CLOUDY CONDITIONS FOR ASOS STATIONS IS THE SUM OF THE CEILOMETER AND SATELLITE DATA FOR THE SUNRISE TO SUNSET PERIOD.

GENERAL CONTINUED:
CLEAR INDICATES 0 - 3 TENTHS, PARTLY CLOUDY INDICATES 4 - 7 TENTHS, AND CLOUDY INDICATES 8 OR MORE TENTHS. WHEN AT LEAST ONE OF THE ELEMENTS (CEILOMETER OR SATELLITE) IS MISSING, THE DAILY CLOUDINESS IS NOT COMPUTED.
WIND DIRECTION IS RECORDED IN TENS OF DEGREES (2 DIGITS) CLOCKWISE FROM TRUE NORTH. "00" INDICATES CALM. "36" INDICATES TRUE NORTH.
RESULTANT WIND IS THE VECTOR AVERAGE OF THE SPEED AND DIRECTION.
AVERAGE TEMPERATURE IS THE SUM OF THE MEAN DAILY MAXIMUM AND MINIMUM TEMPERATURE DIVIDED BY 2.
SNOWFALL DATA COMPRISE ALL FORMS OF FROZEN PRECIPITATION, INCLUDING HAIL.
A HEATING (COOLING) DEGREE DAY IS THE DIFFERENCE BETWEEN THE AVERAGE DAILY TEMPERATURE AND 65° F.
DRY BULB IS THE TEMPERATURE OF THE AMBIENT AIR.
DEW POINT IS THE TEMPERATURE TO WHICH THE AIR MUST BE COOLED TO ACHIEVE 100 PERCENT RELATIVE HUMIDITY.
WET BULB IS THE TEMPERATURE THE AIR WOULD HAVE IF THE MOISTURE CONTENT WAS INCREASED TO 100 PERCENT RELATIVE HUMIDITY.

HEATING DEGREE DAYS (base 65°F) 1993 TULSA, OKLAHOMA (TUL)

YEAR	JUL	AUG	SEP	OCT	NOV	DEC	JAN	FEB	MAR	APR	MAY	JUN	TOTAL
1964-65	0	0	18	162	385	797	775	711	752	73	1	0	3674
1965-66	0	0	15	122	283	556	992	722	395	227	67	0	3379
1966-67	0	0	13	202	376	859	776	724	362	100	101	0	3513
1967-68	0	0	37	184	498	781	892	803	479	184	67	0	3925
1968-69	0	0	1	160	543	864	863	652	680	127	24	2	3916
1969-70	0	0	0	241	498	789	1088	642	625	174	26	18	4101
1970-71	0	0	18	217	577	692	878	721	463	176	37	0	3779
1971-72	0	0	53	60	446	653	932	670	373	161	47	0	3395
1972-73	0	0	19	183	634	964	954	700	321	233	42	0	4050
1973-74	0	0	24	95	343	824	951	591	341	137	5	0	3311
1974-75	0	0	74	94	473	777	773	780	610	205	19	0	3805
1975-76	0	0	57	146	429	762	855	402	407	126	109	0	3293
1976-77	0	0	16	317	648	858	1173	511	309	99	1	0	3932
1977-78	0	0	1	118	412	801	1236	989	541	110	67	0	4275
1978-79	0	0	0	121	406	834	1293	972	391	164	47	0	4228
1979-80	0	0	0	90	525	632	812	801	513	154	22	0	3549
1980-81	0	0	13	172	438	703	843	598	360	48	58	0	3233
1981-82	0	0	23	178	402	817	967	747	322	208	11	5	3680
1982-83	0	0	23	146	437	635	794	611	492	321	50	0	3509
1983-84	0	0	19	89	378	1179	941	533	509	229	47	0	3924
1984-85	0	0	73	130	438	628	1073	809	330	103	7	0	3591
1985-86	0	0	46	111	510	936	680	602	322	127	13	0	3347
1986-87	0	0	5	148	632	771	893	544	413	149	0	0	3555
1987-88	0	0	1	189	416	727	928	739	483	187	9	0	3679
1988-89	0	0	8	218	393	662	663	921	487	155	53	0	3560
1989-90	0	0	67	126	375	1029	580	527	376	194	54	0	3328
1990-91	0	0	8	172	271	813	933	459	327	83	17	0	3083
1991-92	0	0	35	121	570	628	682	423	311	156	53	0	2979
1992-93	0	0	9	151	565	812	903	755	556	280	57	0	4088
1993-	0	0	40	294	611	695							
POR= 57 YRS	0	0	19	141	471	761	879	666	473	169	40	0	3619

COOLING DEGREE DAYS (base 65°F) 1993 TULSA, OKLAHOMA (TUL)

YEAR	JAN	FEB	MAR	APR	MAY	JUN	JUL	AUG	SEP	OCT	NOV	DEC	ANNUAL
1969	0	0	0	29	185	312	656	496	307	77	0	0	2062
1970	0	0	0	50	209	382	555	619	307	39	0	0	2161
1971	0	0	3	40	97	442	471	444	298	65	7	0	1867
1972	0	6	11	99	144	446	487	524	339	64	0	0	2120
1973	0	0	0	35	124	357	508	452	249	101	5	0	1831
1974	0	0	47	48	232	270	641	419	71	40	2	0	1770
1975	0	0	9	77	156	335	509	542	192	97	12	0	1929
1976	0	6	7	28	52	307	520	461	256	48	0	0	1685
1977	0	1	6	84	248	486	619	525	327	38	0	0	2334
1978	0	0	7	73	180	388	713	605	476	79	14	0	2535
1979	0	0	9	48	167	388	577	527	298	137	6	0	2157
1980	0	0	0	43	200	533	833	774	419	69	6	4	2881
1981	0	5	4	145	96	456	658	452	296	57	1	0	2170
1982	0	0	28	44	266	300	601	637	319	106	10	5	2316
1983	0	0	3	40	120	353	615	725	396	80	20	0	2352
1984	0	0	0	25	132	464	534	556	272	100	9	2	2094
1985	0	0	19	59	185	333	564	523	340	57	0	0	2080
1986	0	0	20	60	157	448	676	415	303	31	0	0	2110
1987	0	0	2	102	290	421	532	567	230	18	19	0	2181
1988	0	0	2	30	200	454	555	564	262	23	1	0	2091
1989	0	0	6	107	191	300	475	483	183	105	14	0	1864
1990	0	0	17	38	137	521	571	581	416	63	21	0	2365
1991	0	0	29	53	293	458	622	562	274	108	3	0	2402
1992	0	0	5	63	140	298	526	369	251	29	0	0	1681
1993	0	0	1	7	95	360	609	579	153	27	0	0	1831
POR= 25 YRS	0	0	8	56	171	391	585	535	289	65	5	0	2105

SNOWFALL (inches) 1993 TULSA, OKLAHOMA (TUL)

YEAR	JUL	AUG	SEP	OCT	NOV	DEC	JAN	FEB	MAR	APR	MAY	JUN	TOTAL
1964-65	0.0	0.0	0.0	0.0	0.0	T	0.3	1.5	0.6	0.0	0.0	0.0	2.4
1965-66	0.0	0.0	0.0	0.0	0.0	T	4.3	5.1	T	0.0	0.0	0.0	9.4
1966-67	0.0	0.0	0.0	0.0	T	3.1	0.7	0.9	1.1	0.0	0.0	0.0	5.8
1967-68	0.0	0.0	0.0	T	0.9	1.6	0.6	2.1	11.8	0.0	0.0	0.0	17.0
1968-69	0.0	0.0	0.0	0.0	T	1.4	T	5.3	1.3	0.0	0.0	0.0	8.0
1969-70	0.0	0.0	0.0	0.0	0.0	5.8	4.7	T	9.9	T	0.0	0.0	20.4
1970-71	0.0	0.0	0.0	0.0	T	0.0	T	6.5	T	0.0	0.0	0.0	6.5
1971-72	0.0	0.0	0.0	0.0	2.0	1.0	0.8	4.9	T	0.0	0.0	0.0	8.7
1972-73	0.0	0.0	0.0	0.0	5.6	1.7	4.3	2.2	0.0	0.3	0.0	0.0	14.1
1973-74	0.0	0.0	0.0	0.0	T	1.8	T	T	T	T	0.0	0.0	1.8
1974-75	0.0	0.0	0.0	0.0	1.7	T	T	3.0	1.8	T	0.0	0.0	6.5
1975-76	0.0	0.0	0.0	0.0	0.8	1.3	T	T	T	0.0	0.0	0.0	2.1
1976-77	0.0	0.0	0.0	0.0	0.5	T	10.5	0.3	0.0	0.0	0.0	0.0	11.3
1977-78	0.0	0.0	0.0	0.0	T	0.0	5.4	6.3	T	0.0	0.0	0.0	11.7
1978-79	0.0	0.0	0.0	0.0	0.0	2.8	12.7	3.4	0.0	T	0.0	0.0	18.9
1979-80	0.0	0.0	0.0	0.0	T	0.0	0.4	3.8	T	0.0	0.0	0.0	4.2
1980-81	0.0	0.0	0.0	0.0	T	0.0	T	0.9	T	0.0	0.0	0.0	.9
1981-82	0.0	0.0	0.0	0.0	0.0	T	0.3	5.6	T	0.0	0.0	0.0	5.9
1982-83	0.0	0.0	0.0	0.0	T	T	3.8	1.4	T	0.0	0.0	0.0	5.2
1983-84	0.0	0.0	0.0	0.0	T	3.0	4.6	0.2	T	0.0	0.0	0.0	7.8
1984-85	0.0	0.0	0.0	0.0	0.0	6.6	3.3	4.3	0.0	0.0	0.0	0.0	14.2
1985-86	0.0	0.0	0.0	0.0	T	2.5	0.0	4.9	0.0	0.0	0.0	0.0	7.4
1986-87	0.0	0.0	0.0	0.0	0.0	0.0	8.7	4.6	0.0	0.0	0.0	0.0	13.3
1987-88	0.0	0.0	0.0	0.0	T	6.7	11.0	T	0.5	0.0	0.0	0.0	18.2
1988-89	0.0	0.0	0.0	0.0	0.4	2.7	3.4	0.3	9.7	0.0	0.0	0.0	16.5
1989-90	0.0	0.0	0.0	0.0	0.0	2.0	0.0	0.0	0.2	0.0	0.0	0.0	2.2
1990-91	0.0	0.0	0.0	0.0	0.0	4.6	T	1.4	T	0.0	T	0.0	6.0
1991-92	0.0	0.0	0.0	0.0	0.2	0.1	0.8	0.0	T	T	0.0	0.0	1.1
1992-93	0.0	0.0	0.0		3.5	1.1		6.7	T	T	0.0		
1993-	0.0	0.0	0.0	0.3	0.0	0.0							
POR= 58 YRS	0.0	0.0	0.0	T	0.4	1.6	3.1	2.3	1.4	T	T	0.0	8.8

PENDLETON, OREGON

Pendleton is located in the southeastern part of the Columbia Basin, that low country of northern Oregon and central and eastern Washington which is almost entirely surrounded by mountains. This Basin is bounded on the south by the high country of central Oregon, on the north by the mountains of western Canada, on the west by the Cascade Range and on the east by the Blue Mountains and the north Idaho plateau. The gorge in the Cascades through which the Columbia River reaches the Pacific is the most important break in the barriers surrounding this basin. These physical features have important influences on the general climate of Pendleton and the surrounding territory.

The Weather Service Office at Pendleton Airport is located in rolling country which slopes generally upward toward the Blue Mountains about 15 miles to the east and southeast. The Columbia River approaches the area from the northwest to its junction with the Walla Walla River at an elevation of 351 feet and some 25 miles north of Pendleton, then turns southwestward to be joined a few miles below by the Umatilla River. Both the Walla Walla and Umatilla Rivers have their sources in the Blue Mountains and flow westward to the Columbia. The observation station is at an elevation of nearly 1,500 feet, about 3 miles northwest of downtown Pendleton. The city of Pendleton lies in the shallow east-west valley of the Umatilla River, approximately 400 feet lower than the airport.

Precipitation in the Pendleton area is definitely seasonal in occurrence with an average of only 10 percent of the annual total occurring in the three-month period, July-September. Most precipitation reaching this area accompanies cyclonic storms moving in from the Pacific Ocean. These storms reach their greatest intensity and frequency from October through April. The Cascade Range west of the Columbia Basin reduces the amount of precipitation received from the Pacific cyclonic storms. This influence is felt, particularly, in the desert area of the central part of the Basin. A gradual rise in elevation from the Columbia River to the foothills of the Blue Mountains again results in increased precipitation. This increase supplies sufficient moisture for productive wheat, pea, and stock raising activity in the area surrounding Pendleton.

The lighter summertime precipitation usually accompanies thunderstorms which often move into the area from the south or southwest. On occasion, these storms are quite intense, causing flash flooding with resultant heavy property damage and even loss of life.

Seasonal temperature extremes are usually quite moderate for the latitude. The last occurrence in spring of temperatures as low as 32 degrees is mid-April, and the average last occurrence in the fall of 32 degrees is late October. At the city station, where cool air settles in the valley on still nights, temperatures of 32 degrees have been recorded later in the spring and earlier in the fall. Under usual atmospheric conditions, air from the Pacific, with moderate temperature characteristics, moves across the Cascades or through the Columbia Gorge resulting in mild temperatures in the Pendleton area. When this flow of air from the west is impeded by slow-moving high pressure systems over the interior of the continent, temperature conditions sometimes become rather severe, hot in summer and cold in winter. During the summer or early fall, if a stagnant high predominates to the north or east of Pendleton, the hot, dry conditions may prove detrimental to crops during late May and June, and cause fire danger in the forest and grassland areas during late summer and early fall. During winter, coldest temperatures occur when air from a cold high pressure system in central Canada moves southwestward across the Rockies and flows down into the Columbia Basin. Under this condition the heavy cold air sometimes remains at low levels in the Basin for several days while warmer air from the Pacific flows above it, causing comparatively mild temperatures at higher elevations. Extreme winter temperatures are not particularly common in the Pendleton area. Below zero readings are recorded in approximately 60 percent of winters. Maximum temperatures usually reach 100 degrees or slightly higher on a few days during the summer.

NORMALS, MEANS, AND EXTREMES

PENDLETON, OREGON

LATITUDE: 45°41'N LONGITUDE: 118°51' W ELEVATION: FT. GRND 1482 BARO 1507 TIME ZONE: PACIFIC WBAN: 24155

	(a)	JAN	FEB	MAR	APR	MAY	JUNE	JULY	AUG	SEP	OCT	NOV	DEC	YEAR
TEMPERATURE °F:														
Normals														
-Daily Maximum		39.7	46.9	54.2	61.3	70.0	79.5	87.8	86.2	76.3	63.7	48.9	40.5	62.9
-Daily Minimum		27.2	31.6	35.4	39.4	45.8	52.9	58.0	57.7	49.9	41.0	34.1	27.9	41.7
-Monthly		33.5	39.2	44.8	50.3	57.9	66.2	72.9	72.0	63.1	52.4	41.5	34.3	52.3
Extremes														
-Record Highest	58	68	72	79	91	100	108	110	113	102	92	77	67	113
-Year		1974	1986	1964	1977	1986	1961	1939	1961	1955	1980	1975	1980	AUG 1961
-Record Lowest	58	-22	-18	1	18	25	35	42	40	30	11	-12	-19	-22
-Year		1957	1950	1993	1936	1954	1991	1971	1980	1970	1935	1985	1983	JAN 1957
NORMAL DEGREE DAYS:														
Heating (base 65°F)		977	722	626	441	226	71	15	23	145	391	705	952	5294
Cooling (base 65°F)		0	0	0	0	6	107	260	240	88	0	0	0	701
% OF POSSIBLE SUNSHINE														
MEAN SKY COVER (tenths)														
Sunrise - Sunset	48	8.4	8.0	7.3	6.8	6.1	5.4	3.1	3.5	4.1	5.7	7.8	8.4	6.2
MEAN NUMBER OF DAYS:														
Sunrise to Sunset														
-Clear	58	2.3	2.7	4.8	5.3	7.5	9.7	19.3	18.0	15.2	10.1	3.7	2.6	101.1
-Partly Cloudy	58	5.2	5.6	7.5	9.5	10.8	10.1	7.7	7.9	7.8	7.9	6.4	4.5	90.9
-Cloudy	58	23.5	19.9	18.7	15.3	12.7	10.2	4.1	5.2	7.0	13.0	19.9	23.8	173.2
Precipitation														
.01 inches or more	58	12.2	10.5	10.8	8.9	7.8	6.5	2.8	3.1	4.2	7.1	11.4	12.4	97.8
Snow, Ice pellets, hail														
1.0 inches or more	58	2.7	1.1	0.4	0.1	0.0	0.0	0.0	0.0	0.0	0.1	0.5	1.4	6.1
Thunderstorms	56	0.0	0.*	0.2	0.9	1.8	1.9	1.9	2.0	1.1	0.3	0.1	0.*	10.2
Heavy Fog Visibility														
1/4 mile or less	56	7.4	4.9	1.9	0.3	0.2	0.1	0.0	0.*	0.2	1.0	6.0	8.6	30.7
Temperature °F														
-Maximum														
90° and above	58	0.0	0.0	0.0	0.*	0.9	4.6	14.0	10.6	2.7	0.*	0.0	0.0	32.8
32° and below	58	9.3	2.9	0.3	0.0	0.0	0.0	0.0	0.0	0.0	0.*	2.1	7.4	22.0
-Minimum														
32° and below	58	21.4	15.7	9.5	2.4	0.1	0.0	0.0	0.0	0.1	2.5	12.5	19.5	83.6
0° and below	58	1.6	0.7	0.0	0.0	0.0	0.0	0.0	0.0	0.0	0.0	0.1	0.6	3.0
AVG. STATION PRESS. (mb)	20	966.2	964.6	961.6	962.5	961.7	961.4	961.8	961.4	963.0	964.8	964.7	966.4	963.4
RELATIVE HUMIDITY (%)														
Hour 04	52	80	79	74	71	69	65	54	54	61	72	79	82	70
Hour 10 (Local Time)	54	77	72	59	51	47	42	34	36	42	55	72	78	55
Hour 16	54	75	65	50	42	37	32	23	26	32	46	69	78	48
Hour 22	51	80	77	69	63	58	52	38	41	51	66	78	81	63
PRECIPITATION (inches):														
Water Equivalent														
-Normal		1.51	1.14	1.16	1.04	0.99	0.64	0.35	0.53	0.59	0.86	1.58	1.63	12.02
-Maximum Monthly	58	3.92	3.03	2.82	2.78	3.18	2.70	1.45	2.58	2.34	2.79	3.76	4.68	4.68
-Year		1970	1940	1983	1978	1991	1947	1993	1977	1941	1947	1973	1973	DEC 1973
-Minimum Monthly	58	0.21	0.07	0.24	0.01	0.03	0.03	T	0.00	T	T	0.04	0.21	0.00
-Year		1949	1964	1941	1956	1964	1986	1967	1969	1993	1987	1939	1989	AUG 1969
-Maximum in 24 hrs	58	1.29	1.09	1.33	1.24	1.52	1.49	1.19	2.19	1.23	1.88	1.35	1.25	2.19
-Year		1956	1959	1983	1990	1972	1947	1948	1993	1981	1982	1971	1978	AUG 1993
Snow, Ice pellets, hail														
-Maximum Monthly	58	41.6	15.8	4.9	2.2	T	0.0	T	0.0	0.0	3.2	14.9	26.6	41.6
-Year		1950	1936	1971	1975	1993		1993			1973	1985	1983	JAN 1950
-Maximum in 24 hrs	58	13.3	9.7	4.0	2.2	T	0.0	T	0.0	0.0	3.2	8.0	9.9	13.3
-Year		1950	1949	1970	1975	1993		1993			1973	1977	1948	JAN 1950
WIND:														
Mean Speed (mph)	40	7.8	8.2	9.2	9.9	9.6	9.6	9.0	8.6	8.4	7.6	7.7	7.8	8.6
Prevailing Direction through 1963		SE	SE	W	W	W	W	WNW	SE	SE	SE	SE	SE	SE
Fastest Obs. 1 Min.														
-Direction (!!)	38	23	25	29	27	27	29	28	27	27	25	27	29	27
-Speed (MPH)	38	49	54	63	77	48	62	46	40	47	49	62	63	77
-Year		1990	1955	1956	1960	1959	1956	1968	1961	1954	1959	1959	1959	APR 1960
Peak Gust														
-Direction (!!)	10	SW	SW	SW	SW	W	W	W	W	W	NW	W	W	SW
-Speed (mph)	10	76	52	74	61	60	59	62	55	56	51	58	62	76
-Date		1990	1988	1991	1987	1988	1992	1990	1990	1984	1991	1989	1990	JAN 1990

PRECIPITATION (inches) — PENDLETON, OREGON

YEAR	JAN	FEB	MAR	APR	MAY	JUNE	JULY	AUG	SEP	OCT	NOV	DEC	ANNUAL
1964	1.07	0.07	0.66	0.34	0.03	1.01	0.64	0.21	0.15	0.80	1.93	3.23	10.14
1965	3.08	0.37	0.29	0.65	0.57	1.10	0.51	1.21	0.23	0.19	1.95	0.27	10.42
1966	2.19	0.83	0.96	0.08	0.07	0.55	0.79	0.17	0.43	0.75	2.09	2.65	11.56
1967	1.59	0.15	0.89	1.05	0.56	0.41	T	T	0.40	0.64	0.63	0.45	6.77
1968	0.59	1.82	0.47	0.17	0.66	0.89	0.17	0.61	0.57	1.03	2.06	2.19	11.23
1969	2.88	0.88	0.57	2.05	1.40	0.86	0.02	0.00	0.42	1.13	0.36	1.88	12.45
1970	3.92	1.48	0.99	0.63	0.32	0.57	0.08	0.03	0.78	0.81	1.78	0.80	12.19
1971	0.84	0.69	1.11	1.15	1.41	1.73	0.32	0.14	1.03	0.70	2.73	2.59	14.44
1972	0.96	1.08	1.47	0.68	1.97	0.80	0.58	0.36	0.16	0.58	0.70	2.31	11.65
1973	0.50	1.09	0.43	0.27	0.67	0.15	0.01	0.08	1.34	1.71	3.76	4.68	14.69
1974	0.79	1.57	0.81	2.13	0.26	0.19	0.90	T	T	0.29	1.00	1.59	9.53
1975	3.53	1.30	0.65	0.97	0.30	0.28	0.73	0.67	0.00	1.80	0.84	1.98	13.05
1976	1.77	1.00	1.65	1.09	0.92	0.33	0.16	1.77	0.18	0.54	0.19	0.44	10.04
1977	0.48	0.64	1.51	0.18	1.87	0.37	0.06	2.58	1.17	0.51	2.00	2.42	13.79
1978	2.82	1.60	1.03	2.78	0.63	0.76	0.77	2.21	0.92	T	2.37	1.86	17.75
1979	1.43	1.72	1.18	1.17	0.39	0.21	0.09	1.40	0.30	1.68	1.83	0.62	12.02
1980	2.48	1.39	1.60	0.59	2.14	1.12	0.77	0.03	0.59	1.22	0.84	1.20	13.97
1981	0.89	1.35	1.43	1.20	1.59	1.53	0.94	0.03	1.31	0.86	1.91	2.31	15.35
1982	1.54	0.77	1.22	0.84	0.31	0.63	0.51	0.24	1.47	2.67	0.34	2.20	12.74
1983	0.86	1.57	2.82	0.70	0.73	1.44	0.52	0.56	0.46	0.84	1.67	3.42	15.59
1984	0.53	1.74	1.83	1.70	1.02	1.13	0.06	0.44	0.39	1.02	2.14	0.92	12.92
1985	0.44	1.33	1.13	0.37	0.44	0.69	0.34	0.26	2.10	0.89	2.11	1.27	11.37
1986	1.66	2.58	1.13	0.43	1.18	0.03	0.48	0.02	1.28	0.80	2.12	0.82	12.53
1987	1.48	0.64	1.39	0.47	0.85	0.38	0.34	0.05	0.03	T	0.76	1.23	7.62
1988	1.86	0.12	0.95	2.47	1.56	0.31	0.01	T	0.31	0.10	2.16	0.37	10.22
1989	1.86	1.36	1.72	1.57	1.47	0.57	0.09	1.25	0.12	0.84	1.27	0.21	12.33
1990	0.77	0.28	1.14	1.54	1.83	0.58	0.18	0.62	T	0.78	0.87	0.84	9.43
1991	0.98	0.57	1.00	0.71	3.18	2.14	0.24	0.42	T	0.92	2.68	0.67	13.51
1992	0.41	1.04	0.26	1.21	0.07	0.94	0.70	0.43	0.42	1.32	1.15	0.73	8.68
1993	1.79	0.80	1.49	1.85	1.51	0.71	1.45	2.19	T	0.22	0.93	0.92	13.86
Record Mean	1.55	1.29	1.22	1.06	1.13	0.94	0.34	0.46	0.69	1.06	1.53	1.56	12.84

AVERAGE TEMPERATURE (deg. F) — PENDLETON, OREGON

YEAR	JAN	FEB	MAR	APR	MAY	JUNE	JULY	AUG	SEP	OCT	NOV	DEC	ANNUAL
1964	40.3	41.1	43.5	48.5	56.8	64.9	72.2	68.4	62.7	51.9	40.1	32.9	51.9
1965	35.4	41.1	40.6	52.9	58.0	66.0	73.8	71.5	60.1	57.5	44.7	36.9	53.2
1966	38.3	39.7	45.4	52.0	59.9	64.6	71.0	72.4	66.6	54.0	45.1	41.1	54.2
1967	42.4	42.5	43.5	45.8	58.5	69.7	76.4	79.7	69.9	54.9	41.1	36.8	55.1
1968	37.3	42.8	48.5	49.6	59.7	67.5	77.2	70.9	65.9	50.8	42.6	33.3	53.8
1969	22.0	35.5	44.6	49.8	61.7	69.8	72.5	70.1	64.7	49.3	43.2	34.9	51.5
1970	32.3	39.5	43.5	45.8	57.8	68.7	74.8	72.5	56.3	47.4	40.4	35.7	51.2
1971	40.0	39.8	40.5	49.4	60.5	63.3	76.1	76.8	59.1	51.4	43.7	36.9	53.1
1972	34.0	37.4	47.8	47.6	60.9	68.3	74.7	76.2	61.1	51.1	42.6	27.1	52.4
1973	31.3	38.4	45.8	50.3	61.3	66.9	75.3	71.7	64.0	52.8	42.6	41.5	53.5
1974	30.4	43.8	46.4	51.7	57.3	71.1	73.3	75.5	67.5	54.8	44.8	40.6	54.8
1975	37.1	39.0	45.2	47.5	59.3	65.8	78.4	70.1	67.0	54.3	42.3	40.5	53.9
1976	39.2	37.9	42.8	50.2	58.8	63.7	73.4	67.7	67.3	53.1	42.7	35.9	52.7
1977	26.3	41.5	44.2	55.3	55.1	69.1	70.3	74.9	58.5	50.0	38.3	34.8	51.5
1978	32.2	39.3	45.7	48.0	54.4	66.3	72.2	69.4	60.5	51.7	33.5	29.5	50.2
1979	15.3	37.7	46.0	50.4	59.5	66.6	72.8	70.6	65.5	54.3	34.7	38.2	51.0
1980	25.6	36.1	41.3	51.9	56.4	60.4	72.1	66.9	63.3	51.3	42.0	39.2	50.6
1981	36.2	38.9	45.7	50.4	56.0	61.6	69.2	74.3	63.8	50.6	44.2	37.2	52.3
1982	35.0	38.1	43.5	47.6	56.8	67.6	71.1	71.5	60.7	50.7	37.3	35.7	51.3
1983	40.8	43.8	47.8	49.0	58.9	62.7	68.4	72.7	58.9	52.5	45.9	23.2	52.1
1984	34.6	39.7	46.8	48.2	54.7	62.1	72.9	72.2	60.4	49.1	41.8	30.4	51.1
1985	26.3	33.5	43.2	53.1	58.5	65.6	77.4	68.1	57.0	50.3	26.5	19.5	48.3
1986	35.9	39.0	48.8	50.0	58.6	70.0	67.6	75.8	58.9	54.0	42.2	31.5	52.7
1987	30.4	39.1	46.4	53.9	59.7	67.2	68.9	70.6	66.2	54.1	42.6	32.7	52.7
1988	32.4	41.1	44.1	51.9	56.8	63.9	72.0	70.0	63.4	58.4	44.3	33.9	52.7
1989	38.3	25.1	42.5	52.9	55.9	65.9	70.3	68.8	63.6	51.8	44.6	33.2	51.1
1990	39.6	37.9	45.7	54.8	56.4	64.7	75.2	72.2	68.2	51.3	45.4	25.8	53.1
1991	31.2	44.7	42.6	49.6	53.9	59.6	71.5	73.3	64.9	51.6	41.2	36.9	51.8
1992	38.7	42.4	47.7	52.8	62.4	70.4	71.9	72.6	61.9	54.2	39.8	32.0	53.9
1993	25.1	28.2	41.9	50.3	61.8	62.9	65.4	68.0	64.3	54.6	34.6	35.6	49.4
Record Mean	32.5	37.9	44.9	51.3	58.4	65.6	72.9	71.4	63.1	52.5	41.3	35.0	52.2
Max	39.4	46.0	55.0	63.4	71.5	79.5	89.2	87.2	77.4	64.7	49.5	41.6	63.7
Min	25.5	29.8	34.8	39.2	45.3	51.6	56.7	55.6	48.7	40.3	33.0	28.5	40.7

REFERENCE NOTES — PENDLETON, OREGON

GENERAL
T - TRACE AMOUNT.
BLANK ENTRIES DENOTE MISSING/UNREPORTED DATA.
\# INDICATES A STATION OR INSTRUMENT RELOCATION.

SPECIFIC

PM - INCLUDES LAST DAY OF PREVIOUS MONTH
ASOS - AUTOMATED SURFACE OBSERVING SYSTEM IN OPERATION DURING THESE MONTHS.

(a) - LENGTH OF RECORD IN YEARS, ALTHOUGH INDIVIDUAL MONTHS MAY BE MISSING.
0.* OR * - THE VALUE IS BETWEEN 0.0 AND 0.05
NORMALS - BASED ON THE 1961-1990 RECORD PERIOD.
EXTREMES - DATES ARE THE MOST RECENT OCCURRENCE
WIND DIR. - NUMERALS SHOW TENS OF DEGRESS CLOCKWISE FROM TRUE NORTH. "00" INDICATES CALM.
RESULTANT DIRECTIONS ARE GIVEN TO WHOLE DEGREES.
BOLD VALUES INDICATE EXTREME VALUES WHICH OCCURRED AFTER THE ASOS SYSTEM WAS COMMISSIONED.

RECORD = PERIOD OF RECORD
RECORD MEAN PRECIPITATION IS THE MEAN OF ALL DAILY PRECIPITATION AMOUNTS DURING THE PERIOD OF RECORD.
RECORD MAX(MIN) TEMPERATURE IS THE MEAN OF ALL DAILY MAX(MIN) TEMPERATURES DURING THE PERIOD OF RECORD.
RECORD MEAN TEMPERATURE IS THE SUM OF THE RECORD MAX AND RECORD MIN DIVIDED BY 2.
AVERAGE TEMPERATURE IS THE SUM OF THE MEAN DAILY MAX AND MIN TEMPERATURE DIVIDED BY 2.

EXCEPTIONS

RECORD MEANS ARE THROUGH THE CURRENT YEAR, BEGINNING IN 1900 FOR TEMPERATURE
1900 FOR PRECIPITATION
1936 FOR SNOWFALL
BEGINNING IN MAY 1989, SNOWFALL DATA COMPRISE ALL FORMS OF SOLID PRECIPITATION INCLUDING HAIL.

HEATING DEGREE DAYS Base 65 deg. F PENDLETON, OREGON

SEASON	JULY	AUG	SEP	OCT	NOV	DEC	JAN	FEB	MAR	APR	MAY	JUNE	TOTAL
1964-65	6	30	92	397	742	990	912	664	750	357	223	44	5207
1965-66	15	19	153	226	602	865	820	702	597	382	194	75	4650
1966-67	19	10	48	333	590	736	691	621	659	571	218	21	4517
1967-68	0	0	24	306	711	866	850	638	505	462	174	46	4582
1968-69	0	15	73	434	664	977	1327	820	623	450	140	32	5555
1969-70	0	11	79	480	646	926	1007	707	660	568	228	83	5395
1970-71	0	1	260	540	731	903	767	698	755	460	169	95	5379
1971-72	11	9	182	428	633	868	955	793	528	515	171	29	5122
1972-73	5	4	165	422	663	1170	1036	738	588	434	169	73	5467
1973-74	1	16	97	372	666	721	1064	589	573	391	241	29	4760
1974-75	8	0	39	313	600	750	857	721	609	517	194	57	4665
1975-76	0	12	43	332	673	751	791	782	679	436	206	89	4794
1976-77	4	42	31	363	660	896	1192	653	639	299	301	26	5106
1977-78	20	35	200	461	792	927	1011	714	593	504	322	46	5625
1978-79	7	41	146	403	936	1094	1533	757	582	432	184	62	6177
1979-80	12	0	43	326	902	823	1210	829	728	388	267	141	5669
1980-81	4	33	88	438	681	794	886	724	593	435	275	126	5077
1981-82	20	1	128	440	617	855	919	747	662	515	256	72	5232
1982-83	22	7	171	435	825	901	741	588	528	470	242	95	5025
1983-84	42	1	180	381	569	1292	935	729	558	496	316	134	5633
1984-85	4	0	182	490	692	1065	1196	876	665	351	224	65	5810
1985-86	4	22	242	452	1149	1402	898	722	497	446	277	25	6136
1986-87	33	0	213	335	675	1031	1065	717	571	332	201	71	5244
1987-88	25	12	65	334	668	995	1004	689	637	387	264	126	5206
1988-89	22	4	120	208	616	957	821	1113	691	354	279	42	5227
1989-90	11	17	76	403	607	978	781	752	591	299	262	89	4866
1990-91	9	13	11	419	583	1211	1039	564	689	454	338	162	5492
1991-92	4	2	52	418	707	865	810	649	527	362	127	36	4559
1992-93	11	28	129	333	752	1015	1231	1025	709	432	153	98	5916
1993-94	27	35	114	318	908	903							

COOLING DEGREE DAYS Base 65 deg. F PENDLETON, OREGON

YEAR	JAN	FEB	MAR	APR	MAY	JUNE	JULY	AUG	SEP	OCT	NOV	DEC	TOTAL
1969	0	0	0	0	45	183	238	177	76	0	0	0	719
1970	0	0	0	0	11	201	313	243	4	0	0	0	772
1971	0	0	0	0	36	50	363	379	12	13	0	0	853
1972	0	0	0	0	50	134	314	358	55	0	0	0	911
1973	0	0	0	0	63	137	327	232	72	0	0	0	831
1974	0	0	0	0	9	219	272	332	122	4	0	0	958
1975	0	0	0	0	27	88	423	179	109	8	0	0	834
1976	0	0	0	0	20	53	270	129	103	3	0	0	578
1977	0	0	0	16	3	152	190	348	16	0	0	0	725
1978	0	0	0	0	1	93	236	182	16	0	0	0	528
1979	0	0	0	0	21	114	261	186	65	3	0	0	650
1980	0	0	0	2	5	13	232	101	44	20	0	0	417
1981	0	0	0	4	2	28	155	297	101	0	0	0	587
1982	0	0	0	0	7	158	219	215	47	0	0	0	646
1983	0	0	0	0	60	32	155	246	6	0	0	0	499
1984	0	0	0	0	7	55	256	231	51	3	0	0	603
1985	0	0	0	0	28	91	394	127	7	0	0	0	647
1986	0	0	0	2	88	184	121	341	35	1	0	0	772
1987	0	0	0	8	41	145	152	194	108	4	0	0	652
1988	0	0	0	0	16	98	246	164	78	9	0	0	611
1989	0	0	0	0	5	76	182	143	41	0	0	0	447
1990	0	0	0	0	4	92	330	245	114	3	0	0	788
1991	0	0	0	0	0	8	214	267	56	9	0	0	554
1992	0	0	0	1	52	204	229	275	45	4	0	0	810
1993	0	0	0	0	59	42	47	136	99	4	0	0	387

SNOWFALL (inches) PENDLETON, OREGON

SEASON	JULY	AUG	SEP	OCT	NOV	DEC	JAN	FEB	MAR	APR	MAY	JUNE	TOTAL
1964-65	0.0	0.0	0.0	0.0	0.2	4.9	7.0	0.5	2.5	0.0	0.0	0.0	15.1
1965-66	0.0	0.0	0.0	0.0	T	0.1	11.5	1.6	0.2	T	0.0	0.0	13.4
1966-67	0.0	0.0	0.0	T	0.4	2.9	2.3	0.4	3.3	T	0.0	0.0	9.3
1967-68	0.0	0.0	0.0	0.0	0.8	2.5	1.3	T	T	T	0.0	0.0	4.6
1968-69	0.0	0.0	0.0	0.0	T	11.9	27.4	2.7	T	0.0	0.0	0.0	42.0
1969-70	0.0	0.0	0.0	0.0	T	3.5	9.9	3.8	1.3	T	T	0.0	18.5
1970-71	0.0	0.0	0.0	0.0	1.6	2.3	4.0	0.6	4.9	T	T	0.0	13.4
1971-72	0.0	0.0	0.0	1.9	T	11.8	3.6	6.2	0.1	1.1	0.0	0.0	24.7
1972-73	0.0	0.0	0.0	T	T	12.6	2.2	5.9	T	0.1	0.0	0.0	20.8
1973-74	0.0	0.0	0.0	3.2	9.1	5.3	2.6	0.5	T	T	0.0	0.0	20.7
1974-75	0.0	0.0	0.0	0.0	T	T	16.6	3.3	T	2.2	T	0.0	22.1
1975-76	0.0	0.0	0.0	0.0	5.2	3.0	0.3	0.3	0.1	0.0	0.0	0.0	8.9
1976-77	0.0	0.0	0.0	0.0	0.0	1.0	3.1	0.5	0.4	0.0	0.0	0.0	5.0
1977-78	0.0	0.0	0.0	0.0	8.5	11.5	6.1	T	3.9	0.0	T	0.0	30.0
1978-79	0.0	0.0	0.0	0.0	9.0	7.4	14.7	2.2	T	0.0	0.0	0.0	33.3
1979-80	0.0	0.0	0.0	0.0	4.3	T	16.6	0.9	3.9	0.0	0.0	0.0	25.7
1980-81	0.0	0.0	0.0	0.0	2.0	2.7	3.6	1.2	0.0	0.0	0.0	0.0	9.5
1981-82	0.0	0.0	0.0	0.0	0.6	5.1	5.7	1.5	1.9	T	0.0	0.0	14.8
1982-83	0.0	0.0	0.0	0.0	T	1.6	0.2	0.9	0.0	0.0	0.0	0.0	2.7
1983-84	0.0	0.0	0.0	0.0	T	26.6	1.0	1.2	T	T	0.0	0.0	28.8
1984-85	0.0	0.0	0.0	0.0	T	6.2	0.8	12.7	0.6	T	0.0	0.0	20.3
1985-86	0.0	0.0	0.0	0.0	14.9	9.1	T	7.6	0.0	0.0	T	0.0	31.6
1986-87	0.0	0.0	0.0	0.0	1.2	6.8	5.8	0.0	T	0.0	0.0	0.0	13.8
1987-88	0.0	0.0	0.0	0.0	0.3	2.3	10.6	0.0	1.5	0.0	0.0	0.0	14.7
1988-89	0.0	0.0	0.0	0.0	T	T	4.3	4.9	4.0	0.0	T	0.0	13.2
1989-90	0.0	0.0	0.0	0.0	0.0	1.0	T	2.0	1.3	0.0	0.0	0.0	4.3
1990-91	0.0	0.0	0.0	0.0	T	6.4	1.6	0.0	0.6	T	0.0	0.0	8.6
1991-92	0.0	0.0	0.0	2.3	1.0	T	0.8	T	0.0	0.0	0.0	0.0	4.1
1992-93	0.0	0.0	0.0	0.0	0.2	7.6	25.1	14.8	1.8	T	T	0.0	49.5
1993-94	T	0.0	0.0	0.0	0.7	0.4							
Record Mean	T	0.0	0.0	0.1	1.7	4.0	7.3	3.5	1.0	0.1	T	0.0	17.7

PORTLAND, OREGON

The Portland Weather Service Office is located 6 miles north-northeast of downtown Portland. Portland is situated about 65 miles inland from the Pacific Coast and midway between the northerly oriented low coast range on the west and the higher Cascade range on the east, each about 30 miles distant. The airport lies on the south bank of the Columbia River. The coast range provides limited shielding from the Pacific Ocean. The Cascade range provides a steep slope for orographic lift of moisture-laden westerly winds and consequent moderate rainfall, and also forms a barrier from continental air masses originating over the interior Columbia Basin. Airflow is usually northwesterly in Portland in spring and summer and southeasterly in fall and winter. The Portland Airport location is drier than most surrounding localities.

Portland has a very definite winter rainfall climate. Approximately 88 percent of the annual total occurs in the months of October through May, 9 percent in June and September, while only 3 percent comes in July and August. Precipitation is mostly rain, as on the average there are only five days each year with measurable snow. Snowfalls are seldom more than a couple of inches, and generally last only a few days.

The winter season is marked by relatively mild temperatures, cloudy skies and rain with southeasterly surface winds predominating. Summer produces pleasantly mild temperatures, northwesterly winds and very little precipitation. Fall and spring are transitional in nature. Fall and early winter are times with most frequent fog.

At all times, incursions of marine air are a frequent moderating influence. Outbreaks of continental high pressure from east of the Cascade Mountains produce strong easterly flow through the Columbia Gorge into the Portland area. In winter this brings the coldest weather with the extremes of low temperature registered in the cold air mass. Freezing rain and ice glaze are sometimes transitional effects. Temperatures below zero are very infrequent. In summer, hot, dry continental air brings the highest temperatures. Temperatures above 100 degrees are infrequent, but 90 degrees or higher are reached every year, but seldom persist for more than two or three days.

Destructive storms are infrequent in the Portland area. Surface winds seldom exceed gale force and rarely in the period of record have winds reached higher than 75 mph. Thunderstorms occur about once a month through the spring and summer months. Heavy downpours are infrequent but gentle rains occur almost daily during winter months.

Most rural areas around Portland are farmed for berries, green beans, and vegetables for fresh market and processing. The long growing season with mild temperatures and ample moisture favors local nursery and seed industries.

Based on the 1951-1980 period, the average first occurrence of 32 degrees Fahrenheit in the fall is November 7 and the average last occurrence in the spring is April 3.

NORMALS, MEANS, AND EXTREMES

PORTLAND, OREGON

LATITUDE: 45°36′N LONGITUDE: 122°36′ W ELEVATION: FT. GRND 21 BARO 27 TIME ZONE: PACIFIC WBAN: 24229

	(a)	JAN	FEB	MAR	APR	MAY	JUNE	JULY	AUG	SEP	OCT	NOV	DEC	YEAR
TEMPERATURE °F:														
Normals														
-Daily Maximum		45.4	51.0	56.0	60.6	67.1	74.0	79.9	80.3	74.6	64.0	52.6	45.6	62.6
-Daily Minimum		33.7	36.1	38.6	41.3	47.0	52.9	56.5	56.9	52.0	44.9	39.5	34.8	44.5
-Monthly		39.6	43.6	47.3	51.0	57.1	63.5	68.2	68.6	63.3	54.5	46.1	40.2	53.6
Extremes														
-Record Highest	53	63	71	80	87	100	100	107	107	105	92	73	65	107
-Year		1986	1988	1947	1957	1983	1992	1965	1981	1988	1987	1975	1993	AUG 1981
-Record Lowest	53	-2	-3	19	29	29	39	43	44	34	26	13	6	-3
-Year		1950	1950	1989	1955	1954	1966	1955	1980	1965	1971	1985	1964	FEB 1950
NORMAL DEGREE DAYS:														
Heating (base 65°F)		787	599	549	420	249	91	28	35	102	326	567	769	4522
Cooling (base 65°F)		0	0	0	0	0	46	127	147	51	0	0	0	371
% OF POSSIBLE SUNSHINE	44	28	38	47	52	57	56	69	66	62	44	28	23	48
MEAN SKY COVER (tenths)														
Sunrise - Sunset	45	8.4	8.2	8.1	7.8	7.2	6.7	4.8	5.2	5.5	7.1	8.2	8.7	7.1
MEAN NUMBER OF DAYS:														
Sunrise to Sunset														
-Clear	45	2.9	2.8	3.1	3.5	4.8	6.2	12.6	11.4	10.3	5.5	2.8	2.1	68.0
-Partly Cloudy	45	3.6	3.8	5.0	5.7	7.2	7.6	8.6	9.5	8.1	7.4	4.3	3.3	74.4
-Cloudy	45	24.5	21.6	23.0	20.7	19.0	16.1	9.8	10.1	11.5	18.1	22.9	25.6	222.8
Precipitation														
.01 inches or more	53	18.1	15.7	17.0	14.2	11.9	9.1	3.9	4.8	7.5	12.3	17.8	18.6	150.9
Snow, Ice pellets, hail														
1.0 inches or more	53	1.1	0.3	0.1	0.0	0.*	0.0	0.0	0.0	0.0	0.0	0.1	0.5	2.2
Thunderstorms	53	0.*	0.1	0.5	0.9	1.5	0.9	0.8	1.0	0.7	0.4	0.3	0.1	7.2
Heavy Fog Visibility 1/4 mile or less	51	4.2	3.7	2.4	1.1	0.2	0.1	0.1	0.2	2.7	7.3	6.1	5.0	33.1
Temperature °F														
-Maximum														
90° and above	53	0.0	0.0	0.0	0.0	0.3	1.2	3.6	3.8	1.8	0.1	0.0	0.0	10.8
32° and below	53	2.2	0.3	0.*	0.0	0.0	0.0	0.0	0.0	0.0	0.0	0.2	0.9	3.6
-Minimum														
32° and below	53	13.3	8.2	4.7	1.0	0.1	0.0	0.0	0.0	0.0	0.6	5.2	9.6	42.6
0° and below	53	0.*	0.*	0.0	0.0	0.0	0.0	0.0	0.0	0.0	0.0	0.0	0.0	*
AVG. STATION PRESS. (mb)	21	1018.4	1016.6	1015.2	1016.8	1016.3	1016.1	1016.2	1015.2	1015.5	1017.1	1017.3	1018.6	1016.6
RELATIVE HUMIDITY (%)														
Hour 04	53	86	86	86	86	85	84	82	84	87	90	88	87	86
Hour 10 (Local Time)	53	82	80	74	69	66	65	62	64	67	78	82	84	73
Hour 16	53	75	67	60	55	53	49	45	46	48	62	74	78	59
Hour 22	53	83	81	78	75	74	71	68	70	75	84	84	85	77
PRECIPITATION (inches):														
Water Equivalent														
-Normal		5.35	3.85	3.56	2.39	2.06	1.48	0.63	1.09	1.75	2.67	5.34	6.13	36.30
-Maximum Monthly	53	12.83	9.46	7.52	5.26	4.57	4.06	2.68	4.53	4.30	8.04	11.57	11.12	12.83
-Year		1953	1949	1957	1993	1945	1984	1983	1968	1986	1947	1942	1968	JAN 1953
-Minimum Monthly	53	0.06	0.72	1.10	0.53	0.10	0.03	0.00	T	T	0.19	0.77	1.38	0.00
-Year		1985	1993	1965	1956	1992	1951	1967	1970	1993	1988	1976	1976	JUL 1967
-Maximum in 24 hrs	53	2.61	2.36	1.83	1.47	1.47	1.82	1.09	1.54	2.38	2.18	2.62	2.59	2.62
-Year		1974	1987	1943	1962	1968	1958	1978	1977	1982	1941	1973	1977	NOV 1973
Snow, Ice pellets, hail														
-Maximum Monthly	53	41.4	13.2	12.9	T	0.6	T	0.0	T	T	0.2	8.2	15.7	41.4
-Year		1950	1949	1951	1993	1953	1981		1989	1949	1950	1955	1968	JAN 1950
-Maximum in 24 hrs	53	10.6	6.4	7.7	T	0.5	T	0.0	T	T	0.2	7.4	8.0	10.6
-Year		1950	1993	1951	1993	1953	1981		1989	1949	1950	1977	1964	JAN 1950
WIND:														
Mean Speed (mph)	45	10.0	9.2	8.3	7.4	7.1	7.2	7.6	7.1	6.5	6.5	8.6	9.5	7.9
Prevailing Direction through 1963		ESE	ESE	ESE	NW	NW	NW	NW	NW	NW	ESE	ESE	ESE	ESE
Fastest Mile														
-Direction (!!!)	41	S	SW	S	S	SW	SW	SW	SW	S	S	SW	S	S
-Speed (MPH)	41	54	61	57	60	42	40	33	29	61	88	56	57	88
-Year		1951	1958	1963	1957	1960	1958	1983	1961	1963	1962	1961	1951	OCT 1962
Peak Gust														
-Direction (!!!)	10	SW	SE	SW	SW	W	W	NW	E	E	SW	SW	SW	SW
-Speed (mph)	10	63	61	52	45	46	32	32	31	39	41	52	60	63
-Date		1990	1989	1991	1992	1993	1989	1992	1993	1985	1990	1984	1992	JAN 1990

PRECIPITATION (inches) PORTLAND, OREGON

YEAR	JAN	FEB	MAR	APR	MAY	JUNE	JULY	AUG	SEP	OCT	NOV	DEC	ANNUAL
1964	9.51	0.78	2.30	1.56	1.04	1.96	0.68	0.90	1.61	0.84	6.78	9.92	37.88
1965	7.44	2.22	1.10	2.20	1.31	0.83	0.44	0.73	0.01	2.03	5.64	7.34	31.29
1966	5.74	1.70	4.71	0.85	0.91	1.02	1.19	0.59	1.70	3.06	5.50	6.89	33.86
1967	6.21	2.02	4.31	2.17	1.02	1.01	0.00	T	0.76	4.72	2.27	4.75	29.24
1968	4.58	6.64	2.68	1.91	3.63	2.20	0.14	4.53	2.20	5.03	6.23	11.12	50.89
1969	7.60	3.14	1.13	2.28	1.61	2.99	0.14	0.04	3.86	3.02	3.18	8.12	37.11
1970	11.81	4.77	2.58	2.94	1.55	0.49	0.05	T	1.10	2.85	5.72	7.49	41.35
1971	7.09	3.36	4.87	2.72	1.00	1.76	0.26	0.95	3.53	2.37	5.76	8.05	41.72
1972	5.71	4.08	5.41	2.98	2.23	0.68	0.56	0.67	3.06	0.87	3.78	8.79	38.82
1973	3.69	1.94	2.45	1.33	1.43	1.45	0.06	1.41	3.29	3.14	11.55	9.93	41.67
1974	8.51	4.61	5.65	1.76	1.74	0.80	2.01	0.07	0.21	2.14	6.73	6.05	40.28
1975	8.43	4.75	3.45	1.88	1.35	1.13	0.43	2.10	T	4.76	4.10	6.68	39.06
1976	5.14	4.92	2.93	2.34	2.29	0.78	0.66	3.29	0.73	1.48	0.77	1.38	26.71
1977	1.07	2.49	3.50	1.04	4.30	0.83	0.39	3.26	3.33	2.28	5.56	8.98	37.03
1978	4.85	3.28	1.49	3.96	3.17	1.69	1.36	2.05	2.07	0.36	3.83	2.51	30.62
1979	2.55	6.53	2.51	2.47	2.41	0.64	0.25	1.18	1.75	4.85	3.38	7.23	35.75
1980	8.51	4.01	3.11	2.58	2.19	2.50	0.19	0.39	1.56	1.18	6.47	9.72	42.41
1981	1.47	3.86	2.33	1.79	2.25	3.23	0.24	0.15	1.86	4.12	4.62	8.37	34.29
1982	6.31	5.98	2.38	3.56	0.46	1.66	0.94	1.66	3.98	4.44	3.51	8.16	43.04
1983	6.23	7.78	6.80	1.87	1.30	1.95	2.68	2.29	0.39	1.95	8.65	5.30	47.19
1984	2.01	3.93	3.19	3.20	3.41	4.06	T	0.09	1.46	3.85	9.74	2.56	37.50
1985	0.06	1.79	3.08	1.07	1.52	2.34	0.55	0.48	2.76	2.75	3.89	2.19	22.48
1986	4.65	5.31	2.60	1.91	2.19	0.23	1.20	0.10	4.30	1.99	6.26	4.30	35.04
1987	6.93	2.45	4.91	1.94	1.63	0.14	1.03	0.35	0.30	0.27	1.96	8.00	29.91
1988	4.95	1.17	3.13	4.57	2.53	2.34	0.69	0.10	1.76	0.19	7.92	2.37	31.72
1989	3.30	2.84	6.73	2.08	2.87	0.78	0.91	1.07	1.48	1.73	3.18	3.08	30.05
1990	7.95	3.43	2.52	2.31	2.37	1.94	0.32	0.95	0.34	4.65	3.68	2.40	32.86
1991	2.56	3.65	4.64	4.05	3.34	2.31	0.07	0.70	0.02	1.51	6.36	4.34	33.55
1992	4.31	4.12	1.87	3.82	0.10	0.60	0.67	0.49	1.12	2.87	4.55	4.98	29.50
1993	3.06	0.72	4.39	5.26	4.36	1.69	2.41	0.37	T	1.59	1.50	5.01	30.36
Record Mean	5.39	3.94	3.64	2.40	2.14	1.57	0.60	0.91	1.64	3.07	5.40	5.88	36.59

AVERAGE TEMPERATURE (deg. F) PORTLAND, OREGON

YEAR	JAN	FEB	MAR	APR	MAY	JUNE	JULY	AUG	SEP	OCT	NOV	DEC	ANNUAL
1964	40.9	40.1	43.8	46.7	52.6	58.7	64.5	63.7	58.4	53.2	41.0	37.0	50.1
1965	40.2	43.4	47.6	51.8	54.3	61.8	69.7	68.6	60.4	57.5	49.7	39.5	53.7
1966	40.3	42.8	47.2	50.6	57.0	62.4	66.4	67.5	64.4	53.7	47.1	44.2	53.7
1967	43.6	43.7	44.0	46.9	57.1	65.9	69.3	72.9	66.4	54.8	46.2	40.4	54.3
1968	39.3	48.2	48.2	48.0	56.3	62.2	68.6	65.8	61.5	52.1	46.5	37.3	52.8
1969	31.9	39.7	46.5	50.1	59.5	66.5	66.6	66.1	63.4	53.3	47.2	42.9	52.8
1970	40.6	46.0	46.9	48.4	57.0	65.9	69.2	68.2	60.7	53.0	47.1	40.0	53.6
1971	40.4	42.8	43.7	49.6	56.8	60.2	69.2	71.6	60.8	52.4	45.5	40.4	52.8
1972	39.2	43.8	49.8	48.0	60.2	64.0	70.9	71.7	61.2	53.0	48.2	37.4	53.9
1973	39.0	44.9	47.9	52.3	59.4	63.9	70.3	65.9	64.4	54.3	44.2	44.7	54.2
1974	38.0	43.0	47.2	51.3	55.7	64.4	67.1	68.9	67.3	55.2	48.1	44.1	54.2
1975	41.5	41.2	45.0	47.3	57.5	61.9	69.0	65.3	65.7	53.5	46.0	42.7	53.1
1976	42.2	42.1	44.4	50.3	56.6	60.4	67.2	65.5	64.2	54.7	47.0	39.5	52.8
1977	35.7	44.6	45.5	52.9	53.8	63.9	66.3	71.7	60.8	53.8	43.3	42.0	52.9
1978	40.1	44.7	49.1	50.5	54.7	65.1	68.4	67.6	60.9	54.7	39.1	35.3	52.5
1979	30.7	42.9	50.8	53.1	60.1	65.1	70.5	68.6	66.3	58.1	45.0	44.4	54.6
1980	35.1	42.5	46.3	53.8	57.3	60.7	68.9	66.4	63.8	56.0	48.5	44.0	53.6
1981	43.9	44.0	48.8	52.5	57.5	61.8	67.5	72.2	64.9	53.3	48.8	42.7	54.8
1982	39.7	43.6	48.5	49.0	57.6	66.0	67.5	68.6	63.2	54.9	44.4	41.7	53.7
1983	44.4	47.3	50.7	52.7	60.4	62.8	66.5	69.1	61.5	54.2	49.3	36.4	54.6
1984	42.2	45.9	51.1	50.4	56.4	62.2	69.1	69.4	63.7	52.9	46.7	38.3	54.0
1985	36.1	41.1	45.8	53.9	58.3	64.4	74.1	69.3	60.8	52.7	37.3	33.0	52.2
1986	42.5	43.7	51.3	50.2	57.6	66.3	65.3	72.3	61.5	57.0	47.7	40.6	54.7
1987	39.6	45.2	48.7	54.2	60.4	66.5	67.2	70.5	65.5	58.2	48.8	39.1	55.3
1988	39.0	44.7	47.2	52.2	56.4	62.4	68.4	68.0	64.0	58.3	47.5	42.0	54.2
1989	42.2	36.0	45.6	56.0	58.0	64.3	65.5	66.1	65.3	54.9	48.6	40.3	53.6
1990	43.4	41.9	49.4	54.5	56.7	63.6	71.2	70.9	67.0	53.9	48.4	34.7	54.6
1991	38.9	48.8	46.2	50.8	54.7	59.9	69.9	70.1	67.4	55.4	47.5	42.7	54.4
1992	44.5	48.1	52.3	55.4	63.1	67.4	70.2	69.8	62.3	55.9	46.3	39.3	56.2
1993	36.5	40.1	47.9	52.6	61.1	62.5	64.3	68.5	65.7	57.4	41.5	41.4	53.3
Record Mean	39.0	43.3	46.7	51.2	57.3	61.4	66.6	66.6	63.0	54.5	45.8	40.6	53.0
Max	44.7	50.5	55.3	60.8	67.4	71.4	78.0	77.9	74.6	63.8	52.4	46.0	61.9
Min	33.2	36.0	38.1	41.6	47.1	51.3	55.2	55.3	51.5	45.1	39.1	35.2	44.1

REFERENCE NOTES PORTLAND, OREGON

GENERAL
T - TRACE AMOUNT.
BLANK ENTRIES DENOTE MISSING/UNREPORTED DATA.
# INDICATES A STATION OR INSTRUMENT RELOCATION.

SPECIFIC

PM - INCLUDES LAST DAY OF PREVIOUS MONTH
ASOS - AUTOMATED SURFACE OBSERVING SYSTEM IN OPERATION DURING THESE MONTHS.

(a) - LENGTH OF RECORD IN YEARS, ALTHOUGH INDIVIDUAL MONTHS MAY BE MISSING.
0.* OR * - THE VALUE IS BETWEEN 0.0 AND 0.05
NORMALS - BASED ON THE 1961-1990 RECORD PERIOD.
EXTREMES - DATES ARE THE MOST RECENT OCCURRENCE
WIND DIR.- NUMERALS SHOW TENS OF DEGRESS CLOCKWISE FROM TRUE NORTH. "00" INDICATES CALM.
RESULTANT DIRECTIONS ARE GIVEN TO WHOLE DEGREES.
BOLD VALUES INDICATE EXTREME VALUES WHICH OCCURRED AFTER THE ASOS SYSTEM WAS COMMISSIONED.

RECORD = PERIOD OF RECORD
RECORD MEAN PRECIPITATION IS THE MEAN OF ALL DAILY PRECIPITATION AMOUNTS DURING THE PERIOD OF RECORD.
RECORD MAX(MIN) TEMPERATURE IS THE MEAN OF ALL DAILY MAX(MIN) TEMPERATURES DURING THE PERIOD OF RECORD.
RECORD MEAN TEMPERATURE IS THE SUM OF THE RECORD MAX AND RECORD MIN DIVIDED BY 2.
AVERAGE TEMPERATURE IS THE SUM OF THE MEAN DAILY MAX AND MIN TEMPERATURE DIVIDED BY 2.

EXCEPTIONS

RECORD MEANS ARE THROUGH THE CURRENT YEAR, BEGINNING IN 1941 FOR TEMPERATURE
1941 FOR PRECIPITATION
1941 FOR SNOWFALL

HEATING DEGREE DAYS Base 65 deg. F PORTLAND, OREGON

SEASON	JULY	AUG	SEP	OCT	NOV	DEC	JAN	FEB	MAR	APR	MAY	JUNE	TOTAL
1964-65	67	81	191	358	711	860	761	599	533	388	325	113	4987
1965-66	22	16	139	227	451	786	759	620	545	425	249	99	4338
1966-67	27	16	56	345	531	635	655	591	647	535	246	50	4334
1967-68	3	0	29	306	558	758	789	482	515	500	261	110	4311
1968-69	17	43	123	395	544	852	1022	703	570	442	178	51	4940
1969-70	17	22	85	357	526	678	751	526	553	493	246	71	4325
1970-71	14	14	130	369	530	771	757	615	653	454	253	149	4709
1971-72	33	5	123	388	578	756	793	607	466	501	174	61	4485
1972-73	10	6	153	363	497	848	799	560	525	378	202	89	4430
1973-74	6	47	59	326	618	624	832	610	545	403	282	72	4424
1974-75	32	16	29	301	500	640	722	660	615	523	240	127	4405
1975-76	24	41	48	354	565	686	698	658	632	437	258	155	4556
1976-77	15	41	47	319	536	783	901	564	596	358	340	68	4568
1977-78	40	19	131	339	644	707	764	561	485	430	317	58	4495
1978-79	29	26	134	312	772	915	1058	615	434	351	162	57	4865
1979-80	8	2	19	214	592	631	920	647	575	329	232	125	4294
1980-81	15	25	64	284	485	644	650	583	494	372	229	108	3953
1981-82	23	5	76	355	478	687	780	596	502	472	229	71	4274
1982-83	22	10	99	307	614	715	635	492	435	363	184	81	3957
1983-84	27	2	109	325	463	880	701	546	425	430	269	115	4292
1984-85	9	2	80	377	539	820	893	664	588	327	213	62	4574
1985-86	0	7	124	373	826	982	691	591	417	437	265	43	4756
1986-87	37	0	148	242	510	750	780	550	495	321	173	51	4057
1987-88	22	2	54	214	479	798	801	581	544	380	272	109	4256
1988-89	33	15	91	208	518	705	699	805	594	263	219	77	4227
1989-90	32	27	44	306	486	759	664	641	476	308	251	78	4072
1990-91	10	5	14	336	492	933	802	446	575	420	310	156	4499
1991-92	4	13	25	295	517	685	627	483	387	282	108	35	3461
1992-93	5	9	107	274	556	789	877	692	522	366	135	94	4426
1993-94	37	17	57	231	698	726							

COOLING DEGREE DAYS Base 65 deg. F PORTLAND, OREGON

YEAR	JAN	FEB	MAR	APR	MAY	JUNE	JULY	AUG	SEP	OCT	NOV	DEC	TOTAL
1969	0	0	0	0	13	102	74	65	43	0	0	0	297
1970	0	0	0	0	8	106	150	120	8	2	0	0	394
1971	0	0	0	0	5	14	170	217	7	3	0	0	416
1972	0	0	0	0	27	39	200	221	44	0	0	0	531
1973	0	0	0	0	34	65	178	81	45	0	0	0	403
1974	0	0	0	0	1	60	102	144	102	0	0	0	409
1975	0	0	0	0	12	39	157	57	75	2	0	0	342
1976	0	0	0	0	4	23	89	66	30	4	0	0	216
1977	0	0	0	0	0	42	90	233	10	0	0	0	375
1978	0	0	0	0	3	69	141	112	18	0	0	0	343
1979	0	0	0	0	18	65	183	124	65	7	0	0	462
1980	0	0	0	1	0	2	141	75	35	12	0	0	266
1981	0	0	0	3	4	16	109	232	82	0	0	0	446
1982	0	0	0	0	4	107	103	127	50	0	0	0	391
1983	0	0	0	0	48	23	80	137	12	0	0	0	300
1984	0	0	0	0	10	34	140	144	47	6	0	0	381
1985	0	0	0	0	11	53	291	145	5	0	0	0	505
1986	0	0	0	0	40	87	52	235	50	0	0	0	464
1987	0	0	0	4	37	102	95	177	77	12	0	0	504
1988	0	0	0	0	10	39	147	115	67	8	0	0	386
1989	0	0	0	0	9	62	53	66	60	0	0	0	250
1990	0	0	0	2	3	45	206	193	83	0	0	0	532
1991	0	0	0	0	0	7	164	176	102	2	0	0	451
1992	0	0	0	1	57	114	174	164	31	0	0	0	541
1993	0	0	0	0	21	24	22	132	80	3	0	0	282

SNOWFALL (inches) PORTLAND, OREGON

SEASON	JULY	AUG	SEP	OCT	NOV	DEC	JAN	FEB	MAR	APR	MAY	JUNE	TOTAL
1964-65	0.0	0.0	0.0	0.0	T	11.0	T	0.0	0.3	0.0	T	0.0	11.3
1965-66	0.0	0.0	0.0	0.0	0.0	T	T	T	0.6	0.0	0.0	0.0	0.6
1966-67	0.0	0.0	0.0	0.0	0.0	0.0	T	T	T	T	0.0	0.0	T
1967-68	0.0	0.0	0.0	0.0	0.0	5.7	5.2	0.0	0.0	T	0.0	0.0	10.9
1968-69	0.0	0.0	0.0	0.0	0.0	15.7	18.3	T	0.0	0.0	0.0	0.0	34.0
1969-70	0.0	0.0	0.0	0.0	0.0	0.0	T	T	T	T	0.0	0.0	T
1970-71	0.0	0.0	0.0	0.0	T	1.4	6.9	1.7	T	T	0.0	0.0	10.0
1971-72	0.0	0.0	0.0	T	0.0	4.6	0.4	T	T	T	0.0	0.0	5.0
1972-73	0.0	0.0	0.0	0.0	0.0	6.1	0.4	T	T	T	0.0	0.0	6.5
1973-74	0.0	0.0	0.0	0.0	T	0.0	T	T	T	0.0	T	0.0	T
1974-75	0.0	0.0	0.0	0.0	0.0	T	T	0.1	T	T	T	0.0	0.1
1975-76	0.0	0.0	0.0	0.0	T	T	T	T	T	T	T	0.0	T
1976-77	0.0	0.0	0.0	0.0	0.0	0.0	T	0.0	T	0.0	T	0.0	T
1977-78	0.0	0.0	0.0	0.0	7.6	T	0.0	0.0	0.1	T	T	0.0	7.7
1978-79	0.0	0.0	0.0	0.0	3.0	2.4	1.9	1.1	T	T	0.0	0.0	8.4
1979-80	0.0	0.0	0.0	0.0	0.0	T	12.4	T	T	T	0.0	T	12.4
1980-81	0.0	0.0	0.0	0.0	T	T	0.0	T	T	T	T	T	T
1981-82	0.0	0.0	0.0	0.0	0.0	2.0	2.1	T	T	T	0.0	0.0	4.1
1982-83	0.0	0.0	0.0	T	T	0.0	0.0	0.0	T	T	T	0.0	T
1983-84	0.0	0.0	0.0	0.0	0.0	2.3	0.1	T	T	0.0	T	0.0	2.4
1984-85	0.0	0.0	0.0	T	0.0	2.8	T	4.8	T	T	0.0	0.0	7.6
1985-86	0.0	0.0	0.0	0.0	3.4	1.6	T	5.8	T	T	T	0.0	10.8
1986-87	0.0	0.0	0.0	0.0	T	0.1	0.0	T	T	T	T	0.0	0.1
1987-88	0.0	0.0	0.0	0.0	0.0	2.9	0.6	0.0	0.0	T	T	0.0	3.5
1988-89	0.0	0.0	0.0	0.0	T	T	0.9	0.3	2.0	T	0.0	0.0	3.2
1989-90	0.0	T	0.0	T	0.0	0.0	T	8.3	T	0.0	0.0	0.0	8.3
1990-91	0.0	0.0	0.0	0.0	0.0	1.3	0.6	0.0	T	T	0.0	0.0	1.9
1991-92	0.0	0.0	0.0	0.0	T	0.0	0.0	0.0	0.0	T	0.0	0.0	T
1992-93	0.0	0.0	0.0	0.0	T	4.6	2.9	6.6	0.0	T	T	0.0	14.1
1993-94	0.0	0.0	0.0	0.0	T	T							
Record Mean	0.0	T	T	T	0.4	1.4	3.3	1.0	0.4	T	T	T	6.6

AVOCA, WILKES–BARRE – SCRANTON PENNSYLVANIA

The Wilkes–Barre Scranton National Weather Service Office is located about midway between the two cities, at the southwest end of the crescent–shaped Lackawanna River Valley. The river flows through this valley and empties into the Susquehanna River and the Wyoming Valley a few miles west of the airport. The surrounding mountains protect both cities and the airport from high winds. They influence the temperature and precipitation during both summer and winter, causing wide departures in both within a few miles of the station. Because of the proximity of the mountains, the climate is relatively cool in summer with frequent shower and thunderstorm activity, usually of brief duration. The winter temperatures in the valley are not severe. The occurrence of sub–zero temperatures and severe snowstorms is infrequent. A high percentage of the winter precipitation occurs as rain.

Although severe snowstorms are infrequent, when they do occur they approach blizzard conditions. High winds cause huge drifts and normal routines are disrupted for several days.

While the incidence of tornadoes is very low, Wilkes–Barre has occasionally been hit with these storms which caused loss of life and great property damage.

The area has felt the effects of tropical storms. Considerable wind damage has occasionally occurred, but the most devastating damage has come from flooding caused by the large amounts of precipitation deposited by the storms. The worst natural disaster to hit the region was the result of the flooding caused by a hurricane.

NORMALS, MEANS, AND EXTREMES

AVOCA, WILKES-BARRE - SCRANTON PENNSYLVANIA

LATITUDE: 41°20'N LONGITUDE: 75°44' W ELEVATION: FT. GRND 930 BARO 959 TIME ZONE: EASTERN WBAN: 14777

	(a)	JAN	FEB	MAR	APR	MAY	JUNE	JULY	AUG	SEP	OCT	NOV	DEC	YEAR
TEMPERATURE °F:														
Normals														
-Daily Maximum		31.8	34.5	45.5	57.8	69.3	77.5	81.8	79.7	72.4	61.0	48.8	36.6	58.1
-Daily Minimum		17.5	19.0	28.3	38.1	48.3	56.8	61.6	60.0	52.8	42.1	33.9	23.4	40.2
-Monthly		24.7	26.8	36.9	48.0	58.8	67.2	71.7	69.9	62.6	51.5	41.4	30.0	49.1
Extremes														
-Record Highest	38	67	71	83	92	93	97	101	94	95	84	80	67	101
-Year		1967	1985	1977	1976	1962	1964	1988	1983	1983	1959	1982	1984	JUL 1988
-Record Lowest	38	-14	-16	-4	14	27	34	43	38	30	19	9	-9	-16
-Year		1985	1979	1967	1982	1974	1972	1979	1982	1974	1972	1976	1989	FEB 1979
NORMAL DEGREE DAYS:														
Heating (base 65°F)		1249	1070	871	510	217	38	0	11	109	423	708	1085	6291
Cooling (base 65°F)		0	0	0	0	25	104	210	163	37	0	0	0	539
% OF POSSIBLE SUNSHINE	38	42	47	50	53	56	61	62	60	54	52	36	34	51
MEAN SKY COVER (tenths)														
Sunrise - Sunset	38	7.5	7.2	7.1	6.8	6.7	6.2	6.2	6.1	6.2	6.2	7.6	7.8	6.8
MEAN NUMBER OF DAYS:														
Sunrise to Sunset														
-Clear	38	4.4	4.5	5.4	6.2	5.9	6.9	6.3	7.1	7.1	8.3	3.9	3.8	69.7
-Partly Cloudy	38	7.2	6.9	7.7	7.3	9.6	10.8	12.6	11.7	9.7	8.5	6.8	6.7	105.4
-Cloudy	38	19.4	16.8	17.9	16.5	15.5	12.3	12.1	12.2	13.3	14.2	19.2	20.6	190.1
Precipitation														
.01 inches or more	38	12.1	11.1	12.8	12.4	12.7	11.8	11.3	11.1	10.0	9.8	11.8	12.8	139.6
Snow,Ice pellets,hail														
1.0 inches or more	38	3.1	2.9	2.7	0.7	0.*	0.0	0.0	0.0	0.0	0.1	0.9	2.6	12.9
Thunderstorms	38	0.1	0.2	0.8	2.0	3.5	5.8	6.8	5.1	2.7	1.0	0.4	0.2	28.6
Heavy Fog Visibility														
1/4 mile or less	38	1.8	2.0	1.8	1.3	1.2	1.2	1.6	1.9	2.8	2.1	1.7	2.3	21.8
Temperature °F														
-Maximum														
90° and above	38	0.0	0.0	0.0	0.1	0.3	1.6	3.2	1.8	0.4	0.0	0.0	0.0	7.5
32° and below	38	15.1	11.6	3.9	0.2	0.0	0.0	0.0	0.0	0.0	0.0	1.2	10.6	42.5
-Minimum														
32° and below	38	28.2	24.8	21.6	8.4	0.6	0.0	0.0	0.0	0.2	4.4	13.9	25.4	127.5
0° and below	38	2.1	1.3	0.1	0.0	0.0	0.0	0.0	0.0	0.0	0.0	0.0	0.7	4.1
AVG. STATION PRESS.(mb)	21	982.5	983.0	981.8	980.6	981.4	981.6	982.4	984.0	984.9	984.9	984.0	983.6	982.9
RELATIVE HUMIDITY (%)														
Hour 01	38	72	71	69	67	72	80	81	83	84	79	75	75	76
Hour 07 (Local Time)	38	75	75	74	72	76	82	83	87	88	84	79	77	79
Hour 13	38	65	63	58	52	52	55	56	58	61	59	64	67	59
Hour 19	38	67	64	59	54	56	60	62	66	70	66	68	70	64
PRECIPITATION (inches):														
Water Equivalent														
-Normal		2.10	2.15	2.55	2.97	3.65	3.98	3.79	3.32	3.31	2.79	3.06	2.51	36.18
-Maximum Monthly	38	6.48	8.06	4.83	9.56	8.02	7.22	7.25	5.69	8.15	8.12	7.69	6.58	9.56
-Year		1979	1981	1977	1983	1989	1982	1986	1990	1987	1976	1972	1983	APR 1983
-Minimum Monthly	38	0.39	0.30	0.49	0.97	0.77	0.27	1.04	1.23	0.82	0.03	0.80	0.35	0.03
-Year		1980	1968	1981	1989	1959	1966	1993	1980	1964	1963	1976	1958	OCT 1963
-Maximum in 24 hrs	38	1.89	3.11	3.02	3.80	2.58	3.61	2.45	3.18	6.52	3.27	2.91	2.86	6.52
-Year		1978	1981	1986	1983	1972	1973	1990	1966	1985	1976	1972	1983	SEP 1985
Snow,Ice pellets,hail														
-Maximum Monthly	38	29.6	22.0	32.0	26.7	2.4	0.0	0.0	T	T	4.4	22.5	33.9	33.9
-Year		1987	1964	1993	1983	1977			1993	1993	1962	1971	1969	DEC 1969
-Maximum in 24 hrs	38	20.1	13.3	20.4	12.2	2.4	0.0	0.0	T	T	4.4	20.5	12.4	20.5
-Year		1964	1961	1993	1983	1977			1993	1993	1962	1971	1969	NOV 1971
WIND:														
Mean Speed (mph)	38	8.9	9.1	9.4	9.5	8.5	7.9	7.3	7.0	7.4	7.9	8.6	8.8	8.4
Prevailing Direction through 1963		SW	SW	NW	SW	WSW	SW	WSW	SW	SW	WSW	WSW	SW	SW
Fastest Mile														
-Direction (!!)	38	SW	W	S	NW	SW	W	NW	NE	SW	E	NW	SW	W
-Speed (MPH)	38	52	60	49	47	46	43	43	50	47	40	49	47	60
-Year		1992	1956	1970	1957	1980	1956	1988	1956	1989	1980	1989	1957	FEB 1956
Peak Gust														
-Direction (!!)	10	SW	W	E	SW	NW	SW	NW	NW	SW	S	SE	SW	SW
-Speed (mph)	10	74	53	56	64	55	58	58	51	52	52	61	64	74
-Date		1992	1990	1993	1985	1992	1993	1988	1990	1989	1990	1992	1991	JAN 1992

PRECIPITATION (inches)

AVOCA, WILKES-BARRE - SCRANTON PENNSYLVANIA

YEAR	JAN	FEB	MAR	APR	MAY	JUNE	JULY	AUG	SEP	OCT	NOV	DEC	ANNUAL
1964	3.40	2.03	3.54	3.82	0.98	5.00	1.23	2.85	0.82	1.13	1.86	3.67	30.33
1965	2.07	1.90	1.83	2.63	2.51	1.22	1.30	5.23	3.13	1.80	1.43	1.30	26.35
1966	1.66	2.31	1.60	2.91	3.32	0.27	1.89	4.76	2.70	2.04	2.97	2.00	28.43
1967	1.11	0.89	3.91	2.09	4.41	4.48	3.61	5.20	2.13	2.58	2.31	2.45	35.17
1968	2.03	0.30	2.73	2.37	4.64	4.82	1.23	1.43	4.20	1.65	3.40	1.95	30.75
1969	0.64	0.96	1.45	3.04	2.42	4.58	6.81	4.47	1.92	2.20	3.77	3.42	35.68
1970	0.52	2.41	2.33	3.07	2.75	2.56	5.19	2.72	3.03	2.24	2.87	1.85	31.54
1971	1.54	3.92	1.93	1.29	3.38	2.44	5.73	4.88	1.93	3.00	3.55	2.08	35.67
1972	2.05	2.42	4.00	3.31	7.33	7.04	1.23	1.64	1.57	3.30	7.69	3.61	45.19
1973	2.13	1.28	1.79	4.38	3.80	5.99	3.87	2.61	3.62	1.97	1.50	6.07	39.01
1974	2.66	1.48	4.75	2.71	1.89	3.85	2.80	3.50	6.85	1.07	2.26	3.40	37.22
1975	2.78	3.26	2.52	1.17	4.01	5.64	3.85	2.78	6.10	3.29	3.00	1.84	40.24
1976	3.25	2.14	2.18	2.27	3.24	5.43	3.20	2.57	3.81	8.12	0.80	1.50	38.51
1977	0.88	1.82	4.83	3.98	1.72	3.16	3.44	4.23	5.97	5.27	3.98	3.44	42.72
1978	5.33	0.93	2.30	1.67	4.30	2.48	2.16	3.28	3.06	3.35	1.02	3.09	32.97
1979	6.48	2.44	1.52	3.69	5.16	2.54	2.97	2.05	5.84	3.68	3.17	1.70	41.24
1980	0.39	0.69	3.72	2.35	2.37	4.36	3.76	1.23	1.43	2.17	2.83	1.24	26.54
1981	0.63	8.06	0.49	3.54	3.00	3.45	4.27	1.75	2.74	3.50	1.84	2.13	35.40
1982	2.71	2.28	2.55	3.48	3.52	7.22	3.32	3.42	1.10	0.84	3.44	1.52	35.40
1983	1.17	1.46	3.28	9.56	3.28	4.81	2.76	1.77	2.12	2.73	3.71	6.58	43.23
1984	1.11	2.92	2.42	4.09	6.70	4.75	5.12	2.81	1.36	2.30	2.63	2.36	38.57
1985	0.61	1.58	2.24	2.00	6.10	3.00	6.09	2.62	7.83	1.92	4.47	1.96	40.42
1986	2.59	2.58	4.25	2.98	2.24	6.77	7.25	3.94	3.07	2.61	3.94	2.04	44.26
1987	2.60	0.68	1.18	4.38	2.22	4.35	5.80	4.16	8.15	2.77	2.24	0.99	39.52
1988	1.41	2.32	1.97	2.65	4.24	0.82	6.26	5.03	1.89	1.93	3.33	1.08	32.93
1989	1.02	1.73	2.23	0.97	8.02	6.10	2.76	2.92	3.92	4.73	3.57	0.96	38.93
1990	3.81	2.70	1.88	2.48	5.27	4.78	4.36	5.69	3.16	4.33	3.33	4.30	46.09
1991	1.54	1.35	2.91	2.69	2.84	1.72	2.45	3.28	2.55	2.41	3.81	2.73	30.28
1992	1.23	1.41	2.65	1.67	4.21	1.45	3.83	2.13	2.65	1.91	3.47	2.91	29.52
1993	1.97	1.24	4.02	7.47	1.38	1.85	1.04	3.82	6.55	3.99	3.32	3.09	39.74
Record Mean	2.30	2.25	2.82	3.12	3.33	3.75	4.03	3.59	3.23	2.90	2.82	2.61	36.74

AVERAGE TEMPERATURE (deg. F)

AVOCA, WILKES-BARRE - SCRANTON PENNSYLVANIA

YEAR	JAN	FEB	MAR	APR	MAY	JUNE	JULY	AUG	SEP	OCT	NOV	DEC	ANNUAL
1964	27.9	23.5	36.9	46.6	62.0	67.4	74.1	68.2	63.8	49.4	44.1	31.6	49.6
1965	23.0	28.1	34.2	45.3	63.7	68.0	71.0	69.5	64.5	49.6	40.4	33.5	49.2
1966	23.8	27.2	39.0	46.0	55.7	70.1	75.0	72.4	60.2	50.2	43.4	30.5	49.4
1967	32.6	23.5	34.9	49.1	52.7	71.1	71.7	68.9	61.6	51.2	36.6	31.7	48.8
1968	20.0	24.1	40.4	52.9	56.3	67.5	73.7	71.0	64.4	53.4	40.7	27.2	49.3
1969	26.0	26.6	34.4	50.5	59.9	68.2	70.8	69.9	62.7	50.6	39.2	25.7	48.7
1970	17.7	25.7	31.8	48.4	60.4	64.9	70.8	69.6	64.2	52.8	41.5	27.3	47.9
1971	19.5	27.2	33.0	45.0	55.9	68.6	69.9	68.3	65.5	56.4	38.8	34.1	48.5
1972	27.6	24.3	32.8	43.5	60.0	62.9	71.5	69.6	61.9	45.3	36.0	32.9	47.4
1973	28.5	24.5	41.9	47.5	53.4	68.3	71.5	71.6	62.4	53.2	41.5	31.3	49.7
1974	27.8	24.2	34.7	49.1	56.2	64.4	70.8	68.5	61.2	48.5	43.0	34.4	48.6
1975	31.8	32.1	35.8	43.9	64.9	68.8	73.7	71.2	59.9	55.8	47.8	31.1	51.4
1976	22.1	35.0	41.0	51.3	56.7	70.4	69.2	69.1	60.9	48.0	37.0	22.9	48.6
1977	15.0	26.9	40.5	48.9	60.0	63.8	71.1	68.7	62.7	48.5	43.1	29.6	48.2
1978	24.4	19.2	33.1	46.0	58.7	65.2	69.4	71.0	60.5	50.7	40.5	29.1	47.3
1979	24.2	16.0	40.7	46.4	58.6	65.1	70.7	70.7	63.2	51.8	45.9	35.6	49.1
1980	27.8	24.2	35.9	51.0	61.8	65.3	73.2	75.2	66.1	49.8	37.6	25.7	49.5
1981	19.5	34.9	36.2	51.0	59.8	68.5	72.2	70.1	62.1	49.1	41.1	29.1	49.5
1982	18.7	27.8	36.0	46.3	61.2	64.3	71.0	66.2	62.4	52.3	44.3	36.7	48.9
1983	27.3	29.4	38.8	45.9	55.7	67.6	72.4	71.6	64.8	52.5	42.8	27.1	49.7
1984	23.0	35.9	30.9	48.3	57.5	69.3	71.6	72.6	61.7	58.0	40.8	37.3	50.6
1985	21.5	29.8	39.1	51.4	60.6	63.8	70.1	69.0	64.0	52.7	44.5	26.7	49.4
1986	27.2	26.1	39.8	49.3	62.7	66.2	71.0	67.4	61.6	51.2	37.3	32.8	49.4
1987	24.7	25.1	39.7	50.7	60.0	68.7	73.5	68.3	61.8	47.4	41.3	32.7	49.5
1988	22.0	27.4	38.1	46.6	60.1	65.5	75.8	72.9	60.4	46.3	43.3	29.8	49.0
1989	31.3	28.0	37.2	45.6	57.6	67.0	70.4	68.5	62.2	52.8	39.7	18.6	48.2
1990	35.3	33.3	40.6	50.2	56.1	67.6	71.7	69.5	61.6	55.3	44.2	36.0	51.8
1991	27.5	33.4	40.4	51.7	65.7	69.5	73.4	72.2	61.8	53.3	41.4	32.9	51.9
1992	28.6	30.3	34.4	47.4	58.7	66.3	71.1	68.4	62.8	49.0	42.2	32.8	49.3
1993	32.0	23.8	33.3	49.9	61.7	68.8	75.5	72.7	61.2	50.0	41.4	30.0	50.0
Record Mean	26.8	27.4	36.8	48.1	59.2	67.4	72.1	69.9	63.0	52.1	41.2	30.3	49.5
Max	34.0	35.3	45.3	57.9	69.8	78.0	82.5	80.1	73.1	61.9	48.7	37.0	58.6
Min	19.5	19.5	28.3	38.2	48.5	56.8	61.7	59.8	52.8	42.3	33.6	23.6	40.4

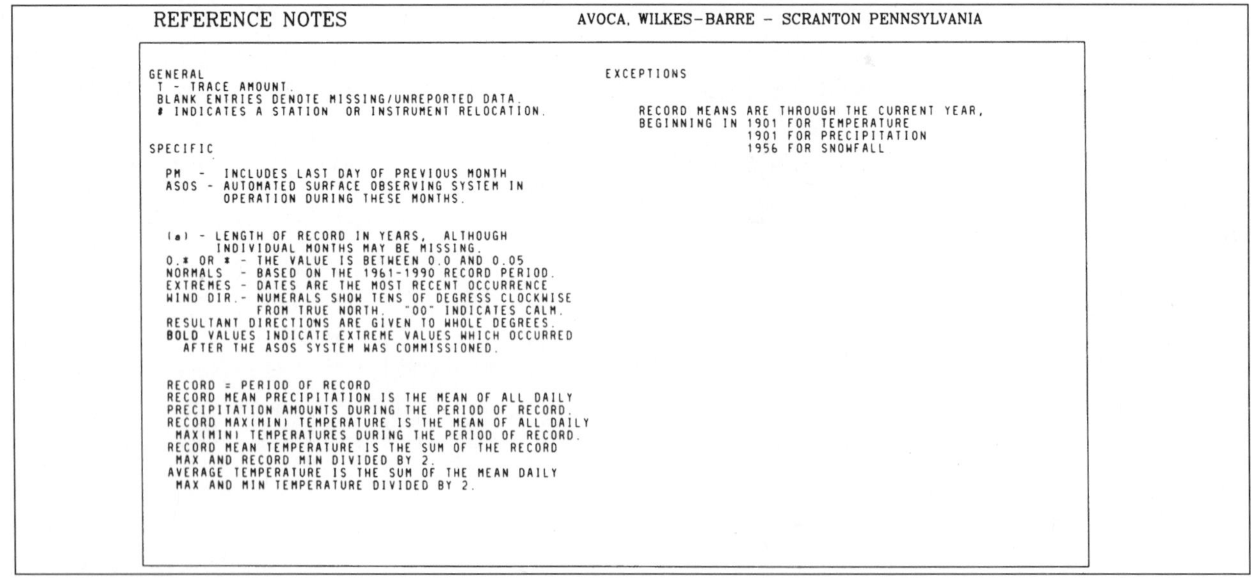

REFERENCE NOTES

AVOCA, WILKES-BARRE - SCRANTON PENNSYLVANIA

GENERAL

T - TRACE AMOUNT.
BLANK ENTRIES DENOTE MISSING/UNREPORTED DATA.
# INDICATES A STATION OR INSTRUMENT RELOCATION.

SPECIFIC

PM - INCLUDES LAST DAY OF PREVIOUS MONTH
ASOS - AUTOMATED SURFACE OBSERVING SYSTEM IN OPERATION DURING THESE MONTHS.

(a) - LENGTH OF RECORD IN YEARS, ALTHOUGH INDIVIDUAL MONTHS MAY BE MISSING.
0.* OR * - THE VALUE IS BETWEEN 0.0 AND 0.05
NORMALS - BASED ON THE 1961-1990 RECORD PERIOD.
EXTREMES - DATES ARE THE MOST RECENT OCCURRENCE
WIND DIR.- NUMERALS SHOW TENS OF DEGRESS CLOCKWISE FROM TRUE NORTH. "00" INDICATES CALM.
RESULTANT DIRECTIONS ARE GIVEN TO WHOLE DEGREES.
BOLD VALUES INDICATE EXTREME VALUES WHICH OCCURRED AFTER THE ASOS SYSTEM WAS COMMISSIONED.

RECORD = PERIOD OF RECORD
RECORD MEAN PRECIPITATION IS THE MEAN OF ALL DAILY PRECIPITATION AMOUNTS DURING THE PERIOD OF RECORD.
RECORD MAX(MIN) TEMPERATURE IS THE MEAN OF ALL DAILY MAX(MIN) TEMPERATURES DURING THE PERIOD OF RECORD.
RECORD MEAN TEMPERATURE IS THE SUM OF THE RECORD MAX AND RECORD MIN DIVIDED BY 2.
AVERAGE TEMPERATURE IS THE SUM OF THE MEAN DAILY MAX AND MIN TEMPERATURE DIVIDED BY 2.

EXCEPTIONS

RECORD MEANS ARE THROUGH THE CURRENT YEAR, BEGINNING IN 1901 FOR TEMPERATURE
1901 FOR PRECIPITATION
1956 FOR SNOWFALL

HEATING DEGREE DAYS Base 65 deg. F AVOCA, WILKES-BARRE - SCRANTON PENNSYLVANIA

SEASON	JULY	AUG	SEP	OCT	NOV	DEC	JAN	FEB	MAR	APR	MAY	JUNE	TOTAL
1964-65	0	31	110	475	621	1028	1293	1027	951	582	100	55	6273
1965-66	7	35	99	471	731	971	1270	1053	799	565	300	41	6342
1966-67	1	0	170	451	642	1063	998	1154	923	475	379	12	6268
1967-68	5	17	139	427	844	1023	1388	1181	754	357	261	42	6438
1968-69	0	28	55	359	725	1165	1204	1068	943	434	188	38	6207
1969-70	6	15	134	440	765	1212	1459	1094	1022	500	176	76	6899
1970-71	2	5	109	371	695	1162	1404	1051	985	593	292	32	6701
1971-72	5	22	90	263	783	951	1152	1175	992	634	168	109	6344
1972-73	21	20	125	603	860	988	1124	1131	704	521	354	25	6476
1973-74	2	11	140	368	699	1036	1145	1135	934	480	291	65	6306
1974-75	5	2	155	503	655	941	1024	913	902	627	88	25	5840
1975-76	0	8	158	291	509	1043	1322	864	737	451	265	31	5679
1976-77	8	25	155	519	834	1297	1546	1058	756	487	206	90	6981
1977-78	14	37	119	505	653	1090	1252	1279	984	562	240	73	6808
1978-79	38	2	153	436	728	1103	1257	1370	747	552	221	66	6673
1979-80	34	31	120	420	568	900	1144	1175	895	414	137	94	5932
1980-81	1	0	82	466	813	1211	1407	835	886	416	195	19	6331
1981-82	2	5	132	485	706	1105	1426	1034	896	554	147	68	6560
1982-83	17	55	112	390	619	870	1158	992	805	569	292	41	5920
1983-84	7	11	119	392	659	1169	1297	837	1052	493	247	34	6317
1984-85	7	6	148	219	719	852	1342	981	799	421	162	78	5734
1985-86	4	11	127	376	610	1181	1163	1083	777	467	140	61	6000
1986-87	16	50	139	428	823	990	1243	1111	779	425	208	20	6232
1987-88	2	34	119	539	706	995	1326	1082	823	546	176	91	6439
1988-89	13	12	156	574	643	1083	1037	1031	853	575	251	39	6267
1989-90	6	31	133	377	750	1433	915	881	757	465	269	44	6061
1990-91	10	13	152	320	619	894	1153	877	757	402	113	23	5333
1991-92	0	0	160	370	699	989	1121	1001	942	521	209	40	6052
1992-93	4	9	132	488	676	993	1017	1148	975	447	136	39	6064
1993-94	0	4	174	460	703	1077							

COOLING DEGREE DAYS Base 65 deg. F AVOCA, WILKES-BARRE - SCRANTON PENNSYLVANIA

YEAR	JAN	FEB	MAR	APR	MAY	JUNE	JULY	AUG	SEP	OCT	NOV	DEC	TOTAL
1969	0	0	0	7	34	141	193	178	73	1	0	0	627
1970	0	0	0	10	40	81	189	159	92	2	0	0	573
1971	0	0	0	0	16	145	160	132	113	4	3	0	573
1972	0	0	0	0	20	53	232	167	42	0	0	0	514
1973	0	0	0	4	0	132	212	223	72	7	0	0	650
1974	0	0	0	10	28	52	194	117	46	0	0	0	447
1975	0	0	0	0	91	146	278	207	13	14	0	0	749
1976	0	0	0	46	16	198	145	159	37	0	0	0	601
1977	0	0	2	13	57	62	208	162	59	0	2	0	565
1978	0	0	0	0	52	84	181	194	26	0	0	0	537
1979	0	0	0	2	32	78	218	214	75	15	0	0	634
1980	0	0	0	0	42	107	263	322	122	3	0	0	859
1981	0	0	0	4	42	131	231	172	55	0	0	0	635
1982	0	0	0	1	34	55	208	98	41	3	5	0	445
1983	0	0	0	4	12	125	243	224	118	9	0	0	735
1984	0	0	0	0	20	165	218	248	58	12	0	0	721
1985	0	0	0	20	32	47	169	142	104	0	0	0	514
1986	0	0	2	0	76	104	205	131	44	8	0	0	570
1987	0	0	0	3	62	138	273	141	30	0	0	0	647
1988	0	0	0	0	34	111	356	266	23	3	0	0	793
1989	0	0	0	0	31	109	179	148	57	4	0	0	528
1990	0	0	8	29	2	127	225	160	56	24	0	0	631
1991	0	0	0	12	142	164	264	230	69	14	0	0	895
1992	0	0	0	0	21	85	201	123	71	0	0	0	501
1993	0	0	0	5	41	158	334	249	66	0	0	0	853

SNOWFALL (inches) AVOCA, WILKES-BARRE - SCRANTON PENNSYLVANIA

SEASON	JULY	AUG	SEP	OCT	NOV	DEC	JAN	FEB	MAR	APR	MAY	JUNE	TOTAL
1964-65	0.0	0.0	0.0	0.2	0.1	4.1	11.5	2.3	9.9	3.8	0.0	0.0	31.9
1965-66	0.0	0.0	0.0	0.6	0.5	1.3	20.7	17.5	3.8	0.7	0.6	0.0	45.7
1966-67	0.0	0.0	0.0	T	T	17.7	8.3	14.4	29.7	4.8	0.4	0.0	75.3
1967-68	0.0	0.0	0.0	T	7.2	13.8	6.0	2.9	2.7	0.0	0.0	0.0	32.6
1968-69	0.0	0.0	0.0	T	10.9	5.8	2.7	14.8	2.5	0.0	0.0	0.0	36.7
1969-70	0.0	0.0	0.0	T	2.7	33.9	9.5	9.5	20.6	0.6	T	0.0	76.8
1970-71	0.0	0.0	0.0	0.3	T	12.3	15.2	12.1	15.6	1.6	0.0	0.0	57.1
1971-72	0.0	0.0	0.0	0.0	22.5	4.1	5.9	19.7	6.6	3.8	0.0	0.0	62.6
1972-73	0.0	0.0	0.0	0.8	7.9	3.9	5.0	3.1	1.9	0.2	0.4	0.0	23.2
1973-74	0.0	0.0	0.0	T	0.4	16.0	12.8	4.5	15.7	2.8	0.0	0.0	52.2
1974-75	0.0	0.0	0.0	0.2	2.2	5.2	13.7	15.2	5.5	1.2	0.0	0.0	43.2
1975-76	0.0	0.0	0.0	0.0	1.3	3.7	13.0	7.5	10.2	0.5	T	0.0	36.2
1976-77	0.0	0.0	0.0	0.0	6.0	6.7	15.7	13.0	11.2	1.4	2.4	0.0	56.4
1977-78	0.0	0.0	0.0	0.6	8.7	9.8	28.8	18.2	6.5	0.9	0.0	0.0	73.5
1978-79	0.0	0.0	0.0	T	4.1	7.9	12.7	14.3	1.1	4.4	0.0	0.0	44.5
1979-80	0.0	0.0	0.0	T	T	5.5	1.4	8.1	10.5	T	0.0	0.0	25.5
1980-81	0.0	0.0	0.0	T	8.6	8.0	11.1	7.0	5.8	T	0.0	0.0	40.5
1981-82	0.0	0.0	0.0	T	1.0	14.2	14.1	13.5	8.7	8.1	0.0	0.0	59.6
1982-83	0.0	0.0	0.0	0.0	0.5	7.4	8.4	12.3	3.8	26.7	0.0	0.0	59.1
1983-84	0.0	0.0	0.0	0.0	3.1	2.7	11.2	4.0	18.4	0.0	0.0	0.0	39.4
1984-85	0.0	0.0	0.0	0.0	3.0	9.2	10.8	9.1	1.4	1.8	0.0	0.0	35.3
1985-86	0.0	0.0	0.0	0.0	1.7	13.4	12.9	11.6	1.1	8.6	0.0	0.0	49.3
1986-87	0.0	0.0	0.0	0.0	8.6	1.4	29.6	6.4	0.9	0.6	0.0	0.0	47.5
1987-88	0.0	0.0	0.0	T	6.4	6.4	13.0	14.9	4.3	0.7	0.0	0.0	45.7
1988-89	0.0	0.0	0.0	T	T	1.1	2.1	3.0	1.1	T	0.0	0.0	7.3
1989-90	0.0	0.0	0.0	T	2.6	8.3	10.8	7.3	6.2	2.1	0.0	0.0	37.3
1990-91	0.0	0.0	T	T	0.4	8.4	6.6	7.6	7.2	1.1	0.0	0.0	31.3
1991-92	0.0	0.0	0.0	0.0	0.1	3.5	5.4	6.3	8.5	0.7	0.0	0.0	24.5
1992-93	0.0	0.0	T	T	0.5	10.0	3.8	12.1	32.0	1.9	0.0	0.0	60.3
1993-94	0.0	T	T	1.9	0.7	8.0							
Record Mean	0.0	T	T	0.2	3.3	8.8	11.2	10.8	9.4	3.1	0.1	0.0	47.0

MIDDLETOWN/HARRISBURG INTL APT
PENNSYLVANIA

No narrative available

NORMALS, MEANS, AND EXTREMES

MIDDLETOWN/HARRISBURG INTL APT PENNSYLVANIA

LATITUDE: 40°12'N LONGITUDE: 76°46' W ELEVATION: FT. GRND 303 BARO 324 TIME ZONE: EASTERN WBAN: 14711

	(a)	JAN	FEB	MAR	APR	MAY	JUNE	JULY	AUG	SEP	OCT	NOV	DEC	YEAR
TEMPERATURE °F:														
Normals														
-Daily Maximum		35.9	39.2	50.3	62.0	72.5	81.2	85.8	83.8	76.3	64.7	52.6	40.6	62.1
-Daily Minimum		21.2	23.3	32.0	41.2	51.1	60.6	65.6	64.3	56.5	44.6	36.1	26.6	43.6
-Monthly		28.6	31.3	41.2	51.6	61.8	70.9	75.7	74.1	66.4	54.7	44.4	33.6	52.9
Extremes														
-Record Highest	55	73	75	86	93	97	100	107	101	102	97	84	75	107
-Year		1950	1985	1945	1985	1942	1966	1966	1944	1953	1941	1950	1984	JUL 1966
-Record Lowest	55	-9	-5	5	19	31	40	49	45	30	23	13	-8	-9
-Year		1985	1979	1984	1982	1966	1980	1945	1976	1963	1969	1955	1960	JAN 1985
NORMAL DEGREE DAYS:														
Heating (base 65°F)		1128	944	738	402	147	9	0	0	59	329	618	973	5347
Cooling (base 65°F)		0	0	0	0	48	186	332	285	101	10	0	0	962
% OF POSSIBLE SUNSHINE	55	49	54	57	58	60	65	68	67	61	57	47	44	57
MEAN SKY COVER (tenths)														
Sunrise - Sunset	43	6.7	6.6	6.6	6.5	6.5	6.1	6.0	5.9	5.8	5.7	6.7	7.0	6.3
MEAN NUMBER OF DAYS:														
Sunrise to Sunset														
-Clear	55	6.7	6.7	7.2	6.4	6.1	6.7	7.2	8.0	8.7	10.0	6.3	6.1	86.0
-Partly Cloudy	55	7.5	7.2	8.2	8.6	10.4	11.5	11.5	11.1	9.5	8.1	8.2	7.5	109.4
-Cloudy	55	16.7	14.4	15.6	15.0	14.5	11.8	12.3	11.9	11.8	12.9	15.6	17.4	169.9
Precipitation .01 inches or more	15	10.5	10.1	11.5	12.4	12.8	10.5	10.0	8.9	9.3	8.6	10.1	10.0	124.7
Snow,Ice pellets,hail 1.0 inches or more	15	2.5	2.3	1.4	0.3	0.0	0.0	0.0	0.0	0.0	0.0	0.4	1.6	8.4
Thunderstorms	50	0.2	0.2	1.1	2.2	5.1	6.2	6.9	5.2	2.9	0.8	0.5	0.2	31.5
Heavy Fog Visibility 1/4 mile or less	50	2.3	2.3	1.7	1.0	0.9	0.6	0.6	0.8	1.5	2.8	1.8	2.4	18.7
Temperature °F														
-Maximum														
90° and above	55	0.0	0.0	0.0	0.3	1.0	4.6	9.0	6.1	1.8	0.1	0.0	0.0	22.9
32° and below	55	9.3	5.9	1.3	0.0	0.0	0.0	0.0	0.0	0.0	0.0	0.2	5.5	22.2
-Minimum														
32° and below	55	26.2	23.1	17.1	3.6	0.1	0.0	0.0	0.0	0.1	2.0	10.9	22.9	105.9
0° and below	55	0.6	0.2	0.0	0.0	0.0	0.0	0.0	0.0	0.0	0.0	0.0	0.1	0.9
AVG. STATION PRESS.(mb)	21	1006.3	1006.2	1004.7	1003.0	1003.3	1003.3	1003.9	1005.4	1006.7	1007.3	1006.8	1007.0	1005.3
RELATIVE HUMIDITY (%)														
Hour 01	51	70	68	67	67	74	79	79	82	81	79	74	71	74
Hour 07 (Local Time)	51	72	71	72	71	74	77	79	83	85	82	77	73	76
Hour 13	50	58	55	52	50	52	53	53	55	56	55	57	58	55
Hour 19	51	63	61	57	54	58	60	60	65	69	67	66	64	62
PRECIPITATION (inches):														
Water Equivalent														
-Normal		2.84	2.93	3.28	3.24	4.26	3.85	3.59	3.31	3.51	2.93	3.52	3.24	40.50
-Maximum Monthly	15	8.01	5.93	6.32	7.96	9.71	8.12	7.20	6.26	8.41	5.59	6.23	7.57	9.71
-Year		1979	1981	1993	1983	1989	1982	1989	1986	1987	1989	1985	1983	MAY 1989
-Minimum Monthly	15	0.43	0.82	1.02	0.45	1.86	1.00	0.97	1.45	0.65	1.34	0.96	0.77	0.43
-Year		1981	1980	1981	1985	1981	1988	1983	1992	1986	1985	1981	1980	JAN 1981
-Maximum in 24 hrs	13	2.09	1.84	1.94	2.06	2.91	2.32	2.58	2.78	3.03	2.19	3.27	2.58	3.27
-Year		1979	1985	1992	1992	1984	1987	1989	1991	1979	1980	1993	1993	NOV 1993
Snow,Ice pellets,hail														
-Maximum Monthly	15	31.5	28.8	22.8	10.2	0.0	T	0.0	T	0.0	T	9.7	12.5	31.5
-Year		1987	1983	1993	1982		1993		1993		1982	1987	1981	JAN 1987
-Maximum in 24 hrs	13	11.2	14.2	20.4	2.6	0.0	T	0.0	T	0.0	T	7.9	9.1	20.4
-Year		1987	1979	1993	1985		1993		1993		1979	1987	1990	MAR 1993
WIND:														
Mean Speed (mph)	51	8.3	9.0	9.5	9.2	7.6	6.9	6.3	5.9	6.1	6.6	7.8	8.1	7.6
Prevailing Direction through 1963		WNW	WNW	WNW	WNW	W	W	W	W	WNW	W	WNW	WNW	WNW
Fastest Obs. 1 Min.														
-Direction (!!)	11	27	31	31	28	29	33	29	35	28	32	31	31	33
-Speed (MPH)	11	44	35	40	35	47	58	35	46	32	37	40	46	58
-Year		1978	1992	1992	1991	1980	1980	1987	1979	1993	1992	1989	1978	JUN 1980
Peak Gust														
-Direction (!!)														
-Speed (mph)														
-Date														

PRECIPITATION (inches)

MIDDLETOWN/HARRISBURG INTL APT PENNSYLVANIA

YEAR	JAN	FEB	MAR	APR	MAY	JUNE	JULY	AUG	SEP	OCT	NOV	DEC	ANNUAL
1964	4.78	3.12	2.94	4.91	0.51	4.20	2.25	3.07	1.77	1.92	1.87	3.11	34.45
1965	2.70	3.29	3.61	1.25	2.38	2.60	3.10	3.99	2.12	3.65	1.63	0.87	31.19
1966	3.57	4.44	1.88	3.44	0.98	0.07	0.81	1.53	6.12	2.12	3.56	3.08	31.60
1967	1.81	1.54	5.26	2.58	4.32	1.90	5.96	5.61	1.80	3.15	2.89	4.27	41.09
1968	1.32	0.53	3.40	2.43	6.55	2.25	1.94	1.77	5.18	2.34	3.38	2.12	33.21
1969	1.06	1.70	2.20	2.13	1.56	2.54	9.72	2.07	2.32	1.63	3.29	6.46	36.68
1970	0.88	3.25	3.64	5.03	2.39	5.80	6.34	2.97	2.12	3.20	4.59	3.50	43.71
1971	2.70	5.62	2.67	1.04	5.30	1.80	2.84	7.77	1.94	2.85	4.96	1.93	41.42
1972	2.65	5.00	2.68	4.10	5.56	18.55	2.26	2.52	1.41	2.03	7.20	5.31	59.27
1973	3.24	2.50	2.00	6.23	6.37	3.34	2.18	2.19	5.73	2.47	1.04	6.52	43.81
1974	3.82	1.36	4.64	3.21	4.38	3.69	2.79	4.13	6.79	1.25	2.30	4.59	42.95
1975	4.12	3.10	3.78	2.80	5.25	6.51	3.13	1.83	14.97	2.62	2.92	3.19	54.22
1976	4.34	1.88	3.43	1.63	5.42	2.42	5.50	3.28	4.79	9.87	0.79	1.96	45.31
1977	1.44	1.75	6.10	4.48	1.00	3.17	3.01	0.93	3.73	3.66	5.61	4.82	39.70
1978	7.44	1.35	3.94	1.97	5.67	5.16	4.35	3.60	1.64	2.51	2.13	3.95	43.71
#1979	8.01	4.74	1.93	3.60	4.66	2.62	3.14	3.24	6.62	3.91	2.67	1.46	46.60
1980	0.90	0.82	5.47	4.27	4.58	2.50	1.59	1.51	1.06	2.94	3.65	0.77	30.06
1981	0.43	5.93	1.02	2.77	1.86	4.66	4.67	4.11	2.20	3.76	0.96	2.41	34.78
1982	3.63	1.92	2.20	4.17	4.89	8.12	2.90	2.47	2.87	1.82	3.37	1.56	39.92
1983	2.26	3.38	4.86	7.96	5.36	?.81	0.97	2.50	1.40	4.21	5.29	7.57	48.57
1984	1.12	4.51	5.36	4.46	6.20	6.36	3.76	2.75	1.49	1.98	3.78	2.28	44.05
1985	1.06	2.91	2.78	0.45	6.29	3.07	2.50	2.14	3.76	1.34	6.23	1.28	33.81
1986	2.24	4.50	3.16	4.10	2.29	1.48	5.17	6.26	0.65	2.59	4.58	4.90	41.92
1987	3.69	1.59	1.43	2.93	3.73	3.46	1.96	2.89	8.41	2.63	4.96	1.84	39.52
1988	2.18	3.28	1.98	2.65	5.79	1.00	4.40	2.67	2.42	1.81	3.67	0.90	32.75
1989	2.29	1.90	3.60	1.10	9.71	6.02	7.20	3.03	2.63	5.59	2.17	1.27	46.51
1990	3.77	2.73	1.76	2.60	7.20	1.10	3.62	6.14	1.65	4.92	2.58	6.05	44.12
#1991	2.61	1.39	3.54	2.00	3.15	1.08	1.99	5.29	1.35	3.15	2.08	3.49	31.12
1992	1.62	1.56	5.13	2.62	3.17	1.90	3.54	1.45	5.65	1.64	4.82	2.42	35.52
1993	2.39	2.32	6.32	6.49	1.96	3.20	3.65	3.45	7.84	2.66	4.17	3.95	48.40
Record Mean	2.79	2.68	3.26	3.07	3.77	3.58	3.61	3.67	3.20	2.91	2.81	2.95	38.29

AVERAGE TEMPERATURE (deg. F)

MIDDLETOWN/HARRISBURG INTL APT PENNSYLVANIA

YEAR	JAN	FEB	MAR	APR	MAY	JUNE	JULY	AUG	SEP	OCT	NOV	DEC	ANNUAL
1964	30.2	28.9	40.5	49.6	64.3	71.4	76.1	71.5	66.2	52.0	45.7	33.9	52.5
1965	26.4	32.5	37.5	50.1	66.5	71.7	75.6	74.6	69.8	53.4	42.2	35.7	53.0
1966	26.3	31.5	43.8	49.0	61.4	74.6	79.9	78.3	66.7	54.7	45.1	31.7	53.6
1967	33.6	26.9	38.8	53.0	55.2	73.9	74.2	71.8	65.3	53.3	39.8	34.8	51.7
1968	24.0	29.2	43.7	53.7	58.0	70.3	77.3	76.7	67.6	56.1	44.9	31.3	52.7
1969	29.9	33.3	38.6	53.4	63.2	72.4	75.3	73.4	65.6	53.8	42.7	31.4	52.8
1970	22.9	30.4	36.7	51.4	65.1	70.7	76.2	75.6	71.6	58.7	46.0	34.8	53.4
1971	26.4	33.2	38.6	50.4	60.0	72.5	75.5	72.2	69.9	60.6	43.5	40.3	53.6
1972	34.5	30.2	40.0	49.6	62.3	67.7	76.2	74.0	68.4	52.1	41.8	36.8	52.8
1973	33.7	31.7	45.2	50.9	57.8	73.4	75.5	76.1	68.6	57.4	46.9	36.2	54.5
1974	34.8	32.3	42.8	56.2	63.0	70.5	77.6	77.1	64.5	51.6	44.9	35.4	54.2
1975	33.3	32.4	38.3	47.4	64.8	70.7	75.3	76.2	63.3	57.7	50.0	34.2	53.7
1976	27.6	39.6	44.2	54.5	59.4	73.4	72.3	72.4	64.8	51.5	39.6	30.0	52.4
1977	20.1	30.4	46.0	54.1	64.5	68.6	75.9	74.3	68.3	52.7	46.1	31.6	52.7
1978	26.2	22.8	38.6	51.0	61.5	69.5	73.1	76.9	67.6	54.4	46.7	36.5	52.1
1979	29.2	22.6	45.1	50.4	62.2	68.5	73.4	72.9	65.5	52.3	46.8	37.6	52.2
1980	30.3	29.1	38.9	52.8	63.3	67.8	76.3	76.1	67.7	51.5	39.4	29.6	51.9
1981	23.7	34.6	38.7	53.7	61.9	71.7	75.7	72.2	63.9	50.7	44.7	31.9	51.9
1982	22.8	30.9	38.6	47.6	62.2	65.1	74.4	70.5	65.3	55.1	47.6	41.4	51.8
1983	33.0	33.4	42.7	49.3	58.4	69.1	75.9	74.9	66.2	53.6	43.9	28.7	52.4
1984	24.8	36.6	33.7	48.0	58.2	72.9	74.3	75.8	64.4	61.5	43.9	41.5	53.0
1985	27.9	34.4	44.5	56.9	65.2	69.4	75.9	74.1	69.2	57.2	47.9	31.0	54.5
1986	31.4	30.0	43.5	53.5	65.6	71.4	76.3	72.0	66.2	56.0	41.2	36.1	53.6
1987	30.0	32.3	44.1	52.3	63.2	72.6	78.2	73.1	65.7	49.4	43.9	36.6	53.5
1988	24.4	31.8	42.4	50.0	62.3	70.8	78.8	76.2	63.5	49.5	43.7	33.3	52.2
1989	34.8	32.4	40.4	50.4	60.0	70.6	73.7	72.6	66.0	55.6	42.7	22.6	51.8
1990	38.2	38.2	44.9	53.1	59.4	71.2	75.2	72.7	65.0	58.2	46.9	38.4	55.1
#1991	31.7	37.4	43.7	53.7	69.1	74.2	78.7	76.2	65.4	56.9	43.7	36.5	55.6
1992	33.0	35.7	40.3	51.8	60.2	69.3	75.0	71.6	65.5	51.3	44.3	35.3	52.8
1993	34.8	28.8	36.6	51.3	64.6	72.1	78.0	75.9	65.6	52.8	43.9	34.0	53.2
Record Mean	30.2	31.3	40.4	50.7	62.1	70.8	75.3	73.4	66.5	55.0	43.6	33.2	52.7
Max	37.1	38.7	48.8	59.6	72.2	80.6	84.9	82.8	75.9	64.3	51.5	40.0	61.4
Min	23.3	23.8	32.0	41.8	52.1	60.9	65.7	63.9	57.0	45.6	35.7	26.4	44.0

REFERENCE NOTES

MIDDLETOWN/HARRISBURG INTL APT PENNSYLVANIA

GENERAL
T - TRACE AMOUNT.
BLANK ENTRIES DENOTE MISSING/UNREPORTED DATA.
# INDICATES A STATION OR INSTRUMENT RELOCATION.

SPECIFIC

PM - INCLUDES LAST DAY OF PREVIOUS MONTH
ASOS - AUTOMATED SURFACE OBSERVING SYSTEM IN OPERATION DURING THESE MONTHS.

(a) - LENGTH OF RECORD IN YEARS, ALTHOUGH INDIVIDUAL MONTHS MAY BE MISSING.
0.* OR * - THE VALUE IS BETWEEN 0.0 AND 0.05
NORMALS - BASED ON THE 1961-1990 RECORD PERIOD.
EXTREMES - DATES ARE THE MOST RECENT OCCURRENCE.
WIND DIR.- NUMERALS SHOW TENS OF DEGRESS CLOCKWISE FROM TRUE NORTH. "00" INDICATES CALM.
RESULTANT DIRECTIONS ARE GIVEN TO WHOLE DEGREES.
BOLD VALUES INDICATE EXTREME VALUES WHICH OCCURRED AFTER THE ASOS SYSTEM WAS COMMISSIONED.

RECORD = PERIOD OF RECORD
RECORD MEAN PRECIPITATION IS THE MEAN OF ALL DAILY PRECIPITATION AMOUNTS DURING THE PERIOD OF RECORD.
RECORD MAX(MIN) TEMPERATURE IS THE MEAN OF ALL DAILY MAX(MIN) TEMPERATURES DURING THE PERIOD OF RECORD.
RECORD MEAN TEMPERATURE IS THE SUM OF THE RECORD MAX AND RECORD MIN DIVIDED BY 2.
AVERAGE TEMPERATURE IS THE SUM OF THE MEAN DAILY MAX AND MIN TEMPERATURE DIVIDED BY 2.

HEATING DEGREE DAYS Base 65 deg. F — MIDDLETOWN/HARRISBURG INTL APT PENNSYLVANIA

SEASON	JULY	AUG	SEP	OCT	NOV	DEC	JAN	FEB	MAR	APR	MAY	JUNE	TOTAL
1964-65	0	4	71	399	570	958	1192	902	847	441	66	27	5477
1965-66	0	7	44	357	677	900	1191	932	648	472	166	12	5406
1966-67	0	0	69	312	592	1024	966	1061	806	364	306	3	5503
1967-68	0	5	85	369	750	931	1266	1032	654	331	216	12	5651
1968-69	0	3	18	277	593	1038	1083	882	809	345	123	8	5179
1969-70	0	0	89	352	662	1036	1299	962	872	407	93	13	5785
1970-71	0	0	39	213	564	931	1192	884	812	432	165	12	5244
1971-72	0	3	40	146	643	759	940	1001	766	457	108	44	4907
1972-73	0	1	25	395	686	865	964	926	607	422	227	7	5125
1973-74	0	1	34	238	534	887	931	910	683	289	133	2	4642
1974-75	0	0	94	414	600	911	977	903	818	520	97	13	5347
1975-76	0	0	87	232	445	951	1150	730	639	354	193	23	4804
1976-77	0	5	75	418	756	1075	1387	966	588	340	106	32	5748
1977-78	0	5	35	377	562	1029	1196	1175	810	414	173	17	5793
1978-79	14	0	48	321	544	876	1104	1182	611	435	123	26	5284
1979-80	12	14	71	393	536	844	1070	1033	799	361	103	48	5284
1980-81	0	0	57	411	761	1091	1277	844	809	339	147	6	5742
1981-82	0	1	94	437	599	1021	1304	948	812	518	128	61	5923
1982-83	7	12	67	318	520	725	985	876	686	468	221	25	4910
1983-84	0	2	103	362	628	1117	1238	817	962	502	240	11	5982
1984-85	0	0	105	131	627	724	1143	849	627	292	87	16	4601
1985-86	0	0	41	237	508	1049	1038	974	664	349	89	9	4958
1986-87	2	17	46	300	705	890	1080	907	643	380	142	2	5114
1987-88	0	8	51	477	627	873	1252	961	693	445	131	41	5559
1988-89	4	5	88	475	633	975	931	912	760	433	196	9	5421
1989-90	1	6	81	292	663	1306	824	744	629	385	175	13	5119
1990-91	5	8	96	248	535	816	1026	769	651	345	69	2	4570
#1991-92	0	0	103	279	634	877	986	842	761	392	170	16	5060
#1992-93	0	3	86	420	615	914	931	1005	875	405	67	15	5336
1993-94	0	2	99	371	628	954							

COOLING DEGREE DAYS Base 65 deg. F — MIDDLETOWN/HARRISBURG INTL APT PENNSYLVANIA

YEAR	JAN	FEB	MAR	APR	MAY	JUNE	JULY	AUG	SEP	OCT	NOV	DEC	TOTAL
1969	0	0	0	3	71	235	327	267	113	11	0	0	1027
1970	0	0	0	7	102	191	353	333	246	24	0	0	1256
1971	0	0	0	0	17	241	331	236	195	17	6	0	1043
1972	0	0	0	0	33	133	357	287	137	3	0	0	950
1973	0	0	0	8	13	266	334	352	148	9	0	0	1130
1974	0	0	0	34	79	176	401	381	88	1	3	0	1163
1975	0	0	0	0	97	192	325	354	44	12	2	0	1026
1976	0	0	0	47	22	283	233	240	73	3	0	0	901
1977	0	0	4	19	95	147	347	297	140	1	3	0	1053
1978	0	0	0	0	69	162	273	377	133	1	0	0	1015
1979	0	0	0	5	43	138	279	264	92	7	0	0	828
1980	0	0	0	0	57	138	355	350	145	0	0	0	1045
1981	0	0	0	6	60	213	339	232	66	0	0	0	916
1982	0	0	0	2	48	70	307	191	83	19	4	0	724
1983	0	0	0	6	22	154	343	315	146	13	0	0	999
1984	0	0	0	0	34	256	292	342	95	35	0	1	1055
1985	0	0	0	55	99	157	345	290	173	4	0	0	1123
1986	0	0	5	12	116	205	360	238	88	27	0	0	1051
1987	0	0	0	9	94	237	418	266	76	0	0	0	1100
1988	0	0	0	0	53	219	439	355	52	4	0	0	1122
1989	0	0	5	0	49	182	279	249	114	9	1	0	888
1990	0	0	14	34	12	205	330	254	102	43	0	0	994
#1991	0	0	0	16	202	284	429	355	118	31	0	0	1435
1992	0	0	0	1	29	151	314	214	108	0	0	0	817
1993	0	0	0	0	63	236	410	348	127	0	0	0	1184

SNOWFALL (inches) — MIDDLETOWN/HARRISBURG INTL APT PENNSYLVANIA

SEASON	JULY	AUG	SEP	OCT	NOV	DEC	JAN	FEB	MAR	APR	MAY	JUNE	TOTAL
1964-65	0.0	0.0	0.0	0.0	T	1.4	13.4	1.7	15.1	0.2	0.0	0.0	31.8
1965-66	0.0	0.0	0.0	T	T	T	24.8	16.8	1.0	T	T	0.0	42.6
1966-67	0.0	0.0	0.0	0.0	0.2	19.9	1.6	16.5	10.2	T	0.0	0.0	48.4
1967-68	0.0	0.0	0.0	0.0	9.7	13.0	3.0	1.8	3.5	0.0	0.0	0.0	31.0
1968-69	0.0	0.0	0.0	0.0	3.0	0.2	1.2	16.8	3.8	0.0	0.0	0.0	25.0
1969-70	0.0	0.0	0.0	T	2.1	28.3	9.8	7.5	12.9	T	0.0	0.0	60.6
1970-71	0.0	0.0	0.0	0.0	0.0	10.9	11.6	5.1	5.3	T	0.0	0.0	32.9
1971-72	0.0	0.0	0.0	0.0	8.8	T	2.6	21.6	0.5	1.1	0.0	0.0	34.6
1972-73	0.0	0.0	0.0	1.2	5.9	0.5	T	5.7	T	T	0.0	0.0	13.3
1973-74	0.0	0.0	0.0	0.0	T	15.3	7.0	5.5	T	T	0.0	0.0	27.8
1974-75	0.0	0.0	0.0	0.0	T	0.5	11.3	13.1	6.1	T	0.0	0.0	31.0
1975-76	0.0	0.0	0.0	0.0	T	2.2	3.6	2.5	10.0	0.0	0.0	0.0	18.3
1976-77	0.0	0.0	0.0	0.0	1.4	5.1	12.2	4.5	0.2	T	T	0.0	23.4
1977-78	0.0	0.0	0.0	T	1.5	5.5	33.5	21.1	9.0	0.0	0.0	0.0	70.6
#1978-79	0.0	0.0	0.0	0.0	4.0	0.3	9.2	26.0	T	T	0.0	0.0	39.5
1979-80	0.0	0.0	0.0	T	T	0.2	3.8	2.7	7.9	0.0	0.0	0.0	14.6
1980-81	0.0	0.0	0.0	0.0	4.0	4.3	5.5	4.4	6.7	0.0	0.0	0.0	24.9
1981-82	0.0	0.0	0.0	0.0	0.8	12.5	18.8	8.4	7.8	10.2	0.0	0.0	58.5
1982-83	0.0	0.0	0.0	T	T	1.1	4.4	28.8	0.4	1.3	0.0	0.0	36.0
1983-84	0.0	0.0	0.0	0.0	T	4.6	9.7	2.3	14.9	T	0.0	0.0	31.5
1984-85	0.0	0.0	0.0	0.0	1.9	2.6	10.6	11.4	T	3.6	0.0	0.0	30.1
1985-86	0.0	0.0	0.0	0.0	T	5.6	7.8	23.1	T	T	0.0	0.0	36.5
1986-87	0.0	0.0	0.0	0.0	T	1.9	31.5	10.1	1.4	1.0	0.0	0.0	45.9
1987-88	0.0	0.0	0.0	0.0	9.7	3.6	9.6	2.8	1.0	T	0.0	0.0	26.7
1988-89	0.0	0.0	0.0	0.0	T	T	6.4	2.2	11.3	0.0	0.0	0.0	19.9
1989-90	0.0	0.0	0.0	0.0	1.8	6.7	4.9	1.3	3.5	1.1	0.0	0.0	19.3
1990-91	0.0	0.0	0.0	0.0	0.0	9.3	5.2	0.7	5.9	T	0.0	0.0	21.1
#1991-92	0.0	0.0	0.0	0.0	0.0	T	1.7	4.6	6.6	0.0	0.0	T	12.9
1992-93	0.0	0.0	0.0	0.0	T	3.9	1.4	18.5	22.8	0.6	0.0	T	47.2
1993-94	0.0	T	0.0	0.0	T	0.9							
Record Mean	0.0	T	0.0	T	1.9	6.6	9.4	9.3	6.5	0.5	T	T	34.3

PHILADELPHIA, PENNSYLVANIA

The Appalachian Mountains to the west and the Atlantic Ocean to the east have a moderating effect on climate. Periods of very high or very low temperatures seldom last for more than three or four days. Temperatures below zero or above 100 degrees are a rarity. On occasion, the area becomes engulfed with maritime air during the summer months, and high humidity adds to the discomfort of seasonably warm temperatures.

Precipitation is fairly evenly distributed throughout the year with maximum amounts during the late summer months. Much of the summer rainfall is from local thunderstorms and amounts vary in different areas of the city. This is due, in part, to the higher elevations to the west and north. Snowfall amounts are often considerably larger in the northern suburbs than in the central and southern parts of the city. In many cases, the precipitation will change from snow to rain within the city. Single storms of 10 inches or more occur about every five years.

The prevailing wind direction for the summer months is from the southwest, while northwesterly winds prevail during the winter. The annual prevailing direction is from the west-southwest. Destructive velocities are comparatively rare and occur mostly in gustiness during summer thunderstorms. High winds occurring in the winter months, as a rule, come with the advance of cold air after the passage of a deep low pressure system. Only rarely have hurricanes in the vicinity caused widespread damage, primarily because of flooding.

Flood stages in the Schuylkill River normally occur about twice a year. Flood stages seldom last over 12 hours and usually occur after excessive thunderstorms. Flooding rarely occurs on the Delaware River.

NORMALS, MEANS, AND EXTREMES

PHILADELPHIA, PENNSYLVANIA

LATITUDE: 39°53'N LONGITUDE: 75°15' W ELEVATION: FT. GRND 5 BARO 63 TIME ZONE: EASTERN WBAN: 13739

	(a)	JAN	FEB	MAR	APR	MAY	JUNE	JULY	AUG	SEP	OCT	NOV	DEC	YEAR
TEMPERATURE °F:														
Normals														
-Daily Maximum		37.9	41.0	51.6	62.6	73.1	81.7	86.1	84.6	77.6	66.3	55.1	43.4	63.4
-Daily Minimum		22.8	24.8	33.2	42.1	52.7	61.8	67.2	66.3	58.7	46.4	37.6	28.1	45.1
-Monthly		30.4	33.0	42.4	52.4	62.9	71.8	76.7	75.5	68.2	56.4	46.4	35.8	54.3
Extremes														
-Record Highest	52	74	74	87	94	97	100	104	101	100	96	81	72	104
-Year		1950	1985	1945	1976	1991	1991	1966	1955	1953	1941	1993	1984	JUL 1966
-Record Lowest	52	-7	-4	7	19	28	44	51	44	35	25	15	1	-7
-Year		1984	1961	1984	1982	1966	1984	1966	1986	1963	1969	1976	1983	JAN 1984
NORMAL DEGREE DAYS:														
Heating (base 65°F)		1073	896	701	378	123	5	0	0	32	283	558	905	4954
Cooling (base 65°F)		0	0	0	0	58	209	363	326	128	17	0	0	1101
% OF POSSIBLE SUNSHINE	51	50	53	55	55	56	62	62	61	59	59	52	49	56
MEAN SKY COVER (tenths)														
Sunrise - Sunset	53	6.6	6.4	6.4	6.4	6.5	6.1	6.0	5.8	5.7	5.5	6.3	6.5	6.2
MEAN NUMBER OF DAYS:														
Sunrise to Sunset														
-Clear	53	7.2	7.2	7.7	7.1	6.2	7.1	7.3	8.3	9.6	10.5	7.2	7.4	92.9
-Partly Cloudy	53	7.9	7.4	8.1	8.8	10.6	11.5	11.7	11.3	9.0	8.7	8.9	8.3	112.2
-Cloudy	53	15.9	13.7	15.2	14.1	14.2	11.4	12.1	11.4	11.4	11.8	13.9	15.2	160.2
Precipitation														
.01 inches or more	53	10.8	9.3	10.9	10.7	11.1	10.0	9.3	9.1	8.2	7.6	9.4	10.1	116.6
Snow, Ice pellets, hail														
1.0 inches or more	53	1.9	1.6	1.0	0.1	0.0	0.0	0.0	0.0	0.0	0.*	0.2	0.8	5.7
Thunderstorms	53	0.2	0.3	1.0	2.0	4.2	5.4	5.7	4.9	2.4	0.8	0.6	0.2	27.5
Heavy Fog Visibility														
1/4 mile or less	53	2.7	2.2	1.7	1.2	1.3	1.0	0.8	1.0	1.5	3.3	2.4	2.5	21.6
Temperature °F														
-Maximum														
90° and above	34	0.0	0.0	0.0	0.4	1.1	4.2	8.9	6.3	1.9	0.0	0.0	0.0	22.8
32° and below	34	8.5	5.4	0.9	0.0	0.0	0.0	0.0	0.0	0.0	0.0	0.1	4.2	19.1
-Minimum														
32° and below	34	25.8	22.4	14.2	2.4	0.*	0.0	0.0	0.0	0.0	1.4	8.3	20.9	95.4
0° and below	34	0.4	0.1	0.0	0.0	0.0	0.0	0.0	0.0	0.0	0.0	0.0	0.0	0.5
AVG. STATION PRESS. (mb)	21	1017.6	1017.5	1015.9	1014.2	1014.4	1014.3	1014.8	1016.3	1017.6	1018.4	1018.1	1018.3	1016.5
RELATIVE HUMIDITY (%)														
Hour 01	34	71	68	69	70	77	79	81	82	82	80	75	72	76
Hour 07 (Local Time)	34	73	71	72	71	75	76	79	81	83	83	78	74	76
Hour 13	34	59	55	52	49	52	53	54	55	56	54	56	59	55
Hour 19	34	65	60	58	55	59	60	63	65	69	69	66	66	63
PRECIPITATION (inches):														
Water Equivalent														
-Normal		3.21	2.79	3.46	3.62	3.75	3.74	4.28	3.80	3.42	2.62	3.34	3.38	41.41
-Maximum Monthly	51	8.86	6.44	7.01	8.12	7.41	7.88	9.44	9.70	8.78	5.21	9.06	7.37	9.70
-Year		1978	1979	1980	1983	1948	1973	1989	1955	1960	1943	1972	1983	AUG 1955
-Minimum Monthly	51	0.45	0.75	0.68	0.52	0.47	0.11	0.64	0.49	0.44	0.09	0.32	0.25	0.09
-Year		1955	1991	1966	1985	1964	1949	1957	1964	1968	1963	1976	1955	OCT 1963
-Maximum in 24 hrs	47	2.70	1.96	2.39	2.76	3.18	4.62	4.49	5.68	5.45	3.85	3.99	3.03	5.68
-Year		1979	1966	1968	1970	1984	1973	1989	1971	1960	1980	1977	1992	AUG 1971
Snow, Ice pellets, hail														
-Maximum Monthly	51	23.4	27.6	13.4	4.3	T	T	0.0	0.0	0.0	2.1	8.8	18.8	27.6
-Year		1978	1979	1958	1971	1963	1993				1979	1953	1966	FEB 1979
-Maximum in 24 hrs	51	13.2	21.3	12.0	4.3	T	T	0.0	0.0	0.0	2.1	8.7	14.6	21.3
-Year		1961	1983	1993	1971	1963	1993				1979	1953	1960	FEB 1983
WIND:														
Mean Speed (mph)	53	10.3	10.9	11.4	10.9	9.5	8.8	8.2	7.9	8.3	8.9	9.6	10.1	9.6
Prevailing Direction through 1963		WNW	NW	N	SW	WSW	WSW	WSW	SW	SW	WSW	WSW	WNW	WSW
Fastest Mile														
-Direction (!!!)	53	NE	NW	NW	SW	SW	NW	SW	E	NE	SW	SW	NW	NW
-Speed (MPH)	53	61	59	56	59	56	73	49	67	49	66	60	48	73
-Year		1958	1956	1989	1958	1957	1958	1980	1955	1960	1954	1958	1988	JUN 1958
Peak Gust														
-Direction (!!!)	10	NW	NW	NW	NW	NW	NW	W	N	W	SW	NW	W	NW
-Speed (mph)	10	59	44	69	43	67	54	60	47	53	55	61	63	69
-Date		1992	1992	1989	1993	1984	1993	1992	1988	1985	1990	1989	1991	MAR 1989

PRECIPITATION (inches)

PHILADELPHIA, PENNSYLVANIA

YEAR	JAN	FEB	MAR	APR	MAY	JUNE	JULY	AUG	SEP	OCT	NOV	DEC	ANNUAL
1964	3.92	2.83	1.94	5.27	0.47	0.21	3.83	0.49	2.42	1.73	1.64	5.13	29.88
1965	2.35	2.18	3.19	2.33	1.23	2.85	3.22	4.05	3.02	2.02	1.05	1.85	29.34
1966	2.82	4.30	0.68	4.35	2.95	0.41	2.35	1.63	8.70	5.12	2.36	4.33	40.00
1967	1.67	1.82	4.53	2.17	3.49	4.12	7.11	7.08	2.96	2.00	1.99	5.88	44.82
1968	2.90	1.40	4.98	1.57	5.17	5.89	2.00	1.24	0.44	3.15	4.17	2.54	35.45
1969	1.57	1.88	1.92	1.68	3.30	7.31	8.33	2.66	4.38	1.13	1.97	7.23	43.36
1970	0.74	2.08	3.83	6.12	2.57	4.60	2.75	3.99	0.82	3.66	4.71	3.27	39.14
1971	2.13	5.43	2.58	1.84	4.10	1.01	4.84	9.61	5.83	3.84	5.37	1.21	47.79
1972	2.34	5.09	2.69	4.08	4.11	5.79	2.62	3.76	1.12	3.77	9.06	5.20	49.63
1973	3.93	2.96	3.52	6.68	4.14	7.88	2.39	2.03	3.39	2.16	0.64	6.34	46.06
1974	2.95	2.14	4.91	2.77	3.21	4.43	2.08	3.83	4.68	1.93	0.81	4.04	37.78
1975	4.00	2.91	4.68	2.97	4.99	7.57	6.32	2.21	7.21	3.24	3.14	2.89	52.13
1976	4.50	1.66	2.38	2.06	4.35	3.42	4.04	2.17	2.44	4.30	0.32	1.63	33.27
1977	2.61	1.33	4.19	5.59	0.70	5.33	1.47	8.70	3.44	3.11	7.76	5.19	49.42
1978	8.86	1.35	4.31	1.76	6.01	1.75	5.27	6.04	1.59	1.20	2.20	5.61	45.95
1979	8.74	6.44	2.43	4.08	3.98	4.34	3.95	5.95	4.89	3.84	2.48	1.67	52.79
1980	2.27	0.96	7.01	4.79	3.22	1.73	6.58	0.80	2.79	5.03	2.85	0.77	38.80
1981	0.50	2.94	1.61	3.60	4.53	4.40	4.54	5.11	2.83	2.68	0.95	4.14	37.83
1982	4.45	3.16	2.66	6.06	4.47	5.76	1.94	2.20	2.32	1.94	3.67	1.80	40.43
1983	2.81	3.53	6.70	8.12	7.03	2.75	0.68	2.57	3.45	3.69	5.71	7.37	54.41
1984	2.22	2.81	6.14	4.25	6.87	2.85	6.99	3.28	1.96	2.56	1.56	2.17	43.66
1985	1.55	2.44	1.95	0.52	4.99	1.88	4.66	2.82	5.78	1.54	6.09	0.98	35.20
1986	4.13	3.38	1.25	4.46	0.70	1.99	4.10	3.70	2.33	2.22	6.27	5.89	40.42
1987	4.58	1.17	1.16	3.63	3.15	2.01	4.82	3.72	2.78	2.62	2.08	1.68	33.40
1988	2.72	4.11	2.24	2.92	3.67	0.57	8.07	3.16	2.62	2.16	5.17	1.00	38.41
1989	2.41	3.25	4.41	2.27	6.76	4.73	9.44	3.92	5.03	3.44	1.79	1.21	48.66
1990	4.09	1.44	2.59	3.16	6.08	3.39	2.62	4.07	1.71	1.68	1.17	3.79	35.79
1991	4.10	0.75	4.13	2.81	1.82	3.36	4.79	3.86	3.58	1.61	1.55	3.86	36.22
1992	0.88	1.31	3.19	1.26	2.74	1.84	5.05	2.00	3.04	1.23	3.26	4.61	30.41
1993	1.97	3.03	6.61	4.20	2.42	1.52	1.98	5.18	6.66	2.69	2.23	3.69	42.18
Record Mean	3.21	3.02	3.53	3.34	3.45	3.55	4.16	4.41	3.39	2.76	3.11	3.20	41.14

AVERAGE TEMPERATURE (deg. F)

PHILADELPHIA, PENNSYLVANIA

YEAR	JAN	FEB	MAR	APR	MAY	JUNE	JULY	AUG	SEP	OCT	NOV	DEC	ANNUAL
1964	33.0	31.8	42.7	50.8	65.1	72.4	76.6	72.2	67.2	52.6	47.1	37.5	54.1
1965	29.2	33.3	37.6	49.0	65.5	70.0	74.1	73.1	69.2	53.7	44.2	37.0	53.0
1966	29.1	31.5	42.5	47.8	59.5	72.1	77.9	74.8	65.2	53.1	46.8	35.5	53.0
1967	36.0	29.0	38.5	51.7	55.9	72.1	76.6	75.1	67.0	56.8	42.8	38.5	53.3
1968	28.9	30.4	44.4	54.6	59.7	71.2	77.1	77.8	69.4	58.1	45.6	32.3	54.1
1969	29.8	32.0	39.7	55.3	64.6	73.4	75.1	75.2	67.2	55.0	44.4	33.5	53.8
1970	24.5	33.1	38.3	51.5	64.9	71.6	76.9	76.7	72.0	60.1	48.2	35.8	54.5
1971	27.8	36.1	40.7	51.6	60.9	74.3	77.4	75.3	71.6	63.5	46.1	41.6	55.6
1972	35.1	32.4	40.7	49.7	63.6	68.7	77.1	76.0	69.2	52.7	43.6	39.9	54.1
1973	34.4	33.6	47.2	53.4	60.3	74.6	77.9	78.8	70.7	59.2	48.0	38.6	56.4
1974	35.9	31.7	43.3	55.8	62.4	70.3	76.9	76.8	68.1	54.8	48.5	39.4	55.3
1975	37.3	35.8	41.2	48.7	66.6	72.2	76.6	77.1	66.6	61.2	52.7	36.9	56.1
1976	28.7	40.9	46.3	56.6	62.7	75.2	75.3	74.8	67.3	52.5	39.9	30.3	54.2
1977	20.0	33.6	48.8	57.2	65.8	68.6	77.8	76.2	69.9	54.3	46.4	32.6	54.3
1978	28.0	24.7	39.0	50.6	61.4	72.6	75.6	79.2	68.5	55.5	47.9	38.6	53.5
1979	32.5	23.0	47.0	52.3	66.4	69.1	76.2	75.5	68.5	54.9	50.1	38.2	54.5
1980	31.8	29.7	40.2	54.7	65.4	70.6	78.5	80.0	72.2	54.9	43.2	32.5	54.5
1981	25.3	37.9	40.0	54.7	62.6	72.0	76.9	74.9	66.8	53.1	45.6	34.6	53.7
1982	24.7	34.4	41.7	50.2	65.9	68.7	76.9	73.5	67.6	56.9	48.4	41.3	54.2
1983	34.1	34.0	43.7	51.0	62.1	72.0	77.9	77.1	69.0	56.6	46.7	33.2	54.8
1984	26.2	38.7	35.5	50.2	60.2	73.0	73.9	75.2	64.7	61.2	44.4	41.9	53.8
1985	27.3	35.3	44.6	55.5	64.5	68.8	75.4	74.1	69.1	59.3	51.3	33.3	54.9
1986	32.8	32.1	44.5	53.3	66.8	73.8	78.1	74.0	68.3	57.8	44.5	37.9	55.3
1987	31.9	32.5	45.7	53.1	63.9	74.6	79.5	75.4	68.8	52.5	48.0	39.2	55.4
1988	27.3	34.6	44.7	51.3	63.6	72.3	80.7	78.3	66.7	51.8	47.7	35.4	54.5
1989	36.5	34.8	42.3	52.4	62.4	74.7	76.3	75.6	69.7	58.3	44.9	25.5	54.5
1990	40.3	41.2	46.1	53.3	61.3	72.2	78.0	75.8	68.0	61.9	49.7	42.1	57.5
1991	35.2	40.0	46.1	55.5	70.8	75.7	79.0	79.0	69.5	58.9	47.3	39.6	58.1
1992	35.7	37.5	41.6	53.2	62.5	71.3	77.1	73.5	68.4	55.2	48.0	38.8	55.2
1993	38.2	31.9	39.8	54.2	66.4	74.4	81.4	78.9	69.7	58.0	49.0	38.4	56.7
Record Mean	32.8	33.8	41.9	52.4	63.2	71.8	76.7	74.9	68.4	57.3	46.3	36.2	54.6
Max	39.9	41.4	50.3	61.8	72.8	81.2	85.5	83.3	77.0	66.1	54.1	43.1	63.0
Min	25.6	26.2	33.4	42.9	53.5	62.5	67.9	66.4	59.8	48.5	38.5	29.2	46.2

REFERENCE NOTES

PHILADELPHIA, PENNSYLVANIA

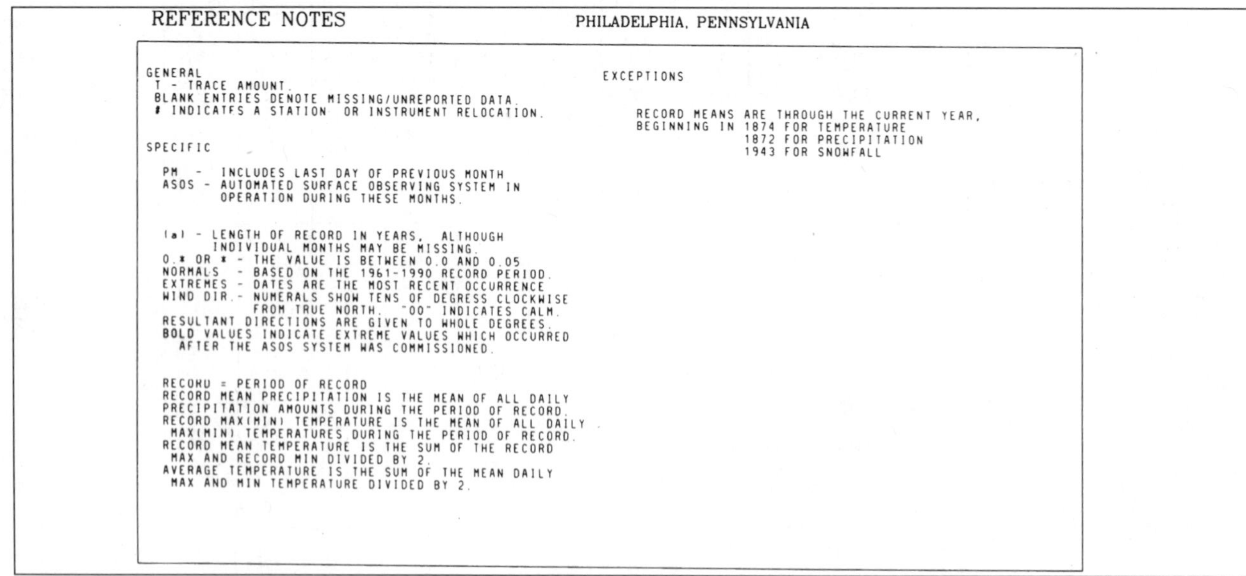

GENERAL
T - TRACE AMOUNT.
BLANK ENTRIES DENOTE MISSING/UNREPORTED DATA.
# INDICATES A STATION OR INSTRUMENT RELOCATION.

SPECIFIC

PM - INCLUDES LAST DAY OF PREVIOUS MONTH
ASOS - AUTOMATED SURFACE OBSERVING SYSTEM IN OPERATION DURING THESE MONTHS.

(a) - LENGTH OF RECORD IN YEARS, ALTHOUGH INDIVIDUAL MONTHS MAY BE MISSING.
0.* OR * - THE VALUE IS BETWEEN 0.0 AND 0.05
NORMALS - BASED ON THE 1961-1990 RECORD PERIOD.
EXTREMES - DATES ARE THE MOST RECENT OCCURRENCE
WIND DIR.- NUMERALS SHOW TENS OF DEGRESS CLOCKWISE FROM TRUE NORTH. "00" INDICATES CALM.
RESULTANT DIRECTIONS ARE GIVEN TO WHOLE DEGREES.
BOLD VALUES INDICATE EXTREME VALUES WHICH OCCURRED AFTER THE ASOS SYSTEM WAS COMMISSIONED.

RECORD = PERIOD OF RECORD
RECORD MEAN PRECIPITATION IS THE MEAN OF ALL DAILY PRECIPITATION AMOUNTS DURING THE PERIOD OF RECORD.
RECORD MAX(MIN) TEMPERATURE IS THE MEAN OF ALL DAILY MAX(MIN) TEMPERATURES DURING THE PERIOD OF RECORD.
RECORD MEAN TEMPERATURE IS THE SUM OF THE RECORD MAX AND RECORD MIN DIVIDED BY 2.
AVERAGE TEMPERATURE IS THE SUM OF THE MEAN DAILY MAX AND MIN TEMPERATURE DIVIDED BY 2.

EXCEPTIONS

RECORD MEANS ARE THROUGH THE CURRENT YEAR, BEGINNING IN 1874 FOR TEMPERATURE
1872 FOR PRECIPITATION
1943 FOR SNOWFALL

HEATING DEGREE DAYS Base 65 deg. F

PHILADELPHIA, PENNSYLVANIA

SEASON	JULY	AUG	SEP	OCT	NOV	DEC	JAN	FEB	MAR	APR	MAY	JUNE	TOTAL
1964-65	0	2	51	377	532	847	1107	883	839	475	66	26	5205
1965-66	0	18	41	342	614	862	1110	931	693	509	207	21	5348
1966-67	0	0	83	362	538	908	893	1001	817	396	280	6	5284
1967-68	0	0	55	271	660	814	1112	995	633	305	170	7	5022
1968-69	0	0	14	234	576	1008	1084	918	782	290	84	2	4992
1969-70	0	0	54	316	611	970	1247	890	821	399	92	0	5400
1970-71	0	0	29	191	499	899	1145	802	746	394	140	3	4848
1971-72	0	0	17	79	576	719	920	941	748	450	86	26	4562
1972-73	0	0	22	378	635	775	940	874	547	359	176	1	4707
1973-74	0	0	18	196	507	810	897	926	667	292	128	11	4452
1974-75	0	0	46	313	500	786	852	812	732	483	66	4	4594
1975-76	0	0	45	152	372	866	1120	692	572	307	119	13	4258
1976-77	0	2	42	387	743	1069	1390	873	505	258	73	36	5378
1977-78	0	0	24	328	558	998	1139	1121	797	423	161	10	5559
1978-79	5	0	41	296	507	811	999	1170	556	378	38	17	4818
1979-80	4	7	28	324	439	823	1021	1016	763	301	72	17	4815
1980-81	0	0	22	320	646	999	1222	752	768	309	129	4	5171
1981-82	0	0	58	364	576	936	1243	850	714	440	50	25	5256
1982-83	0	8	31	277	497	730	951	861	653	423	128	2	4561
1983-84	0	0	70	283	540	981	1196	756	911	438	181	13	5369
1984-85	0	0	92	138	613	709	1161	824	627	306	89	9	4568
1985-86	0	0	38	187	407	975	990	914	628	345	77	6	4567
1986-87	0	21	23	255	609	838	1017	904	591	359	129	1	4747
1987-88	0	0	20	379	504	796	1162	876	624	404	105	32	4902
1988-89	0	0	35	408	513	908	876	840	700	371	138	0	4789
1989-90	0	0	43	220	594	1219	757	662	588	375	127	6	4591
1990-91	2	1	55	171	453	701	920	694	576	296	44	0	3913
1991-92	0	0	42	215	527	778	903	789	720	356	124	9	4463
1992-93	0	1	49	310	504	804	824	920	773	314	47	6	4552
1993-94	0	0	34	219	479	820							

COOLING DEGREE DAYS Base 65 deg. F

PHILADELPHIA, PENNSYLVANIA

YEAR	JAN	FEB	MAR	APR	MAY	JUNE	JULY	AUG	SEP	OCT	NOV	DEC	TOTAL
1969	0	0	0	9	77	259	319	323	126	15	0	0	1128
1970	0	0	0	3	100	204	376	367	247	46	0	0	1343
1971	0	0	0	0	19	292	394	326	223	37	14	0	1305
1972	0	0	3	0	47	143	381	344	153	3	0	0	1074
1973	0	0	0	16	35	294	404	435	193	23	0	0	1400
1974	0	0	0	24	55	179	373	372	145	5	12	0	1165
1975	0	0	0	0	121	224	366	380	98	42	12	0	1243
1976	0	0	0	64	58	326	326	315	115	7	0	0	1211
1977	0	0	10	32	104	150	402	355	175	3	6	0	1237
1978	0	0	0	0	57	244	338	447	153	8	0	0	1247
1979	0	0	6	5	90	146	357	339	137	16	1	0	1097
1980	0	0	0	0	89	194	428	470	244	10	0	0	1435
1981	0	0	0	9	62	224	373	315	119	1	0	0	1103
1982	0	0	0	3	85	142	376	280	115	31	5	0	1037
1983	0	0	0	11	43	217	409	380	199	27	0	0	1286
1984	0	0	0	0	39	260	283	324	90	30	0	0	1026
1985	0	0	0	27	81	133	330	291	166	19	0	0	1047
1986	0	0	0	0	139	278	413	307	129	40	0	0	1306
1987	0	0	0	7	101	295	456	332	142	0	0	0	1333
1988	0	0	0	1	70	259	495	418	93	7	0	0	1343
1989	0	0	1	1	62	298	357	332	192	18	1	0	1262
1990	0	0	9	29	20	226	413	341	152	83	1	0	1274
1991	0	0	1	21	230	327	443	437	183	30	0	0	1672
1992	0	0	0	10	54	205	380	268	158	13	0	0	1088
1993	0	0	0	0	95	298	517	438	181	11	6	0	1546

SNOWFALL (inches)

PHILADELPHIA, PENNSYLVANIA

SEASON	JULY	AUG	SEP	OCT	NOV	DEC	JAN	FEB	MAR	APR	MAY	JUNE	TOTAL
1964-65	0.0	0.0	0.0	0.0	T	2.6	11.9	2.2	6.5	3.0	0.0	0.0	26.2
1965-66	0.0	0.0	0.0	T	0.0	T	16.0	11.4	T	T	0.0	0.0	27.4
1966-67	0.0	0.0	0.0	0.0	T	18.8	0.6	18.4	6.4	0.1	0.0	0.0	44.3
1967-68	0.0	0.0	0.0	0.0	4.9	5.6	1.5	1.7	2.2	0.0	0.0	0.0	15.9
1968-69	0.0	0.0	0.0	0.0	0.4	3.1	1.9	9.5	8.8	0.0	0.0	0.0	23.7
1969-70	0.0	0.0	0.0	0.0	0.2	7.5	7.5	2.7	2.4	T	0.0	0.0	20.3
1970-71	0.0	0.0	0.0	T	0.0	1.1	7.7	0.8	4.4	4.3	0.0	0.0	18.3
1971-72	0.0	0.0	0.0	0.0	T	0.1	3.2	8.2	0.3	0.4	0.0	0.0	12.2
1972-73	0.0	0.0	0.0	T	T	T	T	T	T	T	0.0	0.0	T
1973-74	0.0	0.0	0.0	0.0	T	4.6	4.1	12.1	T	T	0.0	0.0	20.8
1974-75	0.0	0.0	0.0	0.0	T	0.8	3.9	6.6	2.3	T	0.0	0.0	13.6
1975-76	0.0	0.0	0.0	0.0	0.0	1.1	6.4	3.1	6.9	0.0	0.0	0.0	17.5
1976-77	0.0	0.0	0.0	0.0	T	2.8	15.7	0.2	T	0.0	0.0	0.0	18.7
1977-78	0.0	0.0	0.0	0.0	0.2	0.2	23.4	19.0	12.1	T	0.0	0.0	54.9
1978-79	0.0	0.0	0.0	0.0	2.5	T	10.1	27.6	T	T	0.0	0.0	40.2
1979-80	0.0	0.0	0.0	2.1	T	4.9	6.1	0.4	7.4	T	0.0	0.0	20.9
1980-81	0.0	0.0	0.0	0.0	0.2	1.4	5.0	T	8.8	0.0	0.0	0.0	15.4
1981-82	0.0	0.0	0.0	0.0	T	2.8	14.0	3.5	1.1	4.0	0.0	0.0	25.4
1982-83	0.0	0.0	0.0	0.0	0.0	6.8	0.2	26.1	0.9	1.9	0.0	0.0	35.9
1983-84	0.0	0.0	0.0	0.0	0.8	T	10.5	T	10.3	T	0.0	0.0	21.6
1984-85	0.0	0.0	0.0	0.0	T	0.2	11.9	4.4	T	T	0.0	0.0	16.5
1985-86	0.0	0.0	0.0	0.0	0.0	1.5	3.4	11.5	T	T	0.0	0.0	16.4
1986-87	0.0	0.0	0.0	0.0	T	0.4	15.2	10.1	T	T	0.0	0.0	25.7
1987-88	0.0	0.0	0.0	0.0	1.4	1.5	10.6	1.5	T	0.0	0.0	0.0	15.0
1988-89	0.0	0.0	0.0	0.0	0.0	0.4	6.0	2.4	2.4	0.0	0.0	0.0	11.2
1989-90	0.0	0.0	0.0	0.0	4.6	5.3	1.4	0.9	2.4	2.4	0.0	0.0	17.0
1990-91	0.0	0.0	0.0	0.0	0.0	6.4	6.5	1.0	0.7	0.0	0.0	0.0	14.6
1991-92	0.0	0.0	0.0	0.0	T	T	1.2	1.0	2.5	T	0.0	0.0	4.7
1992-93	0.0	0.0	0.0	0.0	T	T	1.0	10.9	12.4	T	0.0	T	24.3
1993-94	0.0	0.0	0.0	0.0	T	0.9							
Record Mean	0.0	0.0	0.0	T	0.6	3.4	6.4	6.4	3.7	0.3	T	T	20.9

PITTSBURGH, GRTR. PITT. AIRPORT
PENNSYLVANIA

Pittsburgh lies at the foothills of the Allegheny Mountains at the confluence of the Allegheny and Monongahela Rivers which form the Ohio. The city is a little over 100 miles southeast of Lake Erie. It has a humid continental type of climate modified only slightly by its nearness to the Atlantic Seaboard and the Great Lakes.

The predominant winter air masses influencing the climate of Pittsburgh have a polar continental source in Canada and move in from the Hudson Bay region or the Canadian Rockies. During the summer, frequent invasions of air from the Gulf of Mexico bring warm humid weather. Occasionally, Gulf air reaches as far north as Pittsburgh during the winter and produces intermittent periods of thawing. The last spring temperature of 32 degrees usually occurs in late April and the first in late October. The average growing season is about 180 days. There is a wide variation in the time of the first and last frosts over a radius of 25 miles from the center of Pittsburgh due to terrain differences.

Precipitation is distributed well throughout the year. During the winter months about a fourth of the precipitation occurs as snow and there is about a 50 percent chance of measurable precipitation on any day. Thunderstorms occur normally during all months, except midwinter, and have a maximum frequency in midsummer. The first appreciable snowfall generally occurs in late November and usually the last occurs early in April. Snow lies on the ground in the suburbs on an average of about 33 days during the year.

Seven months of the year, April through October, have sunshine more than 50 percent of the possible time. During the remaining five months cloudiness is heavier because the track of migratory storms from west to east is closer to the area and because of the frequent periods of cloudy, showery weather associated with northwest winds from across the Great Lakes. Cold air drainage induced by the many hills leads to the frequent formation of early morning fog which may be quite persistent in the river valleys during the colder months.

The Allegheny River flowing south and the Monongahela River flowing north meet to form the Ohio River at Pittsburgh. Heavier rainfall and steeper topography cause the Monongahela River to flood more frequently than the Allegheny River.

Both rivers combine to cause the Ohio River at Pittsburgh to reach the 25 foot flood stage approximately once every four years. The serious flood level of 30 feet is reached much less frequently.

NORMALS, MEANS, AND EXTREMES

PITTSBURGH, GRTR. PITT. AIRPORT PENNSYLVANIA

LATITUDE: 40°30'N LONGITUDE: 80°13' W ELEVATION: FT. GRND 1137 BARO 1213 TIME ZONE: EASTERN WBAN: 94823

	(a)	JAN	FEB	MAR	APR	MAY	JUNE	JULY	AUG	SEP	OCT	NOV	DEC	YEAR
TEMPERATURE °F:														
Normals														
-Daily Maximum		33.7	36.9	49.0	60.3	70.6	78.9	82.6	80.8	74.3	62.5	50.4	38.6	59.9
-Daily Minimum		18.5	20.3	29.8	38.8	48.4	56.9	61.6	60.2	53.5	42.3	34.1	24.4	40.7
-Monthly		26.1	28.7	39.4	49.6	59.5	67.9	72.1	70.5	63.9	52.4	42.3	31.5	50.3
Extremes														
-Record Highest	41	69	69	82	89	91	98	103	100	97	87	82	74	103
-Year		1985	1954	1986	1990	1987	1988	1988	1988	1954	1959	1961	1982	JUL 1988
-Record Lowest	41	-18	-12	-1	14	26	34	42	39	31	16	-1	-12	-18
-Year		1985	1979	1980	1982	1970	1972	1963	1982	1959	1965	1958	1989	JAN 1985
NORMAL DEGREE DAYS:														
Heating (base 65°F)		1206	1016	794	462	214	36	6	14	100	400	681	1039	5968
Cooling (base 65°F)		0	0	0	0	44	123	227	184	67	9	0	0	654
% OF POSSIBLE SUNSHINE	41	32	36	43	46	50	56	57	55	55	51	36	28	45
MEAN SKY COVER (tenths)														
Sunrise - Sunset	41	8.1	7.9	7.5	7.2	6.9	6.5	6.4	6.3	6.2	6.3	7.7	8.2	7.1
MEAN NUMBER OF DAYS:														
Sunrise to Sunset														
-Clear	41	3.0	3.2	4.3	4.5	5.2	5.0	5.3	6.5	7.1	7.7	3.7	2.7	58.3
-Partly Cloudy	41	6.0	6.1	6.9	8.2	9.1	11.7	12.9	11.4	10.2	8.8	6.3	5.6	103.3
-Cloudy	41	22.0	19.0	19.8	17.3	16.6	13.3	12.8	13.0	12.6	14.5	20.0	22.7	203.6
Precipitation														
.01 inches or more	41	16.2	14.0	15.7	13.5	12.6	11.4	10.8	9.6	9.6	10.5	13.1	16.5	153.3
Snow,Ice pellets,hail														
1.0 inches or more	41	3.5	2.8	2.3	0.5	0.*	0.0	0.0	0.0	0.0	0.1	1.0	2.5	12.8
Thunderstorms	41	0.2	0.4	1.7	3.2	5.2	6.7	6.9	5.5	3.1	1.2	0.6	0.3	35.0
Heavy Fog Visibility														
1/4 mile or less	41	1.3	1.2	1.0	0.8	1.1	1.1	1.6	2.2	2.4	1.9	1.4	1.8	17.7
Temperature °F														
-Maximum														
90° and above	34	0.0	0.0	0.0	0.0	0.3	1.6	3.5	1.9	0.6	0.0	0.0	0.0	8.0
32° and below	34	13.7	10.2	3.6	0.1	0.0	0.0	0.0	0.0	0.0	0.0	1.3	9.9	38.8
-Minimum														
32° and below	34	27.0	23.9	19.5	8.2	0.8	0.0	0.0	0.0	0.0	4.2	14.1	24.4	122.0
0° and below	34	2.3	1.4	0.1	0.0	0.0	0.0	0.0	0.0	0.0	0.0	0.*	0.8	4.7
AVG. STATION PRESS.(mb)	21	973.3	973.4	971.9	971.2	971.7	972.3	973.4	974.6	975.1	975.1	974.3	974.0	973.4
RELATIVE HUMIDITY (%)														
Hour 01	33	73	71	70	67	73	78	80	82	82	77	75	75	75
Hour 07 (Local Time)	33	76	75	75	73	76	79	82	86	86	82	79	77	79
Hour 13	33	65	62	57	50	52	52	54	56	57	54	62	67	57
Hour 19	33	67	64	59	53	55	57	60	62	66	62	68	70	62
PRECIPITATION (inches):														
Water Equivalent														
-Normal		2.54	2.39	3.41	3.15	3.59	3.71	3.75	3.21	2.97	2.36	2.85	2.92	36.85
-Maximum Monthly	41	6.25	5.98	6.10	7.61	6.56	10.29	8.71	7.86	6.00	8.20	11.05	8.51	11.05
-Year		1978	1956	1967	1964	1989	1989	1992	1987	1990	1954	1985	1990	NOV 1985
-Minimum Monthly	41	0.77	0.51	1.14	0.48	1.21	0.64	1.62	0.78	0.28	0.16	0.90	0.40	0.16
-Year		1981	1969	1969	1971	1965	1992	1989	1957	1985	1963	1976	1955	OCT 1963
-Maximum in 24 hrs	41	1.69	2.30	2.00	2.15	2.44	2.96	2.97	3.06	2.59	3.56	1.97	2.76	3.56
-Year		1986	1975	1964	1964	1971	1987	1971	1956	1990	1954	1985	1990	OCT 1954
Snow,Ice pellets,hail														
-Maximum Monthly	41	40.2	24.2	34.1	8.1	3.1	T	T	0.0	T	8.5	11.0	21.2	40.2
-Year		1978	1972	1993	1987	1966	1990	1991		1989	1993	1958	1974	JAN 1978
-Maximum in 24 hrs	41	14.0	12.3	23.8	7.7	3.1	T	T	0.0	T	6.6	10.5	12.5	23.8
-Year		1966	1960	1993	1987	1966	1990	1991		1989	1993	1958	1974	MAR 1993
WIND:														
Mean Speed (mph)	41	10.6	10.5	10.7	10.3	8.9	8.0	7.3	6.9	7.4	8.4	9.8	10.4	9.1
Prevailing Direction through 1963		WSW	WSW	WSW	WSW	WSW	WSW	WSW	WSW	WSW	WSW	WSW	WSW	WSW
Fastest Obs. 1 Min.														
-Direction (!!)	41	23	26	25	27	23	27	25	29	26	25	29	25	26
-Speed (MPH)	41	52	58	48	46	44	40	51	46	36	35	45	48	58
-Year		1978	1967	1954	1974	1988	1957	1956	1963	1990	1986	1969	1968	FEB 1967
Peak Gust														
-Direction (!!)	10	SW	W	W	W	SW	W	W	W	W	SW	W	NE	W
-Speed (mph)	10	51	59	60	60	61	52	83	56	48	49	62	55	83
-Date		1992	1990	1985	1991	1988	1990	1992	1986	1990	1990	1992	1990	JUL 1992

PRECIPITATION (inches)

PITTSBURGH, GRTR. PITT. AIRPORT PENNSYLVANIA

YEAR	JAN	FEB	MAR	APR	MAY	JUNE	JULY	AUG	SEP	OCT	NOV	DEC	ANNUAL
1964	2.55	1.73	4.96	7.61	1.77	3.84	4.48	1.79	0.74	1.42	2.74	4.26	37.89
1965	3.84	2.98	3.16	1.79	1.21	2.31	1.82	3.26	4.07	2.82	2.35	0.63	30.24
1966	4.52	3.23	1.88	3.73	2.76	1.72	2.70	5.13	1.92	1.38	3.39	1.70	34.06
1967	1.06	2.54	6.10	4.41	5.21	0.90	4.54	2.67	1.61	2.05	3.07	2.22	36.38
1968	2.83	0.79	4.53	2.33	6.36	2.38	2.36	3.97	3.08	2.13	2.07	3.24	36.07
1969	2.02	0.51	1.14	2.91	1.89	3.74	4.52	2.96	0.91	2.59	2.44	3.95	29.58
1970	1.61	1.92	3.35	3.09	4.36	4.61	3.89	1.55	2.77	4.80	2.64	3.29	37.88
1971	2.29	4.04	3.20	0.48	3.87	1.41	6.82	1.23	3.86	0.84	1.94	3.24	33.22
1972	1.84	3.64	3.68	4.37	1.38	5.08	2.98	1.79	5.42	2.15	4.70	3.04	40.07
1973	2.03	1.80	3.86	4.69	5.87	3.12	2.16	3.40	3.56	4.45	2.65	2.15	39.74
1974	3.47	2.10	3.72	3.26	5.35	5.08	3.30	2.93	4.42	1.12	3.06	4.02	41.83
1975	3.34	4.64	4.62	2.27	1.84	4.58	4.38	7.56	5.06	3.46	1.77	2.90	46.42
1976	3.25	1.74	4.45	1.24	1.99	3.37	4.72	1.25	3.30	3.76	0.90	1.81	31.78
1977	2.06	0.87	4.12	3.26	2.57	2.85	3.38	2.66	3.13	2.44	2.59	3.27	33.20
1978	6.25	0.54	1.65	2.25	4.26	4.11	2.15	3.65	2.64	3.42	1.62	5.24	37.78
1979	4.80	3.12	1.32	3.17	4.49	1.73	4.31	6.84	3.60	2.46	2.43	2.29	40.56
1980	1.56	1.32	5.65	2.94	4.32	4.34	6.76	5.10	1.29	2.42	2.38	1.38	39.46
1981	0.77	4.20	2.12	4.92	2.04	8.20	3.82	0.98	4.13	1.82	1.50	3.00	37.50
1982	4.44	1.93	3.52	1.44	3.98	3.05	2.36	1.97	2.80	0.40	3.33	2.79	32.01
1983	1.19	1.58	3.50	4.33	5.24	4.82	3.32	3.13	2.42	3.67	3.94	4.27	41.41
1984	1.40	2.05	2.32	3.72	5.22	1.98	3.01	5.15	0.84	3.45	3.14	3.04	35.32
1985	1.43	1.45	3.37	1.64	5.80	2.26	4.06	2.64	0.28	2.27	11.05	2.26	38.51
1986	2.49	3.43	1.38	1.94	1.67	5.24	5.66	3.04	2.33	2.83	3.92	3.47	37.40
1987	2.23	0.71	2.65	5.30	2.41	6.30	2.42	7.86	3.97	0.92	2.02	2.41	39.20
1988	1.49	3.46	2.56	1.97	2.78	1.26	2.82	2.04	2.34	1.40	2.80	2.17	27.09
1989	1.99	3.42	5.52	1.43	6.56	10.29	1.62	1.12	4.57	2.04	1.56	2.39	42.51
1990	3.30	3.31	1.47	3.48	6.19	4.24	6.59	3.59	6.00	3.51	2.05	8.51	52.24
1991	2.55	1.88	2.92	2.56	3.29	3.82	3.74	1.63	3.45	0.55	1.97	3.66	32.02
1992	2.13	1.73	3.54	2.30	2.31	0.64	8.71	4.77	2.91	1.47	3.31	2.83	36.65
1993	2.99	2.92	4.14	3.66	2.85	3.35	2.85	2.44	3.87	2.77	4.30	2.12	38.26
Record Mean	2.84	2.46	3.27	3.07	3.39	3.75	3.99	3.21	2.69	2.46	2.47	2.78	36.39

AVERAGE TEMPERATURE (deg. F)

PITTSBURGH, GRTR. PITT. AIRPORT PENNSYLVANIA

YEAR	JAN	FEB	MAR	APR	MAY	JUNE	JULY	AUG	SEP	OCT	NOV	DEC	ANNUAL
1964	31.4	27.0	40.0	51.7	62.7	67.9	72.3	67.1	63.7	50.4	45.5	34.0	51.1
1965	28.2	28.4	35.2	49.0	65.9	66.9	69.9	69.1	64.7	48.1	41.3	37.5	50.4
1966	23.1	30.3	40.9	47.9	56.1	70.4	75.6	71.1	61.3	50.8	42.8	31.4	50.1
1967	32.3	25.6	40.2	52.2	54.3	73.0	71.5	68.8	61.1	52.5	36.8	34.8	50.3
1968	23.4	22.2	40.4	51.2	54.7	66.9	72.4	71.8	64.8	52.2	41.3	27.6	49.1
1969	26.7	29.5	34.3	51.7	60.2	69.3	72.7	69.7	63.0	52.9	39.2	26.7	49.7
1970	20.7	27.7	35.5	52.5	63.9	68.2	71.6	71.6	67.8	54.9	42.2	32.1	50.7
1971	23.7	30.4	34.3	46.0	56.6	71.4	70.2	69.6	68.5	59.5	40.4	38.8	50.8
1972	29.6	26.5	36.4	48.5	61.8	63.8	71.2	70.6	65.3	48.4	39.3	37.2	49.9
1973	29.7	28.8	48.3	49.3	56.4	70.9	73.2	73.2	66.5	56.1	44.1	33.3	52.5
1974	34.0	29.9	41.2	51.8	58.3	65.2	73.1	72.8	62.2	52.4	43.9	32.5	51.4
1975	32.6	32.1	36.3	44.3	63.0	67.8	72.8	73.0	58.8	53.3	46.3	32.9	51.1
1976	23.5	37.2	45.2	50.6	55.6	68.4	67.4	65.3	59.9	45.9	33.1	23.9	48.0
1977	11.4	26.9	43.7	50.8	63.0	63.8	71.8	68.1	64.7	50.5	45.6	31.1	49.3
1978	22.6	20.9	36.9	51.0	60.2	69.4	73.0	71.4	66.2	49.1	43.0	32.7	49.7
1979	21.4	18.0	43.1	49.7	59.1	67.7	70.3	69.6	63.4	50.9	44.7	34.6	49.4
1980	26.9	24.2	35.6	48.1	60.3	66.2	75.0	74.5	67.1	49.5	38.6	28.6	49.5
1981	20.5	31.4	35.6	51.9	58.4	68.8	72.1	69.7	61.9	49.4	40.3	29.4	49.1
1982	20.9	28.4	38.4	45.3	64.7	63.7	72.4	68.2	63.4	54.4	44.7	39.9	50.4
1983	30.0	32.6	40.7	47.1	55.8	67.8	73.0	72.8	64.4	53.0	43.5	25.4	50.5
1984	23.2	36.4	32.2	49.2	55.3	69.7	68.5	70.8	61.4	58.3	40.2	39.3	50.4
1985	22.1	27.7	42.1	55.0	60.6	64.2	70.5	69.6	65.3	55.2	47.1	27.4	50.6
1986	28.3	31.3	41.1	53.1	62.0	68.3	73.3	68.6	66.6	54.2	40.4	33.1	51.7
1987	28.0	32.6	41.9	50.0	63.0	70.9	75.7	71.8	65.1	47.8	46.2	35.1	52.3
1988	26.6	29.0	39.3	49.4	61.4	68.5	76.9	75.1	63.5	46.6	44.2	31.9	51.0
1989	35.5	27.8	41.1	47.0	58.0	69.0	74.1	71.6	64.8	53.3	40.6	19.2	50.2
1990	36.8	36.9	44.0	51.3	57.7	68.3	71.7	70.5	63.7	55.0	45.5	38.0	53.3
1991	29.7	35.4	43.0	54.5	68.7	72.6	75.4	74.4	64.6	55.7	41.6	35.3	54.2
1992	30.5	34.3	38.8	51.3	59.1	66.0	72.4	67.9	63.7	50.1	42.9	33.9	50.9
1993	35.1	27.8	37.6	50.0	61.9	68.9	75.7	75.4	63.3	51.7	43.0	31.7	51.8
Record Mean	30.0	31.1	39.9	51.0	61.7	70.1	74.3	72.5	66.2	54.7	43.1	33.3	52.3
Max	37.6	39.3	49.0	61.1	72.3	80.4	84.3	82.4	76.3	64.4	50.9	40.3	61.5
Min	22.4	22.9	30.8	40.8	51.1	59.8	64.2	62.5	56.1	44.9	35.3	26.3	43.1

REFERENCE NOTES

PITTSBURGH, GRTR. PITT. AIRPORT PENNSYLVANIA

GENERAL
T - TRACE AMOUNT.
BLANK ENTRIES DENOTE MISSING/UNREPORTED DATA.
# INDICATES A STATION OR INSTRUMENT RELOCATION.

(a) - LENGTH OF RECORD IN YEARS, ALTHOUGH INDIVIDUAL MONTHS MAY BE MISSING.
0.* OR * - THE VALUE IS BETWEEN 0.0 AND 0.05
NORMALS - BASED ON THE 1961-1990 RECORD PERIOD.
EXTREMES - DATES ARE THE MOST RECENT OCCURRENCE
WIND DIR.- NUMERALS SHOW TENS OF DEGRESS CLOCKWISE FROM TRUE NORTH. "00" INDICATES CALM.
RESULTANT DIRECTIONS ARE GIVEN TO WHOLE DEGREES.
BOLD VALUES INDICATE EXTREME VALUES WHICH OCCURRED AFTER THE ASOS SYSTEM WAS COMMISSIONED.

RECORD = PERIOD OF RECORD
RECORD MEAN PRECIPITATION IS THE MEAN OF ALL DAILY PRECIPITATION AMOUNTS DURING THE PERIOD OF RECORD.
RECORD MAX(MIN) TEMPERATURE IS THE MEAN OF ALL DAILY MAX(MIN) TEMPERATURES DURING THE PERIOD OF RECORD.
RECORD MEAN TEMPERATURE IS THE SUM OF THE RECORD MAX AND RECORD MIN DIVIDED BY 2.
AVERAGE TEMPERATURE IS THE SUM OF THE MEAN DAILY MAX AND MIN TEMPERATURE DIVIDED BY 2.

EXCEPTIONS

1. TEMPERATURE DATA MAY BE SUSPECT NOVEMBER 1977 THROUGH JULY 1978 DUE TO INTERMITTENT INSTRUMENT MALFUNCTION.

   RECORD MEANS ARE THROUGH THE CURRENT YEAR, BEGINNING IN 1875 FOR TEMPERATURE
   1872 FOR PRECIPITATION
   1953 FOR SNOWFALL

HEATING DEGREE DAYS Base 65 deg. F PITTSBURGH, GRTR. PITT. AIRPORT PENNSYLVANIA

SEASON	JULY	AUG	SEP	OCT	NOV	DEC	JAN	FEB	MAR	APR	MAY	JUNE	TOTAL
1964-65	1	51	99	447	577	954	1134	1018	920	476	63	53	5793
1965-66	9	40	99	518	702	848	1293	963	741	510	289	34	6046
1966-67	2	6	156	435	659	1035	1007	1097	765	387	332	4	5885
1967-68	10	13	146	391	840	931	1284	1232	758	406	313	60	6384
1968-69	8	31	54	400	703	1152	1181	988	944	394	182	35	6072
1969-70	0	8	127	383	770	1183	1370	1039	908	390	127	31	6336
1970-71	5	1	69	318	678	1013	1277	961	949	562	264	6	6103
1971-72	1	6	41	184	729	807	1093	1112	881	489	128	96	5567
1972-73	20	11	63	508	767	853	1087	1006	508	474	264	2	5563
1973-74	2	8	55	274	621	978	957	978	729	403	223	54	5282
1974-75	0	0	124	384	630	1001	997	916	881	617	116	48	5714
1975-76	0	0	192	362	554	989	1278	801	605	453	301	24	5559
1976-77	15	59	159	587	953	1268	1655	1060	658	436	138	102	7090
1977-78	11	41	78	442	583	1043	1307	1229	860	412	209	38	6253
1978-79	4	3	80	485	656	993	1346	1311	671	458	219	38	6264
1979-80	23	26	111	438	601	935	1175	1177	906	500	172	71	6135
1980-81	0	5	48	476	787	1117	1372	936	904	391	223	18	6277
1981-82	3	10	159	475	736	1098	1361	1017	819	586	82	67	6413
1982-83	9	23	119	336	605	770	1080	904	746	535	280	44	5451
1983-84	10	2	126	365	639	1223	1293	823	1008	471	305	16	6281
1984-85	12	7	165	214	734	790	1322	1038	701	334	163	65	5545
1985-86	3	9	116	300	531	1160	1131	936	737	368	148	37	5476
1986-87	1	40	65	346	733	983	1139	904	710	451	145	22	5539
1987-88	4	20	61	529	560	920	1181	1040	792	461	149	64	5781
1988-89	5	3	83	570	619	1018	905	1033	739	532	260	25	5792
1989-90	1	14	102	364	723	1414	869	781	657	439	229	49	5642
1990-91	4	1	116	314	577	829	1085	820	674	337	63	5	4825
1991-92	0	0	127	308	698	913	1063	880	805	417	210	50	5471
1992-93	1	17	116	457	657	956	920	1037	841	445	135	43	5625
1993-94	0	0	118	407	654	1028							

COOLING DEGREE DAYS Base 65 deg. F PITTSBURGH, GRTR. PITT. AIRPORT PENNSYLVANIA

YEAR	JAN	FEB	MAR	APR	MAY	JUNE	JULY	AUG	SEP	OCT	NOV	DEC	TOTAL
1969	0	0	0	2	42	170	245	162	72	14	0	0	707
1970	0	0	0	21	100	133	215	213	162	11	0	0	855
1971	0	0	0	0	13	204	171	158	153	17	0	0	716
1972	0	0	0	0	34	68	219	192	76	0	0	0	589
1973	0	0	0	10	5	185	264	269	108	5	0	0	846
1974	0	0	0	13	19	66	258	247	45	5	4	0	657
1975	0	0	0	0	60	137	248	257	12	7	0	0	721
1976	0	0	1	25	14	134	99	73	12	0	0	0	358
1977	0	0	3	14	83	75	231	141	72	0	4	0	623
1978	0	0	0	0	69	178	260	207	122	0	0	0	836
1979	0	0	0	9	41	125	193	175	70	7	0	0	620
1980	0	0	0	0	34	115	317	306	118	0	0	0	890
1981	0	0	0	5	25	139	230	160	72	0	0	0	631
1982	0	0	0	0	79	33	246	127	77	15	3	0	580
1983	0	0	0	3	3	135	263	251	115	0	0	0	770
1984	0	0	0	3	12	165	127	194	63	13	0	0	577
1985	0	0	0	41	33	49	181	160	130	4	0	0	598
1986	0	0	3	20	65	144	265	157	121	20	0	0	795
1987	0	0	0	6	93	204	342	240	72	0	1	0	958
1988	0	0	0	0	44	174	381	322	47	7	0	0	975
1989	0	0	5	0	49	154	291	225	100	9	0	0	833
1990	0	0	14	37	9	153	218	179	83	13	0	0	706
1991	0	0	0	27	184	239	333	298	124	27	0	0	1232
1992	0	0	0	9	33	87	233	112	86	3	0	0	563
1993	0	0	0	2	45	166	337	327	73	1	1	0	952

SNOWFALL (inches) PITTSBURGH, GRTR. PITT. AIRPORT PENNSYLVANIA

SEASON	JULY	AUG	SEP	OCT	NOV	DEC	JAN	FEB	MAR	APR	MAY	JUNE	TOTAL
1964-65	0.0	0.0	0.0	T	1.6	6.1	10.6	10.4	13.3	0.2	0.0	0.0	42.2
1965-66	0.0	0.0	0.0	0.2	0.2	1.8	24.6	6.9	8.5	2.7	3.1	0.0	48.0
1966-67	0.0	0.0	0.0	0.0	5.1	7.8	4.5	21.7	20.0	0.5	0.0	0.0	59.6
1967-68	0.0	0.0	0.0	T	10.1	7.9	15.4	6.1	11.0	T	0.0	0.0	50.5
1968-69	0.0	0.0	0.0	T	2.7	13.3	6.5	4.0	3.9	0.0	T	0.0	30.4
1969-70	0.0	0.0	0.0	0.4	7.9	20.6	12.6	13.0	16.1	0.1	0.0	0.0	70.7
1970-71	0.0	0.0	0.0	T	0.1	10.1	12.1	20.6	16.8	0.2	0.0	0.0	59.9
1971-72	0.0	0.0	0.0	0.0	10.5	0.7	4.9	24.2	9.8	1.8	0.0	0.0	51.9
1972-73	0.0	0.0	0.0	1.8	6.1	2.9	3.4	6.1	4.6	1.4	T	0.0	26.3
1973-74	0.0	0.0	0.0	0.0	0.8	4.8	4.9	2.2	2.3	1.6	T	0.0	16.6
1974-75	0.0	0.0	0.0	T	2.6	21.2	10.1	13.9	9.8	1.1	0.0	0.0	58.7
1975-76	0.0	0.0	0.0	0.0	1.9	3.8	21.8	3.3	4.3	0.5	0.0	0.0	35.6
1976-77	0.0	0.0	0.0	T	6.6	7.9	26.5	6.4	0.9	1.3	T	0.0	49.6
1977-78	0.0	0.0	0.0	T	3.3	9.1	40.2	5.4	4.0	0.2	0.0	0.0	62.2
1978-79	0.0	0.0	0.0	0.0	2.3	3.2	18.2	13.7	2.0	1.4	0.0	0.0	40.8
1979-80	0.0	0.0	0.0	T	1.1	1.1	7.8	6.2	7.9	T	0.0	0.0	24.1
1980-81	0.0	0.0	0.0	T	9.7	6.3	12.5	11.9	7.6	T	0.0	0.0	48.0
1981-82	0.0	0.0	0.0	T	0.6	11.5	13.4	3.6	12.2	3.8	0.0	0.0	45.1
1982-83	0.0	0.0	0.0	T	0.1	8.8	3.9	12.0	4.3	1.0	0.0	0.0	30.1
1983-84	0.0	0.0	0.0	0.0	6.1	10.5	10.8	11.4	10.4	T	0.0	0.0	49.2
1984-85	0.0	0.0	0.0	0.0	1.5	4.8	14.6	8.1	0.2	7.2	0.0	0.0	36.4
1985-86	0.0	0.0	0.0	0.0	T	15.3	11.1	12.4	4.8	2.7	0.0	0.0	46.3
1986-87	0.0	0.0	0.0	0.0	1.0	0.9	11.6	1.1	7.3	8.1	0.0	0.0	30.0
1987-88	0.0	0.0	0.0	T	4.1	7.9	5.5	6.9	9.8	0.9	0.0	0.0	35.1
1988-89	0.0	0.0	0.0	0.2	1.1	4.0	4.2	4.1	7.5	0.6	T	0.0	21.7
1989-90	0.0	0.0	T	0.2	1.6	12.5	7.7	2.5	0.6	3.3	0.0	T	28.4
1990-91	0.0	0.0	0.0	0.0	T	4.6	4.8	3.6	4.2	T	0.0	0.0	17.2
1991-92	T	0.0	0.0	0.0	2.1	3.1	12.9	2.4	10.6	2.8	T	0.0	33.9
1992-93	0.0	0.0	0.0	1.3	1.5	14.1	2.1	18.5	34.1	0.5	0.0	0.0	72.1
1993-94	0.0	0.0	0.0	8.5	2.6	10.4							
Record Mean	T	0.0	T	0.4	3.3	8.3	11.3	9.3	8.7	1.7	0.1	T	43.1

SAN JUAN, PUERTO RICO

San Juan, located on the north coast of the island of Puerto Rico, is surrounded by the waters of the Atlantic Ocean and San Juan Bay. Local custom assigns the name San Juan to the old city which lies right on the coast, but the modern metropolitan area extends inland about 12 miles. These inland sections have a temperature and rainfall regime significantly different from the coastal area. Isla Verde Airport, where weather observations are made, lies on the coast about 7 miles east of old San Juan. The surrounding terrain is level with a gradual upslope inland. Mountain ranges, with peak elevations of 4,000 feet, extend east and west through the central portion of Puerto Rico, and are located 15 to 20 miles east and south of San Juan. These mountain ranges have a decided influence on the rainfall of the San Juan metropolitan area, and on the entire island in general.

The climate is tropical maritime, characteristic of all tropical islands. The predominant easterly trade winds, modified by local effects such as the land and sea breeze and the particular island topography, are a primary feature of the climate of San Juan and have a significant influence on the temperature and rainfall. During daylight hours the wind blows almost constantly off the ocean. Usually, after sunset the wind shifts to the south or southeast, off land. This daily wind variation is a contributing factor to the delightful climate of the city. The annual temperature range is small with about a 5–6 degree difference between the temperatures of the warmest and coldest months. The inland sectors have warmer afternoons and cooler nights. In the interior mountain and valley regions even greater daily and annual ranges of temperature occur. The highest temperatures recorded in Puerto Rico have exceeded 105 degrees and the lowest have been near 40. Sea water temperatures range from 78 degrees in March to about 83 degrees in September.

Although rainfall in San Juan is nearly 60 inches, the geographical distribution of rainfall over the island shows the heaviest rainfall, of about 180 inches per year, in the Luquillo Range, only 23 miles distant from San Juan. The driest area, with annual rainfall of 30 to 35 inches, is located in the southwest corner of the island. Rain showers occur mostly in the afternoon and at night. The nocturnal showers, usually light, are a characteristic feature of the San Juan rainfall pattern. Rainfall is generally of the brief showery type except for the continuous rains occuring with the passage of tropical disturbances, or when the trailing edge of a cold front out of the United States reaches Puerto Rico. This normally occurs from about November to April.

Puerto Rico is in the tropical hurricane region of the eastern Caribbean. The hurricane season begins June 1 and ends November 30. Only a few hurricanes have passed close enough to San Juan to produce hurricane force winds or damage.

Mild temperatures, refreshing sea breezes in the daytime, plenty of sunshine, and adequate rainfall make the climate of San Juan most enjoyable for tourists and residents alike.

NORMALS, MEANS, AND EXTREMES

SAN JUAN, PUERTO RICO

LATITUDE: 18°26'N LONGITUDE: 66°00'W ELEVATION: FT. GRND 13 BARO 69 TIME ZONE: ATLANTIC WBAN: 11641

	(a)	JAN	FEB	MAR	APR	MAY	JUNE	JULY	AUG	SEP	OCT	NOV	DEC	YEAR
TEMPERATURE °F:														
Normals														
-Daily Maximum		83.2	83.6	84.4	85.8	87.2	88.6	88.5	88.7	88.8	88.3	85.9	83.8	86.4
-Daily Minimum		70.8	70.6	71.6	72.9	74.5	76.1	76.8	76.7	76.2	75.5	74.0	72.4	74.0
-Monthly		77.0	77.1	78.0	79.4	80.9	82.3	82.6	82.7	82.5	81.9	80.0	78.1	80.2
Extremes														
-Record Highest	39	92	96	96	97	96	97	95	97	97	98	96	94	98
-Year		1983	1983	1983	1983	1980	1988	1981	1980	1981	1981	1981	1989	OCT 1981
-Record Lowest	39	61	62	60	64	66	69	69	70	69	67	66	63	60
-Year		1962	1968	1957	1968	1962	1957	1959	1956	1960	1959	1969	1964	MAR 1957
NORMAL DEGREE DAYS:														
Heating (base 65°F)		0	0	0	0	0	0	0	0	0	0	0	0	0
Cooling (base 65°F)		372	339	403	432	493	519	546	549	525	524	450	406	5558
% OF POSSIBLE SUNSHINE	38	68	71	76	71	63	64	68	67	62	63	61	60	66
MEAN SKY COVER (tenths)														
Sunrise - Sunset	38	4.9	5.0	5.0	5.4	6.6	6.2	5.9	5.8	6.2	6.1	5.7	5.5	5.7
MEAN NUMBER OF DAYS:														
Sunrise to Sunset														
-Clear	38	8.7	7.2	9.1	7.0	3.5	4.0	4.9	5.3	3.8	4.4	5.3	6.4	69.7
-Partly Cloudy	38	18.1	16.6	17.6	16.7	15.6	15.9	17.4	17.4	16.9	17.0	17.8	18.4	205.4
-Cloudy	38	4.2	4.4	4.4	6.3	11.9	10.1	8.7	8.2	9.3	9.6	6.9	6.1	90.2
Precipitation														
.01 inches or more	38	16.9	13.0	12.4	12.7	16.5	15.4	18.7	18.2	17.3	17.1	18.3	19.1	195.7
Snow, Ice pellets, hail														
1.0 inches or more	38	0.0	0.0	0.0	0.0	0.0	0.0	0.0	0.0	0.0	0.0	0.0	0.0	0.0
Thunderstorms	38	0.2	0.3	0.3	1.1	4.5	4.8	5.2	6.1	8.3	7.4	3.1	0.8	41.9
Heavy Fog Visibility														
1/4 mile or less	38	0.*	0.0	0.0	0.0	0.0	0.0	0.0	0.0	0.0	0.0	0.0	0.0	*
Temperature °F														
-Maximum														
90° and above	38	0.3	0.8	2.0	3.4	5.7	9.4	8.1	10.1	10.7	9.2	1.8	0.5	62.1
32° and below	38	0.0	0.0	0.0	0.0	0.0	0.0	0.0	0.0	0.0	0.0	0.0	0.0	0.0
-Minimum														
32° and below	38	0.0	0.0	0.0	0.0	0.0	0.0	0.0	0.0	0.0	0.0	0.0	0.0	0.0
0° and below	38	0.0	0.0	0.0	0.0	0.0	0.0	0.0	0.0	0.0	0.0	0.0	0.0	0.0
AVG. STATION PRESS. (mb)	21	1014.9	1014.7	1014.2	1013.1	1013.0	1014.4	1015.0	1013.8	1012.3	1011.4	1011.9	1013.9	1013.5
RELATIVE HUMIDITY (%)														
Hour 02	38	82	80	80	80	84	84	84	84	85	85	84	82	83
Hour 18 (Local Time)	38	82	80	77	75	77	78	79	79	79	80	81	81	79
Hour 14	38	64	62	60	62	66	66	67	66	67	66	67	66	65
Hour 20	38	76	74	73	74	77	77	78	78	78	79	78	77	77
PRECIPITATION (inches):														
Water Equivalent														
-Normal		2.81	2.15	2.35	3.76	5.93	4.00	4.37	5.32	5.28	5.71	5.94	4.72	52.34
-Maximum Monthly	39	7.60	6.69	5.41	10.37	14.99	10.96	9.35	11.76	14.83	15.06	15.96	16.81	16.81
-Year		1977	1982	1958	1988	1965	1965	1961	1955	1989	1970	1979	1981	DEC 1981
-Minimum Monthly	39	0.61	0.20	0.72	0.28	0.44	0.29	1.12	1.93	1.73	1.17	1.91	0.68	0.20
-Year		1978	1983	1970	1984	1972	1985	1974	1982	1987	1979	1980	1963	FEB 1983
-Maximum in 24 hrs	39	5.08	2.75	3.91	7.20	4.74	3.55	2.91	5.08	8.84	5.04	7.07	8.40	8.84
-Year		1969	1989	1969	1988	1986	1965	1993	1955	1989	1985	1979	1981	SEP 1989
Snow, Ice pellets, hail														
-Maximum Monthly	39	0.0	0.0	0.0	0.0	0.0	0.0	0.0	0.0	T	0.0	0.0	0.0	T
-Year										1989				SEP 1989
-Maximum in 24 hrs	39	0.0	0.0	0.0	0.0	0.0	0.0	0.0	0.0	T	0.0	0.0	0.0	T
-Year										1989				SEP 1989
WIND:														
Mean Speed (mph)	38	8.5	8.8	9.2	8.9	8.4	8.9	9.6	8.8	7.5	6.8	7.5	8.2	8.4
Prevailing Direction through 1963		ENE	ENE	ENE	ENE	ENE	ENE	ENE	ENE	ENE	ENE	ENE	ENE	ENE
Fastest Obs. 1 Min.														
-Direction (!!)	8	09	08	07	06	01	12	08	09	34	07	09	11	34
-Speed (MPH)	8	24	23	23	23	25	35	24	23	77	23	25	29	77
-Year		1989	1992	1984	1993	1992	1987	1987	1992	1989	1993	1988	1984	SEP 1989
Peak Gust														
-Direction (!!)	10	E	ESE	E	SE	N	SW	E	E	NW	SE	E	E	NW
-Speed (mph)	10	36	37	36	38	39	38	36	37	92	35	39	41	92
-Date		1993	1989	1989	1989	1992	1984	1991	1989	1989	1986	1985	1984	SEP 1989

PRECIPITATION (inches)

SAN JUAN, PUERTO RICO

YEAR	JAN	FEB	MAR	APR	MAY	JUNE	JULY	AUG	SEP	OCT	NOV	DEC	ANNUAL
1964	2.02	1.70	1.27	6.38	3.96	4.50	7.03	6.71	5.10	3.13	3.39	2.35	47.54
1965	2.62	0.79	0.86	2.19	14.99	10.96	5.88	8.66	4.80	5.08	3.93	5.05	65.81
1966	1.34	1.64	4.63	5.62	5.69	3.26	4.21	3.41	7.20	8.99	7.99	6.21	60.19
1967	3.07	2.93	1.46	0.85	4.15	3.38	4.79	4.20	5.12	4.47	5.00	3.13	42.55
1968	2.15	1.60	1.79	0.50	6.31	5.98	5.25	7.36	5.26	2.33	11.11	3.56	53.20
1969	7.49	3.97	2.89	2.42	5.79	4.04	7.49	6.89	4.86	6.99	6.70	2.28	61.81
1970	2.94	1.33	0.72	1.15	7.98	9.26	3.58	4.66	5.66	15.06	8.00	5.98	66.32
1971	2.18	3.67	1.78	2.93	3.87	1.24	1.69	5.18	2.19	4.61	2.31	3.93	35.58
1972	2.76	2.00	3.40	2.79	0.44	1.58	2.24	3.06	3.68	5.46	2.78	7.53	37.72
1973	2.27	0.92	4.66	8.48	0.48	4.71	2.44	7.00	3.13	3.29	3.01	4.16	44.55
1974	2.92	0.82	1.92	1.20	2.42	2.34	1.12	6.57	3.67	8.23	6.55	3.92	41.68
1975	2.69	0.71	1.13	1.01	1.04	2.64	3.35	4.08	9.29	6.60	10.90	7.82	51.26
1976	1.50	2.18	2.05	3.94	2.96	2.96	2.48	5.12	11.44	7.69	2.77	2.11	47.20
1977	7.60	1.02	1.73	0.96	4.04	1.49	4.64	4.42	4.71	5.94	12.44	3.82	52.81
1978	0.61	1.56	3.52	8.27	7.14	2.86	3.46	3.21	6.34	4.88	5.40	2.61	49.86
1979	1.29	1.80	2.25	4.28	12.13	5.76	6.61	9.38	10.11	1.17	15.96	3.81	74.55
1980	1.75	1.67	1.47	2.55	5.19	1.31	2.19	3.17	4.85	6.71	1.91	3.18	35.95
1981	2.55	2.72	4.39	2.89	11.02	5.48	7.04	3.32	2.98	9.32	4.94	16.81	73.46
1982	2.53	6.69	0.98	1.01	10.26	5.24	2.33	1.93	2.87	2.06	4.34	4.76	45.00
1983	0.69	0.20	1.47	8.54	3.85	1.91	6.53	5.15	2.75	4.06	3.25	3.50	41.90
1984	1.96	3.13	0.82	0.28	3.75	6.85	2.66	6.04	3.16	5.10	5.65	4.69	44.09
1985	2.80	2.40	1.84	1.02	5.95	0.29	2.85	4.33	5.44	11.10	4.54	2.80	45.36
1986	2.18	1.13	1.61	8.93	12.80	1.52	1.94	5.19	1.98	8.54	5.87	3.59	55.28
1987	2.16	1.20	5.17	8.88	12.17	7.07	3.26	2.48	1.73	2.70	7.49	7.69	62.00
1988	3.83	2.27	1.76	10.37	6.06	1.45	4.02	11.31	5.49	4.12	5.68	4.07	60.43
1989	2.96	6.05	3.39	2.63	4.88	2.97	5.54	7.88	14.83	2.09	4.95	2.50	60.67
1990	4.56	3.02	3.14	1.05	2.44	4.32	5.76	3.42	2.23	8.65	5.33	5.03	48.95
1991	2.57	2.26	1.99	1.76	3.23	2.77	3.30	1.94	5.00	1.84	6.16	2.71	35.53
1992	4.03	1.19	1.47	2.12	8.76	5.55	4.38	4.00	5.35	1.74	11.98	4.72	55.29
1993	2.35	0.51	0.78	6.55	4.48	5.46	7.34	3.01	4.36	2.78	4.34	3.00	44.96
Record Mean	2.96	2.27	2.25	3.79	6.29	4.55	4.77	5.65	5.60	5.55	5.86	4.81	54.35

AVERAGE TEMPERATURE (deg. F)

SAN JUAN, PUERTO RICO

YEAR	JAN	FEB	MAR	APR	MAY	JUNE	JULY	AUG	SEP	OCT	NOV	DEC	ANNUAL
1964	76.6	77.5	78.8	78.5	80.9	81.6	81.8	82.2	82.2	80.6	79.0	75.7	79.6
1965	74.7	75.9	77.7	77.7	78.9	80.3	81.7	81.5	82.2	81.5	79.8	77.4	79.1
1966	77.4	76.7	78.1	78.5	79.5	81.0	82.1	82.6	81.1	80.0	77.5	77.1	79.3
1967	76.7	76.3	75.9	78.0	79.7	81.8	82.1	82.2	81.8	81.4	80.4	77.5	79.5
1968	76.4	76.5	76.2	77.0	79.9	80.4	81.2	82.0	81.8	81.6	79.5	77.5	79.2
1969	75.4	75.0	77.8	79.6	80.7	82.0	80.9	81.1	81.2	80.9	78.7	77.1	79.2
1970	76.5	76.2	77.9	80.0	80.6	81.6	82.4	82.3	82.2	81.9	80.2	78.2	80.0
1971	77.6	77.4	78.9	79.7	81.3	83.0	82.9	83.2	83.9	81.9	80.6	78.8	80.8
1972	77.7	77.8	78.7	80.1	81.7	83.8	83.9	83.4	82.9	82.6	81.1	79.2	81.1
1973	78.9	78.3	78.6	80.0	82.9	83.2	83.4	83.2	82.7	83.5	80.7	77.9	81.1
1974	77.3	78.0	78.5	79.6	81.4	83.4	83.7	83.2	82.9	82.5	80.0	78.3	80.7
1975	76.9	77.2	78.4	79.6	81.0	82.9	83.0	82.7	82.1	81.6	79.8	77.5	80.2
1976	76.3	76.6	76.8	78.5	80.5	81.7	83.1	83.5	83.3	82.5	80.9	78.3	80.2
1977	77.0	77.6	78.3	80.2	80.9	81.9	80.6	81.0	81.1	81.9	80.3	79.3	80.0
1978	78.3	79.2	79.8	80.1	80.8	82.3	83.1	83.2	83.9	82.7	81.8	79.6	81.2
1979	78.5	78.7	77.8	79.4	81.3	83.8	83.5	83.0	81.8	83.0	80.6	78.7	80.8
1980	78.2	78.6	79.2	80.8	83.8	85.1	85.2	85.1	84.5	84.4	82.2	80.7	82.3
1981	79.8	79.4	80.9	80.3	83.4	84.2	85.0	83.8	84.3	83.3	81.6	78.7	82.1
1982	78.5	77.8	78.0	80.4	81.0	82.9	83.3	84.6	84.6	83.8	80.2	78.0	81.1
1983	78.5	79.9	82.2	81.8	83.2	85.4	84.2	84.0	84.3	83.6	81.4	79.9	82.4
1984	78.1	77.8	80.2	81.8	81.1	82.4	82.6	82.6	82.2	81.3	78.7	77.3	80.5
1985	76.1	77.3	76.7	78.3	80.4	83.0	83.5	83.4	81.7	79.6	79.0	76.8	79.7
1986	75.5	76.0	77.4	79.0	79.1	81.6	82.0	82.2	82.5	81.4	79.1	77.7	79.5
1987	76.7	77.4	78.0	81.2	81.6	81.7	82.7	83.7	83.8	83.3	80.6	79.7	80.9
1988	76.9	76.6	77.8	80.4	82.4	84.3	83.6	82.8	82.2	81.6	79.8	76.9	80.4
1989	76.2	76.0	76.1	78.8	80.3	81.2	81.8	82.3	82.3	81.7	80.0	79.2	79.7
1990	77.1	76.4	76.5	79.1	81.8	82.4	82.6	82.9	83.4	82.1	80.7	77.5	80.2
1991	77.0	77.8	78.6	79.2	81.0	83.2	83.1	83.9	83.3	82.4	79.9	77.0	80.5
1992	77.1	78.2	78.9	80.8	81.3	83.4	82.4	82.7	82.3	84.0	80.8	79.3	80.9
1993	77.3	78.5	79.3	80.3	82.1	83.3	82.8	84.2	83.0	82.7	80.9	78.9	81.1
Record													
Mean	76.6	76.7	77.6	79.0	80.6	82.0	82.2	82.5	82.2	81.6	79.7	77.8	79.8
Max	82.9	83.2	84.2	85.5	86.9	88.3	88.2	88.6	88.6	88.2	85.8	83.6	86.2
Min	70.3	70.2	71.0	72.5	74.2	75.6	76.2	76.3	75.7	75.0	73.6	71.9	73.5

REFERENCE NOTES

SAN JUAN, PUERTO RICO

GENERAL
T - TRACE AMOUNT.
BLANK ENTRIES DENOTE MISSING/UNREPORTED DATA.
# INDICATES A STATION OR INSTRUMENT RELOCATION.

SPECIFIC

PM - INCLUDES LAST DAY OF PREVIOUS MONTH
ASOS - AUTOMATED SURFACE OBSERVING SYSTEM IN OPERATION DURING THESE MONTHS.

(a) - LENGTH OF RECORD IN YEARS, ALTHOUGH INDIVIDUAL MONTHS MAY BE MISSING.
0.* OR * - THE VALUE IS BETWEEN 0.0 AND 0.05
NORMALS - BASED ON THE 1961-1990 RECORD PERIOD.
EXTREMES - DATES ARE THE MOST RECENT OCCURRENCE
WIND DIR.- NUMERALS SHOW TENS OF DEGRESS CLOCKWISE FROM TRUE NORTH. "00" INDICATES CALM.
RESULTANT DIRECTIONS ARE GIVEN TO WHOLE DEGREES.
BOLD VALUES INDICATE EXTREME VALUES WHICH OCCURRED AFTER THE ASOS SYSTEM WAS COMMISSIONED.

RECORD = PERIOD OF RECORD
RECORD MEAN PRECIPITATION IS THE MEAN OF ALL DAILY PRECIPITATION AMOUNTS DURING THE PERIOD OF RECORD.
RECORD MAX(MIN) TEMPERATURE IS THE MEAN OF ALL DAILY MAX(MIN) TEMPERATURES DURING THE PERIOD OF RECORD.
RECORD MEAN TEMPERATURE IS THE SUM OF THE RECORD MAX AND RECORD MIN DIVIDED BY 2.
AVERAGE TEMPERATURE IS THE SUM OF THE MEAN DAILY MAX AND MIN TEMPERATURE DIVIDED BY 2.

EXCEPTIONS

FASTEST MILE WINDS ARE THROUGH MAY 1983.

RECORD MEANS ARE THROUGH THE CURRENT YEAR, BEGINNING IN 1951 FOR TEMPERATURE
1951 FOR PRECIPITATION

HEATING DEGREE DAYS Base 65 deg. F — SAN JUAN, PUERTO RICO

SEASON	JULY	AUG	SEP	OCT	NOV	DEC	JAN	FEB	MAR	APR	MAY	JUNE	TOTAL
1983-84	0	0	0	0	0	0	0	0	0	0	0	0	0
1984-85	0	0	0	0	0	0	0	0	0	0	0	0	0
1985-86	0	0	0	0	0	0	0	0	0	0	0	0	0
1986-87	0	0	0	0	0	0	0	0	0	0	0	0	0
1987-88	0	0	0	0	0	0	0	0	0	0	0	0	0
1988-89	0	0	0	0	0	0	0	0	0	0	0	0	0
1989-90	0	0	0	0	0	0	0	0	0	0	0	0	0
1990-91	0	0	0	0	0	0	0	0	0	0	0	0	0
1991-92	0	0	0	0	0	0	0	0	0	0	0	0	0
1992-93	0	0	0	0	0	0	0	0	0	0	0	0	0
1993-94	0	0	0	0	0	0							

COOLING DEGREE DAYS Base 65 deg. F — SAN JUAN, PUERTO RICO

YEAR	JAN	FEB	MAR	APR	MAY	JUNE	JULY	AUG	SEP	OCT	NOV	DEC	TOTAL
1969	328	287	401	447	496	517	501	506	493	500	417	382	5275
1970	362	321	409	460	490	506	548	540	523	528	461	416	5564
1971	398	353	438	445	511	545	562	573	577	531	473	438	5844
1972	400	376	431	458	525	569	592	578	543	554	490	446	5962
1973	438	379	428	458	562	553	578	570	539	579	475	406	5965
1974	390	368	424	442	511	558	586	575	544	549	455	418	5820
1975	375	346	420	446	501	543	565	556	521	519	450	395	5637
1976	357	342	375	413	485	506	566	579	557	548	485	419	5632
1977	382	360	419	463	499	514	491	502	487	532	469	452	5570
1978	420	404	464	462	499	526	566	570	575	555	513	459	6013
1979	426	393	404	436	512	571	582	564	511	569	477	432	5877
1980	414	402	446	479	590	610	633	628	591	608	522	494	6417
1981	467	407	499	468	578	584	626	587	588	574	505	429	6312
1982	423	364	412	470	504	543	573	615	593	590	466	405	5958
1983	426	424	541	509	573	621	604	593	583	582	502	468	6426
1984	415	377	479	508	503	528	553	553	522	517	417	389	5761
1985	352	349	368	403	483	547	579	577	508	459	429	371	5425
1986	329	315	390	428	444	501	535	538	534	517	429	401	5361
1987	366	354	407	490	521	508	556	588	571	575	477	464	5877
1988	377	341	403	470	547	587	581	558	523	522	453	375	5737
1989	354	313	353	421	482	495	529	543	525	526	456	443	5440
1990	383	325	362	430	526	526	551	561	559	539	478	392	5632
1991	379	363	428	430	503	551	571	593	558	547	455	380	5758
1992	383	393	435	479	512	556	547	555	524	596	482	454	5916
1993	391	383	450	469	535	557	561	603	550	557	483	440	5979

SNOWFALL (inches) — SAN JUAN, PUERTO RICO

SEASON	JULY	AUG	SEP	OCT	NOV	DEC	JAN	FEB	MAR	APR	MAY	JUNE	TOTAL
1971-72	0.0	0.0	0.0	0.0	0.0	0.0	0.0	0.0	0.0	0.0	0.0	0.0	0.0
1972-73	0.0	0.0	0.0	0.0	0.0	0.0	0.0	0.0	0.0	0.0	0.0	0.0	0.0
1973-74	0.0	0.0	0.0	0.0	0.0	0.0	0.0	0.0	0.0	0.0	0.0	0.0	0.0
1974-75	0.0	0.0	0.0	0.0	0.0	0.0	0.0	0.0	0.0	0.0	0.0	0.0	0.0
1975-76	0.0	0.0	0.0	0.0	0.0	0.0	0.0	0.0	0.0	0.0	0.0	0.0	0.0
1976-77	0.0	0.0	0.0	0.0	0.0	0.0	0.0	0.0	0.0	0.0	0.0	0.0	0.0
1977-78	0.0	0.0	0.0	0.0	0.0	0.0	0.0	0.0	0.0	0.0	0.0	0.0	0.0
1978-79	0.0	0.0	0.0	0.0	0.0	0.0	0.0	0.0	0.0	0.0	0.0	0.0	0.0
1979-80	0.0	0.0	0.0	0.0	0.0	0.0	0.0	0.0	0.0	0.0	0.0	0.0	0.0
1980-81	0.0	0.0	0.0	0.0	0.0	0.0	0.0	0.0	0.0	0.0	0.0	0.0	0.0
1981-82	0.0	0.0	0.0	0.0	0.0	0.0	0.0	0.0	0.0	0.0	0.0	0.0	0.0
1982-83	0.0	0.0	0.0	0.0	0.0	0.0	0.0	0.0	0.0	0.0	0.0	0.0	0.0
1983-84	0.0	0.0	0.0	0.0	0.0	0.0	0.0	0.0	0.0	0.0	0.0	0.0	0.0
1984-85	0.0	0.0	0.0	0.0	0.0	0.0	0.0	0.0	0.0	0.0	0.0	0.0	0.0
1985-86	0.0	0.0	0.0	0.0	0.0	0.0	0.0	0.0	0.0	0.0	0.0	0.0	0.0
1986-87	0.0	0.0	0.0	0.0	0.0	0.0	0.0	0.0	0.0	0.0	0.0	0.0	0.0
1987-88	0.0	0.0	0.0	0.0	0.0	0.0	0.0	0.0	0.0	0.0	0.0	0.0	0.0
1988-89	0.0	0.0	0.0	0.0	0.0	0.0	0.0	0.0	0.0	0.0	0.0	0.0	0.0
1989-90	0.0	0.0	T	0.0	0.0	0.0	0.0	0.0	0.0	0.0	0.0	0.0	T
1990-91	0.0	0.0	0.0	0.0	0.0	0.0	0.0	0.0	0.0	0.0	0.0	0.0	0.0
1991-92	0.0	0.0	0.0	0.0	0.0	0.0	0.0	0.0	0.0	0.0	0.0	0.0	0.0
1992-93	0.0	0.0	0.0	0.0	0.0	0.0	0.0	0.0	0.0	0.0	0.0	0.0	0.0
1993-94	0.0	0.0	0.0	0.0	0.0	0.0							
Record Mean	0.0	0.0	T	0.0	0.0	0.0	0.0	0.0	0.0	0.0	0.0	0.0	T

PROVIDENCE, RHODE ISLAND

The proximity to Narragansett Bay and the Atlantic Ocean plays an important part in determining the climate for Providence and vicinity. In winter, the temperatures are modified considerably, and many major snowstorms change to rain before reaching the area. In summer, many days that could be uncomfortably warm are cooled by refreshing sea breezes. At other times of the year, sea fog may be advected in over land by onshore winds. In fact, most cases of dense fog are produced this way, but the number of such days is few, averaging two or three days per month. In early fall, severe coastal storms of tropical origin sometimes bring destructive winds to this area. Even at other times of the year, it is usually coastal storms which produce the severest weather.

The temperature for the entire year averages around 50 degrees with 70 degree temperatures common from near the end of May to the latter part of September. During this period, there may be several days reaching 90 degrees or more. Temperatures of 100 degrees and more are rare.

Freezing temperatures occur on the average about 125 days per year. They become a common daily occurrence in the latter part of November, and become less frequent near the end of March. The average date for the last freeze in spring is mid-April, while the average date for the first freeze in fall is late October, making the growing season about 195 days in length. Sub-zero weather in winter seldom occurs, averaging less than one day for December and one or two days each for January and February.

Measurable precipitation occurs on about one day out of every three, and is fairly evenly distributed throughout the year. There is usually no definite dry season, but occasionally droughts do occur.

Thunderstorms are responsible for much of the rainfall from May through August. They usually produce heavy, and sometimes even excessive amounts of rainfall. However, since their duration is relatively short, damage is ordinarily light. The thunderstorms of summer are frequently accompanied by extremely gusty winds, which may result in some damage to property.

The first measurable snowfall of winter usually comes toward the end of November, and the last in spring is about the middle of March. Winters with over 50 inches of snow are not common. The area normally receives less than 25 inches. The month of greatest snowfall is usually February, but January and March are close seconds. It is unusual for the ground to remain well covered with snow for any long period of time.

NORMALS, MEANS, AND EXTREMES

PROVIDENCE, RHODE ISLAND

LATITUDE: 41°44'N LONGITUDE: 71°26' W ELEVATION: FT. GRND 51 BARO 58 TIME ZONE: EASTERN WBAN: 14765

	(a)	JAN	FEB	MAR	APR	MAY	JUNE	JULY	AUG	SEP	OCT	NOV	DEC	YEAR
TEMPERATURE °F:														
Normals														
-Daily Maximum		36.6	38.3	46.1	57.0	67.3	76.9	82.1	80.7	74.3	64.1	53.0	41.2	59.8
-Daily Minimum		19.1	20.9	28.8	37.7	47.3	56.8	63.2	61.9	53.8	43.0	34.9	24.4	41.0
-Monthly		27.9	29.7	37.4	47.4	57.3	66.9	72.7	71.3	64.1	53.6	44.0	32.8	50.4
Extremes														
-Record Highest	40	66	72	80	98	94	97	102	104	100	86	78	70	104
-Year		1974	1985	1989	1976	1992	1988	1991	1975	1983	1979	1993	1984	AUG 1975
-Record Lowest	40	-13	-7	1	14	29	41	48	40	33	20	6	-10	-13
-Year		1976	1979	1967	1954	1956	1980	1988	1965	1980	1976	1989	1980	JAN 1976
NORMAL DEGREE DAYS:														
Heating (base 65°F)		1150	988	856	528	246	31	0	8	90	359	630	998	5884
Cooling (base 65°F)		0	0	0	0	7	88	239	203	63	6	0	0	606
% OF POSSIBLE SUNSHINE	40	57	57	58	56	58	61	63	61	62	60	50	52	58
MEAN SKY COVER (tenths)														
Sunrise - Sunset	40	6.2	6.3	6.5	6.6	6.7	6.4	6.4	6.2	5.9	5.5	6.4	6.2	6.3
MEAN NUMBER OF DAYS:														
Sunrise to Sunset														
-Clear	40	9.6	7.9	8.6	7.3	6.4	6.7	6.8	8.3	9.5	10.9	8.2	8.4	98.5
-Partly Cloudy	40	6.8	7.1	7.7	8.1	9.9	10.3	11.9	10.4	8.1	7.9	6.8	7.8	102.9
-Cloudy	40	14.6	13.3	14.8	14.5	14.6	13.1	12.3	12.3	12.4	12.2	14.9	14.8	163.7
Precipitation														
.01 inches or more	40	10.9	10.0	11.9	11.1	11.4	10.7	9.1	9.4	8.4	8.7	10.8	12.0	124.3
Snow,Ice pellets,hail														
1.0 inches or more	40	2.8	2.5	2.0	0.3	0.*	0.0	0.0	0.0	0.0	0.1	0.3	2.1	10.0
Thunderstorms	40	0.3	0.2	0.6	1.2	2.6	3.7	4.4	3.6	1.6	1.0	0.8	0.2	20.2
Heavy Fog Visibility														
1/4 mile or less	40	2.0	2.0	2.1	2.0	2.1	2.4	1.9	1.5	1.7	3.0	2.0	2.0	24.8
Temperature °F														
-Maximum														
90° and above	30	0.0	0.0	0.0	0.1	0.7	1.9	3.8	2.5	0.8	0.0	0.0	0.0	9.8
32° and below	30	11.0	7.6	1.4	0.*	0.0	0.0	0.0	0.0	0.0	0.0	0.2	6.0	26.2
-Minimum														
32° and below	30	27.9	24.4	19.5	5.5	0.2	0.0	0.0	0.0	0.0	3.6	12.7	24.4	118.2
0° and below	30	1.3	0.6	0.0	0.0	0.0	0.0	0.0	0.0	0.0	0.0	0.0	0.3	2.2
AVG. STATION PRESS.(mb)	21	1014.3	1014.6	1013.6	1012.2	1013.1	1012.4	1013.0	1014.8	1016.2	1016.4	1015.6	1015.4	1014.3
RELATIVE HUMIDITY (%)														
Hour 01	30	69	68	70	71	78	82	82	84	84	80	75	72	76
Hour 07 (Local Time)	30	71	70	71	70	73	75	77	80	82	80	77	74	75
Hour 13	30	56	54	53	49	52	56	56	56	56	54	57	58	55
Hour 19	30	63	61	61	60	64	67	68	71	74	71	69	66	66
PRECIPITATION (inches):														
Water Equivalent														
-Normal		3.88	3.61	4.05	4.11	3.76	3.33	3.18	3.63	3.48	3.69	4.43	4.38	45.53
-Maximum Monthly	40	11.66	7.20	8.84	12.74	8.38	11.08	8.08	11.12	7.92	11.89	11.01	10.75	12.74
-Year		1979	1984	1983	1983	1984	1982	1976	1955	1961	1962	1983	1969	APR 1983
-Minimum Monthly	40	0.50	0.39	0.56	1.48	0.71	0.39	1.00	0.71	0.77	1.53	0.81	0.58	0.39
-Year		1970	1987	1981	1966	1964	1957	1970	1984	1959	1992	1976	1955	FEB 1987
-Maximum in 24 hrs	40	3.34	3.14	4.53	4.45	5.17	5.03	4.83	6.71	4.89	6.63	4.18	3.85	6.71
-Year		1962	1978	1968	1983	1984	1984	1976	1979	1961	1962	1983	1969	AUG 1979
Snow,Ice pellets,hail														
-Maximum Monthly	40	28.7	30.9	31.6	7.6	7.0	0.0	0.0	0.0	0.0	2.5	8.0	19.8	31.6
-Year		1965	1962	1956	1982	1977					1979	1989	1963	MAR 1956
-Maximum in 24 hrs	40	10.8	27.6	16.9	7.6	7.0	0.0	0.0	0.0	0.0	2.5	8.0	11.9	27.6
-Year		1978	1978	1960	1982	1977					1979	1989	1981	FEB 1978
WIND:														
Mean Speed (mph)	40	11.1	11.5	12.0	12.0	10.7	9.9	9.4	9.3	9.4	9.6	10.4	10.8	10.5
Prevailing Direction through 1963		NW	NNW	WNW	SW	S	SW	SW	SSW	SW	NW	SW	WNW	SW
Fastest Obs. 1 Min.														
-Direction (!!)	40	20	16	18	20	20	20	34	11	18	14	18	14	11
-Speed (MPH)	40	46	46	60	51	42	40	35	90	58	41	52	48	90
-Year		1978	1972	1959	1956	1956	1957	1964	1954	1960	1954	1957	1957	AUG 1954
Peak Gust														
-Direction (!!)	10	S	SW	SW	SE	S	SE	SW	E	S	NE	SW	NW	S
-Speed (mph)	10	53	55	60	54	49	54	43	63	81	58	54	51	81
-Date		1992	1989	1986	1984	1990	1989	1984	1991	1985	1991	1992	1988	SEP 1985

PRECIPITATION (inches)

PROVIDENCE, RHODE ISLAND

YEAR	JAN	FEB	MAR	APR	MAY	JUNE	JULY	AUG	SEP	OCT	NOV	DEC	ANNUAL
1964	5.65	3.15	2.26	5.34	0.71	2.34	2.63	2.38	3.95	2.11	2.43	5.46	38.41
1965	3.46	3.77	1.72	2.43	1.08	1.91	1.28	1.90	1.64	2.75	2.08	1.42	25.44
1966	3.40	4.30	2.40	1.48	3.85	2.31	2.77	3.37	5.23	2.60	3.93	3.04	38.68
1967	1.60	2.51	5.49	4.19	7.27	2.72	3.95	3.24	3.17	2.25	2.75	7.36	46.50
1968	3.50	1.31	7.83	1.49	3.54	4.74	1.49	1.61	1.14	1.79	6.22	6.70	41.36
1969	2.23	4.30	3.10	3.95	2.41	1.23	2.98	2.58	3.09	1.62	6.35	10.75	44.59
1970	0.50	5.34	4.75	3.91	3.03	4.25	1.00	6.59	1.79	4.41	5.31	4.54	45.42
1971	2.01	5.36	3.81	2.31	3.83	1.64	3.48	3.03	2.54	2.88	5.16	2.37	38.42
1972	1.85	5.19	6.70	3.71	5.73	6.83	4.25	2.98	7.31	4.36	8.45	7.70	65.06
1973	3.06	3.55	2.78	7.16	3.99	3.48	2.92	5.17	3.04	3.17	2.29	7.63	48.24
1974	4.45	3.04	4.51	2.86	2.74	3.28	1.64	3.10	6.15	2.79	1.56	4.54	40.66
1975	6.78	3.29	3.07	2.99	2.06	4.73	3.51	2.19	6.15	4.66	6.29	5.11	50.83
1976	6.38	2.91	3.44	2.00	2.53	1.60	8.08	7.01	1.57	6.52	0.81	3.47	46.32
1977	3.90	2.87	5.62	3.35	3.43	3.92	2.04	2.12	5.60	6.90	3.24	5.85	48.84
1978	9.01	3.20	3.10	2.53	5.27	1.97	2.63	6.46	1.82	3.22	2.61	5.19	47.01
1979	11.66	4.08	2.21	5.12	7.62	1.44	1.65	10.09	4.08	3.94	4.49	1.81	58.19
1980	1.40	1.16	8.11	6.18	1.78	3.85	2.03	1.99	0.90	3.41	3.73	1.57	36.11
1981	0.77	4.79	0.56	4.10	1.92	2.31	3.75	2.65	2.58	3.38	3.20	6.36	36.37
1982	6.09	3.08	3.76	3.64	1.61	11.08	3.51	3.67	3.61	3.08	4.32	1.81	49.26
1983	4.32	4.81	8.84	12.74	4.67	1.91	2.14	2.71	2.16	4.50	11.01	7.71	67.52
1984	2.00	7.20	5.77	4.30	8.38	4.09	5.16	0.71	1.77	4.25	1.95	3.16	48.74
1985	1.18	1.57	3.08	1.65	4.76	4.70	2.88	8.57	1.69	1.78	7.14	1.42	40.42
1986	5.88	3.18	2.86	2.10	2.29	3.27	5.95	3.29	0.97	2.48	5.77	8.09	46.13
1987	4.73	0.39	5.62	6.91	1.80	2.00	1.20	2.58	7.47	2.28	3.40	2.29	40.67
1988	2.69	5.29	4.09	3.11	2.83	0.91	5.73	0.94	2.38	1.77	7.60	1.03	38.37
1989	1.17	2.69	4.13	5.30	6.07	5.84	5.59	6.14	4.75	8.37	4.35	1.66	56.06
1990	5.01	2.93	2.01	5.57	5.70	1.13	3.52	3.74	2.28	4.96	2.45	5.48	44.78
1991	3.44	2.31	6.61	4.80	3.30	0.93	2.76	5.98	5.09	2.65	4.65	3.17	45.69
1992	4.82	2.10	4.04	2.34	1.42	4.61	3.59	6.06	5.09	1.53	5.05	6.83	47.48
1993	2.42	5.06	6.99	5.02	1.12	1.40	2.18	1.23	4.08	3.55	3.35	5.76	42.16
Record Mean	3.73	3.29	3.86	3.75	3.25	3.02	3.17	3.70	3.34	3.20	3.87	3.89	42.08

AVERAGE TEMPERATURE (deg. F)

PROVIDENCE, RHODE ISLAND

YEAR	JAN	FEB	MAR	APR	MAY	JUNE	JULY	AUG	SEP	OCT	NOV	DEC	ANNUAL
1964	30.6	27.9	37.8	46.1	60.3	66.3	71.7	66.6	62.5	52.6	44.6	33.2	50.0
1965	25.0	28.4	36.1	45.4	60.0	67.0	71.6	71.6	64.1	52.1	41.1	35.4	49.8
1966	28.8	29.9	38.8	43.8	54.4	67.4	72.7	70.7	61.3	51.4	45.5	32.8	49.8
1967	33.7	25.7	33.3	44.8	51.2	66.8	72.8	70.6	62.7	53.7	39.5	34.5	49.1
1968	24.5	24.6	38.1	49.9	55.7	65.0	73.1	70.6	64.8	55.9	42.4	30.2	49.6
1969	28.8	28.7	35.0	49.7	57.7	68.2	71.5	74.3	64.0	53.3	42.4	30.5	50.4
1970	19.6	29.3	35.0	47.8	58.2	65.6	74.1	72.3	64.4	54.2	44.7	28.5	49.5
1971	22.9	30.9	36.7	45.9	58.1	69.0	74.3	73.0	68.7	59.2	40.4	35.0	51.2
1972	30.8	28.0	36.4	44.3	57.7	64.9	72.6	70.6	65.1	49.6	40.9	34.3	49.6
1973	31.1	29.6	43.7	50.0	56.7	70.3	73.6	75.0	63.4	54.2	43.8	38.3	52.5
1974	31.6	29.0	38.7	50.6	55.6	65.3	72.6	72.6	63.2	48.2	43.7	35.7	50.5
1975	34.1	30.4	35.5	44.5	61.4	66.0	74.3	71.4	61.0	55.3	48.0	32.1	51.2
1976	23.5	35.5	39.0	52.6	58.0	70.0	70.0	70.0	61.6	48.7	37.9	25.4	49.4
1977	20.9	29.8	43.6	50.6	61.2	66.7	74.3	73.0	64.1	52.9	45.9	31.6	51.2
1978	25.1	22.1	33.8	46.7	57.8	68.0	71.7	71.3	59.5	51.5	42.3	33.4	48.6
1979	30.0	19.7	40.4	46.8	60.3	65.1	73.5	70.2	64.0	53.0	48.3	37.3	50.7
1980	29.7	26.8	37.1	49.5	60.3	64.5	74.8	73.4	64.9	49.8	41.0	28.5	50.0
1981	20.3	37.4	38.7	51.4	58.5	69.4	75.6	70.0	62.4	49.1	43.0	31.1	50.6
1982	21.5	31.5	38.8	47.8	58.9	63.9	73.6	69.2	64.1	53.2	47.5	38.6	50.7
1983	31.4	32.9	40.4	49.9	56.9	70.2	76.6	74.3	69.6	55.3	46.0	32.5	53.0
1984	26.4	37.1	33.8	47.6	57.4	69.1	71.5	73.5	62.1	56.3	43.6	37.9	51.4
1985	22.5	32.1	40.8	51.0	60.2	64.8	73.0	71.1	65.2	54.6	45.9	30.4	51.0
1986	31.1	29.0	39.9	49.4	59.4	66.4	71.0	69.3	62.3	53.0	41.6	35.4	50.7
1987	29.0	28.6	39.8	48.4	59.3	68.4	72.2	69.6	64.3	51.4	43.0	35.1	50.8
1988	26.8	31.8	39.4	47.0	58.0	66.9	74.3	75.3	63.0	48.9	45.2	32.4	50.8
1989	33.8	29.9	37.5	46.2	59.3	68.7	72.3	72.1	65.3	54.1	42.5	21.8	50.3
1990	36.3	34.3	40.1	48.1	56.0	67.7	73.0	73.5	63.7	58.6	46.5	39.5	53.1
1991	29.6	35.1	41.3	51.8	63.9	69.3	74.2	73.6	63.1	56.1	45.4	36.3	53.3
1992	31.4	33.0	36.6	46.5	57.6	67.3	70.3	70.1	64.0	51.7	43.0	34.2	50.5
1993	31.4	26.3	35.8	49.6	61.8	69.3	74.5	73.8	65.1	51.5	44.0	33.7	51.4
Record Mean	29.1	29.6	37.8	47.8	58.1	67.0	72.8	71.1	63.8	53.7	43.5	32.7	50.6
Max	37.0	37.7	46.1	57.0	67.8	76.7	82.0	80.2	73.2	63.2	51.6	40.4	59.4
Min	21.1	21.4	29.5	38.6	48.3	57.3	63.6	62.0	54.5	44.2	35.3	25.0	41.7

REFERENCE NOTES

PROVIDENCE, RHODE ISLAND

GENERAL
T - TRACE AMOUNT.
BLANK ENTRIES DENOTE MISSING/UNREPORTED DATA.
# INDICATES A STATION OR INSTRUMENT RELOCATION.

SPECIFIC

PM - INCLUDES LAST DAY OF PREVIOUS MONTH
ASOS - AUTOMATED SURFACE OBSERVING SYSTEM IN OPERATION DURING THESE MONTHS.

(a) - LENGTH OF RECORD IN YEARS, ALTHOUGH INDIVIDUAL MONTHS MAY BE MISSING.
0.* OR * - THE VALUE IS BETWEEN 0.0 AND 0.05
NORMALS - BASED ON THE 1961-1990 RECORD PERIOD.
EXTREMES - DATES ARE THE MOST RECENT OCCURRENCE
WIND DIR.- NUMERALS SHOW TENS OF DEGRESS CLOCKWISE FROM TRUE NORTH. "00" INDICATES CALM.
RESULTANT DIRECTIONS ARE GIVEN TO WHOLE DEGREES.
BOLD VALUES INDICATE EXTREME VALUES WHICH OCCURRED AFTER THE ASOS SYSTEM WAS COMMISSIONED.

RECORD = PERIOD OF RECORD
RECORD MEAN PRECIPITATION IS THE MEAN OF ALL DAILY PRECIPITATION AMOUNTS DURING THE PERIOD OF RECORD.
RECORD MAX(MIN) TEMPERATURE IS THE MEAN OF ALL DAILY MAX(MIN) TEMPERATURES DURING THE PERIOD OF RECORD.
RECORD MEAN TEMPERATURE IS THE SUM OF THE RECORD MAX AND RECORD MIN DIVIDED BY 2.
AVERAGE TEMPERATURE IS THE SUM OF THE MEAN DAILY MAX AND MIN TEMPERATURE DIVIDED BY 2.

EXCEPTIONS

RECORD MEANS ARE THROUGH THE CURRENT YEAR,
BEGINNING IN 1905 FOR TEMPERATURE
1905 FOR PRECIPITATION
1954 FOR SNOWFALL

HEATING DEGREE DAYS Base 65 deg. F — PROVIDENCE, RHODE ISLAND

SEASON	JULY	AUG	SEP	OCT	NOV	DEC	JAN	FEB	MAR	APR	MAY	JUNE	TOTAL
1964-65	9	24	125	377	605	981	1231	1018	891	581	182	67	6091
1965-66	3	29	99	395	711	907	1115	975	806	630	326	57	6053
1966-67	1	1	135	417	577	994	963	1093	976	598	424	48	6227
1967-68	0	7	103	356	761	937	1246	1166	827	447	281	74	6205
1968-69	2	16	59	295	672	1072	1117	1010	923	452	241	22	5881
1969-70	2	4	119	365	673	1065	1399	996	924	509	214	60	6330
1970-71	0	0	102	342	602	1124	1298	949	868	566	212	34	6097
1971-72	0	7	42	181	736	922	1054	1064	879	616	226	55	5782
1972-73	8	10	64	473	717	945	1044	984	653	451	268	16	5633
1973-74	2	3	125	331	632	819	1028	1003	808	433	313	62	5559
1974-75	0	0	114	512	634	899	951	962	907	606	160	64	5809
1975-76	0	13	132	298	506	1013	1283	850	798	403	223	39	5558
1976-77	2	23	124	501	806	1219	1361	983	653	434	176	51	6333
1977-78	0	6	103	368	568	1030	1231	1192	964	542	238	26	6268
1978-79	8	8	180	412	673	970	1075	1261	755	540	162	52	6096
1979-80	11	25	94	380	496	849	1088	1104	857	459	158	93	5614
1980-81	0	1	120	465	715	1125	1379	769	808	405	228	13	6028
1981-82	0	20	119	486	651	1044	1343	932	802	510	190	91	6188
1982-83	1	26	78	363	518	809	1038	892	755	449	254	13	5196
1983-84	0	4	62	323	563	1001	1190	802	961	513	236	36	5691
1984-85	1	0	125	270	637	832	1309	914	743	417	177	63	5488
1985-86	0	6	78	321	567	1065	1045	999	772	460	216	57	5586
1986-87	14	25	113	380	697	911	1111	1014	772	494	228	23	5782
1987-88	2	25	70	414	653	921	1177	954	787	532	238	67	5840
1988-89	8	10	89	491	587	1003	960	975	847	557	181	22	5730
1989-90	2	9	89	332	668	1329	882	854	761	511	275	24	5736
1990-91	6	0	107	242	549	781	1090	829	726	400	121	29	4880
1991-92	1	0	125	275	581	884	1034	919	876	549	246	27	5517
1992-93	11	4	100	404	652	951	1036	1077	901	455	118	32	5741
1993-94	1	0	102	413	623	966							

COOLING DEGREE DAYS Base 65 deg. F — PROVIDENCE, RHODE ISLAND

YEAR	JAN	FEB	MAR	APR	MAY	JUNE	JULY	AUG	SEP	OCT	NOV	DEC	TOTAL
1969	0	0	0	0	23	125	211	299	94	9	0	0	761
1970	0	0	0	0	13	86	289	237	91	14	0	0	730
1971	0	0	0	0	3	157	296	263	158	8	5	0	890
1972	0	0	0	1	7	60	248	190	76	1	0	0	583
1973	0	0	0	8	17	181	272	318	84	3	0	0	883
1974	0	0	0	7	27	79	242	244	66	0	1	0	666
1975	0	0	0	0	55	100	300	218	16	4	1	0	694
1976	0	0	0	40	13	196	163	183	33	3	0	0	631
1977	0	0	0	5	68	108	295	260	85	0	0	0	821
1978	0	0	0	0	25	126	224	211	24	0	0	0	610
1979	0	0	0	0	26	59	279	190	74	12	0	0	640
1980	0	0	0	0	21	84	312	272	122	0	0	0	811
1981	0	0	0	2	33	152	335	183	47	0	0	0	752
1982	0	0	0	0	11	64	276	165	59	3	2	0	580
1983	0	0	0	1	8	177	367	298	206	30	0	0	1087
1984	0	0	0	0	6	164	206	272	47	7	0	0	702
1985	0	0	0	5	34	65	256	203	90	5	0	0	658
1986	0	0	0	0	51	105	207	164	38	14	0	0	579
1987	0	0	0	0	57	130	231	177	53	0	0	0	648
1988	0	0	0	0	26	131	302	336	37	2	0	0	834
1989	0	0	0	0	10	141	237	237	103	0	0	0	728
1990	0	0	0	8	1	114	262	272	74	49	2	0	782
1991	0	0	0	12	96	166	295	276	73	8	0	0	926
1992	0	0	0	0	27	103	183	169	75	1	0	0	558
1993	0	0	0	0	26	167	303	281	110	1	1	0	889

SNOWFALL (inches) — PROVIDENCE, RHODE ISLAND

SEASON	JULY	AUG	SEP	OCT	NOV	DEC	JAN	FEB	MAR	APR	MAY	JUNE	TOTAL
1964-65	0.0	0.0	0.0	0.0	T	6.9	28.7	2.7	6.6	T	0.0	0.0	44.9
1965-66	0.0	0.0	0.0	0.0	T	1.9	16.1	9.1	8.1	T	0.0	0.0	35.2
1966-67	0.0	0.0	0.0	0.0	T	7.2	1.3	23.1	24.9	1.6	0.0	0.0	58.1
1967-68	0.0	0.0	0.0	0.0	0.8	19.0	13.5	4.6	5.1	0.0	0.0	0.0	43.0
1968-69	0.0	0.0	0.0	0.0	0.1	2.7	0.5	26.7	6.0	0.0	0.0	0.0	36.0
1969-70	0.0	0.0	0.0	0.0	T	15.4	6.5	6.8	15.7	1.1	0.0	0.0	45.5
1970-71	0.0	0.0	0.0	T	0.0	17.8	11.0	5.0	6.1	1.9	0.0	0.0	41.8
1971-72	0.0	0.0	0.0	0.0	T	4.7	2.2	13.7	8.7	0.7	0.0	0.0	30.0
1972-73	0.0	0.0	0.0	0.7	0.3	4.1	2.0	3.2	0.6	0.4	0.0	0.0	11.3
1973-74	0.0	0.0	0.0	0.0	T	T	15.1	11.1	0.4	1.3	0.0	0.0	27.9
1974-75	0.0	0.0	0.0	0.0	0.3	2.1	2.0	18.2	2.2	0.2	0.0	0.0	25.0
1975-76	0.0	0.0	0.0	T	1.2	7.5	15.6	3.7	9.5	0.0	0.0	0.0	37.5
1976-77	0.0	0.0	0.0	0.0	T	9.8	14.0	11.4	4.4	T	7.0	0.0	46.6
1977-78	0.0	0.0	0.0	0.0	1.3	3.9	20.5	28.6	15.9	T	0.0	0.0	70.2
1978-79	0.0	0.0	0.0	0.0	2.3	2.4	6.0	5.5	T	1.1	0.0	0.0	17.3
1979-80	0.0	0.0	0.0	2.5	0.0	T	0.6	3.8	5.3	0.0	0.0	0.0	12.2
1980-81	0.0	0.0	0.0	0.0	4.1	3.6	12.9	0.6	0.3	0.0	0.0	0.0	21.5
1981-82	0.0	0.0	0.0	T	T	16.4	13.4	4.3	5.7	7.6	0.0	0.0	47.4
1982-83	0.0	0.0	0.0	0.0	0.0	7.3	3.8	21.3	T	T	0.0	0.0	32.4
1983-84	0.0	0.0	0.0	0.0	T	4.5	17.9	T	13.7	T	0.0	0.0	36.1
1984-85	0.0	0.0	0.0	0.0	T	2.0	9.8	10.0	0.6	T	0.0	0.0	22.4
1985-86	0.0	0.0	0.0	0.0	1.8	2.6	0.7	13.0	0.5	T	T	0.0	18.6
1986-87	0.0	0.0	0.0	0.0	4.4	8.0	21.5	4.7	1.6	1.1	0.0	0.0	41.3
1987-88	0.0	0.0	0.0	0.0	8.0	7.8	13.5	6.7	2.7	T	0.0	0.0	38.7
1988-89	0.0	0.0	0.0	0.0	T	1.2	0.2	7.3	1.9	0.3	0.0	0.0	10.9
1989-90	0.0	0.0	0.0	0.0	8.0	15.8	10.8	10.5	9.3	1.8	0.0	0.0	56.2
1990-91	0.0	0.0	0.0	0.0	T	6.9	6.4	6.0	5.3	0.0	0.0	0.0	24.6
1991-92	0.0	0.0	0.0	0.0	T	4.8	2.4	4.9	8.2	2.0	0.0	0.0	22.3
1992-93	0.0	0.0	0.0	T	T	3.6	5.4	12.7	17.8	0.2	0.0	0.0	39.7
1993-94	0.0	0.0	0.0	0.0	T	10.1							
Record Mean	0.0	0.0	0.0	0.1	1.0	7.0	9.4	9.6	7.6	0.7	0.2	0.0	35.7

CHARLESTON, SOUTH CAROLINA

Charleston is a peninsula city bounded on the west and south by the Ashley River, on the east by the Cooper River, and on the southeast by a spacious harbor. Weather records for the airport are from a site some 10 miles inland. The terrain is generally level, ranging in elevation from sea level to 20 feet on the peninsula, with gradual increases in elevation toward inland areas. The soil is sandy to sandy loam with lesser amounts of loam. The drainage varies from good to poor. Because of the very low elevation, a considerable portion of this community and the nearby coastal islands are vulnerable to tidal flooding.

The climate is temperate, modified considerably by the nearness to the ocean. The marine influence is noticeable during winter when the low temperatures are sometimes 10-15 degrees higher on the peninsula than at the airport. By the same token, high temperatures are generally a few degrees lower on the peninsula. The prevailing winds are northerly in the fall and winter, southerly in the spring and summer.

Summer is warm and humid. Temperatures of 100 degrees or more are infrequent. High temperatures are generally several degrees lower along the coast than inland due to the cooling effect of the sea breeze. Summer is the rainiest season with 41 percent of the annual total. The rain, except during occasional tropical storms, generally occurs as showers or thunderstorms.

The fall season passes through the warm Indian Summer period to the pre-winter cold spells which begin late in November. From late September to early November the weather is mostly sunny and temperature extremes are rare. Late summer and early fall is the period of maximum threat to the South Carolina coast from hurricanes.

The winter months, December through February, are mild with periods of rain. However, the winter rainfall is generally of a more uniform type. There is some chance of a snow flurry, with the best probability of its occurrence in January, but a significant amount is rarely measured. An average winter would experience less than one cold wave and severe freeze. Temperatures of 20 degrees or less on the peninsula and along the coast are very unusual.

The most spectacular time of the year, weatherwise, is spring with its rapid changes from windy and cold in March to warm and pleasant in May. Severe local storms are more likely to occur in spring than in summer.

The average occurrence of the first freeze in the fall is early December, and the average last freeze is late February, giving an average growing season of about 294 days.

NORMALS, MEANS, AND EXTREMES

CHARLESTON, SOUTH CAROLINA

LATITUDE: 32°54'N LONGITUDE: 80°02' W ELEVATION: FT. GRND 40 BARO 47 TIME ZONE: EASTERN WBAN: 13880

	(a)	JAN	FEB	MAR	APR	MAY	JUNE	JULY	AUG	SEP	OCT	NOV	DEC	YEAR
TEMPERATURE °F:														
Normals														
-Daily Maximum		57.8	61.0	68.6	75.8	82.7	87.6	90.2	89.0	84.9	77.2	69.5	61.6	75.5
-Daily Minimum		37.7	40.0	47.5	53.9	62.9	69.1	72.7	72.2	67.9	56.3	47.2	40.7	55.7
-Monthly		47.8	50.5	58.1	64.9	72.8	78.3	81.5	80.6	76.4	66.8	58.4	51.2	65.6
Extremes														
-Record Highest	51	83	87	90	94	98	103	104	102	99	94	88	83	104
-Year		1950	1989	1974	1989	1989	1944	1986	1954	1944	1986	1961	1972	JUL 1986
-Record Lowest	51	6	12	15	29	36	50	58	56	42	27	15	8	6
-Year		1985	1973	1980	1944	1963	1972	1952	1979	1967	1976	1950	1962	JAN 1985
NORMAL DEGREE DAYS:														
Heating (base 65°F)		548	414	239	66	0	0	0	0	0	74	233	439	2013
Cooling (base 65°F)		15	8	25	63	242	399	512	484	342	130	35	11	2266
% OF POSSIBLE SUNSHINE	34	56	60	65	70	69	66	67	63	61	63	59	56	63
MEAN SKY COVER (tenths)														
Sunrise - Sunset	44	6.3	6.1	6.0	5.3	6.0	6.3	6.5	6.4	6.2	5.2	5.3	5.9	5.9
MEAN NUMBER OF DAYS:														
Sunrise to Sunset														
-Clear	45	8.9	8.7	9.2	11.2	8.0	6.0	5.1	5.5	6.8	11.6	11.8	9.6	102.3
-Partly Cloudy	45	6.3	6.4	8.0	7.9	11.0	11.4	12.3	12.9	10.5	8.3	6.6	7.0	108.6
-Cloudy	45	15.8	13.2	13.8	11.0	12.1	12.6	13.6	12.6	12.7	11.2	11.6	14.4	154.3
Precipitation .01 inches or more	51	9.9	8.8	10.0	7.6	9.0	10.8	13.3	12.8	9.5	6.0	6.9	8.3	112.9
Snow, Ice pellets, hail 1.0 inches or more	51	0.0	0.1	0.*	0.0	0.0	0.0	0.0	0.0	0.0	0.0	0.0	0.1	0.2
Thunderstorms	51	0.8	1.1	2.3	2.9	6.7	9.9	13.3	11.7	5.3	1.4	0.7	0.5	56.5
Heavy Fog Visibility 1/4 mile or less	44	4.2	2.0	2.4	2.1	2.1	1.5	0.7	1.2	1.8	2.5	3.6	3.7	27.8
Temperature °F														
-Maximum														
90° and above	51	0.0	0.0	0.*	0.8	3.9	11.3	16.9	14.7	5.4	0.4	0.0	0.0	53.4
32° and below	51	0.2	0.1	0.*	0.0	0.0	0.0	0.0	0.0	0.0	0.0	0.0	0.1	0.3
-Minimum														
32° and below	51	10.6	7.5	2.7	0.2	0.0	0.0	0.0	0.0	0.0	0.1	3.0	8.9	33.1
0° and below	51	0.0	0.0	0.0	0.0	0.0	0.0	0.0	0.0	0.0	0.0	0.0	0.0	0.0
AVG. STATION PRESS. (mb)	21	1018.8	1017.9	1016.2	1015.3	1014.7	1014.8	1015.8	1016.1	1016.1	1017.5	1018.6	1019.5	1016.8
RELATIVE HUMIDITY (%)														
Hour 01	51	80	78	81	83	88	89	90	91	90	87	85	81	85
Hour 07 (Local Time)	51	83	81	83	84	85	86	88	90	90	88	86	83	86
Hour 13	51	56	52	51	49	53	58	62	63	62	55	53	55	56
Hour 19	51	71	67	66	65	70	74	77	79	80	78	76	73	73
PRECIPITATION (inches):														
Water Equivalent														
-Normal		3.45	3.30	4.34	2.67	4.01	6.43	6.84	7.22	4.73	2.90	2.49	3.15	51.53
-Maximum Monthly	51	8.92	6.35	11.11	9.50	9.28	27.24	18.46	16.99	17.31	9.12	7.35	7.09	27.24
-Year		1993	1983	1983	1958	1957	1973	1964	1974	1945	1959	1972	1953	JUN 1973
-Minimum Monthly	51	0.63	0.33	0.99	0.01	0.68	0.96	1.76	0.73	0.18	0.08	0.48	0.66	0.01
-Year		1950	1947	1963	1972	1944	1970	1972	1980	1990	1943	1966	1984	APR 1972
-Maximum in 24 hrs	51	3.90	3.28	6.63	4.10	6.23	10.10	5.81	5.77	8.84	5.77	5.24	3.40	10.10
-Year		1993	1944	1959	1958	1967	1973	1960	1964	1945	1944	1969	1978	JUN 1973
Snow, Ice pellets, hail														
-Maximum Monthly	51	1.0	7.1	2.0	T	0.0	T	T	0.0	0.0	0.0	T	8.0	8.0
-Year		1977	1973	1969	1985		1989	1993				1950	1989	DEC 1989
-Maximum in 24 hrs	51	0.8	5.9	2.0	T	0.0	T	T	0.0	0.0	0.0	T	6.6	6.6
-Year		1966	1973	1969	1985		1989	1993				1950	1989	DEC 1989
WIND:														
Mean Speed (mph)	44	9.1	9.8	10.0	9.7	8.6	8.3	7.9	7.4	7.8	8.0	8.1	8.5	8.6
Prevailing Direction through 1963		SW	NNE	SSW	SSW	S	S	SW	SW	NNE	NNE	N	NNE	NNE
Fastest Obs. 1 Min.														
-Direction (!!)	18	20	30	21	19	25	32	33	08	21	18	15	24	21
-Speed (MPH)	18	40	38	46	36	32	40	37	35	52	30	37	39	52
-Year		1978	1991	1993	1983	1978	1991	1986	1988	1989	1976	1985	1975	SEP 1989
Peak Gust														
-Direction (!!)	10	SW	NW	SW	S	W	NW	W	N	SW	NW	SE	SW	SW
-Speed (mph)	10	51	48	69	48	49	55	59	64	98	41	48	44	98
-Date		1992	1991	1993	1988	1984	1990	1992	1986	1989	1986	1985	1993	SEP 1989

PRECIPITATION (inches) — CHARLESTON, SOUTH CAROLINA

YEAR	JAN	FEB	MAR	APR	MAY	JUNE	JULY	AUG	SEP	OCT	NOV	DEC	ANNUAL
1964	6.53	6.32	4.40	2.72	4.77	6.95	18.46	7.67	4.11	7.53	0.52	3.01	72.99
1965	1.69	5.49	7.99	3.10	1.32	6.68	8.90	5.90	4.66	6.23	0.87	1.20	54.03
1966	6.68	4.61	2.65	2.83	7.71	6.03	11.48	3.45	2.20	1.70	0.48	3.76	53.58
1967	4.93	3.12	2.81	0.84	8.91	4.06	9.19	3.74	1.39	0.52	1.35	2.79	43.65
1968	2.25	1.27	1.35	1.99	2.54	9.41	7.77	4.42	1.66	6.86	2.67	3.65	45.84
1969	1.19	2.05	5.14	3.46	2.34	4.88	5.34	11.84	5.37	1.50	5.49	3.52	52.12
1970	2.51	2.86	7.72	1.34	3.78	0.96	5.93	10.64	2.53	4.08	0.67	2.90	45.92
1971	5.45	4.71	4.05	4.11	4.15	4.07	6.04	16.32	0.53	7.22	1.61	2.28	60.54
1972	4.13	5.18	2.52	0.01	5.67	5.29	1.76	4.52	1.82	0.25	7.35	4.36	42.86
1973	4.59	5.57	6.15	2.55	1.83	27.24	3.60	6.66	7.93	0.63	0.84	4.58	72.17
1974	1.42	2.96	3.04	0.86	4.82	9.45	3.09	16.99	4.80	0.40	3.78	3.00	54.61
1975	4.92	3.54	4.54	3.74	5.06	5.96	9.34	7.18	5.16	1.97	1.43	3.35	56.19
1976	1.62	0.95	2.33	0.62	8.87	5.59	4.48	5.22	6.03	4.10	3.57	5.12	48.50
1977	2.72	1.38	5.31	0.45	4.66	2.12	3.86	8.13	2.48	2.49	1.76	5.88	41.24
1978	4.31	1.82	3.25	1.97	4.68	3.42	6.19	4.01	5.06	0.18	1.87	4.13	40.89
1979	3.43	3.04	3.01	3.81	8.09	2.23	8.35	0.88	15.36	3.87	3.29	2.62	57.98
1980	3.99	1.25	7.99	3.43	5.85	3.15	6.97	0.73	2.60	1.52	2.19	1.25	40.92
1981	0.93	2.23	2.38	1.87	4.02	6.04	12.66	9.30	1.27	1.95	1.06	5.73	49.44
1982	2.18	3.64	1.26	6.51	3.04	9.16	5.40	4.10	3.92	2.42	1.19	4.20	47.02
1983	4.86	6.35	11.11	3.57	0.75	2.37	8.89	2.90	3.50	2.36	3.08	4.35	54.09
1984	5.12	3.51	5.63	6.30	6.89	2.96	4.87	1.96	5.27	1.67	1.39	0.66	46.23
1985	0.87	2.70	1.50	1.12	2.79	7.02	12.06	8.48	2.53	4.58	5.49	1.21	50.35
1986	2.05	4.17	2.67	0.83	0.93	2.51	5.07	13.41	4.60	2.95	4.03	5.21	48.43
1987	7.17	4.58	5.55	1.31	2.29	5.64	2.92	6.97	14.49	0.56	3.65	1.57	56.70
1988	2.76	2.38	1.78	3.21	1.86	2.32	4.13	11.88	9.72	0.73	1.08	0.72	42.57
1989	2.31	1.17	2.87	4.84	2.14	7.26	1.93	9.18	13.35	4.08	1.85	4.74	55.72
1990	3.96	1.68	6.63	1.65	1.91	3.12	5.95	6.32	0.18	7.29	3.75	2.69	45.13
1991	7.78	0.94	4.66	4.59	5.37	4.54	7.38	8.09	2.29	0.77	1.64	1.62	49.67
1992	4.93	2.23	3.59	2.75	5.07	6.22	4.36	9.55	3.04	4.87	5.76	1.50	53.87
1993	8.92	3.08	5.80	2.72	2.67	3.70	4.21	7.69	5.01	3.00	3.59	2.30	52.69
Record Mean	3.14	3.23	3.75	2.77	3.54	5.17	7.07	6.77	5.09	3.10	2.33	2.87	48.84

AVERAGE TEMPERATURE (deg. F) — CHARLESTON, SOUTH CAROLINA

YEAR	JAN	FEB	MAR	APR	MAY	JUNE	JULY	AUG	SEP	OCT	NOV	DEC	ANNUAL
1964	48.5	47.5	57.6	66.0	73.1	80.0	78.0	79.6	75.4	62.5	60.5	52.9	65.1
1965	48.4	51.2	54.5	64.5	75.3	76.1	79.0	79.6	75.9	65.2	57.6	49.3	64.7
1966	43.9	49.6	53.9	63.2	70.6	73.7	79.6	80.0	75.8	67.4	56.3	48.9	63.6
1967	50.6	48.5	60.0	67.1	71.3	75.6	79.9	79.5	69.9	62.6	53.8	53.4	64.4
1968	43.5	41.8	55.7	65.7	71.7	77.8	81.5	81.5	75.1	67.1	53.7	46.5	63.5
1969	44.6	45.2	50.6	63.3	69.9	80.3	82.7	77.5	73.7	68.2	53.4	46.5	63.0
1970	41.0	48.5	57.1	66.3	72.7	78.4	82.5	80.6	77.3	67.5	54.1	52.1	64.8
1971	49.9	49.8	51.9	62.7	71.1	80.4	80.3	79.6	77.1	70.8	57.1	58.8	65.8
1972	54.8	48.9	56.9	64.0	69.8	74.0	80.1	80.4	76.4	67.3	56.8	55.7	65.5
1973	48.0	46.1	61.0	61.5	71.7	78.4	82.6	81.0	79.6	69.6	61.4	51.3	66.0
1974	61.8	51.5	62.0	63.6	74.0	75.4	78.2	79.3	75.0	61.8	55.5	51.0	65.8
1975	53.8	54.7	56.9	62.3	75.1	78.5	79.2	81.5	76.8	69.0	59.3	49.7	66.4
1976	44.8	55.9	62.3	64.0	70.3	75.8	81.0	77.2	73.9	61.4	50.9	48.8	63.9
1977	38.7	46.3	60.6	66.4	72.8	81.2	83.8	81.4	78.7	63.5	61.3	5.0	65.4
1978	43.5	42.7	55.2	66.5	72.0	78.6	81.1	81.3	77.4	65.7	63.3	52.7	65.0
1979	45.4	46.8	57.4	64.9	72.4	75.9	82.0	81.4	76.5	66.0	59.4	48.7	64.7
1980	48.7	45.9	54.6	64.3	71.4	78.4	82.4	82.1	79.8	65.0	55.4	47.5	64.6
1981	41.6	50.8	54.3	67.5	70.8	82.7	83.5	80.3	74.8	64.1	55.4	46.2	64.3
1982	45.1	51.5	59.2	61.8	72.2	78.8	81.2	80.0	74.5	65.1	60.9	57.0	65.6
1983	45.6	49.0	56.4	61.0	71.7	76.9	82.8	82.9	75.5	68.9	57.4	48.8	64.8
1984	46.1	52.8	57.6	64.0	71.7	78.8	79.9	81.1	73.0	71.3	54.2	57.2	65.6
1985	42.6	50.5	60.7	67.8	73.6	79.6	80.9	79.9	75.8	72.2	67.3	47.9	66.6
1986	45.8	55.5	58.0	66.1	74.3	81.4	86.1	79.9	78.6	68.8	63.1	52.8	67.5
1987	47.2	48.8	56.8	62.6	73.3	80.1	83.0	83.5	77.8	61.0	60.1	53.5	65.6
1988	43.2	49.2	57.4	64.4	71.9	76.7	81.8	82.0	76.3	62.7	61.0	50.6	64.8
1989	55.6	55.0	59.7	65.3	72.3	80.4	82.8	80.7	76.6	68.7	60.6	43.2	66.7
1990	55.4	59.2	62.5	66.0	74.4	81.0	83.6	82.5	79.2	70.5	60.4	56.4	69.3
1991	50.8	54.9	60.5	67.6	76.3	78.9	83.6	82.0	77.4	67.6	56.0	54.3	67.5
1992	49.5	55.0	57.9	63.6	70.3	77.5	83.9	80.6	76.2	65.1	60.4	51.0	65.9
1993	53.7	49.7	55.9	61.6	72.5	79.5	85.5	82.0	78.3	67.3	59.3	48.5	66.2
Record Mean	49.7	51.5	57.5	64.6	72.6	78.7	81.3	80.6	76.5	67.2	58.0	51.0	65.8
Max	58.6	60.6	66.7	73.8	81.1	86.5	88.8	87.9	83.8	75.7	67.3	60.1	74.2
Min	40.8	42.4	48.4	55.3	64.0	70.8	73.8	73.2	69.2	58.6	48.6	42.0	57.3

REFERENCE NOTES — CHARLESTON, SOUTH CAROLINA

GENERAL
T - TRACE AMOUNT.
BLANK ENTRIES DENOTE MISSING/UNREPORTED DATA.
# INDICATES A STATION OR INSTRUMENT RELOCATION.

SPECIFIC

PM - INCLUDES LAST DAY OF PREVIOUS MONTH
ASOS - AUTOMATED SURFACE OBSERVING SYSTEM IN OPERATION DURING THESE MONTHS.

(a) - LENGTH OF RECORD IN YEARS, ALTHOUGH INDIVIDUAL MONTHS MAY BE MISSING.
0.* OR * - THE VALUE IS BETWEEN 0.0 AND 0.05
NORMALS - BASED ON THE 1961-1990 RECORD PERIOD.
EXTREMES - DATES ARE THE MOST RECENT OCCURRENCE
WIND DIR.- NUMERALS SHOW TENS OF DEGRESS CLOCKWISE FROM TRUE NORTH. "00" INDICATES CALM.
RESULTANT DIRECTIONS ARE GIVEN TO WHOLE DEGREES.
BOLD VALUES INDICATE EXTREME VALUES WHICH OCCURRED AFTER THE ASOS SYSTEM WAS COMMISSIONED.

RECORD = PERIOD OF RECORD
RECORD MEAN PRECIPITATION IS THE MEAN OF ALL DAILY PRECIPITATION AMOUNTS DURING THE PERIOD OF RECORD.
RECORD MAX(MIN) TEMPERATURE IS THE MEAN OF ALL DAILY MAX(MIN) TEMPERATURES DURING THE PERIOD OF RECORD.
RECORD MEAN TEMPERATURE IS THE SUM OF THE RECORD MAX AND RECORD MIN DIVIDED BY 2.
AVERAGE TEMPERATURE IS THE SUM OF THE MEAN DAILY MAX AND MIN TEMPERATURE DIVIDED BY 2.

EXCEPTIONS

RECORD MEANS ARE THROUGH THE CURRENT YEAR, BEGINNING IN 1874 FOR TEMPERATURE
1871 FOR PRECIPITATION
1943 FOR SNOWFALL

HEATING DEGREE DAYS Base 65 deg. F CHARLESTON, SOUTH CAROLINA

SEASON	JULY	AUG	SEP	OCT	NOV	DEC	JAN	FEB	MAR	APR	MAY	JUNE	TOTAL
1964-65	0	0	0	135	153	385	507	392	340	95	0	0	2007
1965-66	0	0	0	95	225	481	644	427	338	119	15	2	2346
1966-67	0	0	0	51	280	498	442	460	194	50	29	4	2008
1967-68	0	0	15	112	334	367	657	667	307	67	4	0	2530
1968-69	0	0	0	80	334	564	624	551	444	90	6	0	2693
1969-70	0	0	1	50	349	567	735	454	249	82	9	0	2496
1970-71	0	0	11	42	324	392	465	424	404	127	16	0	2205
1971-72	0	0	0	13	261	220	317	463	249	113	8	0	1644
1972-73	0	0	0	33	268	302	520	524	167	141	18	0	1973
1973-74	0	0	0	34	158	428	131	378	150	114	2	0	1395
1974-75	0	0	5	136	299	432	350	294	273	152	0	0	1941
1975-76	0	0	0	40	221	466	624	265	146	94	15	3	1874
1976-77	0	0	0	159	418	501	808	516	186	58	17	0	2663
1977-78	0	0	0	112	175	459	663	616	309	52	18	0	2404
1978-79	0	0	0	57	83	399	602	505	241	70	2	0	1959
1979-80	0	0	0	68	203	500	495	555	321	82	17	0	2241
1980-81	0	0	0	80	287	537	719	393	333	55	16	0	2420
1981-82	0	0	3	88	291	577	611	372	214	132	3	0	2291
1982-83	0	0	0	102	154	276	596	440	264	146	2	0	1980
1983-84	0	0	4	24	230	500	578	347	240	92	16	0	2031
1984-85	0	0	9	13	337	249	692	418	183	47	4	0	1952
1985-86	0	0	2	16	54	526	586	261	244	74	4	0	1767
1986-87	0	6	0	56	128	376	545	446	272	131	7	0	1967
1987-88	0	0	0	135	188	358	669	458	239	85	7	2	2141
1988-89	0	0	0	107	145	442	286	312	220	121	14	0	1647
1989-90	0	0	1	50	169	669	294	189	137	67	0	0	1576
1990-91	0	0	0	65	152	280	432	293	185	34	0	0	1441
1991-92	0	0	0	41	281	349	472	293	234	119	28	0	1817
1992-93	0	0	3	70	197	430	353	421	279	132	1	0	1886
1993-94	0	0	3	49	206	504							

COOLING DEGREE DAYS Base 65 deg. F CHARLESTON, SOUTH CAROLINA

YEAR	JAN	FEB	MAR	APR	MAY	JUNE	JULY	AUG	SEP	OCT	NOV	DEC	TOTAL
1969	0	0	1	46	165	465	555	394	268	158	6	0	2058
1970	0	0	9	126	253	410	552	487	384	130	3	1	2355
1971	2	5	5	65	215	469	480	457	369	199	31	32	2329
1972	7	3	5	93	163	275	475	488	351	110	30	22	2022
1973	1	0	50	42	233	412	554	501	445	184	56	10	2488
1974	41	7	63	80	288	319	417	450	312	46	18	3	2044
1975	8	13	26	74	318	414	449	516	361	171	58	0	2408
1976	2	9	73	70	187	329	502	384	274	52	2	1	1885
1977	0	1	54	107	263	493	588	518	417	71	71	1	2584
1978	0	0	13	106	242	414	505	514	378	86	40	21	2319
1979	0	2	9	71	241	335	533	514	354	105	40	0	2204
1980	0	9	7	69	221	407	549	539	451	87	5	1	2345
1981	0	0	9	138	199	539	582	481	307	66	9	0	2330
1982	0	2	42	42	232	420	510	475	293	111	36	34	2197
1983	0	0	6	32	217	362	559	567	322	149	10	4	2228
1984	0	1	19	67	228	420	471	509	254	212	21	10	2212
1985	7	17	57	136	276	445	501	470	332	245	129	5	2620
1986	0	2	36	114	300	499	662	474	414	182	78	5	2766
1987	0	0	26	62	269	459	567	580	389	18	48	9	2427
1988	0	2	12	74	229	359	529	534	349	43	30	4	2165
1989	5	37	64	136	246	470	561	493	358	173	44	0	2587
1990	4	34	65	105	302	487	583	548	430	238	24	21	2841
1991	0	20	52	118	356	426	584	531	379	128	18	25	2637
1992	0	7	20	83	199	381	592	495	345	79	68	5	2274
1993	7	0	4	37	241	440	644	536	410	127	42	0	2488

SNOWFALL (inches) CHARLESTON, SOUTH CAROLINA

SEASON	JULY	AUG	SEP	OCT	NOV	DEC	JAN	FEB	MAR	APR	MAY	JUNE	TOTAL
1970-71	0.0	0.0	0.0	0.0	0.0	0.0	T	T	T	0.0	0.0	0.0	T
1971-72	0.0	0.0	0.0	0.0	0.0	0.0	0.0	0.0	0.0	0.0	0.0	0.0	0.0
1972-73	0.0	0.0	0.0	0.0	0.0	0.0	T	7.1	0.0	0.0	0.0	0.0	7.1
1973-74	0.0	0.0	0.0	0.0	0.0	T	0.0	0.0	0.0	0.0	0.0	0.0	T
1974-75	0.0	0.0	0.0	0.0	0.0	0.0	0.0	0.0	0.0	0.0	0.0	0.0	0.0
1975-76	0.0	0.0	0.0	0.0	0.0	0.0	0.4	0.0	0.0	0.0	0.0	0.0	0.4
1976-77	0.0	0.0	0.0	0.0	0.0	0.0	1.0	0.3	0.0	0.0	0.0	0.0	1.3
1977-78	0.0	0.0	0.0	0.0	0.0	0.0	T	0.4	T	0.0	0.0	0.0	0.4
1978-79	0.0	0.0	0.0	0.0	0.0	0.0	0.0	1.8	0.0	0.0	0.0	0.0	1.8
1979-80	0.0	0.0	0.0	0.0	0.0	0.0	0.0	T	1.3	0.0	0.0	0.0	1.3
1980-81	0.0	0.0	0.0	0.0	0.0	3.8	0.0	0.0	0.0	0.0	0.0	0.0	3.8
1981-82	0.0	0.0	0.0	0.0	0.0	0.0	T	0.0	0.0	0.0	0.0	0.0	T
1982-83	0.0	0.0	0.0	0.0	0.0	0.0	0.0	0.0	T	0.0	0.0	0.0	T
1983-84	0.0	0.0	0.0	0.0	0.0	0.0	T	0.0	0.0	0.0	0.0	0.0	T
1984-85	0.0	0.0	0.0	0.0	0.0	0.0	T	0.0	0.0	T	0.0	0.0	T
1985-86	0.0	0.0	0.0	0.0	0.0	0.0	0.5	0.0	0.0	0.0	0.0	0.0	0.5
1986-87	0.0	0.0	0.0	0.0	0.0	0.0	T	0.0	T	0.0	0.0	0.0	T
1987-88	0.0	0.0	0.0	0.0	0.0	0.0	0.4	0.0	0.0	0.0	0.0	0.0	0.4
1988-89	0.0	0.0	0.0	0.0	0.0	T	0.0	0.9	T	0.0	0.0	T	0.9
1989-90	0.0	0.0	0.0	0.0	0.0	8.0	0.0	0.0	0.0	0.0	0.0	0.0	8.0
1990-91	0.0	0.0	0.0	0.0	0.0	0.0	0.0	T	0.0	0.0	0.0	0.0	T
1991-92	0.0	0.0	0.0	0.0	0.0	0.0	0.0	0.0	0.0	0.0	0.0	0.0	0.0
1992-93	0.0	0.0	0.0	0.0	0.0	0.0	0.0	0.0	T	0.0	0.0	0.0	T
1993-94	T	0.0	0.0	0.0	0.0	T							
Record Mean	T	0.0	0.0	0.0	T	0.3	0.1	0.2	0.1	T	0.0	T	0.7

RAPID CITY, SOUTH DAKOTA

Rapid City, which is not far from the geographical center of North America, experiences the large temperature ranges, both daily and seasonal, that are typical of semi-arid continental climates.

The city is surrounded by contrasting landforms, with the forested Black Hills rising immediately west of the city, and rolling prairie extending out in the other directions. From 40 to 70 miles southeast lie the eroded Badlands. The Black Hills, many of which are more than 5,000 feet above sea level, with a number of peaks above 7,000 feet, exert a pronounced influence on the climate of this area. The rolling land to the east of the city is cut by the valleys of the Box Elder and Rapid Creeks, which flow generally east-southeastward. The station is located on the north slope of the irrigated Rapid Valley. An east-west ridge 200 to 300 feet higher than the airport separates the station from the Box Elder Creek Valley.

The principal agricultural products in the area are cattle and wheat, and ranchers and farmers are dependent on the current weather forecasts, which are at times of vital interest in the protection of livestock.

Although the annual precipitation is light at lower elevations, the distribution is beneficial to agriculture with the greatest amounts occurring during the growing season. The heaviest snows are expected in the spring, which helps to furnish moisture for the early maturing crops such as wheat, while heavy winter snows at the higher elevations provide irrigation water for the fertile valleys.

Summer days are normally warm with cool, comfortable nights. Nearly all of the summer precipitation occurs as thunderstorms. Hail is often associated with the more severe thunderstorms, with resultant damage to vegetation as well as other fragile material in the path of the storms. Autumn, which begins soon after the first of September, is characterized by mild, balmy days, and cool, invigorating mornings and evenings. Autumn weather usually extends into November and often into December.

Temperatures for the winter months of December, January, and February are among the warmest in South Dakota due to the protection of the Black Hills, the frequent occurrence of Chinook winds, and the fact that the winter tracks of arctic air masses usually pass east of Rapid City. Rapid City has become the retirement home for many farmers and ranchers from the western half of the state because of the cool summer nights and the relatively mild winters.

Snowfall is normally light with the greatest monthly average of about 8 inches occurring in March. Cold waves can be expected occasionally, and one or more blizzards may occur each winter.

Spring is characterized by unsettled conditions. Wide variations usually occur in temperatures, and snows may fall as late as May.

Based on the 1951-1980 period, the average first occurrence of 32 degrees Fahrenheit in the fall is September 29 and the average last occurrence in the spring is May 7.

NORMALS, MEANS, AND EXTREMES

RAPID CITY, SOUTH DAKOTA

LATITUDE: 44 °03'N LONGITUDE: 103 °04' W ELEVATION: FT. GRND 3162 BARO 3169 TIME ZONE: MOUNTAIN WBAN: 24090

	(a)	JAN	FEB	MAR	APR	MAY	JUNE	JULY	AUG	SEP	OCT	NOV	DEC	YEAR
TEMPERATURE °F:														
Normals														
-Daily Maximum		33.8	38.2	45.9	57.9	68.1	77.8	86.2	85.1	74.4	62.5	46.7	35.6	59.4
-Daily Minimum		10.7	15.2	22.2	32.2	42.3	51.7	58.2	56.1	45.5	34.9	22.8	12.7	33.7
-Monthly		22.3	26.7	34.1	45.1	55.2	64.8	72.2	70.6	60.0	48.7	34.8	24.2	46.6
Extremes														
-Record Highest	51	76	75	82	93	98	106	110	106	104	94	78	75	110
-Year		1987	1988	1993	1989	1969	1988	1989	1988	1978	1993	1990	1965	JUL 1989
-Record Lowest	51	-27	-24	-17	1	18	31	39	38	18	-2	-19	-30	-30
-Year		1950	1989	1962	1975	1950	1951	1987	1992	1985	1991	1959	1990	DEC 1990
NORMAL DEGREE DAYS:														
Heating (base 65°F)		1324	1072	958	597	311	103	18	31	211	505	906	1265	7301
Cooling (base 65°F)		0	0	0	0	7	97	241	205	61	0	0	0	611
% OF POSSIBLE SUNSHINE	51	56	60	63	62	60	65	72	74	69	66	55	55	63
MEAN SKY COVER (tenths)														
Sunrise - Sunset	51	6.3	6.4	6.6	6.6	6.3	5.5	4.4	4.3	4.5	5.1	6.2	6.1	5.7
MEAN NUMBER OF DAYS:														
Sunrise to Sunset														
-Clear	51	8.0	6.5	6.4	5.9	6.8	9.1	12.8	13.7	13.3	12.1	7.7	8.4	110.6
-Partly Cloudy	51	7.8	8.2	9.3	9.5	10.8	11.4	12.8	11.7	8.7	8.2	8.5	8.3	115.2
-Cloudy	51	15.2	13.6	15.4	14.6	13.3	9.5	5.5	5.6	8.0	10.7	13.8	14.3	139.5
Precipitation														
.01 inches or more	51	6.6	7.2	8.7	9.3	11.8	12.4	9.4	7.8	6.4	5.1	5.9	6.0	96.5
Snow,Ice pellets,hail														
1.0 inches or more	43	1.3	2.5	2.6	2.0	0.2	0.*	0.0	0.0	0.1	0.4	1.7	1.8	12.6
Thunderstorms	51	0.0	0.0	0.1	1.2	5.9	10.8	11.7	8.7	3.4	0.4	0.*	0.*	42.3
Heavy Fog Visibility														
1/4 mile or less	51	1.5	2.1	2.5	1.7	0.9	1.2	0.5	0.6	0.6	0.6	2.0	1.9	16.0
Temperature °F														
-Maximum														
90° and above	51	0.0	0.0	0.0	0.1	0.5	3.3	11.4	11.5	3.6	0.3	0.0	0.0	30.6
32° and below	51	12.9	9.9	6.6	0.7	0.*	0.0	0.0	0.0	0.0	0.4	5.1	10.8	46.4
-Minimum														
32° and below	51	30.2	26.9	27.0	14.9	2.7	0.1	0.0	0.0	1.6	10.4	24.7	29.9	168.5
0° and below	51	8.0	4.4	2.0	0.0	0.0	0.0	0.0	0.0	0.0	0.*	1.1	4.4	19.8
AVG. STATION PRESS.(mb)	21	904.5	904.7	902.1	902.8	902.7	903.4	905.2	905.4	905.8	905.8	904.4	904.3	904.3
RELATIVE HUMIDITY (%)														
Hour 05	43	68	72	74	73	75	77	73	71	68	66	69	69	71
Hour 11 (Local Time)	43	59	59	55	48	49	51	45	42	41	42	52	59	50
Hour 17	43	63	61	54	46	47	48	41	37	38	45	59	64	50
Hour 23	43	68	71	72	68	71	73	65	62	60	62	68	68	67
PRECIPITATION (inches):														
Water Equivalent														
-Normal		0.39	0.52	1.03	1.89	2.68	3.06	2.04	1.67	1.23	1.10	0.56	0.47	16.64
-Maximum Monthly	51	1.77	2.46	3.02	5.16	7.35	7.00	6.13	4.83	3.94	3.82	2.22	1.65	7.35
-Year		1944	1953	1945	1967	1946	1968	1969	1982	1946	1982	1985	1975	MAY 1946
-Minimum Monthly	51	0.01	0.06	0.12	0.02	0.33	0.64	0.38	0.10	0.03	T	0.03	0.01	T
-Year		1952	1985	1981	1987	1966	1973	1988	1943	1975	1960	1945	1986	OCT 1960
-Maximum in 24 hrs	51	1.26	1.00	2.19	3.01	3.40	4.01	2.51	2.60	2.13	2.49	1.09	1.04	4.01
-Year		1944	1953	1945	1946	1965	1963	1944	1982	1966	1982	1944	1975	JUN 1963
Snow,Ice pellets,hail														
-Maximum Monthly	51	24.0	23.7	30.7	30.6	11.6	3.6	T	T	2.0	10.2	33.6	17.9	33.6
-Year		1949	1953	1950	1970	1950	1951	1993	1990	1970	1971	1985	1975	NOV 1985
-Maximum in 24 hrs	51	16.3	10.0	14.9	16.0	13.4	3.6	T	T	2.0	7.6	9.4	9.8	16.3
-Year		1944	1953	1973	1970	1967	1951	1993	1990	1970	1971	1977	1975	JAN 1944
WIND:														
Mean Speed (mph)	43	10.8	11.1	12.7	13.3	12.4	10.9	10.2	10.3	11.0	11.2	10.9	10.6	11.3
Prevailing Direction through 1963		NNW	NNW	NNW	NNW	NNW	NNW	NNW	NNW	NNW	NNW	NNW	NNW	NNW
Fastest Obs. 1 Min.														
-Direction (!!)	10	33	32	34	32	34	25	34	23	32	33	34	33	25
-Speed (MPH)	10	52	45	53	51	46	54	51	41	52	44	45	46	54
-Year		1987	1988	1988	1992	1988	1990	1991	1987	1991	1988	1993	1993	JUN 1990
Peak Gust														
-Direction (!!)	10	N	NW	N	NW	NW	W	NW	NW	S	NW	NW	NW	NW
-Speed (mph)	10	68	61	66	67	61	66	72	69	70	67	63	66	72
-Date		1988	1984	1988	1992	1987	1990	1984	1985	1985	1988	1993	1993	JUL 1984

PRECIPITATION (inches)

RAPID CITY, SOUTH DAKOTA

YEAR	JAN	FEB	MAR	APR	MAY	JUNE	JULY	AUG	SEP	OCT	NOV	DEC	ANNUAL
1964	0.35	0.83	0.63	1.24	2.52	4.69	0.77	1.87	0.69	0.50	0.30	0.78	15.17
1965	0.61	0.22	0.46	1.50	6.97	3.56	0.60	1.46	1.46	0.57	0.15	0.12	17.68
1966	0.24	1.00	1.78	2.50	0.33	1.31	3.93	3.24	2.84	1.50	0.95	0.79	20.41
1967	0.47	0.59	0.82	5.16	3.20	6.78	1.07	0.95	2.10	0.28	0.28	0.89	22.59
1968	0.43	0.35	0.21	1.82	1.68	7.00	2.44	2.46	0.89	0.14	0.46	0.58	18.46
1969	0.11	0.73	0.66	1.60	2.20	2.04	6.13	0.31	0.35	0.85	0.35	0.57	15.90
1970	0.73	0.54	1.48	4.63	2.41	2.16	1.04	0.67	1.57	1.23	0.80	0.61	17.87
1971	1.18	1.00	1.25	2.86	3.70	1.92	1.46	0.52	2.32	2.02	0.79	0.15	19.17
1972	0.22	0.44	0.47	2.78	3.28	4.11	1.67	2.49	0.24	0.77	0.38	0.34	17.19
1973	0.11	0.31	2.71	2.69	2.37	0.64	1.46	0.74	1.44	1.38	0.73	0.54	15.12
1974	0.16	0.30	0.34	1.55	1.32	1.10	0.68	1.37	0.88	1.18	0.12	0.12	9.12
1975	1.05	0.35	2.45	1.37	1.23	5.63	1.57	0.87	0.03	0.69	0.57	1.65	17.46
1976	0.28	0.47	0.33	2.70	2.74	4.81	1.05	1.31	0.28	0.21	0.61	0.41	15.20
1977	0.83	0.25	2.63	1.57	2.49	1.76	2.98	1.79	2.86	1.06	0.82	0.36	19.40
1978	0.19	0.84	0.40	2.19	3.12	2.01	4.08	1.42	0.18	0.26	0.63	0.25	15.57
1979	0.49	0.33	0.47	0.31	1.17	3.60	4.11	2.32	0.07	0.90	0.15	0.07	13.99
1980	0.20	0.51	0.86	1.13	1.58	4.75	1.78	2.38	0.48	2.28	0.57	0.66	17.18
1981	0.14	0.09	0.12	0.32	2.81	1.89	4.47	1.74	0.16	1.81	0.23	0.35	14.13
1982	0.39	0.37	1.35	0.69	6.50	2.89	1.81	4.83	2.69	3.82	0.27	0.36	25.97
1983	0.34	0.18	0.84	1.00	2.18	3.01	1.94	2.39	0.33	1.74	1.07	0.47	15.49
1984	0.10	0.18	0.69	3.10	1.57	4.72	1.57	1.00	0.74	0.67	0.51	0.38	15.23
1985	0.46	0.06	1.55	0.32	1.24	1.58	1.03	1.86	1.57	0.98	2.22	0.77	13.64
1986	0.49	0.92	0.88	4.74	1.43	4.56	0.91	1.32	3.14	1.64	1.40	0.01	21.44
1987	0.04	1.71	1.14	0.02	3.39	1.37	0.83	2.37	0.68	0.26	0.30	0.31	12.42
1988	0.17	0.34	0.52	0.60	3.25	1.09	0.38	1.98	0.56	0.76	0.81	0.46	10.92
1989	0.02	0.34	0.96	1.46	1.40	1.04	0.82	1.70	3.09	1.49	0.43	0.82	13.57
1990	0.22	0.37	1.17	0.77	4.87	1.42	1.94	1.87	2.44	0.61	0.44	0.33	16.45
1991	0.32	0.77	0.63	2.99	4.40	3.27	1.97	0.58	0.59	1.00	0.73	0.04	17.29
1992	0.29	0.16	1.92	0.71	2.47	2.17	3.25	0.47	0.42	0.68	0.39	0.57	13.50
1993	0.68	0.61	0.82	3.05	2.16	3.39	4.31	1.18	1.46	0.90	0.70	0.53	19.79
Record Mean	0.41	0.47	1.00	1.91	3.06	3.21	2.27	1.61	1.25	1.02	0.61	0.51	17.33

AVERAGE TEMPERATURE (deg. F)

RAPID CITY, SOUTH DAKOTA

YEAR	JAN	FEB	MAR	APR	MAY	JUNE	JULY	AUG	SEP	OCT	NOV	DEC	ANNUAL
1964	28.4	28.1	29.9	46.3	58.5	64.9	76.7	69.5	59.0	51.7	33.7	18.9	47.1
#1965	25.4	25.6	21.2	47.0	54.7	64.5	72.1	70.7	49.7	54.8	38.2	33.3	46.4
1966	14.2	19.3	35.0	38.7	56.0	65.3	76.6	65.9	61.3	48.6	34.6	26.7	45.2
1967	27.9	27.5	35.2	44.1	49.8	60.0	70.6	70.6	63.4	50.1	34.6	22.5	46.3
1968	23.4	27.4	40.4	42.6	50.8	63.0	69.2	67.0	59.8	51.0	35.5	18.5	45.7
1969	16.0	25.4	27.8	49.6	57.5	59.8	71.0	73.8	64.8	40.6	38.7	28.2	46.1
1970	17.8	30.8	27.5	39.2	55.6	65.6	72.7	73.8	59.1	44.1	34.2	21.9	45.2
1971	17.5	22.6	32.6	46.0	53.6	66.4	68.0	73.9	57.4	46.1	34.5	23.3	45.2
1972	17.3	24.0	36.5	43.6	55.2	64.7	65.6	69.1	59.4	43.8	31.0	18.6	44.1
1973	26.8	28.9	37.5	42.9	53.7	64.7	70.7	74.3	57.1	51.3	32.3	25.4	47.1
1974	21.9	32.5	37.6	47.2	53.8	66.6	77.3	67.7	57.6	51.7	36.4	28.9	48.3
1975	23.7	17.6	27.6	40.5	54.0	62.2	74.7	70.3	58.5	49.2	33.8	29.4	45.1
1976	23.9	34.6	34.4	46.9	55.4	64.3	72.8	72.6	63.3	45.4	31.7	26.8	47.7
1977	12.7	34.6	36.4	49.5	60.3	69.0	73.4	66.0	61.0	48.8	33.3	21.9	47.3
1978	11.0	15.3	35.4	45.2	55.1	65.1	71.1	69.7	66.2	50.5	29.2	17.1	44.2
1979	7.4	16.8	35.4	44.4	53.6	65.4	70.4	68.5	66.3	50.9	33.0	33.2	45.4
1980	21.0	27.1	31.5	48.9	57.4	67.1	74.9	68.6	61.6	48.9	39.3	30.3	48.0
1981	32.6	29.4	40.0	51.5	54.9	64.9	72.0	70.0	63.5	47.7	40.4	25.8	49.4
1982	11.9	23.9	33.0	42.1	53.3	59.7	70.7	70.2	58.7	47.2	32.7	28.6	44.3
1983	32.1	37.3	36.4	40.7	52.0	63.1	73.6	78.0	60.8	49.4	34.9	8.1	47.2
1984	28.0	36.1	34.3	43.8	53.6	62.8	72.2	74.8	57.2	47.2	37.5	21.4	47.4
1985	21.6	23.8	35.9	52.0	61.8	62.1	74.6	69.0	55.6	47.3	16.0	21.0	45.1
1986	29.8	21.5	43.0	44.2	54.9	67.6	70.9	69.6	55.0	48.7	30.6	30.5	47.2
1987	31.1	32.4	32.6	51.6	59.5	67.1	75.4	68.1	61.4	47.1	40.3	28.9	49.6
1988	21.7	26.9	35.6	47.1	60.0	75.6	76.1	72.5	60.4	49.7	36.4	28.4	49.2
1989	28.7	14.4	31.1	45.8	55.4	64.0	77.0	73.1	61.0	48.8	36.4	19.4	46.3
1990	32.4	28.9	36.4	45.0	53.2	66.6	71.7	73.8	65.9	48.2	40.5	17.8	48.4
1991	18.4	36.0	38.5	46.3	56.6	67.2	72.9	74.0	61.1	46.4	30.0	32.7	48.3
1992	33.6	36.3	40.9	47.1	57.4	62.6	64.3	65.9	62.6	49.3	32.4	19.0	47.6
1993	16.0	15.2	37.6	43.5	56.1	60.3	65.1	68.6	56.6	48.2	32.4	31.5	44.3
Record Mean	22.9	25.5	33.4	45.0	55.1	64.6	72.2	70.8	60.6	49.2	35.7	26.3	46.8
Max	34.5	36.9	44.9	57.0	66.9	76.6	85.4	84.4	74.2	62.1	47.3	37.5	59.0
Min	11.3	14.1	21.9	33.1	43.3	52.6	59.0	57.3	47.1	36.3	24.1	15.1	34.6

REFERENCE NOTES

RAPID CITY, SOUTH DAKOTA

GENERAL
T - TRACE AMOUNT.
BLANK ENTRIES DENOTE MISSING/UNREPORTED DATA.
# INDICATES A STATION OR INSTRUMENT RELOCATION.

SPECIFIC

PM - INCLUDES LAST DAY OF PREVIOUS MONTH
ASOS - AUTOMATED SURFACE OBSERVING SYSTEM IN OPERATION DURING THESE MONTHS.

(a) - LENGTH OF RECORD IN YEARS, ALTHOUGH INDIVIDUAL MONTHS MAY BE MISSING.
0.* OR * - THE VALUE IS BETWEEN 0.0 AND 0.05
NORMALS - BASED ON THE 1961-1990 RECORD PERIOD.
EXTREMES - DATES ARE THE MOST RECENT OCCURRENCE
WIND DIR.- NUMERALS SHOW TENS OF DEGRESS CLOCKWISE FROM TRUE NORTH. "00" INDICATES CALM.
RESULTANT DIRECTIONS ARE GIVEN TO WHOLE DEGREES.
BOLD VALUES INDICATE EXTREME VALUES WHICH OCCURRED AFTER THE ASOS SYSTEM WAS COMMISSIONED.

RECORD = PERIOD OF RECORD
RECORD MEAN PRECIPITATION IS THE MEAN OF ALL DAILY PRECIPITATION AMOUNTS DURING THE PERIOD OF RECORD.
RECORD MAX(MIN) TEMPERATURE IS THE MEAN OF ALL DAILY MAX(MIN) TEMPERATURES DURING THE PERIOD OF RECORD.
RECORD MEAN TEMPERATURE IS THE SUM OF THE RECORD MAX AND RECORD MIN DIVIDED BY 2.
AVERAGE TEMPERATURE IS THE SUM OF THE MEAN DAILY MAX AND MIN TEMPERATURE DIVIDED BY 2.

EXCEPTIONS

RECORD MEANS ARE THROUGH THE CURRENT YEAR, BEGINNING IN 1900 FOR TEMPERATURE
1900 FOR PRECIPITATION
1943 FOR SNOWFALL

HEATING DEGREE DAYS Base 65 deg. F

RAPID CITY, SOUTH DAKOTA

SEASON	JULY	AUG	SEP	OCT	NOV	DEC	JAN	FEB	MAR	APR	MAY	JUNE	TOTAL
1964-65	0	64	198	410	931	1419	1218	1098	1351	534	327	55	7605
#1965-66	3	27	461	312	797	978	1573	1273	923	784	285	103	7519
1966-67	0	83	158	504	905	1180	1143	1042	917	622	473	162	7189
1967-68	31	19	129	464	902	1311	1285	1083	755	669	432	107	7187
1968-69	26	46	176	428	881	1438	1516	1102	1145	458	264	176	7656
1969-70	0	0	62	750	781	1135	1461	950	1157	767	293	74	7430
1970-71	2	0	245	644	918	1330	1463	1182	996	563	344	35	7722
1971-72	43	2	267	578	909	1284	1473	1182	877	634	322	74	7645
1972-73	74	43	193	649	1010	1436	1181	1008	847	659	350	83	7533
1973-74	16	0	246	416	972	1223	1329	905	840	530	343	87	6907
1974-75	1	42	242	407	849	1112	1274	1318	1151	728	343	119	7586
1975-76	3	16	206	493	929	1096	1269	878	940	535	295	98	6758
1976-77	3	6	132	606	991	1177	1616	846	877	459	165	17	6895
1977-78	1	48	163	494	944	1330	1669	1383	912	588	312	91	7935
1978-79	17	40	111	443	1068	1480	1781	1348	910	614	362	82	8256
1979-80	3	25	64	433	952	982	1359	1094	1032	483	251	54	6732
1980-81	1	18	144	510	763	1070	998	993	765	402	311	65	6040
1981-82	21	7	108	531	730	1209	1646	1146	985	682	358	170	7593
1982-83	7	21	226	545	962	1119	1012	772	880	723	407	113	6787
1983-84	8	0	208	474	896	1762	1139	832	948	626	366	101	7360
1984-85	0	0	268	546	820	1344	1341	1148	895	393	146	144	7045
1985-86	8	27	327	544	1466	1358	1083	1211	672	617	317	35	7665
1986-87	5	12	296	497	1025	1059	1045	907	997	408	199	46	6496
1987-88	10	49	147	545	736	1111	1340	1103	905	533	195	17	6691
1988-89	3	18	163	470	850	1127	1120	1414	1047	586	303	116	7217
1989-90	3	6	182	495	847	1410	1004	1004	880	597	363	68	6859
1990-91	10	5	112	514	730	1462	1440	807	815	556	269	16	6736
1991-92	2	6	183	581	1045	997	964	828	742	539	262	107	6256
1992-93	67	83	138	493	973	1418	1515	1390	841	636	269	158	7981
1993-94	56	26	256	522	972	1035							

COOLING DEGREE DAYS Base 65 deg. F

RAPID CITY, SOUTH DAKOTA

YEAR	JAN	FEB	MAR	APR	MAY	JUNE	JULY	AUG	SEP	OCT	NOV	DEC	TOTAL
1969	0	0	0	0	35	29	193	280	63	0	0	0	600
1970	0	0	0	0	7	96	248	279	78	5	0	0	713
1971	0	0	0	0	0	81	142	284	43	0	0	0	550
1972	0	0	0	0	21	70	98	178	34	0	0	0	401
1973	0	0	0	0	7	80	202	295	15	0	0	0	599
1974	0	0	0	1	3	143	390	132	28	0	0	0	697
1975	0	0	0	0	9	41	314	188	19	12	0	0	583
1976	0	0	0	0	4	83	251	248	87	3	0	0	676
1977	0	0	0	0	25	143	270	85	51	0	0	0	574
1978	0	0	0	0	9	99	214	193	154	0	0	0	669
1979	0	0	0	4	15	99	179	141	110	2	0	0	550
1980	0	0	0	6	25	123	315	136	48	14	0	0	667
1981	0	0	0	3	5	67	243	170	74	0	0	0	562
1982	0	0	0	0	3	18	189	190	41	0	0	0	441
1983	0	0	0	0	9	62	282	407	88	0	0	0	848
1984	0	0	0	0	18	41	234	309	42	2	0	0	646
1985	0	0	0	10	53	64	312	158	51	0	0	0	648
1986	0	0	0	0	11	124	192	164	0	0	0	0	491
1987	0	0	0	13	33	118	341	152	45	0	0	0	702
1988	0	0	0	2	46	341	355	255	33	2	0	0	1034
1989	0	0	0	15	9	95	380	265	70	0	0	0	834
1990	0	0	0	2	4	120	226	282	147	3	0	0	784
1991	0	0	0	3	16	89	256	294	76	15	0	0	749
1992	0	0	0	9	36	41	51	118	72	11	0	0	338
1993	0	0	0	0	0	25	66	146	9	7	0	0	253

SNOWFALL (inches)

RAPID CITY, SOUTH DAKOTA

SEASON	JULY	AUG	SEP	OCT	NOV	DEC	JAN	FEB	MAR	APR	MAY	JUNE	TOTAL
1964-65	0.0	0.0	0.0	0.0	2.6	7.8	4.3	1.9	4.6	5.5	8.8	0.0	35.5
1965-66	0.0	0.0	1.5	0.0	0.8	0.7	2.4	10.0	16.5	10.0	0.4	0.0	42.3
1966-67	0.0	0.0	T	2.1	6.4	8.5	4.0	7.4	7.6	14.0	3.1	0.0	53.1
1967-68	0.0	0.0	0.0	0.0	2.2	9.1	4.0	3.4	1.3	13.7	T	0.0	33.7
1968-69	0.0	0.0	0.0	0.0	2.7	7.5	1.2	7.9	6.3	5.2	T	0.5	31.3
1969-70	0.0	0.0	0.0	4.1	2.9	5.7	5.5	6.0	14.8	30.6	T	0.0	69.6
1970-71	0.0	0.0	2.0	5.7	4.5	7.8	13.2	15.7	13.8	5.3	0.0	0.0	68.0
1971-72	0.0	0.0	0.0	10.2	6.9	2.0	2.6	8.0	1.2	1.0	T	0.0	31.9
1972-73	0.0	0.0	0.0	0.7	3.6	6.0	2.0	3.1	16.9	1.9	0.0	0.0	34.2
1973-74	0.0	0.0	0.0	1.4	9.7	5.6	2.0	4.0	1.7	4.7	0.0	0.0	29.1
1974-75	0.0	0.0	0.0	T	1.5	1.4	13.7	6.1	27.4	1.3	0.0	0.0	51.4
1975-76	0.0	0.0	0.0	4.6	8.4	17.9	2.0	6.5	4.3	3.5	0.0	0.0	47.2
1976-77	0.0	0.0	0.0	0.5	7.0	6.1	11.1	2.6	26.0	3.4	0.0	0.0	56.7
1977-78	0.0	0.0	0.0	0.8	10.6	7.4	3.1	15.0	3.0	2.6	T	0.0	42.5
1978-79	0.0	0.0	0.0	T	9.8	4.0	6.1	4.4	2.6	1.8	2.8	0.0	31.5
1979-80	0.0	0.0	0.0	T	1.8	0.3	3.0	10.1	8.6	5.4	0.0	0.0	29.2
1980-81	0.0	0.0	0.0	1.4	6.9	6.1	1.2	1.3	T	T	0.0	0.0	16.9
1981-82	0.0	0.0	0.0	1.6	1.2	3.8	6.2	5.0	11.5	5.5	0.0	0.0	34.8
1982-83	0.0	0.0	0.0	1.4	1.2	4.0	2.9	0.3	6.5	4.3	4.3	0.0	24.9
1983-84	0.0	0.0	0.3	0.9	6.9	7.1	1.9	2.5	6.1	22.1	0.2	0.0	48.0
1984-85	0.0	0.0	1.3	0.7	2.0	4.9	3.8	0.7	16.2	0.4	0.0	T	30.0
1985-86	0.0	0.0	1.4	0.6	33.6	10.2	5.7	10.7	6.0	12.7	0.0	0.0	80.9
1986-87	0.0	0.0	0.0	T	12.6	0.1	0.5	21.5	10.9	0.3	0.0	0.0	45.9
1987-88	0.0	0.0	0.0	1.7	T	4.7	2.7	3.6	10.6	6.1	0.0	0.0	29.4
1988-89	0.0	0.0	0.0	0.0	2.2	9.0	0.4	7.3	10.7	6.4	0.0	0.0	36.0
1989-90	0.0	T	0.0	3.9	4.6	10.9	3.1	5.0	9.2	3.0	0.5	T	40.2
1990-91	0.0	T	0.0	1.5	1.0	6.2	6.3	8.2	3.6	11.1	4.9	T	42.8
1991-92	T	0.0	T	4.0	6.7	0.8	5.2	1.2	8.2	3.5	0.0	0.0	29.6
1992-93	T	0.0	0.0	0.9	5.0	12.4	13.6	9.0	1.0	12.2	0.0	0.0	54.1
1993-94	T	0.0	T	2.4	11.4	5.5							
Record Mean	T	T	0.1	1.6	5.1	5.1	5.0	6.4	8.8	6.1	0.8	0.1	39.1

SIOUX FALLS, SOUTH DAKOTA

Sioux Falls is located in the Big Sioux River Valley in southeast South Dakota. The surrounding terrain is gently rolling. The land slopes upward for about 100 miles north and northwest to an elevation about 400 feet higher than the city. To the southeast, the land slopes downward 200 to 300 feet over the same distance. Little change in elevation occurs in the remaining directions.

The climate is of the continental type. There are frequent weather changes from day to day or week to week as the locality is visited by differing air masses. Cold air masses arrive from the interior of Canada, cool, dry air from the northern Pacific, warm, moist air from the Gulf of Mexico, or hot, dry air from the southwest.

Temperatures fluctuate frequently as cold air masses move in very rapidly. During the late fall and winter, cold fronts accompanied by strong, gusty winds drop temperatures by 20 to 30 degrees in a 24-hour period. Severe cold spells usually last only a few days. The winter months of December through February have experienced cold spells with average temperatures under 8 degrees and more than 60 consecutive days below 32 degrees.

Temperatures of 100 degrees and above occur about one in every three years, and will most likely happen in July. Summer nights are usually comfortable with temperatures below 70 degrees.

Rainfall is heavier during the spring and summer with lighter amounts in winter. Nearly 64 percent of the normal yearly precipitation falls during the growing season of April through August.

One or two very heavy snows usually fall each winter. Eight to 12 inches of snow may fall in 24 hours. There have been a few snows in excess of 15 inches and almost 30 inches have fallen during a severe winter storm. Strong winds often cause drifting snow, and blizzard conditions may block highways for a day or so.

Southerly winds prevail from late spring to early fall with northwest winds the remainder of the year. Strong winds of 70 mph with gusts to 90 mph have occurred.

Thunderstorms are frequent during the late spring and summer with June and July the most active months. The thunderstorms usually occur during the late afternoon and evening with a secondary peak of activity between 2 and 5 in the morning. Some of the most severe thunderstorms with damaging winds, hail and an occasional tornado, occur most frequently June.

There is occasional flooding in the lower areas of Sioux Falls along the Big Sioux River and Skunk Creek. Runoff from the melting snow in the spring often causes substantial rises in the rivers. A diversion canal around Sioux Falls has reduced the threat of damaging floods.

Based on the 1951–1980 period, the average first occurrence of 32 degrees Fahrenheit in the fall is October 1 and the average last occurrence in the spring is May 10.

NORMALS, MEANS, AND EXTREMES

SIOUX FALLS, SOUTH DAKOTA

LATITUDE: 43°35'N LONGITUDE: 96°44' W ELEVATION: FT. GRND 1418 BARO 1432 TIME ZONE: CENTRAL WBAN: 14944

	(a)	JAN	FEB	MAR	APR	MAY	JUNE	JULY	AUG	SEP	OCT	NOV	DEC	YEAR
TEMPERATURE °F:														
Normals														
-Daily Maximum		24.3	29.6	42.3	59.0	70.7	80.5	86.3	83.3	73.1	61.2	43.4	28.0	56.8
-Daily Minimum		3.3	9.7	22.6	34.8	45.9	56.1	62.3	59.4	48.7	36.0	22.6	8.6	34.2
-Monthly		13.8	19.7	32.5	46.9	58.4	68.3	74.3	71.4	60.9	48.6	33.0	18.3	45.5
Extremes														
-Record Highest	48	66	70	87	94	100	110	108	108	104	94	76	61	110
-Year		1981	1982	1968	1962	1967	1988	1989	1973	1976	1963	1978	1984	JUN 1988
-Record Lowest	48	-36	-31	-23	5	17	33	38	34	22	9	-17	-28	-36
-Year		1970	1962	1948	1982	1967	1969	1971	1950	1974	1972	1964	1990	JAN 1970
NORMAL DEGREE DAYS:														
Heating (base 65°F)		1587	1268	1008	543	240	50	10	22	165	508	960	1448	7809
Cooling (base 65°F)		0	0	0	0	35	149	298	220	42	0	0	0	744
% OF POSSIBLE SUNSHINE														
MEAN SKY COVER (tenths)														
Sunrise - Sunset	48	6.4	6.5	6.9	6.5	6.3	5.6	4.9	5.0	5.1	5.5	6.7	6.6	6.0
MEAN NUMBER OF DAYS:														
Sunrise to Sunset														
-Clear	48	8.1	7.0	6.3	7.2	7.3	8.7	11.7	11.8	11.8	11.1	6.9	7.6	105.6
-Partly Cloudy	48	7.7	6.6	7.6	8.2	9.9	10.9	11.7	10.6	8.0	7.9	7.3	7.0	103.4
-Cloudy	48	15.1	14.6	17.0	14.7	13.8	10.4	7.6	8.6	10.3	12.0	15.8	16.4	156.3
Precipitation														
.01 inches or more	48	6.1	6.5	8.7	9.4	10.5	10.9	9.7	9.0	8.1	6.1	6.4	6.2	97.6
Snow,Ice pellets,hail														
1.0 inches or more	48	2.0	2.1	2.5	0.6	0.0	0.0	0.0	0.0	0.0	0.1	1.6	2.0	11.0
Thunderstorms	48	0.*	0.1	0.9	3.0	6.2	9.0	9.5	8.0	5.4	1.8	0.4	0.1	44.3
Heavy Fog Visibility														
1/4 mile or less	48	2.5	3.0	2.8	0.9	0.8	0.5	0.7	1.2	1.4	1.5	2.7	3.6	21.4
Temperature °F														
-Maximum														
90° and above	30	0.0	0.0	0.0	0.2	0.7	4.0	10.2	7.3	1.7	0.0	0.0	0.0	24.1
32° and below	30	20.7	15.3	7.0	0.4	0.0	0.0	0.0	0.0	0.0	0.2	6.8	18.6	68.9
-Minimum														
32° and below	30	30.9	27.6	25.6	12.2	2.0	0.0	0.0	0.0	1.3	11.9	25.7	30.7	167.8
0° and below	30	12.7	7.8	1.5	0.0	0.0	0.0	0.0	0.0	0.0	0.0	1.4	7.8	31.2
AVG. STATION PRESS.(mb)	21	966.4	966.8	963.3	962.7	962.3	962.3	963.9	964.7	965.0	965.4	964.9	966.0	964.5
RELATIVE HUMIDITY (%)														
Hour 00	30	76	78	79	73	72	75	76	79	78	75	80	80	77
Hour 06 (Local Time)	30	77	80	82	81	81	82	83	86	86	81	83	81	82
Hour 12	30	68	68	64	54	53	55	54	55	57	55	66	71	60
Hour 18	30	72	70	63	51	49	51	51	54	56	57	71	76	60
PRECIPITATION (inches):														
Water Equivalent														
-Normal		0.51	0.64	1.64	2.52	3.03	3.40	2.68	2.85	3.02	1.78	1.09	0.70	23.86
-Maximum Monthly	48	1.71	4.05	3.60	5.79	8.26	8.43	8.41	9.09	9.26	5.73	2.95	2.62	9.26
-Year		1969	1962	1977	1984	1993	1984	1992	1975	1986	1973	1983	1968	SEP 1986
-Minimum Monthly	48	0.05	0.05	0.14	0.17	0.61	0.91	0.25	0.53	0.29	T	0.02	T	T
-Year		1958	1986	1967	1969	1981	1988	1947	1970	1956	1952	1980	1986	DEC 1986
-Maximum in 24 hrs	48	1.61	2.00	1.96	2.64	3.92	4.32	3.39	4.59	4.02	4.54	1.62	1.44	4.59
-Year		1960	1962	1956	1953	1972	1957	1992	1975	1966	1973	1972	1955	AUG 1975
Snow,Ice pellets,hail														
-Maximum Monthly	48	19.6	48.4	31.5	18.4	0.2	T	T	0.0	0.9	10.0	21.9	41.1	48.4
-Year		1969	1962	1951	1983	1954	1993	1993		1985	1991	1985	1968	FEB 1962
-Maximum in 24 hrs	48	11.8	26.0	18.9	9.0	0.2	T	T	0.0	0.9	8.8	11.8	16.6	26.0
-Year		1960	1962	1956	1957	1954	1993	1993		1985	1991	1979	1968	FEB 1962
WIND:														
Mean Speed (mph)	45	11.0	11.0	12.5	13.2	11.9	10.7	9.8	9.8	10.3	10.7	11.5	10.8	11.1
Prevailing Direction through 1963		NW	NW	NW	NW	S	S	S	S	S	S	NW	NW	S
Fastest Obs. 1 Min.														
-Direction (!!)	45	32	30	02	25	11	23	36	29	16	27	36	36	23
-Speed (MPH)	45	47	44	60	48	46	70	69	52	50	60	52	46	70
-Year		1990	1972	1950	1955	1950	1952	1982	1956	1953	1949	1975	1982	JUN 1952
Peak Gust														
-Direction (!!)	10	NW	NW	NW	SW	SE	E	NW	E	N	NW	W	NW	E
-Speed (mph)	10	67	55	56	64	53	71	66	47	53	53	58	53	71
-Date		1990	1984	1991	1985	1992	1990	1991	1986	1990	1984	1986	1992	JUN 1990

PRECIPITATION (inches)

SIOUX FALLS, SOUTH DAKOTA

YEAR	JAN	FEB	MAR	APR	MAY	JUNE	JULY	AUG	SEP	OCT	NOV	DEC	ANNUAL
1964	0.34	0.08	2.12	4.03	1.29	1.68	4.03	3.87	4.06	0.09	0.38	0.59	22.56
1965	0.24	1.46	1.09	3.35	7.29	4.91	1.49	1.29	4.91	1.05	0.26	0.60	27.94
1966	0.54	0.99	0.70	1.71	1.94	2.68	1.54	2.12	6.34	1.43	0.20	0.65	20.84
1967	0.75	0.44	0.14	3.90	0.72	4.26	0.53	3.46	0.87	0.39	0.03	0.91	16.40
1968	0.33	0.09	0.61	4.34	2.69	4.10	2.37	1.70	4.01	4.57	0.39	2.62	27.82
1969	1.71	2.55	1.09	0.17	2.43	4.85	2.73	5.07	2.41	2.05	0.34	1.18	26.58
1970	0.37	0.10	2.03	3.75	4.83	3.81	2.98	0.53	3.14	3.13	2.17	0.54	27.38
1971	0.13	0.90	0.85	1.59	1.06	6.10	2.92	0.71	3.23	3.06	2.45	0.64	23.64
1972	0.18	0.40	0.97	2.73	7.25	2.09	3.49	2.65	1.75	1.78	1.89	1.25	26.43
1973	0.43	0.43	3.52	2.12	1.93	2.38	3.50	1.05	5.61	5.73	1.01	0.48	28.19
1974	0.13	0.30	1.65	1.33	3.11	2.79	1.27	5.16	0.58	0.34	0.27	0.10	17.03
1975	1.35	0.22	1.95	2.45	1.66	4.48	0.62	9.09	1.35	0.49	2.25	0.19	26.10
1976	0.41	0.48	1.60	2.15	1.02	1.02	1.53	1.31	0.76	0.71	0.07	0.36	11.42
1977	0.19	0.83	3.60	2.17	3.17	1.73	3.64	5.63	5.63	2.36	1.80	0.87	31.62
1978	0.47	0.33	0.56	3.98	3.47	2.91	4.79	3.08	2.45	0.14	0.48	0.51	23.17
1979	1.14	0.41	3.47	2.75	4.90	3.01	3.13	4.35	4.03	3.30	1.72	0.04	32.25
1980	0.18	0.47	0.70	0.77	2.52	2.17	1.63	2.92	0.79	1.36	0.02	0.29	13.82
1981	0.12	0.33	1.86	0.58	0.61	3.90	3.89	2.28	0.50	2.45	1.21	0.38	18.11
1982	0.76	0.13	1.17	1.87	4.72	1.18	4.60	5.23	3.49	5.18	2.94	1.99	33.26
1983	0.52	0.22	3.35	2.88	2.92	6.75	1.82	2.00	1.92	0.71	2.95	0.73	26.77
1984	0.37	1.10	1.83	5.79	2.95	8.43	1.63	0.76	1.62	4.11	0.03	1.02	29.64
1985	0.45	0.05	2.37	5.18	3.29	2.52	2.70	4.07	3.34	0.75	1.97	0.47	27.16
1986	0.72	0.05	1.50	5.15	2.42	3.93	2.59	2.77	9.26	1.22	0.89	T	30.50
1987	0.19	0.26	3.27	0.28	2.94	1.78	3.16	1.36	2.05	0.31	1.66	1.40	18.66
1988	1.54	0.25	0.63	3.00	1.54	0.91	0.49	4.02	4.39	0.02	1.98	0.37	19.14
1989	0.23	0.51	1.07	1.59	1.42	2.50	1.37	2.46	3.38	0.10	0.91	0.25	15.79
1990	0.08	0.31	1.57	1.86	4.07	4.86	1.77	1.17	0.47	1.82	0.61	0.61	19.20
1991	0.22	0.34	0.86	2.21	6.20	6.36	2.26	1.41	3.95	1.65	1.78	0.20	27.44
1992	0.75	1.76	2.36	2.01	1.80	2.44	8.41	5.29	3.06	2.72	1.04	0.83	32.47
1993	0.70	0.81	2.04	2.61	8.26	6.43	7.86	3.10	1.88	0.62	1.50	0.30	36.11
Record Mean	0.60	0.76	1.45	2.49	3.53	4.13	3.04	3.08	2.74	1.58	1.07	0.71	25.17

AVERAGE TEMPERATURE (deg. F)

SIOUX FALLS, SOUTH DAKOTA

YEAR	JAN	FEB	MAR	APR	MAY	JUNE	JULY	AUG	SEP	OCT	NOV	DEC	ANNUAL
1964	23.0	26.9	26.6	48.1	61.6	70.1	77.3	68.3	59.3	48.7	32.7	15.5	46.5
1965	12.0	13.0	21.7	45.9	59.0	65.5	70.8	69.4	51.5	51.7	32.8	28.4	43.5
1966	5.1	17.3	37.7	41.1	54.3	68.5	78.7	68.8	59.9	48.3	31.0	19.4	44.2
1967	17.6	15.3	37.1	46.0	53.1	66.3	71.7	69.9	61.3	47.2	32.7	21.9	45.0
1968	16.8	18.9	39.8	47.8	52.6	69.6	71.8	72.7	61.0	49.4	33.5	16.2	45.9
1969	8.8	19.0	20.5	48.4	59.6	61.4	73.5	73.3	62.3	43.4	33.4	19.5	43.6
1970	4.7	19.4	26.4	44.8	59.9	69.0	73.3	72.5	61.9	46.2	32.0	15.6	43.8
1971	8.3	18.8	31.2	47.8	55.3	71.3	69.3	73.0	61.5	51.7	33.3	17.4	44.9
1972	8.9	11.5	31.5	43.8	59.1	66.7	70.2	70.5	59.5	44.4	31.9	14.8	42.7
1973	18.5	23.1	39.7	46.4	56.9	68.9	74.4	76.7	60.1	52.9	34.7	17.1	47.5
1974	12.8	24.3	34.5	48.9	55.7	65.9	79.2	67.6	57.7	51.4	33.9	23.6	46.3
1975	17.1	16.5	25.5	41.4	61.1	67.6	78.5	72.7	57.0	52.1	33.5	20.4	45.3
1976	15.6	29.5	34.8	51.0	57.1	71.5	76.7	75.2	62.9	44.3	27.6	16.6	46.9
1977	4.7	25.6	36.0	53.8	66.8	71.1	77.0	68.1	61.9	47.7	31.3	16.3	46.7
1978	1.9	8.6	30.5	44.3	57.7	66.6	70.9	71.1	66.7	47.8	31.3	14.6	42.7
1979	1.8	7.5	28.2	44.1	55.2	67.8	74.0	69.9	64.3	48.2	30.2	27.1	43.2
1980	18.1	18.1	31.7	50.1	58.4	68.8	74.2	71.1	62.0	45.5	36.7	21.2	46.3
1981	22.3	26.0	38.4	53.5	58.3	70.4	75.5	71.1	63.0	48.7	39.5	18.0	48.8
1982	3.8	20.2	32.8	43.9	59.6	62.6	74.4	71.3	60.0	48.8	30.3	24.5	44.3
1983	20.1	26.2	33.1	41.5	55.1	66.7	77.1	78.3	63.5	49.6	34.9	2.1	45.7
1984	17.4	27.8	24.6	45.8	55.9	68.1	73.6	74.2	57.2	50.4	36.2	20.4	46.0
1985	13.4	19.9	37.8	52.8	62.7	64.2	71.5	66.3	58.2	46.6	20.7	9.5	43.6
1986	20.7	16.9	36.9	48.2	58.8	69.6	75.0	66.5	59.6	48.6	28.7	25.2	46.2
1987	24.0	32.8	37.8	52.6	64.9	71.4	77.0	68.8	62.8	43.9	38.1	24.4	49.9
1988	9.6	15.0	36.4	46.4	65.1	76.3	77.4	74.8	62.6	44.6	34.2	22.1	47.0
1989	25.5	9.2	29.8	47.8	58.0	66.9	77.3	72.0	60.2	49.5	29.5	11.5	44.8
1990	28.2	24.9	36.7	46.4	56.4	70.1	71.2	72.9	66.5	48.0	35.6	15.3	47.7
1991	13.7	29.8	37.0	50.0	62.5	73.5	73.1	72.8	62.0	46.1	25.7	26.0	47.7
1992	26.5	30.0	36.7	43.7	60.5	67.0	65.5	66.1	60.3	48.7	30.4	19.2	46.2
1993	14.0	15.0	29.0	44.1	57.1	65.1	71.4	71.4	56.8	47.1	29.9	21.9	43.6
Record Mean	15.3	20.6	32.3	47.1	58.9	68.5	74.2	71.7	61.7	49.8	33.1	20.3	46.1
Max	25.3	30.6	42.2	58.9	71.1	80.3	86.1	83.5	73.6	61.7	42.9	29.6	57.1
Min	5.2	10.6	22.4	35.3	46.7	56.6	62.2	59.9	49.8	37.8	23.3	11.0	35.1

REFERENCE NOTES

SIOUX FALLS, SOUTH DAKOTA

GENERAL
T - TRACE AMOUNT.
BLANK ENTRIES DENOTE MISSING/UNREPORTED DATA.
# INDICATES A STATION OR INSTRUMENT RELOCATION.

SPECIFIC

PM - INCLUDES LAST DAY OF PREVIOUS MONTH
ASOS - AUTOMATED SURFACE OBSERVING SYSTEM IN OPERATION DURING THESE MONTHS.

(a) - LENGTH OF RECORD IN YEARS, ALTHOUGH INDIVIDUAL MONTHS MAY BE MISSING.
0.* OR * - THE VALUE IS BETWEEN 0.0 AND 0.05
NORMALS - BASED ON THE 1961-1990 RECORD PERIOD.
EXTREMES - DATES ARE THE MOST RECENT OCCURRENCE
WIND DIR.- NUMERALS SHOW TENS OF DEGRESS CLOCKWISE FROM TRUE NORTH. "00" INDICATES CALM.
RESULTANT DIRECTIONS ARE GIVEN TO WHOLE DEGREES.
BOLD VALUES INDICATE EXTREME VALUES WHICH OCCURRED AFTER THE ASOS SYSTEM WAS COMMISSIONED.

RECORD = PERIOD OF RECORD
RECORD MEAN PRECIPITATION IS THE MEAN OF ALL DAILY PRECIPITATION AMOUNTS DURING THE PERIOD OF RECORD.
RECORD MAX(MIN) TEMPERATURE IS THE MEAN OF ALL DAILY MAX(MIN) TEMPERATURES DURING THE PERIOD OF RECORD.
RECORD MEAN TEMPERATURE IS THE SUM OF THE RECORD MAX AND RECORD MIN DIVIDED BY 2.
AVERAGE TEMPERATURE IS THE SUM OF THE MEAN DAILY MAX AND MIN TEMPERATURE DIVIDED BY 2.

EXCEPTIONS

RECORD MEANS ARE THROUGH THE CURRENT YEAR,
BEGINNING IN 1921 FOR TEMPERATURE
1891 FOR PRECIPITATION
1946 FOR SNOWFALL

HEATING DEGREE DAYS Base 65 deg. F SIOUX FALLS, SOUTH DAKOTA

SEASON	JULY	AUG	SEP	OCT	NOV	DEC	JAN	FEB	MAR	APR	MAY	JUNE	TOTAL
1964-65	0	55	210	499	965	1528	1639	1452	1340	568	195	41	8492
1965-66	2	37	405	408	964	1129	1856	1331	838	709	343	49	8071
1966-67	0	41	188	508	1016	1406	1462	1385	858	563	399	37	7863
1967-68	36	32	141	549	963	1328	1490	1331	776	511	380	53	7590
1968-69	14	14	152	489	938	1511	1742	1283	1373	493	217	143	8369
1969-70	2	2	117	668	941	1404	1867	1274	1192	603	206	46	8322
1970-71	16	3	195	577	986	1526	1754	1288	1041	511	297	17	8211
1971-72	29	12	177	409	945	1470	1737	1551	1031	628	236	50	8275
1972-73	29	43	194	631	984	1555	1440	1166	775	549	256	19	7641
1973-74	1	0	178	373	902	1481	1616	1133	939	477	303	85	7488
1974-75	2	39	240	419	927	1279	1476	1351	1217	701	157	51	7859
1975-76	3	5	271	407	937	1377	1528	1023	929	418	261	23	7182
1976-77	1	0	142	643	1114	1495	1867	1097	891	341	38	4	7633
1977-78	0	22	125	530	1000	1503	1957	1576	1063	613	252	78	8719
1978-79	11	18	104	525	1004	1554	1960	1607	1134	622	321	40	8900
1979-80	0	28	103	512	1038	1168	1448	1349	1027	464	243	32	7412
1980-81	1	14	157	602	841	1354	1318	1087	816	353	230	5	6778
1981-82	5	5	114	497	758	1452	1899	1247	991	632	174	105	7879
1982-83	0	28	188	494	1035	1249	1385	1082	982	699	317	67	7526
1983-84	1	0	160	476	894	1947	1468	1072	1247	569	285	23	8142
1984-85	2	12	265	451	857	1376	1594	1260	836	378	124	101	7256
1985-86	5	44	269	562	1327	1721	1363	1341	865	498	204	17	8216
1986-87	0	54	180	504	1082	1227	1265	896	835	387	96	23	6549
1987-88	5	54	110	649	801	1252	1715	1448	878	554	83	1	7550
1988-89	0	22	126	628	916	1321	1219	1559	1083	514	235	61	7684
1989-90	0	5	192	481	1056	1655	1131	1117	871	586	268	39	7401
1990-91	11	7	109	527	875	1538	1587	977	859	455	192	7	7144
1991-92	6	3	180	583	1171	1200	1186	1009	871	636	187	35	7067
1992-93	35	63	159	500	1030	1414	1576	1397	1109	621	244	74	8222
1993-94	2	19	257	557	1046	1331							

COOLING DEGREE DAYS Base 65 deg. F SIOUX FALLS, SOUTH DAKOTA

YEAR	JAN	FEB	MAR	APR	MAY	JUNE	JULY	AUG	SEP	OCT	NOV	DEC	TOTAL
1969	0	0	0	0	58	43	270	265	41	4	0	0	681
1970	0	0	0	6	54	172	280	241	108	2	0	0	863
1971	0	0	0	4	1	211	167	268	79	2	0	0	732
1972	0	0	0	0	60	108	197	219	35	0	0	0	619
1973	0	0	0	0	13	143	300	370	38	8	0	0	872
1974	0	0	0	2	23	118	450	126	26	6	0	0	751
1975	0	0	0	0	44	134	428	252	36	16	0	0	910
1976	0	0	0	2	24	226	370	324	85	9	0	0	1040
1977	0	0	0	11	101	197	382	123	40	0	0	0	854
1978	0	0	0	0	32	133	202	213	163	0	0	0	743
1979	0	0	0	3	25	131	289	189	87	0	0	0	724
1980	0	0	0	23	46	153	290	207	74	6	0	0	799
1981	0	0	0	14	27	175	342	203	61	0	0	0	822
1982	0	0	0	4	12	42	298	230	45	0	0	0	631
1983	0	0	0	0	15	122	381	420	120	2	0	0	1060
1984	0	0	0	0	10	120	276	305	36	4	0	0	751
1985	0	0	0	19	59	85	212	93	72	0	0	0	540
1986	0	0	0	0	20	163	318	108	25	0	0	0	634
1987	0	0	0	20	100	219	381	178	53	0	0	0	951
1988	0	0	0	1	94	349	393	330	61	0	0	0	1228
1989	0	0	0	6	25	125	387	228	56	7	0	0	834
1990	0	0	0	31	11	198	209	258	160	7	0	0	874
1991	0	0	0	11	119	265	264	249	100	5	0	0	1013
1992	0	0	0	4	53	103	58	103	25	5	0	0	351
1993	0	0	0	0	5	85	208	223	16	9	0	0	546

SNOWFALL (inches) SIOUX FALLS, SOUTH DAKOTA

SEASON	JULY	AUG	SEP	OCT	NOV	DEC	JAN	FEB	MAR	APR	MAY	JUNE	TOTAL
1964-65	0.0	0.0	0.0	0.0	3.9	6.5	3.3	21.1	13.3	0.4	0.0	0.0	48.5
1965-66	0.0	0.0	0.0	0.0	1.6	0.1	6.2	1.8	4.6	0.9	T	0.0	15.2
1966-67	0.0	0.0	0.0	0.4	2.3	9.3	6.0	11.8	1.0	T	0.1	0.0	30.9
1967-68	0.0	0.0	0.0	0.5	0.4	2.5	4.6	0.9	T	0.1	0.1	0.0	9.1
1968-69	0.0	0.0	0.0	0.7	1.9	41.1	19.6	28.5	2.9	0.0	0.0	0.0	94.7
1969-70	0.0	0.0	0.0	T	2.9	15.2	5.9	1.5	19.3	3.0	T	0.0	47.8
1970-71	0.0	0.0	0.0	5.1	0.5	8.5	1.9	1.7	4.7	0.3	0.0	0.0	22.7
1971-72	0.0	0.0	0.0	T	4.4	10.6	1.8	10.6	5.0	0.8	0.0	0.0	33.2
1972-73	0.0	0.0	0.0	0.2	2.5	6.2	5.5	7.4	0.3	T	0.0	0.0	22.1
1973-74	0.0	0.0	0.0	T	0.1	11.6	1.9	2.9	5.1	3.3	0.0	0.0	24.9
1974-75	0.0	0.0	0.0	0.0	2.5	1.1	18.3	3.1	17.9	T	0.0	0.0	42.9
1975-76	0.0	0.0	0.0	T	13.2	2.5	6.5	6.6	7.9	T	0.1	0.0	36.8
1976-77	0.0	0.0	0.0	3.4	0.7	6.7	2.7	1.9	13.5	T	0.0	0.0	28.9
1977-78	0.0	0.0	0.0	0.9	8.6	8.0	7.6	6.5	5.5	0.6	0.0	0.0	37.7
1978-79	0.0	0.0	0.0	0.0	2.9	9.5	19.0	7.3	13.2	1.5	0.0	0.0	53.4
1979-80	0.0	0.0	0.0	T	15.2	0.3	2.9	5.5	5.8	T	0.0	0.0	29.7
1980-81	0.0	0.0	0.0	0.8	0.4	4.6	1.4	3.1	T	0.5	0.0	0.0	10.8
1981-82	0.0	0.0	0.0	0.8	8.9	5.5	16.9	1.0	1.8	7.5	0.0	0.0	42.4
1982-83	0.0	0.0	0.0	3.3	4.1	17.6	4.7	3.6	18.8	18.4	0.0	0.0	70.5
1983-84	0.0	0.0	0.0	T	19.0	13.7	5.0	11.9	19.4	6.0	0.0	0.0	75.0
1984-85	0.0	0.0	T	T	T	4.7	7.4	0.7	16.1	2.5	0.0	0.0	31.4
1985-86	0.0	0.0	0.9	0.2	21.9	9.1	9.1	0.9	8.2	0.3	0.0	0.0	50.6
1986-87	0.0	0.0	0.0	T	5.4	T	2.4	0.3	T	T	0.0	0.0	8.1
1987-88	0.0	0.0	0.0	0.1	7.5	13.3	17.9	7.3	2.5	11.3	0.0	0.0	59.9
1988-89	0.0	0.0	0.0	T	10.9	2.2	2.0	10.0	16.0	0.7	T	0.0	41.8
1989-90	0.0	0.0	0.0	0.0	2.4	4.0	0.2	5.8	0.7	T	0.0	T	13.1
1990-91	0.0	0.0	0.0	1.2	8.4	8.8	5.4	5.4	3.2	T	T	T	32.4
1991-92	0.0	0.0	0.0	10.0	10.8	0.2	3.8	11.2	8.4	3.5	T	T	47.9
1992-93	0.0	0.0	0.0	T	4.7	8.4	8.6	13.1	14.9	2.2	T	T	51.9
1993-94	T	0.0	T	T	8.8	4.6							
Record Mean	T	0.0	T	0.7	5.4	7.2	6.4	8.1	9.6	2.2	T	T	39.7

KNOXVILLE, TENNESSEE

Knoxville is located in a broad valley between the Cumberland Mountains, which lie northwest of the city, and the Great Smoky Mountains, which lie southeast of the city. These two mountain ranges exercise a marked influence upon the climate of the valley. The Cumberland Mountains, to the northwest, serve to retard and weaken the force of the cold winter air which frequently penetrates far south of the latitude of Knoxville over the plains areas to the west of the mountains.

The mountains also serve to modify the hot summer winds which are common to the plains to the west. In addition, they serve as a fixed incline plane which lifts the warm, moist air flowing northward from the Gulf of Mexico and thereby increases the frequency of afternoon thunderstorms. Relief from extremely high temperatures which such thunderstorms produce serves to reduce the number of extremely warm days in the valley.

July is usually the warmest month of the year. The coldest weather usually occurs during the month of January. Sudden great temperature changes occur infrequently. This again is due mainly to the retarding effect of the mountains. Summer nights are nearly always comfortable.

Rainfall is ample for agricultural purposes and is favorably distributed during the year for most crops. Precipitation is greatest in the wintertime. Another peak period occurs during the late spring and summer months. The period of lowest rainfall occurs during the fall. A cumulative total of approximately 12 inches of snow falls annually. However, this usually comes in amounts of less than 4 inches at one time. It is unusual for snow to remain on the ground in measurable amounts longer than one week.

The topography also has a pronounced effect upon the prevailing wind direction. Daytime winds usually have a southwesterly component, while nighttime winds usually move from the northeast. The winds are relatively light and tornadoes are extremely rare.

NORMALS, MEANS, AND EXTREMES

KNOXVILLE, TENNESSEE

LATITUDE: 35°49'N LONGITUDE: 83°59'W ELEVATION: FT. GRND 979 BARO 994 TIME ZONE: EASTERN WBAN: 13891

	(a)	JAN	FEB	MAR	APR	MAY	JUNE	JULY	AUG	SEP	OCT	NOV	DEC	YEAR
TEMPERATURE °F:														
Normals														
-Daily Maximum		45.9	50.9	61.3	70.4	77.6	84.5	87.1	86.7	81.2	70.6	59.9	50.1	68.9
-Daily Minimum		26.0	29.1	36.6	44.6	53.1	61.8	66.0	65.3	59.0	46.0	37.5	30.0	46.3
-Monthly		36.0	40.1	49.0	57.5	65.4	73.2	76.6	76.0	70.1	58.4	48.7	40.1	57.6
Extremes														
-Record Highest	52	77	83	86	92	94	102	103	102	103	91	84	80	103
-Year		1950	1977	1963	1942	1962	1988	1952	1944	1954	1953	1948	1982	SEP 1954
-Record Lowest	52	-24	-2	1	22	32	43	49	49	36	25	5	-6	-24
-Year		1985	1958	1980	1987	1986	1956	1988	1946	1967	1987	1950	1983	JAN 1985
NORMAL DEGREE DAYS:														
Heating (base 65°F)		899	697	496	234	94	0	0	0	18	238	489	772	3937
Cooling (base 65°F)		0	0	0	9	106	246	360	341	171	33	0	0	1266
% OF POSSIBLE SUNSHINE	51	40	47	53	62	64	65	63	63	61	61	49	40	56
MEAN SKY COVER (tenths)														
Sunrise - Sunset	51	7.1	6.7	6.7	6.1	6.1	5.8	5.9	5.6	5.6	5.0	6.2	6.8	6.1
MEAN NUMBER OF DAYS:														
Sunrise to Sunset														
-Clear	51	6.2	6.7	7.2	8.2	7.8	7.5	7.2	8.4	9.5	12.3	8.7	7.0	96.6
-Partly Cloudy	51	6.6	6.0	7.3	8.6	10.1	12.3	12.8	12.3	9.5	7.9	6.9	6.6	106.9
-Cloudy	51	18.2	15.6	16.5	13.2	13.1	10.1	11.0	10.3	11.0	10.8	14.4	17.4	161.7
Precipitation														
.01 inches or more	51	12.3	11.3	12.7	10.9	11.0	10.2	11.3	9.5	8.4	7.8	9.9	11.0	126.3
Snow, Ice pellets, hail														
1.0 inches or more	51	1.3	1.0	0.5	0.1	0.0	0.0	0.0	0.0	0.0	0.0	0.1	0.5	3.5
Thunderstorms	51	0.7	1.4	3.3	4.3	6.7	8.0	9.6	7.0	3.2	1.3	1.0	0.5	47.0
Heavy Fog Visibility 1/4 mile or less	51	2.8	1.8	1.6	1.1	2.4	2.1	2.1	3.5	3.9	4.7	3.2	2.6	31.7
Temperature °F														
-Maximum														
90° and above	33	0.0	0.0	0.0	0.*	0.8	5.1	11.1	8.5	2.8	0.0	0.0	0.0	28.3
32° and below	33	3.3	1.3	0.2	0.0	0.0	0.0	0.0	0.0	0.0	0.0	0.1	1.2	6.0
-Minimum														
32° and below	33	20.1	16.5	8.6	1.8	0.*	0.0	0.0	0.0	0.0	1.0	8.0	17.5	73.4
0° and below	33	0.4	0.*	0.0	0.0	0.0	0.0	0.0	0.0	0.0	0.0	0.0	0.1	0.6
AVG. STATION PRESS. (mb)	21	984.7	983.7	981.6	981.1	980.9	981.5	982.6	983.0	983.5	984.5	984.6	985.2	983.1
RELATIVE HUMIDITY (%)														
Hour 01	33	77	74	72	72	83	86	87	88	88	85	80	78	81
Hour 07 (Local Time)	33	81	80	80	81	87	88	90	92	92	90	84	83	86
Hour 13	33	63	59	55	51	57	59	61	61	60	55	59	64	59
Hour 19	33	66	60	56	53	61	63	65	67	68	65	66	69	63
PRECIPITATION (inches):														
Water Equivalent														
-Normal		4.17	4.06	5.09	3.72	4.13	3.97	4.67	3.13	3.07	2.84	3.75	4.54	47.14
-Maximum Monthly	52	11.74	9.38	10.42	7.20	10.98	8.21	10.09	8.88	9.19	6.67	10.36	11.63	11.74
-Year		1954	1944	1975	1970	1974	1989	1967	1942	1989	1949	1948	1961	JAN 1954
-Minimum Monthly	52	0.95	0.74	1.69	0.39	0.74	0.20	0.70	0.77	0.42	T	0.97	0.45	T
-Year		1986	1968	1986	1976	1970	1944	1957	1954	1985	1963	1942	1965	OCT 1963
-Maximum in 24 hrs	52	3.89	3.42	4.85	3.65	3.40	3.57	4.69	3.25	5.08	2.44	4.06	4.89	5.08
-Year		1946	1991	1973	1977	1984	1972	1942	1959	1944	1961	1948	1969	SEP 1944
Snow, Ice pellets, hail														
-Maximum Monthly	52	15.1	23.3	20.2	10.7	T	0.0	0.0	0.0	0.0	T	18.2	12.2	23.3
-Year		1962	1960	1960	1987	1945					1993	1952	1963	FEB 1960
-Maximum in 24 hrs	52	12.0	17.5	14.1	10.7	T	0.0	0.0	0.0	0.0	T	18.2	8.9	18.2
-Year		1962	1960	1993	1987	1945					1993	1952	1969	NOV 1952
WIND:														
Mean Speed (mph)	51	7.8	8.1	8.6	8.5	6.8	6.4	6.0	5.5	5.7	5.7	6.8	7.2	6.9
Prevailing Direction through 1963		NE	NE	NE	WSW	SW	SW	WSW	NE	NE	NE	NE	NE	NE
Fastest Obs. 1 Min.														
-Direction (!!)	19	27	23	22	29	30	07	36	32	36	27	23	20	23
-Speed (MPH)	19	35	37	36	39	31	35	35	29	26	28	40	39	40
-Year		1978	1990	1977	1988	1989	1975	1985	1983	1989	1988	1988	1988	NOV 1988
Peak Gust														
-Direction (!!)	9	SW	SW	W	W	W	NW	NE	N	W	SW	W	SW	W
-Speed (mph)	9	46	53	53	59	48	58	46	44	39	39	64	58	64
-Date		1989	1990	1989	1985	1989	1989	1985	1989	1989	1988	1988	1988	NOV 1988

PRECIPITATION (inches)

KNOXVILLE, TENNESSEE

YEAR	JAN	FEB	MAR	APR	MAY	JUNE	JULY	AUG	SEP	OCT	NOV	DEC	ANNUAL
1964	4.71	4.09	5.75	6.98	3.96	0.97	3.70	5.75	1.10	2.10	2.80	4.02	45.93
1965	3.94	3.25	9.31	4.16	3.13	4.84	3.49	2.18	2.48	1.08	2.50	0.45	40.81
1966	3.88	4.68	2.72	2.88	2.92	2.27	5.44	4.09	4.41	4.80	5.12	2.66	45.87
1967	2.67	4.58	4.08	2.00	4.10	6.53	10.09	4.06	2.70	2.33	5.57	6.95	55.66
1968	4.13	0.74	4.78	4.12	3.01	3.97	2.57	1.29	2.53	3.40	2.00	3.22	35.76
1969	4.11	5.54	2.89	2.41	1.33	7.58	3.51	6.72	3.03	1.56	2.56	7.74	48.98
1970	3.04	2.86	3.18	7.20	0.74	4.26	3.11	4.89	2.75	5.33	1.40	4.67	43.43
1971	5.03	4.93	4.21	3.87	3.78	3.73	8.76	3.05	3.41	1.98	2.21	5.48	50.44
1972	7.35	4.19	4.98	2.54	4.49	5.02	6.76	1.61	4.70	5.99	3.36	7.02	58.01
1973	3.24	2.59	10.24	5.15	5.71	5.26	4.38	2.31	3.28	3.48	5.01	7.38	58.03
1974	7.05	5.24	6.15	5.77	10.98	2.70	2.92	3.14	3.33	2.35	5.18	4.52	59.33
1975	4.66	4.68	10.42	2.43	2.98	2.43	2.25	1.61	3.28	4.02	2.92	3.59	45.27
1976	3.86	2.18	5.22	0.39	5.53	3.46	3.75	1.98	2.87	5.33	3.45	4.42	42.44
1977	2.55	1.52	6.08	6.96	1.16	6.49	1.08	5.78	6.91	4.04	5.06	3.30	50.93
1978	5.22	1.01	4.42	4.10	3.44	5.27	5.06	2.44	1.26	0.82	3.62	5.91	42.57
1979	6.18	4.17	4.21	4.30	7.21	3.80	9.47	2.29	2.64	1.97	5.73	1.92	53.89
1980	5.54	1.78	8.72	3.30	3.80	1.94	3.57	2.34	2.38	1.53	3.78	1.78	40.46
1981	1.05	3.62	2.83	4.84	3.02	5.53	2.03	3.48	6.09	4.15	3.01	4.14	43.79
1982	6.03	4.88	6.36	3.26	5.52	3.93	6.60	2.68	2.68	2.66	5.21	4.89	54.70
1983	1.58	2.90	1.99	5.88	5.42	3.26	3.18	3.89	0.95	3.34	4.40	5.69	42.48
1984	2.26	4.42	3.79	3.37	10.14	4.34	9.03	1.72	0.85	3.26	2.87	2.49	48.54
1985	3.17	4.11	1.98	2.86	1.60	4.77	2.63	4.07	0.42	3.04	5.39	2.36	36.40
1986	0.95	3.90	1.69	2.25	2.40	0.69	1.89	3.37	3.59	3.84	3.83	4.08	32.48
1987	4.68	4.63	2.91	2.18	4.62	2.66	4.67	1.08	1.93	0.60	1.21	3.49	34.66
1988	4.29	2.94	2.42	2.34	2.35	0.51	3.60	3.20	2.68	1.52	4.82	3.99	34.66
1989	4.96	6.26	3.82	3.50	5.31	8.21	2.68	3.16	9.19	1.47	4.92	2.74	56.22
1990	5.88	6.90	5.73	2.56	4.71	1.72	7.56	3.02	2.68	3.64	1.77	8.99	55.16
1991	2.53	6.99	6.36	3.97	3.10	6.02	3.45	6.13	3.14	1.10	5.24	10.23	58.26
1992	3.87	3.36	3.99	2.11	3.20	3.07	4.62	4.22	1.77	3.05	4.29	6.68	44.23
1993	4.09	2.20	6.16	2.50	3.78	0.90	2.03	6.04	4.77	2.25	3.33	7.04	45.09
Record Mean	4.54	4.53	5.08	4.04	3.82	4.00	4.48	3.66	2.87	2.64	3.43	4.47	47.57

AVERAGE TEMPERATURE (deg. F)

KNOXVILLE, TENNESSEE

YEAR	JAN	FEB	MAR	APR	MAY	JUNE	JULY	AUG	SEP	OCT	NOV	DEC	ANNUAL
1964	36.3	36.1	47.7	60.5	66.9	75.1	75.7	73.7	70.0	55.5	52.3	43.5	57.8
1965	40.1	39.7	46.8	62.4	72.3	73.9	78.0	77.5	73.5	59.0	51.7	43.0	59.9
1966	34.0	41.6	50.4	58.9	66.1	74.3	79.3	75.0	68.9	57.5	49.1	40.0	57.9
1967	41.9	38.1	54.7	62.7	63.5	73.2	71.8	73.2	65.6	58.2	44.2	44.6	57.6
1968	37.1	33.3	49.9	59.0	65.3	73.6	77.2	78.4	69.1	58.8	48.1	37.0	57.3
1969	36.5	39.4	42.1	59.5	67.3	74.5	78.9	74.5	69.3	59.1	45.5	37.7	57.0
1970	30.6	39.3	48.7	61.2	68.6	73.4	78.5	77.1	75.3	62.8	48.1	44.1	59.0
1971	38.5	39.4	45.6	58.5	63.9	75.9	75.4	76.0	73.3	65.3	48.7	50.4	59.2
1972	42.5	39.4	48.2	59.5	64.9	70.8	75.5	75.9	71.9	56.8	47.5	44.8	58.1
1973	38.0	39.9	55.8	56.4	63.5	74.8	76.7	76.2	73.8	62.4	52.4	41.1	59.2
1974	49.3	43.1	55.2	59.8	68.1	70.5	77.7	76.5	69.8	58.6	50.8	41.9	60.1
1975	43.3	45.5	46.6	57.5	70.1	74.6	77.6	78.8	68.9	60.1	50.2	41.1	59.5
1976	34.3	48.2	52.6	58.9	63.4	73.9	76.2	74.9	67.7	54.5	43.2	37.5	57.1
1977	27.2	41.4	55.0	62.9	69.8	75.3	80.3	78.9	74.0	57.4	52.6	40.2	59.6
1978	29.4	34.6	49.0	61.1	66.6	75.4	78.7	77.1	74.8	58.2	54.4	42.8	58.5
1979	33.0	36.7	53.1	59.9	66.9	72.8	75.0	77.6	72.2	58.3	51.4	42.2	58.3
1980	41.6	36.6	47.6	59.1	68.1	75.2	82.1	81.7	73.7	56.0	47.3	40.1	59.1
1981	33.4	41.9	46.8	63.5	63.9	77.1	81.4	78.3	70.2	58.9	49.4	38.7	58.6
1982	33.8	43.1	53.0	55.2	69.3	72.6	77.6	76.7	70.0	59.5	50.9	46.4	59.0
1983	38.0	41.1	49.7	53.2	65.4	72.5	78.5	79.6	70.3	60.2	47.4	36.4	57.7
1984	35.3	43.4	47.7	57.3	62.8	74.8	73.3	74.1	67.1	67.6	46.3	47.5	58.1
1985	29.4	37.1	50.2	58.6	65.7	72.5	76.5	75.1	68.5	63.7	56.8	34.8	57.4
1986	35.0	43.9	48.7	58.6	68.1	77.2	81.4	76.7	72.8	60.2	52.4	39.1	59.5
1987	36.8	42.2	49.2	55.0	71.3	75.5	78.5	79.6	70.1	52.8	50.2	43.5	58.7
1988	33.9	39.4	50.1	57.2	65.0	74.4	78.7	79.6	71.3	52.7	49.7	40.4	57.7
1989	42.8	41.3	53.5	57.8	62.4	73.3	77.5	76.8	70.9	59.4	48.1	32.2	58.0
1990	44.7	48.9	53.6	57.9	65.9	75.4	78.0	77.9	72.1	59.9	52.1	45.1	61.0
1991	41.2	43.8	52.0	62.8	72.0	74.9	79.3	76.5	71.4	61.0	47.1	43.5	60.5
1992	40.5	45.8	48.3	59.0	64.0	72.2	77.9	73.7	71.3	57.4	48.3	40.0	58.2
1993	43.5	39.5	45.7	56.2	67.0	76.0	83.0	78.7	70.6	57.9	48.4	40.2	58.9
Record Mean	39.0	41.8	49.5	58.7	67.2	74.8	77.8	76.8	71.4	59.7	48.4	40.7	58.8
Max	47.6	51.1	59.8	69.7	78.1	85.1	87.7	86.7	81.8	70.9	58.5	49.2	68.8
Min	30.4	32.4	39.1	47.7	56.3	64.4	68.0	66.9	60.9	48.5	38.3	32.1	48.8

REFERENCE NOTES

KNOXVILLE, TENNESSEE

GENERAL
T - TRACE AMOUNT.
BLANK ENTRIES DENOTE MISSING/UNREPORTED DATA.
# INDICATES A STATION OR INSTRUMENT RELOCATION.

SPECIFIC

PM - INCLUDES LAST DAY OF PREVIOUS MONTH
ASOS - AUTOMATED SURFACE OBSERVING SYSTEM IN OPERATION DURING THESE MONTHS.

(a) - LENGTH OF RECORD IN YEARS, ALTHOUGH INDIVIDUAL MONTHS MAY BE MISSING.
0.* OR * - THE VALUE IS BETWEEN 0.0 AND 0.05
NORMALS - BASED ON THE 1961-1990 RECORD PERIOD.
EXTREMES - DATES ARE THE MOST RECENT OCCURRENCE
WIND DIR.- NUMERALS SHOW TENS OF DEGRESS CLOCKWISE FROM TRUE NORTH. "00" INDICATES CALM.
RESULTANT DIRECTIONS ARE GIVEN TO WHOLE DEGREES.
BOLD VALUES INDICATE EXTREME VALUES WHICH OCCURRED AFTER THE ASOS SYSTEM WAS COMMISSIONED.

RECORD = PERIOD OF RECORD
RECORD MEAN PRECIPITATION IS THE MEAN OF ALL DAILY PRECIPITATION AMOUNTS DURING THE PERIOD OF RECORD.
RECORD MAX(MIN) TEMPERATURE IS THE MEAN OF ALL DAILY MAX(MIN) TEMPERATURES DURING THE PERIOD OF RECORD.
RECORD MEAN TEMPERATURE IS THE SUM OF THE RECORD MAX AND RECORD MIN DIVIDED BY 2.
AVERAGE TEMPERATURE IS THE SUM OF THE MEAN DAILY MAX AND MIN TEMPERATURE DIVIDED BY 2.

EXCEPTIONS

RECORD MEANS ARE THROUGH THE CURRENT YEAR,
BEGINNING IN 1871 FOR TEMPERATURE
1871 FOR PRECIPITATION
1943 FOR SNOWFALL

HEATING DEGREE DAYS Base 65 deg. F KNOXVILLE, TENNESSEE

SEASON	JULY	AUG	SEP	OCT	NOV	DEC	JAN	FEB	MAR	APR	MAY	JUNE	TOTAL
1964-65	0	8	9	308	374	657	765	701	559	125	0	0	3506
1965-66	0	0	13	200	393	674	956	650	452	217	59	9	3623
1966-67	0	0	9	232	472	767	709	748	330	112	121	8	3508
1967-68	1	0	63	229	617	626	860	912	467	191	66	0	4032
1968-69	0	0	5	215	501	859	879	710	704	175	50	4	4102
1969-70	0	0	11	200	579	840	1063	712	496	139	45	0	4085
1970-71	0	0	13	109	497	640	813	710	596	209	76	0	3663
1971-72	0	0	0	53	496	450	692	735	516	211	47	11	3211
1972-73	0	0	9	251	522	622	828	697	283	272	97	0	3581
1973-74	0	0	10	135	373	734	481	606	304	190	41	10	2884
1974-75	0	0	23	215	439	713	666	542	563	257	9	0	3427
1975-76	0	0	42	172	437	733	944	485	380	203	91	0	3487
1976-77	0	0	19	320	651	845	1166	658	319	110	33	2	4123
1977-78	0	0	3	242	374	764	1097	846	487	148	74	0	4035
1978-79	0	0	0	210	310	681	985	786	376	167	46	0	3561
1979-80	0	0	0	220	407	700	715	815	529	185	32	1	3604
1980-81	0	0	23	284	523	761	974	641	556	104	94	0	3960
1981-82	0	0	32	196	461	809	959	606	384	295	20	0	3762
1982-83	0	0	30	228	416	577	829	662	472	356	50	3	3623
1983-84	0	0	51	163	523	878	912	619	530	240	139	5	4060
1984-85	0	0	44	30	556	536	1095	776	459	208	51	13	3768
1985-86	0	0	44	86	250	927	922	582	499	206	51	0	3567
1986-87	0	2	0	197	377	797	863	631	483	313	13	0	3676
1987-88	0	0	15	370	437	660	956	734	458	247	66	9	3952
1988-89	0	0	3	384	454	755	681	660	360	258	148	1	3704
1989-90	0	1	36	204	499	1011	622	443	358	239	68	0	3481
1990-91	0	0	26	182	382	612	730	589	405	93	16	0	3035
1991-92	0	0	46	159	538	660	753	549	512	225	113	6	3561
1992-93	0	0	13	229	494	769	659	708	592	270	38	2	3774
1993-94	0	0	37	232	495	761							

COOLING DEGREE DAYS Base 65 deg. F KNOXVILLE, TENNESSEE

YEAR	JAN	FEB	MAR	APR	MAY	JUNE	JULY	AUG	SEP	OCT	NOV	DEC	TOTAL
1969	0	0	0	15	125	294	438	304	147	23	0	0	1346
1970	0	0	0	33	162	258	427	384	326	46	0	0	1636
1971	0	0	0	20	50	333	328	350	252	69	13	3	1418
1972	0	0	0	53	51	193	332	347	223	4	2	0	1205
1973	0	0	4	19	56	298	369	355	282	60	2	0	1445
1974	0	0	9	39	142	179	399	365	171	19	17	0	1340
1975	0	0	0	39	173	293	397	434	168	26	0	0	1530
1976	0	3	1	26	48	273	356	314	107	5	0	0	1133
1977	0	5	14	57	188	317	483	440	283	14	10	0	1811
1978	0	0	0	37	130	319	432	384	302	8	0	0	1612
1979	0	0	15	20	111	242	317	399	224	23	4	0	1355
1980	0	0	0	16	136	315	538	525	290	12	0	0	1832
1981	0	0	0	62	65	373	512	421	193	14	1	0	1641
1982	0	0	17	6	157	233	396	372	187	65	2	8	1443
1983	0	0	4	6	71	235	425	462	217	23	0	0	1443
1984	0	0	0	12	77	306	263	290	116	120	2	0	1186
1985	0	0	11	20	81	247	363	322	155	53	11	0	1263
1986	0	0	0	21	156	374	517	373	241	55	6	0	1743
1987	0	0	0	18	215	321	427	460	172	0	0	0	1613
1988	0	0	3	19	74	297	431	458	200	9	0	0	1491
1989	0	2	10	47	76	257	395	374	219	35	0	0	1415
1990	0	1	13	32	101	316	410	406	245	32	1	0	1557
1991	0	0	9	32	239	306	453	364	244	42	6	2	1697
1992	0	0	0	49	91	230	410	279	206	0	0	0	1265
1993	0	0	0	10	106	339	566	432	212	21	3	0	1689

SNOWFALL (inches) KNOXVILLE, TENNESSEE

SEASON	JULY	AUG	SEP	OCT	NOV	DEC	JAN	FEB	MAR	APR	MAY	JUNE	TOTAL
1964-65	0.0	0.0	0.0	0.0	T	T	6.3	6.9	4.4	0.0	0.0	0.0	17.6
1965-66	0.0	0.0	0.0	0.0	T	T	14.2	T	0.5	0.0	0.0	0.0	14.7
1966-67	0.0	0.0	0.0	0.0	T	3.1	2.2	5.7	0.0	0.0	0.0	0.0	11.0
1967-68	0.0	0.0	0.0	0.0	0.0	T	5.9	4.7	1.9	0.0	0.0	0.0	12.5
1968-69	0.0	0.0	0.0	0.0	0.3	T	0.5	7.7	5.2	0.0	0.0	0.0	13.7
1969-70	0.0	0.0	0.0	0.0	T	8.9	12.9	4.6	T	0.0	0.0	0.0	26.4
1970-71	0.0	0.0	0.0	0.0	T	6.3	1.3	6.4	3.6	7.0	0.0	0.0	24.6
1971-72	0.0	0.0	0.0	0.0	T	T	0.4	4.2	6.7	0.0	0.0	0.0	11.3
1972-73	0.0	0.0	0.0	0.0	T	T	9.0	T	1.9	T	0.0	0.0	10.9
1973-74	0.0	0.0	0.0	0.0	0.0	2.0	T	T	1.8	0.0	0.0	0.0	3.8
1974-75	0.0	0.0	0.0	0.0	T	1.6	1.3	T	2.5	0.0	0.0	0.0	5.4
1975-76	0.0	0.0	0.0	0.0	T	T	0.3	2.8	0.0	0.0	0.0	0.0	3.1
1976-77	0.0	0.0	0.0	0.0	1.0	2.1	7.9	0.2	0.0	0.0	0.0	0.0	11.2
1977-78	0.0	0.0	0.0	0.0	0.1	0.6	11.3	5.5	1.8	0.0	0.0	0.0	19.3
1978-79	0.0	0.0	0.0	0.0	0.0	T	4.7	18.4	T	0.0	0.0	0.0	23.1
1979-80	0.0	0.0	0.0	0.0	T	T	0.5	11.0	3.5	T	0.0	0.0	15.0
1980-81	0.0	0.0	0.0	0.0	T	T	5.0	2.5	T	0.0	0.0	0.0	7.5
1981-82	0.0	0.0	0.0	0.0	T	0.1	4.4	0.1	1.1	T	0.0	0.0	5.7
1982-83	0.0	0.0	0.0	0.0	0.0	3.0	1.1	3.4	0.7	2.0	0.0	0.0	10.2
1983-84	0.0	0.0	0.0	0.0	0.0	0.7	2.8	3.5	T	0.0	0.0	0.0	7.0
1984-85	0.0	0.0	0.0	0.0	0.0	T	14.2	8.3	0.0	0.0	0.0	0.0	22.5
1985-86	0.0	0.0	0.0	0.0	0.0	0.4	3.6	5.0	T	0.0	0.0	0.0	9.0
1986-87	0.0	0.0	0.0	0.0	T	T	7.5	T	1.6	10.7	0.0	0.0	19.8
1987-88	0.0	0.0	0.0	0.0	T	T	9.2	0.9	T	0.0	0.0	0.0	10.1
1988-89	0.0	0.0	0.0	0.0	T	2.6	1.8	2.8	0.0	0.0	0.0	0.0	7.2
1989-90	0.0	0.0	0.0	T	T	1.1	T	T	T	0.0	0.0	0.0	1.1
1990-91	0.0	0.0	0.0	0.0	0.0	T	T	1.2	0.7	T	0.0	0.0	1.9
1991-92	0.0	0.0	0.0	0.0	0.2	T	T	0.0	T	T	0.0	0.0	0.2
1992-93	0.0	0.0	0.0	0.0	0.0	0.3	T	1.0	15.1	T	0.0	0.0	16.4
1993-94	0.0	0.0	0.0	T	0.0	0.3							
Record Mean	0.0	0.0	0.0	T	0.6	1.6	3.9	3.6	1.8	0.4	T	0.0	11.8

MEMPHIS, TENNESSEE

Topography varies from the level alluvial area in east-central Arkansas to the slightly rolling area in northwestern Mississippi and southwestern Tennessee.

Agricultural interests are varied, with major crops being cotton, corn, hay, soybeans, peaches, apples, and a considerable number of vegetables. The climate is quite favorable for dairy interests, and for the raising of cattle and hogs.

The growing season is about 230 days in length. The average date for the last occurrence of temperatures as low as 32 degrees is late March. The average date of the first temperature of 32 degrees or below is early November.

Precipitation of nearly 50 inches per year is fairly well distributed. Crops and pastures receive, on the average, an adequate supply of moisture during the growing season, with lesser amounts during the fall harvesting period.

Sunshine averages slightly over 70 percent of the possible amount during the growing season. Relative humidity averages about 70 percent for the year.

Memphis, although not in the normal paths of storms coming from the Gulf or from western Canada, is affected by both, and thereby has comparatively frequent changes in weather. Extremely high or low temperatures, however, are relatively rare.

NORMALS, MEANS, AND EXTREMES

MEMPHIS, TENNESSEE

LATITUDE: 35 °03'N LONGITUDE: 90 °00' W ELEVATION: FT. GRND 258 BARO 271 TIME ZONE: CENTRAL WBAN: 13893

	(a)	JAN	FEB	MAR	APR	MAY	JUNE	JULY	AUG	SEP	OCT	NOV	DEC	YEAR
TEMPERATURE °F:														
Normals														
-Daily Maximum		48.5	53.5	63.2	73.3	81.0	89.3	92.3	90.8	83.9	74.3	62.3	52.5	72.1
-Daily Minimum		30.9	34.8	43.0	52.4	61.2	68.9	72.9	71.1	64.5	51.9	42.7	34.8	52.4
-Monthly		39.7	44.2	53.1	62.9	71.2	79.1	82.6	81.0	74.2	63.1	52.5	43.7	62.3
Extremes														
-Record Highest	52	78	81	85	94	99	104	108	105	103	95	85	81	108
-Year		1972	1962	1986	1987	1977	1954	1980	1943	1954	1954	1955	1982	JUL 1980
-Record Lowest	52	-4	-11	12	29	38	48	52	48	36	25	9	-13	-13
-Year		1985	1951	1943	1987	1944	1966	1947	1946	1949	1952	1950	1963	DEC 1963
NORMAL DEGREE DAYS:														
Heating (base 65°F)		784	582	383	127	25	0	0	0	10	131	380	660	3082
Cooling (base 65°F)		0	0	14	64	217	423	546	496	286	72	0	0	2118
% OF POSSIBLE SUNSHINE	35	50	54	56	64	69	74	74	75	69	70	58	50	64
MEAN SKY COVER (tenths)														
Sunrise - Sunset	43	6.8	6.4	6.5	6.0	5.9	5.4	5.3	5.0	5.1	4.6	5.6	6.4	5.8
MEAN NUMBER OF DAYS:														
Sunrise to Sunset														
-Clear	41	7.9	7.8	7.8	8.5	8.5	9.7	10.3	11.6	12.3	14.5	10.2	9.0	118.0
-Partly Cloudy	41	5.8	5.8	6.6	7.3	9.6	11.1	12.0	11.8	7.5	7.0	6.2	5.6	96.3
-Cloudy	41	17.3	14.7	16.7	14.2	12.9	9.2	8.7	7.6	10.1	9.5	13.6	16.4	151.0
Precipitation														
.01 inches or more	43	10.0	9.5	10.9	10.2	9.4	8.5	8.5	7.6	7.4	6.4	8.7	9.8	106.7
Snow, Ice pellets, hail														
1.0 inches or more	43	0.8	0.5	0.3	0.0	0.0	0.0	0.0	0.0	0.0	0.0	0.*	0.1	1.7
Thunderstorms	43	1.9	2.4	4.4	6.4	6.8	7.4	8.3	6.2	3.5	2.1	2.3	1.6	53.5
Heavy Fog Visibility														
1/4 mile or less	43	2.0	1.3	0.7	0.3	0.2	0.2	0.3	0.3	0.6	1.0	1.3	1.7	10.0
Temperature °F														
-Maximum														
90° and above	52	0.0	0.0	0.0	0.1	3.1	14.5	21.7	18.5	8.0	0.6	0.0	0.0	66.5
32° and below	52	3.1	1.3	0.2	0.0	0.0	0.0	0.0	0.0	0.0	0.0	0.1	1.4	6.0
-Minimum														
32° and below	52	17.7	12.3	5.3	0.3	0.0	0.0	0.0	0.0	0.0	0.3	5.8	14.4	56.2
0° and below	52	0.1	0.*	0.0	0.0	0.0	0.0	0.0	0.0	0.0	0.0	0.0	0.1	0.2
AVG. STATION PRESS. (mb)	21	1011.4	1009.9	1006.5	1005.6	1004.7	1005.2	1006.3	1006.7	1007.4	1009.1	1009.5	1011.0	1007.8
RELATIVE HUMIDITY (%)														
Hour 00	54	75	73	70	71	76	78	79	80	80	77	74	74	76
Hour 06 (Local Time)	54	79	78	76	78	82	82	84	86	86	83	80	78	81
Hour 12	54	63	60	56	53	55	56	57	57	56	51	56	61	57
Hour 18	54	67	62	57	54	57	57	58	60	62	60	63	67	60
PRECIPITATION (inches):														
Water Equivalent														
-Normal		3.73	4.35	5.41	5.46	4.98	3.57	3.79	3.43	3.53	3.01	5.10	5.74	52.10
-Maximum Monthly	43	12.21	10.51	12.08	17.13	11.58	7.50	8.84	9.65	7.61	7.75	10.52	13.81	17.13
-Year		1951	1989	1975	1991	1953	1992	1959	1978	1958	1984	1988	1982	APR 1991
-Minimum Monthly	43	0.57	1.12	1.50	1.39	0.83	0.04	0.43	0.43	0.19	T	0.75	1.05	T
-Year		1986	1980	1966	1992	1977	1953	1954	1953	1953	1963	1965	1955	OCT 1963
-Maximum in 24 hrs	43	3.89	4.24	5.95	4.35	4.94	4.76	4.71	4.04	4.63	3.40	5.65	5.42	5.95
-Year		1974	1989	1975	1985	1958	1980	1980	1978	1957	1981	1988	1978	MAR 1975
Snow, Ice pellets, hail														
-Maximum Monthly	43	12.4	8.3	17.3	T	T	0.0	0.0	0.0	0.0	T	1.5	14.3	17.3
-Year		1985	1985	1968	1993	1993					1993	1976	1963	MAR 1968
-Maximum in 24 hrs	43	8.1	5.8	16.1	T	T	0.0	0.0	0.0	0.0	T	1.2	14.3	16.1
-Year		1985	1960	1968	1993	1993					1993	1976	1963	MAR 1968
WIND:														
Mean Speed (mph)	45	10.0	10.1	10.8	10.3	8.8	7.9	7.5	6.9	7.4	7.7	9.1	9.7	8.9
Prevailing Direction through 1963		S	S	S	S	S	S	S	S	E	S	S	S	S
Fastest Obs. 1 Min.														
-Direction (!!)	17	34	24	16	24	34	02	34	20	36	28	23	30	24
-Speed (MPH)	17	35	38	40	46	40	40	37	35	39	40	40	36	46
-Year		1976	1993	1973	1979	1979	1977	1990	1980	1972	1984	1979	1972	APR 1979
Peak Gust														
-Direction (!!)	5	N	NW	NW	SW	SE	SE	W	SE	N	W	NW	NW	SE
-Speed (mph)	5	40	49	49	69	48	71	45	39	43	59	43	49	71
-Date		1984	1984	1984	1991	1990	1993	1992	1993	1993	1984	1992	1992	JUN 1993

PRECIPITATION (inches)

MEMPHIS, TENNESSEE

YEAR	JAN	FEB	MAR	APR	MAY	JUNE	JULY	AUG	SEP	OCT	NOV	DEC	ANNUAL
1964	3.73	3.50	7.34	11.03	3.28	1.39	6.14	5.76	2.74	2.21	2.59	7.97	57.68
1965	4.79	6.78	5.35	2.05	7.42	0.98	1.60	3.98	7.38	0.54	0.75	1.17	42.79
1966	2.84	6.88	1.50	5.42	5.69	0.52	2.18	4.28	3.23	1.92	1.57	5.21	41.24
1967	2.23	2.33	4.65	4.46	6.38	1.70	6.01	5.17	1.86	2.38	1.90	7.37	46.44
1968	5.57	1.98	6.52	5.15	5.21	3.76	2.69	1.61	5.58	2.87	4.89	6.04	51.87
1969	3.14	3.20	2.63	8.29	1.34	1.60	1.92	6.62	0.90	1.24	4.19	7.05	42.12
1970	1.16	3.87	5.32	7.08	3.70	5.76	4.99	1.78	3.80	6.20	2.62	3.71	49.99
1971	2.15	7.21	3.64	2.89	3.90	3.82	2.90	6.00	3.42	0.06	1.49	6.71	44.19
1972	4.73	2.23	4.80	3.51	4.55	5.50	4.89	1.94	5.46	3.92	8.05	9.37	58.95
1973	4.62	3.62	7.63	9.44	6.23	1.00	4.49	4.88	5.06	3.37	8.49	5.35	64.18
1974	8.90	4.65	3.40	6.34	7.76	6.30	6.33	4.78	3.45	2.67	4.96	5.03	64.57
1975	4.65	5.53	12.08	4.98	8.72	2.42	2.26	2.03	2.62	2.69	7.77	2.93	58.68
1976	2.85	4.41	7.68	2.41	4.73	4.06	3.82	0.86	5.40	5.66	1.83	1.79	45.50
1977	2.57	1.99	4.13	5.42	0.83	3.38	3.41	1.62	6.43	2.02	6.01	3.39	41.20
1978	8.13	1.31	4.05	2.14	8.14	4.45	3.89	9.65	1.52	1.82	5.56	13.12	63.78
1979	5.98	5.66	6.60	11.47	7.78	4.93	3.12	5.92	4.49	2.60	7.42	4.92	70.89
1980	3.23	1.12	10.86	7.53	4.43	5.75	4.73	1.23	5.32	3.14	5.23	1.86	54.43
1981	1.38	3.66	4.98	3.67	7.06	2.93	1.71	4.21	0.61	5.83	2.12	1.84	40.00
1982	6.61	4.16	4.47	6.76	5.50	6.68	4.13	3.11	1.92	5.23	6.43	13.81	68.81
1983	2.32	2.61	3.66	8.84	9.58	3.50	3.83	0.61	1.52	2.94	9.56	8.68	57.65
1984	1.88	4.37	6.07	5.24	9.06	1.12	4.59	5.00	1.96	7.75	5.85	4.35	57.24
1985	3.78	4.10	4.96	6.51	2.23	4.55	3.50	3.50	4.03	3.36	3.87	3.27	47.66
1986	0.57	2.50	1.90	3.72	4.63	3.80	1.21	2.74	1.21	3.75	8.67	3.92	38.62
1987	1.76	5.81	3.38	3.78	2.96	3.66	2.06	4.12	2.01	1.96	10.45	11.39	53.34
1988	4.25	3.49	4.20	2.85	2.38	2.15	5.21	0.85	4.73	3.62	10.52	5.99	50.24
1989	7.91	10.51	5.50	2.13	2.36	7.20	7.55	1.43	6.08	2.37	3.65	2.20	58.89
1990	3.97	8.99	5.65	6.93	4.55	2.68	2.21	1.18	5.21	4.37	3.44	10.61	59.79
1991	2.90	6.46	3.68	17.13	5.10	1.42	1.92	2.06	1.47	4.39	5.54	7.04	59.11
1992	1.78	2.18	7.07	1.39	3.68	7.50	5.38	2.44	3.62	4.01	4.82	3.28	47.15
1993	3.59	2.46	3.14	6.20	4.56	4.20	0.86	3.69	3.73	1.91	4.07	5.59	44.00
Record Mean	4.82	4.37	5.20	5.16	4.37	3.69	3.41	3.21	3.00	2.89	4.45	4.81	49.40

AVERAGE TEMPERATURE (deg. F)

MEMPHIS, TENNESSEE

YEAR	JAN	FEB	MAR	APR	MAY	JUNE	JULY	AUG	SEP	OCT	NOV	DEC	ANNUAL
1964	41.1	40.2	51.7	64.0	71.9	79.3	80.6	78.6	72.9	58.9	54.4	44.3	61.5
1965	43.4	42.9	44.0	66.4	74.7	78.1	81.8	80.2	73.7	60.8	55.8	45.8	62.3
1966	34.2	42.2	52.8	60.6	67.9	76.6	84.7	76.9	70.8	58.1	53.7	41.4	60.0
1967	42.2	39.2	56.7	66.5	68.8	78.3	77.7	76.0	70.3	62.4	49.1	45.0	61.0
1968	38.9	37.3	50.9	62.7	69.7	79.5	80.8	82.0	71.3	62.2	50.9	41.7	60.7
1969	41.2	43.3	45.0	62.9	72.1	78.8	84.9	79.3	72.9	62.9	49.0	40.1	61.1
1970	35.3	41.7	48.7	65.0	72.3	77.3	79.7	81.2	77.9	61.7	49.8	46.4	61.4
1971	39.6	43.5	48.4	60.5	66.6	80.6	80.6	78.6	76.1	69.3	50.9	50.7	62.1
1972	42.3	44.7	52.2	63.1	69.7	77.5	79.4	79.7	75.9	61.4	45.5	40.0	60.9
1973	38.6	40.5	57.3	59.8	68.3	81.0	83.2	79.6	76.1	67.6	57.3	43.3	62.7
1974	45.7	45.6	58.7	61.8	72.1	74.7	82.5	79.2	68.5	62.4	53.3	45.2	62.5
1975	45.9	46.2	49.9	61.9	73.5	78.8	81.1	81.2	70.9	65.8	53.8	44.1	62.8
1976	39.5	53.8	58.5	63.6	65.6	76.4	81.5	78.9	73.0	58.9	45.5	41.9	61.5
1977	30.7	45.1	58.6	66.9	76.4	81.9	84.7	82.6	79.0	62.2	55.1	44.1	64.0
1978	32.7	35.0	50.3	66.3	70.9	79.8	83.8	80.9	77.7	62.5	57.7	44.0	61.8
1979	30.9	38.5	54.3	63.0	70.0	77.9	82.6	80.9	73.4	65.8	50.7	45.4	61.1
1980	43.2	39.5	49.4	60.9	72.5	80.9	88.8	87.2	80.5	62.7	53.3	45.9	63.8
1981	40.9	47.3	54.3	70.2	70.0	82.5	84.6	81.8	74.0	62.5	53.8	40.9	63.6
1982	36.6	40.5	55.5	58.5	74.5	78.0	85.0	82.9	73.3	63.7	53.4	49.5	62.6
1983	40.4	45.3	51.9	56.8	68.2	77.2	83.6	84.9	75.2	66.2	53.1	34.7	61.5
1984	35.9	47.6	51.1	61.0	69.5	80.9	80.9	79.8	71.9	68.4	50.9	53.8	62.6
1985	32.4	40.6	57.7	65.0	71.8	78.9	82.2	80.2	73.6	67.2	57.6	36.9	62.0
1986	41.9	48.0	55.2	64.4	72.5	81.0	86.5	79.2	79.1	64.2	51.1	42.6	63.8
1987	39.6	47.1	54.7	62.2	76.5	80.0	82.5	83.6	75.3	59.2	54.4	46.7	63.5
1988	36.8	42.2	52.3	62.8	71.8	80.3	81.6	83.7	76.3	59.1	54.6	44.9	62.2
1989	47.3	40.0	53.8	62.6	69.5	77.6	80.7	81.2	72.4	64.2	54.2	33.6	61.4
1990	48.5	52.0	55.3	61.4	68.3	80.7	82.5	82.0	77.9	61.3	57.1	45.8	64.4
1991	41.2	48.0	55.4	65.0	74.6	80.3	83.3	80.9	75.3	65.5	49.2	46.8	63.8
1992	42.2	49.9	53.7	63.0	70.4	76.9	82.5	76.8	73.2	63.8	50.7	43.8	62.2
1993	42.7	42.6	51.1	59.3	69.9	79.2	86.4	83.6	73.5	62.2	50.2	44.8	62.1
Record Mean	40.9	44.1	52.5	62.3	70.6	78.4	81.5	80.2	74.3	63.5	51.8	43.5	62.0
Max	48.9	52.6	61.5	71.6	79.8	87.4	90.3	89.1	83.6	73.6	60.9	51.5	70.9
Min	32.9	35.6	43.5	52.9	61.3	69.3	72.7	71.3	64.9	53.3	42.7	35.6	53.0

REFERENCE NOTES

MEMPHIS, TENNESSEE

GENERAL
T - TRACE AMOUNT.
BLANK ENTRIES DENOTE MISSING/UNREPORTED DATA.
# INDICATES A STATION OR INSTRUMENT RELOCATION.

SPECIFIC

PM - INCLUDES LAST DAY OF PREVIOUS MONTH
ASOS - AUTOMATED SURFACE OBSERVING SYSTEM IN OPERATION DURING THESE MONTHS.

(a) - LENGTH OF RECORD IN YEARS, ALTHOUGH INDIVIDUAL MONTHS MAY BE MISSING.
0.* OR * - THE VALUE IS BETWEEN 0.0 AND 0.05
NORMALS - BASED ON THE 1961-1990 RECORD PERIOD.
EXTREMES - DATES ARE THE MOST RECENT OCCURRENCE
WIND DIR.- NUMERALS SHOW TENS OF DEGRESS CLOCKWISE FROM TRUE NORTH. "00" INDICATES CALM.
RESULTANT DIRECTIONS ARE GIVEN TO WHOLE DEGREES.
BOLD VALUES INDICATE EXTREME VALUES WHICH OCCURRED AFTER THE ASOS SYSTEM WAS COMMISSIONED.

RECORD = PERIOD OF RECORD
RECORD MEAN PRECIPITATION IS THE MEAN OF ALL DAILY PRECIPITATION AMOUNTS DURING THE PERIOD OF RECORD.
RECORD MAX(MIN) TEMPERATURE IS THE MEAN OF ALL DAILY MAX(MIN) TEMPERATURES DURING THE PERIOD OF RECORD.
RECORD MEAN TEMPERATURE IS THE SUM OF THE RECORD MAX AND RECORD MIN DIVIDED BY 2.
AVERAGE TEMPERATURE IS THE SUM OF THE MEAN DAILY MAX AND MIN TEMPERATURE DIVIDED BY 2.

EXCEPTIONS

RECORD MEANS ARE THROUGH THE CURRENT YEAR,
BEGINNING IN 1875 FOR TEMPERATURE
1872 FOR PRECIPITATION
1951 FOR SNOWFALL

HEATING DEGREE DAYS Base 65 deg. F **MEMPHIS, TENNESSEE**

SEASON	JULY	AUG	SEP	OCT	NOV	DEC	JAN	FEB	MAR	APR	MAY	JUNE	TOTAL
1964-65	0	0	13	202	335	634	666	614	645	72	0	0	3181
1965-66	0	0	22	162	275	590	947	634	382	175	47	5	3239
1966-67	0	0	9	227	344	732	707	715	301	60	35	0	3130
1967-68	0	0	34	144	469	613	803	795	444	114	21	0	3437
1968-69	0	0	1	149	423	716	733	601	608	103	12	0	3346
1969-70	0	0	0	151	473	768	917	648	500	97	20	0	3574
1970-71	0	0	7	150	455	571	781	593	509	171	50	0	3287
1971-72	0	0	9	13	432	435	698	582	391	146	27	0	2733
1972-73	0	0	12	172	583	766	809	679	237	200	32	0	3490
1973-74	0	0	8	67	244	665	599	535	235	150	1	0	2504
1974-75	0	0	28	121	367	607	591	521	463	180	2	0	2880
1975-76	0	0	40	90	352	643	783	326	238	100	58	0	2630
1976-77	0	0	0	231	581	708	1056	547	212	61	4	0	3400
1977-78	0	0	0	123	313	640	995	835	454	74	47	0	3481
1978-79	0	0	0	116	230	643	1049	734	345	121	23	0	3261
1979-80	0	0	0	76	426	598	669	733	478	156	7	0	3143
1980-81	0	0	5	146	362	586	739	492	342	18	23	0	2713
1981-82	0	0	9	153	331	739	873	680	324	215	2	0	3326
1982-83	0	0	20	134	352	500	759	543	406	273	25	0	3012
1983-84	0	0	27	73	368	935	894	499	426	162	24	0	3408
1984-85	0	0	37	48	423	367	1004	683	254	100	6	0	2922
1985-86	0	0	17	54	257	864	708	475	307	102	8	0	2792
1986-87	0	0	0	102	413	687	782	492	322	154	0	0	2952
1987-88	0	0	0	186	324	559	867	657	393	108	0	0	3094
1988-89	0	0	1	202	314	619	544	694	369	174	41	0	2958
1989-90	0	0	24	102	337	966	503	363	321	181	38	0	2835
1990-91	0	0	11	182	249	593	728	471	329	57	7	0	2627
1991-92	0	0	23	90	481	556	699	433	347	144	30	0	2803
1992-93	0	0	15	87	428	650	685	617	433	200	15	2	3132
1993-94	0	0	14	164	447	618							

COOLING DEGREE DAYS Base 65 deg. F **MEMPHIS, TENNESSEE**

YEAR	JAN	FEB	MAR	APR	MAY	JUNE	JULY	AUG	SEP	OCT	NOV	DEC	TOTAL
1969	0	0	0	48	240	422	627	449	243	91	0	0	2120
1970	3	0	0	104	251	375	463	509	400	51	6	2	2164
1971	0	0	3	46	107	474	489	426	349	154	14	0	2062
1972	0	0	3	95	179	383	449	464	346	66	6	0	1991
1973	0	0	4	48	143	486	571	458	350	156	19	0	2235
1974	6	0	46	59	228	299	550	445	138	46	23	0	1840
1975	8	0	3	93	272	421	507	510	224	121	23	2	2184
1976	0	7	44	64	84	349	519	438	247	48	0	0	1800
1977	0	0	23	123	362	516	619	551	426	41	20	0	2681
1978	0	0	6	122	235	452	590	501	387	46	18	0	2357
1979	0	0	19	68	184	394	553	499	259	108	4	0	2088
1980	0	0	0	40	249	480	744	695	476	80	18	2	2784
1981	0	5	20	181	184	532	614	527	285	80	2	0	2430
1982	0	1	36	26	305	399	623	563	275	100	14	25	2367
1983	0	0	7	32	131	373	584	622	338	116	17	0	2220
1984	0	1	4	51	169	482	502	462	249	162	5	23	2110
1985	0	6	30	107	224	425	540	478	285	129	42	0	2266
1986	0	3	12	91	247	487	673	448	427	81	4	0	2473
1987	0	0	9	78	366	458	549	584	315	12	13	0	2384
1988	0	0	7	52	221	469	518	586	347	24	8	0	2232
1989	0	2	27	109	186	386	496	510	254	84	20	0	2074
1990	0	7	27	83	146	477	550	534	404	71	18	2	2319
1991	0	0	34	62	309	464	576	500	339	113	13	0	2410
1992	0	0	5	92	204	363	551	375	268	55	4	0	1917
1993	0	0	8	38	173	436	669	584	275	84	13	0	2280

SNOWFALL (inches) **MEMPHIS, TENNESSEE**

SEASON	JULY	AUG	SEP	OCT	NOV	DEC	JAN	FEB	MAR	APR	MAY	JUNE	TOTAL
1964-65	0.0	0.0	0.0	0.0	T	T	T	3.3	4.6	0.0	0.0	0.0	7.9
1965-66	0.0	0.0	0.0	0.0	0.0	0.0	12.2	T	T	0.0	0.0	0.0	12.2
1966-67	0.0	0.0	0.0	0.0	T	0.7	0.6	T	0.3	0.0	0.0	0.0	1.6
1967-68	0.0	0.0	0.0	0.0	0.0	T	2.0	4.5	17.3	0.0	0.0	0.0	23.8
1968-69	0.0	0.0	0.0	0.0	0.0	0.0	T	T	T	0.0	0.0	0.0	T
1969-70	0.0	0.0	0.0	0.0	T	0.1	3.3	0.2	T	0.0	0.0	0.0	3.6
1970-71	0.0	0.0	0.0	0.0	T	1.0	T	6.7	1.6	T	0.0	0.0	9.3
1971-72	0.0	0.0	0.0	0.0	0.8	0.0	0.3	0.1	T	0.0	0.0	0.0	1.2
1972-73	0.0	0.0	0.0	0.0	T	T	1.4	T	0.0	0.0	0.0	0.0	1.4
1973-74	0.0	0.0	0.0	0.0	0.0	0.2	0.9	0.5	T	0.0	0.0	0.0	1.6
1974-75	0.0	0.0	0.0	0.0	T	0.2	3.9	0.5	1.4	0.0	0.0	0.0	6.0
1975-76	0.0	0.0	0.0	0.0	0.0	0.1	0.3	T	0.0	0.0	0.0	0.0	0.4
1976-77	0.0	0.0	0.0	0.0	1.5	0.3	3.5	T	0.0	0.0	0.0	0.0	5.3
1977-78	0.0	0.0	0.0	0.0	0.0	T	4.3	3.2	T	0.0	0.0	0.0	7.5
1978-79	0.0	0.0	0.0	0.0	0.0	T	3.0	7.4	0.0	0.0	0.0	0.0	10.4
1979-80	0.0	0.0	0.0	0.0	T	0.0	1.3	1.5	0.8	0.0	0.0	0.0	3.6
1980-81	0.0	0.0	0.0	0.0	T	T	T	T	0.0	0.0	0.0	0.0	T
1981-82	0.0	0.0	0.0	0.0	0.0	T	4.5	0.7	1.2	0.0	0.0	0.0	6.4
1982-83	0.0	0.0	0.0	0.0	0.0	T	7.3	T	0.2	0.0	0.0	0.0	7.5
1983-84	0.0	0.0	0.0	0.0	0.0	0.8	2.0	T	0.5	0.0	0.0	0.0	3.3
1984-85	0.0	0.0	0.0	0.0	0.0	T	12.4	8.3	0.0	0.0	0.0	0.0	20.7
1985-86	0.0	0.0	0.0	0.0	0.0	T	T	2.0	0.0	0.0	0.0	0.0	2.0
1986-87	0.0	0.0	0.0	0.0	0.0		T	T	0.4	0.0	0.0	0.0	
1987-88	0.0	0.0	0.0	0.0	0.0	T	8.2	3.0	T	0.0	0.0	0.0	11.2
1988-89	0.0	0.0	0.0	0.0	0.0	T	T	0.3	T	0.0	T	0.0	0.3
1989-90	0.0	0.0	0.0	T	T	0.4	0.0	0.0	0.0	T	0.0	0.0	0.4
1990-91	0.0	0.0	0.0	0.0	0.0	0.4	T	T	1.0	0.0	0.0	0.0	1.4
1991-92	0.0	0.0	0.0	0.0	0.6	0.0	T	0.0	T	0.0	0.0	0.0	0.6
1992-93	0.0	0.0	0.0	0.0	T	T	T	T	T	T	T	0.0	T
1993-94	0.0	0.0	0.0	T	0.0	0.0							
Record Mean	0.0	0.0	0.0	T	0.1	0.6	2.3	1.3	0.8	T	T	0.0	5.2

NASHVILLE, TENNESSEE

The city of Nashville is located on the Cumberland River, in the northwestern corner of the Central Basin of middle Tennessee near the escarpment of the Highland Rim. The Rim, as it is called, rises to the height of 300 to 400 feet above the mean elevation of the basin, forming an amphitheater about the city from the southwest to the southeast, with the south being more or less open but undulating.

Temperatures are moderate, with great extremes of either heat or cold rarely occurring, yet there are changes of sufficient amplitude and frequency to give variety.

Based on the 1951-1980 period, the average first occurrence of 32 degrees Fahrenheit in the fall is October 29 and the average last occurrence in the spring is April 5.

Humidity is an important phase of climate in relation to bodily health and comfort. The Nashville records show that the average relative humidity is moderate as compared with the general conditions east of the Mississippi River and south of the Ohio.

Nashville is not in the most frequented path of general storms that cross the country, however, it is in the zone of moderate frequency of thunderstorms. The thunderstorm season usually begins in the latter part of March and continues through September.

NORMALS, MEANS, AND EXTREMES

NASHVILLE, TENNESSEE

LATITUDE: 36°07'N LONGITUDE: 86°41' W ELEVATION: FT. GRND 590 BARO 630 TIME ZONE: CENTRAL WBAN: 13897

	(a)	JAN	FEB	MAR	APR	MAY	JUNE	JULY	AUG	SEP	OCT	NOV	DEC	YEAR
TEMPERATURE °F:														
Normals														
-Daily Maximum		45.9	50.8	61.2	70.8	78.8	86.5	89.5	88.4	82.5	72.5	60.4	50.2	69.8
-Daily Minimum		26.5	29.9	39.1	47.5	56.6	64.7	68.9	67.7	61.1	48.3	39.6	30.9	48.4
-Monthly		36.2	40.4	50.2	59.2	67.7	75.6	79.3	78.1	71.8	60.4	50.0	40.5	59.1
Extremes														
-Record Highest	54	78	84	86	91	97	106	107	104	105	94	84	79	107
-Year		1972	1962	1982	1989	1941	1952	1952	1954	1954	1953	1971	1982	JUL 1952
-Record Lowest	54	-17	-13	2	23	34	42	51	47	36	26	-1	-10	-17
-Year		1985	1951	1980	1982	1976	1966	1947	1946	1983	1987	1950	1989	JAN 1985
NORMAL DEGREE DAYS:														
Heating (base 65°F)		893	689	469	193	59	0	0	0	21	195	450	760	3729
Cooling (base 65°F)		0	0	10	19	143	318	443	406	225	52	0	0	1616
% OF POSSIBLE SUNSHINE	51	41	47	52	59	60	65	63	63	63	62	50	42	56
MEAN SKY COVER (tenths)														
Sunrise - Sunset	53	7.0	6.7	6.6	6.1	6.0	5.6	5.6	5.3	5.3	4.9	6.1	6.8	6.0
MEAN NUMBER OF DAYS:														
Sunrise to Sunset														
-Clear	52	6.4	7.0	7.4	8.3	8.1	8.2	8.2	10.0	10.6	12.8	8.8	7.1	102.9
-Partly Cloudy	52	6.3	5.8	7.1	8.5	9.9	12.5	13.1	12.0	9.0	8.0	6.8	7.0	105.9
-Cloudy	52	18.4	15.4	16.4	13.3	13.0	9.4	9.7	9.0	10.4	10.2	14.4	16.9	156.4
Precipitation														
.01 inches or more	52	10.9	10.6	11.8	10.7	10.9	9.3	10.2	8.7	8.1	7.0	9.5	11.0	118.6
Snow,Ice pellets,hail														
1.0 inches or more	52	1.2	1.2	0.5	0.*	0.0	0.0	0.0	0.0	0.0	0.0	0.1	0.5	3.5
Thunderstorms	52	1.2	1.7	4.1	5.1	7.3	8.1	9.5	7.7	3.7	1.6	1.7	1.1	52.8
Heavy Fog Visibility														
1/4 mile or less	52	2.4	1.3	1.0	0.5	1.0	0.9	1.1	1.6	1.8	2.1	1.7	1.8	17.1
Temperature °F														
-Maximum														
90° and above	28	0.0	0.0	0.0	0.1	1.0	9.5	17.4	12.4	5.4	0.1	0.0	0.0	45.9
32° and below	28	4.8	2.2	0.1	0.0	0.0	0.0	0.0	0.0	0.0	0.0	0.1	1.8	9.1
-Minimum														
32° and below	28	21.6	16.8	9.3	1.7	0.0	0.0	0.0	0.0	0.0	1.1	8.2	17.1	75.8
0° and below	28	0.7	0.2	0.0	0.0	0.0	0.0	0.0	0.0	0.0	0.0	0.0	0.2	1.1
AVG. STATION PRESS.(mb)	21	999.1	997.9	995.2	994.5	994.0	994.4	995.4	995.9	996.6	998.0	998.1	999.1	996.5
RELATIVE HUMIDITY (%)														
Hour 00	28	75	73	71	72	82	83	85	85	85	81	77	76	79
Hour 06 (Local Time)	28	80	80	78	81	86	87	89	90	90	86	82	80	84
Hour 12	28	63	59	53	51	56	55	57	57	58	53	59	63	57
Hour 18	28	65	60	54	52	59	59	62	62	64	60	64	67	61
PRECIPITATION (inches):														
Water Equivalent														
-Normal		3.58	3.81	4.85	4.37	4.88	3.57	3.97	3.46	3.46	2.62	4.12	4.61	47.30
-Maximum Monthly	54	13.92	10.31	12.35	8.41	11.04	9.37	7.75	8.31	11.44	6.13	9.04	13.63	13.92
-Year		1950	1956	1975	1984	1983	1960	1950	1942	1979	1959	1945	1978	JAN 1950
-Minimum Monthly	54	0.19	0.64	1.18	0.52	0.69	0.45	0.71	0.69	0.28	T	0.54	0.98	T
-Year		1986	1968	1987	1986	1941	1988	1954	1968	1956	1963	1949	1985	OCT 1963
-Maximum in 24 hrs	54	4.40	4.73	4.66	3.29	4.27	4.91	4.32	5.34	6.68	3.75	3.74	5.12	6.68
-Year		1946	1989	1975	1979	1984	1960	1992	1963	1979	1975	1973	1978	SEP 1979
Snow,Ice pellets,hail														
-Maximum Monthly	54	18.8	18.9	16.1	1.1	0.0	T	0.0	T	0.0	0.4	9.2	13.2	18.9
-Year		1948	1979	1960	1971		1993		1989		1993	1950	1963	FEB 1979
-Maximum in 24 hrs	54	8.1	8.3	8.8	1.1	0.0	T	0.0	i	0.0	0.4	9.2	10.2	10.2
-Year		1988	1979	1951	1971		1993		1989		1993	1950	1963	DEC 1963
WIND:														
Mean Speed (mph)	52	9.1	9.3	9.9	9.3	7.7	7.1	6.6	6.2	6.5	6.8	8.4	8.9	8.0
Prevailing Direction through 1963		S	S	S	S	S	S	S	S	S	S	S	S	S
Fastest Obs. 1 Min.														
-Direction (!!)	18	34	32	13	18	36	36	34	02	34	36	15	23	13
-Speed (MPH)	18	32	35	41	35	41	35	33	40	33	32	39	41	41
-Year		1985	1980	1987	1993	1984	1990	1978	1983	1977	1986	1984	1987	MAR 1987
Peak Gust														
-Direction (!!)	10	W	SW	SE	W	NW	SW	N	NW	N	N	W	SW	NW
-Speed (mph)	10	46	47	56	67	55	49	51	70	47	48	60	54	70
-Date		1984	1988	1987	1991	1984	1988	1988	1990	1989	1986	1985	1987	AUG 1990

PRECIPITATION (inches)

NASHVILLE, TENNESSEE

YEAR	JAN	FEB	MAR	APR	MAY	JUNE	JULY	AUG	SEP	OCT	NOV	DEC	ANNUAL
1964	3.70	3.26	5.92	5.86	5.04	1.21	2.16	4.56	2.65	1.83	3.67	5.15	45.01
1965	2.98	4.71	6.13	5.72	3.12	2.74	3.32	2.53	5.02	0.57	1.82	1.01	39.67
1966	3.93	3.63	1.39	5.08	3.99	1.09	2.70	5.29	3.87	2.50	2.76	5.69	41.92
1967	1.62	1.78	4.44	3.40	6.98	4.23	7.46	2.06	1.93	1.57	3.87	5.88	45.22
1968	3.50	0.64	4.47	3.57	6.28	2.26	6.87	0.69	2.76	3.92	5.39	3.58	43.93
1969	4.96	4.48	2.12	6.03	4.81	3.34	5.33	2.27	2.06	2.01	1.83	8.03	47.27
1970	1.16	4.36	3.87	6.81	5.90	6.73	3.61	2.99	2.76	2.94	2.20	3.60	46.93
1971	2.66	4.70	2.95	3.34	2.93	3.47	5.00	5.87	2.11	1.27	1.18	5.17	40.65
1972	5.15	3.45	4.34	3.58	3.52	2.54	6.40	4.30	3.71	4.06	5.22	8.14	54.41
1973	3.40	3.63	9.88	7.00	5.72	4.80	7.67	1.79	1.56	3.32	7.78	3.23	59.78
1974	9.45	3.01	5.25	3.97	5.04	6.80	2.10	4.13	10.44	1.47	6.23	2.81	60.70
1975	4.67	5.22	12.35	3.55	6.52	2.22	2.96	4.69	5.42	5.86	3.00	4.12	60.58
1976	4.11	2.28	5.32	1.53	6.19	4.72	4.01	8.05	5.08	5.17	1.30	1.81	49.57
1977	2.53	3.27	5.83	7.87	1.65	4.29	1.15	4.65	5.04	4.22	5.96	4.25	50.71
1978	5.95	1.57	4.88	2.42	8.03	1.46	4.03	3.81	1.37	2.28	4.01	13.63	53.44
1979	7.13	4.01	4.92	7.80	8.18	2.79	4.27	4.59	11.44	3.97	5.98	5.04	70.12
1980	2.59	1.38	7.27	3.67	6.14	2.89	3.53	1.24	1.09	1.17	2.55	1.40	34.92
1981	1.60	3.83	3.38	4.78	3.05	8.05	3.49	3.10	1.37	2.82	3.83	2.38	41.68
1982	6.50	4.80	3.00	4.36	4.19	2.28	5.47	3.46	3.23	1.91	3.87	6.36	49.43
1983	2.56	2.93	3.44	6.80	11.04	3.93	1.71	1.36	0.45	2.77	6.98	7.75	51.72
1984	1.79	2.38	5.14	8.41	9.68	4.49	6.63	2.42	0.97	6.00	6.20	2.38	56.49
1985	3.02	3.30	2.70	2.91	2.65	1.53	2.00	3.91	2.52	1.59	3.81	0.98	30.92
1986	0.19	3.59	2.29	0.52	3.36	2.38	0.77	3.38	2.19	2.19	7.43	3.31	31.60
1987	1.61	4.87	1.18	1.03	4.41	2.82	2.56	0.73	1.95	0.21	3.40	5.46	30.23
1988	3.73	2.02	2.18	2.09	1.86	0.45	3.26	2.39	2.45	1.54	5.49	3.95	31.41
1989	4.52	9.36	5.31	2.68	4.61	7.87	3.18	3.67	6.30	3.62	3.94	1.97	57.03
1990	2.76	4.73	3.26	1.60	2.80	2.37	4.86	3.12	2.13	4.41	4.29	10.76	47.09
1991	2.92	5.44	4.25	3.35	5.63	1.25	2.82	1.79	5.47	3.88	2.87	7.27	46.94
1992	2.97	2.60	4.50	0.77	3.12	4.31	5.89	3.25	3.45	1.62	4.48	2.88	39.84
1993	2.76	3.33	5.50	3.33	4.50	5.31	3.64	1.76	2.90	2.20	2.53	6.62	44.38
Record Mean	4.55	4.12	5.06	4.13	4.07	3.77	3.93	3.35	3.28	2.51	3.61	4.06	46.44

AVERAGE TEMPERATURE (deg. F)

NASHVILLE, TENNESSEE

YEAR	JAN	FEB	MAR	APR	MAY	JUNE	JULY	AUG	SEP	OCT	NOV	DEC	ANNUAL
1964	38.9	37.2	49.0	62.6	69.7	77.7	78.7	77.2	71.3	56.7	51.7	42.7	59.4
#1965	40.0	39.8	41.9	60.9	71.7	75.1	78.6	79.0	74.1	59.3	51.9	44.8	59.7
1966	32.3	41.3	50.5	58.8	65.3	75.1	82.3	76.5	69.5	57.0	50.7	40.2	58.3
1967	42.3	37.5	57.0	63.9	66.3	76.3	75.7	72.6	66.8	59.3	44.3	42.6	58.7
1968	34.0	32.4	47.8	58.7	66.3	74.9	77.8	79.5	69.9	59.5	48.7	38.1	57.3
1969	37.2	39.8	42.6	60.9	68.9	77.2	82.7	78.1	70.8	60.6	46.5	37.3	58.6
1970	32.4	38.4	46.8	61.3	68.4	73.6	77.2	79.2	76.9	61.0	47.5	43.2	58.8
1971	35.6	38.7	44.6	57.9	63.3	77.5	76.8	76.4	74.4	66.7	49.9	49.2	59.3
1972	41.8	41.8	50.2	60.5	67.4	73.0	77.3	77.2	75.7	60.2	47.3	42.8	59.6
1973	38.0	39.7	56.8	56.4	64.2	76.1	78.7	78.1	76.2	66.2	54.7	40.5	60.5
1974	45.4	41.8	54.9	58.6	70.0	71.4	78.0	77.6	67.5	59.4	50.0	42.6	59.8
1975	43.4	44.6	47.3	58.5	70.4	76.0	78.5	79.1	67.9	62.4	52.1	42.8	60.2
1976	36.7	50.5	55.9	59.9	64.0	73.3	76.4	74.4	66.8	53.9	40.9	36.6	57.5
1977	24.5	40.6	53.9	63.0	71.9	77.2	82.2	79.5	74.0	57.0	50.8	38.6	59.4
1978	27.6	29.2	46.9	61.0	66.7	76.2	80.5	78.7	75.5	57.4	53.6	42.4	58.0
1979	29.7	33.4	50.7	57.8	66.3	73.7	77.6	77.0	70.5	60.3	48.6	41.5	57.3
1980	39.7	35.7	46.3	57.3	67.8	75.5	82.8	81.7	76.0	57.8	48.5	41.0	59.2
1981	35.5	42.6	47.5	64.0	64.2	77.5	79.8	76.6	69.1	60.4	49.9	38.3	58.7
1982	34.0	39.5	52.5	54.6	71.0	73.3	79.8	76.1	69.6	61.1	51.4	48.2	59.3
1983	38.8	42.7	50.3	54.5	64.8	75.5	80.5	83.2	73.7	62.4	49.9	34.0	59.2
1984	32.2	43.4	46.1	58.2	64.2	77.4	76.1	76.5	68.6	66.7	46.0	49.6	58.8
1985	27.8	36.5	53.2	61.9	68.4	75.7	80.2	77.2	70.8	64.4	56.9	34.2	58.9
1986	37.2	44.7	50.8	60.8	68.6	76.5	82.4	76.7	74.9	61.0	49.9	39.9	60.3
1987	36.1	43.1	51.8	57.7	73.4	77.5	80.2	81.1	72.2	54.6	52.4	44.1	60.4
1988	34.4	38.7	49.3	57.1	67.3	77.3	81.4	81.9	72.8	54.2	51.1	42.4	59.0
1989	44.9	39.0	52.6	59.3	65.7	74.7	79.1	78.0	70.5	61.0	51.4	29.5	58.8
1990	45.8	49.9	53.6	58.4	66.4	78.2	80.4	79.6	74.7	60.1	54.3	43.7	62.1
1991	39.2	43.9	52.5	63.8	74.2	78.2	81.1	78.3	72.3	61.2	47.2	44.5	61.4
1992	40.0	45.9	50.1	59.6	65.8	72.4	79.9	74.9	70.9	59.4	49.5	41.2	59.1
1993	41.6	39.3	47.1	56.7	67.6	75.9	83.3	81.0	71.0	58.6	47.4	40.3	59.2
Record Mean	38.5	41.0	49.7	59.4	68.1	76.2	79.5	78.3	72.2	60.8	49.1	41.0	59.5
Max	47.2	50.2	59.6	69.9	78.5	86.3	89.3	88.2	82.6	72.0	58.7	49.6	69.3
Min	29.9	31.8	39.7	48.9	57.7	66.1	69.6	68.3	61.7	49.6	39.4	32.4	49.6

REFERENCE NOTES

NASHVILLE, TENNESSEE

GENERAL
T - TRACE AMOUNT.
BLANK ENTRIES DENOTE MISSING/UNREPORTED DATA.
# INDICATES A STATION OR INSTRUMENT RELOCATION.

SPECIFIC

PM - INCLUDES LAST DAY OF PREVIOUS MONTH
ASOS - AUTOMATED SURFACE OBSERVING SYSTEM IN OPERATION DURING THESE MONTHS.

(a) - LENGTH OF RECORD IN YEARS, ALTHOUGH INDIVIDUAL MONTHS MAY BE MISSING.
0.* OR * - THE VALUE IS BETWEEN 0.0 AND 0.05
NORMALS - BASED ON THE 1961-1990 RECORD PERIOD.
EXTREMES - DATES ARE THE MOST RECENT OCCURRENCE.
WIND DIR. - NUMERALS SHOW TENS OF DEGRESS CLOCKWISE FROM TRUE NORTH. "00" INDICATES CALM.
RESULTANT DIRECTIONS ARE GIVEN TO WHOLE DEGREES.
BOLD VALUES INDICATE EXTREME VALUES WHICH OCCURRED AFTER THE ASOS SYSTEM WAS COMMISSIONED.

RECORD = PERIOD OF RECORD
RECORD MEAN PRECIPITATION IS THE MEAN OF ALL DAILY PRECIPITATION AMOUNTS DURING THE PERIOD OF RECORD.
RECORD MAX(MIN) TEMPERATURE IS THE MEAN OF ALL DAILY MAX(MIN) TEMPERATURES DURING THE PERIOD OF RECORD.
RECORD MEAN TEMPERATURE IS THE SUM OF THE RECORD MAX AND RECORD MIN DIVIDED BY 2.
AVERAGE TEMPERATURE IS THE SUM OF THE MEAN DAILY MAX AND MIN TEMPERATURE DIVIDED BY 2.

EXCEPTIONS

RECORD MEANS ARE THROUGH THE CURRENT YEAR, BEGINNING IN 1871 FOR TEMPERATURE
1871 FOR PRECIPITATION
1942 FOR SNOWFALL

HEATING DEGREE DAYS Base 65 deg. F NASHVILLE, TENNESSEE

SEASON	JULY	AUG	SEP	OCT	NOV	DEC	JAN	FEB	MAR	APR	MAY	JUNE	TOTAL
#1964-65	0	3	18	265	398	685	768	698	711	168	3	0	3717
1965-66	0	0	26	198	386	618	1007	657	452	234	78	7	3663
1966-67	0	0	13	255	423	763	697	763	300	106	69	1	3390
1967-68	0	3	58	216	615	688	952	941	531	205	64	1	4274
1968-69	0	0	4	220	484	825	855	700	692	149	38	3	3970
1969-70	0	0	10	201	551	854	1005	737	556	156	51	0	4121
1970-71	0	0	13	159	522	671	902	733	624	227	101	0	3952
1971-72	0	0	0	39	462	483	713	667	454	193	36	6	3053
1972-73	0	0	10	168	533	682	830	702	261	275	83	0	3544
1973-74	0	0	8	84	316	753	601	641	320	227	28	3	2981
1974-75	0	0	48	196	464	685	665	567	547	241	6	0	3419
1975-76	0	0	68	138	398	683	870	417	303	183	94	0	3154
1976-77	0	0	31	349	718	872	1250	679	350	129	28	1	4407
1977-78	0	0	3	255	425	813	1152	996	556	164	92	0	4456
1978-79	0	0	1	240	338	695	1088	877	449	213	57	0	3958
1979-80	0	0	5	180	487	723	777	848	571	240	38	0	3869
1980-81	0	0	9	259	487	739	909	621	537	97	96	0	3754
1981-82	0	0	42	175	445	820	956	707	416	309	8	0	3878
1982-83	0	0	30	194	413	537	806	620	458	322	71	0	3451
1983-84	0	0	45	121	447	956	1009	621	578	220	106	0	4103
1984-85	0	0	59	63	564	473	1146	794	383	145	25	6	3658
1985-86	0	0	30	91	264	948	854	561	432	171	55	0	3406
1986-87	0	3	0	175	447	773	889	608	401	242	6	0	3544
1987-88	0	0	7	317	376	640	941	756	485	242	43	2	3809
1988-89	0	0	5	343	408	693	618	721	397	258	90	0	3533
1989-90	0	0	36	158	408	1095	590	422	373	245	65	1	3393
1990-91	0	0	21	195	323	654	791	586	402	80	9	0	3061
1991-92	0	0	42	166	535	628	768	544	456	217	85	2	3443
1992-93	0	0	26	181	461	731	717	713	552	252	32	4	3669
1993-94	0	0	27	227	528	759							

COOLING DEGREE DAYS Base 65 deg. F NASHVILLE, TENNESSEE

YEAR	JAN	FEB	MAR	APR	MAY	JUNE	JULY	AUG	SEP	OCT	NOV	DEC	TOTAL
1969	0	0	0	33	165	378	554	416	191	74	0	0	1811
1970	0	0	0	56	163	265	386	446	374	40	1	1	1732
1971	0	0	0	23	55	380	374	360	293	101	16	1	1603
1972	0	0	1	62	117	250	385	387	341	24	6	0	1573
1973	0	0	14	25	61	339	432	412	351	128	8	0	1770
1974	0	0	16	39	191	203	410	399	130	30	22	0	1440
1975	3	0	3	55	183	341	424	444	164	62	19	0	1698
1976	0	1	28	36	68	257	363	299	92	10	0	0	1154
1977	0	0	11	74	253	371	543	458	281	13	4	0	2008
1978	0	0	1	50	152	344	489	432	324	13	2	0	1807
1979	0	0	11	5	103	264	393	381	175	44	0	0	1376
1980	0	0	0	17	131	322	562	527	344	44	1	0	1948
1981	0	0	1	71	81	383	464	366	145	42	0	0	1553
1982	0	0	37	4	199	256	470	352	177	84	12	21	1612
1983	0	0	9	12	69	320	488	568	315	49	2	0	1832
1984	0	0	0	21	87	382	352	364	173	121	0	1	1501
1985	0	2	24	59	137	335	479	386	206	79	29	0	1736
1986	0	0	1	52	174	352	551	371	304	59	0	0	1864
1987	0	0	0	31	272	381	479	507	227	3	7	0	1907
1988	0	0	5	17	120	380	515	531	246	17	0	0	1831
1989	0	0	21	93	120	298	446	408	208	39	8	0	1641
1990	0	4	26	51	115	401	485	458	315	52	10	0	1917
1991	0	0	22	50	300	403	507	419	268	57	4	0	2030
1992	0	0	0	60	115	233	471	311	208	15	2	0	1415
1993	0	0	1	9	121	336	573	506	215	33	7	0	1801

SNOWFALL (inches) NASHVILLE, TENNESSEE

SEASON	JULY	AUG	SEP	OCT	NOV	DEC	JAN	FEB	MAR	APR	MAY	JUNE	TOTAL
1964-65	0.0	0.0	0.0	0.0	T	0.0	1.2	2.9	3.4	0.0	0.0	0.0	7.5
1965-66	0.0	0.0	0.0	0.0	T	0.0	11.4	T	T	0.0	0.0	0.0	11.4
1966-67	0.0	0.0	0.0	0.0	7.2	4.3	1.2	T	T	0.0	0.0	0.0	12.7
1967-68	0.0	0.0	0.0	0.0	0.0	8.4	7.2	2.9	8.5	0.0	0.0	0.0	27.0
1968-69	0.0	0.0	0.0	0.0	T	T	5.2	6.9	4.8	0.0	0.0	0.0	16.9
1969-70	0.0	0.0	0.0	0.0	0.3	3.8	5.6	3.0	T	0.0	0.0	0.0	12.7
1970-71	0.0	0.0	0.0	0.0	T	1.2	1.2	6.5	3.0	1.1	0.0	0.0	13.0
1971-72	0.0	0.0	0.0	0.0	0.1	T	0.4	0.5	0.9	T	0.0	0.0	1.9
1972-73	0.0	0.0	0.0	0.0	0.1	0.6	4.8	T	0.2	0.1	0.0	0.0	5.8
1973-74	0.0	0.0	0.0	0.0	0.0	2.4	T	0.3	T	0.0	0.0	0.0	2.7
1974-75	0.0	0.0	0.0	0.0	T	2.1	4.2	T	T	T	0.0	0.0	6.3
1975-76	0.0	0.0	0.0	0.0	T	T	1.1	2.3	T	0.0	0.0	0.0	3.4
1976-77	0.0	0.0	0.0	0.0	1.2	1.8	18.5	T	0.0	T	0.0	0.0	21.5
1977-78	0.0	0.0	0.0	0.0	T	0.1	12.9	9.8	2.4	0.0	0.0	0.0	25.2
1978-79	0.0	0.0	0.0	0.0	0.0	T	8.0	18.9	0.6	0.0	0.0	0.0	27.5
1979-80	0.0	0.0	0.0	0.0	T	T	0.3	6.6	3.1	0.0	0.0	0.0	10.0
1980-81	0.0	0.0	0.0	0.0	T	T	1.2	1.7	T	0.0	0.0	0.0	2.9
1981-82	0.0	0.0	0.0	0.0	0.0	0.2	4.8	3.7	1.0	0.0	0.0	0.0	9.7
1982-83	0.0	0.0	0.0	0.0	0.0	0.4	0.3	0.8	T	0.0	0.0	0.0	1.5
1983-84	0.0	0.0	0.0	0.0	0.0	0.7	5.3	3.7	T	0.0	0.0	0.0	9.7
1984-85	0.0	0.0	0.0	0.0	0.0	0.8	9.8	8.0	0.0	0.0	0.0	0.0	18.6
1985-86	0.0	0.0	0.0	0.0	0.0	0.5	0.4	2.1	T	0.0	0.0	0.0	3.0
1986-87	0.0	0.0	0.0	0.0	0.0	T	1.4	1.3	1.6	T	0.0	0.0	4.3
1987-88	0.0	0.0	0.0	0.0	T	T	8.6	1.4	T	0.0	0.0	0.0	10.0
1988-89	0.0	0.0	0.0	0.0	0.0	1.6	T	5.2	0.0	0.0	0.0	0.0	6.8
1989-90	0.0	T	0.0	T	T	0.4	T	T	0.4	0.0	0.0	0.0	0.8
1990-91	0.0	0.0	0.0	0.0	0.0	0.3	T	0.6	1.1	0.0	0.0	0.0	2.0
1991-92	0.0	0.0	0.0	0.0	T	0.0	T	0.0	1.0	0.0	0.0	0.0	1.0
1992-93	0.0	0.0	0.0	0.0	T	0.3	T	5.9	2.8	T	0.0	T	9.0
1993-94	0.0	0.0	0.0	0.4	T	0.3							
Record Mean	0.0	T	0.0	T	0.4	1.5	3.8	3.1	1.4	T	0.0	T	10.3

1993 AMARILLO, TEXAS (AMA)

The station is located 7 statute miles east northeast of the downtown post office in a region of rather flat topography. The Canadian River flows eastward 18 miles north of the station, with its bed about 800 feet below the plains. The Prairie Dog Town Fork of the Red River flows southeastward about 15 miles south of the station where it enters the Palo Duro Canyon, which is about 1,000 feet deep. There are numerous shallow Playa lakes, often dry, over the area, and the nearly treeless grasslands slope downward to the east. The terrain gradually rises to the west and northwest.

Three-fourths of the total annual precipitation falls from April through September, occurring from thunderstorm activity. Snow usually melts within a few days after it falls. Heavier snowfalls of 10 inches or more, usually with near blizzard conditions, average once every 5 years and last 2 to 3 days.

The Amarillo area is subject to rapid and large temperature changes, especially during the winter months when cold fronts from the northern Rocky Mountain and Plains states sweep across the area. Temperature drops of 50 to 60 degrees within a 12-hour period are not uncommon. Temperature drops of 40 degrees have occurred within a few minutes.

Humidity averages are low, occasionally dropping below 20 percent in the spring. Low humidity moderates the effect of high summer afternoon temperatures, permits evaporative cooling systems to be very effective, and provides many pleasant evenings and nights.

Severe local storms are infrequent, although a few thunderstorms with damaging hail, lightning, and wind in a very localized area occur most years, usually in spring and summer. These storms are often accompanied by very heavy rain, which produces local flooding, particularly of roads and streets. Tornadoes are rare.

Based on the 1951-1980 period, the average first occurrence of 32 degrees Fahrenheit in the fall is October 29 and the average last occurrence in the spring is April 14.

NORMALS, MEANS, AND EXTREMES FOR 1993

AMARILLO, TX (AMA)

LATITUDE: 35° 13′ 10″ N LONGTITUDE: 101° 42′ 20″ W ELEVATION (FT): GRND: 3604 BARO: 3591 TIME ZONE: CENTRAL (UTC+06) WBAN: 23047

	ELEMENT	POR	JAN	FEB	MAR	APR	MAY	JUN	JUL	AUG	SEP	OCT	NOV	DEC	YEAR
TEMPERATURE °F	NORMAL DAILY MAXIMUM	30	49.0	52.8	61.6	71.5	79.1	87.6	91.7	89.1	81.8	72.5	59.7	50.1	70.5
	MEAN DAILY MAXIMUM	54	48.6	53.1	61.1	70.9	78.7	87.7	91.1	91.1	83.9	73.8	60.1	51.8	71.0
	HIGHEST DAILY MAXIMUM	53	81	88	94	98	102	108	105	106	102	95	87	81	108
	YEAR OF OCCURRENCE		1950	1963	1971	1989	1953	1990	1981	1944	1983	1954	1980	1955	JUN 1990
	MEAN OF EXTREME MAXS.	46	71.3	75.3	81.9	88.9	93.8	99.8	99.6	98.4	94.5	89.1	78.3	72.0	86.9
	NORMAL DAILY MINIMUM	30	21.2	25.5	32.7	42.1	51.6	60.7	65.5	63.8	56.4	44.5	32.3	23.7	43.3
	MEAN DAILY MINIMUM	54	21.8	26.1	32.0	42.0	51.5	61.1	65.6	65.3	57.6	46.1	32.5	25.0	43.9
	LOWEST DAILY MINIMUM	53	-11	-14	-3	14	28	42	51	49	30	12	0	-8	-14
	YEAR OF OCCURRENCE		1984	1951	1948	1945	1954	1955	1990	1956	1984	1993	1976	1989	FEB 1951
	MEAN OF EXTREME MINS.	46	3.0	8.2	14.4	27.1	37.8	50.0	58.1	56.4	42.8	30.1	15.6	7.6	29.2
	NORMAL DRY BULB	30	35.1	39.2	47.1	56.8	65.4	74.1	78.6	76.5	69.1	58.5	46.0	36.9	56.9
	MEAN DRY BULB	54	35.2	39.6	46.6	56.5	65.1	74.4	78.4	78.2	70.8	60.0	46.3	38.4	57.5
	MEAN WET BULB	44	28.7	32.3	37.3	45.2	53.9	62.1	65.1	64.4	58.5	48.5	37.4	30.5	47.0
	MEAN DEW POINT	44	18.7	22.4	25.2	33.0	44.7	54.6	58.1	58.0	51.5	39.5	27.8	20.8	37.9
	NORMAL NO. DAYS WITH:														
	MAXIMUM ≥ 90°	30	0.0	0.0	0.1	1.0	4.7	12.8	21.1	16.5	6.4	1.0	0.0	0.0	63.6
	MAXIMUM ≤ 32°	30	4.5	2.8	0.9	*	0.0	0.0	0.0	0.0	0.0	*	0.8	3.6	12.6
	MINIMUM ≤ 32°	30	27.5	21.8	14.7	3.5	0.1	0.0	0.0	0.0	0.2	1.8	14.5	26.7	110.8
	MINIMUM ≤ 0°	30	1.1	0.4	0.0	0.0	0.0	0.0	0.0	0.0	0.0	0.0	*	0.7	2.2
H/C	NORMAL HEATING DEG. DAYS	30	927	722	555	266	89	6	0	0	26	226	570	871	4258
	NORMAL COOLING DEG. DAYS	30	0	0	0	20	102	279	422	357	149	25	0	0	1354
RH	NORMAL (PERCENT)	30	58	59	52	48	54	56	53	58	61	56	59	59	56
	HOUR 00 LST	30	64	65	58	56	63	65	61	67	70	64	66	66	64
	HOUR 06 LST	30	70	72	68	68	74	77	74	78	80	73	72	70	73
	HOUR 12 LST	30	49	50	42	38	43	45	42	46	49	43	47	49	45
	HOUR 18 LST	30	46	43	35	31	37	39	38	43	45	42	48	50	41
S	PERCENT POSSIBLE SUNSHINE	52	69	68	73	75	73	78	79	78	74	76	73	68	73
W/O	MEAN NO. DAYS WITH:														
	HEAVY FOG(VISBY ≤ 1/4 MI)	52	3.3	4.2	3.3	1.9	2.1	0.7	0.5	0.7	2.0	2.5	2.7	2.8	26.7
	THUNDERSTORMS	52	0.2	0.5	1.6	3.5	8.4	9.6	9.2	9.0	4.2	2.4	0.6	0.2	49.4
CLOUDINESS	MEAN:														
	SUNRISE-SUNSET (TENTHS)	1		7.0	5.0	5.0	4.0		3.0	3.0	2.0	4.0	4.0	3.0	
	MIDNIGHT-MIDNIGHT (TENTHS)	1		7.0	5.0	5.0	4.0		3.0	4.0	2.0	4.0	4.0	3.0	
	MEAN NO. DAYS WITH:														
	CLEAR	1	5.0	10.0	15.0	8.0	12.0	12.0	14.0	16.0	19.0	13.0	10.0	19.0	153.0
	PARTLY CLOUDY	1	6.0	3.0	3.0	4.0	8.0	6.0	2.0	3.0	2.0	2.0	6.0	7.0	52.0
	CLOUDY	1	8.0	12.0	7.0	5.0	3.0		4.0	3.0	3.0	6.0	5.0	4.0	
PR	MEAN STATION PRESSURE(IN.)	21	26.35	26.32	26.23	26.25	26.25	26.30	26.37	26.38	26.37	26.37	26.33	26.35	26.32
	MEAN SEA-LEVEL PRES. (IN.)	44	30.07	30.02	29.91	29.87	29.84	29.84	29.90	29.92	29.95	29.99	30.03	30.06	29.95
WINDS	MEAN SPEED (MPH)	30	12.7	13.7	15.4	15.4	14.4	14.1	12.9	12.2	12.7	12.8	12.8	12.8	13.5
	PREVAIL.DIR(TENS OF DEGS.)	30	23	36	21	18	18	19	18	18	18	20	20	23	18
	MAXIMUM 2-MINUTE:														
	SPEED (MPH)	1	31	48	44	43	43	46	45	43	40	38	39	51	51
	DIR. (TENS OF DEGS.)	1	03	25	06	26	14	20	20	05	32	02	24	32	32
	YEAR OF OCCURRENCE		1993	1993	1993	1993	1993	1993	1993	1993	1993	1993	1993	1993	DEC 1993
	MAXIMUM 5-SECOND:														
	SPEED (MPH)	1	36	55	51	52	48	52	52	53	51	43	46	57	57
	DIR. (TENS OF DEGS.)	1	02	24	06	25	14	20	19	31	31	02	25	31	31
	YEAR OF OCCURRENCE		1993	1993	1993	1993	1993	1993	1993	1993	1993	1993	1993	1993	DEC 1993
PRECIPITATION	NORMAL TOTAL (IN.)	30	0.50	0.61	0.96	0.99	2.48	3.70	2.62	3.22	1.99	1.37	0.69	0.43	19.56
	MAXIMUM TOTAL (IN.)	53	2.33	1.83	3.99	3.74	9.81	10.73	7.59	7.55	5.02	7.64	2.26	4.52	10.73
	YEAR OF OCCURRENCE		1968	1948	1973	1942	1951	1965	1960	1974	1950	1941	1961	1959	JUN 1965
	MINIMUM TOTAL (IN.)	53	0.00	T	T	T	0.04	0.01	0.12	0.28	0.03	0.00	0.00	T	0.0
	YEAR OF OCCURRENCE		1986	1991	1950	1964	1984	1953	1946	1983	1977	1952	1989	1976	NOV 1989
	MAXIMUM IN 24 HOURS (IN.)	53	1.74	1.28	2.27	1.99	6.75	6.15	4.74	4.26	3.42	3.45	1.53	3.11	6.75
	YEAR OF OCCURRENCE		1968	1971	1973	1985	1951	1960	1982	1945	1941	1948	1980	1943	MAY 1951
	NORMAL NO. DAYS WITH:														
	PRECIPITATION ≥ 0.01	30	3.9	4.4	5.2	4.9	7.9	8.9	7.7	8.7	6.5	4.7	3.6	4.1	70.5
	PRECIPITATION ≥ 1.00	30	*	0.1	0.1	0.1	0.5	0.9	0.7	0.9	0.5	0.2	*	0.0	4.0
SNOWFALL	NORMAL TOTAL (IN.)	30	3.8	4.6	2.9	0.6	0.*	0.0	0.0	0.0	0.*	0.3	1.9	2.8	16.9
	MAXIMUM TOTAL (IN.)	53	14.5	17.3	14.7	6.4	0.5	T	0.0	0.0	0.3	3.9	13.6	15.3	17.3
	YEAR OF OCCURRENCE		1983	1971	1961	1947	1978	1992			1984	1976	1952	1987	FEB 1971
	MAXIMUM IN 24 HOURS (IN.)	53	9.8	13.5	9.8	5.1	0.5	T	0.0	0.0	0.3	3.2	12.2	11.3	13.5
	YEAR OF OCCURRENCE		1983	1971	1957	1947	1978	1992	1993	1993	1984	1976	1952	1987	FEB 1971
	MAXIMUM SNOW DEPTH (IN.)	44	10	14	10	6	T	T	0	0	T	1	9	13	14
	YEAR OF OCCURRENCE		1987	1983	1957	1973	1988	1949			1984	1970	1952	1987	FEB 1983
	NORMAL NO. DAYS WITH:														
	SNOWFALL ≥ 1.0	30	1.4	1.3	1.0	0.2	0.0	0.0	0.0	0.0	0.0	0.1	0.6	0.8	5.4

PRECIPITATION (inches) 1993 AMARILLO, TEXAS (AMA)

YEAR	JAN	FEB	MAR	APR	MAY	JUN	JUL	AUG	SEP	OCT	NOV	DEC	ANNUAL
1964	T	1.37	0.03	T	1.69	1.90	0.94	5.69	3.95	0.08	1.53	0.79	17.97
1965	0.55	0.47	0.72	0.23	1.88	10.73	1.54	1.71	0.79	1.02	0.07	0.38	20.09
1966	0.43	0.69	0.01	0.87	0.19	4.62	1.37	3.77	2.40	0.29	0.08	0.19	14.91
1967	T	0.15	0.42	1.95	1.40	2.55	3.70	1.81	2.47	1.61	0.28	0.51	16.85
1968	2.33	0.73	0.45	0.93	2.84	1.68	2.96	3.35	0.62	0.90	0.92	0.26	17.97
1969	0.02	0.50	1.15	0.30	2.93	4.09	2.55	4.51	2.77	2.56	0.34	0.83	22.55
1970	0.02	0.02	2.10	1.33	0.23	1.54	1.39	1.27	0.34	1.06	0.26	T	9.56
1971	0.10	1.65	0.10	0.77	0.91	4.17	1.75	3.33	4.70	2.59	2.08	0.89	23.04
1972	0.21	0.11	0.11	0.03	2.81	3.87	2.59	1.73	0.71	1.66	1.19	0.32	15.34
1973	0.56	0.42	3.99	1.88	1.43	0.84	4.08	2.31	1.22	1.05	0.10	0.17	18.05
1974	0.33	0.24	0.60	0.04	4.06	3.33	1.31	7.55	1.65	3.44	0.12	0.42	23.09
1975	0.28	1.33	0.51	1.02	2.47	4.15	5.19	3.97	0.76	0.33	0.92	0.15	21.08
1976	T	0.10	0.79	1.65	1.36	2.94	1.77	1.78	4.28	1.14	0.43	T	16.24
1977	0.64	0.53	0.24	2.74	4.01	2.06	3.14	4.94	0.03	0.26	0.32	0.27	19.18
1978	0.63	0.80	0.21	0.55	5.76	6.50	1.82	1.61	2.42	0.97	0.47	0.27	22.01
1979	0.92	0.28	1.46	1.29	3.94	3.19	2.03	5.08	0.52	1.28	0.40	0.07	20.46
1980	0.85	0.55	1.38	0.82	2.88	1.30	0.65	1.80	1.55	0.42	0.84	0.35	13.39
1981	0.11	0.23	1.87	0.90	2.11	1.04	2.73	5.22	3.47	1.79	1.50	0.03	21.00
1982	0.15	0.39	0.52	0.43	1.96	4.75	6.23	0.55	1.37	0.71	0.75	0.79	18.60
1983	1.78	1.19	0.98	0.83	2.85	1.76	0.74	0.28	0.37	3.23	0.33	0.64	14.98
1984	0.56	0.37	0.98	1.18	0.04	6.76	0.83	2.28	0.95	3.19	1.09	1.00	19.23
1985	0.99	0.77	1.49	2.79	0.86	3.08	2.07	1.67	4.96	3.07	0.39	0.26	22.40
1986	0.00	1.02	0.60	0.30	3.28	3.70	3.52	7.04	1.45	1.94	1.82	0.66	25.33
1987	1.26	0.84	0.92	0.57	4.28	3.29	0.83	3.28	3.40	1.17	0.43	1.75	22.02
1988	0.33	0.04	1.19	2.22	6.02	3.68	3.30	3.59	3.15	0.71	0.29	0.17	24.69
1989	0.16	0.55	0.52	0.75	2.51	6.07	2.74	3.22	1.80	0.74	0.00	0.49	19.55
1990	1.22	1.61	2.56	1.10	0.90	0.14	3.28	2.79	2.72	0.46	0.50	0.23	17.51
1991	0.86	T	0.41	0.04	3.08	2.47	2.20	1.28	2.04	0.64	0.66	2.24	15.92
1992	0.50	0.30	1.11	1.60	3.10	7.57	2.36	2.27	0.16	0.31	0.80	0.55	20.63
1993	0.76	0.36	1.29	0.35	1.92	2.76	3.36	4.64	1.00	0.53	0.51	0.95	18.43
POR= 54 YRS	0.55	0.57	0.87	1.16	2.80	3.42	2.73	3.03	1.89	1.59	0.64	0.64	19.90

AVERAGE TEMPERATURE (˚F) 1993 AMARILLO, TEXAS (AMA)

YEAR	JAN	FEB	MAR	APR	MAY	JUN	JUL	AUG	SEP	OCT	NOV	DEC	ANNUAL
1964	37.2	32.1	44.8	57.9	68.9	76.5	81.9	78.1	69.6	60.6	47.5	39.1	57.8
1965	41.0	37.6	38.4	59.4	66.9	72.1	78.6	76.9	68.5	59.5	52.5	42.9	57.9
1966	27.8	34.1	50.0	54.5	66.0	74.2	82.9	73.5	68.5	57.7	51.6	35.5	56.4
1967	40.7	40.6	53.4	60.6	63.4	73.7	77.2	75.0	68.3	60.9	46.6	35.4	58.0
1968	38.3	38.0	48.7	55.3	63.4	74.9	77.0	77.0	69.1	62.1	45.4	36.9	57.2
1969	41.4	40.4	38.8	59.9	67.2	72.8	82.6	80.2	71.1	54.5	46.7	38.4	57.8
1970	33.2	43.2	41.7	56.0	68.8	74.5	80.7	79.1	70.9	54.0	46.6	43.4	57.7
1971	37.8	38.8	48.3	55.7	64.9	75.9	76.9	72.2	67.1	57.2	45.6	37.6	56.5
1972	35.7	40.9	51.7	59.5	63.2	73.6	74.5	73.9	69.2	57.9	36.9	32.9	55.8
1973	33.4	39.5	47.1	50.3	62.9	75.1	78.1	78.8	68.7	62.0	50.8	38.6	57.1
1974	35.0	42.2	53.1	60.2	71.5	75.0	79.3	73.6	62.9	59.0	45.7	36.1	57.8
1975	37.1	35.3	45.0	54.9	64.5	73.3	75.5	76.7	65.8	61.1	45.8	40.4	56.3
1976	36.9	47.8	46.5	56.8	60.2	72.2	74.8	75.1	66.5	49.9	38.5	37.5	55.2
1977	30.1	43.8	48.7	57.8	67.3	78.1	80.7	77.5	74.3	60.7	47.4	39.9	58.9
1978	29.0	30.1	47.2	61.4	63.7	75.4	80.7	76.1	70.7	59.4	45.6	32.7	56.0
1979	24.9	40.0	46.6	54.5	62.2	70.9	77.1	73.6	69.8	60.1	40.5	38.8	54.9
1980	34.9	37.7	43.9	52.4	61.9	78.3	82.9	78.5	70.7	56.6	42.7	41.4	56.8
1981	37.9	42.2	48.8	63.1	65.6	78.5	81.3	74.4	69.0	56.6	49.1	40.1	58.9
1982	37.1	35.9	47.3	53.8	63.3	72.2	78.8	78.7	71.1	57.3	45.6	36.1	56.4
1983	33.4	36.2	45.3	50.9	60.3	70.4	80.0	81.0	73.6	60.5	47.9	24.7	55.4
1984	31.6	40.3	44.0	51.8	66.9	74.6	75.6	75.3	65.7	56.9	47.0	40.5	55.9
1985	31.5	37.2	49.5	60.0	68.1	75.1	80.1	79.6	68.9	56.9	43.5	34.0	57.0
1986	42.5	40.4	52.7	59.4	65.1	73.3	80.6	74.4	68.8	55.7	42.7	37.1	57.7
1987	34.0	42.0	44.6	54.8	64.5	72.1	77.2	75.3	67.6	57.9	45.4	34.6	55.8
1988	32.2	38.3	44.3	54.1	63.6	73.3	75.8	76.4	67.7	59.0	47.6	38.5	55.9
1989	40.7	32.3	51.2	59.9	67.3	69.4	76.2	76.0	66.3	60.4	47.9	31.4	56.6
1990	39.2	40.8	47.0	55.9	63.6	81.3	76.4	76.3	72.0	57.7	49.7	33.2	57.8
1991	32.6	45.9	49.7	58.2	68.5	74.7	76.5	76.2	67.1	58.5	41.2	39.0	57.3
1992	38.0	45.0	50.6	58.7	63.3	70.8	76.6	73.5	70.2	60.1	39.3	34.2	56.7
1993	33.1	36.0	46.1	54.4	64.5	74.0	79.1	74.9	67.9	54.6	40.9	38.7	55.4
POR= 54 YRS	35.3	39.6	46.6	56.5	65.2	74.4	78.4	76.9	69.5	58.9	45.5	37.7	57.0

REFERENCE NOTES:

THE TEMPERATURE GRAPH SHOWS NORMAL MAXIMUM AND NORMAL MINIMUM DAILY TEMPERATURES (SOLID CURVES) AND THE ACTUAL DAILY HIGH AND LOW TEMPERATURES (VERTICAL BARS).

H/C INDICATES HEATING AND COOLING DEGREE DAYS.
RH INDICATES RELATIVE HUMIDITY
W/O INDICATES WEATHER AND OBSTRUCTIONS
S INDICATES SUNSHINE.
PR INDICATES PRESSURE.
CLOUDINESS [illegible] IS THE SUM OF THE CEILOMETER AND SATELLITE DATA NOT TO EXCEED TEN TENTHS.
MAXIMUM SNOW DEPTH IS THE DEPTH MEASURED AT 12 UTC.

GENERAL:
T INDICATES TRACE PRECIPITATION, AN AMOUNT GREATER THAN ZERO BUT LESS THAN THE LOWEST REPORTABLE VALUE.
+ INDICATES THE VALUE ALSO OCCURS ON EARLIER DATES.
BLANK ENTRIES DENOTE MISSING OR UNREPORTED DATA.
NORMALS ARE 30-YEAR AVERAGES (1961 - 1990).
ASOS INDICATES AUTOMATED SURFACE OBSERVING SYSTEM.
PM INDICATES THE LAST DAY OF THE PREVIOUS MONTH.
POR (PERIOD OF RECORD) INDICATES THE NUMBER OF YEARS USED TO COMPUTE THE MEAN. INDIVIDUAL MONTHS WITHIN THE POR MAY BE MISSING.
WHEN THE POR FOR A NORMAL IS LESS THAN 30 YEARS, THE NORMAL IS PROVISIONAL AND IS BASED ON THE NUMBER OF YEARS INDICATED.
0.* OR * INDICATES THE VALUE OR MEAN DAYS WITH IS BETWEEN 0.00 AND 0.05.
CLOUDINESS FOR ASOS STATIONS DIFFERS FROM THE NON-ASOS OBSERVATION TAKEN BY A HUMAN OBSERVER. ASOS STATION CLOUDINESS IS BASED ON TIME-AVERAGED CEILOMETER DATA FOR CLOUDS AT OR BELOW 12,000 FEET AND ON SATELLITE DATA FOR CLOUDS ABOVE 12,000 FEET.
THE NUMBER OF DAYS WITH CLEAR, PARTLY CLOUDY, AND CLOUDY CONDITIONS FOR ASOS STATIONS IS THE SUM OF THE CEILOMETER AND SATELLITE DATA FOR THE SUNRISE TO SUNSET PERIOD.

GENERAL CONTINUED:
CLEAR INDICATES 0 - 3 TENTHS, PARTLY CLOUDY INDICATES 4 - 7 TENTHS, AND CLOUDY INDICATES 8 OR MORE TENTHS. WHEN AT LEAST ONE OF THE ELEMENTS (CEILOMETER OR SATELLITE) IS MISSING, THE DAILY CLOUDINESS IS NOT COMPUTED.
WIND DIRECTION IS RECORDED IN TENS OF DEGREES (2 DIGITS) CLOCKWISE FROM TRUE NORTH. "00" INDICATES CALM. "36" INDICATES TRUE NORTH.
RESULTANT WIND IS THE VECTOR AVERAGE OF THE SPEED AND DIRECTION.
AVERAGE TEMPERATURE IS THE SUM OF THE MEAN DAILY MAXIMUM AND MINIMUM TEMPERATURE DIVIDED BY 2.
SNOWFALL DATA COMPRISE ALL FORMS OF FROZEN PRECIPITATION, INCLUDING HAIL.
A HEATING (COOLING) DEGREE DAY IS THE DIFFERENCE BETWEEN THE AVERAGE DAILY TEMPERATURE AND 65˚ F.
DRY BULB IS THE TEMPERATURE OF THE AMBIENT AIR.
DEW POINT IS THE TEMPERATURE TO WHICH THE AIR MUST BE COOLED TO ACHIEVE 100 PERCENT RELATIVE HUMIDITY.
WET BULB IS THE TEMPERATURE THE AIR WOULD HAVE IF THE MOISTURE CONTENT WAS INCREASED TO 100 PERCENT RELATIVE HUMIDITY.

HEATING DEGREE DAYS (base 65˚F) 1993 AMARILLO, TEXAS (AMA)

YEAR	JUL	AUG	SEP	OCT	NOV	DEC	JAN	FEB	MAR	APR	MAY	JUN	TOTAL
1964-65	0	0	48	149	517	795	740	762	820	194	56	7	4088
1965-66	0	0	73	191	376	676	1145	857	456	312	99	1	4186
1966-67	0	23	22	250	395	908	743	675	356	159	135	9	3675
1967-68	0	1	23	185	544	911	820	777	504	290	109	0	4164
1968-69	0	0	6	159	583	865	726	681	808	176	69	24	4097
1969-70	0	0	1	374	543	817	981	602	713	280	50	33	4394
1970-71	0	0	47	359	544	661	837	726	524	290	89	0	4077
1971-72	1	0	120	245	575	843	900	692	409	203	106	0	4094
1972-73	13	2	48	274	833	987	972	706	548	438	113	0	4934
1973-74	0	0	56	154	420	813	922	633	368	190	17	0	3573
1974-75	0	0	119	199	571	890	853	826	612	323	67	16	4476
1975-76	0	0	104	158	569	757	861	492	567	253	171	0	3932
1976-77	0	0	59	464	790	846	1075	592	499	215	22	0	4562
1977-78	0	0	1	150	522	768	1107	972	551	136	139	6	4352
1978-79	0	0	33	197	574	992	1236	697	561	319	144	30	4783
1979-80	0	2	28	186	727	806	926	788	649	373	146	0	4631
1980-81	0	0	35	280	662	723	832	630	496	111	65	0	3834
1981-82	0	0	26	271	469	765	849	803	534	340	96	2	4155
1982-83	0	0	23	252	575	888	972	800	603	421	171	32	4737
1983-84	0	0	40	175	506	1241	1028	709	642	390	56	0	4787
1984-85	0	0	125	262	531	752	1034	769	474	169	37	5	4158
1985-86	0	0	111	249	640	957	691	681	379	203	72	0	3983
1986-87	0	2	26	290	665	858	954	634	624	315	70	9	4447
1987-88	0	8	18	226	584	936	1010	765	633	323	102	4	4609
1988-89	0	7	32	197	517	815	747	909	429	219	59	27	3958
1989-90	0	0	91	185	507	1037	795	672	551	276	140	0	4254
1990-91	0	0	11	234	454	981	994	529	467	208	53	1	3932
1991-92	0	0	71	258	709	798	833	576	437	203	98	10	3993
1992-93	0	0	21	171	765	949	984	808	577	317	82	5	4679
1993-	0	2	39	332	717	810							
POR= 53 YRS	0	1	41	217	576	843	911	711	564	269	92	10	4235

COOLING DEGREE DAYS (base 65˚F) 1993 AMARILLO, TEXAS (AMA)

YEAR	JAN	FEB	MAR	APR	MAY	JUN	JUL	AUG	SEP	OCT	NOV	DEC	ANNUAL
1969	0	0	0	30	147	264	550	478	190	54	0	0	1713
1970	0	0	0	14	176	327	495	446	231	24	0	0	1713
1971	0	0	13	18	94	334	381	232	189	10	0	0	1271
1972	0	0	4	44	59	265	313	285	182	60	0	0	1212
1973	0	0	0	3	53	310	414	435	173	67	1	0	1456
1974	0	0	6	52	228	306	449	274	61	20	0	0	1396
1975	0	0	0	24	61	273	330	367	134	46	0	0	1235
1976	0	0	0	13	32	223	312	318	110	5	0	0	1013
1977	0	0	0	10	100	399	493	389	287	22	0	0	1700
1978	0	0	6	33	108	324	497	351	209	28	0	0	1556
1979	0	0	0	12	64	218	380	276	177	41	0	0	1168
1980	0	0	0	4	58	408	562	429	211	26	0	0	1698
1981	0	0	1	59	87	410	512	299	154	16	0	0	1538
1982	0	0	0	9	52	225	437	432	213	22	0	0	1390
1983	0	0	0	2	31	201	473	502	306	41	3	0	1559
1984	0	0	0	1	121	298	331	325	151	17	0	0	1244
1985	0	0	2	27	143	315	473	458	235	6	0	0	1659
1986	0	0	3	45	87	256	489	299	144	10	0	0	1333
1987	0	0	0	19	64	227	386	334	105	11	0	0	1146
1988	0	0	0	3	67	263	340	366	120	19	0	0	1178
1989	0	0	10	75	136	164	354	347	138	51	0	0	1275
1990	0	0	0	9	101	494	359	358	229	17	1	0	1568
1991	0	0	0	12	166	298	364	358	144	66	0	0	1408
1992	0	0	0	19	52	188	366	271	186	25	0	0	1107
1993	0	0	0	6	77	283	443	315	134	15	0	0	1273
POR= 25 YRS	0	0	0	21	94	290	419	357	176	28	0	0	1385

SNOWFALL (inches) 1993 AMARILLO, TEXAS (AMA)

YEAR	JUL	AUG	SEP	OCT	NOV	DEC	JAN	FEB	MAR	APR	MAY	JUN	TOTAL
1964-65	0.0	0.0	0.0	0.0	T	0.5	5.6	3.8	2.3	0.0	0.0	0.0	12.2
1965-66	0.0	0.0	0.0	0.0	0.0	1.4	7.2	0.4	0.1	0.0	0.0	0.0	9.1
1966-67	0.0	0.0	0.0	T	T	1.8	T	1.1	0.4	0.0	0.0	0.0	3.3
1967-68	0.0	0.0	0.0	T	2.1	6.1	0.6	8.0	2.9	0.0	0.0	0.0	19.7
1968-69	0.0	0.0	0.0	0.0	0.3	1.8	0.2	2.9	10.3	0.0	0.0	0.0	15.5
1969-70	0.0	0.0	0.0	0.0	T	7.1	0.1	T	14.1	1.8	0.0	0.0	23.1
1970-71	0.0	0.0	0.0	3.9	2.6	T	0.8	17.3	1.0	T	0.0	0.0	25.6
1971-72	0.0	0.0	0.0	0.0	T	7.9	1.6	2.0	0.6	0.0	0.0	0.0	12.1
1972-73	0.0	0.0	0.0	0.4	9.9	2.8	7.0	4.2	0.5	5.7	0.0	0.0	30.5
1973-74	0.0	0.0	0.0	0.0	0.4	1.5	3.6	1.2	T	0.0	0.0	0.0	6.7
1974-75	0.0	0.0	0.0	0.0	T	1.5	3.8	11.7	1.2	T	0.0	0.0	18.2
1975-76	0.0	0.0	0 0	0.0	0.4	1.8	T	T	4.2	0.0	0.0	0.0	6.4
1976-77	0.0	0.0	0.0	3.9	4.3	T	6.4	3.7	T	T	0.0	0.0	18.3
1977-78	0.0	0.0	0.0	0.0	1.3	0.2	8.2	9.4	1.5	T	0.5	0.0	21.1
1978-79	0.0	0.0	0.0	0.0	2.0	3.3	5.9	1.9	T	T	0.0	0.0	13.1
1979-80	0.0	0.0	0.0	1.6	2.2	0.3	1.4	5.2	1.0	T	0.0	0.0	11.7
1980-81	0.0	0.0	0.0	0.0	8.6	T	1.1	0.1	0.1	0.0	0.0	0.0	9.9
1981-82	0.0	0.0	0.0	0.0	T	0.3	1.1	4.7	1.7	T	0.0	0.0	7.8
1982-83	0.0	0.0	0.0	0.0	4.5	1.9	14.5	13.0	8.1	5.9	0.0	0.0	47.9
1983-84	0.0	0.0	0.0	0.0	T	5.2	7.0	3.5	2.5	0.0	0.0	0.0	18.2
1984-85	0.0	0.0	0.3	0.0	0.1	0.3	7.4	0.3	0.2	0.0	0.0	0.0	8.6
1985-86	0.0	0.0	T	0.0	T	2.8	0.0	10.9	1.0	0.0	0.0	0.0	14.7
1986-87	0.0	0.0	0.0	T	0.2	3.3	12.1	3.1	6.4	0.1	0.0	0.0	25.2
1987-88	0.0	0.0	0.0	0.0	0.7	15.3	4.3	0.5	8.5	4.2	0.0	0.0	33.5
1988-89	0.0	0.0	0.0	0.0	2.4	2.2	T	0.1	4.2	0.1	T	T	9.0
1989-90	0.0	0.0	T	0.0	0.0	5.4	8.5	3.0	0.0	0.0	0.0	0.0	16.9
1990-91	0.0	0.0	0.0	0.0	2.2	3.8	5.0	T	1.0	0.0	T	T	12.0
1991-92	0.0	0.0	T	3.2	T	2.0	1.0	0.2	T	0.3	T	T	6.7
1992-93	0.0	0.0	0.0	T	9.0	10.0	2.5	2.2	2.1	T	T	0.0	25.8
1993-	0.0	0.0	0.0	T	T	0.5							
POR= 54 YRS	0.0	0.0	T	0.2	1.8	2.8	3.9	3.6	2.5	0.6	T	T	15.4

DALLAS – FORT WORTH, TEXAS

The Dallas–Fort Worth Metroplex is located in North Central Texas, approximately 250 miles north of the Gulf of Mexico. It is near the headwaters of the Trinity River, which lie in the upper margins of the Coastal Plain. The rolling hills in the area range from 500 to 800 feet in elevation.

The Dallas–Fort Worth climate is humid subtropical with hot summers. It is also continental, characterized by a wide annual temperature range. Precipitation also varies considerably, ranging from less than 20 to more than 50 inches.

Winters are mild, but northers occur about three times each month, and often are accompanied by sudden drops in temperature. Periods of extreme cold that occasionally occur are short–lived, so that even in January mild weather occurs frequently.

The highest temperatures of summer are associated with fair skies, westerly winds and low humidities. Characteristically, hot spells in summer are broken into three–to–five day periods by thunderstorm activity. There are only a few nights each summer when the low temperature exceeds 80 degrees. Summer daytime temperatures frequently exceed 100 degrees. Air conditioners are recommended for maximum comfort indoors and while traveling via automobile.

Throughout the year, rainfall occurs more frequently during the night. Usually, periods of rainy weather last for only a day or two, and are followed by several days with fair skies. A large part of the annual precipitation results from thunderstorm activity, with occasional heavy rainfall over brief periods of time. Thunderstorms occur throughout the year, but are most frequent in the spring. Hail falls on about two or three days a year, ordinarily with only slight and scattered damage. Windstorms occurring during thunderstorm activity are sometimes destructive. Snowfall is rare.

The average length of the warm season (freeze–free period) in the Dallas–Fort Worth Metroplex is about 249 days. The aver .ge last occurrence of 32 degrees or below is mid March and the average first occurrence of 32 degrees or below is in late November.

NORMALS, MEANS, AND EXTREMES

DALLAS - FORT WORTH, TEXAS

LATITUDE: 32°54'N LONGITUDE: 97°02'W ELEVATION: FT. GRND 551 BARO 575 TIME ZONE: CENTRAL WBAN: 03927

	(a)	JAN	FEB	MAR	APR	MAY	JUNE	JULY	AUG	SEP	OCT	NOV	DEC	YEAR
TEMPERATURE °F:														
Normals														
-Daily Maximum		54.1	58.9	67.8	76.3	82.9	91.9	96.5	96.2	87.8	78.5	66.8	57.5	76.3
-Daily Minimum		32.7	36.9	45.6	54.7	62.6	70.0	74.1	73.6	66.9	55.8	45.4	36.3	54.6
-Monthly		43.4	47.9	56.7	65.5	72.8	81.0	85.3	84.9	77.4	67.2	56.2	46.9	65.4
Extremes														
-Record Highest	40	88	88	96	95	103	113	110	108	106	102	89	88	113
-Year		1969	1986	1991	1990	1985	1980	1980	1964	1985	1979	1989	1955	JUN 1980
-Record Lowest	40	4	7	15	29	41	51	59	56	43	29	20	-1	-1
-Year		1964	1985	1980	1989	1978	1964	1972	1967	1984	1993	1959	1989	DEC 1989
NORMAL DEGREE DAYS:														
Heating (base 65°F)		670	484	286	75	0	0	0	0	0	51	275	566	2407
Cooling (base 65°F)		0	5	29	90	246	480	629	617	372	119	11	5	2603
% OF POSSIBLE SUNSHINE	15	53	54	60	62	59	67	76	73	69	62	57	52	62
MEAN SKY COVER (tenths)														
Sunrise - Sunset	40	6.2	5.8	5.8	5.9	5.9	5.0	4.3	4.3	4.7	4.7	5.3	5.7	5.3
MEAN NUMBER OF DAYS:														
Sunrise to Sunset														
-Clear	40	9.7	9.6	9.9	8.8	8.1	10.7	14.9	14.7	12.6	13.8	11.9	11.0	135.5
-Partly Cloudy	40	5.8	5.6	7.6	8.2	10.4	11.5	9.6	10.1	8.9	7.3	5.9	6.1	96.9
-Cloudy	40	15.5	13.1	13.5	13.1	12.6	7.8	6.5	6.2	8.5	9.9	12.3	13.9	132.8
Precipitation														
.01 inches or more	40	7.3	6.5	7.2	7.9	8.8	6.5	4.7	4.8	6.8	6.1	5.8	6.5	78.9
Snow,Ice pellets,hail														
1.0 inches or more	40	0.5	0.3	0.1	0.0	0.0	0.0	0.0	0.0	0.0	0.0	0.*	0.1	1.1
Thunderstorms	40	1.1	1.8	4.3	5.9	7.5	6.3	4.8	4.5	3.6	3.0	1.9	1.1	45.9
Heavy Fog Visibility														
1/4 mile or less	40	2.5	1.5	1.0	0.6	0.3	0.1	0.0	0.*	0.1	0.9	1.5	2.4	10.9
Temperature °F														
-Maximum														
90° and above	30	0.0	0.0	0.2	0.8	4.0	19.7	27.7	26.3	14.5	2.7	0.0	0.0	95.9
32° and below	30	1.5	0.7	0.1	0.0	0.0	0.0	0.0	0.0	0.0	0.0	0.0	0.8	3.1
-Minimum														
32° and below	30	14.5	8.8	2.6	0.2	0.0	0.0	0.0	0.0	0.0	0.1	2.9	9.7	38.8
0° and below	30	0.0	0.0	0.0	0.0	0.0	0.0	0.0	0.0	0.0	0.0	0.0	0.*	*
AVG. STATION PRESS.(mb)	21	999.6	997.8	993.9	993.1	991.8	992.6	994.2	994.1	994.8	996.5	997.2	998.9	995.4
RELATIVE HUMIDITY (%)														
Hour 00	30	73	72	70	73	79	74	67	67	74	73	74	73	72
Hour 06 (Local Time)	30	80	79	80	82	87	86	81	80	85	83	81	79	82
Hour 12	30	60	58	56	56	60	55	49	49	55	54	57	59	56
Hour 18	30	58	54	51	52	57	51	44	45	53	55	58	59	53
PRECIPITATION (inches):														
Water Equivalent														
-Normal		1.83	2.18	2.77	3.50	4.88	2.98	2.31	2.21	3.39	3.52	2.29	1.84	33.70
-Maximum Monthly	40	4.54	6.20	6.39	12.19	13.66	8.75	11.13	6.85	9.52	14.18	6.23	8.75	14.18
-Year		1990	1965	1968	1957	1982	1989	1973	1970	1964	1981	1964	1991	OCT 1981
-Minimum Monthly	40	T	0.15	0.10	0.11	0.99	0.40	0.00	T	0.09	T	0.20	0.17	0.00
-Year		1986	1963	1972	1987	1977	1964	1993	1980	1984	1975	1970	1981	JUL 1993
-Maximum in 24 hrs	40	3.11	4.06	4.39	4.55	5.34	3.15	3.76	4.05	4.76	5.91	2.83	4.22	5.91
-Year		1990	1965	1977	1957	1989	1989	1975	1976	1965	1959	1964	1991	OCT 1959
Snow,Ice pellets,hail														
-Maximum Monthly	40	12.1	13.5	2.5	T	T	0.0	0.0	0.0	0.0	T	5.0	2.6	13.5
-Year		1964	1978	1962	1990	1990					1993	1976	1963	FEB 1978
-Maximum in 24 hrs	40	12.1	7.5	2.5	T	T	0.0	0.0	0.0	0.0	T	4.8	2.5	12.1
-Year		1964	1978	1962	1990	1990					1993	1976	1963	JAN 1964
WIND:														
Mean Speed (mph)	40	10.9	11.7	12.7	12.4	11.0	10.5	9.7	8.9	9.2	9.7	10.7	10.8	10.7
Prevailing Direction through 1963		S	S	S	S	S	S	S	S	S	S	S	S	S
Fastest Obs. 1 Min.														
-Direction (!!)	40	36	36	29	32	14	32	36	36	11	30	34	32	36
-Speed (MPH)	40	55	51	55	55	55	52	65	73	53	44	50	53	73
-Year		1985	1962	1954	1970	1955	1955	1961	1959	1961	1992	1957	1968	AUG 1959
Peak Gust														
-Direction (!!)	10	N	S	W	SE	N	NW	NE	NW	S	W	W	S	NW
-Speed (mph)	10	66	54	53	58	54	58	54	81	51	63	68	55	81
-Date		1985	1985	1992	1992	1993	1989	1989	1985	1986	1992	1992	1988	AUG 1985

PRECIPITATION (inches)

DALLAS - FORT WORTH, TEXAS

YEAR	JAN	FEB	MAR	APR	MAY	JUNE	JULY	AUG	SEP	OCT	NOV	DEC	ANNUAL
1964	3.53	1.17	3.35	2.71	2.85	0.40	0.25	2.43	9.52	0.62	6.23	1.25	34.31
1965	2.77	6.20	1.45	2.15	8.97	1.50	0.09	2.26	5.04	1.97	2.43	1.73	36.56
1966	1.68	2.84	1.38	10.74	3.13	5.47	3.26	3.38	4.23	1.48	0.53	1.17	39.29
1967	0.28	0.32	2.09	3.84	4.02	0.72	2.20	0.48	5.94	4.19	0.92	2.30	27.30
1968	3.60	1.48	6.39	2.41	6.02	3.50	1.88	2.71	2.53	2.18	4.58	1.20	38.48
1969	1.26	1.99	3.62	3.40	7.12	0.63	0.77	2.56	4.55	5.82	1.22	2.75	35.69
1970	0.72	4.78	3.49	4.68	3.62	0.61	0.94	6.85	6.25	2.95	0.20	1.01	36.10
1971	0.19	1.32	0.34	2.76	1.88	0.83	3.60	5.70	3.24	7.64	1.77	6.99	36.26
1972	1.09	0.26	0.10	3.25	2.35	1.50	0.59	0.81	2.42	6.89	2.36	0.61	22.23
1973	3.26	1.92	2.28	6.06	3.18	5.88	11.13	0.01	7.16	6.85	2.06	0.83	50.62
1974	1.79	1.01	0.80	2.51	6.00	5.44	0.67	4.19	6.04	5.93	3.32	1.93	39.63
1975	3.34	3.72	1.67	3.40	6.88	1.95	5.06	0.30	0.87	T	0.42	1.49	29.10
1976	0.13	0.52	2.29	5.71	6.03	1.40	3.83	4.75	5.02	3.46	0.50	1.99	35.63
1977	2.39	1.68	5.88	4.31	0.99	0.69	2.20	2.33	1.72	2.96	1.79	0.25	27.19
1978	1.41	3.33	2.66	1.34	8.01	0.77	0.33	1.53	0.93	0.55	2.73	0.78	24.37
1979	3.35	1.52	6.33	2.03	5.90	1.36	1.94	2.47	0.99	3.38	0.43	2.72	32.42
1980	2.52	0.84	1.24	2.23	3.01	1.25	0.71	T	6.54	1.08	1.23	1.43	22.08
1981	0.58	1.44	3.39	2.69	6.24	7.85	1.81	2.32	2.40	14.18	1.53	0.17	44.60
1982	2.33	1.89	1.71	2.71	13.66	4.28	2.73	0.52	0.58	3.36	4.22	2.76	40.75
1983	2.55	1.25	4.36	0.59	5.83	2.07	1.56	5.55	0.22	4.04	2.22	0.83	31.07
1984	1.07	3.11	4.92	1.41	3.04	2.79	0.43	1.47	0.09	6.50	2.97	6.09	33.89
1985	0.81	2.62	3.70	3.75	2.13	3.78	2.40	0.53	3.35	3.91	3.11	0.61	30.70
1986	T	2.49	1.08	5.30	5.52	3.92	0.41	1.63	4.60	1.81	3.25	2.44	32.45
1987	1.22	3.67	1.70	0.11	5.95	3.45	1.77	0.81	1.38	0.12	4.17	2.90	27.25
1988	0.88	1.23	2.03	2.21	2.11	3.23	2.47	0.44	4.04	1.64	2.28	2.48	25.04
1989	2.56	3.70	3.72	1.86	9.62	8.75	2.61	1.89	2.40	2.02	0.49	0.33	39.95
1990	4.54	4.72	5.89	6.90	7.16	1.89	2.60	2.37	1.12	2.81	3.81	1.46	45.27
1991	2.72	2.60	1.35	3.63	6.97	4.26	3.99	4.30	4.61	9.32	1.04	8.75	53.54
1992	3.25	2.40	3.24	2.46	6.93	5.23	2.48	2.08	3.25	3.05	3.56	4.26	42.19
1993	1.74	5.78	3.03	3.49	1.75	3.75	0.00	0.75	3.28	5.10	1.62	2.54	32.83
Record Mean	1.83	2.10	2.43	3.75	4.79	3.04	2.19	2.18	2.87	3.08	2.27	2.05	32.57

AVERAGE TEMPERATURE (deg. F)

DALLAS - FORT WORTH, TEXAS

YEAR	JAN	FEB	MAR	APR	MAY	JUNE	JULY	AUG	SEP	OCT	NOV	DEC	ANNUAL
1964	43.8	43.8	55.6	66.8	73.2	81.0	87.1	85.3	76.9	63.6	57.6	47.1	65.2
1965	47.1	45.8	47.0	68.4	72.9	79.9	86.3	84.1	79.4	66.6	62.9	52.8	66.1
1966	40.3	45.4	56.3	63.8	70.8	79.6	86.3	82.7	75.8	65.0	60.7	45.3	64.4
1967	48.3	46.8	63.3	71.1	71.4	81.4	82.9	83.1	74.1	65.4	55.6	47.0	65.9
1968	44.4	44.2	54.6	63.4	72.4	79.5	81.0	83.5	74.6	67.8	53.9	47.4	63.9
1969	49.0	50.0	49.8	65.4	71.9	79.8	87.9	84.2	77.1	65.3	55.1	49.9	65.5
1970	40.6	48.6	52.1	66.2	71.7	79.1	84.0	85.8	78.2	65.1	54.7	53.6	65.0
1971	46.7	49.2	55.6	64.0	70.5	82.9	84.4	79.5	77.1	70.1	57.0	52.2	65.8
1972	45.0	51.5	62.1	70.1	72.7	81.4	83.1	84.7	80.8	67.5	50.1	44.0	66.1
1973	42.5	47.9	60.0	60.7	71.7	79.3	83.9	82.9	76.1	68.3	59.8	48.4	65.1
1974	43.6	52.3	62.9	65.8	75.7	78.7	86.1	82.9	70.9	69.2	55.5	47.2	65.9
1975	49.0	46.6	53.8	64.7	72.4	80.9	83.6	84.8	75.6	69.8	57.3	49.0	65.6
1976	45.0	58.4	59.4	64.9	68.6	78.8	82.1	84.2	76.1	60.2	49.5	45.0	64.3
1977	34.7	49.4	57.2	66.8	77.4	84.1	87.1	84.9	81.6	66.7	56.4	47.6	66.2
1978	33.8	36.7	54.1	67.1	73.1	82.3	88.4	84.6	80.2	68.9	57.7	46.1	64.4
1979	35.4	42.2	56.7	64.4	69.7	81.0	84.5	82.5	77.0	70.8	52.9	49.4	63.9
1980	45.5	46.6	54.2	63.1	75.0	87.0	92.0	88.5	80.3	65.4	54.9	49.4	66.8
1981	44.6	48.9	55.7	69.2	70.5	80.3	85.9	83.4	76.2	66.1	57.5	47.3	65.4
1982	44.6	44.5	59.8	62.5	72.5	79.2	84.6	86.7	78.1	67.0	55.6	49.2	65.4
1983	43.4	48.5	54.5	60.6	69.5	77.3	83.6	84.9	77.1	67.8	57.3	34.8	63.3
1984	39.3	50.9	56.3	63.7	73.7	82.5	85.5	85.8	76.1	67.0	54.6	52.6	65.7
1985	37.8	45.0	60.8	67.2	74.0	80.2	84.4	87.6	77.7	67.6	56.3	42.3	65.1
1986	48.8	51.2	60.2	67.2	71.5	80.8	86.4	83.4	80.2	65.7	52.4	46.1	66.2
1987	44.5	50.8	53.9	65.0	75.1	79.6	83.4	86.5	77.1	66.5	55.7	47.3	65.5
1988	42.2	47.1	56.0	64.5	72.8	80.4	85.3	87.9	79.2	65.7	58.1	49.1	65.7
1989	50.0	42.2	56.7	66.4	74.3	77.9	82.8	82.3	74.7	69.0	58.2	39.0	64.5
1990	51.8	53.9	57.7	64.0	73.4	84.0	82.5	84.6	80.0	66.4	59.8	44.0	66.8
1991	42.8	53.7	59.8	67.4	75.4	81.0	85.0	82.5	75.2	68.1	51.7	50.3	66.1
1992	46.9	54.4	59.1	66.0	71.1	79.4	84.3	80.2	77.7	69.5	52.7	49.9	65.9
1993	45.1	49.0	56.1	63.3	71.9	81.7	87.3	87.5	78.2	63.8	51.6	49.5	65.4
Record Mean	45.1	48.8	56.9	65.2	72.7	80.9	84.6	84.7	77.8	67.6	56.0	47.5	65.6
Max	55.4	59.4	68.0	75.9	82.7	91.1	95.0	95.3	88.2	78.5	66.5	57.6	76.1
Min	34.8	38.1	45.8	54.5	62.7	70.7	74.2	74.0	67.3	56.6	45.4	37.3	55.1

REFERENCE NOTES

DALLAS - FORT WORTH, TEXAS

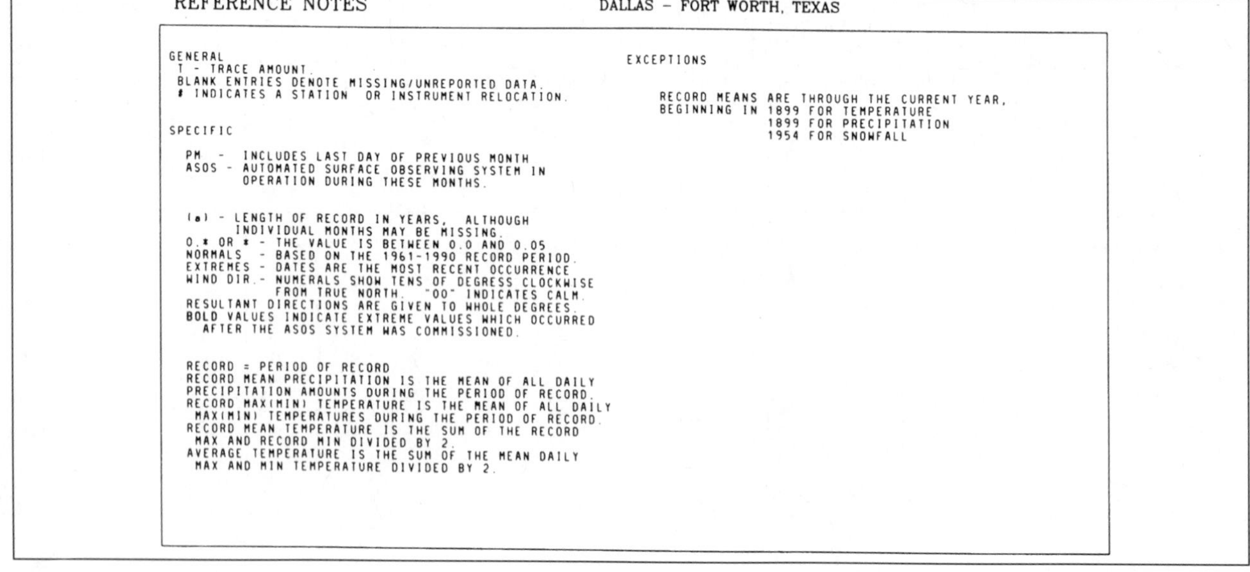

GENERAL
T - TRACE AMOUNT.
BLANK ENTRIES DENOTE MISSING/UNREPORTED DATA.
# INDICATES A STATION OR INSTRUMENT RELOCATION.

SPECIFIC

PM - INCLUDES LAST DAY OF PREVIOUS MONTH
ASOS - AUTOMATED SURFACE OBSERVING SYSTEM IN OPERATION DURING THESE MONTHS.

(a) - LENGTH OF RECORD IN YEARS, ALTHOUGH INDIVIDUAL MONTHS MAY BE MISSING.
0.* OR * - THE VALUE IS BETWEEN 0.0 AND 0.05
NORMALS - BASED ON THE 1961-1990 RECORD PERIOD.
EXTREMES - DATES ARE THE MOST RECENT OCCURRENCE
WIND DIR.- NUMERALS SHOW TENS OF DEGRESS CLOCKWISE FROM TRUE NORTH. "00" INDICATES CALM.
RESULTANT DIRECTIONS ARE GIVEN TO WHOLE DEGREES.
BOLD VALUES INDICATE EXTREME VALUES WHICH OCCURRED AFTER THE ASOS SYSTEM WAS COMMISSIONED.

RECORD = PERIOD OF RECORD
RECORD MEAN PRECIPITATION IS THE MEAN OF ALL DAILY PRECIPITATION AMOUNTS DURING THE PERIOD OF RECORD.
RECORD MAX(MIN) TEMPERATURE IS THE MEAN OF ALL DAILY MAX(MIN) TEMPERATURES DURING THE PERIOD OF RECORD.
RECORD MEAN TEMPERATURE IS THE SUM OF THE RECORD MAX AND RECORD MIN DIVIDED BY 2.
AVERAGE TEMPERATURE IS THE SUM OF THE MEAN DAILY MAX AND MIN TEMPERATURE DIVIDED BY 2.

EXCEPTIONS

RECORD MEANS ARE THROUGH THE CURRENT YEAR, BEGINNING IN 1899 FOR TEMPERATURE
1899 FOR PRECIPITATION
1954 FOR SNOWFALL

HEATING DEGREE DAYS Base 65 deg. F — DALLAS – FORT WORTH, TEXAS

SEASON	JULY	AUG	SEP	OCT	NOV	DEC	JAN	FEB	MAR	APR	MAY	JUNE	TOTAL
1964-65	0	0	6	81	260	550	550	530	551	36	0	0	2564
1965-66	0	0	2	60	103	376	760	542	274	84	26	0	2227
1966-67	0	0	0	79	182	627	514	503	146	15	21	0	2087
1967-68	0	0	13	80	282	548	631	598	330	100	2	0	2584
1968-69	0	0	0	47	348	540	492	416	468	49	6	4	2370
1969-70	0	0	0	116	306	463	756	455	404	63	21	1	2585
1970-71	0	0	7	105	316	369	564	440	307	97	19	0	2224
1971-72	0	0	12	7	270	389	615	398	143	26	1	0	1861
1972-73	0	0	3	96	446	644	690	475	155	182	12	0	2703
1973-74	0	0	1	36	182	509	656	352	173	70	1	0	1980
1974-75	0	0	20	16	296	546	489	508	355	112	0	0	2342
1975-76	0	0	4	33	266	500	616	217	222	48	20	0	1926
1976-77	0	0	0	214	459	614	931	431	241	37	0	0	2927
1977-78	0	0	0	55	257	536	962	786	346	54	41	0	3037
1978-79	0	0	0	27	247	578	911	635	261	78	29	0	2766
1979-80	0	0	0	34	370	478	597	530	339	102	6	0	2456
1980-81	0	0	18	99	330	486	625	448	284	26	23	0	2339
1981-82	0	0	10	116	228	541	625	569	232	140	9	0	2470
1982-83	0	0	1	94	316	495	663	454	324	186	21	2	2556
1983-84	0	0	12	52	269	933	789	401	281	89	11	0	2837
1984-85	0	0	38	66	322	389	837	558	171	37	0	0	2418
1985-86	0	0	19	53	285	696	495	400	164	41	5	0	2158
1986-87	0	0	0	61	376	580	632	387	342	109	0	0	2487
1987-88	0	0	0	55	297	540	703	512	301	70	0	0	2478
1988-89	0	0	0	51	240	487	460	630	294	102	4	0	2268
1989-90	0	0	14	80	251	799	401	306	251	102	19	0	2223
1990-91	0	0	0	100	190	646	681	314	198	37	7	0	2173
1991-92	0	0	12	69	405	456	555	302	182	73	14	0	2068
1992-93	0	0	0	14	366	474	612	445	290	120	4	0	2325
1993-94	0	0	2	145	414	476							

COOLING DEGREE DAYS Base 65 deg. F — DALLAS – FORT WORTH, TEXAS

YEAR	JAN	FEB	MAR	APR	MAY	JUNE	JULY	AUG	SEP	OCT	NOV	DEC	TOTAL
1969	3	3	3	67	228	453	715	602	372	133	17	0	2596
1970	5	0	7	108	236	433	595	653	409	115	12	22	2595
1971	0	6	21	71	195	546	606	456	382	171	36	1	2491
1972	2	14	57	185	249	498	569	618	480	183	4	0	2859
1973	1	0	6	60	230	435	593	559	342	146	33	0	2405
1974	0	2	115	101	341	419	660	563	202	153	20	2	2578
1975	0	0	15	107	236	483	580	620	331	189	39	9	2609
1976	0	32	59	52	138	421	537	602	338	72	0	0	2251
1977	0	0	7	94	391	581	693	626	505	112	6	2	3017
1978	0	0	16	125	301	524	733	614	462	153	37	0	2965
1979	0	1	9	67	179	489	613	551	366	220	14	0	2509
1980	0	0	11	52	320	668	844	737	485	117	35	10	3279
1981	0	5	5	158	200	467	654	577	352	155	8	0	2581
1982	1	2	77	71	252	433	614	679	403	160	40	10	2742
1983	0	0	7	61	171	382	582	626	381	145	46	0	2401
1984	0	0	20	60	288	531	644	652	376	135	16	12	2734
1985	0	5	51	108	287	460	608	706	408	139	29	0	2801
1986	0	19	24	112	212	480	673	578	464	91	3	0	2656
1987	0	0	6	114	318	442	576	674	370	111	23	0	2634
1988	4	0	28	61	247	467	639	714	433	78	39	1	2711
1989	1	0	45	154	297	393	561	542	314	208	52	0	2567
1990	1	2	30	79	286	575	551	617	457	152	41	2	2793
1991	0	3	42	115	335	484	624	550	324	174	14	5	2670
1992	0	2	4	109	213	437	606	480	386	161	4	13	2415
1993	0	0	19	75	223	507	697	701	406	115	20	4	2767

SNOWFALL (inches) — DALLAS – FORT WORTH, TEXAS

SEASON	JULY	AUG	SEP	OCT	NOV	DEC	JAN	FEB	MAR	APR	MAY	JUNE	TOTAL
1964-65	0.0	0.0	0.0	0.0	0.0	T	0.0	T	T	0.0	0.0	0.0	T
1965-66	0.0	0.0	0.0	0.0	0.0	0.0	4.4	2.9	0.0	0.0	0.0	0.0	7.3
1966-67	0.0	0.0	0.0	0.0	0.0	0.0	0.0	T	T	0.0	0.0	0.0	T
1967-68	0.0	0.0	0.0	0.0	0.0	0.0	0.4	2.6	T	0.0	0.0	0.0	3.0
1968-69	0.0	0.0	0.0	0.0	T	0.0	0.0	T	0.0	0.0	0.0	0.0	T
1969-70	0.0	0.0	0.0	0.0	0.0	T	T	0.0	0.8	0.0	0.0	0.0	0.8
1970-71	0.0	0.0	0.0	0.0	0.0	0.0	0.0	T	1.6	0.0	0.0	0.0	1.6
1971-72	0.0	0.0	0.0	0.0	T	0.0	T	T	0.0	0.0	0.0	0.0	T
1972-73	0.0	0.0	0.0	0.0	T	1.4	2.3	T	0.0	0.0	0.0	0.0	3.7
1973-74	0.0	0.0	0.0	0.0	0.0	0.0	T	0.0	0.0	0.0	0.0	0.0	T
1974-75	0.0	0.0	0.0	0.0	T	T	T	3.7	T	0.0	0.0	0.0	3.7
1975-76	0.0	0.0	0.0	0.0	0.0	0.4	0.0	0.0	T	0.0	0.0	0.0	0.4
1976-77	0.0	0.0	0.0	0.0	5.0	0.0	5.4	0.0	0.0	0.0	0.0	0.0	10.4
1977-78	0.0	0.0	0.0	0.0	0.0	0.0	4.1	13.5	T	0.0	0.0	0.0	17.6
1978-79	0.0	0.0	0.0	0.0	0.0	0.8	1.8	0.7	0.0	0.0	0.0	0.0	3.3
1979-80	0.0	0.0	0.0	0.0	0.0	T	0.0	1.6	0.0	0.0	0.0	0.0	1.6
1980-81	0.0	0.0	0.0	0.0	0.0	0.0	T	T	0.0	0.0	0.0	0.0	T
1981-82	0.0	0.0	0.0	0.0	0.0	0.0	0.8	T	0.0	0.0	0.0	0.0	0.8
1982-83	0.0	0.0	0.0	0.0	0.0	T	T	T	0.0	0.0	0.0	0.0	T
1983-84	0.0	0.0	0.0	0.0	0.0	2.0	0.0	0.0	0.0	0.0	0.0	0.0	2.0
1984-85	0.0	0.0	0.0	0.0	0.0	0.0	3.4	1.7	0.0	0.0	0.0	0.0	5.1
1985-86	0.0	0.0	0.0	0.0	0.0	T	0.0	0.8	0.0	0.0	0.0	0.0	0.8
1986-87	0.0	0.0	0.0	0.0	0.0	1.7	T	T	0.5	0.0	0.0	0.0	2.2
1987-88	0.0	0.0	0.0	0.0	0.0	T	0.8	2.7	0.0	0.0	0.0	0.0	3.5
1988-89	0.0	0.0	0.0	0.0	0.0	T	T	0.7	1.1	0.0	T	0.0	1.8
1989-90	0.0	0.0	0.0	0.0	0.0	T	0.0	0.0	0.0	T	T	0.0	T
1990-91	0.0	0.0	0.0	0.0	0.0	0.3	0.3	0.0	0.0	0.0	0.0	0.0	0.6
1991-92	0.0	0.0	0.0	0.0	0.0	0.0	T	0.0	0.0	0.0	0.0	0.0	T
1992-93	0.0	0.0	0.0	0.0	0.0	T	0.0	0.0	0.0	0.0	0.0	0.0	T
1993-94	0.0	0.0	0.0	T	0.3	T							
Record Mean	0.0	0.0	0.0	T	0.1	0.2	1.2	1.0	0.2	T	T	0.0	2.8

EL PASO, TEXAS

The city of El Paso is located in the extreme west point of Texas at an elevation of about 3,700 feet . The National Weather Service station is located on a mesa about 200 feet higher than the city. The climate of the region is characterized by an abundance of sunshine throughout the year, high daytime summer temperatures, very low humidity, scanty rainfall, and a relatively mild winter season. The Franklin Mountains begin within the city limits and extend northward for about 16 miles. Peaks of these mountains range from 4,687 to 7,152 feet above sea level.

Rainfall throughout the year is light, insufficient for any growth except desert vegetation. Irrigation is necessary for crops, gardens, and lawns. Dry periods lasting several months are not unusual. Almost half of the precipitation occurs in the three-month period, July through September, from brief but often heavy thunderstorms. Small amounts of snow fall nearly every winter, but snow cover rarely amounts to more than an inch and seldom remains on the ground for more than a few hours.

Daytime summer temperatures are high, frequently above 90 degrees and occasionally above 100 degrees. Summer nights are usually comfortable, with temperatures in the 60s. It should be noted that when temperatures are high the relative humidity is generally quite low. A 20-year tabulation of observations with temperatures above 90 degrees shows that in April, May, and June the humidity averaged from 10 to 14 percent, while in July, August, and September it averaged 22 to 24 percent. This low humidity aids the efficiency of evaporative air coolers, which are widely used in homes and public buildings and are quite effective in cooling the air to comfortable temperatures.

Winter daytime temperatures are mild. At night they drop below freezing about half the time in December and January. The flat, irrigated land of the Rio Grande Valley in the vicinity of El Paso is noticeably cooler, particularly at night, than the airport or the city proper, both in summer and winter. This results in more comfortable temperatures in summer but increases the severity of freezes in winter. The cooler air in the Valley also causes marked short-period fluctuations of temperature and dewpoint at the airport with changes in wind direction, especially during the early morning hours.

Dust and sandstorms are the most unpleasant features of the weather in El Paso. While wind velocities are not excessively high, the soil surface is dry and loose and natural vegetation is sparse, so moderately strong winds raise considerable dust and sand. A tabulation of duststorms for a period of 20 years shows that they are most frequent in March and April, and comparatively rare in the period July through December. prevailing winds are from the north in winter and the south in summer.

NORMALS, MEANS, AND EXTREMES

EL PASO, TEXAS

LATITUDE: 31 °48'N LONGITUDE: 106 °24' W ELEVATION: FT. GRND 3918 BARO 3932 TIME ZONE: MOUNTAIN WBAN: 23044

	(a)	JAN	FEB	MAR	APR	MAY	JUNE	JULY	AUG	SEP	OCT	NOV	DEC	YEAR
TEMPERATURE °F:														
Normals														
-Daily Maximum		56.1	62.2	69.9	78.7	87.1	96.5	96.1	93.5	87.1	78.4	66.4	57.5	77.5
-Daily Minimum		29.4	33.9	40.2	48.0	56.5	64.3	68.4	66.6	61.6	49.6	38.4	30.7	49.0
-Monthly		42.8	48.1	55.1	63.4	71.8	80.4	82.3	80.1	74.4	64.0	52.4	44.1	63.2
Extremes														
-Record Highest	54	80	83	89	98	104	111	112	108	104	96	87	80	112
-Year		1970	1986	1989	1989	1951	1978	1979	1980	1982	1979	1983	1973	JUL 1979
-Record Lowest	54	-8	8	14	23	31	46	57	56	41	25	1	5	-8
-Year		1962	1985	1971	1983	1967	1988	1988	1973	1945	1970	1976	1953	JAN 1962
NORMAL DEGREE DAYS:														
Heating (base 65°F)		688	473	316	110	7	0	0	0	0	88	378	648	2708
Cooling (base 65°F)		0	0	10	62	217	462	536	468	282	57	0	0	2094
% OF POSSIBLE SUNSHINE	51	77	82	86	88	89	90	81	81	82	84	83	77	83
MEAN SKY COVER (tenths)														
Sunrise - Sunset	51	4.6	4.3	4.2	3.6	3.2	2.8	4.5	4.3	3.4	3.2	3.5	4.3	3.8
MEAN NUMBER OF DAYS:														
Sunrise to Sunset														
-Clear	51	13.9	13.6	15.3	16.6	18.7	19.8	12.2	13.8	17.7	19.0	17.5	15.1	193.2
-Partly Cloudy	51	7.4	7.4	8.2	8.1	8.1	7.5	13.4	12.1	7.2	6.8	6.2	7.3	99.5
-Cloudy	51	9.7	7.3	7.5	5.3	4.3	2.7	5.5	5.1	5.1	5.3	6.2	8.7	72.5
Precipitation														
.01 inches or more	54	4.2	3.0	2.4	1.7	2.5	3.3	8.0	8.1	5.5	4.1	2.8	3.9	49.4
Snow,Ice pellets,hail														
1.0 inches or more	54	0.5	0.3	0.*	0.1	0.0	0.0	0.0	0.0	0.0	0.*	0.3	0.5	1.8
Thunderstorms	54	0.2	0.4	0.5	1.0	2.9	4.5	10.4	10.2	4.1	1.8	0.3	0.2	36.5
Heavy Fog Visibility														
1/4 mile or less	54	0.7	0.2	0.1	0.*	0.*	0.0	0.0	0.0	0.1	0.1	0.3	0.6	2.1
Temperature °F														
-Maximum														
90° and above	33	0.0	0.0	0.0	2.0	12.7	25.9	26.8	23.6	11.9	1.8	0.0	0.0	104.9
32° and below	33	0.3	0.1	0.0	0.0	0.0	0.0	0.0	0.0	0.0	0.0	0.1	0.2	0.6
-Minimum														
32° and below	33	18.9	11.8	4.9	0.8	0.*	0.0	0.0	0.0	0.0	0.4	8.1	18.2	63.2
0° and below	33	0.1	0.0	0.0	0.0	0.0	0.0	0.0	0.0	0.0	0.0	0.0	0.0	0.1
AVG. STATION PRESS.(mb)	21	883.8	882.7	880.1	879.9	879.4	880.2	882.3	882.9	882.8	883.4	883.3	884.0	882.1
RELATIVE HUMIDITY (%)														
Hour 05	33	66	57	47	40	42	46	63	67	68	64	62	66	57
Hour 11 (Local Time)	33	45	37	29	23	23	25	38	42	43	38	38	45	36
Hour 17	33	35	27	21	16	17	18	30	33	34	30	32	38	28
Hour 23	33	56	45	35	28	29	32	47	53	55	52	52	57	45
PRECIPITATION (inches):														
Water Equivalent														
-Normal		0.40	0.41	0.29	0.20	0.25	0.67	1.54	1.58	1.70	0.76	0.44	0.57	8.81
-Maximum Monthly	54	1.84	1.69	2.26	1.42	4.22	3.18	5.53	5.57	6.68	4.31	1.63	3.29	6.68
-Year		1949	1973	1958	1983	1992	1984	1968	1984	1974	1945	1961	1991	SEP 1974
-Minimum Monthly	54	0.00	0.00	T	0.00	0.00	T	0.04	T	T	0.00	0.00	0.00	0.00
-Year		1967	1943	1982	1978	1962	1990	1978	1962	1959	1952	1964	1955	APR 1978
-Maximum in 24 hrs	54	0.61	0.87	1.72	1.08	2.40	1.56	2.63	2.30	2.52	1.77	1.19	1.76	2.63
-Year		1960	1956	1941	1966	1992	1986	1968	1984	1958	1945	1943	1987	JUL 1968
Snow,Ice pellets,hail														
-Maximum Monthly	54	8.3	8.9	7.3	16.5	T	T	T	0.0	T	1.0	12.7	25.9	25.9
-Year		1949	1956	1958	1983	1992	1992	1990		1993	1980	1976	1987	DEC 1987
-Maximum in 24 hrs	54	5.2	7.2	7.3	8.8	T	T	T	0.0	T	1.0	7.8	16.8	16.8
-Year		1992	1956	1958	1983	1992	1992	1990		1993	1980	1961	1987	DEC 1987
WIND:														
Mean Speed (mph)	51	8.3	9.1	11.0	11.0	10.3	9.3	8.3	7.7	7.6	7.5	8.0	7.9	8.8
Prevailing Direction through 1963		N	N	WSW	WSW	WSW	S	SSE	S	S	N	N	N	N
Fastest Obs. 1 Min.														
-Direction (!!)	18	28	26	30	30	13	22	13	13	11	25	24	24	26
-Speed (MPH)	18	40	48	48	42	35	40	37	35	29	35	40	42	48
-Year		1976	1977	1977	1975	1987	1976	1988	1979	1993	1991	1975	1975	FEB 1977
Peak Gust														
-Direction (!!)	10	W	W	SW	W	SW	N	S	SE	SE	W	W	W	W
-Speed (mph)	10	47	60	59	55	48	48	55	48	48	52	49	54	60
-Date		1988	1987	1991	1984	1985	1985	1989	1991	1993	1993	1988	1993	FEB 1987

PRECIPITATION (inches)

EL PASO, TEXAS

YEAR	JAN	FEB	MAR	APR	MAY	JUNE	JULY	AUG	SEP	OCT	NOV	DEC	ANNUAL
1964	T	T	0.99	0.08	0.02	T	0.18	0.76	2.40	0.40	0.00	0.52	5.35
1965	0.19	0.59	0.03	0.01	0.11	0.66	0.17	0.49	2.12	0.18	0.12	0.74	5.41
1966	0.38	0.20	T	1.08	0.04	2.67	1.17	1.85	1.79	0.01	0.01	0.04	9.24
1967	0.00	0.04	0.17	0.03	0.05	1.41	0.84	0.54	1.54	0.09	0.23	0.78	5.72
1968	0.47	1.11	0.85	0.10	T	0.03	5.53	1.71	0.53	0.11	1.35	0.23	12.02
1969	0.05	0.08	0.17	T	0.28	T	1.14	0.28	0.43	0.59	0.63	0.69	4.34
1970	0.03	0.55	0.47	T	0.71	0.73	1.41	0.41	1.01	0.68	T	0.06	6.06
1971	0.17	0.04	0.00	0.42	T	0.01	2.34	1.59	0.96	1.07	0.14	0.50	7.24
1972	0.44	T	T	0.00	0.04	1.62	0.71	2.59	1.60	1.25	0.33	0.42	9.00
1973	1.23	1.69	0.60	0.00	0.29	0.71	2.12	0.73	0.01	0.07	0.08	T	7.53
1974	0.27	T	0.36	0.12	0.05	0.36	2.21	0.63	6.68	1.90	0.50	0.87	13.95
1975	0.70	0.59	0.19	T	0.03	T	1.11	0.45	2.18	0.25	T	0.71	6.21
1976	0.26	0.52	T	0.30	0.74	0.50	3.17	0.23	1.70	1.20	1.20	0.32	10.14
1977	0.57	T	0.17	0.09	0.06	0.04	1.09	1.36	0.16	1.65	0.05	0.26	5.50
1978	0.44	0.47	0.07	0.00	0.57	1.46	0.04	2.18	4.14	2.28	0.45	0.47	12.57
1979	0.77	0.68	T	0.28	0.24	0.03	0.98	2.16	0.41	T	0.04	0.25	5.84
1980	0.54	0.73	0.25	0.31	0.08	T	0.21	1.76	1.90	0.95	0.54	0.04	7.31
1981	1.10	0.36	0.39	0.65	0.72	0.64	2.08	5.26	0.52	0.53	0.30	0.08	12.63
1982	0.34	0.55	T	0.05	0.19	0.18	1.00	0.48	5.28	T	0.29	2.61	10.97
1983	0.35	0.60	0.45	1.42	0.05	0.23	0.43	0.97	1.51	1.48	0.34	0.16	7.99
1984	0.31	0.00	0.44	0.01	0.59	3.18	0.69	5.57	0.58	3.12	0.51	1.17	16.17
1985	0.95	0.19	0.59	0.07	0.01	0.10	1.32	1.46	1.47	1.82	0.13	0.05	8.16
1986	0.01	0.39	0.39	T	0.83	3.05	2.66	0.70	0.85	0.45	1.42	1.42	12.17
1987	0.29	0.30	0.49	0.32	0.24	2.24	0.64	2.22	0.89	0.15	0.29	2.87	10.94
1988	0.25	0.70	0.10	0.23	0.15	0.03	3.35	3.46	1.52	0.59	0.24	0.44	11.06
1989	0.11	0.72	0.62	T	0.65	T	1.23	3.06	0.48	0.23	T	0.16	7.26
1990	0.29	0.14	0.41	0.25	0.10	T	3.96	1.98	3.46	0.58	1.34	0.34	12.85
1991	0.82	0.66	0.10	T	0.23	0.01	2.69	2.06	1.82	0.20	0.50	3.29	12.38
1992	1.14	0.16	0.50	0.30	4.22	0.27	0.65	2.11	0.15	0.27	0.28	1.35	11.40
1993	1.34	0.32	0.01	0.12	T	1.47	0.95	2.73	1.32	0.17	0.49	0.71	9.63
Record Mean	0.45	0.41	0.33	0.25	0.37	0.63	1.67	1.54	1.31	0.80	0.44	0.56	8.75

AVERAGE TEMPERATURE (deg. F)

EL PASO, TEXAS

YEAR	JAN	FEB	MAR	APR	MAY	JUNE	JULY	AUG	SEP	OCT	NOV	DEC	ANNUAL
1964	39.3	40.8	53.6	63.2	73.9	81.5	84.5	82.6	75.2	63.4	51.8	44.0	62.8
1965	48.0	46.7	52.1	65.3	71.8	78.2	84.2	81.1	74.0	63.0	56.8	45.7	63.9
1966	40.1	42.9	56.4	65.1	74.5	79.5	83.6	78.7	73.4	62.1	54.5	42.4	62.8
1967	41.6	48.0	59.6	65.1	70.9	79.1	83.0	78.6	73.3	63.7	53.1	41.5	63.1
1968	42.4	50.4	53.0	61.4	73.0	81.0	79.1	76.5	72.4	65.0	51.0	41.3	62.2
1969	48.6	48.4	49.4	65.8	72.1	81.5	84.9	85.7	77.1	67.7	52.5	48.6	65.2
1970	46.9	52.3	55.6	63.5	72.2	79.7	82.8	81.4	74.2	59.5	51.9	48.0	64.0
1971	44.6	48.4	58.1	62.6	72.1	81.1	82.3	77.0	73.5	62.5	52.1	44.7	63.2
1972	45.2	52.3	61.2	65.2	69.8	78.3	82.2	77.7	72.9	65.7	48.8	46.6	63.8
1973	42.9	47.0	52.4	57.7	68.7	76.6	79.7	79.2	75.9	63.3	53.8	45.7	61.9
1974	44.3	44.8	59.6	65.0	75.6	82.8	79.6	77.0	69.4	63.0	49.9	41.3	62.7
1975	43.1	48.9	55.1	59.7	69.8	80.9	79.8	80.9	72.2	64.0	51.5	44.2	62.5
1976	42.3	52.6	55.9	64.1	69.5	79.4	78.2	78.7	70.5	58.5	44.8	41.9	61.4
1977	44.7	47.3	49.7	61.5	70.7	81.5	82.2	82.5	77.4	64.3	53.7	49.6	63.8
#1978	45.4	48.8	58.6	66.1	73.6	83.4	84.5	80.0	72.3	63.6	55.8	44.6	64.7
1979	41.0	47.1	53.1	63.6	70.1	78.4	85.1	78.8	74.2	66.2	47.9	43.1	62.4
1980	46.8	50.6	54.1	60.6	70.5	86.3	87.2	82.4	75.6	60.3	49.2	48.5	64.3
1981	45.2	50.3	57.2	64.8	73.6	82.6	83.6	79.5	75.9	64.6	54.3	48.7	65.1
1982	42.3	48.7	57.7	64.4	69.6	80.9	84.2	83.5	77.1	64.6	53.2	43.3	64.1
1983	41.6	49.5	54.6	56.3	68.9	77.3	82.9	81.8	78.7	66.6	54.3	45.5	63.2
1984	44.4	47.0	55.7	62.0	75.0	79.5	81.1	80.4	72.9	61.4	51.6	45.7	63.1
1985	40.0	45.6	55.2	64.2	72.1	79.0	79.4	80.6	72.8	61.4	52.9	43.1	62.2
1986	44.7	52.1	55.7	67.3	71.5	77.7	80.0	80.4	74.1	62.4	49.4	42.6	63.2
1987	41.3	46.2	51.2	59.7	68.6	78.1	81.6	79.1	72.1	67.0	51.4	40.5	61.4
1988	42.6	48.4	53.4	61.1	70.3	79.0	80.3	77.6	72.4	66.7	54.0	42.6	62.4
1989	43.6	51.4	58.7	67.4	74.2	81.3	81.8	79.1	73.4	63.2	53.3	41.9	64.1
1990	44.1	49.1	56.1	66.4	73.1	87.1	80.2	76.8	73.9	63.4	52.9	44.8	64.0
1991	44.3	51.1	53.9	64.0	72.6	79.0	78.6	79.5	70.7	65.4	50.3	46.3	63.0
1992	44.0	50.2	58.1	67.9	70.6	81.5	85.1	81.3	77.8	66.5	48.0	44.7	64.6
1993	48.5	51.4	57.9	66.7	74.6	82.7	85.2	82.5	75.8	64.4	52.3	46.9	65.7
Record Mean	44.5	49.3	55.6	63.8	72.1	80.8	82.0	80.3	74.8	64.5	52.3	45.0	63.7
Max	57.2	62.6	69.3	77.8	86.1	94.7	94.1	92.1	87.0	77.9	65.7	57.5	76.8
Min	31.9	35.9	41.8	49.7	58.1	66.8	69.8	68.4	62.5	51.1	38.9	32.6	50.6

REFERENCE NOTES

EL PASO, TEXAS

GENERAL
T - TRACE AMOUNT.
BLANK ENTRIES DENOTE MISSING/UNREPORTED DATA.
# INDICATES A STATION OR INSTRUMENT RELOCATION.

SPECIFIC

PM - INCLUDES LAST DAY OF PREVIOUS MONTH
ASOS - AUTOMATED SURFACE OBSERVING SYSTEM IN OPERATION DURING THESE MONTHS.

(a) - LENGTH OF RECORD IN YEARS, ALTHOUGH INDIVIDUAL MONTHS MAY BE MISSING.
0.* OR * - THE VALUE IS BETWEEN 0.0 AND 0.05
NORMALS - BASED ON THE 1961-1990 RECORD PERIOD.
EXTREMES - DATES ARE THE MOST RECENT OCCURRENCE
WIND DIR.- NUMERALS SHOW TENS OF DEGRESS CLOCKWISE FROM TRUE NORTH. "00" INDICATES CALM.
RESULTANT DIRECTIONS ARE GIVEN TO WHOLE DEGREES.
BOLD VALUES INDICATE EXTREME VALUES WHICH OCCURRED AFTER THE ASOS SYSTEM WAS COMMISSIONED.

RECORD = PERIOD OF RECORD
RECORD MEAN PRECIPITATION IS THE MEAN OF ALL DAILY PRECIPITATION AMOUNTS DURING THE PERIOD OF RECORD.
RECORD MAX(MIN) TEMPERATURE IS THE MEAN OF ALL DAILY MAX(MIN) TEMPERATURES DURING THE PERIOD OF RECORD.
RECORD MEAN TEMPERATURE IS THE SUM OF THE RECORD MAX AND RECORD MIN DIVIDED BY 2.
AVERAGE TEMPERATURE IS THE SUM OF THE MEAN DAILY MAX AND MIN TEMPERATURE DIVIDED BY 2.

EXCEPTIONS

RECORD MEANS ARE THROUGH THE CURRENT YEAR,
BEGINNING IN 1887 FOR TEMPERATURE
1879 FOR PRECIPITATION
1940 FOR SNOWFALL

HEATING DEGREE DAYS Base 65 deg. F — EL PASO, TEXAS

SEASON	JULY	AUG	SEP	OCT	NOV	DEC	JAN	FEB	MAR	APR	MAY	JUNE	TOTAL
1964-65	0	0	0	76	391	643	521	504	397	54	7	2	2595
1965-66	0	0	4	107	240	592	769	612	264	59	4	0	2651
1966-67	0	0	2	126	307	695	718	469	173	56	25	0	2571
1967-68	0	0	2	106	352	720	691	415	377	128	0	0	2791
1968-69	0	0	0	61	414	728	503	464	477	43	24	0	2714
1969-70	0	0	0	62	371	504	556	348	286	94	33	0	2254
1970-71	0	0	39	180	388	519	625	457	254	110	6	0	2578
1971-72	0	0	31	112	381	624	607	364	126	56	3	0	2304
1972-73	0	0	3	87	480	563	679	499	384	218	31	0	2944
1973-74	0	0	7	90	336	592	636	558	178	79	5	0	2481
1974-75	0	0	41	107	445	728	672	445	309	188	13	0	2948
1975-76	0	0	20	66	399	640	696	351	278	91	26	0	2567
1976-77	0	0	7	214	601	709	623	492	469	138	3	0	3256
1977-78	0	0	0	56	328	472	603	449	200	57	22	0	2187
#1978-79	0	0	16	106	272	625	735	494	362	118	26	1	2755
1979-80	0	0	24	56	505	670	555	410	331	157	19	0	2727
1980-81	0	0	2	203	467	503	607	405	233	82	2	0	2504
1981-82	0	0	0	93	313	499	697	449	237	82	17	0	2387
1982-83	0	0	0	88	344	668	720	430	316	284	23	0	2873
1983-84	0	0	0	52	317	599	633	514	285	126	8	0	2534
1984-85	0	0	18	144	404	592	768	537	302	71	5	0	2841
1985-86	0	0	10	125	358	670	621	356	283	47	22	0	2492
1986-87	0	0	1	116	460	687	725	521	420	173	5	0	3108
1987-88	0	0	0	13	405	750	686	474	360	121	16	0	2825
1988-89	0	2	2	17	337	684	661	377	208	52	9	0	2349
1989-90	0	0	2	108	344	708	640	439	271	45	20	0	2577
1990-91	0	2	8	88	354	617	636	383	336	78	3	0	2505
1991-92	0	0	26	66	434	576	644	423	209	49	3	0	2430
1992-93	0	0	0	21	502	624	504	373	222	53	4	0	2303
1993-94	0	0	0	145	375	551							

COOLING DEGREE DAYS Base 65 deg. F — EL PASO, TEXAS

YEAR	JAN	FEB	MAR	APR	MAY	JUNE	JULY	AUG	SEP	OCT	NOV	DEC	TOTAL
1969	0	0	1	71	250	501	627	647	372	155	2	0	2626
1970	0	0	2	57	263	448	559	514	321	19	0	0	2183
1971	0	0	45	45	235	492	543	375	293	43	0	0	2071
1972	0	4	15	70	159	404	543	401	247	120	0	0	1963
1973	0	0	0	7	152	355	459	448	340	44	7	0	1812
1974	0	0	19	84	338	540	459	378	181	54	0	0	2053
1975	0	0	9	35	170	482	469	502	241	41	1	0	1950
1976	0	0	4	71	170	441	418	434	179	18	0	0	1735
1977	0	0	0	39	186	500	540	552	380	43	0	0	2240
#1978	0	0	8	98	295	559	612	474	238	70	2	0	2356
1979	0	0	0	84	190	414	630	432	308	99	0	0	2157
1980	0	0	0	34	198	646	693	546	329	63	0	0	2509
1981	0	2	2	84	275	534	586	455	333	89	0	2	2362
1982	0	0	14	70	167	484	602	583	371	82	0	0	2373
1983	0	0	0	32	151	374	564	527	417	108	6	0	2179
1984	0	0	2	44	324	441	507	482	260	38	8	0	2106
1985	0	0	9	55	233	428	457	488	252	18	0	0	1940
1986	0	3	0	122	228	391	474	485	281	41	0	0	2025
1987	0	0	0	22	121	399	521	446	222	83	2	0	1816
1988	0	0	9	15	186	429	478	399	226	76	16	0	1834
1989	0	2	20	130	300	494	530	442	261	60	0	0	2239
1990	0	1	0	96	278	667	480	374	282	43	0	0	2221
1991	0	0	0	55	245	424	428	455	204	88	0	0	1899
1992	0	0	3	144	182	500	628	511	389	75	0	0	2432
1993	0	0	11	110	306	538	632	550	331	132	2	0	2612

SNOWFALL (inches) — EL PASO, TEXAS

SEASON	JULY	AUG	SEP	OCT	NOV	DEC	JAN	FEB	MAR	APR	MAY	JUNE	TOTAL
1964-65	0.0	0.0	0.0	0.0	0.0	T	0.0	0.3	T	0.0	0.0	0.0	0.3
1965-66	0.0	0.0	0.0	0.0	0.0	T	0.4	T	T	0.0	0.0	0.0	0.4
1966-67	0.0	0.0	0.0	0.0	0.0	T	0.0	T	0.0	T	0.0	0.0	T
1967-68	0.0	0.0	0.0	0.0	0.0	5.6	2.1	2.3	0.8	0.0	0.0	0.0	10.8
1968-69	0.0	0.0	0.0	0.0	7.0	T	0.0	0.0	T	0.0	0.0	0.0	7.0
1969-70	0.0	0.0	0.0	0.0	6.0	1.9	0.3	1.7	T	0.0	0.0	0.0	9.9
1970-71	0.0	0.0	0.0	0.0	0.0	0.0	3.8	T	0.0	T	0.0	0.0	3.8
1971-72	0.0	0.0	0.0	0.0	0.0	1.0	2.5	0.0	0.0	0.0	0.0	0.0	3.5
1972-73	0.0	0.0	0.0	0.0	0.0	T	5.3	4.6	T	0.0	0.0	0.0	9.9
1973-74	0.0	0.0	0.0	0.0	T	0.0	T	T	0.0	0.0	0.0	0.0	T
1974-75	0.0	0.0	0.0	0.0	0.0	5.3	2.2	0.2	2.0	0.0	0.0	0.0	9.7
1975-76	0.0	0.0	0.0	0.0	0.0	T	1.0	0.0	T	T	0.0	0.0	1.0
1976-77	0.0	0.0	0.0	T	12.7	2.0	T	T	0.0	T	0.0	0.0	14.7
1977-78	0.0	0.0	0.0	0.0	0.0	0.0	T	0.0	0.0	0.0	0.0	0.0	T
1978-79	0.0	0.0	0.0	0.0	T	T	T	1.2	0.0	0.0	0.0	0.0	1.2
1979-80	0.0	0.0	0.0	0.0	0.0	0.0	T	3.6	0.0	2.0	0.0	0.0	5.6
1980-81	0.0	0.0	0.0	1.0	4.0	0.0	4.8	0.0	0.0	0.0	0.0	0.0	9.8
1981-82	0.0	0.0	0.0	0.0	0.0	0.0	T	T	0.0	0.0	0.0	0.0	T
1982-83	0.0	0.0	0.0	0.0	0.3	18.2	T	0.0	T	16.5	0.0	0.0	35.0
1983-84	0.0	0.0	0.0	0.0	T	T	T	0.0	6.1	0.0	0.0	0.0	6.1
1984-85	0.0	0.0	0.0	0.0	T	2.9	5.4	1.1	0.0	0.0	0.0	0.0	9.4
1985-86	0.0	0.0	0.0	0.0	0.0	0.9	T	0.9	T	0.0	0.0	0.0	1.8
1986-87	0.0	0.0	0.0	0.0	0.0	0.6	3.4	2.8	0.6	0.0	0.0	0.0	7.4
1987-88	0.0	0.0	0.0	0.0	0.0	25.9	T	6.6	0.0	0.0	0.0	0.0	32.5
1988-89	0.0	0.0	0.0	0.0	T	0.3	0.0	0.0	T	0.0	T	0.0	0.3
1989-90	0.0	0.0	0.0	0.0	0.0	T	T	T	0.0	T	T	0.0	T
1990-91	T	0.0	0.0	0.0	4.3	T	1.5	T	T	0.0	T	0.0	5.8
1991-92	0.0	0.0	0.0	0.0	0.0	0.5	6.9	0.0	T	0.0	T	T	7.4
1992-93	0.0	0.0	0.0	0.0	0.0	1.6	0.0	0.0	0.0	0.0	0.0	0.0	1.6
1993-94	0.0	0.0	T	0.8	0.0	1.6							
Record Mean	T	0.0	T	T	0.9	1.7	1.4	0.8	0.4	0.3	T	T	5.6

HOUSTON, TEXAS

Houston, the largest city in Texas, is located in the flat Coastal Plains, about 50 miles from the Gulf of Mexico and about 25 miles from Galveston Bay. The climate is predominantly marine. The terrain includes numerous small streams and bayous which, together with the nearness to Galveston Bay, favor the development of both ground and advective fogs. Prevailing winds are from the southeast and south, except in January, when frequent passages of high pressure areas bring invasions of polar air and prevailing northerly winds.

Temperatures are moderated by the influence of winds from the Gulf, which result in mild winters. Another effect of the nearness of the Gulf is abundant rainfall, except for rare extended dry periods. Polar air penetrates the area frequently enough to provide variability in the weather.

Records of sky cover for daylight hours indicate about one-fourth of the days per year as clear, with a high number of clear days in October and November. Cloudy days are relatively frequent from December to May and partly cloudy days are the more frequent for June through September. Sunshine averages nearly 60 percent of the possible amount for the year ranging from 42 percent in January to 67 percent in June.

Heavy fog occurs on an average of 16 days a year and light fog occurs about 62 days a year in the city. The frequency of heavy fog is considerably higher at William P. Hobby Airport and at Intercontinental Airport.

Destructive windstorms are fairly infrequent, but both thundersqualls and tropical storms occasionally pass through the area.

NORMALS, MEANS, AND EXTREMES

HOUSTON, TEXAS

LATITUDE: 29°58'N LONGITUDE: 95°21' W ELEVATION: FT. GRND 96 BARO 122 TIME ZONE: CENTRAL WBAN: 12960

	(a)	JAN	FEB	MAR	APR	MAY	JUNE	JULY	AUG	SEP	OCT	NOV	DEC	YEAR
TEMPERATURE °F:														
Normals														
-Daily Maximum		61.0	65.3	71.1	78.4	84.6	90.1	92.7	92.5	88.4	81.6	72.4	64.7	78.6
-Daily Minimum		39.7	42.6	50.0	58.1	64.4	70.6	72.4	72.0	67.9	57.6	49.6	42.2	57.3
-Monthly		50.4	53.9	60.6	68.3	74.5	80.4	82.6	82.3	78.2	69.6	61.0	53.5	67.9
Extremes														
-Record Highest	24	84	91	91	95	97	103	104	107	102	96	89	83	107
-Year		1975	1986	1989	1987	1990	1980	1980	1980	1985	1991	1989	1978	AUG 1980
-Record Lowest	24	12	20	22	31	44	52	62	60	48	29	19	7	7
-Year		1982	1985	1980	1987	1978	1970	1990	1992	1975	1993	1976	1989	DEC 1989
NORMAL DEGREE DAYS:														
Heating (base 65°F)		468	322	187	36	0	0	0	0	0	31	181	374	1599
Cooling (base 65°F)		16	11	50	135	295	462	546	536	396	174	61	18	2700
% OF POSSIBLE SUNSHINE	24	43	49	52	56	60	66	68	67	65	63	51	50	58
MEAN SKY COVER (tenths)														
Sunrise - Sunset	24	7.0	6.5	6.6	6.6	6.4	5.8	5.7	5.6	5.6	5.2	5.9	6.8	6.1
MEAN NUMBER OF DAYS:														
Sunrise to Sunset														
-Clear	24	7.2	7.3	7.1	7.2	6.1	7.3	7.0	6.1	8.3	11.0	9.1	7.5	91.0
-Partly Cloudy	24	5.3	5.6	6.5	7.1	10.7	13.3	15.7	17.0	11.6	9.1	7.1	5.3	114.5
-Cloudy	24	18.5	15.4	17.4	15.7	14.2	9.4	8.3	7.8	10.1	10.9	13.8	18.2	159.7
Precipitation														
.01 inches or more	24	10.7	8.5	9.2	7.3	8.5	9.3	9.4	8.8	9.3	7.4	8.5	9.2	105.8
Snow,Ice pellets,hail														
1.0 inches or more	24	0.1	0.1	0.0	0.0	0.0	0.0	0.0	0.0	0.0	0.0	0.0	0.*	0.3
Thunderstorms	24	2.2	2.0	3.8	3.9	7.2	8.1	10.6	10.2	7.5	3.9	2.8	1.8	63.9
Heavy Fog Visibility														
1/4 mile or less	24	5.0	3.6	3.0	2.8	1.7	0.6	0.2	0.4	1.3	2.9	3.6	4.3	29.5
Temperature °F														
-Maximum														
90° and above	24	0.0	0.*	0.1	0.8	5.1	19.8	26.6	25.6	15.0	2.9	0.0	0.0	96.0
32° and below	24	0.2	0.2	0.0	0.0	0.0	0.0	0.0	0.0	0.0	0.0	0.0	0.3	0.7
-Minimum														
32° and below	24	7.2	4.3	1.3	0.1	0.0	0.0	0.0	0.0	0.0	0.1	1.7	5.1	19.7
0° and below	24	0.0	0.0	0.0	0.0	0.0	0.0	0.0	0.0	0.0	0.0	0.0	0.0	0.0
AVG. STATION PRESS.(mb)	21	1017.1	1015.7	1012.1	1011.1	1009.7	1010.4	1012.3	1011.9	1011.7	1014.0	1015.0	1016.6	1013.1
RELATIVE HUMIDITY (%)														
Hour 00	24	82	83	83	85	87	87	86	87	89	88	85	84	86
Hour 06 (Local Time)	24	86	86	87	89	92	92	93	93	93	91	89	87	90
Hour 12	24	64	61	59	58	60	60	57	57	60	56	60	62	60
Hour 18	24	67	61	60	61	63	63	62	62	66	68	71	71	65
PRECIPITATION (inches):														
Water Equivalent														
-Normal		3.29	2.96	2.92	3.21	5.24	4.96	3.60	3.49	4.89	4.27	3.79	3.45	46.07
-Maximum Monthly	24	9.78	5.99	8.52	10.92	14.39	16.28	8.10	9.42	11.35	16.05	8.91	9.34	16.28
-Year		1991	1992	1972	1976	1970	1989	1979	1983	1976	1984	1982	1991	JUN 1989
-Minimum Monthly	24	0.36	0.38	0.88	0.43	0.79	0.26	0.47	0.31	0.80	0.05	0.41	0.64	0.05
-Year		1971	1976	1987	1983	1977	1970	1993	1990	1975	1978	1988	1973	OCT 1978
-Maximum in 24 hrs	24	2.66	2.22	7.47	8.16	10.36	10.35	3.99	6.83	7.98	9.31	4.19	4.04	10.36
-Year		1992	1985	1972	1976	1989	1989	1973	1981	1976	1984	1986	1991	MAY 1989
Snow,Ice pellets,hail														
-Maximum Monthly	24	2.0	2.8	T	T	T	T	0.0	0.0	0.0	0.0	T	1.7	2.8
-Year		1973	1973	1992	1993	1993	1990					1979	1989	FEB 1973
-Maximum in 24 hrs	24	2.0	1.4	T	T	T	T	0.0	0.0	0.0	0.0	T	1.7	2.0
-Year		1973	1980	1992	1993	1993	1990					1979	1989	JAN 1973
WIND:														
Mean Speed (mph)	24	8.2	8.8	9.3	9.2	8.2	7.8	7.0	6.3	6.9	7.0	8.0	8.0	7.9
Prevailing Direction through 1963		NNW	SSE	SSE	SSE	SSE	SSE	S	SSE	SSE	ESE	SSE	SSE	SSE
Fastest Obs. 1 Min.														
-Direction (!!)	24	33	26	22	14	23	30	10	08	05	27	33	31	08
-Speed (MPH)	24	32	46	35	45	46	45	46	51	37	41	37	35	51
-Year		1993	1984	1989	1978	1983	1973	1969	1983	1982	1988	1972	1973	AUG 1983
Peak Gust														
-Direction (!!)	10	W	W	W	W	W	NE	SE	E	E	W	NW	NW	E
-Speed (mph)	10	44	61	51	56	52	68	52	78	44	58	45	56	78
-Date		1992	1984	1990	1990	1993	1990	1990	1983	1990	1988	1988	1990	AUG 1983

PRECIPITATION (inches)

HOUSTON, TEXAS

YEAR	JAN	FEB	MAR	APR	MAY	JUNE	JULY	AUG	SEP	OCT	NOV	DEC	ANNUAL
1964	2.89	4.97	2.24	1.63	2.25	1.89	1.68	2.61	6.76	2.35	4.28	5.57	39.12
1965	1.87	3.27	0.81	0.95	6.53	3.06	1.57	2.29	3.56	3.09	4.82	6.15	37.97
1966	4.46	7.75	2.20	7.98	11.21	4.42	1.45	7.11	4.01	5.45	1.56	1.53	59.13
1967	2.41	2.17	1.83	4.42	2.54	0.17	7.77	1.60	4.84	3.18	0.50	5.02	36.45
1968	8.02	1.99	2.92	3.02	13.24	11.18	6.49	2.90	3.87	3.91	2.71	1.19	61.44
#1969	2.74	5.31	3.18	3.34	4.73	1.51	3.89	2.67	6.08	3.30	2.13	4.38	43.26
1970	1.93	2.52	5.08	2.21	14.39	0.26	2.28	2.03	6.22	9.09	1.54	0.64	48.19
1971	0.36	2.11	1.21	2.14	3.41	2.42	1.42	6.95	5.17	3.49	1.82	7.33	37.83
1972	3.30	1.20	8.52	2.85	6.99	3.02	2.76	3.90	6.23	3.34	6.49	2.20	50.80
1973	5.00	3.40	3.68	7.15	4.22	13.46	6.77	3.73	9.38	9.31	1.59	2.47	70.16
1974	7.68	0.55	4.20	1.68	5.61	0.59	1.75	6.94	4.51	4.53	7.90	3.35	49.29
1975	1.97	2.63	3.19	4.80	7.57	7.50	5.48	5.72	0.80	5.62	2.08	3.61	50.97
1976	1.39	0.38	1.53	10.92	5.80	2.63	3.93	1.59	11.35	5.83	3.05	6.22	54.62
1977	2.67	1.70	1.95	4.34	0.79	3.55	2.69	4.45	3.92	0.82	5.17	2.89	34.94
1978	7.15	3.07	1.70	0.57	4.15	9.37	2.35	3.66	4.27	0.05	5.99	2.60	44.93
1979	6.30	5.23	2.88	7.79	3.78	1.88	8.10	4.57	9.83	2.80	1.78	4.03	58.97
1980	6.09	2.54	5.39	2.05	5.63	0.92	1.57	1.40	6.00	4.03	2.12	1.25	38.99
1981	2.32	2.21	1.74	2.69	8.75	9.65	4.43	7.01	2.91	6.96	5.26	2.05	55.98
1982	1.82	1.59	1.55	2.28	6.87	1.10	4.32	1.90	0.98	6.64	8.91	4.91	42.87
1983	2.00	3.97	3.85	0.43	7.29	5.37	5.23	9.42	7.23	1.56	3.17	3.69	53.21
1984	3.99	4.37	2.41	0.56	3.13	1.99	3.43	3.52	3.87	16.05	2.28	2.59	48.19
1985	2.10	5.38	4.52	4.31	1.57	5.29	4.93	1.14	4.67	6.54	4.84	3.85	49.14
1986	0.71	2.74	1.44	2.63	4.29	6.34	0.61	3.27	3.70	6.83	6.66	5.71	44.93
1987	2.42	4.26	0.88	0.47	5.39	9.31	4.79	1.48	3.46	0.17	3.41	4.56	40.60
1988	1.27	1.29	4.88	1.26	1.32	2.00	3.23	3.52	1.20	1.29	0.41	1.26	22.93
1989	4.80	0.90	3.96	1.48	13.56	16.28	1.92	2.74	2.69	1.76	1.84	0.80	52.73
1990	3.96	4.54	5.11	6.21	2.23	2.98	4.85	0.31	1.57	3.79	3.01	1.81	40.37
1991	9.78	5.79	1.77	8.06	4.02	7.69	1.31	2.97	2.76	2.57	5.03	9.34	61.09
1992	7.70	5.99	6.28	3.74	7.05	3.38	3.85	2.78	1.08	1.03	5.99	3.46	52.33
1993	5.79	2.67	6.41	7.88	8.50	12.08	0.47	1.82	1.10	5.32	3.27	2.68	57.99
Record Mean	3.79	3.16	2.86	3.48	4.92	4.81	3.96	3.91	4.40	3.91	4.01	4.00	47.20

AVERAGE TEMPERATURE (deg. F)

HOUSTON, TEXAS

YEAR	JAN	FEB	MAR	APR	MAY	JUNE	JULY	AUG	SEP	OCT	NOV	DEC	ANNUAL
1964	51.6	49.4	60.4	70.2	75.8	80.4	83.7	84.4	79.3	67.8	65.0	55.9	68.7
1965	56.0	55.1	58.7	73.5	77.1	83.0	85.1	83.5	81.2	69.4	69.1	58.9	70.9
1966	48.4	52.8	61.5	70.6	75.9	80.0	84.3	82.4	79.6	69.7	64.7	54.2	68.7
1967	54.9	54.5	67.6	75.7	75.9	82.6	82.1	81.1	77.6	70.5	64.1	55.4	70.2
1968	52.7	50.4	59.0	71.1	76.3	80.5	82.5	84.0	78.6	73.5	59.7	55.7	68.7
#1969	56.7	56.9	56.1	70.3	75.4	80.0	84.4	83.2	78.2	71.0	58.5	55.2	68.8
1970	46.7	53.9	56.9	69.3	72.1	78.4	81.4	83.1	78.9	66.7	56.9	60.5	67.1
1971	56.7	55.7	59.4	66.6	74.1	80.3	83.9	80.4	78.3	72.0	60.0	59.9	68.9
1972	56.5	55.2	64.3	71.2	73.7	80.8	80.3	80.3	79.6	69.8	54.7	52.0	68.2
1973	47.4	51.4	63.7	64.6	72.8	79.2	83.0	79.5	78.1	71.8	67.3	53.5	67.7
1974	55.0	56.2	66.8	67.2	76.9	79.9	82.8	81.6	74.6	70.6	60.2	54.6	68.9
1975	56.9	55.4	61.1	68.3	75.9	80.0	81.5	81.1	74.9	69.5	59.7	52.7	68.1
1976	50.6	60.1	62.2	67.7	70.5	78.4	80.5	81.4	76.2	60.6	51.8	49.2	65.8
1977	42.7	53.8	60.9	66.9	74.5	81.0	82.4	83.1	80.0	69.2	61.8	53.7	67.5
1978	40.8	45.1	57.3	67.6	76.0	80.4	83.7	83.1	79.3	68.9	64.7	52.9	66.7
1979	44.1	51.7	62.4	68.7	73.1	79.8	82.6	81.5	75.6	70.7	55.7	52.4	66.5
1980	55.0	53.7	60.9	66.2	77.3	85.1	87.5	86.6	83.2	67.8	58.0	55.2	69.7
1981	51.4	55.4	60.9	74.3	75.3	82.7	84.4	84.4	78.6	72.3	64.4	54.5	69.9
1982	52.9	52.1	64.9	67.8	75.3	83.0	85.4	84.1	79.3	69.5	60.9	55.4	69.2
1983	50.1	52.5	58.3	64.0	73.4	79.0	82.2	82.6	76.6	70.1	63.1	45.7	66.5
1984	47.0	54.0	61.9	67.8	74.9	78.6	81.8	82.9	77.4	74.2	60.0	63.4	68.7
1985	45.7	49.6	64.7	70.0	75.6	81.0	81.6	84.2	79.8	72.5	67.0	51.0	68.6
1986	54.4	59.9	63.3	71.7	75.8	82.0	85.9	82.6	81.8	68.9	62.0	51.7	70.0
1987	51.4	56.1	58.9	67.2	77.1	81.3	83.5	86.2	78.9	68.7	60.5	55.6	68.8
1988	48.1	54.1	61.3	67.6	73.6	80.5	84.4	85.3	80.8	72.0	65.7	55.4	69.1
1989	57.5	52.7	61.3	69.4	77.8	79.9	82.4	81.7	77.0	70.2	62.9	44.4	68.1
1990	57.0	59.1	62.9	69.4	78.1	84.8	82.1	85.1	80.1	68.7	63.4	53.6	70.4
1991	50.4	57.4	63.5	72.2	78.0	82.0	84.0	83.0	77.4	72.3	56.7	56.2	69.4
1992	51.0	58.5	64.0	68.7	73.7	81.7	83.6	80.1	79.3	71.4	56.8	56.7	68.8
1993	53.6	56.7	61.1	65.9	73.4	81.6	85.8	86.5	80.2	69.5	56.9	54.6	68.8
Record Mean	50.9	54.6	61.8	68.3	74.9	80.8	83.2	82.9	78.5	70.0	60.4	54.0	68.3
Max	61.0	65.5	72.7	78.9	84.8	90.7	93.4	93.3	88.6	81.5	71.5	64.7	78.9
Min	40.8	43.7	50.8	57.8	65.0	71.0	73.0	72.5	68.4	58.4	49.3	43.3	57.8

REFERENCE NOTES

HOUSTON, TEXAS

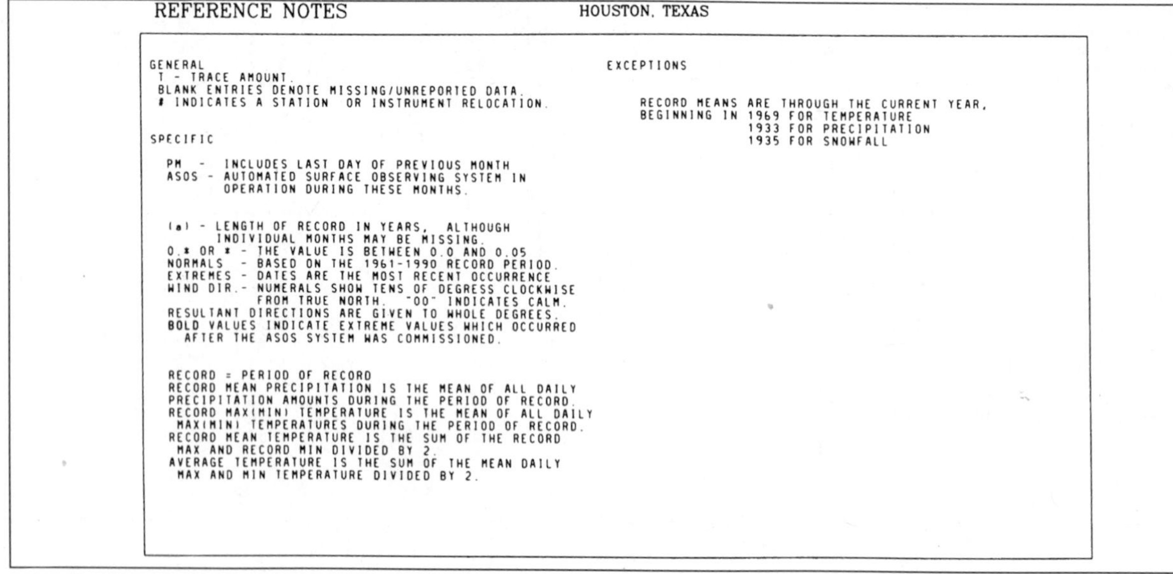

GENERAL
T - TRACE AMOUNT.
BLANK ENTRIES DENOTE MISSING/UNREPORTED DATA.
# INDICATES A STATION OR INSTRUMENT RELOCATION.

SPECIFIC

PM - INCLUDES LAST DAY OF PREVIOUS MONTH
ASOS - AUTOMATED SURFACE OBSERVING SYSTEM IN OPERATION DURING THESE MONTHS.

(a) - LENGTH OF RECORD IN YEARS, ALTHOUGH INDIVIDUAL MONTHS MAY BE MISSING.
0.* OR * - THE VALUE IS BETWEEN 0.0 AND 0.05
NORMALS - BASED ON THE 1961-1990 RECORD PERIOD.
EXTREMES - DATES ARE THE MOST RECENT OCCURRENCE
WIND DIR.- NUMERALS SHOW TENS OF DEGRESS CLOCKWISE FROM TRUE NORTH. "00" INDICATES CALM.
RESULTANT DIRECTIONS ARE GIVEN TO WHOLE DEGREES.
BOLD VALUES INDICATE EXTREME VALUES WHICH OCCURRED AFTER THE ASOS SYSTEM WAS COMMISSIONED.

RECORD = PERIOD OF RECORD
RECORD MEAN PRECIPITATION IS THE MEAN OF ALL DAILY PRECIPITATION AMOUNTS DURING THE PERIOD OF RECORD.
RECORD MAX(MIN) TEMPERATURE IS THE MEAN OF ALL DAILY MAX(MIN) TEMPERATURES DURING THE PERIOD OF RECORD.
RECORD MEAN TEMPERATURE IS THE SUM OF THE RECORD MAX AND RECORD MIN DIVIDED BY 2.
AVERAGE TEMPERATURE IS THE SUM OF THE MEAN DAILY MAX AND MIN TEMPERATURE DIVIDED BY 2.

EXCEPTIONS

RECORD MEANS ARE THROUGH THE CURRENT YEAR, BEGINNING IN 1969 FOR TEMPERATURE
1933 FOR PRECIPITATION
1935 FOR SNOWFALL

HEATING DEGREE DAYS Base 65 deg. F — HOUSTON, TEXAS

SEASON	JULY	AUG	SEP	OCT	NOV	DEC	JAN	FEB	MAR	APR	MAY	JUNE	TOTAL
1964-65	0	0	0	31	114	315	300	284	250	0	0	0	1294
1965-66	0	0	2	20	23	212	516	334	144	12	0	0	1263
1966-67	0	0	0	27	99	359	342	298	68	0	0	0	1193
1967-68	0	0	3	18	99	312	390	415	229	17	0	0	1483
#1968-69	0	0	0	5	199	297	284	234	281	1	0	2	1303
1969-70	0	0	0	29	238	304	579	309	252	51	12	0	1774
1970-71	0	0	0	72	274	209	298	273	219	72	3	0	1420
1971-72	0	0	2	6	195	194	315	295	85	17	0	0	1109
1972-73	0	0	2	50	320	410	540	379	75	117	5	0	1898
1973-74	0	0	0	8	74	364	330	273	95	60	0	0	1204
1974-75	0	0	0	15	196	336	290	270	179	48	0	0	1334
1975-76	0	0	0	26	217	399	441	178	155	26	7	0	1449
1976-77	0	0	0	173	398	484	687	312	166	25	0	0	2245
1977-78	0	0	0	34	150	365	752	553	250	33	17	0	2154
1978-79	0	0	0	22	111	393	646	376	135	23	2	0	1708
1979-80	0	0	0	27	297	389	308	350	169	45	0	0	1585
1980-81	0	0	0	67	255	323	416	291	144	6	1	0	1503
1981-82	0	0	0	50	82	326	409	363	143	79	1	0	1453
1982-83	0	0	0	53	175	328	457	346	219	96	0	0	1674
1983-84	0	0	6	27	138	606	549	325	150	45	2	0	1848
1984-85	0	0	6	12	204	144	591	432	91	22	0	0	1502
1985-86	0	0	5	17	76	434	326	209	99	11	0	0	1177
1986-87	0	0	0	28	175	411	421	245	196	82	0	0	1558
1987-88	0	0	0	16	185	301	525	331	171	35	0	0	1564
1988-89	0	0	0	5	120	309	260	379	210	56	0	0	1339
1989-90	0	0	0	47	160	637	264	177	122	34	0	0	1441
1990-91	0	0	0	61	129	395	448	222	115	8	0	0	1378
1991-92	0	0	0	15	289	303	428	197	95	37	4	0	1368
1992-93	0	0	0	1	270	268	351	235	157	62	0	0	1344
1993-94	0	0	0	76	269	343							

COOLING DEGREE DAYS Base 65 deg. F — HOUSTON, TEXAS

YEAR	JAN	FEB	MAR	APR	MAY	JUNE	JULY	AUG	SEP	OCT	NOV	DEC	TOTAL
#1969	35	13	11	167	328	456	608	569	402	222	48	9	2868
1970	18	3	7	188	238	409	513	567	423	131	38	76	2611
1971	48	18	55	126	292	466	594	485	409	229	52	44	2818
1972	58	20	71	208	275	480	480	482	447	206	17	12	2756
1973	1	4	41	111	253	434	564	458	401	225	151	12	2655
1974	24	33	158	132	374	454	558	519	295	196	60	18	2821
1975	47	8	61	155	342	455	514	505	303	174	68	24	2656
1976	5	43	75	110	182	408	490	520	341	42	9	0	2225
1977	0	5	44	91	302	487	547	565	456	173	58	23	2751
1978	10	5	19	120	369	471	584	568	437	150	108	25	2866
1979	7	13	62	142	261	454	552	519	324	211	26	6	2577
1980	4	31	49	86	388	610	705	677	553	162	52	26	3343
1981	1	28	23	295	330	538	606	609	413	285	71	7	3206
1982	39	11	147	170	329	547	641	599	437	199	60	40	3219
1983	0	0	18	76	268	427	541	554	362	196	87	18	2547
1984	0	13	64	135	315	415	527	562	384	302	62	100	2879
1985	0	6	87	180	335	487	521	602	456	257	143	9	3083
1986	4	71	52	220	341	518	654	553	510	157	92	4	3172
1987	4	4	14	154	383	497	580	661	423	137	54	15	2926
1988	7	20	65	121	274	472	609	637	478	229	144	20	3076
1989	33	44	105	194	405	454	547	526	363	218	105	5	2999
1990	20	19	65	174	413	603	536	630	456	181	87	47	3231
1991	0	14	76	231	408	514	593	565	376	248	47	37	3109
1992	0	17	74	155	281	508	584	476	437	210	32	20	2794
1993	4	10	42	92	267	506	652	674	463	221	31	27	2989

SNOWFALL (inches) — HOUSTON, TEXAS

SEASON	JULY	AUG	SEP	OCT	NOV	DEC	JAN	FEB	MAR	APR	MAY	JUNE	TOTAL
1970-71	0.0	0.0	0.0	0.0	0.0	0.0	T	0.0	0.0	0.0	0.0	0.0	T
1971-72	0.0	0.0	0.0	0.0	0.0	0.0	T	0.0	0.0	0.0	0.0	0.0	T
1972-73	0.0	0.0	0.0	0.0	0.0	0.0	2.0	2.8	0.0	0.0	0.0	0.0	4.8
1973-74	0.0	0.0	0.0	0.0	0.0	0.0	0.0	0.0	0.0	0.0	0.0	0.0	0.0
1974-75	0.0	0.0	0.0	0.0	0.0	0.0	T	0.0	0.0	0.0	0.0	0.0	T
1975-76	0.0	0.0	0.0	0.0	0.0	0.0	0.0	0.0	0.0	0.0	0.0	0.0	0.0
1976-77	0.0	0.0	0.0	0.0	T	0.0	0.0	0.0	0.0	0.0	0.0	0.0	T
1977-78	0.0	0.0	0.0	0.0	0.0	0.0	0.4	0.0	0.0	0.0	0.0	0.0	0.4
1978-79	0.0	0.0	0.0	0.0	0.0	0.0	T	0.0	0.0	0.0	0.0	0.0	T
1979-80	0.0	0.0	0.0	0.0	T	0.0	0.0	1.4	0.0	0.0	0.0	0.0	1.4
1980-81	0.0	0.0	0.0	0.0	0.0	0.0	T	T	0.0	0.0	0.0	0.0	T
1981-82	0.0	0.0	0.0	0.0	0.0	0.0	T	0.0	0.0	0.0	0.0	0.0	T
1982-83	0.0	0.0	0.0	0.0	0.0	0.0	0.0	0.0	0.0	0.0	0.0	0.0	0.0
1983-84	0.0	0.0	0.0	0.0	0.0	0.0	0.0	0.0	0.0	0.0	0.0	0.0	0.0
1984-85	0.0	0.0	0.0	0.0	0.0	0.0	1.4	0.3	0.0	0.0	0.0	0.0	1.7
1985-86	0.0	0.0	0.0	0.0	0.0	0.0	0.0	0.0	0.0	0.0	0.0	0.0	0.0
1986-87	0.0	0.0	0.0	0.0	0.0	0.0	0.0	0.0	0.0	0.0	0.0	0.0	0.0
1987-88	0.0	0.0	0.0	0.0	0.0	0.0	0.0	T	0.0	0.0	0.0	0.0	T
1988-89	0.0	0.0	0.0	0.0	0.0	0.0	0.0	T	0.0	0.0	0.0	0.0	T
1989-90	0.0	0.0	0.0	0.0	0.0	1.7	0.0	0.0	0.0	0.0	0.0	T	1.7
1990-91	0.0	0.0	0.0	0.0	0.0	0.0	0.0	0.0	0.0	0.0	0.0	0.0	0.0
1991-92	0.0	0.0	0.0	0.0	0.0	0.0	0.0	0.0	T	0.0	T	0.0	T
1992-93	0.0	0.0	0.0	0.0	0.0	0.0	0.0	0.0	0.0	T	T	0.0	T
1993-94	0.0	0.0	0.0	0.0	0.0	0.0							
Record Mean	0.0	0.0	0.0	0.0	T	T	0.2	0.2	T	T	T	T	0.4

SAN ANTONIO, TEXAS

The city of San Antonio is located in the south-central portion of Texas on the Balcones escarpment. Northwest of the city, the terrain slopes upward to the Edwards Plateau, and to the southeast it slopes downward to the Gulf Coastal Plains. Soils are blackland clay and silty loam on the Plains and thin limestone soils on the Edwards Plateau. With its location on the NW edge of the Gulf Coastal Plain, San Antonio experiences a modified subtropical climate. Average monthly temperatures range from the 50s in the winter to the 80s in the summer.

During the winter months the area is alternately influenced by a continental climate, when winds blow from the north and west; and by a modified maritime climate, when south and southeast winds blow from the Gulf of Mexico. Mild weather prevails during most of the winter. Below freezing temperatures occur on average about 20 days each year. When cold arctic outbreaks do occur, they cause relatively cold temperatures for this part of the U.S., as the cold north winds block any moderating affects from the Gulf. Some winters may see a mostly cloudy weather pattern that modify daily temperatures, that is cooler days and warmer nights. During sunny winters, the South Texas sun warms daytime temperatures to pleasant levels. On some occasions dry west winds in a mild airmass allow winter temperatures to climb to spring or summerlike levels.

During the summer the climate becomes even more tropical with prevailing south and southeast winds. The moderating effects of the Gulf of Mexico prevent extremely high temperatures; however, summers are usually long and hot with daily maximum temperatures above 90 degrees over 80 percent of the time. In many years summer conditions continue into September and sometimes even October. Occasionally, cool fronts may move through the area, dropping overnight lows into the 50s; however, the cooling unfortunately is brief and in a day or two the minimum temperatures are back up to the 70s. The drier air that is brought in by these cool fronts also allows daily maximum temperatures to rise above normal.

San Antonio is situated, climatically, between a semi-arid area to the west and the tropical area to the east. Such a location allows for large variations in monthly and annual precipitation amounts. The normal annual precipitation for San Antonio is about 30 inches although it may range from 10 to 50 inches from one year to another. Heavy rain may occur with or without thunder in any season. During some of these events, rain has exceeded 5 inches in several hours and caused flash flooding. A year of normal precipitation is sufficient for the production of most crops, although during the drier years irrigation is essential. On average the heaviest rains fall in May and September, while the driest months are December through March, and July. Since rainfall is sporadic, the wettest and driest month in any one year may occur in any season and vary widely from year to year. Precipitation from April through September usually occurs as a result of thunderstorms; however, thunderstorms may occur in any month.

Hail of damaging intensity seldom occurs; however, small hail is frequent with the springtime thunderstorms and has been observed during other seasons. Measurable snow usually occurs only once in three or four years. Snowfall of 2 to 4 inches occurs about every ten years.

Since San Antonio is located only 140 miles from the Gulf of Mexico, tropical storms occasionally affect the city with strong winds and heavy rains. One of the fastest winds recorded, 74 mph, occurred as a tropical storm moved inland east of the city in August 1942.

Relative humidity is above 80 percent during the early morning hours most of the year, dropping to near 50 percent in late afternoon.

San Antonio receives about 50 percent of possible sunshine during the winter months and more than 7 percent during the summer. Stratus clouds frequently develop at night during the summer as Gulf moisture is lifted over the higher terrain. These clouds usually dissipate before noon and lead to partly cloudy to clear skies during the afternoon. During the winter these stratus clouds may be accompanied by fog and drizzle.

Normally the first freezing temperatures occur around December the 1st while the average last freeze occurs in late February. Extreme freeze dates are late October and early April.

NORMALS, MEANS, AND EXTREMES

SAN ANTONIO, TEXAS

LATITUDE: 29°32'N LONGITUDE: 98°28' W ELEVATION: FT. GRND 788 BARO 796 TIME ZONE: CENTRAL WBAN: 12921

	(a)	JAN	FEB	MAR	APR	MAY	JUNE	JULY	AUG	SEP	OCT	NOV	DEC	YEAR
TEMPERATURE °F:														
Normals														
-Daily Maximum		60.8	65.7	73.5	80.3	85.3	91.8	95.0	95.3	89.3	81.7	71.9	63.5	79.5
-Daily Minimum		37.9	41.3	49.7	58.4	65.7	72.6	75.0	74.5	69.2	58.8	48.8	40.8	57.7
-Monthly		49.3	53.5	61.7	69.3	75.5	82.2	85.0	84.9	79.3	70.2	60.4	52.2	68.6
Extremes														
-Record Highest	52	89	97	100	100	103	105	106	108	103	99	94	90	108
-Year		1971	1986	1991	1984	1989	1980	1989	1986	1985	1991	1988	1955	AUG 1986
-Record Lowest	52	0	6	19	31	43	53	62	61	41	27	21	6	0
-Year		1949	1951	1980	1987	1984	1964	1967	1992	1942	1993	1976	1989	JAN 1949
NORMAL DEGREE DAYS:														
Heating (base 65°F)		494	332	167	32	0	0	0	0	0	30	180	409	1644
Cooling (base 65°F)		8	10	64	161	326	516	620	617	429	191	42	12	2996
% OF POSSIBLE SUNSHINE	51	47	51	57	56	56	67	75	74	67	64	54	48	60
MEAN SKY COVER (tenths)														
Sunrise - Sunset	51	6.3	6.2	6.1	6.4	6.4	5.5	5.1	4.9	5.2	4.9	5.5	6.1	5.7
MEAN NUMBER OF DAYS:														
Sunrise to Sunset														
-Clear	51	8.9	8.2	8.7	7.4	6.0	6.9	9.0	10.2	9.3	11.6	10.3	9.6	106.1
-Partly Cloudy	51	5.9	5.9	7.2	7.6	11.3	15.3	15.4	14.8	12.3	10.0	7.0	5.9	118.5
-Cloudy	51	16.2	14.1	15.1	15.0	13.8	7.8	6.6	6.0	8.5	9.4	12.7	15.5	140.7
Precipitation														
.01 inches or more	51	8.1	7.7	7.3	7.3	8.6	6.4	4.4	5.1	7.0	6.2	6.5	7.5	82.1
Snow,Ice pellets,hail														
1.0 inches or more	51	0.1	0.1	0.0	0.0	0.0	0.0	0.0	0.0	0.0	0.0	0.0	0.0	0.2
Thunderstorms	51	1.0	1.6	2.6	4.0	6.6	4.6	3.5	4.0	4.1	2.7	1.7	0.9	37.3
Heavy Fog Visibility														
1/4 mile or less	51	5.1	2.9	2.4	1.4	0.7	0.1	0.1	0.*	0.2	1.4	2.8	4.4	21.5
Temperature °F														
-Maximum														
90° and above	51	0.0	0.1	0.8	2.3	8.5	21.8	28.3	28.2	17.5	4.5	0.1	0.*	112.1
32° and below	51	0.3	0.1	0.0	0.0	0.0	0.0	0.0	0.0	0.0	0.0	0.0	0.1	0.5
-Minimum														
32° and below	51	8.1	4.5	1.5	0.*	0.0	0.0	0.0	0.0	0.0	0.*	2.0	5.8	22.1
0° and below	51	0.*	0.0	0.0	0.0	0.0	0.0	0.0	0.0	0.0	0.0	0.0	0.0	*
AVG. STATION PRESS.(mb)	21	991.8	990.3	986.7	985.8	984.5	985.6	987.5	987.3	987.3	989.2	989.9	991.4	988.1
RELATIVE HUMIDITY (%)														
Hour 00	51	76	75	72	76	81	80	75	74	77	77	77	76	76
Hour 06 (Local Time)	51	80	80	79	83	88	88	87	86	86	84	81	80	84
Hour 12	51	59	57	53	56	59	56	52	51	54	53	55	57	55
Hour 18	51	57	52	47	51	55	52	45	45	51	52	56	57	52
PRECIPITATION (inches):														
Water Equivalent														
-Normal		1.71	1.81	1.52	2.50	4.22	3.81	2.16	2.54	3.41	3.17	2.62	1.51	30.98
-Maximum Monthly	51	8.52	6.43	6.12	9.32	12.85	11.95	8.29	11.14	15.78	9.56	6.01	13.96	15.78
-Year		1968	1965	1992	1957	1987	1986	1990	1974	1946	1942	1977	1991	SEP 1946
-Minimum Monthly	51	0.04	0.03	0.03	0.11	0.17	0.01	T	0.00	0.06	T	T	0.03	0.00
-Year		1971	1954	1961	1984	1961	1967	1993	1952	1947	1952	1966	1950	AUG 1952
-Maximum in 24 hrs	51	3.18	2.44	3.59	4.88	6.53	6.30	6.97	5.57	7.28	5.29	4.87	6.90	7.28
-Year		1968	1986	1992	1977	1972	1986	1958	1950	1973	1942	1977	1991	SEP 1973
Snow,Ice pellets,hail														
-Maximum Monthly	51	15.9	3.5	T	T	T	T	0.0	0.0	0.0	T	0.3	0.2	15.9
-Year		1985	1966	1992	1993	1993	1989				1993	1957	1964	JAN 1985
-Maximum in 24 hrs	51	13.2	3.5	T	T	T	T	0.0	0.0	0.0	T	0.3	0.2	13.2
-Year		1985	1966	1992	1993	1993	1989				1993	1957	1964	JAN 1985
WIND:														
Mean Speed (mph)	51	8.9	9.4	10.2	10.1	9.8	9.8	9.1	8.4	8.4	8.3	8.7	8.4	9.1
Prevailing Direction through 1963		N	NE	SE	SE	SE	SE	SSE	SE	SE	N	N	N	SE
Fastest Obs. 1 Min.														
-Direction (!!)	17	31	31	36	35	02	34	09	20	18	02	33	32	09
-Speed (MPH)	17	35	42	35	39	43	35	48	37	42	31	37	30	48
-Year		1979	1984	1980	1979	1983	1984	1979	1984	1977	1977	1983	1987	JUL 1979
Peak Gust														
-Direction (!!)	10	N	NW	NW	NW	NW	NW	SE	SW	N	N	NW	W	NW
-Speed (mph)	10	51	56	46	47	55	51	41	49	51	43	41	48	56
-Date		1985	1984	1984	1988	1987	1984	1989	1984	1987	1985	1987	1987	FEB 1984

PRECIPITATION (inches)

SAN ANTONIO, TEXAS

YEAR	JAN	FEB	MAR	APR	MAY	JUNE	JULY	AUG	SEP	OCT	NOV	DEC	ANNUAL
1964	3.40	1.89	1.73	1.16	1.79	4.88	0.02	5.19	4.15	1.64	4.81	1.22	31.88
1965	2.40	6.43	2.30	1.97	8.18	2.42	0.08	1.65	3.13	2.69	0.89	4.51	36.65
1966	1.47	2.30	1.14	3.20	3.53	1.78	0.06	4.28	2.13	1.11	T	0.44	21.44
1967	0.18	0.48	2.18	0.94	2.22	0.01	2.12	3.17	11.16	2.00	3.42	1.38	29.26
1968	8.52	1.85	1.27	1.92	2.82	2.63	1.53	0.94	2.99	0.69	4.58	0.66	30.40
1969	1.76	2.90	2.35	2.46	4.61	2.32	0.36	4.19	1.32	5.85	1.02	2.28	31.42
1970	1.10	2.66	1.98	1.13	7.30	0.89	0.91	0.95	4.35	1.31	0.01	0.15	22.74
1971	0.04	0.81	0.04	1.39	1.52	2.74	1.05	9.42	4.57	4.62	2.74	2.86	31.80
1972	1.35	0.40	0.13	1.94	11.24	2.86	3.13	4.24	1.40	1.99	2.37	0.44	31.49
1973	2.77	2.76	1.58	5.41	2.73	10.44	6.91	1.29	13.09	4.85	0.29	0.16	52.28
1974	1.36	0.04	0.94	2.18	4.28	1.02	1.28	11.14	3.85	4.09	5.39	1.43	37.00
1975	1.04	3.30	0.52	2.69	6.91	4.60	1.06	1.28	0.51	2.25	0.03	1.48	25.67
1976	0.56	0.13	1.20	5.67	5.80	1.61	5.39	2.09	3.79	8.48	2.46	1.95	39.13
1977	3.10	0.91	0.88	8.80	1.62	2.26	0.10	0.06	2.11	3.47	6.01	0.32	29.64
1978	0.68	1.76	1.71	3.62	2.45	3.96	1.43	4.97	8.86	0.55	4.91	1.09	35.99
1979	4.07	1.38	3.55	5.34	1.98	5.59	7.38	2.09	0.86	0.11	1.43	2.86	36.64
1980	0.72	0.74	0.98	1.67	6.42	0.52	0.26	2.64	5.05	1.09	3.53	0.61	24.23
1981	2.06	0.96	1.96	2.21	6.43	8.71	0.25	2.41	1.36	8.61	0.72	0.69	36.37
1982	0.72	1.28	0.69	1.23	6.42	1.37	0.14	0.55	0.87	2.84	4.54	2.31	22.96
1983	1.48	1.54	3.89	0.18	4.37	1.27	2.43	2.00	3.86	1.64	3.06	0.39	26.11
1984	1.87	0.54	1.91	0.11	3.76	1.40	T	3.04	1.06	5.94	2.91	3.41	25.95
1985	2.68	1.91	2.85	3.27	2.47	8.20	5.80	0.45	4.80	3.91	5.00	0.09	41.43
1986	0.76	2.52	0.35	0.60	6.29	11.95	0.05	1.86	2.83	6.58	1.83	7.11	42.73
1987	1.13	4.78	1.10	1.48	12.85	7.69	1.21	0.33	2.24	0.44	2.53	2.18	37.96
1988	0.39	0.92	0.86	1.23	0.41	5.50	5.58	1.98	0.83	0.62	0.02	0.67	19.01
1989	2.96	0.29	1.24	2.55	0.33	3.96	0.69	0.48	1.54	5.81	1.93	0.36	22.14
1990	1.17	2.68	5.17	4.52	3.28	1.18	8.29	1.30	3.70	3.71	3.11	0.20	38.31
1991	5.08	2.34	1.06	4.91	5.30	2.28	2.23	2.84	1.42	0.87	0.47	13.96	42.76
1992	5.64	6.37	6.12	3.03	8.15	5.67	1.28	2.56	1.12	0.92	3.47	2.16	46.49
1993	1.31	3.72	1.56	1.81	12.47	6.43	T	0.01	0.52	3.07	0.66	0.44	32.00
Record Mean	1.66	1.74	1.70	2.89	3.66	3.10	2.06	2.32	3.11	2.55	1.96	1.76	28.52

AVERAGE TEMPERATURE (deg. F)

SAN ANTONIO, TEXAS

YEAR	JAN	FEB	MAR	APR	MAY	JUNE	JULY	AUG	SEP	OCT	NOV	DEC	ANNUAL
1964	51.0	49.8	61.5	70.5	77.6	82.4	86.3	86.2	80.0	66.4	62.6	52.3	68.9
1965	54.4	49.8	54.9	71.6	75.0	81.6	84.9	84.0	80.7	66.8	64.5	55.5	68.6
1966	45.4	49.8	60.0	68.6	73.5	78.8	84.2	81.9	77.5	67.0	63.0	50.7	66.7
1967	50.2	51.8	66.9	76.6	76.6	84.5	85.3	82.7	75.5	66.9	60.5	51.0	69.0
1968	49.8	48.3	58.0	68.1	75.3	80.5	82.7	84.2	76.0	72.2	56.4	50.7	66.8
1969	52.5	53.6	54.9	69.0	73.5	81.2	86.8	85.7	79.6	69.8	58.1	55.1	68.3
1970	45.6	54.8	56.8	70.2	72.9	80.7	84.0	85.7	81.1	67.7	58.0	60.1	68.1
1971	56.0	57.4	64.6	69.4	78.1	83.6	85.9	81.2	80.1	73.9	63.2	57.2	70.9
1972	52.8	56.7	66.3	73.7	72.8	80.3	82.2	82.1	82.0	71.9	54.0	50.3	68.8
1973	47.2	51.9	66.1	66.0	74.7	79.2	83.2	82.1	79.3	72.5	65.8	52.2	68.4
1974	51.0	56.5	67.9	69.7	77.3	79.4	83.0	81.2	72.3	68.2	57.3	50.9	67.9
1975	53.2	53.5	61.4	68.4	73.5	80.0	80.9	81.7	76.0	71.1	60.3	53.1	67.8
1976	49.6	61.2	63.8	68.9	71.3	79.8	79.8	81.6	77.5	61.1	52.1	49.9	66.4
1977	44.1	52.8	61.8	66.9	74.8	81.5	84.9	84.7	82.3	71.2	61.4	53.4	68.3
1978	43.4	46.4	59.6	68.9	77.1	82.7	86.1	83.1	78.5	69.3	62.4	51.7	67.5
1979	43.7	52.4	63.3	69.7	73.9	80.9	84.7	83.1	78.7	74.7	58.2	55.4	68.2
1980	52.6	53.7	61.5	67.6	76.1	85.1	88.1	85.3	83.7	70.7	58.3	55.0	69.8
1981	50.8	53.7	60.7	72.9	75.3	81.5	84.2	84.7	79.9	71.9	62.4	53.0	69.2
1982	50.8	49.7	63.1	66.9	74.5	81.6	85.5	86.0	80.1	69.3	59.4	52.4	68.3
1983	48.9	52.1	58.7	65.2	73.6	79.2	82.9	84.5	78.5	70.9	62.5	43.0	66.7
1984	46.7	54.1	64.2	69.7	77.1	82.8	85.0	84.7	77.6	71.2	58.8	59.6	69.3
1985	44.2	50.5	64.1	69.4	76.7	80.2	82.2	85.5	79.4	71.7	64.4	49.9	68.2
1986	53.4	58.0	62.9	72.6	74.6	81.5	85.8	85.7	83.7	69.7	59.4	51.6	69.9
1987	50.7	55.9	57.8	66.1	75.8	80.5	83.8	86.0	79.2	71.2	60.6	54.2	68.5
1988	47.6	54.3	61.3	69.1	76.1	81.2	84.6	86.4	80.7	73.2	65.1	56.0	69.6
1989	56.2	51.6	61.9	70.4	81.7	83.3	86.6	86.0	79.1	71.3	61.8	43.4	69.4
1990	56.4	58.9	61.5	69.7	79.3	87.5	83.4	85.3	80.0	69.3	63.0	51.9	70.5
1991	48.9	56.6	64.0	72.4	77.7	82.8	84.5	85.8	77.8	73.3	57.4	55.5	69.7
1992	50.8	59.1	63.3	69.0	73.7	82.5	84.7	82.2	81.7	73.4	57.3	56.3	69.5
1993	51.2	55.5	61.5	67.3	73.9	81.6	86.1	87.3	81.5	70.7	56.3	55.1	69.0
Record Mean	51.6	55.2	62.2	69.3	75.5	81.6	84.0	84.2	79.4	70.9	60.5	53.5	69.0
Max	62.1	66.1	73.4	80.0	85.5	91.6	94.4	94.9	89.6	81.8	71.1	64.0	79.5
Min	41.1	44.2	50.9	58.6	65.5	71.6	73.6	73.5	69.2	59.9	49.8	43.1	58.4

REFERENCE NOTES

SAN ANTONIO, TEXAS

GENERAL
T - TRACE AMOUNT.
BLANK ENTRIES DENOTE MISSING/UNREPORTED DATA.
# INDICATES A STATION OR INSTRUMENT RELOCATION.

SPECIFIC

PM - INCLUDES LAST DAY OF PREVIOUS MONTH
ASOS - AUTOMATED SURFACE OBSERVING SYSTEM IN OPERATION DURING THESE MONTHS.

(a) - LENGTH OF RECORD IN YEARS, ALTHOUGH INDIVIDUAL MONTHS MAY BE MISSING.
0.* OR * - THE VALUE IS BETWEEN 0.0 AND 0.05
NORMALS - BASED ON THE 1961-1990 RECORD PERIOD.
EXTREMES - DATES ARE THE MOST RECENT OCCURRENCE
WIND DIR.- NUMERALS SHOW TENS OF DEGRESS CLOCKWISE FROM TRUE NORTH. "00" INDICATES CALM.
RESULTANT DIRECTIONS ARE GIVEN TO WHOLE DEGREES.
BOLD VALUES INDICATE EXTREME VALUES WHICH OCCURRED AFTER THE ASOS SYSTEM WAS COMMISSIONED.

RECORD = PERIOD OF RECORD
RECORD MEAN PRECIPITATION IS THE MEAN OF ALL DAILY PRECIPITATION AMOUNTS DURING THE PERIOD OF RECORD.
RECORD MAX(MIN) TEMPERATURE IS THE MEAN OF ALL DAILY MAX(MIN) TEMPERATURES DURING THE PERIOD OF RECORD.
RECORD MEAN TEMPERATURE IS THE SUM OF THE RECORD MAX AND RECORD MIN DIVIDED BY 2.
AVERAGE TEMPERATURE IS THE SUM OF THE MEAN DAILY MAX AND MIN TEMPERATURE DIVIDED BY 2.

EXCEPTIONS

RECORD MEANS ARE THROUGH THE CURRENT YEAR, BEGINNING IN 1885 FOR TEMPERATURE
1885 FOR PRECIPITATION
1943 FOR SNOWFALL

HEATING DEGREE DAYS Base 65 deg. F SAN ANTONIO, TEXAS

SEASON	JULY	AUG	SEP	OCT	NOV	DEC	JAN	FEB	MAR	APR	MAY	JUNE	TOTAL
1964-65	0	0	0	41	155	414	346	419	327	13	0	0	1715
1965-66	0	0	2	62	64	301	607	426	182	39	5	0	1688
1966-67	0	0	0	57	131	456	470	366	80	0	0	0	1560
1967-68	0	0	8	48	164	429	477	478	254	39	0	0	1897
1968-69	0	0	0	9	278	437	394	319	315	5	3	0	1760
1969-70	0	0	0	52	253	299	599	282	266	45	7	0	1803
1970-71	0	0	1	72	247	201	282	239	134	52	1	0	1229
1971-72	0	0	1	0	129	266	382	263	61	7	0	0	1109
1972-73	0	0	0	29	334	457	551	362	29	94	1	0	1857
1973-74	0	0	0	4	85	391	437	257	74	39	0	0	1287
1974-75	0	0	2	19	260	433	389	316	152	41	0	0	1612
1975-76	0	0	1	21	214	394	472	166	143	11	2	0	1424
1976-77	0	0	0	160	382	461	643	336	144	32	0	0	2158
1977-78	0	0	0	19	138	360	667	521	192	27	4	0	1928
1978-79	0	0	0	12	152	413	657	356	109	20	4	0	1723
1979-80	0	0	0	15	243	306	386	333	163	42	0	0	1488
1980-81	0	0	0	62	245	331	437	332	157	10	0	0	1574
1981-82	0	0	2	52	112	368	445	430	171	77	2	0	1659
1982-83	0	0	0	49	237	404	490	356	208	99	1	0	1844
1983-84	0	0	5	20	154	681	563	315	120	21	2	0	1881
1984-85	0	0	9	28	228	203	635	406	109	26	0	0	1644
1985-86	0	0	10	9	112	467	354	232	106	8	1	0	1299
1986-87	0	0	0	14	204	413	443	254	233	98	0	0	1659
1987-88	0	0	0	1	194	339	538	323	179	38	0	0	1612
1988-89	0	0	0	0	122	291	292	392	187	55	0	0	1339
1989-90	0	0	0	42	165	663	283	190	154	32	0	0	1529
1990-91	0	0	0	50	142	422	494	240	96	7	0	0	1451
1991-92	0	0	5	30	271	306	435	188	91	31	5	0	1362
1992-93	0	0	0	0	260	287	421	269	147	42	0	0	1426
1993-94	0	0	0	85	287	323							

COOLING DEGREE DAYS Base 65 deg. F SAN ANTONIO, TEXAS

YEAR	JAN	FEB	MAR	APR	MAY	JUNE	JULY	AUG	SEP	OCT	NOV	DEC	TOTAL
1969	11	5	8	133	273	494	683	652	448	207	53	2	2969
1970	3	3	20	208	259	478	592	651	493	163	40	57	2967
1971	14	36	130	189	414	564	658	509	459	281	81	31	3366
1972	11	31	105	276	252	465	542	539	515	249	12	6	3003
1973	8	0	69	129	310	431	570	536	437	242	114	0	2846
1974	11	22	171	188	387	439	568	506	229	124	34	5	2684
1975	29	1	51	151	273	457	502	524	337	217	80	30	2652
1976	3	62	113	136	202	451	467	521	383	45	0	0	2383
1977	0	3	52	98	311	502	620	618	525	218	38	5	2990
1978	3	7	30	152	384	537	660	567	410	154	79	11	2994
1979	3	13	65	166	285	482	619	570	418	322	42	13	2998
1980	11	14	61	127	355	614	725	635	567	245	51	26	3431
1981	3	24	30	255	324	502	603	619	424	273	41	3	3101
1982	11	5	117	142	304	504	645	659	459	191	72	19	3128
1983	0	0	21	111	276	435	560	611	417	207	84	8	2730
1984	0	8	101	169	383	541	625	618	394	230	46	44	3159
1985	0	8	85	165	368	462	539	641	450	223	101	5	3047
1986	2	45	49	244	304	500	652	646	568	166	40	4	3218
1987	4	5	17	135	340	471	589	658	434	199	67	12	2931
1988	6	19	71	166	352	492	617	671	480	264	131	20	3289
1989	24	23	99	222	524	557	678	656	429	244	75	0	3531
1990	22	26	53	177	450	681	578	635	459	192	91	23	3387
1991	0	10	70	234	402	541	612	654	396	295	49	20	3283
1992	0	23	47	158	281	531	618	542	508	267	34	24	3033
1993	1	7	45	117	283	503	660	698	503	267	31	22	3137

SNOWFALL (inches) SAN ANTONIO, TEXAS

SEASON	JULY	AUG	SEP	OCT	NOV	DEC	JAN	FEB	MAR	APR	MAY	JUNE	TOTAL
1964-65	0.0	0.0	0.0	0.0	0.0	0.2	0.0	T	T	0.0	0.0	0.0	0.2
1965-66	0.0	0.0	0.0	0.0	0.0	0.0	T	3.5	0.0	0.0	0.0	0.0	3.5
1966-67	0.0	0.0	0.0	0.0	0.0	0.0	T	T	0.0	0.0	0.0	0.0	T
1967-68	0.0	0.0	0.0	0.0	0.0	0.0	0.0	T	0.0	0.0	0.0	0.0	T
1968-69	0.0	0.0	0.0	0.0	0.0	0.0	0.0	0.0	0.0	0.0	0.0	0.0	0.0
1969-70	0.0	0.0	0.0	0.0	0.0	T	T	T	0.0	0.0	0.0	0.0	T
1970-71	0.0	0.0	0.0	0.0	0.0	0.0	0.0	0.0	0.0	0.0	0.0	0.0	0.0
1971-72	0.0	0.0	0.0	0.0	0.0	0.0	T	0.0	0.0	0.0	0.0	0.0	T
1972-73	0.0	0.0	0.0	0.0	0.0	T	0.8	2.1	0.0	0.0	0.0	0.0	2.9
1973-74	0.0	0.0	0.0	0.0	0.0	0.0	0.0	0.0	0.0	0.0	0.0	0.0	0.0
1974-75	0.0	0.0	0.0	0.0	0.0	T	T	0.0	0.0	0.0	0.0	0.0	T
1975-76	0.0	0.0	0.0	0.0	0.0	0.0	T	0.0	0.0	0.0	0.0	0.0	T
1976-77	0.0	0.0	0.0	0.0	T	T	0.0	0.0	0.0	0.0	0.0	0.0	T
1977-78	0.0	0.0	0.0	0.0	0.0	0.0	0.0	0.0	T	0.0	0.0	0.0	T
1978-79	0.0	0.0	0.0	0.0	0.0	0.0	T	0.0	0.0	0.0	0.0	0.0	T
1979-80	0.0	0.0	0.0	0.0	T	0.0	0.0	T	0.0	0.0	0.0	0.0	T
1980-81	0.0	0.0	0.0	0.0	T	0.0	T	0.0	0.0	0.0	0.0	0.0	T
1981-82	0.0	0.0	0.0	0.0	0.0	0.0	0.5	0.0	0.0	0.0	0.0	0.0	0.5
1982-83	0.0	0.0	0.0	0.0	0.0	0.0	0.0	0.0	0.0	0.0	0.0	0.0	0.0
1983-84	0.0	0.0	0.0	0.0	0.0	0.0	0.0	0.0	0.0	0.0	0.0	0.0	0.0
1984-85	0.0	0.0	0.0	0.0	0.0	0.0	15.9	T	0.0	0.0	0.0	0.0	15.9
1985-86	0.0	0.0	0.0	0.0	0.0	0.0	T	0.0	0.0	0.0	0.0	0.0	T
1986-87	0.0	0.0	0.0	0.0	0.0	0.0	1.3	0.0	0.0	0.0	0.0	0.0	1.3
1987-88	0.0	0.0	0.0	0.0	0.0	0.0	0.0	0.1	0.0	0.0	0.0	0.0	0.1
1988-89	0.0	0.0	0.0	0.0	0.0	0.0	0.0	0.0	T	0.0	0.0	T	T
1989-90	0.0	0.0	0.0	0.0	0.0	T	0.0	T	T	T	0.0	0.0	T
1990-91	0.0	0.0	0.0	0.0	0.0	T	0.0	T	0.0	T	T	0.0	T
1991-92	0.0	0.0	0.0	0.0	0.0	0.0	0.0	T	T	0.0	0.0	0.0	T
1992-93	0.0	0.0	0.0	0.0	T	0.0	T	0.0	0.0	T	T	0.0	T
1993-94	0.0	0.0	0.0	T	0.0	0.0							
Record Mean	0.0	0.0	0.0	T	T	T	0.5	0.2	T	T	T	T	0.7

SALT LAKE CITY, UTAH

Salt Lake City is located in a northern Utah valley surrounded by mountains on three sides and the Great Salt Lake to the northwest. The city varies in altitude from near 4,200 to 5,000 feet above sea level.

The Wasatch Mountains to the east have peaks to nearly 12,000 feet above sea level. Their orographic effects cause more precipitation in the eastern part of the city than over the western part.

The Oquirrh Mountains to the southwest of the city have several peaks to above 10,000 feet above sea level. The Traverse Mountain Range at the south end of the Salt Lake Valley rises to above 6,000 feet above sea level. These mountain ranges help to shelter the valleys from storms from the southwest in the winter, but are instrumental in developing thunderstorms which can drift over the valley in the summer.

Besides the mountain ranges, the most influential natural condition affecting the climate of Salt Lake City is the Great Salt Lake. This large inland body of water, which never freezes over due to its high salt content, can moderate the temperatures of cold winter winds blowing from the northwest and helps drive a lake/valley wind system. The warmer lake water during the winter and spring also contributes to increased precipitation in the valley downwind from the lake. The combination of the Great Salt Lake and the Wasatch Mountains often enhances storm precipitation in the valley.

Salt Lake City normally has a semi-arid continental climate with four well-defined seasons. Summers are characterized by hot, dry weather, but the high temperatures are usually not oppressive since the relative humidity is generally low and the nights usually cool. July is the hottest month with temperature readings in the 90s.

The mean diurnal temperature range is about 30 degrees in the summer and 18 degrees during the winter. Temperatures above 102 degrees in the summer or colder than −10 degrees in the winter are likely to occur one season out of four.

Winters are cold, but usually not severe. Mountains to the north and east act as a barrier to frequent invasions of cold continental air. The average annual snowfall is under 60 inches at the airport but much higher amounts fall in higher bench locations. Heavy fog can develop under temperature inversions in the winter and persist for several days.

Precipitation, generally light during the summer and early fall, is heavy in the spring when storms from the Pacific Ocean are moving through the area more frequently than at any other season of the year.

Winds are usually light, although occasional high winds have occurred in every month of the year, particularly in March.

The growing season is over five months in length. Yard and garden foilage generally are making good growth by mid–April. The last freezing temperature in the spring averages late April and the first freeze of the fall is mid–October.

NORMALS, MEANS, AND EXTREMES

SALT LAKE CITY, UTAH

LATITUDE: 40°47'N LONGITUDE: 111°57' W ELEVATION: FT. GRND 4221 BARO 4224 TIME ZONE: MOUNTAIN WBAN: 24127

	(a)	JAN	FEB	MAR	APR	MAY	JUNE	JULY	AUG	SEP	OCT	NOV	DEC	YEAR
TEMPERATURE °F:														
Normals														
-Daily Maximum		36.4	43.6	52.2	61.3	71.9	82.8	92.2	89.4	79.2	66.1	50.8	37.8	63.6
-Daily Minimum		19.3	24.6	31.4	37.9	45.6	55.4	63.7	61.8	51.0	40.2	30.9	21.6	40.3
-Monthly		27.9	34.1	41.8	49.7	58.8	69.1	77.9	75.6	65.2	53.2	40.8	29.7	52.0
Extremes														
-Record Highest	65	62	69	78	86	93	104	107	104	100	89	75	67	107
-Year		1982	1972	1960	1992	1984	1979	1960	1979	1979	1963	1967	1969	JUL 1960
-Record Lowest	65	-22	-30	2	14	25	35	40	37	27	16	-14	-21	-30
-Year		1949	1933	1966	1936	1965	1962	1968	1965	1965	1971	1955	1932	FEB 1933
NORMAL DEGREE DAYS:														
Heating (base 65°F)		1150	865	719	464	215	51	0	0	108	373	726	1094	5765
Cooling (base 65°F)		0	0	0	0	23	174	400	329	114	7	0	0	1047
% OF POSSIBLE SUNSHINE	55	45	54	63	68	72	80	83	82	82	72	53	42	66
MEAN SKY COVER (tenths)														
Sunrise - Sunset	58	7.3	7.1	6.7	6.4	5.7	4.3	3.6	3.7	3.6	4.6	6.3	7.2	5.6
MEAN NUMBER OF DAYS:														
Sunrise to Sunset														
-Clear	65	5.6	5.2	6.9	6.8	9.1	13.7	16.8	15.8	16.5	13.9	8.5	6.3	125.0
-Partly Cloudy	65	6.6	6.9	8.2	9.4	10.2	9.9	9.7	10.7	8.3	7.8	7.2	6.5	101.2
-Cloudy	65	18.9	16.1	15.9	13.8	11.7	6.4	4.5	4.6	5.2	9.3	14.4	18.2	139.0
Precipitation .01 inches or more	65	10.0	8.8	9.8	9.4	8.2	5.4	4.5	5.7	5.3	6.3	7.8	9.1	90.6
Snow,Ice pellets,hail 1.0 inches or more	65	4.1	3.2	2.8	1.4	0.2	0.0	0.0	0.0	0.*	0.4	2.0	3.8	17.8
Thunderstorms	65	0.3	0.7	1.4	2.2	5.2	5.4	6.8	7.8	4.2	1.9	0.5	0.3	36.6
Heavy Fog Visibility 1/4 mile or less	65	4.5	2.3	0.3	0.1	0.*	0.0	0.0	0.0	0.0	0.*	0.9	3.6	11.9
Temperature °F														
-Maximum														
90° and above	34	0.0	0.0	0.0	0.0	0.6	8.9	23.1	19.1	3.7	0.0	0.0	0.0	55.5
32° and below	34	10.9	3.7	0.6	0.0	0.0	0.0	0.0	0.0	0.0	0.*	0.7	8.7	24.7
-Minimum														
32° and below	34	27.7	22.7	15.6	6.3	0.7	0.0	0.0	0.0	0.3	4.7	18.2	27.6	123.9
0° and below	34	1.7	0.4	0.0	0.0	0.0	0.0	0.0	0.0	0.0	0.0	0.0	0.8	2.9
AVG. STATION PRESS.(mb)	21	874.8	873.4	869.6	869.7	869.0	869.9	871.2	871.6	872.2	873.6	873.6	874.9	872.0
RELATIVE HUMIDITY (%)														
Hour 05	34	79	78	71	67	65	60	52	55	61	68	75	79	68
Hour 11 (Local Time)	34	71	64	52	44	39	31	27	29	35	43	58	70	47
Hour 17	34	70	60	47	39	33	26	22	23	29	41	59	71	43
Hour 23	34	79	77	68	61	57	50	43	45	54	66	74	78	63
PRECIPITATION (inches):														
Water Equivalent														
-Normal		1.11	1.23	1.91	2.12	1.80	0.93	0.81	0.86	1.28	1.44	1.29	1.40	16.18
-Maximum Monthly	65	3.23	3.22	3.97	4.90	4.76	2.93	2.57	3.66	7.04	3.91	2.63	4.37	7.04
-Year		1993	1936	1983	1944	1977	1947	1982	1968	1982	1981	1985	1983	SEP 1982
-Minimum Monthly	65	0.09	0.12	0.10	0.45	T	0.01	T	T	T	0.00	0.01	0.08	0.00
-Year		1961	1946	1956	1981	1934	1946	1963	1944	1951	1952	1939	1976	OCT 1952
-Maximum in 24 hrs	65	1.36	1.05	1.83	2.41	2.03	1.88	2.35	1.96	2.30	1.76	1.13	1.82	2.41
-Year		1953	1958	1944	1957	1942	1948	1962	1932	1982	1984	1954	1972	APR 1957
Snow,Ice pellets,hail														
-Maximum Monthly	65	50.3	27.9	41.9	26.4	7.5	T	T	T	4.0	20.4	27.2	35.2	50.3
-Year		1993	1969	1977	1974	1975	1993	1991	1993	1971	1984	1985	1972	JAN 1993
-Maximum in 24 hrs	65	10.7	11.9	15.4	16.2	6.4	T	T	T	4.0	18.4	11.0	18.1	18.4
-Year		1980	1989	1944	1974	1975	1993	1991	1993	1971	1984	1930	1972	OCT 1984
WIND:														
Mean Speed (mph)	64	7.5	8.1	9.3	9.6	9.5	9.4	9.5	9.7	9.1	8.5	7.9	7.5	8.8
Prevailing Direction through 1963		SSE	SE	SSE	SE	SE	SSE	SSE	SSE	SE	SE	SSE	SSE	SSE
Fastest Mile														
-Direction (!!)	58	NW	SE	NW	NW	NW	W	NW	SW	W	NW	NW	S	NW
-Speed (MPH)	58	59	56	71	57	57	63	51	58	61	67	63	54	71
-Year		1980	1954	1954	1964	1953	1963	1986	1946	1952	1950	1937	1955	MAR 1954
Peak Gust														
-Direction (!!)	10	N	S	NW	NW	SW	SW	W	SW	NW	NW	SW	S	SW
-Speed (mph)	10	59	54	59	54	69	58	59	67	61	63	54	49	69
-Date		1988	1989	1989	1984	1989	1993	1991	1989	1992	1985	1992	1992	MAY 1989

PRECIPITATION (inches)

SALT LAKE CITY, UTAH

YEAR	JAN	FEB	MAR	APR	MAY	JUNE	JULY	AUG	SEP	OCT	NOV	DEC	ANNUAL
1964	0.94	0.35	2.26	2.69	2.77	2.61	0.26	0.17	0.13	0.45	1.42	3.82	17.87
1965	2.13	1.13	0.14	2.30	2.02	1.87	1.50	2.08	1.93	0.39	1.13	1.81	18.43
1966	0.41	1.19	1.21	1.43	0.51	0.07	0.33	0.22	0.83	1.18	0.75	0.86	8.99
1967	2.05	0.67	1.94	2.08	2.15	2.73	1.14	0.07	0.73	0.66	0.66	1.64	16.52
1968	0.46	2.32	2.21	2.82	2.18	1.58	0.09	3.66	0.56	1.64	1.32	2.27	21.11
1969	1.69	2.84	0.57	1.38	0.18	2.83	1.51	0.34	0.18	1.96	0.92	1.69	16.09
1970	1.24	0.94	1.01	3.25	0.89	1.63	0.86	0.57	2.80	1.61	2.27	2.80	19.87
1971	1.06	2.13	1.01	2.16	1.34	0.64	0.94	2.15	1.75	3.23	1.03	1.35	18.79
1972	1.22	0.48	1.18	3.62	0.14	0.15	0.06	0.21	1.36	2.74	1.36	3.22	15.74
1973	1.49	0.91	2.67	1.64	1.74	0.19	1.07	1.16	4.07	0.67	2.52	2.26	20.39
1974	1.80	1.65	0.97	4.57	0.39	0.28	0.18	0.32	0.03	2.03	0.90	1.34	14.46
1975	1.28	1.24	3.44	2.46	2.58	1.81	0.28	0.10	0.08	1.91	1.71	1.03	17.92
1976	0.63	1.90	1.90	2.47	0.99	1.24	1.55	0.82	0.16	0.57	0.03	0.08	12.34
1977	0.76	0.64	3.10	0.59	4.76	0.06	0.61	1.85	1.85	0.83	1.20	1.42	17.67
1978	2.33	1.96	3.47	2.90	1.57	0.06	0.06	0.92	2.51	T	1.73	0.58	18.09
1979	0.72	1.05	0.80	1.04	0.84	0.35	0.40	0.63	0.05	1.29	0.98	0.55	8.70
1980	2.87	2.25	2.46	0.89	2.70	0.42	1.34	0.26	0.72	1.74	1.17	0.37	17.19
1981	0.64	0.81	2.11	0.45	3.68	1.03	0.33	0.23	0.48	3.91	1.03	1.89	16.59
1982	1.08	0.53	2.39	1.63	1.86	0.66	2.57	0.56	7.04	1.87	0.75	1.92	22.86
1983	1.19	1.36	3.97	1.63	2.58	0.62	1.02	2.64	1.03	1.62	2.23	4.37	24.26
1984	0.50	0.95	1.76	4.43	1.17	1.86	1.72	1.49	1.72	3.70	1.45	0.80	21.55
1985	0.91	0.85	1.80	0.64	2.95	1.30	0.85	0.03	1.98	1.61	2.63	1.42	16.97
1986	0.86	1.28	2.32	4.55	3.39	0.42	0.85	1.32	2.75	0.39	1.17	0.10	19.40
1987	1.53	1.41	1.52	0.79	2.41	0.19	0.79	0.36	0.05	1.18	1.17	1.10	12.50
1988	1.06	0.13	0.94	1.84	2.16	0.03	0.04	0.22	0.07	0.01	2.17	0.62	9.29
1989	0.56	1.57	1.77	0.46	1.83	0.22	0.39	0.90	0.49	1.82	0.73	0.13	10.87
1990	0.57	0.35	2.17	1.14	1.65	0.66	0.64	0.46	0.56	0.69	1.24	0.56	10.69
1991	1.11	0.61	1.11	2.71	2.76	1.09	0.32	0.86	2.55	2.10	2.17	0.40	17.79
1992	0.78	1.24	1.11	0.96	1.86	0.45	0.29	0.35	0.47	1.03	2.46	1.07	12.07
1993	3.23	1.35	1.37		3.99	1.14	1.38	0.46	0.22	2.77	0.54	0.88	
Record Mean	1.28	1.32	1.84	1.98	1.82	0.87	0.63	0.86	0.95	1.43	1.37	1.34	15.69

AVERAGE TEMPERATURE (deg. F)

SALT LAKE CITY, UTAH

YEAR	JAN	FEB	MAR	APR	MAY	JUNE	JULY	AUG	SEP	OCT	NOV	DEC	ANNUAL
1964	21.9	25.8	32.0	45.6	55.8	63.2	77.5	71.9	61.5	53.0	37.8	33.3	48.3
1965	31.0	33.0	36.8	51.0	54.7	64.8	75.0	70.9	57.5	54.5	46.1	30.2	50.5
1966	30.6	29.4	41.6	49.6	62.7	69.2	80.1	74.1	67.5	49.9	43.1	29.2	52.3
1967	29.4	37.5	44.2	46.1	56.3	64.6	78.4	78.6	66.7	52.4	43.0	25.1	51.8
1968	24.5	38.2	44.7	45.4	56.4	67.5	78.3	69.4	61.4	51.7	38.5	26.8	50.2
1969	32.2	28.7	38.4	50.4	64.0	64.8	76.6	77.6	69.7	47.7	39.5	32.4	51.9
1970	34.6	40.4	40.6	44.2	58.8	67.6	76.6	77.7	59.0	47.1	42.6	29.2	51.5
1971	32.4	34.9	40.4	48.2	56.6	67.5	76.4	76.9	59.8	47.5	37.6	26.9	50.4
1972	29.8	37.8	46.9	48.1	60.5	71.9	77.2	75.8	63.9	53.6	39.4	22.7	52.3
1973	19.6	32.3	41.8	47.6	61.6	70.2	76.6	76.6	61.5	54.1	40.5	33.4	51.3
1974	26.7	31.4	45.2	48.1	58.8	73.4	79.2	74.2	66.5	54.7	43.4	31.7	52.8
1975	27.4	35.5	41.1	44.3	54.3	64.8	78.8	73.4	65.4	53.4	37.3	32.9	50.7
1976	27.9	34.1	38.1	49.3	62.2	67.6	78.7	72.3	66.4	51.0	41.8	29.4	51.6
1977	26.8	35.8	37.7	54.1	55.0	73.2	77.3	75.0	66.4	55.6	42.5	37.9	53.2
1978	36.3	39.8	48.0	50.2	56.0	69.2	78.0	74.0	64.0	55.5	41.0	26.8	53.3
1979	22.1	32.5	43.2	51.1	60.2	70.1	78.9	75.6	71.4	56.7	36.5	32.9	52.6
1980	33.7	36.0	41.5	52.7	57.0	67.5	77.6	74.1	66.3	52.6	41.3	33.6	52.8
1981	32.1	38.3	44.1	53.4	57.6	69.6	78.2	78.0	68.5	50.5	44.3	36.4	54.3
1982	29.8	32.3	43.3	46.5	56.7	68.0	75.5	78.4	64.0	48.8	38.1	29.9	51.0
1983	35.2	39.4	44.6	45.9	55.8	67.7	76.6	77.8	67.8	56.0	43.0	31.9	53.5
1984	23.8	25.8	40.1	48.5	61.6	67.3	78.5	77.2	66.5	49.5	42.7	29.9	51.0
1985	24.2	25.6	40.8	55.7	63.9	72.5	80.7	76.5	62.7	53.1	37.4	27.7	51.7
1986	29.0	41.4	47.7	48.8	57.2	73.5	74.2	77.9	60.2	51.3	40.9	29.8	52.7
1987	26.5	36.1	42.8	55.9	62.7	71.6	75.7	74.7	66.5	56.4	40.8	30.5	53.4
1988	25.0	34.8	41.4	52.0	59.6	75.7	80.9	76.5	63.8	60.0	41.1	28.1	53.2
1989	22.3	25.3	45.8	54.8	59.9	69.2	81.1	75.1	66.4	53.4	40.5	31.4	52.1
1990	33.4	32.8	45.0	54.9	57.8	72.0	78.9	76.2	72.0	54.0	41.4	21.0	53.3
1991	24.4	36.5	42.8	47.9	55.6	68.3	79.1	78.4	64.4	53.6	40.0	30.0	51.8
1992	25.6	39.3	49.3	57.1	65.6	70.4	75.4	77.3	66.5	56.0	34.1	27.1	53.6
1993	24.9	29.5	45.5	48.5	63.4	63.7	69.9	72.5	65.5	52.6	34.8	31.5	50.2
Record Mean	28.0	33.3	41.1	49.4	58.4	68.4	77.3	75.5	65.3	53.2	40.4	31.2	51.8
Max	36.1	41.7	50.7	60.3	70.5	81.8	91.2	89.1	78.6	65.1	50.0	39.1	62.8
Min	19.9	24.9	31.5	38.5	46.3	54.9	63.3	61.9	51.9	41.3	30.8	23.3	40.7

REFERENCE NOTES

SALT LAKE CITY, UTAH

GENERAL
T - TRACE AMOUNT.
BLANK ENTRIES DENOTE MISSING/UNREPORTED DATA.
# INDICATES A STATION OR INSTRUMENT RELOCATION.

SPECIFIC

PM - INCLUDES LAST DAY OF PREVIOUS MONTH
ASOS - AUTOMATED SURFACE OBSERVING SYSTEM IN OPERATION DURING THESE MONTHS.

(a) - LENGTH OF RECORD IN YEARS, ALTHOUGH INDIVIDUAL MONTHS MAY BE MISSING.
0.* OR * - THE VALUE IS BETWEEN 0.0 AND 0.05
NORMALS - BASED ON THE 1961-1990 RECORD PERIOD.
EXTREMES - DATES ARE THE MOST RECENT OCCURRENCE
WIND DIR.- NUMERALS SHOW TENS OF DEGRESS CLOCKWISE FROM TRUE NORTH. "00" INDICATES CALM.
RESULTANT DIRECTIONS ARE GIVEN TO WHOLE DEGREES.
BOLD VALUES INDICATE EXTREME VALUES WHICH OCCURRED AFTER THE ASOS SYSTEM WAS COMMISSIONED.

RECORD = PERIOD OF RECORD
RECORD MEAN PRECIPITATION IS THE MEAN OF ALL DAILY PRECIPITATION AMOUNTS DURING THE PERIOD OF RECORD.
RECORD MAX(MIN) TEMPERATURE IS THE MEAN OF ALL DAILY MAX(MIN) TEMPERATURES DURING THE PERIOD OF RECORD.
RECORD MEAN TEMPERATURE IS THE SUM OF THE RECORD MAX AND RECORD MIN DIVIDED BY 2.
AVERAGE TEMPERATURE IS THE SUM OF THE MEAN DAILY MAX AND MIN TEMPERATURE DIVIDED BY 2.

EXCEPTIONS

RECORD MEANS ARE THROUGH THE CURRENT YEAR,
BEGINNING IN 1874 FOR TEMPERATURE
1874 FOR PRECIPITATION
1929 FOR SNOWFALL

HEATING DEGREE DAYS Base 65 deg. F SALT LAKE CITY, UTAH

SEASON	JULY	AUG	SEP	OCT	NOV	DEC	JAN	FEB	MAR	APR	MAY	JUNE	TOTAL
1964-65	0	44	134	365	808	975	1046	889	869	414	316	61	5921
1965-66	0	20	239	317	564	1069	1058	989	717	456	140	40	5609
1966-67	0	4	57	460	649	1101	1097	763	638	564	287	76	5696
1967-68	0	0	57	387	653	1228	1246	772	622	583	276	57	5881
1968-69	3	49	166	407	786	1174	1009	1010	818	433	75	67	5997
1969-70	1	0	17	530	759	1003	935	681	754	619	218	69	5586
1970-71	0	0	218	550	667	1103	1002	836	754	499	258	55	5942
1971-72	0	0	201	535	817	1176	1085	783	556	499	168	2	5822
1972-73	0	0	110	347	761	1307	1400	909	711	515	135	67	6262
1973-74	1	0	140	333	732	975	1181	935	603	502	214	41	5657
1974-75	0	5	54	316	638	1025	1157	819	734	613	334	92	5787
1975-76	0	1	62	365	825	989	1144	890	826	464	112	67	5745
1976-77	0	7	37	432	689	1096	1175	813	838	333	304	0	5724
1977-78	0	11	73	282	670	835	880	697	522	433	293	36	4732
1978-79	0	12	144	284	714	1178	1327	902	666	414	196	57	5894
1979-80	0	0	7	270	846	987	964	835	723	371	250	77	5330
1980-81	0	10	57	379	704	965	1013	742	641	346	233	46	5136
1981-82	0	0	34	444	614	879	1087	909	668	548	259	62	5504
1982-83	7	0	134	495	800	1080	916	710	624	569	314	36	5685
1983-84	6	0	49	276	650	1018	1269	1130	763	493	157	76	5887
1984-85	0	0	98	480	662	1084	1260	1097	740	285	109	17	5832
1985-86	0	0	140	360	821	1151	1110	655	527	477	283	14	5538
1986-87	6	0	203	416	720	1085	1186	803	679	291	123	17	5529
1987-88	0	0	51	260	719	1060	1235	870	723	381	222	3	5524
1988-89	0	0	142	158	711	1138	1318	1105	587	313	193	35	5700
1989-90	0	15	44	355	729	1036	971	895	612	297	232	30	5216
1990-91	0	0	17	347	704	1359	1249	792	682	508	289	32	5979
1991-92	0	0	78	347	742	1078	1220	741	481	247	57	33	5024
1992-93	11	14	42	285	921	1169	1237	986	596	489	151	108	6009
1993-94	19	3	82	391	902	1031							

COOLING DEGREE DAYS Base 65 deg. F SALT LAKE CITY, UTAH

YEAR	JAN	FEB	MAR	APR	MAY	JUNE	JULY	AUG	SEP	OCT	NOV	DEC	TOTAL
1969	0	0	0	1	53	68	366	398	164	0	0	0	1050
1970	0	0	0	0	32	152	365	398	46	0	0	0	993
1971	0	0	0	0	5	136	361	374	50	0	0	0	926
1972	0	0	0	0	34	213	386	340	85	0	0	0	1058
1973	0	0	0	0	38	226	370	367	44	3	0	0	1048
1974	0	0	0	2	31	303	446	298	108	3	0	0	1191
1975	0	0	0	0	9	89	439	269	80	14	0	0	900
1976	0	0	0	0	34	151	431	237	87	3	0	0	943
1977	0	0	0	12	2	254	389	328	123	0	0	0	1108
1978	0	0	0	0	21	167	411	299	120	0	0	0	1018
1979	0	0	0	2	54	214	439	336	208	21	0	0	1274
1980	0	0	0	9	10	159	399	301	99	1	0	0	978
1981	0	0	0	3	12	190	412	409	145	2	0	0	1173
1982	0	0	0	0	11	158	338	423	109	0	0	0	1039
1983	0	0	0	0	37	123	370	405	138	4	0	0	1077
1984	0	0	0	3	58	153	426	383	147	4	0	0	1174
1985	0	0	0	11	78	249	493	364	79	0	0	0	1274
1986	0	0	0	0	47	277	296	407	66	0	0	0	1093
1987	0	0	0	25	60	222	338	309	103	0	0	0	1057
1988	0	0	0	0	61	334	501	363	112	9	0	0	1380
1989	0	0	0	13	43	171	506	337	92	0	0	0	1162
1990	0	0	0	2	19	247	438	351	235	11	0	0	1303
1991	0	0	0	1	3	138	442	425	63	4	0	0	1076
1992	0	0	0	15	81	204	340	401	93	14	0	0	1148
1993	0	0	0	0	108	75	178	246	102	13	0	0	722

SNOWFALL (inches) SALT LAKE CITY, UTAH

SEASON	JULY	AUG	SEP	OCT	NOV	DEC	JAN	FEB	MAR	APR	MAY	JUNE	TOTAL
1964-65	0.0	0.0	0.0	0.0	6.7	6.2	15.7	9.5	1.1	2.4	5.3	0.0	46.9
1965-66	0.0	0.0	2.2	0.0	2.6	12.8	5.9	18.1	17.4	2.8	0.0	0.0	61.8
1966-67	0.0	0.0	0.0	3.6	3.2	8.7	30.4	4.5	11.8	11.4	1.0	0.0	74.6
1967-68	0.0	0.0	0.0	0.0	4.2	27.1	6.8	13.6	8.4	14.2	T	T	74.3
1968-69	0.0	0.0	0.0	T	8.7	33.3	13.7	27.9	5.4	0.2	0.0	0.0	89.2
1969-70	0.0	0.0	0.0	0.1	5.6	16.0	2.8	3.9	5.2	23.6	0.0	0.0	57.2
1970-71	0.0	0.0	0.0	0.3	0.7	25.8	13.6	8.7	8.9	1.7	1.4	0.0	61.1
1971-72	0.0	0.0	4.0	16.6	5.4	17.7	10.5	7.6	1.4	15.0	0.0	0.0	78.2
1972-73	0.0	0.0	0.0	6.0	1.1	35.2	20.9	3.6	17.8	2.6	0.0	0.0	87.2
1973-74	0.0	0.0	0.0	1.3	19.5	19.6	20.1	17.2	6.7	26.4	T	T	110.8
1974-75	0.0	0.0	0.0	T	T	8.8	12.5	7.9	22.8	13.1	7.5	0.0	72.6
1975-76	0.0	0.0	0.0	0.1	18.0	11.8	8.6	15.8	18.7	3.5	0.0	T	76.5
1976-77	0.0	0.0	0.0	0.0	T	1.2	8.6	3.2	41.9	4.8	0.6	0.0	60.3
1977-78	0.0	0.0	0.0	0.2	8.5	8.2	15.6	15.5	6.2	2.5	4.6	0.0	61.3
1978-79	0.0	0.0	1.0	0.0	17.4	8.7	13.8	12.4	3.6	7.7	T	0.0	64.6
1979-80	0.0	0.0	0.0	0.0	4.6	8.5	24.5	2.9	19.9	1.2	T	0.0	61.6
1980-81	0.0	0.0	0.0	T	3.9	3.3	8.9	2.7	11.1	0.3	T	T	30.2
1981-82	0.0	0.0	0.0	4.4	2.4	11.5	15.3	4.5	10.2	9.5	T	T	57.8
1982-83	0.0	0.0	0.0	0.2	1.0	20.1	6.2	1.0	13.3	9.0	5.0	0.0	55.8
1983-84	0.0	0.0	0.0	0.0	5.9	34.2	7.6	18.5	6.7	25.1	T	T	98.0
1984-85	0.0	0.0	T	20.4	6.6	12.9	12.7	11.4	8.0	0.7	0.0	0.0	72.7
1985-86	0.0	0.0	0.0	T	27.2	14.7	3.9	1.7	1.0	5.5	T	0.0	54.0
1986-87	0.0	0.0	T	0.0	4.4	1.7	16.4	9.9	3.0	2.1	0.0	0.0	37.5
1987-88	0.0	0.0	0.0	0.0	0.6	11.0	16.3	0.4	6.1	T	0.9	0.0	35.3
1988-89	0.0	0.0	T	0.0	8.5	12.5	9.4	27.5	2.1	T	0.0	0.0	60.0
1989-90	0.0	0.0	0.0	2.7	2.4	1.7	8.2	8.5	11.8	0.7	T	T	36.0
1990-91	0.0	0.0	T	0.0	4.8	14.3	10.9	1.2	1.9	13.7	T	0.0	46.8
1991-92	T	T	T	2.8	11.4	6.8	12.2	4.7	0.2	0.4	0.0	0.0	38.5
1992-93	0.0	T	0.0	0.0	14.2	16.9	50.3	13.2	T	2.4	1.7	T	98.7
1993-94	0.0	T	0.0	0.0	6.1	8.3							
Record Mean	T	T	0.1	1.3	6.6	12.0	13.5	9.4	9.4	5.0	0.6	T	57.9

BURLINGTON, VERMONT

Burlington is located on the eastern shore of Lake Champlain at the widest part of the lake. About 35 miles to the west lie the highest peaks of the Adirondacks, while the foothills of the Green Mountains begin 10 miles to the east and southeast.

Its northerly latitude assures the variety and vigor of a true New England climate, while thanks to the modifying influence of the lake, the many rapid and marked weather changes are tempered in severity. Due to its location in the path of the St. Lawrence Valley storm track and the lake effects, the city is one of the cloudiest in the United States.

Lake Champlain exercises a tempering influence on the local temperature. During the winter months and prior to the lake freezing, temperatures along the lake shore are often 5-10 degrees warmer than at the airport 3 1/2 miles inland. At the airport the average occurrence of the last freeze in spring is around May 10th and that of the first in fall is early October, giving a growing season of 145 days. This location is justly proud of its delightful summer weather. On average, there are few days a year with maxima of 90 degrees or higher. This moderate summer heat gives way to a cooler, but none the less pleasant fall period, usually extending well into October. High pressure systems moving down rapidly from central Canada or Hudson Bay produce the coldest temperatures during the winter months, but extended periods of very cold weather are rare.

Precipitation, although generally plentiful and well distributed throughout the year, is less in the Champlain Valley than in other areas of Vermont due to the shielding effect of the mountain barriers to the east and west. The heaviest rainfall usually occurs during summer thunderstorms, but excessively heavy rainfall is quite uncommon. Droughts are infrequent.

Because of the trend of the Champlain Valley between the Adirondack and Green Mountain ranges, most winds have a northerly or southerly component. The prevailing direction most of the year is from the south. Winds of damaging force are very uncommon.

Smoke pollution is nearly non-existent since there is no concentration of heavy industry here, however, haze has been on the increase over the years due to the large increase in industry to the north and south. During the spring and fall months, fog occasionally forms along the Winooski River to the north and east and may drift over the airport with favorable winds. In spite of the high percentage of cloudiness, periods of low aircraft ceilings and visibilities are usually of short duration, allowing this area to have one of the highest percentages of flying weather in New England.

NORMALS, MEANS, AND EXTREMES

BURLINGTON, VERMONT

LATITUDE: 44°28'N LONGITUDE: 73°09'W ELEVATION: FT. GRND 332 BARO 350 TIME ZONE: EASTERN WBAN: 14742

	(a)	JAN	FEB	MAR	APR	MAY	JUNE	JULY	AUG	SEP	OCT	NOV	DEC	YEAR
TEMPERATURE °F:														
Normals														
-Daily Maximum		25.1	27.5	39.3	53.6	67.2	75.8	81.2	77.9	69.0	57.0	44.0	30.4	54.0
-Daily Minimum		7.5	8.9	22.0	34.2	45.4	54.6	59.7	57.9	48.8	38.6	29.6	15.5	35.2
-Monthly		16.3	18.2	30.7	43.9	56.3	65.2	70.5	67.9	58.9	47.8	36.8	23.0	44.6
Extremes														
-Record Highest	50	63	62	84	91	93	97	99	101	94	85	75	65	101
-Year		1950	1981	1946	1976	1977	1988	1977	1944	1945	1949	1948	1982	AUG 1944
-Record Lowest	50	-30	-30	-20	2	24	33	39	35	25	15	-2	-26	-30
-Year		1957	1979	1948	1972	1966	1986	1962	1976	1963	1972	1958	1980	FEB 1979
NORMAL DEGREE DAYS:														
Heating (base 65°F)		1510	1310	1063	633	282	58	6	29	199	533	846	1302	7771
Cooling (base 65°F)		0	0	0	0	13	64	176	119	16	0	0	0	388
% OF POSSIBLE SUNSHINE	50	41	48	51	49	54	58	64	60	54	47	31	33	49
MEAN SKY COVER (tenths)														
Sunrise - Sunset	50	7.5	7.3	7.1	7.1	7.0	6.8	6.4	6.4	6.5	7.0	8.2	8.0	7.1
MEAN NUMBER OF DAYS:														
Sunrise to Sunset														
-Clear	50	4.5	4.4	5.8	5.1	4.9	4.7	5.2	5.9	5.9	5.9	2.5	3.0	57.9
-Partly Cloudy	50	6.4	6.8	7.0	7.4	9.2	10.8	12.9	11.8	10.1	7.8	5.4	5.8	101.4
-Cloudy	50	20.1	17.0	18.2	17.4	16.8	14.5	12.8	13.3	14.0	17.4	22.1	22.1	205.9
Precipitation														
.01 inches or more	50	14.4	11.6	13.1	12.4	13.6	12.4	11.8	12.5	11.6	11.9	14.1	14.7	154.0
Snow, Ice pellets, hail														
1.0 inches or more	50	5.2	4.8	3.7	1.2	0.1	0.0	0.0	0.0	0.0	0.1	1.9	5.1	22.0
Thunderstorms	50	0.*	0.0	0.4	0.9	2.5	5.0	6.0	5.2	2.0	0.6	0.3	0.*	23.0
Heavy Fog Visibility														
1/4 mile or less	50	0.9	1.1	1.3	1.2	0.9	1.1	0.8	1.4	2.4	2.0	1.1	1.1	15.4
Temperature °F														
-Maximum														
90° and above	29	0.0	0.0	0.0	0.1	0.6	1.1	2.9	1.2	0.1	0.0	0.0	0.0	6.0
32° and below	29	21.1	17.9	8.7	0.5	0.0	0.0	0.0	0.0	0.0	0.*	4.3	16.2	68.7
-Minimum														
32° and below	29	29.8	26.5	25.7	14.8	2.6	0.0	0.0	0.0	0.6	8.8	18.7	27.6	155.1
0° and below	29	9.8	8.3	2.0	0.0	0.0	0.0	0.0	0.0	0.0	0.0	0.0	4.7	24.8
AVG. STATION PRESS. (mb)	21	1003.8	1004.8	1003.6	1001.9	1002.3	1001.6	1002.4	1004.3	1005.5	1005.8	1004.7	1004.9	1003.8
RELATIVE HUMIDITY (%)														
Hour 01	28	71	72	73	74	77	81	83	85	85	79	76	75	78
Hour 07 (Local Time)	28	72	74	75	74	74	77	79	83	86	81	78	76	77
Hour 13	28	64	62	58	53	51	55	53	57	61	61	66	68	59
Hour 19	28	67	65	62	58	58	61	61	67	73	71	72	72	66
PRECIPITATION (inches):														
Water Equivalent														
-Normal		1.82	1.63	2.23	2.76	3.12	3.47	3.65	4.06	3.30	2.88	3.13	2.42	34.47
-Maximum Monthly	50	4.69	5.38	3.58	6.55	6.31	7.69	6.12	11.54	8.18	6.22	6.85	5.95	11.54
-Year		1978	1981	1972	1983	1983	1973	1972	1955	1945	1959	1983	1973	AUG 1955
-Minimum Monthly	50	0.42	0.21	0.38	0.93	0.29	1.09	1.23	0.72	0.87	0.50	0.63	0.62	0.21
-Year		1989	1978	1965	1966	1977	1949	1979	1957	1948	1963	1952	1960	FEB 1978
-Maximum in 24 hrs	50	1.53	1.93	1.62	2.16	2.26	2.83	2.69	3.59	3.26	2.17	2.48	2.60	3.59
-Year		1978	1981	1971	1968	1955	1972	1985	1955	1983	1983	1990	1950	AUG 1955
Snow, Ice pellets, hail														
-Maximum Monthly	50	42.4	34.3	39.9	21.3	3.9	0.0	T	0.0	0.1	5.1	19.2	56.7	56.7
-Year		1978	1958	1993	1983	1966		1989		1992	1969	1971	1970	DEC 1970
-Maximum in 24 hrs	50	14.5	16.5	22.4	15.6	3.5	0.0	T	0.0	0.1	5.1	10.1	17.0	22.4
-Year		1961	1966	1993	1983	1966		1989		1992	1969	1958	1978	MAR 1993
WIND:														
Mean Speed (mph)	50	9.7	9.4	9.5	9.5	9.0	8.5	8.0	7.6	8.3	8.8	9.7	9.9	9.0
Prevailing Direction through 1963		S	S	N	S	S	S	S	S	S	S	S	S	S
Fastest Obs. 1 Min.														
-Direction (!!)	10	16	17	16	17	29	16	18	17	17	17	16	16	17
-Speed (MPH)	10	38	39	33	30	35	32	35	26	32	31	35	33	39
-Year		1989	1990	1988	1992	1993	1989	1989	1987	1989	1991	1989	1985	FEB 1990
Peak Gust														
-Direction (!!)	10	SE	S	SW	S	S	S	S	W	S	S	SE	W	SE
-Speed (mph)	10	49	54	54	40	54	44	60	41	52	47	62	51	62
-Date		1989	1990	1991	1993	1990	1989	1991	1993	1989	1990	1989	1993	NOV 1989

PRECIPITATION (inches)

BURLINGTON, VERMONT

YEAR	JAN	FEB	MAR	APR	MAY	JUNE	JULY	AUG	SEP	OCT	NOV	DEC	ANNUAL
1964	2.27	0.63	2.64	2.11	4.67	3.00	2.87	4.10	1.49	2.20	2.10	1.63	29.71
1965	0.60	0.93	0.38	2.16	1.05	4.08	2.91	6.27	3.19	3.32	2.65	1.47	29.01
1966	2.02	2.49	2.63	0.93	2.49	2.63	1.92	4.46	3.33	1.41	1.41	2.82	28.54
1967	1.65	0.77	0.51	3.77	3.19	3.12	4.60	3.79	3.06	3.03	2.12	2.61	32.22
1968	1.26	1.28	3.23	3.54	2.43	3.66	2.70	2.36	2.06	2.73	4.37	3.12	32.74
1969	2.43	0.94	1.93	2.93	3.10	4.01	2.40	3.71	1.88	1.62	4.98	4.59	34.52
1970	0.65	1.95	2.01	2.78	3.14	4.38	1.92	3.44	3.93	2.66	2.35	3.77	32.98
1971	1.24	2.98	2.71	2.65	2.97	2.29	4.29	4.85	1.63	2.16	2.29	1.93	31.99
1972	0.93	1.69	3.58	2.26	2.83	6.52	6.12	2.35	1.69	2.60	4.10	3.43	38.10
1973	2.13	1.55	2.09	3.80	5.38	7.69	3.02	5.41	5.02	1.93	2.31	5.95	46.28
1974	1.90	1.54	2.73	3.47	4.61	4.45	3.70	2.60	3.23	0.78	3.60	2.08	34.69
1975	2.20	2.01	2.86	1.71	1.17	2.47	3.77	2.85	4.12	3.85	3.14	2.36	32.51
1976	2.99	2.85	2.35	2.54	5.86	4.04	3.05	4.69	3.77	4.34	1.63	1.97	40.08
1977	1.61	1.78	2.97	3.13	0.29	2.06	3.34	6.27	6.33	5.02	4.22	3.42	40.44
1978	4.69	0.21	2.98	2.51	2.16	4.36	3.50	1.82	2.07	3.72	0.95	2.11	31.08
1979	4.50	0.60	2.15	3.61	3.12	1.39	1.23	3.42	3.84	2.31	3.89	1.50	31.56
1980	0.61	0.67	2.44	2.39	1.61	1.92	6.11	3.83	4.41	2.48	2.92	1.50	30.89
1981	0.49	5.38	1.32	3.05	3.76	3.07	3.22	5.58	6.24	5.26	2.73	2.03	42.13
1982	2.74	1.43	2.31	2.63	1.95	4.95	3.07	3.55	2.12	2.31	3.59	1.69	32.34
1983	3.09	1.66	2.60	6.55	6.31	1.49	3.92	4.31	3.77	4.38	6.85	5.23	50.16
1984	0.81	2.73	1.72	4.25	5.27	1.70	5.11	3.30	2.81	1.89	3.08	3.14	35.81
1985	1.46	1.26	2.46	1.90	3.53	3.76	4.42	2.67	3.30	3.31	3.68	1.59	33.34
1986	3.69	1.68	3.17	0.95	4.11	4.40	4.53	5.82	4.86	2.50	2.99	1.32	40.02
1987	1.91	0.49	1.33	1.42	2.69	4.42	2.79	2.09	3.58	3.28	2.24	1.17	27.41
1988	0.69	1.69	1.55	1.91	1.80	3.26	2.55	4.27	1.50	2.05	4.51	0.90	26.68
1989	0.42	0.67	2.60	1.89	3.19	3.68	3.65	7.30	5.98	2.98	2.41	1.26	36.03
1990	2.36	2.82	1.81	2.97	3.66	3.08	5.12	4.85	2.03	5.99	3.91	3.58	42.18
1991	1.65	0.51	2.55	3.41	3.15	1.28	2.83	4.00	5.14	5.07	1.58	1.35	32.52
1992	1.65	1.56	2.13	2.58	2.38	1.72	4.58	1.89	4.73	3.00	3.67	0.96	30.85
1993	2.17	1.90	1.54	3.76	2.19	3.35	3.34	4.46	3.38	2.93	2.27	1.57	32.86
Record Mean	1.82	1.66	2.16	2.53	3.02	3.45	3.62	3.54	3.39	2.96	2.79	2.07	33.01

AVERAGE TEMPERATURE (deg. F)

BURLINGTON, VERMONT

YEAR	JAN	FEB	MAR	APR	MAY	JUNE	JULY	AUG	SEP	OCT	NOV	DEC	ANNUAL
#1964	21.9	17.2	31.1	43.3	58.6	63.0	69.6	62.9	55.8	45.3	35.7	24.8	44.1
1965	13.7	20.0	27.4	39.3	57.2	62.9	65.1	66.0	58.7	46.8	32.9	28.6	43.2
1966	15.5	17.9	30.3	41.3	51.2	65.3	69.6	67.4	55.7	47.0	40.6	23.4	43.7
1967	23.9	11.7	25.3	40.7	47.6	67.6	70.1	67.0	58.1	48.8	32.9	25.5	43.3
1968	8.4	11.0	29.6	46.2	51.7	60.8	68.7	63.7	61.0	49.8	32.2	17.9	41.8
1969	16.5	18.5	24.3	41.4	51.3	64.1	67.8	68.6	57.9	45.8	36.3	18.6	42.6
1970	3.6	16.9	25.8	42.6	54.1	63.7	70.6	68.4	60.1	50.5	39.0	14.3	42.5
1971	9.7	20.0	24.1	37.3	54.5	64.9	68.9	67.1	63.5	53.8	33.5	24.3	43.5
1972	21.1	17.0	24.8	35.6	56.2	63.1	69.5	65.3	58.7	42.4	32.1	22.5	42.4
1973	21.5	14.6	37.1	44.6	53.6	66.9	70.6	72.1	58.5	49.3	37.2	27.4	46.1
1974	18.7	15.6	29.2	44.4	51.3	66.5	70.2	69.1	58.2	43.4	36.2	28.5	44.3
1975	23.6	20.7	28.0	37.1	62.3	66.4	74.6	69.1	58.0	50.4	42.1	20.1	46.1
1976	11.1	24.6	33.4	47.4	54.7	69.2	68.5	65.7	57.0	43.7	33.0	16.3	43.7
1977	11.1	20.5	37.6	45.3	60.0	64.7	69.6	67.5	58.7	46.6	40.0	22.4	45.3
1978	15.1	9.5	26.0	38.7	60.1	63.9	69.4	68.3	55.2	46.4	34.8	25.2	42.7
1979	18.0	7.5	36.9	43.5	58.5	65.3	72.2	65.9	58.6	48.1	41.3	29.0	45.4
1980	21.2	17.6	31.1	46.5	58.9	64.4	70.6	70.7	57.9	45.0	32.3	15.0	44.2
1981	8.9	32.9	33.5	46.7	58.2	66.1	71.1	67.1	59.3	44.9	36.9	25.3	45.9
1982	9.6	19.1	30.3	43.4	57.3	60.7	69.5	65.9	62.3	50.1	42.3	31.9	45.2
1983	21.0	22.3	33.0	42.3	52.9	66.3	71.3	68.6	62.9	48.2	38.1	22.4	45.8
1984	16.5	28.7	21.9	44.7	52.3	66.0	70.3	71.1	57.2	50.0	38.4	30.3	45.6
1985	13.4	22.5	31.6	44.3	55.8	61.7	69.6	67.5	60.3	49.1	36.9	21.3	44.5
1986	18.5	16.2	33.7	48.5	58.3	62.3	68.5	66.1	58.1	46.9	34.5	27.8	45.0
1987	18.1	15.0	33.3	48.6	55.5	66.3	71.5	66.7	59.5	45.9	37.0	28.5	45.5
1988	19.9	21.4	29.7	44.3	57.9	63.4	73.2	70.7	58.2	44.4	39.6	22.9	45.5
1989	23.7	19.7	28.4	41.6	59.6	67.2	71.7	67.7	61.4	50.3	36.4	7.6	44.6
1990	29.8	23.5	33.8	46.2	52.9	65.9	70.2	69.8	59.4	49.4	39.5	30.1	47.5
1991	18.9	26.5	34.0	49.1	59.3	65.9	70.4	70.5	57.8	50.4	37.6	24.0	47.0
1992	18.6	19.1	26.5	42.3	56.5	64.4	66.1	67.6	60.2	45.5	36.7	28.1	44.3
1993	21.7	10.6	27.4	45.3	56.6	64.7	72.2	70.8	59.1	46.1	36.8	24.7	44.7
Record Mean	17.9	18.6	29.6	43.0	55.5	64.8	69.8	67.4	59.5	48.5	36.7	23.4	44.5
Max	26.5	27.5	38.0	52.2	65.8	74.9	79.9	77.2	68.9	57.2	43.5	30.7	53.5
Min	9.3	9.7	21.2	33.7	45.2	54.7	59.7	57.7	50.1	39.8	29.9	16.0	35.6

REFERENCE NOTES

BURLINGTON, VERMONT

GENERAL
T - TRACE AMOUNT.
BLANK ENTRIES DENOTE MISSING/UNREPORTED DATA.
# INDICATES A STATION OR INSTRUMENT RELOCATION.

SPECIFIC

PM - INCLUDES LAST DAY OF PREVIOUS MONTH
ASOS - AUTOMATED SURFACE OBSERVING SYSTEM IN OPERATION DURING THESE MONTHS.

(a) - LENGTH OF RECORD IN YEARS, ALTHOUGH INDIVIDUAL MONTHS MAY BE MISSING.
0.* OR * - THE VALUE IS BETWEEN 0.0 AND 0.05
NORMALS - BASED ON THE 1961-1990 RECORD PERIOD.
EXTREMES - DATES ARE THE MOST RECENT OCCURRENCE
WIND DIR.- NUMERALS SHOW TENS OF DEGRESS CLOCKWISE FROM TRUE NORTH. "00" INDICATES CALM.
RESULTANT DIRECTIONS ARE GIVEN TO WHOLE DEGREES.
BOLD VALUES INDICATE EXTREME VALUES WHICH OCCURRED AFTER THE ASOS SYSTEM WAS COMMISSIONED.

RECORD = PERIOD OF RECORD
RECORD MEAN PRECIPITATION IS THE MEAN OF ALL DAILY PRECIPITATION AMOUNTS DURING THE PERIOD OF RECORD.
RECORD MAX(MIN) TEMPERATURE IS THE MEAN OF ALL DAILY MAX(MIN) TEMPERATURES DURING THE PERIOD OF RECORD.
RECORD MEAN TEMPERATURE IS THE SUM OF THE RECORD MAX AND RECORD MIN DIVIDED BY 2.
AVERAGE TEMPERATURE IS THE SUM OF THE MEAN DAILY MAX AND MIN TEMPERATURE DIVIDED BY 2.

EXCEPTIONS

FASTEST MILE WIND IS THROUGH NOVEMBER 1983.

RECORD MEANS ARE THROUGH THE CURRENT YEAR,
BEGINNING IN 1893 FOR TEMPERATURE
1884 FOR PRECIPITATION
1944 FOR SNOWFALL

HEATING DEGREE DAYS Base 65 deg. F BURLINGTON, VERMONT

SEASON	JULY	AUG	SEP	OCT	NOV	DEC	JAN	FEB	MAR	APR	MAY	JUNE	TOTAL
#1964-65	12	102	280	601	872	1238	1585	1256	1159	766	257	136	8264
1965-66	43	80	236	558	956	1125	1531	1313	1069	707	432	91	8141
1966-67	17	26	280	551	725	1285	1269	1490	1225	722	533	29	8152
1967-68	11	35	223	495	957	1216	1751	1561	1089	562	407	140	8447
1968-69	32	104	127	472	979	1451	1496	1298	1256	700	422	107	8444
1969-70	41	41	244	589	856	1434	1906	1342	1208	663	341	105	8770
1970-71	10	36	174	444	773	1567	1710	1257	1263	821	336	83	8474
1971-72	12	49	131	344	938	1254	1357	1387	1239	872	281	113	7977
1972-73	26	69	212	694	982	1310	1344	1410	855	608	345	86	7941
1973-74	10	17	256	480	825	1160	1431	1378	1101	618	430	37	7743
1974-75	2	6	224	665	858	1128	1276	1236	1141	831	152	82	7601
1975-76	0	45	208	448	681	1385	1669	1168	973	545	331	50	7503
1976-77	20	68	254	654	954	1505	1667	1240	842	590	223	89	8106
1977-78	24	53	207	564	740	1314	1539	1547	1202	781	225	90	8286
1978-79	49	38	295	571	897	1227	1452	1610	866	641	224	90	7960
1979-80	23	65	213	528	703	1107	1350	1371	1043	550	204	91	7248
1980-81	10	3	240	611	976	1545	1738	894	969	544	239	43	7812
1981-82	13	36	204	617	837	1224	1716	1277	1069	643	255	133	8024
1982-83	30	54	124	455	676	1021	1356	1188	983	675	367	77	7006
1983-84	19	36	148	518	803	1317	1500	1044	1331	602	395	68	7781
1984-85	6	24	241	460	792	1068	1592	1185	1029	615	296	118	7426
1985-86	11	42	169	489	835	1344	1436	1361	966	492	219	113	7477
1986-87	40	60	215	553	906	1144	1446	1397	975	488	328	48	7600
1987-88	19	66	185	584	833	1125	1389	1260	1088	614	236	136	7535
1988-89	15	52	212	635	755	1298	1273	1265	1128	691	188	45	7557
1989-90	2	43	164	451	849	1776	1084	1156	961	577	370	63	7496
1990-91	19	10	180	480	758	1074	1424	1072	954	475	206	59	6711
1991-92	7	11	240	451	813	1266	1434	1327	1187	674	277	83	7770
1992-93	49	33	197	597	843	1137	1335	1517	1159	584	256	80	7787
1993-94	3	12	211	579	839	1243							

COOLING DEGREE DAYS Base 65 deg. F BURLINGTON, VERMONT

YEAR	JAN	FEB	MAR	APR	MAY	JUNE	JULY	AUG	SEP	OCT	NOV	DEC	TOTAL
1969	0	0	0	0	2	86	134	160	38	0	0	0	420
1970	0	0	0	0	11	75	189	150	36	1	0	0	462
1971	0	0	0	0	17	87	138	118	90	4	0	0	454
1972	0	0	0	0	14	64	169	81	30	0	0	0	358
1973	0	0	0	3	0	149	187	243	68	0	0	0	650
1974	0	0	0	5	9	89	171	140	27	1	0	0	442
1975	0	0	0	0	75	131	306	181	5	1	0	0	699
1976	0	0	0	24	19	185	135	97	23	0	0	0	483
1977	0	0	0	7	75	86	174	138	27	0	0	0	507
1978	0	0	0	0	79	64	194	146	6	0	0	0	489
1979	0	0	0	2	29	106	253	101	27	13	0	0	531
1980	0	0	0	0	24	78	189	184	34	0	0	0	509
1981	0	0	0	2	35	85	211	110	39	0	0	0	482
1982	0	0	0	1	24	11	179	90	51	0	0	0	356
1983	0	0	0	0	0	121	223	155	92	6	0	0	597
1984	0	0	0	0	7	106	175	217	15	3	0	0	523
1985	0	0	0	0	15	25	160	123	34	0	0	0	357
1986	0	0	0	4	19	38	156	104	14	0	0	0	335
1987	0	0	0	3	42	92	228	126	30	0	0	0	521
1988	0	0	0	0	19	96	274	238	15	3	0	0	645
1989	0	0	0	0	28	117	216	134	63	0	0	0	558
1990	0	0	0	16	1	95	189	165	18	6	0	0	490
1991	0	0	0	5	35	92	182	186	32	6	0	0	538
1992	0	0	0	3	21	71	91	121	61	0	0	0	368
1993	0	0	0	0	2	79	235	198	39	0	0	0	553

SNOWFALL (inches) BURLINGTON, VERMONT

SEASON	JULY	AUG	SEP	OCT	NOV	DEC	JAN	FEB	MAR	APR	MAY	JUNE	TOTAL
1964-65	0.0	0.0	0.0	0.1	1.2	23.0	11.8	4.3	7.9	1.1	0.0	0.0	49.4
1965-66	0.0	0.0	0.0	0.4	12.4	11.9	41.3	28.5	8.3	4.9	3.9	0.0	111.6
1966-67	0.0	0.0	0.0	T	2.4	36.2	20.5	12.6	6.1	4.7	2.6	0.0	85.1
1967-68	0.0	0.0	0.0	T	10.3	17.1	18.4	24.8	14.5	T	0.0	0.0	85.1
1968-69	0.0	0.0	0.0	T	18.8	28.6	15.8	17.0	12.4	3.7	0.0	0.0	96.3
1969-70	0.0	0.0	0.0	5.1	10.5	50.8	11.1	13.8	10.5	2.4	0.4	0.0	104.6
1970-71	0.0	0.0	0.0	0.1	2.7	56.7	17.1	23.1	33.1	12.6	0.0	0.0	145.4
1971-72	0.0	0.0	0.0	0.0	19.2	19.3	14.3	25.1	21.8	9.2	0.0	0.0	108.9
1972-73	0.0	0.0	0.0	T	12.2	39.0	11.4	18.5	2.3	6.3	0.0	0.0	89.7
1973-74	0.0	0.0	0.0	0.1	2.6	24.1	21.5	9.9	20.9	16.8	0.0	0.0	95.9
1974-75	0.0	0.0	0.0	0.1	11.5	16.8	14.8	22.0	12.4	13.3	0.0	0.0	90.9
1975-76	0.0	0.0	0.0	T	5.3	16.0	28.3	20.4	18.8	0.9	T	0.0	89.7
1976-77	0.0	0.0	0.0	0.9	13.3	11.5	24.2	16.4	9.6	1.8	T	0.0	77.7
1977-78	0.0	0.0	0.0	0.0	16.0	22.6	42.4	4.0	12.5	1.9	T	0.0	99.4
1978-79	0.0	0.0	0.0	T	5.7	24.1	37.9	6.6	1.6	8.4	0.0	0.0	84.3
1979-80	0.0	0.0	0.0	1.5	0.4	6.0	3.0	11.6	16.8	0.3	0.0	0.0	39.6
1980-81	0.0	0.0	0.0	T	12.2	17.5	8.7	11.9	13.3	1.1	0.0	0.0	64.7
1981-82	0.0	0.0	0.0	T	3.9	32.8	19.4	8.3	13.0	4.1	0.0	0.0	81.5
1982-83	0.0	0.0	0.0	T	0.8	5.0	22.5	18.3	11.9	21.3	0.7	0.0	80.5
1983-84	0.0	0.0	0.0	T	4.7	14.4	15.2	13.7	16.1	0.4	T	0.0	64.5
1984-85	0.0	0.0	0.0	0.0	6.0	29.3	25.9	10.9	16.6	2.7	0.0	0.0	91.4
1985-86	0.0	0.0	0.0	T	4.6	21.3	33.6	18.3	8.4	T	T	0.0	86.2
1986-87	0.0	0.0	0.0	T	10.5	7.7	34.4	7.0	6.0	2.1	0.0	0.0	67.7
1987-88	0.0	0.0	0.0	0.6	6.5	12.4	9.2	26.9	6.4	2.4	0.0	0.0	64.4
1988-89	0.0	0.0	0.0	0.3	0.6	12.4	6.6	8.5	9.7	2.3	0.0	0.0	40.4
1989-90	T	0.0	0.0	0.0	5.6	20.7	17.6	20.5	10.2	2.1	0.0	0.0	76.7
1990-91	0.0	0.0	T	T	7.3	10.3	17.8	3.9	3.2	T	0.0	0.0	42.5
1991-92	0.0	0.0	T	T	2.3	14.9	12.2	27.2	14.0	8.6	0.0	0.0	79.2
1992-93	0.0	0.0	0.1	T	2.9	2.6	24.8	33.8	39.9	12.8	0.0	0.0	116.9
1993-94	0.0	0.0	0.0	1.3	7.9	9.1							
Record Mean	T	0.0	T	0.2	6.6	18.1	18.8	16.8	12.4	3.8	0.2	0.0	77.1

NORFOLK, VIRGINIA

The city of Norfolk, Virginia, is located near the coast and the southern border of the state. It is almost surrounded by water, with the Chesapeake Bay immediately to the north, Hampton Roads to the west, and the Atlantic Ocean only 18 miles to the east. It is traversed by numerous rivers and waterways and its average elevation above sea level is 13 feet. There are no nearby hilly areas and the land is low and level throughout the city. The climate is generally marine. The geographic location of the city with respect tc the principal storm tracks, is especially favorable, being south of the average path of storms originating in the higher latitudes and north of the usual tracks of hurricanes and other tropical storms.

The winters are usually mild, while the autumn and spring seasons usually are delightful. Summers, though warm and long, frequently are tempered by cool periods, often associated with northeasterly winds off the Atlantic. Temperatures of 100 degrees or higher occur infrequently. Extreme cold waves seldom penetrate the area and temperatures of zero or below are almost nonexistent. Winters pass, on occasion, without a measurable amount of snowfall. Most of the snowfall in Norfolk is light and generally melts within 24 hours.

Based on the 1951-1980 period, the average first occurrence of 32 degrees Fahrenheit in the fall is November 17 and the average last occurrence in the spring is March 23.

NORMALS, MEANS, AND EXTREMES

NORFOLK, VIRGINIA

LATITUDE: 36°54'N LONGITUDE: 76°12'W ELEVATION: FT. GRND 24 BARO 44 TIME ZONE: EASTERN WBAN: 13737

	(a)	JAN	FEB	MAR	APR	MAY	JUNE	JULY	AUG	SEP	OCT	NOV	DEC	YEAR
TEMPERATURE °F:														
Normals														
-Daily Maximum		47.3	49.7	57.9	66.9	75.3	82.9	86.4	85.1	79.6	69.5	61.2	52.2	67.8
-Daily Minimum		30.9	32.3	39.3	47.1	56.8	65.2	70.0	69.4	64.2	52.9	43.8	35.4	50.6
-Monthly		39.1	41.0	48.6	57.0	66.1	74.1	78.2	77.2	71.9	61.2	52.5	43.8	59.2
Extremes														
-Record Highest	45	78	81	88	97	100	101	103	104	99	95	86	80	104
-Year		1970	1989	1990	1960	1991	1964	1993	1980	1983	1954	1974	1991	AUG 1980
-Record Lowest	45	-3	8	18	28	36	45	54	49	45	27	20	7	-3
-Year		1985	1965	1980	1982	1966	1967	1979	1982	1967	1976	1950	1983	JAN 1985
NORMAL DEGREE DAYS:														
Heating (base 65°F)		803	672	508	249	51	0	0	0	11	164	380	657	3495
Cooling (base 65°F)		0	0	0	9	85	277	409	378	218	46	0	0	1422
% OF POSSIBLE SUNSHINE	29	54	57	60	63	63	67	63	62	62	59	57	56	60
MEAN SKY COVER (tenths)														
Sunrise - Sunset	45	6.3	6.2	6.1	5.8	6.1	5.8	6.0	5.9	5.7	5.4	5.5	6.1	5.9
MEAN NUMBER OF DAYS:														
Sunrise to Sunset														
-Clear	45	8.9	8.1	8.8	8.7	7.8	7.5	7.4	7.7	9.0	11.6	10.4	9.2	105.2
-Partly Cloudy	45	6.5	6.3	7.6	9.3	10.0	11.9	11.9	12.0	9.6	7.1	8.0	7.0	107.1
-Cloudy	45	15.6	13.8	14.7	12.0	13.2	10.6	11.7	11.2	11.4	12.3	11.7	14.8	153.0
Precipitation														
.01 inches or more	45	10.6	10.2	11.0	10.0	9.9	9.1	11.1	10.4	7.9	7.6	8.0	9.2	115.1
Snow, Ice pellets, hail														
1.0 inches or more	45	0.8	0.7	0.2	0.*	0.0	0.0	0.0	0.0	0.0	0.0	0.0	0.3	2.0
Thunderstorms	45	0.4	0.7	1.9	2.7	4.8	5.8	8.3	6.9	2.7	1.3	0.5	0.4	36.3
Heavy Fog Visibility														
1/4 mile or less	45	2.1	2.6	1.9	1.4	1.9	1.0	0.5	1.0	1.2	2.2	1.8	2.2	19.9
Temperature °F														
-Maximum														
90° and above	45	0.0	0.0	0.0	0.4	1.6	6.7	11.9	8.9	2.9	0.1	0.0	0.0	32.5
32° and below	45	2.5	1.2	0.1	0.0	0.0	0.0	0.0	0.0	0.0	0.0	0.0	1.0	4.8
-Minimum														
32° and below	45	16.2	14.2	6.2	0.3	0.0	0.0	0.0	0.0	0.0	0.1	3.0	13.3	53.5
0° and below	45	0.*	0.0	0.0	0.0	0.0	0.0	0.0	0.0	0.0	0.0	0.0	0.0	*
AVG. STATION PRESS. (mb)	21	1018.4	1018.0	1016.4	1015.0	1015.0	1015.0	1015.6	1016.7	1017.6	1018.6	1018.9	1019.2	1017.0
RELATIVE HUMIDITY (%)														
Hour 01	45	73	72	72	73	81	83	84	86	84	82	76	73	78
Hour 07 (Local Time)	45	74	74	74	73	77	79	81	84	83	83	79	75	78
Hour 13	45	59	56	54	50	56	56	59	61	61	59	56	58	57
Hour 19	45	67	65	62	61	66	67	70	74	75	74	70	68	68
PRECIPITATION (inches):														
Water Equivalent														
-Normal		3.78	3.47	3.70	3.06	3.81	3.82	5.06	4.81	3.90	3.15	2.85	3.23	44.64
-Maximum Monthly	45	9.93	6.23	8.50	7.25	10.12	9.72	13.73	14.32	13.80	10.12	7.01	6.10	14.32
-Year		1987	1983	1989	1984	1979	1963	1975	1992	1979	1971	1951	1983	AUG 1992
-Minimum Monthly	45	1.05	0.84	0.75	0.43	0.64	0.37	0.36	0.74	0.26	0.57	0.49	0.67	0.26
-Year		1981	1991	1986	1985	1991	1954	1993	1975	1986	1984	1965	1988	SEP 1986
-Maximum in 24 hrs	45	3.80	2.71	3.18	5.90	3.41	6.85	5.64	11.40	6.79	4.38	3.35	2.76	11.40
-Year		1967	1983	1958	1991	1980	1963	1969	1964	1959	1971	1952	1983	AUG 1964
Snow, Ice pellets, hail														
-Maximum Monthly	45	14.2	24.4	13.7	1.2	0.0	T	0.0	T	0.0	0.0	0.6	14.7	24.4
-Year		1966	1989	1980	1964		1990		1991			1950	1958	FEB 1989
-Maximum in 24 hrs	45	9.1	14.2	9.9	1.2	0.0	T	0.0	T	0.0	0.0	0.6	11.4	14.2
-Year		1973	1989	1980	1964		1990		1991			1950	1958	FEB 1989
WIND:														
Mean Speed (mph)	45	11.5	11.9	12.4	11.8	10.5	9.8	9.0	8.8	9.6	10.3	10.6	11.1	10.6
Prevailing Direction through 1963		SW	NNE	SW	SW	SW	SW	SW	SW	NE	NE	SW	SW	SW
Fastest Obs. 1 Min.														
-Direction (!!)	21	23	36	22	02	28	30	34	35	30	04	21	01	04
-Speed (MPH)	21	39	44	46	41	38	46	46	46	46	48	40	39	48
-Year		1978	1973	1973	1990	1989	1977	1973	1979	1985	1982	1989	1989	OCT 1982
Peak Gust														
-Direction (!!)	10	N	E	SW	N	NW	SW	N	E	NW	N	E	N	N
-Speed (mph)	10	58	56	66	56	66	69	63	63	67	69	55	53	69
-Date		1987	1984	1993	1990	1984	1987	1986	1986	1985	1990	1985	1989	OCT 1990

PRECIPITATION (inches)

NORFOLK, VIRGINIA

YEAR	JAN	FEB	MAR	APR	MAY	JUNE	JULY	AUG	SEP	OCT	NOV	DEC	ANNUAL
1964	4.56	4.56	2.26	2.38	1.56	2.58	7.33	10.58	12.26	5.55	1.14	2.95	57.71
1965	2.73	2.53	2.83	2.24	1.48	4.69	3.46	3.08	0.77	1.29	0.49	1.08	26.67
1966	4.86	3.83	1.50	1.68	5.95	1.82	4.26	5.24	3.39	1.25	1.05	3.13	37.96
1967	5.44	3.56	1.34	1.31	3.25	1.37	7.21	11.19	3.02	0.93	1.75	4.84	45.21
1968	3.62	2.01	4.76	3.17	2.16	3.07	4.23	2.04	1.51	4.44	3.56	3.14	37.71
1969	2.26	2.16	4.88	2.07	2.05	4.13	12.70	5.28	2.72	3.18	2.97	3.93	48.33
1970	2.27	3.97	3.37	3.19	2.58	4.10	5.33	2.04	1.72	1.30	2.34	3.01	35.22
1971	4.03	3.59	3.88	2.18	4.46	2.16	4.81	4.63	5.46	10.12	0.97	1.44	47.73
1972	2.94	3.50	2.55	2.15	3.35	4.93	4.65	1.60	6.91	4.09	5.44	4.12	46.23
1973	2.54	3.21	4.69	3.44	3.62	5.93	4.19	7.92	0.86	1.37	1.90	5.83	45.50
1974	3.52	2.98	5.16	3.34	3.74	4.76	5.47	8.33	4.40	1.23	1.22	3.81	47.96
1975	4.18	4.18	5.72	4.19	3.37	1.16	13.73	0.74	4.82	3.19	1.63	3.62	50.53
1976	2.51	1.50	2.21	0.99	3.74	1.59	5.19	2.62	3.51	2.90	2.38	3.22	32.36
1977	3.33	2.23	4.05	2.20	3.86	2.41	2.70	4.57	3.00	6.09	5.41	3.92	43.77
1978	6.32	1.91	7.80	2.90	5.64	7.84	4.19	1.66	1.17	1.50	4.40	2.31	47.64
1979	6.47	5.01	5.13	7.00	10.12	2.97	4.69	1.79	13.80	1.74	5.26	0.98	64.96
1980	4.54	2.91	4.40	3.25	5.17	1.39	1.85	4.54	1.47	4.21	2.01	2.64	38.38
1981	1.05	2.26	1.88	2.26	2.75	5.00	5.10	6.87	3.18	3.28	1.78	5.77	41.18
1982	3.35	5.81	3.04	1.71	3.07	4.22	5.83	6.51	3.63	4.25	3.43	4.30	49.15
1983	2.21	6.23	4.55	6.13	3.52	3.84	0.77	3.07	4.52	5.29	3.24	6.10	49.47
1984	2.77	4.66	5.09	7.25	6.23	1.50	7.66	2.25	1.94	0.57	2.68	2.22	44.82
1985	3.98	3.53	2.02	0.43	3.23	6.81	6.14	1.89	6.36	3.92	5.71	0.79	44.81
1986	2.52	2.71	0.75	3.31	1.41	1.51	2.59	4.80	0.26	1.67	1.21	3.74	26.48
1987	9.93	3.11	2.30	3.83	2.65	2.98	3.20	2.04	7.00	1.81	3.51	2.33	44.69
1988	3.12	2.70	2.11	3.53	5.49	3.83	2.93	5.69	1.74	2.85	4.02	0.67	38.68
1989	2.70	5.80	8.50	3.62	2.97	5.10	4.86	7.49	5.10	2.94	3.69	3.86	56.63
1990	3.26	2.93	3.49	3.55	3.79	3.51	4.06	11.85	1.00	3.73	1.68	2.67	45.52
1991	4.74	0.84	4.70	6.39	0.64	4.54	6.46	3.77	2.04	4.65	1.72	2.43	42.92
1992	4.48	2.07	2.63	1.26	3.46	2.22	4.52	14.32	2.06	2.85	4.26	3.15	47.28
1993	4.89	2.36	5.91	3.59	2.88	2.79	0.36	1.45	4.14	3.40	0.97	3.29	36.03
Record Mean	3.37	3.34	3.76	3.25	3.68	3.98	5.54	5.35	3.83	3.13	2.66	3.19	45.06

AVERAGE TEMPERATURE (deg. F)

NORFOLK, VIRGINIA

YEAR	JAN	FEB	MAR	APR	MAY	JUNE	JULY	AUG	SEP	OCT	NOV	DEC	ANNUAL
1964	42.3	39.9	49.5	55.2	66.4	74.5	77.3	74.4	70.8	57.7	54.6	46.5	59.1
1965	39.7	41.0	44.4	54.5	69.7	72.8	76.7	77.1	73.6	59.0	51.6	43.5	58.6
1966	35.8	38.6	47.9	54.5	63.6	71.6	78.0	74.9	69.9	59.3	50.5	41.4	57.1
1967	45.7	39.9	47.7	58.0	61.2	71.2	76.3	75.2	66.5	58.7	45.9	44.0	57.5
1968	34.8	34.0	50.0	55.1	64.6	74.9	78.0	80.5	71.5	63.1	52.9	41.4	58.4
1969	38.5	39.8	44.7	59.8	67.4	77.1	79.2	76.2	71.1	62.2	49.1	40.9	58.9
1970	33.9	39.3	44.7	56.7	67.5	74.9	76.9	78.0	74.7	63.7	51.7	47.0	59.1
1971	38.6	44.7	46.9	55.9	65.0	76.0	77.2	75.7	73.2	66.7	52.4	52.3	60.4
1972	46.4	43.2	49.0	56.4	63.5	70.5	77.6	75.8	71.9	59.2	51.6	49.2	59.5
1973	40.5	39.7	52.3	58.5	66.9	76.9	78.3	78.5	75.0	64.2	53.5	46.2	60.9
1974	48.6	43.4	53.1	60.8	66.8	72.8	78.3	77.4	71.4	58.7	53.5	46.0	60.9
1975	46.0	45.4	47.4	52.7	68.3	77.0	78.6	79.6	72.3	63.4	55.7	43.2	60.8
1976	38.9	49.9	53.4	61.9	66.3	75.9	78.2	75.9	71.1	57.7	45.9	41.4	59.7
1977	29.2	41.5	54.7	61.9	68.2	74.3	81.4	81.0	76.3	60.5	54.8	43.5	60.6
1978	37.0	32.6	46.1	57.2	65.6	74.1	76.1	80.5	73.2	60.8	56.0	45.3	58.7
1979	39.4	33.3	49.1	58.1	66.7	70.4	77.1	78.5	72.8	60.4	56.4	44.9	58.9
1980	40.3	34.7	46.5	58.6	67.8	73.9	80.9	80.9	76.1	60.4	49.9	42.3	59.4
1981	32.7	43.1	45.4	61.2	65.1	78.3	79.8	75.1	70.7	59.6	50.7	41.0	58.6
1982	35.4	42.0	48.8	55.0	69.4	73.4	78.6	75.3	70.0	60.2	54.4	48.8	59.3
1983	40.2	40.8	51.0	55.7	65.8	73.0	80.3	79.0	72.8	62.7	52.6	41.6	59.6
1984	35.5	46.7	45.4	55.6	67.8	76.2	76.7	78.4	70.5	66.9	49.9	50.9	60.0
1985	34.9	40.4	51.8	62.0	68.8	74.2	78.2	77.2	73.4	65.9	60.3	41.2	60.7
1986	39.3	42.1	49.9	57.3	67.6	76.1	82.1	76.6	72.4	65.4	54.9	44.8	60.7
1987	39.6	38.7	47.5	54.6	68.3	77.0	82.4	79.6	74.3	56.6	54.3	46.0	59.9
1988	37.3	42.5	49.5	56.5	65.8	73.6	80.1	80.8	70.5	56.9	54.2	42.4	59.2
1989	45.3	43.6	50.1	56.5	65.6	78.5	79.2	77.7	73.9	62.7	53.3	34.8	60.1
1990	47.3	50.2	53.2	58.7	66.6	75.5	80.6	78.0	71.6	65.9	55.0	50.5	62.8
1991	43.5	46.0	52.7	61.6	72.8	76.2	82.0	79.5	72.3	61.9	52.7	47.6	62.4
1992	42.7	45.0	48.8	58.2	62.4	72.0	81.8	75.6	73.5	59.7	53.8	44.6	59.8
1993	44.2	39.1	46.8	57.3	68.5	76.1	83.4	78.9	74.6	61.3	53.5	41.5	60.4
Record Mean	41.2	42.2	48.9	57.5	66.8	74.7	78.8	77.6	72.5	62.1	52.3	43.7	59.8
Max	49.0	50.5	57.8	66.9	75.8	83.3	87.0	85.1	79.8	69.9	60.3	51.4	68.1
Min	33.3	33.9	40.0	48.1	57.7	66.1	70.6	70.0	65.1	54.3	44.2	35.9	51.6

REFERENCE NOTES

NORFOLK, VIRGINIA

GENERAL
T - TRACE AMOUNT.
BLANK ENTRIES DENOTE MISSING/UNREPORTED DATA.
# INDICATES A STATION OR INSTRUMENT RELOCATION.

SPECIFIC

PM - INCLUDES LAST DAY OF PREVIOUS MONTH
ASOS - AUTOMATED SURFACE OBSERVING SYSTEM IN OPERATION DURING THESE MONTHS.

(a) - LENGTH OF RECORD IN YEARS, ALTHOUGH INDIVIDUAL MONTHS MAY BE MISSING.
0.* OR * - THE VALUE IS BETWEEN 0.0 AND 0.05
NORMALS - BASED ON THE 1961-1990 RECORD PERIOD.
EXTREMES - DATES ARE THE MOST RECENT OCCURRENCE
WIND DIR.- NUMERALS SHOW TENS OF DEGRESS CLOCKWISE FROM TRUE NORTH. "00" INDICATES CALM.
RESULTANT DIRECTIONS ARE GIVEN TO WHOLE DEGREES.
BOLD VALUES INDICATE EXTREME VALUES WHICH OCCURRED AFTER THE ASOS SYSTEM WAS COMMISSIONED.

RECORD = PERIOD OF RECORD
RECORD MEAN PRECIPITATION IS THE MEAN OF ALL DAILY PRECIPITATION AMOUNTS DURING THE PERIOD OF RECORD.
RECORD MAX(MIN) TEMPERATURE IS THE MEAN OF ALL DAILY MAX(MIN) TEMPERATURES DURING THE PERIOD OF RECORD.
RECORD MEAN TEMPERATURE IS THE SUM OF THE RECORD MAX AND RECORD MIN DIVIDED BY 2.
AVERAGE TEMPERATURE IS THE SUM OF THE MEAN DAILY MAX AND MIN TEMPERATURE DIVIDED BY 2.

EXCEPTIONS

PERCENT OF POSSIBLE SUNSHINE IS THROUGH 1980.

RECORD MEANS ARE THROUGH THE CURRENT YEAR,
BEGINNING IN 1875 FOR TEMPERATURE
1871 FOR PRECIPITATION
1949 FOR SNOWFALL

HEATING DEGREE DAYS Base 65 deg. F NORFOLK, VIRGINIA

SEASON	JULY	AUG	SEP	OCT	NOV	DEC	JAN	FEB	MAR	APR	MAY	JUNE	TOTAL
1964-65	0	0	4	232	312	575	780	667	635	320	29	15	3569
1965-66	0	6	1	195	398	657	897	734	527	330	121	21	3887
1966-67	0	0	22	191	437	725	588	699	533	244	157	21	3617
1967-68	0	0	36	211	566	644	928	895	471	294	88	0	4133
1968-69	0	0	0	124	361	726	814	697	624	192	44	0	3582
1969-70	0	0	8	131	469	741	960	714	622	263	57	0	3965
1970-71	0	0	16	93	393	552	812	567	555	269	69	0	3326
1971-72	0	0	3	27	391	390	572	628	494	272	81	11	2869
1972-73	0	0	4	197	406	486	752	703	403	217	47	0	3215
1973-74	0	0	0	83	353	575	504	599	377	183	63	0	2737
1974-75	0	0	16	213	371	584	584	547	541	382	47	0	3285
1975-76	0	0	6	98	290	671	804	443	362	186	62	6	2928
1976-77	0	0	0	245	566	726	1104	657	330	150	40	1	3819
1977-78	0	0	0	158	321	661	860	902	580	235	72	3	3792
1978-79	0	0	3	162	268	614	787	879	499	213	52	5	3482
1979-80	0	0	0	190	272	616	759	872	564	196	58	2	3529
1980-81	0	0	11	181	449	699	994	610	605	159	96	0	3804
1981-82	0	0	12	189	423	739	907	636	495	303	21	0	3725
1982-83	0	4	6	177	334	498	762	674	426	295	85	3	3264
1983-84	0	0	27	126	370	718	908	522	601	281	54	3	3610
1984-85	0	0	16	37	450	432	928	686	421	172	21	0	3163
1985-86	0	0	6	61	162	731	790	637	465	228	69	1	3150
1986-87	0	1	8	88	311	620	779	730	538	306	58	0	3439
1987-88	0	0	0	252	320	582	851	646	474	266	86	15	3492
1988-89	0	0	2	265	324	692	602	601	486	282	80	0	3334
1989-90	0	0	12	134	356	928	541	417	410	234	39	3	3074
1990-91	0	0	13	102	301	444	657	527	386	166	19	2	2617
1991-92	0	0	22	132	377	542	686	575	496	262	125	1	3218
1992-93	0	0	9	179	337	623	638	722	555	246	22	5	3336
1993-94	0	0	10	140	353	726							

COOLING DEGREE DAYS Base 65 deg. F NORFOLK, VIRGINIA

YEAR	JAN	FEB	MAR	APR	MAY	JUNE	JULY	AUG	SEP	OCT	NOV	DEC	TOTAL
1969	0	0	0	42	125	369	446	357	199	49	0	0	1587
1970	1	0	0	19	140	303	374	412	311	60	0	0	1620
1971	0	3	0	3	76	336	383	343	259	87	23	5	1518
1972	0	0	8	20	40	183	398	343	217	22	10	2	1243
1973	0	0	16	27	112	363	420	424	307	64	17	1	1751
1974	3	0	16	64	124	244	419	390	213	26	32	0	1531
1975	2	3	0	22	157	366	429	460	233	55	17	0	1744
1976	1	13	11	102	110	337	417	347	193	27	0	0	1558
1977	0	4	16	66	145	289	515	502	347	24	22	0	1930
1978	0	0	0	9	96	286	352	487	257	36	3	9	1535
1979	0	0	11	13	112	171	385	426	239	54	22	0	1433
1980	0	0	0	11	153	274	499	497	351	45	1	1	1832
1981	0	0	0	51	103	407	468	320	189	29	0	0	1567
1982	0	0	1	8	166	257	428	331	164	39	21	4	1419
1983	0	0	0	21	115	250	481	440	265	62	4	0	1638
1984	0	0	0	5	146	345	368	426	188	102	5	2	1587
1985	0	5	20	91	146	284	419	382	267	97	28	0	1739
1986	0	0	2	2	153	343	537	367	237	109	15	0	1765
1987	0	0	0	2	168	364	544	461	285	0	7	0	1831
1988	0	0	1	18	118	280	477	498	173	17	10	0	1592
1989	0	9	30	31	106	412	447	399	286	69	10	0	1799
1990	0	8	52	51	98	324	489	407	218	137	8	5	1797
1991	0	0	13	71	269	347	534	456	248	43	18	11	2010
1992	0	0	0	63	51	220	527	336	270	23	9	0	1499
1993	0	0	0	23	136	345	579	438	305	31	18	0	1875

SNOWFALL (inches) NORFOLK, VIRGINIA

SEASON	JULY	AUG	SEP	OCT	NOV	DEC	JAN	FEB	MAR	APR	MAY	JUNE	TOTAL
1964-65	0.0	0.0	0.0	0.0	T	0.0	10.6	3.9	T	0.0	0.0	0.0	14.5
1965-66	0.0	0.0	0.0	0.0	0.0	T	14.2	0.5	0.0	0.0	0.0	0.0	14.7
1966-67	0.0	0.0	0.0	0.0	T	1.0	4.2	5.1	T	0.0	0.0	0.0	10.3
1967-68	0.0	0.0	0.0	0.0	T	2.0	1.5	2.9	0.9	0.0	0.0	0.0	7.3
1968-69	0.0	0.0	0.0	0.0	T	3.8	T	0.8	1.9	0.0	0.0	0.0	6.5
1969-70	0.0	0.0	0.0	0.0	0.0	T	3.0	2.8	T	0.0	0.0	0.0	5.8
1970-71	0.0	0.0	0.0	0.0	T	T	T	2.4	4.2	T	0.0	0.0	6.6
1971-72	0.0	0.0	0.0	0.0	T	T	0.0	1.8	T	T	0.0	0.0	1.8
1972-73	0.0	0.0	0.0	0.0	T	0.0	9.1	4.7	T	0.0	0.0	0.0	13.8
1973-74	0.0	0.0	0.0	0.0	0.0	1.4	T	0.9	7.5	0.0	0.0	0.0	9.8
1974-75	0.0	0.0	0.0	0.0	0.0	T	0.3	T	0.8	T	0.0	0.0	1.1
1975-76	0.0	0.0	0.0	0.0	0.0	T	T	T	0.0	0.0	0.0	0.0	T
1976-77	0.0	0.0	0.0	0.0	T	1.0	4.7	1.4	0.0	0.0	0.0	0.0	7.1
1977-78	0.0	0.0	0.0	0.0	0.0	T	1.3	9.2	2.3	0.0	0.0	0.0	12.8
1978-79	0.0	0.0	0.0	0.0	0.0	0.0	1.0	12.7	T	0.0	0.0	0.0	13.7
1979-80	0.0	0.0	0.0	0.0	0.0	0.0	9.3	18.9	13.7	0.0	0.0	0.0	41.9
1980-81	0.0	0.0	0.0	0.0	0.0	T	T	0.0	0.3	0.0	0.0	0.0	0.3
1981-82	0.0	0.0	0.0	0.0	0.0	1.8	4.2	0.1	T	T	0.0	0.0	6.1
1982-83	0.0	0.0	0.0	0.0	0.0	0.4	T	3.0	T	T	0.0	0.0	3.4
1983-84	0.0	0.0	0.0	0.0	0.0	T	T	5.2	T	0.0	0.0	0.0	5.2
1984-85	0.0	0.0	0.0	0.0	0.0	T	4.3	0.0	T	0.0	0.0	0.0	4.3
1985-86	0.0	0.0	0.0	0.0	0.0	T	3.6	1.1	T	T	0.0	0.0	4.7
1986-87	0.0	0.0	0.0	0.0	0.0	T	1.6	1.0	1.2	T	0.0	0.0	3.8
1987-88	0.0	0.0	0.0	0.0	0.3	T	4.4	T	T	0.0	0.0	0.0	4.7
1988-89	0.0	0.0	0.0	0.0	0.0	T	T	24.4	T	0.5	0.0	0.0	24.9
1989-90	0.0	0.0	0.0	0.0	0.0	0.5	0.0	0.0	T	0.0	0.0	T	0.5
1990-91	0.0	0.0	0.0	0.0	0.0	T	0.0	T	T	0.0	0.0	0.0	T
1991-92	0.0	T	0.0	0.0	0.0	T	T	0.0	T	T	0.0	0.0	T
1992-93	0.0	0.0	0.0	0.0	0.0	0.0	0.3	1.9	1.7	0.0	0.0	0.0	3.9
1993-94	0.0	0.0	0.0	0.0	0.0	3.9							
Record Mean	0.0	T	0.0	0.0	T	0.9	2.6	2.9	1.0	T	0.0	T	7.5

RICHMOND, VIRGINIA

Richmond is located in east-central Virginia at the head of navigation on the James River and along a line separating the Coastal Plains (Tidewater Virginia) from the Piedmont. The Blue Ridge Mountains lie about 90 miles to the west and the Chesapeake Bay 60 miles to the east. Elevations range from a few feet above sea level along the river to a little over 300 feet in parts of the western section of the city.

The climate might be classified as modified continental. Summers are warm and humid and winters generally mild. The mountains to the west act as a partial barrier to outbreaks of cold, continental air in winter. The cold winter air is delayed long enough to be modified, then further warmed as it subsides in its approach to Richmond. The open waters of the Chesapeake Bay and Atlantic Ocean contribute to the humid summers and mild winters. The coldest weather normally occurs in late December and January, when low temperatures usually average in the upper 20s, and the high temperatures in the upper 40s. Temperatures seldom lower to zero, but there have been several occurrences of below zero temperatures. Summertime high temperatures above 100 degrees are not uncommon, but do not occur every year.

Precipitation is rather uniformly distributed throughout the year. However, dry periods lasting several weeks do occur, especially in autumn when long periods of pleasant, mild weather are most common. There is considerable variability in total monthly amounts from year to year. Snow usually remains on the ground only one or two days at a time. Ice storms (freezing rain or glaze) are not uncommon, but they are seldom severe enough to do any considerable damage. A notable exception was the spectacular glaze storm of January 27-28, 1943, when nearly 1 inch of ice accumulation caused heavy damage to trees and overhead transmission lines.

The James River reaches tidewater at Richmond where flooding may occur in every month of the year, most frequently in March and least in July. Hurricanes and tropical storms have been responsible for most of the flooding during the summer and early fall months. Hurricanes passing near Richmond have produced record rainfalls. In 1955, three hurricanes brought record rainfall to Richmond within a six-week period. The most noteworthy of these were Hurricanes Connie and Diane that brought heavy rains five days apart.

Damaging storms occur mainly from snow and freezing rain in winter and from hurricanes, tornadoes, and severe thunderstorms in other seasons. Damage may be from wind, flooding, or rain, or from any combination of these. Tornadoes are infrequent but some notable occurrences have been observed within the Richmond area.

Based on the 1951-1980 period, the average first occurrence of 32 degrees Fahrenheit in the fall is October 26 and the average last occurrence in the spring is April 10.

NORMALS, MEANS, AND EXTREMES

RICHMOND, VIRGINIA

LATITUDE: 37°30'N LONGITUDE: 77°20' W ELEVATION: FT. GRND 164 BARO 178 TIME ZONE: EASTERN WBAN: 13740

	(a)	JAN	FEB	MAR	APR	MAY	JUNE	JULY	AUG	SEP	OCT	NOV	DEC	YEAR
TEMPERATURE °F:														
Normals														
-Daily Maximum		45.7	49.2	59.5	70.0	77.8	85.1	88.4	87.1	80.9	70.7	61.3	50.2	68.8
-Daily Minimum		25.7	28.1	36.3	44.6	54.2	62.7	67.5	66.4	59.0	46.5	37.9	29.9	46.6
-Monthly		35.7	38.7	48.0	57.3	66.0	73.9	78.0	76.8	70.0	58.6	49.6	40.1	57.7
Extremes														
-Record Highest	64	80	83	93	96	100	104	105	102	103	99	86	80	105
-Year		1950	1932	1938	1990	1941	1952	1977	1983	1954	1941	1993	1971	JUL 1977
-Record Lowest	64	-12	-10	11	23	31	40	51	46	35	21	10	-1	-12
-Year		1940	1936	1960	1985	1956	1967	1965	1934	1974	1962	1933	1942	JAN 1940
NORMAL DEGREE DAYS:														
Heating (base 65°F)		908	736	527	241	61	0	0	0	23	233	462	772	3963
Cooling (base 65°F)		0	0	0	10	92	270	403	366	173	34	0	0	1348
% OF POSSIBLE SUNSHINE	43	54	58	62	66	66	70	68	66	64	63	59	54	63
MEAN SKY COVER (tenths)														
Sunrise - Sunset	48	6.4	6.3	6.2	6.1	6.3	6.0	6.1	6.1	5.8	5.4	5.8	6.2	6.1
MEAN NUMBER OF DAYS:														
Sunrise to Sunset														
-Clear	48	8.3	8.2	8.2	7.8	7.0	6.8	6.9	7.2	9.2	11.5	9.3	9.4	99.8
-Partly Cloudy	48	6.7	6.4	8.2	9.2	10.1	11.9	11.6	11.6	8.6	7.3	7.7	6.4	105.8
-Cloudy	48	16.1	13.6	14.6	13.0	13.9	11.3	12.5	12.2	12.2	12.1	13.0	15.2	159.6
Precipitation														
.01 inches or more	56	10.3	9.2	10.8	9.4	10.7	9.4	11.1	9.7	8.1	7.3	8.3	9.0	113.3
Snow, Ice pellets, hail														
1.0 inches or more	56	1.3	1.1	0.6	0.1	0.0	0.0	0.0	0.0	0.0	0.0	0.1	0.6	3.8
Thunderstorms	56	0.2	0.4	1.6	2.4	5.4	6.7	8.7	6.6	2.9	1.0	0.6	0.3	36.6
Heavy Fog Visibility														
1/4 mile or less	64	2.7	2.0	1.7	1.6	1.9	1.5	2.1	2.5	3.0	3.3	2.2	2.8	27.2
Temperature °F														
-Maximum														
90° and above	64	0.0	0.0	0.1	0.8	2.7	9.4	14.1	11.0	4.5	0.4	0.0	0.0	42.9
32° and below	64	3.2	1.4	0.2	0.0	0.0	0.0	0.0	0.0	0.0	0.0	0.*	1.7	6.5
-Minimum														
32° and below	64	21.3	18.8	10.4	2.1	0.1	0.0	0.0	0.0	0.0	1.8	10.0	20.1	84.5
0° and below	64	0.4	0.1	0.0	0.0	0.0	0.0	0.0	0.0	0.0	0.0	0.0	0.*	0.5
AVG. STATION PRESS. (mb)	21	1012.9	1012.5	1010.8	1009.3	1009.4	1009.5	1010.1	1011.3	1012.4	1013.3	1013.5	1013.7	1011.6
RELATIVE HUMIDITY (%)														
Hour 01	59	77	74	73	74	83	86	88	90	90	87	80	77	82
Hour 07 (Local Time)	59	80	79	78	76	80	82	85	89	90	89	84	81	83
Hour 13	59	57	53	49	46	51	53	56	57	56	53	51	55	53
Hour 19	59	68	63	59	55	65	67	71	75	78	76	69	70	68
PRECIPITATION (inches):														
Water Equivalent														
-Normal		3.24	3.16	3.61	2.96	3.84	3.62	5.03	4.40	3.34	3.53	3.17	3.26	43.16
-Maximum Monthly	56	7.97	5.97	8.65	7.31	8.87	9.24	18.87	14.10	10.98	9.39	7.64	7.07	18.87
-Year		1978	1979	1984	1987	1972	1938	1945	1955	1975	1971	1959	1973	JUL 1945
-Minimum Monthly	56	0.64	0.48	0.94	0.64	0.87	0.38	0.51	0.52	0.26	0.30	0.36	0.40	0.26
-Year		1981	1978	1966	1963	1965	1980	1983	1943	1978	1963	1965	1980	SEP 1978
-Maximum in 24 hrs	56	3.31	2.67	3.43	2.97	3.08	4.61	5.73	8.79	4.02	6.50	4.07	3.16	8.79
-Year		1962	1979	1992	1987	1981	1963	1969	1955	1985	1961	1956	1958	AUG 1955
Snow, Ice pellets, hail														
-Maximum Monthly	56	28.5	21.4	19.7	2.0	T	0.0	0.0	0.0	0.0	T	7.3	12.5	28.5
-Year		1940	1983	1960	1940	1989					1979	1953	1958	JAN 1940
-Maximum in 24 hrs	56	21.6	16.8	12.1	2.0	T	0.0	0.0	0.0	0.0	T	7.3	7.5	21.6
-Year		1940	1983	1962	1940	1989					1979	1953	1966	JAN 1940
WIND:														
Mean Speed (mph)	45	8.1	8.7	9.1	9.0	7.8	7.4	6.9	6.4	6.7	7.0	7.6	7.8	7.7
Prevailing Direction through 1963		S	NNE	W	S	SSW	S	SSW	S	S	NNE	S	SW	S
Fastest Obs. 1 Min.														
-Direction (!!!)	8	23	32	27	21	23	30	23	18	36	36	27	21	23
-Speed (MPH)	8	30	32	41	29	46	32	40	30	37	29	32	32	46
-Year		1992	1987	1989	1990	1989	1987	1992	1991	1989	1990	1989	1988	MAY 1989
Peak Gust														
-Direction (!!!)	9	NW	NW	W	N	SW	NW	N	SW	N	N	SW	SW	SW
-Speed (mph)	9	48	48	67	49	79	53	61	48	49	43	54	49	79
-Date		1985	1987	1989	1992	1989	1987	1986	1992	1989	1990	1988	1988	MAY 1989

PRECIPITATION (inches) RICHMOND, VIRGINIA

YEAR	JAN	FEB	MAR	APR	MAY	JUNE	JULY	AUG	SEP	OCT	NOV	DEC	ANNUAL
1964	4.16	4.46	2.61	2.71	1.14	2.40	6.46	9.88	2.56	3.62	1.98	3.05	45.03
1965	2.51	2.77	3.68	2.13	0.87	3.39	6.33	0.81	4.81	1.38	0.36	0.72	29.76
1966	4.58	3.80	0.94	2.18	2.58	2.54	4.07	1.31	5.06	4.81	1.31	3.07	36.25
1967	1.50	3.35	2.34	1.32	3.71	3.58	5.00	6.65	0.95	1.00	1.76	6.48	37.64
1968	2.53	0.98	4.00	2.93	3.13	2.89	3.41	3.71	1.78	1.59	3.87	2.28	33.10
1969	2.04	3.95	3.95	2.60	3.32	4.36	13.90	9.31	3.89	1.88	1.87	5.26	56.33
1970	1.32	2.37	3.70	2.84	1.84	1.12	4.74	1.69	1.02	1.55	3.10	3.00	28.29
1971	1.84	4.37	2.68	1.76	6.82	4.10	4.40	3.73	2.35	9.39	2.76	0.75	44.95
1972	1.43	5.15	2.11	3.35	8.87	8.82	5.80	3.84	3.35	7.89	5.82	2.91	59.34
1973	2.66	3.11	3.44	4.58	3.56	2.45	3.64	4.34	1.82	2.56	1.27	7.07	40.50
1974	3.21	2.54	3.79	1.58	3.02	1.80	2.25	6.84	4.83	0.39	1.23	4.22	35.70
1975	5.71	2.96	8.04	2.78	2.59	4.00	12.29	2.31	10.98	3.10	2.04	4.51	61.31
1976	3.39	1.35	2.14	1.08	3.76	2.85	2.63	1.35	4.78	6.99	1.88	2.56	34.76
1977	2.22	1.34	2.67	2.33	3.99	1.25	4.20	6.15	2.16	7.88	4.32	5.57	44.08
1978	7.97	0.48	5.67	4.31	3.92	5.26	4.24	5.93	0.26	1.21	4.57	3.80	47.62
1979	6.16	5.97	2.59	3.97	3.80	2.42	4.36	7.08	9.76	3.87	5.50	1.64	57.12
1980	6.05	1.01	5.49	4.28	4.68	0.38	5.18	2.15	2.37	6.96	2.18	0.40	41.13
1981	0.64	2.76	1.52	2.96	6.62	3.69	4.01	2.89	2.70	2.36	0.68	5.04	35.87
1982	2.76	4.44	3.74	2.97	3.48	3.97	9.21	4.39	2.55	2.90	2.70	3.37	46.48
1983	1.59	3.95	6.04	5.21	2.50	5.46	0.51	0.97	3.05	4.02	5.63	4.50	43.43
1984	3.98	3.97	8.65	5.92	4.52	2.01	3.55	4.58	1.86	2.14	3.34	1.52	46.04
1985	3.54	3.20	1.80	0.65	2.36	4.01	5.31	10.58	4.97	5.09	6.99	0.58	49.08
1986	2.69	2.67	1.16	1.16	3.15	1.30	7.01	6.75	0.63	2.43	2.46	5.15	36.56
1987	5.53	2.57	1.65	7.31	2.94	6.29	1.20	1.11	4.43	1.25	3.13	2.86	40.27
1988	2.53	3.08	1.98	2.55	4.81	2.25	7.50	2.95	1.74	2.74	4.34	0.79	37.26
1989	1.88	4.34	5.00	4.27	5.02	5.85	4.00	4.89	5.33	3.54	3.00	2.62	49.74
1990	2.84	2.38	2.54	2.81	6.85	0.97	6.74	5.76	1.92	3.90	1.70	3.52	41.93
1991	3.62	1.09	5.87	0.87	0.91	6.24	3.47	3.32	2.69	2.50	0.67	4.53	35.78
1992	1.57	2.89	5.87	2.21	4.95	2.28	5.68	6.40	2.35	1.94	2.62	2.79	41.55
1993	4.48	2.88	7.24	3.23	4.66	1.75	1.91	3.89	2.97	2.23	3.24	3.77	42.25
Record Mean	3.13	2.99	3.65	2.96	3.77	3.64	5.35	4.87	3.48	3.29	3.17	3.16	43.47

AVERAGE TEMPERATURE (deg. F) RICHMOND, VIRGINIA

YEAR	JAN	FEB	MAR	APR	MAY	JUNE	JULY	AUG	SEP	OCT	NOV	DEC	ANNUAL
1964	38.1	37.2	47.6	55.4	66.4	73.1	75.8	73.1	67.1	53.4	51.5	42.9	56.8
1965	35.6	38.8	43.0	53.9	69.6	70.7	74.9	75.9	70.7	56.1	48.2	41.3	56.6
1966	31.1	37.7	47.5	52.8	63.1	71.4	76.4	74.6	67.2	55.5	49.5	38.0	55.4
1967	40.9	34.8	46.6	58.8	60.7	72.1	76.6	75.5	65.7	57.2	44.0	41.9	56.2
1968	33.9	34.2	52.0	58.8	64.7	74.7	78.9	78.9	70.9	61.9	51.3	37.0	58.1
1969	33.9	36.8	42.3	57.6	65.5	75.7	78.3	75.1	68.1	58.5	46.8	35.5	56.2
1970	30.1	37.1	42.9	58.2	69.1	75.7	78.3	78.0	74.8	62.9	49.9	40.4	58.1
1971	33.8	39.5	44.5	55.0	63.3	74.7	76.6	75.3	71.4	64.6	48.5	48.0	57.9
1972	40.7	37.6	47.2	56.2	64.6	70.1	77.1	75.2	70.1	55.8	47.9	45.9	57.4
1973	37.6	38.5	52.6	57.9	65.1	76.0	77.4	77.5	72.3	60.6	51.3	40.8	59.0
1974	45.8	40.1	50.4	59.9	65.8	70.6	76.9	75.7	67.4	55.4	48.5	41.7	58.2
1975	40.7	41.4	45.3	52.9	67.7	73.6	76.0	78.8	69.3	62.5	53.6	40.0	58.5
1976	35.1	48.5	52.6	60.5	65.2	74.6	77.3	75.7	68.7	54.4	42.7	36.7	57.7
1977	25.3	40.5	53.7	61.1	68.2	73.0	81.4	79.8	74.2	57.3	52.3	39.5	58.9
1978	33.4	30.3	44.5	57.3	65.5	74.7	77.5	80.1	72.9	58.3	52.5	42.5	57.5
1979	36.4	28.6	51.1	58.4	67.1	70.8	76.9	77.8	71.0	58.3	53.3	42.3	57.7
1980	38.8	36.0	47.4	61.1	68.3	72.8	80.0	80.7	74.7	56.9	46.2	38.6	58.5
1981	31.2	42.2	44.6	60.6	64.1	77.9	79.6	75.1	69.4	56.4	49.1	38.0	57.3
1982	31.6	41.7	49.1	55.9	70.4	73.4	78.6	75.0	69.8	59.2	51.9	46.1	58.6
1983	37.8	39.1	50.4	56.1	66.1	75.6	79.4	77.7	68.8	58.1	49.0	36.2	57.9
1984	32.6	44.5	43.6	55.8	65.4	77.7	76.0	77.0	67.5	66.1	46.6	47.7	58.4
1985	32.6	40.2	49.7	62.0	68.0	74.3	79.0	77.5	70.8	62.6	56.6	37.8	59.3
1986	36.2	39.3	50.0	59.2	66.9	76.1	80.9	74.2	70.8	61.8	49.1	40.9	58.8
1987	34.7	37.0	47.1	54.3	67.3	75.8	81.3	78.5	72.3	52.9	51.3	43.0	58.0
1988	32.3	39.1	47.9	56.0	65.8	72.8	79.9	79.8	68.4	53.6	50.6	39.2	57.1
1989	42.3	39.6	47.9	55.8	64.1	76.1	77.7	75.3	70.8	60.2	49.3	31.3	57.5
1990	46.3	48.0	52.1	57.9	65.8	75.0	79.9	76.3	69.5	63.1	52.6	46.3	61.1
1991	40.2	44.0	50.8	60.2	72.1	75.3	80.7	78.6	71.6	59.9	49.6	44.3	60.6
1992	40.7	42.7	47.2	57.8	61.7	70.8	79.5	73.7	70.3	56.3	50.6	40.9	57.7
1993	41.4	37.8	45.9	55.9	67.7	75.0	82.5	78.5	72.5	58.6	50.9	39.0	58.8
Record Mean	37.5	39.5	47.3	57.2	66.3	74.1	78.1	76.5	70.1	58.8	49.1	39.9	57.9
Max	47.3	50.1	58.7	69.6	78.1	85.3	88.4	86.6	80.9	70.6	60.6	50.0	68.9
Min	27.6	28.9	35.9	44.7	54.4	62.9	67.7	66.3	59.3	46.9	37.6	29.8	46.8

REFERENCE NOTES RICHMOND, VIRGINIA

GENERAL
T - TRACE AMOUNT.
BLANK ENTRIES DENOTE MISSING/UNREPORTED DATA.
# INDICATES A STATION OR INSTRUMENT RELOCATION.

SPECIFIC

PM - INCLUDES LAST DAY OF PREVIOUS MONTH
ASOS - AUTOMATED SURFACE OBSERVING SYSTEM IN OPERATION DURING THESE MONTHS.

(a) - LENGTH OF RECORD IN YEARS, ALTHOUGH INDIVIDUAL MONTHS MAY BE MISSING.
0.* OR * - THE VALUE IS BETWEEN 0.0 AND 0.05
NORMALS - BASED ON THE 1961-1990 RECORD PERIOD.
EXTREMES - DATES ARE THE MOST RECENT OCCURRENCE
WIND DIR. - NUMERALS SHOW TENS OF DEGRESS CLOCKWISE FROM TRUE NORTH. "00" INDICATES CALM.
RESULTANT DIRECTIONS ARE GIVEN TO WHOLE DEGREES.
BOLD VALUES INDICATE EXTREME VALUES WHICH OCCURRED AFTER THE ASOS SYSTEM WAS COMMISSIONED.

RECORD = PERIOD OF RECORD
RECORD MEAN PRECIPITATION IS THE MEAN OF ALL DAILY PRECIPITATION AMOUNTS DURING THE PERIOD OF RECORD.
RECORD MAX(MIN) TEMPERATURE IS THE MEAN OF ALL DAILY MAX(MIN) TEMPERATURES DURING THE PERIOD OF RECORD.
RECORD MEAN TEMPERATURE IS THE SUM OF THE RECORD MAX AND RECORD MIN DIVIDED BY 2.
AVERAGE TEMPERATURE IS THE SUM OF THE MEAN DAILY MAX AND MIN TEMPERATURE DIVIDED BY 2.

EXCEPTIONS

RECORD MEANS ARE THROUGH THE CURRENT YEAR, BEGINNING IN 1930 FOR TEMPERATURE
1930 FOR PRECIPITATION
1938 FOR SNOWFALL

HEATING DEGREE DAYS Base 65 deg. F — RICHMOND, VIRGINIA

SEASON	JULY	AUG	SEP	OCT	NOV	DEC	JAN	FEB	MAR	APR	MAY	JUNE	TOTAL
1964-65	0	0	32	352	402	676	909	726	674	339	17	34	4161
1965-66	0	6	25	275	498	726	1043	759	538	371	133	27	4401
1966-67	0	0	47	293	466	833	738	841	560	230	171	17	4196
1967-68	0	0	64	256	623	708	956	887	416	191	86	0	4187
1968-69	0	0	0	161	403	864	957	783	695	237	66	0	4166
1969-70	0	0	45	221	541	907	1076	778	677	231	51	0	4527
1970-71	0	0	12	124	445	756	960	709	627	295	104	3	4035
1971-72	0	0	11	69	512	526	748	788	554	286	58	21	3573
1972-73	0	0	17	285	513	588	843	735	394	247	79	0	3701
1973-74	0	0	5	163	414	744	589	691	455	204	75	5	3345
1974-75	0	0	62	310	513	715	746	654	604	368	44	1	4017
1975-76	0	0	27	121	356	770	917	480	386	227	78	11	3373
1976-77	0	1	15	332	660	869	1227	680	366	176	42	7	4375
1977-78	0	0	4	259	401	784	974	964	627	235	88	5	4341
1978-79	0	0	16	214	366	694	876	1011	439	218	44	4	3882
1979-80	0	0	8	242	353	698	806	835	541	135	47	2	3667
1980-81	0	0	14	267	557	813	1042	633	626	171	107	0	4230
1981-82	0	1	29	273	473	834	1029	645	486	280	6	1	4057
1982-83	0	6	10	213	399	585	836	718	445	282	69	2	3565
1983-84	0	1	86	236	475	887	994	589	657	282	93	3	4303
1984-85	0	0	73	57	546	531	997	692	484	177	35	5	3597
1985-86	0	0	31	114	257	838	886	713	465	187	78	3	3572
1986-87	0	16	24	172	476	741	931	777	550	317	57	0	4061
1987-88	0	0	5	370	409	677	1008	746	527	279	79	32	4132
1988-89	0	0	27	361	425	794	696	709	546	293	108	0	3959
1989-90	0	3	38	181	468	1036	574	472	436	258	50	3	3519
1990-91	0	0	33	146	365	574	762	582	443	193	27	1	3126
1991-92	0	0	25	190	458	637	749	640	545	261	142	10	3657
1992-93	0	0	37	275	427	739	724	757	585	280	24	0	3848
1993-94	0	0	26	213	436	799							

COOLING DEGREE DAYS Base 65 deg. F — RICHMOND, VIRGINIA

YEAR	JAN	FEB	MAR	APR	MAY	JUNE	JULY	AUG	SEP	OCT	NOV	DEC	TOTAL
1969	0	0	0	21	90	328	417	321	147	26	0	0	1350
1970	0	0	0	35	185	328	418	410	313	67	0	0	1756
1971	0	0	0	0	56	297	367	327	209	62	22	5	1345
1972	0	0	7	30	52	180	381	326	178	9	8	0	1171
1973	0	0	13	42	91	338	391	395	231	32	9	2	1544
1974	0	0	10	58	106	180	377	340	141	21	26	0	1259
1975	0	0	0	16	135	267	348	433	165	51	18	0	1433
1976	0	8	9	99	91	307	389	337	133	12	0	0	1385
1977	0	0	22	66	148	258	513	467	289	24	27	0	1814
1978	0	0	0	12	112	302	393	475	263	15	0	1	1573
1979	0	0	16	30	117	188	374	404	195	42	9	0	1375
1980	0	0	1	25	157	243	472	494	313	23	1	0	1729
1981	0	0	1	45	89	395	458	319	169	16	0	0	1492
1982	0	0	0	13	181	259	428	323	157	43	13	7	1424
1983	0	0	0	23	108	325	452	405	207	27	0	0	1547
1984	0	0	0	10	114	392	346	381	154	100	0	2	1499
1985	0	4	20	94	139	290	441	392	213	51	10	0	1654
1986	0	0	8	19	142	344	498	308	205	79	6	0	1609
1987	0	0	0	2	136	329	513	427	227	0	3	0	1637
1988	0	0	3	16	108	269	466	465	137	12	0	0	1476
1989	0	3	24	27	88	341	403	331	218	42	4	0	1481
1990	0	1	43	51	81	312	470	356	177	96	0	2	1589
1991	0	0	10	53	254	316	494	428	227	40	3	0	1825
1992	0	0	0	51	48	192	457	275	202	12	3	0	1240
1993	0	0	0	14	112	307	547	426	261	20	18	0	1705

SNOWFALL (inches) — RICHMOND, VIRGINIA

SEASON	JULY	AUG	SEP	OCT	NOV	DEC	JAN	FEB	MAR	APR	MAY	JUNE	TOTAL
1964-65	0.0	0.0	0.0	0.0	0.4	0.0	12.4	6.6	1.0	0.0	0.0	0.0	20.4
1965-66	0.0	0.0	0.0	0.0	0.0	T	26.2	3.0	0.0	0.0	0.0	0.0	29.2
1966-67	0.0	0.0	0.0	0.0	0.2	12.2	6.3	17.1	T	0.0	0.0	0.0	35.8
1967-68	0.0	0.0	0.0	0.0	T	5.6	2.3	2.4	2.8	0.0	0.0	0.0	13.1
1968-69	0.0	0.0	0.0	0.0	1.2	2.8	T	T	11.9	0.0	0.0	0.0	15.9
1969-70	0.0	0.0	0.0	0.0	0.0	1.8	5.4	0.4	0.0	0.0	0.0	0.0	7.6
1970-71	0.0	0.0	0.0	0.0	0.0	0.9	3.3	2.0	8.4	0.6	0.0	0.0	15.2
1971-72	0.0	0.0	0.0	0.0	T	0.0	T	13.7	0.0	T	0.0	0.0	13.7
1972-73	0.0	0.0	0.0	T	0.6	0.0	4.3	0.4	1.4	0.0	0.0	0.0	6.7
1973-74	0.0	0.0	0.0	0.0	0.0	9.9	T	5.0	T	0.0	0.0	0.0	14.9
1974-75	0.0	0.0	0.0	0.0	0.0	T	2.7	2.9	0.4	0.0	0.0	0.0	6.0
1975-76	0.0	0.0	0.0	0.0	0.0	T	0.2	T	1.0	0.0	0.0	0.0	1.2
1976-77	0.0	0.0	0.0	0.0	1.0	1.7	11.1	T	0.0	0.0	0.0	0.0	13.8
1977-78	0.0	0.0	0.0	0.0	T	T	1.3	5.1	5.0	0.0	0.0	0.0	11.4
1978-79	0.0	0.0	0.0	0.0	0.0	0.0	0.7	19.5	T	0.0	0.0	0.0	20.2
1979-80	0.0	0.0	0.0	T	0.0	T	16.6	7.0	15.0	0.0	0.0	0.0	38.6
1980-81	0.0	0.0	0.0	0.0	0.0	0.2	0.6	0.0	0.2	0.0	0.0	0.0	1.0
1981-82	0.0	0.0	0.0	0.0	T	1.9	8.3	10.8	T	0.2	0.0	0.0	21.2
1982-83	0.0	0.0	0.0	0.0	0.0	7.9	0.1	21.4	0.0	T	0.0	0.0	29.4
1983-84	0.0	0.0	0.0	0.0	0.1	T	1.1	2.8	0.3	0.0	0.0	0.0	4.3
1984-85	0.0	0.0	0.0	0.0	0.0	T	8.3	T	T	0.0	0.0	0.0	8.3
1985-86	0.0	0.0	0.0	0.0	0.0	1.3	3.3	4.4	T	T	0.0	0.0	9.0
1986-87	0.0	0.0	0.0	0.0	0.0	0.0	15.8	5.3	0.7	T	0.0	0.0	21.8
1987-88	0.0	0.0	0.0	0.0	4.5	T	8.1	T	T	T	0.0	0.0	12.6
1988-89	0.0	0.0	0.0	0.0	0.0	1.8	T	13.6	T	T	T	0.0	15.4
1989-90	0.0	0.0	0.0	0.0	1.1	9.9	0.0	T	T	0.2	0.0	0.0	11.2
1990-91	0.0	0.0	0.0	0.0	0.0	T	T	1.9	T	0.0	0.0	0.0	1.9
1991-92	0.0	0.0	0.0	0.0	0.1	T	0.0	0.8	T	T	0.0	0.0	0.9
1992-93	0.0	0.0	0.0	0.0	0.0	0.0	0.5	5.3	3.5	T	0.0	0.0	9.3
1993-94	0.0	0.0	0.0	0.0	0.0	5.1							
Record Mean	0.0	0.0	0.0	T	0.4	2.0	4.9	4.1	2.4	0.1	T	0.0	14.0

ROANOKE, VIRGINIA

The climate of Roanoke is relatively mild. Roanoke is nestled among mountains which interrupt the Great Valley, extending from northernmost Virginia southwestward into east Tennessee. This location, at a point where the valley is pinched between the Blue Ridges and the Alleghenies, offers a natural barrier to the winter cold as it moves southward. It is also far enough inland that hurricanes lose much of their destructive force before reaching Roanoke. Finally, the rough terrain is an inhospitable breeding ground for tornadic activity. The elevation in the vicinity usually produces cool summer nights that make a light cover comfortable for sleeping. Although past records show extremes over 100 degrees and below zero, many years pass without either extreme being threatened.

Roanoke is located near the headwaters of the Roanoke River, which flows in a general southeasterly direction. Numerous creeks and small streams from nearby mountainous areas empty into the Roanoke River. The usual low water stage is 1 to 1.5 feet, and flood stage is 10 feet. Some low-lying streets in Roanoke and nearby Salem have to be blocked off during 7 to 8 foot stages, but damage is minor until the river overflows its banks. The highest stage on record exceeds 19 feet. Damage has been widespread on occasion and has amounted to several million dollars in the city of Roanoke alone.

The growing season averages 190 days. The average date of the last freezing temperature in spring is mid-April and the average date of the first freezing date in the fall is late October.

Rainfall is well apportioned throughout the year. Droughts are so infrequent that quoting actual records would be difficult. Snow usually falls each winter, ranging from only a trace to more than 60 inches.

NORMALS, MEANS, AND EXTREMES

ROANOKE, VIRGINIA

LATITUDE: 37°19'N LONGITUDE: 79°58' W ELEVATION: FT. GRND 1149 BARO 1193 TIME ZONE: EASTERN WBAN: 13741

	(a)	JAN	FEB	MAR	APR	MAY	JUNE	JULY	AUG	SEP	OCT	NOV	DEC	YEAR
TEMPERATURE °F:														
Normals														
-Daily Maximum		43.8	47.3	57.8	67.3	75.7	82.9	86.4	85.3	78.5	68.1	58.0	47.6	66.6
-Daily Minimum		25.0	27.2	35.7	43.8	52.5	60.2	64.8	63.8	56.8	44.8	37.0	28.9	45.0
-Monthly		34.5	37.3	46.8	55.6	64.1	71.5	75.6	74.6	67.7	56.5	47.5	38.3	55.8
Extremes														
-Record Highest	46	78	80	87	95	96	100	104	105	101	93	83	76	105
-Year		1952	1985	1986	1957	1962	1959	1954	1983	1954	1951	1950	1984	AUG 1983
-Record Lowest	46	-11	1	9	20	31	39	47	42	34	22	9	-4	-11
-Year		1985	1970	1993	1985	1966	1977	1988	1986	1983	1976	1950	1983	JAN 1985
NORMAL DEGREE DAYS:														
Heating (base 65°F)		946	776	564	289	105	5	0	0	39	283	525	828	4360
Cooling (base 65°F)		0	0	0	7	78	200	329	298	120	20	0	0	1052
% OF POSSIBLE SUNSHINE														
MEAN SKY COVER (tenths)														
Sunrise - Sunset	45	6.3	6.3	6.3	6.0	6.2	6.0	6.0	5.9	5.7	5.0	5.9	6.2	6.0
MEAN NUMBER OF DAYS:														
Sunrise to Sunset														
-Clear	46	8.2	7.8	8.0	8.6	7.4	7.2	6.9	7.7	9.6	12.8	8.8	8.6	101.6
-Partly Cloudy	46	7.8	7.0	8.6	8.7	10.5	11.8	13.0	12.5	8.9	7.4	8.4	8.0	112.6
-Cloudy	46	15.0	13.5	14.4	12.8	13.1	11.0	11.1	10.8	11.5	10.8	12.8	14.4	151.0
Precipitation														
.01 inches or more	46	10.0	9.7	11.2	10.1	12.0	9.9	11.6	10.5	8.6	7.6	8.7	8.9	118.8
Snow,Ice pellets,hail														
1.0 inches or more	46	1.6	1.9	1.0	0.1	0.0	0.0	0.0	0.0	0.0	0.*	0.5	1.1	6.2
Thunderstorms	46	0.1	0.3	1.1	3.1	6.1	6.3	8.5	6.6	2.6	0.9	0.4	0.1	36.0
Heavy Fog Visibility														
1/4 mile or less	46	2.5	2.8	2.0	1.0	1.7	1.0	1.3	1.5	2.5	1.9	2.2	2.4	22.8
Temperature °F														
-Maximum														
90° and above	29	0.0	0.0	0.0	0.4	0.7	5.2	10.6	7.9	2.2	0.0	0.0	0.0	27.1
32° and below	29	4.7	2.7	0.2	0.0	0.0	0.0	0.0	0.0	0.0	0.0	0.1	2.3	10.0
-Minimum														
32° and below	29	22.9	20.1	12.4	2.6	0.1	0.0	0.0	0.0	0.0	2.7	10.1	19.5	90.4
0° and below	29	0.3	0.0	0.0	0.0	0.0	0.0	0.0	0.0	0.0	0.0	0.0	0.2	0.5
AVG. STATION PRESS.(mb)	21	976.1	975.8	974.4	973.5	974.0	974.8	975.7	976.7	977.3	977.7	977.3	977.0	975.9
RELATIVE HUMIDITY (%)														
Hour 01	29	67	65	65	65	78	83	84	86	87	80	72	69	75
Hour 07 (Local Time)	29	70	69	71	71	80	81	83	87	89	84	76	72	78
Hour 13	29	52	50	48	47	53	54	54	56	57	52	52	54	52
Hour 19	29	58	55	51	49	59	62	64	67	69	64	60	61	60
PRECIPITATION (inches):														
Water Equivalent														
-Normal		2.62	3.04	3.48	3.25	3.98	3.19	3.91	4.15	3.50	3.85	3.19	2.97	41.13
-Maximum Monthly	46	6.12	7.17	7.91	11.35	8.42	7.76	10.09	9.54	11.09	9.89	12.36	7.10	12.36
-Year		1978	1960	1993	1987	1950	1989	1989	1984	1987	1990	1985	1948	NOV 1985
-Minimum Monthly	46	0.29	0.56	0.43	0.48	1.27	0.62	0.45	1.04	0.15	0.04	0.44	0.18	0.04
-Year		1981	1968	1966	1976	1951	1986	1977	1993	1991	1991	1960	1965	OCT 1991
-Maximum in 24 hrs	46	2.71	2.62	3.02	5.57	3.99	3.98	2.74	5.22	6.60	6.41	6.63	3.40	6.63
-Year		1968	1984	1983	1978	1973	1972	1989	1985	1987	1968	1985	1948	NOV 1985
Snow,Ice pellets,hail														
-Maximum Monthly	46	41.2	27.6	30.3	7.3	T	T	0.0	0.0	T	1.0	13.8	22.6	41.2
-Year		1966	1960	1960	1971	1990	1989			1953	1957	1968	1966	JAN 1966
-Maximum in 24 hrs	46	13.7	18.4	17.4	7.3	T	T	0.0	0.0	T	1.0	10.0	16.4	18.4
-Year		1966	1983	1960	1971	1990	1989			1953	1957	1968	1969	FEB 1983
WIND:														
Mean Speed (mph)	45	9.4	9.7	10.0	9.6	7.8	6.9	6.5	6.1	6.1	6.9	8.2	8.7	8.0
Prevailing Direction through 1963		WNW	SE	WNW	SE	SE	SE	W	SE	SE	SE	NW	NW	SE
Fastest Obs. 1 Min.														
-Direction (!!!)	32	30	31	32	32	36	28	34	30	15	34	34	30	32
-Speed (MPH)	32	53	40	52	58	46	46	46	44	35	35	52	40	58
-Year		1964	1972	1967	1963	1962	1966	1980	1975	1989	1963	1963	1970	APR 1963
Peak Gust														
-Direction (!!!)	9	31	NW	NW	NW	NW	SW	NW	NW	SE	W	W	NW	NW
-Speed (mph)	9	56	59	52	77	52	72	38	39	54	39	46	53	77
-Date		1989	1987	1985	1989	1990	1993	1991	1993	1989	1989	1986	1991	APR 1989

PRECIPITATION (inches)

ROANOKE, VIRGINIA

YEAR	JAN	FEB	MAR	APR	MAY	JUNE	JULY	AUG	SEP	OCT	NOV	DEC	ANNUAL
1964	5.20	5.33	1.81	3.54	1.79	1.97	3.37	3.54	2.70	2.80	3.09	2.73	37.87
1965	3.72	3.53	3.93	1.70	3.83	1.83	5.50	1.16	1.97	3.42	0.95	0.18	31.72
1966	4.26	4.78	0.43	2.59	3.49	1.54	3.00	4.73	7.25	4.04	1.73	3.25	41.09
1967	1.25	2.51	4.51	1.67	3.95	3.19	4.05	6.36	1.78	2.42	1.30	4.84	37.83
1968	3.33	0.56	3.03	2.73	1.89	2.11	2.95	5.36	0.44	8.06	2.82	1.80	35.08
1969	1.86	2.74	3.35	1.40	1.58	4.95	5.35	5.41	2.79	2.22	1.40	5.54	38.59
1970	1.31	2.36	1.95	2.80	1.51	4.87	3.28	6.40	1.99	7.51	3.67	2.81	40.46
1971	1.21	5.13	2.28	2.55	7.50	4.84	5.23	4.46	3.87	6.75	2.18	0.83	46.83
1972	2.49	4.80	1.76	3.31	6.00	7.55	4.89	2.62	4.79	3.18	5.63	4.62	51.64
1973	2.60	2.95	5.92	5.39	5.58	3.65	5.10	3.34	1.84	4.28	1.79	5.60	48.04
1974	3.33	2.13	3.12	1.86	3.76	2.93	3.71	4.93	3.04	0.77	1.28	3.16	34.02
1975	3.59	3.05	7.80	2.04	6.65	1.54	5.15	5.68	6.46	3.01	1.77	3.67	50.41
1976	2.16	1.27	4.54	0.48	6.13	5.20	1.24	2.20	3.17	9.72	1.31	2.59	40.01
1977	1.46	0.73	2.61	3.50	1.52	2.41	0.45	2.29	2.71	4.70	6.46	2.49	31.33
1978	6.12	0.65	5.92	7.54	4.85	2.05	4.83	6.33	0.52	0.78	2.55	3.15	45.29
1979	5.27	5.37	3.38	3.99	2.65	5.78	3.97	3.37	9.18	3.56	3.77	1.13	51.42
1980	4.10	0.67	5.41	5.51	2.66	1.81	5.18	2.87	1.66	2.30	1.78	0.60	34.55
1981	0.29	2.43	2.30	1.75	4.56	2.49	2.86	1.32	4.52	3.90	0.68	3.79	30.89
1982	3.76	4.75	2.33	2.01	4.83	4.99	3.98	5.20	2.67	4.13	3.65	2.53	44.83
1983	1.28	4.12	6.41	7.95	3.17	2.38	1.67	2.23	1.52	7.73	4.26	5.61	48.33
1984	1.35	4.85	4.30	3.97	4.49	2.34	4.17	9.54	2.69	1.42	2.67	1.84	43.63
1985	2.45	3.64	1.80	1.75	6.89	2.08	4.18	8.67	1.26	3.77	12.36	0.85	49.70
1986	0.93	2.87	1.36	1.67	4.15	0.62	2.83	4.31	3.04	2.76	3.73	5.48	33.75
1987	4.53	4.55	4.11	11.35	2.68	0.71	3.21	1.08	11.09	1.10	5.00	2.16	51.57
1988	1.87	1.07	0.88	3.40	2.76	3.66	3.75	4.30	3.01	1.26	2.42	1.28	29.66
1989	1.31	2.04	2.96	2.54	6.46	7.76	10.09	1.65	8.94	4.13	3.86	2.60	54.34
1990	2.33	2.76	3.42	2.07	7.45	0.83	3.80	4.42	1.86	9.89	1.08	3.79	43.70
1991	3.55	2.10	7.58	2.49	2.88	2.42	7.22	2.31	0.15	0.04	2.51	3.81	37.06
1992	2.51	3.75	2.54	4.89	6.06	6.87	1.73	2.38	2.07	1.90	5.60	2.62	42.92
1993	3.77	3.44	7.91	2.77	2.37	2.49	1.24	1.04	4.58	2.15	2.60	5.27	39.63
Record Mean	2.72	3.15	3.66	3.30	3.95	3.37	3.72	4.04	3.34	3.41	2.99	3.09	40.75

AVERAGE TEMPERATURE (deg. F)

ROANOKE, VIRGINIA

YEAR	JAN	FEB	MAR	APR	MAY	JUNE	JULY	AUG	SEP	OCT	NOV	DEC	ANNUAL
#1964	37.3	35.6	46.6	56.9	67.4	74.6	75.9	74.0	66.8	54.0	51.1	40.0	56.7
1965	36.0	36.4	41.9	54.9	69.2	69.7	73.9	74.2	69.7	56.0	47.5	41.5	55.9
1966	30.6	35.1	46.7	51.5	63.3	71.1	77.9	73.0	66.1	54.6	47.2	37.8	54.6
1967	40.8	34.8	48.5	59.0	59.0	70.3	73.4	72.6	63.2	54.7	43.4	41.3	55.1
1968	33.0	33.8	51.3	56.5	62.4	71.3	75.6	75.2	66.7	57.4	48.1	33.7	55.4
1969	32.3	37.2	40.7	57.3	65.0	73.1	76.0	73.5	66.7	56.6	44.5	33.6	54.7
1970	29.8	36.9	42.5	56.5	66.8	72.9	76.1	74.1	72.6	59.7	46.3	40.0	56.2
1971	33.9	39.1	43.6	55.5	61.5	72.6	73.5	72.6	69.8	62.1	45.4	45.3	56.3
1972	39.6	36.0	45.6	55.5	62.0	67.7	74.3	73.2	67.6	52.2	45.4	44.5	55.3
1973	37.3	35.8	51.1	53.8	61.1	73.8	75.5	76.0	70.8	59.2	49.3	38.2	56.8
1974	45.3	39.0	50.8	57.2	64.3	68.1	74.5	73.5	64.8	55.0	47.3	38.9	56.6
1975	39.6	40.4	42.2	52.9	66.5	71.5	74.5	77.0	66.6	60.0	51.1	38.8	56.8
1976	33.4	46.7	50.8	57.4	62.3	70.0	74.0	72.1	65.2	50.3	40.2	34.3	54.7
1977	23.6	36.6	52.5	58.9	68.1	71.1	79.7	77.8	70.4	53.6	48.5	35.9	56.4
1978	27.8	29.5	44.2	56.3	63.8	72.7	76.0	77.5	71.4	54.0	49.5	39.5	55.2
1979	31.4	29.4	48.6	55.7	63.8	69.3	73.5	74.0	66.3	54.6	49.6	40.9	54.8
1980	37.5	34.0	43.5	56.7	64.8	70.0	78.1	76.8	71.5	55.5	45.4	38.7	56.1
1981	32.0	38.2	43.1	58.6	60.9	74.0	76.1	73.4	66.1	53.7	45.2	32.8	54.5
1982	28.7	38.1	44.8	50.8	67.5	70.1	75.5	72.3	65.8	57.4	47.8	42.4	55.1
1983	35.6	36.5	47.0	52.4	61.0	70.1	77.0	77.9	68.1	57.1	47.1	34.9	55.4
1984	33.6	43.6	43.3	54.2	63.1	74.2	73.2	74.4	64.1	64.3	46.0	47.1	56.8
1985	31.3	38.6	50.3	61.9	67.1	72.7	76.5	73.8	68.4	60.3	55.4	35.1	57.6
1986	35.2	38.3	47.2	58.8	63.9	74.2	78.8	72.4	68.9	59.0	47.4	38.5	56.9
1987	34.2	36.9	46.6	53.2	67.1	75.0	79.3	77.8	68.9	51.5	49.6	41.4	56.8
1988	30.8	37.9	47.5	55.4	63.4	70.9	77.1	77.5	66.0	51.2	46.7	38.9	55.3
1989	41.3	38.2	47.4	54.3	61.2	73.7	75.9	74.1	68.1	58.5	46.0	29.6	55.7
1990	43.7	45.9	51.5	56.0	64.3	72.6	76.8	74.6	68.4	59.2	52.2	43.8	59.1
1991	39.3	42.7	49.2	57.5	69.6	73.5	77.9	74.8	69.3	59.4	46.8	42.4	58.5
1992	39.6	41.5	46.5	55.5	60.2	68.4	77.0	72.1	68.0	55.5	46.3	38.5	55.8
1993	39.7	36.0	42.1	54.5	65.6	71.9	80.3	76.8	68.6	55.3	47.3	36.2	56.2
Record Mean	35.9	38.3	46.1	56.6	64.7	72.1	76.3	74.8	67.8	57.1	47.1	38.4	56.3
Max	45.1	48.3	56.8	67.7	76.2	83.5	87.2	85.6	78.7	68.6	57.4	47.5	66.9
Min	26.7	28.4	35.4	45.5	53.1	60.6	65.3	64.0	56.9	45.6	36.7	29.2	45.6

REFERENCE NOTES

ROANOKE, VIRGINIA

GENERAL
T - TRACE AMOUNT.
BLANK ENTRIES DENOTE MISSING/UNREPORTED DATA.
# INDICATES A STATION OR INSTRUMENT RELOCATION.

SPECIFIC

PM - INCLUDES LAST DAY OF PREVIOUS MONTH
ASOS - AUTOMATED SURFACE OBSERVING SYSTEM IN OPERATION DURING THESE MONTHS.

(a) - LENGTH OF RECORD IN YEARS, ALTHOUGH INDIVIDUAL MONTHS MAY BE MISSING.
0.* OR * - THE VALUE IS BETWEEN 0.0 AND 0.05
NORMALS - BASED ON THE 1961-1990 RECORD PERIOD.
EXTREMES - DATES ARE THE MOST RECENT OCCURRENCE
WIND DIR.- NUMERALS SHOW TENS OF DEGRESS CLOCKWISE FROM TRUE NORTH. "00" INDICATES CALM.
RESULTANT DIRECTIONS ARE GIVEN TO WHOLE DEGREES.
BOLD VALUES INDICATE EXTREME VALUES WHICH OCCURRED AFTER THE ASOS SYSTEM WAS COMMISSIONED.

RECORD = PERIOD OF RECORD
RECORD MEAN PRECIPITATION IS THE MEAN OF ALL DAILY PRECIPITATION AMOUNTS DURING THE PERIOD OF RECORD.
RECORD MAX(MIN) TEMPERATURE IS THE MEAN OF ALL DAILY MAX(MIN) TEMPERATURES DURING THE PERIOD OF RECORD.
RECORD MEAN TEMPERATURE IS THE SUM OF THE RECORD MAX AND RECORD MIN DIVIDED BY 2.
AVERAGE TEMPERATURE IS THE SUM OF THE MEAN DAILY MAX AND MIN TEMPERATURE DIVIDED BY 2.

EXCEPTIONS

RECORD MEANS ARE THROUGH THE CURRENT YEAR,
BEGINNING IN 1948 FOR TEMPERATURE
1948 FOR PRECIPITATION
1948 FOR SNOWFALL

HEATING DEGREE DAYS Base 65 deg. F — ROANOKE, VIRGINIA

SEASON	JULY	AUG	SEP	OCT	NOV	DEC	JAN	FEB	MAR	APR	MAY	JUNE	TOTAL
#1964-65	0	9	41	338	409	770	892	794	710	305	21	19	4308
1965-66	0	9	38	287	520	722	1058	831	565	409	118	25	4582
1966-67	0	0	51	317	527	837	740	838	505	202	206	28	4251
1967-68	0	0	105	321	643	728	984	902	423	255	111	3	4475
1968-69	0	12	11	244	502	963	1005	772	746	227	77	9	4568
1969-70	0	0	53	274	607	967	1087	783	691	269	66	2	4799
1970-71	1	1	24	194	553	769	959	719	658	285	143	3	4309
1971-72	0	0	12	117	595	603	780	837	594	305	99	31	3973
1972-73	10	1	33	391	582	628	852	812	428	344	144	1	4226
1973-74	0	0	12	196	461	826	607	722	440	255	96	14	3629
1974-75	0	0	84	308	539	801	783	683	699	361	60	12	4330
1975-76	0	0	59	173	415	809	973	523	438	271	126	22	3809
1976-77	0	3	47	452	735	945	1275	786	385	203	56	23	4910
1977-78	0	0	18	350	496	896	1147	989	637	261	112	4	4910
1978-79	0	0	29	335	461	784	1037	992	512	279	88	15	4532
1979-80	3	9	49	329	458	738	848	893	656	266	78	14	4341
1980-81	0	0	30	301	582	807	1016	744	672	212	158	3	4525
1981-82	0	0	58	357	589	991	1121	746	618	421	51	3	4955
1982-83	0	6	61	264	509	695	904	792	551	381	157	14	4334
1983-84	1	0	87	246	531	924	966	614	664	336	123	6	4498
1984-85	0	0	120	74	565	549	1041	734	471	168	39	11	3772
1985-86	0	0	55	171	282	918	917	739	551	206	115	1	3955
1986-87	0	22	22	231	523	813	950	782	562	352	58	0	4315
1987-88	0	0	18	412	455	723	1055	778	535	289	101	46	4412
1988-89	1	0	53	423	543	802	726	743	556	340	172	0	4359
1989-90	0	3	63	234	560	1091	654	528	441	297	77	3	3951
1990-91	0	0	38	200	381	652	787	618	486	245	36	4	3447
1991-92	0	0	49	194	539	695	777	677	567	290	172	18	3978
1992-93	0	2	55	290	552	813	777	807	698	310	52	12	4368
1993-94	0	0	52	300	529	886							

COOLING DEGREE DAYS Base 65 deg. F — ROANOKE, VIRGINIA

YEAR	JAN	FEB	MAR	APR	MAY	JUNE	JULY	AUG	SEP	OCT	NOV	DEC	TOTAL
1969	0	0	0	2	86	256	347	272	107	21	0	0	1091
1970	0	0	0	22	128	246	351	291	261	35	0	0	1334
1971	0	0	0	4	40	239	270	245	163	35	13	1	1010
1972	0	0	0	26	13	118	305	262	118	0	2	0	844
1973	0	0	3	15	29	269	331	346	192	23	0	0	1208
1974	0	0	7	27	82	117	303	267	83	3	12	0	901
1975	0	0	0	5	108	213	301	379	114	27	5	0	1152
1976	0	0	8	53	49	179	285	230	58	1	0	0	863
1977	0	0	7	28	158	214	461	400	185	4	7	0	1464
1978	0	0	0	7	79	243	347	391	228	2	0	0	1297
1979	0	0	10	7	56	150	273	296	97	12	1	0	902
1980	0	0	0	21	78	171	412	374	231	13	0	0	1300
1981	0	0	2	26	39	278	350	267	97	13	0	0	1072
1982	0	0	0	0	137	165	332	242	90	35	0	0	1001
1983	0	0	0	11	41	172	382	407	188	10	0	0	1211
1984	0	0	0	20	71	290	260	301	101	56	0	0	1099
1985	0	1	18	78	112	247	365	280	163	34	3	0	1301
1986	0	0	4	24	84	282	438	257	145	48	0	0	1282
1987	0	0	0	4	130	306	450	403	140	0	0	0	1433
1988	0	0	0	7	58	232	386	395	90	1	0	0	1169
1989	0	0	17	27	61	265	344	293	163	38	0	0	1208
1990	0	0	29	34	61	238	377	305	145	27	3	0	1219
1991	0	0	2	29	188	267	407	311	185	28	1	0	1418
1992	0	0	2	12	29	125	377	230	152	4	0	0	931
1993	0	0	0	2	78	226	481	374	166	8	6	0	1341

SNOWFALL (inches) — ROANOKE, VIRGINIA

SEASON	JULY	AUG	SEP	OCT	NOV	DEC	JAN	FEB	MAR	APR	MAY	JUNE	TOTAL
1964-65	0.0	0.0	0.0	0.0	0.5	T	12.1	4.0	4.1	0.0	0.0	0.0	20.7
1965-66	0.0	0.0	0.0	0.0	T	0.3	41.2	8.4	T	0.0	0.0	0.0	49.9
1966-67	0.0	0.0	0.0	0.0	T	22.6	2.7	15.6	0.8	0.0	0.0	0.0	41.7
1967-68	0.0	0.0	0.0	0.0	T	14.8	15.4	3.8	T	0.0	0.0	0.0	34.0
1968-69	0.0	0.0	0.0	T	13.8	T	0.1	11.4	13.8	0.0	0.0	0.0	39.1
1969-70	0.0	0.0	0.0	0.0	T	16.8	4.4	5.4	T	0.2	0.0	0.0	26.8
1970-71	0.0	0.0	0.0	0.0	2.0	10.8	1.1	3.6	7.3	7.3	0.0	0.0	32.1
1971-72	0.0	0.0	0.0	0.0	10.2	0.2	T	12.8	T	T	0.0	0.0	23.2
1972-73	0.0	0.0	0.0	0.0	T	T	2.4	1.4	5.5	0.2	0.0	0.0	9.5
1973-74	0.0	0.0	0.0	T	T	7.9	T	9.7	T	0.0	0.0	0.0	17.6
1974-75	0.0	0.0	0.0	T	3.3	6.6	4.6	6.3	6.2	T	0.0	0.0	27.0
1975-76	0.0	0.0	0.0	0.0	T	0.1	T	T	2.2	0.0	0.0	0.0	2.3
1976-77	0.0	0.0	0.0	0.0	2.4	6.4	8.9	1.5	T	T	0.0	0.0	19.2
1977-78	0.0	0.0	0.0	T	2.4	0.4	14.5	9.6	10.4	0.0	0.0	0.0	37.3
1978-79	0.0	0.0	0.0	0.0	1.6	T	3.0	19.3	T	0.0	0.0	0.0	23.9
1979-80	0.0	0.0	0.0	0.3	T	0.2	15.1	4.2	12.0	T	0.0	0.0	31.8
1980-81	0.0	0.0	0.0	T	T	T	1.4	T	10.4	0.0	0.0	0.0	11.8
1981-82	0.0	0.0	0.0	0.0	4.0	3.9	8.4	12.2	0.5	1.9	0.0	0.0	30.9
1982-83	0.0	0.0	0.0	T	0.0	6.2	3.8	24.3	0.3	0.4	0.0	0.0	35.0
1983-84	0.0	0.0	0.0	0.0	T	0.6	7.2	1.5	0.3	0.2	0.0	0.0	9.8
1984-85	0.0	0.0	0.0	0.0	T	0.8	2.7	1.2	1.3	T	0.0	0.0	6.0
1985-86	0.0	0.0	0.0	0.0	0.0	1.2	1.7	7.1	T	T	0.0	0.0	10.0
1986-87	0.0	0.0	0.0	0.0	T	T	27.9	19.1	2.7	6.3	0.0	0.0	56.0
1987-88	0.0	0.0	0.0	0.0	1.7	T	6.7	T	T	T	0.0	0.0	8.4
1988-89	0.0	0.0	0.0	T	0.0	3.8	0.7	9.1	0.2	0.2	T	T	14.0
1989-90	0.0	0.0	0.0	0.0	3.3	11.1	T	0.2	1.5	0.0	T	0.0	16.1
1990-91	0.0	0.0	0.0	0.0	0.0	0.8	T	T	0.4	0.0	0.0	0.0	1.2
1991-92	0.0	0.0	0.0	0.0	T	T	0.4	2.2	0.5	1.9	0.0	0.0	5.0
1992-93	0.0	0.0	0.0	0.0	T	0.9	0.1	10.7	16.0	0.3	0.0	0.0	28.0
1993-94	0.0	0.0	0.0	T	T	6.2							
Record Mean	0.0	0.0	T	T	1.5	3.8	6.2	7.0	3.8	0.5	T	T	22.9

SEATTLE, WASHINGTON
SEATTLE – TACOMA AIRPORT

The Seattle–Tacoma International Airport is located 6 miles south of the Seattle city limits and 14 miles north of Tacoma. It is situated on a low ridge lying between Puget Sound on the west and the Green River valley on the east with terrain sloping moderately to the shores of Puget Sound some 2 miles to the west. The Olympic Mountains, rising sharply from Puget Sound, are about 50 miles to the northwest. Rather steep bluffs border the Green River Valley about 2.5 miles to the east and the foothills of the Cascade Range begin 10 to 15 miles to the east of the airport.

The mild climate of the Pacific Coast is modified by the Cascade Mountains and, to a lesser extent, by the Olympic Mountains. The climate is characterized by mild temperatures, a pronounced though not sharply defined rainy season, and considerable cloudiness, particularly during the winter months. The Cascades are very effective in shielding the Seattle–Tacoma area from the cold, dry continental air during the winter and the hot, dry continental air during the summer months. The extremes of temperature that occur in western Washington are the result of the occasional pressure distributions that force the continental air into the Puget Sound area. But the prevailing southwesterly circulation keeps the average winter daytime temperatures in the 40s and the nighttime readings in the 30s. During the summer, daytime temperatures are usually in the 70s with nighttime lows in the 50s. Extremes of temperatures, both in the winter and summer, are usually of short duration. The dry season is centered around July and early August with July being the driest month of the year. The rainy season extends from October to March with December normally the wettest month, however, precipitation is rather evenly distributed through the winter and early spring months with more than 75 percent of the yearly precipitation falling during the winter wet season. Most of the rainfall in the Seattle area comes from storms common to the middle latitudes. These disturbances are most vigorous during the winter as they move through western Washington. The storm track shifts to the north during the summer and those that reach the State are not the wind and rain producers of the winter months. Local summer afternoon showers and a few thunderstorms occur in the Seattle–Tacoma area but they do not contribute materially to the precipitation.

The occurrence of snow in the Seattle–Tacoma area is extremely variable and usually melts before accumulating measurable depths. There are winters on record with only a trace of snow, but at the other extreme, over 21 inches has fallen in a 24–hour period. Usually, winter storms do not produce snow unless the storm moves in such a way to bring cold air out of Canada directly or with only a short over water trajectory.

The highest winds recorded in the Seattle–Tacoma area were associated with strong storms crossing the state from the southwest. Prevailing winds are from the southwest but occasional severe winter storms will produce strong northerly winds. Winds during the summer months are relatively light with occasional land–sea breeze effects creating afternoon northerly winds of 8 to 15 miles an hour. Fog or low clouds that form over the southern Puget Sound area in the late summer, fall, and early winter months, often dominate the weather conditions during the late night and early morning hours with visibilities occasionally lower for a few hours near sunrise. Most of the summer clouds form along the coast and move into the Seattle area from the southwest.

Based on the 1951–1980 period, the average first occurrence of 32 degrees Fahrenheit in the fall is November 11 and the average last occurrence in the spring is March 24.

NORMALS, MEANS, AND EXTREMES

SEATTLE, WASHINGTON SEATTLE - TACOMA AIRPORT

LATITUDE: 47 °27'N LONGITUDE: 122 °18' W ELEVATION: FT. GRND 400 BARO 451 TIME ZONE: PACIFIC WBAN: 24233

	(a)	JAN	FEB	MAR	APR	MAY	JUNE	JULY	AUG	SEP	OCT	NOV	DEC	YEAR
TEMPERATURE °F:														
Normals														
-Daily Maximum		45.0	49.5	52.7	57.2	63.9	69.9	75.2	75.2	69.3	59.7	50.5	45.1	59.4
-Daily Minimum		35.2	37.4	38.5	41.2	46.3	51.9	55.2	55.7	51.9	45.8	40.1	35.8	44.6
-Monthly		40.1	43.5	45.6	49.2	55.1	60.9	65.2	65.5	60.6	52.8	45.3	40.5	52.0
Extremes														
-Record Highest	49	64	70	75	85	93	96	99	99	98	89	74	64	99
-Year		1981	1968	1987	1976	1963	1955	1991	1981	1988	1987	1949	1993	JUL 1991
-Record Lowest	49	0	1	11	29	28	38	43	44	35	28	6	6	0
-Year		1950	1950	1955	1975	1954	1952	1954	1955	1972	1949	1955	1968	JAN 1950
NORMAL DEGREE DAYS:														
Heating (base 65°F)		772	602	601	474	307	144	58	65	156	378	591	760	4908
Cooling (base 65°F)		0	0	0	0	0	21	64	81	24	0	0	0	190
% OF POSSIBLE SUNSHINE	27	26	39	49	52	55	56	64	65	61	43	28	22	47
MEAN SKY COVER (tenths)														
Sunrise - Sunset	49	8.4	8.1	7.9	7.8	7.2	7.0	5.4	5.7	6.0	7.5	8.4	8.6	7.3
MEAN NUMBER OF DAYS:														
Sunrise to Sunset														
-Clear	49	2.8	2.9	3.2	2.8	4.4	5.1	10.3	9.1	8.2	4.1	2.5	2.2	57.6
-Partly Cloudy	49	3.9	4.2	5.8	7.2	8.8	7.8	9.6	9.9	8.6	7.4	4.3	3.8	81.2
-Cloudy	49	24.3	21.2	22.0	20.0	17.8	17.1	10.8	12.1	13.2	19.5	23.2	25.1	226.1
Precipitation														
.01 inches or more	49	18.4	15.6	16.9	14.0	10.4	9.0	5.1	6.2	8.8	13.0	17.9	19.1	154.5
Snow,Ice pellets,hail														
1.0 inches or more	49	1.5	0.6	0.5	0.*	0.0	0.0	0.0	0.0	0.0	0.*	0.3	0.9	3.8
Thunderstorms	49	0.2	0.3	0.7	0.9	0.9	0.7	0.7	0.7	0.7	0.4	0.7	0.3	7.2
Heavy Fog Visibility														
1/4 mile or less	49	5.3	3.5	2.4	1.2	0.7	0.7	1.5	2.6	5.1	7.4	5.6	6.2	42.2
Temperature °F														
-Maximum														
90° and above	34	0.0	0.0	0.0	0.0	0.2	0.4	1.1	1.2	0.3	0.0	0.0	0.0	3.2
32° and below	34	1.0	0.2	0.0	0.0	0.0	0.0	0.0	0.0	0.0	0.0	0.2	1.1	2.6
-Minimum														
32° and below	34	10.0	5.4	2.9	0.2	0.0	0.0	0.0	0.0	0.0	0.2	3.6	8.9	31.2
0° and below	34	0.0	0.0	0.0	0.0	0.0	0.0	0.0	0.0	0.0	0.0	0.0	0.0	0.0
AVG. STATION PRESS.(mb)	21	1001.3	1000.0	999.0	1000.8	1000.8	1000.9	1001.5	1000.5	1000.7	1001.6	1000.4	1001.6	1000.8
RELATIVE HUMIDITY (%)														
Hour 04	34	81	81	83	84	83	82	82	84	86	87	84	83	83
Hour 10 (Local Time)	34	79	77	75	71	68	66	65	68	73	79	80	81	74
Hour 16	34	74	67	62	58	54	53	49	50	56	67	75	78	62
Hour 22	34	78	76	76	74	72	70	68	71	75	81	81	81	75
PRECIPITATION (inches):														
Water Equivalent														
-Normal		5.38	3.99	3.54	2.33	1.70	1.50	0.76	1.14	1.88	3.23	5.83	5.91	37.19
-Maximum Monthly	49	12.92	9.11	8.40	6.53	4.76	3.90	2.39	4.59	5.95	8.95	10.71	11.85	12.92
-Year		1953	1961	1950	1991	1948	1946	1983	1975	1978	1947	1990	1979	JAN 1953
-Minimum Monthly	49	0.58	0.35	0.57	0.33	0.12	0.13	T	0.01	T	0.31	0.74	1.37	T
-Year		1985	1993	1965	1956	1992	1951	1960	1974	1991	1987	1976	1978	SEP 1991
-Maximum in 24 hrs	49	3.22	3.41	2.86	3.32	1.83	2.08	0.85	1.75	2.23	3.74	3.58	2.61	3.74
-Year		1986	1951	1972	1991	1969	1985	1981	1968	1978	1981	1990	1979	OCT 1981
Snow,Ice pellets,hail														
-Maximum Monthly	49	57.2	13.1	18.2	2.3	T	0.0	T	0.0	T	2.0	17.5	22.1	57.2
-Year		1950	1349	1951	1972	1993		1980		1972	1971	1985	1968	JAN 1950
-Maximum in 24 hrs	49	21.4	9.8	7.4	2.3	T	0.0	T	0.0	T	2.0	9.4	13.0	21.4
-Year		1950	1990	1989	1972	1993		1980		1972	1971	1946	1968	JAN 1950
WIND:														
Mean Speed (mph)	45	9.7	9.5	9.7	9.5	8.9	8.7	8.3	7.9	8.1	8.5	9.3	9.5	9.0
Prevailing Direction through 1963		SSW	SW	SSW	SW	SW	SW	SW	SW	N	S	S	SSW	SW
Fastest Mile														
-Direction (!!)	25	S	S	SW	SW	SW	SW	SW	SW	S	SW	S	S	S
-Speed (MPH)	25	47	51	44	38	32	29	26	29	35	38	66	49	66
-Year		1993	1981	1984	1972	1968	1974	1981	1977	1990	1982	1981	1982	NOV 1981
Peak Gust														
-Direction (!!)	10	S	S	S	SW	W	S	S	S	S	S	S	S	S
-Speed (mph)	10	64	46	43	44	39	32	29	38	39	45	52	52	64
-Date		1993	1988	1991	1990	1993	1990	1988	1991	1990	1990	1991	1993	JAN 1993

PRECIPITATION (inches)

SEATTLE, WASHINGTON SEATTLE - TACOMA AIRPORT

YEAR	JAN	FEB	MAR	APR	MAY	JUNE	JULY	AUG	SEP	OCT	NOV	DEC	ANNUAL
1964	9.76	1.66	2.96	1.56	0.91	3.82	0.99	1.23	2.27	1.00	9.65	5.53	41.34
1965	5.27	3.88	0.57	3.73	1.63	0.59	0.38	2.18	0.49	2.76	4.98	7.10	33.56
1966	5.43	2.31	4.38	1.99	1.35	1.15	1.35	0.42	1.77	2.92	6.85	8.31	38.23
1967	9.32	2.72	3.71	2.50	0.38	2.04	0.01	0.02	0.94	6.66	2.56	4.72	35.58
1968	6.90	6.08	5.08	1.33	1.67	3.02	0.83	4.58	1.93	4.32	5.86	8.55	50.15
1969	5.71	3.16	2.20	3.45	2.93	0.91	0.27	0.45	5.57	1.19	2.21	5.68	33.73
1970	8.22	2.26	3.16	3.31	1.17	0.43	0.48	0.32	2.23	2.52	5.03	8.28	37.41
1971	5.32	4.36	7.12	2.39	1.43	2.28	0.68	0.57	3.51	3.57	5.31	6.67	43.21
1972	7.24	8.11	6.74	4.12	0.69	1.81	1.34	1.13	4.10	0.72	3.38	8.98	48.36
1973	4.29	1.89	1.62	1.35	1.60	2.50	0.08	0.27	1.81	3.31	7.99	8.33	35.04
1974	7.78	4.01	5.84	2.39	1.37	1.25	1.51	0.01	0.21	1.99	5.06	6.45	37.87
1975	6.01	5.80	2.87	2.49	1.13	0.84	0.27	4.59	T	7.75	5.07	7.66	44.48
1976	5.55	4.74	2.71	1.67	1.61	0.63	1.17	2.71	1.25	2.06	0.74	1.86	26.70
1977	1.77	1.58	3.80	0.55	3.70	0.54	0.42	3.59	2.55	2.60	5.27	6.47	32.84
1978	4.30	3.59	2.43	4.19	1.79	0.75	1.40	1.19	5.95	0.98	6.05	1.37	33.99
1979	2.25	5.32	1.55	0.81	0.88	0.46	0.73	1.02	2.07	3.38	1.94	11.85	32.26
1980	4.09	5.04	2.10	3.23	0.97	1.77	0.46	0.64	1.43	1.32	7.16	7.39	35.60
1981	2.42	4.45	2.23	1.58	1.33	2.31	1.38	0.25	3.42	6.40	4.07	5.56	35.40
1982	5.35	7.57	3.73	2.07	0.63	1.03	0.59	0.62	1.49	4.07	5.31	6.86	39.32
1983	7.07	4.57	3.81	1.06	2.10	1.85	2.39	1.90	1.85	1.34	7.97	5.02	40.93
1984	3.62	3.91	3.91	2.87	3.38	2.81	0.17	0.13	1.01	2.14	8.09	4.95	36.99
1985	0.58	2.63	2.56	1.30	0.85	2.80	0.10	0.55	1.98	5.74	4.26	1.78	25.13
1986	8.54	4.41	2.67	1.38	1.71	0.68	1.10	0.10	1.89	4.21	7.98	3.67	38.34
1987	5.98	2.05	5.53	2.61	2.38	0.16	0.39	0.29	0.91	0.31	3.21	6.11	29.93
1988	4.07	0.71	3.75	3.20	3.01	1.56	0.50	0.28	1.75	2.24	8.43	3.48	32.98
1989	2.78	3.43	5.79	2.80	2.78	1.14	0.64	0.89	0.54	2.98	6.13	4.79	34.69
1990	9.41	3.72	2.58	2.54	1.98	3.05	0.58	0.71	0.05	5.79	10.71	3.63	44.75
1991	4.46	4.69	4.66	6.53	1.39	1.29	0.28	2.17	T	1.31	5.33	3.31	35.42
1992	7.82	3.09	1.68	4.12	0.12	1.14	0.89	0.66	1.15	2.45	5.57	4.09	32.78
1993	4.09	0.35	4.80	4.54	2.86	2.48	1.27	0.16	0.03	1.54	2.20	4.48	28.80
Record Mean	5.63	4.19	3.70	2.54	1.68	1.51	0.77	1.07	1.88	3.51	5.79	5.82	38.09

AVERAGE TEMPERATURE (deg. F)

SEATTLE, WASHINGTON SEATTLE - TACOMA AIRPORT

YEAR	JAN	FEB	MAR	APR	MAY	JUNE	JULY	AUG	SEP	OCT	NOV	DEC	ANNUAL
1964	40.0	41.3	44.1	46.8	53.2	57.9	63.5	62.6	58.5	53.5	42.1	36.4	50.0
1965	40.2	43.0	47.0	49.5	51.9	60.8	67.8	65.7	58.4	56.4	49.4	40.4	52.6
1966	41.1	43.9	45.1	50.0	54.5	58.7	62.1	64.5	61.5	51.4	45.4	43.5	51.8
1967	42.4	42.8	42.2	46.6	55.4	62.7	66.5	71.1	65.7	54.8	47.3	41.6	53.2
1968	40.9	48.5	48.6	48.7	57.3	60.7	67.0	63.7	59.1	51.5	46.8	36.6	52.5
1969	33.1	42.3	46.9	48.9	58.0	64.3	64.7	64.0	61.0	52.4	46.6	45.2	52.3
1970	41.2	47.0	46.0	46.1	54.7	62.7	64.9	64.5	58.6	50.8	46.5	39.0	51.8
1971	39.7	42.3	41.3	48.9	54.5	55.9	65.5	67.7	57.6	51.0	45.7	37.5	50.6
1972	37.0	41.4	46.9	47.0	58.3	60.1	66.0	66.7	55.4	50.1	46.7	38.1	51.1
1973	38.7	43.9	44.1	48.6	56.5	59.3	64.7	61.6	61.9	52.2	43.7	44.4	51.6
1974	38.7	43.2	46.3	50.3	54.9	62.6	64.0	64.6	64.4	52.5	45.1	42.4	52.4
1975	38.8	40.8	42.9	45.8	54.6	60.7	67.5	63.2	63.0	51.4	44.9	41.5	51.3
1976	41.8	40.9	41.3	49.5	56.4	60.0	65.9	64.1	62.6	54.9	47.8	44.7	52.5
1977	39.4	48.7	45.7	53.6	54.5	63.0	65.1	68.5	58.9	52.2	43.9	42.2	53.0
1978	44.4	46.0	48.6	49.9	54.5	64.3	65.8	65.5	58.8	54.3	41.2	37.5	52.6
1979	37.8	42.3	49.3	50.8	57.2	62.5	67.4	64.0	62.6	54.2	43.9	44.1	53.0
1980	34.8	43.8	44.3	51.6	54.2	57.5	63.8	61.9	59.6	53.9	46.7	44.1	51.4
1981	44.4	44.2	48.8	49.6	54.7	57.5	63.3	68.1	61.1	50.9	47.2	41.7	52.7
1982	39.3	42.1	44.1	47.4	54.7	63.1	62.8	65.1	60.6	52.7	43.2	40.8	51.3
1983	45.0	46.9	49.4	50.7	57.7	59.9	63.3	65.6	58.3	51.7	47.8	36.1	52.7
1984	43.2	44.8	48.5	48.7	52.9	58.8	65.0	64.9	59.9	49.7	44.6	36.8	51.5
1985	37.1	39.0	43.3	49.2	54.8	60.0	68.6	65.2	58.1	51.4	35.8	36.2	49.9
1986	44.9	42.8	49.2	48.1	55.7	62.7	61.7	68.4	59.1	54.3	45.3	42.0	52.9
1987	40.5	46.3	48.9	52.0	56.9	62.6	64.2	66.1	62.6	55.8	48.5	39.2	53.6
1988	40.1	44.4	45.6	50.3	54.9	59.6	65.3	65.4	60.5	55.4	45.4	41.9	52.4
1989	40.5	35.9	43.7	53.4	56.0	63.2	64.5	65.3	64.1	53.1	47.0	42.9	52.5
1990	42.5	40.0	47.1	52.1	54.7	59.8	68.0	67.3	63.4	51.2	46.6	35.3	52.3
1991	40.0	47.7	44.1	49.1	54.3	58.9	66.8	66.6	62.9	52.9	47.3	43.7	52.9
1992	43.9	47.3	50.3	53.1	59.8	65.0	66.7	66.8	60.0	54.4	45.5	38.8	54.3
1993	37.9	42.3	48.1	50.6	59.6	60.6	61.2	65.5	61.9	55.4	42.0	41.4	52.2
Record Mean	39.3	42.7	44.9	49.0	55.3	60.3	64.6	64.6	60.0	52.3	44.7	40.5	51.5
Max	44.3	48.8	52.0	57.2	64.4	69.5	75.0	74.6	69.1	59.4	50.2	45.3	59.1
Min	34.2	36.5	37.7	40.8	46.2	51.1	54.2	54.5	50.9	45.1	39.2	35.7	43.8

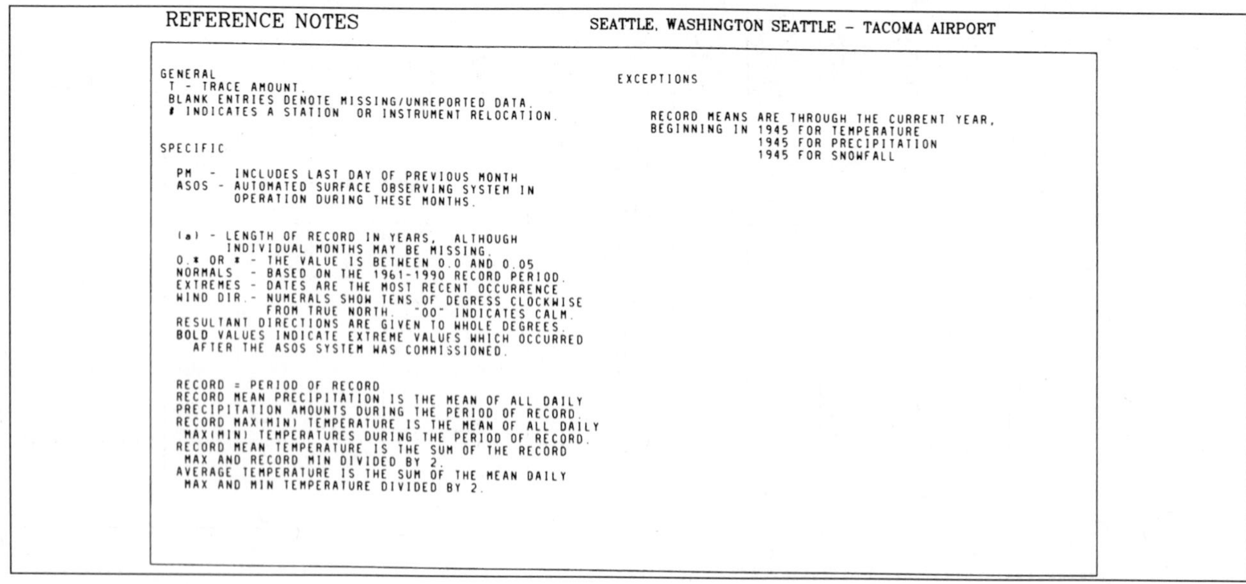

REFERENCE NOTES

SEATTLE, WASHINGTON SEATTLE - TACOMA AIRPORT

GENERAL
T - TRACE AMOUNT.
BLANK ENTRIES DENOTE MISSING/UNREPORTED DATA.
# INDICATES A STATION OR INSTRUMENT RELOCATION.

SPECIFIC

PM - INCLUDES LAST DAY OF PREVIOUS MONTH
ASOS - AUTOMATED SURFACE OBSERVING SYSTEM IN OPERATION DURING THESE MONTHS.

(a) - LENGTH OF RECORD IN YEARS, ALTHOUGH INDIVIDUAL MONTHS MAY BE MISSING.
0.* OR * - THE VALUE IS BETWEEN 0.0 AND 0.05
NORMALS - BASED ON THE 1961-1990 RECORD PERIOD.
EXTREMES - DATES ARE THE MOST RECENT OCCURRENCE
WIND DIR. - NUMERALS SHOW TENS OF DEGRESS CLOCKWISE FROM TRUE NORTH. "00" INDICATES CALM.
RESULTANT DIRECTIONS ARE GIVEN TO WHOLE DEGREES.
BOLD VALUES INDICATE EXTREME VALUES WHICH OCCURRED AFTER THE ASOS SYSTEM WAS COMMISSIONED.

RECORD = PERIOD OF RECORD
RECORD MEAN PRECIPITATION IS THE MEAN OF ALL DAILY PRECIPITATION AMOUNTS DURING THE PERIOD OF RECORD.
RECORD MAX(MIN) TEMPERATURE IS THE MEAN OF ALL DAILY MAX(MIN) TEMPERATURES DURING THE PERIOD OF RECORD.
RECORD MEAN TEMPERATURE IS THE SUM OF THE RECORD MAX AND RECORD MIN DIVIDED BY 2.
AVERAGE TEMPERATURE IS THE SUM OF THE MEAN DAILY MAX AND MIN TEMPERATURE DIVIDED BY 2.

EXCEPTIONS

RECORD MEANS ARE THROUGH THE CURRENT YEAR,
BEGINNING IN 1945 FOR TEMPERATURE
1945 FOR PRECIPITATION
1945 FOR SNOWFALL

HEATING DEGREE DAYS Base 65 deg. F — SEATTLE, WASHINGTON SEATTLE - TACOMA AIRPORT

SEASON	JULY	AUG	SEP	OCT	NOV	DEC	JAN	FEB	MAR	APR	MAY	JUNE	TOTAL
1964-65	76	91	189	349	679	882	761	611	553	459	400	136	5186
1965-66	24	44	194	261	462	754	732	584	610	442	321	190	4618
1966-67	95	54	106	414	585	658	695	614	700	548	292	92	4853
1967-68	16	0	44	310	524	718	737	472	503	485	232	139	4180
1968-69	33	70	179	415	538	871	983	627	554	478	230	71	5049
1969-70	49	49	144	381	547	607	731	499	586	563	314	122	4592
1970-71	53	44	190	435	548	801	778	628	728	472	321	267	5265
1971-72	82	17	214	429	570	843	863	678	557	531	222	144	5150
1972-73	48	32	295	455	544	825	807	586	639	484	272	183	5170
1973-74	70	114	111	388	633	632	809	606	573	433	306	99	4774
1974-75	60	66	74	380	591	690	804	671	678	570	317	144	5045
1975-76	23	73	93	413	594	723	712	693	731	465	265	157	4942
1976-77	24	52	81	307	510	625	786	451	591	335	320	79	4161
1977-78	34	43	178	390	625	701	631	525	498	447	323	78	4473
1978-79	44	42	180	324	706	846	837	630	479	420	235	96	4839
1979-80	27	40	86	327	628	642	929	610	634	395	329	218	4865
1980-81	66	104	158	343	543	639	633	577	494	455	316	220	4548
1981-82	80	28	138	430	530	715	790	636	640	521	312	103	4923
1982-83	93	42	141	373	647	745	613	502	479	422	244	149	4450
1983-84	72	19	196	406	511	890	672	577	507	482	372	183	4887
1984-85	54	42	159	467	603	867	857	719	666	469	310	160	5373
1985-86	8	48	199	413	870	888	618	616	479	502	305	90	5036
1986-87	105	12	196	323	586	707	754	522	491	384	253	105	4438
1987-88	58	37	102	284	485	792	767	590	593	435	316	165	4624
1988-89	60	38	162	291	583	708	749	807	654	340	273	93	4758
1989-90	41	29	68	362	534	677	689	696	547	379	312	158	4492
1990-91	29	23	61	420	546	913	767	475	639	472	322	179	4846
1991-92	24	40	90	368	526	654	645	507	447	351	171	63	3886
1992-93	26	22	151	322	580	805	834	629	517	427	170	135	4618
1993-94	113	48	120	290	685	723							

COOLING DEGREE DAYS Base 65 deg. F — SEATTLE, WASHINGTON SEATTLE - TACOMA AIRPORT

YEAR	JAN	FEB	MAR	APR	MAY	JUNE	JULY	AUG	SEP	OCT	NOV	DEC	TOTAL
1969	0	0	0	0	19	55	44	25	28	0	0	0	171
1970	0	0	0	0	1	60	58	36	6	0	0	0	161
1971	0	0	0	0	4	2	106	107	0	0	0	0	219
1972	0	0	0	0	22	3	85	91	11	0	0	0	212
1973	0	0	0	0	16	19	67	17	21	0	0	0	140
1974	0	0	0	0	0	36	38	62	60	0	0	0	196
1975	0	0	0	0	0	21	108	29	39	0	0	0	197
1976	0	0	0	8	4	14	59	29	15	0	0	0	129
1977	0	0	0	0	0	26	44	158	4	0	0	0	232
1978	0	0	0	0	4	66	76	64	0	0	0	0	210
1979	0	0	0	0	2	27	106	15	21	0	0	0	171
1980	0	0	0	0	0	0	34	15	3	2	0	0	54
1981	0	0	0	0	1	3	35	131	24	0	0	0	194
1982	0	0	0	0	0	53	31	55	15	0	0	0	154
1983	0	0	0	0	24	2	24	44	0	0	0	0	94
1984	0	0	0	0	1	5	62	45	11	0	0	0	124
1985	0	0	0	0	3	17	125	59	0	0	0	0	204
1986	0	0	0	0	22	27	10	124	26	0	0	0	209
1987	0	0	0	0	11	42	39	80	35	5	0	0	212
1988	0	0	0	0	7	10	79	56	36	1	0	0	189
1989	0	0	0	0	2	47	32	45	46	0	0	0	172
1990	0	0	0	0	0	10	129	100	21	0	0	0	260
1991	0	0	0	0	0	0	85	96	34	0	0	0	215
1992	0	0	0	0	18	68	83	85	8	0	0	0	262
1993	0	0	0	0	10	8	1	72	32	0	0	0	123

SNOWFALL (inches) — SEATTLE, WASHINGTON SEATTLE - TACOMA AIRPORT

SEASON	JULY	AUG	SEP	OCT	NOV	DEC	JAN	FEB	MAR	APR	MAY	JUNE	TOTAL
1964-65	0.0	0.0	0.0	0.0	3.3	7.6	7.3	T	T	0.0	T	0.0	18.2
1965-66	0.0	0.0	0.0	0.0	0.0	15.3	2.1	T	5.5	T	0.0	0.0	22.9
1966-67	0.0	0.0	0.0	0.0	0.0	2.0	5.9	T	T	T	0.0	0.0	7.9
1967-68	0.0	0.0	0.0	0.0	0.0	3.6	7.5	0.0	0.0	0.5	0.0	0.0	11.6
1968-69	0.0	0.0	0.0	0.0	0.0	22.1	45.4	T	0.0	0.0	0.0	0.0	67.5
1969-70	0.0	0.0	0.0	0.0	T	0.0	T	0.0	T	T	0.0	0.0	T
1970-71	0.0	0.0	0.0	0.0	T	2.9	9.1	2.2	1.9	T	0.0	0.0	16.1
1971-72	0.0	0.0	0.0	2.0	T	10.6	14.0	0.3	T	2.3	0.0	0.0	29.2
1972-73	0.0	0.0	T	0.0	T	5.6	2.7	T	0.8	T	0.0	0.0	9.1
1973-74	0.0	0.0	0.0	0.0	0.2	0.3	3.7	T	T	0.0	T	0.0	4.2
1974-75	0.0	0.0	0.0	0.0	0.0	9.8	1.3	T	T	0.2	0.0	0.0	11.3
1975-76	0.0	0.0	0.0	0.0	1.6	2.6	T	0.5	0.2	T	0.0	0.0	4.9
1976-77	0.0	0.0	0.0	0.0	0.0	T	1.0	T	0.9	0.0	0.0	0.0	1.9
1977-78	0.0	0.0	0.0	0.0	3.5	T	T	0.0	T	T	0.0	0.0	3.5
1978-79	0.0	0.0	0.0	0.0	4.9	0.2	0.5	0.4	0.0	0.0	0.0	0.0	6.0
1979-80	0.0	0.0	0.0	0.0	0.0	1.2	8.8	2.5	0.1	T	0.0	0.0	12.6
1980-81	T	0.0	0.0	0.0	T	0.3	0.0	1.1	0.0	0.0	0.0	0.0	1.4
1981-82	0.0	0.0	0.0	0.0	0.0	T	7.0	T	2.0	T	0.0	0.0	9.0
1982-83	0.0	0.0	0.0	T	0.0	T	0.0	0.0	0.0	0.0	0.0	0.0	T
1983-84	0.0	0.0	0.0	0.0	T	0.3	T	0.0	0.0	T	0.0	0.0	0.3
1984-85	0.0	0.0	0.0	T	T	2.4	T	5.7	T	T	0.0	0.0	8.1
1985-86	0.0	0.0	0.0	T	17.5	1.7	0.0	1.1	0.0	T	0.0	0.0	20.3
1986-87	0.0	0.0	0.0	0.0	T	0.0	1.4	0.0	0.0	0.0	0.0	0.0	1.4
1987-88	0.0	0.0	0.0	0.0	0.0	T	T	0.0	T	0.0	0.0	0.0	T
1988-89	0.0	0.0	0.0	0.0	T	T	1.0	5.8	7.4	T	T	0.0	14.2
1989-90	0.0	0.0	0.0	0.0	0.0	0.0	T	9.8	T	0.0	T	0.0	9.8
1990-91	0.0	0.0	0.0	0.0	0.0	3.8	0.4	0.0	2.5	T	0.0	0.0	6.7
1991-92	0.0	0.0	0.0	0.0	0.0	0.0	0.0	0.0	0.0	0.0	0.0	0.0	0.0
1992-93	0.0	0.0	0.0	0.0	T	6.7	1.3	1.4	0.0	0.0	T	0.0	9.4
1993-94	0.0	0.0	0.0	0.0	T	0.0							
Record Mean	T	0.0	T	T	1.2	2.5	5.0	1.6	1.4	0.1	T	0.0	11.8

SPOKANE
WASHINGTON

Spokane lies on the eastern edge of the broad Columbia Basin area of Washington which is bounded by the Cascade Range on the west and the Rocky Mountains on the east. The elevations in eastern Washington vary from less than 400 feet above sea level near Pasco where the Columbia River flows out of Washington to over 5,000 feet in the mountain areas of the extreme eastern edge of the State. Spokane is located on the upper plateau area where the long gradual slope from the Columbia River meets the sharp rise of the Rocky Mountain Ranges.

Much of the urban area of Spokane lies along both sides of the Spokane River at an elevation of approximately 2,000 feet, but the residential areas have spread to the crests of the plateaus on either side of the river with elevations up to 2,500 feet above sea level. Spokane International Airport is situated on the plateau area 6 miles west-southwest and some 400 feet higher than the downtown business district.

The climate of Spokane combines some of the characteristics of damp coastal type weather and arid interior conditions. Most of the air masses which reach Spokane are brought in by the prevailing westerly and southwesterly circulations. Frequently, much of the moisture in the storms that move eastward and southeastward from the Gulf of Alaska and the eastern Pacific Ocean is precipitated out as the storms are lifted across the Coast and Cascade Ranges. Annual precipitation totals in the Spokane area are generally less than 20 inches and less than 50 percent of the amounts received west of the Cascades. However, the precipitation and total cloudiness in the Spokane vicinity is greater than that of the desert areas of south-central Washington. The lifting action of the air masses as they move up the east slope of the Columbia Basin frequently produces the cooling and condensation necessary for formation of clouds and precipitation.

Infrequently, the Spokane area comes under the influence of dry continental air masses from the north or east. On occasions when these air masses penetrate into eastern Washington the result is high temperatures and very low humidity in the summer and sub-zero temperatures in the winter. In the winter most of the severe arctic outbursts of cold air move southward on the east side of the Continental Divide and do not affect Spokane.

In general, Spokane weather has the characteristics of a mild, arid climate during the summer months and a cold, coastal type in the winter. Approximately 70 percent of the total annual precipitation falls between the first of October and the end of March and about half of that falls as snow. The growing season usually extends over nearly six months from mid-April to mid-October. Irrigation is required for all crops except dry-land type grains. The summer weather is ideal for full enjoyment of the many mountain and lake recreational areas in the immediate vicinity. Winter weather includes many cloudy or foggy days and below freezing temperatures with occasional snowfall of several inches in depth. Sub-zero temperatures and traffic-stopping snowfalls are infrequent.

Based on the 1951-1980 period, the average first occurrence of 32 degrees Fahrenheit in the fall is October 6 and the average last occurrence in the spring is May 4.

NORMALS, MEANS, AND EXTREMES

SPOKANE WASHINGTON

LATITUDE: 47°38'N LONGITUDE: 117°32' W ELEVATION: FT. GRND 2357 BARO 2360 TIME ZONE: PACIFIC WBAN: 24157

	(a)	JAN	FEB	MAR	APR	MAY	JUNE	JULY	AUG	SEP	OCT	NOV	DEC	YEAR
TEMPERATURE °F:														
Normals														
-Daily Maximum		33.2	40.6	47.7	57.0	65.8	74.7	83.1	82.5	72.0	58.6	41.4	33.8	57.5
-Daily Minimum		20.8	25.9	29.6	34.7	41.9	49.2	54.4	54.3	45.8	36.0	28.8	21.7	36.9
-Monthly		27.1	33.3	38.7	45.9	53.9	62.0	68.8	68.4	58.9	47.3	35.1	27.8	47.3
Extremes														
-Record Highest	46	59	61	71	90	96	101	103	108	98	86	67	56	108
-Year		1971	1958	1960	1977	1986	1992	1967	1961	1988	1980	1975	1980	AUG 1961
-Record Lowest	46	-22	-17	-7	17	24	33	37	35	24	10	-21	-25	-25
-Year		1979	1979	1989	1966	1954	1984	1981	1965	1985	1991	1985	1968	DEC 1968
NORMAL DEGREE DAYS:														
Heating (base 65°F)		1175	888	815	573	344	139	30	56	223	549	897	1153	6842
Cooling (base 65°F)		0	0	0	0	0	49	148	161	40	0	0	0	398
% OF POSSIBLE SUNSHINE	45	28	41	54	61	64	66	80	78	72	55	29	23	54
MEAN SKY COVER (tenths)														
Sunrise - Sunset	46	8.3	7.9	7.4	7.1	6.6	6.1	3.9	4.2	4.8	6.3	8.1	8.4	6.6
MEAN NUMBER OF DAYS:														
Sunrise to Sunset														
-Clear	46	3.0	3.4	4.3	4.5	5.7	7.2	16.1	15.1	12.3	8.0	3.3	2.8	86.0
-Partly Cloudy	46	4.2	4.9	7.7	8.2	10.2	10.3	8.4	8.5	8.3	7.7	5.0	3.9	87.3
-Cloudy	46	23.8	20.0	19.0	17.2	15.1	12.5	6.5	7.3	9.3	15.3	21.7	24.3	191.9
Precipitation														
.01 inches or more	46	14.0	11.3	11.3	8.9	9.3	7.8	4.7	4.8	5.6	7.5	12.7	14.7	112.5
Snow,Ice pellets,hail														
1.0 inches or more	46	5.2	2.8	1.6	0.2	0.*	0.0	0.0	0.0	0.0	0.1	2.1	5.0	17.0
Thunderstorms	46	0.*	0.*	0.3	0.7	1.6	2.9	2.5	2.2	0.7	0.3	0.1	0.0	11.1
Heavy Fog Visibility														
1/4 mile or less	46	9.4	7.3	3.1	1.2	0.8	0.5	0.2	0.3	0.8	4.0	8.5	11.9	48.0
Temperature °F														
-Maximum														
90° and above	34	0.0	0.0	0.0	0.*	0.3	2.1	8.3	7.2	0.9	0.0	0.0	0.0	18.8
32° and below	34	14.6	4.6	0.9	0.0	0.0	0.0	0.0	0.0	0.0	0.1	4.1	13.9	38.2
-Minimum														
32° and below	34	26.5	22.4	20.6	10.4	1.7	0.0	0.0	0.0	0.8	9.3	20.1	26.7	138.6
0° and below	34	2.4	0.6	0.*	0.0	0.0	0.0	0.0	0.0	0.0	0.0	0.3	1.9	5.1
AVG. STATION PRESS.(mb)	20	934.0	933.0	930.0	931.1	930.6	930.8	931.8	931.5	932.8	933.9	932.9	934.2	932.2
RELATIVE HUMIDITY (%)														
Hour 04	34	85	85	81	77	77	74	65	63	71	79	87	88	78
Hour 10 (Local Time)	34	84	80	69	57	53	49	41	43	51	65	83	86	63
Hour 16	34	79	69	55	44	41	36	28	28	34	48	76	83	52
Hour 22	34	84	81	74	66	63	58	46	46	56	70	85	87	68
PRECIPITATION (inches):														
Water Equivalent														
-Normal		1.98	1.49	1.49	1.18	1.41	1.26	0.67	0.72	0.73	0.99	2.15	2.42	16.49
-Maximum Monthly	46	4.96	3.94	3.75	3.08	5.71	3.06	2.33	1.83	2.05	4.05	5.10	5.13	5.71
-Year		1959	1961	1950	1948	1948	1964	1990	1976	1959	1950	1973	1964	MAY 1948
-Minimum Monthly	46	0.38	0.35	0.31	0.08	0.20	0.16	T	T	T	0.03	0.22	0.60	T
-Year		1985	1988	1965	1956	1982	1960	1973	1988	1990	1987	1976	1976	SEP 1990
-Maximum in 24 hrs	46	1.48	1.11	0.96	1.01	1.67	2.07	1.80	1.09	1.12	0.98	1.41	1.60	2.07
-Year		1954	1963	1989	1982	1948	1964	1990	1959	1973	1955	1960	1951	JUN 1964
Snow,Ice pellets,hail														
-Maximum Monthly	46	56.9	28.5	15.3	6.6	3.5	T	0.0	0.0	T	6.1	24.7	42.0	56.9
-Year		1950	1975	1962	1964	1967	1993			1991	1957	1955	1964	JAN 1950
-Maximum in 24 hrs	46	13.0	11.0	6.1	4.9	3.5	T	0.0	0.0	T	6.1	9.0	12.1	13.0
-Year		1950	1993	1989	1964	1967	1993			1991	1957	1973	1951	JAN 1950
WIND:														
Mean Speed (mph)	46	8.8	9.2	9.6	10.0	9.3	9.2	8.6	8.2	8.3	8.1	8.6	8.6	8.9
Prevailing Direction through 1963		NE	SSW	SSW	SW	SSW	SSW	SW	SW	NE	SSW	NE	NE	SSW
Fastest Mile														
-Direction (!!)	46	SW	SW	SW	SW	W	SW	SW	SW	SW	SW	SW	SW	SW
-Speed (MPH)	46	59	54	54	52	49	44	43	50	38	56	54	51	59
-Year		1972	1949	1971	1987	1957	1986	1970	1982	1961	1950	1949	1956	JAN 1972
Peak Gust														
-Direction (!!)	10	SW	S	W	SW	W	SW	SW	W	SW	SW	SW	SW	SW
-Speed (mph)	10	56	51	52	62	53	49	51	47	47	62	56	51	62
-Date		1986	1987	1988	1987	1986	1989	1989	1993	1987	1991	1990	1991	OCT 1991

PRECIPITATION (inches)

SPOKANE WASHINGTON

YEAR	JAN	FEB	MAR	APR	MAY	JUNE	JULY	AUG	SEP	OCT	NOV	DEC	ANNUAL
1964	3.15	0.98	1.53	0.98	0.45	3.06	0.39	1.46	1.03	0.46	2.89	5.13	21.51
1965	2.82	1.13	0.31	2.35	1.02	0.74	0.69	1.73	0.28	0.05	1.71	1.63	14.46
1966	1.94	0.50	2.43	0.13	0.49	0.70	0.95	0.15	0.51	0.36	3.01	2.96	14.13
1967	2.44	0.40	1.72	1.71	1.31	1.99	0.06	T	0.24	1.18	0.82	2.02	13.89
1968	1.57	2.12	0.71	0.10	1.16	0.87	0.23	1.35	0.63	2.24	2.35	2.93	16.26
1969	4.08	1.21	0.53	2.16	0.54	1.17	0.03	T	0.71	0.45	0.37	2.45	13.70
1970	4.15	1.83	1.30	0.93	0.94	1.60	0.59	0.10	0.48	2.13	2.04	1.43	17.52
1971	2.11	0.88	2.11	1.85	1.39	2.46	0.50	0.59	1.37	0.82	1.51	2.89	18.48
1972	1.74	1.13	1.05	1.09	1.99	1.56	0.25	0.87	0.86	0.19	0.88	1.92	13.53
1973	2.05	0.48	0.77	0.42	1.34	0.57	T	0.19	1.44	0.97	5.10	3.78	17.11
1974	3.79	1.79	2.22	0.80	1.03	0.23	0.71	0.04	0.18	0.12	2.59	2.54	16.04
1975	2.53	3.12	1.83	1.78	1.41	1.45	1.60	0.93	0.03	2.23	1.94	2.42	21.27
1976	1.28	2.04	0.83	0.97	1.24	0.78	0.79	1.83	0.05	0.59	0.22	0.60	11.22
1977	0.75	0.52	1.15	0.13	1.71	1.45	0.11	1.25	1.42	0.44	2.12	4.52	15.57
1978	2.53	1.64	0.77	2.62	2.81	1.22	1.76	1.71	0.93	0.13	2.02	1.05	19.19
1979	1.11	2.19	1.03	0.69	1.60	0.78	0.85	1.01	0.78	1.22	1.15	1.94	14.35
1980	1.96	1.90	0.91	1.06	2.34	0.99	0.21	0.79	0.84	0.64	1.67	3.72	17.03
1981	1.00	1.41	1.57	0.85	2.02	1.92	0.51	0.04	0.59	1.53	0.96	2.51	14.91
1982	1.61	1.67	1.49	2.23	0.20	0.85	1.05	0.25	1.77	1.48	1.86	2.79	17.25
1983	1.89	2.07	2.20	0.61	0.92	2.84	1.85	0.96	0.79	1.33	4.80	2.38	22.64
1984	0.99	1.37	1.80	1.75	2.01	1.89	0.07	0.27	0.56	0.76	4.26	2.28	18.01
1985	0.38	0.93	1.39	0.28	1.13	0.67	0.26	0.19	1.64	1.40	2.23	0.71	11.21
1986	3.08	2.02	1.58	1.33	1.08	0.48	0.44	0.15	1.65	0.46	2.25	1.03	15.55
1987	1.59	0.88	2.18	1.12	0.90	0.59	2.27	1.81	0.01	0.03	1.37	4.93	17.68
1988	1.76	0.35	1.57	2.15	1.50	1.12	0.23	T	1.63	0.11	4.35	1.75	16.52
1989	0.82	1.34	2.87	0.72	2.17	0.41	0.40	1.61	0.18	1.58	1.66	0.95	14.71
1990	2.45	1.01	0.85	1.34	3.11	1.91	2.33	1.03	T	3.05	0.84	1.69	19.61
1991	1.72	0.81	2.31	1.35	1.72	1.13	0.58	0.17	0.01	0.34	3.08	1.23	14.45
1992	2.12	1.76	0.43	0.65	0.28	1.51	1.09	0.33	0.36	0.81	3.02	2.16	14.52
1993	1.40	0.86	1.13	1.90	1.36	0.48	2.08	1.24	0.28	0.42	0.68	1.80	13.63
Record Mean	2.05	1.57	1.36	1.10	1.36	1.27	0.57	0.62	0.81	1.20	2.06	2.21	16.17

AVERAGE TEMPERATURE (deg. F)

SPOKANE WASHINGTON

YEAR	JAN	FEB	MAR	APR	MAY	JUNE	JULY	AUG	SEP	OCT	NOV	DEC	ANNUAL
1964	29.3	29.2	35.7	44.5	52.9	60.4	68.3	62.8	55.2	47.9	32.2	24.0	45.2
1965	28.6	32.1	34.4	47.2	52.4	61.3	70.1	67.9	53.8	52.7	38.0	30.0	47.4
1966	29.7	32.8	38.7	46.0	55.9	58.8	68.2	68.2	64.6	47.3	36.9	33.4	48.4
1967	33.9	36.2	37.1	42.3	52.8	63.5	70.6	74.5	65.3	48.4	35.4	27.8	49.0
1968	27.8	37.8	42.1	43.0	53.8	61.2	71.1	65.1	58.9	45.2	34.9	24.6	47.1
1969	16.3	26.1	35.6	46.2	57.4	65.2	67.4	67.1	59.8	43.7	36.3	29.4	45.9
1970	25.9	36.3	37.0	41.6	54.9	66.2	72.5	70.2	54.2	44.9	36.0	27.7	47.3
1971	31.8	33.6	35.2	45.3	56.3	58.2	69.7	74.1	55.2	44.2	35.4	25.8	47.0
1972	22.6	30.7	41.4	42.0	56.9	62.0	68.1	71.1	55.4	47.2	38.3	25.4	46.8
1973	27.0	34.9	41.1	46.2	56.5	62.0	71.2	69.1	59.7	47.2	33.7	33.3	48.5
1974	24.1	35.4	38.5	46.4	50.2	66.0	67.8	68.2	60.5	48.0	36.4	30.5	47.7
1975	23.6	24.7	34.0	41.7	52.7	59.2	72.4	64.1	61.0	46.9	33.8	30.9	45.4
1976	29.6	32.1	35.1	45.2	54.5	58.5	68.8	65.4	63.4	46.8	35.8	29.6	47.1
1977	22.0	35.1	38.2	50.9	51.6	65.0	67.0	71.2	55.1	46.5	34.0	26.2	46.9
1978	27.6	34.0	42.2	45.7	51.4	62.7	68.3	65.9	56.6	46.6	28.7	19.0	45.7
1979	10.5	28.8	40.4	45.5	54.7	62.7	70.4	70.0	63.1	51.1	30.5	35.2	46.9
1980	20.7	34.5	38.6	51.7	55.8	57.8	69.2	64.1	58.4	47.4	36.3	33.2	47.3
1981	32.8	33.9	40.9	45.7	52.0	57.0	65.1	71.5	59.7	45.9	39.9	29.7	47.8
1982	26.0	32.1	40.3	43.5	54.2	66.5	67.6	69.8	59.5	46.1	31.7	27.3	47.0
1983	35.8	38.1	43.0	46.3	57.1	61.9	65.5	72.3	57.1	49.7	39.3	16.2	48.5
1984	30.5	34.5	41.7	44.0	50.1	59.2	69.1	70.1	56.7	43.4	35.8	20.4	46.3
1985	21.4	24.9	35.9	48.0	56.2	61.8	75.0	64.9	53.3	44.7	19.5	19.3	43.7
1986	30.1	31.6	42.8	44.9	55.3	66.2	64.0	72.6	54.8	49.0	34.8	26.3	47.7
1987	26.5	35.1	41.8	51.1	57.2	65.1	66.6	66.2	62.8	49.5	38.1	25.9	48.8
1988	24.7	35.4	39.7	48.9	54.6	61.1	68.7	68.4	58.9	53.3	36.3	27.0	48.1
1989	28.8	21.8	36.6	48.9	53.1	64.3	68.7	64.8	60.1	47.0	38.0	31.0	46.9
1990	33.4	30.2	40.9	49.7	52.8	60.7	70.4	68.5	65.3	45.1	39.0	21.1	48.1
1991	25.7	39.2	36.8	45.8	51.6	56.6	68.7	70.2	61.8	46.2	34.2	32.8	47.5
1992	31.8	38.9	45.5	48.8	58.9	68.0	67.8	69.6	57.4	49.5	34.3	22.9	49.5
1993	21.9	25.4	37.8	45.5	59.8	60.2	60.2	64.2	58.7	50.0	29.4	30.9	45.3
Record Mean	26.8	31.8	39.5	47.6	55.6	62.4	69.8	68.6	59.4	48.5	36.5	29.7	48.0
Max	32.6	38.9	48.4	58.5	67.3	74.5	83.9	82.7	72.3	59.3	43.0	35.0	58.0
Min	20.9	24.7	30.5	36.7	43.8	50.3	55.7	54.5	46.4	37.7	30.0	24.4	38.0

REFERENCE NOTES

SPOKANE WASHINGTON

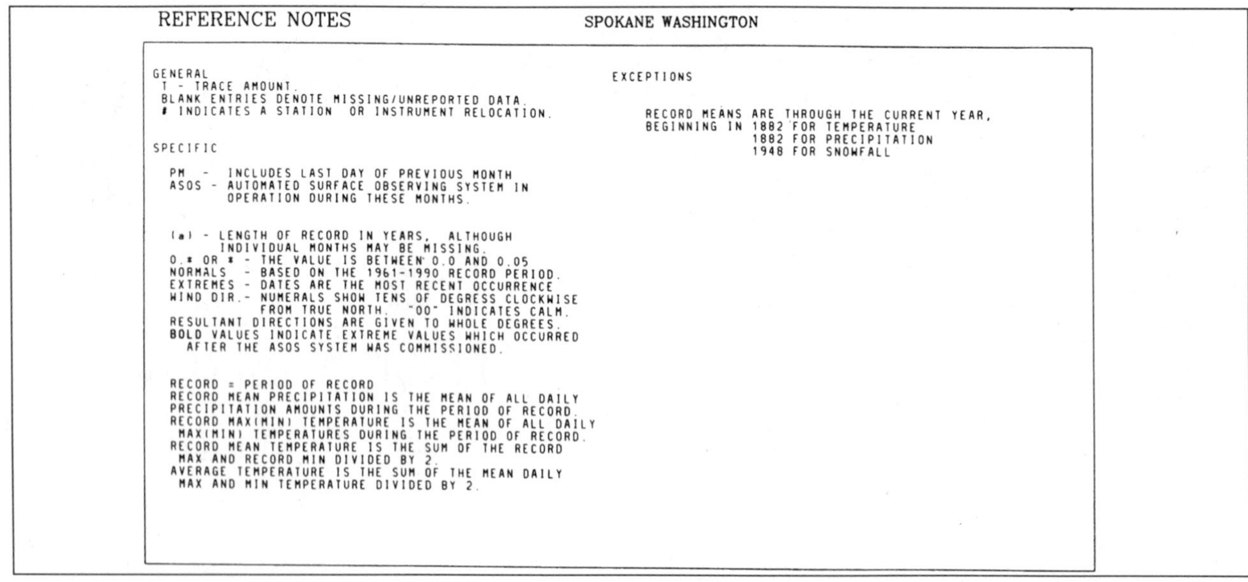

GENERAL
T - TRACE AMOUNT.
BLANK ENTRIES DENOTE MISSING/UNREPORTED DATA.
\# INDICATES A STATION OR INSTRUMENT RELOCATION.

SPECIFIC

PM - INCLUDES LAST DAY OF PREVIOUS MONTH
ASOS - AUTOMATED SURFACE OBSERVING SYSTEM IN OPERATION DURING THESE MONTHS.

(a) - LENGTH OF RECORD IN YEARS, ALTHOUGH INDIVIDUAL MONTHS MAY BE MISSING.
0.* OR * - THE VALUE IS BETWEEN 0.0 AND 0.05
NORMALS - BASED ON THE 1961-1990 RECORD PERIOD.
EXTREMES - DATES ARE THE MOST RECENT OCCURRENCE.
WIND DIR. - NUMERALS SHOW TENS OF DEGRESS CLOCKWISE FROM TRUE NORTH. "00" INDICATES CALM.
RESULTANT DIRECTIONS ARE GIVEN TO WHOLE DEGREES.
BOLD VALUES INDICATE EXTREME VALUES WHICH OCCURRED AFTER THE ASOS SYSTEM WAS COMMISSIONED.

RECORD = PERIOD OF RECORD
RECORD MEAN PRECIPITATION IS THE MEAN OF ALL DAILY PRECIPITATION AMOUNTS DURING THE PERIOD OF RECORD.
RECORD MAX(MIN) TEMPERATURE IS THE MEAN OF ALL DAILY MAX(MIN) TEMPERATURES DURING THE PERIOD OF RECORD.
RECORD MEAN TEMPERATURE IS THE SUM OF THE RECORD MAX AND RECORD MIN DIVIDED BY 2.
AVERAGE TEMPERATURE IS THE SUM OF THE MEAN DAILY MAX AND MIN TEMPERATURE DIVIDED BY 2.

EXCEPTIONS

RECORD MEANS ARE THROUGH THE CURRENT YEAR,
BEGINNING IN 1882 FOR TEMPERATURE
1882 FOR PRECIPITATION
1948 FOR SNOWFALL

HEATING DEGREE DAYS Base 65 deg. F SPOKANE WASHINGTON

SEASON	JULY	AUG	SEP	OCT	NOV	DEC	JAN	FEB	MAR	APR	MAY	JUNE	TOTAL
1964-65	31	118	290	524	976	1268	1121	915	942	528	387	129	7229
1965-66	31	62	330	377	804	1078	1088	896	808	561	291	190	6516
1966-67	30	42	67	544	838	975	956	799	859	677	370	96	6253
1967-68	8	2	71	508	882	1146	1149	783	702	654	343	138	6386
1968-69	19	89	199	607	897	1245	1504	1080	905	559	236	88	7428
1969-70	40	44	192	655	855	1097	1208	797	859	696	305	101	6849
1970-71	13	5	321	614	864	1146	1022	873	918	584	270	215	6845
1971-72	64	19	297	641	882	1208	1308	991	726	684	274	127	7221
1972-73	36	18	292	545	795	1219	1171	838	734	558	286	152	6644
1973-74	17	47	193	546	933	978	1265	824	814	554	455	97	6723
1974-75	41	22	134	519	852	1062	1276	1122	953	694	375	173	7223
1975-76	22	75	136	554	933	1048	1091	946	922	588	317	213	6845
1976-77	20	71	74	556	871	1089	1324	832	824	436	409	66	6572
1977-78	57	56	289	563	921	1197	1154	862	701	576	412	101	6889
1978-79	37	97	252	562	1083	1424	1684	1011	756	577	313	134	7930
1979-80	41	4	91	423	1029	918	1365	880	809	392	283	211	6446
1980-81	19	77	195	543	854	977	992	867	741	570	395	243	6473
1981-82	73	7	209	584	747	1088	1202	912	761	639	328	76	6626
1982-83	62	17	193	582	996	1163	897	747	672	558	285	113	6285
1983-84	55	2	230	468	765	1508	1065	880	715	621	460	194	6963
1984-85	21	18	264	662	870	1381	1345	1117	895	501	280	128	7482
1985-86	0	64	343	622	1363	1409	1076	927	680	595	357	67	7503
1986-87	81	4	311	488	902	1193	1186	831	710	417	253	86	6462
1987-88	51	50	116	474	799	1206	1240	850	775	477	330	173	6541
1988-89	47	16	240	361	856	1171	1113	1205	873	473	364	65	6784
1989-90	22	76	149	554	805	1048	976	968	739	454	373	166	6330
1990-91	37	42	54	610	774	1356	1212	716	866	568	406	248	6889
1991-92	15	16	108	574	918	992	1024	750	598	477	206	61	5739
1992-93	32	60	232	481	916	1297	1331	1102	834	578	192	165	7220
1993-94	151	83	217	457	1063	1051							

COOLING DEGREE DAYS Base 65 deg. F SPOKANE WASHINGTON

YEAR	JAN	FEB	MAR	APR	MAY	JUNE	JULY	AUG	SEP	OCT	NOV	DEC	TOTAL
1969	0	0	0	0	7	99	121	112	40	0	0	0	379
1970	0	0	0	0	3	143	253	175	2	0	0	0	576
1971	0	0	0	0	10	17	216	306	9	0	0	0	558
1972	0	0	0	0	28	41	138	213	10	0	0	0	430
1973	0	0	0	0	31	67	216	177	39	0	0	0	530
1974	0	0	0	0	0	137	134	127	7	0	0	0	405
1975	0	0	0	0	0	7	256	57	20	0	0	0	340
1976	0	0	0	0	0	24	143	93	33	0	0	0	293
1977	0	0	0	18	2	72	126	254	0	0	0	0	472
1978	0	0	0	0	0	42	144	131	9	0	0	0	326
1979	0	0	0	0	1	73	217	166	39	0	0	0	496
1980	0	0	0	1	3	2	156	56	6	3	0	0	227
1981	0	0	0	0	0	9	82	213	60	0	0	0	364
1982	0	0	0	0	2	128	148	171	32	0	0	0	481
1983	0	0	0	0	46	26	77	235	1	0	0	0	385
1984	0	0	0	0	3	28	155	181	23	1	0	0	391
1985	0	0	0	0	15	36	317	68	0	0	0	0	436
1986	0	0	0	0	65	109	57	247	8	0	0	0	486
1987	0	0	0	8	20	94	110	97	53	1	0	0	383
1988	0	0	0	0	12	63	169	128	67	0	0	0	439
1989	0	0	0	0	0	49	145	78	9	0	0	0	281
1990	0	0	0	0	0	42	213	157	68	0	0	0	480
1991	0	0	0	0	0	0	139	187	20	0	0	0	346
1992	0	0	0	0	25	159	124	209	11	8	0	0	536
1993	0	0	0	0	36	27	11	64	34	0	0	0	172

SNOWFALL (inches) SPOKANE WASHINGTON

SEASON	JULY	AUG	SEP	OCT	NOV	DEC	JAN	FEB	MAR	APR	MAY	JUNE	TOTAL
1964-65	0.0	0.0	0.0	T	15.2	42.0	20.1	2.3	2.0	0.1	0.0	0.0	81.7
1965-66	0.0	0.0	0.0	T	6.3	15.4	13.9	1.6	7.2	T	T	0.0	44.4
1966-67	0.0	0.0	0.0	T	0.9	9.0	6.5	3.1	6.4	0.8	3.5	0.0	30.2
1967-68	0.0	0.0	0.0	T	4.8	12.7	11.8	0.4	T	T	T	0.0	29.7
1968-69	0.0	0.0	0.0	0.0	1.2	19.8	48.7	5.4	2.0	0.4	0.0	0.0	77.5
1969-70	0.0	0.0	0.0	0.0	T	10.4	19.4	2.8	6.9	0.3	0.1	0.0	39.9
1970-71	0.0	0.0	0.0	T	6.8	12.0	6.1	5.5	1.5	T	0.0	0.0	31.9
1971-72	0.0	0.0	0.0	3.1	4.0	34.2	17.2	5.9	2.5	0.2	0.0	0.0	67.1
1972-73	0.0	0.0	0.0	0.8	T	4.7	6.5	3.5	0.5	T	0.0	0.0	16.0
1973-74	0.0	0.0	0.0	0.8	23.6	9.1	15.0	4.4	2.5	0.4	0.4	0.0	56.2
1974-75	0.0	0.0	0.0	0.0	0.3	16.6	30.9	28.5	7.6	5.1	T	0.0	89.0
1975-76	0.0	0.0	0.0	3.9	11.4	6.9	15.3	6.3	4.6	0.4	0.0	0.0	48.8
1976-77	0.0	0.0	0.0	0.0	0.1	4.2	6.8	2.5	2.7	T	T	0.0	16.3
1977-78	0.0	0.0	0.0	0.0	11.2	30.3	19.1	6.6	2.2	T	T	0.0	69.4
1978-79	0.0	0.0	0.0	0.0	15.4	14.8	16.5	10.6	3.4	T	T	0.0	60.7
1979-80	0.0	0.0	0.0	0.0	3.9	10.4	16.6	5.9	1.1	0.4	0.0	0.0	38.3
1980-81	0.0	0.0	0.0	0.0	1.2	6.8	2.6	3.3	T	T	0.3	0.0	14.2
1981-82	0.0	0.0	0.0	T	0.8	13.0	23.3	2.2	2.1	6.0	T	0.0	47.4
1982-83	0.0	0.0	0.0	T	5.4	17.4	8.1	5.5	T	0.2	T	0.0	36.6
1983-84	0.0	0.0	0.0	0.0	5.7	24.8	5.3	8.0	1.9	1.3	0.8	0.0	47.8
1984-85	0.0	0.0	0.0	1.1	12.0	24.7	4.6	14.8	9.6	T	T	0.0	66.8
1985-86	0.0	0.0	0.0	0.4	23.7	8.3	14.7	13.8	T	0.2	T	0.0	61.1
1986-87	0.0	0.0	0.0	0.0	5.0	7.9	11.7	1.1	T	T	T	0.0	25.7
1987-88	0.0	0.0	0.0	0.0	1.5	20.3	9.1	1.2	1.6	T	T	0.0	33.7
1988-89	0.0	0.0	0.0	0.0	10.9	16.3	10.5	19.0	9.4	T	T	0.0	66.1
1989-90	0.0	0.0	0.0	T	5.2	1.1	10.3	18.0	2.6	3.5	T	0.0	40.7
1990-91	0.0	0.0	0.0	0.0	1.2	14.3	15.9	1.1	9.5	0.2	0.0	0.0	42.2
1991-92	0.0	0.0	T	0.8	4.9	2.4	9.0	1.4	0.0	T	0.0	0.0	18.5
1992-93	0.0	0.0	0.0	0.0	11.1	40.2	18.8	15.1	2.1	T	T	T	87.3
1993-94	0.0	0.0	0.0	T	3.7	6.4							
Record Mean	0.0	0.0	T	0.4	6.2	15.1	16.2	7.7	4.1	0.6	0.1	T	50.5

CHARLESTON, WEST VIRGINIA

Charleston lies at the junction of the Kanawha and Elk Rivers in the western foothills of the Appalachian Mountains. The main urban and business areas have developed along the two river valleys, while some residential areas are in nearby valleys and on the surrounding hills. The hilltops are around 1,100 feet above sea level, about 500 feet higher than the valleys. The Kanawha Airport is just over 2 miles northeast of the center-city area, on an artificial plateau constructed from several hilltops.

Weather records are maintained at the Kanawha Airport by National Weather Service personnel. This site tends to be slightly cooler than the river valleys during the afternoons. Conversely, the valleys can become cooler than the hilltops during clear, calm nights. The weather at Charleston is highly changeable, especially from mid-autumn through the spring.

Winters can vary greatly from one season to the next. Snow does not favor any given winter month, heavy snowstorms are infrequent, and most snowfalls are in the 4-inch or less category. Snow and ice usually do not persist on valley roads, but can linger longer on nearby hills and outlying rural roads.

Afternoon temperatures in the 40s and morning readings in the 20s are common during the winter. Yet, every winter typically has two or three extended cold spells when temperatures stay below freezing for a few consecutive days. Northwesterly winds are associated with the cold weather. Air reaching Charleston from the northwest can cause cloudiness and flurries, even when there is no nearby organized storm system. Winter conditions are much more severe over the higher mountains less than 50 miles to the northeast through the southeast. Temperatures warm rapidly in the spring and are accompanied by low daytime humidities.

Summer and early autumn have more day-to-day consistency in the weather. Sunshine is more abundant than in winter. Summer precipitation falls mostly in brief, but sometimes heavy, showers. Flash flooding can occur along small streams, but flooding is rare on the dam-controlled Kanawha and Elk Rivers.

Afternoon summer temperatures are mostly in the 80s. Readings above 95 degrees are rare. However, during a hot spell, haze and humidity can add to the unpleasantness and indoor air conditioning is recommended. Cooler and less humid air often penetrates the area from the north to end a hot spell.

Early morning fog is common from late June into October. Industrial and vehicular pollutants can contribute to limited visibility any time of the year, especially when cooler air becomes trapped in the valleys. Autumn foliage is generally at its peak during the second and third weeks of October. By the end of October, the first 32 degree temperature has usually arrived.

Ample precipitation is well distributed throughout the year. July is quite often the wettest month of the year, while October averages the least rain. Droughts severe enough to limit water use are scarce. Any dry spells during the spring or autumn can cause conditions favorable for brush fires in outlying areas.

NORMALS, MEANS, AND EXTREMES

CHARLESTON, WEST VIRGINIA

LATITUDE: 38°22'N LONGITUDE: 81°36' W ELEVATION: FT. GRND 1016 BARO 1019 TIME ZONE: EASTERN WBAN: 13866

	(a)	JAN	FEB	MAR	APR	MAY	JUNE	JULY	AUG	SEP	OCT	NOV	DEC	YEAR
TEMPERATURE °F:														
Normals														
-Daily Maximum		41.2	45.3	56.7	66.8	75.5	83.1	85.7	84.4	78.8	68.2	57.3	46.0	65.8
-Daily Minimum		23.0	25.7	35.0	42.8	51.5	59.8	64.4	63.4	56.5	44.2	36.3	28.0	44.2
-Monthly		32.1	35.5	45.9	54.8	63.5	71.4	75.1	73.9	67.7	56.2	46.8	37.0	55.0
Extremes														
-Record Highest	46	79	78	89	94	93	98	104	101	102	92	85	80	104
-Year		1950	1977	1990	1990	1991	1988	1988	1988	1953	1951	1993	1982	JUL 1988
-Record Lowest	46	-15	-6	0	19	26	33	46	41	34	17	6	-12	-15
-Year		1985	1968	1980	1982	1966	1972	1963	1965	1983	1962	1950	1989	JAN 1985
NORMAL DEGREE DAYS:														
Heating (base 65°F)		1020	826	592	312	129	10	0	0	44	299	546	868	4646
Cooling (base 65°F)		0	0	0	6	83	202	313	276	125	26	0	0	1031
% OF POSSIBLE SUNSHINE														
MEAN SKY COVER (tenths)														
Sunrise - Sunset	46	7.7	7.5	7.3	6.9	6.6	6.4	6.5	6.3	6.2	6.0	7.2	7.6	6.9
MEAN NUMBER OF DAYS:														
Sunrise to Sunset														
-Clear	46	3.9	4.3	4.8	5.8	6.1	4.9	4.6	5.2	6.7	8.8	5.2	4.7	65.0
-Partly Cloudy	46	6.3	5.9	7.5	7.8	9.9	12.8	13.5	14.2	11.1	9.3	7.0	6.3	111.5
-Cloudy	46	20.8	18.0	18.7	16.4	15.0	12.2	12.9	11.6	12.2	12.9	17.8	20.1	188.8
Precipitation														
.01 inches or more	46	15.4	13.7	15.0	13.9	13.2	11.3	12.8	10.8	9.6	9.5	12.0	14.0	151.2
Snow, Ice pellets, hail														
1.0 inches or more	46	3.3	2.6	1.5	0.2	0.0	0.0	0.0	0.0	0.0	0.*	0.8	1.8	10.2
Thunderstorms	46	0.5	0.8	2.3	4.1	6.7	7.7	9.7	7.1	3.2	1.1	0.7	0.3	44.2
Heavy Fog Visibility														
1/4 mile or less	46	3.9	3.0	2.8	2.9	7.7	11.8	14.7	18.3	16.1	10.6	4.5	3.7	100.1
Temperature °F														
-Maximum														
90° and above	46	0.0	0.0	0.0	0.3	1.1	4.8	8.3	5.6	2.2	0.*	0.0	0.0	22.3
32° and below	46	7.1	4.5	0.9	0.*	0.0	0.0	0.0	0.0	0.0	0.0	0.5	4.3	17.3
-Minimum														
32° and below	46	22.9	19.9	14.6	4.7	0.4	0.0	0.0	0.0	0.0	3.4	12.7	20.8	99.3
0° and below	46	0.9	0.3	0.*	0.0	0.0	0.0	0.0	0.0	0.0	0.0	0.0	0.3	1.5
AVG. STATION PRESS. (mb)	21	984.2	983.7	981.7	980.9	981.0	981.7	982.7	983.7	984.3	984.9	984.5	984.6	983.2
RELATIVE HUMIDITY (%)														
Hour 01	46	74	72	68	67	80	87	90	91	89	84	75	75	79
Hour 07 (Local Time)	46	77	77	75	75	83	87	90	92	91	88	80	78	83
Hour 13	46	63	59	53	47	51	54	59	58	56	54	56	62	56
Hour 19	46	65	61	54	49	56	61	66	69	71	66	62	66	62
PRECIPITATION (inches):														
Water Equivalent														
-Normal		2.91	3.04	3.63	3.31	3.94	3.59	4.99	4.01	3.24	2.89	3.59	3.39	42.53
-Maximum Monthly	46	9.11	6.89	6.80	6.46	6.79	7.54	13.54	10.45	7.61	6.49	8.45	8.02	13.54
-Year		1950	1956	1967	1965	1989	1989	1961	1958	1971	1983	1985	1978	JUL 1961
-Minimum Monthly	46	1.09	0.64	1.30	0.50	0.84	0.70	1.98	0.66	0.65	0.09	0.64	0.45	0.09
-Year		1981	1968	1987	1976	1977	1966	1993	1957	1959	1963	1965	1965	OCT 1963
-Maximum in 24 hrs	46	1.91	2.45	2.86	2.72	3.31	2.24	5.60	4.17	2.40	2.48	2.88	2.47	5.60
-Year		1961	1951	1967	1948	1982	1962	1961	1958	1956	1961	1991	1978	JUL 1961
Snow, Ice pellets, hail														
-Maximum Monthly	46	39.5	21.8	20.4	20.7	0.6	T	T	T	T	2.8	25.8	18.6	39.5
-Year		1978	1964	1993	1987	1989	1993	1990	1989	1989	1961	1950	1962	JAN 1978
-Maximum in 24 hrs	46	15.8	11.2	17.1	11.3	0.6	T	T	T	T	2.8	15.1	11.2	17.1
-Year		1978	1983	1993	1987	1989	1993	1990	1989	1989	1961	1950	1967	MAR 1993
WIND:														
Mean Speed (mph)	46	7.4	7.5	8.1	7.5	6.0	5.4	5.0	4.4	4.7	5.1	6.6	7.0	6.2
Prevailing Direction through 1963		WSW	WSW	WSW	SW	SW	SW	S	S	S	S	SW	SW	SW
Fastest Obs. 1 Min.														
-Direction (!!)	44	25	19	32	27	25	32	29	29	20	25	29	25	25
-Speed (MPH)	44	45	40	46	45	55	50	46	50	35	45	40	55	55
-Year		1951	1981	1955	1953	1953	1951	1957	1952	1956	1950	1954	1953	MAY 1953
Peak Gust														
-Direction (!!)	10	SW	S	NW	SW	W	NW	NW	SW	W	SW	W	W	SW
-Speed (mph)	10	66	56	53	66	49	49	56	47	44	38	49	62	66
-Date		1992	1986	1985	1991	1988	1993	1986	1991	1990	1990	1992	1987	JAN 1992

PRECIPITATION (inches)

CHARLESTON, WEST VIRGINIA

YEAR	JAN	FEB	MAR	APR	MAY	JUNE	JULY	AUG	SEP	OCT	NOV	DEC	ANNUAL
1964	2.58	3.58	3.65	3.20	0.95	3.82	2.76	3.23	2.53	0.59	2.95	3.14	32.98
1965	4.65	2.02	4.52	6.46	1.90	2.18	2.46	4.38	3.21	2.09	0.64	0.45	34.96
1966	3.57	2.78	1.51	5.06	1.52	0.70	2.94	3.31	3.74	1.72	3.05	2.53	32.43
1967	1.21	2.95	6.80	3.21	6.45	1.83	4.59	1.85	1.68	2.09	4.30	4.72	41.68
1968	2.01	0.64	4.79	2.58	6.59	2.83	4.02	5.42	3.32	3.16	2.47	2.38	40.21
1969	1.50	1.27	1.43	2.35	1.95	2.43	6.13	8.20	3.27	1.52	2.22	4.85	37.12
1970	1.15	3.51	4.23	3.19	1.13	2.35	3.53	4.84	3.55	5.19	2.34	3.81	38.82
1971	2.35	3.40	1.97	1.19	5.17	2.58	6.59	2.12	7.61	1.30	2.83	1.71	38.82
1972	5.47	5.51	2.17	5.16	2.55	4.33	4.13	4.13	3.61	2.48	5.26	6.35	51.15
1973	1.52	2.41	3.40	5.44	5.36	4.48	6.88	2.07	3.91	4.75	5.42	3.68	49.32
1974	4.67	2.50	4.54	3.05	6.06	5.07	2.16	4.22	2.64	1.64	3.72	3.19	43.46
1975	4.84	3.10	6.01	4.03	6.44	4.25	2.71	5.14	4.99	3.08	2.66	3.74	50.99
1976	2.89	2.11	4.21	0.50	3.66	4.24	6.93	2.23	5.37	5.44	1.02	2.18	40.78
1977	1.90	1.08	3.16	4.06	0.84	5.93	4.92	6.58	1.14	4.16	3.78	2.07	39.62
1978	5.59	1.31	2.67	3.31	3.99	2.96	9.83	8.21	1.45	2.68	2.26	8.02	52.28
#1979	6.48	3.76	3.00	3.82	3.87	3.54	5.17	4.78	3.95	3.67	4.02	2.81	48.87
1980	2.85	2.25	5.32	4.49	2.67	2.17	8.47	10.32	2.37	2.03	3.02	1.85	47.81
1981	1.09	4.59	1.80	4.04	3.78	6.46	3.02	2.24	2.36	2.43	1.29	2.71	35.81
1982	3.74	3.23	4.96	1.14	6.19	7.00	2.68	2.65	2.58	1.65	4.65	2.71	43.18
1983	1.24	2.72	3.15	3.96	5.98	2.77	4.19	2.54	1.33	6.49	4.80	3.19	42.36
1984	1.67	2.56	2.72	4.00	3.71	2.56	4.37	4.57	2.95	3.28	4.73	3.78	40.90
1985	3.07	2.32	4.23	1.84	5.88	3.07	3.22	2.02	0.71	3.65	8.45	2.71	41.17
1986	2.12	4.35	1.87	1.39	4.86	2.36	7.61	4.71	3.51	2.20	6.88	3.89	45.75
1987	3.23	3.34	1.30	4.05	2.49	3.38	4.23	3.56	3.89	1.10	2.71	4.13	37.41
1988	1.62	2.50	2.71	2.17	2.59	0.94	3.00	2.86	3.46	1.87	5.02	2.66	31.40
1989	2.92	6.05	5.81	4.13	6.79	7.54	3.04	5.62	7.28	4.09	2.87	1.83	57.97
1990	2.86	3.74	1.94	2.89	4.87	3.01	5.35	2.54	4.26	3.51	2.07	7.01	44.05
1991	2.68	2.98	6.07	3.49	1.47	2.49	2.84	2.95	5.51	1.10	5.00	5.89	42.47
1992	1.94	2.72	4.79	2.93	4.66	3.21	6.41	4.41	1.38	0.94	3.15	3.50	40.04
1993	1.87	2.98	6.68	1.78	1.98	5.01	1.98	2.71	5.99	3.50	3.95	3.23	41.66
Record Mean	3.57	3.27	4.04	3.57	3.78	3.87	4.90	4.11	3.07	2.76	3.22	3.36	43.51

AVERAGE TEMPERATURE (deg. F)

CHARLESTON, WEST VIRGINIA

YEAR	JAN	FEB	MAR	APR	MAY	JUNE	JULY	AUG	SEP	OCT	NOV	DEC	ANNUAL
1964	35.8	33.2	46.7	58.5	67.0	72.9	75.0	73.1	67.5	53.2	49.0	39.2	55.9
1965	33.3	35.6	39.6	55.1	69.2	70.0	73.2	72.5	69.3	52.6	46.1	39.8	54.7
1966	27.1	36.6	47.7	54.1	62.1	72.0	77.3	73.5	66.5	55.0	48.2	35.5	54.6
1967	38.5	31.6	48.5	56.3	58.3	71.6	71.1	70.2	62.1	55.9	41.3	38.9	53.7
1968	29.1	27.1	47.5	56.4	61.0	70.6	74.2	74.1	66.3	56.0	46.8	34.2	53.6
1969	32.7	35.2	38.7	56.2	64.1	73.7	76.6	72.1	64.1	53.9	41.3	32.3	53.4
1970	28.5	36.2	43.3	58.2	66.9	73.1	74.6	73.6	70.0	57.4	46.0	38.4	55.5
1971	29.4	35.2	39.7	51.9	59.9	73.5	72.4	71.9	70.7	63.8	45.9	47.3	55.2
1972	38.7	35.2	43.8	54.5	63.7	64.9	73.4	72.7	68.7	52.5	43.4	42.1	54.5
1973	34.3	35.1	52.2	53.8	60.8	73.3	74.5	74.6	70.1	58.9	46.8	38.0	56.0
1974	43.5	37.1	49.1	56.9	64.2	67.8	74.2	73.6	63.2	52.4	45.2	36.8	55.3
1975	35.7	38.0	39.8	50.2	66.1	71.7	74.2	76.7	63.9	57.6	50.2	38.6	55.2
1976	31.7	45.8	51.6	55.2	61.9	71.9	72.4	70.2	63.3	49.5	37.6	31.0	53.5
1977	18.6	33.2	49.8	58.4	67.0	68.6	76.9	73.6	70.2	53.4	49.1	35.1	54.5
1978	24.4	24.2	42.6	56.7	63.1	70.9	73.8	74.9	71.0	53.8	49.4	39.0	53.6
1979	28.1	27.9	50.5	55.1	63.0	68.8	72.9	73.4	67.0	54.6	47.5	38.3	54.0
1980	34.1	29.7	42.0	53.3	63.6	68.8	76.6	76.3	69.8	53.6	43.2	36.3	54.0
1981	28.0	37.2	41.4	59.1	60.4	73.2	75.7	72.8	66.5	54.2	45.3	34.6	54.0
1982	29.8	36.1	47.2	51.5	68.6	68.8	76.2	71.1	65.9	57.7	49.0	44.8	55.6
1983	34.0	37.7	47.0	52.1	61.1	71.6	77.0	78.0	68.4	58.1	47.4	32.0	55.4
1984	30.6	41.5	41.1	54.2	61.4	75.3	73.2	74.9	65.4	64.4	44.6	46.9	56.1
1985	27.2	34.0	49.4	60.8	66.3	71.0	75.8	74.0	69.6	62.3	55.5	33.8	56.6
1986	34.1	40.5	47.1	57.9	65.3	72.2	77.2	71.9	69.5	57.9	46.4	36.4	56.4
1987	33.0	37.2	47.0	52.7	68.4	73.5	77.1	77.0	67.1	50.3	49.0	39.8	56.0
1988	31.1	35.2	46.1	54.1	63.2	71.0	78.6	77.4	66.6	49.3	47.0	37.4	54.8
1989	41.1	34.9	47.8	52.8	59.4	71.7	75.7	73.2	67.0	56.7	46.4	26.0	54.4
1990	42.3	45.2	51.7	55.1	62.9	72.3	75.8	74.1	68.7	58.2	50.7	43.6	58.4
1991	36.5	40.3	47.4	60.3	71.7	73.9	77.9	75.2	68.4	59.1	45.8	41.3	58.2
1992	35.6	41.8	45.4	55.7	61.2	68.8	76.0	70.9	67.4	54.1	47.4	37.9	55.2
1993	40.2	34.0	41.8	55.0	64.9	71.4	79.0	76.4	66.6	55.1	47.1	36.6	55.7
Record Mean	35.7	37.7	46.0	55.9	64.7	72.1	76.0	74.7	69.0	57.5	46.7	38.0	56.1
Max	45.6	48.4	57.8	68.7	77.4	84.0	87.3	86.0	81.0	70.0	57.9	47.8	67.6
Min	25.7	26.9	34.3	43.1	52.0	60.1	64.6	63.4	56.9	44.9	35.5	28.2	44.6

REFERENCE NOTES

CHARLESTON, WEST VIRGINIA

GENERAL
T - TRACE AMOUNT.
BLANK ENTRIES DENOTE MISSING/UNREPORTED DATA.
# INDICATES A STATION OR INSTRUMENT RELOCATION.

SPECIFIC

PM - INCLUDES LAST DAY OF PREVIOUS MONTH
ASOS - AUTOMATED SURFACE OBSERVING SYSTEM IN OPERATION DURING THESE MONTHS.

(a) - LENGTH OF RECORD IN YEARS, ALTHOUGH INDIVIDUAL MONTHS MAY BE MISSING.
0.* OR * - THE VALUE IS BETWEEN 0.0 AND 0.05
NORMALS - BASED ON THE 1961-1990 RECORD PERIOD.
EXTREMES - DATES ARE THE MOST RECENT OCCURRENCE
WIND DIR.- NUMERALS SHOW TENS OF DEGRESS CLOCKWISE FROM TRUE NORTH. "00" INDICATES CALM.
RESULTANT DIRECTIONS ARE GIVEN TO WHOLE DEGREES.
BOLD VALUES INDICATE EXTREME VALUES WHICH OCCURRED AFTER THE ASOS SYSTEM WAS COMMISSIONED.

RECORD = PERIOD OF RECORD
RECORD MEAN PRECIPITATION IS THE MEAN OF ALL DAILY PRECIPITATION AMOUNTS DURING THE PERIOD OF RECORD.
RECORD MAX(MIN) TEMPERATURE IS THE MEAN OF ALL DAILY MAX(MIN) TEMPERATURES DURING THE PERIOD OF RECORD.
RECORD MEAN TEMPERATURE IS THE SUM OF THE RECORD MAX AND RECORD MIN DIVIDED BY 2.
AVERAGE TEMPERATURE IS THE SUM OF THE MEAN DAILY MAX AND MIN TEMPERATURE DIVIDED BY 2.

EXCEPTIONS

RECORD MEANS ARE THROUGH THE CURRENT YEAR, BEGINNING IN 1902 FOR TEMPERATURE
1901 FOR PRECIPITATION
1948 FOR SNOWFALL

HEATING DEGREE DAYS Base 65 deg. F — CHARLESTON, WEST VIRGINIA

SEASON	JULY	AUG	SEP	OCT	NOV	DEC	JAN	FEB	MAR	APR	MAY	JUNE	TOTAL
1964-65	0	13	40	364	474	791	974	820	780	299	24	15	4594
1965-66	0	15	58	382	561	776	1166	793	538	354	147	25	4815
1966-67	0	1	44	315	507	910	815	932	517	275	217	17	4550
1967-68	4	6	124	297	704	802	1104	1095	539	263	141	15	5094
1968-69	2	11	35	298	541	946	994	828	807	264	98	9	4833
1969-70	0	0	95	352	703	1007	1125	801	666	239	82	1	5071
1970-71	3	0	40	246	563	817	1097	828	778	387	184	2	4945
1971-72	0	1	13	78	578	543	809	856	649	333	90	81	4031
1972-73	16	2	14	378	642	701	945	832	394	351	157	4	4436
1973-74	0	1	19	202	541	833	659	775	500	277	115	25	3947
1974-75	0	0	110	388	590	869	899	749	772	445	59	4	4885
1975-76	0	0	106	227	441	813	1025	549	427	342	142	4	4076
1976-77	0	9	84	475	814	1047	1432	888	482	242	81	52	5606
1977-78	0	2	19	357	482	919	1249	1138	691	258	137	23	5275
1978-79	0	0	18	344	462	797	1137	1031	456	308	125	19	4697
1979-80	5	10	39	331	519	820	951	1017	707	349	106	27	4881
1980-81	0	0	33	356	650	882	1138	774	727	207	175	2	4944
1981-82	0	1	76	335	585	936	1086	801	545	405	36	2	4808
1982-83	1	2	69	268	480	626	955	757	554	388	153	16	4269
1983-84	4	0	66	227	521	1019	1059	674	734	346	171	5	4826
1984-85	1	0	98	74	613	563	1164	860	488	192	54	18	4125
1985-86	0	0	51	127	294	960	954	679	554	249	83	7	3958
1986-87	0	23	23	255	550	880	989	770	549	374	63	4	4480
1987-88	0	0	37	447	473	774	1043	859	577	326	112	38	4686
1988-89	2	0	37	484	534	849	735	837	536	367	221	2	4604
1989-90	0	7	72	270	553	1203	697	549	446	323	111	8	4239
1990-91	0	0	59	230	428	655	876	685	558	192	21	1	3705
1991-92	0	0	80	229	576	729	904	670	602	319	170	24	4303
1992-93	0	1	67	335	522	834	760	862	713	306	73	24	4497
1993-94	0	0	64	307	540	873							

COOLING DEGREE DAYS Base 65 deg. F — CHARLESTON, WEST VIRGINIA

YEAR	JAN	FEB	MAR	APR	MAY	JUNE	JULY	AUG	SEP	OCT	NOV	DEC	TOTAL
1969	0	0	0	7	79	277	368	227	75	15	0	0	1048
1970	0	0	0	40	147	251	310	273	197	18	0	0	1236
1971	0	0	0	0	32	265	237	219	190	49	11	5	1008
1972	0	0	0	24	56	85	283	247	132	0	0	0	827
1973	0	0	4	22	34	256	304	305	181	22	2	0	1130
1974	0	0	14	43	99	118	292	275	62	6	1	0	910
1975	0	0	0	7	99	212	291	372	82	7	4	0	1074
1976	0	1	17	58	54	218	238	175	39	1	0	0	801
1977	0	0	18	50	148	165	373	277	180	4	12	0	1227
1978	0	0	0	16	88	207	279	314	205	4	1	0	1114
1979	0	0	13	18	69	138	257	277	105	17	0	0	894
1980	0	0	0	6	71	147	370	358	182	9	0	0	1143
1981	0	0	2	38	41	256	340	251	126	5	0	0	1059
1982	0	0	0	6	154	122	355	196	101	47	5	6	992
1983	0	0	2	6	39	222	385	407	177	18	0	0	1256
1984	0	0	0	27	64	318	261	312	116	65	7	8	1178
1985	0	0	9	72	105	204	339	285	194	52	14	0	1274
1986	0	0	4	41	100	227	384	244	167	43	0	0	1210
1987	0	0	0	13	177	268	381	379	108	0	2	0	1328
1988	0	0	3	9	64	225	430	392	91	4	3	0	1221
1989	0	0	11	6	55	211	339	273	140	23	2	0	1060
1990	0	0	41	33	54	232	342	286	174	28	7	0	1197
1991	0	0	17	60	236	273	408	324	190	53	5	0	1566
1992	0	0	2	47	57	143	347	192	145	4	0	0	937
1993	0	0	0	14	76	222	444	364	119	7	8	0	1254

SNOWFALL (inches) — CHARLESTON, WEST VIRGINIA

SEASON	JULY	AUG	SEP	OCT	NOV	DEC	JAN	FEB	MAR	APR	MAY	JUNE	TOTAL
1964-65	0.0	0.0	0.0	0.0	1.3	0.9	13.7	6.7	8.5	T	0.0	0.0	31.1
1965-66	0.0	0.0	0.0	T	T	2.7	19.8	8.0	1.7	T	0.0	0.0	32.2
1966-67	0.0	0.0	0.0	T	3.8	6.0	3.6	20.6	2.2	0.0	0.0	0.0	36.2
1967-68	0.0	0.0	0.0	0.0	0.2	16.6	13.3	9.2	2.0	0.0	0.0	0.0	41.3
1968-69	0.0	0.0	0.0	T	4.3	4.7	2.0	1.3	4.8	0.0	0.0	0.0	17.1
1969-70	0.0	0.0	0.0	0.0	4.3	9.5	12.6	14.2	2.9	T	0.0	0.0	43.5
1970-71	0.0	0.0	0.0	0.0	0.2	10.9	11.6	10.5	11.7	T	0.0	0.0	44.9
1971-72	0.0	0.0	0.0	0.0	4.2	0.8	4.0	9.8	3.5	T	0.0	0.0	22.3
1972-73	0.0	0.0	0.0	0.9	6.9	1.4	3.4	2.9	4.8	0.9	0.0	0.0	21.2
1973-74	0.0	0.0	0.0	0.0	T	6.5	0.3	13.0	0.9	1.2	0.0	0.0	21.9
1974-75	0.0	0.0	0.0	0.6	2.7	8.3	18.1	2.4	8.1	0.1	0.0	0.0	40.3
1975-76	0.0	0.0	0.0	0.0	T	4.0	14.3	2.6	5.4	0.0	0.0	0.0	26.3
1976-77	0.0	0.0	0.0	T	4.7	7.4	22.2	11.1	1.0	1.5	0.0	0.0	47.9
1977-78	0.0	0.0	0.0	0.0	4.4	5.4	39.5	15.6	11.7	0.0	0.0	0.0	76.6
#1978-79	0.0	0.0	0.0	0.0	T	1.5	27.5	20.1	5.5	T	0.0	0.0	54.6
1979-80	0.0	0.0	0.0	T	0.9	0.4	11.7	12.7	10.5	T	0.0	0.0	36.2
1980-81	0.0	0.0	0.0	T	0.5	2.6	9.1	6.8	7.5	T	0.0	0.0	26.5
1981-82	0.0	0.0	0.0	T	0.5	8.2	12.1	6.4	7.4	1.0	0.0	0.0	35.6
1982-83	0.0	0.0	0.0	0.0	T	2.9	5.8	15.0	5.2	0.1	0.0	0.0	29.0
1983-84	0.0	0.0	0.0	0.0	0.3	3.8	12.8	9.7	2.4	0.0	0.0	0.0	29.0
1984-85	0.0	0.0	0.0	0.0	T	3.7	17.6	20.1	0.9	1.7	0.0	0.0	44.0
1985-86	0.0	0.0	0.0	0.0	0.0	8.9	13.1	17.7	3.7	T	0.0	0.0	43.4
1986-87	0.0	0.0	0.0	0.0	0.2	0.1	16.3	9.7	3.9	20.7	0.0	0.0	50.9
1987-88	0.0	0.0	0.0	T	2.4	5.7	8.3	7.8	4.6	T	0.0	0.0	28.8
1988-89	0.0	0.0	0.0	T	T	6.9	1.7	4.6	T	1.4	0.6	0.0	15.2
1989-90	0.0	T	T	T	2.0	14.1	11.0	3.8	6.6	1.1	0.0	0.0	38.6
1990-91	T	0.0	0.0	0.0	0.0	1.2	3.5	6.5	5.3	T	0.0	0.0	16.5
1991-92	0.0	0.0	0.0	0.0	4.1	0.7	5.6	1.1	8.6	3.6	T	T	23.7
1992-93	0.0	0.0	0.0	T	2.5	3.7	0.4	12.0	20.4	T	0.0	T	39.0
1993-94	0.0	0.0	0.0	1.5	0.4	12.4							
Record Mean	T	T	T	0.2	2.2	5.1	10.1	8.7	5.1	0.9	T	T	32.2

MADISON, WISCONSIN

Madison is set on a narrow isthmus of land between Lakes Mendota and Monona. Lake Mendota (15 square miles) lies northwest of Lake Monona (5 square miles) and the lakes are only two-thirds of a mile apart at one point. Drainage at Madison is southeast through two other lakes into the Rock River, which flows south into Illinois, and then west to the Mississippi. The westward flowing Wisconsin River is only 20 miles northwest of Madison. Madison lakes are normally frozen from mid-December to early April.

Madison has the typical continental climate of interior North America with a large annual temperature range and with frequent short period temperature changes. The range of extreme temperatures is from about 110 to -40 degrees. Winter temperatures (December-February) average near 20 degrees and the summer average (June-August) is in the upper 60s. Daily temperatures average below 32 degrees about 120 days and above 40 degrees for about 210 days of the year.

Madison lies in the path of the frequent cyclones and anticyclones which move eastward over this area during fall, winter and spring. In summer, the cyclones have diminished intensity and tend to pass farther north. The most frequent air masses are of polar origin. Occasional outbreaks of arctic air affect this area during the winter months. Although northward moving tropical air masses contribute considerable cloudiness and precipitation, the true Gulf air mass does not reach this area in winter, and only occasionally at other seasons. Summers are pleasant, with only occasional periods of extreme heat or high humidity.

There are no dry and wet seasons, but about 60 percent of the annual precipitation falls in the five months of May through September. Cold season precipitation is lighter, but lasts longer. Soil moisture is usually adequate in the first part of the growing season. During July, August, and September, the crops depend on current rainfall, which is mostly from thunderstorms and tends to be erratic and variable. Average occurrence of thunderstorms is just under 7 days per month during this period.

March and November are the windiest months. Tornadoes are infrequent. Dane County has about one tornado in every three to five years.

The ground is covered with 1 inch or more of snow about 60 percent of the time from about December 10 to near February 25 in an average winter. The soil is usually frozen from the first of December through most of March with an average frost penetration of 25 to 30 inches. The growing season averages 175 days.

Farming is diversified with the main emphasis on dairying. Field crops are mainly corn, oats, clover, and alfalfa, but barley, wheat, rye, and tobacco are also raised. Canning factories pack peas, sweet corn, and lima beans. Fruits are mainly apples, strawberries, and raspberries.

NORMALS, MEANS, AND EXTREMES

MADISON, WISCONSIN

LATITUDE: 43°08'N   LONGITUDE: 89°20' W   ELEVATION: FT. GRND 858 BARO 860   TIME ZONE: CENTRAL   WBAN: 14837

	(a)	JAN	FEB	MAR	APR	MAY	JUNE	JULY	AUG	SEP	OCT	NOV	DEC	YEAR
TEMPERATURE °F:														
Normals														
-Daily Maximum		24.8	30.1	41.5	56.7	68.9	78.2	82.4	79.6	71.5	59.9	44.0	29.8	55.6
-Daily Minimum		7.2	11.1	23.0	34.1	44.2	54.2	59.5	56.9	48.2	37.7	26.7	13.5	34.7
-Monthly		16.0	20.6	32.3	45.4	56.5	66.2	71.0	68.3	59.8	48.9	35.4	21.7	45.2
Extremes														
-Record Highest	54	56	61	82	94	93	101	104	102	99	90	76	62	104
-Year		1989	1981	1986	1980	1975	1988	1976	1988	1953	1976	1964	1984	JUL 1976
-Record Lowest	54	-37	-28	-29	0	19	31	36	35	25	13	-11	-25	-37
-Year		1951	1985	1962	1982	1978	1972	1965	1968	1974	1988	1947	1983	JAN 1951
NORMAL DEGREE DAYS:														
Heating (base 65°F)		1519	1243	1014	588	294	68	12	38	168	499	888	1342	7673
Cooling (base 65°F)		0	0	0	0	30	104	198	141	12	0	0	0	485
% OF POSSIBLE SUNSHINE	47	48	51	52	52	58	64	67	65	60	54	39	40	54
MEAN SKY COVER (tenths)														
Sunrise - Sunset	45	6.7	6.6	6.9	6.8	6.5	6.1	5.8	5.8	5.8	6.0	7.3	7.1	6.5
MEAN NUMBER OF DAYS:														
Sunrise to Sunset														
-Clear	47	7.4	7.1	6.3	6.3	6.9	7.2	8.7	9.3	9.4	9.4	5.5	6.3	89.9
-Partly Cloudy	47	6.5	6.0	7.4	7.7	9.2	10.0	11.1	10.6	8.1	7.4	6.0	6.2	96.2
-Cloudy	47	17.0	15.2	17.3	16.0	14.8	12.8	11.2	11.2	12.4	14.2	18.6	18.5	179.2
Precipitation														
.01 inches or more	45	10.1	8.0	11.0	11.6	11.4	10.4	9.7	9.4	9.4	9.0	9.8	10.0	119.7
Snow, Ice pellets, hail														
1.0 inches or more	45	2.8	2.4	2.5	0.6	0.*	0.0	0.0	0.0	0.0	0.*	1.3	3.3	13.0
Thunderstorms	45	0.2	0.2	1.9	3.5	5.2	7.0	7.3	6.5	4.8	2.0	0.8	0.4	39.8
Heavy Fog Visibility														
1/4 mile or less	47	2.3	2.0	2.7	1.3	1.3	0.9	1.3	2.0	1.8	1.7	1.9	2.9	22.1
Temperature °F														
-Maximum														
90° and above	34	0.0	0.0	0.0	0.*	0.3	3.0	5.0	2.8	0.6	0.1	0.0	0.0	11.8
32° and below	34	21.0	15.3	6.0	0.4	0.0	0.0	0.0	0.0	0.0	0.*	3.9	16.8	63.4
-Minimum														
32° and below	34	30.1	27.2	25.7	13.7	3.2	0.*	0.0	0.0	1.3	10.0	21.6	28.9	161.7
0° and below	34	10.7	6.5	1.2	0.*	0.0	0.0	0.0	0.0	0.0	0.0	0.1	5.4	23.9
AVG. STATION PRESS. (mb)	21	985.7	986.4	983.8	982.9	982.9	982.9	984.3	985.5	985.8	985.7	984.7	985.6	984.7
RELATIVE HUMIDITY (%)														
Hour 00	34	78	78	78	76	77	80	84	87	87	81	82	81	81
Hour 06 (Local Time)	34	79	80	82	81	80	82	86	91	91	86	85	83	84
Hour 12	34	69	66	62	55	54	56	57	59	61	59	67	72	61
Hour 18	34	73	70	65	56	54	56	59	62	69	68	75	77	65
PRECIPITATION (inches):														
Water Equivalent														
-Normal		1.07	1.08	2.17	2.86	3.14	3.66	3.39	4.04	3.37	2.17	2.09	1.84	30.88
-Maximum Monthly	54	2.45	2.77	5.04	7.11	6.26	9.95	10.93	9.49	9.51	5.63	5.13	4.09	10.93
-Year		1974	1953	1973	1973	1960	1978	1950	1980	1941	1984	1985	1987	JUL 1950
-Minimum Monthly	54	0.14	0.08	0.28	0.96	0.64	0.81	1.38	0.70	0.11	0.06	0.11	0.25	0.06
-Year		1981	1958	1978	1946	1981	1973	1946	1948	1979	1952	1976	1960	OCT 1952
-Maximum in 24 hrs	45	1.27	1.58	2.52	2.83	3.64	3.67	5.25	2.90	3.57	2.78	2.36	2.19	5.25
-Year		1960	1981	1973	1975	1966	1963	1950	1965	1961	1984	1985	1990	JUL 1950
Snow, Ice pellets, hail														
-Maximum Monthly	45	26.9	20.9	25.4	17.4	3.0	T	T	T	T	3.1	18.3	32.8	32.8
-Year		1979	1975	1959	1973	1990	1992	1991	1992	1993	1990	1985	1987	DEC 1987
-Maximum in 24 hrs	45	11.6	10.3	13.6	12.9	3.0	T	T	T	T	3.0	9.0	17.3	17.3
-Year		1971	1950	1971	1973	1990	1992	1991	1992	1993	1990	1985	1990	DEC 1990
WIND:														
Mean Speed (mph)	47	10.5	10.4	11.2	11.4	10.0	9.2	8.1	8.0	8.7	9.6	10.8	10.3	9.8
Prevailing Direction through 1963		WNW	WNW	NW	NW	S	S	S	S	S	S	S	W	S
Fastest Mile														
-Direction (!!)	46	E	W	SW	SW	SW	W	NW	W	W	SW	SE	SW	SW
-Speed (MPH)	46	68	57	70	73	77	59	72	47	52	73	56	65	77
-Year		1947	1948	1954	1947	1950	1947	1951	1955	1948	1951	1947	1949	MAY 1950
Peak Gust														
-Direction (!!)	10	SW	NW	S	W	SW	W	N	N	NW	NW	S	NE	N
-Speed (mph)	10	46	62	67	53	63	70	83	64	64	62	52	58	83
-Date		1988	1987	1990	1984	1988	1984	1991	1989	1985	1990	1988	1987	JUL 1991

PRECIPITATION (inches) MADISON, WISCONSIN

YEAR	JAN	FEB	MAR	APR	MAY	JUNE	JULY	AUG	SEP	OCT	NOV	DEC	ANNUAL
1964	0.93	0.26	2.12	3.15	3.87	2.28	4.28	2.52	1.85	0.08	1.94	0.34	23.62
1965	1.80	0.74	2.51	2.94	1.86	2.31	3.30	6.77	9.22	1.69	1.96	2.50	37.60
1966	1.07	1.36	2.11	1.54	4.31	2.91	3.24	3.83	0.51	1.65	1.28	2.62	26.43
1967	1.63	1.17	1.49	2.57	3.53	6.46	2.51	2.71	2.68	5.52	1.83	1.89	33.99
1968	0.56	0.49	0.59	4.18	2.02	7.82	2.54	2.58	4.45	0.85	1.74	2.89	30.71
1969	2.26	0.18	1.47	2.72	3.45	7.96	4.28	0.96	1.35	2.65	0.70	1.66	29.64
1970	0.44	0.16	1.17	2.53	6.09	2.26	2.42	0.97	8.82	2.65	1.06	2.12	30.69
1971	1.48	2.59	1.52	2.42	0.98	2.27	1.65	3.96	1.87	1.30	3.48	3.64	27.16
1972	0.40	0.42	2.23	2.02	2.83	1.65	3.49	7.47	5.26	2.42	0.86	1.91	30.96
1973	1.54	1.20	5.04	7.11	5.27	0.81	2.68	2.53	3.59	2.30	1.48	1.98	35.53
1974	2.45	1.17	3.43	4.24	5.77	3.86	2.69	4.60	1.08	3.18	1.79	1.80	36.06
1975	0.98	1.54	3.09	4.19	4.57	4.30	6.05	5.25	0.84	0.64	2.79	0.29	34.53
1976	0.56	1.72	4.75	4.80	1.95	1.38	1.46	1.99	0.50	1.49	0.11	0.37	21.08
1977	0.53	1.44	3.03	2.59	2.52	2.63	6.63	5.19	2.84	1.41	2.12	1.60	32.53
1978	1.03	0.24	0.28	3.50	3.96	9.95	4.54	1.63	5.44	1.11	3.05	1.71	36.44
1979	1.69	0.90	2.67	2.46	2.70	2.53	2.80	4.96	0.11	3.10	2.27	1.93	28.12
1980	1.11	0.64	0.68	2.36	2.08	3.43	2.67	9.49	7.84	1.13	1.33	1.62	34.38
1981	0.14	2.47	0.33	3.42	0.64	4.99	4.81	7.06	3.10	2.68	1.71	0.75	32.10
1982	1.42	0.17	2.11	3.26	4.34	3.40	3.47	2.67	1.42	1.46	4.21	3.65	31.58
1983	0.53	2.26	2.70	2.23	4.21	1.85	1.92	5.05	2.85	2.59	3.18	2.30	31.67
1984	0.36	1.26	1.15	3.86	3.32	7.01	1.96	1.89	2.79	5.63	1.83	2.66	33.72
1985	1.43	1.89	3.13	1.52	3.35	3.06	4.48	2.98	5.00	4.58	5.13	2.39	38.94
1986	1.02	2.72	1.55	2.27	1.97	3.24	4.31	4.38	6.82	1.85	1.03	0.69	31.85
1987	0.68	0.62	1.99	2.46	3.90	1.17	3.26	7.16	3.61	1.24	3.24	4.09	33.42
1988	1.82	0.46	1.20	2.65	0.92	2.06	2.44	2.95	3.33	1.60	3.58	1.56	24.57
1989	0.61	0.57	1.69	1.69	1.72	1.67	4.97	6.46	0.89	1.88	0.98	0.26	23.39
1990	1.60	0.99	4.18	1.90	5.35	4.88	2.61	6.03	1.64	2.25	1.65	3.46	36.54
1991	1.17	0.44	4.24	4.89	2.20	3.75	5.18	2.34	3.96	5.35	3.86	1.71	39.09
1992	0.78	1.34	1.90	3.17	1.12	1.53	5.54	2.48	5.99	1.06	4.83	2.39	32.13
1993	1.60	1.18	3.29	5.33	3.81	6.67	9.34	5.57	3.74	0.91	1.55	0.35	43.34
Record Mean	1.17	1.06	2.13	2.90	3.23	3.95	3.82	3.74	3.26	2.19	2.12	1.64	31.22

AVERAGE TEMPERATURE (deg. F) MADISON, WISCONSIN

YEAR	JAN	FEB	MAR	APR	MAY	JUNE	JULY	AUG	SEP	OCT	NOV	DEC	ANNUAL
1964	24.9	24.9	30.8	47.5	62.6	68.5	73.1	66.9	59.6	46.9	38.6	18.8	46.9
1965	15.9	18.7	25.0	43.7	59.6	64.2	68.3	66.7	58.3	49.2	35.6	29.8	44.6
1966	10.0	21.3	35.4	42.0	50.3	66.6	71.1	66.2	57.1	47.7	36.0	23.2	43.9
1967	22.2	14.7	33.3	45.6	50.2	66.2	67.1	62.0	57.6	48.0	33.0	25.1	43.7
1968	19.6	19.0	39.2	47.8	54.3	66.2	68.9	68.8	60.1	50.7	35.6	22.6	46.1
1969	14.8	23.6	27.9	47.0	56.4	59.5	69.6	70.3	59.5	46.4	33.1	21.3	44.1
1970	9.9	20.1	31.1	47.9	58.5	66.5	70.6	68.5	60.0	51.0	36.3	22.4	45.2
1971	9.6	19.9	28.6	45.4	55.1	71.7	68.5	68.3	65.1	55.9	35.2	26.8	45.9
1972	12.7	16.5	28.7	41.3	59.2	62.8	68.3	69.2	59.4	45.8	34.6	17.3	43.0
1973	23.4	24.0	41.6	44.9	54.4	67.9	71.6	70.6	60.7	54.1	36.6	21.5	47.6
1974	19.2	18.4	33.1	48.7	54.1	64.0	72.1	66.8	57.4	50.5	37.1	26.8	45.7
1975	21.9	21.3	26.1	41.0	62.5	69.2	72.4	70.6	57.5	52.2	41.9	25.5	46.8
1976	15.7	28.4	36.5	49.3	54.3	68.3	73.4	68.8	58.0	43.7	28.1	13.2	44.8
1977	3.7	22.4	39.8	51.9	65.2	64.9	73.6	64.6	59.7	47.6	34.0	19.6	45.6
1978	10.5	12.4	29.4	44.5	57.9	65.9	69.7	69.5	63.8	47.3	33.5	21.3	43.8
1979	6.9	11.7	32.1	42.4	56.7	66.0	69.8	66.6	61.1	47.5	35.1	28.8	43.7
1980	17.3	15.7	28.0	45.5	57.8	65.3	73.4	70.3	59.9	43.7	35.4	22.6	44.6
1981	20.5	25.3	36.9	48.7	55.3	67.4	70.6	68.7	59.1	46.6	36.7	22.0	46.5
1982	8.0	19.1	30.6	41.7	60.8	59.6	70.9	66.3	59.0	50.6	34.2	28.8	44.1
1983	21.4	26.3	33.1	41.6	51.9	67.5	75.0	72.2	60.1	48.2	37.3	10.8	45.5
1984	14.8	30.2	26.7	45.6	53.4	67.5	70.2	71.3	59.3	52.0	33.9	26.4	45.9
1985	12.2	19.0	37.7	52.2	60.7	63.8	70.0	66.4	61.6	49.4	31.0	11.3	44.6
1986	18.2	19.4	36.2	49.8	58.4	65.9	73.2	64.8	61.6	49.7	31.2	25.5	46.2
1987	22.6	30.5	37.2	49.9	60.8	70.4	74.5	68.7	60.6	43.4	40.0	28.4	48.9
1988	13.8	17.4	34.6	46.0	60.5	69.5	74.1	74.5	63.0	43.5	38.8	24.6	46.7
1989	27.6	14.6	30.1	44.7	56.1	65.7	72.3	68.6	58.7	50.8	33.1	14.2	44.7
1990	28.6	25.8	37.7	48.5	53.6	67.6	70.6	69.9	63.7	48.3	41.0	21.4	48.1
1991	15.1	26.5	36.8	49.4	63.6	71.1	72.3	70.2	60.0	49.4	31.4	26.3	47.7
1992	25.5	29.3	34.8	43.6	58.0	64.9	67.2	65.3	60.4	48.4	34.7	24.9	46.4
1993	21.8	21.2	31.5	43.7	59.6	65.9	72.0	72.1	56.7	47.9	35.2	26.6	46.2
Record Mean	17.3	21.4	32.3	46.3	57.3	66.8	71.5	69.5	60.6	49.9	35.4	22.6	45.9
Max	26.1	30.6	41.7	57.7	69.6	79.0	83.6	81.4	72.3	61.2	43.9	30.6	56.5
Min	8.5	12.2	22.8	34.8	44.9	54.6	59.4	57.5	48.8	38.5	26.8	14.5	35.3

REFERENCE NOTES MADISON, WISCONSIN

GENERAL
T - TRACE AMOUNT.
BLANK ENTRIES DENOTE MISSING/UNREPORTED DATA.
# INDICATES A STATION OR INSTRUMENT RELOCATION.

SPECIFIC

PM - INCLUDES LAST DAY OF PREVIOUS MONTH
ASOS - AUTOMATED SURFACE OBSERVING SYSTEM IN OPERATION DURING THESE MONTHS.

(a) - LENGTH OF RECORD IN YEARS, ALTHOUGH INDIVIDUAL MONTHS MAY BE MISSING.
0.* OR * - THE VALUE IS BETWEEN 0.0 AND 0.05
NORMALS - BASED ON THE 1961-1990 RECORD PERIOD.
EXTREMES - DATES ARE THE MOST RECENT OCCURRENCE
WIND DIR.- NUMERALS SHOW TENS OF DEGRESS CLOCKWISE FROM TRUE NORTH. "00" INDICATES CALM.
RESULTANT DIRECTIONS ARE GIVEN TO WHOLE DEGREES.
BOLD VALUES INDICATE EXTREME VALUES WHICH OCCURRED AFTER THE ASOS SYSTEM WAS COMMISSIONED.

RECORD = PERIOD OF RECORD
RECORD MEAN PRECIPITATION IS THE MEAN OF ALL DAILY PRECIPITATION AMOUNTS DURING THE PERIOD OF RECORD.
RECORD MAX(MIN) TEMPERATURE IS THE MEAN OF ALL DAILY MAX(MIN) TEMPERATURES DURING THE PERIOD OF RECORD.
RECORD MEAN TEMPERATURE IS THE SUM OF THE RECORD MAX AND RECORD MIN DIVIDED BY 2.
AVERAGE TEMPERATURE IS THE SUM OF THE MEAN DAILY MAX AND MIN TEMPERATURE DIVIDED BY 2.

EXCEPTIONS

RECORD MEANS ARE THROUGH THE CURRENT YEAR,
BEGINNING IN 1940 FOR TEMPERATURE
1940 FOR PRECIPITATION
1949 FOR SNOWFALL

HEATING DEGREE DAYS Base 65 deg. F MADISON, WISCONSIN

SEASON	JULY	AUG	SEP	OCT	NOV	DEC	JAN	FEB	MAR	APR	MAY	JUNE	TOTAL
1964-65	13	68	216	556	789	1427	1517	1294	1234	631	208	79	8032
1965-66	27	69	231	486	878	1086	1702	1220	911	684	454	83	7831
1966-67	11	40	252	533	862	1290	1321	1407	978	574	462	46	7776
1967-68	61	120	239	535	955	1229	1401	1327	792	510	330	76	7575
1968-69	34	66	159	460	873	1305	1548	1152	1143	535	282	197	7754
1969-70	13	9	202	579	951	1346	1705	1252	1044	521	244	73	7939
1970-71	28	18	196	431	853	1310	1718	1258	1124	582	312	22	7852
1971-72	28	21	131	293	885	1179	1616	1401	1119	705	212	117	7707
1972-73	44	42	188	587	905	1475	1279	1143	720	596	325	15	7319
1973-74	4	25	180	349	847	1342	1416	1298	979	494	347	90	7371
1974-75	1	37	253	443	829	1179	1329	1220	1198	714	150	43	7396
1975-76	18	11	236	412	687	1217	1520	1056	877	477	333	32	6876
1976-77	4	40	236	656	1102	1602	1898	1188	772	409	110	95	8112
1977-78	6	95	161	533	925	1404	1688	1466	1096	608	269	59	8310
1978-79	19	22	130	543	940	1348	1800	1489	1013	671	283	52	8310
1979-80	14	62	144	546	890	1112	1471	1424	1138	586	255	84	7726
1980-81	2	11	178	651	881	1303	1373	1107	864	482	307	30	7189
1981-82	16	27	193	566	842	1327	1765	1281	1059	688	155	172	8091
1982-83	5	66	230	444	918	1117	1346	1078	978	693	400	57	7332
1983-84	11	6	193	519	823	1678	1550	1006	1181	575	358	20	7920
1984-85	9	21	215	397	927	1191	1632	1287	839	418	155	96	7187
1985-86	12	36	198	475	1012	1661	1444	1272	888	462	220	73	7753
1986-87	7	59	145	471	1007	1218	1309	963	857	452	192	27	6707
1987-88	3	45	150	661	743	1127	1586	1377	938	565	176	53	7424
1988-89	4	18	107	661	777	1242	1153	1404	1076	602	290	68	7402
1989-90	5	22	207	437	952	1568	1122	1092	835	519	349	46	7154
1990-91	7	12	133	511	713	1349	1539	1072	868	467	173	22	6866
1991-92	8	11	222	476	1002	1195	1216	1031	929	634	244	73	7041
1992-93	26	68	176	514	903	1236	1333	1220	1032	633	196	74	7411
1993-94	0	9	260	525	887	1182							

COOLING DEGREE DAYS Base 65 deg. F MADISON, WISCONSIN

YEAR	JAN	FEB	MAR	APR	MAY	JUNE	JULY	AUG	SEP	OCT	NOV	DEC	TOTAL
1969	0	0	0	0	25	39	161	179	45	11	0	0	460
1970	0	0	0	12	47	125	210	133	53	4	0	0	584
1971	0	0	0	0	13	229	144	131	140	20	0	0	677
1972	0	0	0	0	41	61	156	180	27	0	0	0	465
1973	0	0	0	0	2	112	215	207	58	19	0	0	613
1974	0	0	0	9	17	68	228	102	31	2	0	0	457
1975	0	0	0	0	81	176	256	190	18	21	0	0	742
1976	0	0	0	14	6	136	270	165	34	2	0	0	627
1977	0	0	0	24	123	99	278	88	10	0	0	0	622
1978	0	0	0	0	56	92	171	168	102	0	0	0	589
1979	0	0	0	0	33	88	168	115	33	13	0	0	450
1980	0	0	0	8	39	100	268	183	31	0	0	0	629
1981	0	0	0	0	13	107	198	148	19	0	0	0	485
1982	0	0	0	0	29	16	194	114	53	3	0	0	409
1983	0	0	0	0	0	138	327	237	52	6	0	0	760
1984	0	0	0	1	5	102	177	224	50	0	0	0	559
1985	0	0	0	40	29	66	175	84	102	0	0	0	496
1986	0	0	0	13	24	105	269	59	49	0	0	0	519
1987	0	0	0	8	69	194	304	165	26	0	0	0	766
1988	0	0	0	0	43	194	296	315	54	0	0	0	902
1989	0	0	0	0	21	97	237	141	25	3	0	0	524
1990	0	0	0	32	2	132	191	171	100	1	0	0	629
1991	0	0	0	8	136	210	241	180	80	3	0	0	858
1992	0	0	0	0	33	76	100	86	42	5	0	0	342
1993	0	0	0	0	33	111	223	240	18	5	0	0	630

SNOWFALL (inches) MADISON, WISCONSIN

SEASON	JULY	AUG	SEP	OCT	NOV	DEC	JAN	FEB	MAR	APR	MAY	JUNE	TOTAL
1964-65	0.0	0.0	0.0	0.5	3.7	3.5	18.3	4.7	19.4	0.8	0.0	0.0	50.9
1965-66	0.0	0.0	T	0.0	T	5.7	9.6	3.8	5.5	0.1	0.7	0.0	25.4
1966-67	0.0	0.0	0.0	T	0.1	10.1	9.4	13.9	4.5	T	T	0.0	38.0
1967-68	0.0	0.0	0.0	0.9	0.7	2.4	3.9	3.9	0.5	0.4	0.0	0.0	12.7
1968-69	0.0	0.0	0.0	0.0	0.5	11.4	9.7	1.7	10.1	T	T	0.0	33.4
1969-70	0.0	0.0	0.0	0.0	1.0	19.5	6.4	1.7	7.0	1.9	0.0	0.0	37.5
1970-71	0.0	0.0	0.0	0.0	0.2	20.8	21.9	3.7	20.1	0.7	0.0	0.0	67.4
1971-72	0.0	0.0	0.0	0.0	8.8	8.9	3.6	6.3	18.8	3.9	0.0	0.0	50.3
1972-73	0.0	0.0	0.0	T	1.3	16.3	1.9	6.0	1.1	17.4	T	0.0	44.0
1973-74	0.0	0.0	0.0	0.0	0.4	10.9	10.5	14.1	6.6	0.4	T	0.0	42.9
1974-75	0.0	0.0	0.0	0.0	3.0	15.4	5.2	20.9	10.0	5.9	0.0	0.0	60.4
1975-76	0.0	0.0	0.0	0.0	5.5	2.8	10.1	10.4	2.0	T	0.0	0.0	30.8
1976-77	0.0	0.0	0.0	T	1.1	5.8	8.7	2.6	5.8	2.3	0.0	0.0	26.3
1977-78	0.0	0.0	0.0	0.0	10.4	24.6	13.5	4.7	3.0	0.5	0.0	0.0	56.7
1978-79	0.0	0.0	0.0	0.0	6.2	23.0	26.9	8.7	4.0	7.3	0.0	0.0	76.1
1979-80	0.0	0.0	0.0	0.2	4.4	1.3	4.9	7.5	5.6	7.1	0.0	0.0	31.0
1980-81	0.0	0.0	0.0	T	3.5	9.2	2.9	9.2	1.7	0.0	0.0	0.0	26.5
1981-82	0.0	0.0	0.0	0.1	2.0	7.2	19.4	2.4	8.6	10.3	0.0	0.0	50.0
1982-83	0.0	0.0	0.0	0.0	0.3	3.3	6.5	13.0	14.1	4.2	0.0	0.0	41.4
1983-84	0.0	0.0	0.0	0.0	2.1	22.6	6.0	0.8	6.8	3.9	0.0	0.0	42.2
1984-85	0.0	0.0	0.0	0.0	0.5	15.8	19.9	7.4	8.2	1.9	0.0	0.0	53.7
1985-86	0.0	0.0	0.0	0.0	18.3	24.0	13.9	13.3	2.7	0.2	0.0	0.0	72.4
1986-87	0.0	0.0	0.0	T	8.6	8.0	8.7	0.3	8.9	T	0.0	0.0	34.5
1987-88	0.0	0.0	0.0	0.4	3.9	32.8	16.3	6.4	1.1	1.3	0.0	0.0	62.2
1988-89	0.0	0.0	0.0	0.2	5.5	8.2	2.6	9.7	9.3	0.2	0.5	T	36.2
1989-90	0.0	0.0	0.0	0.7	4.4	4.3	10.1	11.7	0.1	0.5	3.0	T	34.8
1990-91	0.0	0.0	0.0	3.1	4.5	23.0	14.5	5.0	3.6	1.3	0.0	0.0	55.0
1991-92	T	0.0	0.0	0.5	8.0	10.2	4.5	12.3	6.9	0.1	0.0	T	42.5
1992-93	0.0	T	0.0	2.1	3.9	10.5	12.5	12.1	21.6	8.5	0.0	0.0	71.2
1993-94	0.0	0.0	T	0.2	1.2	2.5							
Record Mean	T	T	T	0.2	3.7	11.0	9.7	7.3	8.4	2.2	0.1	T	42.7

MILWAUKEE, WISCONSIN

Milwaukee possesses a continental climate characterized by a wide range of temperatures between summer and winter. Precipitation is moderate and occurs mostly in the spring, less in the autumn, and very little in the wintertime. Rainfall is well distributed for agricultural purposes, although spring planting is sometimes delayed by wet ground and cold weather.

Milwaukee is in a region of frequently changeable weather and its climate is influenced by general easterly-moving storms which traverse the nations midsection. The most severe winter storms, which produce in excess of 10 inches of snow, develop in the southern Great Plains and move northeast across Illinois and Indiana.

Occasionally during the cold season, frigid air masses from Canada push southeast across the Great Lakes region. These arctic air masses account for the coldest winter temperatures. Very low temperatures, zero degrees or lower, most often occur in air that flows southward to the west of Lake Superior before reaching the Milwaukee area. If northwesterly wind circulation persists, repeated incursions of arctic air will result in a period of bitterly cold weather lasting several days.

Summer temperatures, which reach into the 90s but rarely exceed 100 degrees, occur with brisk southwest winds that carry hot air from the plains and lower Mississippi River Valley across the city. A combination of high temperatures and humidity occasionally develops, usually building up over a period of several days when persistent southerly winds transport moisture from the Gulf of Mexico into the area.

The Gulf is a major source of moisture for Milwaukee in all seasons, but the type of precipitation which results is dependent upon the time of year. Cold-season precipitation (rain, snow, or a mixture) is usually of relatively long duration and low intensity, and occasionally persists for two days or more, whereas in the warm season, relatively short-duration and high-intensity showery rainfall, usually lasting a few hours or less, predominates.

The Great Lakes significantly influence the local climate. Temperature extremes are modified by Lake Michigan and, to a lesser extent, the other Great Lakes. In late autumn and winter, air masses that are initially very cold often reach the city only after being tempered by passage over one or more of the lakes. Similarly, air masses that approach from the northeast in the spring and summer are cooler because of movement over the Great Lakes.

The influence of Lake Michigan is variable and occasionally dramatic, especially when the temperature of the lake water differs strongly from the air temperature. During the spring and early summer, a wind shift from a westerly to an easterly direction frequently causes a sudden 10 to 20 degree temperature drop. When the breeze off the lake is light, this effect reaches inland only a mile or two. With stronger on-shore winds, the entire city is cooled. In the winter the relatively warm water of the lake moderates the temperature during easterly wind situations. Lake-induced snows usually occur a few times each winter, but snow accumulation is rarely heavy.

Topography does not significantly affect air flow, except that lesser frictional drag over Lake Michigan causes winds to be frequently stronger along the lake shore, and often permits air masses approaching from the north to reach shore areas one hour or more before affecting inland portions of the city.

NORMALS, MEANS, AND EXTREMES

MILWAUKEE, WISCONSIN

LATITUDE: 42°57'N LONGITUDE: 87°54' W ELEVATION: FT. GRND 672 BARO 691 TIME ZONE: CENTRAL WBAN: 14839

	(a)	JAN	FEB	MAR	APR	MAY	JUNE	JULY	AUG	SEP	OCT	NOV	DEC	YEAR
TEMPERATURE °F:														
Normals														
-Daily Maximum		26.1	30.1	40.4	52.9	64.3	74.9	79.9	77.8	70.6	58.7	44.7	31.2	54.3
-Daily Minimum		11.6	15.9	26.2	35.8	44.8	55.0	62.0	60.8	52.8	41.8	30.7	17.5	37.9
-Monthly		18.9	23.0	33.3	44.4	54.6	65.0	70.9	69.3	61.7	50.3	37.7	24.4	46.1
Extremes														
-Record Highest	53	62	65	82	91	93	101	101	103	98	89	77	63	103
-Year		1944	1976	1986	1980	1991	1988	1955	1988	1953	1963	1950	1982	AUG 1988
-Record Lowest	53	-26	-19	-10	12	21	33	40	44	28	18	-5	-20	-26
-Year		1982	1951	1962	1982	1966	1945	1965	1982	1974	1981	1950	1983	JAN 1982
NORMAL DEGREE DAYS:														
Heating (base 65°F)		1429	1176	983	618	338	82	14	27	123	456	819	1259	7324
Cooling (base 65°F)		0	0	0	0	16	82	197	160	24	0	0	0	479
% OF POSSIBLE SUNSHINE	53	45	47	49	53	59	65	69	66	59	54	39	38	54
MEAN SKY COVER (tenths)														
Sunrise - Sunset	53	6.8	6.8	7.0	6.7	6.3	6.0	5.4	5.4	5.7	5.9	7.2	7.2	6.4
MEAN NUMBER OF DAYS:														
Sunrise to Sunset														
-Clear	53	7.1	6.4	6.0	6.2	7.2	7.5	9.6	10.0	9.3	9.2	5.4	6.2	90.1
-Partly Cloudy	53	6.4	6.3	7.7	7.8	9.8	10.4	11.3	10.8	9.0	8.5	6.1	6.0	100.2
-Cloudy	53	17.5	15.5	17.3	16.0	14.1	12.0	10.1	10.2	11.6	13.3	18.5	18.8	175.0
Precipitation														
.01 inches or more	53	11.2	9.5	11.8	12.1	11.6	10.7	9.7	9.1	9.2	9.1	10.5	11.0	125.4
Snow,Ice pellets,hail														
1.0 inches or more	53	3.6	2.7	2.5	0.4	0.*	0.0	0.0	0.0	0.0	0.1	0.9	3.1	13.3
Thunderstorms	53	0.3	0.3	1.5	3.4	4.5	6.3	6.5	5.6	4.0	1.6	1.1	0.3	35.3
Heavy Fog Visibility														
1/4 mile or less	53	2.1	2.0	3.2	3.0	3.2	2.5	1.2	1.6	1.3	2.0	2.2	2.1	26.5
Temperature °F														
-Maximum														
90° and above	33	0.0	0.0	0.0	0.*	0.1	2.1	4.0	2.5	0.6	0.0	0.0	0.0	9.3
32° and below	33	19.8	15.1	6.2	0.5	0.0	0.0	0.0	0.0	0.0	0.0	2.6	14.9	59.2
-Minimum														
32° and below	33	29.5	26.2	23.3	9.5	1.0	0.0	0.0	0.0	0.1	4.1	17.7	27.7	139.2
0° and below	33	7.1	3.3	0.2	0.0	0.0	0.0	0.0	0.0	0.0	0.0	0.1	3.0	13.6
AVG. STATION PRESS.(mb)	21	991.9	992.8	990.3	989.5	989.5	989.3	990.6	991.7	992.1	992.1	991.1	992.0	991.1
RELATIVE HUMIDITY (%)														
Hour 00	33	75	74	76	75	75	77	80	83	82	78	78	78	78
Hour 06 (Local Time)	33	76	77	79	78	77	79	82	86	86	82	81	80	80
Hour 12	33	68	67	65	61	60	60	61	62	63	62	67	71	64
Hour 18	33	71	70	68	64	61	62	63	67	71	70	74	75	68
PRECIPITATION (inches):														
Water Equivalent														
-Normal		1.60	1.45	2.67	3.50	2.84	3.24	3.47	3.53	3.38	2.41	2.51	2.33	32.93
-Maximum Monthly	53	4.04	3.94	6.93	7.31	7.56	8.28	7.66	9.05	9.87	7.03	7.11	5.42	9.87
-Year		1960	1986	1976	1973	1990	1954	1964	1987	1941	1991	1985	1987	SEP 1941
-Minimum Monthly	53	0.31	0.05	0.31	0.81	0.50	0.70	0.95	0.46	0.02	0.15	0.62	0.29	0.02
-Year		1981	1969	1968	1942	1988	1988	1946	1948	1979	1956	1949	1976	SEP 1979
-Maximum in 24 hrs	53	1.73	1.67	2.57	3.11	3.11	3.13	4.35	6.84	5.28	2.60	2.18	2.24	6.84
-Year		1985	1960	1960	1976	1978	1950	1959	1986	1941	1959	1943	1982	AUG 1986
Snow,Ice pellets,hail														
-Maximum Monthly	53	33.6	42.0	26.7	15.8	3.2	T	T	T	T	6.3	16.1	27.9	42.0
-Year		1979	1974	1965	1973	1990	1992	1990	1989	1993	1989	1977	1978	FEB 1974
-Maximum in 24 hrs	53	13.8	16.7	11.2	11.6	3.2	T	T	T	T	6.3	10.6	13.1	16.7
-Year		1990	1960	1961	1973	1990	1992	1990	1989	1993	1989	1977	1987	FEB 1960
WIND:														
Mean Speed (mph)	53	12.6	12.4	12.9	12.8	11.6	10.4	9.7	9.5	10.4	11.4	12.5	12.3	11.5
Prevailing Direction through 1963		WNW	WNW	WNW	NNE	NNE	NNE	SW	SW	SSW	SSW	WNW	WNW	WNW
Fastest Obs. 1 Min.														
-Direction (!!)	11	02	02	19	23	36	25	30	30	26	24	24	04	30
-Speed (MPH)	11	35	36	39	45	44	38	54	44	35	35	38	40	54
-Year		1985	1984	1990	1983	1983	1990	1984	1989	1987	1984	1988	1987	JUL 1984
Peak Gust														
-Direction (!!)	10	SW	NE	SW	SW	SW	W	NW	NW	SW	NW	NW	NE	NW
-Speed (mph)	10	54	46	77	64	54	56	81	64	58	53	56	59	81
-Date		1989	1990	1991	1984	1985	1990	1984	1989	1986	1990	1989	1987	JUL 1984

PRECIPITATION (inches)

MILWAUKEE, WISCONSIN

YEAR	JAN	FEB	MAR	APR	MAY	JUNE	JULY	AUG	SEP	OCT	NOV	DEC	ANNUAL
1964	1.18	0.41	3.05	3.81	2.57	1.70	7.66	2.62	1.74	0.17	2.29	0.98	28.18
1965	3.33	1.04	3.61	3.47	2.12	0.85	2.64	6.15	6.85	2.68	2.02	3.73	38.49
1966	2.06	1.27	3.61	2.67	2.00	1.68	3.32	3.27	0.48	1.76	2.70	2.31	27.13
1967	1.49	1.31	1.35	2.70	1.80	7.38	1.35	1.23	1.69	2.70	1.52	1.33	25.85
1968	0.98	0.56	0.31	2.90	3.28	7.79	3.59	2.59	3.36	0.94	2.56	2.65	31.51
1969	1.83	0.05	1.05	3.42	3.05	7.53	6.61	0.53	2.18	4.48	1.14	1.18	33.05
1970	0.41	0.13	1.62	2.71	3.41	3.92	1.93	0.64	6.94	2.09	2.03	3.02	28.85
1971	1.37	2.50	2.83	1.31	0.90	2.67	2.60	2.28	1.30	1.90	2.45	4.34	26.45
1972	0.75	0.86	2.57	2.76	2.33	3.33	4.60	4.82	7.57	3.28	1.34	2.47	36.68
1973	1.12	1.51	2.86	7.31	3.39	1.96	1.55	0.95	4.50	2.97	1.83	3.80	33.75
1974	3.61	3.10	4.29	3.83	4.10	3.48	3.51	2.54	0.50	1.96	1.86	2.10	34.88
1975	2.25	2.53	3.01	4.08	2.01	3.99	1.14	3.89	1.00	0.72	2.83	1.70	29.15
1976	1.16	2.65	6.93	5.01	3.77	2.27	2.12	2.05	1.70	2.82	0.65	0.29	31.42
1977	0.90	0.59	4.56	2.09	0.90	5.78	5.99	3.82	4.11	2.02	2.56	3.27	36.59
1978	2.03	0.55	1.08	4.41	4.66	4.52	5.98	3.43	6.81	2.22	2.13	2.92	40.74
1979	3.00	0.97	4.17	5.43	1.82	2.84	1.06	4.85	0.02	1.77	2.67	2.27	30.87
1980	1.65	1.75	0.77	4.02	1.81	4.67	3.39	5.06	3.57	1.63	1.57	3.52	33.41
1981	0.31	2.88	0.51	4.87	3.05	2.39	4.35	4.26	5.47	2.71	2.05	1.03	33.88
1982	2.92	0.29	3.20	4.47	2.76	3.06	3.88	3.33	0.64	3.17	4.74	4.10	36.56
1983	0.75	2.23	4.12	4.66	5.83	1.41	1.34	4.70	2.79	2.65	4.10	2.89	37.47
1984	0.79	1.20	2.17	5.04	4.21	4.07	3.39	2.93	2.51	5.30	3.74	4.25	39.60
1985	1.94	2.34	4.11	1.93	2.73	1.27	2.18	2.23	3.44	5.39	7.11	2.62	37.29
1986	0.91	3.94	1.85	1.83	2.74	4.51	6.15	8.82	7.26	2.24	0.89	1.03	42.17
1987	1.22	1.22	1.74	4.26	3.76	2.23	4.20	9.05	2.22	1.09	2.73	5.42	39.14
1988	3.25	1.29	1.30	4.12	0.50	0.70	1.53	3.25	4.94	2.97	5.15	1.43	30.43
1989	0.86	0.69	3.03	1.33	2.86	1.89	6.16	5.19	3.25	2.67	1.90	0.47	30.30
1990	2.57	1.90	2.75	2.67	7.56	4.97	3.02	4.68	1.89	2.65	3.54	2.66	40.86
1991	1.55	0.38	4.06	3.70	4.25	2.13	4.34	2.27	4.34	7.03	3.36	1.94	39.35
1992	1.09	1.54	2.61	2.41	0.60	3.13	5.64	3.50	4.13	1.45	5.40	2.45	33.95
1993	2.63	0.98	3.19	6.64	1.56	6.39	4.22	4.20	3.91	0.44	1.98	0.70	36.84
Record Mean	1.80	1.56	2.51	2.93	3.17	3.48	3.03	3.02	3.18	2.35	2.16	1.86	31.06

AVERAGE TEMPERATURE (deg. F)

MILWAUKEE, WISCONSIN

YEAR	JAN	FEB	MAR	APR	MAY	JUNE	JULY	AUG	SEP	OCT	NOV	DEC	ANNUAL
1964	26.1	25.3	31.7	44.8	60.3	66.5	72.3	67.7	61.2	48.2	40.4	23.2	47.3
1965	19.5	21.2	25.3	42.7	58.6	63.1	68.9	66.8	61.7	50.8	38.5	32.9	45.8
1966	13.9	22.3	35.4	42.3	49.6	67.0	73.5	66.8	59.1	48.9	38.0	24.5	45.1
1967	24.5	17.5	33.2	44.9	50.2	66.5	68.6	66.0	60.8	50.4	35.2	28.9	45.6
1968	21.8	20.7	40.3	47.6	53.2	66.3	69.5	71.4	63.5	52.7	38.1	25.6	47.5
1969	18.6	27.3	29.8	44.9	55.3	58.9	67.8	70.9	62.0	47.5	34.3	25.1	45.2
1970	13.3	22.6	30.5	46.2	56.0	65.3	73.3	71.8	62.0	52.5	37.3	24.3	46.2
1971	12.7	21.6	28.6	40.9	51.1	67.5	68.0	67.0	64.9	55.5	37.3	29.5	45.4
1972	15.9	19.8	27.7	39.4	55.0	61.6	69.3	69.1	61.3	47.5	36.2	20.2	43.6
1973	24.7	25.4	39.9	42.7	51.0	69.2	71.4	72.5	63.9	54.6	38.5	25.5	48.3
1974	21.6	22.9	33.8	46.1	50.6	62.4	71.5	67.3	58.0	49.9	38.6	29.1	46.0
1975	24.0	23.5	28.6	37.7	57.1	65.7	71.7	71.2	58.5	54.1	44.5	27.9	47.0
1976	18.5	31.1	38.6	48.7	52.6	68.2	72.6	69.9	62.6	45.9	29.5	16.3	46.2
1977	8.3	23.7	39.2	48.9	61.3	62.5	73.1	67.2	61.9	49.0	37.1	22.8	46.2
1978	15.4	16.4	29.8	42.5	55.2	65.2	68.6	69.9	65.8	49.5	38.2	23.8	45.0
1979	11.6	15.1	33.2	42.1	54.9	64.7	70.9	68.8	64.7	51.1	38.2	31.4	45.6
1980	20.7	20.3	30.5	45.3	57.2	61.3	71.2	69.7	61.1	45.7	37.7	24.4	45.4
1981	18.9	25.3	35.6	46.5	51.5	65.2	67.3	67.8	59.1	45.8	37.4	24.2	45.4
1982	9.7	19.4	31.5	41.2	58.5	59.8	71.1	67.3	60.8	52.7	38.0	33.2	45.3
1983	26.4	29.4	35.0	41.7	50.2	66.3	76.2	74.4	62.9	52.0	39.9	14.4	47.4
1984	18.9	33.4	29.2	45.5	54.9	68.7	71.7	73.3	60.9	52.9	37.7	29.1	48.0
1985	15.2	21.3	37.9	50.8	58.8	63.8	72.4	68.4	64.3	50.7	36.7	15.7	46.3
1986	21.9	23.3	38.1	48.5	56.1	63.3	72.5	67.1	63.8	51.6	35.1	29.2	47.5
1987	24.8	32.0	37.8	48.0	60.1	72.2	74.8	69.9	63.3	46.2	41.9	31.4	50.2
1988	18.3	20.1	34.8	45.7	58.7	70.2	75.4	75.7	63.5	45.8	40.7	26.6	48.0
1989	30.4	18.0	32.4	43.2	54.9	64.4	71.6	68.8	60.2	52.7	35.1	16.7	45.7
1990	31.1	28.9	38.8	49.3	52.8	67.6	70.5	71.2	66.0	51.5	44.5	26.9	49.9
1991	20.1	29.9	38.2	49.7	63.2	70.7	74.4	73.5	63.2	52.3	35.1	29.6	50.0
1992	27.9	31.9	35.4	42.9	56.7	63.0	67.7	67.4	61.6	49.8	37.3	28.2	47.5
1993	25.7	24.4	32.5	43.0	56.9	63.8	73.0	73.6	60.6	51.0	39.5	29.9	47.8
Record Mean	20.8	23.4	33.0	44.5	54.6	64.7	70.9	69.8	62.5	51.2	37.7	25.9	46.6
Max	28.0	30.5	40.0	52.5	63.7	73.8	79.5	77.9	70.7	59.1	44.5	32.5	54.4
Min	13.6	16.3	25.9	36.4	45.5	55.5	62.3	61.6	54.4	43.3	30.8	19.3	38.7

REFERENCE NOTES

MILWAUKEE, WISCONSIN

GENERAL
T - TRACE AMOUNT.
BLANK ENTRIES DENOTE MISSING/UNREPORTED DATA.
# INDICATES A STATION OR INSTRUMENT RELOCATION.

SPECIFIC

PM - INCLUDES LAST DAY OF PREVIOUS MONTH
ASOS - AUTOMATED SURFACE OBSERVING SYSTEM IN OPERATION DURING THESE MONTHS.

(a) - LENGTH OF RECORD IN YEARS, ALTHOUGH INDIVIDUAL MONTHS MAY BE MISSING.
0.* OR * - THE VALUE IS BETWEEN 0.0 AND 0.05
NORMALS - BASED ON THE 1961-1990 RECORD PERIOD.
EXTREMES - DATES ARE THE MOST RECENT OCCURRENCE
WIND DIR.- NUMERALS SHOW TENS OF DEGRESS CLOCKWISE FROM TRUE NORTH. "00" INDICATES CALM.
RESULTANT DIRECTIONS ARE GIVEN TO WHOLE DEGREES.
BOLD VALUES INDICATE EXTREME VALUES WHICH OCCURRED AFTER THE ASOS SYSTEM WAS COMMISSIONED.

RECORD = PERIOD OF RECORD
RECORD MEAN PRECIPITATION IS THE MEAN OF ALL DAILY PRECIPITATION AMOUNTS DURING THE PERIOD OF RECORD.
RECORD MAX(MIN) TEMPERATURE IS THE MEAN OF ALL DAILY MAX(MIN) TEMPERATURES DURING THE PERIOD OF RECORD.
RECORD MEAN TEMPERATURE IS THE SUM OF THE RECORD MAX AND RECORD MIN DIVIDED BY 2.
AVERAGE TEMPERATURE IS THE SUM OF THE MEAN DAILY MAX AND MIN TEMPERATURE DIVIDED BY 2.

EXCEPTIONS

FASTEST MILE WINDS ARE THROUGH JUNE 1982.

RECORD MEANS ARE THROUGH THE CURRENT YEAR, BEGINNING IN 1875 FOR TEMPERATURE
1871 FOR PRECIPITATION
1941 FOR SNOWFALL

HEATING DEGREE DAYS Base 65 deg. F — MILWAUKEE, WISCONSIN

SEASON	JULY	AUG	SEP	OCT	NOV	DEC	JAN	FEB	MAR	APR	MAY	JUNE	TOTAL
1964-65	7	47	177	515	730	1290	1404	1222	1226	664	232	123	7637
1965-66	25	51	149	438	793	987	1579	1189	915	674	473	88	7361
1966-67	4	41	198	496	804	1249	1249	1325	978	596	458	47	7445
1967-68	46	53	164	460	888	1112	1333	1277	758	521	363	74	7049
1968-69	31	23	82	403	799	1214	1434	1053	1087	596	317	215	7254
1969-70	34	5	143	539	913	1228	1600	1180	1062	561	301	104	7670
1970-71	7	7	145	383	823	1259	1615	1211	1122	716	421	65	7774
1971-72	20	37	119	308	824	1097	1518	1305	1149	758	305	139	7579
1972-73	40	32	133	534	859	1381	1242	1101	769	659	426	6	7182
1973-74	10	5	111	324	788	1218	1340	1173	959	560	448	106	7042
1974-75	0	20	237	461	786	1103	1260	1157	1122	814	267	69	7296
1975-76	17	4	203	353	610	1144	1438	978	813	507	382	43	6492
1976-77	2	21	124	589	1056	1504	1754	1152	790	490	173	151	7806
1977-78	8	47	106	485	827	1302	1531	1356	1086	667	335	83	7833
1978-79	21	5	76	473	796	1273	1654	1391	980	681	322	91	7763
1979-80	20	25	70	436	797	1036	1368	1290	1063	594	259	154	7112
1980-81	8	9	140	590	812	1250	1423	1106	905	548	417	69	7277
1981-82	44	21	187	590	820	1257	1712	1272	1032	707	215	172	8029
1982-83	3	44	170	381	802	983	1186	990	925	692	453	81	6710
1983-84	10	0	148	405	748	1565	1424	910	1103	579	318	35	7245
1984-85	3	7	179	373	812	1103	1542	1215	831	461	222	96	6844
1985-86	2	13	139	436	843	1523	1328	1161	827	494	302	128	7196
1986-87	13	34	98	407	891	1106	1242	917	839	502	236	19	6304
1987-88	12	28	91	576	686	1037	1442	1294	930	571	245	55	6967
1988-89	3	7	87	587	720	1183	1065	1307	1006	649	324	85	7023
1989-90	0	16	166	381	890	1493	1040	1004	805	502	375	51	6723
1990-91	21	9	93	418	612	1173	1385	980	822	467	201	26	6207
1991-92	0	1	160	394	889	1091	1141	955	914	655	278	104	6582
1992-93	27	35	145	472	825	1132	1211	1132	1004	654	245	104	6986
1993-94	1	2	158	428	757	1080							

COOLING DEGREE DAYS Base 65 deg. F — MILWAUKEE, WISCONSIN

YEAR	JAN	FEB	MAR	APR	MAY	JUNE	JULY	AUG	SEP	OCT	NOV	DEC	TOTAL
1969	0	0	0	0	24	38	126	197	59	5	0	0	449
1970	0	0	0	4	29	119	270	227	60	4	0	0	713
1971	0	0	0	0	0	148	120	105	123	20	0	0	516
1972	0	0	0	0	3	42	180	166	26	0	0	0	417
1973	0	0	0	0	0	140	216	247	84	6	0	0	693
1974	0	0	0	3	6	36	210	98	32	1	0	0	386
1975	0	0	0	0	30	98	230	203	16	21	0	0	598
1976	0	0	0	24	5	144	247	181	62	4	0	0	667
1977	0	0	0	12	65	81	264	122	20	0	0	0	564
1978	0	0	0	0	40	97	138	164	109	0	0	0	548
1979	0	0	0	0	16	87	209	147	68	11	0	0	538
1980	0	0	0	9	25	50	207	164	29	0	0	0	484
1981	0	0	0	2	3	84	121	112	16	0	0	0	338
1982	0	0	0	0	21	24	199	121	51	5	0	0	421
1983	0	0	0	0	0	127	364	299	92	9	0	0	891
1984	0	0	0	1	11	152	216	270	63	3	0	0	716
1985	0	0	0	42	35	68	240	127	127	0	0	0	639
1986	0	0	3	7	31	84	251	105	70	0	0	0	551
1987	0	0	0	2	87	244	323	189	47	0	1	0	893
1988	0	0	0	0	57	215	333	344	48	0	0	0	997
1989	0	0	2	0	16	76	214	144	29	4	0	0	485
1990	0	0	2	38	5	135	198	210	132	7	1	0	728
1991	0	0	0	13	150	204	300	268	114	7	0	0	1056
1992	0	0	0	0	25	49	117	119	50	4	0	0	364
1993	0	0	0	0	5	73	258	277	35	3	0	0	651

SNOWFALL (inches) — MILWAUKEE, WISCONSIN

SEASON	JULY	AUG	SEP	OCT	NOV	DEC	JAN	FEB	MAR	APR	MAY	JUNE	TOTAL
1964-65	0.0	0.0	0.0	T	1.4	8.1	23.6	10.1	26.7	4.1	0.0	0.0	74.0
1965-66	0.0	0.0	0.0	T	T	14.5	24.6	7.7	2.8	1.3	0.1	0.0	51.0
1966-67	0.0	0.0	0.0	0.0	2.0	9.9	13.1	27.1	7.4	T	T	0.0	59.5
1967-68	0.0	0.0	0.0	0.8	0.4	1.2	4.6	3.5	1.2	0.4	0.0	0.0	12.1
1968-69	0.0	0.0	0.0	0.0	0.3	11.6	11.1	0.7	6.2	0.0	T	0.0	29.9
1969-70	0.0	0.0	0.0	T	0.7	14.9	6.0	2.0	10.7	5.2	0.0	0.0	39.5
1970-71	0.0	0.0	0.0	0.0	0.6	19.6	15.8	2.5	18.1	0.7	T	0.0	57.3
1971-72	0.0	0.0	0.0	0.0	6.1	2.7	6.8	10.2	14.9	1.2	0.0	0.0	41.9
1972-73	0.0	0.0	0.0	T	3.4	13.7	0.2	9.9	1.8	15.8	T	0.0	44.8
1973-74	0.0	0.0	0.0	0.0	T	19.6	14.2	42.0	7.4	T	0.0	0.0	83.2
1974-75	0.0	0.0	0.0	T	2.0	9.1	3.5	12.2	15.1	10.4	0.0	0.0	52.3
1975-76	0.0	0.0	0.0	0.0	8.4	12.2	14.8	7.6	2.1	0.1	T	0.0	45.2
1976-77	0.0	0.0	0.0	4.0	3.6	5.3	15.6	5.6	12.4	2.1	0.0	0.0	48.6
1977-78	0.0	0.0	0.0	T	16.1	20.8	25.7	13.3	4.8	T	0.0	0.0	80.7
1978-79	0.0	0.0	0.0	0.0	5.3	27.9	33.6	9.1	6.2	0.8	0.0	0.0	82.9
1979-80	0.0	0.0	0.0	T	2.1	0.6	11.6	22.8	6.3	3.6	T	0.0	47.0
1980-81	0.0	0.0	0.0	T	2.3	17.5	4.9	15.7	1.5	T	0.0	0.0	41.9
1981-82	0.0	0.0	0.0	T	2.0	8.3	29.2	3.0	13.0	11.7	0.0	0.0	67.2
1982-83	0.0	0.0	0.0	T	0.4	3.1	6.3	13.5	13.8	1.0	0.0	0.0	38.1
1983-84	0.0	0.0	0.0	0.0	0.3	13.3	9.6	1.2	8.2	0.5	T	0.0	33.1
1984-85	0.0	0.0	0.0	0.0	T	19.0	20.8	15.3	9.0	2.5	0.0	0.0	66.6
1985-86	0.0	0.0	0.0	0.0	3.5	13.5	10.4	14.0	0.7	0.3	0.0	0.0	42.4
1986-87	0.0	0.0	0.0	T	2.4	2.5	11.4	T	5.2	0.4	0.0	0.0	21.9
1987-88	0.0	0.0	0.0	0.6	0.4	19.9	10.2	20.7	2.9	T	0.0	0.0	54.7
1988-89	0.0	0.0	0.0	T	2.7	7.1	2.7	13.1	13.3	0.4	0.6	0.0	39.9
1989-90	T	T	0.0	6.3	11.6	7.4	19.9	17.9	0.2	1.2	3.2	0.0	67.7
1990-91	T	0.0	0.0	0.0	0.4	10.5	15.2	2.4	1.1	0.4	0.0	0.0	30.0
1991-92	0.0	0.0	T	T	4.8	14.7	4.3	5.3	11.1	0.8	0.0	T	41.0
1992-93	0.0	0.0	0.0	1.2	0.4	8.4	12.2	11.6	12.7	3.4	T	0.0	49.9
1993-94	0.0	0.0	T	T	8.0	1.2							
Record Mean	T	T	T	0.2	3.0	10.4	12.8	9.6	8.7	1.7	0.1	T	46.6

CHEYENNE, WYOMING

The city of Cheyenne is located on a broad plateau between the North and South Platte Rivers in the extreme southeastern corner of Wyoming at an elevation of approximately 6,100 feet. The surrounding country is mostly rolling prairie which is used primarily for grazing. The ground level rises rapidly to a ridge approximately 9,000 feet in elevation about 30 miles west of the city. This ridge is known as the Laramie Mountains, one of the ranges of the Rockies, and extends in a north-south direction. Because of this ridge, winds from the northwest through west to southwest are downslope and produce a marked chinook effect in Cheyenne which is especially noticeable during the winter months. Also, winds from the north through east to south are upslope and may cause fog or low stratus clouds in the Cheyenne area throughout the year. Because of this terrain variation, the wind direction plays an important role in controlling the local temperature and weather.

Cheyenne experiences large diurnal and annual temperature ranges. This is due to the advent of both warm and cold air masses and the relatively high elevation of the city which permits rapid incoming and outgoing radiation. The daily temperature range averages about 30 degrees in the summer and 23 degrees in the winter. Many cold air masses from the north during the winter months miss Cheyenne. Because of the downslope of land to the east and the prevailing westerlies, some of the cold air masses do move over the city, but only about 13 percent of the days in an average January, the coldest month of the year, show temperatures dropping to zero or below. Temperatures during the winter months average a few degrees higher than over the Mississippi and Missouri Valleys at the same latitude.

Windy days are quire frequent during the winter and spring months. Since the wind is usually strongest during the daytime it is a very noticeable weather element. Usually the strong winds are from a westerly direction and this tends to raise the temperature because the air is moving downslope.

Most of the air masses reaching this area move in from the Pacific and since the mountains to the west are quite effective moisture barriers the climate is semi-arid. Fortunately, about 70 percent of normal annual precipitation occurs during the growing season. In the summer months, precipitation is mostly of the shower type and occurs mainly with thunderstorms. Hail is frequent and occasionally destructive in some thunderstorms. Most of the snow falls during the late winter and early spring months. It is not uncommon to have heavy snow in May.

The growing season in Cheyenne averages about 132 days a year and extends from around May 18th to September 27th. Freezing temperatures have occurred as late in the spring as mid-June, and as early in the fall as late August.

Relative humidity averages near 50 percent on an annual basis with large daily variations. Very seldom is the relative humidity above 30 percent when the temperature is above 80 degrees.

NORMALS, MEANS, AND EXTREMES

CHEYENNE, WYOMING

LATITUDE: 41°09'N LONGITUDE: 104°48' W ELEVATION: FT. GRND 6130 BARO 6129 TIME ZONE: MOUNTAIN WBAN: 24018

	(a)	JAN	FEB	MAR	APR	MAY	JUNE	JULY	AUG	SEP	OCT	NOV	DEC	YEAR
TEMPERATURE °F:														
Normals														
-Daily Maximum		37.7	40.5	44.9	54.7	64.6	74.4	82.2	80.0	71.1	60.0	46.8	38.8	58.0
-Daily Minimum		15.2	18.1	22.1	30.1	39.4	48.3	54.6	52.8	43.7	33.9	23.7	16.7	33.2
-Monthly		26.5	29.3	33.6	42.5	52.0	61.3	68.4	66.4	57.4	47.0	35.2	27.8	45.6
Extremes														
-Record Highest	58	66	71	74	83	90	100	100	96	93	83	73	69	100
-Year		1982	1962	1986	1992	1969	1954	1939	1979	1960	1992	1954	1939	JUN 1954
-Record Lowest	58	-29	-34	-21	-8	16	25	38	36	8	-1	-16	-28	-34
-Year		1984	1936	1943	1975	1947	1951	1952	1975	1985	1991	1993	1990	FEB 1936
NORMAL DEGREE DAYS:														
Heating (base 65°F)		1194	1000	973	675	403	150	31	44	251	558	894	1153	7326
Cooling (base 65°F)		0	0	0	0	0	39	136	87	23	0	0	0	285
% OF POSSIBLE SUNSHINE	54	64	66	67	63	61	66	69	68	70	69	61	60	65
MEAN SKY COVER (tenths)														
Sunrise - Sunset	58	5.8	6.2	6.3	6.5	6.6	5.5	5.0	5.1	4.6	4.8	5.6	5.7	5.6
MEAN NUMBER OF DAYS:														
Sunrise to Sunset														
-Clear	58	8.9	7.1	7.0	5.7	4.8	8.5	9.5	9.7	13.1	12.8	9.5	9.5	106.2
-Partly Cloudy	58	9.5	9.0	9.8	10.3	12.0	12.3	15.0	13.2	8.5	8.9	9.2	9.1	126.8
-Cloudy	58	12.9	12.1	14.1	13.9	14.3	9.2	6.5	8.0	8.4	9.3	11.3	12.6	132.6
Precipitation														
.01 inches or more	58	5.7	6.3	9.4	9.6	12.0	10.9	11.0	10.1	7.4	5.8	6.3	5.7	100.2
Snow, Ice pellets, hail														
1.0 inches or more	58	2.1	2.0	3.6	2.4	0.8	0.1	0.0	0.0	0.3	1.3	2.5	2.0	16.9
Thunderstorms	58	0.0	0.1	0.2	2.2	7.8	11.4	13.3	10.7	4.5	0.9	0.*	0.0	51.0
Heavy Fog Visibility														
1/4 mile or less	58	1.0	1.8	3.1	3.0	2.9	1.9	1.2	1.4	1.9	2.0	1.9	1.4	23.4
Temperature °F														
-Maximum														
90° and above	34	0.0	0.0	0.0	0.0	0.*	1.2	5.2	2.2	0.2	0.0	0.0	0.0	8.9
32° and below	34	9.4	7.1	5.2	1.3	0.*	0.0	0.0	0.0	0.1	0.7	4.4	8.8	37.0
-Minimum														
32° and below	34	28.9	26.4	27.4	17.7	3.6	0.0	0.0	0.0	2.0	12.2	24.7	28.6	171.6
0° and below	34	4.3	2.5	1.0	0.1	0.0	0.0	0.0	0.0	0.0	0.1	0.6	3.1	11.7
AVG. STATION PRESS. (mb)	21	809.0	809.2	807.3	809.0	810.3	812.8	815.3	815.5	814.5	813.3	810.1	809.3	811.3
RELATIVE HUMIDITY (%)														
Hour 05	34	57	62	66	68	72	72	70	69	67	61	61	58	65
Hour 11 (Local Time)	34	46	46	47	42	42	40	36	36	37	38	44	46	42
Hour 17	34	50	48	47	42	44	41	38	38	38	41	51	53	44
Hour 23	34	58	61	64	65	67	64	63	63	62	59	60	59	62
PRECIPITATION (inches):														
Water Equivalent														
-Normal		0.40	0.39	1.03	1.37	2.39	2.08	2.09	1.69	1.27	0.74	0.53	0.42	14.40
-Maximum Monthly	58	2.78	2.16	3.65	5.04	5.67	5.32	5.01	6.64	4.52	3.57	2.48	1.68	6.64
-Year		1949	1953	1990	1942	1981	1955	1973	1985	1973	1942	1979	1937	AUG 1985
-Minimum Monthly	58	T	T	0.12	0.34	0.11	0.07	0.58	0.03	0.01	0.03	T	0.03	T
-Year		1952	1983	1966	1992	1974	1980	1969	1944	1992	1964	1965	1959	FEB 1983
-Maximum in 24 hrs	58	1.41	1.60	1.88	1.94	2.07	2.68	3.42	6.06	2.75	1.70	1.66	1.19	6.06
-Year		1949	1953	1946	1984	1991	1955	1973	1985	1973	1947	1979	1979	AUG 1985
Snow, Ice pellets, hail														
-Maximum Monthly	58	35.5	19.9	39.2	31.8	30.4	8.7	T	0.5	7.4	21.3	31.1	21.3	39.2
-Year		1980	1953	1990	1984	1943	1947	1992	1993	1985	1969	1979	1958	MAR 1990
-Maximum in 24 hrs	58	12.7	14.0	15.6	17.4	15.0	8.7	T	0.5	5.8	8.6	19.8	11.7	19.8
-Year		1992	1953	1973	1984	1942	1947	1992	1993	1985	1990	1979	1979	NOV 1979
WIND:														
Mean Speed (mph)	36	15.3	14.6	14.5	14.2	12.6	11.4	10.4	10.4	11.2	12.3	13.5	14.7	12.9
Prevailing Direction through 1963		WNW	W	WNW	WNW	WNW	WNW	WNW	W	W	W	WNW	WNW	WNW
Fastest Obs. 1 Min.														
-Direction (!!)	12	28	27	29	30	26	29	28	32	30	29	31	27	30
-Speed (MPH)	12	49	48	51	58	48	41	46	42	46	46	46	49	58
-Year		1989	1988	1982	1982	1988	1990	1993	1983	1992	1990	1986	1992	APR 1982
Peak Gust														
-Direction (!!)	10	W	27	W	NW	W	W	W	NW	NW	SW	W	W	W
-Speed (mph)	10	77	70	69	62	71	58	79	59	62	71	69	71	79
-Date		1990	1986	1985	1992	1986	1993	1993	1989	1992	1985	1986	1992	JUL 1993

PRECIPITATION (inches)

CHEYENNE, WYOMING

YEAR	JAN	FEB	MAR	APR	MAY	JUNE	JULY	AUG	SEP	OCT	NOV	DEC	ANNUAL
1964	0.03	0.24	0.58	1.30	0.84	1.01	1.00	0.28	0.33	0.03	0.14	0.16	5.94
1965	0.57	0.26	0.76	0.57	3.11	4.03	0.89	1.54	1.32	0.75	T	0.22	14.02
1966	0.11	0.22	0.12	0.48	0.21	1.95	3.38	2.78	2.12	0.68	0.29	0.08	12.42
1967	0.45	0.54	0.76	2.15	4.04	2.63	1.71	0.99	0.88	0.46	0.32	0.46	15.39
1968	0.04	0.30	0.31	2.34	3.54	0.87	1.25	1.21	0.20	0.86	0.71	0.28	11.91
1969	0.23	0.25	0.27	0.82	1.77	2.70	0.58	0.99	0.84	2.04	0.23	0.21	10.93
1970	0.10	0.04	1.32	0.85	3.13	2.42	0.82	0.14	1.10	1.30	0.30	0.31	11.83
1971	0.51	0.62	1.08	2.81	2.38	0.97	1.08	1.41	1.76	1.16	0.05	0.07	13.90
1972	0.36	0.02	0.79	0.80	2.76	1.71	1.35	1.83	1.01	0.42	0.59	0.40	12.04
1973	0.23	0.07	1.85	1.75	0.31	1.20	5.01	0.27	4.52	0.06	1.25	1.06	17.58
1974	0.48	0.03	1.24	0.50	0.11	2.81	1.41	1.29	0.50	0.91	0.49	0.10	9.87
1975	0.40	0.17	1.17	0.47	2.27	1.49	2.62	0.39	0.52	0.49	0.20	0.52	10.71
1976	0.32	0.71	0.32	1.79	2.07	0.68	2.39	1.40	0.77	0.15	0.28	0.10	10.98
1977	0.14	0.08	1.21	1.86	2.50	2.44	3.49	1.07	0.19	0.08	0.35	0.24	13.65
1978	0.58	0.78	0.35	0.52	3.98	0.63	0.98	1.38	0.12	0.50	0.45	0.54	10.81
1979	0.27	0.14	1.34	0.77	2.90	3.32	1.83	1.86	0.32	0.46	2.48	1.50	17.19
1980	2.71	0.73	1.36	0.93	2.39	0.07	2.00	1.55	0.97	0.51	0.46	0.08	13.76
1981	0.30	0.20	0.70	0.73	5.67	1.66	2.85	2.90	0.31	0.85	0.09	0.45	16.71
1982	0.41	0.19	0.17	0.53	3.56	4.52	2.71	1.81	2.87	1.20	0.43	0.83	19.23
1983	0.02	T	2.96	4.45	2.31	2.81	2.12	1.95	0.78	0.49	2.34	0.46	20.69
1984	0.54	0.84	1.28	3.71	0.78	2.43	2.57	2.84	0.65	1.55	0.11	0.34	17.64
1985	0.66	0.19	0.36	1.10	1.05	1.59	3.99	6.64	1.78	0.94	0.84	0.80	19.94
1986	0.13	0.50	0.54	2.26	1.03	2.42	1.04	1.55	2.47	1.78	0.66	0.18	14.56
1987	0.09	0.90	1.25	0.68	4.43	1.80	2.04	1.23	0.93	0.33	0.76	0.85	15.29
1988	0.52	0.65	1.34	1.84	3.09	2.03	1.79	1.79	1.66	0.09	0.42	0.53	15.75
1989	0.27	1.26	0.49	0.48	1.37	2.51	1.70	1.79	1.62	0.41	0.14	0.69	12.73
1990	0.35	0.69	3.65	1.66	3.37	1.03	3.64	1.98	0.80	1.35	0.72	0.39	19.63
1991	0.36	0.12	0.43	1.15	3.84	4.56	3.39	1.49	1.87	0.44	0.87	0.13	18.65
1992	1.18	0.11	1.75	0.34	1.86	2.11	1.87	1.90	0.01	0.46	1.69	0.49	13.77
1993	0.35	0.81	0.63	2.49	1.92	3.32	0.64	2.21	3.16	1.85	1.23	0.30	18.91
Record Mean	0.43	0.54	1.05	1.74	2.44	1.86	2.01	1.58	1.19	0.88	0.57	0.45	14.72

AVERAGE TEMPERATURE (deg. F)

CHEYENNE, WYOMING

YEAR	JAN	FEB	MAR	APR	MAY	JUNE	JULY	AUG	SEP	OCT	NOV	DEC	ANNUAL
1964	26.1	22.3	27.4	40.8	54.6	60.5	70.9	64.3	56.9	48.7	35.4	29.5	44.8
1965	32.1	26.0	22.2	45.7	50.8	59.3	68.2	64.7	49.6	52.0	41.4	32.1	45.4
1966	25.8	26.8	37.7	39.6	55.6	61.5	74.5	66.2	59.9	47.8	38.8	31.0	47.1
1967	31.4	31.1	39.0	44.1	49.1	57.7	67.3	66.0	58.4	49.3	35.1	22.5	45.9
1968	28.7	32.6	38.0	38.9	49.2	62.6	68.2	64.5	57.6	49.2	34.0	28.0	46.0
1969	31.4	32.0	28.7	48.1	55.7	57.0	71.5	70.7	61.2	37.1	36.4	31.3	46.8
1970	28.7	34.6	28.9	37.8	54.3	60.9	69.5	70.7	55.0	41.2	35.7	29.1	45.5
1971	29.7	25.8	32.4	41.0	49.2	63.4	65.5	68.7	53.1	44.3	36.0	29.1	44.8
1972	25.3	33.2	39.3	42.5	51.2	63.2	64.3	64.6	56.6	45.5	29.5	21.0	44.7
1973	23.7	29.7	31.9	37.3	51.4	62.9	65.8	68.4	54.1	49.3	35.3	29.4	44.9
1974	24.1	31.9	37.1	43.3	55.0	64.1	70.1	65.2	55.3	48.3	35.6	26.6	46.4
1975	25.5	25.0	30.2	37.5	48.4	57.9	67.3	66.3	56.0	48.1	34.2	32.6	44.1
1976	26.9	32.9	30.9	42.7	51.1	59.7	69.2	65.0	57.7	43.4	33.5	30.6	45.3
1977	22.4	32.9	32.1	44.7	53.4	65.2	68.2	63.5	60.7	48.3	34.4	29.0	46.3
1978	22.1	25.0	37.7	43.9	49.0	61.0	68.7	64.3	59.6	47.9	33.5	21.1	44.5
1979	17.3	31.6	36.0	44.9	49.9	61.5	69.9	65.9	62.9	49.8	29.5	32.9	46.0
1980	22.2	29.4	33.0	42.3	51.2	65.5	71.4	66.5	60.4	46.7	36.8	38.5	47.0
1981	33.4	32.2	36.8	50.1	50.5	63.7	69.0	65.2	61.2	46.1	40.7	30.7	48.3
1982	25.5	28.2	36.1	41.8	50.5	57.5	67.7	69.1	56.7	45.1	31.4	28.3	44.8
1983	32.8	33.5	32.0	34.8	47.4	57.3	67.8	70.2	59.0	48.6	32.3	15.0	44.2
1984	24.3	28.4	32.4	35.7	53.6	59.4	68.4	66.6	53.0	40.0	35.0	27.0	43.7
1985	19.5	23.3	35.2	45.6	54.3	61.1	69.3	66.8	52.8	45.1	26.2	26.1	43.8
1986	37.0	30.1	42.2	43.9	50.6	64.5	68.5	67.0	55.3	44.6	34.3	28.7	47.2
1987	29.1	31.6	32.4	46.7	54.5	63.3	69.2	64.9	58.0	46.9	36.7	25.7	46.6
1988	21.5	28.4	32.3	44.4	53.3	67.4	69.7	68.7	57.5	50.3	35.3	28.7	46.5
1989	30.2	17.3	37.4	44.3	54.3	60.3	70.6	67.0	57.5	46.5	38.7	24.3	45.7
1990	31.5	28.7	31.9	42.8	49.3	64.1	65.0	66.4	62.2	46.7	38.7	20.8	45.7
1991	25.0	36.2	36.4	41.1	52.4	62.5	67.7	67.7	58.0	46.1	31.7	31.6	46.4
1992	30.5	36.7	38.6	48.6	55.0	60.8	64.6	63.8	60.0	49.2	30.9	25.5	47.0
1993	26.1	24.9	37.2	42.1	53.4	58.7	66.1	64.8	54.3	44.1	29.2	30.7	44.3
Record Mean	26.1	28.0	32.8	41.6	51.2	61.1	67.8	66.3	57.4	46.4	35.0	28.4	45.2
Max	37.3	39.2	44.1	53.6	63.5	74.6	81.8	80.2	71.4	59.4	46.6	39.3	57.6
Min	15.0	16.7	21.4	29.6	38.8	47.6	53.8	52.5	43.4	33.4	23.4	17.5	32.8

REFERENCE NOTES

CHEYENNE, WYOMING

GENERAL
T - TRACE AMOUNT.
BLANK ENTRIES DENOTE MISSING/UNREPORTED DATA.
# INDICATES A STATION OR INSTRUMENT RELOCATION.

SPECIFIC

PM - INCLUDES LAST DAY OF PREVIOUS MONTH
ASOS - AUTOMATED SURFACE OBSERVING SYSTEM IN OPERATION DURING THESE MONTHS.

(a) - LENGTH OF RECORD IN YEARS, ALTHOUGH INDIVIDUAL MONTHS MAY BE MISSING.
0.* OR * - THE VALUE IS BETWEEN 0.0 AND 0.05
NORMALS - BASED ON THE 1961-1990 RECORD PERIOD.
EXTREMES - DATES ARE THE MOST RECENT OCCURRENCE
WIND DIR.- NUMERALS SHOW TENS OF DEGRESS CLOCKWISE FROM TRUE NORTH. "00" INDICATES CALM.
RESULTANT DIRECTIONS ARE GIVEN TO WHOLE DEGREES.
BOLD VALUES INDICATE EXTREME VALUES WHICH OCCURRED AFTER THE ASOS SYSTEM WAS COMMISSIONED.

RECORD = PERIOD OF RECORD
RECORD MEAN PRECIPITATION IS THE MEAN OF ALL DAILY PRECIPITATION AMOUNTS DURING THE PERIOD OF RECORD.
RECORD MAX(MIN) TEMPERATURE IS THE MEAN OF ALL DAILY MAX(MIN) TEMPERATURES DURING THE PERIOD OF RECORD.
RECORD MEAN TEMPERATURE IS THE SUM OF THE RECORD MAX AND RECORD MIN DIVIDED BY 2.
AVERAGE TEMPERATURE IS THE SUM OF THE MEAN DAILY MAX AND MIN TEMPERATURE DIVIDED BY 2.

EXCEPTIONS

FASTEST MILE WINDS ARE THROUGH MARCH 1981.

RECORD MEANS ARE THROUGH THE CURRENT YEAR, BEGINNING IN 1871 FOR TEMPERATURE
1871 FOR PRECIPITATION
1936 FOR SNOWFALL

HEATING DEGREE DAYS Base 65 deg. F — CHEYENNE, WYOMING

SEASON	JULY	AUG	SEP	OCT	NOV	DEC	JAN	FEB	MAR	APR	MAY	JUNE	TOTAL
1964-65	2	95	239	500	883	1095	1012	1088	1320	569	435	169	7407
1965-66	11	47	454	397	702	1016	1208	1061	841	758	291	143	6929
1966-67	0	51	166	526	781	1049	1036	945	800	622	490	221	6687
1967-68	12	45	202	481	891	1308	1117	932	833	777	487	107	7192
1968-69	40	82	221	481	924	1137	1034	919	1118	498	297	248	6999
1969-70	3	3	113	859	854	1038	1115	846	1113	811	326	168	7249
1970-71	3	5	302	732	874	1108	1087	1093	1007	713	481	99	7504
1971-72	56	6	364	633	863	1108	1226	916	791	668	419	61	7111
1972-73	85	75	248	599	1056	1358	1275	980	1017	824	414	122	8053
1973-74	80	4	323	482	883	1098	1264	922	862	643	304	110	6975
1974-75	4	55	302	509	873	1180	1215	1115	1070	819	506	212	7860
1975-76	11	39	274	515	920	998	1175	924	1048	661	425	158	7148
1976-77	11	44	224	664	937	1059	1314	894	1014	602	352	44	7159
1977-78	21	74	150	511	910	1108	1324	1115	840	627	491	157	7328
1978-79	28	73	200	523	937	1358	1471	933	893	597	459	139	7611
1979-80	2	62	105	468	1058	990	1321	1027	984	673	424	65	7179
1980-81	0	41	151	558	840	812	974	913	868	440	445	95	6137
1981-82	21	50	120	580	722	1058	1216	1025	892	687	446	227	7044
1982-83	29	7	264	608	1002	1131	992	875	1016	898	538	233	7593
1983-84	23	0	202	502	974	1547	1259	1058	1002	870	348	177	7962
1984-85	6	15	365	769	892	1171	1403	1163	917	576	323	162	7762
1985-86	11	37	364	612	1158	1199	862	970	698	629	440	71	7051
1986-87	4	20	286	630	914	1121	1102	928	1002	542	321	78	6948
1987-88	27	79	214	554	841	1213	1343	1056	1008	611	361	42	7349
1988-89	12	18	236	449	884	1116	1075	1332	851	615	334	180	7102
1989-90	4	18	236	566	779	1257	1037	1012	1021	662	480	106	7178
1990-91	75	28	127	558	784	1364	1231	799	879	712	385	95	7037
1991-92	26	17	217	586	993	1031	1062	813	811	488	307	131	6482
1992-93	63	92	161	484	1014	1216	1198	1118	856	680	351	202	7435
1993-94	45	58	322	642	1068	1059							

COOLING DEGREE DAYS Base 65 deg. F — CHEYENNE, WYOMING

YEAR	JAN	FEB	MAR	APR	MAY	JUNE	JULY	AUG	SEP	OCT	NOV	DEC	TOTAL
1969	0	0	0	0	14	12	211	185	9	0	0	0	431
1970	0	0	0	0	2	52	149	189	11	0	0	0	403
1971	0	0	0	0	0	58	77	128	13	0	0	0	276
1972	0	0	0	0	0	11	69	69	2	0	0	0	151
1973	0	0	0	0	0	65	112	116	0	0	0	0	293
1974	0	0	0	0	4	88	173	67	17	0	0	0	349
1975	0	0	0	0	0	7	90	86	10	0	0	0	193
1976	0	0	0	0	0	7	145	50	15	0	0	0	217
1977	0	0	0	0	0	59	126	38	29	0	0	0	252
1978	0	0	0	0	1	43	150	59	44	0	0	0	297
1979	0	0	0	0	1	42	160	100	49	0	0	0	352
1980	0	0	0	0	0	88	205	94	21	0	0	0	408
1981	0	0	0	0	0	59	156	64	15	0	0	0	294
1982	0	0	0	0	0	8	120	140	21	0	0	0	289
1983	0	0	0	0	0	10	115	169	28	0	0	0	322
1984	0	0	0	0	1	14	118	72	8	0	0	0	213
1985	0	0	0	0	0	52	150	98	8	0	0	0	308
1986	0	0	0	0	0	62	118	89	0	0	0	0	269
1987	0	0	0	0	0	35	164	83	9	0	0	0	291
1988	0	0	0	0	4	122	166	140	18	0	0	0	450
1989	0	0	0	0	7	46	188	86	19	0	0	0	346
1990	0	0	0	0	0	86	84	79	49	0	0	0	298
1991	0	0	0	0	2	28	119	106	13	4	0	0	272
1992	0	0	0	1	2	15	58	63	16	0	0	0	155
1993	0	0	0	0	0	19	89	60	6	0	0	0	174

SNOWFALL (inches) — CHEYENNE, WYOMING

SEASON	JULY	AUG	SEP	OCT	NOV	DEC	JAN	FEB	MAR	APR	MAY	JUNE	TOTAL
1964-65	0.0	0.0	0.0	0.0	2.0	1.6	8.5	5.5	10.0	2.5	1.4	0.0	31.5
1965-66	0.0	0.0	2.0	T	T	2.4	1.3	2.7	1.1	3.6	T	0.0	13.1
1966-67	0.0	0.0	T	4.5	2.3	0.8	5.4	8.0	3.4	15.9	11.0	0.0	51.3
1967-68	0.0	0.0	0.0	0.4	3.6	4.8	0.2	2.5	2.8	15.4	2.2	0.0	31.9
1968-69	0.0	0.0	0.0	0.5	6.0	5.5	3.0	4.7	2.9	3.0	0.0	T	25.6
1969-70	0.0	0.0	0.0	21.3	1.8	2.4	1.2	1.5	19.4	8.3	T	T	55.9
1970-71	0.0	0.0	T	11.0	4.7	4.9	8.6	9.3	15.2	13.0	1.2	0.0	67.9
1971-72	0.0	0.0	7.4	8.1	0.9	1.4	7.4	0.4	10.6	8.5	0.3	0.0	45.0
1972-73	0.0	0.0	T	5.0	8.8	7.6	4.6	0.6	27.0	12.8	1.2	0.0	67.6
1973-74	0.0	0.0	T	0.5	17.4	13.9	5.0	0.8	16.3	8.0	0.0	0.0	61.9
1974-75	0.0	0.0	1.9	1.4	2.4	1.5	5.8	4.3	14.0	5.4	0.8	0.0	37.5
1975-76	0.0	0.0	0.6	5.5	4.7	8.4	6.0	8.5	9.0	6.7	T	T	49.4
1976-77	0.0	0.0	0.0	1.5	3.5	1.2	2.5	0.8	12.9	7.0	T	0.0	29.4
1977-78	0.0	0.0	0.0	0.4	4.3	5.6	7.0	12.0	2.5	1.0	18.3	0.0	51.1
1978-79	0.0	0.0	0.1	2.0	9.3	17.6	6.7	2.2	21.1	4.0	14.1	T	77.1
1979-80	0.0	0.0	0.0	3.6	31.1	15.6	35.5	10.7	17.8	3.4	3.8	0.0	121.5
1980-81	0.0	0.0	0.0	1.1	6.3	2.1	3.4	2.9	9.0	2.0	0.8	0.0	27.6
1981-82	0.0	0.0	0.0	4.6	0.8	5.8	5.6	2.4	1.7	2.0	4.0	0.0	26.9
1982-83	0.0	0.0	0.0	12.2	7.9	13.1	0.1	T	31.9	25.7	10.1	0.0	101.0
1983-84	0.0	0.0	T	0.2	27.2	7.0	7.9	12.1	13.0	31.8	T	0.0	99.2
1984-85	0.0	0.0	1.6	3.8	1.5	5.6	9.8	1.9	3.6	2.6	0.4	0.0	30.8
1985-86	0.0	0.0	7.4	6.0	12.4	13.0	1.3	4.9	5.6	11.3	3.8	0.0	65.7
1986-87	0.0	0.0	0.0	9.2	6.9	2.2	1.1	9.9	13.7	4.4	T	0.0	47.4
1987-88	0.0	0.0	0.0	1.3	4.5	16.1	9.0	7.5	16.0	7.5	2.2	0.0	64.1
1988-89	0.0	0.0	0.2	0.0	4.5	7.2	4.4	17.6	5.0	4.3	T	T	43.2
1989-90	T	T	2.6	3.4	1.9	9.7	5.6	11.6	39.2	5.6	1.3	T	80.9
1990-91	T	T	T	12.3	8.8	6.6	7.7	1.6	3.7	10.5	T	T	51.2
1991-92	T	T	T	7.5	9.1	2.0	18.2	0.8	11.3	0.7	4.4	0.5	54.5
1992-93	T	T	0.0	2.1	25.5	10.9	7.1	14.6	6.6	11.3	T	0.5	78.6
1993-94	0.0	0.5	5.5	3.1	18.0	5.7							
Record Mean	T	T	0.8	3.7	7.4	6.2	6.4	5.9	12.1	9.0	3.4	0.3	55.1

General Index

A

B

C

I

J

K

L

M

N

O

P

Y